Encyclopaedia
of the
SOCIAL
SCIENCES

Encyclopaedia of the SOCIAL SCIENCES

EDITOR-IN-CHIEF
EDWIN R. A. SELIGMAN

ASSOCIATE EDITOR
ALVIN JOHNSON

VOLUME FIFTEEN

Trade Unions–Zwingli

THE MACMILLAN COMPANY
MCMXXXVII   NEW YORK

Copyright, 1934, by The Macmillan Company
All rights reserved—no part of this book may be reproduced in any form
without permission in writing from the publisher except
by reviewers who wish to quote brief passages in
connection with a review written for
inclusion in magazines or
newspapers
Published June, 1935

Reissued, November, 1937.

THE MACMILLAN COMPANY
NEW YORK · BOSTON · CHICAGO · DALLAS
ATLANTA · SAN FRANCISCO

MACMILLAN & CO., Limited
LONDON · BOMBAY · CALCUTTA
MELBOURNE

THE MACMILLAN COMPANY
OF CANADA, Limited
TORONTO

: Printed in the United States of America :

EDITORIAL STAFF

EDITOR-IN-CHIEF

EDWIN R. A. SELIGMAN

Professor Emeritus of Political Economy in Residence, Columbia University; LL.B., Ph.D. and LL.D.; Hon. D., University of Paris and Heidelberg University; Corresponding Member of the Institut de France and of the Masaryk Sociological Society, Czechoslovakia; Member of the Accademia dei Lincei, of the Russian Academy of Science, of the Norwegian Academy of Science, of the Cuban Academy of Political and Social Science and of the Accademia delle Scienze Morali e Politiche; Laureat of the Belgian Academy of Science; Foreign Correspondent of the Royal Economic Society; Ex-President of the American Economic Association, of the National Tax Association and of the American Association of University Professors

ASSOCIATE EDITOR

ALVIN JOHNSON, Ph. D.

Director of the New School for Social Research

ASSISTANT EDITORS

LEWIS COREY	FLORENCE MISHNUN
ELSIE GLÜCK	KOPPEL S. PINSON
LOUIS M. HACKER	NATHAN REICH
SOLOMON KUZNETS	WILLIAM SEAGLE
IDA CRAVEN MERRIAM	JOSEPH J. SENTURIA
GLADYS MEYERAND	BERNHARD J. STERN
EDWIN MIMS, Jr.	HELEN SULLIVAN

ELIZABETH TODD

Advisory Editors

American

Anthropology
A. L. Kroeber

Economics
Edwin F. Gay
Jacob H. Hollander
E. G. Nourse

Education
Paul Monroe

History
Sidney B. Fay
A. M. Schlesinger

Law
Roscoe Pound

Philosophy
John Dewey

Political Science
Charles A. Beard
Frank J. Goodnow

Psychology
Floyd H. Allport

Social Work
Porter R. Lee

Sociology
William F. Ogburn
W. I. Thomas

Statistics
Irving Fisher
Walter F. Willcox

Foreign

England
Ernest Barker
J. M. Keynes
Sir Josiah Stamp
R. H. Tawney

France
Charles Rist
F. Simiand

Germany
Carl Brinkmann
H. Schumacher

Italy
Luigi Einaudi
Augusto Graziani

Switzerland
W. E. Rappard

Constituent Societies
and
Joint Committee

AMERICAN ANTHROPOLOGICAL ASSOCIATION
    Robert H. Lowie and Clark Wissler

AMERICAN ASSOCIATION OF SOCIAL WORKERS
    Philip Klein and Stuart A. Queen

AMERICAN ECONOMIC ASSOCIATION
    Clive Day and Frank A. Fetter

AMERICAN HISTORICAL ASSOCIATION
    Carl Becker and Clarence H. Haring

AMERICAN POLITICAL SCIENCE ASSOCIATION
    William B. Munro and John H. Logan

AMERICAN PSYCHOLOGICAL ASSOCIATION
    Georgina S. Gates and Mark A. May

AMERICAN SOCIOLOGICAL SOCIETY
    Harry E. Barnes and Kimball Young

AMERICAN STATISTICAL ASSOCIATION
    R. H. Coats and Robert M. Woodbury

ASSOCIATION OF AMERICAN LAW SCHOOLS
    Edwin W. Patterson and Edwin D. Dickinson

NATIONAL EDUCATION ASSOCIATION
    E. L. Thorndike and J. A. C. Chandler

Board of Directors

Academic

Franz Boas
Walter Wheeler Cook
John Dewey
John A. Fairlie

Carlton J. H. Hayes
Jacob H. Hollander
Alvin Johnson
Wesley C. Mitchell
John K. Norton

Edwin R. A. Seligman
Mary van Kleeck
Margaret Floy Washburn
Howard B. Woolston

Lay

James Couzens
Thomas W. Lamont

John J. Raskob
Robert E. Simon
Jesse I. Straus

Silas H. Strawn
Owen D. Young

Contributors to Volume Fifteen

Amery, G. D.
  University of Oxford
Anderson, Nels
  Columbia University
Antonelli, Étienne
  University of Lyons
Armstrong, Barbara Nachtrieb
  University of California

Babinger, Franz
  University of Berlin
Bachi, Riccardo
  Regio Istituto Superiore di Scienze Economiche e Commerciali, Rome
Barnes, Gilbert Hobbs
  Ohio Wesleyan University
Barnes, Harry E.
  New York City
Batson, H. E.
  London School of Economics and Political Science
Becker, Carl
  Cornell University
Beckman, Theodore N.
  Ohio State University
Beer, Max
  London
Bettermann, Wilhelm
  Archiv der Brüder-Unität, Herrnhut
Blom, D. van
  University of Leyden
Bonbright, James C.
  Columbia University
Bourgin, Georges
  Archives Nationales, Paris
Bradley, Phillips
  Amherst College
Brailsford, H. N.
  London
Brewer, John M.
  Harvard University
Brierly, J. L.
  University of Oxford
Brinton, Crane
  Harvard University
Brubaker, Howard
  Greens Farms, Connecticut

Budge, Siegfried
  Frankfort
Burr, George L.
  Cornell University

Carlyle, A. J.
  University of Oxford
Carstens, C. C.
  Child Welfare League of America, New York City
Cassau, Theodor
  Berlin
Cheyney, Edward P.
  University of Pennsylvania
Cobban, Alfred
  University of Durham at New Castle upon Tyne
Codignola, Ernesto
  Regio Istituto Superiore di Magistero, Florence
Cole, G. D. H.
  University of Oxford
Collinet, Paul
  University of Paris
Colm, Gerhard
  Graduate Faculty of Political and Social Science, New School for Social Research
Condliffe, J. B.
  Canterbury College, Christchurch, New Zealand
Coupland, R.
  University of Oxford
Croce, Benedetto
  Naples
Cunow, Heinrich
  University of Berlin
Curti, Merle E.
  Smith College

Daggett, Stuart
  University of California
Danielian, N. R.
  Harvard University
Daniels, G. W.
  University of Manchester

de los Ríos, Fernando
    University of Madrid
Dewey, Davis R.
    Massachusetts Institute of Technology
Dietz, Frederick
    University of Illinois
Dilliard, Irving
    St. Louis, Missouri
Dodd, William E.
    Berlin
Douglas, Dorothy W.
    Smith College
Du Bois, W. E. B.
    Atlanta University

Eckhart, Franz
    University of Budapest
Elbogen, Ismar
    Hochschule für die Wissenschaft des Judentums, Berlin
Emin, Ahmet
    Istanbul

Falnes, Oscar J.
    New York University
Faulkner, Harold U.
    Smith College
Faÿ, Bernard
    Collège de France
Fay, Sidney B.
    Harvard University
Feller, A. H.
    Harvard University
Fetter, Frank Whitson
    Haverford College
Finkelstein, Moses I.
    Encyclopaedia of the Social Sciences
Fitzpatrick, John C.
    Washington, D. C.
Flexner, Jean Atherton
    Children's Bureau, United States Department of Labor
Ford, Grace
    Southampton, England
Franke, Otto
    University of Berlin
Fraser, Lindley M.
    University of Oxford
Friedrich, A. A.
    New York University
Fritzsche, Hans
    University of Zurich

Garner, James Wilford
    University of Illinois

Garrison, F. H.
    Johns Hopkins University
Gaus, John M.
    University of Chicago
Gelesnoff, V.
    Moscow
Georgievsky, P. I.
    Prague
Gilson, Mary Barnett
    University of Chicago
Glück, Elsie
    Encyclopaedia of the Social Sciences
Goodrich, Carter
    Columbia University
Goodrich, L. C.
    Columbia University
Goodsell, Willystine
    Columbia University
Gosnell, Harold F.
    University of Chicago
Gottschalk, Louis
    University of Chicago
Goyau, Georges
    Académie Française

Hail, William James
    College of Wooster
Halphen, Louis
    École des Hautes Études, Paris
Hammond, John Lawrence
    Hemel Hempsted, England
Handelsman, Marceli
    University of Warsaw
Hankins, Frank H.
    Smith College
Haring, H. A.
    Woodland, New York
Harsin, Paul
    University of Liége
Hartung, Fritz
    University of Berlin
Hearnshaw, F. J. C.
    University of London
Heaton, Herbert
    University of Minnesota
Heberle, Rudolf
    University of Kiel
Heichelheim, Fritz
    Cambridge, England
Heuss, Theodor
    Hochschule für Politik, Berlin
Hicks, Granville
    Rensselaer Polytechnic Institute
Himes, Norman E.
    Colgate University

Contributors to Volume Fifteen

Hintze, Hedwig
Berlin
Hitti, Philip K.
Princeton University
Homan, Paul T.
Cornell University
Hook, Sidney
New York University
Hugelmann, Karl Gottfried
University of Vienna
Hyma, Albert
University of Michigan

Irsay, Stephen d'
École des Hautes Études Sociales, Paris

Jaffe, L. L.
Supreme Court of the United States
James, M.
London School of Economics and Political Science
Janowsky, Oscar I.
College of the City of New York
Joad, C. E. M.
Hampstead, England
Johnson, Alvin
New School for Social Research
Jolowicz, H. F.
University of London
Jones, Howard Mumford
University of Michigan
Jones, Rufus M.
Haverford University
Jordan, H. Donaldson
Clark University

Kandel, I. L.
Columbia University
Kleeck, Mary van
Russell Sage Foundation
Knight, Frank H.
University of Chicago
Knubben, Rolf
Bielefeld, Germany
Koch, Woldemar
Cologne
Kocharovsky, K.
Belgrade
Köhler, W.
University of Heidelberg
Kohn, Hans
Smith College
Konkle, Burton Alva
Swarthmore, Pennsylvania

Kosminsky, E. A.
Moscow
Krzywicki, Ludwik
University of Warsaw

Ladas, Stephen P.
New York City
Laistner, M. L. W.
Cornell University
Landtman, Gunnar
Helsingfors
Laski, Harold J.
London School of Economics and Political Science
Lee, Robert Warden
University of Oxford
Lehmann, Fritz
Graduate Faculty of Political and Social Science, New School for Social Research
Lerner, Max
Sarah Lawrence College, Bronxville, New York
Levin, Max
Encyclopaedia of the Social Sciences
Lévy-Bruhl, Henri
University of Paris
Lhéritier, Michel
École des Hautes Études Sociales et Internationales, Paris
Liesse, André
Institut de France
Livingston, J. A.
New York City
Lore, Ludwig
New York City
Lorwin, Lewis L.
The Brookings Institution, Washington, D. C.
Lowie, Robert H.
University of California

McBride, George McCutchen
University of California at Los Angeles
McClintock, Miller
Harvard University
MacIver, R. M.
Columbia University
Mackenzie, Catherine
New York City
McMurray, Orrin K.
University of California
Mannheim, Karl
London School of Economics and Political Science

Marett, R. R.
: University of Oxford
Marschak, Jakob
: University of Oxford
Marshall, George
: New York City
Marshall, T. H.
: London School of Economics and Political Science
Martino, Pierre
: University of Poitiers
Mayer, Gustav
: University of Berlin
Mead, Elizabeth
: Chicago
Mead, Margaret
: American Museum of Natural History, New York City
Meyerand, Gladys
: Encyclopaedia of the Social Sciences
Miliukov, Paul
: Paris
Miller, Harry E.
: Brown University
Mills, R. C.
: University of Sydney
Mishnun, Florence
: Encyclopaedia of the Social Sciences
Mitchell, Broadus
: Johns Hopkins University
Monroe, A. E.
: Harvard University
Morison, S. E.
: Harvard University
Morris, Richard B.
: College of the City of New York
Morrow, Felix
: New York City
Moulton, Harold G.
: The Brookings Institution, Washington, D. C.
Munro, William B.
: California Institute of Technology

Nathan, Otto
: Princeton University
Neumann, Sigmund
: Wesleyan University
Niboyet, J. P.
: University of Paris
Nilsson, Martin P.
: University of Lund

Orchard, Dorothy Johnson
: New York City

Pagni, Carlo
: Università Bocconi, Milan
Paxson, Frederic L.
: University of California
Peake, Harold J. E.
: Boxford, Berkshire, England
Perlman, Selig
: University of Wisconsin
Perreau, E.-H.
: University of Toulouse
Person, H. S.
: Taylor Society, New York City
Pinson, Koppel S.
: Encyclopaedia of the Social Sciences
Pirenne, Henri
: University of Ghent
Ploscowe, Morris
: Harvard University
Plucknett, Theodore F. T.
: London School of Economics and Political Science
Pribram, Karl
: The Brookings Institution, Washington, D. C.
Procopovicz, S.
: Prague
Pruette, Lorine
: New York City
Puech, J. L.
: Paris

Radin, Max
: University of California
Reed, Thomas H.
: University of Michigan
Rees, J. F.
: University College of South Wales and Monmouthshire
Reich, Nathan
: Encyclopaedia of the Social Sciences
Ricci, Umberto
: Egyptian University, Gizeh
Robinson, Howard
: Miami University, Oxford, Ohio
Rohden, Peter Richard
: University of Berlin
Rosenberg, Arthur
: University of Liverpool
Roubakine, N.
: Institut International de Psychologie Bibliologique, Lausanne
Ruggiero, Guido de
: Regio Istituto Superiore di Magistero, Rome

Contributors to Volume Fifteen

Salin, Edgar
 University of Basel
Salvemini, Gaetano
 Harvard University
Schiller, A. Arthur
 Columbia University
Schmidt, Louis Bernard
 Iowa State College
Schnabel, Franz
 Technische Hochschule, Karlsruhe
Schneider, Herbert W.
 Columbia University
Schuman, Frederick L.
 University of Chicago
Schumpeter, Joseph A.
 Harvard University
Scott, Austin W.
 Harvard University
Scott, James Brown
 Washington, D. C.
Seagle, William
 Encyclopaedia of the Social Sciences
Seligman, Edwin R. A.
 Columbia University
Senturia, Joseph J.
 Encyclopaedia of the Social Sciences
Sewny, V. D.
 Encyclopaedia of the Social Sciences
Silva, Pietro
 Regio Istituto Superiore di Magistero, Rome
Slesinger, Donald
 University of Chicago
Slonimsky, H.
 Jewish Institute of Religion
Smith, Robert S.
 Duke University
Solntsev, S.
 Academy of Sciences, Leningrad
Sommer, Louise
 University of Geneva
Souvarine, Boris
 Paris
Speier, Hans
 Graduate Faculty of Political and Social Science, New School for Social Research
Steiner, W. H.
 Brooklyn College
Stenton, F. M.
 University of Reading, England
Stern, Bernhard J.
 Encyclopaedia of the Social Sciences

Stewart, Ethelbert
 Washington, D. C.
Strickland, C. F.
 London

Taranovsky, Theodor
 University of Belgrade
Thompson, Warren S.
 Miami University, Oxford, Ohio
Trotter, Reginald G.
 Queen's University

Vallaux, Camille
 Paris
Van Metre, T. W.
 Columbia University
Vasiliev, A. A.
 University of Wisconsin
Vesey-Fitzgerald, Seymour
 University of London
Vierkandt, A.
 University of Berlin
Vinacke, Harold M.
 University of Cincinnati
Vleugels, Wilhelm
 University of Bonn

Wade, Herbert T.
 New York City
Ware, Norman J.
 Wesleyan University
Warner, Wellman J.
 Ohio Wesleyan University
Watkins, Frederick Mundell
 Harvard University
Watkins, Myron W.
 New York University
Weber, Wilhelm
 University of Berlin
Weill, Georges
 University of Caen
Weinstein, Alexander
 Johns Hopkins University
Wendel, Hermann
 Neuilly-sur-Seine
Whitten, Robert
 New York City
Whittlesey, Charles R.
 Princeton University
Wiedenfeld, Kurt
 University of Leipsic
Williams, E. T.
 University of California
Wilson, George Grafton
 Harvard University

Wolfson, Theresa
Brooklyn College
Workman, H. B.
London
Woytinsky, Wladimir
Paris

Zielenziger, Kurt
Paris
Zimmermann, Erich W.
University of North Carolina
Zulueta, F. de
University of Oxford

Contents

Contributors to Volume Fifteen — ix

Articles

TRADE UNIONS
  INTRODUCTION — *Elsie Glück*
  UNITED KINGDOM AND IRISH FREE STATE — *G. D. H. Cole*
  GERMANY — *Theodor Cassau*
  AUSTRIA, SWITZERLAND AND HOLLAND — *Theodor Cassau*
  SCANDINAVIAN COUNTRIES AND FINLAND — *Rudolf Heberle*
  SUCCESSION STATES AND BALKAN COUNTRIES — *Karl Pribram*
  FRANCE — *Georges Bourgin*
  BELGIUM — *Georges Bourgin*
  SPAIN AND PORTUGAL — *Georges Bourgin*
  ITALY — *Georges Bourgin*
  RUSSIA — *Woldemar Koch*
  FAR AND NEAR EAST — *Dorothy Johnson Orchard*
  UNITED STATES AND CANADA — *Norman J. Ware*
  AUSTRALIA, NEW ZEALAND AND SOUTH AFRICA — *Carter Goodrich*
  LATIN AMERICA — *Max Levin and Joseph J. Senturia*
  INTERNATIONAL ORGANIZATION — *Lewis L. Lorwin*

TRADEMARKS AND NAMES — *Stephen P. Ladas*
TRADES UNION CONGRESS, BRITISH — See TRADE UNIONS, section on GREAT BRITAIN
TRADING WITH THE ENEMY — *Frederick L. Schuman*
TRADITION — *Max Radin*
TRADITIONALISM — *Peter Richard Rohden*
TRAFFIC REGULATION — *Miller McClintock*
TRANSCENDENTALISM — *Herbert W. Schneider*
TRANSIT DUTIES — *Otto Nathan*
TRANSIT, INTERNATIONAL — *Phillips Bradley*
TRANSPORTATION — *Kurt Wiedenfeld*
TRANSPORTATION OF CRIMINALS — *Harry E. Barnes*
TRAVEL — See TOURIST TRAFFIC
TREASON — *Morris Ploscowe*
TREATIES — *Frederick L. Schuman*
TREATY PORTS — See SPHERES OF INFLUENCE
TREITSCHKE, HEINRICH VON — *Sigmund Neumann*
TREVELYAN, GEORGE OTTO — *John Lawrence Hammond*
TRIAL MARRIAGE — See COMPANIONATE MARRIAGE
TRIBE — See SOCIAL ORGANIZATION
TRIBUTE — *Fritz Heichelheim*
TRIKOUPIS, CHARILAOS — *Michel Lhéritier*

xv

TRISTAN, FLORA CÉLESTINE THÉRÈSE HENRIETTE	J. L. Puech
TROELSTRA, PIETER JELLES	D. van Blom
TROELTSCH, ERNST	Karl Mannheim
TRONCHET, FRANÇOIS-DENIS	E.-H. Perreau
TROPICAL MEDICINE	See ACCLIMATIZATION; COMMUNICABLE DISEASES, CONTROL OF
TRUCE AND PEACE OF GOD	Louis Halphen
TRUCK FARMING	See FRUIT AND VEGETABLE INDUSTRY
TRUST COMPANIES	W. H. Steiner
TRUSTS	Paul T. Homan and Myron W. Watkins
TRUSTS AND TRUSTEES	Austin W. Scott
TUBERCULOSIS	See COMMUNICABLE DISEASES, CONTROL OF; PUBLIC HEALTH
TUCKER, GEORGE	Harold U. Faulkner
TUCKER, JOSIAH	J. F. Rees
TUCOVIĆ, DIMITRIJE	Hermann Wendel
TUGAN-BARANOVSKY, MIHAIL IVANOVICH	S. Solntsev
TULL, JETHRO	T. H. Marshall
TURATI, FILIPPO	Gaetano Salvemini
TURGENEV, NIKOLAI IVANOVICH	V. Gelesnoff
TURGOT, ROBERT JACQUES	Paul Harsin
TURNER, FREDERICK JACKSON	Frederic L. Paxson
TURNER, JAMES MILTON	Irving Dilliard
TYLER, MOSES COIT	Howard Mumford Jones
TYLOR, SIR EDWARD BURNETT	R. R. Marett
TYRANNY	Frederick Mundell Watkins
TZ'Û HSI	Harold M. Vinacke
ULLOA, BERNARDO DE	Robert S. Smith
ULLSTEIN FAMILY	Kurt Zielenziger
ULPIAN	A. Arthur Schiller
ULYANOV, VLADIMIR ILICH	Harold J. Laski
UNDERWRITING	See INSURANCE; INVESTMENT BANKING
UNEARNED INCREMENT	Gerhard Colm
UNEMPLOYMENT	Karl Pribram
UNEMPLOYMENT EXCHANGE	See EMPLOYMENT EXCHANGES
UNEMPLOYMENT INSURANCE	Mary Barnett Gilson
UNFAIR COMPETITION	Myron W. Watkins
UNFAIR LIST	See BOYCOTT
UNGER, JOSEPH	Karl Gottfried Hugelmann
UNIFORM LEGISLATION	A. H. Feller
UNINCORPORATED ASSOCIATIONS	See VOLUNTARY ASSOCIATIONS
UNION LABEL	See TRADE UNIONS, section on UNITED STATES AND CANADA
UNION-MANAGEMENT COOPERATION	See LABOR-CAPITAL COOPERATION
UNIVERSITIES AND COLLEGES	Stephen d'Irsay
UNIVERSITY EXTENSION	Donald Slesinger and Elizabeth Mead

Contents

UNWIN, GEORGE	*G. W. Daniels*
UPPER CHAMBERS	*See* BICAMERAL SYSTEM
URBANIZATION	*Warren S. Thompson*
USENER, HERMANN	*Martin P. Nilsson*
USPENSKY, FEDOR IVANOVICH	*A. A. Vasiliev*
USURY	*Edgar Salin*
UTILITARIANISM	*Crane Brinton*
UTILITY	*See* VALUE AND PRICE; ECONOMICS, section on MARGINAL UTILITY
UTOPIA	*Karl Mannheim*
UVAROV, COUNT SERGEY SEMENOVICH	*N. Roubakine*
UZTÁRIZ, JERÓNIMO DE	*Robert S. Smith*
VACARIUS	*F. de Zulueta*
VACATIONS	*See* SHORT HOURS MOVEMENT
VACCINATION	*See* COMMUNICABLE DISEASES, CONTROL OF
VAGRANCY	*Nels Anderson*
VAIL, THEODORE NEWTON	*Catherine Mackenzie*
VALENTI, GHINO	*Umberto Ricci*
VALLA, LORENZO	*Guido de Ruggiero*
VALORIZATION	*Charles R. Whittlesey*
VALUATION	*James C. Bonbright*
VALUE AND PRICE	*Frank H. Knight*
VALUES	*See* ETHICS; MORALS
VÁMBÉRY, ARMIN	*Franz Babinger*
VAN CLEAVE, JAMES WALLACE	*Jean Atherton Flexner*
VANDAL, COMTE ALBERT	*Louis Gottschalk*
VANDERBILT FAMILY	*T. W. Van Metre*
VANDERKINDERE, LÉON	*Henri Pirenne*
VANDERLINT, JACOB	*J. F. Rees*
VANE, SIR HENRY	*F. J. C. Hearnshaw*
VARLIN, LOUIS EUGÈNE	*Boris Souvarine*
VASCO, GIAMBATTISTA	*Riccardo Bachi*
VASILCHIKOV, PRINCE ALEXANDR ILARIONOVICH	*K. Kocharovsky*
VASILEVSKY, VASILY GRIGOREVICH	*A. A. Vasiliev*
VATTEL, EMMERICH DE	*Rolf Knubben*
VAUBAN, SEIGNEUR SÉBASTIEN LE PRESTRE DE	*Edwin R. A. Seligman*
VAUGHAN, RICE	*A. E. Monroe*
VEBLEN, THORSTEIN BUNDE	*Alvin Johnson*
VENEREAL DISEASES	*See* PROSTITUTION; SEX EDUCATION AND SEX ETHICS
VENUE	*L. L. Jaffe*
VERBŐCZY, ISTVÁN	*Franz Eckhart*
VERGENNES, COMTE DE	*Bernard Faÿ*
VERGNIAUD, PIERRE VICTURNIEN	*Hedwig Hintze*
VERRI, PIETRO	*Carlo Pagni*
VESTED INTERESTS	*Max Lerner*
VETERANS	*A. A. Friedrich*
VETO	*William B. Munro*
VEUILLOT, LOUIS	*Georges Goyau*
VICO, GIOVANNI BATTISTA	*Benedetto Croce*
VICTOR EMMANUEL II	*Pietro Silva*

VIDAL DE LA BLACHE, PAUL MARIE JOSEPH	*Camille Vallaux*
VIJNANEṢVĀRA	*Seymour Vesey-Fitzgerald*
VILLAGE	See RURAL SOCIETY
VILLAGE COMMUNITY	*Harold J. E. Peake*
VILLARD, HENRY	*Stuart Daggett*
VILLARI, PASQUALE	*Gaetano Salvemini*
VILLENEUVE-BARGEMONT, VICOMTE DE	*Georges Weill*
VILLERMÉ, LOUIS RENÉ	*André Liesse*
VILLIERS, CHARLES PELHAM	*J. F. Rees*
VILLIERS, FIRST BARON JOHN HENRY DE	*Robert Warden Lee*
VINCENT DE PAUL, SAINT	*Georges Goyau*
VINCENT, HENRY	*Max Beer*
VINOGRADOFF, SIR PAUL	*William Seagle*
VIOLENCE	*Sidney Hook*
VIOLLET, PAUL	*Henri Lévy-Bruhl*
VIRCHOW, RUDOLF	*Theodor Heuss*
VISA	See PASSPORT
VISIT AND SEARCH	See PRIZE
VISITING NURSES	See NURSING; PUBLIC HEALTH
VITAL STATISTICS	See BIRTHS; MORTALITY; POPULATION, section on HISTORY AND STATISTICS; DEMOGRAPHY
VITALISM	See MECHANISM AND VITALISM
VITORIA, FRANCISCO DE	*James Brown Scott*
VITTORINO DA FELTRE	*Ernesto Codignola*
VIVEKĀNANDA, SWAMI	*Florence Mishnun*
VIVES, JUAN LUIS	*Fernando de los Ríos*
VLADIMIRSKY-BUDANOV, MIHAIL FLEGONTOVICH	*Theodor Taranovsky*
VOCATIONAL EDUCATION	*I. L. Kandel*
VOCATIONAL GUIDANCE	*John M. Brewer*
VOCATIONAL PSYCHOLOGY	See VOCATIONAL GUIDANCE
VOGEL, SIR JULIUS	*J. B. Condliffe*
VOGELSANG, FREIHERR KARL VON	*Hans Speier*
VOLLMAR, GEORG VON	*Heinrich Cunow*
VOLTAIRE, FRANÇOIS-MARIE AROUET DE	*Carl Becker*
VOLUNTARY ASSOCIATIONS	*Florence Mishnun*
VORONTSOV, VASSILY PAVLOVICH	*K. Kocharovsky*
VOTING	*Harold F. Gosnell*
VOTING TRUST	See TRUSTS AND TRUSTEES
WACH, ADOLF	*Hans Fritzsche*
WAGE REGULATION	See WAGES
WAGES—THEORY AND POLICY	*Jakob Marschak*
HISTORY AND STATISTICS	*Wladimir Woytinsky*
WAGNER, ADOLF HEINRICH GOTTHILF	*Gerhard Colm*
WAITZ, FRANZ THEODOR	*Robert H. Lowie*
WAITZ, GEORG	*Fritz Hartung*
WAKEFIELD, EDWARD GIBBON	*R. C. Mills*
WAKLEY, THOMAS	*Norman E. Himes*
WALKER, AMASA	*Harry E. Miller*
WALKER, FRANCIS AMASA	*Davis R. Dewey*
WALLACE, ALFRED RUSSEL	*C. E. M. Joad*
WALLACE, HENRY and HENRY CANTWELL	*Louis Bernard Schmidt*

Contents

WALLACE, ROBERT	J. F. Rees
WALLAS, GRAHAM	R. M. MacIver
WALPOLE, ROBERT	Frederick Dietz
WALRAS, ANTOINE AUGUSTE	Étienne Antonelli
WALRAS, MARIE ESPRIT LÉON	Étienne Antonelli
WALTER FAMILY	H. Donaldson Jordan
WANG AN-SHI	Otto Franke
WAR	Alvin Johnson
WAR ECONOMICS	Alvin Johnson
WAR FINANCE	Gerhard Colm
WAR GUILT	See WORLD WAR
WAR PROFITS TAX	See EXCESS PROFITS TAX
WAR PSYCHOLOGY	See PROPAGANDA; MORALE
WAR RISK INSURANCE	See VETERANS
WARBURG, PAUL MORITZ	Edwin R. A. Seligman
WARD, LESTER FRANK	Bernhard J. Stern
WAREHOUSING	H. A. Haring
WARFARE, LAWS OF	James Wilford Garner
WARREN, JOSIAH	Dorothy W. Douglas
WARYŃSKI, LUDWIK TADEUSZ	Ludwik Krzywicki
WASHINGTON, BOOKER TALIAFERRO	W. E. B. Du Bois
WASHINGTON, GEORGE	John C. Fitzpatrick
WASTE	H. S. Person
WASTE DISPOSAL	See SANITATION
WATER LAW	Orrin K. McMurray
WATER POWER	See ELECTRIC POWER
WATER SUPPLY	Thomas H. Reed
WATERWAYS, INLAND	Harold G. Moulton
WATERWAYS, INTERNATIONAL	See INTERNATIONAL WATERWAYS
WATKIN, SIR EDWARD WILLIAM	Reginald G. Trotter
WATSON, ELKANAH	Louis Bernard Schmidt
WATSON, JAMES	Max Beer
WAUGH, BENJAMIN	C. C. Carstens
WEALTH	See NATIONAL WEALTH
WEALTH, NATIONAL	See NATIONAL WEALTH
WEAVER, JAMES BAIRD	Louis Bernard Schmidt
WEBER, MAX	Hans Speier
WEBSTER, DANIEL	Merle E. Curti
WEIGHTS AND MEASURES	Herbert T. Wade
WEISMANN, AUGUST	Alexander Weinstein
WEISS, ANDRÉ	J. P. Niboyet
WEITLING, WILHELM	Gustav Mayer
WELCH, WILLIAM HENRY	F. H. Garrison
WELCKER, KARL THEODOR	Theodor Heuss
WELD, THEODORE DWIGHT	Gilbert Hobbs Barnes
WELFARE CAPITALISM	See WELFARE WORK, INDUSTRIAL
WELFARE WORK, INDUSTRIAL	H. S. Person
WELLESLEY, MARQUIS RICHARD COLLEY	Howard Robinson
WELLHAUSEN, JULIUS	Moses I. Finkelstein
WELLINGTON, FIRST DUKE OF	F. J. C. Hearnshaw
WELLS, DAVID AMES	Edwin R. A. Seligman
WENTWORTH, WILLIAM CHARLES	Howard Robinson
WERGELAND, HENRIK ARNOLD	Oscar J. Falnes
WESLEY, JOHN	Wellman J. Warner
WESTERNIZATION	See EUROPEANIZATION

WESTINGHOUSE, GEORGE	N. R. Danielian
WESTLAKE, JOHN	A. H. Feller
WEYDEMEYER, JOSEPH	Ludwig Lore
WEYL, WALTER EDWARD	Howard Brubaker
WHATELY, RICHARD	Lindley M. Fraser
WHEATLEY, JOHN	Frank Whitson Fetter
WHEATON, HENRY	George Grafton Wilson
WHIG PARTY	See PARTIES, POLITICAL, sections on GREAT BRITAIN and UNITED STATES
WHITE, ANDREW DICKSON	George L. Burr
WHITE LIST	See CONSUMERS' LEAGUES
WHITE SLAVERY	See PROSTITUTION
WHITEFIELD, GEORGE	Wellman J. Warner
WHITLEY COUNCILS	See INDUSTRIAL RELATIONS COUNCILS
WHITMAN, WALT	Granville Hicks
WHITNEY, ELI	Broadus Mitchell
WHOLESALING	Theodore N. Beckman
WICHERN, JOHANN HINRICH	Theodor Heuss
WICKSELL, KNUT	Fritz Lehmann
WICKSTEED, PHILIP HENRY	H. E. Batson
WIDOWS' PENSIONS	See MOTHERS' PENSIONS
WIELOPOLSKI, ALEKSANDER	Marceli Handelsman
WIESER, FRIEDRICH VON	Wilhelm Vleugels
WILAMOWITZ-MOELLENDORFF, ULRICH VON	Wilhelm Weber
WILBERFORCE, WILLIAM	R. Coupland
WILKES, JOHN	John M. Gaus
WILLARD, EMMA HART	Willystine Goodsell
WILLARD, FRANCES ELIZABETH	Lorine Pruette
WILLIAM I	F. M. Stenton
WILLIAM I	Franz Schnabel
WILLIAMS, ROGER	Felix Morrow
WILLS	See SUCCESSION, LAWS OF
WILSON, JAMES	Burton Alva Konkle
WILSON, JOSEPH HAVELOCK	Grace Ford
WILSON, (THOMAS) WOODROW	William E. Dodd
WINCKELMANN, JOHANN JOACHIM	Wilhelm Weber
WINDOW TAX	See HOUSE AND BUILDING TAXES
WINDSCHEID, BERNHARD	H. F. Jolowicz
WINDTHORST, LUDWIG	Arthur Rosenberg
WINKELBLECH, KARL GEORG	See MARLO, KARL
WINSTANLEY, GERRARD	M. James
WINTHROP, JOHN	S. E. Morison
WIRTH, MAX	Siegfried Budge
WISE, ISAAC MAYER	H. Slonimsky
WITCHCRAFT	See MAGIC
WITT, JOHAN DE	Albert Hyma
WITTE, GRAF SERGEY YULIEVICH	Paul Miliukov
WOLF, FRIEDRICH AUGUST	Wilhelm Weber
WOLFF, CHRISTIAN	Koppel S. Pinson
WOLFF, HENRY WILLIAM	C. F. Strickland
WOLLSTONECRAFT, MARY	H. N. Brailsford
WOLOWSKI, LOUIS FRANÇOIS MICHEL RAYMOND	Paul Harsin

Contents

WOLSEY, THOMAS	Edward P. Cheyney
WOLTMANN, LUDWIG	Frank H. Hankins
WOMAN, POSITION IN SOCIETY—Primitive	Margaret Mead
Historical	Bernhard J. Stern
WOMAN'S CHRISTIAN TEMPERANCE UNION	See Prohibition; Temperance Movements
WOMEN IN INDUSTRY—General Principles	Mary van Kleeck
Problems of Organization	Elsie Glück
WOMEN'S ORGANIZATIONS	Gladys Meyerand
WOOD INDUSTRIES	Erich W. Zimmermann
WOODHULL, VICTORIA CLAFLIN	Gladys Meyerand
WOODS, ROBERT ARCHEY	Gladys Meyerand
WOOL	Herbert Heaton
WOOLMAN, JOHN	Rufus M. Jones
WORDSWORTH, WILLIAM	Alfred Cobban
WORKERS' EDUCATION	Selig Perlman
WORKING MEN'S CLUBS	See Mutual Aid Societies
WORKMEN'S COMPENSATION	Barbara Nachtrieb Armstrong
WORKS COUNCILS	See Industrial Relations Councils
WORLD COURT	See Permanent Court of International Justice
WORLD WAR	Sidney B. Fay
WORMS, RENÉ	V. D. Sewny
WRIGHT, CARROLL DAVIDSON	Ethelbert Stewart
WRIGHT, FRANCES	Theresa Wolfson
WRITING	Bernhard J. Stern
WRITS	Theodore F. T. Plucknett
WROŃSKI-HOENE, JÓZEF MARJA	Nathan Reich
WU T'ING FANG	E. T. Williams
WUNDT, WILHELM MAX	A. Vierkandt
WYCLIFFE, JOHN	H. B. Workman
WYTHE, GEORGE	Richard B. Morris
XENOPHON	M. L. W. Laistner
XENOPOL, ALEXANDRU	Florence Mishnun
XIMÉNES DE CISNEROS, FRANCISCO	Florence Mishnun
YAMAGATA, PRINCE ARITOMO	Harold M. Vinacke
YANG CHU	L. C. Goodrich
YANSON, YULY EDUARDOVICH	P. I. Georgievsky
YANZHUL, IVAN IVANOVICH	E. A. Kosminsky
YĀQŪT IBN'ABD-ALLĀH AL-RŪMI AL-ḤAMAWI	Philip K. Hitti
YARRANTON, ANDREW	J. A. Livingston
"YELLOW DOG" CONTRACT	See Labor Contract
YERKES, CHARLES TYSON	George Marshall
YOGA	See Mysticism
YOSHIDA TORAJIRŌ	Harold M. Vinacke
YOUNG, ALLYN ABBOTT	Joseph A. Schumpeter
YOUNG, ARTHUR	G. D. Amery
YOUNG, BRIGHAM	Nels Anderson
YOUTH MOVEMENTS	Hans Kohn
YRJÖ-KOSKINEN, YRJÖ SAKARI	Gunnar Landtmann
YUAN SHIH-KAI	William James Hail
YVES OF CHARTRES	A. J. Carlyle

ZACHARIAE VON LINGENTHAL, KARL-EDUARD	Paul Collinet
ZACHARIAE VON LINGENTHAL, KARL SALOMO	Sigmund Neumann
ZADRUGA	*See* VILLAGE COMMUNITY
ZAGHLUL PASHA, SAAD	Hans Kohn
ZANGWILL, ISRAEL	Oscar I. Janowsky
ZAPATA, EMILIANO	George McCutchen McBride
ZELGEIM, VLADIMIR NIKOLAEVICH	S. Procopovicz
ZETKIN, CLARA	Arthur Rosenberg
ZIA PASHA	Ahmet Emin
ZINCKE, GEORG HEINRICH	Louise Sommer
ZINZENDORF, COUNT NIKOLAUS LUDWIG VON	Wilhelm Bettermann
ZIONISM	Hans Kohn
ZITELMANN, ERNST	William Seagle
ZOAR	*See* COMMUNISTIC SETTLEMENTS
ZOLA, ÉMILE	Pierre Martino
ZONING	Robert Whitten
ZORN, PHILIPP	Theodor Heuss
ZOUCHE, RICHARD	J. L. Brierly
ZUNZ, LEOPOLD	Ismar Elbogen
ZWINGLI, HULDREICH	W. Köhler

INDEX, VOLUMES 1–15   *Page* 545

Encyclopaedia

of the

SOCIAL SCIENCES

Encyclopaedia of the Social Sciences

TRADE UNIONS
    INTRODUCTION...ELSIE GLÜCK
    UNITED KINGDOM AND IRISH FREE STATE..............G. D. H. COLE
    GERMANY...THEODOR CASSAU
    AUSTRIA, SWITZERLAND AND HOLLAND.................THEODOR CASSAU
    SCANDINAVIAN COUNTRIES AND FINLAND...............RUDOLF HEBERLE
    SUCCESSION STATES AND BALKAN COUNTRIES...........KARL PRIBRAM
    FRANCE..GEORGES BOURGIN
    BELGIUM...GEORGES BOURGIN
    SPAIN AND PORTUGAL..................................GEORGES BOURGIN
    ITALY...GEORGES BOURGIN
    RUSSIA..WOLDEMAR KOCH
    FAR AND NEAR EAST.....................DOROTHY JOHNSON ORCHARD
    UNITED STATES AND CANADA............................NORMAN J. WARE
    AUSTRALIA, NEW ZEALAND AND SOUTH AFRICA.........CARTER GOODRICH
    LATIN AMERICA..MAX LEVIN
                                      and JOSEPH J. SENTURIA
    INTERNATIONAL ORGANIZATION.......................LEWIS L. LORWIN

INTRODUCTION. The influence on the forms and policies of trade unions deriving on the one hand from the objective factor of the stage of capitalism and the level of industrial development and on the other from the particular complex of social, economic and political factors determining the character of the working class in a specific country has already been outlined (*see* LABOR MOVEMENT) and is exemplified in detail in the succeeding articles on trade unionism in specific countries.

As a result of the operation of the first influence there may be observed a rather striking similarity of successive stages of trade union structure and policy in the principal industrial countries. This development was marked first by more or less inchoate sporadic and short lived uprisings of labor in general; then by the emergence of local "trades unions" composed of wageworkers drawn not so much from the factory system itself as from the skilled craftsmen and artisans who depended on mutual benefits and control of the supply of workers to enforce their demands; and finally by the rise of the industrial union, which included the semiskilled along with the skilled in factory, mine and transport. Along with this development on occupational and industrial lines there appeared in the second half of the nineteenth century first the local federation in a given municipality designed to protect and advance the supertrade and general interests of all organized groups; and then, as the occupational and industrial groupings achieved national organization, the national federation combining both the national unions and the city central councils, "trades unions" or *bourses du travail*.

In a general way too it was true that in every country the skilled mechanics and those in small enterprises were more highly organized than the factory workers. Even in Germany, despite the adoption of the industrial form of organization, large scale industry was practically untouched by unionism in the pre-war period. Organization was weak among the black coated or white collared proletariat and among agricultural wageworkers. Since these less well organized trades represented the dominant occupations for women, the latter were everywhere far less effectively organized than men. The government employees represented a strong factor in the total trade union membership only in one country, France, where curiously enough the movement was most anti-*étatiste*. The strength of the unions of agricultural workers in Australia was due as much to the capitalistic organization of agriculture as to the character of the working class. In the Latin countries the organizations of agricultural workers took on the character either of sporadic, revolutionary syndicalist organizations or more often of Christian unions.

But this evolution by no means proceeded on a uniform basis with general unions giving way to craft unions, which in turn were succeeded by industrial unions. In the first place, such an advance was hindered by the uneven incidence of industrialization in varying occupations and industries. In certain occupational groupings craft unionism, presumably the hallmark of a past era, found even at the end of the nineteenth century a certain objective basis for its continuance. Moreover varying types of development led even among the industrial unions to the adoption of different bases for organization: the industry (coal mining), the material worked (wood and metal), the type of service rendered (including perhaps allied industries, as in the transport industry) or the character of ownership (government unions). Even the general union, without craft or industrial divisions but distinguished from the general labor movement of the first stage in that it had trade union goals, found a basis for existence in certain localities and among certain groups of workers. At the end of the nineteenth century therefore there were to be found in most trade union federations all forms of unions with varying policies, economic and political. Moreover in the day to day operations of trade unions, in specific industries, regardless of country, there was to be found a similarity caused by objective economic factors; for example, the unions in the construction, printing, coal and garment industries all over the world resembled one another in organization, internal government and relations with employers as much as the movements of a specific country differed from one another. It was no accident therefore that the first impulse to international trade union organization arose in specific crafts rather than among the federations as a whole. The nature of the enterprise and of the market likewise determined to some extent internal organization and government. In the craft unions, particularly in the construction industry, strikes and trade agreements were within the jurisdiction of the local and more particularly of the "business agent." Indeed in most craft organizations the necessity for national organization derived from the migration of workers rather than as in industrial unions from the possibility of the shifting of production from a union to a non-union center. But the conservatism of the craft locals on the one hand and the need for centralization of authority in the national industrial unions on the other confronted both with the problem of internal democracy.

The persistence of the forms described above may be attributed to still another factor inherent in trade unionism—its voluntaristic nature. New forms and policies cannot be created arbitrarily but must grow out of the forces basic to the organized movement itself. It was in large part because of the voluntary action of the groups themselves that the isolated crafts gradually amalgamated or even gave way to industrial unions. So fundamental has been this element of democratic voluntarism that when the national trade union federations were formed, they were given at the outset mainly advisory powers, which would in no way limit the constituent trade unions with respect to either their internal government or their policy on the industrial front. The character of the federation, in other words, was itself the result of the preceding development of isolated occupational and industrial groupings. Only in the realm of what the Germans call *Socialpolitik* were the general working class aims and the influence even of non-proletarian political labor elements perceptible. The one outstanding exception to this rule was the Knights of Labor, which, because of its very disregard of the policies of the stable craft unions and its centralization of executive power and also because it sought to cast aside not only trade but industrial grouping and to return to the earlier form of the general union, met with the opposition not only of the craft unions but of the industrial unions of the coal miners. It is true that the character of none of the federations formed in the last quarter of the nineteenth century was such as to make possible the inclusion of all groups which claimed to be trade unions. The groups which created the federation of German "free" unions were already committed to alliance with the socialist party, and the Christian and liberal trade unions were neither eligible to nor desirous of affiliation with this federation. On the other hand, the craft basis of the American Federation of Labor and the dangers of dual unionism in the United States resulted in the exclusion from membership of those groups which insisted on the extension of another method of organization or policy to the trade union movement as a whole, without the consent of the majority of the constituent federations. Thus the original constituency of the American Federation of Labor not only supplied its initial character but determined its future course. If the working class had already formed strong industrially organized units, the surviving federation might have had another development despite the problems raised by the existence of large masses of immigrant, Negro and women workers among the semiskilled and skilled. As it was, craft exclusiveness was reenforced by the heterogeneous character of the American wageworking population. At this point the character of the working class in the formative period of trade union organization determines not the single and exclusive trade union type or policy but the dominant one. The German and British federations included conservative and exclusive craft unions and the most stable and effective unit within the syndicalist French federation was that of the printers, whose structure and policies resembled the Anglo-Saxon rather than the French type of organization. Nor were these movements free of jurisdictional disputes or the dominance of the most strongly organized group—the skilled workers. In the United States, however, only a few industrial unions developed within the federation: in the mining industries, where the claims of the craft unions over the few skilled engineering craftsmen in each isolated pit town collapsed in the face of the industrial organization of the miners; and in the garment unions, influenced as they were by the European background of the workers, the absence of exclusive craft unionism and the highly competitive nature of the industry. But neither of these unions pressed for the spread of industrial unionism. When the demand for industrial unionism was combined with the demand for revolutionary policy, as in the case of the Industrial Workers of the World, the union found itself outside the dominant federation. The railroad brotherhoods, however, remained aloof from the A. F. of L., in part because of the latter's use of the strike weapon. Undoubtedly this combination of craft exclusiveness with an undeniable militancy in most A. F. of L. unions gave the violently anti-union American industrialists an opportunity to effect a spread of company unionism far greater than in any of the European countries.

The case has been similar with respect to classification of unions as "business," "uplift" or "revolutionary." This classification, made by Hoxie for American trade unions, would group within the first two categories most of the craft unions in the federation, leaving the third only to those outside the federation. But a study of the practises in the field of industrial relations of unions outside the United States would prove that many of them are classifiable as "business" unions as well. Moreover, as Hoxie pointed out, these characteristics describe dominant but not exclusive trends within a given union and are not necessarily true of its entire history. Nor is it correct to identify business unionism with craft unionism and political neutrality; the coal miners' union in the United States was the outstanding protagonist of the "sacredness" of the trade union agreement and despite a strong socialist minority was never a socialist organization. On the other hand, a union committed in the field of *Socialpolitik* to a socialist doctrine might not differ substantially in its bargaining or strike activities from the business union. The militancy of the industrial unions was in most cases a matter of the extent to which they represented small or large group interests, not of their use of certain weapons in contradistinction to those of the craft unions.

Indeed the commitment of a specific union or a trade union federation to a political labor policy was of a lesser direct significance in the field of industrial relations than has commonly been supposed. The dominance of the economic over the political ends in the trade union movement was in point of fact always a source of conflict between the trade union movement and the political labor parties. The trade union movements of both France and the United States, for quite different reasons, rejected the political organization entirely; and it was only because of the victory of the principle of trade union autonomy that the alliance between the economic and political branches of the labor movement in England and in certain continental countries was maintained, the political movement concentrating in the main on certain democratic rights already granted in form in the Anglo-Saxon countries and in France. Generally speaking, even the socialist trade unions have been wary of state intervention, from which indeed they have sought mainly the rights of freedom of association and, in varying degrees, protective legislation. In the United States the fear not only of the basic governmental limitations but also of government intervention has resulted in restricting protective legislation to special groups—women and children. The acceptance of governmental intervention in the form of the English trade boards for the setting of minimum wages is due more to a recognition of realities in the "sweated trades" than to a basic change in philosophy. Vis-à-vis the government the trade unions followed a laissez faire policy which included a keen resentment of legislation that might give the government control over the internal government, policies and finances of the unions. In Australia, which was an exception in this respect, the Labour party was in actual control of the government, and intervention restricted but did not prohibit the right to strike. In countries of new capitalism, especially those of a colonial or semicolonial character, as in Latin America and the Far and Near East, protective legislation has been motivated not by trade union activity but, like Bismarck's social legislation in Germany, by the desire to circumvent trade union organization.

In the period prior to the World War the outstanding characteristic of the trade union movement was its variety among groups in a given country as well as among general federations. Indeed it was not so much a general movement as a series of related groups, except as has been noted in the field of social legislation. The prevalence of one form over another and the tendency to attain certain minima of wages and working conditions were attributable more to voluntary adoption than to fiat or rule. It is true that when menaced by a strong united opposition on the part of employers or by some action of the government, the movement of a particular country responded as a whole; but this response was in the nature of mutual aid and did not commonly involve the use of the weapon of the general strike.

This characteristic nineteenth century development was, however, profoundly affected by the World War and its aftermath. Wartime governmental control of wages and working conditions and the setting up of industrial relations councils sponsored and directed by the state, both a cause and a reflection of the growth of unionism, in favorable circumstances made for a certain standardization. The trade unions in this period assumed a quasi-public character, with the government as an important third party. In the Germanic and in the Scandinavian countries, where labor either was in power or represented a substantial majority in the post-war period, the continuance of this system met with no great opposition. Even more startling was the acceptance of this role by the formerly anti-*étatiste* French labor movement. On the other hand, in the United States and even in England such state "paternalism" declined in the post-war period. The trade unions pressed for governmental intervention, control or even socialization only in the "dying" and the depressed industries. With the onset in 1929 of the period of intense and widespread unemployment the necessity for governmental intervention was accepted generally by trade unions in the United States, apparently in contravention of their traditional attitude. Undoubtedly governmental intervention and social legislation have exerted a leveling influence upon the trade unions and have led them to attempt to work out a more unified common policy.

Even more profound in their effects on traditional trade unionism have been the developments resulting from the rise of fascism and communism. Because both in fascist countries and in Soviet Russia the trade unions are completely controlled by the authoritarian state, which in turn is governed by a single party, and because in both the weapon of the strike hitherto regarded by trade unionism as basic to its existence has been prohibited either directly or indirectly, it has frequently been asserted that the term trade union cannot properly be applied to the bodies which in these countries represent the workers in given occupations or industries. Granted the common loss of autonomy and voluntarism in both fascist and communist countries, the effects and significance are obviously quite different under fascism, where private capitalism is actually in control.

The issue is of significance not only within these countries directly involved but outside of them. Where no authoritarian state has yet been established, trade unions deny that increasing governmental intervention and regulation necessarily represent the seeds of fascism, provided democratic forms of government and the right to strike are maintained. They are in fact more distrustful of communist influence. For the communist parties, reenforced by the defeat of Social Democratic trade unionism in Germany and Austria, refuse to submit to the secondary role played by social democratic parties in the labor movement, with the result that their organized minority groups formerly engaged in "boring from within" the trade unions have been converted into separate communist trade unions. If the influence of these communist trade unions was slight in Germany and is for the present at least negligible in Great Britain and still more so in the United States, where governmental regulation has resulted in the recognition of only one union in a given jurisdiction, it is far more powerful in the countries of "new capitalism." While it is true that in colonial and semicolonial countries of the Far and Near East and in Latin America the craft and neutral unions represent the only groups which have survived political and social upheavals and governmental suppression, the mass labor revolts of these countries present under communist and nationalist leadership possibilities more akin to those of the prerevolutionary Russian labor movement.

Despite the challenge on the right by fascism and on the left by communism and despite the fact that world depression has effected a profound alteration in the relations between trade unions and the state, the mass of the organized wageworkers in Great Britain and its dominions, in the Scandinavian countries, in Holland, Switzerland and in the United States still regard the autonomous voluntary trade union as the basic instrument by which they can maintain and improve their status as workers under capitalism and a democratic form of government. But the need for common action to meet the menace of unemployment as well as the attacks upon trade union rights undoubtedly has given greater significance to the concept of a unified labor movement rather than to that of the loose federation of individual groups which has prevailed in the past. Whatever form this change may take, it is likely profoundly to alter the character of trade unionism even if economic recovery makes possible the continuance of existing forms of capitalism and democratic government.

ELSIE GLÜCK

UNITED KINGDOM AND IRISH FREE STATE. In Great Britain trade unionism, already in existence in certain of the skilled trades throughout the eighteenth century, attained considerable strength with the great growth of wealth and industrial activity which accompanied the earlier stages of the industrial revolution. To a statute of Edward VI (1549), which remained in force and under which all combinations of artificers and craftsmen were prohibited, there were added during the eighteenth century a number of special acts prohibiting combination in particular trades. These prepared the way for the general Combination acts of 1799 and 1800. Passed at a time when the governing class had been scared by the French Revolution, by the rebellion in Ireland and by the naval mutinies of 1797 as well as by the development of unrest in Great Britain over rising war prices and disturbances caused by the industrial revolution, these acts were directed rather against working class combinations which might have a revolutionary political tendency than against mere trade unions as such. Thus in actual enforcement working class combinations in the new textile factory and mining areas were rigidly suppressed, but small trade clubs of urban craftsmen were for the most part left undisturbed and even continued collective bargaining activities with the employers, although it was always possible for a prosecution to be launched in these cases as well. The success of the agitation which led in 1824 to a comprehensive act repealing all the prohibitions against combination was too considerable to last in face of the temper of the time, and an amending act was passed in 1825 recognizing the right of combination but severely restricting its exercise by penal provisions. In the following years trade unionism grew rapidly, aided by the unrest which accompanied the agitation for political reform and by the growth of Owenite socialism. The great outburst of union activity was, however, delayed until after the passing of the Reform Act in 1832. In that year the Builders' Union, consolidating all the separate societies among the various building crafts, was organized; and in the autumn of 1833 Owen's Grand National Consolidated Trades Union, in which he attempted to link up all the trade unions in Great Britain with his own cooperative and socialist movement, was first organized, acquiring a definite constitution in February, 1834. The Grand National after a series of sectional strikes and lockouts collapsed by October, 1834, dragging down with it the Builders' Union and most of the other existing large societies. But many of the societies which had been included in the G.N.C.T.U. remained in being as separate bodies, and within a few years the trade union movement was again growing rapidly. The next attempt to build up an inclusive organization for the whole movement came with the creation of the National Association of United Trades for the Protection of Labour in 1845, a body which combined the aim of mutual assistance in labor disputes with that of establishing cooperative organizations for the employment of labor. Meanwhile in the early 1840's there had been a marked increase of organization among the coal miners, and under the leadership of Martin Jude and others the National Miners' Association was brought into being in 1841, only to fall asunder at the end of the decade into a number of separate county associations. The next great step forward was the creation in 1850–51 of the Amalgamated Society of Engineers, which linked up a number of previously existing societies of skilled engineers and which was regarded as a new model because it was based on high contributions and the provision of substantial friendly benefits as well as on direct action and collective bargaining. It first attained prominence in the great engineering lockout of 1852, in which the employers attempted its destruction by presenting the "document" calling upon their employees to leave the union; but although many workers were compelled to sign the document they did not actually renounce membership, and the A.S.E., which had been greatly aided in the struggle by the Christian Socialists, continued to grow. In the course of the next two decades a number of other "amalgamated societies" were formed on the model of the A.S.E. The leaders of these societies gradually consolidated their position at the head of the trade union movement, especially in connection with the struggle for the extension of the franchise—which led to the Reform Act of 1867 —and for fuller legal recognition of trade unions, which was achieved in the trade union acts of 1871 and 1876, after the renewed repressive measures embodied in the Criminal Law Amendment Act of 1871 had been repealed as the result of agitation in 1875. During the 1860's and 1870's the unions gained many advances in industrial legislation; but the great depression of the later 1870's and the 1880's considerably lessened their fighting strength and compelled them to seek for peace at almost any price. Already in the early 1870's there had been an attempt to extend the scope of the movement beyond the skilled workers represented by the amalagmated societies to the less skilled, and Joseph Arch had succeeded for a few years in the early 1870's in organizing the agricultural laborers. These less skilled workers were unable to maintain their organization during the depression, but with the recovery of 1888–89 there was a fresh wave of organization among the less skilled as well as among the "black-coated" workers, in which the newly recreated British socialist movement took a leading part. The formation of the Miners' Federation of Great Britain in 1888 and the London dock strike of 1889 are the outstanding landmarks of this new period of activity. Although the older leaders prophesied that as soon as trade decreased the less skilled workers' organizations would collapse no less rapidly than they had grown up, this did not happen, and after 1889 British trade unionism came to represent a far wider section of the working class than at any time since 1834. During the 1890's the movement, despite some setbacks, continued to expand and in 1900 the socialists were at length successful in persuading the unions to join in creating the Labour Representation Committee, which in 1906 took the name of Labour party. The first decade of the twentieth century was a period mainly of political agitation; but in face of stationary wages and rising prices and of the influence of syndicalist and industrial unionist ideas imported from the continent and the United States, there was a great wave of labor unrest in the years immediately before the World War. The transport workers' and railwaymen's strikes of 1911 and the national miners' strike of 1912 were the outstanding incidents of this period, but there was also an unprecedentedly large number of small strikes, often called without the sanction of the official leaders. The war interrupted this activity; but under the influence of the wartime demand for labor there was an exceedingly rapid growth of trade union membership, and in the later stages of the war considerable unrest developed in consequence of the "combing out" of men for the army and of the introduction of "dilution" schemes designed to speed up production. When the war ended there was a renewed wave of industrial unrest in the early months of 1919, but the government and the employers, at the price of substantial concessions, succeeded in buying it off until there had been time to complete the process of demobilization; and with the coming of the slump of 1921 the unions were worsted in the great mining struggle of that year, in which the Triple Alliance of Miners, Railwaymen and Transport Workers collapsed. For the next few years the activity of the unions was mainly political, leading up to the Labour government of 1924. After its fall there was a renewal of industrial action which culminated in the national mining dispute and the general strike of 1926. The defeat of this movement and the continuance of trade depression compelled the unions, which had suffered a serious reduction in membership, to follow a cautious policy and to enter into negotiations for better relationships with a group of employers headed by Sir Alfred Mond, which, however, led to no substantial result.

TRADE UNION MEMBERSHIP IN GREAT BRITAIN AND NORTHERN IRELAND, 1892–1932*

Year	Total Number of Unions	Total Membership (In 1000)	Trades Union Congress Number of Societies Represented	Trades Union Congress Number of Members Represented (In 1000)
1892	1233	1576	225	1220
1900	1323	2022	184	1250
1905	1244	1997	205	1541
1910	1269	2565	212	1648
1913	1269	4135	207	2232
1915	1229	4359	215	2682
1919	1360	7926	262	4532
1920	1375	8346	215	6505
1923	1181	5428	194	4369
1925	1165	5505	205	4351
1928	1130	4804	196	3875
1930	1105	4839	210	3744
1932	1060	4441	209	3613

* This membership also includes Irish Free State and oversea branches of unions with headquarters in Great Britain or Northern Ireland. In 1932 total membership of this type numbered 55,000.
Source: For total figures: Great Britain, Ministry of Labour, *Ministry of Labour Gazette*, vol. xli (1933) 361–62. For congress figures: Great Britain, Trades Union Congress, *64th Annual Report 1932* (London 1932) p. 4.

As indicated in the accompanying table, the trade union movement in Great Britain had in 1932 a membership of about 4,500,000 workers, of whom over 3,500,000 belong to unions affiliated with the Trades Union Congress. Of the total membership there are about 750,000 women. The strength of the unions is largely concentrated, although to a somewhat smaller extent than formerly, in certain leading industries. Thus the coal miners account for about 600,000, the cotton workers for nearly 325,000, the engineers for about 475,000, the builders for over 300,000 and the railway workers for about 400,000. There is also a large membership in other forms of transport, but this cannot be ascertained accurately, as the Transport and General Workers' Union includes others besides transport workers. There has also been a great increase in recent years in the number of non-manual workers enrolled in trade unions. Employees of the national and local government, including the Post Office, account for over 350,000, teaching for over 200,000 and distribution for not far short of 200,000. Under the trade union act of 1927, which was passed as a consequence of the general strike and imposed extensive new penal provisions upon the trade unions, non-manual workers in the government service are not allowed to belong to unions including other workers or to affiliate with the T.U.C. or any similar body. Civil servants are well organized in a numerical sense; but their associations have no strike funds and few friendly benefits and are therefore comparatively loose, except in the case of the Post Office and the lower clerical grades. Agricultural organization is very weak, the large post-war trade union movement among the agricultural workers having collapsed in the course of the subsequent depression. Women are strongly unionized only in the textile and clothing trades. In general organization is stronger among the skilled than among the less skilled workers and has shown greater stability in face of the depression, although membership in the mining industry has suffered severely as a result of the struggle of 1926, and membership in the engineering trades has fallen sharply with the contraction of these trades after their wartime expansion.

The trade union movement in Great Britain, unlike those in many of the continental countries but like that in the United States, grew up gradually before the coming of an organized socialist movement. Consequently there has been no imposition of a uniform pattern of trade union organization such as occurred in Germany under Social Democratic influence. The unions have developed separately and then established closer relations, especially since the creation of the Trades Union Congress in the 1860's. The congress, however, has never claimed any extensive jurisdiction over its affiliated bodies, and there is nothing in Great Britain corresponding to the jurisdictional authority of the American Federation of Labor. The T.U.C. since its reorganization immediately after the war has attempted to deal with interunion disputes and to prevent "poaching" for members, but it does not claim the right to decide upon the forms which union organization is to take or to compel its constituent unions to accept an imposed pattern.

Consequently unions of many different kinds exist side by side in Great Britain. The Miners' Federation and the National Union of Railwaymen are the outstanding illustrations of the type of organization by industry, in which the skilled and unskilled belong mainly to the same organization; whereas the Amalgamated Engineering Union (formed as a result of the amalgamation of the A.S.E. and a number of other societies after the war) and the various societies in the printing, building and cotton trades stand for the craft or kindred craft type of organization. A third group consists of the great "general labor" unions. As a result of recent amalgamations these have now been reduced to two: the

National Union of General and Municipal Workers (originally the Gas Workers and General Labourers' Union formed in 1889) and the Transport and General Workers Union (which descends with the aid of amalgamations from the Dockers' Union formed in the same year). The former includes a widely differentiated membership of less skilled workers in many different industries, while the latter consists predominantly of workers in road transport and at the docks but has also a large general labor section with some agricultural workers as well as a substantial membership of clerks and supervisory workers, especially in the waterside trades. Demarcation disputes between trade unions are fairly common but are not usually pushed to an extreme point; and for the most part unions formed on different principles remain without undue jostling inside the T.U.C. Thus the National Union of Railwaymen, as an all grades union, exists side by side with the Associated Society of Locomotive Engineers and Firemen, representing a majority of the footplate grades, with the Railway Clerks' Association and with the numerous craft unions which have members in the railway locomotive and carriage shops; all these unions together with the N.U.R. are affiliated with the T.U.C. In many industries there exist fairly strong federations of trade unions for collective bargaining with the employers' associations. Examples are the Printing and Kindred Trades Federation, the Engineering and Shipbuilding Trades Federation and the National Federation of Building Trades Operatives. The Miners' Federation is of rather a different type, as it consists mainly of local miners' unions in each coal field and not of separate grade associations.

The T.U.C. was for a long time mainly a debating body, designed rather to bring pressure to bear upon Parliament for the removal of grievances and the improvement of industrial legislation than to coordinate industrial action. Until after the war it was governed between congresses by a parliamentary committee concerned mainly with deputations to ministers and similar activities. Only after the war was the congress reorganized as an industrial federation and equipped with a new body, the General Council, possessing a fairly wide but still to a large extent undefined authority over the affiliated unions. The General Council was the body which in 1926 was in effect responsible for declaring the general strike in aid of the miners, although it convened a special conference of trade union executives for the purpose of actually declaring the strike; and it is now recognized as the representative organization of the movement in an industrial sense, the political activities of the T.U.C. having been for the most part transferred to the Labour party.

There is also a smaller body attempting to federate the British trade union movement: the General Federation of Trade Unions, which in return for stipulated contributions provides monetary assistance on fixed scales to unions involved in trade disputes. The G.F.T.U. includes only a fraction of the membership enrolled in the T.U.C. and practically all its larger affiliated bodies are in the congress as well. The G.F.T.U. was, however, until after the war the only British body affiliated to the International Federation of Trade Unions, a position from which it has now been displaced by the T.U.C.

Unlike the situation in many other countries, there are no separate trade unions organized under the auspices of rival movements or tendencies on any considerable scale. Thus there are no separatist Catholic unions; nor are there separate communist unions, although there have been created among members of the ordinary unions a number of left wing unofficial organizations of communist tendency, against which the official trade union movement and the Labour party wage constant war. These groups have succeeded in building up a substantial following among the unemployed, especially through the National Unemployed Workers' Movement. There is also a body, largely communist, called the Minority Movement, which aims at developing left wing opinion inside the trade unions.

Trade unions in practically all industries in Great Britain are recognized by the employers' associations and pursue regular methods of collective bargaining through trade agreements. These are in some cases local, but there has been a growing tendency, especially since the war, to regulate wages, hours and conditions of labor by national bargaining, leaving only supplementary details to be filled in by local negotiations. Certain important firms, especially in the motor trade and other newer industries, refuse to recognize trade unions. The outstanding disputes over recognition in recent years have been in the mining industry, where the employers decline to negotiate with the Miners' Federation as a national body and insist on dealing separately with its constituent county unions. Moreover in some cases local bodies of mine owners in particular coal fields have refused to recognize the county unions and have assisted in the formation of rival unions, which they have subsidized and given preference in employment. This action could hardly have been sustained but for the abnormal depression from which the mining industry has been suffering in recent years.

Where organization is weak and wages have been abnormally low, trade boards and the State Wages Board regulating agricultural wages fix minimum rates of pay and certain conditions of labor; but even in the industries so regulated the unions may agitate or strike for improved conditions. In addition to these two methods of regulating labor conditions there are in existence a large number of joint industrial councils brought into being by the Whitley scheme. The bargaining conducted by these bodies does not differ materially in scope from that carried on by ordinary negotiation before the war. Resort may be had, when the ordinary process of bargaining breaks down, to the system of conciliation and arbitration provided by law. Since the act of 1927, which not only makes "general" strikes definitely illegal but has also restricted to a degree left exceedingly obscure the right of sympathetic strike action, the entire law relating to strikes and trade unions has remained very ambiguous.

Originally the trade unions endeavored to forward their objects in a political sense mainly by deputations to ministers and by lobbying in the House of Commons. The advent of the Labour party, based mainly upon the affiliation of the unions, has altered this situation and caused the unions to undertake political action chiefly through the party, while reserving their right to approach the government directly on any matter in which they are concerned. Generally speaking, relations between the T.U.C. and the Labour party are close. The two bodies together with the Labour members of Parliament are linked together in a National Joint Council, which is the authority for making pronouncements on vital questions of labor and socialist policy, subject to reference to the annual or special meetings of the T.U.C. and the Labour Party Conference.

The trade unions began to take direct political action in promoting their own candidates for Parliament immediately after the Reform Act of 1867, and carried on this activity uninterruptedly until the Osborne judgment in the House of Lords in 1909 held that such activities were unlawful. The effect of this judgment was altered by the trade union act of 1913, which again permitted political activities by the unions, subject to the taking of a ballot and the granting of exemption from payment to the special political fund out of which all payments for political purposes had to be made. The law was changed once more in 1927, when the principle of "contracting in" was substituted for that of "contracting out"; in other words, members had now to sign a form stating their desire to contribute to the political fund before political contributions could lawfully be collected from them. The unions have succeeded in practise in adjusting themselves fairly successfully to this change in the law, and the position of the Labour party has not been materially damaged by it, although of course the collection of political funds has been made more difficult.

With the cooperative movement the trade unions have no direct connection; most of them, however, patronize the Cooperative Wholesale Bank and make arrangements for advances to their members from cooperative societies in prolonged strikes. The Cooperative party has a close working arrangement with the Labour party, and the Cooperative members of Parliament sit there as Labour members, so that the political connection between the cooperative and and trade union movements is close.

The British trade union movement extends to Northern Ireland, except that the Northern Irish textile workers, chiefly in the linen trade, have a separate society of their own, and that a certain number of workers, especially in waterside and road transport, belong to the Irish Transport and General Workers' Union with headquarters in Dublin. A few other Free State unions have members in Northern Ireland, but the main body of the railwaymen and shipyard workers, which are the strongest groups, belongs to the British unions. In the Irish Free State the movement is divided between British and Irish societies; the railwaymen belong chiefly to the British unions, but the Irish Transport and General Workers' Union has most of the remaining transport workers; and the postal workers are also organized in a separate Irish society. The Irish unions, whose membership dropped from 90,000 in 1925–30 to 68,000 in 1931, and many of the branches or districts of the British unions are federated in the Irish Labour party and T.U.C., which has seven representatives in the Lower House of the Free State Parliament. There have been in recent years a number of splits from the British unions resulting in the formation of separate Irish societies. Trade unionism in Ireland has been fairly strong in relation to the comparatively low stage of industrial development. The best remembered incident in Irish trade union history is the famous Dublin transport strike of 1913 led by James Larkin. Irish labor has always been closely associated with the nationalist movement and has in recent years been allied with the De Valera government against the Cosgrave party.

In general British trade unionism, after a great and short lived outburst in the first half of the nineteenth century followed by a serious setback, began to advance steadily among the skilled workers, including the textile operatives and the miners, between 1850 and 1875. It met with a further setback in the great depression of the 1870's and 1880's, grew again rapidly so as to include a large number of the less skilled workers after 1889 and joined with the socialists in forming the Labour party in 1900. In the years immediately preceding the war it passed through a period of active unrest, expanded in membership between 1914 and 1920 and thereafter suffered a substantial decline in consequence of prolonged industrial depression and changes in the structure of industry which lessened the relative importance of the older industries, where trade unionism had its chief strength. The high water mark of trade union membership was reached in 1920, when the movement had nearly 8,500,000 members. From this inflated total, affected by war conditions, it has sunk to less than 5,000,000 as compared with a total wage earning and salaried population of 20,000,000 and an insured population under the unemployment insurance acts of about 13,000,000. But its strength, especially among the manual workers in the leading industries, is much greater than these figures would suggest. It is still by far the most highly organized trade union movement in any important capitalist country.

G. D. H. COLE

See: CHARTISM; FABIANISM.

GERMANY. The revolutionary movement of 1848 in Germany brought forth only tentative steps toward the founding of trade unions. The beginnings of industrialization, although marked by abuses less harsh than those in early capitalist England, created conditions resulting in discontent among the workers, while the differentiation between the interests of the proletarian and those of the artisan remained obscure. The two important associations established at that time upon workers' initiative were the organization of the book printers and that of the cigar makers. The former was built on century old guild traditions and on the viaticum, or travel subsidy fund, an institution which prevailed in a number of skilled craft groups; the latter arose in a new industry. It was characteristic that Stephan Born, the most important labor leader of the time, who led a strike of the Berlin book printers, should have created a general labor organization without setting trade union tasks for it. With the suppression of the 1850's all independent labor organizations were practically wiped out.

More significant beginnings of trade unionism manifested themselves in the middle 1860's with the acceleration of Germany's industrial growth as a capitalist nation. Politically this development was reflected in the creation of the German Empire, which provided for a higher degree of economic unification than was possible in the Zollverein. On the social side the growth of industrialism led to a clear separation of interests between the bourgeoisie on the one hand and the factory workers and a large proportion of the journeymen on the other, to the beginnings of class struggle.

But the continued predominance of political demands in the economic field resulted in a parallel primacy of parties over trade unions; the three outstanding national trade union organizations founded in 1868 were established from above and were essentially political. Two of these were socialistic—the Marxian led by Bebel and the Lassallean led by Schweitzer. The third, the Hirsch-Duncker organization, was closely allied with the progressive party. The program of the Bebel group, with its attempt to balance local and national centers and its provisions for strike control, wage agreements and employment exchanges, was, in contrast to the more centralized and politically oriented Schweitzer group, nearest to the type of national trade union movement ultimately established. Nevertheless, the only significant trade union organizations formed on occupational lines were those of the book printers and tobacco workers, reestablished after 1865. The merging of the two socialist parties after the Gotha congress of 1875 checked the disintegration in trade union ranks which had resulted from their rivalry; but even in 1877 of the 33,000 marks paid in monthly dues by a recorded total membership of 50,000, more than two thirds was contributed by the book printing and tobacco trades.

This slow development cannot be accounted for entirely by legal restrictions; thus the absence of the right of collective bargaining until 1869 hindered only the possibility of striking and not unionization as such. Again, while such political and economic labor organization as had been achieved in this period was apparently destroyed by the antisocialist laws inaugurated in 1878, actual reconstruction proceeded rapidly through local craft societies. That a general mass movement developed in this period (1878–90) is shown by the fact that when the laws were repealed, trade union membership had risen to 121,000. Moreover, although strikes were suppressed by the government, they persisted; and the necessity for cooperation led to the national combination of local societies.

The repeal of the antisocialist laws and the legalization of independent unions made possible the formation in 1890 of the Generalkommission der Gewerkschaften, which was in 1919 transformed into the Allgemeiner Deutscher Gewerkschaftsbund. This commission was the outcome of interunion cooperation in the struggle against the May, 1890, lockout in Hamburg. Although the movement advanced but slowly and its value was underestimated by the Social Democratic party, which had greatly increased its membership under the antisocialist laws, the first trade union congress at Halberstadt, called in 1892 by the Generalkomission declared itself independent of the party.

In the middle 1890's, with the beginning of the great economic upturn in Germany, the trade union movement grew at a rapid rate. The expansion of Germany's heavy industry was accompanied politically by a trend toward imperialism, which in the field of domestic policy incidentally led to social legislation beneficial to the workers. Toward the trade unions themselves the bourgeoisie and the government showed an indecisive attitude. The laws regulating associations annoyed the unions without seriously hampering them. Thus, while unions could be sued but did not enjoy the corresponding right of bringing suit, prosecutions were infrequent and the unions contrived to manage their financial affairs through the medium of trustees. In the same way, although the law provided special punishments for offenses committed in connection with strikes and indeed entrusted the entire handling of strikes to the arbitrary will of the police, a bill for the imprisonment of strikers was defeated by the Reichstag on its first reading in 1899.

Despite many adverse court decisions the unions grew amazingly in the two decades before the World War, carried on many important strikes and concluded trade agreements covering a majority of their membership. The predominance of the "free" (Social Democratic) unions over the Hirsch-Duncker unions continued, but after 1900 the Christian unions developed rapidly. On wage struggles the three groups generally stood together, after each had established its position, and organizationally they were similar in every detail. All three union movements were represented in the Reichstag by leading members of the related parties, which enjoyed great influence in the unions partly because of their parliamentary status. This period likewise was marked by a final entente between the "free" trade unions and the Social Democratic party. At first certain elements in the party saw in the unions the rise of a new independent power which would rival its leadership and narrow its influence in the field of *Sozialpolitik*. But whereas the party congress of 1896 disclosed such antagonism and the congress of 1905 developed into a bitter struggle on the issue of the general strike—the trade unions fearing, with reason, that they would suffer from the purely political application of their basic weapon by an organization lacking their dearly bought experience—in the following year both groups arrived at an understanding which was mutually satisfactory. Cooperation was more easily achieved since every leading trade unionist was a party member and most party leaders continued membership in their respective unions.

The numerical strength of trade unions after 1890 is shown in the following table. The degree of organization of all workers can be estimated roughly if this membership is compared with the total number of workers reported in the occupational census. On this basis the percentage of trade union organization in 1882 was 1; in 1895, 3.5; in 1907, 20; in 1925, 34. For women workers the corresponding percentages for 1907 and 1925 were 6 and 26. These figures show a remarkable expansion of trade unions from 1895 to 1907. On the other hand, they indicate that, despite the tremendous influx during the period of post-war inflation, which accounts for the relative increase of 70 percent from 1907 to 1925, important sectors of the working population were never brought into the unions.

Membership of German Trade Unions, 1891–1931

Year	Free Trade Unions — Associations	Free Trade Unions — Number of Members (in 1000) Total	Free Trade Unions — Number of Members (in 1000) Women	Hirsch-Duncker Unions — Associations	Hirsch-Duncker Unions — Number of Members (in 1000) Total	Hirsch-Duncker Unions — Number of Members (in 1000) Women	Christian Trade Unions* — Associations	Christian Trade Unions* — Number of Members (in 1000) Total	Christian Trade Unions* — Number of Members (in 1000) Women
1891	62	278		18	66				
1896	51	329	15	17	72			8	
1900	58	680	23	20	92		23	79	
1905	64	1345	74	20	117		18	188	12
1910	53	2017	162	23	123		22	295	22
1913	49	2574	230	23	107	6	25	343	28
1919	52	5479	1193	19	190	18	25	858	160
1920	52	7890	1711	17	226	22	25	1077	215
1921	49	7568	1518	17	225	23	19	986	232
1922	49	7895	1688	21	231	20	19	1049	263
1923	44	7138	1526	21	185	16	18	938	230
1924	41	4618	921	20	147	13	18	613	154
1925	40	4156	752	21	158	12	19	588	137
1926	38	3977	659	18	163	12	19	532	113
1927	38	4150	651	22	168	13	18	606	122
1928	35	4654	712	22	168	13	18	647	124
1929	35	4906	723	24	169	13	18	673	126
1930	31	4822	685	22	198	12	18	659	113
1931	30	4418	618	23	181	11	18	578	94

* Affiliated with the Christian trade unions beginning in 1925 is the Gesamtverband deutsches Verkehrs und Staatsbediensten with an additional membership of about 120,000 not included in these figures.

Source: For free trade unions: Allgemeiner Deutscher Gewerkschaftsbund, *Jahrbuch 1931* (Berlin 1932) p. 298–99. For Hirsch-Duncker unions, 1891–1925, and for Christian trade unions, 1896 to 1905: Cassau, J., *Die Arbeitergewerkschaften* (Halberstadt 1927) statistical Appendix, p. 1. For Hirsch-Duncker unions, 1926–31: Germany, Statistisches Reichsamt, *Statistisches Jahrbuch für das Deutsche Reich* for 1929–32. For Christian trade unions, 1905–31: *Jahrbuch der christlichen Gewerkschaften, 1932* (Berlin 1932) p. 52.

The greatest organizational strength prior to the World War was among the skilled workers in shops employing from 10 to 1000 hands; that is, in small and middle sized plants. Such labor was well organized not only in the large cities but also in smaller cities and towns. Apprenticed assistants to well organized skilled workers were sometimes organized in the same local unions or less frequently in special helpers' unions, as in the book printing trade. In the transport industry and in commerce apprenticed helpers were organized in metropolitan areas. Municipal employees were more thoroughly organized than those in the federal, postal and railroad services. Workers in the heavy industries, women workers and agricultural wageworkers were relatively unorganized.

A comparable survey of organization by industries is impossible by reason of the very structure of the unions. Such a comparison would be feasible, it is true, in the case of the national industrial unions. But some unions were organized on the basis of materials involved (woodworkers and metal workers); others were craft organizations (bookbinders, printers, machinists, painters); and still others were general unions (factory workers). Indeed the problem of organizational structure and differentiation has been the subject of frequent controversy in trade union congresses, with the metal workers persistently demanding compulsory industrial unionism, while the majority of the national unions advocated voluntary mergers and amalgamations, supplemented by cooperation in the negotiation of wage agreements. The latter position was finally adopted by the movement as a whole. In point of fact the number of national unions steadily diminished through mergers, so that finally pygmy and giant unions were to be found side by side.

In 1929 of the 4,906,000 members of the free trade unions the metal workers accounted for 965,000, or about 20 percent; public employees and transport 700,000, or 14 percent; the federation of building workers 490,000, or 10 percent (together with the roofers, painters, building carpenters, 14 percent); and factory workers 470,000, or 9.6 percent. Other large unions were those of the miners (198,000), railroad employees (251,000), woodworkers (315,000), food and beverage workers (179,000) and textile workers (297,000). At the other extreme were the precious stone setters with a membership of 3000, the coppersmiths with 7300, the barbers with 4500 and other small craft unions. In the Christian unions, whose aggregate membership amounted to 673,000, the largest unions were the metal workers (124,000) and the miners (103,000). These industries account for the majority of the membership of the Hirsch-Duncker unions as well. Over half of the 712,000 women in the "free" unions were distributed among the textile workers (171,000), the factory workers (94,000), the public employees (81,000) and the metal workers (71,000).

The structure and policies of the national unions were worked out in the pre-war period. They developed sound financial systems, raised their dues, introduced new types of membership benefits and generally expanded their activities. Despite the fear that the introduction of social insurance would deprive the unions of important spheres of activity, experience showed that union benefits, such as those supplementing the public sickness insurance systems, tended to insure steadiness of membership and to swell treasury reserves. Moreover unions early provided certain benefits not available through public funds: travel subsidies, accident and emergency insurance, legal defense, strike allowances, now and then tool insurance and to an increasing extent unemployment insurance.

In the national unions, whether organized along industrial or craft lines, the basic unit was the craft local, in which the vocation of the individual worker was the criterion determining his membership. The municipal employees alone represented a not wholly successful effort to organize along industrial lines. Within a given locality, however, the members of the craft locals of one central organization were territorially united. All members employed in one shop or factory constituted a unit which had its own delegate or shop steward. Between the local and the national organization stood the district organization. The power to determine policies in wage agreements and strikes varied with the nature of the industry and the union; but in general, with the increasing need for a unified wage and strike policy throughout the Reich, there was a strong tendency toward centralization in the national unions, subordinate functions being parceled out to district and local executives and shop functionaries. The leaders of these unions, both local and national, were generally elected every two or three years by the congress of the union or the membership of the town, and in every case were workers who had risen from the ranks. Coupled with the realization that the fighting strength of the union depends upon the confidence of the membership in the leaders this was sufficient to compel the adoption of policies approved by the majority, even though in details the leadership could override the rank and file. The power of the leaders in national unions was so great that they were disinclined to subordinate it to an interunion organization; before the World War the latter resembled joint advisory boards rather than genuine executive bodies.

Trade agreements, which had been known to the book printers for decades, were introduced in the well organized industries about 1900, usually as the result of severe struggles, especially strikes. Labor struggles were aimed especially at shortening hours of labor, but wage rises also were often obtained. In part these were achieved not through strikes alone but also through the skilful utilization of the labor exchanges early set up by trade unions; eventually these agencies were in many cases placed under the joint administration of the union and the municipality. The rapid spread of strikes at the end of the first decade of the twentieth century induced the government to intervene in major controversies and to force the adoption of agreements. Similarly the Reich Bureau of Statistics soon began to devote particular attention to drawing up and submitting wage schedules. These agreements were made mainly with employers' organizations which, as bodies dealing with industrial relations rather than as general associations of industrialists or as craft guilds, developed later than the trade union movement. Only in the heavy and large scale industries was the policy of employers' associations one of unconditional struggle against the unions, but even in some of these, as in the iron and textile industries, occasional concessions were won. In the mining and steel industries the influence of the unions was an indirect one; in prosperous times the employers had to meet their organized workers halfway and could not avoid the influence of general wage increases. Indeed the "pace maker" system by which well organized and strategic crafts, chiefly in the building trade, pulled other groups along with them as they obtained increases played an important role in all wage struggles in the pre-war period.

The World War on the whole caused no drastic change in trade union policies. It resulted at first in a complete tie up of union activities because of the *Burgfrieden* and unemployment. But with the expansion of the war industries, governmental wage fixing in the interests first of munitions production and later as a general system of industrial arbitration as well as the introduction of worker representatives in all factories imposed new and important tasks upon the unions. On the other hand, an attitude of aloofness from purely political activity developed in the "free" unions because of the split in the Social Democratic party in 1917, a split from which they, unlike the other two union federations, suffered.

The developments in the field of governmental wage fixing during the war and even further in the revolutionary period marked a new role for the unions both in direct industrial relations and in the field of *Sozialpolitik*. The revolution produced simultaneously a mass influx into the unions and a potential threat to their strength from the workers' councils (*see* INDUSTRIAL RELATIONS COUNCILS). These councils, made up of workers' representatives in each factory, were in 1918 called workers' councils, after the Russian model. The unions, materially aided by their established tradition, quickly succeeded in adapting the councils to their own needs and in transforming them into a new organizational base. The shop councils law (decree of 1918, law of 1920), which gave to workers wide protection against discharge, strengthened the unions and relieved officials of many tasks by introducing into all factories a system of training in industrial self-government for delegates who had a more intimate knowledge of factory conditions than was possible for any trade union functionary and who, vested with full discretionary powers, were able to take the initiative in dealing with questions of detail. Far more difficult than this problem was that of absorbing permanently the influx of new members into the unions.

Other fields of union activity were also opened up. The least fruitful was that resulting from the heated controversies over the socialization of industry: the unions were too occupied with problems arising from their large new membership and too hesitant to accept the economic responsibility involved. Although during the inflation period they did participate in export control, the only enduring result of attempts at industrial democracy was the participation of the miners' union in the administration of the coal and the potash industries. A similar participation in the iron industry never became firmly established. This very activity, however, led to continued dissensions, because other unions maintained that miners' representatives were more concerned with the interests of their particular groups than with the interests of the trade union movement as a whole. Eventually this type of activity, although it was continued, became entirely removed from the purview of the masses. A more significant and effective task was the participation of the unions in the National Economic Council; basically, however, it did not differ from the advisory participation of Social Democratic members of the Reichstag in the drafting of industrial legislation in the previous decades.

The outstanding results of the revolution for the trade union organizations were in the field of social legislation. The legislative eight-hour day freed them at one blow from the need of fighting for shorter hours. This was a gift of the times for which they did not have to battle and which they could not retain in full. Even more important was the new legislation on trade agreements introduced in 1918, which authorized the minister of labor to extend, under certain conditions, the force of an agreement to unorganized workers and which made impossible individual underbidding of a general trade agreement. Collective agreements which prior to the war had covered about 1,400,000 persons rose to a high point in 1922, when they included 14,250,000 workers.

Through these various measures, including the shop councils legislation, the free trade unions gained a much stronger position politically in the Social Democracy and consequently in the eyes of the general public. In the short period of its post-war existence the Independent Social Democratic party met with little success in its efforts to capture the unions. Even less successful were the Communists, who, after attempting to bore from within by establishing separate cells in every shop and local, embarked on a policy of dual unionism, setting up rival organizations among clothing workers, miners, building workers and railwaymen. When the A.D.G.B. adopted the policy of expulsion, the Communist tactics were again reversed and the separate unions dissolved (1924), a portion of their membership again becoming part of the free unions.

In the period following the stabilization of 1924 the political power of the unions was very limited, a significant factor in view of the increasing importance of social legislation. Government action taken with respect to the eight-hour day, wage rates and unemployment relief—the three dominant issues of social policy—was influenced by economic conditions, especially as reflected in the unemployment situation. Immediately after stabilization unemployment was still held within restricted limits. Although it showed signs of increase in 1926, the following two years brought noticeable improvement. From 1929, however, there was a catastrophic rise in the number of unemployed trade union members. Whereas in 1924 of the membership of the free unions 8.1 percent were wholly and 6.5 percent partially unemployed, in 1929 the percentages had risen to 20.3 and 8.2, in 1930 to 31 and 16.3 and in 1933 to 45.6 and 22.2, with only 32.3 of the membership totally employed, and this despite the loss of almost half the membership of the early post-war period.

Unemployment relief, which had been so outstanding an achievement of the revolution, viewed both as support for the unemployed and as a weapon in wage struggles, was applied with more and more restrictions in the crisis years. Dissatisfaction with the relief situation caused considerable disquiet among the trade union rank and file, who saw the new developments as an unmitigated retreat, despite the fact that even in its altered form relief remained a bulwark of the general wage level. Similar retreats seemed unavoidable on the other two issues. The eight-hour law of 1918 was considerably limited by the ordinance of December 21, 1923, and only in well organized industries and in times of prosperity could the workers maintain their status in this respect. The increase in part time employment during the crisis robbed this issue of its immediate importance. Finally, money wage rates, which during the years 1925–27 had kept pace with the cost of living and which had risen more rapidly from 1928 through 1930, began to decline in 1931. Although the greater decline in the cost of living index meant in effect an actual increase in real wages, the money wage decrease irritated the union rank and file, especially as it was accompanied by a reduction in the hours of employment, a steady rise of total and partial unemployment and failure of the union efforts in "creation of work," which for some time had been their chief slogan.

The unions, unable to maintain the high membership figures of the inflation period, underwent a steady decline until 1926, when a rise set in. Membership figures held up well until 1931, although as early as the summer of that year a third of all members of the independent unions were unemployed. The income of the independent unions in 1930 no longer covered expenditures, despite the fact that their income in 1931 was larger than that in 1927. In 1933 there began a new decline. The seizure of the independent unions on May 2, 1933, under the Nazi dictatorship and the subsequent capture of the other trade union groups occurred without opposition. The entire trade union apparatus, apparently intact, passed into the hands of the National Socialists, who merged trade unions and employers' federations as a unit in the groups of the *Arbeitsfront*.

THEODOR CASSAU

See: ARBEITSGEMEINSCHAFT; NATIONAL SOCIALISM, GERMAN.

AUSTRIA, SWITZERLAND AND HOLLAND. The trade union movements of Austria, Switzerland and Holland developed somewhat later than that of Germany because of the later industrialization of these countries and in the pre-war period were characterized by more divisions, due to special problems in each country, such as Czech separatism in Austria and a powerful syndicalist tendency in Holland. From the beginning of the twentieth century the free trade unions in all three countries followed closely in structure and policy the German socialist unions, attaining, except in Holland, a position of dominance in the economic field as well as in social legislation.

Although as early as 1848 revolutionary workers' organizations stressed the problem of unemployment and put forward economic demands, trade unionism in Austria did not develop to any considerable extent until the end of the century. Factors which hindered its growth were not only a late and dispersed industrial development and legislation restricting workers' freedom of association but also a high rate of illiteracy among the masses and the existence of diverse and conflicting nationalities. Even after 1867, when the right of association was formally granted, innumerable obstacles were placed in the path of the trade unions by the government. It was not until the 1890's, after the resolution of conflicts within the political labor movement through the reorganization of the Social Democratic party and following a period of economic expansion, that the trade union membership, which in 1892 was estimated at 47,000, was united under a trade union commission similar to that set up in Germany for the free trade unions. The movement was, however, considerably hampered not only by continued official persecution but by internal dissension on organizational principles and by conflicts between the German-Austrian and the Czech trade unionists. Although the latter had already been given a degree of autonomy, they split off in 1897. Despite the close ties between the Austrian and the German "free" trade unions the German organizational scheme was taken over only gradually. But after 1903 the total trade union membership rose from 135,000 to 482,000 in 1908, of which perhaps 20,000 were accounted for by a number of Christian trade unions which had sprung up at the turn of the century and were federated in 1902. The free trade unions thus included over a fifth of the total wage and salaried population of the country, and in such trades as printing the percentage of organized workers rose to over 90. Other well organized groups were those of the miners, the harbor workers, the building and textile workers. At the outbreak of the World War the free trade unions were in a strong position and had put through wage contracts covering an important part of their membership. A third trade union grouping arose in 1908 under the sponsorship of the German nationalist workers' protective league, including chiefly railroad workers and commercial employees.

The prestige of the trade unions, which increased throughout the war despite many difficulties, resulted under the republic in a series of measures creating shop councils, regulating wage agreements and setting up chambers of labor, to which all legislative enactments were submitted before their introduction into parliament. The membership of the free trade unions had risen by 1921 to a peak of over a million, or over half of the total working population. Although this number had declined to 828,000 in 1924 and to 750,000 in 1929, the free trade unions still accounted for over 80 percent of the total trade union membership, as compared with about 8 percent for the Christian unions and less than 5 percent each for the nationalist and neutral unions. Included in the ranks of the free trade unions were virtually all of the organized industrial wage earners, over 75 percent of the organized salaried employees in private employment, 50 percent of the organized public employees and over 25 percent of the organized household and agricultural workers. The Christian, nationalist and neutral unions drew their membership mainly from public, household and agricultural employment. In 1927 an attempt of the Heimwehr movement to set up trade union affiliates resulted in the establishment of only a few insignificant groups. Nor was there any considerable weakening of the free trade unions by communist influence. Nevertheless, this powerful movement, reenforced by well organized benefit, educational and credit institutions, was dissolved in February, 1934, after the struggle between the government and the Social Democratic forces; in its place the government is attempting to create under its own domination a single trade union movement.

As early as the 1830's and 1840's Swiss workers came in contact with the radical political currents originating in Germany. But the development of a Swiss trade union movement was hampered by the dominance of handicrafts and homework. The so-called Grütli organizations included non-proletarian elements and were class collaborationist in character. Only among the book printers, the workers in the watch industry and to a lesser extent the embroidery workers were effective non-political organizations with trade union aims created prior to the 1870's, and in these unions both factory and homeworkers were included. In other crafts and industries the foundations were laid by local craft societies, which gradually federated. An attempt to set up a Swiss Workers' Congress in 1873 failed to include the two most powerful unions and split on political issues arising out of the First International. It was only with the founding of the Allgemeiner Schweizerischer Gewerkschaftsbund in 1880 as an interunion organization of the socialistic unions that trade unionism began to develop on any considerable scale. Although this organization in 1900 declared itself politically neutral, Christian trade unions founded at the turn of the century formed their own federation in 1907. The growth of the free trade unions was especially marked in the two years preceding the World War, and after the war there was a strong trend toward amalgamation of related unions. The influence of revolutionary currents in Germany and Austria led to a temporary radicalization of the Swiss unions manifested most seriously in the capture of control of the Basel trade union center by Communists. In 1930 the free trade union federation had over 200,000 members, the quasi-evangelical group 6000, the Christian nationalist unions 23,000 and a nationalist federation founded in 1919 only 2000 members. Among the free trade unions the largest single unit is that of the clock and watch workers with 61,000 members, followed by the union of building and woodworkers, the railway workers' union and public service organizations.

In addition to the hampering factors of belated industrial development and restrictive legislation the Dutch trade union movement has suffered from the outset from divisions along both political and religious lines. Although mutual aid and educational societies were established among the typographers even prior to the granting of freedom of association in 1872, continual political dissension between Marxian and syndicalist groups delayed the founding of free trade unions of the type which prevailed in the Germanic countries. Among the Catholic workers local trade union groups arose as early as 1888. In 1893 under syndicalist influence the Nationaal-Arbeids Secretariaat was founded, but its membership of nearly 16,000 was almost completely lost after the failure of a general strike in 1903. As a result of this development it was not until 1906 that there was set up the Nederlandsch Verbond van Vakvereenigingen with the powerful, independent diamond workers' union as its core and with a membership of about 19,000. In 1909 the Catholic trade unions federated into a central body, and there was also established a federation of trade unions among the evangelical workers' organizations.

As in other countries, the year 1920 witnessed a considerable growth in membership of all groups; the free trade unions numbered 250,000 members, the Catholic organization 158,000, the evangelical organizations 76,000 and the revived syndicalist union 49,000. In 1924 a Communist trade union federation was established, but it had no appreciable following. The persistence of the divisions in the Dutch trade union movement is shown by the figures for 1930, when the total membership was 624,500, representing over a third of the total employed population. The independent unions accounted for about 40 percent, the Catholic unions for over 21 percent, the evangelical groups for 11 percent, the syndicalists for 3 percent, the neutral federations for about 6 percent, the non-affiliated trade unions for 18 percent and the Communist trade unions for less than 1 percent.

THEODOR CASSAU

SCANDINAVIAN COUNTRIES AND FINLAND. A mass trade union movement developed later in the Scandinavian countries than in the great industrial states. Indeed the former, poor in coal and lying on the periphery of the west European economic sphere, had no industrial proletariat until the last quarter of the nineteenth century. At about the turn of the century, with the industrial exploitation of the iron mines in the north of Sweden and the great water power resources of Norway and the development of the pulp and paper industry in Finland and Sweden, trade unions began to take on importance. Even today, however, the proportion of the population of these countries engaged in industry is still relatively small and the principal industries are territorially scattered. The oldest sectors of the trade union movement arose among the skilled urban craftsmen, whose psychology has given the Scandinavian movement its characteristic features. A real agrarian proletariat exists only in southern Sweden and Finland. There has developed, however, as a result of the heavy population increase in the nineteenth century a semiproletariat of poor small and tenant farmers who supplement their income by working for well to do peasants or in the lumber and road building industries.

The trade union organizations of Sweden, Norway, Denmark and Finland have from the outset maintained close contact with one another since the first inter-Scandinavian labor congress in 1886 and have tended in some respects to develop uniformly. After a preliminary period marked by liberal ideology their political concepts came to be influenced primarily by the German Social Democracy, although English models have had greater influence upon trade union tactics and practical politics, especially in Sweden and Norway.

Trade unions appeared first in Denmark during a period of economic prosperity in the early 1870's but were almost wiped out in the ensuing crisis. The movement was revived in the 1880's under Social Democratic leadership. By 1898, when the national craft unions established a central federation (De Samvirkende Fagförbund i Danmark), approximately one third of the industrial workers were organized. After the great lockout of 1899 an understanding was reached with the employers' organizations, which included trade union recognition and the establishment of voluntary arbitration tribunals. This is still the basis of the Danish labor law. During the next twenty years, which witnessed a further development of the system of legalizing and regulating labor disputes, there was less interference from revolutionary labor tendencies in Denmark than in the other Scandinavian countries. Neither syndicalists nor communists have been able to win a significant following in the Danish unions. The Social Democratic party, on the other hand, has had a most decisive influence, although the organizational connection has been less close than in the other Scandinavian countries. In recent years legislative action and judicial attitudes, including the introduction of a form of the labor injunction, have led to restrictions upon trade union activity.

Despite the earlier industrialization of Sweden the trade union movement, with the exception of a few craft unions, did not develop until the rise of the Social Democracy in the 1880's. The party emphasized trade union organization because plutocratic electoral laws at that time restricted its political effectiveness. Not only was it the centralizing agency for the trade unions in their early years, but even after the founding of a central trade union federation (Landsorganisation i Sverige) in 1898 the connection remained very close: the local trade unions were collectively affiliated with the party, and the problem of the non-socialist members was solved after 1908 by their exemption from the payment of party dues. Neither the Svenska Arbetareforbund formed in 1899 on the Hirsch-Duncker model nor the "yellow" unions gained any considerable membership. The former never had more than 15,000 members and practically disappeared after its participation in the general strike of 1909, which decimated the ranks of the Landsorganisation as well.

Syndicalist tendencies, however, obtained considerable sway after 1905 and in 1910 were organized into the Sveriges Arbetares Centralorganisation. Its membership, which in 1927 reached 37,000, was recruited from among migratory and unskilled workers—lumberjacks, loggers, road workers, miners in the Lapland pits—essentially the same groups which constituted the I.W.W. in the United States. In the beginning of 1928 of its 28,000 members 16,000 were in the construction industry. The Landsorganisation in 1928 made an unsuccessful attempt to absorb the syndicalist federation, but it did ally some groups, and syndicalist unions declined from 37,000 members in 1927 to 19,600 at the end of 1928. The first revolutionary faction in the Social Democratic unions, organized in 1917 by the Zimmerwaldian left and known since 1919 as the Fackliga Propaganda Förbund, also had syndicalist leanings and later became the channel for Communist ideology. The Communists, who had split off from this opposition in 1921, acquired a considerable following during the deflation crisis, especially in the new and rapidly developed industries. But when the Communist party itself split in 1929, at a time when it claimed a membership of some 90,000 workers in the opposition, its influence was lessened considerably. Although the Communists retained followers in the largest unions, those of the metal workers, the factory workers and the sawmill workers, the Social Democratic forces became stronger than ever before. In the cities of southern Sweden 80 to 100 percent of the trade unionists in 1929 were members of the Social Democratic party; in the north the proportion was smaller. The Swedish trade unions, unlike those in other industrial countries, have added to their post-war gains in membership.

A movement more serious in its potential socio-political implications has arisen through the alliance of the semiproletarian peasants with industrial employers. This class, dependent on part time employment in the lumber and road building occupations, was adversely affected by the policy not only of the "closed shop" but of the "closed union" adopted, despite its rejection by the Landsorganisation, by some unions because of the intensified competition for jobs, especially in industries producing for the domestic market. In 1923 therefore they formed an organization known as the Freedom of Labor, attacking the trade unions sporadically by food strikes and other forms of direct action. The employers who saw their reserve of cheap labor threatened took sides with the peasants, farmers and landlords in the south and joined the "freedom" movement in order to break the agricultural laborers' union; in 1928 a general press campaign was opened against "trade union monopolism," an employers' defense fund was established and several amendments to the labor laws restricting the unions' freedom of action were successfully sponsored. The consequences of this situation become clear when it is realized that the still weak National Socialist movement has won its support mainly from these elements and that in the other Scandinavian countries a similar combination of forces has led to attacks on trade unionism. Although Sweden since the fall of 1932 has had a Social Democratic government, it is a minority government; and in the spring of 1933 it had to face a united right front, undeniably fascist in character.

The tardy development of the Norwegian trade union movement may be attributed to the later rise of large capitalist industrialism and to the fact that until Norway's separation from Sweden in 1905 the independence movement deflected interest from social questions. Furthermore the political labor movement had the wind taken out of its sails by the reformist policies of the powerful left bourgeois party, *Venstre*. It was the trade unions which inspired the establishment in 1887 of the *Norske Arbeiderparti*; this labor party in its first twenty years resembled the British Labour party more closely than it did the Social Democratic parties in Sweden and Denmark but was thereafter more radical than either. Radicalization in the unions resulted from the influence both of American industrial unionism and of anarcho-syndicalist ideas propagated by the Swedish migratory workers. The left wing, which gained strength after the great lockout of 1911 and was organized in 1913 in the Norske Fagopposition, won a greater following than did the analogous Swedish opposition. And when, during the second period of industrial expansion in the years immediately before and after the World War, trade unionism increased its membership among the workers in the new industries, this radical tendency was strengthened. Although the moderate wing continued in control of the trade union central body (Arbeidernes Faglige Landsorganisation, founded in 1899), the opposition in 1918 captured the leadership of the labor party. In 1919 the party joined the Third International. Even after its expulsion therefrom in 1923 the existence of continued splits within the party, which would have endangered the trade union front, led the trade union central to dissolve its organizational contact. Despite the fact that in 1927 the Social Democrats, who had organized in a reformist wing in 1919, reunited with the labor party and that cooperation between the trade union and the party has since been reestablished, collective party membership of the unions has not been restored.

In Norway too the crisis has resulted in fascist tendencies particularly in the peasant party. An antiboycott law of the spring of 1933 especially aimed to guarantee the provision of lumber to industries and to extend the liability of trade unions.

The trade union movement of Finland emerged in the 1890's simultaneously with the Social Democratic party but was hindered by its necessity to fight not only the Finnish bourgeoisie but the Russian czarist government. When in 1905 some of the legal restrictions were removed, the Finnish trade union league founded in 1907 was confronted with well organized employers' associations. During the World War the labor shortage and the tolerant attitude of the government favored the growth of the trade unions, whose high point was reached after the Russian Revolution of 1917, when the Social Democratic party despite its adhesion to the resolutions of the Zimmerwald Conference joined a coalition government, in which the chairman of the trade union league was premier. This position of power was not long maintained. After the Russian Bolshevist Revolution the White military forces in control in the north attacked the radical labor organizations. The counter movement of revolutionary workers, which established a workers' government in Helsingfors, was crushed in April, 1918. After a half year of complete suppression of trade unions a transition was made late in 1918 to parliamentary democracy. The reorganized trade unions won some successes in the field of social reform, such as the adoption of the eight-hour day and recognition of the right of agricultural workers to organize. In 1920 a powerful Communist faction acceded to power in the trade union league; in 1928 of the 90,000 organized members 70,000 were reported as Communists. The rise of the Lappo movement inaugurated a period of general suppression and persecution of the unions because of their connection with the Communist party, which had been illegal since 1923. With the achievement of relative calm after the elections of 1930 the Social Democrats founded a new, non-political trade union league with a membership of about 30,000, whose expansion, however, was restricted by the crisis. Moreover the patriotic league which replaced the suppressed Lappo movement in the spring of 1933 has renewed the fight against Social Democracy and the trade unions.

The following table shows the growth of trade union membership in the four countries as well as the degree of centralization in the federations. The proportion of this trade union membership to the working population in 1930 was as follows: of the non-agricultural workers, employees and officials more than 70 percent were organized in Denmark and Sweden, some 50 percent in Norway and at most 33 percent in Finland. The organization of the agricultural and forestry workers and domestic employees is much weaker. Employees and officials are not so widely organized as they were in Germany before 1933, and not all of their unions are

GROWTH OF TOTAL TRADE UNION AND OF CENTRAL FEDERATION MEMBERSHIP IN SCANDINAVIAN COUNTRIES
1906–31
(In 1000)

	SWEDEN TOTAL	SWEDEN CENTRAL FEDERATION	DENMARK TOTAL	DENMARK CENTRAL FEDERATION	NORWAY TOTAL	NORWAY CENTRAL FEDERATION	FINLAND TOTAL
1906	180	144	98*	89*	25		
1913	136	97	152	114		64	27
1915	152	111	174	134		78	30
1920	402	280	355	273		143	59
1923	363†	313	299	233	93	86	47
1928	530	469	314	156	108	106	90
1931	639	589	354	269		145	20

* For 1907, the earliest figures available.
† The survey on which this figure is based was taken in 1923–24.
Source: For Sweden: Total figures for 1928 and 1931 and all central federation figures from Landsorganisationen i Sverige, Stockholm, *Berättelse* for 1907, p. 4, for 1929, p. 2, for 1931, p. 5, and for 1933, p. 377; other total figures from *Internationales Handwörterbuch des Gewerkschaftswesens*, vol. ii (Berlin 1932) p. 1423, Woytinsky, W., *Die Welt in Zahlen*, vol. ii (Berlin 1925) p. 92, 132, and Hansson, S., *The Trade Union Movement of Sweden*, International Trade Union Library, no. 6 (Amsterdam 1927) p. 41. For Denmark: Statistiske Departement, *Statistisk Aarbog* for 1908, p. 132, for 1915, p. 140, for 1917, p. 160–61, for 1923, p. 134, for 1925, p. 128–29, for 1929, p. 125–26, and for 1932, p. 130–32. For Norway: Total figures for 1906 and 1923 and central federation figures for 1913 from Woytinsky, W., *Die Welt in Zahlen*, vol. ii (Berlin 1925) p. 92, 94; total figure for 1928 from *International Trade Union Movement*, vol. x (1930) 86; central federation figures for 1915–31 from Statistiska Centralbyrå, *Statistisk årbok for kongeriket Norge* for 1916, p. 107, for 1924, p. 162, and for 1933, p. 145. For Finland: Bureau Central de Statistique, *Annuaire statistique* for 1933, p. 276 (includes only legal trade unions).

affiliated with the central organizations. All the central bodies except that of Norway belong to the International Federation of Trade Unions (Amsterdam International). Some individual Norwegian unions are affiliated with sections of the Amsterdam International, while others are connected with the Red Trade Union International.

As in most countries, the federated and amalgamated union has gradually replaced the craft unions. But the principle of industrial unionism, despite energetic propaganda by the radical groups, has been adopted only in a few industries. The unions of Norway, Sweden and Denmark are marked by a high degree of centralization of authority in the executives, both in the individual unions and in the federations, well elaborated relief systems and comprehensive labor cultural activities. The unions are also in close contact with the consumers' cooperative organizations.

In these three countries the system of regulated collective agreements is general, although in Norway it is opposed in principle by the left wing and in practise is limited to short term contracts. For some time it was threatened in Sweden by the use even in reformist unions of syndicalistic tactics carried on by small groups of key workers. In Finland, despite legislative provision for collective contracts, both the radical union leadership and the employers' organization oppose this institution. In connection with the regulated collective agreements there are provisions for the adjudication of disputes in labor courts before strikes and lockouts are declared as well as for government conciliation with regard to agreements in the process of negotiation; in Sweden such conciliation may be initiated at the request of only one of the parties to the dispute. Generally speaking, the trade unions enjoy representation in the labor courts and in the public commissions on social legislation. Recent legislation, however, has tended to increase the liability of the unions and at the same time to hamper their freedom of action.

RUDOLF HEBERLE

SUCCESSION STATES AND BALKAN COUNTRIES. Of the 2,500,000 trade union members in all of these states in 1932 Czechoslovakia and Poland accounted for 1,500,000 and 750,000 respectively. The limited development of the labor movement in the other countries may be attributed to a number of factors. With the exception of Rumania and to a lesser extent Hungary the non-agricultural proletariat in each of the other countries numbers less than half a million, and among the considerably larger agrarian masses attempts at organization have been defeated by reforms which deflected the class interests of these groups or, more commonly, by governmental suppression of all trade union activity. This suppression was intensified by the post-war situation. Coupled with profound territorial and population changes requiring a readjustment of production to completely altered marketing conditions there were severe currency disturbances in all the countries under discussion except Czechoslovakia. Revolutionary communist ideology was not without influence among the masses returning from the battle lines; this was particularly true of the regions which had been part of the Russian Empire. Communist influence not only divided the trade unions into revolutionary and reformist factions but offered reactionary governments an opportunity to curtail even reformist trade union activity. A united working class front was further hindered by the existence in most of these countries, which were created out of or augmented by sections of the former Austro-Hungarian and Russian empires, of separatist organizations reflecting national antagonisms. The inheritance and creation of denominational trade unions and the setting up of government fostered organizations further divided working class forces.

The strength of trade unionism in each of these states is therefore related not only to the size and character of the proletariat and to the divisions among its ranks but even more to the extent to which freedom of association is permitted by the governments. This exists most fully in Czechoslovakia, to a lesser extent in Poland. In Rumania and Greece, while trade unions are legally recognized, because of prevailing economic conditions they enjoy only limited freedom. In Hungary, Jugoslavia, Bulgaria and the Baltic states the government has either entirely suppressed trade unions or placed them under rigorous police supervision.

Pre-war Hungarian trade unions were granted the right of association by the industrial code of 1872 but were treated nevertheless as political organizations and subjected to careful police control, especially after the limitation in 1878 of the right to strike; nevertheless, under Social Democratic influence they rose to a membership of over 100,000. The advantageous position of these organizations during the war, when they were represented in governmental wage fixing bodies, resulted in a rise of membership in 1917 to 215,000. Under the Communist republic the total number of organized workers for the second quarter of 1919 is reported to have been 1,400,000 out of a total wage earning population of perhaps 1,750,000. After the collapse of the Communist regime the number sank to 150,000 in 1920, and the reintroduction by the regency of wartime regulations and of the criminal code of 1878 has reduced the membership of the independent unions to 89,000 in 1932 despite the expansion of industry. Christian trade unions, which enjoy the favor of the government, count 50,000 members, mainly recruited from elements outside large scale industry.

Such trade union organization as exists in Rumania derives its chief strength from Transylvania (formerly a part of Hungary), which prior to the war had 80,000 members, and Bukovina, whose trade unions were affiliated with the Vienna center. In old Rumania the trade union movement, which began in 1905, never attained a membership in excess of 15,000. Strong communist influence in the post-war period led to the general strike of October, 1920, at a time when more than 167,000 workers were organized. Rigid regulation after the collapse of the strike reduced this membership in 1922 to 65,000, and continued communist influence resulted in 1923 in a further split, so that the reformist General Workers' League founded in 1926 had in 1932 a membership of only 30,000 out of a total working population of perhaps 3,000,000, two thirds of this number being agricultural wageworkers.

The situation in Jugoslavia is somewhat similar to that in Rumania. In old Serbia, with a predominantly peasant population, no trade union movement was possible until after the overthrow of the Obrenović dynasty in 1903. Such pre-war trade unionism as existed sprang from movements with nationalistic tendencies in areas which were part of the Austro-Hungarian Empire. At the outbreak of the World War there were 14,000 workers organized in Serbia, 5200 in Croatia and 2800 in the Slovenian districts. At the present time about 45,000 workers are organized, representing some 6 percent of the total wage earning population in industry and crafts. Of these 42,000 belong to the independent trade unions, which grew out of a union of neutral and reformist federations, and the balance to Christian trade unions. A communist federation which in 1921 rallied 20,000 followers has been suppressed. Although the right to organize and to strike is materially limited by the law of 1921, there have been since 1922 elective workers' representatives in the "chambers of labor" and, since the industrial code of 1931, in the "corporative bodies."

Despite their predominantly agrarian character trade unionism is stronger in Bulgaria and Greece, partly because of the absence of the problem of nationalities. In both countries the spread of communist ideas has resulted in governmental restrictions. In Bulgaria communist influence leading to a general strike in December, 1919, reached its apogee in 1923 in a trade union league with a membership of 34,000 only to be suppressed that year together with its affiliated cooperatives including some 70,000 members. Although the reformist union affiliated with the International Federation of Trade Unions (Amsterdam International) made attempts to win over members of the suppressed organizations, it had no more than 2100 members by 1932. State employees and those in public works, although denied the right to strike, have formed semigovernmental organizations comprising about 30,000 members.

Greek trade unionism emerged in 1910 out of the political developments which instigated the Venizelos measures for the protection of labor. The movement, as reorganized by the Social Democratic party in 1911, led in 1918 to the founding of a central federation; this in turn was split as a result of widespread spontaneous strikes initiated by communist unions in 1920, and severe governmental restrictions followed. In 1928 the Communists set up separate unions. Of the 90,000 workers who remained in the central organization affiliated with the Amsterdam International, more than 40 percent broke away when in 1930 some of the union executives made an alliance with the Social Democratic party. Government interference has modified the tempo of organization among the 500,000 wage earners; early in 1932 the total union membership included only 72,000 workers.

Lowest in organizational achievements are the Baltic states, Estonia, Lithuania and Latvia, formerly part of the Russian Empire. In some of these areas politically directed unions had an important if much interrupted career in the years immediately before and after the war. The introduction by the counter-revolutionary governments of some agrarian reforms, which tended to transform the greater part of the agrarian proletariat into small peasants, and the suppression of communist activities have all but destroyed trade unionism in these countries. Early in 1932 there were only 22,000 members of trade unions in Estonia, of whom only a third were affiliated with the Amsterdam International; barely 1200 in Lithuania; and 23,800 members of independent unions in Latvia.

The situation in Czechoslovakia, where trade unions in 1932 had 1,500,000 members, constituting some 40 percent of the total working population, offers a sharp contrast to that in other succession states. Indeed were it not for the divisions along nationalistic lines, the movement might be comparable to that of pre-Hitlerite Germany. Nationalistic differences are in part an inheritance from pre-war days and in part a result of the inclusion of new minorities. A separatist Czech organization emerged within the Austrian Empire as early as 1897. Although it developed under the aegis of the Social Democratic party, the nationalistic splits within the party itself led to a similar break between the Czech and the German unions despite the disapproval of the Amsterdam International. In 1913 there were some 318,000 organized workers in the industrial provinces of Bohemia, Moravia and Silesia. These were divided into four groups: the independent Czech unions with a membership of 70,000, which despite their Social Democratic tendencies were ruled out of the Amsterdam International; the German independent unions, which acknowledged the authority of the Vienna center; a number of organizations, including mainly commercial and transport workers, which established a separate organization in 1897 under the influence of the anti-German National Socialist party; and several denominational groups also nationalistic in character.

Because Czechoslovakia quickly managed to establish an ordered economic system, the continued development of these organizations proceeded with comparatively little opposition. In 1921, which marked the apex of the trade union growth, about 50 percent of all workers were organized: the various Czechoslovak unions had an aggregate membership of 1,100,000, the German 331,000 and the Communist 196,000. The national cleavages continued even in the Social Democratic organization until 1926, when a union was effected, with the German minority proportionally represented. The Communist unions alone, except for a brief period, have been free of nationalist divisions.

Thus at the beginning of 1932 among the 1,500,000 organized workers there were 13 separate federations. About 611,000, or 40 percent of the total, were members of the "independent" federation affiliated with the Amsterdam International; of this number 218,000 belonged to the German branch. Five Christian unions, including a Slovak as well as two German groups, accounted for 214,000 members, the federation of Czech national socialist trade unions for 228,000, the Communist unions for 131,000 and the remaining groups for about 276,000.

Freedom to organize is guaranteed to all employees, including those of the state. Since 1921 a shop councils law has protected workers against discharge for religious or political activity; at the same time the so-called antiterror law makes it impossible for unions to compel workers to join, as they did in the early post-war period. The development of the craft type of organization was stimulated by the unemployment insurance law of July 19, 1921, which, following the Ghent system, makes benefit payment by the state contingent upon that provided by a craft union. Although collective contracts have thus far not been subjected to legislative regulation, they are instrumental in the control of working conditions in most branches of heavy industry and in mining. Three separate regional arbitration commissions organized along bipartisan lines deal with labor conflicts; and the law of July 4, 1931, provides that the labor courts also may function as conciliation boards. Trade union central bodies are represented in the governmental Advisory Council for Economic Affairs established in 1921.

In Poland, with its more homogeneous population, nationalistic differences are relatively unimportant; the splits are rather along lines of social policy and are carried over largely from pre-war times. In the important industrial sector of Congress Poland, formerly part of the Russian Empire, trade union organization, possible to a limited extent after 1905, was divided three ways. The first group, with about 50,000 members, originally Social Democratic in tendency, later became receptive to Communist ideas. The second, similar in size, was preponderantly nationalistic and was most powerful among the textile workers of Łódź. A third group, almost exclusively Jewish, numbered about 20,000, recruited mainly from home and small shop industry; however, part of the Jewish Socialist Bund, founded in 1897, remained separate from the first because of the Bund's struggle for autonomy within the Social Democratic party. In the Austrian sector, Galicia, there were about 20,000 members in independent unions, affiliated with the Vienna central body but with a special provincial trade union secretariat. In Prussian Poland Social Democratic influence was virtually nil: the so-called Bochum central organization with about 80,000 members and the Polish trade union league in Upper Silesia were markedly nationalistic.

Trade union reconstruction after the war was more difficult in Poland than in Czechoslovakia, not only because the state of war lasted until late in 1920 but because separation from Russia cut off its principal markets. The greater influence of communism resulted in far more restrictive legislation. While the right to organize and to engage in politics is granted to all workers, including employees of the state and public utilities, a legislative decree of October 27, 1932, subjects them to rigid official control. Communist unions are now illegal.

Early in 1932 out of a total working population of 3,500,000 about 750,000 were organized; 170,000 were agricultural laborers representing over 10 percent of the total agrarian proletariat. Trade union membership is divided among four principal groups. The Polish Trade Union League, affiliated with the Amsterdam International, absorbed the several previously unattached independent trade union groups: the German trade unions of Poznań, the Upper Silesian unions and the Jewish unions, the last named, however, retaining some autonomy. The league, which in 1921 had a membership of 450,000 including 110,000 agricultural workers, declined until in 1932 it numbered only 215,800 members, of whom fewer than 40,000 were agricultural workers. Many conflicts have occurred between the reformist central executive body and the affiliated locals with communist tendencies, especially in Congress Poland. The Alliance of Polish Trade Unions, the successor to the Bochum alliance, is essentially Christian and nationalistic; in 1932 it had 204,000 members, among them 86,000 agricultural workers. A third group with 102,000 members is also predominantly Christian. Non-manual workers, including employees of the state and of the public utilities, are organized in several separatist federations with about 200,000 members. In addition there are a number of smaller unions, some revolutionary, others reformist.

The central trade union bodies are represented on the several governmental advisory councils as well as in the administration of various social welfare institutions. Governmental regulation of the collective agreements, which have become common in heavy industry and in agriculture, has been proposed but not yet enacted. In addition to special legislation for agricultural conflicts there is provision for conciliation and arbitration, which in certain instances may be made compulsory.

KARL PRIBRAM

FRANCE. The restrictions on trade union activity inaugurated by the Le Chapelier law of 1791 were not finally revoked until 1884, and even then the legislation provided for a degree of police supervision. Nevertheless, workers' associations, including those of a purely vocational nature, mutual aid societies and revolutionary semipolitical organizations were by no means lacking during the intervening period; weavers' societies took part in the uprisings in Lyons in the 1830's; the compagnonnages, or journeymen's societies, did not fall into complete decadence until the epoch of the July Monarchy; and it was the participation of workers' societies in the revolutionary uprisings of 1848 which led to the restoration of all the repressive measures against them. For a brief period under the liberal empire craft organizations, or *chambres syndicales*, were tolerated. In 1862 a delegation of workers was sent to the universal exposition at London to study trade unionism, and its favorable findings had some influence on the law of May 25, 1864, according to which agreements to stop work were no longer held to be criminal. The implicit recognition of the freedom of association in the law of 1864 was officially confirmed in 1868 and until the Paris Commune workers' organizations gained some influence, especially in the textile and metallurgical industries. The participation of these organizations in the Commune and the spread of the International Working Men's Association led to the adoption of the law of 1872, which under pretext of crushing the International forbade among other things any organization aiming at the cessation of work.

But even after the removal of restrictions independent trade unionism developed slowly. Industrial and craft federations and the Fédération Nationale des Syndicats founded in 1886 were dominated by a socialist leadership which placed primary emphasis on parliamentary action rather than on an industrial program. Reaction from this leadership led to the founding of the syndicalist *bourses du travail* and the Confédération Générale du Travail and to the merging of these two organizations in 1902. The program of this movement as embodied in the Charter of Amiens (1906) rejected parliamentary cooperation with the Socialist party and at the same time opposed the building up of strongly centralized craft and industrial unions aiming at collective bargaining and immediate economic gains. Instead it stressed syndicalist-revolutionary activity (see SYNDICALISM) which looked to the overthrow of the existing order of society by a series of general strikes and antimilitarist activities and its replacement by a new order toward which education and propaganda should be directed. A Christian trade union movement to offset these tendencies among Catholic workmen was formed as early as 1886.

As compared with the growth of trade union membership in other industrial countries in the period before the World War, the French movement was numerically very insignificant. Although membership figures of the C.G.T. often included workers who did not pay their dues regularly, they were extremely low: 150,000 in 1904, 203,000 in 1906, 294,000 in 1908, 358,000 in 1910 and 400,000 in 1912. Together with the Catholic unions they accounted for a very small proportion of the total wage and salaried population, which was estimated in 1911 on the basis of the 1906 census to be no less than 10,200,000, of whom non-agricultural workers accounted for about 8,000,000.

One reason put forward in explanation of the slow development of trade unionism is the relatively small proportion of wage earners as compared with the total gainfully occupied population. The wage earners except in a few instances were scattered in small workshops, and at least one eighth of their number were employed directly or indirectly by the government through its ownership of many public utilities and monopolies. On the other hand, the number of employers and self-employed was estimated in 1911 as 8,500,000. The attitude of this large middle class, which refused except in the government regulated mining industry to enter into collective negotiations with the workers' organizations, was considered by the workers as the dominant influence in the government; for this reason among others the C.G.T. refused to support such social legislation as the old age pension law proposed in 1910.

The influence of the C.G.T. as a revolutionary educational and propaganda organization was far greater than its numbers would indicate, and its leadership of widespread general strikes made it a power to be reckoned with. At the outbreak of the World War, however, the C.G.T. officials apparently abandoned their antimilitarist, antigovernmental attitude and participated in the various governmental commissions, including the Ministry of Munitions headed by the Socialist Thomas. The French government responded not only by comparative moderation in its dealings with the intransigent antimilitarists in the labor movement but by a comprehensive program of social legislation and insurance, which included the legalization of trade agreements and the adoption of the eight-hour day in 1919, the establishment of public employment bureaus and a system of social insurance and labor representation on important governmental commissions. Some of these measures were embodiments of the new program of the C.G.T. of 1918, which in demanding socialization of the means of production was more radical than the Socialist party but was no longer as revolutionary as in pre-war times.

The membership of the C.G.T. mounted to a new peak of 2,500,000 at the end of 1919. It soon declined, however, in part as a result of the disastrous general strike of 1920, initiated by a revolutionary minority in the railway men's federation, in part through the splitting off of large minorities and in part because of the economic depression. As in other countries, the vigorous strikes of 1919–21 were concerned mainly with economic ends.

At the present time the French trade union movement is divided into three principal groups: the C.G.T., affiliated with the Amsterdam International, with an estimated membership in 1932 of 890,000 members; the Confédération Générale du Travail Unitaire (C.G.T.U.), founded in 1922 and affiliated with the Moscow International, with a membership of about 350,000; and the Confédération Française des Travailleurs Chrétiens, founded in 1919, with a membership of about 120,000 Catholic workers. The syndicalist group, which is not affiliated with either of the major federations, has no more than 10,000 members and is largely propagandist in character. Two organizations under employers' control claimed in 1924 memberships of 60,000 and 90,000 each; even the more powerful, the Confédération National du Travail, now has only a small membership. At best the French trade union movement has never represented more than one eighth of the total working population.

Although the C.G.T. still maintains formal adherence to the Charter of Amiens, it has undergone a profound change. It no longer places reliance on the general strike and direct action, the classic weapons of the French working class; and even the revolutionary C.G.T.U. has rejected these tactics in favor of civil war. The C.G.T. now sponsors the usual trade union program of amelioration, not, it insists, in the spirit of compromise but as a method of freeing the working class for its ultimate task of reconstruction. It has reoriented its educational program and in cooperation with the federation of consumers' cooperatives and the union of technicians has participated in economic planning boards. Its internal government has been changed with the vesting of increased responsibility in the central body and the introduction in 1923 of a system of proportional representation, long urged by many of the stronger but less revolutionary unions. But an even greater change in the C.G.T. is the increasing rapprochement with the government. This is expressed not only in the willingness of the federation to participate in social legislation and its administration but in the consideration accorded the C.G.T. by the government in its program of reconstruction of the devastated areas and in its tolerant attitude toward unionization of government employees, despite the absence of explicit legal permission for such association. Organization of state employees began in 1906 and has spread steadily since the war. Government employees, who in 1932 numbered about one eighth of the total wage earning population, constituted probably no less than one third of the total trade union membership; and if the workers in mining, public utilities and public monopolies are included, the proportion is still higher. In 1927 only one fourth of the total membership of the C.G.T. and one half of that of the C.G.T.U. represented workers in purely private undertakings. The C.G.T. has large membership groups only in the printing and textile industries, and the C.G.T.U. in the metal and building industries, which have always been the strongholds of traditional revolutionary syndicalism. The C.F.T.C. draws its membership largely from commercial employees, including many women. Of the 3,000,000 agricultural laborers probably not more than 30,000 are trade unionists. The employing class, on the other hand, is highly organized. In 1924 there were 6596 employers' associations with 496,360 members, of whom a large proportion were in the small scale food industries and trades. The most powerful group, however, is in the metal and mining industries. It is in the textile and metal industries, where stable unionism has made no headway and where elaborate welfare programs have been initiated by the employers, that revolutionary labor activity of the pre-war type is most in evidence. There seems little doubt, especially in the light of the powerful united front shown recently by the working class against the threat of fascism, that the trade union movement is now proceeding on a strong and stable basis.

GEORGES BOURGIN

See: BOURSES DU TRAVAIL; CONFÉDÉRATION GÉNÉRALE DU TRAVAIL.

BELGIUM. Despite its small territory Belgium has attained considerable industrial development, marked by intensive urbanization and concentrated enterprise, especially in metallurgy, textiles, glassworks and transport. At the present time its wage earning and salaried population approximates 2,000,000, of whom perhaps 800,000 are organized in trade unions.

Legislative prohibitions against the freedom of association derived from the French legislation of 1791, when Belgium was under French domination. The law against combinations was not abrogated until 1866, at which time, however, article 310, forbidding strikes, was introduced into the penal code. Despite these prohibitions workers' organizations developed, first in the form of mutual aid societies, even before the creation of the independent Belgian kingdom in 1830, and later as "societies of resistance," whose unemployment reserves were in reality strike funds, in the period 1840–60. Of great influence after 1867 in winning the workers to revolutionary ideas was the International Working Men's Association, which gained a considerable following especially in Brussels and the valley of the Vesdre. The extreme poverty of the Belgian proletariat resulted in a series of bloody strikes and famine riots, beginning in 1886 at Charleroi, where there was a powerful organization among the miners and glassworkers modeled on the American Knights of Labor, and spreading throughout the country. Although these were severely repressed, the government was forced to modify article 310; protective labor legislation also dates from this period.

A new impetus was given to working class organization by the creation in 1885 of the Belgian Labor party as a result of the amalgamation of various labor groups with the Belgian Socialist party, which in its turn was a fusion of César de Paepe's Brabantine party with Anseele's Flemish party. For unlike other labor parties the Belgian party fostered from the outset trade unions, producers' and consumers' societies, mutual aid societies, credit institutions and a central educational organization with schools, libraries, people's houses, militia for workers' defense and sport clubs. In 1898 the Labor party formed the Commission Syndicale, which in the beginning was open only to socialist unions but gradually admitted neutral unions as well. Despite a prolonged controversy which arose from the desire of a minority for the complete separation of the commission from the party, the reciprocal influence of the two has remained very great. It was not until 1905 that the commission achieved virtual autonomy, although its general council includes two delegates of the Labor party and it is similarly represented in the Labor party council. The membership of the commission grew from over 13,000 in 1898 to 42,500 in 1906 and to 116,000 at the outbreak of the World War.

As in other countries, the unions experienced enormous expansion after the war, the total trade union membership of all types reaching a peak of 718,410 in 1920. When in November, 1918, the Belgian Labor party was asked to participate in the government, it accepted on condition that universal manhood suffrage and freedom of association for the workers in both public and private employ be granted and that article 310 be repealed. Despite the fulfilment of this program in May, 1921, trade union membership began to decline. Strikes against the increased cost of living which drained union treasuries and the development of a powerful and resolute employers' organization were in part responsible. Nor was the movement entirely free from Communist dissension. The trade union membership halted in 1928 at 508,658, and by the end of 1932 the number had risen to about 600,000. Along with this growth there has been an increasing tendency toward the replacement of craft and local bodies by central industrial federations, which now number 28. The metal workers' union had a membership of about 111,000 in 1932; the central union of building workers, furniture and allied industries rose from 86,000 to almost 100,000; the textile central union increased from 69,000 to 91,000; employees of the municipalities and the government in 5 unions numbered over 90,000 in 1924. The miners' union alone, because of the crisis in that industry, showed a decrease from 75,000 to 53,000.

The legislative achievements of the period 1921–27, which included government subsidies to trade union unemployment funds, old age pensions, the setting up of joint economic councils and commissions for study of wages and working conditions, and the inauguration of a general system of collective agreements have tended to lead to an emphasis by trade union leadership on peaceful industrial relations. But because of the severe economic crisis the strike movement has been not inconsiderable. The present program of the trade union movement adopted in 1927 includes a complete and coherent system of social insurance, extension to seamen of all protective labor laws, improvement of labor legislation and of its enforcement machinery and a whole series of demands concerning rationalization, socialization, workers' control, minimum wage and the like. Despite the opposition of employers' organizations the trade union movement, reenforced by its educational and mutual aid activities and a powerful labor press, has been able to maintain its membership and to push its claims.

While the division among the working class with regard to language has gradually been overcome, religious differences persist. The Catholic party, a dominant factor in Belgium since 1884, has fostered a separate movement among the peasants, the agrarian proletariat and the industrial workers. Until the World War the Christian trade unions had only a fragmentary existence. But the creation of the Ligue des Travailleurs Chrétiens in 1921 as part of the unified Catholic movement furnished central control. In its form of organization the league patterns itself on the Belgian Labor party. Since 1926 it has operated a central strike fund, the existence of which, although it causes grave concern to the conservative leaders of the Union Catholique, demonstrates the recognition of the need for such funds if workers are to be kept from joining the socialist trade unions, with which they have frequently made common cause in strikes. The membership of the Christian trade unions rose from 70,000 in 1911 to 155,079 in 1929; they now cover 15 industrial federations with a third of their members in the textile industry. The total membership of unions not affiliated with any central body does not aggregate more than 50,000 workers.

GEORGES BOURGIN

SPAIN AND PORTUGAL. In these predominantly agrarian countries, characterized by a semi-feudal system and scarcely touched by industrial capitalism, there is no large trade union movement of the type established elsewhere by the urban proletariat. Before the World War it was estimated that of a total of 20,000,000 inhabitants in Spain the wage earning population barely exceeded 3,000,000, almost 60 percent of these being agricultural wageworkers and 10 percent household employees. Industry, mainly small scale, employed no more than 550,000; coal, iron and copper mines about 85,000; transport 80,000; trade and public employment 50,000. It is doubtful whether even with the twentieth century development of the automobile, electrical and machine industries under the impetus of foreign capital the total number of industrial workers has been increased appreciably, although the distribution has been changed and there are more large and middle sized enterprises, especially in northern Spain. In Portugal with its 6,000,000 inhabitants and a wage earning population of about 1,000,000 the proportion of industrial workers was even smaller. Even after the World War the only important industry in the country, textile manufacture, employed hardly more than 45,000 workers. With a precarious legal status under governments which frequently were dictatorial, trade unions could not maintain a stable existence among a population with a high degree of illiteracy and no organizational forms except along religious lines. Yet despite the strength of organized religion confessional organization, although attempted especially after the papal encyclical of 1891, has never gained a following comparable to that in other Latin and in the Germanic countries. This is to be accounted for partly by the fact that those workers who are amenable to organization have been for over half a century under the influence of strongly anticlerical anarcho-syndicalism. Indeed, although reformist trade unionism has had a small but steady development mainly among industrial workers, there has arisen in both countries a far larger anarcho-syndicalist movement, affecting the agrarian masses and playing a vital part in the recurring political upheavals through propaganda, strikes and revolutionary organs.

As early as 1840 the labor movement in Spain had its inception in connection with the rise of republicanism and federalism; while the textile workers of Barcelona were forming an association, there were serious agrarian uprisings in Andalusia. The democratic revolution of 1868 provided the opportunity for the introduction of the International Working Men's Association and the secret Alianza de la Democracia Socialista, both dominated almost completely by Bakuninism. Although the former was outlawed in 1872, the latter organization claimed a membership of 300,000 in the following year. It was dissolved in 1888. While the anarchists continued their agitation, it was not until 1911 that the dominant anarcho-syndicalist organization, the Confederación Nacional de Trabajo (C.N.T.) was formed at Barcelona, the chief industrial center. It was suspended in 1913.

Significant socialist organization dates from 1879, when a socialist party was founded by the Marxian minority which had seceded from the Bakuninist organization. In 1889 the Unión General de Trabajadores (U.G.T.), the economic counterpart of the party although the two were not formally affiliated, was established with a membership of 3000. In 1910 the U.G.T. numbered only 41,000 members, but in the following year the number increased to about 71,000 as a result of the affiliation of the railway workers. The union played an important role through its participation in the work of the Instituto de Reformas Sociales (founded 1903), which initiated much noteworthy social legislation.

The war and post-war periods were marked by rapid industrialization and by the spread of Russian revolutionary doctrines. In 1917 there was a revolutionary general strike in which the U.G.T. united with the C.N.T., which had been revived in 1916 and which predominated in the strike. Partly as a result of this activity the C.N.T. in 1919 claimed a membership of almost 1,000,000, of whom 25 percent were in Catalonia. Its organization was still based almost completely on regional rather than on occupational units and as such was well adapted to its predominantly agrarian membership. In the same year the U.G.T. numbered less than 220,000, slightly over 25 percent being agricultural workers. In the meantime the employers had organized in 1914 and now sought to counter strike violence with a terrorism of their own; their paid bands were reenforced by the military and the government. There were also organized in Catalonia, mainly on the initiative of the clericals although without confessional obligation, so-called *sindicatos libres*. It was partly to foster these "free" unions and partly to end the bloody strife that the government adopted legislation which required the more important enterprises to deal with labor unions. The unions, however, were required to register with the government and submit to its supervision, and a system of joint committees was set up for the obligatory settlement of disputes. A futile attempt was made in 1920 to unite the U.G.T. and the C.N.T. in order to meet the offensive action of the employers and the government. The coup d'état of Primo de Rivera in 1923 resulted among other things in the dissolution of the C.N.T.; on the other hand, the U.G.T., whose membership had declined to slightly over 200,000, consented to participate in the various corporate bodies set up by the dictatorship in 1926, patterned on earlier legislation and on the Italian model. A rival aspirant to representation of labor was the federation of the *sindicatos libres* established in 1924, which claimed a membership of over 100,000 in 1928 and 274,000 at the beginning of 1931. The corporate system, however, never gained a complete hold, partly because of the opposition of the employers.

With the fall of the dictatorship the *sindicatos libres* and the Catholic unions dwindled to insignificance, but the revived C.N.T. claimed a new peak of 1,000,000 members in 1933, encroaching upon the power of the U.G.T. in some territories. Under the leadership of the anarcho-syndicalists and the numerically insignificant but active Communist element ambitious strikes were undertaken. They resulted in a series of failures, however, and the hold of the C.N.T. became so precarious that without the continuous pressure of the Federación Anarquista Ibérica it might have been swept by reformism. On the other hand, the U.G.T., which gained temporarily from this situation and claimed a membership of 1,000,000 in October, 1932, also began to lose prestige. The participation of its most conspicuous leader, Francisco Largo Caballero, as minister of labor in the Azaña government—which maintained the essentials of governmental control over labor, including restrictions on strikes, enacted emergency legislation suspending the constitutional guaranties and at the same time failed to reduce widespread unemployment—led to a withdrawal of working class confidence in the U.G.T. Since the accession of a conservative government Largo Caballero has advocated a new united proletarian front. The U.G.T. is affiliated with the Amsterdam International and the C.N.T. with the International Working Men's Association (the syndicalist international).

In Portugal developments in the nineteenth century were similar to those in Spain. After 1891 an important workers' movement was begun. When the Workers' Congress of July, 1909, allied itself with the rather weak Socialist party, the anarcho-syndicalists withdrew and formed an autonomous organization, which in 1911 claimed 35,000 members. After the revolution of 1910 there were widespread strikes and syndicalist uprisings even in the rural districts, which the government put down by force. In 1913 the reformist and anarcho-syndicalist groups united in the Uniao Operario Nacional with a membership of 90,000. The gains of the post-war period raised this number to over 100,000 and the union, which had changed its name to Confederaçao Geral de Trabalho, joined the syndicalist international. As a result of political events which served to discredit the leaders and because of conflicting ideologies the total membership, which in 1926 was no more than 20,000, split into four groups, of which the anarchists were the largest. The union was dissolved by the dictatorship established in 1926, which in its constitution of 1933 provided for a corporate system along fascist lines. Despite the governmental ban labor and revolutionary activities are manifested mainly in frequent strikes.

GEORGES BOURGIN

ITALY. The structure of the Italian trade unions in the period before the World War bore a superficial resemblance to that of the French. Even prior to 1860 a workers' mutual aid movement had been initiated and craft organization among the printers had developed. After the unification of Italy and following a period of brutal suppression from 1868 to 1873 "societies of resistance" and workers' congresses were organized, and in 1880 there appeared the first workers' "consulate," which sought to coordinate the cooperative and mutual aid associations with the vocational labor movement. The first chamber of labor, in many respects similar to the French *bourse du travail*, was organized in 1891. In the same year there was founded the first of the Catholic trade unions. A federation of the chambers of labor, formed in 1893 and dissolved after its participation in revolutionary strikes, was subsequently reorganized. Finally a secretariat created by the chambers of labor and the various craft national federations gave rise in 1906 to the Confederazione Generale del Lavoro, which marked a new phase in trade union history.

The actual development of the Italian trade union movement, however, differed widely from that in France. From the very outset the non-Catholic trade unions were closely bound up with the Socialist party and with the cooperative movement. Following recurrent strikes in 1901–04 the moderate government of Giolitti encouraged trade unionism. The membership of the Catholic unions and of the Confederazione rose steadily. The program of the latter was essentially reformist; it participated in the various commissions formed to administer the program of social legislation, in the employment exchanges and in the drafting of regulated collective agreements. The government aided the development more directly by according favorable consideration to the trade unions and the producers' cooperatives in its expansive program of public works. The revolutionary syndicalists who derived from Sorel formed a separate organization, which ultimately became the Union Sindicale Italiana.

Trade union organization met with great success among the agricultural proletariat, who outnumbered the workers in industry and commerce. At the outbreak of the World War after a period of widespread strikes 70 percent of the 962,000 trade unionists were organized in the socialist C. G. del L., 13.1 percent in the Catholic unions and 16.6 percent in other unions, chief among which was the syndicalist. Of some 4,500,000 agricultural laborers 489,000 were organized and of about 3,000,000 industrial and commercial workers 473,000. Both the syndicalists and the Catholic unions were stronger among the agricultural than among the industrial workers.

Despite the dominant reformist tendency in the Italian labor movement it was affected after the World War far more by revolutionary and communist influence than the French syndicalist movement had been. At the outbreak of the war an antiwar group had organized itself separately into an "interventionist" fraction, and in 1918 a further split developed through the formation of a liberal, antirevolutionary organization, the Union Italiana del Lavoro, which in 1920 claimed 200,000 members. As a result of the unprecedented strike movement of 1919–20 trade union membership rose to a peak of almost 4,000,000, of whom 2,200,000 were in the C. G. del L., which held a dominant position in every important industrial enterprise. The revolutionary impulse, particularly in the industrial north, led to the occupation of factories and among the agrarian population to the movement for partition of the landed estates.

The rise of Fascism (*q.v.*) marks a new period in Italian labor history. The first Fascist trade union appeared in January, 1921, and in November of that year comprised no more than 152,000 members, the majority of them recruited from the salaried classes, as contrasted with the 3,100,000 workers in non-Fascist organizations, divided as follows: the C. G. del L., 1,129,000; the Catholic unions, 989,000; the autonomous federations of seamen and railway workers, 501,000; the anarcho-syndicalists, 389,000; and the "liberal" unions, 116,000. The Fascist unions developed more rapidly with the political successes of the Fascist party and its destruction by violence of the entire apparatus of revolutionary socialism. After the march on Rome in October, 1922, when Mussolini had become master of state power, the principle of class struggle had to be abandoned and the state recognized as the final arbiter in all industrial conflicts. The membership of the Fascist trade unions had risen to 857,611 by the end of 1922, whereas that of the C. G. del L. dropped to 212,000 and that of the rest of the non-Fascist trade union organizations to perhaps 1,500,000. After the agreements of December 19, 1923, between the general (industrial) employers' federation and the general federation of Fascist corporations and the rigorous suppression of the non-Fascist unions membership in Fascist unions rose, reaching 2,000,000 in 1925. But in 1932, despite their almost compulsory character, the total trade union membership according to official statistics included only about half of the 6,477,000 "represented" workers.

Although so-called independent trade unions are tolerated alongside the Fascist unions, police surveillance of such organizations was established by the laws of January, 1924, and of November 6, 1926. Up to the end of 1926 some of the independent unions tried to carry on a de facto existence despite the attacks upon them, but on January 4, 1927, the executive council of the C. G. del L. decided to dissolve. A number of its leaders embraced Fascism; some joined the political refugees abroad and still others retired entirely. The Catholic union movement likewise has ceased to exist. As early as October 9, 1925, the moderate elements of this movement announced their adherence to Fascism; but since not more than one vocational organization is permitted in a single profession, the separate Catholic societies have dissolved. The Catholic organizations apparently authorized by the Lateran Concordat of 1929 have never been set up.

In Fascist Italy trade unions are organized along industrial lines, but no association combines manual workers and salaried employees. Special regulations have been imposed on associations of state employees, and the liberal professions have been enrolled in compulsory organizations. It is an open question whether the Fascist organizations can be called trade unions in the usual sense of the word, since they are subordinated to the Fascist executive power and the Fascist concept of the role of labor in the totalitarian system. Formally the unions are endowed with certain powers. There is legal recognition of a single organization for each category or profession; each union is empowered to conclude collective contracts, which have binding force even on non-members in the field. But the officials of the unions are in fact appointed by governmental authority vested in the Ministry of Corporations, created in 1926 to supervise and correlate the central federations of employers and employees. It is the task of this ministry to apply the labor charter, promulgated in April, 1927, according to which the collective contract is based on an authorized just price. Strikes and lockouts are forbidden, and labor disputes are subject to the authority of obligatory labor courts. Although there are separate employers' and employees' federations, there exist also intersyndical committees, instituted in 1928 under the control of the Fascist party; these are headed by the Council of Corporations, which has been charged by Mussolini with the task of effecting a new unified organization in each branch to coöperate in the production of a given commodity. Theoretically these corporations have been given a new function in the state, that of providing representation in the national government on an economic rather than a political basis. In fact, however, so far as the trade union federations are concerned, control rests in the last analysis with the Fascist party and with its executive.

Whatever the claims of Italian Fascism as to its services on behalf of the workers, its occasional decisions against employers, its policy of public land reclamation, which has tended to reduce unemployment, its support of educational and sport organizations, like Dopolavoro, the entire system has meant in practise a complete suppression of freedom of association, speech and press and through the equalization of conditions of work in agriculture, commerce and industry has resulted in a uniformly low wage standard. Under the circumstances it is impossible to ascertain the actual attitude of the Italian workers toward the system, and it is not surprising that the labor representatives of the Fascist corporations have encountered consistent distrust on the part of labor delegates of other countries to the International Labor Office.

GEORGES BOURGIN

See: FASCISM.

RUSSIA. The Russian proletariat was brought into being with the rapid, almost explosive industrialization dating from the last quarter of the nineteenth century. Large scale and giant factories were established in a few large cities; and this concentration, coupled with the fact that the workers were predominantly of peasant origin and thus not encumbered by conservative craft tradition, favored the rise of a strong proletarian class consciousness. That the resultant elemental labor revolts, typical of all early industrial developments, did not gradually give way to a peaceful movement was due primarily to two other factors. One was the policy of the czarist government, which undertook a number of social reforms only to nullify them by administrative action as soon as labor unrest had subsided. Even those trade unions of the late 1890's which were purely economic in character were suppressed or replaced by organizations instigated by the government, such as that founded by Zubatov in 1901. The second factor, growing out of the complex political and economic set up, was the utilization of this situation by the revolutionary intelligentsia, especially the leaders of the Social Democratic factions. The first broad organization of the workers took place between 1905 and 1907 and was immediately taken in tow by the socialist parties, even though formally it was independent of them. In 1907 membership in the unions reached a peak of 123,000, over a third being concentrated in the two capitals. This growth was a consequence of the decree of March 17, 1906, permitting trade union assemblages, although with many restrictions. It was almost immediately counteracted, however, by administrative measures which destroyed the majority of these unions. Not until 1911–14 was there a new upsurge of trade unions, but in the main these were likewise short lived strike organs in the service of the revolutionary movement. Completely lacking any organizational continuity in the period before the World War, it was impossible for these associations to develop functions common to stable trade unions or to foster the growth of a conservative officialdom.

After the revolution of February, 1917, the unions expanded rapidly. At the beginning of the revolution there were in existence only a few weak local trade unions, but by the middle of 1917 the trade union membership was estimated to have reached 693,000. After the October revolution the unions became part of the party and state apparatus: their membership, structure, functions and rights were adapted to the changes required by the successive stages of the Soviet economy and the policies of the Communist party. These stages may roughly be classified as follows: war communism (1918–21), the NEP period and its aftermath up to 1929 and the period of the first Five-Year Plan.

In the first period the trade unions played an important role; they took over the administration of important branches of industry, participated in naming the officials of the state economic councils and contributed recruits to the army. The officers of the unions were appointed by the party. Membership reached a total of 8,500,000 in July, 1921.

Drastic changes were effected in January, 1922, at the initiative of Lenin. Voluntary affiliation and payment of dues were reintroduced and externally the unions transformed themselves into sellers of labor power. The difference between them and the west European unions consisted in the priority given by the trade union leadership to class interests; that is, to the interests of the state economy rather than to those of the membership. Many of the functions previously exercised by the unions were transferred to the state officialdom.

In the first nine months of the NEP membership dropped to 4,546,100. Since then it has increased continuously with the industrialization and later the collectivization of agriculture. Beginning with the inauguration of the first Five-Year Plan in 1929, the character of the trade unions has become increasingly that of state agencies for wage regulation and work discipline. On the eve of the ninth trade union congress held in April, 1932, the union membership was 16,500,000; in 1933 it had risen to 17,377,000. The proportion of organized workers to the total number was about 90 percent in 1923–28; by April, 1931, despite the increase in trade union membership, it had declined to 73 percent but it subsequently rose to over 80 percent. The proportion in individual industries varies: at the end of 1932 it was about 85 percent in the metallurgical industry but only 40 percent in the sugar industry.

As they are at present constituted, the trade unions in the Soviet Union are functionally not comparable with those in capitalistic states. Externally the structure does not differ very much from that of the west European unions, particularly the old German socialist industrial organizations. There is typically one union, including all workers, executives and officials in each branch of production or administration. The movement was rigidly concentrated into 23 unions until 1931, when the number was increased to 45 by the breaking up of the largest unions—such as those of the metal, agricultural and mine workers—into subdivisions representing the special industries in each. There is a hierarchy of councils in the trade unions, the lowest being the factory unit, and the highest the convention and central committee. At the head of the whole movement is the Trade Union Congress, in practise the central trade union council elected by the Congress; this organization is duplicated in the several economic regions of the Soviet Union. Legally the council is the supreme authority; individual unions are created by it, their most important decisions are invalid without its approval and their leading personnel and finances are subject to its control. Since June, 1933, the central trade union council has had transferred to it all the functions of the Commissariat of Labor.

Theoretically the principles of democracy are adhered to: all trade union organs are elective; officers can be recalled by the members at any time; criticism of the leaders by the rank and file has been raised to a principle. But demagogic eulogies of democratic forms are accompanied by absolute power on the part of the leadership, which is far greater than in the trade unions of capitalistic countries. The principal difference between the Soviet unions and those of corporative states—aside from the differences in their ultimate goals—is that the majority of the Italian unions and all the German unions have dispensed with democratic embellishments and are admittedly based on personal leadership. Control in the Soviet unions is maintained through the fact that the leadership has at its disposal a patronage far in excess of that of trade unions in capitalistic countries because of its role in the state apparatus—the assignment of jobs, dwellings, admissions to convalescent homes, advancement of the worker and the like. "Self-criticism" in reality serves to reveal to the highest leaders, themselves beyond criticism, the mistakes of the lower union organs and to aid in the weeding out of heretics.

Indeed party control is the decisive factor in the trade unions as in every branch of the Soviet state. Only in the period 1922-28 were the unions able to achieve a certain independence in their daily tasks, because of the comparative stability of their officialdom. It is true that from the outset the party regarded it as important to disguise this control and made no mention of it in union statutes. But whenever serious conflicts arose between the party and the union leadership, as in 1921 and 1929, the latter were dismissed without resistance. In recent years the dependence of the unions has reached its maximum. As is general throughout all organs of the state, party members are not placed in all, but only in the most important posts. Whereas among the factory councils the proportion of party members and candidates in 1928 was 42.2, among the delegates to the eighth trade union congress it was 72.5 and to the ninth congress 76.1. The party, whose membership is limited, uses the trade unions, first, to gain added support among the labor masses by making them feel that they are participating in political and economic administration and, secondly, to exercise a measure of control in transactions with the state administration. The unions thus make possible a division of powers in the Soviet state and by aiding in selecting workers for functionaries' posts play a role in choosing those destined for higher careers. In general they constitute an essential part of the state apparatus, upon which they are in fact dependent.

Three functions are usually ascribed to the trade unions in the U.S.S.R.: furthering production, cultural activity and protection of the workers. The most significant aspect of cultural work is the popularization and inculcation of Communist ideology through a network of welfare and educational institutions, in the latter of which increasing emphasis is being placed on technical education. Protection is concerned only secondarily with unfair discharge and primarily with production; it is therefore protection against defects in working conditions making for inefficiency and the interruption of production. While strikes are not prohibited, as in Italy, they are de facto penalized. The drafting of wage agreements with the state and with the authorities in charge of economic enterprises, a monopoly of the trade unions, is directed toward the same end. The wage fixing policy is strongly centralized in the upper authorities and represents the result of compromises between various authoritative organs. Its principal goal is the adjustment of wages to the development of the Soviet economy along the lines laid down by the party, thus marking a complete retreat since 1929 from the policy of exploitation of the market situation for the benefit of trade unionists. For this reason there has been an effort to advance wages particularly in the industries manufacturing producers' rather than consumers' goods, an effort which since 1930 has met with considerable success. Moreover despite occasional lapses the trade unions have since 1921 completely abandoned the early revolutionary postulate of equalization of wages. Piecework and the bonus system are relied upon to increase output, and the necessary acquisition of skill is encouraged by an ever increasing spread between the wages of skilled and of unskilled labor.

It is the chief task of the trade unions therefore to counteract the deficiencies in Soviet economy which arise from the absence of private property and free competition, especially the lack of incentives which these institutions might offer to directors of economic enterprises, and from the low technical efficiency of a largely unskilled mass of workers. The trade unions participate in drawing up the economic plans, although the extent of their influence varies from time to time and was greatest in the early years of the revolution. Nevertheless, the thesis, constantly emphasized, that the workers are the owners of the Soviet economy and therefore interested in its prosperity is necessary to reenforce labor discipline and to stimulate the workers in collaborating in the perfecting of the economic organization. The organizational forms which serve these aims are manifold and are steadily increasing; they include the various activities designated as socialist competition, especially the shock brigades, the control commissions and the advisory committees on production, which are really miniature economic parliaments convoked to propose improvements in the factory organization. Although the number of participants is reported to mount into the millions, facilitating the selection of alert and talented workers for posts of leadership in the administration, this very process of rapid social rise leads to a sharpening of conflicts between various levels within Soviet society—between trade union officials and economic administrators, between workers and "specialists," between various elements among the workers—which bear some resemblance to class conflicts in other countries.

WOLDEMAR KOCH

See: RUSSIAN REVOLUTION.

FAR AND NEAR EAST. *Japan*. Western industrialism in the course of the past seventy-five years has been transforming a still predominantly agricultural Japan into one of the important industrial countries of the world; and at the same time it has brought in its wake a labor movement introduced and promoted by the intellectuals, themselves under the influence of occidental social revolutionary doctrines. The development of trade unionism, however, has been handicapped by the policy of severe governmental restriction and by the changing and clashing currents of social revolutionary activity among its leaders. The existence, especially in the dominant textile industry, of a large proportion of female and child labor housed in factory dormitories and the prevalent feudal paternalism in industry are additional restraining factors.

The first labor organizations date back to 1883, when Tokyo ricksha men united; but these early associations were more in the nature of mutual aid societies with political rather than economic aims, and whenever they gave promise of becoming at all powerful, they were quickly suppressed by the government. In 1900 the government enacted article 17 of the Public Peace Police Regulations, which in effect denied the right to strike and seriously delayed the development of trade unionism.

Shortly after the passage of the first factory act Yuai Kai was founded in 1912. It was then a laborers' mutual aid society; but later from its activities came the General Federation of Japanese Labor, which has been the parent body of the labor movement. Real progress in unionism began with the period of the World War, when tremendous industrial expansion led to shortage of industrial labor and increased prices led to collective wage demands. A further stimulus to organization came at this time as a result of the general upheaval of social ideas throughout the world and of contact through the conferences of the International Labor Organization. Labor unions now came into being through the initiative of the workers, and leaders began to rise from the ranks. The membership, which was estimated at 30,000 in 1919, increased to about 228,000 by 1924.

The student antimilitarist and anticapitalist movement helped to spread radical ideas among the wage earners, introducing them to every shade of revolutionary doctrine—syndicalism, socialism, communism—and forming antagonistic groups of adherents. As a result internal dissension has marked the movement from 1924. With the advent of universal manhood suffrage in 1926 both the labor movement and the tenant farmer movement turned to political action and in some instances combined forces in joint political parties. The disunity in the economic movement was transmitted to the political movement, and at the first general election in 1928 there were four major proletarian political parties competing for the proletarian vote. They polled altogether fewer than 500,000 votes and secured only 8 of the 466 seats in the Diet. Continued dissension and government repression have weakened the parties, and in 1932 the proletarian vote had dropped to 270,000 and the number of representatives in parliament to 5.

The communist wing of the movement has been seriously depleted by the imperial ordinance of 1928 which made radical plotting against the political system of Japan punishable by heavy penalties including death. At that time the Communist union known as the Council of Japanese Trade Unions was dissolved and forced underground. Periodic police raids upon alleged communists since then had placed under arrest by October, 1933, 29,646 persons, of whom 1247 had been indicted. The ascendancy of militarism following the Manchurian incident of 1931 brought forth a national socialist element at the extreme right of the political movement. It is a divided movement lacking strength, but it has drawn its membership from the right and center wings of the labor movement. Weakened by desertions, these two wings in 1932 composed their differences and in the political field merged the remnants of their several parties, thus creating the present Social Mass party (*Shakai taishu to*).

The economic labor movement was at the same time unified in the Japanese Trade Union Congress (Nihon Rodo Kumiai Kaigi), which was formed in September, 1932, and now controls about 80 percent of the trade union membership. It includes such substantial organizations as the General Federation of Japanese Labor, the Japan Seamen's Union, the General Federation of Workers in State Undertakings, the National Labor Union Federation, the Confederation of Japanese Labor Unions, the Merchant Marine Officers' Association and five smaller federations. The seamen's group operates a system of free employment exchanges, owns seamen's homes and has developed arbitration machinery. The General Federation has labor schools, a savings bank, several small workers' factories and some cooperative enterprises.

The total trade union membership in 1932 was 377,625, or about 8 percent of the industrial population. Of this membership 95 percent are male workers. Organization has been by industry rather than by craft and chiefly among skilled workers; 39 percent of the membership are transport workers and 25 percent are in the machine and tool industry. The textile industries are less than 5 percent organized. Despite considerable social legislation trade unions have not been legally recognized, and trade union activities are closely watched by the police.

China. Although some large scale industrial undertakings were started in China at the end of the nineteenth century, industrialization has been very slow, and it is only since the revolution and especially since the World War that any appreciable progress has been made. Political revolution rather than the industrial revolution has given the spur to labor organization. Before 1911 it was the revolutionary secret societies that spread socialist doctrines among the workers; after the founding of the republic Sun Yat Sen and his revolutionaries sought to organize workers and peasants as part of the Kuomintang strategy in the struggle for control of the government, and it is from this source that the labor movement has developed. The literary revolution also has been an important factor. Beginning about 1916 it roused the literati to an active interest in the conditions of labor, and within a few years more than two hundred publications were brought out dealing with the various social and revolutionary doctrines of the West. Influenced by this renaissance, the student movement, which arose in 1919 agitating against Japanese control of Shantung and the weak government in Peking, carried the new social ideas to the workers and urged them to organize, to strike and to boycott.

Organization did not begin in the large undertakings. The first labor union was a workers' friendly society in Hongkong, organized in 1909. From there it spread to Canton and founded the present well known Mechanics' Union. The seamen began to organize about 1913. Laborers returning from France after the World War brought back experience in trade unionism, and scattered unions began to form. The successful mechanics' strike in Hongkong in 1920 demonstrated the power of union organization, and within a few months over 100 new unions were formed in the southern province of Kwangtung, where the industrial establishments are small workshops. In 1922 the success of the seamen's union in Hongkong in calling a general strike against that government's order for the suppression of the union disclosed the power of united labor and incidentally the vulnerability of the British colony to boycott by the Chinese. Influenced by the circumstances of this strike, the Kuomintang government in Kwangtung repealed the section of the provincial penal code which prohibited strikes. By 1922 under Kuomintang tutelage a labor movement had begun, and the First National Labor Conference was held at Canton with delegates from 12 cities representing 400,000 workers. In the north there was severe repression of unionism by local authorities, especially on the railways.

Communist influence, especially among the literati and the students, began to be felt about 1920. Systematic propaganda among the workers and peasants followed the arrival from Russia in 1923 of Michael Borodin, who injected into the labor movement of the Kuomintang an antiforeign virus which had far reaching political consequences in the strikes and boycotts of 1925 to 1927. The Kuomintang admitted communists into the party in 1924, and for a short period thereafter the communists were in control of the labor movement: hundreds of communist unions were formed and there was intense labor unrest, which increased throughout the country as the revolutionary army advanced northward. These communist unions were formed not only in the big factories of the industrial centers but in the handicraft workshops and small establishments everywhere. The national labor conference at Canton in 1926 claimed representation of 1,264,000 organized workers, and in 1927 at the time of the communist world labor conference in Hankow the number was said to be 3,000,000; but this figure includes non-dues-paying adherents and sympathizers. During the communist regime at Hankow the labor unions were used primarily for political ends, and at Shanghai in 1927 they paved the way with a general strike for the occupation of the city by the Kuomintang army. With the downfall of the Hankow government the communist Pan-Pacific Trade Union Secretariat, which was founded in that city, moved to Shanghai; and since the suppression of communism by the Kuomintang it has operated among the workers in secret. Communist activity in China is now centered among the peasants.

When the Kuomintang early in 1927 expelled the communist elements from the party, the trade union movement was ruthlessly purged of communists and reorganized under right wing direction. A labor union law promulgated in 1929 sought to regulate all labor organization and required Kuomintang approval before registration of any union. National and general unions were prohibited. They exist, but the Shanghai General Federation of Labor is refused registration and the national aspect of the mechanics', seamen's and other unions is not recognized. Under Kuomintang domination the labor movement lacks initiative and is a weapon of the party rather than of the working classes. The subsidies to unions from factory owners are actually tribute to the Kuomintang.

Besides the devitalizing effect of control by the Kuomintang there are other obstacles to the development of a labor movement inherent in the Chinese proletariat. They are the extreme poverty and illiteracy of a dominant proportion of the workers, the large body of female and child labor, the small workshop and apprentice labor, the recruiting system, the migratory character of industrial labor and the contractor system prevalent in mining, dock work, match factories and elsewhere among the unskilled. The total membership in 1933 was scarcely more than 400,000. There has been disintegrating dissension within the movement and few unions have a continuous history of any length. The Mechanics' Union at Canton goes back to the first union and is an exception. It claims a membership of 200,000, including oversea members. It has written agreements with employers and has established some schools. The Chinese Seamen's Union has been reorganized many times and has been seriously weakened by conflicts with communist elements as well as with the authorities. The Commercial Press Employees' Union began in 1917 as a guild and was one of the best organized unions in China before its destruction in the Shanghai incident of 1932. Some of the tobacco workers' unions have written agreements and workers' schools, and the post office employees have a mutual benefit scheme. The seeds of unionism have been sown, but there is at present no large scale trade union movement with a constructive program of its own to serve the working masses in China.

India. The industrial population of India, that engaged in mining, industry and transport, is estimated at 25,000,000 persons, of whom between 3,000,000 and 5,000,000 are employed in mines, plantations and organized industrial establishments having 10 or more employees; and more than 1,550,000 are in establishments under the factory act. The textile mills employ about 700,000 workers; industrialized agriculture in the tea, coffee and rubber plantations employs about 1,000,000. Until 1915 plantation labor was practically slave labor under a system of indenture with penal sanctions. On the plantations and in the factories workers are housed in company dwellings, and a large proportion are women and children. The development of trade unionism is handicapped not only by these factors but by poverty, illiteracy, caste and religious animosities and by the seasonal and migratory character of much of the factory labor.

Industrialization began in the second half of the nineteenth century, and by 1875 there was agitation for factory legislation, which resulted in the first factory law of 1881. In that period attempts were made to organize labor in order to influence legislation, but these early unions did not survive long; and prior to the World War organization scarcely extended beyond the better paid, better educated railway workers, printers and employees of the postal, telegraph and government services, in which a number of Europeans and Anglo-Indians were employed.

The rise of unionism in the post-war period of industrial expansion, when wages lagged behind prices, was accompanied by widespread strikes and influenced by the International Labor Conference of 1919 and the swaraj (independence) movement, from which came leaders for the labor movement. Recognition of the need for national organization led to the formation in 1920 of the All-India Trade Union Congress, which in turn provided the impetus for the creation of many other unions. A further impetus came with the legislative reforms and the inclusion in the assembly and councils of a few labor representatives. In 1919–22 membership in the labor movement was estimated at 500,000, but many of the unions were primarily strike organizations.

The second period of intense labor activity, 1928–30, was stimulated by the spread of communism and by the non-cooperation campaign of the nationalists. To counteract the communist activity deportation of all non-Indian communists and strict supervision of all agitators were ordered in 1929 by the government's Public Safety Ordinance. The Trades Disputes Act of the same year, besides providing for conciliation machinery, aimed at the prevention of general strikes and provided punishment for lightning strikes and lockouts in certain public utility services. Labor disputes, which in 1928 and 1929 involved 1,000,000 workers in 334 strikes, have since affected about 200,000 annually.

Trade union membership is small and divided. Besides the communists it has the liberal wing and the extreme nationalists. In order to unify the movement the extreme nationalists, including the All-India Trade Union Congress, the All-India Railwaymen's Federation and a number of local unions, amalgamated in 1932 with the liberal All-India Trade Union Federation. That year trade union membership was estimated at 400,000, including both registered and non-registered unions. The membership in registered unions, which comprise the majority of the vigorous organizations, was less than 220,000 in 1931. Of the industrial areas trade unionism is strongest in Bombay and weakest in Bengal. In the large sections untouched by modern industry it is practically non-existent. Organization has been local and generally industrial in structure. The Ahmedabad Textile Labour Association, a strong union with schools, libraries, hospitals and cheap grain shops, is a federation of craft unions. There are also strong unions among the railway workers, seamen, dock workers and government employees. Leadership is supplied by the educated classes, who have been influenced by western socialism and Indian nationalism. Refusal by both British and Indian employers to recognize "outside leadership" led to bitter controversy resulting in the Trade Unions Act of 1926, which recognized registered unions and sanctioned outside leadership. The movement is neither self-reliant nor financially self-sustaining.

Other Far Eastern Areas. In the less industrialized areas adjoining Japan, China and India there is practically no trade union movement. In Korea the advent of Japanese control has introduced some modern industry and there is a small trade union movement involving about 65,000 workers. Both this movement and the tenant farmers' unions have strong communistic and nationalistic elements, which the Japanese keep under observation and suppress from time to time.

The trade union movement in the Netherlands East Indies exists chiefly among the skilled mechanics and in the cities. After the railway strike of 1923 the penal code was amended to prevent political strikes with the result that it practically prohibits all strike activity. Trade union agitation in 1926–27 was suppressed by the government when it became communistic. The communists have tried to organize plantation workers, but the system of indentured labor has been a serious barrier. In 1931 the Dutch government issued an ordinance for the gradual and progressive abolition of penal sanctions on contract labor.

In French Indo-China there is a beginning of labor consciousness. In 1928 a campaign was begun by anti-French elements against the recruiting of contract labor, and in 1929–30 communist activities in industry and on plantations resulted in a number of strikes.

In Malaya mining and industrialized agriculture on rubber estates involve large numbers of workers, but no labor movement of importance has developed as yet. In Ceylon also the attempt to organize plantation coolies has not met with success. The workers in the various trades in Colombo, however, have been organized on the one big union plan and a genuine start has been made in trade unionism. In 1931 an ordinance was enacted to provide for the settlement of industrial disputes.

Labor in the Philippine Islands is somewhat better organized. Trade unions date from about 1902 and the first labor congress was convened in Manila in 1913. The labor movement is centered in Manila, its membership of about 75,000 being mainly cigar and cigarette workers and seamen. Since 1917 there has developed a movement to organize tenant farmers and farm laborers in the provinces.

Near East. Palestine is the only country in the Near East with an important trade union movement. Despite its predominantly agrarian character a strong labor movement has developed there, mainly among the Jewish workers, most of whom have entered the country since 1919 bringing with them a trade union and socialist background. From the outset, because of the limited opportunities in private employment both in industry and on the plantations, the movement has concentrated on colonization in agricultural communes, financed largely by Zionist funds. Since 1920, when the General Federation of Jewish Labor was organized, the labor movement has been in effect an arm of the Jewish Agency and as such has gained power and prestige. In 1933 it claimed a membership in excess of 35,000, amounting to 17 percent of the Jewish population and over 75 percent of the total number of Jewish workers in industry, trade, the professions and agriculture, both on the plantations and in the collectives and cooperative small holders' settlements. The federation is formed on the one big union basis, with strong centralized control over the constituent national and local unions. It is affiliated with the Amsterdam International and is politically nonpartisan. Actually, however, leadership and direction are furnished by a majority labor party, affiliated with the Socialist International. Membership in this party and in the two left opposition labor parties, which are represented proportionately in the legislative organs of the federation, is confined to trade union members. The Communist party has been outlawed. The federation does not confine itself to the usual trade union tasks or to Palestine. It organizes and trains youth groups throughout the world and arranges through the Agency for their entry into Palestine. A colonizing arm of the Zionist enterprise, it has organized a network of agricultural marketing, consumers' credit and housing cooperatives and controls a labor bank; it sets up urban producers' cooperatives, guilds and contracting organizations in the building and in the orange growing industry. It has its own system of schools, health and welfare organization. The labor movement forms a majority in the Jewish National Assembly and in 1926 captured the municipal government of Tel Aviv.

Organization among the Arabs is very slight despite the aid extended by the Jewish Federation and the attempts of Arab nationalist movements to set up unions. A successful joint Arab-Jewish organization in the government railways, post and telegraph service has been ordered by the British government to dissociate itself from the federation. Strikes by Arab workers have been aided by the federation, which aims to set up an Arab federation analogous to the Jewish, joining both in an international federation for Palestine.

The federation has encountered considerable opposition from plantation employers and from the British government in its effort to place Jewish immigrants. Recently there has been an attempt to destroy the prestige of the federation by the creation of an extreme nationalist-fascist labor movement.

In the other countries of the Near East trade unionism has made little progress. While the governments of Egypt, Turkey, Persia, Iraq and Syria have set up tariff barriers to encourage the development of modern industries, they have just begun actual industrialization. Egypt has more of a trade union movement than the others. The labor syndicates, as they are called, are mainly in Cairo and among the railway workers. In 1931 the General Federation of Egyptian Labor Syndicates was established to bring about unity in the movement. Syndicates are not yet legally recognized. In Syria, where the low standards of Armenian labor constitute a serious problem in the labor market, a few trade unions have been organized and in Iraq a trade union movement has been stimulated by the International Labor Office. The government has opposed the movement and local unions have been disbanded. The agitation for labor organization began in 1931, when large groups of workers were thrown out of employment.

DOROTHY JOHNSON ORCHARD

See: KUOMINTANG; IMPERIALISM.

UNITED STATES AND CANADA. *United States.* The characteristics of American trade unionism—limited occupational and industrial penetration, instability of membership, craft and racial exclusiveness, absence of a permanent political labor front—are to be explained largely by several conditions peculiar to the history of the country. The first of these was until recently the almost unlimited possibilities of economic and social expansion. The opening up of the public domain, often with government aid, made possible both an internal migration and an ever expanding area of opportunity for both capital and labor. The industrial worker who moved west seldom retained his original status or, when he did, found himself a part of a diversified community largely dominated by farmers. Another factor of importance was the absence of a feudalistic background and the more complete and earlier realization of the democratic revolution; this explains in part the persistent hold of the traditional individualism of American life and institutions, even after political and social equality ceased to be characteristic of economic and social groupings within the nation. The third factor is the lack of homogeneity in the working class; this became particularly marked after the Civil War, when there set in a mass heterogeneous immigration of labor coupled with the emergence of a free Negro laboring population handicapped doubly by color and previous condition of servitude. The fourth factor is the development in the last quarter of the nineteenth century of trustified industry which looked largely to immigrants without trade union background for its main source of unskilled labor supply. Finally, there is the influence of unprecedentedly rapid technological change in industry.

The effect of these factors on trade unionism up to the late 1880's, when the American Federation of Labor unions fixed the present pattern of organization, was somewhat as follows: until 1820 unionism was confined largely to skilled local groups in the principal industrial centers along the Atlantic coast. In the following two decades these local craft societies, which in 1836 were estimated to include about 300,000 members in 160 local unions in the 5 principal industrial centers, made several attempts to set up regional federations as well as national organizations in individual crafts. They also participated in the recurrent working men's parties and farmer-labor groups whose programs emphasized general measures of social and political equality and whose demands reflected antimonopoly rather than proletarian aims. With the expansion of the market there began in 1850 the development of national unions of workers in a single craft: the typographers (1850), the journeymen stonecutters (1853), the hatters (1854), the iron molders (1859), the locomotive engineers (1863), the cigar makers (1864), the bricklayers, masons and plasterers (1865) and so on. Roughly these unions included the building crafts, the railroad workers and a few other skilled divisions of labor. Despite the inroads on stable organization made by the Civil War, the Homestead Act (1862) and the law permitting contract immigrant labor the period 1866–69 witnessed a new revival of unionism to an estimated membership of about 400,000. It was in this period that the National Labor Union was founded (1866), which despite its dominant trade union membership had other than trade union goals. The period was also marked by agitation for the eight-hour law and other types of protective labor legislation. Although the crisis of 1873 saw the downfall of this and other political labor groups, the national craft unions maintained themselves. No fewer than 16 of the most powerful craft unions of the early twentieth century were founded prior to 1880.

Preserving their autonomy and limited field of craft interests these craft unions remained outside the Knights of Labor (*q.v.*) when that organization took on the form of a general union with but limited autonomy for craft and industrial groupings. The appeal of the American Federation of Labor (*q.v.*) after its reorganization in 1886 to these national trade unions lay precisely in the degree of independence guaranteed them by its loose, federative structure, which at the same time protected them from dual unionism. Nevertheless, the railroad brotherhoods, after their experience with the Knights of Labor, preferred to maintain their independent character as organizations which discouraged the use of the strike. Indeed because of the exclusiveness of crafts and the insistence of many national trade unions upon preservation of their autonomy the A. F. of L. had an amazingly small membership up to the period of industrial expansion following the Spanish American War. In the late 1890's the trade union membership of the country had dropped from 1,000,000 in 1887 to between 400,000 and 500,000, of which the A. F. of L. could claim only slightly more than half. After 1897 the rapid growth of the coal miners' union and the affiliation of the building crafts unions, several of which had previously remained outside the federation, raised the A. F. of L. membership from 264,825 in 1897 to 1,676,200 in 1904, forming in the latter year over 80 percent of the total trade union membership of 2,072,700. The onset of the depression which lasted from 1904 to 1909; the institution of widespread wage cuts; the development of a strong employers' offensive, which resulted in the rupturing of important trade agreements, the punitive antiboycott court decisions in the Danbury Hatters' and the Buck's Stove and Range cases; the McNamara case of 1911, which contributed to the withdrawal of public favor enjoyed by labor in the earlier antitrust agitation; and the incursions of the Industrial Workers of the World among certain sectors of the A.F. of L., all these factors led to a loss of membership, felt most keenly by the unions affiliated with the federation. With the economic upswing of the period from 1910 to 1914 there was a new spurt of activity, which included the expansion of the clothing unions, industrial and semi-industrial, and the growth of the coal miners' unions as well as of the craft federations. On the one hand, the challenge of the I.W.W. and the rise in influence of the industrial unions and, on the other, the movement toward amalgamation dominated by the strong craft rather than by the industrial unions had brought about in the previous decade the creation of departments within the federation, which sought to reconcile and coordinate the interests of craft unions within a single industry. Outside the A. F. of L. the I.W.W. conducted spectacular strikes in the textile and metal mining industries. A strong prolabor swing was reflected not only in the large socialist vote of 1912 but in the appointment of a labor man, W. B. Wilson, to the newly created post of secretary of labor. Legislative gains, such as restrictions on the sale of prison made goods, limitation of immigration, the Clayton Act of 1914 and the Seamen's Act of 1915, were outward signs of the new power of trade unionism in the American scene. This development made it possible for the trade unions to take advantage of their strategic position in the period of labor shortage during the World War. The representation of labor on governmental bodies, the organization of large masses of semiskilled and unskilled workers in the industries which gained through wartime activities, the Adamson Eight Hour Act of 1916, which applied to the railroads—all had repercussions in the rise of total union membership in 1920 to over 5,100,000, of which the A. F. of L. claimed nearly 4,100,000 (Table I).

TABLE I

TRADE UNION MEMBERSHIP IN THE UNITED STATES*

YEAR	TOTAL	UNIONS AFFILIATED WITH A. F. OF L.
1897	447,000	264,825
1900	868,500	548,321
1904	2,072,700	1,676,200
1906	1,958,700	1,454,200
1910	2,184,200	1,562,112
1913	2,753,400	1,996,004
1917	3,104,600	2,371,434
1919	4,169,100	3,260,068
1920	5,110,800	4,078,740
1921	4,815,000	3,906,528
1922	4,059,400	3,195,635
1923	3,780,000	2,926,468
1924	3,536,600	2,865,799
1925	3,567,700	2,877,297
1926	3,504,700	2,803,966
1927	3,498,200	2,812,526
1928	3,449,100	2,896,063
1929	3,444,000	2,933,545
1930	3,407,600	2,961,096
1931	3,298,000	2,889,550
1932		2,532,261

*Including members in Canada, Porto Rico, Hawaii and the Virgin Islands.
Source: Total membership figures for 1897 to 1922 from Wolman, Leo, *The Growth of American Trade Unions, 1880–1923* (New York 1924) p. 33; for 1923–31 from President's Research Committee on Social Trends, *Recent Social Trends in the United States*, 2 vols. (New York 1933) vol. ii, p. 832; for A. F. of L. membership figures from American Federation of Labor, *Report of Proceedings*, vol. liii (1933) 33.

Even with this growth the trade union organization, which in 1910 had accounted for only 10.9 percent of non-agricultural wage earners, included only 20.8 percent of the total in 1920. While no careful estimate has been made for 1930, the proportion probably declined to slightly above that of the 1910 basis. An analysis of trade union membership by industries shows a decided and growing concentration in the transportation, building and mining industries, which in 1910 accounted for 55 percent, in 1920 for 50 percent, in 1925 for 60 percent and in 1930 for 57 percent of the total trade union membership in the United States (Table II). The relative decline of the building trades membership in 1920 at the same time that the metal, machinery and shipbuilding group increased was due to the wartime stimulation of the latter industries and the decline of the former. The amazing decline in the mining and quarrying group from 1910 to 1930 was due as much to internal dissension in the United Mine Workers—the most powerful industrial union in the United States—as to economic conditions in the industry itself.

TABLE II

PERCENTAGE DISTRIBUTION OF TRADE UNION MEMBERSHIP DISTRIBUTED BY INDUSTRY GROUPS, 1910–30

GROUP	1910	1920	1925	1930
Transportation	22.0	24.6	25.0	25.9
Building	21.0	17.4	23.5	26.5
Metal, machinery and shipbuilding	9.0	16.8	5.6	5.9
Food, liquor and tobacco	5.3	2.3	2.0	1.7
Paper, printing and bookbinding	4.1	3.2	4.4	4.8
Chemical, clay, glass and stone	2.8	1.0	1.2	1.0
Mining and quarrying	12.6	8.2	11.5	4.6
Leather	2.1	2.2	1.5	1.3
Clothing	4.4	7.1	7.8	7.3
Public service	2.7	3.2	5.4	7.8
Textile	0.9	2.9	1.0	1.0
Theaters	2.8	1.9	4.6	5.1
Restaurants and trade	2.7	2.8	1.7	1.8
Lumber and woodworking	1.3	0.5	0.3	0.4
Miscellaneous	6.3	5.9	4.5	4.9

Source: President's Research Committee on Social Trends, *Recent Social Trends in the United States*, 2 vols. (New York 1933) vol. ii, p. 834.

A more significant picture of the strength of trade unionism in various industries and occupational groups in 1910 and 1920 is presented in Table III. Details for some of the groups under

TABLE III

PERCENTAGE OF WAGE EARNERS ORGANIZED IN MAJOR INDUSTRIAL DIVISIONS, 1910, 1920 AND 1930

INDUSTRY OR OCCUPATION	1910	1920	1930
Extraction of minerals	27.3	41.0	24.5
Transportation	17.1	37.3	29.6
Building trades	16.4	25.5	29.5
Manufacturing industries:			
total	11.6	23.2	12.5
clothing	16.9	57.8	43.6
food	7.6	19.4	12.7
iron and steel	10.4	28.1	8.9
leather	14.6	29.4	17.9
liquor and beverages	67.6		
printing and publishing	34.3	50.1	46.1
textile	3.7	15.0	6.6
Clerical occupations	1.8	8.3	5.0
Public service	2.5	7.3	5.8
Professional services	4.6	5.4	5.8
Domestic and personal service (including hotels, restaurants)	2.0	3.8	3.2
Trade	1.0	1.1	0.4

Source: For 1910 and 1920, Wolman, Leo, *The Growth of American Trade Unions, 1880–1923* (New York 1924) p. 86, 88; for 1930, estimate by C. R. Daugherty in *Labor Problems in American Industry* (Boston 1933) p. 501–02.

manufacturing industries show, as does Table II, that the great increases in both absolute numbers and proportion of organized workers took place in the clothing and textile industries and in printing and publishing. The decline in the liquor and beverage industry was largely accounted for by prohibition; this led to the virtual extinction of the brewery workers' union, the second largest industrial union in the A. F. of L. The rise in public service unionism is not as significant as that in other groups, since its basis lies in political bargaining rather than in trade union activities in the economic field.

The only important groups outside the federation were the railroad brotherhoods, whose stand on compulsory arbitration diminished the possibility of affiliation, and the Amalgamated Clothing Workers' Union, which had been expelled in 1914 on a charge of dual unionism but was readmitted in 1933. Despite the gains of the A. F. of L. with unskilled and semiskilled workers, the remarkable growth of organization among governmental clerical employees, which led to a white collar membership of over 200,000, and the new spirit of interunion cooperation there was a continued decline in the trade unions from 1920 on. This retrogression may be attributed to various developments, among them the failure of the steel strike and the weakness of the campaign in the automobile industry, the neglect of industries in which women or Negroes predominated; the opposition of most sectors of the A. F. of L. to the continuation of the wartime system of government intervention; the antiradical legislation of the post-war period often invoked against union organizers and, finally, the employers' open shop and "welfare" campaigns. Company unions and employee representation plans increased from a membership of about 400,000 in 1919 to nearly 1,370,000 in 1926. In the face of this situation the upsurge of "one big unionism" in the northwest and in Canada, which culminated in the Seattle general strike; the activities of Communists in the "progressive" industrial or semi-industrial unions, of the miners and the needle trades, whose strength had already been reduced by underemployment, overproduction and cut-throat competition, these factors caused a swing away from progressive trends embodied in such manifestations as industrial unionism, workers' education, the type of policy exemplified by the Plumb Plan and the miners' proposal for nationalization and an enlarged interest in political labor movements.

Confronted by new challenges the labor unions turned to trade union-employer cooperation in order to encourage employers to deal with them. Labor-management cooperation schemes were initiated among railroad shopmen and in the clothing and hosiery industries, joint unemployment benefit schemes were established in the garment industries, and in general there was adopted the doctrine that increases in wages must be postulated on labor's contributions to increased production. This new strategy operated, however, only within those industries which were already organized, and little or no progress was made in the unorganized fields; the increasing importance of non-union areas in the coal and women's garment industries reduced the membership of these two A. F. of L. unions to a level lower than that which had obtained at the beginning of the century. Losses in trade union membership became even more severe after the onset of the depression in 1929. Hour and wage standards in organized industry were broken down, and wages for those who still had work were by 1932 about 60 percent below the 1929 level.

Nevertheless, in any review of the trend since 1900 certain qualifications must be made with respect to particular unions and to the A. F. of L. The first is that, despite the political conservatism of most of the American as contrasted with European unions, the former have shown a marked aggressiveness in the economic field through an application of comprehensive trade agreements and shop rules. Nor have they been lacking in readiness to strike whenever conditions were favorable. Notwithstanding the usual classification of American trade unions as craft unions it should be made clear that of 102 national or international unions (the term international is used because of the inclusion of Canadian unions) in the A. F. of L. in 1932 about 25 were of the pure craft union type, 50 were compound craft unions, 25 were amalgamated craft unions which operated as industrial units (as in the needle trades and textile industries), and the others, as in the mining and brewery industries, were pure industrial unions. The 307 local trade and federal labor unions with a membership of 11,368 in 1932, affiliated directly with the A. F. of L., consisted of craft unions with no national body and of mixed groups of workers of different crafts. The very existence of an almost complete sovereignty in each international union has made possible the widest variety of industrial and political policies. The needle trades unions have been strongly influenced by political labor movements and have often endorsed measures, such as social insurance and unrestricted immigration, opposed by the federation. The unions vary also in their accessibility to Negro workers, and despite the ban on dual unionism, which constitutes the chief hold of the federation over its affiliated bodies, internationals, notably in the needle trades, have given aid to and allied themselves with the Amalgamated Clothing Workers' Union. Nor is there any unanimity of practise with regard to the introduction of machinery or of production standards. Unions in the printing and garment trades in particular have agreed to both, subject to union participation and control; whereas the cigar makers' union has steadfastly refused to accept the machine.

Even the resistance of American trade unions to governmental provision of social insurance and of regulation has gradually given way, and recognition of the advisability of such measures has spread gradually from the progressive unions to the federation as a whole. The measures for workmen's compensation and old age benefits sponsored largely by socialistic groups have become acceptable to trade unions and in 1932 the federation reversed itself on unemployment insurance. The inauguration of the New Deal of the Roosevelt administration marked an even further departure. The federation had endorsed the 30-hour law as a measure to combat unemployment but had opposed comprehensive minimum wage legislation. The setting of such minima, however, under the National Industrial Recovery Act was not in principle opposed by the federation. The affirmative attitude toward independent collective bargaining (but not to the closed union shop) of section 7a of the act spurred a number of the more aggressive industrial unions, especially the miners and the needleworkers, to begin organization campaigns which laid the basis for favorable codes. A vigorous campaign was initiated also in the steel industry. Organization campaigns on an industrial rather than a craft basis were launched in the electrical, automobile and rubber industries. In September, 1933, although the dues paying membership of the A. F. of L. was still only 2,526,796, the actual membership was nearer 4,000,000. About 300,000 workers have been organized in the 1300 new federal labor unions and 50,000 new recruits are enlisted in the existing federal unions. The national and international organizations affiliated with the federation had added 450,000 new members, and 300,000 newcomers were organized in new or recently admitted international unions, such as the Amalgamated Clothing Workers' Union. Still another 100,000 were exempt from dues because of unemployment. The new membership was responsible for a strong movement for industrial unionism, but the resolution embodying this demand in 1933 was defeated because the initiates were not entitled to vote. At the present time there is developing a renewed struggle between craft and industrial unionism as a result of the attempt by certain of the craft internationals to break up the new federal labor unions.

The almost certain conviction in the first six months of 1933 that the favorable aspects of the National Industrial Recovery Act would give trade unionism a new quasi-public status has received a considerable setback with the toning down of section 7a in the automobile code, the subsequent decision with respect to multiple representation handed down by President Roosevelt in setting up the Automobile Labor Board, the antitrade union attitude of some of the members of the National Recovery Administration and the continuance of antilabor decisions by local courts. Company unions have more than doubled their membership. There is little indication that the employers' anti-union offensive has been tempered. The pronouncement of certain labor leaders at an earlier stage as to the inadvisability of strikes and their agreement to the proposal that disputes be referred to regional labor boards have not served to diminish the number of strikes, and with the exception of the railroad brotherhoods the trade unions have unanimously opposed compulsory governmental arbitration.

Whatever the outcome of the New Deal, American trade unionism today is keenly aware that the period of economic and industrial expansion is over; that technological improvements and the limitation of both the foreign and the domestic markets will involve a more or less permanent reservoir of unemployed labor. The shift to the plea for greater consuming power through higher wages and shorter hours and the endorsement of unemployment insurance are signs of a new orientation within the ranks of the A. F. of L.

Outside the federation and the railroad brotherhoods the "independent" trade unions and those connected with radical political parties have shown little stability. The affiliation of the Amalgamated Clothing Workers, representing over 125,000 workers, with the A. F. of L. in 1933 marked the end of strong independent unionism in the pre-NRA period. Pending the struggle over the issue of industrial unionism, several of the newly organized or revitalized unions, like those among the public utility workers and in the automobile industry, have chosen to remain outside the A. F. of L., at least temporarily. The future of certain "guilds" and associations of professional workers which came into being with the NRA is more uncertain from a trade union point of view.

Radical unionism has shown still greater fluctuations. The always unstable ranks of the I.W.W. were decimated by the withdrawal of the Western Federation of Miners, by the postwar criminal syndicalism laws and the conversion of some groups to communism. After the decision in 1928 to set up dual unions the Communists established four such national bodies, but in 1931 their Trade Union Unity League claimed a total membership of only 30,485. The National Miners' Union, which at one time reported a membership of 20,000, is now practically dead, as is the National Textile Workers' Union. Although the league claimed a membership of almost 125,000 in 1934, it has an appreciable following only in the New York fur industry. The decision in the codes for certain industries in which the league had previously had some membership, for example, in the women's garment and the shoe industries, to permit representation of only one body has led the Communist party to return to its policy of "boring from within" both in the A. F. of L. and in independent unions, at the same time that it maintains its skeleton dual unions and attempts to reach the Negroes, the unemployed and the field workers in industrialized agriculture. An insurgent movement among the coal miners of Illinois and the southwest, the National Progressive Miners' Union, while originally affiliated with the Conference for Progressive Labor Action, has since become "conservative" and as a result of the workings of the code is likely to have its membership reabsorbed by the United Mine Workers' Union.

While undoubtedly there has been a rise in radical sentiment within the last year among certain groups and while there is an apparent change in attitude even among conservative unions, there is little indication on the whole of any powerful political revolutionary trend in the American trade union movement. But the National Industrial Recovery Act of 1933, section

7a, has improved the position of labor in one important respect. It has given to the unions, and especially to the formerly unorganized workers in mass production industries, a new feeling of assurance in demanding recognition, higher wages, lower hours and "conditions." The illegal denial by some companies of collective bargaining and the uncertain course of the government in attempting to enforce the law are not so important as the new militancy of labor, growing as it does out of a feeling, perhaps mistaken, that the government is labor's friend.

Canada. Because of the predominance of agriculture in the national economy the trade union movement of Canada is comparatively small. The first impulses toward organization in the pre-industrial period came from British craftsmen who set up local trade unions first among printers and shoemakers and later among building, engineering, clothing and food workers. While some of these locals were for a time affiliated with British unions, independent Canadian unions were more common. The Provincial Workmen's Association, established in 1879 among the miners of Nova Scotia, had a considerable hold for forty years. With the rise of national unionism in the United States and the realization of the community of economic interests between the workers of the two countries the dominant trend was toward the establishment of Canadian locals of these American unions. In 1886, with the encouragement of the American Federation of Labor, there was formed a Trades and Labor Congress of Canada consisting of unions affiliated with the A. F. of L. In addition to the purely Canadian unions, which federated in the early part of the twentieth century, and those affiliated with the A. F. of L. there developed after 1900 among the French Canadian elements of the population a Catholic trade union movement. Insurgent unionism as represented by the Industrial Workers of the World also manifested itself, and the One Big Union movement, which gained strength along the western coast after the Winnipeg general strike of 1919, has obtained a greater foothold in the Canadian lumber camps than in the United States. After 1930 the Communist Workers' Unity League also made its appearance in Canada. The total trade union membership of the country rose from 133,000 in 1911 to 378,000 in 1919; it dropped to 261,000 in 1924 but increased again to 322,400 in 1930. The latter figure, however, includes a considerable portion of non-paying unemployed workers. By 1932 the number had decreased to about 283,500, or about 10 percent of the total number of wageworkers in factories, workshops, mines and lumber camps. The proportionate strength of the various industrial groups is strikingly similar to that in the United States, except for the fact that public employees constitute a rather large proportion of the total membership and that almost 25 percent are grouped under the heading "miscellaneous trades and industries." The comparative strength of the various groups in 1932 was as follows: unions affiliated with the Trades and Labor Congress of Canada, 127,264; the All Canadian Congress of Labor, representing independent Canadian unionism, 50,356, of which the One Big Union accounted for 23,340; the Catholic unions 25,000; the Communist groups 12,500; unaffiliated Canadian Central bodies, 19,332; independent local units 15,596; and unions affiliated with American groups but not with the A. F. of L. (railway workers, clothing workers, I.W.W. and so on) 33,628. Thus organizations without international connections accounted for 107,489 members, and those with such affiliations numbered 176,087. The Canadian trade unions represent a far less unified movement than do those of the United States. Despite the dominance of the American policy in the economic field in the sphere of legislation and political activity the movement tends to follow the example of British labor on a provincial and municipal scale, while the newly organized Cooperative Commonwealth Federation—a socialistically inclined third party—appears to be increasing and extending its political influence.

NORMAN J. WARE

See: AMERICAN FEDERATION OF LABOR; INDUSTRIAL WORKERS OF THE WORLD; KNIGHTS OF LABOR.

AUSTRALIA, NEW ZEALAND AND SOUTH AFRICA. The trade union movements of these three "new" countries differ greatly in age as well as in strength and policy. Australia had functioning local craft unions even in the 1830's, when Sydney was half convict, and can trace an unbroken record of organization from the mid-century. These first unions and the larger bodies of urban artisans and coal miners which developed after the gold rush followed conservative British models, although demands for land reform and the successful fight for Chinese exclusion betrayed more characteristic Australian concerns. The late 1880's broadened the range of interests and the base of organization. Socialist ideas received wide circulation; and a remarkable series of organizing campaigns welded migratory sheepshearers into a strong union, enlisted many of the unskilled and made Australia the most completely unionized country in the world. But the very rapidity of these changes apparently bred overconfidence in the labor leaders and stiffened the employers' resistance; and when in 1890 a trivial dispute on shipboard developed into a prolonged and widespread sympathetic strike, the unions went down to complete defeat.

After the maritime strike the workers promptly discovered their political power, but the unions did not regain their previous size until after 1900. Their revival was closely linked with the introduction and extension of compulsory arbitration. The total membership, which was below 100,000 when New South Wales organized its court in 1901, nearly quadrupled within a decade, exceeded half a million during the war years, passed 900,000 in the late 1920's and even in 1931 remained well over 750,000, or about one half of the total of employees of all sorts. In this number are included not only craftsmen and miners and the urban unskilled but also a great body of pastoral workers, more than a third of all women employees and surprisingly large sections of the white collar class. The proportion of union members to total population—over 14 percent at the peak—is the highest in the world.

Forms of organization are as diverse as the sources of membership. Industrial unionism is the accepted doctrine—the Australian Workers' Union began in 1894 with a nucleus of shearers and absorbed a strange assortment of other groups, and the agitation for a radical One Big Union received a surprising amount of temporary support—yet a large number of craft and even local bodies still exist. Trades councils in the capital cities have long been the most important links between organizations, but occasional trade union congresses and an Australasian Council of Trade Unions formed in 1927 have not succeeded in giving the industrial movement a national unity comparable with that of the Labour party.

Australian unionism cannot be understood apart from its relationship to the party and the system of arbitration. To the latter it owes much of its size, since several organized groups could not maintain themselves without governmental encouragement, and much of its characteristic quality. Although two or three powerful bodies shun the courts almost entirely and others employ the policy of "arbitration plus strikes," the great majority of wage rates and working rules are nevertheless set by arbitration. Unions become "litigious" organizations, and the main business of the leader is the preparation, negotiation and argument of claims before the court and the policing of the subsequent awards. Often his only other function of comparable importance is participation in the control and criticism of the political movement. It was, for example, pressure from the unions that forced the party to adopt in 1921 the "objective" of "socialization." But even when the "industrialists" most bitterly attack the "politicians," the real issue turns not on an I.W.W. or communist demand for the repudiation of the party but on the question of how directly the unions shall determine its policy and control its personnel.

Although it is to the party that the Australian worker looks for the principal improvements in his condition, the unions provide its chief support and most of its leadership; and there is no capitalistic country in which the combined labor movement wields greater power. This fact is to be explained not merely by racial homogeneity and the importation of British Chartist, trade union and socialist ideas but also by the occupational distribution of the people. Since early regulations and the much more fundamental factors of climate made the Australian frontier inhospitable to small man settlement as a possible outlet for disappointed gold diggers or later wage earners, there resulted an extraordinary concentration of population in the capital cities and an early accentuation of class differences both in them and on the great sheep stations.

Resentment against similar conditions played a large part in the early history of the New Zealand movement. Wage earners and urban unemployed joined in agitations against "land monopoly" and "sweating" during the 1880's; six union leaders entered Parliament in the political upset of 1890; and the trades councils provided much of the impetus, although little conspicuous leadership, for the Liberal government's program of land and labor legislation. Even more completely than in Australia the subsequent history of unionism centers around that of the arbitration system. Union membership, which was only about 10,000 when the law of 1894 was passed, doubled before 1901, climbed steadily to wartime figures of about 70,000, passed 100,000 in the late 1920's and declined from 91,000 in 1931 to 79,000 in 1932. The unions demonstrated their support of arbitration during its first decade by an almost complete avoidance of strikes. But with less sympathetic administration and a check to rising prices awards began to yield fewer wage increases; and, on the other hand, more radical leaders from Great Britain, Australia and the American I.W.W. inspired the workers to a more militant unionism. The result was a brief period of violent industrial strife in which an anti-arbitrationist Alliance of Labor held the ascendancy in the movement. There was a bitter strike of miners at Waihi in 1912, and the next year a watersiders' dispute at Wellington led to a brief general strike at all the dominion ports. Both, however, were broken by "free" laborers under strong government protection, and labor turned again to political action as its principal weapon. The unions resumed a reliance upon the arbitration court much more complete than that of the Australian movement. When compulsory arbitration was attacked by farming interests in 1928 and overthrown in 1932, it was for the preservation of the unions that their leaders rallied with virtual unanimity to the defense of the system.

Much of New Zealand unionism may be broken down unless the prop of arbitration is restored, and both the campaign and its result show that the movement is much weaker than the Australian. The two made similar gains when large scale sheep raising was the principal industry in both countries; but since refrigeration and dairying transformed New Zealand into a land of small working farmers, the younger movement has not been able to keep the Australian pace.

South Africa had neither wage paying pastoralists nor substantial industry at the time the labor movements were emerging in the other two countries; and even gold mining, which was just opening up in 1890, gave little occasion for unionism in its early years. A small force of highly skilled British miners supervised masses of cheap native labor, and the high wages won by the former tended to spread to the few other occupations employing European wage earners. Substantial organization did not develop until after white monopoly of semiskilled occupations had been threatened by the increasing competence of natives and the temporary competition of Chinese labor, and until there had grown up a class of "poor whites" who could neither secure skilled employment nor compete for unskilled work on the native standard (*see* NATIVE POLICY).

A successful gold fields strike in 1913 stimulated a wave of organization which was only partly checked by a defeat on the railways in the following year, and membership rose steadily from 12,000 in 1914 to 135,000 in 1920. After 1915 the Chamber of Mines, representing the most powerful employers, dealt regularly with the unions; but in 1922 they attempted to reduce costs by substituting several thousand natives in positions held by whites. This precipitated the most notable labor dispute in South African history, and for a time the armed commandos of the strikers controlled almost the whole length of Witwatersrand. Suppression of the uprising turned the workers to more active use of the Labour party and to alliance with the Nationalists to defend their racial privileges. Unionism rose slowly again from 80,000 in 1922 to a doubtful 200,000 in 1927 and a more certain 115,000 in 1929. Part of this growth represents the encouragement of organization by the Conciliation Act of 1924. The largest figure, however, reflects the peak attained by a remarkable native organization, a sort of Bantu Knights of Labor, called the I.C.U. (Industrial and Commercial Workers' Union), which claimed 100,000 members before it disintegrated. Although this last attempt may represent a significant portent, so far the main body of the movement remains strictly limited to white labor and, in the Cape alone, to mulattoes. Its most characteristic weapon is the enforcement, by convention or trade agreement or in certain occupations by law, of a color bar.

The three movements are alike in their profession of socialist principles and in their readiness to use the machinery of the state and the instrumentality of a labor party to further their trade union aims. Isolation has made all three rather indifferent to organizations extending beyond their borders, and they are not affiliated with the trade union internationals. They do not, however, show conspicuous similarities arising directly from their position as "new," or "frontier," countries. The strength of Australian labor indeed results largely from an occupational structure early approximating that of an "old" country. In New Zealand alone, and there only since 1890, has labor been affected by a movement to a small man's frontier at all comparable with that which has determined so much of the history of the United States and Canada. The South African situation is characterized by the struggle of the white workers against a few large employees on the one hand and the native masses on the other, and the movement represents an aristocracy of labor more exclusive than the American and in sharp contrast to the organizations of the unskilled in Australia and New Zealand. Yet the South African color bar has exactly the same roots as the exclusion of orientals from the other countries. In each case the comparative scarcity of white workers had given them an unusually high standard of living; and the most fundamental common characteristic of these new country labor movements is their determination to preserve that standard against the competition of cheaper labor.

CARTER GOODRICH

LATIN AMERICA. Economic development beginning in the latter part of the nineteenth century, marked by the growth of transportation facilities, increased exploitation of mineral resources, the introduction of some industries and the growth of a number of large cities, provided the basis for the trade union movement in Latin America. The first form of labor organization was generally the mutual aid society. As a result of the influx of immigrants acquainted with unionism, the return of migratory workmen from the United States (to Mexico and Cuba) or the influence of a few native or foreign agitators the movement acquired more of a trade union character. In most Latin American countries the emergence of trade unionism dates from around 1900. About that time depreciated currencies and new protective tariffs raised living costs and produced demands for higher wages; at the same time urbanization accompanied by greater diffusion of general education helped union organization. Politicians began to realize the utility of labor agitation as a means of embarrassing the government, while in some countries the small capitalists, professionals and government functionaries supported labor in order to destroy the alliance of the ruling class with outside capital so as to gain control themselves. The trade union movement generally reached its peak during the period of the World War, when immigration was cut off and native industry stimulated. After 1920 a serious decline set in. Considerable advances were subsequently made, but economic difficulties and the resulting governmental reaction have again seriously weakened the movement. It is too early to determine the effect of the recent revolutions upon trade unionism.

Even at its peak the trade union movement, except in a few countries, failed to enlist important percentages of the working classes. The basic reason for the backwardness of the movement is the fact that in the countries of Latin America the mass of the proletariat is nonindustrial. The usual difficulties of organizing the agrarian proletariat are augmented by the widespread use of seasonal migratory labor and the semiservile state of peonage which still obtains in certain regions. The dependence upon one or two natural products—sugar in Cuba, nitrates in Chile—which leads to marked fluctuations in national economic conditions, has accentuated the instability of the trade union movement. Even where large scale industrial activity exists, lack of facilities for communication and education, extreme poverty and almost total ignorance of organizational methods militate against permanent or centralized organization. In addition the proletariat is of a heterogeneous ethnic character; communication and cooperation are difficult among indigenous elements unable to speak the official language, Spanish speaking native groups and immigrants. Unionism has been characterized by a general absence of national trade unions; local organizations of diverse crafts and industries have tended to affiliate directly with the central federations, where such have existed, rather than through national craft or industrial unions. Conflicting ideologies have led to serious divisions and great fluctuations in membership. Anarcho-syndicalist influences, introduced mainly by Spanish and Italian immigrants, have led to the light hearted use of the general strike. Another detrimental factor has been the disloyalty and dishonesty of many trade union leaders.

In almost all the countries genuine trade unionism has been opposed by both central and local governments, especially by the dictatorships. Particularly in agriculture, where ownership is largely in native hands, attempts to organize have been immediately suppressed. The firm hold of employers upon the governments is not confined to native capitalists. Nevertheless, almost everywhere trade unions have thrived upon nationalistic sentiment directed against alien capitalistic domination, and almost all their victories have been at the expense of foreign owners. Even when hard pressed by labor demands, the employer class has preferred to deal with such questions by social legislation rather than by collective bargaining. The enactment of advanced legislation, however, does not necessarily mean its enforcement. The constitutional guaranties of freedom of association and the special laws establishing the right to organize have been steadily nullified in both law and practise, as has the right to strike. A widespread and effective method of repression has been the summary deportation of alien leaders. On the other hand, governments have encouraged mutualistic, cooperative or "yellow" organizations, which have attracted more workers than the genuine trade unions. The influence of the church has been in the same direction, although Catholic trade unions proper have only a very limited influence.

Membership statistics for Latin American trade unions are highly unreliable. It may be said, however, that the anarchists, who were among the early organizers and had a wide influence, are definitely moribund. The syndicalists, who gained strength before the World War and reached their peak during the war or shortly afterwards, have lost considerably. The International Federation of Trade Unions has had an important affiliate only in Argentina, but the Mexican Confederación Regional Obrera Mexicana (C.R.O.M.) and a number of the important Cuban unions may perhaps be included in this orientation. The communists have gained control of the main central organization in Chile and Cuba; they also claim more or less organized trade union movements in Uruguay, Argentina, Peru, Brazil and Mexico.

Mexico has had the strongest trade union movement in Latin America. Under the dictatorship of Díaz all genuine unions were subject to brutal oppression; certain organizations did develop, however, notably that of the railroad workers. The revolution, assuming the character of a nationalist uprising against foreign capitalistic domination, opened the way for the expansion of the labor movement. As early as 1912 the Casa del Obrero Mundial, more a propaganda center than a federation, was organized. When Huerta renewed the severe repression of labor organizations, the Casa signed an alliance with Carranza under which it organized Red battalions to fight for him against Huerta in return for promises of aid. These promises were soon forgotten by Carranza. Article 123 of the constitution of 1917 set up a liberal labor code including the right to organize and to strike. From the first, a small group of leaders (*grupo acción*) dominated the Mexican labor movement, much as did the "Junta" in the British trade union movement during the 1860's and 1870's.

Their organization, the C.R.O.M., established in 1918, grew slowly in the face of governmental and employer opposition. It supported Obregón against Carranza, and the former rewarded its leaders with government posts. The organization grew rapidly during Obregón's administration and reached the height of its power in the first two years of the Calles administration, which backed it not only against employers but against rival unions. In 1927 it claimed a membership of 2,250,000. Probably more than three quarters of the members were loosely organized peasants and agricultural laborers. Its most active membership consisted of textile workers, printers, stage workers and government employees. In policy the C.R.O.M. had receded considerably from its original revolutionary program; its increasing conservatism was traceable to its alliance with the government, maintained chiefly for the purpose of securing and safeguarding legislation enforcing article 123, as well as to its connections with the American Federation of Labor, which were effectively used, for instance, to secure American support for the government against the de la Huerta revolt in 1923. Outside the C.R.O.M. were the important railway brotherhood (Confederación de Sociedades Ferrocarrileras) founded in 1920, the dwindling anarcho-syndicalist Confederación General de Trabajadores, Catholic unions strong in the states of Jalisco and Michoacán and scattered communist groups, particularly important in Vera Cruz and Yucatan.

Toward the end of Calles' term the C.R.O.M. began to lose influence and to show signs of disintegration. Its leaders have been accused of corruption. The C.R.O.M. itself has been charged with using intimidation and governmental agencies to force independent groups to affiliate with it, as in the case of the street railway workers of Mexico city. Certain of its constituent organizations have been taxed with irresponsibility in their relations with the employers. More important reasons for the decline of the C.R.O.M. were peasant opposition and the increasingly conservative attitude of the government. It was credited by the International Labor Office with a membership of 500,000 on January 1, 1932. In September, 1932, the Cámara del Trabajo was organized, mainly by labor in the Federal District, as a rival to the C.R.O.M. The federal labor law of 1931 makes collective agreements with registered unions compulsory for employers.

Cuba. The cigar makers, the first to organize

and probably the most stable group of unionists, and the railway and port workers have constituted the nucleus of the trade union movement, which manifested itself earlier in Cuba than elsewhere in Latin America; dates prior to 1870 have been set for its origin. However, genuine trade unionism scarcely existed before independence was won, while since then its growth has been fitful and its leadership divided. The reasons are many: Cuba is peculiarly exposed to the most diverse influences from Europe, Latin America and the United States; the powerful Spanish clubs, which pursue mutualistic aims, have attracted the immigrant group, which is extremely important in trade and industry; the remaining Spanish element has been anarchistic; and the particularly corrupt political atmosphere has been fatal to honest leadership. Finally, the government, fearing American intervention or any interference with the basic sugar crop, has maintained the antiquated Spanish legislation pertaining to trade unions. While the movement received occasional aid from native politicians as well as assistance from Samuel Gompers, it was really the wartime sugar boom and the revolution of 1917 which provided the opportunity for union growth. In 1919 every trade was reported by the Pan-American Federation of Labor to be organized. Agitators had even appeared at the sugar plantations, but the government had taken action against them. The immediate post-war period was marked by a wave of general strikes, but a reaction came after the fall of the price of sugar in 1920. As sugar prices rose in 1923 and the presidential elections of 1924 approached, union activity began to revive. The harbor workers' Federación de la Bahía de la Habana engaged in an important strike which gave rise to a general strike in 1924; the railway workers established the moderate Hermandad Ferroviaria; and the long established cigar makers' Federación de las Sociedades de Torcedores de las Provincias de la Habana y Pinar del Río, with a membership of about 5000 or 6000, carried forward its efforts to establish a truly national federation of the industry. The project of organizing the sugar mills and fields was revived and severely repressed. Finally the Confederación Nacional Obrera de Cuba (C.N.O.C.) was formed in August, 1925; it joined the Red International of Labor Unions (R.I.L.U.). Despite the efforts of a strong communistic minority the tobacco workers' federation refused to affiliate with it. According to Carleton Beals, the C.N.O.C. had 8000 members in Havana and the organized tobacco workers 30,000 throughout the country before the final sugar crisis and Machado's dictatorship played havoc with the labor movement. The C.N.O.C. was outlawed in 1930; most of the organizations which survived were mere shells taken over or founded by the president's satellites. Such were the railway brotherhood and the Federación Cubana del Trabajo (established in 1927), which claimed memberships at the beginning of 1929 of 12,780 and 40,406 respectively. A schism in the latter gave rise in 1930 to another paper organization, the Unión Federativa Nacional Obrera, which the *International Labour Office Year-Book 1932* (Geneva 1933) credits with 20,000 members in 1932. The end of the dictatorship in 1933, precipitated immediately by a general strike, gave rise to widespread labor agitation in part antiforeign and even to the seizure of establishments by workers. The C.N.O.C. reemerged with the overthrow of Machado and assumed an important part in the labor movement. The Mendieta government, facing a serious strike wave in 1934, restricted the right to strike, imposed compulsory arbitration and dissolved unions. With the passing of this immediate crisis its attitude moderated somewhat.

Argentina. The marked economic development, accompanied by the influx of great numbers of immigrants, which has placed Argentina in the forefront of Europeanized countries of Latin America and has made Buenos Aires one of the world's largest cities, has given rise to a trade union movement of considerable importance. Trade union organizations began to appear in the 1880's in Buenos Aires; apparently the first was La Fraternidad, established by the railway workers in 1887. Economic and political disturbances beginning in 1890 furthered the growth of organizations, which sprang up in various cities. Two short lived federations, socialistic in orientation, were founded during the decade 1890–1900. Anarchistic propaganda was intensified toward the end of the decade and the first permanent central organization, the Federación Obrera Regional Argentina (F.O.R.A.), although founded in 1901 as a neutral body was dominated from the first by the extremist element. The government replied to the increasing threat from radical labor with the *ley de residencia* of 1902, which gave the police summary powers to expel alien agitators. Although its abrogation was long one of the chief aims of the labor movement, it remained on the statute books until 1922. In fact it was followed by more hampering action and legislation especially in 1910. Meantime the schismatic tendency which, because of both internal and external pressure, long marked the movement began to manifest itself; and although the reformist organizations, backed by the well disciplined Socialist party, constantly sought to establish unity on the basis of neutrality, the extremist elements tended to gain the upper hand within the new body. Such was the fate of the Unión General de Trabajadores, founded in 1903, which was absorbed by the Confederación Obrera Regional Argentina, established in 1909. This in turn was absorbed by the F.O.R.A. in 1914 under the syndicalist banner, but in 1915 the organization divided into the anarchist F.O.R.A. of the fifth congress and the syndicalist F.O.R.A. of the ninth congress. The latter played the leading role in the years 1916–20, when in addition to the favorable conditions created by the war labor enjoyed the support of Irigoyen, the first president elected by the middle and working classes, and engaged successfully in a series of important strikes. The strongest element within the F.O.R.A. was the Federación Obrera Marítima (F.O.M.), which extended its influence into Uruguay and Paraguay. The tide turned, however, in 1921, when a strike of the F.O.M., which developed into a general tie up, was sternly suppressed with the aid of yellow unions. When its membership declined as a result of defeat, the leaders of the syndicalist F.O.R.A. together with a number of anarchist and autonomous organizations formed in 1922 the Unión Sindical Argentina (U.S.A.) with a membership estimated at 30,000. It was soon dominated by the anarcho-syndicalists and constantly lost ground. On the other hand, the socialistic and reformist organizations, notably the Confraternidad Ferroviaria, established in 1920 and comprising La Fraternidad and the Unión Ferroviaria, became the leading force in the labor movement and established the Confederación Obrera Argentina (C.O.A.) with 79,000 members in 1926. The C.O.A. also included among others the cutters' and tailors' union with 3650 members in 1927 and the union of the municipal workers of Buenos Aires, which had 3000 members in 1927. In 1930 the C.O.A. combined with the U.S.A. to form the Confederación General del Trabajo, a free organization affiliated with the I.F.T.U. and claiming a membership of over 200,000. The anarchistic F.O.R.A. has shrunk to negligible proportions. The *círculos de obreros católicos*, the first of which was established in 1892, have a mixed membership. They are federated and affiliated with the White International; in 1927 their membership was estimated at 30,000.

Uruguay. The growth of Montevideo accompanied by an influx of immigrants brought the trade union movement to Uruguay about 1895–96; the street car workers, bricklayers, bakers and port workers organized ostensibly as mutual aid societies and engaged in strikes for better conditions. The police handled these early conflicts in a manner wholly satisfactory to the employers; but support for the trade unions developed among the politicians, notably José Batlle y Ordóñez, who enlisted large masses of the immigrant proletariat under the banner of the *Partido colorado*, with a program of democracy, social legislation and state ownership and operation. As president from 1903 to 1907 Batlle displayed the widest tolerance even in the case of the anarchists, whose leaders were mostly Europeans expelled from Argentina. Batlle's successor, Williman, a member of the same party, seems to have been less tolerant. The first two years of Batlle's second term (1911–15), during which he began to emphasize the social and economic aspects of his program, were marked by a great number of strikes, including a general tie up in Montevideo (1911) sponsored by the anarchistic Federación Obrera Regional Uruguaya (F.O.R.U.). At the time the government refused to concede the right of state employees to strike. As elsewhere, the war gave the trade unions the opportunity to achieve genuine importance; their membership is said to have reached 25,000 in 1918–19. The great strikes in Argentina had their repercussions, and the Federación Obrera Marítima of Uruguay, which cooperated with its sister organization in Argentina, was the center of growth. Employees of the state port and street car administrations were involved in these strike movements, but the directors of these bodies reiterated the earlier policy and refused to recognize "outside" representatives of these workers. The post-war reaction apparently was not serious, for the Oficina Nacional del Trabajo set the trade union membership for 1922 at 28,011 in Montevideo and 5873 elsewhere; among government employees there were 1600 customs house laborers, 900 hospital employees and 800 employees of the Montevideo street cleaning service. A series of schisms in the central organizations began about 1921: the neutral Unión Sindical Uruguaya, soon dominated by the anarcho-syndicalists, was established in 1923; the Confederación General del Trabajo, which affiliated with the R.I.L.U., was founded in 1929; the Unión General de Trabajadores del Uruguay was organized in 1930 by printers, marine engineers and industrial workers with an orientation toward the I.F.T.U. In that year the Uruguayan labor office credited the C.G.T., U.S.U. and F.O.R.U. with 14,370, 3920 and 1350 members respectively.

Brazil. Trade unionism in Brazil, where there is considerable industrial development, is weak in comparison with that in Argentina. Unions began to develop about 1900 under the influence of immigrants and to some extent were aided by politicians. As elsewhere, the World War favored their growth. Government reaction began in 1920 and culminated in 1927 with a law, designed ostensibly to suppress communism, which permitted the police to dissolve workers' organizations regarded as dangerous to public order. However, trade union activity is reported to have revived in recent years. Important unions are those of the harbor and transport workers at Rio de Janeiro and at Santos, the country's coffee outlet. Although a national labor federation was set up as early as 1906, the vast territory of the country makes the survival of such organizations extremely difficult. In 1929, however, a Confederação Geral do Trabalho was founded by communist unions, which in 1932, according to the statistics of the International Labor Office, had a membership of 8600. In 1931 there was established a União Geral dos Trabalhadores do Brasil, claiming about 15,000 members in 1932. The latter opposed the system of "recognized" trade unions set up by the law of March 19, 1931, on the ground that it infringed upon the right of association. The Brazilian employees' associations, which limit themselves to mutualistic or cooperative undertakings, such as the Associação dos Empregados no Commercio of Rio de Janeiro with about 30,000 members, have enjoyed much greater prosperity than the trade unions, especially since the government has long sponsored the formation of such organizations.

Chile. Drawing much strength from the political aspirations of the middle classes, which include the white collar groups, Chilean trade unionism has developed on the railways, at the various ports, in the industries, in the copper, coal and iron mines and in sheep raising in the far south. But the most restless laboring element has existed at the northern nitrate deposits, where high wages have been more than offset by excessive living costs and difficult living conditions. The general unrest has been augmented by antagonism aroused by foreign exploitation and the presence of a goodly number of Peruvian and Bolivian laborers. The earliest important strikes in the country were probably fomented by President Balmaceda in connection with the parliamentary revolution of 1891, but they helped to give rise to a trade union movement, particularly after 1900. Mutual aid societies sometimes engaged in such activities, but a closer approximation to trade unions was provided by the *mancomunales*, which functioned during the first decade of the twentieth century and were said to cover the entire country. Their program consisted largely of mutualism and cooperation, demands for higher pay, sound currency, restriction of the company store system and better working conditions. Their failure to survive was probably the result in part of governmental persecution. The original program of the first permanent national federation, the Gran Federación Obrera de Chile, which was founded by railway workers in 1909, was primarily mutualistic. In the next few years the membership basis was widened and the organization strengthened. But it was the influence of the Socialist Labor party, founded in 1912; the influx of foreigners from Argentina into the far south; the disturbances in the basic nitrate industry, which were accentuated by the war; the wartime industrial growth; and the final disintegration of the old political system as indicated by the election of the middle and working class presidential candidate in 1920, which caused the great expansion of trade union membership and radically altered its viewpoint. Thus the Industrial Workers of the World is said to have enlisted 25,000 workers, primarily in the ports, by 1919, while at the same time the coal and nitrate miners entered the labor federation. The influx of such elements caused a schism, but the conservative group, which retained the original name, soon disappeared. The Federación Obrera de Chile (F.O.Ch.), the organization of the other group, gained wide influence. After the F.O.Ch. joined the R.I.L.U. in 1921, the railwaymen withdrew, but their Federación Ferroviaria maintained close relations with the former and eventually joined the latter. The F.O.Ch. did not escape the universal post-war setback, but with improving economic conditions and continued political unrest it began to grow again. In 1928 its membership was placed at approximately 136,000 and that of the railway federation and of the I.W.W. at 22,000 and

7000 respectively. Meanwhile the trade union spirit had spread to the white collar workers, and at the end of 1924 their organizations formed the comparatively radical Unión de Empleados de Chile with a membership of 7000 in 1928. Fear of labor and the influence of the white collar class led to the enactment of an extensive body of social legislation, which included a voluntary trade union measure (1924) designed to woo the workers from their radicalism. This law set up two types of unions: *sindicatos industriales*, similar to the American company unions, with profit sharing provisions, and *sindicatos profesionales*, which are registered and have the right to conclude collective agreements. In 1924 strike procedure also was regulated. As political instability continued and economic depression set in (1926–27), the workers failed to abandon their old organizations. Hence the dictator Ibañez dissolved all radical unions in 1928, required all trade associations to follow a policy of collaboration and established official supervision of these bodies. Only such organizations as the Catholic Confederación de Sindicatos Blancos, founded in 1925 and possessing a membership of 7000 in 1928, escaped repression; but a new national confederation of trade unions having as one of its objects the defense of freedom of association was established in 1930. With the overthrow of Ibañez in July, 1931, the F.O.Ch. reemerged, having lost a great many members to the "official" unions. At the hands of the various governments which succeeded one another in 1931–32 it suffered considerable persecution. The number of trade union members is placed at 66,663 in President Alessandri's message of May, 1934.

MAX LEVIN
JOSEPH J. SENTURIA

INTERNATIONAL ORGANIZATION. The origins of international organization among trade unionists may be traced to the setting up of trade secretariats of the various national unions in specific industries or crafts. The first of these international trade secretariats was that of the printers (1889), the second that of the miners (1890). The origins of this type of international trade unionism lay in the migration of workers from country to country and in the desire of the unions to aid each other in strikes. A similar motive had led in 1886 to the formation of an inter-Scandinavian federation of trade unions. With the growth in number of trade unionists in the 1890's and the setting up of national centers or federations there developed a movement to found an all comprehensive International Secretariat of National Trade Union Centers which would supplement and unify the trade secretariats and aid as well in the cause of political democracy and world peace. The creation of such an international body in 1903 was assisted by the Second (Socialist) International, whose congresses supplied a meeting ground for socialist trade unionists of various countries. It was realized that on the international scale as on the national trade union organization must be autonomous and distinct from the political party grouping. In 1904 the membership of this comprehensive international trade union secretariat was about 2,500,000 in 14 countries of Europe, over one half being accounted for by the Social Democratic unions of Germany and Austria. In 1906 these 14 countries contributed over 3,500,000 out of a total trade union membership of 9,500,000 in 30 countries, including the United States, Australia and New Zealand. The alliance of the American Federation of Labor in 1909 raised the membership considerably, gave the secretariat an intercontinental scope and also led it to change its name to the International Federation of Trade Unions.

By 1913 the I.F.T.U. claimed a membership of almost 8,000,000 in 16 European countries and the United States out of a total trade union membership of 16,152,000 in 30 countries of the world. The only other international trade union organization in existence was the International Secretariat of Christian Trade Unions, established in 1908 on the model of the I.F.T.U. but emphasizing its own particular ideals.

Before the World War, despite the broad coverage of the I.F.T.U. and its international secretariats, its activity was comparatively narrow in scope and its main achievement was the establishment of contacts between the trade unions of different countries and the interchange of trade union documents and information. It also furnished moral and material aid on occasions of mass struggles, such as the general strike of 1909 in Sweden, that of 1913 in Belgium and the London dock strike of 1911. Because of the principle of admission of only one trade union center in each country the separatist Czech movements in Austria were excluded, as was also the Industrial Workers of the World in the United States. Although the I.F.T.U. under the leadership of German trade unionists represented the outlook of the evolutionary international socialist movement, it included the "neutral" American Federation of Labor and the syndicalist Confédération Générale du Travail of France.

The World War caused a collapse of international trade unionism, although formal affiliations and the headquarters at Amsterdam were still maintained. With the coming of peace and the rapid growth of trade unionism in all countries in the immediate post-war period the I.F.T.U. entered upon a new era of influence. Between 1919 and 1921 over 20 international trade union secretariats were formed. The I.F.T.U. reached a peak membership in December, 1919, of over 23,000,000 in 21 countries out of a total trade union membership of 42,000,000 in 30 countries.

In this period the I.F.T.U. was one of the main factors in the establishment and work of the International Labor Office of the League of Nations and it played an important role in the League as a whole. It carried on a boycott of Hungarian goods during the White terror, gave aid to Vienna in 1919–20 and took action against the transport of munitions to Poland to be used against Soviet Russia.

Beginning, however, with 1921 a number of factors contributed to weaken the position of the I.F.T.U. The first of these was the withdrawal of the A. F. of L., which had three years previously organized a "neutral" international organization among the trade unions of Latin America, the Pan-American Federation of Labor, with headquarters at Washington. Although this withdrawal was followed by the affiliation of the Canadian unions and by the retention of membership on the part of several national unions in the trade secretariats, the important Mexican federation and the trade union centers of the other Latin American countries remained aloof from the I.F.T.U. The second adverse factor was the split between the Socialists and the Communists, which had reverberations in the trade union movement of every European country and in the rising labor movements of the East, especially after the creation in 1921 by the Third (Communist) International of the Red International of Labor Unions. The question of relations with the R.I.L.U. led to an internal split in the secretariat of the I.F.T.U. as well. The liquidation of "free" trade unionism in Italy and other fascist and semifascist countries served still further to undermine the strength of the federation. Also in 1923 the syndicalists created the International Working Men's Association with headquarters in Berlin, which included large groupings in Spain and Portugal as well as smaller groups in Germany, Holland and Sweden, and in Latin America.

In 1923 there were no fewer than 5 international trade union organizations, with 70 affiliated or subordinate bodies. All 5 suffered a marked decrease in membership and influence between 1923 and 1925 because of the steadily diminishing trade union membership in most capitalistic countries. The Pan-American Federation of Labor, as a result of certain developments in Mexican political life, is now largely a paper organization. The rise in the number of members of the R.I.L.U. represents an increase in the membership of Soviet trade unions rather than a growing sphere of influence in capitalistic countries. Indeed its figures of affiliated trade union centers as well as of sympathizing groups or minorities within the "free" or the "neutral" unions show great fluctuation and instability. At one time they were indicative mainly of Communist activity in the Orient, but at the present they represent for the most part the organized centers of Communist trade union activity in France and Czechoslovakia. According to the International Labor Year Book for 1932, of the 17,000,000 members of the R.I.L.U 16,500,000 are in the Soviet Union. France, Brazil and Japan are the only other countries which show any considerable membership. Although the R.I.L.U. has collected funds for the assistance of strikers in various countries, its chief work has been to spread propaganda of the Communist concepts of trade union strategy.

In 1932 the membership of the I.F.T.U. seemed to indicate a new upward trend. It had sunk in 1929 to 13,573,000 out of a total trade union membership estimated at 45,000,000; this total, however, included perhaps 10,000,000 who were organized in government or employer controlled, national socialist and fascist unions. In 1932 the membership had risen to over 15,000,000 in 32 countries. But Hitler's advent to power in Germany in 1933 not only necessitated the removal of the headquarters of the I.F.T.U. to Paris, of the I.W.M.A. to Holland and of several of the trade secretariats to other countries but destroyed the German unions, which had dominated both the I.F.T.U. and the Christian International. The subsequent setting up of fascist or semifascist dictatorships in Austria, in Bulgaria and in several of the Baltic states dealt another blow to all the international trade union organizations. Recent developments in Spain indicate that the gains achieved by the

I.W.M.A. through the Spanish Revolution may soon disappear.

During the period of their greatest development, between 1920 and 1929, the international trade union organizations were concerned with such issues as the type of structure best suited to the promotion of international labor action, forms of international collective bargaining, cooperation between trade union and political internationals, international labor legislation and large questions of world economic policy. At present these issues have been pushed into the background by the supreme question of the capacity of these organizations to survive. The question has two aspects. To the extent to which controlled economy is developing in various countries, it is modifying the structure and functions of national trade unions in such a way as to weaken their interest in international problems. At the same time the growth of nationalistic dictatorships is blocking the international contacts of labor. Under these conditions the various trade union internationals are interested primarily in fighting the common enemy—nationalist fascism. There would seem to be ground here for united action on their part, but the animosities and divisions have so far been an insuperable obstacle.

LEWIS L. LORWIN

See: LABOR; LABOR MOVEMENT; JOURNEYMEN'S SOCIETIES; FRIENDLY SOCIETIES; FACTORY SYSTEM; INDUSTRIAL REVOLUTION; INDUSTRIALISM; PROLETARIAT; CLASS STRUGGLE; CLASS CONSCIOUSNESS; SOCIALISM; GUILD SOCIALISM; SYNDICALISM; LABOR PARTIES; SOCIALIST PARTIES; COMMUNIST PARTIES; SOVIET; CHRISTIAN LABOR UNIONS; COOPERATION; PRODUCERS' COOPERATION; COLLECTIVE BARGAINING; TRADE AGREEMENTS; BUSINESS AGENT; BENEFITS, TRADE UNION; CLOSED SHOP AND OPEN SHOP; DUAL UNIONISM; LABOR BANKING; WORKERS' EDUCATION; SHORT HOURS MOVEMENT; INDUSTRIAL DEMOCRACY; LABOR-CAPITAL COOPERATION; INDUSTRIAL RELATIONS; EMPLOYERS' ASSOCIATIONS; WELFARE WORK, INDUSTRIAL; PERSONNEL ADMINISTRATION; COMPANY UNIONS; PROFIT SHARING; STRIKES AND LOCKOUTS; DIRECT ACTION; GENERAL STRIKE; BOYCOTT; SABOTAGE; INTIMIDATION; CRIMINAL SYNDICALISM; DETECTIVE AGENCIES, PRIVATE; POLICING, INDUSTRIAL; BLACKLIST, LABOR; LABOR INJUNCTION; ARBITRATION, INDUSTRIAL; CONCILIATION, INDUSTRIAL; COURTS, INDUSTRIAL; LABOR LEGISLATION AND LAW; LABOR CONTRACT; LABOR, GOVERNMENT SERVICES FOR; INTERNATIONAL LABOR ORGANIZATION; SOCIAL INSURANCE; MINIMUM WAGE; WAGES; UNEMPLOYMENT; HOURS OF LABOR; MIGRATORY LABOR; CASUAL LABOR; HOMEWORK, INDUSTRIAL; WOMEN IN INDUSTRY; NEGRO PROBLEM; NATIVE POLICY; CONTRACT LABOR; IMMIGRATION. See also articles on individual industries and occupations.

Consult: In addition to bibliography following LABOR MOVEMENTS: International Surveys: Kulemann, Wilhelm, *Die Berufsvereine*, 6 vols. (2nd ed. Jena 1908–13); *Internationales Handwörterbuch des Gewerkschaftswesens*, ed. by Ludwig Heyde, 2 vols. (Berlin 1931–32); International Labour Office, "Freedom of Association," and "Conciliation and Arbitration in Industrial Disputes," *Studies and Reports*, ser. A, nos. 28–32, 34 (Geneva 1927–32); Woytinsky, W., *Die Welt in Zahlen*, 7 vols. (Berlin 1925–28) vol. ii; International Federation of Trade Unions, *Statistical Year Book*, nos. 1–6 (Amsterdam 1922–30).

FOR UNITED KINGDOM AND IRISH FREE STATE: Citrine, W. M., *The Trade Union Movement of Great Britain*, International Trade Union Library, ser. i, no. 2/3 (Amsterdam 1926); Cole, G. D. H., *Organized Labour* (London 1924); Lloyd, C. M., *Trade Unionism* (London 1915, 2nd ed. 1921, 3rd ed. 1928); *Trade Union Documents*, ed. by W. Milne-Bailey (London 1929); Trades Union Congress, *Report of Proceedings*, nos. 1–65 (Manchester 1868–1933).

FOR GERMANY: Cassau, Theodor, *Die Gewerkschaftsbewegung* (Halberstadt 1925); Cassau, Jeanette, *Die Arbeitergewerkschaften; eine Einführung* (Halberstadt 1927); Seidel, Richard, *The Trade Union Movement of Germany*, International Trade Union Library, ser. i, no. 7/8 (Amsterdam 1928); Müller, Hermann, *Geschichte der deutschen Gewerkschaften bis zum Jahre 1878* (Berlin 1918); Schildbach, Bernhard, *Verfassung und Verwaltung der freien Gewerkschaften in Deutschland* (Leipsic 1910); Braun, Adolf, *Die Gewerkschaften* (Nuremberg 1914); Bourceret, Albert, *Les associations professionnelles ouvrières en Allemagne* (Paris 1933).

FOR AUSTRIA, SWITZERLAND AND HOLLAND: Deutsch, Julius, *Geschichte der österreichischen Gewerkschaftsbewegung*, 2 vols. (2nd ed. Vienna 1929–32); Straas, Eduard, *The Trade Union Movement of Austria*, International Trade Union Library, ser. i, no. 9 (Amsterdam 1930); Meister, M., *Fifty Years of Trade Unionism in Switzerland*, International Trade Union Library, ser. i, no. 10 (Berlin 1933); Farner, Hans, *Die Geschichte des schweizerischen Arbeiterbundes* (Zurich 1923); Stucki, Walter, *Der schweizerische Gewerkschaftsbund in der Kriegszeit, 1914–1920* (Berne 1928); Oudegeest, J., *De geschiedenis der zelfstandige vakbeweging in Nederland* (History of the independent trade union movement in the Netherlands), 2 vols. (Amsterdam 1926–32); Smits, H., *De nederlandsche arbeidersbeweging in de negentiende eeuw* (Dutch labor movement in the 19th century) (Rotterdam 1902).

FOR SCANDINAVIAN COUNTRIES: Landorganisation i Sverge, Omorganisationskommittén, *Fackföreningsrörelsen i Sverge, Norge, Danmark* (Trade union movement in Sweden, Norway, Denmark), 3 vols. (Stockholm 1912); Engelstoff, Povl, and Jensen, Hans, *Bidrag til arbejderklassens og arbejderspörgsmaalets historie i Danmark fra 1864–1900* (History of the working class and labor problems in Denmark from 1864 to 1900), Institutet for Historie og Samfundsökonomi, Skrifter, vol. ii (Copenhagen 1931); Hansson, S., *Den svenska fackföreningsrörelsen* (Swedish trade union movement) (4th ed. Stockholm 1932); Heberle, Rudolf, *Zur Geschichte der Arbeiterbewegung in Schweden*, Kiel Universität, Institut für Weltwirtschaft und Seeverkehr, Probleme der Weltwirtschaft, vol. xxxix (Jena 1925); Kausch, K. F. W., *Zur Ge-*

schichte der norwegischen Arbeiterbewegung (Kiel 1931); Ursin, N. R., and Wiik, K. H., "Die Arbeiterbewegung in Finnland" in *Archiv für die Geschichte des Sozialismus und der Arbeiterbewegung*, vol. xii (1926) 23-104.

FOR SUCCESSION STATES AND BALKAN COUNTRIES: Oberschall, Albin, "Die Gewerkschaftsbewegung in der tschechoslowakischen Republik" in *Archiv für Sozialwissenschaft und Sozialpolitik*, vol. liv (1925) 775-92; Kotek, J., *Odborové hnutí zaměstnanců* (Trade union movement of workers), Czechoslovakia, Sociální Ústav, Publikace, no. 50 (Prague 1930); Fulde, Herbert, *Die polnische Arbeitergewerkschaftsbewegung*, Volkswirtschaftstheoretische Abhandlungen, no. 12 (Weinfelden 1931); Biro, Karl, *Die ungarische Arbeiterbewegung seit dem Sturz der Räterepublik, 1914-1925* (Hamburg 1925); Chiulea, N., "Les syndicats ouvriers en Roumanie" in Association Française pour la Lutte contre le Chômage et pour l'Organisation du Marché du Travail, Documents du travail, no. 97/98 (1925) 11-40.

FOR FRANCE AND BELGIUM: Saposs, David, *The Labor Movement in Post-War France*, Columbia University, Council for Research in the Social Sciences, Social and Economic Studies of Post-War France, vol. iv (New York 1931); Martin St. Léon, Etienne, *Les deux C.G.T., syndicalisme et communisme* (Paris 1923); Louis, Paul, *Le syndicalisme français d'Amiens à Saint-Étienne* (Paris 1924); Wirz, J. Paul, *Der revolutionäre Syndikalismus in Frankreich*, Zürcher volkswirtschaftliche Forschungen, no. 18 (Zurich 1931); Garmy, René, *Histoire du mouvement syndical en France*, vol. i- (Paris 1933-); Vandervelde, Émile, *Le parti ouvrier belge 1885-1925* (Brussels 1925) pt. iii; Misson, Achille, *Le mouvement syndical, son histoire en Belgique de 1800 à 1914* (Namur 1921).

FOR SPAIN AND PORTUGAL: Marvaud, A., *La question sociale en Espagne* (Paris 1910); Madariaga, S. de, *Spain* (London 1930) ch. xiii; Nettlau, Max, "Zur Geschichte der spanischen International und Landesföderation (1868-1889)" in *Archiv für die Geschichte des Sozialismus*, vol. xiv (1929) 1-66, and vol. xv (1930) 73-125; Largo Caballero, F., *Presente y futuro de la Unión General de Trabajadores de España* (Madrid 1925); Campos Ferreira Lima, H. de, "Movimento operario en Portugal" in *Instituto*, vol. lii (1905) 385-99, 518-27, 588-95, 650-64, 712-22, and vol. liii (1906) 8-15, 73-80, 148-51, 209-14, 273-85.

FOR ITALY: Hirschberg-Neumeyer, M., *Die italienischen Gewerkschaften*, Münchener volkswirtschaftliche Studien, n.s., no. 2 (Jena 1928); Michels, Roberto, *Italien von heute* (Zurich 1930) p. 148-57; Pitigliana, F., *The Italian Corporative State* (London 1933); Silone, I., *Der Fascismus, seine Enstehung und seine Entwicklung* (Zurich 1934); Buozzi, B., and Nitti, V., *Fascisme et syndicalisme* (Paris 1930).

FOR RUSSIA: Grinewitsch, W., *Die Gewerkschaftsbewegung in Russland*, vol. i- (Berlin 1927-); Vsesoyuzno Tsentralnyi Sovet Professionalnikh Soyuzov, *Professionalnie soyuzi v proshlom i nastoyashchem* (Trade unions in the past and present) (Moscow 1927); Koch, W., *Die bol'sevistischen Gewerkschaften*, Sozialwissenschaftliche Bausteine, vol. v (Jena 1932); Jakobson, M., *Die russischen Gewerkschaften* (Berlin 1932); Dunn, R. W., *Soviet Trade Unions* (New York 1928); Freeman, J., *The Soviet Worker* (New York 1932).

FOR FAR AND NEAR EAST: Articles in *International Labour Review*, published monthly in Geneva since 1921; Heller, Leo, *Gewerkschaftliche Bewegung in den Kolonien und Halbkolonien des Ostens*, Rote Gewerkschafts-Internationale, Bibliothek, vol. xvii (Berlin 1923); Orchard, John E. and D. J., *Japan's Economic Position* (New York 1930); Katayama, Sen, *The Labor Movement in Japan* (Chicago 1918); Lowe, Chaun-Hua, *Facing Labor Issues in China* (Shanghai 1933); Tso, S. K. Sheldon, *The Labor Movement in China* (Shanghai 1928); Fang Fu-an, *Chinese Labour* (Shanghai 1931); Chen, Ta, "Fundamentals of the Chinese Labor Movement" in American Academy of Political and Social Science, *Annals*, vol. clii (1930) 196-205, and "Labor in China during the Civil Wars" in *Monthly Labor Review*, vol. xxxi (1930) 1-19; Tchou, M. T., "The Present-Day Industrial Situation and the Labour Movement" in *China Today through Chinese Eyes*, ed. by T. C. Chao, 2nd ser. (2nd ed. London 1927) ch. ii; Lamb, Jefferson D. H. (Lin Tung-hai), *The Labour Movement and Labour Legislation in China* (Shanghai 1933) ch. viii; Great Britain, Royal Commission on Labour in India, *Report*, Cmd. 3883, 11 vols. (1931); Joshi, N. M., *The Trade Union Movement in India* (Bombay 1927); Burnett-Hurst, A. R., *Labour and Housing in Bombay*, London School of Economics, Studies in Economics and Political Science, no. 75 (London 1925); Anstey, Vera, *The Economic Development of India* (London 1929) ch. xii; Schrader, Karl, and Furtwängler, F. J., *Das werktätige Indien, sein Werden und sein Kampf* (Berlin 1928); Philip, André, *L'Inde moderne, le problème social et politique* (Paris 1930), tr. by C. G. Schlumberger as *India, a Foreign View* (London 1932) pt. i, chs. i-ii; "Labor Conditions in the Philippine Islands" in Philippine Islands, Bureau of Labor, *Labor*, vol. viii (1927) no. 26; Fock, Dirk, "The Labour Problem in the Dutch East Indian Archipelago" in *Asiatic Review*, vol. xxiii (1927) 625-35; Dutch East Indies, Kantoor van Arbeid, "Rapport over de arbeidstoestanden in de metaalindustrie te Soerabaja," its *Publicaties*, no. 1 (Weltevreden 1926); Dingley, S., *The Peasants' Movement in Indonesia*, Farmers and Peasants International, Library of the Revolutionary Farmers and Peasants Movement, no. 2 (Berlin 1927); General Federation of Jewish Labour in Palestine, Executive Committee, *Documents and Essays on Jewish Labour Policy in Palestine* (Tel Aviv 1930); Wolman, Leo, "The Labor Movement and Cooperation" in Joint Palestine Survey Commission, *Report of the Experts* (Boston 1928) pt. ii; Butler, H. B., *Report on Labour Conditions with Suggestions for Future Social Legislation* (Cairo 1932); Zewie, I ben, "The Labour Movement in Egypt" in *International Trade Union Movement* vol. v (1925) 30-35.

FOR UNITED STATES AND CANADA: Lorwin, L. L. (Levine, Louis), *The American Federation of Labor*, Brookings Institution, Institute of Economics, Publication no. 50 (Washington 1933); Wolman, Leo, and Peck, Gustav, "Labor Groups in the Social Structure" in President's Research Committee on Social Trends, *Recent Social Trends in the United States*, 2 vols. (New York 1933) vol. ii, ch. xvi; Wolman, Leo, *The Growth of American Trade Unions, 1880-1923*, National Bureau of Economic Research, Publication no. 6 (New York 1924); Pollak, Heinrich, *Die Gewerkschaftsbewegung in den Vereinigten Staaten* (Jena

1927); Philip, André, *Le problème ouvrier aux États Unis* (Paris 1927); Slichter, Sumner H., "Labour under the National Recovery Act" in *Harvard Business Review*, vol. xii (1933–34) 142–63; Daugherty, C. R., *Labor Problems in American Industry* (Boston 1933); Logan, Harold A., *The History of Trade-Union Organization in Canada* (Chicago 1928); Skelton, O. D., "General Economic History 1867–1912," and Coats, R. H., "The Labour Movement in Canada" in *Canada and Its Provinces*, ed. by Adam Shortt and Arthur G. Doughty, 22 vols. (Toronto 1914–17) vol. ix, p. 93–355; Latham, A. B., *The Catholic and National Labour Unions of Canada*, McGill University, Publications, 15th ser., Economic Studies, no. 10 (Toronto 1930).

For Australia, New Zealand and South Africa: Sutcliffe, J. T., *A History of Trade Unionism in Australia* (Melbourne 1921); Goodrich, Carter, "The Australian and American Labour Movements" in *Economic Record*, vol. iv (1928) 193–208; Heaton, Herbert, *Modern Economic History* (3rd ed. Adelaide 1925) chs. xvi–xvii; Portus, C. V., "The Australian Labour Movement" in *Australia, Economic and Political Studies*, ed. by M. Atkinson (Melbourne 1920) ch. iv; Métin, Albert, *Le socialisme sans doctrines* (2nd ed. Paris 1910); Clark, Victor S., *The Labour Movement in Australasia* (New York 1906); Condliffe, J. B., *New Zealand in the Making* (London 1930) ch. xi; Reeves, W. P., *State Experiments in Australia and New Zealand*, 2 vols. (London 1902); Union of South Africa, Economic and Wages Commission, *Report, 1925* (Cape Town 1926) p. 283–84; Leubuscher, Charlotte, *Der südafrikanische Eingeborene als Industriearbeiter und als Stadtbewohner* (Jena 1931) p. 173–95; Gitsham, E., and Trembath, J. F., *A First Account of Labour Organisation in South Africa* (Durban 1926); Kadalie, C., "The Old and the New Africa" in *Labour Monthly*, vol. ix (1927) 624–31; "The African Labour Problem" in *Round Table*, vol. xviii (1927–28) 498–521.

For Latin America: Iglesias, Santiago, "Labor Organization in Latin America" in *Current History*, vol. xxvi (1927) 928–32; Schück, W., "Politische und wirtschaftliche Lage der Arbeiterschaft in Südamerika" in *Gesellschaft*, vol. vi, pt. ii (1929) 275–86; Tannenbaum, Frank, *Whither Latin America?* (New York 1934); Pan-American Federation of Labor, *Reports of Proceedings*, 1st-5th (New York, Mexico and Washington 1918–27). See also: *Trabajador latino-americano*, published fortnightly in Montevideo since 1928. Mexico: Gruening, E., *Mexico and Its Heritage* (New York 1928) p. 335–42; Tannenbaum, Frank, *Peace by Revolution* (New York 1933) ch. xxi; Walling, W. E., *The Mexican Question* (New York 1927) pt. ii; Retinger, J. H., *Morones of Mexico* (London 1926). Cuba: Beals, Carleton, *The Crime of Cuba* (Philadelphia 1933) p. 246–50; Clark, Victor S., "Labor Conditions in Cuba" in United States, Labor Bureau, *Bulletin*, vol. vii (1902) 663–793. Argentina: Weil, Felix, *Die Arbeiterbewegung in Argentinien* (Leipsic 1923); Unsain, A. M., *Legislación del trabajo*, 3 vols. (Buenos Aires 1925–28); Palacios, Alfredo L., *El nuevo derecho* (2nd ed. Buenos Aires 1928); Ferrarrazzo, E. J., "La acción obrera" in *Revista de ciencias económicas*, ser. ii, vol. xiv (1926) 677–86, 761–75, 1038–45, vol. xv (1927) 23–42, 139–44, 271–88, 409–25, 571–82. Brazil: Schück, W., "Gewerkschaftliche Anfänge in Brasilien" in *Gesellschaft*, vol. iv, pt. ii (1927) 555–61; Rowan, J., "Trade Union Movement and Wages in Brazil" in *Monthly Labor Review*, vol. xxi (1925) 467–77. Chile: Poblete Troncoso, M., *La organización sindical en Chile* (Santiago 1926); United States, Bureau of Labor Statistics, "Labor Organizations in Chile" by M. Poblete Troncoso, *Bulletin*, no. 461 (1928).

TRADEMARKS AND NAMES. The goodwill of a manufacturer's or trader's business is at present peculiarly dependent upon means of identification of such business since personal contact between customer and producer has largely disappeared with the expansion of trade beyond definite local boundaries. The purchaser may often ignore the actual producer of a commodity, depending rather on a symbol identifying the product which has given him satisfaction and which he wishes to continue to purchase. This symbol, or means of identification of a commodity, may be a trademark, a trade name or an indication of place of origin. A trademark is a mark or device affixed to or used in connection with a commodity. A trade name is the name of a manufacturer or trader or the name of a business house, shop or factory. An indication of place of origin is the name of a place, community or region which is used by producers to indicate that their products come from a certain locality.

There are indications that trademarks and trade names were employed in ancient times, but their use does not appear to have had a legal basis, a development which dates only from the beginnings of modern trade. Trademarks served special functions in the Middle Ages, either as proprietary marks identifying the owner or as obligatory marks imposed by state, municipal or guild regulation. Primarily, these marks were designed to maintain standards of workmanship and tended to protect the goodwill of the guild or to trace "foreign" goods encroaching upon the guild monopoly. Secondarily, they came to designate origin with or craftsmanship of a particular producer. This historical origin still affects in large measure the law of the present time, although the real function of a trademark or name has largely ceased to be the indication of origin or ownership of goods; it serves rather as the symbol of a standard of quality or make or selection which has given satisfaction.

Trademark recognition and protection in modern times began in England in the last quarter of the eighteenth century, but it was not until the middle of the nineteenth century that adequate relief was granted. At about this time statutes were passed in various states of the United States, and the first federal act was enacted in 1870. Similarly in other countries of the world legislative enactments regulating trademarks and names appeared gradually from 1850 on. But it was not until the more recent multiplication of businesses and products that trademarks and names acquired great importance. Thus in the United States, in the thirty-four years from 1837 to 1870, an average of 2 cases was reported in collections of court decisions, while in the period before the World War 200 cases came up each year, and more recently there has been a much larger number. Trademark registrations in the United States numbered little more than 100 during 1870; they reached 5000 during 1913 and rose to almost 15,000 in 1929 but dropped to approximately 10,000 in 1932. The development in other countries was similar.

Apart from the interest of every producer or trader in the protection of his goodwill, the law of trademarks and names protects the interest of the consumer in safety from deceit or confusion and the general social interest in the promotion of fair dealing and honesty in business. These same interests are involved in the law of unfair competition, of which trademark and trade name law is merely a branch. But while the general law of unfair competition has not always kept pace with the Protean transformations of fraud and dishonesty, handicapped as it has been by the fact that the legal materials at hand do not afford sufficient elasticity and by the fear of interference with lawful competition, trademark law has reached a certain degree of maturity. For trademarks permit the formulation of definite criteria for the observance of the general principle of fairness and honesty which forms the foundation of the law of unfair competition.

Although a trademark is primarily a mark which distinguishes a commodity of one producer from a similar one of another, it is also selected with a view to psychological factors. If it is to induce an original purchase and a continuance of purchases, it must be attractive, recognizable and easy to remember. Its selection must be based upon careful study of the casual purchaser and his characteristics and of the public's reactions to the particular class of goods. From this point of view trademarks constitute valuable assets, but they may involve the social danger, brought about especially through intense advertising, that producers will be able to overcome free competition and to build up monopolies by substituting for known materials and products their own trademarks and names.

Trademark law is not uniform in the various countries of the world, except that in all the British countries the law is nearly identical and constitutes a system apart. The United States, France and Germany each have a different system. Belgium, Italy, Rumania, Turkey, part of Latin America, Tunis, Morocco and Syria follow France. The law of Austria, Czechoslovakia, Hungary and Jugoslavia is quite similar. In other countries the law cannot be classified under a single system. Even within the countries which have the same general system there are many differences.

The general requirement for a trademark is that it be distinctive, that is, capable of distinguishing the goods of one producer from those of another, for otherwise the grant of exclusive right in the use of a mark would be unwarranted. The application of this principle, however, presents great varieties in the different countries, sometimes because of trade traditions and usages or as a result of legislative policy with regard to competition. Marks in common use or descriptive of products, their quality, quantity, origin or value are generally not protected as trademarks, since no one may claim exclusive rights in a mark which everyone may use with equal justice to describe his products accurately. But again the conception of descriptiveness varies in the different countries.

In British countries even a suggestive mark is ordinarily not a valid trademark, while in the United States mere suggestive marks are protected and in some countries even descriptive marks may be protected. Producers are often inclined to adopt disguisedly descriptive or suggestive marks with the aim of interjecting into their trademarks some intimation of excellence or with the intention of monopolizing an expression close to the common description of goods. The law looks askance at this attempted monopoly in language which may lead to an eventual monopoly in manufacture. When, however, a mark which may not be distinctive or which is descriptive per se has become distinctive in fact by long and exclusive use by one producer with reference to his articles, the law in certain countries undertakes to protect existing rights and to discourage commercial fraud by preventing other persons from using the mark in question on similar goods. This is the so-called secondary meaning theory. The mark is held to have acquired a secondary significance, denoting in addition to its primary dictionary meaning the articles of the particular producer who uses it.

Practically all countries today provide for registration of trademarks with the view to giving notice of claims therein. Formerly use alone was deemed to give sufficient notice, for the market within which the mark was used was confined within a limited area so that competitors could not fail to take notice. But nowadays, when the market of a producer is always changing and is within no definite limits, use alone is not a sufficient notice to all possible competitors. Moreover the stock of available trademarks presenting psychological advantages in certain classes of products is seriously restricted today, and unintentional infringement may occur if notice of prior claims is not given by registration.

The administrative procedure in registration of trademarks varies. In the common law countries the administration examines the question whether the trademark is registrable and not anticipated by prior trademarks and acts affirmatively by publishing the mark for opposition by interested parties. If no opposition is raised or if it is dismissed, the trademark is granted registration. At the other extreme is the French system, in which the administration merely certifies to the deposit of a trademark without any examination of the question of prior publication. Between these two extremes are many other kinds of procedure with varying degrees of administrative intervention in the determination of the validity of claims. Thus Germany examines the registrability of a trademark and invites owners of prior registrations to oppose, but if the latter do not oppose, the administration grants the registration. Switzerland does not even invite the prior registrant; it merely advises the applicant of the prior registration and he is free to maintain or withdraw the application. In many Latin American republics the mark is advertised for opposition as soon as the application for registration is filed, and unless the mark is opposed the administration proceeds with the grant.

The prevailing administrative system usually affects the nature of the right obtained by registration. Thus in France and the other countries where no examination is undertaken by the administration and no provision is made for opposition to the grant the ownership of a trademark is acquired by prior adoption and use. Registration, which merely declares the right, entitles the registrant to the special remedies available to owners of registered trademarks. In the British Empire and many other countries the registrant is considered *prima facie* owner of the trademark, and when his registration has not been contested for a number of years (varying from six months in Portugal to seven years in Great Britain) it ordinarily becomes conclusive. In the remaining countries registration is the basis of ownership in a trademark, so that a subsequent user by registering a trademark obtains exclusive rights as against a prior user of the same mark. The ownership theory of registration is very important from the point of view of international trade. It enables pirates obtaining knowledge of the use of a valuable trademark in a foreign country to register such mark and thus prevent the extension of the market of the true owner unless he is prepared to pay dearly for the right to registration. This situation is most common among the Latin American republics, including Argentina, Brazil, Colombia, Guatemala and Chile (to some extent), and prevails also in Germany, Poland, Norway and Sweden.

The trademark law of most countries provides for both criminal and civil remedies for infringement of trademarks. The equitable remedy of injunction in the common law countries is most potent and effective in ordinary infringement cases. In countries where injunction is not available and the civil remedy of damages is a very lengthy, costly and complicated proceeding, there is an inducement to proceed before the criminal courts. However, the courts in countries where the standards of commercial honesty are not high feel disinclined to impose criminal punishment on trademark infringers unless there is clear intention of fraud. The best remedy available to trademark owners in such countries is the opportunity to oppose an infringing application or to cancel a registration whenever cancellation proceedings may be instituted before administrative authorities.

The American trademark law has certain peculiarities due to federal difficulties. The Supreme Court has decided that Congress has no power to legislate on the subject of trademarks except where these are used in interstate or foreign commerce, and there are now federal statutes providing for the registration of trademarks employed in such commerce. Registration in the United States does not affect substantive rights. The same protection and remedies are enjoyed by registered as by unregistered trademarks. Registration, however, enables the trademark owner to sue in the federal courts, to obtain increased damages, to impound the importation of infringing products by recording the registered trademark at ports of entry and to apply for registration in foreign countries which require home registration as a prerequisite. The federal statutes do not provide for criminal remedies, which, however, exist under almost all state statutes on the subject. The failure to compel registration of claims in trademarks and to give registrants conclusive rights after the lapse of a certain period of time makes the American law very unsatisfactory. A registration may be declared invalid after many years on proof that the same or a similar mark has been used in interstate commerce by another, even though such use was very limited and unimportant.

The regulation of trademarks by international conventions is almost indispensable, and many have been concluded since the middle of the last century. Practically all purport to secure national treatment to the trademark owners in the other contracting country. In 1883 the international Union for the Protection of Industrial Property was created. The convention creating this union, to which forty countries are party today and which was last revised at The Hague in 1925, in addition to stipulating national treatment for foreign trademark owners, contains what may be deemed to be international legislative provisions for the uniform regulation of trademark questions in the union. Thus the right of the prior user of a trademark is secured under certain conditions; the validation is secured of trademark rights acquired in the country of origin; the obligations of the trademark owner are mitigated and special effective remedies for infringement are provided. Moreover trade names are protected without obligation of deposit or registration and false indications of place of origin are prohibited under certain conditions. Furthermore a large part of the member countries of the international union entered into two important special arrangements at Madrid in 1891. By the first, indications of place of origin are more broadly protected, especially appellations of origin of products of the vine. By the second, persons who have registered their trademarks in their own country may register them also at the International Bureau of the union at Berne. By such registration the mark is protected in the twenty countries party to the arrangement, unless such mark should be denied protection by any of these countries within one year after the date of registration at Berne.

The international regulation of trademarks has not, however, kept pace with the expansion of modern commerce. Trademark owners must still rely for protection chiefly on the domestic law. The differences among the laws of the various countries continue to be very great. The right of the foreign prior user of a trademark is not fully secured. Marks which are perfectly valid in their country of origin are not always validated in foreign countries, a fact which may lead to the destruction of valuable assets of a business in a foreign country. The law of assignment of trademarks is still very strict in many countries, while modern forms of economic and commercial organization require a freer transfer of the ownership or use of trademarks and permission for use by interrelated concerns. Furthermore the international protection of trademarks remains a very costly and complicated affair. Usually only large corporations can afford to take steps which will insure full protection. After registration trademark owners must continue to watch for infringements, since no enterprise prospers without being threatened by business parasites. Action against infringements is in many countries too costly. Almost all of the European countries have joined the Madrid Arrangement for International Registration of Trade Marks, and their nationals obtain great saving and convenience by thus securing protection in twenty countries through the central registration at the Berne bureau. The United States and the British countries are not party to this arrangement. It would seem that some of their objections are valid by reason of the state of the domestic law, but these could probably be met by proper amendments of the arrangement.

STEPHEN P. LADAS

See: ADVERTISING; GOODWILL; CONSUMER PROTECTION; CAVEAT EMPTOR; RESALE PRICE MAINTENANCE; UNFAIR COMPETITION; COPYRIGHT; PATENTS.

Consult: Schechter, F. I., *The Historical Foundations of the Law Relating to Trademarks*, Columbia University, Legal Studies, vol. i (New York 1925); Kohler, Josef, *Warenzeichenrecht* (2nd ed. Mannheim 1910); Pouillet, Eugène, *Traité des marques de fabrique* (6th ed. by André Taillefer and Charles Claro, Paris 1912); Kerly, Duncan M., *The Law of Trade Marks and Trade Names* (6th ed. by F. G. Underhay and T. W. Morgan, London 1927); Hopkins, J. L., *The Law of Trademarks, Tradenames and Unfair Competition* (4th ed. Cincinnati 1924); Nims, H. D., *The Law of Unfair Competition and Trade Marks* (3rd ed. New York 1929); Ladas, S. P., *The International Protection* of *Industrial Property*, Harvard University and Radcliffe College, Studies in International Law, no. 2 (Cambridge, Mass. 1930) chs. xxii–xxviii, and *The International Protection of Trade Marks by the American Republics*, Harvard University and Radcliffe College, Studies in International Law, no. 1 (Cambridge, Mass. 1929); Paynter, R. H., *A Psychological Study of Trade-Mark Infringement*, Columbia University, Contributions to Philosophy and Psychology, Archives of Psychology, no. 42 (New York 1920); Schechter, F. I., "The Rational Basis of Trademark Protection" in *Harvard Law Review*, vol. xl (1926–27) 813–33; Handler, M., and Pickett, Charles, "Trade Marks and Trade Names—an Analysis and Synthesis" in *Columbia Law Review*, vol. xxx (1930) 168–201, 759–88; Isaacs, Nathan, "Traffic in Trade-Symbols" in *Harvard Law Review*, vol. xliv (1930–31) 1210–21.

TRADES UNION CONGRESS, BRITISH. See TRADE UNIONS, section on GREAT BRITAIN.

TRADING WITH THE ENEMY. As long as war was the sport of kings, carried on with small professional armies, and did not affect the daily lives of the bulk of the population, there was little governmental interference with commerce between the nationals of belligerent states. Although many authorities hold that such commerce has always been prohibited in time of hostilities and although from the early eighteenth century there have commonly been decrees forbidding private trade with nationals of an enemy state, it is only in the last 150 years that governments have in general definitely enunciated and seriously attempted to enforce the principle that there must be no trading with the enemy. As late as 1785 a treaty between the United States and Prussia provided that in the event of war there should be no interruption whatever of commerce and navigation between the signatories. Changes in the technology and economics of warfare, however, have led to the conception of war as a struggle between whole peoples and consequently to increasing stress upon economic weapons in warfare.

The prohibitions of trade with the enemy rest not upon international law but upon the municipal legislation of belligerent governments. In continental jurisprudence, with the notable exception of French theory, an outbreak of war does not ipso facto render illegal all trade with persons in enemy territory or with the nationals of hostile countries, for such commerce is legitimate until expressly forbidden. In Anglo-American jurisprudence, on the other hand, the fact of war itself is held to prohibit such trade, unless it is expressly authorized [*The Hoop*, 1 c. Rob. 196 (1799); Griswold v. Waddington, 16 Johns, 438 (1819); Porter v. Freudenberg, 1 K.B. 857 (1916)]. But this difference exists only in theory, for it is now the general practise of belligerent governments to forbid trading with the enemy. In the continental view enemy character is generally determined by nationality. According to Anglo-American legal theory it is determined by residence or by place of doing business. In the World War, however, there were many deviations from these principles.

The complexity of modern commercial and financial relations has given rise to many problems of definition and administration in respect to trading with the enemy legislation. Such legislation had its widest development during the World War. The French decree of September 27, 1914, forbade all commerce with residents of Germany and Austria-Hungary and with all their subjects wherever resident. The German ordinances of 1914 and the subsequent measures of retaliation contained similar prohibitions, but they were in general milder and were not applied to enemy nationals residing in neutral territory. The British government in 1914 forbade trade only with residents of enemy countries, but under authority of the Act of December 23, 1915, a blacklist was prepared of over 1500 persons and firms of enemy nationality or having associations with hostile nations but located in neutral countries, with which British subjects were forbidden to trade. This was a departure from the orthodox British view of enemy character, and the United States, as a neutral, protested against the procedure. In 1917, however, after the United States had entered the World War, its War Trade Board listed some 1600 firms and persons in Latin America with which Americans were not to trade, a list which was later extended to include some 5000 names in both European and Latin American countries. Moreover the American Trading with the Enemy Act of October 6, 1917, forbade trade with an "enemy" and with an "ally of an enemy," and included enemy subjects wherever resident and residents of territory occupied by the enemy. It likewise authorized the alien property custodian to impound the property of enemy aliens within the United States. In recent times the trade which is forbidden is generally held to consist of financial transactions, insurance, navigation, transportation and communication, whether directly with enemy nationals or with neutral intermediaries.

All forms of non-commercial intercourse also are prohibited.

During the World War the Allied Powers restricted exports by their nationals not only to hostile countries but also to neutral territory, in order to prevent any indirect delivery of commodities to the enemy. In 1914 such restrictions were effected in Holland by the establishment of the Overzeesche Handels Matschappij and in 1915 in Switzerland through the Société Suisse de Surveillance Économique. These corporations, which were controlled by the Allies, received all merchandise sent by their nationals and made certain that it was not distributed into channels through which it might reach enemy territory. Varying arrangements were made with other neutral states including limitation of exports to the pre-war figure.

The practise of licensing transactions for specific purposes, as exceptions to the general prohibition of trade with the enemy, is common. In the Crimean War the British and French governments permitted their nationals to trade with non-blockaded Russian ports in non-contraband goods carried in neutral vessels. In the World War Great Britain, France, the United States and Germany permitted the payment of fees to enemy governments to protect patents, trademarks and copyrights. The United States granted the American Red Cross the exclusive privilege of sending letters, food and money to American prisoners in Germany. Under the Act of October 6, 1917, the War Trade Board was authorized to issue licenses for trade, the secretary of the treasury licenses for insurance transactions and the Federal Trade Commission licenses for patents. The total amount of licensed trade between enemies in the World War was negligible, as was the amount of unlicensed trade.

The assumption basic to the ban on trade with the enemy is obviously that the enemy will be injured more by such a prohibition than will the state imposing it. Wherever the nature of economic intercourse is such that the assumption is invalid, the ban is relaxed. This is often the case in hostilities between the imperial powers and backward states which are rich market areas. In the opium wars against China, Great Britain and France fought to open the Chinese market to their nationals. In the Manchurian hostilities of 1931–32 Japan, far from forbidding its nationals to trade with the enemy, bombarded and occupied Shanghai to prevent Chinese interference with such trade. Where a nation is dependent upon foreign supplies, its government may also hesitate to oppose trade with the enemy, as was the case in Germany in 1914. Because of the prospective losses to their own merchants and investors from a ban on trade with aggressor states governments are reluctant to resort to boycotts or economic sanctions as a means of preventing war in situations where their own national interests are not vitally involved. The recent practise of carrying on hostilities without inaugurating a formal state of war further complicates the problem, as does the increasingly frequent resort to embargoes and other trade prohibitions as weapons of economic nationalism in peace time.

FREDERICK L. SCHUMAN

See: BLOCKADE; EMBARGO; BOYCOTT; ENEMY ALIEN; MERCHANTMEN, STATUS OF; WARFARE, LAWS OF.

Consult: Fauchille, Paul, *Traité de droit international public*, 2 vols. (8th ed. by Henry Bonfils, Paris 1921–26) vol. ii, p. 75–86; Meyer, Pierre, *De l'interdiction du commerce entre les belligérants* (Paris 1902); Scott, Leslie, *Trading with the Enemy; the Effect of War on Contracts* (2nd ed. London 1914); Bentwich, Norman, *The Law of Private Property in War* (London 1907) ch. v; Phillipson, Coleman, *The Effect of War on Contracts* (London 1909); Baty, T., "Intercourse with Alien Enemies" in *Law Quarterly Review*, vol. xxxi (1915) 30–49; Garner, J. W., *International Law and the World War*, 2 vols. (New York 1920) vol. i, chs. viii–ix; Cassin, René, "L'interdiction du commerce et des relations économiques avec l'ennemi" in *Revue de droit international privé*, vol. xiv (1918) 5–43, 388–420, and vol. xv (1919) 38–66; Huberich, C. H., *The Law Relating to Trading with the Enemy* (New York 1918); Brodnitz, Georg, *Das System des Wirtschaftskrieges* (Tübingen 1920); Curti, Arthur, *Der Handelskrieg von England, Frankreich und Italien gegen Deutschland und Österreich-Ungarn* (Berlin 1917).

TRADITION. If the term tradition were understood in its literal sense of transmission, all elements of social life would be traditional, except those relatively few novelties which each age creates for itself and those immediate borrowings from other societies which can be observed while the process of diffusion is taking place. But only some of the inherited or transmitted customs, institutions, speech, dress, laws, songs and tales are traditions; and the use of the term implies a judgment about the value of the transmitted element. Customs, for example, are ways of acting which have become habitual in a certain area or among a certain people. Frequently they extend over many generations but they are passively received. Their value is not insisted upon; those who follow the customs may admit that they are unimportant or even deplorable. Similarly an institution is a form of social organization which requires a functional classification of persons. The functions performed and the method of classification are often transmitted from a previous generation, but this fact alone does not constitute a tradition. The institution becomes traditional when it is recalled that it existed in past times and when at least some persons now desire to continue it. What is really a tradition therefore is not the institution but the belief in its value. Even in the case of legends, which in popular speech are regarded as synonymous with tradition—in the Romance languages the two words are interchangeable—there is a tendency to reserve the word for those stories which have indefinite origin and are orally transmitted and which have a certain permanence because they are attached to specific places, like aetiological myths or illustrations of a local or a national ideal or some group quality or trait. Strictly and properly speaking therefore, a tradition is not a mere observed fact like an existing custom, nor a story that exhausts its significance in being told; it is an idea which expresses a value judgment. A certain way of acting is regarded as right; a certain order or arrangement is held desirable. The maintenance of the tradition is the assertion of this judgment.

In Christianity, Islam, Judaism and Buddhism there is a traditional element in the literal sense of something transmitted from previous ages which is definite and concrete. It consists of a sacred scripture which is treated as something of supreme value, as the verbal revelation of a god, or so closely associated with divine beings that everything about it, the very material on which it is written, becomes in a measure sanctified. The transmission of this scripture means that the tradition has become identified with a specific embodiment of itself. There is involved in these cases the application of tradition in its historical sense, because it is only a tradition that this book is the historical source imputed to it by pious members of the creeds involved. A further tradition has, however, developed and taken on an independent existence, so that for theology the term tradition has come to have a specific technical meaning.

The word is here applied in a somewhat different sense. For not only can *tradere* be used with the general meaning to transmit, so that tradition is that which has been handed down, if not through all generations, at least through more than one; it can mean also to hand over for safe keeping as a deposit, as it is used in Roman law. This figure of speech, which compares the traditional element to a deposit, to a precious thing delivered to a particular person worthy of confidence, is the basis of theological discussion of the term, and the details of the figure are followed with some care. For example, the need that the depository must be carefully chosen, that the deposit must remain absolutely intact, neither diminished nor increased nor modified, the feeling that the maintenance of the deposit is the highest of duties, all of which attitudes characterize the legal aspects of the Roman law *depositum*, are consciously utilized in the religious aspects of tradition. It is important to note further that the deposit notion is one of the oldest and most widespread sources of moral duty in the world and that the failure to accept, return or cherish a deposit was in popular belief a serious dereliction long before it became a legal one.

Tradition then in its religious aspect became the delivering of a precious deposit, whose source is held to be divine, to a specially selected person or persons. In orthodox Christianity the chain of tradition is connected with the notion of an apostolic succession. The various persons who have transferred one to the other the tradition of the true faith are named. This is likewise the case with the process of renewing the Torah, which created the Jewish Talmud; it is similarly the basis of the Islamic Hadith. In all these instances the subject of the tradition is a body of ideas, practises and judgments often having no immediately apparent connection with the scripture which it is assumed to be the real function of the tradition to preserve. The custodians of the tradition are definite individuals who frequently form a closed sacerdotal corporation. But since their professed character is that of depositories, the idea involved can be maintained successfully only by a formal declaration that whatever is announced as part of the tradition is in fact as old as the specific written document which is the basis of the religion itself. The dogma of the Immaculate Conception, the dogma that the pope is infallible when he speaks ex cathedra on matters of faith and the dogma that the clergy must be celibate are therefore asserted by many to be as old as the primitive church, in spite of the tardy formulation of these doctrines and the particularly late inclusion of them in the official list of dogmas. Similarly, orthodox Jews accept as implicit in the Mosaic revelation complicated series of personal rules drawn up in later centuries. In no case were these dogmas invented by those who formulated them; they had been in existence long before and had an origin about which no precise statement could be made, even by their opponents. These conditions of an indeterminate and relatively ancient source are favorable to the creation of traditions.

Another important example of a traditional deposit may be found in the artificial standards of correct speech which have been established in certain language groups. In some cases, as in France, a definite organization like the Académie Française has as one of its primary concerns the maintenance of a standard of both pronunciation and diction. In the English and German groups the depositories have been a much vaguer and more fluctuating group. Among Germans it has been accepted that the language of the stage is, if not the standard, at least the guide of speech. Since about 1870 conventions of phoneticians, philologists and dramatic artists have undertaken to settle disputes in such matters and to announce permissible variations. In England, where the nearest approach to a standardized speech was the tradition that English was spoken best in the two older universities of Oxford and Cambridge, an artificial and more or less standard English has recently been agreed upon and will doubtless be committed for transmission to successive generations of schoolmasters and radio speakers.

When tradition is associated not with religion but with historical matters, it sometimes becomes the handmaiden and associate of the religious tradition. A generation eager to receive proofs of the value of the religious deposit finds them in abundance, as, for example, in the traditions that Seneca was to some extent a Christian and that the fourth eclogue of Vergil was a messianic prophecy. Other partly historical traditions may serve a different purpose. In antiquity as in modern times a sense of nationalism may create characteristics not only for persons but for entire groups. Often enough these characteristics deal with apparently trivial matters. There are traditions about food, about costumes, about gestures. But these traditions have definite symbolic significance. When roast beef is spoken of as the traditional food of England, there is implicit the English judgment that roast beef is a good food to eat and that it gives Englishmen a sturdiness of body and mind of which they like to boast. The traditional politeness of the French implies that Frenchmen regard their manners as distinguishing them favorably from other people. These examples serve to indicate how this function of tradition assists in building a national ideal and therefore helps to create the complex of nationalism. A national ideal usually means a flattering self-portrayal on the part of a people in which certain traits are singled out as especially characteristic and the possession of those traits and the judgment that they are good are confirmed by tradition. The mythopoeic element in tradition is immediately called upon to create or to restate historical events so that they will seem to be instances of these traits. The importance of these ideals for nationalism lies in the readiness with which they can be converted into symbols that can be used to stimulate national expansion or to resist foreign aggression. Without the mechanism of tradition, that is, without the transmitted judgment that certain events happened and that certain traits are admirable, it would be difficult to create a symbolic value for the traits themselves and to use them as instruments.

Usually the traits that are treated as desirable are those which indicate superiority. Side by side with them and necessarily supplementary to them is the group of traditions about neighbors and enemies which represent them as inferior or evil. The tradition of the Romans' forthrightness and directness was emphasized by the tradition that the Carthaginians were perfidious, the Gauls treacherous, the Greeks mendacious. It is rare for a nation to maintain a tradition of national defects. Sometimes, however, an acknowledgment of a defect is an indirect form of self-glorification. The English are wont to dwell on the tradition that they are blunderers in order to bring out their belief in their saving common sense, and Germans have insisted on the tradition of their diplomatic incapacity as a way of asserting their claims to a special sort of honesty in international relations. One group may impose traditions upon another. A minority group living under depressed conditions amidst a dominant people is not unlikely to accept for itself the traditions of its own defects, sometimes in defiance of demonstrable historical facts. Here the facts of dependence and political inferiority are the cardinal ones, which the tradition in a measure explains and emphasizes.

Nationalism can scarcely be understood except as based in some fashion on a common tradition. The effort to create a national unity in Germany during the nineteenth century entailed a struggle to find a common tradition for all Germans in spite of the contrary tradition of separatism. The fact of the common language, since it was a mere fact and not an idea or a value judgment, was far from enough. Enthusiastic nationalists sought to derive from separatism itself a common traditional ideal of freedom which might serve as the basis of a new tradition while professedly continuing the old one. The members of the Young Ireland group, who in the nineteenth century sought to form an Irish nation, avowedly set themselves to create an Irish tradition which was to continue the intellectual standards of an older aristocracy and to apply their methods to distinctively Irish subject matter.

Besides its function in developing nationalism tradition plays a large part in directing the policy of a nation and in determining the limits within which certain developments must take place. It is customary, for example, to speak of an English tradition of free speech comparable to an Athenian tradition of the same sort. Evidently what is meant is the transmitted belief that Englishmen are in the habit of speaking their minds without much legal restriction and that this is an excellent thing to do. Whether in fact this has been the case among Englishmen is irrelevant. The existence of the tradition is indisputable and this is sufficient to make the establishment of a censorship, at any rate of an undisguised censorship, difficult or impossible and to prevent the constantly renewed agitation for severe libel laws from being effective. Likewise the Roman tradition that the title *rex* was abhorrent to a true Roman gave support to the aristocratic opposition to the principate and forced even Caesar to disguise his unmistakably monarchic leanings.

In such cases the traditions are widely known and are part of the culture of an entire national group. While the traditions are often utilized for selfish and partisan purposes, no special group of men may be considered the guardians or bearers of this type of tradition. Perhaps the relatively new guild of journalists may become the custodians of it, since they must frequently appeal to it and since the character of their work makes a facile method of popular exhortation a necessity. But the range of many traditions is considerably narrower as far as the persons affected are concerned, although it is quite possible that an entire age will be colored by the existence of traditions which strictly speaking are the traditions of a group or class. The institution of chivalry in the Middle Ages developed rules of honor and of courtesy which had little currency outside of a very limited group of courtiers and did not extend even to the lower ranks of the landed gentry. In the courtly period of the Middle Ages and much later in the literature that became the chief entertainment of the luxurious courts of the Renaissance two notions were accepted as chivalric traditions: one the judgment that honor was more valuable than life, and the other the convention that in the courtship of men and women the pretense must be maintained that the man is the humble and submissive slave of the lady's caprices. It is extremely unlikely that these traditions represented the real conduct of men and women in any epoch; but when they became the traditions of literature, they determined the subject matter of plays, poems and novels for a long time. There can be little doubt that these traditions were reflected to a certain extent in actual conduct among those whose intellectual nourishment was largely the literature which these traditions dominated.

It was in the name of the Roman tradition of freedom that Rienzi attempted to recreate the Roman Republic, although republican institutions had disappeared from Rome fourteen centuries previously. It was felt that the imagined liberty of the ancient *civis romanus* was better than the feudal organization of mediaeval Europe and especially better than the existing domination of a few powerful families. This was not a custom or an institution and was not even remembered as a custom or institution. It was, even in the ancient days of the republic, an ideal, itself derived from a mythical golden age of rugged Arcadian liberty. But it was accepted as something which had in reality existed, an excellent thing which should be restored. As a tradition in ancient Rome it served as an effective hindrance to many movements in obvious contradiction of it. As a tradition in mediaeval Rome it kept alive a feeling which on several occasions led to a rebellion, and at all times it created a limit which has been disregarded only in the most recent period.

The tradition of the free Roman citizen upon which Rienzi based his abortive attempt illustrates a significant characteristic of tradition. Customs are matters of fact; they exist only as long as they are widely practised and generally recognized, and when a custom is merely a memory it ceases to be a custom. But a tradition may well be merely a memory, retained by an extremely small number of persons. In fact it is generally when the tradition is no longer a description of actual fact and when it has become somewhat evanescent as a rule of conduct that it most clearly justifies its name and performs its real functions. Those who remember are often a dwindling group and may even disappear altogether for a time. But if the idea or the judgment is embodied in some institution or in a concrete monument, memory can be stimulated and the tradition revived. The tradition of Greek art or Roman dominance never waned completely, even when no one used Greek temples as models and when Rome was a half deserted and turbulent city. The ubiquitous memorials of the ancient tradition made it probable that at various stages some persons would recall it and would attempt to make it an effective mainspring of conduct.

Perhaps the most striking illustration of the way in which a tradition can bridge the gaps of centuries, if the concrete memorials are present, is in the rise of the papacy. The general recognition in the West of the claim of the Roman patriarchs to the headship of the church may in large measure be ascribed to the tradition that Rome was the center of authority. But the city of Rome had ceased to be the seat of the actual government long before Constantine; and when the power of the papacy began to show a marked acceleration of growth, fully three centuries had elapsed since an imperial mandate had issued from the Palatine. None the less the overwhelming evidence of imperial grandeur which Rome presented even in desolation made possible the recollection which seems to be the essence of tradition. In the same way institutions that remain in existence in spite of an almost total lapse of their proper function may become the nuclei of powerful movements which consciously base themselves on forgotten traditions. The fact that an Estates General was still remembered in France at the end of the eighteenth century and remembered as the bearer of an ancient tradition gave the French Revolution its first impulse. Similarly, authoritarian governments always attempt to wipe out all vestiges of popular control; but the tradition of democracy remains as long as some occasions of voting and assembling are retained, however limited and perfunctory they may be.

That tradition when revived is formulated in statements which are not quite historically true does not impair its value or change its character. The tradition of Greek and Roman life which the Renaissance attempted to revive was false, according to more scientific and critical opinion. Romantic tradition depicted the Christian Middle Ages in a manner which now seems puerile to trained historians. But there was in both cases a restatement of ancient judgments about values in life and society which as a matter of fact was not wholly inaccurate even as history. The Renaissance tradition of a social ideal according to which the members of a highly cultivated aristocracy would develop their bodies and minds toward an exquisite perfection was not different from some formulations accepted in ancient society, and the romantic ideal of a world peopled by mystics and lovers would have been intelligible to many classes of mediaeval society. If the idea which the tradition attempts to recall is utterly foreign either to the source from which it seeks to draw its inspiration or to the age in which an attempt is made to apply it, it fails completely as a tradition. The spread of competitive sports in Europe has not therefore based itself on an imaginary ancient tradition but has correctly assumed the form of a conscious borrowing from England, even to the extent of using English terms.

It is perhaps in the arts, particularly in painting and literature, that men have been most conscious of tradition and at greatest pains to understand it. As long as art is a part of the general life of the people, that is, as long as there is no real distinction between the fine and the applied arts, tradition affects art as it does human activities. Transmitted judgments are valued as judgments and applied because of a reverence for the source of the transmission or because of the half-conscious fear of discarding the accumulated emotions which the transmitted idea has gathered about itself. In religious art, for example, a stylized treatment of the most sacred elements continues after freer treatment has become common for the less sacred. The xoanon form was retained longer for cult statues in ancient Greece than for other kinds. The early Renaissance painters used a formalized outline for the features of the madonna, while making naturalistic experiments in their backgrounds. Such a procedure may sometimes be attributed simply to the inertia of conservatism or to the presence of superstition, but in so far as it implies a conscious judgment that the older methods are the best it represents the ordinary working of tradition.

When the fine arts are differentiated from the applied arts and have become the special intellectual occupation of a sophisticated upper class, the existence of a tradition presents difficulties. The more specialized the artistic segment of the community, the greater will be the demand for novelty of stimulation, not simply because of a craving for excitement but because in such a specialized upper class both the creative and the appreciative groups participate in the artistic process and the need of experiment is felt by both. In art tradition is set against experiment; the imitation of methods already valued as beautiful is opposed to the attempt to discover new forms of beauty. Here too tradition is not quite the same as conservatism, which concerns itself less with the imitation of older standards than with the continued enjoyment of them.

Experiment can degenerate, and often does, in wilful and arbitrary paradoxes, and interest in experiment may be an uncritical following of current fashions; but a particular fashion may gain so strong a hold and spread so widely into newer circles of appreciators that it may itself become a tradition. The traditional romantic novel, for example, was in its day a conscious experiment, and its long continued vogue testifies to the fact that each section of society in turn had to acquire literary sophistication. In each generation a newly literate class was content to accept the values of those who had formerly been their intellectual as well as their social superiors. But when novel reading became all but universal, there inevitably developed a desire for experiment and novelty.

As long therefore as the words traditional and tradition are used loosely, they are little more than synonyms for old and long established or perhaps obsolete. For the western world traditional religion means Christianity, traditional metaphysics usually refers to the metaphysics of Plato or Aristotle and the traditional form of legislature is bicameral, because the English Parliament, the oldest European legislature, has two chambers. Tradition has a social significance only when the old or the long established idea becomes something of value in the estimation of some or all of the members of a community and its age or its origin is referred to only as an assurance of its value. It produces in a nation or in a group an exalted group consciousness and is therefore most effective in creating groups or in reestablishing them. In all its aspects it retains enough of its primary characteristics of vagueness, remoteness of source and wide ramification to make it seem peculiarly strong to those who have recourse to it and peculiarly weak to those who mean to reject it.

Max Radin

See: Custom; Conventions, Social; Continuity, Social; Conservatism; Diffusionism; Communication; Culture; Ceremony; Folkways; Literature; Religion; Art; Classicism; Romanticism.

Consult: Bacon, Francis, "De dignitate et augmentis scientiarum" in his *Philosophical Works*, tr. by R. L. Ellis and James Spedding, ed. by J. M. Robertson (London 1905) bk. vi, ch. ii; Bacher, Wilhelm, *Tradition und Tradenten in den Schulen Palästinas und Babyloniens*, ed. by Ludwig Blau, Gesellschaft zur Förderung der Wissenschaft des Judentums, Schriften (Leipsic 1914); Lowie, Robert H., "Oral Tradition and History" in *Journal of American Folk-Lore*, vol. xxx (1917) 161–67; Sorley, W. R., *Tradition* (Oxford 1926); Harnack, Adolf von, *Lehrbuch der Dogmengeschichte*, 3 vols. (4th ed. Tübingen 1909–10), tr. by N. Buchanan and others, 7 vols. (London 1894–99), especially vol. ii, p. 319–32, vol. iii, p. 207–33, and vol. vii, p. 80–86; Ducati, B., "Rationalismus und Tradition im mohammedanischen Recht" in *Islamica*, vol. iii (1927–28) 214–28; Huch, Ricarda O., *Deutsche Tradition* (Weimar 1931); Yeats, William B., "Poetry and Tradition" in his *Essays* (London 1924) p. 304–22; London, City Literary Institute, *Tradition and Experiment in Present-Day Literature* (London 1929); Parodi, D., *Traditionalisme et démocratie* (2nd ed. Paris 1924).

TRADITIONALISM. The naïve conservatism of ordinary individuals, who desire only to live and die as their fathers lived and died and who therefore recoil from any radical social transformation, becomes converted into conscious conservatism or traditionalism under the impact of a revolution. Traditionalism arises as a reaction to the attempt of a revolution to reconstruct state and society *ab ovo* upon rational foundations. What made the French upheaval of 1789 really a revolution was its subjection of all political and social institutions to the tribunal of individual reason. Under such circumstances the social cosmos ceases to be merely a part of nature, something granted by fate, to which the individual must yield as he does to rain and sunshine. The institutional milieu in which man is reared is no longer justified by its mere existence. A normative element takes the place of the mere factor of existence. The individual sets up the criteria of right or wrong for all political and social institutions. Man as such possesses certain definite inalienable rights. These "rights of man" take precedence over all positive statutes and therefore provide the norm by which a political order is judged to be right or wrong.

As against these ideas of 1789, according to

which the individual is the measure of all things, the traditionalist ideology sets up the thesis of the primacy of society, the view that every man is born into a society which is nationally and temporally conditioned. He exists as a social being only through these bonds of destiny. The French Revolution started from man as such and assigned to him certain rights which were valid for all times and in all regions. This timeless humanism looked upon national and temporal differences as attributes, external dressings or even as prejudices. The purely human element beneath these disguises was considered the immutable and essentially valuable factor. Traditionalism represents precisely the opposite viewpoint. It denies the existence of man as such and looks upon the individual as a link in the chain of generations. Man's existence conditioned by national and temporal factors thus is no longer an attribute but a mode of life. One *is* an American, German, Frenchman or Englishman just as one *is* a man thirty or forty years of age.

The first important political theorist who united these views with a definitely counterrevolutionary tendency was Burke. Burke considered himself a disciple of Montesquieu, who had already indicated the dependence of social and political institutions upon physiological and moral factors. When Montesquieu, however, speaks of the influence of climate upon political attitudes or when he attempts to prove that the roots of the three forms of state (despotism, monarchy, democracy) are found in three different moral "principles" (fear, honor, virtue), he still is a rationalist *philosophe*. In his view the thinking person if not the acting individual can always free himself from these prejudices, since behind fear, honor and virtue ultimately stands human reason. This means that even here the dictate of reason remains the last standard which the individual may or may not follow. The wise lawgiver, argues Montesquieu, will therefore not expect too much of the individual. Only with "trembling hand" and the greatest caution will he venture to touch the social institutions in which reason and prejudice are so strangely blended.

Burke goes far beyond this "opportunistic conservatism" and regards human understanding as a function of instincts which are rooted deep in the origins of the race. Man, says Burke, is a creature who lives with prejudices which are the intellectual and moral heritage of many generations. When he thinks, he does so as an American, a German, an Englishman or a Frenchman. When this national and temporal conditioning of the individual is removed from consideration, only the physical being is left and not the *Homo sapiens*, the rational man. Proceeding from this point Burke developed his theoretical criticism of the ideas of 1789. He reproached the French for their systematic negation of historical experience and their rejection of the past and tradition. Revolutionary faith in the progress of mankind Burke considered self-deception. The attempt to refashion state and society according to abstract formulae seemed to him not only absurd but synonymous with the destruction of all foundations of law and order.

Similar ideas were developed in Germany independently of and even prior to Burke. The thought of the classical humanist era in Germany was concerned with the ideal of the self-realized personality and unique individuality. What distinguished the German ideal of humanity from the French Enlightenment was its stress on the idea of becoming, the element of time, which came to occupy a central position in the intellectual movements of the nineteenth century. For rationalism the succession of epochs as well as the differentiation between nations is only a superficial phenomenon. The thought of the Enlightenment was "unhistorical": it knew only the "today" and the "always." Even the greatest works of eighteenth century historiography were considered valuable only as storehouses of examples whereby the immutability and changelessness of human nature could be demonstrated.

As opposed to this timeless conception of the world the German humanistic epoch set up the idea of man as conditioned by his time. An artistic presentation of this view is to be found in Goethe's *Wilhelm Meister*. Goethe depicts the genetic process whereby an individual gradually attains the realization of his latent personality within the framework of a succession of significant events. Goethe's theme, however, is the spiritual evolution of an individual, and the suprapersonal factors serve merely as the background against which the fate of the individual is revealed. Nevertheless, the German classical ideal of personality contained within it the potentialities of a deeper comprehension of national existence. For once the unique individual became the subject of theoretical or artistic presentation, it was no longer difficult to look upon the individual, from the standpoint of time, as a transition point in a succession of generations and, from the standpoint of space, as a member of a national community.

Goethe himself never made the step from the cult of the individual to that of the nation. The German romanticists, guided above all by Herder, developed fully the idea of nationalities as collective personalities. The individual was conceived as a part of a whole beyond which he has no significant existence. He becomes integrated into the national group, which existed before him and will exist after him; for it alone is history and has a history.

The extent of this process of transvaluation is best demonstrated in the evolution in meaning of the single word Gothic. For the Enlightenment the word Gothic was synonymous with the outworn and outmoded. Gothic represented all the prejudices from which man had to free himself if he was to become enlightened. For the romanticists, however, the word Gothic was associated with the idea of reverence for antiquity, for grandeur; in short, for all that is aged and therefore divine. Gothic cathedrals they regarded as the sense images of the folk spirit which gave rise also to folk songs and heroic sagas. With some romanticists, like Friedrich Schlegel and Adam Müller, love of the past degenerated into a flight from the present. They idealized the Middle Ages in order to escape from the demands of their own times. The romantic concept of the organic growth of political and social institutions bears within it the germs of political quietism and pure inertia. The chief difference between political romanticism and traditionalism consists in the method of argument. The romanticist proceeds from aesthetic categories. Usually he is a man to whom his own soul has become too great a burden and who, shrinking from individual responsibility, seeks refuge in a suprapersonal individuality, such as the nation or the church. The traditionalist, on the other hand, thinks in activist terms and in legal categories. He sees the nation primarily as a political community and only secondarily as a cultural group. Thus Haller, whose *Restauration der Staatswissenschaften* (6 vols., Winterthur 1816–34) gave the name to the epoch in which he lived, was more a traditionalist than a romanticist because he looked upon the state as primarily a legal construction.

In the case of the French traditionalists Bonald and de Maistre were outstanding in the juridical precision of their argument. Both asserted the claims of the rights of God as against the Declaration of the Rights of Man of 1789. In order to shield the divine rights from the "caprices of human reason" they subjected all political and social institutions to the criteria of permanence. This argument not only annuls once and for all the adjudication of individual reason but, as a further development of Catholic natural law, leads to the thesis of the primacy of society over the individual. Above all the argument of permanence minimizes the contrast between the temporal and the permanent upon which the absolutist doctrine of Bossuet had based its distinction between state and church. The political sphere too no longer belongs simply to the realm of changing and passing phenomena, as in the older Catholic natural law. It too is part of that *fixité* of which the church is the most perfect expression.

In the writings of the French traditionalists there is an element of the counter-revolutionary crusade. Not only did de Maistre and Bonald represent the theoretical counterpart to the ideas of 1789, but they sought in every way to stand for the "opposite of the Revolution." The revolution was anti-aristocratic, anticlerical and antimonarchic; thus the traditionalists must be aristocratic, clerical and monarchic. It is interesting to note the manner in which they established the "alliance between throne and altar," so characteristic of the period of the Restoration. Bonald and de Maistre aimed to bind the church to a monarchic form of government. When Bonald discussed theism and absolute monarchy, deism and constitutional monarchy and atheism and anarchy as correlative concepts, the logical conclusion was that the king of France freed from constitutional restrictions could be matched only by an infallible pope free from conciliar control. A half century after the appearance of de Maistre's *Du pape* (2 vols., Lyons 1819) the Vatican Council proclaimed the infallibility of the pope.

In recent times political traditionalism has been most strongly developed in France, in the works of Brunetière, Paul Bourget, Maurice Barrès and above all in the writings of Charles Maurras and the Action Française group. In Germany it is a dominant element in the works of Moeller van den Bruck and National Socialist theorists and in Italy it is one of the chief props of Fascist ideology.

PETER RICHARD ROHDEN

See: TRADITION; CONSERVATISM; AUTHORITY; CLASSICISM; ROMANTICISM; NATIONALISM; REGIONALISM; FASCISM; NATIONAL SOCIALISM, GERMAN; PAN-MOVEMENTS; REVOLUTION AND COUNTER-REVOLUTION;

ANTIRADICALISM; MONARCHY; INTELLECTUALS; SOCIAL ORGANISM; CONTINUITY, SOCIAL.

Consult: Cobban, Alfred, *Edmund Burke and the Revolt against the Eighteenth Century* (London 1929); Laski, H. J., *Authority in the Modern State* (New Haven 1919); Kluckhohn, Paul, *Persönlichkeit und Gemeinschaft*, Deutsche Vierteljahrsschrift für Literaturwissenschaft und Geistesgeschichte, vol. v (Halle 1925); Metzger, W., *Gesellschaft, Staat und Recht*, ed. by Ernst Bergmann (Heidelberg 1917); Schmitt, Carl, *Politische Romantik* (2nd ed. Munich 1925); Platz, Hermann, *Geistige Kämpfe im modernen Frankreich* (Munich 1922); Curtius, E. R., *Maurice Barrès und die geistigen Grundlagen des französischen Nationalismus* (Bonn 1921); Jones, Percy M., *Tradition and Barbarism; a Survey of Anti-Romanticism in France* (London 1930); Parodi, D., *Traditionalisme et démocratie* (2nd ed. Paris 1924); Gurian, W., *Der integrale Nationalismus in Frankreich, Charles Maurras und die Action française* (Frankfort 1931); Maurras, Charles, *L'avenir de l'intelligence* (2nd ed. Paris 1917); Moeller van den Bruck, Arthur, *Das dritte Reich* (3rd ed. by Hans Schwarz, Hamburg 1931), tr. by E. O. Lorimer (London 1934).

TRAFFIC REGULATION. Urban areas must be provided with mechanisms for the movement of persons and commodities from one district to another and for connection with the surrounding territory. One such mechanism is the public street system. In their daily social and economic activities all active citizens are compelled to use the public streets, and the safety and convenience of these thoroughfares are therefore of universal import to urban dwellers.

Beginning about 1920 the street traffic problem developed a number of very serious aspects. Streets which previously had been relatively convenient and safe became congested and hazardous. The causes were several in number. Urban population grew rapidly during the first two decades of the present century, and increasing numbers of people demanded the use of public streets. Again, the population arranged itself in residential, commercial and industrial patterns which tended to aggravate the street problem. Multiple family dwellings brought about greater traffic concentration in restricted dormitory areas, while multistoried office and commercial structures tended to cause even more serious concentration in central business districts.

A second contributive factor may be characterized briefly as the "automotive revolution"; that is, the motorizing of urban populations. From 1910 to 1920 automobile registrations in the United States, including passenger cars and trucks, rose from 468,500 to 9,231,941; in 1932 they numbered 24,136,879. Approximately 80 percent of these vehicles were owned by urban dwellers. There was thus a demand for much greater street capacity for individual utilization than would otherwise have been the case. The volume of vehicles increased tremendously, and at the same time the space occupied by the individual in movement became much greater than that required in mass transportation.

It was natural that an individual, having given up pedestrianism and the use of mass transportation, should nevertheless continue to follow his typical livelihood and social habits. Thus the growing flood of traffic demand was complicated by very severe area and time concentrations. The relatively few principal routes of travel in cities became seriously overloaded. Central business districts, the normal destination of a large section of the population, became very congested. Community habits added greatly to the seriousness of the problem in the principal concentration areas, for there is considerable uniformity in business hours. Most establishments open between eight and nine o'clock in the morning and close between five and six in the evening; at such times traffic activity reaches its peak, so that the pressure is frequently two or three times as intense as in other hours of the day.

This increased traffic volume and density had two very serious effects, which became apparent early in the 1920's: a critical congestion and inconvenience in street use and a very rapid rise in accidents and fatalities. The result was widespread popular and official demand for improvement. Public administration, however, was ill equipped to provide relief, both because of an absence of proper technique in traffic regulation and because of the more or less fixed limitations of the street pattern, so that from 1929 on the problem became acute.

Traffic congestion has had significant economic consequences. It has resulted in a large waste in the capital investment in automotive machinery. Vehicles capable of moving safely at a speed of from forty-five to sixty miles per hour or even at higher ranges under free roadway conditions have been forced to operate at speeds scarcely in excess of those maintained by horse drawn vehicles. Thus speed potentials, which make up a considerable part of the value of a motor vehicle, cannot be fully utilized.

The tempo of city life has been accelerated constantly, and many urban activities in their current organization are dependent upon the maintenance of and indeed the increase in individual and commodity transportation processes. It is hazardous to assign specific monetary values to lost time. That time does, however, have value for urban dwellers is obvious, an assertion which is substantiated by the fact that billions of dollars have been spent for motor vehicles, improved street facilities and transportation development in general. The National Conference on Street and Highway Safety estimated in 1930 that congestion cost the American public more than $1,000,000,000 a year. Non-productive gasoline consumption by vehicles idling in traffic congestion constitutes in itself a very important loss. Increasing congestion frequently necessitates the employment of additional commercial vehicles. The staff of salesmen and other employees engaged in field work must also often be enlarged, thus further augmenting distribution costs.

Another effect of traffic congestion has been the decentralization of many commercial activities. In the early 1920's central business district establishments found that their locations were less accessible to the buying power of the community because of the tediousness of protracted automobile trips and also because of parking difficulties. Women shoppers who had become accustomed to the use of the automobile were among the first to seek alternative markets in more accessible areas. The automobile gave the prospective buyer of goods or services a wide freedom of choice. Where two markets offer identical values it is axiomatic that the market with the greater accessibility will be generally preferred. The vigorous growth of secondary business districts was aided by competition among business enterprises for more conveniently located trade connections. The result was a widespread establishment of department store branches, independent department stores, specialty shops and branch banking or independent banks in secondary business districts. It was felt by many that this decentralization was highly desirable and that it indicated a healthy trend in the trade pattern of American cities. Much may be said in support of this contention; but it should be pointed out that the decentralizing movement represented a more or less radical change in community habits and practises and therefore was pathological to the extent that it sprang from a form of traffic disease which was not altogether beyond remedy.

The traffic accident problem has humanitarian and social as well as economic aspects. In 1911, 2043 persons were killed in the United States registration area in motor vehicle accidents. Fatalities had risen to 12,557 in 1920 and were estimated at 29,000 for the whole United States in 1932. Fatal accidents were most numerous in 1931, when 34,400 were killed; in the same year it was estimated that in addition almost 1,000,000 persons suffered physical injury. The number of traffic accidents causing only property loss and the extent of this loss have never been reported nor can they be easily estimated. It is known, however, that such accidents are far more numerous than those involving personal injury or death. In 1930 the National Conference on Street and Highway Safety estimated the economic loss in traffic accidents at approximately $1,000,000,000 a year.

European cities have shared with American cities almost all of the problems relating to traffic convenience and public safety. Their experiences, however, have been much less intensive than those of the typical city in the United States, because the European per capita registration of motor vehicles is so much lower. Approximately 75 percent of the total number of automobiles in use throughout the world are in the United States.

There are two principal relief measures which have been employed in the United States and Europe in an attempt to solve or at any rate to alleviate street traffic difficulties. The first is improved traffic regulation for the purpose of providing a safer and more orderly movement on existing streets. The second involves the reorganization of the street system and the construction of new facilities for traffic use. Both have been employed in America and in Europe; but in the following discussion emphasis is placed on practises developed in the United States, because the severity of the problem in this country has in most cases necessitated more elaborate plans.

The expression traffic regulation may be said to include legal rules governing street use, their enforcement by the police, the adjudication of violations by the courts and the employment of mechanical devices for the promulgation of rules or as a substitute for police direction.

Until the early 1920's traffic regulation was almost exclusively a police matter. Traffic rules were made either by the police or by city councils upon police recommendation, although private interests were not without influence in guiding legislative action. In the first critical period of traffic difficulties, starting in 1923, it became apparent that police methods, unaided, would be entirely incapable of dealing with the situation. There was rapidly developed a technique which may be described as street traffic engineering. The cities undertaking competent and factual engineering analyses of their problems, and basing rules and regulations upon such surveys, found that they were in advance of others using more traditional methods. The demand for traffic engineers was supplied by engineering schools and other technical agencies. This branch of engineering grew so rapidly that in 1930 the Institute of Traffic Engineers was organized, and by 1933 it had a membership of sixty persons actually engaged in traffic engineering, although the total number of those performing such work either full or part time may be estimated at more than five hundred.

So serious had the problem become in 1924 that Secretary of Commerce Hoover called the first National Conference on Street and Highway Safety. Subsequent meetings of this conference, composed of several hundred representatives of public and private agencies, were held in 1926 and in 1930. The purpose of the gatherings was to determine the causes of traffic difficulty and to prepare standard regulations to meet them. It was the anticipation that these regulations would be of direct value in individual communities and would also effect greater uniformity in the various jurisdictions throughout the country. As a result of its three meetings the conference issued comprehensive motor vehicle codes covering almost every aspect of the problem and the entire field of legislative action ranging from statutes to city and town ordinances. The hopes entertained for the conference have been fulfilled; while there can be no question that there is still wide variation in specific provisions among the various jurisdictions, there has been a substantial and gratifying trend toward uniformity. Where a local ordinance departs markedly from standard practises in such matters as speed control, enforcing agencies tend to nullify the exceptional provisions by interpreting them in accordance with generally prevailing usage.

Three essentials characterize good traffic regulation in cities. First, the rules should be in harmony with national uniform standards, unless peculiar local conditions make exception desirable; secondly, the rules should be as simple as the subject matter permits, since a local traffic code expressed in complicated legal terminology can never serve as a textbook for the average driver; thirdly, the rules should be rational, that is, they should be adjusted to existing and apparent needs. A local traffic code should become the basis for community conduct and habit in the use of public streets. This can never be the case and the regulations cannot be enforced adequately, no matter how much police pressure may be brought to bear, if they appear to the average citizen as arbitrary, unnecessary and irrational. The desideratum regarding this cannot be assured by casual observation or guesswork regarding traffic needs, and it is here that the traffic engineer plays an important role in the accurate determination of facts.

Something of the complexity of traffic regulation may be understood from a review of typical conditions. The regulation of speed is now generally the exclusive province of the state legislature, city officials being prohibited from such stipulation except under certain special conditions. The recent years have shown a marked and, it is believed, a desirable tendency away from statutes fixing definite speed limits. Provisions have been substituted for the punishment of those acts which, combined with speed, result in hazard.

The regulation of the proper action to be followed by two drivers about to cross each other's path at an intersection has always been troublesome. The rule almost universally obtaining at the present time is that an operator of a motor vehicle should allow the vehicle on his right to pass. This apparently important guide for the avoidance of collision, at least where only two cars are involved, if actually carried out would without doubt result in the elimination of one serious type of hazard. It is, however, almost universally disregarded in both operation and enforcement, drivers determining their priority by mutual agreement in each instance.

Right and left turning movements are a source of confusion and many accidents. Vehicles making right turns, either with or against a signal, must cross at least one lane of potential pedestrian travel. Vehicles making left turns cause similar pedestrian interference and must likewise cross an opposite stream of vehicular traffic. This condition has led numerous cities to prohibit left turns at the more congested intersections or even over considerable areas. In some cases right turns are likewise prohibited or restricted.

Traffic moves most smoothly where the vehicles have approximately uniform speed characteristics. For this reason there is a natural desire to segregate truck traffic from passenger car traffic. Such separation has been accomplished to only a slight degree in most cities, as there are relatively few routes which may be reserved exclusively for the use of passenger vehicles without involving an undue inconvenience to commercial traffic. The most frequent segregation of traffic is in the exclusion of trucks from boulevards, park drives and parkways.

One-way streets, employed with success in New York City and Philadelphia, do not seem to be generally used. The rule has very considerable value in highly congested districts where streets are relatively narrow, street car traffic is absent or operates in only one direction and where immediately adjacent streets may be paired for opposite movements.

Parking regulations have become essential both to keep congested streets relatively free for moving traffic and to provide an equitable distribution of curb parking space. Parking regulations are of three general types. Some are time limit regulations, under which the maximum time a vehicle may be parked is specified; others reserve certain curb lengths for the exclusive use of vehicles while loading and unloading; while still other regulations may exclude parking altogether. The first two types are as a rule to be found in most cities; the third is used only where there are especially severe conditions in particular streets or areas. The largest area of parking prohibition is to be found in Chicago, where vehicles may not be parked in any part of the so-called Loop district.

The relationship between motor vehicles and pedestrians has always been a source of great difficulty. More than half of the traffic fatalities result from pedestrians being struck by motor vehicles. Pedestrians, in turn, by their casual and unregulated use of public streets, cause inconvenience and irregularity in the movement of vehicles. The National Conference on Street and Highway Safety in its standard regulations proposed that pedestrians, at controlled intersections, be required to obey traffic directions. Few cities have been able to apply the regulation successfully, in most instances because citizens have not been impressed with the reasonableness and necessity of traffic volume and the method of control. The outstanding exception to this experience is to be found in Los Angeles, where intersection crossings for pedestrians have been regulated since 1925.

Experience shows that sound regulations are self-enforcing as far as approximately 95 percent of the street users are concerned. Disobedience arises through the ignorance, confusion or antisocial character of the individual. Thus, with the best regulations available and with most thorough promulgation, there is still need for continuing police direction and enforcement. The more successful police departments have concentrated on directive and educational rather than on punitive activities, viewing their problem as a question of transportation rather than of crime. In the larger cities police departments now regularly maintain traffic divisions with trained personnel and special equipment.

Traffic assignments may be described as stationary or mobile. Stationary assignments are for intersection duty, either to direct the movements of traffic by hand or to cooperate with indications given by traffic control signals. Mobile assignments are for patrolmen engaged in parking enforcement or for men with motorized equipment who are assigned to apprehend those engaged in dangerous practises, particularly speed violations. The motor cycle continues to be the principal vehicle used in mobile assignments, although there is a tendency to substitute automobiles because they are both safer and suited to all weather use. Mounted squads, which are still maintained in some cities, are not well adapted to the handling of motorized traffic, although they are useful in emergency situations involving large crowds of pedestrians.

It is safe to say that police officers, unaided by mechanical devices, would never have been able to cope with the traffic problem in the larger cities during the past ten years. There has been developed a very comprehensive system of traffic signs, signals and markings as an aid in directing and regularizing the movement of traffic. Traffic signs are composed of text, with sometimes the addition of a symbol, usually of fixed aspect. They may be equipped with illumination or with flashing lights. Traffic signals are traffic indicators with a changing aspect and are designed for the purpose of alternating the flow of traffic at intersections. Standard traffic signals may be operated manually by police officers, as is more frequently the case in European than in American cities, or automatically by electric systems. The standard traffic signal in use in the United States gives its indications through colored lenses, red meaning "stop," amber meaning "wait" and green meaning "go." The duration, or interval, for each indication and the cycle, or the time required for the appearance of all three colors, is normally controlled by a pretimed electrical mechanism. The first recorded fixed assignment of police officers to traffic duty was in 1903 in New York City. Traffic light signals first appeared in Cleveland in 1914 and were installed in San Francisco in 1915, in Salt Lake City in 1916 and in New York City in 1918.

There are several types of traffic signal operation. Traffic actuated signals have their durations and cycles controlled by roadway contact pads, sometimes called detectors, which are operated by the passage of vehicles. Under this system signals respond strictly to the traffic requirements. Independent automatic signals are operated by a pretimed mechanism without reference to signals at other intersections. Simultaneous timing results when a series of signals along a route of travel are interconnected and operated in such a manner that all show the same indication to the route at the same time. In progressive timing, the "go" indication in each signal is so fixed in relation to adjacent signals that it will be given at a time equal to that required for travel, at a pre-estimated rate of speed, from the next adjacent signal. Accurately designed progressive signal timing makes possible the uninterrupted movement of a vehicle through the entire series of signals, provided the driver maintains the rate of speed for which the system is operated.

Police departments have done notable work in public education and in the control of certain specialized traffic problems, as in the protection of school children. So-called schoolboy patrols, now common in American cities, have been organized under the direction of the police departments and other interested agencies and have been unusually successful in reducing fatality rates among school children.

Traffic violations, classified by statute as felonies, normally result in a summary arrest of the apprehended violator. For all other violations in the misdemeanor classification the apprehending officer gives the violator, after his identity has been established, a summons, or "ticket," directing him to appear before the suitable judicial agency. In the case of parking violations it is now customary to affix the summons to the vehicle in the absence of the operator, a practise which is of doubtful legality in jurisdictions requiring personal service.

Traffic misdemeanor cases are so numerous that they tend to flood the calendar of the police courts and to render impossible even ordinary summary procedure. This difficulty has been solved in a number of cities, such as Detroit, Chicago, Los Angeles and San Francisco, by the establishment of a traffic fines bureau. Minor, non-hazardous violations are classified and a fixed schedule of penalties is assigned. A violator is summoned in accordance with regular practise and may use his discretion as to whether he will demand a regular judicial hearing or will take advantage of the abbreviated procedure. In the latter case he appears at the traffic fines bureau within the time fixed, pays the prescribed penalty and thus ends his obligations. Traffic fines bureaus usually maintain records of offenders and additional penalties are imposed on repeaters; after three or more offenses within a period of time the violator, with a record of his violations, may be cited before the regular court. There has been an increasing tendency for cities to credit traffic fines and forfeitures to a special fund set aside for improved traffic regulations and facilities.

Traffic regulation as described above gives some assurance that existing streets may be made safer and that it may be possible to avoid the more acute aspects of traffic congestion. Regulation alone, however, can never accurately adjust existing street facilities to the requirements of a thoroughly motorized society. City planning and replanning together with the design of special facilities are the only ultimate hope for efficiency and safety in urban travel. Zoning also is important but, inasmuch as it is ideally designed to provide for a normal, functional allocation and distribution of urban activities, it must be regarded as dependent upon free and natural circulation for its full achievement rather than as in itself a means of traffic relief.

Most city streets were constructed and are still rebuilt for the needs of slow moving, horse drawn traffic. Street widenings and extensions are in many instances necessary to relieve local conditions, although they can never be considered as final solutions. The arcading of sidewalks, whereby they are moved back until they come under the upper stories of abutting buildings so that the entire space between buildings can be utilized for vehicular traffic, has been suggested as a method of traffic congestion relief. This treatment of sidewalks is not expensive and is particularly adapted to warm climates, where the arcades shelter pedestrians from the sun. But although the plan has been widely discussed, its adoption has been slow largely because of objections by shopkeepers.

In the metropolitan centers at least both speed and safety in the major movements of traffic demand that local traffic be completely segregated from high speed, large volume, through movements. This may be accomplished only by the application to the street problem of the same principles which have been followed in the construction of rapid transit for mass transportation; that is, through an elevation or depression of the main route and the complete segregation of movements on it from cross and local traffic requirements. This logical tendency is illustrated in the partially completed west side elevated express highway along the shore of the Hudson River in New York City. The plan calls for a highway about fourteen miles in length which will be connected by ramps with main crosstown streets and will provide access to the Holland Tunnel, the proposed Thirty-ninth Street and Weehawken tunnels and the ferries, freight terminals and industrial and shipping centers of the city. The highway crosses the Sixtieth Street terminal of the New York Central Railroad and will continue into Bronx borough on a steel structure over the railroad tracks lying below Riverside Park. Similar highways have been proposed for Boston and Chicago. An example of a depressed highway constructed through a metropolitan area is that of the Bronx River Parkway in Westchester county, New York, which passes through a series of built up communities. A vehicular tunnel, extending the full width of Manhattan borough, New York, has been given serious consideration in recent years.

MILLER McCLINTOCK

See: MUNICIPAL TRANSIT; MOTOR VEHICLE TRANSPORTATION; MOTOR VEHICLE ACCIDENTS; SAFETY MOVEMENT; POLICE; ROADS; CITY AND TOWN PLANNING; ZONING.

Consult: National Conference on Street and Highway Safety, Reports, nos. 1–3 (Washington 1924–30); McClintock, Miller, Street Traffic Control (New York 1925), Report and Recommendations of the Metropolitan Street Traffic Survey (Chicago 1926), and A Report on the Street Traffic Control Problem of San Francisco (San Francisco 1927); McClintock, Miller, and Williams, S. J., Municipal Organization for Street Traffic Control, Municipal Administration Service, Publication no. 16 (New York 1930); Harvard University, Albert Russell Erskine Bureau for Street Traffic Research, A Report on the Street Traffic Control Problem of the City of Boston (Boston 1928); Lewis, H. M., and Goodrich, E. P., "Highway Traffic" in Regional Plan of New York and Its Environs, Regional Survey of New York and Its Environs, 8 vols. (New York 1927–31) vol. iii; Watson, Henry, Street Traffic Flow (London 1933); "Planning for City Traffic," American Academy of Political and Social Science, Annals, vol. cxxxiii (Philadelphia 1927); Eno, W. P., Fundamentals of Highway Traffic Regulation (Washington 1926), and Simplification of Highway Traffic (Washington 1929); European Conference on Road Traffic, Geneva 1933, Records and Texts, League of Nations, Publications, 1931. VIII. 15 (Geneva 1931); Dikanski, M. G., La ville moderne; la circulation, l'habitation, le travail (Paris 1927); Giese, E., and Paetsch, H., Polizei und Verkehr (Berlin 1926); Kulow, A., Der Strassenverkehr (Lübeck 1925); Institute of Traffic Engineers, Proceedings, published annually in New York since 1931; National Safety Council, Accidents Facts, published annually in Chicago since 1928; National Automobile Chamber of Commerce, Facts and Figures of the Automobile Industry, published annually in New York since 1919; Traffic Digest, published monthly in New York since May, 1931; Verkehrstechnik, published bimonthly in Berlin since 1921.

TRANSCENDENTALISM. Although transcendentalism as a philosophic doctrine has a long history, as a social movement it was confined largely to the influence of romantic idealism in Great Britain and America during the first half of the nineteenth century. In theology the doctrine of a transcendent deity is opposed to any doctrine which holds God to be immanent in the world or in history. In classic logic and metaphysics non-empirical sources or principles of knowledge are called transcendent or transcendental. Kant made a sharp distinction between a "transcendent" realm of revelation, which he denied, and the "transcendental," or a priori, factors as opposed to the empirical, or sensational, factors within knowledge. This distinction laid the foundation for an idealism— developed by Schelling, Novalis, Fichte, Schleiermacher and Goethe—which discovered a transcendental reason, or God, operating within human experience and history, not derived from sense experience and yet immanent in the human mind or soul. These transcendentalists regarded their philosophy as a revival of Platonism, as a unification of the subject and object of reason and as a reconciliation of religious tradition with evolutionary science. It gave to the rationalism of the German Enlightenment a romantic self-assertion and an interest in national culture which was in distinct contrast to the sensationalism and cosmopolitanism of the French Enlightenment.

The introduction of this philosophy into England had important consequences for social thought and movements. It fed the general reaction against the French Revolution and against the sensationalistic rationalism of the Benthamites. Coleridge used it to give a "spiritual" meaning to the British nation and its institutions: that is to say, above the realm of science, or "understanding," is the realm of reason, or spirit; above the secular state with its Parliament is the religious unity of the people represented by the Church of England; above the aims and interests of the liberals are the eternal ideas of reason expressing themselves in morality and faith. Coleridge drew heavily on Schelling, especially in his theology. Carlyle gave the movement further impetus by popularizing Goethe and by ridiculing the principles and aims of the utilitarians, of the "dismal science" and of empirical and evolutionary method in general. Wordsworth's poetry, although less transcendental in its philosophic orientation, was congenial to the transcendental mood and gave the movement an emotional appeal which carried it beyond the ranges of philosophic or theological debate. Growing steadily until it culminated in the philosophy of T. H. Green, transcendentalism in England undermined both the empiricist or utilitarian movement and the Scottish common sense philosophy. It created a new philosophy for a new liberalism, less democratic, less individualistic and less bourgeois than the old.

In the United States transcendentalism ran a different course and drew on a greater variety and confusion of intellectual traditions. The movement began in the 1820's, when some of the Unitarians, especially George Ticknor, George Bancroft and Edward Everett, recently returned from Göttingen, discovered Herder, Schleiermacher and the romantic German literature, but it did not spread until the 1830's, when the writings of Coleridge became a dominant influence. In theological circles in New England Coleridge was regarded as the height or depth of liberalism; by the Unitarians his philosophy was welcomed as the basis for a more adequate conception of the human spirit than Unitarianism had derived from the rationalism of the French and English Enlightenment; by the orthodox it was feared as surrendering the faith to a vague intuitionism and a doubtful theory of nature. Transcendentalism therefore implied in America a radical religious and social reform. In 1836 Orestes A. Brownson organized the Society for Christian Union and Progress and in 1838 founded the *Boston Quarterly Review*. Through him and some of his associates a strong element of French influence was introduced into American transcendentalism, especially Saint-Simonianism and the writings of Constant, Cousin and Jouffroy. Victor Cousin, whose philosophy was a loose mixture of Scottish intuitionism and Kantianism, had a great vogue, and his influence accounts in part for the eclecticism and confusion which reigned in the minds of American transcendentalists, enabling them to combine the conservative and uncritical intuitionism of the Scottish philosophy with the "subjectivism" and the romanticism of the idealists.

The best expression and high water mark of the movement was the *Dial*, a quarterly magazine published from 1840 to 1844. Its chief contributors were A. Bronson Alcott, W. H. Channing, James Freeman Clarke, R. W. Emerson, Margaret Fuller, Theodore Parker, George Ripley and Henry Thoreau. Into its already vague gospel Alcott and Thoreau introduced oriental elements, especially the philosophic ideas of Brahmanism; Ripley and Channing introduced an enthusiasm for Fourierism and for social utopianism in general; and Margaret Fuller introduced feminism. In addition there were liberal amounts of Swedenborgianism, mysticism, Platonism and abolitionism.

Transcendentalism was preoccupied primarily with "self-culture," and its social doctrines were merely means to this end. It encouraged a variety of social reforms, from vegetarianism to abolitionism, but only in so far as they were related to its theory of spiritual freedom. The majority of its members were extremely critical of New England society and its traditions and welcomed opportunities for withdrawing from conventional society and politics and founding small circles of self-culture or, as in the case of Thoreau, renouncing society in general to live in nature and in books. The attempts to found transcendental communities, notably Fruitlands and the Brook Farm experiment, were based on romantic ideas of agricultural labor and on the belief that small agricultural or handicraft groups offered the most favorable environment for literary discussion, moral education and self-culture. They were motivated only secondarily by the socialism of Fourier, which Albert Brisbane wished to introduce in detail. After the failure of such utopian schemes American transcendental philosophy became increasingly individualistic, culminating in Emerson's gospel of self-reliance.

As a consequence American transcendentalism was confined to a limited group whose chief aim was to be spiritually free and culturally elect. It became increasingly inchoate, esoteric and pretentious, and its adherents were unable to agree on any practical social program and were out of touch with those forces in American life which after the Civil War produced a reorientation of social philosophy. Emerson, who undoubtedly enjoyed a popular prestige, owes his influence largely to the fact that he buried most of his transcendentalism under a shrewd Yankee individualism which was pragmatically intelligible quite apart from its philosophic foundations. Idealism in both England and America was refashioned by the Hegelian influence, which was more congenial than transcendentalism to recent physical science, to nationalism, to socialism, as well as to conservative ideas of morality and religion.

HERBERT W. SCHNEIDER

See: IDEALISM; ROMANTICISM; PLATO AND PLATONISM; ENLIGHTENMENT; FOURIER AND FOURIERISM; UTILITARIANISM; COMMUNISTIC SETTLEMENTS.

Consult: Coleridge, Samuel Taylor, *Aids to Reflection* (7th ed. by Derwent Coleridge, London 1854), and *Unpublished Letters of Samuel Taylor Coleridge*, ed. by E. L. Griggs, 2 vols. (London 1933); Masson, David, *Recent British Philosophy* (3rd ed. London 1877) chs. ii–iii; Neff, E. E., *Carlyle* (New York 1932) ch. iv; Frothingham, O. B., *Transcendentalism in New England* (New York 1876); Christy, Arthur, *The Orient in American Transcendentalism*, Columbia University, Studies in English and Comparative Literature (New York 1932); Girard, William, *Du transcendantalisme considéré sous son aspect social*, University of California, Publications in Modern Philology, vol. viii, no. 2 (Berkeley 1918); Goddard, Harold C., *Studies in New England Transcendentalism*, Columbia University, Studies in English, 2nd ser., vol. ii, no. 3 (New York 1908), and his chapter "Transcendentalism" in the *Cambridge History of American Literature*, ed. by W. P. Trent and others, 4 vols. (New York 1917–21) vol. i, p. 326–48, and bibliography p. 546–51; Gohdes, C. L. F., *The Periodicals of American Transcendentalism*, Duke University, Publications (Durham, N. C. 1931); Leighton, Walter, *French Philosophers and New England Transcendentalism* (Charlottesville, Va. 1908); Parrington, V. L., *The Romantic Revolution in America, 1800–1860*, Main Currents in American Thought, vol. ii (New York 1927) p. 379–434, and bibliography p. 480–81; Swift, Lindsay, *Brook Farm; Its Members, Scholars, and Visitors* (New York 1900). Of the writings of Emerson see especially "Nature," "The Transcendentalist," and "New England Reformers" in his *Complete Works*, 12 vols. (Centenary ed. by E. W. Emerson, Boston 1903–12) vol. i, p. 1–78, 327–59, and vol. iii, p. 249–85; Girard, William, *Du transcendantalisme considéré essentiellement dans sa définition et ses origines françaises*, University of California, Publications in Modern Philology, vol. iv, no. 3 (Berkeley 1916).

TRANSIT DUTIES are taxes which are imposed upon goods passing through a country on their way to their final destination in another country. In general either they are levied for purely financial purposes, forming a source of revenue for the government, the state or the municipality in question; or they are intended to hinder the export trade of other countries, in which case they constitute a more or less powerful weapon of competition and are supposed to act as a stimulus to the export trade of the levying country. In the latter instance they are similar to transit prohibitions, which are, however, usually more effective, unless the duties are extraordinarily high and thereby prohibitive.

In recent years transit prohibitions have assumed more importance than transit duties. The latter were of great significance in the past, particularly during the Middle Ages. Even in the eighteenth century they were an important issue in the German states, where they were not abolished until 1861. In France, although more liberal regulations were adopted in the early eighteenth century, transit duties were not finally and entirely removed until 1842. In recent times, except during the World War and in China, such duties have been levied only in minor, isolated cases.

In China, besides other transit dues, the likin, essentially a transit duty, was introduced after 1850 and has since played an important role both internally and in its foreign relations. There is no uniform system, but a great variety of rates and methods. The likin was attacked from the beginning by both Chinese and foreign business people as a hindrance to economic development; but its abolition proved very difficult, since for a long time it furnished the principal source of revenue for the Chinese provincial governments. New efforts toward removal of the likin were made after the World War as part of the reorganization of the customs and taxation systems. Although the Washington Conference of 1922 between China and a number of foreign powers resolved that immediate steps should be taken for a speedy abolition of the likin, such a step was again delayed. By January, 1931, other transit dues had been abolished and the likin was gradually disappearing.

The widespread abolition of transit duties during the nineteenth century was in part a reflection of the gradual liberalization of commercial policy. In addition the national transportation systems became increasingly interested in preventing the diversion of freight, from the carriage of which they would benefit by transit duties or other artificial measures. A number of commercial treaties concluded since the middle of the nineteenth century made special stipulations as to freedom of transit in the territories covered. Similar provisions were incorporated into the peace treaties after the World War and into a number of separate agreements following the war. The League of Nations sponsored a conference on freedom of transit at Barcelona in 1921. The Convention and Statute on Freedom of Transit signed at this conference stipulates that in the countries concerned "traffic in transit shall not be subject to any special dues in respect of transit (including entry and exit)." Only dues intended solely to defray expenses of supervision and administration entailed by such transit may be levied, and these must correspond as nearly as possible with the expenses which they are intended to cover. This convention came into force on October 31, 1922, ratified by most of the thirty-five signatory states. Other countries, principally Germany, acceded later; and by January, 1934, thirty-two countries had ratified it. The United States has not joined the convention.

OTTO NATHAN

See: CUSTOMS DUTIES; TRANSIT, INTERNATIONAL.

Consult: Gruntzel, Josef, *System der Handelspolitik* (3rd ed. Vienna 1928) p. 289–97; Fisk, G. M., and Peirce, P. S., *International Commercial Policies* (New York 1923) p. 64–65, 74; Buell, R. L., *International Relations* (rev. ed. New York 1929) p. 128–29; Plant, T., "Durchfuhrzölle und Durchfuhrverbote" in *Handwörterbuch der Staatswissenschaften*, vol. iii (Jena 1926) p. 309–15; Morse, H. B., *The Trade and Administration of China* (3rd ed. London 1921), especially p. 119–35; See, C. S., *The Foreign Trade of China*, Columbia University, Studies in History, Economics and Public Law, no. 199 (New York 1919); Great Britain, Department of Overseas Trade, *Economic Conditions in China* (1930), and *Trade and Economic Conditions in China* (1933).

TRANSIT, INTERNATIONAL. The treatment of "traffic in transit" has constituted a persistent problem since trade first overflowed parochial limits. From earliest times the frontier has been the focal point of traffic control. Trade strangulation through local transit barriers reached its highwater mark during the Middle Ages, when tolls on bridge, cart, river, ford, and (most general) *péage*, foot traffic toll, as well as a great variety of *douanes*, or taxes, on transit of special products, such as wines, were frequent and numerous. Several factors, however, tended to mitigate the severity of these restrictions. The concessions often obtained by the monasteries for their products in transit to nearby markets tended to be extended to other groups. The development of markets and fairs stimulated a greater volume of traffic, which eventually swept away some of these exactions, and with the restoration of central authority in the sixteenth and seventeenth centuries governmental intervention suppressed many others.

Since the industrial revolution, with the greatly increased volume of trade and the rise of nationalism, freedom of transit has become an even more imperative requisite of international intercourse. Its political importance in the general relations between states is not to be minimized. Freedom of transit may be even more important to cordial commercial relations than tariffs, since its interruption usually affects directly a large number of normal economic relationships, the beneficiaries of which may bring strong pressure to bear on their governments to take retaliatory measures. That this is peculiarly true of the landlocked nations is evidenced by their constant pressure for ocean outlets under their own sovereignty. During the nineteenth century the attempts of Bolivia to obtain a seaport and Russia's policy regarding the Bosporus and an ice free port in the Pacific were inspired by this demand. It was recognized in the peace treaties of 1919–23 in the grant to Poland of access to the sea via the Polish Corridor, the lease of "free ports" by Germany to Czechoslovakia in Hamburg and Stettin, the guaranty to Austria and Hungary of freedom of transit to Adriatic ports. The general interest in preventing a single state from impeding freedom of transit has resulted in such incidents as the controversy over the Danish Sound dues, in the internationalization of canals and straits at Suez, Kiel and the Bosporus and in the imposition of international servitudes regarding freedom of transit on the defeated powers by the peace treaties, the establishment of the Free City of Danzig and the final acceptance by Italy of a similar principle at Fiume.

The nineteenth century saw a number of practical experiments in international control of freedom of transit as not only tariffs but river and port regulations, sanitary regulations and quarantine embargoes, shipping bounties and freight rate concessions, devised as auxiliary weapons in the struggle for markets, proved an increasing burden upon commerce and stimulated efforts for their control.

The earliest field in which action was taken was that of international waterways (*q.v.*). Since the establishment of the first organized system of control on the Rhine in 1804 every international river of navigable importance has been brought within some system of international control or opened to navigation either by treaty or by the unilateral action of the riparian states. New and less easily settled conflicts of interest arose with the use of such streams for irrigation or power.

The disruption of normal transit facilities after the World War made all these problems acute and resulted in their being placed within the scope of activity of the League of Nations. Since 1921 the Organization for Communications and Transit of the League, an autonomous agency representative of member and non-member states, has elaborated a series of conventions and "statutes" dealing with a wide variety of traffic problems. River traffic was handled in the conventional agreements of 1921 concerning Freedom of Transit and the Regime of Navigable Waterways (7 L.N. Treaty Series 11, 35), in those of 1923 concerning the Development of Hydraulic Power Affecting More Than One State, and the Transmission in Transit of Electric Power (36 L.N.T.S. 75; 58 L.N.T.S. 315). Other questions of importance both to inland and to ocean transport have also been codified. The convention of 1925 on Measurement of Vessels Employed in Inland Transportation (67 L.N.T.S. 63) completes and to some degree supersedes an earlier European convention of 1898 on the same subject (28 Martens, N.R.G., 2nd ser., 733). In 1921 a declaration relating to the Recognizing the Right to a Flag of States Having no Seacoast was signed (7 L.N.T.S. 73). In 1923 a convention concerning the International Regime of Maritime Ports (58 L.N.T.S. 284) established the principle of the non-discriminatory treatment of foreign shipping. Numerous other questions, such as the unification of river law, uniformity of shipping signals, the competition of railway and river traffic, specific recommendations on the development of inland waterways in Poland, China and Siam, have been dealt with by the Communications and Transit Organization.

No less important have been its activities with regard to land transit. Numerous railroad conventions, beginning with those signed at Berne in 1886 dealing with the Technical Unity of Railways and the Sealing of Railway Wagons and those of 1890 concerning the Transport of Goods by Rail, have been consolidated and completed by the convention of 1923 on the International Regime of Railways (47 L.N.T.S. 55) and that of 1924 on the Transport of Goods by Rail (77 L.N.T.S. 367). The Central Office for International Transport set up in 1924 by the railroad systems of most of the countries of Europe and the League Organization cooperate at many points but have not as yet found it feasible to merge.

For highway traffic an international convention of 1909 was revised and extended in 1926 by conventions concerning Road Traffic (97 L.N.T.S. 83) and Motor Traffic (108 L.N.T.S. 123). Three further conventions, dealing with lost licenses, unification of road signals (not yet in force) and taxation of foreign motor vehicles, were drafted in 1931 by the European Conference on Road Traffic, under the authority of the organization, which in 1924 set up a Permanent Committee on Road Traffic. In the western hemisphere a pan-American convention of the Regulation of Automotive Traffic was signed in 1930.

Finally, air transit is regulated by the convention of 1919 (11 L.N.T.S. 173) and the succeeding amendments and supplementary agreements. In 1926 a Spanish American convention on aerial navigation and in 1928 a pan-American convention on commercial aviation (Final Act of Sixth International Conference of American States) completed regional international legislation in this field.

Most of these conventions lay down general principles of action and require consultation between the contracting states, without establishing complete international administration. But they mark two important advances. In the first place, they set up international standards and bring the subject within the scope of international jurisdiction. In the second place, they provide an international forum, usually the Permanent Court of International Justice, for the settlement of disputes as to their interpretation and application.

In addition numerous conventions setting up international control of national police regulations in various fields have had direct effect upon international transit. Among these may be mentioned the conventions of 1890, 1908, 1919 and 1925 concerning the supervision of the international traffic in arms; the conventions prior and subsequent to the basic convention of 1903 (and including a pan-American convention of 1924) dealing with quarantine regulations for persons and goods in transit; the liquor traffic conventions of 1919 relating to Africa and of 1925 concerning contraband traffic in the Baltic; the narcotic drugs manufacture and traffic conventions of 1912 and 1925; the conventions of 1910 and 1923 which deal with suppression of the traffic in obscene publications and of 1904 and 1921 regarding the traffic in women and children; the post-war conventions dealing with the international transit and treatment of refugees and *Heimatlosen*.

The number and variety of private associations interested in various aspects of international transit have also steadily increased. International tourist traffic, reaching unprecedented totals during the 1920's, has had repercussions on both public policy and opinion and on private activities in such fields as shipping, railways and educational exchanges.

Despite this internationalization of many transit problems the steady trend of the post-war period toward economic nationalism has been reflected in a reversal of the movement toward greater freedom of transit, as evidenced, for instance, by the practical failure of the convention on the Abolition of Import and Export Prohibitions and Restrictions of 1927 (97 L.N.T.S. 391) to affect the policy of the majority of the signatories. Restriction of freedom of transit for nationalist ends, economic or military, has been sharpened by new threats of war. Whether autarchy will become the settled policy of the great powers for the next few years is perhaps undetermined; if greater freedom of intercourse and exchange is restored as a world policy, the developments outlined above will form the inevitable starting point of future action in the field of international transit.

PHILLIPS BRADLEY

See: TRANSPORTATION; COMMUNICATION; COMMERCE; BOUNDARIES; TRANSIT DUTIES; FREE PORTS AND FREE ZONES; INTERNATIONAL WATERWAYS; PORTS AND HARBORS; RAILROADS; MOTOR VEHICLE TRANSPORTATION; AVIATION, section on LAW OF; ELECTRIC POWER; POLISH CORRIDOR; ARMS AND MUNITIONS TRAFFIC; LIQUOR TRAFFIC; OPIUM PROBLEM; PASSPORTS.

Consult: McClure, W. M., *World Prosperity as Sought through the Economic Work of the League of Nations* (New York 1933); Graf, Ernst, *Internationale Verkehrsfragen und ihre Regelung in der Nachkriegszeit* (Constance 1929); Balaske, Arpad, *Le droit international de l'accès aux marchés mondiaux* (Paris 1927); Hostie, Jean, "Examen de quelques règles du droit international dans le domaine des communications et du transit" in Académie de Droit International, *Recueil des cours*, vol. xl (1932) 403–524; Chavan, Pierre, *Les communications internationales par voies ferrées et le problème de la souveraineté de l'état* (Lausanne 1927); Slavko, Raikovitch, *Le régime international des voies ferrées et la Société des Nations* (Paris 1925); Ogilvie, P. M., *International Waterways* (New York 1920); Smith, H. A., *The Economic Uses of International Rivers*, London School of Economics and Political Science, Studies in Economics and Political Science, no. 108 (London 1931); Hill, C. E., *The Danish Sound Dues and the Command of the Baltic* (Durham, N. C. 1926); Colegrove, K. W., *International Control of Aviation* (Boston 1930); League of Nations, Conference on Freedom of Communications and Transit, Barcelona, 1921, *Verbatim Reports and Texts Relating to the Convention on Freedom of Transit* (Geneva 1921), and *Records and Texts* for Second, Third and Fourth Conferences, 5 vols. (Geneva 1924), 4 vols. (Geneva 1927), and 2 vols. (Geneva 1931).

TRANSPORTATION. The transportation system is the sum of all technical instruments and organizations designed to enable persons, commodities and news to master space. Its form at any given time responds to the complex of human needs, economic, social, cultural, ecclesiastical and political; conversely, it has a vital influence on all human relations. Regardless of the sphere of human activity from which they derive, transport requirements lead to the development of new means of transportation and these in turn stimulate new demands for transportation.

This interrelationship invests the question of the capacity and efficiency of the transportation system and of its component parts with a social significance unequaled in any other technical field. At the same time it complicates the technical aspect. Standards must vary with the diversity of needs, and different values must be ascribed at different times to the technical and operating elements in particular means of transportation as well as in the entire system. Speed and safety, capacity and cheapness, regularity and dependability, territorial diffusion and special services for different commodities are in general the factors which have regulated the organization of the means of transportation throughout its development. In a particular instance one transport requirement is generally stressed at the expense of another. The efficiency of a means of transportation should therefore be measured not by absolute technical or economic ideals but by concrete conditions and objectives. The most perfect technique can miscarry in the absence of a proper economic basis for its utilization, while emphasis on economic ends may be misdirected in cases where some other general social need demands satisfaction. Routes, means of locomotion and vehicles, however, must always be considered as an operating whole in any attempt to evaluate various means of transportation.

PRIMITIVE TRANSPORTATION TECHNIQUES still prevail in regions much greater in area, if not in total population and general importance, than those which possess railroads, channeled streams and other technically advanced means of transportation. Asia, Africa and Australia, large sections of Central and South America and even of eastern Europe and North America are still served by modern transportation agencies only at their borders and along navigable streams; in the main these regions are limited to the most primitive transportation techniques.

In the case of land routes topography, climate, seasonal variations and even temporary changes in the weather are decisive in determining the feasibility of transport operations. Thick woods, swamps and torrential rivers can make traffic impossible. The grassy plains, in favorable seasons the best terrain for extensive voyages and marches, are largely swamp land in spring and fall or in the rainy season. The extreme cold of the northern winter and the burning heat of the tropical dry season are less to be feared than the uncertainties at other periods of the year. Every river forces the traveler to take a roundabout route in order to reach a fordable point. Even a slight rise in the water level resulting from a storm can delay travel for days or weeks. Tea caravans which were supposed to travel from the central Yangtze region to the Irbit fair in the Urals within a year's time often did not reach their destination until a second year had passed and sometimes were forced to spend a third year on the short but hazardous lap to the Nizhni Novgorod fair.

Under very primitive natural conditions land routes do not offer a permanent beaten track but merely set the direction of movement, so that the efficiency of the means of transportation is necessarily limited. Man has often been the bearer of both burdens and news, especially when he could be disposed of as a slave at the end of the journey. Mule, camel, donkey and horse were early utilized in the steppes and mountains of Asia, whence their use spread to other continents. The wagon next appeared in the steppes; this innovation, for all its unwieldiness, was of universal importance as the first expression of a technical principle with great possibilities of development—the separation of the carrier from the motive force. At first, however, its utility was limited. A wagon can bear only a light load if the drawing power of the animal is not to be overtaxed, and long pauses at short intervals are needed to restore the strength of man and beast.

A further cause of the slowness of the carriage of freight was the transport method imposed by the conditions of the roads. Since individuals could not cope with all the dangers and uncertainties involved in travel, they began to move in caravans. This involved certain serious difficulties. Breaking camp and setting out on the journey became cumbersome procedures, and there was increased dependence on camp sites and watering places. The unit with the lowest efficiency limited the performance of the entire body. Moreover all transportation was as a rule bound up with fixed traditional periods, and there might be further delays if the procession set out only once a year. Goods or people destined for points beyond the normal destination of the caravan had to wait an indefinite period at the crossroads for the formation of a new caravan, which sometimes involved a complete change of means of transportation. It was at such intersections that many fairs developed.

Under primitive conditions water routes are not much more dependable. In mountainous streams the water level varies so markedly that a storm along the upper reaches of a river can prevent any use of the mountainous section. Dangerous whirlpools and cliffs may render passage permanently impossible. On the plains the bed of the stream changes so frequently that even where there is plenty of water, as in the Mississippi or the Congo, no accurate forecast as to navigability is possible. Even the Rhine, which was unusually free of such natural obstacles, did not offer a regularly navigable route before the nineteenth century. The Kama River, carrying most of the waters of the Urals to the Volga, is a stream of considerable magnitude; but its upper course is closed to sizable craft except during the spring when the heavy snow melts. If the snowfall has been too light, goods destined for transport on the river must often wait a full year. In such cases the crews settle on the river banks, prepared to sow and harvest a crop during the long period of waiting until the next thaw sets in.

The problem of transportation upstream was always serious before modern motive techniques were developed. Primitive man attempted to travel upstream with oars and sails and later used horses, donkeys or men to tow his craft.

But such devices were unavailing against even a moderate current. In such cases skiffs and rafts had to be disposed of as old wood at the end of the trip downstream, and the possibility of selling the members of the crew as slaves instead of having them make the return journey on foot constituted a distinct advantage. Since in such circumstances no return movement of commodities was possible, traffic downstream was necessarily very limited. Even under more favorable conditions the size of the transport vehicles had to be kept down, for otherwise the power of men and beasts would be insufficient for the current. At best transportation of persons or goods by river was always restricted.

Canals were also affected by these natural conditions, since they were designed for the most part to connect one natural waterway with another. The invention of locks proved a great advantage in that it permitted the linking up of an entire river system regardless of differences in water level. The Elbe-Oder canals during the seventeenth century were, however, navigable only by craft with burdens under forty tons; even as late as the nineteenth century the canals of England and the old Erie Canal were not capable of handling vessels with a capacity greater than this figure.

Waterways are thus not necessarily superior to land routes under primitive conditions; they are used where there are no land routes or where the slope is not too great to permit transport back and forth. Where speed and dependability are of prime importance, as, for example, in the postal service, land routes have apparently always been preferred. The post wagon in Siberia is still days faster than the mighty streams, which, while navigable by steamboat, are unreliable.

Travel on the open seas was the most uncertain and inadequate transport means in primitive times. There was no regular intercourse even between neighboring points. Until the invention of the compass in the thirteenth century seamen in European waters, especially the Mediterranean, almost invariably remained within sight of the coast and passed the night on shore with their craft. In the Aegean Sea travel was aided by the fact that as far down as Crete there is no point from which several islands or the mainland may not be seen. Beyond Sicily and Sardinia, however, there was no traffic on the Mediterranean. The sea route from Rome to Spain—the land route was generally preferred—followed the Italian and Galician coasts; and even in the eastern Mediterranean it was considered an accomplishment when Caesar took the direct route from Brindisi to Egypt via Crete. In the Baltic the Hanseatic League pushed out along the southern coast from Lübeck as far as Novgorod and developed in Visby, on the island of Gottland off the Swedish coast, a center of commerce comparable in its situation to ancient Zanzibar or modern Hongkong. As late as the fifteenth century the Portuguese very slowly felt their way along the west African coast to the southern tip of the continent. By virtue of the regularity of their winds and currents the monsoon regions, especially the western part of the Indian Ocean, probably served earliest as an intercoastal link over wide distances. From the most ancient times, long before the *periplus Maris Erythraei*, there was a sail route directly across from the west coast of India to east Africa and back. Not until the nineteenth century, however, did seamen understand how to utilize the regularity of the trade winds and the south Atlantic currents, although these had already led to the discovery of Brazil.

The dangers of travel upon the high seas resulted in a phenomenon comparable to that characterizing primitive land voyages: the caravan or convoy. At fixed times, generally once a year, the ships of the Hanseatic merchants gathered in the Baltic regions. Later, in the Indian and American trade, the Spanish fleets and those of the great transatlantic companies were likewise assembled for mass voyages. The fact that the infrequent convoy system was used indicates that this traffic had not yet become an essential component of the life of the community. The decline of the convoy and the predominance of individual voyages in the Baltic demonstrate clearly the relatively greater importance to Europe of the Baltic over the transoceanic trade as late as the eighteenth century.

The constructed road, first cut into rocks through mountain ranges by the empires of Asia and South America and later developed by the Romans as the *via calciata* even on the plain, constituted an essential advance over primitive transport conditions (*see* ROADS). Such roads largely eliminated natural obstacles to travel. They could be used in any kind of weather and their substantial bridges permitted the crossing of rivers at all times. The conquest of space became a regular, calculable operation.

The development of the constructed road increased the speed of movement of man and beast and made the wagon, now usable in many regions for the first time, the most important universal means of transport. A greater volume could now be conveyed, since the motive power required on a good highway was about one tenth of that needed on an unbeaten path. Goods also were less subject to breakage from shock, although the wagon was still springless. Finally, travelers were much more comfortable in wagons than in the saddle. Since the road itself offered no dangers, individual transport rather than the caravan became the rule, and speed was further facilitated. Despite all these advantages constructed roads were far from widespread even at the beginning of the nineteenth century. Only later in the same century was the highway a universal phenomenon; at the same time, however, it served largely as a feeder for railroads and as a purely local means of transportation.

One institution of ancient times reveals characteristics similar to those of modern transportation—the postal service (*q.v.*). Of course this too was conditioned by the general technical level of the region and period. But just as the needs of the postal service generally provided the stimulus for highway construction, so its actual functioning, through special forms of operation, was marked by the highest efficiency possible at the time.

The importance of transportation even for those long centuries prior to the introduction of steam must not be underestimated. Provinces remotely distant from one another enjoyed economic, political and cultural contacts even under conditions of primitive transportation technique.

Economic life was least affected by external contacts. If anything, these intensified the peculiarities of individual areas. "World trade," as an exchange of commodities naturally associated with particular places of production, existed at the dawn of history. Even in most ancient times there were established trade routes between distant countries (*see* COMMERCIAL ROUTES). Even before the rise of Rome the merchant was a regular traveler on all routes, for in every empire officials and garrisons on distant service imported goods from their native country. Even the great migrations did not wipe out such mercantile relations. In the Frankish empire Italian and even Syrian merchants pursued their profession regularly. The role played by the crusades in the intensification of European-Asiatic commodity exchange is as well known as that of the Hanseatic League in the north. There are still instances of remote and inaccessible regions which are linked to the rest of the world in an economic sense. Stanley, when he sought and found Livingstone and Emin Pasha in darkest Africa, traversed the pathways of Arab slave and ivory merchants. Innermost South America became an important source of rubber supply for the entire world long before there was any attempt to apply plantation methods to the accessible coastal and inland regions of India. From the heart of central Asia great quantities of wool and sausage skins have been shipped to Europe and North America.

All this world trade, however, did not create an integrated economic system which was depended upon for the necessaries of daily life or a unified price structure covering all regions. In an outstanding commercial city like Renaissance Florence the great mass of the population apparently had but the slightest contact with the world trade operations of the upper class. Under primitive commercial conditions the foreigner broke into a locally determined economic life as buyer and seller only once a year, performing a relatively small function in the domestic economy. Under primitive transport technique economic life is characterized not by territorial liberty but by territorial bondage.

This is not so, however, with political life. The beginnings of political combinations are connected with agricultural economy and raise almost no problem of transportation. But very early a number of rivers played a significant role as bearers of forces for state building and state expansion: the Nile, the Hwang Ho, the Tigris-Euphrates and the Indus. If the empires founded along their banks did not at once reach into the mountainous upper courses, they did overcome the difficulties of rapids and headlands. The Chinese, Egyptian and Persian empires, the later Mongolian Empire and the great states of Central and South America demonstrate that even deserts and mountain ranges are not insuperable barriers to the will of a state. Rome became a maritime power at a time when travel on the Mediterranean, at least in the west, was still extremely hazardous; it even advanced over the Alps and across the channel to Britain. Charlemagne reversed the process by pressing down from the north to Italy. France, by means of its postal service, laid the foundation for its alliance with Turkey and established its claim as protector of the Christian populations throughout the Near East. Central and South America were governed from Spain and Portugal for centuries when safe and regular transatlantic voyages were unknown. The great Chinese Empire is proof that the very uncertainty of steppe and desert routes, once they have come into commercial use, can stimulate political expansion. By means of so-called "highway colonization" gaps in population were filled in from the Hwang Ho region outward as far as the Tarim basin and Turkestan. Similarly, even before its hordes of peasants streamed over the Urals, Russia definitely annexed Siberia politically by establishing Cossack stations on the postal highway as far as Lake Baikal and the Mongolian frontier, in order to manage the postal service and to serve as a border guard. Thanks to their horses, the North American Indians were able to maintain great confederations with some degree of uniform culture. Primitive transportation techniques were always sufficient to build an apparatus for public communication and travel which securely established the connections between the central government and the widely scattered provinces. They also sufficed for mass migratory expeditions, which disturbed and even crushed various states (*see* MIGRATIONS).

Many advances in early transportation technique developed out of the needs of warfare. Among the forward steps attributable to military necessity were the improvement of the wagon on the basis of the Persian military chariot, the breeding of the dromedary into a fast saddle animal and the building of fixed highways to guarantee reenforcements in unopened regions.

Most effective in conquering space in primitive times were movements of culture. While it is true that these were not caused by instruments of transportation, they would have been impossible without brisk traffic and a steady exchange of ideas. Indeed it is possible that the cultural inflexibility of Byzantium and the relative immobility of the old civilizations of eastern Asia were somehow bound up with the difficulties of extensive transportation.

MODERN TRANSPORTATION TECHNIQUES. The introduction of steam and electricity, later supplemented by the internal combustion engine, effected a marked change in traffic institutions. The forces of nature lost their controlling power and were reduced almost universally to the status of elements of cost. The spanning of distances, however long, became a regular operation whose duration could be calculated in advance.

The origins of this process may be traced to the first decades of the nineteenth century, when England and the United States, followed somewhat later by countries in the western and central parts of the European continent, established railways and steamship lines. The development reached world proportions with the completion of the first transcontinental railroad in North America in the summer of 1869 and with the opening in the fall of the same year of the Suez Canal, which brought the Indian Ocean and its hinterland close to Europe. Despite these advances, however, as late as 1880 ocean sailing vessels still represented about the same transport capacity as ocean steamers. Outside of Europe and eastern North America the railroads which had been built were merely disconnected stretches of track, and a world cable network was still in an embryonic stage. Not before the turn of the twentieth century was there any real justification for the phrase world traffic.

The principal supports of the modern transportation system are the railroads and the maritime steamship lines. Railroad trains move on roadbeds and steel rails constructed exclusively for them; consequently it is possible to run the entire operation according to a fixed schedule. Ocean liners utilize natural routes, which they must share with other types of ocean traffic, but the open sea rarely restricts technical improvements or freedom of motion. Harbors and canals are largely adapted to the special requirements of liners.

The entirely novel aspect of modern transportation is the endeavor to preserve a schedule even over the longest runs. Conquest of space can now be reckoned in advance, even for tremendous distances. Anyone in the heart of Europe or North America can, within a very narrow margin of error, calculate the time it will take for a person, object or communication to reach him from the other end of the world.

The adaptation of the route to the requirements of the vehicle has increased both speed and load. This is especially true of railroads, since the locomotive is a separate unit. The relation between route and vehicle is exactly the reverse of that prevailing under primitive conditions. The route no longer determines the maximum capacity of the vehicle, for the type of route which the latter requires can always be supplied by modern technique. Thus progressively heavier locomotives and cars have been utilized to increase speed or load or both. Similarly, modern machinery for making steel plates permits the construction of giant liners which can carry on a single voyage large numbers of persons and an enormous volume of goods and mail.

The vast capacity of transportation vehicles

implies a substantial decrease in the cost of and generally in the charge for each transportation operation, despite the large expenditures necessary for the construction of roadbeds and harbors as well as for operating machinery. These means of transportation, however, possess no absolute superiority over other land and sea types. The high fixed cost structure in fact constitutes a disadvantage which makes it possible for inland waterways to compete with railroads and ocean tramps with liners.

At least in the case of railroads considerable adaptation to diverse transportation tasks is possible. As soon as traffic demands, express service is set apart from those types whose essence is cheapness; and each group is further differentiated according to the degree to which speed or low cost is stressed. The entire transportation mechanism is graded according to intensity of employment; there are main and subsidiary lines, wide and narrow gauge tracks, each built with a view to the profit to be derived from the prospective traffic. The capacity of each line is increased with the rate of use. Special cars, such as tank, refrigerator, coal and cattle cars, are built for particular types of traffic. Topographically no obstacle is insuperable; where friction is insufficient to hold a train going up a grade, cogwheels and wire ropes are used; even the view that friction lines, like canals, must always avoid grades and curves has been discarded. Railroads are laid in ever closer nets over the broadest areas, including many sections in which natural conditions restrict inland waterways to a narrow belt. The railroads lead directly from the point of origin to the destination; and even in difficult terrain, such as a mountain range or a desert, their capacity can more easily be adapted to existing traffic needs and potentialities. Only the ordinary highway is superior in this respect.

Ocean liners also are adaptable to diverse transportation tasks. Express steamers have long been differentiated according to size and speed. Some carry only passengers and mail and occasionally extremely valuable freight. Slower mail steamers also take bulky freight; while freighters, which may carry passengers at times, emphasize cheapness rather than speed and approximate the tramp steamers in their manner of travel. As in the case of freight cars, special freighters are built to handle particular cargoes exclusively. The channels in many ports have been deepened and straightened; artificial channels have been built, as at Amsterdam, Rotterdam and Manchester; and ocean canals, such as those at Suez, Panama and Kiel, have been constructed. The study of water and wind currents, the widespread scientific charting of fixed ocean lanes and the marking of dangerous coastal stretches, by increasing speed and safety, have benefited liner travel in particular. Except for the two polar seas no part of the ocean is not being constantly traversed by steamship lines. The monopolistic central position which until 1890 London occupied with reference to the entire world was shared first by the continental ports of northwest Europe and later also by New York. Since the World War there are no longer any strongly marked central points for world transportation.

The news and communications apparatus fits into the transportation structure as a sort of crossbeam. It has developed its own technique in the telephone and telegraph (*q.v.*) and the radio (*q.v.*) and its own organizational forms in news agencies (*see* PRESS), in stock exchange ticker services and in newspaper systems. Aiming primarily at speed, it endeavors also to achieve dependability. Since, however, this technique cannot convey an actual signature, it must be supplemented for certain purposes by the postal service; that is, by freight transportation.

Aside from peculiarly specialized transport agencies, such as oil pipe lines, the remaining modern means of transportation—inland waterways, ocean tramps, highways and airways—do little more than fill in gaps and perform special tasks in accordance with territorial or organizational peculiarities. This supplementary character is seen most clearly in the case of ocean tramps. These are individual steamers or sailing vessels, bound by no schedule and limited to no particular part of the sea, which offer to carry freight wherever and whenever the amount awaiting shipment is too great for the regular liners. There are many opportunities all around the world for bulk freight cargoes. Although finer goods are also carried occasionally when speed is not essential, tramp service is important and influences the price levels of liners only with respect to bulk goods. Generally tramps use the long and more dangerous routes around the Cape of Good Hope and Cape Horn in order to avoid the tolls at the Suez or Panama Canal. In the tramp service therefore sailing vessels can still compete with steamers.

Inland water service supplements railways in a fundamentally different manner. The common statement that waterways enjoy an advantage in the transport of cheap bulk freight while railroads are more suited to the transport of valuable piece goods and passengers is untrue in general. Local conditions determine which type of goods will predominate at any time on a particular means of transportation. The traffic on the Rhine, for example, is entirely different from that on the Elbe, while the traffic on each is similar to that on the railways paralleling it. Such a relationship exists also between the Mississippi and the Hudson and their corresponding railways. Railroads always seek to obtain the profits of bulk freight shipments by offering attractive rates, while waterways try to attract both piece goods shipments and passenger travel by installing express steamer service.

In this competition the railroads are favored by their unlimited capacity for diffusion. They can transport a commodity from any one point to another without reloading. Even when natural waterways are supplemented by canals, they can reach directly only a very limited territory, so that supplementary operations of another type are usually necessary. In all such cases the state of the existing technical appliances for reloading on railroads (only Germany with its state railway system provides rail connections at all inland ports) and the charges for such service are crucial factors, which tend to obviate any natural cost advantages of waterways.

Whether natural waterways, except where they are very powerful and regular, as in the case of the North American Great Lakes, actually are cheaper is a matter of dispute among marine and railroad technicians. That a disadvantage arises as soon as large expenditures must be made to regulate the flow of water or even to construct a canal is hardly open to challenge. Thus in undeveloped regions, as on the Nile and Congo, it is considered preferable to resort to railways, despite the difficulty of reloading, rather than to correct the currents. Only where the state or some other public institution undertakes to pay for the original cost of channels and equipment and for their maintenance, as in Germany, France and the United States, can such waterways compete with railways.

Inland waterways enjoy a natural field of operation in highly developed areas as supplements to railroads for traffic which requires no reloading. In new countries which cannot support a railroad network inland waterways handle traffic wherever technical improvements on waterways are unnecessary. How effective such waterways can be as pioneers of economic and cultural interrelations is perhaps most clearly illustrated by the great rivers of western Siberia. Before the building of branch railway lines they acted as feeders for the Siberian trunk line from regions thousands of miles northward and southward and so effectively that a region as remote as the Altai steppe, which produces large quantities of butter, became an integral part of world economy a whole generation ago. On the other hand, the minor function which an elaborate rail network leaves to inland waterways may be observed in the history of the Erie Canal and the Mississippi River. All the technical improvements made on these waterways in recent years have not increased their use in comparison with the growth in railroad traffic in the same period. Germany and France, which pay most attention to waterways, have not developed their rivers and canals to the same capacity in all regions, while railroads have the same gauge throughout the two countries and throughout Europe. In the transportation plans of Soviet Russia prime emphasis is placed upon the railroads, although important canals, such as the Baltic-White Sea passage (*Belomorstroy*), have been undertaken and completed.

Highways are now very much more important than inland waterways. They serve short local stretches and function as feeders for railroads and waterways. In conjunction with the automobile moreover they have recently attained a new interregional and international importance. Their great advantage lies in the fact that they are even more adaptable to any terrain than the railroads, and that the highways may be laid even more closely and penetrate into otherwise inaccessible regions. Furthermore no special expenditures are necessary for ports or terminals for passengers and freight.

Not only does this elimination of large special investments reduce the total cost as compared with railroad costs, but the expenses for the roadbed itself and for the laying of rails for street traction lines are generally not so high as in the case of railways. On the other hand, since highway traffic is composed of many different elements—pedestrians and various types of vehicles—neither the speed nor the capacity of individual vehicles can be utilized to the technical maximum. Highways and the rails laid along them are therefore not built for maximum performance. Lower investment is thus achieved largely at the cost of speed and capacity. There is lacking that reciprocal adaptation of roadway and vehicle which constitutes the essence of railroad technique.

As a result the cost of an individual transport operation is lower on railroads, despite the higher investment involved, than on street railways, whenever the former are used to full capacity, so that total costs are divided among a great number of passengers and freight loads. Even the smallest railroad, however, can operate profitably only if there is considerable traffic. The exact amount required may vary according to the nature of the terrain, but below that amount the highway has the advantage with respect to cost. The border line cannot be determined by a study of the actual arrangements; competition, especially between railroads and automotive services, is not on a technically equal basis, since railroad roadbed costs must be paid by the railroads themselves, while those of highways used by motor vehicle transport services are defrayed by public bodies supported by taxes. Furthermore railroads are burdened with materially heavier operating and liability obligations.

Special highways exclusively for automobile traffic have been built in the United States by the federal and state governments, and similar highways are now being constructed in Germany by state enterprise. Such roads will permit greater loads and increased speeds and can be built with such objectives. Should the costs of building and maintaining such highways be shouldered entirely by the users, it may perhaps be demonstrated whether, combined with the operating costs of a particular journey, they are lower or higher than those of railroad transportation. Even then, however, differences due to special obligations will have to be taken into account. The railroads will have been deprived by the new highways of part of their traffic, and so long as the total traffic is not increased, their equipment will not be used to the accustomed extent; thus the fixed charge per unit transported will be relatively greater. In any socioeconomic estimate these increased railroad costs must be added to the cost of automobile highway traffic.

Airways, the most rapid means of transportation, are now both safe and regular. Since, however, airports require great level open spaces and high visibility they must necessarily be located outside of cities. As a result there are always relatively long supplementary transportation operations, so that airplanes are preferable to trains only for long distances. A further handicap resulting from these technical airport requirements is the fact that, although airplanes can traverse mountain ranges, they cannot easily have stations in them. Even in level territory airports cannot be nearly so frequent as railroad stations. The most critical feature is the fact that little room is available on the plane for profitable load in addition to the space occupied by the motors. Thus far it has not been possible to separate a motive plane from the load carrier, although experiments with trains composed of a motive plane and several gliders have been carried out successfully. The possibility of classifying the total air traffic in terms of diverse requirements and of constructing a multiplicity of types of airplanes is also limited. Since these basic facts restrict air travel to the speedy conveyance of passengers and mail as well as of very delicate and perishable goods, the high investment costs for airports and the equally high operating expenses must be borne by a small number of profitable loads. The number is in fact too small to permit the cost of individual air transport operations to be brought down to the level of that of other means of transportation, and the factor of speed therefore remains the decisive competitive advantage of air travel.

The development of transportation agencies involving tremendous capital investments and requiring large traffic volume brought about a fundamental change in the economic organization of transportation. Before the advent of railroads and steamers the merchant as a general rule furnished and owned his own means of transport. Even on the railroads the cars were at first for a brief time provided by the shipper. With the increasingly large scale capitalization and capacity of railroads and steamship lines merchant or shipper ownership declined and independent transportation companies developed. Only a few shippers, such as the United Fruit Company, the Ford Motor Company and the Cooperative Wholesale Society, still own transport agencies on a large scale. The use of the truck has restored the old system only to a limited extent, but the development of the passenger automobile has tremendously increased the number of individuals who travel in their own conveyances. With the passing of shipper ownership those who were able to own or control transport agencies often possessed a tremendous advantage which they could use to embarrass and even to destroy their competitors. In the American combination movement, for example, the control of transportation played an important role. This was perhaps most strikingly demonstrated in the case of the Standard Oil Company, which owned pipe lines and other specialized transport facilities and obtained valuable rebates from the railroads.

The significance of the modern transportation system stands out clearly in the economic interdependence which characterizes all fully developed regions. This is best described by the expression "world market economy," which, unlike the purely geographical phrase world economy, emphasizes not the territorial expansion of commodity exchange relations but rather the transformation brought about in these relations by modern means of communication. This change is expressed primarily in the fact that in whole regions elementary human needs are no longer satisfied by local production of the necessary raw materials but by production in distant regions, and that conversely the existence of an outside market for large quantities of raw materials becomes a controlling factor in the entire productive process of exporting regions. Hence countries requiring supplies from outside must develop the export of their own products in order to pay for the imports. Nor can regions producing raw materials avoid the introduction of the means of production, among which are the means of transportation themselves. This reciprocal dependence is intensified rather than diminished in the course of development. With the increase of population and capital equipment even raw material producing countries begin to fabricate their own raw products and, in many cases, to substitute exports of semi-finished or finished products for raw materials. This tendency was especially evident in the mid-nineteenth century in the relations between England and Germany and was characteristic of the last decade of the nineteenth century in the relations between the United States and western and central Europe. In the present century it has affected other continents with increasing rapidity since the World War. Pre-war developments created an international division of labor in agriculture as well as in industry, which finally produced complete universal interdependence of all sections of the earth. The prerequisite of this transformation was large scale regular freight transportation.

In addition the regularity of commodity exchange and the rapid diffusion of all news of any economic importance have made the price structure basically international. Remoteness remains important as an element in cost and therefore continues to cause price differences. But identical forces of production and consumption affect price movements with equal force universally, and the trend of prices everywhere consequently depends on the direction and intensity of one international market process. The uniformity of price trends is not decisively modified even by the various customs tariffs, which tend to operate merely as a tax on commodity exchange. The price quotations on the internationally important raw material exchanges offer a particularly clear illustration of this general situation.

Again, large scale transportation, by lowering freight rates, has reduced price differences between localities. According to the movement of the respective commodity markets this may benefit producers in exporting regions by increasing their profit, or it may benefit consumers in importing countries by decreasing the price. Conversely, it will burden the consumers in the exporting country or the producers in the importing country. In any case for the world economy a decrease in transportation costs means a rise in productivity, even though the profits of transportation enterprises decline because freights are low and the investors in such enterprises are forced to bear part or all of the burden of the lower rates. The interests of individual countries or provinces may of course lie in the opposite direction. The new protective tariff movement, sweeping the world with increasing force since the 1870's, is due not least of all to the fact that transportation developments have repeatedly injected into the world market agricultural and industrial enterprises of newly developed countries and, through the fall in freight rates, have largely robbed distance of its natural protective character. Although the erection of barriers against world market economy has been the result chiefly of phenomena of the productive processes, freight developments have played a significant role even in the post-war period.

Regular and dependable transport relations with a constantly expanding market both for the sale of finished products and for the supply of raw materials have permitted individual plants to grow to their present gigantic size. Certainty of obtaining adequate supplies of foodstuffs from distant lands was a necessary prerequisite to the development of overwhelmingly industrialized countries, such as England. Similarly the growth of large cities even in such agricultural export countries as the United States rests upon frequent and regular shipment to the cities of enormous supplies of fresh meats, vegetables and dairy products.

The urbanization which the railroads have been instrumental in developing has its indispensable support in metropolitan transportation facilities. The size of the population which can be unified locally in one community is conditioned of course by the particular habits of life and type of dwelling and consequently varies greatly from place to place. But there always arises at a relatively early stage the necessity of providing not only territorial and administrative unity but a genuine communal life. This would be virtually impossible without mass transportation (street railways and autobuses) and communication (telephone). The separation of residential from business quarters in the modern city is inconceivable without the modern communication system. The demand for means of mass transportation is heightened as the movement cityward necessarily gives rise to a counter movement toward the country.

The new transportation developments have multiplied the cultural and social links which are characteristic of modern life. Thanks to the railroads, intracontinental migrations have become both extensive and regular. With the completion of the Trans-Siberian Railway and connecting steamer facilities Russian peasant families poured into the Altai steppes at the rate of 500,000 to 1,000,000 persons annually in the first decade of the twentieth century. Almost as many families of farmers migrated from the United States to the newly opened western portions of Canada. It has been estimated that the cityward movement observable in all industrialized nations is still more extensive.

Transatlantic emigration, numerically less important at present than overland migration, populated the middle west and the far west of North America in the course of the nineteenth century. The technical role of transportation in modern life is reflected still more vividly in a transoceanic type of migratory labor which developed toward the end of the last century. Great numbers of farm hands from southern Europe used to travel to the United States and to South America for the cultivating season, returning to their native lands after the harvest. Similarly, large groups of Chinese and Japanese regularly made the trip to the plantations and factories of the Indian archipelago and Australia and to the west coast of the United States for a stay which was only temporary, although it might extend over more than one production period. This migratory labor movement was so considerable that anti-immigration agitation was directed primarily against it. Finally, voyages across the ocean have scattered enterpreneurs from Europe and North America over the entire earth and from eastern Asia at least over southern Asia. Generally such entrepreneurs settle for long periods, sometimes effecting a profound transformation of the local social structure.

Where travel is regularized and the means of communication bring news from all parts of the world, no level of the population can escape the influence of alien cultural forces. How universal these connections have become is evidenced most clearly by fashions in dress, which throughout most of the world have eliminated local costumes from daily use and which tend to bring the latest styles into the tiniest village. At the same time international standardization has wiped out almost the last remnant of individuality. The same influences find expression in the world wide diffusion of national literatures and arts, with the inevitable result that production is aimed at an international public and therefore tends to be superficial.

Cultural internationalism, on the other hand, has in no way diminished the importance of national peculiarities. Expectations of the abolition of international conflict, voiced at the dawn of the age of railroads and steamships, whether in poetic enthusiasm or in sober discussion, have proved entirely erroneous. The nineteenth century is recognized as an era of heightened nationalism throughout the world. This is true not least of all of the United States, where state and populace have sought to create a new unified nation, and where the means of transportation themselves serve to stamp a mighty empire with its own unique character. Each nation has clung to its basic mores, its general laws, the typical features of its own philosophy; and each has become more self-conscious than before as men and their views have come into direct contact with one another.

In political relations these paradoxical trends have been brought out with striking clarity. On the one hand, the development of transportation has made increasingly necessary the protection of all traffic against arbitrary interference and the achievement of uniformity across all border lines by international agreements—the international telegraphic union, the postal union, the establishment of fixed ocean routes, the international agreements with regard to railroad and inland waterway traffic as well as airways, the innumerable special bilateral treaties regulating such matters as railroad connections and automobile traffic. On the other hand, cultural differences among nations have so intensified the consciousness of national antagonisms that even small nations demand independence despite the resulting economic hardships. Considerations of national defense and of potential foreign attack, which have been important factors in the development of transport facilities within individual countries, have tended to some extent to restrict transit facilities between countries. Such considerations, for example, have been important in the rejection of the project for a tunnel under the English Channel to connect England and France.

The effects of transportation on domestic political life are easier to understand. There is scarcely a state which has not influenced the building of its modern transportation apparatus by legislative and economic means. Even the government of the United States, which until recently maintained a policy of non-interference in business affairs, not only put the postal system under federal control but assisted private railroad companies by enormous land grants and gave considerable cash subsidies to merchant marine companies. In its colonies and even in Ireland, England used its resources to build railroads and cable connections, and later it employed them in the mother country itself to develop the merchant marine. Throughout the British Empire the central authority has long controlled postal and telegraphic communications. Air travel enjoys state subvention everywhere, as do steamship lines in many countries. The system of state railroad operation, which existed even before the World War, has become general since the war. Where railroads are in private hands, the state not only supervises the management of the plant and its operation in the interests of security but it also controls rate schedules and tariffs. The public administration is entrusted further with the construction of artificial and the maintenance of natural inland waterways as well as with the upkeep of the highways. By reason of its profound importance in all aspects of social life the modern transportation system is universally a field of public trust and regulation rather than a purely private economic matter.

KURT WIEDENFELD

See: COMMERCE; COMMERCIAL ROUTES; INTERNATIONAL TRADE; ROADS; MOTOR VEHICLE TRANSPORTATION; RAILROADS; WATERWAYS, INLAND; INTERNATIONAL WATERWAYS; SHIPPING; PORTS AND HARBORS; TERMINALS; AVIATION; EXPRESS COMPANIES; POSTAL SERVICE; COMMUNICATION; TELEPHONE AND TELEGRAPH; RADIO; PRESS; LOCATION OF INDUSTRY; TOURIST TRAFFIC; COMMON CARRIER; RATE REGULATION; GOVERNMENT OWNERSHIP; EMPIRE.

Consult: Wiedenfeld, Kurt, *Transportwesen*, Grundriss der Sozialökonomik, sect. 5, pt. iii (Tübingen 1930); Borght, R. van den, *Das Verkehrswesen*, Hand- und Lehrbuch der Staatswissenschaften, no. 1 (3rd ed. Leipsic 1925); Pirath, Carl, *Die Grundlagen der Verkehrswirtschaft* (Berlin 1934); Blum, Otto, *Der Weltverkehr und seine Technik im 20. Jahrhundert*, 2 vols. (Stuttgart 1921); Kirkaldy, Adam W., and Evans, Alfred D., *The History and Economics of Transport* (3rd ed. London 1924); Daggett, Stuart, *Principles of Inland Transportation* (New York 1928); Brun, René, *Précis de transports commerciaux*, 2 vols. (Paris 1931); Foville, A. de, *La transformation des moyens de transport et ses conséquences économiques et sociales* (Paris 1880); Colson, Clement, *Transports et tarifs* (3rd ed. Paris 1907), especially ch. iv, abridged translation ed. by Charles Travis (London 1914); Willey, M. M., and Rice, S. A., *Communication Agencies and Social Life*, Recent Social Trends Monographs (New York 1933); Hassert, K., *Allgemeine Verkehrsgeographie*, 2 vols. (2nd ed. Berlin 1931); Fürst, Arthur, *Das Weltreich der Technik*, 4 vols. (Berlin 1923–27; vol. i 2nd ed. 1929); Witte, Bernhard, *Eisenbahn und Staat*, Weltwirtschaftliches Archiv, Ergänzungsheft, vol. iv (Jena 1932); Hennig, Richard, *Grundzüge einer militärischen Verkehrspolitik*, Verkehrswissenschaftliche Abhandlungen, vol. iii (Berlin 1917).

TRANSPORTATION OF CRIMINALS. Punishment by exile, labor in the mines and imprisonment in fortresses, long provided for in the law of Iberian countries, gave the basis for the practise of transportation of criminals as a form of punishment by these countries in the period of their colonial expansion.

Portugal, which first sent criminals to work on fortifications or to aid in the defense of Ceuta, the north African post taken from the Moors in 1415, continued to transport them throughout its colonial history. Criminals and vagrants were often transported as settlers to the Cape Verde Islands, St. Thomas and Mozambique, and the earliest settlers of Brazil were largely deserters, mutineers and transported convicts abandoned on the coast and left to shift for themselves. As colonization to Brazil became more systematic about the middle of the sixteenth century, transportation flourished; legislation indicates that during the eighteenth century efforts were made to send to the various colonies the types of convict laborers and artisans actually needed. The transported criminals were subjected to severe military discipline the rigor of which was tempered only in a minor degree until the latter half of the nineteenth century, when attempts were made to effect fundamental changes. The code of 1852 contained provisions for transportation to India and to east and west Africa; with the abolition of the death penalty in 1867 transportation assumed larger proportions. A system of transportation combined with imprisonment was set forth in the code of 1886, and in 1892 the penalty was extended to recidivists and could be applied to vagrants. In military colonies organized in Angola some prisoners were permitted to have their wives and children with them and at the expiration of their servitude some were given land; commutation of sentence and repatriation were also provided for. The transportation of convicts to the Portuguese colonies was opposed by free colonists.

In Spain Ferdinand and Isabella decreed as early as 1497 that all who had been convicted of crimes punishable by exile and of crimes not subject to the death penalty should be transported to Hispaniola, primarily to provide labor for the mines. Transportation to oversea possessions was, however, never carried out on a large scale by Spain; some authorities in fact deny that it existed as an organized practise; criminals were instead employed in galleys and on public works at home. But transportation to military fortresses in north Africa began early in the sixteenth century and increased with the abolition of punishment in the galleys. At Ceuta, which became part of the Spanish Empire in 1580, a colony grew up in close connection with the prison fortress; a rudimentary progressive system developed in the course of time and prisoners, when not occupied with governmental work, were permitted to be employed by private individuals. The African prisons were ordered abolished in 1907 so that their inmates might be used for internal colonization purposes and Ceuta was closed in 1911.

In England transportation of criminals was devised largely as a substitute for labor in the galleys; the first law authorizing transportation, passed in 1597, was elaborated by an order of the Privy Council in 1617. As early as 1670 Virginia passed an act prohibiting the importation of convicts, and as a result of the vigorous agitation by the colonists Great Britain confirmed the act and extended it for a brief period to other colonies. In 1717, however, it authorized the transportation of convicts for seven years and, in cases where the penalty for the crime was death, for fourteen years. At the outset the movement for transportation appears to have been motivated by the desire to rid England of criminals, including political prisoners, paupers and common felons, rather than to provide the colonies with man power, one of its later functions. By 1775 England was sending about 2000 convicts annually to its colonies in America, mostly as indentured servants; conservative estimates place the total number at approximately 50,000. Maryland received a larger quota than any other colony, the number reaching about 20,000; fewer criminals were transported to New England than to the southern colonies, by reason of the fact that they sold at higher rates in the southern markets.

After the American Revolution had put an end to the transportation of criminals to America from England, a few were sent to Africa; but as they perished when exposed to the tropical diseases of that area, that destination was abandoned. In 1787 the practise began of transporting convicts, including many who were guilty merely of petty offenses and also persons who were exiled for political opinions and rebellion, to the newly discovered areas in Australasia—Australia, Tasmania and Norfolk Island. This involved a considerable change in methods of transportation. Masters of merchant vessels had been responsible for the transport and disposal of convicts as bond servants to colonial planters in communities in America, where such servants formed an unimportant minority of the population. In Australasia the majority of the colonists were convicts under direct control of the government, which founded the colony for their disposal; and contractors were engaged at a per capita fee to transport the convicts, who were often chained in pairs in dank, disease ridden ships. Upon arrival the convicts were put to work in penal colonies under military control at the heavy labor of clearing and breaking land, at mining and at burning lime. Chain gangs, gruesome floggings and other brutalities were the rule; scant clothing and a scarcity of food, which sometimes approached actual famine, occasioned much suffering; homosexuality was prevalent. When they were not employed by the government the convicts were assigned to farmers, who were usually convicts whose time had expired and who, finding it almost impossible to return to England, had become settlers; in the service of these emancipists most of the convicts were in virtual peonage. The government officials administering the colonies were often corrupt;

when Maconochie, in defiance of the traditional callous attitude toward the prisoners, attempted at Norfolk Island to introduce reforms, including a scheme of commutation for good behavior which was later adopted in other parts of the world, he was removed from office. As many as 1500 juveniles had been transported between 1842 and 1853, when an act abolishing transportation for sentences of less than fourteen years checked the practise. Approximately 160,000 convicts had been sent to Australia by 1867. At that time transportation was virtually abandoned, largely because of the insistent pressure of the non-convict population, which had increased by migration with the discovery of gold and of the possibilities of sheep raising and wheat cultivation, and because of the influence of the humanitarian movement and the construction of large prisons in England for the convict population. Transportation is still being practised within the British Empire; since 1858 life and long term convicts and at times political prisoners have been sent from India to the penal settlement on the Andaman Islands, which in 1932 had a population of over 7600 prisoners.

France in 1791 had legislated transportation for life to a penal colony on Madagascar for all convicts twice convicted of a felony, but the destruction of the French navy prevented the execution of this plan. In 1851 the project of transporting criminals was revived by Louis Napoleon, who established a penal colony in French Guiana in 1852. A scheme was finally legalized in 1854 by which criminals sentenced to forced labor for less than eight years were to remain in the colony for an equal period after their release, while those serving longer terms were to stay there for life. A few convicts were to be allowed to work for themselves and to receive grants of land in reward for good conduct. New Caledonia was selected in 1863 as the place to which criminals were to be transported, and between 1867 and 1887 it was the destination for transported white convicts. By 1908 a total of 21,841 convicts had been sent out, the number in the island at any one time never being much in excess of 7000. The system was basically the same as in the Australian colonies; the convicts were placed in camps of 15 to 30 and labored in the forests and mines and on the roads, often chained together in pairs. After some time individual convicts were assigned to farmers or permitted to establish themselves on the land. Political offenders who had been sent first to the Marquesas Islands were, after the insurrection of 1871, sent to New Caledonia; approximately 4000 were sent from France beginning in 1872. By a law passed in 1885 exiled recidivists were also transported to New Caledonia and Guiana; between 1887 and 1897 the number of these recidivists in New Caledonia never exceeded 2800. Attempts to make New Caledonia a huge convict farm failed; economic, social and moral standards on the island became utterly degraded. After 1897 no more convicts were transported to the island, but by 1919 approximately 4000 convicts still remained there. In spite of the failure of New Caledonia as a penal colony sentiment for transportation continued to be strong in France. In 1900 the International Colonial Congress under French influence decided that convicts should be sent to all colonies in which there was a shortage of labor. Convicts are still being transported to French Guiana and Devil's Island; recent investigations have revealed that indefensibly brutal practises prevail in these prison camps.

Early in the nineteenth century the king of Naples, by agreement with Portugal, sent convicts to Angola; soon after the unification of Italy agricultural penal colonies to which convicts were transported were established on islands off the Tuscan coast. The non-agricultural prison colonies on the islands near Sicily, to which the Fascist government has transported thousands of political prisoners, are characterized by the traditional gross inhumanities associated with colonies for transported convicts. Holland transported criminals to Batavia, the Moluccas and Penguin Island from the sixteenth to the eighteenth century; Denmark undertook and soon abandoned transportation to Greenland; in South America, Chile and Ecuador have had penal colonies on Pacific islands. In 1824–25 the Grand Duchy of Mecklenburg-Schwerin allowed convicts to go to Brazil as agriculturists, artisans and soldiers. In czarist Russia the transportation of criminals to Siberia was begun in the sixteenth century and to Turkestan by Alexander II; in these settlements convicts were herded in chain gangs and brutally flogged. Since the revolution the Soviet government has transported criminals on a large scale, but its prison colonies have been transformed and the new ones which it has established have followed the most advanced and humane innovations in the field of contemporary penology.

Transportation has been defended with reservations by eminent criminologists of the positivistic school, such as Garofalo and Ferri. The former stressed the value of the practise as a method of intimidating the criminal and increasing the deterrent influence of punishment; the latter upheld transportation on the grounds that it aided the elimination of the hopeless and non-reformable criminals and served as a colonizing agency for the less serious criminals; neither defended the abuses that have been connected with transportation.

HARRY E. BARNES

See: CRIME; PUNISHMENT; PENAL INSTITUTIONS; EXILE; FORCED LABOR.

Consult: Ives, G., *A History of Penal Methods* (London 1914) ch. iv; Brésillion, A., *De la transportation* (Paris 1899); Capello Franco Frazão, José, "Quel rôle peut jouer la transportation dans un système de répression?" in Internationale kriminalistische Vereinigung, *Mitteilungen*, vol. vi (1897) 446–54; Dorado y Montero, Pedro, *El derecho protector de los criminales*, 2 vols. (new ed. Madrid 1916) vol. ii, p. 269–398; Cadalso y Manzano, Fernando, *Principios de la colonización y colonias penales* (Madrid 1896), and *Colonias penales exteriores* (Madrid 1909); Salillas, Rafael, *La vida penal en España* (Madrid 1888) p. 244–66; Heindl, Robert, *Meine Reise nach den Strafkolonien* (Berlin 1913); Butler, James D., "British Convicts Shipped to American Colonies" in *American Historical Review*, vol. ii (1896) 12–33; Jernegan, M. W., *Laboring and Dependent Classes in Colonial America, 1607–1783*, University of Chicago, Social Service Monographs, no. 17 (Chicago 1931) ch. iii; Gillespie, J. E., "The Transportation of English Convicts after 1783" in *Journal of Criminal Law and Criminology*, vol. xiii (1922–23) 359–81; Roberts, Stephen H., *History of Australian Land Settlement (1788–1920)*, Melbourne University, Publications, no. 3 (Melbourne 1924); Scott, Ernest, *A Short History of Australia* (Oxford 1916); Scholes, Alexander G., *Education for Empire Settlement*, Imperial Studies, no. 6 (London 1932) ch. i; Gibb, E., *Thrilling Incidents of the Convict System in Australasia* (London 1895); White, C., *Convict Life in New South Wales and Van Diemen's Land* (Bathurst 1889); Rashleigh, Ralph, *Adventures of an Outlaw: Memoirs of Ralph Rashleigh, a Penal Exile in Australia, 1825–1844* (London 1929); Roberts, Stephen H., *History of French Colonial Policy (1870–1925)*, 2 vols. (London 1929) vol. ii, p. 516–26; Niles, B., *Condemned to Devil's Island* (New York 1928), and *Free* (New York 1930); Fani, Angelo, *La deportazione* (Perugia 1896); Nitti, F. F., *Escape* (New York 1930); Rosenfeld, Ernst, "Verschickung freiwillig auswandernder Insassen der Gefängnisse von Mecklenburg nach Brasilien in den Jahren 1824 und 1825" in *Zeitschrift für die gesamte Strafrechtswissenschaft*, vol. xxiv (1904) 412–25; Edwards, Agustin, *My Native Land* (London 1928) p. 267–74; Dizhur, S., "Russkaya ssilka, eya istoriya i ozhidaemaya reforma" (Russian transportation; its history and anticipated reform) in *Russkoe bogatstvo* (1900) no. 4, p. 45–64; Kennan, George, *Siberia and the Exile System*, 2 vols. (New York 1891); Smith, A. E., "The Transportation of Convicts to the American Colonies in the Sixteenth Century" in *American Historical Review*, vol. xxxix (1933–34) 232–49.

TRAVEL. *See* TOURIST TRAFFIC.

TREASON is essentially a violation of allegiance to the community; it is the one natural crime, punishable at all times and in all types of social organization. In early history the concept of treason was sufficiently broad to include along with betrayal to an external enemy any act which threatened the safety of the group. For instance, *perduellio*, the earliest Roman conception of treason, was, literally, the act of a base or evil enemy, of one who assumed a state of war toward his community, and the *perduellis* was either hanged or thrown from the Tarpeian rock. As Roman power developed, to *perduellio* there was added *crimen majestatis populi romani imminutae*, which encompassed acts injuring the honor or majesty of the Roman people. For a time these two crimes covered the field of offenses against the state. The vagueness of both concepts made possible under either head the punishment of many acts, including attacks upon any important state official. But the scope of *crimen majestatis* was wider than *perduellio* and in the course of time absorbed it. In the later period of Roman history the term *perduellio* remained only as an archaic survival, sometimes used to indicate more serious cases of *crimen majestatis*. When Rome became an empire, the safety, welfare and majesty of the state were personified in the emperor and *crimen majestatis* was regarded as an offense against the interests of the Roman emperor as well as those of the state. Despots like Nero, Tiberius and Caligula made injury to the emperor the all important aspect of this crime. Since the estate of the convicted offender was confiscated, fiscal considerations stimulated such prosecutions; while a harsh procedure, including the free use of torture, which developed in the later empire, made convictions almost a matter of course. Death, the usual penalty, might be inflicted in horrible forms.

In Germanic law treason was conceptually a breach of loyalty. It consisted of betraying the community to an enemy or summoning or leading the enemy to the community's lands. The punishment for this crime was outlawry. In the law of the various Germanic nations fleeing the land also came to be regarded as a form of treason, probably because perpetual hostilities existed between neighboring states and the flight of a comrade to an adjacent territory meant in effect an increase in the enemy's fighting strength. Another treasonable act was desertion from the army in war, since it resulted in aiding the enemy. In feudal law any breach of the loyalty which a vassal owed his lord was treason. The idea of the king as the personification of the state and of any act directed against him or his family as high treason first developed among the Franks and later in the other monarchies. It received great impetus with the revival of Roman law.

The Roman conception of *crimen majestatis* as found in the Digest (XLVIII: 4) and the Code of Justinian (IX: 8), with its attendant misinterpretations, dominated the continental law of treason from the time of the revival of Roman law studies down to the latter part of the eighteenth century. The absolutist rulers of France and Germany identified the interests of the state with their own personal welfare, just as did the Roman emperors. Nor did the monarchs of France and Germany overlook the advantages of *crimen majestatis* as an instrument for legally executing unwelcome enemies and for replenishing an empty treasury, for the traitor forfeited his property to the crown.

The rationalistic philosophy of the eighteenth century refused to accept the identification of the state with the sovereign and distinguished attacks upon his personal interests from attacks upon the state. This distinction appears in the codifications of the nineteenth and twentieth centuries. On the continent concepts of offenses against the state seek to maintain the existing form of government, to provide security against foreign enemies and in monarchies to protect the head of the state. The chief offenses against the internal security of the state are, first, killing the king, inflicting bodily injury upon him, restricting his physical freedom or hindering him in the performance of his functions; second, acting in like manner against the heir to the throne, the queen and other members of the royal family and, in Fascist Italy, the head of the government (*il capo del governo*); third, attempting to change the form of government or the order of succession to the throne by illegal methods; fourth, seeking to deliver the territory of a country, in whole or in part, to foreign domination or to promote secession. These offenses constitute high treason and are equivalent to the German *Hochverrat*. Others, endangering the external security of the state and known in German as *Landesverrat*, include aiding a foreign enemy by enlisting in its military forces or supplying it with arms, money or men or betraying to it state and military secrets. Some European countries attempt to avoid violations of peaceful relations with other states by provisions forbidding such hostile acts of private citizens against foreign governments, their heads and representatives as might expose the state to war or reprisals. Since the National Socialist revolution in Germany the law of treason has been considerably widened in scope and its penalties have been made much more severe.

The English law of treason developed differently from the continental, partly because it was fixed at a much earlier date. Its basis is the Statute of Treasons passed in 1350 during the reign of Edward III (25 Edw. III, c. 2), which was intended to restrain the king's courts from capriciously terming as treason any act displeasing to the monarch. High treason, according to this statute, is to "compass or imagine the death of our lord the King, or of our Lady his Queen or of their eldest son and heir"; to "levy war against our lord the King in his realm"; to adhere to the king's enemies; to counterfeit the king's seal or his money; to bring false money into the realm; to kill the chancellor, the treasurer or any of the king's justices; to violate the queen or the king's eldest daughter, unmarried, or the wife of the king's eldest son and heir. It defines as petit treason the killing of a master by his servant, of a husband by his wife and of a prelate by "a man secular or religious."

This statute contains an admixture of Roman and Germanic elements. The identification of the king with the state, so that it becomes treason to attack him, counterfeit his money or kill his high officers, shows the Roman influence. But distinctly Germanic is the distinction between high and petit treason, which comes from the notion that allegiance may be owed to others than the king and that it is always treachery to violate it. Petit treason was abolished in 1828 (9 Geo. IV, c. 31, pt. 2). The provisions regarding the violation of the royal ladies also are Germanic and feudal. Such acts were regarded as particularly atrocious breaches of the duty of loyalty to the king as overlord.

Edward's statute makes no mention of attempts to injure, maim, depose or imprison the king or of plotting to levy war against him. Nor does the statute distinguish between political uprising against a king's government within the country and furthering war against him by assistance to a foreign enemy. A good part of the subsequent history of treason in England has been concerned with filling the gaps in the fundamental law. Supplementary statutes were passed in almost every reign, but they were enacted during periods of excitement and were usually repealed when the occasion for them disappeared. The insufficiency of the Edwardian statute was evident especially in Elizabeth's reign. The danger to the queen's life from Roman Catholic plots and the belief that the orderly development of England was bound up in her safety led the nation to acquiesce in strong measures for her protection. But it was not so much legislative enactment as judicial interpretation which fashioned the Statute of Treasons into an instrument designed to safeguard the modern state.

The construction which the courts put upon two clauses in the statute was of especial importance in enlarging its application. The clause relating to compassing and imagining the death of the king does not cover attempts to depose him. Yet in the case of Lord Essex the judges stated that "in every Rebellion the law intendeth as a consequent the compassing the death and deprivation of the king as foreseeing that the rebel will never suffer that king to live or reign, who might punish or take revenge of his treason and rebellion" [2 State Trials, (1600) 1333, 1355]. Subsequent judicial interpretation, continuing through the eighteenth century, extended the meaning of the clause to include "anything whatever which under any circumstances may possibly have a tendency, however remote, to expose the king to personal danger or to the forcible deprivation of any part of the authority incidental to his office."

The other clause which underwent a curious extension was "levying war against the King." Aid to a foreign enemy was obviously covered by this and the third clause of the statute, but the judges interpreted any internal violence in opposition to the king's authority as "levying war against the King." Under this construction the leaders in any forceable resistance to the enforcement of a particular law were liable to the charge of treason. In Messenger's case [6 State Trials, (1668) 879] a mob tore down some brothels, broke open a prison and released some prisoners. This was held to be treason. In 1710 in the case of Dammarree (15 State Trials, 521) the rioters, opposing the Toleration Act, pulled down four dissenting meeting houses, crying "down with the Presbyterians." This too was held to be treason.

In 1795 a law (36 Geo. III, c. 7) was passed which expressly recognized by statute the judicial constructions put upon the Statute of Treasons (see also 57 Geo. III, c. 6). A statute of 1848 (11 & 12 Vict., c. 12), however, made it possible to treat as felonies all treasonable offenses, except compassing the death, bodily harm, imprisonment or restraint of the person of the king. But one of its provisions reads, "That nothing herein contained shall lessen the Force of or in any Manner affect anything enacted by the Statute passed in the twenty-fifth Year of King Edward the Third." It was thus made possible to regard the same act as either felony or treason. In England as on the continent treason was punishable by a particularly cruel death, but in 1870 all exceptional features of execution for treason were abolished, including attainder and forfeiture. Hanging is the present punishment, although the law still permits quartering and beheading if ordered by royal warrant.

The framers of the Constitution of the United States were aware of the fact that constructive treasons had been employed to exterminate political offenders in England. In order to prevent such abuses the framers inserted in the constitution a very restrictive definition of treason, providing that "treason against the United States shall consist only in levying war against them, or in adhering to their enemies, giving them aid and comfort" (art. III, sect. 3). Similar definitions of treason are found in state constitutions and statutes.

In the treason trial of Aaron Burr (4 Cranch 470), however, Chief Justice Marshall indicated that the term levying war in the constitution was a technical term employed by the framers in the sense which had been affixed to it by English law. This interpretation impliedly adopts the constructive extension of the phrase as worked out by the courts of England and appears in strange contradiction to the wishes of the framers of the constitution. Thus treason against the United States in war time includes any act by a citizen which furthers the hostile designs of the enemies of the United States, by either strengthening the former or weakening the power of the latter to resist [United States v. Fricke, 259 Fed. 673 (1919)]. In time of peace treason may consist not alone in any forceable attempt to overthrow the government but also in organized violent resistance to the execution of any law of the United States. This doctrine was applied in a number of cases, especially in those arising out of the

Whiskey Rebellion [2 U.S. 348 (1795); 2 U.S. 346 (1795)] and the execution of the Fugitive Slave laws (Fed. Cas. 18263; Fed. Cas. 18276). Treason may be punished by death or by imprisonment of not less than five years and a fine. Like the English law, the American requires two witnesses to the overt act of treason or a confession in open court. This requirement, however, is more strictly construed in the United States. Here two direct witnesses to the whole overt act are necessary [United States v. Robinson, 259 Fed. 685 (1919)]; in England one witness to each of two different acts is sufficient. As in England, treason does not include all offenses against the state. Federal statutes punish as ordinary felonies such acts as inciting or engaging in rebellion or insurrection against the United States, correspondence with a foreign government with intent to influence its conduct in relation to disputes with the United States, seditious conspiracies to overthrow the government, enlisting in foreign service within the territory of the United States and hostile expeditions against people at peace with the United States.

MORRIS PLOSCOWE

See: LESE MAJESTY; SEDITION; ALLEGIANCE; CONSPIRACY, POLITICAL; POLITICAL OFFENDERS; INSURRECTION; MILITARY LAW; COURT MARTIAL.

Consult: Schizas, P. M., *Offences against the State in Roman Law* (London 1926); Mommsen, Theodor, *Römisches Strafrecht*, Systematisches Handbuch der deutschen Rechtswissenschaft, ed. by H. Brunner and others, pt. iv (Leipsic 1899) p. 537–94; Greenidge, A. H. J., "The Conception of Treason in Roman Law" in *Juridical Review*, vol. vii (1895) 228–40; Brunner, Heinrich, *Deutsche Rechtsgeschichte*, 2 vols. (2nd ed. Leipsic 1906–28) vol. ii, p. 881–86; Mitteis, Heinrich, "Politische Prozesse des früheren Mittelalters in Deutschland und Frankreich" in Heidelberger Akademie der Wissenschaften, Philosophisch-historische Klasse, *Sitzungsberichte* (Heidelberg 1927) no. 3; Epstein, Max, *Der Landesverrat in historischer, dogmatischer und rechtsvergleichender Darstellung*, Strafrechtliche Abhandlungen, no. 12 (Breslau 1898); Frind, Joseph W., *Der Landesverrat im deutschen Strafrecht*, Strafrechtliche Abhandlungen, no. 298 (Breslau 1931); Liszt, Franz von, *Lehrbuch des deutschen Strafrechts* (25th ed. by E. Schmidt, Berlin 1927) p. 754–79; Calker, Fritz van, "Hochverrat und Landesverrat; Majestätsbeleidigung" in *Vergleichende Darstellung des deutschen und ausländischen Strafrechts, Besonderer Teil*, 16 vols. (Berlin 1905–09) vol. i, p. 1–255; Perrot, E., *Les cas royaux* (Paris 1910); Garraud, R., *Traité théorique et pratique du droit pénal français*, vols. i–v (Paris 1913–24) vol. iii, p. 475–608; Florian, Eugenio, "Delitti contro la sicurezza dello stato" in *Trattato di diritto penale*, 5 vols. (new ed. Milan 1911–15) vol. ii, pt. i; Urysohn, I., *Das Verbrechen des Hochverrats im russischen Strafrecht*, Strafrechtliche Abhandlungen, no. 69 (Breslau 1906); Robinson, Thomas R., "Treason in Modern Foreign Law" in *Boston University Law Review*, vol. ii (1922) 34–36, 98–113; Holdsworth, W. S., *A History of English Law*, 10 vols. (3rd ed. London 1922–32) vol. iii, p. 287–93, vol. viii, p. 307–33; Stephen, James F., *A History of the Criminal Law of England*, 3 vols. (London 1883) vol. ii, ch. xxiii; Thornley, I. D., "Treason by Words in the Fifteenth Century," and Rezneck, S., "Early History of the Parliamentary Declaration of Treason" in *English Historical Review*, vol. xxxii (1917) 556–58, and vol. xlii (1927) 497–513; Kenny, C. S., *Outlines of Criminal Law* (new ed. by G. G. Phillips, Cambridge, Eng. 1933) p. 271–95; Bishop, J. P., *Bishop on Criminal Law*, 2 vols. (9th ed. by J. M. Zane and Carl Zollmann, Chicago 1923) vol. ii, ch. xlvi; Warren, Charles, "What Is Giving Aid and Comfort to the Enemy?" in *Yale Law Journal*, vol. xxvii 1917–18) 331–47.

TREATIES. The making of written agreements between states is apparently as old as states and state systems themselves. When and where the practise first originated is uncertain. The earliest treaty of which any written record remains was an arbitration treaty for the settlement of a boundary dispute between the kings of Umma and Lagash (city-states of Mesopotamia) concluded about 3000 B.C. The earliest treaty of which the full text is preserved is a treaty of peace, alliance and extradition between Rameses II, king of Egypt, and Hattushilish III, king of the Hittites, dating from 1280 B.C. The negotiation of treaties of peace, alliance, commerce, arbitration, extradition and the like was a regular feature of international relations in all the state systems of the ancient Near East and of the Mediterranean basin. Elaborate ceremonials of treaty making were developed by the Greeks and were likewise observed by the Romans. The sanctity of treaties (*pacta sunt servanda*) and the personal safety and immunity of negotiators were among the first principles of international law to receive general recognition in the ancient world. Treaty making was resumed at an early period in the development of the mediaeval state system and has become the customary form of concluding contractual agreements between the sovereignties composing the western state system in the modern age.

During the past three centuries treaties between the western states have gradually increased in number, complexity and scope of subject matter, until at the present time the sixty odd sovereignties in the world are bound together by some 10,000 treaties, covering every imaginable type of international interest. The United States alone has signed more than 850 treaties since the establishment of its independence. Of these 89 were concluded between 1778 and 1838, 134 during the next thirty years, 190 during the following three decades and over 500 since 1900.

Many modern treaties are multilateral rather than bilateral in form. The Treaty of Westphalia of 1648, concluded at the close of the Thirty Years' War, signified the emergence of a genuine society of European states, meeting in congress through their representatives to lay down the public law of the continent. Great international congresses, representing most of the states of Europe and incorporating the military and diplomatic results of shifts in the balance of power in complex multilateral engagements, were held at Utrecht in 1713–14, at Vienna in 1815 and at Paris in 1919. The Treaty of Versailles, consisting of over 400 articles worked out by the 58 technical commissions of the Peace Conference, meeting in no less than 1646 sessions between January and June, was signed on June 28, 1919, by representatives of 27 states. General international conferences have been resorted to increasingly as treaty making agencies, not only for purposes of working out major territorial settlements after wars but also for codifying international law, facilitating administrative cooperation, limiting armaments, coping with commercial, financial and industrial relations between states and protecting a bewildering variety of social, humanitarian, aesthetic and scientific interests transcending national frontiers.

Since all treaties impose legally binding obligations upon the contracting parties and are indeed the primary source of international law whereby the rights and duties of signatories may be ascertained, a large body of legal principles has developed with regard to treaty making. The name treaty is often applied loosely to all types of international engagements other than executive agreements (*q.v.*). Treaties and conventions are legally indistinguishable. The term protocol is often applied to any type of agreement less formal than a treaty or convention. A declaration is usually a multilateral engagement setting forth certain legal principles to which the parties agree to subscribe, as, for example, the Declaration of Paris of 1856. Sponsions are agreements signed by delegates in excess of their authority and subject to subsequent approval. Cartels and armistices are agreements between belligerents. A *compromis* is an agreement for the submission of a dispute to arbitration. All of these types of engagements as well as letters, memoranda and exchanges of notes have the legal effect of treaties if they have been properly signed and ratified as binding state agreements.

If a treaty is to be legally valid, a well established and highly formalized sequence of procedure must be followed. The first step is the meeting of the negotiators named by the governments concerned and the "exchange of full powers" between them, each negotiator examining the documentary credentials of the others. The negotiators have traditionally been members of the diplomatic service of the states concerned, although governments in recent decades have increasingly entrusted important treaty negotiations to ad hoc plenipotentiaries, to special delegations, to their foreign ministers and even to their chief executives. Multilateral treaties are more frequently negotiated by special delegations in international conferences than are bilateral treaties. Ad hoc political conferences are of great antiquity. In the past half century periodical conferences for dealing with legal, economic, technical and administrative questions have become a characteristic feature of international procedure, as in the Hague peace conferences, the pan-American conferences and the numerous periodical conferences of the various international unions. The annual assemblies and the quarterly councils of the League of Nations, coupled with the numerous special conferences under League auspices, represent the most highly institutionalized development of conference procedure.

The second major step in treaty making is the actual negotiation of the agreement, usually behind closed doors, since premature publicity renders compromise difficult and endangers the success of the discussion. Such considerations prompted President Wilson at the Paris Peace Conference to abandon his original insistence on "open covenants openly arrived at" and to agree to secret negotiation with full publicity for the final results. When an agreement is arrived at by negotiators, the text of the treaty is drafted and signed. Before the nineteenth century treaty texts usually began with an invocation of the Deity and contained a preliminary pledge of perpetual peace between the parties. At present treaty texts ordinarily begin with a simple preamble setting forth the general purposes of the agreement and giving the names of the heads of the signatory states and of the negotiators. The numbered articles of the compact follow. At the end the conditions of ratification are indicated, along with the place and date of signature and the signatures and seals of the negotiators. Abstract statements of moral principles or judgments, such as the so-called treaty of Holy Alliance of September 26, 1815, are usually omitted in modern treaties, although the Allied and Associated Powers at the Paris Peace Conference saw fit to adjudge Germany and its allies morally guilty of "aggression" (art. 231, Treaty of Versailles) and to make this judgment the basis of demands for reparations.

The next necessary step is the ratification of the agreement thus signed. In modern practise treaties are not regarded as legally binding without the formal approbation of the executive agency constitutionally authorized to ratify international engagements. This agency was the king in the era of monarchical absolutism. British and Italian treaties are still made in the name of and ratified by the king; Japanese treaties in the name of and by the emperor; French, German and American treaties in the name of and by the president. The formal act of ratification is universally an act of the highest executive authority. The constitutions of the western democracies, however, ordinarily require some form of legislative approval before the chief executive can constitutionally ratify an engagement. In the United States the president makes treaties "by and with the Advice and Consent of the Senate . . . provided two-thirds of the Senators present concur" (art. II, sect. 2, par. 2, of the constitution). In France treaties relating to territory, peace, commerce, finances and personal and property rights of Frenchmen abroad (but not political alliances and military conventions) may be ratified by the president only with the approval of a majority of the senators and deputies. In Great Britain the practise of cabinets varies, but important treaties are usually submitted for approval to the House of Commons prior to ratification by the crown. In Switzerland certain treaties may be submitted to a popular referendum before ratification. These developments in democratic control have accompanied the transition from the conception of a treaty as a personal bargain between sovereigns to that of an agreement between whole political communities. In the dictatorships treaty ratification is exclusively an executive act, although the meaningless forms of legislative approval are sometimes still observed. Prior to ratification amendments or reservations may be attached by the legislature or by the executive, but they are not binding unless accepted by the other signatory. While a state is never legally bound to accept a treaty signed by its plenipotentiaries, it is often regarded as morally obliged to do so. This attitude lies behind the resentment frequently caused abroad by the practise of the United States Senate in rejecting or amending treaties submitted to it by the president.

Following ratification there takes place the exchange of ratifications—a formal ceremony in which the parties deliver to one another the ratifying acts and prepare a *procès verbal* registering this fact. The exchange of ratifications brings the treaty into force, usually as from the date of signature, unless some other date is specified. The final step is the actual execution of the agreement. In the United States this is preceded by a formal proclamation of the treaty in the name of the president. American constitutional arrangements make secret treaties impossible for the United States. All American treaties are published in pamphlet form in the United States treaty series of the Department of State as soon as they are proclaimed. Most other states likewise publish official treaty series. Before 1914, however, secret political engagements were common in Europe. Criticism of "secret diplomacy" led to the incorporation of article 18 into the League of Nations Covenant, according to which no treaties or international engagements of League members are binding until registered with the Secretariat. The League of Nations treaty series is now the most comprehensive collection of treaties in existence since the World War, containing the texts of more than 3000 treaties in over 130 volumes. Complete publicity, however, has not been assured. The post-war alliances between France, Belgium, Poland and the Little Entente were registered, but certain of the agreements between the general staffs for military cooperation remain secret. Secret diplomacy has again become fashionable in recent years, particularly in the dictatorships. The progressive abandonment of democracy has terminated legislative participation in treaty making and has promoted a return to the ancient practise of secret bilateral negotiations and secret international engagements.

Not only must the formalities indicated be complied with in order to insure the validity of a treaty, but certain other conditions must be observed. The parties must be legally competent to contract the engagement; namely, they must be independent sovereignties and the engagement must not conflict with earlier treaties still binding on the parties. The treaty must be a proper state agreement, entered into freely by authorized negotiators, without fraud, bribery or personal coercion (the coercion of state by state does not invalidate a treaty), and it must be constitutionally ratified and executed by both parties. It must be in conformity with international law and must not infringe on the rights of other states. Outside states are not bound in any way by a treaty, although they are free to express their "approbation," their "adherence" (an expression of willingness to abide by its principles) or their "accession." Only in the last case do they become parties. The Kellogg-Briand Pact was signed at the Quai d'Orsay on August 27, 1928, by representatives of 15 states. It was subsequently acceded to by almost all other states.

The enforcement of treaties depends upon the good faith of the parties, sometimes reenforced by fear of the consequences of non-fulfilment. Violations can be protested legally only by those whose rights are thereby injured; that is, by the other signatories. National self-help remains the ultimate method of protecting national interests. The community of states has not yet developed to a point where the collective enforcement of engagements is possible through international executive agencies. The collective political and economic sanctions contemplated in article 16 of the League Covenant have proved unworkable, even with regard to multilateral engagements which are world wide in scope. The Stimson doctrine of January 7, 1932, embodying international non-recognition of the fruits of treaty violation (a moral and legal sanction), has likewise been ineffective in compelling the observance of treaties in the Far East. The enforceability of political treaties continues to depend upon the ability of their beneficiaries to compel observance.

Treaties may be terminated by the expiration of a specified time limit, as is customary in commercial treaties. They may be terminated also by the complete fulfilment of their terms, by the disappearance of one of the parties (e.g. Texas in 1845, Austria-Hungary in 1918) or by a new treaty expressly superseding the earlier one. An outbreak of war terminates political treaties between the belligerents, suspends the functioning of non-political treaties until the close of hostilities and brings into operation such agreements as relate to the conduct of war. Non-observance of treaty terms by one party permits the other to protest and, if its representations are ignored, to regard the treaty as voidable by its own action.

The revision and abrogation of treaties involve controversial questions of politics as well as of law. Ordinarily a treaty containing no provision for revision or termination at the option of either party cannot lawfully be modified or abrogated by one party without the consent of the other. Under the Constitution of the United States, Congress or the president or both may constitutionally denounce a treaty without the consent of the other signatory. The justifiability of this procedure, however, from the point of view of international law is most dubious. Under the doctrine of *rebus sic stantibus* it has been contended that fundamental changes of conditions authorize one party to a treaty to terminate it by unilateral action. China has sought to make use of this doctrine to escape from the obligations of the "unequal" treaties of the last century. But the injured party almost always protests under these circumstances, and it cannot be said that the doctrine is part of international law. In its statement to the Japanese government of April 30, 1934, with regard to Japan's assertion of hegemony over China, the Department of State of the United States asserted: "Treaties can lawfully be modified or be terminated only by processes prescribed or recognized or agreed upon by the parties to them." This may be considered an accurate statement of existing international law on the subject.

It is clear, however, that insistence upon the static and unchangeable character of political treaties in a dynamic state system in which national interests and relationships of power are constantly shifting produces a state of maladjustment between international public law, as embodied in treaties, and the realities of international politics. If negotiations fail to secure the consent of the beneficiaries of the status quo to its modification, its victims have no alternative save illegal unilateral abrogation, accompanied by defiance and danger of war. Such situations exist in acute form in the Far East and in post-Versailles Europe. Article 10 of the League Covenant, by guaranteeing "as against external aggression the territorial integrity and existing political independence of all Members of the League," constituted an effort to perpetuate for all time the territorial settlements of the Paris Peace Conference. Article 19 took cognizance of the impossibility of realizing such an ambition in declaring that "the Assembly may from time to time advise the reconsideration by Members of the League of treaties which have become inapplicable." The Assembly, however, can only "advise"; it has no authority to modify treaties. In fact it has never taken effective action under article 19. The withdrawal of Japan and Germany from Geneva in 1933 was in part due to the persistent refusal of certain powers to modify existing treaties sufficiently to satisfy these "unsatiated" states. In such situations the revisionist states would seem to have no recourse save force, actual or potential, as a means of compelling treaty changes. Here is the most serious defect in what has been called the international legislative process. This defect is obviously fatal to the development of an orderly system of flexible international law and reflects the dilemma of a state system in which national attitudes and policies are motivated by the exclusive pursuit of national interests on the part of independent sovereignties rather than by any effective international "constitutional consensus."

Apart from this imperfection, which has little application to the great bulk of non-political treaties, it may be said that modern treaties have furnished the legal basis for the pacific regulation of a great variety of international interests. Wherever public sentiment on opposite sides of a frontier has been in agreement with regard to the furtherance of some common enterprise or the attainment of some common objective, the procedure of treaty making has furnished a convenient and effective instrument for the achievement of the goal. By treaty international law has been clarified and developed, international controversies have often been peaceably settled and some measure of security for all states has been guaranteed. The national societies of the western state system have been knit together through a closely integrated network of reciprocal rights and obligations into some semblance of a world community. Where general multilateral treaties have been made without the support of a genuine consciousness of common purposes on the part of the peoples of the world community, they have failed to achieve their ends, just as bilateral treaties and even national statutes must fail under similar circumstances. Where the obstacles imposed by political emotions and ambitions have been acknowledged, the procedure of treaty making has led to the results desired. If the world community in the epoch of fascist imperialism is still inchoate, if it is still menaced with conflict and disaster by recurrent ethnocentrism and chronic national megalomania, the cause lies less in the inherent limitations of the treaty making process than in the circumstance that law itself, as a technique of control, is but a means to an end and can never lead mankind closer to the good life than politics and ethics will permit.

FREDERICK L. SCHUMAN

See: INTERNATIONAL LAW; INTERNATIONAL ORGANIZATION; INTERNATIONAL RELATIONS; INTERNATIONAL LEGISLATION; DIPLOMACY; LEAGUE OF NATIONS; PERMANENT COURT OF INTERNATIONAL JUSTICE; ARBITRATION, INTERNATIONAL; AGREEMENTS, INTERNATIONAL; GUARANTIES, INTERNATIONAL; COMMERCIAL TREATIES; EXECUTIVE AGREEMENTS.

Consult: Crandall, S. B., *Treaties, Their Making and Enforcement* (2nd ed. Washington 1916); Hoijer, O., *Les traités internationaux*, 2 vols. (Paris 1928); *The Great European Treaties of the 19th Century*, ed. by A. Oakes and R. B. Mowat (Oxford 1918); Phillipson, Coleman, *Termination of War and Treaties of Peace* (London 1916); Bittner, Ludwig, *Die Lehre von den völkerrechtlichen Vertragsurkunden* (Berlin 1924); Kaufmann, Erich, *Das Wesen des Völkerrechts und die Clausula Rebus sic stantibus* (Tübingen 1911); Yü Tsung-Chi, *The Interpretation of Treaties*, Columbia University, Studies in History, Economics and Public Law, no. 294 (New York 1927); Fleming, D. F., *The Treaty Veto of the American Senate* (New York 1930); Dangerfield, R. J., *In Defense of the Senate* (Norman, Okla. 1933); Miller, D. H., *Reservations to Treaties* (Washington 1919); Hill, N. L., *The Public International Conference* (Stanford University, Cal. 1929); Dunn, F. S., *The Practice and Procedure of International Conferences*, Johns Hopkins University, Studies in Historical and Political Science, extra vols., n.s., no. 9 (Baltimore 1929); *A History of the Peace Conference of Paris*, ed. by H. W. V. Temperley, 6 vols. (London 1920–24); Hill, C. E., *Leading American Treaties* (New York 1922); *The International Conferences of American States, 1889–1928*, ed. by J. B. Scott (New York 1931); *The Hague Conventions and Declarations of 1899 and 1907*, ed. by J. B. Scott (3rd ed. New York 1918); Wright, Quincy, "The Legal Nature of Treaties," and "Conflicts between International Law and Treaties" in *American Journal of International Law*, vol. x (1916) 706–36, and vol. xi (1917) 566–79; Hyde, C. C., "The Interpretation of Treaties by the Permanent Court of International Justice," Harley, J. E., "The Obligation to Ratify Treaties," Kellogg, F. B., "Effect of Reservations and Amendments to Treaties," and Williams, J. F., "The Permanence of Treaties" in *American Journal of International Law*, vol. xxiv (1930) 1–19, vol. xiii (1919) 389–405, 767–73, and vol. xxii (1928) 89–104; Dunn, F. S., "International Legislation" in *Political Science Quarterly*, vol. xlii (1927) 571–88; Malkin, H. W., "Reservations to Multilateral Conventions" in *British Year Book of International Law*, vol. vii (1926) 141–62. For the older treatises as well as additional periodical literature, see: Hershey, A. S., *The Essentials of International Public Law and Organization* (rev. ed. New York 1927) ch. xxi; Oppenheim, L., *International Law*, 2 vols. (3rd ed. London 1920) vol. i, pt. iv. The most important treaty collection is the *Recueil Martens* (first series, 7 vols., Göttingen 1791–1801; last series, still being published, vols. i–

xxiii, Leipsic 1909–31). For post-war treaties, see: League of Nations series. For American treaties, see: Myers, Denys P., *Manual of Collections of Treaties and of Collections Relating to Treaties* (Cambridge, Mass. 1922).

TREATY PORTS. *See* Spheres of Influence.

TREITSCHKE, HEINRICH VON (1834–96), German historian and political writer. Treitschke, the son of an army officer, was born in Dresden. An accident in his youth caused him to turn from the prospects of a military career to the pursuit of history and politics, and eventually he became at once the most popular and the most frequently attacked German historian in the nineteenth century. A representative of the Prussian school of political historians, he illustrated most clearly the greatness but also the defects of this historical school. In contradistinction to Ranke and his ideal of perfect historical objectivity Treitschke pursued history with the pragmatic purpose of furthering the political ideas current in his time. All his numerous essays as well as his most important work, the history of Germany in the nineteenth century, were written with the avowed purpose of advancing the cause of German national unification under the militant and aggressive leadership of Protestant Prussia. His zeal, vivid imagination and rhetorical talents made him the admired teacher of the academic youth at Freiburg, Heidelberg and Berlin.

Treitschke was one of the first German professors of political science. His lectures on politics, based on Aristotle and influenced by Machiavelli, Dahlmann, Stahl and de Tocqueville, sought to expound a political system of historical and ethical laws in opposition to the prevailing theory of fixed natural laws and above all to show the unique importance of the state whose essence is power (*Machtpolitik*). Treitschke maintained therefore that history is made by strong individual personalities. He often spoke of liberty and liberalism, but political liberty meant for him a liberty politically limited by the state. This position is reflected in his repudiation of the classical humanism of Humboldt and in the metamorphosis of his cosmopolitan liberalism into national liberalism.

Treitschke was very active politically as a publicist and was for many years editor of the most important national liberal periodical, *Preussische Jahrbücher*. He was also an active member of the German Reichstag. His political development was characteristic of many members of the German middle classes. In his youth an enthusiastic supporter of the Revolution of 1848 and an outspoken opponent of Bismarck and his domestic policy, he finally became a devoted apologist even for the latter's internal policy. The priority of foreign policy, the idea of the powerful state (*Machtstaatsgedanke*) and the readiness to abandon political privileges for foreign successes—these were the principles that became the political basis of the German middle classes.

In internal politics Treitschke bitterly attacked Catholics, Jews and socialists. His sharp denunciation of the socialists of the chair illustrates not only his rejection of every kind of socialism but his lack of understanding of economic and social forces. This attitude, like his opposition to universal suffrage, corresponded with his aristocratic conception of liberty. His racial antisemitism in particular had a lasting effect, especially in academic circles.

In consequence of his conception of the all powerful state and his heroic ideal of education Treitschke has been attacked in the countries of western Europe as one of the spiritual inspirers of the World War. In post-war Germany too the intellectual circles took sides for or against Treitschke. But apart from all conflicting judgments as to his personality he remains outstanding as Germany's most vigorous and effective teacher.

Sigmund Neumann

Important works: *Deutsche Geschichte im 19. Jahrhundert*, 5 vols. (Leipsic 1879–94), tr. by E. and C. Paul, 7 vols. (New York 1915–19); *Historische und politische Aufsätze*, 3 vols. (Leipsic 1865–97; new ed. 1886–97); *Zehn Jahre deutscher Kämpfe* (Berlin 1874, 2nd ed. 1879); *Deutsche Kämpfe; der Socialismus und der Meuchelmord* (Berlin 1878); *Der Socialismus und seine Gönner* (Berlin 1875); *Ein Wort über unser Judentum* (Berlin 1880); *Die Gesellschaftswissenschaft* (Leipsic 1859); *Politik*, ed. by Max Cornicelius, 2 vols. (Leipsic 1897–98), tr. by B. Dugdale and Torben de Bille, 2 vols. (London 1916); *Reden im deutschen Reichstage 1871–1884*, ed. by O. Mittelstädt (Leipsic 1896).

Consult: Petersdorff, H. von, in *Allgemeine deutsche Biographie*, vol. lv (Leipsic 1910) p. 263–326; Hausrath, A., *Zur Erinnerung an Heinrich v. Treitschke* (Leipsic 1901), tr. as *Treitschke; His Doctrine of German Destiny and International Relations* (New York 1914); Davis, H.W. C., *The Political Thoughts of Heinrich von Treitschke* (New York 1915); Meinecke, F., *Die Idee der Staatsräson* (2nd ed. Munich 1925) p. 488–510; Westphal, O., "Der Staatsbegriff H. v. Treitschkes" in Meinecke, F., *Deutscher Staat und deutsche Parteien* (Munich 1922) p. 155–200; Gooch, G. P., *History and Historians in the 19th Century* (London 1913) p. 147–55.

TREVELYAN, GEORGE OTTO (1838–1928), English statesman and historian. Trevelyan was the son of Sir Charles Trevelyan, who was famous both for his reforms in India, where he served as finance minister, and for his leading part in the creation of the British Civil Service; and the nephew of the historian Macaulay. At one time it seemed as though his chief interest would be politics. Gladstone gave him office as civil lord of the admiralty three years after he had entered Parliament. A speech he made in 1868 on army reform, in which he criticized the royal princes, caused the queen to urge his dismissal. Gladstone defended him with his usual generosity in such matters, but in 1870 Trevelyan resigned on a disagreement with the government on its Education Bill. He was given office again in Gladstone's government of 1880, and after the murder of Lord Frederick Cavendish in 1882 he was sent to Ireland as chief secretary. He was rewarded for his wise and courageous administration with cabinet office in 1884, when he became chancellor of the duchy of Lancaster. Up to this time he had been one of the radical leaders, interested chiefly in army reform, in land reform and in the enfranchisement of the agricultural laborer. When Gladstone took up home rule in 1886, he followed Chamberlain and resigned office. But he was unhappy outside the Liberal party, and the Round Table Conference, at which he and Chamberlain discussed the whole problem with Harcourt, Morley and Herschell, ended in his acceptance of home rule. When Gladstone formed his last government in 1892, Trevelyan sat in his cabinet as secretary for Scotland.

If Trevelyan's political career disappointed earlier expectations, his literary triumph gave him ample compensation. His *The Life and Letters of Lord Macaulay* (2 vols., London 1876) received a resounding welcome, in which Carlyle, Morley, Leslie Stephen and Froude joined, and put him at once in the front rank of historians. Lord Acton praised his *The Early History of Charles James Fox* (London 1880) as worthy of Macaulay; no living man understood Fox's world better. When Trevelyan retired from Parliament in 1897, instead of completing his life of Fox he devoted himself to the history of the American Revolution (*The American Revolution*, 4 vols., London 1899–1907; and *George the Third and Charles Fox; the Concluding Part of the American Revolution*, 2 vols., London 1912–14). Henry James acclaimed this history as a "work of civilisation" which, he believed, would help to "build the bridge across the Atlantic."

JOHN LAWRENCE HAMMOND

Consult: Trevelyan, George Macaulay, *Sir George Otto Trevelyan; a Memoir* (London 1932); Hirst, F. W., "Recollections of Sir George Trevelyan" in *Contemporary Review*, vol. cxli (1932) 581–88; Williams, B., "Sir George Otto Trevelyan, Bart." in British Academy, *Proceedings*, vol. xvi (1930) 383–91.

TRIAL MARRIAGE. See COMPANIONATE MARRIAGE.

TRIBE. See SOCIAL ORGANIZATION.

TRIBUTE. As in most levies the payment of tribute has its source in political power. Unlike other forms of fiscal revenue, however, tribute refers only to the standing obligations of political groups which are not fully incorporated into a conquering state and which in return for the payment of an impost are permitted to retain a modicum of self-government. The exaction of tribute is not infrequently accompanied by reciprocal service on the part of the recipient state, which may, for instance, undertake to protect those who pay tribute from outside aggression.

The practise of levying tribute upon weaker tribes and peoples by groups endowed with superior political and military force is as old as organized political life. From the beginning of history martial pastoral peoples, like the west Mongols and many African Negro tribes; semi-nomadic peoples, like the Indo-Germans, Semito-Hamites and east Mongols; maritime peoples, like the Vikings; and hunting tribes, like the Indians, have exacted tribute from the more settled and less bellicose agricultural peoples of the old and new worlds. In the urban civilizations of pharaonic Egypt and older Babylonia tribute was collected not only from the areas under permanent subjection to the empire but occasionally also from tribes as far distant as east Africa, Arabia and Asia Minor which were reached by military trade expeditions dispatched by the rulers. The system was further developed in some great ancient empires of the Orient, as in the Hittite Empire of the second millennium B.C.; in the Assyrian Empire of the first millennium B.C., in whose budget tributes figured as a regular and most important source of revenue; in the Lydian Empire, particularly in its relation to the Hellenic city-states of Asia Minor; in the Median and neo-Babylonian empires as evidenced in their relations to the kingdom of Judea. The tribute system had its greatest development, however, in the Persian Empire under the Achaemenian dynasty. Darius I levied upon the twenty satrapies into which his empire was divided fixed graduated payments in money and commodities suitable for the needs of the empire. The total money collected by the Persian rulers, in addition to the very considerable payments in kind, approximated the value of $17,000,000, representing a purchasing power many times that of contemporary gold currency. The Persian Empire furthermore surpassed the earlier empires in that its tributes were levied according to a well balanced plan, which influenced the Orient and which in many of its features was incorporated into the tax systems of the Greek *polis*.

While the Homeric period testifies to the existence of tribute payments to princes and ruling tribes among the early Greeks, such levies were not very common in intercity relations of archaic Hellas. Except for the tributary obligations of the peri-oecic cities around Sparta, which were a remnant of the earlier times, the Hellenic intercity alliances of this period, like the Spartan Peloponnesian League, were voluntary war alliances and involved no payment of tribute. Similarly the Attic Delian maritime league of the fifth century B.C. was a war alliance which received into its membership on an equal basis the Aegean Hellenic city-states, hitherto tributaries to the Persian king. Only gradually did the so-called *phoros* evolve from a voluntary financial settlement of the obligation of every *polis* to provide soldiers and ships into a compulsory tribute levied systematically at Athens and, beginning with the age of Pericles, assessed by the hegemonic city itself. Carvings from the Athenian Acropolis covering several decades record the details of the changing periods of assessments of the Attic maritime league, the names of the city-states which paid tribute from time to time, the varying amounts contributed and the rise and decline of the Attic empire of the Periclean age in general. The Attic *phoros* system, which ceased to operate in the Peloponnesian War, continued in the attenuated form of a *syntaxis*, in theory a voluntary contribution, in the Hellenic leagues of the fourth and third centuries B.C. Among these were the later Spartan league, the second Attic maritime league, the empire of Syracuse and the *polis* leagues established by Philip, Alexander and the Diadochian princes for their Greek subjects. Among the non-Greeks of the Alexandrian empire as well as in numerous suzerain regions under the hegemony of the Diadochian states, and especially for a long period in the provinces of the Seleucid empire and the Parthian kingdom which succeeded the Diadochi in Irania and Mesopotamia, an improved form of the Persian tribute system continued in force.

Rome from the very outset levied upon the conquered Italic peoples the *stipendium*, a contribution to cover military expenses incurred in war or conquest. With the extension beyond Italy of the sphere of influence of the Roman Republic, the *stipendium* was collected regularly in all the new provinces, except from autonomous or privileged confederates and dependent principalities and nationalities, and acquired all the characteristics of a tribute. The Latin term *tributum*, it is true, originally referred to a head tax levied on Roman citizens in cases of special need. Only later, when the abundant flow of revenue from subject regions made it no longer necessary to collect the head tax, was the term applied unofficially to the *stipendium*. Beginning with Augustus the *stipendium* was broken up into a form of head tax (*tributum capitis*) and a land tax (*tributum soli*) levied in regular assessments on non-Roman subjects; in a modified form these evolved into the central tax of late antiquity levied on all citizens of the empire. The suzerain princes and peoples outside the provincial divisions and the settlements of subjugated barbarians (*laeti, inquilini*), who frequently were required to render military service but did not enjoy Roman civic rights, continued to pay tribute in the modern sense of the term. Islam also began by levying a head tax (*jizya*) and a land tax (*kharāj*) on conquered and subject non-Moslems. As in Rome, these developed into regular taxes levied upon the different classes of the population, including to some extent even Moslems.

The Mediterranean and near eastern empires of the early Christian epoch were not merely recipients of tribute. Although nominally presented as gifts, tributes were paid by the Roman emperors to barbarian tribes endowed with superior military force; such payments were made to the Dacians in the first century and to the Germans in the third and later still more extensively to Germans, Slavs, Arabs and Huns. A similar relation often prevailed between the Arsacid and Sassanian empires of Persia and the Romans, Byzantines and Huns; between the later Islamic states and the Turks and Mongols; between the states of India of the post-Christian epoch and the Huns, Turks and Mongols. Tributes were paid also by the Christian states of eastern Europe, the Near East and even central Europe to the Huns and in later periods to the Hungarians, Turks, Tartars, Mongols and related tribes. Throughout the Christian era down to the sixteenth and seventeenth centuries there arose in the Mongolian storm center of inner Asia, whose martial, nomadic shepherd peoples preserved their military prowess longer than any others in the old world, ever new states covering enormous areas. Loosely held together, except for the Osmanli Empire and the Indian Empire of the Great Mogul, their chief object was booty and tribute for the dominant group. These developments, so important in the history of cultural relations between eastern Asia and the rest of the old world, culminated in the Mongolian Empire, which, beginning with Genghis Khan, levied tribute from time to time on almost all Asia and on eastern Europe as far as the German border, collecting an income many times greater than that of the Persian Achaemenian Empire.

In Europe after the fall of Rome the migrating Germans, among them the rulers of the empire of the Franks and of the Norsemen, levied tribute on subjugated peoples, as had been customary among Indo-Germans from antiquity. Generally the tribute was payable in kind, as in Saxony, Thuringia and Franconia. In addition there were subject tributary settlement groups (*Lassen*, or bondsmen) analogous to the *laeti* of the Roman Empire. In the late Middle Ages the feudal system and the germinating bureaucratic state offered new forms for the incorporation of subject groups into a conquering state, and the system of tribute payments continued only with respect to heathen peoples, particularly Islamic and Slavic. Venice held sway over the older Adriatic cities by a system of tributary obligations in money and in kind as well as in military service; but later, with the expansion of its power, payment of tribute gave way to general fiscal obligations characteristic of the mercantilistic period.

In the modern colonial empires of the Spanish, Portuguese, Dutch, French, Russians and English tribute payments in precious commodities and coin played an important role in the finances of the respective mother countries. The system still survives in the less developed colonial regions, as in the African colonies of the European powers, and to some extent in India, Indo-China and the Dutch East Indies. In the earlier periods of its history China exacted tribute from the subjugated barbarian peoples on the Chinese frontier chiefly in commodities not available in eastern Asia. This Chinese system began to decline at the beginning of the revolutionary period in 1912. A similar system had been in vogue at the time of the conquest of the Japanese and Korean empires.

Tribute in its strict meaning must be regarded today, in so far as it exists at all, as a vestige of an extinct form of public economy. On the other hand, contributions, fixed with respect to both the duration of the period of obligation and the amount of the absolute total payable, have continually been exacted from conquered peoples from the stone age, the empires of the cuneiform peoples, the Egyptians and the ancient Chinese down to the treaties which closed the World War. Such contributions have occasionally, even in modern times, been referred to as tribute. Never in history, however, has such tribute possessed the long time financial importance for the state budget which is associated with tribute in the narrower sense.

FRITZ HEICHELHEIM

See: REVENUES, PUBLIC; EMPIRE; CONQUEST; INDEMNITY, MILITARY; REPARATIONS.

Consult: Thurnwald, R., *Die menschliche Gesellschaft in ihren ethno-soziologischen Grundlagen*, 3 vols. (Berlin 1931–32) vol. iii, ch. ii, sects. 2–12; Andreades, A. M., *Historia tes helleniches demosias oikonomias* (2nd ed. Athens 1928), tr. and ed. by Carroll N. Brown as *A History of Greek Public Finance*, vol. i– (Cambridge, Mass. 1933–) bk. ii; Nesselhauf, H., *Untersuchungen zur Geschichte der delisch-attischen Symmachie*, Klio, Supplement no. 30 (Leipsic 1933); Marquardt, Joachim, *Römische Staatsverwaltung*, Handbuch der römischen Alterthümer, pt. v, 3 vols. (2nd ed. Leipsic 1881–85) vol. ii, p. 282–87; Abbott, F. F., and Johnson, A. C., *Municipal Administration in the Roman Empire* (Princeton 1926) chs. v, ix; Kötzschke, R., *Allgemeine Wirtschaftsgeschichte des Mittelalters* (Jena 1924); Kulischer, J., *Russische Wirtschaftsgeschichte*, vol. i– (Jena 1925–) p. 19–22; Franke, Otto, *Geschichte des chinesischen Reiches*, vol. i– (Berlin 1930–); Schröder, R., *Lehrbuch der deutschen Rechtsgeschichte* (6th ed. Berlin 1922) p. 208, 588–89; Kretschmayr, Heinrich, *Geschichte von Venedig*, 2 vols. (Gotha 1905–20).

TRIKOUPIS, CHARILAOS (1832–96), Greek statesman. After studying in Athens and Paris, Trikoupis entered the diplomatic service. He was attached to the legation in London from 1853 and negotiated the cession of the Ionian Islands from England to Greece. In 1866 he was appointed minister of foreign affairs, a post which he occupied again in 1877. As head of the Radical party he was prime minister almost continuously from 1882 to 1895.

Trikoupis was the outstanding Greek statesman of the nineteenth century. His great merit was his recognition of the fact that Greece needed above all to be reorganized along modern lines in order to realize its national aspirations. This idea dominated both his foreign and his domestic policy. He felt that until reorganization was achieved Greece must refrain from an expansionist program which would have little chance of success and which, if defeated, might mean a serious setback. Nevertheless, he showed marked independence toward the great powers and was careful not to expose Greece to danger for the advantage of other countries. One of his chief aims was to maintain peace with Turkey.

In internal affairs the period from 1882 to 1885 especially was devoted to reorganization and industrial development. Through a series of laws he endeavored to reform political customs and to constitute a corps of permanent civil servants independent of political vicissitudes. Army and navy schools were organized and changes were made in education and in the teaching personnel. Road systems and railroads were built and foreign assistance was obtained for the development of the country. To sustain his policy Trikoupis was forced to increase taxes and raise loans. His financial system and his lack of chauvinism made him unpopular and from time to time he was forced from power. Although in the intervals when Trikoupis was out of the government many of his reforms were reversed by his opponent Deligiannis, modern Greece owes much to his leadership.

MICHEL LHÉRITIER

Consult: Bourchier, J. D., in *Fortnightly Review*, vol. lxvi (1896) 36–47; Driault, Édouard, and Lhéritier, Michel, *Histoire diplomatique de la Grèce*, 5 vols. (Paris 1925–26) vol. iv, p. 164–94; Mavrogordato, John, *Modern Greece* (London 1931) p. 66–71.

TRISTAN, FLORA CÉLESTINE THÉRÈSE HENRIETTE (1803–44), French socialist writer and feminist. Flora Tristan was born in Paris and was married at the age of eighteen to André Chazal, a painter for whom she had worked as a colorist. The marriage proved unhappy and she separated from her husband before the birth of her third child. From Peru, where she went in an effort to reclaim property belonging to her father, she gathered material for her *Pérégrinations d'une paria* (2 vols., Paris 1838), which met with considerable success but which her husband held to be slanderous of himself. His anger was expressed in an attempt upon her life, as a result of which he was condemned to forced labor. Flora Tristan took advantage of the notoriety to publish her curious novel, *Méphis* (2 vols., Paris 1838). In 1839 she made a fourth trip to England and wrote her *Promenades dans Londres* (Paris 1840).

The social views contained in these three works, particularly in the last mentioned, reflect the author's interest in the English Chartist movement and in the ideas of Robert Owen. Moved by the wretched condition of the working classes of France and England, she became convinced that only through organization could workers improve their lot. This was the basic theme of her *Union ouvrière* (Paris 1843, 3rd ed. 1844), a well documented and clearly reasoned book with which she sought to gain a hearing among the workers in Paris and in the provinces. She advocated an assessment, very small but to be paid by all the workers, with which they might finance the establishment of "Palaces of the Workers' Union" (hospitals, schools and meeting places where the interests of the masses would be centralized) and pay the salary of a defender of the working class in parliament as the unhappy Irish paid their deputy O'Connell.

In order to spread this "new gospel," Flora Tristan undertook a trip in which she followed the route of the journeymen in their tour of France; after having visited the chief cities from Paris to Lyons, Marseille and Toulouse, she contracted typhoid fever and died at Bordeaux. The workers gave her an impressive funeral.

Flora Tristan subscribed neither to Saint-Simonianism nor to Fourierism nor to communism, although her ideas bore resemblance to all three. She may be regarded as a precursor of the mutualists, of the syndicalists, of the cooperators and, finally, of the school of solidarists. She was the first to herald the International of workers, since her *Union ouvrière* antedated the propaganda of Karl Marx.

As a feminist Flora Tristan emphasized the economic and social condition of women, although she was not uninterested in the political aspect of the problem. She was a champion of women's education, of divorce and of the campaigns against prostitution and capital punishment.

J. L. PUECH

Consult: Blanc, Eléonore, *Biographie de Flora Tristan* (Lyons 1845); Puech, J. L., *La vie et l'oeuvre de Flora Tristan* (Paris 1925); Thibert, Marguerite, *Le féminisme dans le socialisme français de 1830 à 1850* (Paris 1926); Beard, Mary R., *On Understanding Women* (New York 1931) p. 509–11.

TROELSTRA, PIETER JELLES (1860–1930), Dutch socialist leader. Troelstra was one of the founders and the uncontested leader of the Social Democratic Workers' party (S.D.A.P.) of the Netherlands. He was a Frisian by origin and inclination, and the democratic tendencies and religious sentiment characteristic of his people may account for his development as a force for the unification of the various currents in the labor movement: orthodox Marxism, trade unionism, opportunistic revisionism and religious socialism. As a young barrister, struck by the misery of the rural proletariat in Friesland, he made its cause his own and proclaimed himself a socialist. This led to a break with his conservative father and to the sacrifice of a promising legal and political career. As a propagandist of the new socialist movement Troelstra suffered real poverty for several years. He rejected the more dynamic and revolutionary aspects of Marxism, merely accepting it as a scientific method of investigation. He early freed the socialist party of the anarchist influences of Domela Nieuwenhuis and in 1909 expelled from the party the left wing organized around the newspaper *Tribune*, which ten years later joined the Communist International. His political career was ended in November, 1918, when after the successful revolution in Germany he attempted to secure power but was deserted by his colleagues. Troelstra was for years leader of the parliamentary fraction and a member of the Bureau of the Second Socialist International. At the International Socialist Congress at Stuttgart in 1907 he urged the formulation of a more concrete and practical program for the realization of the socialist commonwealth; in this demand, however, Troelstra received the support of none of the other leaders except Jaurès.

D. VAN BLOM

Works: *Gedenkschriften*, 4 vols. (Amsterdam 1927–31).

TROELTSCH, ERNST (1865–1923), German historian and sociologist. Troeltsch belongs to that group of scholars who first gave to sociology the stamp of an academic science in Germany. After one year as lecturer at Göttingen University he became professor of theology at Bonn in 1892 and two years later professor in the same faculty at Heidelberg. He held this post until 1915, when he became professor of philosophy at the University of Berlin.

During his stay at Heidelberg he came into contact with Max Weber, who had a decisive influence upon Troeltsch's future work. In a certain sense his most significant sociological empirical investigation, *Die Soziallehren der christlichen Kirchen und Gruppen* (Tübingen 1912; tr. by O. Wyon, 2 vols., London 1931), may be considered a supplement to the works of Max Weber. In this treatise Troeltsch set himself the task of solving the problem of how far the origin, growth and modifications of Christianity as well as the arrest of that growth in modern times were sociologically determined. He drew his material only from the teachings of the Christian church and sects; that is, from ethico-social theories. All religious, dogmatic and theological factors he considered reflex functions of the sociological conditions under which they arose.

As historian and theologian he was a student of Treitschke, Lagarde and Ritschl; to the last named he owed his insight into the psychology and logic of the growth of Christian doctrine. As a philosopher he drew heavily on the neo-Kantian theory of knowledge and upheld the existence of an a priori in the sphere of religion. But the more he sought to do justice to the specific content of religion and the more in so doing he grew aware of the historical manifold nature and creative power of social factors, the more difficult it became for him to reach a nontemporal starting point. Accordingly he approached the conception of historical dialectics and historicism. His ambitious work *Der Historismus und seine Überwindung* (Berlin 1924; tr. into English as *Christian Thought; Its History and Application*, London 1923) belongs among the foremost contributions to the history of German philosophical ideas. In his chapters on Marxist dialectic Troeltsch analyzed in a penetrating manner the advantages and disadvantages of Marx' dialectical method. His philosophical works are characterized by minute attention to every aspect of a problem, but they never developed into a well rounded and complete system. This may be explained partly by the fact that Troeltsch was a dynamic type of thinker who sought always to reflect the spiritual and social forces operating around him.

Troeltsch was a keen observer of wartime and post-war events in Germany, as is evidenced in his *Spektator-Briefe* (ed. by H. Baron, Tübingen 1924). A convinced democrat, he was elected to the Prussian diet in 1919 and became parliamentary undersecretary to the Prussian minister of education, in which position he exercised considerable influence on the trend of the educational and church policy of the Prussian government.

KARL MANNHEIM

Works: *Gesammelte Schriften*, 4 vols. (Tübingen 1912–25); *Die Bedeutung des Protestantismus für die Entstehung der modernen Welt*, Historische Bibliothek, vol. xxiv (Munich 1911), tr. by W. Montgomery as *Protestantism and Progress* (London 1912).

Consult: Spiess, Emil, *Die Religionstheorie von Ernst Troeltsch* (Paderborn 1927); Mannheim, Karl, "Historismus" in *Archiv für Sozialwissenschaft und Sozialpolitik*, vol. lii (1924) 16–30; Salis, J. R. de, "La théorie de l'histoire selon Ernst Troeltsch" in *Revue de synthèse historique*, vol. xliii (1927) 1–13; Hintze, Otto, "Troeltsch und die Probleme des Historismus" in *Historische Zeitschrift*, vol. cxxxv (1926–27) 188–239; Christie, F. A., "Spiritual Values in the Work of Ernst Troeltsch" in *Methods in Social Science*, ed. by Stuart A. Rice (Chicago 1931) p. 415–23.

TRONCHET, FRANÇOIS-DENIS (1726–1806), French jurist. Tronchet was admitted to the Paris bar in 1745 and won great fame as a consultant. In 1789 he was elected to the Estates General, where he was known as a moderate constitutionalist. He took a prominent part in the debates on the reorganization of the judicial system and was instrumental in eliminating a plan for jury trials in civil cases. The National Assembly appointed him to the commission which examined the king after the latter's arrest at Varennes. Tronchet's sense of justice made a profound impression upon Louis XVI, who entrusted him with his defense before the Convention. In this task he was associated with Malesherbes and Sèze.

Suspected of counter-revolutionary tendencies, Tronchet had to go into hiding during the Terror but under the Directory he returned to the practise of law and was elected to the Council of Elders. In 1800 the First Consul appointed him president of the Tribunal of Cassation and shortly thereafter he was made a member, together with Maleville, Portalis and Bigot de Préameneu, of a commission charged with the preparation of a new draft for a civil code, the first three projects having failed to meet with approval. The four commissioners set themselves the task of determining the outstanding conceptions of ancient French law. In cases of divergence between the Roman law and the customary law Tronchet tried to make the latter predominate, observing that it reflected more faithfully the national traditions of France. His influence was especially marked in the sections of the code dealing with succession and community property. Once the project was prepared, Tronchet defended it before the Council of State with such ardor and intelligence that Napoleon considered his opinions the very core of the discussion. At present his statements at the sessions of the councils, as preserved in the proceedings, are held to be an authoritative source for the interpretation of the Civil Code.

E.-H. PERREAU

Consult: Royer, "Discours . . . sur la vie et les travaux de M. Tronchet, ancien président du Tribunal de Cassation" in France, *Moniteur universel, Journal officiel de l'Empire français* (1853) 1222–24; Delamalle, G. G., *Plaidoyers choisis et oeuvres diverses*, 4 vols. (Paris 1827); Sagnac, P., *La législation civile de la Révolution française* (Paris 1898) p. 390–94.

TROPICAL MEDICINE. *See* ACCLIMATIZATION; COMMUNICABLE DISEASES, CONTROL OF.

TRUCE AND PEACE OF GOD. The Truce of God should be distinguished clearly from the Peace of God. The latter institution, the earlier of the two, aimed to place under permanent shelter from the scourge of feudal wars all churches and clergy and the peaceful elements of the population in general. The Truce of God, which did not appear until about 1025, tended to limit feudal wars by prohibiting fighting on certain days. Both proceeded from the desire of the church to lessen the risks to which these wars subjected Christian society.

The first measures against war were carried out at the initiative of the church at the end of the tenth century in a series of bishops' councils in France, Burgundy and particularly Viennois. At first they were of a more general character and were valid only for the dioceses in which they were promulgated. Anathema was pronounced upon all those who committed acts of violence resulting in loss to churches, monasteries and peasants. At the beginning of the eleventh century, however, fraternities of peace were organized under the auspices of the clergy for the protection of churchmen; subsequently these were extended to embrace all those who did not belong to the military class. A pact of peace (*pactum pacis*) involving an oath upon holy relics bound the adherents in definite terms to respect the possessions and buildings of the churches and peasants throughout the diocese. Sometimes also other social groups, such as pilgrims, travelers and the like, or other types of possessions, such as mills, tools, cattle and beasts of burden, were expressly included under the Peace of God. Occasionally also the adherents to the pact undertook to support the bishop in his attempt to enforce the observance of the pact. In 1038 at a council in Bourges a peace militia was organized for this purpose. All of the faithful above the age of fifteen were obliged to join the militia of the diocese and were charged with punishing violators of the peace.

Such propaganda for peace had scarcely any success. The popes, however, did not desist from extending to all of Christendom the measures for the general protection of the non-military population. In 1095, at the Council of Clermont, Pope Urban II extended the Peace of God to the possessions of the crusaders and made it obligatory upon all the faithful. The Lateran Council of 1139 specified that the Peace of God should cover not only churches, monasteries and cemeteries but also priests, clerics, monks, pilgrims, traders and peasants, going and coming or while at work, their fields and the animals they used for work or transportation.

The idea of a truce of God (*treuga Dei*) first appeared as a diocesan measure at the Synod of Elne held in 1027. Throughout the diocese of Elne "it was prohibited for any inhabitant to attack his enemy during the period between nine o'clock Saturday to one o'clock Monday." This measure was designed to enable "each one to render what he owes to God during the Lord's Day."

The truce, although at first limited to Sunday, was gradually extended to other days of the week and there was increasing propaganda in favor of it. In 1041 the archbishop of Arles, the bishops of Avignon and Nice together with Odilo, the abbot of Cluny, addressed to all the clergy of Gaul and Italy a pressing exhortation to rally to the principle of a truce of God, extending each week from Wednesday evening to Monday morning, in commemoration of the Thursday of Ascension, the Friday hallowed by the sufferings of Christ, the Saturday sanctified by His burial and the Sunday upon which He was resurrected. All violators of this long truce were subject to excommunication. The idea was immediately taken up by the bishops' synod of Montriond in the diocese of Lausanne and the truce was extended from Advent and Christmas to the first Sunday of Epiphany and finally from the third Sunday before Lent to the first Sunday of Easter. It was adopted in the same year in Normandy, where the period was extended to include the time between the Rogation Days and the end of the eighth day of Pentecost. In 1054 in the diocese of Narbonne it covered the week of Pentecost, all festivals of the Virgin Mary, of St. John the Baptist, of St. Peter, St. Lawrence, St. Michael and St. Martin and, finally, the fast days of the ember days. Evidently the idea was to cut down the time reserved for war until fighting became virtually impossible. Pope Urban II made the measure general at the Council of Clermont in 1095 and it was finally confirmed at the Lateran Council of 1139; in all Christendom war was definitely prohibited from Advent to the eighth day of Epiphany and from the third Sunday before Lent to the eighth day of Easter, from the first of the Rogation Days to the eighth day of Pentecost and at all times from Thursday sundown to Monday sunrise. It has been calculated that the feudal lords were thus permitted only about ninety days a year for combat.

These measures, which with various modifications were also adopted in 1068 in Spain, about 1080 in Germany and in the last years of the eleventh century in Italy, did not prove very effective, since there were no means of enforcement except the sanctions of the ecclesiastical order. Even the desire of the popes to permit no exceptions could not triumph over the warlike spirit of the feudal classes. The leagues of peace soon disintegrated. With the emergence of the idea of the state and of royal authority in the twelfth century, the king's peace tended gradually to replace the peace of the church. As early as the first half of the eleventh century Robert the Pious in France and Henry II in Germany entertained the hope of imposing a peace upon the world and seriously discussed the question at an assembly held at Mouzon in 1023. In the following century king Louis VI of France used the diocesan peace militia for the defense of the country; in the course of the twelfth century the kings of France and Germany in particular attempted by every means to stop feudal wars. It was only in the thirteenth century, however, that St. Louis of France and Frederick II of Hohenstaufen were able to enforce such prohibition.

LOUIS HALPHEN

See: SANCTUARY; WAR; PEACE MOVEMENTS; CHRISTIANITY; CLUNIAC MOVEMENT.

Consult: Huberti, Ludwig, *Studien zur Rechtsgeschichte der Gottesfrieden und Landfrieden* (Ansbach 1892); Sémichon, Ernest, *La paix et la trêve de Dieu*, 2 vols. (2nd ed. Paris 1869); Manteyer, Georges de, "Les origines de la maison de Savoie en Bourgogne (910–1060). La paix en Viennois (Anse [17 juin?] 1025) et les additions a la Bible de Vienne (ms. Berne A9)" in Société Scientifique du Dauphine, *Bulletin*, 4th ser., vol. vii (Grenoble 1904) p. 87–189; Poupardin, René, *Le royaume de Bourgogne (888–1038)*, École Pratique des

Hautes Études, Bibliothèque. Sciences historiques et philologiques, no. 163 (Paris 1907).

TRUCK FARMING. *See* FRUIT AND VEGETABLE INDUSTRY.

TRUST COMPANIES. In contrast to the concept of trusteeship the trust company is distinctly an American growth whose development coincided with the growth of capital accumulation and the rise of the corporate form of business organization. It originated as a collateral feature of life and fire insurance, as in the case of the Massachusetts Hospital Life Insurance Company, chartered in 1818, and the Farmers Fire Insurance and Loan Company, organized in New York in 1822. The real rise of the trust company, however, began only well after the Civil War. In 1875 the comptroller of the currency reported the existence of only 35 trust companies, all located in New York, Philadelphia and New England, whereas in 1900 he reported over 290, widely distributed geographically. This spread indicates in part the increased trust business for individuals resulting from the cumulative growth, both in number and in size, of private fortunes. It also reflects the multiplication of trust company activities in connection with security issues, arising from the phenomenal development of the corporation.

The alliance of trust business with insurance was gradually superseded by that with general banking. The trust companies invaded in particular the field of commercial banking, although they long continued to hold time deposits in excess of their demand deposits. The state courts gradually sanctioned the extension of trust company activities. On their part the banks retaliated by incursions into the trust field. A few commercial banks organized affiliated trust companies, but most of them established trust departments. National banks were first permitted to assume limited trust powers by the Federal Reserve Act. After the constitutionality of the provision had been upheld, the amendment of September 26, 1918, increased the list of trust powers and permitted the Federal Reserve Board to grant permission for their exercise in states in which competing state institutions possessed such powers. No comprehensive data are available to show the growth and present extent of trust work carried on by both national and state charted institutions, although it is known that they are steadily supplanting the individual as trustee.

Elsewhere the trust company has made much less headway. Its development was earliest and greatest in British colonies. A Trustee and Executor Company was established in south Africa in 1832, while in Australia the 20 or so specialized trust companies (doing no banking) originated in 1878. In New Zealand a Public Trustee Office was established as early as 1872. The first Canadian trust company dates from 1882. In 1929 there were at least 62 such companies in Canada; the business of these enterprises is intermediate between that of the Australian trustee companies and that of the American trust companies. In England there has been rapid progress along several lines—trust companies dating from 1887 to 1888, followed by insurance companies, banks and the Public Trustee Office in London established in 1908. The English investment trusts include trust business among their operations. Following the example of the United States the first German trust company was organized in 1890 and was followed by the establishment of similar enterprises. The development of trust companies in Germany was interrupted by the financial disorganization caused by the inflationary movement after the World War which weakened the older, large companies and encouraged the mushroom growth of small establishments whose primary business was public accounting and auditing rather than trust work proper. Most of the big trust companies in Germany are affiliated with the larger banks. Trust companies are found also in Switzerland, Austria and Denmark and are of growing significance in the financial organization of Japan.

The modern trust company developed to fill certain gaps in an incomplete financial system. Its seemingly diverse trust, or fiduciary, activities, when subject to thorough analysis, reveal it both as an investing institution and as one which renders certain needed services. In fact its investment activities arose from the necessity of administering considerable funds in the course of trust services. These services, bound together largely by their similar legal bases, have shifted and expanded considerably in response to the needs of economic life. Their ramifications have led to the rapid growth of the trust company and to combination of trust work with the other financial activities cited.

The essential features of a trust are the separation of the use of property from its ownership and the placing upon the user by reason of this fact of certain legal responsibilities toward the owner. The trustor surrenders certain property to a trustee, the latter to administer it for the benefit of a specified beneficiary, who may be the trustor. Legal title rests with the trustee as such, equitable title with the beneficiary. The trust instrument specifies the terms under which the trust estate, or corpus, is to be administered, subject to the state law. The law seeks to emphasize the sacred and binding character of a trust; hence it does not permit the trustee to administer the trust for his own benefit, while it requires him to use reasonable care to act in accordance with the terms of the trust instrument, under liability of an action at law by the beneficiary. In addition the trust company also carries on agency relations. These are created by contract in which the agent is employed and authorized to represent and act for the principal in business dealings with third persons but in which the agent does not have title to property. Considerable differences exist between the various classifications of trust work which have been attempted. The difficulty arises to some extent from the rapid growth of agency work. Furthermore the services rendered to individuals and to corporations overlap at certain points, although the general distinction between personal and corporate trusts is reasonably clear.

The trust company may serve an individual during his lifetime and his estate after his death. The former class—living or voluntary trusts—are of more recent origin than testamentary or court trusts but have grown more rapidly in recent years, both in number and in variety. They may be established for the benefit of the donor or of others. Testamentary trusts, however, are still more important as a class. The trust company acts as executor and trustee under a will or as administrator by court appointment in the absence of a will or of an executor.

Two interesting special forms of such trusts may be mentioned. The life insurance trust, while dating in the United States from 1877, has had its real development only since 1920. It consists in general of life insurance policies the proceeds of which are paid out to the trustee, to be invested by him and the income distributed according to the testator's wishes. The community trust provides funds, usually handled by a trust company or group of trust companies, to promote charitable, educational and research activities for the benefit of the community.

In their administration of both living and testamentary trusts other than those involving mere settlement of estates investment is a central trust company service. Unless the trustee is allowed no voice in the selection of investments, the trust company must prepare a special investment program adapted to the needs of the particular trust. Some trusts restrict the trustee to what are designated by state law as legal trustee investments, but in others the trust instrument specifically grants the trustee discretion in making investments. The former class of trust is subject to the same ultraconservative canons as those governing mutual savings bank investment. In some states, as, for example, Massachusetts, common law as interpreted by the surrogate's court takes the place of the legal list of investments; the trustee possesses wide discretionary powers in the absence of instructions in the trust instrument and is responsible only for losses incurred when he fails to act in good faith and to exercise caution or sound discretion. A well known authority observes that "in the hands of a good trustee the Massachusetts rule is undoubtedly superior, since it gives him a large opportunity to use his skill and ability as a financier for the advantage of his beneficiaries, but undoubtedly the English rule, or the New York rule, is better adapted to inexperienced or ignorant trustees, as much less is left to their discretion" (Loring, A. P., *A Trustee's Handbook*, 4th ed. Boston 1928, p. 140). Much attention has been given by trust companies to investment problems in the twofold effort to maintain the principal intact and to obtain the best yield compatible with such safety. In an attempt to secure more effective administration of small trust funds trust companies have created commingled trust funds which avoid the necessity of separate investment of each fund.

For the individual the trust company has also developed numerous agency services. Expert physical care and handling of securities are widely provided, while a few trust companies also give investment advice for a fee—an activity similar to that of a living trust, except that the trust company acts purely in an advisory capacity.

The trust company performs a number of services which facilitate the functioning of corporate enterprise. It acts as trustee in the issue of corporate bonds and the indenture under which such issue is made, specifies the duties of the trustee in event of the debtor's default or any other non-compliance with the terms of the deed. As transfer agent the trust company keeps an accurate record of all changes in the ownership of stock, while as registrar it acts as a check upon the transfer agent, to assure that stock outstanding does not exceed the amount authorized and issued by the corporation. Bonds as well as stock may be registered. A trust company may also be named as depositary under reorganization agreements, voting trust agreements, escrow agreements and the like. Finally, the trust company may take general or special charge of the finances of a corporation, acting, for example, as treasurer in charge of all receipts and disbursements or as agent for payment of coupons, interest and dividends.

Except for their banking departments trust companies were at the outset subject to little control. In respect to the former, first in the 1870's and 1880's, then after 1907, the laws were strengthened, and control now is similar to that imposed on national and state banks. Since charters have been broad, trust work has remained chiefly subject to the state laws and decisions relating to trust and agency business in general; but these have on the whole proved adequate to insure faithful performance of such duties. National banks are subject to the state law in the conduct of their trust departments, with regard to deposit of securities with state officers, investment of trust funds and inspection, although the trust department is also audited by regular national or Federal Reserve examiners. Segregation of the trust funds and keeping of separate records are also required, so that trust funds cannot be mingled with those of the institution proper.

The social and economic significance of the trust company is twofold. In the first place, in its individual trust work it represents a leading investment organization, which places large sums of capital in the channels of conservative industry and trade. In so doing, although the time during which its services may be rendered is limited by law, it helps to preserve private wealth and to perpetuate large estates. While directly it serves those of means, indirectly it serves all, through the effect of its operations and through its educational activities. At the same time, as an important and expert investor it is of value in determining the course of industry and trade and in tending to stabilize investment. In the second place, through its corporate trust work it promotes the use of corporate securities. It acts as a "clearing house of equities." Its service facilitates a wider distribution of ownership of industry. Thus indirectly it assists the corporation to raise permanent capital; it manages some of the corporation's affairs as a going concern; and it safeguards the interests of both creditor and security holder in event of insolvency and reorganization. It therefore aids the investor no less than the corporation and may well be considered the handmaiden of investment banking.

W. H. STEINER

See: INVESTMENT; INVESTMENT TRUSTS; INSURANCE; BANKING, COMMERCIAL; FEDERAL RESERVE SYSTEM; STATE BANKS, UNITED STATES; TRUSTS AND TRUSTEES; AGENCY; INHERITANCE.

Consult: Smith, J. G., *The Development of Trust Companies in the United States* (New York 1927), with extensive bibliography p. 487–563; Herrick, Clay, *Trust Companies* (2nd ed. New York 1915); American Bankers Association, *Year Book*, published in New York since 1933, and *Reports* of earlier Regional Trust Conferences; Ertel, H. A., *Treuhänder und Treuhandgesellschaften in Deutschland* (Berlin 1925); Hintner, Otto, *Das Treuhandwesen in der deutschen Volkswirtschaft* (Munich 1926); Gassmann, Hans, *Die schweizerische Treuhandgesellschaft* (Zurich 1913).

TRUSTS

EARLY DEVELOPMENT. The term trust has been so variously defined that its connotations remain unprecise. In connection with industrial combinations it commonly refers only to forms of organization in manufacturing and mining industries motivated by the desire to escape the limiting force of competition. It has not generally been applied to large scale organizations or combinations in the fields of finance and the so-called natural monopolies, although the terms money trust and power trust are sometimes heard. In some uses the term is broad enough to cover the various types of monopolistic agreements and pools (cartels in European terminology) which have existed in American industry. More precisely it refers to forms of organization —"trust proper," corporate mergers, holding company groups or combines—wherein a formal concentration of control is achieved over previously competing business units on a large scale and with monopolistic intent or result. In relation to the general movement toward industrial combination the term may be said to exclude large scale organizations into which the purpose or result of control of the market does not enter. Vertical combination, however complete, would not impress upon an enterprise the stamp of a trust unless the horizontal combination at some point of contact with the market were sufficient to create the prospect of control.

All attempts to define a trust precisely are in

the nature of the case bound to fail, however, since the forms and degrees of control of the market are so numerous and various. On the one hand, while the modes in which markets operate are usually described in terms of the antipodal systems of competition and monopoly, the facts seldom correspond clearly to either. On the other hand, while the fusion or federation of numerous erstwhile competitive enterprises usually affords some degree of domination in a market, the growth of a single concern may give it a commanding position in the trade overtowering not only that of independent rivals but also that of consolidations. It may perhaps be said, nevertheless, that there is some approximation toward agreement upon confining the term to industrial situations or set ups characterized by a relatively permanent form of organization, an element of combination and a substantial degree of market control.

The monopolistic tendency in American industry (on other than a local scale) had discernible beginnings in the decade following the Civil War, primarily in agreements—for limiting production, fixing prices, centralizing selling and allocating quotas—in industries which had adopted factory methods for the mass production of goods having relatively standardized specifications. Through the remainder of the century such agreements were applied to an increasing area of industry, although because of the secrecy with which most of them were administered it is impossible to say how widely ramified they were. It is known that they existed in the salt, cordage, gunpowder, distilling, cotton yarn, sugar refining, coal mining, oil refining and other industries, including the various branches of the iron and steel industry. Many were limited to restricted geographical areas, which tended, however, to expand with the development of railways.

The scope of the agreements varied, as was true of European cartels. The forms too were numerous, ranging from the simple word of tanners to damp no hides for three months to elaborate and solemnly attested documents covering rate of output, market territories, prices, penalties, supervisory agencies and similar matters in the anthracite coal industry. The more formal types have commonly been called pools, but in the midst of such variety no clear line of distinction between pools and simple agreements is discernible. The policies, whatever their character, converged on the maintenance of satisfactory market prices.

The ubiquity of such associations has suggested to all writers on industrial combinations the need for some general explanation of their existence, as distinct from the peculiar circumstances obtaining in particular industries. The most common points of reference in such explanations are the rising importance of fixed capital investment, the steady accumulation of new capital funds despite the chronic existence of unused productive capacity, the gradual disappearance of the frontier and settlement of the country with a corresponding decline in the rate of industrial expansion, the instability of prices and of general economic activity, the development of new techniques and substitute commodities. It is probable that the adequate explanation lies much more in the direction of attempted maintenance of profitable operation in the face of a highly dynamic technological and marketing situation than in that of deliberate monopolistic exploitation of consumers.

However this may be, as a device for controlling the market, whether upon a prudential or upon a predatory basis, such associations were highly unsatisfactory. Most of them were of brief duration; but although they broke down frequently, after an interval of severe competition they were usually restored in some new form. This has been variously explained on grounds of the congenital inability of American business men to cooperate for a long pull; of the inherent instability of the economic situation within which the agreements were functioning; and of the peculiarities of American law. This last point needs to be developed.

As cases involving agreements for monopolistic control of the market came before the courts of the various states, the common law principles relating to unreasonable restraint of trade were at the outset applied almost uniformly, so that the terms of the agreements became invalid as contracts and non-enforceable at law. There was moreover a possibility that the common law of conspiracy might be invoked. The failure of such agreements to attain a contractual status effectively undermined the possibility of permanency, since each party thereto was at all times legally a free agent. The incentives to act as such were, for some members of almost every association, at times too strong to be resisted. Various devices were developed to overcome this centrifugal tendency, including leasing of plants, joint ownership of marketing corporations and the achievement of communities of interest through interlocking stock ownership and interlocking directorates. The problem of unity of action was not, however, solved by such devices. Furthermore the invasion of interlopers could not legally be blocked. A legally unexceptionable form of permanent association was therefore sought, one affording as well greater powers of resistance to outside attack. This was found in the equity device of trusteeship.

The first great monopolistic trust was the Standard Oil Trust, the form of organization of which in 1882 provided the whole movement with the name of trust. Under the trust agreement stockholders in the various refining, pipe line and other associated companies assigned their stock to a board of trustees at an agreed valuation, receiving trust certificates in exchange. The trustees attained legal title and voting rights over the stock, while the stockholders secured a fractional pro rata beneficial interest in the total income realized from the properties jointly held and administered by the trustees. The various corporations and firms retained their respective identities. Nominally the trustees merely received dividends or profits and disbursed income to certificate holders. Actually they were in a position to, and did, establish a unified control over the policies and activities of all the underlying companies. Furthermore the enhanced prestige and increased financial power of this type of combination made it, not only in the oil industry but elsewhere, a far more formidable factor in disposing of threatening or actual interlopers than the loosely organized, secret pool. It is therefore not surprising that the trust pattern was copied within a few years in numerous industries, including among others distilling, white lead manufacture and sugar refining.

Public agitation over the monopolistic tendencies exhibited by these new giants in the industrial world led to a testing of the legality of the trust form of organization. In a series of cases in the state courts it was held illegal, mainly on the grounds, first, that entrance into such an association by corporations, even though carried out by private stock transactions, was a corporate act *ultra vires*, justifying forfeiture of charter; and, secondly, that the action of any enterprise joining with others to form a monopolistic combination was contrary to public policy and void at common law. By 1891 the trust agreement had virtually been outlawed as an agency of industrial concentration.

Meanwhile legislative attention was being given to a more effective program for the prevention and suppression of monopolies. Popular agitation against big business had originally centered, particularly in agricultural communities, on the railways and collateral enterprises, such as grain warehouses. Various states passed Granger laws during the 1870's fixing maximum rates, prohibiting discrimination in rates and attempting to prevent pooling operations. The federal Interstate Commerce Act of 1887, in so far as it was concerned with rate discrimination, was in effect a bulwark raised against the growth of industrial monopoly. Various states in the late 1880's passed anticombination laws of varying degrees of severity. Whether such statutes added anything to the common law protection against industrial monopolies already existing has been a moot point. In any case, since the operations of large enterprises or associations transcended the boundaries of single states, the application of state laws was hardly an adequate means of meeting the problem, even if they had been stringently enforced.

In spite of some expert economic opinion that monopolistic tendencies were inherent in modern industrialism and ought to be controlled not prohibited, popular opposition to the tendencies emerged in the Sherman Anti-Trust Act of 1890. Sections 1 and 2 of this act, which to the present day define the basic policy of the United States toward monopolistic combinations, state that "Every contract, combination, . . . or conspiracy, in restraint of trade or commerce among the several States, . . . is . . . illegal" and that "every person who shall monopolize, or attempt to monopolize, or combine or conspire with any other person or persons, to monopolize any part of the trade or commerce among the several States . . . " is guilty of a misdemeanor. Both criminal penalties and civil liabilities are provided.

Clearly the law was inspired by the predatory competitive tactics of the great trusts, and its primary purpose was the maintenance of the competitive system in industry. The evidence indicates no intention that the law apply to railroads, already subject to the act of 1887, and but slight appreciation, particularly among its supporters, of the significance of its broad terms in relation to labor organizations. Nevertheless, both railroads and labor were later made subject to it by judicial rulings. Vaguely worded, the varying subsequent influence of the Sherman Act upon American industrial organization has depended mainly upon the cumulative interpretation of its meaning by the Supreme Court of the United States. With respect to the various types of agreements for raising prices above the competitive level, entered into by independent enterprises, the Supreme Court has until recently uniformly found that they violate the act and has thus served to reenforce the state laws in driving cartel activities into secret channels or subterfuges. A few leading cases in which activities of trade unions have been curbed have led to bitter opposition to the law in labor circles, particularly in view of its failure, as will hereinafter be shown, to prevent huge corporate combinations.

With respect to the growth of proprietary consolidations in some form, or big business, which undoubtedly constituted the principal target at which the Sherman Act was aimed, the history of its application is peculiar. At the time the law was passed the great trusts were fleeing from the outlawed trust form of organization. The Standard Oil Trust dissolved into a community of interest based on interlocking stock ownership until 1899, when a holding company was formed. The sugar trust went through a holding company form into a consolidated corporation. The whisky trust went directly to the consolidated form. The new combinations, which sprang up in great number between 1897 and 1900, were almost exclusively corporate consolidations. Thereafter the holding company form came into extensive use. This whole movement was facilitated by the radical changes in the policy of certain states toward chartering corporations, exemplified by the New Jersey general corporation law of 1888 (extended by amendments in 1889 and 1893), whereunder corporations could be organized with the widest latitude in defining their own powers and especially with full sanction for the acquisition of stock in other corporations. Moreover these new style state incorporation laws gave slight ground for fear of vigilant supervision or effective control. There was then, as in 1934, no general federal incorporation act.

It was generally believed in business and legal circles that corporate combinations could not be reached by the law. The grounds for this anomalous belief were that, under constitutional guaranties, the right of the owners of industrial plants or of the stocks of manufacturing corporations to dispose of them to anyone whom they might choose could not be limited by statute. It was reasoned that the Sherman Act, resting as it did expressly upon the congressional power to regulate interstate commerce, could not be held to apply to a transaction involving simply the transfer of title to industrial properties situated within the boundaries of particular states and in every instance consummated within those boundaries. It seemed plain from this standpoint that the act could be upheld only if its application were restricted to agreements and contracts dealing with the trade in the products of these industrial plants, which products did of course customarily move to market over state boundaries.

The widely held opinion based upon this line of reasoning was fortified by the decision in the E. C. Knight case [United States v. E. C. Knight Company, 156 U.S. 1 (1895)], which validated the purchase of stock in competing corporations by the American Sugar Refining Company in spite of the fact that acquisition of the stock gave the company almost complete control of the cane sugar refining capacity of the country. Furthermore there were other grounds which seemed to lend support to the view that corporate consolidations were immune from the prohibitions of the law. The mere existence of monopoly was clearly not illegal. Patent monopolies, for instance, were not deprived of their privileges by the Sherman Act. It was only "monopolizing" which had been forbidden. And there were precedents from which it might be concluded that monopolizing consisted not in the uniting of competitors but only in practises of a nature designed to eliminate competitors against their will.

These and other not less persuasive arguments and precedents combined to afford the promoters of the great industrial combinations a sense of legal security from which they were rudely jostled by the decision dissolving the Northern Securities Company in 1904 (Northern Securities Company v. United States, 193 U.S. 197). The illusion had lasted long enough, however, in conjunction with complacency or discouragement in the attorney general's office, to permit that wave of comprehensive corporate combinations which took place around the turn of the century and gave to American industry its characteristic twentieth century concentration of control. There had been organized in many of the mass production industries amalgamated enterprises of outstanding size, not usually indeed capable by themselves of controlling the market but easily able to exert a sufficient pressure upon so-called independents to insure that their market leadership would be followed, at least for considerable periods and over considerable areas. In this way they undoubtedly modified the play of competitive forces, if indeed they did not become the nuclei of clandestine cartels. The most spectacular combination of the period was the formation in 1901 of the United States Steel Corporation, capitalized at more than $1,000,000,000, which secured control of a number of underlying trusts in the various branches of the iron and steel industry. The degree of control achieved was, however, less than that in a number of financially less imposing combinations.

It is not difficult to list reasons for the timing and extent of this movement, although the relative importance of the causes is impossible of statement. The legal situation was presumptively favorable to corporate combination and not to cartelization. The preceding business depression had given severe object lessons in the devastation of competitive warfare. The improvement in business created an investment market which could absorb securities upon an unprecedented scale. Equities accordingly not only could be disposed of widely in an open market, for the first time in America, but they had to be pressed into service to supply the seemingly inexhaustible grist required by the financial mill. At the same time railroad securities, previously a large outlet for investment funds, were no longer in favor. In the higher realms of industry and finance the profit making merits of large scale combination had gained broad acceptance and now awaited a favorable opportunity for further expression. This belief, supported by the success of a few great combinations, inspired an imitative movement of wide scope which was encouraged by promoters and financiers who stood to gain from promoters' fees and underwriting operations. About this time too the fillip to trade provided by a short and successful war furnished a spur to the introduction of new forms of enterprise. Skeptical industrialists were driven into line both by the prospect of a competitive war of extermination with a powerful combination if they declined to join the procession, and by the promise of unexampled profits if they did.

As the movement developed, however, serious weaknesses and limitations became manifest at various points. Capitalization of the combinations was commonly much in excess of the reasonably capitalized earning capacity of the underlying enterprises, and the early operating profits were often disappointing or non-existent. Where large fixed interest charges were present, this led in many cases to the necessity for corporate reorganization. Where such charges were not present, the payment of unearned dividends led, as Dewing has shown, to financial difficulties by impairing working capital. Low profits and the dwindling market for new securities, evidenced in the stock market panic of 1903, marked the necessary end of the movement. In retrospect it appears a reasonable judgment that few if any of the combinations achieved sufficient economies to make them proof against independent competition, and only a small number acquired a sufficient degree of control of the market to give more than a temporary respite from competition. Even in the absence of legal restraints it is problematical therefore to what extent the menace of uncontrolled corporate monopoly was real, except in a few specially favored industries. In any case the later history of the movement records a diminishing control over most industries by the outstanding combinations within them.

This outcome is, however, no doubt to be explained in part by the state of public opinion and of the law. The financial abuses which came to light, the coercive methods used to force independent competitors into line and the mounting fear of monopolistic exploitation on the part of the public were associated with a more general sentiment that the concentration of economic power was overthrowing the traditional structure of American social life, wherein the ideal points of reference were equality of opportunity and economic independence. It was this tide of opinion which inspired and supported President Theodore Roosevelt's "trust busting" activities, although a more accurate expression of it came ten years later in President Wilson's policies.

PAUL T. HOMAN

SINCE 1910. The dissolution of the Northern Securities Company brought an abrupt end to the prevailing sense of corporate invulnerability. The terms of the decision, giving plausibility to the theory that the union of any competitors might be deemed in restraint of trade, effectively stopped further important combinations for the time being. But if corporate amalgamations were notably less frequent and less comprehensive in the decade following the Northern Securities decision than they had been in the preceding decade, it is by no means certain that the same can be said of monopolistic tendencies. The available evidence indicates rather that the combination movement may have simply been driven underground, manifesting itself in an increasing resort to secret sub rosa agreements and the looser forms of confederation. Whether, in so far as this was the outcome, the diligent enforcement of antitrust policy yielded benefits to the public interest commensurate with the strenuous efforts put forth or indeed any net benefits is problematical. For not only is combination in these loose forms unrestrained by some of the salutary, albeit weak, economic factors which tend to curb the rapacity of big business units operating more or less in the open, but their furtive and ephemeral character undoubtedly aggravates the inherent instability of capitalistic industry.

There developed at the same time a profound change in the tactics of the trusts. The policy of exterminating rivals or keeping them down at all costs which had characterized the early years of trustification, notably in such industries as tobacco, sugar, oil, cash register, starch and glucose, photographic materials and gunpowder, was gradually abandoned, and there was a perceptible improvement in the temper and plane of business competition. There were of course significant exceptions: industries in which trusts continued to carry on a sort of guerrilla warfare against independents and interlopers, as in the shipping trade and in meat packing. But in general there was substituted for the old policy, which had brought so much opprobrium upon the trusts, one which was more far sighted, elastic and tolerant. This has frequently been described as the "live and let live policy," although the phrase doubtless suggests somewhat fuller conformity with the popular ideal and the legislative standard of a "fair field and no favors" in trade competition than was actually contemplated, to say nothing of what was realized in practise. Among the industrial leaders sponsoring this shift in strategy Elbert H. Gary of the United States Steel Corporation was conspicuous; and generally it was the men who came into power, both in industry and in finance, after the turn of the century, who showed the keenest appreciation of the advisability of a shift in the basic strategy of big business. There can be little doubt that the revival of antitrust agitation in the Progressive movement and the vigorous trust busting campaign which eventuated from it impressed pointedly upon these leaders the expediency of trimming their sails to the freshening winds from this quarter. It may be added at once, however, that this explanation of the shift in strategy is incomplete; it requires supplementary reference to the excessive costliness of business buccaneering as demonstrated by bitter experience.

It should not be overlooked that the change in strategy did not imply a change of goal. The goal of the trust movement from the beginning had been to enable business to escape the rigors of free competition. In such episodes as the Gary dinners in the steel industry and the bathtub pool in the plumbing fixtures industry it was made abundantly clear that the new policy of the trusts did not involve abandonment of efforts to control the market. If bludgeoning tactics were to be dropped or perhaps better laid on the shelf, it was only for a price. The little fellows must play the game—not their old game of forthright business rivalry, but the trust's game of business "stability," insuring the maximum profits consistent with safety.

The reform of the trusts, such as it was, under the pressure of an aroused public opinion and the dread of legal penalties, began very soon to give indications of its abundant justification. In the field of business practise it demonstrated time after time, as in the corn products and window glass industries, its superiority for profit making over the old all-or-none policy, at least under twentieth century conditions.

In respect of legal status also the new policy of tolerance and leadership very shortly yielded signs of justification. The first clear signal that not all types of industrial combination, not even all consolidations acquiring a dominant position in any market, were to be considered subject to dissolution was the obiter distinction, enunciated in the Standard Oil and American Tobacco cases in 1911 [Standard Oil Company of New Jersey v. United States, 221 U.S. 1 (1911), and United States v. American Tobacco Company, 221 U.S. 106 (1911)], between reasonable and unreasonable restraints of trade. While holding that both of these trusts, among the oldest, most powerful and most unscrupulous examples of industrial concentration, had in their formation and continuously in their operation violated the express prohibitions of the Sherman Act, the Supreme Court went out of its way nevertheless to reassure "good trusts." Those trusts which refrained from the abuses which had characterized the establishment and growth of the defendants in these cases were told in effect that they need not fear condemnation. The opinion of the court plainly disclosed to any discerning lawyer that the judicial conception of an "attempt to monopolize" comprehended primarily devices for ruining independent competitors or preventing their establishment, such as local price wars, harassing litigation, exclusion from trade channels or from transportation facilities or credit accommodations.

The expansion of the judicial conception of the legitimate limits of industrial combination, dramatically proclaimed in the enunciation of the rule of reason in the oil and tobacco cases, was only the beginning, however, of the accommodating flexure of legal policy to meet the gesture of reform in trust strategy. In the very next year the court held in the case of United States v. Terminal Railroad Association of St. Louis [224 U.S. 383 (1912)] that even a combination which had been guilty of just such acts of oppression and exclusion as had, in the judicial view, established an "intent to monopolize" in the oil and tobacco cases might be released from the penalties of the law if it could be shown that it was also capable of being used for legitimate ends. In other words, a combination which might be helpful in the advancement of the public interest was not to be disturbed simply because it had in practise shown itself on occasion susceptible of perversion to other purposes. The practical import of the introduction of the rule of reason appeared to be that, whereas in the terms of the antitrust statute and under its original construction the crucial assumption of probity and moderation in business concerts was flatly negatived, this assumption was now admissible. It remained then only for the trusts to make out a case for being "trusted" with the privilege of concerted power to win for themselves substantial immunity from the law.

How this might successfully be done was demonstrated in the United Shoe Machinery litigation. In these cases, a criminal action disposed of in 1913 (United States v. Winslow, 227 U.S. 202) and a civil suit for injunction decided in 1918 (United States v. United Shoe Machinery Company, 227 U.S. 32), the defendant was in both adjudged innocent of any infraction of the antitrust law, despite the facts: first, that it had acquired through amalgamation a predominant position in the industry; second, that some at least of the sponsors of the original merger had openly avowed a purpose to control the whole trade; third, that it had persistently followed the policy of discouraging the use by its patrons of any shoe machines not acquired from it; and, finally, that it had, on the only occasion upon which formidable competition had threatened, promptly forestalled it by the purchase of the entire assets of the would be competitor, under suspicious circumstances. To overcome the damning force of these several factors the Shoe Machinery Corporation relied principally upon the broad privileges accorded it as a patentee, the character testimony of its patrons regarding its standards in commercial dealing and evidence of technological advance and specific technical advantages under its concentrated form of organization and mode of business conduct.

This line of defense, which might be summarized as an argument to establish legal reasonableness from economic legitimacy, was upheld also in the United States Steel Corporation case in 1920 (United States v. United States Steel Corporation, 251 U.S. 417). As a justification for the new trust strategy of seeking legal safety through a more tolerant, less predatory commercial policy this case is of even more significance. For the steel trust could not rely upon the judicial leniency toward patentees. It had to win its vindication from the charge of monopolizing simply on its record as a good trust. And this was not easy. It was handicapped by the admitted purposes of its original organization and by the evidence of continuing efforts to control the market, sometimes by collusion, as in the Gary dinners, sometimes by exclusion, as in the extensive ore leases and in the Tennessee coal and iron transactions. Nevertheless, the defense again prevailed. The increased stability of the industry following the formation of the trust was stressed. Much was made also of the disorganization and losses which would attend a dissolution of the combination. The upshot of these cases was to establish beyond speculation that corporate consolidations of dominant size were not to be outlawed in the future development of American industry. Business men were not slow to appreciate the full import of this modification of legal policy. The merger movement of the 1920's was in effect simply a capitalization of the opportunities made available by the judicial legislation of 1911 as amplified and clarified by the outstanding decisions of the ensuing decade.

Meanwhile new legislation and the experience of the World War had intervened to play a part in the molding of public opinion, making the traditional antitrust attitude less intransigent and allaying the popular clamor. The Wilson administration had been committed to a policy of vigorous efforts to restore genuinely free competition in trade and industry. It represented a determined, if not the final, resurgence of the handicraft and frontier tradition of individual economic independence, a desperate demand of the small entrepreneurs for preservation and a share in the profits of business prosperity. This was the meaning of the New Freedom. The Clayton Act and the Federal Trade Commission Act of 1914 were the legislative expression of this policy. The former was truly an omnibus measure, carrying sections relating to the railroads, banks and labor; but four sections were applicable to the organization and conduct of business. These condemned, with much verbiage and confusing qualifications, certain practises, among them local price discriminations, tying contracts and interlocking directorates, by which the trusts were supposed to have consolidated their power. Perhaps the most important of these sections, at least until it was emasculated [Western Meat Company v. Federal Trade Commission, 272 U.S. 554 (1926); and International Shoe Company v. Federal Trade Commission, 280 U.S. 291 (1930)] by judicial construction of its ill drafted terms, was the one prohibiting the acquisition by one corporation of stock interest in another in the same line of trade.

Far more important for the subsequent course of industrial development was the act establishing the Federal Trade Commission. By section 5 of this act "unfair methods of competition" were forbidden, and the commission was constituted an administrative agency for the enforcement of this prohibition. In addition it superseded the Bureau of Corporations as an investigatory body. While the energy and resourcefulness displayed in the discharge of these functions have varied from period to period, the work of the commission over two decades has not succeeded in reinvigorating antitrust policy. It has not retarded the growth of giant mergers. It has not prevented the insidious spread of the network of financial interconnection and trade cooperation whereby the essential policies of whole fields of industry are manipulated by powerful interests, often operating behind the scenes with a minimum of direct proprietary responsibility. In a word, it has not restored free competition in the markets.

There is no single explanation of this miscarriage of the New Freedom. It has connections, perhaps somewhat remote, with the indefeasible tendency toward coordination, integration (in the non-technical sense) and systematization under the compelling sway of the machine technique. So long as mechanization of industrial processes marches forward, artlessly accepted as the embodiment of progress, so long will the scope of competition as a mode of regulating and giving direction to these processes continue to be more and more narrowly circumscribed. Not only are the habits of thought engendered by the machine technique incompatible with the spontaneous higgling and hit or miss adjustment which are the essence of free competition, but the very nature of the increasingly elaborate instrumental equipment of mechanized industry imposes the necessity of a steady routine in its utilization.

Another factor tending to thwart the realization of the aims of the refurbished antitrust policy has been the apathetic, if not antipathetic, attitude toward this policy of the three administrations which in turn followed that of Wilson. The leaders of the Republican party, riding the crest of the post-war prosperity wave, were indisposed to undertake forthright efforts to preserve competition. That might have hampered big business; that is, conflicted with the interests of those aggressive concerns already at the top, whose mounting profits were the object of their solicitude and the accepted index of national prosperity. There was no pronounced disposition, it is true, to repeal the antitrust laws, partly no doubt because their efficacy as a curb on the power of labor organizations was beginning to be thoroughly appreciated but chiefly, it appears, because under the current construction of the laws the largest and most influential business interests, which stood close to the administration in the post-war decade, considered them if not innocuous at least far less menacing than the alternatives which, once the issue was again raised, might have replaced them. These interests had no wish to risk reawakening the crusading spirit from which in 1914 they had so narrowly escaped unscathed.

Probably the chief factor, however, in the miscarriage of the New Freedom was the onset of the war so soon after the enactment of the 1914 legislation. By that event all interest was diverted from the attempt to regulate business to the striving to win a military victory. Indeed the necessities of war dictated a policy not only of official connivance with existing forms of industrial concentration, but actually of fostering an even closer concert of action in every field. New agencies, such as the War Industries Board, the Food Administration and the like, were instituted with the specific design of achieving this object, quite regardless of the limitations of the antitrust laws. Moreover the Federal Trade Commission was in practise relieved from all responsibility for preventing or suppressing monopoly and was in substance sent off on a wild goose chase. It became a sort of statistical agency for compiling cost data and information upon prices—as a means, presumably, of combating the spiral ascent of prices. This picayune task, doomed to futility by virtue of the government's own inflationary program, did much to discredit the Federal Trade Commission in the crucial years immediately following its formation.

The war had more than a negative significance, however, in placing the antitrust laws in abeyance and in giving the Federal Trade Commission a bad start. It provided, as it were, a licensed training school in trade cooperation. It taught business men of every kind and variety of antecedents the forms and the advantages of concerted action. Moreover the rapid rise in prices induced by the inflationary policy of financing the war tended to take the emphasis off the more nefarious and disreputable aspects of trade combination. In these circumstances business leaders were easily persuaded that to neglect or to resist opportunities for united action was to obstruct the realization of social benefits. What had before the war been regarded as a questionable method of getting rich at the expense of society now came to be looked upon as a laudable avenue of profit making, a source of gain all around. Doubtless an unbiased account would disclose qualifications upon the accuracy no less of the pre-war view than of the post-war view, the former tending to overlook some potentialities of genuine economic advantage, the latter to slough over some potentialities of perversion. But for present purposes what is significant is the change in the susceptibility of business men to tempting invitations to combination.

Perhaps even more decisive for the future course of antitrust policy was the experience of the war period for the public generally; that is, for the consumer interest. Public opinion had fought stubbornly against the rising cost of living during the two decades preceding the war. Not a little of the popular clamor against the trusts had been nourished by the belief that they were largely responsible for this untoward development. So long as living costs mounted piecemeal and sporadically this illusion had much to recommend it, and trust busting continued to have in the common sense of the community a vital *raison d'être*. But the sudden, general and extraordinary upward leap of the cost of living during the war effectively dissipated the old popular illusion. Monetary factors were plainly enough at the bottom of this movement, and trust baiting no longer seemed to offer any promise of relief.

In another way too the experience of the war abated popular interest in antitrust policy and deprived the law of its indispensable emotional backing. The orgy of patriotic fervor and blind hero worship brought in its train prolonged disillusionment, profound apathy and unwonted depths of cynicism. Now the policy of opposing the trusts, of attempting to regulate business in the public interest, had always involved or rather depended upon a certain kind of chivalry. Those who would marshal the forces of progressivism for an attack had to be in some sense crusaders. But the post-war public had had enough of crusading.

In addition there must be mentioned the more subtle but in the end perhaps controlling influence of industrial technology. Revolutionary improvements in productive processes did not come simultaneously in all fields of industry nor have they been of the same character everywhere. But the cumulative effect of better mechanical expedients here, improved chemical processes there, new raw materials somewhere else, has been to make the way of the independent enterpriser more and more difficult. There is a growing burden of overhead costs; the risks of obsolescence have steadily mounted; improvements in transportation, communication and power generation have intensified the interdependence of enterprises and industries.

In view of the aggregate force of all these influences—changes in judicial interpretation, in political administration, in trust strategy, in business outlook and in popular attitude, all interacting and combining with transformations in technology to produce a new orientation of public policy—there is perhaps less occasion for wonder that the antitrust laws have suffered eclipse than that they still stand as the nominal definition of the legally sanctioned method of organizing American trade and industry.

The new direction of policy was evidenced at first by an increasing resort, particularly during the war period, to the device of the consent decree. By this expedient many trusts, without contesting the alleged illegality of their practises or their organization, conceded their liability under the law to the extent of consenting to the imposition of certain penalties. Sometimes they were placed on probation. Sometimes there was a *pro forma* dissolution which amounted to no more than a sale of some obsolete plant or of a minor branch of the business. More frequently the offender was simply required to renounce dubious trade practises. Occasionally there were restrictions on expansion, the legality of which was at least questionable. Later the eclipse of the antitrust laws was signaled no less patently by the institution of the device of advance sanction. Under the Coolidge administration it became possible to secure from the law enforcement officers of the government an advance opinion upon the lawfulness of a projected merger. If the plan was not deemed objectionable, the promoters obtained what amounted to a guaranty against prosecution; and if it was rejected, revision was always possible.

It was under this obliging dispensation, fortified by the lenient judicial policy exemplified in the steel decision, that the resurgence of the merger movement occurred in the 1920's. While the combinations of this period were in general less comprehensive and spectacular than those of a quarter century earlier, perhaps just because the basic industries had already been merged so extensively, they were far more numerous. It has been estimated that over five hundred mergers were consummated during the Coolidge administration alone. It may be mentioned that while the consolidation tendency at this time was most conspicuous in the field of the public utilities, particularly in the electrical industry, it embraced also mercantile trade, food purveyance (milk, bread, restaurants, hotels), amusements and financial institutions of all kinds in addition to ordinary manufacturing industries.

The growing popular indifference to the public policy of preserving active competition in trade is evidenced also by the successful agitation of trade associations for a wider scope of permissible action in concerted regulation of the markets. The looser forms of business federation had undoubtedly continued judicially suspect for some time after the "light of reason" had enabled the courts to see elements in proprietary consolidations which condoned any abuses of which they might have been susceptible. As late as 1921 the Supreme Court had condemned a lumber manufacturer's organization (American Column and Lumber Company *v.* United States, 257 U.S. 377) chiefly on the ground that the mode of conducting a statistical interchange service evinced a conspiracy to raise prices. But the unremitting pressure of business interests for greater privileges of (collective) self-regulation and the waning interest of the public in antitrust repressive measures eventually led to a modification of the strict construction of the Sherman Act prohibitions even in this field. By 1925 (Maple Floor Manufacturing Association *v.* United States, 268 U.S. 563) it had been established that in the absence of positive evidence of outright agreement or collusive action to fix prices or restrict output trade associations could not be molested in their efforts to standardize market policies and stabilize market conditions through such activities as cooperative cost finding, statistical interchange, joint determination of credit terms and the like. Eight years later the license was extended still further, and the benefits which the trusts as such had derived from the rule of reason were made available in substantial measure to business concerns, i e. cartels. In the Appalachian Coals case [Appalachian Coals, Inc., *v.* United States, 288 U.S. 344 (1933)] it was held that even the organization of a joint sales agency for the announced purpose of controlling the prices of members, who together produced approximately 75 percent of the output of an important kind of fuel, did not in itself, that is, without proof of unreasonable abuses in rigging the market, violate the antitrust law.

It is not always recognized that through this added license the trusts themselves acquired vastly greater power to control the markets in their own interests vis-à-vis consumers' interests, even if not in their special interests as compared with the outside, nominally independent producer. In other words, the Appalachian decision affords the trusts the privilege of cooperating with the independents for their mutual advantage no less than it gives the independents the opportunity of working together either to forfend trustification or to resist trust encroachments. With this concession to business interests, the most significant vestiges of the original antitrust policy are the curbs upon labor organizations and upon trade boycotts, as represented in such cases as the Eastern States Retail Lumber Dealers' Association *v.* United States [234 U.S. 600 (1914)], the Pathe Exchange [Binderup *v.* Pathe Exchange, Inc., 263 U.S. 291 (1923)] and the First National Pictures cases [Paramount Famous Lasky Corporation *v.* United States; and United States *v.* First National Pictures, Inc., 282 U.S. 30 and 44 (1930)] as well as, in a manner, in the resale price maintenance cases.

Finally, the current efforts under the New Deal of Franklin D. Roosevelt to reorganize industry for the ostensible purpose of accomplishing recovery from the immediate business depression appear to mark the total eclipse of the traditional antitrust policy. Although it is too early to determine the full import of the new policy represented by the National Industrial Recovery Act of 1933, it is already manifest that the old faith in free competition has vanished. Reliance is being more and more directed toward some form of arbitrary regulation of the market, although it should be recognized that this takes place solely within each particular industry as a separate field of regulatory jurisdiction and involves no elements, beyond an empty pretense, of comprehensive socio-economic planning. Just how much public responsibility and governmental supervision the new "codes of fair competition" will involve cannot yet be stated. The share of consumers' interests in the actual administration of industry under the new regime is still problematical. Above all it remains to be seen in what respects the specific devices being experimented with may prove transient. But in view of the gradual lapsing or disintegration of the public policy embodied in the antitrust laws, as here traced, it cannot be doubted that the industrial policy of the United States is undergoing profound modification.

The antitrust laws expressed the faith of the nineteenth century in free enterprise and free competition. But their very enactment was a recognition of the fact that in practise the competitive organization of industrial control did not work well, that it afforded imperfect protection to vital interests of the community. The antitrust program was in essence an effort to remedy the evils of free capitalistic enterprise by depriving it of some of its freedom; that is, limiting the concentration of control. The aim was to enforce competition if and whenever that was necessary. The anomalies of such a policy are plain, depending on free enterprise to organize and give direction to industry but setting legal bounds, that is, bounds dissociated from industrial considerations and therefore incomprehensible to business men, to the pursuit of profits. But the antitrust policy was not only anomalous, it was anachronistic. In a frontier society living by agriculture, the handicrafts and petty trade it might have functioned very well—chiefly because under those conditions it would have been superfluous. In a developed industrial society exploiting the machine technique, the credit system of high finance and world markets it was already moribund when it achieved belated legislative expression.

Whether the primary role in stimulating the onward sweep of the trust movement and the concomitant decline of the antitrust movement belongs to the objective factor of machine technology or to the subjective factor of capitalistic cupidity, it would now be pointless to inquire. That mechanized industry requires for its full fruitfulness or even tolerably efficient utilization some type of unified management, some control in the most literal sense, is now generally conceded. Together these two powerful thrusts in modern industry, so long as they were left untouched, precluded the possibility of enduring success for an antitrust policy, however well conceived and zealously administered.

MYRON W. WATKINS

See: COMBINATIONS, INDUSTRIAL; CARTEL; TRADE ASSOCIATIONS; RESTRAINT OF TRADE; UNFAIR COMPETITION; FEDERAL TRADE COMMISSION; GOVERNMENT REGULATION OF INDUSTRY; MONOPOLY; COMPETITION; LARGE SCALE PRODUCTION; CORPORATION; HOLDING COMPANIES; INTERLOCKING DIRECTORATES; RATE REGULATION; PRICE REGULATION; RESALE PRICE MAINTENANCE; BASING POINT PRICES; PRICE DISCRIMINATION; STABILIZATION, ECONOMIC; TRUSTS AND TRUSTEES.

Consult: Seager, H. R., and Gulick, C. A., *Trust and Corporation Problems* (New York 1929); Jones, Eliot, *The Trust Problem in the United States* (New York 1921); Jenks, Jeremiah, and Clark, Walter E., *The Trust Problem* (5th ed. New York 1929); *Trusts, Pools, and Corporations*, ed. by W. Z. Ripley (rev. ed. Boston 1916); Durand, E. D., *The Trust Problem* (Cambridge, Mass. 1915); Clark, John Bates and J. M., *The Control of Trusts* (enlarged ed. New York 1912); Watkins, Myron W., *Industrial Combinations and Public Policy* (Boston 1927); Clark, John D., *The Federal Trust Policy*, Johns Hopkins University, Studies in History and Political Science, extra vols., n.s., no. 15 (Baltimore 1931); Keezer, D. M., and May, Stacy, *The Public Control of Business* (New York 1930); Laidler, Harry W., *Concentration of Control in American Industry* (New York 1931); Fetter, Frank A., *The Masquerade of Monopoly* (New York 1931); Clark, John M., *Social Control of Business* (Chicago 1926); Veblen, Thorstein B., *Absentee Ownership and Business Enterprise in Recent Times* (New York 1923); Thompson, Merle R., *Trust Dissolution* (Boston 1919); Walker, Albert H., *History of the Sherman Law* (New York 1910); National Industrial Conference Board, *Mergers and the Law* (New York 1929); Berman, Edward, *Labor and the Sherman Act* (New York 1930); "The Anti-Trust Laws of the United States," American Academy of Political and Social Science, *Annals*, vol. cxlvii, no. 236 (Philadelphia 1930); Watkins, M. W.,

"Trustification and Economic Theory" in *American Economic Review*, vol. xxi, supplement no. 1 (1931) 54–76; National Conference on the Relation of Law and Business, *First Session, with Specific Emphasis on the Anti-Trust Laws* (New York 1931); *The Federal Anti-Trust Laws, a Symposium*, ed. by Milton Handler (Chicago 1932).

TRUSTS AND TRUSTEES. A trust is a device by which one person or group of persons is enabled to deal with property for the benefit of another or others. It is not, however, the only instrument which the law offers for this purpose. An owner may employ another as his agent to sell or manage or deal in other ways with his property. An owner of a chattel may deliver it to another as a bailee, to keep it for him or otherwise to dispose of it. If property is owned by a person under legal incapacity, as, for example, an infant or an insane person, a guardian may be appointed to take charge of the property and to administer it in the interest of the ward. When the owner of property dies, an executor or administrator is appointed to distribute his estate. The agent, the bailee, the guardian and the executor or administrator are fiduciaries and are subject to many duties not unlike those imposed upon trustees. But the relationships between them and those in whose interest they act differ in many ways from the relationship between the trustee and the beneficiary of a trust. The former relationships are to be found in all mature systems of law; the trust is a peculiar product of the Anglo-American legal system. Maitland has said that the development of the trust idea is the greatest and most distinctive achievement performed by Englishmen in the field of jurisprudence.

Because of the development of the trust in English equity it is difficult to find the proper place to assign to it in any analytical system of jurisprudence. The beneficiary of a trust undoubtedly acquires rights against the trustee. At first it was held that he acquired only rights against the trustee personally. Ultimately, however, it came to be held that if the trustee disposed of the property in breach of trust, the beneficiary could follow and reclaim the property if it had not come into the hands of a bona fide purchaser. In other words, the beneficiary had something more than a right of action against the trustee to compel him to do what conscience required: he acquired an equitable interest in the trust property. Here, however, a fiction came into play; the courts continued to say that the trustee and not the beneficiary was the owner of the trust property. Indeed some jurists still hold this view. As a result of the use of the fiction that the beneficiary is not the owner of the property, the courts of equity felt free to mold the character of the beneficiary's rights and to refrain from applying the rules of the strict law which were applicable to ownership of property.

In consequence of the anomalous position of the trust in the English system of jurisprudence it was possible to evolve an entirely new kind of ownership. The kinds of ownership permitted under the strict law had already been more or less clearly limited and the incidents of such ownership had been fairly well settled. Interests in land were governed by the principles of the feudal land law. No one except the king could actually own land, all others holding as tenants either of the king or of some intermediate overlord. Various feudal burdens rested upon tenants long after the feudal system itself had fallen into decay. Instead of waiting until the law should be modernized by act of Parliament, the chancellor introduced and superimposed a new system of interests in property. The legal title to the property would be vested in the trustee, or feoffee to uses, as he once was called, and his title was subject to the rules of the strict law; but a new kind of interest was created in the beneficiary of the trust, the cestui que use or cestui que trust, as he was designated. In molding this new kind of interest, the equitable interest, the chancellor felt free to apply to it such principles as seemed to be more just and in closer accord with the spirit of the times than those of the strict law. It is true that he did not depart entirely from established legal rules; in many matters he applied the maxim that equity follows the law. But actually he was creating a new kind of ownership with incidents very different from those which attached to legal interests.

There has been some difference of opinion among legal historians as to the origin of the "use" out of which the modern trust has been evolved. It was once thought that it was derived from concepts of the Roman law, particularly the fideicommissum; but although there is a certain resemblance between the two concepts, it is now conceded that the use is not of Roman origin. The prevailing opinion today is that it was derived largely from the Germanic *Salman*, or *Treuhand*, whose position was not unlike that of a feoffee to uses, or a trustee. It must be remembered, however, that the use or trust was developed through a gradual process of evolution. As Sir Francis Bacon said, it "grew to strength and credit by degrees." The enforcement of uses and trusts has been one of the chief heads of equity jurisdiction for five hundred years. The trust might have been evolved from its Germanic prototype even if there had been no separate courts of law and equity; but in that case it would undoubtedly have been something quite different and not so comprehensive or so flexible as the courts of equity made it.

The history of the use or trust can be divided into four periods. The first extended from the twelfth to the fifteenth century. During this period it became increasingly common for a landowner to convey his land to another person to hold it for the use of the grantor or for the use of a third person. The use during this period, however, was not enforceable in any court, except perhaps occasionally in the ecclesiastical courts; and the undertaking by the feoffee was regarded as nothing more than a gentleman's agreement. The second period began early in the fifteenth century when the chancellor undertook to give a remedy to the cestui que use against the feoffee to uses and continued until the enactment of the Statute of Uses [27 Henry VIII, c. 10 (1535–36)]. The use or trust now passed from the domain of morals into that of law. At first relief was given only against the trustee personally; but before the end of this period the chancellor held that in equity the cestui que use was the owner of the land, and he therefore compelled third persons to whom the trustee had conveyed the land to surrender it to the cestui que use, unless indeed it was not unconscientious for the third person to hold the land, as where he was a purchaser for value and without notice of the use. Now that the cestui que use was entitled to judicial protection of his interest, feoffments to uses became very common, so common in fact that it was said that at the end of the fifteenth century most of the land in England was held by the legal owners to the use of others. The third period covers the century after the enactment of the Statute of Uses. This famous statute provided that where one person should be seised to the use of another, the other should have the seisin; in other words, that the legal title should automatically vest in the equitable owner, thus "executing" the use. The purpose was to destroy the system of double ownership, the separation of the legal and the equitable titles, not by invalidating the rights of the beneficiary but by making them legal rights. During this period uses were employed merely as a means of conveying legal ownership and were dealt with by the courts of law rather than by the courts of equity. The fourth period began with the revival of trusts in the seventeenth century. The view was taken that the Statute of Uses did not entirely put an end to the separation of legal and equitable interests. It was held that a trust of chattels or of leasehold interests in land was not executed by the Statute of Uses; nor was a trust executed where the trustee had active duties imposed upon him; nor, curiously enough, did the statute execute a use raised on a use, as, for example, where a conveyance was made to the use of the transferee or another, but upon trust nevertheless for a designated beneficiary.

During this period the modern trust began to develop and to assume its present form. The old reasons for creating uses, such as the avoidance of feudal burdens and of forfeiture for treason, the evasion of the mortmain acts, the desire to make a testamentary disposition of land, which had been impossible under the old feudal law, had ceased to operate, and the former objections to the creation of uses had disappeared; but for other reasons it was still found desirable to separate the legal and the equitable ownership.

Indeed apart from limitations of public policy the purposes for which the trust may be employed are almost unlimited. The trust has played a great part as an instrument of law reform, for its use has made possible avoidance of the application of technical or outworn rules of law. But the trust has frequently also been employed for unlawful purposes. So frequently indeed has this been the case that, as Sir Francis Bacon said, the parents of the trust were fraud and fear although a court of conscience was its nurse. Perhaps the most common fraudulent use of the trust is to evade the claims of creditors. As early as 1376 Parliament passed a statute (50 Edw. III, c. 6) condemning conveyances for the use of the transferor when made for the purpose of defrauding his creditors. In the same century it became necessary also to enact a statute to prevent the use of the trust device to defeat the policy of the mortmain statutes, which forbade the holding of land by religious and other corporations.

The principal private purpose for which trusts are employed today is to promote the interests of the family. A man of property who will be survived by a widow and children frequently does not wish to leave the property outright to be divided among them. He therefore bequeaths the property to a trustee with directions to pay the income or a part of it to the widow for her life and to pay income and ultimately the principal to the children, or perhaps he postpones the final distribution so as to give the property ultimately to his grandchildren. Until the final distribution is made the property will be managed by the trustee. The testator cannot, however, postpone the final distribution indefinitely, since this would be in contravention of the rule against perpetuities, but he can control the disposition of the property for a generation or two.

It was through the use of the trust that married women in England first obtained some degree of economic independence. At common law a woman's personal property vested in her husband, and he was entitled to the use and enjoyment of her land. The courts of equity held, however, that property could be vested in trustees for the wife's separate use and that the beneficial interest thus given her could not be reached by her husband. It was not until the nineteenth century that statutes were enacted which permitted a married woman to have the separate ownership of property without the necessity of the creation of a trust.

A trust can be created by a disposition *inter vivos* as well as by will. A family settlement upon marriage is much more common in England than in the United States. Such a settlement usually includes the creation of a trust for one or both of the spouses and for the prospective children of the marriage. In the United States it has become quite common for the owner of property to create a trust during his lifetime, a living trust, as it is commonly called, under which the income may be made payable to him during his lifetime and to various members of his family after his death. Not infrequently one of the purposes in creating such a trust is to avoid the payment of income or inheritance taxes, but changes in the tax laws have made this difficult. The principal advantage to the owner of property resulting from the creation of such a trust is that it subjects the property to the management and control of a competent person or organization and allows him to arrange before he dies for its disposition after his death. In recent years insurance trusts have become increasingly common. A man takes out insurance policies on his life; but instead of making the policies payable directly to the intended beneficiaries, he makes them payable to a trustee, whose duty it becomes to collect the policies and to hold the proceeds in trust. In some cases the insured person also transfers to the trustee securities or other income producing property in trust, so that the latter may apply the income to the payment of the premiums upon the policies and upon the death of the insured may hold the securities and the proceeds of the policies in trust. Such a trust is called a funded insurance trust.

The creator of a trust may desire not merely to give the management of the property to the trustee but also to prevent the beneficiary from anticipating the income, so as to protect him against his creditors. In a majority of the states of the United States a provision that the beneficiary shall not assign his interest under the trust and that his creditors shall not reach it is held to be valid. Such a trust is called a "spendthrift trust." In a number of states there are statutes permitting this type of trust, although in some of them only so much of the income as is needed by the beneficiary for his support is exempt from the claims of his creditors. In England it is held that the creator of the trust has no power to exempt the interest of the beneficiary from the claims of his creditors, on the ground that it is against public policy to permit him to have property which he can enjoy but with which he need not pay his debts.

The trust has been employed to a large extent, particularly in the United States, for business purposes. As Isaacs has said, "Trusteeship has become a readily available tool for everyday purposes of organization, financing, risk-shifting, credit operations, settling of disputes, and liquidation of business affairs." Thus not infrequently the trust is used instead of the ordinary corporate device for the carrying on of a business: the property employed in the undertaking is held by a group of trustees, and the interests of the beneficial owners are represented by transferable certificates. Where a corporation borrows money and issues bonds secured by a mortgage upon the property of the corporation, a mortgage or deed of trust is executed to a trustee and not directly to the bondholders. The trust device is employed also in financing the purchase of railroad equipment and to some extent in purchases of commodities at home or abroad. The trust has been employed for the purpose of distributing the risk of loss in the making of investments by the creation of investment trusts, although frequently today so-called investment trusts employ the corporate device rather than the trust. Sometimes it is used in order to assure control over the voting power of the stockholders of a corporation by the setting up of a voting trust. The use of the trust device to suppress competition among corporations by vesting the shares of all the corporations in a single body of trustees has become so notorious that the term trust has been popularly applied to all forms of monopolies, although the particular device may be the creation of a holding company or the establishment by merger or otherwise of a single corporation.

Another important field in which trusts have been employed is the promotion of charity. A charitable trust differs from a private trust in that there need be and ordinarily there are no definite beneficiaries, and that a charitable trust may continue for an indefinite or unlimited period. The charitable trust has been for centuries a great instrumentality for the promotion of eleemosynary, educational and religious enterprises and others beneficial to the community. In modern times, however, particularly in the United States, it has become more common to create corporations for charitable purposes.

The trust has been used also as a means of giving property to unincorporated associations, not charitable in character, and thus has had an important role in promoting the right of association by making it possible for unincorporated social clubs, fraternal organizations, trade unions and the like to maintain themselves. At common law associations were not regarded as legal entities, and they could not take the legal title to land or other property. Where an association is composed of a large and shifting membership, it is impracticable to vest the title to the property in the individual members. The property can be vested in trustees in trust for the benefit of the association. Today, however, it has become increasingly easy and common for such organizations to incorporate.

In the United States much more than in England the administration of trusts has become a business or profession. In some communities it is the custom of many persons of large means in creating trusts of their property to select one or more trustees from among a small number of persons who have established a reputation for sagacity in the administration of trusts. More commonly today, however, a trust company or bank is selected as trustee. Probably the earliest corporation authorized by its charter to administer trusts was created in New York in 1822. Since that time there has been a constant development of corporate trusteeship. In 1913 national banks were authorized to act as trustees. In the year ending June 30, 1933, it was reported by the comptroller of the currency that national banks were administering over 100,000 individual trusts with assets aggregating over $6,000,000,000 and were handling corporate trusts and acting as trustees under security issues aggregating over $10,000,000,000. No exact figures are available in regard to the amount of trust business of state banks and trust companies. For many years banking institutions have been very active in seeking business of this character. In England many trusts are managed by a public official, the so-called public trustee.

Trusts are usually divided into three classes: express, resulting and constructive trusts. Express trusts are those which arise as a result of a manifestation of intention to create them, and it is these trusts which have been thus far discussed. A resulting trust arises where a person transfers property under such circumstances that it appears that he did not intend the person to whom the property is transferred to have a beneficial interest in the property, or where property is transferred upon an express trust which fails in whole or in part or which is fully accomplished without exhaustion of the entire property. In such cases the trustee holds the property or what remains of it for the benefit of the person who created the trust or of his estate if he is dead. Thus if a testator devises land in trust to pay the income to another person and the latter predeceases the testator, the trustee holds the land upon a resulting trust for the heir or residuary devisee of the testator. Another common situation in which a resulting trust arises is where property is purchased and the purchase price is paid by one person and by his direction the property is transferred by the vendor to another person; in such a case the transferee holds the property upon a resulting trust for the person who paid the purchase money, unless indeed it appears that the latter intended to make a gift of the property to the transferee or unless the transferee was his wife or child or other near relative, in which case the intention to make a gift is presumed. In the case of land an express trust is not enforceable in most states unless the trust is declared in a written instrument properly signed; but a resulting trust may arise out of an oral transaction.

Constructive trusts have little in common with express trusts except the name. A constructive trust arises whenever one person holds property which he will be compelled in equity to surrender to another for some equitable reason. In other words, a constructive trust is merely a remedial device. Thus if land is obtained by fraud, the fraudulent party can be compelled to reconvey the land to the defrauded party; and prior to such reconveyance he is said to hold the land upon a constructive trust. So also it is held in many states that when a devisee of land murders the testator, he holds the land upon a constructive trust for the testator's heirs; and if an heir murders his ancestor, he holds the land which he acquires by the death intestate of the ancestor upon a constructive trust for the person who would have been heir if he had predeceased the intestate. If a person misappropriates the property of another and exchanges the property for other property and makes a profit thereby, he is chargeable as constructive trustee of the property so received. In short, whenever one person is permitted by a suit in equity specifically to recover property from another, in order to prevent the latter from profiting by a wrong or from otherwise being unjustly enriched the latter holds the property upon a constructive trust.

AUSTIN W. SCOTT

See: OWNERSHIP AND POSSESSION; TRUSTS; INVESTMENT TRUSTS; MASSACHUSETTS TRUSTS; CHARITABLE TRUSTS; PERPETUITIES; GUARDIANSHIP; AGENCY.

Consult: Lewin, Thomas, *Practical Treatise on the Law of Trusts* (13th ed. by Walter Banks, London 1928); Underhill, Arthur, *The Law Relating to Private Trusts and Trustees* (8th ed. London 1926); Godefroi, Henry, *The Law of Trusts and Trustees* (5th ed. by H. G. Hanbury, London 1927); Perry, J. W., *A Treatise on the Law of Trusts and Trustees*, 2 vols. (7th ed. by R. C. Baldes, Boston 1929); Bogert, G. G., *Handbook of the Law of Trusts* (St. Paul 1921); Loring, Augustus P., *A Trustee's Handbook* (4th ed. Boston 1928); Smith, James G., *The Development of Trust Companies in the United States* (New York 1928); Dunn, W. C., *Trusts for Business Purposes* (Chicago 1922); Stephenson, G. T., *Living Trusts* (New York 1926); Sears, J. H., *Trust Estates as Business Companies* (2nd ed. Kansas City 1921), and *A Treatise on Trust Company Law* (Chicago 1917); Madden, J. L., *Wills, Trusts and Estates* (New York 1927); Lepaulle, Pierre, *Traité théorique et pratique des trusts* . . . (Paris 1932); Roth, Hermann M., *Der Trust in seinem Entwicklungsgang vom Feoffee to Uses zur amerikanischen Trust Company*, Arbeiten zum Handels-, Gewerbe- und Landwirtschaftsrecht, no. 48 (Marburg 1928); Brunner, Max, *Wesen und Bedeutung der englisch-amerikanischen Treuhand*, Abhandlungen zum schweizerischen Recht, n.s., no. lxii (Berne 1931); Hein, Johannes, *Grundriss des Treuhandrechts* (Berlin 1929); Holmes, O. W., "Early English Equity" in *Law Quarterly Review*, vol. i (1885) 162–74; Ames, J. B., "The Origin of Uses and Trusts," and Holdsworth, W. S., "The Political Causes Which Shaped the Statute of Uses" in *Harvard Law Review*, vol. xxi (1907–08) 261–74, and vol. xxvi (1912–13) 108–27; Wilgus, H. L., "Corporations and Express Trusts as Business Organizations" in *Michigan Law Review*, vol. xiii (1914–15) 71–99, 205–38; Isaacs, Nathan, "Trusteeship in Modern Business" in *Harvard Law Review*, vol. xlii (1928–29) 1048–61; Phillips, E. I., "Life Insurance Trusts" in *University of Pennsylvania Law Review*, vol. lxxxi (1932–33) 284–312, 408–33; Smith, Marion, "Limitations on the Validity of Voting Trusts" in *Columbia Law Review*, vol. xxii (1922) 627–37; Finkelstein, Maurice, "Voting Trust Agreements" in *Michigan Law Review*, vol. xxiv (1925–26) 344–69; Bergerman, M. M., "Voting Trusts and Non-Voting Stock" in *Yale Law Journal*, vol. xxxvii (1927–28) 445–67; Bernays, M. C., "The Validity of Voting Trusts of the Stock of National Banks" in *Illinois Law Review*, vol. xxii (1927–28) 587–612; Berle, A. A., Jr., "Corporate Powers as Powers in Trust" in *Harvard Law Review*, vol. xliv (1930–31) 1049–74; Scott, A. W., "The Trust as an Instrument of Law Reform" in *Yale Law Journal*, vol. xxxi (1921–22) 457–68, and "The Restatement of the Law of Trusts" in *Columbia Law Review*, vol. xxxi (1931) 1266–85; Arnold, Thurman, "The Restatement of the Law of Trusts" in *Columbia Law Review*, vol. xxxi (1931) 800–23; Lepaulle, Pierre, "Civil Law Substitutes for Trusts" in *Yale Law Journal*, vol. xxxvi (1926–27) 1126–47, and "An Outsider's Viewpoint of the Nature of Trusts" in *Cornell Law Quarterly*, vol. xiv (1928–29) 52–61; Bates, L. T., "Common Law Express Trusts in French Law" in *Yale Law Journal*, vol. xl (1930–31) 34–52.

TUBERCULOSIS. See COMMUNICABLE DISEASES, CONTROL OF; PUBLIC HEALTH.

TUCKER, GEORGE (1775–1861), American economist and historian. Tucker served a Virginia district as a representative in Congress from 1819 to 1825, when he was appointed by Jefferson as the first professor of moral philosophy at the University of Virginia. Of his numerous works, which include poetry, fiction, philosophy, economics, history and biography, that which is probably consulted most commonly today is his *Progress of the United States in Population and Wealth in Fifty Years* (New York 1843), a compendium, with comments and interpretations, of the census reports from 1790 to 1840, which was republished in 1855 to include the census of 1850. His most important historical effort was his *History of the United States . . . to the End of the Twenty-Sixth Congress in 1841* (4 vols., Philadelphia 1856–57). Because Tucker himself had played a part in the history of the period and knew personally most of the chief actors, the book is still of interest; and it is significant as the first important effort to write the history of the United States from the southern viewpoint. His *Life of Thomas Jefferson* (2 vols., Philadelphia 1837), written with an intimate familiarity with the subject and discriminating sympathy, was likewise the first important life of the great statesman.

Tucker's greatest contribution, however, was in economic theory, where he easily ranked among the foremost Americans of the pre-Civil War period. He criticized Ricardo's theories of rent, wages and value, adhering generally to the subjective concept of value. Although he was profoundly influenced by the Malthusian economics, particularly the concept of rent, Tucker believed that Malthus had overrated the propensity of mankind to increase and had underestimated the checks to population. Unlike other southern writers, he saw clearly the diminishing returns from slave labor and asserted that slavery "cannot exist in the most advanced stages of society." His writings on finance, characterized by clarity and understanding, favored in general the system exemplified by the Second United States Bank.

HAROLD U. FAULKNER

Other important works: *Essays on Various Subjects of Taste, Morals and National Policy* (Georgetown 1822); *Laws of Wages, Profits and Rent, Investigated* (Philadelphia 1837); *The Theory of Money and Banks Investigated* (Boston 1839); *Correspondence with Alexander H. Everett on Political Economy* (n.p. 1845); *Banks or No Banks* (New York 1857); *Political Economy for the People* (Philadelphia 1859); *Essays Moral and Metaphysical* (Philadelphia 1860).

Consult: Turner, J. R., *The Ricardian Rent Theory in Early American Economics* (New York 1921) ch. v; Dunglison, Robley, "An Obituary Notice of Professor George Tucker" in American Philosophical Society, *Proceedings*, vol. ix (1862) 64–70.

TUCKER, JOSIAH (1712–99), English economist and theologian. Tucker was born at Langhame in Carmarthenshire and entered St. John's College, Oxford, in 1733. He took orders and eventually became dean of Gloucester. He combined an ecclesiastical career with an active interest in political and economic affairs. His first tract on an economic subject was *A Brief Essay on the Advantages and Disadvantages Which Respectively Attend France and Great Britain with Regard to Trade* (London 1749, 3rd ed. 1753), which in its general treatment marks him as in all essentials a mercantilist: in his references to the theory of the balance of trade, to the importance of a large population fully employed, to projects for fostering the silk and fishing industries and for fitting the colonies into an economic scheme profitable to the mother country. There are acute observations on the need for improved inland transport, particularly by means of canals, on the value of tourist traffic and the promotion of immigration by naturalization of foreigners. The *Essay*, which ran through a number of editions, established Tucker's reputation as a writer on economic questions and he was induced to undertake *The Elements of Commerce and Theory of Taxes* (p.p. Bristol 1755), one of the first comprehensive treatises on economics. Here he set out to deduce general principles from the postulate of "self-love"; but he was not persistent in the conduct of his analysis, being too apt to indulge in digression. The detailed examination and condemnation of monopolies, both domestic and for the furtherance of foreign trade, deserve special notice. But the work is incomplete: the parts devoted to such topics as money and taxation are merely represented by chapter headings. Part of what Tucker intended to include in it was published as *Instructions for Travellers* (p.p. London 1757, first published Dublin 1758), which contains much that is valuable on the state of English agriculture and industry in the middle of the eighteenth century. During the Seven Years' War Tucker exposed the folly of resorting to war as an instrument for the expansion of trade in *The Case of Going to War, for the Sake of Procuring, Enlarging, or Securing of Trade, Considered in a New Light* (London 1763). He prophesied that the British conquest of Canada would snap the bond of self-interest which bound the American colonies to the mother country. As the dissension became more acute Tucker attracted wide attention by advocating complete political separation, which he held would have no adverse effect on English trade since it was based on mutual advantage. He believed indeed that the colonies rather than the mother country would suffer. His most important tracts on this subject were *A Letter from a Merchant in London to His Nephew in North America, Relative to the Present Posture of Affairs in the Colonies* (London 1766) and *The True Interest of Great Britain Set Forth in Regard to the Colonies* (Norfolk 1774).

Tucker was by no means an unqualified supporter of laissez faire. While he condemned such legislation as the Statute of Artificers, the navigation acts, the usury laws and the settlement acts, he considered that the self-interest of particular merchants might conflict with general national policy and that the state ought to take steps to prevent such disharmony. He favored paternal legislation on a variety of subjects, in particular to maintain population and to penalize idleness and promote industry. Tucker's writing was discursive and voluminous; he had a weakness for repetition and was always too apt to be involved in controversy over current events.

J. F. REES

Works: Josiah Tucker; a Selection from His Economic and Political Writings, ed. by R. L. Schuyler (New York 1931), which publishes for the first time the complete text of *The Elements of Commerce and Theory of Taxes*, p. 51–219.

Consult: Clark, Walter E., *Josiah Tucker, Economist; a Study in the History of Economics*, Columbia University, Studies in History, Economics and Public Law, no. 49 (New York 1903), with a very full list of Tucker's published writings, p. 241–58.

TUCOVIĆ, DIMITRIJE (1881–1914), Serbian socialist leader. Tucović was born in Gostilje (Užice) of a family of ecclesiastics and was destined by his parents for the church. As a student he became a convinced and thorough Marxist even before there was a socialist party in Serbia. When immediately after the overthrow of the Obrenović regime in the summer of 1903 the Serbian Social Democratic party was formed, Tucović at once assumed a leading role in the movement. He was well versed in the works of Marx and Engels, corresponded with Kautsky and modeled his activity upon that of his prototype, Viktor Adler, the leader of the Austrian Social Democracy. Like Adler, Tucović was active both as a theoretician and as a practical leader; and similarly also he combined energy with prudence and enthusiasm with self-criticism, thus developing a wide sphere of influence. He was secretary of the socialist organization, delegate of the party to the International Bureau, teacher in the Belgrade workers' school, editor of the daily *Radničke novine* (Labor news) and editor of the scientific weekly *Borba* (Fight). He addressed hundreds of meetings, wrote numerous articles, wrote propaganda pamphlets and historical and political essays and translated Bebel's *Die Frau und der Sozialismus* and *Die Studenten und der Sozialismus* and works of Kautsky. He also carried on agitation in Old Serbia and Macedonia, which were still under Turkish rule, and was a candidate in two electoral districts.

Tucović's social outlook was Marxist in the German sense of the term, but without dogmatism. Through socialism he sought to find a way out of the threatening dangers of the Balkan situation. In 1909 he participated in the Laibach conference of socialists of the South Slav sections of the Danubian monarchy and the next year he initiated the first Socialist Balkan conference of representatives from Serbia, Bulgaria, Bosnia-Herzegovina, Croatia, Turkey, Slovenia and part of Rumania. Tucović worked unceasingly for the adoption of the policy, which had already been proposed by Svetozar Marković, of creating a Balkan federation of free Balkan states which should act as a bulwark against the imperialism of the great powers in southeastern Europe.

The World War, however, was a force in the opposite direction. Although Tucović was unconditionally opposed to war and was instrumental in causing the socialists to reject the Serbian military credits, he fought with distinction as a reserve officer against the Turks, the Bulgars and the Austrians and was killed in the battle of Kolubara in the fourth month of the war.

HERMANN WENDEL

Works: Socijaldemokratska agitacija (Belgrade 1911); *Srbija i Albanija* (Belgrade 1914); *Celokupna Djela Dimitrija Tucovića* (Complete works), vol. i– (Belgrade 1924–).

Consult: Lapčević, Dragiša, *Istorija socijalizma u Srbiji* (Belgrade 1922); Wendel, Hermann, in *Aus der Welt der Südslawen* (Berlin 1926) p. 211–16.

TUGAN-BARANOVSKY, MIKHAIL IVANOVICH (1865–1919), Russian economist. Tugan-Baranovsky was originally trained in the natural sciences and mathematics but after his graduation from the University of Kharkov he shifted his interest to the social sciences. Except for a few forced interruptions he taught economics from 1895 to 1917. After the October revolution he served for a time as minister of finance in the Ukraine. His first great work which attracted international attention was *Promishlennie krizisi v sovremennoy Anglii* (St Petersburg 1894, 3rd ed. as *Periodicheskie promishlennie krizisi*, 1914; tr. by J. Schapiro as *Les crises industrielles en Angleterre*, Paris 1913), in which he ascribed the cause of modern crises to the recurring disproportion between the flow of funds into the field of production of capital goods and into that of consumption goods. This disproportion, he held, arises out of the nature of capital accumulation and capital investment under a system of private individual enterprise; while capital is accumulated and saved slowly and by degrees, the investment of capital is usually carried through precipitately and in large amounts. The advanced stage of the boom is usually marked by active investment and consequent exhaustion of available savings, which result in scarcity of funds and lead up to a collapse of investment values. During the depression which follows the crisis capital gradually becomes again abundant; investors at first hesitate to invest their funds and only after the interest rate and rediscount rate drop considerably does the accumulated capital burst through the dam which obstructed its flow into production. The process of investment proceeds to the point where the money funds again become depleted, giving rise to a new crisis, which signalizes the beginning of the next cycle.

Tugan-Baranovsky's second great work, *Russkaya fabrika* (St. Petersburg 1898, 2nd ed. 1900; tr. by B. Minzès as *Geschichte der russischen Fabrik*, Berlin 1900), presented an analysis of the rise of the factory system and the development of industrial capitalism in Russia from the end of the eighteenth century and marked the culmination of the prolonged discussion among Russian economists as to whether the development of capitalism in Russia exhibited the same tendencies as in western Europe; Tugan-Baranovsky strongly attacked the populist doctrine of the uniqueness of Russian capitalism. Although *Russkaya fabrika* was written in a Marxian spirit, the author soon began to attack the formulations of Marxism in a series of publications. Foremost among these is his *Teoreticheskiya osnovi marksizma* (St. Petersburg 1905; tr. as *Theoretische Grundlagen des Marxismus*, Leipsic 1905), in which along the lines of Bernstein's revisionism he criticized sharply the philosophical and sociological views of Marx. In his economic views Tugan-Baranovsky, as evidenced in his *Osnovi politicheskoy ekonomii* (Foundations of political economy, St. Petersburg 1908, 3rd ed. 1915), was an eclectic and attempted to reconcile the theory of marginal utility with the Marxian labor theory of value. He did not accept the Marxian theory of exploitation; profits, he believed, are due to technical productivity, but the magnitude of the profit share is determined by the relative strength of the social groups. This doctrine also underlies his theory of wages.

Although he was not a Marxist, Tugan-Baranovsky was a socialist; but his socialism, as expressed in his *Ocherki iz istorii politicheskoy ekonomii i sotsializma* (Essays on the history of political economy and socialism, St. Petersburg 1905) and in *Sovremenniy sotsializm v svoem istoricheskom razvitii* (St. Petersburg 1906; tr. by M. I. Redmount as *Modern Socialism in Its Historical Development*, London 1910), was in sympathy with the views of the great utopians and stressed above all the element of moral consciousness. Tugan-Baranovsky also devoted considerable attention to the problems of cooperation; he edited the publication *Vestnik kooperatsii*, organized cooperative institutes at Moscow and Kiev and published *Sotsialniya osnovi kooperatsii* (Social foundations of cooperation, Moscow 1916, 2nd ed. Berlin 1921), which contains a valuable study of the theory of cooperation. Other notable works are his *Sotsialnaya teoriya raspredeleniya* (Moscow 1913; tr. as *Soziale Theorie der Verteilung*, Berlin 1913) and *Bumazhnie dengi i metall* (Paper money and metal, Moscow 1917, rev. ed. 1919).

S. SOLNTSEV

Consult: Gringauz, S., *M. I. Tugan-Baranowsky und seine Stellung in der theoretischen Nationalökonomie* (Kovno 1918); Moiseev, M., "L'évolution d'une doctrine. La théorie des crises de Tougan-Baranovsky et la conception des crises économiques" in *Revue d'histoire économique et sociale*, vol. xx (1932) 1–43.

TULL, JETHRO (1674–1741), British agriculturist. Between 1699, when he began farming, and 1714 Tull evolved what he believed to be an original system of cultivation and in 1730 he was finally persuaded to write an account of it. The next year his *New Horse-Houghing Husbandry* was published in London; in 1733 a greatly enlarged work containing plates of the implements was published under the title *Horse Hoing Husbandry*, and this was followed by additional notes and comments down to 1739. Tull's system amounted to adapting for field crops the gardener's practise of dibbling seed in straight rows and repeatedly hoeing around the young plants as they grew. Since large scale operations demanded mechanization, he invented his drill and horse hoe as the essential implements of the new culture. Others had tried to invent similar machines, not entirely without success; Tull's originality lay in the way he combined them and in his explanation of the principles governing their use. The gardeners drilled to simplify hoeing and hoed to kill the weeds. Tull pointed out, first, that mechanical sowing gave to each seed the depth and space it needed for perfect growth and, second, that hoeing, by pulverizing the soil, brought the food of the plant into contact with its roots. These principles have remained basic to good farming ever since.

Unfortunately Tull tried to find scientific justification for his methods and elaborated an entirely false theory of plant physiology just when that science was making steady progress at the hands of such men as Nehemiah Grew and Stephen Hales. He denied that there was any scientific basis for the rotation of crops and that manures supplied any essential food to plants; and to prove his theories he grew wheat for thirteen years in succession on the same land without manure. Practical farmers were naturally skeptical; but large landowners like Charles, second Viscount Townshend, and Thomas Coke of Norfolk, who could afford to experiment, gradually sifted the good from the bad in Tull's teachings. They showed that the drill was of universal value, that both the hand hoe and the horse hoe were excellent for turnips and that Tull's two soundest principles of regular sowing and constant cultivation by the hoe could be combined with rotation and manures. Meanwhile progress was being made in the invention and manufacture of machines which farmers could buy and use without risk, so that by the end of the century Tull's work was beginning to have its true effect upon British agriculture.

T. H. Marshall

Consult: Cathcart, A. F., "Jethro Tull; His Life, Times, and Teaching" in Royal Agricultural Society of England, *Journal*, 3rd ser., vol. ii (1891) 1–40; Marshall, T. H., "Jethro Tull and the 'New Husbandry' of the Eighteenth Century" in *Economic History Review*, vol. ii (1929–30) 41–60; Macdonald, William, *Makers of Modern Agriculture* (London 1913) ch. i; Ernle, Lord (Prothero, R. E.), *English Farming, Past and Present* (4th ed. London 1926) ch. vii.

TURATI, FILIPPO (1857–1932), Italian Socialist leader. A member of a well to do family of Lombardy, he at first participated in the democratic movement but soon was attracted by socialistic thought. In 1883 he published a study *Il delitto e la questione sociale* (Milan 1883), the gist of which may be put in Quetelet's epigram: "Society creates criminals in order to punish them." In 1885 he associated himself in life and thought with Anna Kuliscioff, a Russian nihilist who, having emigrated to western Europe, had there adopted the doctrines of Marxian socialism; she was a woman of great intelligence and of heroic character. In 1890 he assumed the editorship of a semimonthly review entitled *Cuore e critica*, the name of which he changed to *Critica sociale*, making it the organ of the socialist intelligentsia. When in 1892 the *Partito socialista italiano* was formed under the Marxian banner, he was the leader with the greatest authority. In 1896 he was elected a deputy to parliament from a working class district in Milan. In 1898 a military tribunal sentenced him to sixteen years' imprisonment. Anna Kuliscioff was sentenced in the same trial to two years' imprisonment. Many other citizens received similar sentences. But at the end of 1899 the government was obliged to free all of those convicted, as a result of the pressure of the voters, who in many cities of Italy elected many of them as deputies and communal councilors.

In the dissensions which divided the right wing from the left wing Socialists in Italy from 1902 to the World War, Turati was the leader of the right wing, or reformist, Socialists. He asserted that the working class must abandon the illusion of revolutionary tactics and adopt the tactics of legal action and gradual conquests. In the economic sphere it should seek to extend and make more effective the network of its unions, cooperative societies and educational institutions. In the political sphere it should seek to gain control of the central Parliament and the local bodies, allying itself with those other parties which might be disposed to respect the liberty of the unions and introduce into Italy a body of social legislation similar to that which already existed in Germany and England. In the international sphere he was a pacifist but conceded that the Socialists must defend their country if it should be attacked. In accordance with these principles he condemned in 1911 the war for the conquest of Libya. When the World War broke out, he wanted the Italian government to associate itself with the other neutral governments in order to impose upon the belligerents the cessation of the slaughter and in May, 1915, he opposed Italy's entry into the war. But after November, 1917, when the country suffered the calamity of the Austrian invasion, he reaffirmed the duty of the Socialists to defend the fatherland. In 1919 and 1920 he vigorously resisted the wave of revolutionary excitement by which the Socialist party was carried away. When this agitation began to subside, at the end of 1920, he found himself overwhelmed by a new wave of violence: that of Fascism. All the institutions which the Italian working class had created in the preceding forty years by his counsel and with his aid were demolished one after the other. In December, 1925, Anna Kuliscioff died. In November, 1926, the Socialist party was declared illegal and the *Critica sociale* suppressed. In December, 1926, ill and menaced by arrest, he evaded from Italy by night in a small motor boat, which carried him in a tempestuous sea from the coast of Liguria to Corsica. He died in Paris.

GAETANO SALVEMINI

Consult: Lazzeri, Gerolamo, *Filippo Turati* (Milan 1921); Rosselli, Carlo, "Filippo Turati in *Giustizia libertà*, no. 3. (1932) 1–42; Michels, Roberto, *Storia critica del movimento socialista italiano* (Florence 1921), and *Sozialismus in Italien* (Karlsruhe 1925).

TURGENEV, NIKOLAI IVANOVICH (1789–1871), Russian political and social reformer and writer on finance. Turgenev studied economics and finance at Göttingen under the ardent Smithian Sartorius and between 1813 and 1815, while serving on the civil staff of the anti-Napoleonic coalition, came under the influence of Baron vom Stein. His *Opit teorii nalogov* (Essay on a theory of taxation, St. Petersburg 1818), published after his return to Russia, was the first work on the subject to appear in that country. Its wide acclaim was due to no small extent to the interspersed sections on serfdom, which was by implication shown to be economically inexpedient. In one of the memoranda which he presented to Alexander I during the period (1816–24) of his membership in the imperial bureaucracy Turgenev again pleaded for the amelioration of the status of the serfs. His prominence in the activities of the northern secret societies seems beyond doubt, despite his own testimony to the contrary; and after the unsuccessful revolution which occurred while he was abroad in December, 1825, he was sentenced to death. Henceforth an émigré, living after 1830 in Paris, he became the only articulate liberal critic of the regime of Nicholas I.

After 1825 Turgenev's earlier more compromising attitude toward the serf question became increasingly radical. But while he demanded not only personal emancipation but the allotment of land to the freed serfs and opposed compensation to the expropriated landowners, he differed from the majority of Russian liberals in advocating the restriction of the allotments to parcels of land far smaller than those previously worked by the serfs. He foresaw with equanimity that the emancipated peasantry would constitute an agricultural proletariat. The essential moderation of his entire political and social outlook, at least in his mature years, is manifest in his memoirs, *La Russie et les Russes* (3 vols., Paris 1847), which like his diary, *Arkhiv bratev Turgenevikh* (Archives of the brothers Turgenev, 6 vols., St. Petersburg 1911–21), constitutes a valuable historical document. In the former work he insists that the introduction of representative government and of civil liberties should come as the culmination of the reform movement and that the immediate objective should be the gradual mitigation of absolutism by the elimination of specific abuses. In addition to the abolition of serfdom his proposed reforms included the strict separation of the judicial system from the administrative, the establishment of jury trial for both criminal and civil cases, the development of a competent legal profession and the abandonment of corporal punishment. In the sphere of administration he stressed particularly the need for local self-government; in public finance he advocated as early as 1818 the substitution of property taxes for the poll and consumption taxes. He followed the Smithian doctrines in condemning limitations upon free trade but on the other hand objected to any attempt to promote the conversion of Russia into an industrial and commercial nation.

V. GELESNOFF

Consult: Wischnitzer, Markus, *Die Universität Göttingen und die Entwicklung der liberalen Ideen in Russland*, Historische Studien, no. 58 (Berlin 1907), and "Nikolaj Turgenews politische Ideale" in *Beiträge zur russischen Geschichte*, ed. by Otto Hoetzsch (Berlin 1907) p. 214–40; Masaryk, T. G., *Russland und Europa*, 2 vols. (Jena 1913), tr. by E. and C. Paul as *The Spirit of Russia* (London 1919) vol. i, especially p. 127–28; Kornilov, A. A., *Ocherki po istorii obshchestvennago dvizheniya i krestyanskago dela v Rossii* (Essays on the history of the social movement and the peasant question in Russia) (St. Petersburg 1905) p. 1–118.

TURGOT, ROBERT JACQUES (1727–81), French statesman and economist. Turgot was born in Paris. He studied theology at the Sorbonne but in 1750 abandoned the cassock for a judicial career. He held successively the posts of deputy counselor to the procureur general, counselor to the Parlement and *maître des requêtes*. From this period of his life date his relations with the *encyclopédistes* and physiocrats. His first published economic writing was a letter to the abbé of Cicé in 1749, which was a criticism of Law's views on paper money. Turgot studied intensively the most diverse subjects, frequented the most celebrated salons of his time, published two letters on toleration, which made quite a stir, collaborated on the *Encyclopédie* and translated into French the works of Josiah Tucker. He became intimate with Gournay, from whom he got his ideas on freedom of enterprise, and with François Quesnay, whose theory of the *produit net* profoundly influenced the ideas of the future minister. Turgot, however, cannot be considered a pure physiocrat. His most comprehensive work on economics was his *Réflexions sur la formation et la distribution des richesses*, which was written in 1766 but first published in the *Éphémérides* in 1769–70 (tr. into English, London 1898). This work may be placed beside that of Quesnay as the first scientific exposition of political economy. It was written nine years before Adam Smith's *Wealth of Nations*, and the extent to which it influenced the illustrious Englishman is difficult to determine. It is undeniable, however, that many of Smith's ideas, such as division and productivity of labor, freedom of enterprise, competition and the like, are mentioned explicitly by Turgot.

In 1761 Turgot was named intendant of Limoges; his reforms in that city were incalculable. He improved the system of tax collection, constructed new roads, increased the facilities for grain trading, established freedom for the exercise of certain professions, created bureaus of charity and increased educational facilities. These reforms brought him such renown that upon the advent of Louis xvi he was raised to power by enthusiastic public opinion.

In July, 1774, he was named secretary of state for the navy and soon thereafter comptroller general of finance. Upon entering the latter office he was confronted with an almost hopeless situation. Refusing to resort to bankruptcy, which several of his predecessors had found convenient, he attempted to save the state without increasing taxes and without further borrowing. By a policy of strict economies he prosecuted abuses, abolished privileges, sought to substitute a tax administration for the farming out system and succeeded in reducing the deficit. On September 13, 1774, he abolished grain restrictions so that grain could circulate freely throughout France. The coincidence of a bad harvest, however, caused public opinion to oppose this measure and gave rise to widespread pilfering. Despite growing dissatisfaction Turgot set out to push his ideas to the limit. After having recommended in a memoir to the king the organization of municipalities, which would bring about the cooperation of all the citizens in provincial and local administration, he presented in January, 1776, several decrees which were promulgated despite the resistance of Parlement and the privileged groups. The most important of these abolished the trade corporations, restoring the free exercise of industrial and commercial professions, and suppressed the corvée, which worked hardships only on the peasants, attempting to distribute taxation among all orders. On May 12, 1776, under pressure from the exasperated privileged groups Louis xvi asked for Turgot's dismissal. Most of his measures were revoked almost immediately upon his retirement from public life.

It is difficult to say whether or not Turgot's work, if he had been allowed to carry it to completion, might have prevented the financial bankruptcy of the old regime. By virtue of the soundness of his doctrines and the purity of his motives, however, Turgot occupies today an honored place among the great ministers of France.

PAUL HARSIN

Works: *Oeuvres*, ed. by P. S. Dupont de Nemours, 9 vols. (Paris 1808–11; new ed. by G. Schelle, 5 vols., 1913–23).

Consult: Neymarck, Alfred, *Turgot et ses doctrines*, 2 vols. (Paris 1885); Feilbogen, S., *Smith und Turgot* (Vienna 1892); *The Life and Writings of Turgot*, ed. by W. W. Stephens (London 1895); Say, Léon, *Turgot* (2nd ed. Paris 1891), tr. by M. B. Anderson (Chicago 1888); Fengler, Otto, *Die Wirtschaftspolitik Turgots und seiner Zeitgenossen im Lichte der Wirtschaft des Ancien Régime* (Leipsic 1912); Lafont, Jean, *Les idées économiques de Turgot*, Université de Bordeaux, Faculté de Droit (Bordeaux 1912); Shepherd, R. P., *Turgot and the Six Edicts*, Columbia University, Studies in History, Economics and Public Law, no. xlvii (New York 1903); Higgs, Henry, *The Physiocrats* (London 1897) p. 91–97; Lodge, E. C., *Sully, Colbert, and Turgot* (London 1931) ch. xii.

TURNER, FREDERICK JACKSON (1861–1932), American historian. Turner received his doctorate from Johns Hopkins University in 1890 and was professor of history at the university of his native state of Wisconsin when he presented his famous frontier hypothesis, in an essay entitled "The Significance of the Frontier in American History," at the World's Columbian Exposition in 1893. He served as president of the American Historical Association in 1910 and in the same year accepted a chair in history at Harvard University. Upon his retirement from Harvard in 1924 Turner returned to Madison, Wisconsin, to live; three years later, however, he became a research associate of the Henry E. Huntington Library at San Marino, California, and there Turner remained until his death in 1932.

In his essay "The Significance of the Frontier

in American History" Turner suggested that the development of the United States through three centuries owed much to a unique factor in its environment, namely, an accessible area of usable farm land which might easily be possessed by the individual farmer of small means. Along the frontier separating the land under plow from the area unoccupied by whites—the "hither edge of free land," as he called it—occurred the social processes of American growth. Here, as nowhere else in recorded history, the individual set up institutions relatively free from coercion by either law or habit. The uniform conditions of poverty and hard work created an atmosphere favorable to the development of democracy. Also in the absence of antecedent society the frontier became a social laboratory in which old institutions were tested and new experiments were tried. The significance of this analysis of frontier forces was appreciated at once, almost without critical test, and Turner was for the rest of his life a recognized leader in historical research and interpretation. It can be said with justice that in the forty years following its enunciation a great part of the writing of American history was reorganized around Turner's frontier hypothesis.

Never a voluminous writer, Turner nevertheless produced for the American Nation Series one of its most original volumes, *The Rise of the New West* (New York 1906), in which he set forth the play of sectional forces in the period 1820 to 1830; and he left at his death in almost finished form *The United States, 1830–1850: The Nation and Its Sections* (New York 1933). In his later years Turner's studies were broadened to cover American sectionalisms of all kinds as well as the social forces deriving from them. A volume of his monographs and articles was printed as *The Frontier in American History* (New York 1920); and posthumously there appeared a second volume of similar reprints, *The Significance of Sections in American History* (New York 1932), which was awarded the Pulitzer Prize for history for 1932.

FREDERIC L. PAXSON

Consult: Becker, Carl, "Frederick Jackson Turner" in *American Masters of Social Science*, ed. by H. W. Odum (New York 1927) ch. ix; Curti, Merle E., "The Section and the Frontier in American History: the Methodological Concepts of F. J. Turner" in *Methods in Social Science*, ed. by S. A. Rice (Chicago 1931) p. 253–67; Paxson, F. L., "A Generation of the Frontier Hypothesis, 1893–1932" in *Pacific Historical Review*, vol. ii (1933) 34–51; Hacker, L. M., "Sections—or Classes" in *Nation*, vol. cxxxvii (1933) 108–10.

TURNER, JAMES MILTON (1840–1915), American Negro leader. Born on a plantation near St. Louis, Missouri, Turner was delivered from slavery in his fourth year on payment of $50 by his father, a veterinarian, who previously had freed himself. He showed interest in schooling and at the age of fourteen enjoyed a rare privilege for a member of his race at that time—enrolment in the preparatory department of Oberlin College.

Education of Negroes was his first concern. In 1866, a year after the Missouri constitution had provided that Negroes should be taught in public schools, he was employed as a teacher by the Kansas City school board. During the Civil War, while a servant to a Union officer, he had promoted the idea of an educational institution for Negroes. This was realized in the establishment of Lincoln Institute at Jefferson City—now the state supported Lincoln University—for which Turner solicited funds and acted as trustee.

An eloquent speaker, Turner quickly became a political leader of his people and in 1871, on appointment by Grant, went to Liberia as minister resident, the first Negro to hold a diplomatic post. Serving at Monrovia until 1878, he strongly advised philanthropists against sending colonies of American Negroes to Liberia. He observed that they were unable to stand the climate and he held that the way to help Liberia was to assist native tribes. He was an able writer and his dispatches from Liberia gave a vivid picture of the turbulent conditions there in the 1870's.

Upon his return to the United States Turner took up the claims of the freedmen of several Indian nations to a share in congressional grants. An appropriation of $75,000 for Cherokee freedmen in 1889 was largely the result of his work as their representative. Although his name is virtually forgotten even by his own race, Turner was a significant contributor to Negro advancement in the early years of emancipation, and he himself was one of those who left his slave origin farthest behind.

IRVING DILLIARD

Consult: Dilliard, Irving, "James Milton Turner: a Little Known Benefactor of His People" in *Journal of Negro History*, vol. xix (1934) no. 4.

TYLER, MOSES COIT (1835–1900), American historian. Tyler graduated from Yale College and entered the ministry, which, however, he soon abandoned. After a period of uncertainty he found his true vocation when he was appointed in 1867 to the faculty of the University of Michigan, where with interruptions he served as professor of English literature until 1881; from that year until his death he was professor of American history at Cornell University. Tyler's importance in the historical field is to be attributed to his masterly surveys of the early periods of American literature: *A History of American Literature during the Colonial Time* (2 vols., New York 1878; new ed. 1897) and *The Literary History of the American Revolution* (2 vols., New York 1897; vol. i, 2nd ed. 1898). These four volumes first applied to American literary history the technique and critical examination of sources characteristic of the best German scholarship of the period. With less success they sought to discover in the explication of American cultural history interpretative formulae determining the thought of the writers. In this respect the influence of Buckle upon Tyler was strong. It was his intention not to write "mere" literary history, but to trace tendencies of thought expressive of the social milieu; Tyler believed that "a spirit of the age" ruled "the evolution of the events of the age" and used statesmen and writers "as the tide uses chips that are carried upon its top." Admiration for the critical methods of Sainte-Beuve kept Tyler from the oversimplification of literary history found in Taine. As history was for his generation mainly political narrative, economic motives are not stressed in his work although they are often implicit. Tyler was especially sound in his treatment of the ideology of the American Tories, but failing to understand economic motivation he misread New England theological development. His power of portrait painting, sympathetic analysis and clear synthesis of ungrateful material is immense.

HOWARD MUMFORD JONES

Other important works: *Patrick Henry*, American Statesmen series (Boston 1887, new ed. 1898); *Three Men of Letters* (New York 1895).

Consult: *Moses Coit Tyler*, ed. by J. T. Austen (New York 1911); Jones, H. M., *The Life of Moses Coit Tyler* (Ann Arbor, Mich. 1933); Casady, T. E., in *Michigan History Magazine*, vol. xiii (1929) 55–73.

TYLOR, SIR EDWARD BURNETT (1832–1917), English anthropologist. Tylor, the father of anthropology in all its British developments, was of Quaker parentage and therefore could not obtain a university education under the then existing regulations. Uncertain health during adolescence caused him to abandon his work in his father's brass foundry and to travel abroad. A casual encounter at Havana in 1856 with Henry Christy, an enthusiast for prehistoric research, led to a tour in Mexico, the fruits of which are embodied in his first book, *Anahuac: or, Mexico and the Mexicans, Ancient and Modern* (London 1861). Four years later in *Researches into the Early History of Mankind* (London 1865; 3rd ed. Boston 1878) he achieved a classic. *Primitive Culture* (2 vols., London 1871; 7th ed. New York 1924), a masterpiece of patient research and luminous exposition, which established Tylor's fame, retains a timeless quality. Those who criticize it for taking savage custom too much at its face value as an expression of living processes, social and mental, rather than as the outcome of historical conditions inevitably resting more on inferences than on positive records have failed to supply an adequate substitute despite the further discoveries of more than sixty years. Tylor did not treat as a fetish a single method of interpreting human life and its many aspects; he stressed the fact that if mankind is to know itself it must study culture, that is, its own efforts at self-cultivation, not piecemeal but as a whole. Beliefs and institutions formed his chief interest and especially in respect to their psychological inspiration. Tylor's name is bound up particularly with his theory of animism as a "bare and meagre definition of a minimum of religion," first enunciated in the *Fortnightly Review* (vol. vi, 1866, p. 71–86) and later developed in *Primitive Culture*. Time has shown that this theory does not cover all the facts relating to the beginnings of mythology and religion, but it nevertheless has furnished a standpoint of commanding outlook, as is seen in its effects in inspiring the work of Frazer and many others. Tylor was likewise a pioneer in the study of cultural distributions and the proofs of contact and diffusion founded thereon; his numerous articles on myths, games, plows, face brasses, Tasmanian implements and American totem poles show unbiased judgment when dealing with questions of independent origin and diffusion. He initiated the application of statistics to the evolutionary treatment of social facts, and his suggestions in his article "On a Method of Investigating the Development of Institutions" (*Journal of the Anthropological Institute*, vol. xviii, 1888–89, p. 245–72) did much to shape the later work of Steinmetz and Hobhouse. Tylor from 1883 until his last years continuously lectured and organized at Oxford; and its

School of Anthropology, the working principles of which have been freely copied elsewhere, owes its inception to him.

R. R. MARETT

Consult: Lang, Andrew, "Edward Burnett Tylor," and bibliography of Tylor's writings by B. Freire-Marreco in *Anthropological Essays Presented to Edward Burnett Tylor*, ed. by N. W. Thomas (Oxford 1907) p. 1–15, and 375–409; Lowie, R. H., "Edward B. Tylor," and Hodgen, M. T., "The Doctrine of Survivals: the History of an Idea" in *American Anthropologist*, vol. xix (1917) 262–68, and vol. xxxiii (1931) 307–24.

TYRANNY. In current usage the word tyranny has no very precise meaning and may be defined simply as an oppressive abuse of power. Where a specific standard of rightful conduct is lacking, the term remains wholly indefinite and is accordingly seldom used, save in a historical connection, by contemporary political scientists. As a historical phenomenon, however, the concept of tyranny commands an interest which is entirely disproportionate to its current scientific significance, for at various times in the past it has been much less nebulous and has played a significant part in the development of political thought and institutions.

The name tyrant was first applied to the series of monocrats who wielded power in many Greek cities in the course of the seventh century B.C. The stress of class warfare and the imminence of barbarian invasion gave rise during this period to recurrent crises which demonstrated the incompetence of the reigning oligarchies, thus placing a premium on the efficiency of one-man rule. Various talented individuals, usually supported by the lower classes, forcibly seized power and established a personal absolutism which dealt effectively with the problems of the moment. The power of the oligarchs was broken, barbarian invaders were repulsed and a tolerable measure of social solidarity was reestablished. Despite their brilliance, however, the reigns of the various tyrants were comparatively brief. Once crucial difficulties had been overcome, the Greek city-state betrayed a persistent tendency to develop along democratic lines; and monocratic rule proved but a transitory stage in Greek constitutional evolution, continuing after the sixth century only in outlying portions of the Hellenic world where barbarian power remained a constant menace. Considered as a historical fact Greek tyranny is simply a rather commonplace instance of the temporary emergence of monocratic rule under the stress of unusually trying circumstances.

In the subsequent democratic period, however, the concept of tyranny began to develop along somewhat unexpected lines. Originally nothing more than a Lydian word for king, the appellation tyrant at first carried no sort of stigma, being used even in the worship of the gods. But since the tyrants were their immediate antagonists, the democrats gradually made the word tyranny the focus of all their hatred of monocratic rule. This hatred found striking expression in the institution of ostracism and in the elevation of tyrannicides to the rank of heroes. Particular emphasis was laid on the fact that the tyrants, unlike the monarchs of the heroic age, had exercised a usurped rather than a legitimate authority. From this point it was but a step to assert that capricious lawlessness was characteristic of the exercise as well as of the origin of tyrannical power. Although many of the great tyrants had been prudent rulers whose authority rested on a broad basis of popular consent, tyranny came to be associated exclusively with the arbitrary abuse of monocratic authority. This established usage was followed both by Plato and by Aristotle, who classified tyranny among the perverse forms of government. Through this historically false identification with selfish and arbitrary rule the word tyrant became an important instrument of democratic propaganda, serving to marshal public opinion against all attempts at the restoration of monocracy.

It was only with the introduction of the doctrine of natural law, however, that the concept of tyranny acquired a systematic philosophical basis. If there exist certain immutable and rationally discoverable principles of justice, the characteristic wickedness of tyranny may be defined in terms of the negation of those principles. This formed the basic criterion of the Platonic and Aristotelian distinction between good and perverse forms of government. Cicero and the stoics followed the same tradition; and wherever the doctrine of natural law persisted, the violation of its principles became one of the primary means of distinguishing tyranny from monarchy. This idea of natural law entered into the writings of the Christian fathers and was variously combined with the more specific precepts of the revealed law of God. In this way the ancient concept of tyranny, supplemented with new religious elements, was handed down to later ages as an integral part of the Christian tradition.

Although the opinions of the fathers exercised the highest authority during the Middle Ages, the mediaeval idea of tyranny was notably modified through the infusion of Germanic elements. The barbarian conquerors of the Roman Empire conceived of law wholly in terms of immemorial custom. Since the idea of creative legislative sovereignty remained virtually non-existent throughout the mediaeval period, traditional systems of customary law seemed to possess an eternal validity wholly comparable with that possessed by the law of nature. It thus became usual to describe as tyrannical not only those actions which transgressed the comparatively nebulous precepts of divine and natural law but also those more readily definable acts contravening the specific provisions of positive law. Thus the concept of tyranny became closely linked with the denial of a specific traditional system of law and government and, as such, was destined to serve as a powerful defense of customary usages against the forces of innovation.

With regard to the practical conclusions to be derived from this principle, however, the writings of the early fathers provided support for two contradictory opinions. St. Gregory was the outstanding advocate of the position that the power even of evil rulers comes from God and must be obeyed under all circumstances. St. Isidore, on the other hand, believed that, inasmuch as the purpose of the state is to maintain justice, the tyrant's failure to serve that end deprives him of all claim upon the obedience of his subjects. Since the absolutist principles of Gregory were fundamentally incompatible with certain basic contractual elements in the Germanic political system, mediaeval political theory tended to lean heavily toward St. Isidore's point of view. Mediaeval kings reigned not simply by hereditary right but also on the basis of election, and the conditions of their appointment were clearly set forth in the coronation oath. It was only natural that power conferred under such terms should be considered to lapse upon failure to fulfil those conditions. An unjust king was therefore generally believed to have forfeited his kingship. In the ordinary usage of mediaeval writers the word tyrant is employed to describe a ruler who either never had or never ceased to have any claim on the obedience of his subjects.

This position gave rise to the celebrated doctrine of tyrannicide. It was generally agreed that a tyrant might be resisted and if necessary put to death. Some writers, most notably John of Salisbury, even advocated private assassination in such cases. A more typical point of view is represented by St. Thomas, who thought that anyone might kill a usurper but that the tyranny of legitimate rulers should be dealt with only by organized public authorities. This points to the fact that various feudal courts and other corporate institutions existed during the Middle Ages alongside the king as legally constituted organs of the community. According to feudal principles it was possible to appeal to them for justice even against the king, and it was upon them that the duty of resisting tyranny and if necessary of deposing tyrants ultimately rested. Remedies against unconstitutional abuses were sought primarily within the framework of legitimate constitutional action.

The concept of tyranny was first raised to a position of central controversial importance during the period of rapid constitutional development which was ushered in by the Renaissance. Sweeping innovations were involved in the creation of the modern territorial state, so that any thoroughgoing devotion to customary law was rendered impracticable. The concept of legislative sovereignty gradually gained currency. Monocratic power was concentrated in the hands of princes, and an appeal was made to the classical tradition of state absolutism through the general reception of Roman law. Many interests were injured by these changes, however, and the religious wars produced dissatisfaction with prevailing state policies on the part of numerous dissentient religious bodies. From these centers of opposition arose an important group of political theorists known as the monarchomachs, who made notable use of the concept of tyranny in their efforts to stem the rising tide of royal absolutism.

Despite the liberal employment of classical allusions the monarchomachs' use of the word tyrant was fundamentally mediaeval in spirit. In the city-states of Italy, to be sure, incessant class warfare had given rise to a horde of usurping monocrats who are comparable to the tyrants of ancient Greece. Their excesses produced a truly republican reaction, and in the *Apologia* of Lorenzino de' Medici, for example, tyrannicide is justified in terms of a devotion to liberty which is antique in spirit as well as in form. The princes with whom the monarchomachs were concerned, however, were generally possessed of an admittedly legitimate authority; and the crucial problem was to prevent, through the maintenance of those constitutional safeguards with which legitimate kingship had traditionally been associated, the tyrannical abuse of that authority. In full accordance with mediaeval usage, tyranny was found to consist primarily in the violation of the law of God (as interpreted by the various religious groups of the period) or of the customary law of the realm. Resistance and even tyrannicide were considered admissible, but at the same time there was a strong preference for action by estates and other constituted organs of the community rather than by irresponsible individuals. In a slightly more classical guise the arguments of mediaeval theologians opposed the current movement toward state absolutism.

The tendency to monocratic centralization ultimately proved too strong for the forces of conservative constitutionalism, and royal absolutism became an almost universal fact. But the victory of the Whigs permitted the ideas of the monarchomachs to persist in England. Preserved most notably in the writings of Locke, the mediaeval concept of tyranny became a source of inspiration for later anti-authoritarian movements. It was used freely by the supporters of the American and less extensively by those of the French Revolution. Through this and other channels the political thought of the Middle Ages exercised profound influence on the formation of modern libertarian ideology. Nevertheless, the importance of the concept of tyranny has decreased steadily since the seventeenth century. Successive generations have been ever less awed by the sanctity of legal tradition, while the disappearance of any general consensus of ethical and religious opinion decreases the significance of natural law. Deprived of its connection with any specific legal or philosophical system, the once potent word tyrant has tended to degenerate into an ill defined term of abuse. The modern word "unconstitutional" most nearly approximates the emotional power of the mediaeval "tyrannical," but with a comparative mildness which marks the decline of traditionalistic forces in modern society. None of the earlier meanings of tyranny can be said to be entirely dead. But the conditions which once made it one of the most potent of political myths have long since passed away.

FREDERICK MUNDELL WATKINS

See: MONARCHY; OLIGARCHY; ABSOLUTISM; AUTOCRACY; DICTATORSHIP; SUCCESSION, POLITICAL; DIVINE RIGHT OF KINGS; MONARCHOMACHS; NATURAL RIGHTS; NATURAL LAW; CONSTITUTIONALISM; SOCIAL CONTRACT; ASSASSINATION; OSTRACISM.

Consult: Wade-Gery, H. T., "The Growth of the Dorian States," and Adcock, F. E., "Athens under the Tyrants" in *Cambridge Ancient History*, vol. iii (Cambridge, Eng. 1925) p. 548–58, and vol. iv (1926) ch. iii; Glotz, Gustave, *La cité grecque* (Paris 1928), tr. by N. Mallinson (London 1929) p. 107–16; Ure, P. N., *The Origin of Tyranny* (Cambridge, Eng. 1922); Barker, Ernest, *The Political Thought of Plato and Aristotle* (London 1906) p. 313–14, 492–96, 515–16; Heintzeler, Gerhard, *Das Bild des Tyrannen bei Platon*, Tübinger Beiträge zur Altertumswissenschaft, no. iii (Stuttgart 1927); Carlyle, R. W. and A. J., *A History of Medieval Political Theory in the West*, vols. i–v (Edinburgh 1903–28) vol. i, chs. xiii–xiv, xvii–xx, vol. ii, pt. i, ch. vii, pt. ii, ch. vii, and vol. v, pt. i, chs. iii–viii; *The Statesman's Book of John of Salisbury*, tr. and ed. by John Dickinson (New York 1927) p. lxvi–lxxx, and bk. viii; *Humanism and Tyranny; Studies in the Italian Trecento*, tr. and ed. by Ephraim Emerton (Cambridge, Mass. 1925) p. 3–21; Ercole, F., *Da Bartolo all' Althusio* (Florence 1932) pt. iv; Burckhardt, J. C., *Die Kultur der Renaissance in Italien* (16th ed. by Walter Goetz, Leipsic 1927), tr. by S. G. C. Middlemore (new ed. London 1929) pt. i, chs. i–iv, vi; Laski, H. J., "Historical Introduction" to his ed. of Languet's *A Defense of Liberty against Tyrants* (London 1924) p. 1–60; Allen, J. W., *A History of Political Thought in the Sixteenth Century* (London 1928) p. 285–92, 302–42; Treumann, Rudolf, *Die Monarchomachen*, Staats- und völkerrechtliche Abhandlungen, vol. i, no. 1 (Leipsic 1895).

TZ'Û HSI (1835–1908), Chinese empress. Of Manchu birth, Tz'û Hsi became a secondary wife of the emperor Hsien Fêng and as his favorite and the mother of the heir to the throne her position was second only to that of the empress consort. After the death of the emperor in 1861 she succeeded in instituting a joint regency with Tz'û An, during the minority of T'ung Chih (1861–72). She governed as sole regent from the time of T'ung Chih's death in 1875 until 1889, when Kuang Hsü, whom she had placed on the throne, attained his majority. During the period of the latter's nominal rule the "Old Buddha," as Tz'û Hsi was popularly called, retained control over the appointment and dismissal of officials. Her coup d'état of 1898 directed against Kuang Hsü and his reforms was successful, and thereafter until her death she ruled China in the name of the emperor.

As a ruler Tz'û Hsi possessed undoubted gifts, maintaining Manchu authority in the face of widespread rebellion and difficult foreign relations. Her limitations were set by her confinement to the palace, her completely classical education and her inability to shake off prevalent superstitious beliefs. Under her rule the evil of interference in public affairs by eunuchs, with the concomitant traffic in offices, reached a high point and weakened the Manchu position correspondingly. Her inherent autocracy and conservatism made it difficult for her to appreciate adequately the new forces which were at work and to use them to strengthen and modernize China. In this respect her natural tendencies were confirmed by the hostility to foreigners engendered by her experiences after 1861. When she regained control of the government in 1898 she made a desperate attempt to withstand foreign economic and political penetration and to restore the old Chinese system of decentralization in administration. The failure of the Boxer movement, which she supported in part because her superstitions caused her to overestimate its possibilities of success, convinced her, however, of the necessity of changes along western lines. Accordingly, despite her natural inclinations, she undertook to reform the civil service and the traditional educational system and even promised a constitutional government. Lack of confidence in the sincerity of her professions was one factor in the development of revolutionary opposition. Tz'û Hsi's guiding principle, divide and rule, carried out by the balancing of appointments between Manchus and Chinese and between important Chinese factions, aided the maintenance of Manchu rule—perhaps beyond its time. As her autocratic tendencies were confirmed by prolonged rule, however, she departed from the principle, and her disregard of the southern faction in particular strengthened anti-Manchu feeling and thus promoted the revolution of 1911.

HAROLD M. VINACKE

Consult: Bland, J. O. P., and Backhouse, E., *China under the Empress Dowager* (London 1910); Steiger, G. N., *China and the Occident* (New Haven 1927), especially chs. v–vi.

ULLOA, BERNARDO DE (died 1740), Spanish economist. Ulloa's only extant work, *Restablecimiento de las fábricas y comercio español* (Madrid 1740), falls into common mercantilist errors. Although he grasped the quantity theory of money, he outlined an economic policy whose objective was the retention of American treasure and the acquisition of gold and silver from foreign countries by a favorable balance of trade. He asserted that foreigners despoiled Spain of its wealth by exchanging goods for specie. Likening looms to a magnet for the precious metals, Ulloa advanced measures for the revival of the textile and other industries, such as removal of internal trade barriers, improvement of transportation and drastic revision of the rates and abolition of the farming of customs duties. Holding a subsistence theory of wages, Ulloa believed that the competitive position of Spanish manufacturers would be improved by a reduction of taxes on the necessaries of laborers. With the exception of iron, which was abundant in Spain, he urged lower duties on imported raw materials, even if this involved competition with native grown staples; he advocated raising the duties on all other imports "to the highest level possible under the terms of treaties." Only nominal duties should be placed upon exports of textiles and other manufactures. In contrast with Uztáriz' program for the revival of shipping Ulloa proposed to reorganize the fleet system for American trade; to establish differential duties on goods carried in native bottoms; and, by terminating the asientos—exclusive trade concessions—in slaves and tobacco to foreigners who used such privileges as a cover for general smuggling, to check interloping, which he considered as deserving of the death penalty as counterfeiting. He suggested measures for stimulating fisheries, not only to prevent the drain of specie resulting from the consumption of foreign fish but to develop able seamen. Accepting Uztáriz' view that depopulation did not cause the decline of manufactures but that the neglect of industry led to a reduction of population, Ulloa faced the problem of a drop in population in the West Indies as a consequence of rigid prohibitions against the establishment of manufactures. His conviction that this market should be maintained intact for Spanish goods prevented him from suggesting a more effective remedy than the cultivation of spices in America.

ROBERT S. SMITH

Consult: Wirminghaus, Alexander, *Zwei spanische Merkantilisten*, Sammlung nationalökonomischer und statistischer Abhandlungen des Staatswissenschaftlichen Seminars zu Halle, vol. iv, no. 2 (Jena 1886).

ULLSTEIN FAMILY, German publishers. The publishing enterprise of the Ullstein family was among the largest in the world. Its founder, Leopold Ullstein (1826–99), was the son of a Bavarian wholesale paper merchant. In 1848 Leopold settled in Berlin; he opened his own wholesale paper business, served for six years as a liberal member of the Berlin municipal assembly and in 1877 bought the newly founded *Neues Berliner Tageblatt*. In the same year he formed the Ullstein Aktiengesellschaft. Shortly thereafter he took over the *Berliner Zeitung* and merged it with the *Tageblatt* to form a thoroughly liberal organ, whose democratic attitude quickly won many subscribers. One of its relatively novel features, at least for Germany, was the policy of illustrating the paper and of issuing special supplements. The chief editorial writer was Hans Ullstein, son of the founder, who was trained as a lawyer. It was under his direction, while he was a member of the left wing of the liberal group in the Berlin municipal assembly, that the paper adopted a sharply critical tone and was frequently suppressed by the government. In 1887 the *Berliner Abendpost*, appealing especially to provincial readers, was founded. In 1894 the *Berliner illustrirte Zeitung* was acquired; this paper was to become Germany's greatest picture newspaper, with a circulation of 1,800,000. In September, 1898, there first appeared the *Berliner Morgenpost*. Designed by the Ullsteins as a typical democratic paper for the petty bourgeoisie, it achieved the largest circulation of all German papers.

Leopold Ullstein's five sons developed the business further after his death. Each of the brothers took charge of a special sphere of the work. In October, 1904, the *Berliner Zeitung* first began to publish an extra noon edition, the *B. Z. am Mittag*, which became the largest and most popular midday paper of Germany. In 1906 the *Berliner allgemeine Zeitung* was taken over, and in 1913 the *Vossische Zeitung*, the oldest newspaper of Berlin and one of Germany's leading journals, was acquired. Beginning in 1927 the firm published the *Grüne Post*, a Sunday sheet for rural readers; every issue was soon selling more than 1,000,000 copies.

All the Ullstein papers expounded a decidedly liberal and democratic policy, and after the revolution of 1918 they were extremely powerful forces in the life of the Weimar republic. With the National Socialist overturn of March, 1933, however, there was a marked transformation in the policies of every Ullstein newspaper. All the former important editors who were close to the republican parties were forced out of the organization, which was "coordinated" with the Nazi regime.

In addition to political newspapers the firm of Ullstein published a great chain of periodicals devoted to the household, fashions, the fine arts and science, and various engineering and trade journals. The Ullstein book publishing department was likewise an important enterprise. It popularized contemporary literature by means of the cheap *Ullsteinbuch*. The Propyläen-Verlag owned by the house of Ullstein led in the publication of fine editions; its history of fine art became a standard in that field. The works of well known composers were popularized through the periodical *Musik für Alle*. Instruction in languages was given through a series of books which won wide popularity throughout Germany. In May, 1934, the Ullstein family sold its interests in the firm.

On its fiftieth anniversary in 1927 the house of Ullstein employed a total of over 8000 people, among whom were 200 editors, while the Ullstein news agency had some 250 correspondents throughout the world. The Ullsteins rode the crest of the great tide of popular enlightenment which swept Germany after the 1850's. In addition to the use of the most modern technical and commercial methods their success was based on an extraordinary gift for understanding and meeting middle class needs.

KURT ZIELENZIGER

Consult: *50 Jahre Ullstein, 1877–1927* (Berlin 1927); Buchholtz, Arend, *Vossische Zeitung* (Berlin 1904).

ULPIAN (died 228), Roman jurist. Ulpian, whose Roman name was Domitius Ulpianus, was born at Tyre or at least was of Tyrian stock. He is first mentioned as a member of the council of the jurist Papinian (203?–11). Ulpian occupied the highest legal post at Rome from 222 until his death and was the constant companion and adviser of the emperor Alexander Severus; but even his prominence did not protect him from death at the hands of the praetorian guard, whose enmity he had incurred.

All of Ulpian's juristic writings seem to have been penned in the reign of Caracalla (211–17). His great commentaries upon the praetorian and civil law, the *Libri ad edictum* and the *Libri ad Masurium Sabinum* are particularly significant; the former was a complete treatment of Julian's Perpetual Edict; both works were filled with innumerable citations and extracts from earlier jurists. Among his didactic works was the *Responsa*, a collection of cases from Ulpian's own activity as a jurist. There are also two elementary law works of merit entitled *Libri regularum*. One of these, a "single book," is known from a manuscript work to be dated shortly after 320; Arangio Ruiz has recently attempted to show that this was nothing more than an epitome of a second edition of Gaius' Institutes rather than a work of Ulpian largely based on Gaius, as had previously been held. Albertario has advanced the view that it was an epitome of various writings of Ulpian, but Schulz seems to have found favor with the view that it is not a collection of fragments of one or more classical jurists but a postclassical recasting of classical texts. Ulpian, who seems to have contemplated covering the whole field of Roman law, is further noted for his many writings upon the various offices, particularly his *De omnibus tribunalibus*, and for his monographs, for example, *De fideicommissis*.

The view has long prevailed that Ulpian marked the beginning of the decadence of the classical Roman law; it has been said that he was nothing more than a compiler. Pernice has gone so far as to say that Ulpian's work was not even a mosaic. Jörs, however, has pointed out that Pernice limited his study to the *Libri ad edictum* and that there is a relative scarcity of citation of others in Ulpian's works on the various magistrates. Even in his commentaries, although these are compilations from the older writers, Ulpian had to choose the view he favored and support it with recent decisions and legislative materials. Moreover Ulpian did not use any one author at length but employed rather a small number of works as prime sources, consulting in the original a great number of other works. No other jurist has such a wealth of material from various sources, and a good part of this must be credited to Ulpian's own research. It is true, however, that Ulpian had neither the creative ability of Labeo or Julian nor the acumen of Papinian. Yet it is beyond doubt that he was well thought of in postclassical times; one third of the whole Digest of Justinian consists of extracts from his works.

A. ARTHUR SCHILLER

Consult: Jörs, P., "Domitius" in *Paulys Real-Encyclopädie der classischen Altertumswissenschaft*, ed. by Georg Wissowa and Wilhelm Kroll, vol. v (new ed. Stuttgart 1905) cols. 1435–1509; Krüger, P., *Geschichte der Quellen und Litteratur des römischen Rechts*, Systematisches Handbuch der deutschen Rechtswissenschaft, vol. i, pt. ii (2nd ed. Munich 1912) p. 239–50, 280–82; Ledlie, J. C., in *Great Jurists of the World*, ed. by J. Macdonell and E. Manson, Continental Legal History series, vol. ii (Boston 1914) p. 32–44; Pernice, A., "Ulpian als Schriftsteller" in Preussische Akademie der Wissenschaften, *Sitzungsberichte*, (1885) 443–84; Roby, H. J., *An Introduction to the Study of Justinian's Digest* (Cambridge, Eng. 1886) p. cxcvi–cci; Arangio Ruiz, V., "Sul' liber singularis regularum," and Albertario, E., "Tituli ex corpore Ulpiani" in Istituto di Diritto Romano, Rome, *Bolettino*, vol. xxx (1921) 178–219, and vol. xxxii (1922) 73–130; *Die Epitome Ulpiani des Codex Vaticanus Reginae 1128*, ed. by F. Schulz, Juristische Texte für Vorlesungen und Übungen, no. 3 (Bonn 1926) p. 1–21.

ULYANOV, VLADIMIR ILICH (Nikolay Lenin) (1870–1924), Russian revolutionary leader and social philosopher. Lenin has unassailable claims to be regarded as the greatest practical revolutionary in modern history.

The son of an inspector of schools and of the daughter of a small landowner, he was one of a family of six children, all of whom devoted themselves to the Russian Revolution; his eldest brother was hanged in 1887 for his share in an abortive conspiracy against Alexander III. Lenin was educated at the universities of Kazan and St. Petersburg, from the latter of which he graduated; and he was called to the bars of Samara and St. Petersburg, although he never practised. From his arrival in St. Petersburg in 1893 until his death his life was that of a professional revolutionary devoted to the cause of proletarian emancipation.

His career may be usefully divided into four periods. In the first (1893–1900) he was serving his apprenticeship to the revolution. At this time he acquired his extraordinary knowledge of Marxian theory, his remarkable insight into the mentality of the Russian proletariat and the peasantry, his experience of imprisonment and Siberian exile (1895–1900) and his conviction that the revolutionary party should be dominated by a trained group of professional revolutionists whose one objective was to be leadership in the inevitable proletarian revolution. In this period also his outstanding qualities became widely known to his contemporaries and his position in the front rank was universally recognized. In 1900 he was sent abroad for organizational and propaganda purposes by the Russian Social Democratic party and he remained in western Europe, save for a brief return during the revolution of 1905, until the great events of 1917.

In the first period Lenin was one of those who fought strongly for a socialist party free from the peasant romanticism of the *narodniki* and the paralyzing theory of proletarian "spontaneity," which made the "economists" futile as leaders of a revolution. The second period of his life (1900–03) may be described as one in which he was fighting to transform the Social Democratic party into a rigorous and disciplined instrument of proletarian revolution that would not compromise with any victory short of the full Marxian demand. This involved the conflict of 1903, when at the London conference of the party he split it, winning a temporary majority on the Central Committee, which he lost, largely through the defection of Plekhanov, almost immediately afterwards. From that conference dates the foundation of the Bolshevik party. By this time Lenin had become the acknowledged leader of the extreme left of the revolutionaries, and all the energies of his mind were devoted to the single task of making his group an adequate instrument for the purposes he had in view.

The third period of his life (1903–17) was concerned with the direction of his group, the adjustment of its attitude to the revolution of 1905, to the experience of the Duma and to the implications of the World War. His leadership in the revolution, which he saw at once could not successfully assume a socialist character, was marked by his perception of two principles vital to his later thinking. First, only the working class was a genuine revolutionary force; the bourgeoisie, both great and small, would end the revolution as soon as czardom was overthrown. It was necessary therefore to break with the bourgeoisie once it was victorious and go on to the proletarian revolution. Second, the peasants were a united class only against the landowners; once czarism was overthrown, they would divide into rich and poor, and the latter could be made the natural allies of the industrial proletariat. Lenin also drew from the revolution of 1905 the inference that the dividing line between his party and the other socialist groups was a decisive one. The latter took the view that revolution grows from below and that socialists cannot impose their leadership upon it. Lenin, on the contrary, insisted that the defeat of the czar would be followed by an era of civil dissension the outcome of which would be decided by the quality of leadership in the contending parties, granted only that the material for proletarian revolution was there. The non-Bolshevik socialists, that is, would exert pressure on a liberal bourgeois government without hoping to extract more than concessions from it. Lenin's policy was built on the belief that a united and determined socialist party could conquer power.

The defeat of the revolution of 1905 seemed to make these discussions academic, although Lenin did not at once acknowledge defeat. From 1905 to 1914 his energies were largely absorbed in seeking a basis of socialist reunion upon the common ground (admitted after the failure) of the need for armed insurrection and in devising the strategy of the Bolshevik fraction in the Duma. He stayed in Russia and Finland from 1905 to 1907; but thenceforward he was in exile again and the years of exile were difficult. He had to face criticism from the Mensheviks, who could not understand his resolute refusal to pursue opportunist tactics through the Bolshevik representatives in the Duma, and, on the other hand, attack from within his own party, led by Bogdanov and Lunacharsky, which urged boycott of the Duma (failing to realize, as he did, its value as a platform from which to address the working class) and sought on philosophic grounds to transform the metaphysical basis of socialism from materialism to a form of Kantian idealism. The years from 1907 to 1914 were important to Lenin for two reasons. On the one hand, through his relations with the Bolshevik working men in the Duma he became widely known to the revolutionary industrial proletariat; and, on the other, by his defeat of the attempted revisionism in debate, although only after a long and difficult struggle, he immensely strengthened his grasp upon the essentials of revolutionary theory and consolidated beyond challenge his leadership of the party.

Keen as was his interest in European socialism (he had attended three of the international congresses and was a Russian representative from 1907 to 1914 on the International Socialist Bureau) Lenin was absorbed by Russian problems in the years before the outbreak of the war; and his part in the European movement had been largely confined to supporting the effort of Rosa Luxemburg at the Stuttgart conference in 1912, who insisted that the duty of socialists in the event of war was, as Marx had always maintained, to seek to transform a war between nations into a civil war. He was naturally therefore profoundly chagrined by the chauvinism displayed by most socialists, including even Plekhanov, in 1914. He insisted at once that the Second International was dead; and from then on his effort was directed toward the building of a new international which should seek the realization of socialist principles.

From 1914 until his return to Russia after the February revolution Lenin's mind was occupied with two things. On the one hand, he was clear that the war would bring revolution, especially in Russia, in its train and sought to prepare for it; on the other, he worked feverishly to bring home to socialists his view of the war as simply the expression of the inherent contradictions of capitalism in its imperialist phase. From his activities (on the formal initiative of the Italian socialists) proceeded the two famous conferences of Zimmerwald (1915) and Kienthal (1916) which defined the Communist attitude to the war. Without direct effect, save that they led Liebknecht to the formation of the Spartakusbund in Germany, the conferences were nevertheless of decisive importance, because they not only provided the basis upon which the Third International was founded in 1919 but declared a frontal attack on those socialists who displayed patriotic leanings during the war. It was in his remarkable research into the nature of economic imperialism during these years that Lenin discovered the formulae of that world revolution to whose imminence he began confidently to look forward.

The revolution of February, 1917, proceeded along the lines Lenin had always predicted. Although it was followed by the wide creation of councils of soldiers and workmen or peasants (soviets), power although in semi-anarchic conditions was effectively in the hands of the bourgeoisie; and they were supported by the Menshevik leaders of the soviets on the ground, which had always been the basis of their outlook, that a bourgeois revolution must necessarily precede the transition to the socialist state. The Menshevik leaders demanded a "democratic peace without annexations or indemnities"; but they were prepared to continue the war in the belief that the revolution must be defended against German aggression, and they were prepared to postpone all economic reforms until a constituent assembly had decided upon a form of government for the new Russia.

Lenin was not able to return to Russia at once; he was on the blacklist of the Allies, and although the soviets demanded his return, it appears that the Russian Foreign Office showed less than friendliness to its facilitation. After the discussion of many plans a left wing Swiss socialist, Platten, persuaded the German authorities to transport him (with other émigrés) back to Russia in a sealed train in the belief that the return of the international socialists would injure the prospect of further fighting by Russia. Lenin accepted the offer and arrived in Petrograd in April, 1917. It was this journey which led to the foolish accusation, for some weeks a serious weapon against him, that Lenin was in the pay of Germany.

Once Lenin was back, his leadership of the Bolsheviks was beyond question. He persuaded the party to adopt his view of the war, to insist that "a democratic peace was impossible without the overthrow of capitalism." The immediate task in Russia was the transfer of power to the workers and the poor peasants. The Provisional Government was capitalist and must be overthrown. The soviets were the nucleus of a new revolutionary order, and they must be used (although socialism could not be introduced at once) to confiscate the land in favor of the peasants, to nationalize the banks and to control production and distribution.

During the months from April until October, 1917, while often in hiding from the Kerensky government, not seldom in danger of his life, opposed by all socialists outside his party and not a few of the most distinguished within it, he never wavered in the views he held. His was the policy and his was the strategy that made the Bolsheviks the one party in the chaos of Russian politics which both knew its own mind and could convey its purposes to a people anxious above all for peace, bread and the land. He saw that the continuance of the Kerensky government endangered the very existence of the revolution, that unless it was overthrown democracy in Russia would simply become the capitalist democracy of the Allies; from his angle therefore the revolution would be deprived of its essential significance. He therefore devoted all his energies to persuading his party to seize power. Events were on his side. The Kornilov revolt, the risings of the peasantry against the Provisional Government, the increasing strength of the Bolsheviks as displayed in election returns, all indicated that mastery in the state would pass to Lenin's party. Consummately planned, its attack on the Kerensky government was successful almost without loss of life. On October 25, 1917, Lenin found himself installed as the head of the Bolshevik government; he remained the head of the Russian state until his death in 1924.

The last seven years of Lenin's life were on any showing remarkable. His realistic insight brought the revolution successfully through the war, the long and costly period of intervention (1918–21) and the famine. If the price was enormous, he nevertheless fulfilled his promise to the people—peace and the land for the peasants. Certain of his achievements, the courage which compelled the signing of the Brest Litovsk Treaty (1918) and the objective sagacity which determined upon the temporary retreat of the New Economic Policy in 1921 are now recognized as measures of statesmanship of the first order. In the fields of culture and of industrial organization, in party direction, in the solution of national problems within the Soviet Union, he showed unexampled fertility and resource of mind. His only error, if it can be called an error, was his excessive faith in the proximity of European revolution. He undoubtedly underestimated the power of capitalism in western countries to recover from so momentous a blow as the war. But his title to be considered the most remarkable architect of Russian history is from any angle beyond discussion.

Lenin is likely to remain for many years the outstanding figure in the history of socialism. His grasp of doctrine was unsurpassed; and as the strategist of revolution no difference of view can conceal the fact that he was unequaled. Remarkable as were many of the men who aided him, above all Trotsky and Stalin, his preeminence among them was unchallenged. No doubt he was able to exploit historic conditions that were unique; but his genius is shown by the unerring power with which he took instant and complete advantage of those conditions.

His writings have been preserved with great fulness. Distinction of style they do not possess. But they display a clarity, a realistic insight, a power of weighing men and ideas, unsurpassed by anyone in the revolutionary tradition. Some of them, especially the famous *Gosudarstvo i revolutsiya* (Petrograd 1918, tr. as *State and Revolution*, London 1919), already have a permanent place in political literature. He was less an originator of ideas than a great architect of their application. From this angle none of his works, not even his brief letters, are insignificant. Together they form a textbook of revolutionary practise more formidable than the work of any other man.

The secret of his character lay in a number of qualities. Above all he had iron courage and endless resolution. He was wholly devoid of personal ambition. He had a power which amounted to genius for working with types as different as Trotsky and Stalin and imposing himself upon them without creating resentment. While not a great orator, he had a forcible directness in speech to the power of which endless observers have borne testimony. Devotion, singlemindedness, a sense of the movement of mind in ordinary people, the ability to blend theory and practise into coherent and decisive policy—these become more obvious the more carefully his achievement is studied.

The core of his doctrine may be described as the quintessence of Marxism projected into the imperialist epoch. It assumes the inevitability of violent revolution, in which the workers are directed by a party of trained revolutionaries, the dictatorship of the proletariat, the ruthless destruction of all attempts at counter-revolution, the maintenance of dictatorship until the transition to complete socialism has been effected. Lenin believed that the shattering of the bourgeois state apparatus (civil service, police, judiciary, armed forces) is inescapably necessary and that the Soviet system would take the place of parliamentary government, which he regarded as useless for revolutionary ends since it expressed the needs of the bourgeoisie. He assumed that socialism would be born of an epoch of imperialist wars, each of which would require transformation in the country of each participant into a civil war. He regarded the present phase of capitalism as the one in which its contradictions had become finally manifest. The building of communist parties therefore was the necessary prelude to the successful achievement of revolution. Social Democrats he looked upon as the allies of capitalism; and he was prepared to cooperate with them only up to the point where their own accession to power made more effectively possible the movement to the final struggle.

Whether one agrees or disagrees with his principles, it is clear that he is likely to remain one of the half dozen supreme figures in modern history; for from a Russia in chaos he built a powerful modern state upon foundations strong enough to make it a decisive challenge to capitalist civilization.

HAROLD J. LASKI

Works: *Sochineniya*, 30 vols. (2nd-3rd ed. Moscow 1926-32), authorized English translation, vols. iv, xiii, xviii, xx-xxi (New York 1927-33). For a complete bibliography of English, German and French translations of Lenin's writings, see: Institut Lenina, Moscow, *Lenin na inostrannikh yazikakh* (Lenin in foreign languages), ed. by M. A. Savelev (Leningrad 1931).

Consult: Krupskaya, N., *Vospominaniya o Lenine* (new ed. Moscow 1932), tr. by E. Verney as *Memories of Lenin*, 2 vols. (London 1930); Yaroslavsky, E., *Zhizn i rabota Lenina* (Life and work of Lenin) (5th ed. Leningrad 1926); "Arkhivnie dokumenti k biografii V. I. Lenina" (Archive documents for the biography of Lenin) in *Krasny arkhiv*, vol. lxii (1934) 53-248; Fox, Ralph W., *Lenin; a Biography* (London 1933); Stalin, I. V., *Voprosi Leninisma* (9th ed. Moscow 1933), tr. by E. and C. Paul as *Leninism*, 2 vols. (London 1932-33); Trotsky, L., *Lenin* (London 1925); Dutt, R. Palme, *The Life and Teachings of V. I. Lenin* (New York 1934); Mirsky, D. S., *Lenin* (Boston 1931). See also: Communist Academy, Moscow, *Lenin and Leninism. An Alphabetical and Subject Index to the Collection of the Communist Academy* (Moscow 1928); *Ezhegodnik leninskoy i istoriko-partiynoy bibliografii* (Bibliographical yearbook for Lenin and party history), published in Moscow since 1932.

UNDERWRITING. *See* INSURANCE; INVESTMENT BANKING.

UNEARNED INCREMENT. The concept of unearned increment was originally formulated by John Stuart Mill. It stems directly from the Ricardian theory of rent, according to which unequal costs in the production of agricultural commodities in the face of equal prices in the market, as set by the highest cost producer, yield differential rents, which in capitalized form constitute a source of unearned increment for the owners of the more fertile or more advantageously located agricultural lands. The owners may realize this increment either as current income or, in capitalized form, as an accrual of property value. As used by the followers of the classical school the term had more than mere analytical importance, for it served as a justification of the liberal economic system by implying that except for income derived from land rent all other types of income, such as wages, interest and profits under a system of private ownership of means of production, are "earned"; that is, represent just compensations for actual services. Thus only the landowners "grow richer, as it were in their sleep, without working, risking, or economizing" (Mill, John Stuart, *Principles of Political Economy*, new ed. London 1909, p. 818).

The differential principle adopted by Ricardo proved to be a most fruitful method of analysis, and its application to other economic phenomena soon revealed the existence of elements of "unearned increment" in virtually all spheres of economic activity. Ricardo himself recognized the existence of mining rent. John Stuart Mill referred to industrial differential profits similar to rent in the case of production of patented goods. Von Thünen pointed to advantageous location of land as a source of differential rent. From agricultural rent there was an easy transition to urban land rent, the difference between the two consisting, according to von Wieser, in the fact that while the former is due to varying costs of production of equal commodities, the latter arises because land of a similar kind serves different purposes commanding various prices in accordance with its location. With the process of rapid urbanization that characterized the economic development of the nineteenth century land in the vicinity of growing population centers, which had occupied a marginal or even submarginal position in agricultural production, soon acquired rapidly increasing value as building ground. The owners of such lands thus enjoyed an enormous appreciation of their possessions without making any active contribution, precisely in the manner described by John Stuart Mill as applying to agricultural rent. In Marshall's system the differential principle was raised to the rank of a general principle of price theory. The success of the principle in its application to theory, however, undermined the socio-ethical thesis of classical economics, according to which all incomes with the exception of rent are just equivalents for services.

The concept of unearned increment was broadened considerably when it came to be linked up with the general phenomenon of monopoly. The Ricardian theory of rent had already implied that land can become a source of rent income only because it is not reproducible; that is, it enjoys a monopoly position. It is only because of this position that, according to the labor theory of value—the corner stone of classical economics—land can command a price above the value of invested labor and capital and thus provide a differential residuum giving rise to unearned increment to the owner of land. But as monopolistic elements are present in all factors of production, all kinds of income may contain elements of unearned increment. Even certain differences in income derived from labor and services are traceable to the monopoly of education which certain groups enjoy under the prevailing system of economic organization. The most general application of the monopoly concept to that of unearned increment is offered by the Marxian theory of surplus value. Because of the chronic oversupply of labor in relation to available jobs as expressed in the Marxian doctrine of the industrial reserve army, the entrepreneurs enjoy a monopolistic position with regard to the workers and are enabled to purchase the labor power of the latter below its use value to the entrepreneur. The Marxian concept of "surplus value," which refers to the appropriation by the entrepreneur of the difference between the amount paid to the laborer and the value of his product, is merely a generalization of the concept of unearned increment designed to explain an exploitative profit economy as distinguished from its classical use as a description of an exceptional phenomenon in an otherwise just economic order.

As economic theory departed from the analysis of natural value to that of market value, the restriction of the concept of unearned increment to one factor of production became more and more untenable. Cumulative experience with cyclical price fluctuations led economists to conclude that under changing market conditions equal expenditures of cost may yield unequal returns and that these may accrue variously, to labor, to the entrepreneur or to the owner of capital. All other gains which arise out of special market conditions, such as war profits, inflationary profits, in short, all forms of "accretions to the real value of people's property that are not foreseen by them and are not in any degree due to efforts made, intelligence exercised, risks borne, or capital invested by them," also belong in the category of unearned increment (Pigou, A. C., *A Study in Public Finance*, London 1928, p. 177). This definition of unearned increment, although not very different from that of John Stuart Mill, comprises a much wider range of phenomena than Mill envisaged. Against this formulation of the concept, particularly against the inclusion of profits resulting from market fluctuations, it was urged that such gains are as a rule offset by losses occasioned by similar market forces. The answer clearly must depend on the direction of the secular trend of economic development. Furthermore the objection is valid only if accidental profits and losses accrue to the same people. To the extent, however, that the loss of the entrepreneur is shifted to other economic agents or is assumed by the state, the profits which accrue to the entrepreneur as a result of especially favorable market conditions fall within the category of unearned increment.

The original rigidity of the concept of unearned increment was further undermined by the growing discrepancy between the functional and the personal distribution of income. To Ricardo land rent was not an abstract concept but a concrete income of the landowning class. This, however, was changed with the shift in the sociological structure. Agricultural land and particularly urban land began to change hands more frequently. Rent was capitalized in the purchase price. To the buyer of land who paid for it out of his earnings the income which he derived therefrom was no longer unearned increment in Mill's sense but interest on capital invested. On the other hand, if the original seller of the land invested in securities the money realized from the sale, the dividends or interest accruing to him would still constitute unearned increment. Thus the distinction between rent and interest, at least from the viewpoint of personal distribution, was completely obliterated. The rent concept did not thereby lose its usefulness as an instrument of price theory, but it could no longer assist in the determination of the nature of individual income streams. The current differentiation between earned and unearned income—the former referring to income from services, the latter to that from property—is a purely arbitrary device primarily for differential taxation and is not intended as a means of evaluating the "justness" of the system of distribution.

The treatment of rent as unearned increment led to the formulation of demands for the abolition of private ownership of land, the source of rent payments. It was in accord with the philosophy of natural rights that private property should have been recognized in the products of land resulting from a man's labor but not in land itself. "The essential principle of property being to assure to all persons what they have produced by their labour and accumulated by their abstinence, this principle cannot apply to what is not the produce of labour, the raw material of the earth" (Mill, John Stuart, *Principles of Political Economy*, p. 229–30). Starting from this assumption land reformers agitated for the abolition of private property in land. Similar demands were voiced whenever other sources of unearned enrichment appeared. The theory of surplus value as a species of unearned increment led to the campaign for socialization of industry, and the theory of monopoly rent to insistence upon nationalization or municipalization of monopolies.

Less radical demands acquiesced in the retention of private property in land but called for the appropriation by the state of at least part of the rent. John Stuart Mill offered this compromise on the ground that it was impossible to separate the capital improvement from the original properties of land. Henry George urged the appropriation of the rent through taxation rather than through the nationalization of the land itself. From the viewpoint of classical economics the appropriation of rent by the state not only is a device for raising revenue but is economically justified on the ground that it taps an income which bears no corresponding economic function and that therefore it involves no interference with processes of production. Since it is a tax on differential income, it does not reach the marginal producer and thus is not shiftable.

In the practical proposals of John Stuart Mill as well as in those of German land reformers, however, the idea of taxing away land rent was dropped. A tax assessed on the value of land would hit interest as well as rent. The yield of a piece of land comprises an element of interest, as is clearly revealed by the fact that the marginal land, which according to Ricardo yields no differential rent, commands a certain value and would be subject to a land tax. It was proved also that because of the mobility of land rent and interest would become interchangeable. A land value tax without corresponding taxes on other sources of earnings would therefore constitute a discriminatory burden upon a particular kind of investment. Land taxes undoubtedly reach rent, but they do not affect rent alone or the whole of rent. The heavier taxation of the absentee owner, as practised in Australia, may be justified; it cannot, however, be maintained that such a tax is aimed at unearned increment, as the rent has already been capitalized in the sales price by the previous owner of the particular estate and either consumed or placed in another investment. John Stuart Mill confined his proposals to a tax on future rents as capitalized in the value increment of the land.

This convincing proposal waned in importance in Europe, where the farmers were forced by oversea agricultural developments into the position of marginal or even submarginal producers. In the decades prior to the World War the problem of taxing agricultural land rent in Europe was discussed only in connection with rises in land values as a result of increases in agricultural tariffs. Consequently the arguments of Henry George, which arose from the rapidly mounting values of agricultural land in the United States, were diverted in Europe to the phenomenon of urban land rent. The growth of cities and the advance of transportation facilities resulted in such an increase of urban land values that the idea of taxing the increment in the value of urban land found wide acceptance. Unlike the problem of agricultural land rent, in the case of urban land ground value was not difficult to separate from that of improvements. The "trend" was unmistakably upward and there were therefore no losses to offset the "unearned" gains. In spite of the wide support accorded these tax proposals the tax, which at the time would have had important fiscal and social effects, was not actually introduced until the rate of increase of land values had slowed down considerably and the future development was already being discounted by speculation. The actual low return of these taxes in no way detracts from the arguments of those who early recognized the idea of incremental taxation; but indeed it serves to reproach those legislators who under the influence of landed interest delayed the employment of this source of taxation.

One of the earliest instances of increment taxation of urban land values is to be found in the French law of 1807 which provided for a tax of as much as 50 percent of the increase in value caused by public improvements. The tax could be paid in cash or in the form of a rent charge on the land; or the owner might relinquish a part of the property. A hundred years later a similar tax was introduced by the city of Frankfort. In 1909 Great Britain established an impost on increments of land value, which was, however, never enforced and was soon repealed, and in 1911 Germany followed suit. The German imperial tax was abolished in 1913, but it became the model for similar taxes in the individual states and communities in Germany. The tax was levied on the transfer of land and was graduated according to the length of time during which the land had remained in the seller's possession and according to the percentage of increase; it was thus a tax on realized value increment. In 1898 the German leased territory of Kiaochow decreed a tax on land value increments even in cases where there was no transfer of property. The taxing of unrealized increment was the subject of considerable dispute. Its proponents pointed out that as opposed to a tax on realized increment the tax on unrealized increment would not retard the exchange of property. It could easily be paid through the imposition of a rent charge upon the taxable property. In the post-war period with its monetary fluctuations the question of methods of separating nominal from real values was debated at length but not solved.

The taxation of realized and unrealized value increments can be effected by means of other taxes than those on special increment; this is exemplified in the income tax of the city of Basel, Switzerland, which, based on Schanz' concept, comprises all realized and unrealized income. Germany in 1913 introduced a general property increment tax which of course included increment of land value. The tax was levied on increments that occurred in three years. No other tax was so violently disputed as this levy, which taxed indiscriminately "unearned increment" and increments derived from savings, inheritance, gifts and the like. The tax was revised in 1922 and suspended in 1925 on the ground that it might discourage the habit of saving. Inheritance taxes and stock transfer taxes also have at times been regarded as taxes on unearned increment. A variant of an increment tax is to be noted in the special assessments whereby the owner of property which benefits from public improvement contributes to the cost involved and is thus prevented from appropriating what would constitute an unearned increment.

The theoretical extension of the concept of unearned increment to other gains, such as profits arising out of especially favorable market conditions and war profits, led to attempts to tax these as well. Almost all countries which participated in the World War and some neutral states instituted war or excess profit taxes (see EXCESS PROFITS TAX). In countries which experienced drastic inflationary fluctuations the problem of taxation of inflationary profits attracted considerable attention. At the end of the inflationary period the federal government of Germany enacted a law whereby the states were obliged to impose taxes on property owners whose fixed financial obligations had been drastically reduced by monetary depreciation, for the purpose of capturing part of the accrued benefits for the state and of using the revenue to stimulate the construction of housing. This, however, was only a levy on special inflationary gain; a general tax on inflationary profit was discussed but not introduced. On the contrary, under conditions of depreciating currency the taxpayers gained an unearned increment at the expense of the public fisc by paying in depreciated currency, thus appropriating the difference in the value of money between the date of assessment and that of actual payment of the tax. In other instances nominal increments based merely on the depreciation of money were taxed.

During the depression which set in after 1929 some countries introduced taxes intended to reach excessive profits which might arise as a result of special legislation enacted in an effort to overcome the crisis. Belgium, for instance, imposed a tax in 1932 on the special profits which might follow the introduction of the quota system for imports. In the United States the National Industrial Recovery Act of 1933 provided for an excess profit tax under certain circumstances. Similar provisions exist also in German legislation. The tax levied by the state of Rhode Island on all profits in the liquor industry exceeding 9 percent belongs in the same category; the same holds true of the 25 percent tax levied by the Dominion of Canada in 1934 on the difference between the statutory and the current value of gold and of the 50 percent tax levied by the government of the United States on the profit realized by the holders of silver following the enactment of the Silver Purchase Act of 1934. While all these specific taxes on windfall profits as well as the established practise of differentiating between earned and unearned income with a view to subjecting the funded income to heavier taxation are measures in the direction of a more just distribution of income, they nevertheless have only limited significance. By no means do they indicate the realization of the goal envisaged by John Stuart Mill; namely, the establishment of an equitable economic system through the elimination of unearned increment.

GERHARD COLM

See: LAND SPECULATION; SPECULATION; APPRECIATION; RENT; SINGLE TAX; EXCESS PROFITS TAX; LAND TAXATION; TAXATION.

Consult: Scheftel, Yetta, *The Taxation of Land Value* (Boston 1916); Kumpmann, Karl, *Die Wertzuwachssteuer*, Zeitschrift für die gesamte Staatswissenschaft, supplement no. 24 (Tübingen 1907); Bauckner, Arthur, *Die Wertzuwachsbesteuerung in Deutschland* (Munich 1919); Lefebvre, Roger, *L'impôt sur les plus-values d'après les récents projets français* (Paris 1927); Pigou, A. C., *A Study in Public Finance* (London 1928) ch. xvi; Germany, Reichsfinanzministerium, "Denkschrift über den Ausbau der Besteuerung von Inflationsgewinnen" in Germany, Reichstag, *Verhandlungen*, vol. cd (1924–25) no. 803; Stamp, Josiah C., *Taxation during the War*, Carnegie Endowment for International Peace, Economic and Social History of the World War, British series (London 1932).

UNEMPLOYMENT may be defined briefly as the negative aspect of the economic process, for an unemployed person is one who, despite his willingness and capacity to work, is unable to do so for reasons inherent in the organization of commodity production. Persons permanently or temporarily incapable of work (the sick, the aged, the injured, the mentally incompetent) are not to be classed as unemployed, nor are those workers or employees who are engaged in a strike. Unemployment is a condition of the labor market in which the supply of labor power is greater than the number of available openings. Because of an unorganized or inadequately organized labor market some degree of unemployment may be caused by lack of knowledge of available jobs or by the overcrowding of a particular trade while other trades are in need of workers. Such cases, however, which present problems really administrative in nature, obviously do not touch the crux of the question of mass unemployment.

Mass unemployment is a peculiarity of modern capitalist economy with its extreme division of labor, its methods of production, distribution and income accumulation all conditioned by the mechanism of market and price, and its complex credit system. In an authoritarian economy, in which each individual was assigned a fixed place in the economic structure, a lasting disoccupation of large population groups could develop only as the result of a natural disturbance of the means of production, such as crop failures, or as a consequence of wars, banditry or the like. Not until price, profit and the market came to dominate the productive process and its trends did unemployment become a phenomenon controlled by strictly economic forces. The question of why the market mechanism fails is the central problem of unemployment in a capitalist economy.

There are three forms of unemployment: seasonal, cyclical and "normal." The first is brought about by seasonal changes in production; in its worst forms it includes casual labor on the docks, in many luxury trades and in the harvesting of certain crops. Cyclical employment, in which the number of unemployed rises markedly as a result of economic crises and depressions, affects particularly the industries producing capital goods. While the incidence of unemployment is related to the intensity of the crisis, its duration depends upon the length of the depression period. Normal unemployment is an inevitable concomitant of any economic system based upon a free labor market, in which the even distribution of all seekers for employment among the available openings can never be achieved as long as the worker is free to move to another place. Consequently there exists a universal condition, described by Beveridge as "an irreducible minimum of unemployment" and by Pigou as "an intractable minimum below which the percentage of unemployment never falls." In so far as this normal, unavoidable unemployment, measured over long periods, affects only a small percentage of workers (1 to 2 percent), it presents no special problem, since it may be assumed that every unemployed individual can once more find an occupation after a relatively brief time. A substantially higher percentage is a critical symptom of economic conditions in a country where economic expansion is on the decline. In addition to these forms of unemployment involving a total loss of labor and earnings for the workers there is the partial unemployment of part time work, which involves a reduction of wage earnings proportional to the shrinkage in hours of work. Clearly observable correlations exist between the extent and duration of part time work and the trend of seasonal and cyclical unemployment.

The disastrous consequences of prolonged unemployment, both for the individual and for society, can be indicated only briefly here. Loss of income from labor means suffering and misery for the unemployed worker and his family, even when some measure of public support guarantees against outright starvation. The fewer the savings available from better times, the more severe are the suffering and misery. Homes are broken up. The number of children who become inmates of state institutions rises sharply, and malnutrition becomes widely prevalent among those who remain in the schools. It has been estimated that in the United States by 1932 the health of one fifth of the children had been impaired as a direct result of the depression. One of the worst aspects was the emergence of an army of 200,000 to 300,000 homeless children, among them many girls, who wandered over the nation, destitute and demoralized. There is some slight mitigation of the misery of unemployment in countries which have systems of unemployment assistance; in other countries the unemployed must submit to the humiliation of accepting charity. In many cases exclusion from regular, disciplined work deprives the unemployed worker of the indispensable basis of an orderly existence and robs him of the opportunity to practise the craft he has mastered. Younger elements among the unemployed often turn to restless, aimless wandering, as a result of which they lose all moral and social restraint, so that even when an opportunity to work is at length available, they find it difficult to adapt themselves to an orderly existence. Among the older and more settled workers with family responsibilities prolonged unemployment, after inspiring rebelliousness at the outset, later breeds a wild desperation regarding the society and the institutions which condemn the unemployed, through no fault of their own, to moral and physical decay. The desperation is often intensified by the fact that the unemployed worker sees no chance, especially if he is advanced in age, of ever reestablishing himself in the trade he has learned and thus regards himself as definitely declassed. Such feelings often enough lead the unemployed to join social revolutionary parties or movements. In many cases, however, the attitude of revolt seems to give way after a time to a sullen resignation. Whether or not the discontent produced by unemployment ends in revolution depends upon the combination of many other factors. But it is a fact that in almost all countries where unemployment has become serious the fear of revolutionary outbreaks has led to an extraordinary strengthening of the repressive powers of the state. The state has been the decisive support of the capitalist economic order, despite the view, widespread not only in labor circles but to a great extent also in bourgeois intellectual circles, that the terrible evil of unemployment can be abolished only through a profound transformation of the existing economic organization and the introduction of some form of planned economic control.

One of the important aspects of the problem of unemployment is the statistical determination of who and how many are unemployed. From this viewpoint the methods of calculating unemployment may be divided into two main groups, primary and secondary. Among the primary methods is the direct census of the unemployed. In the United States such inquiries were made in 1890, 1900 and 1910; since 1915 numerous special investigations have been conducted, in some cases covering wide areas, in others only small localities, the most comprehensive being in 1930. Such inquiries afford a picture of unemployment for a particular sample day. The selection of the sample day determines the nature of the results, and there are numerous other sources of error. In times of prolonged depression many of the unemployed who have become unsettled move away from their homes; the permanently unemployed can be differentiated only very roughly from those who expect to be reinstated in their trade when the state of business improves; the classification of unemployed by branches of industry is impaired by the fact that vocational data given by the unemployed frequently afford no indication of their future relation to the labor market. The gathering of direct data may be supplemented by inquiries as to the rate of unemployment. The results, however, in no way determine the total number of unemployed or the state of the labor market, although they do reveal the percentage of employment fluctuations in the enterprise covered by the particular inquiry.

Since such investigations must, for technical reasons, be limited largely to carefully selected large scale factories of particular branches of industry, the fluctuations in the rate of employment are calculable for at most 30 or 40 percent of the total working population. Consequently the extent to which the results may be used to estimate the general condition of the labor market depends upon how far they may be regarded as typical; not infrequently the variations in the rate of employment are quite different in small factories or in branches of an industry not included in the inquiry. Before the World War regular studies of this character were undertaken only in England and the United States. Since the war they have been introduced in Canada, South Africa, Germany, Poland and Sweden. In combination with data obtained from an occupational census, they make possible—with numerous reservations—estimates of shifts in the level of unemployment and provide statistical data important for the determination of cyclical fluctuations.

The most complete type of secondary statistical data is ordinarily that obtained from periodic statements on unemployment issued in those countries in which state systems of unemployment insurance or unemployment relief are to be found (Great Britain, Germany, Austria). In this case the conception of unemployment depends on the nature of the legal basis for a claim to benefit. Ordinarily the provisions are rather broad. But there is always an "invisible" unemployment which is not covered by the insurance statistics, and whose extent is often subject to severe fluctuations. Since, on the other hand, every unemployed worker who had any claim to support registers at a relief bureau, these statistics have occasionally been attacked on the grounds that they tend to exaggerate the extent of unemployment.

The same completeness is impossible under the Ghent system, whereby the trade unions receive from the state or local government allowances supplementing contributions made by them for the support of unemployed members. The unemployed who have no claim to trade union support are not included in the statistics, which are valuable in proportion to the perfection of the organization of labor. These exist in Czechoslovakia, Belgium, the Netherlands, the Scandinavian states and several other countries. Changes in the relief system can effect far reaching transformations in the data on unemployment. This is true likewise of the analogous data of trade unions in countries in which no supplementary allowances from the public treasury are provided; as, for example, Great Britain and Germany. Naturally trade union reorpts of the state of the labor market which are based simply on estimates have a much more limited value. The data provided by public employment agencies have some significance only as indices of the direction of trends in the labor market; but in periods of prolonged depression, when there is slight prospect of employment, many who are out of work do not register with the employment bureau. In some cases, however, such registration is required before claims to unemployment relief are granted. Data on part time work are gathered by means of special inquiries conducted by trade unions, state labor department inspectors and similar bodies.

Seasonal unemployment can be measured exactly by special methods which separate the variations due to seasonal factors and those arising from cyclical influences and the effects of the general movement in prices, production and demand. Average unemployment is computed by months over a long period of time, and the figures are correlated with a general monthly average worked out for the entire period. After all reservations have been made in comparing data from several countries, available statistics for the years 1922–29 reveal clearly the slight extent of seasonal variations in unemployment in Great Britain as contrasted with other countries (Table 1). Winter unemployment is twice as great as summer unemployment in Germany, Belgium, Sweden and Norway and almost three times that in Holland and Canada. On the other hand, the low general monthly average for Belgium in comparison with the extraordinarily high average for Denmark shows that there is no observable connection between the trend of seasonal variations and the general intensity of unemployment. The extent of seasonal unemployment is moreover seriously affected by the business cycle. In Germany the annual decrease in the number of registered unemployed between the low point of the year and the end of June was 806,000 in 1928, 1,810,000 in 1929, 725,000 in 1930, 1,018,000 in 1931, 653,000 in 1932 and 1,191,000 in 1933.

Studies of particular branches of industry in the United States have demonstrated that seasonal variations are especially extreme in those producing unstandardized consumption goods with relatively elastic demand and of course in those branches of industry, such as construction, mining and manufacture of agricultural equipment and fertilizer, which are strongly dependent upon the state of the weather, from the viewpoint either of the productive process or of demand trends.

The question as to how far seasonal fluctuations in employment might be eliminated has been the subject of study only in the United States, and only there have there been some practical efforts at solutions. In individual branches of industry, especially construction, it has been possible to make the continuity of production partly independent of the influence of weather by means of certain technical innovations. Some efforts have been made by large scale factories to take up side lines, or "fillers," in the dead season to supplement declining demand for the main product and thereby to maintain a fairly constant rate of employment throughout the year. The method of budgetary control has also had some successes. In producing durable goods for mass consumption, where the total demand can be approximately

TABLE I

SEASONAL VARIATIONS IN UNEMPLOYMENT AND AVERAGE UNEMPLOYMENT IN SELECTED COUNTRIES, 1922–29

	GREAT BRITAIN	GERMANY	BELGIUM	NETHERLANDS	DENMARK	SWEDEN	NORWAY	CZECHOSLOVAKIA	CANADA
Seasonal index: January	112	140	156	192	157	141	135	131	136
February	104	135	136	142	156	135	134	134	127
March	98	107	105	141	131	128	122	120	118
April	90	99	99	74	98	112	112	102	108
May	100	76	94	59	75	85	93	91	92
June	101	75	86	66	69	78	81	81	70
July	103	73	85	66	68	73	66	75	54
August	104	65	75	66	67	68	76	78	59
September	104	77	75	67	67	68	83	84	59
October	104	85	76	68	75	71	91	88	75
November	106	108	86	100	98	96	99	99	105
December	104	141	128	149	151	139	125	125	126
Percentage of average unemployment	11.2	9.8	1.4	8.4	18.4	11.2	19.6	2.1	5.5

Source: Computed mainly from figures assembled by the International Labour Office.

forecast, annual schedules of production are drawn up and the production is distributed over the entire year as evenly as possible. In other cases efforts have been made to educate dealers and consumers to a steady consumption of goods, especially by means of seasonally adjusted prices. Such methods are, however, limited, because they can be used only by very large enterprises, and only if in their own interest by reducing expenses. In Europe they have thus far scarcely been attempted.

Normal unemployment requires particularly careful examination, not simply because of its absolute significance—it never disappears even at the peak of the business cycle—but also because of its effect upon the trend of cyclical unemployment. While the available statistical material is limited, it permits two striking conclusions: first, in the United States before the World War the quantity of normal unemployment was much greater than in the industrial countries of Europe; second, in many, although not in all, countries the percentage of normal unemployment has been substantially higher in the post-war than in the pre-war period.

In the United States, according to Douglas, normal unemployment (including, however, that due to illness and other individual causes) in the manufacturing, transportation, mining and construction industries amounted to an average of 10 percent for the period 1897–1926. The average rate for all manufacturing branches was 8 percent; while in periods of depression unemployment in the four groups rose as high as 20 percent. On the other hand, trade union statistics for the decade preceding the war show that the yearly average of unemployment in Great Britain ranged from a high of 7.8 percent in

TABLE II
NUMBER OF FULLY UNEMPLOYED WORKERS, 1921–32
(In 1000)

Country	1921	1922	1923	1924	1925	1926	1927	1928	1929	1930	1931	1931 (end)	1932 (end)	Percentage Change from 1931 to 1932
Germany	354	213	751	978	636	2010	1327	1368	1679	3144	4573	5668	6014	+ 6.1
Great Britain and Northern Ireland	1589	1599	1294	1180	1346	1512	1162	1290	1262	1994	2719	2670	2955	+10.7
France	362	182	142	240	266	243	729	365	144	194	624	797	880	+10.4
Italy	591	415	246	165	110	113	278	324	300	425	734	982	1225	+24.7
Austria	14	55	129	112	176	209	206	186	196	244	303	396	450	+13.6
Czechoslovakia	106	202	355	136	65	89	69	50	58	138	379	639	970	+51.8
Poland	123	153	98	156	249	355	245	163	171	295	389	406	333	—18.0
Belgium	178	62	23	27	43	33	43	38	35	90	249	367	408	+11.2
Netherlands	35	52	76	64	59	58	60	54	53	74	138	246	351	+42.5
Denmark	146	147	98	85	111	160	172	145	123	107	139	238	323	+35.7
Sweden	263	244	137	109	118	133	130	116	112	127	178	276	324	+17.2
Norway	95	99	62	51	74	138	146	112	90	95	101	152	192	+26.3
Switzerland	58	67	33	15	11	14	12	8	8	13	24	51	82	+60.8
Finland	2	2	1	2	3	2	2	2	5	10	14	21	27	+28.6
Estonia	1	1	1	3	3	3	4	3	4	4	4	11	16	+45.4
Latvia	7	6	4	2	3	4	4	6	7	6	11	27	21	—22.2
Rumania	25	20	30	40	30	33	22	66	48	50	72	99	62	—37.8
Jugoslavia	12	10	13	15	12	13	11	15	17	16	20	29	29	
Hungary	33	30	40	54	66	52	32	30	32	44	57	66	89	+34.2
Danzig	2	2	3	4	9	16	13	11	13	18	25	33	39	+18.1
Saar	1	1	1	2	3	5	3	4	7	9	21	35	45	+28.8
Irish Free State	77	75	79	76	75	78	78	67	66	69	76	93	104	+11.8
Canada	268	164	107	153	158	113	107	98	124	236	358	426	536	+25.8
United States	5124	4129	1838	2778	2130	2003	2466	4247	4247	4359	7854	10,304	12,100	+17.4
Australia	142	123	93	93	121	103	109	160	160	297	413	416	415	— 0.1
New Zealand	13	12	10	10	14	13	20	26	20	27	42	50	56	+12.0
Japan	228	351	338	333	330	318	314	307	412	557	628	729	743	+ 1.9
Total for above countries	9849	8416	6002	6883	6221	7823	7764	9261	9393	12,642	20,145	25,227	28,789	+14.1

Source: Based on compilation by A. Aghte published in Verein für Sozialpolitik, *Schriften*, vol. clxxxv, pt. i (Munich 1932) p. 148–49, revised by K. Pribram.

1908 to 2.1 percent in 1913, in Germany between 1.2 percent in 1906 and 2.9 percent in 1908 and 1913. The percentages in Denmark and in some other countries were somewhat higher, the former reaching 10.7 in 1910. In Australia the rates ranged between 4.7 in 1910 and 6.7 percent in 1906. The corresponding percentages in the post-war period, omitting the period of inflation and of severe crisis, are considerably higher. Unemployment never dropped below 9.7 percent (1927) in Great Britain, 6.7 percent (1925) in Germany, 12.7 percent (1923) in Denmark and 7 percent (1927) in Australia. There was a similar tendency toward a rise in normal unemployment in the United States, although it was not so marked as in most European countries, and it was even less marked in such small industrial countries as Belgium and Switzerland. Unemployment since the World War has shown an extraordinary increase in amount and fluctuation. The rise in the number of unemployed in the countries listed in Table II from 6,002,000 in 1923 (a year of prosperity) to 9,393,000 in 1929 (a year of prosperity) is indicative of terrific economic dislocation; this is also true of the increase of those affected by cyclical unemployment from 9,849,000 in 1921 to 28,789,000 at the end of 1932.

Ordinarily cyclical unemployment refers to the increase in the number of jobless workers in periods of depression. It is the aim of the present discussion, however, to interpret the concept of cyclical unemployment in a broader sense and to extend it to those types of unemployment which, while they are in no way cyclically conditioned, nevertheless do appear as clearly identifiable reactions to general falls in price levels. Thus in the post-war deflationary crises which in all countries followed stabilization of the currency after periods of monetary inflation, there set in without exception a rise of unemployment similar to that observable in the cyclical periods of crisis and depression. Beveridge, Pigou, Fisher and others have demonstrated the existence of interesting correlations between price movements and changes in unemployment. Fisher's calculations reveal a striking identity in the course of the curves of price movements and unemployment.

While periods of cyclical unemployment in pre-war times were more or less simultaneous in all countries, this identity was not maintained in the first decade after the war because of the diverse currency policies of the various industrial countries. In most of them, it is true, the world wide fall in prices which followed the short boom of 1919–20 resulted in an exceptional rise in unemployment; this occurred in Great Britain, Norway, Sweden, Denmark, Australia and Canada. In those countries, however, in which the inflationary rise of prices continued, as in Germany, Austria, Czechoslovakia and Poland, unemployment was temporarily stationary. These states began to experience it when, with the stabilization of their currencies, a reaction set in against the upward trend of prices: in Czechoslovakia in 1922, in Austria in 1923, in Germany in 1924. Similar reactions were to be observed in France and Italy in 1927.

The effects of deflationary policy were felt in 1925 in Great Britain, Denmark and Norway, when the currency was stabilized at the pre-war par (Table III). A steady annual price decline was attended by a steady annual rise in unemployment from 1924 to 1927. A world wide process of monetary and credit contraction began in 1929 and in the course of one year had led to a 10 to 14 percent decline of the wholesale trade index in all industrial countries. This contraction introduced a period of declining prices and unrestrainable rise in unemployment, which did not come to an end until a new rise in price levels. It is interesting to note that the percentage rise (17.3) in unemployment for Europe as

TABLE III

FLUCTUATIONS IN PRICES AND UNEMPLOYMENT, JUNE 1920–21 AND JUNE 1924–27

COUNTRY	WHOLESALE PRICE INDEX						PERCENTAGE OF UNEMPLOYMENT					
	1920	1921	1924	1925	1926	1927	1920	1921	1924	1925	1926	1927
Great Britain	330	198	163	157	147	141	1.2	17.8	9.4	12.2	14.6	8.9
Denmark	380	253	220	206	141	142	2.1	16.1	5.0	9.1	15.6	17.9
Norway	382	294	264	258	195	159	0.8	20.6	4.9	8.9	22.1	22.5
Sweden	366	222					3.4	27.7				
Canada	258	165					2.1	13.2				
Australia	233	170					6.2	12.5				

Source: International Labour Office, Studies and Reports, ser. C, no. 16 (Geneva 1931) p. 111, 113–14, 117.

a whole for the year 1932 is approximately the same as that for the United States. Despite the undeniable connection between changes in the price level and cyclical unemployment it has not yet been possible to present a statistical picture that would exclude the influence of other circumstances which help to determine the trend of unemployment.

The costs of unemployment are ordinarily understood to mean simply the resultant shrinkage in the wages of labor. This includes both losses from unemployment and wage cuts. The Institut für Konjunkturforschung estimated the decline in the total earnings of German labor between 1929 and 1932 as 13 percent from unemployment and part time work and 7 percent from wage and salary cuts. From an income standpoint, however, some of the wage losses are offset by unemployment insurance or ordinary charity relief. According to estimates of Colin Clark the total earnings of the insured population in Great Britain fell from £1,840,000,000 in 1929 to £1,709,000,000 in 1931, a total loss of about £131,000,000. More than half of this decline was balanced by the fact that the amount of unemployment relief distributed rose from £44,000,000 in 1929 to £115,000,000 in 1931. There is of course no other country in which the unemployed are in so favorable a situation as in England. In the United States, where prior to the National Industrial Recovery Act the unemployed were dependent almost wholly upon local charity relief, the combined salary and wage income, according to the Department of Commerce, was 40 percent lower in 1932 than in 1929 (property income was only 30 percent lower); but wage income alone, in industries where it could be isolated, was 60 percent lower. There are likewise losses in vocational standards and health. In countries with a high percentage of normal unemployment several months or more often go by, even in periods of economic expansion, before an unemployed worker finds a new job, if he finds one at all.

According to inquiries by the British Ministry of Labour in 1929, when unemployment reached 10 percent, the average period of unemployment (omitting mining, which is marked by a high degree of permanent unemployment) was under three months for 33.5 percent of the men and 51.1 percent of the women; three to six months for 31.3 percent of the men and 30.9 percent of the women; six to nine months for 20.9 percent of the men and 11.6 percent of the women; and over nine months for 14.2 percent of the men and 6.3 percent of the women. Another inquiry early in 1931, when unemployment reached 20 percent, showed about the same ratios. I. Lubin of the Brookings Institution conducted a survey in a number of key industrial cities in the United States to ascertain what became of workers discharged because of technological changes. The survey revealed that 41 percent had been out of work more than six months. The situation of the workers above forty-five years in age was especially serious. The most comprehensive material bearing on technological unemployment is contained in a study by David Weintraub of the National Bureau of Economic Research. The data presented by him disclose a high rate of displacement by increasing efficiency in American industry (Table IV). During the period 1920–31 over 3,000,000 wage earners were displaced in manufacturing industries alone because of increases in technological and managerial efficiency. In spite of the rapid growth of the physical volume of production there were 841,000 fewer workers employed in 1928 than in 1920. Even in the peak year of 1929 there were 1,000,000 fewer workers employed in the manufacturing industries, in railway transportation and in coal mining than had been employed in the same industries in 1920.

In England and the United States there was, prior to the depression, considerable discussion of what measures might be used to ease the situation of workers dismissed as a result of increased technological efficiency. Some suggested staggering the introduction of new methods over a long period; or others proposed that enterprises establish special reserve funds out of which discharged workers might receive compensation. Such dismissal wages were introduced in one or two American union industries. The crisis, however, ended all such discussion and action.

One explanation of the cause of unemployment is to be found in theories of the static equilibrium of economic life. Such theories characterize crises as disturbances of the normal economic process which can be brought about only by external developments, particularly circumstances which hamper free competition or the unrestrained movement of capital and labor. Economic life appears as a system whose relations are automatically regulated by free competition. Through this mechanism the marketing of all goods produced is constantly guaranteed;

TABLE IV
Displacement of Workers by Changes in Efficiency and Output, United States, 1921–31
(In 1000)

Year	Manufacturing Industries — Changes in Employment — Due to Changes in the Output per Man Hour	Due to Changes in the Physical Volume of Output	Net Change — During Current Year	Since 1920	Class I Railways — Changes in Employment — Due to Changes in the Output per Service Hour	Due to Changes in the Physical Volume of Output	Net Change — During Current Year	Since 1920
1921	—163	—2045	—2208	—2208	+ 2	—494	—492	—492
1922	—935	+1759	+ 824	—1384	—36	+100	+ 64	—428
1923	—183	+1350	+1167	— 217	—52	+286	+234	—194
1924	—276	— 584	— 860	—1077	—47	—103	—150	—344
1925	—495	+ 948	+ 453	— 624	—82	+ 80	— 2	—346
1926	— 93	+ 211	+ 118	— 506	—39	+ 93	+ 54	—292
1927	— 68	— 204	— 272	— 778	+ 9	— 67	— 58	—350
1928	—503	+ 440	— 63	— 841	—74	— 5	— 79	—429
1929	—116	+ 541	+ 425	— 416	—26	+ 39	+ 13	—416
1930	+197	—1762	—1565	—1981	+12	—233	—221	—637
1931	—467	— 936	—1403	—3384	+ 1	—273	—272	—909

Year	Bituminous and Anthracite Coal Industry — Changes in Employment — Due to Changes in the Output per Man Day	Due to Changes in the Physical Volume of Output	Net Change — During Current Year	Since 1920	Totals for the Group of Industries — Changes in Employment — Due to Changes in Technological and Managerial Efficiency	Due to Changes in the Physical Volume of Output	Net Change — During Current Year	Since 1920
1921	—15	—165	—180	—180	—176	—2704	—2880	—2880
1922	—27	— 62	— 89	—269	—998	+1797	+ 799	—2081
1923	—15	+224	+209	— 60	—250	+1860	+1610	— 471
1924	+ 8	— 94	— 86	—146	—315	— 781	—1096	—1567
1925	— 7	— 19	— 26	—172	—584	+1009	+ 425	—1142
1926	+ 5	+102	+107	— 65	—127	+ 406	+ 279	— 863
1927	—11	— 66	— 77	—142	— 70	— 337	— 407	—1270
1928	—21	— 25	— 46	—188	—598	+ 410	— 188	—1458
1929	—12	+ 29	+ 17	—171	—154	+ 604	+ 455	—1003
1930	—23	— 70	— 93	—264	+186	—2065	—1879	—2882
1931					—466*	—1209*	—1675*	—4557*

* Not including the 1931 figures for the coal industry.
Source: Weintraub, David, in American Statistical Association, *Journal*, vol. xxvii (1932) 396–97.

any decline in the demand for goods of any branch of industry and any consequent reduction in its rate of employment must be balanced by a corresponding rise in another branch of industry. The demand of workers for goods is more or less unchanging regardless of their number and can grow only in proportion to the increasing productivity of industry. Any serious influence on market conditions is denied even to that type of unemployment which results from technological changes. These are attributable chiefly to the introduction of new, labor saving machines. There is more intense competition in the labor market between the discharged workers and those still employed, which in turn leads to a fall in wages, a corresponding decline in all prices and thus to an increased demand for the cheapened commodities. In this way the absorption of the discharged workers in the process of production is made possible. According to this theory of compensation the best and only means of avoiding unemployment is therefore absolutely free competition in all markets. The theory was preeminently fitted to justify the liberal economic policy of the era of competitive capitalism. Unemployment, even where it appeared on a large scale, was not a matter for special concern, and there were at best occasional attempts to mitigate it with ineffective palliatives (emergency work and the like). The insufficiency of the theory was brought to light after the World War, when unemployment, normal and cyclical, increased tremendously.

A second group of theoreticians also proceeds from the principle that the mechanism of price produces a tendency toward the establishment of a static equilibrium and that therefore the causes of the disturbance of the normal course of economic life can lie only in non-economic events. But they view crises and depressions and the unemployment growing out of them, in so far as they are not the result of observable "accidental" occurrences of a special character, as components of a regularly recurring process expressing itself in a cyclical movement, which consequently can have its determining causes only in analogous factors which develop periodically. Adherents of this view are responsible for the discovery of the so-called long cyclical waves, which on the down curve show particularly sharp depression phenomena and increased unemployment. If crises are thus conceived as an integral component of the cyclical trend which characterizes a highly developed industrial economy, there can hardly be serious hope of finding effective measures whereby cyclically recurring unemployment may successfully be counteracted within the limits of capitalism.

A third group comprises all the so-called disproportionality theories. These also see crises and depressions and the resulting unemployment as part of an economic cycle, but they do not regard any single factor as a cause. They find the origin of the cyclical trend mainly in the disproportionate development of particular branches of industry during a boom period. No cycle is exactly like another, and the important task is descriptive analysis of the fluctuations. There is no unanimity as to the importance of particular types of causes of unemployment. It is agreed, however, that unemployment related to cyclical fluctuations cannot be abolished without a transformation in the dominant economic order so basic as to be likely to destroy it in its present form. Reforms must be limited to measures which will lend greater stability to economic life. Some exponents of the disproportionality theory have come to the conclusion that only the most extreme separation of internal economy from foreign entanglements can provide a modicum of security against crises.

A fourth and very distinct group of theoreticians includes all investigators who are inclined to consider cyclical phenomena and all other aspects of economic life as primarily the effects of monetary influences. They argue that booms are brought about by credit expansions undertaken by the banks; a crisis develops when banks, finding their liquidity threatened, cannot continue to expand credit. The periodicity of the cyclical movement may be explained by the nature of the banking organization; the intensity of the reaction and hence also the extent and duration of cyclical unemployment are defined by the degree of credit expansion. According to this conception, if unemployment is an effect of the contraction of the volume of the means of payment in times of crisis and depression, then the only conceivable way to stabilize economy involves the most accurate constant adjustment of the volume of the means of payment to economic needs. There is no unanimity, however, as to the method whereby this adjustment is to be achieved.

A fifth group stresses maladjustments between production and consumption. This idea was already advanced in the criticisms of the "anarchy of capitalist production" offered by the first socialist opponents of the classical school of economics. In the modern formulations of similar nature it is argued that there exists what John A. Hobson calls "a general tendency in the economic system for productive capacity to outrun the expansion of markets, ... attributable to a distribution of money income which upsets the true balance between saving and spending, production and markets."

Crises come about, then, because the purchasing power of labor, that is, of the overwhelming body of consumers, does not suffice even during periods of prosperity to absorb the output resulting from the expansion of production, while the share of the national income obtained by the capitalist increases. These theories provide no answer to several crucial questions. Whence comes this "natural tendency" toward immoderate expansion of production capacity? Why do crises first break out in heavy industries and only subsequently affect consumption goods industries? Why does unemployment not grow incessantly, once it has begun to destroy the consuming power of the worker, and lead ultimately to the collapse of the capitalistic economic system?

As stated by Karl Marx and utilized as a scientific basis for socialist thought, the theory of the maladjustment between production and consumption has an entirely different character. According to Marx the decisive role is played by changes in the composition of capital. More fixed capital and raw materials with relatively less labor are used to produce a larger mass of commodities, which find inadequate markets because of the relative restriction of wages, while an "industrial reserve army" of workers discharged as a result of the introduction of new machines exercises a constant pressure on wages. In the Marxist theory of crises the existence of a relatively great army of unemployed as a permanent phenomenon—a "surplus population" —is an essential characteristic of capitalist economy. The industrial reserve army, however, might, without necessitating any essential change in the argument, arise and be perpetuated by other causes than technical advances, such as a flight from the land resulting from a growth of large scale agricultural enterprises and the like. From this standpoint only the introduction of socialist planned economy can bring salvation from the misery of crises and unemployment. The idea of fighting unemployment by abolishing or "leveling" cyclical fluctuations is feasible only from the standpoint of those theories which regard cyclical fluctuations simply as result of poor organization and functioning of the credit system and not as something inherent in the capitalist economy.

The causes of seasonal unemployment, which gains extraordinary significance only in combination with other forms of unemployment, present no special theoretical problems. Much more difficult is the establishment of the causal relations between normal and cyclical unemployment. It goes without saying that every decline in demand for goods must lead to a contraction of production in the respective enterprises. But whether such contraction means prolonged unemployment depends on whether the decline is or is not balanced by a corresponding increase in the demand for other goods, thus leading to the hiring of the discharged workers, as the compensation theory states in principle. There is no compensation when the changes in demand do not offer new employment to the discharged workers.

In the decades immediately preceding the World War these fluctuations apparently came about so slowly and gradually in European countries that nowhere did they induce any large normal unemployment. Aside from seasonal unemployment only cyclical unemployment really aroused the interest of social research workers and social reformers. A good organization of employment exchanges was regarded as the best and indeed the only remedy for normal unemployment; such a system was, it is true, lacking in most countries.

Capitalist production after the war adapted itself quickly and successfully to great fluctuations in demand involved in the sudden transition from a war to a peace economy. But in particular branches of European industry where, as a result of the tremendous demand for war materials, large capital sums had been invested and productive capacity greatly increased, the contraction of demand came about too quickly for accommodation to new market conditions. Serious disturbances ensued in such industries as iron and steel, machinery, shipbuilding, electrical manufacturing, coal mining, potash, chemicals, cotton and wool, silk and artificial silk and sugar refining. The loss of earlier markets perhaps dealt the most serious blow to the important branches of the British export industry; especially in the oversea markets of Asia and America they were pressed by the competition of enterprises founded in those countries under the protection of wartime tariffs. Widespread unemployment in all the important export industries has become characteristic of the British economy in general (Table v); they are no longer

TABLE V

UNEMPLOYMENT IN CERTAIN EXPORT INDUSTRIES COMPARED WITH GENERAL UNEMPLOYMENT, GREAT BRITAIN, 1923–28

END OF	GENERAL PERCENTAGE OF UNEMPLOYMENT	COAL INDUSTRY	PERCENTAGE OF UNEMPLOYMENT IN ENGINEERING AND ALLIED INDUSTRIES*	COTTON INDUSTRY
September, 1923	11.6	3.1	17.8	20.1
March, 1924	9.7	2.1	15.7	15.4
September, 1924	10.5	8.2	14.4	14.3
March, 1925	10.8	11.9	11.9	7.2
September, 1925	11.7	23.6	11.7	10.2
March, 1926	9.5	9.4	11.8	9.7
September, 1926	13.5	†	16.8	24.3
March, 1927	9.7	16.8	11.3	6.0
September, 1927	9.2	19.1	9.0	9.3
March, 1928	9.6	17.2	9.2	9.2
September, 1928	11.5	21.6	9.9	14.3

* Includes the following classifications: (1) engineering; engineers' iron and steel founding; (2) electrical engineering; (3) marine engineering and so on; (4) constructional engineering; (5) general iron founding; (6) electrical cable, wire and electric lamp manufacture; (7) heating and domestic engineering.
† Stoppage in industry.
Source: Adapted from Clay, Henry, The Post-War Unemployment Problem (London 1929) p. 41.

able to absorb the steady increase in the working population. Where there has been an observable decline in unemployment in the export industries, this has been the result not of an expansion of production but of the migration of the permanently unemployed to other branches of industry. The situation of many branches of Austrian industry was similar if more hopeless. In the case of Great Britain the unemployment in its export industries reflects profound changes in the world market.

Technological advance has already been mentioned as an important factor. The classical theory assumed that workers displaced by technological changes were absorbed by the expansion of production. The introduction of labor saving machinery under free competition meant lower costs and lower prices and therefore an increase in demand and production. Workers were thrown out of work. But this, it was assumed, was temporary. According to the theories of the classical school the unemployed in all branches of production would, assuming perfectly free competition in the labor market, exert pressure to bring down wages. There would then ensue a general fall in the costs of production, a drop in price levels and a rise in the relative purchasing power of the consumers. This in turn would cause an approximately equal rise in demand for all products, resulting in absorption of the displaced workers. In recent discussions of "technological" unemployment the condition of free competition in the labor market presupposed by the classical school is often tacitly replaced by the more realistic recognition of a more or less rigid wage system. When wages remain unchanged, the cheapening of costs resulting from technical advances is not reflected in the prices of other goods. There is a rise in demand in so far as part of the purchasing power, previously absorbed by the now cheapened products, is liberated. This leads to the hiring of new workers at some other point. But the marginal productivity of these workers is less, should they be employed at the same wage level, than it would be if they were employed in the rationalized industries. More workers are discharged than a rise in production can cause to be reemployed. The reabsorption of absolutely all workers in such a rigid wage system would be possible, theoretically speaking, only after a multitude of unforeseeable obstacles had been overcome and only if technical advances were being applied equally in all branches of production, so that there might be a relatively uniform general decline in prices.

Technical advances and rationalization played an especially vital rôle in the United States and Germany in the period immediately preceding the world economic crisis. In the United States between 1914 and 1927 the productivity of workers in certain branches, calculated in terms of one hour of work, was enormously increased. Productivity in the petroleum refining industry rose 82 percent, in open hearth steel 103 percent, in automobile construction 178 percent and in automobile tires 292 percent. While the volume of manufacturing production was 24 percent higher in 1926 than in 1920, the rate of employment—the number of workers employed —declined almost 6.5 percent (Table VI). Despite a sharply accelerated rise in production in 1929 this number remained constant. Thus that portion of the population which reached working age during this period had either to displace the older generation in order to find occupation or to depend upon the expansion of other branches of industry.

TABLE VI

Index Numbers of Production, Employment, Productivity and Wages, United States, 1920–29*

(1923–25 average = 100)

Year	Manu-facturing Production	Factory Employment	Output per Worker	Factory Pay Rolls	Wage per Worker
1920	87	108	87	118	109
1921	67	82	82	77	94
1922	86	90	96	81	90
1923	101	104	97	103	99
1924	94	96	98	96	100
1925	105	100	105	101	101
1926	108	101	107	104	103
1927	106	99	107	102	103
1928	112	97	115	102	105
1929	119	101	118	108	107

* The indices of manufacturing production, factory employment and factory pay rolls are those compiled by the Federal Reserve Board and published in the *Federal Reserve Bulletin*. The index of output per worker is obtained by dividing manufacturing production by factory employment, and the index of wage per worker by dividing factory pay rolls by factory employment.

A wave of rationalization and technological change began to sweep most branches of Germany's large scale industries after the inflation period. In relation to the amount of goods produced in the key mass production industries the number of hours of labor worked declined steadily after 1925 (Table VII). The average annual increase in labor productivity from 1925 to 1932 was about 5 percent. The data for 1929 are especially noteworthy. They reveal a decline in the number of hours of work performed despite a rise in the volume of production. In the same year, that is, before the beginning of the world economic crisis, there was a slight rise in unemployment. The process of displacement of human labor continued during the crisis with the declining volume of production.

TABLE VII

INDEX OF PRODUCTION, EMPLOYMENT AND PRODUCTIVITY IN INDUSTRY, GERMANY, 1925–32

YEAR	OUTPUT	LABOR HOURS	OUTPUT PER LABOR HOUR	PERCENTAGE CHANGE IN PRODUCTIVITY FROM PRECEDING YEAR
1925	81.1	92.9	87.8	
1926	77.9	79.0	98.6	+12.9
1927	98.4	97.5	100.9	+ 2.3
1928	100.0	100.0	100.0	− 0.9
1929	100.6	94.4	106.6	+ 6.6
1930	88.8	76.8	115.6	+ 8.4
1931*	72.1	59.6	121.0	+ 4.7
1932*	60.2	48.4	124.4	+ 2.8

* Tentative figures.
Source: Institut für Konjunkturforschung, Berlin, *Wochenbericht*, July 5, 1934.

Similar figures for Great Britain, where the speed of technical advance was not nearly so marked, are also characteristic. As Table VIII indicates, the increase of production from 1924 to 1929 by over 11 percent must be credited exclusively to augmented labor productivity. The fateful effect upon the labor market exercised by technical advances combined with wage policies, undoubtedly true also of other countries, can be indicated with some statistical accuracy only for Germany. Wage policies pursued energetically by German trade unions since the end of the inflation period were partly based on the idea that an important benefit of high wages is that they stimulate employers to a more rapid adoption of technical advances and thoroughgoing methods of rationalization. This idea ignores the fact that no decrease in prices can be brought about by economies involving the discharge of workers, for such a move is made for the purpose of balancing higher wage costs.

TABLE VIII

INDEX OF PRODUCTION, EMPLOYMENT AND PRODUCTIVITY IN INDUSTRY, GREAT BRITAIN, 1927–29
(1924 = 100)

YEAR	PHYSICAL VOLUME OF OUTPUT	EMPLOYMENT	OUTPUT PER WORKER
1927	106.8	100.2	106.6
1928	105.5	98.7	106.9
1929	111.6	100.6	111.1

Source: International Labour Office, *Hours of Work and Employment* (Geneva 1933) p. 173.

In Germany the introduction of labor saving processes increased the productive capacity especially of industries manufacturing producers' and export goods; the economic results of the extraordinary advance in productive power were lost, however, to a large degree. As a consequence of the protectionist policies of importing countries, rises in wages, the expense of foreign loans and heavy tax burdens every decrease in cost achieved by industrial reorganization was more than compensated for. Last but not least, while the supply of capital was sufficient to finance basic technological reorganization, it was exhausted before an equivalent expansion of productive capacities in complementary branches of industry could be accomplished. Thus the advantages of economies which might have been derived from a full exploitation of the increased capacity were to a great extent canceled out.

Reithinger's study covering many groups of industry compares the increase of labor productivity with the trend of wages and other factors on the basis of conditions in 1926, the year in which the rationalization process set in. He finds that in those branches of industry in which labor productivity was greatly enhanced because of changes in methods of production the share of wages in the value of the product remained unchanged, so that, as far as the wage factor in costs was concerned, no decline in prices was possible. On the other hand, since the same wage increases were effected in other branches of industry, regardless of any rise in labor productivity, wages in most cases became a greater part of total costs; and since this item could hardly be compensated for by a decline in other factors of cost, it was bound to send prices up. Even the wage decreases of 1931 scarcely balanced this development except in a few fields. Furthermore, as A. Rustow has shown, in the machine industries there was at the same time temporary decline in unemployment. Reithinger estimates that of the industrial workers unemployed in 1931 some 500,000 lost their jobs by reason of contraction in the volume of production, while about 1,000,000 were thrown out of work through technical advances which made possible savings in labor.

Beveridge, Pigou, Clay and many others have argued that the high degree of normal unemployment characteristic of British economy ever since the end of the brief post-war boom may be credited largely to the fact that the wages of labor, especially in sheltered industries, did not entirely share in the price fall of 1921–22, remained quite rigid after 1923 and did not follow the subsequent additional fall in prices. The

French economist Rueff has pointed to the correlation of the curves of real wages and unemployment as a proof of the causal connection between wage conditions and unemployment in England. This proof is not entirely convincing, however, since Rueff has not been able to discount the influence which other factors can always exercise on the trend of the two curves. A similar comparison for Germany has produced no clear results.

The rise of other elements entering into the total cost of production can have an effect on the rate of employment similar to that of real wages. This applies above all to taxes, social services, interest on long term obligations, the cost of raw materials and half finished materials; for example, when these are made more costly by protective tariffs whether domestic or foreign, which must be borne by the domestic manufacturer. A similar stepping up of production costs as a result of cartel price policy can come about in those branches of industry which must purchase raw materials or half finished products controlled by cartels (steel, iron, copper, aluminum, cellulose, lime, cement and so on). The weight of cartelized products in Germany is estimated at not less than 40 percent of the total industrial production. If the prices of 1913 be taken as 100, the index figure of fixed (cartelized) prices in Germany in May, 1930, was about 105, while that of raw materials, whose prices were unfixed and which freely adjusted themselves to the level of the world market, was about 85. Even greater of course is the influence of price fixing on the intensification of cyclical unemployment.

Finally, among the decisive costs of the whole economic system there must be mentioned the rate of interest on capital, whose decline makes possible the use of means of production which otherwise would not have been profitable, while its rise generally reduces the rate of employment.

The natural increase in the population capable of working is absorbed easily in countries where industrial development is rapid. If the rate of capital accumulation is higher than the rate of growth of the population, the expansion of industrial production is dependent on the increase in the number of workers. This is demonstrated by the development of the capitalist economy, which in the course of the nineteenth century permitted a doubling of the population of Europe along with a material raising of the standard of living. The population increase of the United States was even greater. Today the increase of population in the industrial countries of Europe is comparatively small, about 5 or 6 for every 1000 annually; in the United States it is greater, about 16 for every 1000 inhabitants.

Given definite living standards and a fixed rate of capital growth, relative overpopulation, that is, a permanent supply of labor power too great in comparison with the demand, can result from population increase only if sudden changes occur in the rate of increase of the population seeking employment, without those compensating tendencies which indirectly effect a constant adjustment of production to the state of the labor market through the wage and price mechanism. In recent decades such sudden changes have come about as a result of limitations on immigration. In some countries the abolition of general conscription has induced a rise in the demand for work. Moreover the labor market has been glutted by increasing numbers of women not previously engaged in industry. Changes in the age levels of the population which raise the proportion of the older generation and decrease that of the younger in the laboring population impair mobility in the search for work and make more difficult the adjustment of wages to price levels. The density of population and population growth apparently have no further influence on the structure of the labor market.

The general effects of credit restriction are the first important factors to be considered in connection with the causes of cyclical unemployment. If the restriction of the means of payment and the volume of credit which sets in with a crisis causes a general fall of prices, it is disastrous to the productive process. Numerous elements of cost remain unaltered for a time and the price drop continues in the commodity markets in varying degrees. The greater the differentiations in the price trends, the sharper usually are the contraction of the volume of production and the fall in the rate of employment. Industries manufacturing producers' goods are more severely affected than those producing consumers' goods (Table IX). While the rapid advance of the crisis in Germany swept the heavy industries in the fall of 1929, the rate of employment in consumers' goods industries remained fairly steady well into the winter and sank much more slowly.

Credit restriction resulting in unemployment need not necessarily, however, be of a cyclical nature. Even a contraction of the volume of money following a purely inflationary increase

TABLE IX

PERCENTAGE OF FULLY EMPLOYED TRADE UNION MEMBERS IN PRODUCERS' GOODS AND CONSUMERS' GOODS INDUSTRIES, GERMANY, 1927–31

PERIOD	IN PRODUCERS' GOODS INDUSTRIES	IN CONSUMERS' GOODS INDUSTRIES
Average 1927	88.9	89.2
Average 1928	89.4	86.1
May 1929	89.7	82.4
November 1929	82.8	83.1
December 1929	73.7	78.1
May 1930	74.3	79.2
May 1931	60.5	68.0

Source: Compiled from Institut für Konjunkturforschung, Berlin, *Vierteljahrsheft*, vol. v (1930) no. 2, pt. B, p. 57, and vol. vi (1931) no. 2, pt. B, p. 49.

in the means of payment causes disturbances to the productive process; this is true also of all reductions in the supply of capital. The supply of foreign capital is especially exposed to fluctuations; political events above all may bring about a sudden withdrawal. The extraordinary fluctuations in the unemployment curve of Germany since 1925 can hardly be explained without reference to the often very precipitate transitions from influx to stoppage and withdrawal of foreign loans. The announcement of the Hoover moratorium in the summer of 1931 induced a precipitate flight of foreign capital, which caused unemployment to increase more than 4 percent between July and September.

Phenomena very similar to those characteristic of cyclical unemployment are produced in a country with heavy export interests when there is a decline in the value of its currency relative to foreign currencies. The depression which followed the stabilization of the English pound presents a classic example: stabilization was undertaken in 1925 at a rate of exchange which considerably raised the dollar value of the pound. Consequently British exporters received about 14 percent less for their goods in the third quarter of 1927 than they had before stabilization, while this was balanced only to the extent of some 25 percent by a cheapening of the prices of imported raw materials, such as cotton. The competing manufacturers in other countries, notably France, Belgium and Italy, which selected a favorable exchange rate for the stabilization of their currencies enjoyed the advantage of comparably lower internal production costs, which slowly approximated world market prices. The prolonged unemployment in England's export industries was undoubtedly responsible in part for that country's abandonment of the gold standard.

The curve of unemployment is not only a barometer of economic well being but also a measure of the social burden of labor. An important feature of the crisis which set in after 1929 is the marked tendency to shift economic and social burdens from one population group to another, from one class to another, from one country to another. Undoubtedly a multitude of political, economic and social factors combine to this end. The circumstances which play a vital part in making unemployment so much more widespread in the present crisis than in any other cyclical slump can be divided most appropriately into two groups: those which have intensified the crisis as a specifically cyclical phenomenon, and those which have hampered its liquidation because they have helped to block the adjustment of costs to falling prices. The first group pertain of course especially to the field of monetary phenomena. In periods of decline falling prices and rising interest rates tend to intensify crises and to prolong depression periods. The general trend of economic development is slowed down. World economy, it has been maintained, was under the influence of a declining long wave from 1914 to 1921; an analogy may be found only in the crisis of the 1870's, which occurred approximately at the break of the preceding long cyclical wave. One contributing factor is the maldistribution of gold, which makes the reciprocal approximation of the price systems of various countries extremely difficult.

These disorganizing tendencies have been aided by the uneven movement in the international flow of capital in the post-war period in contrast to its very steady development in the pre-war decades, in which it was chiefly under the domination of the English financial market. In the United States, which has become the creditor country of the whole world, there have been explosive expansion and contraction of capital supply. Since the extraordinary expansion of credit in the boom period served in part to finance consumption, the contraction of credit which very quickly involved all debtor countries was all the more sudden. Many political developments also helped to shake confidence in the credits to debtor countries. The effects of this flight of capital could be ameliorated on the whole only by sharp limitations on trade in securities and foreign exchanges. The price fall which resulted from this unusual restriction in the means of payment and the volume of credit was further aggravated by the fact that the process of mechanization of production since the end of the war had also involved to an increasing degree the production of raw materials, especially in agriculture. The endeavor of many governments to restrain the threatening collapse of agricultural prices by interventionist measures made for an even greater drop in prices when the decline could no longer be prevented. In the United States, with 1926 as 100, the index of wholesale trade fell to about 60 from the end of 1929 to the beginning of 1933, while the index of highly flexible prices dropped to about 30. Since the prices of industrial goods did not sink to the same extent, it was possible to buy the same amount of agricultural goods with a much reduced amount of industrial goods. Thus the purchasing power of the agricultural population contracted and along with it the market for industrial products and the rate of employment in industry. As a result of the very sharp contraction in capital investment the market for means of production was reduced to a fraction of its capacity (in the case of the iron and steel industries, on a world scale, to less than one half). The entire income pyramid began to sway.

The prolonged resistance to the downward trend by prices of industrial products was closely bound up with the fact that in most countries industry's fixed charges constituted a large part of the costs of production. This may be attributed to the immobility of great capital invested in large industrial enterprises, whose fixed costs mount progressively with the decline in the rate of utilization of productive capacity; to the immobility of the wage system; to the heavy burdens on industry in the form of taxes, contributions for social insurance, high interest rates, the fixing of prices by cartels and other combinations of important raw materials and half finished goods. The more other prices fell, the more important did the fixed elements in costs become.

Efforts to limit the extent of the price decline, and thus at least partly to compensate for the insufficient elasticity of the economic system, were supported by the most persevering measures of protectionist commercial policy (raising of tariffs, import embargoes and quotas). The total value of world trade in the third quarter of 1932 was only about one third that in 1929. The condition of the balance of trade of individual countries and its effects on the rate of employment in export industries are determined much less by government commercial policy than by other factors. These are chiefly international migration of capital supply, devaluation of currencies and limitation of trade in securities. The improvement of the balance of trade of those countries which exported capital during the crisis, despite all the other modifying influences, is as clearly discernible as the opposite development in countries which attracted capital.

There is little likelihood that there will be an early and drastic liquidation of unemployment in Europe, particularly in view of the absence of the condition most essential to an intensive stimulation of production: the prospect of comprehensive, profitable, long term productive investments. The struggle against unemployment is handicapped chiefly by the fact that the factors which disturb the balance between production and consumption of products often work entirely independently of one another, cutting across those very tendencies which open the way to a restoration of the balance. At bottom there is only one method of combating unemployment which has no direct connection with its causes, but it is for this very reason limited in scope. That is, the organization of unemployment exchanges combined with the creation of work which can render important services also through its auxiliary aspects: vocational guidance of young people, resettlement of unemployed in regions in which they can find steady work, reeducation of workers who have no further prospect of employment in their old trades, planning and execution of public works, organization of emigration and similar measures.

Public works are advocated not only to "make work" but as a means of stimulating the capital expenditures necessary for revival. Public initiative is to rectify the failure of private enterprise. Especially in countries with state systems of unemployment relief it is frequently maintained that it is better to use state funds for public works than in the form of entirely unproductive relief, which, should unemployment last long, becomes a regular state annuity, or "dole." If this kind of state action is to be effective, if it is to make idle capital active or lead the way to credit expansion, thus producing revival and an increase in employment, the public works program must be based on other considerations than that of emergency works designed to give employment to the jobless. Nearly all industrial countries—the United States, France, Italy, Germany, Sweden, Czechoslovakia, Japan and Chile—have spent millions on public works, partly as a means of making work, partly as a means of stimulating revival. Only England took no such measures. But while programs of public works have provided some employment for the jobless, they have not resulted in any substantial upward movement of revival and recovery.

KARL PRIBRAM

See: BUSINESS CYCLES; OVERPRODUCTION; DISTRIBUTION; INDUSTRIALISM; INDUSTRIAL REVOLUTION; TECHNOLOGY; LABOR; LABOR TURNOVER; MIGRATORY LABOR; CASUAL LABOR; UNEMPLOYMENT INSURANCE; PUBLIC WORKS; STABILIZATION, ECONOMIC; NATIONAL ECONOMIC PLANNING; RATIONALIZATION; EMPLOYMENT EXCHANGES; HOURS OF LABOR; SHORT HOURS MOVEMENT; POOR LAWS; POVERTY; SOCIAL INSURANCE; LABOR MOVEMENT; SOCIALISM; PROLETARIAT.

Consult: Berridge, W. A., *Cycles of Unemployment in the United States, 1903–1922*, Pollak Foundation for Economic Research, Publications, no. 4 (New York 1923); Beveridge, W. H., *Unemployment; a Problem of Industry* (*1909 and 1930*) (new ed. London 1930); Clay, Henry, *The Post-War Unemployment Problem* (London 1929); Bibby, J. P., *Unemployment* (London 1929); Douglas, Paul H., *Real Wages in the United States, 1890–1926*, Pollak Foundation for Economic Research, Publications, no. 9 (Boston 1930); Douglas, Paul H., and Director, Aaron, *The Problem of Unemployment* (New York 1931); *Unemployment as a World Problem*, ed. by Quincy Wright, University of Chicago, Norman Wait Harris Memorial Foundation, Lectures, 1931 (Chicago 1931); World Social Economic Congress, Amsterdam, 1931, *International Unemployment* (The Hague 1932); International Labour Office, *Hours of Work and Unemployment* (Geneva 1933); *Die Arbeitslosigkeit der Gegenwart*, ed. by Manuel Saitzew, Verein für Sozialpolitik, Schriften, vol. clxxxv, pts. 1–3, 3 vols. (Munich 1932–33); International Labour Office, "Unemployment Problems in 1931," and "Unemployment Problems in the United States," by H. B. Butler, *Studies and Reports*, ser. C, nos. 16 and 17 (Geneva 1931); National Bureau of Economic Research, *Business Cycles and Unemployment* (New York 1923); Conference on Unemployment, Washington, D. C., 1921, Committee on Recent Economic Changes, *Planning and Control of Public Works*, National Bureau of Economic Research, Publications, no. 17 (New York 1930); Demant, V. A., *This Unemployment* (4th ed. London 1932); Great Britain, Royal Commission on Unemployment Insurance, *Report*, Cmd. 4185 (1932); "Unemployment Insurance and Relief in Overseas Countries" in Great Britain, Ministry of Labour, *Labour Gazette*, vol. xli (1933) 128–29; Lederer, Emil, *Technischer Fortschritt und Arbeitslosigkeit* (Tübingen 1931); Weintraub, David, "The Displacement of Workers through Increases in Efficiency and Their Absorption by Industry, 1920–1931" in American Statistical Association, *Journal*, vol. xxvii (1932) 383–400; Lubin, Isador, *The Absorption of the Unemployed by American Industry*, Brookings Institution, Pamphlet series, vol. i, no. 3 (Washington 1929); Corey, Lewis, *The Decline of American Capitalism* (New York 1934) pt. v; Marx, Karl, *Das Kapital*, 2 vols. (ed. by B. Kautsky, Leipsic 1929), bk. i tr. by E. and C. Paul (London 1928), and bks. ii–iii tr. by E. Untermann, 2 vols. (Chicago 1906–09); Hobson, J. A., *The Economics of Unemployment* (rev. ed. London 1931), and *Rationalisation and Unemployment* (London 1930); Bielschowsky, Georg, "Business Fluctuations and Public Works" in *Quarterly Journal of Economics*, vol. xliv (1929–30) 286–319; International Labour Office, "Unemployment and Public Works," *Studies and Reports*, ser. C, no. 15 (Geneva 1931); Fricke, Rolf, *Die Ursachen der Arbeitslosigkeit in Deutschland* (Berlin 1931); Lampe, Adolf, *Notstandsarbeiten oder Lohnabbau?* (Jena 1927); Lukas, Eduard, *Das wahre Wesen und die wahren Aufgaben der Arbeitslosenversicherung* . . . (Graz 1926); Mahr, Alexander, *Hauptprobleme der Arbeitslosigkeit*, Wiener staats- und rechtswissenschaftliche Studien, vol. xx (Leipsic 1931); Martin, P. W., *Unemployment and Purchasing Power* (London 1929); Pigou, A. C., *Industrial Fluctuations* (2nd ed. London 1929), and *The Theory of Unemployment* (London 1933); Reithinger, Anton, "Stand und Ursachen der Arbeitslosigkeit in Deutschland" in *Vierteljahrshefte zur Konjunkturforschung*, Sonderheft xxix (Berlin 1932); Wedemeyer, Rudolf, *Mit Lohnsenkungen gegen die Arbeitslosigkeit?* (Berlin 1930); International Labour Office, "Methods of Statistics of Unemployment," *Studies and Reports*, ser. N, no. 7 (Geneva 1925); National Federation of Settlements, Unemployment Committee, *Case Studies of Unemployment*, University of Pennsylvania, Wharton School of Finance and Commerce, Industrial Research Department, Research Studies, vol. xii (Philadelphia 1931); Calkins, Clinch, *Some Folks Won't Work* (New York 1930); Wunderlich, Frieda, "New Aspects of Unemployment in Germany" in *Social Research*, vol. i (1934) 97–110.

UNEMPLOYMENT EXCHANGE. *See* EMPLOYMENT EXCHANGES.

UNEMPLOYMENT INSURANCE. The term unemployment insurance is generally used to describe governmental schemes, both voluntary and compulsory, which now form part of the social insurance systems of most European countries. On the basis of regular contributions —under voluntary schemes by workers jointly with the state and under most compulsory contributory schemes including employers—benefits for a stipulated period are paid to insured workers involuntarily unemployed who have fulfilled certain requirements and come within certain occupational and age groupings. Occasionally the term is used also to designate non-governmental unemployment benefit plans; these consist of trade union funds, financed entirely by the workers; company plans, financed by employers and sometimes also by the workers; and in a few instances of joint employer-trade union schemes, jointly financed. Up to July, 1934, the only type of unemployment benefit existing in the United States was non-governmental. As originally conceived unemployment benefit schemes were insurance not against unemployment itself but against the distress caused by unemployment, and the idea of mutual sharing of risks and the payment of stipulated amounts as a contractual right was advanced as preferable to public or private charitable relief. Despite their dominantly ameliorative purpose most trade union and public plans have included certain preventive features. Their usual correlation with a system of public exchanges has made for a better organization of the labor market and has served to cut down preventible unemployment. Less directly a system of regulated benefits has helped to prevent the undercutting of wage standards of the employed and has contributed toward the maintenance of purchasing power. Another constructive feature has been the provision of adequate statistical data as to the nature and incidence of unemployment; such information is necessary not only for the operation of a system of unemployment insurance but for the planning of other measures to relieve unemployment, such as public relief supplementary to insurance, public works and the like. However, proponents of public unemployment insurance in the United States have recently tended to stress the preventive rather than the ameliorative aspect in the belief that certain types of unemployment insurance would furnish employers with a powerful incentive to stabilize employment.

The attitude implicit in all plans of unemployment insurance, that involuntary unemployment is caused through no fault of the worker and that the distress it entails must therefore be alleviated or prevented, represents a recent development in public opinion and policy. Even after the rise of modern industrialism with its recurrent mass unemployment public authorities continued to regard loss of work as indication of personal shortcoming. And both in the punitive vagrancy laws and in those dealing with "able bodied" poor which were inherited from another type of economic society the central motive was to force the unemployed to work. When major unemployment crises developed, there were added to these measures extended provisions for poor relief, both public and private, which involved not only humiliating "means" tests but in some communities an accompanying loss of citizenship rights.

As in other types of social insurance, the origins of public unemployment insurance are to be found in the benefit systems established by trade unions. Early in the nineteenth century some trade unions in most industrialized countries began to set up a correlated system of placement service, traveling and unemployment benefits. As early as 1824 in England the Journeymen's Steam Engine Makers' Society and in Belgium in 1846 the Brussels Printers' Union began to pay out of work benefits.

Since, however, the trade unions in the nineteenth century were mainly composed of skilled workers in the most strategic positions and often outside the factory system proper, the unorganized mass of the working population, commonly the lowest paid and the most insecure, was still forced to resort to poor relief in times of unemployment. In Great Britain, where the trade union movement developed earliest and most rapidly, the total number of workers covered by such plans was about 500,000 at the end of the nineteenth century; in Germany (in 1904) about 454,000 were thus provided for and in France about 30,000. Moreover the amounts paid were small and the period of payment was brief. Even when unionism was established in the latter half of the nineteenth century among a section of the factory, mine and transport workers, the magnitude of the problem of unemployment—seasonal, cyclical and technological—and the limited resources of the unions made impossible a system of trade union benefits. Instead these unions stressed division of work in slack times with occasional trade union relief funds to supplement oppressive poor relief.

The catastrophic rise of unemployment in the last decade of the nineteenth century in most of the industrialized countries of Europe led the trade unions, whose funds were being drained, and the growing political labor parties to demand from their governments work or public support. The insistence on public responsibility led to the appointment in a number of continental countries of commissions to investigate the possibilities of governmental participation in these trade union funds. The inauguration in the late 1880's by Germany of a nation wide compulsory scheme of workmen's accident compensation set a valuable precedent for the consideration of public subsidies to unemployment insurance.

Nevertheless, governmental participation in unemployment funds began first on a municipal basis, mainly through subsidies to existing trade union funds. The pioneer experiments in this field were made not in Germany, the classic land of social insurance, but in Switzerland. As early as 1789 the town of Basel had proposed a system of voluntary insurance for lace makers, but it was never carried into effect. Following the depression of 1890–91, which led to the submission to the federal chancellor of a resolution sponsored by the Swiss socialists wherein the right of work was demanded for every citizen, the first modern experiment in unemployment insurance was inaugurated. In 1893 the town of Berne established a fund which was to provide benefits for insured persons unemployed through no fault of their own. It was administered by public authorities, and provision was made for annual subsidies to trade union and mutual aid society benefit funds. It was to be built up in part from voluntary contributions from employers and in part from gifts from individuals. The workers made their contributions to their trade union funds; and since the employers' contributions and the voluntary gifts were not forthcoming, the actual burden was divided between the workers and the municipality. For this reason and also because the scheme attracted mainly workers in occupations with a high percentage of unemployment, benefits were soon restricted to winter months and even then the fund could not meet its obligations. Similar schemes launched by municipalities in other countries (Cologne and Bologna in 1896 and Leipsic in 1903) encountered the same difficulties. The somewhat more successful plans of Dijon (1896), Limoges and Liége (1897) were based from the outset on public subsidies from public funds to trade unions with established plans. An even more daring experiment was made by the Swiss canton of St. Gallen, which in 1894 instituted the first scheme of compulsory public insurance; this, however, survived for only two years.

The first really successful plan for voluntary public insurance was established in 1901 in the Belgian city of Ghent. The Ghent plan placed its system on a permanent basis and established a public commission to handle the funds and allocate them to unions or to individuals who fulfilled certain stipulated requirements. The number of trade union members covered by the Ghent funds rose to 12,000 in 1902 and 17,000 in 1907. A number of other Belgian communes adopted the plan and in 1907 it was made applicable to the entire country. France in 1905, Norway in 1906 and Denmark in 1907 also adopted the Ghent plan for the nation as a whole; in other continental countries it was taken over by the municipalities.

The Ghent plan was essentially a system of public subsidies to trade union funds, with some measure of public control over requirements and administration. Although membership was open to individuals, including persons not affiliated with a union, in practise the plan was limited mainly to members of those trade unions which had functioning benefit funds. Employers were not required to make any contribution. Such a system served to encourage the establishment of self-help institutions by the workers themselves, and it had the additional advantage of requiring a minimum of administrative machinery. On the other hand, its effectiveness in coverage depended not only on the numerical strength of the unions but on the extent to which they had qualified for membership. At the outbreak of the World War 62.2 percent of the trade union membership in Belgium, 86 percent in Denmark, 51.4 percent in Norway and 22.6 percent in France were covered by such funds. But of the total wage earning population, excluding agricultural workers, the percentages were 7.1, 56.1, 20.6 and .04 respectively. Thus Belgium and France, which were more highly industrialized than the other two countries, covered only a small fraction of the workers.

It was partly because of the foregoing considerations that Great Britain in 1911 chose the method of compulsory insurance. Unlike most continental countries, England had no municipal voluntary schemes and its workers had had to depend largely on poor relief. The British plan, when it began operating in 1912, applied to about 2,500,000 workers—several times as many as were covered by all the public voluntary schemes in other countries. After the war, under the stress of mass unemployment, national public unemployment insurance was widely advocated throughout Europe. Although several other countries, as shown by the following table, eventually adopted voluntary public insurance, the number of workers in countries with compulsory plans was ten times as great. At the beginning of 1919 of the 4,500,000 to 5,000,000 wageworkers covered by unemployment insurance plans 3,750,000 were in Great Britain, then the only country with a compulsory scheme. In 1931 of about 39,000,000 insured 35,500,000 were under compulsory schemes. In 1933 totals had risen to 42,000,000 and 38,000,000 respectively. The Soviet Union, which in 1922 enacted a comprehensive compulsory scheme, is excluded from the table because the plan was suspended in 1930 with the liquidation of unemployment.

Although unemployment insurance was not

COVERAGE OF PUBLIC UNEMPLOYMENT INSURANCE, 1931

COMPULSORY PLANS

Country	First Adopted	Number Insured	Percentage of Gainfully Employed	Percentage of Wage-Workers
Great Britain	1911	12,290,000	63.5	75
Italy	1919	4,250,000	23.0	
Irish Free State	1920	283,000	16.0	
Austria	1920	1,181,000	38.0	54
Australia*	1922	170,000	52.4	
Poland	1922	1,206,000	9.0	
Bulgaria	1925	307,000	12.0	
Switzerland†	1925–30‡	150,000		
Germany	1927	15,600,000	48.7	75

VOLUNTARY PLANS

Country	First Adopted	Number Insured	Percentage of Gainfully Employed	Percentage of Wage-Workers
France	1905	300,000	1.5	
Norway	1915**	36,000	3.3	
Netherlands	1916	450,000	16.0	35
Finland	1917	69,000	5.0	
Spain	1919††			
Belgium	1920**	641,000	20.0	25
Denmark	1921**	288,000	21.0	35
Czechoslovakia	1921	1,734,000	28.0	40
Switzerland	1925–30‡	165,000		

* Queensland only.
† Nine cantons.
‡ The Swiss plans, compulsory and voluntary (323,754 workers), cover 17.5 of the gainfully employed and 40 percent of the wageworking public.
** These are the dates of the amended, not the original plans.
†† Not in operation.
Source: United States, Bureau of Labor Statistics, *Monthly Labor Review*, vol. xxxiii (1931) 48–74.

limited to countries with strong labor movements but was adopted as well by other countries including even Fascist Italy, actually the balance of political and economic forces is demonstrated by the proportion of the population covered as well as by the amount, duration and type of benefits. Even in countries with a strong trade union movement and adequate plans administration has varied with the type of government in power. The somewhat tardy entrance of Germany in the field is attributable to a number of factors: in the pre-war period the existence of well established trade union benefits often combined with municipal subsidies and a comparatively low rate of unemployment; in the post-war years the enactment of emergency relief measures as a preliminary toward unemployment insurance, which was temporarily delayed by the absorption of the unemployed in the period of inflation. When it was eventually adopted, the German system of unemployment insurance provided for a more complete coverage than that of any other country.

Failure to adopt public unemployment insurance in the United States must be explained on altogether different grounds. It has been estimated by Douglas that in the pre-war period the average yearly rate of unemployment was far higher than in any European country. Only a small proportion of the trade union movement, which in turn represented less than 10 percent of the industrial wage earners, was affected by trade union plans. Both the structure of the government and the character of public opinion operated against the acceptance of the idea of unemployment insurance. It is true that the British scheme, especially in the first years of its operation, aroused some interest; but this was manifested concretely only in Massachusetts in 1916, when a bill was introduced in the state legislature. Despite the high rate of unemployment there persisted even through the worst periods of unemployment a belief in eventual recovery. After the war talk of unemployment insurance was revived during the depression of 1921 but with little effect. For one thing, unlike European countries, the United States had no system of public exchanges requisite to the operation of unemployment insurance. The trade unions too were largely opposed to such proposals. Furthermore there was no widespread experience with private schemes, for at the very height of their development trade union, employer and joint union-employer schemes never affected more than 200,000 workers. In 1932 only 3 international unions had benefit schemes covering altogether 1000 members; 39 local union plans covered an additional 42,000. Employers' plans applied to about 73,000—the membership was reduced to 32,000 in 1933—and trade union-employer plans, the first of which on a small scale was launched in 1894, covered 47,000 workers, mainly in the men's and women's garment industries. When these industries had set up such plans in 1921, a far greater number had been included. Even after the beginning of the depression in 1929 the movement for unemployment insurance developed only slowly, and the American Federation of Labor did not endorse it until 1932. By this time certain developments in the British scheme led to a concerted opposition; not only were the traditional arguments advanced, but in addition the supposed malignant effects of the British "dole" were now publicized. Because of prejudice thus aroused many proponents of unemployment insurance measures have endeavored to depart from the British precedent.

Because of the extensive discussion as to the British experience it is advisable at this point to describe the English scheme in some detail. Prior to the enactment of the unemployment insurance bill of 1911 the British government had set up a coordinated system of public employment exchanges. On the basis of the data yielded by these exchanges and supplemented by trade union statistics on unemployment the plan was originally applied to workers in industries where unemployment was severe but not strictly seasonal. The trades selected comprised about 2,500,000 workers and were characterized by a yearly average rate of unemployment of 8.6 percent as compared with an average for all industries of 6 percent. On the basis of these figures a fund was set up to which contributions were made by employers, workers and the national Treasury. The share of employers and workers, equally divided, amounted to three quarters of the total. Both the contributions of the workers and the benefits paid them were flat; no distinction was made as to earnings, sex or age. The entire system was contractual; the number of benefits paid was in proportion to contributions made by the insured worker (a ratio of 1:5), and the duration of the benefits was limited to 15 weeks in any one year. Provisions were also included allowing rebates to employers who supplied continuous employment and to workers over sixty who had paid in at least 500 weekly contributions and had not drawn out an equivalent amount in benefits. The workings of the law required only a few simple rules as to testing of qualifications: proof that the insured applicant for benefits had not refused suitable employment at a public exchange; elimination of those unemployed through strikes and lockouts and of certain age groups. Administration was vested in the Ministry of Labour, and the system operated through the public employment exchanges at which workers registered.

This scheme, instituted at a time of relatively stable employment, was able to accumulate during the war years a large surplus, which amounted to over £18,000,000, or enough to cover an additional number of 1,250,000 upon demobilization. Actually, however, the needs of unemployed ex-service men and civilians were met not from this fund but from an emergency Out-of-Work Donation fund created in 1918. It was in connection with this latter fund, not administered on an insurance basis but working also through the exchanges, that the term dole was applied.

Unemployment, which at the beginning of 1919 was as low as 2.4 percent of trade union members and perhaps 4.5 percent of the total population, rose rapidly. By November, 1919, the Out-of-Work Donation fund went out of existence, and by 1921 the ex-service fund also was abolished. In 1920, when the unemployed constituted 7.8 percent of the insured population, the insurance scheme was extended to all wageworkers between the ages of sixteen and sixty-five, with the exception of those in agriculture, domestic service, certain public jobs which enjoyed security of tenure and non-manual workers whose rate of payment exceeded £250 per annum. The coverage was thus increased from about 4,000,000 to over 11,000,000. Benefits were raised from 7 to 15 shillings per week for men and to 12 for women, with proportionately greater contributions from all three parties, while the proportion of benefits to contributions was modified to 1:6. In other respects the basic features of the 1911 act were retained. The statutory conditions and disqualifications for benefit were almost exactly the same. And since the reserves had risen to over £22,000,000, the fund would even now have been able to meet its obligations if the rate of unemployment had not increased.

But the concurrent elimination of the emergency fund and rapid rise in unemployment led the government in 1921 to pass amendments which in effect relaxed the previous requirements as to the relation between contributions and benefits. Benefits could now be paid or "extended" in advance of contributions to unemployed persons who were in trades or occupations where there was a likelihood of reemployment or to persons in insurable trades who had exhausted their benefits. These extended benefits were, however, payable only under certain conditions, which in some instances amounted to "means" tests set at the discretion of the Ministry of Labour. Additional allowances were made for dependents of all beneficiaries, involving further recognition of "need." Benefits were raised one third and their duration was almost doubled. As a result of the heavy drain entailed by these changes the reserves of the fund were soon exhausted and the Exchequer was called upon for large loans. The number of unemployed and therefore of claimants rose rapidly, from 1,065,000 in January, 1921, to 2,015,000 in January, 1922; after a drop in January, 1924 to 1,374,000 it began to increase again.

The unemployment situation, undoubtedly a factor in the victory of the Labour party in 1924, confronted the short lived Labour government with serious difficulties. It inaugurated changes which set more rigid requirements—all applicants had to prove that they were "genuinely seeking work"—and at the same time it abolished the principle of "ministerial discretion" for extended benefits and increased both the amount and the duration of benefits. The rules for the return of unused contributions were abolished. The government's contribution was raised from one fourth to one third, so that now all three parties paid an equal share. Finally, provision was made for a thorough investigation of the system.

The act of 1927 incorporating many of the suggestions of the Blanesburgh investigating committee abolished extended benefits and made all benefits standard. No limit, however, was set for the duration of benefits; the restriction of benefits in proportion to contributions was canceled and the requirement of 30 contributions during the two years preceding unemployment was made virtually ineffective. The rates of contributions were again increased, but the proportion of the state was lowered. Benefits were likewise raised. At the time this act was passed it was assumed on the basis of the committee's report that the peak of the crisis had been reached and that there would be a yearly unemployment average of 6 percent instead of the actual average of 13 percent.

Actually, however, there was no decrease in unemployment, and upon the return of the Labour government in 1929 there was further liberalization. The applicant was given the benefit of doubt in his search for work, the provision for "a reasonable period of insurable employment during the past two years" was abolished, benefit rates for the age group seventeen to nineteen were raised and the minimum age requirement was lowered from sixteen to fifteen. Despite the provision for the increase of the share of the Exchequer again to one third of the total these changes involved augmented liabilities of some £8,000,000. The borrowings of the fund were finally limited in 1930 to £70,000,000.

The fall of the Labour government in 1931 resulted in the passage of the Economy Act by the National Ministry. At the same time that contributions were raised to 10s each from the contributing agencies—four times the original contribution of workers and employers under the act of 1911—benefits were reduced and standard benefits were limited to 26 weeks in a year. The means test was again applied to extended benefits, the cost of which was now met entirely by the government. Despite all these cuts, however, the fund was exhausted, and in 1931 the principle was adopted of meeting deficiencies with direct parliamentary grants. The steady rise of unemployment—the peak was reached in January, 1933, when 2,903,065 out of an insured population of approximately 12,900,-000 were registered at the employment exchanges—led to further hardships. Although the number was still over 2,000,000, benefit cuts instituted in 1931 were restored in July, 1934.

The British Unemployment Insurance Act of 1934 inaugurates a significant experiment in the discretionary relief of able bodied destitution beyond the range of insurance. Whereas hitherto the national government had confined its direct administrative functions to social insurance involving contractual rights, it now embarked upon national relief according to status. True, the national Treasury had previously paid for the discretionary relief on the basis of need by local authorities. The application of the means test by local authorities, who were frequently the poor law administrators, had been the basis of violent protests. The new act sets up for the purpose of administering discretionary relief to able bodied unemployed who are ineligible for unemployment insurance an Unemployment Assistance Board and centralized service which has no connection with nor obligation to local government. The experiment, a direct result of the rapidly growing sentiment that unemployment should be a national and not a local charge, may nevertheless cause much confusion and overlapping because of the setting up of two wholly separate centralized services for the same purpose.

In Germany unemployment insurance was established when post-war unemployment was at its peak, so that the system had to withstand even greater tests than the British. Socialist agitation for federal unemployment insurance in Germany began as early as 1895; by that time 15 of the 40 free trade unions had accumulated out-of-work benefits, and in 1896 the congress of these unions voted to grant assistance to unemployed members. Actually, however, the responsibility for relieving the bulk of the unemployed was left to the local poor authorities. In 1902 an investigation was initiated by the Reichstag as to the possibilities of a federal plan. Trade union opinion favored the Ghent system, which after 1907 had been inaugurated in a number of municipalities. The association of local public employment exchanges, the first of which had been set up in 1840, expressed a preference for compulsory insurance. In the face of strong opposition on the part of employers, especially in the heavy industries, no action was taken by the federal government. By the outbreak of the war about 25 municipalities had set up Ghent insurance plans.

The post-war period brought to the fore the problem of caring for 6,000,000 returned soldiers. The reduced territory of Germany and its depleted finances led therefore to emphasis on a program of "productive" relief through public works, "made" work by the welfare agencies and the customary poor relief. The Weimar constitution guaranteed to every citizen "the right to work or to financial support"; and after the first quarter of 1919 there was a steady improvement in the employment situation, which continued throughout the entire period of inflation. During this time plans were being formulated for the transformation of relief into an insurance system. An important step was taken in 1922 with the national coordination of the public employment exchanges. In 1923 under emergency orders an insurance system was to be set up on the basis of employer-employee and local community contributions to include all workers covered by health insurance. The commune was to bear one fifth of the cost and the other two parties were to divide the balance. Federal and state subsidies were to be utilized only for emergency relief funds. At the end of 1923 stabilization of the mark led to an increase in the number of the unemployed; over 2,000,000 workers were enrolled at the exchanges and in 1924 no fewer than 1,500,000 were recipients of public relief. Attempts were made to increase "productive" relief and rules were formulated to deal with layoffs imposed by the employer. The situation was aggravated in 1926 by the depression resulting from the waste of war, the burden of reparations, the loss of foreign markets and high tariff barriers.

Finally after nine years of experimentation it was realized that unemployment insurance must replace relief and that it must be national in scope. On July 16, 1927, the Employment Exchanges and Unemployment Insurance Act was passed. The costs of administration and maintenance were to be borne entirely and equally by employers and workers up to a maximum of 3 percent of wages. The federal government made no donations to the fund, but it did help to defray the expenses of the central office in Berlin and to contribute toward an emergency benefit fund. The bill covered all persons participating in the health and salaried employees' insurance schemes; it was not limited to German citizens, but it did exclude from the compulsory provision certain agricultural, forestry and fishery workers, those in home industries except domestic workers and those who had an income above a certain level. Workers involved in strikes and lockouts were ineligible to benefits, and there was the usual provision with respect to acceptance of suitable employment. Certain exceptions were also made for casual workers and for employees of the Zeiss firm, whose voluntary compensation scheme dated back to the pre-war period. Workers' contributions were proportional to earnings and benefits varied according to 11 wage classes (the lowest group receiving 75 percent of its representative wage, the highest 35 percent); supplementary benefits were allowed for dependents in amounts which would keep these proportions within the limits of 80 and 60 percent. The basis of classification was occupational. The entire scheme was interrelated with the other forms of social insurance, both workers and employers making their contributions along with health insurance premiums. Administration was vested in an autonomous body, the Reichsanstalt für Arbeitsvermittlung und Arbeitslosenversicherung, removed from political influences and conducted on a tripartite basis, with the balance of control held by the employers and the workers. The same was true of the courts of appeal. In contrast to the original British plan, which made previous contributions a basis of benefits, the German law defined as eligible only those involuntarily unemployed workers who had been employed at least 26 weeks in the previous year in an industry covered by compulsory insurance. From the outset provision was made for extension of benefits under certain conditions. By qualified aid to part time workers part time employment was encouraged. Emergency unemployment insurance for German citizens who had exhausted their benefits was provided for entirely by public funds, but applicants were subject to the means test.

Under conditions of mass unemployment, with no reserve and no provision for government contributions to the regular fund, the system by 1928 was forced to borrow from the federal government. In 1929 the number of jobless had increased to over 3,000,000; as a result more agricultural, industrial homeworkers and casual workers were excluded, so that the unemployed in these groups were shifted to relief funds. By April, 1930, the loans, which had reached $148,000,000, were canceled by the Reichstag but with the proviso that no further loans or subsidies were to be made. In September benefits were reduced, the duration was cut down to 13 weeks, a means test was introduced for extended unemployment, the qualifying period of previous employment was raised to 52 weeks in the preceding two years, and contributions were increased from $3\frac{1}{2}$ percent of the pay rolls to $6\frac{1}{2}$ percent. Emphasis was more and more shifted to relief work supported by local communities with additional federal subsidies for localities in special need. In November, 1931, when the number of the unemployed had somewhat decreased but was still above 5,000,000, there was passed a fourth emergency decree designed to reduce production costs, prices and the cost of living. Whereas from October, 1927, to March, 1928, 73 percent of the unemployed were receiving unemployment insurance, from April to December, 1932, the percentage was only 40. The average number receiving ordinary benefit fell from 67.5 percent of the insured unemployed for the fiscal year 1929 to 15 percent in 1932, while the recipients of emergency benefit increased from 15.3 percent in 1931 to 25 percent in 1932, leaving 12 percent of the unemployed without any benefit or relief in 1931 and 20 percent in 1932. Moreover in June, 1932, by a decree issued by Hindenburg, benefits were reduced by 23 percent, a means test was introduced for regular benefits after a period of 36 days and surpluses from regular benefit funds were applied to other forms of unemployed relief. A peak of unemployment reaching 6,128,000 in February, 1933, led to a relaxation of some of these orders, but the tendency persisted toward supporting the mass of the jobless through other means than insurance. With the accession to power of the National Socialists the coverage of the act was further reduced to exclude all female domestic workers (May, 1933) and all agricultural workers (October, 1933). At the latter date the financing of the emergency as well as of the ordinary benefits was shifted entirely to employers and workers.

In both Great Britain and Germany the attack on unemployment insurance related in the main to inclusion of groups not strictly classifiable on an insurance basis. But in Great Britain for the year ending March 31, 1930, transitional benefits constituted less than 7 percent of the total disbursements of £53,400,000 for unemployment benefits, and at their peak (in December, 1930, when the number in receipt of such benefits had risen from 140,000 to 400,000) about one fifth of the total disbursements. The situation was far more serious in Germany: in December, 1931, of the 5,608,000 unemployed 29 percent were drawing regular benefits, 27 percent were covered by emergency grants, 28 percent were getting community relief and 16 percent were receiving no aid at all.

Despite the hardships encountered by the two major systems of unemployment insurance there have been no serious proposals in Great Britain or in Germany for their abandonment. It is true that numerous investigations have brought out many criticisms and suggestions for reform. The British critics in their testimony before the Royal Commission on Unemployment Insurance appointed in December, 1930, indicated a number of deficiencies and questioned certain policies. The argument was advanced that the system tends artificially to maintain the wage rate, since any attempt to lower benefits has been vigorously fought because of its probable effect on the wages of the employed. It has been charged that workers have refused to accept employment, preferring to live on their benefits; but such assertions are patently ridiculous in view of the small amount of the benefit payments as compared with the average or even the lower than average wage levels. Far more important were criticisms as to the basis upon which insured groups were chosen and the maintenance of the essential contractual insurance elements, the necessity for the distinction between insurance and relief and the wisdom of a general fund which distributed the costs of insurance without distinction among highly casual and continuous industries, "dying" and "live" enterprises, foresighted and careless employers and workers.

It is this last point which brings out the chief difference between the European plans and the so-called American plan, first proposed in 1921 during the depression of that year by Professor John R. Commons of Wisconsin. Subsequently it was sponsored by the American Association for Labor Legislation and introduced in modified form in a number of states.

The "American" plan of unemployment insurance is perhaps best understood by the term unemployment compensation frequently applied to it. It is based on the notion that unemployment is an industrial hazard which, like industrial accidents, can be greatly lessened through foresight on the part of individual employers and that unemployment compensation, like workmen's (accident) compensation, should be so planned as to distinguish between the foresighted and the careless employer. Financing should be borne entirely by the employers, and contributions should be placed not in a general treasury but in separate funds for each employer, with provision for a reduction of the rate with decreased employment in each plant. Specifically the Wisconsin plan, which finally went into effect in July, 1934, includes the following provisions. Employers make contributions to an unemployment insurance fund amounting to 2 percent of their respective pay rolls. The benefit, paid after a waiting period of 2 weeks, is not to exceed 50 percent of the average weekly earnings of the unemployed worker or $10 a week; and only $100 may be paid to a beneficiary in a single year. If an employer by reducing unemployment can accumulate reserves amounting to an average of $55 per employee, the rate of contribution is to be cut down to 1 percent; and if the reserves reach an average of $75, the contributions are to be temporarily eliminated as long as that reserve is maintained. If, however, in a specific fund the average per employee falls below $55, the rate is not to be increased but the benefit to the worker is to be cut proportionally. The state is custodian of the funds and provision is made for tripartite representation on advisory and administrative boards.

The Wisconsin plan has served as the basis of plans advocated by several governmental and non-governmental commissions; and it has been accepted in principle by the American Federation of Labor. Under the sponsorship of the American Association for Labor Legislation, which launched its American Plan for Unemployment Reserves in 1930, it was introduced in a number of states in 1930–32. Its sponsors hold that the plan has several points in its favor: it requires no direct contributions from the workers or from the state; its provisions make its administration comparatively simple; and its basic concept removes the inequalities which have led in England, according to Sir William Beveridge, to the "subsidizing of dying industries by more prosperous ones, thus retarding the solution of the problem of unemployment in the dying industries."

Until 1932 practically all plans proposed in the United States were based on the Wisconsin idea of unemployment reserves. In that year, however, the report of the Ohio Commission on Unemployment Insurance included in its recommendation the draft of a bill on somewhat more traditional lines. Instead of separate funds it advocated a general fund which was to be built up by contributions from workers as well as employers. By implication therefore the report did not accept the theory of the individual employer's responsibility for unemployment but treated it as a concern of industry and of the working class. Because of the objection which public subsidies would arouse the report did not include provision for state contributions but only for state assumption of the cost of the plan. The commission advocated the general fund on the ground that true insurance involved a spreading of the risk and offered more protection to those who through no fault of their own worked in a plant or industry with a high rate of unemployment and therefore easily exhausted reserve funds. The commission did suggest, however, that differentiation of rates of contribution for employers or industries be based on careful statistical studies and actuarial experience, which could be put into effect without abandonment of the general pool. Workers' contributions were recommended on the ground that they would establish the worker's right to participate in the administration and conservation of funds, spread the risk among all workers and make possible a higher rate of benefit. After a careful study of all available unemployment figures for 1923–31 the commission suggested a contribution to be divided equally between workers and employers and to amount to 4 percent of the total pay rolls of the industries and groups involved. This rate would allow for adequate reserves for emergency, since the actuarial calculations of the cost of benefits called for a rate of 3 percent. Benefits, to be paid after a waiting period of three weeks, were to be limited as in the Wisconsin plan to 50 percent of the previous average wage; but the maximum was set at $15 and the duration at 16 weeks, thus allowing a yearly maximum of $240. The commission estimated that if such a plan had been adopted by Ohio in 1921, benefits in the first two years of the depression would have been available to the amount of $200,000,000.

Although the Ohio plan failed to pass the state senate in 1933, it served as the model for 120 bills introduced in state legislatures in that year. Nor was it without influence on the

American plan. In 1933 the proponents of the latter introduced modifications to compel pooling of the individual funds "when the administrative authority after investigation and public hearing finds that it is desirable in order to safeguard the general reserves." The rate of contributions was raised to 3 percent, with provisions for a reserve per employee of $65 before reduction to 1 percent and $100 before discontinuance. The maximum duration was also raised to the same level as in the Ohio plan.

The method of enacting legislation by states has of course considerably retarded the progress of unemployment insurance in the United States and has raised the usual charge of unfair competition between states with and without such schemes. The Wagner-Lewis bill, introduced into Congress in 1934, was designed to stimulate the passage of state measures. It proposed a 5 percent tax on all employers' pay rolls, with the stipulation that employers' contributions to state unemployment insurance funds be credited against this federal tax. It did not endorse either the American or the Ohio plan, leaving the choice to the individual state. The bill, however, failed of passage. In the meanwhile advocates of both plans have suggested various possibilities of experimentation.

Perhaps the most basic problem encountered in the field of unemployment insurance is that of obtaining pertinent statistics to supply the basis for a sound insurance system. A careful classification of such data should also serve to mark off groups and industries in which the distress caused by unemployment must be met by supplementary public relief rather than by insurance measures. Statistical data should if possible cover several successive business cycles and should separate by wage and occupational groupings the rate and duration of unemployment, the total number of jobless persons and the average length of unemployment per person, the total number of claims and their annual duration under a number of possible plans. It is true that because of the still all too vague knowledge of trade cycles and the many variables which have not yet been defined and measured, the causes of unemployment are more complex than those of any other single risk. The catastrophe hazard is also imponderable. But these difficulties do not furnish insuperable obstacles to plans worked out experimentally. Indeed the necessary correlation of public employment exchanges with compulsory unemployment insurance schemes and of adequate trade union statistics with voluntary subsidized schemes has in European countries furnished far more accurate and continuous data with respect to the extent and incidence of unemployment than are available in the United States.

It remains true nevertheless that not all groups among the unemployed can be covered by insurance plans in the strict sense of the word. Specific exemptions are not made in most voluntary publicly subsidized schemes, because such schemes are limited to groups which already have weeded out the greatest risks. Spain, however, does specifically exempt domestic workers and civil servants. The latter are ineligible in other countries as well because of governmental pension provisions. Only Denmark and Spain exclude persons with an income above a set amount.

Compulsory subsidized plans, on the other hand, usually cut out certain groups. Domestic workers are excluded specifically in Austria, Great Britain, the Irish Free State, Italy, the state of Wisconsin and Germany since 1933. Similarly agricultural wageworkers are for the most part excluded. Only in Germany up to the spring of 1933 were they included. Although voluntary schemes do not exclude them, only in Czechoslovakia, Denmark and the Netherlands, where separate insurance societies are set up aside from the trade unions, are agricultural workers included and then only in small proportions. In both voluntary and compulsory schemes seasonal workers are usually restricted to benefits during the work season. This is usually true in voluntary funds as well. Another restriction that usually excludes the seasonal workers arises out of the clauses which stipulate a stated previous period of employment in the industry or a definite number of contributions to the fund. The period of time for employment in the industry is most frequently one year, although since the recent depression the time has been shortened in some countries. In Germany, although the ordinary rules concerning qualification for benefit apply to seasonal workers, the latter must have been employed for at least 26 weeks in their avowed occupation during the 52 weeks preceding their registration as unemployed. In Great Britain a seasonal worker must give proof that within each of the preceding two years he has been employed in some other insurable occupation during the off season or has a reasonable chance of being so employed. At the other end of the scale men manual workers with incomes above a certain limit are excluded in

Germany and Italy, and in Great Britain and Soviet Russia both manual and non-manual workers with incomes above certain amounts are likewise deprived of benefits. Finally, most countries provide that workers are ineligible if they receive any income other than earnings. A limitation frequently found in American proposals concerns the size of the establishment; most American plans set a minimum of from 3 to 10 workers; among European countries only Poland (until 1933) used this standard.

In addition to occupational exclusions there are those of age; minima vary greatly among countries of voluntary as well as subsidized insurance. Germany and Great Britain relate their minimum age requirement to the age when compulsory schooling ends, fourteen years. Other countries vary from a minimum of fifteen (Bulgaria, Finland and Italy) to eighteen (Denmark and Queensland). In Switzerland with its varying cantonal laws the range is from sixteen to twenty. There is also an upper limit, often correlated with the year at which old age provision begins: sixty in Denmark, Finland, Poland (non-manual workers) and Bulgaria; sixty-five in Great Britain, Spain and Italy.

Most countries make provisions in regard to the type of work which the jobless must accept if offered by the employment exchange. In Czechoslovakia a claimant may be obliged to take any employment which will not hinder his return to his original occupation. In France and Spain he is not required to depart from his own trade; in Belgium, Denmark, Finland, Norway and Switzerland and under most American proposals he must accept any work within a reasonable radius of distance and offering wages and working conditions equal to those prevailing in the locality. In Spain he need not take employment which necessitates a change in residence, while in Czechoslovakia he is entitled to free transportation to the new place of work. In Bulgaria, Austria and Great Britain he must accept any work offered by the exchange, after a certain period. Most countries provide that the unemployed person must be physically fit for the kind of employment offered, and several stipulate that it must not be injurious to health and morals. In most countries persons who leave work voluntarily without good reason or who are discharged for misconduct are not eligible for benefits, although Austria, Belgium, Germany, Great Britain, the Irish Free State, Italy, Poland and Spain restrict such disqualification to periods varying from one to two months.

Another provision usually relates to unemployment due to strikes and lockouts and to the refusal of available work in such instances. In almost all schemes persons directly involved in industrial disputes are not eligible for benefits. The Wisconsin act and the laws of some European countries provide, however, that a worker who is not directly involved in a strike or lockout but who is unemployed because of it is eligible for benefits. In other instances, as in Belgium, refusal by employers of governmental conciliation or a governmental award renders workers eligible for benefits. In order, however, to maintain their role of neutrality most governments have stipulated that refusal by unemployed workers of employment in undertakings involved in strikes or lockouts does not constitute refusal of suitable employment.

Finally, there is always a specified waiting period before benefits may be claimed. Except in France and in the Netherlands a minimum period, varying from 3 days in Switzerland to 2 weeks in Queensland and Wisconsin, is set by both compulsory and voluntary public plans. In some countries the waiting period varies with the type of benefit or according to the number of dependents.

An important factor in the administration of the entire system of insurance, and especially in the application of the provisions with respect to suitable employment, is the public employment exchange, at which unemployed persons must register. Such exchanges are usually better developed in countries with compulsory schemes, since under the voluntary plans the trade unions perform the greater part of this function. It is through the exchanges moreover that workers who lack skill or whose occupations appear to be permanently depressed are given vocational training. The Wisconsin plan, by granting an additional benefit of one dollar per week, encourages unemployed workers in receipt of benefits to attend courses of vocational training. In Great Britain the training service was formerly applicable only to juveniles, but in 1930 it was extended to adults. Italy has made use of such instruction chiefly to transfer workers from depressed occupations to large government projects. Belgium since May, 1933, requires all recipients of emergency benefits over twenty-one to attend vocational schools or to work on local relief projects. Germany has set up work camps for juveniles where they learn methods of agriculture, in addition to the other training courses held in connection with exchanges in cities.

It is thus to be seen that in every country not all the unemployed are eligible for insurance and that even among the insured certain conditions are set for eligibility for benefits. The size of the insured population in various countries is indicated in the above table. The coverage as well as the amount and duration of benefits is an important factor in determining the method of financing the unemployment insurance fund. Another important factor, however, is the prevailing political structure. Thus in Fascist Italy not only are coverage, amount and duration of benefits very limited, but the state makes no contribution to the compulsory fund. At the other extreme the Soviet scheme and the Wisconsin plan require the employers to carry the entire cost. In practise, however, these two provisions have varied in their effects. The Soviet scheme applied almost entirely during the NEP period, when private employers met the cost. When most industries were nationalized, the government assumed the entire burden. In most countries with compulsory insurance the state, the employers and the workers all contribute to the funds. In the countries and regions where voluntary subsidized insurance prevails only the workers and the government contribute. Denmark provides for employers' contributions to a central unemployment fund which is used only in times of emergency.

The size and the duration of benefits are largely conditioned by the wage level of the employed, which of course varies from country to country with the economic results of war and tariffs, exploitation of workers, the strength of the trade union movement and many other factors. Two important methods are used to set the amount of benefit to and contribution from the worker. In Great Britain the original scheme was based on a flat contribution and a flat benefit. Later this arrangement was altered so that differentiation was based on age and sex, women and younger claimants having a lower rate of contributions and benefits. The German scheme, on the other hand, took account of varying wage groups. Adaptations of this principle are to be found in Austria, Italy, Poland, Queensland and the Netherlands. The American proposals more nearly follow the German precedent. While originally the British plan made no additional provisions for either married claimants or their dependents, at the present time almost all laws grant additional benefits on this basis.

It is true that even where insurance limitations have been relaxed in the face of continued depression, supplementary programs for relief have had to be instituted. Nevertheless, the countries which provide for some sort of unemployment insurance have been better able to care for their unemployed than has the United States, where long winded arguments in opposition to such plans have accompanied the chaotic and sporadic outpouring of huge sums of money often in unsystematic and demoralizing ways. Yet even the most enthusiastic proponents of unemployment insurance as the most dignified, feasible and systematic method of relieving some of the distress caused by lack of work are confronted with important questions. If the present catastrophic unemployment situation is abnormal, obviously a compulsory unemployment insurance scheme must be set up to cover the majority of workers regularly employed in "normal" times. Along with insurance there should be devised also a systematic plan for emergency relief to be financed by public funds and administered on the basis of need and adequate case work. This was essentially the procedure followed in Great Britain from 1913 to 1919. But if most highly industrialized capitalist countries never return to predepression conditions, it may be impossible for democratic countries with strong labor movements to adhere strictly to pure insurance principles so that relaxation of limitations becomes inevitable. In such a situation public policy must adopt a much broader view unless it is willing to face the alternative of increasing general pauperization.

It is significant that even the radical critics of unemployment insurance, who point out that the Soviet Union has been the only country able to liquidate unemployment and therefore the necessity for unemployment insurance, still press for broader schemes of unemployment insurance in capitalist countries. Moreover it has become increasingly clear that those who hold that a return to "normal" conditions of employment is both possible and inevitable must look upon public compulsory unemployment insurance as a means in times of emergency unemployment of insuring that return and of meeting ordinary demands under "normal" times.

MARY BARNETT GILSON

See: UNEMPLOYMENT; SOCIAL INSURANCE; LABOR LEGISLATION AND LAW; LABOR, GOVERNMENT SERVICES FOR; EMPLOYMENT EXCHANGES; MINIMUM WAGE; STANDARDS OF LIVING; LABOR, METHODS OF REMUNERATION FOR; WAGES; PROFIT SHARING; EMPLOYEE STOCK OWNERSHIP; LABOR; LABOR MOVEMENT;

TRADE UNIONS; LABOR PARTIES; INDUSTRIAL RELATIONS; LABOR-CAPITAL COOPERATION; TRADE AGREEMENTS; WELFARE WORK, INDUSTRIAL; LABOR TURNOVER; CASUAL LABOR.

Consult: Bibliographies: International Labour Office, "Bibliography of Unemployment . . . Covering the Period 1920–1929," *Studies and Reports*, ser. C, no. 14 (2nd ed. Geneva 1930); Morley, L. H., *Unemployment Compensation; a Chronological Bibliography of Books, Reports and Periodical Articles in English, 1891–1927* (New York 1928), and *Supplement on Unemployment Insurance, . . . 1928–1931* (New York 1932); United States, Library of Congress, Division of Bibliography, *List of Recent References on Unemployment Insurance*, Select lists, nos. 1264, 1278 (1932–33).
GENERAL: International Labour Office, *Studies and Reports*, ser. C, Employment and Unemployment, nos. 1, 5, 10, 14 (Geneva 1920–30); International Labour Conference, Seventeenth Session 1933, *Unemployment Insurance and Various Forms of Relief for the Unemployed*, Third Item on the Agenda (Geneva 1933); University of Minnesota, Employment Stabilization Research Institute, *An Historical Basis for Unemployment Insurance* (Minneapolis 1934); Armstrong, B. N., *Insuring the Essentials* (New York 1932) pt. iii, sect. v; Epstein, Abraham, *Insecurity; a Challenge to America* (New York 1933) pts. iii–v; Wolfenden, H. H., *Unemployment Funds; a Survey and Proposal* (Toronto 1934); United States, Bureau of Labor Statistics, "Unemployment-Benefit Plans in the United States and Unemployment Insurance in Foreign Countries," *Bulletin*, no. 544 (1931); Metropolitan Life Insurance Company, *Monograph . . . Series on Social Insurance*, nos. i–xiii (New York 1931–33) nos. i, v–xii; Manes, Alfred, *Versicherungswesen*, 3 vols. (5th ed. Leipsic 1930–32) vol. iii, pt. B, ch. v.
FOR GREAT BRITAIN: Davison, R. C., *The Unemployed; Old Policies and New* (London 1929), and *What's Wrong with Unemployment Insurance?* (London 1930); Gilson, M. B., *Unemployment Insurance in Great Britain; the National System and Additional Benefit Plans* (New York 1931); Great Britain, Royal Commission on Unemployment Insurance, *First Report, . . . Final Report*, Cmd. 3872, 4185, 2 vols. (1931–32), *Minutes of Evidence*, 40 vols. (1931–32), *Appendices*, 9 pts. (1931–32), and *Guide and Index* (1933); Cohen, J. L., *Insurance against Unemployment* (London 1921), and *Insurance by Industry Examined* (London 1923); Morley, Felix, *Unemployment Relief in Great Britain; a Study in State Socialism* (Boston 1924); Astor, J. J., and others, *The Third Winter of Unemployment* (London 1923); Beveridge, William, *Unemployment; a Problem of Industry (1909 and 1930)* (new ed. London 1930), and *The Past and Present of Unemployment Insurance* (London 1930); Gsell, Emil, *Die Arbeitslosenversicherung in Grossbritannien*, Zürcher volkswirtschaftliche Forschungen, no. 12 (Zurich 1927).
FOR GERMANY: Carroll, M. R., *Unemployment Insurance in Germany* (2nd ed. Washington 1930); National Industrial Conference Board, *Unemployment Insurance and Relief in Germany* (New York 1932); Germany, Gutachterkommission zur Arbeitslosenfrage, *Gutachten zur Arbeitslosenfrage*, 3 vols. (Berlin 1931), tr. as Great Britain, Ministry of Labour, *The Unemployment Problem in Germany* (1931); Wiggs, K. I., *Unemployment in Germany since the War*, London School of Economics, Studies in Economics and Commerce, no. 1 (London 1933). FOR AUSTRIA: Carroll, Mollie Ray, *Unemployment Insurance in Austria*, Brookings Institution, Institute of Economics, Pamphlet series, no. 10 (Washington 1932). FOR FRANCE: Héreil, G., *Le chômage en France* (Paris 1932). FOR BELGIUM: Kiehel, C. A., *Unemployment Insurance in Belgium* (New York 1932); Spates, T. G., and Rabinovitch, G. S., *Unemployment Insurance in Switzerland* (New York 1931); Teuscher, Hugo, *Die Arbeitslosenunterstützung in der Schweiz* (Lachen 1929); Morren, H. J., *De practijk der werkloosheidsverzekering in Nederland* (Alphen 1932). FOR SCANDINAVIA: Ratzlaff, C. J., *The Scandinavian Unemployment Relief Program* (Philadelphia 1934).
FOR UNITED STATES: Douglas, P. H., *Standards of Unemployment Insurance*, Social Service Monographs, no. 19 (Chicago 1933); American Academy of Political and Social Science, "Social Insurance," ed. by C. A. Kulp in *Annals*, vol. clxx (1933); Laidler, Harry W., *Unemployment and Its Remedies*, League for Industrial Democracy, Publications, no. 22 (New York 1931); United States, Congress, Committee on Education and Labor, *Unemployment in the United States; Hearings*, 70th Cong., 2nd sess. (1929); Rubinow, I. M., *The Quest for Security* (New York 1934); Stewart, Bryce M., and others, *Unemployment Benefit Plans in the United States* (New York 1930); American Federation of Labor, *Unions Provide against Unemployment* (Washington 1929).
FOR PERIODICALS AND GOVERNMENT PUBLICATIONS: International Labour Office, *Industrial and Labour Information*, published weekly in Geneva since 1922, and *International Labour Review*, published monthly in Geneva since 1921; Great Britain, Ministry of Labour, *Labour Gazette*, published monthly since 1917; Germany, Reichsanstalt für Arbeitsvermittlung und Arbeitslosenversicherung, *Arbeit und Arbeitslosigkeit*, published weekly in Berlin since 1927; United States, Bureau of Labor Statistics, *Monthly Labor Review*, published since 1915; *American Labor Legislation Review*, published quarterly in New York since 1911.

UNFAIR COMPETITION. The economic conditions of human life are such as to insure struggle. Social institutions may either curb or displace, in a measure, individual rivalries generated by the inadequacy of "all good things" to surfeit everyone. But no social institution can eradicate the fundamental condition of human life and no society can free itself from pervasive and persistent competition with other societies in the ubiquitous contest for livelihood and power. Moreover whatever basis of sharing and whatever system of selection for the distribution of functions within a society may be adopted, there is no escape from the rewarding of some at the expense of others, the preferment of some and the rejection of others.

In these circumstances there inevitably emerge in all societies standards by which individuals judge the tolerableness of the livelihood afforded and the justice of the distribution of rewards. Sometimes these standards of living become so rigidly fixed and the rules for assuring their preservation so inelastic that they take on the character of a divine sanction. The society becomes ossified. Ethics, the consideration of what it is "right" to do, comes to throttle economics, the consideration of what it is expedient to do. But the conditions of life do not admit of the indefinite "suppression of competition." Eventually from without or from within there is a reassertion of the urge to reshape the standards and reformulate the rules of behavior in ways which will afford expression to new interests and scope for newly discovered powers.

It is manifest that what is regarded as unfair competition in one society or in a given historical period is not likely to coincide with the content of the concept in other societies or periods. This alone is certain: no society will be found devoid of restrictions upon the methods employed in the winning of livelihood and power. From the course of history it appears, however, that in societies in which the disposable surplus above the minimum necessary for subsistence is small the curbs upon individual discretion in the choice of methods of relieving want or of achieving plenty are numerous and strict, while contrariwise there are few if any methods of competition regarded as unfair in the struggle with other societies for survival. Wherever the ratio of population to available resources and current output becomes comparatively favorable for economic ease, on the other hand, the standards of fair play in the intratribal contest for ascendancy become correspondingly lax. But at the same time there tend to develop more definite conceptions of what is fair and legitimate by way of exploitation of neighboring societies. Societies come to acknowledge a duty to respect the territorial integrity of their neighbors, even rights founded upon priority of occupation, or at least an obligation to find a pretext for disregarding these vested interests.

If the foregoing speculations are provisionally admissible, they help to account for the extraordinary dissolution of conventional standards of fair tactics in trade which marked the rise of business, that is, of a capitalistic economy, in early modern times. The age of geographical exploration and discovery coupled with the cumulative advances in technology had finally so far widened the margin above the necessary means of subsistence according to traditional standards in western countries that the sense of the paramount need for asserting the fraternal obligations of each to all was impaired. For the first time in any considerable area economic life became an adventure, not too unsafe. Business was born. It is amazing to note the comparatively weak resistance to the dissolution of a whole code of ethical, group regarding norms in trade which had been laboriously built up and sedulously maintained through centuries of collective effort. Standards of just price, tolerable interest rates, decent wages, merchantable quality and fair dealing, which limited the tendency toward overreaching of self-seeking individuals in the competition of the market, were, in historical perspective, almost summarily swept aside. But in view of the unprecedented widening of men's horizons and the attendant increase in their sense of opportunity in the sixteenth and seventeenth centuries it is not difficult to understand the general acquiescence in the shift of standards by which conduct in the market was to be judged.

The law, ever reflecting, even though tardily, changes in popular sentiment, gradually permitted the old standards of fair competition in trade to fall into desuetude and abeyance. The rule of caveat emptor became the chief guide to market conduct and judicial decision. Indeed so attenuated did the legal circumscription of market conduct become that by the beginning of the nineteenth century in England the doctrine of unfair competition had taken on a narrow technical meaning confined to the prohibition of deceitful diversion of patronage. In plain terms what this connoted was that the law was little concerned with what a trade competitor did by way of taking advantage of virtually defenseless employees or gullible customers so long as he did not by stealth injure a business rival in his coordinate right of exploitation of the market. There was recognized neither a public nor a private right to enjoin a dealer on the market to honest representation of goods and fair, nondiscriminatory terms of sale.

In the course of the nineteenth century the doctrine of unfair competition was broadened by degrees, both in England and in America, to cover many ingenious artifices for poaching upon the goodwill of competing traders beyond imitation of their trademarks. Precedent, however, did not admit of its extension to the protection of non-business interests from the irresponsible and unconscionable conduct of business. In the game of business, as the law had come to recognize and sanction it, profits were the prize and keen wits with a minimum of scruples were the meritorious talents deserving them. The courts might adapt the rules to the changing tempo of the game and style of play. They could not, or at least did not, attempt to change the whole objective and character of the game. Such a change awaited legislation, which in turn awaited a profound and general alteration in public opinion.

Meanwhile the conditions pointing to and encouraging such a shift in public sentiment were visibly in process of development. The ratio of population to available resources was everywhere increasing and the sense of security afforded by abundant opportunity was being weakened. Moreover experience was becoming an ever more convincing teacher of the impotence for self-defense of individual consumers and workers. Business organized in giant corporations for the more effective utilization of the machine technique through large aggregates of fixed capital and mass production was in a position if not to dictate terms at least to make bargaining a one-sided process, whether in the labor market or in the product market. The resources of business for insidious propaganda and high pressure salesmanship left little room for prudent, circumspect bargaining by self-reliant individuals. In these circumstances profits were at least commonly enough amassed with such magical ease, such bewildering celerity and in such stupendous amounts as to arouse widespread skepticism of the adequacy and justice of the standards of fair dealing which made their competitive acquisition possible. By the beginning of the twentieth century the essential elements of unfair competition were manifestly in need of redefinition.

It was the growth of the trusts and the revelation of the unscrupulous methods by which under the existing law they might, and did in many instances, fortify and extend their power that aroused popular agitation for a reorientation of public policy in this field. The conviction was widespread that the nefarious competitive tactics of the trusts were chiefly responsible for their dominance. Such notorious examples as the local price cutting policy of the Standard Oil, the bogus independent device of the American Tobacco, the exclusive dealer arrangement of the Corn Products and American Thread combines and the persistent resort to discriminatory railway rate favors kindled popular indignation against the "malefactors of great wealth" and stimulated the demand for more effective curbs upon their rapacity. The progressive movement canalized this revolt into the demand for a reformation of the policies of big business and the maintenance of a square deal. The movement was backed for the most part by small scale business men, the petty bourgeoisie, who still had faith that the state could purify business without emasculating the system of profit seeking enterprise.

This agitation finally crystallized in the federal legislation of 1914, prohibiting certain tactics for ruining competitors and establishing administrative regulation of marketing policies. The Clayton Act defined and forbade price discrimination, so-called tying contracts and exclusive dealer arrangements, although with provisos designed to preserve the freedom of action of small enterprises which rather effectively precluded their enforcement even against the intended targets, the trusts. The Federal Trade Commission Act sweepingly condemned all "unfair methods of competition," however, besides setting up the commission as an investigatory and supervisory agency. Nevertheless, this legislation was not penal. It was essentially prophylactic. The commission was given no power under its organic act to prosecute in the first instance. After hearing it could merely issue orders to "cease and desist" from the methods found unfair, and only upon subsequent defiance of its orders could it appeal to the courts for enforcement. In the judicial proceedings only the facts established by the administrative findings were to be incontrovertible, and these had to be backed by adequate evidence. The interpretation of the legal consequences of the facts was reserved to judicial determination.

The commission has not been fortunate in the preservation of even this circumscribed jurisdiction. The courts have on numerous occasions employed the pretext of lack of evidence to set aside the commission's findings, particularly as to the economic consequences of practises the unfairness of which was controverted. Nevertheless, the province of public regulation of competitive methods has been appreciably broadened in the course of two decades. Most noteworthy, misrepresentation and misbranding of products have been reached in a mass of proceedings extending from impotent hair tonics to secondhand trucks sold as new. Commercial bribery has also been successfully attacked in a great number of instances, although judicial limitation of the administrative jurisdiction in respect to this practise has latterly deprived the regulation of much of its salutary significance. But the attack of the commission upon harassing tactics of various kinds by which genuine independent competition is throttled has been discouragingly weak. This may be due in part to the practical success of the law in forestalling resort to trade warfare. There are grounds for believing, however, that if buccaneering policies in business are less drastic and less prevalent than formerly, this may be accounted for as a consequence of the enlarged scope for business consolidation and confederation under the judicial modification of the basic antitrust policy in recent years. There is also to be taken into account the circumstance that the fighting tactics of big business tend to become more refined, less boldly brutal, with the passage of time. Above all, however, the diversion of the thrust of administrative regulatory policy from unfairness to trade competitors to unfairness to trade customers reflects the general shift in public opinion from the trust busting sentiment of a previous generation to resignation to the inevitableness of economic concentration and to the endeavor to find such protection as may be had in the exercise of public control rather than in the restoration of free competition.

This changing attitude finds its neatest expression in the legislative sanction of "codes of fair competition" by the National Industrial Recovery Act of 1933. The codes which have been drafted by trade associations and have received the approval of the president in accordance with the terms of the statute contain in the main two groups of provisions. Those dealing with employment relations need not be discussed here, but those relating to trade practises represent a new attempt to define unfair competition. The rationale of this codification of trade practises lies in the assumptions, first, that each industry has fairly distinct boundaries; second, that the conditions and problems within each industry are peculiar to it and require special regulation; and, third, that business men are competent to define and administer rules governing their own trade behavior.

A study of the trade practise provisions of the codes, some 450 in number, adopted during the first year of operation under the act is enlightening, even if not conclusive, as to the validity of these assumptions. One enterprise was subject to the provisions of fifty-nine different codes, because of the fact that the range of industrial operations did not in this case or commonly fall into neatly defined categories of mutually exclusive compass. Although the provisions of the sundry codes vary almost indefinitely, most of them do cover in some way price policies, trade channels and product standards. The salient fact, however, concerning all of the trade practise provisions in the codes generally is that what is considered unfair is anything that impairs the vested interests of established traders. Thus it has suddenly become "unfair" in a great many lines of business to reduce prices, whatever the motive. It has become unfair too to buy or sell outside of the regular channels of trade, and experiments in remodeling the mercantile structure are penalized. Again, such definition of product standards as has found its way into the codes is predominantly concerned with setting maximum limits of quality and quantity of goods offered at certain prices rather than with minimum requirements, the failure to maintain which has traditionally been regarded as unfair trading.

It is manifest that behind a pretentious façade of blatant moralizing the "reconstruction" of industry is going busily forward. If it is already evident that the structure is to contain plenty of dark rooms where the arts of skullduggery may flourish unmolested, the responsibility lies less with the craftsmen who are building it than upon the architects who drew the plans. In truth the concept of unfair competition was never before so flagrantly prostituted to the defense of the special interests of a ruling class as it is at present in the United States. If ethical notions or norms are ever to be vindicated as something more than deceptive instruments of rulership, the time is surely at hand for their positive reaffirmation and militant reassertion. For the endeavor to maintain free enterprise in trade can be invigorated and sustained only upon the basis of a general belief in the fairness of the competitive process which such a public economic policy postulates. But if experience teaches anything, it is that save in exceptional circumstances, such as occurred in Europe in the sixteenth and seventeenth centuries and two centuries later in America, free enterprise will not lead to fair competition, in accordance with the generally accepted ethical standards of the community, in the absence of forthright measures to protect the economically weak from the economically strong, the prudent from the imprudent. In the light of the historical record it appears nothing less than fatuous folly to suppose that such protection will be afforded by the self-government of a privileged class in whose hands economic power is already largely centered. Of course the magicians so busily engaged in pouring new wine into old bottles may work miracles, but again they may not. Meanwhile there are some, it may be surmised, who prefer old wine in new bottles to counterfeit wine or no wine at all.

MYRON W. WATKINS

See: COMPETITION; CUT-THROAT COMPETITION; MONOPOLY; COMBINATIONS, INDUSTRIAL; TRUSTS; TRADE ASSOCIATIONS; FEDERAL TRADE COMMISSION; GOVERNMENT REGULATION OF INDUSTRY; CONSUMER PROTECTION; CAVEAT EMPTOR; BUSINESS ETHICS; RESALE PRICE MAINTENANCE; PRICE DISCRIMINATION; RESTRAINT OF TRADE.

Consult: Stevens, W. H. S., *Unfair Competition* (Chicago 1917); United States, Bureau of Corporations, *Trust Laws and Unfair Competition* (1916); Henderson, G. C., *The Federal Trade Commission* (New Haven 1924); National Industrial Conference Board, *Public Regulation of Competitive Practices* (2nd ed. New York 1929); Reed, H. B., *The Morals of Monopoly and Competition* (Chicago 1916); Taeusch, C. F., *Policy and Ethics in Business* (New York 1931); Kohler, Josef, *Der unlautere Wettbewerb* (Berlin 1914); Chenevard, Charles, *Traité de la concurrence déloyale*, 2 vols. (Geneva 1914); Morozov, N., *La concurrence illicite en droit suisse* (Lausanne 1930); Valenstein, Lawrence, and Weiss, E. B., *Business under the Recovery Act* (New York 1933); Mason, E. S., "Controlling Industry" in Brown, D. V., and others, *The Economics of the Recovery Program* (New York 1934) p. 38–63.

UNFAIR LIST. See BOYCOTT.

UNGER, JOSEPH (1828–1913), Austrian jurist and statesman. The son of a Jewish merchant of Vienna, Unger late in life embraced the Roman Catholic faith, having gradually become deeply absorbed in German culture, particularly German idealistic philosophy and music. He received his legal education at the University of Vienna and after teaching at Prague for a number of years became professor at Vienna, where he remained for almost three decades. As early as 1867, when the constitution of the old Austria received its final form, he turned to active political life: as a member of the German Liberal party he served in the Lower Austrian diet and then in the lower house of the Imperial Council. After he had surrendered this mandate he was called by the emperor in 1869 to the house of lords, where he took a leading part in all legislative labors, especially in facilitating Klein's reform of civil procedure. His strongly pronounced political convictions were coupled with a great measure of tolerance for others. He himself defended the existing dual structure of the Austro-Hungarian monarchy, opposing federal schemes.

Unger was a pioneer in the field of Austrian private law, both as a teacher and as a scholar. The publication of his *System des österreichischen allgemeinen Privatrechts* (3 vols., Leipsic 1856–64) marked the liberation of the science of Austrian civil law from the narrow bonds of the purely exegetical method and its integration with the stream of German legal science. He accomplished this result by leaning heavily on Romanistic studies, a procedure which was contrary to the prevailing scientific tendency of the time. In subsequent works of a monographic character, however, he also took cognizance of the Germanistic conceptions of the Austrian civil law. While the system of Savigny was the inspiration and starting point of his work, he was more a dogmatic than a historical jurist, and in his later years he was allied with Jhering.

Unger's objectivity fitted him particularly to occupy judicial office. From 1881 until his death he was president of the Imperial Court, the highest Austrian tribunal, which had to adjudicate questions of public law. The fact that he was able to discharge the duties of this office in a brilliant manner is proof of the breadth of his endowment.

KARL GOTTFRIED HUGELMANN

Consult: Stintzing, R. von, and Landsberg, E., *Geschichte der deutschen Rechtswissenschaft*, 3 vols. (Munich 1880–1910) vol. iii, pt. ii, p. 917–24; Jellinek, Georg, *Ausgewählte Schriften und Reden*, 2 vols. (Berlin 1911) vol. i, p. 255–65; Zweig, Egon, in *Biographisches Jahrbuch und deutscher Nekrolog*, vol. xviii (1913) 187–215; Wlassak, M., in Vienna, Akademie der Wissenschaften, *Almanach*, vol. lxiii (1913) 483–99; Strohal, E., in *Jherings Jahrbücher für die Dogmatik des bürgerlichen Rechts*, 2nd ser., vol. xxviii (1914) 1–30.

UNIFORM LEGISLATION. One of the great advantages of the federal state is that individual units furnish so many laboratories for legal and social experimentation. Yet diversity has its evils as well as its virtues. In commercial law it results in uncertainty where certainty is believed to be desirable in the interests of security of transactions and the free flow of commerce. In criminal matters diversity of law may often act to defeat the administration of justice. Even in regard to social legislation, where adaptability to local conditions and mores is of prime importance, the complexities of a competitive economic system may require a certain measure of uniformity to equalize competition.

It is obvious that the problem of uniformity

of legislation should be of greatest moment in the United States, not only because of the great number of jurisdictions within it but also because the powers of the federal government are severely limited. As early as 1842 an attempt to secure uniformity in commercial law through judicial action was initiated by the decision of the United States Supreme Court in Swift *v.* Tyson (41 U. S. 1). Irrespective of whether or not this doctrine of a "federal common law" was desirable, there can be little question that few substantial gains for the cause of uniformity have been achieved through it.

The organized movement for uniform state legislation began in 1889 with the appointment of a Committee on Uniform State Laws by the American Bar Association. In the next year the New York legislature passed an act authorizing the appointment of "commissioners for the promotion of uniformity of legislation in the United States." Similar acts were soon passed in several other states, and in 1892 the first Conference of Commissions for the Promotion of Uniformity of Legislation in the United States was held, representatives from nine states attending. Since then conferences have been held annually, and all the states and Alaska, Hawaii, Philippine Islands, Porto Rico and the District of Columbia are now represented. The conference is known at present as the National Conference of Commissioners on Uniform State Laws, and its object is "to promote uniformity in state laws on all subjects where uniformity is deemed desirable and practicable."

The efforts of the conference have not always met with conspicuous success. By 1933 it had drafted and approved sixty-six acts, of which thirteen were subsequently declared obsolete, superseded or withdrawn. Two of the uniform acts have secured almost universal acceptance, the Negotiable Instruments Act, which is in force in fifty-three jurisdictions, and the Warehouse Receipts Act in forty-eight. The Sales Act and the Veterans' Guardianship Act have been adopted in thirty-four jurisdictions, the Bills of Lading Act in twenty-nine and the Stock Transfer Act in twenty-four. A number of the acts are in effect in only a very few states; the Business Corporations Act has become law in four states, and since its approval by the conference several important states, notably Michigan, California and Illinois, have adopted corporation acts of their own drafting. Nevertheless, it cannot be denied that the uniform act has had some influence in the drafting of these acts.

If the task of securing adoption of the uniform acts by state legislatures has proved difficult, much more serious obstacles have been encountered in the attempt to secure uniformity of judicial decision under these statutes. Most of the acts contain a clause similar to the following: "This act shall be so interpreted and construed as to effectuate its general purpose to make uniform the law of those states which enact it." Not infrequently, however, courts have been prone to disregard this clause and to perpetuate diversity where uniformity is desired. It is hoped that the restatements of law prepared by the American Law Institute will bring about greater uniformity of judicial decision.

The slowness and the inadequacies of the process of adopting uniform acts in the states have brought forth demands for more vigorous use of federal legislative power. The federal taxing powers and the power over interstate commerce have been invoked to bring about uniformity where the older method has failed. A decided check was given to this movement by Supreme Court decisions holding unconstitutional federal child labor legislation based on the interstate commerce and taxing powers. More recently, however, federal legislative power has been brought into play in the enactment of the federal Securities Act of 1933, and laws of this character will doubtless be enacted in increasing numbers. Through the constitutional amendment also a degree of uniformity may be attained.

The American experiment in organizing the movement for uniform legislation has been followed in Canada, where a Conference on Uniformity of Legislation has met annually since 1918. A number of acts have been drafted which have secured widespread, although by no means universal, acceptance in the provinces.

In other federal states, where the powers of the federal government are broader, the problem is not so acute. Thus in Germany after 1871 civil, commercial, penal and procedural codes were enacted for the whole empire. Before 1871 the problem of uniformity presented great difficulties. Only in the case of bills of exchange was it possible to secure the adoption of a uniform statute by all of the states of the German Confederation. Switzerland now boasts a unified civil and commercial law.

Uniform legislation as an international problem long antedates the federal state. In the Middle Ages the problem was apparent in the law of the sea, and the solution was found in a sort of common sea law based on several compilations of laws, particularly the laws of Oléron, of Wisby and the *Consolato del mare*. Much the same development of a universal customary law took place with regard to certain aspects of commercial law. Furthermore the Roman and canon laws were a potent force for uniformity of civil law, although local customs offered considerable resistance in many countries.

These tendencies toward uniformity became increasingly less effective with the rise of the modern system of states. There is indeed a fundamental similarity in the Anglo-American law prevailing in many countries, since their legal systems are all based upon the English common law; and in the nineteenth century a partial return toward uniformity became evident through the imitation of the Napoleonic codes in many countries of Europe and South America. This tendency toward imitation continued to grow, the laws of Germany and France serving as models. In Scandinavia it was given a definite direction with the adoption, late in the nineteenth century, of a number of identical laws in Norway, Sweden and Denmark.

The process of haphazard imitation was supplemented by direct efforts toward securing international action. Commencing with the International Telegraphic Conference held at Paris in 1864 there has been continuous international legislation through multipartite treaties, which have dealt with almost every matter concerned in international intercourse, including communications, transportation, patents, trademarks, weights and measures, postal matters, navigation. In some instances the movement for uniformity was aided by private institutions, such as the International Law Association and the International Chamber of Commerce. The establishment of the League of Nations and the International Labor Organization gave immense impetus to the process. Between 1919 and 1929 some 229 multipartite treaties had been concluded, many of them dealing with matters which would formerly have been left to action by the legislation of the individual states. From the standpoint of the technique of uniform legislation the most conspicuous of these treaties were probably those regarding the unification of laws on bills of exchange, promissory notes and checks. The form adopted was that of a uniform law, which the states ratifying or adhering to the convention agree to incorporate into their national laws.

In addition to the attempt to secure world wide uniform legislation there have been movements, promoted by governments or jurists, for the enactment of unitary legislation within a regional or allied group of countries. Thus in 1916 a commission was created for the formulation of laws to be adopted by both Austria-Hungary and Germany. The World War also gave rise to the Union Législative entre des Nations Alliées et Amies. The movement for the unification of Italian and French law has gained considerable strength. Likewise efforts have been made to establish uniform commercial and other legislation in the pan-American and Hispanic American countries. Recently a movement has been initiated for uniformity in merchant shipping legislation and Admiralty jurisdiction throughout the British Commonwealth of Nations. In 1929 a Conference on the Operation of Dominion Legislation and Merchant Shipping Legislation recommended such uniformity, and these recommendations were adopted by the Imperial Conference in 1930.

A. H. FELLER

See: CONFLICT OF LAWS; CODIFICATION; FEDERATION; FULL FAITH AND CREDIT CLAUSE; COMPACTS, INTERSTATE; COMMERCIAL LAW; INTERNATIONAL LAW; INTERNATIONAL LEGISLATION; INTERNATIONAL LABOR ORGANIZATION; COMITY.

Consult: Rey, Charles, *La commission américaine d'uniformité des lois d'états*, Institut de Droit Comparé de Lyon, Bibliothèque, Études et Documents, vol. xvii (Paris 1927); Barratt, J. A., "The Tendency to Unification of Law in the United States, 1868–1922" in Society of Comparative Legislation, *Journal*, 3rd ser., vol. v (1923) 227–33; Kenner, S., "The Function of Uniform State Laws" in *Indiana Law Journal*, vol. i (1926) 127–34; Pope, Herbert, "The Federal Courts and a Uniform Law" in *Yale Law Journal*, vol. xxviii (1918–19) 647–55; Ailshie, J. F., "Limits of Uniformity in State Laws" in *American Bar Association Journal*, vol. xiii (1927) 633–36; National Conference of Commissioners on Uniform State Laws, *Handbook*, published annually since 1891, and originally designated as *Proceedings* of State Boards of Commissioners for Promoting Uniformity of Legislation; Moore, J. B., "The Passion for Uniformity" in *University of Pennsylvania Law Review*, vol. lxii (1913–14) 524–44; Kan, Joseph van, "L'unification du droit et les résistances des jurisconsultes sous l'ancien régime" in Société d'Histoire du Droit, *Mélanges Paul Fournier* (Paris 1929) p. 363–74; *The Progress of Continental Law in the Nineteenth Century*, ed. by J. H. Wigmore, Continental Legal History series, vol. xi (Boston 1918) pt. iii; Demogue, René, *L'unification internationale du droit privé* (Paris 1927); Lyon-Caen, Charles, "L'unification du droit commercial et l'Académie internationale de droit comparé" in International Academy of Comparative Law, Berlin, *Actorum Academiae universalis jurisprudentiae comparativae*, vol. i (1928) 158–64; Hudson, M. O., Introduction to *International Legislation*, ed. by M. O. Hudson, 4 vols. (Washington 1931) vol. i, p. xiii–lx; Hudson, M. O., and Feller, A. H., "The International Unification of Laws concerning Bills of Exchange" in *Harvard Law Review*, vol. xliv (1930–31) 333–77; Larnaude, F., *Rapport à Monsieur le Garde des sceaux, Ministre de la Justice sur l'unification législative entre la France et l'Italie* (Paris 1929); Block, Anton Leo de, *Scandinavische samenwerking inzake wetgeving* (The Hague 1927); Cosentini, F., "The Integral Unification of American Civil Law" in *Tulane Law Review*, vol. v (1930–31) 515–34; Burchell, C. J., "Uniformity of Merchant Shipping Legislation and Admiralty Jurisdiction throughout the British Empire" in *Canadian Bar Review*, vol. x (1932) 179–81.

UNINCORPORATED ASSOCIATIONS. See VOLUNTARY ASSOCIATIONS.

UNION LABEL. See TRADE UNIONS, section on UNITED STATES AND CANADA.

UNION-MANAGEMENT COOPERATION. See LABOR-CAPITAL COOPERATION.

UNIVERSITIES AND COLLEGES. The primary aim of universities is to spread higher learning and to provide both the foundations and the technical knowledge for the learned professions. Since propagation of true learning is impossible without original investigation, an equally important function of universities has been to conduct scientific research. On the other hand, colleges have been devoted to general education preparatory to advanced study; the emphasis on instruction has endowed them with certain of the characteristics of institutions of secondary education. Colleges have formed and still form component parts of universities, but in many instances they are autonomous institutions.

Antiquity had important schools, such as the philosophical schools of Athens and the literary and rhetorical schools of Rome; but it had no universities in the accepted sense, for no permanent organizations for the transmission of learning existed. The establishment of universities toward the middle of the twelfth century may be attributed to two major factors. In the first place, the range of knowledge and of intellectual curiosity had been greatly enhanced by closer contact with Arab civilization, by the growth of cities and by the steadily increasing level of general education among churchmen. In the second place, corporations had developed as a form of social organization. Schools of young clerks attached to the cathedrals, under the control of the bishops and connected with monasteries, had safeguarded and transmitted the meager knowledge inherited from Hellenistic Rome, comprising the elements of the seven liberal arts: grammar, logic and dialectic (the literary group, or *trivium*) and arithmetic, astronomy, geometry and music (the scientific group, or *quadrivium*). These provided the foundation of the learning cultivated in the faculty of arts, transformed after the middle of the thirteenth century into the faculty of philosophy. The schools of Laon, Reims and Chartres were eclipsed by the cathedral school of Paris, to which William of Champeaux and Abélard drew large numbers of students in the twelfth century with the result that it became the approved center for the study of theology. When it was incorporated as the University of Paris, between 1198 and 1215, it comprised the faculties of theology, arts and medicine.

The University of Bologna founded in the mid-twelfth century, through the voluntary association of law students attracted there by the teaching of Irnerius in civil law and of Gratian in canon law, differed from that of Paris in that it was a university of students and not, like the latter, one of masters. For a university in early mediaeval times merely designated a well defined community; the word did not acquire its modern connotation until about 1250. Mature, financially independent law students made up the majority of the student body in Bologna and these controlled the university through rectors chosen from their ranks; whereas in Paris it was the masters who governed and not the students, who were young men dependent on their parents or on scholarships.

Medicine became a university discipline at the University of Montpellier, situated in a prosperous trading center at the crossroads of Hellenistic and Latin as well as Spanish-Arab civilizations. By the end of the twelfth century a free group of scholars, working under the authority of the bishop of Maguelonne, obtained from the papacy much the same sort of privileges as were enjoyed by the Parisians and the Bolognese. To prevent the exercise of medicine by charlatans the state authorities required examinations and degrees, and thus by 1272 universities came to function for the first time as organs of the state.

Also in this early period scholars who sought instruction for learning's sake or for professional training in theology, law or medicine established Oxford, controlled in the name of the bishop of Lincoln by the chancellor of the diocese, Orléans in France and Coimbra in Portugal. Several universities were founded early in the thirteenth century by scholars who had been obliged to leave other universities: Cambridge by Oxonians, Padua by emigrants from Bologna and Angers by Parisians. After about 1220 universities were formed no longer by scholars but by the rulers of various territories to meet political and social needs arising in their respective states; the University of Naples was established in 1224 by Emperor Frederick II to train men for his administration, and the University of Toulouse in 1229 by Count Raymond VII in order to combat the Albigensian heresy. These examples were followed in rapid succession during the fourteenth and fifteenth centuries by rulers of rival states: Prague (1347), Cracow (1362), Vienna (1365), Heidelberg (1386) and others in Germany, Copenhagen and Uppsala in Scandinavia and St. Andrews, Glasgow and Aberdeen in Scotland. Spain, where the two important universities at Salamanca and Valladolid had flourished from the thirteenth century, was the first to introduce legislation in matters of teaching through the code known as the *Siete partidas*, written under the direction of Alfonso the Wise around 1256.

The mediaeval university during its best period in the middle of the thirteenth century showed remarkable conditions of intellectual freedom; unhampered by property, it was able to resist any attempt to tamper with its autonomous jurisdiction. In many respects because of its international clientele and because of the authority it commanded as an intellectual world power—as *studium*, alongside the temporal and spiritual powers, empire and papacy—it served as a sort of tribunal not only in intellectual but also in political matters; at the Council of Constance, for example, the universities sat in judgment.

The universities had only one kind of property at this time and this was in the form of scholarship endowments connected with the colleges. Colleges were originally hostels for the poor students; the first, the College of the Eighteen, was founded by the cathedral chapter of Paris around 1180. Colleges multiplied rapidly: the Sorbonne in Paris, Balliol, Merton and University colleges in Oxford and Peterhouse in Cambridge all arose in the middle of the thirteenth century. The universities absorbed them all on the continent; in England, on the contrary, the colleges, which tended to dominate the universities, provided a nearly complete curriculum and became teaching institutions rather than mere hostels. Grants, donations and endowments enabled most universities to acquire during the fifteenth century real property consisting of lands, buildings and libraries.

The early universities were important factors in determining the character of the culture of their period: mediaeval philosophy was born in the great schools as were some of the great religious movements which shook mediaeval Europe and divided its unity. Wycliffism, for example, took root in Oxford and Hussitism developed in Prague. When humanism made new demands upon schools and pressed for a change of curriculum away from philosophy, especially Aristotelian philosophy, toward a study of classical literature and rhetoric, it encountered resistance on the part of the professional faculties, which were strictly training schools for the professions of the theologian, the lawyer, the administrator of church or state and the physician. On the other hand, the faculties of arts in old universities and particularly in the new universities founded in Italy—Pavia, Ferrara, Pisa, Florence and Rome—and in the Netherlands became centers of the literary Renaissance. During the fifteenth century Greek and Latin as well as Hebrew studies flourished in Italy and the great printers settled in university towns. Early in the sixteenth century Erasmus made Louvain one of the leading institutions of learning in the world. In Paris several colleges adopted humanism enthusiastically; the Collège de France, which developed from a series of lectureships in the University of Paris, was created especially to conduct humanistic studies. In England such studies were equally well received, as is evidenced in the work of Linacre, Colet and Grocyn, and were supported by the patronage of Sir Thomas More and Cardinal Fisher. The chief centers of the German Renaissance were the universities of Basel, Vienna and Erfurt, which resisted innovations in the philosophical and even more in the religious field but fostered linguistic and literary studies. Thus between 1450 and 1520 purely intellectual ideals gained ground; literary work and scientific research were centered in the universities, and for a short time the demands of professional training were neglected. The University of Alcalá (now Madrid) in Spain was founded in 1508, particularly to promote the study of literature.

With the Reformation there came a decisive change in the outlook and scope of universities;

henceforth they were instruments of the states, which were becoming aware of their sovereign powers. Their traditional autonomy and freedom disappeared; the professors became state employees; censorship and strict discipline were imposed. The university was regarded as an institution to train functionaries for the state and for the national church attached to it. Marburg (1527), Königsberg (1543) and Jena (1558) were conceived in this spirit. In Geneva (1559), where a theocracy ruled, the university was bound up in the Calvinistic concept with the moral education of the people. The Counter-Reformation entered the field of higher studies with the foundation of several universities, of which the most notable examples were Würzburg (1582) and Graz (1585). The Council of Trent revived the ancient traditions of the church by creating episcopal schools to train the clergy, who could not utilize the existing theological faculties on account of the length and costliness of the courses. German universities were at this time either strictly Catholic or Protestant, depending upon the allegiance owed to the ruler of their respective territories; instruments of policy, they were not able to give much attention to disinterested research or to continue humanist traditions.

The municipalities of Leyden (1575), Edinburgh (1583) and Strasbourg (1566 and 1621), however, founded universities on a rationalist basis. Edinburgh was controlled for some time by the local clergy; Strasbourg was founded by Sturm, who was a Protestant clergyman as well as a man of letters; and Leyden had strong Calvinist leanings. These universities did not participate in the religious battles of the time but devoted their attention to the sciences and letters. The centers of scientific research during the sixteenth century were the Italian universities, principally Padua and Pisa, where Galileo and Vesalius did their work. Scientific teaching rose to a high standard in Leyden in the seventeenth century; with Lipsius and Scaliger this university also became one of the first centers of oriental scholarship and literary erudition as these terms are now understood. Spanish, Italian and Dutch scholars (Vitoria, Gentile, Grotius) also created international law, a discipline which emerged between 1550 and 1650 as a sort of constructive counterblast against the destruction of the Thirty Years' War; Pavia, Bourges, Leyden and Oxford were among the first to study in and elaborate this field. The Dutch universities (Leyden, Utrecht, Groningen) equipped themselves with observatories and laboratories and fostered scientific discovery. The primary function of the university, however, remained teaching and not research; because the two functions were considered to be incompatible, learned societies were established. In the eighteenth century, however, universities as such became actively engaged in scientific investigation after the philosophical and religious crises of the preceding period (Cartesianism, Methodism, Jansenism, Pietism). The utilitarianism of the age of Enlightenment made for a wider interpretation of the university's functions; many new disciplines were wedged into the traditional frame, for new needs were felt in a growing and expanding society. The rise of the professions of diplomacy, political economy and engineering was reflected in the regius professorships of history, in the king's scholarships in modern languages in Oxford and Cambridge and in the founding of chairs of administrative sciences (first in Halle in 1729, then in Uppsala in 1740). The development of medical sciences witnessed the endowment of special chairs in the universities of Leyden, Edinburgh, Vienna and Göttingen.

These universities adapted themselves to the immediate needs of society and attempted to teach the varied subjects requisite to professional training. In some countries, however, as in France, teaching methods remained antiquated; the universities were still powerful corporations which feared that innovations might interfere with their age long privileges. The English university corporations were at the service of the ruling class; although scientific progress made headway under the influence of such men as Newton and Locke, the universities could not adapt themselves fully to the exigencies of contemporary society as a whole. In the states where enlightened despotism prevailed university instruction was in general further advanced.

When the French Revolution abrogated the rights of the privileged corporations it included the universities. The scheme of national education, which culminated in Napoleon's founding of the University of France, was a centralized system in which the interests of the state were paramount. It prevailed throughout the Restoration, the July Monarchy, the Second Empire and the Third Republic and in form at least it still exists today.

There were important innovations in universities during the first half of the nineteenth century. The University of Berlin (1810), established by Humboldt, Fichte and Schleiermacher, was the first to be designed as a research as well as a teaching institution and thus served as a model not only for the German but also for the Dutch, Scandinavian and Swiss universities. The founders realized that no advanced teaching is possible without active participation in the development of knowledge by the teachers. Furthermore they distinguished clearly the limits of secondary and higher education and restricted the university to the latter. Thus the German university of the early nineteenth century served as the generator of modern scientific teaching; and its hospitals, laboratories and institutes were eagerly imitated in other countries.

The universities of the period were not only scientific but also political centers. By fostering national sentiments they played a significant role in the political evolution of the various countries. German universities, such as Berlin and Breslau, led the nationalistic movement during the War of Liberation (1813–14); their professors and students through organizations such as the *Burschenschaft* educated the general public politically and spread the idea of national unity. Heidelberg and Freiburg were at the forefront of the liberal movement; Kiel raised the problem of Schleswig-Holstein. Guizot, Cousin and Villemain in Paris aided in the liberalization of French politics. Italian universities formed strongholds of resistance against foreign despotism and served as rallying points of the Risorgimento. Spanish universities were instrumental in the downfall of Napoleon and in the spreading of liberal doctrines. Copenhagen and Christiania (now Oslo) universities, the latter founded in 1811, were centers of Danish and Norwegian nationalism, Warsaw and Vilna of Polish and Pest of Hungarian. Moscow, Kazan, Kharkov, St. Petersburg and Kiev (founded in 1755, 1804, 1805, 1819 and 1833 respectively) promoted Slavic studies and were the nuclei of intellectual as well as political pan-Slavism.

Universities, like other institutions, spread beyond Europe along with Old World civilization in general. The first universities erected in the New World were Spanish: Mexico (1551) and Lima (the University of San Marcos, 1553). During the sixteenth and seventeenth centuries similar universities were established in Bogotá, Quito, Cordova, Santo Domingo and Manila. In English speaking North America the movement began with Harvard College (1636), founded as "The School" by Cambridge men chiefly from Emmanuel College. Only denominational colleges existed until 1785, when the first state university, that of Georgia, was founded. Harvard was first Congregational and later Unitarian; Yale ("The Collegiate School," 1701) Congregational; Columbia (King's College, 1754) and William and Mary (1693) Episcopal; Brown (College of Rhode Island, 1765) Baptist; Princeton (1746) Presbyterian. State institutions often developed from the denominational colleges; and when the question of disestablishment was eventually raised the University of Virginia, founded by Jefferson in 1816, set the first liberal example. New universities and colleges were established as the population spread westward; their numbers increased very rapidly because of the peculiar conditions offered by a young nation with democratic institutions. Before the Civil War there already existed in the United States 182 colleges and universities, of which 21 were state institutions. Universities with large endowments from private sources began to be established in the latter half of the nineteenth century; one of the most important of these is the University of Chicago, which was founded in 1892.

By the end of the nineteenth century the universities in Europe, in America and in the East where western civilization had penetrated were closely bound up with the public. In England, where the two ancient universities had maintained their exclusive character almost down to contemporary times, rival institutions were created in the spirit of liberalism and democracy. London University (University College, London, 1826–34) was established through the influence of Bentham and Grote in order to provide an intellectual home for Catholics and Nonconformists, who were excluded from Oxford and Cambridge. The universities of Manchester, Leeds, Liverpool and Wales, which were formed during the nineteenth century and the early twentieth, were meant to serve the public; and accordingly a utilitarian tendency was more marked in them than in Oxford and Cambridge, where the emphasis was primarily upon the so-called liberal education, the rounded training of a gentleman. Modern universities now tend to disregard the traditional limits set for their intellectual activities; technical subjects of all sorts, sometimes of a purely empirical or utilitarian character, have been introduced particularly in the United States. In the intellectual capitals of different countries there have arisen a few vast institutions, such as Columbia University in New York and the universities of Paris, London and Berlin, which in many respects are related to the needs and desires of the public. There has been a movement away from professional training of restricted groups toward the education of an entire nation.

Modern universities belong, from the point of view of their origins and social relations, to one of three categories: either they are institutions of the church or of the state or they are established by private groups. The last type has flourished only in the United States; elsewhere state institutions predominate. In France the principle of freedom of teaching, that is, the right to establish and maintain schools and institutions of learning, was asserted by the revolution (constitution of the year III, 1795, article 300) and confirmed in 1830 and again in 1848. The working of this principle, inherent in liberal doctrine, was impeded because of the place given the university in the Napoleonic system of education. The University of France is an administrative entity under the authority of the minister of public instruction and is divided into educational districts, called academies, each conducted by a rector; in these academies are found the university faculties as well as primary and secondary educational institutions. Since 1896 the isolated faculties in each academy have been reunited into universities proper, but the administrative system still prevails. The state alone has a right to grant degrees and in this way controls the teaching profession as well as the other learned professions. To counteract this monopoly the law of 1850 (*Loi Falloux*) and subsequent acts reaffirmed the liberty of teaching, the Catholic church being foremost in availing itself of this right. Thus five Catholic universities supported by contributions of church members have grown up in France since 1875, in Paris, Lille, Angers, Toulouse and Lyons.

The struggle for freedom in teaching was one of the most powerful factors in the achievement of Belgian independence. Between 1814, when the Kingdom of the Netherlands was established under the Dutch rule, and 1830, when Belgium became independent, state monopoly of education, which the Belgians considered detrimental to their national (French-Walloon) civilization as well as to their Catholic faith, consolidated and reenforced the opposition against the Dutch regime. After the revolution of 1830 the right of freedom in teaching was established. The Catholics founded the University of Louvain, the rationalists the Université Libre in Brussels; and quite recently the Flemish formed a university in Ghent. Belgium is the only country on the continent which has established free universities entitled to confer degrees.

Whenever the state monopolizes teaching, it endeavors to assert its official principles, whether these be orthodoxy, rationalism, agnosticism, monarchy, democracy, socialism, fascism or totalitarianism or doctrines of racial or national superiority. The states have at their disposal various means whereby they can make the universities serve the ends of national education, based on national doctrines. The European universities and their counterparts in the Near and Far East and in South America are entirely dependent on the state for their support. Even in England the Treasury or the local authorities subsidize the various universities, acting through the University Grants Committee. In 1933 the annual grant in England amounted to £1,800,000; in the new universities the students pay only three tenths of the expenses of their education. The trend everywhere is away from fees and toward increased financing by the state. High fees are apt to put a university in the hands of a well to do class, conservative in thought and outlook (the Russian minister Uvarov as early as 1840 conceived of high tuition as a method of maintaining an educational monopoly of a reactionary ruling class); a democratic society will not accept such an arrangement. Private benefactions likewise tend to secure to various private interests an influence upon education.

Other means of pressure are of an administrative nature, arising from the fact that universities throughout the continent are governed by ministries, whose direct influence is especially marked in dictatorial countries. In Germany the recently created post of federal minister of education (Prussia, Bavaria, Saxony, Württemberg, Hamburg, Mecklenburg-Schwerin, Thuringia, Baden and Hesse had their several ministries of education until 1934) controls all appointments, while the faculties have a merely consultative voice, which is often disregarded. Formerly academic freedom was guaranteed by the institution of *Privatdozenten*; lecturers were appointed by the faculties in which their specialties were located, and the government had merely the power of confirmation. Whatever the tendencies toward meddling on the part of the government, they were offset by the presence of these lecturers, who were appointed only on their merits and from among whom the professors were almost invariably chosen. In Germany as well as in Italy the rectors and deans, instruments of government policy, rule the universities, in which therefore the teaching and even the direction of research has to conform to the will of the government. In the Soviet Union also a university director determines what researches are to be undertaken.

For a university to maintain its independence from the state and from public opinion, expressed otherwise than through government channels, becomes increasingly difficult. Much depends on disinterested private benefactions and public subscriptions. From the financial point of view also popular subscriptions seem to be, in times of crisis and inflation, particularly advantageous. But more important than financial independence and administrative autonomy is the fact that only in an atmosphere of free discussion can the objectives of a university be fulfilled.

There remains the question whether the primary function of the university should be teaching or research. Especially since the founding of the University of Berlin, which developed as a reaction against eighteenth century utilitarianism, it has been widely believed that disciplines and skills which have primarily a practical value should not be taught in a university. During the nineteenth century the universities tried to keep out such utilitarian studies as business administration and engineering. Nevertheless, these disciplines made their way, while at the same time the practical aspects of legal and medical studies came to be stressed and administrative and financial studies were established as an integral part of a jurist's education. Agriculture found its place in Oxford in 1796 (the Sibthorpian chair) and in Edinburgh in 1792. Engineering has been taught in English universities, although tradition demands that engineering sciences have a special home of their own (the polytechnic institutes in Europe or the institutes of technology in the United States). The French Revolution replaced the traditional university with a group of utilitarian professional schools. The Russian Revolution has done likewise; in the Soviet Union medicine is now under the Commissariat of Health, teachers' training under the Commissariat of Education and various branches of engineering are under the commissariat of heavy or of light industry. Quite recently, however, there has been a tendency to reconstitute the unity of learning.

Specialization, called forth by the rapid multiplication of professions, is characteristic of contemporary universities. In England the tripos examination and the honors system are utilized early in the undergraduate's training. In German universities graduate specialization begins immediately after the termination of secondary studies. In Soviet universities special emphasis is placed on technical specialization. The university has to face the problem of how far it can and should go in giving technical education for professional purposes without neglecting the border line studies between the sciences and the fundamental principles inherent in all of them which guarantee an organic unity of things learned and their proper assimilation. The solution seems to lie in a delay of specialization, as in the universities in the United States, where specialization is a postgraduate affair. The university is something more than a research institution and its function is greater than that of affording adequate technical equipment to the professionals it trains; its basic purpose is to raise the intellectual and cultural standards of society. English and American colleges have cultivated also an esprit de corps through campus life, which is absent in Scotland and on the continent; student hostels in Scotland and Germany, the *cité universitaire* in Paris and similar *cités* in Clermont-Ferrand and Madrid represent efforts to encourage such developments. As a result of the intensification of nationalism and of the economic crisis, modern universities are no longer international communities as were mediaeval universities, although an interchange of university students and teachers still occurs to a limited extent.

STEPHEN D'IRSAY

See: EDUCATION; ENDOWMENTS AND FOUNDATIONS; LEARNED SOCIETIES; RESEARCH; ACADEMIC FREEDOM; TEACHING PROFESSION; PROFESSIONS; INTELLECTUALS; UNIVERSITY EXTENSION; ADULT EDUCATION; CO-EDUCATION.

Consult: Irsay, S. d', *Histoire des universités*, 2 vols. (Paris 1933–34); Rashdall, Hastings, *The Universities of Europe in the Middle Ages*, 2 vols. (Oxford 1895); Erman, Wilhelm, and Horn, Ewald, *Bibliographie der deutschen Universitäten*, 3 vols. (Leipsic 1904–05); Liard, Louis, *L'enseignement supérieur en France, 1789–1889*, 2 vols. (Paris 1888–94); Tewksbury, D. G., *The Founding of American Colleges and Universities before the Civil War*, Columbia University, Teachers College, Contributions to Education, no. 543 (New York 1932); Haskins, C. H., *The Rise of the Universities* (New York 1923); Tillyard, A. I., *A History of University Reform, from 1800 A.D. to the Present Time* (Cambridge, Eng. 1913); Robertson, Charles Grant, *The British Universities* (London

1930); Newman, John Henry, *The Idea of a University* (London 1852); Spranger, Eduard, *Wandlungen im Wesen der Universität seit 100 Jahren* (Leipsic 1913); *Die Universitätsideale der Kulturvölker*, ed. by C. Hoffmann and R. Schairer (Leipsic 1925); Barker, E., *Church, State and Study* (London 1930); Flexner, A., *Universities, American, English, German* (2nd ed. New York 1930); Ortega y Gasset, José, *Misión de la universidad* (Madrid 1930); Mannhardt, J. W., *Hochschulrevolution* (Hamburg 1933).

UNIVERSITY EXTENSION. The university extension movement must be evaluated against the background of the rapid rise of interest in adult education in countries where political democracy and the complexity of industrial society made literacy essential and gave knowledge social unity. In England, where the movement developed earlier than it did in the United States, the adult education that preceded it had three characteristic approaches: the church sought to educate workers for permanent membership; the Mechanics Institutes, motivated by humanitarianism, attempted to raise the level of the workers by vocational training; and the Chartists and the People's Colleges were concerned with the education of their fellow workers for its own sake. Most of the material presented in courses or lectures was of a practical nature whether the end was religious, political or vocational. Until 1845, when an attempt was made to provide for the admission of members of the working class to Oxford, the universities did not participate in adult education, although there was a general feeling that any educational movement too far separated from them was destined to be weak. In 1855 Lord Arthur Hervey proposed the establishment of circuit professors and in 1858 Oxford and Cambridge agreed to administer local examinations for the Society of Arts, certifying the completion of work at the Mechanics Institutes. As a result of the success of a series of lectures by James Stuart beginning in 1867 university extension lectures were first officially established in England in 1873; they were given in Nottingham, Leeds, Derby and Leicester by fellows of Cambridge University. Oxford joined the movement in 1878; it added traveling libraries to its lectures and after ten years of experimentation instituted resident summer meetings. By 1881 more than nine university colleges had been formed in British industrial centers.

The curriculum offered was chiefly a popularization of the regular university courses in spite of their remoteness from the needs of the workers. While the traditional conservatism of the universities had yielded, the curriculum went no farther than the middle class supporters of university extension demanded and the courses remained largely cultural. In this way a movement intended to promote education among the working class became an instrument of popular middle class education.

University extension in the United States had a comparable development, although the fact that universal education had always been regarded as desirable made the entrance of universities into extension work less difficult. As early as 1830 Columbia University offered popular lectures with no loss of dignity. However, the beginnings of American adult education were independent of the universities. The success of the lyceum, which was first organized in 1826 and had by 1834 approximately three thousand branches, indicates that there was a powerful demand for educational opportunity. Commercial organizations, such as the Redpath Lyceum and the Chautauqua Circuit, which employed all the techniques later used in university extension including lectures and correspondence courses, put adult education on a paying basis.

The adult education movement showed vitality but it lacked direction. It was neither working class nor middle class education; much of it was of the order of refined entertainment. In an attempt to improve its character Melville Dewey, with the cooperation of a number of university professors, proposed in 1888 the organization of extension work under the American Library Association in New York. The following year the Wisconsin Agricultural College and Teachers College, Columbia University, formally inaugurated extension courses, and in the next fifteen years such courses became part of the curriculum of universities in all parts of the country. This may have been a manifestation of a more democratic interpretation of the function of universities, an acknowledgment that they were no longer to be merely at the disposal of a single class of society. Yet while the universities extended their activities, they did not adapt their courses to the needs of the new audiences; they popularized them, but relatively few people were interested in what they had to offer. As a result interest in the movement declined, and from 1894 until 1906 university extension work barely survived. Then followed a marked revival, which may be attributed to the fact that the promoters of university extension patterned their courses after those offered by the lyceums, circuits and institutes. The growth of university extension from 1906 to 1917 was accelerated during the World War because the government made liberal use of university extension divisions to present its war aims to the country, and the universities were not slow to consolidate the resulting gains.

The renewed interest in university extension activities was a consequence not only of the new content of the courses but also of the application of new methods. Courses are now given by lecture, discussion, correspondence and radio and are illustrated by motion pictures and other visual devices. Through their extension divisions the American universities reach a vast public. They are no longer cloistered institutions devoted to learning for its own sake and to the transmission of knowledge to a few trustees of culture; they compete with newspapers and the radio in the formation of public opinion. In 1919 the United States Bureau of Education reported that over 2,000,000 people were reached by university extension lectures in this country; by 1930 the number had mounted to almost 3,000,000, exclusive of the auditors of radio broadcasts under the auspices of universities. The number taking formal courses rose during the same period from about 35,000 to 250,000. The National University Extension Association reported in 1933 that enrolment in the extension classes of twenty-one larger universities from 1920 to 1932 had more than doubled in spite of a decrease in the last two years caused by the economic crisis. During the peak year, 1929–30, extension income of these universities was $3,000,000. Twenty-one institutions reported a peak of over 200,000 course enrolments in 1928–29. The range of expenditures in 1931–32 was from over $500,000 at the University of Wisconsin to less than $7500 by the University of New Mexico; the total expenditures usually exceeded income by about one third, the balance being made up by state or institutional appropriations. The highest proportion of subsidy amounted to 86.4 percent; Syracuse University and Texas Technological College, on the other hand, were entirely self-supporting in 1931–32. The number of individuals taking credit courses in a single university extension division, excluding the correspondence section, ranged from over 7500 to under 100, with the median at over 1000.

The practise of giving credit toward degrees for courses taken gives university extension competitive advantage in the field of adult education. Most universities insist on a minimum period of residence for each student before degrees are granted, but much of the work can be taken off the campus in extension. This procedure has had a disintegrating effect on academic education and causes constant friction between the several branches of many institutions which have not yet determined what ends they ought to serve. In some institutions the extension students outnumber regular students.

On the continent the organization of adult education has been less bound up with the universities than in England or the United States and is not therefore properly a part of university extension. The universities, however, through their scholars have cooperated closely with various movements. In Switzerland university men and women aid and encourage folk education as they did in England in the middle of the last century. In Germany the folk schools are part of the state system of education, and members of university faculties and scientific institutes serve on the boards. In Denmark the schools are part of the state system but are permitted a large degree of self-government. The Danish schools are chiefly agricultural in their emphasis, while those in Germany and Switzerland are industrial as well as agricultural. The continental type of adult education is not primarily middle class as in England and the United States of America. Peasants and workers not only benefit by but frequently support their own folk schools.

The advisability of combining extension courses with the usual university functions may be questioned. The technique of administering adult education is specialized, and institutions now exist, unconnected with universities, which are doing good work in this field. These institutions have the advantage of being closer to the needs of working classes and special interest groups in contrast with universities and their extension divisions, which are essentially middle class; they can be flexible, for no traditional values are damaged when they yield to a demand. Such institutions derive benefits from cooperation with the universities which furnish them with their subject matter, their theory and the answers to many of their questions. The wisdom of their being organically connected with universities and the desirability of moves on the part of universities to take over their functions may, however, be doubted. The ability to advance knowledge and the skill of presenting it popularly are not necessarily correlated, and when the same institution attempts to do both it often works to mutual disadvantage. On the other hand, a new and more democratic conception of the university may make popular adult education its chief function, with the task of increasing knowledge relegated to institutes or schools organized exclusively for research.

Donald Slesinger
Elizabeth Mead

See: Adult Education; Education; Correspondence Schools; Universities and Colleges.

Consult: Hall-Quest, A. L., *The University Afield* (New York 1926); Price, Richard R., "University Extension" in *Higher Education in America*, ed. by Raymond A. Kent (Boston 1930) ch. xii; Bulkeley, J. P., *Adult Education* (*University Extra-Mural Teaching in England and Wales*), India, Bureau of Education, Occasional Reports, no. 10 (Calcutta 1922); Hodgen, M. T., *Workers' Education in England and the United States* (London 1925); Mansbridge, Albert, *An Adventure in Working-Class Education* (London 1920); *The Way Out*, ed. by Oliver Stanley (London 1923); Draper, W. H., *University Extension ... 1873–1923* (Cambridge, Eng. 1923); Flexner, A., *Universities: American, English, French, German* (New York 1930); Peffer, Nathaniel, *New Schools for Older Students* (New York 1926); World Association for Adult Education, *International Handbook of Adult Education* (London 1929); Thompson, C. O., *The Extension Program of the University of Chicago* (Chicago 1933); United States, Bureau of Education, "The University Extension Movement," by W. S. Bittner, and "College and University Extension Helps in Adult Education," by L. R. Alderman, *Bulletin*, no. 84 (1919), and no. 10 (1930); Shaw, W. B., *Alumni and Adult Education* (New York 1929).

UNWIN, GEORGE (1870–1925), English economic historian. Unwin in 1910 was appointed professor of economic history at the University of Manchester, occupying the first such chair to be established in Great Britain. Although his historical researches were of fundamental importance, he was primarily a social philosopher. His main interest was in the process whereby human beings seek to build up a society which will be at once an expression of their inherent qualities and a means to their further development. Unwin held that the data of economic history provide a more objective and scientific line of approach to a study of this process than the data of political history. His basic faith was in the operation of the principle of voluntary association, and it was in relation to this principle that he estimated the social value of the guild organizations, the later companies, the early trade unions and the organizations of his own day. Thus he considered that in mediaeval times it was in the guild organizations that the principle of voluntary association found its most typical and widespread embodiment. He regarded these organizations in their early stages as a dynamic force in society but, as they grew in strength and sought political authority with its implied coercive power, he saw them become a static force. Of this kind of association between economic organizations and political authority he was extremely critical, and much of his work on English economic history consists of an examination of its causes and consequences. Necessarily his critical attitude extended to the historical writings which have sought to show that the social and economic progress of nations has been consequent upon a judicious alliance of economic interests and political power in pursuit of a consistent and strongly directed national policy. Instead of such a policy in English history he found a series of opportunist expedients, usually inspired by sectional interests; and he insisted that the expedients had not been the cause of progress, but that progress took place in spite of them. To this authoritarian view of progress, which, he contended, finds its basis in statutes, state papers and similar official documents, Unwin opposed an approach founded upon local records, the records of individual lives, families, business firms and the numerous organizations in which individuals voluntarily associate and play their part in the building up of society.

G. W. Daniels

Important works: *Industrial Organisation in the Sixteenth and Seventeenth Centuries* (Oxford 1904); *Gilds and Companies of London* (London 1908, 2nd ed. 1925); *Finance and Trade under Edward III*, University of Manchester, Publications, no. cxvii (Manchester 1918); *Studies in Economic History*, ed. with a memoir by R. H. Tawney (London 1927).

Consult: Daniels, G. W., *George Unwin; a Memorial Lecture*, Manchester University Lectures, no. xxiv (Manchester 1926).

UPPER CHAMBERS. See Bicameral System.

URBANIZATION is characterized by movements of people from small communities concerned chiefly or solely with agriculture to other communities, generally larger, whose activities are primarily centered in government, trade, manufacture or allied interests. Although there were earlier eras, as, for example, in Greece during the age of Pericles and during the later Roman Empire, when the movement of people to the cities presented serious social problems, the phenomenon has become especially important since the onset of the industrial revolution. Urbanization depends largely on the extent to which industrial and mercantile products are divorced from agriculture. This statement is borne out by quantitative data for recent years, assembled in the adjoining table, which suggest a correlation between non-agricultural activities and concentration of population in large cities.

EMPLOYMENT IN NON-AGRICULTURAL PURSUITS AND DISTRIBUTION OF POPULATION BY SIZE OF COMMUNITY

Country	Year	Percentage of Gainfully Employed Engaged in Non-agricultural Pursuits	Percentage of Population in Communities Under 20,000	100,000 and Over
England and Wales	1931	93.2*	35.2	39.8
United States	1930	78.0	58.1	29.6
Netherlands	1920	76.4	54.3	24.2
Germany	1925	69.5	57.8	29.6
France	1931	61.7†	69.1	15.7
Sweden	1932	59.3‡	77.2	14.6
Japan	1932	44.8‡	70.8	22.3
Italy	1931	43.9*	63.3	17.4
India	1921	27.7	94.5	2.6
Russia	1926	13.3	88.0	6.5

*Figure for 1921.
†Figure for 1926.
‡Figure for 1920.

Source: Figures for gainfully employed from League of Nations, *Statistical Yearbook 1931-32* (Geneva 1932) p. 44-45. Figures for distribution of population calculated from official statistical yearbooks and similar government sources.

Although trade, manufacture and government, which have always been the functions of urban communities, permit almost indefinite elaboration, until very recent times the proportion of the community which could live away from the land and thus the size of cities as well were limited by the inadequacy of the methods available for the production of raw materials and foodstuffs. Likewise as long as all goods had to be moved by relatively small boats propelled by sails or by man power or by pack animals and packmen, the difficulties of transport were of the utmost importance in checking the growth of cities. It seems doubtful therefore whether any of the cities of the world prior to the steam age ever contained more than about 1,000,000 inhabitants, and probably none but capitals of great empires, such as Rome and Peking, ever exceeded a few hundred thousands. The situation in India throws light on the conditions prevailing in the western world prior to the industrial revolution. Even as late as 1881, after steam transport by water had begun to affect the size of the cities of India, Calcutta and Bombay had but 829,000 and 773,000 inhabitants respectively; at that time only nineteen other Indian cities comprising, with Calcutta and Bombay, only 1.98 percent of the population had over 100,000 inhabitants, while only six had over 200,000. The extent of urbanization in England since the industrial revolution is indicated by the fact that the ratio of the urban to the entire population increased from about 10 percent at the beginning of the nineteenth century to 80 percent in 1921. Similar although not as drastic cityward drifts in population have occurred throughout the western world.

The form of aggregation in cities also is determined largely by production techniques. The highly centralized mononucleated city as it has evolved in modern times could not develop as long as man had to depend on his own power for manufacture and transport. In the Orient the cities, including the semimodernized seaports, are still polynucleated, as all cities must have been before steam power came into use. Here much of the manufacturing is carried on in or near the shop where the product is sold. The only form of centralization observable, except in the ports, is the tendency for like industries to congregate in a particular quarter. Some concentration of governmental functions must have developed early in the great capitals of the world near the abode of the monarch. But as a rule and even in relatively small provincial cities living quarters, factories and shops are more or less indiscriminately mingled. Paris, Rome, Vienna and even Berlin and London, although tending in recent times toward a centralized form, still exhibit many characteristics of the polynucleated form of oriental cities.

Until quite recently steam power, which must be used close to the point of generation, tended to concentrate population in large cities. When larger plants were needed, it was generally more economical to build additional units near the existing steam plant than to build an entirely new plant elsewhere. Steam was also not well adapted for use in small transport units or for conveyances traveling on variable routes, except between seaports. Likewise in the days before the telephone became common, the management of a business centered in one large factory was decidedly simpler than that of a similar business made up of several smaller units located considerable distances apart. As long as the use of the telephone was largely local, it acted as a centralizing force because it permitted the separation of office from factory and warehouse, but only within the local telephone area; it thus made possible the great concentration of the office work, of certain types of retailing and of professional service in the downtown areas of cities. The telegraph also tended to encourage greater centralization of cities, because it was more useful in extending trade areas than in providing the means whereby productive processes could be managed at a distance. It was not until it became possible to use the telephone or teletype for conversational communication over long distances, to distribute electric power cheaply over wide areas and to employ the internal combustion engine to attain a wholly new flexibility in transportation that it became practicable to decentralize most types of businesses and thus to break up the compact city dependent on steam.

Largely because of the pressure of vested interests which would be affected adversely by decentralization, there has been little tendency as yet to make use of cheap long distance communication and more flexible sources of power to reform the steam city. The use of the new agents to concentrate office work and the general management of industry at considerable distances from the field or production units accounts for the tremendous and continued growth of such cities as London, Paris, Berlin, New York, Chicago, Tokyo and Moscow. The possibilities inherent in electricity and the gas engine are beginning to be actualized, as is seen in the rapid growth of the suburbs around large cities, the increased number of subcenters developing within these cities and the tendency to move factories out to lower rent areas. Although these new forces have as yet exerted little influence in changing the form of the nineteenth century city, it seems highly probable that the congested mononucleated city will soon begin to disintegrate. The city of the future will derive its form from the use of electricity for communication and power and from reliance upon the internal combustion engine for transportation. In the place of the highly compact city great areas or districts will probably be so organized that people can live near their work and yet be able to enjoy the benefits of living in a semirural environment. It is no longer necessary to crowd people together in densely populated urban areas to attain the close personal contact and instantaneous communication essential to high efficiency. In addition to the dispersal of urban populations stimulated by changing sources of power and the improvement of means of transportation and communication, there has been in the United States and in western Europe since the beginning of the economic crisis in 1929 a cessation of the migratory movement toward urban centers and a distinct trend back to rural regions, due to the inability of the urban community to provide employment.

Although the decline in the general death rate of western countries during the nineteenth century may perhaps be attributed in part to the more efficient productive methods of urban as compared with rural economy, the direct effect of urbanization appears to have been to retard population growth. It seems almost certain, from what is known of English cities in the eighteenth century and of the present day Indian and Chinese cities, that until the industrial revolution was well under way deaths were more numerous than births in practically all urban populations. In the past, cities grew or maintained their numbers only because of the large immigration of young adults from the rural districts. For a time after modern sanitation came into use in the cities there was an excess of births over deaths. But more recently in many western cities the birth rate has declined so rapidly that there is now only an apparent natural increase—apparent because migration has resulted in a population of an age composition favorable to low death rates and high birth rates. In 1928 in nine large cities in the United States the "true" rate of natural increase of the white population was such that without immigration their populations would decrease in numbers by 5.1 per 1000 each year when their populations reached a stable age composition about a generation hence, if the same specific birth rates and death rates were to prevail. But since birth rates are still declining, it will probably be only a few years until crude birth rates are lower than the crude death rates. This is already the case in San Francisco and in many of the larger German cities, where in 1932 the birth rates and death rates respectively were: Berlin 8.1, 11.1; Hamburg 10.3, 10.5; Munich 10.5, 11.7; Dresden 8.2, 10.8. For the entire population of all cities in Germany of over 100,000 the rates were 10.8 and 10.1. Thus these large cities, which contain 30.2 percent of Germany's population, have a crude natural increase of only 0.7. Although the mortality rate among urban populations is generally higher than among rural populations in the United States, the gross illness rate appears to be approximately the same in the country as in the city; differences appear, however, when the rates are considered by age. A study conducted from 1928 to 1931 by the United States Public Health Service under the auspices of the Committee on the Costs of Medical Care of 9000 white families, observed for twelve consecutive months in 130 localities in seventeen states and the District of Columbia, revealed that country children between the ages of one and ten and persons over sixty-five years of age were sick less frequently than persons of similar ages living in cities, while at all ages between ten and sixty-five the rural morbidity rate was in excess of the urban. The notoriously congested housing conditions characteristic of many urban centers present more significant declines in morbidity and mortality rates, although their death rate is still higher than in the country, in spite of prodigious advances in urban medical and public health services.

The social and economic effects of modern urbanization are only beginning to be understood. Although it is erroneous to dismiss folk culture in rural areas as of no consequence or to assume that a high degree of culture and great size in cities are causally related, there is little doubt that intellectual activities have flourished more in towns and cities than in the country. The concentration of wealth in cities permits larger expenditure for educational and recreational activities and other public services which improve living standards. In spite of extreme disparities of opportunity there is a wider variety of possibilities for the manifestation of an individual's potentialities in urban communities by reason of the more detailed division of labor and the greater number of social contacts possible; Odin, Cattell and Holmes in their studies of eminent men have supported this conclusion by giving statistical evidence that the chances of an individual's attaining eminence are much greater in urban than in rural areas. Extremes of private wealth and poverty are much more apparent in the cities than in rural districts, because concentration of the population dramatizes the contrasts. Notwithstanding greater social stratification, the horizontal mobility and the possibility of labor organization which urban life affords improve the status of city workers and make them less subservient to the will of employers than are workers on farms or in farm villages, who are subject to constant supervision. These advances in personal and political freedom of the masses associated with the increase of urbanization explain in part the vast cultural and economic progress which marked the last century.

WARREN S. THOMPSON

See: CITY; METROPOLITAN AREAS; INDUSTRIAL REVOLUTION; LOCATION OF INDUSTRY; HOUSING; SLUMS; SANITATION; RECREATION; BACK-TO-THE-LAND MOVEMENTS; MOBILITY, SOCIAL; MIGRATIONS; POPULATION; NEIGHBORHOOD.

Consult: Weber, A. F., *The Growth of Cities in the Nineteenth Century*, Columbia University, Studies in History, Economics and Public Law, no. 29 (New York 1899); Clerget, Pierre, "Urbanism; a Historic, Geographic, and Economic Study" in Smithsonian Institution, *Annual Report, 1912* (Washington 1913) p. 653–67; Bücher, Karl, "Die Grossstädte in Gegenwart und Vergangenheit" in *Die Grosstadt*, ed. by Theodor Petermann, Jahrbuch der Gehe-Stiftung zu Dresden, vol. ix (Dresden 1903) p. 1–32; Schlesinger, A. M., *The Rise of the City, 1878–1898* (New York 1933), with bibliography; Brunhes, Jean, *La géographie humaine*, 3 vols. (3rd ed. Paris 1925), tr. by T. C. LeCompte, 1 vol. (Chicago 1920); Ratzel, Friedrich, "Die geographische Lage der grossen Städte" in *Die Grosstadt*, ed. by Theodor Petermann, Jahrbuch der Gehe-Stiftung zu Dresden, vol. ix (Dresden 1903) p. 33–72; Aurousseau, M., "Recent Contributions to Urban Geography," and Jefferson, Mark, "Distribution of the World's City Folks" in *Geographical Review*, vol. xiv (1924) 444–55, and vol. xxi (1931) 446–65; Preuss, Hugo, *Die Entwicklung des deutschen Städtewesens* (Leipsic 1906); Geisler, Walter, *Die deutsche Stadt*, Forschungen zur deutschen Landes- und Volkskunde, vol. xxii, no. 5 (Stuttgart 1924); Park, R. E., Burgess, E. W., and McKenzie, R. D., *The City*, University of Chicago, Studies in Urban Sociology (Chicago 1925), with bibliography p. 161–228; McKenzie, R. D., *The Metropolitan Community*, Recent Social Trends Monographs (New York 1933); *Decentralisation of Population and Industry*, ed. by Herbert Warren and W. R. Davidge (London 1930); Wright, F. L., *The Disappearing City* (New York 1932); Douglass, H. Paul, *The Suburban Trend* (New York 1925); Chase, Stuart, "The Future of the Great City" in *Harper's Magazine*, vol. clx (1929–30) 82–90; Ward, Lester F., *Applied Sociology* (Boston 1906) p. 169–98; Thompson, J. G., *Urbanization; Its Effects on Government and Society* (New York 1927); Baker, O. E., "Rural-Urban Migration and the National Welfare" in Association of American Geographers, *Annals*, vol. xxiii (1933) 59–126; Bogardus, E. S., "The City; Spatial Nearness and Social Distance" in *Sociology and Social Research*, vol. xiii (1928–29) 572–77; Beard, Charles A., "The City's Place in Civilization" in *American City*, vol. xxxix, no. 5 (1928) 101–03; Thompson, W. S., *Population Problems* (New York 1930) chs. xvi-xix; Sydenstricker, E., *Health and Environment*, Recent Social Trends Monographs (New York 1933) ch. iv; Howe, F. C., *The Modern City and Its Problems* (New York 1915); Woolston, H. B., "The Urban Habit of Mind" in *American Journal of Sociology*, vol. xvii (1911–12) 602–14.

USENER, HERMANN (1834–1905), German classical philologist and historian of religions. Usener exercised a profound influence as professor at Bonn between 1866 and 1902. Among his numerous important philological writings *Epicurea* (Leipsic 1887) contributed greatly to the appreciation of this school of philosophy.

Most significant, however, was his work in the history of religion. Following a philological method in *Götternamen* (Bonn 1896, 2nd ed. 1929) he arrived at a theory of the origin of the concept of gods comparable to that of the anthropological school. His terms *Augenblicksgötter* and *Sondergötter* have been widely used, the former signifying the agent believed to have produced a single phenomenon, as, for example, lightning, the latter the agent producing a certain class of phenomena, such as the thunderstorm. From a psychological point of view the *Augenblicksgötter* correspond to the awe, caused by an impressive phenomenon, in which many scholars find the original source of religion; the *Sondergötter* correspond to the numerous and various demons of polydemonism; the Roman gods of the *Indigitamenta*, which Usener considered as *Sondergötter*, are, however, not true *Sondergötter* but an outcome of theological and juridical speculation. He contended that when the name of a god is no longer comprehensible because of the development of language the *Sondergott* may become a personal god.

Usener, who had a profound knowledge of ancient ecclesiastical writings and was deeply interested in folklore, tried to prove that pagan customs and myths had been taken over by Christianity, that St. Pelagia, for example, was a disguised Aphrodite and Ticonius a Priapus (*Der heilige Tychon*, Leipsic 1907). In his best known work, *Das Weihnachtsfest* (Bonn 1888, 2nd ed. 1911), he showed that the Christian festival is a direct continuation of the pagan festival of the birthday of the sun god, formerly celebrated on the old day of the winter solstice, December 25, and introduced by Pope Liberius between 354 and 360 A.D. into Rome, whence it rapidly spread through the Christian world.

MARTIN P. NILSSON

Consult: Deubner, L., in *Biographisches Jahrbuch*, vol. xxxi (1908) 53–74; Dieterich, Albrecht, in *Archiv für Religionswissenschaft*, vol. viii (1905) i–xi.

USPENSKY, FEDOR IVANOVICH (1845–1928), Russian historian. Uspensky was professor of European history at the University of Odessa from 1879 to 1894 and director of the Russian Archaeological Institute in Constantinople from 1894 to 1914. After Turkey's entrance into the World War he left for Petrograd, where he was appointed editor of the *Vizantiisky vremennik*, a journal edited by the Academy of Sciences and devoted to Byzantine studies. In his numerous works on different phases of the history of the Byzantine Empire he was particularly interested in the question of landownership and peasantry as well as Slavonic influence on the internal life of the empire; in this connection he undoubtedly exaggerated the role of the Slavs in the social evolution of Byzantium. His *Istoriya vizantiiskoi imperii*, covering the period from the fourth century A.D. to the end of the eighth, presents a synthesis of the many sided problems studied in his previous works. A convinced adherent of the particular importance of the history of the Byzantine Empire for the history of Russia and the Slavonic peoples of the Balkan Peninsula, he could not refrain from discovering in the past of Byzantium some "lessons" for modern times. Although Uspensky failed to solve satisfactorily all the social and economic problems he advanced and discussed, his works still remain a point of departure for further studies in the social structure of the Byzantine Empire.

A. A. VASILIEV

Important works: *Obrazovanie vtorogo bolgarskago tsarstva* (Foundation of the second Bulgarian kingdom) (Odessa 1879); "Znachenie vizantiiskoi i yuzhno-slavyanskoi pronii" (Significance of Byzantine and South-Slavonic pronoia) in *Sbornik statei po slavyanovedeniyu v chest V. I. Lamanskogo* (St. Petersburg 1883) p. 1–23; *Ocherki po istorii vizantiiskoi obrazovannosti* (Essays on the history of Byzantine civilization) (St. Petersburg 1891); *Istoriya krestovikh pokhodov* (History of the crusades) (St. Petersburg 1900); *Istoriya vizantiiskoi imperii* (History of the Byzantine Empire), vols. i–ii (St. Petersburg-Leningrad 1914–26); *Vazelonskie akti; materiali dlya istorii krestyanskogo i monastirskogo zemlevladeniya v Vizantii XIII–XV vekov* (The acts of Vazelon; materials on the history of peasant and monastery landownership in Byzantium from the thirteenth century to the fifteenth) (Leningrad 1926), in collaboration with V. N. Beneshevich; *Ocherki po istorii trapezuntskoi imperii* (Outlines of the history of the empire of Trebizond) (Leningrad 1929).

Consult: Akademiya Nauk, S.S.S.R., *Pamyati akademika Fedora Ivanovicha Uspenskogo* (To the memory of F. I. Uspensky, member of the Academy) by V. N. Beneshevich and others (Leningrad 1929); Diehl, Charles, "L'oeuvre de Théodore Uspenskij" in *L'art byzantin chez les slaves*, Orient et Byzance, ed. by G. Millet, vol. iv, pt. i (Paris 1930) p. vii–x.

USURY. In the course of its history the concept of usury has covered a variety of meanings. Originally it referred to all returns derived from the lending of capital and carried no moral opprobrium. With the growing condemnation of the financial abuses of the moneylenders the term came to be confined to credit transactions carrying excessive charges and thus acquired a distinct ethical connotation. In the Middle Ages all direct payments for loans were deemed usurious and condemned as sinful. In modern times the term was again narrowed down and now it refers only to excessive loan charges, while the payment of moderate rates is covered by the more neutral term interest. As usury is essentially a price for the use of capital and thus a specific manifestation of the general principle of price, the term has occasionally been extended to include all exchange transactions in which the stronger party takes advantage of the weaker in order to derive undue profit. Thus the term *Wucher*, the German equivalent for usury, applies to all forms of economic abuse; and German literature treats profiteering, wage exploitation and excessive rentals as specific manifestations of the general phenomenon of usury. While there is a logical and to some extent a historical justification for the use of the term usury in this widest sense, the overwhelming practise, at least in English speaking countries, favors the confinement of the concept to moneylending exclusively.

The ethical nature of the concept of usury renders it impossible to formulate permanent and definite criteria of what constitutes a usurious transaction. As long as freedom of contract remains the corner stone of economic organization, it is not the economist but the legislator who must decide at what point a voluntary economic transaction constitutes an abuse of economic freedom and thus an act of usury. Transactions which were condemned in the Middle Ages as usurious became recognized in subsequent centuries as normal economic practises, while usages which were outlawed and punished in one country were at the same time freely permitted in another. Moreover in certain periods the moral views of the legislative bodies were identical with those of the majority of the people, while at other times there was a wide divergence in this respect, so that usages which were officially outlawed were nevertheless sanctioned in economic life. Thus while concepts such as price, wage, interest, are economic categories transcending time, usury is a historical category understood only in the light of the moral and legal norms prevailing in a particular period.

The theory of usury was shaped by the conceptions developed by the ancient Greek and Roman philosophers on the one hand and the Jewish and Christian theologians on the other. The earliest prohibition of usury is to be found in the Mosaic code (*Leviticus* XXV: 36, and *Deuteronomy* XXIII: 20). The restriction, however, applied only to Jews; the taking of interest from aliens was permitted. In Athens the legislation of Solon, intended to ease the financial burden of the agricultural population, limited the rate of interest. In Rome the Twelve Tables established a maximum of 10 percent. From that time until the empire various legislative acts attempted to enforce the lawful rate of interest. In 342 B.C. there was even promulgated a law, the *Lex genucia*, which prohibited the taking of any payment for loans. Although there is no record of its abolition, this act was never enforced. The fact that the usual restrictions did not apply to the *foenus nauticum*—a loan advanced to finance maritime trade—probably facilitated a general evasion of anti-usury legislation; and there is no doubt that the wealthy bourgeois class under the early empire in Italy and in the provinces derived its economic origin and financial strength from "usurious" operations. Subsequently Justinian reduced the legal rate considerably, to 6 percent for general loans, 8 percent for manufacturers and merchants, 4 percent for persons in high positions and 12 percent for the *foenus nauticum*. The more drastic restrictions of the Justinian code were inspired by the growing influence of the teachings of the ancient philosophers and of the young Christian church.

The negative attitude toward usury adopted by the ancient Attic philosophers was not due to their ignorance of the principles of capitalistic economy. Plato and Aristotle were perfectly aware of the importance of the Attic "banks" to the economy of the fourth century B.C. But they realized also the social danger inherent in a system which encourages the pursuit of gain for gain's sake, and by condemning moneylending they hoped to strike at the very roots of profit economy. The ban on gains derived from moneylending was also influenced by the naturalistic conception of money and interest which permeated the teaching of Aristotle and through him the thinking of mediaeval theologians. This is well expressed in the Greek term for usury τοκος, meaning the offspring of an organic being. Money, Aristotle held, is an inorganic object used as a medium of exchange and therefore cannot breed new coins. He who demands payment for the lending of money causes money to beget money and thus acts contrary to the laws of nature.

The antichrematistic tone of the ancient philosophers was in perfect accord with the teachings of the rising church. While the attitude of the church was based primarily on the Scriptural command *Mutuum date nihil inde sperantes* (Lend, hoping for nothing again, *St. Luke* VI: 35), the theologians drew freely upon the anti-usury arguments of the philosophers. Thus Gregory of Nyssa admonished the faithful not to seek gain from gold and other precious metals; that is, from objects which cannot produce offspring. In the Roman church Ambrose of Milan formulated the principle which dominated ecclesiastic teaching for almost a thousand years: everything which accrues to the capital constitutes usury. While couched primarily in moral terms, this rigorous prohibition derived its social justification from the fact that under conditions of a primitive economy most loans were contracted by the needy for purposes of consumption and the borrower usually found himself in a worse position at the end than at the beginning of the loan period. Moreover because of the absence of business opportunities in the early Middle Ages, when the usury doctrine of the church took shape, the holder of funds did not forego any loss of profit by parting temporarily with his capital. The absolute prohibition of usury was further justified in terms of contemporary economic theory; it was argued that a loan transaction involving the transfer of ownership of the sum of money to the borrower really constituted a sale in which in accordance with the mediaeval principle of equivalence of exchange the lender, that is, the seller of money, might expect in return only the exact equivalent of the amount originally advanced. The fact that a period of time intervened between the offering and the return of the sum was dismissed with the argument that time is divine and can therefore command no price. Unlike the situation in ancient Greece and Rome, it was no longer necessary to determine at what rate a charge for money loan became usurious and punishable; all charges above the principal were held usurious. Usury was no mere transgression of the law but a mortal sin punishable by excommunication. This rigid measure originally applied only to the clergy but was subsequently extended to all lay Christians.

While the church consistently prohibited the charging of a price for loans throughout the Middle Ages, a person in need of money who was willing to shoulder the cost was never deprived completely of the possibility of borrowing money. Aside from the various devices designed to evade the anti-usury laws, as, for instance, the practise of sale and resale whereby the prospective lender fictitiously sold to the borrower a commodity on credit at a high price and simultaneously repurchased it for cash at a lower price, the difference constituting an interest charge for an actual loan, the mediaeval borrower could turn to the Jewish moneylenders and pawnbrokers, who did not come under the jurisdiction of the church and were tolerated in their moneylending operations. Later Christian traders, notably the Lombards and the Caorsini, engaged to an increasing extent in the banking business; and although they were generally condemned as usurers, they came in time to enjoy the privileges of the princes and even of the church. Under the impact of economic necessity the church authorities themselves began to reinterpret the all comprehensive concept of usury in favor of a more liberal policy toward financial transactions. Thus while it denied to the creditor the right to charge a price for his loans, the church permitted the collection of a fine in case the debtor did not return the principal at the time specified in the loan agreement. There developed the practise of inserting a penal clause (*poena conventionalis*) into the loan agreements whereby a nominal, brief, gratuitous loan period was set; after its expiration the debtor automatically was liable for the payment of the fine in addition to the repayment of the principal. But even in the absence of a penal clause the creditor was allowed, by invoking the principle *damnum emergens*, to recover for any damages he might have suffered as a result of the loan. It was but one step further to the application of the principle of *lucrum cessans*, whereby the lender had a right to indemnity if he could prove that he had to forego a potential profit as a result of the loan; this proof was rendered easier with the growth of investment opportunities, and later it was waived for merchants and manufacturers. Still another escape from the ban on commercial moneylending was eventually made available through the institution of partnership. After Aquinas the church voiced no objection to the practise of investing money in the form of partnership and drawing a profit, provided that the person supplying the capital shared in the losses as well as in the profits. The insistence on sharing the risk as an indispensable element in a partnership agreement rendered this form of investment unsuitable to the moneylender, who was interested primarily in the safety of his principal and in a fixed return on his capital. He could, however, protect his investment by insuring the principal against loss, which was legal, and assure a fixed rate of return by selling a future uncertain profit for a certain definite return, which was also legal. There was no reason why the three contracts—the partnership agreement, the insurance contract and the sale of a future uncertain profit—each one legal in itself, should be presumed to be illegal when entered into by the same two persons. This so-called triple contract (*contractus trinus*), which became an established practise in the latter part of the fifteenth century, was in effect an agreement with all the implications of a modern loan transaction. In some countries, for example, Germany, the purchase of rents provided wide opportunities for the investment of funds. In others the churches themselves established the *montes pietatis*; that is, funds which were used in advancing small loans to the needy in return for a small charge sufficient to cover the cost of administration.

The more liberal attitude of the church toward interest and usury was reflected in contemporary theological writings. While the official position remained as expressed by Gerson in the fifteenth century, namely, that it is contrary to nature for money to breed money, other writers began to distinguish between usury proper and non-usurious forms of gain. Thus the Franciscan Bernardino of Siena and the Dominican Antonino of Florence, the two great preachers of the early Renaissance, endeavored to define cases in which gain could be permitted without being usurious. In a commentary to the *Summa* of Aquinas, Cardinal Cajetan renounced the principle of sterility of money and thus provided the moral justification for the financial practises of early capitalism.

In the sixteenth and seventeenth centuries the jurists continued to struggle against the prohibition and they succeeded in restricting the concept of money and thereby the applicability of anti-usury laws. Charles de Moulin and above all Salmasius, who attempted to differentiate between interest and usury, exerted a most profound influence in Europe; the latter in a hypothetical case actually sought to justify a rate of interest of 36 percent.

Under the impact of capitalistic development the original conceptions of the church fathers receded into the background. By the eighteenth century the status of moneylending came to resemble that prevailing in ancient Rome; the question was no longer whether it was permissible to charge a price for capital but at what rate the charge became excessive and therefore usurious. Most states attempted to fix maximum rates of interest. But soon even such restrictions drew the attack of the advocates of the newly emerging doctrine of freedom of enterprise. In England William Petty in 1682 and in France Turgot a century later pleaded for freedom in credit operations. Of greatest significance, however, was the demand for complete freedom put forward by Jeremy Bentham in his famous *Defence of Usury* (London 1787). In the name of personal liberty Bentham demanded the same degree of freedom for money trade as that prevailing in commodity trade. Taking as his point of departure the familiar argument that every rational person knows best how to defend his interests and that there is therefore no reason for government interference, he maintained that the state which aims to aid the poor by restricting the interest rate excludes them at the same time from the sources of credit. Similarly impressive was the common contention that a restriction of the rate of interest necessarily results in a shortage of capital and consequently in an increase in the cost of credit. But it was not only in the interest of the individual but also for the sake of the state that it was held necessary to suspend the operation of the anti-usury laws; thus Keynes has pointed out that the continuance of the 5 percent maximum rate in England rendered it impossible to institute a modern discount policy and that the Bank of England could initiate such a policy only after the abolition of the rate restriction in 1839.

The advances of economic liberalism wiped the anti-usury laws from the statute books of most countries. England removed its ban on usury in 1854, Holland in 1857, Belgium in 1865 and Prussia and the North German Federation in 1867. In the United States the overwhelming majority of the states still retain their anti-usury laws, but these have little effect on the actual movement of interest rates. The sweeping repeal of the anti-usury laws did, however, produce in most countries a flood of credit abuses, sufficient to warrant the prompt reintroduction of protective measures. In the latter part of the nineteenth century Germany, Austria and other countries and England in 1900 found it necessary to enact measures covering all cases in which the moneylender took undue advantage of the inexperience or carelessness of the borrower, particularly when the latter was led to accept excessive financial charges through fraud or misrepresentation on the part of the former. In some countries and in the various states of the United States the whole field of small loans, most of which are in the nature of consumption loans, was placed under the special protection of the law to prevent financial exploitation of the small and as a rule economically weak borrower.

The future of usury legislation is closely related to the general fate of economic liberalism. Recent economic history and particularly experience since the World War reflect a waning faith in the automatic adjustment of economic processes and a greater reliance upon a conscious interference with the workings of the economic mechanism. The growing recognition of the fact that the individual is frequently helpless in the face of organized powerful economic groups and must therefore be protected in his economic dealings against exploitation will undoubtedly again focus the attention of the legislator upon the necessity of protecting the borrower against abuses in the field of credit. In pursuing this aim the legislator will be aided by the growing popular opposition to the regime of unrestrained economic individualism which has manifested itself since the turn of the century, and it may be that in the near future new anti-usury laws will be the common sign of a doomed capitalism.

EDGAR SALIN

See: INTEREST; DEBT; LOANS, PERSONAL; SMALL LOANS; PAWNBROKING; JUST PRICE.

Consult: Endemann, W., *Die Nationalökonomischen Grundsätze der canonistischen Lehre* (Jena 1863); Funk, F. X., *Zins und Wucher* (Tübingen 1868), and *Geschichte des kirchlichen Zinsverbots* (Tübingen 1876); O'Brien, G. A. T., *An Essay on Mediaeval Economic Teaching* (London 1920) p. 159–83; Ashley, W. J., *An Introduction to English Economic History and Theory*, 2 vols. (4th ed. London 1906–09) vol. i, pt. i, p. 148–63, pt. ii, p. 377–488; Chorinsky, C., *Der Wucher in Oesterreich* (Vienna 1877); Endemann, Wilhelm, *Studien in der romanisch-kanonistischen Wirtschafts- und Rechtslehre bis gegen Ende des 17. Jahrhunderts*, 2 vols. (Berlin 1874–83); Peschke, K., *Was ist Zinswucher?* (Berlin 1926); "Der Wucher auf dem Lande," and "Verhandlungen . . . Generalversammlung des Vereins für Socialpolitik über den ländlichen Wucher" in Verein der Socialpolitik, *Schriften*, vol. xxxv (Leipsic 1887), and vol. xxxviii (Leipsic 1889); Ryan, F. W., *Usury and Usury Laws* (Boston 1924); Schneider, Fedor, "Neue Theorien über das kirchliche Zinsverbot," and Salin, E., "Kapitalbegriff und Kapitallehre von der Antike zu den Physiokraten" in *Vierteljahrschrift für Social- und Wirtschaftsgeschichte*, vol. v (1907) 292–307, and vol. xxiii (1930) 401–40.

UTILITARIANISM. The term, more precise than most abstractions, refers to the doctrines held by a relatively small, well organized group of nineteenth century Englishmen, whose chief theorists were Bentham, James Mill, Ricardo, J. S. Mill, Austin and Sidgwick and whose chief political agents were Francis Place, Joseph Hume, Roebuck, Grote, Buller and Molesworth. Although the utilitarians were ardent individualists and although John Mill proudly denies that they formed a "school," they seem in retrospect to have had a great deal of cohesion. Their sympathetic historian, Leslie Stephen, speaks of them as a "sect." Nor were their ideas modified greatly in the seventy odd years of their existence as a self-conscious group; John Mill was a subtler psychologist than Bentham, had a tempting glimpse of mysticism, from which he recovered, and toward the end of his life under the influence of sympathy for the working classes modified his trust in economic individualism. Yet the fundamentals of the faith remained unchanged. Utilitarian ideas in less dogmatic form did indeed gain widespread hearing, and there is a loose sense of the word utilitarian, implying a prosaic attachment to material ends, which has passed into common English.

The philosophical antecedents of utilitarianism are briefly: Epicureanism, or classical hedonism, a doctrine always suspect to good Christians but increasingly popular from the Renaissance to the eighteenth century; English and French rationalism from Locke to the *encyclopédistes* and especially the famous *De l'esprit* of Helvétius; the *Wealth of Nations*; and the work of such eighteenth century humanitarians as Shaftesbury, Beccaria, Howard and the Adam Smith of the *Moral Sentiments*. Those who hold racial or national theories in such matters commonly add to this list the general tradition of English empiricism. In actual fact the consciousness of a traditional English distrust of metaphysics affected the utilitarians chiefly by sharpening their fear that they were after all metaphysicians and by increasing their sense of isolation and importance. For utilitarianism is an absolute empiricism, to be distinguished from absolute idealism only by the devoutly professional philosopher.

The physical antecedents of utilitarianism are to be found in the England of the early industrial revolution. The principle of utility and particularly the notion that self-interest is identical with common interest were admirably fitted to the purpose of the more active leaders of the new industrial England, who found in them at once a means of undermining the power of the feudal gentry and a justification for their own industry. This ideology helped them to get things done, make converts, pass laws, and—not least important—it gave them a consciousness of being right. Utilitarianism, always the doctrine of a small minority, was never in its purer form held by ordinary middle class Englishmen. But the utilitarians were the thin end of the wedge which overturned the old regime in England. They carried through that English revolution of 1832 which is so like the moderate French revolution of 1789. Indeed the fundamental similarity between Girondists and utilitarians is striking. Both represent the youthful optimism of the leaders of a crusading bourgeoisie; both in their ardor outdistance the main body of their troops, occupied in the comfortable consolidation of existing gains.

The utilitarians based their whole system, with all its ramifications into economics, politics, jurisprudence, penology, education and religion, on one grand principle, Bentham's great discovery that man is ruled by two sovereign masters, pleasure and pain. Actually the famous principle of utility was not very novel; what made it new in Bentham's hands was his use of it to cement the alliance with a deified science and thereby to make utilitarianism a faith. The religious impulse toward self-annihilation appears in Bentham in its characteristically modern form, the form in which certain types of "knowledge" are embraced as wholly objective and independent of the knower's desires. Whereas, according to Bentham, previous thinkers, especially in the political and social spheres, had been accustomed to deal in generalities, such as "right" and "justice," which each man stained with his private emotions, the principle of "utility" removed politics into the serene impersonality of mathematics. If the scientist observes men objectively, his mind cleansed of moral and religious preconceptions, he sees that all men seek pleasure and avoid pain; he must therefore conclude that pleasure is "good" and pain "evil." These pleasures and pains, which in a rough way all individuals have equal capacities to experience, can be treated as mathematical quantities and weighed against each other through the application of the so-called hedonistic calculus. A maximum of men enjoying a maximum of pleasures minus a minimum of men afflicted with a minimum of pains equals the greatest good of the greatest number. The principle of utility does not equate "good" with crude sensual satisfaction, and it does not exclude from "good" the higher pleasures of imagination and taste. John Mill used to grow very indignant over the accusation that the utilitarians had a porcine notion of pleasure and that their utility was the simple usefulness of machinery. All this meant of course that the school by no means succeeded in escaping from the necessity of making value judgments. The utilitarians, especially those of the first generation, failed notably to penetrate the psychological depths of human motivation. Nor could they maintain quite consistently their assurance that the enlightened self-interest of the individual is identical with the enlightened self-interest of all other men. Bentham's metaphysical atomism made it impossible for him to solve what Élie Halévy has called the problem of the "artificial identification of interests." But he did provide his fellows with a measuring rod for existing institutions.

This measuring rod they applied to English life with doctrinaire rigor and found that Englishmen, ignorant of the principle of utility, had for generations pursued pleasure and avoided pain unintelligently. The utilitarians proposed to set them right. Bentham gathered about himself a little group which wrote, preached and gradually edged into journalism and politics. The Benthamites became the "philosophical radicals," represented in the House of Commons by a small but able and determined group. As journalists and politicians the philosophical radicals hastened and gave shape to a number of important reforms.

Utilitarian economics is simply classical economics. Ricardo, M'Culloch, John Mill, were all of the inner circle of the elect. Utility in the field of economics dictates free trade, cheap but efficient government and low taxes, abolition of guilds and all other forms of monopoly, unlimited competition; for if all men are permitted to follow without hindrance their enlightened self-interest in buying in the cheapest and selling in the dearest market, their individual selfishnesses will mutually cancel out and a maximum of goods will be produced and distributed. In early nineteenth century England, the utilitarians claimed, the corn laws gave to the unproductive landed gentry in the form of rent an artificially increased share of other men's production; the prolific breeding of the laboring classes kept them constantly pressing on the means of subsistence; and the survival of all sorts of feudal prejudices prevented the full extension to economic life of the career open to talents. These three defects were the main objects of utilitarian attack. The philosophical radicals helped destroy the corn laws and make business a noble life. The population problem gave them more trouble, practically because the English laboring classes found the utilitarian preaching for the most part rather wearisome, logically because to restrict the number of working men was to restrict competition in the labor market and to make a concession to the spirit of monopoly. In his declining years John Mill in fact began to desert orthodox utilitarian economics, and in the end he admitted that workers united in unions not only could but ought to raise wages.

In jurisprudence the utilitarians are acknowledged to have attained their most striking results. In criminal jurisprudence utility saw in punishment neither divine nor social vengeance but a means of preventing crime and, if possible, reforming the criminal. The criminal should feel just a shade more pain from punishment than pleasure—that is, profit—from his crime. Too much pain would embitter him, turn him against society, and too little would encourage him to further crime. In its details absurd, this hedonistic calculus was applied by Bentham and his disciples to the disordered cruelties of English penology with excellent results. Again, utility saw in civil law no mystic inheritance from the fathers, no accumulation of unquestionable if occasionally inconvenient regulations but simply a means of enabling men to deal securely and efficiently with one another. Law, like any other arrangement, could be made anew and in the tangled state of Eldon's law should be so treated. The Benthamites never achieved the English code they set up as their ideal, although they helped draft many codes outside England, in South America, Spain and even Russia. But working first through Romilly and then through Mackintosh they did attain piecemeal a considerable reform of English law in the direction of simplicity, clarity and lessening of conflict.

The utilitarians had the highest hopes in popular education. If democratic experiments like the French Revolution had been failures, the reason was that ignorant men had not known how to use their freedom. Universal education, guided by utilitarian philosophers, would open a way for the untrammeled operation of the principle of utility. The philosophical radicals supported Lancaster in his quarrel with Bell, founded University College, London, the first English institution of higher learning wholly free from Christian religious tests and teaching, encouraged Mechanics Institutes and preached education everywhere. But it must be admitted that here their achievement fell far short of their aims, and the later spread of popular education in England owes more to other groups than to the utilitarians.

Politically the philosophical radicals were democratic republicans; but so long as kings and queens were useful, they were willing to tolerate them, at least in England. Bentham professed great scorn for the metaphysical nonsense of the Rights of Man; but utility inspired a political program only slightly different from that of the impractical French, for it included universal manhood suffrage, equal electoral districts, rotation in office, freedom of speech and of the press, the inviolability of individual property rights and all the familiar apparatus of nineteenth century democracy. Democracy was perhaps not the best form of government, but in contemporary England only the people could be trusted to embrace the truths of utilitarianism. Bentham had learned that the upper classes were not to be converted. His followers led the agitation for the Reform Bill of 1832, thinking it at least a step toward the ultimate goal of democracy. The useful government, however, is the efficient government, and Austinian doctrines of sovereignty show that the utilitarians never really abandoned the authoritarian basis from which Bentham set out.

In religion the utilitarians were practically what later came to be called secularists. But they were all thoroughly respectable men, hardly daring to defy British religious conventions, and they therefore attacked Christian superstitions with something less than bravado. The aged Bentham and the young Grote collaborated in a book on religion, cautiously signed "Philip Beauchamp" (*Analysis of the Influence of Natural Religion on the Temporal Happiness of Mankind*, London 1822), in which the pleasures and pains of anticipation of an afterlife, of God's judgment, of prayer, are carefully balanced and utility made to decide against superstition. Yet most of the utilitarians were of a believing or even dogmatic temperament, and it is not insignificant that John Mill should have died in a tepid Manichaeanism.

Having helped build up the England of laissez faire, utilitarianism helped destroy it. By repulsion utilitarian ideology strengthened the opposing idealisms which aimed at state or group intervention in economic and social life. Leading the attack against the "pig philosophy" was

Carlyle, never a very scrupulous fighter and in his presentation of utilitarian judgments of value generally quite unfair. But Carlyle possessed the mystic graces and possibly that insight into ordinary men which the utilitarians most certainly lacked. By the turn of the twentieth century the utilitarians had ceased to be prophets. Even liberalism, through the medium of T. H. Green, was drawing inspiration from German idealism. Secondly, by attraction important elements in utilitarian ideology passed over into Marxism and were turned against laissez faire. The indebtedness of Marx to the classical economists for his labor theory of value and to the Ricardian socialists for his theory of surplus value—not to mention other technical borrowings—is of course well known. But the significant relation between utilitarianism and Marxism, at least in its vulgar form, is a spiritual one: both make economic relations the basic fact of social organization, both are class conscious, both are piously materialistic and both very profitably confuse their desires with a supernatural force which they are unwilling to call God.

CRANE BRINTON

See: INDIVIDUALISM; HEDONISM; ALTRUISM AND EGOISM; EPICUREANISM; RATIONALISM; HUMANITARIANISM; POSITIVISM; ECONOMICS, section on THE CLASSICAL SCHOOL; LAISSEZ FAIRE; CRIMINOLOGY.

Consult: Halévy, Élie, *La formation du radicalisme philosophique*, 3 vols. (Paris 1901–04), tr. by M. Morris as *The Growth of Philosophic Radicalism*, 1 vol. (London 1928), with critical bibliography; Stephen, Leslie, *The English Utilitarians*, 3 vols. (London 1900); Albee, Ernest, *A History of English Utilitarianism* (London 1902); Davidson, W. L., *Political Thought in England; the Utilitarians, from Bentham to J. S. Mill* (London 1915); Brinton, Crane, *English Political Thought in the Nineteenth Century* (London 1933) p. 14–30, 89–103; Kent, C. B. R., *The English Radicals* (London 1899) p. 168–249, 322–414; Wallas, Graham, *The Life of Francis Place* (rev. ed. London 1918); Dicey, A. V., *Lectures on the Relation between Law and Public Opinion in England during the Nineteenth Century* (2nd ed. London 1914) lectures vi, ix; Pollock, Frederick, *An Introduction to the History of the Science of Politics* (new ed. London 1923) p. 101–11, 118–33; Veblen, Thorstein, "The Preconceptions of Economic Science," and "The Socialist Economics of Karl Marx and His Followers" in his *The Place of Science in Modern Civilisation and Other Essays* (New York 1919) p. 130–44, 409–56; Schumpeter, J. A., "Epochen der Dogmen- und Methodengeschichte" in *Grundriss der Sozialökonomik*, vol. i, pt. i (2nd ed. Tübingen 1924) sect. iii; Cahnmann, Werner, *Der oekonomische Pessimismus und das ricardosche System* (Halberstadt 1929) ch. B; Guyau, M. J., *La morale anglaise contemporaine* (4th ed. Paris 1900); Cazamian, L. F., *Le roman social en Angleterre (1830–1850)* (2nd ed. Paris 1904) ch. ii; Neff, E. E., *Carlyle and Mill* (2nd ed. New York 1926).

UTILITY. *See* VALUE AND PRICE; ECONOMICS, section on MARGINAL UTILITY.

UTOPIA. The word utopia, a coinage from the Greek, meaning literally "nowhere," was first used by Sir Thomas More in 1516 as the name of a far distant island on which, according to his fiction, there existed an ideal commonwealth. Since the publication of More's *Utopia* its title has been appropriated to designate more or less indiscriminately literary works of all ages which seek, whether through the medium of the dialogue, the novel or some similar form, to conjure up a society or state free from human imperfections. In recent years, however, the term has come also to be used in a more strictly sociological sense. The analysis of a particular type of intellectual outlook and thought pattern which is now designated as the utopian mind or the utopian spirit has become one of the most fruitful fields of inquiry for contemporary sociologists. It is coming to be realized that a clear understanding of the structure and characteristics of this psychological type is important not only in itself but also because it throws light on the social process as a whole no less than on intellectual development in its broader aspects.

As a literary genre the utopian fiction made its appearance many centuries before More. It was Plato who furnished, notably in his *Republic*, the general model to which all later utopian fictions have been heavily indebted. But whereas the writings of Plato were motivated primarily by an authoritarian desire to buttress, in as rational terms as possible, a static and hierarchically ordered social and political system, the utopian writings of More and his fellow humanists during the Renaissance were the expression of a wave of intellectual and social release. Steeped in the spirit of the classical revival and at the same time living in detachment from the broader currents of life about them, these small groups of humanists could arrive at an objective attitude toward current social norms and institutions. It is in fact the humanist way of life which accounts for both the rigidly systematic quality of the characteristic Renaissance utopia and the often paradoxical and fantastic nature of many of its conclusions. In More, for example, a trenchant criticism of social injustice as manifested in the period of transition between feudalism and capitalism is combined with a nostalgic mediaevalism; in Bacon's *New Atlantis* (1627) an aggressive faith in the liberating role of science with a predilection for authoritarianism; in Campanella's *Civitas soli* (1623) the pious superstition of an orthodox Calabrian monk with an antipathy to tyranny and an untrammeled intellectual search for means to eradicate social evil. The most realistic of the humanist utopias was Harrington's *The Common-Wealth of Oceana* (1656), which was later to exert a marked influence on the constitution makers in the United States. Drawing upon his travels and his humanistic studies, Harrington undertook during Cromwell's regime a comparative study of constitutions to discover the form of government most ideally suited to his troubled country.

The third great climate of opinion in which utopian fictions played a significant role was that which prevailed during the eighteenth and the early nineteenth century. The widespread social unrest engendered by the economic and political readjustments which culminated in the bourgeois revolutions found natural expression in the succession of heterogeneous utopias modeled on the work of the earlier humanists. In the period following the French Revolution the literary utopias were by comparison oriented more consistently toward a single political ideal. Thus Engels in his *Die Entwicklung des Sozialismus von der Utopie zur Wissenschaft* could more or less plausibly group together Morelly, Babeuf, Saint-Simon, Fourier, Cabet and Owen and, despite their minor variations of approach, dub them indiscriminately "utopian socialists." In branding these antibourgeois reformers with the epithet utopian Engels meant to rebuke them for their addiction to the sentimental delusions of the eighteenth century *philosophes*, who naïvely fancied that they could bring their fellow men to carry through a reorganization of society merely by placing before them certain abstract ideals. Since, according to Engels, the starting point of scientific socialism is the realization of the definite objectives which can be carried through at a given stage of history and in a given social complex, he called upon social reformers to abandon the a priori fabrication of ideal societies and to devote their energies instead to precise analyses of current social forces. Having done this they would naturally proceed to identify themselves with the proletariat, that class which alone can carry through such a reorganization of society.

While the making of utopias by no means came to an end with the utopian socialists, the subsequent examples, although frequently meeting with considerable literary success, cannot be said to have attained, as did their predecessors, a broader social significance. And yet until the development of sociology they continued to provide a substitute of sorts for the scientific analysis of social phenomena.

In the sociological approach to the problem of the utopian mind and the utopian spirit the attempt is made to ascertain the psychological genesis of this type of mental outlook, the principal phases of its historical development and its functional significance. The term utopian, as here used, may be applied to any process of thought which receives its impetus not from the direct force of social reality but from concepts, such as symbols, fantasies, dreams, ideas and the like, which in the most comprehensive sense of that term are non-existent. Viewed from the standpoint of sociology, such mental constructs may in general assume two forms: they are "ideological" if they serve the purpose of glossing over or stabilizing the existing social reality; "utopian" if they inspire collective activity which aims to change such reality to conform with their goals, which transcend reality. There is thus a close bond which connects the social process itself with intellectual development and the formation of the mind. Not only the mental structure of existing social groups but the destiny of an entire social scheme may depend upon the nature of the unreal or reality transcending concepts originally embraced by these groups, upon the manner in which the original ideas have been assimilated into the social stream and, finally, upon the ultimate outcome of the interaction between the utopian element and the other elements and the mind.

From the psychological point of view the history of the utopian mind involves an evolutionary process which begins with the primitive mythical mind and leads gradually to the comprehension of reality. Fragmentary traces of this development may be discerned in the growth of the child as well as in the evolution of mankind. Sometimes accelerated by the concrete social situation and sometimes interrupted by forces of retrogression, the process of development leads, however unevenly, not only to a definite realism but to a progressive rationalism. It is characteristic of the primitive or mythical mind that it offers escape from reality in the form of symbolic equivalents which bring to satisfaction impulses and desires frustrated by social realities. Such a tendency of mind operates directly to fuse the unreal subjective and symbolic wish fulfilment fictions with elements of objective reality and in fact cannot distinguish between the two. This phenomenon, characteristic of children and the dream experiences of normal human beings, is found moreover not only in certain types of neurotic individuals and primitive peoples but also occasionally among certain strata of contemporary society which have not progressed far beyond the primitive and under stress of circumstance give way readily to atavistic urges.

The function of the myth as contrasted with the daydream, which at most can represent an interplay between two individuals, is to project and collectivize those subjective ecstasies and symbolic equivalents for the wish fulfilment idea which survive in a particular society. But even in the primitive variety of myth it may be observed that with the differentiation of social groups the oppressed classes make different use of their religious ecstasy and their symbolic equivalents from that made by the ruling classes and in particular that they fuse them with social resentment. Hence the religious aspects of the myth already tend to give way to the social. Whereas the ruling group, as it progresses toward rationalistic attitudes, gradually converts the symbolic equivalents originally common to the entire collectivity into instruments which can be consciously manipulated to support its authority, and so transforms them into a protective coloring of ideology, the masses oftentimes evolve from the same matrix a utopia which subverts the status quo. Whenever the myth stereotypes, under the guise of ideology, fail to maintain the stability of the social order against the disintegrating force of economic, political or other change, the ingredients of the myth tend to be metamorphosed into eschatological and chiliastic conceptions. The strata which are most victimized by social tabus and oppression are in such cases moved as much by the impulses springing from symbols as by social objectives which can be immediately realized. At this moment the reality transcending element, hitherto merely a wish fulfilment equivalent, becomes the force which welds the masses into a collectivity and spurs them to group action; and in turn the action, by bringing them into contact with actual concrete situations and by necessitating collective adaptation, gradually becomes the instrument through which reality is disclosed to an ever greater degree. Thus with the aid of utopian fictions the rationalization of consciousness follows a course altogether different from that of the rationalization of society by the ruling groups.

One of the principal phases in the progressive rationalization of the western mind through the medium of the utopia is represented by the teachings of the Jewish prophets. Their enunciation of the doctrine that collective evil is not to be exorcized through ritualistic magic and that any change in social destiny must be wrought on the basis of individual responsibility marked the completion of the process whereby the mere expression of religious ecstasy became an ethical criticism of society. The ethical rationalization of particular behavior patterns and the transformation of the will to change society into a deep inward force were furthered also by the work of Jesus. Through Him ethical salvation, an idea which the later prophets had extended to the Gentiles, was to be sought by all mankind. In His case as in that of the prophets it is significant that the individualization and ethical rationalization of religion were the work of isolated individuals rather than of the official priestly caste. Among the postexile prophets the enforced absence from the traditional paraphernalia of ritual service was a factor which served to place emphasis on the significance of religion as an inner experience of the individual. In the early years of the modern era the eschatological-chiliastic utopia again made its appearance, as may be seen most clearly in the efforts of Thomas Münzer to fuse religious ecstasy with social pressure. The first phase of the subsequent uprisings fomented by the masses also bore a resemblance to the Peasants' War in that it aimed at the immediate realization of the millennium; while the later forms of the utopian mind as typified in the "liberal utopia" of the emergent bourgeoisie, where the emphasis was shifted to the "idea," can be accounted for only as a reflection of the gradual sublimation of social struggle and religious expectation. Thus in various ways it may be shown that the utopian fiction constitutes an integral part of the spiritual and intellectual equipment of the different social groups, and by orienting their activity in terms of this reality transcending element these groups, each in its own way, discover social reality. Therefore the utopian element may be said to operate not only as a collectivizing force in political activity but also as an underlying thread which knits together the conception of reality as held by the different classes of a collectivity. It is this utopia, this ultimate point of reference, which determines what questions shall be posed as to social events. In it are rooted not only the basic concepts which man creates in order to comprehend social phenomena but also the diverse forms of the "historical stage of existence" of various groups.

KARL MANNHEIM

See: COMMUNISTIC SETTLEMENTS; FOURIER AND FOURIERISM; OWEN AND OWENISM; SAINT-SIMON AND SAINT-SIMONIANISM; COMMUNISM; SOCIALISM; ANARCHISM; PRIMITIVISM.

Consult: Dermenghem, E., *Thomas Morus et les utopistes de la Renaissance* (Paris 1927); Hertzler, J. O., *The History of Utopian Thought* (New York 1923); Gerlich, Fritz, *Der Kommunismus als Lehre vom tausendjährigen Reich* (Munich 1920); Lichtenberger, A., *Le socialisme utopique* (Paris 1898); Prys, J., *Der Staatsroman des 16. und 17. Jahrhunderts und sein Erziehungsideal* (Würzburg 1913); Girsberger, Hans, *Der utopische Sozialismus des 18. Jahrhunderts in Frankreich und seine philosophischen und materiellen Grundlagen*, Zürcher volkswirtschaftliche Forschungen, no. 1 (Zurich 1924); Schomann, E., *Französische Utopisten des 18. Jahrhunderts und ihr Frauenideal* (Berlin 1911); Voigt, A., *Die sozialen Utopien* (Leipsic 1906); Engels, Friedrich, *Die Entwicklung des Sozialismus von der Utopie zur Wissenschaft* (4th ed. Berlin 1891), tr. by E. Aveling (London 1892); Mannheim, K., *Ideologie und Utopie* (Bonn 1929); Vida Nájera, Fernando, *Estudios sobre el concepto y la organización del estado en las "Utopías"* (Madrid 1928); Reiner, J., *Berühmte Utopisten und ihr Staatsideal* (Jena 1906); Doren, Alfred, "Wunschräume und Wunschzeiten" in Bibliothek Warburg, Hamburg, *Vorträge 1924–1925* (Leipsic 1927) p. 158–205; Massó, Gildo, *Education in Utopias*, Columbia University, Teachers College, Contributions to Education, no. 257 (New York 1927).

UVAROV, COUNT SERGEY SEMENOVICH (1786–1855), Russian official. Uvarov, a member of the landed aristocracy, studied at the University of Göttingen, where he came in contact with the Humboldts, Goethe and Madame de Staël. At the age of fifteen he was an attaché in the Ministry of Foreign Affairs and in 1809 became secretary to the Russian Legation in Paris. From 1811 to 1822 he served as curator of the school district of St. Petersburg and from 1833 to 1849 as minister of education. He attained a reputation as a scholar and wrote many historical, literary and philosophical works.

Uvarov started out as a pronounced liberal, but after the Decembrist revolt of 1825 he adopted the autocratic views of Nicholas I and enforced strict government regulation of public education, science, literature and the press. He based his educational philosophy on the three fundamental tenets of Russian absolutism: orthodoxy, autocracy and nationalism; as minister of education he shaped the educational institutions in strict conformity with these principles. Primary education was almost completely neglected. The curricula of the secondary schools were purged of such "superfluous" subjects as philosophy and natural sciences, while the teaching of the orthodox religion was made more intensive. Uvarov initiated the teaching of the classics in the secondary schools; toward the end of his administration the authorities restricted this branch of instruction, believing that the political experiences of the Greeks were conducive to the development of liberalism and republicanism. The institutions of higher learning were reserved to the ruling classes and were looked upon as training schools for government officials. Although Uvarov applied his principles in a ruthless manner, he failed to stem the tide of liberalism, which reached ever widening circles of Russian intellectuals. Moreover by sending the most gifted students abroad to study and then nominating them to university posts Uvarov himself was instrumental in spreading those very ideas against which his efforts were ostensibly directed. When in 1849 the Russian government became still more reactionary, he was forced to resign; he was thus victim of the movement which he had initiated.

N. ROUBAKINE

Consult: Pogodin, M., "Dlya biografii grafa Uvarova" (For a biography of Count Uvarov) in *Russky arkhiv*, vol. ix (1871) 2078–2112; Miliukov, P. N., *Ocherki po istorii russkoy kulturi* (Outlines of the history of Russian culture), 3 vols. (new ed. Paris 1930–31) vol. ii, pt. ii, p. 782–96; Schmid, Georg, "Zur russischen Gelehrtengeschichte" in *Russische Revue*, vol. xxvi (1886) 77–108; Koyré, Alexandre, *La philosophie et le problème national en Russie au début du XIXe siècle*, Institut Français de Leningrad, Bibliothèque, vol. x (Paris 1929) ch. vii; Darlington, T., *Education in Russia*, Great Britain, Board of Education, Special Reports on Educational Subjects, vol. xxiii (1909), especially p. 76–79; Hans, Nicholas, *History of Russian Educational Policy* (London 1931) ch. iii.

UZTÁRIZ, JERÓNIMO DE (1670–1732), Spanish economist. Uztáriz was a member of the Real Junta de Comercio y de Moneda and of the Consejo de Indias. His *Theórica y práctica de comercio y de marina* (Madrid 1724, rev. ed. 1742; tr. by J. Kippax, 2 vols., London 1751) did exert a profound influence upon Spanish economic thought and state policy for half a century, but the praise bestowed upon it by commentators and translators has been extravagant. Repeatedly identifying wealth and treasure, Uztáriz held that economic recovery was attainable through industrial and commercial policies designed either to attract specie to Spain or to prevent its exodus. While he was familiar with the effect of invisible items in international payments, he devoted his attention primarily to means of maintaining a favorable commodity balance, insisting that "advantageous commerce" is achieved by "selling to foreigners more than we buy from them." The measures recommended to secure the prerequisite industrial rehabilitation bear a typical mercantilist stamp. Nominal duties should be placed upon imports of textile machinery and desirable raw materials; while high export duties on native staples, such as wool and silk, would stimulate their consumption by home industries. High tariffs on imports and low duties on exports of finished goods would further assist the renascent Spanish manufactures in supplanting foreign products in the domestic, American and even European markets. Diagnosing correctly some causes of industrial stagnation, Uztáriz strongly urged the removal of the remaining internal customs barriers and a reduction in the exorbitant turnover taxes on most agricultural and manufactured goods. He recognized the necessity of developing an adequate navy and merchant marine, cited with approval the navigation acts of the Catholic kings and offered a few positive suggestions for the revival of shipping, such as the reduction of taxes on materials for shipbuilding, in which he considered Spain self-sufficient. Rejecting depopulation as an explanation of economic decadence, Uztáriz anticipated the Malthusian view that population depends upon subsistence and production. He praised Colbert unstintedly and urged Spain to adopt commercial policies similar to those of France, England and Holland.

ROBERT S. SMITH

Consult: Castillo, Andrés Villegas, *Spanish Mercantilism; Gerónimo de Uztáriz—Economist* (New York 1930); Mounier, André, *Les faits et la doctrine économiques en Espagne sous Philippe v. Gerónimo de Uztáriz (1630–1732)* (Bordeaux 1919); Wirminghaus, Alexander, *Zwei spanische Merkantilisten*, Sammlung nationalökonomischer und statistischer Abhandlungen des staatswissenschaftlichen Seminars zu Halle, vol. iv, no. 2 (Jena 1886).

VACARIUS, twelfth century Lombard civilian. Vacarius studied civil law at Bologna in the age of the Four Doctors, was brought to England by Archbishop Theobald about 1145 and became a pioneer of civilian learning. He taught with great success and produced his so-called *Liber pauperum* in 1149; afterward King Stephen suppressed the civil law. Subsequently he wrote a disquisition on Our Lord's human nature (*De assumpto homine*) and, probably about 1156, a canonistic *Summa de matrimonio*. Prebendary of Southwell from about 1165, he was confidential agent of Roger of York in the Becket controversy and was also often employed as ecclesiastical judge. In 1198 he was commissioned by the pope to preach a crusade in the north.

The *Liber pauperum*, produced in response to a demand for a cheap and compendious textbook, consists of a liberal selection of extracts from Justinian, arranged substantially in the Code order, but drawn at least in equal degree from the Digest. To this text Vacarius added in the gloss further texts, including some taken from or based on the Novels, original explanatory notes and an apparatus of cross references, which last have become merged in a mass of minor and for the most part later glosses. These represent almost all that is known of academic Anglo-Norman jurisprudence of the period. Their contents justify the inference that Vacarius resumed teaching after Stephen's death, and it was probably then and not as early as 1149 that he taught at Oxford. The book was so well designed to meet a practical need that it constitutes a landmark, although its scientific quality could hardly be of the first order. Its conception is original, the execution reveals systematic grasp, and his glosses show Vacarius as a clear and independent thinker. Although it was barely heard of outside England and Normandy, it is typical early glossator work: extremely specialized, uninfluenced by contemporary law whether canon or English, it is not sufficiently individual to permit any tracing of its practical effect, which must, however, have been considerable in its local sphere.

F. DE ZULUETA

Consult: "Magistri Vacarii Summa de matrimonio," ed. by F. W. Maitland, in *Law Quarterly Review*, vol. xiii (1897) 133–43, 270–87; *The Liber pauperum of Vacarius*, ed. by Francis de Zulueta, Selden Society, Publications, vol. xliv (London 1927) p. xiii, no. 1, with bibliography of older literature; Stölzel, Adolf, "Glossenapparat des Vacarius Pragensis zu den Digestentiteln 43, 24.25 und 39, 1." in University of Berlin, Juristische Fakultät, *Festschrift für Heinrich Brunner* (Munich 1914) p. 1–35; Kantorowicz, Hermann, "Magister Vacarius" in *Zeitschrift der Savigny-Stiftung*, Romanistische Abteilung, vol. xlix (1929) 63–73; Senior, W., "Roman Law MSS. in England" in *Law Quarterly Review*, vol. xlvii (1931) 337–44.

VACATIONS. *See* SHORT HOURS MOVEMENT.

VACCINATION. *See* COMMUNICABLE DISEASES, CONTROL OF.

VAGRANCY is a legal term commonly applied with reference to persons who have neither definite domicile nor visible means of support. Vagrancy represents a form of delinquency, so rated for the inconvenience caused society by the indigency of vagrants. The category of persons included in the term vagrant varies from statute to statute. During the Elizabethan period, for example, it included singers, fencers, fortune tellers, players of interludes, itinerant booksellers, mendicant scholars and monks as well as the group variously known as vagabonds. At other times prostitutes, disorderly persons and street fakers were termed vagrants. Often, however, these persons were classed as vagrants for reasons other than their apparent dependency: they were feared as potential robbers or as soldiers to be recruited by an enemy.

Vagrants and mendicants have been present in every society, frequently tolerated and assigned uncongenial tasks, such as grave digging. In certain oriental countries in addition to the beggar castes customarily serving as scavengers there have always been various religious beggars, pilgrims to shrines and keepers of vows, greatly feared for their power to curse or revered as holy men. These types, including crippled and handicapped mendicants, do not, however, fall within the modern category of vagrancy. The latter, particularly in England and America, comprises such popularly designated types as tramps, hobos, panhandlers, "bums" and in certain seasons migratory workers.

As now used the term vagrancy seems to have emerged with the rise of the wage system and the institution of private property. The decline of feudalism and the guild system made it impossible to keep lordless men from wandering abroad in large numbers, and vagrancy became a pressing problem. A shortage of labor and rising wage rates following the Black Death of the fourteenth century tempted men to run away from their masters; at this time laws were passed designed to force the serfs to remain with their masters at former wage rates. A century or so later, when the feudal estates were enclosed for sheep pastures and the peasants driven out, there was another great exodus to the towns or the open road; but now there was considerable unemployment and attempts were made by law to prevent the wholesale eviction of the peasants. None of these efforts could withstand the force of economic transitions then under way. The vagrancy resulting from these was a mass phenomenon, and similar manifestations continue to appear with every serious disruption of the equilibrium of society, including wars, panics, famines and crop failures. There is evidence of an unmistakable increase of vagrancy in England following the industrial revolution, which sent thousands of hand spinners and weavers to the road in quest of a livelihood. Likewise during the period following the Napoleonic wars on the continent discharged soldiers who roamed the countryside in search of work or adventure swelled the ranks of the vagrants. More recent examples are the vagrant children common in Soviet Russia after the revolution and the appearance of a similar group in the United States during the economic depression beginning in 1929.

Besides being a symptom of sudden economic and political change, vagrancy may also reflect certain less dramatic changes brought about by invention. It is well known, for instance, that every improvement in the means of transportation has widened the range of mobility of vagrant groups, who have been very ready to utilize both roads and vehicles. On the other hand, new devices have often lifted the transient person temporarily out of the vagrant class into that of the migratory worker, affording means of transportation to sections of the country where opportunity for temporary employment in seasonal industries may exist. In the new countries, especially Australia, South Africa and the United States, the vagrant classes have carried a considerable share of the burden of pioneering. In clearing of land, prospecting, road building and railroad construction the tramp and the vagrant were familiar figures. With the passing of the frontier they continued their role as migratory and seasonal laborers in the harvest fields, in lumber camps and on sheep ranches.

The classification of vagrants and homeless persons has tempted observers since earliest times. Lawmakers, aware of the close relationship between vagrancy and crime, have been especially concerned about distinctions as a basis for meting out punishment or prescribing relief. This is reflected in the early English differentiation between the "sturdie beggar" and the "impotent beggar." The first was to be whipped or branded and "passed" on his way to his home parish; the second was often given a beggar's license with instructions to use it only in his own community. Many ex-soldiers, sailors, wandering students and pilgrims were given licenses to beg en route. The early classifications were basically similar to those of the present day.

Vagrant persons are rated, on the one hand, according to their ability to care for themselves or with respect to the devices which they use to obtain a livelihood and, on the other hand, according to the extent to which they may burden the community.

Socially ostracized as they are, vagrants have generally responded by forming their own society, which varies in completeness with the degree of isolation. At one extreme are the gypsies with virtually a culture of their own, and at the other are the American hobos whose vagrancy is generally sporadic and whose isolation is rarely permanent. A completely isolated vagrant population tends to have its own customs, traditions and cant language and, as among certain Old World beggars, its own family life. The latter feature has not as yet become characteristic of the New World homeless; in fact until recently women and children were conspicuously absent from the American hobo population.

In all countries the vagrant population is becoming, to an increasing degree, an urban class. Although the search for adventure or jobs may lure these wanderers out of the city, they usually return, like sailors to their port. Even the tramps and hobos who roam about the countryside during the summer months desert their jungles or roadside camps with the first approach of winter. In metropolitan centers they tend to foregather in their own areas, forming there a type of voluntary ghetto. Where there is a large vagrant and migrant labor population, as in the United States, the areas of the homeless are likely to become quite conspicuous. The Bowery in New York City is one of the most widely known of the vagrant "hobohemias." Here are found the low price lodging houses; lunch rooms; barrooms; free soup kitchens; bread lines; barber colleges, which exchange student practise for free shaves; and evangelical missions, where relief is sometimes given in the course of saving souls. But the chief function of the street of the homeless is that of a labor market for casual and migratory workers.

The difficulty of obtaining figures as to the extent of vagrancy is apparent from the very nature of the problem. In the United States, aside from scattered statistics gathered by individual cities and private agencies, only general estimates of the number of vagrants have been made. Between 1901 and 1905 nearly three fourths of the 49,200 persons killed and injured on railroads were vagrants, while in 1910 close to half a million tramps were said to be using the railroads of the country. Since the World War the popularity of "hitch hiking," coupled with the rise in unemployment, has greatly augmented the volume of vagrancy. According to one student of the problem Chicago alone harbors some 75,000 homeless each winter. In England the number of persons with no settled abode and no means of subsistence is said to be approximately 40,000 in times of industrial activity and 70,000 to 80,000 in times of depression.

Without home or family ties, with no clearly articulated objective, the vagrant is an elusive subject for social treatment. The ancient method of passing him on, whether to his home or elsewhere, generally served the ends of the vagrants rather than the aims of the law. Inherent in the passing on system is a confession of failure and of unwillingness to deal with the problem. Likewise punishment, even branding, whipping, enslavement, transportation and the gallows, brought only negative results. However severe the antivagrancy laws were made, repressive measures had little effect in diminishing the extent of vagrancy. With the opening of the London Bridewell (1615) as a house of industry emphasis turned toward penal treatment. On the assumption that vagrants have an incorrigible aversion to labor and that all are potential if not actual criminals, the workhouse became popular in England and later in the United States. In France the earlier practise of condemning vagrants to the galleys or of transporting them to the colonies was superseded in the nineteenth century by a system of *dépôts de mendicité*, where beggars and vagabonds were confined for stated periods and forced to work. This same period witnessed the rise of the labor, or farm, colony in central Europe, a notable example of which was the Wilhelmsdorf colony founded in 1882 by Pastor Friedrich von Bodelschwingh at Bielefeld, Germany, where vagrants of all types were admitted and obliged to earn their shelter, food and clothing by working on the farm attached to the colony. The success of the experiment led to the establishment of similar colonies in other countries. Within recent years the system of penal farm and labor colonies in Holland, Switzerland and Germany has reached a high degree of efficiency with a well developed program for the rehabilitation of vagrants, including detention, discipline and industrial or agricultural training. Except as an unproved experiment in a few states, notably New York, Pennsylvania and Illinois, the farm colony has had no vogue in the United States.

The nineteenth century marked the beginning of certain humanitarian movements in the interest of vagrants and other homeless persons, especially sailors. The earlier efforts, chiefly evangelistic, were followed by movements to establish model lodging and boarding houses and free employment agencies. In a few cities industrial centers were organized where shelter, food and employment were furnished as a means of rehabilitating the vagrant. The hotel and industrial program of the Salvation Army in many cities of the world is perhaps the most advanced and representative example of such privately promoted humanitarian enterprises for the homeless. Beginning about 1880 and largely in response to private initiative a number of the larger cities of Europe and the United States established municipal lodging houses for the non-vagrant and partially vagrant homeless.

The religious and humanitarian movement was sympathetic to the vagrant but lacked understanding of causative factors and devices for guiding and controlling rehabilitation. Too frequently, as the literature on the subject reveals, interest in the romantic aspects of vagrancy as a wandering existence has hindered efforts to deal objectively with the problem. There has been too little recognition of the relation between the vagrant and the employment situation or between vagrancy and the personal problems of the particular vagrant. These shortcomings have greatly concerned the more able students of the problem, and during the past three decades serious attempts have been made to examine the factors underlying vagrancy. In the course of these studies the role of economic forces has become increasingly apparent. Nevertheless, while recognizing the fact that the vagrant is often the victim of a casual and laissez faire labor market, sociologists, penologists and other students of vagrancy are asking why certain persons and not others are drawn into this class; why certain types eventually settle down while others become habitual vagrants. In France, where the phenomena of the labor market are less important than the individual causes of vagrancy, there have been numerous unrelated attempts to study vagrants as psychopathic cases. This approach to the question in terms of individual factors is likewise gaining headway in the United States through the medium of social work. Although there are as yet no comprehensive findings, there is evidence that mental and physical defects, educational or industrial inadequacy and racial handicaps are often contributory causes of vagrancy. One of the more hopeful consequences of the case work approach is the realization that vagrancy cannot be isolated from the social and economic maladjustments of which it is the product and that, before any solution of the problem is possible, such related evils as bad housing, unemployment and lack of adequate health, recreational and educational facilities must be dealt with. Furthermore vagrancy is now recognized to be less of a local and more of an intercommunity problem. Any treatment that does not go beyond passing the vagrant on or imposing punishment is generally conceded to be futile. Yet most communities burdened with vagrants, particularly transients, have no alternative, and consequently the passing on practise has continued. Certain European countries require transient vagrants to carry identification cards and thus are better able to control transiency. In England an effort at regulation was made in 1906, when a departmental committee on vagrancy was appointed. The report of this committee included recommendations for uniform treatment of all homeless poor in casual wards or common lodging houses, the establishment of detention colonies or certified labor colonies for the reclamation of habitual vagrants and assistance to able bodied workers through the organization of labor exchanges and public employment bureaus. A departmental committee set up in 1929 made similar recommendations, some of which have been realized while others await enabling legislation. In the United States there was no program for the care of transient and homeless persons until 1933, when the federal government under the Federal Emergency Relief Administration initiated a number of transient camps and shelters. In these camps, established in forty-five states and operated by trained workers, the transients are given clothing, food, shelter and medical care as well as a small weekly allowance.

NELS ANDERSON

See: MIGRATORY LABOR; CASUAL LABOR; BEGGING; LABOR TURNOVER; EMPLOYMENT EXCHANGES; LODGING HOUSES; LABOURERS, STATUTES OF.

Consult: Becker, Otto, *Die Regelung der Wanderarmenfürsorge in Europa und Nordamerika*, Verband deutscher Arbeitsnachweise, Schriften, no. 14 (Berlin 1918); Ribton-Turner, C. J., *History of Vagrants and Vagrancy* (London 1887); Pagnier, Armand, *Le vagabond* (Paris 1909); Gillin, J. L., *Social Pathology* (New York 1933) ch. xix; Lewis, O. F., *Vagrancy in the United States* (New York 1907); Willard, J. F.

(Josiah Flynt), *Tramping with Tramps* (New York 1899); Dawson, W. H., *The Vagrancy Problem* (London 1910); Anderson, Nels, *The Hobo* (Chicago 1923); Mullin, G. H., *The Adventures of a Scholar Tramp* (New York 1925); Great Britain, Ministry of Health, Departmental Committee on the Relief of the Casual Poor, *Report*, Cmd. 3640 (1930); London School of Economics, *New Survey of London Life and Labour*, 5 vols. (London 1930–33) vol. iii, ch. xii; Webb, S. and B., "English Poor Law History" in their *English Local Government*, 9 vols. (London 1906–29) vol. vii, ch. vi, and vol. ix, p. 771–78, 945–62; Sturm, K., *Die Landstreicherei*, Strafrechtliche Abhandlungen, vol. cv (Breslau 1909); Rolfes, H., *Der wandernde Erwerbslose* (Bernau 1932); Solenberger, Alice W., *One Thousand Homeless Men* (New York 1911); Willard, Eugene B., "Psychopathic Vagrancy" in *Welfare Magazine*, vol. xix (1928) 565–73; Anderson, Nels, "The Juvenile and the Tramp" in American Institute of Criminal Law and Criminology, *Journal*, vol. xiv (1923–24) 290–312; Astrofsky, Ralph, "'Trombenicks' or Jewish Hoboes" in *Jewish Social Service Quarterly*, vol. iv (1928) 226–34; Park, Robert E., "Human Migration and the Marginal Man" in *American Journal of Sociology*, vol. xxxiii (1928) 881–93; Lisle, John, "Vagrancy Law" in American Institute of Criminal Law and Criminology, *Journal*, vol. v (1914–15) 498–513.

VAIL, THEODORE NEWTON (1845–1920), American capitalist. Vail was the dominant figure in the development of American communications. He received little formal education; two years' employment in a drug store which housed the local telegraph office gave him his start as a telegraph operator. At twenty-three he went to Wyoming as night operator on the Union Pacific Railroad. After his appointment in 1869 as railroad mail clerk Vail initiated notable work in revising and simplifying methods of postal routing. This and his share in inaugurating civil service reform and the first fast mail resulted, through successive promotions, in his appointment as general superintendent of the railway mails in 1876. Two years later he abandoned the security of this government position to become general manager of the Bell Telephone Company, then a speculative and struggling enterprise. Vail, one of the most important pioneers of the amalgamation movement, extended the scope of this company until it was firmly intrenched. He showed a masterly knowledge of both the technical and the financial needs of a new industry. The American Telephone and Telegraph Company, which dominates the Bell Telephone system, was his creation. Vail's resignation as president in 1887 and his retirement from the telephone industry in 1889, formally attributed to ill health, should probably be attributed to conflict over policies. In the next two and a half years, with intermittent travel abroad, he devoted himself to promotion of a scheme for centralized municipal heating; this venture, one of the examples of a lifelong and often mistaken faith in inventions, brought him close to ruin. Presently, however, Vail launched a new and brilliantly successful enterprise in the development of electric power for street railways in South America.

After an absence of twenty years Vail returned as president of the American Telephone and Telegraph Company. He reorganized and refinanced the company so effectively that it easily weathered the panic of 1907. The company grew in facilities and power, nationally and internationally, toward Vail's consistent goal of "one policy, one system, universal service." Vail's attempt to absorb the Western Union Telegraph Company (1910–13) was, however, frustrated by the intervention of the federal government. While Western Union was under his company's control, he introduced improvements in the service, inaugurating night and day letters, cable letters and week end cables. He anticipated wireless telephony and concentrated its development under the aegis of his company. Consolidation of service, conciliation of rivals, taking the enemy into camp, were basic policies of Vail's program. In his lifetime Vail personified the strength and stature of his company, and public confidence in it was identified with his vital and commanding figure.

CATHERINE MACKENZIE

Consult: Paine, Albert Bigelow, *Theodore N. Vail; a Biography* (New York 1929); Vail, Theodore Newton, *Views on Public Questions; a Collection of Papers and Addresses by Theodore Newton Vail* (p.p. New York 1917).

VALENTI, GHINO (1852–1920), Italian economist. Valenti began his career by collaborating in the famous *Inchiesta agraria*, an agricultural inquiry instituted by the Italian Parliament in 1877 under the direction of Stefano Jacini. For many years he was engaged in the management of his landed estate in Macerata, and at about the age of forty he settled in Rome, where he lectured at the university, and in 1895 became general secretary of the Società degli Agricoltori Italiani. From 1897 to 1920 he occupied chairs of economics successively at the universities of Modena, Padua and Siena. While at Padua he succeeded in convincing the minister of agriculture, Cocco-Ortu, of the necessity for reform of the agricultural statistics of the kingdom—a measure made doubly important by the impending establishment of the International Institute of Agriculture in Rome. Valenti was entrusted with this task, and as chief of the department of agricultural statistics in the Ministry of Agriculture from 1907 to 1910 he succeeded in laying the foundations of the Italian *Catasto agrario*. The conquest of Libya by Italy drew his attention to colonial problems; he studied the new Italian possession as well as the old colony of Erythraea and set forth his observations in *La colonia Eritrea* (Rome 1913) and in *Il problema sociale della colonizzazione* (Rome 1913). Immediately before the World War, when in anticipation of the renewal of commercial treaties the Italian federation of industries organized a committee for the study of tariffs, Valenti was made director of the agricultural section of the committee and in this capacity prepared reports on the trade in agricultural products.

Valenti's most important contributions were in the field of agricultural economics; the best of these studies are collected in *Studi di politica agraria* (Rome 1914), including a most original and penetrating monograph *La Campagna romana* and a valuable sketch of the agricultural history of the Kingdom of Italy in its first fifty years. He did not, however, neglect problems of general economic theory, particularly those bearing on agriculture. He was a keen student of the theory of rent and upon close investigation denied the validity of the law of diminishing returns. He was the author of a widely used text, *Principi di scienza economica* (Florence 1906; 3rd–4th ed., 2 vols., 1921–25); and earlier in his career he demonstrated his interest in the history of economic doctrine in *Le idee economiche di G. D. Romagnosi* (Rome 1891), in *Lavoro produttivo e speculazione* (Rome 1892), a study of the development of ideas concerning productive labor and speculation, and in *La proprietà della terra e la costituzione economica* (Bologna 1901), a refutation of Loria's theories.

UMBERTO RICCI

Consult: Bonfante, P., in *Rivista d'Italia*, vol. xxiv (1921) 348–58; Rocca, G., "Un economista agrario: Ghino Valenti" in *Riforma sociale*, vol. xxxii (1921) 137–51; Virgilii, F., "Ghino Valenti nella vita e nella scienza" in *Studi senesi*, vol. xxxvi (1921–22) 1–20; Graziadei, A., "Economia politica pura ed applicata" in *Rivista italiana di sociologia*, vol. xi (1907) 254–65; Ricci, U., "Osservazioni critiche su un nuovo libro del Prof. Valenti" in *Giornale degli economisti*, 2nd ser., vol. xxxii (1906) 440–57.

VALLA, LORENZO (1406–57), Italian humanist. Valla was professor of rhetoric at Pavia and Rome and secretary to King Alfonso V of Aragon and of Naples; later he was attached to the Curia under popes Nicholas V and Calixtus III. One of the initiators of modern philological and historical criticism, he exposed in his *De falso credita et ementita Constantini donatione declamatio* (1440) the mediaeval forgery of the Donation of Constantine, upon which the popes had founded their temporal claims. This work also served as one of the bases for the Lutheran polemic against the Church of Rome. Valla applied his standards of criticism to the Vulgate and the Apostles' Creed. His other writings, like *De elegantia latinae linguae* (1444) and *Dialecticae disputationes contra Aristotelicos* (1439), employed the criteria of humanistic philology in the reform of Latin style, logic and rhetoric. His *De voluptate ac de vero bono* (1431), which represents the first modern attempt to determine hedonistic and utilitarian principles of human action, is of particular philosophical and sociological importance. This work upholds the doctrine of Epicureanism against the ethics of the stoics. Valla did not propose to issue a generic praise of pleasure but rather to formulate a rational reply to the question whether the good consists in the pleasure (*voluptas*) of the Epicureans or in the virtue (*virtus*) of the stoics. He strove to show that pleasure as opposed to honorable conduct is in conformity with nature and to find a hedonistic motive for all acts apparently prompted by altruistic and virtuous motives. Valla held that Cato and Scipio did not kill themselves because of love of virtue but because life under Caesar had become distasteful to them. In other noble acts as well virtuous pretense dissimulates love of glory, which also belongs to the category of pleasures. Infamy, on the other hand, is shunned not because it is inherently bad or indecent but out of fear of the scorn of others. Hedonism, however, is not blind impetuosity but a doctrine that implies reason and discernment, by which the wise person prefers minor to major injury and greater to lesser good. Hedonistic valuation extends also from the particular individual to all of society. Utility in fact is the basis of governments, laws and punishments (which Valla regards as a worthy means of social intimidation). Valla's hedonism attempts also to justify the Christian religion in contrast to the pessimistic asceticism of the Middle Ages. The paradise that Christianity promises to the faithful is a place where sublime pleasures prevail. The anticipation of this happy life completes terrestrial pleasure by making it eternal, thus fortifying man against the discomforts of earthly existence.

GUIDO DE RUGGIERO

Works: Opera (Basel 1540, new ed. Venice 1592).

Consult: Voigt, Georg, *Die Wiederbelebung des classischen Alterthums*, 2 vols. (3rd ed. by M. Lehnerdt, Berlin 1893), especially vol. i, p. 460–77; Mancini, Girolamo, *Vita di Lorenzo Valla* (Florence 1891); Monnier, Philippe, *Le quattrocento*, 2 vols. (5th ed. Paris 1912) vol. i, p. 186–89, 274–89; Rossi, Vittorio, *Il quattrocento*, Storia Letteraria d'Italia, vol. vi (3rd ed. Milan 1933), especially p. 80–90; Ruggiero, G. de, "Rinascimento, riforma e controriforma" in his *Storia della filosofia*, 8 vols. (Bari 1920–33) pt. iii, vol. i, p. 104–09, 195–97.

VALORIZATION. The term valorization was introduced into English speaking countries about 1906 from Brazil where it (*valorizaçao*) had been applied to measures regulating the marketing of coffee. In its original meaning it signified the act or process of raising the price of a commodity by governmental interference above a level regarded as uneconomically low but not above the price that would in the long run be set by free competition. Valorization is presumably temporary in character, and it is significant that when Brazil inaugurated a permanent plan for the control of coffee in 1922, this was described as "defense" of coffee and not as valorization.

Since the World War the meaning of the term has been extended so widely as seriously to impair its usefulness. It is now commonly but improperly applied to any effort through governmental measures other than import tariffs to raise the market value of a commodity through limitation of the supply entering the market; it is frequently used to describe attempts, with or without governmental participation, of monopolies, cartels or trade associations to raise prices; it is sometimes applied (especially revalorization) to plans for the conversion of defaulted debts; and it is occasionally used to describe a change in the legal value of a currency, as in the expression "the devalorization of the franc."

The word valorization is of significance to economic terminology only if employed in its relatively restricted sense. In this use valorization consists fundamentally in the attempt to regularize supplies and stabilize prices at the long run equilibrating level, and it embraces measures involving governmental action to raise the price of a commodity by the purchase and withholding from the market of part of the supply or by the reduction of the quantity produced. It does not, however, include measures to raise prices by cartels, trade associations, import duties or monetary manipulation. The best known instances of valorization in the international field (with the dates when the more important restrictions were imposed) are the control of coffee by Brazil (1905, 1917, 1920, defense 1922), cacao by Ecuador (1912), henequen by Mexico (1922), rubber by British Malaya and Ceylon (1922), sugar by Cuba (1925) and later by a group of countries (1931), long staple cotton by Egypt (1915, 1921), currants by Greece (1895, 1904) and citrate of lime by Italy (1910). In addition valorization has been applied to numerous commodities in a purely domestic market, a familiar example being the efforts of the Federal Farm Board to raise the price of wheat in the United States.

Valorization differs from a government monopoly, such as the control of camphor by Japan or of quicksilver by Spain and Italy, in that it is designed primarily to benefit competing private producers rather than the government; it differs from agreements such as the international steel cartel, the quinine convention and the sulphur syndicate in that these are monopolistic associations of producers; and it differs from government aided monopolies, such as nitrates and potash, and from import restrictions in that it aims to restore prices to what is regarded as normal rather than to maintain them permanently at artificially high levels.

Valorization usually originates in a condition of continued low prices. If supply and demand are relatively inelastic, if domestic demand is only a small part of the total demand, if a single country or group of countries provides a large proportion of the supply and if there are no satisfactory substitutes, conditions are favorable for the introduction of valorization. The measures are ordinarily designed to meet the situation by reducing the supply offered for sale, often with the intention, after price has been restored, of releasing the supplies withdrawn from the market.

Various means have been used to limit the available supply of valorized products. In coffee valorization Brazil relied chiefly upon the purchase of the commodity and its withdrawal from the market. Under the programs of 1905, 1917 and 1920 most of this coffee was held abroad; but after 1922 extensive warehouses were erected in Brazil, and coffee held by the government is now stored chiefly within the country. Continued low prices during the depression of the early 1930's led to the destruction of large quantities of coffee which had been acquired under the coffee defense scheme (*see* PLANTATION WARES). Henequen, which had been withheld from the market by Mexico under the valorization measures begun in 1922, was later sold; and purchasers of the new crop were required to take a certain proportion of the old, which had deteriorated. In those cases in which valorization aims merely at raising the price in the domestic market all or part of the supply withdrawn may be dumped on the foreign market for whatever it will bring, as in the case of wheat by the United States Federal Farm Board, of sugar by Brazil and of grain by Bulgaria. Another common practise has been the limitation of production. The International Sugar Agreement (Chadbourne plan) provided both for the limitation of exports and for the direct restriction of production. The supply entering the world market is sometimes checked by means of a tax on exports, as has been done various times in the case of coffee; Greece accomplished the same result by diverting part of the output of currants to industrial uses within the country.

Funds for administering valorization are often obtained through export taxes, which may or may not be an essential part of the control mechanism, on the commodity in question. This was done in the case of cacao in Ecuador, coffee in Brazil and rubber in British Malaya. Sometimes the supplies withheld from the market are used as security for a foreign loan, as was repeatedly done with coffee, and at other times the funds are obtained by general taxation or by borrowing within the country. Brazil's coffee valorization of 1917–18 is probably unique in that it was financed chiefly by the issue of paper money.

The first and second Brazilian coffee valorization plans must be regarded as highly successful; they accomplished the purposes for which they were instituted and were then abandoned. In general, however, valorization schemes have collapsed either because they were ineffective in materially influencing price or more often because the original aims were forgotten and prices were raised to monopolistic levels, thus stimulating production and reducing demand. These difficulties have sometimes been aggravated by a bumper crop or by a decline in demand due to cyclical factors. Valorization measures have as a rule exerted first a buoying and then a stabilizing influence on price, as should be expected from measures directed toward evening out the supply on the market. In the case of rubber the stabilizing influence was short lived, and subsequently there were extreme swings in price with a general downward tendency; in other cases also prices have ultimately shown a drastic decline. Perhaps the most important lessons gained from experience with valorization are that it is folly to attempt to maintain average prices above the equilibrium level and that it is necessary to establish a flexible rather than a fixed price.

Where valorization has led all producers to restrict output, the effect has usually been to raise the unit cost of production. Such increase in price as occurs will presumably fall chiefly on consumers, but by avoiding the waste due to alternate overinvestment and overelimination a wisely administered program of valorization would in the long run be likely to reduce the cost to consumers. In this it contrasts sharply with the other forms of price control mentioned, which are designed either to exact monopoly prices from consumers or to assist relatively inefficient producers.

The primary significance of governmental participation is that it permits a degree of control that would not otherwise be possible. It introduces, however, a political element, which has on several occasions in the past led to international friction. Valorization has been attacked on the ground that it places in the hands of the producing country undue power over foreign industries dependent upon the controlled raw material. Inasmuch as import restrictions may prove equally serious to producers situated in some other country, this is a criticism of trade restrictions in general and not of raw material controls.

The aims of valorization, properly construed, are to correct aberrations of price, to check overinvestment at one time and underinvestment at another, to avoid the elimination of a large part of the productive equipment that will subsequently be needed and to ease such adjustments in supply as may be genuinely necessary. These are all economically and socially desirable. The modesty of its aims and its presumably temporary character establish a strong presumption in favor of valorization as compared with other forms of price control, but this presumption is considerably abated by the tendency toward monopolistic abuses. Valorization has frequently worked badly from the standpoint of both producers and consumers. But this has been due largely to lack of knowledge as to its functions and limitations and to inexperience in applying it. Such results are inevitable in the evolution of a new economic device under the direction of practical men; they cannot be accepted as proof that valorization is economically unwise. The attempts, whether they succeed or fail, are significant steps in the gradual evolution of a more ordered economic society, and it is altogether probable that the future will see even greater experimentation with valorization than has obtained in the past.

CHARLES R. WHITTLESEY

See: SUGAR; RUBBER; NITRATES; PLANTATION WARES; RAW MATERIALS; MONOPOLY; CARTEL; PRICES; PRICE REGULATION; OVERPRODUCTION; INTERNATIONAL TRADE; EXPORT DUTIES; FARM RELIEF.

Consult: Wallace, B. B., and Edminster, L. R., *International Control of Raw Materials*, Brookings Institution, Institute of Economics (Washington 1930); Rowe, J. W. F., "Studies in the Artificial Control of Raw Material Supplies" in Royal Economic Society, *Memorandum*, nos. 23, 29, 34 (London 1930–32); United States, Bureau of Foreign and Domestic Commerce, "Foreign Combinations to Control Prices of Raw Materials," *Trade Information Bulletin*, no. 385 (1926); United States, Department of Agriculture, *World Trade Barriers in Relation to American Agriculture*, 73rd Cong., 1st sess., Senate Document, no. 70 (1933); Culbertson, W. S., "Raw Materials and Foodstuffs in the Commercial Policies of Nations" in American Academy of Political and Social Science, *Annals*, vol. cxii (1924) 1–145; Whittlesey, C. R., *Governmental Control of Crude Rubber*, Princeton University, Department of Economics and Social Institutions, International Finance Section, Publications, vol. ii (Princeton 1931); Viner, Jacob, "National Monopolies of Raw Materials" in *Foreign Affairs*, vol. iv (1925–26) 585–600; Bernhard, Erich, *Baumwollvalorisierung und die amerikanischen Pläne zur Valorisierung anderer Agrarprodukte* (Tübingen 1930); Scherrer, Hans, *Die Kaffeevalorisation und Valorisationsversuche in anderen Artikeln des Welthandels* (Jena 1919).

VALUATION as the term is used here is a synonym for appraisal; that is, the theory and process of estimating the value of any given property at a specific place and date. In a derived sense it refers to the value placed upon the property as a result of an appraisal. The present discussion is limited to legal valuation under the auspices of a court or an administrative commission.

Under any system of private property valuation is an essential device of the law for settling disputes between property owners and for determining claims between private owners and government. In Anglo-American law it has been of special significance because of the prevailing resort in the common law to money damages rather than to specific performance as a means of redress. But the most numerous occasions for a legal appraisal have been created by the modern systems of taxation. Damage law, used in a broad sense to include compulsory takings under the law of eminent domain, and tax law supply most of the legal traditions as to the meaning of value and as to the methods by which this value shall be proved.

Within recent years the development of corporate wealth and the acceptance of concepts of fair price as distinct from unregulated, market made prices have brought other types of valuation into prominence. In the United States regulation of public utility and railroad rates under the rulings of the courts has called for measurement of fair profits by reference to a "reasonable return on the fair value of the property." In company reorganizations, through foreclosure sales, the courts now fix an "upset price" below which no sale will be confirmed, and which is supposed to represent the minimum value of the property. In a corporate merger, under the laws of various jurisdictions, dissenting stockholders are entitled to a cash settlement based on an independent appraisal of the assets. Where corporations issue stock with a par value in exchange for property other than cash, the stockholders are liable, with qualifications, to creditors on stock issued in excess of a good faith valuation of the property as of the date when the stock was issued. Even in the United States, which has been notoriously lax in safeguarding investors against fraud by corporate directors and promoters, the courts have become somewhat more alert in holding responsible officers and auditors liable for overvaluations of assets on the balance sheets, and the liability has been greatly extended by the passage of the Federal Securities Act in 1934.

This list of the newer and older types of legal valuations is by no means complete; but it indicates the multiplicity of purposes for which appraisals are made and the vital importance of satisfactory principles and methods of valuation as a means of controlling business conduct. Unfortunately the courts have not kept pace in their theory and technique of valuation with the developing requirements of the situation. Especially in the fields of eminent domain and of rate making criticism of the legal processes of valuation has become more and more widespread. Demand for reform has been most insistent in the latter field, where popular resentment against the prolonged litigation over rate making values and excessive valuations enforced by the courts has led to a new wave of interest in government ownership.

The fundamental problem of legal valuation concerns the meaning that should be placed upon the phrase value of the property. Economic treatises have usually identified value with market value, which in turn has been defined as the price that the commodity in question will command if offered for sale. In the great majority of cases, particularly in the fields of damage law, eminent domain and property taxation, the courts also have stated that value at law means market value. But they have either failed to give any precise definition to the term, or else they have construed it to mean different things in different cases. Sometimes it has been used in the classical economic sense, as meaning the price at which the property could actually be sold as of valuation date, generally with the qualification that a forced sale must not be assumed. At other times the term market value has been employed in what economists call an "imputed sense," as meaning a price derived from the current unit prices of similar property actually sold on the market. This latter concept of market value is often applied in the assessment of large blocks of securities for inheritance tax purposes. The fact that the property could not be sold except at a heavy discount from current market prices is disregarded in the appraisal. In other instances market value is identified in effect with replacement cost. This has been true of the valuation of chattels in most damage cases.

Further confusion as to the meaning of market value has been introduced by the traditional legal definition of value as the price at which the property would sell "as between a willing buyer and a willing seller." This evasive phrase has been generally applied in the appraisal of real property under the laws of eminent domain and of taxation. In its narrowest sense it is designed merely to preclude a valuation based on an assumed forced sale; the property must be appraised at what it would probably bring if the owner allowed a reasonable opportunity for negotiations. But the courts have often invoked a mythical willing buyer to justify a valuation higher than any attainable sale price.

Properties especially adapted to their owners' uses are typically worth more to them than their market value. Indeed where the market values of these properties are merely nominal, as with churches, hospital buildings and schoolhouses, the courts have generally held that value to the owner or some apparent synonym, like "real value," is the proper basis of appraisal. But the strong legal tradition in favor of a market value standard has led to its nominal retention save with highly peculiar types of property. A hypothetical market is assumed, which includes a fictitious willing buyer whose use of the property is not clearly distinguished from that of the owner himself. This attempt to bridge the gap between actual market value and value to the owner has resulted in serious confusion. The law pays a heavy price for its tendency to apply universal standards in so many different situations.

Still another controversial question as to the meaning of market value is raised where the current market price of the property is thought to be abnormally and temporarily inflated by a boom or deflated by a slump. The issue has become acute in cases involving compensation for property condemned during the prevailing business depression. The usual rule of market value as of the date of the taking would seem to require a valuation at whatever price the property might have commanded if offered for sale at that time. Yet the owners have claimed either that this standard is inapplicable in these times or else that it means "fair market value," which in turn indicates a more stable and normal price than would be fixed in the current market. The few decisions that have so far been rendered on the point are in conflict. In earlier cases, however, the courts seldom accepted the arguments of a condemnor that prices prevailing during a boom period should be disregarded.

Legal valuation raises not merely the problem of the meaning of value but also that of estimating it after it has been clearly defined. The former question is one of substantive law, while the latter is one of evidence. The two issues, however, are not clearly distinguished in the reported opinions, for the judicial definitions of value are so ambiguous that most of the substantive law itself must be found in the treatment of the evidence.

Opinion testimony on value by real or so-called experts is likely to form the basis of the evidence presented to a judge or jury, especially in real estate valuation under the law of eminent domain. Since the witnesses derive their fees from the one or the other party to the controversy, the trial often amounts to a mere battle of lies. To some extent the exaggerations and prevarications of the witnesses are discounted by the tribunal as a result of the cross examinations. But few juries and judges are equipped to form independent judgments on matters of such a technical nature, and the award is often a meaningless compromise between the values testified to on both sides. There is a crying need in the United States for the use of skilled commissions and specially trained judges in the trial of important valuation cases.

Aside from opinion testimony the following facts or opinions about the property constitute the most frequently offered evidence of value: actual sales of or occasionally bids or offers for the same or similar property; original cost; replacement cost with or without deductions for depreciation; and capitalized income, realized or prospective. So complex and confusing are the rulings of the courts as to admissibility of these types of evidence, that an attempt to summarize the law is more misleading than helpful. By and large the courts have approved the data and methods of valuation that are used by the professional appraiser, but in their desire to avoid confusion to an inexpert tribunal and to prevent undue prolongation of the trial they have set many limits to the admission of facts that would seem highly material to the expert.

From the viewpoint of modern appraisal theory the most serious defect in the American law of evidence and, to a lesser extent, in the British law is to be found in the undue weight given by the courts to current replacement costs as a measure of value. Almost uniformly, to be sure, the reported opinions make a verbal distinction between value and replacement cost, insisting that the latter is relevant only as evidence of the former and that it is to be considered along with other, possibly countervailing data. In practise, however, judges like laymen find it difficult to avoid the unjustified assumption that because a building or a machine could be reproduced only at great expense, it must have a high value. Allowances not only for functional depreciation, such as obsolescence and inadequacy, but even for physical depreciation, while not completely ignored, are quite generally understated.

This tendency is strikingly disclosed in the cases on valuation for fire insurance purposes. Until recently the lower New York courts held here that structures should be valued without reference to obsolescence. Only physical depreciation was thought to be deductible. Lately this absurd position was abandoned as a result of an opinion by the New York Court of Appeals in McAnarney v. Newark Fire Insurance Company [247 N.Y. 176 (1928)]. The same tendency is illustrated by the case of the Washington Mills Emery Company, which concerned a Boston building destroyed by fire: both the Massachusetts Supreme Court [Washington Mills Emery Mfg. Co. v. Weymouth & Braintree Mutual Fire Ins. Co., 135 Mass. 503 (1883)] and a federal district court [Washington Mills Emery Mfg. Co. v. Commercial Fire Ins. Co., 13 Fed. 646 (1882)] declined to recognize the claim of the insurers that the value placed upon the structure should be abated because shortly before the fire the owner had conveyed the land to the city, under an agreement whereby he might move the building within a given time. The courts did not deny that this liability to relocation greatly impaired the value of the building to the owner as well as its market value, but they stated that the intrinsic value of the structure remained unaffected. Evidently the law has not yet rid itself of the myth that a thing can have an intrinsic value independent of the uses to which it is capable of being put. Many of the American awards of compensation in compulsory takings reveal shocking illustrations of overvaluations, made in disregard of the fact that the improvements on the land, while costly to reproduce, were of little value as business assets.

The use of original, or actual, cost of property as a measure of value has given rise to a legal controversy no less than has that of current replacement cost. The courts have uniformly held that value must be distinguished from cost, but they have also declared that under certain circumstances cost is admissible as evidence of value and sometimes that it is the best available measure of it. Where market value is the supposed objective, the price actually paid for the property by the owner is sometimes held to be relevant for either of two reasons: if the purchase has been made recently, it may be given the same weight that any recent actual sale of the same or similar property would be given; or the actual cost may be taken as evidence of current replacement cost, which in turn may be accepted as an index of the price at which the property could now be sold. Both of these theories of the relevancy of actual cost have been accepted in real estate valuation under the law of eminent domain and in taxation. In public utility valuation for rate making the bearing of actual cost on fair value is a highly controversial question. Some courts have held that this cost is utterly irrelevant except as a possible check on estimated replacement cost, while others have stated or implied that actual cost should be given weight in a rate base even though it obviously diverges from replacement cost. The dicta of the United States Supreme Court are more consistent with the latter position, while the actual decisions of this court are more consistent with the former.

A further problem in the law of evidence in a valuation case concerns the use of capitalized earnings as a measure of value. Recent schools of economic theory, of which Professors Fetter and Fisher are the most prominent representatives in the United States, have emphasized that the value of any object of wealth is simply a capitalization of the services or income which actual or potential owners of the property expect to derive from it. This point of view has greatly influenced the current literature of the appraisal profession, as is illustrated by F. M. Babcock's book, *The Valuation of Real Estate* (New York 1932). The courts, however, have been very chary of accepting prospective or even realized earnings as a measure of value. They have generally held in real estate appraisals under the law of eminent domain that the profits of a business enterprise may not be adduced as evidence of the value of the premises in which the business is located, although they have usually admitted actual rentals as evidence of the value of rented property. In stock watering cases there is an imposing line of opinions led by See v. Heppenheimer [69 N.J. Eq. 36, 61 Atl. 843 (1905)], holding that prospective earnings are inadmissible as evidence of the value of the corporate assets. In the valuation of inactive securities earning power, realized or prospective, has generally been considered along with other data, such as book value and occasional sales.

The reluctance of the courts to accept earning power as a basis of valuation may be explained upon the grounds of the speculative character of estimates of future earning power and the difficulty of attributing to a specific business asset, such as the real estate of a corporation, any specific share in the profits made by the entire enterprise. Mindful of these two practical objections to the use of capitalized earnings, most courts have preferred to rely on other data, such as estimated replacement costs and actual sales.

The most vital and controversial question in legal valuation and indeed in the entire field of appraisal concerns the extent to which the meaning of "value of the property" is affected by the particular purpose for which the valuation is made. Referring to this problem as applied to a public utility rate case Justice Brandeis of the United States Supreme Court remarked in his dissenting opinion in Southwestern Bell Telephone Company v. Public Service Commission [262 U.S. 276 (1923)]: "Value is a word of many meanings. That with which commissions and courts in these proceedings are concerned, in so-called confiscation cases, is a special value for rate making purposes, not exchange value."

That the law has in fact construed value in various senses and that it has chosen different meanings partly by reference to the different purposes of the appraisal is undoubtedly true. But the distinctions have been obscured in the reported opinions. Among orthodox judges and lawyers there is a strong tendency to deny that value at law has more than one basic meaning or at least to belittle the differences in meaning. In consequence the reader of the cases must discover the distinctions for the most part by noting the differences in the judicial treatment of the evidence rather than by looking for definitions frankly distinguishing value for various purposes.

One of the major aims of a valuation is to measure the money indemnity due to an owner for property from some party liable for its destruction or alienation. Substantially all appraisals under the law of damages and of eminent domain have this objective. It would seem to follow that in these cases value to the owner is the only relevant value, and indeed precisely this interpretation has been accepted by the courts with respect to unique and unmarketable properties. With most types of property, however, the courts have held that market value is the measure of indemnity. No doubt the difficulty of estimating what the property may have been worth to a particular individual has been primarily responsible for this practise. But market value, if uniformly interpreted to mean just one thing, such as the price at which the owner could have sold the property, would often not even roughly measure value to him. Accordingly the courts have used market value first in one sense, then in another, and they have tended to choose that meaning which presumably makes it the most satisfactory index of value to the owner. Thus in a damage case involving the loss of merchandise in the hands of a retailer market value is generally interpreted to mean replacement cost; but where there is abundant indication that the retailer could not have replaced the property in time to avoid missing his market, some courts have identified market value with retail selling price. A similar tendency so to construe market value as to make it serve as a measure of indemnity may be found in the field of eminent domain. In this same field of law it may also be noted that "value to the taker" has been rejected as a basis of compensation. In the language of the United States Supreme Court, "the question is what has the owner lost, not what has the taker gained" [Boston Chamber of Commerce v. City of Boston, 217 U.S. 189 (1910)].

The most striking contrast between indemnity cases and tax cases is to be found where the tax valuation is designed to measure taxable income rather than to serve as an assessment under a property tax. The assets of a business are here valued for the purpose, among others, of determining a base against which deductible, annual depreciation may be calculated. But they are generally although not invariably valued at original cost, no matter how much that may vary from the current sale price or going concern value of the assets. In short, what is called value is really cost—such a cost as would never be accepted by a court as a measure of damages or of compensation under the law of eminent domain.

Even under the property taxes value is often interpreted to mean something quite different from what it means in an indemnity case. Some courts, for example, have held that the assessment of real estate under the general property tax must be based on market value in the strict sense of selling price, even though the property is obviously worth much more to its owner. The Wisconsin courts have been most explicit in taking this position, as is illustrated by the holding that a recently constructed golf course should be assessed at mere meadowland value, since no purchaser for other uses could have been found [State v. Petrick, 172 Wis. 82 (1920); see also State v. Weiher, 177 Wis. 445 (1922)]. This Wisconsin rule has not been followed in New York and other jurisdictions [People ex. rel. New York Stock Exchange Bldg. Co. v. Cantor, 221 App. Div. (N.Y.) 193 (1927) aff'd 248 N.Y. 533 (1928)]. There is no doubt moreover that even the Wisconsin courts would apply a different rule if the property were to be valued in order to determine compensation under the law of eminent domain.

Within recent years valuation of railroad and public utility properties as a basis of rate control has given rise to more discussion than any other problem in the American law of appraisal. Except for Canada, which has been mildly infected by the United States' precedents, the United States is probably the only country which purports to fix utility rates by reference to the return earned on the present value of the property. This basis of regulation is the outgrowth of a series of decisions by the United States Supreme Court. After holding at first that rate making was a matter for the legislature, not for the courts, the court later held that the Fifth and Fourteenth amendments of the federal constitution, forbidding the taking of property "without due process of law," would be violated if the government were permitted to fix the charges of private utility companies so as to preclude the earning of a "reasonable return on the fair value of the property used and useful in the public service." This fair value doctrine was first announced in Smyth v. Ames [169 U.S. 466 (1898)] and has been adhered to in later cases down to the present time.

While the opinion in Smyth v. Ames enumerated several factors that were to be considered as elements or evidence of value, notably original cost of the property, replacement cost, market value of outstanding securities and earning power under reasonable rates, it did not define the meaning of this value. This deficiency has never been remedied in subsequent cases, and there is still much dispute as to what is meant by value for rate making purposes and as to the difference between this kind of value and the market value that is presumed to measure compensation under the law of eminent domain.

The economics profession seems to agree unanimously that the determination of reasonable profits by reference to the value of the property in any customary sense of the term would involve a vicious circle fallacy. A business property, such as a public utility, has value as private property only to the extent that it is expected to yield interest and dividends to security holders. But the earning capacity of the property is itself dependent on the rates that may be charged. With this point in mind many students of public utility law contend that the Supreme Court must be identifying value with some form of cost—replacement cost or original cost or some compromise figure. Certain it is that the principles of valuation accepted by the courts cannot result in an appraisal that measures the commercial or market value of the utility enterprise or of the assets used by that enterprise. But the rulings have been so confused and so inconsistent that it is doubtful whether the Supreme Court has any well considered standard of value in mind.

A series of opinions delivered several years before the business depression which started in 1929 seemed to indicate that the Supreme Court was gradually coming to identify value with the replacement cost of the property, minus certain deductions for depreciation and plus arbitrary allowances for intangible values, called "going value." A more recent case, Los Angeles Gas & Electric Corporation v. Railroad Commission of California [289 U.S. 287 (1933)], suggests the possibility that the court may now be reverting to original cost as the dominant factor in valuation. But the significance of this case is not clear and the whole issue is still in doubt.

While there is general agreement among specialists in the theory of rate regulation that value is not a proper basis of rate control, much difference of opinion prevails as to the desirable alternative basis. The predominant opinion apparently favors actual legitimate cost or prudent investment as the more satisfactory rate base, although the case for replacement cost minus depreciation is strongly defended by a minority of economists.

Advocates of the prudent investment principle uphold it primarily on two grounds: first, that it avoids the serious delays resulting from the necessity of a revaluation of property prior to an order by a public service commission changing the existing rates; and, secondly, that it rids utility securities of the wildly speculative character which they have attained in the United States because of the uncertainties of a changing rate base. Defenders of replacement cost insist that securities are less speculative under this base than under the actual cost base, since the money income earned on the property will rise and fall with changing general price levels and hence will result in greater stability of real income. They have also argued that during periods of low reconstruction costs public utilities will not find it practicable to maintain their charges so as to yield a return on the higher original costs of the property, and that competition of new utility enterprises together with the force of public opinion would prove too strong for resistance. A more subtle argument in favor of replacement cost rate making, based upon the classical economic theory of competitive prices, has been advanced by some of the academic economists, notably by Harry Gunnison Brown.

JAMES C. BONBRIGHT

See: RATE REGULATION; PUBLIC UTILITIES; RAILROADS; MUNICIPAL TRANSIT; LAND VALUATION; CAPITALIZATION; FAIR RETURN; PRICE REGULATION; GOVERNMENT REGULATION OF INDUSTRY; INTERSTATE COMMERCE COMMISSION; DUE PROCESS OF LAW; EMINENT DOMAIN; DAMAGES; ASSESSMENT OF TAXES.

Consult: Bonbright, J. C., *The Valuation of Property* (New York 1934), and "The Problem of Judicial Valuation" in *Columbia Law Review*, vol. xxvii (1927) 493–522; Friday, David, "An Extension of Value Theory" in *Quarterly Journal of Economics*, vol. xxxvi (1921–22) 197–219; Mathews, Nathan, "The Valuation of Property in the Early Common Law" in *Harvard Law Review*, vol. xxxv (1921–22) 15–29; Webb, Clarence A. and N. A., *Valuation of Real Property* (5th ed. London 1931); Rifkind, S. H., "What Is Fair Value in Taxation?" in National Tax Association, *Proceedings*, vol. xix (New York 1927) p. 305–25; Cooley, Thomas M., *The Law of Taxation*, 4 vols. (4th ed. by Clark A. Nichols, Chicago 1924) vol. ii, sects. 811–16, vol. iii, sects. 1134–63; Tunell, G. G., "Value for Taxation and for Rate Making" in *Journal of Political Economy*, vol. xxxv (1927) 1–38; Ballantine, A. A., "Valuations for Income Tax Purposes" in American Bar Association, *Journal*, vol. xv (1929) 14–18; Orgel, Lewis, *Valuation under the Law of Eminent Domain* (New York 1934); Nichols, Philip, *The Law of Eminent Domain*, 2 vols. (2nd ed. Albany 1917) vol. i, ch. xiv; Lewis, John, *A Treatise on the Law of Eminent Domain in the United States*, 2 vols. (3rd ed. Chicago 1909) vol. ii, chs. xx and xxiv; Hale, R. L., "Value to the Taker in Condemnation Cases" in *Columbia Law Review*, vol. xxxi (1931) 1–31; Bonbright, J. C., and Katz, David, "Valuation of Property to Measure Fire Insurance Losses" in *Columbia Law Review*, vol. xxix (1929) 857–900; Bauer, John, and Gold, Nathaniel, *Valuation of Public Utility Properties* (New York 1934); Whitten, R. H., and Wilcox, D. F., *Valuation of Public Service Corporations*, 2 vols. (2nd ed. New York 1928); Gray, John H., and Levin, Jack, *The Valuation and Regulation of Public Utilities* (New York 1933); Jones, Eliot, and Bigham, T. C., *Principles of Public Utilities* (New York 1931) ch. v; Hale, Robert L., *Valuation and Rate-Making*, Columbia University, Studies in History, Economics and Public Law, no. 185 (New York 1918); Bauer, John, *Effective Regulation of Public Utilities* (New York 1925) chs. iv–viii; Mosher, W. E., and Crawford, F. G., *Public Utility Regulation* (New York 1933) chs. xiii–xv; Bonbright, J. C., "The Problem of Valuation; the Economic Merits of Original Cost and Reproduction Cost" in *Harvard Law Review*, vol. xli (1927–28) 593–622, "Depreciation and Valuation for Rate Control" in *Columbia Law Review*, vol. xxvii (1927) 113–31, and "The Breakdown of 'Present Value' as a Basis of Rate Control" in Academy of Political Science, *Proceedings*, vol. xiv (1930–32) 75–80; Brown, Harry G., *Transportation Rates and Their Regulation* (New York 1916) p. 169–71, 234–40, 289–90, and "Railroad Valuation and Rate Regulation" in *Journal of Political Economy*, vol. xxxiii (1925) 503–30 and vol. xxxiv (1926) 500–08; Reiter, Prosper, *Profits, Dividends and the Law* (New York 1926); Weiner, J. L., and Bonbright, J. C., "Theory of Anglo-American Dividend Law: Surplus and Profits" in *Columbia Law Review*, vol. xxx (1930) 330–58 and 954–85; Locklin, D. P., *Regulation of Security Issues by the Interstate Commerce Commission*, University of

Illinois, Studies in the Social Sciences, vol. xiii, no. 4 (Urbana 1927) ch. vi; Bonbright, J. C., *Railroad Capitalization*, Columbia University, Studies in History, Economics and Public Law, no. 215 (New York 1920) p. 21–31; Bonbright, J. C., and Pickett, Charles, "Valuation to Determine Solvency under the Bankruptcy Act" in *Columbia Law Review*, vol. xxix (1929) 582–622; Weiner, J. L., "Conflicting Functions of the Upset Price in a Corporate Reorganization," and "Payment of Dissenting Stockholders" in *Columbia Law Review*, vol. xxvii (1927) 132–56 and 547–65; Dodd, D. L., *Stock Watering* (New York 1930).

VALUE AND PRICE. Modern economics is a study of the system of social-economic organization which functions through and in connection with the pricing process; price and pricing therefore constitute one of the central topics of economics. Three main sets of prices are generally distinguished: the prices of consumption goods and services; the prices of productive services, or of the uses of productive agencies; and the sale prices of productive agencies or in a non-slaveholding society of property which, unlike human beings, can be bought and sold. Theoretically property prices are merely the capitalized prices of the uses which property yields, although the large speculative element in the knowledge of future services and their expected price makes the matter much more complicated in fact.

Since price is always the price of something and is a quantity or number, it is natural to think of it as the measure of some quality or attribute in the thing which bears a price. This quality or attribute measured by price is the simplest conception of value. Indeed it is this value concept which constitutes one of the two notions of value in a sense distinct from price in the *Wealth of Nations*, as in most economic writing before and since. The second and very different value concept is related to social policy. The economic doctrine of Adam Smith and of the classical school as a whole is a mixture of a more or less scientific analysis of a price economy with what is really political propaganda for laissez faire; and the advocacy of any specific policy implies some ideal of the end of social policy in general and a hierarchy of values based upon it. This broader concept of value is also involved in the thought of most economists of the other schools, for they too have combined scientific analysis with propaganda.

Modern systematic discussion of the phenomena of value (in the scientific sense) and price may be said to have begun with the classical school. It proceeded from two general theories which go back to the earliest speculations on the subject among the Greeks—the theories which emphasize respectively "use value," or utility, and cost. The classical economists dismissed use value as a cause of price on the ground that there seemed to be no correspondence in fact between the two. Smith used the illustration of water and diamonds, which had appeared in the literature before, to show that the highest use value may go with the lowest price and conversely. But in centering attention on cost as the determinant of price Smith employed in different portions of his work two distinct conceptions of the nature of cost. In certain passages he obviously referred to absolute cost in labor, pain or sacrifice, while in others he implied relative or alternative cost, a reflection of the competition of different uses for productive capacity. He never saw the relation between the two cost concepts, and he gave the predominant place to a labor cost view. His first great successor, Ricardo, whose work gave the characteristic form to economic theory for the greater part of the nineteenth century, was concerned mainly with giving unity and consistency to Smith's system by developing the labor cost theory to the exclusion of the other conception. Even more exclusive emphasis was placed on labor cost as the basis of value by the post-Ricardian socialistic schools of thought.

Thus throughout most of the nineteenth century both orthodox and socialistic economics treated price as tending to measure or express value, more perfectly so as a longer run was taken into view, and found the essence of value in pain cost. It may well be suspected that the primitive idea of the curse of labor, as found in the book of *Genesis*, had something to do with this attitude. At bottom the issue between the two cost conceptions reflects a confusion between ethics and science, between the defensible but not necessarily sound ethical principle that labor or sacrifice ought to be the basis of value, or at least of economic income, and the doctrine that in a competitive price economy price in fact is determined by or tends to correspond with sacrifice cost. The second position can be characterized only as an error, in view of the conditions of production which obtain generally in the modern world. A labor cost theory would have considerable validity if each commodity were produced by a different laborer or different kind of labor incapable of producing any other. But the truth is that in general each kind of labor competes for employment in connection with the production of a great many commodities, and that production generally involves agencies other than labor similarly transferable with more or less freedom from one use to another. In so far as productive resources are freely transferable but perform complementary functions in each use, the relative price of any two products depends upon the quantities of fluid resources used to produce a unit of each, and the relative price of any two transferable productive resources depends upon the quantities of products added to output by a unit of each productive resource. Non-transferable resources get a price-determined, differential or residual payment, a rent in the theoretical sense. If the essential resources are transferable to nearly every productive use, all prices become interconnected into a system and any one price can be explained only in terms of economic equilibrium, which takes into account all the general conditions of economic life in the given system: the tastes of consumers; the supplies of the different kinds of resources and their distribution of ownership; and technology as known and applied. True, in such a system prices are affected by effort and intelligence, which may at least in part be considered as ethical factors, but they are also affected, and much more decisively, by considerations of economic power.

As the classical writers recognized, price may arise from any cause limiting supply. It is limitation and the resulting necessity of balancing one thing against another in choice which generate the idea of equivalence underlying the concept of price. The latter has no necessary connection with cost of production. It depends on relative attractiveness, which depends on relative supply. Where production is involved, it affects prices through determination of relative supply, which in turn is conditioned by the allocation of productive resources among industries turning out different goods or services. This phenomenon is best studied at the point of equilibrium, where resources are allocated among the different uses in such a way as to equalize their productive values; it is this equivalence which is reflected in both prices and costs. Thus the cost of producing a unit of any commodity is the non-production of a determinate amount of other commodities. The pain or pleasure involved in production is operative only to the extent that it varies from one employment to another, and it has in fact little to do with prices. In so far as the owners of the resources have no preference as to their uses, it is irrelevant to the explanation of price whether the resources are property or free laborers and whether their functioning is painful or pleasant or unconscious.

Historically breakdown of the pain cost theory of value and establishment of a more realistic doctrine were by-products of the subjective value revolution. Although at first all cost theory was discarded in favor of the marginal utility explanation of value, gradually it came to be recognized that while price immediately depends on marginal utility, under competitive conditions of production it is ultimately determined by cost in the sense just indicated. But the identification of value with marginal utility raised new problems, in the handling of which social values and the propaganda interest played a part. A typical problem of this sort is the "rich-man-poor-man" difficulty, the fact that the price paid by the rich for food to waste is the same as that paid by the poor for food to sustain life.

As a scientific question the problem of economic utility is simply that of the comparative motivation of purchasers of a commodity. Since economic theory had grown up in the intellectual milieu of the hedonistic interpretation of human nature, the motivation stressed was the desire to increase pleasure and reduce pain. The pleasure theory, however, was always more or less ambiguous as between psychological and ethical hedonism; it did not make clear whether maximum pleasure to the individual is actually and necessarily the determining motive of every act or whether maximum pleasure in some of many possible and conflicting interpretations is the end toward which all conduct ought to be directed. Even ethical hedonism is ambiguous, since it may refer to a moral duty of the individual or to an end at which social policy should be aimed.

For the purposes of explanatory analysis, however, ethical hedonism is obviously irrelevant. And psychological hedonism, the theory of pleasure as the universal motive, is becoming increasingly untenable. Clearly the motive underlying actual purchases must at least be modified from the pleasure which actually results to that which is anticipated, unless it can be assumed that the two always coincide, as they proverbially do not. From the question as to just what is anticipated, what later consequence of any behavior constitutes its motive, one naturally proceeds to inquire just what part conscious anticipation in any form plays in the actual determination of conduct. This is the question of rationality. Critical students are more and more doubtful not only as to the degree to which people really foresee the consequences of their acts but even as to the extent to which choices are consistently made with a view to any intended result, especially any result desired for its own sake. In modern psychology there is an increasing emphasis on unconscious motivation as well as on the "prejudice" and caprice in the conscious motives of men; again, it is recognized that the immediate, concrete aims of action are desired as symbols of social relations or social position. To the extent that rational action plays a part in economic life and social conduct at large its motives are increasingly regarded as analogous to the motives of a game in which the capture of opponents' pieces or the gain of points is desired not for itself but with a view to winning the game. This is far removed from such tangible and concrete results as are suggested by terms like utility or want satisfaction in the consumption of goods and services.

In any event a growing recognition that many problems of economics are independent of any particular conception of the nature of motivation has resulted in an increasing tendency to treat motivation as a datum and to leave the discussion of its character to specialists in fields other than economics. The one fact which is essential to economics as a science is the law of the variation of relative intensity of the incentive or attraction to any particular line of activity as this is carried on in competition with other lines. Acceptance of this conclusion amounts to an interpretation of economic behavior on the analogy of mechanics, with motive as the "force" which produces the act. It is doubtful, however, whether motive in this sense affords any place for the notion of value. Moreover the concept of force in mechanics has itself been recognized as metaphysical rather than scientific in a strict sense. Again, the interpretation of motive as force is subject to serious objections. In mechanics forces are known and measured through their effects alone; consequently there is no ambiguity in the information about them, such as it is. In the field of human conduct motives are not inferred merely from the observation of behavior; there seems to exist, on the contrary, a kind of direct knowledge of motivation through the process of social intercommunication—and the two sources of knowledge disagree. As a result of direct experience it is known that behavior does not correspond to intent as accurately as the effect in mechanics is assumed to correspond to the force producing it; the relation between motive and act is vitally affected by error absent from mechanical process.

For these reasons there has been a movement in economics to dispense with motivation altogether. Although utility doctrine is still ably defended in one of its early homes by Hans Mayer and his school at Vienna, efforts have been made, notably by Gustav Cassel, to build up a system of price theory without making use of utility or value theory in any form.

In general, if explanation of economic behavior in terms of motives is to be abandoned, a number of alternative possibilities are open. Perhaps the simplest is the one analogous to a trend in physics—to do away with all "explanation" and merely to formulate empirical laws; the result is statistical economic theory, having for its content the objective phenomena of commodities and prices alone. A second line of development away from the types of value theory represented by classical or utility economics centers around the emphasis on the social control of economic life with clearly implied advocacy of such control. In the past generation this trend has been most marked in Germany (socialism of the chair), in England (Fabianism and left wing liberalism) and in the United States (as a phase of institutionalist economics).

The third alternative to explanatory theory is that of treating economic phenomena as essentially historical, which of course must be done in any case if the concrete content of economic life at a particular time and place is to be explained. Historical economics again subdivides into as many varieties as there are basic conceptions of history and historical method. Two such varieties stand out. The first treats history as far as possible in objective, empirical terms and may use statistics for the discovery and analysis of trends; logically this procedure contrasts sharply with the search for repetitive laws, analogous to those of natural science, which characterizes statistical economic theory, but in practise the two conceptions run together in the work of statistical economists. The second variety of historical economics uses the more familiar humanistic conceptions of political and social history—individual ambitions, efforts and failures in a given social-psychological setting. It represents essentially a revival or continuation of the historical schools of the nineteenth century, especially prominent in Germany. In so far as it arrives at generalizations, it may be described as institutional economics, a term which has come into use particularly in the United States. The related contemporary movement in the German literature is referred to as neohistorical or sociological economics, with Sombart and Max Weber as its most prominent leaders.

At the root of the differences and disputes between the old and the new economics as well as among the three new lines of theoretical development noted above are two problems: the relation between description and explanation and the relation between statement of fact and critical evaluation. The first, inescapable in any thinking about human conduct, is fundamentally the problem of the reality of choice or "freedom of the will." It involves the essence of the value problem in the sense of individual values and is at bottom the problem of the relation between individual man and nature. The second basic problem has to do with the relation between the individual and society.

The crucial fact in connection with the first problem is that if motive or end in any form is granted any real role in conduct, it cannot be that of a cause in the sense of causality in natural science. This is the supreme limitation alike of statistical and of historical economics. For if motive or end is used to explain behavior, it must in turn be brought into the same relation with events and conditions antecedent to it, and then the motive becomes superfluous; the behavior will be fully accounted for by these antecedents. Motive cannot be treated as a natural event. A fundamental contrast between cause and effect in nature and end and means in human behavior is of the essence of the facts which set the problem of interpreting behavior. There seems to be no possibility of making human problems real without seeing in human activity an element of effort, contingency and, most crucially, of error, which must for the same reason be assumed to be absent from natural processes.

Thus motive or intent forces itself into any relevant discussion of human activity. But the subject of behavior cannot be simplified even to the point of reducing it to a dualism. At least three basic principles must be introduced into its interpretation. The typical human action is explained in part by natural causality; in part by an intention or desire which is an absolute datum and is thus a "fact" although not a natural event or condition; and in part by an urge to realize "values" which cannot be reduced entirely to factual desires, because this urge has no literally describable objects. Interpretation in terms of factual desires is the procedure of economics as represented by the bulk of the theoretical literature, in so far as it is objective in outlook. Yet this second principle of explanation is perhaps the most vulnerable of the three. It is doubtful whether any desire is really "absolute," whether there exists any desire that does not look to achievement of some change in a growing system of meanings and values; this is a different thing from changes in physical nature, even though rearrangements in physical nature are the only means by which values can be realized. Every act, in the economic sense, changes the configuration of matter in space. But this does not exclude the possibility of "acts" which change meanings and values without changing natural configuration, since reflection may yield new insight and effect a change of personal tastes. More fundamentally, it is doubtful whether one configuration is in itself preferable to another.

People report and feel two different types of motivation for their acts. There is the wish or preference which is treated by the actor and by outsiders as final, as a brute fact. On the other hand, people make value judgments of various sorts in explanation of their acts; and explanation runs into justification. In other words, no one can really treat motive objectively or describe a motive without implications of good and bad. Thus not only do men desire more or less distinctly from valuing, but they desire because they value and also value without desiring. Indeed the bulk of human valuations, in connection with truth, beauty and morals, are largely or altogether independent of desire for any concrete thing or result. That individual economic motivation itself typically involves some valuation and not merely desire is established by two other considerations: first, what is chosen in an economic transaction is generally wanted as a means to something else, which involves a judgment that it "really" is a means to the result in question; and, second, what is ultimately wanted for its own sake can rarely, if ever, finally be described in terms of physical configuration but must be defined in relation to a universe of meanings and values. Thus there is an element of valuation in the notion of efficiency in the realization of a given end; and in addition the real end contains as an element a value concept.

The dual conception found in motivation is reflected also in the more narrowly economic concept of value. The latter contains definitely more than the notion of a quality measured by price; it is always imperfectly measured under actual conditions. Price "tends" to coincide with value, but the notion of value also involves a norm to which price would conform under some ideal conditions. This norm includes two ideas: that of a goal aimed at but only more or less approximately realized because of errors of various kinds (which tend to be corrected); and that of a "correct" goal of action in contrast with incorrect goals as well as the actual goal. In a society based upon competition as an accepted principle the competitive price, or price equal to necessary costs of production, is the true value in both senses; aberrations are to be attributed to two sets of causes—accidental miscalculations and wrong objectives of action. This statement overlooks of course the existence of different technical conceptions of competitive price relative to the short run or local conditions; and a deeper ethical criticism may condemn given conditions other than the tastes of consumers which fix competitive price, especially the distribution of income and economic power.

To make the main point clear it is necessary to notice the difference in the conception of ideal conditions in economics and in mechanics. In the latter field the most notable of the ideal conditions is the absence of friction; and apparently similar conception of ideal conditions is one of the familiar features, almost a cliché, in economic theory. As generalized description the conception of perfect competition, reached by abstraction from the features of the economic situation which make competition imperfect, is like the conceptions of frictionless mechanics and is similarly justified. But to assume that the specific thing abstracted from in the theory of perfect competition bears the same relation to behavior as does friction to mechanical process would be utterly misleading. Friction in mechanics involves a transformation of energy from one form to another, according to a law just as rigid and a conservation principle just as definite as the law and conservation principle which hold good for mechanical changes where no energy disappears. There is nothing corresponding to any of this in the economic process. What is abstracted in equilibrium price theory is the fact of error in economic behavior. Perfect competition is, among other things irrelevant here, errorless competition; fundamentally it is not comparable to a frictionless machine. The familiar "tendency" of competition to conform to the theoretical ideal is no mere possibility of experimental approximation but a real tendency in so far as men are supposed to endeavor with some success to learn to behave intelligently. It cannot be treated as a tendency toward an objective result but only as a tendency to conformity with the intent of behavior, which intent cannot be measured or identified or defined in terms of any experimental data. The ideal conditions of economics involve perfect valuation in a limited sense, perfect economic behavior which assumes the end or intention as given. The correctness of the intention is an ethical question, from which the economist abstracts just as he abstracts from error which causes the behavior to end otherwise than according to the intent.

Thus far two levels of interpretation of economic behavior have been discussed. The first is that at which behavior is reduced as far as possible to principles of regularity by statistical procedure; it may or may not be thought convenient to impute behavior to some "force," but if it is so adjudged, the force must be assumed to correspond with the behavior observed. The second is the interpretation of behavior in terms of motivation, which must center on the difference between motive and act and on the fact of error. It is at the third level of interpretation that the intentional end of action itself is submitted to valuation or criticism from some point of view. Here the relation between individual and society, the second main problem suggested above, and the concept of value as related to social policy become central topics of discussion.

In fact even at the second level two forms of social reference must be recognized: the individual ends as they are given are chiefly social in origin and content; and in societies in which economic thinking has any relevance there is a large social-ethical acceptance and approval of individual motivation in the abstract. Modern society, for instance, has accepted the right and even the duty of the individual to pursue his own ends within wide limits; in other words, individual liberty itself is a social value and not merely a fact. Thus the second level of interpretation tends to break down. If the notion of economic behavior is effectively separated from mechanical process, if the ends are regarded as ends and not merely as physical effects, the discussion is already in large part at the third level. Factual ends as desired cannot be maintained unless they are given a large element of valuation in addition to desire. The desires for economic goods and services cannot be held to be final or to have a self-contained, independent reality. The least scrutiny shows that they are very largely rather accidental manifestations of desire for something of the nature of liberty or power. But such objects of desire are forms of social relationship and not things, and the notion of economic efficiency has only a limited applicability to their pursuit and attainment. Treatment of such activities, if it is to have any general, serious appeal, must be a discussion of social policy relative to social ends or norms and social procedure in realizing them.

The serious difficulty in economic theory in this connection has been the tendency to confuse advocacy of a policy of political non-interference (or the opposite) with description of a social organization based on free contract. Even when the authors have not deliberately intended to preach as well as to analyze, the difficulties of keeping the two types of discussion separate have been too great, especially in view of the requirements of an exposition which would be intelligible, not to say appealing, to any considerable reading public. In this field the interest in values and especially in social policy is in fact predominant. Thus economic theory, growing up in an atmosphere of reaction against control, clearly overemphasized this side of the case and neglected the other. It is now just as obvious that there are equally sweeping and complex limitations to the principle of liberty in the economic sense; that is, to the organization of economic life exclusively through free contract among individuals using given resources to achieve given individual ends. Society cannot accept individual ends and individual means as data or as the main objectives of its own policy. In the first place, they simply are not data but are historically created in the social process itself and are inevitably affected by social policy. Secondly, society cannot be even relatively indifferent to the workings of the process. This would be ultimately destructive of society and individual alike. This conclusion is strongly reenforced by the fact that the immediate interest of the individual is largely competitive, centered in his own social advancement relative to other individuals. In such a contest it is the function of the public authority to enforce the rules impartially and still more to make such rules as would tend to keep the "game" on the highest possible level. To this end it must maintain a standpoint distinctly different from the interest in which the individual, always more conscious of conflicts of interests than of community of interest with the social body as a whole, tends to be absorbed.

These reflections point to a logical error underlying the value theory typical of the classical economists. It was not ostensibly their contention that liberty as such is a good. Notoriously they were hedonists; their argument for liberty made it instrumental to pleasure, on the ground that the individual is a better judge than government officials of the means to his happiness. It is not denying weight to this argument to point out that liberty itself is unquestionably a good to the individual and in addition an ethical good more or less apart from the degree to which the individual actually prizes it. Certainly an individual may desire liberty and claim a right to it without contending that he will uniformly make decisions more wisely than they would be made for him, from the standpoint of his own material comfort and security. And just as certainly it can be maintained that the individual should within limits make his own decisions and abide by their consequences even if he may not choose to do so. In other words, the classical economists did not realize, and the "scientific" spirit of the age has made economists generally reluctant to admit, that liberty is essentially a social value, at least when it is advocated or opposed, as is any other social system or social relation.

The actual interests or desires expressed in economic behavior are to an overwhelming extent social in genesis and in content; consequently they cannot be described apart from a system of social relations which itself cannot be treated in purely objective, factual terms. To a limited extent they can be conceived by an individual in such terms; they may even be described by one individual to another as matter of fact. But the parties to such a communication place themselves in the role of spectators rather than members of society or participants in the phenomena. Thus any published discussion, presupposing a general appeal to readers as members and participants, necessarily takes the form of stating a case for a policy, possibly with more or less equal attention to both sides. In this conflict between the spectator's interest in seeking and understanding and the participant's interest in action and change, the philosopher or methodologist cannot possibly take sides. The question whether economics as such should be one or the other is to be answered only by recognition that it must be both, with more or less emphasis one way or the other according to the aims of a particular treatment; but always by implication it must be both, however one-sided the emphasis, since each interest presupposes and is relative to the other, and every writer and reader as a human being is motivated by both interests. What is desirable is that in any statement the relation between the two sets of interests should be clear. But what tends to happen is the reverse: he whose interest is primarily in truth tends to reenforce his statements by identifying truth and value, and he whose interest is in values tends to strengthen his statements by giving them the quality of truth.

While in the period of development of the classical economics the practical social interest centered almost exclusively on liberation from an antiquated system of control, at present the pendulum has swung definitely the other way. The new problem raised by the confusion of scientific and evaluative interests is enormously more difficult than the old. Society is positively seeking a basis of unity and order instead of negatively attempting to abandon an unsatisfactory basis. Moreover the current standards of thinking have come under extreme domination of the scientific ideal, which has little if any applicability to the problem. The ultimate foundation of group unity must be of the nature of morale and sentiment rather than knowledge. There is no intellectual solution of conflicts of interest. Only values can be discussed, but the discussion does not necessarily lead to agreement; and disagreement on principles seems morally to call for an appeal to force. It is also significant that the tendency to "rationalization" causes conflict of interest and disagreement on principles each to take on the quality of its opposite, and that in practise they are inseparably mingled.

The extremist wings in the advocacy of change recognize the inapplicability of purely intellectual knowledge. Both fascist and communist schools incline to treat the truth or falsity of propositions in economics as a matter of indifference or even as illusory, judging the doctrines only by their conduciveness toward the establishment of the desired type of social order. This view is of course "untrue" from a narrower "scientific" point of view; in any social order the results of certain choices affecting production and consumption, by whomever made, come under certain abstract, essentially mathematical principles which express the difference between economy and waste. At the other extreme—at the first and second levels of interpretation indicated above—there is an equally energetic movement in the interest of a rigorously "scientific" treatment of economics. Analysis at the first level, disregarding motivation and considering only the results of action in the form of commodity statistics, leaves no real place for any concept of economy. Moreover it cannot be carried out even literally, for commodities must be named and classified and the treatment must take account of similarities and differences in use as well as physical characteristics. And economics at the second level, treating desires as facts, is subject to very narrow limitations. Desires really have no very definite content, and of what they have the student can possess no definite knowledge. The conception can be made the basis of a purely abstract theory, but it has little application to reality. To give the data any content the desires must be identified with the goods and services in which they find expression, and the second method then is reduced to identity with the first. Moreover the only desires which can be treated as at all akin to scientific data are purely individual, and any discussion of social policy must draw on values or ideals entirely outside of such a system.

FRANK H. KNIGHT

See: ECONOMICS; PRICES, section on THE PRICE SYSTEM; DEMAND; SUPPLY; COST; VALUATION; FAIR RETURN; LAND VALUATION; METHOD, SCIENTIFIC.

Consult: FOR HISTORY AND CRITIQUE OF VALUE THEORIES: Turgeon, C. and C.-H., *Premières études. La valeur d'après les économistes anglais et français* (3rd ed. Paris 1925); Kaulla, Rudolf, *Die geschichtliche Entwicklung der modernen Werttheorien* (Tübingen 1906); Zuckerkandl, Robert, *Zur Theorie des Preises* (Leipsic 1889); Fetter, F. A., "The Definition of Price" in *American Economic Review*, vol. ii (1912) 783–813; Davenport, H. J., *Value and Distribution* (Chicago 1908); Diehl, Karl, "Die Entwicklung der Wert- und Preistheorie im 19. Jahrhundert" in *Die Entwicklung der deutschen Volkswirtschaftslehre im neunzehnten Jahrhundert*, 2 vols. (Leipsic 1908) vol. i, ch. ii; Whitaker, A. C., *History and Criticism of the Labor Theory of Value in English Political Economy*, Columbia University, Studies in History, Economics and Public Law, no. 50 (New York 1904); Wicksell, Knut, *Über Wert, Kapital und Rente nach den neueren nationalökonomischen Theorien* (Jena 1893); Veblen, Thorstein, "Professor Clark's Economics," and "The Limitations of Marginal Utility" in his *The Place of Science in Modern Civilisation* (New York 1919) p. 180–251; Boucke, O. F., *A Critique of Economics* (New York 1922); Hamilton, Walton H., "The Place of Value Theory in Economics" in *Journal of Political Economy*, vol. xxvi (1918) 217–45, 375–407; Liefmann, Robert, *Grundsätze der Volkswirtschaftslehre*, 2 vols. (Stuttgart 1917–19); Cassel, Gustav, *Theoretische Sozialökonomie* (5th ed. Leipsic 1932), tr. by S. L. Barron, 2 vols. (new ed. London 1932); Gottl-Ottlilienfeld, Friedrich von, *Die wirtschaftliche Di-*

mension (Jena 1923); "Wert und Preis" in *Die Wirtschaftstheorie der Gegenwart*, ed. by Hans Mayer and others, 4 vols. (Vienna 1927–32) vol. ii, p. 1–239; Mises, Ludwig von, *Grundprobleme der Nationalökonomie* (Jena 1933); *Probleme der Wertlehre*, ed. by Ludwig von Mises and Arthur Spiethoff, Verein für Sozialpolitik, Schriften, no. clxxxiii, 2 vols. (Munich 1931–33); Young, Allyn A., "Some Limitations of the Value Concept" in his *Economic Problems, New and Old* (Boston 1927) ch. x; Clark, J. M., and Anderson, B. M., Jr., "The Concept of Value" in *Quarterly Journal of Economics*, vol. xxix (1914–15) 663–723; Knight, F. H., "Cost of Production and Price over Long and Short Periods" in *Journal of Political Economy*, vol. xxix (1921) 304–35. See also bibliography of Economics.

For the Value Problem in Social Science: Weber, Max, "Die Objektivität sozialwissenschaftlicher und sozialpolitischer Erkenntnis," and "Der Sinn der 'Wertfreiheit' der soziologischen und ökonomischen Wissenschaften" in his *Gesammelte Aufsätze zur Wissenschaftslehre* (Tübingen 1922) p. 146–214, 451–502, and his *Wissenschaft als Beruf* (3rd ed. Munich 1930); Spranger, Eduard, "Die Stellung der Werturteile in der Nationalökonomie" in *Schmollers Jahrbuch*, vol. xxxviii, no. ii (1914) 557–81; Sombart, Werner, *Die drei Nationalökonomien* (Munich 1930); Falk, Werner, *Das Werturteil* (Berlin 1932); Frohnhäuser, E., *Das Werturteil in der Volkswirtschaftslehre* (Munich 1929), with bibliography; Knight, F. H., "Ethics and the Economic Interpretation," and "Economic Psychology and the Value Problem" in *Quarterly Journal of Economics*, vol. xxxvi (1921–22) 454–81, and vol. xxxix (1924–25) 372–409, and "Statik und Dynamik" in *Zeitschrift für Nationalökonomie*, vol. ii (1930–31) 1–26.

VALUES. See Ethics; Morals.

VÁMBÉRY, ARMIN (1832–1913), Hungarian orientalist and publicist. Vámbéry studied at secondary schools but was early compelled to support himself by tutoring. He became interested in oriental languages and in 1857 went to teach at Constantinople, where he was well received by Turkish society and had an opportunity to familiarize himself with Turkish customs and language. Aided by the Hungarian Academy of Sciences, in 1863 he traveled disguised as a dervish through the little known region of Turkestan, including Khiva, Bokhara and Samarkand, returning to Europe through Persia. Later he visited England, where he gained a large following. In 1865 Vámbéry was appointed professor of oriental languages at the University of Budapest. Much of his attention was devoted to philological research in Turkish languages, particularly old Osmanli, and he helped to found scientific Turkology. He was the author of a number of historical works based on original sources.

Vámbéry's literary productivity was amazing. In addition to his scientific studies he published in the periodical press of Hungary, Germany, England and France hundreds of articles on near and middle eastern political and economic developments, and his popular books were translated into many languages. Consistently he stressed the conflict of interests between Russia and England and the danger to British India inherent in Russian expansion in the Middle East. He proposed the extension of British authority as opposed to that of Russia, on the ground that England had established the best features of western civilization in all its spheres of influence. Islam, according to Vámbéry, was as capable as Christianity of giving rise to important cultural and scientific achievement, and he urged the abandonment of traditional western hatred of the "infidel." His knowledge of Turkish and Islamic affairs and his friendship with successive sultans lent great weight to his opinions in diplomatic circles, and to a marked extent influenced the policies of various nations toward the Near and Middle East.

Franz Babinger

Chief works: *A magyarok eredete* (Budapest 1882), tr. as *Hungary* (London 1886); *A török* (Budapest 1885), German translation as *Das Türkenvolk* (Leipsic 1885); *Der Islam im 19. Jahrhundert* (Leipsic 1875), in Hungarian and German; *Geschichte Bocharas*, 2 vols. (Stuttgart 1872), English translation (London 1873); *Russlands Machtstellung in Asien* (Budapest 1871), in Hungarian and German; *Zentralasien und die englisch-russische Grenzfrage* (Leipsic 1873), tr. by F. E. Burnett (London 1874); *The Coming Struggle for India* (London 1885); *Westlicher Kultureinfluss im Osten* (Berlin 1906), English translation (London 1906).

Consult: Munkácsi, B., in *Ungarische Rundschau*, vol. iii (1914) 513–32, vol. iv (1915) 88–113, 386–408; Pröhle, Vilmos, in *Keleti Szemle*, vol. xiv (1913–14) 1–3; Vámbéry, A., *Arminius Vámbéry; His Life and Adventures* (new ed. London 1885), and *Story of My Struggles*, 2 vols. (London 1904).

VAN CLEAVE, JAMES WALLACE (1849–1910), American industrialist. Van Cleave was one of the most belligerent advocates of the open shop and was active in organizing employers against union labor. He entered the stove manufacturing business in Louisville soon after the Civil War and in twenty years had established himself as a successful industrialist. Although the Buck's Stove and Range Company, with which Van Cleave was associated from 1888, was one of the largest concerns in its line, it employed only 700 men. But its trade was country wide and Van Cleave as its president was an influential national figure among manufacturers, because of his views on labor. In May, 1906, Van Cleave was elected president of the National Association of Manufacturers, succeeding David M. Parry, whose hostility to organized labor he shared and whose policies he continued. He was already prominently identified with the Citizens' Industrial Association of America, which John Kirby, Jr., had helped to organize and which was inaugurating an active open shop movement. During his presidency of the National Association of Manufacturers Van Cleave called upon the business men of the country to raise a fund of $1,500,000 to establish the open shop. The result was an intensification of the antagonism between organized labor and capital. In 1907 Van Cleave organized the National Council for Industrial Defense, later the National Industrial Council, which became the organ of the National Association of Manufacturers for legislative and lobbying purposes. This council, which existed only on paper, soon acquired an extensive membership. Each member association in joining signed a power of attorney empowering James A. Emery to act as its counsel and to represent its views before legislatures and Congress. Six years later the council's lobbying activities were exposed by a congressional investigation. Under Van Cleave's direct instigation the Buck's Stove and Range Company in 1907 filed suit against the American Federation of Labor and some of its member unions to restrain them from publishing the company's name on the unfair list. A sweeping injunction was issued and three officials of the American Federation of Labor, Samuel Gompers, John Mitchell and Frank Morrison, were later sentenced to prison terms, varying from six months to a year, for contempt of court in violating some of the terms of the injunction. After Van Cleave's death in 1910, when the company had a new management more friendly to the unions, both suits were dismissed by the Supreme Court as moot cases.

JEAN ATHERTON FLEXNER

Consult: Bonnett, C. E., *Employers' Associations in the United States* (New York 1922) p. 41–42, 327–29, 356–57; Kirby, John, Jr., in *American Industries*, vol. x (1909–10) no. 11, p. 9–13; Gompers, Samuel, "Justice Wright's Decision and Sentence in the Gompers, Mitchell, and Morrison Case" in *American Federationist*, vol. xvi (1909) 438–59, and vol. xvii (1910) 516. See also: *American Industries*, the organ of the National Association of Manufacturers, *Report of Proceedings* of the American Federation of Labor, and *Proceedings of the Annual Convention* of the National Association of Manufacturers, for the years 1906–09.

VANDAL, COMTE ALBERT (1853–1910), French historian. Vandal, the son of Napoleon III's postmaster general, studied under Albert Sorel and between 1877 and 1887 was a member of the Conseil d'État. His first serious historical undertaking, *Louis xv et Élisabeth de Russie* (Paris 1882), was made possible by the opening of the archives of the French Ministry of Foreign Affairs and was inspired by rapidly mounting French interest in Russia. In analyzing the futile efforts of the czarina Elizabeth to effect a Russo-French alliance during the preceding century, Vandal proposed to show "that at no time in its history did France have the right to be indifferent to the problems that agitate the north and east of Europe" (p. xv). Shortly after the publication of this volume he was invited to give courses on the near eastern question at the École Libre des Sciences Politiques, where he entered into closer association with Sorel and soon became one of the school's most popular lecturers. Several essays on the near eastern problem came from his pen in the next few years. At the same time the Franco-Russian rapprochement kept alive his interest in the previous associations of these two countries and stimulated him to produce his exhaustive *Napoléon et Alexandre Ier: L'alliance russe sous le premier empire* (3 vols., Paris 1891–96). Based upon Russian as well as French sources, this work attempted to set forth *des avis et des leçons* (vol. i, p. xvii) to be learned from past failures. It won the *prix* Gobert in 1893 and again in 1894 and led to Vandal's election to the Académie Française in 1897. It also revived his Bonapartist sympathies and resulted in his writing *L'avènement de Bonaparte* (2 vols., Paris 1902–07), the first serious study of the consulate since Thiers. Here Vandal tried to show that the advent of Napoleon was the inevitable consequence of the popular reaction to the painful shortcomings of the Directory, and that the First Consul's work of reconstruction and reconciliation was the result of a gradual evolution. Upon Sorel's death in 1906 Vandal succeeded to his master's chair in diplomatic history, but illness and premature death soon followed.

LOUIS GOTTSCHALK

Other works: *En karriole à travers la Suède et la Norwège* (Paris 1876); *Le pacha Bonneval* (Paris 1885); *Une ambassade française en Orient sous Louis xv: la mission du Marquis de Villeneuve (1728–1741)* (Paris 1887); *Louis xiv et l'Égypte* (Paris 1886); *L'odyssée d'un ambassadeur: les voyages du Marquis de Nointel (1670–1680)* (Paris 1900).

Consult: Gooch, G. P., *History and Historians in the*

Nineteenth Century (London 1913) p. 266–70; Monod, G., in *Revue historique*, vol. cv (1910) 348–52; Leroy-Beaulieu, Anatole, in *Annales des sciences politiques*, vol. xxv (1910) 589–92; Ségur, M. de, in *Revue des deux mondes*, 5th ser., vol. lx (1910) 241–76.

VANDERBILT FAMILY, American capitalists. The founder of the family fortune, Cornelius Vanderbilt (1794–1877), was the son of a poor farmer; he was later called "the Commodore" because of his large shipping interests. His most pronounced characteristic, which became evident at an early age and apparently grew stronger throughout his long life, was an insatiable desire for riches. Along with his acquisitive instinct he possessed an uncanny ability to discern opportunities for financial reward, and he likewise had the shrewdness, the persistence, the unscrupulousness and the physical vitality requisite for their exploitation.

Although most of the Vanderbilt fortune was to come from railroads, the Commodore was not a pioneer in railroad development. He took his tides at the flood, like the other captains of industry of his age, who developed industries but were rarely pioneers. His earliest business venture, begun when he was sixteen, was the operation of a small sailboat in which he carried freight and passengers between Staten Island and Manhattan, in New York. Within a few years he owned a small fleet of sloops and schooners employed in the coastwise and the local harbor trade. In 1817 he turned to the steamboat. He worked as captain on boats owned by Thomas Gibbons for some twelve years, after which he invested his entire capital in a steamboat business of his own. For thirty years the Commodore was one of the leading steamboat operators of New York, most of his vessels being engaged in the trade of Long Island Sound and Hudson River cities. One of his most profitable ventures, however, was the service he established between New York and San Francisco by way of Nicaragua after the discovery of gold in California. For a few years also he owned a transatlantic steamship line.

In 1859, having accumulated a fortune of some $15,000,000, Cornelius Vanderbilt sold out his steamboat business and turned his attention almost exclusively to railroads. Throughout his career in railroad finance he was ably assisted by his son, William Henry (1821–85), whose ability, demonstrated by success as a farmer and as receiver and manager of the Staten Island Railroad, finally won the Commodore's much belated recognition and eventually his complete trust and confidence. The first Vanderbilt road was the New York and Harlem, complete control of which was acquired in 1863 by means of a corner of its stock which yielded huge profits. The New York and Hudson River Railroad was obtained the following year and combined with the Harlem. Both developments involved sharp financial and political manipulations. In 1867 the Vanderbilts forced their way into the New York Central and two years later consolidated it with their other lines, doubling the stock capitalization of the combined roads in anticipation of future earnings. As president and vice president respectively and as chief stockholders the Commodore and his son completely dominated the affairs of the company. After acquiring control of the New York Central the Commodore engaged in a losing battle with Jay Gould, Jim Fisk and Daniel Drew for control of the Erie Railroad; this struggle involved stock juggling, the use of corrupt judges and resort to violence.

While the Vanderbilts do not seem to have been any more scrupulous in business deals than the railroad financiers of the Drew-Fisk-Gould variety, they differed in one important particular from these contemporaries in that they regarded railroads as agencies of transportation as well as vehicles of speculation. They rebuilt the New York Central system completely and made it a highly successful business enterprise. In the early 1870's the Vanderbilts under pressure of rate wars and the fierce competition for business obtained control of the Lake Shore and Michigan Southern and the Michigan Central, thereby assuring the New York Central of adequate connections with Chicago. In later years the West Shore, the New York, Chicago and St. Louis (Nickel Plate), the Cleveland, Cincinnati, Chicago and St. Louis (Big Four) and the Boston and Albany were added to the New York Central system, and the Chicago and Northwestern also became known as a Vanderbilt road. By 1900 the Vanderbilt system was the third largest in the country, with 19,517 miles of track; the first two were dominated by Morgan and Harriman.

When the Commodore died he had probably realized his ambition of becoming the richest man in America. Nine tenths of his fortune, which amounted to more than $100,000,000, he bequeathed to his son, William Henry, who continued to give evidence of his father's keen judgment in the management of business affairs. The other children bitterly resented the unequal division of the money and forced some minor adjustments. Two of William Henry's sons, Cornelius (1843-99) and William Kissam (1849-1920), were for several years prominent in the management of the New York Central properties, and other members of the family served as directors and officers in the numerous Vanderbilt corporations. Beginning with 1879, when William Henry secured the services of J. Pierpont Morgan to sell some Central stock in England, the Vanderbilts' relations with banking interests became increasingly close, while the expansion of their railroad system and the institutionalization of its management slowly but surely thrust the family into the background. Since the latter part of the nineteenth century the family has been less and less active in business, although very prominent in social life.

The chief benefaction of the family was Vanderbilt University, toward the establishment of which the Commodore gave $1,000,000 shortly before his death. His descendants contributed additional sums from time to time. William Henry also gave the land and $300,000 for the construction of the buildings of the College of Physicians and Surgeons in New York.

T. W. VAN METRE

Consult: Smith, A. D. H., *Commodore Vanderbilt* (New York 1927); Meyers, Gustavus, *History of the Great American Fortunes*, 3 vols. (Chicago 1908-10) vol. ii, chs. iii-viii; Adams, Charles Francis, *A Chapter of Erie* (Boston 1869).

VANDERKINDERE, LÉON (1842-1906), Belgian historian and anthropologist. Vanderkindere studied at the University of Brussels and later in Germany, where he became imbued with political and economic liberalism and developed strong anti-French and pro-German leanings. His early scholarly interests were devoted to anthropology. He published several works on the races and ethnographical characteristics of Belgium and was one of the founders of the Société d'Anthropologie de Bruxelles. In 1872 he was appointed to the chair of mediaeval history at the University of Brussels, and thenceforth his chief interest was in historical research. His *Le siècle des Artevelde* (Brussels 1879) marked a significant development in Belgian historiography, for in it he presented the first social history of Flanders and Brabant; this was likewise the first work in which the achievements of the German historical school were utilized for the understanding of the national past of Belgium. In his *Introduction à l'histoire des institutions de la Belgique au moyen âge* (Brussels 1890) Vanderkindere traced the development of Belgian history and society up to the end of the Carolingian epoch. He emphasized the importance of economic factors in history and gave particular attention to historical geography; in this respect his great work *Histoire de la formation territoriale des principautés belges au moyen âge* (2 vols., Brussels 1899-1902; vol. i, 2nd ed. 1912) was of fundamental importance. In 1904 he published an excellent edition of the very important chronicle of Gislebert of Mons. At the same time he began to investigate the difficult problem of the origin of urban institutions. Unfortunately he was inspired in these studies by the older theories of Wilhelm Arnold and von Maurer. All his works are distinguished by clarity and logic, and it was these qualities which made Vanderkindere also an incomparable teacher. The ardor with which he expressed his liberal and anticlerical convictions also impelled him to take part in political affairs. He was a member of the left group in the Chamber of Representatives from 1880 to 1884 and again from 1892 to 1894 and in 1890 was made burgomaster of the commune of Uccle.

HENRI PIRENNE

Consult: Pirenne, Henri, in Académie Royale des Sciences, des Lettres et des Beaux Arts de Belgique, *Annuaire*, vol. lxxiv (1908) 73-120, with a full list of his writings; Leclère, Léon, and Marez, G. des, in Brussels, Université Libre, *Revue*, vol. xii (1906-07) 401-64, with bibliography.

VANDERLINT, JACOB (d. 1740), English economic writer. Little is known of Vanderlint except that he published in 1734 a long pamphlet entitled *Money Answers All Things; or, an Essay to Make Money Sufficiently Plentiful amongst All Ranks of People* (ed. by J. H. Hollander, Baltimore 1914). The essay apparently attracted but slight attention at the time; references to it were not frequent until the nineteenth century, when there was a tendency to overestimate its importance mainly because Vanderlint advocated the removal of restrictions on commerce. The main argument of the essay is that the current trade depression could be overcome if the rates of wages were lowered. Since in his view these rates depended on the prices of necessaries, they could be reduced if the supply of necessaries were greatly increased. To this end the area of land under cultivation should be extended; for Vanderlint held that the workers were badly distributed over the available occupations and some were not employed because with the increase of population sufficient waste land had not been brought into use. The stress on land as the ultimate source of wealth and taxation gives him some claim to be regarded as a forerunner of the physiocrats. His contention that every person is by nature entitled to the land he can cultivate is probably derived from John Locke. The object of reducing the general price level within the country is that England shall obtain a competitive advantage in foreign trade. Vanderlint differs from the many contemporary economic writers who argue in favor of low wages on this ground in that he does not contemplate a worsening of the conditions of the workers. They do not in his opinion consume half as much as they ought, and he insists on the importance to the country of their demand for necessaries. Here as elsewhere, however, he is inconsistent, for he assumes that the level of wages is that of bare subsistence and does not show how the standard of life can be raised. While he wishes to reduce the internal price level to stimulate exports and so in the mercantilist manner insure a favorable balance of trade, he inadvertently suggests a refutation of this argument. A nation which attracts money, he points out, will find its price level rising while the one which loses it will have falling prices. But he does not regard this as automatic. Abundance must be fostered to "fetch the money back again," and apparently he conceives that this may be done indefinitely. His treatment of money is unsatisfactory. He assumes that prices depend on the ratio between the quantity of money and the size of the population. At one moment he fears a shortage of money (should the balance of trade be unfavorable), and at another he is so concerned about a possible excess of the precious metals that he suggests that encouragement should be given to their employment in the arts.

J. F. REES

Consult: Monroe, Arthur Eli, *Monetary Theory before Adam Smith*, Harvard Economic Studies, vol. xxv (Cambridge, Mass. 1923); Furniss, Edgar S., *The Position of the Laborer in a System of Nationalism* (Boston 1920).

VANE, SIR HENRY, the younger (1613–62), British statesman. At the age of fifteen the younger Vane, usually called "Sir Harry" to distinguish him from his father, who was an unscrupulous and time serving minister of Charles I, became a convert to an extreme form of Puritanism. Finding the life of both the royal palace and the paternal manor house increasingly uncongenial, he sailed for Massachusetts in 1635. His rank and influence at once made Vane an important personage in New England, and in 1636 he was elected governor of Massachusetts. The furious controversy aroused during his tenure of office by the religious views of Anne Hutchinson enabled him to come forward as the champion of one of his two leading ideas —religious toleration. He maintained that the civil power should leave spiritual concerns entirely to the individual conscience and throughout his life opposed all forms of state establishment or governmental control of religion. Defeated on this issue in Massachusetts, he returned to England in 1637 and soon threw himself into the struggle between king and Parliament. As a strong parliamentarian he developed and strove to realize his second great idea—the sovereignty of the people. From the death of Pym in 1643 until 1653 he was the civil leader of the resistance to the royalists, as Cromwell was the military leader. Unsympathetic with the military dictatorship set up by Cromwell in 1653, he withdrew from public life until after the Protector's death. His efforts between 1658 and 1660 to prevent the Restoration were such that on the return of Charles II he was expressly exempted from the general amnesty, and was executed in 1662.

F. J. C. HEARNSHAW

Consult: Hearnshaw, F. J. C., *Life of Sir Henry Vane the Younger* (London 1910); Willcock, J., *Life of Sir Henry Vane the Younger* (London 1913); Ireland, W. W., *Life of Sir Henry Vane the Younger* (London 1905); Hosmer, J. K., *The Life of Young Sir Henry Vane* (Boston 1888); Gooch, G. P., *English Democratic Ideas in the Seventeenth Century* (2nd ed. by H. J. Laski, Cambridge, Eng. 1927).

VARLIN, LOUIS EUGÈNE (1839–71), French labor leader. Varlin, a bookbinder by trade, was one of the most militant as well as one of the most cultured and able leaders of the French labor movement under the Second Empire. In a general way he was involved in every phase of this movement, and he played a major role in the strike wave of the period. In 1857 he helped to found the first bookbinders' mutual aid society and in 1865 the Parisian section of the First International. He had an important part in the organization of two consumers' coöperatives, La Ménagère (1866) and La Marmite (1868). He collaborated in the newspaper *Travail*, in Henri Rochefort's *Marseillaise* and in the *Socialiste*, organ of the Parisian federation of chambers of workers' societies; this last association, of which Varlin served as secretary in 1869, was the embryo of the future trade union organization. In addition he was cofounder of three labor newspapers, the *Tribune ouvrière*, the *Presse ouvrière* and the *Fourmi*. Besides participating in the conference of the First International at London in 1865 he was a representative at the first and fourth congresses convened respectively at Geneva (1866) and at Basel (1869). On the occasion of the second prosecution of the International at Paris in 1868 Varlin was sentenced to prison for three months. The third prosecution in 1870 brought him a year's sentence; this time, however, he escaped to Belgium. Returning to France after the proclamation of the republic, he was elected member of the Commune of Paris and was appointed to the committee on finance and the commission on supplies. Regarded as one of the "moderates" of the municipal assembly, he voted with the minority against the creation of the Committee of Public Safety. Having vainly used every resource to save the hostages during the "bloody week," he remained at the barricades with the last defenders. After the battle he was denounced by a priest and immediately executed. Varlin left no writings except his newspaper articles and his letters, some of which have been preserved; but the memory of his heroic and entirely disinterested service constitutes in itself a valuable legacy to the labor movement.

BORIS SOUVARINE

Consult: Clémence, Adolphe, "Eugène Varlin" in *Revue socialiste*, vol. i (1885) 415–26; Clère, Jules, *Les hommes de la Commune* (4th ed. Paris 1871) p. 191–95; Dommanget, Maurice, *Eugène Varlin* (Paris 1926); Faillet, Eugène, *Biographie de Varlin* (Paris 1885); Bourgin, Georges, *Histoire de la Commune* (Paris 1907) p. 171, 178–80; Lissagaray, Prosper, *Histoire de la Commune de 1871* (new ed. by A. Dunois, Paris 1929), tr. by E. M. Aveling (London 1886); Descaves, Lucien, Varlin, Eugène, Keller, Charles, and Guillaume, James, in *Vie ouvrière*, vol. v, pt. i (1913) 514–88.

VASCO, GIAMBATTISTA (1733–96), Italian economist. Vasco, a native of Mondovi in Piedmont and a priest, was well acquainted with the works of Turgot and Adam Smith and despite persecution adhered consistently to the tenets of economic liberalism. In "Delle università delle arti e mestieri" (1793) he advocated the abolition of trade guilds and of all privilege in industry and commerce. His *Mémoire sur les causes de la mendicité et sur les moyens de la supprimer* (1788), inspired partly by the example of the system of charity in force in Lombardy, studied the causes of mendicancy and made suggestions for the relief of the unemployed as well as of men incapable of work. In *La felicità pubblica considerata nei coltivatori di terre proprie* (1767) he advocated peasant ownership. *L'usura libera* made a plea for freedom of contract as the best means of lowering the interest rate, but the analysis of interest which it presented lacked the originality displayed by Galiani. In *Del setificio* (1788), a dissertation on employment in the silk industry, Vasco recommended freedom of trade and of migration and on certain occasions the mitigation of unemployment by public works. All the foregoing essays or books were written in response to questions posed respectively by the Academy of Verona, of Valence and of St. Petersburg, by Joseph II and by the Academy of Turin. Vasco's well known *Della moneta; saggio politico* (1772) condemned bimetallism, favored the use of copper as a standard because of its durability and low maintenance cost, opposed governmental attempts to regulate the value of money and depicted the evils resulting from the debasement of coinage, notably from the point of view of the wage earners; the work as a whole, however, is inferior to the writings of Galiani, Carli and Costantini on monetary theory. Perhaps Vasco's most important work was a short anonymous essay on paper money, written probably in 1790 but published only in 1915 by Giuseppe Prato ("Saggio politico della cartamoneta" in Reale Accademia delle Scienze di Torino, Classe di Scienze Morali, Storiche e Filologiche, *Memorie*, 2nd ser., vol. lxv, 1916, no. 2). With an acuteness far superior to other contemporary writings on the subject this essay clearly divides paper currency into the three categories of bills of exchange, convertible and non-convertible banknotes, expounds the theory of foreign exchange and analyzes the causes of state issues in the light of current experience. Especially noteworthy are the sections dealing with the demand for money in relation to the quantity of national wealth and the flow of national income. Most of Vasco's works are included in the Custodi collection (Parte Moderna, vols. xxxiii–xxxv, Milan 1804).

RICCARDO BACHI

Consult: Pecchio, G., *Storia della economia pubblica in Italia* (3rd ed. Lugano 1849); Monroe, A. E., *Monetary Theory before Adam Smith*, Harvard Economic Studies, vol. xxv (Cambridge, Mass. 1923); Prato, Giuseppe, *Problemi monetari e bancari nei secoli XVII e XVIII*, R. Università di Torino, Laboratorio di Economia Politica "S. Cognetti di Martiis," Documenti finanziari degli stati della monarchia piemontese, 1st ser., vol. iii (Turin 1916) p. 38–48, 65–69, 81–87.

VASILCHIKOV, PRINCE ALEXANDR ILARIONOVICH (1818–81), Russian writer on agrarian problems and local government. Although Vasilchikov belonged to a wealthy aristocratic family which had attained distinction in the state service, he associated himself with liberal and populist activities. After the introduction of the zemstvo he served as member of the district and provincial zemstvo assemblies in Novgorod. From 1871 until his death he was the guiding spirit of the St. Petersburg division of the committee for the promotion of rural savings and loan associations and producers' cooperatives, which was an important center of Russian cooperation before the revolution.

Of Vasilchikov's published works the two treatises on self-government and on land proprietorship and cultivation are outstanding. In the first, *O samoupravlenii* (3 vols., St. Petersburg 1869–71; 3rd ed. in 2 vols., 1872), he combined the Slavophile thesis concerning the independence of the real life of the people from the centralized state with a study of the experience in local self-government of western countries, particularly England. He concluded that democratization of local government in Russia and the broadening of its program to provide for popular schools, promote artels and credit cooperatives and arrange for livestock and fire insurance would assist materially in solving the agrarian question at the root of all social problems. In the second treatise, *Zemlevladenie i zemledelie* . . . (2 vols., St. Petersburg 1876; 2nd ed. 1881), he started with the assumption that the people are fundamentally averse to a system of wage labor and that the work of a small independent producer is in every way superior to work for hire. He proposed therefore a comprehensive policy for modernization of small scale agriculture, which involved easing the tax burden of the peasants, financing their purchase of land, settling state lands, improving the system of communal landownership, promoting new types of cooperation, such as rural credit societies and the like.

Both as a practical reformer and as a student of Russian conditions Vasilchikov stressed collective spontaneous local effort, particularly through zemstvo governments and rural cooperatives, which he held would prevent the proletarization of the masses by the encroachments of a system similar to western capitalism. He was thus the first ideologist of the zemstvo and cooperation, the two creative forces in rural Russia of the postreform and prerevolutionary epoch.

K. Kocharovsky

VASILEVSKY, VASILY GRIGOREVICH (1838–99), Russian historian. The son of a village priest in the government of Yaroslavl, Vasilevsky received his primary education at the Divinity School of Yaroslavl and graduated from the University of St. Petersburg. He was professor of mediaeval history at the University of St. Petersburg from 1870 to his death. Concentrating on the history of Byzantium he became the founder of scientific study of Byzantine history in Russia and created a school of Russian Byzantinists. The characteristic feature of Vasilevsky's work is his astounding knowledge of primary sources and secondary works referring to his subject as well as his fine analytical ability. His studies embrace many important problems in the external history of Byzantium as well as in the history of its administration, social structure and literature; a considerable number of his works are devoted to political relations between Byzantium and Old Russia. Vasilevsky was a pioneer in many of the subjects he discussed. His masterly study on *Vizantiya i Pechenegi* has become indispensable to any student of the history of the first crusade; his penetrating treatise on landholding and taxation in Byzantium, with striking parallels from analogous phenomena in Old Russia, has opened up new horizons for the understanding of Byzantine social and economic structure. Vasilevsky was the first to show convincingly the essential importance of Arabic sources for the history of Russia in the tenth century. His writings on the lives of Byzantine saints revealed the great significance of this branch of literature for Byzantine history. Although Vasilevsky wrote exclusively in Russian, his works have been used extensively by west European scholars.

A. A. Vasiliev

Important works: "Vizantiya i Pechenegi" (Byzantium and the Pechenegs), "Varyago-russkaya i varyago-angliyskaya druzhina v Konstantinopole XI i XII vekov" (The Varangian-Russian and the Varangian-English company in Constantinople in the eleventh and twelfth centuries), "Russko-vizantiyskie otrivki" (Russo-Byzantine fragments), "Zakonodatelstvo ikonobortsev" (Legislation of the iconoclasts), studies originally published as articles in *Zhurnal ministerstva narodnago prosveshcheniya* through the 1870's; "Iz istorii Vizantii v XII veke" (On the history of Byzantium in the twelfth century) in *Slavyansky sbornik*, vol. ii (1875) 210–90, and vol. iii (1876) 372–400. These studies, together with others by Vasilevsky, were published under the auspices of the Academy of Sciences as *Trudi*, 4 vols. (St. Petersburg-Leningrad 1908-30).

Consult: Bezobrazov, P., in *Vizantiysky vremmenik*, vol. vi (1899) 636-58; Grevs, I., "V. G. Vasilevsky kak uchitel nauki" (Vasilevsky as a teacher of science), and Uspensky, F., "Akademik V. G. Vasilevsky" (Academician Vasilevsky) in *Zhurnal ministerstva narodnago prosveshcheniya*, vol. cccxxiv (1899) pt. iii, p. 27-74, and vol. cccxxv (1899) pt. ii, p. 291-342; Kurtz, E., in *Byzantinische Zeitschrift*, vol. ix (1900) 330-34.

VATTEL, EMMERICH DE (1714-67), Swiss diplomat and international jurist. Vattel represented Saxony at Berne. His celebrated *Le droit des gens* (2 vols., London 1758; text and tr. by C. G. Fenwick, Classics of International Law, no. iv, 3 vols., Washington 1916), a classic in the literature of international law, for decades exercised a decisive influence upon statesmen. In his very first work, *Défense du système leibnitien* (Leyden 1741), Vattel had proclaimed his adherence to the school of Leibniz and Wolff. Wolff, following Leibniz, had sought to employ the mathematical method which the latter had taken over from Descartes for the purpose of distinguishing positive international law from the natural law of nations, deducing the characteristics of both from self-evident maxims. But Wolff invented also the fiction of a supreme world state (*civitas maxima*) which, resting upon the tacit consent of all states, might be said in a sense to impose voluntary rules of international law as distinguished from the compulsory rules of the natural law of nations. Within the sphere of the voluntary law of nations Wolff distinguished between customary international law, based upon real although tacit agreement, and consensual international law, representing the express will of the individual states.

Vattel, however, abandoned the mathematical method and the idea of a world state, which to practical statesmen seemed chimerical. Moreover he believed that it was possible to discover the ultimate basis of all legal institutions, including the natural law of nations, in the notions of utility derived from the postulates of ideal reason. Each state, he held, is in conscience and in justice bound to cooperate in the preservation of other states but is also justified in seeking its own self-preservation. But he excluded enforcement by violence of these natural rights and duties on the ground that the frequent collisions of interest would lead to *bellum omnium contra omnes*. This prohibition of war Vattel founded upon a fictitious agreement of all states, which he thus regarded as voluntary international law. Nevertheless, he allowed war for the enforcement of those rights and duties which were derived from customary or consensual international law.

Vattel's success is to be attributed to his eclecticism. He rejected the extreme claims of the natural law of nations which went back to Aquinas, returning rather to Zouche, who had regarded international law as a *jus inter gentes*. He recognized, however, that the universal law of nature might have subsidiary force when customary or consensual international law was silent. Vattel's theory was clearly in closer harmony with the practise of statesmen.

ROLF KNUBBEN

Consult: Mallarmé, A., in *Les fondateurs du droit international*, ed. by A. Pillet (Paris 1904) p. 481-601; Rolin, A., "Grotius et Vattel" in Académie Royale de Belgique, Classe des Lettres et des Sciences Morales et Politiques, *Bulletin* (1920) 385-407; Staub, Hans, *Die völkerrechtlichen Lehren Vattels im Lichte der naturrechtlichen Doktrin* (Berlin 1922); Knubben, R., "Völkerrechtspositivismus und Völkernaturrecht" in *Wörterbuch des Völkerrechts und der Diplomatie*, ed. by Julius Hatschek and Karl Strupp, 3 vols. (Berlin 1924-29) vol. iii, p. 281-82.

VAUBAN, SEIGNEUR SÉBASTIEN LE PRESTRE DE (1633-1707), French engineer, soldier and publicist. Vauban served in almost all the wars of Louis XIV as a military engineer, constructing and repairing a number of fortresses and successfully laying siege to many towns. In 1668 he was made governor of Lille, in 1678 general commissioner of fortifications and in 1703 marshal of France. He was responsible for the adoption of improved types of bayonet and musket. A warm supporter and a favorite of the king, he made unavailing efforts to procure the recall of the Huguenots. In the course of his engineering career he became interested in the economic and social condition of various localities as a basis for their military possibilities and prepared a large number of reports. Many of his fortification plans—over two hundred in number—contained comprehensive geographic and economic information. In some instances he prepared separate economic and fiscal surveys, the most important of which was the *Description géographique de l'élection de Vézelay* (written 1696; printed in Vauban's *Oisivetés*, ed. by A. M. Augoyat, 3 vols., Paris 1842-45, vol. i, Memoir x).

Vauban was a typical representative of enlightened absolutism. His ideal was a strong, well populated and prosperous country united under the highly centralized authority of a benevolent monarch. He was seriously concerned with the welfare of the masses and was alarmed over the growing economic deterioration of France during the closing decades of the century. Convinced that the cause was to be found in large measure in the unfortunate fiscal conditions, he advanced at various times proposals for tax reform, which culminated in the comprehensive plan of fiscal reorganization outlined in his *Projet d'une dixme royale* (Paris 1707; English translation, 2nd ed. London 1710).

Vauban's fiscal program started with the proposition that all the subjects of the king are under a natural obligation to contribute to his support in proportion to their income and their industry. On this assumption he based his demand for uniformity and universality of taxation, claiming that every privilege or exemption constitutes an injustice and an abuse. He proposed to abolish all the existing taxes except the import and export duties and to replace them with four "funds." The first, designed to raise about one half of the entire public revenues, was the "royal tenth," or tax in kind on the gross produce of the soil at a rate of 5 percent. The second was a tax of 5 to 10 percent on house rents together with a similar tax on wages, government salaries and securities and commercial and industrial profits. The third was to consist of a low but completely generalized and fixed salt tax. The fourth comprised the customs, the so-called "voluntary" taxes on tobacco, drinks, coffee, tea and the like and a variety of minor revenues. His work also contained a detailed estimate of the probable yield as compared with that of the taille and the tithe and a refutation of the possible objections to his plan.

Although Vauban's project was immediately proscribed, it nevertheless initiated a discussion which flared up at intervals and led the government to make repeated attempts at reform, which culminated in the revolution of 1789.

EDWIN R. A. SELIGMAN

Consult: For a bibliography of works by and about Vauban, see Gazin, F., *Essai de bibliographie. Oeuvres concernant Vauban. Écrits personnels du maréchal* (Paris 1933); Michel, Georges, *Histoire de Vauban* (Paris 1879); Halévy, D., *Vauban* (Paris 1923); Rochas d'Aiglun, Albert de, *Vauban, sa famille et ses écrits. Ses Oisivetés et sa correspondance*, 2 vols. (Paris 1910); Michel, Georges, and Liesse, André, *Vauban économiste* (Paris 1891); Dreyfus, Ferdinand C., *Vauban économiste* (Paris 1892); Vignes, J. B. M., *Histoire des doctrines sur l'impôt en France. Les origines et les destinées de la dixme royale de Vauban* (Paris 1909); Lohmann, Friedrich, *Vauban, seine Stellung in der Geschichte der Nationalökonomie und sein Reformplan*, Staats- und socialwissenschaftliche Forschungen, no. 58 (Leipsic 1895); Mann, Fritz K., *Der Marschall Vauban und die Volkswirtschaftslehre des Absolutismus* (Munich 1914).

VAUGHAN, RICE, seventeenth century English barrister and economist. Vaughan was admitted to Gray's Inn in 1638 and subsequently held a number of positions in the courts, his last post being in north Wales. He was the author of *A Plea for the Common-Laws of England* (London 1651)—an attack on the legal reforms proposed by Hugh Peters in *Good Work for a Good Magistrate* (London 1651)—and of a guide to practise in Welsh courts, *Practica Walliae* (London 1672), published shortly after his death. His principal work was *A Discourse of Coin and Coinage*, written in the second quarter of the century but not published until 1675. It is a historical, technical and theoretical treatise on money, probably the first of its kind in English.

The treatment of prices in the book is strongly reminiscent of Bodin's. High prices are due to two causes: abundance of gold and silver and the "raising," or debasement, of money. Changes in the value of money cannot be discovered by a study of the price of any given commodity, since this is affected by special circumstances. The one factor that "carries with it a constant resultance of the Prices of all other things which are necessary for a Mans life" is laborers' wages. This observation of a group of prices, indirect though it is, is probably the earliest forerunner of the index number. The values of the precious metals depend on world conditions—"the general consent of neighboring nations"—and hence are beyond the control of particular governments. Vaughan discusses Gresham's law from various angles and devotes much attention to the coinage ratio. The ratio to be adopted should assure the abundance of both gold and silver, but especially the latter, since most commerce and all inland trade are conducted on a silver basis. Vaughan's analysis of the effects of monetary instability upon the different classes in the community, although embodying many ideas which were already conventional, contains some interesting refinements. He exposes with considerable skill the futility of various monetary devices designed to bring specie into the kingdom. Although Vaughan leaned heavily on other writers, he was a thinker of much independence and originality, and his book deserves a prominent place in the early literature of money.

A. E. MONROE

Consult: Monroe, A. E., *Monetary Theory before Adam*

Smith, Harvard Economic Studies, vol. xxv (Cambridge, Mass. 1923); Hoffmann, Friedrich, *Kritische Dogmengeschichte der Geldwerttheorien* (Leipsic 1907) p. 20–22.

VEBLEN, THORSTEIN BUNDE (1857–1929), American economist and social philosopher. The son of Norwegian immigrants, Veblen was born in a Wisconsin farm community where the Norwegian language, religious organization and social customs prevailed in antagonism to the American and Americanizing influences of town and city—a circumstance that helps to explain the cosmopolitan and provocative character of his thought. He was educated in Carleton College (1877–80), Johns Hopkins (1881), Yale (1881–84) and Cornell (1890–92). In 1892 he became teaching fellow in economics at the University of Chicago, in 1896 instructor and in 1900 assistant professor. He was appointed to an associate professorship in Stanford University in 1906, and in 1911 he became lecturer at the University of Missouri. In 1918 he joined the staff of the New School for Social Research, where he remained until his retirement from teaching in 1927.

His bent toward philosophy may be accounted for in part by the philosophic-theological controversies evoked in the 1870's and 1880's by the advance of evolutionary doctrines, especially as presented in the works of Herbert Spencer. While a student at Carleton Veblen read widely in philosophy, advancing through Spencer to the eighteenth century philosophers, of whom Hume and Kant appealed to him most powerfully. His impetus to economic study originated in the popular equalitarian current of ideas of that time, with its antithesis of the classes and the masses, its fierce hatred of monopoly and the money power, its attacks upon political parties and political authority as venal, its contempt for journalism, the colleges and often the churches as satellites of the interests. In college Veblen read the standard textbooks on economics and followed with interest courses by John Bates Clark, but there is no evidence that then or at any later time orthodox economics appeared to him anything better than an apology for the dominant order. Nor was he drawn toward Marxism. A Kantian by training and instinct, he had little interest in the Hegelian dialectic either in its original idealistic form or in the materialistic adaptation by Marx. The Marxian antithesis of capitalist and proletariat, both defined in strictly economic terms, unsupported by any convincing sociological and psychological analysis of the character of these classes, appeared to Veblen too simple and abstract to be useful. Yet he had no interest in programs of reform. These were palliatives, mechanical inventions, not organic growths rooted in the institutional evolutionary process.

Beginning with *The Theory of the Leisure Class* (New York 1899, new ed. 1918) Veblen published a succession of remarkable books: *The Theory of Business Enterprise* (New York 1904); *The Instinct of Workmanship and the State of the Industrial Arts* (New York 1914, new ed. 1918); *Imperial Germany and the Industrial Revolution* (New York 1915); *An Inquiry into the Nature of Peace* (New York 1917, new ed. 1919); *The Higher Learning in America* (New York 1919); *The Place of Science in Modern Civilisation* (New York 1919); *The Vested Interests and the State of the Industrial Arts* (New York 1919); *The Engineers and the Price System* (New York 1921); *Absentee Ownership and Business Enterprise in Recent Times; the Case of America* (New York 1923). The general objective of these works was to present, from different angles, an evolutionary analysis and a critique of the existing economic system, which Veblen conceived of as essentially a price system, a pecuniary economy, rather than as a system of capitalism or as a system of individualism and laissez faire.

As an evolutionary social philosopher Veblen saw the whole history of civilization characterized by the conflict between the predatory and the industrious, this conflict, however, shifting its forms with protean facility and varying from phase to phase in the degree of naked force and fraud displayed or in the ingenuity with which predation is veiled by an appearance of ethical legitimacy and observance of the general interest. Thus the pirate chieftain of one epoch becomes the captain of industry of another; the robber baron levying upon peaceful trade becomes the financial magnate. The elaborateness of the structure of predation depends on the fruitfulness of the productive process, its capacity to yield an appropriable surplus; and this in turn depends on the state of the industrial arts. Thus the profits of high finance, which orthodox economics imputes to the function of efficient organization of the factors of production and which Marxian economics treats as a deduction from the product of labor, are to Veblen the usufruct of a rich and versatile industrial technique developed out of ancient germs by the proficiency of modern science.

The price system now dominant is in Veblen's opinion incapable of long survival. The recurrence of crises of constantly increasing intensity is proof of a failure of adjustment which is inherent in the system and therefore irremediable. Veblen is never entirely explicit as to the nature of the economic organization that is to succeed the price system, but his latest works suggest a system in which production and distribution will be controlled by the engineers, conceived of as a profession immensely extended so as to include virtually the whole of the initiating and executive functions of social life.

In spite of his prodigious learning and the wealth of original ideas published in his articles and books Veblen found few readers and fewer disciples among academic economists until late in his life. The issues which he raised had little apparent bearing on current controversies either in theory or in applied economics. Accordingly the effect of his writings was baffling to the professional economist, who was unable to follow him in his evolutionary and philosophical twistings and turnings. The difficulty was enhanced by the fact that Veblen created for himself an idiosyncratic style, very copious and precise, full of turns of expression that have since become widely used but that at first seemed wantonly obscure. It remains true to this day that a relatively small number of American economists know Veblen well. He is little known to English economists and virtually unknown to scholars on the European continent.

From the outset, however, Veblen exerted an important influence upon philosophers, sociologists and historians, who found his approach to the problems of economic life and his methods of analysis more closely related to modern scientific thought than the economics of the schools. In the last two decades Veblen's influence has been greatly extended through the work of his students. While none of them has assumed the role of disciple or interpreter, they have taught an increasing body of students to turn to Veblen for suggestions and stimulus.

ALVIN JOHNSON

Consult: Dorfman, Joseph, *Thorstein Veblen and His America* (New York 1934), the only comprehensive account of Veblen and his works; Taggart, Richard V., *Thorstein Veblen*, University of California, Publications in Economics, vol. ix, no. i (Berkeley 1932); Homan, Paul T., *Contemporary Economic Thought* (New York 1928) p. 105–92; Anderson, Karl L., "The Unity of Veblen's Theoretical System" in *Quarterly Journal of Economics*, vol. xlvii (1932–33) 598–626; Jaffé, William, *Les théories économiques et sociales de Thorstein Veblen* (Paris 1924); Masoero, A., "Un Americano non edonista" in *Economia*, vol. ix (1931) 151–72; Innes, Harold A., "A Bibliography of Thorstein Veblen" in *Southwestern Political and Social Science Quarterly*, vol. x (1929–30) 56–68.

VENEREAL DISEASES. *See* PROSTITUTION; SEX EDUCATION AND SEX ETHICS.

VENUE means place of trial and must be distinguished from jurisdiction, which refers to the capacity of a court to make an enforceable judgment. Objections to the hearing of a litigation on the ground that it has not been started in the proper place territorially can be pleaded only before any other defense, whereas attacks based on the lack of jurisdiction are in order whenever the effectiveness of the judgment is asserted and may be urged by any party or by the court.

The selection of a particular judicial district within a territory is regulated almost universally by statute; as between separate states or territories the choice is usually made by the courts according to principles which they lay down. In the United States both statute and judge made law reflect the influence of early common law origins. In the common law all actions were originally triable only by a jury gathered from the vicinity where the happenings in controversy were supposed to have occurred. When the juror's function became separate from that of the witness, however, the need for trying every action in its immediate locale disappeared; gradually by the use of legal fictions there arose in civil cases a broad distinction between local and transitory actions for purposes of place of trial. Real or local actions consist of those related to real property titles and must be tried where the property is located. In this class are included administration of estates and such matters as the regulation of intramural corporate affairs. In transitory or personal actions, that is, those in which claims are asserted against particular persons, the proper venue is usually the defendant's residence or domicile, although in some of the states of the United States it may be supplemented or superseded by the place where the defendant is served with summons or even where the plaintiff lives, a solution which gives predominant consideration to the latter's convenience. In various jurisdictions it is provided that an action on contract may be brought at the place of its making or performance and that a tort action may be brought at the place where the tort occurred, regardless of the domicile or residence of the parties to the action.

The above outline, including the distinction between local and transitory actions, is descriptive not only of the United States but of many European and South American states. Each judicial structure reflects in its rules of venue the composite effect of such factors as the convenience of litigants and witnesses; special competences of judges and juries in local matters; and even, as, for example, where suits against insurers are specially permitted at the plaintiff's residence, specific social policies, which take account of inequalities, fostering or discouraging certain litigations. In addition every system represents an attempt to apportion the financial burdens of administration over the whole territory and to prevent, to a degree, jockeying by the parties for favoring tribunals. To correct the occasionally too rough approximations of justice in the balancing of various considerations there is the device of change of venue. In England centralization of administration makes it possible for each case to be assigned by the High Court of Justice as it sees fit, and the earlier common law rules are at best suggestive guides.

Greater difficulty and diversity obtain in the determination, in certain cases, whether there is any proper venue at all within the territorial jurisdiction or system or courts invoked, a matter still decided by the judges without aid of statute. In all jurisdictions it is held that there is no proper venue in a local action when the subject which gives it local character is outside of the territory. Most American courts will entertain a transitory action even if the defendant is a non-resident; an increasing number of courts, however, will refuse the suit where the plaintiff is also a non-resident and the cause of action is of foreign origin, a rule which prevails in England, Germany and France, unless in the last named country the plaintiff, although a non-resident, is a French national. In modern times, when the areas of travel and business have been extended so widely, the indiscriminate reception of transitory actions, no matter how distant the seat of the evidence or the resources of the defendant, may result in unreasonable inconvenience and unjust judgments; courts should develop the doctrine that there is an ambit within which they are free to refuse to entertain a suit. When a suit is brought in the wrong local unit within a territory, statutes often provide that it may be transferred to the proper unit without compelling the plaintiff to begin anew and to serve the defendant again, which he may not be able to do. But where the suit is brought in the wrong state, no interstate understandings provide for its transfer; a court might refuse to dismiss the suit unless the defendant agreed to accept service in the proper jurisdiction, but very few courts have worked out such a procedure. The injustice which is likely to result from this inflexibility may find illustration in actions for trespass to real property. These are personal actions and service must be had on the defendant; but most American courts, following the older common law, hold that for venue purposes they are local, being intimately related to real property titles. Thus unless the defendant can be found and served within the territory where the land is located, the plaintiff is without remedy.

Expressly or by implication forty-two of the state constitutions in the United States guarantee a criminal defendant trial in the county where the crime has been committed, and the courts have supported this common law doctrine. This practise is a survival from a time when the jury gave its verdict of its own knowledge; even now the evidence is available most easily and cheaply at the place where the offense has been committed. A splitting up of certain crimes, as, for example, the original larceny and the resulting illegal possession, has to some extent broadened criminal venue. In England, where there are no constitutional guaranties, the counties of commission, apprehension, custody and appearance are all proper. In France trials for contraventions are limited to the locality of the offense, while for *crimes* and *délits* the districts of commission, apprehension and residence of the accused are proper, as they are in Germany. A number of countries hold that their courts have jurisdiction where the accused or the victim is one of its nationals or the accused is apprehended within the state or where these conditions are combined. These rules have developed in part as a result of the failure of extradition in certain cases and the consequent necessity of dealing with criminal populations.

State constitutions and statutes in the United States provide for a change of venue in civil suits upon the application of either party, in criminal cases upon the application of the defendant and sometimes of the prosecution and occasionally upon motion of the court. The formulation of grounds varies: convenience of witnesses; prejudice of the judge or the inhabitants of the county; the general impossibility of securing a fair trial; and, in four states, danger of mob violence. Unfortunately the device of change of venue is of limited and uncertain value where race prejudice subjects judicial administration to virtually irresistible stress. Where prejudice of the county or fear of mob violence is claimed as the basis for a different venue, the change is usually within the court's discretion; where the statutes are mandatory, the court may determine whether the evidence supports the claim. In either case an elected judge may hesitate to balk the county of the offended kin seeking revenge. In a very few states change is automatic upon the filing of a petition supported by affidavits of interested and credible parties, usually a given number of citizens; in Missouri this procedure is limited to counties of under 75,000 inhabitants, a fact which implies recognition that the problem of prejudice is apt to be more difficult in small communities. The suggestion has been made that in states where race prejudice is intense the trial, when the charge is murder or rape of a white person by a Negro, should be transferred automatically from the county of the crime. Unfortunately the threat of removal may in itself provoke a lynching, and also, as has been demonstrated in the famous Scottsboro Case, prejudice may be so widespread that it becomes difficult to find a substitute county. Furthermore many of the statutes give the defendant a right to but one change of venue, although doubtless a court in its discretion might grant another. In a society divided by enormous social inequalities or torn by class warfare change of venue, like many legal safeguards, provides little real protection.

L. L. JAFFE

See: JURISDICTION; PROCEDURE, LEGAL; COURTS; CRIMINAL LAW; LAWLESSNESS; LYNCHING.

Consult: Halsbury's Laws of England, vols. i-xii (2nd ed. by D. M. H. Hailsham, London 1931–34) vol. ix, p. 65–76; Holdsworth, W. S., "The Rules of Venue, and the Beginnings of the Commercial Jurisdiction of the Common Law Courts" in Columbia Law Review, vol. xiv (1914) 551–62; Scott, Austin Wakeman, Fundamentals of Procedure in Actions at Law (New York 1922) ch. i; Foster, Roger S., "Place of Trial in Civil Actions" in Harvard Law Review, vol. xliii (1929–30) 1217–48; Blair, P., "The Doctrine of Forum Non Conveniens in Anglo-American Law" in Columbia Law Review, vol. xxix (1929) 1–34; Stephen, J. F., A History of the Criminal Law of England, 3 vols. (London 1883) vol. i, p. 275–80; Harris, S. F., Principles and Practice of the Criminal Law (14th ed. by A. M. Wilshere, London 1926) bk. iii, ch. v; Clark, W. L., Handbook of Criminal Procedure (2nd ed. by W. E. Mikell, St. Paul 1918) ch. i; Chadbourn, J. H., Lynching and the Law, University of North Carolina, Social Study series (Chapel Hill 1933) ch. ix; Répertoire général alphabétique du droit français, ed. by E. L. P. Fuzier-Herman, 37 vols. (Paris 1886–1906) vol. ii, p. 405–19; Goldschmidt, James, "Zivilprozessrecht" in Enzyklopädie der Rechts- und Staatswissenschaft, vol. xvii (Berlin 1929) p. 61–65; Lilienthal, Karl von, "Strafprozessrecht" in Enzyklopädie der Rechts- und Staatswissenschaft, vol. xxi (Berlin 1923) p. 12–16; Garraud, René, Précis de droit criminel (14th ed. Paris 1926) p. 713–23.

VERBŐCZY, ISTVÁN (1458–1540), Hungarian statesman and jurist. Verbőczy studied in Italy and became familiar with both Roman and canon law. He was very active in politics as the leader in the Diet of the gentry who were opposing the great lords. He held high offices in the judiciary and headed several missions which sought to enlist the help of European countries in Hungary's struggle against Turkey. In 1525 he was elected palatine of Hungary. Twenty years earlier he had been instrumental in the passage of a resolution by the nobility which favored the interests of the pretender John of Zápolyai as opposed to the Hapsburgs; after the battle of Mohács in 1526 Verbőczy aided John in his accession to power and during the period of the dual kingdom was his confidant and counselor.

In fifteenth century Hungary there existed no collection of laws or legal manual, so that there was a pressing need for a thorough study of the customs and statutes upon which the courts based their judgments. Verbőczy was commissioned to prepare a code, and although it was finished in 1514 and won the approbation of the king and Diet, it was never promulgated and as a result did not obtain the force of law. Three years later, however, Verbőczy published his study entitled Tripartitum opus iuris consuetudinarii inclyti regni Hungariae (Vienna 1517; Latin and Hungarian ed. by S. Kolosvári and K. Óvári, Budapest 1897), and within a short time the maxims of this unique work were generally accepted in the courts. The code, which dominated Hungarian law until 1848, equalized the rights of all the nobility and protected their privileges against the king and the peasants, whose perpetual servitude it established.

The work took the form of a manual and presented theoretical discussions as well as statements of law. While it deals chiefly with private law and procedure, it treats some questions of public law, such as the relations of the church and the king and the privileges of the nobles. Verbőczy also developed within the limitations of the estate-democratic conceptions of his time a theory of the holiness of the crown. According to this theory the nation, that is, the association of nobles, had transferred its right to legislate, adjudicate and enfeoff to the crown and through it to the king. Those, however, who were invested with the estate of nobility by the king obtained thereby the right to share in the offices of the crown (*membrum sacrae regni coronae*) and accordingly should take part in political functions, especially in legislation.

Verbőczy exercised a profound influence upon the spiritual life of the Hungarian nation, for the *Tripartitum* maintained the unity and national character of Hungarian legal development under the most adverse political conditions. On the other hand, it contributed to the inflexible conservatism of the Hungarian estates, which for centuries opposed social and legal reforms.

FRANZ ECKHART

Consult: Fraknoi, Vilmos, *Werbőczi István*, Magyar történeti életrajzok, vol. xv (Budapest 1899); Almási, A., *Ungarisches Privatrecht*, 2 vols. (Berlin 1922–23) vol. i, p. 16–18; Timon, Ákos, *Magyar alkotmány- és jogtörténet* (4th ed. Budapest 1910), tr. into German by F. Schiller as *Ungarische Verfassungs- und Rechtsgeschichte* (2nd ed. Berlin 1909) p. 643–46; Illés, Jozsef, *Bevezetés a magyar jog történetébe* (Introduction to Hungarian legal history) (2nd ed. Budapest 1932).

VERGENNES, COMTE DE, CHARLES GRAVIER (1717–87), French diplomat and statesman. Scion of a noble but not very influential family, Vergennes was sponsored in his diplomatic career by a distant relative, Théodore de Chavigny, in whose retinue he served at Lisbon in 1740 and at Frankfort in 1742. He was appointed minister to Treves in 1750, where he showed such promise that he was transferred to Hanover and later to Mannheim. In 1755 he was sent as an ambassador to Constantinople and despite serious obstacles succeeded in winning the cooperation of the Ottoman government, even to the point of supporting France's war policies. As minister to Sweden (1771–74) he encouraged the royalist anti-English revolution of August, 1772, which placed supreme power in the hands of Gustavus III and reestablished French influence in the Baltic.

On the strength of this brilliant success Maurepas persuaded Louis XVI to appoint Vergennes minister of foreign affairs. Dedicating himself to the task of restoring the international prestige which France had lost during the period from 1757 to 1763, the new minister pursued a conciliatory diplomatic policy in Europe, as evidenced in the Peace of Teschen (1779); a firm pro-American policy at a time when the other ministers of Louis XVI were hesitant; a liberal commercial policy, which reached its climax in the bold treaty of 1786 with England, establishing in effect a regime of free trade. His unswerving support of the United States was in keeping with the traditional foreign policy of France, which consisted in reducing in so far as possible the number and influence of the great empires and in multiplying medium sized and independent powers. The last great minister of the French monarchy, Vergennes was the only one, with the exception of Richelieu, who correctly understood the role of international opinion.

BERNARD FAŸ

Consult: Meng, John J., *The Comte de Vergennes; European Phases of His American Diplomacy* (Washington 1932), with critical bibliography p. 113–21; Ormesson, Wladimir d', *Portraits d'hier et d'aujourd'hui* (Paris 1925) p. 53–166; Doniol, Henri, *Politiques d'autrefois. Le Comte de Vergennes et P.-M. Hennin* (Paris 1898); Corwin, Edward S., *French Policy and the American Alliance* (Princeton 1916); Faÿ, Bernard, *L'esprit révolutionnaire en France et aux États-Unis à la fin du XVIIIe siècle* (Paris 1925), tr. by Ramon Guthrie (New York 1927); Van Tyne, C. H., "Influences Which Determined the French Government to Make the Treaty with America, 1778" in *American Historical Review*, vol. xxi (1915–16) 528–41; Nussbaum, F. L., "The Revolutionary Vergennes and Lafayette versus the Farmers General" in *Journal of Modern History*, vol. iii (1931) 592–604.

VERGNIAUD, PIERRE VICTURNIEN (1753–93), French revolutionary statesman. Vergniaud, the most famous orator and one of the most brilliant leaders of the Girondist party, was influential in the period between the opening of the Legislative Assembly in October, 1791, and the overthrow of the Girondists on June 2, 1793. He came from an old established bourgeois family of Limoges and as a statesman represented the ideals of the rising French middle class, but with more enthusiasm than logic. His characteristic inconsistency was manifest in his speech of July 3, 1792, the most celebrated of his orations in the Legislative Assembly, which sealed the doom of the monarchy, although Vergniaud himself was still unprepared to take that step. In the Convention his attitude toward the trial of the king manifested similar lack of clarity. That he would have liked to save the king is obvious from his great speech of December 31, 1792; lacking the courage to support acquittal, however, he advocated the evasive and impracticable policy of referring the question to the people and eventually cast his ballot for the death penalty. The word recurring most frequently in his addresses was "humanity," a concept which, as used by the chosen representative of the Girondist mercantile coterie, was of course circumscribed by the class interests of the bourgeoisie. In company with Brissot, Vergniaud, the lover of mankind, inflamed his countrymen to undertake the propaganda war in the name of the future "universal brotherhood." But after this unreflective enthusiasm had precipitated the war, Vergniaud was as incapable as the other Girondists of conducting it and could only attempt to block the economic and political dictatorship of the Mountain which the war had rendered inevitable. He opposed most of the emergency measures, such as the employment of representatives on mission to control the generals, the erection of a revolutionary tribunal, the requisition policy, the laws of the maximum and progressive taxation. The charge of federalism upon which he and twenty of his comrades were condemned to the guillotine by the Revolutionary Tribunal on October 31, 1793, was unfounded, if the term implies, as it did for the Mountain, that they plotted against the "unity and indivisibility of the Republic." But to the extent that the Girondists obstructed regimentation and aroused the propertied and cultured bourgeoisie of the departmental capitals against the central government the accusation had a certain justification. In the last analysis, however, Vergniaud was the victim of his own illusions, which he epitomized in his speech of April 10, 1793, when he declared that he had "wished to carry out the revolution" not through terror but "through love."

HEDWIG HINTZE

Consult: Vernon, Guy de, Vergniaud (Limoges 1858); Raismes de Verdière, L. de, Biographie de Vergniaud (Paris 1866); Lintilhac, E. F., Vergniaud; le drame des Girondins (Paris 1920); Aulard, F. V. A., "Vergniaud et les Girondins proprement dits" in his Les orateurs de la Révolution, la Législative et la Convention, 2 vols. (2nd ed. Paris 1906–07) vol. i, bk. v; Mathiez, A., "Robespierre et Vergniaud" in his Girondins et Montagnards, Études d'histoire révolutionnaire, vol. i (Paris 1930) p. 20–69.

VERRI, PIETRO (1728–97), Italian economist and statesman. The son of a high Milanese official, Verri was influenced to study economics by the English economist Lloyd. His first work in this field, Elementi di commercio (Vienna 1760), attracted the attention of the Austrian government, which enlisted him in its service at Milan, where he rose rapidly. He promoted some of the major reforms introduced in that state, among them the abolition of the method of leasing tax collection to private agencies (fermiers généraux) in 1770 and the reduction and simplification of the tariff in 1786.

Verri's writings were an important element in the liberal movement of the period. From 1764 to 1766 he and his brother Alessandro published a liberal journal, the Caffè, to which some of the best Milanese economists and scientists, like Beccaria and Frisi, contributed. His economic works were a strong plea for laissez faire, but, unlike the physiocrats and Smith, Verri sought freedom only for internal trade. Fundamental to his economic system was his advocacy of lower prices, resulting from an increase in the number of sellers relative to the number of purchasers. He argued that an outflow of money constitutes a loss of national wealth because it diminishes the internal circulation of goods and raises prices, and he therefore favored restriction of imports and encouragement of exports. Verri's monetary theory is based upon the paradox that an increase in the amount of money, when it comes from commerce or passes directly into the hands of the producers and is not derived from mines or when it is gradual, lowers rather than raises prices. He admitted the possibility of conflict between public and private interest, but believed they could be reconciled by persuasion and guidance rather than by constraint.

While there were many points of agreement between Verri and the physiocrats, the Italian differed from their principle of the produit net, holding that taxes are paid by all consumers in the act of consumption and not from land—a principle which points to the modern theory of shifting of taxes. His canons of taxation were very similar to those of Smith, except for the fact that Verri believed that taxation should be paid directly by a few individuals and be passed on by them to consumers through the market mechanism.

Verri's most significant theoretical ideas are probably to be found in occasional parenthetical clauses: the definition of economic wants as "an excess in the valuation of the goods one desires over those one wishes to sell"; the recognition that price, or value, is set by both utility and scarcity; the embryonic concept of economic equilibrium; the distinction between economic production, or the creation of utility, and technical production, or the creation of things; and the psychological basis of the economic calculus. Einaudi has justly termed Verri one of the greatest economists of his age and certainly the greatest Italian economist of the eighteenth century.

CARLO PAGNI

Works: Meditazioni di economia politica (Milan 1771);

Dialogo sul disordine delle monete nello stato di Milano (Milan 1762); *Bilanci del commercio dello stato di Milano* (Milan 1764; new ed. by L. Einaudi, Turin 1932); *Memorie storiche sull' economia pubblica dello stato di Milano* (Milan 1768); *Riflessioni sulle leggi vincolanti, principalmente nel commercio de' grani* (Milan 1769). Verri's chief works have been reprinted in *Scrittori classici italiani di economia politica. Parte moderna*, vols. xv–xvii (Milan 1804).

Consult: Bouvy, Eugène, *Le comte Pietro Verri, ses idées et son temps* (Paris 1889); Manfra, M. R., *Pietro Verri e i problemi economici del tempo suo*, Biblioteca Storica del Risorgimento Italiano, n.s., no. 1 (Milan 1932); Valeri, Nino, "Un revoluzionario del settecento: Pietro Verri" in *Nuova antologia*, vol. ccclxxiii (1934) 3–28, 170–201, 348–74, 537–68, and vol. ccclxxiv (1934) 48–79, 206–32; Einaudi, Luigi, "Introduzione" in his edition of Verri's *Bilanci del commercio dello stato di Milano*, Piccola collezione di scritti inediti o rari di economisti, vol. i (Turin 1932) p. 11–36; Ferrara, Francesco, *Esame storico-critico di economisti e dottrine economiche del secolo XVIII e prima metá del XIX*, 2 vols. (Turin 1889–91) vol. i, pt. i, p. 300–05, 357–61, 371–75; Ricca Salerno, G., *Storia delle dottrine finanziarie in Italia* (Palermo 1896) p. 276–82; Macchioro, Gino, *Teorie e riforme economiche, finanziarie ed amministrative nella Lombardia del secolo XVIII* (Città di Castello 1904); Negri, Luigi, "Saggio bibliografico su Pietro Verri" in *Archivio storico lombardo*, 6th ser., vol. liii (1926) 136–51, 337–51, 499–521; Verri, Pietro and Alessandro, *Carteggio dal 1766 al 1797*, ed. by A. Giulini, E. Greppi, and F. Novati, vols. i–vi (Milan 1910–   ).

VESTED INTERESTS. When an activity has been pursued so long that the individuals concerned in it have a prescriptive claim to its exercise and its profits, they are considered to have a vested interest in it. When this interest is given legal sanction it becomes a vested right. The prescriptive claim may be enforced against other individuals or even against the state itself seeking to encroach upon it. In this broadest sense vested interests and vested rights are as old as human history and as broad as social life. Property may be traced back ultimately to the vesting of ownership or other proprietary rights in individuals and groups who have carved out their claim by conquest or effort or ingenuity and have made it secure by force or continued exercise of it. Roman law, however tenacious of the sanctity of property rights, recognized *usucapio*, the taking by continued use, in order that there might be no sustained uncertainty about ownership. The whole of legal history may be regarded as the sequence of vesting rights in individuals whose claims for one reason or another come to be regarded as sufficient.

The rise and fortunes of capitalism in the western world have given the concept the most specific consequence for social thought. Feudalism was a system of frozen rights and relationships; and while it sanctioned the established, it did not, except through a certain residual continuity with Roman law, smile upon more newly acquired rights. With its disintegration scope was given to the exercise of arbitrary power over private property by the prince and the creation of a system of aristocratic privilege. The whole effort of a rising capitalism in the sixteenth and seventeenth centuries, as exercised through the natural law jurists of that period, was to place bounds around the dynastic power and privilege and to open a path for the vesting of the claims which a new merchant class was pressing. On the continent this struggle found intellectual expression in the writings of Grotius, Pufendorf and other natural rights philosophers. In England it conditioned the constitutional conflict of the seventeenth century, with its insistence upon subjecting an arbitrary monarch to the rule of law. The culmination of both movements of thought was the eighteenth century natural rights philosophy of the French and English intellectuals, finding its most significant formulation in Locke's definition of property as whatever a man has mixed his labor with. This flung the gates open for a legitimation of the claims of the capitalist class as rapidly as they were acquired; and once the rights were vested, it placed barriers against the encroachment of the state upon them. The vested interests of a rising capitalist class were written into the English common law as they were written into natural rights philosophy, and by the latter part of the eighteenth century Lord Mansfield declared it an established doctrine that vested rights must be protected. As capitalism matured in nineteenth century England, the task of removing the disabilities which political inequality imposed upon the vesting of new interests was completed by the reform movements and Benthamite jurisprudence in the period between 1832 and 1870.

The *locus classicus* of the vested interests, however, is American business enterprise and its accompanying body of constitutional law. In fact the history of American constitutional law is most clearly intelligible as a record of the varying legal sanctity of the vested interests. The Constitutional Convention itself may be seen as a concerted attempt to intrench the vested interests against agrarian discontent and the lingering revolutionary *élan*. In the judicial interpretation of the constitution a series of bulwarks was erected against the interference of state legislatures with this property conscious intent of the framers. The mechanism was the establishment of judicial supremacy and the power of judicial review of legislative enactments. The doctrine principally relied upon before the Civil War was that of vested rights. While this doctrine sought to secure the constitutional guaranty of equal protection of the laws and the constitutional prohibition of the impairment of the obligation of contracts, it had no substantial underpinning within the constitution for negating hostile state legislation and had to seek it outside the constitution in the theory of implied limitations on state power. These limitations were found to be implied in natural law, in the social compact, in the character of republican government and in the genius of American institutions. Ultimately of course they were nowhere more clearly implied than in the genius of an expanding American capitalism.

The first important statement of the doctrine of implied limitations as the basis for vested rights is given by Justice Chase as an *obiter dictum* in Calder v. Bull [3 U.S. 386 (1798)]. Chief Justice Marshall in his first great decision, Marbury v. Madison [5 U.S. 137 (1803)], showed the trend of his thought in this direction by saying: "The government of the United States has been emphatically termed a government of laws, and not of men. It will certainly cease to deserve this high appellation, if the laws furnish no remedy for the violation of a vested legal right." His statement of the doctrine reached its most significant form in Fletcher v. Peck [10 U.S. 87 (1810)], when he refused to inquire into the reputedly corrupt circumstances surrounding the Yazoo land grants on the ground that they had created a vested right, and Dartmouth College v. Woodward [17 U.S. 518 (1819)], when he declared rights vested by a state charter of incorporation irrevocable. Marshall's tenacity of purpose and the clarity with which he saw the stakes of the conflict were given substance and circumstance by the erudition of his friend Justice Story and of Chancellor Kent. The latter set down in his opinions in the New York court and in his *Commentaries* (4 vols., New York 1826–30), delivered as the lectures of a law professor, the fullest and most reasoned exposition of the doctrine of vested rights before Cooley. From the end of Marshall's dominance over the Supreme Court until after the Civil War the vested rights philosophy was thrust into the background by the Jacksonian supremacy, the slavery conflict and the needs of federal expansion. It continued, however, almost uninterruptedly in state judicial review in another form—that of the due process clause, which, while unavailable in the federal constitution against state legislation, was available in the state constitutions. The New York court, which invalidated a whole series of statutes between 1840 and 1860, set the pattern for other states.

After the Civil War the swift expansion of business energies and business power brought again the threat of control by hostile state legislatures. To meet this threat the due process clause of the Fourteenth Amendment was conscripted into service by the Supreme Court for the protection of vested rights, and it was used with greatest effect in those cases where the denial of due process was alleged to constitute a deprivation of liberty of contract. Actually the concept of vested rights, along with that of due process, is vague and malleable. Vested rights have had a varying sanctity in the functioning of the judicial process. In a significant sense the history of American constitutional law is the record of advances and retreats on the battle ground of vested rights, the contending forces being those groups who have sought to extend the area of state control and those who have sought to limit it. At bottom these conflicts have been between economic interest groups. But the reality of the battle has been considerably obscured by the rhetoric of democracy thrown over it—in Marshall's day nationalism and after the Civil War individual liberty.

Heartened by its triumph American business enterprise in the 1880's and after turned from the defensive and sought a free field for industrial mergers and the concentration of power. What had previously been mainly a desire to protect existing vested rights against state encroachment became, in a period of monopoly capitalism, an effort to wrest and hold power for new vested interests. This alternation of periods of defense and aggression, of the protection of existing vested rights and the creation of new vested interests, is integral to the history of capitalism. In America the new vested interests not only broke the competitive pattern of the older economic society but threatened the established political forms. Accordingly two successive generations—in the late 1880's and at the turn of the century—threw themselves into the task of curbing the vested interests. The culmination of the efforts of the first generation was the Interstate Commerce Act and the Sherman Anti-Trust Act; of the second, Roosevelt's trust busting, Wilson's New Freedom and the Pujo investigation into the money trust. The legislative efforts were largely frustrated by Supreme Court policy, especially as formulated in the rule of reason with respect to monopolies; and the official attacks and investigations served only to put the vested interests on the defensive again until after the World War.

The attack on the vested interests was a phase of the muckraking era. Denunciations of the "interests" were common in the 1880's and 1890's, especially in the western agrarian movements, the fiction of Frank Norris and the writings of Henry Demarest Lloyd. But with the turn of the century they became epidemic in the influential magazines and produced a unique periodical literature. Ida M. Tarbell's "History of the Standard Oil Company" (*McClure's Magazine*, 1902–04) and Thomas W. Lawson's "Frenzied Finance" (*Everybody's Magazine*, 1904) were the opening guns of the campaign. C. E. Russell, Upton Sinclair, David Graham Phillips, Alfred Henry Lewis, Burton J. Hendrick, Ray Stannard Baker and Lincoln Steffens all had a hand in exposing the power of the vested interests and the malignancy of the "system." Their attacks became the foundation of magazine fortunes and writing reputations. The tone of the articles was often as frenzied as the financial operations they described; there was generally more heat than analysis in them; and several of the writers later joined or returned to the fold that they had depicted as wolves in disguise. The entire movement was probably as episodic in the span of American life as it turned out to be in the lives of the principals. Yet it left some impress on politics, and it subsequently furnished the basis for more detached analysis of the new phases of business enterprise.

The high point of such an analysis was achieved in the writings of Thorstein Veblen. He took the term vested interests out of the popular literature of the muckraking period and gave it a laborious and yet ironic precision. His definition of a vested interest as "a marketable right to get something for nothing" (*The Vested Interests*, p. 100) has, however, a greater sharpness in itself than is contained in his actual analysis. The latter suffers from being at once too broad and too narrow, the reference being now to the whole of business enterprise and now to the strategic position of being able to make use of the technique of "sabotaging," or "conscientious withdrawal of efficiency," in the pursuit of maximum profit. With Veblen as with the more popular writers of the muckraking era the term vested interests must be regarded not as a sharply analyzed concept but as a symbol with a shifting reference.

Yet Veblen's analysis has taken on an increased meaning in the period of corporate growth and banker control in the 1920's and in the wrack and reconstruction of the depression period in the 1930's. While the doctrine of vested rights arose originally to protect a socially valid claim against the encroachment of other individuals and was as such sanctioned by the state, it has become increasingly a matter of vesting the right against the state itself. In an era of corporate concentration vested rights have paralyzed the effective functioning of state control and overshadowed the very existence of the state. A communist state finds no place for them. A fascist state, however, after rooting out certain dissident or dangerous vested rights by its totalitarian power, intrenches those that remain more securely than in a democracy. So much have vested interests come to be part of the legal and constitutional fabric that even proletarian movements, such as that of the English Labour party, include in their plans for a seizure of power the compensation of vested interests. In the current schemes of economic planning for a controlled capitalism vested interests enter as an important factor: the Tugwell drug control bill was opposed by some on the ground that if the consumer knew in advance all the conditions of marketing, valuable vested interests in advertising would be lost; on the other hand, the liquor control set up under President Franklin D. Roosevelt expressly provided that nothing contained therein could be later construed as having created vested interests which could be defended against governmental action. Latterly among democratic thinkers a tendency has shown itself not so much to fight the vested interests as to extend vested rights and thereby secure a stake in social stability to the lower middle class and the skilled worker. This may well become an important factor in the future in meeting the threat of revolution. But whatever the drift, the idea of vested interests, whether as reality or as symbol, will remain of value so long as a capitalist economic system continues to create legal sanctions for its own operations.

MAX LERNER

See: PROPERTY; INTERESTS; NATURAL LAW; NATURAL RIGHTS; LIBERTY; DUE PROCESS OF LAW; FREEDOM OF CONTRACT; CONTRACT CLAUSE; LAW; CAPITALISM.

Consult: Veblen, Thorstein, *The Vested Interests and*

the State of the Industrial Arts (New York 1919), The Theory of Business Enterprise (New York 1904), and Absentee Ownership and Business Enterprise in Recent Times (New York 1923); Haines, C. G., The Revival of Natural Law Concepts, Harvard Studies in Jurisprudence, vol. iv (Cambridge, Mass. 1930), especially ch. iv; Hamilton, W. H., "Property—According to Locke" in Yale Law Journal, vol. xli (1931–32) 864–80; Tawney, R. H., Equality (London 1931) p. 105–19; Corwin, E. S., "A Basic Doctrine of American Constitutional Law" in Michigan Law Review, vol. xii (1913–14) 247–76, and "The Doctrine of Due Process of Law before the Civil War" in Harvard Law Review, vol. xxiv (1910–11) 366–85, 460–79; Mott, R. L., Due Process of Law (Indianapolis 1926) ch. xi; Boudin, L. B., Government by Judiciary, 2 vols. (New York 1932); Lerner, Max, "The Supreme Court and American Capitalism" in Yale Law Journal, vol. xlii (1932–33) 668–701; "The Variable Quality of a Vested Right" in Yale Law Journal, vol. xxxiv 1924–25) 303–09; Smith, Bryant, "Retroactive Laws and Vested Rights" in Texas Law Review, vol. v (1926–27) 231–48; Regier, C. C., The Era of the Muckrakers (Chapel Hill, N. C. 1932) chs. ix–x; Chamberlain, John, Farewell to Reform (2nd ed. New York 1933) ch. iv; Lippmann, Walter, The Method of Freedom (New York 1934).

VETERANS. The extent to which disbanded soldiers organized as a more or less distinct pressure group constitute a political problem depends upon a number of factors. Among these the more important are the ease with which veterans are absorbed into productive employments; the make up of the army, depending on whether it is limited wholly to an upper class with a fixed economic status or whether it includes the lower classes with a shifting and uncertain basis of livelihood; and, lastly, the duration and destructiveness of wars. In ancient Rome the breakdown of Latin agriculture as a result of the import of grain from the provinces and the continuous wars of expansion resulted in the creation of a large class of disbanded soldiers who at the end of the wars were thrown into the landless proletariat of the city of Rome. As early as the time of the Gracchi the unrest and clamor of this group forced an abortive attempt to readjust the land laws to the end that the large concentrated landholdings might be broken up for distribution among veterans. From this time on the veterans, ready to give their political loyalty to any military adventurer who promised them plunder from conquest, were a continuous threat to the established order. To placate this group by securing land for them became one of the congeries of problems which made the political history of Rome a succession of internal social crises. Under the Caesars other and more successful attempts were made to find land for disbanded soldiers not only in Italy but also in the colonial dependencies. The seriousness of the pressure of veterans is indicated by the ambitious attempt of one of the Roman emperors to drain and clear the Italian swamps to secure land for veteran distribution. Then as now one of the basic problems was to find a way to satisfy the demands of a largely propertyless but powerful pressure group without disturbing existing property rights or too greatly burdening the propertied classes with taxes and levies.

In mediaeval society war was one of the vocational pursuits of the landed nobility. In view of the fact that the maintenance of a feudal noble and his household was not dependent upon his participation in productive labor but was the perquisite of a hereditary status, disablement as a result of war activity did not jeopardize his economic security or that of his dependents. Even toward the end of the feudal period and into the early modern period, when wars had become monarchical enterprises using common soldiers and sailors drawn from the lower classes, the care and maintenance of the maimed and disabled veterans were left to the captains and local overlords into whose service they had been pressed. Such feudal aid was supplemented by the charitable efforts of various religious orders.

Such quasi-feudal, local relief of disbanded soldiers became, however, progressively more inadequate as the size of the armies and the scale and destructiveness of warfare increased. As early as the reign of Queen Elizabeth captains complained that the maintenance and care of the disabled soldiers "laid heavily upon them." The enclosure of peasant holdings in Great Britain, the severely restrictive regulations of craft guilds and local corporations, made impossible an orderly absorption into productive employment of the tens of thousands of soldiers disbanded after each war. The plight of those who, as a public official of the seventeenth century characterized them, "have little or nothing to maintain themselves, their wives and children but by their own labors" was such that many resorted to brigandage, piracy, thievery and beggary. A popular English ballad of the seventeenth century was called *The Maunding Soldier; or the Fruit of War Is Beggary*. Although there were during these early centuries of the modern age no mass political groups of organized veterans such as are found in modern nations, the constituted authorities were not free from the irritations of sporadic violence and clamor.

Although the details vary, reflecting the differences in national traditions and in the tempo of the development of modern economic and political institutions, certain common factors were operative in the new national states throughout the seventeenth, eighteenth and nineteenth centuries creating a "veterans" problem and ways of dealing with it which in their larger aspects are similar. The nationalization of political life, the development of standing armies under the control of the central government, the inclusion of the propertyless masses to provide the man power of military forces, the dependence of disbanded common soldiers and sailors upon the sale of their labor power for their livelihood, the frequency and growing scale of warfare, the destructiveness of military weapons and the skill of medical technique, which kept pace with the destructiveness of war, created in varying degrees and convergence a situation in which the pressure of demands by ex-soldiers and the inadequacy of local aid and self-help forced upon central governments the responsibility of taking financial care of disabled soldiers and of veterans generally. The nationalization of pensions was, however, a slow growth over several centuries. The earliest instance of central governmental action with reference to pensions was the series of acts of Queen Elizabeth in the last decade of her reign. Under these acts the central government fixed general compensation rates for disabled soldiers and those in service twenty years or more but entrusted their financial administration and enforcement to local counties. The full financial and administrative responsibility of central government was not firmly established in Great Britain until well into the eighteenth century.

At the present time as an aftermath of the World War there exist in all the belligerent nations, under central governmental control and financing, elaborate systems for the care of veterans. In all countries hospitalization and medical care are given the war maimed to restore them to such health as their injuries will permit. For those who were injured in such fashion that they cannot return to civil occupations on the pre-war basis special training is provided to reeducate them in new techniques by which they may employ their time usefully and perhaps gainfully. Financial compensation is paid to the disabled and their dependents on the basis of a complex system of ratings which includes not only the degree of disability with reference to gainful employment but, varying with countries, other considerations, such as the number of dependents, the type of customary employment in civil life whether in unskilled, skilled or managerial work (Germany) or the rank held in the army as in France. In most countries veterans are the beneficiaries of preferences in competition for public employment, in securing land or housing and in numerous other ways. The French government, for example, gives certain classes of pensioners rebates of taxes, provides them with small loans to set up in business and makes special grants to enable them to acquire cheap homes. In France private enterprises beyond a certain minimum size are required by law to give employment to partially disabled veterans up to a certain percentage of their employed personnel. The British government sought to accomplish a similar reabsorption of partially disabled veterans by a voluntary appeal to employers and added persuasion to the appeal by confining contracts for governmental work to employers who had agreed to the reemployment of disabled veterans. To encourage the settlement of ex-service men in agriculture the British government offered ex-service officers and the better educated common soldiers free training in farming with a yearly maintenance allowance, scholarships in university departments of agriculture and grants for oversea training. In all countries veterans' organizations and private charitable endowments provide homes and workshops for the disabled veterans.

Care and maintenance of invalid veterans by the government were an accepted practise in the American colonies. Very shortly after the outbreak of the Revolutionary War the Continental Congress established invalid and widows' pension rates for service incurred injuries and deaths. Lacking resources of its own the Congress authorized the state legislatures to provide for the pension payments and to charge them to the account of the central government. Upon its establishment the federal government assumed direct financial and administrative responsibility for pensions. The emphasis in discussing the American pension system therefore lies not with the development of its nationalization but rather with the process as a result of which the system of pensions in the United States, with reference both to the rate of pensions granted and to the basis of entitlement to pension, attained a standard of liberality far exceeding that of any other contemporary nation.

Excluding pensions applying to the administration of the regular army, European governments generally limit governmental aid to those veterans and the direct dependents of veterans who have suffered death or physical disability as a result of injuries or sickness incurred in actual service. The French government offers an exception to the European pattern in recognizing as a pensionable claim service or assignment to service in certain combat units. It is further characteristic of European pension systems that the pension expenditures gradually diminish after passing a peak period shortly after the closing of hostilities. Like the European systems, the pension system in the United States provides for the disabled and their dependents. The minimum compensable disability is lower than is generally true of European countries and the financial rating of disablement is higher. Hospitalization and rehabilitation are on a much larger scale and the basis of entitlement is much wider, including not only injuries and sickness directly traceable to war service but also those cases for which statutory definition establishes a presumptive connection. But unlike European systems, the expenditures of the United States government for its veterans service goes largely to veterans unscathed by military service. War service as such has in the United States been established as a compensable claim. The methods of rewarding war service moreover are such that the veterans expenditures continue to rise many years after the end of the war. It is estimated, for example, that, assuming no further liberalizations of the World War pension laws, the peak of expenditures will be reached in 1958, two years before the British World War pensions will be totally extinguished. Although the number of sick and wounded in service was far smaller than is true of any other large power, the expenditures on World War veterans in the United States are greater than those of any other of the belligerent nations. In the year 1931–32 the total expenditure of the United States was greater than the combined totals of France, Germany and the United Kingdom.

The history of pensions in the United States is an account of the accumulative demands of well organized veteran groups, the solicitation of the political favor of these groups by candidates and holders of political office and the exploitation of the governmental acquiescence in granting the demands of veterans by claim attorneys and sundry other individuals for pecuniary gain. The convergent and generally successful pressures of these interests upon the financial benevolence of the federal government rather than the crystallization of underlying principles and standards explain the peculiarities of the American pension system.

The first instance of group pressure to secure grants of governmental funds to reward military service as distinct from maintenance of invalids injured in military service is the effort of officers of the revolutionary army to secure half pay for life on condition of service to the end of the war. As ready as the Continental Congress was to grant invalid pensions, it was reluctant to establish what it regarded as the privileges of a military aristocracy. The officers, however, persisted in their agitation, repeatedly petitioning Congress, threatening to resign individually and in groups and banding together into societies, of which the most prominent was the secret Society of the Cincinnati. Suggestive of the bonus army assembled in Washington in 1932 was a similar assembly of officers in convention where they threatened to stay until their demands were met. Ultimately a reluctant Congress partly granted their demands.

This incident initiated the pattern which characterizes the history of the American pension system and defines the role of mass organization of veterans in the political life of the United States. These organizations, quick to form after each war, have pursued with tenacity and single minded devotion the securing and enlarging of pensions. Of participation in the larger issues of political life they have been free, centering and specializing their efforts on one objective. The varying circumstances of prosperity and depression seemed equally conducive to liberalization; when the government in periods of prosperity had a surplus, it was argued as only just that veterans should participate in the increasing wealth of the country; in periods of depression the poverty of ex-soldiers was offered as a sufficient reason for additional pension grants. After each of the several wars in which the United States has engaged the numerous veterans' organizations which sprang up succeeded in extending the list of pensioners to include not only the disabled but all soldiers and their widows, mothers and children as well. The fact that the federal government was still paying pensions arising out of Revolutionary War claims 125 years after the close of the war and that there are still pensioners on the list of the War of 1812 attests to the success with which veterans have pressed their cause.

Upon the entrance of the United States into the World War an attempt was made to forestall political pressure for pensions by establishing in advance of the close of the war a pension and insurance system. Under the War Risk Insurance Act (October 6, 1917) provisions were made for the maintenance of the dependents of soldiers in service, partly by compulsory deductions from the pay of the men and partly by governmental grants. In addition there were compensation provisions for injuries incurred in military service, for hospitalization, medical care and for rehabilitation. And, lastly, the government offered insurance protection against permanent disablement of the veteran and against death for the maintenance of dependents at peacetime rates. It was hoped that this system would take pensions out of the realm of political manoeuvring and would make them independent of the pecuniary enterprise of claim agents and of veterans' organizations.

It was almost a quarter of a century before the Grand Army of the Republic, representing the Civil War veterans, had become efficiently active. But within five years following the declaration of peace after the World War nearly one hundred changes, most of them removing restrictions, had been legislated into the basic act at the instance of the American Legion, the strongest of the World War veterans' organizations. The most far reaching liberalization of the World War pension system occurred upon the passing of the World War Adjusted Compensation Act. This act gave all veterans who had served in the army for more than sixty days after April 5, 1917, and before July 1, 1919, a bonus amounting to $1.00 a day for every day of home service and $1.25 a day for every day of foreign service. If the credit to the veteran was less than $50.00, it was paid in cash; if above $50.00, the veteran received a paid up twenty-year endowment insurance certificate with a face value equal to that amount of endowment insurance which his bonus credit plus 25 percent, considered as a single net premium, could buy from a commercial insurance company, with interest at 4 percent and compounded annually. Under the provisions of this act more than 3,500,000 policies were issued with a maturity value of more than $3,500,000,000. In 1931 the American Legion asked for a 50 percent advance loan on the certificates to be paid immediately, and Congress acquiesced, passing the loan measure over the veto of the president.

In 1932 an attempt was made to secure for veterans the full cash value of the bonus certificates. Thousands of unemployed veterans, variously estimated from 12,000 to 20,000 ex-soldiers, their wives and children, assembled in Washington from all parts of the United States and threatened to stay until the bonus certificates were fully paid. In this instance, however, Congress resisted their demands, and after several months of futile demonstrations the bonus army was dispersed by military action. This act of resistance to veterans' demands was followed by legislation in 1933, upon the initiative of President Roosevelt, which narrowed the base of entitlement for invalid pensions, particularly with reference to those disablements arising from injuries or sickness with merely presumptive connection with military service, and which reduced pension rates in the lower disability brackets.

To account for the pecuniary acquisitiveness of veterans' groups in the United States and for their success in deflecting governmental funds into pensions and gratuities is a problem in the field of conjecture. It is worth noting, however, that the behavior of veterans' organizations is similar in character to that of other minority groups who secure effective representation of their interests in governmental circles. The success of railroad promoters in obtaining land grants, of manufacturers in securing high tariffs, the exploitation of political office for the pecuniary aggrandizement of politicians and their associates, fall alongside organized veterans and their acquisition of public funds as characteristic features of American political life. If there is any distinction to be noted, it is that war service pensions and gratuities give the governmental largess a somewhat wider mass dispersion than is true of the other instances cited. Attention should also be called to the probability that much of the provocation to the demands of veterans and much of the force of their pressure would be lost if there were in existence a national system of unemployment and social insurance.

Except in the interest of pension getting the organized ex-soldiers in the United States have engaged in very little other political activity. In European countries, on the other hand, the large post-war veterans' organizations have been active in the revolutionary politics of Germany, Italy and Russia. Mussolini built the Fascist organization largely on the mass support of ex-soldiers. In Germany the Stahlhelm played a determining role in the course of events which swept Hitler into power. In both cases the organized veterans supported an antisocialistic and strongly nationalistic program. Similarly in France the veterans' organizations have begun to take active part in fostering a strongly nationalistic and conservative program.

A. A. FRIEDRICH

See: PENSIONS; LAND GRANTS; LAND SETTLEMENT; REHABILITATION; CRIPPLES; SOCIAL INSURANCE; ARMY; MOBILIZATION AND DEMOBILIZATION; WAR; AMERICAN LEGION.

Consult: Pierce, Bessie L., *Citizens' Organizations and the Civic Training of Youth*, American Historical Association, Report of the Commission on the Social Studies, pt. iii (New York 1933) chs. iii-iv; Hayes, C. J. H., *France; a Nation of Patriots* (New York 1930) p. 220–23; Felix, Georges, *Les droits des anciens combattants et victimes de la guerre* (Paris 1930); Oliver, John W., *History of the Civil War Military Pensions, 1861–1885*, University of Wisconsin, History Series, vol. iv, no. 1 (Madison 1917); Glasson, William H., *History of Military Pension Legislation in the United States*, Columbia University, Studies in History, Economics and Public Law, no. 32 (New York 1900), and *Federal Military Pensions in the United States* (New York 1918); Weber, Gustavus A., and Schmeckebier, Laurence F., *The Veterans' Administration; Its History, Activities, and Organization*, Service Monographs of the United States Government, no. 66 (Washington 1934); James, Marquis, *A History of the American Legion* (New York 1923); Duffield, Marcus, *King Legion* (New York 1931); Mayo, Katherine, *Soldiers What Next!* (Boston 1934). See also: United States, Veterans' Bureau, *Annual Report of the Director*, published from 1922 to 1930, and the *Annual Report of the Administrator of Veterans' Affairs*, published since 1931.

VETO. Although the term veto goes back to the form in which the tribune of the plebs in ancient Rome sometimes countermanded orders of other officials, the modern use of the executive veto originated in England as part of the legislative process. At the outset of its history the House of Commons took no part in the formal enactment of legislation but merely petitioned the crown to make laws. Early in the fifteenth century, however, the House adopted the plan of presenting its petitions in the form of bills all ready to be enacted, and thereafter the crown simply gave or denied the royal assent. Thus there developed the absolute veto which was so freely exercised by the Tudor and Stuart monarchs. With the subsequent growth of ministerial responsibility the royal veto dwindled in importance; since the veto of the Scotch Militia Bill in 1708 it has never been exercised. In theory it still exists, but since all acts of the crown are guided by the advice of the prime minister, who controls a majority in the House of Commons, the need for a veto never arises.

While the royal veto was losing ground in England, it held its own in the American colonies, whither it had been translated from England. In the royal colonies the governors frequently vetoed acts of the colonial legislatures, and the English king occasionally disallowed measures which the governors had approved. Thus the first complaint in the Declaration of Independence states that George III had "refused his assent to laws the most wholesome and necessary for the public good."

In the Constitutional Convention of 1787 there was considerable discussion concerning the nature of the veto power which should be lodged in the hands of the president. Members of the convention were not prepared to give the president an absolute veto, such as the governors had possessed in colonial days; on the other hand, they did not think it proper to let Congress make laws without any executive check whatsoever. Accordingly they compromised upon a qualified executive veto, somewhat like the provision adopted by Massachusetts in 1776. Article 1, section 7, of the federal constitution provides that with the exception of a vote to adjourn all legislative bills, orders, resolutions and votes which require the concurrence of both houses must be submitted to the president for his approval. In practise, however, two exceptions to the requirement of presidential approval have been recognized: constitutional amendments and concurrent resolutions, as distinguished from joint resolutions. The constitution also sets forth in detail the procedure to be followed when the president does not approve a measure, including the arrangement for passing it over his veto by a two-thirds vote and the provision that a bill automatically becomes a law if it is neither approved nor disapproved within ten days after it is presented to him provided that Congress is still in session at the end of the period. The last qualification has made possible the so-called pocket veto in case Congress adjourns before the president has had ten days in which to take action. In such a case the president can veto the bill absolutely by simply refusing to sign it.

The earlier presidents used their veto power sparingly. During the initial forty years of the republic only 9 congressional measures failed to receive executive approval. In every case moreover the veto was based upon some inherent defect of the measure, not upon the president's personal objections to it. President Jackson set a new record by vetoing more bills than had all his predecessors combined. He claimed that the veto power was intended as a device with which the hand of Congress might be stayed whenever its action ran counter to the president's own views, and he utilized the power accordingly. Jackson's interpretation was criticized as a usurpation, but in due course it came to be accepted generally.

Although Tyler vetoed 9 measures in a single term, more than any president before him in an equal period of time, presidential vetoes were not again a source of serious controversy until President Johnson began to use them freely in his quarrel with Congress. Grant vetoed bills at about the same rate as Johnson but created less stir. The use of the veto reached its high point under Cleveland, who vetoed 115 bills in the year 1886, over 300 in his first term and over 40 in his second. Most of the bills which Cleveland vetoed were private pension bills. Other presidents have used their prerogative to a considerable extent, but in proportion to the total number of bills submitted to them there were fewer vetoes during the early decades of the twentieth century than in the first quarter of the nineteenth. Obviously the frequency of its use depends upon whether Congress and the president represent the same or different political parties. Under normal conditions the qualified veto power of the president tends to become absolute, for only in exceptional cases can the necessary two-thirds majority in both houses be mustered to override the president's action. Since Johnson's term, when Congress overrode 15 of his 21 vetoes, the requisite two-thirds majority has been attained on only twenty-seven occasions.

From the national constitution the qualified veto passed into the constitutions of the states, slowly in the case of the original states but more rapidly in the new states. It is now established in all the states except North Carolina. The arrangements relating to the governor's veto differ somewhat from state to state, especially with respect to the number of days during which the executive signature may be delayed and to the provision for the pocket veto, which exists in some states but not in others. Vetoes have been more common in the states than in the federal government and have been used more frequently in some states than in others.

Vetoes are most numerous where the governor has the power of item veto, or of rejecting individual sections or items in bills. The president of the United States does not have this power but must accept or reject each measure as a whole. The limitation is particularly serious in the case of appropriation bills, where the president must frequently tolerate obnoxious individual items because his rejection of the entire bill would delay the provision of funds urgently needed for the carrying on of the work of administration. This privilege of item veto, which exists in two states (Washington and South Carolina) for all bills and in more than half the states for appropriation bills only, gives the governor almost complete control over state expenditures. Objection to it has been raised on the ground that it enables the state executive to put undue pressure upon legislators who are deeply interested in particular appropriations. Occasionally moreover it encourages the governor's opponents to insert items which the governor will have to strike out, thereby incurring considerable popular odium.

From the state constitutions the executive veto has passed into the charters of most cities which have the mayor and council form of government. In some city charters moreover the mayor's authority has been strengthened by his being given an absolute veto over any budget increases. The pocket veto does not exist in cities. The tendency in both state and municipal government is to enlarge the veto power, thus increasing the powers of the executive and concentrating responsibility.

In European countries the absolute veto has virtually lapsed with the growth of ministerial responsibility. In England it has been lost through lack of use. In Sweden it was surrendered by the king only after a bitter struggle which lasted many years. In France the constitution permits the president to withhold his assent from a bill and to refer it back to the legislative body for reconsideration, but this prerogative has never been exercised. Some of the democratic constitutions adopted in Europe in the years immediately after the World War provided for a modified form of presidential veto. Under the Weimar constitution the president of the German Reich might instead of promulgating a law submit it to popular referendum, but this provision was never invoked. The Latvian president can, under the constitution, either return a bill to the Saeima for reconsideration or call for a public referendum on the measure. Only the constitutions of Czechoslovakia and Lithuania provide for a qualified presidential veto similar to that in the United States; repassage is possible in Czechoslovakia by an absolute majority of both houses or a three-fifths majority of all the members of the lower house and in Lithuania by a two-thirds vote of the Seimas. In Lithuania, however, the dictatorship renders the provision meaningless.

Aside from Czechoslovakia and Lithuania, the qualified veto has been adopted only by the Latin American republics. Most of these have incorporated in their constitutions a veto provision modeled on that of the United States, but in practise the provision has not operated similarly. The qualified veto is a logical device only in governments based upon the principle of separation of powers, which has found its most rigid application in the United States.

WILLIAM B. MUNRO

See: SEPARATION OF POWERS; LEGISLATIVE ASSEMBLIES; EXECUTIVE; DEADLOCK; LEGISLATION; GOVERNMENT; PREROGATIVE; CONGRESSIONAL GOVERNMENT.

Consult: Mason, E. C., *The Veto Power*, ed. by A. B. Hart, Harvard University, Historical Monographs, no. 1 (2nd ed. Boston 1891); Black, H. C., *The Relation of the Executive Power to Legislation* (Princeton 1919) ch. v; Hill, J. P., *The Federal Executive* (Boston 1916); Taft, W. H., *Our Chief Magistrate and His Powers*, Columbia University, George Blumenthal Foundation Lectures, 1915 (New York 1916) p. 14–28; Willoughby, W. W., *The Constitutional Law of the United States*, 3 vols. (2nd ed. New York 1929) vol. ii, p. 657–64; Greene, E. B., *The Provincial Governor in the English Colonies of North America*, Harvard University, Historical Studies, vol. vii (New York 1898); Fairlie, John A., "The Veto Power of the State Governor" in *American Political Science Review*, vol. xi (1917) 473–93; Holcombe, A. N., *State Government in the United States* (2nd ed. New York 1926); Mathews, J. M., *American State Government* (New York 1924) p. 222–28; Bates, F. G., and Field, O. P., *State Government* (New York 1928) p. 164, 210–12, 275–76; Story, R. M., *The American Municipal Executive*, University of Illinois, Studies in the Social Sciences, vol. vii, no. 3 (Urbana 1918) p. 131–39, 143–48, 196–98; Reed, T. H., *Municipal Government in the United States* (New York 1926) p. 54, 62, 68–69; Munro, W. B., *The Government of American Cities* (4th ed. New York 1926) p. 273–74; Bompard, Raoul, *Le veto du président de la République et la sanction royale* (Paris 1906); Zurcher, A. J., *The Experiment with Democracy in Central Europe* (New York 1933) p. 146.

VEUILLOT, LOUIS (1813–83), French journalist. Veuillot, a man of humble origin and little formal education, worked as a lawyer's clerk before beginning his journalistic career in 1831. In 1838, while at Rome, he became an enthusiastic convert to Catholicism and five years later assumed the editorship of the Catholic newspaper, the *Univers*. Through this organ he championed the cause of Catholicism with all the impulsive energy and violence of a man of the people. Inspired by an intransigent conviction which drew him into bitter controversies, he recognized only one standard for judging the various political parties and regimes: their attitude toward the church. It was because he believed Napoleon III to be the protector of Catholicism that he became under the Second Empire an uncompromising advocate of political absolutism. His castigation of any form of liberalism often recalls de Maistre, as does his defense of papal power. Veuillot's writings helped to raise French Catholics, particularly the lower clergy, to a position of influence and played a major part in the campaigns of Pope Pius IX for temporal power. The liberal Catholics repeatedly charged him with exaggeration, while the bishops sometimes regarded him as a lay intruder. But the Syllabus of Errors and the decree of papal infallibility by the Vatican Council of 1870 set an official seal upon his ideas, giving a new impetus to his social and religious influence. Two of Veuillot's works, *Les libres penseurs* (Paris 1848, 4th ed. 1866) and *Odeurs de Paris* (Paris 1866, new ed. 1867), constitute an indispensable record of French opinion between 1848 and 1870. His *Mélanges* (18 vols., Paris 1856–75; n.s., 4 vols., 1908–09), a collection of all his journalistic writings, is in effect a chronicle of the church during the pontificate of Pius IX. In his *Correspondance* the less militant side of his nature and his sensitiveness to social evils are expressed with the characteristic verve to which he owed much of his power as a journalist.

GEORGES GOYAU

Works: *Oeuvres complètes*, ed. by François Veuillot, vols. i–xxx (Paris 1924–34).

Consult: Veuillot, Eugène, *Vie de Louis Veuillot*, 4 vols. (Paris 1899–1914); Soltau, R., *French Political Thought in the Nineteenth Century* (London 1913), especially p. 176–88; Gurian, Waldemar, *Die politischen und sozialen Ideen des französichen Katholizismus (1789–1914)* (München-Gladbach 1929); Fernessole, Pierre, *Les origines littéraires de Louis Veuillot* (Paris 1923).

VICO, GIOVANNI BATTISTA (1668–1744), Italian philosopher. Vico, who was born in Naples in the midst of great poverty, secured in 1698 a minor teaching appointment for rhetoric at the university; this post together with his private teaching enabled him to subsist. The gradual development of Vico's ideas may be traced in some of his university lectures, principally *De nostri temporis studiorum ratione* (1709), in his metaphysical work *De antiquissima Italorum sapientia* (1710), in certain related polemics (1711–12) and in his vast treatise *De universi iuris uno principio et fine uno* (1720). His system is recapitulated and brought to perfection in the *Principî di una scienza nuova intorno alla commune natura delle nazioni* (1725) and especially in the second *Cinque libri de' principî di una scienza nuova* (1730, new ed. 1744).

Vico was bound to the philosophical traditions of humanism and the Renaissance, Italian political science and the historical interpretation of Roman law. He opposed vigorously the philosophy of Descartes, which was then being widely received in Europe. Descartes, Vico held, was entirely intellectualistic, and his philosophy disparaged history and poetry. Nevertheless, like Descartes, Vico found it necessary to withdraw into the spirit; the principle of knowledge which he opposed to the Cartesian principle of evidence was his profound interpretation of the statement that "we know only what we do" and that accordingly "action and truth are mutually convertible." Thus he recognized the wholly arbitrary and conventional character of mathematics and the reality of historical knowledge, humanity's living consciousness of what it has done. This was the basis of his conception of a *scienza nuova*; that is, his dialectical and historical conception of the spirit or, as he says, of the human mind. In spite of the intellectualistic tendencies of his own time and of the entire eighteenth century Vico gave prominence to the role of the imagination in humanity and in history and sketched a logic of poetry—an aesthetics as it was later called—an associated philosophy of language and a theory of the myth. On the other hand, he gave equal prominence to the period of force preceding the moral or ethical period, in which states representing subjection by the strong are founded. In his view of the historical development of mankind he shed new light on primitive language, consisting in imagination, rhythm and song; on the primitive thinking characterized by myths; on the primitive and genuine poetry of Homer in antiquity and of Dante in Christian times as distinct from the intellectualistic poetry of unpoetic eras and of the eighteenth century. In contrast to the stylized tales of contemporary historians he interpreted the barbaric character of ancient Greece, the nature of primitive Rome and its aristocratic institutions, and he conceived the Middle Ages as a return to primitive conditions of agricultural economy, of violence and subjection, of feudal relationships, serfdom or vassalage, of fierce and warlike religiosity, of aristocratic monarchies, of picture language and hieroglyphics, of heroic poetry. He was absorbed in the contemplation of the spiritual cycle in history: emergence from the bestial into the barbarian age, subsequent spiritual refinement through intellect and custom, the transition to the era of humanity, gradual enfeeblement in vital energy, corruption and relapse and then the resumption of the cycle. Vico accordingly remained impervious to the idea of simple and rectilinear progress which was the concept of the new century. Despite the pessimism which isolated him in an age of great revolutionary impetus the substance and the particular characteristics of his thought presented an ensemble of doctrines and of historical interpretations which were destined to integrate, correct and transform the rationalism of the eighteenth century. To his singular and perhaps unique position in the history of philosophy, an anachronism by virtue of his excess of genius, may be traced the almost complete ineffectiveness of his work in his own time.

Early in the nineteenth century the discovery of Vico aroused the astonishment and the admiration of Italian philosophers, politicians, historians and jurists, who had noted the philosophic, political and historical weakness of the Enlightenment and Jacobinism. From Italy his thought spread to France, where it became known principally through Jules Michelet. Elsewhere it was unheard of, misunderstood or disregarded down almost to the present time; now it is again claiming the attention of German and English scholars. There is much in Vico's work which still requires elaboration. Even where it may seem antiquated, however, it retains the educational value of original thought in its original form.

BENEDETTO CROCE

Works: *Opere*, ed. by G. Ferrari, 6 vols. (Milan 1835–37, 2nd ed. 1852–54); *Opere*, critical edition by F. Nicolini, vols. i–v (Bari 1911–31). *Scienza nuova* has been translated into German by Erich Auerbach (Munich 1924).

Consult: Croce, B., *La filosofia di Giovanni Battista Vico*, his Saggi filosofici, vol. ii (3rd ed. Bari 1933), tr. by R. G. Collingwood (London 1913); Werner, Karl, *Giambattista Vico als Philosoph und gelehrter Forscher* (Vienna 1879); Labanca, B., *G. B. Vico e i suoi critici cattolici* (Naples 1898); Peters, Richard, *Der Aufbau der Weltgeschichte bei Giambattista Vico* (Stuttgart 1929); Flint, Robert, *Vico* (Edinburgh 1884); Vaughan, C. E., *Studies in the History of Political Philosophy*, University of Manchester, Publications, nos. 166–67, 2 vols. (Manchester 1925) vol. i, p. 205–53; Croce, B., "Bibliographia vichiana" and supplements in Accademia Pontaniana, Naples, *Atti*, vols. xxxiv, xxxvii, xl (1904–10), in *Critica*, vols. xv–xix (1917–21), and in Accademia di Scienze Morali e Politiche, Naples, *Atti*, vols. li, lv (1927–32).

VICTOR EMMANUEL II (1820–78), Italian king. Victor Emmanuel II personified in the Italian Risorgimento the ideals of the monarchical current of the national liberal movement. The son of Charles Albert of Savoy, king of Sardinia and of Piedmont, he ascended the throne in March, 1849, after his father, defeated in the war with Austria, had abdicated and gone into exile. The first period of his reign (1849–59) was particularly difficult; the position of the little Savoyard state was precarious, as a result partly of the loss of the war, partly of the menace of Austria, which was dominant in the rest of northern Italy and was suspicious of Piedmont, where constitutional liberty was maintained and liberals from other parts of the peninsula could find refuge. But Victor Emmanuel, assisted by his great ministers Massimo d'Azeglio and Camillo di Cavour, successfully passed through this hazardous period. He improved economic and financial conditions, encouraged the productive forces and maintained the liberal constitutional regime, although absolutism and reaction held sway throughout the rest of Italy. As a result the Italians came to regard him as the symbol of the liberal national monarchy, and he gained the confidence of the great western powers France and England, which were his allies in the Crimean War (1854–56).

The fruits of this capable and liberal policy were gathered by Victor Emmanuel from 1859 to 1861, when, first with the assistance of Napoleon III in the war against Austria (1859) and then with the cooperation of the national movement promoted by Mazzini and Garibaldi in central and southern Italy, he extended his kingdom to include a large part of the peninsula and he took the title of king of Italy (March, 1861).

These great achievements were completed and consolidated in the following period of his reign. In 1866 through a new war against Austria, in which he was allied with Prussia, Victor Emmanuel succeeded in liberating Venetia; in 1870 the fall of Napoleon III, who had been the chief defender of the temporal power of the pope in Rome, permitted him to abolish that temporal power, which had existed for a thousand years, and to fulfil another part of the national program by moving the national capital to Rome. These great successes assured the definitive triumph of the monarchic current in the Italian Risorgimento as against the republican movement.

PIETRO SILVA

Consult: Bersezio, V., *Il regno di Vittorio Emanuele II*, 8 vols. (Turin 1878–95); Massari, G., *La vita ed il regno di Vittorio Emanuele II*, 2 vols. (new ed. Milan 1896); Rosi, M., *Vittorio Emanuele II*, 2 vols. (Bologna 1930); Godking, G. S., *Life of Victor Emmanuel II* (new ed. London 1880); King, Bolton, *History of Italian Unity, 1814–71*, 2 vols. (London 1899).

VIDAL DE LA BLACHE, PAUL MARIE JOSEPH (1845–1918), French geographer. Vidal de la Blache first devoted himself to history, but his stay at the French schools of Rome and of Athens as well as his reflections upon the events of 1870 led him to forsake history for geography. In 1873 Vidal de la Blache was appointed professor at the University of Nancy, in 1877 director of lectures at the École Normale Supérieure and in 1898 professor at the University of Paris.

His early work in geography led to notable improvements in the teaching of the subject, which in France had fallen to a very low plane. He then turned more and more to research, especially in the field of human geography; and the points of contact between his work and the sociological sciences constantly increased. Among his major contributions was the application of the regional method to geographical studies. This method was essentially synthetic, since it postulated the inseparability of geographic and sociological data in a specific, objectively defined region. For twenty years this method has served as the basis for the reform projects put forward by French regionalists. Vidal de la Blache also studied and developed the environmental theory previously outlined by Montesquieu, Vico and Buckle. He demonstrated the relative and variable elements in this theory and emphasized that the effect of human societies upon physical environment is no less significant than the influence of natural causes upon society and that, in densely populated and highly civilized lands, the equilibrium of the living world is a function of man himself and of the natural forces which he disciplines. His conclusion was that "geographical causes influence man only through the medium of social facts." Vidal de la Blache's greatest contributions are the studies which he made toward the end of his life on large human groups, although he did not have time to present these in definitive form. As a tribute to the importance of his work he was awarded in 1915 the gold

medal of the American Geographical Society.
CAMILLE VALLAUX

Principal works: *Atlas général géographique et historique* (Paris 1894); *Tableau de la géographie de la France*, Histoire de France, ed. by E. Lavisse, vol. i, pt. i (Paris 1903); *La France de l'est* (Paris 1917); *Principes de géographie humaine*, ed. by E. de Martonne (Paris 1922), tr. by M. T. Bingham (New York 1926).

Consult: Gallois, L., "Paul Vidal de la Blache" in *Annales de géographie*, vol. xxvii (1918) 161–73; Bourgeois, Émile, "Notice sur la vie et les travaux de M. Paul Vidal de la Blache" in Académie des Sciences Morales et Politiques, *Séances et travaux . . . Compte rendu*, vol. lxxxi (1921) pt. i, p. 221–54.

VIJNANESVĀRA (1076–1127), Hindu jurist. Vijnanesvāra's activity coincided with the reign of the Chālukya king, Vikramāditya VI of Kalyāna (Deccan). His principal work, the *Mitākshara*, or concise treatise (ed. by L. Nyayalankára, Calcutta 1829), serves as the foundation of law for all Hindus except Bengalis. In Gujarat and the island of Bombay it has been supplanted by a later work of the same school, the *Vyavahāra Mayukha* of Nilkantha Bhatta (text and translation by J. R. Gharpure, Collections of Hindu Law Texts, nos. xiv–xv, Bombay, n.d.); in the Madras Presidency the *Smrti Chandrika* of Devanna Bhatta (text and translation by J. R. Gharpure, Collections of Hindu Law Texts, nos. xi–xii, Bombay, n.d.) was preferred before British rule, but the *Mitākshara* is now predominant. Neither of these writers differs greatly from Vijnanesvāra.

The *Mitākshara*, following Yājnavalkya, is divided into three parts, discussing respectively religious observances, civil law and penances. The subsection on inheritance has been translated by H. T. Colebrooke and is included in the *Two Treatises on the Hindu Law of Inheritance* (Calcutta 1810; reprinted in *Hindu Law Books*, ed. by W. Stokes, Madras 1865; and other selections in West, R., and Majid Abdul, *A Digest of the Hindu Law*, 4th ed. London 1919, p. 1087–90); the entire first part has been translated by Rai Bahadur Srisa Chandra Vidyārnava (Allahabad 1918), and the second part by J. R. Gharpure (Bombay 1920). In form the *Mitākshara* is a gloss, sentence by sentence, on the Yājnavalkya *Smrti*, with copious quotations from other sources. By finely drawn logical distinctions, etymological argument and reconciliation of conflicting texts the writer achieved a synthesis of pre-existing legal material which enjoyed wide legislative authority, but it is arguable that some of his innovations are not revivals of pre-sastric tradition. He explains away texts giving the father absolute powers of disposition by saying that they refer only to self-acquired property; in property inherited from their father or father's father sons acquire an indefeasible ("unobstructed") right by birth, and they can, again in the face of express *Smrti* texts, compel a partition of the property even in the father's lifetime. The father, although still described by titles implying sole ownership of the family property, is only *primus inter pares*: of the patria potestas in its property aspect there remain only a power to make trifling gifts of joint family property to a daughter or for a religious purpose and the pious duty of the sons to pay their father's debts if not abnormal (*avyāvahārik*) in character. In the same spirit of family communism Vijnanesvāra endeavored to cut down the peculia of the sons. Manu and Yājnavalkya had allowed the gains of learning or of the sword to be private property. Vijnanesvāra added the condition "provided they have been gained without detriment to joint family funds." He was also to some extent a feminist; although in his legal system (in contrast to the Bengal law) a woman can have no share in the joint family property, Vijnanesvāra endeavored by another fictitious interpretation of his text to enlarge her private property rights. In this, however, he failed, perhaps because of the troubled conditions in the centuries which followed. Inheritance in Vijnanesvāra's scheme is even more strongly agnatic than in the Bengal school; no cognate, except the daughter's son, can succeed until all agnates are exhausted. In spite of this fact, it is commonly said that his criterion for inheritance is consanguinity, or in his own phrase "community of particles of the same body." He does, it is true, apply this principle as one of his grounds for preferring the mother to the father as an heir. But the obscure passage on which a general theory of consanguinity has been based occurs not in the chapter on inheritance but in the chapter dealing with prohibited degrees in marriage. It is doubtful how far the resulting chaos of cognate inheritance which British courts have evolved can be justified by anything in the *Mitākshara*.

SEYMOUR VESEY-FITZGERALD

Consult: Kane, P. V., *History of Dharmaśāstra*, Bhandarkar Oriental Research Institute, Government Oriental series, Class B, no. 6, vol. i– (Poona 1930–) vol. i, p. 287–93; Ghose, J. C., *The Principles of Hindu Law* (2nd ed. Calcutta 1906); Venkatarama Aiyar, S., *Outlines of Hindu Law* (Madras 1931).

VILLAGE. *See* RURAL SOCIETY.

VILLAGE COMMUNITY. The village community consists of a group of related or unrelated persons larger than a single family, occupying a large house or a number of dwellings placed close together, sometimes irregularly, sometimes in a street, and cultivating, originally in common, a number of arable fields, dividing the available meadowland between them and pasturing their cattle upon the surrounding waste land, over which the community claims rights as far as the boundaries of adjacent communities. In historic times most such villages were under the rule of a lord, who governed the people and administered justice, receiving in return the labor of the community for the cultivation of his share of the land. It has been asserted by many authorities that the institution of the lordship is of relatively recent origin and that it was superimposed upon an originally lordless community.

Research into the nature and origin of village communities began in the middle of the nineteenth century. The earliest studies were devoted to the institution among primitive peoples and led to the development of theories of the village community, many of which derived their impetus largely from the eighteenth century glorification of the free primitive man and his equitable social system. Olufsen and other Danish writers described the original coownership and common cultivation of the soil in Denmark and Holstein by village communities, but the subject became better known through the works of Georg L. von Maurer, whose first work on the origin of the German mark, *Einleitung zur Geschichte der Mark-, Hof-, Dorf- und Stadtverfassung und der öffentlichen Gewalt* (Munich; 2nd ed. by H. Cunow, Vienna 1896), appeared in 1854. Although he took cognizance of similar institutions among all European peoples, including Germans, Scandinavians, Celts and Slavs, as well as among certain Asiatic peoples and the Mexicans in America, his concern was chiefly with the village community in Germany. When he wrote, most of the common fields and all signs of common cultivation had disappeared but many features of the village communities still survived. Maurer believed that the mark was a large clearing made in the woodland by a group of early pastoral Teutons who settled in a land formerly uninhabited. His thesis was that for the sake of security this group of related individuals or families placed their houses close together in the center of the clearing and cultivated in common the surrounding arable fields, while they allowed their beasts to graze on the waste beyond. As the population increased they added more common fields, which sometimes numbered three, four, five or even six, enlarging the clearing until it met those of other groups. With the continued growth in population there was a tendency to found other smaller and subsidiary villages in the waste and sometimes in later periods isolated houses with enclosed lands held in severalty. Ultimately the mark came under the rule of a king, who received tribute in kind and sometimes passed on many of his dues and responsibilities to one of his nobles. Thus the members of the originally free community became serfs of a landlord.

In 1861 Sir Henry Maine, apparently in ignorance of these earlier works on the village community, published his *Ancient Law* (London), in which, basing his argument partly on practises in Russia and other Slavonic countries, partly on survivals in the Roman law but mainly on the land system in India, he argued that land was originally held in common by groups of people, for the most part of common descent but including strangers who had been adopted. Ten years later he published *Village Communities in the East and West* (London 1871, 7th ed. 1895), which contained a more complete study of the Indian village. Between 1865 and 1872 the problem of village communities was treated by Haxthausen, Gierke, Elton, Stemann, Innes and especially by Fustel de Coulanges, in his *La cité antique* in 1864 (Paris; tr. by W. Small, 12th ed. Boston 1901). In 1869 Nasse's study of the agricultural community in England, *Über die mittelalterliche Feldgemeinschaft und die Einhegungen des 16. Jahrhunderts in England* (Bonn; tr. by H. Ouvry, 2nd ed. London 1872), had appeared.

In *De la propriété et de ses formes primitives* (Paris 1874; tr. by G. Marriot, London 1878) Laveleye reviewed the village communities in Russia, Java, Switzerland and many other countries and noted that the same institution was found among all the Slavonic nations and in China and India, while it had formerly existed in Germany and among the nations of antiquity. He believed that all peoples utilized this economic form as they passed from a pastoral to an agricultural state and that communal ownership was natural at this phase of development. Throughout the work he sympathized with the equality in wealth which he implied in the village communal system and contrasted it with contemporary inequality, which he considered a danger to the state. His views were ardently seized upon by the advocates of socialistic doctrines, who pointed to communal ownership and equality as fundamental and natural social institutions. The scientific study of village communities had thus been checked by polemical discussions when Fustel de Coulanges published his great work, *Histoire des institutions politiques de l'ancienne France* (6 vols., Paris 1875-92), in which after careful research he denied the whole conception of the free self-governing German mark with its common ownership of the land. This work aroused wide opposition, and Glasson attempted to answer it in *Les communaux et le domaine rural à l'époque franque: réponse à M. Fustel de Coulanges* (Paris 1890). In 1892 Baden-Powell described the land system in India (*The Land System of British India*, Oxford), criticizing the views advanced by Maine, and four years later published a fuller account entitled *The Indian Village Community* (London 1896) with a more detailed criticism of Maine. The view that communal ownership of agricultural land was the primitive system was questioned also by Ashley (*An Introduction to English Economic History and Theory*, 2 vols., London 1894), by Pollock and Maitland (*History of English Law before the Time of Edward I*, 2 vols., Cambridge, Eng. 1898) and again by Maitland in *Domesday Book and Beyond* (Cambridge, Eng. 1897). Lewinski's *The Origin of Property* (London School of Economics, Studies, no. 30, London 1913) stated the case more fully, and it has been restated more recently by Sanderson (*The Rural Community*, Boston 1932).

Meanwhile in 1883 Seebohm published *The English Village Community* (London, 4th ed. 1890), in which, avoiding the question of the communal or individual origin of landed property, he endeavored to show that in England the village community had developed from a semipastoral system in vogue in the west of the British Isles, perhaps under Roman influence. He followed this with two volumes on the tribal organization of the Saxons and Welsh, while Gomme produced an interesting work on village communities in general entitled *The Village Community* (London 1890). Guiraud in *La propriété foncière en Grèce jusqu'à la conquête romaine* (Paris 1893) discussed the evidence from ancient Greece, concluding that clan ownership of land had existed among the early Greeks; similar institutions were ascribed to the Romans before the agrarian laws by Maine, Laveleye and H. E. Seebohm. Jubainville wrote on the organization of the Celt (*La famille celtique*, Paris 1905), Slater discussed the British common fields (*The English Peasantry and the Enclosure of Common Fields*, London 1907), and between 1892 and 1907 Vinogradoff produced a series of works dealing with the English manor. A number of other volumes also appeared, mainly on the village system in Russia and other Slavonic lands and in Scandinavian countries.

One of the outstanding works on the village community was Meitzen's *Siedelung und Agrarwesen der Westgermanen und Ostgermanen* (3 vols., Berlin 1895), in which he discussed the different types of villages, dividing them into "nucleated villages" and "scattered homesteads." He noted the difference in plan between the villages of Teutonic and those of Slavonic origin and thought the scattered homesteads were the work of the Celts. The latter view has now been abandoned, for the scattered homesteads seem always to be found where the land is or was formerly wooded; it seems likely also that many scattered homesteads are relatively late, dating from the decay of the village community.

Village communities have been noted in many parts of the world and are thought to have existed in others where they are no longer extant. The evidence has been well summarized by Sanderson, who classifies such communities under three headings. His first series he calls the migratory agricultural village, which cannot properly be described as a village community, since the people are seminomadic and live in fixed abodes for periods usually measured by months. Under this heading he cites many of the more primitive peoples of the Malay Peninsula, on the authority of Skeat and Blagden, and certain tribes living in the Amazon region. In the next series, the semipermanent agricultural villages, the settlements are made for fifteen, ten or even fewer years; but eventually the fertility of the soil becomes exhausted and the village community seeks fresh lands. Such semipermanent communities existed in the past among the American Indians, including the Iroquois, and are at present to be found throughout southeastern Asia and Melanesia and in large parts of Africa. The best known contemporary examples are among the pagan tribes in Borneo, as described by Hose and McDougall, the Fangs in west Africa and the Nagas of Assam, as described by Hutton. The third type, the permanent agricultural settlement, which is the basis of the true village community, is also widespread. It prevailed and still persists in many parts of Europe, India and China. It is found today in southeast Asia, among the Mafulus in British New Guinea, among the Nagas of Manipur and among the Basutos and was formerly the unit of organization among the Hurons in America.

Village communities exist all over China, except in Szechwan, where scattered homesteads are the rule; recent archaeological discoveries show that such villages date from the neolithic age in the third millennium B.C. A modern Chinese village community is usually inhabited by several joint families belonging to the same clan, although sometimes several clans are represented among the occupants of one village. The houses of the village are grouped together and the villagers possess well defined rights in the common pasture. Where two or more clans are found in a village, the commons are generally clan rather than communal lands. No family can alienate its land without the consent of its clan.

In India the village community dates from at least the Vedic period; Maine stated that it was general throughout India in his time. Baden-Powell showed, however, that less than a third of the cultivated soil was communally held while more than two thirds was occupied by ryotwari villages, where individual ownership of arable was the rule. In the latter the landowners of the village had rights in the commons; although these are now regarded as the property of the government and no new settlements may be established upon them without its consent, the rights of the villagers in them are still recognized to a limited extent. In the other villages, which are either jointly owned or under the jurisdiction of a landlord, allotments in the arable are regarded as shares in the jointly held land, while the waste is the property of the community. Kennett has suggested that village communities existed in Palestine under the monarchy, and that since the invading Hebrews continued to be mainly pastoral, these were of Canaanite origin.

In Europe the most persistent communities occur among the Slavonic peoples, who recently imagined that this system was their exclusive prerogative. The literature on this subject is extensive. The Russian mir was first described in Haxthausen (*Studien über die innern Zustände; das Volksleben*, 3 vols., Hanover 1847–52), but soon afterwards Chicherin in a survey of the Russian *obshchina* denied that this form of community was primitive, asserting that it was a creation of the government designed to facilitate tax collection. A number of works appeared on the subject. These were summarized by Kovalevsky (*Modern Customs and Ancient Laws of Russia*, London 1891), who argued that this type of village community was ancient in Russia, since it was mentioned in the *Pravda* of Yaroslav at the end of the eleventh century. It was held by a community of kinsmen, the shares being usually unequal since each householder's portion became divided among his sons. Such communities were the rule in north Russia, where they were often of great antiquity, and were found in south Russia on either side of the Dnieper. During the sixteenth and seventeenth centuries colonists crossed to the east of that river to occupy the open steppes in the government of Chernigov, founding villages on the old model. For a time they brought fresh land under cultivation each year and abandoned it after harvest, but with closer settlement this practise ceased. In 1719 Peter the Great abolished the land tax and introduced a capitation tax; this led to the periodic redistribution of land among households and eventually among individuals, so that in time a certain number of acres were allotted to each individual. In Little Russia the communities seem to have had no lords until a feudal nobility and the institution of serfdom were introduced by Catherine II. In the central governments a two-field system may be traced back to 1511; later a three-field system became more general and the redistribution of lands took place every third or sixth year. In Siberia, as Lewinski has shown, the pastoral tribes when they began to lead an agricultural life first took up land individually; as in time this led to great inequalities in wealth, the poorer members of the tribe petitioned the government to introduce the community system that was general in European Russia. Kocharovsky, arguing from the Siberian experience as well as from statistical and historical material, holds that the modern Russian land commune did not evolve from earlier kinship collectives and that it did not develop primarily as a result of serfdom or taxation. It was, he believes, preceded by the more individualistic system of hereditary family occupancy tenures and was due to the growing pressure of population, which led to a diminution in the size of holdings and more intensive agriculture. The process of transformation was given a decided impetus by the factors attendant upon the abolition of serfdom, and despite the efforts of the Soviet government after 1928 to eradicate it the land commune in the U.S.S.R. showed a tendency to persist.

Until recently there were to be found in Serbia family organizations known as zadrugas. Troyanovitch says that the zadruga was a large family or clan, organized on a patrilineal basis, dwelling in one large house and holding all its land, livestock and money in common. These zadrugas continued for several generations without division, often including as many as one hundred individuals. They were ruled by an elder (*stareshina*), usually the oldest member of the household capable of exerting authority, who apportioned the work among the different members, each having an allotted task. When a zadruga broke up, the stores were divided equally among all the members, but the lands among the males only. This system obtained also in Montenegro, in Croatia and with some difference in north Albania, and Cvijic says in *La péninsule balkanique* (Paris 1918) that it extended from the Adriatic well into Bulgaria, although it was not general in that country. Laveleye gave a full account of this system, which seems to have been common to all the Southern Slavs, and it has been argued that there is evidence of its former existence among the Czechs and Poles and even among the Russians; communal houses were certainly common in the Ukraine at one time. The presence of the communal house in Albania, however, suggests that a similar organization may have existed in the Balkans before the arrival of the Slavs. In Albania the chief is the patrilineal head of the family.

Very similar to the system described among the Southern Slavs is that which obtained until the Middle Ages in the west of the British Isles. The Irish system was described by Maine and the customs of the west Highlands of Scotland by Skene and Seebohm. In these regions the family lived together, holding the land in common for four generations and usually dividing it in the fifth. In Ireland such households sometimes lived in villages, but in most parts of Wales they occupied homesteads which were either scattered or clustered in small groups. In Wales each male was allotted five *erws*, or acres, in Ireland, thirty to sixty acres; these holdings were cultivated jointly. Each male of the same generation held the same number of acres, and these at his death were divided equally among his sons; but at the death of the last member of a generation the entire arable was redivided equally among the surviving males. The fields were divided into long strips known as rigs; in Scotland and Ireland the method of cultivation was called the rundale, or runrig, system. In Wales the people were mainly pastoral and plowed up only sufficient of the waste to meet their needs, allowing it to relapse at the end of the year or after three years; this has been called "co-aration of the waste." It is doubtful, however, whether the term village community should be applied to such impermanent communal organizations as those of Wales. Many writers have regarded the Welsh system as a survival of the original Celtic community, a view expressly stated by Vinogradoff. As in the case of other survivals in western Britain, the question has arisen whether it should not be traced back to pre-Celtic times.

The French evidence, although touched upon by Laveleye, was first fully treated by Bloch in *Les caractères originaux de l'histoire rurale française* (Oslo 1931). Bloch noted three systems of village communities. The system of enclosed fields was found west of a line drawn from the mouth of the Seine to Navarre, except for the region near the mouth of the Loire; it existed also in the region of the Perche. The second system, containing open fields divided into nearly square irregular patches, was evident for the most part south of the Loire; there appears to have been no communal cultivation of these. The third system, which consists of open fields divided into long strips, was customary north of the Loire, except in the Pays de Caux, and extended also throughout Burgundy. In this area the three-field system obtained, while in the second area the two-field system was more general. Although landholding in France has become almost completely individualized, considerable communal feeling persists, especially in Brittany.

Studies of village communities in Germany have been made by many writers; the best summary is by Seebohm in *English Village Community*, based on the work of Landau, Hanssen and Meitzen; according to this presentation various systems appear to have existed. In some of the mountainous parts of Germany and Switzerland there was a type of community closely resembling that of Wales, known as *Feldgraswirthschaft*, which involved the coaration of the waste. If the description of Germany given by Tacitus is trustworthy, this system was widespread in his time. Reference has already been made to the scattered homesteads noted by Meitzen in Westphalia and elsewhere; these are found most frequently in wooded regions and are probably relatively late in origin. Elsewhere the nucleated village, with its common fields, seems to have prevailed, although, as Meitzen has pointed out, the villages settled by the Slavs are of more regular form, with the houses built on a street. There is a striking difference between the north and the south of the country, for in the area south of the Lippe and the Teutoburger Wald there were three common fields divided into strips, while north of this line and in Saxony as well as in Belgium, Holland and Denmark a one-field system predominated. The communities seem to have consisted originally of related individuals and were usually, at any rate in the Middle Ages, under a lord, who had received his rights from the king. There were, however, exceptions, the most notable of which were the communities in Frisia, Drenthe and the district of Dithmarschen in Holstein, in Westerwald between Drenthe and the Ems, in the country around Delbrück in the east of Westphalia and in the forest cantons of Switzerland. The Dithmarschen communities have been described by Laveleye. They consisted of related groups which had come from Frisia and Saxony and been placed under the overlordship of the bishop of Bremen; the latter exercised no authority over them but left them to be governed by forty-eight elected councilors. In the fourteenth century they were said to be living without a lord or chief. Communities similar to those of north Germany existed in Denmark and south Sweden and in some parts of Norway, where, however, because of geographical conditions and perhaps because of late settlement the scattered homesteads were more usual.

The English community was studied by Nasse, Seebohm, Maitland, Slater and Vinogradoff. The most usual village in England, especially in the southeastern half of the country, was the valley village. Just above the flood plain, on which lay its water meadows, the village proper was located and around it were the common fields, usually three in number, divided into a number of acre strips, a furlong in length and four poles in width. Beyond extended the waste, woodland, heath or downland, reaching usually to the top of the slope, where it met the waste belonging to a village in the next valley. Such an area was a township, sometimes incorrectly called a tithing, a name which more accurately signifies its inhabitants. Besides these valley villages there were hill villages, in some cases later in origin, although dating back to Saxon times; in others perhaps survivals of an earlier type. Finally, some townships had no villages but a number of scattered homesteads; these were usual in areas formerly densely wooded and were probably even later in origin than the hill villages, although they existed before the Norman Conquest. Crawford has pointed out that air photographs show signs of the former existence of hill villages with a number of small rectangular enclosures; these, which he believes were occupied between 450 B.C. and 450 A.D., he has called Celtic lynchets ("Air Survey and Archeology" in *Geographical Journal*, vol. lxi, 1923, p. 342–66).

When Maurer and Laveleye were writing, anthropologists believed that all mankind had passed or was passing through identical stages of culture, such as the hunting, pastoral and agricultural phases. Even the most convinced opponent of the diffusion school would not subscribe to that doctrine today; indeed there is evidence that the earliest inhabitants of Susa and Anau cultivated grain but had no domesticated beasts. Again at that time it was believed that the Aryans had introduced grain and cattle into a Europe either uninhabited or peopled solely by savages in the hunting stage; and it was assumed that they must have been responsible for the first village communities, although as early as 1890 Gomme suggested a pre-Aryan origin.

Moreover at that time nothing was known of prehistory, nor had much been discovered about prehistoric villages even when Lewinski wrote. Since then the labors of many archaeologists in central Europe, the results of whose work were summarized by Childe in *The Dawn of European Civilization* (London 1925) and *The Danube in Prehistory* (Oxford 1929), have supplied information. According to Peake, agriculture, with which the permanent community is indissolubly tied, seems to have arisen in or near Syria and spread thence to Egypt, Mesopotamia and Asia Minor. From Mesopotamia it passed to Persia and thence to the Indus basin, while from Asia Minor it was carried to Turkestan, to the "black earth" lands of southwest Russia and Transylvania, to Thessaly and to the middle Danube basin. In each of these areas arose villages, of such a size as to postulate the presence of a community. About the middle of the third millennium B.C. and again on later occasions the pastoral peoples from the steppes between the Dnieper and the Hindu Kush invaded the agricultural areas and may well have established themselves as lords over the peasants. The Danubian culture spread to the valley of the Rhine, but further west the knowledge of agriculture spread from Spain, whither it had been brought from Greece about 2400 B.C.; Jacquetta Hawkes has suggested, however, on the basis of certain evidence that it arrived two centuries earlier in the south of France and thence spread over the west, where the people seem to have been mainly pastoral folk, growing small crops of grain. Toward the close of the second millennium B.C. the culture of central Europe was carried to both the Baltic and the Atlantic coasts.

It is obvious that village communities, especially in Europe, possess many similar features, some or all of which are occasionally absent; it seems unwise to assume, however, that all of these are features of the earliest communities or that all have the same origin. Except in the case of scattered homesteads, which seem to be a late development, and in some of the semipastoral communities of the west of Britain people appear to have lived in nucleated villages since the dawn of agriculture. The communities were always on a kindred basis, except in England, where the family tie seems to have been broken by oversea migration. These kindreds were usually tribally organized on a patrilineal basis, often under a chief, or headman; this organization may well have been an Aryan feature. Sometimes the community was under the rule of a lord, who was not the tribal chief but a delegate of the king; this is certainly true of England in the later centuries of Saxon rule. Nevertheless, free communities survived, as at Dithmarschen. Except among the semipastoral communities of west Britain a characteristic of the village community was the common open fields; a one-field system obtained in the plain of north Germany and a three-field system in an area stretching from England across northeastern France to the Danube basin and extending eastwards to Transylvania, where in 1863 Boner noted the system in Szekler villages at Buczacz and near Sepsiszentgyörgy. These fields were divided into irregular or rectangular plots or else into long narrow strips, usually an acre in extent. Bloch associated these strips in northeastern France with the wheeled plow, which, according to Pliny, was introduced into the west in the early iron age from Rhaetia. Thus the evidence points to the Danube basin as the place of origin of the three-field system and the wheeled plow. Karslake has suggested that this plow was introduced into Britain by the Belgae, and the discoveries made in 1933 by Birkbeck and Stuart of the presence of Belgic pottery in the turned over soil on a long strip of cultivation near Winchester seem to support his view.

HAROLD J. E. PEAKE

See: AGRICULTURE; PEASANTRY; RURAL SOCIETY; LAND TENURE; MANORIAL SYSTEM; FEUDALISM; SERFDOM; COMMUNISM; SOCIAL ORGANIZATION; SMALL HOLDINGS.

Consult: Peake, H. J. E., *The Origins of Agriculture* (London 1928); Hawkes, J., "Aspects of the Neolithic and Chalcolithic Periods in Western Europe" in *Antiquity*, vol. viii (1934) 24–42; Karslake, J. B. P., "Plough Coulters from Silchester" in *Antiquaries Journal*, vol. xiii (1933) 455–63; Feist, Sigmund, *Kultur, Ausbreitung und Herkunft der Indogermanen* (Berlin 1913) p. 123–46; Hildebrand, Richard, *Recht und Sitte auf den primitiveren wirtschaftlichen Kulturstufen* (2nd ed. Jena 1907) p. 43–189; Maine, H. S., *Lectures on the Early History of Institutions* (London 1875) chs. iii–iv; Fustel de Coulanges, N. D., "Le problème des origines de la propriété foncière" in *Revue des questions historiques*, vol. xlv (1889) 349–439, tr. by M. Ashley with an introduction by W. J. Ashley (London 1891); Vinogradoff, P., *Outlines of Historical Jurisprudence*, 2 vols. (London 1920–22) vol. i, p. 321–43; Landau, G., *Die Territorien in Bezug auf ihre Bildung und ihre Entwicklung* (Hamburg 1854); Kennett, Robert Hatch, *Ancient Hebrew Social Life and Custom as Indicated in Law, Narrative and Metaphor* (London 1933) p. 73–82; Pöhlmann, Robert von, *Geschichte der sozialen Frage und des Sozialismus in der antiken Welt*, 2 vols. (3rd ed. by Friedrich Oertel, Munich 1925) vol. i, chs. i–ii; Seebohm, H. E., *On the Structure of Greek Tribal Society* (London 1895) ch. iv; Kovalevsky, Maxim, *Ekonomicheskiy rost Evropi do vozniknoveniya kapitalisticheskago khozyaystva*, 3 vols. (Moscow 1898–1900), tr. by Leo Motzkin and others as *Die ökonomische Entwicklung Europas bis zum Beginn der kapitalistischen Wirtschaftsform*, 7 vols. (Berlin 1901–14) vols. i–iii; Elton, C. I., *A Treatise on Commons and Waste Lands* (London 1868); Hanssen, Georg, "Zur Geschichte der Feldsysteme in Deutschland" in his *Agrarhistorische Abhandlungen*, 2 vols. (Leipsic 1880–84) vol. i, p. 123–387; Meitzen, August, "Die Ausbreitung der Deutschen in Deutschland und ihre Besiedelung der Slawengebiete" in *Jahrbücher für Nationalökonomie und Statistik*, vol. xxxii (1879) 1–59, and "Georg Hanssen, als Agrar-Historiker" in *Zeitschrift für die gesammte Staatswissenschaft*, vol. xxxvii (1881) 371–417; Maurer, Georg Ludwig von, *Geschichte der Markenverfassung in Deutschland* (Erlangen 1856), *Geschichte der Fronhöfe, der Bauernhöfe und der Hofverfassung in Deutschland*, 4 vols. (Erlangen 1862–63), and *Geschichte der Dorfverfassung in Deutschland*, 2 vols. (Erlangen 1865–66); Gierke, Otto von, *Rechtsgeschichte der deutschen Genossenschaft*, his Deutsche Genossenschaftsrecht, vol. i (Berlin 1868) p. 12–218, 514–30, 581–637; Lamprecht, K., *Deutsches Wirtschaftsleben im Mittelalter*, 3 vols. (Leipsic 1885–86) vol. i, pt. i; Sering, Max, *Erbrecht und Agrarverfassung in Schleswig-Holstein*, Landwirtschaftliche Jahrbücher, vol. xxxvii, supplement v, pt. ii (Berlin 1908); Dopsch, A., *Die ältere Wirtschafts- und Sozialgeschichte der Bauern in den Alpenländern Oesterreichs*, Instituttet for sammenlignende Kulturforskning, Oslo, Publikationer, ser. A, no. 11 (Oslo 1930); Skene, W. F., *Celtic*

Scotland, 3 vols. (Edinburgh 1876–80) vol. iii; Innes, C. N., *Lectures on Scotch Legal Antiquities* (Edinburgh 1872) ch. vi; Seebohm, F., *Tribal Custom in Anglo-Saxon Law* (London 1902), *The Tribal System in Wales* (2nd ed. London 1904), and *Customary Acres and Their Historical Importance* (London 1914); Vinogradoff, P., *The Growth of the Manor* (3rd ed. London 1920), *Villainage in England* (Oxford 1892) p. 223–409, and *English Society in the Eleventh Century* (Oxford 1908) p. 219–479; Peake, H. J. E., *The English Village* (London 1922); Gray, H. L., *English Field Systems*, Harvard Historical Studies, vol. xxii (Cambridge, Mass. 1915); Gonner, E. C. K., *Common Land and Inclosure* (London 1912); Scrutton, Thomas E., *Commons and Common Fields* (Cambridge, Eng. 1887); Steenstrup, J. C. H. R., *Studier over Kong Valdemars Jordebog* (Copenhagen 1874) ch. iii; Stemann, C. L. E., *Den danske Retshistorie* (Copenhagen 1871); Lauridsen, P., "Om gamle danske Landsbyformer" in *Aarbøger for nordisk Oldkyndighed og Historie*, 2nd ser., vol. xi (1896) 97–170; Taranger, A., *Udsigt over den norske rets historie*, 2 vols. (Christiania 1898–1904); Bogišić, Baltazar, *Zbornik sadašnjih pravnih običaja kod Južnih Slovena* (Collection of present day legal customs in southern Slovenia) (Zagreb 1874); Demelić, F., *Le droit coutumier des Slaves méridionaux d'après les recherches de M. V. Bogišić* (Paris 1876) p. 23–63, 130–38; Dopsch, Alfons, *Die ältere Sozial- und Wirtschaftsverfassung der Alpenslaven* (Weimar 1909); Krauss, F. S., *Sitte und Brauch der Südslaven* (Vienna 1885) p. 64–128; Peisker, J., *Die älteren Beziehungen der Slawen zu Turkotataren und Germanen und ihre sozialgeschichtliche Bedeutung* (Stuttgart 1905); Boner, Charles, *Transylvania; Its Products and Its People* (London 1865) chs. viii–ix; Troyanovitch, S., "Manners and Customs" in *Servia by the Servians*, ed. by Alfred Stead (London 1909) ch. xii; Robinson, G. T., *Rural Russia under the Old Regime* (New York 1932); Chicherin, B., "Obzor istoricheskago razvitiya selskoy obshchini v Rossii" (A survey of the historical development of the land commune in Russia) in his *Opiti po istorii russkago prava* (Moscow 1858) p. 1–58; Haxthausen, August von, *Die ländliche Verfassung Russlands* (Leipsic 1866); Tschuprow, Alexander, *Die Feldgemeinschaft*, Abhandlungen aus dem staatswissenschaftlichen Seminar zu Strassburg, no. 18 (Strasbourg 1902); Kaufman, A. A., *Russkaya obshchina v protsesse eya zarozhdeniya i rosta* (The Russian village community in the process of its formation and growth) (Moscow 1908), *Krestyanskaya obshchina v Sibiri* (The peasant commune in Siberia) (St. Petersburg 1897), and *Sbornik statey: obshchina, pereselenie, statistika* (Collection of articles: the village community, population, statistics) (Moscow 1915); Kachorovsky, K. R., *Russkaya obshchina* (The Russian land commune), vol. i– (2nd ed. Moscow 1907–), "Burokraticheskyi zakon i krestyanskaya obshchina" (Bureaucratic law and the peasant commune) in *Russkoe bogatstvo*, vol. vii (1910) 121–42, and vol. viii (1910) 44–62, and *Narodnoe pravo* (Folk law) (Moscow 1906); Veniaminov, P., *Krestyanskaya obshchina* (The peasant commune) (St. Petersburg 1908); Izgoev, A. S., *Obshchinnoe pravo* (Communal law) (St. Petersburg 1906); Vorontsov, V. P., *Krestyanskaya obshchina* (The peasant commune) (St. Petersburg 1892); Pershin, P. N., *Zemelnoe ustroystvo dorevolutsionnoy derevni* (The land organization of the prerevolutionary countryside) (Moscow 1928); Morachevsky, V., *Uspekhi krestyanskago khozyaystva v Rossii* (Progress of peasant economy in Russia) (St. Petersburg 1910); Mukerjee, Radhakamal, *Land Problems of India* (London 1933) chs. i–iv; Banerjea, Pramathanath, *A Study of Indian Economics* (2nd ed. London 1915) p. 49–57; Hose, Charles, and McDougall, W., *The Pagan Tribes of Borneo*, 2 vols. (London 1912) vol. i, p. 39–41, 63–72; Hutton, J. H., *The Angami Nagas* (London 1921) p. 109–42; Skeat, W. W., and Blagden, C. O., *Pagan Races of the Malay Peninsula*, 2 vols. (London 1906).

VILLARD, HENRY (1835–1900), American journalist and financier. Villard emigrated to the United States from Germany in 1853. Shortly afterward he began his journalistic career as editor of a small German paper in Racine, Wisconsin. In 1857 he came east and subsequently distinguished himself as a newspaper correspondent and as an active promoter of civil service reform.

Transferring his energies from newspaper work to finance Villard in 1874 visited the Pacific coast as a representative of German investors in Oregon railroads. He soon came to exert a dominating influence in the transportation affairs of the northwest through the backing of German capital and the bold use of his own rapidly growing wealth. At one time he was president of the Oregon Railway and Navigation Company and of the Northern Pacific Railroad. Under his direction the transcontinental line of the Northern Pacific was completed in 1883; but the excessive cost resulted in a collapse of the railroad, in which Villard lost his position of preeminence in railway matters and a large part of his fortune. His interest in electricity, particularly in the inventions of Thomas A. Edison, led him in 1889 to organize the Edison General Electric Company, which was the beginning of the enormously successful General Electric Company of later years. Somewhat earlier, in 1881, he had been able to purchase and combine the New York *Evening Post* and the *Nation* under the joint management of Carl Schurz, Horace White and Edwin L. Godkin. That both papers became a force in liberal journalism in the United States was due in no small measure to the editorial independence which Villard's ownership made possible.

STUART DAGGETT

Works: *Memoirs of Henry Villard*, 2 vols. (Boston 1904).

Consult: "Henry Villard" in *Nation*, vol. lxxi (1900) 380–83; Halstead, Murat, "Some Reminiscences of Mr. Villard" in *American Monthly Review of Reviews*, vol. xxiii (1901) 59–63; Hedges, James Blaine, *Henry Villard and the Railways of the Northwest* (New Haven 1930).

VILLARI, PASQUALE (1827–1917), Italian historian. Villari was born in Naples, the son of a lawyer. He was appointed professor of history at the University of Pisa in 1859 and at the Istituto di Studi Superiori in 1862. He served in the Chamber of Deputies and the Senate and was minister of public instruction in 1891–92. Villari's most important historical works are concerned with mediaeval and Renaissance history. In his youth he was a Hegelian, but he soon turned to positivism. "The intimate nature of the soul, of the mind, of God," he wrote in 1868, "is still unknown to us, or at least the philosophers do not agree among themselves on these matters. Let us study moral phenomena, their history and their laws, without at the present trying to possess an absolute knowledge of the soul, the reason and so forth. We shall proceed as far as we can; but at least we shall have definite facts on which all are agreed." Yet the complete renunciation of every effort toward absolute knowledge appeared to him impossible. Man will ever be asking himself about the nature of the soul, whether it is immortal and whether there is a God, "even if he cannot give a scientifically certain answer to these questions." Villari preached the duty of submitting to the discipline of what was then coming to be known as the historical method and therefore of renouncing any ambition to compile those syntheses, as arbitrary as they were grandiose, which paraded under the name of "philosophy of history." But he maintained that the historian must not confine himself to the criticism of sources and the verification of isolated facts. This is fragmentary erudition, not history. After all the facts have been ascertained in accordance with all the safeguards suggested by the historical method, the historian must concatenate them in conformity with the principle of causality.

Villari took an active interest in problems of both higher and lower education. He conducted investigations into the conditions of the lower classes in Naples, of the workers in the sulphur mines of Sicily and of the rural population as well as into emigration and other kindred subjects. Although conservative by both temperament and philosophy, he did not hesitate to reprove the upper classes in Italy for their inertia in the face of social problems. His historical and social writings were consequently not infrequently employed by the Socialists in their political propaganda. His social philosophy may be summed up by the following proposition, repeatedly encountered throughout his works: the better part of man consists not in intelligence but in moral character.

GAETANO SALVEMINI

Important works: *La storia di Girolamo Savonarola e de' suoi tempi*, 2 vols. (Florence 1859–61, new ed. 1926), tr. by Linda Villari, 2 vols. (London 1888); *Niccolò Machiavelli e i suoi tempi*, 3 vols. (Florence 1877–82, 3rd ed. Milan 1912–14), tr. by Linda Villari, 2 vols. (rev. ed. London 1892); *Le lettere meridionali ed altri scritti sulla questione sociale in Italia* (Florence 1878, 2nd ed. Turin 1885); *I primi due secoli della storia di Firenze*, 2 vols. (Florence 1894–98), tr. by Linda Villari (London 1894); *Le invasioni barbariche in Italia* (Milan 1901, 3rd ed. 1920), tr. by Linda Villari, 2 vols. (London 1902); *Scritti sulla questione sociale in Italia* (Florence 1902); *Scritti sulla emigrazione* (Bologna 1909); *L'Italia da Carlo Magno alla morte di Arrigo VII* (Milan 1910), tr. by Costanza Hulton (London 1910); *Storia, politica e istruzione* (Milan 1914); *Saggî storici i critici* (Bologna 1890), tr. by Linda Villari (London 1907).

Consult: Sforza, G., "Commemorazione di Pasquale Villari" in Reale Accademia delle Scienze di Torino, *Atti*, vol. liii (1917–18) 1081–1302; Panella, A., *Commemorazione di Pasquale Villari con la bibliografia dei suoi scritti* (Florence 1918); Alazard, Jean, in *Revue internationale de l'enseignement*, vol. lxxii (1918) 417–28; Armstrong, E., in *English Historical Review*, vol. xxxiii (1918) 197–209.

VILLENEUVE-BARGEMONT, VICOMTE DE, JEAN PAUL ALBAN (1784–1850), French economist. Villeneuve-Bargemont followed an administrative career under Napoleon I and then under the Restoration. He took a keen interest in social questions and was at first a stanch disciple of Adam Smith and later of Jean-Baptiste Say. In 1828 he became prefect of the Nord, one of the first industrial departments of France; there he was shocked by the misery prevailing among the proletariat. In the chief center, Lille, half the population was entered on the list of indigents maintained by the bureau of charities. Like Sismondi before him, Villeneuve-Bargemont promptly severed all connections with liberal economics. In 1830 he refused, as a legitimist, to serve the new monarchy and for a brief time even went so far as to favor the revolt of the duchess of Berry; soon, however, he began to devote himself entirely to the furthering of his social theories. In his great work *Économie politique chrétienne* (3 vols., Paris 1834) he recounted his experiences in the Nord and insisted that under the influence of the Christian spirit the law should curb the formidable triumph of capitalism. His *Histoire de l'économie politique* (Brussels 1839) developed the same ideas. He devoted some sympathetic attention to certain systems which were opposed to his own; he held Malthus in great esteem; and instead of scoffing at the utopias of Fourier he noted therein more than one fruitful idea. For a short time he served as deputy under Louis Philippe and in this capacity contributed to the votes in favor of the law of 1841 which prohibited labor of children under eight years of age in factories. He developed an interest also, in the early days of the Second Republic, in the charitable societies founded by the Catholics, attacking at the same time the materialism of the orthodox disciples of Jean-Baptiste Say. Ignored during his lifetime, Villeneuve-Bargemont was later to be admired by the social Catholics as one of their forbears.

GEORGES WEILL

Consult: Théry, Adolphe, *Un précurseur du catholicisme social. Le vicomte de Villeneuve-Bargemont* (Paris 1911); Waha, Raymund de, *Die Nationalökonomie in Frankreich* (Stuttgart 1910) p. 192–94.

VILLERMÉ, LOUIS RENÉ (1782–1863), French physician and statistician. After receiving his early education at Lardy, Villermé studied medicine in Paris, entered military service in 1804 and obtained his medical degree in 1814. His twofold interest in the laboring classes and in social and economic statistics led to a wide range of published works. He produced studies on prisons, textile workers, labor organizations, housing for workers, the influence of prosperity and poverty on mortality, the distribution of the French population in relation to sex and civil status, and the value of vital statistics. He was elected a member of the Académie de Médecine in 1823 and of the Académie des Sciences Morales et Politiques in 1832. In 1829 he founded the *Annales d'hygiène publique et de médecine légale*, being one of the first in France to emphasize the value of statistics in the fields of public health and hygiene. In 1848 he was appointed a member of the Conseil Supérieur de l'Hygiène.

When the manufacturers of Mulhouse took the initiative in calling public attention to the child labor prevalent in the silk mills, the Académie des Sciences Morales et Politiques invited Villermé to make an investigation of the conditions. His report, published in 1840, served as the basis for the law of 1841 extending a measure of protection to children in industry.

ANDRÉ LIESSE

Works: *Mémoire sur la mortalité dans les prisons* (Paris 1829); *Tableau de l'état physique et moral des ouvriers employés dans les manufactures de coton, de laine et de soie*, 2 vols. (Paris 1840); "Mémoire sur la distribution de la population française, par sexe et par état civil ..." in Académie des Sciences Morales et Politiques, *Mémoires*, 2nd ser., vol. i (1837) 79–112; *Des associations ouvrières* (Paris 1849); *Les accidents produits dans les ateliers par les appareils mécaniques* (Paris 1850); "Considérations sur les tables de mortalité" in Académie des Sciences Morales et Politiques, *Séances et travaux ... Compte rendu*, vol. xxvi (1853) 395–424.

Consult: Guérard, Alphonse, in *Annales d'hygiène publique et de médecine légale*, 2nd ser., vol. xxi (1863) 162–77; Chevalier, M., *De l'industrie manufacturière en France* (Paris 1841).

VILLIERS, CHARLES PELHAM (1802–98), British statesman. Villiers was educated at the East India College, Haileybury, and at St. John's College, Cambridge; later he came into contact with the followers of Jeremy Bentham and adopted the utilitarian position. He was appointed an assistant commissioner under the Royal Commission of the Poor Laws of 1832–34. In his able report he suggested that the poor should be made a national instead of a parochial charge; although the commissioners agreed that such a measure would remove vexatious restrictions and promote mobility of labor, they rejected it on other grounds. In 1835 Villiers was returned to the House of Commons as a member for Wolverhampton, which he represented for the remainder of his life. He advocated the total repeal of the corn laws in the election of 1837, and in March, 1838, he made the first of his annual motions in favor of it in the House of Commons. In his view commercial liberty had become as essential to the well being of the country as civil and religious liberty had been considered to be in the past. When the Anti-Corn Law League was founded in 1839, Villiers was naturally accepted as the parliamentary leader of the movement, although later he was somewhat eclipsed by Richard Cobden and John Bright. Villiers had an opportunity to reveal the anomalies of the existing fiscal arrangements when he became chairman of the Committee on Import Duties which was appointed in 1840. The committee's recommendation that duties should be confined to a small number of articles productive of revenue greatly influenced Sir Robert Peel in his tariff reform.

The repeal of the corn laws in 1846 completed

the task to which Villiers had devoted his energies. He was appointed judge advocate general in 1853, and in 1859 Palmerston offered him the post of president of the Poor Law Board with a seat in the cabinet. He was thus able to undertake some useful reforms; the most important was the Union Chargeability Act of 1865, which placed the entire expenditure of the guardians on the common fund of the union, each parish in the union bearing its share according to its ratable value. This measure broke down parochial autonomy and practically solved the vexed questions of settlement and removal. Under Villiers the medical service was also greatly improved and a medical officer of the board appointed. In dealing with the distress caused in Lancashire by the cotton famine during the American Civil War Villiers was instrumental in the granting of loans amounting to nearly £2,000,000 to local authorities.

J. F. REES

Works: *The Free Trade Speeches of the Rt. Hon. Charles Pelham Villiers with a Political Memoir*, ed. by a member of the Cobden Club, 2 vols. (London 1883).

Consult: Webb, Sidney and Beatrice, *English Poor Law History; the Last Hundred Years*, their English Local Government series, vol. ix (London 1929); Morley, John, *Life of Richard Cobden*, 2 vols. (new ed. London 1908) vol. i; Trevelyan, G. M., *The Life of John Bright* (2nd ed. London 1925); Barnes, D. G., *A History of the English Corn Laws from 1660-1846*, London School of Economics, Studies in Economics and Social History (London 1930) chs. x-xi.

VILLIERS, FIRST BARON JOHN HENRY DE (1842-1914), South African judge. De Villiers is an outstanding figure in the history of the law of South Africa. Like Bynkershoek he abandoned theology for law. He became chief justice in the colony of the Cape of Good Hope at the age of thirty-one and, when in 1910 Cape Colony was absorbed in the Union of South Africa, served as the first chief justice of the union, retaining this office until his death. From 1897 he sat when in England as a member of the Judicial Committee of the Privy Council, which hears appeals from all the outlying parts of the British Empire. As chief justice De Villiers enjoyed a position of unique authority. The modern law of South Africa, so far as it is contained in judicial decisions, is largely his creation. With a wise discrimination he knew how to adapt the ancient structure of the Roman-Dutch law to the needs of a new age. He had studied law in England, where he was called to the bar by the Inner Temple, and therefore brought to his task as chief justice a competent knowledge of the two legal systems which have been in contact or conflict in British South Africa. A wise rather than a learned judge, he was more concerned to administer justice than to explore the intricate passages of the law. He is reported to have said to a colleague: "You read too many books. What you want is to get hold of a good conception of justice and apply it." His judgments are of this character, for the most part short and terse, and more interested in justice than in jurisprudence. In politics De Villiers exercised a considerable though indirect influence, and he never lost an opportunity to promote the union of the four governments of South Africa, which he lived to see realized under the British Crown.

ROBERT WARDEN LEE

Consult: Walker, Eric A., *Lord De Villiers and His Times, South Africa, 1842-1914* (London 1925).

VINCENT DE PAUL, SAINT (1581-1660), French humanitarian. As a young man Vincent, who had been ordained priest at the age of nineteen, was captured near Marseille by the Tunisian pirates and sold into slavery. Having regained his freedom, he became curate at Clichy near Paris in 1612. Five years later, after a sojourn in the provinces had given him an opportunity to observe the miserable living conditions of the rural lower classes, he founded in the small country parish of Châtillon the first *confrérie de la charité*, consisting of a group of parish women who undertook to care for the sick poor. Out of these experiences grew the three great charitable associations which he established at Paris. In 1625 the Congregation of the Priests of the Mission was created by Vincent, with the financial assistance of his patroness Madame de Gondi, for the purpose of evangelizing the poor people of the rural districts and of bringing spiritual aid to convicts. The priory of St. Lazare, its headquarters after 1632—whence the name of Lazaristes which was applied to Vincent's disciples—played an important part in the religious revival of the reign of Louis XIII, serving as a center for laymen, young clerics, mature ecclesiastics and wealthy philanthropists. In 1629 and 1630 Vincent founded the society of the Ladies of Charity, while the third organization, which was later to become known as the Daughters of Charity, was instituted in 1633 by Louise de Marillac, who was under Vincent's immediate influence.

Through these various groups Vincent carried on a widely diversified campaign for the mitigation of suffering. By their visits and ministrations to patients the Ladies and Daughters of Charity completely transformed the atmosphere of Parisian hospitals; abandoned children were adopted by Vincent and provided for by the Ladies of Charity; the home of the Name of Jesus was opened for aged men, who were allowed to work at their vocations in return for a small wage; the Daughters of Charity tended the insane and performed menial services for convicts. The Lazaristes as well as the two other organizations brought relief to the victims of the *Fronde*. Vincent moreover inspired the queen mother Anne of Austria to see that episcopal offices were filled by men interested in works of charity. Although his own pioneering efforts in the field of foreign missions proved abortive, the Lazaristes are today scattered throughout Asia, Africa and America; and the Daughters of Charity, which in the past hundred years has also grown into a world wide organization, numbers about 37,500 members and 3500 establishments. Vincent's renown began to revive in the early stages of the French social Catholic movement of the nineteenth century, and his name was given to the great charitable organization founded by Ozanam. Only within recent years, however, has the history of his work been investigated adequately.

GEORGES GOYAU

Works: *Correspondance, Entretiens, Documents,* ed. by Pierre Coste, 14 vols. (Paris 1920–25).

Consult: Coste, Pierre, *Le grand saint du grand siècle, Monsieur Vincent,* 3 vols. (Paris 1932), and *La Congrégation de la Mission dite de Saint-Lazare* (Paris 1927); Feillet, Alphonse, *La misère au temps de la Fronde et Saint Vincent de Paul* (4th ed. Paris 1868); Goyau, Georges, *Les Dames de la Charité de Monsieur Vincent* (Paris 1918); Celier, L., *Les Filles de la Charité* (Paris 1929); Coste, Pierre, Baussan, Charles, and Goyau, Georges, *Les Filles de la Charité* (Paris 1933); Sanders, E. K., *Vincent de Paul, Priest and Philanthropist, 1576–1660* (London 1913); Emanuel, C. W., *The Charities of St. Vincent de Paul; an Evaluation of His Ideas, Principles and Methods* (Chicago 1923).

VINCENT, HENRY (1813–79), English Chartist. Obliged to earn his own living at the age of eleven Vincent became a compositor, and while still a boy he was active in political agitation. In 1838–39 he took a leading part in organizing the Chartist movement. He centered his activities mainly in Wales, where through his lectures he was successful in organizing a large number of working men's associations among the miners. At Bath he published a weekly, the *Western Vindicator*, and at Newport he delivered speeches which, in the opinion of the authorities, were calculated to excite disaffection. He was sentenced to a year's imprisonment in Monmouth Gaol and later received an additional sentence of eight months; the rigorous treatment to which he was subjected was one of the causes of the Chartist riot at Newport in November, 1839. After his release from prison he devoted himself to lecturing from a liberal point of view on politics, ethics, temperance and parliamentary reform. During the American Civil War he advocated the cause of the North and was therefore welcomed in the United States of America on his lecture tours in 1866–67, 1867–68, 1868–69 and 1875–76. He appears to have been popular with American audiences, and he won the friendship of Wendell Phillips and William Lloyd Garrison.

MAX BEER

Consult: Dorling, W., *Henry Vincent; a Biographical Sketch* (London 1879); Gammage, R. G., *History of the Chartist Movement* (London 1894) p. 10–12; Rosenblatt, F. F., *The Chartist Movement,* Columbia University, Studies in History, Economics and Public Law, no. 171 (New York 1916) p. 135, 147, 190–92; Beer, Max, *A History of British Socialism,* 2 vols. (London 1919–20) vol. ii, p. 8–9.

VINOGRADOFF, SIR PAUL (1854–1925), Anglo-Russian historian and jurist. The son of a Moscow school director, Vinogradoff studied at the university there and then attended seminars of Mommsen and Brunner in Berlin. The quest of learning took him also to Italy and England. Returning to Russia in 1884, he was appointed to the chair of history at Moscow, which he held until 1901, when he resigned in protest against the measures of the government. After his resignation he came to England again and in 1903 he was appointed to the Corpus chair of jurisprudence at Oxford, where during his first visit he had achieved fame by rediscovering Bracton's notebook. At Oxford Vinogradoff established a seminar where he trained pupils who spread his fame at home and abroad. Many of them contributed volumes to the *Oxford Studies in Social and Legal History* (vols. i–ix, Oxford 1909–27), which Vinogradoff edited. He also became the first literary director of the Selden Society. By virtue of his remarkable command of ancient and modern languages he was peculiarly fitted to fill the important role of liaison officer between the worlds of continental and English scholarship. An excellent example of his work in this capacity is his *Roman Law in Mediaeval Europe* (London 1909, 2nd ed. Oxford

1929), a little volume on the reception which made available in English the results of continental research.

Vinogradoff's most important work was done in the field of mediaeval agrarian organization and related legal antiquities. His first major work in this field, *Villainage in England* (Oxford 1892), is his most brilliant book; it was generously described by Maitland as by far the greatest achievement in English legal history. From the abundant evidences of the practise of villenage in the twelfth and thirteenth centuries he argued in favor of the free origin of the English village community. In *The Growth of the Manor* (London 1905, 3rd ed. 1920) he attempted to describe the institution which he regarded as the most characteristic of mediaeval civilization. He was inclined to ascribe to Celtic survivals a rather larger influence than was generally admitted, but on the whole the book is less an attempt at discovery than a coordination and sifting of existing views, for since the publication of Vinogradoff's work on villenage there had been much investigation of agrarian antiquities by Maitland, Round and Seebohm. Of least general interest is Vinogradoff's *English Society in the Eleventh Century* (Oxford 1908). Not only is this a highly technical commentary on the Domesday survey but the writing is confused and the trend of the argument is not always clear. Of Vinogradoff's essays, assembled in his *Collected Papers* (2 vols., Oxford 1928), the most important perhaps is the one on folkland, in which he demonstrated as against the united opinion of many illustrious authorities that this type of holding was not *ager publicus* but land held by private individuals according to the folk, or customary, law.

The judgment of Vinogradoff's work has been somewhat varied. As a historian of legal antiquities he was perhaps less acute than Maitland. Holdsworth has complained that Vinogradoff's lack of familiarity with the post-mediaeval development of English law prevented him often from appreciating the significance of ideas which later became important. Vinogradoff's authority as a historian of agrarian economics has been more universally conceded, although it is stressed that he excelled rather in the evaluation of evidence than in the projection of new ideas.

Vinogradoff's *Outlines of Historical Jurisprudence* (2 vols., London 1920–22), which was intended to run to many more volumes but was interrupted by his death, was to have been his great contribution as a philosophical jurist of the historical school. He aimed apparently at the construction of a new theory of law based upon the identification of various historical types. "Historical jurisprudence" he conceived to be "ideological jurisprudence." But the writing does not make it clear exactly how this differs from mere legal history.

WILLIAM SEAGLE

Consult: Kovalevsky, Maxime, "Early English Land Tenures" in *Law Quarterly Review*, vol. iv (1888) 266–75; Seebohm, F., "Villainage in England" in *English Historical Review*, vol. vii (1892) 444–65; Baildon, A. Paley, "Vinogradoff on the Manor" in *Law Quarterly Review*, vol. xxi (1905) 294–300; Pound, Roscoe, in *Harvard Law Review*, vol. xxxv (1921–22) 774–83; Isaacs, Nathan, in *Yale Law Journal*, vol. xxxiii (1923–24) 676–80; Kocourek, Albert, in *Yale Law Journal*, vol. xxxviii (1928–29) 833–87; Pares, Bernard, "Sir Paul Vinogradoff" in *Slavonic Review*, vol. iv (1926) 529–51; Zulueta, F. de, "Paul Vinogradoff, 1854–1925" in *Law Quarterly Review*, vol. xlii (1926) 202–11; Powicke, F. M., "Sir Paul Vinogradoff" in *English Historical Review*, vol. xli (1926) 236–43; Schechter, Frank I., "Paul Vinogradoff—the Pontiff of Comparative Jurisprudence" in *Illinois Law Review*, vol. xxiv (1929–30) 528–46; Fisher, H. A. L., *Paul Vinogradoff; a Memoir* (Oxford 1927); Holdsworth, W. S., *The Historians of Anglo-American Law* (New York 1928) p. 84–91.

VIOLENCE. In the social context violence may be defined roughly as the illegal employment of methods of physical coercion for personal or group ends. It must be distinguished from force, or power, which is a purely physical concept having direction and intensity but, apart from human ends, no intention, and also from might, which has legal sanction and which expresses itself in the imposition of physical constraints as well as in the use of less conspicuous but more effective social pressures, such as discriminatory economic, cultural and administrative measures. The use of physical coercion by duly constituted government, either as a method of defense or as a means of consolidating its rule, collecting taxes and the like, raises no particular problem of social ethics—once the sovereignty of the government is accepted—but only a question of expediency. Physical coercion or the threat of physical coercion is of the very nature of state rule; there can be difference only upon its occasion and degree. The really troublesome issues over the use and justification of violence arise out of the problems faced by a politically subordinate group, whether minority or not, which seeks to capture political power or to compel the acceptance of some specific measure. On certain occasions these issues have taken acute form, especially among those groups which have justified their revolt against the existing government on the ground that it had exercised terrorism against its own citizens. A recurrent theme which runs through the literature of social reform, especially that of prerevolutionary Russia, concerns itself with the spiritual predicaments which flow from the attempt to meet violence with greater violence. If violent action against man is wrong, is it any less wrong to use violent action against the men who practise it? Approached from the moral angle the paradox cannot be resolved except by the formal statement that where devotion to the values of peace and spiritual serenity is higher than devotion to life itself and all the other values which life makes possible, the use of violence against violence cannot be sanctioned; where other values are considered as intrinsically desirable as serenity or blessedness, the use of violence may be extenuated as the necessary, even if painful, means of achieving them.

Practically all movements of social revolt which have proved to be successful have been compelled to use violence at some point in the process of acquiring power. Even primitive Christianity, which conquered ostensibly with the slogans of love and the technique of non-resistance, destroyed pagan temples and hounded pagan priests wherever it had the support of community sentiment. The critical rationalism of the French *philosophes*, although accepted by the Jacobins, was not regarded by them as incompatible with the vigorous measures of defense and offense adopted during the course of the revolution. In the face of the violent opposition of the counter-revolution the terrorism of action on the part of its own partisans was regarded as a practical corollary of the terrorism of reason. Those who oppose violence on the grounds of humanity, love or reason have always justified their own violent activities by the simple theoretical device of regarding the human beings upon whom they visit violence as no longer a genuine part of the community and therefore subject to the same treatment as other material obstacles to the realization of the communal good as interpreted by the revolting group.

It is not hard to understand why violence seems to be an invariable concomitant of all mass movements of social reform. First of all, it symbolizes in dramatic fashion the issues involved and focuses upon them the attention of those elements in the community which cannot be stirred into activity by rational appeal. The Boston tea party was planned by the leaders of the escapade as a far more effective way of forcing the question of taxation upon public consciousness than any other available. Carry Nation with her saloon smashing hatchet crystallized a type of opposition to liquor consumption which could never have survived if the debate had been kept on the level of rational argument. In a large mass movement the appeal to action must be made on several planes. There always seem to be more individuals susceptible to the emotionalism bound up with the immediacies of action—its thrill, its imaginative appeal and the ultimate sacrifices which make the cause sacred —than to the validity of arguments, even in those rare cases where arguments are relevant to fundamental conflicts of social interest. Some theorists, such as Sorel, offer as the only practical justification of the poetic cult of violence its usefulness in dramatizing the conflict of ethical values. Even in periods of political and economic stability, when problems of social justice are not acute, they recommend violence as providing the ideal opportunity for expressing the heroic virtues of sacrifice, honor and courage. Secondly, whatever the nature of the social process, its ultimate constituents consist of a series of individual actions by individual men. The ultimate transfer of power is from man to man and not by the development of concepts or the movement of forces. At the critical points in the social and political process where profound conflicts come to a head, their resolution almost always involves "the laying of hands upon" something or someone, especially if there is resistance or fear of resistance. Thirdly, a systematic and consistent refusal to use violence, no matter how extreme the provocation, would doom every movement of social reform to futility if it were faced by an intransigent foe whose liberty of action was not bound by the fetish of non-resistance. Even where there is no real intention to use violence, the threats of violence have won occasional concessions which would hardly have been granted out of admiration for the non-resistant spirit. Finally, the history of "peaceful" social reform demonstrates that the shadow or threat of more violent action has been the prime catalyst of "sweet reasonableness" upon the part of groups which possess power. The oldest and strongest—but by no means invariably persuasive—argument for social reform has always been that it would obviate "revolution or worse." Whether it is King John granting reforms to his nobles in order to save his throne or the English Tories yielding to the mass pressure of the Chartist movement on the question of the reform bills, the fear that the consequences of refusal would be more onerous than the humiliation of acceding is the most powerful, but not exclusive, factor in accelerating peaceful reforms. Such fear cannot be experienced where there are no storm signals of violent action visible on the political horizon.

The two chief considerations, aside from questions of ethical principle, which make for self-imposed curbs on violent activity in any mass movement flow from the desire to escape persecution and repression and from the necessities of intelligent strategy. The probability that any movement aiming at ultimate violent action will gain a foothold, develop and thrive wherever it is confronted by a strong state power is inversely proportional to the degree to which it preaches and practises violence in its early phase. The notion that repression cannot effectively crush revolutionary movements for long periods is a monstrous superstition which cannot stand up under historical analysis. Tactically, however, widespread use of violence is suicidal, unless it directly precedes open civil war. Yet at the same time the theoretical and public renunciation of the use of violence under all circumstances deprives a social movement not only of its fighting power but also of its negotiating power.

The nature and role of violence in Marxian theory and practise represent an attempt to mediate between the dual impracticalities of pacifism and "putschism." Before the influence of Marx and Engels made itself felt on the socialist movement, the dominant political tendencies within it subscribed either to the philosophy of moral force or to that of direct action. Marx' philosophy of the state and his conception of political tactics, which made the main line of revolutionary strategy dependent upon objective social conditions, cut under both of these tendencies. Against those who pinned their faith solely upon moral force Marx pointed to the non-moral reality of the state as the governmental arm of the nation's industry and to its source of power in the existence of special bodies of armed men not part of the working population but standing over against it. It followed that any attempt to capture state power must be prepared to meet the state forces if necessary on their own ground. Against the direct actionists and all believers in the propaganda of the deed Marx argued that violence could succeed only when the social conditions ripe for a new order were at hand; that it must cap the process of organization of labor and not precede it; that if it took the customary individual form rather than a social form it invariably played into the hands of the reaction. Advocacy of such tactics could therefore be characterized either as the expression of irresponsible petty bourgeois anarchism or as downright police provocation. It would perhaps be no exaggeration to say that it was due to the spread of Marxist ideas among the working classes that individual acts of terror and violence almost disappeared from the labor movement in western Europe. In Russia the spread of Marxism among the prerevolutionary intellectuals at the turn of the century and thereafter also led to a marked decline in terrorism. In Latin countries, like Italy and Spain, where Marx' ideas did not strike deep root, anarcho-syndicalist notions prevailed and labor disturbances took on an incipient revolutionary character. Even in the United States labor disputes which were carried through without the guidance of a broad social philosophy were accompanied by spontaneous individual violence which surpassed in ferocity anything known abroad.

Marxism holds that the chief objection to individual expressions of violence or premature violent action on the part of working class groups is that such expressions invariably facilitate the policy of government repression. The objective presupposition of any violent action is a revolutionary situation defined as one in which there is chaos in economic life and in which the traditional psychology of all classes is demoralized. Revolutionary action is not begun unless there is reason to believe that a majority of the population stands behind the representative councils of the workers and the producers in whose name power is taken. The amount of violence which must be employed is a function of the intensity of resistance which is encountered. For Marxism the moral and social justification of the use of violence consists in the fact that it is a measure of defense on the part of the majority of the community against the horrors of war, poverty and political repression and aims to establish the political conditions under which the transition from a profit to a use economy may be effected.

There are two great dangers in the use of violence which, if not guarded against, may easily defeat the ends, no matter how exalted, in whose behalf violence is employed. Wide scale use of violence results in a brutalization of those who employ it, an insensitiveness to special conditions and to the distinctive features of familiar situations which can be adjusted by finesse and tact rather than by force. There is further the danger that violence will be employed to settle conflicts of a scientific, philosophical or cultural nature which are irrelevant to politics. Secondly, unless very stringent control is exercised by representative organs of the community over the forces and instruments of violence, the latter may set themselves up as the ruling power and oppress the community in the name of their ultimate interests. The issues which arise among the victors may become the occasions of violent conflict instead of democratic discussion. Before its force is drawn into proper institutional channels, successful violence may devour its own offspring. Although there is no guaranty that violence may not go berserk and create objective situations which call for more violence, this relative danger must by no means be construed as an absolute argument against its use. But the danger is real enough to show that only a great philosophy can ever justify its use—and even then only unwillingly, as a matter of last resort in the face of worse evils and as subordinate to a conception of a free society in which violence has no place or justification.

SIDNEY HOOK

See: REVOLUTION AND COUNTER-REVOLUTION; CONFLICT, SOCIAL; CLASS STRUGGLE; SOCIALISM; SOCIALIST PARTIES; BOLSHEVISM; COMMUNIST PARTIES; ANARCHISM; SYNDICALISM; INDUSTRIAL WORKERS OF THE WORLD; CRIMINAL SYNDICALISM; TERRORISM; DIRECT ACTION; GENERAL STRIKE; PASSIVE RESISTANCE AND NON-COOPERATION; SECTS.

Consult: Dewey, John, "Force and Coercion" in *International Journal of Ethics*, vol. xxvi (1915–16) 359–67; Engels, F., *Herrn Eugen Dührings Umwälzung der Wissenschaft* (4th ed. Stuttgart 1901) sect. 2, chs. ii–iv; Hook, Sidney, *Towards an Understanding of Karl Marx* (New York 1933) chs. xvii–xix; Niebuhr, R., *Moral Man and Immoral Society* (New York 1932) chs. vii–viii, and *Reflections on the End of an Era* (New York 1934) chs. xii–xiv; Masaryk, T. G., *Russland und Europa*, 2 vols. (Jena 1913), tr. by E. and C. Paul as *The Spirit of Russia* (London 1916); Trotsky, Leon, *The Defence of Terrorism* (London 1921); Russell, B., *Bolshevism, Practice and Theory* (London 1920); Lenin, N., *Gosudarstvo i revolutsiya* (Petrograd 1918), tr. as *State and Revolution* (London 1919).

VIOLLET, PAUL (1840–1914), French jurist. Viollet was librarian of the law faculty of the University of Paris, professor of the history of civil and canon law at the École des Chartes and a member of the Académie des Inscriptions et Belles-Lettres. His scientific activity was devoted to French public and private law.

Among the most important of Viollet's achievements was his edition of the *Établissements de Saint Louis* (4 vols., Paris 1881–86), a famous compilation of mediaeval customs, which he showed authoritatively to have been not an official but a private collection. In his *Précis de l'histoire du droit français* (Paris 1885; 3rd ed. with title *Histoire du droit civil français*, 1905) he surveyed the sources and chief institutions of French private law. His chief work, however, was the monumental *Droit public. Histoire des institutions politiques et administratives de la France* (3 vols., Paris 1889–1903), dealing with the public institutions of France. This he supplemented in a fourth volume, *Le roi et ses ministres pendant les trois derniers siècles de la monarchie* (Paris 1911). He thus covered almost the whole of French public law from the earliest period to the revolution.

Viollet's work is notable for its documentation, as is to be expected since he was an archivist. Nevertheless, despite his sincere efforts to be objective his writing often suffers from the injection of opinion. He was a convinced individualist and a liberal Catholic and he tended to find the origins if not the counterparts of many so-called modern institutions in the Middle Ages. The last three centuries of the French monarchy he regarded as virtually devoid of constitutional development, the unifying tendency under the royal power simply continuing in a sterile manner.

HENRI LÉVY-BRUHL

Consult: Fournier, Paul, in *Nouvelle revue historique de droit français et étranger*, vol. xxxviii (1914–15) 816–27; Delaborde, H. F., in *Bibliothèque de l'École des Chartes*, vol. lxxix (1918) 147–75.

VIRCHOW, RUDOLF (1821–1902), German scientist and political leader. As a young physician Virchow was sent in 1847 to make a study of a typhoid fever epidemic in Upper Silesia. The impressions gained in this experience were a determining factor in the development of his political views. He became an enemy of feudalism and a faithful supporter of liberalism and democracy. He lost his teaching position in Berlin because of his participation in the movement of 1848 but was recalled in 1856, and after 1859 he was active both in the field of science and in the world of public affairs.

As a scientist Virchow made his greatest contribution to medicine. He developed the science of anatomy, laid the foundations for the study of cellular pathology, was instrumental in the founding of several important medical journals and was also active in the organization of hospitals and institutions of public health and sanitation. Virchow's scientific interests also extended to anthropology and prehistory. He did important work in physical anthropology, especially in connection with measurement of skulls and bodily dimensions, and was active in the organization of the Deutsche Anthropologische Gesellschaft, the Berliner Gesellschaft für Anthropologie, Ethnologie und Urgeschichte and the *Zeitschrift für Ethnologie*.

Virchow also became active in politics. In 1861 he helped found the German *Fortschrittspartei* (Progressive party). From 1862 until his death he was a member of the Prussian *Landtag* and from 1880 to 1893 of the German Reichstag. He was a follower of Eugen Richter and an opponent of the Bismarckian policy of the 1860's. His industry was amazing. Apart from his scientific and academic work he gave conscientious attention to his parliamentary duties and became a specialist in budgetary matters. Parliamentary control of the Prussian budget was in large measure a result of his efforts, and he served as chairman of the committee for many years. It was Virchow who coined the expression Kulturkampf for Bismarck's conflict with the Catholic church in 1873. He was not an original political thinker. Essentially a humanitarian, progressive liberal, of independent and courageous character, he typifies the highest conception of public service.

THEODOR HEUSS

Consult: Posner, C., *Rudolf Virchow* (2nd ed. Vienna 1921); Waldemeyer, W., in Preussische Akademie der Wissenschaften, *Abhandlungen* (1903) no. i; Luschan, F. von., in *Virchows Archiv*, vol. ccxxxv (1921) 418–43. For a complete bibliography of Virchow's works, see: Schwalbe, J., *Virchow Bibliographie* (Berlin 1901).

VISA. *See* PASSPORT.

VISIT AND SEARCH. *See* PRIZE.

VISITING NURSES. *See* NURSING; PUBLIC HEALTH.

VITAL STATISTICS. *See* BIRTHS; MORTALITY; POPULATION, section on HISTORY AND STATISTICS; DEMOGRAPHY.

VITALISM. *See* MECHANISM AND VITALISM.

VITORIA, FRANCISCO DE (c. 1480–1546), Spanish theologian and jurist. Vitoria entered the Dominican order in his youth and after completing his early theological and classical studies at Burgos was sent in 1506 to study at Paris. He returned to Spain in 1523 and for three years was connected with the University of Valladolid. In 1526 he became chief professor of theology at the University of Salamanca, a post which he filled with great distinction until his death. It was the custom of his day to choose texts from the *Sententiae* of Peter Lombard and to comment upon them. Vitoria preferred, however, the writings of the Dominican Thomas Aquinas, and through his influence the *Summa theologica* of St. Thomas was substituted for the *Sententiae* of Peter Lombard, with the result that a new school of theology came into being in Spain. Conceiving the domain of theology to be very broad Vitoria held that it included the legal sciences; that as law had a moral and spiritual content, it could be properly understood, interpreted and applied only by one versed in theology as well as in the law of his church and in other branches of law.

During Vitoria's lifetime the discovery of the New World, the subsequent conquests of Spain and the consolidation of its empire in the Americas gave rise to new questions in international relations. To these questions and the law applicable to them he gave particular attention and in so doing inaugurated a scientific system of international law.

As principal professor of theology Vitoria delivered annually a public reading on some phase of the course which he had offered to his students. These public readings, often dealing with current questions, are masterpieces of the scholastic method and indeed mark the rebirth of scholasticism. Twelve of them were published at Lyons in 1557 under the title *Relectiones theologicae* and included disquisitions on the civil power, on the ecclesiastical power and on matrimony, the last dealing with the divorce of Henry VIII of England from Catherine of Aragon. But his most important lectures were on the Indians and on the law of war, which taken together comprise an outline, perfect in form and adequate in detail, of the modern law of nations and, in the opinion of many, of future international law. The first, written in 1532, forty years after the discovery of the New World, discusses not only the alleged legal foundations of Spain's dominion over the Indians and their lands but also the laws of peace, developing the concept of an international community in which not merely Christian nations but non-Christian states, such as the American "principalities," were included on an equal basis and admitted to the law of Christendom, binding upon all countries. This law, derived from natural and moral law according to Vitoria and added to by custom and treaty, was accepted by a majority of nations. His conception of the international community is stated in perfect form in the earlier reading on the civil power: "International law has not only the force of a pact and agreement among men, but also the force of a law; for the world as a whole, being in a way one single state, has the power to create laws that are just and fitting for all persons, as are the rules of international law. Consequently, it is clear that they who violate these international rules, whether in peace or in war, commit a mortal sin; moreover, in the gravest matters, such as the inviolability of ambassadors, it is not permissible for one country to refuse to be bound by international law, the latter having been established by the authority of the whole world."

In the lecture on war Vitoria maintained, on the authority of St. Augustine, that the only just cause of warfare was "a wrong received," and this only because there was no court for redress between states as there was between individuals.

JAMES BROWN SCOTT

Chief works: Relecciones teológicas del Maestro Fray Francisco de Vitoria, ed. by P. Mtro. Fr. Luis G. Alonso Getino (Madrid 1933); *De Indis et de iure belli relectiones*, with an introduction by Ernest Nys, followed by an English translation of the Latin text by J. P. Bate and a revised text by H. F. Wright, has been published by the Carnegie Institution of Washington, Classics of International Law series, no. 7 (Washington 1917); *Comentarios a la secunda secundae de Santo Tomás*, ed. by R. P. Vincente Beltrán de Heredia, Biblioteca de Teólogos Españoles, vols. i–iv (Salamanca 1932–34).

Consult: Getino, Luis G. Alonso, *El maestro Fr. Francisco de Vitoria, su vida, su doctrina e influencia*, Asociación Francisco de Vitoria, Publications (2nd ed. Madrid 1930); Barcia Trelles, Camilo, "Francisco de Vitoria et l'école moderne du droit international" in Academy of International Law, *Recueil des cours*, vol. xvii (1927) 113–342; Barthélemy, J., in *Les fondateurs du droit international* (Paris 1904) p. 1–26; Scott, James Brown, *The Spanish Origin of International Law; Francisco de Vitoria and His Law of Nations* (Oxford 1933) pt. i, with appendix containing relevant translations; Phillipson, Coleman, "Franciscus a Victoria (1480–1546)" in Society of Comparative Legislation, *Journal*, n.s., vol. xv (1915) 175–97; Catholic University of America, *Francisco de Vitoria; Addresses in Commemoration of the Fourth Centenary of His Lectures "De Indis" and "De jure belli"* (Washington 1932); Beuve-Méry, H., *La théorie des pouvoirs publics d'après François de Vitoria et ses rapports avec le droit contemporain* (Paris 1928); Baumel, Jean, *Le droit international public, la découverte de l'Amérique et les théories de Francisco de Vitoria* (Montpellier 1931); Wright, Herbert, "The 'De potestate civili' of Vitoria" in American Catholic Philosophical Association, *Proceedings of the Seventh Annual Meeting* (1931) 85–95.

VITTORINO DA FELTRE (Vittorino de' Rambaldoni) (1378–1446), Italian humanist and educator. Vittorino was born in Feltre and studied at the University of Padua. A disciple and friend of the greater humanists of his time and in particular of Gasparino Barzizza and of Guarino da Verona, he taught first in the private schools in Venice and Padua and later in the University of Padua. In 1423 he went to Mantua, where Gianfrancesco Gonzaga entrusted him with the education of his children. He took over the Zoiosa (a place for social meetings and amusements), which was near the royal palace, renamed it La Casa Giocosa and transformed it into a famous educational institute and center of study. Here he taught not only the children of the prince but a most select group of scholars, who spread the fame of his piety, his quality of human compassion and his knowledge throughout the world. La Casa Giocosa was the most original and expressive creation of the new humanistic education. Here Vittorino by his remarkable intuition and serene spontaneity and harmony realized the aspiration of early Italian humanism—the reconciliation of Christian ethics, now stripped of all mediaeval rigidity and narrowness, with classical culture and the achievement of an integrated human personality.

The new spirit animating the Italian culture of the time exercised such irresistible power that Vittorino, notwithstanding his piety and sincere devotion to the Catholic faith, devoted all his attention to the promotion of the spontaneous development of the personality of his pupils through games, gymnastics, sports, literary and scientific exercise and music. He conceived of religion as a force for creating energy and reviving the spirit as it had been during the period of Christianity's expansion. His profound respect for natural ability establishes Vittorino as the first great educator of the modern era and definitely sets him apart from the mediaeval pedagogical tradition. Vittorino's institute also was the first model in Europe of the intermediate school, filling the gap between elementary and university instruction. To this day it remains the soundest educational institution of the major European countries.

ERNESTO CODIGNOLA

Consult: Rosmini, Carlo de', *Idea dell'ottimo precettore nella vita e disciplina di Vittorino da Feltre e de' suoi discepoli* (Bassano 1801); Luzio, A., and Renier, R., "I Filelfo e l'umanismo alla corte dei Gonzaga" in *Giornale storico della letteratura italiana*, vol. xvi (1890) 119–217; Woodward, W. H., *Vittorino da Feltre and Other Humanist Educators* (Cambridge, Eng. 1897), and *Studies in Education during the Age of the Renaissance, 1400-1600* (Cambridge, Eng. 1906); Saitta, G., *L'educazione dell'umanismo in Italia* (Venice 1928); McCormick, P. J., "Two Medieval Catholic Educators: I, Vittorino da Feltre" in *Catholic University Bulletin*, vol. xii (1906) 453–84.

VIVEKĀNANDA, SWAMI (1862–1902), Indian religious leader. Vivekānanda, whose real name was Narendra Nath Dutt, was a high caste Hindu of wealthy family. He attended Duff College in Calcutta, where he became interested in the rationalistic teachings of the Brahmo Samaj. Soon after his graduation in 1884 his father died and the attendant financial ruin of the family forced him to abandon his plan of a career at the bar. In his college days he had come into contact with Rāmakrishna, the Hindu ascetic who believed in the Vedanta philosophy but preached that all religions had truth; during this crucial period Dutt turned to Rāmakrishna, whose beliefs he was later to construct into a philosophic system.

Upon his teacher's death in 1886 Dutt founded the Rāmakrishna order and lived with his brother monks for several years. In 1890 after a number of shorter excursions he set out on a long pilgrimage, which terminated in 1893 when his followers in Madras sent him to the Parliament of Religions at Chicago. In the Occident he hoped to spread the gospel of Rāmakrishna and to receive for India the material help it required. On the eve of his departure he adopted the name of Vivekānanda, by which he became famous.

Vivekānanda was in a sense the unconscious prophet of the new Indian nationalism, whose ideology shows the impress of his doctrines. Following several generations of Hindus who had envisaged India's salvation only in terms of the adoption of occidental standards, he synthesized the doctrines of Hinduism and sounded a defiant note of pride in the heritage of his country. His speeches at the sessions of the Chicago parliament and upon other occasions were the first militant answer of orthodox Hinduism to the Christian missions. They emphasized the divinity of man and the essential unity in all religious thought. Each religion, Vivekānanda asserted, is a path to God, but Hinduism, the most eclectic and tolerant, has a spiritual content which surpasses that of all others. It is based upon principles, while Christianity and Islam depend primarily upon personalities. Every element in the Hindu religion has its value and what is needed is not reform but a continuing expansion to embrace any doctrine which may add to its spiritual strength. The diffusion of Hindu spirituality in the West is the duty of the Indian people, but the latter in turn should utilize the material achievements of the Occident. The vividness of the swami's personality added to the effectiveness of his message. During the three years which he spent in the United States and Europe he succeeded in gathering a number of disciples and in founding Vedanta societies.

The effect of his western experiences upon Vivekānanda's thought became obvious after his triumphant return to India. Even before his departure he had begun to feel that the chief task of his order must be the regeneration of the Indian masses rather than personal meditation. Now he definitely stressed the prime necessity of proselytism and of social and educational work. For this purpose he founded the Rāmakrishna Mission, which was to coordinate the efforts of monastic and lay supporters, while monasteries were established to train monks for their work. The mission became an important philanthropic organization.

FLORENCE MISHNUN

Works: *The Complete Works of the Swami Vivekananda*, 7 vols. (Mayavati, Almora 1922–31).

Consult: Rolland, Romain, *La vie de Ramakrishna*, 2 vols. (Paris 1930), tr. by E. F. Malcolm-Smith as *Prophets of the New India* (New York 1930); Virajananda, Swami, *The Life of the Swami Vivekananda*, 3 vols. (Calcutta 1912–15); Bannerjea, D. N., in *India's Nation Builders* (London 1919) p. 128–45; Farquhar, J. N., *Modern Religious Movements in India* (New York 1915) p. 195–207.

VIVES, JUAN LUIS (1492–1540), Spanish philosopher, pedagogue and publicist. When he was seventeen years old an epidemic in Valencia sent him to Paris, from where he went to Bruges. He was a professor at the universities of Louvain and Oxford and tutor of the princess Mary, the daughter of Henry VIII of England.

As a philosopher Vives is considered the predecessor of Bacon in that he oriented his thought in experience, used the methods of the natural sciences and upheld the inductive method. He is regarded as the creator of modern psychology because he separated the psychological fact from the speculative, theological and physical, applying the descriptive method to the examination of the facts of consciousness. His influence upon Descartes is well known. The relation between soul and life Vives considered to be intimate, but he attributed to the soul the quality of generator of all organic life and not merely of that of consciousness. The soul is not satisfied with the perceptible finite: it seeks the infinite and this reveals its divine origin. His principal philosophical works are *De disciplinis* (Cologne 1532) and *De anima et vita* (Basel 1538).

In the field of pedagogy the significance of Vives has been estimated as superior to that of Comenius and Ratke. He based pedagogy upon psychology and ethics and gave to the world of perceptible intuitions a value that only Pestalozzi was to develop. His conception of a school involves teachers who make every child the object of individual observations and see to it that those who do not excel cease studying in order that the superior students may be trained to constitute a true aristocracy. The teachers are to be paid by the state. His principal works on pedagogy are found in the philosophical works already cited and in *De ratione studii puerilis* (Paris 1536), *Introductio ad sapientiam* (Louvain 1524) and *De subventione pauperum sive de humanis necessitatibus* (Bruges 1526).

In the politico-social sphere Vives has been less important. Vives assumes the existence of community of property in the state of nature. The present inequalities of wealth are the consequence of corruption by the passions. It is the mission of the Christian to rectify this inequality in so far as it conflicts with the preaching of the Evangelists. He describes the evils which poverty engenders and outlines norms of politico-social action: registration of the poor, indicating the number of children and the causes which bring them to need or beggary; erection of "hospitals," or public establishments in which the sick are fed and cared for and the needy support themselves, where children of both sexes are educated, abandoned infants raised, the insane confined and the blind housed.

The obligation of teaching all a trade and supplying them with work led Vives to put forth a plan of municipal workshops, and to indicate to the artisans the duty of admitting into their workshops certain workers designated by the public authorities. The rest should be fed for a time, but they must also work in order not to acquire habits of laziness.

FERNANDO DE LOS RÍOS

Works: *Opera*, 2 vols. (Basel 1555); *Opera omnia*, 8 vols. (Valencia 1782–90).

Consult: Hoppe, Gerhard, *Die Psychologie des Juan Luis Vives* (Berlin 1901); Parmentier, Jacques, "Jean-Luis Vives; de ses théories de l'éducation et de leur influence sur les pédagogues anglais" in *Revue internationale de l'enseignement*, vol. xxv (1893) 441–55; Bonilla y San Martin, A., *Luis Vives y la filosofía del Renacimiento*, 3 vols. (2nd ed. Madrid 1929); Carriazo, Juan de M., *Las ideas sociales de Juan Luis Vives* (Madrid 1927); Watson, Foster, *Luis Vives; el gran valenciano*, Hispanic Notes and Monographs, no. 4 (Oxford 1922), and "The Father of Modern Psychology" in *Psychological Review*, vol. xxii (1915) 333–53; Thorndike, Lynn, "John Louis Vives: His Attitude to Learning and to Life" in *Essays in Intellectual History* (New York 1929) p. 329–42.

VLADIMIRSKY-BUDANOV, MIKHAIL FLEGONTOVICH (1838–1916), Russian legal historian. Although Vladimirsky-Budanov was born in central Russia, he studied at the University of Kiev and was associated with it as professor from 1875 on. Influenced by his teacher Ivanishev and by the general interest in Slavic nationalities which was characteristic of Kiev in his day, he followed the comparative Slavic method in Russian legal history; thus he escaped the extremes of the German historical school, with whose philosophy he was in general agreement. His attention was early attracted to Polish-Lithuanian history; in his first work (*Nemetskoe pravo v Polshe i Litve*, St. Petersburg 1868) he dealt with the reception of Magdeburg law, maintaining that it exerted a negative influence because of its incompatibility with the Slavic "cultural historical" type. In later writings on Lithuanian law (*Ocherki iz istorii litovsko-russkogo prava*, 3 vols., Kiev 1889–93) he displayed more interest in social and economic aspects; thus he treated the law of family relations as determined almost entirely by economic factors, and in tracing the law of real property he discerned a general evolutionary tendency for feudal restrictions upon individual ownership to disappear.

Vladimirsky-Budanov's greatest distinction as a jurist is to be found in his lifelong work on historical sources. As chief editor of the Commission on the Publication of Ancient Documents in Kiev he concentrated on the sources for southwestern Russia, his independent investigations being concerned mainly with the sixteenth century; yet he also published and analyzed two Dalmatian statutes of Kastva and Veprinač (in *Zhurnal Ministerstva Narodnago Prosveshcheniya*, 1881, no. iii, pt. 2, p. 93–138) and together with Paul Vinogradoff edited a collection of sources of ancient western laws (3 vols., Kiev 1906–08). His anthology of Russian legal documents to the end of the seventeenth century (3 vols., Yaroslavl 1872–75; 4th-6th ed. Kiev 1908–15), supplied with annotations and comments, was widely used as a scholarly compilation incorporating the results of the latest research; while his general survey of Russian legal history (Kiev 1886, 7th ed. 1915) was a systematic treatise much superior to a university textbook. Vladimirsky-Budanov ranked with Sergeyevich as a central figure in the science of Russian legal history. In his special field—Lithuania and southwestern Russia—his work has been continued by a number of distinguished pupils.

Theodor Taranovsky

Consult: Yakovkin, I., in *Zhurnal Ministerstva Narodnago Prosveshcheniya*, 1916, no. xi, pt. iv, p. 35–48; Taranovsky, T., in *Uridicheskiy vestnik*, vol. xiv (1916) no. 2; Malinovsky, T. A., in *Varshavskiya universitetskiya izvestiya* (1917) no. 1.

VOCATIONAL EDUCATION. The term vocational education may be applied broadly to any form of education which prepares an individual directly for the efficient pursuit of a remunerative occupation. In practise, however, it does not include training in industrial or practical arts as a part of general education or preparation in colleges or universities for the so-called liberal professions.

The history of vocational education reflects the changing character of the economic organization of the world and, in the case of women, their changing status. The oldest form of vocational education was apprenticeship (*q.v.*), which ceased to be practicable in those industries which could best be carried on in factories and by machinery. The organization of large scale industry, which proceeded with increasing rapidity throughout the nineteenth century, accompanied as it was by mechanization, standardization and specialization, tended to reduce the amount and variety of skill needed by an operative and consequently the degree of preliminary training required. Apprenticeship could, however, survive in the occupations which did not lend themselves to mass production or in those to which entrance was restricted by well organized unions or, again, in those which required some training in the fine arts. The increasing application of science to industry and agriculture, the growth of specialized technologies and inventions, while pointing on the one hand to a reduction in the amount of training needed for the mass of workers, emphasized on the other the importance of training for occupations requiring additional skill and knowledge or preparation for supervisory and managerial positions.

Proposals for the creation of trade schools were first made in the eighteenth century. In 1708 Johann Georg Leib in his *Von Verbesserung Land und Leuten* urged the establishment of an academy for the development and improvement of manufactures. Leibniz and others advocated the provision of trade schools. The trade school established in 1706 by Semler at Halle found a number of imitators, the best known of which was Hecker's Realschule, opened in Berlin in 1747. These movements were supported actively by Frederick William and Frederick the Great. In France Descartes was one of the first to suggest schools for masters who would train artisans and make new discoveries in the arts. About 1750 the *Encyclopédie* undertook "to secure for the mechanical arts the place that belongs to them in a modern state," while d'Alembert and Diderot anticipated the later methods of "job analysis" for the improvement of apprenticeship training. In England and the United States the movement did not begin until the next century, when it was associated with the creation of mechanics institutes largely by private enterprise, a development which contrasted with that in France, where the earliest trade schools were set up under public auspices. The more rapid organization of vocational education began after the middle of the nineteenth century and paralleled the intensification of national and international competition. Attention was directed to its importance in the competition for markets by the early expositions at London in 1851, Paris in 1867 and Philadelphia in 1876. The methods of organization varied in different countries with the extent to which apprenticeship had survived; in Germany apprenticeship training was supplemented by general education in continuation schools; in France vocational schools gave both practical and theoretical instruction; in England practical skill was expected to be acquired on the job, while the schools provided instruction in theory; in the United States the urgency for vocational education was not felt so long as industry could count on a flow of labor, skilled and unskilled, from abroad.

At present the problem of vocational education is assuming a new aspect. There is everywhere an increasing and generally accepted belief that it is the duty of public authorities to provide vocational as well as general education in the interests both of the individual and of national economy. Because industry with few exceptions is unwilling to assume the burden of training in an era of great mobility of labor and because the young worker must be protected from exploitation, the task can no longer be left to private agencies or to industry itself. The problem, however, is becoming aggravated by three factors: the growing unemployability of adolescents in modern industry, the relatively small amount of training needed at the lower levels and increasing specialization at the upper levels. Additional complications arise out of the frequent technological dislocation of labor, which affects the character of initial training and introduces the need of providing centers for retraining (see REHABILITATION). These factors have brought out the necessity of studying the whole question of occupational distribution as an essential basis for vocational guidance (q.v.), a task which is being considered in most countries and at all levels (cf. for example, the conference held in Geneva in August, 1933, on overproduction of intellectuals). In the United States the problem is being studied by the National Occupational Conference under the direction of Dr. Franklin J. Keller.

There is further the problem of discovering an appropriate adjustment between vocational and general education. The individual is first a citizen and then a worker; education in citizenship and training for a vocation are equally essential for social welfare. The unemployability of adolescents provides the opportunity for extended educational supervision. There still remains, however, the question whether general and vocational education should be blended or parallel or whether vocational should follow general education. The inevitable reduction in the hours of labor and the increasing amount of leisure emphasize the importance of continued general education for the cultivation of recreational and avocational interests. The tendency at present seems to favor an extended general education followed by vocational courses and by the elaboration of a program of adult education (q.v.). So far as the organization of vocational education is concerned, it is recognized that not all vocations require the same length of preparation and that opportunities must be provided for "upgrading" courses. The chief difficulties perhaps are the reproduction in schools of the conditions which prevail in factories in an economy of mass production and disposal of the manufactured product; the second of these has been solved in France by the sale of the product of trade schools to public institutions. There is, finally, the question raised by a number of idealists, usually unfamiliar with machine occupations, whether vocational training can cultivate human values and promote the creative impulse in industry to offset the deadening and nerve racking routine of mechanized industry. By some it is considered that Soviet Russia, which has solved the dualism between general and vocational education by vocationalizing all education, has made an important contribution to this problem, in so far as the individual worker is supposed to feel himself no longer an insignificant cog in a vast machine but an essential element in a large, social undertaking.

The vocational education and employment of girls and women present today exactly the same problem as in the case of boys and men. The fact that the majority of women expect to become home makers was for a long time used as an argument against providing vocational training for them and for relegating them to relatively unskilled employment or to occupations, like needle industries or food preparation, which were regarded as natural to them. The developments of the last thirty years, accompanied by the increased provision for the general education of girls and the emancipation of women, have in many countries removed the prejudices against their employment in skilled occupations, many of which have been definitely relegated to women and are leading to the acceptance of their employment after marriage. The fullest implications of this trend are to be found in Soviet Russia, where but little difference is made between men and women either in vocational preparation or in employment. The traditional attitude, however, has been revived in Nazi Germany and Fascist Italy in the demand that women leave occupational careers to men and return to what is regarded as their natural sphere, the home. Whether this reactionary point of view will be accepted by women or by modern industry even in Germany is still uncertain. The vocational education of girls and women is today a part of the general problem; and in so far as it requires separate consideration, the task is to survey the opportunities open to them, to discover the appropriate training on the same principles as for boys and men and to provide as part of their general education preparation for home making.

The provision of vocational education varies in different countries. Private training has survived longest in the field of commercial or business education for the preparation of clerical workers; it is disappearing in the field of agricultural education; and in trade and industrial education it is found only in a small number of "works" schools in England and "corporation" schools in the United States. The tendency to organize vocational education at public expense, which is shared by the state and local authorities, is widespread. On the European continent, where the mobility of labor from one level to another is slight, appropriate vocational schools are organized for the various levels, but definite educational standards are set up for admission to each type. In Italy general prevocational work is given in the *scuola complementare*, which prepares selected pupils between the ages of ten and fourteen for trade, agriculture, industry and commerce and may be followed up after a further selection by study in the technical school organized in 1931 or in a trade school for girls or in vocational continuation schools (*corsi per maestranza*) or in the two four-year courses of the Istituto Tecnico. In Germany part time vocational education is compulsory where schools have been established for boys and girls between the ages of fourteen and eighteen; these schools, the old continuation schools (*Fortbildungsschulen*), are now known as *Berufsschulen* and organize their courses around the pupils' occupations. Full time vocational courses are provided in a great variety of occupations and range in length from one to three years; some require the completion of an elementary course, others an intermediate and still others a secondary education; in all cases a certain period of practical experience in the occupation to be studied is a prerequisite. In France, although arts and crafts schools were first established during and after the revolution, an organized system was not created until the end of the nineteenth century and was supplemented in 1919 by the *Loi Astier*. Under this law apprentices are required to attend vocational courses, for the maintenance of which a tax on employers was imposed in 1925 with exemptions for those who wish to contract out and provide the training themselves or through industrial associations and chambers of commerce. Practical schools of industry and commerce for boys and girls provide the lower level type of full time courses; the second grade is made up of a number of national vocational schools offering four-year courses to selected students; higher vocational training below university grade is given in national schools of arts and crafts and in special institutes. The characteristics of vocational education in France are the long school sessions and the combination in the same course of general education and workshop practise. Vocational education in England is in the main part time and is based on the principle that the school must provide the theoretical training and the occupations the practical. Accordingly the majority of students are found in evening schools which offer graded courses of instruction adapted in general to the occupational needs of a locality. Out of the effort which was made in 1918 to introduce compulsory continuation schools a few voluntary continuation schools have survived. Full time courses are provided in junior technical schools also adapted to local needs and offering two or three-year courses to boys and girls between thirteen and seventeen. Above these are the technical schools and colleges, which offer part time and full time instruction to students above sixteen, who in some cases must have had practical experience.

In no country has the problem been so simplified as in the Soviet Union, where vocational education is definitely coordinated with a planned economy. Not only has socially useful labor been made a constituent part of education, but all education above the primary has been vocationalized. Its organization includes lower vocational schools based on four years of primary school; factory and technical schools offering two and three-year courses above the seven-year schools for training skilled workers, administrative personnel and technical staff; and industrial academies and higher institutes, with two to five-year courses on a foundation of ten years of education. There is thus an articulated system arranged according to the needs of the industrial plan as a whole and drafting recruits in accordance with the probable demands of industry and agriculture.

Vocational education in the United States is of fairly recent origin. Mechanics institutes and manual labor colleges in the first half of the nineteenth century and private schools, correspondence schools and manual training high schools in the last quarter attempted to meet the need, but it was not until 1906 that the urgency of the problem was recognized. In that year the National Society for the Promotion of Industrial Education and the *Report* of the Massachusetts Commission on Industrial and Technical Education concentrated attention on the subject and led to a number of state surveys. Through the efforts of industrial and educational associations a movement was begun to attack the problem on a national basis and culminated in the passing of the Smith-Hughes Act in 1917, which provided federal grants to promote, in cooperation with the states, education in agriculture, trades and industries, commerce and home economics. Later extensions of the act increased the appropriations and made possible a program of vocational rehabilitation. Administration of the act is entrusted to the Federal Board for Vocational Education. At the present time vocational education is provided in part time continuation classes with general courses, evening classes, trade extension courses and trade preparatory or cooperative vocational courses. Full time vocational education is available in special schools or more generally in high schools under conditions prescribed by the Federal Board. Between 1918 and 1932 the number of pupils enrolled in vocational courses of federally controlled schools increased from 164,123 to 1,176,162. During the same period the total expenditure of federal, state and local funds for vocational education and teacher training rose from $3,039,061 to $33,402,402. Under the terms of the Smith-Hughes Act federal funds must be matched by state or local appropriations or both, but in actual fact at the present time the average state or local contribution is approximately $3 for every federal dollar. According to the sixteenth *Annual Report* of the Federal Board for Vocational Education (1932) some 9000 agricultural and home economics schools were given federal aid for the year ending June 30, 1932, while the total number of teachers employed in specified types of vocational schools sharing in federal support was 28,372. The economic depression since 1929 has led to the provision in many cities and states of short, intensive, full time courses for training displaced adults, part time courses to prepare unemployed persons for jobs and extension training or upgrading courses for adults. In 1931 the Federal Board for Vocational Education undertook a study of the relation of vocational education to unemployment with particular reference to the possibility of retraining workers who lose their jobs. Other agencies, such as the American Vocational Association, organized in 1906 to promote vocational education throughout the country, have likewise concerned themselves with the question of social and economic shifts as they are reflected in occupational displacement and technological unemployment and with the development of measures designed to meet the problem through an expanded and more flexible system of vocational education.

I. L. Kandel

See: Vocational Guidance; Education; Workers' Education; Industrial Education; Business Education; Agricultural Education; Adult Education; Continuation Schools; Correspondence Schools; Folk High Schools; Manual Training; Apprenticeship; Rehabilitation.

Consult: *Objectives and Problems of Vocational Education*, ed. by Edwin A. Lee (New York 1928); Snedden, David S., *Vocational Education* (New York 1920); Anderson, L. F., *History of Manual and Industrial School Education* (New York 1926); Sears, W. P., *The Roots of Vocational Education* (New York 1931); Prosser, C. A., and Allen, C. R., *Vocational Education in a Democracy* (New York 1925); Payne, A. F., *Administration of Vocational Education* (New York 1924); United States, Bureau of Labor Statistics, "Organization and Scope of Vocational Education in the United States," and "Vocational Training and Unemployment" in *Monthly Labor Review*, vol. xxxiii (1931) 1–19, and vol. xxxiv (1932) 275–79; Cooley, E. G., *Vocational Education in Europe*, 2 vols. (Chicago 1912–15); Réville, Marc, *Enseignement technique et apprentissage* (Paris 1913); Kandel, I. L., *Comparative Education* (Boston 1933); Columbia University, Teachers College, International Institute, *Educational Yearbook*, ed. by I. L. Kandel, vol. v (1929) pt. ii; Abbott, Albert, *Education for Industry and Commerce in England* (London 1933); *Year Book of Education*, ed. by E. S. C. Percy, published in London since 1932; Diamond, Thomas, "Technical Education in Great Britain" in *Industrial Arts and Vocational Education*, vol. xx (1931) 1–4, 39–42; Great Britain, Board of Education, *Education for Industry and Commerce*, Educational Pamphlets, no. 64, Industry series, no. i (London 1928); Abbott, Albert, and Dalton, J. E., *Trade Schools on the Continent*, Great Britain, Board of Education, Educational Pamphlets, no. 91, Industry series, no. xi (London 1932); Kerschensteiner, G. M. A., *Grundfragen der Schulorganisation* (4th ed. Leipsic 1921) ch. ii; *Die Berufserziehung des Arbeiters*, Gesellschaft für Soziale Reform, Schriften, nos. 70–72, 3 vols. (Jena 1920–21); *Handbuch für das Berufs- und Fachschulwesen*, ed. by Alfred Kühne (2nd ed. Leipsic 1929); Pınkevich, A. P., *Pedagogika*, 2 vols. (2nd ed. Moscow 1925), tr. by N. Perlmutter as *The New Education in the Soviet Republic*, 1 vol. (New York 1929) ch. xv; International Labour Office, *Vocational Education in Agriculture*, Studies and Reports, Ser. K, no. 9 (Geneva 1929). See also United States, Federal Board for Vocational Education, *Annual Report*, issued since 1917, and "Vocational Training and Unemployment," *Bulletin*, no. 159 (1931).

VOCATIONAL GUIDANCE was organized initially as a social service calculated to assist young people in choosing their occupations. In its present scope it consists of systematic effort to inform, counsel or furnish experiences to persons who seek to discover their occupational interests and abilities, to learn about the problems and opportunities of employment, to choose general or special fields of service, to secure preparation for a particular type of work, to obtain suitable employment or to make successive adjustments toward a satisfactory economic status.

The rise of the movement for vocational guidance may be traced to a number of factors. First among these was the gradual removal from the home of industrial, commercial and personal service processes, so that young people were left without the experiential and cognitive backgrounds required for intelligent occupational decisions. Second, the growing complexity of industrial and commercial technology made sampling experiences and accurate information difficult to obtain. Third, there was marked waste of vocational training upon pupils who had enrolled in expensive and highly specialized curricula without careful appraisal of their talents and plans. Fourth, industrial specialization increased the difficulties of finding appropriate employment. Fifth, the greatly extended enrolment of pupils of diverse backgrounds in secondary schools forced upon the educational system the problems of later adjustment which were undreamed of when schools offered merely preparatory training for college. Sixth, the dissemination of democratic ideals created a most difficult problem, namely, the distribution, on the basis of decisions made by individuals themselves, of vocational services calculated to satisfy the complex needs of the social whole.

An analysis of the task of vocational guidance is suggested by its definition. Certain steps must be taken by the individual, and these break up into a number of separate phases in each of which the teacher-pupil relationship is apparent.

Discovery of the interests and abilities of the individual should take place for most pupils at about the junior high school level. This problem involves the question of inborn aptitudes and acquired abilities. Some psychologists hold that the use of tests will reveal general and special abilities, even if there has been no background of experience. Others advocate the setting up of shops and classrooms offering samples of work, so that abilities may be explored and tested by trial and success. As vocational guidance has gained recognition among educators, there has been a gradual transformation of manual training rooms into "general shops"; simple tasks are now provided in wood and metal working, plumbing, electrical wiring, automobile mechanics, printing and the like. "Junior business training," a comprehensive course including many kinds of elementary exercises drawn from commercial transactions together with work in gardening and in home making situations, serves to round out a wide scope of vocational exploration. Moreover extracurricular activities develop abilities in human relations, a factor of paramount importance in occupational success. Still other means for the discovery of abilities are available: experiences in actual jobs, activities in scouting and organized play, development of hobbies, counseling, observation of workers, reading and opportunities to assist workers. Success in certain studies points more or less directly toward specific forms of vocational service.

Study of the occupational field, its opportunities and problems supplies the other half of the requisite background. Early experiments led to the imparting of such information in connection with English composition, lectures by successful adults and visits to places of employment. Methods of this sort have usually proved inadequate unless coordinated with opportunity for systematic study, such as is now frequently furnished through regular classes in vocational information, for which numerous courses of study have been drawn up. Well trained teachers are rare and supervision is generally inadequate. The survey made in 1929 by the White House Conference on Child Health and Protection revealed that about half of the American cities were maintaining such courses. Perhaps a score of colleges are offering class work in occupational opportunities.

The third phase of vocational progress relates to a decision of some sort, at least to the choice of the general area of an individual's vocational investment. Possessed of self-knowledge and vocation knowledge, he may consider agriculture, commerce, industry or a profession. Many educational institutions provide counselors or deans to assist students in such decisions. Research is now being conducted, largely by psychologists, with a view to helping counselors and students. Tests have been devised, criticized, validated and standardized, and inventories of interests and of personality characteristics have been provided. Record blanks furnish cumulative evidence. Counseling, still valuable in the consideration of alternatives, clarification of purposes and development of morale, has tended to make increasing use of carefully kept records and test results.

Vocational education may be effective only when rational choice has been made. In view of the large number of pupils who leave school early, however, some forms of juvenile training seem necessary. The continuation school offers such assistance, and there are signs that an intensification of the experimental idea may provide pupils of fifteen to eighteen years of age with an equipment of diverse skills which will prove adequate for initial contacts and may lead to better positions. Vocational guidance has made several contributions to vocational education. It serves to gauge the wisdom of the pupil's enrolment, furnishes him with a vestibule experience as a basis for selecting his specialization within the school, teaches him about the opportunities and problems ahead and develops in his thought and practise the "wisdom factor" requisite for his success and for his cooperation in bettering economic society.

While the typical child worker secures jobs in a variety of ways, progress is being made toward maintaining centralized placement offices to facilitate the process of transition from school to work. Such offices obtain records and other specifications relating to the individual and compare them with the stated characteristics of the job. State and federal agencies assist in the problem of securing work, juvenile and adult employment being separately organized.

Seldom does a person's record present an orderly progress through the five steps just described. In any event occupational shifts and individual changes of objective make readjustment a necessary phase in the development of plans. A few school systems maintain a follow-up and employment supervision service, designed to review with worker and employer accomplishments, plans and problems relating to success, promotion and further education. Employers maintain services which assist in the readjustment process, and many professional, semi-educational, labor and social service organizations, such as the National Federation of Business and Professional Women's Clubs, the Southern Women's Educational Alliance, Rotary, Kiwanis, Altusa, the Young Men's Christian Association, the Young Women's Christian Association, Pioneer Youth, trade unions and social settlements, furnish advice to young men and women in vocational adjustment.

Some forms of vocational guidance are as old as the division of labor. Plato, Montaigne, Herbart, Pascal, Henry MacKenzie and many others wrote of the need, and Dickens in Chapter XIII of *Bleak House* gave an excellent picture of the problem of choice without guidance. Various early writers offered occupational information, and one volume dated 1836 (Hazen, Edward, *The Panorama of Professions and Trades: or Everyman's Book*, Philadelphia) contains questions in textbook form and states that such material should be studied in schools. Meanwhile the sophists in phrenology, physiognomy, astrology, palmistry and character analysis attempted to advise upon choice of vocation.

In the United States the movement which led to the present effort to supply vocational guidance was originated by a publicist and social worker, Frank Parsons, professor of law in Boston University. In a social settlement, Civic Service House, Parsons organized in 1908 the Vocation Bureau of Boston, concerned primarily with counseling young people in regard to choice of career but also with the collection of occupational information and the spread of the guidance idea. He used the expression vocational guidance, suggested the several phases of the work and insisted that it should be taken over by school systems. Meyer Bloomfield, who succeeded Parsons, popularized the plan and set up a training course for counselors at Harvard University Summer School and at Boston University. In 1917 the bureau was transferred to Harvard University and later became the Bureau of Vocational Guidance of the Graduate School of Education. Vocational guidance was early introduced into the public schools, and, beginning with Boston, Brooklyn and Grand Rapids, the movement spread throughout the country. Pennsylvania, New York, Ohio, California, Washington and Virginia have made some progress toward a state wide plan and together with four or five cities have set up standard qualifications for the counselor's position. In some communities county or regional plans have been tried. At the present time a considerable number of universities and teachers colleges maintain curricula for the preparation of counselors. In the development of vocational guidance, whether under educational or other auspices, psychology and mental testing have played an important part; in addition there has been close correlation between guidance and scientific management and job analysis. The movement for educational guidance was an outgrowth of that for vocational guidance. Within recent years some of the techniques used in vocational guidance have been applied to other fields of life activity and have thus influenced education in general. In the case of a few public school systems vocational counseling is oriented with a comprehensive course in guidance which includes analysis and study of educational, social, recreational and avocational interests as well as vocational aptitudes, with a view to the more satisfactory adjustment of the pupil to society.

The first national conference on vocational guidance was held in Boston in 1910; and three years later the National Vocational Guidance Association was organized, a body which has contributed markedly to the clarification of the aims and procedures of the movement. In 1915 a periodical was started which later became the *Vocational Guidance Magazine*, the organ of the association. In 1933 through a grant from the Carnegie Corporation there was formed the National Occupational Conference, a group interested in furthering the magazine, renamed *Occupations; the Vocational Guidance Magazine* (published at Cambridge, Mass., 9 issues per year), and in conducting and sponsoring researches and conferences.

Because of the extent to which social, class and family traditions still function as determinants of an individual's career, vocational guidance in European and Asiatic countries has not been so widely developed as in the United States. Nevertheless, special bureaus have been established in the larger cities, and in nearly every country some type of vocational guidance is under way.

In England vocational guidance was until recently empirical in character and existed as an informal service conducted by the juvenile advisory committees under the Ministry of Labour or by the juvenile employment committees and "aftercare" committees under local educational authorities. It was designed chiefly for boys and girls leaving school between the ages of fourteen and eighteen, to advise them in regard to opportunities for and selection of employment in trade and industry. Little use was made of technical methods of vocational guidance, including the utilization of psychological tests. Recently, however, under the auspices of the National Institute of Industrial Psychology in London a system of vocational service for youth has been worked out on the basis of scientific tests and counseling.

In France vocational guidance has been developed largely as a result of the work of the Institut National d'Orientation Professionnelle, which was established in 1928 to conduct research and to train vocational counselors. Somewhat earlier informal vocational guidance bureaus had been established in several of the larger industrial centers and a commission for vocational guidance created under the auspices of the Ministry of Public Instruction.

During the period following the World War and prior to the Nazi revolution Germany had developed a fairly wide system of vocational guidance with offices and bureaus in some five hundred cities, most of them in connection with government employment exchanges. Much valuable work was done in the analysis of occupations and in the preparation of psychological tests and questionnaires. In many cities steps were taken to enlist the cooperation of school authorities and parents. Special emphasis was laid on the general economic situation in addition to a study of applicants' interests and abilities. The agencies in control of vocational guidance included the Zentralinstitut für Erziehung und Unterricht, the Reichsamt für Arbeitsvermittlung and the Reichsarbeitsverwaltung.

Japan has made a beginning in vocational guidance both through its schools, where lectures are given to teachers to enable them to advise pupils in regard to choice of vocation, and through public employment exchanges. In several cities plans have been made for the appointment of special vocational guidance advisers who will devote all their time to the guidance of young people and who will encourage cooperation between industrial and educational authorities, employment exchanges and parents. These advisers will give assistance not only in the selection of occupations but will also supervise young workers after their placement.

In Soviet Russia vocational guidance exists not so much as a separate service but rather as an integral part of the nation wide system of vocational training which dominates all education. Since the latter is directed chiefly toward industrialization of the country, there is accordingly less need for vocational guidance than in countries characterized by the absence of a planned economy.

Bureaus for investigation and service in the field of "psycho-technics" have been established in several countries, and guidance offices of an educational nature exist in Switzerland, Czechoslovakia, Belgium, Spain, Italy, Austria, China and three South American countries. The International Labor Office has from time to time published reports of practises in vocational guidance as a part of its services in the field of labor relations.

An estimate of the results of vocational guidance is exceedingly difficult because of the complexity of the problems with which it deals. Even in the relatively simple matter of measuring the results of the dissemination of occupational information in school classes the statistical findings, while favorable, are not outstandingly clear. Case studies indicate that vocational guidance is often applied effectively and suggest that broadening the work will not interfere with liberal or general education but will lead to wiser occupational decisions, aid the individual in developing a social viewpoint, effect economies through rationalizing programs of vocational education and prepare the individual for cooperation in the necessary reorganization of industrial society. For the future, vocational guidance must take into account changing social and economic conditions and their relation to the problems of occupational shift, unemployment and the extension of leisure both voluntary and involuntary. In countries such as the United States the limitations imposed by an unorganized labor market and the absence of public employment exchanges also constitute important factors; unless these are recognized, no system of vocational guidance can be entirely effective.

JOHN M. BREWER

See: VOCATIONAL EDUCATION; CHILD; CONTINUATION SCHOOLS; MENTAL TESTS; CAREER; OCCUPATION; PERSONNEL ADMINISTRATION.

Consult: Myers, George E., *The Problem of Vocational Guidance* (New York 1927); Brewer, John M., *The Vocational Guidance Movement* (New York 1918), and *Education as Guidance* (New York 1932); *Principles and Problems in Vocational Guidance*, ed. by F. J. Allen (New York 1927); Cohen, I. D., *Principles and Practices of Vocational Guidance* (New York 1929); Neuberg, Maurice J., *Principles and Methods of Vocational Choice* (New York 1934); Earle, F. M., *Methods of Choosing a Career* (London 1931); Jones, A. J., *Principles of Guidance* (rev. ed. New York 1934); Proctor, W. M., *Educational and Vocational Guidance* (Boston 1925); Lipmann, O., Burt, C., and Thurstone, L. L., "Principles of Vocational Guidance" in *British Journal of Psychology*, vol. xiv (1923–24) 321–61; Hättenschwiller, A., *Berufsberatung* (Lucerne 1923); Schwarz, M., *Das Berufsproblem* (München-Gladbach 1923); Payne, A. F., *Organization of Vocational Guidance* (New York 1925); *Practice in Vocational Guidance*, ed. by F. J. Allen (New York 1927); National Vocational Guidance Association, *Basic Units for an Introductory Course in Vocational Guidance*, ed. by W. B. Jones (New York 1931); Kitson, H. D., "Training for Vocational Counselors" in *Vocational Guidance Magazine*, vol. v (1926–27) 313–15; White House Conference on Child Health and Protection, sect. III: Education and Training, Report of Sub-Committee on Vocational Guidance, *Vocational Guidance* (New York 1932); Allen, Richard Day, *Organization and Supervision of Guidance in Public Education* (New York 1934); Trumbull, Frederick M., *Guidance and Education of Prospective Junior Wage Earners* (New York 1929); United States, Children's Bureau, "Vocational Guidance and Junior Placement," *Publications*, no. 149 (1925); Hatcher, O. L., *Guiding Rural Boys and Girls* (New York 1930) pt. iii; Koos, L. V., and Kefauver, Grayson N., *Guidance in Secondary Schools* (New York 1932); Maverick, Lewis A., *The Vocational Guidance of College Students*, Harvard Studies in Education, vol. viii (Cambridge, Mass. 1926); "Vocational Guidance and Vocational Education for the Industries," ed. by A. H. Edgerton in National Society for the Study of Education, *Twenty-Third Yearbook* (Bloomington, Ill. 1924) pt. ii; Keller, Franklin J., *Day Schools for Young Workers* (New York 1924), and "Guidance in Vocational Training" in *Industrial Psychology*, vol. i (1926) 781–87; Kitson, Harry D., *The Psychology of Vocational Adjustment* (Philadelphia 1925); Lipmann, Otto, *Wirtschaftspsychologie und psychologische Berufsberatung*, Schriften zur Psychologie der Berufseignung und des Wirtschaftslebens, no. 1 (2nd ed. Leipsic 1921); Lorge, Irving, "The Chimera of Vocational Guidance," and Kitson, H. D., "Vocational Guidance Is Not Fortune Telling; a Reply to Dr. Lorge" in *Teachers College Record*, vol. xxxv (1933–34) 359–76; Bingham, W. V., and Moore, B. V., *How to Interview* (New York 1931). See also: *Occupations; the Vocational Guidance Magazine*, published monthly in Cambridge, Mass., since 1922.

VOCATIONAL PSYCHOLOGY. *See* VOCATIONAL GUIDANCE.

VOGEL, SIR JULIUS (1835–99), New Zealand statesman and imperialist. Born and educated in London, Vogel as a young man emigrated to Australia. At the time of the gold rush in 1861 he went to New Zealand and engaged in journalism at Dunedin. Before long he was active in both provincial and national politics, entering Parliament in 1863 and becoming colonial treasurer in 1869. In this capacity he inaugurated a policy of extensive borrowing for public works and immigration, a landmark not only in New Zealand history but in the development of British capital exports. While local political and economic circumstances were the main reasons for his policy, Vogel pressed his schemes as a means of imperial expansion. He endeavored also to force the British government to forestall German expansion in the Pacific islands, urging on many occasions that these islands should be united in a federation under New Zealand's leadership.

Vogel was an important influence in shaping both the constitutional development and the political policies of New Zealand in the transitional period after the gold rushes and in assisting immigration which broke down the exclusiveness of the first settlements. He abolished the provincial system in 1876 and laid the foundations of centralized administration. Besides the national education system, established in 1877 shortly after his premiership, he was largely responsible for the public trust office, the system of land transfers through state registration, the government life insurance department, the first efforts at forest conservation and the subsidizing of oversea cable and steamer connections with England through America. He was a pioneer advocate of tariff protection for local industries and of woman suffrage. In these steps toward state enterprise, protection and complete democracy he prepared the way for the later experiments in state socialism, just as in his imperialist policies he foreshadowed subsequent attempts at imperial cooperation.

In addition to editing the *Official Handbook of New Zealand* (2nd ed. London 1875) Vogel was the author of *Great Britain and Her Colonies* (London 1865), *New Zealand and the South Sea Islands* (London 1878) and a novel, *Anno Domini 2000* (London 1889).

J. B. CONDLIFFE

Consult: Reeves, W. Pember, *The Long White Cloud* (3rd rev. ed. London 1924) ch. xix; Condliffe, J. B., *New Zealand in the Making* (London 1930), especially p. 31–34, 103–06; Parsons, F., *The Story of New Zealand* (Philadelphia 1904) p. 98–119, 615–16.

VOGELSANG, FREIHERR KARL VON (1818–90), Austrian social reformer and publicist. Born in Germany, Vogelsang came from an old Protestant family of the landed aristocracy and became an official in the Prussian civil service. Under the personal influence of Bishop Ketteler he was converted to Catholicism in 1850. In 1864 he emigrated to Austria, where he engaged in wide publicistic activity. He developed his Christian social ideas in the *Vaterland*, the organ of the clergy and the nobility, and in the *Monatsschrift für christliche Sozialreform*, which he founded in 1879. As an Austrian federalist he was strongly opposed to the Prussian political system and the German Empire. But neither his loyalty to the Austrian emperor nor his social and intellectual connections with the Catholic nobility could induce him to take part in the struggle against the "anarchists," whose radicalism he considered but a consequence of capitalistic economy.

Vogelsang's works developed among Catholics an understanding of the social problems involved in the capitalist system. He obtained the approval of Pope Leo XIII and gained adherents in Switzerland, Belgium, France and Germany. He was involved, however, in various controversies with the German Catholic party, partly because the latter was more inclined to a liberal course in Catholic politics and partly because it did not wish to raise the questions of social reform during the *Kulturkampf* with Bismarck. In Austria, however, Vogelsang became one of the intellectual inaugurators of the Christian Socialist party.

Vogelsang considered capitalism a complete disorder which arose from the "revolution of the higher social groupings against the Christian social order" once realized in the Middle Ages and later destroyed by the Renaissance, the Reformation and the reception of Roman law. As the social agents of the present system he fought, above all, the liberals and the Jews. On the basis of Christian natural law combined with national juridical traditions Vogelsang sought to reestablish an economic system compatible with and subject to the social principles of Roman Catholic dogma. Instead of the class system he advocated a society vertically stratified and corresponding to the occupational division of labor. Minimizing the gap in interests between small and large scale production he conceived of a corporate society built in harmony with the "natural law of man" and the principle of estates. He urged the imposition of trenchant measures upon economic organization by the state and was therefore often reproached with being a state socialist. In order to transform the private property system in agriculture into one of cooperative ownership he proposed to begin with governmental administration of the entire mortgage on landed property, aiming at complete liberation from debt. He also suggested cooperative organizations of handicrafts, considering peasants and independent craftsmen as the fundamental classes in society. He sought to bridge the gap between the industrial worker and the entrepreneur by connecting the worker more closely with the plant.

The most romantic features of Vogelsang's theory were his suggestions to bring about a shrinkage of money economy as well as foreign trade. Attempting to revive the old usury law of the church he wanted to substitute deliveries in kind for several money taxes and restrict the interest rate for credits. Foreign trade he considered unethical, politically destructive and unsocial. His ideal was a state of economic self-sufficiency, or autarchy.

HANS SPEIER

Works: *Gesammelte Aufsätze über socialpolitische und verwandte Themata*, pts. 1–7 (Augsburg 1885–86); *Vogelsang. Extrait de ses oeuvres. I. Morale et économie sociale. II. Politique sociale*, 2 vols. (Paris 1905).

Consult: Klopp, Wiard, *Leben und Wirken des Sozialpolitikers Karl Freiherrn von Vogelsang* (Vienna 1930), and *Die sozialen Lehren des Freiherrn Karl von Vogelsang* (St. Pölten 1894); Schwalber, Joseph, *Vogelsang und die moderne christlich-soziale Politik* (Munich 1927).

VOLLMAR, GEORG VON (1850–1922), German Social Democratic leader and parliamentarian. Vollmar was born in Munich of an old family of state officials and received a strict Catholic upbringing. He attended the school of the Benedictines at Augsburg and then as a cadet entered a regiment of Bavarian cuirassiers. At the outbreak of the Franco-Prussian War he volunteered for the German army and was seriously wounded at Blois. He went to Paris and Zurich and turned to the study of social and political science; in this way he developed an interest in the socialist movement and became active as a journalist. Vollmar took over the direction of the socialist *Dresdner Volkszeitung* and soon thereafter was elected to the Saxon *Landtag*, the German Reichstag and the Bavarian *Landtag*.

At first Vollmar joined the Bebel group, but he gradually went over to the so-called revisionists. He believed that all social progress is realized only through slow transition and that preoccupation with the future is therefore idle. The Social Democrats, he held, should concentrate all their agitation upon greater protection of labor, extension of trade union rights, increased wages and the like.

With this turn to the right Vollmar came into more and more opposition to the Marxist wing of the party. This conflict culminated in the violent debate between Vollmar and Bebel at the Dresden Party Congress of 1903. Outvoted and hindered by his physical condition from making any energetic counter attack, Vollmar gradually withdrew from political life. He remained a member of the Social Democratic party but he rarely made a public appearance.

HEINRICH CUNOW

Consult: Saenger, Alwin, in *Deutsches biographisches Jahrbuch*, vol. iv (1929) 276–89 with full bibliography.

VOLTAIRE, FRANÇOIS-MARIE AROUET DE (1694–1778), French man of letters, historian and *philosophe*. Educated at the Collège Louis-le-Grand, Voltaire soon became known as a wit, was received in the circle of the duchesse du Maine, wrote two tragedies and before the age of twenty-six was twice "exiled" from Paris and once sent to the Bastille for lampoons on prominent people. In 1725, countering a witty insult from the chevalier de Rohan by one more finished, he was beaten in the streets by the chevalier's lackeys, challenged the chevalier to a duel, was sent to the Bastille and after a fortnight, at his own request, allowed to retire to England. In England (1726–29), where he was cordially received by the Walpoles, Pope, Congreve and other distinguished people, he was profoundly impressed with the contrast between France and a country where every one chose his "own road to heaven," where nobles were "great without insolence," the people "share in government without disorder" and a professor of mathematics (Newton) "is buried like a king." Returning to France with a full purse, a European reputation, settled ideas on all *les grands sujets* and a bag full of manuscripts, he completed *Henriade* (Geneva 1723), printed privately *Charles XII* (2 vols., Rouen 1731), produced *Brutus* and *Zaïre* (1730 and 1732) and published *Lettres philosophiques . . . sur les anglais* (Amsterdam 1734), an indirect but powerful attack on French political and ecclesiastical intolerance which added much to his fame and contributed more than any other work to making English literature and institutions popular in France.

Foreseeing the official condemnation of this work, Voltaire had already retired to Lorraine, where he set up house with Madame du Châtelet at Cirey. Here during the next fifteen years he did much of his best writing: *Essai . . . sur les moeurs* (7 vols., Geneva 1756) and *Le siècle de Louis XIV* (2 vols., Berlin 1751); *Alzire* and *Mérope* (produced in 1736 and 1743) and, with the collaboration of Madame du Châtelet, *Élémens de la philosophie de Newton* (Amsterdam 1738). Employed in connection with the fêtes attending the dauphin's marriage, he was rewarded, through the influence of Madame du Pompadour, with the office of historiographer royal at a salary of 2000 livres (1745) and in 1746 was admitted to the Academy. The death of Madame du Châtelet (1749) and the loss of royal favor induced him to accept the invitation of Frederick the Great, many times extended, to establish himself at Berlin (1750–53). Admiring each other at a distance, the two incompatible great men exhibited their worst qualities when brought together. If their puerile billingsgate battles and revenges are judged on their demerits, dishonors were doubtless even; but the facile wit and sly dishonesty of the king of letters were in the end forced to yield to the authority and brutality of the king of Prussia. Secretly escaping from his royal prison Voltaire managed to return to France, only to find that the unauthorized publication of part of the *Essai* (1754) made him no more welcome at Paris than at Berlin. He therefore cannily established himself, first at Les Délices outside the gates of Geneva, then at Ferney just inside the frontier of France, where, within easy distance of four independent political jurisdictions, he lived until 1778.

Voltaire's great wealth—partly inherited, partly acquired—enabled him to live at Ferney on the scale of a grand seigneur, keeping open house to the stream of people who came from all parts of Europe and America to visit the most famous man of letters of the century. During these last years, as always, he wrote ceaselessly, keeping abreast of his swelling correspondence and publishing, besides a multitude of lesser works, *La Pucelle* in 1755, the first authorized edition of the *Essai*, and *Candide* in 1759. Having seemingly attained the height of fame and influence by his writings, Voltaire now added to both by his deeds. In 1761 the Parlement of Toulouse, swayed by the religious passions of the community, condemned the Huguenot Jean Calas to torture and death for the alleged murder of his son and deprived his family of their property and civil rights. Convinced that Calas was innocent, Voltaire employed all his talent, influence and furious zeal to make the *affaire Calas* a European *cause célèbre* and after three years of unremitting effort obtained a reversal of the verdict and a restoration of rights and property (1762–65). The French were quick to see a dramatic fitness in Voltaire's championship of the Calas family, since their sufferings flagrantly exemplified the evils of religious intolerance, the stupidity of mass emotion and the barbarous inhumanity of the prevailing legal procedure—the very conditions which Voltaire had denounced in his writings, the essence of that "Infamous Thing" which he had insisted must be "crushed." Henceforth his name was a household word, even among the ignorant masses; and in 1778, when he came to Paris for the last time, crowds followed the "savior of Calas" in the streets, and in the theater he was crowned with laurel.

Voltaire's *Oeuvres complètes* (ed. by Beaumarchais, Condorcet and Decroix, Kehl 1785–89) comprises seventy volumes of poetry, plays, tales, histories, works of popularization, polemics and private letters. In point of merit the letters are nearest perfection. The best of his works in the different *genres* are perhaps *Zaïre* and *Mérope*; *Candide* and *Zadig*; *Lettres . . . sur les anglais* and *Philosophie de Newton*; *Charles xii* and *Le siècle de Louis xiv*. The *Essai sur les moeurs* (which in later editions includes *Le siècle de Louis xiv* and *Le siècle de Louis xv*) was the longest and most ambitious of his works and perhaps also the most influential, since it was an event in historiography as well as a tract for the times. As an event in historiography, it contributed toward the development of a more critical handling of historical sources and did much to shape the modern trend toward *Kulturgeschichte*. As a tract for the times, it made of "God's Universe," as Carlyle said, "a greater Patrimony of St. Peter, from which it were well and pleasant to hunt out the Pope"; it surveyed the history of mankind in such guise as to demonstrate that the progress of civilization is incompatible with political oppression and ecclesiastical intolerance. The virtues and defects of the *Essai* are those of Voltaire himself, of all his works and of his century. If there is not in all his seventy volumes a profound or an original idea, neither is there any that is irrelevant to the immediate interests and problems of his time. He accepted at first sight and without reservation all the characteristic faiths and skepticisms of the Enlightenment: its aversion to "superstition" and its dislike of "dim perspectives"; its preoccupation with the world that is evident to the senses; its passion for freedom and its humane sympathies; its profound faith in the efficacy of reason for resolving all mysteries and for harmonizing the ideas, the conduct and the institutions of men with the imprescriptible laws of nature and of nature's God. Accepting these ideas without reservation, he could express them with conviction and in writing which, for clarity, precision, wit and movement as swift and effortless as sunlight passing over rippling water, has surely never been equaled. It was Voltaire's supreme virtue and the source of his immense influence that, by raising to the level of genius the art of delivering ideas struggling to be born, he became the authentic and inspired voice of the age in which he lived.

CARL BECKER

Works: *Oeuvres complètes de Voltaire*, 52 vols. (new ed. Paris 1877–85); *The Works of Voltaire*, 42 vols. (New York 1901).

Consult: Desnoiresterres, G. Le B., *Voltaire et la société française au XVIIIe siècle*, 8 vols. (Paris 1871–76); Morley, J., *Voltaire* (New York 1878); Brandes, G. M. C., *François de Voltaire*, 2 vols. (Copenhagen 1916–17), tr. by O. Kruger and P. Butler (New York 1930); Collins, J. C., *Voltaire . . . in England* (London 1908); Chase, C. B., *The Young Voltaire* (New York 1926); Torrey, N. M., *Voltaire and the English Deists*, Yale Romantic Studies, vol. i (New Haven 1930); Sainte-Beuve, C. A., *Causeries du lundi*, 15 vols. (Paris 1857–62) vol. vii, p. 105–26, vol. xiii, p. 1–38, and vol. xv, p. 219–45; Brunetière, F., *Études critiques sur l'histoire de la littérature française*, ser. 1–9 (new ed. Paris 1890–1925) ser. iii, p. 259–90, ser. iv, p. 267–324; Faguet, E., *Dix-huitième siècle* (Paris 1894); Fueter, E., *Geschichte der neueren Historiographie*, Handbuch der mittelalterlichen und neueren Geschichte, vol. i (Munich 1911) p. 349–63; Ritter, M., "Studien über die Entwicklung der Geschichtswissenschaft . . . . Das 18. Jahrhundert" in *Historische Zeitschrift*, vol. cxii (1914) 29–131; Bengescu, G., *Voltaire; Bibliographie de ses oeuvres*, 4 vols. (Paris 1882–90); Mornet, Daniel, *Les origines intellectuelles de la Révolution française* (Paris 1933) p. 28–32, 82–89; Brunot, Ferdinand, *Histoire de la langue française des origines à 1900*, vols. i–viii (Paris 1905–33) vol. vi, pt. 2, ch. i.

VOLUNTARY ASSOCIATIONS. The voluntary association is an unincorporated group of persons organized for some common purpose. The application of the term voluntary to an organization of this type is a reflection of the theory that it comes into being through the will of its members, whereas the state creates the corporation. Voluntary associations may be established for profit or for social, charitable or other non-commercial ends; and from an early period this essential difference in purpose led, in English law, to the development of two different sets of legal principles, applicable respectively to profit and non-profit associations. Both bodies of law are, however, dominated by the concept that no unincorporated association has legal personality and that rights and liabilities arising in connection with such an association can be only the rights and liabilities of its members. Many departures from this conception, in effect if not always in theory, have, however, taken place especially in recent years. But the pace has been uneven, and the change has been more marked in regard to business associations than to non-profit organizations.

Voluntary business associations include partnerships, limited partnerships, joint stock companies, partnership associations, business trusts and certain types of de facto corporations. The business trust has a distinctive character as compared with other unincorporated associations for profit and will therefore be discussed separately.

Historically the complex partnership, the joint stock company and even the partnership association, a creation of statutory law, may be considered developments of the simple partnership; and according to orthodox common law theory their legal position and that of their members are based essentially upon the law governing partners. Thus a voluntary association is said to partake of the disadvantages of a partnership: namely, unlimited personal liability of members, inability to achieve perpetual existence, diffusion of management resulting from the rule that each partner may bind his associates, and difficulties in taking and conveying real property. Furthermore, since an association is not an entity, suits cannot be brought by or against the association as such, the necessary parties being the individual members. Finally, although a stockholder may enforce his rights against a corporation in an action at law, this remedy is not available to a shareholder in an association as against either the association or his comembers. However, since voluntary associations, other than the simple partnership, developed with a view to meeting the demand for large, heavily capitalized enterprises, in which the burden of risk and liability might be divided among many participants, it was inevitable that their position in law should be made less onerous. Prior to the nineteenth century members of associations, because of the difficulty of obtaining corporate status, were unable to evade by incorporation the disabilities attaching to associations. Later, incorporation was avoided so as to escape from the restrictions of charters and state supervision and taxation.

From an early date relief from some of the disadvantages characteristic of the voluntary association was given in courts of equity through representative suits in situations where it was impossible to make all the associates parties and through settlement of the claims of individual partners against the association by an accounting. Much was accomplished by statutory changes, induced by the pressure of business interests, and also by judicial support of agreements between members of an association. In fact the similarity between the association and the corporation, both in organization and in activities, led irresistibly to a confusion of the two related bodies of law in the judicial mind and to the resultant reception of corporate concepts into the law of associations.

In England the Bubble Act of 1720 (6 Geo. I. c. 18) and the uncertainty of the common law in the matter of the transferability of shares in unincorporated companies gave them an equivocal position at law. Nevertheless, a large number of voluntary companies had come into existence by the end of the eighteenth century; during the nineteenth they became very popular, obtaining by legislative act many of the advantages of the corporation and at the same time becoming subject to increasing governmental supervision. They were, however, reduced to insignificance by the Companies Act of 1862 (25 & 26 Vict. c. 89), which not only facilitated incorporation but made it compulsory thereafter for all business associations consisting of more than twenty persons and for all banking organizations of more than ten. Limited partnerships were authorized by the act of 1907 (7 Edw. VII. c. 24).

In the United States, where the Bubble Act was not considered part of the common law, the unincorporated association has flourished, gradually acquiring corporate attributes. Continuity of existence and concentration of management are obtained in large partnerships and joint stock companies by agreements between members, while difficulties in the conveyance and taking of real property are avoided in many instances by trust devices. In most states statutes authorize suits against voluntary associations either in the firm name through service upon one or more of the officers or against the officers as representing the associates; in the latter situation individual shareholders may sometimes be joined. In such suits execution can issue only against the joint assets of the associates or at best against the individual assets of the members served. Some states also permit suits in the name of the association or in that of its officers. It is of course in relation to the question of liability that the courts cling most tenaciously to the theory that an association is only the aggregate of its several members. Nevertheless, it is possible at present for shareholders in unincorporated companies to attain by contract limitation of liability. Agreements between members of an association and strangers that the latter will look only to the joint assets of the associates for payment have been upheld, although the courts are chary of granting the associates protection on this basis unless the stipulation is an express part of the particular contract involved. Limited liability may also be obtained for certain of the members of a limited partnership, a special type of statutory unincorporated association. Here too the limitation of liability is precarious, for any failure to conform to the statute may convert the special partner into a general partner with unlimited personal liability. Not only limitation of liability but almost all other corporate features can be realized in the partnership association, which is permitted in five states, including Pennsylvania and Michigan. This form of organization has, however, been held by a federal court to constitute a limited partnership for purposes of jurisdiction [Great Southern Fire Proof Hotel Company *v.* Jones, 193 U.S. 532 (1903)].

The type of voluntary association which became the most effective rival of the corporation, however, is one which derives from both the partnership and the common law trust. The use of the Massachusetts, or business, trust for large scale enterprises spread rapidly from the latter part of the nineteenth century in the United States and to a lesser extent in England. It appeared to combine all the benefits of incorporation without its many disadvantages. Through a trust a trustee or group of trustees may organize a business in which perpetual succession is assured and in which shareholders, whose certificates are freely transferable, have technically the status of beneficiaries of the trust. Management is concentrated in the trustees, while conveyances of property are effected as easily by trustees as by corporations. Actions at law are brought by or against the trustees; a beneficiary may contract with a trustee and sue upon such an agreement. In order to protect themselves and the beneficiaries from personal liability trustees may provide in their contracts with third parties that liability on obligations will be limited to the extent of the trust fund. Moreover for a time the trust, like other unincorporated associations, appeared to enjoy a special prerogative; under the privileges and immunities clause of the constitution the trustee, as a citizen of a state, was allowed to do business in a foreign state under the same conditions as the local citizen, while the corporation, an artificial person without the rights of citizenship, was generally forced to submit to special burdens.

But the law could not for long ignore the persistent realities of this situation. The trust was too obviously a means of evading governmental control and at the same time escaping from the responsibilities placed upon the members of unincorporated associations by the common law. The courts accordingly began to hold that where a so-called trust agreement gave control of the trustees to the beneficiaries, the organization would be considered a partnership and liability would be governed by the rules relating to partners. On the other hand, in Hemphill v. Orloff [48 Sup. Ct. 577 (1928)] the Supreme Court of the United States affirmed the holding of a Michigan court to the effect that as a prerequisite to doing business in that state a foreign trust must comply with the statutes regulating the admission of foreign corporations. The law in question stated that for purposes of the statute corporations were "all associations, partnership associations and joint stock companies having any of the powers or privileges of corporations, not possessed by individuals or partnerships . . . ." In its decision the Supreme Court said: "The real nature of the organization must be considered. If clothed with the ordinary functions and attributes of a corporation, it is subject to similar treatment." Impliedly all voluntary associations enjoying such attributes have now lost the advantage they had over corporations in doing business in foreign states.

The realistic point of view taken by the Supreme Court in Hemphill v. Orloff has found expression in other decisions and in legislation regulating and taxing voluntary associations, including trusts, in the same manner and almost as extensively as corporations. Because of these conditions and because of the still uncertain state of the law concerning trusts, the latter have begun to decline in importance and corporations have become the most favored type of organization for both large and small business units.

The changes in the legal principles governing voluntary associations appear to have created for them a special status in law, somewhere between that of the simple partnership and that of the corporation. This status is apparently a recognition that neither the unitary nor the aggregate aspect of business associations can be ignored without denying the requirements of business and of public control. Realistic justice is insistent that cognizance be taken of both.

Non-profit making voluntary associations include social clubs, family and religious societies, fraternal orders, socialistic communities, trade unions, employers' associations and mutual benefit associations, with or without insurance features. The obviously private nature of most of these types of organization, particularly of those which developed earliest historically, and which were chiefly influential in the common law, led the courts to apply legal principles differing in many important respects from those regulating unincorporated business associations.

The properties of most such societies, except charitable and religious organizations which have large trust funds, are usually negligible, and the right of each member in the common property consists only of the right to enforce its application to the purposes of the association. Upon the death or withdrawal of a member his right in the property accrues to the survivors, while upon dissolution the assets are divided among those who are then members. Of course where the property has been given to an association for a particular purpose, the courts will enforce the trust and there will be no division upon dissolution.

The relationship between members of voluntary non-profit organizations is not one of partnership; the constitution and by-laws to which a member subscribes upon joining embody the terms of the contract between him and the other members of the society. The courts are loath to interfere with the relationship between members, and they tend to support the rules and tribunals of the society. Accordingly in cases of wrongful expulsion the courts will grant specific relief only when a property interest is involved. It must be shown moreover that the rules and proceedings of the association relating to expulsion were arbitrary, that the expulsion was not carried out in accordance with the rules or that it was not done in good faith. The courts have gone very far in discovering a property interest where the expulsion results in only a trifling pecuniary loss and in some cases have disregarded the question of property interest entirely, an attitude which indicates a desire to protect rights of personality. Actions for damages also are possible where there has been a wrongful expulsion.

The objects and activities of an association may be changed by the unanimous consent of the membership or, if the by-laws so provide, by a majority. Such changes, in the case of religious societies with large property holdings, have given rise to a great deal of litigation and there have been many conflicting decisions. The leading English case, Free Church of Scotland v. Overtoun [(1904) A. C. 515], decided that a change in a fundamental doctrine by a religious body was *ultra vires* and that any minority group which still subscribed to the original tenets of the association was entitled to the property. The American law is guided by Watson v. Jones [80 U.S. 679 (1871)], in which the Supreme Court attempted to differentiate certain situations and to state rules for them. It held that where property is given in trust for a religious body or society to support a particular doctrine, it cannot be used for the support of a new dogma. Where it is granted to a society simply for its use, rights in it depend upon the type of the organization: if the society is a self-governing group, such as a Congregational church, the right to the use of the property is determined by the rules of the association; but if the particular group which changes its views is a subordinate part of a hierarchy in which the superior body adheres to the original doctrine, the property belongs to the membership that remains loyal to the superior organization.

The liability of members of non-profit societies toward the organization and toward strangers has been carefully limited. A member is liable to the society only for the amount of his subscription and dues; the latter may not be increased except in accordance with the rules of the association to which the individual has consented as a condition of membership. The member's liability to outsiders is based not upon the law of partnership but of agency. Thus he is liable on contracts made by officers or agents only if he authorized or ratified them. Even where ratification has taken place, his liability may be limited by the consent of the contracting party to look only to the funds of the association for payment.

Some states have statutes permitting actions by and against associations, but otherwise the common law rule obtains that the parties to suits must be the individual members. A distinct departure from this rule occurred in two famous trade union cases, the Taff Vale Railway Company v. The Amalgamated Society of Railway Servants [(1901) A. C. 426] and the United Mine Workers of America v. Coronado Coal Company [259 U.S. 344 (1921)]. In the first case the English court held that the special privileges given registered trade unions made them quasi-corporations and that therefore actions for damages might be brought against them as units, with recovery out of joint funds. So far as English trade unions are concerned the rule of this case was nullified by the Trade Disputes Act of 1906 (6 Edw. VII. c. 47), which stated that neither unions nor employers' associations could be held liable for torts. This statute was modified by the Trade Disputes and Trade Unions Act of 1927 (17 & 18 Geo. v. c. 22), which restored the liability of the unions and employers' associations for injuries committed in contemplation of or in the course of an illegal strike or lockout, these being defined by the act.

In the Coronado case the United States Supreme Court, influenced by the Taff Vale decision, ruled that since a union is recognized as an entity in various congressional acts, it may be sued for the torts of its officers and members committed in pursuit of activities authorized by the union. This decision has been regarded by some legal scholars as affecting only trade unions. If this is so, the decision would appear to be a startling example of class judicial legislation. It is more likely, however, that the Coronado case has implications for all voluntary associations which have been accorded specific statutory recognition or perhaps more narrowly for those organized to obtain pecuniary benefits, whether or not they are technically associations for profit. The narrower interpretation would be warranted by the emphasis which the court placed upon the character of a union as a "business entity," although theoretically it is in the nature of a non-profit association. In fact the opinion employs in certain parts phraseology applicable only to profit organizations. But whatever the future interpretation of the Coronado decision, it represents an important addition to the body of statute and case law creating a special position for such so-called non-profit associations as mutual insurance companies, stock exchanges, trade unions and others, thus recognizing that they must be distinguished in law, as they are in fact, both from the ordinary business association and from purely social organizations.

FLORENCE MISHNUN

See: ASSOCIATION; CORPORATION; PARTNERSHIP; JOINT STOCK COMPANY; TRUSTS AND TRUSTEES; MASSACHUSETTS TRUSTS; PERPETUITIES; CHARITABLE TRUSTS; CLUBS; FRATERNAL ORDERS; MUTUAL AID SOCIETIES; FRIENDLY SOCIETIES; TRADE UNIONS; LIABILITY; CONTRACT; TORT; AGENCY.

Consult: Maitland, F. W. *The Collected Papers*, 3 vols. (Cambridge, Eng. 1911) vol. iii, p. 271–84, 304–404; Laski, H. J., "The Personality of Associations" in

Harvard Law Review, vol. xxix (1915–16) 404–26; Wrightington, Sidney R., *The Law of Unincorporated Associations* (2nd ed. Boston 1923); Smith, Herbert A., *The Law of Associations, Corporate and Unincorporate* (Oxford 1914); Owens, Richard N., *Business Organization and Combination* (New York 1934) chs. ii–iii; Formoy, R. R., *The Historical Foundations of Modern Company Law* (London 1923); Warren, E. H., *Corporate Advantages without Incorporation* (New York 1929); Dodd, E. M., Jr., "Dogma and Practice in the Law of Associations" in *Harvard Law Review*, vol. xlii (1928–29) 977–1014; Sturges, W. A., "Unincorporated Associations as Parties to Actions" in *Yale Law Journal*, vol. xxxiii (1923–24) 383–405; Wertheimer, J., *Law Relating to Clubs* (4th ed. by A. W. Chaster, London 1913); Chafee, Zechariah, Jr., "Internal Affairs of Associations Not for Profit" in *Harvard Law Review*, vol. xliii (1929–30) 993–1029; Hedges, R. Y., and Winterbottom, A., *The Legal History of Trade Unionism* (London 1930) chs. v–vi; McDonough, J. B., "Liability of an Unincorporated Labor Union under the Sherman Act" in *Virginia Law Review*, vol. x (1923–24) 304–11; Berman, Edward, *Labor and the Sherman Act* (New York 1930).

VORONTSOV, VASSILY PAVLOVICH (1847–1918), Russian economist known as V.V. A physician by training, Vorontsov practised medicine for several years as a zemstvo employee and later engaged in statistical research for the railways. Beginning in the early 1880's, however, he devoted himself entirely to free lance journalism on economic topics. At first he was in close contact with the populist movement, contributing to *Vpered* (Forward), a magazine published abroad by Lavrov; but as the populists turned increasingly to terrorism in practise and to revolution in theory, Vorontsov, who believed in peaceful evolution based on cultural uplift of the peasant masses, broke with them. He was generally regarded nevertheless as the ideologist of Russian populism in the economic sphere, perhaps more important and certainly more prolific than his contemporary Danielson (*q.v.*).

In a number of works, the most important of which is *Sudbi kapitalizma v Rossii* (The fortunes of capitalism in Russia, St. Petersburg 1882), Vorontsov maintained—and buttressed his contention with elaborate statistical "proof" —that capitalism could not dominate the Russian economy. Because capitalism distributes insufficient purchasing power to assure its subsistence exclusively on the demand in the home market, export outlets must be relied upon to avoid crises of overproduction. As the youngest rival for foreign markets Russian capitalism must encounter the formidable competition of the older and technologically more advanced countries. Therefore, he argued, Russian capitalism, which thus far had been an artificial growth fostered by protection, would never resemble the sturdy and expansive western European type. Virtually limited to the home market, it could not develop large scale and efficient production; it would remain merely a system of exploitation, subjecting the population to the insecurity of recurring crises. Although this analysis was condemned by the Russian Marxists, particularly Plekhanov and Lenin, as an adaptation from Sismondi enriched here and there by bits from Marx and Rodbertus and although the chief argument as to the impossibility of capitalism confined to the domestic market was flatly denied, Vorontsov's prognosis proved to be partly correct. The bourgeois mode of production as it developed in Russia was not a constructive force and it made no headway in Russia's basic industry, agriculture.

The critics who concentrated on the "burning question" of Russian capitalism missed Vorontsov's really important contribution—the comprehensive statistical and descriptive treatment of the peasant economy, including both agriculture and the handicrafts, and of the cooperative institutions deeply imbedded in it which assured its social and technical progress without the separation of production and consumption necessitated by capitalism. The most important of Vorontsov's works in this field is *Krestyanskaya obshchina* (Itogi ekonomicheskago izsledovaniya Rossii podannim zemskoy statistiki, vol. i, Moscow 1892), a veritable historical and statistical encyclopaedia of the land commune; this was supplemented by a study of the progressive trends in the peasant economy (*Progressivniya techeniya v krestyanskom khozyaystve*, St. Petersburg 1892) and by a number of books on the artel, particularly with regard to its operation in the peasant handicraft industries.

K. KOCHAROVSKY

Consult: Simchowitsch, W. G., "Die sozial-ökonomischen Lehren der russischen Narodniki" in *Jahrbücher für Nationalökonomie und Statistik*, vol. lxix (1897) 641–78.

VOTING is the process whereby an individual member of a group registers his opinion and thus participates in the determination of the consensus among the group with regard to either the choice of an official or the decision upon a proposal. As such it is the procedure implied in all elections (*q.v.*) as well as in all parliamentary or direct legislation. Under a dictatorial form of government the individual may be called upon to express his opinion as to the choices already made by the dictator; various devices, however, render this procedure an empty formality. Voting finds its principal sphere and its predominant importance under democratic governments and under conditions of maximum freedom of choice and suffrage.

Many theories have been advanced as to the function of voting in democratic countries. It has been looked upon as a social safety valve which relieves tensions in times of stress, as a method of securing obedience to the governing authorities, as a means of adjusting social conflicts, as a process by which right decisions may be made under right conditions, as a system of uncovering social needs and dissatisfactions and as a safeguard against the exclusion of minorities from the benefits of the state. Certain antidemocratic groups, such as the French Action Française, have expressed their opposition to democracy by refusing to vote in elections. Similarly antipolitical anti-*étatist* organizations, such as the French revolutionary syndicalists and their Spanish and Italian counterparts, have disdained the utilization of the ballot as a means of advancing their cause and have urged voters to remain away from the polls. In general, however, it remains true that in a democracy one group after another seeks the right to vote; and the political history of democratic countries has recorded the grant of the suffrage to increasingly broad groups of the population as these groups have become powerful enough to demand political recognition.

In recent years, however, considerable attention has been devoted to the extent to which those who are entitled to vote actually take the trouble to go to the polls. The United States has never had an official complete registration of all the eligible voters, as certain European countries have. Consequently all estimates as to the popular participation in elections in the United States have been based upon the decennial census figures. Various calculations show that in the presidential election of 1896 about 80 percent of the eligible voters went to the polls. No such level of interest has since been reached. In 1920 and 1924 only 50 percent of the electorate voted and in 1928 and 1932 only 60 percent.

The decline in percentage since 1896 has been attributed to a variety of causes, such as woman suffrage, lack of issues and growing disillusionment about democracy. Writers like Walter Lippmann used to attribute it to prosperity, which, it was considered, created too many interests competing with politics. The fact that participation in the 1932 election, despite the depression that set in in 1929, was about the same as in the 1928 election indicates that this theory is not a complete explanation, even if allowance is made for the fact that many unemployed adults may have been disfranchised in 1932 because they had no legal residence.

Interest in presidential elections has varied to some extent with the vitality of the issues and the uncertainty of the results. The Bryan-McKinley contest brought out an unusually high vote because it raised vital issues. More money was spent, particularly on behalf of the Republican ticket, than in any previous election. The fact that, except for 1912 and 1916, the Republicans had comparatively easy going after 1896 tended to discourage voting. When the Republican party was split in 1912, Wilson won by a minority of the votes cast; and in 1916 Wilson scored a great personal triumph but failed to make many permanent converts to the Democratic party. The one-sided party situation existing in the country at large was one reason for the small vote in 1924. Increased voting in 1928 represented largely a response to the challenges put forward by the candidacy of Alfred E. Smith. In 1932 there was a high participation partly because of the important economic issues involved but also because the various straw votes indicated that the Republican party was likely to be unseated. An analysis by states brought out even more clearly the relation between the closeness of the struggle and the size of the poll. In the so-called one-party states popular participation is almost always low.

Concerted attempts have been made by various civic and business organizations, newspapers, magazines, ministers and others to "get out the vote." A National-Get-Out-the-Vote Club has been organized, with headquarters in Washington and branches in various states. Unlike the party organizations, which are interested in getting out only their own voters, these organizations are theoretically interested in getting all electors to vote, regardless of the nature of their party affiliation. This non-partisan effort, however, has proved of little avail. As compared with certain other democratic countries interest in voting in the United States has remained low, particularly in the period since the World War.

Since 1916 at least 70 percent of the eligible voters have taken part in practically every national election in Great Britain, France, Austria, Denmark, Belgium and Switzerland. These high voting records have been the result of such factors as efficient election administration, intensive party organization and disturbing economic and social conditions. Permanent official registration, short ballots and list systems of proportional representation are some of the legal devices used by these countries to stimulate voting. While such mechanical aids make it convenient for voters who have opinions to register them, they do not furnish the driving power. The World War effected a profound change in economic conditions and discussion of such vital issues as national security, inflation, unemployment and the high cost of living has kept the interest of the voters at a high level. The party organizations have been in close touch with different economic groups and have been zealous in seeing that their supporters vote.

In these European countries the individual citizens who are entitled to vote need expend comparatively little effort to see that their names are put on the lists of qualified voters, whereas in the United States inconvenient systems of registration have kept many citizens from voting (*see* REGISTRATION OF VOTERS). Furthermore various studies have indicated that there is a marked relation between the system of representation and the size of the poll. The election returns for Great Britain, France and the United States show that the system of choosing legislators by single member districts tends to discourage voting in those areas where the party struggle is one-sided. When the Swiss adopted a list form of proportional representation in 1919, there was an increase of almost 40 percent in the size of the vote at national council elections, and most of this increase has been maintained. The adoption in the United States of some form of proportional representation for the election of congressmen and state legislators and the apportionment of presidential electoral votes according to the popular vote would probably increase the interest in elections.

Again, in most European countries the burden placed upon the voter is not an impossible one. Except in Switzerland the number of elective officials is not large. In the United States the variation in the vote cast for different officers is clear proof that too great a burden is placed upon the voter. In general the highest polls are recorded in presidential elections, although a contest for governor or United States senator may sometimes bring out a bigger vote in a given state than that for president. As a rule the vote for state and local officers, particularly in non-presidential years, is much lower than that for president. An analysis of the returns for certain municipal elections showed that on the average 5 to 20 percent fewer voters participate in city elections than in presidential elections. The vote for minor administrative candidates is usually much less than the vote for the important political officers on the same ballot. The vote on propositions in some places has been as low as 20 percent of the registered vote. Frequently where a great number of choices is submitted to the voters at the same election, the vote on the first choices is much larger than that on the last; the voter's attention soon flags when he is confronted with the necessity of making many decisions. A short ballot movement was initiated in the United States in 1909 with the express purpose of eliminating most of the administrative positions from the ballot and concentrating power in the hands of a few responsible authorities.

The highest voting records in democratic countries are found in those which have adopted compulsory voting. Thus in Belgium, Holland, Czechoslovakia and Australia nine tenths or more of the electors take part in national elections. While the idea of compulsory voting appears to have been incorporated in several early American colonial statutes, it was first given a thorough trial by the canton of St. Gallen in Switzerland. In 1835 the canton passed a law punishing absence from the district assembly elections without sufficient excuse by a small pecuniary fine. This law was reenacted in 1867 and 1890 and a series of legally valid excuses enumerated, including illness in the family, mourning for a relative, absence from the canton, birth in the family and official business. In the five German Swiss cantons where compulsory voting has been in operation longest, the interest of the voters in elections has been uniformly higher than in the rest of the country. The device has been useful in notifying the Swiss citizens of their electoral duties. It has also tended to lighten the burden of the party organizations in getting out the vote.

Compulsory voting was introduced in Baden and Bavaria in 1881, in Bulgaria in 1882 and in Belgium in 1893. In Bavaria the system applied to indirect elections and a unique method was worked out whereby the abstainers, if they constituted more than one third of the total electorate, were charged with the expense of a new election. The most thorough trial of compulsory voting has been made in Belgium. Under the old regime of limited suffrage the number of non-voters in Belgium was not excessive as compared with the number in England or France at the same time; but when the universal suffrage law went into effect, the Belgian publicists were impressed with the problem of how to handle the new masses of voters. The conservatives wanted to make sure that the moderate elements polled their full strength. The politicians looked upon compulsory voting as a means of saving them the trouble of keeping after the voters. The device was regarded also as a guaranty of the secrecy of the vote, since some party agents had bribed opposition voters to stay away from the polls. The opponents of compulsory voting argued that the suffrage was a right which the voter should be free to exercise or not as he wished, that the difficulties of enforcement might disorganize the system of justice and that the ignorant should not be compelled to register choices at random.

The Belgian system of compulsory voting has undoubtedly produced remarkable results. Over nine tenths of the voters take part in national, provincial and municipal elections. The penalties worked out for the law were of three kinds: money fines, public reprimands and disfranchisement. The prosecutions have not been very numerous but the system has been effective. One of the reasons for its success has been the fact that it required a thorough organization of the entire election process. An effort was made to register all the eligible voters and to inform them of their impending obligations. Official notices or convocations were sent to the voters before each election. The number of blank ballots cast has not been excessive. The Belgian people seem to be well satisfied with the system and regard its educational features as especially valuable.

While there have been other plans of compulsory voting, the money fine plan has been the system usually adopted, the highest fines being imposed in Australia. New Zealand in 1893 and Tasmania in 1901 provided for disfranchisement as the sole sanction for unexcused absence from the polls. The money fine plan was adopted in parts of Austria and in Spain in 1907, in Argentina in 1912 and in Holland in 1917. Since the World War the plan has been adopted by Bulgaria, Czechoslovakia, Rumania, Luxemburg, Australia, Hungary and Greece. The success of the system has varied somewhat with such factors as the efficiency of the administrative machinery, the literacy of the population and the character of party organizations; but in general the introduction of the plan has brought marked increases in the poll. Its failure to do so in Spain may be attributed in part to the laxity of the Spanish administrative system. Since the war the plan has been especially successful in reducing non-voting in Bulgaria, Czechoslovakia and Australia.

While there has been some agitation for compulsory voting in the United States, the movement has not gone very far. The Kansas City charter of 1889 provided that a poll tax should be levied upon every adult male resident but exempted from payment of this tax all those who voted at the general election. In 1896 the Supreme Court of Missouri declared this provision unconstitutional on the ground that it was a discriminatory tax and an invasion of the citizen's "sovereign right of suffrage." Compulsory voting was made permissive by the constitution of North Dakota in 1898 and by the Massachusetts constitution in 1918, but neither state has taken any steps to implement the constitutional provision. Proposals for obligatory voting have been rejected by the voters of Oregon and California. On the other hand, a number of states have adopted a very mild form of compulsory voting, cancellation of registration for failure to vote within a certain period. This device is intended to stimulate voting and check fraud.

Whether or not compulsory voting is regarded as desirable depends upon particular theories of democracy and upon certain practical considerations. If it is believed that democracy is an inferior form of government and that organized thinking by the masses is impossible, then compulsory voting and like devices are meaningless. Many German citizens who had never voted came out to take part in the 1933 election which was to end the experiment with democracy in their country. The poll at the election was higher than any previous poll and a majority of the voters decided to abdicate their powers. In the United States a hostile view toward compulsory voting has been taken by some for other reasons. Isolated voting studies made in the United States and in parts of Europe seem to indicate that non-voting is related to such factors as marked mobility, inferior educational opportunities, undesirable occupations and inexperience in political affairs. These findings have led some to discourage movements designed to increase the size of the vote. This point of view fails to take into consideration the fact that the party organizations in the United States enlist many ignorant and illiterate voters and by rendering them special favors persuade them to vote for organization candidates. The character of those who refrain from voting is not so important a matter as the methods employed to get out the vote. If political organizations with special and sometimes corrupt interests to promote are the main agents which bring the voters to the polls, then something may be said in favor of having the government assume more responsibility for the administration of the election process.

HAROLD F. GOSNELL

See: ELECTIONS; SUFFRAGE; DEMOCRACY; MAJORITY RULE; PARTIES, POLITICAL; MACHINE, POLITICAL; PRIMARIES, POLITICAL; SHORT BALLOT MOVEMENT; PROPORTIONAL REPRESENTATION; REGISTRATION OF VOTERS; ABSENT-VOTING; STRAW VOTES; INDEPENDENT VOTING.

Consult: Braunias, Karl, *Das parlamentarische Wahlrecht*, Institut für ausländisches öffentliches Recht und Völkerrecht, Beiträge, no. 18, 2 vols. (Berlin 1932); Merriam, C. E., and Gosnell, H. F., *Non-Voting; Causes and Methods of Control* (Chicago 1924); Gosnell, H. F., *Getting Out the Vote* (Chicago 1927), and *Why Europe Votes* (Chicago 1930); Bock, E., *Wahlstatistik* (Halle 1919); Ségot, R., *De l'abstention en matière électorale* (Angers 1906); Barthélemy, Joseph, *L'organisation du suffrage et l'expérience belge* (Paris 1912), and in France, Assemblée Nationale, Chambre des Députés, Ordinary sess., Annexe no. 4738, *Documents parlementaires* (1922) vol. iii, p. 2317–32; Schlesinger, A. M., and Eriksson, E. M., "The Vanishing Voter" in *New Republic*, vol. xl (1924) 162–67; Deeter, Paxon, *Prize Essay on Compulsory Voting* (Philadelphia 1902); Donaldson, W. T., *Compulsory Voting and Absent Voting with Bibliographies*, Ohio, Legislative Reference Department, Bulletin no. 1 (Columbus 1914); Robson, W. A., "Compulsory Voting" in *Political Science Quarterly*, vol. xxxviii (1923) 569–77; Giraud, Émile, in *Revue du droit public*, vol. xlviii (1931) 473–95; Merriam, C. E., "Government and Society" in President's Research Committee on Social Trends, *Recent Social Trends in the United States*, 2 vols. (New York 1933) vol. ii, ch. xxix; Munro, W. B., "Is the Slacker Vote a Menace?" in *National Municipal Review*, vol. xvii (1928) 80–86; Lippmann, Walter, *Men of Destiny* (New York 1927) ch. iii.

VOTING TRUST. *See* TRUSTS AND TRUSTEES.

WACH, ADOLF (1843–1926), German jurist. Wach was professor of civil procedure and criminal law. After teaching for short periods at the universities of Königsberg, Rostock, Tübingen and Bonn he went to Leipsic in 1876, where he remained almost to the end of his long life. He was one of the most celebrated members of the Leipsic law faculty, which during his time reached the summit of its fame. In addition to his teaching and research work he found time for extensive political, philanthropic, artistic and church activities.

As a criminalist Wach was an adherent of the classical school of criminal law. His important work was done in procedure. At an early age he wrote a monograph which attracted considerable attention, *Der italienische Arrestprocess* (Leipsic 1868), wherein he stressed the study of the Italian town laws with their Germanic and Roman elements as the starting points of the canonical and hence the modern law of procedure. Wach was prompt to realize also the significance of the same sources as well as the work of Albertus Gandinus for the study of the history of the modern European criminal law.

His great opportunity came with the publication of the new German Code of Civil Procedure in 1877, which was intended to replace the more formalized common law procedure. It was Wach's task to apply to the exposition of the new code the results of a whole century of brilliant dogmatic, historical and critical development of procedural science. His *Vorträge über die Reichs-Civilprozessordnung* (Bonn 1879) won immediate and sensational success. It became virtually the "institutes" of the new procedure for the next decade. Thus it was natural for Wach to undertake a definitive treatise on procedure, the first volume of which appeared as *Handbuch des deutschen Civilprozessrechts* (Systematisches Handbuch der deutschen Rechtswissenschaft, sect. ix, pt. ii, vol. i, Leipsic 1886). Although it remained incomplete, the work was recognized as fundamental for all further treatment of the new procedure. Wach failed to finish it not only because of his other activities but probably also because he was discouraged by a mounting volume of criticism of the code. Thereafter his energies were devoted to the defense of its principles against modernism, eclecticism and imitation of the newly created Austrian procedure. His *Grundfragen und Reform des Zivilprozesses* (Berlin 1914) represents the most important expression of this defense.

HANS FRITZSCHE

Consult: Schmidt, Richard, "Adolf Wach, Erinnerungsblätter" in *Zeitschrift für deutschen Zivilprozess*, vol. li (1926) i–xiv.

WAGE REGULATION. *See* WAGES.

WAGES

THEORY AND POLICY. *Definitions*. In the analysis of modern capitalistic society certain properties usually ascribed to wages are not necessarily connected one with another. Their simultaneous presence in the great majority of wage contracts or wage payments is merely an institutional fact rather than a rigorously logical necessity.

Like interest and rent, wages are *contractual incomes*: wage rates, whether piece rates or time rates or whether fixed in money or in goods, are agreed upon by the payers and the recipients of wages before the product is sold. Occasional gains accruing to wage earners in consequence of favorable changes, especially in the form of price fluctuations, in the period between the fixing of the contract and the purchase of goods by the wage earner are supposed to be offset in the long run by corresponding losses in times of opposite changes. In this respect wages and other contractual incomes differ from the so-called speculative incomes; these accrue, more or less continually, to all who are able to anticipate more accurately than others the nature of price and other changes which are likely to occur between the fixing of contractual incomes and the sale of the product. Entrepreneurial profits are said to be at least in part speculative incomes. In most cases, as far as highly developed industrial societies are concerned, wages and speculative gains are earned by different classes of persons.

Wages are *remuneration for labor*. The difference between wages and other contractual incomes is based on the traditional distinction between the "original factors of production." This distinction has already been successfully criticized by Cairnes and F. H. Knight and is by no means as rigid as it appeared in its original formulation. In the long run there is a certain degree of interchangeability between the traditional "labor" and "capital." On the other hand, there are strong barriers between different kinds of labor. The addition of skill to the labor capacity of a hitherto unskilled worker requires "waiting" in the same way if not in the same degree as the worker's replacement by a machine. The substitution of one man for another is in certain cases as difficult as the substitution of land for labor. Furthermore the distinction between the three "factors" loses much of its alleged logical necessity if it is remembered that a slave is a form of capital to his owner, who may use him directly or lend him to a third person. Here again the distinction is institutional rather than logical. A legally free labor contract between the employer and the employee is supposed to be a necessary institutional characteristic of wages. But the products of the employees on the one hand and of the self-employed, such as farmers, small shopkeepers, handicraftsmen and their cooperating family members, on the other compete vigorously with each other. For this reason the wage theorists have had to split the income of the self-employed into wages and other incomes and to evaluate the employers' wages in terms of remuneration paid for labor of comparable kind. All these difficulties of definition are, however, scarcely essential either for the purely theoretical analysis or for its application to concrete problems. A general theory of distribution must hold good for any number of productive agents with any degree of mutual interchangeability. The degree of interchangeability of a pair of agents is measurable: by the change in their exchange ratio necessary to bring about a given change in their quantity-proportions, a magnitude called in modern terminology elasticity of substitution; and by the amount of time required to produce this effect. With a general theory of distribution as a basis, the combination of all the single productive elements into groups is merely a matter of convenience, as is also the determination of the extent to which the purely quantitative criterion of interchangeability is to be supplemented by other principles of classification, physical, sociological and the like. Thus an important peculiarity of free labor stressed by Knight seems to be its inseparability from the person of the owner.

This relativistic aspect of the definition of wages proves also to be necessary with regard to the distinction between wages as the *income of the manual or poor workers* and the remuneration of non-manual workers. All these incomes are usually treated in economic theory as wages, sometimes with the important exception of payment for managerial services. (This remuneration is of course to be distinguished theoretically from speculative gains, although such a distinction turns out to be difficult in practise.) Yet the competition between high salaried employees and wage earners or low salaried employees is rather imperfect. The substitution may require a period of one human generation—not much less and sometimes more than the life of a machine. Furthermore the great differences in the type and distribution of expenditures and their reaction on income changes of the poor and the rich are shown to be among the determinants of the supply of and demand for labor and capital respectively. Should these differences be explicitly emphasized by restriction of the term wages to the manual or to the poor (manual and clerical) workers, or would such classification prove inexpedient? Actually the vast majority of modern workers are poorer than the majority of non-workers; whatever the terminology, the economist is expected not to neglect the special effects of this fact. Indeed traditional and recent wage discussions deal not only with the remuneration of labor but to a great extent also with the incomes of the poor, although these two areas do not coincide but merely overlap. It appears that the limited degree of interchangeability between and the sociological peculiarities of the productive agencies in modern industrial societies warrant the confinement of the theory of wages to the relatively low paid employees, whether or not they are manual workers. On the other hand, any alternative definition could also be fitted into the general theory without great difficulties.

Theory. Wage rates are connected, as causes or effects, with a number of other economic magnitudes: the number of workers employed and the duration of work, the amount of capital used, the amount of managerial services required, the price of capital, the salaries of the managers, the price of land, the price and output of the product and the like. A theory of wages is logically consistent if it can be expressed by a set of relationships whose number equals the number of those magnitudes which are considered as variable, i.e. not as independent data fixed from the outside. Thus on the assumption that all but one or two of the magnitudes enumerated above are independent data, relatively simple theories of wages, each consisting respectively of one or two or three relationships only, have been constructed. The extent, however, to which these theories are not only logically consistent but also true depends on whether the assumed relationships are true and whether the magnitudes assumed to be independent in theory are essentially so in reality.

If it be assumed, for instance, that the demand for labor is a fixed datum, in the sense that a rigid "lump of work" is to be done, the wage rates are easily explained if it is proved that increasing labor supplies always follow increasing wage rates: the wage rate would then cease to increase when the labor supply equaled the (rigid) labor demand. Thus the "iron law of wages," or Ricardo's equation, wages = subsistence minimum, presents an explanation of wage rates by two relationships only; namely, by a statement of the following "supply and demand schedules" of labor: first, the higher the wage rates, the larger the working population; and, second, the quantity of labor demanded is independent of the wage rates. It remains to be seen whether these relationships are true and whether they are empirically sufficient. It is also logically consistent to assume the labor supply to be independent of wage rates and to confine the theory of wages to this assumption and to the statement of the relationship existing between increasing wage rates and decreasing numbers of workers profitably employable. Again, unless the assumption made is proved empirically, these relationships alone cannot exhaust the problem.

The last named assumption may, however, be used as a convenient start. Let it be assumed that not only labor but all productive factors are employed in a given industry in fixed absolute quantities. The variables are then: the prices of labor, capital, managerial activities and so on; the quantity of the commodity produced; and its price. The number of the necessary relationships must therefore be the number of the factors plus two. If there is full competition in the markets where the factors are hired, these necessary relationships are easily determined. They are: (1) the demand schedule of the product—at each possible price definite quantities of the product can be sold, if there is no change in the structure of demand, e.g. in the tastes of the various income groups and in the relative shares of these groups; (2) the production function—each possible combination of the factors produces a definite quantity of the product, if there is no change in technical knowledge and in the workers' ability. And, finally, (3) for each factor equality must have been reached between the entrepreneurs' money outlay for the marginal increment of this factor and the increase of the money receipts caused by such an increment. If, for example, the marginal outlay for labor is greater than the marginal receipts, the entrepreneurs are compelled by losses to reduce employment in order to increase the marginal product of labor. If, on the other hand, the marginal outlay falls short of the marginal receipts, profits induce an expansion of employment until equality is restored. This equality of marginal receipts to marginal outlays implies that the cost per unit of output is at its minimum. Any of the factors may be thought of as "entrepreneurial," i.e. as hiring the other factors (Wicksell) and making no speculative gains. The decrease of returns of consecutive portions of a factor may be the consequence of a hiring of portions with poorer and poorer qualities: inferior land, less efficient workers, less competent managers. But even where the portions of each factor show no differences of quality, different quantitative combinations of factors would produce different outputs, as shown by the production function. The assumption of diminishing returns is not compatible with all possible forms of production functions.

The discussion thus far has proceeded on the basis of certain *assumptions* which may be summarized as follows: the amount of each factor offered per time unit is independent of the reward for this and the other factors; the shape of the production function is independent of the payments to the factors; the structure of the demand for the product also is independent of the rewards to the factors; the law of diminishing returns is in operation; full competition prevails in the labor market; and speculative gains and losses are absent. In order that theoretical considerations may be brought into closer conformity with observable phenomena it is proposed now to drop these more or less arbitrary assumptions one by one in the order enumerated above.

Before proceeding, however, to the gradual dropping of the assumptions and thus augmenting the number of the variables involved, a brief statement concerning the *elasticity of demand for labor* or any other factor is pertinent. This is defined as the ratio of a small relative increase of the wage rates to the corresponding relative decrease of the labor demanded. Since the mere dismissal of laborers may in general be supposed to require less time than a replacement of labor by other factors, especially by fixed capital, the notion of a short period demand elasticity for labor applies to the case in which all the factors except labor continue to be used, after the wage increase, in the same quantities as before. In practise certain portions of the capital—circulating capital—are more or less rigidly proportional to the amount of labor employed. Accordingly the short period demand elasticity for labor would be more conveniently defined under the assumption that only "fixed" capital but not "circulating" capital is kept constant. The border line is, however, not always clear. If the quantities of all factors have been allowed sufficient time to adjust themselves to the new wage level, the ratio of the relative decrease of the labor demanded to the relative wage increase is the long period demand elasticity for labor. In any of the elasticity concepts the demand for labor is the less elastic (i.e. the dismissals caused by a given wage rise are the less numerous), the steeper the increase of the marginal labor products with decreasing output and the less elastic the demand for the product. The first of these two conditions makes for the physical, the second for the value component of the value of the marginal product. The first condition implies, according to Pigou, that during depression (work under capacity) the short term labor demand elasticity is probably greater than in periods of boom (work over capacity). The second condition indicates that industries producing commodities for which there are easy substitutes, e.g. competing with foreign goods, have a relatively elastic labor demand; the demand for, say, the manual labor of all trades in a country not exposed to foreign competition or the demand for the world's total labor is considerably less elastic. Still, even the elasticity of short term demand for labor in general is considered by some (Pigou and Douglas, if the latter's definition is rightly interpreted) to be surely more than 1; the long term elasticity would be still greater (Hicks). If these evaluations are true, then under the assumptions enumerated above a small increase in wage rates causes more than a proportionate decrease in employment and consequently a decrease in aggregate wages.

A few words on the *wage fund theory* are appropriate here. This theory cannot seriously be interpreted as assuming a constant ratio between capital and either aggregate wages or total output. These interpretations would indeed presuppose very peculiar shapes of the production function and would imply respectively: either that the elasticity of short period demand for labor were 1, which is unfounded; or that labor's marginal product, i.e. the wage rate, were 0, which is absurd. The idea possibly hidden in Mill's phrases but hinted at particularly by Taussig, Böhm-Bawerk and Wicksell is instead a profound reformulation of the production function itself. The output can be conceived as determined not by labor and capital amounts as mutually independent variables but by the shape of the time distribution of labor, i.e. by the labor amounts invested at different time-distances from the consumption act. Marginal increments of product due to slight changes of the total amounts of labor or of waiting respectively, and caused by minor changes of the time distribution, explain the level of wage and interest rates. In so far as the time distribution of labor is fixed by outside causes (e.g. agricultural seasons, payment periods), the discounted wages are indeed proportionate to capital. As, however, a fixed time distribution is peculiar to certain parts of circulating capital only and as the interest rate at which the wages would be discounted depends, with a given production function, on the labor supply, the wage fund theory does not exhaust the wage problem. It is a capital not a wage theory.

The analysis may now be continued if the first assumption, concerning the rigid flow of capital and other factors, is dropped. Let it be assumed instead that the *supply of each factor* instead of being fixed from outside *depends* in some definite way *on its reward*. The whole system continues to be a determinate one, since to the additional set of new variables (the amounts of the factors used per time unit) there will correspond an equal number of additional relationships (the supply schedules of the factors). There will be, with n factors, $2n+2$ variables and an equal number of relationships. In such a system wages will depend not only on the character of the labor supply schedule but also on the character of the supply schedule of capital and the supply schedule of managerial services. Account must be taken also of the influence not only of reward rates per unit of factor and time but also of the aggregate rewards earned per unit of time by a factor and possibly affecting the supply schedule of this factor as well as of the other factors. Since the aggregate rewards are products of reward rates and amounts used, no new variables are involved in this further complication.

The *labor supply schedule* mentioned above as the iron law was based on the assumption that change in population, i.e. the difference between births and deaths, moves in accordance with wage earnings. This is of course a long run schedule; and the "lag" between cause and effect is greater where social aid delays the effect of wages on mortality and where child labor restrictions retard the effect of increased births on wages. Yet even in the long run the validity of such a supply schedule is doubtful. The influence of wage earnings on mortality can be mitigated largely by hygienic measures of public bodies. And the relationship between incomes and births has in the last decades seemed to contradict the iron law. As stated in terms of the familiar theory of value, it appears that the subjective undervaluation (Böhm-Bawerk's *perspektivische Verkleinerung*) of the future costs of upbringing, as compared with the present subjective value of those competing pleasures lying outside sex and family, varies with the poverty of the parents. Only with relatively higher incomes do those pleasures acquire higher subjective values or even become at all enjoyable; and higher incomes lead at the same time to a more rational attitude—less *perspektivische Verkleinerung* and more birth control. Since change of habits requires time, the negative influence on the birth rate of a rise in income would of course involve a lag, but this lag itself might be highly variable. This negative correlation between income and birth rates, as stated among others by L. Brentano for Germany before the World War, may, however, again give way to a positive correlation, as brought out by Burgdörfer for large German cities after the war, as soon as the rationalized conduct and the pleasure scales of the relatively better off are imitated by the relatively poor as a result of mass information and mass production prices (Douglas). Besides there can be no doubt that wage differences between countries and differences between earnings of workers and of other social groups may, in the long run, induce important migration and occupational shifts.

The behavior of the short run supply of labor is also subject to conflicting tendencies. On the one hand, it might be thought that higher wage rates stimulate willingness to work or increase the amount of work time offered. On the other hand, higher hourly wages may be used to buy leisure for the worker in the form of shorter hours and early retirement or for his family in the form of longer school attendance and thus may decrease the aggregate effort. It is probable that the attitude is different among the various income classes. Again, as in the case of birth rates, the gradual imitation of the changed habits of the more prosperous by the poorer groups, and the different time lags between any individual income rise and the adjustment to the prevailing habits of the income group entered, make the causal relationship between an income rise and the labor supply complicated and liable to changes in time. From material gathered in the United States Paul Douglas infers the predominance of the negative influence of wage rates on labor supply over the positive. His conclusion and the numerical elasticities of the short term labor supply ($-\frac{1}{4}$ to $-\frac{1}{3}$) obtained by him should be subject to correction if there were shifts, of uniform or of fluctuating character, between the periods or towns observed. In particular the size of the worker's reserves, an important cause of such shifts, depends on the former income of the worker but also on the condition of his parents, who may belong, especially in the case of clerical workers, to the middle class. This nexus with the non-workers may differ markedly according to time and place.

The *supply schedule of capital* represents the interdependence of interest rates and current investments, the latter being the total expenditure for factors engaged in producing additions to the instruments and other commodity stocks of the nation. In the absence of speculative gains and losses the unconsumed part of the factor rewards is always invested. In any consideration of the influence of interest rates on saving it must be noted that while a stimulating effect of the interest rate on the amount saved, being the result of several mutually opposed attributes, is not likely to be considerable (and perhaps may even be negative), an increase of the aggregate interest payments may stimulate savings considerably; since the saved percentage of incomes shows, even with constant interest rates, a steep increase with increasing incomes, an income rise shifts the capital supply schedule upward. These high incomes consist in large part of interest revenues and not of wages. An increase in the wage rate and a decrease in the interest rate may therefore affect savings unfavorably in two ways: by increasing aggregate wages if the elasticity of the short period demand for labor is less than 1, and by increasing aggregate interest payments if the elasticity of the short period demand for capital is less than 1 or at least not much above 1 (if a small direct stimulation of savings by interest rates is not wholly excluded).

It is sometimes said that the influence of interest rates on savings cannot be of great importance for the supply of capital, since it affects only the rate of increase of capital, not the total existing supply. A decrease of savings does not mean decreased capital supply unless the savings become negative. The same is of course true, with regard to labor supply, of changes in the birth rate. What matters for the determination of the relative reward rates of capital and labor is, however, not the absolute amount of either but, with a given production function, the ratio of their marginal products. Thus a capital increase of 3 percent proves to be of great consequence to the distribution of the national income only if the simultaneous increase of the working population has not been such as to diminish labor's marginal product in the same proportion in which the 3 percent capital increase has reduced the capital's marginal product.

So long therefore as one ignores speculative gains and losses, an increase of wage rates above the marginal product (conditioned by the actual state or the justifiable prospects of technique and ability) may in extreme cases, while decreasing the output, simultaneously increase the consumption to the point where it makes savings negative, i.e. renders adequate current replacement of fixed plants impossible. This would of course reduce the output still more. Moreover since the main concessions of managers to trade unions and to shareholders are likely to occur simultaneously, viz. toward the end of a boom, a genuine capital destruction may ensue. In a world, however, where lack of foresight causes speculative losses and gains, it is not always possible to ascribe such capital destruction to an increase in the wage rate.

Finally, there is the *supply schedule of managerial services*. Is the entrepreneur's or manager's "willingness to work" stimulated or paralyzed by a decrease of the reward rate? In Hicks' opinion a decrease in the rate of reward is less likely to stimulate willingness to work on the part of persons with higher incomes than in the case of persons with low incomes. A decrease in the rate of reward of a wealthy person may result in a reduction of savings or of other parts of his budget which are easily sacrificed, rather than in an increase of his productive efforts. If, on the other hand, phrases like "the bracing air of free competition" (Marshall) have any meaning, they suggest that an actual or expected decrease of the employer's income—which in this connection necessarily had previously included monopolistic or "frictional" elements—induces him to use his abilities to better advantage. Thus an income variation may work as a stimulus which "merely shakes the frictional elements out of the existing situation, and oils things into their true places" (Stamp). Adjustments of all kinds, including in particular the mutual substitution of factors in response to changed reward rates, may be stimulated with a favorable result for the total output. In addition income variation may also serve as a direct "increment in incentive" to work in the form of shorter week ends for employers and managerial staff and other adjustments.

Of greater importance is the effect of change in the rates of rewards of the productive factors on the method of production. In a discussion of this topic, however, it is necessary to remove the assumption of the independence of the production function from the rate of reward and to assume instead that the production function showing the output produced by any given combination of the factors (the human efforts being measured in man days) is subject to changes of form under the influence of wage changes, either because of induced changes in *production methods* in general or because of direct changes in *workers' ability*.

In modern terminology (Pigou, Hicks, Douglas) and on the basis of two factors only an *invention* may be labor saving, capital saving or neither. If after the invention any combination of factors were to produce a doubled output, the ratios of the marginal products and the relative shares of the factors would not have changed. If, however, as may more reasonably be presumed, the potential outputs of different combinations do not increase in strict proportion, the invention will cause a decrease of the relative share either of labor or of capital, so that it will be labor saving or capital saving. These definitions may be extended to any number of factors: there are "manual labor saving" devices (as distinct from "supervising saving") or "land saving" (skyscrapers). It is by no means true that all invention is labor saving, as is sometimes supposed. The reduction of wage costs per unit of output and of interest costs per unit of output may be called labor spreading and capital spreading respectively; they may or may not be combined in the same invention. On the other hand, labor saving and capital saving as defined above cannot occur simultaneously (except for a change in some third factor). A capital spreading device may or may not be accompanied by labor saving. While reducing the total costs per unit of output it may even increase the labor costs per unit of output, at least in theory. Capital spreading devices are to be found among those inventions and reorganizations which speed up chemical or other processes of transformation, transport, sales, banking operations and so on and which do not introduce much durable apparatus or which cut down workers' waiting time (conveyor), reduce the volume of stocks in relation to output and reduce the value of instruments and stocks by the use of constructional and other raw materials cheapened by devices such as those enumerated. Those capital spreading devices which do not imply considerable labor spreading are likely to be capital saving devices. This is true especially if in the new, accelerated production process, as compared with the old, a relatively greater proportion of the labor employed is used in the finishing stages of production.

If a labor saving device reduces labor's relative share more than it increases output, labor's absolute share will decrease. This may occur not only for a single industry or for a transition period but for the nation as a whole (Wicksell); it is supposed, however, that the latter development is improbable as long as capital grows more rapidly than labor, as it has in the last hundred years (Hicks). On the other hand, it appears that during the transition period of adaptation of all prices and incomes to the new methods and of the consequent migration and substitution of factors speculative losses may occur, and that the fear of further speculative losses may decrease the output and labor's absolute share.

It is sometimes supposed that a wage increase must induce employers to seek labor saving inventions and an interest increase to seek capital saving inventions, over and above that replacement of the costlier factor by the cheaper which would have taken place with unimproved technical knowledge. Thus after the marginal product of labor had reached, because of dismissals and substitution, the increased wage rate, further reduction of the unit costs down to or below the old level would, according to this hypothesis, go the way of labor saving inventions in preference to capital saving inventions. Theoretically there is no reason for such a preference, any more than there is in the case of an entrepreneur who casts about for new improvements under the pressure of a general tax. The empirical truth, however, is that the impulse toward substitution provided by a wage increase (or by a special tax on specific materials) will usually not stop at that point, and that in a world of advancing knowledge almost any act of substitution is inextricably tied up with new methods. It follows that the elasticity of labor demand, if the assumption of unchanging technical knowledge is superseded by the fact of continually changing knowledge, becomes considerably higher. The remarks made above regarding the difficulties of transition seem to imply that as far as these technological displacements are concerned, the elasticity of labor demand would be greater in the short period than in the long—unlike the short and long demand elasticities previously discussed.

It is generally agreed that wage increases may enhance the *working ability* of the laborer or of his offspring, and that this influence is likely to have less effect upon better paid workers who have left the physiological minimum far behind them than upon the poorly paid (and is therefore out of question in the case of managers). All this applies to a period which is not too short but sufficient for adaptation of the worker's budget to an increased income. Quantitative measurements of this relationship are hampered by the difficulty of disentangling statistically changes of ability from changes in technical methods.

With the removal of the assumption of the independence of the production function from the rates of remuneration of the productive factors the system has remained formally determined. The number of variables has not changed. Nor has the number of relationships; some of them—production functions—have merely developed a more complicated form, so that the output now depends not only on the amounts of the factors employed but also on their reward rates. (A statistical expression of these functions would, however, imply predictability of the "behavior" of inventors, which is hardly possible even with the strongly rationalized invention activities characteristic of certain fields.)

More predictable, however, are the relationships dealing with the *behavior of consumers*. It is proposed now to drop the assumption of rigidity of demand in the face of changing consumers' incomes and to analyze the effect of such changes on the demand for different types of goods. The incomes of workers, employers and receivers of interest are spent in different ways, mainly because of variations in the size of the income. The change in rewards must therefore influence the demand for single commodities. At a given price more or less of a commodity will be purchased according to changes in the distribution of income. The system remains determined. With one commodity only, and n factors, the number of relationships and of variables is, as before, $2n+2$. With m commodities, it is $2m+mn+n$. With the aid of budgets and of income distribution statistics it would be possible to evaluate the long run changes in total consumption caused by a given wage increase, assuming that no considerable changes of tastes occur during the adaptation period. With the further aid of cost statistics two principal questions might then be attacked: first, to what extent would a transfer of income to the workers favor or penalize industries working with more or less steeply increasing (or even with decreasing) costs; and, second, to what extent would it favor industries with a high or a low proportion of labor costs?

Theoretically it would be in the interest of the community to favor industries with decreasing (or relatively slightly increasing) costs at the expense of the others. What industries should these be? Are they to be found among those producing luxuries of the poor, which are especially favored by an increase of the low incomes? Or rather shall they be sought among the industries penalized by a decrease of the expenses of the rich? The answer to these questions depends entirely on the historical situation. In 1766 Messance described how decreasing prices of corn and rising money wages enabled the poor to buy more meat, how farmers were consequently induced to increase their livestock and how the resulting abundance of manure further enhanced the harvests. Whether these internal economies in agriculture were or were not offset by a loss in external economies or technical innovations which might otherwise have been stimulated in the manufacturing industries producing luxuries for the rich landowners is undetermined. Today the manufacture and marketing of those mass products, especially of non-agricultural products, which are likely to be purchased with the wage increments of the best paid manual and clerical workers may indeed promise internal and external economies or serve as a fertile soil for improvements in technique and organization. This is indeed true of radio, rayon textiles and automobiles. The luxuries of the rich are on the whole more highly individualized. The rich are, however, also savers. The non-consumed portions of interest and managerial salaries are certainly spent in the most mechanizable industries in so far as they are used to add to the nation's industrial equipment.

The cost of commodities purchased with the income derived from wage increments consists probably to a lesser degree of wage costs than does the cost of consumers' goods previously purchased with the marginal portions of employers' and capitalists' incomes. The difference is minimized, however, if account is taken of the new investment goods financed largely by the savings of the rich. Some difference nevertheless may remain; the effect is similar to that of a labor saving invention.

The *assumption of diminishing returns* which prevailed in the above reasonings is obviated if it is accepted that entrepreneurs do not always, or at least not very quickly, proceed to such adjustments of the quantities of factors used as are necessary to insure in changed circumstances the lowest unit costs possible. But even if all firms reach the optimum size, a full distribution of the product to the factors according to their marginal products, that is, the elimination of any surplus for the entrepreneur beyond the value of the marginal return of his managerial activity, would presuppose that such enterprises "are still numerous enough for perfect competition to be maintained," so that "either . . . new entrepreneurs enter the industry, or . . . those already engaged in it will establish more than one concern each" (Wicksell). The factor acting as entrepreneur is at the present time the manager. Besides the natural scarcity of managerial abilities there are doubtless social limitations, although they are probably subject to broad historical fluctuations. It is well known to what extent the incomes of the managers' class (including the socially connected groups, liberal professions and civil service, which are interchangeable with the managerial factor) were endangered, with respect to their status and security, after the post-war revolution and inflation in central Europe reduced the educational and posteducational de facto privileges of the propertied class. The existence of social barriers warrants the presumption that either the existing firms do not always represent optimal factor combinations or that, even if the optimum is reached, the reward rates of the hired factors may be increased within a certain margin without affecting equilibrium. (This does not mean of course that a wage increase would necessarily be the proper means of diminishing the barriers and at the same time of insuring the optimum.) Another aspect, with less appeal to social frictions, is afforded by "external economies." A slight increase in the size of a firm may augment the total product of the industry concerned or of the whole nation by more than the marginal increment of the firm's product. Thus the private marginal product of labor may be below its social marginal product (Pigou, Hicks); a wage rate between both does not lead to a reduction of the total output.

The fifth assumption to be removed is that stipulating widespread operation of *free competition in the labor market*. Such competition is in fact restricted by lack of mobility or by ignorance on the part of the bargaining parties, by silent or outspoken arrangements between employers and between employees and occasionally by state intervention. Lack of mobility is characteristic not only of workers but also of the fixed portions of capital. Ignorance which may prevent different units of a factor from getting uniform rewards has probably affected workers in the past, but it is scarcely of great significance at present. Much more important are the organizations of employees and employers and state intervention. The small number of employers as compared with the great number of workers in a given industry made silent elimination of their competition possible, probably long before the earliest outspoken unionization of labor took place in England; the organization of employers was a subsequent development. In a unionized labor market both the employment figure and the wage rates differ from those which would exist under competition. Wages may then deviate considerably both from the marginal product which the last worker employed under free competition would have produced, and from the marginal product which is actually produced by the last of the restricted number of workers employed. Instead of the marginal product the determining fact is now the evaluation of the expected strike sacrifices to each of the fighting parties as compared with the positive or negative advantages of a wage change. The cost and gain balance of each party determines, however, only the upper and lower limits of the possible wage rates (Hicks, Zeuthen). The positions within this range are strongly affected not only by the more or less measurable magnitudes, the size of the union's and the employer's reserves and the magnitude of the losses threatening both per strike day and not only by the subjective values assigned by each party to its measurable gains and losses, but also by the extent to which each of the opponents may forecast the other's and his own behavior from the beginning to the end of the strike. This conjectural factor in bargaining is probably stronger on the employer's side, as is to a certain extent his position with regard to the subjective value of the lost portions of the income. On the other hand, the position of the workers has been strengthened by social legislation, like unemployment insurance. The results of arbitration must be determined in the long run by the same forces as the results of a strike; but the range of possible solutions is broader, since the net advantage to each party is increased by the saving of strike costs.

Finally, it is necessary to drop the last assumption, namely, that of the absence of *speculative gains or losses*. The existence of such gains and losses in modern economy implies that the sum of contractual money incomes may be greater by the amount of losses or smaller by the amount of gains than the sum spent by the recipients of contractual incomes for consumption goods or for investment, i.e. for financing additions to instruments and stocks (Keynes, Myrdal). It follows that the current investments should not be regarded as the unconsumed part of the contractual incomes but as this amount plus speculative gains or minus speculative losses. It is relevant to the theory of wages to note that in this connection money wages are a contractual income, while the speculative gains are as a rule attached to and administered by managers; and that wages are earned by the poor and thus more likely to be consumed than other incomes.

With the prevailing lack of foresight the adjustment of factor combinations to precisely known actual or future changes of circumstances (the business of the manager as described above) cannot be separated from adjustments to those changes which are merely conjectured; these are perhaps better grasped by managers than by others yet are not revealed perfectly even to the former. If managers build their conjectures of the future on the basis of their current experience, present gains may induce them to undertake greater expansion and present losses lead them to more drastic reduction of the quantities of the factors hired than would be the case with adjustments based on changes foretold precisely in advance. Thus the optimal factor combinations would not be reached. An increase of contractual incomes to offset speculative gains and the decrease of the former to offset speculative losses would therefore reduce those fluctuations of the employment of factors which are attributable to the manager's projection into the future of current gains and losses. (It must of course be borne in mind that while the existence of such an attitude on the part of management is not merely psychologically plausible but an established fact, it is far from being the only logical possibility.) A mitigation of speculative gains in the particular case of technical progress may assume two forms, depending on the monetary and the incomes policy chosen. Either the money reward rates to factors are stabilized, with the final prices left to a free fall under the competition of managers, or a price index is stabilized by a monetary authority while the money rewards to the factors are augmented in accordance with increased physical marginal returns. The first way is unencumbered by difficulties of administrative intervention, assuming that effective competition is at work; but during the free fall of prices dangerous speculative losses may develop, aggravating the fluctuation at least for an indefinitely long transition period. The second way is unhampered by this drawback but implies a difficult double control of prices and incomes; it even suggests control of the quantities produced (at least for the commodities with a rather rigid demand, like food), since with increasing money incomes the demand for different commodities changes in different proportions, without regard to the necessarily constant relative weights assigned in the price index to the commodities.

Apart from the contrast between contractual incomes and speculative gains, there is a contrast between the low incomes (mostly wages) and other incomes. The unfavorable influence of equalization of incomes on savings has been mentioned above. Yet wage increases cannot be considered as the sole cause of a diminished investment when the existence of speculative losses or gains is no longer excluded by assumption. Diminished investments may, in accordance with what has already been said, be the expression not of increased consumption but of increased speculative losses; and these may be due to any change in relations between the contractual money incomes and the expenditures made by the receivers of these incomes, unfavorable to and not foreseen by entrepreneurs. Further diminution of investments may be induced if managers project these present losses into the future. In this situation as in that of capital destruction an increasing inequality of incomes would of course reduce consumption. But it would not reduce speculative losses, even if all the amounts previously consumed by workers were to be invested by receivers of interest and high salaries. It is therefore questionable whether the increase of output involved in a restoration of wage rates to their competitive level (if such level as required by the actual state or the well founded prospect of technique and ability had previously been exceeded) and in a transfer of incomes from non-savers to savers would or would not be offset by the decrease of output induced by continuing speculative losses. The presumption that speculative losses may be of greater import than absolute wages is particularly strong in times of great and widespread technical improvements. Such improvements, while generally raising the competitive level of wage rates, inaugurate at the same time, except in the case of a price stabilizing monetary policy, a transitional period of falling prices. Since speculative losses are perpetuated by abstinence from investment, the transitional period is shortened either by the supply of additional money to those who will certainly invest it (public works) or by its provision to those who will certainly spend it for consumption, i.e. the poor. Broadly speaking, keeping down in periods of deflation and technical progress the contractual incomes with exception of the incomes of the poor means lower interest rates and reduced salaries. But the difficulties of diagnosis and the danger of errors in measurement and control are of course obvious.

Wage Policy. In a fully competitive labor market a wage rate for a single and absolutely interchangeable worker in an absolutely interchangeable working place cannot be fixed except at a level determined by the magnitudes which are described above and are certainly less flexible than such an individual wage rate. But this is much less true in the case of imperfect mobility of workers and entrepreneurs, such as has always existed in reality. It is still less true in the regime of bilateral monopoly in a unionized labor market. Even then, however, prolonged unemployment caused by the fact that obtainable wage rates exceed the competitive level, determined with due regard to the potential changes in population, technique, ability, demand structure and so on, after a time exhausts the financial and certainly the psychological strength of a trade union. (This does not necessarily imply that the aggregate income of employed and unemployed must decline.) The union's loss of strength may be represented by the shift of concession schedules of employers and employees (the numbers of strike days which are considered to compensate for given amounts of wage changes) in favor of the former. A new wage rate fixed under these conditions is of course not necessarily equal to the competitive level as it existed at the time the old wage rate was fixed; but it is lower than the old wage rate. Trade unions will therefore set the wage rate they sincerely desire somewhere between the competitive level (in the sense defined above) and the highest obtainable level. The elasticity of demand for labor determines the point within this range at which the aggregate wage of employed and unemployed will reach its maximum.

The margin between the competitive and the highest obtainable rate is obviously wider for a wage fixing public authority than for trade unions. It is, however, not limitless because of the possibility of evasions. Again the elasticity of demand for labor will determine whether a given obtainable rate is or is not advantageous for the employed and unemployed workers of the trade or region concerned and for the *working class as a whole*. Another consideration for the public authority is the effect of a wage change on the *national output as a whole*.

The determinants of the labor demand elasticities have been mentioned above. It has been shown also that a simple observation of wage rates and employment figures, either simultaneous or "lagged" by any time amounts, does not immediately yield the theoretical demand elasticities, although, on the assumption that the complicating causes occurred at random while the elasticities sought did not undergo considerable fluctuations, a statistical regression may come near to a theoretical relationship. (Very different results have been obtained, for wages and employment, and for production in England, by J. Rueff and J. Tinbergen respectively.)

The competitive wage level as qualified above, i.e. with regard to potential changes of the supply of factors, of the production function and of the demand structure, corresponds to an optimal output. Thus a wage increase will augment the output if the wage rate was previously below the competitive level. This might have been the case either because employers had been relatively more powerful or more completely organized than workers; or because changes in the supply of factors, production function and demand structure, elevating the competitive wage level, had anticipated actual wage changes. Special consideration must also be given to the problem of reducing the costs of business fluctuations to the nation, in connection with what has been said of the speculative gains and losses affected by changes in contractual incomes and in low incomes.

The two criteria—the workers' aggregate wages and the total national output—may conflict with each other. A striking example is the labor saving technique if it goes so far as to impair not only the relative but the absolute share of labor. This may be counteracted on the monetary level; neither ethical considerations which may put equality above aggregate wealth nor the conception of "welfare" in terms of subjective values which makes the money losses of the rich appear smaller than equivalent money gains of the poor (Pigou) would then be involved. Wages are not the sole form of income distribution. A system of public taxes and expenditures may effect a partial transfer to the poor of the accruals of output arising from technical change. Unlike a wage increase, the tax would not induce dismissals if it were not paid per head of employed. A reduction of output due to decreased rewards to employers may or may not ensue; even if it does, the reduction will not necessarily be as great as it would in the case of substitution of expensive workers by other factors or so drastic as to reach the level of the output prior to the introduction of the new invention. Similarly if the ethical criterion of equality or the requirements of a subjective total welfare be acknowledged, a general tax would often prove a more simple procedure than a wage increase. Considerations such as these serve to support the statement presented at the beginning of this discussion. Wages are a historical category. The cooperation of employers and employees—buyers and sellers of manual or other low paid forms of labor, conditioned more or less definitely by their respective marginal products but also by the forecasting abilities of the employing class as a whole—is not and never has been the only possible form of production and distribution.

JAKOB MARSCHAK

HISTORY AND STATISTICS. *Methods of Wage Statistics.* Wages are at once the price of labor power considered as a commodity, an important expense of production and a form of income for large masses of people. There are accordingly three types of wage statistics, which must never be confused even though they may appear in combination.

Statistical measurement of wages as the price of labor power utilizes the ordinary methods of price statistics. There are of course innumerable kinds of labor power which are compensated at different rates, but this is a difficulty encountered also in other branches of price statistics. In observing the prices of goods in the market the statistician selects the typical grades or brands of the various goods and accepts the officially recorded quotations for the latter or their average as the price of the particular group of goods per unit of weight, length, volume and so forth. As applied to wages this method calls for the ascertainment of the "normal," or officially recorded, wages paid in occupations which are both typical and numerically important in the labor market. The base to which wages are related is the one generally employed in the country; thus hourly, daily or weekly wage rates are obtained for industrial workers, weekly or monthly salaries are obtained for white collar employees and seasonal or annual wages for farm laborers. Piece rates present no special problem because they are easily convertible into time rates.

The statistics of wages as the price of labor power may be described as wage rate statistics. They are not concerned with the length of the working week, part time employment and similar questions. Nor are the differences between actual wage earnings of individual workers and normal rates taken into account. It is safe to ignore these differences so long as they remain a stable component of the wage situation, similar to the discrepancies between the price paid by a particular buyer of merchandise and the prevailing market price for it. When, however, conditions undergo a radical change so that ostensible minimum wage rates become in practise maximum rates or when collective wage agreements are substantially disregarded by employers, statistics of normal wage rates lose their significance. In general wage rate statistics are the more useful the more readily it can be assumed that "other things remain equal"; thus they are quite reliable in the study of month to month changes or of general wage trends over longer periods, provided the individual deviations from the normal are not too important as compared with fluctuations in the normal. But in periods of rapid economic change statistics of this type are apt to prove misleading; in a crisis, for instance, normal wage rates may remain unchanged while actual wages decline because of underpayment and elimination of overtime; conversely, during a revival actual wages may rise before collective wage agreements are officially revised.

For countries and industries where collective bargaining is common the wage schedule of the trade agreement is the important source of wage rate statistics. Elsewhere reliance is placed upon reports of public bodies and of representative employers as to typical rates paid. The raw material of wage rate statistics is non-statistical in character since it is not derived from mass observation. Yet on the basis of rates thus obtained, averages—often weighted by the number of people to whom the rates apply—are computed for occupations, major industrial groups, regions and the like. In current statistics a simpler and somewhat more illuminating procedure is adopted: only current changes in wage rates are recorded. This method is favored particularly in Great Britain, where monthly reports are compiled on changes in weekly wage rates and on the number of workers affected by them. In the United States the Bureau of Labor

Statistics compiles monthly figures on the number of wage earners affected by a rise or decline in wage rates. Until 1932 the "free" trade unions in Germany published annual data which covered the number affected by wage rate changes and attempted to measure the change in wage incomes of those employed under trade agreements.

The statistics of wages as an element of production costs are concerned not with normal rates or with rates paid to individual workmen but with total wages paid, or pay roll outlays. Such data obtained in production censuses or through current reports by cooperating establishments afford no information regarding the differentiation of wages by sex, age, skill and the like. Frequently they do not segregate salaries from wages, a particularly undesirable practise if the salaries of officers and executives are also included (as in German production censuses). The simplest form in which pay roll statistics are used is that of current index numbers, as compiled, for example, by the United States Bureau of Labor Statistics. Wage figures of this type may serve to measure labor cost per unit of output, as in the mining and metallurgical industries. Such computations are impracticable for other industries where the statistician must content himself with the ratio of wage outlay to the gross value of product or "value added by manufacture."

Pay roll data are utilized also in estimates of per capita earnings. For annual figures the base may be the average number of persons employed, derived from monthly reports or from figures recording employment on a particular day in each month. The result shows the average earnings of those actually employed and tends to vary with the change in the average number of hours or days of work per employed person. An alternative procedure is to use as the base the quotient of the total number of man days of labor for the establishment in question by the normal number of labor days in the year, say 300; the result indicates the average earnings of a hypothetical fully employed worker, not of those actually employed. By whatever method they are obtained averages of this type are likely to be misleading in comparisons over time because of a change in the composition of the labor force; they may show, for instance, a rise of wages in depression because of a reduction in the number of less skilled and lower paid workers, whom it is customary to lay off first, or, conversely, a fall of wages in prosperity.

The statistics of wages as a source of individual or family income are concerned not with averages or totals but with the individual incomes and their distribution in typical groups. Since the subject of observation is the actual wage income, wage rates cannot here be separated from hours of work; and estimates of wage income derived by multiplying rates by hours worked are likely to prove misleading.

The two main sources of wage income statistics are family budgets and pay roll sheets. Budgets show not only the wage income of the head of the family but also his supplementary income and the earnings of the other members of the household. They are open nevertheless to grave theoretical and practical objections: in addition to being complicated and expensive, they are not ordinarily typical and afford no clue to the composition of the wage received (normal wage, pay for overtime, bonuses and so on). More important are pay roll sheets, labor books or pay envelopes, which show how the actual wage is computed and contain information as to the occupation, age and sex of the wage recipient.

In this type of statistics it is essential not to overlook that part of the wage which may be paid in kind and such irregular additions as holiday gifts, compensation for injury or illness and the like. On the other hand, the regular contributions of the employer to social insurance funds are not properly a part of the wage income of the worker, although in a calculation of production costs they would be regarded as a form of expenditure on labor. The "invisible income" of the wage earner from free services by the state, municipality or private philanthropies is not wage income, although this would be taken into account in a comparison of the status of wage earning groups in different countries or periods.

A substitute for wage income figures is sometimes obtained from per capita wages derived through a division of pay roll outlays by the average number employed. Such per capita earnings are reduced by a percentage measuring unemployment in the particular industry, occupation or region. The result, however, is a bare average which sheds no light on the composition of the group whose central tendency it purports to represent; moreover experience indicates that the wage fluctuations it reflects are virtually identical with those shown in pay roll statistics. This type of wage income information is used in Australia and occasionally elsewhere.

The statistics of real wages differ from the three types of wage statistics outlined above. Their purpose is to make possible the comparison of the real values of wages despite changes in the prices of the goods in the purchase of which the wage is usually spent. A primitive measure of real wages is that used by the historian when he relates the money wage to the price of wheat and thus ascertains the wheat equivalent of the daily or weekly wage. For the recent period real wages are expressed in terms of a money unit of fixed purchasing power or more often in index numbers.

The comparison of real wages for different localities must take into account the regional and urban-rural differences in the cost of living. Since, however, the requisite statistics are available only in a few countries, in most instances reliance is placed upon quasi-statistical substitutes obtained from small sample studies. For the purpose of comparisons over time the influence of price changes is eliminated with the aid of a cost of living index. This is calculated on the assumption that the commodity budget is not appreciably affected by price fluctuations. The validity of this assumption, however, is dubious, particularly for comparisons extending over several decades as well as for shorter periods in which radical price changes occur. Such changes may be expected to induce a rational adaptation of the commodity budget to the new price situation—an expanded consumption of goods with smaller than average price increases or larger than average price declines and a contracted consumption of goods with comparatively large price increases or slight drops in price. If this expectation is realized, the wage earner gains more from a fall in the cost of living and loses less from an increase than is suggested by an index based on the assumption of a fixed budget; in other words, the ordinary indices tend to depress the trend of real wages.

The method of living cost index can be used also in comparing wage trends in different countries, as was done by the International Labor Office. The ordinary procedure cannot, however, be employed for international comparisons of wage levels, because the national cost of living indices cannot be reduced to a common base. An approach to such comparisons is made possible by the device of an international commodity budget, which will be discussed below.

History of Wages. Since wages are paid out of current income and constitute a part of the aggregate output of the economy, the upper limit to wages is set by the condition of the productive forces of society. This varies with technological development and may also be influenced by demographic and political factors, such as overpopulation and colonial exploitation. In any event in ascertaining the maximum level which wages may conceivably reach attention should be paid not to the productivity of labor in this or that branch of production but to the magnitude of the social product and the number of active participants in production. The lower limit of wages is the minimum of subsistence, which is not simply a physiological minimum but is relative to current notions regarding the necessaries of existence. Actual wages fluctuate within these limits, according to the comparative bargaining position of workers and employers.

Broadly speaking, the character of the wage bargain and of the bargaining power exercised therein has passed through three stages of development. The first was that of a business bargain between the sellers and the buyers of labor power, in which bargaining position was a direct function of the supply of and demand for labor power; a shortage of labor raised wages to so high a level that little "surplus value" was left to the employer, and an oversupply of labor reduced wages to the point where the wage earner could scarcely afford the barest necessities of life. The second stage may be called that of the social wage bargain, wherein the parties in the labor market confront each other as conflicting social forces; this stage began with the rise of trade unionism and has been characteristic of most capitalist countries since the middle of the nineteenth century. The third stage, that of the political wage bargain, is marked by the increasing intervention of government as the largest employer of labor and the arbitrating authority in wage disputes. The democratic government of today, unlike the absolute ruler of the sixteenth century, cannot limit itself to protecting labor against the "exaggerated and disproportionate" demands of employers; it must attempt to equalize the position of the parties to the wage bargain. Wage regulation, the implications of which are just beginning to be realized, has become an established practise; it is an essential prerequisite of a farsighted social policy as well as of an effective economic policy.

Historical sources yield only fragmentary indications of the level of actual wages. In general it may be said that in the slaveholding societies of antiquity, where only skilled work was done by free men for a wage, wages were high and the standard of living maintained by wageworkers was much superior to the subsistence minimum of that epoch, the level at which slaves lived. Since the supply of free labor was limited, an increase in demand for it not infrequently entailed government intervention for the protection of the employer. Moreover considerable differentiation of wages by occupations, sex and age had already set in. Virtually the same situation persisted through the Middle Ages. Despite the primitive industrial technique and wage differentiation wage earners enjoyed a standard of living much above that of the peasants, who constituted the great bulk of the population. The economic revolution of the sixteenth century which opened the vast reservoirs of labor outside the city walls to the manufacturing employer spelled the doom of free handicraft. Because of overpopulation and the radical shift in the labor market wages showed a tendency to fall to a level of barest subsistence. Real wages had already begun to drop—in the fifteenth century in Germany and at the beginning of the sixteenth in England and France—but the victory of the new organizational forms of production accelerated and intensified the decline. Real wages had sunk to a very low level by the middle of the eighteenth century; their movement was reversed in the nineteenth century by technological improvements, which raised the productivity of labor, and by the development of labor organization, which enhanced its bargaining power.

An account of wage trends in the principal countries in the last hundred years can be based on fairly complete statistical data. On the whole wages have risen, but the increase has not been continuous. Money wages have as a rule followed changes in commodity prices. For the periods of high prices it is not always easy to tell whether the increase in wages merely offset the rise in the cost of living or exceeded it; for the periods of falling prices it is quite certain that with a few exceptions the reduction of money earnings did not depress the level of real wages. In general the data suggest that the share of labor in the value of output remained more or less constant over decennial periods and that real wages kept pace with the productivity of labor. A partial confirmation of this generalization has been supplied for the United States by G. F. Warren and F. A. Pearson, who found that in the period 1840–1914 the average annual increase in real wages (the quotient of an index of money wages over an index of wholesale prices) was 1.71 percent and that the average annual increase in the physical volume of output per capita was 1.73 percent.

For the United States sufficient data are available to carry the record of money wage rates back to 1840. The figures assembled in Table 1

TABLE I

INDEX OF NOMINAL WAGE RATES IN THE UNITED STATES, 1840–1932

(1913 = 100)

Year	Wages per Hour Exclusive of Agriculture	Farm Wage Rates
1840	33	—
1844	32	—
1849	36	—
1854	37	—
1859	39	—
1864	50	53*
1869	66	52
1874	67	57
1879	59	57
1884	64	63
1889	68	63
1894	67	59
1899	70	65
1904	80	73†
1909	90	92
1914	102	97
1919	184	198
1920	234	230
1921	218	144
1923	217	160
1925	226	162
1927	231	163
1929	233	161
1930	229	143
1931	217	109
1932	186	81
1933	184	79

* Figure for 1866.
† Figure for 1902.
Source: *Monthly Labor Review*, vol. xxxii (1931) 398, and vol. xxxvii (1933) 632; International Labour Office, *I.L.O. Year-Book, 1933* (Geneva 1934) appendix ii.

show that non-agricultural wage rates increased considerably during the Civil War and the following quinquennium, fluctuated about this level until the end of the nineteenth century, rose markedly in the period 1909–14, more than doubled during the years of the World War and the post-war boom and increased slightly during the prosperity of 1923–29, declining thereafter to a low point in 1932. Farm wages rose much more than industrial rates before the World War but slumped badly in the post-war decade. While the general trend of wages has been upward, it would be rash to conclude that wage earnings have increased nearly as much or as steadily as wage rates; working hours have been greatly reduced since 1840 and there have been several periods of widespread total or partial unemployment. The behavior of real wages be-

TABLE II
INDEX OF REAL WAGES IN THE UNITED STATES, 1890–1926
(1890–99 = 100)

| YEAR | WEEKLY RATES ||||||| ANNUAL EARNINGS OF FULLY EMPLOYED, ALL INDUSTRIES ‡ |
	AVERAGE, ALL INDUSTRIES *	MANUFAC- TURING INDUSTRIES †	BUILD- ING TRADES	BITUMINOUS COAL INDUSTRY	RAILWAY WORKERS	UNSKILLED LABOR	FARM LABOR	
1890	98	96	97	106	97	97	99	100
1894	102	101	102	108	103	102	97	98
1899	99	100	100	97	98	99	102	99
1904	99	98	102	123	95	95	110	101
1909	103	98	111	126	99	100	118	106
1914	100	95	105	122	98	94	111	107
1919	101	96	82	139	99	109	125	115
1920	103	97	91	134	106	101	124	116
1921	109	104	111	168	112	92	93	118
1922	114	107	111	178	117	96	97	124
1923	121	112	120	181	114	106	107	131
1924	123	113	129	170	116	107	107	131
1925	124	113	132	149	117	109	107	132
1926	125	112	138	147	118	109	108	135

* Includes in addition to industries listed in following columns also anthracite coal miners, railway clerks, seamen, postal employees, federal employees, teachers and ministers.
† Includes foundries and machine shops, marble and stonework, baking, book and job printing, newspaper printing, millwork, cotton goods, woolen goods, hosiery and knit goods, men's clothing, boots and shoes, slaughtering and meat packing, iron and steel, sawmills.
‡ Weighted for each year by the number employed in each industry.
Source: Douglas, P. H., *Real Wages in the United States 1890–1926* (Boston 1930) p. 130, 137, 144, 168, 177, 187, 211 and 392 supplement.

fore 1890 cannot be described with any degree of certainty for lack of adequate data on hours of work and cost of living, but for 1890–1926 real weekly wage rates were computed by Paul H. Douglas on the basis of information regarding hourly rates, hours per week and living costs. These figures, presented in Table II, show no uniform trends for different industries and occupations. The movement of the average of weekly wage rates for all industries indicates that little progress was made from 1890 to 1914, but that in the years following 1920 real weekly rates increased by 25 percent. The average of real annual earnings, derived mainly from census data, confirms this conclusion for the post-war years but suggests in addition an increase of 7 percent before the World War. After taking into account gains resulting from the changing of occupations, an expansion of free services rendered by governmental and philanthropic institutions, a reduction in unemployment and a decrease in the number of dependents Douglas concludes that from 1890–99 to 1926 the real income of the working class increased on the average by 55 percent. The situation after 1926 is reflected in the following indices of real hourly and weekly wage rates in manufacturing industries (on a 1923 base) computed by the International Labor Office from money wage and cost of living series compiled by the National Industrial Conference Board, an employers' organization:

YEAR	HOURLY WAGE RATES	WEEKLY WAGE RATES
1926	101	99
1927	105	102
1928	107	104
1929	109	107
1930	113	101
1931	120	98
1932	118	83

For England the history of wages can be traced back to the thirteenth century. According to Thorold Rogers English wages in the mediaeval period were comparatively high. In the middle of the fourteenth century the Black Death effected a sharp reduction in the supply of labor and raised its price, while food became cheap because of the decimation of the population. This inaugurated the golden age of English labor, which persisted over into the first quarter of the sixteenth century. Then a reaction set in. Living costs rose and labor was hamstrung by the Statutes of Labourers, which provided for governmental fixation of wage maxima and outlawed labor organization. Real wages were particularly low in the eighteenth century because of a steep rise in commodity prices accompanied by only a mild increase in money wages. Not

Wages

TABLE III

Index of Weekly Wage Rates in the United Kingdom, 1880–1913*

(1900 = 100)

Year	Building Trades	Coal Mining	Engineering	Textile	Agriculture	Average of Preceding Groups Including Agriculture	Average of Preceding Groups Excluding Agriculture
1880	86	62	88	90	91	83	81
1885	84	63	90	90	91	84	82
1890	87	86	93	95	92	91	90
1895	92	73	93	95	94	89	88
1900	100	100	100	100	100	100	100
1905	100	81	100	103	103	97	96
1910	100	90	102	107	105	101	100
1913	104	100	105	112	111	107	105

* The averages in the table are compiled as follows: building trades—mean of 74 rates relating to bricklayers, carpenters and joiners, and masons; coal mining—weighted percentage changes in hewers' wages in principal districts; engineering—mean of 36 rates relating to fitters, turners, ironmolders and pattern makers; textile—cotton spinners and weavers, and linen and jute operatives.
Source: Great Britain, Board of Trade, Department of Labour Statistics, *Seventeenth Abstract of Labour Statistics of the United Kingdom* (1915) p. 66.

until the nineteenth century with the growth in the productivity of labor, repeal of anti-union laws and progressive factory legislation did real wages begin to rise again, in some instances reaching the fifteenth century level. The same story is told by Gustav Schmoller, who equates the average weekly wage in England to 35 kilograms of wheat in the thirteenth century, 60–80 kilograms in the second half of the fourteenth and the fifteenth, 30–40 kilograms in the latter half of the sixteenth, 24–32 kilograms in the seventeenth, 40 kilograms in 1725–50 and 30 kilograms during the two generations prior to 1850.

British wage statistics, however, do not go back further than the 1880's. The data assembled in Table III indicate that on the average weekly wage rates increased by about 30 percent in the course of the thirty-five years preceding 1914; since the value of the index of wholesale prices was approximately the same in 1913 as in 1880, it is probable that real wage rates increased as much as the nominal rates. During the World War and the following two years money wages experienced a very large increase caused by an enhanced demand for labor and a rise in the cost of living. This is shown in Table IV illustrating current wage statistics in Great Britain based on union wage rates applicable to a normal work week. With the onset of the post-war depression wages fell rapidly; within two years they were 35 to 40 percent below the high point established in 1920. Although living costs declined at the same time, real wages at the end of 1922 were probably from 5 to 10 percent lower than in the last pre-war month. Since that time fluctuations in nominal wages have been much narrower, but the general trend has been downward; the cost of living, however, has declined even more, so that the real wages of those fully employed have increased. At the end of 1929 real wages were about 5 percent higher and before the abandonment of the gold standard in 1931 from 14 to 17 percent higher than in 1914; at present they are stabilized at this level.

In prerevolutionary France real wages were extremely low. While prices in terms of gold were as high as in the 1880's, money wages were 50 to 60 percent less. Under the regime of assignats real wages were of course subject to violent fluctuations. In the nineteenth century with the economic development of the country and a shift in the political and social balance of power the condition of the working classes gradually improved. At the opening of the nineteenth century money wages were from 40 to 50 percent higher than before the revolution; since commodity prices were only 20 to 30 percent above the prerevolutionary level, it is fair to assume that real wages increased by about 25 to 30 percent. In the following fifty years money wages remained practically stationary, while living costs declined. From 1850 to the World War nominal wage rates and money earnings increased continually except for the period 1880–95, which was marked by declining prices and stable wages. The general movement of French wages after 1896 is summarized in Table V. This compilation suggests that if, as may readily be assumed, retail prices were the same in July, 1914, as in 1911, the real value of hourly wage rates in 1932 was 30 to 40 percent and that of

TABLE IV
Changes in Wages in Great Britain and Northern Ireland, 1914–1933*

Year	Approximate Number of Individuals (in 1000) Reported as Affected by — Net Increase	Net Decrease	Estimated Net Weekly Amount of Change (in £1000) in Rates of Wages — Net Increase	Net Decrease	Estimated Net Weekly Increase (+) or Decrease (−) in Rates of Wages of All Work People Affected
1914	960	—	13	—	+ 13
1915	3470	—	678	—	+ 678
1916	3593	—	637	—	+ 637
1917	5029	—	2307	—	+2307
1918	5998	—	2988	—	+2988
1919	6240	—	2547	—	+2547
1920	7867	—	4793	—	+4793
1921	78	7244	14	6075	−6061
1922	74	7633	11	4221	−4210
1923	1202	3079	169	486	− 317
1924	3019	481	616	62	+ 554
1925	873	851	81	159	− 78
1926	420	740	133	84	+ 49
1927	282	1855	31	388	− 358
1928	217	1615	22	164	− 142
1929	142	917	13	92	− 79
1930	768	1100	59	116	− 57
1931	47	3010	5	406	− 401
1932	33	1949	3	252	− 249
1933	171	896	16	82	− 66

* Exclusive of changes affecting agricultural laborers, government employees, domestic servants, shop assistants and clerks. The figures are based mainly on reports from unionized industries.
Source: Great Britain, Ministry of Labour, *Gazette*, vol. xxiv (1916) 4, vol. xxv (1917) 4, vol. xxvi (1918) 4, vol. xxvii (1919) 3, vol. xxviii (1920) 3, and vol. xlii (1934) 5.

TABLE V
Wages and Prices in France, 1896–1932

Year	Hourly Wage Rates (1911 = 100) — Men's in 38 Trades outside Paris	Men's in 22 Trades in Paris Region	Women's in 7 Trades outside Paris	Daily Wages of Coal Miners (1911 = 100)	Retail Prices of 13 Articles (July, 1914 = 100) — In Paris	Outside Paris
1896	85	83	65	80	—	—
1901	89	90	87	94	—	—
1906	96	97	91	93	—	—
1911	100	100	100	100	100	100
1921	502	401	509	413	337	374
1926	700	580	809	599	554	571
1927	720	582	787	671	557	559
1928	750	597	857	655	557	538
1929	833	693	983	725	611	583
1930	883	755	1053	783	614	607
1931	883	751	1053	756	611	613
1932	868	725	1022	696	536	532

Source: France, Statistique Générale, *Annuaire statistique 1932* (Paris 1933) p. 131*, 151*–53*.

weekly earnings 20 to 25 percent higher than before the war.

The above account of wage trends in France is confirmed by François Simiand in his comprehensive study covering the period 1789–1930. This work deserves attention not only because of the wealth of material assembled therein but also because of the methods used. Instead of computing a general wage index, as is usually done, Simiand plots on the same chart a whole series of indices for various wage rates and wage earnings and thus establishes the trend common to all of them. The charts are drawn to a logarithmic scale and the comparability of the indices is assured by utilizing a common base, 1890–91. The four principal charts relate to men and women in Paris and in the rest of France. The general conclusions are that in the period covered wages were subject to considerable variation with a predominance of changes upward; that the movement was neither uniform nor cyclical but passed through several phases; that the major upward movements occurred in the periods 1850–80 and 1900–30, while in the intervening years the major trends were slightly upward, stationary or downward. The study contains also a detailed investigation concerning the relationship between the succession of phases in the movement of wages and that of the long cycles in prices. It appears that the relation between wages and wholesale prices is clearer than that between wages and retail prices. Nevertheless, the response of wages to price changes is by no means automatic and direct but is mediated by the changed position of employers and workers in the struggle for the division of the social product.

The trend of wages in Germany has been similar on the whole to that in Great Britain. As compared with grain prices wages were quite high in the Middle Ages, declined by about one third in the fifteenth century and by one half in the sixteenth and have been rising slowly since the seventeenth. Both nominal and real wages increased considerably in the second half of the nineteenth century and particularly in the last quarter. Thus from 1872 to 1900 hourly wage rates rose from 40 to 50 percent and weekly earnings from 30 to 40 percent; the cost of living was lower in 1900 than in the 1870's. In the pre-war decade the rise of nominal wages continued —the net earnings of mine workers, for instance, increased from 10 to 25 percent depending on occupation—but living costs increased simultaneously, so that real wages probably remained unchanged. In the war years real wages declined; the attempt made in 1917 to raise them in the war industries succeeded for but a short time and even then for only a few favored occupations. Although statistical measurement is difficult, there is no doubt that the decline in real earnings during the period of post-war inflation was very marked, particularly for skilled workers and salaried employees; earnings in those years scarcely sufficed to cover a bare physiological minimum. At the end of 1923, when the mark was stabilized, wage rates were so fixed that their real value was far below that of 1914; but in the following years normal and real wage rates increased, exceeding eventually the pre-war level (Table VI). If account is taken

TABLE VI

UNION WAGE RATES IN INDUSTRY AND COST OF LIVING, GERMANY, 1924–30

(1913 = 100)

January of Year	Hourly Men's Wage Rates Skilled	Hourly Men's Wage Rates Unskilled	Weekly Men's Wage Rates Skilled	Weekly Men's Wage Rates Unskilled	Cost of Living
1924	88	111	81	99	126
1925	116	138	108	123	136
1926	138	166	128	145	140
1927	139	167	130	147	145
1928	151	187	140	160	151
1929	161	202	149	172	153
1930	166	209	153	178	152

Source: Computed from data in Germany, Statistisches Reichsamt, *Statistisches Jahrbuch für das Deutsche Reich* (Berlin 1927) p. 297, 318, 320, and for 1930 (Berlin 1930) p. 275, 299.

of the enhanced invisible income (social insurance paid for by the employer, free services by public welfare agencies), it will be recognized that before the beginning of the present depression real weekly earnings were higher than in the pre-war period, perhaps by 10 to 20 percent for skilled labor and by 20 to 30 percent for unskilled. In the years following 1929 money wages were reduced by the elimination of overtime work, by systematic violation of the wage schedules of collective agreements as well as by a formal revision downward of the latter and finally by the phenomenal spread of part time employment. Living costs declined in 1930–32 by about 20 percent. While official hourly wage rates dropped in about the same proportion, the reduction in money earnings of the fully employed workers attributable to other causes, subject though it is to extreme variation by occupation, may be estimated to have amounted on the average to from 10 to 15 percent; the average decline in earnings for all employed workers caused by part time employment may be set at another 10 to 15 percent. The real weekly wage in 1933 was therefore scarcely above the very low level established immediately after currency stabilization in a country seriously impoverished by war and inflation.

In the nineteenth century Italy was the lowest wage country in Europe. According to the reports of the British consuls the daily wage of unskilled labor in Italy was 4 pence in 1835 and 8 pence in 1865 as contrasted with 20–26 pence in England, 8–16 pence in Germany, 15–20 pence in France and 42–74 pence in the United States.

This low level was caused by the backwardness of the Italian economy, particularly its agriculture; the poverty of the rural population, which exercised a steady pressure on the labor market; and the prevalence of low living standards, which could be tolerated because of the mild climate. As Italy advanced economically real wages increased, although they never reached the standard prevailing in most capitalist states on the continent. Regulation by the Fascist government did not raise the general wage level, nor did it radically change the wage relationships of the various industries and occupations.

For Russia wage statistics date only from the beginning of the twentieth century. According to reports of factory inspectors the average annual earnings of workers in manufacturing establishments subject to inspection rose from $110 in 1900 to $125 in 1908; an important factor in this increase was the change in the political situation after 1905 and the vigorous labor movement which helped to bring it about. The average daily wage at the outbreak of the World War was 55 cents; while there was a rise during the years of war and revolution, living costs increased even more, so that by the end of 1917 real wages were 37 percent less than in 1913. In the period of war communism and civil war the country was greatly impoverished and the real value of money wages sank so low that survival would have been impossible without payments in kind, which were much more important than cash pay. As compared with an average monthly wage of 22 rubles in 1913 the monthly wage in 1917–21 expressed in terms of 1913 commodity rubles was as follows:

	1917	1918	1919	1920	1921
Money payments	16.60	4.73	1.40	0.49	0.96
Payments in kind:					
food	0.69	1.47	2.42	2.62	2.85
clothing		0.80	0.86	1.31	0.94
dwelling and the like	0.50	1.99	2.09	2.18	2.20
Total	17.79	8.99	6.77	6.60	6.95

Under the NEP payments in kind were abolished and real wages, which at first barely equaled a third of the pre-war wage, increased rapidly. In 1926 the official index of real wages on a 1913 base stood at 128.8 in Moscow and 94.6 in the rest of the country. With the replacement of the NEP by the policy of "the general line," aiming at the complete nationalization of the Russian economy, the fixing of money wages throughout the country was centralized in Moscow. The Soviet government has attempted to keep wages high, but it has not been entirely successful because of the general destitution of the country, the low productivity of labor and the poor organization of production. During the first Five-Year Plan moreover part of the national income which ordinarily would have been available in the form of wages and salaries was considerably reduced by the enormous investment in capital equipment. Nominal monthly earnings increased nevertheless by about 17 percent from 1928 to 1930, but this rise was more than offset by the drop in the purchasing power of the ruble. Averages, however, are less significant for wage statistics in Russia than elsewhere because of the unusual differentiation of wages by industry and occupation, even within each craft. Thus a study in 1929 of 835,800 individual wage earners revealed that while average monthly earnings were 74.93 rubles (as compared with 77.85 rubles for the country as a whole), 21.4 percent of the total number covered earned less than 50 rubles and 22.6 earned more than 100 rubles; in the same year average monthly earnings by industries varied from 46.34 rubles in linen textiles to 103.29 in machine construction, while the average for all manufacturing industries was 77.85 rubles. Such differentiation is to be accounted for in part by the strenuous effort to utilize wages as an incentive to greater productivity; the basic piece rates are supplemented by an extensive system of bonuses for better quality of work, less waste of material, prompt execution of the quota and the like. The differentiation in real wages is even greater, for in the absence of a free market the purchasing power of the ruble varies not only from time to time and from one locality to another but also from one group of workers to the next, depending upon the quantity of consumers' goods which the government allocates to each and the prices charged therefor. It is consequently very difficult to present a statistical evaluation of either nominal or real wages in modern Russia; and the use of Russian statistics for international comparisons is further inhibited by the fact that the invisible income of the worker in the Soviet Union is much greater than in any other country.

Some mention should be made of Australia, which in addition to the United States is the outstanding country of high wages and possesses moreover wage statistics that are not only well developed but methodologically interesting. As indicated in Table VII, the real wage of a fully

Wages

TABLE VII
Index of Nominal and Real Wages in Australia, 1901–31
(1911 = 100)

Year	Nominal Weekly Wages, Adult Males	Retail Prices	Real Wage Rates	Percentage Unemployed	Real Wages Allowing for Unemployment
1901	84.8	88.0	96.4	6.6	94.5
1906	86.6	90.2	96.0	6.7	94.0
1911	100.0	100.0	100.0	±4.7	100.0
1916	114.4	132.4	86.4	5.8	85.4
1921	182.6	169.7	107.6	11.2	100.2
1926	191.4	178.6	107.2	7.1	104.5
1927	194.6	176.6	110.2	7.0	107.5
1928	196.3	176.0	111.5	10.8	104.4
1929	197.2	182.2	108.2	11.1	100.9
1930	193.9	168.3	115.2	19.3	97.6
1931	175.2	147.9	118.5	27.4	90.3
1932	163.9	140.2	116.9	29.0	87.1
1933	158.4	134.6	117.7	26.1	92.5

Source: Australia, Commonwealth Bureau of Census and Statistics, *Official Year-Book of the Commonwealth of Australia, 1932* (Canberra 1933) p. 786; *Quarterly Summary of Australian Statistics* (March, 1934) p. 89.

employed worker in Australia increased from 1911 to 1929 more than in Great Britain but less than in the United States. In the present depression real wages for full time work have continued to increase because of the drop in the cost of living, but the condition of the working class as a whole is worse than in 1911 on account of widespread unemployment.

Wages and the Value of Output. The measurement of the share of labor in the value of output may be carried out in two ways: the wage and salary outlay may be related to the gross value of products, so that the quotient shows the percentage of total expense allocated to labor; or the wage and salary outlay may be related to the new value created in the process of manufacture, with the quotient indicating the share of labor in the specific output of the industry. The first of these quotients is subject to extreme variation and is influenced by the proximity of the industry to the stage of raw material extraction or cultivation. The second quotient, much more stable and significant, is conditioned by the composition of capital in the industry, the level of wages, the tax burden carried by the industry and so on.

The value and derivation of these ratios for the census groups of industry in the United States are shown in Table VIII. It is subject to two corrections. Salaries, which grow in importance with technological progress, increase in the scale of operations and the spread of modern organizational forms of production, must be

TABLE VIII
Wages and the Value of Output in Manufacturing Industries, United States, 1929
(In $1,000,000,)

Industry Groups	Value of Products	Cost of Materials*	Value Added by Manufacture	Wages	Percentage which Wages Form of Total Value of Products	Percentage which Wages Form of Value Added by Manufacture
Food and kindred products	12,024	8,632	3,391	902	7.5	26.6
Textiles	9,243	5,104	4,139	1,733	18.7	41.9
Forest products	3,592	1,586	2,006	939	26.1	46.8
Paper and allied products	1,892	1,093	800	287	15.2	35.9
Printing and publishing	3,170	766	2,404	636	20.1	26.4
Chemicals and allied products	3,759	1,971	1,789	354	9.4	19.8
Products of petroleum and coal	3,648	2,547	1,101	229	6.3	20.8
Rubber products	1,117	579	539	207	18.5	38.4
Leather and its products	1,906	1,132	774	359	18.8	46.4
Stone, clay and glass products	1,561	526	1,035	433	27.7	41.8
Iron and steel	7,138	3,863	3,275	1,381	19.3	42.2
Non-ferrous metals	3,597	2,465	1,132	443	12.3	39.1
Machinery	7,043	2,694	4,349	1,634	23.2	37.6
Transportation equipment	6,047	3,683	2,364	943	15.6	39.9
Railroad repair shops	1,270	548	722	637	50.2	88.2
Miscellaneous	3,426	1,359	2,067	501	14.6	24.2
All industries	70,435	38,550	31,885	11,621	16.5	36.4

* Includes cost of containers for products, fuel and purchased electric energy.
Source: United States, Bureau of the Census, Fifteenth Census of the United States, *Census of Manufactures: 1929*, vol. ii (1933) p. 36–37.

added to wages in computing labor's share of gross or net value of output. And in relating the labor outlay to new value created by the industry allowance must be made in the base for the transfer of value from the capital equipment to the product; that is, "value added by manufacture" should be reduced by the amount representing capital amortization. If capital amortization per annum is assumed to have averaged 7 percent of the investment in the period 1889–1919, for which the census collected data on capital investment, and 5 percent of the total value of products in 1921–29, the percentage ratio of wages and salaries to net value output for manufacturing industries in the United States will appear to have been as follows:

Year		Year	
1889	59	1919	61
1899	54	1921	67†
1899	57*	1923	61
1904	59	1925	59
1909	60	1927	59
1914	65	1929	56

* This and the following figures exclude hand and neighborhood industries.
† This and the following figures exclude establishments with an annual output less than $5000.

The percentage ratios suggest an upward trend until 1921 and a declining one since, but in view of the roughness of the estimating procedure it is not clear whether much significance can be attached to this impression.

The share of labor in the specific product of mines and quarries tends to be much larger. United States census data show that the percentage of the value of net product—computed as the difference between value of products on the one hand and cost of supplies and materials, fuel, purchased energy and contract work on the other, reduced further by an amount equal to 5 percent of the value of products to allow for capital depreciation—expended in wages and salaries was 77 in 1909, 76 in 1919 and 74 in 1929. Also for blast furnaces and steel mills in the United States the percentage ratio of wages to value added by manufacture is higher than for manufacturing industries as a whole. According to census data it averaged about 52 percent in 1879–1929; it was particularly low in the prosperous years 1899, 1909 and 1929 (43, 47 and 45 respectively) and particularly high in the depression year 1921 (66 percent). If value added by manufacture is reduced by an allowance for capital amortization, the average percentage for the period is raised to over 60; it would be still higher if salaries were added to wages in computing the ratio.

Other countries for which similar computations can be made are Canada, the Union of South Africa, Australia, New Zealand and Finland. Canadian statistics treat value added by manufacture as the difference between value of products and cost of materials, not including the cost of fuel and purchased energy; on this basis the percentage ratio of wages and salaries to value added appears to have varied in 1918–30 within the narrow range of 39.8 to 44.5. If allowance is made for capital depreciation by deducting, say, 7 percent of the capital investment from value added, the percentage ratio will obviously be raised; for the ratio computed on the latter basis the range of variation in the period 1870–1930 is from 45 to 62. Similar ratios for the other countries are: if value added is computed as the difference between value of products and cost of materials, 49 to 56 for South Africa in 1923–27, 53 to 56 for Australia in 1926–30 and 51.3 to 52.0 for New Zealand in 1926–30; if allowance is made for capital depreciation, 51 to 57 in South Africa, 60.3 to 61.5 in Australia and 59.5 to 60.2 in New Zealand. In Finland the share of wages in the net product of industry is somewhat lower. According to 1931 data the value of industrial output less the cost of raw materials was 4,487,400,000 Finnish marks; the value of net product, after allowance is made for the cost of fuel and purchased energy as well as for capital amortization, may be estimated at 3,800,000,000 marks. Wages amounted to 1,484,800,000 marks, or about 39 percent of the value of net product; if salaries are estimated at 30 percent of wages, the corresponding ratio is raised to 51 percent.

On the basis of the above data it may be concluded that for industry as a whole the share of labor in net value output constitutes in each country a fairly stable proportion, although it is subject to considerable variation from one branch of industry to the next. If the share of labor is regarded as the sum of wages and salaries and net value output is interpreted strictly, then the ratio of the former to the latter is about 60 percent for manufacturing industries and appreciably higher for mining; if no allowance is made for capital amortization, the ratio is reduced to between 40 and 50 percent. For wages alone the ratio is from 35 to 45 percent, and if capital depreciation is not eliminated from the net value output it sinks even lower.

Wage Differentiation. National wage averages constitute merely the central points in the distribution of wage rates and earnings of the various groups of workers. A considerable amount of wage differentiation is to be observed in every country. It follows the lines of division between major branches of production, industries, occupations, and takes cognizance of the sex and age of workers; again, within each of these groups wages vary with the ability of the individual wage earner. Differences of the latter type are not recorded in statistics of wage rates or in pay roll statistics; it is through special wage investigations based on a study of pay roll sheets or labor books that such variations may be observed. The conclusions to which such studies lead are that individual differentiation is more pronounced among skilled workers than among the semiskilled, among the latter as compared with the unskilled, among adult male workers as compared with women and children and among those receiving piece rate wages as compared with those paid on a time basis. This is illustrated in Table IX, which summarizes the results of four German wage studies and indicates the composition of the groups in terms of deviations from the group average. The table suggests that the lower the group average the greater is the clustering about the average.

Variation in wages as between the major branches of production can be explained largely by the differences in the structure of the labor market—in the organization of labor, its customary living standards, the extent of competition among employers and the like. Many of these differences are a carry over from the past or a product of temporary conditions; yet a

TABLE IX

Wage Groups in Selected Industries, Germany, 1927–29

Industry and Occupation	Average Weekly Earnings (in Marks)	Average Class Interval (in Marks)	2 Class Intervals Below the Average	1 Class Interval Below the Average	Average Class Interval	1 Class Interval Above the Average	2 Class Intervals Above the Average
Metals, October, 1928							
Skilled male, time wage	53.61	50–55	10.2	16.7	19.9	18.4	10.6
Semiskilled male, time wage	43.74	40–45	5.4	18.7	30.2	19.3	11.9
Skilled male, piece wage	56.16	55–60	8.9	16.4	21.6	18.4	12.0
Semiskilled male, piece wage	51.21	50–55	10.4	20.2	22.7	16.4	9.6
Chemicals, June, 1928							
Semiskilled male, time wage	47.95	45–50	9.3	16.4	18.0	17.1	14.6
Semiskilled male, piece wage	55.74	55–60	13.9	14.3	16.1	15.7	9.2
Female, time wage	26.40	25–30	35.2*		38.1	20.7	4.6
Female, piece wage	31.20	30–35	15.4*	26.4	30.4	16.2	8.7
Skilled, time wage	60.60	60–65	11.1	12.9	13.3	13.8	12.5
Skilled, piece wage	68.14	65–70	8.2	13.1	16.0	19.9	18.4
Textiles, September, 1927							
Skilled male	42.22	40–44	10.5	14.9	16.3	13.9	10.6
Helpers male	33.78	32–36	8.9	26.3	24.2	16.8	9.7
Skilled female	30.25	28–32	12.6	21.1	25.1	13.8	10.0
Helpers female	22.40	20–24	24.4*		41.4	25.4	7.0
Boots and shoes, March, 1929							
Adult male, time wage	42.09	40–44	9.3	12.4	19.1	14.1	9.8
Adult male, piece wage	48.68	46–50	9.4	9.7	10.5	11.1	10.0
Adult female, time wage	29.64	28–32	9.1	13.9	32.1	19.5	8.4
Adult female, piece wage	33.35	32–36	12.0	13.9	17.6	16.0	10.9
Male, 18–21 years, time wage	30.01	28–32	9.8	13.1	21.0	23.9	10.8
Male, 18–21 years, piece wage	36.43	34–38	10.5	18.5	15.8	15.9	9.8
Female, 18–21 years, time wage	21.97	20–24	29.0*		43.8	19.1	5.6
Female, 18–21 years, piece wage	27.27	26–30	25.2*	19.8	21.0	14.2	9.2
Male, 16–18 years, time wage	21.24	20–24	15.2*	19.3	35.3	25.4	3.4
Female, 16–18 years, piece wage	20.52	18–22	11.7	24.1	22.8	17.3	10.2

* Includes also classes below second class interval.
Source: Germany, Statistisches Reichsamt, *Wirtschaft und Statistik*. vol. viii (1928) 164–65, and vol. ix (1929) 155–56, 840, 847–49, 1001, 1004–05.

complete equalization of wages in the major branches of production can never be achieved because of ineradicable differences in the composition of the labor force as to skill and strength. Lowest wages prevail generally in agriculture: living in the open country is cheaper than in the city; labor power flows to the city chiefly from rural regions where rate of natural population increase is higher than in urban sections. Table x shows that farm labor receives in most countries from one half to three quarters of the wages of unskilled urban labor. Where farm wages are particularly low, as in Denmark, statistics do not account for payments in kind. In Australia and Finland agricultural and industrial wages differ little because of the scarcity of agricultural labor, but for British India the high ratio of rural to urban wages means only that coolie labor in the cities lives on the ragged edge of existence. For many countries farm wages compare unfavorably with those of the industrial worker, because the farm laborer hires out also his wife and children.

Industrial differentiation in wages, although less marked than between agriculture and industry, is nevertheless quite pronounced. In certain industries, such as mining and textiles, wages are generally low; in others, like construction, higher than the national average. Usually these differences rest upon rational grounds, at

TABLE X
COMPARISON OF FARM WAGES AND INDUSTRIAL WAGES, 1930–31

COUNTRY	PERCENTAGE RATIO OF FARM TO INDUSTRIAL WAGES	FARM WAGE, MALE DESCRIPTION	AMOUNT	WAGE OF UNSKILLED INDUSTRIAL LABOR DESCRIPTION	AMOUNT
United States	59	Average weekly wage*	$12.96	Average 24 manufacturing industries, per week	$21.91
Canada	53	Annual wage and board	$559	Average annual earnings in manufacturing	$1038
British India	82	Monthly wage for field workers in Bombay Presidency†	Rup. 11.6	Monthly wage of coolies in the building trades, Central Provinces	Rup. 14
Australia	90	Average weekly rate	Sh. 87.4	Average weekly rate, all industrial groups	Sh. 96.9
England	75	Average weekly wage‡	Sh. 31.6	Union weekly rate for laborers in engineering trades	Sh. 42.1
Germany	37	Annual cash wage of unmarried workers	Rm. 575	Average annual earnings of helpers in textile industry	Rm. 1650
France	67	Average daily wage of day laborers	Fr. 22.50	Most common daily wage of helpers outside Paris	Fr. 33.56
Poland	55	Average earnings per day	Zl. 3.3	Average daily wage of helpers in metal industry**	Zl. 6.0
Switzerland	70	Day's wage for field work	Swiss Fr. 6.97	Unskilled, average for industry	Swiss Fr. 9.90
Denmark	45	Day's wage for laborer in summer	Kr. 4.78	Unskilled, average for industry**	Kr. 10.56
Finland	80	Average daily cash wage	Fm. 25.7	Helpers in metal industry**	Fm. 32
Norway	40	Average daily cash wage	Kr. 3.9	Helper's daily wage	Kr. 9.8

* Excluding room and board.
† Daily wage converted into monthly.
‡ Including payments in kind.
** Hourly wage converted into daily on the basis of 8 hours per day.

Source: FOR THE UNITED STATES: United States, Bureau of Foreign and Domestic Commerce, *Statistical Abstract of the United States 1931* (1931) p. 360. FOR CANADA: Canada, Dominion Bureau of Statistics, *The Canada Yearbook 1933* (Ottawa 1933) p. 259, 798. FOR BRITISH INDIA: Bombay, Labour Office, *Labour Gazette*, vol. xii (1932–33) 279; Central Provinces, Commerce and Industry Department, *Report on the Working of the Department of Industries, 1930* (Nagpur 1931). FOR AUSTRALIA: Australia, Commonwealth Bureau of Census and Statistics, *Official Year-Book ... 1933* (Canberra 1934) p. 717. FOR ENGLAND: Great Britain, Board of Trade, *Statistical Abstract for the United Kingdom ... 1913 and 1919 to 1932* (1934) p. 122–23. FOR GERMANY: Germany, Statistisches Reichsamt, *Statistisches Jahrbuch für das Deutsche Reich 1931* (Berlin 1931) p. 281, 291, 296. FOR FRANCE: France, Statistique Générale, *Annuaire statistique ... 1930* (Paris 1931) p. 247, 250. FOR POLAND: Poland, Office Central de Statistique, *Statystyka pracy*, vol. xii (1933) 129. FOR SWITZERLAND: Switzerland, Bureau Fédéral de Statistique, *Annuaire statistique ... 1931* (Berne 1932) p. 299. FOR DENMARK: Denmark, Statistiske Departement, *Statistisk Aarbog 1933* (Copenhagen 1933) p. 117–18. FOR FINLAND: Finland, Sosiaaliministeriö, *Socialinen aikakauskirja*, vol. xxvi (1932) 92. FOR NORWAY: Norway, Statistiske Centralbyrå, *Årbok ... 1931* (Oslo 1931) p. 150–51.

other times upon historical continuity and tradition. In the textile industry the importance of women workers depresses the wages of men and leads to work for wives and daughters. In mining the wages, paid at the same rate as for skilled labor in manufacturing, set the maximum for compensation; and accordingly other occupations rate less pay. In construction industries there are skilled and hazardous occupations, work is irregular, so that despite high daily wages annual earnings are no greater than in other skilled trades.

The difference in compensation between skilled and unskilled labor has always been considerable and rather stable. In periods of labor shortage, however, as during the World War, the span between the two is narrowed. Since the war the normal differential—about 30 percent in terms of the average wage rate for the skilled worker—has been restored in the United States; but in a number of European countries, including Great Britain, Germany and France, the difference is less now than it was in 1913. There is reason to believe that statistical measurement underestimates the actual difference in compensation. Because data on earnings are scarce, wage rates are used; and these do not take account of the greater regularity of employment of the skilled worker, his greater ability to benefit by temporary labor shortages, the larger pay which he draws for overtime and similar advantages. Another statistical factor reducing the difference is failure to segregate the semiskilled into a separate category. If the wage rates for the semiskilled are added to those of the skilled, the average for the whole group is smaller than it should be, and if semiskilled are combined with the unskilled, the average for the latter group is raised; whichever procedure is used the difference between the averages of wage rates for the skilled and for the unskilled is not so large as the actual differences supposedly measured by it.

Another important criterion of wage differentiation is that of sex and age, although intervening differences in skill and occupation make direct comparison for the sexes almost impossible. Even with men and women at the same type of work, as in weaving and spinning where both tend identical machines, women's wages are lower but not greatly so; piece rates are alike for both. Generally women willing to work at a lower wage tend toward lower paid employment, chiefly because of expectation of marriage; the stop gap character of their career as wageworkers creates a traditional obstacle to training for an entry into the more skilled occupations, makes the establishment of trade union organization among women more difficult and strengthens the age old notion as to the lower value of women's work. The difference in pay is not so large in some countries as in others; in the United States the average hourly rates for women in 24 manufacturing industries in 1923–29 were somewhat above 80 percent of those for unskilled male labor, whereas the percentage ratio of hourly rates in France (outside Paris) was only 51 to 59 and the percentage ratio of weekly earnings for skilled work in Australia in 1927–29 only 52 to 53. Since the World War the difference in compensation between men and women has been somewhat reduced in France and Germany.

The wage differential for adult and child labor tends to become less significant with the gradual elimination of factory employment of children in the more advanced countries. For youths up to eighteen years of age statistical determination of the differential is difficult, for much of this employment is combined with apprenticeship. It is probably correct to assume that the wages of youths rarely exceed one half of the lowest adult male wage in the same occupation.

The difference between wages and salaries parallels in a sense the differentiation of wages by occupations, for the salaried employees and officials constitute merely the upper layer of the social class whose income is derived from selling labor services. Salaries are on the whole higher than wages, but the trend in recent years has been toward a gradual equalization of the two. Salaries tend to be depressed by the increased employment of women in clerical positions; the absolute and relative growth in the number of subordinate technical jobs; the spread of education, which permits the recruiting of young employees from among the sons and daughters of wage earners; and the steady supply of candidates for salaried work, who find that the superior social status of such employment compensates for the low pay. Table XI illustrates this trend for the United States; in every instance except that of school teachers the differential between salaries and wages was much greater in the pre-war years than in the post-war period.

In all countries the structure of salaries is greatly influenced by the salary scale in public employment, because the government is the largest employer of white collar labor. At the same time the government can afford to pay lower salaries than private business, for it offers greater security of tenure; the differential, how-

TABLE XI

AVERAGE ANNUAL EARNINGS OF SALARIED EMPLOYEES IN THE UNITED STATES, 1890–1926

YEAR	SALARIED EMPLOYEES IN MANUFACTURING INDUSTRIES	RAILWAY CLERKS	GOVERNMENT EMPLOYEES IN THE DISTRICT OF COLUMBIA	POSTAL EMPLOYEES	PUBLIC SCHOOL TEACHERS	WAGE EARNERS IN MANUFACTURING INDUSTRIES
1890	$ 872	$ 635		$ 878	$ 256	$ 439
1894	961	668	$1110	919	283	386
1899	1046	686	1017	924	318	426
1904	1106	708	1066	931	377	477
1909	1188	721	1106	1021	476	518
1914	1323	829	1140	1157	564	580
1919	1999	1363	1520	1618	810	1158
1920	2243	1681	1648	1844	936	1358
1921	2236	1613	1593	1870	1082	1180
1922	2164	1540	1625	1844	1188	1149
1923	2223	1547	1658	1870	1224	1254
1924	2299	1576	1708	1934	1247	1240
1925	2348	1587	1776	2051	1263	1280
1926	2428	1604	1809	2128	1277	1309

Source: Douglas, P. H., *Real Wages in the United States 1890–1926* (Boston 1930) p. 246, 361, 375, 378, 382.

ever, cannot be large if the quality of the personnel in the public service is to be comparable with that in private employment. Since the World War there has been an increase in the real earnings of public employees; until 1929 it was not so large as that in real wages, but after that year real wages in many countries declined drastically despite a reduction in the cost of living, while the real value of government salaries increased considerably despite temporary "economy" salary cuts. This fact illustrates the general proposition that nominal salaries are less readily affected by cyclical fluctuations than wages and that salaried employees are apt in times of depression to gain more by a decline in living costs than they lose by salary reductions. The postwar increase in real earnings of government employees was unevenly distributed. Social considerations and political pressure have produced in most countries a clearly marked tendency toward a differential increase in the compensation of the lower paid government employees. Thus the salary ratio between the highest class of civil service employees in Germany and the lowest class varied in 1913 from 6.1 to 6.9; the range in 1932, however, was from 4.5 to 5.3.

International Wage Comparisons. Non-statistical comparisons of wages have a long history. Even prior to the industrial revolution travelers and investigators often observed not only customs and manners but also material living standards, prices and wages. In the nineteenth century British and American consuls used to relay to their home offices a miscellany of economic information, including data on wages. The first systematic and comprehensive investigation, however, was carried out in 1905–09 by the British Board of Trade; it covered on a uniform program building, engineering and printing trades in 94 cities in Great Britain, 33 cities in Germany, 30 cities in France, 15 cities in Belgium and 28 cities in the United States. An independent student, Carl von Tyszka, summarized the principal findings of this investigation in the form of indices with England as a base. The indices are:

	UNITED STATES	GERMANY	FRANCE	BELGIUM
Average daily wage	230	83	75	63
Average length of working day	96	111	117	121
Average hourly wage	240	75	64	52
Cost of living	141	111	104	93
Average real wage per day	163	75	72	68
Average real wage per hour	170	68	62	56

In the post-war years the rapid and frequently violent fluctuations in foreign exchange rates, prices and wages stimulated an interest in current international comparisons of real wages. The British Ministry of Labour made an attempt to provide a basis for such comparisons by compiling a monthly series of wage rates for 17 occupational groups in a number of European capitals and a few non-European cities covering the period from July 1, 1923, to June 1, 1924; nominal wage rates were converted into real wages by the use of an index of living costs based on the commodity budget employed in British statistics (Table XII). At the suggestion of the British government the continuation of this index was transferred to the International Labor Office in the middle of 1924. In addition to its other functions, including the compilation of wage statistics gathered by the various countries, the promotion of uniformity in methods of collection, the execution of independent wage studies on an international scale (the best known study of this type is the investigation of the wages in coal mines in seven European states, Canada and Japan in 1925, 1927, 1929 and 1931, which deals among others with such questions as the composition of the wage and labor cost per ton of coal sold), the statistical division of the International Labor Office thus assumed the task of current international comparison of real wages.

Since 1924 international wage comparisons have had an eventful history. At first the International Labor Office proposed to follow substantially the British method improving only the procedure of calculating the purchasing power of money in the different countries. At this point it was necessary to take account of the fact that the commodity budgets of working class families vary from country to country; appreciable differences exist between the north and the south, agrarian and industrial regions. Instead of using a single commodity budget for the purpose of computing the cost of living indices the office devised six typical commodity budgets—for Great Britain, for France and Belgium, for Scandinavian countries and the Netherlands, for central Europe, for southern Europe and for non-European countries—which were used in compiling six cost of living indices for each of the cities involved. Nominal wage relatives with London in July, 1924, as a base were then converted into real wage relatives through division by each of the six cost of living indices; the average of the six real wage relatives, further corrected for differences in house rentals, was assumed to yield an index of real wages for the particular city which is comparable with similar measures for the other cities as of the same date and with those for the same city on other dates. Monthly figures on this program were collected quarterly from July, 1924, to January, 1929, in a

TABLE XII

INDEX OF REAL WAGES FOR A FORTY-EIGHT-HOUR WEEK IN SELECTED OCCUPATIONS AND SELECTED CITIES, JUNE 1, 1924

(LONDON = 100)

Occupation	Amsterdam	Berlin	Brussels	Christiania	Stockholm	Vienna
Building trades						
Mason	86	70	54	70	106	49
Bricklayer	86	70	54	70	106	49
Carpenter	86	70	58	67	106	52
Joiner	86	70	59	67	106	44
Plumber	91	69	51	67	83	
Painter	85	74	48	74	105	55
Unskilled	93	79	45	88	128	53
Engineering trades						
Fitter	92	56	66	85	75	50
Ironmolder	80		66	85	75	
Pattern maker	86	53	88	79	70	50
Turner	92	56	67	85	75	54
Unskilled	95	64	68	111	90	49
Furniture trades						
Cabinetmaker	71	84	56	67	76	39
Printing and bookbinding trades						
Compositor: hand	72	52	52	66	72	40
machine	75	56	51	61	74	43
Machine minder	72		53	66	72	40
Bookbinder	80	57	56	77	73	38
Average	84	65	58	76	88	47

Source: Great Britain, Ministry of Labour, *Gazette*, vol. xxxii (1924) 304.

TABLE XIII
Index Numbers of Comparative Real Wages in Selected Cities, 1924–29
(London in July, 1924 = 100)

City	July, 1924	July, 1925	July, 1926	July, 1927	July, 1928	January, 1929
Amsterdam	89	83	92	92	88	88
Berlin	55	63	70	71	77	77
Brussels	59	54	48	50	57	52
Copenhagen	—	93	114	112	—	—
Dublin	—	—	100	108	111	106
Lisbon	32	31	35	33	31	33
Łódź	—	54	44	44	49	47
London	100	99	102	106	110	105
Madrid	57	53	57	57	60	57
Milan	46	46	48	55	51	50
Ottawa	172	162	152	166	175	163
Paris	73	—	—	56	61	59
Philadelphia	213	180	169	189	197	206
Prague	56	48	51	49	49	—
Riga	—	42	48	51	—	53
Rome	46	45	44	46	48	44
Stockholm	85	78	89	98	92	93
Sydney	—	138	133	—	156	—
Tallinn	—	36	42	48	44	—
Vienna	47	42	44	43	47	47
Warsaw	—	43	46	39	46	48

Source: *International Labour Review*, vol. xix (1929) 572.

considerably larger number of cities than those covered by the British Ministry of Labour (Table XIII).

International statistical comparisons of this type could not fail to arouse strong opposition; they furnished labor groups in low wage countries with a forceful argument for higher wages and the governments of high wage countries with a telling argument in tariff negotiations. The opposition seized upon the imperfection of the methods employed in the investigation. And faults could easily be detected in them; they failed, for example, to distinguish rates from actual earnings, ignored forms of compensation other than cash payment and confined commodity budgets to food items. To meet some of these criticisms the comparisons carried out in June–July, 1929, January, 1930, and July, 1930, were based on expanded commodity budgets, including heat, light and laundry, and on a larger number of cities for each country covered; these improvements, however, made little difference in the final index figures, particularly for the larger industrial countries. Opposition continued as vociferous as before; it was argued now that international wage comparisons were impossible in principle because the labor services rendered by workers in different countries were incommensurable, as were the living standards which they customarily maintained. The International Labor Office was thus forced to abandon real wage comparisons. In January, 1931, it merely compiled data on wage rates for 30 occupational groups in 71 cities, which it published together with a table of retail prices for foodstuffs and household articles. It expanded the program of investigation in October, 1931, and in October, 1932. The results of the latter include a number of valuable details and may readily be used for an international comparison of nominal and real wages; but the office has not attempted to draw up a summary which might resemble an international series of real wages.

WLADIMIR WOYTINSKY

See: Labor; Labor, Methods of Remuneration for; Employee Stock Ownership; Profit Sharing; Minimum Wage; Family Allowances; Standards of Living; Cost of Living; Family Budgets; Prices; Distribution; Consumption; Income; National Income; Interest; Production; Population; Poverty; Unemployment; Unemployment Insurance; Social Insurance; Labor Legislation and Law; Labor Movement; Trade Unions; Collective Bargaining; Strikes and Lockouts; Labor Disputes; Conciliation, Industrial; Arbitration, Industrial.

Consult: For Theory and Policy: Hicks, J. R., *The Theory of Wages* (London 1932); Douglas, P. H., *The Theory of Wages* (New York 1934); Dobb, Maurice, *Wages*, Cambridge Economic Handbooks, vol. vi (London 1928); Isles, K. S., *Wages Policy and the Price Level* (London 1934); Robbins, Lionel, *Wages* (London 1925); Pigou, A. C., *The Economics of*

Welfare (4th ed. London 1932), and *The Theory of Unemployment* (London 1933); Robertson, D. H., *Economic Fragments* (London 1931) p. 42–57; Dalton, Hugh, *Some Aspects of the Inequality of Incomes* (2nd ed. London 1925); Rowe, J. W. F., *Wages in Practice and Theory*, London School of Economics and Political Science, Studies, no. 94 (London 1928); Simiand, F., *Le salaire, l'évolution sociale et la monnaie*, 3 vols. (Paris 1932); Strigl, Richard, *Angewandte Lohntheorie*, Wiener staatswissenschaftliche Studien, n.s., vol. ix (Leipsic 1926); Zeuthen, F., *Problems of Monopoly and Economic Warfare* (London 1930) ch. iv; Robinson, Joan, *The Economics of Imperfect Competition* (London 1933) bks. vii–x; Johnson, Alvin, "The Effect of Labor-Saving Devices upon Wages" in *Quarterly Journal of Economics*, vol. xx (1905) 86–100; Ricci, U., "Die Arbeit in der Individualwirtschaft" in *Wirtschaftstheorie der Gegenwart*, 4 vols. (Vienna 1927–32) vol. iii, p. 113–31; Valk, W. L., *The Principles of Wages* (London 1928); Frisch, R., *New Methods of Measuring Marginal Utility*, Beiträge zur ökonomischen Theorie, no. 3 (Tübingen 1932) ch. x; Landauer, Carl, *Grundprobleme der funktionalen Verteilung des wirtschaftlichen Wertes* (Jena 1923); Lederer, Emil, *Wirkungen des Lohnabbaus* (Tübingen 1931); Marschak, J., *Die Lohndiskussion*, Recht und Staat in Geschichte und Gegenwart, no. 75 (Tübingen 1930); Heimann, Eduard, *Soziale Theorie des Kapitalismus* (Tübingen 1929) ch. iv, pt. ii; Webb, Sidney and Beatrice, *Industrial Democracy* (new ed. London 1920); Walker, F. A., *The Wages Question* (New York 1876); Taussig, F. W., *Wages and Capital* (New York 1896), and *Outlines of a Theory of Wages* (Cambridge, Mass. 1910); Carver, T. N., *The Distribution of Wealth* (New York 1904), and *Essays in Social Justice* (Cambridge, Mass. 1915) ch. vii; Wicksteed, P. H., *An Essay on the Coordination of the Laws of Distribution* (London 1894); Marshall, Alfred, *Elements of Economics of Industry* (4th ed. London 1909); Wicksell, K., *Vorlesungen über Nationalökonomie*, 2 vols. (Jena 1913–22) vol. i, pt. ii; Brentano, Lujo, *Ueber das Verhältniss von Arbeitslohn und Arbeitszeit zur Arbeitsleistung* (2nd ed. Leipsic 1893), tr. by W. Arnold (London 1894); Herkner, H., *Die soziale Reform als Gebot des wirtschaftlichen Fortschrittes* (Leipsic 1891); Wood, Stuart, *The Theory of Wages*, American Economic Association, Publications, vol. iv, no. 1 (Baltimore 1889); Thompson, H. M., *The Theory of Wages* (London 1892).

For the Method of Wage Statistics: Cheysson, Émile, "Rapport sur la statistique des salaires ... au nom du Comité du Travail" in Institut International de Statistique, *Bulletin*, vol. vi (1891) pt. i, p. 174–78; Schmoller, Gustav, "Die historische Lohnbewegung von 1300–1900 und ihre Ursachen," Zahn, Friedrich, "Die deutsche Arbeiterstatistik," and Mandello, Julius, "Zweck und Methode der historischen Lohnstatistik" in Institut International de Statistique, *Bulletin*, vol. xiv (1903–05) pt. iii, p. 223–40, 241–60, and 261–78; Huber, Michel, "Statistique des salaires et de la durée du travail," and Bowley, A. L., "Report of the Commission on 'Les salaires comme éléments du coût de production'" in Institut International de Statistique, *Bulletin*, vol. xxii (1925–26) pt. ii, p. 318–44, and vol. xxiii (1927–28) pt. ii, p. 452–96; International Labour Office, *Methods of Statistics of Wages and Hours of Labour*, Studies and Reports, ser. N, no. 2 (Geneva 1923); International Labour Office, *Report of the International Conference of Labour Statisticians, 1st–3rd*, Studies and Reports, ser. N, nos. 4, 8, 12 (Geneva 1924–26), and "The Fourth International Conference of Labour Statisticians" in *International Labour Review*, vol. xxiv (1931) 1–23; Mitchell, W. C., "Methods of Presenting Statistics of Wages" in American Statistical Association, *Publications*, vol. ix (1904–05) 325–43; Moore, H. L., "The Variability of Wages" in *Political Science Quarterly*, vol. xxii (1907) 62–73; Hansen, A. H., "The Best Measure of Real Wages" in *American Economic Review*, vol. xvi (1926) supplement, p. 5–16; Bowley, A. L., *A New Index-Number of Wages*, London and Cambridge Economic Service, Special Memorandum, no. 28 (London 1929); Douglas, P. H., *Real Wages in the United States, 1890–1926* (Boston 1930); Woytinsky, W., "Das Tarifwesen und der Kampf um den Lohn," and "Probleme der Tarif- und Lohnstatistik" in *Arbeit*, vol. vii (1931) 1–16 and 179–89; "Die Nachprüfung und Neubearbeitung der amtlichen Tariflohnstatistik" in Germany, Statistisches Reichsamt, *Vierteljahrshefte zur Statistik des Deutschen Reiches*, vol. xl (1931) pt. ii, p. 94–109; Nixon, J. W., "Index-Numbers of Wages" in Institut International de Statistique, *Revue*, vol. i (1933) 39–53; Zwiedineck-Südenhorst, Otto von, "Lohnstatistik" in *Handwörterbuch der Staatswissenschaften*, vol. vi (4th ed. Jena 1925) p. 375–96; Woytinsky, W., "Statistik der Arbeit" in *Internationales Handwörterbuch des Gewerkschaftswesens*, 2 vols. (Berlin 1931–32) vol. ii, p. 1574–80.

For the History of Wages: International Labour Office, "Wage Changes in Various Countries, 1914 to 1921," "Wage Changes in Various Countries, 1914 to 1922," and "Wage Changes in Various Countries, 1914 to 1925," Studies and Reports, ser. D, nos. 2, 10, and 16 (Geneva 1922–26); Kuczynski, R., *Arbeitslohn und Arbeitszeit in Europa und Amerika, 1870–1909* (Berlin 1913); Tyszka, C., "Löhne und Lebenskosten in Westeuropa im 19. Jahrhundert" in Verein für Sozialpolitik, *Schriften*, vol. cxlv (1914) pt. iii. For United States: United States, Commissioner of Labor, *Eleventh Annual Report, 1895–96* (1897), and *Nineteenth Annual Report, 1904* (1905); Wright, Carroll D., "The Course of Wages in the United States since 1840" in Institut International de Statistique, *Bulletin*, vol. viii (1893) pt. ii, p. 108–19; Brissenden, P. F., *Earnings of Factory Workers, 1899 to 1927; an Analysis of Pay-Roll Statistics*, United States, Bureau of the Census, Census Monographs, no. 10 (1929); Douglas, P. H., *Real Wages in the United States, 1890–1926* (Boston 1930). For Great Britain: Great Britain, Board of Trade, *Report of an Inquiry into the Earnings and Hours of Labour of Workpeople*, 8 vols. (1909–13), *Statistical Tables and Charts Relating to British and Foreign Trade and Industry, 1854–1908* (1909) section x; Great Britain, Board of Trade, Commercial, Labour, and Statistical Department, *Report on Changes in Rates of Wages and Hours of Labour*, published annually from 1911 to 1913; Rogers, J. E. Thorold, *Six Centuries of Work and Wages; the History of English Labour*, 2 vols. (London 1884); Bowley, A. L., "Statistics of Wages in the United Kingdom during the Last Hundred Years" in Royal Statistical Society, *Journal*, vol. lxi (1898) 702–22 and vol. lxix (1906) 148–92. For Other Countries: France, Statistique Générale, *Salaires et coût de l'existence à diverses époques jusqu'en 1910* (1911); Simiand, F., *Le salaire, l'évolution sociale et la monnaie*, 3 vols. (Paris 1932); Kuczynski, R., *Die Entwicklung der gewerblichen Löhne seit der Begründung des Deutschen Reiches* (Berlin 1909); Ashley, W. J., *The Progress of the German Working Classes in the Last Quarter of a Century* (London 1904); Strumilin, S. G., *Zarabotnaya plata i proizvoditelnost truda v russkoy promishlennosti za 1913–1922 goda* (Workers' wages and the productivity of labor in Russian industry from 1913 to 1922) (Moscow 1923).

For International Wage Comparisons: Young, E., *Labor in Europe and America; a Special Report on the Rates of Wages, the Cost of Subsistence and the Condition of the Working Classes in Great Britain, Germany, France, Belgium and Other Countries of Europe, also in the United States and British America* (Washington 1875); Shadwell, A., *Industrial Efficiency; a Comparative Study of Industrial Life in England, Germany and America*, 2 vols. (London 1906) vol. ii, ch. viii; Great Britain, Board of Trade, *Cost of Living of the Working Classes. Report of an Enquiry ... into Working-Class Rents and Retail Prices, together with the Rates of Wages in Certain Occupations in Industrial Towns of the United Kingdom, German Empire, France, Belgium and United States of America*, 5 vols. (1908–11); Tyszka, Carl von, *Die Lebenshaltung der arbeitenden Klassen in den bedeutenderen Industriestaaten: England, Deutschland, Frankreich, Belgien und Vereinigten Staaten von Amerika* (Jena 1912); Richardson, J. H., "International Comparisons of Real Wages" in Royal Statistical Society, *Journal*, vol. xciii (1930) 398–423; Zahn, F., "Weltlohnniveau? Eine Antwort der internationalen Statistik" in *Allgemeines statistisches Archiv*, vol. xxi (1931) 1–26, and "Der Preis der menschlichen Arbeit in seiner Bedeutung für Produktion und Verbrauch" in Institut International de Statistique, *Bulletin*, vol. xxv (1931) pt. iii, p. 835–76; Social Science Research Council, *International Wage Comparisons; Documents Arising out of Conferences Held at the International Labour Office in January, 1929 and May, 1930* (Manchester 1932).

WAGNER, ADOLF HEINRICH GOTTHILF (1835–1917), German economist. Wagner was professor of economics at a number of universities before his appointment to the University of Berlin, where he taught for forty-seven years. In his economic views he steered a middle course between the theoretical and highly abstract approach of the school of Menger and the historical approach represented by the Schmoller group. Trained in the tradition of classical economics, he combined theoretical treatment with a keen understanding of the complexity and manifoldness of economic reality. His interests covered virtually the entire range of economic problems. While he made important contributions to general theory, banking and statistics, his greatest achievement lies in the field of public finance. He freed German financial literature from its mainly fiscal administrative character which it had inherited from the period of cameralism and attempted to integrate fiscal phenomena with the totality of economic and social conditions. His chief work, *Finanzwissenschaft*, which presents a masterly treatment of factual and statistical material in the light of contemporary economic and social theory, remained the standard work for almost half a century and exerted its influence beyond the borders of Germany.

Wagner was one of those conservatives who believed that the existing social and economic order can survive only if subjected to a thoroughgoing process of social reform, extending beyond the measures advocated by most of the contemporary economists. He held that economic development tends toward a gradual extension of public or municipal ownership at the expense of private ownership; that the function of the fiscal system is not merely to provide revenues with which ordinary public expenditure may be met but rather to effect a redistribution of wealth, thus reducing what he regarded as intolerable economic and social inequalities; and more specifically that "unearned" increment derived from appreciation of urban property should accrue to the public rather than to the private owner. In this spirit of "conservative socialism" Wagner participated in the organization of the Verein für Sozialpolitik and in the activities of the Christian Socialist party and of the Protestant-Social Congress and worked in the Prussian Diet. As a teacher he influenced a generation of Prussian officials.

Gerhard Colm

Important works: *Finanzwissenschaft* (4 vols., Leipsic 1877–1901; vol. i, 3rd ed. 1883; vols. ii–iii, 2nd ed. 1880–1912; based originally on Rau's *Finanzwissenschaft*); *Grundlegung der politischen Oekonomie*, Lehr- und Handbuch der politischen Oekonomie, pt. i, 2 vols. (3rd ed. Leipsic 1892–94); *Die Geld- und Credittheorie der peel'schen Bankacte* (Vienna 1862); *Der Staat und das Versicherungswesen* (Tübingen 1881); *Die Gesetzmässigkeit in den scheinbar willkührlichen menschlichen Handlungen vom Standpunkte der Statistik* (Hamburg 1864), "Staat in nationalökonomischer Hinsicht" in *Handwörterbuch der Staatswissenschaften*, vol. vii (3rd ed. Jena 1911) p. 727–39; *Wohnungsnot und städtische Bodenfrage*, Soziale Streitfragen, no. xi (Berlin 1901); *Agrar- und Industriestaat* (Jena 1901, 2nd ed. 1902); *Die Strömungen in der Sozialpolitik und der Katheder- und Staatssozialismus* (Berlin 1912); *Über Verstaatlichung der Eisenbahnen und über sociale Steuerreform, zwei Landtagsreden* (Berlin 1883).

Consult: Schumacher, H., in *Deutsches biographisches*

Jahrbuch, vol. ii (Berlin 1928) p. 173-93; Rendu, André, *La loi de Wagner et l'accroissement des dépenses dans les budgets modernes* (Paris 1910); Bürger, G., *Adolph Wagner als Statistiker*, Ergänzungshefte zum deutschen statistischen Zentralblatt, no. xi (Leipsic 1929); Thier, E., *Rodbertus, Lassalle, Adolph Wagner; ein Beitrag zur Theorie und Geschichte des deutschen Staatssozialismus* (Jena 1930); *Social Reformers*, ed. by D. O. Wagner (New York 1934) ch. xxii.

WAITZ, FRANZ THEODOR (1821–64), German psychologist and anthropologist. Waitz, who was professor of philosophy at Marburg, is best known for his *Anthropologie der Naturvölker* (6 vols., vols. i–iv Leipsic 1859–64; vols. v–vi, ed. by G. Gerland, 1865–71). In 1863 the Anthropological Society of London selected the first volume of this book for translation as the most adequate presentation of the contemporary state of knowledge in the field of anthropology. The remainder of the work has become antiquated in the light of the accumulated data derived from later field researches, but the summary of Polynesian social conditions as witnessed by early explorers has lasting value. The first volume, however, remains a landmark in the history of anthropology. With nice discrimination Waitz attacked the moot problems of the specific unity of mankind and the alleged hereditary differences of the several races and often anticipated present day theories, such as Eduard Hahn's and Eugen Fischer's view of man as a domesticated animal. While weighting environmental factors heavily, Waitz deprecated overestimation of climate and fully accepted hereditary differences of individuals. He concluded that there was a gap between Negroes and Caucasians anatomically but that in view of intraracial variability no significant physiological differences existed. He also refuted the assertion that mixed races are less viable than "pure" types. He did not dogmatize as to the specific unity of mankind but found the theory fraught with fewer difficulties than the theory of multiple origin. He recognized that craniometry alone could not solve the riddles of race classification and demanded attention to other somatological characters. In dealing especially with the relation of cultural grade and native racial capacity Waitz exposed the fallacy, still current in some quarters, that there was any simple connection between the two. While granting differences in individual native ability, he pointed out that the capacity of a people is an empty, unsound abstraction: "There is no agent, real or substantive, which can be considered as the spirit of a people or of humanity; individuals alone are real." He argued that what is mistaken for racial capacity is not a constant but something which varies with the mutual relations of the constituent individuals; that since extreme favorable variations occur among every people, none can be denied the potency for progressing to higher levels. On the one hand, the culturally rudest tribes belong to distinct races; on the other, the favored races of modern times vary in cultural achievement in time and in different geographical areas. Waitz cites the case of the Arabs, who declined from their supremacy in art and science without any detrimental mixture with alien elements to account for the difference in achievement. Waitz' treatise is a classic which may be regarded as an ampler precursor of Boas' *The Mind of Primitive Man*.

ROBERT H. LOWIE

Other important works: *Lehrbuch der Psychologie als Naturwissenschaft* (Brunswick 1849); *Allgemeine Pädagogik* (Brunswick 1852; 3rd ed. by O. Willman, 1883).

Consult: Gebhardt, Otto, *Theodor Waitzs pädagogische Grundanschauungen in ihrem Verhältnis zu seiner Psychologie, Ethik, Anthropologie und Persönlichkeit* (Leipsic 1906); Zeller, Eduard, *Vorträge und Abhandlungen*, 3 vols. (Leipsic 1875-84) vol. ii, p. 363-72.

WAITZ, GEORG (1813–86), German historian. Waitz was one of the earliest disciples of Leopold von Ranke, under whose influence he edited the *Jahrbücher des deutschen Reichs unter . . . Heinrich I* (Berlin 1837, 3rd ed. Leipsic 1885). He was professor at the University of Kiel from 1842 to 1848. The Schleswig-Holstein movement brought him into politics and he represented Kiel at the Frankfort Assembly of 1848–49. Together with Droysen and Dahlmann he took an active part in the constitutional committee. This political activity found literary expression in his *Schleswig-Holsteins Geschichte* (2 vols., Göttingen 1851–54), *Kurze schleswig-holsteinsche Landesgeschichte* (Kiel 1864) and *Grundzüge der Politik nebst einzelnen Ausführungen* (Kiel 1862). From 1849 Waitz devoted himself almost exclusively to mediaeval history. As professor at Göttingen from 1849 to 1875 he led numerous disciples who devoted themselves to the critical edition of the newly discovered mediaeval source materials. His seminar attracted mediaevalists from all over Europe. After the death of Pertz in 1875 Waitz assumed the direction of the *Monumenta Germaniae historica* in Berlin and reorganized its activities. During the same period he published *Lübeck unter Jürgen Wullenwever* (3 vols., Berlin 1855–56) and was editor of the *Forschungen zur deutschen Geschichte* from 1862 to 1886. Waitz is best known for his new edition of the *Quellenkunde zur deutschen Geschichte* (Göttingen 1869), which was started by Dahlmann. This work, since known as "Dahlmann-Waitz," has become the standard bibliographical guide to German history. Waitz' most important scientific work, however, is his *Deutsche Verfassungsgeschichte* (8 vols., Kiel 1844-78), the first presentation of German constitutional history viewed simply from a historical viewpoint and free from subordination to legal history. While it is extreme in renouncing juristic clarity of conceptions, it is noteworthy for its complete mastery and critical treatment of the sources.

FRITZ HARTUNG

Consult: Steindorff, Ernst, *Bibliographische Uebersicht über Georg Waitz' Werke* (Göttingen 1886); Waitz, Eberhard, *Georg Waitz; Ein Lebens- und Charakterbild* (Berlin 1913); *Historische Aufsätze dem Andenken an Georg Waitz gewidmet*, ed. by Oswald Holder-Egger (Hanover 1886); Gooch, G. P., *History and Historians in the Nineteenth Century* (London 1913) p. 117-22; Bresslau, Harry, *Geschichte der Monumenta Germaniae historica*, Gesellschaft für ältere deutsche Geschichtskunde, Neues Archiv, vol. xlii (Hanover 1921) chs. vii-viii.

WAKEFIELD, EDWARD GIBBON (1796-1862), English empire builder. From 1814 Wakefield held a series of minor diplomatic posts on the continent, but the possibility of a successful diplomatic career ended in 1827 with his conviction for the abduction of a schoolgirl heiress. During his three years in prison he developed his theory of colonization, the principles of which he set forth first, under the name of Robert Gouger, in *A Letter from Sydney* (London 1829; new ed. by R. C. Mills, 1929) and later amplified in *England and America* (2 vols., London 1833) and *A View of the Art of Colonization* (London 1849; new ed. by James Collier, Oxford 1914).

Three proposals made up the Wakefield "theory" of "systematic colonization," for which its author claimed a scientific precision sadly at variance with facts. Colonial waste lands were to be sold at a price sufficiently high to prevent laborers from immediately becoming landowners. The presence of a laboring class and the possibility of increases in land prices would make investment in the colonies attractive to capitalists. Incidentally pastoral lands were to be leased for short periods so that they could be converted to agricultural use as required. The money raised by land sales was to be used for assisting selected immigrants, with the purpose of encouraging settlement by both sexes and improving the moral and social conditions of the colonies. Finally, colonies whose prosperity had thus been assured were to be treated as civilized offshoots of Britain and encouraged to remain within the empire by the grant of responsible government.

Wakefield devoted his great natural abilities to putting the theory into practise in the hope of reviving the spirit of British colonization and of regenerating British colonial policy. Keeping in the background so far as possible he organized the National Colonization Society and until 1852, when he left England to become a colonist in New Zealand, busied himself with importuning reluctant politicians, pacifying hostile officials, persuading skeptical capitalists and encouraging prospective colonists in pursuit of his plans. Practical colonial administrators scoffed at the theory but borrowed from it the working rules of land sales and assisted immigration. The application of these rules wrought a revolution in eastern Australia between 1830 and 1850, for through Wakefield's propaganda transportation of convicts ceased and the convict element was submerged in a tide of subsidized immigration.

In the face of official inertia Wakefield by his persistent efforts led to the founding of the colony of South Australia based in large part upon his theory and in 1839 to the establishment of a settlement in New Zealand, forcing the British government to assert sovereignty there just in time to prevent French dominion. He lived to see his dream of responsible government, realized by Lord Durham for Canada, come true also in Australia. In 1838 he had gone to Canada as an unofficial secretary to Durham, and the latter's famous report embodied Wakefield's theories of colonial self-government and of land settlement, somewhat modified to conform with the Canadian situation.

R. C. MILLS

Consult: Garnett, Richard, *Edward Gibbon Wakefield* (London 1898); Mills, R. C., *Colonization of Australia 1829-42*, London School of Economics and Political Science, Studies, no. 44 (London 1915), especially chs. iv-xi; Siegfried, André, *Edward Gibbon Wakefield et sa doctrine de la colonisation systématique* (Paris 1904); Macdonnell, U. N., *Gibbon Wakefield and Canada Subsequent to the Durham Mission 1839-42*, Queens University, Departments of History and Political and Economic Science, Bulletin, no. 49 (Kingston, Ontario 1925).

WAKLEY, THOMAS (1795-1862), English medical journalist and social reformer. In 1823, partly through William Cobbett's influence,

Wakley retired from the practise of medicine in London and founded the *Lancet*, which became a leading British medical journal. Through its columns he waged a vigorous campaign for the reform of medical education and practise.

In Wakley's youth the Royal College of Surgeons admitted none to its fellowship save graduates of Oxford and Cambridge and members of the Church of England. Hospital appointments in London were treated as family livings and were bestowed by nepotism or purchase. The brilliant but poor medical student could ill afford the high fees of attendance at compulsory lectures controlled by the surgeons, who were by no means always the most competent men available. In the *Lancet* Wakley fought as mercilessly the corruption, arbitrary authority and inefficiency of the college as he did quackery, malpractise and incompetence. His publication of hospital lectures raised a storm of protest and led even to injunctions.

In Parliament, where he served from 1835 to 1852, Wakley continued his reform campaign. Although some of his bills did not immediately become law, the major portion of his demands were eventually enacted. He was directly responsible for substituting physicians for lawyers as coroners, for the registration of qualified medical practitioners, for a considerable decline in food adulteration, for improvement in poor law administration, for better treatment of the sick in workhouses and for more humane laws relating to the insane.

If promotion by merit is now more general than in the early nineteenth century; if the organization of medical associations is more democratic; if many abuses in hospital administration have been swept away; if high grade medical journalism and education have led to improvements in the healing art, Wakley deserves no small portion of the credit.

NORMAN E. HIMES

Consult: Sprigge, S. S., *Life and Times of Thomas Wakley* (London 1897); *Lancet* (1895) no. ii, p. 1660–64, and (1923) no. ii, p. 687–706; "A Great Medical Reformer" in *British Medical Journal* (1899) vol. i, p. 283–85.

WALKER, AMASA (1799–1875), American economist. After a period of school teaching and varied business experience Walker became a successful merchant in Boston. He retired from business in 1840 because of illness but continued to be active in civic life. He helped to organize the Boston Lyceum in 1829; he was an early advocate of railroad development; he held a prominent position in the temperance and anti-slavery movements; and he acted as vice president of two international peace conferences abroad. From 1842 until 1848 he taught political economy at Oberlin College, which he had been instrumental in founding. Later he served as lecturer in political economy at Amherst and as examiner at Harvard. Walker aided in the formation of the Free Soil party in 1848 and served at various times as Massachusetts secretary of state and member of the legislature. He played a leading role in 1859 in revising the Massachusetts banking laws, and when elected to Congress in 1862 he was again active in discussion of financial matters and sponsored the bill that led to the issue of interest bearing notes.

In 1857 Walker began to write articles for *Hunt's Merchants' Magazine* on the currency question. Following the crisis of 1857 he published a pamphlet on *The Nature and Uses of Money and Mixed Currency* (Boston 1857), which together with his widely used book *Science of Wealth* (Boston 1866), written in collaboration with his son, Francis A. Walker, placed him in the forefront of American followers of the currency school, of which he was a more steadfast advocate than either Gouge or Raguet. In his book Walker advocated free trade and was generally orthodox in his economics, except for his rejection, common in the United States, of Malthus' principle of population and of some aspects of the theory of rent. The book reflected his particular interest in currency and finance and is noteworthy chiefly for its rigorous support of the currency principle and its exposition of the quantity theory. He now recognized, as he had not in 1857, that bank loans may mischievously "manufacture currency" in the form of deposits as well as notes. To prove his thesis that "general prices are determined by the quantity of the currency," after giving due consideration to velocity of circulation, he made use of charts that compared crude annual price aggregates with movements in the per capita volume of media of payments.

HARRY E. MILLER

Consult: Walker, F. A., *Memoir of Hon. Amasa Walker*, LL.D. (Boston 1888); Turner, John R., *The Ricardian Rent Theory in Early American Economics* (New York 1921) p. 165–78; Miller, H. E., *Banking Theories in the United States before 1860*, Harvard Economic Studies, vol. xxx (Cambridge, Mass. 1927).

WALKER, FRANCIS AMASA (1840–97), American economist, educator and public administrator. In his boyhood Walker enjoyed a wide range of stimulating influences. His father, Amasa Walker, retired early from business and devoted his life to social reforms, taking part in the antislavery, temperance and international peace movements. He also had a keen interest in the economic controversies of his day, particularly those relating to money and banking. Francis Walker graduated from Amherst College in 1860, studied law, entered military service in 1861 as sergeant major and served during the Civil War with rapid promotion to brevet brigadier general. Upon discharge he engaged in teaching and assisted his father in the latter's writing of *The Science of Wealth* (Boston 1866, 5th ed. 1869).

In 1868 Walker joined the editorial staff of the *Springfield Republican* and in the following year was called to Washington to assist David A. Wells in the administration of the Bureau of Internal Revenue and to serve as chief of the Bureau of Statistics. This position led to his appointment as Superintendent of the Census of 1870. In 1871 he was made Commissioner of Indian Affairs. A year later he became professor of political economy at the Sheffield Scientific School of Yale University. He had no previous specialized academic training in his chosen field; his knowledge came from experience and association with a well read father.

In 1876 appeared *The Wages Question* (New York), in 1878 *Money*; in 1883 the treatises *Political Economy* (3rd ed. New York 1888) and *Land and Its Rent* (Boston). These volumes quickly established Walker's reputation as an economist. In addition he supervised the census of 1880, probably the most elaborate statistical survey of a nation's activities ever published.

In 1881 he assumed the presidency of the Massachusetts Institute of Technology. This, however, did not interrupt his previous specialized interests, to which he added valuable contributions in the field of education. *First Lessons in Political Economy* was published in New York in 1889. Walker's texts were adopted in many colleges in the United States and were used also in England.

His exposition of economics was a combination of realistic illustration, drawn from his varied contacts with public affairs, and a clear cut theory of distribution of the product of economic work. In his earlier writings Walker decisively rejected the wage fund theory of wages, which up to that time had been generally accepted in English and American texts; although he was not the first to criticize it adversely, his analysis was a final blow which changed subsequent exposition. He distinguished sharply between interest and profits as independent factors and held profits as well as rent to be a differential by the same reasoning that Ricardo applied to rent. This analogy between profits and rent did not find general acceptance. Walker's vigorous promotion of this theory, however, was a powerful stimulus in subjecting prevailing theories of distribution to fresh analysis.

Walker took an active part in the current discussion of monetary questions. He gave broad scope to the term money, including banknotes; he introduced the term "common denominator in exchange" as a substitute for the phrase "measure of value"; he followed his father in his opposition to the so-called banking school. He accepted the quantity theory of money and attributed the fall of prices between 1873 and 1896 to an insufficient supply of gold. While recognizing the evils of inflationism, he was deeply impressed with the danger of contracting the sound money supply in a time of expanding industry. These views he developed in *Money in Its Relations to Trade and Industry* (New York 1879) and more exhaustively in *International Bimetallism* (New York 1896).

As a realist Walker did not take an extreme theoretical position in current economic controversies. He thus approved of a moderate tariff, favored the restriction of immigration and recognized the benefit of trade unions at a time when sympathy was rare. In education he stood for manual training and, for those who had the aptitude, technical training of a higher order. Such training he regarded not only as an educational factor and a means of conserving economic and industrial forces which otherwise might go to waste but as a bulwark to the laborer, helping him to resist pressure and making of competition a beneficial force.

DAVIS R. DEWEY

Other works: *The Indian Question* (Boston 1874); *History of the Second Army Corps in the Army of the Potomac* (New York 1886, 2nd ed. 1891); *General Hancock* (New York 1894); *Discussions in Economics and Statistics*, ed. by D. R. Dewey, 2 vols. (New York 1899), a selection of magazine articles and addresses; *Discussions in Education*, ed. by J. P. Munroe (New York 1899); "Bibliography of the Writings and Reported Addresses of Francis A. Walker" in American Statistical Association, *Journal*, vol. v (1896–97) 276–90.

Consult: Munroe, J. P., *A Life of Francis Amasa Walker* (New York 1923); Laughlin, J. L., in *Journal of Political Economy*, vol. v (1896–97) 228–36; Wright, C. D., in American Statistical Association, *Journal*, vol. v (1896–97) 245–75; Tyler, H. W., "The Educational Work of Francis A. Walker" in *Educational Review*, vol. xiv (1897) 55–70.

WALLACE, ALFRED RUSSEL (1823–1913), English naturalist and social reformer. Wallace's chief claim to fame rests upon his formulation of the theory of evolution independently of Darwin. He made his well known journey to the Amazon in 1848–52 and in 1854 went to the Malay Archipelago, where he carried on his scientific work for the following eight years. An important result of this journey was the discovery of Wallace's line, dividing the archipelago into two groups of islands, a western group with oriental and an eastern with Australian affinities, each having its distinct and divergent mammalia. The rest of his long life was spent mainly in arranging and studying his various collections, in writing and lecturing and from middle age onward in vigorous propaganda for social reform.

While still a boy he was impressed by the works of Robert Owen. Six years' practical experience of land surveying gave him considerable knowledge of the laws relating to public and private property and incidentally revealed to him the iniquity of the enclosures of common lands then taking place. Wallace as a result became an ardent social reformer and advocate of land nationalization. Influenced by Henry George's *Progress and Poverty*, he urged continually that the recovery by the community of the land filched from it was an essential condition of a return to general prosperity. He believed that the evils of society were attributable to a system of universal competition for the means of existence, to economic antagonism, to the monopoly by private individuals of land and capital and to the social injustice which allows wealth to be inherited by a favored few in each generation. These evils were to be corrected by a complete reversal of policy, by means of which alone the existing "immoral environment" could be changed into a moral one. No detailed application of this policy was ever worked out by Wallace, but he advocated at various times legislation to establish a system of general cooperation and friendly economic relations, to give freedom of access to land and capital to all and to enable the state to inherit wealth in trust for the community. In *Studies, Scientific and Social* he proposed a system of industrial colonization whereby each would have a reasonable share in the products of his own labor. When discussing education Wallace urged the training of individual talent and vocational as well as general teaching for all; he suggested that if each man and woman were possessed of technical skill in two or more occupations there would be more fluidity of labor and consequently less unemployment and monotony.

C. E. M. JOAD

Important works: *Travels on the Amazon and Rio Negro* (London 1853, new ed. 1900); *Contributions to the Theory of Natural Selection* (London 1870, 2nd ed. 1871); *Land Nationalisation* (London 1882, 5th ed. 1909); *Bad Times* (London 1885); *Darwinism* (London 1889, 3rd ed. 1902); *The Wonderful Century* (London 1898, new ed. 1903); *Studies, Scientific and Social*, 2 vols. (London 1900); *Man's Place in the Universe* (London 1903, 4th ed. 1904); *My Life*, 2 vols. (London 1905); *Social Environment and Moral Progress* (London 1913); *The Revolt of Democracy* (London 1913).

Consult: *Alfred Russel Wallace; Letters and Reminiscences*, ed. by James Marchant, 2 vols. (London 1916); Hogben, L. T., *Alfred Russel Wallace; the Story of a Great Discoverer* (London 1918).

WALLACE, HENRY (1836–1916) and HENRY CANTWELL (1866–1924), American agriculturists. Henry Wallace, who was of Scotch-Irish descent, was educated for the ministry and licensed to preach. After serving for a number of years as pastor of Presbyterian churches in Rock Island, Illinois, and Morning Sun, Iowa, he was compelled by ill health to give up the ministry. In 1877 he moved to Winterset, Iowa, and took up farming. A student of public affairs and a zealous advocate of the farmer's cause, Wallace attained considerable local prominence, which led him to enter the field of agricultural journalism while continuing the practise of farming. In 1883 he became the contributing editor and later part owner of the *Iowa Homestead*, with which he was associated until 1895, when with his sons, Henry C. and John P., he founded *Wallace's Farmer*. "Uncle Henry," as he came to be known by his generation, set a high standard in farm journalism and made his paper one of the leading agricultural periodicals of the country. Through it he urged diversified farming, crop rotation, good roads, agricultural education and the general improvement of rural living conditions. In addition to his editorial activity he was the author of several books on practical farming and on problems related to farm life: *Clover Culture* (Des Moines 1892), *Clover Farming* (Des Moines 1898), *Trusts and How to Deal with Them* (Des Moines 1899), *The Skim Milk Calf* (Des Moines 1900) and *Letters to the Farm Boy* (first published in

Wallace's Farmer; 4th ed. New York 1902).

His son, Henry Cantwell Wallace, attended Iowa State College of Agriculture and shortly after his graduation in 1892 was appointed assistant professor of agriculture in the same institution. In 1916 he succeeded his father as editor of *Wallace's Farmer.* He continued the established policy in dealing with farm problems in their economic, political, social and educational aspects. His influence and leadership in farm organizations, notably the Corn Belt Meat Producers' Association, of which he was secretary for fourteen years, led to his appointment as secretary of agriculture in 1921. His son, Henry Agard Wallace, who likewise became editor of *Wallace's Farmer,* was destined later (1933) to succeed him in the cabinet. Henry Cantwell held the cabinet appointment until his death in 1924. During his incumbency he carried on a systematic campaign for increased efficiency in production, for improved systems of marketing and for the conservation of natural resources. He reorganized the Department of Agriculture and established the Bureau of Agricultural Economics and the Bureau of Home Economics. He took an active part in agricultural legislation and supported the principles of the McNary-Haugen bill. *Our Debt and Duty to the Farmer* (New York 1925), published posthumously, reveals his keen insight into the problems of agricultural economics.

LOUIS BERNARD SCHMIDT

Consult: Wallace, Henry, *Uncle Henry's Own Story of His Life,* 3 vols. (Des Moines 1917–19); Pammel, L. H., *Prominent Men I Have Met; Henry Cantwell Wallace* (Ames, Iowa 1930); "Secretary Wallace" in *Outlook,* vol. cxxxviii (1924) 350–52.

WALLACE, ROBERT (1697–1771), British writer on population. Born in Scotland and educated at the University of Edinburgh, Wallace in 1733 entered the Presbyterian ministry and later served as moderator of the General Assembly. To him was largely due the scheme of the ministers' widows' fund, which subsequently became a legal provision.

Wallace is remembered chiefly for his contributions to the discussion of population problems. In a paper read to the Philosophical Society of Edinburgh he ranged himself with those who held that the world had been more densely populated in antiquity than it was in modern times. David Hume reviewed classical literature for such evidence as it afforded and in his essay "Of the Populousness of Antient Nations" (in his *Political Discourse,* Edinburgh 1752, ch. x) expressed his skepticism on the question. In reply Wallace was induced to publish his paper, with an appendix in which he attempted to refute Hume's contentions, under the title *Dissertation on the Numbers of Mankind in Ancient and Modern Times* (Edinburgh 1753). He returned to the population question in his *Various Prospects of Mankind, Nature and Providence* (London 1761) and raised an issue which was destined to have a profound effect on later discussion. He postulated a perfect form of government for mankind, by which he meant a high degree of social equality and a more even distribution of wealth, and then suggested that such a condition could not be attained because the increase of population which would be stimulated by a movement in that direction would necessarily frustrate such efforts. Each generation, he argued, could more than double itself if the fecundity of mankind were not countered by destructive wars, poverty and vice. William Godwin in his *Enquiry concerning Political Justice* (2 vols., London 1793) devoted a chapter to the consideration of this obstacle to the perfectibility of man; and, as is well known, it was in discussing this question with his father that T. R. Malthus conceived the idea which he developed in the first edition of his *Essay on the Principle of Population as It Affects the Future Improvement of Society* (London 1798). Godwin took Wallace as the typical exponent of the opinion he was attempting to refute, and Malthus as the critic of Godwin naturally went back to the same source; there he found in broad outline the idea of the limit to the fertility of the earth and of the preventive checks to the increase of population which he then proceeded to elaborate.

J. F. REES

Consult: Bonar, James, *Theories of Population from Raleigh to Arthur Young* (London 1931) p. 175–78; Stangeland, C. E., *Pre-Malthusian Doctrines of Population,* Columbia University, Studies in History, Economics and Public Law, no. 56 (New York 1904) p. 275–80; Beer, Max, *A History of British Socialism,* 2 vols. (London 1919–20) vol. i, p. 84–87, 118–19.

WALLAS, GRAHAM (1858–1932), English political scientist and sociologist. Wallas was an eclectic thinker and teacher who by reason of his wide sympathies, his realistic sense of social situations and his zest for social exploration made influential and pioneering contributions in a number of directions. His study *The Life of Francis Place* (London 1898, rev. ed. 1918) helped to lay the foundations for the historical understanding of English working class movements. This was followed by *Human Nature in Politics* (London 1908, 3rd ed. 1914), a work in which the long maturing insight gained by Wallas in London municipal elections and also as a very active member of the London School Board and the London County Council was applied to the interpretation of the problems of democracy. It was really an essay in the political psychology of the common man, although Wallas characteristically did not draw the anti-intellectualist conclusions which have since been frequently associated with this approach.

Wallas was not content to rest with the shrewd and tolerant understanding of political behavior offered in this early work, which was probably the most influential of his writings. He had the attitude of a reformer. He was for twenty years one of the leaders of the English Fabian movement. He was always impressed with the need for social reorganization and always sought the constructive principles on which such reorganization might be based. This quest took direction in the volume *The Great Society* (London 1914), in which he faced the question of how human nature responds to the conditions of the complex urbanized environment which industrial and technological advance has created, and how the art of living and of thinking can be socially organized to meet these new conditions. It was here that Wallas developed the idea that the native dispositions of human nature are balked by the restrictions of a civilization to which they are not biologically adjusted. But his discussion of the type of social organization which would bring a new harmony of life and environment did not advance much beyond some luminous suggestions as to the need for it. In his later years he made renewed tentatives in the quest for a coherent scheme of social reconstruction. This is the motive of the somewhat miscellaneous series of lectures published as *Our Social Heritage* (London 1921), approached from another side in *The Art of Thought* (London 1926). But Wallas was not the kind of thinker who builds a consistent system, although he remained acutely conscious of the challenge to do so.

Wallas was professor of political science at the University of London, and his power to provoke thought and to suggest avenues of intellectual exploration found perhaps a more adequate expression in his lectures than in his books.

R. M. MacIver

Consult: Stamp, Josiah, and others, "Graham Wallas" in *Economica*, vol. xii (1932) 395–412; Laski, Harold J., "Lowes Dickinson and Graham Wallas" in *Political Quarterly*, vol. iii (1932) 461–66; Barnes, Harry E., "Some Typical Contributions of English Sociology to Political Theory" in *American Journal of Sociology*, vol. xxviii (1922) 179–204.

WALPOLE, ROBERT, EARL OF OXFORD (1676–1745), first British "prime minister." Brought to power in 1721 as a result of his skill in dealing with the South Sea Company crash, Walpole, in conformity with his principle of letting "sleeping dogs lie" as the best way of promoting material prosperity, sought to avoid difficulties at home and abroad. In foreign affairs, where "any peace was preferable to even a successful war," Walpole, cooperating with Cardinal Fleury of France, kept England out of European conflicts until 1739, when he was forced to enter upon the War of Jenkins's Ear against Spain. In his policies Walpole was influenced by budgetary limitations. The landed gentry had to be conciliated by a low land tax; the mercantile interests were granted the removal or reduction of tariff duties; and a factious opposition, led by such men as Viscount Bolingbroke and William Pulteney, manifested its refusal to permit any thoroughgoing fiscal reform by forcing the abandonment of the excise bill of 1733. So strong was Walpole's conviction of the impossibility of revising the budget that after 1733 he made good his deficits by regularly drawing upon the sinking fund, which he had devised in 1717.

In an age when political parties were loose confederations of factions, the cabinet was an association of ministers of various political complexions holding office through the favor of the king because their control of votes in the House of Commons assured the smoother functioning of government, and the House, independent of popular sentiment, a body of henchmen of political chieftains, Walpole evolved the principles of the cabinet system. He achieved the unitary cabinet by persuading the king to dismiss all cabinet members who were not strictly subject to his control. The king's favor, still a prerequisite of tenure of office, was retained by Walpole's unswerving support of the Hanoverian succession, by generous financial settlements and by the cooperation of George II's queen, Caroline. A closely knit majority in the House of Commons, the court Whigs, now a definite political party under the control of the prime minister, was maintained by bribery at elections, manipulation of patronage and contracts and judicious distributions from the secret service fund. Finally, on losing command of the Commons in 1742 Walpole introduced the simple practise of resignation in favor of the opposition, and thus obviated the clumsy device of impeachment as a means of forcing ministers to give way to new majorities.

FREDERICK DIETZ

Consult: Coxe, William, *Memoirs of the Life and Administration of Sir Robert Walpole*, 3 vols. (new ed. London 1800); Morley, John, *Walpole* (London 1889); Robertson, John Mackinnon, *Bolingbroke and Walpole* (London 1919); Oliver, F. S., *The Endless Adventure*, vols. i–ii (London 1930–31); Michael, Wolfgang, *Englische Geschichte im achtzehnten Jahrhundert*, vols. i–ii, pt. i (Hamburg and Berlin 1896–1920) vol. ii, pt. i; Taylor, G. R. S., *Robert Walpole and His Age* (London 1931); Brisco, N. A., *The Economic Policy of Robert Walpole*, Columbia University, Studies in History, Economics and Public Law, no. 72 (New York 1907); Vaucher, Paul, *Robert Walpole et la politique de Fleury (1731–1742)* (Paris 1924).

WALRAS, ANTOINE AUGUSTE (1801–66), French economist. Auguste Walras' significance rests upon his *De la nature de la richesse, et de l'origine de la valeur* (Évreux 1831), in which he rejected both of the doctrines which in his time sought to determine the origin of value—one in utility, the other in labor or in the costs of production—and found it instead in *rareté*, which he defined as the "relationship between the total of limited goods and the total of the needs demanding satisfaction. Utility is a condition of quality or nature. Rarity is a condition of number or of quantity." From this quantitative conception Walras concluded that "political economy ought to be a mathematical science." This work also contained important developments of several ideas, at that time quite new and promising, which were later to be taken up and developed more thoroughly by Cournot, Stanley Jevons, Léon Walras, Carl Menger and Irving Fisher. These concerned the relations between value and property and between value and price and the distinction between money as a unit of account and measure of value and money as a medium of exchange.

In a second work, entitled *Théorie de la richesse sociale; ou, résumé des principes fondamentaux de l'économie politique* (Paris 1849), particularly in the seventh and eighth chapters, which remained unpublished until the appearance of Louis Modeste Leroy's edition, Walras set forth the principles of a doctrine of property which, written before John Stuart Mill, A. R. Wallace, Henry George and Léon Walras, contained all the fundamentals of the modern doctrines of "nationalization of land." He distinguished two forms of ownership, private and public, holding that some objects of property lend themselves to either form of ownership, others to private and still others to public ownership. Land, he believed, belongs in the last category.

ÉTIENNE ANTONELLI

Works: "Considération sur la mesure de la valeur et sur la fonction des métaux précieux dans l'appréciation de la richesse sociale" in *Revue mensuelle d'économie politique*, vol. iv (1836); "De la richesse sociale, ou de l'objet de l'économie politique" in *Revue étrangère et française de législation et d'économie politique*, vol. v (1838) 101–25, 348–66; "Mémoire sur l'origine de la valeur d'échange" in Institut de France, Académie des Sciences Morales et Politiques, *Séances et travaux . . . Compte rendu*, vol. xvi (1849) 201–33; *Esquisse d'une théorie de la richesse* (Pau 1863).

Consult: Walras, Léon, "Un initiateur en économie politique, A. A. Walras" in *Revue du mois*, vol. vi (1908) 170–83; Leroy, L. M., *Auguste Walras, sa vie, son oeuvre* (Paris 1923); Antonelli, Étienne, "Un économiste de 1830; Auguste Walras" in *Revue d'histoire économique et sociale*, vol. xi (1923) 516–38.

WALRAS, MARIE ESPRIT LÉON (1834–1910), French economist. Walras abandoned training for the profession of mining engineer to become a free lance journalist and champion of the cause of social and economic reform. Before his appointment to the chair of political economy at the University of Lausanne in 1870 he had shown particularly active interest in cooperation. It was the desire to lay a scientific basis for reform which turned him to pure economic theory; in this field he was influenced by Cournot, whose *Recherches* he studied as a youth, and by his father, Auguste Walras. He retired from active teaching in 1892, when he was succeeded by Vilfredo Pareto.

Walras was the first to apply mathematical analysis to the study of a case of general economic equilibrium under a regime of individual private property and absolute free competition. The problem of equilibrium with which he dealt may be summarized as follows: Let the rarity (r) of a commodity be defined as the ratio of the increase in satisfaction accruing from the consumption of an additional very small quantity of the commodity to this quantity, and the effective utility (u) of a particular quantity of a commodity as the sum total of satisfaction obtained from its consumption. For two commodities, A and B, the equations of effective utility can be written as $U_a = \varphi_a(q_a)$ and $U_b = \varphi_b(q_b)$ and the equations of rarity as $r_a = \dfrac{d\varphi_a(q_a)}{dq_a} = \varphi'_a(q_a)$ and

$r_b = \dfrac{d\varphi_b(q_b)}{dq_b} = \varphi'_b(q_b)$, where q stands for quantity. Rarity, the derivative of effective utility, is assumed to decline with an increase in the quantity consumed; effective utility therefore increases but not as much as the quantity. On the assumption that the exchange of some quantity of A against some quantity of B occurs under conditions of maximizing utility for the owner of either commodity exchange is governed by the equation $\dfrac{d\varphi_a(q_a)}{dq_a} dq_a + \dfrac{d\varphi_b(q_b)}{dq_b} dq_b = 0$ or $r_a dq_a + r_b dq_b = 0$, which is also the equation of demand for or supply of either commodity, since the demand for one commodity is tantamount to the supply of the other. When developed for more than two commodities, one of which assumes also the role of a standard of value, this equation permits the complete determination of equilibrium in exchange. The addition of equations which express the conditions governing production—and therefore exchange in markets for producers' goods—capitalization and credit yields a system of equations that provides a general solution of the problem of economic equilibrium.

Walras will scarcely be remembered for his contribution to social reform. His name was closely allied with the advocacy of land nationalization, a proposal rooted in the social philosophy which he inherited from his father. Starting with the proposition that man never existed outside society, this doctrine recognized the individual and the collectivity, or the state, as two coordinate social types, both of which must share in the distribution of wealth; natural wealth, it concluded, should belong to the state and human faculties, including all that issues from them, to the individual. Walras was also regarded as a bimetallist, but he was in effect an early exponent of managed currency. In order that the marginal utility of the monetary commodity might vary in proportion to the average marginal utility of the social product he proposed that gold currency be supplemented by a token currency of silver, the issue of which was to be regulated with reference to price level fluctuations.

ÉTIENNE ANTONELLI

Important works: Éléments d'économie politique pure, 2 pts. (Lausanne 1874–77, 4th ed. 1900; definitive ed. Paris 1926); Théorie mathématique de la richesse sociale (Lausanne 1883); Études d'économie politique appliquée (Lausanne 1898).

Consult: Pareto, V., in Economic Journal, vol. xx (1910) 137–40; Schumpeter, J., in Zeitschrift für Volkswirtschaft, Sozialpolitik und Verwaltung, vol. xix (1910) 397–402; Antonelli, É., Principes d'économie pure (Paris 1914) pt. i; Osorio, Antonio, Théorie mathématique de l'échange, tr. from the Portuguese by J. d'Almada, with introduction by V. Pareto (Paris 1913) chs. ii, v–vii; Leone, E., "Léon Walras und die hedonistischmathematische 'Schule von Lausanne'" in Archiv für Sozialwissenschaft und Sozialpolitik, vol. xxxii (1911) 36–71; Boven, P., Les applications mathématiques à l'économie politique (Lausanne 1912) p. 103–33; Moret, Jacques, L'emploi des mathématiques en économie politique (Paris 1915) p. 105–13, 162–94; Bompaire, F., Du principe de liberté économique . . . (Paris 1931) pts. ii–iii; Marget, A. W., "Léon Walras and the 'Cash-Balance Approach' to the Problem of the Value of Money" in Journal of Political Economy, vol. xxxix (1931) 569–600.

WALTER FAMILY, founders and proprietors of the London *Times*. John Walter (1739–1812), formerly a coal merchant and underwriter of London, started the *Daily Universal Register* in 1785 primarily as a vehicle for the use of the invention known as logographic printing (the employment of fonts of groups of letters). Although logography was not successful and had to be abandoned, Walter was able eventually as a supporter of Pitt to make a moderate success of the paper, which in 1788 was renamed the *Times*. It was his second son, however, John Walter (1776–1847), who was the real founder of the *Times* as "the leading journal of Europe." He became full manager of the paper in 1803 and scarcely relaxed his attention for forty years. As early as the 1820's the *Times*' claims to preeminence were becoming recognized, and by 1840 there was no doubt of its superiority over all rivals. Walter was possibly the first newspaper owner with no other thought than to raise his journal to prosperity and power, and this fact is in large part the explanation of his success. The policies which he applied are easily summarized: every possible exertion to obtain the significant news earlier and more accurately than other newspapers; a particular attention to the collection of foreign news; an editorial tone skilfully following and leading the opinion of the paper's constituency; absolute independence of party and of government officials; the acceptance of favors but never the granting of them; and genuine enterprise in dealing with the business problems of manufacture and production. In addition Walter had good fortune and good judgment in the choice of his editors and writers, chief of whom were Thomas Barnes and J. T. Delane; very little evidence exists as to any real interference on his part with their work.

The second John Walter had had time to become a country gentleman and a member of Parliament, and his eldest son, John Walter (1818–94), succeeded him in these capacities as well as in that of chief proprietor of the *Times*. Continuity of policy was not broken when the ownership passed in 1847, but the new manager's reins seem to have been loosely held except in regard to mechanical matters. In this respect the second and third Walters were pioneers, and their efforts from the beginning of the *Times'* use of steam printing in 1814 to the perfection of the Walter press in 1868 are an important phase of newspaper history. The third John Walter gave up the active management of the paper shortly after 1847 and seems largely to have dissociated his public and even his private life from its daily conduct. During the first twenty years of his ownership the *Times*, edited by Delane, attained new heights in British journalism. But nothing was done to adapt it to changing conditions and, while its prestige continued enormous, by 1890 the paper was virtually insolvent. A long struggle under Moberly Bell and John Walter's second son, Arthur F. Walter (1846–1910), was unsuccessful and in 1908 control passed to Lord Northcliffe. In 1922 the *Times* once more became an independent newspaper through its acquisition by John Jacob Astor and John Walter, great-great-grandson of the founder. The new owners in 1923 legally made the *Times* a national institution by setting up a committee of five notables which was to pass on any future transfers of the controlling shares.

H. Donaldson Jordan

Consult: Bowman, W. Dodgson, *The Story of "The Times"* (London 1931); The Times, *The Times; Past, Present, Future* (London 1932); "The 'Times' from Delane to Northcliffe" in *Quarterly Review*, vol. ccxxxix (1923) 83–108.

WANG AN-SHI (1021–86), Chinese statesman. After receiving the customary education in the Chinese classics Wang entered the provincial administrative service. In 1058 he became a high official in the central Ministry of Finance and in the same year offered to Emperor Jen Tsung his suggestions for the reorganization of the administrative system.

Wang hoped to improve the situation of the Sung empire, which throughout his lifetime was threatened by two great states, the Tungusian Khitan and the Tibetan Hsi Hsia. Struggles for power and intrigues by various cliques were rife at the court as well as in the provinces. Recognizing the danger inherent in these conditions. Wang saw clearly that a thorough revision of the unstable internal political system was essential and that it was conditioned upon the development of a better trained and honest officialdom. In his memorial he demanded basic changes in the administrative service, including professional education instead of the traditional literary training for candidates and higher salaries for officials which would serve as a deterrent to bribery.

Wang realized also the necessity of strengthening state finances and of improving and stabilizing the national economy. Accordingly, when he became minister of state in 1069, he launched his great economic and financial reforms, which had as their guiding principle state regulation of the price of necessaries. This was to be effected by state control of such products as grain, salt, tea and wine. Huge warehouses were to be established and stocked with provisions derived from tax payments in kind and government purchases of surplus supplies. Market prices were to be equalized by the purchase or release of goods as conditions required. State loans were to be made to cultivators each spring; they were to be repaid with moderate interest, in grain or in money, after the harvest. By this system of state socialism Wang hoped to assure to the state an augmented income, to the farmer stable prices for his produce and to the population as a whole a secure basis of existence. He also inaugurated a redistribution of land and attempted to substitute for forced labor a new tax based upon wealth.

Wang An-shi was a revolutionary born before his time. Even during the reign of his patron, Shên Tsung, the impossibility of executing Wang's system was recognized. His reforms failed primarily because he was unable to establish an expert and honest officialdom. Nor was the time ripe for a transformation which touched the very basis of Chinese civilization and which aroused the bitter opposition of almost all the Confucianists.

Otto Franke

Consult: Ferguson, John C., in Royal Asiatic Society, China Branch, *Journal*, vol. xxxiv (1903–04) 65–75; Tchéou Hoan, *Le prêt sur récolte institué en Chine au XIe siècle* (Paris 1930); Franke, O., "Staatssozialistische Versuche im alten und mittelalterlichen China," and "Der Bericht Wang Ngan-schis von 1058" in Preussische Akademie der Wissenschaften, Philosophisch-historische Klasse, *Sitzungsberichte* (1931) 218–42, and (1932) 264–312; Ivanov, A. I., *Wang an-Shih i ego reformi* (St. Petersburg 1909).

WAR. The term war is generally applied to armed conflict between population groups conceived of as organic unities, such as races or tribes, states or lesser geographic units, religious or political parties, economic classes. Armed conflict between states that legally enjoy complete and unlimited sovereignty is in modern thought treated as typically war. Within such a state armed conflict between provinces, sections, religious groups, political parties, economic classes, is defined in its inchoate condition as insurrection or rebellion against the sovereign state, guardian and guarantor of the peace. When prolonged and representing a power, actual or potential, sufficient to challenge the authority of the state either in its entirety or in some part of its territory, the conflict is known as civil war. Further there are numberless border line cases often treated as essentially war. Thus the mobilization of a powerful force at the boundary state, designed to force specific action on the part of that state, is often treated as a form of war. So also is the more or less peaceful penetration of the forces of a powerful nation into the territory of a weaker nation, as, for example, the invasion of Mexico by American forces in pursuit of Villa, the American seizure of Vera Cruz, which was designed to apply pressure for the ousting of Huerta, the seizure of Greek soil by the Allies in the early part of the World War and the Japanese expedition to Shanghai. In all such cases the events are likely to be regarded as war by the weaker party but as some unusual form of pacific enterprise by the stronger party.

Naturally a term covering so vast a volume of human experience has been peculiarly subject to metaphorical application. So writers speak of class war, meaning the opposition of class interests, whether these classes confront each other in open conflict, as in strikes and lockouts, or express their opposition in the numberless forms of silent sniping and sabotage. One speaks of the war of the generations, of the sexes, of mental types, of physical stocks even within a unified population. The term is interpolated into the descriptions of animal and even plant life. The red squirrel carries on a ruthless warfare against the gray squirrel, the Japanese black rat against the European brown rat, the evergreen trees against the deciduous trees, the corn against the weeds, bacteria against the race of man and so on without limit. As is commonly the case when a clear cut conception, corresponding to a genuine reality, is corrupted to the service of miscellaneous metaphor, this promiscuous use of the term has operated to obscure the definition and confuse the theory of war itself.

It is still generally assumed that the life of primitive man was one of incessant warfare of tribe against tribe. This view is based mainly upon the alleged behavior of savage tribes in the period of recorded history. As a rule, however, these tribes have been corrupted by the adjacent civilizations with their thirst for gold and other valuable natural products and their demand for slaves. The African tribes south of the Sahara appear to have lived mostly in peace prior to the opening of the modern slave trade. The Indians of North America were prevailingly peaceful until the white man came with his demand for furs, his supplies of guns and ammunition, trinkets and rum. No doubt wherever it was possible to accumulate wealth, such as flocks and herds, stores of agricultural products, there arose robber tribes, like the east African Masai of the present time or the Suevi of Tacitus' *Germania*. It is worth noting that all the earliest centers of culture appear in spots sheltered by national barriers against incursions by hostile tribes. Mountain valleys, as in southern France and Spain, the Caucasus, Mexico, Peru; the high ground in the midst of extensive swamps, as in the delta of the Nile, in the Euphrates-Tigris valley, along the Indus and the Ganges, the Yangtze and the Hwang Ho, served as the nuclei of early cultures, which later were able to extend their sway under the shelter of defensive works.

Warlike forays aiming at the seizure of movable wealth played a considerable role in human history down to comparatively recent times. The cities of the coastal regions of north Africa have been subject to raiding by Kabyle tribesmen from the founding of Carthage down to the last generation. The Syrian coast civilization was always exposed to Bedouin raids from the Arabian grasslands; the Balkan Peninsula and the region south of the Caucasus were anciently harassed by Scythians from the steppes; and the Chinese centers of culture have been subject to frequent attacks by the wild horsemen of Mongolia and Siberia.

This type of war, which reached its highest point of development in the invasion of Europe by the Huns and the great campaigns of Genghis Khan in eastern and southern Asia, has disappeared almost completely in consequence of the development by the culture centers of an overwhelming technique of mechanical warfare. Only vestiges remain in the brigandage of Kabyles, Bedouins, Himalayan and Mongolian tribes.

A second type of war which has played a vast role in history is the conflict that attends the displacement of one people by another. The succession of palaeolithic cultures in western Europe and the disappearance of various skeletal types suggest that wars of extermination characterized the close of the glacial period. The third millennium B.C. was marked by the movement of the Semitic peoples from the east into Mesopotamia, Arabia and Syria, attended by wars of extermination against the earlier populations; the second millennium was marked by the movements of the so-called Aryan peoples into India and Persia and into southern and western Europe; the millennium from 300 B.C. to 700 A.D. was characterized by the westward and southward movement of the Germanic tribes; and the period from the thirteenth well into the seventeenth century by the movement into Asia Minor and southwestern Europe of the Turkish tribes. Similar movements may be traced in aboriginal America and Africa. The wars attending these movements have been among the most ruthless of history, since their objective has been the complete extermination of whole populations.

It is generally assumed that this type of war has disappeared for all time. The peoples of today that are most powerful in war are those of the highest material culture, and these have no need to seize the lands of weaker peoples with a view to population displacement. Through intensive cultivation and foreign trade a dense population may be maintained on the home soil; occasional population pressures can be relieved by emigration. It is, however, to be noted that present day tendencies toward economic nationalism and toward restricting the movement of population over national boundaries raise the question whether pressure for population outlets may not again play a sinister role in the relations of the peoples. The pressure of the German population toward the southeast, the pressure of the Italian population toward the sparsely peopled lands of Algeria and Morocco and the pressure of the Japanese population toward the Asiatic mainland are recognized as potentially disturbing factors in world peace.

In contrast to the wars arising out of the expansive power of populations are those arising out of the expansive power of political systems. In such centers of population as the Nile valley and Mesopotamia the most powerful city early attempted to extend its sway to the limit of the cultural area and beyond, until its forward thrust was weakened by distance, difficulty of supplying armies or the presence of a powerful enemy. Thus Assyria carried its power as far as Syria, where it encountered the power of Egypt, and as far as Armenia, where it encountered the power of the Hittite empire. At such points border warfare was waged inconclusively generation after generation. When the better organized and better equipped Persian Empire displaced the Assyrian power, the limits of imperial subjugation were carried forward through Egypt and to the Hellespont. On the southeast the Persian boundary was securely fixed among the pacific peoples of the Indus; on the northeast it extended deep into Bactria to the forbidding uplands, which could not maintain a population capable of challenging even a feeble frontier guard. The weak points in the Persian border were the Caucasus, menaced by the hordes of horsemen from the northern steppes, and the Straits and the Aegean, easily crossed by warlike Thracians and Greeks. The disastrous expedition of Darius across the Danube which brought the Persians into conflict with the Greeks of the European mainland was an ungeographical attempt to strike at the Scythian hordes in their own country and thus to secure the peace of Armenia.

From the time of Cyrus to the fall of the Roman Empire the objective that determined the character of war was the same: to subject to control the centers of culture and wealth and to establish a tenable frontier behind which empire could live in peace. At the time of the flowering of the Persian Empire this objective had been attained except for the two weak points noted above. Alexander, having assured himself of the Greek cities, could attain to a momentary completion of the design of empire such as the Persians had never attained. In the meantime the Romans, through centuries of persistent effort, had succeeded in consolidating the better part of Italy under their sway. After prolonged efforts to arrive at a stable boundary between themselves and the Carthaginians, in Sicily and Spain, they were drawn into a life and death struggle with Carthage, from which they issued as contenders for empire, now enlarged to include the western Mediterranean. Once they had attained to empire their effort was to stabilize the boundaries, on the Firth of Forth, the Rhine and Danube, the

Caucasus and the Euphrates, the uplands of Ethiopia, the Sahara and the Atlas Mountains. If on occasion Roman generals passed beyond these limits, in the lands between the Rhine and the Elbe, in what is now Hungary and Rumania, in the Crimea and in Mesopotamia, it was not with a view to a permanent extension of the empire but in the hope of breaking up dangerous hostile forces.

The motives of war making throughout classical antiquity were essentially the same: plunder and tribute. Where the defensive was highly developed, as in the city-states of Greece, Asia Minor and the western Mediterranean, wars were entered upon with much hesitation and were far more likely to be directed against helpless dependencies than against the well walled metropolitan cities. By developing the art of the siege the Persians found it possible to bring vast areas under a homogeneous organization; the Macedonians under Alexander commanded an immensely superior technique for breaking through city walls and so were able in a very short space of time to consolidate their hold on the littoral of Asia Minor and Syria and thus to proceed with security through Mesopotamia into Persia itself. This engineering technique of the Macedonians and Greeks was taken over by the Romans and carried to such a point of efficiency that a walled city came to be rather a trap for the enemy forces than an obstacle in the conqueror's path.

It was inevitable that in the case of each of the three great empires the progress toward world rule should have been punctuated by civil war. The financing of war rested on plunder; the success of military adventure depended on a technique which the several conquering generals had in common. Any general might hope, through sacking cities within reach or levying ransom upon them, to build up a power that might place dominion in his own hands. Persia was never long secure against insurrections like that of Cyrus the Younger. Alexander's empire broke up on his death; Caesar's power was established only after a desperate struggle with Pompey; Brutus and Cassius first and later Antony had to be crushed before the Roman Empire was actually consolidated. Even after the long reigns of Augustus and Tiberius the empire was never secure against revolting generals. It was in no small degree that this danger from generals who had become too powerful gave rise to the policy of the stabilized frontier. There were no technical reasons why the Roman Empire might not have carried its boundaries on into India, if the generals on the Euphrates had received the full backing of Rome. But the accumulated treasures of the Indus and the Ganges would too greatly have aggrandized the generals in command of the East.

After the stabilization of the Roman frontiers the epoch of classical imperial wars may be treated as closed. No new accumulations of treasure were available for the support of ambitious campaigns. The empire had to be maintained from the revenues of provinces that had been skimmed of their accumulated resources by the original conquest and by a succession of plundering proconsuls. The available gold and silver in the empire was drained away to the East by the demand for luxuries: silks from China; textiles and embroideries, metal work and inlaid furniture, cloth of gold and gems, from the Indies; perfumes and spices from the Archipelago. In the end the empire could not find resources even to fight a defensive war against barbarians not technically so well equipped for fighting but capable of living off the country and more eager to win lands for settlement than to gain easy treasures.

The declining period of Rome was marked by a type of war reminiscent of those which had ushered in the period of recorded history. Just as the Hellenes ousted the autochthonous population from the richer plains of Greece and gradually assimilated the population of the forests and mountains, so the Anglo-Saxons ousted the Britons, the Franks ousted the Gauls, the Visigoths and Vandals the Celtiberians, the Lombards the Romanized Celts, from the best available lands, pressing the original population into the hills and swamps. But unlike the invasions at the dawn of history, the invasions of the German tribes could supply only a relatively small population for settlement. It was not possible for them to occupy considerable areas solidly. For the most part the invaders seized the best lands but as a rule depended on the original population to operate them. The newcomers, in other words, confined themselves largely to the privileged positions. Unlike settlement groups, whose requirements were easily satisfied, the hunger for privilege was insatiable; hence the conquerors were driven to fight among themselves, with the resulting chronic warfare that marked the early Middle Ages. The pattern of the Roman Empire remained, however, to stir princes like Charlemagne to tremendous though futile efforts for universal conquest. The vestiges of Roman administration helped to create a sense of legality and hence to promote civil stability in various parts of the area that had been conquered by the barbarians. In the later Middle Ages there was a considerable number of states which lived peaceably as a rule within their recognized boundaries. This tendency toward stabilization, however, was again disturbed by the crusades.

In the period immediately preceding the first crusade the motive leading to war had been almost exclusively the desire of princes and nobles to extend their personal dominions. The underlying populations of serfs and craftsmen were not concerned in these struggles, except in so far as they were drafted for auxiliary military service or found their homes destroyed in the progress of campaigns. There was no factor to correspond with the later nationalist spirit. A Norman prince might oust a French or Sicilian or Greek prince with no serious objection on the part of the subject class. The crusades reintroduced in a remote way the conception of war as a struggle of peoples. The contestants were not indeed peoples in the sense of nations, but at the outset at least the interest of Christendom was set against that of the whole range of Moslem peoples. It made an overwhelming difference to the underlying populations of Syria and of the Islamic territories of Spain whether they remained under rulers of their own faith or were transferred to rulers sworn to force another faith upon them. For technical reasons fighting remained largely a business of the knights and their trained retainers; but the motif of desperate resistance on the part of the mass of the population, characteristic of later national wars, began to emerge.

What was an even more important contribution of the crusades to the development of the institution of war was the rise of motives that flowered later in the era of colonial conquests and rivalries. The four Latin principalities established in Syria by the first crusade exposed to western Europe, particularly to the Italians, the possibility of seizing accumulations of wealth which according to mediaeval standards were enormous. Venice and Genoa particularly rose to wealth and power on the basis of the plunder won not only from the Moslem Levant but from the helpless Byzantine Empire. The imperial cities were prepared to fight for this plunder, like the western maritime powers in the sixteenth century. In the thirteenth and fourteenth centuries the more westerly cities (Marseille, Barcelona and by the fifteenth century Lisbon) exhibited an inclination to fight for a share of the Levantine loot. Indeed this element in crusading enterprise may be conceived of as continuing into the enterprise of discovery and conquest in America and the Indies.

The other element, the defense of Christendom against the infidel, also developed a continuity in the resistance to the advance of the Turks. Christian disunion did indeed permit the Turks to subjugate the weak Byzantine Empire, Bulgaria, Serbia, Wallachia and Moldavia and finally Greece. But a combination of Christian states broke the Turkish sea power in the battle of Lepanto (1571), and armies of Poles and Germans defeated the Turks before Vienna in 1683. From that date down to the present century pressure against the receding Turkish Empire in Europe has produced war after war, usually involving the combination of several Christian states. But the most significant development from the crusading impulse is closely connected with the successful Spanish struggle to expel the Moors. In this struggle two objectives stand out: religious unification and national unification. The interplay of these objectives characterizes the history of war from the latter part of the fifteenth century to the beginning of the eighteenth century.

The complex of war objectives through this period included also the reactionary aim of universal empire, as typified by the military ambitions of the Spanish-Austrian empire and in a modified sense by the French ambitions of the period of Louis XIV. Increasingly important also was the struggle for colonial dominion with the immediate plunder to be had by the acquisition of centers of accumulated treasure, as in Central and South America, the East Indies and the Far East; and later the attempt to control colonial commerce, either directly through colonial dominion or indirectly through shipping.

In any considerable war of the period all these objectives were likely to manifest themselves, along with such minor objectives as the maintenance of military forces through the business of war and the pursuit of military glory by commanders in a position to determine questions of war and peace. Thus the long struggle of the Netherlands against Spain arose primarily from resistance to religious oppression, but in the course of its development became more importantly a struggle for national independence and still more importantly a struggle for control of the seas and the consequent control of colonial plunder and commerce. The Thirty Years' War, likewise a religious war at the outset, soon involved the whole range of dynastic and nationalistic ambitions of the time, with the result that Catholic France was supporting the Protestant party and Protestant Sweden was warring upon Protestant Denmark. In addition the struggle was complicated by the activities of great masses of professional soldiers under freebooting leaders, of whom the greatest was Wallenstein. To these men war was merely a business; the political, social and religious objectives were irrelevant.

By the end of the seventeenth century religion had become virtually a negligible factor in the objectives of war; the development of industry and trade, on the other hand, aggravated the tendency toward the assertion of supremacy at sea and the control of the vast colonial areas of the world. Dynastic ambitions still figured heavily among the causes of war, but the commercial motive made use of these ambitions for its own purposes. In the meantime grave tensions were developing between the rising middle class and a more or less effete aristocratic order, tensions that finally resulted in the violent explosions of the British and French revolutions which, with attendant European wars, ushered in a new epoch of war motives. The colonial commercial motive, after Napoleon's abortive conquest of Egypt and the failure of his designs against India, assumed secondary importance, while the strivings for national independence and union assumed a primary importance. Thus the American War of Independence; the revolt of the Spanish colonies in America; the wars against Denmark, Austria and France attending the unification of Germany; the Greek war of independence; the wars of independence of Serbia, Bulgaria, Rumania; the Italian war for independence and unification; the American Civil War, to preserve the Union and to suppress slavery, were primarily motivated by the nationalistic impulse. The World War of 1914–18 with its actual achievements, the liberation of the South Slavs, the Czecho-Slovaks, Poles, Lithuanians, Estonians, Finns, Arabs, with the return of Alsace-Lorraine to France and the annexation by Italy of the Italian speaking territories on the Adriatic and in the Trentino, may be regarded in one aspect as the final flowering of the nationality motive in war.

In the second half of the nineteenth century the development of high capitalism with its dependence on foreign supplies of raw materials and on foreign markets gave new value, in the eyes of statesmen, to colonial dominion. Colonies could be handled as closed trading areas, if necessary. Hence a new imperialism, which resulted in the swift partition of Africa, the extension of British and French dominion in the Indo-Chinese peninsula, extensive schemes for the partition of China and a disposition on the part of the stronger powers to wrest colonial dominions from the weaker ones. Among the results of this imperialistic movement were the Sino-Japanese and the Russo-Japanese War, the Boer War and the Spanish American War. The Fashoda incident came near involving France and England in war, as the Morocco dispute came near involving Germany in war with England and France.

This imperialistic tendency was quite as significant as nationalism in the issues of the World War. The industrial and commercial interests of Germany had long been discontented with the distribution of colonial dominion, which cramped German commercial expansion and threatened to cramp it more seriously in the future. By joining the interests of German high capitalism with the traditional dynastic ambitions of Austria it appeared possible to press forward into the Levant, through the weak state of Serbia and the friendly states of Bulgaria and Turkey to the Persian Gulf. Such an area, held together by commercial treaties and still further consolidated by capital invested in development enterprises, like the Bagdad Railway, might be expected to become a unified economic and political empire, which would challenge the British control of India and which would forever exclude the traditional Russian goal of a position on the Aegean. The defense of Serbian nationalism and redress of the wrong to Belgium were from this general point of view only the concrete forms in which the allied powers accepted the challenge of German capitalistic imperialism.

Prior to the epoch of nationalism every important modern war exhibited some of the elements of civil war. Huguenot elements in France might fight on the side of the British against their fellow countrymen; Italians fought on the side of Austria against other Italians; Germans could be enlisted against other Germans. The nationality movement unified whole peoples. The French Revolution introduced the principle of the nation in arms, a principle universally accepted by the national states of the nineteenth century. A foreign war became a clear cut issue between the peoples.

With the development of capitalism this national unity began to show signs of disintegration through the differentiation of economic classes. The more extreme working class parties officially adopted the view that nationalistic and imperialistic wars represented an exclusive interest of the capitalist class. At the outbreak of the World War this class conception was so widely held that it caused concern to the governments over the possibility of serious passive or even active resistance on the part of a considerable body of citizens. The event proved that the nationalistic schooling of a century lay deeper in the consciousness of the working class than the relatively new doctrines of class interest. With the exception of certain extremist left groups the socialist party of every belligerent country supported its war policy. This tendency, however, broke down in Russia, where the extreme left was able to seize power and dictate peace. Since the Russian Revolution the statesmen of every European power have been compelled to admit into their calculations the possibility that national solidarity might break down under a prolonged war.

It may be noted that many of the forces that in earlier epochs made for war remain in the present epoch. The war making tendency of population displacement is represented by the pressure of too dense populations, like those of Italy, Germany and Japan, toward contiguous or adjacent territory from which the existing population might be expelled. The tendency toward world empire which marked the period from the Assyrian monarchy down through the Roman Empire, the adventures of the Mongol conquerors and the policy of the early modern Spanish-Austrian dynasty was thrust into the background by the nationality movement but finds its counterpart in the aggressive tendency of the Soviet Union in central and eastern Asia. The concept of Mitteleuropa presented by Naumann during the World War, a vast grouping of peoples nationally discrepant but economically united, bears certain resemblances to the earlier dreams of world empire. The war making force of differences in religion has disappeared from the greater part of the world but retains a certain vitality on the fringe between Moslem and Christian civilizations. The tendency toward national independence and unification manifests itself dangerously in the Danube valley and the Balkans, where political boundaries fail to coincide with the boundaries of nationality, and in India and China. War for loot and tribute is hardly conceivable at the present time, but the motives of commercial competition and monopoly are still powerful forces menacing the peaceful relations among the nations.

It is often assumed that the ultimate force making for war is the necessity of expansion on the part of increasing populations, and hence that war is merely a special manifestation of the biological struggle for existence. This may have been true of the wars of population displacement of prehistory and of the period around the opening of the Christian era. Even here we have little evidence that it was actually pressure of population and not the temptation of easy wealth, exposed by trade, that set the barbarians in motion toward the centers of civilization. Pressure of population had nothing to do with the wars between the Mesopotamian empires and Egypt nor with the Persian, Macedonian and Roman conquests nor with the wars of the crusades, the colonial and national wars of early modern times. Some element of concern over population pressures may have entered into the calculations of statesmen in the period just preceding the World War. Yet throughout western Europe the rate of population increase was declining rapidly, indicating the establishment of a stationary population long before defect in the means of subsistence could become severe. It is notable that the two countries in which the pressure of population was greatest, China and India, have never exhibited any tendency toward conquest.

Increase in population has indeed frequently affected the military equilibrium and thus may indirectly have made for war. The more rapid increase of the German population was disturbing to French statesmen in the period from 1850 to the outbreak of the World War, and the still more rapid increase in the population of Russia was disturbing to German statesmen. In this respect increasing population may be counted among the causes of international unrest, along with increasing wealth, technical proficiency and armaments.

It is also commonly assumed that antipathies between peoples differing in race, culture or language have played a large part in the causation of war. History offers singularly little evidence upon which such a view can be based. The wars of the Hebrews against the peoples occupying Palestine, the alleged contempt of the Greek for the barbarian, the hatred of Romans for Carthage, are cited as ancient instances; the antagonism of the British to the Spanish and French down to the nineteenth century and the mutual dislike of Frenchmen and Germans since the time of Napoleon serve as modern instances.

But a closer analysis exposes the inadequacy of any explanation of war based upon popular antipathy. Such antipathies in any significant degree of development appear rather to be a result than a cause of war. Where the interests of nations or peoples clash, each party naturally launches a propaganda, consciously or unconsciously, against the other. Thus the Greeks made the most of instances of Persian treachery, although the numerous amicable arrangements between the Persians and the Greek cities and the generous behavior of Alexander toward the conquered Persians indicate that the antipathy was not deep seated. The Roman charge of "Punic perfidy" was mainly a consequence of the determination of the Romans to rid themselves of a commercial rival. So the mutual recriminations of British and French in more recent times have been hushed or exacerbated according as the two nations conceived of their interests as identical or conflicting.

A realistic view of the immediate causation of war involves an examination of the organs of society in which the war making power is lodged and the considerations controlling the bellicose determinations of those organs. In the oriental empires the war making organ was the king or perhaps more properly the group of satellites surrounding the king, who played on his instinct for glory in order to further their own greed for wealth and power. Some such organization needs to be assumed if the somewhat rational character of the strategy of the Mesopotamian kings is to be explained. This involved a persistent reaching for the control of trade routes converging in Syria; the same objective was pursued by the Egyptian and Hittite monarchies. In his brief period of empire King David struck for control of these trade routes. The war making power of Persia was held by the great king and a clique of military and civil adventurers for whom conquest offered a career. In the Greek cities the war power might be lodged in a democracy, as in Athens; an oligarchy, as in Sparta; a tyrant, as in many of the cities of Asia Minor and Graecia Magna. With the exception of Sparta there does not appear to have been any Greek city in which a project of war could command the adhesion of all parties; hence the remarkable vacillation in policy as one party succeeded another in control. In Rome during the republic the war making power was vested in the Senate, which was seldom a unit in sentiment except in the case of a defensive war. Even after the rivalry of Rome and Carthage for naval and commercial control of the western Mediterranean had become intense and Carthage had given evidence of intention to expel the Roman influence from territories granted to Rome by treaty, years of agitation by the war party were required to involve the republic in war.

After the consolidation of the imperial power the war making power was theoretically concentrated in the emperor. In fact, however, the various provincial governors or the commanders of legions on the frontier often provoked and carried on war on their own account, trusting to success to cancel any disapprobation of the emperor. Similar manifestations of the military free hand were frequent in the modern era of colonial conquest.

Through the feudal period not only the suzerain but the great vassals also exercised the right to raise military forces and to carry on war. With the rise of the absolute monarchy such powers were absorbed by the king, who might make war to advance his own glory, or more frequently served as an instrument in the hands of ambitious parties at court, eager for opportunities of advancement or in the employ of powerful commercial interests seeking profit through colonial dominion.

With the establishment of the liberal parliamentary state the war making power came to be vested theoretically in the people as a whole, as represented in parliament. In practise, however, popular control down to the present day has been everywhere subject to numerous restrictions. Certain items of policy which may involve war are commonly excluded from parliamentary oversight. Thus the Monroe Doctrine, first proclaimed by the president, is in effect a limitation upon the free choice of the people of the United States as to peace or war. The seizure of territory on the American continent by a European or Asiatic power would until recently have been accepted as a casus belli. Probably it would still be potent enough to draw America into war, however distasteful war might be to the great majority. All through the nineteenth century it was the settled policy of England to checkmate the progress of Russia toward the Aegean; any British government could appeal to this policy to justify acts leading necessarily to war. The maintenance of the independence of the Netherlands and Belgium was another point in British policy to be maintained by war if necessary, without regard to the current state of public sentiment. Moreover the nineteenth and the early twentieth century developed a whole network of treaties, some publicly known, some secret, that might demand the sanction of war irrespective of parliamentary action.

In virtually every modern country a department of foreign affairs handles the details of foreign relations with considerable latitude and therefore may work toward war or peace without any certain control on the part of the representative arm of government. There is also always the possibility that the military organization, which likewise maintains secrecy with respect to its ultimate plans, may exert an undue influence upon the policy of government. Finally, there are powerful private interests that may profit from war or the threat of war, such as the armament and munitions industries, and may through a propaganda of suspicion prepare the way for war.

In view of the foregoing considerations it is impossible to say with certainty whether in all history any people as a whole or by an actual majority has willed to make war. A war situation arises in which the only possible alternatives appear to be victory or defeat; and however little the majority of the citizens of one state may desire to crush another state, they are still less willing to contemplate being crushed. After war is on, the union of the great majority in support of the war is effected, mainly by the inherent force of the situation but in part by propaganda. It is by this ex post facto consent, given unavoidably, that wars inaugurated by minority interests or in response to traditional policies present a pseudo-popular character.

Down to comparatively recent times any considerable military preparations were assumed on every hand to have an offensive purpose. The building up of highly organized cavalry forces by the Medes and Persians was just as definite a part of the offensive against the Mesopotamian empire as the actual invasion; so were the military preparations of Thebes under Epaminondas, the organization of the phalanx by Philip, the enrolment of legions by Rome. When military forces were organized on a considerable scale in the England of the Edwards, it was taken for granted that a descent upon France was contemplated. The military preparations of Louis XIV and Frederick the Great were always recognized as having a definite offensive purpose, as were those of Napoleon. After the Sino-Japanese War, when the Japanese felt that the fruits of victory had been snatched from them at the instance and in the interest of Russia, Japan entered upon a prolonged effort of military preparations, designed ultimately to thrust Russia out of Korea and the Liaotung Peninsula. Prior to the World War the lengthening of the term of military service by France and the capital levy by Germany for military expenditures were generally recognized as definite moves toward war, as were also the competing naval developments of England and Germany. So severe had this competitive race of armaments become by the opening of the twentieth century and so intolerable the fiscal burdens involved, that the peace of the world was widely conceived as jeopardized by the very weight of the instrumentalities of war, even in default of any genuine conflict of interest between the states. Hence the organization of the peace conference at The Hague in 1899, summoned at the instance of the czar of Russia and designed to remove the causes of war, particularly those causes springing from competing armaments. From that time on it has been generally accepted that reduction in armaments would work toward peace. Numerous international conferences have been held with the object of disarmament in view; one of the most important was the Washington Conference, which fixed naval ratios as among the United States, Great Britain and Japan, presumptively on such terms as to preclude a crushing superiority of any of the three parties except in home waters.

What has most seriously complicated the problem of disarmament is the inescapable confusion of offensive and defensive. A military historical view, such as commonly dominates the diplomacy of the great powers, conceives of the causes of war in terms of the strength of the offensive and the weakness of the defensive. Seldom in history has any power entered upon a war of aggression except with a confident expectation of success. Power of resistance, if adequate, operates to dissuade a country inclined toward aggression from an undertaking that may turn out disastrously. Hence armament, so long as it remains essentially defensive, is conceived to be an insurance of peace.

Attempts to define defensive armament have been numerous but never highly successful. It is an accepted principle that an attacking power must have stronger armaments than a defending power. The superior command of the terrain on land, the possibility of establishing fortified points, the superior facility of supply services on shorter lines, offer the defense an advantage which has varied historically from perhaps 3:1 to 2:1. At sea the possession by the defensive of bases for refueling, remunitioning and repair ward from Italy, so did the system of warehousing. The Hanseatic merchants had warehouses in most of the great trading centers, including some in Russia. The growth of colonial trade led to the building of similar establishments in India, Africa and the American settlements. With the growth of capitalist enterprise, mass markets and wholesale trade the warehouse became an increasingly important economic factor.

As warehouses depend upon trade, they are inseparably identified with the development of transportation. Railroads created the need for a new type of warehouse. The task of assembling and distributing carloads of goods led to the development of the railroad freight depot. When, however, the railroads reached their capacity as transporters of goods, a separation of the transporting and storing functions became necessary. The railroads assessed storage and demurrage charges, devised car service, levied a toll for extra handling and vigorously discouraged the use of railroad facilities for storing beyond the necessary "free time" for loading and unloading. In addition discrimination and favoritism in railroad storage, whether in cars or in depots, was an element in the system of secret rates and rebates which big producers used to oppress the smaller. Finally the protests of injured shippers led to congressional legislation (the Hepburn Act of 1906) and, under direction of the Interstate Commerce Commission, to a further separation of transporting and warehousing. This separation has emphasized the importance of warehousing as an entirely distinct industry.

It had become apparent that storing is to some extent an inseparable part of the transportation service; for although the two functions are easily separable in theory, they have proved to be closely associated in fact. This situation has been acknowledged by the public, the railroads and the many regulatory commissions. On the other hand, although warehousing is not separable from the movement of freight, the warehousing function of a common carrier is everywhere recognized as distinct from its carrying function.

As an equalizer of supply and demand warehousing must save from a time of plenty to a time of need. Warehouses are filled at the stroke of nature's clock and must serve as reservoirs of supply until the next striking hour. In an industrial economy this process comes to include nonagricultural goods, because of various factors in production and distribution. The fluctuations of supply and demand bring to the warehouse as the reservoir of goods first a heavy inflow of commodities and then a slow process of withdrawal, until the store is entirely depleted at the end of the year. Or for irregular demand the inflow of goods may be fairly even throughout the year and the withdrawals may occur within a single month. Much waste is prevented by this leveling of supply and demand. Storing adjusts the time lag between producing and consuming. Thus warehousing tends to flatten out many of the violent swings of price formerly caused by the irregular supply of goods for a fairly regular market. It is no longer necessary for the producer to accept a ruinously low price when the market is glutted or, at the opposite end of the year, for the consumer to pay ridiculously high prices for whatever goods are available.

As the number of products has increased and trade has become more widespread and complex, warehousing services have been greatly specialized in line with the peculiar requirements of the goods in store. The industry recognizes the following four classifications: first, furniture and household goods; second, agricultural commodities (cotton, grain, tobacco, wool, sugar, coffee, rice, peanuts, beans, potatoes, broom corn); third, cold storage (temperature 45° F and under); fourth, merchandise (most manufactured goods, with subdivisions for yard and ground storage, dock and wharf and farm implements) and field warehouses. As a general rule warehouses are independent business enterprises; in many cases, however, manufacturers, department stores and chain stores maintain their own warehouses for special purposes.

The law in all countries holds the warehouseman responsible for goods while they remain in store. Upon proper demand he must deliver them out of store in the same condition as when received by him. The Uniform Law of the United States stipulates that: "A warehouseman shall be liable for any loss or injury to the goods caused by his failure to exercise such care in regard to them as a reasonably careful owner of similar goods would exercise, but he shall not be liable, in the absence of an agreement to the contrary, for any loss or injury to the goods which could not have been avoided by the exercise of such care."

The warehouseman's integrity accordingly becomes the security of the owner of the goods. The warehouseman is not in any strict sense, however, a banker. Unlike the latter, the warehouseman has no right to use or to loan the merchandise in his possession, which he holds, under the law of bailment, merely for the performance of stated acts. He must return the identical goods—not their equivalent value—untouched and unaltered. He may not even mingle one owner's goods with another's, except in the single case of goods "fungible" under the law (staples susceptible of definite grading and which actually have been so graded and do not suffer from being commingled, chief among them being grain and rice, pig iron and bar copper, cotton and hay, potatoes and oranges, wool and tobacco, beans and broom corn).

So vital a factor is the warehouseman's integrity as a guaranty that the goods will be neither harmed nor abstracted that supervision and bonding have been instituted as safeguards. One type of bonding is that of customhouse storage, which involves the warehousing of merchandise still subject to customs duty or internal revenue. Here rigid supervision and heavy bonding redound to the exclusive benefit of the government. Another type of bonding and supervision prevails among those warehouses which have been made regular by the commodity exchanges. Here in addition to governmental requirements the exchanges assume strict supervision and demand ample bonds. Another group in the United States comprises warehouses operating under the Federal Warehouse Act of 1916, which provides for federal license with inspection and bonding. The system includes only a small proportion of warehouses in the United States, for federal licenses are available only for the storing of agricultural products. Finally, to protect the general public nearly all of the states require the posting of a bond as a condition precedent to the granting of a license to do business; this is a guaranty of reliability and a tangible source of recovery for damages.

Thus the warehouseman becomes an ideal third party, wholly disinterested in the goods he holds and able to serve as an intermediary between buyer and seller or between borrower and lender. His receipt for the goods is accepted everywhere, for either selling or borrowing, as a symbol for the merchandise itself. Thus the warehouse becomes the physical support for all trading on the commodity exchanges. This development is thoroughly modern. In the ancient and mediaeval world physical presence of the goods on the market place was absolutely necessary. Men could neither buy nor sell without the presence of visible and tangible substances. Transfer of ownership was by delivery from hand to hand, so that the size of the market and the volume of trading were severely limited. A larger market became possible only when, in response to the growth of capitalist industry and trade with their increasingly far flung and complex markets, a symbol was accepted by both parties as representative of the goods. Then larger quantities could be traded, and transactions could spread over greater distances.

The modern commodity exchange deals in goods seldom seen by either party. This requires standardization of products, or grading, which occurs after they reach the warehouse. Once graded there can be no tampering and one grade cannot be mixed with another. The warehouse receipt guarantees to the holder not only the goods but also their quantity unchanged and their quality intact. Thus the exchange can recognize the lot of goods as a unit, with the receipt as its symbol. Exchanges have established their own supervision over the warehouses; only those which satisfy the requirements are approved as "regular" and only the receipts from "regular" warehouses are good for delivery on the exchange. Making a warehouse "regular" is the equivalent of listing a security on the stock exchange.

On all such exchanges contracts are completed not by delivery of the commodity itself but by the transfer of warehouse receipts representing the proper quantity. The receipt is so completely accepted as a symbol for the goods that it is preferred even as security for bank loans. This use of the receipt is not limited to agricultural products but extends also to manufactured goods. Loans on merchandise are known as commodity or merchandise loans as distinguished from loans against corporate securities. In the United States the Federal Reserve Board has authorized preferential rates of discount for these loans, which range from $\frac{1}{2}$ to 1 percent, a maturity of six months against the usual limit of ninety days, and permission to member banks to loan to a single borrower up to 50 percent of the bank's capital and surplus instead of the usual 10 percent.

Under the roof of the manufacturer or jobber, goods, whether raw or finished, are in law as well as in fact part of the general assets and not a separate entity. An additional $10,000 worth of goods swells the inventory account, but it does not correspondingly increase the owner's ability to borrow. The borrower has such complete control over the additional goods that the bank's security is not increased to any appreciable extent. If, however, the additional $10,000 worth of goods is stored in a warehouse, it can be used as collateral for borrowing; for in the warehouse the goods are segregated from other goods of the borrower, who is deprived of their control, which is now vested in a disinterested third party. The lot cannot be used, sold or even touched by the borrower without the previous and written order of the bank. Thus it becomes perfect security for a loan, specifically insured, beyond reach of attachment or any server of legal process; and it is not involved in the borrower's bankruptcy or financial difficulties, being beyond his reach until the loan is satisfied. Thus the producer or distributor is able to convert into liquid form otherwise temporarily dead stock.

There is less risk of fire in warehouses than in the factory, and insurance rates are correspondingly lower. Moreover there is a practical guaranty against the temptation of a hard pressed merchant or manufacturer to convert unsalable merchandise into cash by setting fire to his establishment. In self-protection against this moral risk banks regularly require certain borrowers to separate their holdings of goods by storing them in public warehouses, with the bank controlling all withdrawals.

Beginning about 1905 the warehouse assumed new functions tending to promote the more rapid handling of goods from factory to final consumer. It undertook to enable the manufacturer, through a system of spot stock of goods in a warehouse, to make local deliveries as rapidly as he could through a branch house or jobber. In addition to simplifying distribution this has been an important factor in the efforts of manufacturers to sell directly to the dealer. Manufactured goods in carload or in cargo lots are shipped from the factory to a warehouse centrally located in a marketing zone. The manufacturer's salesmen then solicit orders. Delivery of goods is effected from the nearby spot stock rather than by shipment from the distant factory. The manufacturer merely instructs the warehouse to fill the order, with shipment either by rail or by truck.

By shipping bulk lots of goods from factory to warehouse the manufacturer benefits by the carload freight rate, which is less than the less-than-carload rate for a small lot to the dealer. The dealer profits from the shorter time of delivery from a neighboring warehouse, for his orders are more quickly filled, he is able to operate with smaller capital, and the small lot frequently ordered supports as large a total volume of sales as a greater volume ordered at longer intervals. All this is worth the ex-warehouse price he must pay—the cost of the goods plus an adjusted freight rate and a rather nominal fee for the privilege of ordering in tiny lots. The manufacturer gains by shipping in carload lots, for he pockets the difference, or spread, between the carload and the less-than-carload freight rate. This difference for nearly all commodities under nearly all circumstances is sufficient to pay all costs of the additional handling in and out of store, the warehouse's charge for storing and the incidental items. The manufacturer is able to serve his customer better, to retain close contact with his market and yet suffer no net expense, for the saving in the freight rate more than compensates for all minor costs.

By a further refinement of this method manufacturers file with the warehouseman an accredited list of regular customers in good standing. Each customer is then privileged to make his own requisition upon the warehouse for goods (sometimes with restrictions), without waiting to place an order with the manufacturer. Immediate delivery follows. Each day the warehouseman reports to the manufacturer the day's withdrawal, vouchered by signed delivery slips, and the manufacturer invoices against the customer in the same manner as though shipment had gone from the factory. The effect is greatly to speed up distribution. Since goods can be withdrawn weekly, daily or even several times in a day, a business may be operated with a minimum of stock actually on hand. This procedure has encouraged small lot ordering and hand to mouth buying among retailers. Particularly since the World War, both in the United States and in Canada, it has become widespread as an alternative to selling on consignment. The main causes were at first the wide fluctuations in prices and later intensified competition and more changeable consumer demands. This method developed rapidly in 1921–22 west of the Mississippi, when banks were failing and credit was seriously disturbed. At that time a manufacturer hesitated to ship goods to a merchant on open account. To put them out on consignment was little better, because of the costliness of repossession. Yet there existed all the time a real demand for goods. To meet the situation merchants stocked with minimum lots, barely enough for display and demonstration. They were instructed to requisition a warehouse for further goods. Then with a sale in prospect the merchant could present evidence to warrant credit, or in extreme instance he would accept merchandise on the C.O.D. basis.

So successful has been the accredited list in buttressing the market with goods, that it has become an outstanding feature of warehousing manufactured goods. It has largely displaced consignment selling—always fraught with evils—because it avoids the risks of the consignment while supplying every outlet with merchandise. The same method is used and to a very large extent between manufacturer and wholesaler, particularly among the newer types of specialty jobber. The result has been to increase the warehouse's handling costs by augmenting the number of small lot deliveries. Many warehousemen have complained that they were asked to make too many deliveries. Another result has been a marked growth in the number of conveniently located warehouses. In 1927–30 the value of new warehouse construction amounted to $98,694,000, or over 6 percent, of a total of $1,554,986,000 for all types of industrial construction.

In many cases storing goods at the factory becomes almost a necessity. A factory may be located far from a suitable warehouse, or the entrepreneur may find that it is uneconomical to transport the merchandise to a city where a warehouse exists. To meet this situation the warehouseman extends his services from the city to the outlying factory, providing the field warehouse, a distinctly American development. In the case of canned foodstuffs, one of the typical commodities which call for field warehousing, the fruits or vegetables or fish must be canned at the time of harvest. As the canneries are necessarily at outlying points, the shipment of goods to a city would involve transportation. The expense is often prohibitive, for profit margins are threatened by waste. Yet the cannery must as a rule borrow against its pack, all the costs of which demand payment within a single month, although sales stretch out over the year to come. It is seldom moreover that canned goods are labeled at the time of packing. The filled cans are accordingly tiered in immense stacks, grade by grade but unlabeled and uncased. The field warehouseman takes over one building on the canner's property, usually under a lease. This is set aside as a warehouse, securely protected, with a custodian installed who is an employee of the warehouse. As canned goods are packed they are stacked within this warehouse, so completely isolated that even the cannery owner is denied access under any pretext. The goods are insured. Then with the resultant warehouse receipt running in the name of the bank as collateral the cannery is able to borrow. The terms are more liberal than if the cannery retained title to the pack, especially as the loan is eligible for rediscount on the preferential rating. This form of commodity paper has been approved by the Federal Reserve Board.

Throughout the United States a uniform warehouse receipts law has been enacted. The warehouse receipt is the contract. It gives evidence that the goods described have been deposited with the warehouse, and it contains the terms under which they were so deposited and the conditions under which they will be released. The principal requirements relate to unequivocal description of the goods and identification of the warehouse, a plain and complete statement of the warehousing charges and, if the warehouse has any financial interest in the goods, a statement of that fact. There is a negotiable form of warehouse receipts passed by endorsement; but, unlike negotiable commercial paper, the endorser guarantees only that the receipt is genuine so far as he knows and that he holds legal right to it. In order to obtain delivery of the goods under a negotiable receipt, this itself must be surrendered for cancellation. The negotiable receipt is little used except for the storage of staple commodities which are traded on the commodity exchanges. The non-negotiable form is ordinarily employed, and it is merely evidence of an ordinary contract under bailment. The owner may withdraw from store all or a portion of his goods without surrender of the receipt. Possession of the receipt does not carry title to the goods. To obtain the goods the registered holder may issue against the warehouse any sort of written order which definitely expresses his wishes, much as he writes a check against a bank deposit. Title to the goods remains with him. The risk of fraudulent possession of the receipt by another is very small, because the warehouseman knows that the receipt itself is not transferable. In all states of the United States it is a criminal offense for a warehouseman to issue a receipt for goods not actually received into the warehouse, to describe goods falsely, to issue a receipt for goods of which he is owner in whole or in part without stating this fact or to deliver goods under a negotiable receipt without first obtaining a return of that document for cancellation. In addition to their general importance as a link in distribution, warehouses have a large direct economic importance by virtue of their capital investment. While run as profit enterprises under capitalism warehouses would be necessary even in a non-profit economy (although perhaps on a less extensive scale, if industry were considerably decentralized), for where goods are produced on a large scale for mass markets some form of storage is indispensable.

H. A. HARING

See: MARKETING; WHOLESALING; RETAIL TRADE; AGRICULTURAL MARKETING; FOOD SUPPLY; PORTS AND HARBORS; TERMINALS; GRAIN ELEVATORS; REFRIGERATION; GRADING; COMMODITY EXCHANGES; LIEN; BAILMENT.

Consult: Haring, H. A., *Warehousing* (New York 1925), *Corporations Doing Business in Other States* (New York 1927), and *New Business for Warehouses* (New York 1931); United States, Bureau of Statistics, "Warehousing Industry in the United States" in *Monthly Summary of Commerce and Finance of the United States*, ser. 1903-04, no. iv (1903) 1033-95; MacElwee, R. S., and Taylor, T. R., *Wharf Management, Stevedoring and Storage* (New York 1921); Cricher, A. L., *The Merchandise Warehouse in Distribution*, United States, Bureau of Foreign and Domestic Commerce, Trade Promotion series, no. 15 (1925); Lyon, Leverett S., *Hand-to-Mouth Buying* (Washington 1929); Campbell, William, *Wholesale and Retail Trade. What Services the Warehouseman and the Shopkeeper Render*, ed. by J. G. Smith (London 1929); Rideout, Eric H., "The Development of the Liverpool Warehousing System" in Historic Society of Lancashire and Cheshire, *Transactions*, vol. lxxxii (1932) 1-41; Bruegelmann, H. F., *Systematische Darstellung von Lagerschaft und Lagerscheinwesen* (Oberhausen 1930); Abraham, H. J., *Der Lagerschein* (Berlin 1933); Cartechini, Fernando, *I magazzini generali* (new ed. Turin 1920). See also series of articles by H. A. Haring under the general subject of "Public Warehousing and Economic Distribution" in *Distribution and Warehousing*, vol. xxiv (1925), and vol. xxxiii (1934).

WARFARE, LAWS OF. Laws of warfare constitute the procedure by which war is carried on by the opposing belligerents engaged therein. This procedure embraces the methods adopted, the instruments employed and the rules governing the conduct of war.

It was characteristic of ancient warfare that the parties who engaged in it were subject to few or no internationally binding rules. Treachery and perfidy were permissible methods, and instrumentalities of destruction which are now forbidden by international law were employed without scruple. Enemy aliens were made prisoners and sometimes even put to death and their property was confiscated. Captives were mutilated, tortured, killed or sold into slavery. The municipal law of some ancient states, however, occasionally imposed limitations on the conduct of their military forces. Thus in India the Code of Manu forbade the use of barbed or poisoned arrows, the killing of a suppliant enemy or of one who had thrown down his arms. Likewise among the Greek peoples there was developed a body of custom which set limitations upon the conduct of war as between themselves, although not in their wars with non-Greek peoples. The Romans developed a still more definite body of war law (*jus belli*) but its rules, especially in respect to the treatment of enemies, were scarcely less cruel or severe. The *jus fetiale* enunciated certain ceremonial and procedural rules governing, among other things, declarations of war, and it recognized only four legitimate causes of warfare.

Throughout the Middle Ages the conduct of war was generally characterized by harshness and cruelty. The practise was sometimes softened, especially among Christian nations, by the pacific and humane teachings of the great church fathers and by the influence of the doctrines of the church. The high standards of honor which were the basis of the code of chivalry may also have exerted a moderating influence on the procedure of warfare, but the extent of this influence has probably been exaggerated.

A more important stage in the development of the idea that the power of belligerents in waging war is not unlimited was reached in the sixteenth and seventeenth centuries when the modern system of international law began to take form in the treatises of Vitoria, Grotius, Pufendorf and others. Stirred by the atrocities of the Thirty Years' War and the license which characterized the conduct of the belligerents engaged in it, Grotius appealed to the law of nature as a system of law binding upon nations as upon individuals and which set humanitarian limits upon them in the conduct of war with one another.

But aside from occasional stipulations in bipartite treaties relating to such matters as the treatment of enemy aliens in respect of their persons and property, the capture of ships, exercise of search at sea and the articles which should be regarded as contraband the laws of war consisted mainly of usages and customs which had grown up in the course of centuries, the evidences of which were found in the histories and treatises of text writers. Today, however, while a considerable portion of the law of war is still based on custom and usage, much of it, especially the law of land warfare, is found in multipartite treaties or conventions and in the manuals or ordinances promulgated by states for the guidance of their military forces.

The starting point in the movement which brought about this transformation may be said to have been the adoption of the Declaration of Paris in 1856 at the close of the Crimean War. This declaration laid down four brief but important rules dealing with privateering, blockade and the immunity from capture of enemy private property on neutral ships and of non-contraband neutral property on enemy ships. The rules regarding blockade and the immunity of neutral goods under an enemy flag were in the main merely declaratory of the existing doctrine and practise. But those abolishing privateering and exempting from capture enemy goods under a neutral flag enunciated new law. The declaration is incomplete in that it is limited to a very brief statement of a few general principles, makes no attempt to define enemy character or contraband and does not lay down the rules to be applied in determining the liability of contraband to capture or deal with various matters relative to blockade which became a matter of controversy during the World War. This declaration, signed by the seven powers participating in the Congress of Paris, was the first of a series of important multipartite conventions dealing with the laws of war, and by the time of the outbreak of the World War in 1914 it had been either formally acceded to or accepted in practise by all the important maritime powers of the world. The prize courts of all the belligerent states which had occasion during the war to apply its rules held it to be an established part of international law and therefore binding upon them. It was applied in the decision of the British Prize Court in the case of the *Marie Glaeser* [1 Lloyd 56 (1914)] and in that of the German Prize Court in the case of the *Indian Prince* [1 Entsch. 87 (1916)].

The Declaration of Paris was shortly followed by the conclusion of the first Red Cross convention in 1864. This convention, consisting of nineteen articles, laid down a series of rules whose purpose was to ameliorate the condition of the sick and wounded in war by providing certain immunities for the doctors, nurses and other persons charged with caring for them and by securing protection for hospitals, ambulances and other instrumentalities employed in such service. By one of the Hague conventions of 1899 its principles were adapted and extended to apply to maritime warfare. In 1906 the convention of 1864 was replaced by a new and more detailed one, likewise concluded at Geneva, containing thirty-three articles. Some of the articles in the convention of 1906 were new; others were revisions of the corresponding articles of the convention of 1864; while in various articles a new and more scientific nomenclature was employed. Finally in 1929 the convention of 1906 was superseded by one still more detailed, concluded by an international conference held at Geneva. This convention retains in principle the substance of its predecessors but lays down a number of new rules, the need for which had been demonstrated by the experience of the World War.

Another although less important landmark in the development of the conventional law of war was the Declaration of St. Petersburg of 1868, framed by a conference of the powers called by the czar of Russia for the purpose of securing an agreement among them to refrain from the employment by their military forces of a type of bullet which inflicted needless suffering. The declaration bound the parties to renounce in case of war between any of them the use of "any projectile of less weight than 400 grammes (about 14 ounces) which is explosive or charged with fulminating or inflammable substances." The preamble to the declaration asserted the general proposition that "there are technical limits at which war ought to yield to the requirements of humanity" and that "the progress of civilization should have the effect of alleviating as much as possible the calamities of war; that the only legitimate object which States should endeavor to accomplish during war is to weaken the military forces of the enemy; that for this purpose it is sufficient to disable the greatest possible number of men; that this object would be exceeded by the employment of arms which needlessly aggravate the sufferings of disabled men or render their death inevitable." It is significant that the declaration was framed by a conference composed entirely of military officers and experts. Although the general principle enunciated in the preamble has been criticized as practically obsolete, it found its way into the military manuals of many states and was incorporated by reference in the *règlement* (art. 23) respecting the laws and customs of war on land adopted by the Hague conferences of 1899 and 1907.

The charges and counter charges made by both belligerents during the Franco-Prussian War of 1870–71, relative to violations of allegedly established customary rules of warfare, and the controversies which arose as to what those rules required of belligerents and prohibited aroused considerable sentiment among jurists and military men in favor of an effort to reach an agreement among states upon those matters concerning which there was controversy. The czar of Russia, who sympathized with the idea, was accordingly induced to call an international conference. The British government, which was rather unsympathetic and skeptical, finally agreed to participate, provided that the conference would confine its effort to a codification of the existing customary rules of land warfare and not deal with the subject of naval warfare. The conference was held at Brussels in 1874, the delegates for the most part being military men. At the outset irreconcilable differences of opinion were manifested between the representatives of the larger military powers and those of the smaller states, especially with regard to the rights of military occupants. In spite of the differences, however, agreement was reached on many points, the results being embodied in the draft of a declaration consisting of fifty-six articles. But the British government declined to ratify the declaration on the alleged ground that it was not limited to a statement of the existing customs and usages but embodied various new rules which would give an advantage to the great continental military powers. In consequence of Great Britain's refusal to ratify the declaration it never came into force, although it exerted a strong moral influence upon the conduct of belligerents during the wars which followed. Many of its rules were in fact incorporated into the manuals of instructions issued by various states for the guidance of their military commanders during war, and it became the basis of the Hague convention of 1899 respecting the laws and customs of war on land.

The high water mark in the movement to codify the laws and customs of warfare was attained in the work of the two Hague conferences of 1899 and 1907. Of the conventions and declarations agreed upon and adopted by the first conference five related to the conduct of war, their general purpose being to define more precisely the rules by which belligerents should be bound and to impose limitations upon them in respect to the methods which they might employ and the instrumentalities which they might use in the waging of war. The most important of these acts was the convention respecting the laws and customs of war on land, in sixty articles, dealing with the qualifications which armed forces must possess in order to be recognized as lawful combatants, the treatment of prisoners of war, the means which a belligerent may employ to overcome the enemy, forbidden weapons and agencies, the powers of military commanders in occupied enemy territory, the status of spies and other matters. The conference recognized that the rules embodied in the convention did not cover the whole field, since it had proved impossible to reach an agreement on all points. In order therefore to remove the foundation for a possible claim that any matters not covered by the convention might be determined by military commanders without regard to the law, the conference took the precaution to insert in the preamble a statement to the effect that it was not the intention of the parties that such matters should be left to the arbitrary judgment of military commanders and that until a more complete code of the laws of war should be agreed upon and accepted by the states of the world, "inhabitants and belligerents should remain under the protection and the rule of the principles of the law of nations, as they result from the usages established among civilized peoples, from the laws of humanity, and the dictates of the public conscience." An important provision of the convention was that contained in article 1 which imposed upon the contracting parties an obligation to issue instructions to their armed forces which should be in conformity with the regulations annexed to the convention. A manual of this kind, the first ever issued, had already been promulgated by President Lincoln in 1863. It was known as the *Instructions for the Government of the Armies of the United States in the Field* and was prepared by Francis Lieber at the request of the president. These instructions remained in force until 1914, when they were superseded by a new manual entitled *Rules of Land Warfare* prepared and issued by the War Department. They were largely a revision of the instructions of 1863, with such additions and omissions as were necessary to bring them into harmony with the Hague conventions and the Red Cross convention of 1906. Some states complied with the obligation imposed by the Hague convention and issued similar manuals or ordinances, while others did not. One of the best known was the German *Kriegsbrauch im Landkriege* (tr. by J. H. Morgan as *The German War Book . . . by the Great General Staff*, London 1915), prepared by the German General Staff and promulgated in

1902. The *Kriegsbrauch* was widely criticized for its extreme views in regard to the rights of military commanders and for its non-conformity with the Hague regulations. The French manual, *Les lois de la guerre continentale* (4th ed. Paris 1913), was largely a reproduction of the rules of the Hague conventions. The British manual issued in 1908 likewise embodied the Hague regulations, with chapters on various matters of military interest including one on the laws and usages of war on land prepared by Edmonds and Oppenheim. While it was not required by the Hague convention, a good many states issued similar manuals for the guidance of their naval forces. Thus in 1900 a naval code prepared by Admiral Stockton was issued by the government of the United States but was revoked in 1905 by President Theodore Roosevelt, mainly on the ground that while it restricted the powers of American naval commanders, the naval forces of other states were not bound by similar rules. In 1917, however, a new manual of *Instructions for the Navy of the United States Governing Maritime Warfare* in 113 articles was issued by the Navy Department. It lays down numerous rules for the guidance of naval officers in the conduct of maritime war. Of a somewhat similar character was the German Prize Code of 1909 (*Prisenordnung*), the French manual of instructions for the guidance of French naval commanders issued in 1912 and reissued in revised form in 1916, the Austro-Hungarian naval regulations of 1913 and those of Italy of 1917. As yet the British government has never issued a code or manual for the guidance of the British naval forces.

The issuance of such instructions represented an important step toward defining and reducing to written form the rules governing the conduct of war, although being unilateral acts they had no international binding force and were subject to revision or abrogation at any time by the governments issuing them.

The Hague conventions of 1899 relative to the conduct of war were revised and extended by a second conference in 1907, which adopted nine new conventions and declarations dealing with various matters not considered at the first conference or concerning which no agreement had been reached, such as the beginning of hostilities, conversion of merchant vessels into warships, status of enemy merchant vessels in port at the outbreak of war, naval bombardments, the use of submarine mines, the discharge of projectiles from balloons, restrictions on the right of capture in maritime warfare, the rights and duties of neutrals in time of war and the establishment of an international prize court. Altogether these conventions constituted the most elaborate body of conventional war law ever adopted, although there were a good many points on which no agreement had been reached and others upon which the agreements represented unsatisfactory compromises. Unfortunately in many instances in which the conventions purported to impose obligations upon belligerents these were largely nullified by qualifying phrases such as "where circumstances permit," "when the exigencies of military necessity permit" and the like. Moreover, as a result of the so-called solidarity clause in all of the conventions to the effect that they were not applicable except between the contracting parties and then only when all the belligerents were parties thereto, none of the conventions of 1907 were binding on any of the belligerents during the World War, because several of them had never ratified any of the conventions. The convention of 1899, however, respecting the laws and customs of war on land, of which the corresponding convention of 1907 was mainly a revision, had been ratified by all the belligerents and was therefore binding upon all of them. Those provisions of the 1907 conventions which were merely declaratory of existing customs and usages, as was true of many of them, were binding as customary law independently of the status of the conventions of which they were a part.

When the Second Hague Conference assembled in 1907, there was no conventional law dealing with the conduct of maritime warfare, aside from the brief rules contained in the Declaration of Paris of 1856. The first conference had not occupied itself at all with the subject. The program of the second conference apparently envisaged the preparation of a code of maritime war law which would supplement the rules governing land warfare adopted by the first conference; but although several conventions dealing with particular questions of maritime war were adopted, no comprehensive work of codification comparable to the land warfare convention was attempted.

The adoption of a convention providing for the establishment of an international prize court to apply "the rules of international law" in the absence of applicable treaty provisions accentuated the necessity for an agreement among the naval powers as to the rules of international law relative to maritime war since in the absence of such agreement the court itself would have to determine what those rules were. Great Britain in particular was unwilling that such power should be entrusted to a court composed of judges a majority of whom would certainly be opposed to the traditional views of that country. In order to settle controverted questions of maritime law and to provide a code of rules which the Prize Court would be bound to apply, a conference was held in London (1908–09) which framed the Declaration of London, dealing with the subjects of contraband, blockade, continuous voyages, destruction of neutral prizes, unneutral service and transfers of ships to neutral registries. An agreement was reached on all but two points of the program. Unfortunately the declaration never came into force, and the conventional law of maritime warfare has therefore remained unchanged. Those rules of the declaration which merely state the existing principles of customary law are, however, binding upon states without regard to the status of the declaration as a treaty.

The many controversies which were raised during the World War, especially in regard to the rights of neutrals, revealed the need of an agreement among the naval powers upon various matters of maritime war law. But a proposal by Senator Borah in 1928 for the calling of an international conference to codify the law did not meet with general favor and nothing came of it. In fact since the World War there has been little sentiment in favor of further attempts to codify the laws of warfare, the general feeling being that world effort should be directed toward the prevention of war rather than to attempts to regulate the processes by which it is carried on. Nevertheless, the horror aroused by the employment of certain instrumentalities and methods of destruction during the World War led to several attempts to outlaw their use by international agreements. Thus by an article of the treaty for the limitation and reduction of armaments signed at the Washington Disarmament Conference in 1922 the destruction of merchant vessels by submarines was condemned except when the crews and passengers of the former have been taken off and placed in safety. The treaty likewise condemned as a violation of international law the use in war of asphyxiating, poisonous or other gases and all analogous liquids, materials or devices. Because of France's failure to ratify the treaty it never came into force. At the London Conference of 1930 for the limitation and reduction of naval armament the condemnation of the employment of submarines was renewed (art. 22 of the treaty concluded), although without the provision for the punishment of violators on the same basis as pirates. In the meantime, by the so-called Poison Gas Protocol signed at Geneva in 1925, the condemnation of the use of gases, liquids and other materials mentioned in the Washington Treaty of 1922 was renewed and "bacteriological substances" were added. This protocol has been ratified by thirty-three states, including France. The Senate of the United States, however, refused to consent to its ratification, although urged by General Pershing and other high military and civil personages. In consequence of the failure of the United States to ratify it, the provisions of the protocol would not be binding on the United States in a war with one of the ratifying states.

The only other post-war achievements in the field of international regulation of the conduct of warfare were the conventions on the treatment of prisoners of war and for the amelioration of the condition of the wounded and sick of armies in the field, both signed at Geneva in 1929. They were framed by a conference of representatives of forty-seven countries called for the purpose of revising, in the light of the experience of the World War, the Hague regulations on the treatment of prisoners and the Geneva Red Cross convention of 1906. The convention on the treatment of prisoners of war is a veritable code of ninety-seven articles, many of which embody new rules whose general purpose is to set the highest standards of just and humane treatment of prisoners. Among other new rules laid down by the convention one forbids the practise of reprisals upon prisoners, which had been resorted to by some belligerents during the World War. The Red Cross convention, in thirty-nine articles, likewise aims to extend the safeguards of the earlier conventions of 1864 and 1906, both of which it supersedes. An important provision of both agreements is the stipulation that in case one of the belligerents is not a party to the convention, its provisions shall nevertheless be binding as between belligerents who are parties. Unlike the Hague conventions of 1907, they do not therefore cease to be binding on all belligerents the moment a state not a party becomes a belligerent.

There is little conventional international law and, by reason of its short history, little customary law for the conduct of aërial warfare. Airplanes were used for the first time during the

Turco-Italian War (1911–12) and the Balkan Wars (1912–13) for purposes of observation, signaling, transportation of dispatches and the distribution of proclamations and propaganda literature. During the World War they were employed for the first time on an extensive scale for attack and particularly for the dropping of bombs on towns and military works. The prediction is now commonly made by military experts that the wars of the future will be waged in large part in or from the air, and consequently it is highly important that the conduct of this mode of warfare should be regulated by internationally binding agreements. As yet, however, there are no international conventions dealing with the subject, aside from a declaration adopted by the Hague Conference of 1899, renewed in 1907, prohibiting the launching of projectiles and explosives from aircraft for a limited time, and article 25 of the Hague convention of 1907 respecting the laws and customs of war on land, which prohibits bombardments by whatever means of "undefended" towns, villages, dwellings or buildings. The convention of 1919 relative to international air navigation does not deal at all with the use of aircraft in war. A commission of jurists authorized by the Washington Conference of 1922, which sat from 1922 to 1923, drafted and adopted an excellent "code" of rules governing the conduct of air warfare, but no action has been taken upon it by any of the states represented on the commission. There seems in fact to be little disposition on the part of governments to take up the matter, apparently for the reason that any regulations which might be agreed upon would restrict the employment of an instrument whose potency and future possibilities were abundantly demonstrated during the World War. At present the only effective conventional rule in force which limits the use of aircraft for war purposes is the Poison Gas Protocol of 1925, which by implication forbids the aircraft of the signatory powers from disseminating gases, liquids and bacteriological substances as means of attack. As stated above, the United States has not as yet ratified this agreement. If the wars of the future are to be conducted in accordance with rules of law, there is an urgent need for revision, extension and adaptation of the existing rules to the new conditions under which they will have to be applied.

JAMES WILFORD GARNER

See: WAR; INTERNATIONAL LAW; DECLARATION OF PARIS; DECLARATION OF LONDON; HAGUE CONFERENCES; RED CROSS; NEUTRALITY; BELLIGERENCY; PRISONERS OF WAR; PRIZE; PRIVATEERING; ARMED MERCHANTMEN; CONTRABAND OF WAR; ANGARY; FREEDOM OF THE SEAS; ENEMY ALIEN; REPRISALS; ATROCITIES; LIMITATION OF ARMAMENTS; AVIATION, section on INTERNATIONAL ASPECTS.

Consult: Redslob, Robert, *Histoire des grands principes du droit des gens* (Paris 1923) p. 87–94, 150–57; Phillipson, C., *The International Law and Custom of Ancient Greece and Rome*, 2 vols. (London 1911) vol. ii, chs. xxii–xxvii; Hershey, A. S., *The Essentials of International Public Law and Organization* (rev. ed. New York 1927) p. 33–56 and pt. v; Walker, T. A., *A History of the Law of Nations* (Cambridge, Eng. 1899) p. 122–35, 188–95; Basdevant, Jules, *La Révolution française et le droit de la guerre continentale* (Paris 1901); Baty, T., and Morgan, J. H., *War; Its Conduct and Legal Results* (London 1915), especially pt. ii; Pillet, Antoine, *Les lois actuelles de la guerre* (2nd ed. Paris 1901); Bentwich, Norman, *The Law of Private Property in War* (London 1907); Wehberg, H., *Das Beuterecht im Land- und Seekriege* (Tübingen 1909), tr. by J. M. Robertson (London 1911); Spaight, J. M., *War Rights on Land* (London 1911); Hall, John A., *The Law of Naval Warfare* (2nd ed. London 1921); Dupuis, Charles, *Le droit de la guerre maritime d'après les doctrines anglaises contemporaines* (Paris 1899); Garner, J. W., *Prize Law during the World War* (New York 1927), *International Law and the World War*, 2 vols. (London 1920), *Recent Developments in International Law* (Calcutta 1925) p. 43–140, 164–81, 189–396, 723–52, 775–818, and "International Regulation of Air Warfare" in *Air Law Review*, vol. iii (1932) 103–26, 309–23; Comité International de la Croix-Rouge, *La protection des populations civiles contre les bombardements*, by A. Hammerskjöld and others (Geneva 1930); Fauchille, P., "Le bombardement aérien" in *Revue générale de droit international public*, vol. xxiv (1917) 56–74; Spaight, J. M., *Aircraft in War* (London 1914), *Air Power and War Rights* (2nd ed. London 1933), and *Air Power and the Cities* (London 1930).

WARREN, JOSIAH (1798–1874), American philosophical anarchist. Warren left Boston at the age of twenty for the west and had already established himself successfully as a self-made inventor, musician and small business man when Robert Owen's preaching drew him to the colony at New Harmony, Indiana. Two years of failure there led him to repudiate Owenite communism and to formulate his own opposite philosophy of "the sovereignty of the individual."

Warren took over Owen's theory of labor notes and was the first to put it into practise in a series of "equity stores." He also founded several relatively long lived anarchist communities of "sovereign individuals." He educated his own and other people's children with a freedom elsewhere unknown. All these activities he regarded merely as illustrations of his method.

Warren's philosophy was indigenous to pioneer America struggling against the invasion of industrial capitalism. He believed that each individual can be set free to pursue his own ends, free from economic monopoly and from government. To this end both the policeman and partnerships must go, for the "Sovereignty of the Individual over his or her Person, Time, Property and Reputation" is possible only when "the natural government of consequences is free to operate," i.e. when each person is being sovereign "at his own cost." Even community services must be furnished by individual enterprise. No individual, however, can be allowed to monopolize either natural resources or the fruits of talent. Demand is an unfair guide to men's needs—a tenet which Warren practised consistently, declining to hold land for appreciation and refusing to patent his inventions. The price and profit system, he held, must be altered to a basis of "cost the limit of price," i.e. with price never more than a reasonable reward for production costs, including time and expenses of training. Warren illustrated this principle in his equity store in Cincinnati, where each article was listed at its cost price plus a small overhead and the customer was charged extra by the clock for the storekeeper's actual time in handling.

Warren's philosophy is elaborated by Stephen P. Andrews in *The Science of Society* (2 vols., 3rd ed. New York 1854). Of his own writings there remain only the brief but pungent *Equitable Commerce* (New Harmony 1846; 3rd ed. by S. P. Andrews, New York 1852) and *True Civilization* (Boston 1863; 5th ed. by S. P Andrews, Princeton, Mass. 1875).

DOROTHY W. DOUGLAS

Consult: Bailie, William, *Josiah Warren* (Boston 1906); Conway, M. D., "Modern Times, New York" in *Fortnightly Review*, vol. i (1865) 421–34.

WARYŃSKI, LUDWIK TADEUSZ (1856–89), Polish socialist. Waryński, the founder of the socialist movement in Russian Poland, was born of Polish parents in the province of Kiev and was imbued with the tradition of Poland's struggles for independence. After studying for some time at the Technological Institute at St. Petersburg and at the agricultural institute at Puławy he worked under an assumed name as a fitter's apprentice in a factory in Warsaw in order to be near the workers and to influence them. From that time onward he devoted all his energies to disseminating the principles of socialism. Courageous to the point of recklessness, genial of manner and endowed with a capacity for forceful expression, he was instrumental in spreading the revolutionary movement from small groups of students to the entire working class. He was pursued by the Russian authorities and fled to Galicia, where he continued his revolutionary activities. In 1879 he was tried before the Austrian court in Cracow; ordered to leave Austrian territory he went to Geneva, where during a celebration of the fiftieth anniversary of the Polish insurrection of 1830 he made an impassioned protest against purely nationalistic ideals, insisting on the primacy of the social revolution. In 1881 he reappeared in Warsaw and began to work for the reconstruction of the socialistic movement, which had been completely undermined by four years of incessant arrests and reprisals. He was now under the influence of the Russian terrorist Narodnaya Volya. Conditions in his section of Poland were not, however, propitious for the prosecution of political terror, and Waryński substituted economic terror as the equivalent of strikes. This doctrine he introduced into the program of the recently formed revolutionary-socialistic party known as *Proletaryat*. His activities were widespread, supported as they were by the clumsy tactics of the Russian authorities, who suppressed an orderly strike at Żyrardów in which a number of workers were killed. Waryński was again arrested in 1883, when he was sentenced to sixteen years of imprisonment. He was kept in solitary confinement in the fortress of Schlüsselburg, where lack of food and insanitary prison conditions caused him to contract tuberculosis, from which he died. The influence of Waryński's ideas among the Polish socialists continued until 1894, when they discarded his negative attitude toward the struggle for Polish political independence and his policy of terrorism against industrial executives.

LUDWIK KRZYWICKI

Consult: Jędrzejewski, B. A., in *Światło*, vol. ii (1899) 97–115; Mazowiecki, Mieczysław, *Historya ruchu socyalistycznego w zaborze rosyjskim* (History of the socialist movement in Russian Poland), Polska Partya Socyalistyczna Proletaryat, no. 7 (Cracow 1903) chs. i–ii; Perl, F., *Dzieje ruchu socjalistycznego w zaborze rosyjskim* (History of the socialist movement in Russian Poland) (2nd ed. Warsaw 1932); Volkovicher, I., *Nachalo sotsialisticheskago rabochego dvizheniya v bivshey russkoy Polshe* (Origin of the socialist workers' movement in former Russian Poland) (Moscow 1925).

WASHINGTON, BOOKER TALIAFERRO (c. 1859–1915), American Negro educator and social reformer. Washington, who was a mulatto, was born a slave and educated at Hampton Institute. He grew up during the days of reconstruction and in 1881 became principal of Tuskegee Institute, then a small state school for Negroes in Alabama. American Negroes had long been trying to use their newly acquired political power in order to gain education and social advancement, but when their efforts were partially frustrated by the political developments of 1876 a period of bitter disillusion followed. In 1895 Washington at Atlanta enunciated a new economic philosophy for Negroes, urging them "to dignify and glorify common labor, and put brains and skill into the common occupations of life." In speeches made throughout the country he minimized political power and emphasized industrial education. For this purpose he collected money for Tuskegee, which he developed into a large and flourishing institution.

Difficulties arose, however, in the fulfilment of Washington's program. His truce with the whites was met in the south by a radical demand for a system of color caste instead of acceptance of the Negro as a citizen with eventual political rights. The Negro was practically disfranchised and segregated with inferior treatment and accommodations; a public stigma of inferiority was put legally on all persons of Negro blood. Many Negroes bitterly resented disfranchisement and the caste system and held Washington partly responsible for them. Negro labor was used as a non-union substitute for white labor at lower wages, which gave the unions an excuse for their already wide practise of excluding Negroes as members. Furthermore the changing techniques of industry throughout the United States led to the displacement of individual trades by machinery and mass production, so that it became increasingly difficult for industrial schools such as Tuskegee to teach current techniques. The condition of Negroes in industry did not improve therefore as rapidly as Washington's philosophy had anticipated.

Washington's net contribution was thus psychological rather than economic. He instilled into the Negroes a new respect for labor and impressed upon the whites the value of the Negro as a worker. His earnestness, shrewd common sense and statesmanlike finesse in interracial contacts mark his greatness; and Tuskegee Institute stands as his magnificent monument.

W. E. B. Du Bois

Works: *Up From Slavery* (New York 1901); *Selected Speeches*, ed. by E. D. Washington (New York 1932).
Consult: Scott, Emmett J., and Stowe, Lyman B., *Booker T. Washington; Builder of a Civilization* (New York 1916); Thrasher, M. B., *Tuskegee; Its Story and Its Work* (Boston 1900); Howe, M. A. De Wolfe, *Causes and Their Champions* (Boston 1926) ch. vii.

WASHINGTON, GEORGE (1732–99), first president of the United States. Washington's real education began with the disorganization of the family following his father's death; for several years thereafter, having no permanent home, he divided his time among his relatives on the lower Potomac, his mother's farm on the Rappahannock and his elder half brother's Mount Vernon estate. His early experiences with the Fairfax domain and as official surveyor of Culpeper county impressed upon him the importance of land as a source of wealth and power; and it was but natural, at a time when most large business enterprises of Virginia were land schemes of "gentlemen adventurers," that the scion of a family interested in the old Ohio Company should come to regard land as the honorable means of establishing family prestige and influence. These early impressions account for the later growth of Washington's comprehension of the importance of developing the western territory and for the place that the policy held in his public career. Living at a period when the governmental principles of England were being scrutinized and nowhere more searchingly than in the American colonies, Washington displayed a vigor of logic and a receptiveness equal to those of his most advanced contemporaries. Much of this receptiveness was due to personal experience with a stubborn royalist governor, to large commercial transactions with English merchants and to the minor, everyday legal controversies on which he sat in judgment as a colonial justice. His sense of right made him increasingly aware of the inefficiency, injustice and indifference of the crown toward the colonists and colonial affairs, and his military service on the Virginia frontier in protecting the inhabitants early developed in him the habit of thinking and laboring for the welfare of a people. The struggle to obtain the cooperation of Maryland and Pennsylvania in this frontier defense dissolved his provincialism and accustomed him to the idea of colonial union. Once convinced that the welfare of the colonies necessitated a greater degree of political liberty than was accorded by England, Washington devoted himself with unswerving singleness of purpose to achieving this objective. In the Revolutionary War his struggle with Congress to obtain an effective army is the most important chapter in the history of that movement. Hampered repeatedly by short-sighted and selfish factions in Congress and state legislatures, by the jealousy and personal ambitions of some of his subordinates, he maintained an indomitable fortitude and faith in the ultimate success of the American cause.

In victory his integrity and foresight guaranteed to the people the constitution which came from the convention over which he presided, and in whose deliberations he served as the balance wheel. His natural inclination to retire from the active political scene to his Virginia estates was overbalanced by the unanimity of the call of the people for his services as first president. In the new governmental experiment he succeeded, without the aid of guiding precedents, in giving the American democracy a healthy foundation and directional growth. In a situation which demanded above all else stability of government the new president had little sympathy with controversies over abstract principles of political theory and deprecated the Hamilton-Jefferson feud mainly because it stultified the national services of two competent men. He was intolerant of the personal animus involved. Since the revolution had been carried through successfully only by means of suppressing personal differences and by resort to compromise, it was incomprehensible to Washington that similar sacrifices could not be made when it was a question of the welfare of the nation which the revolution had created. He remained unimpressed by the doctrinaire radicalism of the Jeffersonians and came more and more to throw his influence on the side of the Federalists. The end of his public career saw the government he had been so largely instrumental in creating firmly established among the nations of the world.

JOHN C. FITZPATRICK

Works: *The Writings of George Washington*, ed. by W. C. Ford, 14 vols. (New York 1889–93); *The Writings of George Washington*, ed. by J. C. Fitzpatrick, vols. i–xii (Washington 1931–34); *The Diaries of George Washington*, ed. by J. C. Fitzpatrick, 4 vols. (Boston 1925).

Consult: Ford, P. L., *The True George Washington* (Philadelphia 1896); Lodge, H. C., *George Washington*, 2 vols. (Boston 1899); Ritter, Halsted L., *Washington as a Business Man* (New York 1931); Fitzpatrick, J. C., *George Washington Himself* (Indianapolis 1933); Farrand, Max, *The Fathers of the Constitution*, Chronicles of America series, vol. xiii (New Haven 1921); Wrong, G. M., *Washington and His Comrades in Arms*, Chronicles of America series, vol. xii (New Haven 1921); Prussing, Eugene E., *Estate of George Washington* (Boston 1927); Haworth, P. L., *George Washington, Farmer* (Indianapolis 1915).

WASTE is failure to utilize, or to utilize with equitable, prudent and maximum effectiveness, the means made available by nature for the satisfaction of human wants. It is through use of energies embodied in material things, such as foodstuffs, coal and raw materials of industry, and in human mental and manual skills that such wants are satisfied. Nature is a mass of energies and does not itself waste them, although it provides energy in only a limited number of forms suitable directly to satisfy human wants. In compensation nature has given man that distinguishing form of energy, intelligence, which empowers him to arrange other forms of energy. His failure to utilize his intelligence to that end creates the problem of waste, for man's wants have increased faster than his manifested competence to apply abundant natural energies to supplying them. The more important concrete forms of waste, or failure to appropriate and manipulate energies, may be summed up under the following classes: failure to utilize energies when they are available; to utilize them competently; to use a collateral energy released at the time a principal energy is utilized; to arrange energies in appropriate forms and at the proper times and places; to employ them in a quantity indicated by prudent requirement and use; to regard other energy losses accompanying the use of particular energies; to make suitable qualitative and quantitative combinations of energy; to balance present against future energy reserves and uses; to balance individual against collective uses of energy; to apply effectively in co-operative arrangement the collective use of that most valuable of all energies, man's own intelligence. These and other failures result in restricted realization of the want satisfactions potential in the energies made available by nature.

The distinction between waste and loss offers difficulties. For instance, a pioneer destroys a forest in order to get at fertile soil for crops. From his generation's point of view there is immediate net benefit and neither waste nor loss. Half a century later it is realized that for the long run social benefit it would have been better to preserve the forest. Some authorities classify the act as a social waste; others as a social loss but not a social waste. It is a matter of assumptions in definition.

Waste elimination is a problem fundamental to all social sciences. Since income is the simplest and most fundamental concept of economic science, elimination of the waste of sources of income is the very essence of the art of economics. Because such elimination involves choice, it is important also to ethics; and because proportion is involved, it has significance for aesthetics. Waste elimination is important likewise to sociology, inasmuch as social processes and relations are determined primarily by the modes of realizing income and the resultant weal.

It is one of those paradoxes of history that serious concern for waste as a social problem should have appeared only after society had entered upon an economy of potential abundance. In earlier periods of scarcity the opposites of waste, economy and thrift, were recognized as virtues but were regarded as an individual rather than a social matter. Not until well into the age of power machines, indirect methods of production, monetary valuations, traffic in incomplete products and vendibility as the primary object of production was it realized by many individual producers that the benefits of increasing production were being offset by the costs of increasing waste, and by social scientists that the total output of want satisfactions was progressively disproportionate to energy consumption and that these want satisfactions were not being distributed in a manner which promoted the highest potential standard of living.

The first noteworthy group concern for waste was evidenced by industrial owners and managers about the beginning of the twentieth century. They were interested in waste not as a social but as an individual plant problem. Somehow their margin between costs and sales income was becoming too narrow, and they were stimulated both to increase the salable products from a given lot of raw materials and to reduce their costs. The physical sciences, particularly chemistry, were summoned to the aid of industry; these taught industry how to salvage byproducts whose use values were previously unknown. The management movement, to the aid of which scientific management had brought measurement and analysis, was called upon to reduce the unit costs of processes and of management itself. Elimination of waste through research, standardization, planning, better knowledge of materials and improved control of production operations became the central interest of the management movement. In 1921 Herbert Hoover, as first president of the American Engineering Council, initiated a study of waste in industry. A sampling of six industries led to the conclusion that wastes were widespread, were the result of practises of long standing in industry and took the forms principally of low production caused by faulty management of materials, plant, equipment and men; interrupted production caused by idle men, idle materials and idle equipment; restricted production intentionally caused on the one hand by management's refusal to overproduce what the market would absorb at a price and on the other hand by labor's sabotage and strikes because of unsatisfactory working conditions; and lost production caused by ill health, physical defects and industrial accidents. In so far as assessment of responsibility could be made, the average for the six industries was determined to be approximately: management, 68 percent; labor, 16 percent; other influences, 16 percent.

Shortly after the beginning of the century there developed also a concern for waste as a social problem. This was manifested by specialists in public administration and in education, who focused attention on forest, mineral and other exhaustible natural resources; and by socialists, who seized upon the growing interest in waste as a new avenue of appeal for their doctrines. The agitation of these groups appears to have made but a slight impression at the time. Waste as a major social problem was not brought sharply to the fore until the World War, which was voracious in its consumption of materials, destroyed free international exchange of commodities and threw the participating countries back squarely on their own resources. It was then that the fact of waste was driven deep into the public mind.

During the period following the war the study of waste has been further intensified and the discussion raised to a higher plane. The depression which began in 1929 has caused statesmen as well as students to give more attention to the question of the waste caused by dissipation of human energy through absence of proper organization and coordination of the institutions and processes of the economic system. Not only have want satisfactions since 1929 amounted to only a fraction of what had been realized in more productive years, but strong evidence is being brought forward to show that they might have been far greater even in the most industrially active times and that the resultant satisfactions have progressively been less and less equitably distributed. Because of this and other aspects of the problem waste elimination has become a major social concern.

H. S. PERSON

See: PRODUCTION; LARGE SCALE PRODUCTION; EFficiency; Scientific Management; Conservation; Natural Resources.

Consult: Federated American Engineering Societies, Committee on Elimination of Waste in Industry, *Waste in Industry* (New York 1921); National Joint Council, Committee of Inquiry into Production, *The Waste of Capitalism* (London 1924); Labor College, Philadelphia, Conference for the Elimination of Waste in Industry, Symposium on Waste Elimination in *American Federationist*, vol. xxxiv (1927) 664–744; Koller, Theodor, *Handbuch der rationellen Verwerthung, Wiedergewinnung und Verarbeitung von Abfallstoffen jeder Art* (2nd ed. Vienna 1900), tr. as *The Utilization of Waste Products* (3rd ed. London 1918); Carver, T. N., *The Economy of Human Energy* (New York 1924); Taylor, Horace, *Making Goods and Making Money* (New York 1928); Talbot, Frederick A., *Millions from Waste* (London 1919); Chase, Stuart, *The Tragedy of Waste* (New York 1929), and *The Economy of Abundance* (New York 1934); Withers, Hartley, *Poverty and Waste* (2nd ed. London 1932); Hobson, J. A., *Work and Wealth* (new ed. London 1933); Howe, F. C., *The High Cost of Living* (New York 1917); Ely, Richard T., and others, *The Foundations of National Prosperity* (New York 1917); Nourse, Edwin G., and others, *America's Capacity to Produce*, Brookings Institution, Institute of Economics, Publication, no. 55 (Washington 1934); Gilbert, C. G., and Pogue, J. E., *America's Power Resources* (New York 1921); Van Hise, C. R., *The Conservation of Our Natural Resources* (rev. ed. enlarged by Loomis Havemeyer and others, New York 1930); Tugwell, Rexford Guy, *Industry's Coming of Age* (New York 1927); Columbia Commission, *Economic Reconstruction. Report* . . . (New York 1934); President's Committee on Social Trends, *Recent Social Trends in the United States*, 2 vols. (New York 1933) vol. i, ch. ii.

WASTE DISPOSAL. *See* Sanitation.

WATER LAW. Early records of man's culture include rules respecting the use of water. The Code of Hammurabi contained legislation dealing with dams, canals and water wheels; and Herodotus centuries before the Christian era contrasted the institutions of Egypt, Assyria and Persia dealing with irrigation. The experience of the Mediterranean peoples, generalized under the philosophical concepts of the classical Roman jurists and transmitted to the western world through the codification of Justinian, has guided the settlement of conflicts involving the use of springs, rivers, lakes and seas and the solution of the varied problems that arise from the nature of water.

Basic in the developed Roman law is the idea of property. All things, the Institutes declare, are the property of someone or of no one; by the law of nature the air, running water and the sea are common to all, *res communes*. The post-classical Roman jurists included also within this category the shores of public rivers and of the sea. Access to the seashore was open to all; and shelters might be built on the shore for purposes connected with the use of the sea, although the builder obtained no right to the soil. While the Roman jurists' theory of the community nature of running water and the sea continues to dominate modern law, the views expressed as to the seashore are not followed in England or in countries whose jurisprudence is based on the English common law. It is true that Bracton, writing in the thirteenth century about the laws and customs of England, included the seashore, with the air, the sea and running water, as *res communes*, but he was probably copying rather blindly from Roman texts. It is now well settled under the common law that the title to the shore between high and low water mark is in the proprietor of the land contiguous to the sea. The public may not enter without trespass. Access to the sea for fishing, bathing or other purposes may not be had without the owner's consent, express or implied. Beyond low water mark the title in England is in the crown and in the United States in the state. Littoral proprietors may construct wharves and other structures for the benefit of commerce and navigation, but in the absence of a grant from the sovereign such structures are subject to abatement by the sovereign as purprestures. Wharves or other projections which interfere with commerce are also subject to abatement as nuisances at the suit of private persons injured as well as through an action by the attorney general. The law of France and of other countries whose legal systems have been more influenced by Rome than has that of England continues with modifications to follow the Roman texts.

English law has abandoned also the Roman law distinction between public and private rivers and has classed rivers as navigable and non-navigable. The test of navigability has been involved in some doubt. Some judges and legal authors have said that only those streams in which the tide ebbs and flows are navigable. A more liberal rule has been adopted, especially in the United States, whereby rivers and lakes navigable in fact although not tidal are classed as navigable. An important result has been that the great fresh water lakes and rivers of the United States have been brought under the admiralty jurisdiction. The rights of the public in respect to navigation and fishing in such streams and lakes have been extended, while the federal government has secured the power to control and regulate such waters in the general interest. With respect to the title of the beds of navigable streams diversity exists among the states of the union. Most of the states hold that the title is in the state, but there are several in which the riparian proprietor owns the bed of the stream to the middle of the river. It may thus happen that riparian proprietors on opposite sides of streams forming state boundaries may have different rights in the bed. Problems upon which Ulpian, Paul and Celsus differed with respect to the ownership of islands formed in midstream are presented to the courts in the United States. Anglo-American law has been to some extent confused with respect to the law of the foreshore and navigable waters by the injection of political claims in texts possessing authority. A seventeenth century tract, *De jure maris*, frequently attributed to Sir Matthew Hale but condemned by some as the work of an unknown author, is especially chargeable with causing doubt and difficulty.

While there may be some uncertainty with respect to the riparian proprietor's rights of ownership in beds of navigable streams, the law with respect to his rights in those of nonnavigable streams is clear. His ownership is extended to the bed of the middle of the stream or, if he owns both banks, to the whole bed of the stream within his boundaries. He may exclude all persons from entering any portion of the river for fishing, bathing or other purposes. He enjoys a monopoly of these privileges resulting from the position of his land with respect to the river. The gradual recession of the stream will not rob him of his advantages. On the other hand, while he is entitled to additions to his land made gradually and imperceptibly, the benefit of accretion or alluvion is offset to some extent by the risk that the stream may suddenly change its course. Within reasonable limits he may protect his banks against the possibility of injury, but he must be careful not to injure his neighbors by such protective measures. His rights in this respect are correlative with those of other riparian proprietors.

The correlative nature of the riparian occupier's rights is strongly illustrated by a consideration of his rights as to the use of the water running in a stream over or in front of his land. Every other occupier of lands upon the stream may demand that the former's use of the water shall not materially affect its natural flow and may insist upon the maxim *aqua currit, et debet currere ut currere solebat ex jure naturae*, even though he suffer no actual damage from his neighbor's use of the waters. A riparian proprietor may use a reasonable quantity of water from the stream for purposes connected with his occupation of the land—for domestic needs, for watering his cattle, irrigating his land or running his mill—but he may not sell any part of the water to third persons or carry it to lands of his own which do not constitute a parcel of the land contiguous to the stream. He must return to the stream the residue of water that he has taken for irrigating his crops or for running his mill, and he must not pollute the stream so that the water will be useless or injurious for other occupiers on the stream. If he conveys his frontage on the stream he loses all privilege as to the use of the water; if he retains a frontage, however small, he may continue to use the water upon his land. The doctrine of correlative rights in water applies under the law of England only to occupiers and owners upon rivers or streams. It has no application to so-called percolating waters, underground waters not flowing in a defined course. The English courts have gone so far as to hold that a man may sink a well upon his property with the sole motive of destroying a neighbor's well supplied from percolating waters. Some American courts have refused to follow this declaration respecting percolating waters and have held that such waters should be governed by the principle of correlative rights of user by the proprietors of the overlying land.

The maxim *debet currere* has application only to running water. Rain water falling upon an occupier's land may be stored; while stored it ceases to be *res communis* and becomes the property of the captor. But the right of property is qualified, like that of capture of a wild beast. If it escapes, another may take it; and the first captor has no claim for its recovery. The French *Code civil* as originally adopted, which was largely influenced by Pothier's speculations, applied the principles respecting rain water to springs issuing upon one's land. The owner of the land whence the spring issued might use the water as he pleased or sell it to others. In 1898 legislation reduced his right to the privilege of using the water upon his own land and forbade its sale to third persons. Judicial decisions, legislation and the rules of administrative tribunals have further modified the spring owner's privileges by authorizing its taking for the use of urban communities, leaving him a claim for indemnity. The extensive rights of use and ownership, recognized in the *Code civil*, have thus been limited in practise to springs of minor importance.

The story of the law regarding springs under the *Code civil* is typical of modern tendencies in the law of waters. The riparian proprietor's right to demand that water flow past his land substantially unimpaired in volume was not unsuited to a settled agricultural community where there was abundant rainfall and little need for conservation of water. With the growth of great cities, incident to the development of machinery, the necessity arose for the avoidance of waste of water; and inevitably the control of natural resources tended to fall into the hands of administrative bodies representing the public interest. This tendency, although it has been operating for a long time, has since the beginning of the present century proceeded with accelerated force and has been in harmony with political and economic theories concerning social obligations and the distribution of property. An example of a code of water law embodying modern principles is the *Wassergesetz* of Prussia. There is scarcely a country, however, which has not by its legislation established rules, with boards and officials to enforce them, regarding the use and control of water.

The system of correlative rights to the use of flowing waters is known as the system of riparian right. It was not settled as the law of France until the adoption of the *Code civil*; and it seems that it was then given currency in the United States by Story and Kent, who were both acquainted with the writings of the civilians. As a result it became also the law of England but not until almost the middle of the nineteenth century. The acceptance of the doctrine of riparian right by the English courts is thus an example of English reception of American law. Because of this international assimilation the law of waters in both common and civil law countries shows few fundamental divergences. In Germany, unlike France, the law of waters is not governed by the general Civil Code but is left to regulation by the individual German states.

Contrasted with the system of riparian right is the system of prior appropriation. This developed in some of the arid and semi-arid regions of the United States and is an interesting example of the evolution of legal rules from physical conditions and necessities. Under this system the person who first puts water to a beneficial use, as by raising crops or washing ore, retains his right to use the water so long as he continues such use. He may diminish the flow of the stream or carry it away from its watershed so that its benefits are lost to other owners or occupiers on the stream. Under this system the first in time is first in right, but his right may be lost by failure to make use of his privilege. If the riparian system is based upon equality and correlative rights among landowners on a stream, the appropriation system rests upon the assertion of the rights of the individual based upon a claim by capture. The appropriation system could develop only in a state of society where the notion of individualism was strongly emphasized and where rights of property were faintly recognized. In fact it was born upon the public lands of the United States, where the policy of the government favored settlers, even if they entered upon the lands without express authority. Necessity forced the recognition of the first taker, the miner who staked his claim without any other claim of right than his discovery of ore and with his own hands dug canals or built rude sluice boxes to conduct from a neighboring stream the water necessary for his simple mining operations. The customs of pioneer mining camps recognized the claims of prior occupation and labor devoted to a useful end; and what the customs established was subsequently made legal by an act of Congress passed in 1866, recognizing the rights of settlers on the public lands of the United States to divert water from the streams for beneficial use. It is not a matter for surprise that a system which was the offspring of pioneer individualism in its most extreme form tends to develop into monopoly, with its exclusion of individual activity, where water is diverted for large undertakings, such as the supply of water and power for urban and industrial needs. Collective or public control of the water supply becomes an essential need to effect some degree of fairness in distribution of water between town and country, between farmer and industrialist, and to preserve a proper balance in the development of the community. The law of waters gives way to the administration of the water supply.

ORRIN K. McMURRAY

See: IRRIGATION; FLOODS AND FLOOD CONTROL; WATERWAYS, INLAND; TERRITORIAL WATERS; RECLAMATION; WATER SUPPLY.

Consult: Ossig, Alfred, *Römisches Wasserrecht* (Leipsic 1898); Costa, Emilio, *Le acque nel diritto romano* (Bologna 1919); Buckland, W. W., *A Text-Book of Roman Law* (2nd ed. Cambridge, Eng. 1932) p. 262–67; Picard, A. M., *Traité des eaux*, 5 vols. (Paris 1890–

95; vols. i–ii, 2nd ed. 1896); Schmidt, Walter, "Wasserrecht," and "Gewässer, öffentliche" in *Handwörterbuch der Rechtswissenschaft*, ed. by F. Stier-Somlo and Alexander Elster, 7 vols. (Berlin 1926–31) vol. vi, p. 788–99, and vol. ii, p. 904–07, and bibliography there cited; Planiol, M. F., *Traité élémentaire de droit civil*, 3 vols. (9th ed. Paris 1922–24) vol. i, p. 748–53; Colin, A. V. C., and Capitant, Henri, *Cours élémentaire de droit civil français*, 3 vols. (5th–6th ed. Paris 1928–30) vol. i, p. 728–43; Vitale, Antonio, *Il regime delle acque nel diritto pubblico e privato italiano* (Milan 1920); Cruzado Sanz, Félix, *Legislación y jurisprudencia de aguas* (Madrid 1916); Angell, J. K., *A Treatise on the Law of Watercourses* (7th ed. by J. C. Perkins, Boston 1877); Pomeroy, J. N., *A Treatise on the Law of Water Rights* (rev. ed. by H. C. Black, St. Paul 1893); Gould, J. N., *A Treatise on the Law of Waters* (Chicago 1900); Farnham, H. P., *The Law of Waters and Water Right*, 3 vols. (Rochester 1904); Wiel, Samuel Charles, *Water Rights in the Western States*, 2 vols. (3rd ed. San Francisco 1911); Moore, S. A., *A History of the Foreshore and the Law Relating Thereto* (London 1888); Fitzgerald, J. V. V., *The Law Affecting the Pollution of Rivers and Water Generally* (London 1902); Coulson, H. J. W., *The Law Relating to Waters* (4th ed. by H. S. Moore, London 1924); Walton, D. T., "Origin and Growth of Western Irrigation Law" in *Illinois Law Review*, vol. xxi (1926–27) 127–41; Treadwell, E. F., "Modernizing the Water Law" in *California Law Review*, vol. xvii (1928–29) 1–18; Hawkins, Wallace, "Water Rights in United States-Mexico Streams" in *Temple Law Quarterly*, vol. v (1930–31) 193–207; Carman, E. C., "Is There a New Era in the Law of Interstate Waters?," and "Sovereign Rights and Regulations in the Control and Use of American Waters" in *Southern California Law Review*, vol. v (1931–32) 25–35, and vol. iii (1929–30) 84–100, 152–72, 266–319; Bannister, L. W., "Interstate Rights in Interstate Streams in the Arid West" in *Harvard Law Review*, vol. xxxvi (1922–23) 960–86; Lasky, Moses, "From Prior Appropriation to Economic Distribution of Water by the State—Via Irrigation Administration" in *Rocky Mountain Law Review*, vol. i (1928–29) 161–216, 248–70, and vol. ii (1929–30) 35–58; Shields, J. F., "The Federal Power Act" in *University of Pennsylvania Law Review*, vol. lxxiii (1924–25) 142–57; Wiel, S. C., "'Priority' in Western Water Law" in *Yale Law Journal*, vol. xviii (1908–09) 189–98, "Running Water" in *Harvard Law Review*, vol. xxii (1908–09) 190–215, "Public Control of Irrigation" in *Columbia Law Review*, vol. x (1910) 506–19, "Public Policy in Western Water Decisions," and "A Short Code of Underground Water" in *California Law Review*, vol. i (1912–13) 11–31, and vol. ii (1913–14) 25–33, "Theories of Water Law" in *Harvard Law Review*, vol. xxvii (1913–14) 530–44, "Water Titles of Corporations and Their Consumers," and "What Is Beneficial Use of Water?" in *California Law Review*, vol. ii (1913–14) 273–90, and vol. iii (1914–15) 460–75, "Mingling of Waters" in *Harvard Law Review*, vol. xxix (1915–16) 137–57, "Origin and Comparative Development of the Law of Watercourses in the Common Law and in the Civil Law," "Political Water Rights," "Europeanizing the State Constitution—the Water and Power Amendment," "Unregistered Water Appropriations at Law and in Equity," "The Pending Water Amendment to the California Constitution and Possible Legislation" in *California Law Review*, vol. vi (1917–18) 245–67 and 342–71, vol. x (1921–22) 111–19, vol. xii (1923–24) 454–62, vol. xiv (1925–26) 427–40, vol. xvi (1927–28) 169–207 and 257–80, "Need of Unified Law for Surface and Underground Water" in *Southern California Law Review*, vol. ii (1928–29) 358–69, "The Recent Attorneys' Conference on Water Legislation" in *California Law Review*, vol. xvii (1928–29) 197–213; Brown, R. G., "The Conservation of Water-Powers" in *Harvard Law Review*, vol. xxvi (1912–13) 601–30, "The Golden Rule as a Maxim of the Modern Law of Water Rights" in *American Law Review*, vol. lvi (1922) 401–21, and "The Water-Power Problem in the United States" in *Yale Law Journal*, vol. xxiv (1914–15) 12–33; Taft, H. W., "State Control of Navigable Waters" in *Columbia Law Review*, vol. xv (1915) 417–32; Coudert, F. R., "Riparian Rights; a Perversion of Stare Decisis" in *Columbia Law Review*, vol. ix (1909) 217–37; Bannister, L. W., "The Question of Federal Disposition of State Waters in the Priority States" in *Harvard Law Review*, vol. xxviii (1914–15) 270–93; Fairlie, J. A., "Public Regulation of Water Power in the United States and Europe" in *Michigan Law Review*, vol. ix (1910–11) 463–83; Parsons, G. S., "Public and Private Rights in the Foreshore" in *Columbia Law Review*, vol. xxii (1922) 706–35; Clayberg, J. B., "The Law of Percolating Waters" in *Michigan Law Review*, vol. xiv (1915–16) 119–34; Hunt, W. H., "Law of Water Rights" in *Yale Law Journal*, vol. xvii (1907–08) 585–88; Howell, Roger, "Federal Power of Legislation as to the Development of Water Power" in American Law Review, vol. l (1916) 883–900; Hornbeck, S. K., "Federal Control of Water Power in Switzerland" in *American Political Science Review*, vol. iii (1908–09) 86–87; Hess, R. H., "Arid-Land Water Rights in the United States" in *Columbia Law Review*, vol. xvi (1916) 480–95.

WATER POWER. *See* ELECTRIC POWER.

WATER SUPPLY. In primitive times men always selected their abodes with reference to some natural supply of pure fresh water. In the semi-arid Mediterranean world of antiquity the original sites of cities were more than ordinarily influenced by the scarcity of natural sources of supply. At an early period men learned the art of digging wells, but without modern well boring machinery locations for hand dug wells were limited. Some ancient wells were, it is true, of great size and depth. "Joseph's Well" in Cairo was 297 feet deep; for the first 165 feet it was 18 by 24 feet, and for the rest of its depth it was 9 by 15 feet. China had wells reputed to be 1500 feet in depth. But these were exceptional. Some cities developed cisterns for the storage of rain water; the underground reservoirs of ancient Carthage were justly celebrated.

It remained, however, for the Romans to develop the art of water supply to the point where cities could be freed from the limitations upon their growth imposed by the poverty of local water resources. Until about the fourth century B.C. Rome obtained its water from the Tiber and from local springs and wells. The first Roman aqueduct was built about 312 B.C. and the last about 305 A.D. Between these dates 14 aqueducts were constructed having an aggregate length of 359 miles, about 50 miles of which were supported on arches. During the early days of the empire the daily per capita consumption, according to a conservative estimate, was 50 gallons; this compares favorably with the daily consumption of many European cities of today.

The Roman conduits varied in size from 3 to 8 feet in height and from $2\frac{1}{2}$ to 5 feet in width. The sides were straight and the roof was slightly arched. Ordinarily the conduits were built of masonry and finished on the inside with a smooth impervious cement. The water was brought from the mountains to the city, where it passed as a rule into sedimentation basins, from which it was carried to small reservoirs or cisterns, which had numerous outlets. These in turn supplied the great number of public fountains and baths at which most of the population obtained water; private house connections were few. The quality of the water furnished by different aqueducts varied greatly, but the distributing cisterns were so arranged that only the better waters were used for domestic purposes. Another interesting feature of the Roman water system was the overlapping of the supply from different sources, so that an aqueduct could be shut off for repairs without depriving any part of the city of water. Some of the aqueducts are still in use. Besides these large works for Rome itself the Romans built many other important water supply systems for cities throughout the empire. Paris, Lyons, Metz, Segovia and Seville all had water systems. Part of the system for Metz is still in use after 1800 years. During the Middle Ages the waterworks of most of these cities fell into ruin. Generally speaking, the cities of the Middle Ages got their water from local sources which were insufficient in quantity and frequently seriously polluted. It was not until the end of the sixteenth century that there was renewed progress in water supply.

The development of pumps was of course a necessary preliminary to large public water supplies in flat countries. The first pumps were installed at Hanover in 1527. In 1582 a water power pump was set up on London Bridge, and it supplied water to that city through lead pipes. Similar pumps were constructed in Paris in 1608; and in 1624 an aqueduct was completed which brought 200,000 gallons of water to the city daily. At the end of the seventeenth century the Paris water supply amounted to $2\frac{1}{2}$ quarts per capita per day. In 1619 the New River Company was incorporated to supply London with water from the New River. At this time the practise of furnishing water to individual houses was inaugurated. The eighteenth century contributed the steam pump to the extension of waterworks. The first such installation was in London in 1761 and was followed by two in Paris in 1781 and 1783 and a second in London in 1787. It remained for the nineteenth century, however, to provide the great modern water supplies which make urban living tolerable today.

The development of satisfactory water systems for large cities has been accompanied by the supplanting of private by public enterprise. The fact that until the twentieth century the great metropolis of London had no satisfactory supply of this prime necessary indicates the relative timidity of private initiative with regard to the problem. At present virtually every large city in the world is supplied with water by public enterprise. A city must have an abundant supply of water whether this can be made commercially profitable or not. The capital investment necessary is very large and social and sanitary reasons call for the sale of water at low rates. Furthermore the city is always a very large user of water for public purposes, and a "stand by" service—a surplus over the needs for all other purposes—must be maintained for fire protection. The administration of a water department, once the plant has been provided, is relatively simple. All these considerations have prevailed to make water supply a public business. In no field of public endeavor have greater vision and courage been demonstrated than in the development of the water systems of cities like New York, Glasgow and Los Angeles.

In a modern city water must be supplied for four distinct uses. First, it is required for domestic use; that is, for drinking, cooking, bathing, washing and general household needs as well as for watering lawns and gardens. The amount of water consumed daily for domestic purposes varies greatly with the different classes of residential property. The poorest districts will have a daily per capita consumption of 15 to 20 gallons, while the wealthiest districts will use 60 to 70 gallons or more. Apartment houses have a high rate of consumption equal to or exceeding the rate for first class dwellings. Ordinarily with metered service the daily domestic consumption for a city as a whole is between 20 and 50 gallons per capita with a tendency toward the higher figure.

A second important use is for industry and commerce. Average figures for this class are of slight significance because the consumption varies greatly with the type of industry. Commercial establishments in large cities show a relatively stable consumption, falling ordinarily between 8 and 12 gallons per capita. Industrial consumption, on the other hand, varies from 10 to 50 or more gallons per capita depending on the nature and extent of the industry.

The third demand is for fire protection. In fact relatively little water is thus consumed, but there must be a permanent, or stand by, provision in excess of the maximum requirements for other purposes. Except in the very smallest places, however, fire protection depends not on the size of the supply but on a distribution system so arranged as to conduct a sufficient amount of water to every potential fire. Separate systems of mains carrying a pressure as high as 300 pounds per square inch are employed for fire protection in the business districts of some cities. Sea water or water from polluted sources can be used for this purpose; the high pressure system is usually maintained by the fire department independently of the normal water supply of the city.

Water is needed, in the fourth place, for other public purposes—schools, hospitals, public buildings, public or private charitable institutions, parks, cemeteries, street and sewer flushing and various minor uses. The amount consumed for such purposes varies to a large extent with the amount required for street and sewer flushing. From 5 to 15 gallons per capita is a reasonable limit for public uses, the average being about 10 gallons per capita.

In addition an appreciable portion of the water supply is lost or wasted; and under the most efficient management about 20 percent of the water will be unaccounted for. The normal leakage even in new pipe is 100 gallons or more per day per mile for every inch diameter of pipe. New York City aqueduct specifications limit such leakage to 240 gallons a day per mile per inch diameter. Added to this is the leakage that will develop in the system as it grows older, as a result of settling, worn valves and hydrants and undetected breaks. There are further losses where the service is unmetered and carelessness on the part of consumers results. The advantages of the use of meters over a system of flat rate charges are obvious. These are shown by the excessive consumption averages in cities without meters, on the one hand, and by the reduction in per capita consumption after meters have been installed, on the other. The effects of metering on water consumption are shown in the following table.

The usual sources of water for a large city are surface water, which is obtained from streams or lakes, and ground water, which is derived from wells. Ground water as a rule is clear and palatable, but it also frequently contains large quantities of mineral matter in solution; this latter characteristic renders it objectionable for cooking, laundry and some industrial uses. The bacteria content of ground water is ordinarily low, so that from the health aspect little purification is needed. Ground water, however, is not often found in sufficient quantities to meet the needs of any large community. Surface water contains less mineral matter in solution than ground water, but it is more turbid and usually more contaminated from sewage or from human

AVERAGE DAILY CONSUMPTION OF WATER IN VARIOUS AMERICAN CITIES, 1890, 1905, 1920

CITY	1890 PERCENTAGE METERED	1890 CONSUMPTION PER CAPITA (IN GALLONS)	1905 PERCENTAGE METERED	1905 CONSUMPTION PER CAPITA (IN GALLONS)	1920 PERCENTAGE METERED	1920 CONSUMPTION PER CAPITA (IN GALLONS)
Detroit	2.1	161	9.0	188	97.4	144
Boston	5.0	80	5.0	151	73.0	126
Cleveland	5.8	103	68.0	137	98.0	121
San Francisco	41.4	61	21.0	96	100.0	60
Cincinnati	4.1	112	12.0	130	98.0	119
Nashville	0.8	146	52.0	148	87.0	99
Beloit, Wis.	10.0	64	—	130	100.0	82
Melrose, Mass.	1.7	71	3.0	112	100.0	61

Source: Turneaure, F. E., and Russell, H. L., *Public Water-Supplies* (3rd ed. New York 1924) p. 23.

habitations on the watershed from which it is drawn. Surface water also is likely to be discolored when it originates on watersheds covered with dense vegetation. The lakes and streams near large cities or in any thickly populated area are always seriously polluted, so that many cities are obliged either to purify a local water supply or to draw water from a great distance. Cities located on the Great Lakes or on the major rivers of the United States usually depend on the purification of the abundant supply close at hand. Detroit, Cleveland, Chicago, Pittsburgh and St. Louis belong in this class. Other cities, of which New York, Boston, Los Angeles and San Francisco are examples, have gone to great expense to impound the waters of distant watersheds. These comparatively pure water supplies need little if any additional treatment.

There are four elements of impurity which are ordinarily present in water in some degree, any or all of which it may be desirable to remove; these are turbidity, color, mineral salts and bacteria. Turbidity and color may not be harmful to health, but as a rule they are eliminated to comport with modern standards of cleanliness. Water containing mineral salts may not be unpalatable; but if the mineral content is too large, the water will be objectionable to industrial users and will damage pipes and domestic appliances. The most important impurity of course is the presence of bacteria. The relation of pure water to public health has been appreciated only since the general acceptance of the germ theory of disease; it is interesting, however, to note that the means of purification were all in use and had been tested in practise before the presence of germs was known.

Perhaps the oldest treatment of water has been by sedimentation. The Romans used it to some extent, particularly for turbid waters. Sedimentation consists of stopping or reducing the flow of the water to allow sand, clay and other inorganic matter held in suspension to settle. Coagulants are ordinarily used after a short period of plain sedimentation has allowed the coarser matter to settle. By the use of coagulants a high percentage of suspended matter can be removed in a few hours. The coagulant also eliminates considerable quantities of bacteria. Sedimentation with or without coagulants is usually insufficient in itself to remove enough bacteria to make the water safe if seriously polluted, and additional means of purification are ordinarily employed.

The customary treatments for bacteria are filtration and disinfection. Disinfection usually is accomplished by the use of chloride of lime and, more recently, by liquid chlorine. The process of purification by means of chlorine is still something of a mystery, but it has proved effective on waters of low bacterial content. Chlorination is inexpensive and easy to apply. Ozone, or atmosphere which has been subject to high voltage electrical charges, is also used as a disinfectant in a few European cities. It is effective when it can be brought in contact with the bacteria, but satisfactory mixing devices have not been developed and the cost of the process is high. Ultraviolet rays may also be used as a sterilizing agent; but the equipment is costly and demands constant attention, so that the method is employed only on a small scale, in swimming pools, hotels and the like.

Filtration is now used almost everywhere to purify the supply when derived from surface water. Early in the nineteenth century filters on a small scale were employed at Paris to purify water taken from the Seine. The first large sand filter, similar to those now in use, was placed in operation by the Chelsea Water Company in London in 1829. After 1875 the use of filters spread rapidly throughout Europe; in the United States this development took place largely after 1900. Whereas in 1890 only 1.5 percent of the country's urban population was supplied with filtered water, by 1914 the proportion had reached 40 percent.

The principal purposes of filtration are the removal of visible suspended matter, that is, turbidity, and of bacteria. For both of these purposes filtration is effective. Two types of filter are in general use. The slow sand filter, in which the water is flowed on to large beds of graded sand gravel and rock, through which it percolates by gravity or under very slight pressure, operates at a rate of from 2,000,000 to 6,000,000 gallons per acre per day. The rapid filter, consisting of air tight metal tanks containing beds of sand and gravel through which water is forced, operates at from 100,000,000 to 125,000,000 gallons per acre per day. With a rapid filter a coagulant must be used to remove the major part of the suspended matter. Where the water is of high turbidity, a coagulant is necessary with either type of filter; and since the rapid filter costs less to construct and requires less space, it is gradually displacing the slower type.

The efficiency of the two types of filter in

removing bacteria is approximately equal. A bacterial efficiency of better than 99 percent is to be expected from a well operated filter of either class. A bacterial count of less than 100 per cubic centimeter is generally considered to be a good result. Evidence of the bacterial efficiency of filters is to be found in the decrease in the morbidity rates from typhoid fever.

Besides the removal of suspended matter and bacteria, it is sometimes necessary to eliminate certain mineral salts because of the odor, flavor, color or the quality of hardness which they may impart to the water. These salts are usually bicarbonates and sulphates of magnesium and calcium. Various chemicals may be employed to remove these salts by reacting with them to form insoluble salts which will precipitate. Lime in the form of milk of lime is quite commonly used for this purpose. For small industrial and domestic plants zeolite is used; in the process the water is passed through a filter of this material and the magnesium or calcium is replaced by sodium. The zeolite can be regenerated if the process is reversed and a solution of common salt is used. The existence of iron compounds in the water is even more objectionable than other minerals in its effect on color and taste; where these are present the so-called "iron bacteria," or *Crenothrix polyspora*, will be found. These bacteria cause deposits in the pipes which may seriously disrupt the distribution system as well as create a disagreeable odor and taste. Aëration is the most common means of removing such iron compounds; here the oxygen in the air reacts with the iron compound to form an insoluble precipitate.

Aëration is used also to remove other disagreeable odors or flavors. It may be accomplished by a number of different means, depending on the amount of oxygen which must be introduced into the water. Exposure in settling basins or passage over weirs may be sufficient. Common devices involve introduction of oxygen under pressure or passing the water through a system of sprayers.

The counterpart of the removal of bacteria for the protection of public health is the addition of iodine to prevent goiter, particularly in regions where that disease is prevalent. The experiment has been tried in Rochester, Sault Ste. Marie, Cleveland and Cincinnati, but it has not been carried out long enough to supply conclusive results. It is known, however, that goiter is common where the iodine in the water supply is low. It is a question whether the consumption of iodine with food is not more efficacious than treatment of water supply.

In planning a water supply system the seasonal, daily and hourly variations in consumption must be considered as well as the average daily consumption. These variations depend to a great extent on the character and location of the city, so that no general rule is of much value. Of course consumption during the daylight hours is much greater than at night. The minimum consumption ordinarily occurs between one and four a.m. and is about 50 to 60 percent of the average for the day, while the maximum is usually between eight and ten a.m.; consumption then drops off slowly until five or six p.m., when the rate falls rapidly until about midnight. The maximum hourly rate will be about 160 percent of the average for the day and about 200 to 225 percent of the yearly average.

The monthly or seasonal variation differs greatly with location and climatic conditions. Ordinarily there will be a period of heavy consumption during the summer months because of lawn and street sprinkling. There is also a secondary peak of consumption during the winter months in cold climates because of the waste of water to prevent freezing. The maximum monthly consumption will seldom be more than 125 percent of the average, although under unusual circumstances it may be considerably higher. The maximum daily and weekly rates will ordinarily be reached during the month of maximum consumption.

A knowledge of these variations for a particular city is essential to the design of a water supply system on an economical basis. The system must be capable of furnishing water at the maximum rate of consumption, but it would be uneconomical to construct pumps and filters and the like of sufficient size to operate at this maximum rate where the variation is large. Storage facilities are necessary to tide over the periods of high consumption for either long or short intervals.

The administration of water supply in American cities has usually been entrusted to a board of from three to seven members, appointed by the chief executive, frequently for long and overlapping terms. A tendency, however, has been manifest in recent years, especially in connection with the newer forms of city government, to substitute for the board a single commissioner, or director. The construction of great water systems has sometimes been carried on by the regular water department of the city but very often by special boards appointed for the purpose. A board is valuable chiefly in the developmental stage, when important questions are to be decided. The daily administration of a water system is one of the simpler tasks of city administration and can readily be handled by a single head. A relatively small staff of engineers to deal with the technical problems of filtration, a few workmen to perform the labor at the filter, the necessary inspectors to check waste in the use of water, a repair gang or gangs, a corps of meter readers and a bookkeeping and office force sufficient to make out water bills and receive collections are all the personnel required; the last two categories represent the great majority of employees in water departments.

Water rates should ordinarily be so fixed that the income from them balances the outlay for operation and debt service. Rates are nearly always regressive, so that the larger users of water pay a lower unit price. This is commonly considered good practise, both because unit cost tends to decrease as use increases and because it encourages the growth of industry in the city. Since water is essential to health and sanitation, it may be advisable in some cities with large slum areas to encourage its use by reducing rates to less than the operating costs. In such cases the rate should not be based on ability to pay but should be a straight unit rate and the deficit should be made up out of tax revenues. Where meters are not in use, various rough expedients are employed to arrive at water rates, such as the frontage of the property, the number of taps, floor space of buildings, the number of occupants or various combinations of such criteria. Metered service at reasonable rates is a deterrent to waste of water but does not discourage its proper use.

The collection of water rates is enforced in two ways: first, by shutting off the water of delinquent users; second, by adding the unpaid water bill of the owner of the property at the end of the tax year to the next year's tax bill. The first method is much the more efficacious but is forbidden for sanitary reasons by the laws of some states. It is not unusual to offer a premium for the prompt payment of bills and to add penalties when payment is delayed.

Waterworks construction is generally financed by long term bonds. These bonds are usually a general obligation of the city, although in some instances they are secured by a mortgage on the water system. The better practise is to pay principal and interest from earnings, but paying them from taxation is not uncommon. It is not usually considered necessary for publicly owned waterworks to earn money to cover depreciation as well as to pay off their bonds, complete reproduction of the plant being cared for by new bond issues. For this reason and also because cities need earn no profit for stockholders and can in normal times borrow money at low rates of interest, water rates can be kept low; these factors also make water bonds an unusually safe investment.

THOMAS H. REED

See: SANITATION; PUBLIC HEALTH; COMMUNICABLE DISEASES, CONTROL OF; CITY; METROPOLITAN AREAS.

Consult: Turneaure, F. E., and Russell, H. L., *Public Water-Supplies* (3rd ed. New York 1924); Horwood, M. P., *The Sanitation of Water Supplies* (Springfield, Ill. 1932); Burton, W. K., *The Water Supply of Towns*, 2 vols. (4th ed. London 1928); Babbitt, H. E., and Doland, J. J., *Water Supply Engineering* (New York 1929); Alban, F. J., *Organization and Administration of the Waterworks Undertaking* (London 1926); Garnett, William, *A Little Book on Water Supply* (Cambridge, Eng. 1922); Munro, William B., *Municipal Government and Administration*, 2 vols. (New York 1923) vol. ii, ch. xxix; Gross, Erwin, *Handbuch der Wasserversorgung* (2nd ed. Munich 1930); Clar, Wilhelm, *Wasserversorgung und Abwässerbeseitigung* (Potsdam 1921); Frick, P., *Considérations sur l'établissement des projets de distribution d'eau potable dans les communes* (Paris 1919); Fournier, Eugène, *Études sur les projets d'alimentation, le captage, la recherche et la protection des eaux potables*, France, Service de la Carte Géologique, Bulletin, no. 94 (Paris 1903); Halbfass, W., *Das Wasser im Wirtschaftsleben des Menschen* (Frankfort 1911), and "Die Siedelungen des Menschen in ihrem Verhältnis zur Versorgung mit Trink- und Brauchwasser" in *Geographische Zeitschrift*, vol. xxvi (1920) 169–77, 229–43; Beardsley, J. C., "History of Water Supply" in Cleveland Engineering Society, *Journal*, vol. xii (1919) 25–42; Semple, E. C., "Domestic and Municipal Waterworks in Ancient Mediterranean Lands" in *Geographical Review*, vol. xxi (1931) 466–74; Ewbank, Thomas, *A Description and Historical Account of Hydraulic and Other Machines for Raising Water* (16th ed. New York 1870); *Water Supply Statistics of American Municipalities*, ed. by T. R. Kendall and E. L. Sloan (2nd ed. New York 1930).

WATERWAYS, INLAND. Water transportation has played a role of tremendous significance in economic evolution. Coastal and ocean transportation were of prime importance in the rise of the Phoenician, Carthaginian, Iberian, Norse and British civilizations; and the discovery of the ocean routes between the Orient and the Occident by way of Cape Horn and the Cape of Good Hope constituted one of the vital factors in the transformation of world relationships. In a similar although less romantic way inland water transportation has influenced profoundly the course of internal economic development.

The earliest form of extensive inland water transportation was by river, and civilization developed in large degree along these water courses. Nearly everywhere, in all climes and in all ages, settlement, trade, industrial development and political and military history have been determined materially by the location of navigable streams. During the Middle Ages and as late as the nineteenth century water courses constituted the chief arteries of commerce in Europe and the avenues along which population and economic activity proceeded.

In South America civilization developed along the Plata, Paraguay, Paraná, Amazon and Orinoco rivers. In North America it was by way of the St. Lawrence, the Great Lakes and the Mississippi and its tributaries that Marquette and La Salle led their followers to the heart of an unexplored continent. Considerations of transportation confined the early Atlantic seaboard settlements to the banks of the coastal rivers. The three great routes to the land beyond the Alleghenies—the first by way of the Hudson and Mohawk river valleys to the Great Lakes; the second by the transverse valleys of Pennsylvania, and the Susquehanna, Juniata and Allegheny rivers to the Ohio gateway; and the third by the Cumberland Gap opening on the south through the mountains of Tennessee—necessarily conditioned the trend of settlement. In the great middle west in turn the early pioneers always kept close to the banks of rivers, following their winding courses as the frontier pushed out across the prairies. The establishment of virtually every city of importance in the eastern half of the United States and the original location of almost all of the country's industries were determined by possibilities of water transportation.

Transportation by artificial inland waterways, or canals, dates in the modern era from the last half of the eighteenth century. The first great era of inland canal development began in Great Britain with the opening of the Bridgewater Canal in 1761. This canal had a romantic origin. The young duke of Bridgewater, disappointed in love, determined to devote himself to the public service by building as a philanthropic enterprise a canal from the mines at Worsley to the city of Manchester. The canal was so great an improvement over land transport that it yielded enormous profits, and by 1772 the route was continued to Liverpool. The success of the Bridgewater Canal led to the inauguration of other projects; between 1790 and 1794 as many as 81 canal acts were passed by Parliament, many of these being unfortunately of a speculative character. By 1830 there were as many as 69 canals and 71 canalized rivers in England and Wales, with a total length of 3639 miles. From Liverpool, Manchester, Birmingham and London canals radiated in all directions, while through connections enabled goods to travel the entire length of the country by boat. At one time it was a common boast that every town in England was within 20 miles of a navigable water route.

In the United States canal construction began in a small way in Virginia and the New England states shortly before 1800. It was not until the second quarter of the nineteenth century, however, that canal transportation became important. The invention of the steamboat in 1807 accelerated the movement by water and pointed the way to the realization of the dreams of men like Washington and Clinton for the connection of the Atlantic seaboard with the middle west by means of all water routes. The Erie Canal, completed in 1825, led to a period of very rapid canal development not only in those states which were in need of lines of communication with the west, but within the western and southern states themselves. This waterway movement, particularly between 1825 and 1838, was linked up with comprehensive schemes for internal development, in which many state governments embarked upon a "planned system" of transportation consisting of canals, turnpikes and the newly invented railways. In nearly a score of states such systems were laid out, and many of the units in them were actually constructed. By 1838 in eighteen states indebtedness had been incurred to the extent of $60,201,551 for canals, $42,871,084 for railways and $6,618,868 for public roads. In only a few states, notably New Jersey and Delaware, were canals constructed by private enterprise.

In all these early projects both in Great Britain and in the United States it was assumed that financial profits would be realized through the levy of tolls. In Pennsylvania, for example, "it was predicted that the tolls would support the government and educate every child in the Commonwealth." In Michigan it was declared that not only would the returns from the investments prove sufficient to pay off the state debt speedily but there would be a surplus of funds so great as to free the inhabitants of that state forever from the burdens of taxation. In fact, however, few if any of the canals yielded returns sufficient to cover capital charges and maintenance expenses. The panic of 1837 and the ensuing depression wrecked the hopes of deriving large financial revenues from canal and other transportation systems. The Pennsylvania canals proved a complete financial failure and in 1857–58, when most of them were sold to railroad companies, the net loss to the state amounted to approximately $60,000,000. The burden of indebtedness resulting from these enterprises in the western and southern states was largely responsible for the destruction of state credit and the insertion in constitutions, after 1840, of articles prohibiting states from engaging in transportation enterprises.

The deepening and improvement of river channels did not become important until after the advent of the steamboat. So long as commerce was handled by canoes, keel boats and barks, river obstructions were of no great significance. Fulton and Livingston established a regular steamboat service on the Mississippi in 1817, and three years later Congress authorized a survey of the Ohio and Mississippi rivers with a view to determining the most practicable method of improving these streams for navigation purposes. The first federal appropriation for river improvements, amounting to $75,000, was made in 1824; but until 1880 expenditures for this purpose were comparatively small.

In general it may be said that the canal system, in the United States as well as in other countries, reached the apex of its development in the third quarter of the nineteenth century. In the United States canal projects began to be abandoned before the Civil War, and as many as 314 miles had been given up as early as 1860. In 1880 the Tenth Census stated that 1956.56 miles had already been abandoned, while a large portion of the remaining 2515.04 miles was not paying expenses. The New York canal system carried its greatest traffic in 1872, and 1882 was the peak year on the Illinois and Michigan Canal. The same was true of river transportation. As arteries of commerce the Ohio and the Mississippi rivers met with virtually no competition until 1850. New Orleans was the great entrepôt of traffic for the interior of the country, while Cincinnati and St. Louis were the primary assembling points for commerce moving out. In 1840 New Orleans was the fourth port in the world; as late as 1850 the population of Cincinnati was nearly four times and that of St. Louis about two and one half times that of Chicago. Within twenty years after the Civil War, however, most of the high grade traffic was lost to the river carriers, and before the end of the century both canal and river transportation had dwindled to relative insignificance. The one important exception was the carriage of coal on the Monongahela and Ohio rivers. The disappearance of canal and river traffic in Europe closely followed the same phenomenon in the United States. Before the end of the century the old barge canal system of Great Britain had ceased to be important, and river transportation had also greatly declined; a similar situation had come to prevail on the continent.

The virtual passing of inland water transportation was due directly to the development of the railways. The invention of the steel rail and the steel locomotive, the latter with its great load capacity, ushered in another revolution in inland transportation; for not only were the railways able to carry traffic at rates lower than those existing on the waterways, but they created a vastly more flexible transportation system. Thanks to the railway carriers industrial enterprise, which hitherto had clung close to the banks of the waterways, now was able to move out from the river valleys over the entire area of a country. By means of sidings and spur lines the railroads also found it possible to reach into almost every recess of great urban communities as well as into the heart of mining districts, where the depressions caused by exhausted mines had made canal building practically impossible. Thus the rapid and economical shipment of goods was no longer confined to trunk line water routes aided by such additional canalized highways as the physical character of a country might allow; and by virtue of the standard gauge it became possible to send commodities to any destination, however distant from the original place of origin, without transshipment.

The decline of river and canal traffic in the 1860's and 1870's in the United States and Europe led to agitation for the preservation of water transportation. Governments, yielding to these demands, took the first step by abolishing tolls. New York discarded tolls on its state canal system in 1883 and Congress abolished tolls on all federal rivers and canals in 1884. During this period similar action was being taken in Europe, both in countries where railroads were under public ownership or close public supervision and in those where private railroad operation existed. Moreover, in order to insure the continuance of water borne traffic, some governments established railroad rates on competitive traffic at a level approximately 20 percent above the water rates. Even when the overhead costs of water transportation were thus transferred from shippers to the general taxpayers, water routes continued unable to maintain any considerable volume of traffic. It was then concluded that the failure of water transportation was due to the inadequate depth of existing canals and river channels.

Hence about the turn of the century a great movement was inaugurated in the United States and in European countries for the rehabilitation and the deepening of inland waterways. Since 1900 most of the waterways of Germany, France, Holland and Belgium have been improved at considerable cost. Great expenditures have also been made in the United States. Between 1890 and 1930 internal waterway developments in the United States, exclusive of those affecting the Great Lakes and seacoast harbors, have cost the American people $1,177,000,000. In recent years money has been appropriated for the improvement of literally hundreds of rivers and connecting channels involving the expenditure of more than $100,000,000 annually.

Beginning in 1918 the federal government undertook an interesting experiment in government operation, with the express purpose of demonstrating the feasibility of water transportation. Originally two federal barge line services were created, one on the Mississippi River below St. Louis and the other on the Warrior River (New Orleans to Birmingham, Alabama). These services were placed under the supervision of the United States Railroad Administration until 1920; for the next four years they were under the control of the Inland and Coastwise Waterways Service of the War Department; and from June 1, 1924, the enterprise was carried on by the semi-independent Inland Waterways Corporation. By 1933 the corporation was also carrying freight on the upper Mississippi, the Missouri and Illinois rivers.

The slow rate of development of traffic on these routes was ascribed in part to the failure of the railroads to cooperate in the matter of through rates. Accordingly in 1928 Congress passed the Denison Act, which provided that the railroads were to join with inland waterway carriers in through routes and joint rates, on the basis of a reasonable division of revenue between the two types of carriers. The transportation charges on the waterways averaged about 5 mills per ton mile in 1931, providing a differential of from 10 to 20 percent below rail rates for similar types of low grade traffic.

As has already been indicated, by the 1880's governments had found it necessary to abolish tolls in order to preserve traffic on inland canals and rivers. Both interest on the capital investment and annual maintenance charges were thereafter shifted from the shipper to the taxpayers; this portion of the costs was concealed from the public view, being absorbed in the general budget figures of the government. As a result few people have had any conception of the magnitude of the water transportation costs assumed by the taxpayers. It is only when the subsidies in question are dug out of government archives and translated into terms of ton mile rates on particular water routes that the true situation is revealed.

The prevailing method of comparing the costs of rail and water transportation is simply to cite the rates charged to the shippers. The fallacy in this proceeding may be illustrated from the following. Railroad rates must provide means of meeting: first, interest and dividends on investment in railway properties and rolling stock; second, maintenance of roadbed, track, terminals and equipment; third, taxes on real estate properties, equipment and corporate income; and, fourth, the direct cost of transporting goods. The water rates, on the other hand, must offer the means of meeting only interest and dividends on the investment in boats, the maintenance of boats, the direct costs of transporting goods and the taxes on boats and boat company income. With all the overhead costs in the second case borne by the government it is obvious that rate comparisons afford no real measure of the relative costs.

The inclusive cost of transportation by inland waterways is in fact much higher than transportation costs by rail for similar classes of traffic. The following data with reference to a number of specific projects show the rate charges plus the charges assumed by the government. On the New York State Barge Canal system in 1931 interest and maintenance charges borne by the taxpayers of the state, when spread over the ton miles of traffic, amounted to 7.84 mills per ton mile. The rate paid by the shippers averaged approximately 4.5 mills, making a total cost of 12.34 mills. Before this can be compared with railway rates, however, the figure has to be increased to accord with the fact that the distance between Buffalo and Albany by rail is only five sixths that by water. The water rate in terms of the rail mileage is equal to approximately 14.81 mills. This may be compared with an average rate for all freight carried by the New York Central Railroad in 1931 of 9.87 mills. Of this total approximately .80 mills went for taxation.

The rail rate represents the average on all classes of freight, high as well as low grade traffic. Rates on grain, petroleum, sand, stone, gravel and other bulky materials, which make up the greater part of waterway tonnage, run very much lower than those on high grade freight. The average rate per ton mile on the Chesapeake and Ohio Railroad, which for the most part carries bulky freight, was 5.97 mills in 1931. It will be seen therefore that the inclusive cost over the New York Barge Canal system was virtually double that by rail for the same kind of traffic.

On the Ohio River in 1931 the taxpayers' subsidy, in terms of a ton mile rate for the traffic handled, amounted to 7.46 mills. This figure was computed on the basis of the total traffic, including the non-commercial sand and gravel tonnage, which constituted nearly 50 percent of the aggregate. The direct cost of moving the traffic on the river was approximately 6 mills per ton mile, making a total cost of 13.46 mills, which became 18.84 mills when allowance was made for the 40 to 50 percent greater distances by water than by rail between given points on the river.

On the Missouri River capital and maintenance charges borne by the government amounted, on the basis of 1929 commercial traffic, to approximately $7900 a ton. The only commercial traffic carried in that year consisted of 750 tons of logs, 10 tons of horses and mules, 6 tons of cattle and hogs, 6 tons of corn, 4 tons of machinery and 3 tons of other goods. Federal expenditures on the lower Mississippi system were made for purposes of both navigation and flood control. If only the former were taken into account, the overhead contribution of the taxpayers in 1930 would amount to about 8 mills per ton mile. If to this rates to shippers were added, averaging approximately 5 mills per ton mile, the total cost would be approximately double that by rail.

In connection with water rates on the Mississippi it should be remembered also that the government's Inland Waterways Corporation is not self-supporting. It pays no interest on the capital donated by the government; little depreciation is charged against equipment; the corporation enjoys certain free privileges, such as postage, wireless service, legal services, government rates on telegrams and office space; and it pays taxes only on an insignificant portion of its $24,000,000 of assets.

The proposed St. Lawrence deep waterway is analogous to the interoceanic canal. The project calls for a 27-foot depth in both the St. Lawrence River and the connecting channels between the Great Lakes. The cost of the combined navigation and power project has been estimated officially at $543,429,000, of which $272,453,000 is assignable to the United States. This estimate covers the improvements in the St. Lawrence River, the interconnecting lake channels and the Welland Ship Canal already completed by Canada. It falls far short, however, of covering all the costs involved. The Joint Board of Engineers has admitted that interest during the period of construction was not included in the estimates. This would amount at 4 percent to $87,000,000. Moreover the estimates make no provision for the deepening of lake harbors and the improvement of port facilities. Since the deepening of the harbors is not necessary for the purpose of lake shipping, the costs have had to be assigned to the St. Lawrence seaway. Toronto has already expended $40,000,000 on harbor improvements in an effort to make that city an ocean port; and there are at least ten lake cities which might have to make expenditures of this general magnitude. It is not improbable therefore that the ultimate cost of the waterway would be in the neighborhood of $1,000,000,000.

The project was conceived in the early years after the World War, when transportation rates were relatively high and railway facilities were not always available as required. Railway congestion disappeared in the 1920's, and the primary issue in 1934 was whether the reduction of rates to shippers would warrant the imposition of the increased taxes which the general public would have to bear. For the seven-year period ending 1931 grain rates between Buffalo and Montreal averaged 5.85 cents a bushel, the entire rate from Duluth to Liverpool being 16.2 cents. Advocates of the project claimed that rate reductions of from 8 to 10 cents a bushel would easily be possible. Since the rate between Buffalo and Montreal in 1933 was considerably less than 5.85 cents, it was apparent that the anticipated savings could not be realized. What little of this could be expected would in fact be confined to savings in the cost of transshipment and would amount to not more than a cent or two a bushel.

The costs imposed upon the taxpayers would, on the most conservative basis of figuring, amount to at least $35,000,000 a year for capital and maintenance charges. If the traffic should reach the "potential" 20,000,000 tons estimated by the United States Department of Commerce, the cost carried by the taxpayers would amount to about $1.75 a ton. In terms of wheat this would be the equivalent of more than 5 cents a bushel. Thus the cost to the taxpayers would be several times as great as the savings to the shippers.

In Germany and other European countries the inclusive costs of inland water transportation, generally speaking, also greatly exceeded those by rail. It has been the government policy in Germany to charge little or no tolls on inland waterways and to fix the rates on government railways sufficiently above those by water to insure the carriage of certain kinds of traffic by this means. As a result it has been possible to develop an extensive water borne commerce. It has been the practise, however, to meet the deficit incurred by the government in connection with the waterways from the profits earned on the railroads. In 1905, a typical year, the annual deficit on canalized rivers and on canals was $6,869,667, or $4555 per mile. In the same year the railways yielded a net revenue to the government of $56,900,000, or $1814 per mile. The only waterway in Germany which may be justifiable economically is the Rhine River, where the costs of canalization have been relatively very small. Even here where transshipment is involved, the inclusive costs are greater than over an all rail route.

The primary explanation of the high costs over inland canals and canalized rivers was to be found in the extremely heavy costs of construction per mile of route. For example, the improvement of the New York State Barge Canal system, carried out between 1903 and 1918, cost $192,803,467, exclusive of interest during construction. The cost per mile was thus nearly $370,000. This may be compared with an investment in all railroads of the eastern district of only $188,000 per mile of road. This railroad figure includes investment in second, third and fourth tracks, the expensive terminal properties in metropolitan areas and rolling stock and equipment of every kind. Of the total investment in railroads more than 25 percent was moreover assignable to passenger traffic.

From 1890 to the middle of 1931 federal expenditures on the Ohio River aggregated $150,000,000, or somewhat more than $200,000 a mile for the rail distance between Pittsburgh and the mouth of the Ohio River. In addition various cities provided free harbor and terminal facilities. The investment per mile in the Chesapeake and Ohio Railroad was $189,000, including of course passenger facilities and terminal properties.

Maintenance charges on canals and canalized rivers also exceed those on railroads. Such charges on the New York Barge Canal system in 1930 were $6286 per mile of canal as compared with $6097 per mile on the Erie Railroad. The latter figure included maintenance charges attributable to passenger traffic, which contributed 18 percent of the revenues. The ton mileage of traffic was nearly twice as great on the railway as on the canal system. On the Ohio River maintenance charges in 1929–30 were $6800 per mile of river exclusive of terminals as compared with $5282 inclusive of terminal costs per mile of road on the Norfolk and Western Railroad. Passenger revenues on this road amounted to only about 6 percent of the total. The density of traffic on the Norfolk and Western was over five times that on the Ohio River. A comparison with the Chesapeake and Ohio shows similar figures.

In European countries much has been made of the argument that inland waterways constitute a necessary asset for purposes of war. It has been pointed out moreover that during the World War extensive use was made by the belligerent countries of their canals and canalized rivers. Even in the United States encouragement was given to water transportation as a war measure. The development of inland canals for military purposes would be sound only if transportation facilities were less costly or more effective than the railroads. It is true that the European canals proved of some value in meeting the excessive traffic demands of the war period; but additional railway facilities might have been developed which would have served the same purpose at less cost. The military argument is of course somewhat different with regard to the Suez, Panama and Kiel canals. Here naval considerations are involved, and under certain conditions the military value of the canals might prove incalculable.

Recently the improvement of rivers has been connected in numerous instances with land reclamation and water power projects. On the

Mississippi flood control is the principal secondary objective; on the St. Lawrence it is water power; and in the Tennessee valley it is both power and land reclamation. The problems of flood control, as an engineering matter, are largely separate and distinct from those of navigation and improvement. In flood control the construction of levees and revetments for the control of channels is involved, while in navigation the chief tasks are the dredging and snagging operations to keep the channels unobstructed. Flood control improvements may bring incidental benefits to navigation, but large additional navigation costs will be incurred in any event. For example, of total expenditures on the lower Mississippi amounting to $268,000,000 as much as $137,454,000 was definitely assignable to navigation.

The relation of power development to navigation may be illustrated by the St. Lawrence project. This involves the incurring of certain costs which can be allocated solely to navigation, other costs which can be charged only to power development and still other costs which would have to be met by both divisions of the enterprise. If the project were conceived solely as a power development, these joint costs would of course have to be assigned exclusively to power; similarly, if the project were conceived merely as a transportation enterprise, they would have to be included as a part of the cost of transportation. If the project is developed with both ends in view, then the simple procedure is to assign half of these joint costs to navigation and half to power. Sound policy requires that the navigation aspects and the power aspects of the St. Lawrence project be tested separately on their respective merits. It is unfortunate that the merging of the two objectives has tended to confuse the issues involved. Depending upon the audience and the section of the country it has been argued, on the one hand, that the transportation will support the power and, on the other, that the power will support the transportation.

The ultimate goal of all transportation policy is to furnish the needed service as cheaply and efficiently as possible. If water transportation over a given route is cheaper, all elements of cost included, than rail, highway or air transportation, obviously that form of transportation should be used. In order that this desired end may be realized, competitive forms of transportation should be placed upon a plane of economic equality. Either tolls sufficient to cover overhead and maintenance charges must be levied upon the waterways, or competing forms of transportation must be relieved of their overhead and maintenance costs. Otherwise traffic will continue to be diverted by an artificial rate situation from more to less economical carriers.

HAROLD G. MOULTON

See: COMMERCE; RAILROADS; TERMINALS; TRANSPORTATION; RATE REGULATION; PORTS AND HARBORS; SHIPPING; INTERNATIONAL WATERWAYS; PANAMA CANAL; SUEZ CANAL; FLOODS AND FLOOD CONTROL; ELECTRIC POWER; PUBLIC UTILITIES.

Consult: Moulton, H. G., *Waterways versus Railways* (rev. ed. Boston 1926), with bibliography p. 459–66; Moulton, H. G., and associates, *The American Transportation Problem* (Washington 1933); Daggett, Stuart, *Principles of Inland Transportation* (New York 1928); Johnson, E. R., and others, *Principles of Transportation* (New York 1928); Cadbury, George, and Dobbs, S. P., *Canals and Inland Waterways* (London 1929); Hepburn, A. B., *Artificial Waterways of the World* (New York 1914); United States, National Waterways Commission, *Reports*, 22 vols. (1909–11), and *Final Report*, 62nd Cong., 2nd sess., Senate Document no. 469 (1912); United States, Commissioner of Corporations, *Report . . . on Transportation by Water in the United States*, 4 vols. (1909–13); United States, Bureau of Foreign and Domestic Commerce, *Inland Water Transportation in the United States*, Miscellaneous series, no. 119 (1923); Esch, E., *Die Binnenschiffahrt der Vereinigten Staaten von Amerika* (Leipsic 1925); *History of Transportation in the United States before 1860*, ed. by B. H. Meyer (Washington 1917); Great Britain, Royal Commission on Canals and Waterways, *Report*, 12 vols. (1906–11); Great Britain, Royal Commission on Transportation, *Final Report . . . Coordination and Development of Transport*, Parliament, House of Commons, Cmd. 3751 (1931); Pratt, E. A., *Canals and Traders* (London 1910); McPherson, L. G., *Transportation in Europe* (New York 1910); Netherlands, Departement van Waterstaat, *Statistiek der scheepvaartbeweging op de rivieren en kanalen in Nederland*, published annually in The Hague since 1878; Sympher, Leo, *Die neuen wasserwirtschaftlichen Gesetze in Preussen* (Berlin 1905); Peters, Max, *Schiffahrtsabgaben* (Leipsic 1907); Rathenau, Walter, and Cauer, W., *Massengüterbahnen* (Berlin 1909); Clapp, E. J., *The Navigable Rhine* (Boston 1911); Joint Board of Engineers on St. Lawrence Waterway Project (United States and Canada), *Report . . . on the Improvement of the St. Lawrence River between Lake Ontario and Montreal* (Washington 1927); International Joint Commission, *Report . . . concerning the Improvement of the St. Lawrence River between Montreal and Lake Ontario*, United States, 67th Cong., 2nd sess., Senate Document no. 114 (1921); United States, Congress, Senate, Committee on Foreign Relations, *Great Lakes—St. Lawrence Deep Waterway Treaty*, 72nd Cong., 2nd sess., Senate Executive Report no. 1 (1933); Canada, Royal Commission to Inquire into Railways and Transportation in Canada, *Report* (Ottawa 1932); United States, Bureau of Foreign and Domestic Commerce, *Great-Lakes-to-Inland-Waterways*, Domestic Commerce series, no. 4 (1927); United States, Chamber of Commerce, Special Committee on Competing Forms of Transportation, *Report* (1933); Security Owners' Association, Inc., *A Study of Transportation by Waterways as Related to Competition with Rail Carriers in Continental United States* (New York 1932); Moulton, H. G., and others, *The St. Lawrence Navigation and Power Project* (Washington 1929). See also United States, Bureau of the Census, *Special Reports: Transportation by Water*, for 1906 (1908), for 1916 (1920), and for 1926 (1929); United States, Army Chief of Engineers, *Annual Reports*, published since 1839; United States, War Department, Inland Waterways Corporation, *Annual Reports*, published since 1925; Germany, Statistisches Reichsamt, "Binnenschiffahrt" in *Statistik des Deutschen Reichs*, n.s., vol. cxxv (1898), vol. cxxxi (1899), vol. cclxiv (1914), and vol. cccxliii (1927); France, Ministère des Travaux Publics, *Guide officiel de la navigation intérieure* (new ed. Paris 1921), and *Statistique de la navigation intérieure*, published annually since 1880; Belgium, Société Anonyme du Canal et des Installations Maritimes de Bruxelles, *Notice sur le port de Bruxelles* (Brussels 1907), and *Rapport présenté par le conseil administratif* (Brussels 1911).

WATERWAYS, INTERNATIONAL. *See* INTERNATIONAL WATERWAYS.

WATKIN, SIR EDWARD WILLIAM (1819–1901), British railway promoter. Watkin entered his father's business, that of cotton merchant, at an early age but abandoned it in 1845 to become secretary of the Trent Valley Railway, engineering the sale of the latter to the London and North Western Railway Company. He served as manager of the Manchester, Sheffield and Lincolnshire Railway from 1853 until 1861 and was its chairman from 1864. During this period he was also chairman of the South Eastern Railway (1866–94) and of the Metropolitan (1872–94) and a director of other important railway companies. Believing that English railways should be amalgamated into two or more great systems competing for all the important traffic, he promoted company consolidations and was instrumental in the opening of important through routes. As a result of his efforts the Manchester, Sheffield and Lincolnshire Railway was developed into the Great Central. Watkin had intended to extend the Sheffield line to Dover and connect it by a channel tunnel to continental railways, but the latter project failed to secure parliamentary sanction. Although he supported dividend interests rather than expert planning and although he frequently engaged in wasteful struggles, Watkin by virtue of his organizing skill and ability to gauge future developments was one of the outstanding figures in British railroad history. From 1864 to 1868 and from 1874 to 1895 he served as a member of Parliament.

Watkin made a number of visits to British North America as superintending commissioner and later president of the Grand Trunk Railway. In this capacity and as promoter of the purchase of control of the Hudson's Bay Company in 1863 by a group prepared to assist in opening up the northwest to transit and settlement, Watkin exercised an unostentatious but important influence which hastened the establishment of the Dominion of Canada and its westward expansion. He devoted his attention to encouraging the construction of the Intercolonial Railway to connect the St. Lawrence with ice free ports of the Maritime Provinces on the Atlantic and of a transcontinental railway running westward to the Pacific. His activities were pivotal in promoting these projects among leaders in the several provinces and among official and financial circles in London, where he had the support of the duke of Newcastle, the colonial secretary. In Parliament he espoused relevant imperial legislation and opposed attempts of the Nova Scotian opposition to block and then to abolish Canadian confederation. For his services in promoting confederation he was knighted in 1868. Twelve years later he was made a baronet.

REGINALD G. TROTTER

Consult: Watkin, E. W., *Canada and the States; Recollections, 1851 to 1886* (London 1887); Cleveland-Stevens, E. C., *English Railways; Their Development and Their Relation to the State* (London 1915) p. 288–311; Trotter, R. G., *Canadian Federation; Its Origins and Achievement* (Toronto 1924) chs. xiii–xv, xx, and "British Finance and Confederation" in Canadian Historical Association, *Annual Report* (1927) 89–96.

WATSON, ELKANAH (1758–1842), American agriculturist. Watson devoted the early part of his life to mercantile pursuits and the promotion of internal improvements, particularly canal building. In 1807 he purchased a mansion house and farm near Pittsfield in Berkshire county, Massachusetts, where at the age of fifty he entered upon his agricultural career. He procured the first pair of Merino sheep to be brought into the state, exhibiting them on the public square, where they attracted so much attention that agricultural fairs and cattle shows became the predominant interest of his life. He was the founder and first president of the Berkshire Agricultural Society, which exerted a great influence on the agricultural development of the county. It became the model for the organization of agricultural societies in New England and New York and in the southern and western states, and its reputation spread to England and other western countries of Europe. The society promoted the fair as a means of interesting the farmer in the development of a better rural economy. The principle on which the society was organized, Watson's son wrote, was "to address the interests and sentiments of the people. The public exhibition of choice animals, while it made them familiar to the farming community, attracted its attention to their beauty and value, and to the importance of their introduction. It aroused the emulation of the farmers and by the brilliant display of premiums excited their self-interest. Competition in crops awakened scientific investigations, and their practicable application. The management and the appliances by which the fortunate competition had secured success, were described and widely adopted. Domestic industry was fostered, and its labors accelerated. Farmers at the fairs and business meetings of the Society were brought into intercourse, and were led to act in concert, and to appreciate the dignity and importance of their vocation" (*Men and Times of the Revolution*). Watson visited Europe on various occasions. He published many pamphlets on agricultural and other subjects. He was a keen critic of current agricultural practises and an earnest promoter of better farming methods and improved living conditions on the farm.

LOUIS BERNARD SCHMIDT

Works: *History of the Rise, Progress, and Existing Condition of the Western Canals in the State of New-York, from September 1788, to . . . 1819. Together with the Rise, Progress, and Existing State of Modern Agricultural Societies, on the Berkshire System, from 1807, to . . . 1820* (Albany 1820); *Men and Times of the Revolution; or, Memoirs of Elkanah Watson*, ed. by Winslow C. Watson (2nd ed. New York 1857).

Consult: Pound, Arthur, *Native Stock* (New York 1931) p. 195–267; Van Wagenen, Jared, "Elkanah Watson—a Man of Affairs" in *New York History*, vol. xiii (1932) 404–12.

WATSON, JAMES (1799–1874), English radical and publisher. A self-educated Yorkshire laborer, Watson at an early age became a freethinker and a follower of Robert Owen. In 1828 he was placed in charge of the first cooperative store in London, where he met William Lovett. Three years later he opened a printing and bookshop for the dissemination of literature on free thought and Owenism. In all the struggles of the stormy decades 1820–50, which witnessed the final victory of liberal thought and the beginning of the political rise of the working class, Watson proved himself one of the sturdiest, truest and most self-sacrificing fighters for free speech, free press, free association and the rights of labor. Undaunted by many years of imprisonment and many hundreds of pounds in fines he continued to spread free thought periodicals and unstamped newspapers, such as Carlile's *Republican* and Hetherington's *Poor Man's Guardian*, and to republish Tom Paine's works, Mirabaud's (pseudonym for Holbach) *System of Nature* and Shelley's revolutionary poems. In 1837–38 as one of the leaders of the National Union of the Working Classes he served on the committee appointed to draw up the Charter and thus to launch the Chartist movement.

MAX BEER

Consult: Linton, W. J., *James Watson; a Memoir* (Manchester 1880); Hovell, Mark, *The Chartist Movement*, University of Manchester, Publications, Historical series, no. xxxi (Manchester 1918) p. 58–59.

WAUGH, BENJAMIN (1839–1908), English social reformer. While serving as a Congregational minister at Greenwich Waugh became interested in the problem of the neglected child. He established a day nursery for the children of working mothers and launched a program for the care of juvenile first offenders, who would otherwise have been committed to prison. In 1870 he was elected a member of the London School Board, after carrying on a poster campaign in behalf of neglected children. His personal investigations of the handicaps which the children of London suffered led him to publish *The Gaol Cradle—Who Rocks It?* (London 1873), which became a powerful plea for the abolition of juvenile imprisonment.

As editor of the *Sunday Magazine* from 1874 to 1896 he took note of the beginning of the movement for the protection of children in the United States through the New York Society for the Prevention of Cruelty to Children. Upon his initiative a great meeting was held in 1884, which resulted in the founding of the London Society for the Prevention of Cruelty to Children. Waugh was made secretary and afterward director of this society. Five years later it became the National Society for the Prevention of Cruelty to Children with one purpose and one policy, the linking of all towns, villages and hamlets throughout the British Isles in the movement to protect children. Mainly through his personal efforts in 1885 the power was given to magistrates to take evidence of children too young to understand the nature of an oath. In 1889 Waugh succeeded in securing passage of the act for the prevention of cruelty to children, which established in England for the first time the right of a child to an endurable existence in his own home. Out of his experience with this statute came important contributions to both the form and the content of the Infant Life Protection Act of 1897 and the great Children Act of 1908.

C. C. CARSTENS

Consult: Waugh, Rosa, *Life of Benjamin Waugh* (London 1913); Higgins, H., "The Champion of the Child" in *Sunday Magazine*, vol. xxxiv (1904–05) 661–65; Picton, H., "Benjamin Waugh und die Kinderschutzbewegung" in *Süddeutsche Monatshefte*, vol. xxvi (1928–29) 222–25.

WEALTH. See NATIONAL WEALTH.

WEALTH, NATIONAL. See NATIONAL WEALTH.

WEAVER, JAMES BAIRD (1833–1912), American political reformer. After his graduation from the Cincinnati law school in 1856 Weaver practised law in Iowa, identifying himself with the Republican party in its first national campaign. During the Civil War he enlisted in the Union army; he was promoted rapidly and in 1865 was breveted brigadier general of volunteers "for gallant and meritorious service." At the close of the war he resumed his legal practise in Iowa, achieving considerable success at the bar. In the political field he became a recognized leader of the Republican party.

His political career reached a turning point in 1875, when he was tricked out of the Republican nomination for governor because of his advanced stand against the liquor interests and against the influence of big business. It became obvious that the party managers would never permit him to obtain a political office and that the Republican party had lost its early idealism. Accordingly in 1877 Weaver became affiliated with the Greenback party, which elected him to the House of Representatives the following year. In 1880 he received the Greenback nomination for the presidency and in 1884 and again in 1886 was reelected to Congress. Later he became a leader of the Populist party and in 1892 was its presidential nominee, receiving 1,027,329 popular votes and twenty-two electoral votes. The Populist was the most significant third party movement in American history subsequent to the formation of the Republican party, but the nomination of Bryan by the Democratic party in 1896 signalized its decline. Weaver supported Bryan and thenceforth identified himself with the Democratic party.

Weaver was a pioneer in American politics. One of the first "progressives," he defined and interpreted the leading issues which engaged the attention of both state and national governments for many years. His was a platform of social and industrial democracy: the political reforms he advocated included prohibition of speculation in government lands; regulation of corporations; government ownership of railroads; free coinage of silver; a graduated income tax; establishment of postal savings banks; the initiative and the referendum; the election of United States senators by popular vote; an eight-hour labor law; federal standards in industry, comprising factories, mines and workshops; child labor legislation; regulation of interstate commerce by Congress; regulation of the liquor traffic; woman suffrage; and the Australian ballot. With the notable exception of government ownership of railroads and the free coinage of silver all of these political reforms have to some extent been enacted into law by the major parties.

LOUIS BERNARD SCHMIDT

Consult: Haynes, F. E., *James Baird Weaver* (Iowa City 1919); Harlan, Edgar R., *A Narrative History of the People of Iowa*, 5 vols. (Chicago 1931) vol. ii, p. 79–85, vol. v, p. 3–5; Nixon, H. C., "The Populist Movement in Iowa" in *Iowa Journal of History and Politics*, vol. xxiv (1926) 3–107.

WEBER, MAX (1864–1920), German sociologist and political economist. Weber, the son of a prosperous National Liberal politician, studied law and with the publication of a work on Roman agrarian history in 1891 established himself in Berlin as a jurist. After the appearance of his widely acclaimed study "Die Verhältnisse der Landarbeiter im ostelbischen Deutschland" (Verein für Sozialpolitik, *Schriften*, vol. lv, Leipsic 1892) he was called to the chair of political economy at Freiburg. From 1897 on, except for rather protracted interruptions due to ill health, he taught at Heidelberg and later at Munich. Weber was one of the founders of the Deutsche Gesellschaft für Soziologie and editor of the *Archiv für Sozialwissenschaft und Sozialpolitik*, in which practically all of his sociological writings were first published.

As defined by Weber sociology is concerned with the social activities of human beings; that is, with activities oriented to those of others. If the structural forms, such as the state, the church, the joint stock company, which the other social sciences treat as units in themselves, be reduced to their elements they are all found to center about social activity; the reality of all structural forms rests upon the chance of occurrence of certain (definite) actions. Sociology treats social activity from the point of view of its meaning, which either was purposefully intended by the agent or would have had to be intended if the action had been consciously pursued. It is as a science of understanding that sociology is differentiated from the natural sciences, where neither the motive nor the meaning of events is taken into account; for this reason it must employ a method peculiar to itself. Weber's methodology, evolving under the influence of Rickert, posits a connection between causal explanation and the understanding of meaning, on the ground that a knowledge of the meaning of activity is a prerequisite of the causal correlation of facts, for otherwise there could be nothing but a description of meaningless facts. The difference between the natural and the cultural sciences becomes particularly apparent in their divergent views as to the nature of laws. Whereas in the natural sciences the discovery of laws is the end in itself, in sociology laws are merely a means of facilitating the discovery of the causal interrelationship of historical phenomena. The concepts which the sociologist uses to formulate his working hypotheses were designated by Weber as ideal types. These are neither average types nor ideals but non-normative standards built up by the deliberate selection and combination of particular elements of reality.

The cultural importance of the phenomena with which sociology deals depends upon the relation of these phenomena to values. It is impossible to derive values from the material of knowledge itself, as do, for example, the exponents of the idea of progress, since values lie beyond the realm of science and acquire their binding force from personal decision. Nor can science ever resolve the eternal conflict between such values as power, justice and peace. Weber, who carried on a zealous struggle for the strict separation of what is from what ought to be, of empirical knowledge from prophecy, of universally valid scientific analysis from value judgments, ascribed to science the task of intensifying the awareness of this conflict and thereby of imparting to the active individual a stronger sense of responsibility based upon the consciousness that in the pursuit of his own values he must inevitably infringe upon the values of others.

Weber's sociological studies are founded upon a thorough knowledge of economic, social and legal history, political and military development, religious and intellectual evolution, as revealed in a wide range of oriental as well as occidental civilizations. Alongside his political and sociological studies of contemporary society are to be found works on agrarian conditions in antiquity, on the history of mediaeval trading associations, on the psychophysics of industrial labor, and critical treatises on methodology. His masterpiece, *Wirtschaft und Gesellschaft*, a posthumous work edited from part of the papers left behind at his death, includes, besides the systematic presentation of his conceptual apparatus in the field of sociology, a sociology of economics and a series of extended treatises, notably those dealing with the historical sociology of the city, with the rational foundations of music, with class, state, nation and party and with the sociology of law. Among the typological studies of the forms of political sovereignty his masterly analyses of bureaucracy, feudalism and charismatic authority have been accorded particular acclaim. Above all else Weber was preoccupied with the problem of tracing the process of rationalization which for centuries has been operating more and more in all spheres of occidental life. In posing this problem without any trace of mere speculation and in demonstrating its bearing on the problem of personal freedom in modern civilization Weber's work acquired genuine philosophical significance. Jaspers has characterized Weber as the philosopher of his age because he gave expression to its moral doctrine.

It is from this point of view that Weber's sociology of religion is likewise to be understood. In the famous essays entitled *Die protestantische Ethik und der Geist des Kapitalismus* (first published in *Archiv für Sozialwissenschaft und Sozialpolitik*, 1904–05; 2nd ed. as vol. i, pt. i of Weber's *Gesammelte Aufsätze zur Religionssoziologie*; tr. by Talcott Parsons, London 1930) and *Die protestantischen Sekten und der Geist des Kapitalismus* (first published in *Christliche Welt*, 1906; reprinted as vol. i, pt. ii of *Gesammelte Aufsätze zur Religionssoziologie*) he reached the conclusion that Calvinism, on the basis of the idea of the calling as developed by Luther, had elevated this-worldly asceticism to an ideal of conduct and that the obligation of the godly man to pursue this ideal constituted one of the main springs of capitalism. More specifically this-worldly asceticism tended to identify spiritual salvation with business success and so created the capitalistic spirit, which by reason of the inertia of institutions retained its vitality even after its religious sources had evaporated. By way of rounding out and testing his theories in the sociology of religion Weber subsequently analyzed Confucianism, Taoism, Hinduism, Buddhism and ancient Judaism, tracing the interplay between the economic ethics of these religions and the forms of social life.

As a statesman Weber remained aloof from the partisanship of the political arena. In his youth he had belonged to the Pan-German League and sympathized with its nationalistic program. But he had soon resigned because of the attitude of assiduous indifference which the league, acting in the interests of the large landowners, adopted toward the national and social menace presented by cheap migratory labor from Poland. Weber's love of country was based upon his sense of national honor and power—power neither as an end in itself nor as a means of promoting the interests of privileged economic groups but rather as a safeguard of German and European culture. No existing class seemed to Weber capable of leading the people as national interest demanded. The *Junkers* had developed into capitalistic entrepreneurs and had thereby lost the requisite leisure for political activity; the bourgeoisie prized the state only in so far as they could use it as an instrument against the laboring class; the proletariat was led by men of petty bourgeois ideals. Weber had little sympathy for the irresponsible, autocratic policy of the kaiser, which had discredited Germany in the eyes of the world.

In the period before the World War Weber's ideas made a deep impress upon Friedrich Naumann and the circle of National Socialists. Yet despite his extraordinarily keen political insight Weber failed to exert any appreciable influence upon governmental policy. His candidacy for the German National Assembly was blocked by functionaries of the Democratic party. In 1920 he abandoned this party because he disapproved of its concessions to the Social Democratic program of socialization. He accompanied the German delegation to the Versailles Conference and delivered an opinion on the war guilt clause. Although he argued against the ratification of the Versailles Treaty because of the impossibility of carrying out its provisions and because of the moral humiliation which it involved for Germany, he always remained hostile to chauvinism and reaction. The provision in the constitution of the German Republic for the popular election of the president was adopted upon the recommendation of Weber, who sat on the committee which drafted the constitution. He insisted also upon the right of the parliamentary minority to carry out investigations as a curb upon the omnipotence of the bureaucracy.

Although Weber has been represented as the intellectual spokesman of the bourgeoisie of his time, he had in fact little sympathy with that class. The search on the part of the German youth movement for a substitute for religion drew from him the observation that the doors of the church were still open to those who could not live without faith and were willing to sacrifice their intellectual integrity. For those who were not Weber, who avowed that he was neither areligious nor irreligious, advised that they live free from illusion, face frankly the fact that religious power was paralyzed in the West and yet guide their actions according to the dictates of knowledge and a realization of their responsibility to the future. Weber's influence as an educator was and still is hardly less far reaching, although perhaps it is more intangible, than his importance in the moral and social sciences of Germany, which have yet to utilize to the full the problems he raised and the knowledge he amassed.

HANS SPEIER

Works: *Gesammelte Aufsätze zur Wissenschaftslehre* (Tübingen 1922); *Gesammelte Aufsätze zur Religionssoziologie*, 3 vols. (Tübingen 1920–21, 2nd ed. 1922–23), vol. i, pt. i tr. by T. Parsons as *The Protestant Ethic and the Spirit of Capitalism* (London 1930); *Gesammelte Aufsätze zur Sozial- und Wirtschaftsgeschichte* (Tübingen 1924); *Gesammelte Aufsätze zur Soziologie und Sozialpolitik* (Tübingen 1924); *Wirtschaft und Gesellschaft*, Grundriss der Sozialökonomik, pt. iii (Tübingen 1922; 2nd ed., 2 vols., 1925); "Die Börse" in *Göttinger Arbeiterbibliothek*, vol. i (1894–95) 17–48, vol. ii (1896–1900) 49–80; *Wirtschaftsgeschichte*, ed. by S. Hellmann and M. Palyi (Munich 1923, 2nd ed. 1924), tr. by F. H. Knight as *General Economic History* (New York 1927); *Gesammelte politische Schriften* (Munich 1921); "Zur Lage der bürgerlichen Demokratie in Russland," and "Russlands Übergang zum Scheinkonstitutionalismus" in *Archiv für Sozialwissenschaft und Sozialpolitik*, vol. xxii (1906) 234–353, and vol. xxiii (1906) 165–401.

Consult: "Chronologisch geordnetes Verzeichnis der Schriften von Max Weber" in Weber, Marianne S., *Max Weber* (Tübingen 1926) p. 713–19; Jaspers, Karl, *Max Weber* (Oldenburg 1932); Grab, Hermann J., *Der Begriff des Rationalen in der Soziologie Max Webers*, Sozialwissenschaftliche Abhandlungen, vol.

iii (Karlsruhe 1927); Löwith, Karl, "Max Weber und Karl Marx" in *Archiv für Sozialwissenschaft und Sozialpolitik*, vol. lxvii (1932) 53–99; Steding, Christoph, *Politik und Wissenschaft bei Max Weber* (Breslau 1932); Walther, Andreas, "Max Weber als Soziologe" in *Jahrbuch für Soziologie*, vol. ii (Karlsruhe 1926) p. 1–65; Landshut, Siegfried, *Kritik der Soziologie* (Munich 1929) p. 2–10, 34–63, 77–82; Wolf, Erik, "Max Webers ethischer Kritizismus und das Problem der Metaphysik" in *Logos*, vol. xix (1930) 359–75; Schelting, Alexander von, *Max Webers Wissenschaftslehre* (Tübingen 1934); Salomon, Albert, "Max Weber's Methodology" in *Social Research*, vol. i (1934) 147–68; Abel, T. F., *Systematic Sociology in Germany*, Columbia University, Studies in History, Economics and Public Law, no. 310 (New York 1929) ch. iv; Robertson, H. M., *Aspects of the Rise of Economic Individualism*, Cambridge Studies in Economic History (Cambridge, Eng. 1933).

WEBSTER, DANIEL (1782–1852), American lawyer and statesman. Although he was the son of a poor New Hampshire farmer, Webster rose to prominence and power by serving the shipping, financial and industrial interests of New England. Influenced by Harrington, he upheld the Federalist doctrine of economic determinism, maintaining that the form and character of political institutions are determined by the distribution and security of property and that the property interest of each individual should determine the weight of his political power. In his early career as a member of Congress, when he represented the dominant commercial interest, Webster adhered in practise as well as in theory to the laissez faire doctrines of Adam Smith by his resolute opposition to protective tariffs and to any extension of governmental interference with individual initiative. When manufacturing became a dominant interest, however, he reversed his position, and became an outspoken advocate of governmental aid to industry.

Although as a Federalist Webster opposed the War of 1812 and defended the doctrine of states' rights, he reversed his attitude when the planters of the South tried to advance their economic interests by resort to states' rights and nullification. In the Senate and as a popular orator Webster defended the doctrine, borrowed largely from Story, that the federal constitution was a fundamental law resting on an executed and irrevocable contract between individuals acting collectively in which the states as such had no part. This nationalistic doctrine was legalistic, expedient and sentimental rather than historical. As a practising attorney before the federal Supreme Court Webster upheld the sanctity of contracts and the vested interests of corporations and a loose construction of the constitution which was favorable to an expanding capitalistic economy. As secretary of state he took important steps to protect and extend Pacific trade and was thus a pioneer in economic imperialism. He was also a belligerent exponent of national self-consciousness.

A believer in the Ricardian labor theory of value and genuinely interested in the well being of the working classes, Webster none the less denounced collective bargaining and the idea of a class struggle, advocating instead class collaboration. The only humanitarian crusade which enlisted the support of this institutionalistic defender of the family, the church and the national state was that of popular education, which he believed to be an excellent insurance against social unrest and revolution. Webster was bitterly denounced by abolitionists for his political opportunism and readiness to compromise with the slavocracy in its demand for stringent fugitive slave laws and access to western territory for the expansion of slavery. This compromise, however, not only served the immediate interest of the New England industrialists who derived profit from their alliance with cotton planters; possibly it also prevented an appeal to arms until the industrial North was better prepared for the struggle.

MERLE E. CURTI

Works: *The Writings and Speeches of Daniel Webster*, 18 vols. (Boston 1903).

Consult: Fuess, Claude Moore, *Daniel Webster*, 2 vols. (Boston 1930); Carey, Robert L., *Daniel Webster as an Economist*, Columbia University, Studies in History, Economics and Public Law, no. 313 (New York 1929); Parrington, Vernon L., *Main Currents in American Thought*, 3 vols. (New York 1927–30) vol. ii, p. 304–16.

WEIGHTS AND MEASURES. To measure time, distance, area, space, mass or any other physical quantity a fundamental unit is required; when realized in concrete form, this unit becomes a standard and other units can be derived from it for convenient uses. The unit may be determined by natural phenomena, such as the time of revolution of a heavenly body, the length of a great circle of the earth, the length of some member of the human body, the length or weight of one or more grains or seeds or the capacity of a certain type of shell; or it may be selected arbitrarily. A system of weights and measures is the interrelation of units on a fixed ratio.

Ancient Babylon and Egypt had linear measures based on the cubit and the foot, while the earliest unit of weight was doubtless determined arbitrarily from some convenient object and used in a crude form of balance. The weight of a cube of water where each dimension was the unit of length was later employed, as in the case of the Babylonian talent derived from the cubed foot. Units of capacity were likewise defined in terms of cubic contents. It was soon realized that systems of weights, measures and standards must be simple and convenient for use, capable of development into a logical and symmetrical arrangement and invariable in regard to time and place. On such bases systems were developed, usually by the rulers, with the object of securing fairness in all commercial transactions.

Systems of weights and measures became diffused by conquest and commercial relations, as is illustrated in the widespread use in international trade of the British measures, which as early as the thirteenth century had been standardized locally. It is estimated that at the end of the eighteenth century, when France undertook needed reforms, there were still in Europe 391 different units of weight corresponding to the term pound, 370 of which were superseded by the kilogram, while the word foot applied to 282 different units of length. Similar diversity exists even at present in the Orient and impedes the marketing of products beyond the local community.

As early as 1670 Gabriel Mouton had suggested a decimal system of linear measures based not on a conventionalized or legalized body measure but on the arc of one minute of a great circle of the earth with an appropriate subdivision defined in terms of the length of a pendulum. Nothing was accomplished until 1790, when Talleyrand asked the National Assembly to consider metrological reforms. In 1795 following the adoption of the revolutionary calendar a plan for a new system of weights and measures was accepted, with the meter, one ten millionth of the earth's quadrant, as the fundamental unit and with the franc as a new unit of coinage. Legally adopted in 1797, the metric system became increasingly used in France, until in 1840 all other measures were outlawed. Belgium and the Netherlands adopted the metric system in 1816, Greece in 1836, Spain in 1849 and Portugal in 1852; in 1872 it became compulsory throughout the German Empire.

An International Conference on Weights and Measures met at Paris in 1870 and two years later established a permanent scientific organization to redetermine and construct new prototype standards for the meter and kilogram and to distribute accurate and authentic copies. The metric convention, which was signed at Paris in 1879 by representatives of seventeen nations, definitely established the metric system on an international basis and founded the International Bureau of Weights and Measures, where the standards are preserved. Later the bureau also determined the meter in terms of the wave length of the red light of cadmium vapor, and 1,553,164.13 wave lengths were formally adopted as standard in 1927; the reproduction of the standard was thus made possible at any time by precise optical methods. The metric system, which came to be used universally for scientific research and experiment, made possible the foundation of an international system of units and standards for all electrical measurements, both theoretical and practical; this system has been in universal use since 1893.

The claims of the metric system to universality in trade and industry have encountered opposition in English speaking countries, although for many years the system has been permitted by law. It is admitted that decimalization is advantageous for calculation and records, but it is argued that it is less useful for construction and commercial purposes than a binary or duodecimal system, which affords 3 as well as 2 as a factor. In both Great Britain and the United States early in the industrial age there was assimilation to the same fundamental standards demanded in accurate work, particularly in the manufacture of machinery, where the various components are constructed to mate with one another and to be used interchangeably. As a result there were developed in both nations methods and machinery based on the Anglo-Saxon measures, involving large capital outlay and establishing trade processes and standards. Arguments addressed to the English speaking peoples in favor of the metric system which outline international advantages, convenience in measurement and computation and like considerations have been countered with statements that American and British trade and industry have predominated throughout the world in spite of such alleged handicaps; that ordinary business and construction prefer a binary to a decimal system; that the cost of new weighing and measuring devices, machinery, patterns, conversion tables and other items and the inconvenience of the change would be far greater than any benefits; and that the weights and measures of a civilized country, although regularized by government, cannot be revolutionized as they are indissolubly connected with its past.

Simplification of systems of weights and measures and the elimination of unnecessary and special units and arbitrary trade sizes have been the trend of metrological progress. The United States, whose weights and measures were received from England in colonial days, did not follow the British reforms of 1824, when the imperial measures were adopted, but retained the Queen Anne gallon of 231 cubic inches established in 1707 and the Winchester bushel of Henry VII of 2150.42 cubic inches established in 1495. These discrepancies between British and American measures have caused confusion in foreign trade, and at the same time there has been a growing tendency in the United States to discontinue the bushel and other capacity measures and to follow the European practise of selling bulk commodities exclusively by weight.

Equity in trade and efficiency in industry depend upon correct and standardized weights and measures. Errors of weighing or measuring in any commercial transaction, great or small, are a tax collected on the gross amount involved and mean overpayments by the buyer or losses by the seller. Industries using interchangeable parts are dependent on accurate standards of measures, on which all specifications are based and to which, within the required tolerances, they must conform. The gauges, patterns and jigs must represent the requisite precision secured by accurate reference not merely to shop standards but to fundamental standards affording universal measures. Standardization of industrial products and processes of course depends upon precise measurement, which may result from cooperative action by industry or may be developed and controlled by the state.

In practically all countries the primary control of weights and measures is an attribute of sovereignty and, like the issuing of money, is located at the center of government, usually as a part of a ministry of trade, industry or commerce with subordinate functions at times assigned to local agencies. The control involves the mechanical inspection and comparison of weights and measures and supervisory functions, which deal with methods to insure observance of necessary regulations and sound practises. The range of activity is constantly being broadened by legislation; it now includes specifications for and inspection of various types of containers, thermometers, water, gas and electric meters and gasoline pumps.

In the United States, although the constitution authorizes Congress to fix the standard of weights and measures, federal legislation in this field has been limited and far more has been accomplished by executive order than by statutory enactment. By the failure of Congress to exercise its constitutional prerogative the supervision of weights and measures has come to be the responsibility of the individual states. Left free to enact such statutes as are deemed necessary or expedient, the states differ widely in the amount and kinds of regulation of weights and measures and in their enforcement. In 1901 the National Bureau of Standards was established at Washington as a national clearing house and source of technical authority on weights and measures. It has the custody of the fundamental standards of the United States and is a scientific bureau charged with comparison and research of high precision in metrology as well as in other fields. In Great Britain the Standards Department is a bureau of the Board of Trade, but local weights and measures administration is in the hands of the county and borough councils, which appoint the inspectors and provide their equipment. The Board of Trade has the custody of the national standards, approves the devices for weighing and measuring used in trade, examines candidates for the post of inspector, verifies local standards, formulates regulations and issues information to the local inspectors who enforce the weights and measures acts of Parliament as well as official regulations. In France control of weights and measures is exercised by the national government through the Direction des Affaires Commerciales et Industrielles in the Ministère du Commerce et de l'Industrie. Under a director at the Paris office there are chief inspectors in charge of districts with local offices manned by inspectors and assistant inspectors. In general the regulation of weights and measures shows the same variations as do other manifestations of the police power in different countries, ranging from complete central control to varying degrees of local authority.

HERBERT T. WADE

See: CONSUMER PROTECTION; STANDARDIZATION; INSPECTION; ASSIZES; CALENDAR.

Consult: Petrie, W. M. Flinders, *Ancient Weights and Measures* (London 1926); Bigourdan, Guillaume, *Le système métrique des poids et mesures* (Paris 1901); Guillaume, Charles E., *Le récent progrès du système métrique*, 3 vols. (Paris 1907–13); Hallock, William, and Wade, H. T., *Outlines of the Evolution of Weights* and *Measures and the Metric System* (New York 1906); National Industrial Conference Board, *The Metric versus the English System of Weights and Measures* (New York 1921); Halsey, Frederick A., *The Metric Fallacy* (rev. ed. New York 1919); United States, Bureau of Standards, *History of the Standard Weights and Measures of the United States*, by L. A. Fischer, Miscellaneous Publications, no. 64 (new ed. 1925); Chaney, Henry James, *Our Weights and Measures* (London 1897); Watson, Charles M., *British Weights and Measures* (London 1910); Nicholson, Edward, *Men and Measures* (London 1912); United States, Bureau of Standards, *Federal and State Laws Relating to Weights and Measures*, Miscellaneous Publications, no. 20 (3rd ed. rev. by William Parry, 1926), and *Weights and Measures Administration*, by R. W. Smith, Handbook series, no. 11 (1927).

WEISMANN, AUGUST (1834–1914), German zoologist. Weismann was professor at the University of Freiburg. Partly because an impairment of vision interfered with his microscopic work, he devoted himself largely although not exclusively to theoretical analyses of biological problems, especially heredity and evolution.

In his microscopic researches Weismann had been struck by the distinction between the reproductive (germ) cells and the other (somatic) cells of the individual. The fertilized egg from which an individual starts is a union of two reproductive cells, egg and sperm; it divides into numerous cells, some of which remain reproductive cells and are passed on to the next generation, while others become somatic cells and die with the individual. The reproductive cells thus constitute a continuous stream of protoplasm from generation to generation; they are potentially immortal; and it is through them that the hereditary material must be transmitted. A variation in a reproductive cell may affect the somatic cells derived from it; but an acquired character, which is a variation occurring first in somatic cells, cannot be transmitted to the next generation since somatic cells do not give rise to reproductive cells. The theory of the heritability of acquired characters was held by many of Weismann's contemporaries, including Darwin and Spencer. Weismann showed that the supposed instances of such inheritance were either incorrect or explicable in other ways; and largely as a result of his work the theory has been practically abandoned.

In a strict sense the hereditary material, or germ plasm, is only part of the reproductive cell. Weismann identified the germ plasm with the chromosomes; he predicted that the number of chromosomes in the mature reproductive cells would be found to be half as great as in the somatic cells, since the number is constant in successive generations of a species; and he deduced the fact that the hereditary material is composed of units as numerous as the traits that may separate in heredity. These conclusions have been verified and incorporated into modern genetical theory. But Weismann's system of units and subunits, which comprised four orders in all, was more complicated than the Mendelian system now in use. Weismann elaborated his theory without any knowledge of Mendel's work but attempted to harmonize the two systems after the rediscovery of Mendelism in 1900.

Heritable variations were attributed by Weismann to the formation of new combinations of genes in sexual reproduction and in a more fundamental sense to changes in the units themselves. The causes of these changes were then unknown, but he admitted the possibility, since demonstrated by H. J. Müller and Edgar Altenburg, that the changes might be brought about by the direct action of the environment on the reproductive cells. Weismann also realized that "the influences of the environment must always have a powerful effect upon the soma of the individual," including both physical and mental traits. He pointed out, for example, that the way in which genius expresses itself depends on the conditions of the time. What he denied was that the somatic effects of the environment can be transmitted to subsequent generations through the germ cells.

Weismann accepted Darwin's theory of evolution by natural selection of random variations. He developed it ingeniously and critically, applying it not only to physical but to mental characters, including the mind of man. In accordance with his selectionist views he was a mechanist in his biological philosophy.

ALEXANDER WEINSTEIN

Important works: *Studien zur Descendenz-Theorie*, 2 vols. (Leipsic 1875–76), tr. and ed. by Raphael Meldola as *Studies in the Theory of Descent* (London 1882); *Aufsätze über Vererbung und verwandte biologische Fragen* (Jena 1892), tr. as *Essays upon Heredity and Kindred Biological Problems*, ed. by Edward B. Poulton, Selmar Schönland, and Arthur E. Shipley, 2 vols. (Oxford 1889–92); *Das Keimplasma; Eine Theorie der Vererbung* (Jena 1892), tr. by W. Newton Parker and Harriet Rönnfeldt as *The Germ-Plasm; a Theory of Heredity*, Contemporary Science Series, vol. xxii (London 1893); *Vorträge über Descendenztheorie*, 2 vols. (Jena 1902, 3rd ed. 1913), tr. by J. Arthur and M. R. Thomson as *The Evolution Theory* (London 1904); "The Selection Theory" in *Darwin and Modern Science*, ed. by A. C. Seward

(Cambridge, Eng. 1909) p. 18–65, amplified in German as *Die Selektionstheorie* (Jena 1909).

Consult: Gaupp, Ernst, *August Weismann; sein Leben und sein Werk* (Jena 1917), with bibliography; Poulton, E. B., "August Friedrich Leopold Weismann" in Royal Society of London, *Proceedings*, ser. B, vol. lxxxix (1915–17) xxvii–xxxiv; Parker, W. N. and H., in Linnean Society of London, *Proceedings*, Session 127 (1914–15) 33–37.

WEISS, ANDRÉ (1858–1928), French jurist. At first professor at Dijon, Weiss subsequently occupied the chair of international law, both public and private, at Paris. He was a member of the Institut de France and member and president of the Institute of International Law. He served also as judge and vice president of the Permanent Court of International Justice at The Hague; he was jurisconsult in the French Ministry of Foreign Affairs until 1920 and was a member of the Académie Internationale de Droit Comparé and of similar institutions.

Weiss' most important contribution was in the field of private international law. His chief work is his *Traité théorique et pratique de droit international privé* (5 vols., Paris 1892–1905; 2nd ed., 6 vols., 1907–13). For students he also wrote an elementary text, *Manuel de droit international privé* (1st ed. with title *Traité élémentaire de droit . . .*, Paris 1885; 9th ed. 1925), which proved extremely popular. It was his great contribution to have written in the nineteenth century the first fundamental work in French of a general character concerned with private international law which was noteworthy from the point of view not only of doctrine but of documentation—and this in a period when the available literature was not as extensive as it is today.

Throughout his life Weiss played a very authoritative role, and he had numerous disciples. As chief of the school of the personality of law and as propagandist of the doctrine of the Italian Mancini, which he upheld consistently, he was considered an important figure in France. At the present time, however, his views are somewhat outmoded. The idea of the personality of law, however generous in its conception, contradicts the very structure of the state. For this reason it has never been accepted by Americans and it has now almost no supporters even in France.

J. P. NIBOYET

Consult: Bartin, Étienne, in *Journal du droit international*, vol. lv (1928) 849–52; Niboyet, J. P., "Trois jurisconsultes: Pillet, Weiss, Jordan" in *Revue de droit international privé*, vol. xxiv (1929) 577–91; Capitant, Henri, "Notice sur la vie et les travaux de M. André Weiss" in Institut de France, Académie des Sciences Morales et Politiques, *Séances et travaux . . . Compte rendu*, vol. xci, pt. ii (1931) 10–50.

WEITLING, WILHELM (1808–71), German communist. Weitling was the most important German figure in pre-Marxian communism and its first proletarian leader. The illegitimate son of a German servant and a French officer, he learned the tailor's craft, fled from Prussian military service and, as was customary among journeymen, took to wandering. During an extended stay in Paris he became a revolutionary egalitarian under the influence of Babeuf, Fourier and Lamennais. In the years 1838–44 in Paris and later in Switzerland he carried on effective oral and written agitation among the German journeymen, especially through his books: *Die Menschheit, wie sie ist und wie sie sein sollte* (Paris 1838, 2nd ed. Berne 1845) and his chief work, *Die Garantien der Harmonie und Freiheit* (Vevey 1842; new ed. by F. Mehring, Berlin 1908). The prospectus of his *Das Evangelium eines armen Sünders* (Zurich 1843, 2nd ed. Berne 1845) led to his imprisonment in Zurich in 1843, but the published report of his trial won many new supporters to communism. Switzerland turned Weitling over to the Prussian government, which in order to rid itself of an agitator permitted him to emigrate to the United States. Before he left in 1846 he visited London and Brussels, there coming into contact with Marx, who expressed considerable regard for Weitling's role among the revolutionary proletariat.

Weitling's influence on the later communist movement derived rather from his antimilitarism and antinationalism than from his radical egalitarianism. During the period up to 1844, when his contribution was of significance, he considered his writings as the collective achievement of his class. But his ideas, which grew out of the soil of handicraft, did not correspond to the needs of the rising industrial workers; certain pathological aspects of his personality became more marked; and his theories based on "natural law" were superseded by the "scientific" communism of Marx and Engels. Although Weitling revisited Germany during the revolutionary years 1848–49, he realized that his influence was waning and returned to the United States.

Among the German workers in the United States the agitation which he conducted particularly for labor exchange banks left no permanent mark, and his literary work, carried on mainly through the *Republik der Arbeiter* (New York 1850–55), showed that he had nothing further to contribute to the revolutionary movement.

GUSTAV MAYER

Consult: Introduction by F. Mehring to his edition of *Garantien der Harmonie und Freiheit* (Berlin 1908); Barnikol, Ernst, *Wilhelm Weitling*, Christentum und Sozialismus; Quellen und Darstellungen, vols. i–v (Kiel 1929–31); Brugger, Otto, *Geschichte der deutschen Handwerkervereine in der Schweiz, 1836–43. Die Wirksamkeit Weitlings*, Berner Untersuchungen zur allgemeinen Geschichte, vol. iii (Berne 1932); Commons, J. R., and associates, *History of Labour in the United States*, 2 vols. (New York 1918) vol. i, p. 512–16; Adler, Max, *Wegweiser* (5th ed. Vienna 1931) p. 287–313.

WELCH, WILLIAM HENRY (1850–1934), American pathologist, bacteriologist and hygienist. A graduate of Yale in 1870 and of Columbia Medical School in 1875, Welch devoted three years to postgraduate study in the German universities and in 1879 became professor of pathology in the Bellevue Hospital Medical College, where he established the first pathological laboratory in the United States. Having been recommended by Billings and Cohnheim for the chair about to be established in the Johns Hopkins Medical School, he put in another year of bacteriological training in Europe, principally under von Flügge, and thus brought the advanced laboratory technique of Koch to Baltimore. Up to 1900 he devoted himself mainly to research work and to teaching. His principal contributions to pathology were monographs on pulmonary oedema, glomerulo-nephritis, thrombosis and fever. In 1891 he discovered the bacillus *Aërogenes capsulatus*, or Welch bacillus, which activates gas gangrene in wounds, and the white streptococcus which infests wounds by way of the skin. Subsequently he became a leading member of the State Board of Health of Maryland, serving as its president from 1898 to 1922. Up to the World War his interests were in the main concentrated upon public health and social welfare, notably mental hygiene and the prevention of tuberculosis. He served in uniform as an inspector of camps and military hospitals during the war and was rewarded with the brevet of brigadier general. The creation of the School of Hygiene and Public Health in Baltimore, which he directed between 1916 and 1926, was the culmination of Welch's activities in public health and applied sanitation. He founded the *Journal of Experimental Medicine* and edited it from 1896 to 1905 and was a founder in 1921 of the *American Journal of Hygiene*. Active in the establishment of the Rockefeller Institute for Medical Research, he was president of its board of directors during the last three decades of his life and was a trustee of the Carnegie Institution of Washington, a member of the International Health Board and a principal adviser of the China Medical Board of the Rockefeller Foundation and of the Milbank Memorial Fund. Welch was a recipient of many honors and distinctions, notably the presidency in 1915–16 of the National Academy of Sciences. The Welch Medical Library, erected in his honor, was opened in 1929.

F. H. GARRISON

Works: *Bibliography of William Henry Welch*, ed. by Walter C. Burket (Baltimore 1917).

Consult: Garrison, F. H., in *Scientific Monthly*, vol. xxxviii (1934) 579–82; *William Henry Welch at Eighty*, ed. by V. O. Freeburg (New York 1930).

WELCKER, KARL THEODOR (1790–1869), German political theorist. Welcker played a decisive role in the development of the ideology of German bourgeois liberalism. He was born in Hesse and as a very young man became professor of political science at the University of Kiel. Later he taught at Bonn with Arndt and in 1823 became associated with Karl von Rotteck at the University of Freiburg. Rotteck and Welcker became the leaders of the opposition in the Baden *Landtag*. Because of their publicist activities they were ousted from their teaching positions in 1832 and became the most influential representatives of liberal and national propaganda during the period prior to 1848. The period during which Welcker occupied a position of importance in Germany began in 1830 when he introduced into the Bundestag at Frankfort on the Main a motion for the establishment of full freedom of the press throughout the German Confederation. The motion was unsuccessful; as a result of it Welcker was persecuted, although he acquired renown throughout Germany. After the suppression of his own paper, the *Freisinniger*, he collaborated with Rotteck in the publication of the *Staats-Lexicon* (19 vols., Altona 1834–49; 3rd ed., 14 vols., Leipsic 1856–66), which served as a political text for two generations of the educated classes of Germany. In 1848 Welcker represented Baden at the Frankfort Assembly, where he joined the group of moderate liberals and took an active part in the elaboration of the fundamental principles. He took a decisive step when, contrary to his earlier "greater German" views, which allowed for the retention of Austria in the German federal state, he introduced a motion in 1849 to the effect that the imperial crown be offered to the king of Prussia. Welcker was an idealist and a skilful popularizer rather than an original thinker. His general attitudes were shaped by the experiences and institutions of the Anglo-Saxon world. Personally of unimpeachable character, he was zealous in his belief that bourgeois freedom represented the arcanum of political power and national political development. Welcker exerted a much greater influence as a teacher than as a scientist or political figure.

THEODOR HEUSS

Consult: Wild, Karl, *Karl Theodor Welcker* (Heidelberg 1913); Zehnter, Hans, *Das Staatslexikon von Rotteck und Welcker*, List-Studien, no. iii (Jena 1929).

WELD, THEODORE DWIGHT (1803–95), American abolitionist. Weld grew up in western New York, where he became an evangelist in Charles G. Finney's Presbyterian revival. Through Finney, Weld met the New York philanthropists led by Arthur and Lewis Tappan, who were backing Finney's revival, and became their agent in various projects for social reform.

Through his friendship with Charles Stuart, British advocate of emancipation in the West Indies, Weld became an abolitionist. It was at his suggestion that the New York philanthropists organized the American Anti-Slavery Society when in 1833 Parliament abolished slavery in the British West Indies. The society adopted the British motto of "immediate emancipation" in order to link its cause with the British movement; this was interpreted everywhere as a program of immediate freedom for the slaves, and the society's propaganda not only failed to win the east but often provoked hostility.

Weld saved the abolition movement from disaster. He and students whom he had won to the cause, acting as agents of the American Anti-Slavery Society, preached emancipation as a revival in religious benevolence with extraordinary success and established the movement securely in Ohio, western Pennsylvania, New York and many districts in the east. The antislavery areas in the west in the main coincided with the field of Weld's labors. He made converts of many men who later became prominent leaders in the abolition movement and in Republican party politics, and antislavery sentiment among New-School Presbyterians may be ascribed largely to his agitation among the ministers.

By 1836 the success of Weld's agents was so apparent that the American Anti-Slavery Society turned all its resources to enlarging Weld's band. Weld himself selected seventy new agents and gave them a Pentecostal training in the gospel of abolitionism. During the next few years "the Seventy" consolidated the antislavery movement throughout the north. The most widely distributed tracts of the movement, although published either anonymously or under the signatures of other authors, were all written by Weld. In addition he directed the national campaign for presenting antislavery petitions to Congress. When his converts in the House of Representatives—Giddings, Gates, Andrews and others—determined to break with the Whig party on the slavery issue, they summoned Weld to Washington to act as their lobbyist. For two crucial years, 1841 and 1842, Weld directed their campaign; and when an antislavery bloc within the party was well established, he withdrew from public life.

Weld's anonymity in history may be attributed to his almost morbid modesty. He accepted no office, refused all honors, attended no conventions and would not permit his speeches or his letters to be printed. During his long life he refused to let friends write of his achievements.

GILBERT HOBBS BARNES

Works: *The Bible against Slavery* (New York 1837, new ed. Pittsburgh 1864); "Wythe," *The Power of Congress over the District of Columbia*, Anti-Slavery Examiner, no. 5 (New York 1837, 4th ed. 1838); Thome, J. A., and Kimball, J. H., *Emancipation in the West Indies*, rewritten and condensed by T. D. Weld, Anti-Slavery Examiner, no. 7 (New York 1838, 2nd ed. 1839); *American Slavery As It Is*, American Anti-Slavery Society (New York 1839); *The Correspondence of Theodore Weld*, ed. by G. H. Barnes and D. L. Dumond (New York 1934).

Consult: Barnes, Gilbert H., *The Antislavery Impulse, 1830–1844* (New York 1933).

WELFARE CAPITALISM. See WELFARE WORK, INDUSTRIAL.

WELFARE WORK, INDUSTRIAL. This term is used to describe the voluntary efforts of an employer to establish, within the existing industrial system, working and sometimes living and cultural conditions of his employees beyond what is required by law, the customs of industry and the conditions of the market. It has come into disuse in the United States, because most earlier and some later forms have been paternalistic and inquisitorial or because the apparent motive of some—the desire to avoid wage increases—has made the term repugnant to organized labor and therefore indiscreet for employers to use and more particularly because its substantial content has been incorporated into a comprehensive, organized managerial function identified by such new terms as labor management and personnel administration. In the United Kingdom, on the other hand, the term is still in vogue, both because labor there has been more accustomed to class distinctions and paternalistic relations and also because the recent development has been limited chiefly to physical factors within a framework of established relations with strongly organized labor and has manifested characteristic British adeptness in adjustment to dominant conditions.

Industrial welfare work has taken numerous forms. Those dealing with immediate working conditions are special provisions for adequate light, heat, ventilation, toilet facilities, accident and occupational disease prevention, lunch rooms, rest rooms, maximum hours, minimum wages. Those concerned with less immediate working conditions and group interests are gymnasiums, clubrooms, playgrounds, gardens, dancing, music, house organs, mutual aid societies, vacations with pay, profit sharing, stock ownership, disability and unemployment funds, pensions, savings banks, provision for conciliation and arbitration, shop committees and works councils. Still others are designed to improve community conditions: housing, model dwellings, retail stores, churches, schools, libraries, kindergartens, domestic science, day nurseries, dispensary and dental service, lectures, motion pictures, athletic contests, picnics, summer camps. The combination in which such elements of welfare work are found in any given situation is a result of the interrelation of the employer's motives, the requirements of the situation, the reaction of the employees and the ability of the enterprise to bear the costs. Only rarely, however, has more than a small fraction of the list characterized the welfare work of a particular enterprise.

Conscious and organized welfare work has not been typical of all industrial enterprises. It is today quite common in large organizations, where personal contacts are least intimate, where the problem of winning individual interest and good will is more difficult because the unfavorable forces of mass psychology find free play, and where the per capita cost of such work may be distributed over a large output. In the smaller and more numerous enterprises only the simpler types are undertaken and in a less formal way. Such organizations continue to rely on the strength of intimate personal contacts to secure and maintain the interest and good will of workers.

A generalization concerning the motives which induce employers to establish welfare work would be misleading. In individual cases one or more of the following may dominate: humanitarianism, or social mindedness; the striving for efficiency and greater output; the necessity of attracting workers to a decentralized locality; the necessity of attracting a higher grade of workers; the attempt to smooth the way for mechanization; the aim of combating organization of employees by outside influence; the desire to avoid payment of a tax on surplus; exhibitionism and advertising. In particular instances the motives are usually composite—conduct of employers in this respect is as varied as human conduct in other respects. Yet in broad historical perspective certain motivating characteristics appear to dominate successive periods of the development of the movement.

Forerunners of some of the present forms of welfare work are to be found in studies of the guild, manorial and even earlier periods of employer-employee relationships. The inference seems fairly reasonable that there have always existed, first, a variety of temperaments among employers which has led some of them to take advantage of differential opportunities for securing worker good will and application; and, second, a margin for exploitation between the model employer-employee relationship of a period and an economically feasible, more cooperative, more productive and more profitable relationship. This may account adequately for the fact that some prototype of present day welfare work has always existed.

Welfare work as a movement began in the early years of the industrial revolution. It appears at that time to have been a reaction of social minded employers both to the shocking conditions of work which developed in the first years of the factory system and to the concept of scientific meliorism represented by such philosophers as Comte, John Stuart Mill, the Martineaus and George Eliot. In the first quarter of the nineteenth century Robert Owen openly declared that he sought formation of character in his employees through shorter hours, a minimum wage, schools, churches, decent housing, medical attendance, sick benefits and such devices. In the second quarter Leclaire in France introduced profit sharing, jointly administered benefits and aid and other democratic factors. The influence of Owen was reflected in the first noteworthy welfare work in the United States in the second quarter of the century under the leadership of Francis Cabot Lowell and Nathan Appleton at Lowell, Massachusetts. Generally the characteristics of this first period of the movement were humanitarianism and a belief in human perfectibility and the possibility of reconstruction of character. It was unquestionably paternalistic and arbitrary, and a major theme was the graciousness of fortunate superiors to unfortunate inferiors.

From then on until close to the end of the century welfare work as a movement lagged, became less idealistic and reflected the point of view of more self-interested employers. Either because the doctrine of perfectibility of human nature had not proved its validity in practise or more probably because, in the United States especially, workers as well as employers were concerned with pursuit of the full dinner pail and a rapid rise to wealth, and looked upon working discomforts as belonging only to a temporary situation, better in any case than the woods and farms and the conditions of pre-immigration days, the movement lost acceleration and its humanitarian characteristics. Of course individual employers departed from model employer-employee relations to bestow benefits upon workers in varying degrees as permitted by the profitableness of each enterprise. In Europe the movement was influenced by the appearance of socialism. The Krupp contribution in Germany in the third quarter of the century is fairly representative of the continental development of that period. Because of the inadequacy of local conditions for proper community life in the Essen district and as part of the general homeopathic treatment of the socialistic movement in Germany at the time, there was initiated at the Krupp works an extensive paternalistic community welfare program, involving housing, cooperative stores, a thrift campaign, guaranties against the results of accident, sickness and other incapacities, old age pensions, life insurance and technical education. Thus while in the United States the relief work movement became quiescent, the counter socialist movement in Europe promoted a special manifestation of its development.

About the turn of the century the movement in the United States showed a renewed vigor which reflected changing conditions and a new class of managerial problems. The machine age then really appeared—the first century following the industrial revolution had been only an incipient machine age. Prior to the railroad construction of the 1870's and 1880's in the United States markets were local; even the world markets of England were but an aggregate of local markets, each with its particular form and style demands. But with the consolidation by transcontinental railroad systems of the market of the United States, a market with apparently limitless demands for both capital goods and consumer goods, a previously uneconomic degree of mass selling and large scale production became practicable. Increase in size of plants, in variety and capacity of machines and in the number of workers per plant followed rapidly. New problems of management emerged; a management movement was generated; and the concepts of organization, system and efficiency became the concern of industrial employers. Organization and mechanisms were the order of the day, and even a worker came to be regarded by many employers as not merely a man with a certain amount of energy and an incidental skill but as a special kind of human, delicately adjusted machine which would yield a greater output per labor hour if, as it were, properly oiled, greased and otherwise kept in prime condition. Humanitarianism, at which most hard headed business men had looked askance as an inadequate reason for spending money on welfare activities, was now replaced in their minds by a genuinely economic justification: more efficient performance and lower unit costs. Thus better light, heat and ventilation, better toilet facilities and wash rooms, lunch rooms, lockers for clothing, technical education, productivity wage systems and similar factors became the concern of a labor maintenance department—the functionalized counterpart of the functionalized plant and equipment maintenance department. The welfare secretary appeared as the personal representative of the employer in labor maintenance activity. At the same time organized labor, struggling for higher wages, entertained the suspicion that welfare efforts were intended to serve chiefly as a blanket with which the wage issue might be obscured. For this reason and because of frequent evidences of paternalism welfare work did not at the time win the sympathetic interest of labor; never in fact until the content of welfare work had become integrated into the management structure and the term itself with its disagreeable connotations was discarded did labor extend tolerant approval to the movement.

The most recent period of the development of welfare work in the United States began with the World War and continued for a decade thereafter, becoming part of a more highly organized managerial function commonly identified as personnel administration. Several influences hastened this evolution, of which four are outstanding. In the first place, during the war the drafting of many experienced and skilled workers into the army, at the very time when circumstances required a stepping up of production, made necessary the filling of factories with unskilled, diluted labor. Output was accordingly dependent upon the maintenance of employees' good will through appeals to patriotism and other emotions and upon the training of this diluted labor for the required kinds and degrees of skilled work. Every known device for stimulation of the emotions and for organization of work was employed. Labor management became the concern of functionalized departments under major executives. Most of the activities of conventional welfare work were taken over by the new functionaries; but they stressed a new approach: training in skills and cultivation of interests, motives and good will. In the second place, during the decade following the war mass selling and mass production received an additional impetus, so much so that new sources of power were developed, multiple purpose machines were replaced by huge single purpose machines, and the organization and system of a factory came to be a network of coordinated and finely adjusted procedures. Uninterrupted flow of work to keep costly capital investment continuously productive became imperative. It was discovered that although the machine had replaced labor as a source of power and as the embodiment of many kinds of skill, nevertheless maintenance of labor adept in managing the machines, in governing their adjustment during operations and especially in the routines of the operating system was a more critical problem than ever. Labor turnover came to be recognized as a measurable cost; labor ill will also, through sabotage of expensive machines and tools, was becoming progressively much easier, more subtle and more costly. It was perceived that a new kind of worker was required: intelligent, alert, trained, capable of correct perception, quick reaction and sustained attention. Labor as a source of power and an embodiment of specialized skills was replaced by labor as an embodiment of alert intelligence, good will and cooperation. In the third place, the researches of scientific management and of industrial psychology were presenting abundant evidence of natural differences among individuals and of the need of selection, training and wise placement; of the nature of physical and especially emotional fatigue and methods of avoiding them; of the power of non-financial as well as financial incentives; and in general of the part played in every organization by the psychology of the total situation. As soon as science had indicated the significance of both the total personality and the total situation, much of what had once been called welfare work received new evaluation and new attention as a vital part of the integrated structure of management. And, finally, labor came out of the World War with additional strength of organization; thus sometimes as a means of adjustment to this condition and at other times as a method of opposition, depending on the motivation of the particular management, increasing attention was given to welfare work as one element of the new function of personnel administration.

Welfare work and social legislation have progressed side by side but with unequal pace. There are some who see in welfare work the origins of social legislation. By definition welfare work is in advance of social legislation. There is evidence also that welfare work has suggested what forms social legislation should take; that it is the field where individual initiative puts on record its ideas and experiments in improvement of management looking toward the establishment of local working and living conditions which later come to be models for application on a social scale. However, with noteworthy exceptions industrialists generally are not leaders in social legislation. Owen's conception of welfare work as a means of reforming individual and social character gave way to the industrialist's present conception of the movement as good management offering a differential advantage over competitors who ignore it. Social legislation has been enacted through the humanitarian and social minded effort of non-industrial reformers organized into consumers' leagues, child welfare associations and similar groups; through the vision of the occasional statesman who perceives and interprets social trends; through the opportunistic, sometimes demagogic, appeals of small caliber politicians for class support; and especially through the pressure of organized labor. In Soviet Russia, in Germany and Austria of the post-war decade and in Fascist Italy the translation into social legislation of various forms of welfare work has been the result of political revolutions. In the United Kingdom and in the United States progress in social legislation has been more deliberate because of industry's skill in regulating the pace by appeals to the dominant spirit of individualism and by the manipulation of the processes of democracy.

There appears to be little ground for concluding that the costs of welfare work have been either taken out of wages or added to the unit costs of production. There have been numerous instances of the wastes of impracticable and irritating developments of its forms and even of the outright failure of enterprises which could not bear the costs, but by and large this has undoubtedly been more than offset by a tapping of new levels of interest, energy and skill and by economies of cooperation which otherwise would not have been realized. This is especially true with respect to present day welfare work, which personnel administration has subjected to the discipline of research and evaluation, eliminations and additions. It should be borne in mind that the industrial world has been operating in an economy of relative scarcity, in which, with an apparatus and a technique introduced a century and a half ago, it has been striving to secure command of the deeper forces of animate as well as inanimate nature, to accumulate a stock of capital goods and a fund of free capital and to bring all individual activities in the enterprise into a technical framework of ever greater productivity. In such an economy the devices of welfare work in stimulating individual and group capacity for utilizing human intellectual and manual energies have served a social function corresponding to that served by the privileges allowed custodians and manipulators of savings. It is likely that in the long run society will continue to permit some degree of individual managerial initiative in the exploitation of the margin between the modal and the best in industrial relationships, to serve its function of experiment and to discover what forms of welfare work are most suitable for incorporation into social regulations. But it appears equally likely, in view of the problems created by a potential economy of abundance and as is indicated by current social and political trends, that such individual experimentation will be brought more and more under social direction and that the process of translating its approved results into standardized social procedures will be accelerated.

H. S. PERSON

See: PERSONNEL ADMINISTRATION; MANAGEMENT; INDUSTRIAL RELATIONS; INDUSTRIAL DEMOCRACY; EMPLOYEE STOCK OWNERSHIP; PROFIT SHARING; EMPLOYEE REPRESENTATION; COMPANY UNIONS; COMPANY HOUSING; COMPANY TOWNS; GARDEN CITIES; LABOR-CAPITAL COOPERATION; LABOR, METHODS OF REMUNERATION FOR; TRADE UNIONS; PENSIONS; INDUSTRIAL HYGIENE; SAFETY MOVEMENT; PUBLIC WELFARE; LABOR LEGISLATION AND LAW.

Consult: Boettiger, Louis A., *Employee Welfare Work* (New York 1923); *Welfare Work in Industry*, ed. by Eleanor T. Kelly (London 1925); Proud, E. Dorothea, *Welfare Work* (3rd ed. London 1918); Mayo, Elton, *The Human Problems of an Industrial Civilization* (New York 1933); Tolman, William H., *Social Engineering* (New York 1909); Todd, A. J., *Industry and Society* (New York 1933); Frankel, Lee K., and Fleisher, Alexander, *The Human Factor in Industry* (New York 1920); Commons, John R., *Industrial Goodwill* (New York 1919); Commons, J. R., and others, *Industrial Government* (New York 1921); Hepner, Harry Walker, *Human Relations in Changing Industry* (New York 1934), especially chs. xiii–xv; "Personnel and Employment Problems in Industrial Management," ed. by Meyer Bloomfield and Joseph H. Willits, in American Academy of Political and Social Science, *Annals*, vol. lxv (1916); *Linking Science and Industry*, ed. by Henry C. Metcalf (Baltimore 1925); National Industrial Conference Board, *Industrial Relations Programs in Small Plants* (New York 1929), and *Industrial Relations; Administration of Policies and Programs* (New York 1931); Rowntree, B. Seebohm, *The Human Factor in Business* (2nd ed. London 1925); *Business Leadership*, ed. by Henry C. Metcalf (New York 1930); Tead, Ordway, and Metcalf, Henry C., *Personnel Administration* (3rd ed. New York 1933); Scott, Walter Dill, Clothier, R. C., and Mathewson, S. B., *Personnel Management* (2nd ed. New York 1931) ch. xxiv; Willoughby, W. F., "Industrial Communities" in United States, Department of Labor, *Bulletin*, vol. i (1895–96) 223–64, 335–59, 479–517 and 567–609; Cadbury, E., *Experiments in Industrial Organization* (London 1912); Williams, Iolo A., *The Firm of Cadbury, 1831–1931* (London 1931); Tusil, Erich, *Die Betriebswohlfahrtseinrichtungen in der deutschen Brauindustrie* (Berlin 1931); United States, Bureau of Labor Statistics, "Employers' Welfare Work" by E. L. Otey, *Bulletin*, no. 123 (1913), "Industrial Health and Efficiency. Final Report of the British Health of Munition Workers' Committee," *Bulletin*, no. 249 (1919), and "Welfare Work for Employees in Industrial Establishments in the United States," *Bulletin*, no. 250 (1919); "Indoor Recreation for Industrial Employees" in *Monthly Labor Review*, vol. xxv (1927) 465–78; Herring, H. L., *Welfare Work in Mill Villages* (Chapel Hill, N.C. 1929).

WELLESLEY, MARQUIS RICHARD COLLEY (1760–1842), British colonial administrator. Intended for the presidency of Madras

Wellesley was transferred to Calcutta in 1797 when Pitt deemed it best to send Cornwallis to Dublin. Wellesley became governor general of India at a critical time. With the temperament and ideas of a Warren Hastings and a ministerial viewpoint akin to that of his friend Pitt, it is not surprising that Wellesley added largely to British India. French officers and emissaries at the various native courts served as agents provocateurs for his exceptional energy and imperious temper. Two days after learning of Bonaparte's landing in Egypt Wellesley ordered the governor of Madras to prepare for war with Tippu, the sultan of Mysore. This vainglorious Moslem prince, on terms with the French, soon lost his throne and life; henceforth Mysore was a subordinated state with the shadow of a rajah as the screen for British aggrandizement. By the treaty Mysore, deprived of half its territory, granted a large annual subsidy to the East India Company for protecting the remainder. The overlordship of the British in southern India was greatly increased during the next few years by similar subsidiary treaties with Tanjore, Hyderabad, Surat and the Carnatic. The government of the Carnatic was taken over on the pretext of its relations with Tippu.

The most questionable of Wellesley's actions was the forced deposition in 1801 of the ruler of Oudh and the acceptance by that state of a subsidiary treaty, on the ground of possible Afghan attacks. The attempted conquest of central India from the marauding Mahratta chieftains, Sindia and Holkar, was less successful in a military way, although the British obtained Delhi and the person of the blind emperor. Military defeats in central India, dislike by the company of Wellesley's forward policy, a dismaying increase in the company's debt, led to the governor general's recall in 1805, his replacement by Cornwallis and the resumption temporarily of the policy of non-interference in the affairs of the Indian native states.

Wellesley was foreign secretary from 1809 to 1812. He favored free trade and the removal of Catholic disabilities, differing sharply from his younger brother, the duke of Wellington, in these views. In 1821 Wellesley was appointed lord lieutenant of Ireland but felt it necessary to resign when Wellington became prime minister in 1828. Wellesley concurred in the Reform Bill of 1832.

HOWARD ROBINSON

Consult: *The Despatches, Minutes and Correspondence of the Marquess Wellesley*, ed. by Montgomery Martin, 5 vols. (London 1836–37); *The Life and Correspondence of Richard Colley Wellesley*, 2 vols. (London 1914); Hutton, W. H., *The Marquess Wellesley* (London 1893); Roberts, P. E., *India under Wellesley* (London 1929); *Cambridge History of India*, vol. v ed. by H. H. Dodwell (Cambridge, Eng. 1929).

WELLHAUSEN, JULIUS (1844–1918), German Semitist and historian. In 1870 he was appointed *Privatdozent* for Old Testament history at Göttingen, where he had studied under Ewald, and in 1872 he became professor at Greifswald. Because of his role in the higher criticism movement Wellhausen realized that promotion to the theological faculty of a larger university was closed to him, and he voluntarily withdrew in 1882 to become *Privatdozent* in Semitics at Halle. In 1885 he became professor of Semitics at Marburg, and from 1892 until his retirement in 1913 he taught at Göttingen. Beginning with his studies on the composition of the Hexateuch in 1876 Wellhausen identified himself with the higher criticism movement, and in 1878 he published his *Geschichte Israels* (vol. i, Berlin 1878), later revised as *Prolegomena zur Geschichte Israels* (6th ed. Berlin 1905; tr. by J. S. Black and A. Menzies, Edinburgh 1885). The so-called Grafian hypothesis, which maintained that the Priestly Code, which provides the backbone and general tone of the Hexateuch, was actually the latest element in the Hexateuch, had made little headway despite the work of Vatke and Graf in Germany and Kuenen in Holland. In Wellhausen's *Prolegomena* it received its most complete exposition, and he immediately became the spearhead of the entire movement. Despite the storm of opposition from orthodox Christians and Jews alike the power of Wellhausen's exposition soon brought a majority of Biblical scholars over to his view. He followed this work with his *Israelitische und jüdische Geschichte* (Berlin 1894, 8th ed. 1921), in which on the basis of his critical analysis of the Old Testament he reconstructed the history of the Hebrews from their coming to Egypt up to the rise of Christianity. As a historian Wellhausen shows a remarkable critical ability in the use of source materials and considerable detachment from theological bias but fails to overcome certain a priori notions, as, for example, regarding the role and ideas of Jesus. Furthermore his conception of history was almost exclusively politico-religious. Today his main ideas are still accepted but his work has been broken down in many places. The most significant and most valid criticism is of his disregard for new discoveries in the ancient Orient. Although he was not ignorant of this new material and admitted that the Hebrews can no longer be studied as an isolated group, Wellhausen distrusted these finds and failed to make use of them. Much of his picture of the growth of Israelite religion from primitive animism to monotheism and the rise of Judaism can no longer be accepted. But his defense of Graf, the central theme in his work, still stands despite the recent attacks of Koenig, Kegel and others, who have reaffirmed the traditional view of the Mosaic Torah. Wellhausen was attracted to Islamic history by its similarities with Jewish history. His contributions were of the same nature, a painstaking reconstruction of the literary sources for early Islam, followed by a history in which he traced its development from animism to monotheism. His chief work in this field, *Das arabische Reich und sein Sturz* (Berlin 1902; tr. by M. G. Weir, Calcutta 1927), is also entirely politico-religious. But here Wellhausen was not hampered by his religious beliefs and the result is much more valid, even in its details. In his New Testament work Wellhausen made a similar critical examination of the Gospels, discarding much as not genuine. In general his contributions to New Testament history are his least significant works.

Moses I. Finkelstein

Other important works: Die Pharisäer und die Sadducäer (Greifswald 1874, 2nd ed. Hanover 1924); Skizzen und Vorarbeiten, 6 vols. (Berlin 1884–99), especially vol. iii, Reste arabisches Heidentums gesammelt und erläutert (2nd ed. Berlin 1897); Einleitung in die drei ersten Evangelien (Berlin 1905; 2nd ed. 1911). For a complete bibliography to 1914, see Rahlfs, A., in Studien zur semitischen Philologie und Religionsgeschichte Julius Wellhausen . . . gewidmet . . ., ed. by K. Marti (Giessen 1914) p. 351–68.

Consult: Baumgartner, W., "Wellhausen und der heutige Stand der alttestamentlichen Wissenschaft" in Theologische Rundschau, n.s., vol. ii (1930) 287–307; Smith, H. P., *Essays in Biblical Interpretation* (Boston 1921) ch. xii; Sellin, E., in Deutsches biographisches Jahrbuch, vol. ii (1928) 341–44, and Archaeology versus Wellhausenism, Aftermath series, no. 6 (Nashville 1924); Schwartz, E., in K. Gesellschaft der Wissenschaften zu Göttingen, Nachrichten. Geschäftliche Mitteilungen (1918) 43–73; Becker, C. H., in Islam, vol. ix (1919) 95–99.

WELLINGTON, FIRST DUKE OF, Arthur Wellesley (1769–1852), British soldier and statesman. Wellington began his military career in 1787 as an ensign and until 1793 served as aide-de-camp to successive lords lieutenant of Ireland. In 1794 he was called upon for service in the war against France and for nearly a year fought under the incompetent command of the duke of York. From 1797 to 1805 he served in India, where as a general in command he established a great military reputation by his brilliant campaigns against native leaders.

On his return to England he sat for a short time in the British Parliament and from 1807 to 1809 acted as chief secretary for Ireland. But the great Napoleonic wars called him imperatively to the continent, where his succession of victories in Portugal and Spain placed him in the front rank of military leaders. After the fall of Napoleon in 1814 he served as ambassador in Paris and plenipotentiary at the closing sessions of the Congress of Vienna. Upon Napoleon's escape from Elba he assisted the allies in formulating those plans of campaign which resulted in the crowning victory at Waterloo. After the completion of the peace treaties Wellington remained on the continent for nearly three years in command of the army of occupation in northeastern France.

The business of war having now been settled, Wellington addressed himself to the problems of international and domestic politics. As British delegate at the Congress of Verona in 1822 he strongly asserted the principle of non-intervention in the internal affairs of civilized states. His general international policy was directed toward the maintenance of peace on the basis of the status quo ante; he opposed the recognition of the independence of the Spanish American colonies (1824), tried to preserve the integrity of the Turkish Empire, in 1826 advocated the sending of British troops to Portugal to avert a Spanish invasion of that country and deplored the revolt of the Belgians in 1830. As prime minister from January, 1828, to November, 1830, Wellington was not a success. He did not understand party government; he could not tolerate opposition; he showed himself obscurantist and reactionary in policy. But while he held strong opinions, he was always prepared to retreat from an unpopular principle as he would from an indefensible fortress. Thus having denounced Catholic emancipation he carried it through in 1829, and having condemned parliamentary reform he led his followers out of the House of Lords and allowed the first Reform Bill to become law in 1832. Similarly in 1846 he asserted his belief in the corn laws yet assisted Sir Robert Peel to remove them from the statute book. After the fall of Peel's cabinet, of which he had been member without portfolio, he retired into private life, although he reemerged in 1848 to organize defense measures against an anticipated Chartist rising. By the time of his death the mistakes and vacillations of his politics had been entirely overshadowed in the public mind by the memory of his superb military gifts, his patriotism and his personal qualities.

F. J. C. HEARNSHAW

Consult: Maxwell, Herbert, *The Life of Wellington*, 2 vols. (2nd ed. London 1900); Morris, W. O., *Wellington, Soldier and Statesman, and the Revival of the Military Power of England* (New York 1904); Guedalla, Philip, *Wellington* (New York 1931); Halévy, Élie, *Histoire du peuple anglais au XIXe siècle*, 4 vols. (Paris 1912–26), tr. by E. I. Watkin and D. A. Barker (London 1924–29), especially vol. i, p. 73–81, vol. ii, p. 257–60, 296–306; Fortescue, J. W., *Wellington* (London 1925); Oman, C. W. C., *Wellington's Army, 1809–1814* (London 1912).

WELLS, DAVID AMES (1828–98), American economist. Wells graduated from the Lawrence Scientific School, Cambridge, in 1851. He published several widely used manuals on geology and chemistry. At a time when the fortunes of the Civil War were at a low ebb he delivered a lecture on *Our Burden and Our Strength* (New York 1864), in which he argued that the credit of the North was still unimpaired and that a wise use of its undoubtedly superior resources would in the end bring victory. The lecture attracted wide attention, and as a result Wells was appointed a member of the United States Revenue Commission and in 1866 was made special commissioner of revenue. His *Reports of the Special Commissioner of the Revenue*, 1866, 1867, 1868, 1869, have become classics on the subject of indirect taxes and his advice on fiscal matters was generally followed, especially as to the use of stamps in the collection of the tobacco and liquor taxes. Because of his adoption of the extreme free trade view, however, his position was abolished in 1870. He thereupon became chairman of the New York state tax commission and prepared the first and second reports of the commissioners (1871–72; the first report revised as *Local Taxation*, New York 1871) on the problems of state and local taxation, the earliest treatment of the subject to appear in the United States. During the remainder of his life he published works on the tariff, the money problem—especially paper currency and later silver—the merchant marine and public revenue. His chief works were *Practical Economics* (New York 1885), *Recent Economic Changes* (New York 1889) and the posthumous *Theory and Practice of Taxation* (ed. by W. C. Ford, New York 1900), all of them distinguished by a rare command of statistical material and by an eminent common sense.

Wells remained to the end an extreme individualist and an advocate of laissez faire, as is revealed in his *The Relation of the Government to the Telegraph* (New York 1873) and *The Relation of the Federal Government to the Railroads* (New York 1874), in his *Freer Trade Essential to Future National Prosperity and Development* (New York 1882), in his bitter controversies with General Francis A. Walker on wages and money, in "The Communism of a Discriminating Income-Tax" (*North American Review*, vol. cxxx, 1880, p. 236–46) and later in his unqualified opposition to a federal income tax. In fiscal theory he will be remembered for his criticism of the general property tax, which was, however, not based on any wide historical or philosophical grounds; for his acceptance of the diffusion theory of taxation; and for his sturdy opposition to anything savoring of the broader social point of view in public finance.

EDWIN R. A. SELIGMAN

Consult: Hollander, J. H., "David Ames Wells. 1827–1898. Report of a Memorial Meeting of the Economic Conference of the Johns Hopkins University" in Johns Hopkins University, *Circulars*, vol. xviii (1898–99) 35–38.

WENTWORTH, WILLIAM CHARLES (1793–1872), Australian political leader. Wentworth was born on Norfolk Island, where his father had gone as assistant surgeon of a convict ship. Young Wentworth was educated in England and there admitted to the bar in 1822. In the meantime he had pioneered in the writing of Australian history by his *A Statistical, Historical and Political Description of the Colony of New South Wales* (London 1819, 3rd ed., 2 vols., 1824). In 1824 he returned to New South Wales and entered on an active political career. Wentworth's influence was aided by his establishment in that year of a newspaper, the *Australian*, which as organ of the emancipists championed freedom of the press, trial by jury and representative institutions. He was never a member of the nominated Legislative Council, instituted in 1823, but became the leader of the opposition when he was elected for the city of Sydney to a council that had been enlarged in 1842 by the addition of elected members.

During the next ten years Wentworth was actively engaged in demanding responsible government, although, like Robert Lowe, who was a fellow council member at the time, Wentworth disclaimed democracy and sought local self-government in behalf of a landed gentry class. He even upheld the attempted reintroduction of transportation in 1848. With the separation of Victoria from New South Wales in 1850 and the acquiescence of the home government in the preparation locally of colonial constitutions, Wentworth was made chairman (1853) of a committee to prepare the constitution of New South Wales. Although his desire for a hereditary upper house was not acceptable to the colony, he was the acknowledged leader in the successful effort to attain responsible government. He went to London as an advocate of the new constitution. Henceforth he lived mostly in England, disliking, as did Lowe, colonial democratic tendencies.

Wentworth was one of the earliest advocates of Australian federation. In 1848 he proposed a general assembly of the Australian colonies. When in England he established in 1855 a General Association for the Australian Colonies. Two years later this group presented to the home government an unsuccessful draft bill for an Australian federal assembly. While still in Australia Wentworth successfully fathered a bill (1849) for the founding of the University of Sydney; as the first of the Australian universities it was inaugurated in 1852.

HOWARD ROBINSON

Consult: Rusden, G. W., *History of Australia*, 3 vols. (London 1883); Martin, A. P., *Life and Letters of the Right Honourable Robert Lowe, Viscount Sherbrooke*, 2 vols. (London 1893); Allin, C. D., *The Early Federation Movement in Australia* (Kingston, Ont. 1907); Dunbabin, Thomas, *The Making of Australasia* (London 1922); Sweetman, Edward, *Australian Constitutional Development*, University of Melbourne, Publications, no. 4 (Melbourne 1925); *Cambridge History of the British Empire*, vol. vii, pt. i (Cambridge, Eng. 1933).

WERGELAND, HENRIK ARNOLD (1808–45), Norwegian man of letters, publicist and patriot. A voluminous writer and modern Norway's first distinguished poet, Wergeland played an important role in the development of the Norwegian national movement. The universal prevalence of Danish cultural traditions—championed by Wergeland's opponent Welhaven—among the burgher, official and intellectual classes, served only to intensify his patriotism. He worked for a national culture, to be sustained especially by the more indigenous yeoman peasantry. This class, as he several times implied in passages on historical subjects, had preserved many national qualities even during the centuries of union with Denmark. Among the rural elements he discerned traces of a national folklore and he drew upon rural speech to enrich his literary medium; he was one of the early figures in the efforts to make the language more national.

But Wergeland was committed to the peasant's cause in no exclusive sense. He saw in the Norwegian nationality a serious cleavage between the upper and lower classes, which he strove to eliminate by stimulating patriotism and public spirit. As a liberal and humanitarian he was interested in prison reform and in temperance and he pleaded the cause of the socially outcast and of religious dissenters living under legal disabilities. He took the initiative in agitating for the removal of the constitutional exclusion of Jews from the kingdom. He sought constantly to extend the range of popular enlightenment, promoting rural loan libraries and, on occasion, teaching, editing newspapers and pamphlets and giving homely advice on matters of husbandry and conduct. With the passing of time Wergeland's name has become a national slogan and his career a symbol of sterling Norwegian patriotism. A spiritual debt to him has been acknowledged by such outstanding national figures as J. Sverdrup, B. Björnson and J. E. Sars.

OSCAR J. FALNES

Works: *Samlede skrifter, trykt og utrykt*, ed. by Herman Jaeger and D. A. Seip, vols. i–xix (Oslo 1918–33).

Consult: Koht, Halvdan, *Henrik Wergeland, ei folkeskrift* (Christiania 1908); Laache, Rolv, "Henrik Wergeland og hans strid med prokurator Praëm" in Norske Videnskaps-Akademi i Oslo, Historisk-Filosofisk Klasse, *Skrifter* (1927) no. 5 and (1929) nos. 1–2; Bull, Francis, and Paasche, Fredrik, *Norsk litteraturhistorie*, vols. i–iv (Oslo 1923–33) vol. iii, p. 113–319; Elviken, Andreas, *Die Entwicklung des norwegischen Nationalismus*, Historische Studien, no. 198 (Berlin 1930); Gjerset, Knut, *History of the Norwegian People*, 2 vols. (New York 1915) vol. ii, p. 464–75.

WESLEY, JOHN (1703–91), English clergyman and founder of Methodism. Educated at Charterhouse and Christ Church, Oxford, Wesley was elected a fellow of Lincoln in 1726. He was ordained to the priesthood of the Church of England in 1728, and on the strength of this fact in 1784 he took the decisive step of exercising the episcopal right to ordain others, when it became necessary to provide the American Methodists with authoritative leadership. His early Oxford associations, his experiences in Georgia and his contacts with Moravians were formative influences. From his first society in 1739 to his death the Methodist movement grew to number nearly half a million adherents and developed an existence independent of the Established Church. The ideology behind the religious experience which he propagated was a simple description of a process by which man's impulses and will were transformed through self-abandonment to and faith in the power in Christ. His theology was epitomized in the doctrine of perfectionism of will and disposition. Its emphasis upon experience and ethical results shared with other evangelical preaching an immense success.

Wesley's political theory was conservative in phrase, but much of the political effect of his work was disruptive. He rejected emphatically the theory of representative government and contractual rights as immoral, first, because of popular incompetence and, secondly, on principle. Civil society did not, as Locke claimed, originate in human self-interest. It was providential and ethical. The function of government is moral, and for the performance of that function governors are responsible not to the people but to God. Political obligation is therefore religious in quality and there exists no right of revolution, even if the governors violate their trust. Although Christian and non-Christian alike are under the law, the Christian is obedient by character and loyal by impulse. Wesley did not see that this metaphysical theory of the state failed to reflect existing practise and the needs of an emerging society or that it endowed all government, regardless of its ethical character, with divine prescription. But it rationalized Wesley's conservatism, tended to concentrate the energy of the masses upon personal problems instead of political agitation and helped to give the movement a hard won status of respectability. The net result, however, was to promote change. Self-respect and self-assertion were nurtured in those dispossessed groups which were certain to repudiate unresponsible and outmoded political institutions. The period of Wesley's death and the French Revolution therefore saw dissension in which radicals were thrust out from the main organization to work elsewhere, while the official body, seeking to avoid political activity, in fact supported the conservative position of the divine prescription of all government.

The work of Wesley not only coincided with the accelerated change to an industrial society but also promoted that transition. The town and industrial population provided his followers, while skilled workmen and tradesmen supplied a major part of his leadership. His ethics of economic activity was perfectly adapted to the new economic process. Divine ownership of all property included time and energy no less than money. The pursuit of gain therefore became a religious obligation, industriousness a Christian virtue; and since ownership is a moral trust, frugal living and saving were imperative in order to provide for necessary business and family needs or to give to those in distress. This religious sanction of the economic virtues had two consequences. On the one hand, it provided a disciplined and eagerly sought labor supply for the expanding economic needs and furnished the incentive and qualities ideally suited for initiative in business enterprise. On the other, Methodists tended to prosper and in doing so gained social and economic prestige, acquired changed standards of living and the organized group pursued an increasingly conservative policy.

The main contribution of Wesley to humanitarian reform was indirect. The movement formed a type of character to which the relief of distress became a habitual impulse. But since its philosophy promoted private rather than political action Wesleyanism furnished none of the leadership for politically implemented reform movements of the period, although all of them called heavily upon Methodist support. Wesley attacked the slave trade, and his societies were centers of propaganda against it as well as for prison reform and popular education. The rising standard of hygiene and improved care of the sick owed much to the powerful influence of Wesley and his organization.

WELLMAN J. WARNER

Important works: *The Works of the Rev. John Wesley*, 14 vols. (new ed. London 1872); *The Journal of the Rev. John Wesley*, ed. by Nehemiah Curnock, 8 vols. (London 1909–16).

Consult: Tyerman, Luke, *The Life and Times of the Rev. John Wesley*, M.A., 3 vols. (2nd ed. London 1871–72); Warner, Wellman J., *The Wesleyan Movement in the Industrial Revolution* (London 1930); Edwards, M. L., *John Wesley and the Eighteenth Century* (London 1933); Dimond, Sydney G., *The Psychology of the Methodist Revival* (London 1926); Lee, Umphrey, *The Historical Backgrounds of Early Methodist Enthusiasm*, Columbia University, Studies in History, Economics and Public Law, no. 339 (New York 1931); Wilson, Woodrow, *John Wesley's Place in History* (New York 1915); Prince, John W., *Wesley on Religious Education* (New York 1926).

WESTERNIZATION. *See* EUROPEANIZATION.

WESTINGHOUSE, GEORGE (1846–1914), American inventor and capitalist. The work of Westinghouse revolutionized the railway transportation and electric power industries. His technical contributions to transportation, all developed between 1869 and 1888, include a straight air brake, the automatic air brake with the quick action triple valve, an electropneumatic system of interlocking railway signals and the friction draft gear used in coupling cars, which eliminated the danger of broken trains. These devices, which were rapidly adopted by the railroads, made it possible to hold trains together, stop them at convenience and quickly and control their movements without danger of collision.

In the early 1880's the electric light industry under the leadership of Thomas Edison had adopted the direct current method of generation and distribution. As a result transmission voltages and distances were extremely limited. In 1884 Westinghouse perceived that the alternating current system was more economical, more flexible and above all amenable to long distance transmission, thus making water power available to industrial markets. Westinghouse encountered strong opposition but won his initial victories with the lighting of the World's Columbian Exposition in Chicago in 1893 and the construction of the electrical apparatus for the Niagara Falls power development in 1892–95, both on the alternating current system. Today nearly 95 percent of all electric service is on alternating current. The development of the new method involved the invention and perfection of many devices, including the transformer, a rotary converted to change alternating to direct current, Nikola Tesla's polyphase alternating current motor and the turbogenerator. Westinghouse was the first to conceive and develop every detail of his inventions only in two instances; in general he profited by the efforts of precursors and the assistance of brilliant young engineers.

He was one of the few inventors who was also a successful manufacturer and promoter. He erected works to produce his own devices, and these grew with the widening of his interests. His works were models of technical organization and efficiency and early included the development of laboratories.

In the 1890's there were important litigations between the Westinghouse Electric and Manufacturing Company and the General Electric Company, involving patents about alternating current machinery and filament bulbs. At the conclusion of these contests Westinghouse emerged master in the alternating current field, while General Electric established its monopoly over the manufacture of electric bulbs. Thenceforth the two companies agreed to exchange patent privileges, thus establishing a practical duopoly in the field of electrical apparatus. In the manufacture of railway brake and signal equipment Westinghouse companies have remained supreme in the United States.

The financial interests of Westinghouse spread far and wide throughout the world, with many establishments in foreign countries. In order to provide a market for equipment Westinghouse also acquired large interests in electric utilities. In the panic of 1907 the Westinghouse Electric and Manufacturing Company was forced into receivership; although George Westinghouse himself assisted in its reorganization, he was ultimately forced out of his dominant position. For his services Westinghouse received decorations from many governments and scientific societies.

N. R. DANIELIAN

Consult: Leupp, Francis E., *George Westinghouse; His Life and Achievements* (Boston 1918); Prout, Henry G., *A Life of George Westinghouse* (New York 1921); Terry, C. A., *Early History of Westinghouse Electric and Manufacturing Company* (East Pittsburgh, Pa. 1925).

WESTLAKE, JOHN (1828–1913), English jurist. Westlake studied at Cambridge and was admitted to the bar in 1854. He practised law until his appointment in 1888 to the Whewell chair of international law at Cambridge, a post which he held for twenty years. He served also as a member of the Permanent Court of Arbitration from 1900 to 1906 and was one of the founders and editors of the *Revue de droit international et de législation comparée*, to which he contributed frequently. In 1873 he helped to establish the Institut de Droit International.

Westlake was one of the foremost students of international law in his time. His early efforts were devoted to private international law; the *Treatise on Private International Law, or the Conflict of Laws* (London 1858; 7th ed. by N. Bentwich 1925) was the first attempt to bring order out of the chaos of the English conflicts of laws which had developed haphazardly on the basis of Story's study. His application of the analytical method and of the theories of Savigny and other German scholars to the scattered empiricism of the English cases exercised a great influence upon the development of this branch of the law and led to its systematization in England.

Even more important was his work in public international law. Westlake was a rare combination of philosopher and practical lawyer, and during an era of thoroughgoing positivism he forecast the trends of a later generation which was to react against the extremes of nineteenth century law. To him the foundation stone of international law was the community of states. The dogma of sovereignty he relegated to a subordinate position; he also contended that although states were the creators of international law, individuals as well as states were its subjects. Possessing a thorough knowledge of the practise of states and an ability to apply it with masterful technique, he considered reason, "for the seekers after international right," as well as practise a source of the law of nations. Thus he envisaged a dynamic system of international law evolving with the growth of an organized international community. This philosophic vision was strengthened by Westlake's practical interests in the codification of international law and the establishment of international tribunals. His most significant books in this field are *International Law* (2 vols., Cambridge, Eng. 1904–07; 2nd ed. 1910–13) and *The Collected Papers of John Westlake on Public International Law* (ed. by L. Oppenheim, Cambridge, Eng. 1914). Westlake was not a great systematizer, and the principles implicit in his writings have been developed more extensively by other writers; but his work remains preeminent in its exactness of information and clarity of expression.

A. H. FELLER

Consult: Lauterpacht, H., "Westlake and Present Day International Law" in *Economica*, vol. v (1925) 307–25; *Memories of John Westlake*, ed. by J. F. Williams (London 1914), contains a bibliography of Westlake's writings.

WEYDEMEYER, JOSEPH (1818–66), German-American political theorist, propagandist and journalist. Weydemeyer was born in Münster, Germany, and served for several years as artillery officer in the Prussian army. He was one of a group of Prussian military men who in the late 1840's were dismissed from the service for their communist opinions. His journalistic work brought him into contact with Marx and Engels, with whom he remained closely associated throughout his life.

Exiled because of his support of the Revolution of 1848, Weydemeyer in 1851 went to America, where he at once entered into political work. Largely as a result of his activity the Amerikanischer Arbeiterbund was created in New York in 1853 for the "political union of all workers in the United States . . . for working class reform." In the same year a convention of English speaking labor groups met in Washington and organized the Nationale Arbeiterassociation, in which Weydemeyer played a leading part. In its platform the new organization demanded political action for federal labor legislation, collective ownership of the public domain, the ten-hour workday and the prohibition of child labor. At about the same time a group of "Forty-eighters" in New York founded a weekly periodical, *Reform*, which was by far the clearest and most intelligent of the many labor publications which appeared briefly in that period. Weydemeyer as its associate editor secured the regular cooperation of German émigrés from all parts of Europe and contributed valuable material for the popularization of Marxist ideas. In the previous year Weydemeyer had attempted the publication of a weekly magazine, *Revolution*, for the second and last issue of which Marx wrote his famous "The Eighteenth Brumaire of Louis Bonaparte."

In 1856 Weydemeyer went to Milwaukee to engage in journalism and surveying; then he went to Chicago, returning to New York in 1860 to direct the surveying of Central Park. When the Civil War broke out he joined Captain Frémont's body guard and was mustered out as lieutenant colonel in 1865. In St. Louis Weydemeyer again took up journalism, becoming for a time editor of the *Neue Zeit*. In the fall of 1865 he was elected auditor of that city. Weydemeyer's life was one of tireless effort on behalf of labor; he was the spiritual leader of the first attempt to create a national labor party in the United States.

LUDWIG LORE

Consult: Schlüter, Hermann, *Die Anfänge der deutschen Arbeiterbewegung in Amerika* (Stuttgart 1907) p. 157–60; Sorge, F. A., in *Pionier, Illustrirter Volks-Kalender* (New York 1897) p. 54–60.

WEYL, WALTER EDWARD (1873–1919), American economist and writer on industrial problems, labor conditions and world politics. Weyl conducted investigations for the United States Department of Labor in Europe, Mexico and Porto Rico and he served as statistical expert on internal commerce for the Treasury Department. He was an associate editor of the

New Republic from its inception and was the author of many articles in that and other journals. His book *The New Democracy* (New York 1912), a penetrating survey of political and economic tendencies, won him a place in the first rank of American publicists. Appearing in 1912, the year of the Progressive party campaign, it had great influence in shaping the thought of that tumultuous period and many of Weyl's specific suggestions were incorporated in Theodore Roosevelt's platform. Despite the defeat of the party these economic and political principles were approved by millions of citizens and they found expression in the domestic policies of Woodrow Wilson. With the outbreak of the World War Weyl inevitably turned from national to international problems. In *American World Policies* (New York 1917) he made a masterly analysis of the economic rivalries which caused the war, of the place of the United States among the nations and of the slow growth of an economic internationalism which alone can insure peace. *The End of the War* (New York 1918), published during American participation, was a courageous plea for a just, democratic peace with political security and a free economic life for all nations. Weyl lived to see that hope betrayed in the Versailles Treaty, which he denounced as an inglorious end of Wilson's quest of a new world. In 1919 Weyl visited the Orient and made a prophetic study of those economic forces which were to lead Japan into a policy of expansion and conquest. After his death a collection of his essays was brought out under the title *Tired Radicals and Other Papers* (New York 1921).

HOWARD BRUBAKER

Consult: Walter Weyl; an Appreciation (Philadelphia 1922).

WHATELY, RICHARD (1787–1863), English divine. Whately's early adult life was largely spent in Oxford, his later life in Ireland. In 1829, while principal of St. Alban Hall (a small collegiate institution within Oxford University, which has since disappeared), he was appointed Senior's successor as professor of political economy and held this post until he became Anglican archbishop of Dublin in 1831.

Although most of his published works dealt with religious subjects, Whately found time for several philosophical and sociological investigations. His *Elements of Logic* (London 1826, 9th ed. 1850) and *Elements of Rhetoric* (London 1828, 7th ed. 1846)—originally contributed to the *Encyclopaedia Metropolitana*—represented useful studies of the formal science of thought and the art of discussion. In economics his only important work was the *Introductory Lectures on Political Economy* (London 1831, 4th rev. ed. 1855). This book is concerned chiefly with the scope and nature of economics, which Whately refused to define as the study of wealth, proposing instead the title "catallactics," or the science of exchanges. It includes also an illuminating examination of the phenomenon of increasing returns and its significance as a stimulus to the division of labor. But the central problems of value and distribution are not touched, and perhaps the most valuable parts of the work are contained in the appendices, in which are republished various articles and addresses on such subjects as the tithe system and the reform of the penal code. Whately opposed the transportation of criminals to the colonies, both in the interests of the colonies themselves and on the ground that since it probably represented an improvement in the economic status of those transported, it could have no efficacy as a deterrent to crime.

In ecclesiastical matters Whately was a strong Protestant and deplored the Romeward tendency of the Oxford movement. With regard to the abolition of slavery he advocated a policy of gradualness.

LINDLEY M. FRASER

Consult: Whately, E. J., *The Life and Correspondence of Richard Whately* (3rd ed. London 1875); Martineau, Harriet, *Biographical Sketches* (London 1869) p. 169–81. For a full bibliography of works by and about Whately, see Rigg, J. M., in *Dictionary of National Biography*, vol. lx (London 1899) p. 423–99.

WHEATLEY, JOHN, nineteenth century English economist. Wheatley is known chiefly for his writings on money and foreign exchange during the controversy over the restriction of cash payments by the Bank of England at the time of the Napoleonic wars. His best known works are his *Remarks on Currency and Commerce* (London 1803) and the first volume of *An Essay on the Theory of Money and Principles of Commerce* (London 1807). Wheatley expounded the theory that the quantity of money required for a country was that necessary to maintain its prices in equilibrium with those of other countries; that the issue of paper currency in excess of this amount brought depreciation to approximately the same extent both internally and on the foreign exchanges (thus presenting one of the earliest formulations of the recently revived doctrine of purchasing power parity); and that the transfer of foreign subsidies was effected by commodity movements caused by changes in prices. He was a severe critic of mercantilist views on money and foreign trade. In 1822 Wheatley brought out the second volume of *An Essay on the Theory of Money and Principles of Commerce*, which dealt principally with the population problem. He defended large landed estates and advocated greater freedom of trade in grain. His other writings were *Thoughts on the Object of the Foreign Subsidy* (London 1805), *A Letter to Lord Grenville on the Distress of the Country* (London 1816), *A Report on the Reports of the Bank Committees* (Shrewsbury 1819) and *A Letter to . . . the Duke of Devonshire on the State of Ireland and the General Effects of Colonization* (1824). Wheatley had a cumbersome literary style and was intolerant in his judgments of those with whom he disagreed. Despite his prior statement of much of the theory which has come to be associated with the bullion report of 1810 and David Ricardo, he received little contemporary recognition, and the theoretical significance of his work has been generally overlooked by later economists.

FRANK WHITSON FETTER

Consult: Hollander, J. H., "The Development of the Theory of Money from Adam Smith to David Ricardo" in *Quarterly Journal of Economics*, vol. xxv (1910–11) 463–67.

WHEATON, HENRY (1785–1848), American jurist, statesman and historian. Wheaton made greater contributions to the science and history of international law than any man of his period. His legal and diplomatic experience and his wide contact with affairs and men gave him an exceptional basis for sound treatment of international topics.

Wheaton was graduated from Rhode Island College, now Brown University, in 1802. He was admitted to the bar in 1805 and later studied in Europe, engaging in legal research in France; after returning to the United States in 1806 he practised law in Providence for some years and also wrote upon political questions. In 1812 he moved to New York City and assumed the editorship of the *National Advocate*, a Republican party organ, which brought him into contact with differing opinions and many leading men of the time. Encouraged by Judge Story, he first showed his aptitude in the field of international law by publishing *Digest of the Law of Maritime Captures and Prizes* (New York 1815), which received much favorable recognition at home and abroad. He was commissioned a division judge advocate of the army in 1814 and reporter of decisions of the Supreme Court of the United States in 1816. His reports (1816–27), because of the extremely learned character of their annotations, brought Wheaton wide recognition among American jurists. During this period Wheaton held other important offices in New York state.

Thus Wheaton had had a varied experience when in 1827 President Adams appointed him to the post of chargé d'affaires to Denmark. He succeeded in negotiations on claims which had long been a subject of controversy arising from seizure and "erroneous or unjust condemnation by Danish tribunals" of American vessels during the Napoleonic wars. In 1831 he published *History of the Northmen* (London), which later he expanded in a French translation stimulating interest in Scandinavian history in Europe. In 1835 Wheaton was appointed chargé d'affaires to Prussia. On his advice the American representative was raised to the rank of minister in 1837; he negotiated many important treaties with the German states before his service terminated in 1846.

Wheaton is most widely known for his *Elements of International Law* (Philadelphia 1836) and his *History of the Law of Nations in Europe and America* (New York 1845), which had appeared in French in a less extended form in 1841. Both works have been translated into many languages and the *Elements* has passed through many editions including Chinese and Japanese editions. Wheaton regarded international law as a form of customary law; his *Elements* has long been the standard treatise and is still frequently cited in court decisions and diplomatic papers. This first extended work upon international law by an American has been a potent influence in determining American and foreign views and practise upon many matters of international concern.

GEORGE GRAFTON WILSON

Consult: Hicks, F. C., *Men and Books Famous in the Law* (Rochester 1921) ch. viii, and p. 245, containing a bibliography of the literature on Wheaton; Benson, A. B., "Henry Wheaton's Writings on Scandinavia" in *Journal of English and Germanic Philology*, vol. xxix (1930) 546–61.

WHIG PARTY. See PARTIES, POLITICAL, sections on GREAT BRITAIN and UNITED STATES.

WHITE, ANDREW DICKSON (1832–1918), American educator, historian, diplomat. Andrew D. White was born in central New York the son of Horace White, financier, and of Clara Dickson, only daughter of a village magnate, and soon removed with his family to Syracuse, where his father gained wealth. Having studied at Hobart and Yale, in France and in Germany, he was at twenty-four professor of history in the University of Michigan. While at home settling his father's estate, his Syracuse townsmen in 1863 sent him to the state senate, where as chairman of its educational committee he took part in codifying the school laws and creating new normal schools. But nearer his heart lay university betterment. Abroad he had been struck by the wider curriculum, the greater freedom of teaching, the more scientific spirit, not least by the attention to political and social studies. At Michigan he had warmly supported President Tappan's broadening efforts; and when in 1862, upon coming into his share of his father's wealth, he laid before his fellow liberal Gerrit Smith a plan for "a new university worthy of the State of New York," it breathed this spirit. To the founding of such a university he stirred his fellow senator Ezra Cornell, who made White its president; and in the "plan of organization" for the new Cornell University a "department of History, Political and Social Science" had a specially large place. But the young university, "land poor," barely weathered the panic of 1873. In the planned department history alone had a chair to itself, political economy but a course. Not until 1881 could Herbert Tuttle be called for international law and H. C. Adams for economics, while F. B. Sanborn did not begin his course in social science until 1884. But White's own lectures as professor of history had been rich in social suggestion; and the university's heresies—its democracy of studies, its attention to science, pure and applied, its freedom as to race and sex, its non-sectarian faculty and pulpit—made it a social achievement. Attack these brought also, and White's reply was a lecture that grew to a booklet, then to two thick volumes, *A History of the Warfare of Science with Theology in Christendom* (New York 1896), showing how every forward step in human research had thus been fought by the timid in religion's name and how religion as well as science had thereby suffered. Now too from his lectures on the French Revolution he gave to the press his study on *Paper-Money Inflation in France* (New York 1876; new ed. as *Fiat Money Inflation in France*, 1933). Public duties he did not escape. In 1871 he had been sent as a commissioner to Santo Domingo, in 1878 to the Paris Exposition, in 1879–81 as American minister to Germany. In 1884 he was the first president of the American Historical Association. In 1885, dogged by ill health, he resigned from Cornell, although he was soon to endow the university with his rich historical library. In 1892–94 he was minister to Russia, in 1895–96 member of President Cleveland's commission on the Venezuela-Guiana boundary, in 1897–1903 ambassador to Germany; and during this last service he headed the American delegation to the First Hague Conference (1899), where he worked hard for the creation of a world court. Retiring at the age of seventy he found time to complete his *Autobiography* and to edit a volume of his lectures (*Seven Great Statesmen in the Warfare of Humanity with Unreason*, New York 1910).

GEORGE L. BURR

Consult: White, Andrew D., *Autobiography*, 2 vols. (New York 1905).

WHITE LIST. *See* CONSUMERS' LEAGUES.

WHITE SLAVERY. *See* PROSTITUTION.

WHITEFIELD, GEORGE (1714–70), English evangelist. The son of a Gloucester innkeeper, Whitefield received the bachelor's degree from Pembroke College, Oxford, in 1736. Under the influence of the Wesleys and the "Holy Club" he underwent the typical evangelical conversion in 1735 and at twenty-two was ordained in the Established Church. His preaching was an immediate sensation. Urged by John Wesley (*q.v.*) he went to Georgia in 1738 and thereafter devoted himself to evangelism alternately in Great Britain and in the American colonies. The work of Whitefield was that of an evangelist, not of a theologian or an organizer. His nominal Calvinism after 1739 tended only temporarily to isolate his work from that of the Wesleyans. He helped found Calvinistic Methodism in 1743, and whenever he was in England he served as moderator until 1749, when he withdrew to concentrate upon traveling preaching. His appointment as chaplain to the countess of Huntingdon in 1748 indicated the extension of the movement to the upper social strata as well as to the masses. As a preacher Whitefield's influence in propagating the typical revival experience was wider than that of any other figure of the period. He made seven visits to the American colonies, preaching from Georgia to New England with results similar to those in England. Much of Whitefield's success is attributable to his ability to identify himself with nonconformity. His work also prepared the way for the later spread of Wesleyan Methodism in America.

In politics and economics Whitefield made no contribution except indirectly in the form of the pious and disciplined character which was the stamp of the revival. He was absorbed in a specific form of individual religious experience, not in social reform. He did protest under provocation that his followers were the firmest supporters of established political authority, and even claimed divine support for British arms. He was not aware of a moral issue in slavery, declaring at one time that "God has put it into the hearts of my *South-Carolina* friends, to contribute liberally towards purchasing . . . a plantation and slaves, which I purpose to devote to the support . . ." of the Georgia orphanage.

WELLMAN J. WARNER

Important works: *Works*, ed. by J. Gillies, 6 vols. (London 1771–72); *Journals*, 7 vols. (London 1738–41).

Consult: Tyerman, L., *The Life of the Rev. George Whitefield*, 2 vols. (London 1876–77); Hall, T. C., *The Religious Background of American Culture* (Boston 1930) p. 151–56; Schneider, H. W., *The Puritan Mind* (New York 1930); Belden, A. D., *George Whitefield, the Awakener* (London 1930).

WHITLEY COUNCILS. See INDUSTRIAL RELATIONS COUNCILS.

WHITMAN, WALT (1819–92), American journalist and poet. Prior to the publication of the first edition of *Leaves of Grass* in 1855 Whitman was employed chiefly in newspaper work. In his editorials in the Brooklyn *Daily Eagle* from 1846 to 1848 (collected and republished as *The Gathering of the Forces*, ed. by C. Rodgers and J. Black, 2 vols., New York 1920) and in the Brooklyn *Daily Times* from 1857 to 1859 (collected and republished as *I Sit and Look Out*, ed. by E. Holloway and V. Schwarz, New York 1932) Whitman opposed the extension of slavery, recommended gradual emancipation and rebuked the extreme abolitionists for their indifference to all evils but slavery. He spoke constantly of the greatness, present and future, of America and favored territorial expansion. He advocated prison reform, the abolition of capital punishment, improvements in the hours, conditions and wages of labor and the development of public education. His belief in democracy, almost mystical in its intensity, expressed itself in attacks on European despotisms as well as in proposals for the extension of democratic practise in America.

The various elements of Whitman's thought were given a kind of personal and emotional unity by the discovery of Emerson's transcendentalist theory of self-reliance. Although much confusion remained, he was able to regard with singleness of vision the diversities and complexities of American life. *Leaves of Grass* attempted to embrace the whole of America, and Whitman imaginatively identified himself with every type of American. Each poem expressed his faith in the United States, in democracy and in the common people. In *Democratic Vistas* (Washington 1871) he tried to give a rational exposition of this faith, but its poetic expression remains more convincing. Closer to the realities of American life than Emerson, he fused the latter's idealism with the more concrete aspirations of the common man.

After devoting some time to caring for wounded soldiers during the Civil War Whitman was from 1865 to 1873 a clerk in the office of the attorney general. As time passed he became more critical of governmental institutions and especially of current business practises. To the end he was a mystic and an individualist, but, according to Horace Traubel (*With Walt Whitman in Camden*, 3 vols., Boston and New York 1906–14), his strong humanitarianism led to a growing sympathy with socialism.

GRANVILLE HICKS

Works: *Complete Writings*, ed. by R. M. Bucke and others, 10 vols. (New York 1902).

Consult: Parrington, V. L., *Main Currents in American Thought*, 3 vols. (New York 1927–30) vol. iii, p. 69–86; Mumford, Lewis, *The Golden Day* (New York 1926) p. 121–37; Calverton, V. F., *The Liberation of American Literature* (New York 1932) p. 275–98.

WHITNEY, ELI (1765–1825), American inventor and manufacturer. Whitney graduated from Yale College in 1792; unable to secure the teaching position for which he had gone to Georgia, he became the guest of the widow of General Nathaniel Greene at her plantation on the Savannah River. In the spring of 1793, hearing some planters express the hope that a mechanism might be devised to separate the lint from the tenacious green seed of upland cotton, Whitney set to work and soon produced his gin. It consisted of a wooden cylinder with wire teeth set annularly and revolving through slots in a bar; when the seed cotton was pressed against the opposite side of the bar the teeth pulled away the lint, which was cleaned from the teeth by brushes revolving in an opposite direction and several times as rapidly as the wire studded cylinder. The device was operated by a hand crank, and Whitney asserted that if driven by a horse his gin would clean fifty times as much cotton in a day as a man could with his fingers.

The Whitney gin was patented March 4, 1794, but not before a number of machines on his principle had been made by local blacksmiths. Hodgen Holmes, a mechanic of Augusta, Georgia, received a patent May 12, 1796, for a gin which substituted circular saws for the wire teeth. After fourteen years of expensive litigation Whitney's patent was upheld; but he and his partner, Phineas Miller, had meantime disposed of their rights in three cotton states for $90,000 appropriated by the legislatures. Whitney built a factory near New Haven, Connecticut, where he manufactured muskets on government contract; it was here that the principle of interchangeable parts was first applied with perfect success.

The cotton gin caused a sudden prodigious increase in cotton cultivation. The crop of the United States rose from 1,500,000 pounds in 1790 to 35,000,000 pounds in 1800 and 85,000,000 pounds in 1810; in 1860 cotton production totaled more than 2,000,000,000 pounds. It had the effect of destroying manufacturing enterprise in the South and wedded the section to commercial agriculture with slave labor. These developments were chiefly responsible for the economic and political differences between North and South which led to the Civil War.

BROADUS MITCHELL

Consult: Olmsted, Denison, *Memoir of Eli Whitney* (New Haven 1846); Blake, W. P., "Sketch of the Life of Eli Whitney" in New Haven Historical Society, *Papers*, vol. v (1894) 109–31; Tompkins, D. A., *Cotton and Cotton Oil* (Charlotte, N. C. 1901) chs. i–ii; Scherer, J. A. B., *Cotton as a World Power* (New York 1916) chs. xxxi–xxxiii.

WHOLESALING covers the marketing functions incident to the sale of all goods except those sold to ultimate users for personal or home consumption. It comprises all activities relating to the sale of goods at wholesale by producers, wholesalers or functional middlemen, such as brokers and selling agents. The goods may be sold to a retailer, a wholesaler or an industrial consumer so long as the purpose of the customer in buying such goods is to resell them in one form or another or to use them for business needs as supplies or equipment.

Wholesaling is consequently performed on several different planes, depending upon the type of customer to whom the commodities are sold. In the case of manufactured goods, as, for example, sugar, a producer may sell to wholesalers or to jobbers. He may choose to sell all or part of his product directly to retailers or directly to makers of confectionery, with or without the intervention of a broker, through a wholesale sales branch of his own or direct from the refinery. The wholesaler in turn may sell the sugar, which he purchased directly from the refinery or through a broker, to retailers or to industrial consumers, such as manufacturers of soft drinks, confectionery and other products in which sugar is used in considerable quantities. In the case of farm products there are wholesale organizations which buy goods from farmers in the local growers' markets for shipment to central or secondary wholesale markets, where they are disposed of at wholesale either to retailers or to flour millers, maltsters, packers and other industrial consumers.

In determining the volume of wholesale trade and in computing data for the construction of wholesale price indices it is of utmost importance that the distinction between the various planes of wholesaling be maintained. Prices of a given commodity are usually different at any given time on each of the planes of wholesaling, and their variability differs greatly with the plane involved.

The beginnings of wholesaling are lost in antiquity. In its earlier form wholesale trade was associated with caravans; as boats became stancher and mariners hardier, it entered the fluvial phase; later it was connected principally with oceanic shipments. For many centuries wholesale trade was closely associated with the movement of goods over long distances and particularly with foreign trade. During the Egyptian, Babylonian and Phoenician periods wholesaling was connected largely with importing and exporting but was also rather closely tied up with retailing. In the period of Greek supremacy separate wholesale districts developed and wholesalers were definitely distinguished from retailers. According to Plato the *emporos* imported foreign goods and sold them to other wholesalers, to smaller traders or to agents similar to brokers; he usually also owned ships. The *kapelos*, on the other hand, was the retail dealer. The closest prototype of the present day wholesaler in the days of Roman domination was the *negotiator*, who dealt both in merchandise and in money. He was usually an independent Greek shipowner who tramped from port to port, personally buying and selling whatever cargo promised the greatest profits. Storing of goods by wholesale dealers in large warehouses (*horrea*) located at strategic points became an important function at this time.

With the decline of Rome the wholesaler again disappeared, as his functions were integrated with those of the retailer. Dealers sold both *en gros* and *en détail* until late in the Middle Ages, when the wholesaler reappeared as a distinct middleman. During the Middle Ages and through the handicraft stage of economic development agricultural production was limited, manufacturing highly localized and on an exceedingly small scale and retailing was confined largely to markets held weekly or at frequent intervals. In domestic trade direct contact between producer and retailer or producer and consumer was the rule. The limited amount of wholesaling in inland trade was carried on by itinerant or traveling merchants with pack horse trains and by some established wholesale houses, through fairs held at intervals of from three to twelve months and occasionally through auctions and exchanges, such as the candle auction on the Antwerp exchange. In foreign trade the merchant companies, regulated and joint stock, were most important. Early in the fourteenth century England permitted merchants from foreign countries to "safely come with their merchandise into all cities, towns, and ports, and sell the same by wholesale only, as well to natives as to foreigners," with the exception of haberdasheries and groceries, which could also be sold "by retail."

Under the putting out system the wholesaler assumed a position of considerable importance; it was he who organized production and took over control of the selling of the goods. In addition to itinerant merchants there appeared many general merchants (wholesalers), jobbers, brokers and factors. Adam Smith frequently refers to regular wholesalers and in one place he mentions wholesale merchants in the grocery trade "who carry a stock of ten thousand pounds at a profit of only eight to ten per cent as compared with a profit of forty to fifty per cent for the small grocer." While such wholesalers were generally regarded as warehouse keepers, they rendered many other important services. The London wholesalers in the cloth trade, in the words of Daniel Defoe, "not only furnish the country shopkeepers, but give them large credit and sell them great quantities of goods by which they again are enabled to trust the tailors who make the clothes."

With the development of the factory system and with improvements in transportation and communication the wholesaler ceased to be the organizer of production. Manufacturers extended their scale of operation and began to specialize; products multiplied; the banking system made it possible for producers and retailers to rely less on the wholesaler's financial assistance. As a result the wholesaler was faced with new problems and the need of making new adjustments.

In the United States the first wholesalers were importers who also dealt in some domestic goods. Apparently the first wholesale house that was entirely divorced from the import business (presumably dealing in dry goods) was established in 1808 in Eaton, Ohio, by Cornelius Vanausdal. At the close of the War of 1812 wholesale houses were founded in a number of lines of trade, including boots and shoes, meats and groceries; and about 1850 wholesaling was definitely and generally divorced from retailing. Furthermore it became specialized by lines of merchandise, and many different types of middlemen appeared—brokers, jobbers, commission houses as well as regular wholesalers.

Accurate and complete data on wholesaling in the United States are available only for the year 1929, as a result of the first nation wide Census of Distribution taken in 1930. The Census of American Business taken in 1934 covering the year 1933, although it does not cover sales from producers' plants, adds further light on the subject. During 1929 there were 169,702 wholesale establishments reporting a volume of business of approximately $69,000,000,000. In addition manufacturers sold directly to retailers approximately $12,000,000,000 worth of merchandise and to industrial consumers another $20,000,000,000 worth of goods. Thus the total volume of wholesale trade during the year approximated $100,000,000,000, an amount nearly twice as large as the sales reported by retail stores. In 1933 there were approximately 263,000 wholesale establishments reporting a volume of business of about $32,000,000,000 as against retail store sales of around $26,500,000,000. The excess of wholesale trade over retail store sales is explained partly by the fact that wholesale trade includes exports and sales to industrial and institutional users and partly by the duplication which results from the sale of the same goods by two or more wholesale organizations successively. A similar excess in the volume of wholesale over that of retail trade is to be noted also in other countries. In Germany the estimated wholesale trade during 1928 amounted to 48,000,000,000 RM, as compared with 35,000,000,000 RM for the retail trade. According to the Canadian Census of Merchandising and Service Establishments, the trade of the dominion in 1930 as reported by 13,140 wholesale establishments approximated $3,300,000,000, which was about 16 percent higher than its retail trade.

The wholesale establishments located throughout the United States in 1929 and in 1933 consisted of a number of different types, which may be classified in several ways. According to ownership of the goods handled there are merchant middlemen, i.e. full service wholesalers, cash and carry houses, drop shippers, wagon distributors and bulk tank stations, who take title to the goods; and functional middlemen, including auction companies, commission merchants, brokers and agents of all kinds, who do not take such title. According to the ownership of the establishments there are independent wholesale organizations, sales branches owned by manufacturers, chain store warehouses owned by retail institutions, cooperative marketing associations and various types of wholesale chains, including bulk tank stations, line elevators, centralized and federated cooperatives. Wholesale organizations may also be classified on the basis of services rendered as full service wholesalers, drop shippers and so forth; on the basis of the domestic territory covered, as local, semisectional, sectional and national; according to whether they engage in foreign or domestic trade; on the basis of integration of wholesaling either with manufacturing (manufacturing wholesalers and wholesaling manufacturers) or with retailing (semijobbers). Finally, wholesale organizations usually are classified on the basis of the variety of merchandise handled—into general merchandise houses, general line concerns and specialty firms.

The relative importance of each of these types of wholesale organization is shown in Table I. Table II presents a bird's eye view of the relative importance of all wholesale organizations and of

TABLE I

WHOLESALE TRADE OF THE UNITED STATES AND CANADA BY TYPE OF ESTABLISHMENT*

Type of Establishment or Organization	United States Number of Establishments	United States Percentage of Total Volume	Canada Number of Establishments	Canada Percentage of Total Volume
Total	169,702	100.0	13,140	100.0
Wholesalers proper	79,840	42.6	5,108	33.4
Wholesale merchants (full function service wholesalers)	70,896	35.5	4,031	26.7
Converters	204	0.3		
Exporters	754	2.2	110	1.1
Importers	2,262	2.6	809	4.9
Limited function wholesalers	2,292	0.9	73	0.2
Supply and machinery distributors	3,432	1.1	85	0.5
Bulk tank stations	19,587	3.0	3,602	5.6
Chain store warehouses	559	2.8	79	4.9
Manufacturers' sales branches	16,515	21.4	1,428	16.7
Assemblers and country buyers	34,143	6.7	740	5.0
Cooperative marketing associations	4,078	1.6	68	0.3
Elevators (independent and line)	8,181	1.7	72	3.9
Assemblers and country buyers (other than cooperatives and elevators)	21,884	3.4	600	0.8
Functional middlemen	18,388	20.6	1,745	17.2
Brokers	3,689	5.8	191	4.5
Commission merchants	3,479	6.8	220	3.1
Manufacturers' agents	6,987	2.6	825	3.8
Selling agents	3,260	3.8	64	1.3
Other agents and brokers	973	1.6	445	4.5
All other types	670	2.9	385	17.2

*Total of wholesale trade for the United States, $60,291,547,000; for Canada, $3,325,210,000.
Source: For the United States: United States, Bureau of the Census, "Wholesale Distribution" in *Fifteenth Census of the United States 1930: Distribution*, vol. ii (1933) p. 81. For Canada: Dominion Bureau of Statistics, Census of Merchandising and Service Establishments, *Wholesale Trade in Canada 1930* (1934).

TABLE II
WHOLESALE TRADE BY KIND OF BUSINESS

LINE OF TRADE	ALL WHOLESALE ESTABLISHMENTS*	"WHOLESALERS ONLY"*
Amusement and sporting goods	0.70	0.58
Automotive	3.26	4.68
Chemicals, drugs and allied products	2.97	3.21
Dry goods and apparel	8.59	9.53
Electrical	3.51	2.86
Farm products (not elsewhere specified)	17.36	12.67
Farm supplies (except machinery and equipment)	1.30	2.00
Food products (not elsewhere specified)	13.73	14.66
Forest products (except lumber)	0.30	0.36
Furniture and house furnishings	1.43	1.68
General merchandise	0.86	1.53
Groceries and food specialties	13.76	14.23
Hardware	1.25	2.42
Iron and steel scrap and other waste materials	0.80	1.61
Jewelry and optical goods	0.71	1.28
Leather and leather goods (except gloves and shoes)	0.66	0.76
Lumber and building materials (other than metal)	3.09	4.34
Machinery, equipment and supplies (except electrical)	4.41	4.02
Metals and minerals (except petroleum and scrap)	8.08	4.57
Paper and paper products	1.63	2.38
Petroleum and petroleum products	4.86	3.05
Plumbing and heating equipment and supplies	1.18	1.69
Tobacco and tobacco products (except leaf)	2.44	2.90
All other	3.11	2.98

*Total of trade for all wholesale establishments was $69,291,547,000; for "wholesalers only" $29,556,155,000.
Source: United States, Bureau of the Census, "Wholesale Distribution" in *Fifteenth Census of the United States 1930: Distribution*, vol. ii (1933) p. 66–80.

regular or conventional wholesalers respectively in each of 24 trade groups.

The wholesale organization performs a variety of economic functions. For agricultural commodities wholesaling begins at the local growers' markets, where the goods must first be concentrated in quantities large enough for economical handling and shipment to distant markets. The production of farm commodities on a small scale and at a distance from consumption centers makes necessary local provision for storing, grading, packing, weighing and loading. Such functions are usually carried out by assemblers and country buyers, although some farmers ship directly to city markets. If farm products are in the form of consumers' goods and do not require further processing, they are shipped next to central wholesale markets, where they may be reshipped or otherwise resold to operators in the secondary wholesale markets for further distribution to retailers. If the farm products consist of raw materials, the secondary wholesale markets and the retail markets are eliminated.

In the marketing of consumers' goods the conventional type of wholesaler, designated in the Census of Distribution as wholesale merchant, is the general wholesaler—the wholesale grocer, the wholesale druggist, the hardware wholesaler, the electrical wholesaler, the dry goods jobber. He performs all of the principal wholesale functions: he buys goods on his own account, carries stocks in his place of business, assembles in large lots and redistributes to retailers or other dealers through salesmen, who keep them posted on market conditions, sometimes grades and standardizes the goods prior to sale, grants credit to his customers, makes deliveries and helps the retailers in financial distress. By buying in large quantities he secures price concessions from his sources of supply and effects economies in transportation, which through competition are passed on at least in part to the retailer. The services which the wholesaler normally renders his customers are many and varied; were it not for the facilities thus made available, the average retailer could not possibly remain in business.

The wholesaler also renders invaluable services to the manufacturer. Being a specialist in distribution, he obviates the need of the manufacturer to make a market survey to determine what can be sold profitably in a given territory and in what amounts. The wholesaler establishes connections with retail outlets for the manufacturer, so that the latter can operate with a small sales force or with none at all. He cultivates the field intensively; his salesmen cover every village and hamlet and call upon all kinds of retailers, large and small alike. To a considerable extent the wholesaler relieves the manufacturer of the storing function; he pays cash within a short time after purchase, frequently places his orders in advance of production thus enabling the manufacturer to forecast demand, simplifies the manufacturer's accounting problems and reduces his cost of credit granting. The wholesaler may also aid the manufacturer financially by endorsing the latter's notes or by direct cash advances.

In the case of one large and increasingly important group of goods, industrial, or producers', goods, the functions of the wholesaler have been of limited scope. As compared with consumers' goods the number of purchasers of industrial goods is small, purchases are substantial in amount, are made largely on a performance basis by individuals who are not generally influenced by emotional appeals, the goods are frequently highly technical and the demand varies considerably with the business cycle, particularly in the case of machinery and equipment. The most important channel in the distribution of such goods leads directly from producer to industrial consumer. Next in importance is the channel that involves one functional middleman, usually a manufacturers' agent. A substantial amount of industrial goods, however, is still handled through wholesalers, commonly designated as industrial distributors or mill supply houses. A twilight zone relates to sales made to institutions (educational and governmental), to hotels and restaurants, to contractors, to public utilities, to services (barber shops) and to the professions (dentists). Whether such sales are to be considered as sales of producers' or of consumers' goods is still a debatable question, although the consensus of authoritative opinion leans to the former point of view.

Since the World War numerous attempts have been made to eliminate the wholesaler from the chain of distribution. The organization of wholesaling follows somewhat similar lines in most modern industrial countries, but the rate of change is greatest in the United States and it is there that the wholesaler has faced the most serious difficulties. As manufacturers grew in size and financial strength, many of them attempted to perform the wholesaling functions themselves, either through the maintenance of sales branches or directly from the main offices. The growth of large scale retailing, notably the phenomenal expansion of chain stores; the development of group buying on the part of the smaller independent retailers; the establishment of retailer owned voluntary chains, sometimes known as cooperative wholesaling; the growing importance of style merchandise, which requires direct distribution; and the increased use by manufacturers of public warehouse facilities as local depots for the immediate delivery of goods to retailers have all contributed to the difficulties of the wholesaler.

The roots of these new developments may be traced primarily to the growth of large scale production and the creation of a surplus that could not be disposed of at remunerative prices. Supply caught up with the demand and markets became glutted. Mass production therefore called for mass distribution. This gave rise to branding and advertising, which in turn made it possible for the producer to control, within certain limits, the market for his goods. In his desire to approach the consumer as closely as possible he turned away from the wholesaler to direct distribution. At the same time the large scale retailers set up their own organizations for the performance of the wholesaler's functions.

To meet the various repeated attempts to eliminate him the wholesaler resorted to a number of expedients. He adopted private brands in order to become independent of any one producer. At the same time he began to modify his functions in order to reduce his costs of doing business. This procedure gave rise to new types of wholesalers, like cash and carry houses, which neither deliver goods nor grant credit to customers and confine their stocks to staples and to drop shippers, who do not handle the goods but have them shipped from plant directly to the retailer. The wagon distributor came into prominence again; during the nineteenth century this type of wholesaler, known as the wagon peddler or perambulating wholesaler, was of considerable importance. Many wholesalers attempted to integrate their functions with retailing or with manufacturing or both. The policy of hand to mouth buying adopted by many retailers aided the wholesaler, since no retailer can follow such a policy without a reservoir of goods in the vicinity for immediate supply when the stock in his store runs low. Some wholesalers entered the voluntary chain movement, particularly in the grocery trade, where the competition from regular chains was keenest. There are two types of voluntary grocery chains: retailer cooperative chains and wholesaler-retailer or wholesaler sponsored cooperative chains, with the latter apparently growing most rapidly up to 1932.

Among the other tendencies now discernible are the apparent movement back from specialty wholesaling to general line wholesaling, the use of specialty salesmen by general line wholesalers and the attempt on the part of wholesalers to increase the efficiency of their operations. The leading wholesalers are endeavoring to reduce the number of items and parallel lines carried; to select their customers rather than to sell promiscuously; to reduce the size of their territory, substituting profit territories for sales territories; to reduce the volume of broken package business; to increase the size of the sales order; and to advertise more effectively. Instead of being a distributor the wholesaler tends to become a merchandiser and a creator of demand for his goods. The Census of Distribution figures indicate, however, that some of the newer types of wholesalers are faced with a higher cost of doing business than the wholesale merchant and that when manufacturers undertake to perform the wholesalers' functions through their own sales branches, the cost is often greater than it would have been had they relied on wholesalers, particularly during a depression, as shown by the Census of American Business for 1933. Table III throws much light on the relative costs of doing business of the different types of wholesale organizations.

In conclusion it should be noted that the elimination of the service, or conventional, wholesaler does not involve the elimination of his functions, many of which at least are inescapable in a highly specialized industrial society. The question then is whether the wholesaler, who is presumably a specialist, can perform them more economically and more effectively than either the manufacturer or the retailer. The answer to this question is indicated by existing statistics and by an analysis of the benefits and disadvantages of specialization, but it will largely depend also on the willingness and ability of the wholesaler of the future to effect such modifications in his methods of doing business as are warranted by constantly changing economic conditions.

THEODORE N. BECKMAN

TABLE III

OPERATING EXPENSES BY TYPE OF WHOLESALE ESTABLISHMENT

TYPE OF ORGANIZATION	PERCENTAGE OF NET SALES
For all kinds of business combined	
Regular wholesalers	
Wholesale merchants (service wholesalers)	12.39
Converters	10.80
Exporters	3.79
Importers	6.98
Cash and carry wholesalers	5.69
Drop shippers	6.52
Mail order wholesalers	22.64
Wagon distributors	18.79
Supply and machinery distributors	16.48
Bulk tank stations	16.04
Chain store warehouses	4.34
Manufacturers' sales branches	9.39
Assemblers and country buyers	
Cooperative marketing associations	4.82
Elevators (independent)	4.11
Elevators (line)	2.97
Other assemblers and country buyers	4.69
Functional middlemen	
Brokers	1.32
Commission merchants	2.34
Export agents	4.43
Import agents	9.24
Manufacturers' agents	6.84
Purchasing agents	2.82
Selling agents	4.82
For the grocery trade only	
Retailer owned cooperative chains	4.00
Wholesaler-retailer voluntary chains	9.30
Regular service wholesalers	9.30
Cash and carry wholesalers	5.30
Drop shippers	6.60
Wagon distributors	14.30

Source: United States, Bureau of the Census, "Wholesale Distribution" in *Fifteenth Census of the United States 1930: Distribution*, vol. ii (1933) p. 81–91, and United States, Federal Trade Commission, *Chain Stores; Cooperative Grocery Chains*, 72nd. Cong., 1st sess., Senate Document, no. 12 (1932) p. 160.

See: MARKETING; RETAIL TRADE; MIDDLEMAN; MARKET; COMMODITY EXCHANGES; AGRICULTURAL MARKETING; MERCANTILE CREDIT; WAREHOUSING; TRANSPORTATION; COMMERCE.

Consult: Beckman, T. N., *Wholesaling* (New York 1926); Stephenson, James, *Economics of the Wholesale and Retail Trade* (London 1929) sect. ii; Hirsch, J., *Der moderne Handel*, Grundriss der Sozialökonomik, pt. v, vol. ii (2nd ed. Tübingen 1925); Pintschovius, K., *Der Grosshandel im wissenschaftlichen Urteil* (Berlin 1928); Westerfield, R., "Middlemen in English Business" in Connecticut Academy of Arts and Sciences, *Transactions*, vol. xix (1915) 111–445; Wright, R., *Hawkers and Walkers in Early America* (Philadelphia 1927) ch. v; Hirsch, Julius, *Zeitgemässe Handelsfragen; Kennzahlen zur Handelsforschung* (Berlin 1933); Zeitlin, Leon, "Der deutsche Grosshandel" in *Wirtschafts-Jahrbuch für Industrie und Handel, 1928/29*, vol. i (Leipsic 1928) p. 199–216; Götz, Martin, *Wandlungen des deutschen Grosshandels in der Nachkriegszeit* (Berlin 1933); National Wholesale Conference, *Report of Committee I–IV*, 4 vols. (Washington 1929); United States, Bureau of Foreign and Domestic

Commerce, *Distribution Cost Studies*, nos. 1, 4, 7, 9, 14 (1928–32); United States, Bureau of the Census, *Fifteenth Census of the United States. Census of Distribution: 1930. Wholesale Distribution, Definitions and Classifications* (1931), and *Fifteenth Census of the United States: 1930. Distribution*, Vol. ii. *Wholesale Distribution* (1933); Canada, Dominion Bureau of Statistics, Census of Merchandising and Service Establishments, *Wholesale Trade in Canada 1930* (1934).

WICHERN, JOHANN HINRICH (1808–81), German religious and social reformer. After studying theology at Göttingen and Berlin Wichern returned to his native Hamburg, where he became interested in welfare work and in 1833 opened the Rauhes Haus, an institution for neglected children. Based on the principle of organizing groups of eight to twelve children into "families," each under the direction of a "brother," or member, of the training seminary which Wichern had established in connection with his school, the Rauhes Haus attained considerable fame and served as a model for numerous similar institutions in Germany.

Increasing emphasis was laid by Wichern on practical social welfare work in the missionary program of the church. The publication of his memorial to the German nation in 1848 led to the formation of the Inner Mission (Centraler Ausschuss für die Innere Mission der Deutschen Evangelischen Kirche). Under the influence of his leadership the activities of the Inner Mission spread to all parts of the country. Schools, hospitals, orphan asylums and lodging houses for migratory workers were opened, and welfare work for ex-convicts and delinquent women was undertaken.

In 1851 Wichern was invited by the Prussian government to make suggestions for reforms in the jails and houses of correction. Later, as superintendent of the entire prison system in Prussia, he did a great deal to humanize penal methods. Work among sick and wounded soldiers occupied his attention in 1866 and again in 1870–71. From 1844 until his death he edited *Fliegende Blätter*, the official organ of the Rauhes Haus and the Inner Mission movement.

Theologically and politically a conservative, Wichern was nevertheless one of the first to perceive the effects of capitalism on the structure of society. Unlike Kingsley and other leaders of English Christian Socialism, which was developing almost simultaneously, he advocated no definite program of economic or social change; instead, showing little inclination to deviate from his fundamental religious purpose of saving souls, he stressed Christian ideals. The work of Stöcker, Bodelschwingh, Naumann and others was in part inspired by the ideas and example of Wichern.

THEODOR HEUSS

Works: *Gesammelte Schriften*, ed. by Johannes Wichern and Friedrich Mahling, 6 vols. (Hamburg 1901–08).

Consult: Oldenberg, Friedrich, *Johann Hinrich Wichern; Sein Leben und Wirken*, 2 vols. (Hamburg 1884–87); Gerhardt, Martin, *Johann Hinrich Wichern, ein Lebensbild*, 2 vols. (Hamburg 1927–28), and "Der Begründer der Inneren Mission" in *Süddeutsche Monatshefte*, vol. xxvi (1928–29) 174–79; Rohden, Gustav von, in *Encyklopädisches Handbuch der Pädagogik*, ed. by Wilhelm Rein, vol. x (Langensalza 1910) p. 160–70; Salomon, Alice, *Soziale Führer*, Wissenschaft und Bildung, vol. cclxxix (Leipsic 1932) p. 45–54; Pörksen, Martin, *Johann Hinrich Wichern und die sozialen Fragen* (Rendsburg 1932); Eberhard, O. G., *Die Kräfte der Lebenserziehung in Falks und Wicherns Pädagogik*, Beiträge zur Kinderforschung und Heilerziehung, no. 186 (Langensalza 1922).

WICKSELL, KNUT (1851–1926), Swedish economist. Wicksell studied philosophy and mathematics at the University of Uppsala but later turned his interests to economics. He studied in England, Germany, Austria and France and served as professor at the University of Lund from 1900 to 1916.

Wicksell, although not a socialist, was an ardent friend of the workers. He believed that Sweden, like most of the European countries, was overpopulated and therefore held both emigration and birth control to be necessary. As an economic theoretician he was in the main a follower of Walras and Böhm-Bawerk. From Walras he took over the use of algebraic formulae and geometric constructions; from Böhm-Bawerk, on the other hand, the material problems. Through his keen and rich conceptual analysis Wicksell contributed much to economic theory.

Wicksell developed many of the details of the concepts of value and exchange. He emphasized the point that free competition might well secure the maximum of production but not the maximum general satisfaction of needs. Wicksell also belongs to the first who developed a theory of distribution out of the theory of marginal utility by emphasizing the central significance of marginal productivity in determining the shares of labor, capital and land. In his explanation of interest Wicksell followed Böhm-Bawerk. He believed that capital represents stored up contributions not only of labor but also of land and that interest will arise even when the lengthening of the production period does not result in a steadily increasing productivity. Wicksell clearly formulated the concept of the incidence of taxation involving the problem of how, with given expenditures of revenue, various forms of taxation affect the volume of production and its distribution among labor, land and capital. He considered the most important condition for the realization of equitable taxation to be that every measure involving public expenditure be accompanied by one calling for corresponding public revenue and that both be passed by overwhelming majority. In this way those favored by the expenditures will also contribute to the revenues.

Wicksell's most significant and epoch making contributions are in the fields of money and credit theory. The doctrine that high interest rates result in lowering prices and low interest rates cause a price increase does not tally with statistical figures. High interest rates often coincide with high prices, as do low interest rates with low prices. Wicksell called attention to the fact that the question is not of the absolute but of the relative rate of interest. Interest is relatively high when, under existing expectation of profits, it offers no inducement to expand production; and it is relatively low when it stimulates an increase in business activities. Possibilities of profits correspond to real interest; that is, to the interest which would result when labor, land and capital are exchanged directly without the medium of money. The rate of the real interest is determined among other things by the advance in technology. Increased prices may coincide with increased rates of interest when the money interest has not increased as much as the real interest and there is therefore an inducement for the producers to use additional capital for the expansion of production. If real interest falls faster than money interest, production must be restricted and prices fall. The long term interest rate is decisive for production; and since the discount rate of the central bank of issue determines long term interest rate, it also determines the price level. Wicksell, even before 1900, advocated a monetary system in which the banks of issue would maintain the stability of the value of money by their discount policy. As long as the currency is based upon the value of metal, Wicksell held that no monetary stability could be achieved. Wicksell's views exerted a strong influence on European monetary theories and banking and currency policies.

FRITZ LEHMANN

Important works: Über Wert, Kapital und Rente nach den neueren nationalökonomischen Theorien (Jena 1893), reprinted as no. 15 of London School of Economics and Political Science, Series of Reprints of Scarce Tracts (London 1933); Geldzins und Güterpreise. Eine Studie über die den Tauschwert des Geldes bestimmenden Ursachen (Jena 1898) English tr. (London 1934); Föreläsningar i nationalekonomi, 2 vols. (Lund 1901–06; 3rd ed. 1928–29), tr. by M. Langfeldt as Vorlesungen über Nationalökonomie, 2 vols. (Jena 1913–22).

Consult: Sommarin, E., "Das Lebenswerk von Knut Wicksell" in Zeitschrift für Nationalökonomie, vol. ii (1930–31) 221–67; Ohlin, B., "Knut Wicksell (1851–1926)" in Economic Journal, vol. xxvi (1926) 503–12; Schumpeter, J., "Zur Einführung der folgenden Arbeit Knut Wicksells" in Archiv für Sozialwissenschaft und Sozialpolitik, vol. lviii (1927) 238–51.

WICKSTEED, PHILIP HENRY (1844–1927), English economist. Wicksteed is chiefly remembered as a great teacher: at first as a teacher of an increasingly unorthodox theology from the pulpit of an important London Unitarian chapel; then for the last thirty years of his life, through the medium of writings and lectures, as a professional teacher of the two subjects that had been his hobbies while he was still in the Unitarian ministry, Dante and economics.

His original interest in economics sprang from his interest in ethics and social questions. The first great influence on his economic thought was fortunately or perhaps inevitably Jevons, whose *The Theory of Political Economy* (London 1871) he assimilated and re-created in much the same way as he was later to deal with the works of Dante and Aristotle. The earlier Austrians and, after the publication of Pareto's *Manuale di economia politica* (Milan 1906), the Lausanne school also influenced him greatly. His indebtedness to Jevons is shown most clearly in his first economic writings—the controversy with Bernard Shaw about the Marxian theory of value and the earlier articles in Palgrave's *Dictionary* and elsewhere—and his indebtedness to Walras and Pareto in *The Common Sense of Political Economy*, that magnum opus of his with the misleading title and illuminating subtitle which is now his most widely read work, and which will probably continue to be widely read after many of its better known contemporaries are forgotten.

Wicksteed's independent contributions to economic science were quite as significant as those of his masters, modest though the claims were that he himself made for them. His editor, Lionel Robbins, lays chief emphasis on the importance of his work in elucidating the methodological implications of the subjective theory of value, particularly in the famous chapter "Business and the Economic Nexus" in *The Common Sense of Political Economy*. Among his contributions to the technical apparatus of economics perhaps the best known are his resolution of the market supply curve, his peculiarly happy use of the marginal utility concept as a basis for the general equilibrium theory, and his theory of distribution. (It is true that he withdrew the theory put forward in *An Essay on the Co-ordination of the Laws of Distribution*; but there is some doubt as to both the scope of and the necessity for the recantation.)

Among all English economists no longer living he is the most closely allied to Jevons and the Austrians; and perhaps he more than any other single writer has helped to make possible the latest developments of the equilibrium theory in English speaking countries.

H. E. BATSON

Important works: *The Alphabet of Economic Science* (London 1888); *An Essay on the Co-ordination of the Laws of Distribution* (London 1894), reprinted as no. 12 of London School of Economics and Political Science, Series of Reprints of Scarce Tracts (London 1932); *The Common Sense of Political Economy Including a Study of the Human Basis of Economic Law* (London 1910, new ed. with introduction by Lionel Robbins as *The Common Sense of Political Economy, and Selected Papers and Reviews on Economic Theory*, 2 vols., 1933).

Consult: Herford, C. H., *Philip Henry Wicksteed; His Life and Work* (London 1931); Hicks, J. R., *The Theory of Wages* (London 1932) appendix i; Robbins, Lionel, *An Essay on the Nature and Significance of Economic Science* (London 1932).

WIDOWS' PENSIONS. See MOTHERS' PENSIONS.

WIELOPOLSKI, ALEKSANDER, MARQUIS MYSZKOWSKI (1803–77), Polish statesman. Wielopolski studied at Vienna, Warsaw, Paris and Göttingen and was nominated member of the legislative deputation in 1827. In 1830 he was sent by the Polish government as diplomatic agent to London and after his return in 1831 became a member of the diet and chief editor of the extremely conservative publication *Zjednoczenie* (Union). Following the Polish insurrection of 1831 he was exiled, but he soon returned to Poland and after the peasant riots in Galicia in 1846 published his *Lettre d'un gentilhomme polonais sur les massacres de Galicie, adressée au Prince de Metternich* (Paris 1846), in which he proclaimed himself an adherent of pan-Slavism and of Polish-Russian union. In 1861 he was named director of education and of justice and prepared a comprehensive program of reform. The realization of the program was halted for a brief period by his recall to St. Petersburg in December, 1861; but it was, however, soon resumed in 1862 after he had secured from the czar a new plan of organization according to which the brother of the czar became the viceroy and Wielopolski the chief of the civil administration of the country. In the spirit of enlightened despotism he organized a system of modern education, founded an institution of higher learning in Warsaw, established a system of municipal and county self-government, accorded political equality to the Jews and paved the way for the gradual emancipation of the peasants by the purchase of land from the landlords. Wielopolski failed, however, to rally public opinion behind his policies and aroused increasing discontent, particularly among the Polish revolutionary youth, who refused to acquiesce in the Russian domination of Poland and aimed at complete political independence. In the attempt to forestall a violent outbreak among the revolutionary youth Wielopolski ordered compulsory enlistment of young Poles in the imperial army. This drastic measure was promptly countered by an insurrection which broke out on January 22, 1863, marking the complete bankruptcy of Wielopolski's pro-Russian policies. He resigned and left Poland never to return.

MARCELI HANDELSMAN

Consult: Lisicki, Henryk, *Aleksander Wielopolski, 1803–1877*, 4 vols. (Cracow 1878–79), *Domowe sprawy* (Home affairs) (Cracow 1880), and *Le marquis Wielopolski, sa vie et son temps 1803–1877*, 2 vols. (Vienna 1880); Spasowicz, W., *Zhizn i politika Markiza Wielopolskago* (Life and policy of Marquis Wielopolski) (St. Petersburg 1882); Dąbrowski, Józef (J. Grabiec), *Ostatni szlachcic* (The last nobleman), 2 vols. (Warsaw 1924); Grabski, W., *Historya towarzystwa rolniczego, 1858–1861* (History of the agricultural association), 2 vols. (Warsaw 1904); Manteuffel, T., *Centralne władze oświatowe na terenie b. Królestwa Kongresowego (1807–1915)* (Central educational authorities in the former Congress Kingdom), Towarzystwo Naukowe Warszawskie, Rozprawy Historyczne, vol. vi (Warsaw 1929) pt. ii, p. 1–150; Sempołowska, Stefania, *Reforma szkolna 1862 roku* (The school reform of 1862) (Warsaw 1915).

WIESER, FRIEDRICH VON (1851–1926), Austrian economist and sociologist. Wieser was born in Vienna of an old Austrian family. Following his graduation from the University of Vienna he entered the service of the provincial government but shortly thereafter returned to the study of economics at the universities of Heidelberg, Jena and Leipsic. In 1884 he was appointed professor of economics at the German University in Prague and from 1903 he occupied Carl Menger's chair at the University of Vienna. In 1917 he was made minister of commerce but resumed teaching after the breakdown of the Austro-Hungarian Empire.

Wieser was one of the leading exponents of the Austrian, or "subjective," school of economics. He was the first to apply the principle of marginal utility to the phenomenon of cost by attempting to prove that cost, that is, the value of the factors of production, is determined by the least important of all economic uses to which the productive factors are applied. He demonstrated his doctrine with two simple algebraic formulae in connection with his theory of computation (*Zurechnung*), the corner stone of his general price theory. It was characteristic of Wieser that in dealing with special economic problems he always attempted to place them in their relationship to the totality of economic phenomena, imparting to economic theory a degree of integration previously unknown.

He was, however, more than an economist. In his economic works he early revealed a thorough appreciation of the importance of the social milieu within which economic phenomena operate, and of which they are but a part. On the basis of an extended analysis of the various systems of social organization he formulated in his chief sociological work, *Das Gesetz der Macht* (Vienna 1926), the law of small numbers, according to which the many are always governed by the few through outright domination or other forms of leadership. He characterized historical development as the combination of two main tendencies: the continuous redistribution of political power among the various classes of society and the gradual, although not uninterrupted, decrease in the use of force as a means of adjusting conflicting interests of the various groups composing society. He held that forms of social organization are conditioned by the political and cultural maturity of the people. His criticism of the new democracies established after the World War and his prediction that they would give place to dictatorships which would put an end to the wrangle of political parties were almost prophetic.

WILHELM VLEUGELS

Important works: *Über den Ursprung und die Hauptgesetze des wirtschaftlichen Werthes* (Vienna 1884); *Der natürliche Werth* (Vienna 1889), tr. by C. A. Malloch (London 1893); *Die deutsche Steuerleistung und der öffentliche Haushalt in Böhmen* (Leipsic 1904); *Über Vergangenheit und Zukunft der österreichischen Verfassung* (Vienna 1905); *Die Theorie der städtischen Grundrente* (Vienna 1909); *Recht und Macht* (Leipsic 1910); *Theorie der gesellschaftlichen Wirtschaft*, Grundriss der Sozialökonomik, Abteilung 1, pt. ii (Tübingen 1914, 2nd ed. 1924); *Österreichs Ende* (Berlin 1919). Wieser's most important articles are collected in *Gesammelte Abhandlungen*, ed. by F. A. Hayek (Tübingen 1929), with bibliography p. xxv–xxix.

Consult: Mayer, Hans, "Friedrich Wieser zum Gedächtnis" in *Zeitschrift für Volkswirtschaft und Sozialpolitik*, n.s., vol. v (1927) 633–45, and in *Neue österreichische Biographie*, vol. vi (Vienna 1929) p. 180–98; Menzel, Adolf, *Friedrich Wieser als Soziologe* (Vienna 1927); Morgenstern, O., in *American Economic Review*, vol. xvii (1927) 669–74; Roche-Agussol, M., *Un économiste sociologique; Friedrich von Wieser* (Paris 1930); Schams, E., "Friedrich Freiherr von Wieser und sein Werk" in *Zeitschrift für die gesamte Staatswissenschaft*, vol. lxxxi (1926) 432–48; Vleugels, Wilhelm, *Die Lösungen des wirtschaftlichen Zurechnungsproblems bei Böhm-Bawerk und Wieser*, Königsberger gelehrte Gesellschaft, Geisteswissenschaftliche Klasse, Schriften, 7th year, vol. v (Halle 1930), and "Ertragswert und Kostenwert" in *Zeitschrift für Nationalökonomie*, vol. iii (1931–32) 692–703.

WILAMOWITZ-MOELLENDORFF, ULRICH VON (1848–1931), German classical philologist. Wilamowitz was born in Posen of noble Prussian ancestry; he studied at Bonn and Berlin and taught at Greifswald, Göttingen and Berlin. His first work was his *Zukunftsphilologie* (2 vols., Berlin 1872–73), in which he attacked Nietzsche's *Geburt der Tragödie aus dem Geiste der Musik* (1872). From then on he fought consistently against all romanticism and classicism. He rejected the intuitions of the poet philosopher as well as the works of Ernst Curtius and Jacob Burckhardt, and he carried on a bitter struggle against dulness and ignorance and against the false *Schwärmerei* of miniature epigoni. He was impulsive, sober, clear, versatile, often sophistical, always open to new impressions and constantly engaged in recasting his knowledge; and his work naturally bore the impress of his dynamic personality. Applying Mommsen's epigraphic method to the most varied problems of Greek literature, he excelled in the most minute researches as well as in broad, sweeping works. Thanks to his marvelous memory he was able to command an ever increasing body of knowledge. As a young man he had already surveyed the entire field from Homer to the late Greek epoch. He worked continuously, studied inscriptions and coins, papyri and literature and surveyed all the results of discoveries and archaeological excavations. With deep understanding he penetrated into the forms of religion and state, literature and philology, although he never fully appreciated the plastic arts. In his editions of important works of the classical tradition he showed himself the equal of the greatest textual editors by his general knowledge of the language, his specific knowledge of the author and his meticulousness of method and keen critical sense. His *Homerische Untersuchungen* (Berlin 1884) and *Die Ilias und Homer* (Berlin 1916) stimulated a multitude of new investigations. His bold and brilliant *Die griechische Literatur des Altertums* (Die Kultur der Gegenwart, sect. i, pt. viii, Leipsic 1905; 3rd ed. 1912) was the first attempt to survey over fifteen hundred years of Greek life. He displayed a complete mastery of the material in this field as well as a grandiose universal conception. He admired Droysen's presentation of Hellenistic history and urged the further investigation of Hellenistic culture. In numerous articles and in his *Hellenistische Dichtung in der Zeit des Kallimachos* (2 vols., Berlin 1924) he gave a powerful impetus to these studies. He was heir to Böckh in his energetic work on the corpus of Greek inscriptions for the Academy of Sciences. In his *Aristoteles und Athen* (2 vols., Berlin 1893) and in *Staat und Gesellschaft der Griechen und der Römer . . .* (Die Kultur der Gegenwart, sect. ii, pt. iv, vol. i, Leipsic 1910; 2nd ed. 1923) he presented a broad synthesis of Greek political life. No scholarly task overawed him, and he soberly encompassed the totality of Greek life in all its reality and all its transformations. In this historical interpretation of Hellenism he was a pupil of Theodor Mommsen and his entire work represents the Greek counterpart of Mommsen's work on Rome. He believed that "great men make the nation." He acknowledged also that man can learn to comprehend the aims and influence of genius although he can never explain rationally the underlying causes of the existence of genius, which "remains the secret of God." Thus he preserved a reverence for what was beyond the limits of understanding, and it was not by chance that his last work was *Der Glaube der Hellenen* (2 vols., Berlin 1931–32), a treatise on Greek religious ideas.

Wilhelm Weber

Consult: Wilamowitz-Moellendorf, U., *Erinnerungen 1848–1914* (2nd ed. Leipsic 1928), tr. by G. C. Richards (London 1930); Hiller von Gaertringen, F., *Wilamowitz-Bibliographie 1868–1929* (Berlin 1929).

WILBERFORCE, WILLIAM (1759–1833), British statesman and humanitarian. Born of a well to do commercial family in Hull, Wilberforce entered the House of Commons in 1780 together with his intimate friend the younger Pitt. His ready if loose knit eloquence and his beautiful voice quickly won him a front place in debate, while his wit and charm made him a favorite of fashionable society. In 1785 he underwent an evangelical "conversion," adopted a life of strict although never unctuous piety and would probably have abandoned politics if he had not felt a call to join the movement for abolishing the slave trade. It was mainly by reason of his personality and persistence that the British share of the trade was abolished in 1807. Thenceforward one of the most famous Englishmen of the time, Wilberforce used his influence abroad to press for the universal abolition of the trade and at home to support, although he became too old to lead, the campaign against slavery itself. The bill emancipating over 700,-000 slaves in British ownership was passing through Parliament when he died. Preaching also the positive duty of bringing civilization to backward races Wilberforce supported "legitimate" trade in Africa, the Sierra Leone colony and, above all, Christian missions. He was a founder of the Church Missionary Society and the British and Foreign Bible Society and did much to open British India to missionaries.

In politics he became like Pitt a moderate Tory, although after his conversion he was never a strong partisan. He favored Catholic emancipation and parliamentary reform and on such social questions as the condition of the poor, the penal system and popular education he took a liberal view; but his support of Sidmouth's repressive measures exposed him to the radical sneer that the victims of oppression could gain his sympathy only if their skins were black. Although the collaboration of other philanthropists was essential to his success, Wilberforce was and is still regarded as the foremost figure in British humanitarianism. So great was his prestige that in public life he became in a sense the keeper of the nation's conscience; and perhaps his greatest achievement was the part he played in elevating the moral temper of his class and period. Many thousand copies of his *Practical View* (London 1797), an exposition of his evangelical creed, were sold in England and abroad; and the power which he and a group of close friends, known as "the Saints" or "the Clapham Sects," wielded in Parliament was an example of the effect of a candid profession of religion as the guiding principle in politics.

R. Coupland

Consult: Wilberforce, Robert I. and Samuel, *Life of*

William Wilberforce, 5 vols. (London 1838–39); *Correspondence*, ed. by R. I. and Samuel Wilberforce, 2 vols. (London 1840); Coupland, R., *Wilberforce* (Oxford 1923); Mathieson, W. L., *British Slavery and Its Abolition, 1823–1838* (London 1926), *Great Britain and the Slave Trade, 1839–1865* (London 1929), and *British Slave Emancipation, 1839–1849* (London 1932); Klingberg, F. J., *The Anti-Slavery Movement in England*, Yale University, Historical Publications, Miscellany, vol. xvii (New Haven 1926), especially chs. iii–vi; Coupland, R., *The British Anti-Slavery Movement* (London 1933) p. 70–88, 91–121.

WILKES, JOHN (1727–97), British publicist and political figure. As a Whig follower of Pitt, Wilkes in 1757 entered Parliament, where his attacks upon Bute and George III led to his prosecution by the government, the search of his house and the seizure of his papers. There followed expulsion from the House, ostensibly because of his notorious *Essay on Woman* (1763), and outlawry during his residence in Paris. Upon his return to England in 1768 Wilkes was reelected to the House as a member for Middlesex. The outlawry was reversed on a technicality but he was imprisoned for a term upon other convictions. He was twice again rejected by the House but was seated upon a third election in 1774. The protracted quarrel is reflected in Edmund Burke's brilliant pamphlet *Thoughts on the Cause of the Present Discontents* (London 1770) and in the *Letters of Junius* (1769–72). Wilkes had become popular in Britain and the colonies as a defender of the rights of the people (a Pennsylvania town, Wilkes-Barre, was named for him and his colleague) and was elected sheriff, lord mayor and chamberlain in the City of London.

"Few objects of intolerance have touched such a low level of thought and action, few have rendered more numerous and more valuable services to liberty than John Wilkes," says Chafee, who enumerates these as establishing in his resistance to the government of the day the immunity of political criticism from prosecution, the publicity of legislative debates, the abolition of outlawry of a man through condemnation in his absence, the protection of house and property from unreasonable search and seizures (written into the Constitution of the United States in the Fourth Amendment) and the right of a duly elected representative of a constituency to sit in the legislature unless disqualified by law, regardless of the personal objections of his colleagues to his opinions and writings or of his previous conviction for sedition.

JOHN M. GAUS

Consult: Bleackley, H. W., *Life of John Wilkes* (London 1917); Postgate, R. W., *That Devil Wilkes* (New York 1929); Sherrard, O. A., *Life of John Wilkes* (London 1930); Chafee, Zechariah, Jr., *Freedom of Speech* (New York 1920) ch. vi.

WILLARD, EMMA HART (1787–1870), pioneer in the education of American women. Emma Hart was born in Connecticut, where she was educated in the district school of Kensington and in the academy at Berlin. At the age of seventeen she began to teach school, and in 1807 she took charge of the girls' academy in Middlebury, Vermont. A few years after her marriage to Dr. John Willard in 1809 her husband met with financial reverses, and in order to restore the family fortunes she opened a girls' boarding school at her home in Middlebury. Her famous *Plan for Improving Female Education* (Middlebury 1819) presented to the state legislature of New York in 1819 made the audacious proposal that legislatures appropriate funds for the education of girls, hitherto neglected. That same year Mrs. Willard's school was moved to Waterford, New York, and in 1821 to Troy, where the city council provided funds for the establishment of Troy Female Seminary. Under her leadership this institution became famous for the breadth and thoroughness of its educational work and for its training of future teachers. In 1838 she retired to Kensington, where she rendered valuable aid to Henry Barnard in his campaign for improvement of the public schools. Later she made a tour of New York counties, addressing teachers' institutes, and in 1846 she traveled through the west and the south lecturing on problems of education and teaching.

Emma Willard's educational reforms attacked the worst evils in girls' education of her day. She urged consistently that women's education be placed on a sound economic basis; that the curriculum in girls' schools be enriched; that sounder methods of instruction be instituted; and that professional training for teachers be provided. Finally, she wrote a series of improved textbooks, including *History of the United States or the Republic of America* (New York 1828, rev. ed. 1856); *A System of Universal History* (Hartford 1835); *A System of Universal Geography* (Hartford 1822, new ed. 1861) in collaboration with William C. Woodbridge; and *Guide to the Temple of Time and Universal History for Schools* (New York 1849).

WILLYSTINE GOODSELL

Consult: Lord, John, *Life of Emma Willard* (New York 1873); Lutz, Alma, *Emma Willard, Daughter of Democracy* (Boston 1929); *Pioneers of Women's Edu-*

cation in the United States, ed. by Willystine Goodsell (New York 1931) p. 15–108; Fowler, Henry, "Educational Services of Mrs. Emma Willard" in *American Journal of Education*, vol. vi (1859) 125–68; Bartlett, Ellen S., in *New England Magazine*, vol. xxv (1901) 555–76.

WILLARD, FRANCES ELIZABETH (1839–98), American temperance reformer. Frances Willard was born in New York state of New England parentage and passed her early years in Wisconsin and in Evanston, Illinois. After her graduation from Northwestern Female College in 1859 she taught school for several years, finally becoming president of Evanston College for Ladies. Upon the merger of this institution with Northwestern University, of which her former fiancé was president, she was made dean of women and professor of aesthetics. Before long, however, she came into conflict with the president on matters of college administration and resigned in 1874.

At this time the "praying bands" of women in Ohio had begun to harry the saloon keepers, often with astonishing success. In the work of the newly organized Woman's Christian Temperance Union Frances Willard found an outlet for her remarkable energies and genuine ability and she devoted the remainder of her life to the cause of prohibition. Believing that the temperance crusade taught women their power to transact business and opened their eyes to the need of the republic for their enfranchisement, she espoused the cause of woman suffrage and allied reforms, although she considered them of subsidiary importance.

She wrote with great rapidity and voluminously. In addition to editing the *Union Signal*, official organ of the temperance movement, she found time to produce numerous pamphlets and magazine articles on prohibition and to write her autobiography, *Glimpses of Fifty Years* (Chicago 1889). In collaboration with Mary A. Livermore she edited a series of biographical sketches, *American Women* (2 vols., New York 1897).

LORINE PRUETTE

Consult: Gordon, A. A., *Frances E. Willard; a Memorial Volume* (Chicago 1898); Strachey, R. C., *Frances Willard; Her Life and Work* (London 1912); Bradford, G., *Portraits of American Women* (Boston 1919) p. 195–225; Dibble, R. F., *Strenuous Americans* (New York 1923) p. 183–256; Howe, M. A. De Wolfe, *Causes and Their Champions* (Boston 1926) p. 80–118.

WILLIAM I (the Conqueror) (c. 1027–87), king of England. The illegitimate son of Robert, duke of Normandy, William succeeded to the duchy in 1035 as a child under the protection of his feudal lord, Henry I, king of France. His rule in Normandy was marked by the gradual establishment of public order and by hostilities with adjacent powers, culminating in the conquest of the county of Maine in 1060. He received from his childless cousin, Edward the Confessor, king of England, a promise of the succession to the English kingdom, and asserted his claim when the English nobility recognized Harold, earl of Wessex, as king on Edward's death in 1066. His enterprise was favored not only by the temporary weakness of his rivals in France but also by the fact that the uncanonical position of Stigand, archbishop of Canterbury, led pope Alexander II to support the Norman claimant, whose expedition thereby acquired to some extent the character of a crusade. Early in 1066 William collected an army from every part of northern France and in September crossed from Saint-Valery to Pevensey without serious opposition from the English fleet. As a result of the defeat and death of Harold at the battle of Hastings there was no single candidate around whom the whole English nation could combine. William was crowned king on the Christmas Day after the battle and in the following years suppressed with little difficulty English revolts, Danish invasions and such disaffection as arose among his own French followers.

William ruled in England as the heir of Edward the Confessor, using the English administrative system and insisting that each Frenchman who received land in England should occupy the exact legal position of the Englishman whom he had supplanted. The great transference of land which followed the Conquest was accomplished gradually and in accordance with the accepted principles of law. The settlement of England in church and state proceeded under the king's immediate supervision. The church was ruled by his personal friend Lanfranc, archbishop of Canterbury, and the great barons were used in the business of government under William's direct control. Under him England became the first centralized state in western Europe. Only a monarchy of most unusual strength could have carried out the elaborate survey of which the results were summarized in *Domesday Book*, and the effectiveness of government which made this undertaking possible was essentially due to the king's own power and initiative. As a military commander William was not in advance of his time; his later warfare was ineffective, and in 1087 he was killed in the course of an obscure raid on Mantes arising out of a personal quarrel with the king of France. His unique place in history is due to the statesmanship through which he became the real founder of the mediaeval English monarchy.

F. M. STENTON

Consult: Freeman, E. A., *The History of the Norman Conquest of England*, 6 vols. (Oxford 1867–79); Davis, H. W. C., *England under the Normans and Angevins* (London 1905) chs. i–ii; Stenton, F. M., *William the Conqueror* (London 1908).

WILLIAM I (1797–1888), German emperor and king of Prussia. Throughout his life William remained essentially a soldier. He took part in the campaign in France in 1814, became leader of the corps of guards in 1825 and attained recognition as a military expert. He considered an active army the only efficient military weapon and a reliable instrument in the hands of the crown. He devoted his life to these military and political aims and opposed the constitutional plans of his older brother, later Frederick William IV. With the early success of the March Revolution of 1848 he withdrew to England. He returned again in June, 1848, and the next year commanded the Prussian troops which entered Baden to crush the uprising. As military governor of Rhenish Prussia and Westphalia he remained in opposition to his brother even when in the 1850's the latter had fallen completely under the influence of reaction. The National Liberals therefore looked to William as their leader. In 1857 he was invested with the direction of affairs during the illness of Frederick William IV, in 1858 he was made prince regent and in 1861, after his brother's death, was crowned king of Prussia.

The beginning of his reign marked a new era for Prussia, since he called in a liberal ministry. But when together with War Minister Roon he sought to execute his long cherished plan for army reform both the Landtag and the ministry refused to support him. On September 24, 1862, he called Bismarck to the office of prime minister. Bismarck carried through the reform for an increase in the active army and an extension of the power of the crown against the will of parliament. Thus under the rule of William and with the army created by him Prussia achieved the victories of 1864, 1866 and 1870 and the national unification of Germany under Prussian leadership. The imperial proclamation of January 18, 1871, brought William the title of German emperor. From 1871 he followed the leadership of Bismarck, although he often raised objections to his policy. He opposed the German-Austrian alliance of 1879 and the Kulturkampf. The designation "the Great," bestowed upon him by William II, never gained acceptance, for the political achievements of this era were largely the work of Bismarck and the military achievements of Moltke.

FRANZ SCHNABEL

Consult: Marcks, Erich, *Kaiser Wilhelm I* (8th ed. Munich 1918); Wiegler, Paul, *Wilhelm der Erste; sein Leben und seine Zeit* (Dresden 1927), tr. by C. Vesey (London 1929).

WILLIAMS, ROGER (1603–83), colonial religious leader and founder of Rhode Island. Williams was the son of a London merchant. He became a minister and Puritan partisan and had to flee to Boston in 1631. He was then no longer a Puritan but a separatist, demanding a break with the Church of England. By 1636, when he was expelled from Massachusetts Bay, he denied that the authority of the state extended to religion. During the rest of his life he developed his principles in a number of controversial writings, which had more influence on his English contemporaries than on the colonists or posterity. His originality consisted in his sharp distinction between religious toleration, which is consistent with a favored church, and religious liberty, which holds all religions equal before civil law, and in his development of the political implications of religious freedom as a doctrine of the limitations of civil authority. Williams' general orientation was that of the lower middle class sects with their suspicion of church and state. After publishing his most radical writings in England Williams was given a charter for Rhode Island by the English Puritans, who also warned the New England Puritans not to molest him. The community between the English Puritans and Williams is apparent from his friendship and association with many of the leaders, including Cromwell, Milton and Vane. Williams' place in seventeenth century society becomes clearer if it is remembered that from the doctrine that civil authority may not interfere with religion he drew the corollary that evil economic practises, such as usury, are no concern of the church. It may be said that when the Puritan oligarchy of Massachusetts expelled Williams in 1636, it was developing precisely those aspects of Puritanism which were already disappearing from the main Puritan stream. The Massachusetts oligarchy was finally overwhelmed by an influx of the lower middle class groups for which Williams provided the revolutionary expression. It was these succeeding waves of immigration, bringing a multiplicity of sects of which none was dominant, that insured American religious liberty. The honor of having founded Rhode Island as the first community practising complete religious liberty must be credited to Williams, but his achievement was not a significant factor in bringing about the separation of church and state in the United States.

FELIX MORROW

Consult: Ernst, James E., *The Political Thought of Roger Williams*, University of Washington, Publications in Language and Literature, vol. vi, no. i (Seattle 1929), and *Roger Williams, New England Firebrand* (New York 1932); Adams, James Truslow, *The Founding of New England* (Boston 1921) chs. vii and xi; Hall, Thomas Cuming, *The Religious Background of American Culture* (Boston 1930) chs. viii-ix; Parrington, V. L., *Main Currents in American Thought*, 3 vols. (New York 1927–30) vol. i.

WILLS. *See* SUCCESSION, LAWS OF.

WILSON, JAMES (1742–98), American jurist and statesman. Wilson was born near St. Andrews in Fifeshire, Scotland. After studying at St. Andrews, Glasgow and Edinburgh universities he went to New York in 1765 while the Stamp Act Congress was in session. He soon removed, however, to Philadelphia, where he became a tutor in the College of Philadelphia and shortly thereafter began to study law in the office of John Dickinson. He soon acquired the reputation of the greatest lawyer in Pennsylvania and was intimately connected with its politics throughout the revolutionary period.

Wilson was a signer of the Declaration of Independence and was largely instrumental in persuading the Continental Congress to wait for an expression of the popular will, as sovereignty lay in it, before severing the connection of the colonies with Great Britain. He failed of reelection to the Continental Congress in 1777 because he opposed the state constitution of 1776, but served again from 1782 to 1783 and from 1785 to 1787. He was also a member of the Board of War; advocate general for France, in which capacity he worked out the first French consular system for the United States; attorney for Pennsylvania in defeating the claims of Connecticut in the Wyoming Valley Dispute; he was active in bringing about the cession of the Northwest Territory and the incorporation of the Bank of North America. But above all his fame rests upon the great role he played in the framing of the federal constitution and in securing its adoption by Pennsylvania. He was appointed a justice of the new national Supreme Court upon its organization; and it was he who wrote the famous opinion in Chisholm *v.* Georgia. Selected by the College of Philadelphia to do for America what Blackstone had done for England by interpreting the new national and state constitutions and laws, he delivered in 1790 a famous course of law lectures, which were later published by his son. He died in adversity, however, at a comparatively early age, because of losses in the panic years of the 1790's.

It was the rise of the Jeffersonian party which long obscured his fame. Only in recent decades has he come to be regarded as the chief theoretician of the revolution. In arguing that a connection with the British crown existed although Parliament could not legislate for the colonies, he was the first to give expression to the modern theory of the British constitution, as stated by Bryce and Lord Hailsham, the latter on July 4, 1934. Much of the very language of the Declaration of Independence has been traced to his pen. In the constitutional convention only Madison's work compares in importance with Wilson's. The latter is credited with having formulated the clause against the impairment of the obligations of contracts. He elaborated in effect the doctrine of implied powers, stressing the sovereignty of the nation as a necessary consequence of the sovereignty of the people. He favored the people far more than the other framers, for he supported the popular election of the Senate and president and opposed equal representation in the Senate as well as property qualifications for voting. In his law lectures indeed he enunciated the very arguments used later by Marshall in establishing the right to declare an act of Congress unconstitutional. Despite the fact that some of his more liberal views were rejected, he may be regarded as the chief architect of the constitution.

BURTON ALVA KONKLE

Works: *Works*, ed. by Bird Wilson, 3 vols. (Philadelphia 1804; new ed. by J. D. Andrews, 2 vols., Chicago 1896); *Selected Political Essays*, ed. by Randolph G. Adams (New York 1930); *Life and Writings of James Wilson*, ed. by B. A. Konkle, vols. i–ii (New York 1934).

Consult: McLaughlin, Andrew C., "James Wilson in the Philadelphia Convention" in *Political Science Quarterly*, vol. xii (1897) 1–20; Harlan, John M., "James Wilson and the Formation of the Constitution" in *American Law Review*, vol. xxxiv (1900) 481–504; Alexander, L. H., "James Wilson, Patriot, and the Wilson Doctrine" in *North American Review*, vol.

clxxxiii (1906) 971–89, and "James Wilson, Nation-Builder" in *Green Bag*, vol. xix (1907) 1–9, 98–109, 137–46, 265–76; Konkle, Burton Alva, and others, "The James Wilson Memorial" in *University of Pennsylvania Law Review*, vol. lv (1907) 1–46; Klingelsmith, M. C., "James Wilson" in *Great American Lawyers*, ed. by W. D. Lewis, vol. i (Philadelphia 1907) p. 151–221, and "James Wilson and the So-called Yazoo Frauds" in *University of Pennsylvania Law Review*, vol. lvi (1908) 1–27; Adams, Randolph G., "The Legal Theories of James Wilson" in *University of Pennsylvania Law Review*, vol. lxviii (1919–20) 337–55.

WILSON, JOSEPH HAVELOCK (1859–1929), English labor leader. Born into seafaring traditions, Wilson at the age of eleven left home to become a seaman. His experiences with sailing ships, primitive steamships, crimping houses and casual port labor gave him that ruthless doggedness which influenced the whole of his career. He faced with pioneer courage the insuperable difficulties of organizing seamen and in 1887 founded the National Amalgamated Sailors' and Firemen's Union of Great Britain and Ireland. Litigation, imprisonment and bankruptcy forced upon him by the shipowners failed to prevent his building up an effective national organization. This struggle ended in 1917 when as members of the National Maritime Board Wilson and the shipowners agreed to a system of joint control for the recruitment of seamen.

Wilson was never a socialist; he distrusted state socialism and looked only to combination as the means by which seamen might obtain their share of the profits of the industry. He was, however, persuaded to spend much of his time in political lobbying and later to enter Parliament by his friend Plimsol, who wanted a seaman to help him with his shipping legislation. Wilson entered Parliament as a Liberal in 1892, but when in 1922 he was spectacularly defeated he felt that the logic of his earlier theory was vindicated.

By opposing the Labour party, by fighting the political tendencies of the Trades Union Congress and by alliance with the shipowners against both unorganized seamen and all competing unions Wilson aroused the fiercest hostility in the labor movement. Although he worked in isolation, he kept intact a national organization for seamen, of which he remained the autocratic head until his death.

GRACE FORD

Consult: Wilson, J. H., *My Stormy Voyage through Life* (London 1925). See also the annual *Reports* of the Labour party, vols. i–xxix (1901–29), and of the Trades Union Congress, vols. xx–lxi (London 1887–1929), and the files of the *Seaman*, official organ of the National Union of Seamen, published fortnightly in London since 1912.

WILSON, (THOMAS) WOODROW (1856–1924), president of the United States. Wilson graduated from Princeton in 1879 and after a year's work in the Law School of the University of Virginia opened a law office in Atlanta. Becoming dissatisfied with his prospects, he went to Johns Hopkins University in 1883, where he wrote a doctoral thesis, *Congressional Government*. After a short career at Bryn Mawr and at Wesleyan he became in 1890 professor of jurisprudence and political economy at Princeton and at once took rank among the foremost political scientists of his time. Although he was a conservative in social philosophy, he leaned more and more toward the radical viewpoint in national affairs. In 1902 he was elected president of Princeton and quickly became second only to President Eliot of Harvard as an educational leader. There was opposition to his policy after 1905, but he obtained large gifts from wealthy friends and was about to recast the character of the institution in 1910 when a large gift was offered to Princeton on condition that Wilson's program be abandoned. His position became untenable.

Already the president of Princeton was beginning to be widely discussed as a probable candidate for the presidency of the United States. He was urged upon the public by George Harvey as a conservative Democrat of the east in the hope of defeating William J. Bryan. That meant that Tammany Hall, the James Smith machine of New Jersey and the Thomas F. Ryan capitalists of the east would unite behind a university president in the expectation of controlling the United States. Harvey and his allies managed to nominate Wilson for governor of New Jersey in September, 1910, and their favorite was elected the following November by a surprising majority. Within a few months the new governor became chief of all the "progressive" executives, and there was grave concern in conservative circles that Wilson would be a more "dangerous" president of the United States than Bryan himself. Wilson frankly acknowledged that the support of his powerful eastern friends was a liability. A break followed, and during the early months of 1912 Bryan and Wilson, till then supposed to be opponents, became allies. When the Republicans divided into two factions in June, 1912, it became evident that the Democratic nominee would almost certainly become president. A bitter struggle ensued, and the Democrats in their Baltimore convention, after nearly a week of balloting between the reactionary and the liberal forces, nominated the New Jersey liberal. Wilson was elected by a popular vote of almost 6,300,000 as against 7,600,000 divided between Taft and Roosevelt. The new president, supported by a Democratic Congress, undertook to apply a semirevolutionary policy in the early spring of 1913 and at once revealed a power and an art of leadership unmatched in the history of the country since Jefferson's embargo failure in 1808.

It was an opportunity of world wide significance. The imperialistic policy that followed the Spanish American War, the industrial-financial overlordship and the unbroken railway control of large blocs of national life demanded drastic subordination if democracy were to survive in the United States. Wilson procured the acceptance of the Federal Reserve Act, under which some control of national finance was assumed by the government. The protective tariff system was radically reformed. A new antitrust law designed to protect the small business man or corporation was enacted, and the federal government reapplied the national income tax system of the Civil War period. Between April, 1913, and the summer of 1914 the new president moved forward with his domestic reforms in a manner which presaged a violent campaign in the autumn of 1914. Nor were Wilson's moves in foreign policy less appealing. In October, 1913, he announced to the world at Mobile that the United States was abandoning the "big stick" policy and recasting the Monroe Doctrine, which was resented all over Latin America. In May, 1914, as the tense European situation gave evidence once more of breaking into open conflict, he sent Colonel Edward M. House to Berlin to persuade the German militarists to unite their country with the United States, England and France in a sort of four-power pact to keep the peace of the world. With the outbreak of the World War Wilson declared the United States neutral, but the whole Wilson program changed. He held his own in the congressional election of 1914; but all America talked about the war, while millions of workers gradually turned their attention to the production and shipment of supplies to warring Europe.

From August, 1914, to June, 1916, Wilson and his party contended in vain for the rights of neutrals. Reelected in 1916 on the strength of having "kept us out of war" Wilson at once called upon the warring peoples of Europe to come to some reasonable terms on which the struggle might be concluded. But neither the Central nor the Allied Powers were ready for a "peace without victory." Following the announcement on January 31, 1917, that Germany would immediately apply a submarine blockade to all the ports of its enemies, Wilson reluctantly asked the recall of the German ambassador and asked Congress to declare an armed neutrality. On April 2 he called upon Congress and the country to declare war.

From the entrance of the United States into the great struggle until the signing of the Armistice on November 11, 1918, Wilson was the soul of the allied cause. He would save the German people from the oppressions of their autocratic masters. The Allies must forego all claims to new territory. All peoples must be free to govern themselves, and there should be no indemnities. His program was summed up in the famous "Fourteen Points"—a new creed for mankind. But the leaders of Europe were not enamored of their new ally. Every national group had definite aggrandizements in view, and large groups of Americans ridiculed the "idealism" of their second Jefferson. In order to win the president required a new mandate in the autumn of 1918. He asked the country to give him a Democratic majority. Republicans resented the appeal. Millions of German voters would not forgive Wilson for entering the war. The Irish were equally resentful because the president had not beaten the English, and hundreds of thousands of Negroes in northern industrial areas voted solidly against the southern "aristocrat." The result was a Republican majority in the House of Representatives and a tie vote in the Senate. Wilson was no longer the democratic autocrat of the world. He was terribly depressed; but early in December, 1918, he left Congress to organize against him, a few Democratic Senators joining the Republicans to defeat the chief who had not always distributed patronage to their liking.

When Wilson appeared in Paris on December 14, he was received with an acclaim unparalleled in a hundred years. He visited London and Rome, where the masses seemed ready to worship him. But when the delegations to the Peace Conference sat down together, there was no real approval of his "points." He and David Lloyd George agreed for a moment to ask Russia to send delegates to check the revolutionary sweep in Europe and to get friendly support. But the House of Commons gave Lloyd George contrary orders. The United States Senate continued its warfare. Wilson's power was gone. He returned to Washington late in February and tried unsuccessfully to rally support in the country and in Congress. He went to Paris again after promises of support from Taft and Bryan. The Senate cabled in March that Wilson must put the Monroe Doctrine in the treaty. Taft, Bryan and Elihu Root cabled to similar effect. When Wilson made the proposal, Clemenceau renewed his demands and Foch asked for all Germany west of the Rhine. Japan insisted upon a Monroe Doctrine of the Far East. Contemplating a return to Washington early in April and threatened with a paralytic stroke, Wilson finally decided to remain, sign the best peace he could get in the hope of forestalling a communist revolution and then go home and fight for its adoption. Although most of the Fourteen Points were slowly whittled away, there was to be a League of Nations; Poland was to have its free existence again; the Balkan states were to have their independence; the so-called backward countries of the world were not to be exploited; Germany must disarm and the other powers agreed to do the same. It was not a bad treaty as compared with the treaties of 1648, 1713 and 1763. Wilson returned to ask the Senate's approval. In the early autumn he was fatally stricken, and he never again made an effective speech. In the election of 1920 Wilson's candidate was defeated and another Republican Congress was chosen. The Senate refused to act before Wilson's term closed, and the United States finally decided against adoption.

WILLIAM E. DODD

Works: *Congressional Government* (Boston 1885; new ed. by R. S. Baker, 1925); *The State* (Boston 1889; new ed. by E. Elliott, 1918); *Division and Reunion, 1828–1889* (New York 1893, new ed. 1926); *George Washington* (New York 1896); *A History of the American People*, 5 vols. (New York 1902; enlarged documentary ed., 10 vols., 1918); *Constitutional Government in the United States* (New York 1908); *The New Freedom* (New York 1913).

Consult: Princeton University Library, *Essays towards a Bibliography of Woodrow Wilson*, by H. Clemons, G. D. Brown and H. S. Leach, 3 vols. (Princeton 1913–22); Baker, Ray Stannard, *Woodrow Wilson; Life and Letters*, vols. i–iv (New York 1927–31); *The Public Papers of Woodrow Wilson*, ed. by R. S. Baker and W. E. Dodd, 6 vols. (New York 1925–27); House, Edward M., *The Intimate Papers of Colonel House*, arranged by Charles Seymour, 4 vols. (Boston 1926–28); Dodd, W. E., *Woodrow Wilson and His Work* (4th ed. New York 1921); White, William A., *Woodrow Wilson, the Man, His Times and His Task* (Boston 1924); Daniels, Josephus, *The Life of Woodrow Wilson* (Philadelphia 1924); Seymour, Charles, *Woodrow Wilson and the World War*, Chronicles of America series, vol. xlviii (New Haven 1921); Tumulty, Joseph P., *Woodrow Wilson as I Know Him* (New York 1921); Merriam, C. E., *Four American Party Leaders* (New York 1926) ch. iii; Hollingsworth, William W., *Woodrow Wilson's Political Ideals as Interpreted from His Works* (Princeton 1918); McKown, Paul, *Certain Important Domestic Policies of Woodrow Wilson* (Philadelphia 1932).

WINCKELMANN, JOHANN JOACHIM (1717–68), German historian of classical art. Winckelmann was the most important single force making for the development of nineteenth century classical humanism. During his long sojourns in Rome, Florence and other parts of Italy he collected voluminous material on the life of the Greeks and became thoroughly familiar with all aspects of their literature. Although he lived in the era of rationalist Enlightenment he appreciated the value of enthusiasm and the importance of historical criteria for objective evaluations.

Winckelmann may be said to have discovered the Hellenic world for the German spirit. Lessing, Goethe, Schiller, Humboldt and Hölderlin and successive scholars for over a century reflected the influence of his work on classical art. He never regarded as an end in itself the extraordinary knowledge which he amassed under the greatest hardships. He wrote his first work, *Gedancken über die Nachahmung der griechischen Wercke* (1755; tr. by H. Fuseli, London 1765), in order to stimulate interest in art. He warned his readers that feeling for beauty and form had been destroyed and that the only hope of regaining it lay in following the lines of classical art. All naturalist and baroque forms were disturbing to him; instead he glorified the unity of structure, delicate harmony, proportion, ease of execution and freedom of spirit which he considered characteristic of Greek art.

Winckelmann's most important work was his *Geschichte der Kunst des Alterthums* (2 vols., 1764; tr. by G. Henry Lodge, 4 vols., Boston 1849–73). He subjected all the available materials to careful examination, described them with finesse, boldly worked out period styles, attempted to establish groups of schools and presented the first general picture of the development of classical art. The ideal norms of Greek art as he saw them were "noble simplicity and tranquil loftiness," proportion, order and harmony. Shaftesbury spoke in general of the "refined manner and accurate simplicity of the ancients," but Winckelmann saw among the Greeks the realization of the fusion of nature and man. The impetus which proceeded from his view was tremendous: poets, artists, scholars and teachers from all over the world were inspired by Winckelmann's work, which had an indelible effect upon historiography and classical scholarship.

WILHELM WEBER

Works: *Sämtliche Werke*, ed. by Joseph Eiselein, 12 vols. (Donaueschingen 1825–29).

Consult: Justi, Carl, *Winckelmann und seine Zeitgenossen*, 3 vols. (3rd ed. Leipsic 1923); Dilthey, Wilhelm, "Das achtzehnte Jahrhundert und die geschichtliche Welt" in his *Gesammelte Schriften*, vol. iii (Leipsic 1927), especially p. 257–61; Pater, Walter, *The Renaissance* (London 1873) p. 168–245.

WINDOW TAX. *See* HOUSE AND BUILDING TAXES.

WINDSCHEID, BERNHARD (1817–92), German jurist. In the development of law in Germany Windscheid's work marks the end of an epoch. No other book represents so fully the final achievement of dogmatic jurisprudence on a Roman law basis as does his *Lehrbuch des Pandektenrechts* (3 vols., Düsseldorf 1862–70; 9th ed. by T. Kipp, Frankfort 1906), seven editions of which appeared during his lifetime. In his later years Windscheid was, as he said, "the prisoner of his textbook," the successive editions of which contain in footnotes a critical digest of the mass of contemporary literature. Of his earlier works the most significant was *Die Actio des römischen Civilrechts vom Standpunkte des heutigen Rechts* (Düsseldorf 1856), in which he succeeded in disentangling the Roman expression from its procedural implications and substituted for it the substantive conception of *Anspruch*, or claim, of which full use has been made in the Civil Code. Almost as influential at the time was his theory of the "presuppositions" as developed in his *Die Lehre des römischen Rechts von der Voraussetzung* (Düsseldorf 1850), but this theory was not accepted by the code.

Windscheid was a teacher all his life, holding chairs successively at Bonn, Basel, Greifswald, Munich, Heidelberg and Leipsic; he took little part in politics or practise, but his influence on the practical administration of law was far reaching. His lectures, although abstract in form and difficult to follow, attracted great numbers of students, who knew that they would learn from him the doctrines which swayed the courts, and his textbook may be said to have in large measure taken the place of a code. Toward the Roman texts his attitude was less independent than that of some contemporaries (for instance Jhering), and his greatness lay less in originality than in the careful analysis and skilful formulation of legal rules. From 1874 to 1883 he worked as a member of the Civil Code Commission, but the task was unsuited to a man who had always regarded legislation as a matter outside the sphere of the lawyer. "Jurisprudence," he said, "is the handmaid of legislation." The flood of criticism with which the first draft of the code was received was in part the measure of a revolt against Windscheid's Romanism, but even the code as finally enacted owes much of its substance and terminology to him.

H. F. JOLOWICZ

Consult: Eck, Ernst, *Zur Feier des Gedächtnisses von B. Windscheid und R. von Jhering* (Berlin 1893); Leonhard, R., "Ein Nachruf für Jhering und Windscheid" in *Rechtsgeleerd magazijn*, vol. xii (1893) 249–83; Stintzing, R. von, and Landsberg, E., *Geschichte der deutschen Rechtswissenschaft*, 3 vols. (Munich 1880–1910) vol. iii, pt. ii, p. 854–65; Bekker, E. I., "Vier Pandektisten" in *Heidelberger Universität, Heidelberger Professoren aus dem 19. Jahrhundert*, 2 vols. (Heidelberg 1903) vol. i, p. 187–202; Rümelin, Max, *Bernhard Windscheid und sein Einfluss auf Privatrecht und Privatrechtswissenschaft* (Tübingen 1907); Smith, Munroe, "Four German Jurists" in his *A General View of European Legal History* (New York 1927) p. 110–225; *Bernhard Windscheid, Gesammelte Reden und Abhandlungen*, ed. by P. Oertmann (Leipsic 1904), with bibliography p. 431–34.

WINDTHORST, LUDWIG (1812–91), German political leader. Windthorst was born in Hanover. He became a barrister and afterward a judge at Hanover and from 1851 to 1853 and from 1862 to 1865 served as minister of justice for the same kingdom. He was always a faithful son of the Catholic church and ready to fight for the authority of his religion. Yet his public life was directed by political and not by religious motives. In 1866 Prussia conquered Hanover and Bismarck annihilated the ancient kingdom of the Guelphs. Windthorst, however, could not accept the new organization of Germany and he remained instead a friend of the traditional federalist order of German politics and an adversary of the Prussian hegemony. In 1871 he became the leader of the German Center party, which combined all the elements of western and southern Germany in opposition to the system of Bismarck. The overwhelming majority of these anti-Prussian federalists were Catholics and therefore the Center party became the representative of German Catholicism. An able orator and political leader, Windthorst led the opposition against Bismarck and his empire. He had a large following among the masses of the Catholic peasants and artisans in western and southern Germany and also among some of the Protestant farmers in the former kingdom of Hanover. The Center party extended its activities to organization of the Catholic workers of Germany and helped them in their struggle against capitalist interests. During the Kulturkampf (1871–79) Bismarck persecuted the Catholic church in Germany, for he saw in the Catholic organization the real basis of the anti-Prussian and federalist tendency. At the close of the Kulturkampf Bismarck had not been able to destroy German Catholicism, but Windthorst and his party were constrained to acknowledge the existence of the new German Empire. Windthorst now set out to establish peace with the government, and after 1879 his party voted in the Reichstag for the economic and social measures proposed by Bismarck. It was Windthorst's aim to gain for the Center a position as referee between the conservative and capitalist followers of the government and the radical and socialist opposition. Bismarck, however, refused to give the Catholic federalists this decisive authority and to enter into a permanent alliance with Windthorst. The latter lived long enough to witness Bismarck's dismissal in 1890 and the beginning of the disintegration of the empire under William II.

ARTHUR ROSENBERG

Works: *Ausgewählte Reden 1851–1891*, 3 vols. (Osnabrück 1901–02).

Consult: Hüsgen, E., *Ludwig Windthorst* (Cologne 1907); Bachem, Karl, *Vorgeschichte, Geschichte und Politik der deutschen Zentrumspartei*, 9 vols. (Cologne 1927–32), especially vol. iii, chs. i, iv, vii–viii, vol. iv, chs. i–vi, vol. v, chs. i–vi, vol. vii, chs. iii, viii, and vol. ix, ch. iii.

WINKELBLECH, KARL GEORG. See MARLO, KARL.

WINSTANLEY, GERRARD (1609?–?), English social reformer. Winstanley's personality is revealed mainly in his writings, since remarkably few details of his career are known. While it is clear that he was the inspiration behind the Digger, or True Leveller, movement (*see* LEVELLERS) during the Interregnum, his public activity was limited to a few months during the year 1649 and was then less conspicuous than that of his companion Everard. In April, 1649, following the publication of the first Digger manifesto, which outlived the creed of universal participation in the ownership of land and appealed to the people to rise against their oppressors, Winstanley and Everard, with a little band of followers, began to dig up the common land on St. George's Hill in Surrey. The two leaders of this experiment were summoned to appear before the Council of State. Although Everard, who acted as spokesman, succeeded in convincing the council that the experiment was not an immediate menace to the established order, it is significant that shortly thereafter Winstanley issued a manifesto, *The True Levellers Standard Advanced* (London 1649), embodying a fundamental attack upon private property and its consequences. In July, 1649, he made a second brief public appearance, when he and two of his companions were brought before the court at Kingston for trespass. After the destruction of the Digger settlement in the autumn of 1649, he continued for several years to issue pamphlets giving a full and eloquent exposition of the Digger creed of communism and universal love. It was by his working out of a comprehensive, if sometimes vague and overidealistic philosophy, that Winstanley succeeded in differentiating the Digger movement from earlier attempts at land reform and communism and secured for it a more permanent and far reaching influence. The affinity between some of his principles and those of early Quakerism is throughout clearly apparent, and it has been suggested by G. P. Gooch that during his later years Winstanley joined the Quaker Society.

M. JAMES

Other important works: *A Letter to Lord Fairfax and His Council of War* (London 1649); *The New Law of Righteousness* (London 1649); *A New Year's Gift for the Parliament and Armie* (London 1650); *The Law of Freedom in a Platform* (London 1652); *The Saints' Paradise* (London 1658).

Consult: Berens, L. H., *The Digger Movement in the Days of the Commonwealth* (London 1906); Bernstein, Eduard, *Sozialismus und Demokratie in der grossen englischen Revolution* (4th ed. Berlin 1922), tr. by H. J. Stenning as *Cromwell and Communism* (London 1930) chs. ix–x; Gooch, G. P., *English Democratic Ideas in the Seventeenth Century* (2nd ed. by H. J. Laski, Cambridge, Eng. 1927) p. 182–91; James, M., *Social Problems and Policy during the Puritan Revolution, 1640–1660* (London 1930), especially p. 99–106, 303–08; Freund, M., *Die Idee der Toleranz im England der grossen Revolution* (Halle 1927) p. 272–74.

WINTHROP, JOHN (1588–1649), founder and governor of the Massachusetts Bay Colony. Winthrop, the son of a Suffolk country gentleman, studied at Trinity College, Cambridge, between 1602 and 1604 and in 1626 became attorney at the Court of Wards and Liveries. As a Puritan he disliked the religious, political and economic trends under Charles I. Opportunity came with the formation of the Massachusetts Bay Company, of which he was elected governor in 1629; the following year he headed the Puritan migration to New England. In eleven of the eighteen annual elections during the remainder of his life he was chosen governor, and in the others either deputy governor or assistant; in all three positions he wielded executive, judicial and legislative powers.

Winthrop regarded the Massachusetts Bay Colony, which he hoped would embrace all New England, as an experimental Christian commonwealth based on an implied covenant between the emigrants and God and partaking of the nature of a mediaeval church-state whose New Testament standards of life would be practised and enforced. Hence he promoted a strong community spirit, suppressed what he regarded as seditious criticism or opposition and protected the colony against every attempt at outside interference. His political ideas were derived largely from the Bible, the church fathers and Calvin's *Institutes*. It was sufficient for him that democracy, "amongst most civill nations, accounted the meanest and worst of all formes of Government," had "no warrant in scripture." Prevented from exercising autocratic powers by the insistence of the freemen on their rights under the royal charter, he became reconciled to the resulting "mixt aristocratie." In order to allow the free growth of an indigenous common law without interference from the English government, he wished the judges to have complete discretion as to finding law in both civil and criminal cases, and succeeded in forestalling the establishment of fixed penalties for non-capital offenses. Although temperamentally inclined to mercy, he was converted to the need of stern justice to curb frontier lawlessness and to quell disturbing sects. In his famous *Little Speech on Liberty* he defined civil liberty as "the proper end and object of authority," which "cannot subsist without it; and it is a liberty to that only which is good, just and honest." While holding that the state must enforce the orthodoxy defined by the church, he refused to allow the clergy to meddle in the processes of government. His economic ideas were mediaeval, including a belief in divinely ordained social classes, in the "just price" and in government regulation of prices, wages and production for the good of the community. The commonwealth, which constituted his main interest in life, was a failure from his own point of view, yet of social value to posterity through the educational opportunities that it founded and the civic consciousness that it fostered.

S. E. MORISON

Works: The *Winthrop Papers* are now in course of publication by the Massachusetts Historical Society, vols. i–ii (Boston 1929–31); in the meantime the best compendium is *Life and Letters of John Winthrop*, ed. by R. C. Winthrop, 2 vols. (2nd ed. Boston 1869). The only unexpurgated edition of Winthrop's *Journal* is that by James Savage as *History of New England from 1630 to 1649*, 2 vols. (Boston 1853). *A Modell of Christian Charity*, the key to Winthrop's political theory, *A Little Speech on Liberty*, and *Conclusions for the Plantation in New England* were reprinted in *Old South Leaflets*, nos. 207, 66, and 50 (Boston 1916 and 1896.)

Consult: Morison, S. E., *Builders of the Bay Colony* (Boston 1930) p. 51–104; Johnson, E. A. J., "The Economic Ideas of John Winthrop," and "The Political Thought of John Winthrop" in *New England Quarterly*, vol. iii (1930) 234–50, 681–705.

WIRTH, MAX (1822–1900), German economist. For many years Wirth was engaged in publicist activity in Germany. In 1865 he became director of the Swiss federal statistical bureau in Berne; nine years later he joined the staff of the *Neue Freie Presse* in Vienna. With Prince-Smith, Michaelis and others he was one of the leading exponents of the German Manchester school. His main significance lies in his having combined the theories of the optimistic free trade school in Germany in a systematic treatise, *Grundzüge der Nationalökonomie* (4 vols., Cologne 1856–73; vol. i 5th ed., vol. ii 4th ed., vol. iii 3rd ed., 1881–83), which enjoyed wide acceptance at the time. In a preface to the German translation (3 vols., Munich 1863–64) of Carey's *Principles of Social Science* he declared himself a follower of the American economist, whom he credited with having demolished the "erroneous doctrines of Malthus and Ricardo." As a free trader, however, he was opposed to Carey's protectionist theories, although in later years he departed from the doctrine of extreme free trade in demanding moderate protective tariffs and endorsing public ownership of railroads. Wirth's estimate of the theories of Malthus and Ricardo may be attacked on the same grounds as the arguments of Carey, Bastiat and Prince-Smith. Nevertheless, he correctly stressed the idea that in a given total of population under a system of unlimited competition the position of the worker must improve with the growth of capital accumulation. He did not, however, foresee the rise of monopolistic combines which render invalid any conclusions based on the assumption of free competition. In the *Geschichte der Handelskrisen* (Frankfort 1858, 4th ed. 1890) Wirth associated the phenomenon of commercial crises with a credit economy and pointed out that the main factor making for booms and crises is the recurring tendency for investment to outrun the existing savings resources of society.

SIEGFRIED BUDGE

WISE, ISAAC MAYER (1819–1900), organizer and leader of American Reform Jewry. Growing up in the full tide of Metternich reaction in a small Bohemian village, Wise experienced all the galling restraints put upon a *Schutzjude* of that day and was led early through the writings of Gabriel Riesser, the spokesman of German-Jewish discontent, to that eighteenth century political radicalism which became the guiding doctrine of his life. To the end his interest remained political rather than religious, and he conceived religion in terms of rights and duties rather than as an inner life. Despite considerable formal schooling he was essentially self-taught and anything but scholarly and academic. He was a fighter and organizer, a man of the open road and the frontier, born for the American scene. His freedom from any deep seated loyalty to German traditions made him especially fitted for his historic task of formulating a new tradition on American soil.

He landed in New York in 1846 and found his way to Albany, where he functioned as rabbi until 1854. In that year he was elected to a post in Cincinnati, then the "Queen City of the West," which remained the center of his activity. His problem was to find a decent form of worship and a suitable ideology for the mass of Jewish immigrants. These were mostly peddlers or small storekeepers in the process of consolidating their position economically and socially. Their religious worship was an unthinking orthodoxy without much dignity or decorum. Wise refused to be carried away by the extreme proposals of doctrinaire reform; but he abolished abuses, evolved an American ritual, introduced choir and music and laid stress upon the sermon and upon instruction for the youth. Above all he labored to show that Judaism among all religions is the purest embodiment of high ethical and civic doctrine, uncomplicated by myth or otherworldliness. Wise's great historic achievement was the organization of American Reform Jewry. The Hebrew Union College, the Union of American Hebrew Congregations and the Central Conference of American Rabbis owe their creation entirely to him.

His theology was a curious composite of conservatism and radicalism. He felt he had to insist upon the inviolability of the Bible and therefore maintained that the Pentateuch especially, with its nucleus of Decalogue and codes, was authentic revelation. Everything outside the Bible he called Talmud, and, whether the Talmud of the rabbis or that of the higher critics of modern times, he held himself free to accept or reject as much of it as he required.

H. SLONIMSKY

Works: *Selected Writings*, with a biography by D. Philipson and L. Grossmann (Cincinnati 1900); *Pronaos to Holy Writ* (Cincinnati 1891).

Consult: Wise, I. M., *Reminiscences*, tr. and ed. by D. Philipson (Cincinnati 1901); Marcus, J. R., *The Americanization of Isaac Mayer Wise* (Cincinnati 1931); Philipson, David, *The Reform Movement in Judaism* (new ed. New York 1931) ch. xii; May, M. B., *Isaac Mayer Wise* (New York 1916).

WITCHCRAFT. *See* MAGIC.

WITT, JOHAN DE (1625–72), Dutch statesman. De Witt studied law and mathematics at the University of Leyden and after two years of travel in France was admitted to the practise of law at The Hague. In 1650 he was appointed pensionary of his native city Dordrecht and three years later was unanimously elected council pensionary of Holland. His new position was a curious one, resembling that of Bismarck in the German Empire, except that throughout his term of office there was no reigning prince. Since Holland alone was as wealthy as the other six provinces together, his position as first minister of Holland amounted to a sort of chancellorship of the entire republic. Not long after 1653 he was consulted in all important matters concerning the fate of the United Netherlands.

Both the correspondence of Johan de Witt and the records of the provincial estates of Holland and of the States General of the republic show clearly that he was primarily a diplomat. While at times he underestimated the strength of England and occasionally was outwitted by Louis XIV, his wholehearted devotion to his country, his innate honesty, his robust health and his skilful management of finances enabled him to accomplish even more than Johan van Oldenbarneveldt. He reached his greatest success at the conclusion of the War of Devolution, although it should be noted that the Triple Alliance of 1668 was the result more of Temple's work than of his own.

There is virtually no evidence to show that de Witt was seriously concerned with the development of commerce, industry and the oversea dominions of the republic. This apparent lack of interest may be attributed to the highly decentralized character of the Dutch government. The army, the navy and the merchant marine were supervised by independent bodies, while commerce and industry were entrusted to the more important municipal governments. De Witt was at all times desirous of strengthening the naval forces. He neglected the army, particularly in the time of imminent danger, leaving unheeded numerous warnings from France and England. This neglect, combined with his reluctance to elevate Prince William to the offices held by William II, resulted in his downfall. As the armies of France and its German allies invaded province after province, popular animosity increased until a frenzied mob in The Hague brutally murdered him and his brother. De Witt's political preoccupations did not prevent him from making notable contributions in other fields; he attracted considerable attention as mathematician, and by his elaborate calculations of the prospective life spans which he made in connection with his proposal for the sale of annuities as a means of raising funds he contributed to the development of the principles of life insurance.

ALBERT HYMA

Consult: Japikse, N., *Johan de Witt* (Amsterdam 1915, 2nd ed. 1928), German translation (Leipsic 1917); "Brieven," ed. by R. Fruin, in Utrecht, Historisch Genootschap, 3rd ser., nos. 18, 25, 31, 33, 42, 44, 6 vols. (Amsterdam 1906–22); Wicquefort, A. van, *Histoire des Provinces-Unies des Pais-Bas depuis le parfait établissement de cet état par la Paix de Münster*, 4 vols. (Amsterdam 1861–74); Lefèvre-Pontalis, G. A., *Vingt années de république parlementaire au dix-septième siècle; Jean de Witt, grand pensionnaire de Hollande*, 2 vols. (Paris 1884), tr. by S. E. and A. Stephenson (London 1885); Geddes, J., *History of the Administration of John De Witt* (London 1879); Godee Molsbergen, E. C., *Frankrijk en de Republiek der Vereenigde Nederlanden (1648–62)* (Amsterdam 1902).

WITTE, GRAF SERGEY YULIEVICH (1849–1915), Russian statesman. Upon graduation from Odessa University Witte became a railway functionary and rose within a few years to the position of traffic manager of a large railroad system. In 1888 he entered the service of the state as director of the railway department and in 1892 was appointed minister of finance; he retained the ministerial post until 1903, although Nicholas II, who had succeeded to the throne in 1894, detested his intellectual superiority and straightforwardness.

During this period Witte reorganized Russian finances and exerted a profound influence upon internal policy. By increasing indirect taxation, in part through the establishment of a state liquor monopoly (1895), and by introducing a business income tax he accumulated Treasury surpluses, which were used to finance the expansion of the railway net. In raising customs duties and negotiating commercial treaties he followed the policy of industrial protectionism inaugurated by his predecessors; the favorable trade balance achieved thereby enabled him to reestablish the ruble, devalued by one third, on the gold standard (1895–97). Stabilization of the currency permitted the conversion of outstanding foreign loans and the flotation of new issues, making possible at the same time an influx of large amounts of foreign capital for private investment. Heavy industry, favored also by huge government orders and easy credit from the state bank, achieved phenomenal progress in these years. On the whole Witte's economic program called for rapid industrialization at the expense of landed interests under the benevolent aegis of a bureaucratic monarchy. His attitude toward the peasantry is best illustrated by his activity in the Special Conference on the Needs of the Agricultural Industry (1902–05), over which he presided; to this organization, which through its local committees secured the opinions of over 13,000 people and with the aid of academic experts produced a voluminous set of investigations and reports, he recommended —in addition to the expansion of peasant landholding through increased allotment, better agricultural credit facilities and a system of tenancy—the abolition of the peculiar quasi-feudal status of the peasantry as a legal class under a separate administration.

Witte wished to preserve peace in order to encourage the economic development of the country. He opposed the persistent demand for increased military expenditures and advocated a continental bloc with Germany and France. He was attracted, however, by a scheme for the "peaceful colonization" of Asia and secured a concession for a short cut to Vladivostok through Manchuria (Chinese Eastern Railway). But his plans were thwarted by the influential militarist clique, which deliberately sought a break with Japan, and by the reactionaries who believed that a war would be helpful in averting a revolution. Witte protested in vain and was removed from the Ministry of Finance.

The defeat of Russia and the success of the revolutionary movement in 1905 brought Witte to power once more. Sent to the United States to negotiate with Japan through the mediation of President Theodore Roosevelt, he displayed diplomatic skill of high caliber and enlisted the support of American public opinion; Japan was forced to disavow its demands for a monetary indemnity and to concede peace terms which were justly regarded as advantageous to Russia. Upon his triumphant return Witte accepted the premiership on condition that he be allowed to realize a program which amounted to the establishment of a limited form of representative government protected from autocratic caprice and court intrigue. With the country in the throes of a general strike and the army in Siberia the czar yielded; the manifesto dictated by Witte, which proclaimed civil liberties and promised the extension of the franchise and the grant of legislative authority to the Duma, was promulgated on October 17, 1905 (according to the Julian calendar). But this concession was merely a stop gap. Witte, hated by the czar and the reactionaries, enjoyed no real authority at the court, nor did he inspire confidence in the liberal opposition. As soon as he had succeeded in bringing the army to European Russia and in obtaining a large loan from France, Nicholas II felt free to turn back. Witte retired from the government to round out his career as a member of the State Council (upper chamber). His memoirs published posthumously (*Vospominaniya*, 3 vols., Berlin 1922–23; abridged translation by A. Yarmolinsky, New York 1921) shed a gloomy light upon the failure of his attempt to modernize the political institutions of Russia and to save the monarchy.

PAUL MILIUKOV

Consult: Korostowetz, W. von, *Graf Witte* (Berlin 1929); Tompkins, S. R., "Witte as Minister of Finance" in *Slavonic Review*, vol. xi (1932–33) 590–606; Miliukov, P., and others, *Histoire de Russie*, 3 vols. (Paris 1932–33) vol. iii, chs. xix–xxi.

WOLF, FRIEDRICH AUGUST (1759–1824), German classical philologist. Wolf was born in Hainrode and studied at the University of Göttingen under Heyne. After teaching at Ilfeld and Osterode he was called to the University of Halle in 1783 as professor of philosophy and pedagogy. He was active at Halle until 1806, and from 1807 to 1824 he taught at the University of Berlin.

Wolf's chief aim was to raise philology to an independent science. His writings belong primarily to the period of 1782–1801. He began with an edition of Plato in 1782 and produced successively editions of Hesiod's *Theogonia* (Halle 1783), Homer (2 vols., Halle 1784–85), selections from the dialogues of Lucian (Halle 1791), four classical dramas (Halle 1787), the oration of Demosthenes against Leptines (Halle 1789), Herodian (Halle 1792), Cicero's *Tusculanae disputationes* (Leipsic 1792, 3rd ed. 1825) and his *Orationes quattuor* (Berlin 1801), and above all his *Prolegomena ad Homerum* (Halle 1795; 3rd ed. by Rudolf Peppmüller, 1884). He published no other important works after this period, and the *Prolegomena* has remained his most important work. As an academic teacher he lectured on Greek and Latin literature, antiquities and geography, history, painting and numismatics. At Halle he established the first seminar in classical philology. The greatest scholars of the following generation were influenced by Wolf and he was instrumental in determining the progress of classical scholarship. Schleiermacher, Böckh, Buttmann, Niebuhr, Bernhardi and Bekker as well as many of the teachers in Prussian *Gymnasien* were his pupils. Scholars like Heyne, Ruhnken, Wyttenbach, Elmsley, Sainte-Croix, and literary figures like Klopstock, Goethe, Schiller, Wieland, Voss, the Schlegel brothers and Wilhelm von Humboldt participated in the controversy concerning his views. Acclaimed and assailed he was a guiding spirit in classical learning. His ardent enthusiasm, his enormous erudition, his keen critical sense and his effective presentation reacted upon the younger generation. Drawing upon the topography of the ancient world, antiquities, old records and the great literary masterpieces he painted a picture of the ancient world and its peoples; of these the Greeks were the most perfect and therefore worthy of emulation by all who strove for perfection. The poets and the intellectuals honored and esteemed Wolf as the learned founder of the new humanism.

In his *Prolegomena ad Homerum*, which has been called "one of the cardinal books of the modern world," he subjected the Homeric poems to a critical analysis and asserted that whereas in the year 950 B.C. there was no writing or at least no written literature, these poems had been transmitted by oral tradition and put together much later according to later artistic canons. Wolf held that the artistic unity of the *Iliad* and even more that of the *Odyssey* were not the work of a very ancient poet and that the poems brought together were not created by the same poet. His thesis aroused a bitter struggle which lasted for a century and a half. Although his central theory concerning the tardy use of writing has been successfully challenged, Wolf contributed more than any other writer toward stimulating the critical study of classical records and developing the science of classical philology.

WILHELM WEBER

Consult: Kern, Otto, *Friedrich August Wolf*, Hallische Universitätsreden, no. xxv (Halle 1924); Arnoldt, J. F. J., *Friedrich August Wolf in seinem Verhältnisse zum Schulwesen und zur Pädagogik dargestellt*, 2 vols. (Brunswick 1861–62); Volkmann, Richard, *Geschichte und Kritik der wolfschen Prolegomena zu Homer* (Leipsic 1874); Gooch, G. P., *History and Historians in the Nineteenth Century* (London 1913) p. 26–29; Sandys, J. E., *A History of Classical Scholarship*, 3 vols. (Cambridge, Eng. 1903–08) vol. iii, p. 51–60; Reiter, S., in *Neue Jahrbücher für das klassische Altertum, Geschichte und deutsche Literatur*, vol. xiii (1904) 89–111.

WOLFF, CHRISTIAN (1679–1754), German philosopher. Wolff was born in Breslau and was the son of a tanner. He studied theology, mathematics and law at the universities of Jena and Leipsic and in 1706 became professor of mathematics and natural science at the newly founded University of Halle. Wolff soon incurred the hostility of the Pietist theologians of the university by the rationalism of his philosophic and religious views and after many controversies was finally forced to leave Halle in 1723. It was not until the accession of Frederick the Great in 1740 that Wolff was restored to his post.

Wolff was the most typical philosopher of the German Enlightenment. His system of philosophic, social and political thought is marked by a striving for logical clarity and mathematical precision and breathes a spirit of optimism and utilitarian eudaemonism which is based on a fundamental faith in the principles of natural reason, natural law and natural religion. The state was preceded by an era of natural existence. Unlike Hobbes, however, Wolff conceived of this natural state not as one of war of all against all but as one of full individual freedom regulated by the principles of natural law. The state arose out of a rational contract, and its purpose is to secure for its citizens the greatest welfare and security. It is left to the ruler, however, to determine what the greatest welfare is and he has obligations to nothing but his own conscience and his own interpretation of natural law. The *raison d'état* therefore imposes complete obedience upon the subjects of a state, and Wolff reveals himself as a supporter of the absolutism characteristic of the Age of Enlightened Despots.

Wolff was not an original thinker. His system is based chiefly on Leibniz and the thought of the early British and French rationalists. His importance in German intellectual history is mainly as a systematizer and popularizer of philosophic knowledge among the wider classes of the German bourgeoisie. Wolff has often been called the second *praeceptor Germaniae*. He wrote most of his important works in German instead of in Latin so that they could reach a wider circle of readers. His books went through countless editions, and the Wolffian method of explanation, proof and classification was applied to all sciences and penetrated even into the most everyday aspects of life. Special societies were founded for the "diffusion of truth" after the ideas of Wolff. It was due to the influence of Wolff that theology was supplanted by philosophy as the leading discipline at German universities and the Wolffian system dominated German intellectual life until the time of Kant.

KOPPEL S. PINSON

Chief works: *Vernünftige Gedancken von den Kräften des menschlichen Verstandes und ihrem wichtigen Gebrauch in Erkänntniss der Wahrheit* (Halle 1712, 9th ed. 1738); *Vernünftige Gedancken von Gott, der Welt und der Seele der Menschen* (Frankfort 1719, new ed. 1736); *Vernünftige Gedancken von der Menschen Thun und Lassen zur Beförderung ihrer Glückseligkeit* (Halle 1720, new ed. 1754); *Vernünftige Gedancken von dem gesellschaftlichen Leben der Menschen* (Halle 1721); *Ius naturae methodo scientifica pertractatum* 8 vols. (Leipsic 1740–48).

Consult: Wolff, C., *Lebensbeschreibung*, ed. by H. Wuttke (Leipsic 1841); Ludovici, K. G., *Ausführlicher Entwurf einer vollständigen Historie der wolffischen Philosophie*, 3 vols, (Leipsic 1736–38); Biedermann, K., *Deutschland im achtzehnten Jahrhundert*, 2 vols. (2d ed. Leipsic 1880) vol. ii, pt. i, p. 394–426; Hettner, H., *Literaturgeschichte des achtzehnten Jahrhunderts*, 3 vols. (3d ed. Brunswick 1879–81) vol. iii, pt. i, p. 221–66; Frauendienst, W., *Christian Wolff als Staatsdenker* (Berlin 1927).

WOLFF, HENRY WILLIAM (1840–1931), international cooperative leader. Wolff was born in England and educated in Germany. He was perhaps the first cooperator to visualize the movement as world wide in scope and extremely diverse in form. By virtue of his ability, enthusiasm and command of foreign languages he was able as chairman of the International Cooperative Alliance from 1896 to 1907 to strengthen the bond between the consumers' organizations of Europe and to enlarge their view of cooperative possibilities. Although his effort to bring together the consumers' and the producers' organizations, including those for agricultural credit, was less successful, he rendered great services to the latter. His *People's Banks* (London 1893, 4th ed. 1919) was the first attempt to describe the varied forms of cooperative credit institutions. In 1894 as Plunkett's associate he established the first cooperative credit societies in Ireland. He was a founder in 1900 of the Agricultural Organization Society and an active participant until 1913. His writings had considerable influence in checking proposed British legislation for the reduction of interest on small savings. Although he never visited India, he had a sound grasp of its cooperative problems and by personal contact and correspondence with officials and others from 1894 on he exerted great influence over their policy; his *Co-operation in India* (London 1919) was an important contribution.

Wolff insisted that the cooperative movement should depend as little as possible on state support; for this reason he regarded agricultural mortgage banks, which were invariably granted state aid and privileges, as lying outside the field of genuine cooperation. Again, although he emphasized the moral value of cooperation Wolff rejected the idea of special cooperative societies for such objects as arbitration, health or better living. His first judgment is not adopted by contemporary cooperative opinion and the second, while accepted in Europe and America, has been questioned in Asia, where such societies have been formed in considerable numbers.

C. F. STRICKLAND

WOLLSTONECRAFT, MARY (1759–97), English writer and feminist. Mary Wollstonecraft, the literary pioneer of the emancipation of women, drew from a poignant personal experience the passion and daring that made her the most forceful and original advocate of this cause. The child of a drunken and disreputable father, she was obliged at an early age, with only the most superficial education, to earn her own living and to help a sister ruined in health and fortune by an unhappy marriage. For a time the two young women conducted a school near London, but Mary found the work of writing and translating educational books more congenial. At the age of thirty-three she published the fruit of her reflections on her own struggles, *A Vindication of the Rights of Woman* (London 1792), a plea for the human dignity, the economic independence and the education of women. At the end of this year she went to Paris as much to see the revolution as to perfect herself in French. There she met Gilbert Imlay, an American traveler of some note and a soldier of the War of Independence. He lived with her and in documents acknowledged her as his wife, but they were never formally married. After the birth of their child, Fanny, in 1794 Imlay deserted her, and she attempted to drown herself in the Thames. Friends nursed her back to health, and she became active in the radical literary circle of which William Godwin (*q.v.*) was a member. They contracted an unconventional union in accordance with that philosopher's earlier views, but in March, 1797, at the risk of some inconsistency they were married. Their happy relationship ended in September of that year with Mary's death a few days after the birth of their daughter (also Mary) who was to become Shelley's wife.

Mary Wollstonecraft was a woman of considerable beauty and charm, capable of deep affections and resentments, an ardent lover and a devoted mother. Of her literary work only the *Vindication* (often reprinted) survives, but she was the author also of a charming volume of travel sketches, *Letters Written during a Short Residence in Sweden, Norway, and Denmark* (London 1796), as well as the touching "Letters to Imlay" (in her *Posthumous Works*, 4 vols., London 1798, vols. iii–iv; new ed. by C. Kegan Paul, 1879) and the fragment entitled "Lessons for Children" (in her *Posthumous Works*, vol. ii, p. 169–96), perhaps the most graceful expression in English prose of the physical tenderness of a mother's love.

The *Vindication* has many faults. Written hastily in six weeks it is ill arranged and full of repetitions, yet its directness, its sincerity and the terse militant strength of some passages make it one of the creative books of its age. Its teaching sprang naturally from the revolutionary philosophy of the period, which traced all the imperfections and inequalities of mankind to faulty social and political institutions and errors of education. Holbach had indeed made the inevitable application of these doctrines to women. Condorcet worked them out in his project for the universal public education of both sexes in 1792. Mary Wollstonecraft perhaps had read Holbach but she could not have seen Condorcet's scheme when she composed her *Vindication*. It was original in that it drew from a woman's experience, hotly and with passion, the lesson that a few rare men had already deduced from philosophy. The case which she was the first of her sex to state for its human dignity, its economic independence and its right to equality in education was later to become a commonplace of western civilization. Mary Wollstonecraft wrote without bitterness or hostility to the other sex, and in an age of extravagant individualism it is remarkable that she emphasized the social duties of women no less than their rights. Setting out to destroy the system that compelled women to "live by their charm" she demanded the coeducation of girls and boys, the opening of all suitable trades and professions to women and the ending of the dual standard of morals, and in one brief pregnant sentence she entered a claim for political rights.

H. N. Brailsford

Consult: Godwin, William, *Memoirs of Mary Wollstonecraft* (London 1798; new ed. by W. C. Durant, 1927); Clough, Emma R., *A Study of Mary Wollstonecraft and the Rights of Woman* (London 1898); Taylor, G. R. S., *Mary Wollstonecraft; a Study in Economics and Romance* (London 1911); Linford, Madeline, *Mary Wollstonecraft* (London 1924); Severn Storr, M., *Mary Wollstonecraft et le mouvement féministe* (Paris 1931); James, H. R., *Mary Wollstonecraft; a Sketch* (London 1932); Brailsford, H. N., *Shelley, Godwin and Their Circle* (London 1913).

WOLOWSKI, LOUIS FRANÇOIS MICHEL RAYMOND (1810–76), French economist. Wolowski was born in Warsaw of Polish parents. He participated in the preparations for the Polish insurrection of 1830, for which he was condemned to death by the Russian authorities. Freed from prison at the outbreak of the rebellion, he was sent on a diplomatic mission to Paris; after the collapse of the insurrection he became a naturalized Frenchman. His knowledge of law and economics rapidly won him a great reputation. In 1834 he founded the *Revue de législation et de jurisprudence*, and in 1839 he was appointed to the chair of industrial legislation at the Conservatoire National des Arts et Métiers. He was active in the political arena from the time of the Revolution of 1848 and as a deputy was one of the devoted supporters of Louis Napoleon Bonaparte. He abandoned his partisanship when the prince indicated his imperial ambitions, and he resigned from public life on the morrow of the coup d'état of 1851. Throughout the Second Empire he devoted himself to economic problems; in 1852 he created the Crédit Foncier, in 1855 was made a member of the Académie des Sciences Morales et Politiques and in 1864 was given the chair of political economy at the Conservatoire. Elected by the department of the Seine in 1871, he made himself the champion of free trade in opposition to the protectionist policy of Thiers. A stanch republican, he was appointed senator for life in 1875.

During more than forty years Wolowski wrote copiously on all subjects related to economics. He showed preference for the historical approach in economics and translated into French Roscher's *Grundlinien der Nationalökonomie* (tr. as *Principes d'économie politique*, 2 vols., Paris 1857). He was the first to acquaint the French public with Copernicus' monetary treatise by translating the latter's *De monetae cudendae ratione* (tr. as *Traité de la monnaie*, Paris 1864), including in the same volume a translation of Oresme's *Tractatus de origine, natura, jure et mutationibus monetarum* (tr. as *Traictié de la première invention des monnoies*). He was a specialist on financial questions and his works include studies on joint stock companies, on the mobilization of mortgage credit and on the finances of Russia. He was a supporter of bimetallism and regarded the 15 to 1 ratio as one which would vary but slightly. His book *L'or et l'argent* (Paris 1868) still merits consideration. Wolowski favored the centralization and public control of note issue. As a theorist of free trade he published in 1868 *La liberté commerciale* (Paris 1868), in which he analyzed the results of the commercial treaty of 1860. Finally mention should be made of his last book, *Résultats économiques du paiement de la contribution de guerre en Allemagne et en France* (Paris 1874).

Paul Harsin

Consult: Levasseur, Émile, *La vie et les travaux de Wolowski* (Paris 1877), with extensive bibliography.

WOLSEY, THOMAS (*c.* 1473–1530), English churchman and statesman. The son of a tradesman, Wolsey was educated at Oxford and obtained distinction there in his early manhood. In 1507 he went to court and served Henry VII as chaplain and ambassador. On the accession of Henry VIII in 1509 Wolsey's attractiveness, abilities, industry and ambition made him an intimate friend and indispensable minister of the young king. He advanced rapidly in office and became lord chancellor in 1515. He was given many lucrative church positions and became successively dean and bishop of Lincoln, bishop of Winchester, archbishop of York and, at the request of the king, cardinal and papal legate in England. Twice he was nominated for the papacy but failed of election.

Wolsey's foreign policy was directed toward preserving peace, acquiring for England a prominent position in Europe and encouraging trade. His principal interest, however, was in internal reforms. With a view to the better education of the clergy he founded a new college at Oxford and as a feeder to it a public school at his native town of Ipswich. For the endowment of these institutions he dissolved, with the consent of the king and the pope, some twenty-two small and decayed monasteries and appropriated their lands. He provided for a visitation of the larger monasteries, introduced new regulations for them and made carefully selected appointments to vacancies. He published new constitutions for the province of York and by his authority as legate summoned the clergy of all England to a synod for purposes of reform.

In the midst of these schemes of reform he was halted by the necessity of negotiating with the pope for the king's separation from Catherine in order to marry Anne Boleyn. The failure of these negotiations caused Wolsey to lose the confidence of the king. The enemies he had created by his policy or his overbearing manners came into control; he was deprived of his offices and his property was seized on the pretext that he had acted illegally as legate of the pope. Arrested while on his way to York to resume his clerical duties, he was charged with treason and died before trial at the abbey of Leicester.

His plans of reform died with him. His educational foundations were dissolved or reduced to much smaller proportions; his plans for the reorganization of the church and the university were dropped; his reform of the chancery failed of permanency. The principal weakness of Wolsey's policy, which for a while promised to bring about the Reformation without violence or schism, was its purely personal character and lack of permanent support by a party or the king.

EDWARD P. CHEYNEY

Consult: Pollard, A. F., *Wolsey* (London 1929); Creighton, Mandell, *Cardinal Wolsey* (London 1888); Constant, Gustave, *La réforme en Angleterre*, vol. i– (Paris 1930–); Corcoran, T., "Thomas Cardinal Wolsey, Educator" in *Studies*, vol. xx (Dublin 1931) p. 24–38.

WOLTMANN, LUDWIG (1871–1907), German publicist. In his earlier years Woltmann acquired doctor's degrees in philosophy and medicine and considerable repute as an advocate of revisionism within the Socialist party. While he never repudiated his sympathy with proletarian aspirations, he later shifted his emotional allegiance to the ideologies of the Gobineau cult and social selectionist school as currently represented in the writings of Ammon, Lapouge and H. S. Chamberlain. While he contributed nothing novel to their claims, he made the *Politisch-anthropologische Revue*, which he founded in 1902 and which he edited until his untimely death, an outstanding expression of mystical faith in the providential mission of the tall, blond superman.

His historical importance thus rests on his eager and effective promotion of the rising Teutonomania in Germany before the World War. To him the blond Teuton, whether Goth, Burgundian, Frank, Swabian or Norman, was the born aristocrat, the sole creative racial element in modern history, while round heads and brunets were inert and commonplace. His principal works rest on an extensive study of portraits, whereby he sought to prove that nearly all the great men of the Renaissance and subsequent times in Italy, Spain and France were of Teutonic derivation. Pushing the claims of his predecessors to an extreme he held that "The entire European civilization, even in Slav and Latin countries, is the work of the Teutonic spirit." He failed to win the approval of scientific opinion. So variable were the traits of distinguished men that he was compelled by various ingenious twists of the evidence to include within his galaxy of Teutonic geniuses both blonds and brunets, tall and short, round heads and long heads. In spite of their contradictions, exaggerations and bias his works have exerted considerable influence since the World War, especially through the writings of Hans Günther and Otto Hauser in Germany and Madison Grant in the United States.

FRANK H. HANKINS

Important works: *Politische Anthropologie* (Eisenach 1903); *Die Germanen und die Renaissance in Italien* (Leipsic 1905); *Die Germanen in Frankreich* (Jena 1907).

Consult: "Symposium" in *Politisch-anthropologische Revue*, vol. vi (1907–08) 1–93; Seillière, Ernest, "Une école d'impérialisme mystique. Les plus récens théoriciens du pangermanisme" in *Revue des deux mondes*, 5th ser., vol. l (1909) 196–228; Hankins, F. H., *The Racial Basis of Civilization* (New York 1926) p. 75, 90–92.

WOMAN, POSITION IN SOCIETY

PRIMITIVE. Data regarding the political position of women in primitive society have been employed in social theorizing in two principal ways: in the construction of hypothetical evolutionary sequences in which society is conceived as having evolved from a primordial state of mother right; and in an argument which differs in content rather than in methodology, since it continues to associate present day tendencies with desirable end products in social evolution, in the correlation of human progress and in the progressive emancipation of women. The first argument stresses the few and scattered examples of matriarchy among primitive peoples; the second emphasizes instead the almost universal subordination of women in primitive and ancient societies.

Existing evidence concerning primitive social organization suggests that in the simplest societies of which there are adequate records, such as the Eskimo and the Andamanese, where there is an absence of any type of segmented social organization or institutionalized leadership, the society is under the domination of men. In such societies the accidental assumption of temporary leadership by women with sufficiently dominant personalities would, if it did occur, leave no formal traces in altered social forms, but the simple rigid division of labor between the sexes would reassert itself. It was only with the development of more complicated social forms that matriliny, the organization of society into groups defined by relationship traced through the mother, provided a basis upon which any sort of female dominance could become institutionalized. There is no ground whatever for regarding matriliny as a social form which universally preceded patriliny, although it is very probable that a transition from matrilineal unilateral organization to patrilineal organization is more congenial to human social institutions than the reverse process.

But the incidence of matrilineal social forms in the primitive world has only indirect relevance to the problem of the position of women. Where matriarchy occurs, however, as among the Iroquois, the Zuñi, the Minang Kabau, the Nairs and the Khasi of Assam, it will be found that that form of organization, which may be defined as actual institutionalized female dominance in some if not in all of the important divisions of cultural activity, has developed upon a base of matrilineal organization. It is improbable that a shift of power between the sexes so antithetical to the prevailing human arrangements and conflicting with the more usual division of labor could take place were the society not already committed to an emphasis upon a group defined by the mother rather than the father. Furthermore it is customary to define as matriarchal those societies in which the institutionalized role of the wife and mother is emphasized at the expense of the role of the father and husband. The relationship between husband and wife, however, is not necessarily indicative of the position of women; an examination must also be made of the balance of power between women and their male blood kindred. The Iroquois are perhaps one of the most conspicuous examples of the political power of women in primitive society; women were the electors, official critics and censors of their younger male relatives whom they had selected to hold political power. Yet when examined closely the situation there resolved itself into the dominance of the elder members of the kin group over the younger males. The actual power was in the hands of the men, guided and in some measure controlled by the most responsible and cohesive group within their matrilineal lineage. The existence of a matrilineal reckoning of descent and very probably the greater longevity and lower death rate of women in a warlike culture produced a situation in which women had at best only a formalized extension of the kind of power wielded by influential old women in other societies. Greater longevity of women is an almost constant feature of human societies and is probably accentuated at those social levels in which men are constantly exposed to the exigencies of war and hunting accidents; yet this longevity, which has a high potential social value, has seldom been utilized; and those primitive societies which rely most explicitly upon the greater knowledge and experience of the aged, particularly the Australian tribes, are the very ones which most strenuously disallow any dominant role to women.

A fundamental division of labor may be distinguished, under which men fight, hunt and go to sea and women engage in less dangerous and more circumscribed occupations. This basic division of labor illustrates most aptly the forces which probably operated to give human society its orientation toward a division of activities between men and women and to set a prestige upon men's activities which holds over even in societies where women fish and men do beadwork. It is impossible to distinguish an inevitable sequence in the development of the division of labor. The entrance of men into agriculture with the substitution of animal for human labor may have been the course of development in areas where animals were introduced into horticulture; but in Oceania, where all animal husbandry is lacking, horticulture is shared in by both sexes. The argument presupposes animal husbandry administered by males and developed from hunting, horticulture practised by females and developed from seed and root gathering, and a merging of the two—a course of events which occurred in some societies but is by no means a universal or determined sequence. An examination of the economic occupations which require no great strength, exposure, danger or prolonged and unencumbered absence from the domestic hearth serves to illustrate, first, that any occupation (with the exception of wood, stone and metal work, which seem to have stubbornly preserved their association with activities requiring masculine strength) including the care of children, pottery, weaving, basketry, cooking, shelter building, leather working, may be assigned to both sexes or to either sex; and, second, that those occupations which are traditionally pursued by men are the ones to which prestige is attached.

The infrequent cases where women as a sex possess political power, or even formulate supervising positions within the household, may be regarded as a further extension of an already existing structural matrilineal emphasis, which is not directed toward theories or practise of feminine dominance and does not proceed from them. In Oceania this matrilineal structure often seems to derive from a stressing of the blood bond between brother and sister at the expense of the marriage bond and the bilateral family, an emphasis which may also produce an aggressive form of patrilineal organization. In many North American Indian tribes the ownership of the house by the woman, a condition which in its simplest form need be no more than a reflection of the division of labor in which women make the skin or bark shelter, seems to have provided a basis upon which, with larger residential units, matrilineal organization could develop. The mere existence of any matrilineal structure, however, permits within it such developments as matrilocal residence with a resulting scattering of the married men among closely knit groups of related women. Such a secondary aspect of matriliny provides a base upon which, should political forms develop, additional political powers of women could be elaborated. The opposite result is, however, as likely to occur, as in the Trobriands, where the institution of male chieftainship is maintained among a matrilineal people by various compromises.

Social stratification and more specifically the institution of rank, while they are essentially variants of social organization originally irrelevant to the problem of balance of power between the sexes, serve as a foundation upon which female political and social eminence may develop. All forms of stratification, whether political, social, economic or intellectual, serve to cut across the simple bifurcation of society into sex groups with defined social status. Increasing emphasis upon the privileges of any class tends to extend those privileges to the wives or sisters of the male members of the particular class, just as it formally denies these privileges to male members of other classes. The resulting picture, when viewed from the standpoint of a woman's relative independence of her husband or male kin, may be one of complete feminine subordination, as is the case when a Polynesian woman of noble blood is completely under the control of her male relatives. Nevertheless, one definite institutional rearrangement has been made, the formal admission that some women, by virtue of birth or status, have more prestige than some men in the same society. The transition to the position of chieftainess or queen is then relatively simple, being usually in terms of a temporary scarcity of males in the ruling line or very occasionally in terms of personality. The latter motivation appears at times in Samoa, where personality rather than primogeniture or direct descent is the basis for the selection of incumbents of titles. This illustrates further the dependence of feminine political power upon originally irrelevant structural features in the society. In societies which insist upon direct descent in the ruling line queens and chieftainesses occur only when a woman satisfies these requirements better than any male. Similarly in Samoa, where such formal qualifications are subordinated to a consideration of individual personality traits suitable for office, a woman was nominated only when she possessed such traits to a far more outstanding degree than any available male.

When the royal forms of the primitive state derive from the simpler kinship forms of the family, women as members of the family share automatically in this enhancement of status. Of such a character is the position of the queen mother and her court in west Africa or that of the chief's wife in south Africa, where she is purchased by contributions from the whole tribe and holds an exalted position as the wife of the whole tribe, of which the chief is the symbolic head. This likewise accounts for the position of the sacred chieftainess of Tonga, the female Tuitonga, and her daughter, the Tamaha, who was institutionalized as the sister's child of the whole of Tonga and was therefore the most exalted personage in the Tongan hierarchy. The elevated social status of individual women is also in this instance in no sense related to any fundamental concept of the high position of women but is an accident of social structure, upon which, however, actual power for women might conceivably have developed.

The widespread and biologically defined political disability of women obtains in all societies in which women, as a sex, are not accorded explicit privileges denied to men. As most primitive societies have developed along paths of least resistance toward patrilineal forms, it is usually in the patrilineal societies with social stratification that special powers of individual women rulers occur. Even in societies where in one particular reversals of the usual position between the sexes are found, as in mother-in-law dominance combined with matrilocal residence or where there is house ownership by women, the bulk of the political and economic power and leadership remains in the hands of the men, as in matrilineal Zuñi, and the anomalous institutional superiority of women in a few respects only serves to stress their fundamental social disabilities.

Recent investigations among the Tchambuli tribe of New Guinea suggest that any estimate of the relative power of men and women which is based only upon an analysis of formal institutions may be seriously at fault. The Tchambuli are patrilineally organized; there is bride price, patrilocal residence and a men's tribal secret society from which women are excluded. Institutionally the society contains many of the elements from which the low position of women in primitive society is traditionally argued. Actual analysis of the functioning of the society, however, reveals the fact that all of the real power lay in the hands of the women, who were trained to a position of temperamental dominance directly antithetical to the formal institutions, while the men were educated to be responsive to and dependent upon feminine preferences and decisions. This instance suggests that more penetrating analysis of the actual distribution of power between the sexes in primitive societies might discover many cases where the actual and the institutionally expressed dominances were in contrast rather than in accord.

Extensive participation in formal religious activity by women is sporadic and relatively infrequent. In general it may be said that when religious functionaries are chosen upon a basis of temperamental predisposition to various forms of psychic abnormality or special aptitudes or where the religious functionary is subordinate to rather than master of the situation, as is the case in Manus, where female media interpret situations which male diviners have defined, women tend to play a relatively greater role than elsewhere. Often women's religious disability is a function of their political or economic disability; for example, where religion is primarily oriented toward formal tribal life or individual search for power in such activities as hunting and war, characteristic of so many North American Indian religions. Also among some primitive peoples, notably in Polynesia and Australia, the exclusion of women from religious activity was a function of the definition of female reproductive powers as inherently dangerous. Where it is always assumed that men will engage in the aspects of life which give more prestige, it is not difficult to account for the fact that women appear more often as witches than as priestesses. As in other fields of cultural activity, there are isolated instances where the whole of the religious life is in the hands of women, as in the case of shamanism among the Shasta of California.

In the field of the arts, while women often have in charge the decorative arts appropriate to the various crafts which have fallen to their lot, as in the ornamentation of basketry, pottery and cloth, a great many aspects of primitive art have tended to be associated either structurally, as in the case of wood carving, stone and metal work, or functionally, as parts of religious or social ceremonial, with those departments of life which have been traditionally defined as the domain of the male. Therefore, while it is not at all difficult to find tribes where the women are responsible for the only art practised, as in the instance of basketry in some California tribes, the role of women is negligible in whole departments of highly developed primitive art, as among the northwest coast Indians, the Maori or in west coast Africa.

The various exceptional cases in which women as a sex, as a class or as individuals have achieved conspicuous preeminence in any field of culture beyond the confines of the household and the educational tasks and handicrafts associated with it serve only to point more sharply the general cultural disability under which women live throughout the primitive world. Just as it is possible to explain the exceptions in terms of underlying social forms which have had accidental reverberations in feminine dominance or preeminence, so also the prevailing low social status of women can be attributed to the persistence in explicit social forms and implicit social attitudes of an original division of labor between the sexes which appears to obtain in all unstratified societies. This division of labor, correlated as it is in simple non-agricultural cultures with the biological requirements of pregnancy and child care and the relative unfitness of women for the rigors of warfare and hunting, has persisted as a ground plan for the sexual division of labor in fields in which these primary biological considerations have become increasingly irrelevant.

Primitive data do not provide any basis for the arguments which proceed on the hypothesis that, as human society outgrows a dependence upon mere physical strength and endurance, on the one hand, and, on the other, upon the continuous care of the infant by its mother, the disabilities of women which are characteristic of previous states of society will disappear. This originally appropriate division of labor, which is a social heritage from simpler conditions, persists as an important factor in shaping social institutions. Whenever social struggle makes it advantageous completely to subordinate or disfranchise any group in the population, women as a sex, historically defined as biologically unfitted for equality, present a particularly convenient object. The occasional special privileges or achievements of women in primitive and in modern society always occur in spite of a historical conception to which such privilege is antithetical.

MARGARET MEAD

HISTORICAL. The patriarchal social organization prevailing at the inception of civilization militated against the interests of women and defined their subordinate status for later periods. The core of the social structure, the closely knit patrilocal family in which property was transmitted through the male line, institutionalized the dominance of men over women. Underlying these decisive cultural determinants of the position of women have been the disabilities arising from their physiological make up, especially from the requirements of pregnancy; the significance of the biological factors has varied in different eras, depending upon the economic, social and religious organization of a society and the extent of its scientific and technological knowledge.

Throughout history class lines have cut across sex lines with the result that women of the ruling classes have enjoyed privileges denied to the men as well as the women of the submerged classes; within each class, however, women have been at a disadvantage as compared with the men. Likewise women of dominant races as a rule have had rights and privileges not shared by either the men or the women of minority races. Women's rights are intimately tied up with the larger problem of human rights, and recognition of the rights of the masses and improvement of their conditions stimulate an advance in the status of women. When the prevailing spirit of an era has been liberal, humanitarian and rationalistic, women's rights have been extended, if not always formally through legislation, at least in practise; on the other hand, in periods of counter-revolution restrictions are intensified. Especially in modern times political and economic revolutions have embraced or have been reflected in the struggle for women's rights. War and immediate post-war periods are usually marked by a modification of the customary sanctions that impede woman's participation in social life; such change results largely from the disequilibrium caused by the drastic effects of war upon the social structure and from the need for the services of women in the maintenance of economic activities. The disproportionate number of women to men brought about by the mortality of males in war cannot be regarded as the important initiating factor in post-war movements for the improvement of women's social status, for in communities where the population ratio has been distinctly unfavorable to the males the dominance of the latter as determined by the existing social institutions often remains unchallenged. Changes in technology which modify the existing division of labor and the allocation of the possessions and prestige of members of the family and in particular those which deprive the family of certain functions, as in the case of the industrial revolution, have a potent influence in determining the status of women; and the nature of this influence depends to a large extent on the class structure of the society in which these changes occur. The intensity of the emphasis in different societies upon woman's function in the bearing and rearing of children plays a large part in deciding the extent of her active participation in the wider economic, social and political spheres; wherever the sanctions of state and religion stress women's role in procreation and prohibit or inhibit the utilization of methods to decrease the size of the family, women's activities outside of the family are necessarily hindered. The effectiveness of the sanctions regulating sex expression, marriage and divorce is largely a reflection of woman's economic power. Law, theory and practise are often widely at variance; woman's legal rights may be negated by extralegal social discriminations and, on the other hand, formal disabilities may be evaded and defied with impunity. Whenever women have been indoctrinated with religious views stressing virtues of meekness and self-denial and have sought escape from frustration in emotionalized ritualism, they have been subject to intensified discrimination.

An appraisal of the position of women in society in different historical periods is complicated by the fact that the records deal almost exclusively with the women of the upper classes and are primarily reflections of the prevailing male attitudes rather than objective accounts of woman's status. In the cultures of the ancient world there were varied degrees of subordination and freedom of women. In ancient Babylon patriarchal power within the family was moderated by certain provisions for the protection and maintenance of the wife. A woman could engage in business and in certain cases dispose of property; she appears to have possessed a full legal personality and to have been considered a qualified witness. The independence of Egyptian women was noted by Greek observers; unlike Greek women, some worked outside of their homes at their trades and at manual labor, while women of the commercial and propertied classes had full rights of property with testamentary powers and could protect these rights and guard against arbitrary divorce by means of prenuptial contracts. In ancient Greece the father remained the religious and legal head of the family, representing the wife along with the children and slaves, although the right possessed in early Greek times by a father to sell his daughter and by brothers as guardians to sell their sisters was abolished by Solon except in cases of unchastity. Property was inherited by the male children, and the daughters possessed only the right of maintenance and dowry. Athenian women appear to have received only movables as their dowry; but in military Sparta, where women managed the land while men were fighting, the former could inherit and retain landed estates as their own. Women obtained education under great difficulties in Athens, where there were no schools for girls; the Spartans, however, admitted women to the gymnasium; and commercial centers, such as Miletus, appear also to have afforded them educational opportunities. Certain women, notably among the hetaerae, are said to have wielded significant influence; but the high position of the few merely serves to reveal more sharply the typically subordinate status of Greek womanhood.

Plato expressed liberal views in reference to the potentialities of women in contravention to the existing customs and laws. He argued that since "as far as the state is concerned there is no difference between the natures of man and woman," women ought to be admitted freely to all the duties and rights of man; and he stressed the loss to the state as a result of their restricted sphere of activity. Aristotle, on the other hand, averred that men are by nature superior and that therefore they are fit to rule, while women should be ruled. The Greek dramatists, particularly Euripides, give utterance to many feminist views; by contrast Pericles expressed a judgment not unfamiliar in later periods that women should be well spoken of but kept in their places.

In Rome at the time of the drawing up of the Twelve Tables a woman passed into the family and power of her husband at marriage and had no means of emancipating herself from his *manus*. But through development of marriage by *usus* the bride remained under the nominal guardianship of her father and did not legally become a member of her husband's family, with the result that she acquired complete control of her own property. The disabilities arising from male tutelage of unmarried women also became obsolete in practise. The consent of the woman became a normal requisite to marriage, and divorce became the free choice of either party. Although new restrictions arose during the empire, such as the limitation on a woman's right to become surety, the Roman matron of this period was more independent legally and had more freedom socially than did a wife in any later civilization until very recent times. The satirical accounts of Juvenal and Tacitus of feminine profligacy appear at best to be exaggerated characterizations of behavior among women of the upper classes.

The vigorous denunciations of the freedom of Roman women by the early Christian church fathers were an outgrowth of the attitude of the latter toward sex, which in many instances was undoubtedly pathological. The ascetic ideal of Christianity according to which sexual activity was carnal and marriage was a concession to the flesh resulted in the regarding of woman as the chief vehicle of sin—in Tertullian's words "the devil's gateway"—a view embodied in the penitentials. As Christianity became dominant throughout Europe, women were deprived of that freedom which they had attained in Rome and had enjoyed to some degree under Anglo-Saxon law. Except for the fact that the church extended the doctrine of free courtship and consent in marriage, women and especially wives occupied a position of abject dependence. Women shared in the universal insecurity and cultural and economic poverty that followed the collapse of ancient civilization; under the self-sufficient patriarchal localism of feudal economy the vast majority of women lived in complete subjection not only to their male relatives but to the feudal powers as well. A few exceptional women participated in the meager cultural activity and in philanthropic undertakings through their work in nunneries, but the position of women both in custom and in law was degraded. Chivalric romanticism is but a symptom of this degradation as it affected the upper classes; the exalted formalism and passionate eroticism of knightly gallantry added little to the prestige of womanhood. Canon law institutionalized male dominance, reflecting the influence of the strongly patriarchal family law of the Old Testament and of Germanic law. The wife became completely subject to her husband's authority, deprived of legal rights and independent existence; as marriage was held to be a sacrament, she could have no recourse to divorce. The Reformation liberalized the canonical view of marriage and divorce, but because of its justification of the prerogatives of the husband as the absolute head of the family and its rigid view of sexual morality, lapses from which were punished with grim severity, it did not modify essentially woman's position in society.

In precapitalist economy women as a rule spun and wove in their homes, brewed the ale and performed other domestic tasks. In England almost all of the early customs of the boroughs enabled married women to engage in trade and to go to law and provided that their husbands were not to be held responsible for their debts. Although girls were seldom apprenticed to the guild trades, marriage to a member of a guild conferred upon a woman her husband's rights and privileges as his assistant or partner and she shared in the social and religious life of the guild; as a widow she continued to control and direct the business which she had inherited from her husband. Women held a monopoly in textile spinning and many engaged in the retail and provision trades. Seventeenth century English records indicate that there were a few married women among the pawnbrokers, moneylenders, stationers, shipowners, booksellers, shopkeepers and clothing contractors for the army and navy. As capitalism developed, the wives of the prosperous members of the bourgeoisie tended to become idle and in the words of Mary Astell had "nothing to do but to glorify God and to benefit their neighbors." The women of the richer farmers were able to withdraw from farm work; but the status of the wives of farm wage-workers was lowered, because they were now deprived of gardens and pastures which had previously served as the source of food for their families.

As the technological changes of the industrial revolution transformed the processes of production, the women of the urban proletariat and many of the artisan class were drawn into the factories, mills and mines as unskilled wage-workers (see WOMEN IN INDUSTRY). The majority of women found it necessary to work outside of the household in order to augment the family income. The leisure which the industrial revolution brought to a relatively small number of women of the upper classes was made possible in part by the labor of the women of the proletariat. The latter acquired a certain element of power within family councils by virtue of their contributions to the support of their families; and their employment away from home increased their personal contacts and released them to some extent from domestic controls and thus modified male dominance within the family. The growing urbanization and secularization of life likewise changed the status of women within the family. As the factory took over the industrial functions of the family, the state encroached upon its educational functions and this detracted from the cohesion of the patriarchal family group, which had perpetuated women's inferiority. The acquisitive nature of capitalist society, however, has prevented the release of the potentialities of the new technology for relieving the burdens of the masses of women.

In the struggle of the rising bourgeoisie for political power and social ascendancy the rights of women received only incidental attention, but the ferment engendered by propaganda for democratic rights was expressed to some extent in demands for women's emancipation. In the early part of the eighteenth century Holdberg, and Condorcet and Holbach among the philosophers of the French Revolution, urged unequivocally equal citizenship and educational rights for women. Olympe de Gouges in her polemical tracts, particularly *Les droits de la femme*, contended for absolute equality of both sexes and through a feminist paper and revolutionary clubs sought political and economic justice for women as well as equality in the family and in marriage. When a group of women proposed a Declaration of the Rights of Women to the National Assembly in 1789, it was rejected with scant consideration, in line with Rousseau's judgment that not only women's education but their very existence is of value only in so far as it benefits man. Mary Wollstonecraft's *A Vindication of the Rights of Woman* (London 1792) and Theodor Gottlieb von Hippel's *Über die bürgerliche Verbesserung der Weiber* (Berlin 1792) as well as Amalie Holst's more conservative *Über die Bestimmung des Weibes zur höhern Geistesbildung* (Berlin 1802) were written under the influence of the French Revolution. That the commercial and industrial revolutions had effected no essential modification in the social attitudes toward women is indicated by the hostile reception accorded these books.

In England, the first country to feel the effects of the industrial revolution, the liberals of the Bentham school did nothing on behalf of women's rights. It was the conservative stand taken by James Mill on the position of women that provoked William Thompson, the socialist disciple of Robert Owen, to write his *Appeal of One Half the Human Race, Women, against the Pretensions of the Other Half, Men* (London 1825). The National Union of the Working Classes, organized in 1831 by Lovett and other disciples of Owen as well as Hodgskin and parliamentary radicals like Hume, included in its program a demand for suffrage of all adults of both sexes. In 1838 the Chartists included woman suffrage in the People's Charter, although later they omitted it. With the support of Barbara Bodichon and Emily Davies, who were also instrumental in creating facilities for higher education for women, John Stuart Mill in the course of the debates on the Reform Bill of 1867 introduced an unsuccessful amendment for the enfranchisement of women. His *The Subjection of Women* (London 1869) served as a text for the movement for women's rights throughout the world, particularly in Denmark, Norway and Sweden, where Camilla Collett and Ellen Key became the leading feminists whose influence extended beyond the confines of their respective countries, as did that of Fredrika Bremer earlier in the century. The English movement gained somewhat in size if not in effectiveness in the succeeding decade; in 1897 the National Union of Women's Suffrage Societies was organized. Many advocates of suffrage came to define the problem in terms of "equivalence" as distinct from equality; they argued that although the potentialities of men and women might not be identical, full legal, social and political rights without artificial restrictions were imperative before women could manifest their inherent powers. Although Parliament was repeatedly petitioned for the franchise, woman suffrage did not come to the forefront as a serious issue in English political life until the twentieth century, when attention was focused on the question by the heckling of opponents, by the mass demonstrations and by the hunger strikes of the members of the Women's Social and Political Union organized in England in 1903 by Emmeline Pankhurst and her daughter Christabel. These militant tactics, although discountenanced by the conservative feminist groups, were likewise adopted in other countries and gave wide publicity to the movement. In 1907 women were qualified to vote in municipal elections and to serve as members of municipal bodies.

On the continent the counter-revolution which followed the French Revolution submerged the campaign for women's rights until it developed again as a reflection of the middle class revolutions between 1830 and 1850. In France the Saint-Simonians and George Sand stressed women's emancipation in the marriage relation and urged improvements in women's education. The Fourierist Considérant in 1848 proposed a resolution to bestow equal political rights on women, which was defeated by the constitutional committee of the French parliament; and in 1851 a similar motion by Pierre Leroux in the Chamber suffered the same fate. The Socialist Jeanne Deroin ran as candidate for the National Assembly in the first republican election in 1849 to protest against the omission of women from the provisions of universal suffrage. During the Commune of 1870–71 Louise Michel organized the Union des Femmes for revolutionary purposes. The French League for Women's Rights, composed of members of the republican upper classes, was organized by Maria Deraismes and Léon Richer in 1876. As a protest against the timidity of the first International Feminist Congress called by them in Paris in 1878, which refused to commit itself to suffrage, Hubertine Auclert wrote *Le droit politique des femmes* (Paris 1878). The following year the French Socialist congress went on record in favor of woman's social and political equality, which henceforth became a doctrine of the party. In France the liberal political parties supported the feminist movement to a greater extent than did their counterparts elsewhere in Europe.

In Germany Luise Otto-Peters, who was involved in the revolutionary agitation of 1848, included in her feminist program a demand for the improvement of the condition of working women as well as those of the privileged classes. The Allgemeiner Deutscher Frauenverein was founded in Leipsic in 1865 with a platform built around the demands for woman's right to work and to receive an education. In a message to a labor congress assembled at Gera in 1867 it drew attention to the common oppression of women and the proletariat, a theme later to become dominant in socialist literature on woman's emancipation. The organization subsequently became cautious and conservative, and a distinct cleavage developed between the middle class and the proletarian women's movement in Germany. The breach was widened in 1894 when at the founding of the Bund Deutscher Frauenvereine no invitation was extended to working women's organizations. Although there were from the beginning leaders among the socialists who actively supported the struggle for the emancipation of women, the Socialist party officially delayed in its advocacy of women's rights. Marx had declared in a letter to Kugelmann in 1868 that "Social progress can be measured with precision by the social position of the female sex"; in the following year, however, the Socialist program at Eisenach demanded equal, direct and secret suffrage for men but failed to include a demand for similar rights for women. August Bebel's proposal at the Gotha convention in 1875 that the newly formed Social Democratic party go on record as favoring equal rights for women was rejected on the ground that women were not prepared for such a step. Shortly thereafter Bismarck suppressed all socialist organizations, and it was not until the Erfurt Congress in 1891 that the Social Democratic party supported the movement for women's rights by demanding the "abolition of all laws which in domestic relations operate to the disadvantage of women as compared to men." Bebel's extremely influential book, *Die Frau und der Socialismus* (Zurich 1883), urged organized efforts for the attainment of political and legal rights for women and at the same time argued forcibly that the full emancipation of women could not be realized until the overthrow of capitalist society and the establishment of a socialist society. Under the stimulus of Clara Zetkin's weekly woman's periodical, *Gleichheit*, which eventually attained a circulation of almost 100,000, socialist organizations for women's rights grew in number in the face of the German government's use of the *Vereingesetz* to abolish and discourage them and despite the fact that the government until 1908 banned political activities for women. The Lassallean Universal Working Men's Association in 1867, Vandervelde at the Brussels International Socialist Congress in 1891 and Edmund Fischer in 1905 had opposed socialist agitation for the emancipation of women and had argued against the increasing entrance of women into industry. But Bebel's position that the attraction of women to industry should be encouraged as a progressive fact, since it counteracted the isolation and resulting backwardness of women under the pre-capitalist patriarchal family, and that to exclude women from industry was reactionary became the party doctrine of international socialism. This was the stand taken by Lenin within the party, and it was the principle which later determined his program for women in Russia after the Bolshevik revolution. He and subsequently the Communist International under his leadership saw the struggle for women's rights as an aspect of the class struggle and held women's complete emancipation to be contingent upon the abolition of class exploitation.

In the United States the question of the franchise for women, when considered at the Constitutional Convention of 1787, was referred to the individual colonies. Among the opponents of citizenship rights for women was Thomas Jefferson, who put forth the familiar argument that women should be excluded from political activity in a democracy "to prevent depravation of morals and ambiguity of issues" which would result if they were to mingle with men in public meetings. On the other hand, Charles Brockden Brown popularized the views of Mary Wollstonecraft, and Thomas Paine likewise agitated for women's rights. Frances Wright and Robert Dale Owen included political equality among their demands for women's emancipation, as did Margaret Fuller later in *Woman in the Nineteenth Century* (New York 1845). The organized feminist movement, which was an outgrowth of women's activity in antislavery agitation, had its inception in 1848 at the Women's Rights Convention held at Seneca Falls, New York. At this convention a "Declaration of Sentiments" protested against disfranchisement, legal incapacity arising from marriage, unequal divorce laws, the "double standard of morals," occupational limitations, the denial of educational opportunities and subordination in church government. The subsequent agitation of Lucretia Mott, Elizabeth Cady Stanton, Lucy Stone and Susan B. Anthony for full legal, social and political equality, for industrial, educational and professional opportunities and for equal pay for equal work met with the ridicule and disparagement which were the common lot of pioneer advocates of women's rights universally, but it did secure the support of William Lloyd Garrison, Wendell Phillips, Channing, Whittier and Emerson. The campaign for women's suffrage was laid aside for the struggle for abolition of slavery and for the support of the North in the Civil War, from the outcome of which it was expected that women's suffrage would emerge along with Negro suffrage. But the end of the war found these hopes unfulfilled. The National Labor Union organized in 1867 under the leadership of Sylvis went on record for full political rights for women and for equal pay for equal work. In 1869 an amendment to the federal constitution specifically conferring suffrage on women was defeated in the House of Representatives, as were similar bills in succeeding decades. Pressure upon state legislatures was somewhat more successful; Wyoming, which had adopted suffrage for women in 1868 while still a territory, incorporated this innovation when it became a state twenty years later, and in the early 1890's, when Populism prevailed in the west, Colorado, Utah and Idaho granted the franchise to women. Agitation gained in strength and militancy at the turn of the century. In the United States organized feminism remained a distinctly middle class movement both in membership and in program.

Although women had previously been very active in pacifist agitation, during the World War women's organizations with few exceptions promoted the war work of their respective countries. As a means of securing support of the women for the program of the British government Asquith, who had been consistently opposed to suffrage, introduced in 1917 the Representation of the People Bill, which enfranchised women on a limited scale; voting privileges were not extended to women on the same terms as to men until 1928. Similarly in the United States President Wilson, likewise an antisuffragist, in September, 1918, recommended the passage of the national suffrage amendment to the federal constitution as a measure "vital to the winning of the war"; by the summer of 1920 it had been ratified by the states as the Nineteenth Amendment. The Soviet constitution put into effect immediately after the Russian Bolshevik Revolution in November, 1917, established complete equality between the sexes in all fields of social activity. In 1918 the establishment of the republic gave suffrage rights to German women. Finland had granted suffrage to women in 1906, Norway full parliamentary suffrage in 1913 and Denmark in 1915; but successive attempts to enfranchise women were defeated in the upper house in Sweden until 1921. The French Chamber of Deputies has since the World War repeatedly favored the extension of votes to women, but the Senate has rejected it. In 1925 the election of 10 Communist women candidates in the Paris municipal election was declared void by judicial decision. The *podestà* system of appointment of municipal authorities in Fascist Italy annulled the voting rights of women in municipal elections, which had been granted by the Chamber of Deputies but had never been exercised. After the founding of the Spanish Republic in 1931 franchise rights, which women had acquired to some extent in 1926, were extended.

The status of women throughout Asia is undergoing a drastic transformation largely as a result of the westernization movement, the effects of the World War and the success of the policy of the government in Soviet Asia, where the principle of full equality for women is being put into practise and all traditional disabilities are being removed. Under Islamic law married women were granted property rights not possessed by them under canon law in Christian countries, but the institution of polygamy and the practise of seclusion and of the wearing of the veil had worked to their disadvantage and had become symbols of their subordinate status. In Turkey women began to organize for their rights in 1908, but their entrance into the schools, occupations and professions was not notable until a decade later. The Turkish Civil Code of December, 1925, makes no discrimination between the sexes. Many women in Constantinople and Smyrna have discarded the veil, which still is insisted upon in the interior. In Persia and Afghanistan the women's emancipation movement is also advancing in spite of considerable opposition. In Egypt Qâsim Emîn's feminist writings, particularly his *Tahrîr el-mar'a* (tr. by O. Rescher as *Ueber die Frauenemancipation*, Stuttgart 1928), articulated the growing sentiment for women's rights. Women participated actively in the 1919 revolution against British rule and organized protests when the new constitution did not grant them suffrage rights. Except for a few educational projects of minor significance the British government has done nothing to improve the status of Indian women, particularly in the lower castes. Demands for women's rights have been part of the program of the Indian nationalist movement, in which women have been prominent. In China the patriarchal family and traditional religious controls have been disintegrating under the impact of the individualistic philosophy of western capitalism and of the socialism of the Soviet Union. Rapid gains were made by women between 1922 and 1927 when the strong revolutionary movement supported the demands of women for equal rights, but these have been negated in the territory controlled by the counter-revolutionary policies of Chiang Kai-shek. The Chinese Soviet Republic through the constitution drawn up by the first All-China Soviet Congress in November, 1931, established and is effectively realizing full political, legal and social equality for women within its borders. In Japan, where Buddhism and Confucianism contributed to their inferior status, women have been agitating for rights and privileges for about half a century. In 1898 a series of laws effected some improvement in their legal status. Feminists of the upper classes, organized into the Shinfujin Kukai, or "New Women's Society," and the later Association of Proletarian Women, founded in 1921, have insisted upon full economic, political, legal and educational equality and have often used militant methods in their agitation. When suffrage was extended in Japan in 1926, women were still left without franchise; and under the present reactionary Japanese government many of the activities of the feminist organizations, particularly those of the proletarian groups, have been suppressed.

In the difficult struggle for its attainment many feminists came to regard the franchise as a goal to which all else was subordinate, and its value as an instrument of progressive change was exaggerated in terms of the political philosophy of the eighteenth century. The major political issues in which women have specifically concerned themselves are prohibition, the enactment of measures for the control of prostitution, birth control legislation, independent citizenship for married women and social welfare legislation, such as maternity insurance and protective factory laws for women. On each issue, however, there has by no means been unanimity among women; and at times, as in the case of protective legislation, there has been organized opposition from certain feminist organizations. The vested interests associated with women's economic and religious affiliations have usually prevailed over the interests of sex solidarity. Whenever the results of woman suffrage have been appraised in parliamentary countries, statistical evidence points to an increase in the vote of conservative parties. Although women appear to utilize the ballot to an extent comparable with that of men, relatively few women have been elected to public office. In 1929 there were only 13 women members (2.1 percent) in the British House of Commons; in the United States 8 (1.1 percent) in the House of Representatives and 145 in the state legislatures of thirty-nine states. In 1928 there were 17 (8.5 percent) in the Finnish chamber; 7 (7 percent) in the Dutch chamber; 33 (6.7 percent) in the German Reichstag. More than one half of the women members of parliament in Germany and Finland and all of the 7 (4.3 percent) of the women in the Austrian Nationalrat were Socialist candidates. Wherever fascism has developed, and particularly in Germany, political offices are again closed to women on the ground that it is their essential function to be the "bearers of laborers and fighters." On the other hand, it is regarded as a fundamental tenet of the theory and practise of the Soviet Union that a socialist society cannot function adequately unless women participate as equals with men in political life; women are functioning in increasing numbers not only in village and regional soviets but also in the All-Russian Soviet and the All-Union Soviet. At the Fourteenth Congress of Soviets, held in 1931, 16 percent of the members were women.

While the struggle for women's civic rights was going on, significant advances were made throughout western society in the status of women, particularly in the case of the property rights of married women, in the laws of divorce (q.v.) and in women's educational and professional opportunities. Already in the eighteenth century in England the discriminations against women in common law, which merged the personality of a married woman in that of her husband, could be evaded by women of wealth by means of prenuptial settlements, private agreements and appeals to courts of equity whenever property and substantial economic interests were involved. Working class women were, however, unable to take advantage of the chancery because of their insufficient resources and remained subject to common law. The property of married women, except when protected by settlements, continued to be at the absolute disposal of their husbands until the passage of the married woman property acts of 1870 and 1882. The former law entitled a wife to her earnings; the latter established her as a distinct legal personality by giving her rights to her property in her own name; in 1886 a wife was also given equal rights with her husband in the control of her children. In the United States, Mississippi in 1839 was the first state to emancipate women from tutelage in the matter of property; New York, Indiana and Pennsylvania followed in 1848 and California and Wisconsin in 1850. Married women of six states of the United States still do not possess their earnings as their own, and in twenty-five states they do not have absolute right of contract. In no state has a wife legal right to collect for services performed in her home, nor is she entitled to determine the choice of the family domicile. In eight states a mother does not share equally in the guardianship of her children. Under the French Civil Code the wife has absolute right to one half of her husband's earnings; but she may not alienate property, even if it be her own, without his authority, nor can she sue or make a contract independently even if she be engaged in trade; she is likewise incapable of exercising parental power. The German Civil Code of 1900 put single women on an equal footing with men but gave the husband the right of decision in all matters affecting the common married life. It stipulated that unless the marriage contract made other provisions, the husband should have possession and use of the property of his wife as well as of the property acquired by their common labor, and that the wife should have parental authority only in exceptional circumstances. These laws remained unchanged during the period of the German Republic; National Socialist idealization of women's subordinate role in the home as in all phases of social life has led to their rigid enforcement in the Third Reich. In the Soviet Union the marriage code provides absolute equality in property as well as other rights between man and woman, whether they live in registered or in unregistered marriage, and the government is successfully utilizing its forces to have practise conform to law in the face of an obstinate tradition of male dominance.

In the course of the nineteenth century wherever education became secularized and compulsory public schools developed, it came to be an accepted principle that the same elementary education should be offered to girls as to boys; and provisions were gradually made for secondary and higher education as well. Coeducation, which developed rapidly in the United States after 1850, became popular more because it proved to be economical than for reasons of equality of the sexes. The segregation of boys and girls in separate schools, which is the rule in Europe, particularly in Catholic countries, where there has been vigorous opposition to coeducation, often results in inferior schools for girls, even when the formal curriculum is approximately the same for both sexes. Secondary schools for girls were not provided in France until 1880. In the United States higher education for women began with the opening of Oberlin College as a coeducational institution in 1833 and the establishment of Mount Holyoke Female Seminary in 1837. Women's colleges flourished, largely because of the restrictions against women at endowed and public universities, which were modified only gradually and still prevail in certain institutions, particularly in the graduate professional faculties. A comparison of the statistics of enrolment shows that in 1894 there were 163,000 girls in American secondary schools and 84,000 women in colleges and normal schools; by 1924 the numbers had increased to about 1,963,000 and 450,000 respectively. Higher education is still, however, largely confined to the women of the upper and middle classes.

In England Girton College, Cambridge, was established in 1869 as the first women's college of university rank and the London School of Medicine for Women followed in 1874. London medical schools have opened their doors to women on equal terms with men only within the last decade; no woman was qualified to practise law in England until 1922. In Germany, although women had been granted in rare instances special permission to enter universities as early as the eighteenth century and in the 1890's had been given certain privileges of university study, they were not permitted to matriculate anywhere as regular students until 1901, when Heidelberg and Freiburg granted them that right. All German universities followed within a decade thereafter. By 1910 women had been admitted to the universities of Holland, Belgium, Denmark, Sweden, Norway, Russia, Austria-Hungary, Italy, Switzerland, France, Turkey and Australia. As institutions of higher learning were opened to women, they entered the professions in increasing numbers in the face of persistent opposition in many countries. Recently in fascist countries their attendance at universities has again been restricted and they have been virtually excluded from the professions; the National Socialist government in Germany decreed in 1934 that women may not exceed 10 percent of the total student body of a university. Women in the Soviet Union have entered all schools on an equal basis with men; in 1932 they accounted for 28.9 percent of the enrolment in higher technical schools and in 1934, 74 percent of the 480,000 medical students.

Everywhere in capitalist countries women have shared in the drastic reverses resulting from the crisis which began in 1929. A distinct retrogressive trend is observable and is particularly pronounced in fascist countries, where all rights which women gained during the nineteenth and the early twentieth century are rapidly being annulled. On the other hand, in the Soviet Union, along with the release of the energies of the proletariat of both sexes in a socialized industrial economy, there is marked progress toward the dissipation of the traditional attitudes of condescension and derogation toward women.

BERNHARD J. STERN

See: WOMEN IN INDUSTRY; WOMEN'S ORGANIZATIONS; SOCIAL ORGANIZATION; FAMILY; MARRIAGE; COMPANIONATE MARRIAGE; CONCUBINAGE; CHASTITY; BIRTH CONTROL; MATERNITY WELFARE; FAMILY LAW; FAMILY DESERTION AND NON-SUPPORT; MARITAL PROPERTY; DIVORCE; ALIMONY; DOWRY; COEDUCATION.

Consult: FOR PRIMITIVE: Lowie, R. H., *Primitive Society* (New York 1920), and *The Matrilineal Complex*, University of California, Publications in American Archaeology and Ethnology, vol. xvi, no. 2 (Berkeley 1919); Hartland, E. S., *Primitive Society* (London 1921), and *Matrilinial Kinship and the Question of Its Priority*, American Anthropological Association, Memoirs, vol. iv, no. 1 (Lancaster, Pa. 1917); Goldenweiser, A. A., *Early Civilization* (New York 1922) p. 259–64; Bachofen, J. J., *Das Mutterrecht* (2nd ed. Basel 1897); Morgan, L. H., *Ancient Society* (New York 1877); McLennan, J. F., *Studies in Ancient History* (new ed. London 1886); Tylor, E. B., "On a Method of Investigating the Development of Institutions; Applied to Laws of Marriage and Descent" in Royal Anthropological Institute of Great Britain and Ireland, *Journal*, vol. xviii (1888) 245–72; Westermarck, Edward, *The History of Human Marriage*, 3 vols. (5th ed. London 1921); Briffault, Robert, *The Mothers*, 3 vols. (London 1927); Olson, R. L., *Clan and Moiety in Native America*, University of California, Publications in American Archaeology and Ethnology, vol. xxxiii, no. 4 (Berkeley 1933); Ronhaar, J. H., *Woman in Primitive Motherright Societies* (Groningen 1931); Hahn, Eduard, *Das Alter der wirtschaftlichen Kultur der Menschheit* (Heidelberg 1905); Mason, O. T., *Woman's Share in Primitive Culture* (New York 1894); Sumner, W. G., and Keller, A. G., *The Science of Society*, 4 vols. (New Haven 1927) vol. iii, chs. l–li, and vol. iv, sects. 376–89; Crawley, A. E., *The Mystic Rose*, 2 vols. (new ed. by Theodore Besterman, London 1927).

FOR HISTORICAL: Hobhouse, L. T., *Morals in Evolution* (3rd rev. ed. London 1916) chs. iv–v; Lecky, W. E. H., *History of European Morals*, 2 vols. (3rd ed. London 1877) ch. v; Abensour, Léon, *Histoire générale du féminisme des origines à nos jours* (Paris 1921); Howard, G. E., *A History of Matrimonial Institutions*, 3 vols. (Chicago 1904); Putnam, Emily J., *The Lady* (New York 1910); Beard, Mary, *On Understanding Women* (New York 1931); Braun, Lily, "Die Anfänge der Frauenbewegung" in *Archiv für soziale Gesetzgebung und Statistik*, vol. xiii (1899) 314–81; Cornish, F. W., and Bacon, J., "The Position of Women" in *A Companion to Greek Studies*, ed. by Leonard Whibley (4th rev. ed. Cambridge, Eng. 1931) p. 610–17; Wright, F. A., *Feminism in Greek Literature* (London 1923); Friedländer, Ludwig, *Darstellungen aus der Sittengeschichte Roms*, 4 vols. (10th ed. by G. Wissowa, Leipsic 1920–22), tr. by L. A. Magnus and others as *Roman Life and Manners under the Early Empire*, 4 vols. (London 1908–13) vol. i, ch. v; Bücher, Karl, *Die Frauenfrage im Mittelalter* (Tübingen 1910); Tout, T. F., "The Place of Women in Later Mediaeval Civilisation" in Royal Institution of Great Britain, *Proceedings*, vol. xxvi (1929–31) 68–72; Havemann, Elizabeth, *Die Frau der Renaissance*, Quellenhefte zum Frauenleben in der Geschichte, no. 10 (Berlin 1928); Stricker, Käthe, *Die Frau in der Reformation*, Quellenhefte zum Frauenleben in der Geschichte, no. 11 (Berlin 1927); Tickner, F. W., *Women in English Economic History* (London

1923); Crofts, M. I., *Women under English Law* (2nd ed. London 1928); O'Malley, I. B., *Women in Subjection* (London 1933); Clark, Alice, *Working Life of Women in the Seventeenth Century*, London School of Economics and Political Science, Studies in Economics and Political Science, no. 56 (London 1919); Reynolds, Myra, *The Learned Lady in England, 1650–1760* (Boston 1920); Pinchbeck, Ivy, *Women Workers and the Industrial Revolution, 1750–1850* (London 1930); Brailsford, H. N., *Shelley, Godwin and Their Circle* (London 1913); Strachey, Rachel C., *"The Cause"; a Short History of the Women's Movement in Great Britain* (London 1928); Fawcett, Millicent G., *Women's Suffrage* (London 1912); Blease, W. Lyon, *The Emancipation of English Women* (rev. ed. London 1913); Lang, E. M., *British Women in the Twentieth Century* (London 1929); Richardson, L. M., *The Forerunners of Feminism in French Literature*, The Johns Hopkins Studies in Romance Literatures and Languages, vol. xii (Baltimore 1929); Abensour, Léon, *La femme et le féminisme avant la Révolution* (Paris 1923); Neumann, Ilse, *Die Frauen der französischen Revolution,* Quellenhefte zum Frauenleben in der Geschichte, no. 14 (Berlin 1927); Bonnecase, Julien, *La philosophie du code Napoléon appliquée au droit de famille* (2nd rev. ed. Paris 1928); Thibert, Marguerite, *Le féminisme dans le socialisme français de 1830 à 1850* (Paris 1926); Abensour, Léon, *Le féminisme sous le règne de Louis-Philippe et en 1848* (Paris 1913); Grinberg, S., *Historique du mouvement suffragiste depuis 1848* (Paris 1926); Belot, Gustave, and others, *Les problèmes de la famille et le féminisme* (Paris 1930); Anthony, Katharine, *Feminism in Germany and Scandinavia* (New York 1915); Neumann, A., "Die Entwicklung der sozialistischen Frauenbewegung" in *Schmollers Jahrbuch*, vol. xlv, pt. 3 (1921) 195–257; Puckett, H. W., *Germany's Women Go Forward* (New York 1930) with bibliography; Beard, Miriam, "The Nazis Harness Woman Power" in *Today*, vol. i (May 12, 1934) 6–7; *History of Woman Suffrage*, ed. by Elizabeth Cady Stanton, Susan B. Anthony, and Matilda J. Gage, 6 vols. (New York 1881–1922); Calhoun, Arthur W., *A Social History of the American Family*, 3 vols. (Cleveland 1917–19); American Academy of Political and Social Science, "Women in Public Life," and "Women in the Modern World," *Annals*, vol. lvi (1914), and vol. cxliii (1929); Breckinridge, S. P., *Marriage and the Civic Rights of Women* (Chicago 1931); National League of Women Voters, *A Survey of the Legal Status of Women in the Forty-eight States* (rev. ed. Washington 1930); Branch, Mary S., *Women and Wealth; a Study of the Economic Status of American Women* (Chicago 1934); Pruette, Lorine, *Women and Leisure; a Study of Waste* (New York 1924); Hutchins, Grace, *Women Who Work* (New York 1934); Breckinridge, S. P., *Women in the Twentieth Century* (New York 1933); *Handbuch der Frauenbewegung*, ed. by Helene Lange and Gertrud Bäumer, 5 vols. (Berlin 1901–06); Schirmacher, Käthe, *Die moderne Frauenbewegung* (2nd ed. Leipsic 1909), tr. by C. C. Eckhardt as *The Modern Woman's Rights Movement* (New York 1912); Bernhard, Margarete, "Die Frauen im politischen Leben" in *Zeitschrift für Politik*, vol. xix (1929–30) 142–47; Dutt, R. Palme, "Women in the Class Struggle" in *Woman's Coming of Age*, ed. by S. D. Schmalhausen and V. F. Calverton (New York 1931) p. 550–64; Ameer Ali, Syed, *The Legal Position of Women in Islam* (London 1912); Emin, Ahmed, *Turkey in the World War*, Carnegie Endowment for International Peace, Economic and Social History of the World War (New Haven 1930) ch. xx; Hauswirth, Frieda, *Purdah; the Status of Indian Women* (New York 1932); Halle, Fannina W., *Die Frau in Sowjetrussland* (Berlin 1932), tr. by M. M. Green (London 1933); Smith, Jessica, *Woman in Soviet Russia* (New York 1928); Field, Alice W., *Protection of Women and Children in Soviet Russia* (New York 1932); Kollontai, A. M., *Rabotnitsa i krestyanka v Sovetskoy Rossii* (Petrograd 1921), tr. into German as *Die Arbeiterin und Bäuerin in Sowjet-Russland* (Leipsic 1921). For a comprehensive bibliography of the earlier literature, see: Mehler, H. J., *La femme et le féminisme. Collection de livres . . . sur la condition de la femme et de mouvement féministe* (Paris 1900).

WOMAN'S CHRISTIAN TEMPERANCE UNION. See Prohibition; Temperance Movements.

WOMEN IN INDUSTRY

GENERAL PRINCIPLES. The subject of women in industry is here restricted to women's work in an economy in which production is carried on predominantly by power driven machinery. Since, however, industrialization is nowhere complete and even the most highly industrialized nation is involved in a process of continual change of its methods of production, a discussion of women in industry must take account of various stages of evolution in different nations, in successive decades and in special industries. Certain branches of economy tend to remain unmechanized or to retain the hand as the motive power of the tool or machine. Thus unpaid household tasks and commercial employment of women in their homes, extreme examples of this retardation of both industrialization and organization, are profoundly affected by industrialization, in the economy of which they represent the most undeveloped branch. The subject therefore cannot be limited to wage earning or to gainful employment but must include all aspects of women's activities in the productive and distributive processes of industrialized societies, whatever the extent of their industrialization.

It is precisely out of this dual status of women workers who combine wage earning with unpaid work at home or who pass from one to the other with the rise or fall of the earnings of other wage earners in the family that there arise many of the characteristic inequalities and special problems of women in industry. If there be assumed certain standards of living of workers' families, the rise and fall in the means of maintaining these standards draw women and girls back and forth from home to factory. This fluctuation in family income involves consideration of the whole subject of men's work and its adequacy or inadequacy for the support of families. All the hazards to the economic security of male wage earners—unemployment, sickness, accident and dismissal because of old age—therefore affect the problem of women in industry. Especially significant is unemployment or displacement due to technological changes, which under capitalist industrialism make profitable the substitution of cheap labor by women for men's work.

Until recently industrialism was actually inseparable from capitalism and the employment of women was treated in numerous investigations, official and private, as an evil to be regulated, reformed or even prohibited under injurious conditions regarded by observers as inevitable under industrialization. But the new phenomenon of industrialization in Soviet Russia, that is, under socialism, should, when the data are compiled, make possible comparative studies isolating the effects of capitalism as such on women's work. Indeed new light may be thrown by such comparative studies on the whole subject of the freedom of women, which the feminist movement has made its goal without, however, recognizing its essential economic foundation. In this connection two aspects of women in industry under capitalism require special consideration: first, the place of women in industry when there is, quite aside from wage considerations, an absolute shortage of labor, as for example in war time, and, second, the position of women workers in times of economic crisis when there seems to be a surplus of men workers. The former situation, which reveals the wider scope for women in industrial processes, indicates the forces which in other times limit women to certain occupations, thus intensifying their competitive struggle for jobs. The promise by governments during war time of equal pay for equal work reflects the inequality which has been regarded as "normal" in peacetime industry, but which is in fact the focal point of a fundamental analysis of women's work in industry under capitalism. Similarly the introduction during a period of depression of lower paid but equally competent women workers in jobs held formerly by men indicates the basic futility of the recurrent agitation against the employment of women.

Finally, attention must be given also to the historic conflict now emerging between that stage of capitalism known as fascism and communism, which views women in industry as part of the working class inevitably exploited under capitalism and even more under fascism. In Italy and in Germany alike a whole new social philosophy of women's status and function has been built up by way of removing women from competition with men for the insufficient jobs available during the industrial depression. This philosophy demands that women recognize wifehood and motherhood as their great contribution to society and that they therefore remain at home. In practise, however, this program is merely an intensification of the forces at work in non-fascist industrial capitalism. Women in the professions and in the higher governmental positions are increasingly excluded. The policy which has always created obstacles to the employment of married women, as in the public school systems of the United States and of other countries, has become under fascism a complete system whereby women are denied economic independence. Nevertheless, women are still used for the most onerous and badly paid jobs where modern industry needs them.

In extreme contrast to the policy of fascism and of industrial capitalism is the policy of the Soviet Union. The proportion of women among the gainfully employed in czarist Russia was only 16.9 percent in 1897, whereas the proportion in the Soviet Union in 1932 was given as 29.9. In publishing this figure the State Planning Commission for the second Five-Year Plan announced its intention of increasing the proportion to 33.9 percent by 1937.

It may of course be argued that this new phenomenon of conscious planning for the extension of women's employment in the total national economy is merely an application in a country about to be highly industrialized of what actually took place in capitalistic industrialized countries during the period from 1880 to the first decade of the twentieth century, and that the decline or failure to increase this proportion in the decades since the World War indicates that the peak of industrialization has been attained.

But certain essential differences, quite aside from the important element of conscious planning, must be noted. The Soviet Union aims to socialize industry in order to raise the standard of living of all its workers. As part of this objective women as workers are to be related on an equal basis with men to the whole system of production. And their work at home, hitherto unpaid for, which under capitalism creates the double burden of women wage earners, is to be organized as an integral part of the national economy for the purpose of raising standards of living and freeing women from uncompensated drudgery. Thus the increase in the proportion of women in gainful employment as planned for 1937 signifies that more and more of the unpaid household tasks—cooking, laundry and the more important care of children—will be organized as new or expanding fields of employment for specialists of both sexes. At the same time women's opportunities for work are to be extended in industry, in agriculture and in the professions. The proportion of women among the gainfully employed in other countries has been determined by factors quite different from those operative in the Soviet system. In the main these have been: first, the need of wages for self-support or for the support of a family and, second, the demand for cheap, marginal labor in processes adapted to the employment of women.

The importance of the distinction between women in gainful employment and women in industry under capitalism must be noted. The comparative data for women in gainful employment for various countries as tabulated by Woytinsky (*Die Welt in Zahlen*, vol. ii, Berlin 1926, p. 71) show that the proportion was smaller in the countries marked by the highest development of industrialism than in less industrialized countries. In England and Wales the proportion of women to the total wage earning and salaried population was 29.7 in 1911, in the United States 20.5 in 1910 and in Germany 33.8 in 1907. But in South Africa the proportion for 1911 was 47.6 and in Bulgaria in 1910, 42.2 percent. An examination of the figures for South Africa, which had the largest proportion of women workers of any country in the world, showed that women were employed largely in agriculture, secondly in domestic service and only to a small extent in mechanized industry. In the more highly industrialized countries the proportion of women in agriculture tends to be smaller and employment in industry greater. The proportion in domestic service decreases at the same time that a new demand is created through the drawing of middle class women into paid professional work outside the home. The percentage in industry, however, tends to be modified by the composition of the industrial activities of the particular country: it has been smaller in countries in which heavy industry and mining predominate. But even here technological changes in certain of the so-called heavy industries have led to increasing employment of women at the expense of men workers, at a time when the proportion of women to the total of those gainfully employed has declined, as in the period 1910–20 in Great Britain and the United States.

The employment of women in countries of industrial capitalism has thus been a development arising neither from society's requirement of women's work in industry nor from women's inherent need for work, but in the main from the desire of entrepreneurs to utilize cheap labor for profit making purposes. Even those proposals which are aimed at the raising of men's wages so that they may support their families, thus restricting paid employment of women to those who have no male support or who prefer to work and are in a position to compete equally with men on the basis of skill, fail to take account of this basic role of women workers.

Contrary to popular opinion, the machine created neither the need nor the opportunity for women's work. Every known economic system has utilized and presumably required the work of women, while women obviously "need work" both for their maintenance and for their happiness as human beings and members of society. Actually capitalistic industrialism has resulted in the uprooting of women's work and in their loss of status. At the same time, however, that many of the tasks formerly undertaken in the home were removed to the factory, with the result that the family income now had to be expended on the purchase of goods formerly made in the home, the basic problem of the care of children remained. Naturally it became the aim of working men to earn enough to enable their wives to stay at home. If the increased cost of living necessitated earnings supplementary to their own, it was deemed preferable that daughters and even younger children should work for wages. Industry, seeking to keep down costs of production in order to keep up profits, offered only this supplementary wage to the daughters, while the wages of men were reduced to a level which made it necessary for the daughters to work. In addition to the care of children certain tasks have remained part of the unpaid work of the household and outside the organized economy, solely because they cannot profitably be organized on a wage earning basis. These unpaid workers must necessarily derive their subsistence from the wages paid to men. But when women are forced to follow industrialized occupations, their wage level is affected by the low level of subsistence of the unpaid women workers, who constitute the largest reserve of labor power. In a word, women are "marginal" workers in an industrialized economy, and their work therefore, even when identical with men's, is not equally paid. Thus the unpaid work of women is a competitive drag upon their pay in gainful employment. Moreover their unpaid work is a contribution to the maintenance of the labor power of both men and women, lessening the charge upon industry for the minimum subsistence wage which capital must pay for labor power.

It is true of course that in the search for cheap labor power, where the potentialities of the population have already apparently been exhausted, employers attempt to draw upon other masses from other areas. In the United States such labor was obtained from immigrants from countries with overcrowded populations and limited opportunities and later from the Negro population formerly concentrated in the non-industrialized south. Here too it is the women among the immigrant and Negro workers who suffer most. And where industrial capitalism enters the field of production in foreign or subjugated regions, the position of the women among the colonial workers represents the extreme of low standards.

In countries of industrial capitalism three programs have been advanced for the improvement of the conditions of women workers. The first has been the organization of women into trade unions, which presumably would extend the same protection to women as to men workers. Although the degree of unionization of women workers varies greatly from country to country, being highest in countries like Germany and Great Britain, where there is a comparatively high proportion of women members of trade unions, trade unionism has been effective only to a limited extent. It has hardly touched women in paid household service, who in all countries represent a large proportion of women wage earners. In the consumption industries, in which in the past women have been mainly employed in factories, the tendency has been to make these predominantly women's trades. Since the strength of trade unions has been based largely upon the exclusiveness of skill, with the displacement of the skilled workers by increasing mechanization the proportion of organized male workers in these trades has decreased, a factor which in combination with the traditional helplessness of low paid, semiskilled or unskilled labor has led to a breakdown of traditional craft unionism. Although countries and individual unions vary with respect to their willingness and initiative in admitting women to membership or in cooperative endeavor along organizational fields, the fact remains that despite gains in a number of occupations the problem has barely been touched upon by trade unionism.

In the absence of this traditional form of workers' protection there has been the movement for special protective legislation for women. This movement has lately been subjected to adverse criticism and attack from certain groups in the feminist movement, which has drawn its membership largely from women in the professions or in the leisure class. Urbanization and industrialization brought into the professions and into the new service occupations, especially trade and clerical work, an increasing number of middle class women. The first demand of this feminist movement was for the suffrage. But after 1918, with the granting of this demand in most countries, certain feminist groups turned their energies toward the achievement of economic equality. Thus they opposed special protective legislation for women in factories, on the ground that it would handicap women in securing employment. Although such groups also stress at times the issue of equal pay for equal work, they place far more reliance on the opening up of opportunities, in the struggle for which presumably the principle of free competition on a laissez faire basis is to dominate.

The proponents of protective legislation emphasize, however, that this theoretical freedom to enter paid employment, while it may obtain in the professions and among middle class women, does not hold for the pressing problems of women wage earners, for whom special laws tend in fact to correct inequalities and to regulate industry with its special physical hazards for women and its tendency to exploit them by low wages, long hours and night work.

Neither group has fully grasped the limitations inherent in labor legislation in overcoming women's handicaps, which have persisted in the countries of matured capitalism after a century or more of effort to establish minimum industrial standards through legislation. Such legislation in England, for instance, as in other countries under growing industrialism, was enacted in response to the growing discontent and increasing political power of the working class, supported by a limited but articulate public sentiment which may briefly be described as the expression of a social conscience against child labor, overwork of women and young girls and other excesses of industrialization. Following the World War international scope was given to this movement with the formation of the International Labor Organization at Geneva, established by the Treaty of Versailles as part of the League of Nations. The world wide economic depression that began to be evident in 1929 has, however, revealed the deeper economic problems, which these limited legal regulations, useful as they may be in specific circumstances, are powerless to solve. On the other hand, out of the planlessness and the struggle for markets and for dominance that reach their climax in the economic system in the countries of matured capitalism arise the insecurity, poverty and unwholesome and unhappy conditions of women in industry which labor laws are designed to correct. Enactment and enforcement of labor laws are resisted by these same conflicting interests.

If then these inherent tendencies in capitalism have operated against trade unionism, have counteracted the effects of such protective legislation as has been passed and have revealed the basic weakness of the feminists' plea for equality without consideration of the essential economic factors involved, it follows that efforts to establish equal pay for equal work would meet with even greater failure. This point is best illustrated by experience during the World War, when in contrast to peace time women were presumably in an advantageous bargaining position and when the pressure of events compelled governments to issue edicts embodying the equality principle. The war experience in fact throws light both on the claims of the feminists as to women's capacities and on the role of protective labor legislation. In the war period the theory that women's capacity and physical strength limited their range of occupations, which had been used to justify lower wages and exclusion from skilled trades, was discredited in the face of the feverish desire of industry to produce for the war. Women were drawn into men's work in production and began to handle machines which they had never operated before and to take part in many new tasks in the heavy industries, in metal trades, in the engineering trades and in transportation. In the United States the sudden expansion of munitions plants resulted in efforts to recruit labor, including women, by offers of shorter hours and higher wages. But once women were employed, production made heavy claims upon the physical energies of the workers. For instance, a study of conditions in Bridgeport, Connecticut (Hewes, Amy, *Women as Munition Makers*, Russell Sage Foundation, New York 1917), showed that "neither the shortage of labor nor the labor legislation of the state proved to be a real protection for the unorganized working women against the well-known dangers of long hours and night work." Governmental commissions appointed in the various countries advocated shorter hours on the ground that they not only protected the health of the workers but favorably affected the quantity and quality of output. But the very appointment of these commissions was an indication of the disregard of these factors, and in general their recommendations were not enforced.

The same situation obtained on the promise of equal pay for equal work. In most countries this policy was endorsed by the government. In England a Treasury agreement embodying the policy was so often violated that a special commission was appointed to take it up. Only a minority report prepared by Beatrice Webb maintained that the Treasury agreement should be kept and that the basis for wage determination should be the work and not the sex of the worker.

In the United States the chief of ordnance in 1917 had announced in general orders addressed to arsenal commanders and ordnance contractors that "the standard of wages hitherto prevailing in the process should not be lowered where women render equivalent service." The Women's Branch of the Ordnance Department, however, in its final report after the signing of the Armistice declared: "The facts of actual practise and experience in ordnance plants did not, however, conform to this policy." Of the hundreds of plants manufacturing ordnance the Women's Branch was able to list only eleven which had been reported to have paid equal piece rates to men and women for the same work.

In March, 1919, the Women-in-Industry Service of the Department of Labor in drawing up its standards for the employment of women included "equality with men's wages" and recommended that "women doing the same work as men shall receive the same wages, with such proportionate increases as the men are receiving in the same industry." It is significant, however, that this general recommendation required the following explanation: "Slight changes made in the process or in the arrangement of work should not be regarded as justifying a lower wage for a woman than for a man, unless statistics of production show that the output for the job in question is less when women are employed than when men are employed. If a difference in output is demonstrated, the difference in the wage rate should be based upon the difference in production for the job as a whole and not determined arbitrarily."

Needless to say, violation of this principle increased once the wartime need was over. Equal pay for equal work is usually held to apply only to identical jobs as between men and women. But in peace time the large majority of women are employed in women's occupations paying only women's wages. The equality principle therefore is not sufficiently inclusive, unless it be understood as calling for an identical basis for the determination of wages for both men and women. This was recognized in the following recommendations by the Women-in-Industry Service: "Wages should be established on the basis of occupation and not on the basis of sex. The minimum wage rate should cover the cost of living for dependents and not merely for the individual." In the light of studies made since the war by the United States Department of Labor and by governmental departments in other countries it must be said that these recommendations regarding wages were evidently mere counsels of perfection. They were not fulfilled in the policy of industry except in the new economic system of the Soviet Union.

Freedom to choose an occupation, opportunity to receive training in it, protection against preventable hazards and payment of wages adequate to maintain the rising standard of living which should accompany increasing productive capacity are claims that women cannot make for themselves alone; nor can they be fulfilled for women as a group apart from all workers. This is the weakness of reform movements and of the feminist program. Both have lacked comprehension of the fundamental forces affecting both men and women but pressing more heavily in many respects upon the latter. It is necessary therefore to recognize, on the one hand, the identity of interest of men and women and, on the other, the special problems of women. Women's work under industrialism evidently involves a problem so bound up with the status of workers in the prevailing economic system as to be insoluble except as part of the solution for all workers. The significance of the prevailing economic crisis in revealing the necessity for balance between production and consumption by the raising of standards of living in proportion to productive capacity suggests that only in such a balanced economy can women be accorded equal rank with men. The pressure upon women as marginal workers cannot be lifted either by the community, through labor legislation, or by the labor movement, through trade unions, so long as these operate in an economy characterized by recurrent industrial depressions, insecurity and poverty.

MARY VAN KLEECK

PROBLEMS OF ORGANIZATION. In every industrial country except the Soviet Union women workers have advanced far less toward trade union organization than men. Perhaps the highest degree of organization was achieved in Germany prior to National Socialism and in Austria. In the "free," or Social Democratic, unions of Germany the number of women rose from 15,000 in 1896 to 230,000 in 1913, or from less than 5 percent of the total membership to about 9 percent. In 1919 woman members numbered 1,200,000 and in 1920, 1,711,000, or 21 percent of the membership of the free trade unions. There were also in 1920, 215,000 women in the Christian trade unions and 21,000 in the liberal Hirsch-Duncker unions. After 1921 the number of women in the free trade unions declined. In 1931 it was 617,000, representing 14 percent of the total membership. In the textile unions the proportion of women (56.7 percent) in the total membership approximated very nearly that existing among the wage earners in this industry (58.7 percent). This was true in a lesser degree for the clothing, bookbinding and tobacco industries. The proportion of women in the metal industries, in which in 1920 they constituted 20 percent of the workers, formed a proportion in labor organizations that in 1930 was only 7.3 percent. The broad distribution of trade union membership among German women workers is made evident by the figures for 1925. Out of 752,000 women members in the free trade unions the women textile workers represented the largest single group (136,380, or about 25 percent of the total number of women textile workers). There were 71,000 members in public employment and transport, 72,000 factory workers, 54,350 members in the metal trades (representing almost one half of the total number of women employed in that branch of industry), about 30,000 members in bookbinding and large units of 20,000 or more members in the boot and shoe, printing, food and other industries.

In British trade unionism women never attained to a position of importance comparable with the position to which they had attained in Germany. In 1899, however, women represented almost 10 percent of the total trade union membership. The high point was achieved in 1918 when 18.5 percent of the total trade union membership consisted of women—a rise due largely to organization among the "black-coated proletariat" and in public employment. In 1932 of 746,000 women in trade unions well over a third (258,000) were in the various branches of the textile industry, 50,000 in commerce and distribution, 68,000 in the clothing industry, 38,000 in printing and paper and 26,000 in the boot and shoe industry.

In the United States there were in 1910, 76,748 women trade unionists, representing 3.5 percent of the total trade union membership and 5.2 percent of all women workers in manufacturing and mechanical industries. At the peak of organization in 1920 only 8 percent of the total trade union membership (397,000) consisted of women. The increase had taken place almost entirely in clothing, where woman trade union membership rose from 11.2 percent in 1910 to 46.0 percent in 1920. By 1927 woman trade union membership had declined to 260,095.

This trend is in contrast to that of the Soviet Union, where in 1929 women constituted 33.3 percent of the working force of the country and 29.7 percent of the total trade union membership. The number of women in trade unions grew from about 3,000,000 in 1929 to almost 5,000,000 in 1932, out of 6,000,000 women wage earners.

At the other extreme is the instance of Japan, where in the textile industry, which absorbs the greater part of the wage earning women, the recruitment of women workers or more commonly girl workers is carried on in remote regions under long time contracts. Moreover these workers are housed in company dormitories and are kept at their job for such long hours that they have virtually no freedom of movement. On the other hand, in India, also a country of new imperialist capitalism, where the woman working population is likewise recruited from the peasantry, there has been an amazing response by women to labor organization.

For the older industrial countries the high percentage of women trade union members in Germany and Austria until recently is to be accounted for by the spread of Social Democratic ideals, the greater prevalence of industrial unionism and the fact that from the outset both the socialist and labor movements developed their own feminist groups. These factors were less in evidence in Great Britain and almost entirely absent in the United States.

The first serious attempt to promote the organization of women in England was led by Emma Paterson and her Women's Trade Union League in 1874–86. The movement received another strong impetus from the National Federation of Women Workers formed in 1906. The opening of the unions to women in the period 1886–1906 was also supported by the trade boards in the sweated industries. In the United States, after the first wave of organization in the period preceding and immediately following the Civil War, the organization of women workers was urged both by the National Labor Union in the 1860's and by the Knights of Labor. The predominantly craft character of the unions in the American Federation of Labor was less favorable to the organization of women; and it was not until the formation of unions in the clothing trades after 1909, with leaders and membership under socialist influences, that anything approaching a mass movement among women workers occurred. In this work the national Women's Trade Union League, a fraternal organization within the A. F. of L. and including elements outside of the working class, played an important role. Unlike its British prototype, the Women's Trade Union League has worked to secure protective legislation for women.

The relatively weak position of women in organized labor is to be explained by many special circumstances. At the beginning of industrialization lack of previous training excluded the mass of women workers from the skilled functions in the factories. The skilled workers succeeded in organizing themselves at a comparatively early date. In most countries another half century had to elapse before trade unionism could penetrate to the unskilled and semiskilled and to the industries of mass production where women were chiefly employed. Thus a tradition of lower pay and inferior jobs had been established for the woman worker. Nor were the men workers always hospitable to the advance of women into the skilled and organized trades, where their competition might become a serious problem.

Another point bearing on the problem is the

relative immaturity and instability of the women workers and their consequent weakness in forming and carrying out plans for improving their position in industry. In every industrial country the proportion of workers under twenty-one and in the age group twenty-one to thirty is far greater for women than for men. In Japan 26.6 percent of the women industrial workers are below sixteen, and in the textile industry more than one half of the women workers are below that age. In the United States in 1930, 60 percent of the women workers ranged from sixteen years to thirty-four as against 46 percent for men. The increasing proportion of married women among these workers—in the United States in 1890 one out of seven was married and in 1930 one out of three, with a proportion as high as 40 percent in cotton—while indicating a more mature group, creates its own difficulties because of the peculiar position of the married woman worker as an earner of auxiliary family income. Studies by the federal Women's Bureau indicated that in 1929 in a sample grouping 52.5 percent of the women workers contributed their earnings to the family.

The restriction of women to the less skilled jobs, resulting from tradition, trade union rules in the crafts and more recently from technological changes, makes comparison of general wage standards difficult. But enough evidence exists of discriminatory wage standards in comparable work as well as of the extremely low wages in occupations predominantly left to women. In 1925 in the United States the differential in the cotton textile industry was 28 percent and in the boot and shoe industry 36 percent; in tobacco, where women make up a far greater proportion of the workers, it was as high as 80 percent. In the period 1922–30 women's average earnings ranged from 45 percent to 84 percent of the earnings of men, with an average of 70 percent for three quarters of the cases. In 1915 outside of the professional groups almost one half of the women workers earned less than $6 weekly and three quarters less than $8. The poorest paid factory trades were candy, textile and tobacco, in which women predominated; the highest were clothing, in which women were comparatively well organized, and metal and rubber products, where men and women are mixed.

In Germany by contrast the differential was not nearly so high; but even in the skilled trades in metal there was a 32 percent differential for equal work, and the piece rates of the unskilled women workers were 30 percent lower than those of unskilled men workers. Differential wage payments for women exist even in the Soviet Union, although the margin is narrower. Women's wages average from 81.8 percent in some branches of printing to 93.9 percent in machine construction; and in some tasks in textiles, where women are doing skilled work formerly performed by men, the wages are the same.

Despite the acceptance of the principle of equal pay as a basis for rates under the National Industrial Recovery Act in the United States, such equality was provided for only in the well organized trades or in those in which women were hardly employed at all. Almost 25 percent of the codes provided lower rates for women than for men. Apparently the differential was too wide, with resulting widespread substitution in some industries of women for men. In England the rules of a few of the skilled crafts definitely provide for lower wage rates for women. Dependence is placed on union control to prevent the substitution of women for men.

In view of this tendency it is not surprising that the substitution of women for men in the period of depression and the falling off of trade union strength kept the percentage of unemployment among women lower than among men workers. The reduction in women's wages was more drastic than the reduction in men's wages. Prior to the enactment of minima under the recovery act many factories showed pay rolls of $2 and less for women working 55 hours.

In Germany before the advent of the National Socialists this tendency to cut women's wages and substitute women for men was checked by the strength of trade unionism and by the legalized collective agreements, which included all workers, as well as by the effect of certain provisions in the unemployment insurance legislation. In Great Britain labor organizations were able to exert a measurable control of the situation but could not wholly prevent substitution. Thus the number of women in the manufacturing industries of Great Britain increased by 112,000 between 1923 and 1933, while the number of men decreased by 155,000. The application in the United States of minimum rates of wages, while it has improved the condition of women workers in certain industries, has in the mass production industries, untouched by trade union organization and undergoing rapid technological changes, resulted in some branches in the substitution of women for men.

The recent tendency in the United States toward a drastic reduction of hours, the abolition of child labor and the fixing of higher minimum wages has given an impetus to trade union organization among women and has speeded up the process of protective labor legislation. These tendencies may make for the breakdown of the barriers between men and women workers in industry and a clarification of the basic problem common to both.

ELSIE GLÜCK

See: WOMAN, POSITION IN SOCIETY; TRADE UNIONS; HOURS OF LABOR; MINIMUM WAGE; LABOR LEGISLATION AND LAW; MATERNITY WELFARE; DAY NURSERY; OCCUPATION; CLERICAL OCCUPATIONS; DOMESTIC SERVICE; HOMEWORK, INDUSTRIAL; WOMEN'S ORGANIZATIONS.

Consult: Bebel, August, *Die Frau und der Sozialismus* (new ed. Stuttgart 1910), tr. by M. L. Stern (New York 1910); Clark, Alice, *Working Life of Women in the Seventeenth Century*, London School of Economics and Political Science, Studies in Economics and Political Science, no. 56 (London 1919); Leroy-Beaulieu, Paul, *Le travail des femmes au XIXe siècle* (Paris 1888);Woytinsky, Wladimir, *Die Welt in Zahlen*, 7 vols. (Berlin 1925–28) vol. ii, ch. ii; International Labour Office, "Women's Work under Labour Law; a Survey of Protective Legislation," *Studies and Reports*, ser. I, no. 2 (Geneva 1932); "Wages of Male and Female Workers in Various Countries," and Thibert, Marguerite, "The Economic Depression and the Employment of Women" in *International Labour Review*, vol. xxiii (1931) 558–66, and vol. xxvii (1933) 443–70, 620–30; *Das Familienleben in der Gegenwart*, ed. by Alice Salomon and Marie Baum, Deutsche Akademie für soziale und pädagogische Frauenarbeit, Forschungen über "Bestand und Erschütterung der Familie in der Gegenwart," vol. i (Berlin 1930); "Resolutions Adopted by the First International Congress of Working Women, Washington, Oct. 28–Nov. 6, 1919" in National Women's Trade Union League of America, *Proceedings*, vol. viii (1922) 11–14; Breckinridge, S. P., *Women in the Twentieth Century* (New York 1933); Hutchins, Grace, *Women Who Work* (New York 1934); Abbott, Edith, *Women in Industry* (New York 1910); Henry, Alice, *Women and the Labor Movement* (New York 1923); Wolfson, Theresa, *The Woman Worker and the Trade Unions* (New York 1926); Branch, Mary S., *Women and Wealth; a Study of the Economic Status of American Women* (Chicago 1934); Van Kleeck, Mary, *Women in the Bookbinding Trade* (New York 1913), *Working Girls in Evening Schools* (New York 1914), and *A Seasonal Industry; a Study of the Millinery Trade in New York* (New York 1917); Odencrantz, Louise C., *Italian Women in Industry* (New York 1919); Hutchinson, Emilie J., *Women's Wages*, Columbia University, Studies in History, Economics and Public Law, no. 202 (New York 1919); United States, Women's Bureau, "The New Position of Women in American Industry," "Married Women in Industry," "Facts about Working Women; a Graphic Presentation Based on Census Statistics and Studies of the Women's Bureau," "The Effects of Labor Legislation on the Employment Opportunities of Women," "History of Labor Legislation for Women in Three States," "Chronological Development of Labor Legislation for Women in the United States," "Women in Industry; a Series of Papers to Aid Study Groups," "Wage-Earning Women and the Industrial Conditions of 1930," "Labor Laws for Women in the States and Territories," "Women Workers in the Third Year of the Depression,""The Occupational Progress of Women, 1910 to 1930" and "Women at Work," *Bulletin*, nos. 12, 38, 46, 65, 66, 91, 92, 98, 103, 104, and 115 (1920–33); United States Bureau of the Census, *Women in Gainful Occupations, 1870 to 1920*, Census Monographs, no. 9 (1929); United States, Bureau of Labor Statistics, "Summary of the Report on Conditions of Woman and Child Wage Earners in the United States," *Bulletin*, no. 175 (1916); Pinchbeck, Ivy, *Women Workers and the Industrial Revolution* (London 1930); Neff, Wanda F., *Victorian Working Women* (New York 1929); Hutchins, B. L., *Women in Modern Industry* (London 1915), and *Women in Industry after the War*, Social Reconstruction Pamphlets, no. 3 (London 1917); Webb, Beatrice, "Minority Report. Part I: The Relation between Men's and Women's Wages. Part II: The War Pledges of the Government with Regard to the Wages of Women Taking the Place of Men" in Great Britain, War Cabinet, Committee on Women in Industry, *Women in Industry*, 2 vols. Cmd. 135, 167 (1919) vol. i, p. 254–334; Brittain, Vera M., *Women's Work in Modern England* (London 1928); Great Britain, *A Study of the Factors Which Have Operated in the Past and Those Which Are Operating to Determine the Distribution of Women in Industry*, Cmd. 3508 (1930); Walter, H. R., *Munition Workers in England and France; a Summary of Reports Issued by the British Ministry of Munitions* (New York 1917); Simon, Helene, *Der Anteil der Frau an der deutschen Industrie* (Jena 1910); Lüders, Else, "The Effects of German Labour Legislation on Employment Possibilities for Women" in *International Labour Review*, vol. xx (1929) 385–96; Zahn-Harnack, Agnes von, *Die arbeitende Frau* (Breslau 1924); Braun, Adolph, *Die Arbeiterinnen und die Gewerkschaften* (2nd rev. ed. Berlin 1923); Milhaud, Caroline, *L'ouvrière en France* (Paris 1907); Theimer, Camilla, *Frauenarbeit in Österreich* (Vienna 1909); Gortvay, Georges, "La situation sociale et les conditions de travail de la femme active en Hongrie" in Société hongroise de statistique, *Journal*, vol. viii (1930) 97–149; Ragaz, Christine, *Die Frau in der schweizerischen Gewerkschaftsbewegung*, Soziale Organisationen der Gegenwart, n.s., vol. ii (Stuttgart 1933); Smith, Jessica, *Woman in Soviet Russia* (New York 1928); Freeman, Joseph, *The Soviet Worker* (New York 1932); Henry, P., "Some Aspects of the Labour Problem in China" in *International Labour Review*, vol. xv (1927) 24–50; Fang Fu-an, *Chinese Labour* (Shanghai 1931); United States, Bureau of Labor Statistics, "Labour Conditions of Women and Children in Japan," *Bulletin*, no. 558 (1931); Ayusawa, I. F., "The Employment of Women in Japanese Industry," and Das, R. K., "Woman Labour in India" in *International Labour Review*, vol. xix (1929) 193–204, 385–401, 503–21, and vol. xxiv (1931) 376–409, 536–62; Fischmann, Ada, *Die arbeitende Frau in Palästina* (Tel Aviv 1930); *The Plough Woman; Records of the Pioneer Women of Palestine*, ed. by R. Katzenelson-Rubashow, tr. by Maurice Samuel (New York 1932).

WOMEN'S ORGANIZATIONS. The organization of groups of women in Europe and America during the nineteenth and the early twentieth century, a phenomenon which served at once as a symbol of and a force in woman's growing emancipation, was not without precedent in pre-industrial society. Among certain primitive peoples women are known to have formed secret societies in emulation of similar organizations of men or in connection with the exercise of religious functions or the observance of rites of birth and adolescence. In Rome under the empire women held meetings for the purpose of discussing matters of court etiquette and dress and at one period formed an assembly or senate known as the Conventus Matronarum. Apart from scattered efforts, usually under ecclesiastical direction or auxiliary to existing institutions of the Christian church, there is little record of organized activity among women during the Middle Ages and the Renaissance. It is probable, however, that the salons of the seventeenth and eighteenth centuries contained to some extent the beginnings of what later became women's clubs; for while these assemblages were composed of both men and women, they were often initiated and dominated by the latter, who found in them an opportunity for social intercourse and intellectual discussion.

The widespread social changes ushered in by the industrial revolution gave impetus to the rapidly developing woman's movement and through it to an amazing variety of women's organizations. The changing nature of the family and the extension of leisure for large sections of the population made possible for the first time the emergence of women in the life of the community. In this process they became aware of certain handicaps—their lack of education, their political and social disabilities and their economic dependence—which contributed to or were chiefly responsible for their subordinate position. Out of an effort to overcome these conditions there arose both in Europe and in the United States organizations founded and directed by women; these ranged from purely literary or cultural clubs, usually under genteel influence, to societies established to encourage education, to agitate for woman suffrage or to promote social reform. The latter emphasis, concomitant with the prevailing humanitarianism of the nineteenth century, found its expression in charitable, philanthropic and missionary societies, often under the auspices of the church; in groups seeking to ameliorate the condition of the working class; in organizations particularly in Germany and Scandinavia dealing with delinquent girls and unmarried mothers; in associations to combat venereal disease and prostitution; and in the United States in women's clubs formed to promote education, temperance, pacifism and the abolition of slavery.

Women's organizations in England were especially characteristic of these varied emphases. The demand for education and through it for increased economic opportunity found expression in such organizations as the National Union for Improving the Education of Women and the Society for Promoting the Employment of Women, which endeavored to open new occupations to women other than the traditional needlework and teaching. The establishment in 1841 of a Governesses' Benevolent Institution led seven years later to the opening of Queen's College for Women, London, the first institution offering higher education to women. In 1872 a group of women formed the Girls' Public Day School Company, an important force in the shaping of the education of the English girls of the middle class. The extension of new educational opportunities to women and their increased participation in the reform movement were reciprocal in effect; for as their initiative and independence were developed, women expanded their field of activity and began to seek still further means of bettering their own and their children's position. The Matrimonial Causes Act of 1878, the Married Women's Property Act of 1882, the Guardianship of Infants Act of 1886—measures whose effect was to improve the personal and social status of women—were all to some extent the result of organized effort on the part of women themselves. The repeal of the Contagious Diseases acts in 1886 was brought about largely by women, who under the leadership of Josephine Butler formed the British, Continental and General Federation for the Abolition of Government Regulation of Vice, which became the Fédération Abolitioniste Internationale with affiliations in France, Italy and Switzerland. The Ladies' National Association for the Diffusion of Sanitary Knowledge, which during the middle of the nineteenth century distributed tracts on the importance of fresh air and other simple matters of hygiene, was the forerunner of numerous later developments in public health and sanitation. Concern for the less privileged members of society led middle class women to establish clubs affording means of recreation and self-improvement for working women. The Soho Club and Home for Working Girls, opened in London in 1880, served as a model for several hundred similar societies during the next three decades.

The present day range of women's interests and the extent of their participation in the civic, social and economic life of the community are nowhere better reflected than in the United States, with its profusion of women's clubs and organizations. Their development, while distinctly a product of the late nineteenth and the early twentieth century, had its beginning in the sewing circles, "quilting bees" and informal social gatherings which in colonial and later pioneer days served as the sole diversion for women. Feminine preoccupation with religion and charity found early expression in such organizations as the Female Society for the Relief and Employment of the Poor established in 1798, the Boston Female Society for the Promotion and Diffusion of Christian Knowledge (1800), the Piqua, Ohio, Bible Society (1818) and in countless ladies' aid, Dorcas and missionary societies. Ultimately this religious interest was to give rise to the Women's Home Mission Board (1877) and the Young Women's Christian Association, organized locally in Boston in 1866 and nationally in 1906. Prior to the Civil War the abolition of slavery engaged the attention of women as it did of men, and numerous groups, such as the Philadelphia Female Anti-Slavery Society (1833), voiced their organized protest against the system. The Daughters of Temperance societies, which flourished during the 1840's, eventuated in the Woman's Christian Temperance Union, organized in 1874 for the purpose of abolishing legalized liquor, which attained international scope in 1883 with the establishment of the World's Woman's Christian Temperance Union largely through the efforts of Frances E. Willard.

Opposition to war was likewise a recurrent subject of concern and resulted in the formation of local women's peace societies in the mid-nineteenth century. It was not until the World War, however, that organization on a wide scale was effected. The members of the Women's Peace Party who attended the Hague convention in 1916 set up the United States section of the Women's International League for Peace and Freedom, which in 1930 numbered 10,000 members. Other associations working for peace and disarmament included the Women's Peace Society, the Women's Peace Union and the Conference on the Cause and Cure of War organized in 1923, an American affiliate in which 11 national women's organizations participate.

Culture and self-improvement were, however, the leading incentives to organization. The new leisure that had come to large groups of middle class women coupled with their increasing awareness of their intellectual deficiencies led them to form reading, poetry, library, art and literature circles in a collective quest for culture. The names of some of these organizations—Clio, Athenaeum, Wednesday Culture Club, Browning Circle, Ladies' Library Association—reflect their emphasis. Under the leadership of Sorosis, organized in New York in 1868, 61 such clubs banded together in 1889 to form the General Federation of Women's Clubs. At first only clubs organized for "literary, artistic or scientific culture" were admitted to the federation. But within a few years the increasing preoccupation of women with the social order led to a broadening of emphasis and a corresponding heterogeneity of membership. In the words of one commentator, "Village improvement associations were joined with Shakespeare clubs, and cemetery associations supplemented Monday afternoon societies." The trend toward public welfare became so pronounced that within a few years the federation had established departments of education, home economics, industrial conditions as affecting women and children, and civic improvement; and at its biennial conventions it endorsed a variety of subjects, ranging from forest conservation to sex education, from civil service reform to the abolition of child labor. The literary and cultural note remained uppermost in individual club programs, however, and the federation declined frequently to declare its position on important public questions, particularly those which involved any but a conservative approach. The popularity of the woman's club movement in the United States is apparent from the enormous growth of the federation: in 1928 it comprised 14,000 clubs with a total membership of nearly 3,000,000 women. No single development among middle class women in any other country has reached such astonishing proportions.

Another strikingly leisure class organization of women in the United States is the Association of Junior Leagues, which expanded from a single league formed in New York in 1901 to 109 leagues in 1930, including 1 in Hawaii, 3 in Canada and 1 in Mexico. The membership of the association, which was organized in 1921, consists of some 22,000 young débutantes in the larger cities, who offer their services in a voluntary capacity to social service institutions. They contribute financially toward the upkeep of numerous welfare projects and in a few cities they have established or maintained milk stations for babies, hospital libraries, day nurseries and clinics.

Secret societies and fraternal orders were organized toward the end of the nineteenth century, sometimes auxiliary to or in imitation of existing men's societies, as in the case of the Degree of Honor (1873), Order of the Eastern Star (1876) and Ladies of the Maccabees (1886). Patriotism and the commemoration of war service enlisted the support of American women through such organizations as the Woman's Relief Corps, established in 1883 as an auxiliary of the Grand Army of the Republic; Daughters of the American Revolution (1890); Colonial Dames of America (1891); and the United Daughters of the Confederacy (1894).

The extension of higher education to women is reflected in the development of numerous college organizations, such as sororities, which largely social and recreational in purpose banded together in 1891 to form the National Pan-Hellenic Association; and in the Association of Collegiate Alumnae (1882), which afterward became the American Association of University Women. The latter in 1931 comprised 551 branches with over 36,000 members in all parts of the country. An affiliate of the International Federation of University Women, it aims to further education generally and in particular to promote study and research among college alumnae. To this end it publishes a journal and provides a number of graduate fellowships.

The entrance of women into business and the professions has led to the organization of specialized groups based on occupational interests, such as the Medical Women's National Association (1915), the International Association of Policewomen (1915), the National Federation of Business and Professional Women's Clubs (1919) and numerous other groups, including nursing, home economics and teaching organizations.

Among the groups whose appeal is to racial or religious loyalty and those whose program centers in specialized educational, recreational or welfare work are the National Association of Colored Women, organized in 1896; the National Council of Catholic Women (1920); and the National Council of Jewish Women, the latter an outgrowth of the Parliament of Religions held in connection with the World's Fair in Chicago in 1893. Within recent years Jewish women have enlarged the scope of their activity to international efforts in behalf of the women and children of Palestine. Hadassah, the Women's Zionist Organization of America, founded in 1912, has been responsible for the promotion of health work, child care and education in Palestine.

From the first, woman suffrage served as an especially powerful fulcrum for feminine organization. Sporadic efforts, such as the women's political clubs which appeared in Paris during the French Revolution only to be suppressed by official decree in 1793, the demands of the English Chartists for political equality of the sexes and the work of the "female political associations" in the mid-nineteenth century, led eventually to national and international organizations launched by women for the purpose of securing the franchise. In England the National Society for Woman's Suffrage (1866), the militant group known as the Women's Social and Political Union (1903) and the National Union of Women's Suffrage Societies and in the United States the National American Woman Suffrage Association, representing the merger in 1890 of two earlier societies, won remarkable support and were to no small degree responsible for the ultimate granting of the franchise to women in both countries. Within recent years these organizations have reorganized and directed their efforts toward political education and citizenship training. In England the woman suffrage organization became the National Union of Societies for Equal Citizenship based upon the slogan, "After the Vote, the Education of the Woman Voter." Since 1929 it has pursued an intensive educational policy, one of its chief activities being the formation of Townswomen's Guilds for the improvement of conditions among urban women. By February, 1933, 150 of these guilds had been established, 22 of them in Scotland. In the United States the ratification of the Nineteenth, or woman suffrage, Amendment in 1919 led to the transformation of the woman suffrage organization into the National League of Women Voters, which has branches in 45 states, the District of Columbia and Hawaii with a total membership of approximately 100,000 and which sponsors courses in government and nonpartisan political education. A few years prior to the granting of suffrage the National Woman's Party was launched, an outgrowth of the Congressional Union for Woman Suffrage. This organization represents a politically left wing group whose objective is to secure for women absolute equality with men "under the law and in all human relationships." It is affiliated with the Equal Rights International organized in Geneva in 1930 to work for equality of women throughout the world. The International Alliance of Women for Suffrage and Equal Citizenship grew out of a series of international conferences held between the years 1888 and 1904, the first of which led also to the organization of the International Council of Women. The latter in 1928 included 34 affiliated councils in leading countries of the world.

In France, although woman suffrage was agitated for in the revolutions of 1830 and 1848 and through later organizations, such as the Ligue pour le Droit des Femmes (1880) and the Union Française pour le Suffrage des Femmes (1909), the demand for the franchise has not been of major concern, perhaps because the attention of French women has been centered on problems other than political equality. Through the Société de Protection Maternelle founded in 1856, the Société pour l'Enseignement Professionel des Femmes (1862) and the more recent Conseil National des Femmes Françaises efforts have been made to better the condition of French mothers and children and working women and to effect various social and religious reforms which appear to the French of greater importance than the vote. The conservatism with regard to the franchise is also to be explained in part by the predominance of the Catholic religion. Catholic women, however, while indifferent to suffrage, have worked steadily through their own Féminisme Chrétien and through general organizations to further education and child and maternity welfare. Following the World War the Association de la Mère et de l'Enfant was organized, a merger of several relief societies existing during the war.

Similarly in Germany early feminism concentrated its efforts on the removal of educational, social and economic rather than legal disabilities. Although charitable societies (*wohltätige Frauenvereine*) existed prior to 1850, the first association whose avowed purpose was the emancipation of women was the Allgemeiner Deutscher Frauenverein. Launched in 1865 by Luise Otto-Peters and Auguste Schmidt, this organization grew rapidly and became one of the most influential women's groups in the country. The Letteverein, a more conservative organization, was established in Berlin the next year to promote employment among women through vocational training and the opening of new occupations. The Bund Deutscher Frauenvereine grew out of the World's Congress of Representative Women held at Chicago in 1893 and attended by several German delegates. This organization, which in 1930 embraced over 6000 associations with a membership of nearly 1,000,000, eventually included suffrage in its program. Organizations of German women based solely upon a demand for the franchise included the Deutscher Verband für Frauenstimmrecht, the Deutsche Vereinigung für Frauenstimmrecht and the Deutscher Staatsbürgerinnen Verband, the last named a member until 1933 of the International Alliance of Women for Suffrage and Equal Citizenship. Among the numerous German women's organizations the most articulate if not the most effective was the Deutscher Bund für Mutterschutz und Sexualreform founded in 1905. Its object included the protection of unmarried mothers and their children, the combating of sex prejudice and the reform of the institution of marriage. The attack on legalized prostitution had its beginnings twenty-five years earlier when Frau Gertrud Guillaume-Schack organized the Deutscher Kulturbund. Finally, there were in Germany as in other countries numerous Catholic, Protestant and Jewish organizations of women sponsored by their respective religious bodies as well as women's auxiliaries or divisions organized by political parties, particularly after the extension of the franchise to women following the World War.

In the Scandinavian countries, in Austria, Holland and Switzerland women's organizations followed somewhat the same pattern as in England, France and Germany. Religious societies sprang up under the influence of the churches, feminist groups urged the promotion of women's rights, and reform organizations undertook the amelioration of social evils. In some cases new organizations were established in connection with or in emulation of similar masculine efforts; in others feminine initiative was resorted to in defiance of custom. A significant feature of organized activity among the women of most European countries was a class cleavage apparent almost from the beginning. A difference in point of view between middle and working class women early resolved itself into distinct approaches to the solution of social and industrial problems. In Germany, for example, where working class organizations were almost entirely socialist in emphasis, Frau Guillaume-Schack became interested in the women workers' movement and eventually espoused it to the exclusion of middle class women's organizations, in which she had formerly been active.

The decade following the World War witnessed in nearly every country an extension of women's organizations. In countries where until recent years woman's role had been a subordinate one a new upsurge of feminism, evidenced by the increase of women in the wage earning group and the opening to them of new educational opportunities, has resulted in their emergence into social and economic life and the consequent formation of organizations designed to further their own emancipation or to promote the welfare of the nation generally. Notable examples of this activity among women in Japan are the establishment of a Woman's Medical Association, a Young Women's Buddhist Association, the Women's Primary School Teachers' Association, the Woman's League for Political Rights and the government sponsored Japanese Young Women's Association as well as local branches of the International Council of Women, the World's Woman's Christian Temperance Union and the Young Women's Christian Association, the latter two of course largely the result of missionary enterprise. In Turkey the Woman's League founded in Istanbul in 1924 has been a vigorous supporter of woman's rights. Feminist agitation in South America finds expression in numerous women's organizations, conspicuous among which are the Unión Femenina de Chile and in Argentina the Sociedad de Beneficencia, the Centro Feminista, later the Asociación por Derechos de la Mujer, a recently organized woman's suffrage society, and a women's university association.

There are, however, two exceptions to this new development of women's organizations: Soviet Russia and Nazi Germany. In the case of the former the emphasis of the Soviet regime is upon joint organizations of men and women in which equality prevails. Nevertheless, although women's organizations have been considered superfluous, it has been found practicable under government auspices to encourage their formation to a limited extent in the eastern republics, where women's advancement has been slow. Furthermore under the direction of Zhenotdel, the women's section of the Communist party organized in 1919, a system prevails whereby women engaged in factory, domestic and agricultural work appoint representatives who meet regularly to discuss social and industrial problems. This institution of women delegates, numbering more than 1,000,000, is partially responsible for the successful functioning of the state's provision for the care of mothers and children. The women delegates are also active in promoting education and physical welfare among women through the opening of classes to stamp out illiteracy and the support given to crèches, kindergartens and playgrounds. In the case of Germany the Hitler government has had an adverse effect upon women's organizations. Many of them have been suppressed, while others have had their work disrupted through the removal of their leaders or the compulsion to redirect their program in conformity with National Socialist principles and under party domination.

It is difficult to evaluate women's organizations as a social force because of the diversity of their emphases and the differing milieus in which they function. Certainly the drive of the woman suffrage movement has borne testimony to the capacity of women for joint action. On the other hand, the club movement as exemplified by the General Federation of Women's Clubs has been charged with being dilettante and superficial in its approach, with dissipating its efforts and with promoting a popularized pseudo-culture. In past generations the literary club performed an undeniable educational service for a large body of women whose opportunities had been limited and whose cultural horizons were necessarily circumscribed. Today women's wider educational opportunities and their active participation in the community life of most western nations have led them to specialize, to organize increasingly upon the basis of their economic, professional and occupational interests. For this reason if for no other a movement like the General Federation of Women's Clubs with its heterogeneous appeal must necessarily diminish in importance even as an involuntary form of adult education. This decline will be due not so much to its own limitations as to a changing social and economic environment.

A more serious criticism of organized women's activity is that it fails to appeal to or to enlist the support of farm women. Attempts to meet this problem have been made in the United States through the establishment of women's divisions of the Grange and through the encouragement of farm women's clubs and bureaus sometimes under county or state auspices; in England and

Canada the Women's Institute movement represents a nation wide endeavor to improve conditions of rural life and in particular to promote education and social betterment among farm women.

Another indictment of women's organizations, especially in the United States, has of late been advanced by observers who claim that their preponderantly leisure class membership has served indirectly if not directly to block any attempt at economic or political realignment. The working class women's organizations have in a majority of countries been numerically weaker and less articulate in voicing their objectives, a situation which has been fostered by the paternalistic attitude of upper class women who seek through their more powerful organizations to secure certain benefits for the workers but to prevent any essential change in their status. Such critics usually cite the National Women's Trade Union League as an example. This organization, founded in 1903, from the first included in its membership not only women representatives of trade unions but leisure class women interested in educational and philanthropic activities for workers. Women members of the trade union movement in Europe hold that the American organization places a mistaken emphasis on a women's movement within the ranks of labor instead of on the working class as a whole. The organization of women, according to these critics, must be sought on an economic rather than on a sex basis, and a healthy balance will be reached only by the organization of women workers independently of middle or upper class sponsorship.

GLADYS MEYERAND

See: WOMAN, POSITION IN SOCIETY; WOMEN IN INDUSTRY; CLUBS; BOYS' AND GIRLS' CLUBS.

Consult: Lange, H., and Bäumer, G., *Handbuch der Frauenbewegung*, 5 vols. (Berlin 1901–12, vol. v 3rd ed.); Abensour, L., *Histoire générale du féminisme* (Paris 1921); Ronhaar, J. H., *Woman in Primitive Motherright Societies* (The Hague 1931) ch. xi; Briffault, R., *The Mothers*, 3 vols. (London 1927) vol. ii, p. 545–52; *The Woman Question in Europe*, ed. by Theodore Stanton (New York 1884); Schirmacher, K., *Die moderne Frauenbewegung* (2nd ed. Leipsic 1909), tr. by C. C. Eckhardt (New York 1912); Anthony, K., *Feminism in Germany and Scandinavia* (New York 1915), especially chs. i, iv, vii–viii; Plothow, A. S., *Die Begründerinnen der deutschen Frauenbewegung* (Leipsic 1907); Diers, M., *Die deutsche Frauenfrage* (Potsdam 1920); Puckett, H. W., *Germany's Women Go Forward* (New York 1930), especially ch. vii; Schwabach, E. E., *Die Revolutionierung der Frau* (Leipsic 1928); Brunauer, E. C., "The German Frauenfront" in American Association of University Women, *Journal*, vol. xxvii (1933–34) 131–37; Grinberg, S., *Historique du mouvement suffragiste depuis 1848* (Paris 1926); Thibert, Marguerite, *Le féminisme dans le socialisme français de 1830 à 1850* (Paris 1926); Slater, G., *The Growth of Modern England* (London 1932) p. 450, 552–75; Strachey, R., "*The Cause*"; *a Short History of the Women's Movement in Great Britain* (London 1928); Robertson-Scott, J. W., *The Story of the Women's Institute Movement in England and Wales and Scotland* (Idbury 1925); Webb, C., *The Woman with the Basket; the History of the Women's Co-operative Guild, 1883–1927* (Manchester 1927); Courtney, J. E., *Countrywomen in Council* (London 1933); Halle, F. W., *Die Frau in Sovietrussland* (Berlin 1932), tr. by Margaret M. Green (London 1933) p. 269–89, 378–93; Woody, T., *New Minds, New Men?* (New York 1932) p. 380–81, 388–95; Strozzi, A., "Feminism in Argentina" in Pan-American Union, *Bulletin*, vol. lxvi (1932) 565–67; Croly, J. C., *The History of the Woman's Club Movement in America* (New York 1898); *History of Woman Suffrage*, ed. by E. C. Stanton, S. B. Anthony, M. J. Gage, and I. H. Harper, 6 vols. (Rochester and New York 1881–1922), especially vols. iv–vi; Bruce, H. A., *Woman in the Making of America* (Boston 1912) ch. vii; Woody, Thomas, *A History of Women's Education in the United States*, 2 vols. (New York 1929) vol. ii, ch. ix; Willard, F. E., *Woman and Temperance* (Hartford, Conn. 1883); United States, Department of Agriculture, "Women's Rural Organizations," by A. M. Evans, *Bulletin*, no. 719 (1918); Atkeson, Mary M., *The Woman on the Farm* (New York 1924) p. 238–50, 289–98; Irwin, I. H., *The Story of the Woman's Party* (New York 1921); Wolfson, T., *The Woman Worker and the Trade Unions* (New York 1926); Fisher, Dorothy Canfield, *Why Stop Learning?* (New York 1927) p. 79–115; President's Research Committee on Social Trends, *Recent Social Trends in the United States*, 2 vols. (New York 1933) vol. i, p. 744–50; Irwin, I. H., *Angels and Amazons; a Hundred Years of American Women* (New York 1933) p. 60–79, 181–237; Breckinridge, S. P., *Women in the Twentieth Century* (New York 1933) pt. i, and pt. iii, ch. xvii; Winn, Mary D., *Adam's Rib* (New York 1931) ch. ix; Richardson, A. S., "Is the Women's Club Dying?" in *Harper's Magazine*, vol. clix (1929) 605–12; Cobb, Margaret, "Three Million Women" in *American Mercury*, vol. xix (1930) 319–25; Hutchins, Grace, *Women Who Work* (New York 1934) p. 256–60. For statistics regarding women's organizations see publications or yearbooks of individual clubs; also *Dictionary of Secret and Other Societies*, compiled by Arthur Preuss (St. Louis 1924); *The Official Catholic Year Book*, vol. i (New York 1928) p. 670–81; *American Jewish Year Book*, published in Philadelphia and New York since 1899, especially Kohut, Rebekah, "Jewish Women's Organization in the United States," vol. xxxiii (1931–32) 165–201; *Social Work Year Book*, published in New York since 1930; *Women of Today*, ed. by Ida C. Clarke (New York 1928).

WOOD INDUSTRIES. Wood can be adapted to innumerable uses. It burns readily and lends itself easily to working and shaping. Since the original forest covered much of the land area of the earth, wood, even in primitive times, was abundant for local use. Trees can be cut and utilized with relatively simple tools. Moreover many kinds of wood float and keep well in water; hence long before other materials of similar weight and bulk could be so transported, logs could be moved considerable distances. Wood was thus of paramount importance to peoples living in a precapitalistic economy; they were dependent upon it for warmth, the preparation of food and all the industrial processes in which the application of fire produced heat is necessary, for shelter in many regions and for most tools, implements, weapons and machines, including the means of transportation on both water and land. What steel and coal, petroleum and copper and all the other machine and energy materials are to modern machine civilization, wood alone was to the peoples of vegetable civilization; indeed this is still the case wherever surface and near surface minerals are unavailable.

The versatility of wood in general is increased by the wide range of properties of different kinds of wood, from soft to hard and from light to dark. Soft woods furnish the bulk of the pulpwood and sawmill products; hard woods are most widely used either for fuel—in the tropics often in the form of charcoal—or for special purposes, such as the making of veneer, furniture and railroad ties. In general hard woods are produced mainly in the warmer regions and soft woods in the colder. It is estimated that of the 7,500,000,000 acres of forest land nearly half lie in the tropical mixed hard wood belts, which as yet contribute relatively little to human needs. Normal world timber consumption has been estimated at 56,000,000,000 cubic feet, less than half of which is saw timber. Coniferous, or soft, wood forests furnish about three fourths of all the saw timber and about half of all the timber cut. Wood continues to be the most important domestic fuel; and even in the United States, the largest producer of coal, petroleum and natural gas in the world, probably not much less than a third of all the materials derived from the forest goes to fire making.

Against the advantages of versatility, general availability and renewability of wood must be balanced a number of disadvantages. Most woods cannot be worked with the precision possible in the case of many metals. Moreover despite progress in its production and uses wood still guards many of the secrets which block its scientific utilization. It is still common, although unscientific and primitive, to view a tree merely as the source of a given number of board feet of lumber. Most wood industries are still in the form utility stage. This condition materially limits the economic value of timber, especially as a construction material. The history of shipbuilding illustrates this point clearly. For centuries this industry was seriously handicapped, in fact condemned to virtual stagnation, because of the natural limitations of tree growth. The size of a ship bears a definite relationship to the size of the rudder; its dimensions in turn depend upon the size and strength of the stern post. As this vital part had to be one single piece of wood, its dimensions were definitely determined by the height and thickness of tree trunks whose wood could be used. The making of masts met with similar checks. When iron and later steel were substituted for wood in ship construction, the rapid increase in ship dimensions unequivocally proclaimed the emancipation of shipbuilding from the limitations of the organic nature of wood. An almost identical story is told in the records of the construction of bridges, towers and other buildings. Such defects, however, are being overcome. During the World War Germany, a large producer of iron and steel, required most metals for military purposes. Engineers turned to the forests for structural materials; knowing that the wood joint is the weakest part of a wooden structure, they developed a metal connector, substituting an iron ring inserted into the two wooden members for the customary single bolted joint. This modest supplementation of wood with iron and the careful application of scientific principles marked the most important development in wood construction in a century. Wooden structures as high as 500 feet have since been erected. The present limitations of wood probably are no more permanent than those which affected the use of coal and petroleum a few decades ago. Sawing boards is like skimming crude oil. When wood "refineries" rival petroleum refineries in size and scientific perfection, the organic limitations of wood will appear far less real than today. The rapid growth of the pulp, paper and rayon industries strongly supports this assumption.

It is not true that all replacement of wood in the United States by substitutes is attributable to some inherent weakness of wood. In specific instances of course wood no longer meets modern requirements. Thus charcoal is too soft for use in modern blast furnaces; it cannot support the enormous burdens of monster stacks. Wood is less fire resisting than most metals; unless science overcomes this weakness, the use of wood in large cities may have to be curtailed. Wood does not lend itself to skyscraper construction. As a source of heat it cannot compete with coal, oil or gas in densely populated areas and in treeless prairies. Yet many of the markets in which wood had to yield to substitutes were lost because wood was becoming more expensive in relation to the general price levels, while its more scientifically prepared substitutes—metals, cement, brick compositions, synthetic substances and the like—were becoming cheaper.

This relative increase in the price of wood is not brought about by immutable laws of nature but is largely the result of preventable causes. The worship of scarcity as the chief source of profit, so typical of money economy, came close to wrecking by competition the timber and lumber industries of the United States. For increased scarcity can bring prosperity through higher prices only if the demand can withstand the pressure of price. One cause of the rise in prices was the progressive depletion of timber stands, accompanied by an even more rapid recession of the forest from the lumber market. This increased haulage charges. Whereas in 1914 the average rail haul from the mill to the market was estimated to be 360 miles, by 1924 it had risen to 725 miles. Lumber from the Pacific northwest must travel an average of 2600 miles to the consuming markets of the east, while the water haul from the northwest to points on the Atlantic coast averages about 6000 miles. Today no large lumber consuming area may be called an exclusive marketing territory of any one species or region. More or less all producing areas compete in all consuming areas. Prices therefore tended to rise partly in response to increased scarcity, partly because longer hauls raised the cost to the consumers.

This situation may be changed, however, by certain new developments in the United States. The objective of the reforestation program provided for in the Code of Fair Competition for the Lumber and Timber Products Industries adopted in 1933 is to place the forest areas of the United States eventually on a sustained yield basis. This may prove of great significance for the timber supply of the world, its continuity, size, availability and cheapness. In the absence of human interference timber supply is relatively static in the sense that forests tend to reach a state of equilibrium in which the forces of decay and growth are held in balance. But use is greater than replacement. The net annual increment of the world's forests is 18,000,000,000 cubic feet, or 32 percent less than consumption; and the deficit is due mainly to the destructive methods in vogue in the United States. Thus the American program of reforestation, by assuring a continuous and cheap supply of timber, may mark one of the most vital differences between wood and the minerals in the expansion of use. For there is no reason inherent in the nature of wood why even an industrialized country like the United States should not continue to absorb quantities of lumber far in excess of present consumption, provided the price relationship between wood and minerals and other substitutes is not thrown out of gear by forest devastation and excessive freight charges. Cheap timber from 500,000,000 acres of forests under sustained yield management scientifically adapted to constantly changing market requirements should prove a powerful factor in economic progress and social development.

The amount of wood available in a given market or to a given group of users depends on the extent and yield of accessible forests. A forest can either be treated as a mine and used up by reckless exploitation or it can be regarded as a crop, the annual increment being viewed as the interest on the forest principal, or capital. The actual amounts shipped to a given market depend primarily on the market price. This in turn depends on the size and nature of the demand, in particular its elasticity and intensity. Supply is conditioned by the uses to which wood is put. Only large trees can furnish large boards, while much smaller trees can supply pulpwood, posts or firewood. The number of trees big enough to yield the larger sizes of saw products is much smaller than that of trees which can yield fence posts, lathes, pulpwood and the like. In addition the supply of some species is much more limited than that of others. Broadly speaking, technological progress has rendered the demand for timber less exacting or more catholic. Formerly markets for building lumber could insist on larger sizes. Now construction technique has been adjusted so as to make smaller sizes perform the duty formerly expected only from larger sizes. The pulp industry is learning to manufacture very creditable newsprint from a constantly enlarging variety of soft woods. The utilization of by-products and waste products is progressing.

This change in the nature of the demand reacts on the supply in several ways. When New

England was first exploited for white pine, there was no market for the spruce. Only the white pine was removed, while no particular care was taken of the spruce stands. Later the pulp industry became interested in the spruce and removed that separately. Where both lumber and pulp industries are well developed, similar mixed forests of white pine and spruce or Douglas fir and hemlock can be exploited much more economically. Perhaps the most beneficial effect of the shift to smaller sizes results from the reduction of the time required to bring forests to maturity, i.e. when the trees are ready to be cut. In the southeast of the United States it is not unlikely that large quantities of pine wood can be grown in rotations covering only ten to twenty years, and perhaps still shorter rotations. Such a reduction in the rotation period is of paramount importance everywhere, but particularly in countries in which most forests are privately owned. A larger number of private owners may be prepared to enter the business of timber growing under sustained yield management when the production cycle is limited to ten or fifteen years than under conditions of much longer growing periods.

Plywood furnishes another example of the effect of the discovery of new uses for wood upon supply. The increased use of plywood has invested with economic value a number of tree varieties which formerly were considered worthless, and at the same time it affects the timber market in still another way. It has been estimated that from the point of view of strength a sheet of plywood 3 millimeters thick is equivalent to a plank 12 millimeters thick, indicating a saving of 75 percent. Thus not only does the fabrication of plywood permit the substitution of timber formerly considered unmarketable, but it makes possible the accomplishment of certain purposes with an absolute reduction of timber requirements.

The shift to newer products tends in addition to conserve timber and still further to retard the exploitation of forests. So long as practically all timbers removed from the forest were used either for fuel purposes or for saw timber, practically none of the wood could be re-used. In the case of paper, however, and even more so of fiber board the re-use coefficient is very high, approximately 90 percent of the fiber board manufactured in the United States being made from old fiber board. Some years ago it was estimated that 25 percent of the paper output was manufactured from old paper.

While wood was indispensable in most precapitalist civilizations, it assumed unique political significance after the fifteenth century, when modern European nations emerged from feudalism and began to engage in almost ceaseless warfare over *mare clausum*, colonies and naval supremacy. Down to the battle of Hampton Roads, which spelled the doom of the wooden battleship, timber for both the navy and the merchant marine was the key commodity, the strategic material of national power and wealth. Nations coveted timber resources with the same eagerness which today marks their unbridled interest in the oil fields of the world. Trade—and this came to mean chiefly water borne or sea borne trade—was the magic wand that opened the road to national wealth and power; and trade depended almost exclusively on an adequate timber supply with which ships could be built. For this reason all the great colonial powers down to the middle of the nineteenth century were deeply concerned with the timber problem. It shaped or warped both colonial and commercial policy. The Dutch and Portuguese showed keen interest in the excellent ship timber of tropical regions of Asia, while the Spanish turned mainly to the Caribbean region for similar purposes. Timber supply was one of the guiding purposes of English colonial policy in North America.

During the sixteenth century England imported increasing amounts of lumber and naval stores first from Norway and later from the Baltic regions. Dependence on the Baltic for timber and naval stores was a cause of constant worry to English statesmen who dreaded the day when Elsinore (Helsingör), "the turnstile of the Baltic," would come under the control of a strong hostile naval power. Some of the statesmen saw in the New World an opportunity for relief. Even the Elizabethan voyagers were not wholly absorbed in the quest for precious metals; they had an eye for timber also. Toward the end of the reign of Queen Elizabeth depletion of oak stands began to alarm the Royal Navy, and increasing attention was given to the development of the American lumber trade. At first interest was concentrated on masts and naval stores, but later ever greater amounts of timber were imported. Many of the troubles of the English navy could have been solved by a vigorous development of a trade in southern live oak, cypress, long leaf pine and other varieties of southern timber. But since southern planters found the trade in tobacco and other money crops more profitable, the lumber trade was concentrated almost entirely in New England and only later in the regions farther west and south. Trade began as early as 1609. Up to 1688 the colonists were allowed to develop the lumber industry with little interference from England except for temporary encouragements. Soon after the accession of William and Mary, there began a period of regulation which is to be explained partly by the increasing timber requirements of England as a result of continuous warfare and partly by the spread of mercantilist theories. The mercantilist idea of imperial self-sufficiency encouraged colonial specialization. The West Indies were viewed as sugar colonies, the south was considered a tobacco colony and New England was looked upon as a source of timber. It was hoped that a profitable lumber industry would divert the colonies from such competitive industries as the manufacture of woolen goods. New England had several disadvantages as compared with other sources of English timber supply. The distance from the market was 3000 miles, while Riga was 1000 and Norway only 600 miles away. Freight charges were two to three times as high for the Atlantic voyage, while labor costs were as much as six times as great. Moreover the New England trade was not so well organized as the Baltic trade, and serious prejudices on the part of English shipbuilders had to be overcome. Later England took increasing interest in the south as a source of naval stores, turpentine and resin.

Early lumbering operations in the United States served local needs, met the requirements of nearby shipyards and made material contributions to the export trade. Moreover in many cases they rendered profitable the settlers' chief task—the clearing of land for agricultural purposes. As a large scale commercial venture lumbering began in earnest when improved transportation facilities opened up the great plains for settlement. To people these prairies entire forests were moved hundreds of miles. Farther west the development of the mining industry furnished a similar impetus to gigantic lumber operations both manufacturing and commercial. Closely associated as they were with frontier developments, they could scarcely be expected to continue unabated after the frontiers were closed. The zenith of lumber production was reached in 1906, when 46,000,000,000 feet b.m. were cut and when the per capita consumption reached the extraordinary figure of 525 feet b.m. (Table 1). Then a rather rapid decline set in,

TABLE I

LUMBER PRODUCTION, EXPORTS AND IMPORTS AND CONSUMPTION, UNITED STATES
(In 1,000,000,000 feet b.m.)

YEAR	TOTAL PRODUCTION	EXPORTS	IMPORTS	VISIBLE CONSUMPTION*	APPROXIMATE PER CAPITA CONSUMPTION (in feet b.m.)
1809	0.4	—	—	0.4	55
1849	5.4	—	—	5.4	235
1879	18.1	0.3	0.4	18.2	365
1899	35.1	1.0	0.4	34.5	460
1910	44.5	2.7	1.1	43.0	465
1920	35.0	1.9	1.4	34.5	325
1930	26.1	2.4	1.2	25.7	210
1932	10.2	1.3	0.4	12.0	96

*Changes in lumber stocks are taken into account.
Source: United States, Department of Agriculture, *Yearbook of Agriculture 1933* (1933) p. 748. Figures for 1932 from United States, Bureau of the Census, *Wood Industries: 1932* (mimeographed, 1933).

which was interrupted only during the building boom following 1921 and the period of industrial prosperity ending in 1929. Within a quarter of a century production dropped from 46,000,000,000 feet b.m. to 26,100,000,000 in 1929 and barely 10,000,000,000 feet b.m. in 1932. At the same time the geographical center of lumber operations in the course of a century shifted from New England and other northeastern states first to the lake states, later to the south and finally to the Pacific coast. In 1927 western production, with 42.6 percent of the total lumber output, exceeded that of the south, which supplied 41.7 percent. This westward movement is attributable to progressive denudation of large areas of the southern forest belt. A new crop of trees is, however, maturing in the south.

In spite of this decline in quantity of output the lumber and timber products industries continue to rank among the largest American industries. The lumber industry leads in number of workers employed in the states of Washington, Louisiana, Mississippi, Oregon, Idaho, Arkansas, Florida, Virginia, Alabama, California and Texas. In Washington and Oregon over 50 percent of all wage earners are employed in the lumber industry, around 75 percent in Mississippi, 40 percent in Louisiana, 33 percent in Florida and 25 percent in Alabama. While in Scandinavia and Canada the pulp mills have become the largest consumers of timber, the largest consumer in the United States is still the lumber industry. Of an average yearly lumber output of 54,600,000,000 feet from 1919 to 1926, 38,000,000,000 feet were used for lumber, 7,000,000,000 for fuel wood and only 1,500,000,000 for pulpwood. American lumber companies are, however, showing constantly greater interest in pulp and paper mills. The total number of wage earners in the lumber industry rose from 150,100 in 1869 to 419,100 in 1929, and the value of output increased from $210,400,000 to $1,273,500,000 (Table II). A striking trend

TABLE II

GROWTH OF LUMBER AND TIMBER INDUSTRY, UNITED STATES, 1869–1931*

YEAR	NUMBER OF ESTABLISH-MENTS (in 1000)	NUMBER OF WAGE EARNERS (in 1000)	WAGES PAID (in $1,000,000)	VALUE OF PRODUCT (in $1,000,000)
1869	25.8	150.1	40.1	210.4
1879	25.8	148.3	31.9	233.6
1889	22.6	444.0	117.3	437.9
1899	23.0	413.3	148.0	555.0
1909	33.1	547.2	238.9	753.4
1919	26.1	480.9	489.4	1387.5
1929	12.9	419.1	421.6	1273.5
1931	5.0	196.6	155.9	443.6

*Including logging camps, merchant sawmills, planing mills operated in conjunction with sawmills, veneer mills and cooperage stock mills.

Source: United States, Bureau of the Census, Thirteenth Census 1910, *Manufactures 1909*, vol. x (1913) p. 489, Fourteenth Census 1920, *Manufactures 1919*, vol. x (1923) p. 422, and Census of Manufactures 1931, *Principal Lumber Industries* (1933) p. 3.

toward concentration is revealed in the decline of establishments from 25,800 in 1869 to 12,900 in 1929 and to only 5000 in 1931.

Concentration of production is matched by concentration in the ownership of lumber lands. Approximately 80 percent of the productive timberland in the United States is privately owned. The history of the largest timber holdings is closely linked up with the federal policy of land settlement and with the federal and state policy of encouraging railroad construction. Land laws allegedly passed for the purpose of helping veterans, pioneer settlers, schools and railroad construction companies actually enabled a small number of speculators to acquire some of the largest and richest timber tracts. As a result over half of the privately owned commercial timber of this country is said to be held by not more than 250 companies. The concentration of ownership is particularly pronounced in the west, where the Weyerhaeuser interests were reported in 1929 to control 50 percent of all the timber in Idaho, 37 percent in western Washington and 15 percent in Oregon. The Northern Pacific Railroad and the Anaconda Copper interests are reported to control considerably more than half of all the timber of Montana. In California 23 companies, partly interlocked, are credited with approximately 60 percent of the redwood area, while two companies are said to own over 40 percent of the entire pine region. The pulpwood stands of New England are also rather closely held, the International Paper and Power Company being the largest owner.

A leading authority on American forestry estimated the distribution of ownership of the forest lands of the United States in 1925 as follows: big private interests 220,000,000 acres, or 45.6 percent; smaller private owners and small farm lots 150,000,000 acres, or 33.1 percent, of which the smaller owners accounted for 6.1 percent; federal government 89,000,000 acres, or 18.9 percent; states 10,500,000 acres, or 2.3 percent; municipalities and counties 700,000 acres, or .1 percent.

The small owners, who control about a third of the forest land, frequently prove a disturbing element in periods of falling farm prices, although they are normally unimportant as producers of lumber. At such times the small farmer is apt to turn to his wood lot as a last resort in the fight against famine, and distress sales of lumber are likely to demoralize the lumber market. There is another important contact with agriculture. In some lumbering regions the same labor alternates with farming and lumbering. Through this interchangeability the extremely low wages which have prevailed for some time in American agriculture tend to depress wage rates in the logging camps and lumber mills. The agricultural crisis is adding rapidly to the American forest area as a result of the abandonment of farm land.

In addition to the gradual shrinkage of the market and the slow but steady westward movement of the industry a third important trend in the lumber industry of the United States is the growing importance of large scale producers. In 1929, 753 mills out of a total of nearly 20,000 each cut over 10,000,000 feet annually and together produced almost two thirds of the total output. This development is associated in part with the westward movement, for most of the large operators are concentrated in the western states. During periods of depression many small mills are forced out. Most of the large lumber corporations are integrated concerns, controlling most or all of the stages of production from the tree to the retail yard which sells the finished product. In other words, such a company not only owns timber stands, operates its own logging camps, its own sawmills and auxiliary manufacturing plants, such as planing mills, veneer and plywood plants, mills making by-products, such as lathes, pulpwood or even paper mills, produces its own electric power for both mills and camps and in some cases even many logging railroad and steamship facilities but also controls the marketing through both wholesale and retail outlets. Where, as in the south, smaller mills still play a part, they are organized into sales units; thus 80 percent of them in Alabama are financed by wholesale lumber dealers.

Concentration in large production units has been accompanied by progressive mechanization. Oxen, sleds, snow and ice roads or greased skidways have virtually disappeared, although traces of these once universal devices may still be found in isolated places. Where the sled remains, it is apt to be a huge affair drawn by tractors, which are used also in logging operations, making selective logging economically possible. Most logging operations, however, rely upon elaborate systems of powerful donkey engines and cables. This method has been rapidly modernized. Whereas formerly cables controlled by donkey engines dragged logs over the ground, they now convey them through the air, the cables running over pulley blocks attached to the tips of masts as high as 150 feet. These cables may run as far as 1000 to 1500 feet through the woods. The logs are pulled along these cables, one end bouncing on and off the ground, over gulleys, ravines and canyons. At the loading point power loaders operated by steam or electricity pick up the logs and pile them neatly on the trucks of the logging railroad. There are 30,000 miles of these railroads; some are 100 miles long and have many feeder branches. Giant sawmills cut 1,000,000 board feet of lumber a day. Such mills, which compare with automobile plants in mechanical efficiency, usually have planing, veneer, plywood, specialty and by-product mills attached to them. The conveyor system is universally used, and from the moment the log is dragged from the storage pond until the kiln dried product is loaded on the railway or motor truck electrical machinery performs the sawing, planing, trimming, edging, dressing and handling. At every possible point labor saving devices are installed, constantly reducing the share of labor in the product. In the storage yard mechanical stackers are used.

In spite of this definite drift toward a reduced number of large producers, competition in the lumber industry continues to be keen. Up to the adoption of the Code of Fair Competition the powerful National Lumber Manufacturers Association, one of the strongest trade associations in the United States, for a time supported by the quasi-public Timber Conservation Board, tried to bring order into the chaos caused by cutthroat competition, price cutting, chronically overstocked markets, increasing excess capacity and other factors. These conditions were to some extent inevitable because of the progressive contraction of the lumber market; they were in part concomitants of the geographical shifts and in part attributable to factors lying altogether outside the control of the industry. Frequently lumber mills have felt the need of enlarging operations in order to escape excessive taxation on their timber holdings.

While the United States continues to export considerable amounts of lumber and new timber, it also imports considerable quantities, especially from Canada. In 1931 total exports of wood and manufactures of wood (exclusive of pulp and paper) amounted to $70,600,000, while imports were valued at $32,700,000. If pulp and paper are included, a large excess of imports over exports is evident. Intercontinental trade in lumber is relatively small; in 1925–27 it amounted to only 1,650,000 standards (a standard is approximately 2000 board feet). The total world trade is much larger (Table III).

World softwood production is estimated at roughly 64,000,000,000 board feet, of which North America produces 35,000,000,000 feet and Europe 23,000,000,000. As a producer of wood Europe has several geographical advantages over North America. It does not stretch quite so far north and does not turn its broadest side to the Arctic. Its land mass is more broken up, so that not only are the forests more accessible but the favorable conditions of maritime climate can reach a larger percentage of the land area. Moreover the Gulf Stream creates temperature conditions favorable to timber growth. Europe has no counterpart to the magnificent timber stands of the American Pacific coast, but as a continent it has an added cultural advantage. In most countries possessing important forest areas sustained yield management has been in force for some time and is being further strengthened by more recent legislative acts. In few parts of Europe is serious overcutting going on, while in the United States in years of normal business activity timber depletion has been as much as four or five times as great as the natural growth. While Europe has few remaining virgin forest areas, except in Soviet Russia, there are large areas, especially in Finland and Scandinavia, which contain overmature second growth. This means that the timber cut probably can be increased materially without violation of the prin-

TABLE III

EXPORT AND IMPORT TRADE IN SAWED SOFTWOOD, SELECTED COUNTRIES AND YEARS
(In 1000 standards)

COUNTRY	\multicolumn{5}{c}{EXPORTS}	COUNTRY	\multicolumn{5}{c}{IMPORTS}
	1880	1900	1913	1929	1931*		1880	1900	1913	1929	1931*
Norway	265	235	153	120	65	England	1248	2010	2010	1770	1472
Sweden	633	1007	1046	1123	701	France	91	402	506	500	500
Finland	307	467	781	1101	735	Italy	110	180	340	409	300
Russia†	200	640	1455	811	950	Holland	65	155	265	513	391
Poland				296	252	Germany	170	555	626	588	219
Latvia				195	125	Belgium	71	179	250	293	223
Austria†	192	445	543	378	250	United States‡	260	307	551	715	350
Rumania†	32	21	65	431	270						
United States	149	805	1359	1363	683						
Canada	772	853	751	959	450						

*Preliminary data.
†Pre-war boundaries for pre-war figures.
‡Fiscal years.

Source: Streyffert, Thorsten, in Svenska Handelsbanken, *Index* (March, 1932) p. 68, 70–71.

ciple of sustained yield management. In many parts of northern Europe logging methods closely resemble those of eastern Canada and those which used to be practised in the northeastern part of the United States. Most of the sawmills of Sweden and Finland are located at the mouths of rivers, which permits marked concentration of raw materials and hence encourages large scale mill operations. In addition most of the Scandinavian and Finnish lumber companies also own and operate pulp and paper mills and are thus able to exploit their timber resources in an unusually rational and stable manner.

Lumber can be produced relatively cheaply in northern Europe. Most of Europe's timber regions possess a farming population sufficiently dense to furnish an ample labor supply during the winter months. Moreover topographical and climatic conditions are exceptionally favorable, so that sled logging on snow and ice roads and river driving can be carried on fairly cheaply. The Soviet Union does not fully share these advantages. The timber regions bordering the White Sea, especially the eastern forest sections, are only thinly populated, and labor has to be brought in from the outside. These regions are more distant from the most important consuming centers of western and central Europe than are Scandinavia and Finland. The U.S.S.R. is making systematic efforts to improve these conditions by such measures as the construction of the new Baltic-White Sea Canal, designed to open up the vast timberlands of Karelia for the domestic market of Leningrad and the export markets of central and western Europe and to increase the accessibility of northern Russian and Siberian forests via the Ob and Yenisei rivers and even the Lena. There is being developed a permanent labor force specializing in lumber production. The Soviet Union has the important advantage, however, of enormous stands of untouched virgin forests, which justify the belief that it will become the largest lumber producer in the world. The entire lumber and timber industry is organized into three commissariats, which are under the immediate control of the Supreme Economic Council. The first Five-Year Plan has resulted in a substantial increase in the production and exportation of lumber. Total timber output rose from 41,100,000 cubic meters in 1927 to 98,500,000 cubic meters in 1932 (1 cubic meter equals 35.314 cubic feet and 1 cubic foot equals 12 feet b.m.). Exports increased from 10,400,000,000 cubic meters in 1913, fell to 1,000,000,000 in 1922 and rose to 12,200,000,000 in 1930. The rather sudden and unexpected increase of Soviet exports disturbed the lumber industries of Scandinavia and Finland, with whose exports Soviet lumber is primarily competing. Stumpage values declined materially in these European countries. A number of international conferences have met during recent years under the auspices of the League of Nations with a view to bringing about through international agreements a more stable condition in the European export trade in lumber. The American industry was also seriously disturbed by imports of lumber and pulpwood from the Soviet Union. The so-called convict or forced labor clause of the Smoot-Hawley tariff law passed in 1930 temporarily held up

Russian imports, which were released, however, when investigation failed to substantiate charges of "forced labor."

Labor conditions in American wood industries are in general about the same as in other highly industrial countries. Labor in the forest industry may be divided into two classes: loggers and other workers living in camps and working in the woods and sawyers and other workers employed in sawmills, shingle mills, planing mills and the like. Timber workers are necessarily isolated from population centers. Logging camps moreover are usually temporary establishments, especially in regions not under sustained yield management. Under such circumstances it is difficult, to say the least, to create satisfactory living conditions for loggers. In many cases, however, actual conditions have been possibly worse than such circumstances would seem to warrant.

More or less all logging workers must possess alertness and strength and at times even ingenuity; a proportion of forest workers is classed as semiskilled. Employment is exceptionally unstable. Seasonal variations of employment are important; in the Pacific northwest, for example, men are generally laid off during July and August because dry weather renders the fire hazard excessive, while in mid-winter men are laid off because in very rugged country heavy snowfall hinders logging operations. In other parts of the north temperate zone, such as Canada and Scandinavia, operations depend on ice and snow cover for the movement of logs to streams, although this contingency is being overcome in part by the use of modern transportation devices. The decline of lumber production in the United States rendered employment of labor in logging camps increasingly unstable. This was aggravated by increased mechanization through the use of labor saving and labor speeding devices, to which especially the larger lumber companies have been resorting for some time past in an effort to maximize profits in the face of a shrinking market and fierce competition. Seasonal, normal and cyclical unemployment are increasing. In addition, when forests are not placed under sustained yield management but are "devastated," the basic wood industries are forever on the move. In a migratory industry labor must likewise be highly mobile. Marked geographical shifts may be accomplished when large operators transfer their activity from one area to another. In some cases the capital transfer directly involves labor transfer; in others regional labor shifts are accomplished through the instrumentality of nationally organized labor employment agencies. Thus a considerable number of loggers must be classed as casual or migratory labor. The attitudes of labor employed in logging camps are necessarily affected by this condition.

Labor conditions vary in a vast country like the United States, whose economic and social life is characterized by sharp regional differences. The migratory labor of the lake states, working in wheat fields in the summer and shifting to lumbering in the winter, is necessarily different from the casual labor of the Pacific coast region. Moreover not all loggers can be considered as casual or migratory labor. Even in the Pacific northwest there are the so-called home guard camps, in which simple family and community life exists. Schools on wheels are provided and housing facilities are adapted to the needs of family life. Again, there are the "stump ranchers," who try to turn cut over land into farms and supplement their meager earnings from farming by working in the neighboring logging camps. The diversity of labor conditions is accentuated further by racial heterogeneity. In the south Negro labor predominates, especially in the larger commercial enterprises. In the cypress swamps Negro and Mexican labor is employed almost exclusively. Negroes also furnish most of the labor in the construction camps of the southeast. Many laborers now in the Pacific coast belt have come from the Carolinas and from the lumber camps of Michigan, Minnesota and Wisconsin. Among the foreign born workers Scandinavians and Finns are predominant in the northwest, being preferred in heavy operations, such as falling, bucking and rigging. On construction crews Mexicans, Italians, Croats, Bulgarians and other south European laborers are hired.

In the larger sawmills labor conditions are quite different from those in the logging camps and even from those in the smaller sawmills. Standardization and mechanization have reduced a majority of lumber mill workers to mere machine tenders. Steady nerves rather than skill have become the most important qualification. Many of the larger mills have erected mill towns. In some cases the company in an effort to reduce the costly labor turnover provides schools, churches, parks and playgrounds.

Hours of labor and wages also vary greatly. The census reports that head band sawyers are paid two to four times as much as the average logger, and in the same organization different hours of labor may apply to white and colored labor. Before the war the 10-hour day or the 60-hour week was the rule and up to the adoption of the code for the lumber industry the 8-hour day law had not yet been generally in force. Average wages per year in the lumber and timber products industries amounted to $436, $1017, $1006 and $793 in 1909, 1919, 1929 and 1931 respectively. These figures represent about 15 to 30 percent less than the average annual wage income of all industrial wage earners. Furthermore in any appraisal of wages the high accident rate in several important branches of the lumber and timber industries, notably in logging and in shingle mills, must be taken into account.

Generally speaking, the labor in the forest products industries is poorly organized. Efforts on the part of workers have not been lacking. Indeed some of the greatest labor battles have been fought in lumber towns. Labor organizations are notoriously absent in the south, one of the most important forest regions of the nation. Nor have labor organizations been able to make much headway in California. It is in the Pacific northwest, at present the largest producer, that organizers have been most active and have occasionally met with temporary success. The shingle weavers of the west coast were among the first to attempt union organization. The success of their unions, loosely attached to the American Federation of Labor, has been sporadic. Affiliation with the Industrial Workers of the World was strenuously opposed by the employers and by government agencies. To many of the loggers and affiliated trades, including at times sawmill workers, some of the ideas behind the I.W.W. appealed more strongly than those of the more conservative A. F. of L. One of the outstanding events in the history of the I.W.W. in the Pacific northwest was the unsuccessful Portland, Oregon, strike of 1907, which involved 2000 to 3000 workers. Another was the bloody encounter at Everett, Washington, in which a number of workers were shot and a larger number drowned. During 1917 the I.W.W. was particularly active. Employers answered with "criminal syndicalism" laws in several western states. In the summer of that year strikes were being called by organizers of both the A.F. of L. and the I.W.W., and there was constant warfare between employers and employees. Another bloody encounter between members of the I.W.W. and employers occurred in Centralia, Washington. It resulted in several deaths, lynching and heavy court sentences for several of the workers, who are still in prison despite a substantial movement for their release. The I.W.W. was very active in the south during the years 1910 and 1913, causing a number of battles between labor and company forces. In 1919 the A. F. of L. undertook a vigorous organizational campaign in the south, at one time trying to barter recognition of white unions for the promise not to organize colored labor. The offer was refused by the employers.

When the United States entered the World War there was organized in the Pacific northwest under the leadership of army officers the Loyal Legion of Loggers and Lumbermen, known as the Four L. This was not a labor union but an organization of both employers and employees, whose original objectives were to expedite spruce production for airplane manufacture and to combat radicalism among the forest workers, especially those affiliated with the I.W.W. During the war the organization was quasi-military in character. In 1918 it was reorganized but it gradually lost its hold on both labor and employers. The I.W.W. has likewise been in a state of general disintegration. Labor conditions in the lumber industry may be said to have been scarcely less chaotic than the general economic conditions of the industry itself.

Many of the troubles which at present beset the lumber industry are not dissimilar to those found in other extractive industries. In general it may be said that simple exploitation of natural resources no longer fits readily into the modern economic set up, characterized as it is by the increasing importance of machine equipment and science. Just as the refinery is probably the strategic medium through which order can be brought into the chaotic conditions prevailing in the crude oil industry, so the hope for the timber and lumber industries may likewise lie in the penetration of the industry by organization and science. This involves the general problem of larger economic and social organization; it also points to the specific need for the lumber industry to discard the traditional view that a tree represents a given number of board feet of lumber in favor of the new conception that a tree represents a constantly growing variety of products.

ERICH W. ZIMMERMANN

See: CONSTRUCTION INDUSTRY; SHIPBUILDING; PULP AND PAPER INDUSTRY; FURNITURE; FORESTS; FLOODS AND FLOOD CONTROL; CONSERVATION; NATURAL RE-

SOURCES; PUBLIC DOMAIN; MIGRATORY LABOR; TRADE UNIONS.

Consult: Hiley, W. E., *The Economics of Forestry* (Oxford 1930); Defebaugh, J. E., *History of the Lumber Industry of America*, 2 vols. (Chicago 1906–07); Brown, N. C., *The American Lumber Industry* (New York 1923); Albion, R. G., *Forests and Sea Power*, Harvard Economic Studies, vol. xxix (Cambridge, Mass. 1926); United States, Bureau of Corporations, *The Lumber Industry*, 3 vols. (1913–14); United States, Forest Service, *Timber Depletion, Lumber Prices, Lumber Exports, and Concentration of Timber Ownership* (1920), and *A National Plan for American Forests*, Senate Document no. 12, 2 vols. (1933); Blodgett, J. W., "The Lumber Industry" in *A Century of Industrial Progress*, ed. by F. W. Wile (New York 1928) ch. ii; Bryant, R. C., "The Lumber Industry" in *Representative Industries in the United States*, ed. by H. T. Warshow (New York 1928) ch. xiv; Kellogg, R. S., *The Lumber Industry* (New York 1914); Knappen, T. M., and others, "The Lumber Industry" in *The Development of American Industries; Their Economic Significance*, ed. by J. G. Glover and W. E. Cornell (New York 1932) ch. v; Kellogg, R. S., *Lumber and Its Uses* (4th ed. New York 1931); Hayward, Phillips A., *Wood, Lumber and Timbers* (New York 1930); Streyffert, T., "The World's Staples, Sawn Woodgoods" in Svenska Handelsbanken, *Index*, vol. vii (1932) 62–85; Glesinger, Egon, *Le bois en Europe* (Paris 1932), with a foreword by J. Viner; United States, Tariff Commission, "Report to the President on Lumber," *Reports*, 2nd ser., no. 32 (1932), and *Report to the President upon the Red Cedar Shingle Industry in the United States and Canada* (1927); United States, National Committee on Wood Utilization, *Wood Construction* (New York 1929); Oxholm, A. H., "Fabricated Structural Timber" in *Manufacturers Record*, vol. cii, no. vi (June, 1933) 18–19; Bureau of Railway Economics, *Lumber; Commodity Prices in Their Relation to Transportation Costs*, Bulletin no. 30 (Washington 1928); League of Nations, Economic Organisation, *The Timber Problem; Its International Aspects*, Publications, 1932 II.B.6 (Geneva 1932); International Institute of Agriculture, *Enquête internationale sur la standardisation de la mesure du bois et sur les différents modes de vente du bois* (Rome 1930); Buchholz, E., *Die Wald- und Holzwirtschaft Sowjet-Russlands*, Berichte über Landwirtschaft, supplement no. 56 (Berlin 1932); Dietrich, B. F. A., "European Forests and Their Utilization" in *Economic Geography*, vol. iv (1928) 140–58; Oxholm, A., "Forest Resources, Lumber Industry, and Lumber Export Trade of Finland," "Forest Resources, Lumber Industry and Lumber Export Trade of Norway," and "Swedish Forests, Lumber Industry and Lumber Export Trade," United States, Bureau of Foreign and Domestic Commerce, *Special Agents Series*, nos. 207, 211, 195 (1921–22); Streyffert, T., "Softwood Resources of Europe" in *Economic Geography*, vol. x (1934) 1–13; Cameron, J., *The Development of Governmental Forest Control in the United States*, Institute for Government Research, Studies in Administration, no. 19 (Baltimore 1928); Compton, W., "Out of the Woods: a Program of Industrial Reforestation" in *Forum and Century*, vol. xci (1934) 118–21; United States, Department of Agriculture, "American Forests and Forest Products," *Statistical Bulletin*, no. 21 (1928); Mumford, Lewis, *Technics and Civilization* (New York 1934); Knappen, T. M., "An Old Industry Meets a New Age" in *Southern Lumberman*, vol. cxlv, no. 1822 (March 1, 1932) 25–26, 43–45; United States, Bureau of Labor Statistics, "Industrial Relations in the West Coast Lumber Industry," by C. R. Howd, *Bulletin*, no. 349 (1924); Todes, Charlotte, *Labor and Lumber* (New York 1931); Mittelman, E. B., "The Loyal Legion of Loggers and Lumbermen" in *Journal of Political Economy*, vol. xxxi (1923) 313–41; Parker, C. H., *The Casual Laborer and Other Essays* (New York 1920).

WOODHULL, VICTORIA CLAFLIN (1838–1927), American feminist. Born in Ohio of ignorant, shiftless parents, Victoria Claflin was married at the age of fifteen and led a roving existence as a mental healer and spiritualist medium. In 1869 with her sister, Tennessee Claflin (1845–1923), she opened a brokerage house in New York and shortly afterward launched *Woodhull and Claflin's Weekly* (1870–76) as an organ for their views on finance, labor problems, woman suffrage and sex freedom. In 1871 Mrs. Woodhull's testimony in behalf of woman suffrage before a congressional committee won her the approbation of the woman suffrage leaders who had previously shared in the popular condemnation of her as an adventuress and an exponent of "free love." The association, however, was short lived; and Mrs. Woodhull's attempt to organize disaffected radicals into a new political party under the aegis of the National Woman Suffrage Association was promptly suppressed by Susan B. Anthony.

In 1872 Victoria Woodhull, who with her sister had dominated one of the two American sections of the International Working Men's Association, was nominated for the presidency of the United States by the Victoria League, and her nomination was supported by the Equal Rights party. Late that year, ostensibly on behalf of her campaign for a single standard of morality, she published the details of the Beecher-Tilton scandal in the *Weekly*. Both sisters were imprisoned on charges of obscenity, of which, however, they were acquitted. In London Mrs. Woodhull's lecture on *The Human Body, the Temple of God*, delivered in 1877, attracted considerable attention and led to a series of pamphlets on stirpiculture, the current term for eugenics, and to publication of the *Humanitarian* (1892–1901).

A woman of beauty and charm, with undoubted intellectual and oratorical gifts, Mrs. Woodhull was apparently sincere in her desire to further the emancipation of women and to break down sex prudery. She was one of the first women publicly to agitate for birth control, liberal divorce laws and rational sex education, but her efforts were often vitiated by her craving for publicity and by the curious admixture of crude spiritualism in her ideas. In later life as the wife of a London banker, John Biddulph Martin, she repudiated her early radicalism and with her sister, who had become Lady Cook, established a reputation in England chiefly for philanthropic benefactions.

GLADYS MEYERAND

Consult: Sachs, Emanie, "*The Terrible Siren*," *Victoria Woodhull (1838–1927)* (New York 1928); Oliver, L., *The Great Sensation* (Chicago 1873); Broun, H., and Leech, M., *Anthony Comstock* (New York 1927) ch. vii–viii.

WOODS, ROBERT ARCHEY (1865–1925), American social worker. Woods was born in Pittsburgh and educated at Amherst College and at Andover Theological Seminary. Profoundly interested in the newly developing social settlement movement, he went to London in 1890 and spent six months at Toynbee Hall. Upon his return to the United States he was invited to deliver at Andover a series of lectures on social and humanitarian forces in England, later published as *English Social Movements* (New York 1891). At the same time he was made head of Andover House (now South End House), the first settlement in Boston, a position which he retained until his death.

American settlements at the time were still in a formative stage and Woods' work had considerable influence upon their development. From the first he conceived of the settlement not as an extension of organized charity or of popular education but as an agency for the rehabilitation of home and neighborhood life, disorganized by modern industrialism. His emphasis was on the neighborhood as a unit for social action, and under his leadership the residents and associates of South End House undertook two local community studies—*The City Wilderness* (Boston 1898) and *Americans in Process* (Boston 1902)—which established the value of the survey as a settlement project and served as models for similar investigations in other parts of the country. Several years later Woods took an active part in the Pittsburgh Survey, an elaborate inquiry into the social and industrial conditions of that city.

Woods was one of the chief promoters of the National Federation of Settlements, formed in 1911, and under its auspices he collaborated with Albert J. Kennedy in the publication of *The Handbook of Settlements* (New York 1911), *Young Working Girls* (New York 1913) and *The Settlement Horizon* (New York 1922), the last a comprehensive discussion of the origin and scope of the settlement movement. *The Neighborhood in Nation-Building* (Boston 1923), a collection of Woods' addresses and monographs, reflects not only his identification with settlement and social work but his participation in various civic and municipal reforms including the solution of such problems as housing, unemployment, the saloon and commercialized vice.

GLADYS MEYERAND

Consult: Woods, Eleanor H., *Robert A. Woods, Champion of Democracy* (Boston 1929); Brooks, J. G., "Robert Archey Woods" in *Survey*, vol. liii (1924–25) 732–34.

WOOL. As a staple textile raw material wool ranked first in many non-tropical areas until it was superseded by cotton during the nineteenth century. The hair of goats and camels was sufficiently long or wavy to allow fibers to be spun; the wool of sheep was curly, elastic and covered with serrations, and the fibers therefore clung together when carded or spun, and felted when subjected to heat, moisture and pressure, thus producing a firm strong cloth. Wools with long fiber could be combed, spun to produce a fine yarn and then woven into a smooth fabric which reflected the light and was strong without being heavy. Thus the properties of different animal fibers and the various processes permitted the production of a wide range of wares, from carpets, flannel, felt, knitted garments or Harris tweed, to broadcloth, light worsteds, alpaca and mohair.

The domestication of sheep and goats and the use of wool go back at least to the neolithic age. In Egypt and Mesopotamia woolen fabrics were less important than those made of flax grown locally or of silk and cotton from the East; but in the Levant of the Old Testament and the Greece of Homer and Hesiod the shepherd was a prominent figure and work in wool was part of the routine of rich and poor households alike. Phoenicians made and sold woolen cloth, and in classical and Hellenistic Greece the sheep and goats of Attica, Arcadia, Asia Minor, north Africa and the Levant supplied material for an industry which won its greatest repute in Miletus. In the Roman Empire wool production was important nearly everywhere, but especially on the Apennines, in Gaul, Spain and north Africa, and spread to England and the Rhine frontier. Agricultural writers such as Vergil and Columella were interested in improving sheep breeds, and Spanish merino wool already enjoyed the reputation it was to retain from that time onward. Cloth making was carried on in cottage and villa, but manufacture for sale was highly organized in such towns as Parma, Padua and Cahors, while guilds of fullers, woolworkers and purple dyers existed in the leading textile centers.

In the Middle Ages sheep were part of the manorial economy and manufacture for use continued in cottage, castle and convent; in the gynaeceum of the great feudal household women made cloth and clothes, in some monasteries and nunneries there was great division of labor and a high degree of skill, and the wandering weaver who worked up the yarn spun by a cottage group was not uncommon. The revival of cloth production for market stimulated sheep farming greatly; for the leading textile centers, especially in the Low Countries and Italy, could not obtain all the wool they needed or wool of the desired quality from local farmers. They therefore bought raw cloth made in the wool producing lands and dyed, finished and sold it; or they bought raw wool abroad to supplement the native supply. Both methods called for elaborate organization, much capital and use of credit; both increased the production of wool, especially in Spain and the British Isles. Small farmers contributed a little to this international wool trade; but the large monastic producers played the greater part, especially the Cistercians, whose settlements were usually in remote places fit only for pastoral occupation. Huge flocks of sheep were developed; the English abbey at Meaux had 11,000 in 1270–80 and the abbey at Crowland, relying on its outlying manors for the production of its food, ran its central estate as a vast sheep farm, selling over 9000 fleeces in 1309–10. In Scotland the church was a great flockmaster, and in Spain large ecclesiastical and lay estates on the central and northern plateaus were given over to cattle and sheep. Italian, Flemish and French merchants bought this wool; the Italians went to the fairs of Barcelona, Valencia, Winchester or Stourbridge; but they also penetrated into the producing regions, set up warehouses, purchased the whole clip of an estate, signed contracts to take the yield of the next ten to thirteen years at a fixed price and often paid in advance, since they had capital and the growers had little. They lent money to kings and lords, collected papal revenues and remitted interest or other payments to Italy in the form of wool. Cloth produced in their own workshops and finishing plants and in the homes of artisans to whom they "put out" the material was so good that it found markets even in the Levant. There were few commodities which Asia cared to buy from Europe, but the inferior quality of most Asiatic wool gave Europe an advantage in wool textiles, because of the fine wool of Spain and England and the high technical skill of Italy.

The wool trade was an integral aspect of Italian and Flemish capitalism and of English and Spanish agrarian, commercial and political history. Florence was dominated by capitalists who mingled trade in cloth and wool with banking; Flanders bought foreign wool and sold cloth as far afield as the Mediterranean and the Volga. In the wool producing lands export brought the country into the circle of interregional trade, stimulated a money economy, fostered the rise of a native merchant class and developed the use of credit. Almost every purchase and sale by the Celys, the big English wool merchants of the late fifteenth century, was on credit. Producers and landowners began to commercialize sheep farming; and if wool offered a greater net return than did other commodities, they strove to discourage agriculture, to regain control of land held by tenants, to enclose commons and by other devices to secure the largest possible grazing area. In England this movement was resisted ineffectually by the Tudor state. In Spain it was encouraged, when Ferdinand and Isabella and their successors granted valuable privileges to the Mesta, the guild or association of sheep ranchers. These grants gave the Mesta flocks the right to feed on commons on their migration between summer and winter pastures; they checked enclosure for arable cultivation and handed to sheepmen large tracts taken from the evicted Moriscos. At one time the Mesta flocks numbered over 3,000,000; their owners dominated agrarian policy until the middle of the eighteenth century.

With the development of mercantilism wool and woolens became more subject than ever to political control. While England exported wool, the English kings regarded the trade as a source of revenue and a weapon of diplomacy. Henry III, Edward III and Henry VII prohibited exports to the Low Countries in order to compel the rulers of that textile area to support England in war or to grant some demand. Taxation of wool exports was an easy method of collecting revenue, especially if all the trade was directed through one town. With the growth of economic nationalism from the fifteenth to the seventeenth century most governments sought to foster their own textile industries, to build up the production of the necessary raw material, to prevent native wool from being exported to feed rival looms, to induce foreign craftsmen to enter, while forbidding native workers to take their skill abroad. In Spain Isabella taxed wool exports and cloth imports for protective reasons, and many of her successors followed the same policy; such efforts had little result, however, and wool remained a staple Spanish export. In England, where cloth making grew in importance from the fourteenth century and where the wool trade with Flanders and Italy declined heavily, wool exports were forbidden in 1647 and from 1660 to 1825. The motive for this action was the desire to prevent France, the Low Countries and Germany from obtaining the English long wools needed for making worsted cloths and thus to compel them to buy worsteds from England. The act of 1660 was frequently amended in efforts to check smuggling; but illicit export continued, although the chief beneficiary of the policy was probably the Spanish wool producer and exporter. Every European ruler of the seventeenth and eighteenth centuries sought to foster a local wool textile industry, and imperial powers tried to prevent their colonists from making cloth and thereby becoming independent of the parent land. The English ban in 1698 on Irish exports of wool and cloth to foreign countries ruined a textile industry which was competing with English rivals and crushed a group of sheep farmers who were supplying French and other continental weavers with raw material. The American colonies were the best single customers for English woolens and on the eve of the revolution absorbed approximately one fifth of the total cloth export; as a result the growth of colonial manufactures was discouraged.

In the second half of the eighteenth century revolutionary changes took place in the supply of wool and in the demand for it. Mechanical improvements came more slowly to wool than to cotton manufacture. The older industry was more conservative; its supply of raw material could not easily or rapidly be increased; the market was not capable of such great extension as was that for cotton goods; and the wool fiber did not lend itself to the strain imposed by fast moving machines, especially power looms. For these reasons some processes were not mechanized until 1850 and hand weaving of woolens remained important until after 1870. The sewing machine and the ready made garment industry, which developed after 1850, augmented the demand for woolens of the cheaper grades to clothe a rapidly growing population whose standard of living was steadily rising; wars, such as the Crimean and Franco-Prussian, and periods of rapid pioneer settlement in the cooler parts of the New World caused the woolen industry to boom; improved combing methods allowed the use of short fibered wool in worsted making; while the combination of wool with cotton or silk and the reclaiming of wool from rags gave opportunities for the production of new or cheaper kinds of cloth.

These developments, which came first in Great Britain, then in Belgium, France, Germany, the United States, Japan, Austria-Hungary and Italy, created demands for wool which none of these countries could satisfy from the local supply. England leaned more and more heavily during the eighteenth century on Spain, Ireland, Denmark and Germany. Its own wool supply suffered in quality as sheep breeders, led by Bakewell, improved the mutton producing properties of sheep and found greater profit in mutton than in wool. The new breeds carried fleeces which were coarser than those of old and were therefore less suitable for making fine cloth. Relief came by the transfer of merinos from Spain to other parts of Europe during the last third of the eighteenth century and by their transplantation to the New World in the nineteenth. Between 1765 and 1800 the rulers of England, France, Saxony, Russia and Hungary obtained, by gift or purchase, merinos from the Spanish court and the influence of these animal emigrants was enormous. In France the Rambouillet merino revolutionized French sheep raising and was exported to Australia, south Africa, Germany and North America. In Germany the ruler of Saxony led in the development of merino flocks, and soon Saxon wool was so much better than that of Spain that Spanish breeders imported Saxon rams. Pomerania, Bohemia, Hanover, Mecklenburg, Silesia, Austria and Prussia followed the Saxon lead; governments and banks controlled and financed production and sale, and wool fairs were established at Stettin, Breslau, Berlin, Hamburg, Leipsic, Dresden, Magdeburg, Frankfort, Vienna, Prague and elsewhere. After 1815 the industry grew rapidly; between 1816 and 1837 the number of sheep in Prussia rose from 8,000,000 to 17,000,000 and that of merinos from 700,000 to 3,600,000. Buyers from all parts of western Europe and even from North America flocked to the fairs or the sheep ranches to buy wool. Exports to Great Britain alone rose from 5,000,000 pounds in 1820 to 32,000,000 pounds in the boom year 1836; during the same period Spanish exports dwindled, and Germany became the chief European producer, especially of fine wool.

In England vigorous but futile attempts were made by George III to popularize the merino. In Australia, New Zealand, south Africa, South America and parts of North America, however, the merino found a welcome home; it dispelled the woolworker's fear of a fine wool famine and knit the Antipodes into the European economic system. When the quality of their wool had been brought up to the necessary standard and shipping freight rates had fallen low enough, these regions could more than hold their own in competition with the wools of Europe. By 1810 Australia's flocks had been put upon a firm basis with merinos obtained by Macarthur from south Africa or from the royal flock at Kew, and specimens of fine Australian wool had won praise from English manufacturers. In 1813 the crossing of the Blue Mountains revealed the existence of vast pastures, and in 1818 Australian wool was sold in London at a price nearly double that of the best Spanish product. From 1821 sales by auction at Garroway's Coffee House in London became more frequent—in 1829 over twenty were held in London or Liverpool; in 1830 nearly 2,000,000 pounds of Australian wool reached England, and in 1850 Australia supplied 39,000,000 pounds of the total British imports of 74,000,000 pounds. South Africa and South America each sent over 5,000,000 pounds in that year, and thus two thirds of the total British import came from below the equator. Spain sent only 400,000 pounds and Germany only 9,000,000 pounds, for its clip was now going chiefly to local and continental manufacturers. Fifty years later the British imports were ten times as large as in 1850, and the south temperate areas supplied 80 percent of them. But in addition these areas were feeding looms in France, Germany, Belgium, the United States, Italy and Japan. One half the Australian wool exported between 1901 and 1906 went to non-British consumers; since 1918 the proportion has grown to two thirds, while South American wool has for long been shipped chiefly to continental European ports. The gradual dispersion of wool textile manufactures has widened the market open to the Antipodean producers, and in the period 1925-29 France had the largest net imports of wool, while Japan was buying five times as much as in 1909-13. In 1860 Australia had 20,000,000 sheep; and by 1891 it had over 106,000,000, which yielded 640,000,000 pounds of wool. But a decade of drought, bankruptcy, low prices and other misfortunes cut the flocks down to 54,000,000 in 1902 and not until 1928-29 was the peak of 1891 regained. The yield of wool mounted to 9 pounds per fleece, and Australia now produces about one quarter of the world's total wool supply, nearly two fifths of all the wool made into cloth and half the fine merino wool clip.

When refrigeration made possible the long distance transportation of mutton, New Zealand was the first country to desert the merino in order to rear sheep which would produce food as well as wool; it developed breeds which matured quickly and carried a large medium fibered fleece. In Australia small ranchers and farmers turned to crossbreds wherever soil and climate were suitable, and by 1919-20 one third of the Australian clip was crossbred. In Argentina, where merinos once predominated, crossbreds supplied three fourths of the clip by 1900, and in Uruguay sheep raised for the dual purpose gradually displaced the fine wool breed. Only in South Africa has there been any important attempt in recent years to expand fine wool production; large areas of that country are, like those in Australia, fit only for merinos, but near the coast the production of lamb for export is growing in importance. Meanwhile the merino has passed out of favor in the northern hemisphere, in Spain, Germany and in North America, except in Ohio and on the western ranges. The Soviet republics, which have about 100,000,000 sheep, mostly of inferior quality, have since 1927 imported merinos and are improving the breed of their flocks; but this will probably add to the supply of medium rather than of fine wool. Manufacturers of fine cloths have for the last fifty years been subject periodically to concern over the future of their wool supply. They have had to take what the grower decided would yield him the greatest profit and have paid high prices for the comparatively small fine wool supply which was forthcoming. The competition of rayon since 1920 has led to the establishment of the International Wool Textile Organisation, an association of wool producers, dealers and manufacturers, to foster research and collaboration in solving the problems of wool supply.

Wool producers in the United States never had any important export market; but they had a big local demand from a rapidly growing population, the larger part of which lived in cool latitudes. To the scrub sheep of colonial days improved breeds, both English and Spanish, were added soon after the revolution. While small farmers generally kept a few sheep as part of a mixed farming plan, some areas, such as the hilly regions of Vermont and Ohio and the arid or mountainous lands of the far west, were used chiefly or solely as sheep ranches. By 1885 the far west had more sheep than the rest of the country, and the abundance of open range country allowed flocks to be shepherded from winter lowlands to mountain and forest summer pastures. With the gradual filling up of the pastoral ranges, the competition of cattle, the multiplication of small grazing homesteads, the growth of irrigation and the development of dry farming the character of the western industry changed. Ranchers bought land to assure access to ranges, cultivated fodder crops to replace the food formerly obtained from the winter pastures, which had now been homesteaded, sank wells, made reservoirs, fenced paddocks and generally made the industry more intensive, involving, however, a greater outlay of fixed capital. Meanwhile the smaller ranchers, like farmers elsewhere in the middle west and east, kept crossbreds to serve a double market, and the merino retained its hold only on the far western ranges and the Ohio hills. The product has been protected, except for brief periods, by a substantial tariff on wool and woolens; but prior to 1920 wool production was losing ground, as land became too valuable to be used as pasture or as other products gave better returns. During the last ten years, however, wool production has increased rapidly, since the corn belt and the western states have diversified their farming and the return from cattle has fallen. In 1931 almost the entire demand for wool for cloth was met by the local clip, and the imports were chiefly inferior wools for making carpets.

Wool marketing methods are conditioned by the size of the producing unit and by the great varieties of quality in each fleece, flock, area and breed. There may be eight to ten grades of wool in each fleece; wools from the same breed vary from ranch to ranch, and climatic or soil conditions cause variations. About 2000 recognized kinds of wool are known to the trade; when the British government bought the Australian clip in 1916 the appraisers divided it into 847 classes. Such a commodity cannot be sold by grade in anonymous bulk but must be seen or sampled by the buyer; it cannot have a futures market, except after it has been sorted and in part processed; tops of combed wool for the worsted industry have standards, according to which they are sold by combers and bought by worsted spinners. There are small futures markets for tops at Antwerp, Roubaix and New York; and some observers of the wool trade, such as Shimmin, feel that the industry "should develop a system of marketing which will enable the carrying of wool until it is wanted by a process of hedging against specialized risk-bearers in the open market." Meanwhile raw wool is sold in almost every conceivable way. At one extreme the small producer sells privately or at some fair to a local dealer or to the agent of some large merchant or manufacturer; the dealer sorts the wool gathered from many sources and sells it to manufacturers in lots and qualities to suit their particular needs. Sometimes the dealer buys before the sheep are shorn and finances the grower. At the other extreme the large rancher sorts his wool and sends bales, each containing a special grade, to be sold by sample at public auction. The auction sale developed in London during the first half of the nineteenth century, fed by Spanish, German and Australian consignments. But after 1843 wool brokers in Melbourne and Sydney began to hold auctions in those towns, and now 90 percent of the Australian clip is sold there at auction sales attended by buyers from all the wool working countries.

If he is to gain the benefits of the auction sale, the small producer must have his wool sorted and his small portions of each quality pooled with those of other farmers, thus making lots large enough to be put under the hammer. Sorting and pooling are sometimes done by the broker before auction; on one occasion in 1927, 339 bales of sorted and pooled wool were made up from fleeces sent by 329 owners. Cooperation offers the same service by establishing sorting and bulking facilities and by providing the advantages usually associated with cooperative societies. Since the World War cooperation has made some progress among small growers, but in Australia and New Zealand the efficient service and the powerful grip of the private wool broker make that progress difficult. In France, Scotland, England and South Africa there are cooperative societies. In the United States, where for a century wool was sold unsorted to local wool dealers or to the representatives of Boston, Philadelphia or New York firms, Ohio farmers cooperated in 1918, and other states in the west and east soon followed. Members signed contracts binding themselves to hand over their entire clip for a number of years to be stored, graded and sold by the association. By 1925, 91 wool and mohair cooperative groups had been formed, and in 1929 the National Wool Marketing Corporation was set up on the initiative of the Federal Farm Board to centralize the sale of wool collected by the regional cooperatives. The aim of this corporation was to develop orderly marketing, reduce selling costs, stabilize prices, abolish competition between rival sellers and increase the net return on wool. Its stock was held in 1930 by 26 cooperatives; it could borrow from the Federal Farm Board, the Federal Intermediate Credit Bank and commercial banks and make advances both before shearing and upon delivery of the clip, thus avoiding the charge that the grower could get cash only very slowly when wool was sold through cooperatives. In 1930 it handled 30 percent of the wool clip and 90 percent of the mohair yield; but it could do nothing to mitigate the severe decline in the average price received by producers—from 31 cents per pound in 1929 to 9 cents in 1932—and its advances proved too large.

For decades the wool market has operated under the difficulties caused by the lack of reasonably accurate statistics concerning the probable offerings of wool. Data supplied by growers, fellmongers and others were defective, and serious understatements were made by many landholders. After the World War the joint council of Australian growers and brokers issued figures; but when those of 1927 were found to be far too low, buyers complained of deception and market rigging and refused to take subsequent estimates seriously. The International Chamber of Commerce is attempting to have the collection of statistics properly organized, and government statisticians are striving to reduce the margin of error; but the defects are still serious.

The modern wool manufacturer has not relied solely on the new wool clip. The use of cotton warps began about 1834; in 1836 Sir Titus Salt first became interested in alpaca, and soon he gave the worsted industry a raw material which had been spun and woven by the Andeans before the discovery of America. Mohair was put to use, and the Angora goat which supplied it was transferred to south Africa and North America. Mixtures of wool and silk entered the hosiery and worsted trades. Finally, wool reclaimed from rags, tailors' clippings and old garments began to be used about 1813, at a time when wool was very scarce and costly. The shoddy industry grew rapidly on the basis of this raw material, and rags were collected in all parts of the world. In 1905 British manufacturers used 180,000,000 pounds of rags and 450,000,000 pounds of new wool; but in 1931–32 new wool was so cheap that even the best clippings from tailors' shops were virtually unsalable.

In the early years of the present century students of the wool trade feared that the quantity of raw material would soon be inadequate. The rapid expansion of wool production of the nineteenth century had overreached itself, as the heavy fall in prices revealed; the great pastoral expanses had been filled up, the area devoted to sheep was being reduced by the extension of agriculture and cattle breeding, fine wool was being sacrificed to permit the production of lamb, and a period of drought, low prices and spreading pests had reduced the yield of wool in important countries. The European output in 1920 was little greater than that of sixty years before; Argentina had fewer sheep in 1924 than in 1875; Uruguay's sheep had fallen in number to half the peak figure; in the United States, Great Britain and Canada the wool clip was declining or at a standstill; and it was believed that the Australian sheepmen could never repeat the output of 1890–91. Yet the post-war years proved that the industry was capable of still further expansion, as is shown in the accompanying table. The output of France, Germany and Italy remained the same or dropped between 1926 and 1931, but that of the British Isles increased about 7 percent, while the United States raised its output by one third. This world expansion took place in a period marked by a decline in the growth of population, competition of other fabrics and a reduced demand for warm clothing, including wool hosiery and underwear, because of improved central heating, the advent of the sedan car and changes in fashion. Overproduction resulted and the price collapse began as early as April, 1928. As yet there is little hope that new uses for wool will be found, partly because the price which makes production profit-

ANNUAL PRODUCTION OF WOOL, 1909–31
(In 1,000,000 pounds)

PERIOD	WORLD TOTAL	SOUTHERN HEMISPHERE			EUROPE EXCLUDING RUSSIA	RUSSIA	UNITED STATES
		TOTAL	AUSTRALIA	SOUTH AFRICA			
1909–13	3124	1530	728	158	596	330	314
1923–25	3112	1576	758	198	527	315	284
1929–31	3655	1964	933	305	489	307	411

Source: United States, Department of Agriculture, *Yearbook of Agriculture* (1931) p. 879, and (1933) p. 621; United States, Bureau of Agricultural Economics, *Foreign Crops and Markets* (March 23, 1931) p. 358–61, and (May 15, 1933) p. 537–40.

able is too high to permit the use of wool in bulk and partly because wool can be damaged by moths.

HERBERT HEATON

See: TEXTILE INDUSTRY; GARMENT INDUSTRIES; ENCLOSURES; INDUSTRIAL REVOLUTION; AGRICULTURAL MARKETING; COMMODITY EXCHANGES; AUCTIONS; FAIRS; GRADING; FLAX, HEMP AND JUTE; COTTON; SILK INDUSTRY; LIVESTOCK INDUSTRY; STOCK BREEDING.

Consult: HISTORY OF WOOL MANUFACTURES: Bischoff, James, *A Comprehensive History of the Woollen and Worsted Manufactures*, 2 vols. (London 1842); Burnley, James, *The History of Wool and Woolcombing* (London 1889); Doren, A. J., *Studien aus der Florentiner Wirtschaftsgeschichte*, 2 vols. (Stuttgart 1901–08) vol. i; Espinas, Georges, *La draperie dans la Flandre française au moyen âge*, 2 vols. (Paris 1923); James, John, *History of the Worsted Manufacture in England* (London 1857); Lipson, E., *The History of the Woollen and Worsted Industries* (London 1921); Jubb, Samuel, *The History of the Shoddy-Trade* (London 1860); Heaton, Herbert, *The Yorkshire Woollen and Worsted Industries*, Oxford Historical and Literary Studies, vol. x (Oxford 1930); Clapham, J. H., *The Woollen and Worsted Industries* (London 1907); Cole, A. H., *The American Wool Manufacture*, 2 vols. (Cambridge, Mass. 1926).

HISTORY OF WOOL SUPPLY: Klein, Julius, *The Mesta; a Study in Spanish Economic History, 1273–1836*, Harvard Economic Studies, vol. xxi (Cambridge, Mass. 1920); Power, E. E., "The English Wool Trade in the Reign of Edward iv" in *Cambridge Historical Journal*, vol. ii (1926–28) 17–35, and "The Wool Trade in the Fifteenth Century" in *Studies in English Trade in the Fifteenth Century*, ed. by E. E. Power and M. M. Postan, London School of Economics, Studies in Economic and Social History, vol. v (London 1933) ch. ii; Page, F. M., " 'Bidentes Hoylandie' (A Mediaeval Sheep-Farm)" in *Economic History*, vol. i (1926–29) 603–13; Roberts, S. H., "The Wool Trade and the Squatters" in *Cambridge History of the British Empire*, vol. vii (Cambridge, Eng. 1933) ch. vii; Dyason, E. C., "Bawra" in *Economic Record*, vol. iv (1928) supplement p. 51–67; Smith, John, *Chronicon Rusticum-Commerciale: or, Memoirs of Wool*, 2 vols. (2nd ed. London 1756–57); Collier, James, *The Pastoral Age in Australasia* (London 1911) chs. xxviii–xxix, xxxii; Coghlan, T. A., *Labour and Industry in Australia*, 4 vols. (London 1918), especially vol. i, p. 93–113; Condliffe, J. B., *New Zealand in the Making* (London 1930), especially p. 123–30; Roberts, S. H., *History of Australian Land Settlement (1788–1920)*, University of Melbourne, Publications, no. 3 (Melbourne 1924), especially p. 151–55, 284–86; Shann, E. O. G., *An Economic History of Australia* (Cambridge, Eng. 1930), especially p. 79–96, 126–33, 389–94.

RECENT DEVELOPMENTS AND PRESENT CONDITIONS: United States, Bureau of Foreign and Domestic Commerce, *Commerce Yearbook*, published since 1923, and Department of Agriculture, *Yearbook of Agriculture*, published since 1895; United States, Bureau of Animal Industry, *Special Report on the History and Present Condition of the Sheep Industry of the United States*, by E. A. Carman, H. A. Heath, and John Minto (1892); United States, Tariff Commission, *The Wool-Growing Industry* (1921); Benton, A. H., "Wool Marketing," North Dakota, Agricultural Experiment Station, *Bulletin*, no. 252 (Fargo, N. D. 1931); United States, Department of Agriculture, "Some Factors Affecting the Marketing of Wool in Australia, New Zealand, the Union of South Africa, England and France," by J. F. Walker, *Technical Bulletin*, no. 124 (1929); Smith, M. A., *The Tariff on Wool*, Institute of Economics, Investigations in International Commercial Policies (New York 1926); Wright, C. W., *Wool-Growing and the Tariff*, Harvard Economic Studies, vol. v (Boston 1910); National Association of Wool Manufacturers, *Bulletin*, published monthly and quarterly in Boston since 1869; Australia, Bureau of Census and Statistics, *Official Year Book*, published since 1908; Hawkesworth, Alfred, *Australasian Sheep and Wool* (6th ed. Sydney 1930); Norris, T. C., *Practical Sheep-Farming* (London 1933); Shimmin, A. N., "The World's Staples: v. Wool" in *Svenska Handelsbanken, Index*, vol. vi (1931) 151–64; Frobisher, A., "The World's Wool Markets" in *International Review of Agriculture*, vol. xx, pt. ii (1929) 393–404, 433–43; Great Britain, Ministry of Agriculture and Fisheries, *Report on the Organisation of Wool Marketing*, Economic Series, no. 35 (1932); *Dalgety's Annual Wool Review for Australia and New Zealand*, published in Sydney since 1899; *Wool Year Book*, published in Manchester since 1909; The *Times*, London, *Textile Numbers* (June 27 and September 22, 1913).

WOOLMAN, JOHN (1720–72), American Quaker opponent of slavery and social reformer. A native of New Jersey, Woolman was an extensive traveler, going on repeated journeys through the colonies and making one important trip to England, where he died of smallpox. He traveled always with his eyes open to note the deleterious effects of slavery on both masters and slaves, and he was quick to see its far reaching social and economic consequences. His ideas on the subject, which are summarized in his tract *Some Considerations on the Keeping of Negroes* (2 pts., Philadelphia 1754–62), and his constant exhortations against the practise were chiefly responsible for the generation of an antislavery sentiment among American Quakers in the eighteenth century. Woolman also sponsored the cause of the Indians, whose hardships he observed at first hand during his journey to the Indian settlement of Wehalosing in 1763. His most important constructive essay first appeared in 1793 under the title *A Word of Remembrance and Caution to the Rich* (Dublin 1793), although Woolman had originally called it *A Plea for the Poor*. Here he analyzed with great keenness the causal relationship between the love of luxury on the part of the rich and the general poverty of the masses.

Woolman cannot be understood or rightly estimated without an appreciation of the fact that he was profoundly influenced in his life and thought by the wave of quietism which came into the Society of Friends in the eighteenth century from the continent of Europe. Quietism, of which Woolman was the consummate American example in that century, was characterized essentially by a distrust of human nature and a desire through silence and quiet waiting to find the pure divine will and divine guidance for all practical tasks. Woolman's method of preparation for his assault upon intrenched evils is the most interesting aspect of his life, while the gentleness of his blows is as amazing as is their effectiveness. He always endeavored to identify himself with those who were suffering from injustice or social evils and he aimed, although not quite so successfully, to understand the minds of those who were responsible for the infliction of wrongs. His own sensitiveness to wrong conditions was a peculiarity of his life, and his efforts to purify his own mind and to adjust his own life to social demands form his major contribution. His *Journal* (Philadelphia 1774; new ed. by J. G. Whittier, Boston 1871), written in simple Biblical style, is a unique expression of his personality and social passion and has become a classic in American literature.

RUFUS M. JONES

Consult: *The Journal and Essays of John Woolman*, ed. with introduction by A. M. Gummere (New York 1922); Wilson, E. C., "John Woolman; a Social Reformer of the Eighteenth Century" in *Economic Review*, vol. xi (1901) 170–89; Shore, W. T., *John Woolman; His Life and Our Times* (London 1913); Jones, Rufus M., Sharpless, Isaac, and Gummere, A. M., *The Quakers in the American Colonies* (London 1911), especially p. 391–413.

WORDSWORTH, WILLIAM (1770–1850), English poet. An intimate friend of Coleridge and Southey, Wordsworth was early fired with enthusiasm for the French Revolution. In conjunction with Coleridge he published in 1798 *Lyrical Ballads, with . . . Other Poems*, a volume intended to be the manifesto of the new romantic school in poetry. After much criticism his work was destined to find its place among the greater glories of English literature. Wordsworth's revolutionary ardor waned with the rise of Napoleon, and he was almost the first to proclaim in his "Sonnets Dedicated to Liberty" and in a tract entitled *Concerning the Convention of Cintra* (1809) that the most effective force against Napoleonic imperialism would be the national sentiments of a people striving for independence.

After 1815 Wordsworth's significance in the national life declined, and he was generally regarded as a traitor to his earlier ideals. New problems and policies with which he was out of sympathy had developed. Even now, however, despite his hostility to parliamentary reform, Catholic emancipation and trade unionism, his fear of revolutionary and nationalist movements on the continent of Europe and his sonnets published in 1842 in support of capital punishment Wordsworth still retained some of the more generous sympathies of his youth. The "Postscript" to *Yarrow Revisited and Other Poems* of 1835 contains a noble defense of the principle of the poor laws. He remained to the end of his life a bitter critic of the new industrialism and in 1848 admitted that while he had no respect for the Whigs he had a great deal of the Chartist in him.

ALFRED COBBAN

Works: *The Poetical Works of Wordsworth*, ed. by W. Knight, 11 vols. (Edinburgh 1882–89); *The Prose Works of Wordsworth*, ed. by W. Knight, 2 vols. (London 1896).

Consult: Harper, G. M., *William Wordsworth; His Life, Works and Influence* (3rd ed. London 1929); Batho, E. C., *The Later Wordsworth* (Cambridge, Eng. 1933); Cobban, A. B. C., *Edmund Burke and the Revolt against the Eighteenth Century* (London 1929) p. 133–52; Dicey, A. V., *The Statesmanship of Wordsworth* (London 1917); Brinton, Crane, *The Political Ideas of the English Romanticists* (London 1926) p. 49–65.

WORKERS' EDUCATION in contrast to other types of adult education seeks to help the worker to solve his problems not as an individual but as a member of his social class. It may aim to make him an effective member of his group by giving him a better understanding of his environment and by arousing his cultural interests. It may also aim to give him requisite special training for office in his trade union. Or it may seek to inculcate in him a given body of social, political and economic doctrines. The schools having a purely cultural aim with a general labor orientation are as a rule sponsored by non-labor educational institutions. The workers' schools which seek to train for labor leadership are operated by the various branches of the trade union movement, with emphasis upon organization problems rather than on cultural subjects. The third group of schools, specializing in the training of propagandists, is chiefly under socialist or communist control.

The earliest schools for workers were set up by philanthropists when industrialism was young. These schools were generally of the adult education pattern but in a slight way adumbrated present day workers' education. One was organized in Glasgow, Scotland, in 1800, and another in London in 1823. The London Mechanics' Institute, founded in 1823, was supported by Francis Place and James Mill and his circle.

The rise of the Chartist movement in the 1830's led to a genuine attempt at workers' education. William Lovett, recognizing the need for working class journalists and competent public speakers, organized in 1831 the National Trade Union of the Working Class and Others. In 1836 he founded the London Working Men's Association as a forum for creating an understanding among advanced workers of scientific and political questions. The Working Men's College, founded in London in 1854 by Frederick Denison Maurice, the Christian Socialist leader, sought to draw together workers and advanced middle class intellectuals.

The next important forward step in workers' education was not made until 1899, when three Americans organized and financed Ruskin College, a residential institution closely affiliated with Oxford University. In 1907 the labor movement took over the financing of Ruskin College, the Trades Union Congress inducing a number of unions to make regular grants for scholarships.

In 1903 Albert Mansbridge, a middle class intellectual who had been active in the cooperative movement, organized the National Association for Promoting the Higher Education of Workingmen, which later became the Workers' Educational Association. Branch organizations sprang up in a number of cities, and soon it was the veritable center of the English workers' education movement. The method was to establish tutorial classes meeting twice a week for twenty-four weeks each year for three years. The association drew its support from adult education schools, trade unions, working men's clubs, cooperative societies, universities and public spirited individuals. A national council included representatives of trade unions, cooperative societies and universities. The supervision of the classes was in the hands of a joint committee with equal representation from the universities and working class organizations.

The Workers' Educational Association and Ruskin College attempted to give the worker a richer background for understanding society and politics, but they carefully eschewed partisanship for any definite point of view. At Ruskin College a number of socialist students organized in the Plebs League revolted against neutrality in teaching and, aided by a majority of the alumni, founded in 1909 Central Labour College, also a residential school, with the Plebs League as a propagandist wing. Two years later the school moved to London, where in addition to its evening and Sunday classes it instituted instruction by correspondence. In 1921 the Labour College and Plebs League together with the Scottish Labour College and other groups formed the National Council of Labour Colleges. The schools under the council are committed to Marxian doctrine and vigorously oppose the point of view represented by the Workers' Educational Association. The labor movement blandly ignores the controversy between the two workers' education centers and continues to give financial support to both.

In the United States the movement for independent workers' education did not gain headway until the early 1920's. Labor, however, had pioneered in the movement for free public schools and consistently supported the extension of general educational opportunities. The distrust of intellectuals on the part of the leadership of the American Federation of Labor led to the rejection by its Executive Council in 1901 of a suggestion offered by Walter Vrooman, one of the founders of Ruskin College, that the federation cooperate in establishing a similar institution in the United States. The next year the federation, as a counter move, urged its local bodies to establish schools for the teaching of the principles of trade unionism. The Women's Trade Union League, with a predominant middle class membership, resolved in 1907 to form training schools for organizers and several years later actually established such schools.

The failure of workers' education as a mass movement in the United States has been due essentially to the absence of class consciousness among American workers. The left wing groups, however, have supported educational projects for many years. The socialists and the Industrial Workers of the World conducted lecture courses and classes for their members and sympathizers. The Rand School of Social Science was founded in 1906 by leading socialists with funds bequeathed by a wealthy socialist woman. The majority of the teachers have been socialists, although advanced thinkers who are non-socialists have also been invited to teach. Established at a time when the needle trades workers were actively organizing, it drew a large proportion of its students from these unions. It gave considerable attention to trade union organization problems. The Work Peoples College, a residential school outside of Duluth, Minnesota, controlled by Finnish members and sympathizers of the Industrial Workers of the World, was transformed in 1908 from a theological seminary into a radical labor school, with courses in English, Finnish, public speaking, psychology and economics. The Communists conduct schools as a regular part of their party activities.

A number of international unions have established educational departments which provide systematic lecture courses, concerts and study classes for the membership. The pioneer in this work is the International Ladies' Garment Workers' Union under the leadership of Fannia M. Cohn, which organized an educational department in 1916. In addition a number of universities have organized summer schools for workers. Bryn Mawr began this movement in 1920 with a summer school for women workers and was followed by Wisconsin and Barnard. The summer schools give courses in history, trade unionism, public speaking, English and journalism. No particular point of view is emphasized, although the schools have a general labor orientation.

A number of city central bodies have established labor colleges or trade union classes. These give courses in history, public speaking, economics and labor law, usually one evening a week; and frequently the teachers are drawn from the universities and colleges in the vicinity.

Two residential labor colleges, Brookwood Labor College and Commonwealth College, have been organized. Brookwood gives a two-year course, with a possible arrangement for a third year. Social problems, general and labor history, Marxism, journalism, labor problems and trade union methods are taught. It is supported by donations from individuals and labor organizations and has a board of directors with a trade union majority. In 1927 the school was attacked by leaders of the American Federation of Labor for spreading radical doctrines, and affiliated organizations were strongly urged to discontinue their support. Brookwood's chief supporters have been socialistic and left wing labor groups. Commonwealth College, originally non-factional, has recently inclined toward a semicommunist point of view. Students pay a small tuition fee and are required to work for their support on the farm owned by the institution. Deficits are made up by individual sympathizers. Marxism, history, journalism and similar subjects are taught by an unpaid faculty.

These projects varied so greatly in emphasis, control and financial support that an attempt was made to unify the movement. The Workers' Education Bureau was formed in 1921 by a group of liberals, socialists and trade unionists. It serves as a clearing house for information and an employment exchange for teachers and prepares and recommends textbooks and other classroom material. The American Federation of Labor held aloof until 1922, when it accepted membership on the executive committee, limited to its affiliated unions and the four railway brotherhoods. The bureau refuses to cooperate with left wing schools, its chief emphasis being on turning out trade union organizers and officials.

The resurgence of trade union organization since the inauguration of the National Recovery Administration has given workers' education a new impetus. The International Ladies' Garment Workers' Union has once more set up its classes; the Workers' Education Bureau has extended its system of institutes at conventions and in specific localities; and in centers throughout the country trade unions and other labor groups have founded new labor colleges. Particularly significant is the growth of labor education in the south, initiated by the Southern

Summer School for Women Workers. The inclusion of teachers in the relief projects of the government has led to the formation of adult education classes for both the employed and the unemployed throughout the country. The schools of the various political parties have increased their enrolment.

In Germany the Social Democratic party excelled in systematic mass workers' education after the repeal of the antisocialist laws in 1890—through lectures, leaflets and especially through a network of popular party organs. It was, however, the German trade union federation which organized the first formal labor school. The Berliner Gewerkschaftsschule, offering a six weeks' course of full time instruction and an additional four weeks of technical training for labor secretaries, was organized in 1905. The teachers were drawn from the leadership of the trade union and socialist movements. In the general course the subjects taught were German and foreign labor movements, natural sciences, invalidity and accident insurance, banking, statistics, criminal jurisprudence and industrial hygiene. The course for labor secretaries included labor insurance, legislation, wage agreements and legal procedure before industrial and insurance administrative bodies.

The Mannheim Congress of the Social Democratic party in 1906 authorized a school for party functionaries, which opened in Berlin during the following year. The students were selected by the party executive and the curriculum emphasized party history, economics, historical materialism and other studies for training propagandists for the party.

After the World War, with the widened participation of the labor movement in governmental and industrial administration, the need for an ever increasing body of technically trained labor functionaries became manifest. The trade unions needed trained representatives on the workers' councils. Accordingly after 1919 a three-year course was made available in Berlin by the trade union movement. The first year was devoted to general study, the last two years being given over to strictly technical subjects. The pedagogical method employed stressed independent work by the superior students.

In cooperation with the University of Frankfort, the Akademie der Arbeit was formed in 1920 by the trade unions, aided by a subsidy from the national government. The students were originally appointed by the trade unions; but the persons thus chosen had to qualify by a successful year's work under the extension system, which was followed by two years in residence. The municipality of Düsseldorf financed a residential training school for municipal and trade union and works council functionaries. The curriculum included industrial organization, bookkeeping, general law, employment exchanges, administration and administrative and labor law.

The German metal workers' union operated a school of economics for one month each year for students alternately recruited from the several industries covered by this comprehensive union. The expenditures of the German trade union movement for education were far greater proportionately then those of Great Britain. The large "secret" fund seized by the National Socialists on their accession to power was actually that devoted to trade union education. The entire workers' education system along with the German trade union movement was of course destroyed by the National Socialist regime.

In Holland the Social Democratic party and the trade unions jointly formed in 1924 the Instituut voor Arbeidersontwikkeling. An educational workers' union was formed by the trade unions and the Social Democratic party as early as 1912, but little progress has been made aside from outlining curricula and issuing study material.

The Belgian workers' education movement is one of the oldest and most advanced on the continent. A socialist school was organized by the Belgian Labor party in 1908. The Centrale d'Éducation Ouvrière was opened in 1911 with the avowed aim of preparing workers for a more effective struggle against capitalism. Two years later the institute was placed upon a firm financial basis by Ernest Solvay, who donated 1,000,000 francs. Work was resumed after the war and a women's department was added in 1923. In addition to mass workers' education a residential institution, the École Ouvrière Supérieure in the vicinity of Brussels, gives to promising young people a thirty-six weeks' course, with expenses defrayed by the organizations sending the students. The curriculum consists of economics, bookkeeping and accounting, hygiene, civil law and socialism.

In Austria mass education classes were conducted by local branches of the Socialist party and the trade unions, specializing in party and labor problems in addition to lectures on scientific and literary topics. The Vienna Arbeiterhochschule was the most advanced institution for workers' education with a distinguished faculty of leading Socialist scholars and public men. The course lasted for six months, and the living expenses and tuition were borne by the organizations appointing the student.

Workers' education developed relatively early in Czechoslovakia. Under the leadership of Thomas G. Masaryk the Social Democratic party and the trade unions organized the Prague Labor Academy in 1895. The academy was non-partisan but with a labor orientation. The Higher Socialist School was launched after the war for training leaders and specialists for the labor movement. The faculty is composed mainly of university teachers.

A Workers' Institute to spread independent thinking among the Finnish working class was organized in 1899, but the first important step was made twenty years later when the Social Democratic party, the trade unions and other workers' groups formed the Workers' Educational Federation. The federation organized lecture courses, study circles and libraries. In 1924 a residential institution, the Workers' Academy, was added with a six months' term. Each student is obliged to choose a field of concentration from the following four fields: social and political sciences, natural sciences, humanistic studies and applied subjects. The training of labor functionaries is the main objective.

In Sweden workers' institutes of the adult education type date from the 1880's. It was not, however, until 1912 that formal workers' education began, with the organization of the Workers' Education Federation by the labor party, the trade unions and the cooperative societies and cultural organizations.

The launching of the Workers' High School at Esbjerg by trade unions and Social Democrats in 1916 was the beginning of formal workers' education in Denmark. Elementary and advanced courses are given for men, and a summer school is conducted for women. The curriculum includes courses in labor history, cooperation, economics, labor law and literature. The school is maintained on per capita payments by the trade unions and the Social Democratic party, with aid from the cities and the national government. In 1923 a further step was taken in forming the Workers' Education Federation by the Federation of Trade Unions, and the Social Democratic Youth Organization, with facilities for both mass education and the special training of the chosen. In Norway the socialist party founded in 1920 a school for functionaries in labor law, cooperation, socialism and industrial problems.

The Japanese Federation of Labor organized a school for trade union functionaries in 1921 with labor law, labor legislation and social theories in its curriculum. The school operates three evenings a week for three hours. The Osaka Federation of Labor conducts a similar enterprise of its own. A Workers' Educational Association with headquarters at Tokyo directs country wide training and is divided into the following five departments: publicity, education, home study, legal and advisory.

In contrast with the older major activities of the labor movement, the political, trade union and cooperative, workers' education suffers from lack of definiteness of aim. It is not unlikely that this state of affairs is inherent in the activity itself and will therefore remain permanent. First, there is the division between the "culturists" and the class conscious laborists, the former reenforced in their point of view by general educators and humanitarians. In addition the leadership in the above mentioned standard movement endeavors to stamp the general workers' education movement with its special stamp reflecting the particular objectives and needs of the respective movements and activities. In the final analysis a workers' education movement depends on a thriving general labor movement supporting its activities and offering opportunities for its graduates.

SELIG PERLMAN

See: TRADE UNIONS; LABOR MOVEMENT; EDUCATION; ADULT EDUCATION; VOCATIONAL EDUCATION; INDUSTRIAL EDUCATION; SOCIAL SETTLEMENTS.

Consult: Hansome, Marius, *World Workers' Educational Movements; Their Social Significance*, Columbia University, Studies in History, Economics and Public Law, no. 338 (New York 1931), with complete bibliography; Hodgen, Margaret T., *Workers' Education in England and the United States* (London 1925); Horrabin, J. F. and Winifred, *Working Class Education* (London 1924); Price, T. W., *The Story of the Workers' Educational Association, from 1903 to 1924* (London 1924); Kallen, H. M., *Education, the Machine and the Worker* (New York 1925); Paul, Eden and Cedar, *Proletcult* (London 1921); Hermes, G., *Die geistige Gestalt des marxistischen Arbeiters und die Arbeitsbildungsfrage* (Tübingen 1926); Michel, E., "The Frankfort Academy of Labour and the Problem of Workers' Education," and Nisot, M. T., "Workers' Education in Belgium" in *International Labour Review*, vol. xiii (1926) 157–74, and vol. xxiv (1931) 55–74. See also: *Highway*, the organ of the Workers' Educational Association, published monthly in London since 1909, and other publications and reports of the

W.E.A.; *Plebs*, the organ of the National Council of Labour Colleges, published monthly in Oxford since 1909; and the reports and publications of the Workers' Education Bureau of America.

WORKING MEN'S CLUBS. *See* MUTUAL AID SOCIETIES.

WORKMEN'S COMPENSATION is the term now applied indiscriminately to all legislative systems which provide, without reference to traditional legal responsibility rooted in actual negligence, standardized economic benefits for workers injured in industry. These benefits, which are stipulated by law rather than by the choice of the employer who pays the premium, bear a relation to the financial loss to the workers involved in the specific injuries. It is widely conceded that they fall far short of full compensation for actual loss. This shortcoming is defended upon the ground that the creation by statute of the right to compensation benefits, irrespective of the fault of the worker and without proof of the negligence of the employer, is an advantage to the worker which justifies substantial sacrifice on his part of the potential damage claims he enjoyed under the old law of employers' liability.

With the progress of the machine age industrial injury and industrial death loomed large among the causes of destitution. Through pressure upon public and private funds for relief of the needy the economic problem of industrial injury attracted public attention. The first solutions offered were in the guise of amendments to the existing liability laws and were designed merely to increase the worker's chances of recovery; in any case these proved of but interim merit because of the cost, delay and cumbersomeness of the damage suit at law which was required of the worker. Moreover such legislation failed to eliminate the social problem of maintaining the families of workers crippled through accidents caused by the workers' own negligence. The conviction eventually gained acceptance, first in Germany and a few other European countries and ultimately in virtually all industrial nations of the world, that no adjustment of a system predicated upon damage suits could prove a workable remedy for the socio-economic problems entailed by injuries suffered in modern mechanized industry. From then on, the attempt to force the old liability law into workable shape was abandoned; and the standard was fixed at reasonable immediate compensation of workers for losses resulting from industrial injuries, without regard to the specific cause of the individual case.

A chronological review of workmen's compensation begins with the pioneer country, Germany. Legislation in that country climaxed a period of lawmaking in the several German states which strengthened and aided workers' mutual aid societies and guilds. This legislation was patterned for the most part after the regulations governing the provident funds, which by ancient custom in the mining communities of Germany and other European countries provided benefits for injured and sick workers and their families. The compensation scheme was divided between two systems set up in 1883 and 1884. By the Sickness Insurance Act of 1883 victims of industrial accidents received medical and cash benefits for thirteen weeks of disability; by the so-called Industrial Accident Insurance Law of 1884 compulsory insurance by employers against serious and fatal industrial injuries was required. This second measure was regarded as the real workmen's compensation scheme and the standards which it set up had great influence on later legislation in other countries. Austria followed the example of Germany in 1887; Norway, Finland, France, Denmark and Great Britain legislated in the 1890's; and Spain, the Netherlands, Sweden, Luxemburg, Belgium, Russia, Italy, Hungary and most of the British dominions were added to the list during the first decade of the twentieth century. At the outbreak of the World War Switzerland and several of the states in the United States had become compensation jurisdictions; in the years following most of the Latin American countries, the territories and all but four of the states of the United States, the remaining European nations including those created by the Treaty of Versailles, Japan and China and a number of European colonies in Africa and in the Far East similarly adopted workmen's compensation measures.

The principal standards of the original German law included: a generous definition of industrial accident as covering all injuries occurring during the course of employment; provision of medical and other remedial care; payment of cash benefits both to compensate for wage loss and to cover the funeral costs in the event of fatal accident; continuation of cash benefits throughout the whole period of disability with increase in benefit up to 100 percent of the wage loss when the worker was helpless and in need of attendance; pensions lasting throughout legal dependency for the family of the worker suffering fatal injury; security to the worker that compensation would be paid according to the law, first, through the requirement that employers insure their obligations under the law in industrial mutual insurance associations and, second, through the acceptance by the imperial Treasury of responsibility for the obligations of any association which became insolvent; strict requirement of accident reporting and provision for accident prevention work through enforced safety devices; provision for prompt payment of benefits through the postal authorities; effective administrative machinery including speedy settlement of disputes with right of appeal to a court of arbitration. In most respects the original German measure set up standards which time has demonstrated were rooted in sound principle. The chief shortcomings were found in the coverage provisions, which applied only to listed extra-hazardous industries and to their non-manual workers, who were either "works officials" or technicians with less than a stipulated earning power.

The British and Danish acts of 1897 and 1898 respectively contained unfortunate deviations from the pattern set in the pioneer German legislation. Both measures restricted compensation to accidents not caused by the "gross carelessness of the worker," an innovation which struck at the very foundation of compensation legislation by throwing open to litigation the question of fault. Again, both measures omitted medical benefits altogether. Also in the case of a fatal accident, instead of granting survivors' pensions varying with the number of dependents, the British and Danish laws provided only limited death benefits of three years' and four years' earnings respectively. Denmark moreover limited the maximum amount payable in the case of permanent total disability. Both British and Danish acts omitted any requirement of insurance or substitute security that the legal benefits would be paid in the individual case, merely stipulating that stated compensation benefits were payable in the event of a compensable injury. Lastly, the British act provided no special administrative agency for the enforcement of the law, the worker being left entirely to his own devices without advice from a public officer as to his rights. Some or all of these unfortunate omissions in the British and Danish codes characterized also the later measures adopted by Spain, Italy, the British dominions, the states of the United States and the Latin American countries. In particular the British arbitrarily limited death benefit had a marked influence upon American compensation legislation.

A survey of the sixty odd foreign laws, with special reference to their recent amendments, indicates a continuing liberalizing tendency. In general the coverage clauses show a growing conviction of the fact that "in principle . . . the worker's right to compensation . . . is the same, whether the undertaking be large or small, whether the work carried on therein be considered as dangerous or as involving only an insignificant risk, whether the undertaking be industrial, commercial, or agricultural, whether the worker's pay is low or high, whether or no he is a manual worker, and finally, whether he is the victim of an industrial accident or of an occupational disease" (International Labour Office, *Studies and Reports*, ser. M, no. 2, p. 6). The employment which has been most commonly denied compensation protection has been, as in the early years of compensation history, domestic service. Agricultural enterprise in which machinery is used has been protected in the great majority of cases; all farm labor, however, is still omitted from the scope of about 25 percent of the acts. More than a third of the foreign jurisdictions continue to discriminate against either small industrial plants or non-mechanized plants. Moreover about a fifth of the laws have failed to protect employees in offices, stores and similar establishments. Almost a third have omitted seamen, and the majority have left out home industry labor. Employees both manual and non-manual have been included, without regard to their earnings, in nearly two thirds of the measures—a marked improvement over the earlier situation. Although provisions for medical and other remedial care have remained deficient in a few European countries and in some of the Australian states, medical as well as cash benefits, with hospitalization when needed, have been guaranteed in almost all of the large industrial nations and in most of the lesser ones.

The original German provision whereby two thirds of the wage loss was granted during permanent disability has been duplicated in the majority of the foreign laws. Indeed this ratio was raised to 70 or 75 percent of the basic wage in some acts. Moreover the German provision for increasing the pension to 100 percent in permanent disability cases has been widely followed. Neither time nor money limits were set on these permanent disability pensions. The lower percentage of 50 percent remained the most usual ratio paid in the case of temporary incapacity; recent amendments, however, have provided in some cases 66.6 percent and even 75 percent. Both Great Britain and Denmark have liberalized their death benefit clauses to provide more generously for dependent children, and most of the foreign measures provide continuous pensions throughout dependency for the family of the worker killed in industry. A maximum limit on the weekly compensation allowable is an almost universal feature. There has been a marked tendency away from the type of law initiated by Great Britain, which merely placed upon the employer the obligation to pay compensation, leaving insurance to his discretion. All countries of importance except Great Britain have come to require either insurance or its equivalent. Finally, in the field of administration it is noticeable that accident reporting has received increasing emphasis and that informal special judicial procedure is more commonly provided.

The compensation movement in the United States was a much later development, having been initiated a full decade after the first British law of 1897. A few early experimental measures either proved unconstitutional or, because they were purely optional, were ineffectual. After 1911, however, when nine states enacted compensation laws, there was rapid progress. By 1920, forty-one states as well as the federal government had substituted compensation for the old liability law; and by 1934 three more states and the four territories had accepted compensation, leaving only Florida, South Carolina, Mississippi and Arkansas as adherents to the outworn liability system. The federal government protected harbor workers, but workers in interstate commerce and seamen were still without compensation rights. These groups could recover damages only by successful suit under the Federal Employers' Liability Act.

There was at first considerable doubt on constitutional grounds that the European type of compulsory law would be permissible in the United States. As a result the "elective" compensation law was devised. This gave both the worker and his employer the right to choose between the newly created compensation system and the old damage suit arrangement. Pressure was exerted, however, to prevent rejection of compensation by the employer by providing that such a choice would deprive him of his three defense doctrines of assumption of risk, fellow servant and contributory negligence. Conversely, the worker who chose to adhere to his damage suit rights was handicapped by the restoration of the defenses to his employer. As the Supreme Court of the United States upheld the legal propriety of the compulsory type of compensation law in 1917 (N.Y. Central Ry. Co. v. White, 243 U.S. 188), there was no longer any reason for the elective type of measure.

Most of the American acts started with an undue number of the worst features of the various continental laws. Considerable improvement has, however, been achieved through constant amending of original statutes. It remains true nevertheless that the great majority of American laws still contain a marked number of clauses which make them far less satisfactory compensation measures than the current laws of the important foreign industrial countries. One of the worst of the unfortunate provisions prevalent in American workmen's compensation laws embodies the benefit payable on fatal accident. Of the fifty-one acts operative in American jurisdictions only seven, those of Arizona, Nevada, Oregon, New York, Washington, West Virginia and the Federal Employees Compensation Act, follow the customary continental standard death benefit, which assures the surviving family pensions throughout their entire dependency period. Wisconsin has arrived at much the same result by adding to the basic compensation a sum which varies with the ages of the surviving dependent children. The remaining acts give a death benefit in the form of either a lump sum or, more frequently, a pension which is arbitrarily terminated at the end of a given number of weeks (ranging from two hundred to five hundred in the various laws) or on the payment of a selected sum ranging in two thirds of the laws from $3000 to $8000. All but seven of these laws provide that the death benefit shall be reduced, in cases where the injury does not cause immediate death, by the amount paid out in disability benefits. In cases of fatal injury where a family of young children survives compensation often terminates long before the children are permitted to seek work. The result is that a residue of financial burden is thrown back upon the relief agencies, which must pick up the cases where the compensation laws have dropped them.

Other major shortcomings of many American compensation measures are the following. First, certain codes contain penalty clauses which exclude from benefits or reduce benefits in situations where a variety of types of misconduct or "gross negligence" contributes to the injury. These clauses are to be criticized in that they lead to litigation and also because they shut out from compensation benefits thousands of workers who are injured at their work. Second, in order that the cost of compensation may be kept down, total compensation for all types of injury is limited to an arbitrary sum, regardless of the particular requirements of individual cases. Moreover specific permanent injuries are scheduled with corresponding compensation amounts, which are not adjusted with reference to the age and occupation of the worker. Third, weekly benefits, although usually stated as a percentage of the wage earned, are scaled down, by the inclusion of a low maximum benefit figure, to an amount inadequate to maintain the worker's family even at the lowest current standard of living. Fourth, occupational disease is not compensated as an industrial injury; even in the minority of states which do make provision, compensation only for listed diseases is allowed. Fifth, no provision for a state insurance carrier is made in thirty-one of the acts, so that the "poor risk" employer, whose business is rejected by the commercial companies, is left without any practicable opportunity to protect his workers.

One of the definite tendencies apparent from a survey of amendments to American laws has been the administrative change from the earlier method of leaving the worker to enforce his own compensation rights via a lawsuit to the provision for administration by a board or commission charged with securing the benefits of the compensation law to the workers. Considerable contemporary interest has been shown in the standards of administration set up by these boards. Obviously those which on their own initiative make a real investigation of at least the serious accidents and provide a corps of attorneys or agents to advise workers of their rights and to aid them in securing appropriate compensation are in a class quite apart from the boards which sit passively, giving information only on request and deciding disputes only when these are brought before them. The public conviction is growing that an active aggressive enforcement policy on the part of administrative boards must become the norm, if fraudulent denial of workers' compensation rights is to be eliminated.

There has been continuous debate in the United States as to the advantages of private insurance companies as compared with nonprofit state funds. By 1934 every state except Alabama required the employer either to insure his compensation risks or to give proof of ability to meet them ("self-insurance"). In seven states all compensation risks had to be insured in a state fund; in twenty-seven private insurance companies carried all the insurance; in ten the employer could choose between a state fund and private insurance companies. Many of the arguments concerning the relative advantages of the different insurance arrangements were merely matters of business interest to the employer. It would seem incontrovertible, however, that in the absence of some arrangement by private companies to accept jointly the "poor risks" refused by individual companies the existence of some sort of state fund is essential, since otherwise the workers in industries with an accident hazard so large and uncertain that private insurance companies find them unprofitable have only a nominal compensation protection.

There are emerging, on the basis of provisions to be found in the some 120 compensation codes on the statute books of foreign and American jurisdictions, the outlines of a standard measure capable, in the near future at any rate, of carrying the burden which this branch of social insurance could sustain. Such a standard measure would make insurance of compensation obligations compulsory and provide either a monopoly or a competitive state insurance carrier in which self-employed workers also would be allowed to insure their risks of industrial injury; cover all employments, regardless of occupation or income; compensate all injuries including occupational diseases; include a retroactive waiting period, which, while eliminating trifling accidents, would not reduce the compensation of workers suffering substantial injury; provide full medical, hospital and other remedial care calculated either to cure or to relieve disability or disfigurement; include a minimum compensation figure to prevent the benefits of the low paid worker from falling below a subsistence level; peg the maximum compensation at a figure high enough to offer to employers a real financial incentive for eliminating accidents and to prevent the average working family from becoming dependent; provide additional compensation for the permanently totally disabled worker to cover the salary of an attendant and in case of fatal injuries compensation for the entire dependency period via the family allowance method of pensions varying with the number of surviving dependents; reeducate the worker whose injury prevented pursuit of his usual occupation, financing rehabilitation work at least in part from compensation collected for fatal injury cases where no dependents survived; provide for administration by a board or commission supported by sufficient appropriations to make possible an active and aggressive enforcement of the law for the benefit of the workers; empower the administrative board to make and enforce safety orders predicated upon the adoption of safety rules and mechanical safety devices. Such a standard measure would cope with the social and economic problems caused by industrial injuries as completely as is possible under prevailing standards.

BARBARA NACHTRIEB ARMSTRONG

See: EMPLOYERS' LIABILITY; COMPENSATION AND LIABILITY INSURANCE; LIABILITY; DAMAGES; NEGLIGENCE; STATE LIABILITY; ACCIDENTS, INDUSTRIAL; MINING ACCIDENTS; RAILROAD ACCIDENTS; INDUSTRIAL HAZARDS; SAFETY MOVEMENT; INDUSTRIAL HYGIENE; LABOR LEGISLATION AND LAW; SOCIAL INSURANCE; HEALTH INSURANCE; PENSIONS; REHABILITATION.

Consult: Bowers, E. L., *Is It Safe to Work?*, Pollak Foundation for Economic Research, Publication, no. 12 (Boston 1930); Downey, Ezekiel H., *Workmen's Compensation* (New York 1924); Blanchard, Ralph, *Workmen's Compensation in the United States*, International Labour Office, Studies and Reports, ser. M., no. 5 (Geneva 1926); Armstrong, Barbara N., *Insuring the Essentials* (New York 1932); Michelbacher, G. F., and Nial, Thomas M., *Workmen's Compensation Insurance, Including Employers' Liability Insurance* (New York 1925); Chaney, L. W., *Statistics of Industrial Accidents in the United States to the End of 1927*, United States, Bureau of Labor Statistics, Bulletin no. 490 (1929); United States, Bureau of Labor Statistics, *Workmen's Compensation Legislation of the United States and Canada*, Bulletin no. 496 (1929); Goldberg, Rosamond W., *Occupational Diseases in Relation to Compensation and Health Insurance*, Columbia University, Studies in History, Economics and Public Law, no. 345 (New York 1931); Hamilton, Alice, *Industrial Poisons in the United States* (New York 1925); Collie, John, *Workmen's Compensation; Its Medical Aspect* (London 1933); International Labour Office, *Compensation for Industrial Accidents*, and *Compensation for Occupational Diseases*, Studies and Reports, ser. M, nos. 2 and 3 (Geneva 1925); McCohan, David, *State Insurance in the United States* (Philadelphia 1929); Association of Casualty and Surety Executives, *Digest of Workmen's Compensation Laws in the United States and Territories*, compiled by F. Robertson Jones (13th ed. New York 1933); United States, Bureau of Labor, *Workmen's Insurance and Compensation Systems in Europe*, Twenty-fourth Annual Report of the Commissioner of Labor, 1909, 61st Cong., 2nd sess., House Document no. 132, 2 vols. (1911); Cohen, Joseph L., *Workmen's Compensation in Great Britain* (London 1923); Manes, Alfred, *Die Haftpflichtversicherung* (Leipsic 1902); Hertzfelder, Emil, *Haftpflichtversicherung* (Berlin 1914); Pic, Paul J. V., *Traité élémentaire de législation industrielle; les lois ouvrières* (5th ed. Paris 1922) p. 720–816.

WORKS COUNCILS. *See* INDUSTRIAL RELATIONS COUNCILS.

WORLD COURT. *See* PERMANENT COURT OF INTERNATIONAL JUSTICE.

WORLD WAR. The World War, unparalleled in so many respects, is unparalleled likewise in the wealth of information available as to its causes. At its outbreak or very soon afterward all the leading belligerents published official books —Blue, White, Orange, Yellow, Red—containing some of their diplomatic correspondence during the crisis which preceded the war. These "color books," as they have been called from their covers, were also colored in the sense that the documents were highly selective and in many cases flagrantly edited for propagandist effect. Soon after the war, however, the German Republic began a very complete forty-volume publication of secret material from its archives from 1871 to 1914. Other governments promptly followed suit. In addition there came a vast flood of memoirs, biographies and interpretations. Never before therefore has a generation of fighters been in a position to learn so completely why it fought.

Yet the causes have never been so complex. The political and economic relations of nations had become more interrelated and complicated than ever before. In spite of and partly because of the vast amount of material available the question of the responsibility for the war was perhaps never before so clouded and twisted by national hatreds and propaganda, at least during and immediately after the war. The underlying causes of the war may be grouped for convenience under five headings: nationalism, economic imperialism, militarism and navalism, press and public opinion, and system of secret alliances.

Nationalism was the oldest of the underlying causes. The growing feeling of nationality among the Christian peoples under Turkish misrule was one of the chief disturbing factors in the near eastern question, which contributed to several wars and involved the great powers in dangerous rivalries and jealousies. Similarly the growing consciousness of nationality among the

Slav, Rumanian and Italian oppressed populations in Austria-Hungary, deliberately inflamed by Russia, threatened the disruption of the Hapsburg empire. It explains also the spark—the assassination of the Austrian archduke—which touched off the conflagration of 1914.

Nationalism existed in different forms and under varying names in all the countries of Europe during the half century before the World War. Germany, exultant over the victories which brought about German national unity and vigorous in its rapid industrial development, was ambitious to acquire oversea colonies, expand its commerce and navy and become a world power. These ambitions took an extreme form among the pan-Germans. They made a vociferous noise quite out of proportion to their actual numbers and often embarrassed the German Foreign and Navy offices by their exorbitant pretensions, but their newspaper clamor and other activities sowed dragon's teeth by greatly alarming Germany's neighbors. The latter drew more closely together for self-protection, which in turn nourished in Germany an embittered doctrine that it was being "encircled."

Pan-Slavs proclaimed Russia's historic mission to control Constantinople and the Straits and to dominate the Balkan Peninsula by affording a fostering protection to the lesser Slav peoples along the lower Danube. Pan-Slavism meant conflict with the Ottoman Empire, which would be pushed further along the path to collapse; with the Hapsburg empire, which was threatened with disintegration in the future if Russia succeeded in fostering the establishment of a "Great Serbia"; and with the German Empire, whose new "Berlin-to-Bagdad" interests would be imperiled.

Nationalism in France took the form of *revanche*, the desire to recover the prestige and the provinces lost in 1870. For a generation it remained more a pious sentiment buried in the heart than a political factor endangering peace, except that it prevented any genuine reconciliation and friendship with Germany. In the decade preceding the World War it was revivified, partly through the influence of French nationalist writers and newspapers but more as a result of the resentment of the French at what they regarded as the bullying character of German diplomacy. In the Morocco crises of 1905 and 1911 and the Bosnian crisis of 1908 Germany thumped the green table with the mailed fist to secure diplomatic victories. The French and the Russians were forced to make what they regarded as humiliating concessions because they were not prepared to take up the German challenge. So the desire for *revanche* and the recovery of Alsace-Lorraine revived. There grew up in France the determination that in the future, if Germany made a new threat of force, it would be better to risk war than to accept a fresh humiliation. The new national spirit, determination and self-confidence were greatly increased by friendship with England and the growing conviction that in case of a conflict with Germany there would be a good prospect of victory, the fruits of victory being the recovery of the lost provinces and the end of the nightmare of the German menace. Most of the French leaders, like the mass of the French people, did not want war; but if Germany's desire for the hegemony of Europe and her attempt again to use the mailed fist to force a diplomatic triumph brought on another international crisis, then it would be better for France to fight than to back down.

A new set of international rivalries, which may be called economic imperialism, set in during the last quarter of the nineteenth century. The struggle for markets, raw materials, colonies and fields for investment became more acute during the forty years before the World War, by reason of the fact that Germany and Italy entered the competition. Hitherto politically weak and divided, they had now secured national unity and wished to come forward to share with the other powers in the partitioning of the world. It can hardly be said that any one of the great powers was more responsible than another for the international jealousies, friction and fears which arose out of this economic imperialism. By 1914 all the great powers had secured slices of Africa. In China, Italy alone had failed to gain something for itself. In the field of railway construction, which was one of the most dangerous forms of economic imperialism because it involved political as well as economic interests, the English were building the Cape-to-Cairo railway, the Russians the Trans-Siberian and the Germans the Berlin-Bagdad Railway. The first of these came into conflict with German, French and Belgian interests; the second was in part responsible for the Russo-Japanese War; the third caused endless friction between Germany and the Triple Entente.

Protective tariffs, which usually accompanied the modern industrial system, except in England, were another form of economic imperialism. Tariff wars and retaliatory measures caused irritation between countries, especially in the mind of the man in the street and in newspaper discussion. There was always the danger that great merchants and industrialists and agrarian interests would use official government support to secure economic advantages for themselves. This tended to bring the governments themselves into conflict with one another.

Another important underlying cause of the World War was increased militarism and navalism. Armaments were alleged to be for defense and in the interests of peace, according to the fallacious maxim *si vis pacem, para bellum*. They were intended to produce a sense of security. What they really did create was universal suspicion, fear and hatred between nations. If one country increased its army, built strategic railways and constructed new battleships, its fearful neighbors were straightway frightened into doing likewise. So the mad competition in armaments went on in a vicious circle, especially during and after the Balkan Wars of 1912–13, when it was feared that the great powers might soon be involved.

Militarism also implied the existence of an influential body of military and naval officers in every country, whose whole psychological outlook was naturally colored by the possibility if not the "inevitability" of an early war. In a political crisis precisely when it was most difficult for diplomats to keep their heads clear and their hands free, the militarist leaders were quick to conclude that war was "inevitable" and to exert all their influence to persuade the ruling civilian authorities to consent to an order for general mobilization at the earliest possible moment. But a general mobilization, according to prevailing military opinion, actually did make war inevitable. Once the complicated military machine was set in motion, it was virtually impossible to stop it. This was one of the greatest evils of militarism, as shown by the course of events in July, 1914. Closely akin to this influence of military and naval officers was the pressure exerted on civilian authorities and on public opinion by the munition makers and big business in favor of ever larger armaments.

Too often newspapers and periodicals in all lands tended to poison public opinion by inflaming national feelings, misrepresenting the situation in foreign countries and suppressing factors in favor of peace. In fact there is no single subject which recurs so frequently in the mass of pre-war diplomatic correspondence as this problem of the dangerous tendency of the press in embittering nations toward one another. Ambassadors frequently admitted that they were hampered by the jingoistic attitude of the newspapers in their own country, apologized for it and promised to exert themselves to restrain it, if only other governments would do the same toward their papers. Often these efforts were quite genuine and occasionally successful. At other times, however, politicians sought to score an advantage or to defend their attitude by stirring up their own press and then alleging that their freedom of action was restricted because of the press and public opinion, that if they yielded the point under dispute there would be such an outcry from the newspapers and public opinion that they would be turned out of office.

So the newspapers, whether influenced by governments, by bribes from munition makers, by desires to boost circulation or by supposed patriotic motives, often took up some point of international dispute, exaggerated it, made attacks and counterattacks, until a regular newspaper war was engendered which offered a fertile soil in which the seeds of a real war might easily germinate. A violent press feud broke out between the Austrian and Serbian press after the murder of the Austrian archduke; the governments of the two countries, instead of trying to restrain it, deliberately allowed it to incite public opinion and to arouse indignation and enthusiasm for war in a way which contributed to the actual outbreak of the great conflict.

The fifth and perhaps the greatest single underlying cause of the World War was the system of secret alliances, military and naval understandings and ententes. These began in their pre-war form with Bismarck's formation of the Triple Alliance of Germany, Austria-Hungary and Italy in 1882. To balance this France and Russia came to an understanding ten years later, which was cemented by a very secret military convention in 1894. England, which had stood aloof in "splendid isolation," made an entente with France in 1904 and with Russia in 1907, thus forming the Triple Entente. Thus the six great powers became divided into two groups which were increasingly suspicious of one another and which steadily built up greater and greater armies and navies. The members of each group generally felt bound to mutual support, even in matters where they had no direct interest, because failure to give such support would have weakened the solidarity of the group. Thus Germany often felt bound to back up Austria-Hungary in the Balkans, because otherwise Germany feared to lose its only thoroughly dependable ally and it could place no confidence in the loyalty of Italy. Similarly France had no direct political interests in the Balkans but felt bound to support Russia, because otherwise the existence of the Dual Alliance would have been threatened and the best guaranty of French safety from a German attack would have been lost. Likewise British officials became increasingly convinced that England must support France and Russia in a European war in order to preserve the solidarity of the Triple Entente as a check to the Triple Alliance. In the crisis of July, 1914, it was not merely a question of Austria, Serbia and the Balkans; it was a question of the solidarity and prestige of the two groups of powers into which Europe had become divided.

The immediate event which occasioned the World War was the political assassination of the Austrian heir to the throne, the archduke Franz Ferdinand, and his wife at Sarajevo on June 28, 1914. It was the act of a Bosnian, an Austrian subject of Serb nationality and sympathies, who had been supplied with weapons by Serbian officers in the Serbian capital, Belgrade. It set fire to the combustible material which had been piling up in Europe and it brought to an explosive climax the underlying causes which had been at work for forty years or more.

None of the powers wanted a European war. Their governing rulers and ministers, with very few exceptions—like Count Berchtold of Austria, who wanted a localized war against Serbia, or the Russian Izvolski, who wanted revenge for his humiliation in the Bosnian crisis of 1908–09—all foresaw that it must be a frightful struggle, of which the political results were not absolutely certain but in which the loss of life, the suffering and the economic consequences were bound to be terrible. In the diplomatic crisis following the archduke's assassination nearly all the ministers and ambassadors, with varying degrees of ability and sincerity, worked to avert a European war. But they were swept along by fears, suspicions, militarist influence and the overwhelming pressure of swift events resulting from the perfected technique of the telephone and telegraph. They fell under a severe physical and mental strain of overwork, worry and lack of sleep, whose psychological consequences are too often overlooked in attempts to assess the blame for what took place. If one is to understand how it was that experienced and trained men occasionally failed to grasp fully the contents of the sheaves of telegrams put into their hands at frequent intervals, how their proposals were sometimes confused and misunderstood, how they quickly came to be obsessed with pessimistic fears and suspicions and how in some cases they finally broke down and wept, one must remember the nerve racking psychological effects of continued work and loss of sleep, combined with the consciousness of the responsibility for the safety of their country and the fate of millions of lives.

Was the war "inevitable?" Unfortunately many political leaders and writers before the war had come to think so. Therefore they increased armaments and made other preparations to wage it victoriously when it should come; in so doing they increased the fears and suspicions of their neighbors and thereby tended directly to make it almost "inevitable." But many students think that it was not inevitable. No one can foresee all the imponderable factors which may suddenly change a situation. For instance, the tension between Triple Alliance and Triple Entente might have relaxed if England and Germany, which were on more friendly terms in June, 1914, than they had been for many months previously, had finally signed the treaties already initialed concerning the Berlin-Bagdad Railway and the Portuguese colonies; or if Kiderlen-Wächter had remained in charge of the German Foreign Office instead of suddenly dying at the end of 1912; or if Kokovtsov had remained in office and Izvolski been dismissed; or if Caillaux had not been replaced by Poincaré; or if the archduke Franz Ferdinand, instead of becoming the victim of the fatal chance by which his chauffeur happened to make a mistake as to streets in Sarajevo and stopped just at the point where the assassin was waiting, had lived to put into effect his plans for "trialism" instead of "dualism" in the government of Austria-Hungary. A general European war had indeed been successfully averted during several severe diplomatic crises in the decade preceding 1914, notably during the Balkan Wars of 1912–13.

A war of words has long raged over the question of responsibility for the war. By article 231 of the Treaty of Versailles Germany was forced against its conscience and belief to sign the dictated statement that Germany and its allies were responsible. Two eminent French historians, Camille Bloch and Pierre Renouvin, sought in 1931 to show that this article in the treaty did not mean that Germany had premeditated the war or was morally responsible for it but merely that it was legally liable for reparations payments. There is some evidence to support this technical argument. But if it is regarded in the light of statements made by allied officials during and after the Peace Conference, it is clear that the interpretation of article 231 made in 1919 and generally accepted without question for a dozen years thereafter casts the moral responsibility on Germany and its allies. This view is now generally regarded by persons acquainted with the facts as historically unsound. All the countries were more or less responsible in contributing to both the underlying causes and the immediate events which led to the actual outbreak of war. As to the precise degree of responsibility of each, however, there still remains room for honest differences of opinion.

By August 4, 1914, seven countries were at war: Austria-Hungary and Germany against Serbia, Belgium, Russia, France and Great Britain. Twenty-one other countries—or twenty-four if new states like Poland, Czechoslovakia and Jugoslavia, which arose during the war and were admitted to the Peace Conference, are included—gradually joined in the struggle, either to defend their rights or to realize their nationalistic or other ambitions by adhering to the side which they thought would win.

Japan, eager to seize German possessions and rights in the Shantung peninsula and to take advantage of the opportunity to extend Japanese power in eastern Asia while the European powers were engaged in a life and death struggle, declared war on Germany in August, 1914. Turkey, under pressure of German officials and from traditional enmity to Russia, whose ultimate designs on Constantinople and the Straits were not doubted, joined the Central Powers in November, 1914. Bulgaria followed suit in October, 1915. Italy had been a member of the Triple Alliance; but because of equivocal secret agreements with France and Russia, because of hatred for Austria and desire for "unredeemed" territories inhabited by Italians but ruled by the Hapsburgs and because Italy claimed Austria did not live up to the terms of article 7 of the Triple Alliance, that country at first remained neutral. After bargaining with both sides for several months it finally joined the Entente powers in May, 1915, after being assured in secret treaties that its irredentist ambitions would be generously recognized at the final peace settlement. Rumania followed suit in August, 1916.

The United States, which became "associated" with the Allied Powers in April, 1917, entered the war for reasons which were many and varied in the minds of different persons: defense of neutral rights, indignation at Germany's reported methods of causing and conducting the war, fear of German domination of Europe and consequent danger to the United States, the desire "to make the world safe for democracy" and other motives. The powerful example of the United States encouraged China, Siam, Liberia, Greece and several states in Central and South America likewise to enter the war against Germany.

Germany possessed at first an advantage in the conduct of the war in that its general staff, disregarding the German chancellor and Reichstag, early acquired virtual unity in command and administration. By enjoying the inner line between its adversaries in the east and the west it could quickly transport its army corps by strategic railways to points where they were most needed. Germany's military superiority rapidly gave it virtual control not only over the armies but also over the economic resources of its allies. This advantage of the unified supreme direction of the war Germany retained until its allies successively collapsed in September and October, 1918.

The Entente powers long suffered from the absence of harmonious coordination in command and administration. Their armies remained under their separate national commands, which too often lacked successful unity of action. The Russian armies, widely separated from one another and from their allies on the west front, sadly lacked munitions and any means of importing them and collapsed in July, 1917. This opened the way for the Bolshevist revolution of October, for the Russian withdrawal from the war by the Treaty of Brest Litovsk and for Germany's transfer of troops from the east to the west for Ludendorff's final drive in the spring of 1918. Faced with these dangers and urged by President Wilson, the Allies finally established an Inter-Allied Conference and in November, 1917, created a Supreme War Council with strictly advisory functions. It was not until the initial successes of the Ludendorff drive that they at last achieved real unity of command by giving the supreme strategic direction to General Foch.

In order to attain agreement in the prosecution and objectives of the war England definitely allied with France and Russia; beginning in March, 1915, secret treaties were signed guaranteeing to Russia Constantinople and the Straits, partitioning most of the remainder of Turkey, assuring Italy of its irredentist territories and promising various advantages to the Balkan states and others. The United States, not fully mindful of these secret treaties and being merely associated with the Entente powers, was not bound by these secret treaties. Being largely in contradiction to President Wilson's view of the war objectives as stated in his Fourteen Points of January 18, 1918, they caused great trouble at the Peace Conference. Coordination of effort, however, for mobilizing resources for carrying on the war—food, munitions, shipping and so on —was gradually acquired by the sending of missions to the United States and by the creation of a large number of interallied government agencies.

Within each belligerent country the need for the rapid production of munitions, the coordination of effort and resources and efficiency of administration rapidly led everywhere to a great increase in the functions and control of the central government. New emergency agencies were constantly being created, merged or changed. While these measures doubtless achieved to a large extent the immediate aim in view more rapidly and efficiently than could have been possible under the pre-war system of individualistic effort and more or less free competition, they nevertheless operated with gigantic and often reckless expenditure, with great profits to some and losses to others and with very serious economic and political consequences when decentralization of control came to be undertaken after the war.

The war changed fundamentally and probably permanently the political forms of government over a wide area of Europe. Four great autocratic or semi-autocratic governments were swept away, those in Germany, Austria-Hungary, Russia and Turkey. A wave of republicanism and radicalism swept over Europe. Between 1917 and 1934 twelve new continental republics were created, and socialist, communist and labor governments became common. Together with this there grew up also a widespread distrust of democracy. Among the reasons for this distrust were the inability of the new governments to cope successfully with the complex post-war problems, the crushing burden of taxation, currency instability, the paralyzing effect of reparations and interallied debts upon economic recovery, the upsetting of old social conditions and the shifting of power into the hands of easily influenced masses. Consequently there appeared a number of dictators, who promised to save their peoples from the follies of the past by energetic if despotic measures. Thus there arose such interesting politico-economic experiments as Bolshevism in Russia, Fascism in Italy, National Socialism in Germany and various modifications of these types of dictatorships in many other smaller countries of central and eastern Europe.

In the relations of states with one another the war brought considerable changes. Countries shifted in relative importance. Before 1914 six great powers controlled the European scene. The temporary eclipse and partial ostracism of Germany and Russia, the break up of Austria-Hungary and the emergence of a number of new smaller states augmented the number of actors on the international stage and complicated the solution of international questions. For a dozen years England, France and Italy enjoyed a relatively increased influence. But with the new self-confidence which National Socialism has brought to Germany and with Russia's economic progress and recognition by countries like the United States, these two European states are regaining their former position as first rate powers.

Although secret treaties are forbidden to members of the League of Nations, Europe has tended quickly to divide again into two hostile groups of states. The revisionist group, led by Germany, has sought to effect a revision of the peace treaties as the primary requirement for a sound political foundation of international relations. The antirevisionist group, led by France and warmly supported by the new states created or benefited by the peace treaties, has taken its stand on the League of Nations and insisted that the treaties constitute the sacred legal foundations of Europe. Between the two groups England and to some extent Italy have sought to serve as mediators.

There is much ground for pessimism as to the consequences of the war: increased nationalism especially in economic matters, such as tariffs, quotas and other efforts toward isolationist self-sufficiency; world wide industrial and commercial depression, resulting in part from the gigantic uneconomic expenditures of the war; an annual world outlay of over $4,000,000,000 in preparation for war; failure to achieve any considerable limitation or reduction of armaments; suppression of freedom of thought and personal liberty in many countries; and a legacy of war hatreds, fears and suspicions.

On the other hand, there is reason for thinking that the war ushered in a new phase of political and social development. Statesmen directing countries belonging to the League of Nations now meet periodically in personal and friendly conference to iron out their disagreements, instead of handling them at long range through ambassadors with embarrassing leakages in the press—a new practise which makes for peace. There exists the League of Nations, which in spite of its weaknesses and failures affords a ready made machinery for dealing with international disputes with dignity and without loss of prestige to the parties concerned. Most important of all, the World War revealed more clearly than ever before the futility of war as a means of settling disputes, for it proved that war is almost as disastrous to the victors as to the vanquished. In social development the war and especially the post-war period brought to the youth of many countries a greater sense of responsibility. Peasants and industrial workers acquired more economic and political influence, insisting that governments should keep some of the increased control assumed during the war and that it should be exercised more for the welfare of the masses and less for that of the favored few.

SIDNEY B. FAY

See: NATIONALISM; IRREDENTISM; PAN-MOVEMENTS; ALSACE-LORRAINE; MILITARISM; PROPAGANDA; IMPERIALISM; FOREIGN INVESTMENT; GREAT POWERS; BALANCE OF POWER; ALLIANCE; TREATIES; DIPLOMACY; ARCHIVES; WAR; WARFARE, LAWS OF; WAR ECONOMICS; WAR FINANCE; NATIONAL DEFENSE; ARMAMENTS; MUNITIONS INDUSTRY; ARMS AND MUNITIONS TRAFFIC; MOBILIZATION AND DEMOBILIZATION; RUSSIAN REVOLUTION; BOLSHEVISM; SELF-DETERMINATION, NATIONAL; MINORITIES, NATIONAL; FASCISM; NATIONAL SOCIALISM, GERMAN; INDIAN QUESTION; PAN-ISLAMISM; NEAR EASTERN PROBLEM; EGYPTIAN PROBLEM; FAR EASTERN PROBLEM; MANCHURIAN PROBLEM; POLISH CORRIDOR; MANDATES; LEAGUE OF NATIONS; INTERNATIONAL ORGANIZATION; INTERNATIONAL LEGISLATION; PERMANENT COURT OF INTERNATIONAL JUSTICE; INTERNATIONALISM; DISARMAMENT; REPARATIONS; MIGRATIONS.

Consult: Fay, S. B., *The Origins of the World War*, 2 vols. (2nd ed. New York 1930); Brandenburg, Erich, *Von Bismarck zum Weltkriege* (2nd ed. Berlin 1925), tr. by A. E. Adams (London 1927); Dickinson, G. L., *The International Anarchy, 1904–1914* (London 1926); Gooch, G. P., *Recent Revelations of European Diplomacy* (4th ed. London 1930); Angell, Norman, *The Great Illusion* (4th ed. London 1913); Isaac, Jules, *Un débat historique, 1914. Le problème des origines de la guerre* (Paris 1933); Langer, W. L., *European Alliances and Alignments, 1871–1890* (New York 1931); Moon, P. T., *Imperialism and World Politics* (New York 1926); Renouvin, Pierre, *Les origines immédiates de la guerre (28 juin-4 août 1914)* (2nd ed. Paris 1927), tr. by T. C. Hume (New Haven 1928); Schmitt, B. E., *The Coming of the War*, 2 vols. (New York 1930); Wegerer, Alfred von, *Die Widerlegung der Versailler Kriegsschuldthese* (Berlin 1928), tr. by E. H. Zeydel (New York 1930); Renouvin, P., *La crise européenne et la grande guerre, 1904–1918* (Paris 1934); Seymour, C., *American Diplomacy during the World War* (Baltimore 1934); Carnegie Endowment for International Peace, Division of Economics and History, *Economic and Social History of the World War*, ed. by J. T. Shotwell, vols. i–cxxxii (New Haven 1921–34); Rosenberg, Arthur, *Die Entstehung der deutschen Republik, 1871–1918* (Berlin 1928), tr. by I. F. D. Morrow (London 1931); *Fall of the German Empire, 1914–1918*, ed. by R. H. Lutz, 2 vols. (Stanford University 1932); Glaise-Horstenau, E. von, *Die Katastrophe; die Zertrümmerung Österreich-Ungarns und das Werden der Nachfolgestaaten* (Zurich 1929), tr. by I. F. D. Morrow as *The Collapse of the Austro-Hungarian Empire* (London 1930); Ponsonby, Arthur, *Falsehood in War-Time* (London 1928); Baker, R. S., *Woodrow Wilson and World Settlement*, 3 vols. (New York 1922); *A History of the Peace Conference of Paris*, ed. by H. W. V. Temperley, 6 vols. (London 1920–24); Keynes, J. M., *The Economic Consequences of the Peace* (London 1919), and *A Revision of the Treaty* (London 1922); Bassett, J. S., *The League of Nations* (New York 1928); Shotwell, J. T., *War as an Instrument of National Policy and Its Renunciation in the Pact of Paris* (New York 1929); Salter, J. A., *Recovery; the Second Effort* (London 1932); Cole, G. D. H. and M. I. P., *The Intelligent Man's Review of Europe Today* (London 1933).

WORMS, RENÉ (1869–1926), French sociologist. Worms, the son of the political economist Émile Worms, was born at Rennes. His early studies in the field of philosophy received generous recognition, but his attention was soon diverted to other disciplines, and he approached sociology with an erudition acquired from a thorough training in law, letters, economics and related subjects. Throughout his life he displayed an almost incredible capacity for activity. As a teacher he held positions simultaneously in the University of Paris and in a number of other important institutions. But his chief contribution to the social sciences was as editor and organizer. Worms founded toward the end of 1892 the *Revue internationale de sociologie* and the next year the Institut International de Sociologie, followed by the *Bibliothèque sociologique internationale*. Finally in 1895 he organized the Société de Sociologie de Paris. After thirty years of service to the government he was promoted in 1924 to the office of *conseiller d'état*.

The name of Worms has been associated with the organismic school of sociology. His *Organisme et société* (Paris 1896) followed the course already set by Spencer, Lilienfeld and Fouillée, and to some degree by Schäffle, toward an interpretation of society in the light of the new principles of evolutionary biology, which were then gaining prestige. In this early work Worms propounded the existence of a close analogy between the biological organism and society. Societies and individual organisms, being part of living nature, are subject to the same general laws. But since society is on a higher evolutionary level than the organism, its processes appear more amplified and complex. This is the result of the fact that whereas the elements forming the organism are held together by unconscious bonds, in the case of society the individuals form the whole through conscious mental relations. Thus to Worms the social fact results from the mental contact of individuals in the group; this contact implies an activity in common, a cooperation. The nation at the present evolutionary level is the highest organismic expression of this conscious unity. A nation has a distinct life of its own, which emerges from that of its members, and in turn it is the nation that determines the nature of the life of the individual. The complete identification of the individual with the nation is expressed in times of war when men show a willingness to sacrifice themselves for the state.

Conscious of the growing criticism directed against the organismic approach, Worms in his later works attempted to shift the emphasis from the biological to the psychological factors in his scheme, but the result was little more than a change in terminology.

V. D. SEWNY

Other important works: *Philosophie des sciences sociales*, 3 vols. (Paris 1903–07, 2nd ed. 1913–20); *Les principes biologiques de l'évolution sociale* (Paris 1910); *La sociologie; sa nature, son contenu, ses attaches* (Paris 1921).

Consult: Ouy, Achille, in *Revue internationale de sociologie*, vol. xxxiii (1925) 577–80; Case, C. M., and Woerner, Fred, "René Worms; an Appreciation" in *Sociology and Social Research*, vol. xiii (1929) 403–25; Richard, Gaston, in Institut International de Sociologie, *Annales*, vol. xv (1927) 55–70; Essertier, Daniel, *La sociologie*, Philosophes et savants français du xxe siècle, vol. v (Paris 1930) p. 232–44.

WRIGHT, CARROLL DAVIDSON (1840–1909), American statistician. Wright had a varied career: he was soldier and officer in the Civil War, lawyer and member of the Massachusetts senate, chief of the Massachusetts Bureau of Statistics of Labor from 1873 to 1885 and United States commissioner of labor from 1885 to 1905; he often lectured in various academic institutions and from 1902 until his death was president of Clark College in Worcester, Massachusetts.

Wright was the outstanding figure in the organization of official labor statistics in the United States. As chief of the first bureau of labor statistics he outlined the policies under which economic and statistical research was to be conducted and determined the scope and possibilities of such investigations. Above all he insisted upon strict impartiality, holding that it was the task of statistical research to ascertain objective facts to be used as the basis of legislative and administrative action. He set the standards upon which social and industrial statistical work in other states and in the federal government was subsequently modeled. Dissatisfied with wage rates and averages as measures of the return to labor, he worked toward a more comprehensive collection and more refined analysis of statistical data, particularly those pertaining to actual earnings and standards of living. As United States commissioner of labor he organized the work of the United States Bureau of Labor Statistics, laying down the policies and outlining the methods which it has since continued. He recognized the importance of permanent offices devoted to the accumulation of labor information along systematic lines and from identical establishments. He never started an investigation with preconceived ideas but was always ready to change his opinion in conformity with obtained results. Recognition of his ability in the field of statistics led President Cleveland to appoint him to complete the eleventh census upon the resignation of Robert B. Porter as director.

Wright played a great part in improving the condition of labor, yet he always maintained a non-partisan stand, encouraging trade unions in collective bargaining and arbitration of industrial disputes but decrying excesses by either party. His position was essentially that trade unionism had on the whole justified itself and that some sort of organization of workers was a necessary part of collective bargaining and especially of arbitration of industrial disputes, in which he was particularly interested. As the government representative to investigate the Pullman strike in Chicago, 1894, he handed down a courageous report, for which he was bitterly attacked, although later vindicated. In 1902 he served as adviser to President Roosevelt in the anthracite strike and was made reporter of the tribunal appointed to arbitrate the issue in that industry.

ETHELBERT STEWART

Consult: North, S. N. D., in American Statistical

Association, *Publications*, vol. xi (1908–09) 447–66, with a complete bibliography, p. 550–61; Wadlin, H. G., *Carroll Davidson Wright; a Memorial* (Boston 1911).

WRIGHT, FRANCES (1795–1852), Anglo-American social reformer. Frances Wright was born in Scotland, the daughter of a wealthy political liberal. Orphaned at the age of two and a half, she was brought up with her younger sister in a conservative English household. At nineteen she wrote a defense of Epicureanism, *A Few Days in Athens*, which she dedicated to her friend Jeremy Bentham when it was printed several years later (London 1822). In 1818 she visited the United States, and the account of her two-year stay, *Views of Society and Manners in America* (London 1821), aroused the interest of Lafayette and other liberals. While she was in America her play, *Altorf*, a drama of political liberty (Philadelphia 1819), was produced in New York City.

Upon her return to Europe she lived for a time on the continent working with Lafayette in the interests of the Carbonari movement. In 1824 she and her sister followed Lafayette to America. Convinced that the solution of the slave problem lay in gradual emancipation through industrial education, she purchased some slaves and set up a cooperative colony (Nashoba) in Tennessee in 1825; the experiment ended in failure in 1830. From 1828 to 1830 she lectured throughout the country, edited the *Free Enquirer* with Robert Dale Owen and helped to form the first American labor party, the Working Men's party of New York (1829–39), popularly known as the "Fanny Wright party." She revisited France during the revolution of 1830; a decade before Marx she held that the struggle was in reality a "class" war of universal character. She married William Phiquepal d'Arusmont in 1831 and four years later returned to the United States, continuing to lecture and to write until her death.

Frances Wright was the first woman in the United States to demand political equality for her sex; she challenged traditional religion and was a pioneer in educational reform. But throughout her adventuresome career, which brought her celebrity and repeated persecution, these "minor reforms" were merely incidental to her vision of a reorganized state—suggested in her first book—in which free education and state guardianship of children would insure universal equality.

THERESA WOLFSON

Consult: Waterman, William W., *Frances Wright*, Columbia University, Studies in History, Economics and Public Law, no. 256 (New York 1924); Pope-Hennessy, Una B., *Three English Women in America* (London 1929) p. 28–52, 61, 97–98; Symes, L., and Clement, T., *Rebel America* (New York 1934) p. 21–33, 40–44.

WRITING. Knowledge of the art of tracing signs or symbols which constitute in themselves or in combination words representing objects or ideas came late in human history. It has played such a significant role in the development of culture that the possession of a system of writing is commonly regarded by anthropologists as marking a dividing line between primitive and civilized peoples. Greatly enhancing the extent and fidelity of intercommunication between individuals, areas and generations, it acts as a conserving force which facilitates the accumulation of culture. It tends to standardize trade relations within and outside of the community by enabling a record of transactions and leads to the codification of legal and religious codes and the recording of scientific and technical knowledge in a manner which makes possible progressive systematic elaboration. By means of writing political and economic power could be extended; far flung empires could be managed by central authorities. The development of a written literature has often led to greater community cohesion by serving as a vehicle for the intensification of ethnocentric attachments; on the other hand, writing has provided a means of dissipating provincialisms by affording contacts with the traditions of diverse civilizations. Although writing has often acted as a conservative as well as a conserving force, by making available knowledge of a wide variety of possible types of behavior it has promoted more rapid institutional change; periods in world history in which there has been the greatest ferment have been marked by the revival of the classics, which have preserved traditions that otherwise would have perished, and by the flowering of native literature. In many phases of social life only the written record has legality and authority. Not all aspects of culture respond equally to writing; intimate reflections of the emotional life of a people may elude written records, and the individuality and informality of the art of the raconteur may lose some of its essential appeal when his tale is transcribed. Some religious beliefs defy the logical coherence which writing demands. Priestly authorities almost universally first resisted the recording of religious tradition as a threat to their monopoly of religious knowledge and resulting power, only later to sanctify writing and sacred books. The early scribes became an integral part of the prevailing theocracies and later were found among the secular lawgivers and scholarly officials. Still later the profession of the scribe developed into a purely commercial pursuit in connection with book publishing (large staffs of calligraphers were employed in the scriptoria of ancient Alexandria, of Rome, of the mediaeval monasteries and of Islamic centers, such as Cordova), with trade and with personal correspondence.

There were many precursors of writing among primitive peoples in the form of mnemonic devices such as knots, message sticks, marking pebbles and wampum belts. The beginnings of writing are found in the pictographic ideographs of the stone age of prehistoric Europe and the New World. Ideographic writing was restricted almost entirely to the representation of objects and ideas which lend themselves readily to symbolic portrayal and lacks clarity and precision. The earliest form of phonetic writing was acrophonic writing, which represented not the idea of the object depicted but its name, its first syllable or its initial; its pictures tended to be as ambiguous as the ideograms that continued to be used along with acrophonic texts. Eventually scribes came to regard the graphic devices, which were often mere schematizations of earlier pictures, as characters for syllables. Babylonian cuneiform script reached a syllabic and even a semi-alphabetic stage and the picture script of the Egyptians and the Mayas came to embody conventionalized signs for separate sounds with older syllabic and ideographic signs. The earliest known inscriptions in pure alphabetic writing—the picture being a symbol of the initial sound of the name of the object represented—are the accounts of the Seirite foremen of the copper and turquoise mines on the Sinai peninsula probably written under the influence of the Egyptian scribes accompanying the expeditions of Amenemhet III, who ruled about the nineteenth century B.C. The south Arabic-Minaean alphabet and the northern Canaanite-Phoenician-Aramaic alphabets became differentiated from this parent stock. The latter was carried by the Aramaean traders eastward as far as India, where it became Sanskrit, and spread over western Asia and became differentiated into Hebrew, Syraic and Arabic. It was carried on by the Phoenicians into Greece sometime before the thirteenth century B.C. In the process of diffusion the original pictorial character of the letters of the alphabet became conventionalized signs representing sounds and the alphabet adapted itself to the phonetic peculiarities of the diverse spoken languages.

The many varieties of Greek scripts that developed because of the cultural and political independence of the city-states may be broadly classified as eastern Greek and western Greek. The latter came to be widely distributed along the routes of trade in Europe, to be supplanted only gradually by the Latin alphabet, which was derived from the Greek by way of Etruria about the seventh century B.C. and was carried by the Romans throughout Europe. In 403 B.C. the Ionic style of eastern Greek was officially adopted in Athens and it spread from there, with modifications in the course of time, over the entire Greek world. In the ninth century A.D. the Bulgarians adopted the eastern Greek minuscule called Glagolitic, which came to be used by the Eastern Orthodox church in the transcribing of the Old Church Slavonic language and which survived among the Croats until the seventeenth century. The complicated Cyrillic script, which was based on the Greek uncials in use in the ninth and tenth centuries, developed several centuries after the Glagolitic and through the agency of the Orthodox church it came into use in Jugoslavia, Bulgaria and Russia.

In the meantime there had been significant changes in the Latin script. After the political hegemony of Rome was broken by the Germanic invaders in the fifth century, national scripts arose in Europe reflecting the cultural isolation of mediaeval communities. Inscriptional lettering, book hands and cursive scripts acted and reacted upon one another and produced eclectic scripts. Wherever the Roman legions had gone, the normal medium for recording legal transactions had been the cursive Latin script; and communities which had no scribes, who used the literary book hand, had notaries to record wills and other contracts. The various cursive scripts had the same relation to the formal book hands as dialect had to literary diction. The many local scripts prevailed until the ninth century, when they were practically supplanted by the Caroline minuscule, or small letter, which had been developing since the seventh century and which owed its success to the sanction of Charlemagne and Alcuin, abbot of St. Martin of Tours, and to the wide propagation of the standard texts of the Benedictine Rule and the revisions of the Vulgate and liturgy which Charlemagne had ordered made. Gothic script marked by angularity, compression and fusion developed on the basis of the minuscule in northern France in the eleventh century and was at its best in the thirteenth. The Italian humanists of the fifteenth century reverted to the Caroline minuscule through their interest in the Latin manuscripts of the tenth and the eleventh century. The neo-Caroline script was spread largely by its adoption for papal documents by the apostolic chancery; during this period merchants, bankers and lawyers continued to keep their accounts in the tortuous mercantile or cursive script. Italy's example was followed by France, Holland and England in the sixteenth century.

With the coming of printing the calligraphers vied with the printers in producing artistic texts, and they exercised reciprocal influence on one another. As printing improved the services of calligraphers were gradually dispensed with in the preparation of books (*see* PRINTING AND PUBLISHING). Handwriting styles did not, however, deteriorate at this time, for the reason that it became the fashion among men and women of leisure to perfect their correspondence scripts so that their letters might be displayed for their artistic merit. Nevertheless, the new chancery cursive script was soon corrupted by mannerisms occasioned by ostentatious display.

The increased use of handwriting for commercial purposes along with the expansion and heightened tempo of industrial life and the extension of literacy to the middle classes and finally to the proletariat led to a pronounced simplification of scripts and the elimination of decorative interlacings and ornaments, which persisted among leisure class groups. The Scandinavian countries gave up the use of the Gothic script in the nineteenth century; it still predominates, however, in Germany. With the exception of Greece and other countries where the Orthodox church prevailed the Latin alphabet is used throughout the Occident; and through colonization, conquest and commercial and financial penetration it has been carried to North and South America, Africa, Australia and parts of Asia. The Turks, who had used the Arabic alphabet, which had spread with Islam throughout western Asia, adopted the Latin alphabet in 1928 by act of parliament. There has been agitation in eastern Asia to abandon the complicated ideographic Chinese and Japanese systems of writing for the Latin script. In the Soviet Union the minor nationalities who were previously preliterate are now being taught the Latin script and there is a growing movement for its use throughout the Soviet Union. Within each area and each period there have been mannerisms determined by fashion and individual and class affectations, and distinct handwritings have developed for diplomatic, legal and commercial usage and for correspondence.

The nature of the materials and the tools of writing have had a potent influence upon the styles of writing as well as upon the extent to which writing has been utilized. Stone and bronze in classical times developed highly deliberate shapes. The smooth surface of papyrus permitted fluency; and well pumiced vellum although excellent for permanent record was so expensive that it caused the crowding of the manuscript, which was one of the factors that led to the development of small letters. The use of a hair brush instead of a metal pen in Chinese writing has made calligraphy one of the most important branches of Chinese art. In imitating the technique of the copper engraver the calligraphers of the later sixteenth century in England used a very fine pen that transformed their style of writing. The invention and improvement of paper greatly facilitated the use of writing among the masses, as did the improvement and cheapening of inks and other writing materials.

Scripts are not mere external symbols of reference but take on an emotionalized ritualistic significance. For this reason in the history of writing once a style had found favor it tended to last for centuries with minor changes; the ancient uncial and half uncial scripts and the mediaeval Beneventan, Visigothic and Irish prevailed for five centuries or longer, the Gothic in Germany and Austria over eight centuries. Even when supplanted by other scripts survivals of older forms continue to be utilized for special purposes. While imperialistic expansion tends to obliterate the peculiarities of local scripts, the development of nationalism with its cultural introversion gives heightened tenacity to specialized forms and revives old forms, as in the case of the Irish. Changes of alphabet by edict in some cases have met organized resistance; suggested changes in the Bulgarian alphabet in 1922, for example, led to a political crisis, and the Latinizing of the Turkish alphabet was strenuously opposed particularly in religious circles.

BERNHARD J. STERN

See: COMMUNICATION; LANGUAGE; SYMBOLISM; LITERATURE; ART; CULTURE; LITERACY AND ILLITERACY;

Records, Historical; Sacred Books; Printing and Publishing.

Consult: Delitsch, Hermann, *Geschichte der abendländischen Schreibschriftformen* (Leipsic 1928); Jensen, Hans, *Geschichte der Schrift* (Hanover 1925); American Council on Education, *The Story of Writing*, Achievements of Civilization, no. 1 (Washington 1932); Mason, W. A., *A History of the Art of Writing* (New York 1920); Taylor, Isaac, *The History of the Alphabet* (London 1899); Faulmann, Karl, *Illustrierte Geschichte der Schrift* (Vienna 1880); Clodd, Edward, *The Story of the Alphabet* (New York 1900); Weule, Karl, *Vom Kerbstock zum Alphabet* (Stuttgart 1915); Tylor, E. B., *Researches into the Early History of Mankind* (3rd ed. London 1878) ch. v, and *Anthropology* (London 1881) ch. vii; Kroeber, A. L., *Anthropology* (New York 1923) ch. xi; Sprengling, Martin, *The Alphabet*, Chicago University, Oriental Institute, Communications, no. xii (Chicago 1931); Ullmann, B. L., *Ancient Writing and Its Influence* (New York 1932); Thompson, E. M., *An Introduction to Greek and Latin Palaeography* (Oxford 1912); Lowe, E. A., "Handwriting" in *The Legacy of the Middle Ages*, ed. by C. G. Crump and E. F. Jacob (Oxford 1926) p. 197–226; Morrison, Stanley, "The Development of Handwriting" in Heal, Ambrose, *The English Writing-Masters and Their Copy-Books, 1570–1800* (Cambridge, Eng. 1931) p. xxiii–xl; Hackmann, H., *Der Zusammenhang zwischen Schrift und Kultur in China* (Munich 1928).

WRITS. In its widest aspect a writ is a written command in the name of the sovereign addressed to an official or more rarely a private person, often but not always relating to the administration of justice. The regular use of writs necessarily implies a centralized government, which by this means keeps close control over a large number of distant agents. As soon as it became apparent that most forms of writ could be constantly repeated in similar circumstances, thus creating a regular routine, administration was simplified. The early history of the writ is therefore closely connected with the beginnings of the civil service and the oldest government department, the exchequer.

As the judicial business of the King's Court increased, it borrowed the machinery of the writ together with the useful device of requiring it to be "returned" on a stated day with an endorsement of the action taken upon it. During the twelfth century such writs became common, and before its close Glanvill was able to regard them as fundamental for an understanding of the common law, for each of the old traditional procedures was beginning to be represented by a particular set of writs. From Glanvill's day onward the multiplication of writs is an accurate measure of the expansion of the common law. Local jurisdictions continued to entertain litigation by informal (and apparently unwritten) plaints, unless a royal writ had been obtained with the special object of making them temporary delegates of the crown for that particular case. The crown frequently issued its writs addressed to a sheriff in cases where properly they should have been sent to the lord of a franchise, thus deliberately depriving him of his rights; even the Magna Carta denounced this abuse in vain.

By the time of Bracton no action could be brought in the king's court unless a satisfactory writ had been procured, and so it became a vital question as to who was to compose these writs and who was to have the responsibility of devising new forms when required. Down to Bracton's day the king's advisers often settled new forms of far reaching importance, while minute modifications were made in established forms by the chancery clerks, on the suggestion no doubt of plaintiffs. From Edward I's day new writs were often set out in statutes, but it is a significant fact that the presence of the great seal appended to a solemn command in the sovereign's name was no guaranty that the writ would be accepted by the courts, who might quash it for its grammar, spelling, handwriting and substance, according to their own view of its consonance with established legal principles. The drafting of writs therefore remained in the hands of the profession, bench and bar collaborating in the important task of cautiously varying the forms of writ and thus creating new actions and new substantive law. Under such conditions practitioners had to compile their own collections of those writs whose efficacy was established or which were regarded as likely to stand the scrutiny of the court. There has never been an official register of writs. The mediaeval commentaries on the register were superseded by Fitzherbert's *New Natura Brevium*, which went through twenty editions between 1534 and 1794. Five editions of the register of writs were published from 1531 to 1687. Both works follow the conventional classification of writs as "original," issuing generally from chancery and initiating judicial or administrative proceedings, or as "judicial," issuing from the courts and regulating steps in procedure.

There are two main phases in the development of the writ system after its classical expression in the work of Bracton. The first began shortly after his death with some statutory reforms and continued with further changes wrought by the profession itself. These took the form of modifications of the writ of trespass, which had great procedural advantages. Many sorts of wrong were made actionable in the King's Court by modifying this writ until it became possible to frame a large number of "special cases" in what came to be called "trespass on the case." There then appeared a new variety of "case" called assumpsit, which treated as a trespass the failure of the defendant to do what he had undertaken. Later still other derivatives completed the expansion of trespass from tort into the field of contract. By another line of development many of the real actions for land were replaced for most purposes by ejectment, another variation of trespass.

The second phase, developed in the seventeenth and eighteenth centuries, consisted in the evolution by practitioners of a procedure eliminating original writs altogether. This was made possible by an elaborate series of fictions, devised originally by courts in order to enable them to encroach upon one another's jurisdiction. The Bill of Middlesex is a typical example. The older procedure therefore gradually fell into disuse except in those few cases in which it afforded the only remedy. In the nineteenth century the legislature regularized this situation by abolishing most of the real actions in 1833 and the rest in 1860, by unifying the process in all personal actions in 1832 and by substituting a writ of summons in 1852 for the old original writs and the fictitious devices which often replaced them in practise.

The writ of error deserves special mention. It was the only means of reviewing decisions of law made by the central courts, and its great defect, derived from the Middle Ages, was that it availed only to reverse error on the record of the court below; with the growing artificiality of the record this tended to make many material matters of law not reversible because they did not in fact appear on the record. This troublesome anomaly was abolished in civil proceedings in 1875 and in criminal cases in 1907.

The writs which still generally survive in common law jurisdictions are the prerogative writs; certain judicial writs, especially writs of execution; and some of the old administrative writs, notably those ordering the election of the lower legislative house. The reform of chancery procedure removed the old writ of assistance, which called on the sheriff to aid in enforcing various types of chancery decree. The statutory extension of this writ in the colonies to call on sheriffs to search for and seize goods handled contrary to the navigation acts is a famous incident in the days preceding the American War of Independence.

At the time when American law was taking shape English lawyers were already making great use of the conventional and fictitious procedure noted above, one of the elements of which is the separation of the form of action, which had to be observed, from the original writ, which might be dispensed with. In America this situation was generally reproduced. The forms of action were accepted with varying degrees of precision according to time and place, but a simple summons seems generally to have replaced the original writ. Some of the forms of action, such as dower, entry, replevin and the like, still survive in some jurisdictions, but there is a wide and growing tendency toward their elimination through the adoption of codes of civil procedure. It is noteworthy that although complete reform has not yet been achieved in all the states, partial reform was undertaken in some of them, as in Virginia and Georgia, earlier than the corresponding reforms in England. The prerogative writs are in very general use.

THEODORE F. T. PLUCKNETT

See: JUDGMENTS; PROCEDURE, LEGAL; JUSTICE, ADMINISTRATION OF; COURTS; APPEALS; CERTIORARI; MANDAMUS; HABEAS CORPUS; INJUNCTION; TORT; ADMINISTRATIVE LAW; COMMON LAW.

Consult: Hall, Hubert, *Studies in English Official Historical Documents* (Cambridge, Eng. 1908); Maitland, F. W., *Equity; also the Forms of Action at Common Law* (Cambridge, Eng. 1909), and "The History of the Register of Original Writs" in *Harvard Law Review*, vol. iii (1889–90) 97–115, 167–79, 212–25; Ames, J. B., *Lectures on Legal History* (Cambridge, Mass. 1913); Hepburn, C. M., *The Historical Development of Code Pleading* (Cincinnati 1897); Sutton, R., *Personal Actions at Common Law* (London 1929).

WROŃSKI-HOENE, JÓZEF MARJA (1788–1853), Polish philosopher and scientist. Wroński was born in the province of Posen. He received a military education and at the age of fifteen participated in the defense of Warsaw against the Prussians and later fought under Kościuszko in the Russian-Polish war. Following the final partition of Poland he served in the Russian army, where he quickly attained the rank of major. Learning that a Polish legion was about to be organized abroad, he resigned from the Russian service and left the country never to return. After two years of study in Germany, where he became an ardent disciple of Kant, Wroński settled permanently in France; but instead of joining the legion as he had originally intended, he devoted himself entirely to scholarly work.

Wroński displayed amazing versatility and erudition. He attained considerable renown as a mathematician, made significant contributions in the field of celestial mechanics, busied himself with the designing and construction of machines and wrote widely and brilliantly on philosophy, sociology, politics and economics. Besides thirty-eight volumes in the field of mathematics and physics, he published thirty-five works on philosophical and sociological subjects and was the author of numerous unpublished treatises and pamphlets covering a wide variety of interests. His social philosophy, known as messianism, was based on the assertion that mankind strives persistently toward the discovery of absolute truth and that historical development is merely a manifestation of the various stages along the path to this ultimate goal. He viewed the historical process as the continuous clash of two fundamental and conflicting attitudes: the liberal and the conservative. The former emphasizes experience as the source of knowledge, adopts the mechanical explanation of the universe, is frankly atheistic, assumes a constant widening of the sphere of human knowledge, professes an optimistic view of life and its possibilities and accepts agreement as the source of all law; the latter expresses a belief that God is the source of all knowledge and that mankind, morally imperfect, will forever be prevented from penetrating into the realm of absolute truth. It was the aim of messianism to reconcile the two conflicting attitudes, to synthesize divine law and human law and thus to usher in the new era of absolute truth.

Wroński interpreted the scant response of the western world to messianism as a sign of the decadence of nations grown corrupt and weary of exaggerated civilization. He appealed to the youthful Slav race to assume the task of moral regeneration of the world along the principles of messianism and thus take over the role of early Christianity, which under similar circumstances had rescued the world from a decaying pagan civilization.

NATHAN REICH

Consult: Dickstein, Samuel, *Hoene-Wroński, jego zycie i prace* (Cracow 1896), with extensive list of works by and about Wroński; Daszyńska-Golińska, Z., "Filozofja gospodarcza i społeczna Hoene-Wrońskiego," introduction to her edition of Wroński's *System ekonomiczno-przemysłowy Adama Smitha*, Biblioteka dzieł społeczno-ekonomicznych (Warsaw 1912); Warrain, F., *L'armature métaphysique établie d'après la loi de création de Hoené Wroński* (Paris 1925).

WU T'ING FANG (1842–1922), Chinese statesman. Born in the British colony of Singapore, Wu T'ing Fang was educated at St. Paul's College in Hongkong and at Lincoln's Inn, London. His acquaintance with western culture qualified him to serve his people in international relations, a field to which he was introduced by the veteran politician Viceroy Li Hung Chang, who in 1882 appointed Wu his secretary and deputy commissioner of foreign affairs at Tientsin.

Wu's services at Shimonoseki, where he helped Li make peace with Japan in 1895, led to his appointment as minister to the United States the following year. In 1902 he returned to China to assist in the revision of the commercial treaties and in 1903 was made vice minister in the newly created Board of Commerce. A year later he was entrusted with the revision of the penal code, whose harsh provisions were being cited as justification by the western powers for exterritorial jurisdiction over their nationals in China. With the adoption of the new code the most objectionable features of Chinese criminal law were eliminated. In 1905 Wu T'ing Fang was appointed China's representative at the International Court of Arbitration at The Hague. He served as minister to Washington from 1907 to 1910, signing a treaty of arbitration with the United States in 1908.

Wu was very active in the Chinese Revolution of 1911 and assisted in the conference at Shanghai in 1912 which arranged for the suspension of hostilities between the north and the revolutionaries. He was minister for foreign affairs in the revolutionary government at Nanking, and while holding the same post at Peking in 1916–17 succeeded in bringing China into the World War on the side of the Allied and Associated Powers, despite the opposition of his friend Sun Yat Sen. In 1918, however, he cast his lot definitely with the separatist government at Canton. Four years later he served as civil governor of Kwangtung and endeavored without success to reconcile Canton and Peking, his failure being due to Sun's opposition. Wu was one of the eminent statesmen of the Chinese Revolution and as a diplomat made great strides in furthering occidental understanding of China and in creating a friendly attitude toward that country.

E. T. WILLIAMS

Consult: Taylor, G., "Wu Ting Fang and a Reunited China" in *American Review of Reviews*, vol. lxvi (1922) 513–16.

WUNDT, WILHELM MAX (1832–1920), German philosopher and psychologist. After serving as assistant to Helmholtz, Wundt taught at the universities of Heidelberg, Zurich and Leipsic. He was a man of extraordinary encyclopaedic knowledge. His voluminous works cover a vast range of subjects in philosophy, psychology, natural science and methodology of the social sciences. He is most widely known, however, as the founder of the sciences of experimental psychology and folk psychology. In philosophy he contributed greatly to the shift from positivism and neo-Kantianism to greater emphasis upon totality and organic relations and general conceptual and metaphysical questions. He created a stir with his *Ethik* (Stuttgart 1886, 4th ed., 3 vols., 1912; tr. by E. B. Titchener and others, 3 vols., London 1897–1901), in which he not only assailed utilitarianism but insisted upon the reality of a general will and supported Hegel in the precedence over the individual which he gave to objective forms and institutions, such as the state. He considered psychology as more than a special discipline; to him it was the foundation of all knowledge of the intellectual and spiritual world and the intermediary between natural science and philosophy. His psychological views reflected the change from an atomistic and analytical conception to one which was more unified and organic, and it was along these lines that Wundt influenced the development of German psychology. From the outset he felt that the systematically developed experimental psychology, of which his *Grundzüge der physiologischen Psychologie* (Leipsic 1874, 6th ed. 3 vols., 1908–11; tr. by E. B. Titchener, 2nd ed. London 1910) was a model, needed to be complemented by a cultural-historical and social-scientific approach. Such an "elaboration and continuation of psychology along the lines of social life" he presented in his *Völkerpsychologie* (10 vols., Leipsic 1900–20, vols. i–v, 2nd–4th ed. 1912–21). The subject of this study is human speech in its most general aspects and, for the lower cultures, myth and morals as well as religion, art and law. The basic problem here is "the analysis of those phenomena which arise from the intellectual and spiritual interaction of a multiplicity of individuals." Actually, however, the emphasis is not upon the psychological factors but upon the objective forms of language, morals, religion and so on. Wundt's work may thus be designated as a psychologically colored ethnology and presentation of the science of language. Ethnologically it is still dominated by the older evolutionist approach rather than by the more modern tendency which classifies social phenomena according to individual historical criteria and cultural spheres. The contribution to psychology which Wundt made in this work lies in his improved explanation of facts; relentlessly he attacked the intellectualistic vulgar psychology with its too high evaluation of consciousness and purpose. On the other hand, he did not devote sufficient attention to the significance of personality. The cultural factors too are almost never related to the interplay of forces within the group. Instead the group, particularly the tribe, also appears as one large individual. Wundt himself did not formulate his fundamental ideas in a systematic way. This task was undertaken by Felix Krüger and his school.

A. VIERKANDT

Consult: Petersen, Peter, *Wilhelm Wundt und seine Zeit* (Stuttgart 1925); Titchener, E. B., in *American Journal of Psychology*, vol. xxxii (1921) 161–78; Cattell, J. McKeen, and others, in *Psychological Review*, vol. xxviii (1921) 153–88; Goldenweiser, A. A., in *Freeman*, vol. iii (1921) 397–98; Hall, G. Stanley, *Founders of Modern Psychology* (New York 1912) p. 309–458. For an exhaustive bibliography of Wundt's works, see: Titchener, E. B., and others, "A Bibliography of the Scientific Writings of Wilhelm Wundt" in *American Journal of Psychology*, vol. xix (1908) 541–56, vol. xx (1909) 570, vol. xxi (1910) 603–04, vol. xxii (1911) 586–87, vol. xxiii (1912) 532, vol. xxiv (1913) 586, vol. xxv (1914) 599 and vol. xxxiii (1922) 260–62.

WYCLIFFE, JOHN (*c.* 1328–84), English religious leader. Wycliffe studied at Oxford and entered the service of Edward III. He attached himself to the anticlerical party and in 1374 was sent to Bruges to treat with Gregory XI, who demanded the payment of the tribute exacted from King John by Innocent III in 1213. Wycliffe strongly opposed the papal claims, maintaining that the pope ought to be chief follower of the Christ who abjured all earthly possessions, and that chosen laymen should administer the temporalities of the church. In Wycliffe's theory of dominion (derived from Fitzralph) Christ is the Lord in chief who grants to every creature that which he holds. All lordship is dependent on grace. Wycliffe maintained that the superfluity of ecclesiastical wealth should be divided among the poor. These ideas he embodied in two lengthy treatises, *De dominio divino* (ed. by R. L. Poole, London 1890) and *De civili dominio* (ed. by R. L. Poole, London 1884).

During the years 1377–82 many attacks were

made on Wycliffe by William Courtenay, bishop of London, and by various monks, backed by the pope. Wycliffe was supported by John of Gaunt and the seculars at Oxford. On May 22, 1377, Gregory XI issued bulls against Wycliffe, denouncing him as a heretic and citing him to Rome. Wycliffe was never so strong as in that year when he stood as the national champion against the papacy and expressed the national feeling against the abuses of the church. In 1379 Wycliffe began to deny the orthodox belief as to transubstantiation. He took a strongly realist attitude as opposed to the current nominalism. This position alienated John of Gaunt, who was afraid to countenance an archheretic. It also put a formidable weapon in the hands of his opponents. Consequently in 1380 Wycliffe was condemned as a heretic. He was forced to leave Oxford and to retire to Lutterworth. There Wycliffe ministered as a parish priest. He instructed and dispatched far and wide his poor priests, thus laying the foundations of Lollard thought and practise, which lasted down to the Reformation.

Wycliffe's influence was not confined to England only. Through servants of the Czech queen of Richard II, Anne of Bohemia, his works were carried to Prague, fell into the hands of John Huss and Jerome of Prague and formed the basis of the Hussite movement and the origin of the later Moravians.

One of Wycliffe's most important achievements was his translation of the Bible into English. He was driven to this as a logical outcome of two main ideas. He regarded the Scriptures as the paramount rule of life; and as a reformer he maintained that if man is God's tenant, no intermediary, priest, bishop or pope, can come between the tenant and his Lord in chief.

Wycliffe was also strongly opposed to war. In his *De officio regis* (ed. by A. W. Pollard and C. Sayle, London 1887) he endeavored to determine when a king might be justified in waging war, but he came to the final conclusion that "it is more conformable to the law of Christ not to war." In his English writings he was very critical of the way in which the merchants built up wealth against truth, charity and common profit. His sympathies were altogether on the side of the people. He was opposed to serfdom and was the only mediaeval philosopher who objected to it on principle. Further he demanded that lords should be just, sympathetic and lenient. On the other hand, he required from the laborer hard work and loyal service. He was not responsible directly for the Peasants' Revolt in 1381, although indirectly it embodied his principle.

Wycliffe poured his most reiterated denunciations on the heads of monks and friars. He disapproved of the monks partly because of their vast possessions and partly because they failed in the chief office of a priest—the preaching of God's Word. Shut up behind their walls, they did not maintain any contact with the spiritual life of the people. The friars influenced the religious life of the people by bad methods. They reduced confession to a farce and in their preaching twisted God's Word and pleased their auditors with fables. The English bishops also came under Wycliffe's condemnation because of their assumption of secular offices. They were not as a rule vicious men, but they labored less at the cure of souls than at the king's business, deputing their spiritual functions to archdeacons, who were often alien cardinals. Wycliffe desired the reform of the church from top to bottom. It should be stripped of its endowments and these divided among the poor. Temporalities should be entirely in the hands of the king and secular lords. The preaching of the Gospels should be performed by pastors kept thoroughly evangelical in spirit by their having to depend for clothing and sustenance on the voluntary grants of their flock.

H. B. Workman

Consult: Lechler, G. V., *Johann von Wiclif und die Vorgeschichte der Reformation*, 2 vols. (Leipsic 1873), tr. by P. Lorimer (new ed. London 1884); Workman, H. B., *John Wyclif*, 2 vols. (Oxford 1926); Poole, R. L., *Wycliffe and Movements for Reform* (London 1889); Trevelyan, G. M., *England in the Age of Wycliffe* (new ed. London 1909).

WYTHE, GEORGE (1726–1806), American jurist. Virtually self-educated, Wythe rose to prominence in the Virginia colonial bar and was among the first to advocate the cause of independence. His remonstrance against British policy in 1764, drafted when a member of the House of Burgesses, was, however, too advanced for adoption at that time. With the advent of the revolution Wythe served as a delegate to the Continental Congress and signed the Declaration of Independence. He was a strenuous advocate of the ratification of the federal constitution and as chairman of the Committee of the Whole in the state convention lent all his influence to defeating the obstructionists.

Wythe's most constructive efforts were achieved as a member of the historic committee which revised the laws of Virginia and which presented the code adopted in 1785. This provided for the promotion of education, the gradual emancipation of the slaves, of which Wythe was an earnest personal advocate, the abolition of entails and primogeniture and the establishment of religious liberty. In the division of work Wythe concentrated on the operative effect of British statutes from the time of colonization to the revolution, leaving the other periods to his colleagues Jefferson and Pendleton. His juristic reputation was further enhanced by his services first as one of the three judges and later as sole chancellor of the High Court of Chancery.

Anticipating Marbury v. Madison, Wythe in an opinion rendered in Commonwealth v. Caton [4 Call 5–21 (1782)] asserted by way of dicta the right of the court to resist an unconstitutional act of the legislature, declaring it his duty "to protect one branch of the legislature, and, consequently, the whole community, against the usurpation of the other. . . ." Wythe's views of the power of the judiciary are of special significance when it is remembered that he was the most influential law teacher of eighteenth century America. He occupied a professorship of law at William and Mary College from 1779 to 1789. Among those who learned their law from him were two future presidents, Jefferson and Monroe, and one chief justice of the United States, John Marshall. Of the next generation Henry Clay testified to the value of his youthful contacts with the chancellor.

RICHARD B. MORRIS

Consult: Tyler, L. G., in *Great American Lawyers*, ed. by W. D. Lewis, 8 vols. (Philadelphia 1907–09) vol. i, p. 51–90; Minor, B. B., "Memoir of the Author" in Wythe's *Chancery Reports* (Richmond 1852) p. xi–xl; Anderson, D. R., "Chancellor Wythe and Parson Weems" in *William and Mary College Quarterly*, vol. xxv (1916–17) 13–20, and "The Teacher of Jefferson and Marshall" in *South Atlantic Quarterly*, vol. xv (1916) 327–43; Lingley, C. R., *The Transition in Virginia from Colony to Commonwealth*, Columbia University, Studies in History, Economics and Public Law, no. 96 (New York 1910).

XENOPHON (c. 431–354 B.C.), Greek soldier, historian and essayist. Xenophon's participation in the March of the Ten Thousand had a decisive influence on his life; for his subsequent service under Spartan commanders, especially Agesilaus, caused his banishment from Athens, while the desire to set down his experiences led him to exercise his undoubted literary gifts. His record of the march, *Anabasis*, and the *Hellenica* together provide an account of Greek history from 411 to 362 B.C. After giving up soldiering Xenophon lived for a quarter of a century at Scillus in Elis; his declining years were spent at Corinth. His literary output was most varied. Treatises on the management of an estate, hunting with dogs and horsemanship are the fruits of his experience as a country gentleman. More ambitious were the reminiscences of Socrates, *Memorabilia*, and the education of Cyrus, *Cyropaedia*. The former is more valuable as a reflection of the amiable character, varied interests and practical morality of the author than as a record of the philosopher, with whom Xenophon's acquaintance can have been little more than superficial. The latter, which in form resembles a historical novel, is partly an educational treatise, partly a manual on generalship and the art of war. The system of training boys obviously owes much to that actually practised at Sparta; save for the unique recommendation of "nature study" in the form of elementary botany it is entirely physical and moral. The later parts of the book derive their worth from being based on Xenophon's own experiences as a soldier. Xenophon's reputation in Roman times rested mainly on these two works. His last essay, on the revenues of Athens, may have been composed to support the financial policy of Eubulus. It reveals the writer as a very amateur economist but contains some interesting suggestions for improving the commercial prosperity of Athens by attracting more resident aliens and by exploiting more intensively the silver mines at Laurium. Xenophon is a versatile writer whose charm has always attracted many readers. As a historian he is much inferior to Thucydides and Polybius. His narrative is clear and straightforward but has important omissions. He has an imperfect understanding of the complicated political and diplomatic history of his age. He is at his best in the biographical passages; and in emphasizing this aspect of history he together with Isocrates exercised, for good or ill, a decisive influence on historical composition in the later fourth century and in the Hellenistic age.

M. L. W. LAISTNER

Works: *Xenophontis opera omnia*, ed. by E. C. Marchant, Scriptorum Classicorum Bibliotheca Oxoniensis, 5 vols. (Oxford 1902–20), tr. by H. G. Dakyns, 3 vols. (London 1890–97); *Xenophon*, original Greek and translation by C. L. Brownson, E. C. Marchant, and others, Loeb Classical Library, 7 vols. (London 1914–25).

Consult: Croiset, Alfred and Maurice, *Histoire de la littérature grecque*, 5 vols. (2nd–3rd ed. Paris 1898–

1910) vol. iv, ch. vi, abridged translation by G. Heffelbower, 1 vol. (New York 1904) p. 311–21; Tarn, W. W., "Persia, from Xerxes to Alexander" in *Cambridge Ancient History*, vol. vi (Cambridge, Eng. 1927) ch. i; Glover, T. R., *From Pericles to Philip* (3rd ed. London 1919), especially chs. vi, viii–ix; Münscher, Karl, *Xenophon in der griechisch-römischen Literatur*, Philologue, Supplement xiii, no. ii (Leipsic 1920).

XENOPOL, ALEXANDRU (1847–1920), Rumanian historian. After studying law in Germany Xenopol returned to Rumania in 1871 to enter the legal department of the government. Later he engaged in the private practise of the law. In 1883 he was appointed professor of Rumanian history at Jassy.

As a teacher and writer Xenopol profoundly influenced the intellectual life and the national spirit of Rumania. His most significant writings are in the field of history, where he took as his model the English historian Buckle, allowing less weight, however, to geographical conditions. In addition to articles in the *Revue historique*, the *Revue de synthèse historique* and the *Annales* of the Rumanian Academy he published a number of longer studies. Of these the most outstanding was *Istoria Românilor din Dacia Traiană* (6 vols., Bucharest 1888–93), an abridged version of which appeared in French as *Histoire des Roumains de la Dacie Trajane* (2 vols., Paris 1896). It constituted the first scientific history of the Rumanian people and of the states which they had established. Based upon a critical analysis of such meager source material as was available to him, it evidenced the author's remarkable gift for synthesis and clarified the chief trends in Rumanian history. Although examination of additional sources later revealed many errors of fact, this work still remains one of the important achievements in Rumanian historiography. It supported the theory of the continuity of the Roman element in the Rumanian population, a view which Xenopol had already developed in *Les Roumains du moyen-âge: un énigme historique* (Paris 1885). He stressed the unity of the Rumanians as an amalgamation of Dacians, Romans and Slavs in which the Roman strain dominated. An expanded edition of the *Istoria Românilor* appeared in 1896; the revision upon which Xenopol was engaged at his death was published in three volumes in 1925.

In his later years Xenopol was interested primarily in the philosophy of history. The most complete statement of his own theory is contained in *Les principes fondamentaux de l'histoire* (Paris 1899) and *La théorie de l'histoire* (Paris 1908), the latter an elaboration of the earlier work. He divides the sciences into two categories according to the nature of their material. The material of one category, which includes such sciences as chemistry and biology, consists of phenomena grouped on the basis of similarity. Within each group the facts are essentially alike and are repeated in time. Because of this factor of repetition general laws may be established for such groups, and through these laws recurrences may be predicted. The distinguishing characteristic of the second category, that of the historical sciences, is that the material they utilize is composed of individual facts which are never repeated but merely succeed one another. It is the difference between these facts rather than their similarity which is important. For such phenomena no general laws can be established. Nevertheless, history is a science for, according to Xenopol, the criterion of a science is that its facts may be organized within general frames; in history this is accomplished through the historical series, consisting of a chain of causally related, successive events united by a general idea. There are, in addition, general laws of development in history. Only social events which have consequences affecting a large number of people may be considered historical facts. No series is ever repeated and each forms part of a larger series in an almost infinite process. From the study of historical series future trends may be indicated but not future events.

The methodology of the historical sciences is necessarily different from that employed for repetitive material. Neither induction nor deduction is applicable to successive phenomena. The special logic of history is accordingly inference; that is, the discovery of unknown facts from causally related known facts. The former have the status of hypotheses until they are authenticated by direct evidence. It is also possible by inference to establish causes for series. A historical study which consists of a mere chronicle of events and neglects causal analysis is incomplete and unscientific.

This emphasis upon causality and generalization was perhaps a premature influence in a country where the factual foundations of history had still to be established. But although subsequent historical schools necessarily tended to concentrate upon detailed examinations of source material, Xenopol's theories left their impress upon all social sciences in Rumania.

FLORENCE MISHNUN

Consult: Jorga, N., "Roumanie" in *Histoire et his-*

toriens depuis cinquante ans, 2 vols. (Paris 1927) vol. i, p. 320–40, especially p. 325–28; Vladesco-Rascoassa, G., "La sociologie en Roumanie" in *Revue internationale de sociologie*, vol. xxxvii (1929) 1–22, especially p. 4–7; *Revue historique*, vol. cxxxvi (1921) pt. i, p. 309–10; Bagdasar, N., "Conceptia filosofiei istoriei" in *Archiva pentru stiinta si reforma sociala*, vol. vii (1928) nos. 3–4; Barth, Paul, *Die Philosophie der Geschichte als Soziologie* (3rd–4th rev. ed. Leipsic 1922) p. 91–95.

XIMÉNES DE CISNEROS, FRANCISCO (1436–1517), Spanish ecclesiastic and statesman. Ximénes studied canon and civil law at the University of Salamanca and for several years practised in the ecclesiastical courts at Rome. He returned to Toledo about 1465 with an order from the pope that he was to be appointed to the first vacant benefice, but when a vacancy occurred the archbishop Carrillo proceeded to select his own appointee. Ximénes pressed his claims, however, and as a result was imprisoned for a number of years. Subsequently Mendoza appointed him grand vicar of Sigüenza, an office which he resigned to join the Franciscan order. Although he reentered public life in 1492 upon his appointment as confessor to Queen Isabella, he always remained essentially an ascetic.

Ximénes became archbishop of Toledo in 1495 and continued on a wider scale the work of religious reform which he had undertaken as provincial in Castille for the Franciscan order. His zeal aroused a powerful opposition group; Ximénes, however, supported by the queen, refused to yield. In 1499 he went to Granada in order to convert the Moors, who under the treaty of 1491 had enjoyed civil and religious liberty. His energetic proselytizing and his questionable methods, which included the burning of Moorish manuscripts, provoked a revolt; nevertheless, Ximénes continued his efforts, and in 1501 the Moslems were forced to choose between conversion and banishment. Later he was instrumental in organizing a successful military expedition against the Moors in Africa. He served as inquisitor general of Castille and in 1507 was named by the pope cardinal of Spain.

Ximénes was a generous patron of learning; he founded the University of Alcalá, modeling it upon that of Paris and providing special facilities for the poor. With the assistance of some of the professors, including Greeks and converted Jews, he completed and published the famous polyglot Bible *Vetus testamentum multiplici lingua* (6 vols., Alcalá 1514–17), containing Hebrew, Latin, Greek and Chaldean texts. The old copies of the Vulgate had become corrupted, and Ximénes' work provided a great impetus to textual criticism.

By virtue of his office as archbishop of Toledo Ximénes was grand chancellor of Castille. This position and his friendship with his sovereigns made his opinion important in decisions of state. He encouraged absolutism in the government, consistently urged colonial expansion and fostered religious intolerance. The influence of these doctrines is obvious in the policies of Ferdinand and Isabella.

FLORENCE MISHNUN

Consult: Cedillo, Jerónimo, *El cardenal Cisneros Gobernador del reino* (Madrid 1921); Fernández de Retana, L., *Cisneros y su siglo*, 2 vols. (Madrid 1929–30); *Crónica del certamen histórico-literario, Francisco Jiménez de Cisneros* (Havana 1918); Lyell, James P. R., *Cardinal Ximenes* (London 1917); Porreño, Baltasar, *Dos tratados históricos tocantes al Cardenal Ximénez de Cisneros*, ed. by Jerónimo Cedillo, Sociedad de Bibliófilos Españoles, Libros Publicados, no. 41 (Madrid 1918).

YAMAGATA, PRINCE ARITOMO (1838–1922), Japanese statesman. A Choshu samurai and pupil of Yoshida Shōin, Yamagata organized a non-samurai force before the restoration, thus revealing the possibilities of utilizing the common man in a military machine. In the war to restore the emperor he commanded some of the Choshu forces and in the first restoration government served as undersecretary in the War Department. In 1869 he was sent to Europe for study. Upon his return he became minister of war and in this capacity undertook to organize the modern Japanese army. He introduced conscription and was responsible for the general scheme of organization. It was his conscript army under his direction which put down the Satsuma rebellion (1877) and defeated China in 1894 and Russia in 1904. As minister of the interior in 1887 he established local autonomy.

Always an influential adviser of the emperor, it was only after the promulgation of the constitution that Yamagata turned definitely to politics. This shift was necessary, he felt, in order to insure a conservative application of the constitution and to promote the interests of the army. Yamagata headed the first constitutional government and served thereafter on several occasions as premier and held various cabinet positions. It was due to his efforts that military dominance of the government was established and perpetuated and party influence minimized. He was equally successful in his contest after 1890 with Ito, the leader of the non-militarist faction in the oligarchy which ruled Japan. Retiring from active politics in 1900 he continued to dominate the political scene until his death, working partly through his protégé Katsura but deriving his influence primarily from his recognized position as the leading elder statesman. The modern Japanese military system is Yamagata's legacy to his country.

HAROLD M. VINACKE

Consult: Hall, Josef W., *Eminent Asians* (New York 1929) p. 101–245; Morris, J., *Makers of Japan* (London 1906) ch. xiii; Yamazaki, F., "Prince Yamagata" in *Japan Magazine*, vol. xii (1921–22) 473–83; Vinacke, H. M., *A History of the Far East in Modern Times* (rev. ed. New York 1933) p. 343–49; Fujisawa, R., *The Recent Aims and Political Development of Japan*, Williams College, Institute of Politics (New Haven 1923) p. 29–39.

YANG CHU (4th century B.C.), Chinese philosopher. Little is known of the life of Yang Chu, but it is held that he was a small proprietor in the state of Wei. He lived during the period of the "warring states" when the China of the lower Yellow River valley was in political and social turmoil. Although he is credited with having been a Taoist, or follower of Lao Tzu, he must early have forsaken the mystical teachings of the master to become a pronounced egotist and fatalist.

The writings attributed to him are to be found in the seventh chapter of the *Lieh Tzŭ*, an incorporation of early literature, and are very fragmentary; they have been translated by Forke under the title *Yang Chu's Garden of Pleasure* (London 1912). The philosophy which they express is essentially one of conduct. Happiness, according to Yang Chu, consists in the realization of the individual, which is possible only through the cultivation of the senses. The degradation of human life is the result of the unnatural attempt to curb the senses, due to cravings for longevity, fame, position and wealth, which, he argued, run counter to the "mandates of Heaven." Independent men are "far above earthly things; they have destiny in their own hands and are free from all outward interference." Such sentiments struck at the basis of moral and social control lauded by the Confucians, but Yang Chu went even further. He laughed at the ruler sages of antiquity, figures which were revered by the political philosophers of the day as the truest guides to good government.

These reflections were heresy and roundly denounced as such by the loyal Mencius. They were so much a product of the time, however, that Hirth (*The Ancient History of China*, New York 1908, p. 279) is perhaps right when he points to Yang Chu as an indication of degeneration in the leadership of the more important states and as an influence which made for its bankruptcy a century and a half after Yang Chu's death.

L. C. GOODRICH

Consult: Cranmer-Bying, H., Introduction to *Yang Chu's Garden of Pleasure*, p. 7–35; David, Alexandra, *Les théories individualistes dans la philosophie chinoise, Yang-Tchou* (Paris 1909); Forke, Alfred, *Geschichte der alten chinesischen Philosophie*, Hamburg University, Abhandlungen aus dem Gebiet der Auslandskunde, vol. xxv (Hamburg 1927) p. 356–67, and "Yang Chu, the Epicurean in His Relation to Liehtse, the Pantheist" in Peking Oriental Society, *Journal*, vol. iii, no. 3 (1893) 203–58; Suzuki, D. T., *A Brief History of Early Chinese Philosophy* (London 1914) p. 84–92; Maspero, Henri, *La Chine antique*, Histoire du Monde, vol. iv (Paris 1927) p. 508–15; Legge, James, *The Chinese Classics*, 8 vols. (rev. ed. Oxford 1893–95) vol. ii, ch. iii, sect. 1.

YANSON, YULY EDUARDOVICH (1835–93), Russian statistician. Yanson was a native of Kiev and a graduate of Kiev University. In 1865, after he had taught rural economics for some years at an agricultural institute, he was appointed to the chair of statistics in the University of St. Petersburg, a post which he retained until his death. Although he has been described as the outstanding representative of academic statistics in Russia, Yanson was not primarily a theorist. His textbook (*Teoriya statistiki*, St. Petersburg 1885; 3rd ed. 1889), which influenced an entire generation of Russian authors, excelled in the discussion of practical problems, such as the organization of censal inquiries and of registration, tabulation and graphic presentation, statistical office management and the like; and in his comparative study of population and agriculture in Russia and western Europe (*Sravnitelnaya statistika Rossii i zapadno-evropeyskikh gosudarstv*, 2 vols., St. Petersburg 1878–80; 2nd ed. vol. i, 1893) he avoided all but the most elementary methods of statistical analysis. Yanson's forte was rather applied statistical research and statistical administration. In 1867–68 he investigated on behalf of the Free Economic Society the production and trade in cereals in southwestern Russia and later presented his findings in a number of distinguished reports. In a study published in 1877 (*Opit statisticheskago izsledovaniya o krestyanskikh nadelakh i platezhakh*, St. Petersburg; 2nd ed. 1881) and based on a complete collation of the meager statistical material then available he painted a striking picture of the decay of postreform peasant economy undermined by the inadequacy of land allotments, the heavy burden of redemption payments, the inequity of the tax system and the virtual prohibition of peasant migration; his conclusions were largely confirmed by later zemstvo statistics and the remedial measures he proposed—reduction and redistribution of redemption payments, better credit facilities for land purchase, organized transfer of populations—were adopted in part by the government. From 1881 on Yanson was in charge of the St. Petersburg municipal bureau of statistics established according to his plans; in this capacity he organized, directed and published the results of two comprehensive population censuses of the capital (1881 and 1890), which served as a model for large city censuses throughout the country.

P. I. GEORGIEVSKY

Consult: Georgievsky, P. I., in Russkoe Obshchestvo Okhraneniya Narodnago Zdraviya, *Sobranie* (March 13, 1893); Kaufman, A. A., *Statisticheskaya nauka v Rossii* (Statistical science in Russia) (Moscow 1922) ch. iii.

YANZHUL, IVAN IVANOVICH (1845–1914), Russian economist and publicist. Yanzhul was professor of economics and statistics at the University of Moscow and in 1895 was elected a member of the Academy of Sciences. A follower of the historico-ethical school, he favored a system of state socialism and participated actively in the promotion of various measures of social legislation. In 1882 he was appointed factory inspector but resigned in 1887 in protest against the Russian authorities, which not only ignored all his recommendations but failed to fine the employers for their violation of the labor laws. His report published as *Fabrichniy bit Moskovskoy gubernii* (Factory life in Moscow province, St. Petersburg 1884) was an important source of information on industrial conditions. He recounted his experiences as factory inspector in *Iz vospominaniy i perepiski fabrichnago inspektora* (From the memoirs and correspondence of a factory inspector, St. Petersburg 1907).

Yanzhul's first important work was *Opit izsledovaniya angliyskikh kosvennikh nalogov; aktsiz* (An essay on indirect taxes in England; the excise, Moscow 1874), in which he arrived independently at the Marxian view that the fiscal system was an outcome of class structure and class struggle and had changed in England when power shifted from the landed aristocracy to industrial capitalists. His principal work, *Angliyskaya svobodnaya torgovlya* (English free trade, 2 vols., Moscow 1876–82), which deals with the doctrines of free competition and protection in trade and industry, is based on a thorough knowledge of economic literature from the sixteenth to the middle of the nineteenth century. Yanzhul also contributed to leading periodicals numerous articles on current economic and political problems.

E. A. KOSMINSKY

Consult: Akademiya Nauk, St. Petersburg, *Materiali dlya biograficheskago slovarya deystvitelnikh chlenov Imperatorskoy Akademii Nauk* (Materials for a biographical dictionary of the members of the Imperial Academy of Sciences), 2 vols. (Petrograd 1915–17) vol. ii, p. 273–81, containing a complete list of Yanzhul's publications.

YĀQŪT IBN 'ABD-ALLĀH AL-RŪMI AL-ḤAMAWI (1179–1229), Moslem geographer. Yāqūt was born of Greek parents in Asia Minor. In his youth he was bought by a Moslem merchant domiciled in Bagdad, who after giving him a good education and using him as a traveling clerk enfranchised him in 1200. In order to support himself Yāqūt roamed from place to place copying and selling manuscripts. His journeys carried him to Syria, Egypt, Oman and Persia.

The first draft of Yāqūt's geographical dictionary, *Mu'jam al-Buldān* (ed. by H. F. Wüstenfeld and O. Rescher as *Jacuts geographisches Wörterbuch*, 7 vols., Leipsic and Stuttgart 1866–1928), was completed in 1224 and the final version four years later. In this work he arranged the place names alphabetically, defined their orthography and vocalization and attached a historical sketch to each name. Besides its fund of historical and geographical lore the book contains a great number of archaeological, literary, ethnographic and scientific facts. It established Yāqūt as the chief of Moslem geographers, and it is still the standard work in Arabic geography. The part of the *Mu'jam* relating to Persia was extracted and translated by C. Barbier de Meynard as *Dictionnaire géographique, historique et littéraire de la Perse et des contrées adjacentes* (Paris 1861).

Yāqūt also prepared a geographical dictionary of homonyms, *Al-Mushtarik Waḍ'a w-al-Muftariq Saq'a* (ed. by H. F. Wüstenfeld as *Jacuts Moschtarik*, Göttingen 1846), and compiled an elaborate biographical dictionary of men of letters, *Kitāb Irshād al-Arīb ila Ma'rifat al-Adīb* (ed. by D. S. Margoliouth, 7 vols., Leyden

1907–27), which is surpassed only by the work of ibn-Khallikān.

PHILIP K. HITTI

Consult: Brockelmann, Carl, *Geschichte der arabischen Litteratur*, 2 vols. (Weimar and Berlin 1898–1902) vol. i, p. 479–81; Carra de Vaux, Bernard, *Les penseurs de l'islam*, 3 vols. (Paris 1921–26) vol. ii, p. 14–19; Huart, Clement, *Littérature arabe* (Paris 1902), tr. by Mary Loyd as *A History of Arabic Literature* (London 1903), especially p. 304–05; Sarton, George, *Introduction to the History of Science*, Carnegie Institution of Washington, Publications, no. 376, 2 vols. (Baltimore 1927–31) vol. ii, pt. ii, p. 642–43.

YARRANTON, ANDREW (1616–84?), British economist and engineer. Yarranton began his career as a linen draper, but the "shop being too narrow" for his "large mind," he turned to farming; then he became a soldier, an ironworker, a canal designer and finally a political economist and publicist.

Yarranton's chief work, *England's Improvement by Sea and Land*, was published in 1677. He outlined an integrated plan for the advancement of British trade, embracing six projects: a general system of chartered banking to eliminate the haphazard goldsmith deposit system; a land registry, so that titles could be readily verified and real estate could become acceptable collateral for loans; the improvement and extension of the linen, iron and woolen trades, including production of raw materials and manufacture; the development of inland navigation by canals and by deepening the smaller rivers; the building of granaries to conserve grain and to enable farmers to transfer their grain by means of warehouse receipts; and the enlargement and construction of harbors to accommodate an expansion of shipping.

Yarranton envisioned England's improvement as a totality and toward this end he strove for intensive utilization of British resources and British labor. To develop British manufactures he advocated customs duties to protect growing industries. His system of economic nationalism was an outgrowth of the immediate problem of his time. Britain was beset by competition from the Netherlands—in manufacturing and shipping particularly—and it was Yarranton's purpose to show the British "the true way to beat the Dutch without fighting."

Yarranton's public opposition to the goldsmiths and his labors in behalf of chartered banking were part of the agitation which led to the founding of the Bank of England in 1694, about ten years after his death. His efforts to mobilize real estate and commodities as sound assets for mortgages and loans undoubtedly influenced monetary thought and accelerated the development of the credit system.

J. A. LIVINGSTON

Important works: *Improvement Improved, or the Great Improvement of Land by Clover* (London 1661, 2nd ed. 1663); *England's Improvement by Sea and Land* . . . , 2 pts. (London 1677–81).

Consult: Dove, Patrick E., *The Elements of Political Science, with an Account of Andrew Yarranton, the Founder of English Political Economy* (Edinburgh 1854) p. 402–70; Smiles, Samuel, *Industrial Biography* (new ed. London 1905) ch. iv; Eden, Frederic M., *The State of the Poor*, 3 vols. (London 1797) vol. i, p. 192–96; Cunningham, William, *The Growth of English Industry and Commerce in Modern Times*, 3 vols. (Cambridge, Eng. 1910–12) vol. ii, especially p. 318, 532–33; McCulloch, John R., *The Literature of Political Economy* (London 1845) p. 350.

"YELLOW DOG" CONTRACT. See LABOR CONTRACT.

YERKES, CHARLES TYSON (1837–1905), American capitalist. The son of a banker, Yerkes was one of the few captains of industry of his period who was not born poor. After employment as a clerk in a grain commission house he opened a brokerage office in 1859 and later purchased a bank. His firm failed, and he was found guilty of technical embezzlement for having misappropriated public money received from the sale of bonds of the city of Philadelphia. He served seven months of his sentence in the penitentiary and was then pardoned. After a brief real estate venture in Dakota he settled in Chicago, where he conducted a brokerage and banking business and finally entered upon his extraordinary career as manipulator of Chicago's traction and politics.

Yerkes was probably the first to discover that large profits could be derived from reorganizing and pyramiding street railway companies and capitalizing the franchises of growing cities. While he made some preliminary experiments in Philadelphia, his greatest success was achieved in the chaotically expanding Chicago of the 1880's, when the replacement of horse cars by mechanical power gave impetus to the development and overcapitalization of traction systems. In 1886–87 with the assistance of P. A. B. Widener and Stephen B. Elkins he secured virtual control of Chicago's street railway lines and later strategic sections of the elevated railway, all of which he dominated until 1899. He made tremendous profits by setting up a labyrinth of interlocking holding, operating and construction companies and a system of leases, friendly contracts and watered securities. In return he provided overcrowded service, installed flimsy equipment and, by having two nominally separate companies cover a single route, charged passengers double fares.

Franchises were Yerkes' most valuable asset in his system of manipulation, and to secure them he dominated local politics, which his wealth and the corruptibility of councilmen and legislators made relatively easy. When Governor John P. Altgeld refused his bribe and vetoed his bills, he saw to it that the next governor should be friendly by capitalizing on conservative resentment against Altgeld and his own growing influence in political and financial circles. His attempts, however, to have his franchises extended beyond 1903 finally aroused so much public antagonism that beginning in 1898 a political upheaval led by reformers defeated his bills decisively. Although his key franchises were apparently expiring, Yerkes unloaded his thoroughly deteriorated and heavily watered traction interests on a syndicate headed by his old friend Widener; and after making public the amazing books of his companies, he left Chicago with about $15,000,000 in cash. He moved to England in 1900 and headed the company which secured control of the underground rights for London, constructed subways and drove J. P. Morgan's rival syndicate from the field.

GEORGE MARSHALL

Consult: Russell, C. E., "Where Did You Get It, Gentlemen?," and Lefèvre, Edwin, "What Availeth It?" in *Everybody's Magazine*, vol. xvii (1907) 348–60, and vol. xxiv (1911) 836–48; Hendrick, B. J., *The Age of Big Business*, Chronicles of America series, vol. xxxix (New Haven 1919) ch. v; Civic Federation of Chicago, Committee Report, "Street Railways of Chicago" in *Municipal Affairs*, vol. v (1901) 439–594; Fairlie, J. A., "The Street Railway Question in Chicago" in *Quarterly Journal of Economics*, vol. xxi (1906–07) 371–404. See also: Dreiser, Theodore, *The Financier* (rev. ed. New York 1927), and *The Titan* (New York 1914), of which Yerkes was the prototype.

YOGA. *See* MYSTICISM.

YOSHIDA TORAJIRŌ (1830–59), Japanese scholar. Yoshida Torajirō is popularly known as Shōin. By family succession he became head of the Choshu clan's military school; but although he was a student of military science, his significant doctrines were political. He traveled extensively in Japan, studying military science, broadening his understanding and impressing his views on an ever widening circle. Influenced by the Mito school, which was royalist in sentiment, but especially by Sakuma Shōzan, whose friend and pupil he became in 1851, Yoshida early advocated the restoration of power to the emperor. A trip to the north in 1851, deliberately undertaken before he had received the necessary authority, resulted in the loss of his samurai status, and thus he became, in his own view, a citizen of Japan instead of a clansman. Although he was hostile to intercourse with other countries, Yoshida made two unsuccessful attempts to go abroad in order to acquaint himself with foreign achievements. The second led to his imprisonment for attempted violation of the law. While in confinement at home he was, however, permitted to resume teaching. Among his pupils were many future political leaders, including Ito and Yamagata. Yoshida's views moreover were also impressed on such men as Kido and others who came to advocate the restoration. Because of his active hostility to the shogunate he was taken to Yeddo as a prisoner and beheaded.

Yoshida left his mark on Japan through the influence of his teachings upon Japanese statesmen. Back of his championship of the restoration lay an intense spirit of nationalism. From this evolved his advocacy of imperialism, the restoration and the establishment of the cult of the state being considered the prelude to continental expansion. His ideas were adopted by his clan and by restoration Japan.

HAROLD M. VINACKE

Consult: Coleman, H. E., "The Life of Shōin Yoshida," tr. from the Japanese by I. Tokutomi in Asiatic Society of Japan, *Transactions*, vol. xlv (1917) pt. i, p. 119–88; Morris, J., *Makers of Japan* (London 1906) ch. v.

YOUNG, ALLYN ABBOTT (1876–1929), American economist. Young was professor of economics at a number of universities, including Harvard and the London School of Economics. No enumeration of the chairs held by him or of his services on various committees and organizations dealing with problems after the World War or, finally, of his publications can give an adequate conception of his contribution to economics. He was first and last a creative teacher, and it was through his teaching rather than his writing that he influenced contemporary thought. Most of his work is irretrievably lost or lives on in the work of others to an extent which it is impossible to estimate. Rarely if ever has fame comparable to his been acquired on the basis of so little published work. What there is, consists of mere fragments written in response to chance occasions.

Although Young's many papers and memoranda on questions of current economic policy invariably bear witness to the fertility of his mind, to the breadth of his sympathies and to the width of his cultural horizon, he was primarily a theorist. He was among the first to understand the peculiar stage of transition which economics entered upon at the beginning of this century and both the necessity and difficulty of helping it on toward more exact forms of thought, especially toward the point where statistical material and economic theory could be welded together. His teaching was basically a cross between Marshall on the one hand and Cournot and Walras on the other, which he developed along lines of his own. His famous review of Pigou's *Wealth and Welfare* (in *Quarterly Journal of Economics*, vol. xxvii, 1913, p. 672–86), his paper "Increasing Returns and Economic Progress" (in *Economic Journal*, vol. xxxviii, 1928, p. 527–42) and his contributions to the fourteenth edition of the *Encyclopaedia Britannica* may be cited as samples both of his doctrine and of his scientific temperament. Fourteen other papers he collected in *Economic Problems, New and Old* (Boston 1927); the contribution to the theory of index numbers contained in the last two deserves particular attention. In his later years Young devoted an increasing amount of energy to the field of money, where he came nearest to giving a full exposition of his views. His analytical study of American bank statistics (Cambridge, Mass. 1928; first published in *Review of Economic Statistics*, vols. vi–vii and xi, 1924–27) and some of his papers and addresses as well may be looked upon as component parts of a comprehensive treatise.

JOSEPH A. SCHUMPETER

Consult: Taussig, F. W., and others, in American Academy of Arts and Sciences, *Proceedings*, vol. lxiv (1930) 550–53.

YOUNG, ARTHUR (1741–1820), English agriculturist. Apprenticed in 1758 to Messrs. Robertson, merchants of Lynn, Norfolk, Young in 1761 left the firm "without education, profession or employment." Maternal influence led him to take over a farm on the family estate at Bradfield, Suffolk. Of this early farming he says, "The only real use . . . was to enable me to view the farms of other men with . . . more discrimination"; it was the occasion of his going on the southern, northern and eastern tours (1767–70), thereby creating a new school of agriculturists, those who based their teaching on the observed practises of the best farmers. The publication of these *Tours* placed Young in the front rank of agricultural writers, and he was now launched on a literary career, although he tried two more farming ventures—Samford Hall, Essex, in 1767 and North Mimms, Hertfordshire, from 1768 to 1777—and in 1792 contemplated developing some 4000 acres of waste in Yorkshire.

At this time his energy was prodigious. Within five years appeared *The Farmer's Letters* (London 1767; 3rd ed., 2 vols., 1771), *A Six Weeks' Tour* (London 1768, 3rd ed. 1772), *Letters concerning the Present State of the French Nation* (London 1769), *Six Months' Tour through the North of England* (4 vols., London 1770), *The Farmer's Guide* (2 vols., London 1770), *A Course of Experimental Agriculture* (2 vols., London 1770), *Rural Economy* (London 1770, 2nd ed. 1773), *Farmer's Tour through the East of England* (4 vols., London 1771) and *Farmer's Kalendar* (London 1771; 21st ed. by J. C. Morton, 1862) as well as four pamphlets. This flood of literature temporarily impaired his reputation, and in 1773 he wrote " . . . the rapidity of my publications satiated the world." However, he had acquired an international position; many of his works were translated in whole or part and published on the continent.

Young toured Ireland in 1776, returned there as agent to Lord Kingsborough in 1777–78 and in 1780 published his *Tour in Ireland* (London 1780; new ed., 2 vols., 1892; selections ed. by C. Maxwell, Cambridge, Eng. 1925), recognized as the chief authority for contemporary Irish economic conditions.

The *Annals of Agriculture*, begun in 1784 "as a general channel for information relative to Agriculture," reached the forty-fifth volume in 1808. The next volume was never completed. Although not financially successful this publication was widely read and diffused much valuable information.

The *Travels during . . . 1787, 1788 and 1789* (2 vols., Bury St. Edmunds 1792–94; ed. by C. E. Maxwell, 1 vol., Cambridge, Eng. 1929), today the best known of his writings, is still regarded as the primary source on the economic condition of prerevolutionary France.

In 1793 Young was appointed secretary to Pitt's newly created Board of Agriculture. He threw himself with characteristic vigor into the production of the County Surveys, compiling them for Norfolk, Suffolk, Hertfordshire, Essex, Lincolnshire and Oxfordshire. In the *General Report on Enclosures* (1808) he summed up the advantages of enclosure: "the landlord doubles his income, the farmer trebles his profit; the laboring poor are more regularly employed and better paid." The economic benefits, however, did not blind him to the hardships inflicted in many cases on the laboring poor. *An Inquiry into the Propriety of Applying Wastes to the Better Maintenance and Support of the Poor* (Bury St. Edmunds 1801) drew attention to the beneficial results to be derived from settling the poor on waste land sufficient for a house, a garden and keep for a cow.

Failing eyesight, which developed into complete blindness in 1809, put an end to many of Young's activities; compelled to rely on reader and amanuensis, he became morbidly introspective. However, he worked steadily at his *Elements and Practice of Agriculture*, a manuscript in thirty-four volumes, now in the British Museum.

Young's influence on the development of British agriculture from 1770 to 1820 can hardly be exaggerated. He stoutly advocated every improved practise, especially rotations, including roots and artificial grasses, the use of manures and the abolition of fallows; he stressed the need for new brains and adequate capitalization ("the great error of common farmers is the hiring too much land in proportion to their fortunes"); he preached enclosure as an essential preliminary to progress, and by his writings he familiarized men's minds with the needs of British agriculture. Although his views did not always meet with general acceptance, his writings gave to his work practical influence greater than that of any of his contemporaries.

G. D. AMERY

Consult: *The Autobiography of Arthur Young*, ed. by M. S. Betham-Edwards (London 1898); Haslam, C. S., *The Biography of Arthur Young, F. R. S., from His Birth until 1787* (Rugby 1930); Amery, G. D., "The Writings of Arthur Young" in Royal Agricultural Society of England, *Journal*, vol. lxxxv (1924) 175–205.

YOUNG, BRIGHAM (1801–77), American religious leader. A native of New England, Young received almost no formal education and worked as a carpenter and glazier. In 1832 he joined the newly formed church of Jesus Christ of Latter Day Saints. Four years later he was appointed one of its twelve apostles. He devoted himself energetically to missionary activities and from 1840 to 1841 was in charge of this work in England. When Smith died, Young succeeded to the presidency of the church, which at that time was on the verge of collapse; and it was he who led the exodus to Utah.

Young was the great organizer of Mormonism (*q.v.*). He attempted to realize all of Smith's doctrines and to build a strong empire capable of resisting the persecutions of the "Gentiles." The settlement of Utah was a model of planned colonization, of which he was the directing force. Missionary work received new impetus and thousands of converts were brought to the colony through the utilization of the Perpetual Emigration Fund, to which all Mormons contributed. The best lands were promptly preempted and irrigation was introduced. Cultivation of the land was stressed and Young was successful in preventing his followers from joining the gold rush to California. The Mormons under him attempted unsuccessfully to sever trade relations with the outside world by producing all needed commodities at home. Political and ecclesiastical organization was firmly established. Polygamy, a secret practise under Joseph Smith, was openly acknowledged as a doctrine and was not abandoned by the church until after Young's death. Between 1874 and 1879 Young promoted but failed to maintain a form of communism known as the United Order, which Smith had tried to institute. Unsuccessful in his attempt to isolate the church or to sustain church communism, he was able, however, to establish various cooperatives; most of these have not survived, although they were of great value during the period of settlement.

Young was governor of Utah territory from 1850 to 1857, when he was removed on a charge of insurrection. For the next twenty years he traveled among the settlements, urging the people to strengthen his ecclesiastical empire, which throve in spite of all opposition.

NELS ANDERSON

Consult: Werner, Morris R., *Brigham Young* (New York 1925); Cannon, Frank J., and Knapp, G. L., *Brigham Young and His Mormon Empire* (New York 1913); Tullidge, Edward W., *Life of Brigham Young* (2nd ed. New York 1877); Gates, Susa Young, and Widtsoe, Leah D., *The Life Story of Brigham Young* (New York 1930).

YOUTH MOVEMENTS represent a conscious revolt of the younger generation and serve as a means whereby youth may proclaim its own ideas, values and standards, which are different from and frequently opposed to those of the older generation. In their assumptions and aims they contradict the notion that the experience of the elders, the *gerontes*, can best guarantee the continuity of civilization through authoritarian guidance of the younger generation.

In this sense youth movements are not to be confused with the recreational, educational, religious or even political groups for boys and girls which are sponsored by the older generation in its desire to train young persons to take their proper place in adult life as envisaged by the elders. Basic to all youth movements are a deep dissatisfaction with the existing intellectual, moral, social or political order, a desire to change this order and a confidence in the power of youth to accomplish this change. Thus defined, youth movements are essentially a phenomenon of the twentieth century. Only toward the end of the nineteenth century, after the French Revolution and later the concepts of change and evolution had invaded all spheres of life, was a new consideration accorded to youth. Characteristically, however, youth movements arose in countries where the effects of these changes had not altered the traditional authoritarian social, political and economic structure but where youth, largely through the influence of ideological currents from more emancipated communities, had become aware of its limited possibilities for expansion.

As early as the 1840's there developed under the leadership of Mazzini the Young Europe movement, which had its strongest manifestations in those countries in which the democratic revolution had failed and nationalist aspirations remained unsatisfied. Its aim, however, was purely political and nationalistic; it sought no new ways of life, and it drew its membership not from the generation between fourteen and twenty, like the modern youth movements, but mainly from young men in their twenties and thirties.

Another type of youth movement emerged in the 1860's in Russia. This was nihilism (*q.v.*), at the outset essentially a revolt of the youth of the new intellectual class against the sentimentality and romanticism of their fathers. Its chief spokesman, Pisarev, stressed as did the later German youth movement the liberation of the individual. But whereas the latter was essentially idealistic and even mystical, the Russian youth was materialistic, agnostic and blatantly utilitarian in its outlook. Indeed its antisocial or non-social character and its lack of positive program or organization doomed it to a speedy disappearance, and its remnants were taken over by the revolutionary movement of the succeeding decade.

The German youth movement of the pre-war period found its inspirations in other sources. Following Rousseau and his disciples Ellen Key had proclaimed the "century of the child"; the new pedagogy and the new psychology considered childhood and early youth as important stages in life and not merely as preliminary to adulthood without value in themselves. Along rather different lines Friedrich Nietzsche had earlier cast doubts on the usefulness of experience and tradition. He and other men of his time, including Henrik Ibsen, demanded new standards of morality, attacked the mendacity of the traditional standards of "bourgeois" behavior and stressed the right of the individual as opposed to society and his longing for happiness. At the same time the system of sanctions maintained for many centuries by religion and the church had been considerably weakened; the body with its beauties and its desires, denied or repudiated by Christianity and the other great religions, began to be recognized and even sanctified.

Many factors serve to explain why the youth movement had its greatest appeal in Germany. Unlike the west European nations, Germany had never attained an organic integration of its civilization. Stirred by metaphysics and music, torn by religious wars and lacking unity as did no other nation, suffering under the prevailing relics of a feudal and militaristic order and since 1871 subjected to the drive for material power, the youth of Germany developed a confused but consuming desire for a fuller and richer civilization which should integrate all strata and classes of the population. Thus the pre-war youth movement of Germany was not in any sense economic; it represented groups of young persons in a highly prosperous society who took no part in economic life but who, as the sons and daughters of the well to do, were relatively care free. It was an "idealistic" movement, inspired by philosophy and poetry and manifesting itself through these media. It reflected the desire for a new way of life, for greater liberty, sincerity and beauty as opposed to the materialism, conventionalism and insincerity of Wilhelmine society. Traditions of the romanticists, of the *Burschenschaften*, of German mediaeval mystics, were revived and folk song, folk dances and folklore again came to the fore. A new stream of enthusiasm began to undermine the hard nationalistic utilitarianism of the older generation. The revolt of youth against parents, school and traditional authority culminated in the October celebrations of 1913 at the Hoher Meissner near Kassel. The movement was purely secular, but it was colored by religious or mystical enthusiasm and was often marked by vague irrationalism. It sought to create true and free individuals but at the same time was agitated by a longing for a new and true community, a *Gemeinschaft*, which should be both a symbol of the rebirth of the nation and the only place where such freedom could be made universal. Politically and socially the youth movement had no clear or definite aims. It had no alternative to offer for the existing order which it disliked; it fought against all established authority but it longed for a new authority, for a real *Führer* instead of established bureaucratic leadership. It organized *Scharen* and *Bünde*, fellowships and communities of friends, drawn together by the warmth of emotional life and trusting in a leadership of older comrades. The German youth movement blossomed but never bore fruit. Nevertheless, both because of its content and because of its attraction for large numbers of the German youth it exercised no negligible influence on the ways of life and thought of Germany, on poetry and song and artistic expression. It recognized Nietzsche as its prophet and later Stefan George as its poet. It represented with its wandering, hiking and camping the old precapitalistic unrest of the *Wanderburschen* and the new unrest of dissatisfied German sentimentality within the German political and capitalistic structure.

The pre-war youth movements in the Orient were of a somewhat different character. To the opposition to traditionalism and an obsolete mediaeval social and intellectual order was added the protest against national and economic oppression under the impact of twentieth century imperialist expansion from the West. New ideas penetrated first among the younger generation, the students who in modern schools or in universities abroad became imbued with occidental liberalism. Thus the youth movements in the Orient became in a sense the pioneers of Europeanization in their acceptance of progressive and radical standards of morality and social life as opposed to the traditionalism of the elders. But at the same time there was a definite anti-European trend in the protest against the effects of imperialism and capitalism. The oriental youth movements, of which the Chinese student movement was the most important, laid special emphasis upon the breakdown of traditional culture and morals and fought for and realized a more equal relation between the sexes, a new valuation of the individual, of the body and of art. They broke down the barriers which had existed between the educated classes, the literati and the illiterate masses, and they sought to effect a rejuvenation and a popularization of literature and language.

Different also were the youth movements in Slav, south European and South American countries. These were most akin to Young Europe in that they were purely political and expressed a revolt against the passive attitude of the older generation with respect to the existing political and social order, its incompetent leadership, the prevalence of corruption and the absence of program. Although some of these countries gave rise to movements for national independence, these often served only to conceal the continuation of exploitation by foreign influences. In others national aspirations were only partly fulfilled. The older leaders of such movements were in many cases concerned only with their own position and paid little attention to the future of youth or the backward and illiterate masses. Against some or all of these evils the youth movements of these countries revolted. Among the Jugoslavs and the Czechs the movements were called *Omladina*, a Slavic word meaning rejuvenation. Although they were not unlike the oriental youth movements in their national and social outlook, they developed in a social milieu already Europeanized and therefore lacked the appeal of a complete rupture between the generations.

The element common to these varying types of youth movements was the consciousness that in a given tradition or political or economic situation youth had but limited possibilities of expansion and adjustment. The mediaeval and formalistic tradition of China, the feudal and orthodox tradition of Prussian Germany, the primitive and petty qualities of life in South American republics, gave no scope to the emotions and intellect of a recently awakened youth. The youth movements were often representative of the rising generation of classes which were not accorded a part in the political and economic activity of the country.

The more purely political youth movements which arose in countries under foreign domination or influence in alliance with the native ruling class represented largely a bourgeois youth which could find no basis for its own economic and social development. However, outside of Germany many of these groups were strongly influenced by the revolutionary movement in Russia. Although this was not in any sense of the word a youth movement, it represented a revolt against mediaeval traditionalism, the narrowness of social and cultural life, political autocracy and the feudal economic order. Not only did it absorb the youth of Russia but it also affected the movements of youth in the other Slav countries, in China and even in Japan prior to the World War.

The pre-war youth movements thus were bound together by only two factors. In the first place, they developed only in countries where the revolutions at the close of the eighteenth century had not destroyed the feudal order and had not accomplished the liberation of the individual. In countries where the nation had not yet acquired a substantial measure of freedom they were nationalistic, but at the same time they were radical and individualistic. In the second place, they were animated, like all movements of revolt, by far reaching, missionary ideals: the rise of a new type of man, community or nation better than that produced by the preceding generation. The vagueness, exaggerated self-esteem and lack of experience common to all youth movements were compensated for by enthusiasm and frequently by uncompromising consistency of ideal and action.

After the World War, with the intensification and acceleration of social and political unrest, the youth movements grew in number and at the same time began to lose their character as movements of individualistic revolt. They became indoctrinated with definite political and social theories and were transformed from independent expressions of autonomous youth into tools of state, party or church. The youth movements, formerly the expression of a revolt against society, became fully integrated into the new forms of society whose foundations they had in part helped to lay. Adult leaders began to recognize the pivotal role of youth in the recreation of society. Now every political and ideological group reached directed its appeal to the youth and sought to form its own youth movement. In European countries there developed the most varied types of religious, proletarian and nationalistic youth movements. Fascism and National Socialism especially drew their mass support largely from the youth; as soon as they acquired power they instituted a youthful governmental personnel so that their victory could be proclaimed as the triumph of the youth movement itself. In many European countries the younger generation which had fought in the war tried to invest the political and social life of the nation with the spirit of the trenches and to take leadership either by forming distinct parties or by gaining predominance in the nationalist parties. They made a stirring appeal to heroism and to sacrifice, as a continuation of what was called the true comradeship of the battlefield—the abolition of all class distinctions in the patriotic enthusiasm of the united nation. Many military expressions—"front," "shock brigades," "storm troops"—were carried by this generation into political and social life. In place of the individualism of the pre-war youth movements there now became manifest an anti-individualistic tendency with a strong disciplinarian and authoritarian character.

This new attitude of the youth movement arose out of the realities of the post-war situation, particularly in the economic field. The economic disintegration of the middle classes, from which its membership had largely been recruited, led to a realization of the lack of opportunities offered to youth in the existing economic and political set up. The youth movement could not maintain its attitude of detachment with respect to economic problems nor could it accept the passive or mildly reformistic attitude of its elders. Moreover the outstanding leadership of the pre-war youth movement had been killed in the World War, so that the younger generation found itself in search of guides. Some efforts were made in Germany to continue the work begun in 1913 at the Hoher Meissner. The first "Freideutscher Jugendtag" after the war had proudly declared for internal and external autonomy. An excellent monthly journal, *Junge Menschen*, begun in 1920 by Walter Hammer and Knud Ahlborn, sought to imbue the youth with the older liberal and human spirit. In the autumn of 1923, on the suggestion of Eugen Diederichs, whose publications had largely reflected the pre-war German youth movement, a new youth conference was convoked at the Hoher Meissner. This meeting, called at a crucial period in pre-Hitler Germany—the year of the Ruhr occupation and of extreme inflation—became involved in endless discussion between communistic, religious and nationalistic groups.

What remained of the vague but lofty dreams

of the pre-war youth now centered around the idea of settlements or communes which it was hoped would set an example for a national and social revival. The influences of pre-Marxian and romantic socialism, of Tolstoyan anarchism, of religious sectarianism and of liberal nationalism all contributed to the creation in Germany and Austria of small rural and industrial communities of likeminded young people of both sexes, whose ultimate aim was the regeneration of the social life of the nation. This tendency spread also among the uprooted middle class Jewish youth of central Europe, who had already come under the influence of the pre-war youth movement and who found moral support in the existence of such communes in Palestine.

In the post-war states where new forms of one-party dictatorship had been established—the Soviet Union, Fascist Italy, National Socialist Germany—the new rulers depended upon youth to effect the transition from the old order to the new. The youth movements became official or semi-official organizations and very often the most faithful support of the new regime. The youth organizations were now supplemented by similar organizations of children up to fourteen years. They no longer expressed a revolt against the school, for in these totalitarian states school and youth were subject to the same indoctrination; but they did continue in many cases to represent a revolt against the paternal home. In a sense National Socialism can be considered a product of the German youth movements, from which it inherited its irrationalism, its vague nationalistic sentimentalism, its ideals of the soldier, the *Bund*, the *Führer* and the *Gefolgschaft*. Mediaeval and ancient Teutonic folklore and myths blossomed forth in National Socialism to an extent surprising to western nations. The post-war youth movements of Germany, Italy and the Soviet Union were imitated by the fascist and communist movements in other countries: they stressed *Wehrhaftigkeit*, military discipline and training and they exalted force and arms. But their contempt for humanity and humanitarianism, their lack of respect for human life and dignity, their dislike of reason and liberalism, nowhere reached the passionate extremes attained in Nazi Germany; elsewhere they were generally attacked by pacifist, religious and liberal youth movements.

In countries where the World War had not resulted in complete satisfaction of national aspirations the youth movements kept up their wartime enthusiasm, devotion and recklessness and served as shock troops of extreme nationalistic movements, within which, however, they represented a socially progressive outlook. This was the case in the Balkan countries, in Latin America, in the Orient and in the Zionist movement.

Recent years have witnessed the emergence of an autonomous youth movement in the United States. A conscious revolt against the older generation had been foreshadowed by Randolph Bourne in his *Youth and Life* (Boston 1913). But despite occasional protests against the leadership of "tired elders," particularly during the World War, no stable organization resulted either from Bourne's teachings or from the movement which called itself the Young Democracy. Both the Socialist and the Communist parties have, however, manifested a new realization of the role of youth and have mobilized youth sectors. Other groups of youth in the United States find no authoritarian religious, political or social order to rebel against. Since the depression, however, there has been a new realization that economic opportunities, particularly for middle class youth, are dwindling; and Young America, with its vague program for a new social order, has appealed to this class for support.

Youth movements are always the symptom of a break in the internal order of a nation, of a much quickened pace of change or of the lack of integration of a civilization with the existing social structure. So long as national and social movements continue in their violence and intransigence, youth movements will maintain their influence and strength. The growing instability and insecurity of political and social conditions in many countries are reflected in the increasing vigor of youth movements. Today, however, most of these have shifted their emphasis from the individual to the corporate body, the nation or the class. They have gained perhaps in efficiency and in the attainment of definite economic and political ends, but they have certainly lost the great personal and creative appeal of autonomous freedom, sincerity and human comradeship which distinguished them in the pre-war period.

HANS KOHN

See: BOYS' AND GIRLS' CLUBS; EDUCATION; CIVIC EDUCATION; INTELLECTUALS; IDEALISM; NIHILISM; ZIONISM; SOCIALIST PARTIES; COMMUNIST PARTIES; PATRIOTISM; PAN-MOVEMENTS; NATIONALISM; NATIONAL SOCIALISM, GERMAN; FASCISM; CONSERVATISM; RADICALISM.

Consult: Gründel, E. G., *Die Sendung der jungen*

Generation (Munich 1932); Messer, A., *Die freideutsche Jugendbewegung*, Pädagogisches Magazin, no. 597 (5th ed. Langensalza 1915), and *Die neue Jugend*, ed. by R. Thurnwald, Forschungen zur Völkerpsychologie und Soziologie, vol. v (Leipsic 1927); Siemering, Hertha, *Die deutschen Jugendverbände* (Berlin 1931); Kosok, Paul, *Modern Germany* (Chicago 1933) ch. xii; Stählin, O., *Die deutsche Jugendbewegung* (2nd ed. Leipsic 1930); Blüher, H., *Wandervögel*, 2 vols. (4th ed. Berlin 1919); Wyneken, Gustav, *Der Kampf für die Jugend* (new ed. Jena 1920); Kohn, Hans, *Martin Buber, sein Werk und seine Zeit* (Hellerau 1930); Mehnert, Klaus, *Die Jugend in Sowjetrussland* (Berlin 1932), tr. by Michael Davidson (London 1933); Knoppers, B. A., *Die Jugendbewegung in den Niederlanden* (Emsdetten 1931); Wendel, Hermann, *Aus dem südslavischen Risorgimento* (Gotha 1921) p. 73–102; Hartmann, Hans, *Die junge Generation in Europa* (Berlin 1930); Wang, T. C., *The Youth Movement in China* (New York 1927); High, Stanley, *The Revolt of Youth* (Cincinnati 1923); Kohn, Hans, *Geschichte der nationalen Bewegung im Orient* (Berlin 1928), tr. by M. M. Green (London 1929).

YRJÖ-KOSKINEN, YRJÖ SAKARI (Georg Zachris Forsman) (1830–1903), Finnish historian and politician. Yrjö-Koskinen, who was of Swedish descent, devoted himself to the advancement of the neglected Finnish language and nationality. He was a follower of J. V. Snellman, whose doctrine he tried to put into practise as the leader of the aggressive Fennomen movement directed against the Swedish language and culture. He emphasized the importance of language in national development and led the struggle to have the Finnish language accepted in educational institutions and in official public affairs. Like Snellman he held that the educated among the Swedish population of Finland ought to give up their own language and adopt that of the Finnish majority. From 1863 to 1882 he was professor of history at Helsingfors University and during this period published several important works on the history of Finland, which are marked, however, by nationalist motives. As a member of the ecclesiastical estate of the old diet he won its undisputed support for his ideas. One of his ruling principles as a political leader was to maintain good relations with the Russian government. In 1882 he was nominated a member of the senate of Finland, two years later he was raised to the rank of nobility and in 1897 he was made a baron. During the Russification period in Finland his attitude toward the czarist government was one of submission. He has been most severely criticized for inducing the senate to sanction the "February manifesto" of 1899, which in part revoked the autonomy of Finland.

This move caused the constitutional group of his followers to split off into a separate party.

GUNNAR LANDTMAN

Consult: *Historiallenen aikakauskirja*, vol. xxviii (1930) 257–99; Wuorinen, J. H., *Nationalism in Modern Finland* (New York 1931) p. 127–40.

YUAN SHIH-KAI (1859–1916), Chinese statesman. Yuan Shih-Kai was an outstanding figure in Chinese politics during the late nineteenth and the early twentieth century. For a decade preceding the Sino-Japanese War he served as Chinese resident in Korea. In this capacity he employed every means at his disposal to restore Chinese hegemony after it had been compromised by permitting Japan, followed by the western nations, to deal with Korea as a sovereign state in respect to treaties opening the latter country to foreign intercourse. The Sino-Japanese War terminated his efforts. He sided with the empress dowager in her coup d'état which blocked the reforms that the emperor, under the influence of K'ang Yu-wei, had decreed in 1898, and which virtually dethroned the emperor himself. In 1899 Yuan became acting governor of Shantung and maintained order there throughout the Boxer uprising of 1900. In 1901 he became viceroy of Chihli, where he introduced reforms, drilled a superior army and eventually became a grand councilor and president of the Ministry of Foreign Affairs. Shortly after the death of the empress dowager in 1908 Yuan was dismissed by the regent, who could ill afford this disastrous gratification of a private grudge. When the revolution broke out in 1911 Yuan was recalled and appointed viceroy of Wuchang in the hope that he might secure unity. Either by reason of the situation itself or because of the machinations of Yuan or his representative, T'ang Shao-yi, the Manchus were forced to abdicate. Subsequently Sun Yat Sen retired in Yuan's favor and the latter became president of the Chinese Republic.

Yuan realized the ineffectuality of the old administrative system but had no faith in a Chinese republic or in representative institutions in China. Instead of restoring the recently discarded examinations for candidates for government office, he inaugurated a system of patronage which soon resulted in wholesale corruption. His attention was concentrated upon the reform of Chinese military technique, for he sought to establish an autocracy based upon a strong military force. From the first Yuan antagonized the Kuomintang, and after the abortive rebellion in

1913 he drove their representatives from Parliament. He was well on the road to dictatorship when the famous Twenty-one Demands of Japan, accepted in May, 1915, followed by Yuan's unsuccessful attempt to become emperor, which Japan vetoed, produced a rebellion, forced him to cancel his imperial program, hastened his death and introduced a period of chaos.

WILLIAM JAMES HAIL

Consult: MacNair, H. F., *China in Revolution* (Chicago 1931) chs. ii–iii; Holcombe, A. N., *The Chinese Revolution* (2nd ed. Cambridge, Mass. 1931) p. 101–07; Morse, H. B., *The International Relations of the Chinese Empire*, 3 vols. (London 1910–18) vol. iii.

YVES OF CHARTRES (*c.* 1040–1116), French churchman. Yves was born at Beauvais and was consecrated bishop of Chartres by Pope Urban II in 1090. He occupied a significant position in the Middle Ages, first, as the most important canonist in Europe before Gratian and, secondly, as a representative of moderation in the great conflict between the temporal and spiritual authorities, a position which was probably much more characteristic of the normal attitude of men in the Middle Ages than that of the more extreme partisans on either side.

There were many collections of canons before Yves produced his great compilation which is known as the *Decretum*, but his collection was larger and more comprehensive than any previous one; the smaller work called the *Panormia* would seem to have been of the nature of a handbook, representing what seemed to him the most important elements of the *Decretum*.

Yves intervened in the great question of investiture at two points. In 1097 in a letter to Hugh, the archbishop of Lyons, he maintained that the papal prohibition of royal investiture did not mean that the king should have no place in episcopal appointments, but that as head of the people he might have his place in the election; he had the right of "concessio," and its form was immaterial, for it had no relation to the spiritual office and merely expressed the royal consent to the election or conferred the "temporalities" of the see. Again in 1111 or 1112 he intervened to protest against the condemnation of Pope Paschal II, who had in 1111 under great pressure conceded the right of investiture to the emperor Henry V. He urged, as indeed he had done in the earlier letter, that the question of investiture was not a question about the eternal law, but of what may be called administrative order. He now gave it as his opinion that it would be better that lay investiture should be given up, if this could be done without causing schism; if not, the matter should be postponed. Yves' attitude anticipated the compromise which was finally reached by the Concordat of Worms in 1122, and it was no doubt due to such influences as his that the question was settled in France as in England without the violent conflicts which took place in the empire.

A. J. CARLYLE

Works: The *Decretum* and *Panormia* may be found in *Patrologia latina*, ed. by J. P. Migne, vols. clxi, clxii (Paris 1854–55); the *Epistolae* have been edited by E. Sackur in *Monumenta Germaniae historica*, Libelli de lite, vol. ii (Hanover 1892) p. 640–57.

Consult: Fournier, Paul, "Yves de Chartres et le droit canonique" in *Revue des questions historiques*, vol. lxiii (1898) 51–98, 384–405, and "Les collections canoniques attribuées à Yves de Chartres" in École des Chartres, *Bibliothèque*, vol. lvii (1896) 645–98, and vol. lviii (1897) 26–77, 293–326, 410–44, 624–76; Fournier, Paul, and Le Bras, Gabriel, *Histoire des collections canoniques en Occident*, 2 vols. (Paris 1931–32) vol. ii, ch. ii; Carlyle, R. W. and A. J., *A History of Mediaeval Political Theory in the West*, vols. i–v (Edinburgh 1903–28) vol. ii, and vol. iv, pt. ii, ch. iv.

ZACHARIAE VON LINGENTHAL, KARL-EDUARD (1812–94), German jurist. Zachariae was born in Heidelberg, where his celebrated father, Karl Salomo, was teaching. The son was to become famous as the principal authority on Byzantine law. At Berlin Biener, who had worked on the Novels of Justinian, initiated him in Byzantine law. In 1845, two years after his father's death, he retired to his vast estate, Grosskmehlen, in Saxony; and although he almost entirely lost his sight and hearing, he worked on until his death.

At the time Zachariae began his work Byzantine law was as yet little known, and he began its study by searching the Byzantine manuscripts in all the libraries of Europe, a task which occupied him from 1832 to 1838. Their examination enabled him to publish or republish scholarly editions of his principal sources: the *Ropai* (Heidelberg 1836), the *Procheiros nomos* (Heidelberg 1837), *Anecdota* (Leipsic 1843), the *Supplementum editionis Basilicorum heimbachianae* (Leipsic 1846), the *Ecloga* and the *Epanagoge* (Leipsic 1852), the *Ius graeco-romanum* (7 vols., Leipsic 1856–84), the *Novellae* (2 vols., Leipsic 1881). His first description of Byzantine law as a whole, *Historiae iuris graeco-romani de lineatio*, was published quite early (Heidelberg 1839). His more complete work, *Geschichte des griechisch-römischen Rechts* (3 vols., Leipsic 1856–64; 3rd ed. in 1 vol., Berlin 1892), still remains fundamental. His general viewpoint was that Byzantine law was a further development of Justinian law. Zachariae also wrote articles on Roman law and accounts of his travels in the Orient. His influence was especially potent on Contardo Ferrini, who succeeded him as the great authority on Byzantine law.

PAUL COLLINET

Works: A complete bibliography of Zachariae's works has been compiled by Wilhelm Fischer in *Zeitschrift der Savigny-Stiftung für Rechtsgeschichte, Romanistische Abteilung*, vol. xvi (1895) 320–32, and vol. xvii (1896) 332–34.

Consult: Monnier, H., in *Nouvelle revue historique de droit français et étranger*, vol. xix (1895) 665–92; Ferrini, C., in his *Opere*, 5 vols. (Milan 1929–30) vol. i, p. 461–65; Stintzing, R. von, and Landsberg, E., *Geschichte der deutschen Rechtswissenschaft*, 3 vols. (Munich 1880–1910) vol. iii, pt. ii, p. 483–86.

ZACHARIAE VON LINGENTHAL, KARL SALOMO (1769–1843), German jurist. Zachariae was professor of law at Wittenberg from 1798 to 1807 and at Heidelberg from 1807 to 1843. In 1820 he became a member of the first chamber of Baden and in 1825 of the second chamber, where he exercised an important political influence in a somewhat conservative direction.

In his scientific work Zachariae dealt with almost every branch of jurisprudence and many legal systems, but his numerous publications are uneven in quality. His *Handbuch des französischen Civilrechts* (2 vols., Heidelberg 1808; 8th ed., 4 vols., 1894–95), however, achieved world wide fame and is generally regarded as the best systematic work on French civil law by a German. It demonstrates an amazing combination of the clarity of French thinking and the systematic character of German jurisprudence.

Zachariae's masterpiece, *Vierzig Bücher vom Staate* (5 vols., Stuttgart and Heidelberg 1820–32; 2nd ed., 7 vols., Heidelberg 1839–42)—in its second edition his scientific and political testament—exhibits his strange personality in all its strength and weakness. Zachariae wished to become the German Machiavelli but he lacked the latter's classical calm and profundity. On the other hand, he had much in common with Montesquieu, the same astonishing knowledge and ingenious and witty style; his was a sparkling and sagacious spirit, with a penchant for subtlety and paradoxical affectation and a striving after peculiarity and effect.

Zachariae's writings have a catholicity and brilliance seldom to be found in German scientific works but they generally lack a strong systematic and comprehensive clearness, and German jurisprudence has in consequence rendered varied judgments upon his work and personality. As Robert von Mohl very rightly has pointed out, "He has few equals, but it is difficult to say whether this fact is a subject for regret or for rejoicing."

SIGMUND NEUMANN

Other important works: *Handbuch des kursächsischen Lehnrechts* (Leipsic 1796; 2nd ed. by C. Weisse and F. von Langenn as *Handbuch des königlichen sächsischen Lehnrechts*, 1823); *Die Einheit des Staats und der Kirche, mit Rücksicht auf die deutsche Reichsverfassung* (Leipsic 1797); *Versuch einer allgemeinen Hermeneutik des Rechts* (Meissen 1805); *Die Wissenschaft der Gesetzgebung* (Leipsic 1806); *Das Staatsrecht der rheinischen Bundesstaaten und des rheinischen Bundesrechts* (Heidelberg 1810); *Abhandlungen aus dem Gebiete der Staatswirthschaftslehre* (Heidelberg 1835).

Consult: Brocher, Charles A., *K. S. Zachariae, sa vie et ses oeuvres* (Paris 1870); Mohl, Robert von, *Die Geschichte und Literatur der Staatswissenschaften*, 3 vols. (Erlangen 1855–58) vol. ii, p. 512–28; Stintzing, R. von, and Landsberg, E., *Geschichte der deutschen Rechtswissenschaft*, 3 vols. (Munich 1880–1910) vol. iii, pt. ii, p. 100–10.

ZADRUGA. *See* VILLAGE COMMUNITY.

ZAGHLUL PASHA, SAAD (1850–1927), Egyptian nationalist. Of peasant stock, Zaghlul was educated at Al-Azhar and in his youth was active in the first Egyptian nationalist movement led by 'Arābi. Later he became a lawyer and participated in the rise of a new middle class intelligentsia to political influence.

Before the World War Zaghlul favored democratic and educational reforms. His outstanding ability and integrity were recognized by the British and he served successively as minister of education, minister of justice and vice president of the Egyptian legislative assembly. After the war, when for the first time the peasants consciously participated in the nationalist movement, Zaghlul became the undisputed leader of the united Egyptian nation in its struggle for complete independence. He headed the Wafd, the nationalist delegation, which in 1918 demanded passports in order to visit England and present Egypt's case. The refusal of the British and Zaghlul's deportation led to the Egyptian revolution of 1919. After his release from Malta, Zaghlul went to Europe to further Egyptian interests. His triumphant return in 1921 marked a turning point in the nation's history. In an autocratic country ridden with personal ambitions and rivalries and where standards of public morality were low, he succeeded during the period of his undisputed authority in establishing national unity to a degree rarely attained elsewhere. He was prime minister in 1924 but was forced to resign because of the hostility of the British and the court. As president of the Egyptian parliament from 1926 to 1927 he trained the Egyptians in the use of the machinery of democratic government and forced European politicians to recognize Egyptian ambitions. Under his tutelage the nation attained political maturity and the Wafd party, which Zaghlul created, continued to represent the overwhelming majority of the Egyptian people even after his death.

HANS KOHN

Consult: Kohn, Hans, *Nationalismus und Imperialismus im vorderen Orient* (Frankfort 1931), tr. by M. M. Green (London 1929) p. 78–97, 287; Yeghen, Fouald, *Saad Zaglul* (Paris 1928); Khaivallah, I. A., "The Late Zaghlul Pasha's Struggle for Egyptian Freedom" in *Current History*, vol. xxvii (1927) 147–50; Carra de Vaux, B., *Les penseurs de l'islam*, 5 vols. (Paris 1921–26) vol. v, p. 296–306; Adams, Charles C., *Islam and Modernism in Egypt*, American University at Cairo, Oriental Studies (London 1933), especially p. 226–30.

ZANGWILL, ISRAEL (1864–1926), Anglo-Jewish man of letters and nationalist leader. Zangwill, the son of poor parents who had emigrated from Latvia, was born in London and educated at the Jews' Free School and at the University of London. After some experience with teaching he turned to journalism and literary work, and his literary reputation was made with *The Children of the Ghetto* (Philadelphia 1892), a novel which portrayed Jewish life in London. This was followed by a number of other works dealing with general as well as with Jewish themes. The Jewish characters which Zangwill created, unlike the caricatures so common in literature, were painted true to life; they were neither unregenerate Shylocks nor incorruptible and ever wise Nathans. Zangwill won recognition also as playwright, essayist and poet.

Although he deprecated the evils of exaggerated nationalism, Zangwill was himself a Jewish nationalist. He became an active Zionist soon after the movement was launched by Theodor Herzl, but in 1905 he led an influential minority out of the Zionist Organization because the Zionist Congress of that year refused to accept the offer of the British government of a territory in east Africa. The disaffected group created the Jewish Territorial Organization (I.T.O.) with the following program: "To acquire a territory upon an autonomous basis for those Jews who cannot or will not remain in the lands in which they live at present." This aim remained unrealized because no suitable territory could be found. Zangwill also cooperated with Jacob H. Schiff, the American philanthropist, in the attempt to divert Jewish immigrants headed for the United States from the Atlantic seaboard to the middle west. The World War halted the activities of the I.T.O. and the Balfour Declaration appeared to render the organization entirely superfluous. In 1925 it was disbanded.

Zangwill set forth his views on nationalism and nationality in *The Principle of Nationalities* (New York 1917). He held that the development of nationality, which is "as old as the pyramids," is determined by the "law of contiguous cooperation." Faced with common danger and the need for mutual self-sacrifice, related and cooperating clans are welded into a "simple nationality," with common language, race, religion, culture and territory. This homogeneity is quickly destroyed by conquest, migration and intermarriage, and a complex nationality appears in which the chief bond of union is a "state of mind." However, contiguity and cooperation begin at once to fuse the dissimilar elements into a new unity and a "secondary simple nationality" results. Zangwill's ideal was to free all nationalities from oppression and to unite them in the service of justice and peace.

OSCAR I. JANOWSKY

Consult: Freund, Margit, *Israel Zangwills Stellung zum Judentum* (Berlin 1927); Lowrey, D. M., *Mr. Zangwill and the Jew*, Address before Phi Beta Kappa Society, University of Pennsylvania (Philadelphia 1900); Roth, Samuel, *Now and Forever* (New York 1925); Schneiderman, H., in *American Jewish Year Book, 5688*, vol. xxix (Philadelphia 1927) p. 121–43; Spire, André, *Quelques Juifs* (2nd ed. Paris 1913) p. 17–155.

ZAPATA, EMILIANO (c. 1869–1919), Mexican revolutionist. Zapata was born of Indian ancestry in one of the small agricultural villages of southern Mexico. He became a tenant farmer, but because of his revolutionary tendencies he was sentenced to serve ten years in Díaz' army. He was released in 1910, and after trying by legal processes to have the land of his native village restored to its citizens he led the Indians in attacks upon the haciendas and seized the land by force. He supported the revolutionary movement led by Madero, and when the latter failed to formulate a definite program for land reform, Zapata attempted to carry one out on his own initiative; within a short time the state of Morelos and the adjoining territory were under his control. The war against the *hacendados* was conducted so ruthlessly that Zapata became known as the "Attila of the South," and the campaigns between his followers and the federal troops led to endless bloodshed and destruction. In an attempt to make his revolt nation wide Zapata in 1911 issued the *Plan de Ayala*, calling for the breaking up of the haciendas and the restoration of village lands to the villagers either in severalty or as *ejidos* (commons). The Mexicans rallied to his cause; and although Zapata himself never controlled all of Mexico, agrarian reform became the principal aim as it has been the chief result of the revolution. Illiterate and untutored in political matters, Zapata made no attempt to reform government, his one purpose being to secure land for his fellow Indians and thus to enable them to shake off the shackles of peonage and to rise to the dignified independent status of agriculturists which they had enjoyed before the conquest. He was killed by followers of Carranza before the reforms he advocated had become established.

The most forceful single influence in the agrarian policy of the revolution, Zapata is regarded as the embodiment of the Mexican people's age long aspiration for freedom from the social and economic bondage imposed upon them at the conquest. As a leader of the Indians in their struggle for better living conditions he was responsible in part for the present revival of Indian culture in Mexico. His tomb is held sacred by the Indian people of all southern Mexico, and they regard him as a legendary hero.

George McCutchen McBride

Consult: Araquistaín, L., *La revolución mejicana; sus orígenes, sus hombres, su obra* (2nd ed. Madrid 1930) ch. xi; Gamio, Manuel, *Forjando patria* (Mexico 1916); Tannenbaum, Frank, *The Mexican Agrarian Revolution*, Brookings Institution, Institute of Economics (New York 1929) p. 159–63; Gruening, E. H., *Mexico and Its Heritage* (New York 1928) p. 98–99, 141–44, 310–11.

ZELGEIM, VLADIMIR NIKOLAEVICH (1873–1924), Russian cooperator. While a student at the University of Odessa, Zelgeim was imprisoned for participating in a students' self-educational association. Following his expulsion from the university he went first to St. Petersburg and then to the village of Pavlovo in the province of Nizhni Novgorod, where he joined the producers' cooperative (artel) of cutlery workers. Although this was the only successful cooperative organization of producers in Russia, Zelgeim lost faith in the possibilities of the cooperative organization of producers on a large scale and reached the conclusion that the future of the cooperative movement lay in the association of consumers; the interests of producers are always antagonistic, while the interests of consumers are identical. In Pavlovo Zelgeim organized a consumers' cooperative society and took part in the conference of Russian cooperators, then still few in number, which was held during the all-Russian exhibition at Nizhni Novgorod in 1896 and which originated the plan for the establishment of a central union of consumers' cooperative societies in Moscow. The union was organized in 1898 and in 1901 Zelgeim was elected a member of its executive board. Later he became director of its cultural and educational department and edited its organ *Soyuz potrebitelei* (Consumers' union). Until his departure from Russia in 1919 he was generally recognized as the guiding spirit of the union.

On Zelgeim's initiative the first all-Russian cooperative congress was called in Moscow in 1908. In spite of the obstructions put in its way by the government the congress succeeded in organizing the national cooperative movement on a sound basis and in establishing it as a school of self-government and collective independence. In 1912 Zelgeim took an active part in the organization of the Moscow People's Bank, a credit center for all cooperative organizations. In 1917 under the Provisional Government he was appointed assistant minister in the Department of Food Supply. After the nationalization of the central cooperative organs in 1919 Zelgeim went abroad; in 1923 he was elected president of the Inotsentr (Union of Russian Cooperative Societies Abroad), organized in Berlin. Zelgeim regarded the cooperative movement as one of the chief means whereby man could acquire control over the spontaneous course of economic relations; he held that its aim was to transform economic relations in the field of production and exchange in accordance with the best interests of all. Zelgeim's chief printed work is *Organizatsiya i praktika potrebitelnikh obshchestv* (Organization and work of consumers' societies, Moscow 1913), based on a course of lectures delivered by him in the cooperative section of the Shanyavsky People's University in Moscow.

S. Procopovicz

ZETKIN, CLARA (1857–1933), German revolutionary and feminist leader. Clara Zetkin joined the German Social Democratic party during the period of the Bismarckian antisocialist laws. From the outset she directed her energy not so much toward general socialist politics as toward the special questions of educational and cultural work in the party and of the working women, whose emancipation she visualized as the outcome of socialism. After the repeal of the antisocialist law in 1890 she became the leader of the ever growing organization of socialist women. She founded the *Gleichheit* in 1892, of which she was editor until 1916.

Because she had a profound knowledge of Marxist theory and a clear judgment on contemporary political problems, was an accomplished linguist and a master equally of the written and spoken word, she exercised great influence in the Socialist International. An adherent always of the left revolutionary wing, she began in 1914 an active opposition against the official policy of the German party, especially against the civil truce with the government. In 1917 she left the party to become a member of the newly formed Independent Social Democratic party (U. S. P. D.); after the 1918 revolution she left this group and joined the Communist party. In 1920 she was chosen by the Communist party as its representative in the Reichstag and as editor of the *Kommunisten*. As early as 1921, however, her differences with the Moscow leadership of the Third International over their policy in western Europe led her to join with the opposition group of Paul Levy, who was subsequently expelled from the party. Rather than lose the prestige of her name, the Russian leaders made some concessions to Clara Zetkin and an apparent peace was concluded.

During the last ten years of her life she lived mainly in Russia, returning to Germany only at rare intervals, as when in August, 1932, she presided as the oldest deputy at the opening of the Reichstag. Although she could not agree with the policies of Stalin, she no longer had the energy to fight against the dominating tendency within the Communist International. She was the last great figure of pre-war socialism who remained with the Third International.

ARTHUR ROSENBERG

Works: *Die Arbeiterinnen—und Frauenfrage der Gegenwart*, Berliner Arbeiterbibliothek, 1st ser., vol. iii (Berlin 1889); *Geistiges Proletariat, Frauenfrage und Sozialismus* (Berlin 1902); *Zur Frage des Frauenwahlrechts* (Berlin 1907); *Karl Marx und sein Lebenswerk* (Elberfeld 1913); *Um Rosa Luxemburgs Stellung zur russischen Revolution* (Hamburg 1922); *Trotzkis Verbannung und die Sozialdemokratie* (Berlin 1928); *Reminiscences of Lenin* (London 1929).

ZIA PASHA (1825–81), Turkish author and nationalist. Zia attended the Mektebi-i-Edebyye (School of Humanities) and at an early age became interested in the study and writing of poetry. He was employed in the offices of the grand vizierate and in 1854 became third secretary to Abdul Aziz. At this time he turned to the study of French and translated a long series of French literary and historical works. His poems soon began to show a new orientation: western influences were apparent in both their content and their style.

During this same period Zia became a severe critic of the existing regime and engaged in a bitter campaign against Ali Pasha and Fuad Pasha, who had succeeded Reshed Pasha in the leadership of the reform movement. Convinced that his satirical poems attacking the government's policies would never effect the changes he desired, he became active in 1865 in the organization of the Young Turks, a new secret revolutionary society modeled on the Carbonari. In 1867, following official discovery of the organization, Zia and its other leaders fled to Europe. Here Zia collaborated with Kamál in editing a revolutionary paper, *Ḥurrīyat* (Liberty), and continued his translations and his written attacks upon the Turkish government, offering by way of comparison an idealized picture of the west. In *Ruya* (Dream), written in London in 1869, Zia presented an imaginative picture of a regenerated liberal Turkey.

After his return to Turkey in 1871 he worked for the dethronement of Abdul-Aziz in the hope of initiating a better regime. But Abdul-Hamid, who succeeded to the throne, proved anything but a liberal; fearing Zia's influence, he kept him away from Istanbul by making him governor successively of Syria, Konia and Adana, where he died in despair.

Zia, together with Shinasi, initiated the Turkish literary renascence, concentrating his attention upon the creation of a clear and simple medium of expression. His poems, especially his satirical verses, and his articles on political and social subjects were influential in the cause of reform and helped to introduce western ideas into Turkey.

AHMET EMIN

Consult: Gibb, E. J. W., *A History of Ottoman Poetry*, 6 vols. (London 1900–09) vol. v, ch. iii.

ZINCKE, GEORG HEINRICH (1692–1768), eighteenth century German cameralist. Zincke may be considered a transition figure between the early cameralists J. J. Becher, Hornigk and W. von Schroeder and Justi and Sonnenfels, who represented the science of cameralism as a fully developed academic discipline; next to Dithmar, Zincke was most instrumental in introducing cameralism into university curricula. That Zincke in the main followed the old cameralistic tradition is indicated in his edition (Leipsic 1754) of Becher's *Politischer Discurs*, originally published a century before, which Zincke annotated and brought up to date. He departed, however, from early cameralism in his emphasis on natural law. While the original edition of Becher's *Politischer Discurs*, true to the spirit of the rigid absolutism of its epoch, failed to recognize the existence of prestate rights, Zincke believed that certain original rights had existed prior to the formal organization of society. Thus he helped to establish the concept of civic society as distinct from the organization of the state and attempted to build up an empirical although crude theory of the state by distinguishing between its various component elements. His emphasis on natural law stamps Zincke as an advocate of enlightened absolutism.

Zincke's cameralistic writings are characterized by a measure of systematization which constituted a distinct advance over the general run of cameralistic works of his time. Like all cameralists, he placed the science at the service of the state, its main object being the training of efficient administrators; but he paid more attention to its didactic aspects. His attempt to delimit the subject matter of cameralistics from that underlying other disciplines necessitated a certain degree of abstract treatment, and he established the practise of having the discussion of "the general principles" common to the science of cameralism precede the treatment of its special branches. Novel too was his regrouping of the subject matter, whereby he treated all problems first from the economic, or technological and natural scientific, viewpoint and then from the police, or public administrative, aspect. Zincke's concern for the spread of economic science is attested by numerous textbooks and manuals which he published. He deserves special mention as the editor of *Leipziger Sammlungen von wirthschafftlichen, Policey-Cammer und Finantz-Sachen*, the first important periodical devoted exclusively to problems of cameralism, and for his *Cameraliste-Bibliothek* (4 pts., Leipsic 1751–52), the first systematic bibliography of cameralism in which the works are classified not merely according to subject but also according to degree of scientific merit.

LOUISE SOMMER

Other important works: *Grundriss einer Einleitung zu den Cameralwissenschaften*, 2 vols. (Leipsic 1742); *Anfangsgründe der Cameralwissenschaften*, 2 vols. (Leipsic 1755).

Consult: Small, Albion W., *The Cameralists* (Chicago 1909), especially ch. xi; Roscher, Wilhelm, *Geschichte der National-Oekonomik in Deutschland* (2nd ed. Munich 1924), especially p. 432–41; Stieda, Wilhelm, *Die Nationalökonomie als Universitätswissenschaft*, K. Sächsische Gesellschaft der Wissenschaften, Philologisch-historische Klasse, Abhandlungen, vol. xxv, no. ii (Leipsic 1906) p. 25–32.

ZINZENDORF, COUNT NIKOLAUS LUDWIG VON (1700–60), German religious reformer. Zinzendorf was born in Dresden and was educated in the Pietist schools of Halle. Against the wishes of his family he dedicated himself to a religious career. In 1722 he welcomed on his estate several families of refugees from the old Bohemian Brethren of Moravia. These were soon joined by others and many Pietists, Separatists and members of other mystical sects. In 1727 Zinzendorf organized these settlers into the community of Herrnhut and they were later officially constituted as the Erneuerte Brüderkirche. It was not intended that this be a separate church but rather an institution working for the "community of the children of God" in all evangelical denominations without depriving any group of its peculiar characteristics. Communities of the Moravian church were also established in England and America and a very vigorous missionary activity was carried on among primitive peoples. A far famed model settlement was established in Bethlehem, Pennsylvania, by Spangenberg, the most important disciple of Zinzendorf. All the needs of the community were provided for within the community and the surplus was sold to the surrounding country. The profits were not accumulated but expended for the spiritual activities of the members in their missionary activities. The economic successes of the Moravian communities were due not to an economic program but to the subordination of the economic to the religious life. New methods of economic organization were adopted without prejudice, but every member was inspired above all to sacrifice himself for the good of the whole and especially for the Savior. Worldly labor was considered to be a product of common religious life. It was characteristic of Zinzendorf to work without a program and allow himself to be led by God. This resulted in his great adaptability. Thus also the educational work of the Moravians was started by him even though he had never written a work on pedagogy or attempted to survey the field. Individual expressions of opinion, however, indicate his preoccupation with the subject. "Children are little majesties" and are therefore to be treated with respect; "one should obey the course of nature and sanctify it." Important is also his appreciation of individuality. Educational practise in his church was directed toward the community. He was kindly disposed toward philosophy in so far as it pertained to earthly matters, and he liked to call himself a practical philosopher. He repudiated any influence of philosophy, however, in religion and theology. Understanding was valid only in worldly affairs. Otherwise he was a decided antirationalist. In constructing religious knowledge on feeling he did not mean it to be a faltering and wavering subjectivism but rather another instrument of knowing besides understanding. The chief object of knowledge is the Biblical truth that since man cannot attain to God, God must become man in order to redeem him; that the knowledge of God is only through Christ; and that man as a sinner can find justification only through the grace of God because of the merits of Christ. The doctrine of justification, which he took over from Luther, he developed at times into an exaggerated theology of blood and wounds, in which his unusual sensual images often appear repellent unless their foundation in the doctrine of justification is recognized.

The ideas of Zinzendorf together with the other Pietistic currents were of considerable influence in the molding of religious and general intellectual currents in Germany. The stress on emotionalism, the development of the idea of individuality and the greater emphasis on the feeling of *Gemeinschaft* were important factors in paving the way for the *Sturm und Drang* and romantic movements. Schleiermacher and Novalis in particular reveal the strong impress of the Moravian tradition. Outside of Germany the influence of the Moravians was particularly apparent in the work of John Wesley and the Methodists.

WILHELM BETTERMANN

Consult: Becker, Bernhard, *Zinzendorf und sein Christentum* (2nd ed. Leipsic 1900); Uttendörfer, Otto, *Alt-Herrnhut* (Herrnhut 1925), *Zinzendorfs Weltbetrachtung* (Berlin 1929), *Zinzendorf und die Jugend* (Berlin 1923), and *Das Erziehungswesen Zinzendorfs*, Monumenta Germaniae paedagogica, vol. li (Berlin 1912); Bettermann, W., *Theologie und Sprache bei Zinzendorf* (Gotha 1934); Meyer, H. H., *Child Nature and Nurture* (New York 1928); Hamilton, J. T., *A History of the Church Known as the Moravian Church* (Bethlehem, Pa. 1900); Erbe, Hellmuth, *Bethlehem, Pa. Eine kommunistische Herrnhuter Kolonie des 18. Jahrhunderts*, Deutsche Ausland-Institut, Schriften, sect. A, vol. xxiv (Stuttgart 1929); Pinson, Koppel S., *Pietism as a Factor in the Rise of German Nationalism* (New York 1934), with full bibliography.

ZIONISM is the Jewish national movement which has as its aim the reestablishment of Palestine as a Jewish nation state. It originated in the nineteenth century among the Jews of eastern and central Europe. Numerous currents and different shades of opinion have developed within the Zionist movement and its origins too are traceable to a complexity of factors. Although the organized form of political Zionism, strictly speaking, had its beginnings in central Europe, the intellectual and spiritual background as well as the mass support of Zionism came from the Jews of eastern Europe. Two movements were of particular importance in providing the intellectual milieu for the development of modern Jewish nationalism. Chassidism (*q.v.*), a pietistic and mystical religious movement, proclaimed the value of the uneducated, intellectually untrained masses as against the upper classes of merchants and scholars. It thus acted as a democratic force in raising the self-esteem of the lower classes. Paralleling Chassidism came the *Haskalah*, or Jewish Enlightenment movement, which, originating in the larger cities and among the upper classes of society and touched by the influences of western European Enlightenment, helped to break down the traditional orthodox structure of Jewish society and opened the way to new careers, to secular learning and to participation in the general movement of European ideas. Both movements brought about a newly awakened individualism and instigated a break with the rigid traditionalism of the past; out of their influence followed the regeneration of Judaism in the nineteenth century, a new vigorous activity in all fields of social and cultural life and the birth of a modern Jewish literature in the Hebrew, Yiddish and various European languages.

Although Zionism is a modern nationalist movement, it may be viewed as a continuation of the age old longing of the Jews for a restoration to their homeland, from which Zionism drew its enthusiasm and religious fervor. The Jews had been one of the few peoples in antiquity possessed of a strong racial and national consciousness. After the destruction of the comparatively short lived Jewish state in Palestine the intense national feeling of the Jews survived with undiminished fervor for nearly two thousand years. It dominated their daily prayers, their philosophical and juridical teaching and their poetry. In almost every century of the exile messianic leaders arose to gather the Jews from the ends of the earth and to redeem the land of Israel. National and religious life formed an indissoluble unity in Judaism; both culminated in one hope, the return to Zion. In mediaeval fashion, however, this political ideal had been expressed in religious terms and its realization made dependent upon the will and the grace of God. Zionism represents in modern form a continuation of this deeply rooted feeling of national consciousness among the Jews. It makes its appeal to the uninterrupted and all powerful consciousness of an indissoluble connection with the past among the masses of Jewry. Zionism as a political and secular movement arose among the secularized Jewish intelligentsia of central Europe as a reaction to economic and political factors, but it quickly became the form into which was cast the mediaeval religious Zionist fervor of the eastern European and oriental Jews. Social misery, economic depression and political humiliation among many parts of Jewry strengthened the romantic impulse toward Zionism. On the other hand, Zionism was not the only form of modern Jewish nationalism. Other currents of Jewish nationalism accepted the dispersion as a basic and irreversible fact of Jewish history. They did not look upon the two thousand years as an irrelevant development, a cause for shame, but recognized in the lack of territorial concentration and of governmental power the possibilities of a higher and humanly more progressive form of organization. They even looked with suspicion upon the romantic traits of Zionism. But those currents of Diaspora nationalism never exercised as powerful an attraction upon Jewry as did Zionistic nationalism. They lacked the power of appeal which Zionism drew from the whole Jewish past and from its promise of a fulfilment of the messianic longing for the reestablishment of the splendor of the kingdom of David.

During the first half of the nineteenth century it was commonly held by Jews of central and western Europe that the Jewish problem could be solved by the realization of political emancipation for the Jews in the various European countries and the assimilation of the Jews into the social, political and cultural life of the countries in which they live. Toward the close of the century, however, it became increasingly clearer that under existing social organization assimilation offered a solution at best only in individual cases. There were three main reasons for the failure of assimilation, which gave Jewish nationalism its impetus: first, assimilation and the movement of Europeanization did not reach the great masses of Jews, especially in the countries of eastern Europe, where the legal emancipation of the Jews had not been accomplished. Jewish racial consciousness was in most cases too strong to allow assimilation. The Jewish masses either had no opportunity to assimilate or very often did not wish it. They desired the continuation of Judaism as a corporate religious, national and social body. Second, in western European countries, where assimilation had succeeded to a great extent and where the Jews had entered fully into the social, political and cultural life of the nation, the validity of assimilation was perpetually questioned by the influx of Jews from eastern Europe who sought in Berlin and Vienna, in Paris, London and the United States not only the liberty and cultural atmosphere of large urban centers but also the possibilities of a better economic life. Third, racial aversion, existing in a particularly pronounced form in Germany, and economic competition against the successful rise of the Jew in commerce and the professions led to recurring tides of antisemitism, which acted as a bar to assimilation and reawakened racial consciousness even in the partly or fully assimilated Jews. The relative failure of assimilation led the assimilated central European Jews to Zionism and to a rapprochement with eastern European Jewry, which had not been touched by assimilation. Modern political Zionism began with the rediscovery by the Jewish individual of his membership in the Jewish nation and of the unity of the Jewish nation. It represented an effort to normalize an apparently anormal national situation by territorial concentration. By assimilation the Jews had tried individually to escape the heavy yoke of the Jewish fate, to become "normal" like all other people around them; as assimilation failed Zionism seemed to offer another escape, not individually but as a corporate body, whereby the Jews were to become "normal" like all other nations.

The general European scene was favorable to

such a development. In the first third of the nineteenth century the dominant elements had been liberal individualism, the fight against traditionalism and the belief in humanitarianism; the second third (about 1848–78) was dominated by nationalism, the tendency to liberate and to unite nationalities as corporate bodies; the third period (about 1878–1914) by the expanding tendencies of imperialism and colonization. The impact of the modern theories of nationalism made itself felt among the Jews only comparatively late. Whereas assimilation had been influenced by the European ideas of the first third of the nineteenth century, Zionism almost wholly belongs to the last third of the nineteenth century. In 1862 appeared the first important book of modern Jewish nationalism, *Rom und Jerusalem* (Leipsic; tr. by Meyer Waxman, New York 1918) by Moses Hess. The motivating force in the Zionism of Hess was the desire to maintain Jewish values. His Zionism was based on the necessity to reanimate the creative genius of Israel in the interests of mankind and of the final fulfilment of the messianic promises of the French Revolution. Hess remained a solitary forerunner, but in the beginning of the 1880's more organized forms of Zionism appeared in Russia. At that time a wave of pogroms swept over Russia, and the reactionary regime instituted by Pobedonostsev after the liberal rule of Alexander II seemed to destroy hope for an emancipation of the Jews. At the same time enlightenment and modern capitalism forced their way into Russia and dissolved the foundations of Jewish traditional social and cultural life, filling the hearts of leading Jews with anxiety about the future of Judaism. It was an age of transition, socially, economically and culturally. Europeanization had set in irresistibly among the younger generation, but the traditionalism of the ghetto continued to dominate Jewish life. The *Haskalah* under the influence of German literature and philosophy, especially of Friedrich Schiller, had introduced into Hebrew literature modern forms of thought and feeling. Historical novels and poems depicting the life of Biblical times, such as Abraham Mapu's *Ahavat Zion* (The love of Zion, Vilna 1853), stirred the hearts of the youth in the orthodox Talmudistic schools. Some young people started to study Russian and secular sciences and were touched by the nationalism and romanticism of the Russian literature of the time. The new railways brought the small Jewish towns into contact with the larger cities, and a mass movement of emigration began to the United States and to western Europe. Modern nationalist, liberal and socialist theories took hold of the Jewish intelligentsia, and a literary renaissance set in similar to those at the beginning of all modern national movements. The spoken language of the Jewish masses, Yiddish, became a literary language in which works of popular science, essays, poetry, novels and drama were produced. The old scholastic language, Hebrew, was revivified by romantic nationalism, gained a new power of expression and became again a living language. The Hebrew movement, like the Gaelic movement, proved the vitality of Jewish nationalism and its connection with the past. In 1882 an assimilated Jewish physician in Odessa, Leon Pinsker, published in German an appeal to his western European brethren, which he called *Autoemancipation!* (Berlin 1882; tr. by A. A. L. Finkenstein, London 1891), to save the Jewish people from persecution and the misery of dispersion. He maintained that the Jewish people had to rely only upon its own forces and its own historic will and could not expect help from governments or from the progress of civilization. It was an appeal to national self-consciousness, activity and self-help. It applied the ideas of European secularism and the tendencies of the nineteenth century to the Jewish people and declared the necessity of concentrating the Jews territorially, in Palestine or elsewhere. Pinsker was free from national romanticism—he was entirely secularized; but his appeal found no echo among western European Jewry, to which it was addressed. Only in Russia a small group gathered around him, partly young men and students, partly older men of the more orthodox and traditional type, for whom the modern national movement was a direct continuation of the two thousand years of longing for the ancient homeland, Palestine. The movement took the name of Chovevei Zion (Lovers of Zion); some tens of young people, known as the Bilu, left Russia to start Jewish agricultural colonies in the wilderness of Palestine. Untrained and without sufficient resources, they were soon faced by bankruptcy but were saved by the intervention of Baron Edmond de Rothschild of Paris. A committee was formed in Odessa under Pinsker's presidency to promote the settlement of Jewish agriculturists and artisans in Palestine, and a conference was convoked at Kattowitz in 1884 to organize the movement. But the Chovevei Zion remained a small movement. The settlers remained dependent on philanthropic aid and, against the will of Pinsker, they retained the lower middle class methods and narrow minded psychology of the Russian village. The movement, however, laid the foundations of practical Jewish colonization in Palestine and it offered the opportunity for the constructive criticism of Ahad Ha-am (Asher Ginsberg), the first and most important attempt at a theory of Jewish nationalism and at a fusion of modern nationalism with traditional Zionism. Ahad Ha-am considered as utopian the claims of Zionism as a solution of the Jewish problem by the concentration of the Jewish masses in Palestine. Palestine, however, he thought, offered the possibility for a Jewish cultural center, by the slow and methodic upbuilding of a selective community of Jewish agriculturists, artisans, students and scholars, who would lead their lives on the basis of a rejuvenated Hebrew culture in the spirit of the ancient prophets. Zionism, he declared, was not and could never become a quantitative solution of the problem of Jewry nor a remedy against persecution or antisemitism. It could only be a qualitative solution for the regeneration of Judaism and the reintegration of the Jews into a living Jewish civilization, which would give them new inner forces of resistance and life. It would constitute a cultural unity of the dispersed Jewry with its spiritual center in Palestine, from which influences would radiate into all corners of the Diaspora. A new love of Judaism and of Zion would be awakened in the hearts of the Jews, which would mean for them a moral and intellectual rebirth, and this true "love of Zion" would again strengthen the center in Palestine. But Zionism, according to Ahad Ha-am, had nothing to do with the egoistic wishes of the Jewish individual for economic betterment or greater happiness. The cultural center in Palestine could fulfil its function only by being built out of disinterested love and on the basis of the ethics of the prophets. Ahad Ha-am's Zionism was never adopted by any considerable group, as it did not pretend to offer a solution of the economic and political Jewish problems. But his insistence on the necessity of Hebrew culture permeated first the eastern European Zionists, then after 1905 the whole Zionist movement, and only by that element was it turned into a complete modern national movement conscious of its link with its historic past and embracing all aspects of life.

A new impetus was given to Zionism by Theodor Herzl, who raised the Zionist movement out of the narrow limits of philanthropy and the petty bourgeois ghetto and molded it into a political movement of a general European significance. Herzl was aroused to a keen consciousness of the gravity of the Jewish problem by the widespread antisemitism during the Dreyfus case. He declared assimilation desirable but in view of antisemitism impossible of realization. Against their own wishes the Jews were forced by pressure from outside to form a nation. As a nation they could lead a happy and dignified life only by normalizing their existence through concentration in one territory. Without knowing it Herzl resumed the work of Pinsker, but he did it not from Odessa but from Paris and Vienna, with the impetus of a born leader of men. With the publication of his pamphlet *Der Judenstaat* (Leipsic 1896; tr. by S. d'Avigdor, London 1896), in which he developed his ideas of political Zionism, he became the indefatigable propagandist of this idea. Herzl's Zionism was barren with respect to traditional Jewish values. He had no knowledge of Jewish history and culture nor of the problems of eastern European Jewry. His Zionism, receiving its impetus from antisemitism, did not strive to regenerate the creative forces of Judaism but to provide for those who could not or did not wish to be assimilated a home where they could lead a happy and free life but in no way a specifically Jewish life. He did not consider Palestine as the only necessary place for the Jewish homeland and never contemplated the rebirth of Hebrew as the Jewish national language. Even in his novel *Altneuland* (Leipsic 1902), in a certain way his last will and testament to the movement, he described the future life of the Jews in Palestine as a continuation of the life of assimilated central European Jewry. His Zionism was purely political without Jewish content; but because of his detachment from Judaism and his Europeanization Herzl was able to give to Zionism a modern form and establish it as a democratic political movement. He convoked the first Zionist Congress in Basel in 1897, which drew up a constitution for the Zionist movement. The congress, which met first annually and after 1901 every second year, consisted of delegates elected by the members of the organization by general and direct suffrage. Every male or female member over eighteen years of age was eligible to vote. This congress became the supreme legislative body and elected larger and smaller executive committees, which were responsible to the congress. Thus Zionism was organized as an interterritorial modern democratic nationalist movement, the first organization of its kind in Jewish history. It claimed to represent the Jewish people on the march to its goal of nationhood; its president claimed to speak on behalf of the newly organized Jewish democracy in all countries of the Diaspora, although only a small minority of the Jews were organized in the Zionist movement. But it was the only democratically and interterritorially organized part of Jewry, active and young. In every town of the Diaspora local organizations were created, which were united in each country into a federation. Besides these federations several other nonterritorial federations called *Sonderverbände*, such as the Mizrachi, or strictly religious Zionists, and the Labour Zionists (*Poale Zion* and *Hapoel Hazair*) came to be recognized within the world Zionist organization.

The creation of the Zionist Organization was Herzl's great achievement. Until his death the center of the movement was under his presidency in Vienna. After his death in 1904 it was moved to Germany, where it remained until 1920, when it was removed to London, the seat of the mandatory government over Palestine. With the growth of Zionist colonization in Palestine the headquarters were partly moved to Jerusalem. Until the World War Austrian and German Jews led the movement, but the mass strength of the movement came from Russia. After the World War the leadership passed to Jews of Russian origin living in London or Palestine (the presidents were Chaim Weizmann and Nahum Sokolow), the financial and economic strength of the movement came from the Jews in the United States, the masses of its adherents from Poland and its backbone from the growing settlement in Palestine. Sociologically it remained a movement of the smaller middle class led by a sprinkling of academic intelligentsia. During Herzl's lifetime the struggle between his more modern and western European Zionism and the traditional Zionism of the eastern European Jews filled the history of the world congresses. After his death a compromise was worked out, which constituted Zionism as a full national movement uniting the masses, bound by traditionalism, under a modern leadership. The Zionist Organization developed an active propaganda by orators and pamphlets, created its own newspapers in different languages and its own financial instruments and gave an impetus to what was called a "Jewish renaissance" in the letters and arts. The ideal of Herzl had been a modern secular movement, his ideas being those of the progressive freethinking bourgeoisie of the end of the nineteenth century. The Zionist Organization declared itself neutral in matters of religion; it united strictly orthodox, moderately traditional, indifferent and radically freethinking Jews; but the insistence of the religious groups upon stricter observance of the Jewish religious precepts caused from time to time sharp conflicts, which have continued to the present day. Under Herzl's leadership all work within the Zionist Organization was done without remuneration. After his death, however, a bureaucratic apparatus was created, which after the World War grew to great proportions and tended to control the organization.

The Zionist Congress of Basel in 1897 had declared as the aim of Zionism the creation and international guaranty of a home for the Jewish people in Palestine. Herzl negotiated with the sultan and with different European governments; but lacking the support of Jewish influential circles in western Europe, he did not succeed in getting more than cautious declarations of platonic sympathy, except in Great Britain, where he was offered in 1903 the African territory Uganda for the settlement of Jews as an autonomous community within the British Empire. Herzl was inclined to accept this as at least a temporary solution of the Jewish problem, but the majority of Russian Zionists insisted in their nationalistic orthodoxy upon Palestine as the only homeland of the Jews. The Zionist Congress declined the British offer and a group under the leadership of Israel Zangwill, who for political and geographical reasons did not consider the small and populated Palestine fit to become a Jewish state, split off under the name of Territorialists (I.T.O.) to search for a territory for Jewish settlement.

The Russian events of 1905 changed the situation within the Zionist Organization. The Russian revolution had aroused a revolutionary and nationalistic enthusiasm among the youth of Russia and her non-Russian nationalities. The failure of the revolution, the disillusionment in Jewish emancipation in eastern Europe, the wave of pogroms and the repressive measures of reaction led many young Jews into Zionism. Again as in 1882, but now in growing numbers, young men and women set out for Palestine to live there as the pioneers of the Jewish nationalist movement. They were filled with the ideal of a regeneration of Jewish life and labor on the soil of Palestine. There had been Jewish farmers in Palestine since 1882, but they had worked with Arab labor; now Jews came to work the fields with their own hands. They declared that only by doing all the work themselves could they make Palestine *Erez Israel*, the land of Israel. They were influenced by the often romantic and sometimes anarchistic theories of the Russian Social Revolutionaries and their idealization of the peasant and the laborer. One of the most important of their leaders was A. D. Gordon, who like Tolstoy preached the return to simplicity of life and the healing forces of nature. Organized as the *Hapoel Hazair* (the Young Worker) and as an anti-Marxian, strictly nationalist labor movement, they started to create communistic agricultural settlements similar to the early socialist communities and fought against the employment of "foreign" (Arab) labor. Outside Palestine a Marxian and strongly nationalist labor movement, calling itself *Poale Zion* (the Workers of Zion), under the leadership of Ber Boruchov, gained influence among many Jewish workers. According to Boruchov socialism offered no solution to the Jewish problem so long as the Jews were not constituted as a nation with a normal economic structure and a strong working class basis. Only within an independent national community could the class war fulfil its normal function.

At the same time Jewish life in Palestine had expanded; Hebrew became the language of the youth, Hebrew schools were created and slowly the nucleus of a genuine national community began to emerge. This growing reality in Palestine and the despair in the possibility of diplomatic successes strengthened in the Zionist organization the "practical" tendencies of colonizing activities. The period from 1905 to 1914 was an epoch without outward successes but with a relatively strong intellectual life and manifold cultural activities for Zionism.

The World War marked a decisive turn in Zionism. Herzl's expectations were realized and Zionism was internationally recognized. The Balfour Declaration of November 2, 1917, expressed in a letter of the British foreign secretary to Lord Rothschild the sympathy of the British government for the establishment of *a* Jewish national home in Palestine. This intentionally vague promise fell short of the expectations of the Zionists who had asked for the reconstitution of Palestine as *the* Jewish National Home. Nevertheless, it aroused enthusiastic hopes among Zionists and convinced many Jews, especially among the wealthy classes who had held aloof from Zionism, of its practicability. The Balfour Declaration was endorsed by the principal Allied Powers, and through its acceptance by the Conference of San Remo and its inclusion in the Treaty of Sèvres (1920) it became an integral part of British imperial policy in the Near and Middle East.

At the same time the situation of the Jews had changed in eastern Europe. The White armies during the civil wars following the Russian Revolution had perpetrated pogroms in the Ukraine worse than those of 1905; and the creation or enlargement of many new nation states in eastern and central Europe had, notwithstanding political emancipation, affected adversely the economic and social position of the Jews. With the doors closed by the restrictions upon immigration in the United States and other countries after the war, Palestine loomed up as the great haven of refuge for the suffering Jews. At the same time American Jewish leaders gained an influence which they had never before exercised in Jewish life. They tried to permeate the Zionist movement with American methods of business and organization, but they did not succeed in attaining any directing influence. The conflict between the Americanized Jewish leadership and the old European Zionist leadership, which was in the hands of Jews of Russian origin, ended in 1921 with a victory for the latter. Post-war Zionism was characterized by a growing concentration upon Palestine, with a simultaneous decline in the world Zionist movement, especially in its cultural activity. The growing power of the Jews in Palestine and the intensity of their cultural and social life attracted the attention and the sympathy of wide circles of Diaspora Jewry. The Zionist Organization tried to win the active support of wealthy non-Zionist Jews, especially in the United States; and in August, 1929, the enlarged Jewish Agency was formed to unite, under the leadership of the president of the Zionist Organization, representatives of the Zionist Organization and of non-Zionist groups. But the cooperation of the non-Zionists did not equal the expectations and the Jewish Agency remained a predominantly Zionist body. The Zionist funds, the Keren Hayesod (Palestine Foundation Fund), which financed the colonizing and educational activities of the Zionist Organization in Palestine, and the Keren Kayemeth (Jewish National Fund), which bought land in Palestine to be given to Jewish agriculturists in hereditary lease, appealed for voluntary contributions from Diaspora Jewry; but their income decreased rather than increased during the years following the first period of post-war enthusiasm. Considerable Jewish capital nevertheless was invested in Palestine, especially after 1932. The rapid growth after 1932 was not due primarily to an organic growth of Zionist sentiment or to more active support by non-Zionists. It was due mainly to factors in the general central and eastern European situation, to world economic instability, to the advent to power of the extremely antisemitic National Socialism in Germany with the ensuing exodus of Jewish capital and youth from Germany and to the growth of acute poverty and the destruction of middle class existence in Poland. This growth of Jewish immigration into Palestine since 1932 has therefore led to a deep transformation and crisis in Zionism. While Zionism before the World War was an idealistic and ideological national movement, it became after the Balfour Declaration more and more identified with the realities of the political, economic and social problems of Palestinian Jewry.

Zionist colonization in Palestine after the Balfour Declaration was dominated not only by outward factors in the Jewish world, such as the increasing objective urge toward Palestinian immigration in the situation of world Jewry, especially in Poland, Hitlerite Germany and central Europe, and the rising restrictions against immigration in previous countries of Jewish mass influx, but also by two factors inherent in the situation in Palestine: the limited absorptive capacity of Palestine, which is a small country with few fertile districts; and the existence of a large Arab population, which had become strongly conscious of its national aspirations during and after the World War and which, resenting the influx of Jewish immigrants, rose during the years from 1920 to 1933 four times in revolt against the British Zionist mandate. The mandatory government of Great Britain took these two factors into consideration in its interpretation of the vague Balfour Declaration. From the beginning the British government refused to accept the idea of a Jewish commonwealth. The British high commissioner in Palestine, Sir Herbert Samuel, declared on June 3, 1921, that the Balfour Declaration meant that some Jews should come to Palestine within the limits set by the number and interests of the present inhabitants and help by their means and efforts to develop the country in the interest of all its inhabitants. Although the worthiness and loftiness of the ideals of Zionism and the claim to consideration of the national aspirations of fourteen million Jews were acknowledged, it was maintained that "the degree to which Jewish national aspirations can be fulfilled in Palestine is conditioned by the rights of the present inhabitants." The mandate of the League of Nations for Palestine of July 24, 1922, was restricted by the statement of British policy of June 3, 1922, which was officially accepted by the Zionist Organization. British experts who were sent by the British government to Palestine after 1929 to report on the economic possibilities of land settlement and development declared that at the present stage agricultural Palestine did not afford possibilities for a large settlement without endangering the prospects of the present population. This they declared true especially in view of the fact that the greatest part of the most fertile and economically important lands, such as the maritime plain, the bay of Haifa and the valley of Esdraelon, had already passed into Jewish hands. The Zionist Organization criticized the findings of the experts and strongly protested against the restrictive explanation of the Balfour Declaration and the practise of the mandatory government of curtailing Jewish immigration into Palestine. The political aim of Zionism remained: the reconstitution of Palestine as a Jewish commonwealth, Palestine to comprise not only the territory west of the Jordan but also Transjordania, which according to engagements of Great Britain to her Arab allies in the World War had been constituted as an Arab principality. Two different currents developed in Zionism as to the realization of this aim. One group, led by Dr. Chaim Weizmann and the Zionist Labour party, worked for a close cooperation with Great Britain, for a realistic acceptance of whatever could be attained, coupled with permanent pressure upon Great Britain for a more generous and vigorous fulfilment of the hopes of the Jewish people. They believed in the patient upbuilding of stronger economic and social positions of the Jewish people in Palestine, trusting that these facts would in themselves prove strong enough to mold political realities and at some not too remote time to bring the Jewish state into being. The other, led by the Revisionists, openly opposed the cautious policy of Great Britain and demanded the immediate institution of a political regime which would anticipate the future Jewish state and thus accelerate its coming. The Zionist Labour party represented the interests of the Jewish working class in Palestine and aimed at a cooperative socialist Jewish state in Palestine. The Revisionists represented the smaller middle class elements, who later came to advocate a sort of fascist Jewish state. With the economic destruction of the Jewish middle classes in central and eastern Europe, especially in Poland, the Revisionist temper extended to other Zionist groups, like the Mizrachi, the party of religious orthodox middle class Zionists. At the same time the extreme nationalism in the central and eastern European states influenced the Jewish youth in those countries from which the emigration to Palestine was being mainly recruited. The struggle between the Revisionists and the Labour group has taken on a more and more embittered form. Between those two groups the middle parties, the general Zionists, seem steadily to lose in importance. A group of Zionist intellectuals displayed from 1925 to 1931 some activity as a pacifist group, called Brith Shalom. They recognized the gravity of the moral and political problems presented to Zionism by its attitude against the Arab population of Palestine and its aspirations and wished a reorientation of Zionism in the light of the theories of Ahad Ha-am. They opposed the extreme nationalism of the Revisionists and criticized the politics of the Zionist Labour federation, which insisted upon 100 percent Jewish labor in all Jewish enterprises, public and private.

Jewish colonization in Palestine after the World War can be divided into three distinct periods. During the period from 1920 to 1925 there was an influx of enthusiastic post-war youth, known as the *chaluzim*, from central and eastern Europe. This was an idealistic movement with strong socialistic beliefs; it resulted in the creation of a great number of agricultural workers' settlements, with a preponderance of communistic settlements, known as *kvuzoth*. This period terminated in 1924–25 with a strong influx of Polish middle class elements into Tel Aviv, the new Jewish town near Jaffa, and the rapid development of urban colonization and of modern industry, particularly of the building trades, bringing with it the creation of an urban Jewish working class. During the period from 1926 to 1931 there was a long crisis accompanied by emigration and unemployment, which, however, allowed for an organic consolidation and a strengthening of the existing Jewish economic structure in the towns and agricultural settlements. During this period American influence, which emphasized industrial development and sound business practise, found expression in a number of relatively powerful financial institutions emanating from the group under the leadership of Justice Brandeis and others. From 1932 onward came a new boom by the influx of many immigrants from Poland and Germany together with Jewish capital in search of security and investment. A rapid growth of the Jewish urban colonization in Tel Aviv, Haifa and Jerusalem, of building activity and industrial expansion set in. In agriculture a strong preference was shown for orange plantations. The Jewish urban population grew more quickly than the agricultural population, which by the middle of 1934 could be estimated at only about 25 percent of the whole Jewish population of the country. The idealistic and romantic period of Zionism in Palestine seemed closed, and a spirit of hard economic expansion tended to dominate the situation.

Today Zionism has become an undisputed reality and a factor in the political world. The number of Jews in Palestine is growing rapidly. It amounted in October, 1922 (official census), to 83,794 out of a total of 757,182 inhabitants; in November, 1931 (official census), to 175,006 out of a total of 1,035,154 inhabitants; in June, 1934 (estimate), to 265,000 out of a total of 1,175,000 inhabitants. The Jews, although a minority of about 22 percent, exercise a dominating influence in the economic, social, cultural and political life of Palestine. By their efforts the character of those parts of the country where they have settled has been entirely changed. By their high standards of education and modern efficiency, their ardent nationalism with its strict discipline and exclusiveness in political and economic life and its devoted energy, their wealth and organization they have created most important economic and social positions, against which the Arab population, greatly impoverished for centuries, non-educated and backward, cannot compete. The great differences in standards of life and education accentuate the tension between the two races, especially as the Jewish industries and commercial enterprises have not tried to invite participation of Arab capital and labor in their benefits. The excellent colonizing achievements of Zionism have revealed the great organizing and constructive capacities of the Jews, even as agriculturists and agrarian laborers; but Zionism has up to now been unable to solve the problems inherent in the fact that Palestine is populated by a nationally conscious Arab people.

The realities of the Palestinian situation during and after the World War have deeply changed the character of Zionism as compared with the pre-war years. The achievements of Zionism in the field both of national cultural life and of practical colonization, however, are outstanding in the history of modern nationalism and colonization. As a movement Zionism has undoubtedly been the most important factor in modern Jewish history. Zionism, the national hope of the Jews during the two thousand years of their dispersion, has since the deterioration of their situation in central Europe again become the hope and refuge of many. It has rekindled the fire of Jewish nationalism in the heart of many an assimilated Jew, has taught the Jews a new pride in their history and a new consciousness of their destiny. For many it has provided a new homeland, at least a spiritual and historic homeland. Zionism has also created for the Jewish people its first organization upon a grand scale, revivified Jewish intellectual and spiritual life and opened up new outlets for creative expression. It has once again focused public attention upon the Jewish problem throughout the world. Whether or not it can realize its claims for the solution of the Jewish problem or whether the Jewish problem is essentially incapable of a normal "solution" still remains for many an open question.

HANS KOHN

See: JUDAISM; CHASSIDISM; JEWISH EMANCIPATION; JEWISH AUTONOMY; DIASPORA; GHETTO; MESSIANISM; NEAR EASTERN PROBLEM; MANDATES; LAND SETTLEMENT; COOPERATION, section on BRITISH EMPIRE, COOPERATION IN PALESTINE; NATIONALISM; MINORITIES, NATIONAL; ANTISEMITISM; ASSIMILATION, SOCIAL.

Consult: *Zionistisches Handbuch*, ed. by Gerhard Holdheim (Berlin 1923); Böhm, Adolf, *Die zionistische Bewegung*, 2 vols. (Berlin 1920–21); Schlesinger, Abraham, *Einführung in den Zionismus* (Frankfort 1921); Sokolow, Nahum, *History of Zionism, 1600–1918*, 2 vols. (London 1919); Stein, Leonard J., *Zionism* (London 1925); Bentwich, Norman, *Palestine* (London 1934); Horowitz, P., *The Jewish Question and Zionism* (London 1927); Ruppin, Arthur, *Die Juden der Gegenwart* (2nd ed., Cologne 1911), tr. by M. Bentwich (London 1913), and *The Jews in the Modern World* (London 1934); Kohn, Hans, *L'humanisme juif* (Paris 1931); Ginsberg, Asher, *Ten Essays on Zionism and Judaism* (London 1922); Buber, Martin, *Die jüdische Bewegung* (Berlin 1920); Kohn, Hans, *Martin Buber; sein Werk und seine Zeit* (Hellerau 1930); Birnbaum, Nathan, *Ausgewählte Schriften zur jüdischen Frage*, 2 vols. (Czernowitz 1910), and *Um die Ewigkeit* (Berlin 1920); Bergmann, Hugo, *Jawne und Jerusalem* (Berlin 1919); Tartakower, A., *Toldot tenuat happoalim hajehudit* (History of the Jewish labor movement), 2 vols. (Warsaw 1929–30), and "Zur Geschichte des jüdischen Sozialismus" in *Jude*, vol. vii (1923) 503–16, 591–618, and vol. viii (1924) 16–38, 148–73, 386–99, 455–72, 638–61; Arlosoroff, V. C., *Der jüdische Volkssozialismus* (Berlin 1919); Great Britain, Colonial Office, *Palestine; Report on Immigration, Land Settlement and Development*, by John Hope Simpson, 2 vols., Cmd. 3686–3687 (1930); Jewish Agency for Palestine, *Palestine; Land Settlement, Urban Development and Immigration. Memorandum Submitted to Sir John Hope Simpson* (London 1930); *Survey of International Affairs, 1925*, 2 vols. (London 1927) vol. i, sect. vii, and *Survey of International Affairs, 1930* (London 1931) part iii, sect. iii; Hocking, W. E., *The Spirit of World Politics* (New York 1932); Kohn, Hans, *Nationalismus und Imperialismus im vorderen Orient* (Frankfort 1931), tr. by M. M. Green (London 1932); Stoyanovsky, J., *The Mandate for Palestine* (London 1928); Schwarzenberger, Georg, *Das Völkerbunds-Mandat für Palästina*, Tübinger Abhandlungen zum öffentlichen Recht, no. 21 (Stuttgart 1929); Kampffmeyer, G., "Die Stellung der Araber zur neueren Entwicklung Palästinas und Transjordaniens" in *Zeitschrift des deutschen Palästina-Vereins*, vol. l (1927) 274–88; Kallen, H. M., *Zionism and World Politics* (New York 1921); Seidel, Hans J., *Der britische Mandatsstaat Palestina im Rahmen der Weltwirtschaft* (Berlin 1926); Kohn, Hans, and Weltsch, Robert, *Zionistische Politik* (Mährisch-Ostrau 1927); Andrews, Fannie Fern, *The Holy Land under Mandate*, 2 vols. (Boston 1931); Solow, Herbert, "The Realities of Zionism," and "Camouflaging Zionist Realities" in *Menorah Journal*, vol. xix (1930–31) 97–127 and 223–41; Klatzkin, Jakob, *Probleme des modernen Judentums* (3d ed. Berlin 1930); Margulies, Heinrich, *Kritik des Zionismus*, 2 vols. (Vienna 1920); Borochow, Ber, *Sozialismus und Zionismus* (Vienna 1932); Janowsky, Oscar I., *The Jews and Minority Rights 1898–1919* (New York 1933); Haas, Jacob de, *Theodor Herzl*, 2 vols. (Chicago 1927).

ZITELMANN, ERNST (1852–1923), German jurist. Zitelmann, who was professor successively at Göttingen, Rostock, Halle and Bonn, was one of the brilliant galaxy of dogmatic jurists who flourished under the German Empire. But Zitelmann did not confine himself to the exclusive cultivation of the positive law. Throughout his long life he was attracted also to philosophy and theory. He is really to be classed with the exponents of *allgemeine Rechtslehre* who sought to deal with the general and theoretical problems of the positive law. His particular contribution in this direction, embodied in the recognized classic *Irrtum und Rechtsgeschäft* (Leipsic 1879), stimulated the psychological examination of juristic problems, which was a marked phase of the activity of German jurists under the empire. Zitelmann's unique gift of combining positive law with theoretical studies was again put to notable use in the criticism of the draft of the general part of the German Civil Code and in the exposition of the code after its adoption. Both his *Die Rechtsgeschäfte im Entwurf eines bürgerlichen Gesetzbuches für das Deutsche Reich* (Berlin 1889–90) and his *Das Recht des bürgerlichen Gesetzbuchs* (Berlin 1900) have had an important place in all subsequent treatments of the code.

Zitelmann achieved his greatest fame, however, in the field of private international law with the publication of his *Internationales Privatrecht* (2 vols., Leipsic 1897–1912). This work is an attempt to elaborate a theoretical system of private international law upon international principles. But it would be wrong to claim him as an internationalist exponent of the science in the direct line of Savigny and Bar. For as a positivist he felt constrained to recognize the obligatory force of existing private international law. His private international law was to have only subsidiary application when the positive law was silent or confused. It was this subsidiary system, which he hoped would become in time the normal system, that was to be based upon the international principle of sovereignty. The rules of conflict were to be derived by applying the personal and territorial limitations of the principle of sovereignty. Thus the law to be applied was always that of the state in the sphere of whose sovereignty the effect of a created right was to take place.

The logical coherence and brilliance of Zitelmann's system of private international law have generally been conceded. But most critics have denied that the principle of sovereignty, which as yet applies only to the relations of states, can be accepted as its starting point. On the other hand, such a critic as Ehrlich has attacked Zitelmann for clinging to the positive law. Almost paradoxically he has been praised by some Italians; for in Italy the nationalist school has always been strong, and Zitelmann's results were similar to those derived by the application of the principle of nationality.

WILLIAM SEAGLE

Consult: *Die Rechtswissenschaft der Gegenwart in Selbstdarstellungen*, ed. by Hans Planitz, 3 vols. (Leipsic 1924–29) vol. i, p. 177–214; Bar, Ludwig von, "Neue Prinzipien und Methoden des internationalen Privatrechts" in *Archiv für öffentliches Recht*, vol. xv (1900) 1–49; Marcusen, W., "Innerstaatliches und überstaatliches internationales Privatrecht" in *Zeitschrift für internationales Privat- und Strafrecht*, vol. x (1900) 257–69; Ehrlich, Eugen, "Les tendances actuelles du droit international privé" in *Revue de droit international privé*, vol. iv (1908) 902–24; Gutzwiller, Max, "Zitelmanns völkerrechtliche Theorie des Internationalprivatrechts," and Klein, P., "Ernst Zitelmann" in *Archiv für Rechts- und Wirtschaftsphilosophie*, vol. xvi (1922–23) 468–81, and vol. xvii (1923–24) 504–20; Betti, Emilio, "Ernst Zitelmann e il problema del diritto internazionale privato" in *Rivista di diritto internazionale*, ser. iii, vol. iv (1925) 33–72, 188–231; Pacchioni, Giovanni, *Elementi di diritto internazionale privato* (Padua 1930) ch. v.

ZOAR. *See* COMMUNISTIC SETTLEMENTS.

ZOLA, ÉMILE (1840–1902), French novelist. Few if any literary movements have been so immediately affected by broader intellectual and social currents as was the naturalistic school, of which Zola was the principal apostle. Under the spell of positivistic philosophy and stimulated by the avowed purpose of the recently established Third Republic to translate the positivistic doctrines into political and social reality, Zola determined at an early age to demonstrate the advantages of associating the functions of novelist, scholar and statesman. His *Roman expérimental* (Paris 1880; tr. by B. M. Sherman, New York 1893) was an attempt to demonstrate in theoretical terms how the union of novelist and scientist might be achieved, while his political point of view was formulated in *La république et la littérature* (Paris 1879), wherein he declared that the modern state can be organized only by the "scientific or naturalistic republican."

In the course of the next twenty years Zola's ideas, expressed with varying degrees of intensity, exercised a tremendous influence upon most of the young novelists and upon a large part of the French public. A new portrait of contemporary France was popularized by the twenty-six volumes of *Rougon-Macquart*, *Trois villes* and *Quatre évangiles* (1871–1903). The workaday world and the life of the disinherited classes were thrown into bold relief in Zola's glowing descriptions. He familiarized his readers with the gospel of socialism and implanted in them a faith in the revolution as an inevitable catastrophe which must precede the happier era when rival classes will be supplanted by a society of free individuals bound only by ties of cooperative labor and love. Zola's last novels constitute in effect a body of socialist homiletics.

Not content with the more passive role of the observer, Zola aspired to play a direct part in political life. Thus his participation in the Dreyfus affair was not an accident to be accounted for by his friendship with individuals involved but a deliberate act of faith in science and humanity as well as in the republic, which he continued to uphold despite the divergence between its official ideology and the socialist leanings of his later years. The decisive importance of his gesture was eventually recognized by the government, which in 1908 accorded him the honors of the Panthéon. Although Zola's prestige has waned with the recent reaction against positivism and naturalism, he is still deeply revered in non-conformist, communistic and anarchist quarters.

PIERRE MARTINO

Works: *Oeuvres complètes*, ed. by Eugène Fasquelle, 50 vols. (Paris 1927–29); *Novels*, tr. and ed. by E. A. Vizetelly, 20 vols. (London 1892–1925).

Consult: Martino, P., *Le naturalisme français (1870–1895)* (2nd ed. Paris 1930) chs. ii–vii; Seillière, E., *Émile Zola* (Paris 1923); Barbusse, H., *Zola* (10th ed. Paris 1932), tr. by M. B. and F. C. Green (New York 1933); Josephson, Matthew, *Zola and His Time* (New York 1928).

ZONING as commonly understood refers to the legal regulation by districts or zones of the use of private property. In its specific application, the division of cities into three customary districts—business, industrial and residential—it has to do not only with the use to which the land is put but also with the height of buildings erected thereon and the percentage of ground space which they may occupy. As a supplement to building and housing codes it serves to stabilize property both economically and socially and forms a part of the wider program of city and town planning. Although informal and unofficial zoning was practised in European cities during the Middle Ages through the restriction of trades and commercial activities to certain streets and districts, zoning in its modern sense came into use only with the close of the nineteenth century when several German municipalities enacted legislation designed to keep undesirable manufacturing establishments at a distance from residences. This was followed by the creation of "protected districts" from which all industry was excluded and the development of bulk zoning as a method of planning additions to cities. As early as 1891 Frankfort attempted to control the height and area of new buildings through bulk zoning regulations.

The first comprehensive zoning ordinance adopted in the United States was that of New York City in 1916. The passage of this ordinance was preceded by a thorough study and analysis of the entire problem of urban land and building use regulation by a special Heights of Buildings Commission in 1913 and by the Commission on Building Districts and Restrictions, which had been authorized in 1914 to draft a complete zoning ordinance. Prior to the New York ordinance there had been various partial and comparatively crude attempts at zoning, the most notable of which were in Boston and Los Angeles. In none of these earlier applications, however, is there any record of a conscious effort to approach the problem from the viewpoint of systematic city planning. On the other hand, the reports of the New York commissions evidenced an understanding of the need for a more efficient and orderly apportionment and utilization of the entire land area of the city based upon social and economic considerations.

Zoning spread rapidly throughout the United States because of an increasing public recognition of the evils of haphazard urban growth. Direct stimulus to action, however, often came from one or more specific cases of misplaced development, such as an isolated public garage, filling station, grocery store or milk bottling plant in a residential section or an apartment house in a neighborhood of detached dwellings. From the broad outlook of public policy and city or regional planning there are a number of basic objectives which can be effectively served by zoning regulations. First among these objectives is the prevention of mixed and incongruous building development, which leads to obsolescence of existing structures and to such uncertainty as to the future that a condition of depreciated value and general blight often sets in, resulting in social and economic loss. Second in importance is the protection of the environment of the home. This is accomplished through the setting aside of residential districts from which business and industrial establishments are excluded, by prohibiting apartment houses in the dwelling house areas and by requiring adequate lot sizes and adequate front and rear yards for each residential building. Third, congestion of population may be obviated by limiting the spread of apartment houses, by requiring open space on each apartment house lot proportionate to the floor area or by restricting the number of separate apartments in relation to the area of the lot. Fourth, congestion may be mitigated in metropolitan areas through a better distribution of business and industrial establishments and the regulation of the height and bulk of buildings.

In practise some of these zoning objectives are not fully realized. The failure may be attributed in part to inherent difficulties attendant upon city growth. For example, central business areas must expand, creating a zone of transition, uncertainty and sometimes blight. Again, the problem of the best distribution of industry has not been worked out satisfactorily even in theory. The most disturbing defect, however, is the lack of an enlightened public or official opinion in support of some of the broad social purposes of zoning. Only where the interests of individual property owners happen to coincide with these social objectives are they likely to prevail against the attack of special groups clamoring for amendments and exceptions. The amendment of the zoning map should be left, as in Boston, to a special zoning or planning board rather than as elsewhere to a municipal council, the members of which are usually quite uninformed as to the social implications of the zoning plan and are apt to be swayed by personal or political considerations.

The adoption of the Oneida county, Wisconsin, zoning ordinance of May 16, 1933, marked the first application of the zoning method to a distinctly rural land problem. Other county zoning ordinances had been adopted, but they merely provided for the extension of city zoning objectives and methods to similar urban or semi-urban building development in the county. The Oneida county ordinance, however, is aimed primarily at preventing farm settlement in parts of the cut over area where such scattered settlement would create unwarranted burdens for schools, roads and local administration and would moreover interfere with the best use of the region as a whole, which is believed to be that of forestry and recreation.

State and rural zoning of the future should be based on the acceptance of broad policies in relation to the distribution of population and the utilization of the entire land resources of the community and the nation. It should develop as an integrated part of a regional planning program, and its objectives should include: the reservation of large areas for forestry, recreation and watershed protection; the discouragement of farm settlement on submarginal land and the prevention of the subdivision of land in areas where such subdivision is premature or where a scattered settlement would cause excessive expenditures for public facilities and other community services; the regulation of the cultivation of soils subject to excessive erosion or the zoning of such areas for pasture or forestry; the regulation of development along highways in the interest of both traffic efficiency and protection of the beauty of the countryside.

While certain phases of zoning have been the subject of litigation, the courts have in the main upheld zoning as a proper exercise of police power. Except in cases where the state constitution confers authority on cities, an enabling act is usually necessary to permit the enactment and enforcement of zoning codes. The United States Department of Commerce, through the Building and Housing division of the Bureau of Standards, drew up a Standard State Zoning Enabling Act which by 1930 had been adopted either as a whole or in part by thirty-five state legislatures. The rapid extension of the zoning movement within recent years is further evidenced by the fact that in 1921 there were fewer than 100 zoned municipalities in the United States, while in January, 1930, the number had increased to 856. Similar progress has been apparent in Canada, where at first zoning was practised under the town planning acts of England. Within recent years, however, Canadian cities have tended to draft zoning regulations modeled after those in the United States.

ROBERT WHITTEN

See: CITY AND TOWN PLANNING; BUILDING REGULATIONS; FIRE PROTECTION; TRAFFIC REGULATION; POLICE POWER.

Consult: Hammarstrand, Nils, "The Origins of Zoning" in American Institute of Architects, *Journal*, vol. xi (1923) 64–65; "Zoning in the United States," ed. by W. L. Pollard, American Academy of Political and Social Science, *Annals*, vol. clv (Philadelphia 1931) pt. ii; Bartholomew, Harland, *Urban Land Uses*, Harvard City Planning Studies, vol. iv (Cambridge, Mass. 1932); James, Harlean, *Land Planning in the United States for the City, State and Nation* (New York 1926) p. 231–48; Hubbard, T. K. and H. V., *Our Cities To-day and To-morrow* (Cambridge, Mass. 1929) p. 162–91; Lohmann, K. B., *Principles of City Planning* (New York 1931) p. 249–73; Deland, Frederic A., "City Planning and Zoning" in President's Conference on Home Building and Home Ownership, *Planning for Residential Districts*, Publications, vol. i (Washington 1932) p. 1–45; Rey, A. A., and others, *La science des plans de villes* (Lausanne 1928) ch. x; Adams, Thomas, "The Character, Bulk and Surroundings of Buildings" in Regional Plan of New York and Its Environs, *Regional Survey of New York and Its Environs*, 8 vols. (New York 1927–31) vol. vi, p. 22–200; Ford, George B., *Building Height, Bulk and Form*, Harvard City Planning Studies, vol. ii (Cambridge, Mass. 1931); Comey, A. C., *Transition Zoning*, Harvard City Planning Studies, vol. v (Cambridge, Mass. 1933); Baker, Newman F., *The Legal Aspects of Zoning* (Chicago 1927); Williams, F. B., *The Law of City Planning and Zoning* (New York 1922).

ZORN, PHILIPP (1850–1928), German jurist. Zorn studied in Switzerland and later at German universities. After brief periods of teaching at

Munich and Berne he was appointed professor of law at Königsberg in 1887. From 1900 until his resignation in 1914 he taught at the University of Bonn. A moderate conservative, he was appointed by William II a member of the Prussian upper house, but he took no important part in domestic politics.

Zorn came from the Protestant part of Bavaria, in which the imperial idea was very strong. The union of Germany under Bismarck had made a deep impression upon him in his youth, and his adoration of the first chancellor determined his political views and the direction of his scientific work. His early studies were devoted to ecclesiastical law, his outstanding work being the *Lehrbuch des Kirchenrechts* (Stuttgart 1888), in which he supported the doctrine of a wide sphere of state influence. Later he favored the relative legal autonomy of the churches and recognized as an advance the separation of church and state established by the Weimar constitution.

With Laband and Hänel, Zorn participated actively in the development of the constitutional law of the empire, to which his greatest contribution was his *Das Staatsrecht des Deutschen Reiches* (Lehrbücher des deutschen Reichsrechtes, vols. v–vi, 2 vols., Berlin 1880–83; 2nd ed. 1895–97). He recognized the historical fact of Prussian hegemony and emphasized the rights of the empire over local traditions. In general his work was more positivistic in character than theoretical. Zorn became interested in international law and in 1899 and 1907 served as expert member of the German delegation to the Hague conferences. Originally a firm adherent of strict state sovereignty and a skeptic concerning international agreements, which he believed acquired validity only when they became the law of the separate states, Zorn changed his views in the course of his responsible collaboration at The Hague. He was able in 1899 to persuade the German Foreign Office to rescind its purely negative instructions and won German support for a permanent court of arbitration. He later expressed regret that in 1907 Germany had rejected the idea of a compulsory tribunal while he was attempting to further its development. In *Deutschland und die beiden Haager Friedenskonferenzen* (Stuttgart 1920) he asserted that Germany's attitude toward arbitration at The Hague had been a great factor in arousing the unfriendliness of the rest of the world. Despite his skepticism toward the fundamental ideas of the Weimar constitution and his vigorous criticism of the legal terms of the Versailles Treaty, he came to favor and aid a positive formulation of the laws of international obligations and in *Die Zukunft des Völkerrechts* (Im neuen Deutschland, no. i, Berlin 1918) discussed this problem and that of a league of nations.

THEODOR HEUSS

Consult: Pohl, Heinrich, *Philipp Zorn als Forscher, Lehrer und Politiker* (Tübingen 1928); Giese, Friedrich, "Philipp Zorn als Forscher, Lehrer und Praktiker des Völkerrechts" in *Zeitschrift für Völkerrecht*, vol. xiv (1927–28) 325–36.

ZOUCHE, RICHARD (1590–1661), English jurist and judge. Zouche graduated in civil law at Oxford, became an advocate of Doctors' Commons and in 1620 regius professor of civil law at Oxford. From 1641 until his death (except for a temporary deprivation during the Commonwealth) he was also judge of the High Court of Admiralty. This exclusively civilian training and practise influenced the substance and even more the terminology of his juristic writings.

Zouche's most important work is the *Iuris et iudicii fecialis, sive, iuris inter gentes, et quaestionum de eodem explicatio* (Oxford 1650). This was the culmination of a task begun in his *Elementa iurisprudentiae* (Oxford 1629), in which he surveyed the whole field of jurisprudence. The end of jurisprudence, according to Zouche, is justice; its subject is human society (*communio*); its instruments (*media*) are law (*jus*) and procedure, or remedies (*judicium*). In a series of monographs he discussed the *jus* and *judicium* of certain special *communiones*, the feudal (1634), the sacred, the military, and the maritime (1640) and finally the fecial already mentioned. In each of these he subdivided *jus* and *judicium*, by a misapplication of the Roman classification *personae, res, actiones*, into *personae, res, actus*; and he further complicated this intricate scheme in the *Jus feciale* by devoting most of the part professing to relate to *judicium* to a series of *quaestiones*, so that the substantial division of the subject matter of this work becomes one between well established rules, grouped under *jus*, and controverted points (*judicium*).

Despite the artificiality of its arrangement Zouche's work on international law has great merits. It is, as Scelle has said, "the first manual" on the subject. It discusses concisely, clearly and fairly almost every aspect of the subject. It shows remarkable erudition combined with an almost excessive modesty; for not only does Zouche generously acknowledge his debt to predecessors, especially to Gentili and Grotius, but he prefers on debatable points to state the arguments pro and con and to leave the conclusion to his reader. Zouche's theoretical position is not clearly defined, but his method of deducing the law from precedents instead of using these merely as illustrations and his preference for modern rather than ancient instances make him in a sense a forerunner of the positive school of international lawyers. His work is notable also for the prominence which it gives to the law of peace over that of war. Zouche has been credited with a doctrinal innovation in substituting the term *jus inter gentes* for the traditional *jus gentium*; but although the preference was deliberate, it is unlikely that he attached much significance to it.

J. L. BRIERLY

Consult: Scelle, Georges, in *Les fondateurs du droit international*, ed. by A. Pillet (Paris 1904) p. 269–330; Holland, Thomas Erskine, "Introduction" to his edition of *Jus et iudicium feciale*, original Latin and translation by J. L. Brierly, Classics of International Law, no. 1, 2 vols. (Washington 1911) vol. i, p. i–xvi; Phillipson, Coleman, in *Great Jurists of the World*, ed. by John Macdonell and Edward Manson (London 1913) p. 220–47.

ZUNZ, LEOPOLD (1794–1886), German-Jewish historian and philologist. Zunz was born in Detmold. He was the first Jewish candidate for graduation in the Wolfenbüttel Gymnasium and one of the first Jewish students at the University of Berlin. He is commonly regarded as the father of the science of Judaism. In 1819 he helped organize the Verein für Kultur und Wissenschaft der Juden and served as editor of its *Zeitschrift für die Wissenschaft des Judenthums*. As a pupil of Wolf and Böckh and of the critical theologian de Wette he attempted to bring the critical and systematic study of Judaism within the realm of general scientific endeavor. He conceived it to be the task of this science to investigate Judaism systematically and critically as a historical, social and spiritual phenomenon and believed that Judaism could assure its continued existence in a period of civic equality only by making its own contribution to the general intellectual and spiritual development of mankind. Zunz was convinced that this method of intellectual work would provide strength and reenforcement to Judaism, shaken as it was by its contacts with the new social environment.

Zunz laid the basis for the scientific investigation of Judaism in his first work, *Etwas über die rabbinische Literatur* (Berlin 1818), in which he surveyed the manifold aspects of rabbinic literature and their relations to the various fields of knowledge. His most important work, *Die gottesdienstlichen Vorträge der Juden, historisch entwickelt* (Berlin 1832, 2nd ed. by N. Brüll, Frankfort 1892), took as its point of departure the institution of the reading and interpreting of the Holy Scriptures during the divine service in the synagogue and presented an outline of the intellectual achievements of Judaism from works of the Biblical period up to the homilies and catechisms of his own time. The work aroused extraordinary interest and was acclaimed by scholars as the most significant work produced by a Jew since Spinoza. Zunz also cultivated new fields in lesser writings, such as *Namen der Juden* (Leipsic 1837). This work, prompted by the attempt of the Prussian government to forbid Jews to bear Christian first names, was the first survey of Jewish names. In his *Zur Geschichte und Literatur* (Berlin 1845; partly tr. in *Hebrew Characteristics*, New York 1875, p. 7–43) Zunz analyzed the fundamental aspects of the term "Jewish literature" and presented a series of papers on its various aspects and on auxiliary historical sciences, such as Jewish epigraphy, numismatics and bibliography, which had never before been studied scientifically. Amidst the general widespread enthusiasm for the great literary achievements of the Jews in Spain Zunz drew attention to the more modest but none the less significant literature of the Jews in mediaeval France and Germany. In contrast to the extreme tendencies in Reform Judaism he also emphasized the positive values of Judaism and its historical foundations. His later studies dealt chiefly with synagogal liturgy and related literature. In *Die synagogale Poesie des Mittelalters* (Berlin 1885, 2nd ed. Frankfort 1920; ch. ii tr. as *Zunz on the Sufferings of the Jews*, New York 1907) he presented a general treatment of the development of the synagogue service and its influence on the growth of Hebrew poetry and made available illustrative material in translation. Since many of the synagogue elegies go back to persecutions of the Jews, the book also contained a survey of Jewish martyrology from the Roman period up to 1750. He continued these liturgical studies in his *Die Ritus des synagogalen Gottesdienstes, geschichtlich entwickelt* (Berlin 1859) and in *Literaturgeschichte der synagogalen Poesie* (Berlin 1865).

ISMAR ELBOGEN

Works: *Gesammelte Schriften*, 3 vols. (Berlin 1875–76);

Das Buch Zunz, ed. by Fritz Bamberger (Berlin 1931).

Consult: Kaufmann, David, *Gesammelte Schriften*, ed. by M. Braun, 3 vols. (Frankfort 1908–15) vol. i, ch. xxiv; Maybaum, Siegmund, *Aus dem Leben von Leopold Zunz* (Berlin 1894); Geiger, L., "Zunz im Verkehr mit Behörden und Hochgestalten" in *Monatsschrift für Geschichte und Wissenschaft des Judentums*, vol. lv (1911) 245–62, 321–47; Elbogen, Ismar, "Ein Jahrhundert Wissenschaft des Judentums" in Hochschule für die Wissenschaft des Judentums, *Festschrift zum 50 jährigen Bestehen* (Berlin 1922) p. 101–44.

ZWINGLI, HULDREICH (1484–1531), Swiss religious leader. Zwingli's ideas of religious reform were conditioned largely by his humanistic background. A native of Toggenburg, he was educated at Wesen, Basel and Berne and after a period at the University of Vienna became master of arts at Basel in 1506. While vicar of Glarus during the next decade he continued his humanistic studies and published a number of political poems, through which he argued for a league with the pope, until the disastrous defeat at Marignano coupled with the effects of a visit with Erasmus changed his theme to one of Christian pacifism. The post of people's priest at the shrine of Maria Einsiedeln (1516–18) prepared him for a call to Zurich, where on New Year's Day, 1519, he outlined his great program for the preaching of the gospel in its entirety and according to a rational plan. Inspired largely by the writings of Erasmus and echoing Erasmus' solemn plea for the renovation of Christian ethics on the basis of the Sermon on the Mount, Zwingli assailed ecclesiastical abuses and sought to awaken the faith of his followers in the compassion of God. Yet the change which he contemplated at this time was merely an intellectual and moral reform rather than a practical assault upon the authority of the church. The religious impulse which drove him into open revolt against Rome came not from humanism but from his reading of Luther's tracts in 1518 and 1519, from Luther's audacious attack upon papal supremacy at the Leipsic disputation and from his own spiritual experiences during a serious illness. But while Zwingli agreed with the German reformer with respect to the doctrine of justification by faith and the exclusive authority of Scripture, he never became a Lutheran or abandoned his characteristically humanistic conceptions of God and human nature.

Zwingli's practical policy at Zurich, which under his leadership adopted the Reformation in 1523, revealed him as a true Swiss, predisposed by his national traditions to link religion with political and military activity. Protestant Zurich thus became a theocracy headed by the Christian magistrate and its prophet Zwingli. The close identification of church and state involved a modification of Zwingli's original view that the church was a charismatic body of believers and that the new religion would conquer without coercion by its own spiritual dynamic. Faced with the necessity of combating the more radical Anabaptists on the one hand and the Catholics on the other, Zwingli solved his intellectual dilemma by drawing a distinction between divine and human righteousness and by affirming that in view of human weakness and sinfulness the latter must be enforced by the magistrate who acted in this capacity under divine inspiration. While Zwingli's work of political and social reorganization was prematurely terminated by his death in the battle of Kappel in 1531, he had already given clear indication of a disposition to improve the social status of the masses. The fundamental divergence between his social outlook and that of the conservative Luther was well illustrated by his favorable attitude toward the Peasants' War. During this uprising he proclaimed the emancipation of the serfs, although out of consideration for the practical interests of the states he abolished the titles only in part. By virtue of a decree issued in 1520 (renewed in 1525) Zurich became the first evangelical city to inaugurate public poor relief. The divorce court (founded in 1525), an innovation which Zwingli did not regard as out of harmony with a puritanical moral discipline, may be regarded as the first consistory. Thus in respect of institutional organization as well as in other matters, including the doctrine of predestination, Zwingli was the forerunner of Calvin.

W. KÖHLER

Works: *Sämtliche Werke*, ed. by Emil Egli, G. Finsler, W. Köhler and others, Corpus reformatorum, vols. lxxxviii-xcvii, vols. i-v, vii-xi (Berlin 1905–34); *The Latin Works and the Correspondence of Huldreich Zwingli, Together with Selections from his German Works*, ed. by S. M. Jackson, 3 vols. (New York 1912–29).

Consult: Stähelin, R., *Huldreich Zwingli; sein Leben und Wirken*, 2 vols. (Basel 1895–97); *Das Buch der Reformation Huldrych Zwinglis*, ed. by W. Köhler (Munich 1926); Köhler, Walther, *Ulrich Zwingli und die Reformation in der Schweiz*, Religionsgeschichtliche Volksbücher, 4th ser., nos. 30–31 (Tübingen 1919), *Die Geisteswelt Ulrich Zwinglis*, Brücken, vol. iii (Gotha 1920), *Armenpflege und Wohltätigkeit in Zürich zur Zeit Ulrich Zwinglis*, Zürcherische Hülfsgesellschaft, Neujahrsblätter, no. 119 (Zurich 1919), and *Zürcher Ehegericht und Genfer Konsistorium*,

Zwingliverein, *Quellen und Abhandlungen zur schweizerischen Reformationsgeschichte*, 2nd. ser., vol. vii (Leipsic 1932); Wernle, P., *Der evangelische Glaube nach den Hauptschriften der Reformatoren*, 3 vols. (Tübingen 1918–19) vol. ii; Farner, A., *Die Lehre von Kirche und Staat bei Zwingli* (Tübingen 1930); Herding, Wilhelm, *Die wirtschaftlichen und sozialen Anschauungen Zwinglis* (Erlangen 1917); Lindsay, T. M., *A History of the Reformation*, 2 vols. (New York 1928) vol. ii, ch. ii; Lagarde, Georges de, *Recherches sur l'esprit politique de la réforme* (Paris 1926), especially p. 308–20.

Index

Note Concerning Index	546
Classification of Articles	
LIST OF HEADINGS USED IN CLASSIFICATION	547
CLASSIFICATION OF ABSTRACT TITLES	548
CLASSIFICATION OF BIOGRAPHICAL TITLES	558
Index	572
Index of Contributors	692

Note Concerning Index

The Index has been arranged in three sections: first, a general classification, by titles, of all the articles; second, the main index, which is a reference guide to the contents of articles; and, third, an index of contributors.

The Classification of Articles is designed to schematize as concisely as possible the contents of the fifteen volumes by listing under descriptive headings the titles of all the articles in the Encyclopaedia. The headings used for this purpose are listed on page 547. In order to avoid some of the dangers inherent in the process of schematization each article has been listed under as many headings as are suggested by the general nature of its contents. Even with this measure of flexibility material so diverse cannot be reduced to the rigid confines of categories without some sacrifice of precision, but it is believed that the results will be useful enough to make amends for the unavoidable roughness of detail.

For greater convenience this section has been divided into two parts, the first a classification of abstract titles, and the second a classification of biographical titles, the latter further modified by a subdivision into nationalities under each heading. In some instances, especially for men who lived in the Middle Ages, the indication of nationality is somewhat arbitrary; in others a man's activity, as described in the article, gives him equal claim to two nationalities. The designation "British" includes Scots as well as Englishmen, even though in a few cases it does violence to the realities of history.

The Main Index is primarily analytical, and seeks to make available for reference purposes not only concrete names of persons and things but, even more, the significant aspects of a discussion. Such an undertaking is subject to many and treacherous hazards, is in fact impossible of perfect achievement. But it is believed that even in imperfection it will be more valuable than a simpler aim fully realized.

The keywords, or headings, used in compiling the index have been, as far as possible, the titles of articles in the Encyclopaedia, thus avoiding some of the difficulties of synonyms and haphazard terminology. Every heading printed in capitals is a title of an article, its volume and page-span indicated by the numerals immediately following it; a heading appearing in lower case type will be found discussed in the places where the references indicate, but is not covered in an independent article of that title.

In all cases where there is more than one reference under a given heading the page reference is preceded by the title of the article in which the discussion appears. This title is not always precisely descriptive of the discussion to be found, but it will give some indication of its general nature and will help the reader to eliminate without investigation references which for him are not relevant. Titles within parentheses indicate subdivisions of the article referred to.

References are given only when the discussion is sufficient to make investigation worth the effort. The figures represent volume, page and column and indicate only the beginning of a discussion; it is left to the reader to continue as far as he finds the material relevant to his purposes. Inclusive page references indicate either an entire article or an entire subdivision of an article.

There has been no attempt to make a complete system of cross references within the index. It can readily be understood that each title referred to under any heading can be considered a cross reference and itself examined in the index for further references.

Few abbreviations have been used and those are undoubtedly self-explanatory.

The Index of Contributors is an alphabetical list of all persons whose work appears in the Encyclopaedia, with a list of their articles.

Classification of Articles

For Abstract Titles

Heading of Classification	Page	Heading of Classification	Page
Administration of Justice	548	Literature and the Press	553
Agriculture	548	Marriage and the Family	553
Art	548	Occupations	553
Banking	548	Opinion	553
Business	548	Philosophy	553
Citizenship	549	Political Parties	554
Civil Liberties	549	Primitive Society	554
Civil Opposition	549	Property	554
Commerce	549	Psychology	554
Conduct	549	Public Finance	554
Consumption	550	Public Health	554
Cooperation	550	Public Office	554
Credit	550	Public Welfare	555
Crime	550	Recreation and Amusement	555
Economic Policy	550	Religion	555
Economics	550	Representation	555
Education	550	Science	555
Food and Drink	551	Social Discrimination	555
Government	551	Social Organization	556
Housing	551	Social Process	556
Industry	551	Socialism	556
Insurance	552	Sociology	556
International Relations	552	Statistics	556
Investment and Speculation	552	Tariff	556
Jurisprudence	552	Taxation	556
Labor	552	Transportation	557
Legal Relations	553	War	557
Legislation	553		

For Biographical Titles

Agrarian Reform	558	Nationalism	565
Agriculture	558	Natural Science	565
Anthropology	558	Negro Problem and Slavery	565
Business and Finance	558	Pacifism	565
Colonial Administration	559	Philology	565
Cooperation	559	Philosophy	566
Criminology	559	Political Affairs	566
Economics	559	Political Science	566
Education	560	Psychology	567
Feminism	561	Public Health	567
Financial Administration	561	Religion (Brahmanism and Hinduism)	567
Geography	561	Religion (Christianity before 1500)	567
History	561	Religion (Christianity after 1500)	567
History (Economic)	562	Religion (Islam)	568
History (Legal)	562	Religion (Judaism) (see Jewish Problems and Judaism)	
History (Religious)	562		
Jewish Problems and Judaism	563	Social Philosophy and Sociology	568
Journalism	563	Social Reform	568
Labor	563	Socialism	569
Law	563	Statecraft	569
Literature and Social Criticism	564	Statistics	571

Classification of Articles

Abstract Titles

Administration of Justice

Advisory Opinions; Alienist; Amnesty; Appeals; Arbitration, Commercial; Arbitration, Industrial; Arrest; Assizes; Asylum; Attainder; Audiencia; Bail; Benefit of Clergy; Blood Vengeance Feud; Capital Punishment; Capitulations; Certiorari; Comity; Commutation of Sentence; Compurgation; Conseil d'État; Constitutionalism; Constitutions; Contempt of Court; Contingent Fee; Coroner; Corporal Punishment; Court Martial; Courts; Courts, Administrative; Courts, Commercial; Courts, Industrial; Criminal Law; Damages; Declaratory Judgment; Diplomatic Protection; Domestic Relations Courts; Double Jeopardy; Due Process of Law; Ecclesiastical Courts; Equal Protection of the Law; Equity; Evidence; Excommunication; Exile; Expert Testimony; Exterritoriality; Extradition; Fee Splitting; Fines; Grand Jury; Habeas Corpus; Hunger Strike; Identification; Impeachment; Imprisonment; Indeterminate Sentence; Injunction; Inquisition; Insanity; Judgments; Judicial Interrogation; Judicial Process; Judiciary; Jurisdiction; Jury; Justice, Administration of; Justice of the Peace; Juvenile Delinquency and Juvenile Courts; Labor Injunction; Law Enforcement; Law Merchant; Legal Aid; Limitation of Actions; Lynching; Mandamus; Martial Law; Medical Jurisprudence; Municipal Courts; Ostracism; Outlawry; Pardon; Penal Institutions; Perjury; Permanent Court of Arbitration; Permanent Court of International Justice; Police; Political Police; Prison Labor; Probation and Parole; Procedure, Legal; Prosecution; Public Defender; Punishment; Retroactive Legislation; Rule of Law; Sanctuary; Searches and Seizures; Self-Incrimination; Sheriff; Small Claims Courts; State Liability; Summary Judgment; Supreme Court, United States; Transportation of Criminals; Venue; Writs.

Agriculture

Agrarian Movements; Agrarian Syndicalism; Agricultural Cooperation; Agricultural Credit; Agricultural Economics; Agricultural Education; Agricultural Experiment Stations; Agricultural Fairs; Agricultural Insurance; Agricultural Labor; Agricultural Machinery; Agricultural Machinery Industry; Agricultural Marketing; Agricultural Policy; Agricultural Societies; Agriculture; Agriculture, Government Services for; Agriculture, International Institute of; Allotments; Back-to-the-Land Movements; Cattle Loans; Chambers of Agriculture; Climate; Colonate; Corn Laws; Cotton; Country Life Movement; Crop and Livestock Reporting; Dairy Industry; Dry Farming; Enclosures; Extension Work, Agricultural; Famine; Farm; Farm Bloc, U. S.; Farm Bureau Federation, American; Farm Loan System, Federal; Farm Management; Farm Relief; Farm Tenancy; Farmers' Alliance; Farmers' Organizations; Farmers' Union; Fertility Rites; Fertilizer Industry; Flax, Hemp and Jute; Food Supply; Frontier; Fruit and Vegetable Industry; Grain Elevators; Grains; Grange; Homestead; Irrigation; Land Mortgage Credit (Agricultural); Land Settlement; Land Tenure; Land Utilization; Landed Estates; Latifundia; Livestock Industry; Manorial System; Markets, Municipal; Meat Packing and Slaughtering; Migratory Labor; Milk Supply; Milling Industry; Natural Resources; Nomads; Peasantry; Plantation; Plantation Wares; Reclamation; Refrigeration; Rubber; Rural Industries; Rural Society; Serfdom; Silk Industry; Slavery; Small Holdings; Soils; Stock Breeding; Sugar; Tobacco; Village Community.

See also Classification of Articles (Biographical Titles), AGRARIAN REFORM (p. 558), AGRICULTURE (p. 558).

Art

Amateur; Architecture; Art; Art Collecting; Censorship; City and Town Planning; Civic Art; Civic Centers; Classicism; Dance; Furniture; Glass and Pottery Industries; Handicraft; Industrial Arts; Literature; Modernism; Motion Pictures; Museums and Exhibitions; Music; Ornament; Pottery; Precious Stones; Primitivism; Renaissance; Romanticism; Theater.

Banking

Acceptance; Bank Deposits; Bank Deposits, Guaranty of; Bank Reserves; Banking, Commercial; Banknotes; Banks, Wildcat; Branch Banking; Call Money; Central Banking; Check; Clearing Houses; Credit Control; Farm Loan System, Federal; Federal Reserve System; Financial Organization; Investment Banking; Labor Banking; Labor Exchange Banks; Land Bank Schemes; Liquidity; National Banks, United States; Postal Savings Banks; Savings Banks; State Banks, United States; Trust Companies.

See also Classification of Articles (Abstract Titles), CREDIT (p. 550), INVESTMENT AND SPECULATION (p. 552).

Business

Accounting; Acquisition; Advertising; Agency; Appreciation; Arbitration, Commercial; Auditing; Bankruptcy; Bargaining Power; Bonding; Boom; Bourgeoisie; Business; Business Administration; Business Cycles; Business Education; Business Ethics; Business, Government Services for; Business Taxes; Capitalism; Captain of Industry; Cartel; Caveat Emptor; Chambers of Commerce; Clerical Occupations; Collectivism; Combinations, Industrial; Commercial Law; Commercialism; Competition; Conjuncture; Corporation; Corporation Finance; Corporation Taxes; Cost Accounting; Courts, Commercial; Crises; Cut-Throat Competition; Debt; Depreciation; Economic Incentives; Economic Policy; Economics; Efficiency; Employers' Associations; Employers' Liability; Entrepreneur; Exploitation; Export Associations; Expositions, International; Fair Return; Farm Management; Federal Trade Commission; Financial Statements; Forecasting, Business; Foreign Corporations; Foreign Exchange; Fortunes, Private; Fraud; Frauds, Statute of;

For complete list of headings used in Classification of Articles see page 547.

Goodwill; Government Owned Corporations; Government Ownership; Government Regulation of Industry; Hedging; Holding Companies; Income; Index Numbers; Inflation and Deflation; Insurance; Interlocking Directorates; Joint Stock Company; Just Price; Liquidity; Management; Marketing; Massachusetts Trusts; Monopolies, Public; Monopoly; Moratorium; National Economic Councils; National Economic Planning; Negotiable Instruments; Organization, Economic; Partnership; Personnel Administration; Price Discrimination; Price Regulation; Price Stabilization; Prices; Profit; Profit Sharing; Profiteering; Promotion; Public Contracts; Racketeering; Rate Regulation; Real Estate; Receivership; Restraint of Trade; Retail Trade; Risk; Sales; Sales Tax; Salesmanship; Stabilization, Economic; Trusts; Unfair Competition; Valorization; Vested Interests; Weights and Measures; Wholesaling.

See also Classification of Articles (Abstract Titles), BANKING (*p.* 548), COMMERCE (*p.* 549), CONSUMPTION (*p.* 550), CREDIT (*p.* 550), ECONOMIC POLICY (*p.* 550), ECONOMICS (*p.* 550), INDUSTRY (*p.* 551), INSURANCE (*p.* 552), INVESTMENT AND SPECULATION (*p.* 552), PROPERTY (*p.* 554), SOCIALISM (*p.* 556); (Biographical Titles), BUSINESS AND FINANCE (*p.* 558).

Citizenship

Alien; Allegiance; Americanization; Chauvinism; Citizenship; Civic Education; Civic Organizations; Civil Rights; Deportation and Expulsion of Aliens; Diplomatic Protection; Domicile; Dual Citizenship; Emigration; Enemy Alien; Equal Protection of the Law; Exile; Expatriation; Exterritoriality; Extradition; Identification; Immigration; Individualism; Mass Expulsion; Migrations (Modern); Minorities, National; Nationalism; Nationality; Naturalization; Obedience, Political; Oriental Immigration; Passport; Patriotism; Refugees; Social Contract; Zionism.

See also Classification of Articles (Abstract Titles), CIVIL LIBERTIES (*p.* 549), CIVIL OPPOSITION (*p.* 549), REPRESENTATION (*p.* 555).

Civil Liberties

Academic Freedom; Alien and Sedition Acts; Arms, Right to Bear; Assembly, Right of; Bills of Rights; Cachet, Lettre de; Catholic Emancipation; Civil Liberties; Criminal Syndicalism; Declaration of the Rights of Man and the Citizen; Due Process of Law; Equal Protection of the Law; Freedom of Association; Freedom of Speech and of the Press; Habeas Corpus; Jewish Emancipation; Liberalism; Liberty; Magna Carta; Martial Law; Natural Rights; Petition, Right of; Religious Freedom; Searches and Seizures; Sedition.

See also Classification of Articles (Abstract Titles), CITIZENSHIP (*p.* 549).

Civil Opposition

Action Française; Amnesty; Anarchism; Armed Forces, Control of; Assassination; Attainder; Babouvism; Bolshevism; Brigandage; Cachet, Lettre de; Camorra; Carbonari; Civil War; Comitadji; Commune of Paris; Communist Parties; Conscientious Objectors; Conspiracy, Political; Coup d'État; Direct Action; Exile; Fascism; Force, Political; French Revolution; General Strike; Guerrilla Warfare; Hunger Strike; Indian Question; Industrial Workers of the World; Insurrection; Intransigence; Irish Question; Irredentism; Jacobinism; Kuomintang; Lese Majesty; Martial Law; Massacre; Monarchomachs; Mutiny; National Socialism, German; Obedience, Political; Ostracism; Passive Resistance and Non-cooperation; Political Offenders; Political Police; Praetorianism; Rebellion; Refugees; Revolution and Counter-revolution; Riot; Russian Revolution; Sedition; Socialism; Socialist Parties; Soviet; Syndicalism; Terrorism; Treason; Violence.

See also Classification of Articles (Abstract Titles), SOCIALISM (*p.* 556); (Biographical Titles), NATIONALISM (*p.* 565), SOCIALISM (*p.* 569).

Commerce

Acts of Trade, British; Agricultural Marketing; Arms and Munitions Traffic; Asiento; Auctions; Balance of Trade; Barter; Broker; Casa de Contratación; Caveat Emptor; Chartered Companies; Colonies; Commerce; Commercial Law; Commercial Routes; Commercial Treaties; Commodity Exchanges; Contraband of War; Courts, Commercial; Customs Duties; Dumping; Embargo; Exchange; Export Associations; Export Credits; Export Duties; Expositions, International; Exterritoriality; Fairs; Food Industries (Food Distribution); Foreign Exchange; Free Ports and Free Zones; Free Trade; Fur Trade and Industry; Grading; Grain Elevators; Guilds; Hanseatic League; Instalment Selling; International Trade; Interstate Commerce; Interstate Commerce Commission; Law Merchant; Liquor Traffic; Marine Insurance; Maritime Law; Market; Marketing; Markets, Municipal; Mercantile Credit; Mercantilism; Merchant Marine; Middleman; Neutrality; Open Door; Opium Problem; Piracy; Ports and Harbors; Price Discrimination; Prices (History); Prize; Prohibition; Protection; Railroads; Rate Regulation; Raw Materials; Resale Price Maintenance; Retail Credit; Retail Trade; Sales Tax; Salesmanship; Self-Sufficiency, Economic; Shipping; Smuggling; Trademarks and Names; Trading with the Enemy; Transit, International; Transportation; Valorization; Warehousing; Waterways, Inland; Weights and Measures; Wholesaling.

See also Classification of Articles (Abstract Titles), ECONOMIC POLICY (*p.* 550), TRANSPORTATION (*p.* 557).

Conduct

Acquisition; Altruism and Egoism; Asceticism; Atrocities; Attitudes, Social; Authority; Avoidance; Belief; Birth Customs; Blasphemy; Bribery; Brigandage; Business Ethics; Casuistry; Celibacy; Ceremony; Character; Chastity; Chivalry; Class Consciousness; Coercion; Collective Behavior; Commercialism; Common Sense; Compromise; Conduct; Confession; Conformity; Consciousness; Control, Social; Conventions, Social; Conversion, Religious; Crowd; Custom; Death Customs; Dress; Dueling; Duress; Duty; Economic Incentives; Ethical Culture Movement; Ethics; Etiquette; Extortion; Fanaticism; Fashion; Fasting; Fertility Rites; Feuds; Folkways; Fraud; Free Love; Gentleman, Theory of the; Habit; Hedonism; Honor; Hospitality; Human Nature; Humanitarianism; Imitation; Initiation; Innovation; Instinct; Institution; Interests; Intimidation; Intolerance; Intransigence; Lawlessness; Leadership; Liberty; Magic; Maladjustment; Mob; Morale; Morals; Mysteries; Nihilism; Obedience, Political; Opportunism; Passive Resistance and Non-cooperation; Persecution; Personality; Play; Pressures, Social; Professional Ethics; Ritual; Sacrifice;

For complete list of headings used in Classification of Articles see page 547.

Sanction, Social; Self-Preservation; Service; Sex Education and Sex Ethics; Suicide; Symbolism; Tabu; Taste; Thrift; Value and Price; Youth Movements.
See also Classification of Articles (Abstract Titles), OPINION (p. 553), PSYCHOLOGY (p. 554).

Consumption

Adulteration; Caveat Emptor; Consumer Protection; Consumers' Cooperation; Consumers' Leagues; Consumption; Cost of Living; Demand; Excise; Family Budgets; Food and Drug Regulation; Instalment Selling; Loans, Personal; Luxury; National Income; Nutrition; Overproduction; Prices; Retail Credit; Retail Trade; Saving; Small Loans; Standards of Living; Tourist Traffic.

Cooperation

Agrarian Syndicalism; Agricultural Cooperation; Artel; Building and Loan Associations; Consumers' Cooperation; Cooperation; Cooperative Public Boards; Credit Cooperation; Fourier and Fourierism; Housing, Cooperative; Owen and Owenism; Producers' Cooperation.
See also Classification of Articles (Biographical Titles), COOPERATION (p. 559).

Credit

Acceptance; Agricultural Credit; Banking, Commercial; Banknotes; Bill of Exchange; Brokers' Loans; Building and Loan Associations; Call Money; Cattle Loans; Check; Compensated Dollar; Credit; Credit Control; Credit Cooperation; Credit Insurance; Debt; Export Credits; Farm Loan System, Federal; Federal Reserve System; Financial Organization; Foreign Exchange; Inflation and Deflation; Instalment Selling; International Finance; Labor Exchange Banks; Land Bank Schemes; Land Mortgage Credit; Liquidity; Loans, Intergovernmental; Loans, Personal; Mercantile Credit; Money Market; Moratorium; Mortgage; Negotiable Instruments; Pawnbroking; Pledge; Public Debt; Rent Charge; Retail Credit; Small Loans; Usury.
See also Classification of Articles (Abstract Titles), INVESTMENT AND SPECULATION (p. 552).

Crime

Atavism; Camorra; Conspiracy, Criminal; Crime; Criminal Law; Criminal Statistics; Criminal Syndicalism; Criminology; Detective Agencies, Private; Homicide; Intent, Criminal; Juvenile Delinquency and Juvenile Courts; Lawlessness; Lese Majesty; Mafia; Military Desertion; Perjury; Piracy; Political Offenders; Racketeering; Recidivism; Riot (Legal Aspects); Sedition; Smuggling; Treason.
See also Classification of Articles (Abstract Titles), ADMINISTRATION OF JUSTICE (p. 548); (Biographical Titles), CRIMINOLOGY (p. 559).

Economic Policy

Acts of Trade, British; Agricultural Policy; Agriculture, Government Services for; Agriculture, International Institute of; Asiento; Balance of Trade; Blue Sky Laws; Bounties; Bullionists; Business, Government Services for; Cameralism; Capitulations; Casa de Contratación; Chambers of Agriculture; Chartered Companies; Colonial Economic Policy; Colonial System; Colonies; Commercial Treaties; Concessions; Conservation; Consumer Protection; Continental System; Cooperative Public Boards; Economic Policy; Embargo; Employment Exchanges; Export Credits; Extension Work, Agricultural; Farm Bloc, U. S.; Farm Loan System, Federal; Farm Relief; Federal Trade Commission; Food and Drug Regulation; Food Supply; Forced Labor; Forests; Free Trade; Gosplan; Government Owned Corporations; Government Ownership; Government Regulation of Industry; Grants-in-Aid; Homestead; Imperialism; Inspection; International Advisers; International Labor Organization; Interstate Commerce; Interstate Commerce Commission; Labor, Government Services for; Labor Legislation and Law; Labourers, Statutes of; Laissez Faire; Land Grants; Land Settlement; Licensing; Liquor Traffic; Markets, Municipal; Mercantilism; Merchant Marine; Minimum Wage; Mobilization and Demobilization; Monetary Stabilization; Monetary Unions; Monopolies, Public; Municipal Transit; National Economic Councils; National Economic Planning; Native Policy; Philippine Problem; Postal Savings Banks; Postal Service; Price Regulation; Price Stabilization; Prison Labor; Prohibition; Protection; Public Contracts; Public Domain; Public Finance; Public Utilities; Public Works; Rate Regulation; Reclamation; Regional Planning; Rent Regulation; Revenues, Public; Roads; Self-Sufficiency, Economic; Socialization; Stabilization, Economic; Subsidies; Sumptuary Legislation; Tariff; Taxation; Trusts; Unemployment Insurance; Valorization; War Economics; Waterways, Inland.
See also Classification of Articles (Abstract Titles), PUBLIC FINANCE (p. 554), TARIFF (p. 556), TAXATION (p. 556); (Biographical Titles), FINANCIAL ADMINISTRATION (p. 561).

Economics

Absentee Ownership; Abstinence; Agricultural Economics; Appreciation; Balance of Trade (Hist. of Doctrine); Bargaining Power; Bullionists; Business Cycles; Cameralism; Capital; Capitalism; Church Fathers; Competition; Conjuncture; Consumption; Cost; Demand; Diminishing Returns; Distribution; Economic History; Economic Incentives; Economics; Entrepreneur; Exchange; Exploitation; Geography (Economic); Income; Increasing Returns; Individualism; Interest; International Trade (Theory); Just Price; Laissez Faire; Luxury; Market; Mercantilism; Money; Monopoly; National Wealth; Overhead Costs; Overproduction; Price Stabilization; Prices (Theory and Statistics); Production (Theory); Profit; Public Finance; Rent; Saving; Statics and Dynamics; Supply; Taxation; Unearned Increment; Unemployment; Value and Price; Wages (Theory and Policy).
See also Classification of Articles (Abstract Titles), CREDIT (p. 550), INVESTMENT AND SPECULATION (p. 552), PUBLIC FINANCE (p. 554), STATISTICS (p. 556); (Biographical Titles), ECONOMICS (p. 559), HISTORY (ECONOMIC) (p. 562), STATISTICS (p. 571).

Education

Academic Freedom; Adult Education; Agricultural Education; Apprenticeship; Athletics; Business Education; Case Method; Chautauqua; Civic Education; Coeducation; Continuation Schools; Correspondence Schools; Education; Education, Primitive; Educational Psychology; Extension Work, Agricultural; Folk High Schools; Health Education; Home Economics; Humanism; Industrial Education; Initiation; Legal Profession and Legal Education; Literacy and Illiteracy; Manual Training; Medicine (Medical Education); Military Training; Museums and Exhibitions; Parent Education;

Classification of Articles (Abstract Titles)

Physical Education; Preschool Education; Sex Education and Sex Ethics; Social Work (Training); Teaching Profession; Universities and Colleges; University Extension; Vocational Education; Vocational Guidance; Workers' Education.
See also Classification of Articles (Biographical Titles), EDUCATION (*p.* 560).

Food and Drink

Adulteration; Agriculture; Alcohol; Anti-Corn Law League; Anti-Saloon League; Canning Industry; Corn Laws; Dairy Industry; Famine; Fisheries; Food and Drug Regulation; Food Industries; Food Supply; Fruit and Vegetable Industry; Game Laws; Grains; Hunting; Liquor Industry; Liquor Traffic; Livestock Industry; Markets, Municipal; Meat Packing and Slaughtering; Milk Supply; Milling Industry; Nomads; Nutrition; Plantation Wares; Prohibition; Refrigeration; Restaurants; Salt; Stock Breeding; Sugar; Temperance Movements; Water Supply.

Government

Absolutism; Administration, Public; Administrative Areas; Administrative Law; Advisory Opinions (National); Agreement of the People; Alsace-Lorraine; Amendments, Constitutional; Anarchism; Archives; Aristocracy; Armed Forces, Control of; Articles of Confederation; Audiencia; Authority; Autocracy; Autonomy; Bicameral System; Bills of Rights; Boards, Administrative; Boards, Advisory; Boundaries; Cabinet; Cabinet Government; Caliphate; Cameralism; Central American Federation; Centralization; Checks and Balances; Chinese Problem; City; City Manager; City-State; Colonial Administration; Commission System of Government; Commissions; Commune, Mediaeval; Compacts, Interstate; Concurrent Powers; Confiscation; Congressional Government; Conseil d'État; Constitutional Conventions; Constitutional Law; Constitutionalism; Constitutions; Corruption, Political; Council of the Indies; County-City Consolidation; County Councils; County Government, United States; Courts, Administrative; Decentralization; Declaration of Independence; Declaration of the Rights of Man and the Citizen; De Facto Government; Delegation of Powers; Democracy; Dictatorship; Dominion Status; Egyptian Problem; Eminent Domain; Empire; Executive; Expert; Far Eastern Problem; Fascism; Federalism; Federation; Feudalism; Financial Administration; Force, Political; French Revolution; Gerontocracy; Government; Government Publications; Government Reporting; Guild Socialism; Hanseatic League; Holy Roman Empire; Home Rule; Imperial Unity; Indian Question; Investigations, Governmental; Irish Question; Islam; Jewish Autonomy; Judicial Review; Legislative Assemblies; Liberalism; Local Government; Magna Carta; Majority Rule; Manchurian Problem; Mandates; Metropolitan Areas; Military Occupation; Minorities, National; Monarchy; Morocco Question; Municipal Corporation; Municipal Government; National Socialism, German; Nationalism; Near Eastern Problem; Oligarchy; Organization, Administrative; Pan-Islamism; Pan-movements; Parties, Political; Philippine Problem; Plebiscite; Plutocracy; Police; Police Power; Polish Corridor; Political Science; Politics; Popular Sovereignty; Power, Political; Prerogative; Protectorate; Public Finance; Reason of State; Recognition, International; Reconstruction; Regionalism; Representation; Republicanism; Royal Court; Rule of Law; Russian Revolution; Self-Determination, National; Separation of Powers; Social Contract; Socialism; Sovereignty; State; State Government, United States; State Liability; State Succession; States' Rights; Succession, Political; Territorial Waters; Tyranny.
See also Classification of Articles (Abstract Titles), ECONOMIC POLICY (*p.* 550), INTERNATIONAL RELATIONS (*p.* 552), LEGISLATION (*p.* 553), POLITICAL PARTIES (*p.* 554), PUBLIC FINANCE (*p.* 554), PUBLIC OFFICE (*p.* 554), REPRESENTATION (*p.* 555), SOCIALISM (*p.* 556), TARIFF (*p.* 556), TAXATION (*p.* 556); (Biographical Titles), POLITICAL AFFAIRS (*p.* 566), STATECRAFT (*p.* 569).

Housing

Architecture; Building and Loan Associations; Building Regulations; City and Town Planning; Company Housing; Construction Industry; Furniture; Garden Cities; Home Ownership; Hotels; House and Building Taxes; Housing; Housing, Cooperative; Lodging Houses; Rent Regulation; Slums; Zoning.

Industry

Accidents, Industrial; Agricultural Machinery Industry; Automobile Industry; Aviation; Basing Point Prices; By-Product; Canning Industry; Capitalism; Captain of Industry; Cement; Chemical Industries; Coal Industry; Combinations, Industrial; Company Housing; Company Towns; Conservation; Construction Industry; Continuous Industry; Cost; Dairy Industry; Detective Agencies, Private; Diminishing Returns; Dye Industry; Efficiency; Electric Power; Electrical Manufacturing Industry; Employers' Associations; Factory System; Fatigue; Fertilizer Industry; Fisheries; Flax, Hemp and Jute; Food and Drug Regulation; Food Industries; Fruit and Vegetable Industry; Funerals; Fur Trade and Industry; Furniture (Industry); Garment Industries; Gas Industry; General Strike; Glass and Pottery Industries; Gold; Gosplan; Government Regulation of Industry; Guilds; Handicraft; Heavy Chemicals; Homework, Industrial; Hotels; Increasing Returns; Industrial Alcohol; Industrial Arts; Industrial Democracy; Industrial Hazards; Industrial Hygiene; Industrial Relations; Industrial Relations Councils; Industrial Revolution; Industrialism; Inspection; Invention; Iron and Steel Industry; Labor-Capital Cooperation; Large Scale Production; Laundry and Dry Cleaning Industry; Leather Industries; Liquor Industry; Livestock Industry; Location of Industry; Machinery, Industrial; Machines and Tools; Management; Match Industry; Meat Packing and Slaughtering; Mechanic; Medical Materials Industry; Metals; Milling Industry; Mining; Mining Accidents; Mobilization and Demobilization; Motion Pictures; Municipal Transit; Munitions Industry; National Economic Planning; Natural Resources; Nitrates; Oil Industry; Organization, Economic; Overhead Costs; Overproduction; Paints and Varnishes; Policing, Industrial; Potash; Pottery; Power, Industrial; Precious Stones; Press; Printing and Publishing; Producers' Cooperation; Production; Proletariat; Promotion; Public Utilities; Pulp and Paper Industry; Putting Out System; Quarrying; Radio; Railroads; Rationalization; Raw Materials; Refrigeration; Restaurants; Rubber; Rural Industries; Safety Movement; Salt; Scientific Management; Shipbuilding; Silk Industry; Socialization; Specialization; Stabilization, Economic; Standardization; Sugar; Technology; Telephone and Telegraph; Textile Industry; Tobacco; Trade Associations;

Trusts; Unemployment; Waste; Welfare Work, Industrial; Women in Industry; Wood Industries; Wool.
See also Classification of Articles (Abstract Titles), BUSINESS (*p.* 548), ECONOMIC POLICY (*p.* 550), ECONOMICS (*p.* 550), LABOR (*p.* 552); (Biographical Titles), BUSINESS AND FINANCE (*p.* 558).

Insurance

Agricultural Insurance; Annuities; Automobile Insurance; Bank Deposits, Guaranty of; Benefits, Trade Union; Casualty Insurance; Compensation and Liability Insurance; Credit Insurance; Fire Insurance; Fraternal Orders; Friendly Societies; Group Insurance; Health Insurance; Insurance; Life Insurance; Marine Insurance; Mutual Aid Societies; Social Insurance; Unemployment Insurance; Workmen's Compensation.

International Relations

Advisory Opinions (International); Agreements, International; Alabama Claims; Alliance; Annexation; Arbitration, International; Asylum; Aviation (International Aspects); Backward Countries; Balance of Power; Boundaries; Buffer State; Calvo and Drago Doctrines; Capitulations; Central American Federation; Cession; Clarté Movement; Colonies; Comity; Commercial Treaties; Concert of Powers; Concessions; Conflict of Laws; Conquest; Consular Service; Declaration of London; Declaration of Paris; Diplomacy; Diplomatic Protection; Egyptian Problem; Equality of States; Europeanization; Executive Agreements; Exterritoriality; Extradition; Far Eastern Problem; Filibustering; Foreign Investment; Freedom of the Seas; Great Powers; Guaranties, International; Hague Conferences; Holy Alliance; Immunity, Diplomatic; Imperialism; International Advisers; International Finance; International Labor Organization; International Law; International Legislation; International Organization; International Relations; International Trade; International Waterways; Internationalism; Intervention; Isolation, Diplomatic; Jus Gentium; League of Nations; Limitation of Armaments; Loans, Intergovernmental; Manchurian Problem; Mandates; Mediation; Merchantmen, Status of; Military Occupation; Monroe Doctrine; Morocco Question; National Defense; Near Eastern Problem; Open Door; Outlawry of War; Panama Canal; Pan-Americanism; Peace Movements; Permanent Court of Arbitration; Permanent Court of International Justice; Polish Corridor; Protectorate; Recognition, International; Reparations; Reprisals; Sanction, International; Self-Determination, National; Spheres of Influence; Suez Canal; Transit, International; Treaties; War; Warfare, Laws of; World War.
See also Classification of Articles (Abstract Titles), COMMERCE (*p.* 549), ECONOMIC POLICY (*p.* 550), WAR (*p.* 557).

Investment and Speculation

Absentee Ownership; Accumulation; Agio; Arbitrage; Blue Sky Laws; Bonds; Boom; Brokers' Loans; Bubbles, Speculative; Bucket Shops; Call Money; Calvo and Drago Doctrines; Capital; Capitalization; Commodity Exchanges; Concessions; Corner, Speculative; Debentures; Employee Stock Ownership; Fair Return; Foreign Investment; Fortunes, Private; Hedging; Interest; Investment; Investment Banking; Investment Trusts; Land Speculation; Lotteries; Money Market; Rent Charge; Rentier; Saving; Savings Banks; Speculation; Stock Exchange; Stocks and Stock Ownership; Trust Companies.

Jurisprudence

Administrative Law; American Law Institute; By-Law; Canon Law; Case Law; Case Method; Civil Law; Code Civil; Codification; Commentators; Commercial Law; Common Law; Comparative Law; Conflict of Laws; Constitutional Law; Corpus Juris Civilis; Criminal Law; Customary Law; Family Law; German Civil Code; Glossators; International Law; Islamic Law; Judicial Review; Jurisprudence; Jus Gentium; Justice; Labor Legislation and Law; Law; Law Merchant; Lawgivers; Legal Profession and Legal Education; Legislation; Maritime Law; Medical Jurisprudence; Military Law; Natural Law; Police Power; Prerogative; Procedure, Legal; Public Law; Reception; Retroactive Legislation; Roman Law; Rule of Law; Sovereignty; Uniform Legislation; Water Law; Writs.
See also Classification of Articles (Abstract Titles), ADMINISTRATION OF JUSTICE (*p.* 548), LEGAL RELATIONS (*p.* 553); (Biographical Titles), HISTORY (LEGAL) (*p.* 562), LAW (*p.* 563).

Labor

Absenteeism, Labor; Accidents, Industrial; Agricultural Labor; Allotments; American Federation of Labor; Apprenticeship; Arbeitsgemeinschaft; Arbitration, Industrial; Ateliers Nationaux; Benefits, Trade Union; Blacklist, Labor; Bourses du Travail; Boycott; Business Agent; Casual Labor; Chartism; Child (Labor); Christian Labor Unions; Christian Socialism; Clerical Occupations; Closed Shop and Open Shop; Collective Bargaining; Company Housing; Company Towns; Company Unions; Conciliation, Industrial; Confédération Générale du Travail; Conspiracy, Criminal; Consumers' Leagues; Continuation Schools; Continuous Industry; Contract Labor; Courts, Industrial; Criminal Syndicalism; Direct Action; Domestic Service; Dual Unionism; Employee Stock Ownership; Employers' Liability; Employment Exchanges; Enticement of Employees; Exploitation; Factory System; Family Allowances; Fatigue; Forced Labor; Friendly Societies; General Strike; Group Insurance; Guild Socialism; Health Insurance; Homework, Industrial; Hours of Labor; Indenture; Industrial Democracy; Industrial Education; Industrial Hazards; Industrial Hygiene; Industrial Relations; Industrial Relations Councils; Industrial Workers of the World; International Labor Organization; Intimidation; Journeymen's Societies; Knights of Labor; Labor; Labor Banking; Labor-Capital Cooperation; Labor Contract; Labor Disputes; Labor Exchange Banks; Labor, Government Services for; Labor Injunction; Labor Legislation and Law; Labor, Methods of Remuneration for; Labor Movement; Labor Parties; Labor Turnover; Labourers, Statutes of; Lodging Houses; Longshoremen; Mechanic; Migratory Labor; Minimum Wage; Mining Accidents; National Economic Councils; Negro Problem; Occupation; Oriental Immigration; Peonage; Personnel Administration; Policing, Industrial; Prison Labor; Producers' Cooperation; Profit Sharing; Proletariat; Putting Out System; Rehabilitation; Sabotage; Safety Movement; Scientific Management; Seamen; Short Hours Movement; Slavery; Social Insurance; Socialist Parties; Specialization; Standards of Living; Strikes and Lockouts; Syndicalism; Trade Agreements; Trade Unions; Unemployment; Unem-

ployment Insurance; Vagrancy; Vocational Education; Wages; Welfare Work, Industrial; Women in Industry; Workers' Education; Workmen's Compensation.
See also Classification of Articles (Abstract Titles), INDUSTRY (p. 551), OCCUPATIONS (p. 553), SOCIALISM (p. 556); (Biographical Titles), LABOR (p. 563), SOCIALISM (p. 569).

Legal Relations

Adoption; Agency; Alienation of Property; Alimony; Allegiance; Aviation (Law); Bailment; Bankruptcy; Bargaining Power; Blue Laws; Bonding; Breach of Marriage Promise; Caveat Emptor; Child (Delinquent and Welfare Legislation); Civil Rights; Common Carrier; Common Law Marriage; Confiscation; Consideration; Contract; Contract Clause; Debt; Divorce; Domicile; Dual Citizenship; Dueling; Duress; Eminent Domain; Employers' Liability; Entail; Escheat; Excess Condemnation; Extortion; Foreign Corporations; Fraud; Frauds, Statute of; Freedom of Contract; Freehold; Full Faith and Credit Clause; Gambling (Legal Aspects); Game Laws; Gifts (Law); Goodwill; Guardianship; Homestead Exemption Laws; Illegitimacy (Legal Aspects); Immunity, Diplomatic; Immunity, Political; Insanity; Insurance (Law and Regulation); Labor Contract; Labor Injunction; Labor Legislation and Law; Land Tenure; Land Transfer; Landlord and Tenant; Law; Legal Aid; Lese Majesty; Liability; Libel and Slander; Licensing; Lien; Majority, Age of; Marital Property; Mining Law; Miscegenation; Moratorium; Mortgage; Mortmain; Nationality; Negligence; Negotiable Instruments; Notaries, Public; Nuisance; Ownership and Possession; Partnership; Passport; Patents; Perpetuities; Pledge; Prohibition; Radio (Legal Aspects); Rate Regulation; Receivership; Restraint of Trade; Sales; Seduction; Servitudes; Specific Performance; State Liability; Succession, Laws of; Suretyship and Guaranty; Tort; Trademarks and Names; Trusts and Trustees; Valuation; Voluntary Associations.
See also Classification of Articles (Abstract Titles), ADMINISTRATION OF JUSTICE (p. 548), CRIME (p. 550), JURISPRUDENCE (p. 552), PROPERTY (p. 554).

Legislation

Advisory Opinions (National); Bicameral System; Bloc, Parliamentary; Bundesrat; Checks and Balances; Closure; Committees, Legislative; Congressional Government; Constitutional Law; Deadlock; Debate, Parliamentary; Estates General; Immunity, Political; Impeachment; Initiative and Referendum; Insurgency, Political; International Legislation; Interpellation; Investigations, Governmental; Judicial Review; Legislation; Legislative Assemblies; Lobby; Majority Rule; Minority Rights; Obstruction, Parliamentary; Popular Assemblies; Procedure, Parliamentary; Representation; Retroactive Legislation; Separation of Powers; Sumptuary Legislation; Uniform Legislation; Veto.
See also Classification of Articles (Abstract Titles), POLITICAL PARTIES (p. 554), PUBLIC OFFICE (p. 554); (Biographical Titles), POLITICAL AFFAIRS (p. 566), STATECRAFT (p. 569).

Literature and the Press

Censorship; Classicism; Copyright; Criticism, Social; Encyclopédistes; Folklore; Foreign Language Press; Freedom of Speech and of the Press; Government Publications; Humanism; Journalism; Literature; Modernism; Myth; Press; Primitivism; Printing and Publishing; Public Libraries; Public Opinion; Renaissance; Romanticism; Sacred Books; Theater.
See also Classification of Articles (Biographical Titles), JOURNALISM (p. 563), LITERATURE AND SOCIAL CRITICISM (p. 564).

Marriage and the Family

Abduction; Abortion; Adoption; Alimony; Birth Control; Birth Customs; Breach of Marriage Promise; Celibacy; Chastity; Child (Marriage); Common Law Marriage; Companionate Marriage; Concubinage; Courtship; Divorce; Domestic Relations Courts; Dowry; Family; Family Desertion and Non-support; Family Law; Fertility Rites; Free Love; Guardianship; Home Economics; Home Ownership; Illegitimacy; Incest; Infanticide; Intermarriage; Kinship; Marital Property; Marriage; Maternity Welfare; Miscegenation; Parent Education; Prostitution; Race Mixture; Seduction; Sex Education and Sex Ethics.
See also Classification of Articles (Biographical Titles), FEMINISM (p. 561).

Occupations

Amateur; Begging; Business Ethics; Captain of Industry; Career; Civil Service; Clerical Occupations; Consular Service; Contingent Fee; Dentistry; Diplomacy; Domestic Service; Engineering; Entrepreneur; Espionage; Fee Splitting; Handicraft; Intellectuals; Journalism; Labor; Legal Profession and Legal Education; Management; Mechanic; Medicine; Nursing; Occupation; Priesthood; Professional Ethics; Professions; Public Employment; Public Office; Real Estate; Rehabilitation; Research; Seamen; Social Work (Training); Specialization; Teaching Profession; Vocational Guidance; Women in Industry.

Opinion

Abolition; Action Française; Advertising; Agitation; American Legion; Anticlericalism; Anti-Corn Law League; Antimilitarism; Antiradicalism; Anti-Saloon League; Antisemitism; Apostasy and Heresy; Atheism; Attitudes, Social; Belief; Blood Accusation; Censorship; Chauvinism; Civic Education; Common Sense; Compromise; Conformity; Conscientious Objectors; Consensus; Conservatism; Cosmopolitanism; Criticism, Social; Discussion; Doctrinaire; Dogma; Emancipation; Encyclopédistes; Ethnocentrism; Fanaticism; Fictions; Freedom of Association; Freedom of Speech and of the Press; Freethinkers; Fundamentalism; Hero Worship; Humanism; Individualism; Inquisition; Intellectuals; Intolerance; Intransigence; Ku Klux Klan; Law Enforcement; Liberalism; Majority Rule; Militarism; Minority Rights; Missions; Modernism; Monarchomachs; Morals; Nationalism; Pacifism; Patriotism; Press; Primitivism; Prohibition; Propaganda; Proselytism; Public Opinion; Publicity; Radicalism; Reformism; Regionalism; Religious Freedom; Renaissance; Romanticism; Secularism; Social Christian Movements; Taste; Temperance Movements; Traditionalism; Utopias.
See also Classification of Articles (Abstract Titles), CONDUCT (p. 549).

Philosophy

Atheism; Buddhism; Casuistry; Common Sense; Confucianism; Consciousness; Cynics; Cyrenaics; Determinism; Encyclopédistes; Enlightenment; Epicureanism; Equality; Ethics; Fatalism; Fictions; Freethinkers; Functionalism; Gestalt; Hedonism;

Human Nature; Humanism (Philosophical Aspects); Idealism; Individualism; Justice; Liberty; Logic; Materialism; Mechanism and Vitalism; Mysticism; Natural Law; Naturalism; Nihilism; Philosophy; Political Science; Positivism; Pragmatism; Progress; Rationalism; Realism; Scholasticism; Sophists; Stoicism; Taoism; Transcendentalism; Utilitarianism.
See also Classification of Articles (Abstract Titles), RELIGION (*p.* 555), SOCIOLOGY (*p.* 556); (Biographical Titles), PHILOSOPHY (*p.* 566), RELIGION (*p.* 567), SOCIAL PHILOSOPHY AND SOCIOLOGY (*p.* 568).

Political Parties

Bloc, Parliamentary; Bolshevism; Campaign, Political; Catholic Parties; Caucus; Clubs, Political; Coalition; Communist Parties; Conservatism; Convention, Political; Corrupt Practises Acts; Faction; Farm Bloc, U. S.; Free Silver; Gerrymander; Independent Voting; Insurgency, Political; Kuomintang; Labor Parties; Leadership; Levellers; Liberalism; Machine, Political; Nominations, Political; Ostracism; Parties, Political; Primaries, Political; Reconstruction; Socialist Parties; Soviet; Spoils System.
See also Classification of Articles (Abstract Titles), LEGISLATION (*p.* 553), PUBLIC OFFICE (*p.* 554); (Biographical Titles), POLITICAL AFFAIRS (*p.* 566).

Primitive Society

Abduction; Adoption (Primitive); Age Societies; Agriculture (Primitive); Animism; Anthropology; Archaeology; Art (Primitive); Aryans; Avoidance; Birth Customs; Blood Vengeance Feud; Cannibalism; Ceremony (Primitive); Culture; Culture Area; Death Customs; Diffusionism; Divination; Domestication; Dress; Education, Primitive; Family (Primitive); Fertility Rites; Fetishism; Folklore; Gerontocracy; Gifts (Primitive); Gypsies; Holidays; Hunting; Incest; Initiation; Kinship; Land Tenure (Primitive Societies); Law (Primitive); Magic; Man; Marriage; Migrations (Primitive); Music (Primitive); Myth; Nomads; Ornament; Pottery (Primitive); Prehistory; Priesthood; Ritual; Secret Societies; Slavery (Primitive); Social Organization; Tabu; Totemism; Woman, Position in Society (Primitive).
See also Classification of Articles (Biographical Titles), ANTHROPOLOGY (*p.* 558).

Property

Absentee Ownership; Accumulation; Agrarian Movements; Alien Property; Alienation of Property; Appanage; Appreciation; Assizes; Aubaine, Right of; Bailment; Charitable Trusts; Communism; Confiscation; Copyright; Debt; Eminent Domain; Enclosures; Endowments and Foundations; Entail; Escheat; Excess Condemnation; Fair Return; Forests; Fortunes, Private; Freehold; Frontier; General Property Tax; Gifts; Hoarding; Home Ownership; Homestead; Homestead Exemption Laws; House and Building Taxes; Inheritance; Inheritance Taxation; Land Grants; Land Mortgage Credit; Land Settlement; Land Speculation; Land Taxation; Land Tenure; Land Transfer; Land Valuation; Landed Estates; Landlord and Tenant; Latifundia; Lien; Limitation of Actions; Marital Property; Mining Law; Mortgage; Mortgage Tax; Mortmain; National Wealth; Ownership and Possession; Patents; Perpetuities; Pledge; Plutocracy; Primogeniture; Property; Property Tax; Public Domain; Real Estate; Rent Charge; Rent Regulation; Rentier; Requisitions, Military; Sales; Servitudes; Slavery; Special Assessments; Succession, Laws of; Thrift; Trusts and Trustees; Unearned Increment; Valuation; Vested Interests; Village Community; Water Law.

Psychology

Abnormal Psychology; Adolescence; Alienist; Behaviorism; Character; Child (Psychology *and* Guidance); Comparative Psychology; Conditioned Reflex; Consciousness; Cyrenaics; Educational Psychology; Genius; Gestalt; Habit; Imitation; Instinct; Maladjustment; Mental Defectives; Mental Disorders; Mental Hygiene; Mental Tests; Personality; Play; Psychiatry; Psychoanalysis; Psychology; Social Psychology.
See also Classification of Articles (Abstract Titles), CONDUCT (*p.* 549); (Biographical Titles), PSYCHOLOGY (*p.* 567).

Public Finance

Accounts, Public; Annuities; Assignats; Bills of Credit; Bimetallism and Monometallism; Budget; Bullionists; Central Banking; Coinage; Compensated Dollar; Currency; Devaluation; Education (Finance); Expenditures, Public; Federal Reserve System; Financial Administration; Fiscal Science; Forced Loans; Foreign Exchange; Free Silver; Gold; Grants-in-Aid; Hoarding; Indemnity, Military; Inflation and Deflation; International Finance; Land Bank Schemes; Loans, Intergovernmental; Local Finance; Lotteries; Monetary Stabilization; Monetary Unions; Money; Monopolies, Public; Municipal Finance; Paper Money; Pensions; Public Contracts; Public Debt; Public Finance; Public Works; Rentenmark; Reparations; Repudiation of Public Debts; Revenue Farming; Revenues, Public; Silver; Sinking Fund; Special Assessments; Taxation; Tribute; War Finance.
See also Classification of Articles (Abstract Titles), TARIFF (*p.* 556), TAXATION (*p.* 556); (Biographical Titles), FINANCIAL ADMINISTRATION (*p.* 561).

Public Health

Accidents; Accidents, Industrial; Alcohol; Black Death; Blind; Child; Clinics and Dispensaries; Communicable Diseases, Control of; Cripples; Deaf; Dentistry; Disasters and Disaster Relief; Drug Addiction; Epidemics; Eugenics; Fatigue; Fee Splitting; Food and Drug Regulation; Funerals; Health Centers; Health Education; Health Insurance; Hospitals and Sanatoria; Industrial Hazards; Industrial Hygiene; Insanity; Life Extension Movement; Maternity Welfare; Medical Jurisprudence; Medical Materials Industry; Medicine; Mental Defectives; Mental Disorders; Mental Hygiene; Mental Tests; Milk Supply; Mining Accidents; Morbidity; Mortality; Motor Vehicle Accidents; Nursing; Nutrition; Opium Problem; Physical Education; Prostitution; Psychiatry; Public Health; Railroad Accidents; Resorts; Sanitation; Water Supply.
See also Classification of Articles (Abstract Titles), PUBLIC WELFARE (*p.* 555); (Biographical Titles), PUBLIC HEALTH (*p.* 567).

Public Office

Abdication; Appointments; Assassination; Bureaucracy; Cabinet; City Manager; Civil Service; Consular Service; Contested Elections; Coroner; Corruption, Political; Deification; Diplomacy; Divine Right of Kings; Elections; Executive; Expert; Franking; Immunity, Diplomatic; Immunity, Political; Impeachment; International Advisers; Ju-

For complete list of headings used in Classification of Articles see page 547.

Classification of Articles (Abstract Titles)

diciary; Justice of the Peace; Machine, Political; Mandamus; Nominations, Political; Notaries, Public; Politics; Public Employment; Public Office; Recall; Sheriff; Spoils System; State Liability; Statesmanship; Succession, Political; Teaching Profession.
See also Classification of Articles (Abstract Titles), REPRESENTATION (*p.* 555).

Public Welfare

Allowance System; Almshouse; Animal Protection; Begging; Building Regulations; Charitable Trusts; Charity; Child; City and Town Planning; Civic Centers; Community Organization; Country Life Movement; Day Nursery; Dependency; Disasters and Disaster Relief; Drives, Money Raising; Endowments and Foundations; Family Allowances; Family Desertion and Non-support; Famine; Fire Protection; Floods and Flood Control; Food Supply; Garden Cities; Health Centers; Health Insurance; Housing; Humanitarianism; Inspection; Institutions, Public; Labor, Government Services for; Labor Legislation and Law; Mothers' Pensions; National Wealth; Native Policy; Old Age; Parks; Pensions; Placing Out; Playgrounds; Police; Police Power; Poor Laws; Poverty; Public Health; Public Welfare; Recreation; Red Cross; Regional Planning; Rehabilitation; Safety Movement; Sanitation; Social Insurance; Social Settlements; Social Surveys; Social Work; Unemployment Insurance; Zoning.
See also Classification of Articles (Abstract Titles), PUBLIC HEALTH (*p.* 554); (Biographical Titles), SOCIAL REFORM (*p.* 568).

Recreation and Amusement

Agricultural Fairs; Amateur; Amusements, Public; Athletics; Blue Laws; Boys' and Girls' Clubs; Camping; Chautauqua; Clubs; Community Centers; Dance; Festivals; Gambling; Game Laws; Gangs; Holidays; Hunting; Leisure; Motion Pictures; Parks; Physical Education; Play; Playgrounds; Public Libraries; Radio; Recreation; Resorts; Sports; Theater; Tourist Traffic; Women's Organizations.

Religion

Ancestor Worship; Animism; Anticlericalism; Anti-Saloon League; Apostasy and Heresy; Asceticism; Atheism; Benefit of Clergy; Birth Customs; Blasphemy; Blood Accusation; Blue Laws; Brahmanism and Hinduism; Buddhism; Bull, Papal; Caliphate; Canon Law; Catholic Emancipation; Catholic Parties; Celibacy; Ceremony; Chassidism; Chastity; Chivalry; Christian Labor Unions; Christian Science; Christian Socialism; Christianity; Church Fathers; Cluniac Movement; Comparative Religion; Conciliar Movement; Concordat; Confession; Confucianism; Conversion, Religious; Crusades; Cults; Death Customs; Deification; Deism; Diabolism; Dogma; Dominican Friars; Ecclesiastical Courts; Education (Sectarian); Ethical Culture Movement; Excommunication; Fasting; Fatalism; Fertility Rites; Festivals; Fetishism; Franciscan Movement; Freethinkers; Fundamentalism; Gallicanism; Hero Worship; Higher Criticism; Holidays; Holy Places; Holy Roman Empire; Iconoclasm; Idolatry; Inquisition; Investiture Conflict; Islam; Islamic Law; Jansenism; Jesuits; Jewish Autonomy; Jewish Emancipation; Jihad; Judaism; Magic; Messianism; Military Orders; Missions; Modernism; Monarchomachs; Monasticism; Mormonism; Mortmain; Mysteries; Mysticism; Myth; Pan-Islamism; Papacy; Priesthood; Proselytism; Protestantism; Puritanism; Quakers; Reformation; Religion; Religious Freedom; Religious Institutions, Christian; Religious Orders; Revivals, Religious; Sacred Books; Sacrifice; Scholasticism; Sects; Secularism; Shinto; Social Christian Movements; Taoism; Truce and Peace of God; Zionism.
See also Classification of Articles (Biographical Titles) HISTORY (RELIGIOUS) (*p.* 562), JEWISH PROBLEMS AND JUDAISM (*p.* 563), RELIGION (*p.* 567).

Representation

Absent-Voting; Apportionment; Ballot; By-Elections; Chartism; Constituency; Elections; Functional Representation; Gerrymander; Independent Voting; Initiative and Referendum; Lobby; Majority Rule; Minority Rights; National Economic Councils; Plebiscite; Pluralism; Popular Assemblies; Proportional Representation; Registration of Voters; Representation; Rotten Boroughs; Short Ballot Movement; Soviet; Straw Vote; Suffrage; Voting.
See also Classification of Articles (Abstract Titles), POLITICAL PARTIES (*p.* 554).

Science

Agricultural Economics; Alchemy; Anthropology; Anthropometry; Archaeology; Astrology; Biology; Calendar; Climate; Communicable Diseases, Control of; Comparative Psychology; Comparative Religion; Criminology; Demography; Divination; Ecology, Human; Economic History; Economics; Educational Psychology; Encyclopédistes; Engineering; Enlightenment; Eugenics; Evolution; Fictions; Geisteswissenschaften; Geography; Heredity; Higher Criticism; History and Historiography; Identification; Industrial Revolution; Invention; Jurisprudence; Language; Learned Societies; Logic; Materialism; Mechanism and Vitalism; Medical Jurisprudence; Medicine; Method, Scientific; Museums and Exhibitions; Naturalism; Philosophy; Political Science; Positivism; Pragmatism; Prehistory; Professions; Psychiatry; Psychoanalysis; Psychology; Records, Historical; Research; Science; Social Psychology; Social Work; Sociology; Statics and Dynamics; Statistics; Technology; Universities and Colleges; Weights and Measures. *Also* Introd. to Vol. 1, The Development of Social Thought and Institutions *and* The Social Sciences as Disciplines.
See also Classification of Articles (Abstract Titles), ECONOMICS (*p.* 550), JURISPRUDENCE (*p.* 552), PSYCHOLOGY (*p.* 554), STATISTICS (*p.* 556); (Biographical Titles), CRIMINOLOGY (*p.* 559), ECONOMICS (*p.* 559), GEOGRAPHY (*p.* 561), HISTORY (*p.* 561), LAW (*p.* 563), NATURAL SCIENCE (*p.* 565), PHILOLOGY (*p.* 565), POLITICAL SCIENCE (*p.* 566), PSYCHOLOGY (*p.* 567), SOCIAL PHILOSOPHY AND SOCIOLOGY (*p.* 568), STATISTICS (*p.* 571).

Social Discrimination

Abolition; Alien; Antisemitism; Blacklist; Blood Accusation; Boycott; Catholic Emancipation; Civil Rights; Class Consciousness; Deportation and Expulsion of Aliens; Diaspora; Emancipation; Equal Protection of the Law; Ethnocentrism; Ghetto; Illegitimacy; Intermarriage; Intolerance; Jewish Emancipation; Ku Klux Klan; Lynching; Mass Expulsion; Massacre; Minorities, National; Miscegenation; Nationalism; Native Policy; Negro Problem; Oriental Immigration; Persecution; Pressures, Social; Race Conflict; Refugees; Religious Freedom; Segregation; Slavery; Social Discrimination; Status; Woman, Position in Society.
See also Classification of Articles (Biographical

Titles), FEMINISM (*p.* 561), JEWISH PROBLEMS AND JUDAISM (*p.* 563), NEGRO PROBLEM AND SLAVERY (*p.* 565).

Social Organization

Adoption; Age Societies; Agrarian Movements; Agricultural Societies; Animal Societies; Aristocracy; Association; Authority; Autonomy; Backward Countries; Bourgeoisie; Boys' and Girls' Clubs; Brigandage; Caste; Census; Chivalry; City; City-State; Civic Organizations; Civilization; Class; Class Consciousness; Clubs; Clubs, Political; Collectivism; Colonate; Commune, Mediaeval; Communistic Settlements; Community; Cossacks; Culture; Diaspora; Equality; Ethnic Communities; Family; Family Law; Farm Tenancy; Farmers' Organizations; Feudalism; Fourier and Fourierism; Fraternal Orders; Free Love; Freedom of Association; Friendly Societies; Gangs; Garden Cities; Gentleman, Theory of the; Gerontocracy; Ghetto; Group; Guild Socialism; Guilds; Gypsies; Hero Worship; Incest; Inheritance; Initiation; Institution; Intellectuals; Interests; Intermarriage; Isolation; Jewish Autonomy; Kinship; Labor; Land Tenure; Landed Estates; Latifundia; Learned Societies; Manorial System; Marriage; Masonry; Masses; Middle Class; Military Orders; Mobility, Social; Monasticism; Mutual Aid Societies; Neighborhood; Nobility; Nomads; Occupation; Organization, Economic; Peasantry; Plutocracy; Priesthood; Primogeniture; Professions; Proletariat; Race; Race Conflict; Race Mixture; Religious Orders; Rentier; Revolution and Counter-revolution; Royal Court; Rural Society; Secret Societies; Serfdom; Slavery; Social Discrimination; Social Organism; Social Organization; Socialism; Society; State; Status; Suburbs; Totemism; Trade Unions; Vagrancy; Village Community; Voluntary Associations; Woman, Position in Society; Women's Organizations; Zionism.
See also Classification of Articles (Abstract Titles), PRIMITIVE SOCIETY (*p.* 554), SOCIAL PROCESS (*p.* 556), SOCIOLOGY (*p.* 556); (Biographical Titles), ANTHROPOLOGY (*p.* 558), SOCIAL PHILOSOPHY AND SOCIOLOGY (*p.* 568).

Social Process

Acclimatization; Accommodation; Adaptation; Adjustment; Agitation; Amalgamation; Americanization; Aryans; Assimilation, Social; Atavism; Back-to-the-Land Movements; Births; Change, Social; Civilization; Class Struggle; Climate; Collectivism; Communication; Conflict, Social; Continuity, Social; Control, Social; Culture; Custom; Decadence; Degeneration; Determinism; Dialect; Diffusionism; Domestication; Emigration; Environmentalism; Europeanization; Evolution; Evolution, Social; Folkways; Frontier; Heredity; Human Nature; Imitation; Immigration; Industrial Revolution; Innovation; Institution; Invention; Isolation; Language; Leadership; Leisure; Literature; Maladjustment; Man; Migrations; Mobility, Social; Modernism; Mortality; Population; Pressures, Social; Progress; Public Opinion; Radicalism; Religion; Renaissance; Revolution and Counter-revolution; Sanction, Social; Science; Self-Preservation; Social Organism; Social Process; Statistics (Practise); Symbolism; Tradition; Urbanization; Utopia; War; Writing; Zionism.
See also Classification of Articles (Abstract Titles), SOCIAL ORGANIZATION (*p.* 556), SOCIOLOGY (*p.* 556); (Biographical Titles), SOCIAL PHILOSOPHY AND SOCIOLOGY (*p.* 568).

Socialism

Ateliers Nationaux; Atheism (Modern); Babouvism; Bolshevism; Brook Farm; Christian Socialism; Class Struggle; Collectivism; Commune of Paris; Communism; Communist Parties; Communistic Settlements; Direct Action; Economics (Socialist); Fabianism; Fourier and Fourierism; General Strike; Gosplan; Government Ownership; Guild Socialism; Industrial Workers of the World; Labor Movement; Materialism; National Economic Planning; National Socialism, German; Owen and Owenism; Proletariat; Russian Revolution; Socialism; Socialist Parties; Socialization; Soviet; Syndicalism.
See also Classification of Articles (Biographical Titles), SOCIALISM (*p.* 569).

Sociology

Animal Societies; Anthropology; Anthropometry; Archaeology; Aryans; Atavism; Criminology; Culture; Culture Area; Demography; Determinism; Diffusionism; Ecology, Human; Environmentalism; Evolution, Social; Folklore; Functionalism; Geisteswissenschaften; Geography; Population (Theory); Prehistory; Race; Social Organism; Social Process; Social Psychology; Social Surveys; Sociology.
See also Classification of Articles (Abstract Titles), CONDUCT (*p.* 549), OPINION (*p.* 553), PRIMITIVE SOCIETY (*p.* 554), SOCIAL DISCRIMINATION (*p.* 555), SOCIAL ORGANIZATION (*p.* 556), SOCIAL PROCESS (*p.* 556); (Biographical Titles), ANTHROPOLOGY (*p.* 558), SOCIAL PHILOSOPHY AND SOCIOLOGY (*p.* 568).

Statistics

Average; Births; Census; Child (Mortality); Consumption (Problems of Measurement); Correlation; Criminal Statistics; Crop and Livestock Reporting; Curve Fitting; Demand; Demography; Family Budgets; Forecasting, Business; Frequency Distribution; Index Numbers; Morbidity; Mortality; National Income; Occupation (Statistics); Population; Prices (Statistics); Probability; Production (Statistics); Statistics; Time Series.
See also Classification of Articles (Biographical Titles), STATISTICS (*p.* 571).

Tariff

Ad Valorem and Specific Duties; Anti-Corn Law League; Corn Laws; Customs Duties; Customs Unions; Drawback; Export Duties; Farm Relief; Free Ports and Free Zones; Free Trade; Protection; Tariff; Transit Duties.
See also Classification of Articles (Abstract Titles), ECONOMIC POLICY (*p.* 550), PUBLIC FINANCE (*p.* 554); (Biographical Titles), FINANCIAL ADMINISTRATION (*p.* 561).

Taxation

Aids; Alcabala; Assessment of Taxes; Business Taxes; Capital Levy; Capitalization and Amortization of Taxes; Corporation Taxes; Corvée; Double Taxation; Excess Profits Tax; Excise; Gasoline Tax; General Property Tax; House and Building Taxes; Income Tax; Inheritance Taxation; Land Taxation; Mortgage Tax; Poll Tax; Property Tax; Revenue Farming; Sales Tax; Single Tax; Special Assessments; Tax Administration; Tax Exemption; Taxation; Unearned Increment.
See also Classification of Articles (Abstract Titles), ECONOMIC POLICY (*p.* 550), PUBLIC FINANCE (*p.* 554); (Biographical Titles), FINANCIAL ADMINISTRATION (*p.* 561).

For complete list of headings used in Classification of Articles see page 547.

Transportation

Armed Merchantmen; Automobile Industry; Aviation; Commerce; Commercial Routes; Common Carrier; Continuous Voyage; Express Companies; International Waterways; Interstate Commerce; Interstate Commerce Commission; Marine Insurance; Maritime Law; Merchant Marine; Merchantmen, Status of; Motor Vehicle Accidents; Motor Vehicle Transportation; Municipal Transit; Panama Canal; Piracy; Ports and Harbors; Postal Service; Railroad Accidents; Railroads; Roads; Seamen; Shipbuilding; Shipping; Suez Canal; Terminals; Tourist Traffic; Traffic Regulation; Transit, International; Transportation; Waterways, Inland.

See also Classification of Articles (Abstract Titles), COMMERCE (*p.* 549).

War

Aggression, International; Alien Property; American Legion; Angary; Antimilitarism; Armaments; Armed Forces, Control of; Armed Merchantmen; Armed Neutrality; Armistice; Arms and Munitions Traffic; Army; Atrocities; Aviation (International Aspects); Belligerency; Blockade; Casus Belli; Chivalry; Civil War; Conquest; Conscientious Objectors; Conscription; Continuous Voyage; Contraband of War; Court Martial; Crusades; Declaration of London; Declaration of Paris; Disarmament; Drives, Money Raising; Embargo; Enemy Alien; Espionage; Excess Profits Tax; Fraternizing; Freedom of the Seas; Guerrilla Warfare; Impressment; Indemnity, Military; Jihad; Limitation of Armaments; Mercenary Troops; Militarism; Military Desertion; Military Law; Military Occupation; Military Orders; Military Training; Militia; Mobilization and Demobilization; Morale; Munitions Industry; Mutiny; National Defense; Navy; Neutrality; Neutralization; Outlawry of War; Pacifism; Peace Movements; Prisoners of War; Privateering; Prize; Profiteering; Reconstruction; Red Cross; Reparations; Requisitions, Military; Sanction, International; Trading with the Enemy; Truce and Peace of God; Veterans; War; War Economics; War Finance; Warfare, Laws of; World War.

See also Classification of Articles (Abstract Titles), INTERNATIONAL RELATIONS (*p.* 552); (Biographical Titles), PACIFISM (*p.* 565).

For complete list of headings used in Classification of Articles see page 547.

Classification of Articles

Biographical Titles

Agrarian Reform

AMERICAN—Bryan, W. J.; Evans, G. H.; Kelley, O. H.; Lubin, D.

BRITISH—Collings, J.; Dove, P. E.; Girdlestone, E.; Green, F. E.; Haggard, H. R.; Hales, J.; Ogilvie, W.; Sinclair, J.; Spence, T.; Wallace, A. R.; Winstanley, G.

BULGARIAN—Stamboliĭski, A. S.

CROATIAN—Radić, S.

CZECH—Bráf, A.

FRENCH—Boncerf, P. F.; Méline, J.

GERMAN—Buchenberger, A.; David, E.; Gesell, S.; Goltz, T. von der; Hanssen, G.; Miaskowski, A. von; Thaer, A. D.

IRISH—Davitt, M.; O'Brien, J.

ITALIAN—Neri, Pompeo.

MEXICAN—Zapata, E.

NEW ZEALAND—Grey, G.; McKenzie, J.

ROMAN—Gracchus, T. and G.

RUMANIAN—Cuza, A. J.; Dobrogeanu-Gherea, C.; Haret, S.

RUSSIAN—Chavchavadze, Ilia; Cherkassky, V. A.; Hertzenstein, M. Y.; Kaufman, A. A.; Khomyakov, A. S.; Kiselev, P. D.; Milutin, N. A.; Peshekhonov, A. V.; Samarin, Y. F.; Vasilchikov, A. I.

SPANISH—Aranda, Conde de.

SWISS—Fellenberg, P. E. von.

See also Classification of Articles (Abstract Titles), AGRICULTURE (p. 548).

Agriculture

AMERICAN—Atwater, W. O.; Crèvecoeur, M.-G. J. de; Judd, O.; McCormick, C. H.; Ruffin, E.; Skinner, J. S.; Wallace, H. and H. C.; Watson, E.; Whitney, E.

AUSTRALIAN—Macarthur, J.

BRITISH—Anderson, J.; Bakewell, R.; Caird, J.; Fitzherbert, J.; Henley, W. of; Lawes, J. B.; Marshall, W.; Sinclair, J.; Townshend, C.; Tull, J.; Young, A.

FRENCH—Gasparin, Comte de.

GERMAN—Eyth, M.; Goltz, T. von der; Liebig, J. von; Meitzen, A.; Schubart, J. C.; Schulze-Gävernitz, F. G.; Thaer, A. D.; Thünen, J. H. von.

IRISH—Plunkett, H. C.

ITALIAN—Ridolfi, C.

RUSSIAN—Ludogovsky, A. P.

SWISS—Kraemer, A.

See also Classification of Articles (Abstract Titles), AGRICULTURE (p. 548).

Anthropology

AMERICAN—Abbott, C. C.; Brinton, D. G.; Cushing, F. H.; Gallatin, A.; Gatschet, A. S.; McGee, W. J.; Mason, O. T.; Mooney, J.; Morgan, L. H.; Powell, J. W.; Putnam, F. W.

AUSTRALIAN—Fison, L.; Howitt, A. W.

BRITISH—Beddoe, J.; Codrington, R. H.; Crawley, A. E.; Gomme, G. L.; Hartland, E. S.; Johnston, H. H.; Lang, A.; Lubbock, J.; McLennan, J. F.; Pitt-Rivers, A. H. L.; Prichard, J. C.; Rivers, W. H. R.; Tylor, E. B.

DUTCH—Nieboer, H. J.

FRENCH—Boucher de Crèvecoeur de Perthes, J.; Broca, P.-P.; Démeunier, J.-N.; Deniker, J.; Hubert, H.; Lafitau, J.-F.; Quatrefages de Bréau, J.-L. A. de; Reinach, S.; Topinard, P.

GERMAN—Ammon, A. O.; Andrée, R.; Bastian, A.; Blumenbach, J. F.; Dargun, L. von; Ehrenreich, P.; Gerland, G.; Grosse, E.; Hahn, E.; Lippert, J.; Luschan, F. von; Martin, R.; Post, A. H.; Schurtz, H.; Seler, E. G.; Waitz, F. T.

RUSSIAN—Anuchin, D. N.; Sternberg, L. Y.

SWEDISH—Nordenskiöld, N. E.; Retzius, A. A.

SWISS—Bachofen, J. J.; Bandelier, A. F. A.

See also Classification of Articles (Abstract Titles), PRIMITIVE SOCIETY (p. 554).

Business and Finance

AMERICAN—Appleton, N.; Armour Family; Astor, J. J.; Atkinson, E.; Baer, G. F.; Brice, C. S.; Carnegie, A.; Cooke, J.; Cooper, P.; Field, M.; Fink, A.; Fisk, J., Jr.; Frick, H. C.; Gantt, H. L.; Gary, E. H.; Gilbreth, F. B.; Gould, J.; Grace, W. R.; Gregg, W.; Guggenheim Family; Harriman, E. H.; Havemeyer, H. O.; Hewitt, A. S.; Hill, J. J.; Hunt, F.; Huntington, C. P.; Justi, H.; Keith, M. C.; Kirby, J., Jr.; Kruttschnitt, J.; McCormick, C. H.; Macy, R. H.; Mitten, T. E.; Morgan Family; Parry, D. M.; Pullman, G. M.; Rosenwald, J.; Ryan, T. F.; Schiff, J. H.; Stanford, L.; Stevens, J.; Stewart, A. T.; Stillman, J.; Taylor, F. W.; Vail, T. N.; Van Cleave, J. W.; Vanderbilt Family; Villard, H.; Warburg, P. M.; Westinghouse, G.; Yerkes, C. T.

BELGIAN—Loewenstein, A.

BRITISH—Arkwright, R.; Ashburton, Lord; Brassey, T. (d. 1870); Bridgewater, F. E.; Burlamachi, P.; Cadbury, G.; Cassell, E. J.; Child, J.; Coutts, T.; Cowdray, Lord; Cunard, S.; Denny, W.; Gilbart, J. W.; Goldie, G. D. T.; Gott, B.; Hudson, G.; Ismay, T. H.; Leverhulme, Lord; Lipton, T. J.; Melchett, Lord; Mundella, A. J.; Paterson, W.; Pirrie, W. J.; Pole Family; Reuter, P. J. von; Rhodes, C. J.; Rothschild Family; Salt, T.; Stephenson, G.; Watkin, E. W.

CANADIAN—Allan, H.; Cunard, S.; Fleming, S.; Mackenzie, W.; Mount Stephen, Lord.

FRENCH—Coeur, J.; Dollfus, J.; Harmel, L.; Leclaire, E. J.; Péreire, J.-É.; Schneider, J.-É.

GERMAN—Abbe, E.; Ballin, A.; Brandts, F.; Fugger Family; Hansemann, D. J. L.; Henckel, G.; Krupp, A.; Peutinger, K.; Rothschild Family; Siemens, E. W. von; Stinnes, H.

ITALIAN—Bardi Family; Medici.

JAPANESE—Mitsui.

POLISH—Steinkeller, P. A.; Szczepanowski, A. P. S.

RUSSIAN—Morozov, S.

SPANISH—Güell y Ferrer, J.

SWEDISH—Kreuger, I.; Nobel, A. B.

See also Classification of Articles (Abstract Titles), BANKING (p.

For complete list of headings used in Classification of Articles see page 547.

Classification of Articles (Biographical Titles)

548), BUSINESS (*p.* 548), COMMERCE (*p.* 549), CREDIT (*p.* 550), INDUSTRY (*p.* 551), INVESTMENT AND SPECULATION (*p.* 552).

Colonial Administration

BRITISH—Angas, G. F.; Bentinck, Lord; Bourke, R.; Brooke, J.; Buller, C.; Calvert Family; Carleton, G.; Clive, R.; Cromer, Lord; Curzon, G. N.; Dalhousie, Lord; Duff, A.; Dufferin and Ava, Lord; Durham, Lord; Elgin, Lord; Elphinstone, M.; Goldie, G. D. T.; Grey, G.; Grey, Third Earl; Hastings, W.; Johnston, H. H.; Kirk, J.; Lawrence, H. M. *and* Lord; Livingstone, D.; Lucas, C. P.; Macquarie, L.; Merivale, H.; Milner, A.; Molesworth, W.; Morel, E. D.; Munro, T.; Penn, W.; Phillip, A.; Raffles, T. S.; Rhodes, C. J.; Shepstone, T.; Stanley, H. M.; Wakefield, E. G.; Wellesley, R. C.

DUTCH—Coen, J. P.; Johann Moritz.

FRENCH—Bert, P.; Bugeaud de la Piconnerie, T. R.; Champlain, S. de; Dupleix, J.; Étienne, E.; Faidherbe, L. L. C.; Frontenac, Comte de; Galliéni, J.-S.; Lanessan, J. M. A. de.

GERMAN—Peters, C.

PORTUGUESE—Albuquerque, A. de.

SPANISH—Agia, M. de; Bucareli y Ursúa, A. M.; Campillo y Cossio, J.; Cortés, H.; Gálvez, J. de; Gasca, P. de la; Labra y Cadrana, R. M. de; Las Casas, B. de; Mendoza, A. de; Revillagigedo, Conde de; Toledo, F. de.

See also Classification of Articles (Biographical Titles), STATECRAFT (*p.* 569); (Abstract Titles), GOVERNMENT (*p.* 551), INTERNATIONAL RELATIONS (*p.* 552).

Cooperation

BELGIAN—Mellaerts, J. F.

BRITISH—Greening, E. O.; Holyoake, G. J.; Hughes, T.; Jones, L.; King, W.; Ludlow, J. M.; Maxwell, W.; Mitchell, J. T. W.; Neale, E. V.; Owen and Owenism; Wolff, H. W.

CZECH—Chleborád, F. L.; Šimáček, F.

FRENCH—Beluze, J. P.; Boyve, É. de; Fourier and Fourierism; Godin, J. B. A.

GERMAN—Busch, E.; Elm, A. von; Haas, W.; Huber, V. A.; Ketteler, W. E. von; Pfeiffer, E. von; Raiffeisen, F. W.; Ratzinger, G.; Schulze-Delitzsch, H.

IRISH—Plunkett, H. C.

ITALIAN—Maffi, A.

POLISH—Mielczarski, R.

RUSSIAN—Balakshin, A. N.; Hübner, N. P.; Kulizhny, A. E.; Zelgeim, V. N.

SLOVENIAN—Krek, J.

SWISS—Kraemer, A.; Schär, J. F.

See also Classification of Articles (Abstract Titles), COOPERATION (*p.* 550).

Criminology

AMERICAN—Barrows, S. J.; Brockway, Z. R.; Dwight, L.; Osborne, T. M.

AUSTRIAN—Benedikt, M.; Gross, H.

BELGIAN—Ducpétiaux, É.; Prins, A.

BRITISH—Crofton, W. F.; Du Cane, E. F.; Fry, E. G.; Goring, C. B.; Howard, J.; Maconochie, A.; Molesworth, W.; Romilly, S.

DANISH—Goos, C.

DUTCH—Hamel, G. A. van.

FRENCH—Bérenger, A. M. M. T.; Bertillon, A.; Bonneville de Marsangy, A.; Despine, P.; Tarde, G.

GERMAN—Baer, A. A.; Berner, A. F.; Binding, K.; Birkmeyer, K. von; Feuerbach, P. J. A. von; Grolman, K. von; Liszt, F. E. von.

ITALIAN—Beccaria, C. B.; Carmignani, G.; Carrara, F.; Ferri, E.; Lombroso, C.; Romagnosi, G. D.; Sighele, S.

RUSSIAN—Foynitsky, I. Y.; Kistyakovsky, A. F.

SPANISH—Dorado Montero, P.; Giner de los Ríos, F.

See also Classification of Articles (Abstract Titles), ADMINISTRATION OF JUSTICE (*p.* 548), CRIME (*p.* 550).

Economics

AMERICAN—Adams, C. F. (d. 1915); Adams, H. C.; Atkinson, E.; Baird, H. C.; Cardozo, J. N.; Carey, H. C.; Carey, M.; Colwell, S.; Conant, C. A.; Coxe, T.; Davenport, H. J.; Dunbar, C. F.; George, H.; Hadley, A. T.; Hawley, F. B.; Helper, H. R.; Horton, S. D.; Hourwich, I. A.; Hoxie, R. F.; Kellogg, E.; MacVane, S. M.; Parker, C. H.; Patten, S. N.; Rae, J.; Raymond, D.; Seager, H. R.; Sumner, W. G.; Taylor, F. M.; Tucker, G.; Veblen, T. B.; Walker, A.; Walker, F. A.; Wells, D. A.; Young, A. A.

AUSTRALIAN—Hearn, W. E.

AUSTRIAN—Auspitz, R.; Böhm-Bawerk, E. von; Hertzka, T.; Hock, K. F.; Hornigk, P. W. von; Lieben, R.; Menger, C.; Philippovich von Philippsberg, E.; Sax, E.; Schroeder, W. von; Sonnenfels, J. von; Wieser, F. von.

BELGIAN—Brants, V.; Denis, H.; Laveleye, É. L. V. de; Périn, H. X. C.

BRITISH—Acworth, W. M.; Atkinson, W.; Attwood, T.; Babbage, C.; Bagehot, W.; Bailey, S.; Banfield, T. C.; Barbon, N.; Barton, J.; Baxter, R. D.; Berkeley, G.; Boyd, W.; Buchanan, D.; Cary, J.; Colquhoun, P.; Copleston, E.; Craig, J.; Crombie, A.; Culpeper, T.; Davenant, C.; Decker, M.; Denny, W.; De Quincey, T.; Eden, F. M.; Edgeworth, F. Y.; Fawcett, H.; Fleetwood, W.; Giffen, R.; Gilbart, J. W.; Gonner, E. C. K.; Goschen, Lord; Gray, J.; Hamilton, R.; Harris, J.; Hodgskin, T.; Hume, D.; Hutcheson, F.; Jenkin, H. C. F.; Jevons, W. S.; Jones, R.; Lauderdale, Lord; Law, J.; Levi, L.; Lloyd, W. F.; Locke, J.; Longe, F. D.; McCulloch, J. R.; Macleod, H. D.; Malthus, T. R.; Malynes, G. de; Mandeville, B. de; Marcet, J.; Marshall, A.; Martineau, H.; Massie, J.; Mill, J.; Mill, J. S.; Milles, T.; Misselden, E.; Mun, T.; Newmarch, W.; Norman, G. W.; North, D.; Overstone, Lord; Palgrave, R. H. I.; Paterson, W.; Petty, W.; Price, R.; Ramsay, G.; Ravenstone, P.; Ricardo, D.; Scrope, G. J. P.; Senior, N. W.; Smart, W.; Smith, A.; Steuart, J. D.; Temple, W.; Tooke, T.; Torrens, R.; Tucker, J.; Vanderlint, J.; Vaughan, R.; Wallace, Robert; Whately, R.; Wheatley, J.; Wicksteed, P. H.; Yarranton, A.

BULGARIAN—Popov, K.

CZECH—Bráf, A.; Gruber, J.

DANISH—Scharling, H. W.

DUTCH—Ackersdijck, J.; Beaujon, A.; Bruijn Kops, J. L. de; Cohen Stuart, A. J.; Court, P. de la; Pierson, N. G.

FRENCH—Abeille, L. P.; Agoult, C. d'; Bacalan, A. T. I. de; Bastiat, F.; Baudeau, N.; Baudrillart, H. J. L.; Bellet, D.; Blanqui, J. A.; Block, M.; Bodin, J.; Boisguillebert, P. le P.; Boiteau, D. A. P.; Bourguin, M.; Canard, N. F.; Cantillon, R.; Casaux, C.; Cauwes, P. L.; Cernuschi, H.; Chaptal, J. A.; Chevalier, M.; Clamageran, J. J.; Clément, A.; Clicquot-Blervache, S. de; Con-

For complete list of headings used in Classification of Articles see page 547.

dillac, É. B. de; Coquelin, C.; Courcelle-Seneuil, J. G.; Cournot, A.-A.; Dunoyer, B. C. P. J.; Dupont de Nemours, P. S.; Dupré de Saint Maur, N. F.; Dupuit, A. J. E. J.; Dutot, C. de F.; Forbonnais, F. V. D. de; Foville, A. de; Garnier, G.; Garnier, J. C.; Gasparin, Comte de; Gomel, C.; Gournay, J. C. M. V. de; Gramont, S. de; Graslin, J. J. L.; Guyot, Y.; Jannet, C.; Jourdan, A.; Juglar, C.; Laffemas, B. de; Lavergne, L.-G. L. de; Lavoisier, A. L.; Leroy-Beaulieu, P.; Le Trosne, G. F.; Melon, J. F.; Mercier de la Rivière, P.-P.; Mirabeau, Marquis de; Moheau; Molinari, G. de; Montchrétien, A. de; Morellet, A.; Necker, J.; Oresme, N.; Pecqueur, C.; Quesnay, F.; Say, J.-B.; Stourm, R.; Turgot, R. J.; Vauban, S. le P. de; Villeneuve-Bargemont, Vicomte de; Walras, A. A.; Walras, M. E. L.; Wolowski, L. F. M. R.

GERMAN—Arnd, K.; Bamberger, L.; Baumstark, E.; Becher, J. J.; Bendixen, F.; Bernhardi, T. von; Besold, C.; Biel, G.; Bollmann, J. E.; Bornitz, J.; Braun, K.; Büsch, J. G.; Cohn, G.; Conrad, J.; Conring, H.; Crome, A. F. W.; Darjes, J. G.; Dietzel, K. A.; Dithmar, J. C.; Dühring, E. K.; Ehrenberg, R.; Eiselen, J. F. G.; Engel, C. L. E.; Faucher, J.; Gerlach, O. A. J.; Gesell, S.; Gossen, H. H.; Gothein, E.; Graumann, J. P.; Hagen, K. H.; Held, A.; Helferich, J. A. R. von; Helfferich, K.; Henry of Langenstein; Hermann, F. B. W. von; Heyn, O.; Hildebrand, B.; Hufeland, G.; Jakob, L. H. von; Justi, J. H. G. von; Knapp, G. F.; Knies, K. G. A.; Kraus, C. J.; Laspeyres, E.; Lau, T. L.; Lehr, J.; Leib, J. G.; Leuber, B.; Lexis, W.; List, F.; Lotz, J. F. E.; Lueder, A. F.; Luxemburg, R.; Mangoldt, H. K. E. von; Marx, K.; Mauvillon, J.; Nasse, E.; Nebenius, K. F.; Neumann, F. J.; Obrecht, G. von; Oncken, A.; Osse, M. von; Pesch, H.; Peutinger, K.; Pfeiffer, J. F. von; Pohle, L.; Prince-Smith, J.; Ratzinger, G.; Rau, K. H.; Rodbertus, J. K.; Roscher, W. G. F.; Sartorius von Waltershausen, G.; Schäffle, A. E. F.; Schanz, G. von; Schlettwein, J. A.; Schmoller, G. von; Schönberg, G. F. von; Schulze-Gävernitz, F. G.; Seckendorff, V. L. von; Soden, F. J. H. von; Soetbeer, A. G.; Thünen, J. H. von; Wagner, A. H. G.; Wirth, M.; Zincke, G. H.

GREEK (ANCIENT)—Aristotle.

HUNGARIAN—Horn, E. I.; Kautz, G.; Kovács, G.; Láng, L.; Matlekovits, S.

IRISH—Butt, I.; Cairnes, J. E.; Hancock, W. N.; Ingram, J. K.; Leslie, T. E. C.; Longfield, S. M.; Thompson, W.

ITALIAN—Agazzini, M.; Antonino, St.; Aquinas, T.; Augustinis, M. de; Bandini, S. A.; Barone, E.; Beccaria, C. B.; Bianchini, L.; Boccardo, G.; Bocchi, R.; Botero, G.; Broggia, C. A.; Carli, G. R.; Conigliani, C. A.; Cossa, E.; Cossa, L.; Custodi, P.; Cusumano, V.; Davanzati, B.; De Cesare, C.; Fabbroni, G.; Ferrara, F.; Ferraris, C. F.; Fuoco, F.; Galiani, F.; Genovesi, A.; Gianni, F. M.; Gioia, M.; Lampertico, F.; Martello, T.; Mazzola, U.; Messedaglia, A.; Montanari, G.; Neri, Pompeo; Ortes, G.; Palmieri, G.; Pantaleoni, M.; Pareto, V.; Pascoli, L.; Prato, G.; Ricca-Salerno, G.; Roncali, A.; Rossi, P. L. E.; Scaruffi, G.; Scialoja, A.; Serra, A.; Supino, C.; Valenti, G.; Vasco, G.; Verri, P.

NORWEGIAN—Aarum, P. T.; Ascheoug, T. H.; Einarsen, E.; Hertzberg, E. C. H.; Schweigaard, A. M.

POLISH—Biliński, L.; Cieszkowski, A.; Czerkawski, W.; Lewiński, J. S.; Luxemburg, R.; Popławski, A.; Skarbek, F. F.; Strojnowski, H.; Supiński, J.

PORTUGUESE—Ferreira Borges, J.

ROMAN—Augustine.

RUSSIAN—Bunge, N. C.; Chuprov, A. I.; Dmitriev, V. K.; Hertzenstein, M. Y.; Kablukov, N. A.; Kankrin, E. F.; Karishev, N. A.; Ludogovsky, A. P.; Manuilov, A. A.; Orzhentsky, R. M.; Pososhkov, I. T.; Storch, H. F. von; Tugan-Baranovsky, M. I.; Turgenev, N. I.; Vorontsov, V. P.; Yanzhul, I. I.

SOUTH AFRICAN—Lehfeldt, R. A.

SPANISH—Anzano, T. de; Arriquibar, N. de; Campillo y Cossio, J.; Campomanes, P. R.; Canga Argüelles, J.; Cantos y Benitez, P. de; Carranza, A.; Castro, J. de; Centani, F.; Dormer, D. J.; Ezpeleta, P. A. de; Fernández Navarrete, P.; Flórez Estrada, A.; González de Cellorigo, M.; Güell y Ferrer, J.; Jovellanos, G. M. de; Mariana, J. de; Martínez de la Mata, F.; Moncada, S. de; Ulloa, B. de; Uztáriz, J. de.

SWEDISH—Berch, A.; Chydenius, A.; Wicksell, K.

SWISS—Cherbuliez, A. É.; Herrenschwand, J.; Iselin, I.; Sismondi, J. C. L. S. de.

See also Classification of Articles (Biographical Titles), HISTORY (ECONOMIC) (*p.* 562), STATISTICS (*p.* 571); (Abstract Titles), ECONOMICS (*p.* 550), PUBLIC FINANCE (*p.* 554), STATISTICS (*p.* 556).

Education

AMERICAN—Alcott A. B.; Andrews, E. B.; Angell, J. B.; Armstrong, S. C.; Aycock, C. B.; Barnard, H.; Blow, S. E.; Carter, J. G.; Cooper, T. (d. 1839); Davidson, T.; Douai, A.; Eliot, C. W.; Fernald, W. E.; Gilman, D. C.; Hall, G. S.; Harris, W. T.; Holbrook, J.; Johnson, J. F.; Knapp, S. A.; Lyon, M.; Mann, H.; Parker, F. W.; Peabody, E. P.; Rush, B.; White, A. D.; Willard, E. H.

ARMENIAN—Abovian, K.

AUSTRALIAN—Pearson, C. H.

BOHEMIAN—Comenius, J. A.

BRITISH—Anson, W. R.; Arnold, T.; Ascham, R.; Bacon, F.; Bain, A.; Bell, A.; Birkbeck, G.; Bray, T.; Davies, E.; Duff, A.; Forster, W. E.; Jowett, B.; Kay-Shuttleworth, J.; Lancaster, J.; Locke, J.; Maurice, F. D.; Mulcaster, R.; Raikes, R.

CANADIAN—Dawson, J. W.

DANISH—Grundtvig, N. F. S.

FRENCH—Alcuin; Boutmy, É. G.; Braille, L.; Bréal, M.; Compayré, G.; Demolins, E.; Duruy, J. V.; Fénelon, F. de S. de la M.; Ferry, J. F. C.; La Salle, J. B. de; Lemonnier, É.

GERMAN—Altenstein, K.; Andreae, J. V.; Basedow, J. B.; Beneke, F. E.; Bonitz, H.; Bugenhagen, J.; Diesterweg, F. A. W.; Dörpfeld, F. W.; Ernest I; Francke, A. H.; Fröbel, F.; Gaudig, H.; Gesner, J. M.; Hecker, J. J.; Herbart, J. F.; Humboldt, F. W. von; Jahn, F. L.; Lange, H.; Lietz, H.; Melanchthon, P.; Natorp, P.; Paulsen, F.; Rabanus Maurus, M.; Ratke, W.

HUNGARIAN—Brunswick, T.; Kármán, M.

INDIAN—Ramabai, P.; Sayyid Ahmad Khan.

IRISH—Edgeworth, R. L.

ITALIAN—Angiulli, A.; Aporti, F.; Bosco, G.; Capponi, G. A.; De Sanctis, F.; Vittorino da Feltre.

JAPANESE—Fukuzawa, Y.

LATIN AMERICAN—Gutiérrez, J. M.; Hostos, E. M. de.

NORWEGIAN—Bruun, C. A.

POLISH—Konarski, S.; Popławski, A.

For complete list of headings used in Classification of Articles see page 547.

Classification of Articles (Biographical Titles)

PORTUGUESE—Costa Ferreira, A. A. da.

RUMANIAN—Haret, S.; Lazăr, G.

RUSSIAN—Betsky, I. I.; Filosofova, A. P.; Manuilov, A. A.; Uvarov, S. S.

SERBIAN—Obradović, D.

SPANISH—Giner de los Ríos, F.; Jovellanos, G. M. de; Vives, J. L.

SWISS—Fellenberg, P. E. von; Girard, J.-B.; Pestalozzi, J. H.

See also Classification of Articles (Abstract Titles), EDUCATION (*p.* 550).

Feminism

AMERICAN—Anthony, S. B.; Fuller, S. M.; Howe, J. W.; Lockwood, B. A. B.; Mott, L.; Sewall, M. W.; Shaw, A. H.; Spencer, A. G.; Stanton, E. C.; Stone, L.; Woodhull, V. C.

BRITISH—Anderson, E. G.; Blackwell, E.; Bodichon, B. L. S.; Butler, J.; Davies, E.; Fawcett, M. G.; Jameson, A. B.; Jex-Blake, S.; Macarthur, M. R.; Pankhurst, E. G.; Paterson, E.; Wollstonecraft, M.

EGYPTIAN—Kasim Amin.

FRENCH—Auclert, H.; Deraismes, M.; Deroin, J.; Gouges, O. de; Pisan, C. de; Tristan, F. C. T. H.

GERMAN—Braun, L.; Cauer, M.; Dohm, H.; Guillaume-Schack, G.; Lange, H.; Otto-Peters, L.; Schirmacher, K.; Schmidt, A.; Zetkin, C.

INDIAN—Ramabai, P.; Ranade, M. G.

NORWEGIAN—Collett, C.

RUSSIAN—Filosofova, A. P.

SOUTH AFRICAN—Schreiner, O. E. A.

SPANISH—Arenal, C.

SWEDISH—Bremer, F.; Key, E.

See also Classification of Articles (Abstract Titles), MARRIAGE AND THE FAMILY (*p.* 553).

Financial Administration

AMERICAN—Biddle, N.; Gallatin, A.; Hamilton, A.; Morris, R.

AUSTRIAN—Böhm-Bawerk, Eugen von.

BRITISH—Burlamachi, P.; Gladstone, W. E.; Grenville, G.; Gresham, T.; Huskisson, W.; Liverpool, Lord; Montagu, C.

CANADIAN—Fielding, W. S.

CZECHOSLOVAK—Rašín, A.

FRENCH—Cambon, P. J.; Colbert, J.-B.; Gaudin, M. M. C.; Law, J.; Necker, J.; Say, L.; Sully, Duc de; Turgot, R. J.

GERMAN—Bamberger, L.; Erzberger, M.; Graumann, J. P.; Helfferich, H.; Nebenius, K. F.; Peutinger, K.

ITALIAN—Palmieri, G.

POLISH—Lubecki, F. X.

RUSSIAN—Bunge, N. C.; Kankrin, E. F.; Witte, S. Y.

SPANISH—Canga Argüelles, J.

TURKISH—Javid, M.

See also Classification of Articles (Biographical Titles), STATECRAFT (*p.* 569); (Abstract Titles), GOVERNMENT (*p.* 551), PUBLIC FINANCE (*p.* 554), TARIFF (*p.* 556), TAXATION (*p.* 556).

Geography

AMERICAN—Semple, E. C.

FRENCH—Ailly, P. d'; Champlain, S. de; Reclus, J. É.; Vidal de la Blache, P. M. J.

GERMAN—Büsching, A. F.; Humboldt, A. von; Peschel, O.; Ratzel, F.; Ritter, K.

ITALIAN—Balbi, A.

MOSLEM—Idrīsi, al-; Yāqūt.

PORTUGUESE—Henry the Navigator.

History

AMERICAN—Abbott, F. F.; Adams, C. F. (d. 1915); Adams, G. B.; Adams, H.; Adams, H. B.; Alvord, C. W.; Bancroft, G.; Bancroft, H. H.; Bassett, J. S.; Beer, G. L.; Beveridge, A. J.; Bourne, E. G.; Dunning, W. A.; Eggleston, E.; Fiske, J.; Gross, C.; Hildreth, R.; Holst, H. E. von; Howard, G. E.; Latané, J. H.; Lea, H. C.; Luckenbill, D. D.; McMaster, J. B.; Mahan, A. T.; Motley, J. L.; Osgood, H. L.; Parkman, F.; Parrington, V. L.; Pitkin, T.; Prescott, W. H.; Rhodes, J. F.; Schouler, J.; Sparks, J.; Thayer, W. R.; Tucker, G.; Turner, F. J.; Tyler, M. C.; White, A. D.

ARGENTINE—Bunge, C. O.; Groussac, P.; Gutiérrez, J. M.; López, V. F.; Mitre, B.

AUSTRIAN—Hammer-Purgstall, J. von; Hartmann, L. M.; Hoernes, M.; Jireček, J. K.; Kremer, A. von.

BELGIAN—Vanderkindere, L.

BRITISH—Abrahams, I.; Acton, Lord; Alison, A.; Bateson, M.; Bede; Bryce, J.; Buckle, H. T.; Burnet, G.; Bury, J. B.; Camden, W.; Carlyle, T.; Cramb, J. A.; Dill, S.; Egerton, H. E.; Figgis, J. N.; Finlay, G.; Flint, R.; Fowler, W. W.; Freeman, E. A.; Froissart, J.; Froude, J. A.; Gardiner, S. R.; Gibbon, E.; Gomme, G. L.; Green, J. R.; Grote, G.; Hallam, H.; Haverfield, F. J.; Hume, D.; Hunter, W. W.; Jacobs, J.; Kemble, J. M.; King, L. W.; Lingard, J.; Lucas, C. P.; Macaulay, Lord; Madox, T.; Palgrave, F.; Paris, M.; Pearson, C. H.; Robertson, W.; Round, J. H.; Seeley, J. R.; Smith, G.; Stephens, H. M.; Stubbs, W.; Symonds, J. A.; Tout, T. F.; Trevelyan, G. O.

BULGARIAN—Drinov, M. S.; Paisii of Khilendar.

BYZANTINE—Psellos, M.

CANADIAN—Bourinot, J. G.; Garneau, F. X.

CHILEAN—Lastarria, J. V.; Letelier, V.

CHINESE—Chang Hsüeh-Ch'eng; Cheng Ch'iao; Ku Yen-Wu; Ssŭ-ma Ch'ien; Ssŭ-ma Kuang.

CROATIAN—Rački, F.

CUBAN—Bachiller y Morales, Antonio.

CZECH-SLOVAK—Palacký, F.; Šafařík, P. J.; Tomek, V. V.

DANISH—Erslev, K.; Holberg, L.; Rubin, M.

DUTCH—Beaufort, Louis de; Blok, P. J.; Dozy, R. P. A.; Fruin, R. J.

FRENCH—Aulard, F. V. A.; Basnage, J. C.; Boissier, G.; Boulainvilliers, H.; Champollion, J. F.; Chuquet, A. M.; Clément, J.-P.; Clermont-Ganneau, C.; Cochin, A.; Commines, P. de; De Brosses, C.; Delisle, L. V.; Denis, E.; Dubos, J. B.; Du Cange, C. du F.; Duruy, J. V.; Flach, J.; Fréret, N.; Fustel de Coulanges, N.-D.; Gebhart, N. É.; Giry, A.; Guérard, B.; Guillaume, J.; Guiraud, P.; Guizot, F. P. G.; Houssaye, H.; Jubainville, H. d'A. de; Lacombe, P.; Langlois, C. V.; Lavisse, E.; Luchaire, A.; Mabillon, J.; Martin, B.-L.-H.; Maspero, G. C. C.; Masson, F.; Mathiez, A.; Michelet, J.; Mignet, F. A. M. A.; Monod, G. J. J.; Ozanam, F.; Rambaud, A.; Raynal, G. T. F.; Reinach, T.; Rougé, O. C. E. de; Sorel, A.; Taine, H.-A.; Thierry, J.-N.-A.; Thiers, L. A.; Thomas, A. A.; Thou, J. A. de; Vandal, A.; Voltaire, F.-M. A. de.

GERMAN—Adelung, J. C.; Anton, K. G. von; Arndt, E. M.; Barth,

P.; Beloch, K. J.; Berliner, A.; Bezold, F. von; Biedermann, F. K.; Böckh, A.; Chamberlain, H. S.; Curtius, E.; Dahlmann, F. C.; Delbrück, H.; Delitzsch, F.; Droysen, J. G.; Duncker, M. W.; Ebert, M.; Ewers, J. P. G. von; Fallmerayer, J. P.; Freytag, G.; Friedländer, L.; Gervinus, G. G.; Gothein, E.; Graetz, H.; Grosse, E.; Güdemann, M.; Häusser, L.; Haxthausen, A. von; Haym, R.; Heeren, A. H. L.; Hegel, G. W. F.; Hegel, K.; Herder, J. G. von; Hirschfeld, O.; Hirth, F.; Janssen, J.; Jost, I. M.; Krumbacher, K.; Lamprecht, K.; Leo, H.; Lepsius, K. R.; Lippert, J.; Luden, H.; Marquardt, K. J.; Mascov, J. J.; Maurer, G. L. von; Mehring, F.; Meyer, E.; Mommsen, T.; Möser, J.; Müller, K. O.; Niebuhr, B. G.; Nitzsch, K. W.; Nöldeke, T.; Oncken, W.; Otto of Freising; Pertz, G. H.; Pöhlmann, R. von; Pufendorf, S. von; Rachfahl, F.; Ranke, L. von; Riehl, W. H.; Ritter, M.; Rotteck, K. W. R. von; Schäfer, D.; Schlosser, F. C.; Schlözer, A. L. von; Schrader, E.; Seeck, O.; Sickel, T.; Spittler, L. T.; Steinhausen, G.; Sybel, H. von; Treitschke, H. von; Troeltsch, E.; Waitz, G.; Wilamowitz-Moellendorff, U. von; Winckelmann, J. J.; Wolf, F. A.

GREEK (ANCIENT)—Herodotus of Halicarnassus; Plutarch; Polybius; Thucydides; Xenophon.

HUNGARIAN—Horváth, M.; Kállay, B.; Tagányi, K.

INDIAN—Abul Fazl Allami.

IRISH—Lecky, W. E. H.; Mahaffy, J. P.; Ridgeway, W.

ITALIAN—Amari, M.; Balbo, C.; Capponi, G. A.; Cuoco, V.; Ferrari, G.; Giannone, P.; Guicciardini, F.; Muratori, L. A.; Rossi, G. B. de; Ruffini, F.; Vico, G. B.; Villari, P.

MEXICAN—Ixtlilxóchitl, F. de A.

MOSLEM—Ibn-Khaldūn; Maqrīzi, al-; Mas'ūdi, al-; Miskawayhi, Abū 'Ali Ahmad.

NORWEGIAN—Keyser, R. J.; Munch, P. A.; Sars, J. E. W.

POLISH—Długosz, J.; Krochmal, N.; Lelewel, J.

PORTUGUESE—Barros, João de; Gama Barros, H. de; Herculano de Carvalho e Araujo, A.; Oliveira Martins, J. P. de.

ROMAN—Josephus; Livy; Tacitus.

RUMANIAN—Kogălniceanu, M.; Xenopol, A.

RUSSIAN—Aksakov, K.; Antonovich, V. B.; Ardashev, P. N.; Beliayev, I. D.; Bestuzhev-Riumin, K. N.; Bunge, F. G. von; Dyakonov, M. A.; Granovsky, T. N.; Karamzin, N. M.; Kareyev, N. I.; Kluchevsky, V. O.; Kovalevsky, M. M.; Lappo-Danilevsky, A. S.; Luchitsky, I. V.; Pavlov-Silvansky, N. P.; Pogodin, M. P.; Pokrovsky, M. N.; Savin, A. N.; Semevsky, V. I.; Shchapov, A. P.; Shcherbatov, M. M.; Solovyev, S. M.; Tatishchev, V. N.; Uspensky, F. I.; Vasilevsky, V. G.

SPANISH—Cánovas del Castillo, A.; Lafuente y Zamalloa, M.; Llorente, J. A.; Mariana, J. de; Masdeu, J. F.; Menéndez y Pelayo, M.; Morales, A. de.

SWEDISH—Geijer, E. G.; Hjärne, H.; Malmström, C. G.

SWISS—Burckhardt, J. C.; Fueter, E.; Müller, J. von; Sismondi, J. C. L. S. de.

UKRAINIAN—Kostomarov, N. I.; Lipinsky, V.

See also Classification of Articles (Biographical Titles), HISTORY (ECONOMIC) (*p.* 562), HISTORY (LEGAL) (*p.* 562), HISTORY (RELIGIOUS) (*p.* 562).

History (Economic)

AMERICAN—Callender, G. S.

AUSTRIAN—Inama-Sternegg, K. T. von.

BRITISH—Ashley, W. J.; Cunningham, W.; Gibbins, H. de B.; Knowles, L. C. A.; Rogers, J. E. T.; Seebohm, F.; Toynbee, A.; Unwin, G.; Vinogradoff, P.

CANADIAN—Mavor, J.

DUTCH—Nieboer, H. J.

FRENCH—Babelon, E.; Budé, G.; Levasseur, P. É.

GERMAN—Arnold, W.; Below, G. A. H. von; Büsching, A. F.; Ehrenberg, R.; Hanssen, G.; Hasbach, W.; Heyd, W. von; Meitzen, A.; Schmoller, G. von; Schönberg, G. F. von; Soetbeer, A. G.

HUNGARIAN—Acsády, Ignac; Tagányi, K.

ITALIAN—Cognetti de Martiis, S.; Prato, G.; Salvioli, G.

RUSSIAN—Danielson, N. F.; Efimenko, A. Y.; Luchitsky, I. V.

SPANISH—Colmeiro, M.

See also Classification of Articles (Biographical Titles), ECONOMICS (*p.* 559), HISTORY (*p.* 561), HISTORY (LEGAL) (*p.* 562); (Abstract Titles), ECONOMICS (*p.* 550).

History (Legal)

AMERICAN—Smith, E. M.

BRITISH—Maine, H. J. S.; Maitland, F. W.; Vinogradoff, P.

CROATIAN—Mažuranić, V.

CZECH—Kadlec, K.

FRENCH—Brissaud, J. B.; Chénon, É.; Esmein, A.; Girard, P. F.; Glasson, E. D.; Jubainville, H. d'A. de; Viollet, P.

GERMAN—Brunner, H.; Dahn, F. L. S.; Eichhorn, K. F.; Ficker, C. J. von; Fitting, H. H.; Liebermann, F.; Lipsius, J. H.; Maurer, K. von; Savigny, F. C. von; Schröder, R.; Seckel, E.

ITALIAN—Gaudenzi, A.; Sclopis di Salerano, F.

NORWEGIAN—Hertzberg, E. C. H.

POLISH—Maciejowski, W. A.

RUSSIAN—Leontovich, F. I.; Sergeyevich, V. I.; Vladimirsky-Budanov, M. F.

SPANISH—Cárdenas, F. de; Hinojosa y Naveros, E. de; Martínez Marina, F.

See also Classification of Articles (Biographical Titles), HISTORY (*p.* 561), HISTORY (ECONOMIC) (*p.* 562), LAW (*p.* 563); (Abstract Titles), JURISPRUDENCE (*p.* 552).

History (Religious)

AMERICAN—Jastrow, M.; Schaff, P.

AUSTRIAN—Denifle, H. S.

BELGIAN—Goblet d'Alviella, E. F. A.

BRITISH—Creighton, M.; Davids, T. W. R.; Harrison, J. E.; Müller, F. M.; Robertson, J. M.; Smith, W. R.

DUTCH—Kuenen, Abraham; Tiele, C. P.

FRENCH—Batiffol, P.; De Brosses, C.; Duchesne, L. M. O.; Montalembert, Comte de; Reinach, S.; Renan, E.; Sabatier, P.

GERMAN—Baur, F. C.; Döllinger, I. von; Funk, F. X. von; Gieseler, J. K. L.; Harnack, A. von; Hauck, A.; Hefele, K. J. von; Hegel, G. W. F.; Hergenröther, J.; Kraus, F. X.; Magdeburg Centuriators; Möhler, J. A.; Mosheim, J. L.; Neander, A.; Pastor, L. von; Planck, G. J.; Reimarus, H. S.; Rohde, E.; Sleidan, J.; Spittler, L. T.; Strauss, D. F.; Troeltsch, E.; Usener, H.; Wellhausen, J.; Zunz, L.

HUNGARIAN—Goldziher, I.

ITALIAN—Baronius, C.; Sarpi, P.

For complete list of headings used in Classification of Articles see page 547.

Classification of Articles (Biographical Titles)

ROMAN—Eusebius of Caesarea.

See also Classification of Articles (Biographical Titles), HISTORY (p. 561), JEWISH PROBLEMS AND JUDAISM (p. 563), RELIGION (p. 567); (Abstract Titles), RELIGION (p. 555).

Jewish Problems and Judaism

Aaronson, A.; Abrahams, I.; Basnage, J. C.; Berliner, A.; Bernstein, A.; Boruchov, B.; Crémieux, A. I. M.; Frankel, Z.; Geiger, A.; Ginsberg, A.; Gordon, A. D.; Graetz, H.; Güdemann, M.; Herzl, T.; Hess, M.; Hirsch, M. de; Holdheim, S.; Horn, E. I.; Jacobs, J.; Jastrow, M.; Josephus; Jost, I. M.; Karo, J. ben E.; Krochmal, N.; Liebermann, A. S.; Lilienblum, M. L.; Maimonides, M.; Marshall, L.; Medem, W.; Melchett, Lord; Mendelssohn, M.; Montefiore, M.; Nordau (Südfeld), M. S.; Philippson, L.; Philo Judaeus; Pinsker, J. L.; Riesser, G.; Schechter, S.; Schiff, J. H.; Straus, N.; Syrkin, N.; Wise, I. M.; Zangwill, I.; Zunz, L.

See also Classification of Articles (Biographical Titles), HISTORY (RELIGIOUS) (p. 562); (Abstract Titles), RELIGION (p. 555).

Journalism

AMERICAN—Abell, A. S.; Atkinson, Wilmer; Barron, C. W.; Bennett, J. G. (d. 1872) and J. G. (d. 1918); Blair, F. P.; Bok, E. W.; Bowles Family; Bryant, W. C.; Cameron, A. C.; Cobb, F. I.; Dana, C. A.; De Bow, J. D. B.; Dunbar, C. F.; Evans, G. H.; Freneau, P. M.; Gales, J., Jr.; Godkin, E. L.; Greeley, H.; Harvey, G. B. McC.; Hunt, F.; Judd, O.; Munsey, F. A.; Niles, H.; Pulitzer, J.; Raymond, H. J.; Reid, W.; Scripps, E. W.; Skinner, J. S.; Stone, M. E.; Swinton, J.; Wallace, H. and H. C.

AUSTRIAN—Friedländer, M.

BRITISH—Addison, J.; Baines, E. (d. 1848) and Baines, E. (d. 1890); Borthwick, A.; Cobbett, W.; Defoe, D.; Delane, J. T.; Hetherington, H.; Levy Lawson Family; Massingham, H. W.; Northcliffe, Lord; Reuter, P. J. von; Scott, C. P.; Stead, W. T.; Steele, R.; Strachey, J. St. L.; Walter Family.

CANADIAN—Brown, G.

CZECH—Havlíček, K.

FRENCH—Bertin, L. F.; Clunet, É.; Desmoulins, C.; Fréron, É. C.; Girardin, É. de; Hébert, J. R.; Renaudot, T.

GERMAN—Bachem, Josef and Julius; Bernstein, A.; Cotta, J. F.; Dumont Family; Faber Family; Francke, E.; Görres, J. von; Philippson, L.; Sonnemann, L.; Ullstein Family.

RUSSIAN—Katkov, M. N.

See also Classification of Articles (Abstract Titles), LITERATURE AND THE PRESS (p. 553).

Labor

AMERICAN—Arthur, P. M.; Bagley, S.; Barondess, J.; Buchanan, J. R.; Cameron, A. C.; Debs, E. V.; De Leon, D.; Garretson, A. B.; Gompers, S.; Haywood, W. D.; Hoxie, R. F.; Jones, M.; Kearney, D.; McNeill, G. E.; Mitchell, J.; Most, J.; Parsons, A. R.; Powderly, T. V.; Schlesinger, B.; Sigman, M.; Siney, J.; Sörge, F. A.; Stephens, U. S.; Steward, I.; Stone, W. S.; Swinton, J.; Sylvis, W. H.; Weydemeyer, J.; Wright, C. D.

AUSTRALIAN—Lane, W.; Spence, W. G.

BRITISH—Allan, W.; Anderson, W. C.; Applegarth, R.; Arch, J.; Aves, E.; Benbow, W.; Bray, J. F.; Broadhurst, H.; Burnett, J.; Burt, T.; Campbell, A.; Cremer, W. R.; Doherty, J.; Dunning, T. J.; Hardie, J. K.; Hetherington, H.; Howell, G.; Jones, L.; Lovett, W.; Ludlow, J. M.; MacArthur, M. R.; MacDonald, A.; Morrison, J. (d. 1835); Odger, G.; Owen and Owenism; Paterson, E.; Place, F.; Potter, G.; Schloss, D. F.; Watson, J.; Wilson, J. H.

CROATIAN—Bukšeg, V.

FRENCH—Barberet, J.-J.; Griffuelhes, V.; Keufer, A.; Merrheim, A.; Pelloutier, F.-L.-É.; Thomas, A. A.; Tristan, F. C. T. H.; Varlin, L. E.

GERMAN—Born, S.; Duncker, F. G.; Elm, A. von; Hirsch, M.; Hué, O.; Ihrer, E.; Lange, F. A.; Legien, C.

IRISH—O'Brien, J.

ITALIAN—Lazzari, C.

NORWEGIAN—Thrane, M. M.

See also Classification of Articles (Biographical Titles), SOCIALISM (p. 569); (Abstract Titles), LABOR (p. 552), SOCIALISM (p. 556).

Law

AMERICAN—Ames, J. B.; Baker, H. H.; Benjamin, J. P.; Briesen, A. v.; Carter, J. C.; Cooley, T. McI.; Cushing, C.; Dillon, J. F.; Ellsworth, O.; Field, D. D.; Gibson, J. B.; Gray, J. C.; Hohfeld, W. N.; Kent, J.; Langdell, C. C.; Livingston, E.; Livingston, R. R.; Marshall, J.; Mitchell, W.; Olney, R.; Pomeroy, J. N.; Shaw, L.; Story, J.; Taney, R. B.; Thayer, J. B.; Wheaton, H.; Wilson, J.; Wythe, G.

ARGENTINE—Alberdi, J. B.; Bunge, C. O.; Calvo, C.

AUSTRALIAN—Griffith, S. W.; Higgins, H. B.

AUSTRIAN—Ehrlich, E.; Glaser, J.; Klein, F.; Lammasch, H.; Menger, A.; Unger, J.

BELGIAN—Thonissen, J. J.

BRAZILIAN—Barbosa, R.

BRITISH—Amos, S.; Anson, W. R.; Atkyns, R.; Austin, J.; Bentham, J.; Blackstone, W.; Bracton, H. de; Campbell, J.; Coke, E.; Dicey, A. V.; Eldon, Lord; Ellesmere, Lord; Erskine, Lord; Fortescue, J.; Glanvill, R. de; Hale, M.; Hall, W. E.; Hardwicke, Lord; Harrison, F.; Holland, T. E.; Holt, J.; Ilbert, C. P.; Jessel, G.; Jenkins, L.; Lambarde, W.; Lanfranc; Levi, L.; Littleton, T. de; Lorimer, J.; Maitland, F. W.; Mansfield, Lord; Nottingham, Lord; Oppenheim, L. F. L.; Romilly, S.; Selborne, Lord; Selden, J.; Stephen, J. F.; Stowell, Lord; Vacarius; Westlake, J.; Zouche, R.

CANADIAN—Blake, E.; Denison, G. T.; Lefroy, A. H. F.

CROATIAN—Bogišić, V. A.

DANISH—Goos, C.; Hübner, M.

DUTCH—Bynkershoek, C. van; Grotius, H.; Huber, U.; Jitta, D. J.; Leeuwen, S. V.

FRENCH—Acollas, É.; Argentré, B. d'; Aucoc, J. L.; Baudouin, F.; Beaumanoir, Sire de; Boutillier, J.; Budé, G.; Cambacérès, J. J. R. de; Charmont, J.; Clunet, É.; Coquille, G.; Cujas, J.; Daguesseau, H.-F.; Demolombe, J. C. F.; Domat, J.; Doneau, H.; Douaren, F. le; Duguit, L.; Dumoulin, C.; Durand, G.; Fauchille, P.; Favre, A.; Girard, P. F.; Glasson, E. D.; Godefroy, D. and J.; Hauriou, M.; Hotman, F.; Laferrière, É. L. J.; Lainé, A.; Lamoignon, G. de; Loisel, A.; Loyseau, C.; Pillet, A.; Portalis, J. É. M.; Pothier, R.-J.; Renault, L.; Saleilles, R.; Tronchet, F.-D.; Weiss, A.; Yves of Chartres.

GERMAN—Ahrens, H.; Andlo, P. of; Bähr, O.; Bar, K. L. von; Bekker, E. I.; Bergbohm, K. M.; Berner, A. F.; Beseler, K. G. C.; Beyer, G.; Bierling, E. R.; Binding, K.; Birkmeyer, K. von;

For complete list of headings used in Classification of Articles see page 547.

Bluntschli, J. K.; Brinz, A. von; Bruns, K. G.; Bulmerincq, A. von; Bülow, O.; Burchard of Worms; Carpzov, B.; Cocceji, H. von; Cocceji, S. von; Cohn, G. L.; Conrat(Cohn), M.; Conring, H.; Dahn, F. L. S.; Degenkolb, H.; Dernburg, H.; Ehrenberg, V.; Eichhorn, K. F.; Eisele, F.; Endemann, W.; Feuerbach, P. J. A. von; Friedberg, E. A.; Fuchs, E.; Gans, E.; Gerber, K. F. W. von; Gierke, O. von; Gneist, R. von; Goldschmidt, L.; Grolman, K. von; Haloander, G.; Hälschner, H.; Hänel, A.; Heffter, A. W.; Heineccius, J. G.; Henry of Langenstein; Hinschius, P.; Holtzendorff, F. von; Homeyer, K. G.; Hugo, G.; Jellinek, G.; Jhering, R. von; Kahl, W.; Kaskel, W.; Kirchmann, J. H. von; Kohler, J.; Kreittmayr, Baron von; Krueger, P.; Laband, P.; Leist, B. W.; Leonhard, R. K. G.; Liszt, F. E. von; Martens, G. F. von; Maurer, G. L. von; Mayer, M. E.; Mayer, O.; Merkel, A. J.; Mitteis, L.; Mittermaier, K. J. A.; Mohl, R. von; Mommsen, T.; Moser, J. J.; Osse, M. von; Planck, G.; Planck, J. J. W. von; Post, A. H.; Puchta, G. F.; Pufendorf, S. von; Pütter, J. S.; Rachel, S.; Repgow, E. von; Savigny, F. C. von; Schwarzenberg, J. von; Seydel, M. von; Sohm, R.; Struve, G. A.; Suarez, K. G.; Thibaut, A. F. J.; Thöl, J. H.; Thomasius, C.; Wach, A.; Windscheid, B.; Zachariae von Lingenthal, K.-E.; Zachariae von Lingenthal, K. S.; Zitelmann, E.; Zorn, P.

GREEK (ANCIENT)—Draco; Solon.

HINDU—Jīmūtavāhana; Nārada; Vijnaneṣvāra.

HUNGARIAN—Pulszky, Á.; Verbőczy, I.

ITALIAN—Accursius; Alciati, A.; Andreae, J.; Azo; Azuni; Baldus, P.; Bartolus of Sassoferrato; Carle, G.; Carmignani, G.; Carrara, F.; Chironi, G.; Cino da Pistoia; Ferraris, C. F.; Ferrini, C.; Fiore, P.; Four Doctors; Gentili, A.; Gratian; Gravina, G.; Irnerius; Lampredi, G. M.; Mancini, P. S.; Pessina, E.; Peter Lombard; Placentinus; Raymond de Pennafort; Romagnosi, G. D.; Rossi, P. L. E.; Ruffini, F.; Sclopis di Salerano, F.; Stracca di Ancona, B.

JEWISH—Frankel, Z.; Karo, J. ben E.; Maimonides, M.

MOSLEM—Dā'ūd al-Zāhiri; Ibn-Ḥanbal; Ibn-Taymīya; Mālik ibn-Anas; Māwardi, al-; Shāfi'i, al-.

NEW ZEALAND—Swainson, W.

POLISH—Hube, R.; Jaworski, W. L.; Spasowicz, W.

PORTUGUESE—Ferreira Borges, J.; Gouvea, A. de; Mello Freire, P. J. de.

ROMAN—Gaius; Julianus; Papinianus; Paulus; Tertullian; Ulpian.

RUSSIAN—Bunge, F. G. von; Goldenweiser, A. S.; Kistyakovsky, B. A.; Korkunov, N. M.; Martens, F. F.; Petrazhitsky, L. I.; Pobedonostsev, K. P.; Speransky, M. M.

SERBIAN—Stefan Dušan.

SOUTH AFRICAN—Villiers, J. H. de.

SPANISH—Agustín, A.; Alfonso x; Antequera, J. M.; Ayala, B.; Azcárate, G. de; Costa y Martinez, J.; Covarrubias y Leiva, D.; Dato e Iradier, E.; Dorado Montero, P.; Duran y Bas, M.; Fontanella, J. P.; López de Palacios Rubios, J.; Soto, D. de; Suárez, F.; Vitoria, F. de.

SWEDISH—Cronhielm, G.

SWISS—Burlamaqui, J. J.; Heusler, A.; Huber, E.; Keller, F. L.; Rivier, A.-P.-O.; Vattel, E. de.

See also Classification of Articles (Biographical Titles), HISTORY (LEGAL) (*p.* 562); (Abstract Titles), ADMINISTRATION OF JUSTICE (*p.* 548), JURISPRUDENCE (*p.* 552), LEGAL RELATIONS (*p.* 553), LEGISLATION (*p.* 553).

Literature and Social Criticism

AMERICAN—Bellamy, E.; Bourne, R. S.; Bryant, W. C.; Crèvecoeur, M.-G. J. de; Croly, H.; Curtis, G. W.; Eggleston, E.; Emerson, R. W.; Freneau, P. M.; Fuller, S. M.; Gleason, A. H.; Godkin, E. L.; Hay, J. M.; Helper, H. R.; Hildreth, R.; Howe, J. W.; Parrington, V. L.; Lowell, J. R.; Stowe, H. B.; Thoreau, H. D.; Weyl, W. E.; Whitman, W.

ARMENIAN—Abovian, K.; Arzruni, G.

BRITISH—Addison, J.; Arnold, M.; Bagehot, W.; Beaconsfield, Lord; Blunt, W. S.; Bodley, J. E. C.; Butler, S.; Byron, Lord; Carlyle, T.; Coleridge, S. T.; De Quincey, T.; Dickens, C.; Dryden, J.; Eliot, G.; Harrison, F.; Hazlitt, W.; Hughes, T.; Johnson, S.; Kingsley, C.; Lang, A.; Langland, W.; Mallock, W. H.; Mandeville, B. de; Milton, J.; More, H.; More, T.; Morley, J.; Morris, W.; Ruskin, J.; Scott, W.; Shelley, P. B.; Smith, G.; Southey, R.; Stephen, L.; Swift, J.; Symonds, J. A.; Wordsworth, W.; Zangwill, I.

CANADIAN—Mavor, J.

CZECH-SLOVAK—Kollár, J.

DANISH—Brandes, G. M. C.; Grundtvig, N. F. S.; Holberg, L.

DUTCH—Douwes Dekker, E.; Erasmus, D.

FRENCH—About, E.; Barrès, M.; Beaumarchais, P. A. C. de; Brunetière, F.; Chateaubriand, F. A. R.; Déroulède, P.; Diderot, D.; Dubos, J. B.; Finot, J.; Fontenelle, B. le B. de; France, A.; Fréron, É. C.; Hugo, V.-M.; La Boétie, É. de; Lamartine, A. M. L. de P. de; Mirabeau, Marquis de; Pisan, C. de; Quinet, E.; Rabelais, F.; Sainte-Beuve, C. A.; Saint-Simon, Duc de; Sand, G.; Staël-Holstein, A. L. G. N. de; Taine, H.-A.; Veuillot, L.; Voltaire, F.-M. A. de; Zola, É.

GERMAN—Börne, L.; Freytag, G.; Goethe, J. W.; Heine, H.; Herder, J. G. von; Lessing, G. E.; Moser, F. K. von; Möser, J.; Novalis; Otto-Peters, L.; Richter, J. P. F.; Schiller, J. C. F.; Schlegel, K. W. F. von *and* A. W. von.

GREEK (ANCIENT)—Aristophanes; Euhemeros; Euripides; Lucian; Plutarch; Xenophon.

GREEK (MODERN)—Koraes, A.; Rhigas, K.

HUNGARIAN—Vámbéry, A.

INDIAN—Malabari, B. M.

ITALIAN—Alfieri, V.; Boccalini, T.; Bruni, L.; Carducci, G.; Cattaneo, C.; Colajanni, N.; Dante Alighieri; Delfico, M.; De Sanctis, F.; Giusti, G.; Manzoni, A.; Petrarch, F.

JAPANESE—Fukuzawa, Y.; Mabuchi, K.

LATIN AMERICAN—Alvarez, A.; Lastarria, J. V.; Mariátegui, J. C.; Rodó, J. E.

NORWEGIAN—Björnson, B.; Ibsen, H.

PERSIAN—Malkam Khan.

POLISH—Mickiewicz, A.

PORTUGUESE—Quental, A. T. de.

ROMAN—Cato; Lucretius; Seneca.

RUSSIAN—Aksakov, I.; Aksakov, S. T.; Arsenyev, K. K.; Belinsky, V. G.; Chavchavadze, I.; Chernyshevsky, N. G.; Dobrolubov, N. A.; Dostoevsky, F. M.; Gradovsky, A. D.; Karamzin, N. M.; Korolenko, V. G.; Radishchev, A. N.; Tolstoy, L. N.

For complete list of headings used in Classification of Articles see page 547.

Classification of Articles (Biographical Titles)

SOUTH AFRICAN—Schreiner, O. E. A.

SPANISH—Feijóo y Montenegro, B. J.; Ganivet, A.; Macías Picavea, R.

SWEDISH—Bremer, F.; Geijer, E. G.

SWISS—Mallet du Pan, J.; Sismondi, J. C. L. S. de.

TURKISH—Gök Alp, Z.; Kamál, M. N.; Shinasi, I.; Zia Pasha.

UKRAINIAN—Shevchenko, T.

See also Classification of Articles (Biographical Titles), JOURNALISM (*p.* 563); (Abstract Titles), LITERATURE AND THE PRESS (*p.* 553).

Nationalism

ARMENIAN—Khrimian, M.; Raffi, H. M. H.

BULGARIAN—Drinov, M. S.; Karaveloff, L.; Paisii of Khilendar; Slaveykov, P. R.

CANADIAN—Denison, G. T.; Foster, W. A.; Howe, J.; McGee, T. d'A.

CHINESE—Sun Yat Sen.

CROAT-SLOVENE—Bukšeg, V.; Gaj, L.; Jelačić, J.; Krek, J.; Križanić, J.; Rački, F.; Radić, S.; Starčević, A.; Strossmayer, J. J.; Supilo, F.

CZECH-SLOVAK—Dobrovský, J.; Havlíček, K.; Kollár, J.; Palacký, F.; Rieger, F. L.; Šafařík, P. J.

EGYPTIAN—Arabi, A.; Blunt, W. S.; Jamál; Mohammed 'Abdu; Muṣṭafa Kāmil; Zaghlul Pasha, S.

FINNISH—Arwidsson, A. I.; Snellman, J. V.; Yrjö-Koskinen, Y. S.

FRENCH—Barrès, M.; Boulanger, G. E.; Déroulède, P.; Péguy, C.

GERMAN—Adelung, J. C.; Arndt, E. M.; Chamberlain, H. S.; Droysen, J. G.; Freytag, G.; Gagern, H. von; Görres, J. von; Häusser, L.; Jahn, F. L.; Lagarde, P. de; Luden, H.; Moeller van den Bruck, A.

GREEK (MODERN)—Koraes, A.; Rhigas, K.

HUNGARIAN—Deák, F.; Eötvös, J.; Fényes, E. (A.) C.; Horváth, M.; Kossuth, L.; Széchenyi, I.

INDIAN—Das, C. R.; Gokhale, G. K.; Lajpat Rai, L.; Mohammed 'Ali; Naoroji, D.; Ranade, M. G.; Roy, R. M.; Saraswati, D.; Tilak, B. G.; Vivekānanda, Swami.

IRISH—Butt, I.; Collins, M.; Connolly, J.; Davitt, M.; Flood, H.; Grattan, H.; Griffith, A.; O'Connell, D.; Parnell, C. S.

ITALIAN—Alfieri, V.; Amari, M.; Azeglio, M. d'; Balbo, C.; Cattaneo, C.; Cavour, C. B. di; Cernuschi, H.; Crispi, F.; Cuoco, V.; Foscolo, U.; Garibaldi, G.; Gioberti, V.; Gioia, M.; Giusti, G.; Guerrazzi, F. D.; Manin, D.; Manzoni, A.; Mazzini, G.; Pagano, F. M.; Pius IX; Rosmini-Serbati, A.; Rossi, P. L. E.; Spaventa, S.; Tommaseo, N.

JAPANESE—Mabuchi, K.; Yoshida Torajirō.

LATIN AMERICAN—Artigas, J. G.; Bolívar, S.; Hidalgo y Costilla, M.; Hostos, E. M. de; Lastarria, J. V.; Miranda, F. de; San Martín, J. de.

LETTISH—Kronvalds, A.

MACEDONIAN—Gruev, D.; Matov, K.

NORWEGIAN—Aasen, I. A.; Björnson, B.; Wergeland, H. A.

POLISH—Czartoryski, A. J.; Długosz, J.; Kamieński, H. M.; Kościuszko, T. A.; Mickiewicz, A.; Mierosławski, L.; Mochnacki, M.; Staszic, S. W.; Szczepanowski, A. P. S.

SERBIAN—Karadžić, V. S.; Karageorge, P.; Obradović, D.; Pelagić, V.

SOUTH AFRICAN—Hofmeyr, J. H.; Kruger, S. J. P.

SYRIAN—Buṭrus al-Bustāni.

TURKISH—Enver Pasha; Gök Alp, Z.; Kamál, M. N.; Shinasi, I.; Zia Pasha.

UKRAINIAN—Antonovich, V. B.; Drahomanov, M. P.; Franko, I.; Khmelnitsky, B.; Lipinsky, V.; Shevchenko, T.

See also Classification of Articles (Abstract Titles), CITIZENSHIP (*p.* 549), CIVIL OPPOSITION (*p.* 549), GOVERNMENT (*p.* 551).

Natural Science

AMERICAN—Franklin, B.; Jordan, D. S.; McGee, W. J.; Powell, J. W.

AUSTRIAN—Mach, E.

BRITISH—Bacon, R.; Bateson, W.; Butler, S.; Darwin, C. R.; Galton, F.; Huxley, T. H.; Lawes, J. B.; Lyell, C.; Newton, I.; Priestley, J.; Wallace, A. R.

FRENCH—Broca, P.-P.; Buffon, G. L. L.; Chaptal, J. A.; Descartes, R.; Lamarck, Chevalier de; Pascal, B.; Pasteur, L.

GERMAN—Agricola; Blumenbach, J. F.; Haeckel, E.; Humboldt, A. von; Liebig, J. von; Mendel, G. J.; Weismann, A.

GREEK (ANCIENT)—Aristotle.

ITALIAN—Bruno, G.; Galileo.

POLISH—Copernicus, N.

RUSSIAN—Lomonosov, M. V.

See also Classification of Articles (Biographical Titles), PUBLIC HEALTH (*p.* 567); (Abstract Titles), SCIENCE (*p.* 555).

Negro Problem and Slavery

AMERICAN—Armstrong, S. C.; Birney, J. G.; Chase, S. P.; Child, L. M.; Delany, M. R.; Douglass, F.; Finley, R.; Garrison, W. L.; Helper, H. R.; Jones, A.; Lincoln, A.; Mott, L.; Olmsted, F. L.; Parker, T.; Phillips, W.; Turner, J. M.; Washington, B. T.; Weld, T. D.

BRITISH—Buxton, T. F.; Clarkson, T.; Wilberforce, W.

Pacifism

AMERICAN—Burritt, E.; Dodge, D. L.; Ginn, E.; Jordan, D. S.; Ladd, W.

AUSTRIAN—Fried, A. H.; Lammasch, H.; Suttner, B. von.

BRITISH—Cremer, W. R.; Richard, H.

FRENCH—Crucé, É.; Estournelles de Constant, Baron d'; Lemonnier, C.; Passy, F.; Saint-Pierre, C. I. C. de.

HUNGARIAN—Giesswein, S.

RUSSIAN—Bloch, J. de.

SWEDISH—Nobel, A. B.

Philology

AMERICAN—Gatschet, A. S.

BRITISH—Davids, T. W. R.; Müller, F. M.; Rawlinson, H. C.

CROATIAN—Gaj, L.

CZECH-SLOVAK—Dobrovský, J.; Šafařík, P. J.

FINNISH—Yrjö-Koskinen, Y. S.

FRENCH—Champollion, J. F.; Clermont-Ganneau, C.; Jubainville, H. d'A. de; Rougé, O. C. E. de.

GERMAN—Adelung, J. C.; Delitzsch, F.; Grimm, J. L. K. *and* W. K.; Lepsius, K. R.; Rohde, E.; Schrader, E.; Wilamowitz-Moellendorff, U. von; Wolf, F. A.

GREEK (MODERN)—Koraes, A.

HUNGARIAN—Vámbéry, A.

ITALIAN—Valla, L.

NORWEGIAN—Aasen, I. A.

RUSSIAN—Lomonosov, M. V.

For complete list of headings used in Classification of Articles see page 547.

SERBIAN—Karadžić, V. S.
SYRIAN—Buṭrus al-Bustāni.
TURKISH—Shinasi, I.

Philosophy

AMERICAN—Alcott, A. B.; Edwards, J.; James, W.; Mead, G. H.; Münsterberg, H.; Royce, J.

BRITISH—Bacon, F.; Berkeley, G.; Bradley, F. H.; Herbert of Cherbury, Lord; Hume, D.; Hutcheson, F.; Locke, J.; Martineau, J.; Ockham, W. of; Shaftesbury, Third Earl of; Sidgwick, H.; Tindal, M.; Toland, J.

BYZANTINE—Psellos, M.

CHINESE—Chuang Tzu; K'ang Yu-wei; Mencius; Yang Chu.

DUTCH—Spinoza, B.

EGYPTIAN—Maimonides, M.

FRENCH—Alembert, J. L. d'; Bayle, P.; Boutroux, É.; Condillac, É. B. de; Cousin, V.; Descartes, R.; Destutt de Tracy, A. L. C.; Guyau, J. M.; Helvétius, C. A.; Janet, P.; Lamettrie, J. O. de; Montaigne, M. de; Pascal, B.; Renan, E.; Renouvier, C. B.; Royer-Collard, P. P.

GERMAN—Bauer, B.; Beneke, F. E.; Biel, G.; Büchner, L.; Edelmann, J. C.; Eucken, R. C.; Feuerbach, L. A.; Fichte, J. G.; Haeckel, E.; Hartmann, E. von; Hegel, G. W. F.; Kant, I.; Lange, F. A.; Leibniz, G. W., von; Lotze, R. H.; Mendelssohn, M.; Münsterberg, H.; Natorp, P.; Nelson, L.; Nicholas of Cusa; Nietzsche, F. W.; Paulsen, F.; Reimarus, H. S.; Scheler, M.; Schelling, F. W. J.; Schleiermacher, F. E. D.; Schopenhauer, A.; Steiner, R.; Wolff, C.; Wundt, W. M.

GREEK (ANCIENT) — Aristotle; Plato and Platonism; Socrates.

ITALIAN—Alberti, L. B.; Bruno, G.; Gioberti, V.; Rosmini-Serbati, A.; Spaventa, B.; Valla, L.; Vico, G. B.

MOSLEM—Averroes; Ghazzālī, al-; Miskawayhi, Abū 'Ali Aḥmad.

ROMAN — Aurelius Antoninus; Epictetus; Lucretius; Origen; Philo Judaeus; Seneca.

RUSSIAN—Chicherin, B. N.; Solovyev, V. S.

SPANISH—Balmes, J. L.; Isidore of Seville; Vives, J. L.

SWISS—Secrétan, C.

See also Classification of Articles (Biographical Titles), RELIGION (p. 567), SOCIAL PHILOSOPHY AND SOCIOLOGY (p. 568); (Abstract Titles), PHILOSOPHY (p. 553), RELIGION (p. 555), SOCIOLOGY (p. 556).

Political Affairs

AMERICAN—Adams, H. C.; Aldrich, N. W.; Altgeld, J. P.; Aycock, C. B.; Benton, T. H.; Berger, V. L.; Beveridge, A. J.; Birney, J. G.; Blair, F. P.; Bryan, W. J.; Bryant, W. C.; Cannon, J. G.; Clinton, De W.; Cooper, T. (d. 1839); Dickinson, J.; Donnelly, I.; Eaton, D. B.; Fernow, B. E.; Greeley, H.; Hanna, M. A.; Hay, J. M.; Hooker, T.; Ingersoll, R. G.; Johnson, T. L.; Kelley, W. D.; Knapp, M. A.; La Follette, R. M.; Lathrop, J. C.; McDuffie, G.; Maclay, W.; Morris, R.; Pitkin, T.; Prouty, C. A.; Raymond, H. J.; Schurz, C.; Sterne, S.; Stevens, T.; Toombs, R.; Weaver, J. B.; Wright, C. D.

AUSTRALIAN—Higgins, H. B.; Wentworth, W. C.

AUSTRIAN—Adler, V.; Auspitz, R.; Friedjung, H.; Lueger, K.

BRITISH—Abbot, C.; Acworth, W. M.; Anderson, W. C.; Bateman, A. E.; Bentham, J.; Bright, J.; Broadhurst, H.; Bruce, H. A.; Burdett, F.; Cartwright, J.; Cobden, R.; Courtney, Lord; Eliot, J.; Fawcett, H.; Forster, W. E.; Glasier, J. B.; Hampden, J.; Hardie, J. K.; Hart, R.; Hill, R.; Lilburne, J.; McAdam, J. L.; Melchett, Lord; Montfort, S. de; Morel, E. D.; Morrison, J. (d. 1857); O'Connor, F.; Pole Family; Pym, J.; Sidney, A.; Vane, H.; Wilkes, J.

CANADIAN—Beck, A.; Brown, G.; Denison, G. T.; Gourlay, R. F.

CHINESE — Hung Hsiu-ch'üan; K'ang Yu-wei; Liang Ch'i-ch'ao; Sun Yat Sen.

DUTCH—Gorter, H.; Nieuwenhuis, F. D.; Troelstra, P. J.

FRENCH—Barrot, C.H.O.; Blanc, L.; Boileau, É.; Boulanger, G. E.; Boutmy, É. G.; Brissot de Warville, J.-P.; Clamageran, J. J.; Clemenceau, G.; Cloots, J. B.; Crémieux, A. I. M.; Fouché, J.; Jaurès, J.; Lafayette, Marquis de; Lamartine, A. M. L. de P. de; Lavergne, L.-G. L. de; Lemire, J.; Littré, M. P. É.; Malon, B.; Marat, J.-P.; Marcel, É.; Roland de la Platière, M. J.; Sembat, M. É.; Simon, J.

GERMAN—Arndt, E. M.; Auer, I.; Bachem, Josef and Julius; Ballin, A.; Bamberger, L.; Barth, T.; Bassermann, E.; Bebel, A.; Bennigsen, R. von; Beseler, K. G. C.; Biedermann, F. K.; Bödiker, T.; Braun, K.; Dahlmann, F. C.; David, E.; Delbrück, H.; Duncker, F. G.; Duncker, M. W.; Eisner, K.; Frank, L.; Gentz, F. von; Gerlach, E. L. von; Gneist, R. von; Haase, H.; Hansemann, D. J. L.; Hitze, F.; Hoffmann, J. G.; Jacoby, J.; Jörg, J. E.; Lasker, E.; Liebknecht, K.; Liebknecht, W.; Luxemburg, R.; Mallinckrodt, H. von; Mehring, F.; Mohl, R. von; Moser, F. K. von; Münzer, T.; Naumann, F.; Reichensperger, A. and P. F.; Richter, E.; Riesser, G.; Rössler, C.; Rotteck, K. W. R. von; Schweitzer-Allesina, J. B. von; Singer, P.; Sonnemann, L.; Stein, Ludwig; Stöcker, A.; Treitschke, H. von; Virchow, R.; Vollmar, G. von; Welcker, K. T.; Windthorst, L.; Zetkin, C.

HUNGARIAN — Giesswein, S.; Kunfi, Zsigmond; Martinovics, I. J.

ITALIAN—Bissolati, L.; Guerrazzi, F. D.; Lazzari, C.; Matteotti, G.; Montemartini, Giovanni; Turati, F.

JAPANESE—Goto, S.; Yoshida Torajirō.

PERSIAN—Malkam Khan.

POLISH—Diamand, H.; Kołłątaj, H.; Lelewel, J.; Luxemburg, R.; Spasowicz, W.; Staszic, S. W.

RUSSIAN—Axelrod, P. B.; Chaykovsky, N. V.; Gershuni, G. A.; Gradovsky, A. D.; Martov, L.; Pestel, P. I.; Plekhanov, G. V.; Samarin, Y. F.; Tatishchev, V. N.; Ulyanov, V. I.; Uvarov, S. S.

SOUTH AFRICAN—Jabavu, J. T.

SPANISH—Castelar y Ripoll, E.; Costa y Martinez, J.; Iglesias Posse, P.; Labra y Cadrana, R. M. de; Pi y Margall, F.

SWEDISH—Danielsson, A. F.; Steffen, G. F.

SWISS—Mallet du Pan, J.

See also Classification of Articles (Biographical Titles), NATIONALISM (p. 565), SOCIALISM (p. 569), STATECRAFT (p. 569); (Abstract Titles), GOVERNMENT (p. 551), POLITICAL PARTIES (p. 554), PUBLIC OFFICE (p. 554), SOCIALISM (p. 556).

Political Science

AMERICAN—Adams, J.; Ames, F.; Calhoun, J. C.; Dunning, W. A.; Fitzhugh, G.; Ford, H. J.; Hamilton, A.; Lieber, F.; Madison, J.; Paine, T.; Smith, E. M.; Smith, J. A.; Taylor, J.

Classification of Articles (Biographical Titles)

AUSTRALIAN—Hearn, W. E.

BELGIAN—Laveleye, É. L. V. de; Prins, A.

BRITISH—Bacon, F.; Bagehot, W.; Barclay, W.; Berkeley, G.; Bolingbroke, Lord; Bosanquet, B.; Bryce, J.; Buchanan, G. (d. 1582); Burke, E.; Cartwright, J.; Cartwright, T.; De Quincey, T.; Eliot, J.; Figgis, J. N.; Filmer, R.; Fortescue, J.; Green, T. H.; Halifax, Lord; Harrington, J.; Hoadly, B.; Hobbes, T.; Hooker, R.; Hume, D.; John of Salisbury; Lewis, G. C.; Locke, J.; Lorimer, J.; Maine, H. J. S.; Merivale, H.; Mill, J. S.; Penn, W.; Price, R.; Priestley, J.; Prynne, W.; Ritchie, D. G.; Rutherford, S.; Sidney, A.; Spencer, H.; Stephen, J. F.; Wallas, G.; Wesley, J.

CANADIAN—Bourinot, J. G.

CHINESE—Han Fei-tzǔ; Mencius; Shang Yang; Sun Yat Sen.

CZECH—Palacký, F.

DUTCH—Spinoza, B.

FRENCH—Aegidius Colonna; Agobard, Argenson, Marquis d'; Block, M.; Bodin, J.; Bonald, L. G. A.; Boutmy, É. G.; Constant de Rebecque, H. B.; Destutt de Tracy, A. L. C.; Duguit, L.; Dunoyer, B. C. P. J.; Dupont-White, C. B.; Fénelon, F. de S. de la M.; Gerson, J.; Hauriou, M.; Hincmar of Reims; Hotman, F.; Janet, P.; John Quidort of Paris; Joly, C.; Jurieu, P.; Laboulaye, É. R. L. de; Lamennais, H. F. R. de; Mably, G. B. de; Maistre, J. M. de; Mercier de la Rivière, P.-P.; Michel, H.; Montesquieu, Baron de; Renan, E.; Rousseau, J.-J.; Royer-Collard, P. P.; Saint-Pierre, C. I. C. de; Saint-Simon, Duc de; Sieyès, J. E.; Tocqueville, A. C. H. M. C. de.

GERMAN—Althusius, J.; Andlo, P. of; Bluntschli, J. K.; Clausewitz, C. von; Engels, F.; Fichte, J. G.; Frantz, K.; Gerlach, E. L. von; Gneist, R. von; Haller, K. L. von; Hegel, G. W. F.; Humboldt, F. W. von; Jellinek, G.; Justi, J. H. G. von; Kant, I.; Manegold of Lautenbach; Melanchthon, P.; Mohl, R. von; Müller, A. H.; Preuss, H.; Pufendorf, S. von; Rössler, C.; Schleiermacher, F. E. D.; Seckendorff, V. L. von; Seydel, M. von; Stahl, F. J.; Treitschke, H. von; Wolff, C.; Zincke, G. H.

GREEK (ANCIENT) — Aristotle; Plato and Platonism.

HINDU—Kautilya.

HUNGARIAN—Eötvös, J.

ITALIAN—Aquinas, T.; Bartolus of Sassoferrato; Boccalini, T.; Botero, G.; Contarini, G.; Dante Alighieri; Filangieri, G.; Foscolo, U.; Galluppi, P.; Genovesi, A.; Giannotti, D.; Gioberti, V.; Guicciardini, F.; James of Viterbo; Machiavelli, N.; Marsilius of Padua; Mazzola, U.; Paruta, P.; Pius II.

MOSLEM—Fārābi, al-.

POLISH—Konarski, S.; Modrzewski, A. F.; Skarga Powęski, P.

ROMAN—Augustine; Cicero.

RUSSIAN—Kavelin, K. D.; Korkunov, N. M.; Ostrogorsky, M. Y.; Pobedonostsev, K. P.; Speransky, M. M.

SPANISH—Ayala, B.; Cánovas del Castillo, A.; Donoso Cortés, J.; Mariana, J. de; Pi y Margall, F.; Suárez, F.

SWEDISH—Fahlbeck, P. E.; Kjellén, R.

See also Classification of Articles (Biographical Titles), SOCIAL PHILOSOPHY AND SOCIOLOGY (p. 568); (Abstract Titles), GOVERNMENT (p. 551).

Psychology

AMERICAN—Fernald, W. E.; Hall, G. S.; James, W.; Ladd, G. T.; Mead, G. H.; Münsterberg, H.; Parker, C. H.; Prince, M.; Sidis, B.; Titchener, E. B.

AUSTRIAN—Mach, E.; Mesmer, F. A.

BRITISH—Bain, A.; Galton, F.; Hartley, D.; Maudsley, H.; Rivers, W. H. R.

DANISH—Lange, C. G.

FRENCH—Binet, A.; Charcot, J. M.; Esquirol, J.-É. D.; Le Bon, G.; Pinel, P.; Seguin, E.

GERMAN—Beneke, F. E.; Ebbinghaus, H.; Fechner, G. T.; Gall, F. J.; Griesinger, W.; Hartmann, E. von; Kraepelin, E.; Lazarus, M.; Münsterberg, H.; Preyer, W. T.; Steinthal, H.; Wundt, W. M.

RUSSIAN—Bekhterev, V.

See also Classification of Articles (Abstract Titles), PSYCHOLOGY (p. 554).

Public Health

AMERICAN—Atwater, W. O.; Biggs, H. M.; Billings, J. S.; Carter, H. R.; Fernald, W. E.; Prince, M.; Rush, B.; Salmon, T. W.; Sedgwick, W. T.; Straus, N.; Welch, W. H.

AUSTRIAN—Benedikt, M.; Frank, J. P.; Mesmer, F. A.

BRITISH—Baker, G.; Buchanan, G. (d. 1895); Chadwick, E.; Jenner, E.; Lister, J.; Maudsley, H.; Nightingale, F.; Prichard, J. C.; Simon, J.; Wakley, T.

FRENCH—Bourneville, D. M.; Budin, P.; Charcot, J. M.; Esquirol, J.-É. D.; Pasteur, L.; Pinel, P.; Seguin, E.; Villermé, L. R.

GERMAN—Gall, F. J.; Griesinger, W.; Koch, R.; Kraepelin, E.; Virchow, R.

GREEK (ANCIENT)—Hippocrates and the Hippocratic Collection.

PORTUGUESE—Costa Ferreira, A. A. da.

RUSSIAN—Bekhterev, V.

SWISS—Forel, A. H.

See also Classification of Articles (Abstract Titles), PUBLIC HEALTH (p. 554).

Religion (Brahmanism and Hinduism)

Roy, R. M.; Saraswati, D.; Vivekānanda, Swami.

Religion (Christianity before 1500)

Abélard, P.; Ailly, P. d'; Albertus Magnus; Ambrose; Anselm; Arnold of Brescia; Augustine; Becket, T.; Benedict; Bernard of Clairvaux; Boniface VIII; Chrysostom, J.; Clement of Alexandria; Eusebius of Caesarea; Gelasius I; Gerhoh of Reichersberg; Gerson, J.; Gregory I; Gregory VII; Grosseteste, R.; Henry of Langenstein; Huss, J.; Innocent III; Isidore of Seville; James of Viterbo; Joachim of Flora; John Quidort of Paris; John of Salisbury; Lanfranc; Lull, R.; Nicholas of Cusa; Ockham, W. of; Origen; Peter Lombard; Photius; Pius II; Rabanus Maurus, M.; Raymond de Pennafort; Savonarola, G.; Tertullian; Wycliffe, J.; Yves of Chartres.

See also Classification of Articles (Biographical Titles), HISTORY (RELIGIOUS) (p. 562); (Abstract Titles), RELIGION (p. 555).

Religion (Christianity after 1500)

AMERICAN—Abbott, L.; Beecher, H. W.; Brownson, O. A.; Channing, W. E.; Channing, W. H.; Cotton, J.; Eddy, M. B.; Edwards, J.; Hooker, T.; Mather, I. and C.; Parker, T.; Smith, J.; Williams, R.; Young, B.

BRITISH—Bancroft, R.; Baxter, R.; Booth Family; Bray, T.;

For complete list of headings used in Classification of Articles see page 547.

Browne, R.; Burnet, G.; Cartwright, T.; Chalmers, T.; Cranmer, T.; Cromwell, O.; Fox, G.; Headlam, S. D.; Hoadly, B.; Holland, H. S.; Hooker, R.; Jowett, B.; Knox, J.; Laud, W.; Manning, H. E.; Martineau, J.; Newman, J. H.; Paley, W.; Penn, W.; Prynne, W.; Rutherford, S.; Wesley, J.; Whitefield, G.; Wolsey, T.

CANADIAN—Laval, F. X. de.

DANISH—Grundtvig, N. F. S.

FRENCH—Batiffol, P.; Baudouin, F.; Bossuet, J. B.; Fénelon, F. de S. de la M.; Grégoire, H.; Jurieu, P.; Lacordaire, J. B. H. D.; Lamennais, H. F. R. de; Lemire, J.; Mabillon, J.; Montalembert, Comte de; Pascal, B.

GERMAN—Bugenhagen, J.; Döllinger, I. von; Francke, A. H.; Hefele, K. J. von; Hergenröther, J.; Hontheim, J. N. von; Ketteler, W. E. von; Kraus, F. X.; Luther, M.; Melanchthon, P.; Möhler, J. A.; Mosheim, J. L.; Münzer, T.; Stöcker, A.; Zinzendorf, N. L. von.

ITALIAN—Bellarmine, R. F. R.; Consalvi, E.; Contarini, G.; Leo XIII; Neri, Philip; Paul IV; Pius IX; Ricci, M.

POLISH—Skarga Poweski, P.

RUSSIAN—Samarin, Y. F.

SPANISH—Francis Xavier; Loyola, Ignatius de; Ximénes de Cisneros, F.

SWISS—Calvin, J.; Castellio, S.; Zwingli, H.

See also Classification of Articles (Biographical Titles), HISTORY (RELIGIOUS) (p. 562); (Abstract Titles), RELIGION (p. 555).

Religion (Islam)

Būkhāri, al-; Ghazzālī, al-; Husayn A'li; Ibn-Taymīya; Jamál; Mohammed; Mohammed 'Abdu; Mohammed Ahmad; Mohammed 'Ali; Mohammed ibn 'Abd al-Wahhāb.

Religion (Judaism)

See JEWISH PROBLEMS AND JUDAISM.

Social Philosophy and Sociology

AMERICAN—Adams, B.; Adams, H.; Andrews, S. P.; Cooley, C. H.; Emerson, R. W.; Fiske, J.; Giddings, F. H.; Hadley, A. T.; Hayes, E. C.; Jefferson, T.; Royce, J.; Small, A. W.; Stuckenberg, J. H. W.; Sumner, W. G.; Thoreau, H. D.; Veblen, T. B.; Ward, L. F.; Warren, J.

AUSTRIAN—Hertzka, T.; Ratzenhofer, G.; Wieser, F. von.

BELGIAN—Colins, J. H.; De Greef, G.; Denis, H.; Solvay, E.

BOHEMIAN—Comenius, J. A.

BRITISH—Bagehot, W.; Bentham, J.; Bosanquet, B.; Buckle, H. T.; Bury, J. B.; Davidson, T.; Duns Scotus, J.; Edmonds, T. R.; Ferguson, A.; Flint, R.; Godwin, W.; Green, T. H.; Hall, C.; Hobbes, T.; Hobhouse, L. T.; Hume, D.; Kidd, B.; Malthus, T. R.; Mandeville, B. de; Mill, J. S.; Morley, J.; Owen and Owenism; Ritchie, D. G.; Robertson, J. M.; Ruskin, J.; Smiles, S.; Spencer, H.; Stephen, L.; Townsend, J.; Unwin, G.; Wallace, R.; Wallas, G.

CHINESE—Han Fei-tzǔ; K'ang Yu-wei; Mo Ti.

FRENCH—Ballanche, P. S.; Barrès, M.; Bastiat, F.; Bazard, S.-A.; Bodin, J.; Bonald, L. G. A.; Bossuet, J. B.; Bourgeois, L. V. A.; Brunetière, F.; Buchez, P. J. B.; Bureau, P.; Cabanis, P. J. G.; Chateaubriand, F. A. R.; Chevalier, M.; Comte, I. A. M. F. X.; Condorcet, M. J. A. N. C.; Coste, A.; Cournot, A.-A.; Demolins, E.; Dumont, A.; Durkheim, É.; Espinas, A.; Finot, J.; Fouillée, A. J. É.; Fourier and Fourierism; Gobineau, J. A. de; Guyau, J. M.; Hauriou, M.; Holbach, Baron von; La Boétie, É. de; Lacombe, P.; Le Bon, G.; Leroux, P.; Linguet, S. N. H.; Littré, M. P. É.; Mably, G. B. de; Maistre, J. M. de; Michel, H.; Montesquieu, Baron de; Morelly; Novikov, Y. A.; Pecqueur, C.; Proudhon, P. J.; Reclus, J. É.; Rousseau, J.-J.; Saint-Simon and Saint-Simonianism; Sorel, G.; Tarde, G.; Tourville, H. de; Worms, R.

GERMAN—Achelis, T.; Ammon, A. O.; Baader, F. X. von; Barth, P.; Bastian, A.; Chamberlain, H. S.; Dietzgen, J.; Dilthey, W.; Dühring, E. K.; Engels, F.; Franck, S.; Fröbel, F.; Grosse, E.; Grün, K. T. F.; Heine, H.; Herder, J. G. von; Jhering, R. von; Kant, I.; Kirchmann, J. H. von; Kohler, J.; Leibniz, G. W. von; Lessing, G. E.; Lippert, J.; Marx, K.; Müller, A. H.; Müller-Lyer, F. C.; Natorp, P.; Nicholas of Cusa; Nordau (Südfeld), M. S.; Pesch, H.; Rathenau, W.; Riehl, W. H.; Rodbertus, J. K.; Ruge, A.; Schäffle, A. E. F.; Scheler, M.; Schiller, J. C. F.; Schleiermacher, F. E. D.; Schmoller, G. von; Schopenhauer, A.; Simmel, G.; Stein, Lorenz von; Stein, Ludwig; Stirner, M.; Stuckenberg, J. H. W.; Thomasius, C.; Troeltsch, E.; Weber, M.; Woltmann, L.; Wundt, W. M.

HUNGARIAN—Beöthy de Bessenyo, L.; Giesswein, S.; Pulszky, Á.

IRISH—Ingram, J. K.

ITALIAN—Angiulli, A.; Aquinas, T.; Ardigò, R.; Campanella, T.; Carle, G.; De Sanctis, F.; Ferrari, G.; Galiani, F.; Gioia, M.; Gravina, G.; Labriola, A.; Malatesta, E.; Mamiani della Rovere, T.; Mazzini, G.; Pagano, F. M.; Pareto, V.; Romagnosi, G. D.; Sighele, S.

JAPANESE—Motoöri, N.

LATIN AMERICAN—Echeverria, J. E. A.; Hostos, E. M. de; Ingenieros, J.; Justo, J. B.; Lamas, A.; Letelier, V.; Rodó, J. E.; Sarmiento, D. F.

MOSLEM—Ibn-Khaldūn.

NORWEGIAN—Sundt, E. L.

POLISH—Cieszkowski, A.; Gumplowicz, L.; Jaworski, W. L.; Kamieński, H. M.; Krauz-Kelles, K.; Krochmal, N.; Supiński, J.; Wroński-Hoene, J. M.

PORTUGUESE—Pinheiro Ferreira, S.

ROMAN—Lucretius.

RUSSIAN—Aksakov, K.; Bakunin, M.; Bogdanov, A.; Chaadayev, P. Y.; Chernyshevsky, N. G.; Danilevsky, N. Y.; Dostoevsky, F. M.; Granovsky, T. N.; Khomyakov, A. S.; Kireyevsky, I. V.; Kistyakovsky, B. A.; Korkunov, N. M.; Kovalevsky, M. M.; Kropotkin, P. A.; Lavrov, P. L.; Leontyev, K. N.; Lilienfeld-Toailles, P. F.; Machajski, W.; Mikhailovsky, N. K.; Petrazhitsky, L. I.; Plekhanov, G. V.; Roberty, E. de; Solovyev, V. S.; Tolstoy, L. N.; Ulyanov, V. I.

SPANISH—Arenal, C.; Azcárate, G. de.

SWEDISH—Fahlbeck, P. E.; Steffen, G. F.

SWISS—Iselin, I.; Secrétan, C.

See also Classification of Articles (Abstract Titles) SOCIOLOGY (p. 556).

Social Reform

AMERICAN—Abbott, L.; Altgeld, J. P.; Barton, C.; Beecher, H. W.; Bergh, H.; Bliss, W. D. P.; Brace, C. L.; Briesen, A. v.; Brinkerhoff, R.; Brisbane, A.; Channing, W. E.; Channing, W. H.; Clinton, De W.; Comstock,

Classification of Articles (Biographical Titles)

A.; Cooper, P.; Curtis, G. W.; De Forest, R. W.; Dew, T. R.; Dix, D. L.; Dow, N.; Fels, J.; Gilman, D. C.; Gleason, A. H.; Grady, H. W.; Greeley, H.; Henderson, C. R.; Howe, S. G.; Ingersoll, R. G.; Johnson, T. L.; Kelley, F.; Kelly, E.; Knowlton, C.; Lathrop, J. C.; Lloyd, H. D.; Lockwood, B. A. B.; Lowell, J. S.; Owen, R. D.; Parker, T.; Post, L. F.; Rantoul, R., Jr.; Richmond, M. E.; Schurz, C.; Seager, H. R.; Skidmore, T.; Smith, Z. D.; Spencer, A. G.; Warren, J.; Willard, F. E.; Woods, R. A.; Woolman, J.; Wright, F.

AUSTRALIAN—Lane, W.

AUSTRIAN—Vogelsang, K. von.

BELGIAN—Brants, V.; Solvay, E.

BRITISH—Acland, J.; Attwood, T.; Baines, E. (d. 1848) *and* Baines, E. (d. 1890) Barnardo, T.; Barnett, S. A.; Baxter, R.; Bellers, J.; Bentham, J.; Booth, C.; Bradlaugh, C.; Brassey, T. (d. 1918); Bright, J.; Butler, J.; Cadbury, G.; Carlile, R.; Carpenter, M.; Chadwick, E.; Chalmers, T.; Cooper, T. (d. 1892); Davies, D.; Defoe, D.; Derby, Lord; Devas, C. S.; Dickens, C.; Fawcett, H.; Fox, G.; Gilbert, T.; Gray, J.; Headlam, S. D.; Hill, O.; Holland, H. S.; Hughes, T.; Kay-Shuttleworth, Sir J.; Kingsley, C.; Loch, C. S.; Lovett, W.; Manning, H. E.; Maurice, F. D.; Mill, J.; Milton, J.; More, T.; Morris, W.; Morrison, J. (d. 1857); Mundella, A. J.; Oastler, R.; O'Connor, F.; Owen and Owenism; Raikes, R.; Ruskin, J.; Schloss, D. F.; Shaftesbury, Seventh Earl of; Southey, R.; Toynbee, A.; Villiers, C. P.; Vincent, H.; Waugh, B.; Wilberforce, W.; Wilkes, J.

CANADIAN—Gourlay, R. F.

DANISH—Sörensen, T.

DUTCH—Bosch Kemper, J. de.

FRENCH—Brissot de Warville, J.-P.; Cabet, É.; Cheysson, É.; Dezamy, T.; Dubois, P.; Enfantin, B. P.; Fourier and Fourierism; Godin, J. B. A.; Grégoire, H.; Harmel, L.; Laffemas, B. de; La Rochefoucauld-Liancourt, F. de; La Tour du Pin Chambly, R. de; Lemire, J.; Le Play, P. G. F.; Leroux, P.; Montalembert, Comte de; Mun, A. de; Ozanam, F.; Passy, F.; Renaudot, T.; Saint-Pierre, C. I. C. de; Saint-Simon and Saint-Simonianism; Sand, G.; Villeneuve-Bargemont, Vicomte de; Vincent de Paul.

GERMAN—Andreae, J. V.; Böhmert, K. V.; Brandts, F.; Duncker, F. G.; Faucher, J.; Francke, A. H.; Francke, E.; Guillaume-Schack, G.; Hitze, F.; Holtzendorff, F. von; Ketteler, W. E. von; Kolping, A.; Münsterberg, E.; Nelson, L.; Rodbertus, J. K.; Ruge, A.; Wichern, J. H.

HUNGARIAN—Eötvös, J.

INDIAN—Gokhale, G. K.; Malabari, B. M.; Ranade, M. G.; Saraswati, D.; Sayyid Ahmad Khan.

IRISH—Hancock, W. N.

ITALIAN—Antonino; Leo XIII; Luzzatti, L.; Montemartini, G.; Tommaseo, N.

NORWEGIAN—Sundt, E. L.; Wergeland, H. A.

POLISH—Kołłątaj, H.; Modrzewski, A. F.

RUMANIAN—Kogălniceanu, M.

RUSSIAN—Goldenweiser, A. S.; Pososhkov, I. T.; Turgenev, N. I.

SERBIAN—Marković, S.

SPANISH—Azcárate, G. de; Costa y Martinez, J.; Dato e Iradier, E.; Feijóo y Montenegro, B. J.; Macías Picavea, R.; Sagra y Périz, R. D. de la; Vives, J. L.

SWISS—Dunant, J. H.; Le Grand, D.

Socialism

AMERICAN—Berger, V. L.; Debs, E. V.; De Leon, D.; Douai, A.; Ruthenberg, C. E.; Sörge, F. A.; Weydemeyer, J.

AUSTRALIAN—Lane, W.

AUSTRIAN—Adler, V.; Menger, A.

BELGIAN—Colins, J. H.; Paepe, C. de.

BRITISH—Bax, E. B.; Bray, J. F.; Crane, W.; Glasier, J. B.; Hardie, J. K.; Harney, G. J.; Hyndman, H. M.; Jones, E. C.; Morris, W.; Owen and Owenism.

DUTCH—Gorter, H.; Nieuwenhuis, F. D.; Troelstra, P. J.

FRENCH—Blanc, L.; Blanqui, L. A.; Boissel, F.; Brousse, P.; Considérant, V.; Deroin, J.; Fourier and Fourierism; Fournière, E.; Guesde, J.; Guillaume, J.; Jaurès, J.; Lafargue, P.; Leroux, P.; Linguet, S. N. H.; Malon, B.; Merrheim, A.; Michel, L.; Pecqueur, C.; Proudhon, P. J.; Saint-Simon and Saint-Simonianism; Sembat, M. É.; Sorel, G.

GERMAN—Adler, G.; Auer, I.; Bebel, A.; Braun, L.; Dietzgen, J.; Eisner, K.; Engels, F.; Fichte, J. G.; Frank, L.; Grün, K. T. F.; Haase, H.; Hess, M.; Ihrer, E.; Landauer, G.; Lassalle, F.; Legien, C.; Liebknecht, K.; Liebknecht, W.; Luxemburg, R.; Marlo, K.; Marx, K.; Mehring, F.; Most, Johann; Schippel, M.; Singer, P.; Stein, Lorenz von; Vollmar, G. von; Weitling, W.; Zetkin, C.

HUNGARIAN—Frankel, L.; Kunfi, Z.; Szabó, E.; Táncsics, M.

IRISH—Connolly, J.; O'Brien, J.; Thompson, W.

ITALIAN—Bissolati, L.; Costa, A.; Labriola, A.; Lazzari, C.; Matteotti, G.; Turati, F.

LATIN AMERICAN—Justo, J. B.; Mariátegui, J. C.

POLISH—Diamand, H.; Luxemburg, R.; Waryński, L. T.

RUMANIAN—Dobrogeanu-Gherea, C.

RUSSIAN—Axelrod, P. B.; Bakunin, M.; Chaykovsky, N. V.; Danielson, N. F.; Gapon, G. A.; Gershuni, G. A.; Herzen, A. I.; Lavrov, P. L.; Liebermann, A. S.; Machajski, W.; Martov, L.; Medem, W.; Morozov, S.; Plekhanov, G. V.; Pokrovsky, M. N.; Ulyanov, V. I.

SERBIAN—Marković, S.; Tucović, D.

SPANISH—Iglesias Posse, P.

UKRAINIAN—Franko, I.

See also Classification of Articles (Abstract Titles), SOCIALISM (*p.* 556).

Statecraft

ALBANIAN—Ismail Kemal Bey.

AMERICAN—Adams, C. F. (d. 1886); Adams, J.; Adams, J. Q.; Adams, S.; Benjamin, J. P.; Blaine, J. G.; Bradford, W.; Burlingame, A.; Calhoun, J. C.; Chase, S. P.; Clay, H.; Cleveland, S. G.; Cushing, C.; Davis, J.; Douglas, S. A.; Franklin, B.; Gallatin, A.; Hamilton, A.; Hay, J. M.; Jackson, A.; Jay, J.; Jefferson, T.; La Follette, R. M.; Lincoln, A.; Livingston, E.; Livingston, R. R.; Madison, J.; Mason, G.; Monroe, J.; Olney, R.; Rhett, R. B.; Roosevelt, T.; Seward, W. H.; Stephens, A. H.; Sumner, C.; Washington, G.; Webster, D.; Wilson, J.; Wilson, (T.) W.; Winthrop, J.

AUSTRALIAN—Deakin, A.; Griffith, S. W.; Kingston, C. C.; Parkes, H.; Pearson, C. H.

AUSTRIAN—Aehrenthal, A. L.; Bach, A.; Beust, F. F. von; Bruck, K. L. von; Francis

For complete list of headings used in Classification of Articles see page 547.

Joseph I; Maria Theresa; Metternich-Winneburg, C. W. L.; Schwarzenberg, F. von.

BELGIAN—Leopold II.

BRITISH—Ashburton, Lord; Asquith, H. H.; Balfour, A. J.; Beaconsfield, Lord; Bolingbroke, Lord; Brougham, Lord; Bryce, J.; Burghley, Lord; Burke, E.; Canning, G.; Canning, S.; Castlereagh, R. S.; Chamberlain, J.; Churchill, R. H. S.; Clarendon, E. H.; Cromwell, O.; Cromwell, T.; Derby, Lord; Dilke, C. W.; Dufferin and Ava, Lord; Durham, Lord; Edward I; Elizabeth; Fox, C. J.; George III; Gladstone, W. E.; Goschen, Lord; Grenville, G.; Grey, Lord; Hamilton, G. G.; Henry II; Henry VII; Henry VIII; Huskisson, W.; James I; Liverpool, Lord; Morley, J.; Nicolson, A.; Palmerston, Lord; Peel, R.; Pitt, W. (d. 1778) *and* W. (d. 1806); Russell, Lord; Salisbury, Lord; Shaftesbury, First Earl of; Smith, T.; Temple, W.; Trevelyan, G. O.; Walpole, R.; Wellington, Duke of; William I; Wolsey, T.

BULGARIAN—Geshov, I. E.; Stamboliĭski, A. S.; Stambulov, S. N.

BYZANTINE—Justinian I; Leo III; Theodosius II.

CANADIAN—Baldwin, R.; Cartier, G. É.; Fielding, W. S.; Galt, A. T.; Lafontaine, L. H.; Laurier, W.; MacDonald, J. A.

CHINESE—Chang Chih-tung; Li Hung Chang; Shang Yang; Ssŭma Kuang; Tz'û Hsi; Wang An-shi; Wu T'ing Fang; Yuan Shih-kai.

CROATIAN—Jelačić, J.

DANISH—Bernstorff, A. P.; Bernstorff, J. H. E.

DUTCH—Oldenbarneveldt, J. van; Pierson, N. G.; Witt, J. de.

EGYPTIAN—Mehemet Ali; Zaghlul Pasha, S.

FRENCH—Barère de Vieuzac, B.; Barnave, A. P. J. M.; Bourgeois, L. V. A.; Broglie, A. V.; Cambacérès, J. J. R. de; Cambon, P. J.; Cambon, P. P.; Carnot, L. N. M.; Clemenceau, G.; Colbert, J.-B.; Danton, G.-J.; Delcassé, T.; Dubois, G.; Ferry, J. F. C.; Fleury, A. H. de; Freycinet, C. de; Gambetta, L.; Guizot, F. P. G.; Henry IV; Hospital, M. de l'; Ledru-Rollin, A.-A.; Louis XI; Louis XIV; Mazarin, J.; Méline, J.; Mirabeau, Comte de; Napoleon I; Napoleon III; Philip IV; Philip Augustus; Portalis, J. É. M.; Richelieu, A.-J. du P. de; Robespierre, M.; Royer-Collard, P. P.; Sieyès, J. E.; Sully, Duc de; Talleyrand-Périgord, C.-M. de; Thiers, L. A.; Thomas, A. A.; Turgot, R. J.; Vergennes, Comte de; Vergniaud, P. V.

GERMAN—Bethmann Hollweg, T. von; Beust, F. F. von; Bismarck, O. E. L.; Buchenberger, A.; Bülow, B. H. M.; Caprivi (de Caprara de Montecuculi), G. L. von; Ebert, F.; Ernest I; Erzberger, M.; Frederick II (the Great); Frederick William; Frederick William I; Gagern, H. von; Gentz, F. von; Hardenberg, K. A. von; Helfferich, K.; Hohenlohe-Schillingsfürst, C. K. V.; Holstein, F. von; Karl Friedrich; Kiderlen-Wächter, A. von; Marschall von Bieberstein, A.; Miquel, J. von; Otto I; Preuss, H.; Radowitz, J. M. von; Rathenau, W.; Stein, H. F. K. vom und zum; Stresemann, G.; Tirpitz, A. von; William I (d. 1888).

GREEK (ANCIENT) — Alexander the Great; Demosthenes; Solon.

GREEK (MODERN)—Capodistrias, J.; Trikoupis, C.

HOLY ROMAN EMPIRE—Charlemagne; Charles V; Frederick I; Frederick II; Henry IV (d. 1106); Joseph II.

HUNGARIAN—Andrássy, G.; Deák, F.; Eötvös, J.; Francis Joseph I; Kállay, B.; Kossuth, L.; Tisza, I.; Tisza, K.

INDIAN (ANCIENT)—Asoka.

IRISH—Collins, M.; Flood, H.; Grattan, H.; Griffith, A.; O'Connell, D.

ITALIAN—Azeglio, M. d'; Cavour, C. B. d'; Crispi, F.; Depretis, A.; Gianni, F. M.; Giolitti, G.; Jacini, S. F.; Luzzatti, L.; Mancini, P. S.; Medici; Neri, Pompeo; Ruffini, F.; Sarpi, P.; Scialoja, A.; Spaventa, S.; Victor Emmanuel II.

JAPANESE— Arai Hakuseki; Goto, S.; Itagaki, T.; Ito, H.; Kido, T.; Ōkubo, T.; Ōkuma, S.; Yamagata, A.

LATIN AMERICAN (*see also* MEXICAN)—Artigas, J. G.; Balmaceda, J.; Barbosa, R.; Barrios, J. R.; Batlle y Ordóñez, J.; Bello, A.; Bolívar, S.; Bonifacio de Andrada e Silva, J.; Castilla, R.; Castro, C.; Francia, J. G. R.; García Moreno, G.; Gorostiaga, J. B.; Guzmán-Blanco, A.; Justo, J. B.; Lamas, A.; Mitre, B.; Núñez, R.; Pedro I *and* Pedro II; Portales, D.; Rivadavia, B.; Rosas, J. M. de; San Martín, J. de; Santa Cruz, A.; Sarmiento, D. F.

MEXICAN—Carranza, V.; Díaz, J. de la C. P.; Juárez, B. P.; Madero, F. I.; Obregón, A.

MOSLEM—Enver Pasha; Javid, M.; Köprülü Family; Mahmud II; Midhat Pasha; Mohammed II; Mu'Āwiyah; Omar ibn al-Khattab; Suleiman I.

NEW ZEALAND—Atkinson, H. A.; Ballance, J.; Grey, G.; McKenzie, J.; Reeves, W. P.; Seddon, R. J.; Swainson, W.; Vogel, J.

NORWEGIAN—Nansen, F.; Schweigaard, A. M.; Sverdrup, J.

POLISH—Czartoryski, A. J.; Kościuszko, T. A.; Lubecki, F. X.; Wielopolski, A.

PORTUGUESE—Henry the Navigator; Pinheiro Ferreira, S.; Pombal, Marquez de.

ROMAN—Augustus; Aurelius Antoninus; Caesar; Constantine; Diocletian; Gracchus, T. *and* G.; Julianus; Theodosius I.

RUMANIAN—Bratianu Family; Cuza, A. J.; Ionescu, T.; Kogălniceanu, M.

RUSSIAN—Alexander I; Alexander II; Bunge, N. C.; Capodistrias, J.; Catherine II; Ivan IV; Izvolsky, A. P.; Kankrin, E. F.; Kiselev, P. D.; Milutin, N. A.; Peter I; Radishchev, A. N.; Sazonov, S. D.; Speransky, M. M.; Stolipin, P. A.; Ulyanov, V. I.; Witte, S. Y.

SERBIAN—Karageorge, P.; Milovanović, M.; Obrenović Dynasty; Pašić, N.; Stefan Dušan.

SOUTH AFRICAN—Botha, L.; Khama; Kruger, S. J. P.; Moshesh.

SPANISH—Alberoni, J.; Alfonso X; Aranda, Conde de; Campomanes, P. R.; Canalejas y Mendez, J.; Canga Argüelles, J.; Cánovas del Castillo, A.; Ensenada, Marqués de la; Ferdinand V and Isabella; Floridablanca, Conde de; Jovellanos, G. M. de; Macanaz, M. R. de; Philip II.

SWEDISH—Branting, K. H.; Gustavus I; Gustavus II; Oxenstierna, A. G.

SWISS—Ador, G.

UGANDA—Kagwa, A.

UKRAINIAN—Khmelnitsky, Bohdan.

See also Classification of Articles (Biographical Titles), COLONIAL ADMINISTRATION (*p.* 559), FINANCIAL ADMINISTRATION (*p.* 561), POLITICAL AFFAIRS (*p.* 566); (Abstract Titles), ECONOMIC POLICY (*p.* 550), GOVERNMENT (*p.* 551), PUBLIC FINANCE (*p.* 554), PUBLIC OFFICE (*p.* 554).

For complete list of headings used in Classification of Articles see page 547.

Statistics

AMERICAN—Abbott, S. W.; Billings, J. S.; De Bow, J. D. B.; Jarvis, E.; King, W. A.; Mayo-Smith, R.; Shattuck, L.; Wright, C. D.

AUSTRALIAN—Coghlan, T. A.; Knibbs, G. H.

AUSTRIAN—Czoernig von Czernhausen, K.; Inama-Sternegg, K. T. von.

BELGIAN—Ducpétiaux, É.; Quetelet, A.

BRITISH—Baily, F.; Baines, J. A.; Bateman, A. E.; Booth, C.; Eden, F. M.; Edgeworth, F. Y.; Edmonds, T. R.; Farr, W.; Giffen, R.; Graunt, J.; Hunter, W. W.; Jevons, W. S.; King, G.; Levi, L.; Petty, W.; Sinclair, J.

BULGARIAN—Popov, K.

CANADIAN—Johnson, G.

DANISH—Rubin, M.; Sörensen, T.

DUTCH—Ackersdijck, J.; Beaujon, A.

FRENCH—Benoiston de Chateauneuf, L. F.; Bertillon, J.; Block, M.; Deparcieux, A.; Dupré de Saint Maur, N. F.; Foville, A. de; Laplace, Marquis de; Lavoisier, A. L.; Poisson, S.-D.; Villermé, L. R.

GERMAN—Achenwall, G.; Böckh, R.; Conring, H.; Crome, A. F. W.; Dieterici, K. F. W.; Engel, C. L. E.; Hermann, F. B. W. von; Hoffmann, J. G.; Knapp, G. F.; Laspeyres, É.; Lexis, W.; Lueder, A. F.; Mayr, G. von; Meitzen, A.; Rümelin, G.; Scheel, H. von; Schlözer, A. L. von; Soetbeer, A. G.; Süssmilch, J. P.

HUNGARIAN—Beöthy de Bessenyo, L.; Fényes, E. C.; Jekelfalussy, J.; Keleti, K.; Kőrösy de Szántó, J.; Láng, L.

IRISH—Hancock, W. N.

ITALIAN—Balbi, A.; Bodio, L.; Ferraris, C. F.; Messedaglia, A.

RUSSIAN—Annensky, N. F.; Chuprov, A. A.; Chuprov, A. I.; Fortunatov, A. F.; Kablukov, N. A.; Kaufman, A. A.; Orlov, V. I.; Orzhentsky, R. M.; Peshekhonov, A. V.; Semenov, P. P.; Yanson, Y. E.

SERBIAN—Jakšić, V.

SWEDISH—Sundbärg, A. G.

SWISS—Bernoulli Family.

See also Classification of Articles (Abstract Titles), STATISTICS (*p.* 556).

For complete list of headings used in Classification of Articles see page 547.

Index

Aaronson, A.—i 353.
Aarum, P. T.—i 353.
Aasen, I. A.—i 353.
Abandonment—*see* Exposure.
Abbas Hilmi—v 442 b.
Abbassides—Caliphate iii 146 a; Islam viii 339 a.
Abbe, E.—i 354; Hours of Labor vii 491 a; Profit Sharing xii 488 b.
Abbot, C.—i 354.
Abbott, C. C.—i 355.
Abbott, F. F.—i 355.
Abbott, L.—i 355.
Abbott, S. W.—i 356.
Abd-el-Krim—xi 19 a.
Abdication—i 356–57.
Abduction—i 357–58.
Abdul-Hamid ii—Midḥat Pasha x 418 a; Pan-Islamism xi 542 a.
Abeille, L. P.—i 358.
Abélard, P.—i 358; Introd. Vol. I (The Universal Church) i 67 a; Arnold of Brescia ii 219 a; Canon Law iii 180 b; Scholasticism xiii 579 a.
Abell, A. S.—i 359.
Aberdare, Lord—*see* Bruce H. A.
Aberdeen, Lord—*see* Hamilton, G. G.
Abnormal Psychology—i 360–69; Atavism ii 291 a; Mental Disorders x 313–19; Mental Hygiene x 319–23; Mental Tests x 326 b; Psychiatry xii 578–80; Psychology xii 594 b.
Abolition—i 369–72; Emancipation v 484 a; Quakers xiii 13 a; Slavery xiv 83 a, 89 a. *For biog. references see* Classification of Articles (Negro Problem and Slavery), p. 565.
Abortion—i 372–74; Birth Control ii 559 b.
About, E.—i 374; Anticlericalism ii 114 a.
Abovian, K.—i 375.
Abrahams, I.—i 375.
Absent-Voting—i 376.
Absentee Ownership—i 376–78; Agrarian Movements i 496 b, 500 b, 503 b; Fortunes, Private vi 398 a; Irish Question viii 287 a; Landed Estates ix 141 b; Rent Regulation xiii 293 a.
Absenteeism (Labor)—i 378–80; Morbidity xi 4 b.
Absolutism—i 380–82; Introd. Vol. I (Renaissance and Reformation) i 88 b, (The Rise of Liberalism) i 110 b; Assassination ii 271 b; Authority ii 319–21; Autocracy ii 321–22; Cameralism iii 158–61; Dictatorship v 133–36; Empire v 497–506; Enlightenment v 549 a; Force, Political vi 339 b; Forced Loans vi 346 a; Govt. vii 12 a; Hobbes vii 395 a; Idealism vii 571 a; Legislative Assemblies ix 356 b; Materialism x 211 b; Monarchy x 579–84; Prerogative xii 319 a; Reason of State xiii 143 a; Sovereignty xiv 266 b; Tyranny xv 135–37.
Abstinence—i 382–83; Accumulation i 415–18; Interest viii 132 b.
Abu Bakr—iii 145 b.
Abul Fazl Allami—i 383.
Academic Freedom—i 384–88; Introd. Vol. I (The Social Sciences as Disciplines, Spain) i 297 a, (U. S.) 348 a; Education (Finance) v 430 a; Fundamentalism vi 526 b; Teaching Profession xiv 550 a; Universities and Colleges xv 185 a.
Academies—*see* Learned Societies.
Acceptance—i 388–89; Banking, Commercial ii 434 b; Bill of Exchange ii 540 a, 541 a; Credit iv 547 b; Federal Reserve System vi 160 b; Financial Organization vi 244 b; Mercantile Credit x 330 a; Money Market x 613–18; Negotiable Instruments xi 332–35.
Accident Insurance—*see* Compensation and Liability Insurance.
Accidents—i 389–91; Accidents, Industrial i 391–401; Aviation ii 342 b; Contingent Fee iv 312 b; Motor Vehicle Accidents xi 70–74; Railroad Accidents xiii 71–74; Rehabilitation xiii 221–25; Safety Movement xiii 503–06.
Accidents, Industrial—i 391–401; Absenteeism i 379 a; Alcohol i 627 a; Automobile Industry ii 327 a; Blind ii 588 a; Child (Labor) iii 422 a; Construction Industry iv 270 a; Employers' Liability v 514–18; Fatigue vi 148–51; Industrial Hazards vii 697–705; Iron and Steel Industry viii 316 b, 320 a; Mining Accidents x 508–13; Railroad Accidents xiii 73 b; Rehabilitation xiii 221–25; Safety Movement xiii 503–06; Workmen's Compensation xv 488–92.
Accidents, Mining—*see* Mining Accidents.
Accidents, Motor Vehicle—*see* Motor Vehicle Accidents.
Accidents, Railroad—*see* Railroad Accidents.
Acclimatization — i 401–03; Adaptation i 436 b.
Accommodation — i 403–04; Adaptation i 436 a; Adjustment i 438 b; Civil War iii 524 b.
Accounting — i 404–12; Accounts, Public i 412–15; Agricultural Economics i 537 a; Appreciation ii 141–44; Auditing ii 312–13; Corporation Finance iv 428 a; Cost Accounting iv 475–78; Depreciation v 98–102; Financial Statements vi 247–49; Municipal Finance xi 103 a; National Income xi 213 a; Overhead Costs xi 511–13; Professions xii 477 b.
Accounts, Public—i 412–15; Budget iii 38–44; Financial Administration vi 234–41; Govt. Reporting vii 131 a; Public Contracts xii 596–99.
Accumulation—i 415–18; Acquisition i 420–23; Bourgeoisie ii 655 a; Fortunes, Private vi 389–99; Hoarding vii 393–94; Inheritance viii 37 b, 40 a; Interest viii 136 b; National Economic Planning xi 199 a; National Wealth xi 227–31; Saving xiii 548–52; Thrift xiv 623–26.
Accursius—i 418; Civil Law iii 505 a; Commentators iii 679 b; Glossators vi 681 a.
Achard, F. K.—xiv 451 b.
Achelis, T.—i 419.
Achenwall, G.—i 419; Statistics xiv 356 a.
Ackersdijck, J.—i 419.
Acland, J.—i 420.
Acollas, É.—i 420.
Acquired Characters—*see* Heredity.
Acquisition—i 420–23; Accumulation i 415–18; Art Collecting ii 259–60; Bourgeoisie ii 655 a; Calvin iii 152 b; Capitalism iii 196 b; Commercialism iv 31–34; Economic Policy v 333 b.
Acsady, I.—i 423.
Action Française—i 423–25; Antisemitism ii 123 b; Barrès ii 466 b.
Acton, Lord—i 425; Intolerance viii 244 a; Liberty ix 445 a.
Acts of Trade, Brit.—i 426–29.
Actuaries—ix 468 a.
Acworth, W. M.—i 429.
Adams, B.—i 429.
Adams, C. F. (d. 1886)—i 430.
Adams, C. F. (d. 1915)—i 430.
Adams, C. K.—i 334 a.
Adams, G. B.—i 431.
Adams, H.—i 431; History and Historiography vii 388 a.
Adams, H. B.—i 433.
Adams, H. C.—i 432; Publicity xii 699 a; Revenues, Public xiii 362 a.
Adams, J.—i 434; Introd. Vol. I (The Revolutions) i 135 b.
Adams, J. Q.—i 434; Monroe Doctrine x 630 b.
Adams, S.—i 435.
Adams, T. S.—Mortgage Tax xi 39 a; Taxation xiv 538 b.

572

Index (Aaronson — Agrarian Movements)

ADAPTATION—i 435–37; Acclimatization i 401–03; Accommodation i 403 a; Adjustment i 438 b; Biology ii 553 b; Comparative Psychology iv 131 a; Environmentalism v 561–66; Evolution v 649–56; Immigration vii 591 a; Maladjustment x 61 a; Race xiii 25–36.
ADDISON, J.—i 437.
ADELUNG, J. C.—i 437.
Adjective Law—see PROCEDURE, LEGAL.
ADJUSTMENT—i 438–39; Acclimatization i 401–03; Accommodation i 403–04; Adaptation i 435 b; Maladjustment x 61 a.
Adler, A.—Genius vi 613 a; Personality xii 86 b; Psychoanalysis xii 587 a.
Adler, F.—v 601 a.
ADLER, G.—i 439.
Adler, M.—viii 541 b.
ADLER, V.—i 439.
Administration, Business — see BUSINESS ADMINISTRATION.
Administration, Financial — see FINANCIAL ADMINISTRATION.
Administration of Justice — see JUSTICE, ADMINISTRATION OF.
ADMINISTRATION, PUBLIC—i 440–50. See Classification of Articles (Government), p. 551. See also Introd. Vol. I (The Roman World) i 54 a, (War and Reorientation) 217 b; Accounts, Public i 412–15; Appointments ii 137–38; Budget iii 38–44; Bureaucracy iii 70–74; Business, Govt. Services for iii 113–22; Census iii 295–300; Certiorari iii 317 b; Civil Service iii 515–23; Economic Policy v 333–44; Education v 419 a; Federal Trade Commission vi 165–69; Functional Representation vi 520 b; Gosplan vi 705–13; Grants-in-Aid vii 152–55; Health Centers vii 287–89; Health Education vii 291 a; Inspection viii 71–74; Institutions, Public viii 90–95; Interstate Commerce Commission viii 229–36; Jurisprudence viii 488 b; Labor, Govt. Services for viii 649 b; Labor Legislation and Law viii 660 a; Licensing ix 447–51; Local Finance ix 573 a; Mandamus x 84–87; Monopolies, Public x 621 b; Municipal Finance xi 101 a; Native Policy (N. Amer.) xi 265 a, 268 a; Navy xi 316 a; Parks xi 584 a; Patents xii 20 b; Penal Institutions xii 59 a; Poor Laws xii 230–34; Ports and Harbors xii 258 b; Public Contracts xii 596–99; Public Employment xii 628–37; Public Health xii 651 a; Public Office xii 665–69; Recreation xiii 179 a; Roads xiii 400–11; Sanitation xiii 538–42; Sheriff xiv 20–23; Social Work xiv 169 b, 180 b; Socialization xiv 221–25; Spoils System xiv 301–05; Statistics (Practise) xiv 360–66; Tax Administration xiv 526–28; Traffic Regulation xv 71 b; Water Supply xv 376 b; Weights and Measures xv 391 a. *For biog. references see* Classification of Articles (Statecraft), p. 569.
ADMINISTRATIVE AREAS—i 450–52; County-City Consolidation iv 499–501; County Councils iv 501–04; County Govt., U. S. iv 504–08; Home Rule vii 434–36; Metropolitan Areas x 396–401; Organization, Administrative xi 482 a.
Administrative Boards — see BOARDS, ADMINISTRATIVE.
Administrative Commissions—see COMMISSIONS.
Administrative County of London —x 399 a.
Administrative Courts — see COURTS, ADMINISTRATIVE.
ADMINISTRATIVE LAW—i 452–55; Administration, Public i 448 a; Aucoc ii 309 a; Certiorari iii 317 b; Commissions iv 39 b; Contempt of Court iv 305 b; Courts, Administrative iv 529–33; Interstate Commerce Commission viii 233 a; Judiciary viii 467 b; Laferrière ix 11 b; Licensing ix 447–51; Mandamus x 84–87; Mayer x 236 b; Public Office xii 665–69; Rule of Law xiii 463–66; Separation of Powers xiii 663–67; State Liability xiv 338–43.
Administrative Organization—see ADMINISTRATION, PUBLIC.
Admiralty—see MARITIME LAW.
ADOLESCENCE—i 455–59; Child (Labor) iii 423 a, (Marriage) 395–98; Conversion, Religious iv 354 a; Education, Primitive v 401 b; Gangs vi 564–67; Initiation viii 49–50; Sex Education and Sex Ethics xiv 8–13.
ADOPTION—i 459–63; Conflict of Laws iv 192 b; Law (Chinese) ix 253 a, (Hindu) 259 b; Naturalization xi 305 b; Placing Out xii 145 b.
ADOR, G.—i 463.
ADULT EDUCATION—i 463–66; Introd. Vol. I (The Social Sciences as Disciplines, France) i 256 b, (Gt. Brit.) 241 a; Americanization ii 33 b; Chautauqua iii 359–60; Correspondence Schools iv 444–47; Education (Part Time) v 425–28; Folk High Schools vi 286–88; Museums and Exhibitions xi 142 a; Parent Education xi 573–76; Radio xiii 60 b; University Extension xv 187–89; Workers' Education xv 484–88.
ADULTERATION—i 466–68; Consumer Protection iv 282 b; Food and Drug Regulation vi 297–301; Liquor Industry ix 498 a.
Adultery—x 150 b.

AD VALOREM AND SPECIFIC DUTIES—i 468–69; Customs Duties iv 669 a.
ADVERTISING—i 469–75; Campaign, Political iii 165 a; Consumer Protection iv 282 b; Correspondence Schools iv 446 a; Expositions, International vi 23–27; Food Industries (Confectionery) vi 310 a; Habit vii 238 a; Health Education vii 293 a; Instalment Selling viii 77 a; Lotteries ix 613 b; Press xii 329 b, 335 a, 340 b; Propaganda xii 521–28; Publicity xii 700 b; Radio xiii 58 b, 59–62.
Advisory Ballots—xiv 418 b.
Advisory Boards—see BOARDS, ADVISORY.
ADVISORY OPINIONS—i 475–80 (National 475–78, International 478–80); Declaratory Judgment v 51 b; Govt. (Canada) vii 29 a; Permanent Court of International Justice xii 79 a, 80 b.
Advocate—ix 324–46.
AEGIDIUS COLONNA—i 480.
Aegidius Romanus—viii 368 a.
AEHRENTHAL, A. L.—i 481.
Aeneas Silvius—History and Historiography vii 373 b; Pius II xii 142.
Aeration—xv 376 a.
Aerial Law—Aviation (Law) ii 366–68; Radio (Legal Aspects) xiii 62–66.
Aeroboe, F.—vi 112 b.
Aeronautical Chamber of Commerce—ii 344 a.
Aeronautics Bureau—ii 341 b.
Aeschylus—xiv 600 b.
Afforestation—see Reforestation.
Aftalion, A.—iii 98 b.
AGAZZINI, M.—i 481.
AGE SOCIETIES—i 482–83; Gerontocracy vi 637–38; Schurtz xiii 587 b.
AGENCY—i 483–85; Bailment ii 388–90; Broker iii 9 a; State Liability xiv 339 a.
Agent Provocateur—Detective Agencies, Private v 109 b; Political Police xii 206 a.
Agglutinative Languages — ix 161 b.
AGGRESSION, INTERNATIONAL—i 485–86; Reprisals xiii 317 a; Sanction, International xiii 529 b; War xv 338 a.
AGIA, M. DE—i 486.
AGIO—i 487; Interest viii 134 b.
AGITATION—i 487–88.
AGOBARD—i 488.
AGOULT, C. D'—i 489.
AGRARIAN MOVEMENTS—i 489–515 (Introd. 489–92, Greece 492–94, 513, Rome 494–95, 513, Gt. Brit. 495–97, 513, France 497–98, 514, Germany and Austria 498–99, 514, Italy 500–01, 514, Denmark 501–02, 514, E. C. Eur. and the Balkans 502–04, 514, Europ. Russia 505–07, 514, Poland and Lithuania 507–08, 515, Latvia and Estonia 508,

515, U. S. 508-11, 515, Lat. Amer. 511-13, 515); Introd. Vol. I (Renaissance and Reformation) i 101 a; Agrarian Syndicalism i 515-16; Agric. Policy i 565-69; Agriculture (Mediaeval) i 576 a, (England) 577 b, (Europe) 582 a; Allotments ii 5-7; Black Death ii 575 b; Chambers of Agriculture vi 323-25; Colonate iii 639-41; Enclosures v 523-27; Farm Bloc, U. S. vi 103-05; Farm Bureau Federation, American vi 105-06; Farm Tenancy vi 118 b; Farmers' Alliance vi 127-29; Farmers' Organizations vi 129-32; Farmers' Union vi 132-33; Free Silver vi 438-40; French Revolution vi 472 b; Frontier vi 500-06; Grange vii 150-51; Indian Question vii 670 a; Irish Question viii 287 b, 288 b; Land Settlement ix 53-64; Land Tenure ix 73-127; Landed Estates ix 141 b; Manorial System x 101 a; Peasantry xii 50 a; Reformation xiii 189 a; Small Holdings xiv 103 b. *See also* Agrarian Parties. *For biog. references see* Classification of Articles (Agrarian Reform), p. 558.

Agrarian Parties — Agrarian Movements (U. S.) i 508-11; Parties, Political (Australia) xi 607 a, (Baltic States) 624 b, (Bulgaria) 629 b, (Canada) 605 b, (Irish Free State) 610 a, (Sweden) 622 a, (U. S.) 598 a.

Agrarian Syndicalism—i 515-16.

Agreement of the People—i 516-18; Levellers ix 421 b; Lilburne ix 473 a.

Agreements, International—i 518-20; Advisory Opinions i 478-80; Alliance ii 3-4; Arbitration, International ii 157-62; Balance of Power ii 395-99; Blockade ii 595 b; Boundaries ii 650 a; Business, Govt. Services for iii 117 a, 121 a; Concert of Powers iv 153-54; Executive Agreements v 685-86; Guaranties, International vii 190-92; International Legislation viii 175-77; International Organization viii 177-85; Match Industry x 204 a; Mediation x 272 b; Prisoners of War xii 420 b; Privateering xii 423 b; Radio xiii 65 a; Sanction, International xiii 528-31; Spheres of Influence xiv 297 b; Sugar xiv 454 b; Transit, International xv 79 a; Treaties xv 96-101.

Agreements, Interstate—iv 109-13.

Agricola—i 520.

Agricultural Colonies—*see* Land Settlement.

Agricultural Cooperation—i 521-29; Agrarian Movements (Denmark) i 501 b, (France) 498 a; Agrarian Syndicalism i 515-16; Agric. Credit i 533 a; Agric. Insurance i 546-47; Agric. Marketing i 563 a, 564 a; Agriculture, Govt. Services for i 603 a; Balakshin ii 394 b; Cooperation iv 359-99; Dairy Industry iv 692 a; Farm Bureau Federation, American vi 106 a; Farm Loan System, Federal vi 111 a; Farmers' Organizations vi 129 b; Fruit and Vegetable Industry vi 509 b; Grain Elevators vii 138 b; Grange vii 150 b; Haas vii 232 b; Kraemer viii 596 b; Kulizhny viii 610 a; Meat Packing and Slaughtering (Denmark) x 252 a; Mellaerts x 304 b; Milk Supply x 478 a; Plunkett xii 169 b; Raiffeisen xiii 70 a.

Agricultural Credit—i 529-34; Agrarian Movements i 490 b, (France) 498 a; Agric. Policy i 569 a; Agriculture (India) i 593 a; Agriculture, Govt. Services for i 603 b; Cattle Loans iii 276-77; Cotton iv 490 b; Farm Loan System, Federal vi 106-11; Federal Reserve System vi 160 a; Land Mortgage Credit ix 43-50; Livestock Industry ix 549 a; Loans, Personal ix 562 a; Retail Credit xiii 345 a.

Agricultural Economics — i 534-38; Conrad iv 208 a; Farm Management vi 112 b; Kraemer viii 596 b; Lavergne ix 199 b; Ludogovsky ix 629 a; Thünen xiv 627 a.

Agricultural Education — i 538-42; Agric. Economics i 534-38; Agric. Fairs i 544-45; Agriculture, Govt. Services for i 600 a, 605 a; Extension Work, Agric. vi 31-36; Home Economics vii 429 a; Land Grants (U. S.) ix 34 a.

Agricultural Experiment Stations—i 542-44; Agric. Education i 539 b, 540 b; Agriculture, Govt. Services for i 602 a; Atwater ii 307 a; Farm Management vi 113 b.

Agricultural Extension Work—*see* Extension Work, Agricultural.

Agricultural Fairs—i 544-45; Meat Packing and Slaughtering (U. S.) x 244 b; Stock Breeding xiv 396 a; Watson xv 384 b.

Agricultural Holdings Acts—*see* Allotments; Small Holdings.

Agricultural Insurance — i 546-47; Agric. Cooperation i 527 a; Agriculture, Govt. Services for i 604 a.

Agricultural Journalism—Atkinson ii 302 a; Judd viii 442 a; Skinner xiv 72 b; Wallace xv 325 b.

Agricultural Labor—i 547-51; Agrarian Movements i 489-515; Agric. Machinery i 553 a; Agriculture (Rome) i 575 a, (Mediaeval) 577 a; Agriculture, Govt. Services for i 604 a; Arch ii 163 a; Child (Labor) iii 415 a; Cotton iv 489 a; Fruit and Vegetable Industry vi 511 a; Migratory Labor x 441-45; Negro Problem xi 341 a; Plantation xii 148-53; Serfdom xiii 667-71; Slavery xiv 73-92; Wages xv 314 a.

Agricultural Machinery—i 551-54; Agric. Machinery Industry i 554-58; Agriculture i 597 a; Dry Farming v 253 b; Eyth vi 44 a; Grains vii 142 a; Land Utilization ix 134 a; McCormick ix 648 b; Machinery, Industrial x 5 b; Machines and Tools x 25 a; Whitney xv 410 b.

Agricultural Machinery Industry—i 554-58.

Agricultural Marketing—i 558-65; Agric. Cooperation i 522 b, 525 a; Agric. Credit i 529 b; Agric. Policy i 569 a; Agriculture, Govt. Services for i 603 a; Cotton iv 491 b; Dairy Industry iv 692 b; Food Industries (Food Distribution, Russia) vi 323 b, (U. S.) 315 b, (W. Eur.) 320 b; Fruit and Vegetable Industry vi 509 b; Grading vii 133 b; Grain Elevators vii 136-39; Grains vii 142 b; Markets, Municipal x 139-44; Meat Packing and Slaughtering x 242-63; Refrigeration xiii 196-200; Wholesaling xv 414 a.

Agricultural Policy—i 565-69; Agrarian Movements i 489-515; Agriculture, Govt. Services for i 600-06; Enclosures v 524 b; Farm Loan System, Federal vi 106-11; Farm Relief vi 114-18; Flax, Hemp and Jute vi 275 b; Food Supply vi 334 a; Gosplan vi 708 a; Peasantry xii 49 b; Protection xii 559-67; Russian Revolution xiii 487 a, 488 b; Self-Sufficiency, Economic xiii 658 a; Small Holdings xiv 103 b.

Agricultural Societies—i 570-71; Agric. Fairs i 544-45; Agriculture, International Institute of i 606-07; Dairy Industry iv 692 a; Eyth vi 44 b; Farmers' Organizations vi 129-32; Watson xv 384 b; Women's Organizations xv 464 b.

Agriculture—i 572-600 (Primitive 572-74, 598, Antiquity and the Middle Ages 574-77, 599, England 577-81, 599, Europ. Continent 581-85, 599, U. S. 585-89, 599, China 589-90, 599, Japan 590-92, 599, India 592-93, 599, General Problems 593-600). *See* Classification of Articles (Agriculture), p. 548. *See also* Introd. Vol. I (Greek Culture and Thought) i 17 a, (The Roman World) 56 b; Anthropology ii 80 a, 82 b; Biology ii 556 b; Census iii 299 b; Chinese

Problem iii 433 a; City iii 477 a; Diminishing Returns v 144 b; Domestication v 207 a; Dumping v 276 b; Economics (Physiocrats) v 349 b; Electric Power v 468 a; Employers' Associations v 513 b; Gosplan vi 708 a; Indian Question vii 662 a; Labor viii 617 b; Large Scale Production ix 172 a; Negro Problem xi 341 a; Occupation xi 432 b; Production (Statistics) xii 468 a; Protection xii 561 a; Specialization xiv 283 a; Statistics (Practise) xiv 361 a. *For biog. references see* Classification of Articles (Agriculture), p. 558.

Agriculture, Departments of—Agric. Economics i 534 a; Agric. Societies i 571 a; Agriculture, Govt. Services for i 600 a, 601 a.

AGRICULTURE, GOVT. SERVICES FOR—i 600–06; Agric. Cooperation (U. S.) i 527 b; Agric. Credit i 533 a; Agric. Economics i 534–38; Agric. Education i 538–42; Agric. Experiment Stations i 542–44; Agric. Fairs i 544–45; Agric. Marketing i 563 a, 565 a; Agric. Policy i 565–69; Agric. Societies i 570 b; Agriculture, International Institute of i 606–07; Chambers of Agriculture iii 323–25; Cotton iv 488 b; Crop and Livestock Reporting iv 608 a; Dairy Industry iv 693 b; Extension Work, Agric. vi 31–36; Farm Bloc, U. S. vi 104 a; Farm Loan System, Federal vi 106–11; Grading vii 134 a; Grain Elevators vii 138 a; Irrigation viii 328–32; Land Mortgage Credit ix 45 a, 48 a, 49 a; Land Settlement ix 52–64; Land Utilization ix 135 a; Reclamation xiii 160–64; Statistics (Practise) xiv 361 a.

AGRICULTURE, INTERNATIONAL INSTITUTE OF—i 606–07; Lubin ix 624 a; Statistics (History) xiv 360 a.

Aguesseau, H.-F. d'—*see* DAGUESSEAU, H.-F.

AGUSTÍN, A.—i 607.

Ahad Ha-am—*see* GINSBERG, A.

Ahimsa—Asoka ii 270 a; Indian Question vii 667 b.

Ahmad Khan—*see* SAYYID AHMAD KHAN.

AHRENS, H.—i 608; Public Law xii 659 a.

Aide-Toi, Le Ciel T'Aidera—iii 223 a.

AIDS—i 608–10.

AILLY, P. D'—i 610; Conciliar Movement iv 161 a.

Aingo de Ezpeleta, P.—*see* EZPELETA, P. A. DE.

Air Commerce Act of 1926—Aviation ii 341 b, 353 a, 356 a, 367 a, 368 b.

Air Mail—Aviation ii 341 b, 353 a, 361 a, 365 b.

Airship—Aviation ii 344 a.

Akbar—Abul Fazl Allami i 383 b; Art (India) ii 232 a; Empire v 501 b; Espionage v 594 a.

Akkadian Law—ix 211–19.

AKSAKOVS—i 610.

ALABAMA CLAIMS—i 611–13; Neutrality xi 362 a.

Alamán, L.—i 307 b.

Alamin—xi 287 a.

ALBERDI, J. B.—i 613.

ALBERONI, J.—i 613.

Albert, Prince—vi 23 b.

ALBERTI, L. B.—i 614.

ALBERTUS MAGNUS—i 614; Just Price viii 505 b.

Albigenses—Messianism x 361 b; Sects xiii 625 b.

ALBUQUERQUE, A. DE—i 615.

ALCABALA—i 615–16.

Alcántara—x 463 a.

ALCHEMY—i 616–18; Taoism xiv 511 b.

ALCIATI, A.—i 618; Commentators iii 681 a.

Alcidames—xi 285 b.

ALCOHOL—i 619–28; Anti-Saloon League ii 118–19; Liquor Industry ix 495–502; Liquor Traffic ix 502–09; Prohibition xii 499–510; Temperance Movements xiv 567–70.

Alcohol, Industrial—*see* INDUSTRIAL ALCOHOL.

ALCOTT, A. B.—i 628; Transcendentalism xv 76 b.

ALCUIN—i 628.

ALDRICH, N. W.—i 629; Warburg xv 353 a.

Aldrich Plan—Federal Reserve System vi 155 b.

Aldrich-Vreeland Act—vi 155 b.

Aldus—vii 539 a.

ALEMBERT, J. L. D'—i 629; Encyclopédistes v 527 b.

ALEXANDER I—i 630; Concert of Powers iv 153 b; Holy Alliance vii 419 a.

ALEXANDER II—i 630; Local Govt. ix 576 b.

Alexander V—iv 161 b.

ALEXANDER THE GREAT—i 631; Introd. Vol. 1 (Greek Culture and Thought) i 16 a, 19 b, 31 b, 33 b; Empire v 504 a; Museums and Exhibitions xi 138 a; Stoicism xiv 407 a; War xv 333 a.

Alexander Hamilton Institute—viii 408 a.

Alexanderson, E. F. W.—xiii 55 a.

Alfasi, I.—ix 224 a.

ALFIERI, V.—i 632.

ALFONSO X—i 632; Codification iii 607 b; Price Regulation xii 357 a.

Alfred the Great—xi 313 b.

Algeçiras Conference—Morocco Question xi 18 b; Nicolson xi 371 b.

'Ali—iii 146 a.

ALIEN—i 633–35; Introd. Vol. 1 (Greek Culture and Thought) i 12 b, 14 a; Alien and Sedition Acts i 635–36; Allegiance i 646 a; Americanization ii 33–35; Anthropology ii 97 b; Antisemitism ii 119–25; Aristocracy ii 185 b; Assimilation, Social ii 281–83; Aubaine, Right of ii 307–08; Blood Accusation ii 598 a; Commercial Treaties iv 26 b; Conflict of Laws iv 187–94; Deportation and Expulsion of Aliens iv 95–98; Enemy Alien v 537–39; Ethnic Communities v 607–13; Ethnocentrism v 613–14; Exterritoriality vi 36–39; Foreign Language Press vi 378–82; Gypsies vii 231 b; Hospitality vii 462–64; Immigration vii 587–95; Intermarriage viii 154 a; International Finance viii 160 b; Judaism viii 437 b; Ku Klux Klan viii 607 a; Law (Greek) ix 227 a; Mass Expulsion x 185–89; Militarism x 446 b; Minorities, National x 518–25; Naturalization xi 305–09; Passport xii 13–16; Smuggling xiv 121 a.

Alien, Enemy—*see* ENEMY ALIEN.

ALIEN PROPERTY—i 636–38; Concessions iv 157 a; Enemy Alien v 538 b; International Finance viii 161 a; Land Tenure (Latin America) ix 122 a; Nitrates xi 382 b; Requisitions, Military xiii 324–26.

ALIEN AND SEDITION ACTS—i 635–36; Freedom of Speech and of the Press vi 457 b.

ALIENATION OF PROPERTY—i 639–41; Charitable Trusts iii 338 b; Entail v 553–56; Feudalism vi 207 b; Freehold vi 463 a; Gifts vi 658–61; Law (Cuneiform) ix 217 a; Mortmain xi 40–50; Perpetuities xii 81–83.

ALIENIST—i 641.

ALIMONY—i 641–43.

ALISON, A.—i 643; Population xii 250 a.

ALLAN, H.—i 643.

ALLAN, W.—i 644.

ALLEGIANCE—i 644–46; Alsace-Lorraine ii 10–12; Annexation ii 68 b; Citizenship iii 471–74; Civic Education iii 496–98; Civil War iii 523–25; Dominion Status v 211–16; Dual Citizenship v 257–59; Excommunication v 678 a; Expatriation v 3–5; Feudalism vi 207 b, 216 b; Freedom of Association vi 447–50; Impressment vii 615 a; Nationalism xi 231–49; Nationality xi 249–52; Naturalization xi 305–09; Obedience, Political xi 415–18; Patriotism xii 26–29; Treason xv 93–96.

Allen, R.—viii 414 a.

Allenby, Lord—v 443 b.

ALLIANCE—ii 3–4; Agreements, International i 518–20; Balance of Power ii 395–99; Federation vi 173 a; Hanseatic League vii 261–67; Holy Alliance vii 417–19; Isolation, Diplomatic viii 352 b; National Defense xi 190 b; Protectorate xii 567 b; World War xv 494 b.

Alliance Aluminium Company—x 377 b.
Alliance, Holy—see HOLY ALLIANCE.
Allied Debts—see Interallied Debts.
ALLOTMENTS—ii 5–7; Land Settlement ix 55 b, 59 b; Land Tenure ix 82 b, 89 a.
ALLOWANCE SYSTEM—ii 7.
Alloys—Iron and Steel Industry viii 306 a; Metals x 384 b.
Allport, F.—i 206 b, 218 b.
Almirall, V.—xiii 214 a.
ALMSHOUSE—ii 8–10; Begging ii 494 b; Child (Dependent) iii 399 b; Institutions, Public viii 91 a; Old Age xi 458 a; Poor Laws xii 231 a.
Alodial Tenure—vi 206 a.
ALSACE-LORRAINE—ii 10–12; Autonomy ii 333 a; Ethnic Communities v 608 b.
Altamira, R.—vii 378 b.
ALTENSTEIN, K.—ii 12.
Alternating Current—xv 405 a.
ALTGELD, J. P.—ii 12.
ALTHUSIUS, J.—ii 13; Enlightenment v 548 b; Social Contract xiv 129 a.
ALTRUISM AND EGOISM—ii 14–16; Anthropology ii 97 b; Charity iii 340 b; Dependency v 93–95; Epicureanism v 568 a; Hedonism vii 307–10; Hobbes vii 395 a; Human Nature vii 535 a; Individualism vii 674–80; Service xiii 672–74; Social Christian Movements xiv 126 a; Stirner xiv 393 b; Utilitarianism xv 197–200.
Aluminum—x 375 b, 385 b.
ALVAREZ, A.—ii 16.
ALVORD, C. W.—ii 16.
Amalgamated Assoc. of Iron and Steel Workers—viii 317 b.
Amalgamated Clothing Workers—Garment Industries vi 582 a; Housing vii 516 b; Labor-Capital Cooperation viii 628 b.
Amalgamated Cooperative Apartments—vii 519 a.
Amalgamated Society of Engineers—xv 8 a.
AMALGAMATION—ii 16–17; Assimilation, Social ii 281–83; Race xiii 25–36; Race Mixture xiii 41–43.
Amana Society—iv 96 b.
AMARI, M.—ii 17.
AMATEUR—ii 18–20; Administration, Public i 444 b, 448 b; Athletics ii 300 a; Career iii 225 a; Gentleman, Theory of the vi 617 b; Music xi 164 b; Sports xiv 306 a.
AMBROSE—ii 20; Church Fathers iii 465 b.
Ambulance Chasing—iv 312 b.
AMENDMENTS, CONSTITUTIONAL—ii 21–23; Bills of Rights ii 545 a; Constitutional Conventions iv 245 b; Constitutional Law iv 248 a; Constitutions iv 260 b; Federation vi 175 a; Govt.

(U. S.) vii 16 b; Initiative and Referendum viii 50–52; Prohibition xii 503 b.
Amercement—vi 249–52.
American Assoc. for Adult Education—i 465 b.
American Assoc. of Social Workers—xiv 184 a.
American Assoc. of University Professors—i 386 b.
American Civil Liberties Union—iii 512 a.
American Civil War—see Civil War, U. S.
American Council of Learned Societies—Learned Sociétés ix 299 b; Research xiii 331 b.
AMERICAN FEDERATION OF LABOR—ii 23–30; Automobile Industry ii 327 b; Boycott ii 664 a; Company Housing iv 117 a; Dual Unionism v 259 b; Gompers vi 697 a; Independent Voting vii 648 b; Industrial Workers of the World viii 13 b, 17 a; Knights of Labor viii 583 b; Labor Banking viii 621 b; Labor Movement viii 693 b, 695 a; Negro Problem xi 350 b; Railroads xiii 95 a; Trade Unions xv 4 b, 40 b.
American Federation of Teachers—xiv 551 b.
AMERICAN LAW INSTITUTE—ii 30–31; Codification iii 609 b, 610 b.
AMERICAN LEGION—ii 31–33; Lobby ix 567 a; Veterans xv 246 a.
American Management Association—iii 90 a.
American Party—see Know Nothing Party.
American Peace Society—xii 42 a.
American Plan—Unemployment Insurance xv 169 b.
American Protective Assoc.—viii 608 b.
American Revolution—Burke iii 75 a; Franklin vi 421 a; Land Grants (U. S.) ix 33 a; Liberalism ix 439 a; Morris xi 20 a; Paine xi 530 a; Wilson xv 425 a.
American Telephone and Telegraph Co.—Telephone and Telegraph xiv 562 b, 563 b; Vail xv 208 a.
American Tobacco Co.—xiv 642 a.
AMERICANIZATION—ii 33–35; American Legion ii 31 b; Assimilation, Social ii 281–83; Immigration vii 591 b.
AMES, F.—ii 35.
AMES, J. B.—ii 35; Case Method iii 252 b.
Ammende, E.—x 523 b.
AMMON, A. O.—ii 36; Sociology xiv 238 b.
AMNESTY—ii 36–39.
Amortization—Capitalization and Amortization of Taxes iii 211 b; Mortmain xi 43 b; Public Debt xii 606 b.
AMOS, S.—ii 39; Codification iii 610 b.
Amphictyony—i 14 a.

Amsterdam International—ii 116 a. See also International Federation of Trade Unions.
AMUSEMENTS, PUBLIC—ii 39–46. See Classification of Articles (Recreation and Amusement), p. 555. See also Anthropology ii 89 b; Boom ii 640 a; Lotteries ix 613 a.
Anabaptists—Messianism x 362 a; Passive Resistance and Non-cooperation xii 11 a; Religious Institutions xiii 271 a; Sects xiii 626 b; Socialism xiv 190 b.
Anacharsis Cloots—see CLOOTS, J. B.
Anaconda Copper Co.—x 375 a.
ANARCHISM—ii 46–53; Introd. Vol. 1 (The Revolutions) i 134 b, (Individualism and Capitalism) 158 a; Andrews ii 59 a; Antimilitarism ii 115 b; Bakunin ii 393; Bargaining Power ii 460 a; Chuang Tzu iii 462 b; Communistic Settlements iv 100 b; General Strike vi 608 b; Kropotkin viii 603 a; Labor Movement viii 682 b; Malatesta x 63 b; Most xi 53 a; Passive Resistance and Non-cooperation xii 11 b; Political Offenders xii 202 a; Reclus xiii 164 b; Romanticism xiii 430 b; Sabotage xiii 496 b; Sedition xiii 638 b; Stirner xiv 393 a; Syndicalism xiv 496 a; Terrorism xiv 577 b; Trade Unions (Spain) xv 29 b.
ANCESTOR WORSHIP—ii 53–55; Confucianism iv 198 b; Hero Worship vii 337 a; Law (Hindu) ix 259 b, (Japanese) 254 b.
Anderson, B. M., Jr.—v 392 a.
ANDERSON, E. G.—ii 55.
ANDERSON, J.—ii 55; Masonry x 178 a.
ANDERSON, W. C.—ii 56.
ANDLO, P. OF—ii 56.
ANDRÁSSY, G.—ii 57.
ANDREAE, J.—ii 58.
ANDREAE, J. V.—ii 57; Introd. Vol. 1 (Renaissance and Reformation) i 102 a.
ANDRÉE, R.—ii 58.
ANDREWS, E. B.—ii 58.
ANDREWS, S. P.—ii 59.
Andronicus, L.—xiv 602 b.
ANGARY—ii 59–60.
ANGAS, G. F.—ii 60.
ANGELL, J. B.—ii 60.
Angell, N.—vii 643 a.
ANGIULLI, A.—ii 61.
Anglicanism—Protestantism xii 571 b; Religious Institutions (Protestant) xiii 269 b.
Anglo-Saxonism—Pan-movements xi 550 a.
Animal Magnetism—Mesmer x 355 b.
ANIMAL PROTECTION—ii 61–63; Bergh ii 522 b; Humanitarianism vii 546 b.
Animal Psychology—Behaviorism ii 497 a; Comparative Psychology iv 129–31; Consciousness iv

214 b, 216 b; Dress v 235 a; Psychology xii 593 b; Reimarus xiii 226 b.
ANIMAL SOCIETIES—ii 63–65; Anthropology ii 79 a; Biology ii 556 a; Courtship iv 538 b; Domestication v 206–08; Espinas v 593 b; Property xii 530 a.
ANIMISM—ii 65–67; Anthropology ii 94 b; Fetishism vi 202 a; Fictions vi 227 a; Gambling vi 555 b; Magic x 40 b; Science xiii 594 b.
ANNENSKY, N. F.—ii 67.
ANNEXATION—ii 68–69; Alsace-Lorraine ii 10–12; Filibustering vi 231–33; Imperialism vii 605 b; Plebiscite xii 163–66; Protectorate xii 567–71; State Succession xiv 344–46.
ANNUITIES—ii 69–71; Group Insurance vii 185 a; Life Insurance ix 468 a.
Anseele, E.— iv 379 b.
ANSELM—ii 71.
ANSON, W. R.—ii 71.
ANTEQUERA, J. M.—ii 72.
ANTHONY, S. B.—ii 72.
Anthracite Coal—Coal Industry iii 594 b; Iron and Steel Industry viii 300 a; Mining Accidents x 509 a; Trade Agreements xiv 668 a.
Anthropogeography—see GEOGRAPHY.
ANTHROPOLOGY—ii 73–110 (Introd. 73–75, Biological Aspects 75–77, Psychological Aspects 77, Language 77–79, Culture 79–98, Integration of Culture 98–102, Study of Cultures 102–10); Introd. Vol. I (What Are the Social Sciences?) i 4 b, (Individualism and Capitalism) 162 b, (Nationalism) 170 b, (The Trend to Internationalism) 184 a, (War and Reorientation) 199 a, (The Social Sciences as Disciplines, France) 253 b, (Gt. Brit.) 238 a, 243 b, (Japan) 322 b, (U. S.) 337 b; Anthropometry ii 110–12; Aryans ii 264–65; Atavism ii 290 b; Criminology iv 586 b; Culture iv 621–46; Culture Area iv 646–47; Diffusionism v 139–42; Domestication v 206–08; Evolution, Social v 656–62; Folklore vi 288–93; Functionalism vi 525 b; Human Nature vii 536 a; Language ix 155–169; Method, Scientific x 392 b; Prehistory xii 316–18; Psychology xii 591 a; Race xiii 25–36; Sociology xiv 243 b. See also Primitive Society. For biog. references see Classification of Articles (Anthropology), p. 558.
ANTHROPOMETRY—ii 110–12; Introd. Vol. I (War and Reorientation) i 199 b; Anthropology ii 75 b; Broca iii 7 b; Galton vi 553 b; Martin x 168 a; Race xiii 26 b; Retzius xiii 357 a.

Anthropomorphism—ii 94 b.
Anthroposophy—xiv 382 b.
ANTICLERICALISM — ii 112–14; About i 375 a; Antisemitism ii 123 a; Barrios ii 466 b; Civic Education iii 497 a; Deism v 62 a; French Revolution vi 481 b; Religious Freedom xiii 245 a; Secularism xiii 633 b.
ANTI-CORN LAW LEAGUE—ii 114–15; Introd. Vol. I (The Social Sciences as Disciplines, Gt. Brit.) i 241 b; Bright iii 3 a; Chartism iii 353 a; Cobden iii 603 a; Corn Laws iv 407 b.
Antigonus Gonates—i 36 b.
ANTIMILITARISM—ii 115–16. See PEACE MOVEMENTS.
Antimony—x 387 b.
ANTIRADICALISM—ii 116–18; Action Française i 423–25; American Legion ii 31 b; Antisemitism ii 122 b, 123 a, 124 b; Assembly, Right of ii 276 a; Belief ii 502 b; Censorship iii 290–94; Civil Liberties iii 511 a; Communist Parties iv 94 a; Concert of Powers iv 153 b; Conservatism iv 230–33; Criminal Syndicalism iv 582–84; Deportation and Expulsion of Aliens v 97 a; Employers' Associations v 512 a; Freedom of Speech and of the Press vi 457 b; Higher Criticism vii 348 b; Lynching ix 641 b; Political Offenders xii 202 a; Political Police xii 203–07; Sedition xiii 638 b; Traditionalism xv 67–70.
ANTI-SALOON LEAGUE—ii 118–19; Prohibition xii 501 b.
ANTISEMITISM—ii 119–25; Aryans ii 264–65; Blood Accusation ii 597 a; Crusades iv 615 b; Diaspora v 126–30; Ghetto vi 646–50; Intellectuals viii 120 a; Jewish Emancipation viii 394–99; Mass Expulsion x 186 b; Massacre x 194 a; National Socialism, German xi 225 b.
Antislavery Movements — see ABOLITION.
Antisthenes—iv 680 a.
Antitrust Laws—see TRUSTS.
Antivivisection—Animal Protection ii 62 b; Bergh ii 522 b.
ANTON, K. G. VON—ii 125.
ANTONINO—ii 126; Just Price viii 506 a.
ANTONOVICH, V. B.—ii 126.
ANUCHIN, D. N.—ii 127.
ANZANO, T. DE—ii 127.
APORTI, F.—ii 128; Preschool Education xii 321 a.
APOSTASY AND HERESY—ii 128–30; Introd. Vol. I (The Universal Church) i 66 b; Belief ii 502 a; Franciscan Movement vi 414 b; Inquisition viii 61–64; Religious Institutions (Roman Catholic) xiii 252 b.
APPANAGE—ii 130–31; Feudalism vi 208 b.
APPEALS—ii 131–36; Audiencia ii 311–12; Certiorari iii 317–19;

Courts, Administrative iv 532 a; Equity v 585 b; Judgments viii 443 b; Supreme Court, United States xiv 479 a.
Appert, N.—iii 174 b.
APPLEGARTH, R.—ii 136.
Appleton, L. E.—xii 160 a.
APPLETON, N.—ii 136.
APPOINTMENTS—ii 137–38; Judiciary viii 464 b; Legislative Assemblies (U. S.) ix 363 a; Spoils System xiv 301–05.
APPORTIONMENT—ii 138–41; Census iii 295–300; Gerrymander vi 638–39; Govt. (Gt. Brit.) vii 24 b, (U. S.) 20 a; Legislative Assemblies (History and Theory) ix 359 a, (U. S.) 362 a, 367 b; Rotten Boroughs xiii 443–44.
Appraisal—see VALUATION.
APPRECIATION—ii 141–44; Income vii 623 b; Income Tax vii 629 a.
APPRENTICESHIP—ii 144–47; Business Educ. iii 107 b; Child (Dependent) iii 399 b; Construction Industry iv 274 a; Guilds (Chinese) vii 219 b, (Europ.) 213 b, (Islamic) 215 b; Industrial Educ. vii 693 a; Journeymen's Societies viii 425 a; Labourers, Statutes of ix 4 b; Legal Profession and Legal Educ. ix 336 b; Medicine (Medical Educ.) x 289 a; Printing and Publishing xii 412 b; Vocational Educ. xv 272 a.
Appropriations—see BUDGET.
April Theses—ii 627 a.
AQUINAS, T.—ii 147; Introd. Vol. I (The Growth of Autonomy) i 80 a; Albertus Magnus i 614 b; Catholic Parties iii 272 a; Christianity iii 457 a; Duns Scotus v 282 a; Just Price viii 505 b; Justice viii 510 b; Leo XIII ix 408 b; Natural Law xi 287 a; Public Finance xii 641 b; Rationalism xiii 115 a; Scholasticism xiii 579 b; Secularism xiii 631 b; Service xiii 673 a; Soto, de xiv 264 b.
ARABI, A.—ii 148; Egyptian Problem v 442 a.
ARAI HAKUSEKI—ii 149.
Arakcheyev, A.—i 630 b.
ARANDA, CONDE de—ii 149.
ARBEITSGEMEINSCHAFT—ii 150.
ARBITRAGE—ii 150–51.
ARBITRATION, COMMERCIAL — ii 151–53.
ARBITRATION, INDUSTRIAL — ii 153–57; Conciliation, Industrial iv 165–69; Construction Industry iv 273 a, 276 a; Employers' Associations v 511 b; Garment Industries vi 583 b; Industrial Relations Councils vii 717–22; Justi viii 507 b; Kingston viii 568 a; Labor Disputes viii 636 a; Labor, Govt. Services for viii 646 b; Minimum Wage x 492 b; Mundella xi 85 b; Railroads xiii 96 b;

Strikes and Lockouts xiv 423 a; Trade Unions (Australia, New Zealand) xv 46 b.
ARBITRATION, INTERNATIONAL—ii 157-62; Introd. Vol. 1 (The Trend to Internationalism) i 173 a; Aggression, International i 485 b; Alabama Claims i 611-13; Calvo and Drago Doctrines iii 156 a; Casus Belli iii 268 a; Govt. (Brit. Commonwealth of Nations) vii 42 b; Hague Conferences vii 242 b; International Law viii 170 b; International Organization viii 182 a; League of Nations ix 292 a; Mediation x 272 a; Outlawry of War xi 508-10; Peace Movements xii 41-48; Permanent Court of Arbitration xii 76-78; Permanent Court of International Justice xii 78-81; Repudiation of Public Debts xiii 323 b.
ARCH, J.—ii 163; Agrarian Movements i 496 a.
ARCHAEOLOGY—ii 163-67; Introd. Vol. 1 (War and Reorientation) i 199 b, 224 a, (The Social Sciences as Disciplines, Lat. Amer.) 316 a; Anthropology ii 74 a, 106 a; Art (Primitive) ii 228 b; Boucher de Crèvecoeur de Perthes ii 648 a; Clermont-Ganneau iii 555 a; Continuity, Social iv 316 a; Curtius iv 652 a; Dress v 235 b; History and Historiography vii 379 b; Man x 72 b; Pottery xii 279 b; Prehistory xii 316-18; Records, Historical xiii 173 b.
Archigenes of Apamea—x 285 b.
Archimedes—xiii 597 b.
ARCHITECTURE—ii 167-75; Art ii 223-59; Expositions, International vi 24 b; Functionalism vi 525 b; Modernism x 567 a; Professions xii 477 b.
ARCHIVES—ii 176-81; Introd. Vol. 1 (The Roman World) i 51 a; Government Publications vii 120-22; History and Historiography vii 372 a; Law (Greek) ix 227 a; Madox x 35 b; Palgrave xi 536 a; Public Libraries xii 659-65; Records, Historical xiii 174 b.
ARDASHEV, P. N.—ii 181.
ARDIGÒ, R.—ii 181.
ARENAL, C.—ii 182.
Aretino, L.—see BRUNI, L.
ARGENSON, MARQUIS D'—ii 182.
ARGENTRÉ, B. D'—ii 182; Conflict of Laws iv 188 b.
Aristippus of Cyrene—Cyrenaics iv 685 b; Hedonism vii 307 a.
ARISTOCRACY—ii 183-90; Introd. Vol. 1 (The Roman World) i 46 b, 58 b; Agrarian Movements i 492-515; Amateur ii 19 a; Amusements, Public ii 41 b; Armed Forces, Control of ii 200 b; Art ii 226 a, 248 b, 255 b; Art Collecting ii 259 a; Assassination ii 272 b; Bicameral System ii 534 a; Bourgeoisie ii 654 b; Brahmanism and Hinduism ii 674 b; Bureaucracy iii 70 b; Career iii 225 a; Conservatism iv 230 b; Diplomacy v 147 b; Fashion vi 142 a; Gentleman, Theory of the vi 616-20; Govt. (Gt. Brit.) vii 24 a; Landed Estates ix 140-43; Legislative Assemblies (Gt. Brit. and Dominions) ix 370 a; Leisure ix 403 a; Liberalism ix 436 b; Literature ix 533 b; Middle Class x 409 a; Nobility xi 385-89; Plutocracy xii 175-77; Primogeniture xii 402-05; Renaissance xiii 280 a; Royal Court xiii 448-51.
ARISTOPHANES—ii 190; Theater xiv 601 a.
ARISTOTLE—ii 191; Introd. Vol. 1 (Greek Culture and Thought) i 26 b, 31 a; Albertus Magnus i 614 b; Aquinas ii 147 a; Averroes ii 338 b; Biology ii 550 b; Bruni iii 19 a; Christianity iii 457 a; Common Sense iv 58 b; Communism iv 82 a; Democracy v 78 a; Economics v 347 a; Education v 406 a; Evolution v 650 a; Evolution, Social v 657 a; Human Nature vii 533 b; Just Price viii 504 b; Justice viii 509 b; Logic ix 599 b; Malthus xii 248 b; Materialism x 210 b; Mechanism and Vitalism x 267 b; Natural Law xi 286 a; Philosophy xii 121 a, 124 b; Political Science xii 208 a; Race Conflict xiii 36 b; Rationalism xiii 114 b; Scholasticism xiii 578 a; Science xiii 597 a; Sociology xiv 232 b; Usury xv 194 b; Woman, Position in Society xv 443 b.
Arithmetic Mean—ii 337 b.
ARKWRIGHT, R.—ii 193.
Armaingaud, A.—viii 615 b.
ARMAMENTS—ii 193-99; Arms and Munitions Traffic ii 206-09; Army ii 210-18; Aviation ii 348 b; Balance of Power ii 397 a; Disarmament v 158-61; Iron and Steel Industry viii 296 b; Limitation of Armaments ix 480-86; Militarism x 447 b; Munitions Industry xi 128-34; Navy xi 310-19; War xv 338 a.
Armaments, Limitation of—see LIMITATION OF ARMAMENTS.
ARMED FORCES, CONTROL OF—ii 199-201; Army ii 211 a; Militarism x 449 a; Militia x 474 a; Power, Political xii 302 a; Praetorianism xii 305-07.
ARMED MERCHANTMEN—ii 201-03; Merchantmen, Status of x 352 a.
ARMED NEUTRALITY—ii 203-04; Armed Merchantmen ii 202 b; Arms and Munitions Traffic ii 206-09; Blockade ii 594 b; Neutrality xi 362 a.
ARMISTICE—ii 204-05.
ARMOUR FAMILY—ii 205; Meat Packing and Slaughtering x 245 b.
ARMS AND MUNITIONS TRAFFIC—ii 206-09; Armaments ii 193-99; Embargo v 486 b; Munitions Industry xi 128-34.
ARMS, RIGHT TO BEAR—ii 209-10.
ARMSTRONG, S. C.—ii 210.
Armstrong, W. G.—xi 129 a.
ARMY—ii 210-18. See Military Service.
ARND, K.—ii 218.
ARNDT, E. M.—ii 218.
ARNOLD OF BRESCIA—ii 219.
ARNOLD, M.—ii 219.
ARNOLD, T.—ii 220.
ARNOLD, W.—ii 220.
ARREST—ii 221-22.
ARRIQUIBAR, N. DE—ii 222.
ARSENYEV, K. K.—ii 222.
ART—ii 223-59 (Introd. 223-26, 257, Primitive 226-29, 258, India 229-33, 258, China 233-36, 258, Japan 236-38, 258, Near Eastern 238-40, 258, Classical 240-43, 258, Mediaeval 243-45, 258, Renaissance 246-53, 258, Modern 253-57, 259). See Classification of Articles (Art), p. 548. See also Introd. Vol. 1 (What Are the Social Sciences?) i 7 b; Anthropology ii 89 b; Ceremony iii 315 b; Chinese Problem iii 432 b; Criticism, Social iv 600 a; Culture iv 643 b; Decadence v 41 a; Evolution, Social v 659 a, 660 a; Genius vi 613 a; Gentleman, Theory of the vi 618 b; Grosse vii 175 b; Guyau vii 229 a; Hegel vii 313 b; Jesuits viii 385 b; Luxury ix 637 b; Metals x 367 a; Naturalism xi 305 a; Negro Problem xi 346 a; Nihilism xi 378 a; Philosophy xii 128 a; Ritual xiii 396 b; Ruskin xiii 472 b; Tradition xv 66 b; Woman, Position in Society (Primitive) xv 441 b.
ART COLLECTING—ii 259-60; Art (Roman) ii 242 b; Museums and Exhibitions xi 138-42.
Art, Industrial—see INDUSTRIAL ARTS.
ARTEL—ii 260-61.
Arthasāstra—Kautilya viii 550 b; Law (Hindu) ix 260 a.
ARTHUR, P. M.—ii 261.
ARTICLES OF CONFEDERATION—ii 262-63; Full Faith and Credit Clause vi 515 a; Native Policy (N. Amer.) xi 263 b.
Articles of War—x 454 a.
Artifacts—Archaeology ii 163-67; Man x 73 a; Pottery xii 279 b; Records, Historical xiii 173 b.
Artificers, Statute of—Apprenticeship ii 145 a; Labourers, Statutes of ix 4 b; Mercantilism x 334 b.
ARTIGAS, J. G.—ii 263.
Artisan—Middle Class x 410 b.

Arts and Crafts Movement—Handicraft vii 257 a; Industrial Arts vii 689 a.
ARWIDSSON, A. I.—ii 263.
Arya Samaj—xiii 543 a.
Aryanism—Adelung i 438 a; Antisemitism ii 120 a, 122 a; Aryans ii 264-65; Gobineau vi 683 b; Müller xi 81 b; National Socialism, German xi 225 b; Woltmann xv 438 b.
ARYANS—ii 264-65; Race xiii 27 a. See also Aryanism.
ARZRUNI, G.—ii 265.
ASCETICISM—ii 266; Brahmanism and Hinduism ii 675 b, 677 a; Buddhism iii 33 a; Celibacy iii 284 a; Chastity iii 357-58; Cynics iv 680-85; Fasting vi 144-46; Franciscan Movement vi 410 b; Monasticism x 584 a; Religious Orders xiii 276-78.
ASCHAM, R.—ii 267.
ASCHEHOUG, T. H.—ii 267.
Asclepiades of Bithynia—x 285 b.
ASHBURTON, LORD—ii 267.
Ashe, T.—vii 553 b.
Asher, J. ben—Karo viii 547 b; Law (Jewish) ix 224 a.
Ashley, Lord—see SHAFTESBURY.
ASHLEY, W. J.—ii 268.
ASIENTO—ii 268-70; Migrations x 433 a; Slavery xiv 81 b.
ASOKA—ii 270; Art (India) ii 231 a; Buddhism iii 34 b, 36 b.
ASQUITH, H. H.—ii 270.
ASSASSINATION—ii 271-75; Introd. Vol. I (Renaissance and Reformation) i 97 a; Conspiracy, Political iv 238-41; Gershuni vi 639 b; Mariana x 110 a; Terrorism xiv 577 b; Tyranny xv 136 a.
Assemblies, Legislative—see LEGISLATIVE ASSEMBLIES.
ASSEMBLY, RIGHT OF—ii 275-76; Freedom of Association vi 448 b.
ASSESSMENT OF TAXES—ii 276-79; General Property Tax vi 603 b; House and Building Taxes vii 495 a; Income Tax vii 627 a; Inheritance Taxation viii 45 b; Land Taxation ix 71 a; Mortgage Tax xi 38 b; Slums xiv 94 a; Tax Administration xiv 526 a; Valuation xv 216 a.
Assessments, Special—see SPECIAL ASSESSMENTS.
ASSIGNATS—ii 279-81; Bimetallism and Monometallism ii 548 a; Cambon iii 157 b.
ASSIMILATION, SOCIAL—ii 281-83; Accommodation i 404 a; Amalgamation ii 17 a; Americanization ii 33-35; Civic Education iii 497 b; Conquest iv 207 a; Crusades iv 615 b; Diaspora v 129 a; Foreign Language Press vi 378-82; Immigration vii 591 a; Irredentism viii 326 b; Jewish Emancipation viii 395 a; Judaism viii 440 a; Native Policy xi 252-83; Zionism xv 529 b.

ASSIZES—ii 283-84; Courts iv 521 b.
Associated Press—Press xii 331 a, 335 b; Stone xiv 411 b.
Associated Telephone and Telegraph Co.—xiv 566 b.
ASSOCIATION—ii 284-86; Achelis i 419 a; Age Societies i 482-83; Artel ii 260-61; Civic Organizations iii 498-502; Clubs iii 573-77; Clubs, Political iii 577-80; Collectivism iii 635 a; Cooperation iv 359-99; Corporation iv 414-23; Employers' Associations v 509-14; Freedom of Association vi 447-50; Gierke vi 655 b; Group vii 178-82; Interests viii 147 a; Mazzini x 240 a; Voluntary Associations xv 283-87.
Association of American Law Schools—ii 30 a.
Association of Junior Leagues—xv 461 b.
Association, Right of—see FREEDOM OF ASSOCIATION.
Associationism—Bain ii 390 b; Behaviorism ii 496 a; Habit vii 237 a; Hartley vii 276 b; Psychology xii 589 a.
Associations for the Advancement of Science—see LEARNED SOCIETIES.
Assumpsit—Fraud vi 428 b; Tort xiv 654 a; Writs xv 504 a.
Assumption of Risk—v 515 a.
Assyrian Law—Law (Cuneiform) ix 211-19.
Assyriology—Delitzsch v 69 a; King viii 565 b; Luckenbill ix 626 b; Schrader xiii 583 b.
ASTOR, J. J.—ii 287.
ASTROLOGY—ii 287-89; Science xiii 596 a.
Astronomy—Introd. Vol. I (Renaissance and Reformation) i 86 a; Bruno iii 20 a; Calendar iii 140-44; Copernicus iv 400 b; Galileo Galilei vi 547 b; Science xiii 597 b, 598 b.
ASYLUM—ii 289-90; Exile v 687 a; Extradition vi 41-44; Holy Places vii 420 b; Political Offenders xii 201 a; Refugees xiii 200-05; Sanctuary xiii 534-37.
ATAVISM—ii 290-91; Criminology iv 585 a, 587 a; Lombroso ix 603 b.
Atcherley, L. W.—vii 574 a.
ATELIERS NATIONAUX—ii 291-92.
Ateliers Sociaux—ii 584 a.
Athanasius—iii 465 a.
ATHEISM—ii 292-96; Freethinkers vi 465-71; Religious Institutions (Roman Catholic) xiii 259 b.
Athenaeus of Attalia—x 285 b.
ATHLETICS—ii 296-300; Physical Education xii 129-33; Sports xiv 305-08.
ATKINSON, E.—ii 300.
ATKINSON, H. A.—ii 301.
ATKINSON, WILLIAM—ii 301.
ATKINSON, WILMER—ii 302.

ATKYNS, R.—ii 302.
Atlantic and Pacific Tea Co.—xiii 352 a.
Atomism—Materialism x 209 b.
ATROCITIES—ii 302-04; Massacre x 191-94.
ATTAINDER—ii 304-05; Appeals ii 132 b; Confiscation iv 184 b; Jury viii 493 b.
ATTITUDES, SOCIAL—ii 305-07; Introd. Vol. I (War and Reorientation) i 206 a; Accommodation i 403 b; Folklore vi 291 a; Lawlessness ix 277-79; Modernism x 564-68; Nationalism xi 231-49; Pressures, Social xii 344-48; Primitivism xii 398-402; Romanticism xiii 426-34; Sanction, Social xiii 531-34; Social Psychology xiv 151-57; Taste xiv 523-25; Traditionalism xv 67-70.
Attorney—ix 330 a.
ATTWOOD, T.—ii 307; Chartism iii 352 b.
ATWATER, W. O.—ii 307; Family Budgets vi 77 a.
AUBAINE, RIGHT OF—ii 307-08.
Aubert, A.—iv 588 b.
AUCLERT, H.—ii 308.
AUCOC, J. L.—ii 308.
AUCTIONS—ii 309-11; Agricultural Marketing i 561 b; Food Industries vi 317 b.
AUDIENCIA—ii 311-12.
AUDITING—ii 312-13; Accounting i 404-12; Accounts, Public i 412-15; Financial Administration vi 236 a, 240 b; Municipal Finance xi 103 a.
AUER, I.—ii 313.
AUGUSTINE (d. 430)—ii 313; Introd. Vol. I (The Universal Church) i 65 b, 70 b; Art ii 224 b; Church Fathers iii 465 b; History and Historiography vii 370 b; Intolerance viii 243 b; Just Price viii 505 a; Monasticism x 588 b; Natural Law xi 286 b; Persecution xii 83 b; Rationalism xiii 115 a; Religious Freedom xiii 241 a.
Augustine (d. 604)—x 538 a.
AUGUSTINIS, M. DE—ii 315.
AUGUSTUS—ii 315; Introd. Vol. I (The Roman World) i 53 a, 54 b, 58 a; Monarchy x 580 b; Royal Court xiii 448 b.
AULARD, F. V. A.—ii 316; Mathiez x 228 a.
Aumône—xi 43 b.
Aurangzeb—ii 232 b.
AURELIUS ANTONINUS, M.—ii 317.
AUSPITZ, R.—ii 317; Economics v 367 b; Lieben ix 451 b.
Austin Canons—x 588 b.
AUSTIN, J.—ii 317; Amos ii 39 a; International Law viii 172 a; Jurisprudence viii 481 a; Positivism xii 263 a.
Australian Ballot—ii 411 a.
AUTHORITY—ii 319-21; Absolutism i 380-82; Allegiance i 644-46; Aristocracy ii 183-90; Asso-

ciation ii 285 b; Autocracy ii 321–22; Bribery ii 691 b; Coercion iii 618 b; Conservatism iv 230–33; Dictatorship v 133–36; Dogma v 189–91; Duty v 293–95; Expert vi 10–13; Family vi 68 a; Force, Political vi 338–41; Leadership ix 282–87; Liberty ix 444 a; Masses x 197 b; Obedience, Political xi 415–18; Pluralism xii 170–74; Power, Political xii 300–05; Prerogative xii 318–20; Priesthood xii 388–95; Renaissance xiii 282 b; Rule of Law xiii 463–66; Social Contract xiv 127–31; Society xiv 226 b; Sovereignty xiv 265–69; State xiv 328–32.

AUTOCRACY — ii 321–22; Monarchy x 579–84; Tyranny xv 135–37.

Automatic Electric, Inc.—xiv 564 a.

Automobile—see MOTOR VEHICLE TRANSPORTATION.

Automobile Accidents—see MOTOR VEHICLE ACCIDENTS.

AUTOMOBILE INDUSTRY—ii 322–30; Aviation (Industry) ii 365 b; Instalment Selling viii 76 a; Leather Industries ix 311 b; Rubber xiii 458 a.

AUTOMOBILE INSURANCE—ii 330–32; Agricultural Insurance i 547 a; Casualty Insurance iii 263 a; Compensation and Liability Insurance iv 141 a; Motor Vehicle Accidents xi 73 a.

AUTONOMY—ii 332–36; Association ii 285 b; Dominion Status v 211–16; Federalism vi 169–72; Federation vi 172–78; Govt. (Brit. Commonwealth of Nations) vii 38–43, (Soviet Russia) 67 b; Irredentism viii 327 a; Jewish Autonomy viii 391–94; Local Government ix 574–85; Minorities, National x 518–25; Protectorate xii 567–71; Regionalism xiii 208–18; States' Rights xiv 346–50.

Avebury, Lord—see LUBBOCK, J.

Avenarius, R.—iv 214 a.

AVERAGE—ii 336–38; Index Numbers vii 652–58; Statistics xiv 371 a.

AVERROES—ii 338; Medicine x 286 b.

AVES, E.—ii 338.

AVIATION—ii 339–69 (Historical Development 339–47, 368, International Aspects 347–52, 368, Commercial 352–57, 368, Industry 358–66, 368, Law 366–69); Armaments ii 194 b, 196 a; Business, Govt. Services for iii 119 b; Transit, International xv 79 b; Transportation xv 87 a; Warfare, Laws of xv 363 b.

Aviz—x 463 a.

AVOIDANCE—ii 369–70.

Avunculate—Anthropology ii 86 b; Social Organization xiv 145 a.

AXELROD, P. B.—ii 370; Bolshevism ii 625 a.

Axiometry—see INDEX NUMBERS.

AYALA, B.—ii 371.

AYCOCK, C. B.—ii 371.

Azana, M.—xi 631 a.

AZCÁRATE, G. DE—ii 371.

AZEGLIO, M. D'—ii 372.

Azo—ii 372; Glossators vi 680 b.

AZUNI, D. A.—ii 373.

BAADER, F. X. VON—ii 373.

Baal Shem Tob—iii 355 a.

BABBAGE, C.—ii 374; Specialization xiv 284 a.

Babbitt, I.—Humanism vii 543 b; Humanitarianism vii 548 a.

BABELON, E.—ii 374.

Babeuf, F. N.—see BABOUVISM.

BABOUVISM—ii 375; Communism iv 85 a; French Revolution vi 478 b; Socialism xiv 192 b.

Babson, R. W.—vi 349 b.

Baby Farming—see PLACING OUT.

Babylonian Law—Law (Cuneiform) ix 211–19.

BACALAN, A. T. I. DE—ii 375.

BACH, A.—ii 376.

BACHEM, JOSEF and JULIUS—ii 376.

BACHILLER Y MORALES, A.—ii 377.

BACHOFEN, J. J.—ii 377; Evolution, Social v 658 b.

BACK-TO-THE-LAND MOVEMENTS—ii 378–79; Land Utilization ix 134 b.

BACKWARD COUNTRIES—ii 379–81; Brigandage ii 693 b; Concessions iv 159 a; Forced Labor vi 342 b; Hours of Labor vii 489 b; Imperialism vii 610 a; International Advisers viii 155–59; International Finance viii 162 b; Machinery, Industrial x 12 b; Mandates x 87–93; Native Policy xi 252–83; Protectorate xii 569 a; Spheres of Influence xiv 297–99.

BACON, F.—ii 381; Introd. Vol. I (Renaissance and Reformation) i 102 b, (The Rise of Liberalism) 105 b, (Individualism and Capitalism) 150 b; Academic Freedom i 386 b; Alembert i 629 b; Encyclopédistes v 529 a; Logic ix 601 a; Materialism x 211 a; Positivism xii 261 b.

BACON, R.—ii 383; Nitrates xi 379 b.

Bacteriology—iv 68 a.

Baden-Powell, R. S. S.—ii 667 b.

BAER, A. A.—ii 383.

BAER, G. F.—ii 383.

Baer, K. E. von—Evolution v 651 b; Evolution, Social v 657 b; Haeckel vii 240 b.

Baer of Mezherich—iii 355 a.

BAGEHOT, W.—ii 384; Imitation vii 586 b.

BAGLEY, S.—ii 385.

Bahá'Alláh—see HUSAYN A'LI.

BÄHR, O.—ii 386.

BAIL—ii 386–88; Bonding ii 633 a.

BAILEY, S.—ii 388.

BAILMENT—ii 388–90; Common Carrier iv 49 a; Hotels vii 476 b; Pledge xii 166–68; Warehousing xv 358 b.

BAILY, F.—ii 390.

BAIN, A.—ii 390.

BAINES, E.—ii 391.

BAINES, J. A.—ii 391.

BAIRD, H. C.—ii 392.

BAKER, G.—ii 392.

BAKER, H. H.—ii 393.

BAKEWELL, R.—ii 393; Agriculture i 580 a; Stock Breeding xiv 395 a.

Baking Industry—vi 303–07.

BAKUNIN, M.—ii 393; Introd. Vol. I (Individualism and Capitalism) i 158 b; Anarchism ii 49 a, 51 b; Masses x 196 b.

Balādhuri, al—vii 381 b.

BALAKSHIN, A. N.—ii 394.

Balance of Indebtedness—Balance of Trade ii 402 a, 404 b.

Balance of Payments—Balance of Trade ii 402 a, 405 b.

BALANCE OF POWER—ii 395–99; Alliance ii 3–4; Balance of Trade ii 400 a; Buffer State iii 45–46; Concert of Powers iv 154 a; Great Powers vii 161 a; Isolation, Diplomatic viii 352 b; Protectorate xii 568 a.

BALANCE OF TRADE—ii 399–406; Bullionists iii 60–64; Business, Govt. Services for iii 122 a; Carli iii 228 b; Castro iii 259 b; Chartered Companies iii 350 a; Foreign Exchange vi 361 a; Foreign Investment vi 366 b; Free Trade vi 441 a; International Finance viii 159–164; Mercantilism x 337 b; Misselden x 535 b; Mun xi 84 b.

BALBI, A.—ii 406.

BALBO, C.— ii 406.

Balduinus—see BAUDOUIN, F.

BALDUS, P.—ii 407; Commentators iii 680 a.

Baldwin, B. T.—Adolescence i 456 b; Anthropometry ii 112 a.

Baldwin, J. M.—Accommodation i 403 a; Imitation vii 587 a.

BALDWIN, R.—ii 407.

BALFOUR, A. J.—ii 408; Insurgency, Political viii 115 b.

Balfour Declaration—Zionism xv 533 a, 534 a.

Balkan Problem—see NEAR EASTERN PROBLEM.

BALLANCE, J.—ii 408.

BALLANCHE, P. S.—ii 409.

BALLIN, A.—ii 409.

BALLOT—ii 410–12; Absent-Voting i 376; Elections v 453 b; Machine, Political ix 660 b; Short Ballot Movement xiv 43–44.

Ballou, A.—Christian Socialism iii 451 b; Communistic Settlements iv 97 b.

BALMACEDA, J.—ii 412.

BALMES, J. L.—ii 412.

Balsamo, P.—i 275 a.

Baltimore and Ohio Plan—viii 627 b.

Baltimore Sun—i 359 b.
Bambergensis—xiii 588 b.
BAMBERGER, L.—ii 413.
BANCROFT, G.—ii 413; Introd. Vol. I (The Social Sciences as Disciplines, U. S.) i 328 b; History and Historiography vii 387 a.
BANCROFT, H. H.—ii 414.
BANCROFT, R.—ii 414.
BANDELIER, A. F. A.—ii 414.
BANDINI, S. A.—ii 415.
BANFIELD, T. C.—ii 415.
Banier, A.—vi 288 b.
Banishment—see EXILE.
BANK DEPOSITS—ii 416–17; Bank Deposits, Guaranty of ii 417–19; Bank Reserves ii 419–21; Banking, Commercial ii 421–47; Brokers' Loans iii 12 a; Credit iv 547 b; Currency iv 650 b; Money x 601 b; Savings Banks xiii 555 b.
BANK DEPOSITS, GUARANTY OF— ii 417–19; Bonding ii 633 a; National Banks, U. S. xi 187 a.
Bank of England—Bank Reserves ii 420 b; Banking, Commercial ii 429 b, 431–35; Central Banking iii 305 a; Credit Control iv 552 a; Financial Administration vi 235 b; Foreign Exchange vi 359 b; Gilbart vi 661 a; Montagu x 634 a; Paterson xii 25 b.
Bank of Exchange—see LABOR EXCHANGE BANKS.
Bank of France—Banking, Commercial ii 430 b; Financial Administration vi 237 a.
Bank for International Settlements—Central Banking iii 307 a; Clearing Houses iii 547 b; Financial Organization vi 247 a; International Finance viii 163 b; Monetary Unions x 600 b.
Bank Rate—see Discount Rate.
BANK RESERVES—ii 419–21; Bank Deposits ii 416 b; Banking, Commercial ii 422 b; Banknotes ii 448 b; Banks, Wildcat ii 454–56; Brokers' Loans iii 12 a; Central Banking iii 303 a; Credit Control iv 552 b; Federal Reserve System vi 154–65; Liquidity ix 493 a; National Banks, U. S. xi 187 a.
Bank of the United States, First— Banking, Commercial ii 442 a; Bollmann ii 623 b.
Bank of the United States, Second—Banking, Commercial ii 442 b; Biddle ii 536 b.
BANKING COMMERCIAL—ii 421–47 (Theory 421–23, 445, History 423–31, 445, Modern Banking, United Kingdom 431–35, 446, Continental Eur. 435–41, 446, U. S. 441–44, 447, Canada 444–45). See Classification of Articles (Banking), p. 548. See also Introd. Vol. I (Greek Culture and Thought) i 29 a; Agric. Credit i 532 b;

Bardi Family ii 458; Biddle ii 536 b; Bollmann ii 623 b; Bonding ii 632 b; Brokers' Loans iii 11 a; Burlamachi iii 76 a; Cassell iii 254 a; Colonial Economic Policy iii 650 a; Conant iv 153; Cooke iv 355 a; Corporation Taxes iv 434 a; Coutts iv 540 b; Credit iv 546 a; Crises iv 596 b; Fairs vi 61 a; Fortunes, Private vi 390–92; Fugger Family vi 513 b; Gilbart vi 661 a; Govt. Owned Corporations vii 107 a; Interest viii 141 b; Interlocking Directorates viii 150 b; Investment viii 266 a; Land Mortgage Credit ix 46 a, 50 b; Medici x 282 b; Mercantile Credit x 331 a; Military Orders x 461 a; Mitsui x 549 b; Money Market x 615 a; Negro Problem xi 348 b; Prices (Theory) xii 371 b; Rothschild Family xiii 440 b; Saving xiii 550 a; Small Loans xiv 110 a; Stillman xiv 392 a; Trusts and Trustees xv 125 a; Warburg xv 352 b.
Banking, Investment—see INVESTMENT BANKING.
Banking, Labor — see LABOR BANKING.
BANKNOTES—ii 447–49; Bank Reserves ii 420 b; Banking, Commercial ii 428 b, 432 a, 435 b, 443 a, 445 a; Banks, Wildcat ii 454–56; Central Banking iii 303 a; Credit iv 547 a; Currency iv 649–51; Federal Reserve System vi 154–65; Land Bank Schemes ix 29–32; National Banks, U. S. xi 186 b, 187 b; Paper Money xi 568 b; State Banks, U. S. xiv 333 b.
BANKRUPTCY—ii 449–54; Corporation Finance iv 430 a; Debt v 38 a; International Finance viii 161 a; Receivership xiii 150 a, 152 b.
Banks of Issue—see BANKNOTES and CENTRAL BANKING.
BANKS, WILDCAT — ii 454–56; Banking, Commercial ii 443 a.
Baptism—Birth Customs ii 567 a; Mysteries xi 174 a.
Baptists—Religious Institutions (Protestant) xiii 272 a; Revivals, Religious xiii 365 b; Sects xiii 627 b, 628 a.
Bar—see LEGAL PROFESSION AND LEGAL EDUCATION.
BAR, K. L. VON—ii 456.
Baransky, N. N.—vi 627 b.
Barbarossa, Frederick—see FREDERICK I.
BARBERET, J.-J.—ii 456.
BARBON, N.—ii 456.
BARBOSA, R.—ii 457; Parties, Political xi 634 a.
Barbusse, H.—Clarté Movement iii 531 a; Peace Movements xii 47 a.
BARCLAY, W.—ii 457; Introd. Vol. I (Renaissance and Reformation) i 99 a.

BARDI FAMILY—ii 458; Loans, Personal ix 563 a.
BARÈRE DE VIEUZAC, B.—ii 459.
BARGAINING POWER—ii 459–62; Benefits, Trade Union ii 515 a; Collective Bargaining iii 628–31; Distribution v 172 a; Freedom of Association vi 450 a; Freedom of Contract vi 450–55; Labor Contract viii 629–33; Labor Legislation and Law viii 667 b, 671 b; Wages xv 304 b.
Baring, A.—see ASHBURTON, LORD.
Baring, E.—see CROMER, LORD.
Barker, E.—xii 171 b, 172 b.
BARNARD, H.—ii 462.
BARNARDO, T.—ii 463.
BARNAVE, A. P. J. M.—ii 463.
BARNETT, S. A.—ii 464; Social Settlements xiv 157 b.
Barneveld, J. of—see OLDENBARNEVELDT, J. VAN.
BARONDESS, J.—ii 464.
BARONE, E.—ii 465.
BARONIUS, C.—ii 465.
Barrère, B.—x 466 a.
BARRÈS, M.—ii 466; Regionalism xiii 211 a.
Barrett, G.—ii 390 b.
BARRIOS, J. R.—ii 466; Central American Federation iii 301 b.
Barrister—ix 332 b, 336 b.
BARRON, C. W.—ii 467.
BARROS, J. DE—ii 467.
BARROT, C. H. O.—ii 467.
Barrows, H. H.—vi 621 b.
BARROWS, S. J.—ii 468.
BARTER—ii 468–69; Anthropology ii 83 b; Exchange v 667 a; Labor Exchange Banks viii 637 b; Labor, Methods of Remuneration for viii 677 a.
Barth, C. G.—xiii 607 a.
BARTH, P.—ii 469.
BARTH, T.—ii 470.
Barthélemy, J.—ii 36 b.
Bartholomew—x 193 b.
Bartolists—see COMMENTATORS.
BARTOLUS OF SASSOFERRATO—ii 470; Civil Law iii 505 a; Commentators iii 680 a; Conflict of Laws iv 188 a.
BARTON, C.—ii 471.
BARTON, J.—ii 472.
Baruch, L.—ii 643 a.
BASEDOW, J. B.—ii 472.
Basil of Caesarea—Church Fathers iii 465 b; Monasticism x 585 b.
Basile, J.—see GUESDE, J.
BASING POINT PRICES—ii 473–75; Iron and Steel Industry viii 308 a; Price Discrimination xii 354 a.
BASNAGE, J. C.—ii 475.
BASSERMANN, E.—ii 475.
BASSETT, J. S.—ii 475.
Bastable, C. F.—Revenues, Public xiii 362 a; Taxation xiv 533 a.
BASTIAN, A.—ii 476; Anthropology ii 105 b, 109 b.
BASTIAT, F.—ii 476; Carey iii 226 b; Distribution v 169 b.

Bata, T.—ix 310 b.
BATEMAN, A. E.—ii 477.
BATESON, M.—ii 478.
BATESON, W.—ii 478.
Baths, Public—see RESORTS.
BATIFFOL, P.—ii 478.
BATLLE Y ORDÓÑEZ, J.—ii 479; Trade Unions xv 51 b.
BAUDEAU, N.—ii 479.
BAUDOUIN, F.—ii 480.
BAUDRILLART, H. J. L.—ii 480.
BAUER, B.—ii 481; Edelmann v 396 b.
Bauer, E.—ii 112 a.
Bauer, G.—see AGRICOLA.
Bauer, O.—Minorities, National x 521 a; Socialization xiv 222 a.
Baumes Law—xiii 159 b.
BAUMSTARK, E.—ii 481.
BAUR, F. C.—ii 481.
Bauxite—x 375 b.
BAX, E. B.—ii 482.
BAXTER, R.—ii 482.
BAXTER, R. D.—ii 483.
Bayes, T.—Probability xii 430 a, 431 b, 432 b.
BAYLE, P.—ii 483; Religious Freedom xiii 242 b.
BAZARD, S.-A.—ii 484; Carbonari iii 223 a; Saint-Simon and Saint-Simonianism xiii 510 a.
BEACONSFIELD, LORD—ii 484; By-Elections iii 127 b.
Bear Trading—xiv 291 a.
Beardmore, Wm., and Co.—xi 130 a.
BEAUFORT, L. DE—ii 485.
BEAUJON, A.—ii 486.
BEAUMANOIR, SIRE DE—ii 486.
BEAUMARCHAIS, P. A. C. DE—ii 486; Theater xiv 608 b.
Beauquier, C.—xiii 210 b.
BEBEL, A.—ii 487; Socialist Parties xiv 213 b; Trade Unions xv 12 b; Woman, Position in Society xv 446 b.
BECCARIA, C. B.—ii 488; Introd. Vol. I (The Revolutions) i 137 a, (The Social Sciences as Disciplines, Italy) 274 b; Capital Punishment iii 193 b; Criminal Law iv 576 b; Criminology iv 584 b; Economics v 365 a.
BECHER, J. J.—ii 489; Cameralism iii 159 a.
Bechterew, W.—see BEKHTEREV, V.
BECK, A.—ii 490.
Beck, C.—xii 131 b.
Becker, W. A.—x 146 a.
BECKET, T.—ii 490; Benefit of Clergy ii 512 b.
BEDDOE, J.—ii 491.
BEDE—ii 491; History and Historiography vii 371 b.
BEECHER, H. W.—ii 492.
BEER, G. L.—ii 493.
Beers, C. W.—x 320 a.
BEGGING—ii 493–95; Blind ii 588 b; Charity iii 342 b; Franciscan Movement vi 414 a; Poor Laws xii 230 b; Vagrancy xv 205–08.
Behavior—see COLLECTIVE BEHAVIOR; CONDUCT.

BEHAVIORISM—ii 495–98; Introd. Vol. I (War and Reorientation) i 196 b; Abnormal Psychology i 361 b, 368 a; Adjustment i 438 b; Conditioned Reflex iv 175–76; Consciousness iv 214 a; Educational Psychology v 433 b; Environmentalism v 564 b; Functionalism vi 524 a; Psychology xii 594 a, 595 b; Social Psychology xiv 155 a; Sociology xiv 240 b.
Beirut—Legal Profession and Legal Education ix 327 b.
BEKHTEREV, V.—ii 498; Behaviorism ii 497 a; Conditioned Reflex iv 176 a.
BEKKER, E. I.—ii 499.
BELIAYEV, I. D.—ii 500.
BELIEF — ii 500–03; Common Sense iv 58–61; Conformity iv 196–98; Conversion, Religious iv 353–55; Dogma v 189–91; Fanaticism vi 90–92; Fictions vi 225–28; Fundamentalism vi 526–27; Ritual xiii 396–98.
BELINSKY, V. G.—ii 503.
BELL, A.—ii 503.
Bell, A. G.—xiv 562 a.
Bell, C.—xiii 142 b.
BELLAMY, E.—ii 504.
BELLARMINE, R. F. R.—ii 504.
BELLERS, J.—ii 505.
BELLET, D.—ii 505.
BELLIGERENCY—ii 505–07; Armed Merchantmen ii 201–03; Armistice ii 204–05; Arms and Munitions Traffic ii 206–09; Blockade ii 594–96; Casus Belli iii 266–68; Civil War iii 525 a; Contraband of War iv 321–23; Guerrilla Warfare vii 199 a.
BELLO, A.—ii 507; Introd. Vol. I (The Social Sciences as Disciplines, Lat. Amer.) i 312 a.
BELOCH, K. J.—ii 507.
BELOW, G. A. H. VON—ii 508; Economic History v 322 a.
BELUZE, J. P.—ii 509.
BENBOW, W.—ii 509; General Strike vi 608 a.
BENDIXEN, F.—ii 509.
BENEDICT—ii 510; Introd. Vol. I (The Universal Church) i 65 b; Monasticism x 586 a.
Benedict xv—xiii 260 b.
Benedict of Aniane—x 587 a.
Benedict, F. G.—i 621 a.
BENEDIKT, M.—ii 511; Criminology iv 587 a.
Benefice—xi 563 a.
BENEFIT OF CLERGY—ii 511–13; Becket ii 490 b.
Benefit Societies—see MUTUAL AID SOCIETIES; FRIENDLY SOCIETIES.
BENEFITS, TRADE UNION—ii 513–16; Friendly Societies vi 495 b; Old Age xi 457 b; Unemployment Insurance xv 163 a.
BENEKE, F. E.—ii 516; Psychology xii 591 b.
Bénévent, Prince de—see TALLEYRAND-PÉRIGORD, C.-M. DE.
BENJAMIN, J. P.—ii 516.

Benjamin, P. H.—see ESTOURNELLES DE CONSTANT, BARON D'.
BENNETT, J. G.—ii 517; Press xii 328 b.
BENNIGSEN, R. VON—ii 518.
BENOISTON DE CHATEAUNEUF, L. F.—ii 518.
BENTHAM, J.—ii 518; Introd. Vol. I (The Revolutions) i 134 a, (Individualism and Capitalism) 153 b; Altruism and Egoism ii 14 b; Behaviorism ii 496 a; Codification iii 609 a; Criminology iv 585 a; Democracy v 80 b; Economics v 352 a; Govt. Regulation of Industry vii 124 a; Hedonism vii 308 b; Individualism vii 678 a; Mill x 480 b; Positivism xii 262 b; Priestley xii 395 b; Procedure, Legal xii 453 a; Radicalism xiii 52 b; Usury xv 196 b; Utilitarianism xv 198 a.
BENTINCK, LORD—ii 519.
Bentley, A. F.—xii 347 b.
BENTON, T. H.—ii 520; Homestead vii 437 a.
BEÖTHY DE BESSENYO, L.—ii 520.
BERCH, A.—ii 521.
Berengarius—i 66 b.
BÉRENGER, A. M. M. T.—ii 521.
Bérenger, R.—ii 521 b.
BERGBOHM, K. M.—ii 521.
Bergengren, R. F.—iv 395 a.
BERGER, V. L.—ii 522.
BERGH, H.—ii 522.
Bering Sea Controversy—vi 270 a.
BERKELEY, G.—ii 523; Consciousness iv 213 a; Positivism xii 261 b; Psychology xii 589 b.
BERLINER, A.—ii 523.
Bernard, C.—x 268 b.
BERNARD OF CLAIRVAUX—ii 524; Introd. Vol. I (The Universal Church) i 66 a.
Bernardin of Feltre—xii 34 b.
Bernardino of Siena—viii 506 a.
BERNER, A. F.—ii 524.
BERNHARDI, T. VON—ii 524; Small Holdings xiv 102 b.
BERNOULLI—ii 525; National Income xi 221 a; Probability xii 426 b, 429 a, 430 b, 432 a.
BERNSTEIN, A.—ii 526.
Bernstein, E.—Class Struggle iii 539 b; Economics v 380 a; Socialism xiv 203 a.
Bernstein-Kogan, S. V.—vi 627 b.
BERNSTORFF, A. P.—ii 526.
BERNSTORFF, J. H. E.—ii 526.
Berr, H.—i 222 b.
Berry Press Interests—xii 333 b.
BERT, P.—ii 527; Native Policy xi 271 b.
BERTILLON, A.—ii 527; Identification vii 573 a.
BERTILLON, J.—ii 528; Mortality xi 29 a.
Bertillon System—Identification vii 573 a.
BERTIN, L. F.—ii 528.
Besant, A.—ii 561 b.

Index (Bata — Blind)

Beseler, K. G. C.—ii 529.
Besht—iii 355 a.
Besold, C.—ii 529.
Bessemer Process—viii 301 b.
Bestuzhev-Riumin, K. N.—ii 530.
Bethmann Hollweg, T. von—ii 530.
Béthune, M. de—see Sully, Duc de.
Betsky, I. I.—ii 531.
Better Business Bureaus—iii 112 a.
Betterment Taxes—see Special Assessments.
Beust, F. F. von—ii 531.
Beverage Industry—Food Industries vi 307–09; Plantation Wares xii 154 b. See also Alcohol.
Beveridge, A. J.—ii 532.
Beyer, G.—ii 532.
Beyer, O. S.—viii 627 b.
Beyer, W. C.—vi 75 b.
Bezold, F. von—ii 533.
Bhakti—ii 230 b.
Bianchini, L.—ii 533.
Bible—see Sacred Books.
Bicameral System—ii 533–36; Cabinet Government iii 136 b; Deadlock v 17 a; Federation vi 176 b; Legislative Assemblies ix 358 b, 362 a, 367 b, 369 b, 384 a.
Biddle, N.—ii 536.
Biedermann, F. K.—ii 537.
Biel, G.—ii 537; Natural Law xi 287 a.
Bierling, E. R.—ii 538.
Biggs, H. M.—ii 538; Communicable Diseases, Control of iv 68 a; Health Education vii 290 a.
Bilbao, F.—ix 185 a.
Biliński, L.—ii 539.
Bill, A. C.—iii 449 a.
Bill Broker—Banking, Commercial (United Kingdom) ii 433 b; Bill of Exchange ii 540 b; Broker iii 10 a; Money Market x 615 a.
Bill of Exchange—ii 539–41; Acceptance i 388–89; Banking, Commercial ii 425 a, 433 a; Check iii 362–63; Credit iv 546 b; Fairs vi 61 a; Foreign Exchange vi 358 a; Mercantile Credit x 329 b; Moratorium x 652 a; Negotiable Instruments xi 332–35; Thöl xiv 618 b.
Bill of Lading—Bailment ii 389 b; Credit iv 549 a; Marine Insurance x 113 b.
Billings, J. S.—ii 542.
Bills of Credit—ii 542–44.
Bills of Rights—ii 544–46; Agreement of the People i 516–18; Civil Liberties iii 510 a; Declaration of the Rights of Man and the Citizen v 49–51; Due Process of Law v 265 a; Enlightenment v 550 b; Freedom of Speech and of the Press vi 457 a; Magna Carta x 44–46; Mason x 176 b; Natural Rights xi 301 a; Searches and Seizures xiii 618 a.

Bimetallism and Monometallism—ii 546–49; Bamberger ii 413 a; Bullionists iii 60–64; Cernuschi iii 317 a; Free Silver vi 438–40; Monetary Unions x 596 a; Money x 606 a; Silver xiv 57 b, 59 b.
Binding, K.—ii 549.
Binet, A.—ii 549; Abnormal Psychology i 365 b; Child (Psychology) iii 392 a; Mental Defectives x 312 b; Mental Tests x 323 b.
Bing, S.—ii 256 a.
Biology—ii 550–57; Introd. Vol. 1 (What Are the Social Sciences?) i 7 a; Acclimatization i 401–03; Adaptation i 435–37; Adjustment i 438 b; Adolescence i 455–59; Alcohol i 620–22, 624 b; Amalgamation ii 17 a; Anthropology ii 75–76; Aristocracy ii 186 b; Atavism ii 290–91; Blumenbach ii 605 a; Broca iii 7 a; Buffon iii 46 a; Chastity iii 358 a; Class iii 535 a; Communicable Diseases, Control of iv 66–78; Comparative Psychology iv 129–31; Courtship iv 538–40; Criminology iv 587 a; Darwin v 4; Degeneration v 55–57; Environmentalism v 561–66; Eugenics v 617–21; Evolution v 649–56; Gestalt vi 642–46; Heredity vii 328–35; Human Nature vii 533 a; Instinct viii 82 a; Jurisprudence viii 483 b; Lamarck ix 21 b; Man x 71 a; Materialism x 212 b, 215 a; Mechanism and Vitalism x 267–71; Medicine x 287 b; Psychology xii 592 b; Race xiii 25–36; Science xiii 600 b.
Biometry—see Anthropometry.
Birkbeck, G.—ii 557.
Birkenhead, Lord—xiv 475 b.
Birkmeyer, K. von—ii 558.
Birney, J. G.—ii 558.
Birth Control—ii 559–65; Abortion i 372–74; Births ii 572 a; Carlile iii 229 a; Companionate Marriage iv 113–15; Comstock iv 150; Infanticide viii 27–28; Knowlton viii 585 a; Marriage x 153 b; Owen xi 517 b.
Birth Customs—ii 565–68; Culture iv 631 a; Death Customs v 22 b.
Birth Rates—see Births.
Births—ii 568–72; Birth Control ii 564 a; Child (Hygiene) iii 380–84, (Mortality) 384–90; Family Allowances vi 72 b; Illegitimacy vii 579 b; Marriage x 153 b; Population xii 246 a; Urbanization xv 191 b; Wages xv 295 a.
Bishop — Religious Institutions (Roman Catholic) xiii 250 b, 258 b, (Byzantine) 262 a.
Bismarck, O. E. L.—ii 572; Introd. Vol. 1 (Individualism and Capitalism) i 159 a; Alliance ii 3 a; Alsace-Lorraine ii 10 b; Antisemitism ii 122 b;

Archives ii 178 a; Bennigsen ii 518 a; Beust ii 531 b; Catholic Parties iii 273 a; Health Insurance vii 294 b; Lasker ix 183 a; Lassalle ix 184 b; Militarism x 449 b; National Economic Councils xi 193 b; Parties, Political xi 615 b; Rössler xiii 440 b; Windthorst xv 429 b.
Bismuth—x 387 b.
Bissolati, L.—ii 573.
Bit—Aksakovs i 610 b; Khomyakov viii 562 b; Kireyevsky viii 574 a.
Bituminous Coal—Coal Industry iii 595 b; Mining Accidents x 509 a; Trade Agreements xiv 668 a.
Björnson, B.—ii 574.
Blache, P. M. J. Vidal de la—see Vidal de la Blache, P. M. J.
Black Book of the Admiralty—x 124 b.
Black Death—ii 574–76; Agrarian Movements i 495 b; Agric. Labor i 548 a; Agriculture i 578 a; Begging ii 493 b; Communicable Diseases, Control of iv 66 b, 71 a; Epidemics v 571 a; Labourers, Statutes of ix 3 b; Land Tenure ix 88 a; Monasticism x 589 b.
Black, J. D.—Appreciation ii 141 b, 142 b.
Black, W.—iii 380 b.
Blacklist—ii 576–78; Blacklist, Labor ii 578–79; Blockade ii 595 a; Boycott ii 662–66.
Blacklist, Labor—ii 578–79; Labor Disputes viii 635 a.
Blacklist, War—xv 61 b.
Blackmail—see Extortion.
Blackstone, W.—ii 580; Acquisition i 421 b; Child (Delinquent) iii 407 b; Confiscation iv 185 a; Judicial Review viii 558 b; Kent viii 558 b; Police Power xii 190 b.
Blackwell, E.—ii 581.
Blackwell, L. S.—see Stone, L.
Blackwood, F. T.—see Dufferin and Ava, Lord.
Blaine, J. G.—ii 582.
Blair, F. P.—ii 582.
Blake, E.—ii 583.
Blake, L.—ix 307 b.
Blanc, L.—ii 583; Introd. Vol. 1 (The Social Sciences as Disciplines, France) i 249 a; Ateliers Nationaux ii 291–92; Cooperation iv 360 a; Socialism xiv 195 a.
Bland-Allison Act—ii 548 b.
Blanqui, J. A.—ii 584.
Blanqui, L. A.—ii 584; Anticlericalism ii 113 b; Commune of Paris iv 65 a; Communism iv 85 a; Terrorism xiv 577 a.
Blasphemy—ii 585–86; Freedom of Speech and of the Press vi 458 b.
Blind—ii 587–90; Braille ii 678 b; Franking vi 420 b; Howe vii 523 a; Institutions, Public viii 91 b; Rehabilitation xiii 222 b.

Bliokh, I. S.—see BLOCH, J. DE.
BLISS, W. D. P.—ii 590; Christian Socialism iii 451 b.
Blith, W.—i 579 b.
BLOC, PARLIAMENTARY—ii 591–93; Cabinet Government iii 136 b; Farm Bloc, U. S. vi 103–05; Insurgency, Political viii 114 a; Legislative Assemblies ix 360 a; Majority Rule x 58 a; Parties, Political (France) xi 612 a.
Bloch, C.—xv 495 b.
BLOCH, J. DE—ii 593.
Block Booking—Motion Pictures xi 62 b.
BLOCK, M.—ii 593.
BLOCKADE—ii 594–96; Continental System iv 310–11; Continuous Voyage iv 320–21; Declaration of London v 47 b; Declaration of Paris v 49 a; Mahan x 47 a; Navy xi 315 a; Stowell, Lord xiv 414 b.
BLOK, P. J.—ii 596.
BLOOD ACCUSATION—ii 597–98; Antisemitism ii 121 a.
BLOOD VENGEANCE FEUD—ii 598–99; Feuds vi 220 a; Law (Primitive) ix 203 b, (Germanic) 237 a, (Greek) 228 b, (Slavic) 245 a; Punishment xii 713 a.
BLOW, S. E.—ii 600.
BLUE LAWS—ii 600–02; Sumptuary Legislation xiv 466 a.
BLUE SKY LAWS—ii 602–05.
BLUMENBACH, J. F.—ii 605.
BLUNT, W. S.—ii 605.
BLUNTSCHLI, J. K.—ii 606.
Boarding House—ix 596 a.
Boarding Out—see PLACING OUT.
BOARDS, ADMINISTRATIVE—ii 607–09; Appointments ii 138 a; Boards, Advisory ii 610 a; Commission System of Govt. iv 35–36; Commissions iv 36–40; County Govt., U. S. iv 506 b; Delegation of Powers v 65–67; Functional Representation vi 521 a; Govt. (Canada) vii 27 b, (S. Africa) 35 a, (Soviet Russia) 68 b; Institutions, Public viii 91 b; Metropolitan Areas x 398 a; Police xii 184 b; Separation of Powers xiii 664 b, 666 a; Socialization xiv 222 a.
BOARDS, ADVISORY—ii 609–12; Gosplan vi 709 a; Railroads (Labor) xiii 96 a.
Boas, F.—Introd. Vol. I (The Trend to Internationalism) i 185 b; Anthropometry ii 111 b; Folklore vi 291 a; Ornament xi 497 a.
Boccaccio, G.—xiii 279 b.
BOCCALINI, T.—ii 612.
BOCCARDO, G.—ii 612.
BOCCHI, R.—ii 612.
BÖCKH, A.—ii 613.
BÖCKH, R.—ii 613.
Bodelschwingh, F. von—xv 206 b.
BODICHON, B. L. S.—ii 613.
BÖDIKER, T.—ii 614.

BODIN, J.—ii 614; Introd. Vol. I (Renaissance and Reformation) i 97 b; Absolutism i 380 b; Enlightenment v 549 a; Public Finance xii 642 b; Revenues, Public xiii 361 a; Sovereignty xiv 266 b.
BODIO, L.—ii 616.
BODLEY, J. E. C.—ii 616.
Boétie, É. de la—see LA BOÉTIE, É. DE.
BOGDANOV, A.—ii 617.
BOGIŠIĆ, V. A.—ii 618.
Bogomiles—x 361 b.
BÖHM-BAWERK, E. VON—ii 618; Abstinence i 382 b; Capital iii 189 a; Distribution v 171 b; Economics v 362 a; Interest viii 133 b, 135 b; Laissez Faire ix 17 b.
Böhmer, J. F.—History and Historiography vii 377 b; Janssen viii 373 a.
BÖHMERT, K. V.—ii 619; Profit Sharing xii 488 b.
BOILEAU, É.—ii 619.
BOISGUILLEBERT, P. LE P.—ii 619; Introd. Vol. I (The Rise of Liberalism) i 122 b.
BOISSEL, F.—ii 620.
BOISSIER, G.—ii 620.
BOITEAU, D. A. P.—ii 621.
BOK, E. W.—ii 621.
BOLINGBROKE, LORD—ii 622.
BOLÍVAR, S.—ii 623; Santa Cruz xiii 542 b.
Bolland, J. van—i 142 b.
BOLLMANN, J. E.—ii 623.
BOLSHEVISM—ii 623–30. See SOCIALISM and Soviet Russia.
BONALD, L. G. A.—ii 630; Traditionalism xv 69 a.
Bonaparte, Napoleon—see NAPOLEON I.
Bonaventura—vi 414 a.
BONCERF, P. F.—ii 631.
Bond Houses—see INVESTMENT BANKING.
Bonded Warehouses—xv 356 a.
BONDING—ii 631–34; Automobile Insurance ii 330 b; Bail ii 386–88; Free Ports and Free Zones vi 437 b; Suretyship and Guaranty xiv 485 b; Warehousing xv 356 a.
BONDS—ii 634–36; Corporation iv 420 a; Corporation Finance iv 423–30; Credit iv 548 b; Debentures v 29–30; Land Mortgage Credit ix 43–53; Lotteries ix 613 a; Public Debt xii 605 b; Railroads xiii 84 a; Sinking Fund xiv 68 a; Special Assessments xiv 278 a; Tax Exemption xiv 529 b.
BONIFACE VIII—ii 636; Philip IV xii 107 b; Religious Institutions (Roman Catholic) xiii 256 a.
BONIFACIO DE ANDRADA E SILVA, J.—ii 636.
BONITZ, H.—ii 637.
Bonnard, V. C.—viii 640 a.
Bonnet, C.—ii 409 b.
BONNEVILLE DE MARSANGY, A.—ii 637.

Bonus, Labor—viii 679 a, 680 a.
Bonus, Soldiers'—American Legion ii 32 a; Veterans xv 246 a.
Bookkeeping—see ACCOUNTING.
BOOM—ii 638–41; Land Speculation ix 65 b, 69 a.
Boot and Shoe Industry—Large Scale Production ix 173 a; Leather Industries ix 304–16.
Boot and Shoe Workers International Union—ix 313 b.
BOOTH, C.—ii 642; Aves ii 339 a; Poverty xii 286 a; Social Surveys xiv 163 a.
BOOTH FAMILY—ii 641.
Bootlegging—ix 500 b.
Borah, W. E.—xi 509 a.
Borges, J. F.—see FERREIRA BORGES, J.
Borgia, C.—ix 655 b.
BORN, S.—ii 642; Trade Unions xv 12 b.
BÖRNE, L.—ii 643.
BORNITZ, J.—ii 643.
Borodin, M.—viii 611 b.
Boroughs—see MUNICIPAL GOVERNMENT.
Borovský, K.—see HAVLÍČEK, K.
BORTHWICK, A.—ii 644.
BORUCHOV, B.—ii 644; Zionism xv 533 a.
BOSANQUET, B.—ii 644; Absolutism i 381 b; Association ii 285 a.
Bosch, J. van den—xi 271 a.
BOSCH KEMPER, J. DE—ii 645.
Bosco, G.—ii 646.
Boss, Political—ix 658 b.
BOSSUET, J. B.—ii 646; Introd. Vol. I (The Rise of Liberalism) i 116 a; Gallicanism vi 551 a.
BOTERO, G.—ii 647.
BOTHA, L.—ii 647; Parties, Political xi 608 b.
Bötticher—see LAGARDE, P. DE.
BOUCHER DE CRÈVECOEUR DE PERTHES, J.—ii 648; Archaeology ii 163 b.
BOULAINVILLIERS, H. DE—ii 648; Introd. Vol. I (The Rise of Liberalism) i 117 a; Race Conflict xiii 36 b.
BOULANGER, G. E.—ii 649.
Boulle, A.-C.—vii 688 a.
BOUNDARIES—ii 649–52; Administrative Areas i 450–52; Alsace-Lorraine ii 10–12; Brigandage ii 693 b; Compacts, Interstate iv 111 a; Customs Duties iv 669 b; Frontier vi 500–06; Irredentism viii 325 a; Land Grants (Lat. Amer.) ix 43 a; Nationalism xi 234 a; Polish Corridor xii 196–99; Smuggling xiv 119–23; Territorial Waters xiv 574–75.
BOUNTIES—ii 652–54; Business, Govt. Services for iii 117 b; Drawback v 234 b; Dumping v 276 a; Land Grants ix 32–43; Merchant Marine x 344 b; Protection xii 565 a; Sugar xiv 452 a.
Bourdaloue, L.—viii 372 b.
BOURGEOIS, L. V. A.—ii 654; Economics v 384 a.

BOURGEOISIE—ii 654–56; Antiradicalism ii 117 a; Bolshevism ii 623–30; Commune, Mediaeval iv 61–63; French Revolution vi 471–83; Ghetto vi 648 a; Intellectuals viii 120 b; Liberalism ix 435–42; Literacy and Illiteracy ix 517 a; Middle Class x 407–15; Natural Rights xi 300 a; Plutocracy xii 177 a; Proletariat xii 512 a; Protestantism xii 574 b; Renaissance xiii 281 a; Rentenmark xiii 296–300; Revolution and Counter-revolution xiii 367–76; Royal Court xiii 450 b.
BOURGUIN, M.—ii 656.
BOURINOT, J. G.—ii 656.
BOURKE, R.—ii 657.
BOURNE, E. G.—ii 657.
BOURNE, R. S.—ii 658.
BOURNEVILLE, D. M.—ii 658; Company Housing iv 117 b.
BOURSES DU TRAVAIL—ii 659–60.
BOUTILLIER, J.—ii 660.
BOUTMY, É. G.—ii 660; Declaration of the Rights of Man and the Citizen v 50 a.
BOUTROUX, É.—ii 661.
BOWLES FAMILY—ii 662.
Bowman, I.—ix 55 a.
Boxing—xiv 307 b.
Boy Scouts—ii 667 b.
BOYCOTT—ii 662–66; Antiradicalism ii 117 b; Blacklist ii 576–78; Blacklist, Labor ii 578–79; Garment Industries vi 581 b; Indian Question vii 669 b; Labor Legislation and Law viii 670 a; Sanction, International xiii 529 b.
BOYD, W.—ii 666.
BOYS' AND GIRLS' CLUBS—ii 667–70; Agriculture, Govt. Services for i 602 a; Camping iii 168 b; Extension Work, Agric. vi 34 b.
BOYVE, É. DE—ii 670; Cooperation iv 376 b.
BRACE, C. L.—ii 670.
BRACTON, H. DE—ii 671; Glossators vi 680 b.
BRADFORD, W.—ii 671; Criminology iv 585 a; History and Historiography vii 385 b.
BRADLAUGH, C.—ii 672; Birth Control ii 561 b.
BRADLEY, F. H.—ii 672.
Bradstreet Co.—x 332 a.
BRÁF, A.—ii 673.
BRAHMANISM AND HINDUISM—ii 673–78; Art (India) ii 231 b; Caste iii 255 b; Education v 404 a; Fasting vi 145 a; Fatalism vi 147 a; Indian Question vii 659 a; Law (Hindu) ix 259 b; Mysticism xi 175 b. *For biog. references see* Classification of Articles (Religion—Brahmanism and Hinduism), p. 567.
BRAILLE, L.—ii 678; Blind ii 589 a.
BRANCH BANKING—ii 679–82; Banking, Commercial (Canada) ii 445 a, (United Kingdom) 433 a; Central Banking iii 304 b;
Holding Companies vii 409 b; National Banks, U. S. xi 186 a, 188 b.
Brandeis, L. D.—v 266 b.
BRANDES, G. M. C.—ii 682.
Brandes, H. W.—iii 559 b.
BRANDTS, F.—ii 683.
BRANTING, K. H.—ii 683.
BRANTS, V.—ii 684.
Brass—x 385 a.
BRASSEY, T. (d. 1870)—ii 684.
BRASSEY, T. (d. 1918)—ii 685.
BRATIANU FAMILY—ii 685.
Bratt, I.—ix 507 a.
BRAUN, K.—ii 686.
BRAUN, L.—ii 686.
BRAY, J. F.—ii 686.
BRAY, T.—ii 687.
BREACH OF MARRIAGE PROMISE—ii 688–89.
BRÉAL, M.—ii 689.
Brehon—Law (Celtic) ix 249 a.
BREMER, F.—ii 690.
Brentano, L.—v 352 a.
Brest Litovsk Treaty—xiii 483 a.
Briand, A.—Anticlericalism ii 114 a; Customs Unions iv 676 b; General Strike vi 608 b; Outlawry of War xi 508 a.
BRIBERY—ii 690–92; Corrupt Practises Acts iv 447–48; Corruption, Political iv 448–55.
BRICE, C. S.—ii 692.
Bride Purchase—x 148 b.
Bridgewater Canal—Bridgewater ii 692 b; Waterways, Inland xv 378 a.
BRIDGEWATER, F. E.—ii 692.
BRIESEN, A. v.—ii 693.
Briffault, R.—Family vi 65 a; Incest vii 621 b.
BRIGANDAGE—ii 693–96; Cossacks iv 463–66; Gangs vi 564 b; Guerrilla Warfare vii 197 b; Mafia x 37 a; Nomads xi 392 a.
BRIGHT, J.—iii 3; Anti-Corn Law League ii 115 a; Corn Laws iv 407 b.
BRINKERHOFF, R.—iii 4.
BRINTON, D. G.—iii 4.
BRINZ, A. VON—iii 5.
BRISBANE, A.—iii 5; Brook Farm iii 14 a.
Briscoe, J.—ix 30 a.
BRISSAUD, J. B.—iii 5.
BRISSOT DE WARVILLE, J.-P.—iii 6.
British Association—i 243 a.
British Commonwealth of Nations—Govt. vii 38–43.
British Companies Act of 1908—ii 604 b.
Broad, C. D.—iv 218 a.
Broadcasting—*see* RADIO.
BROADHURST, H.—iii 6.
BROCA, P.-P.—iii 7.
BROCKWAY, Z. R.—iii 7; Indeterminate Sentence vii 650 b.
BROGGIA, C. A.—iii 8.
BROGLIE, A. V.—iii 8; Regionalism xiii 210 a.
BROKER—iii 9–10; Agricultural Marketing i 561 b; Bucket Shops iii 30–31; Food Industries vi 317 b; Insurance viii 102 a; Marine Insurance x 115 a; Money Market x 615 b; Real Estate xiii 136 b; Stock Exchange xiv 399 a.
BROKERS' LOANS—iii 10–13; Call Money iii 149–50; Federal Reserve System vi 162 b; Liquidity ix 492 b; Money Market x 613–18; Stock Exchange xiv 400 b.
Bronterre—*see* O'BRIEN, J.
Bronze—x 364 b.
Bronze Age—Archaeology ii 165 b; Machines and Tools x 15 a.
BROOK FARM—iii 13–14; Communistic Settlements iv 100 a; Transcendentalism xv 76 b.
BROOKE, J.—iii 14.
Brookmire, J. H.—vi 349 b.
Brookwood Labor College—xv 485 b.
Brosses, C. de—*see* DE BROSSES, C.
Brotherhood of Locomotive Engineers—Arthur ii 261 b; Stone xiv 412 a.
Brothers and Sisters of the Free Spirit—ii 47 a.
BROUGHAM, LORD—iii 14; Birkbeck ii 558 a; Charitable Trusts iii 339 b; Literacy and Illiteracy ix 518 b.
BROUSSE, P.—iii 15.
BROWN, G.—iii 15.
BROWNE, R.—iii 16; Natural Law xi 287 b.
BROWNSON, O. A.—iii 16; Transcendentalism xv 76 a.
BRUCE, H. A.—iii 17.
Bruce, J.—*see* ELGIN, LORD.
BRUCK, K. L. VON—iii 17.
BRUIJN KOPS, J. L. DE—iii 18.
BRUNETIÈRE, F.—iii 18.
BRUNI, L.—iii 19.
BRUNNER, H.—iii 19.
BRUNO, G.—iii 20.
BRUNS, K. G.—iii 20.
BRUNSWICK, T.—iii 21.
BRUUN, C. A.—iii 21.
BRYAN, W. J.—iii 22; Free Silver vi 440 a; Philippine Problem xii 110 b.
BRYANT, W. C.—iii 22.
BRYCE, J.—iii 23.
Buade, L. de—*see* FRONTENAC, COMTE DE.
BUBBLES, SPECULATIVE—iii 24–27; Boom ii 638–41; Corporation iv 415 a; Crises iv 596 a; Law, J. ix 270 b.
BUCARELI Y URSÚA, A. M.—iii 27.
BUCHANAN, D.—iii 27.
BUCHANAN, G. (d. 1582)—iii 28.
BUCHANAN, G. (d. 1895)—iii 28.
BUCHANAN, J. R.—iii 28.
BUCHENBERGER, A.—iii 29.
Bücher, K.—Class iii 535 a; Economic History v 328 b; Economics v 371–77; Exchange v 667 a.
BUCHEZ, P. J. B.—iii 29; Carbonari iii 223 a; Cooperation iv 360 a, 377 b.
Büchner, G.—xiv 610 a.
BÜCHNER, L.—iii 30; Freethinkers vi 468 b.

BUCKET SHOPS—iii 30–31.
BUCKLE, H. T.—iii 31; Climate iii 560 b; History and Historiography vii 379 a.
BUDDHISM—iii 32–38; Art (China) ii 234 a, (India) 231 a, (Japan) 236 b; Asoka ii 270 a; Brahmanism and Hinduism ii 675 b; Confucianism iv 199 b; Davids v 10 a; Death Customs v 24 b; Guilds (Indian) vii 216 b; Holidays vii 414 b; Indian Question vii 659 b; Law (Hindu) ix 260 b; Messianism x 357 b; Missions x 536 a; Mysticism xi 175 b; Passive Resistance and Noncooperation xii 10 a; Religious Freedom xiii 240 b; Religious Orders xiii 276 b; Sacred Books xiii 498 b; Shinto xiv 25 a; Taoism xiv 511 b.
BUDÉ, G.—iii 38; Humanism vii 540 a.
BUDGET—iii 38–44; Accounts, Public i 412–15; Expenditures, Public vi 5–10; Financial Administration vi 234–41; Government (Japan) vii 97 b; League of Nations ix 291 b; Local Finance ix 573 a; Municipal Finance xi 102 b; Public Debt xii 600 a.
Budgets, Family — see FAMILY BUDGETS.
BUDIN, P.—iii 44.
BUFFER STATE—iii 45–46.
BUFFON, G. L. L.—iii 46; Evolution v 650 b.
BUGEAUD DE LA PICONNERIE, T. R.—iii 46.
BUGENHAGEN, J.—iii 47.
Building Guilds — Construction Industry iv 277 a; Housing (Eur.) vii 503 b.
BUILDING AND LOAN ASSOCIATIONS—iii 47–52; Cooperation iv 394 b; Home Ownership vii 433 a; Housing (Eur.) vii 499 b.
Building Materials—iv 270 a.
BUILDING REGULATIONS—iii 52–57; Architecture ii 174 a; Fire Protection vi 264 a; Housing (Eur.) vii 500 b, 509 a, (U. S.) 513 a.
Building Taxes—see HOUSE AND BUILDING TAXES.
Building Trades—see CONSTRUCTION INDUSTRY.
Building Trades Councils—iv 272 b.
BŪKHĀRI, AL—iii 57.
BUKŠEG, V.—iii 57.
Bulgarus—vi 401 b.
BULL, PAPAL—iii 57–59; Canon Law iii 181 a.
Bull Trading—xiv 291 a.
Bullard, W. H. G.—xiii 55 b.
BULLER, C.—iii 59.
BULLIONISTS—iii 60–64; Balance of Trade ii 399 a; Malynes x 70 a; Mercantilism x 337 b; Milles x 483 a; Misselden x 535 b; Mun xi 84 b.
BULMERINCQ, A. VON—iii 64; Bergbohm ii 521 b.

BÜLOW, B. H. M.—iii 64; Bethmann Hollweg ii 530 b.
BÜLOW, O.—iii 65.
BUNDESRAT—iii 65–67; German Civil Code vi 635 a; Government vii 53 b; Legislative Assemblies ix 380 a.
Bundestag—iii 65 b.
BUNGE, C. O.—iii 67.
BUNGE, F. G. VON—iii 67.
BUNGE, N. C.—iii 67.
Bunk House—ix 596 b.
Bunyan, P.—Folklore vi 292 b.
Buonarroti, F. M.—ii 375 b.
BURCHARD OF WORMS—iii 68.
BURCKHARDT, J. C.—iii 69; Renaissance xiii 279 a.
BURDETT, F.—iii 70.
Bureau of the Budget—iii 41 b.
BUREAU, P.—iii 70.
Bureau of Standards—iii 119 b.
BUREAUCRACY—iii 70–74; Administration, Public i 444 a; Centralization iii 312 a; Civil Service iii 515–23; Commissions iv 36–40; Fouché vi 401 a; Gosplan vi 712 a; Govt. (Germany) vii 54 b, (Soviet Russia) 69 b; Middle Class x 412 a; Parties, Political xi 595 a; Proletariat xii 517 a; Public Employment xii 628–37; Socialism xiv 209 a; Spoils System xiv 301–05. See also CIVIL SERVICE.
Bürgerliches Gesetzbuch — see German Civil Code.
Burgess, E. W.—i 403 a.
Burgess, J. W.—ii 22 a.
BURGHLEY, LORD—iii 74; Mercantilism x 334 b.
Burglary Insurance—iii 263 a.
Burial Customs—Death Customs v 24 b.
BURKE, E.—iii 74; Introd. Vol. I (The Revolutions) i 139 b; History and Historiography vii 376 a; Liberalism ix 439 a; Minority Rights x 525 b; Natural Law xi 289 b; Parties, Political (Gt. Brit.) xi 603 a; Traditionalism xv 68 a.
BURLAMACHI, P.—iii 76.
BURLAMAQUI, J. J.—iii 76; Equality of States v 581 a.
BURLINGAME, A.—iii 76.
BURNET, G.—iii 77.
BURNETT, J.—iii 77.
Burnham, D.—iii 485 b.
Burnham, Lord—see LEVY LAWSON FAMILY.
BURRITT, E.—iii 78; Peace Movements xii 42 a.
BURT, T.—iii 78.
BURY, J. B.—iii 79.
Bus—see Motor Bus.
BUSCH, E.—iii 79.
BÜSCH, J. G.—iii 79.
BÜSCHING, A. F.—iii 80.
Bushidō—vi 217 b.
BUSINESS—iii 80–87. See Classification of Articles (Business), p. 548. See also Career iii 225 b; Consumer Protection iv 282 b; Contract iv 329–39; Corrup-

tion, Political iv 450 a; Gentleman, Theory of the vi 618 a; Intimidation viii 241 b; Legal Profession and Legal Education ix 341 a; Negro Problem xi 348 a; Pensions xii 68 b; Professions xii 479 b; Spoils System xiv 302 a; Trusts and Trustees xv 124 b. See also Index, Government Regulation. For biog. references see Classification of Articles (Business and Finance), p. 558.
BUSINESS ADMINISTRATION — iii 87–91; Accounting i 404–12; Capitalism iii 203 a; Captain of Industry iii 219 a; Cost Accounting iv 475–78; Efficiency v 437–39; Entrepreneur v 558–60; Interlocking Directorates viii 148–51; Management x 76–80; Personnel Administration xii 88–90; Railroads xiii 90 a.
BUSINESS AGENT—iii 91–92; Construction Industry iv 275 a.
BUSINESS CYCLES—iii 92–106; Introd. Vol. 1 (War and Reorientation) i 213 b; Boom ii 638 b; Crises iv 595–99; Economics v 391 b; Einarsen v 447 a; Engineering v 545 b; Forecasting, Business vi 350 a; Foreign Investment vi 377 a; Housing vii 499 b; Inflation and Deflation viii 32 b; Instalment Selling viii 80 b; Interest viii 141 b; Investment viii 267 a; Labor Movement viii 684 b; Large Scale Production ix 175 b; Machinery, Industrial x 11 b; Overproduction xi 515 b; Pohle xii 179 b; Prices (Theory) xii 370 b, (History) 375–81, (Statistics) 383 b; Public Health xii 650 a; Public Works xii 695 b; Saving xiii 551 a; Sismondi xiv 70 a; Stabilization, Economic xiv 309 b; Statics and Dynamics xiv 354 a; Stock Exchange xiv 401 b; Tugan-Baranovsky xv 128 b; Unemployment xv 152 a, 155 a.
BUSINESS EDUCATION—iii 107–110; Introd. Vol. 1 (The Social Sciences as Disciplines, U. S.) i 345 b; Accounting i 406 b; Johnson viii 408 b; Vocational Education xv 272–75.
BUSINESS ETHICS—iii 111–13; Bargaining Power ii 461 b; Business iii 85 b; Capitalism iii 197 b; Consumer Protection iv 283 b; Fraud vi 427–29; Hunt vii 555 a; Real Estate xiii 139 a; Unfair Competition xv 174–78.
Business Forecasting—see FORECASTING, BUSINESS.
BUSINESS, GOVERNMENT SERVICES FOR—iii 113–22; Chambers of Commerce iii 325–29; Consular Service iv 280 a; Export Credits vi 19–21; Housing (Eur.) vii 502–11, (U. S.) 516 a; Inspection viii 71 a; International Trade viii 195 a; Mer-

chant Marine x 343-50; Nitrates xi 380 b; Price Regulation xii 360 a; Production (Statistics) xii 467-72; Statistics (Practise) xiv 361 a; Subsidies xiv 430-33.
BUSINESS TAXES—iii 122-24; Alcabala i 615-16; Excess Profits Tax v 664-66; General Property Tax vi 607 a; Income Tax vii 632 b; Sales Tax xiii 516-19.
Business Trusts—see MASSACHUSETTS TRUSTS.
Bustāni, Buṭrus al—see BUṬRUS AL-BUSTĀNI.
Butler, Joseph—ii 14 b.
BUTLER, JOSEPHINE—iii 124.
BUTLER, S.—iii 125.
BUṬRUS AL-BUSTĀNI—iii 126.
BUTT, I.—iii 126; Irish Question viii 291 b.
Büttner, C.—ii 605.
BUXTON, T. F.—iii 126.
BY-ELECTIONS—iii 127-28.
BY-LAW—iii 128-29.
BY-PRODUCT—iii 129-30; Cotton iv 491 a; Gas Industry vi 592 b; Heavy Chemicals vii 303 a; Meat Packing and Slaughtering x 248 b, 259 a; Nitrates xi 381 b; Quarrying xiii 18 a.
BYNKERSHOEK, C. VAN—iii 130.
Byrne, E.—Hunger Strike vii 554 a.
BYRON, LORD—iii 130.
Byzantine Church—Introd. Vol. I (The Universal Church) i 63 a; Religious Institutions (Byzantine) xiii 262-65.

Ca' Canny—xiii 495 b.
CABANIS P. J. G.—iii 131.
CABET, É.—iii 131; Communistic Settlements iv 100 a; Dezamy v 118 a.
CABINET—iii 132-34; Cabinet Govt. iii 134-37; Committees, Legislative iv 41 b; Congressional Govt. iv 202 a; Executive v 681 b; Govt. vii 12 b, (Canada) 27 b, (Czechoslovakia) 79 b, (Estonia) 71 b, (Finland) 65 a, (France) 45 b, (Gt. Brit.) 22 a, (Japan) 95 b, (Latvia) 72 b, (Russia, Imperial) 66 a, (Russia, Soviet) 69 a, (S. Africa) 35 a, (Sweden) 64 a; League of Nations ix 290 b; Legislative Assemblies (France) ix 377 b, 379 a, (Germany) 382 b, (Japan) 394 a; Walpole xv 327 b.
CABINET GOVERNMENT—iii 134-37; Bicameral System ii 535 b; Budget iii 43 a; Burke iii 75 a; By-Elections iii 127 b; Cabinet iii 132 a; Coalition iii 600-02; Congressional Govt. iv 202 a; Deadlock v 17 b; Govt. vii 10 b; Interpellation viii 219-20; Legislative Assemblies (Hist. and Theory) ix 360 a.
Cacao—see Cocoa.
CACHET, LETTRE DE—iii 137-38; Arrest ii 222 a.
Cadaster—ix 71 a.

CADBURY, G.—iii 138; Garden Cities vi 570 a.
Cadmium—x 387 a.
CAESAR, G. J.—iii 139; Introd. Vol. I (Greek Culture and Thought) i 16 a, (The Roman World) 44 a, 52 b; Calendar iii 142 b; Law (Celtic) ix 246 b.
Caesarean Operation—x 275 a.
Caesaropapism—Religious Institutions (Roman Catholic) xiii 253 a, (Byzantine) 263 a.
CAIRD, J.—iii 139.
CAIRNES, J. E.—iii 140; Cost iv 468 a; Distribution v 169 b; Economics v 351-57; International Trade viii 206 a.
Cairns, H.—vi 519 a.
Calatrava—x 463 a.
Calderón, F. G.—i 317 a.
Calderón de la Barca, P.—xiv 607 a.
CALENDAR—iii 140-44; Astrology ii 287 b; Bede ii 491 b; Festivals vi 198 b; Holidays vii 414 a.
CALHOUN, J. C.—iii 144; Minority Rights x 526 b; States' Rights xiv 347 b.
California Fruit Growers' Exchange—i 525 b.
CALIPHATE—iii 145-49; Govt. (Turkey) vii 84 a; Islam viii 338 b; Jihad viii 402 b; Mu'āwiyah xi 79 a; Pan-Islamism xi 542-44.
CALL MONEY—iii 149-50; Brokers' Loans iii 10-13; Financial Organization vi 244 b; Money Market x 613-18.
CALLENDER, G. S.—iii 150.
Calles, P. E.—xi 258 b.
Callicles—Natural Law xi 286 a; Sophists xiv 260 b.
Calligraphy—Archives ii 177 a; Art (China) ii 233-36, (India) 232 b, (Japan) 237 b.
CALVERT FAMILY—iii 151.
CALVIN, J.—iii 151; Introd. Vol. I (Renaissance and Reformation) i 95 b; Checks and Balances iii 363 b; Christianity iii 458 a; Education v 415 a; Luther ix 632 b; Reformation xiii 191 a; Republicanism xiii 318 b.
Calvinism—Introd. Vol. I (Renaissance and Reformation) i 96 a, (The Rise of Liberalism) 121 b, (Individualism and Capitalism) 147 b; Edwards v 437 a; Equality v 576 a; Knox viii 585 b; Mather x 227 b; Pragmatism xii 307 b; Protestantism xii 571 b; Reformation xiii 191 a; Religious Freedom xiii 244 a; Religious Institutions (Protestant) xiii 270 a; Republicanism xiii 318 b; Society xiv 228 a; Weber xv 387 b.
CALVO, C.—iii 153; Calvo and Drago Doctrines iii 154 a.
CALVO AND DRAGO DOCTRINES—iii 153-56; Castro iii 259 b; Repudiation of Public Debts xiii 323 b.

CAMBACÉRÈS, J. J. R. DE—iii 157.
CAMBON, P. J.—iii 157.
CAMBON, P. P.—iii 157; Native Policy xi 274 a.
Cambridge Modern History—i 425 b.
Cambridge School, Economics—v 368-71.
Cambridge University—i 231 b, 235 b.
Camden, Lord—xiii 617 b.
CAMDEN, W.—iii 158.
CAMERALISM—iii 158-61; Introd. Vol. I (The Rise of Liberalism) i 123 b, (The Social Sciences as Disciplines, Germany) 258 a; Becher ii 489 a; Darjes v 4 a; Govt. Regulation of Industry vii 124 a; Hornigk vii 461 a; Justi viii 508 a; Lau ix 190 a; Leib ix 399 b; Leuber ix 420 b; Osse xi 501 a; Pfeiffer xii 106 b; Seckendorff xiii 620 b; Zincke xv 527 a.
CAMERON, A. C.—iii 161.
CAMORRA—iii 161-62.
Camp Fire Girls—ii 667 b.
CAMPAIGN, POLITICAL—iii 162-66; Caucus iii 278 a; Clubs, Political iii 578 b; Convention, Political iv 349-51; Corrupt Practises Acts iv 447-48; Franking vi 420 a; Parties, Political xi 594 a, (Gt. Brit.) 604 a.
CAMPANELLA, T.—iii 166; Introd. Vol. I (Renaissance and Reformation) i 102 b.
CAMPBELL, A.—iii 166; Cooperation iv 364 a.
CAMPBELL, J.—iii 167.
CAMPILLO Y COSSIO, J.—iii 167.
CAMPING—iii 168-70.
CAMPOMANES, P. R.—iii 170.
Canadian National Railways—x 28 b.
CANALEJAS Y MENDEZ, J.—iii 170.
Canals—Bridgewater ii 692 b; Commercial Routes iv 23 a; International Waterways viii 213 b; Irrigation viii 329 a; Transportation xv 82 a; Waterways, Inland xv 378 a.
CANARD, N. F.—iii 171; Economics v 365 a.
Cancrin, G.—see KANKRIN, E. F.
Candy and Confectionery—Food Industries vi 309-11.
CANGA ARGÜELLES, J.—iii 171.
Canisius, P.—viii 384 a.
CANNIBALISM—iii 172-73; Morals x 644 b.
CANNING, G.—iii 173.
CANNING INDUSTRY—iii 174-79; Warehousing xv 358 a.
CANNING, S.—iii 174.
CANNON, J. G.—iii 179.
CANON LAW—iii 179-86; Introd. Vol. I (The Universal Church) i 68 b, (The Growth of Autonomy) 78 b; Abdication i 356 b; Andreae ii 58 a; Apostasy and Heresy ii 129 a; Blasphemy ii 586 a; Burchard of Worms iii 68 b; Christianity iii 453 b; Church Fathers iii 464-68;

Civil Law iii 504 b; Codification iii 609 a; Compurgation iv 149 b; Criminal Law iv 572 b; Divorce v 179 a; Ecclesiastical Courts v 307–14; Excommunication v 671–80; Friedberg vi 492 b; Glossators vi 681 b; Gratian vii 156 a; Henry of Langenstein vii 324 a; Hinschius vii 353 a; Lanfranc ix 149 b; Legal Profession and Legal Education ix 329 a; Peter Lombard xii 97 a; Raymond de Pennafort xiii 134 a; Religious Institutions (Byzantine) xiii 264 a; Sohm xiv 250 a; Tertullian xiv 580 a; Yves of Chartres xv 522 a.

Canons Regular—x 588 a.

CÁNOVAS DEL CASTILLO, A—iii 186.

CANTILLON, R.—iii 186; Introd. Vol. I (The Revolutions) i 141 b; Entrepreneur v 558 a.

CANTOS Y BENITEZ, P. DE—iii 187.

CAPITAL—iii 187–90; Abstinence i 382–83; Accumulation i 415–18; Capitalism iii 205 a; Capitalization iii 208–11; Corporation Finance iv 426 b; Depreciation v 98–102; Economics (Physiocrats) v 349 b, (Classical School) 355 a, (Cambridge School) 370 a, (Socialist Economics) 378 b; Income vii 623 b; Income Tax vii 629 a; Inheritance Taxation xii 48 a; Interest viii 131–44; Investment viii 263–68; Laissez Faire ix 19 a; Location of Industry ix 587 a; Money Market x 614 a; National Economic Planning xi 199 a; National Income xi 210 a, 218 a; Public Utilities xii 680 a; Saving xiii 548–52; Unemployment xv 160 b; Wages xv 296 a.

Capital Gains—Income vii 623 b; Income Tax vii 629 a.

CAPITAL LEVY—iii 190–92.

Capital Market—Financial Organization vi 244 a; Foreign Investment vi 368 a, 373 b.

CAPITAL PUNISHMENT—iii 192–95; Benefit of Clergy ii 513 a; Law (Jewish) ix 223 b; Punishment xii 713 b.

CAPITALISM—iii 195–208; Introd. Vol. I (Individualism and Capitalism) i 145–63, (Nationalism) 165 b; Acquisition i 420–23; Antisemitism ii 121 a; Bolshevism ii 626 a; Bourgeoisie ii 654–56; Business iii 83 b; Business Cycles iii 92–106; Calvin iii 152 b; Capital iii 189 b; Captain of Industry iii 216–20; Class iii 534 a; Combinations, Industrial iii 664–74; Communist Parties iv 87 a; Competition iv 141–47; Corporation iv 414–23; Crises iv 595–99; Debt v 35 a; Economic Policy v 333–44; Economics (Socialist Economics) v 377 b; Emancipation v 484 b; Employers' Associations v 509–14; Endowments and Foundations v 534 a; Engineering v 545 a; Entrepreneur v 558–60; Exploitation vi 16–17; Factory System vi 52 a; Fascism vi 137 a; Foreign Investment vi 364–78; Fortunes, Private vi 392–99; French Revolution vi 472 a; Gosplan vi 711 b; Guilds vii 213 b; Imperialism vii 606 a; Industrial Relations vii 710–17; Industrial Revolution viii 3–13; Industrialism viii 24 b; Interest viii 143 a; International Relations viii 187 a; Invention viii 248 b; Investment Banking viii 268 b; Iron and Steel Industry viii 310 a; Judaism viii 437 b; Labor-Capital Cooperation viii 626 a; Labor Movement viii 682–96; Laissez Faire ix 15–20; Large Scale Production ix 170–81; Legal Profession and Legal Education ix 341 a; Luxury ix 636 a; Middle Class x 407–15; Middleman x 415–17; Mining x 496 a; National Economic Planning xi 197–205; Natural Resources xi 294 a; Natural Rights xi 302 a; Organization, Economic xi 486 a; Overproduction xi 515 b; Power, Political xii 302 b; Proletariat xii 510–18; Promotion xii 518–21; Property xii 534 b; Protestantism xii 574 a; Reformation xiii 188 a; Rentier xiii 298 a; Social Christian Movements xiv 123–27; Socialism xiv 188–212; Stabilization, Economic xiv 314 b; Technology xiv 553 a; Unemployment xv 147–62; Vested Interests xv 240–43; Women in Industry xv 452 a.

CAPITALIZATION—iii 208–11; Automobile Industry ii 324 b; Aviation ii 342 a, 362 a; Blue Sky Laws ii 602–05; Bonds ii 635 a; Bubbles, Speculative iii 24–27; Capitalization and Amortization of Taxes iii 211–13; Corporation Finance iv 423–30; Electric Power v 459 b; Electrical Manufacturing Industry v 471 b; Goodwill vi 700 a; Interest viii 134 b; Land Valuation ix 137 a; Valuation xv 215 a.

CAPITALIZATION AND AMORTIZATION OF TAXES—iii 211–13; Business Taxes iii 124 a; Capital Levy iii 190 b; Land Taxation ix 71 b.

Capitation Taxes—see POLL TAX.

CAPITULATIONS—iii 213–15; Commercial Treaties iv 26 b; Egyptian Problem v 442 b; Europeanization v 629 b; Exterritoriality vi 37 a; Holy Places vii 421 b; Islamic Law viii 349 a.

CAPODISTRIAS, J.—iii 215.

CAPPONI, G. A.—iii 215.

CAPRIVI, G. L. VON—iii 216.

CAPTAIN OF INDUSTRY—iii 216–20; Business iii 84 b; Capitalism iii 201–06; Fortunes, Private vi 398 b.

Car Trust Certificates—ii 635 b.

Caraffa, G. P.—see PAUL IV.

Caravel—xiv 33 a.

CARBONARI—iii 220–23; Anticlericalism ii 113 a; Bazard ii 484 b; Blanqui ii 584 b.

CÁRDENAS, F. DE—iii 223.

Cardona, T. de—iii 232 b.

CARDOZO, J. N.—iii 223.

CARDUCCI, G.—iii 224.

CAREER—iii 224–26; Business iii 85 a; Equality v 577 a; Literature ix 535 b; Professions xii 476–80; Vocational Guidance xv 276–79.

CAREY, H. C.—iii 226; Introd. Vol. I (The Social Sciences as Disciplines, U. S.) i 339 a; Baird ii 392 a; Balance of Trade ii 401 b; Bastiat ii 477 a; Distribution v 169 b; National Wealth xi 228 b.

CAREY, M.—iii 227.

CARLE, G.—iii 227.

CARLETON, G.—iii 227.

CARLI, G. R.—iii 228.

CARLILE, R.—iii 228; Birth Control ii 561 a.

CARLYLE, T.—iii 229; Introd. Vol. I (Individualism and Capitalism) i 155 b; Economics v 381 b; Froude vi 506 b; History and Historiography vii 378 b; Transcendentalism xv 76 a.

CARMIGNANI, G.—iii 230.

CARNEGIE, A.—iii 230 b; Endowments and Foundations v 533 a; Frick vi 491 b.

Carnegie Corporation—i 465 b.

Carnegie Steel Co.—viii 307 a.

Carnivals—see FESTIVALS.

Carnock, Lord—see NICOLSON, A.

CARNOT, L. N. M.—iii 231.

CARPENTER, M.—iii 231.

Carpetbaggers — Reconstruction xiii 171 a.

Carpocrates—ii 47 a.

CARPZOV, B.—iii 232.

CARRANZA, A.—iii 232.

CARRANZA, V.—iii 233.

CARRARA, F.—iii 234.

CARTEL—iii 234–43; Cement iii 288 b; Coal Industry iii 590 a; Combinations, Industrial iii 664–74; Crises iv 598 a; Dumping v 275 b; International Trade viii 196 a; Iron and Steel Industry viii 309 b, 314 a; Metals x 374 a, 377 b, 386 b; Middleman x 417 a; Potash xii 274 b; Raw Materials xiii 131 a; Trade Associations xiv 672 a.

CARTER, H. R.—iii 243.

CARTER, J. C.—iii 243.

CARTER, J. G.—iii 244.

Cartesianism—see DESCARTES, R.

Carthusians—x 587 b.

CARTIER, G. É.—iii 244.

Cartography—vi 628 b.

CARTWRIGHT, J.—iii 245.
CARTWRIGHT, T.—iii 245.
Carvalho e Mello, S. J. de—*see* POMBAL, MARQUEZ DE.
Carver, T. N.—i 535 a.
CARY, J.—iii 246.
CASA DE CONTRATACIÓN—iii 246–48.
Casas, B. de las—x 540 a.
CASAUX, C.—iii 248.
CASE LAW—iii 249–51; Carter iii 243 b; Case Method iii 251–54; Common Law iv 54 b; Customary Law iv 663 b; Judicial Process viii 451 b.
CASE METHOD—iii 251–54; Introd. Vol. I (The Social Sciences as Disciplines, U. S.) i 343 a; Ames ii 35 b; Casuistry iii 266 a; Langdell ix 151 b; Legal Profession and Legal Education ix 338 a; Medicine (Medical Education) x 290 b; Social Work xiv 167 b, 173–83.
Case Work, Social—Social Work (Case Work) xiv 173–83.
Cass, L.—xii 239 b.
Cassation, Court of—ii 135 a.
Cassel, G.—Abstinence i 382 b; Economics v 367 b; Foreign Exchange vi 364 a; Inflation and Deflation viii 29 a, 31 b; International Trade (Theory) viii 207 a.
CASSELL, E. J.—iii 254.
Cassiodorus—Introd. Vol. I (The Universal Church) i 67 b, 68 b; History and Historiography vii 371 b; Monasticism x 586 b.
CASTE—iii 254–57; Art (India) ii 230 b; Assimilation, Social ii 281 b; Authority ii 320 a; Brahmanism and Hinduism ii 673–78; Buddhism iii 32 b; Guilds (Indian) vii 217 b; Indian Question vii 659 a; Labor viii 617 b; Priesthood xii 392 b; Segregation xiii 645 b; Status xiv 374 a.
CASTELAR Y RIPOLL, E.—iii 257.
CASTELLIO, S.—iii 257.
Castiglione, B.—vi 617 a.
CASTILLA, R.—iii 258.
CASTLEREAGH, R. S.—iii 258; Holy Alliance vii 418 a.
CASTRO, C.—iii 259.
CASTRO, J. DE—iii 259.
CASUAL LABOR—iii 260–62; Lodging Houses ix 595–98; Longshoremen ix 606–09; Migratory Labor x 441–45; Vagrancy xv 205–08.
CASUALTY INSURANCE—iii 262–65; Automobile Insurance ii 330–32; Health Insurance vii 298 a.
CASUISTRY—iii 265–66.
CASUS BELLI—iii 266–68.
Catchings, W.—Business Cycles iii 99 a; Price Stabilization xii 363 a.
Categorical Imperative—viii 539 b.
Cathari—Messianism x 361 b; Sects xiii 625 b.

CATHERINE II—iii 268; Armed Neutrality ii 203 a.
CATHOLIC EMANCIPATION — iii 269–71; Irish Question viii 289 a; O'Connell xi 436 a.
CATHOLIC PARTIES—iii 271–75; Parties, Political xi 594 b, (Belgium) 613 b, (Netherlands) 620 b, (Switzerland) 620 a.
Catholicism—*see* CHRISTIANITY; Church; RELIGION.
CATO, M. P.—iii 275; Agriculture i 575 a; Latifundia ix 187 a.
CATTANEO, C.—iii 275.
Cattell, J. M.—vi 613 b.
Cattle Industry—*see* LIVESTOCK INDUSTRY.
CATTLE LOANS—iii 276–77; Meat Packing and Slaughtering (U. S.) x 245 a.
CAUCUS—iii 277–79.
CAUER, M.—iii 279.
Causality—Gestalt vi 645 a; History and Historiography vii 361 b; Political Science xii 213 a.
CAUWES, P. L.—iii 279.
CAVEAT EMPTOR — iii 280–82; Consumer Protection iv 283 b; Fraud vi 428 a.
Cavendish, W.—*see* BENTINCK, LORD.
CAVOUR, C. B. DI—iii 282; Azeglio ii 372 b; Ruffini xiii 462 b.
Cecil, R.—ix 287 b.
Cecil, W.—*see* BURGHLEY, LORD.
CELIBACY—iii 283–86; Asceticism ii 266 a; Birth Control ii 560 a; Chastity iii 357–58; Priesthood xii 389 a.
Celsus—Origen xi 495 a.
Celsus, A. C.—Medicine x 285 b.
Celtic Law—Law ix 246–49.
CEMENT—iii 286–90; Quarrying xiii 14 b.
CENSORSHIP—iii 290–94; Birth Control ii 562 b; Blacklist ii 576–78; Comstock iv 150; Copyright iv 402 a; Freedom of Speech and of the Press vi 455–59; Motion Pictures xi 60 b, 66 b; Press xii 333 a; Radio xiii 64 b.
CENSUS—iii 295–300; Baines ii 392 a; Billings ii 542 a; Occupation (Statistics) xi 429 a; Production (Statistics) xii 470 a; Shattuck xiv 16 b; Statistics (Practise) xiv 361 a, 364 b; Unemployment xv 149 a.
Census of Manufactures—Census iii 300 a; Large Scale Production ix 176 a.
CENTANI, F.—iii 300.
Center Party, Germany—Catholic Parties iii 273 a; Parties, Political xi 616 a.
CENTRAL AMERICAN FEDERATION —iii 301–02.
Central American Union—ii 466 b.
CENTRAL BANKING—iii 302–08; Balance of Trade ii 405 b; Bank Reserves ii 420 a; Banking, Commercial ii 423 a; Banknotes ii 448 b; Credit Control iv 550–53; Crises iv 596 b; Economic Policy v 343 b; Federal Reserve System vi 154–65; Financial Organization vi 245 a; Foreign Exchange vi 359 b, 362 b; Gold vi 692 a; International Finance viii 163 a; Liquidity ix 494 b; Money Market x 614 b, 616 b; Price Stabilization xii 363 a.
Central Pacific Railroad—xiv 325 a.
CENTRALIZATION—iii 308–13; Administration, Public i 444 a; Administrative Areas i 450–52; Appointments ii 137 b; By-Law iii 128 b; Cameralism iii 158–61; Civil Service iii 516 b; Coinage iii 623 b; Education v 419 b; Fascism vi 136 a; Foreign Corporations vi 356 a; Govt. (France) vii 43 b, (Germany) 53 a, (Jugoslavia) 80 b, (Soviet Russia) 68 a, (U. S.) 15 b; Grants-in-Aid vii 152–55; Interstate Commerce viii 220–29; Justice of the Peace viii 524 b; Local Govt. ix 580 b; Organization, Administrative xi 481 a; Public Contracts xii 598 b; Regionalism xiii 209 a, 216 a; States' Rights xiv 346–50; Statistics (Practise) xiv 363 b.
Cephalic Index—xiii 27 a.
CEREMONY—iii 313–16; Etiquette v 615–17; Fasting vi 144–46; Gifts vi 657–58; Hospitality vii 463 a; Initiation viii 49–50; Marriage x 151 a; Morale x 641 b; Mysteries xi 172–75; Ritual xiii 396–98; Secret Societies xiii 622 a; Theater xiv 598 b.
CERNUSCHI, H.—iii 316.
CERTIORARI—iii 317–19.
Cerutti, L.—iv 382 a.
CESSION—iii 319–20; Annexation ii 68–69; Plebiscite xii 163–66; State Succession xiv 344–46.
Cestui Que Use—xv 123 a.
Ceva, G.—v 365 a.
Cézanne, P.—ii 254 b.
CHAADAYEV, P. Y.—iii 320.
Chadbourne Plan—Sugar xiv 454 b.
CHADWICK, E.—iii 321; Communicable Diseases, Control of iv 67 b; Public Health xii 647 b.
Chain Stores—Marketing x 136 b; Retail Trade xiii 351 a.
Chaka—xi 52 b.
Chalmers, M. D.—xi 333 b.
CHALMERS, T.—iii 321; Charity iii 343 a, b; Social Work xiv 173 b.
Chamber of Deputies—Legislative Assemblies (France) ix 375 a, (Hungary) 389 b.
CHAMBERLAIN, H. S.—iii 322; Race Conflict xiii 36 b.
CHAMBERLAIN, J.—iii 323; Balfour ii 408 a; Free Trade vi 446 a.
Chamberlen, H.—ix 30 a.

CHAMBERS OF AGRICULTURE—iii 323-25.
CHAMBERS OF COMMERCE — iii 325-29; Arbitration, Commercial ii 152 a; Civic Organizations iii 501 a; Employers' Associations v 510 a; Guilds (Chinese) vii 221 a.
Champerty and Maintenance—iv 311 b.
CHAMPLAIN, S. DE—iii 329.
CHAMPOLLION, J. F.—iii 329; Archaeology ii 163 b; Lepsius ix 412 b.
Chance—Cournot iv 511 a; Materialism (Historical) x 219 b; Renaissance xiii 284 a.
Chancery—see Court of Chancery; EQUITY.
CHANG CHIH-TUNG—iii 330.
CHANG HSÜEH-CH'ENG—iii 330.
CHANGE, SOCIAL—iii 330-34. See relevant titles in Classification of Articles (Social Process), p. 556. See also Bourgeoisie ii 654 b; Bribery ii 691 a; Brigandage ii 694 b; Chinese Problem iii 431-36; Consensus iv 225-27; Conservatism iv 231 a; Criticism, Social iv 599-602; Fatalism vi 147 b; Intellectuals viii 118 b; Reformism xiii 194-95; Social Work xiv 171 a; Socialism xiv 188-212.
Change of Venue—xv 236 b.
CHANNING, W. E.—iii 334.
CHANNING, W. H.—iii 334; Transcendentalism xv 76 b.
Cha-no-yu—ii 237 a.
Chapin, R. C.—vi 75 b.
Chapman, J.—ii 510 b.
CHAPTAL, J. A.—iii 334.
CHARACTER—iii 335-37; Adolescence i 455-59; Honor vii 456 b; Personality xii 85-88.
Charce, Marquis de la—see LA TOUR DU PIN CHAMBLY, R. DE.
CHARCOT, J. M.—iii 337.
CHARITABLE TRUSTS—iii 338-40; Endowments and Foundations v 531-37; Mortmain xi 41 a, 48 b; Perpetuities xii 82 b; Trusts and Trustees xv 125 a.
CHARITY—iii 340-45; Almshouse ii 8-10; Begging ii 494 b; Charitable Trusts iii 338-40; Child (Dependent) iii 398-403, (Neglected) 403-06, (Institutions) 410-12; Chivalry iii 438 b; Christianity iii 453 a; Clinics and Dispensaries iii 562-67; Dependency v 93-95; Drives, Money Raising v 238-41; Endowments and Foundations v 531-37; Institutions, Public viii 90-95; Lodging Houses ix 596 b; Lotteries ix 611 b; National Income xi 208 b; Old Age xi 458 a; Public Welfare xii 687 b; Social Work xiv 165 b.
Charity Organization Movement —Charity iii 343 b; Loch ix 593 a; Richmond xiii 382 a; Social Work xiv 167 a, (Case Work) 173 b.

CHARLEMAGNE—iii 345; Introd. Vol. 1 (The Universal Church) i 64 a; Empire v 505 a; Holy Roman Empire vii 423 a; Monarchy x 581 a; Religious Institutions (Roman Catholic) xiii 254 a.
Charles I—vii 253 b.
CHARLES V—iii 346; Reformation xiii 187 a.
CHARMONT, J.—iii 347.
Charron, P.—v 552 a.
Charte d'Amiens—viii 690 a.
CHARTERED COMPANIES—iii 347-52; Asiento ii 268-70; Balance of Trade ii 399 b; Bubbles, Speculative iii 25 a; Child iii 372 b; Clive iii 568 a; Coen iii 617 a; Colonial Administration iii 641 b; Commerce iv 8 a; Concessions iv 157 b; Corporation iv 414 b; Debt v 35 b; Dupleix v 282 b; Free Trade vi 440 b; Goldie vi 694 a; Imperialism vii 607 a; Indian Question vii 660 b; Joint Stock Company viii 411 a; Mercantilism x 335 a; Middleman x 416 b; Misselden x 535 b; Mun xi 84 b; Native Policy xi 260 a.
CHARTISM—iii 352-54; Attwood ii 307 a; Benbow ii 509 b; Christian Socialism iii 450 a; Cooper iv 359 a; Harney vii 271 b; Hetherington vii 344 a; Jones viii 414 b; Lovett ix 619 b; O'Brien xi 421 a; O'Connor xi 437 a; Petition, Right of xii 100 a; Proletariat xii 516 a; Socialism xiv 197 a; Socialist Parties xiv 213 a; Vincent xv 263 a.
CHASE, S. P.—iii 354.
CHASSIDISM—iii 354-57; Judaism viii 432 a; Zionism xv 528 b.
CHASTITY—iii 357-58; Abortion i 372-74; Celibacy iii 283-86; Morals x 645 a; Seduction xiii 639-41.
CHATEAUBRIAND, F. A. R.—iii 358.
Chatham, Lord—see PITT, W.
CHAUTAUQUA—iii 359-60.
CHAUVINISM—iii 361; Ethnocentrism v 613 b; Nationalism xi 231-49; Patriotism xii 27 b.
CHAVCHAVADZE, I.—iii 361.
Chayanov, A. V.—xii 52 a.
CHAYKOVSKY, N. V.—iii 362.
CHECK—iii 362-63; Bank Deposits ii 417 a; Banking, Commercial ii 432 b; Bill of Exchange ii 541 a; Credit iv 546 b; Negotiable Instruments xi 332-35.
Check Off—iii 569 b.
CHECKS AND BALANCES—iii 363-65; Introd. Vol. 1 (The Roman World) i 50 b; Bicameral System ii 534 a; Legislative Assemblies (U. S.) ix 362 a, 366 a; Municipal Govt. xi 113 b; Separation of Powers xiii 666 a.

Cheka—Political Police xii 204 b; Russian Revolution xiii 483 b.
Chelčický, P.—ii 47 a.
CHEMICAL INDUSTRIES—iii 365-67; Dye Industry v 301-05; Fertilizer Industry vi 193-98; Heavy Chemicals vii 300-04; Industrial Alcohol vii 680-84; Laundry and Dry Cleaning Industry ix 193 b; Machines and Tools x 24 a; Medical Materials Industry x 279-82; Metals x 382 a; Nitrates xi 379-84; Paints and Varnishes xi 530-34; Potash xii 274-77; Pulp and Paper Industry xii 706 a; Salt xiii 525 b.
Chemical Warfare—ix 484 b.
CHENG CH'IAO—iii 367.
CHÉNON, É.—iii 368.
CHERBULIEZ, A. É.—iii 368.
Cherbury, Lord Herbert of—see HERBERT OF CHERBURY, LORD.
CHERKASSKY, V. A.—iii 369.
Chernov, V.—xiii 481 a.
CHERNYSHEVSKY, N. G.—iii 369; Nihilism xi 377 b.
CHEVALIER, M.—iii 371; Carbonari iii 223 a; Monetary Unions x 596 a.
CHEYSSON, É.—iii 371.
Chiang Kai-shek—viii 612 b.
CHICHERIN, B. N.—iii 372.
CHILD—iii 373-431 (Welfare 373-80, 428; Hygiene 380-84, 428, Mortality 384-90, 428, Psychology 391-93, 428, Guidance 393-95, 429, Marriage 395-98, 429, Dependent 398-403, 429, Neglected 403-06, 429, Delinquent 406-09, 429, Institutions 410-12, 430, Labor 412-24, 430, Welfare Legislation 424-27, 431); Abnormal Psychology i 365 b; Adoption i 459-63; Animal Protection ii 62 b; Barnardo ii 463 a; Brace ii 670 b; Carpenter iii 231 b; Cripples iv 592-95; Day Nursery v 13-16; Dickens v 132 b; Educational Psychology v 434 b; Family vi 65-70; Family Desertion and Nonsupport vi 79 a; Guardianship vii 192-95; Health Education vii 291 a; Illegitimacy vii 579-86; Infanticide viii 27-28; Institutions, Public viii 90-95; Juvenile Delinquency and Juvenile Courts viii 528-33; Lathrop ix 186 a; Majority, Age of x 53-55; Mental Hygiene x 321 b; Mental Tests x 323-29; Mothers' Pensions xi 53-57; Motion Pictures xi 68 a; Motor Vehicle Accidents xi 70 b; Parent Education xi 573-76; Placing Out xii 144-46; Play xii 160-61; Playgrounds xii 161-63; Preschool Education xii 320-24; Preyer xii 349 b; Public Health xii 652 b; Social Work xiv 168 b, 178 b; Straus xiv 416 a; Waugh xv 385 b.
Child Labor—Apprenticeship ii 144-47; Canning Industry iii

Index (Chambers of Agriculture — City)

177 b; Child (Labor) iii 412-24; Continuation Schools iv 313-15; Education v 416 b; Glass and Pottery Industries vi 676 a; Hours of Labor vii 481 b, 489 b; Industrial Hazards vii 700 b; Industrial Revolution viii 11 b; Labor, Govt. Services for viii 645 a; Labor Legislation and Law viii 662 b; Leather Industries ix 313 a; Textile Industry xiv 591 b.

CHILD, J.—iii 372; Culpeper iv 618 a; Free Trade vi 441 a.

CHILD, L. M.—iii 373.

Child, R.—i 579 b.

Children's Aid Society—iii 670 b.

Children's Bureau—iii 378 b.

Chinese Eastern Railway—x 80 b.

Chinese Immigration—see ORIENTAL IMMIGRATION.

Chinese Law—Law ix 249-54.

CHINESE PROBLEM—iii 431-36; Burlingame iii 76 b; Europeanization v 633 a; Exterritoriality vi 37 b; Famine vi 86 a; Far Eastern Problem vi 92-100; Govt. (China) vii 98-100; Guilds (Chinese) vii 219-21; Hart vii 275 b; International Waterways viii 212 b; Kuomintang viii 610-14; Li Hung Chang ix 427 b; Literacy and Illiteracy ix 520 b; Local Govt. ix 580 a; Manchurian Problem x 80-84; Municipal Govt. xi 112 b; Open Door xi 468-71; Opium Problem xi 471-76; Rebellion xiii 145 a; Spheres of Influence xiv 297-99; Sun Yat Sen xiv 466 b; Trade Unions xv 36 b.

CHIRONI, G.—iii 436.

CHIVALRY—iii 436-43; Introd. Vol. I (The Growth of Autonomy) i 79 b; Education v 408 b; Feudalism (European) vi 207 a, (Japanese) 217 b; Music xi 158 b; Tradition xv 65 b.

CHLEBORÁD, F. L.—iii 443.

Chocolate—xii 154 b.

Chomiakov, A.—see KHOMYAKOV, A. S.

Chovevei Zion—xv 530 b.

CHRISTIAN LABOR UNIONS—iii 443-46; Dual Unionism v 260 b; Labor Movement viii 695 b; Trade Unions (Belgium) xv 29 a.

CHRISTIAN SCIENCE—iii 446-49; Eddy v 395 b.

CHRISTIAN SOCIALISM—iii 449-52; Ballanche ii 409 b; Bliss ii 591 a; Christianity iii 459 b; Hughes vii 529 b; Kingsley viii 567 b; Ludlow ix 628 b; Maurice x 233 a; Social Christian Movements xiv 127 a; Socialism xiv 195 a.

Christian Socialist Party, Austria—Catholic Parties iii 274 a; Parties, Political xi 627 a.

CHRISTIANITY—iii 452-61. See *relevant titles in* Classification of Articles (Religion), p. 555. See also Art (Mediaeval) ii 243 b; Assassination ii 272 b; Charity iii 341 a; Chinese Problem iii 432 b; Civil Liberties iii 509 b; Communism iv 82 b; Democracy v 78 b; Equality v 575 b; Ethics v 603 a; History and Historiography (Mediaeval Eur.) vii 370 b; Human Nature vii 534 a; Humanitarianism vii 545 a; Justice viii 510 b; Labor viii 616 b; Liberty ix 442 a; Literature ix 537 b; Medicine x 286 a; Pacifism xi 527 a; Passive Resistance and Non-cooperation xii 11 a; Progress xii 496 a; Property xii 534 a; Sanctuary xiii 535 a; Self-Preservation xiii 654 b; Service xiii 673 a; Society xiv 226 a; Stoicism xiv 409 b; Suicide xiv 456 a; Theater xiv 603 b. *See also* Church *and* RELIGION. *For biog. references see* Classification of Articles (Religion—Christianity), p. 567 *and* (History—Religious), p. 562.

Chrodegang of Metz—x 588 a.

Chromium—x 387 a.

CHRYSOSTOM, J.—iii 461; Church Fathers iii 465 b.

Chu Hi—iv 200 b.

Chu Yuan-chang—v 502 a.

CHUANG TZU—iii 462; Taoism xiv 511 a.

CHUPROV, A. A.—iii 462; Statistics xiv 366 b.

CHUPROV, A. I.—iii 463.

CHUQUET, A. M.—iii 463.

Church—*see relevant titles in* Classification of Articles (Religion), p. 555. See also Introd. Vol. I (The Universal Church) i 61-72, (The Growth of Autonomy) 73-83; Aegidius Colonna i 481 a; Agrarian Movements (Italy) i 500 a, (Lat. Amer.) 512 b; Allegiance i 645 a; Amusements, Public ii 44 b; Astrology ii 288 a; Autonomy ii 334 a; Censorship iii 291 b; Charity iii 341 b; Charlemagne iii 345 a; Charles v iii 347 a; Child (Dependent) iii 399 a; Civic Education iii 496 b; Concubinage iv 172 b; Conscientious Objectors iv 210 b; Constantine iv 242 b; Courts iv 519 a; Divorce v 179 a; Döllinger v 193 b; Education v 407 b, 414 a, 421-25; Feudalism vi 206 b; Figgis vi 230 b; Freedom of Association vi 447 b; Galileo Galilei vi 547 b; Giannone vi 651 b; Govt. (Balkan States) vii 83 a; Henry IV (d. 1106) vii 321 b; Illegitimacy vii 579 b; Institutions, Public viii 90 a; Intermarriage viii 152 b; Internationalism viii 214 b; Intolerance viii 243 a; Irish Question viii 285 a; Joseph II viii 417 b; Land Grants (British Empire) ix 37 a, (Lat. Amer.) 41 a; Land Tenure ix 86 a, 102 b, 121 b; Lea ix 281 b; Legal Profession and Legal Education ix 330 a; Literacy and Illiteracy ix 514 a; Marsilius of Padua x 159 b; Massacre x 193 b; Monarchy x 581 a; Music xi 156 b; Negro Problem xi 349 a; Otto I xi 504 a; Philip IV xii 107 b; Political Science xii 214 a; Power, Political xii 302 a; Professions xii 476 b; Prohibition xii 504 a; Slavery xiv 78 a, 79 a; Society xiv 226 a; Teaching Profession xiv 544 a; Theodosius I xiv 615 b; Usury xv 195 a; Woman, Position in Society xv 444 a. *For further biog. references see* Classification of Articles (Religion), p. 567 *and* (History—Religious), p. 562.

CHURCH FATHERS—iii 464-68; Communism iv 83 a; Just Price viii 505 a; Natural Law xi 286 b; Origen xi 494 b; Religious Institutions (Roman Catholic) xiii 248 a; Tertullian xiv 580 a.

Church of England—see Anglicanism.

CHURCHILL, R. H. S.—iii 468; Insurgency, Political viii 115 b.

CHYDENIUS, A.—iii 468.

CICERO, M. T.—iii 469; Introd. Vol. I (The Roman World) i 49 a; Jus Gentium viii 502 b.

CIESZKOWSKI, A.—iii 469.

Cigar Makers' International Union—xiv 643 b.

Cincinnati Social Unit—iv 107 b.

CINO DA PISTOIA—iii 470; Commentators iii 680 a.

Circumcision—ii 567 a.

Cistercians—Introd. Vol. I (The Universal Church) i 66 a; Bernard of Clairvaux ii 524 a; Joachim of Flora viii 405 b; Monasticism x 587 a.

CITIZENSHIP—iii 471-74. See Classification of Articles (Citizenship), p. 549. See also Introd. Vol. I (Greek Culture and Thought) i 12 a; Law (Hellenistic and Greco-Egyptian) ix 231 a; Native Policy (N. Amer.) xi 266 a; Public Employment xii 634 a; Status xiv 374 a; Suffrage xiv 447 b.

CITY—iii 474-82; Amusements, Public ii 42 a; City Manager iii 488-89; City-State iii 489-92; City and Town Planning iii 482-88; Civic Art iii 492-95; Civic Centers iii 495-96; Commune, Mediaeval vi 61-63; County-City Consolidation iv 499-501; Expositions, International vi 24 b; Gangs vi 564-67; Garden Cities vi 569-71; Home Rule vii 434-36; Housing vii 496-517; Land Speculation ix 66 a; Markets, Municipal x 139-44; Metropolitan Areas x 396-401; Municipal Corporation xi 86-94; Municipal Courts xi 94-98; Municipal Govt. xi

105-17; Municipal Transit xi 118-28; Regional Planning xiii 205 a; Sanitation xiii 538-42; Slums xiv 93-98; Specialization xiv 280 b; Suburbs xiv 433-35; Traffic Regulation xv 70-75; Transportation xv 89 a; Urbanization xv 189-92; Water Supply xv 372-77.
City Councils—see MUNICIPAL GOVERNMENT.
City-County Consolidation—see COUNTY-CITY CONSOLIDATION.
City of God—ii 314 a.
City Government—see MUNICIPAL GOVERNMENT.
CITY MANAGER—iii 488-89; Municipal Govt. xi 114 b.
CITY-STATE—iii 489-92; Introd. Vol. I (Greek Culture and Thought) i 9 a, 12 a, 19 a, 31 a, (The Roman World) 42 b, (Renaissance and Reformation) 86 b; City iii 474 b; Colonies iii 654 a; Commune, Mediaeval iv 61-63; Exile v 687 b; Legislative Assemblies ix 355 b; Monetary Unions x 595 b; Municipal Govt. xi 105 a; Naturalization xi 306 b; Ostracism xi 501-03; Political Science xii 207 a; Republicanism xiii 317 b; State xiv 329 b.
CITY AND TOWN PLANNING—iii 482-88; Architecture ii 174 b; City iii 481 a; Civic Art iii 492-95; Civic Centers iii 495-96; Eminent Domain v 495 b; Excess Condemnation v 663-64; Garden Cities vi 569-71; Housing (Eur.) vii 500 b; Parks xi 582-87; Regional Planning xiii 205 a; Traffic Regulation xv 74 b; Zoning xv 538-39.
CIVIC ART—iii 492-95; City and Town Planning iii 482-88; Civic Centers iii 495-96.
CIVIC CENTERS—iii 495-96; Community Centers iv 105-06.
CIVIC EDUCATION—iii 496-98; Americanization ii 33 b; Civic Organizations iii 498-502; Education v 411 a, 421 b.
CIVIC ORGANIZATIONS—iii 498-502; Chambers of Commerce iii 325-29; Civic Art iii 493 a; Govt. Reporting vii 132 a; Municipal Govt. xi 116 b.
Civil Disobedience—Indian Question vii 669 b; Passive Resistance and Non-cooperation xii 9-13.
CIVIL LAW—iii 502-09; Code Civil iii 604-06; Codification iii 607 b; Common Carrier iv 49 b; Common Law iv 51 b; Conflict of Laws iv 189 b; Consideration iv 236 a; Damages iv 697 b; Evidence v 646 a; Family Law vi 83 a; German Civil Code vi 634-37; Jury viii 498-502; Justice, Administration of viii 516 b; Landlord and Tenant ix 145 a, 146 b; Procedure, Legal xii 443 b. See also LAW.
CIVIL LIBERTIES—iii 509-13. See Classification of Articles (Civil Liberties), p. 549. See also Bail ii 386 b; Civil Rights iii 513 b; Company Towns iv 122 a; Deportation and Expulsion of Aliens v 97 b; Govt. (France) vii 46 a, (Italy) 50 a, 52 a, (Russia, Imperial) 67 a; Riot xiii 391 a; Wilkes xv 422 a.
Civil Opposition—see Classification of Articles (Civil Opposition), p. 549.
CIVIL RIGHTS—iii 513-15; Catholic Emancipation iii 269-71; Citizenship iii 471-74; Equal Protection of the Law v 573 b; Jewish Emancipation viii 394-99; Nationality xi 250 a; Natural Rights xi 299-302; Negro Problem xi 338 a; Status xiv 373-78; Suffrage xiv 447-50.
CIVIL SERVICE—iii 515-23; Introd. Vol. I (The Social Sciences as Disciplines, Gt. Brit.) i 233 a; Administration, Public i 442-47; Appointments ii 137-38; Bureaucracy iii 70-74; Civic Organizations iii 500 b; Colonial Administration iii 642 b; Consular Service iv 279-82; Corruption, Political iv 451 b; Eaton v 305 b; Expert vi 11 a; Freedom of Association vi 450 a; Govt. (Australia) vii 30 b, (Canada) 27 b, (France) 46 b, (Germany) 55 a, (Gt. Brit.) 23 a, (New Zealand) 32 b, (Soviet Russia) 69 b, (U. S.) 21 a; Indian Question vii 663 a; Judiciary viii 465 b; Labor, Govt. Services for viii 652 a; League of Nations ix 291 a; Middle Class x 412 a; Public Employment xii 628-37; Spoils System xiv 303 b. See also BUREAUCRACY.
CIVIL WAR—iii 523-25; Belligerency ii 506 a; Guerrilla Warfare vii 198 a; Insurrection viii 117 b; Military Desertion x 453 a; War xv 333 a.
Civil War, U. S.—Agrarian Movements i 510 a; Benjamin ii 516 b; Bright iii 3 b; Calhoun iii 144 a; Conscription iv 221 b; Davis v 12 a; Lincoln ix 487 a; Military Desertion x 453 a; Reconstruction xiii 168-73; States' Rights xiv 347 a.
CIVILIZATION—iii 525-29; Backward Countries ii 379-81; Climate iii 560 a; Commerce iv 3 b; Continuity, Social iv 315-18; Culture iv 621 b; Dress v 237 a; Environmentalism v 561-66; Folkways vi 295 b; Magic x 41 a; Maine x 49 b; Maladjustment x 61 b; Progress xii 495-99; Psychoanalysis xii 585 b; Religion xiii 236 a; Rousseau xiii 445 b; Symbolism xiv 492-95; War xv 340 a.
Claflin, T.—xv 475 b.
CLAMAGERAN, J. J.—iii 529.
Clan—Social Organization xiv 142 b; Totemism xiv 657-61.
Clarendon, Constitutions of — Common Law iv 51 a; Religious Institutions (Roman Catholic) xiii 256 a.
CLARENDON, LORD—iii 530.
Clark, J. B.—Capital iii 189 a; Distribution v 171 a; Economics v 362 a; Profit xii 483 b; Statics and Dynamics xiv 353 a.
Clarke, E. Y.—viii 607 a.
CLARKSON, T.—iii 530.
CLARTÉ MOVEMENT—iii 531.
CLASS—iii 531-36; Introd. Vol. I (The Roman World) i 44 b; Aristocracy ii 183-90; Assimilation, Social ii 281 b; Authority ii 320 a; Bourgeoisie ii 654-56; Caste iii 254-57; Ceremony iii 313 b; Class Consciousness iii 536-38; Class Struggle iii 538-42; Distribution v 170 a; Economics (Socialist Economics) v 379 a; Equal Protection of the Law v 572-74; Fashion vi 142 a; Feudalism vi 209 a; Gambling vi 557 b; Gentleman, Theory of the vi 616-20; Inheritance viii 39 a; Interests viii 147 a; Labor viii 615-20; Labor Movement viii 684 a; Land Tenure (Ancient World) ix 79 a; Leisure ix 402-06; Luxury ix 634 b; Masses x 195-201; Materialism (Historical) x 218 a; Middle Class x 407-15; Militarism x 447 b; Mobility, Social x 554-55; Negro Problem xi 354 b; Nobility xi 385-89; Peasantry xii 48-53; Plantation xii 152 a; Plutocracy xii 175-77; Poverty xii 284-92; Priesthood xii 394 a; Proletariat xii 510-18; Property xii 531 b; Renaissance xiii 280 a; Revolution and Counter-revolution xiii 367-76; Soils xiv 251 a; Sports xiv 305 b; Status xiv 373-78; Taste xiv 523-25.
CLASS CONSCIOUSNESS—iii 536-38; Class iii 534 b; Class Struggle iii 541 a; Clerical Occupations iii 553 b; Clubs iii 576 b; Farmers' Organizations vi 129-32; Labor viii 620 a; Labor Movement viii 682 a; Materialism (Dialectical) x 215 a; Proletariat xii 515 b; Revolution and Counter-revolution xiii 369 a.
Class Legislation — see EQUAL PROTECTION OF THE LAWS.
CLASS STRUGGLE—iii 538-42; Introd. Vol. I (Individualism and Capitalism) i 157 a; Chartism iii 352-54; Class iii 535 a; Communist Parties iv 87-95; Direct Action v 156 b; Fabianism vi 47 a; French Revolution vi 471-83; General Strike vi 607-12; Industrial Relations vii 712 b; Intellectuals viii 120 b;

International Relations viii 187 b; Labor-Capital Cooperation viii 629 a; Literature ix 539 b; Massacre x 193 a; Masses x 195–201; Materialism (Historical) x 219 a; Political Offenders xii 202 a; Proletariat xii 510–18; Revolution and Counter-revolution xiii 367–76; Sabotage xiii 495–97; Socialism xiv 201 b; State xiv 331 b; Syndicalism xiv 497 b; War xv 336 a.

Classical School, Economics—v 351–57.

CLASSICISM—iii 542–45; Architecture ii 168 b; Art (Classical) ii 240–43, (Renaissance) 246–53; Humanism vii 537–44; Literature ix 530 a; Rationalism xiii 114 a; Renaissance xiii 282 a; Romanticism xiii 426 b; Winckelmann xv 428 b.

Classified Property Tax — see PROPERTY TAX.

CLAUSEWITZ, C. VON—iii 545.

CLAY, H.—iii 545; Economics v 383 a.

Clayton Act—Boycott ii 665 a; Interlocking Directorates viii 150 b; Labor Injunction viii 656 b; Labor Legislation and Law viii 670 b; Trusts xv 118 a.

Clayton-Bulwer Treaty—xi 554 a.

CLEARING HOUSES—iii 546–48; Federal Reserve System vi 161 a.

CLEMENCEAU, G.—iii 548; Anticlericalism ii 114 a; Bloc, Parliamentary ii 591 b.

Clement VII—xiii 257 a.

Clement XIV—viii 386 b.

CLÉMENT, A.—iii 549.

CLEMENT OF ALEXANDRIA—iii 549; Church Fathers iii 465 a.

CLÉMENT, J.-P.—iii 550.

Clergy—see PRIESTHOOD.

CLERICAL OCCUPATIONS—iii 550–54; Business Education iii 107–10; Hours of Labor vii 484 b; Occupation xi 433 a.

CLERMONT-GANNEAU, C.—iii 554.

CLEVELAND, S. G.—iii 555; Monroe Doctrine x 631 b.

CLICQUOT-BLERVACHE, S. DE—iii 556.

Clientship—Law (Celtic) ix 248 b.

CLIMATE—iii 556–62; Acclimatization i 401–03; Agriculture i 572 a, 593 b; Anthropology ii 99 a; Communicable Diseases, Control of iv 73 a; Criminology iv 588 b; Determinism v 112 b; Dress v 236 b; Location of Industry ix 587 b; Migrations x 420 a.

CLINICS AND DISPENSARIES—iii 562–67; Birth Control ii 561 b, 562 a; Child (Guidance) iii 394 a; Dentistry v 92 b; Health Centers vii 288 a; Hospitals and Sanatoria vii 469 a; Medicine x 297 a; Social Work (Case Work) xiv 179 a.

CLINTON, DE W.—iii 567.

Clipper Ship—xiv 33 a.

Clisthenes—i 11 b.

CLIVE, R.—iii 567; Indian Question vii 661 a.

CLOOTS, J. B.—iii 568.

CLOSED SHOP AND OPEN SHOP—iii 568–70; Construction Industry iv 274 a; Labor Legislation and Law viii 671 a.

CLOSURE—iii 570–73; Obstruction, Parliamentary xi 422 a.

Clothes—see DRESS.

Clothing Industry—see GARMENT INDUSTRIES.

CLUBS—iii 573–77; Agric. Societies i 570–71; Amateur ii 19 a; Anthropology ii 87 b; Aviation ii 343 b; Boys' and Girls' Clubs ii 667–70; Clubs, Political iii 577–80; Fraternal Orders vi 423–25; Gangs vi 564–67; Secret Societies xiii 621–23; Voluntary Associations xv 285 b; Women's Organizations xv 460–65.

CLUBS, POLITICAL—iii 577–80; Clubs iii 573–77; Conspiracy, Political iv 240 a; French Revolution vi 474 b; Jacobinism viii 360–63.

CLUNET, É.—iii 580.

CLUNIAC MOVEMENT—iii 580–82; Introd. Vol. 1 (The Universal Church) i 66 a; Investiture Conflict viii 260 b; Monasticism x 587 a.

COAL INDUSTRY — iii 582–600; Company Housing iv 115–19; Conciliation, Industrial iv 167 b; Electric Power v 460 b; Gas Industry vi 591 b; Hours of Labor vii 483 b; Iron and Steel Industry viii 299 b, 304 b; Jevons viii 390 a; Labor-Capital Cooperation viii 628 b; Mining x 505 a, 508–13; Mitchell x 547 a; Policing, Industrial xii 194 a; Power, Industrial xii 296 b; Shipping xiv 40 a; Trade Agreements xiv 668 a.

Coal and Iron Police—xii 194 a.

Coaling Stations — see Naval Bases.

COALITION—iii 600–02; Bloc, Parliamentary ii 591 a; Bolshevism ii 626 b; Cabinet Govt. iii 136 a; Legislative Assemblies (France) ix 377 b; Parties, Political xi 592 b.

Cobalt—x 287 a.

COBB, F. I.—iii 602.

COBBETT, W.—iii 602.

Cobden Club—i 241 b.

COBDEN, R.—iii 602; Anti-Corn Law League ii 115 a; Corn Laws iv 407 b; Peace Movements xii 43 a.

Cobergher, W.—xii 35 a.

COCCEJI, H. VON—iii 603.

COCCEJI, S. VON—iii 603.

COCHIN, A.—iii 604.

Cocoa—xii 154 b.

CODE CIVIL—iii 604–06; Cambacérès iii 157 a; Child (Delinquent) iii 408 a; Civil Law iii 506 b; Codification iii 608 b, 611 a; Demolombe v 87 b; Employers' Liability v 515 b; Evidence v 647 a; Family Law vi 83 a; Labor Legislation and Law viii 672 b; Legal Profession and Legal Education ix 335 a; Marital Property x 120 b; Mortgage xi 37 a; Negligence xi 330 a; Pothier xii 278 a; Specific Performance xiv 287 a; Water Law xv 370 b.

Code of Hammurabi—Alimony i 642 a; Apprenticeship ii 144 a; Bribery ii 690 b; Building Regulations iii 52 a; Codification iii 606 b; Courts iv 517 a; Law (Cuneiform) ix 213 b; Lawgivers ix 275 b.

Code of Manu—Codification iii 606 b; Law (Hindu) ix 260 a.

Code Napoléon—see CODE CIVIL.

Codes, Industrial, U. S.—see National Industrial Recovery Act.

Codex Juris Canonici—Canon Law iii 181 b; Codification iii 609 a.

Codex of Justinian—see CORPUS JURIS CIVILIS.

CODIFICATION—iii 606–13; Introd. Vol. 1 (The Roman World) i 47 b, 58 a; American Law Institute ii 30 b; Carter iii 243 b; Case Law iii 249 b; Catherine II iii 268 b; Civil Law iii 502–09; Code Civil iii 604–06; Colbert iii 627 a; Commercial Law iv 17 b; Corpus Juris Civilis iv 435–38; Criminal Law iv 573 b; Cronhielm iv 607 a; Customary Law iv 663 b; Draco v 233 a; Family Law vi 83 b; German Civil Code vi 634–37; Huber vii 525 b; International Law viii 171 b; Islamic Law viii 347 b; Judaism viii 431 b; Karo xiii 547 b; Kreittmayr viii 599 a; Labor Legislation and Law viii 674 a; Lamoignon ix 26 b; Law (General View of Ancient) ix 207 b, (Celtic) 246 b, (Chinese) 251 a, 253 a, (Cuneiform) 213 b, (Germanic) 238 a, (Hindu) 260 a, (Japanese) 255 a, (Jewish) 219 a, 224 a, (Slavic) 241 a; Law Enforcement ix 268 b; Lawgivers ix 276 a; Legislation ix 350 a; Maritime Law x 123 a; Military Law x 454 a; Military Occupation x 458 b; Nārada xi 185 a; Pomeroy xii 230 a; Procedure, Legal xii 443 b, 448 a; Roman Law xiii 420 a, 423 b; Speransky xiv 297 a; Stefan Dušan xiv 379 a; Suarez xiv 430 a; Theodosius II xiv 616 a; Tronchet xv 107 a; Verbőczy xv 237 b; Warfare, Laws of xv 359–64.

CODRINGTON, R. H.—iii 613.

COEDUCATION—iii 614–17.

COEN, J. P.—iii 617.

COERCION—iii 617–19; Blacklist ii 576–78; Blockade ii 594–96; Boycott ii 662–66; Conduct iv

179 a; Conscientious Objectors iv 210–12; Consensus iv 225 b; Drives, Money Raising v 241 a; Duress v 287–90; Economic Policy v 334 a, 339 a; Extortion vi 39–41; Force, Political vi 338–41; Hunger Strike vii 552–55; Imperialism vii 606 a; Intimidation viii 239–42; Morals x 647 b; Obedience, Political xi 416 b; Passive Resistance and Non-cooperation xii 9–13; Persecution xii 83–85; Pressures, Social xii 344–48; Sanction, International xiii 529 a; Sanction, Social xiii 531–34; Violence xv 264–67.
COEUR, J.—iii 619.
Coffee—Business, Government Services for iii 120 a; Plantation Wares xii 155 a; Raw Materials xiii 130 b; Valorization xv 210–12.
Coffin, L.—see MOTT, L.
COGHLAN, T. A.—iii 620.
COGNETTI DE MARTIIS, S.—iii 620.
Cohen, H.—viii 541 b.
COHEN STUART, A. J.—iii 621.
COHN, G.—iii 621.
COHN, G. L.—iii 621.
COINAGE—iii 622–25; Babelon ii 374 b; Compensated Dollar iv 135 a; Currency iv 650 a; Graumann vii 157 b; Metals x 366 b, 368 a; Monetary Unions x 595 b; Money x 603 a; Silver xiv 57 b.
Coinsurance—vi 257 a.
Coke—viii 304 b.
COKE, E.—iii 625; Common Law iv 52 a; Prerogative xii 319 b; Rule of Law xiii 464 b.
COLAJANNI, N.—iii 625; Criminology iv 587 a.
COLBERT, J.-B.—iii 626; Aids i 609 a; Clément iii 550 a; Colonies iii 658 a; Mercantilism x 334 a; Roads xiii 402 b; Sugar xiv 451 b.
Colchester, Lord—see ABBOT, C.
Cold Storage—see REFRIGERATION.
COLERIDGE, S. T.—iii 627; Transcendentalism xv 76 a.
Colet, J.—vii 540 b.
COLINS, J. H.—iii 628.
COLLECTIVE BARGAINING — iii 628–31; Bargaining Power ii 460 a; Benefits, Trade Union ii 515 a; Company Unions iv 123–26; Conciliation, Industrial iv 165–69; Employers' Associations v 509–14; Industrial Relations vii 710–17; Industrial Relations Councils vii 717–22; Iron and Steel Industry viii 320 b; Labor-Capital Cooperation viii 624–29; Labor Contract viii 631 a; Labor Legislation and Law viii 666 a; Labor Movement viii 683 b; Monopoly x 626 b; Railroads xiii 95 b; Trade Agreements xiv 667–70.

COLLECTIVE BEHAVIOR—iii 631–33; Introd. Vol. I (War and Reorientation) i 207 a; Agitation i 487–88; Chauvinism iii 361; Class Consciousness iii 536–38; Communication iv 79 a; Consciousness iv 219 a; Conversion, Religious iv 354 a; Crowd iv 612–13; Fanaticism vi 91 a; Leadership ix 282–87; Le Bon ix 316 b; Masses x 196 b; Mob x 552–54; Propaganda xii 521–28; Revivals, Religious xiii 363–67; Social Psychology xiv 151–57.
Collective Representations—Social Psychology xiv 154 a.
COLLECTIVISM—iii 633–37; Anarchism ii 49 a; Civil Liberties iii 512 b; Communism iv 81–87; Communistic Settlements iv 95–102; Control, Social iv 346 b; Cooperation iv 359–99; Corporation iv 421 b; Land Tenure (Introd.) ix 73 b, (Primitive Societies) 76 a, (Lat. Amer.) 119 a, (Russia) 109 b; Law (Cuneiform) ix 217 a, (Greek) 227 b, (Japanese) 256 b; Levellers ix 423 a; Majority Rule x 55–60; Religion xiii 230 a; Romanticism xiii 430 b; Socialism xiv 188–212; Socialization xiv 221–25; Syndicalism xiv 496 b.
College Settlements—xiv 158 a.
Colleges—see UNIVERSITIES AND COLLEGES.
COLLETT, C.—iii 637.
Collinet, P.—xiii 425 a.
COLLINGS, J.—iii 637.
COLLINS, M.—iii 637.
COLMEIRO, M.—iii 638.
COLONATE—iii 639–41; Agrarian Movements i 495 a; Land Tenure ix 81 b; Latifundia ix 187 b; Manorial System x 97 b.
COLONIAL ADMINISTRATION — iii 641–46. See COLONIES.
COLONIAL ECONOMIC POLICY—iii 646–51. See COLONIES.
COLONIAL SYSTEM—iii 651–53; Acts of Trade, Brit. i 426–29; Colonial Economic Policy iii 647 a; Colonies iii 653–63; Imperialism vii 607 a; Mercantilism x 336 a.
COLONIES—iii 653–63; Introd. Vol. I (Greek Culture and Thought) i 9 b, 31 b; Acts of Trade, Brit. i 426–29; Asiento ii 268–70; Audiencia ii 311–12; Backward Countries ii 380 a; Balance of Power ii 397 b; Budget iii 44 a; Casa de Contratación iii 246–48; Chartered Companies iii 347–52; Colonial Administration iii 641–46; Colonial Economic Policy iii 646–51; Colonial System iii 651–53; Commerce iv 8 b; Conquest iv 206 a; Council of the Indies iv 494–97; Dominion Status v 211–16; Economic Policy v 338 a; Export Duties vi 21 b; Forced Labor vi 342 b; For-

tunes, Private vi 392 a; Fur Trade vi 531 b; Govt. (Lat. Amer.) vii 89 b, (Netherlands) 60 a, (New Zealand) 32 a; Great Powers vii 160 b; Immigration vii 592 a; Imperial Unity vii 604 a; Imperialism vii 605–13; Indenture vii 644–48; Indian Question vii 659–74; Land Grants (Brit. Empire) ix 36–39, (Lat. Amer.) 39–43; Land Speculation ix 68 a; Migrations x 429 b; Miscegenation x 531 a; Missions x 539 b; Native Policy xi 252–83; Navy xi 311 b; Philippine Problem xii 109–16; Plantation xii 148–53; Protectorate xii 569 a; Puritanism xiii 5 b; Quakers xiii 13 a; Slavery xiv 80 b, 84 a; Smuggling xiv 120 a; Sugar xiv 451 a; Transportation of Criminals xv 90–93. *For biog. references see* Classification of Articles (Colonial Administration), p. 559.
Colonna, A.—see AEGIDIUS COLONNA.
COLQUHOUN, P.—iii 663.
Columban—x 589 a.
Columbia Broadcasting Co.—xiii 58 a.
COLWELL, S.—iii 664.
Combes, J. L. E.—ii 114 a.
COMBINATIONS, INDUSTRIAL—iii 664–74; Agric. Machinery Industry i 555 b; Automobile Industry ii 325 a; Aviation ii 356 a, 363 b; Branch Banking ii 679–82; Capitalization iii 209 a; Captain of Industry iii 219 a; Cartel iii 234–43; Cement iii 288 b; Chemical Industries iii 367 a; Corporation iv 422 a; Corporation Finance iv 429 a; Crises iv 598 a; Dye Industry v 303 a; Electric Power v 463 a; Electrical Manufacturing Industry v 472 b, 476 b; Export Associations vi 17–19; Fertilizer Industry vi 197 a; Fire Insurance vi 260 b; Food Industries (Baking, U. S.) vi 305 b, (Confectionery) 310 b, (Grocery Trade) 314 b; Furniture vi 540 b; Gary vi 588 a; Heavy Chemicals vii 304 a; Holding Companies vii 403–12; Increasing Returns vii 640 a; Industrial Alcohol vii 682 a; Industrialism viii 22 b; Interlocking Directorates viii 148–51; International Trade viii 196 a; Investment Banking viii 272 a; Iron and Steel Industry viii 305 b, 306 b, 308 b; Kreuger viii 600 b; Krupp viii 605 b; Laissez Faire ix 18 b; Large Scale Production ix 177 b; Liquor Industry ix 499 a; Loewenstein ix 598 a; Match Industry x 206 a; Meat Packing and Slaughtering (U. S.) x 246 a; Medical Materials Industry x 281 a; Metals x 373 b, 375 a,

377 a, 382 a, 384 a; Middle Class x 409 a; Mining x 502 b; Monopoly x 625 b; Morgan Family xi 11 b; Motion Pictures xi 59 b; Munitions Industry xi 129 b; Nitrates xi 380 b, 383 a; Oil Industry xi 442 b, 448 a; Power, Industrial xii 299 a; Precious Stones xii 314 b; Press xii 333 b; Public Utilities (Eur.) xii 685 b, (U. S.) 680 b; Pulp and Paper Industry xii 709 a; Quarrying xiii 18 b; Radio xiii 55 a; Railroads xiii 79 b; Rationalization xiii 117 b; Raw Materials xiii 125 b; Rubber xiii 458 b; Ryan xiii 494 a; Shipping xiv 39 a; Socialism (Marxian) xiv 200 a; Specialization xiv 283 a; Stinnes xiv 392 b; Telephone and Telegraph xiv 562 b; Tobacco xiv 642 a; Trade Associations xiv 670-76; Trusts xv 111-22.

COMENIUS, J. A.—iii 674; Child iii 376 a, 391 a; Education v 413 a; Preschool Education xii 321 a.

COMITADJI—iii 675-78; Parties, Political (Bulgaria) xi 630 a.

COMITY—iii 678-79; Conflict of Laws iv 189 a; Extradition vi 43 a; Foreign Corporations vi 356 b; Judgments viii 447 a.

Commandeering — see REQUISITIONS, MILITARY.

Commedia del'Arte—xiv 606 b.

COMMENTATORS—iii 679-81; Cino da Pistoia iii 470 b; Civil Law iii 505 a; Doneau v 216 a; Glossators vi 681 b; Jurisprudence viii 479 b; Legal Profession and Legal Educ. ix 329 a.

COMMERCE—iv 3-13. See Classification of Articles (Commerce), p. 549. See also Introd. Vol. I (Greek Culture and Thought) i 9 b, 15 b, (The Roman World) 45 b, 56 a, (The Growth of Autonomy) 75 a; Acceptance i 388-89; Bill of Exchange ii 539-41; Brigandage ii 694 b; Business, Govt. Services for iii 113-22; Cartel iii 238 a; Chambers of Commerce iii 325-29; City iii 477 b; City-State iii 490 a; Colonial Economic Policy iii 646-51; Colonial System iii 651-53; Consular Service iv 279 b; Crusades iv 615 b; Dye Industry (Early Dye Trade) v 296-300; Food Supply vi 333 b; Fortunes, Private vi 389-92; Fruit and Vegetable Industry vi 507 b; Ghetto vi 647 b; Imperialism vii 607 a; Industrial Revolution viii 5 a; Labor Exchange Banks viii 637 b; Law (Cuneiform) ix 217 b; Literacy and Illiteracy ix 513 a; Metals x 366 a; Military Orders x 462 a; Navy xi 310 b; Silk Industry xiv 52 b; Wool xv 476 b. See also INTERNATIONAL TRADE.

Commerce, Departments of—iii 114 b.

Commerce, Interstate—see INTERSTATE COMMERCE.

Commercial Courts—see COURTS, COMMERCIAL.

Commercial Education—see BUSINESS EDUCATION.

COMMERCIAL LAW—iv 14-19; Arbitration, Commercial ii 151-53; Civil Law iii 504 b; Commercial Treaties iv 31 a; Consideration iv 233-36; Corporation iv 414-23; Courts, Commercial iv 533-35; Endemann v 531 a; Foreign Corporations vi 354-58; Goldschmidt vi 694 b; Holt vii 417 a; Law (Cuneiform) ix 217 b, (Japanese) 257 a, (Jewish) 224 b; Law Merchant ix 270-74; Mansfield x 102 b; Maritime Law x 122-31; Negotiable Instruments xi 332-35; Stracca di Ancona xiv 415 a; Thöl xiv 618 b.

Commercial Policy — see ECONOMIC POLICY.

COMMERCIAL ROUTES—iv 19-24; Brigandage ii 694 b; Commerce iv 3-13; Hanseatic League vii 262 b; International Trade viii 192 b; Panama Canal xi 557 a; Roads xiii 400-11; Suez Canal xiv 444-47; Transit, International xv 81 a; Waterways, Inland xv 377-84.

COMMERCIAL TREATIES—iv 24-31; Capitulations iii 213-15; Colonial Economic Policy iii 648 a; Customs Duties iv 668 b; Far Eastern Problem vi 93 b; Foreign Corporations vi 357 a; Free Trade vi 445 a; Open Door xi 468 b; Protection xii 564 b; Tariff xiv 514 b; Transit Duties xv 78 a.

COMMERCIALISM—iv 31-34; Agriculture i 578 b, 588 a, 596 a; Amusements, Public ii 43 b; Aristocracy ii 188 a; Art ii 238 b, 255 b; Art Collecting ii 259 b; Athletics ii 299 a; Calvin iii 152 b; Capitalism iii 197 b; Leisure ix 404 a; Literature ix 535 a; Music xi 161 a; Protestantism xii 574 a; Radio xiii 59-62; Recreation xiii 177 a; Sports xiv 307 b; Theater xiv 613 a.

COMMINES, P. DE—iv 34; History and Historiography vii 373 b.

COMMISSION SYSTEM OF GOVERNMENT—iv 35-36; Municipal Government xi 114 a; Police xii 184 b.

COMMISSIONS—iv 36-40; Administrative Law i 453 a; Delegation of Powers v 65-67; Federal Trade Commission vi 165-69; Government Ownership vii 116 a; Interstate Commerce Commission viii 229-36; Investigations, Governmental viii 251-60; Legislative Assemblies (France) ix 377 b, (U. S.) 369 a; Metropolitan Areas x 398 a; Rate Regulation xiii 110 b; Socialization xiv 222 a.

Committee on the Costs of Medical Care—Medicine x 292 b; Morbidity xi 6 a; Public Health xii 650 b.

Committee of the Whole—Committees, Legislative iv 40 b.

COMMITTEES, LEGISLATIVE — iv 40-44; Caucus iii 278 b; Closure iii 572 b; Legislative Assemblies (History and Theory) ix 359 a, (France) 377 b, (Germany) 381 b, (Gt. Brit. and Dominions) 371 b, (Spain) 392 a, (U. S.) 368 a; Procedure, Parliamentary xii 455 b; Pym xiii 12 a.

Commodity Balance of Trade—ii 403 a.

Commodity Budgets—xv 317 b.

COMMODITY EXCHANGES—iv 44-48; Agric. Marketing i 562 a; Arbitrage ii 150-51; Broker iii 9 b; Bucket Shops iii 30-31; Corner, Speculative iv 408-10; Cotton iv 491 b; Hedging vii 305 b; Raw Materials xiii 127 b; Speculation xiv 290 a; Warehousing xv 356 a.

COMMON CARRIER — iv 48-50; Bailment ii 390 a; Motor Vehicle Transportation xi 74 b; Oil Industry xi 440 b; Rate Regulation xiii 104 b.

COMMON LAW—iv 50-56; Bailment ii 389 a; Blackstone ii 580 a; Bracton ii 671 a; Case Law iii 249-51; Certiorari iii 317-19; Child (Delinquent) iii 407 b; Civil Law iii 505 a; Codification iii 611 b; Coke iii 625 b; Commercial Law iv 14-19; Common Carrier iv 48 a; Compurgation iv 149 b; Confiscation iv 184 b; Conflict of Laws iv 189 a; Consideration iv 233-36; Conspiracy, Criminal iv 236-38; Criminal Law iv 575 b; Customary Law iv 665 b; Damages iv 697 b; Edward I v 435 b; Equity v 584 a; Escheat v 591 b; Evidence v 638 b; Family Law vi 83 a; Guardianship vii 193 a; Henry II vii 321 a; Jury viii 492-98; Justice, Administration of viii 517 a; Kent viii 558 b; Landlord and Tenant ix 145 a; Law Merchant ix 273 b; Legal Profession and Legal Education ix 334 a; Libel and Slander ix 430 b; Lien ix 456 b; Procedure, Legal xii 445 a; Reception xiii 155 b; Rule of Law xiii 463-66; Water Law xv 369 b; Writs xv 503-04. See also LAW.

COMMON LAW MARRIAGE—iv 56-58.

Common Pleas, Court of—see Court of Common Pleas.

COMMON SENSE—iv 58-61; Rationalism xiii 113-17.

Common Stock—xiv 403 b.

Commons, J. R.—Boards, Advisory ii 611 b; Economics v 392 a; Unemployment Insurance xv 169 b.
Commonwealth College—xv 485 b.
COMMUNE, MEDIAEVAL—iv 61-63; Introd. Vol. 1 (The Growth of Autonomy) i 75 a; City-State iii 490 b; Guilds (Europ.) vii 210 b, 212 a; Hanseatic League vii 261-67; Law Merchant ix 272 a; Municipal Govt. xi 106 a; Naturalization xi 306 b.
COMMUNE OF PARIS—iv 63-66; Socialism xiv 197 a; Soviet xiv 269 b.
COMMUNICABLE DISEASES, CONTROL OF—iv 66-78; Blind ii 587 b; Deaf v 18 b; Epidemics v 569-72; Health Education vii 289-94; Life Extension Movement ix 461 a; Medicine x 283-89; Morbidity xi 3-7; Mortality xi 29 b; Nursing xi 405-12; Prostitution xii 555 a; Public Health xii 646-57; Sex Education and Sex Ethics xiv 9 b; Water Supply xv 375 a. *For biog. references see* Classification of Articles (Public Health), p. 567.
COMMUNICATION—iv 78-81; Attitudes, Social ii 305-07; Automobile Industry ii 328 b; Aviation ii 339-69; Continuity, Social iv 316 a; Diplomacy v 147-53; Language ix 155-69; Music xi 143 a; Postal Service xii 269-74; Press xii 325-44; Printing and Publishing xii 406-15; Radio xiii 54-67; Roads xiii 400-11; Symbolism xiv 492-95; Telephone and Telegraph xiv 560-67; Tradition xv 62-67; Transportation xv 80-90; Writing xv 500-03.
COMMUNISM—iv 81-87; Christianity iii 452 b, 457 a; Church Fathers iii 466 b; Communistic Settlements iv 95-102; Land Tenure (Primitive Societies) ix 76 a; Village Community xv 253-59. *See also* SOCIALISM.
Communist International — *see* Third International.
Communist League—xiv 213 a.
COMMUNIST PARTIES—iv 87-95; Bolshevism ii 623-30; Far Eastern Problem vi 96 a; Gosplan vi 712 a; Govt. (China) vii 99 a, (Soviet Russia) 69 a; Industrial Workers of the World viii 16 a; Kuomintang viii 611 b; Labor Movement viii 689 b; Labor Parties viii 697 b; Negro Problem xi 351 a; Parties, Political xi 594 a, 616 b, 629 b; Russian Revolution xiii 482 b, 491 a; Sabotage xiii 497 a; Socialist Parties xiv 217 b; Soviet xiv 269-74; Trade Unions (China) xv 37 a, (Japan) 36 a, (Russia) 34 a, (U. S.) 44 b. *See also* SOCIALISM.

COMMUNISTIC SETTLEMENTS — iv 95-102; Alcott i 628 a; Brook Farm iii 13-14; Cabet iii 131 b; Chaykovsky iii 362 a; Christianity iii 452 b; Communism iv 83 b, 85 a; Fourier and Fourierism vi 403 a; Hughes vii 529 b; Labor, Methods of Remuneration for viii 681 a; Lane ix 148 b; Mormonism xi 15 a; Zinzendorf xv 527 b.
COMMUNITY—iv 102-05; Amusements, Public ii 40 b; Association ii 284-86; City iii 474-82; Community Centers iv 105-06; Community Organization iv 106-08; Ethnic Communities v 607-13; Health Centers vii 287-89; Neighborhood xi 356-57; Recreation xiii 178 a; Social Surveys xiv 162-65; Sociology xiv 233 a.
COMMUNITY CENTERS—iv 105-06; Civic Centers iii 495-96; Community Organization iv 106 b; Social Settlements xiv 157-62.
Community Chest—Community Organization iv 107 a; Social Work xiv 170 a.
COMMUNITY ORGANIZATION — iv 106-08; Drives, Money Raising v 238-41; Health Education vii 292 a; Social Settlements xiv 157-62; Social Work xiv 170 a.
Community Property — Alienation of Property i 639 a; Alimony i 642 b; Income Tax vii 632 a; Inheritance viii 35 a; Marital Property x 120 a; Water Law xv 369 a.
COMMUTATION OF SENTENCE—iv 108-09.
COMPACTS, INTERSTATE—iv 109-13; Irrigation viii 330 b; Metropolitan Areas x 398 b.
Compagnie des Indes—ix 270 b.
Compagnie d'Occident—ix 270 b.
Compagnonnages—*see* JOURNEYMEN'S SOCIETIES.
COMPANIONATE MARRIAGE — iv 113-15.
COMPANY HOUSING—iv 115-19; Company Towns iv 119 b; Factory System vi 53 b; Lodging Houses ix 596 a.
Company Schools—Business Education iii 109 a; Company Towns iv 120 b; Food Industries (Food Distribution, W. Eur.) vi 323 a.
COMPANY TOWNS—iv 119-23; Factory System vi 53 b; Labor, Methods of Remuneration for viii 677 b; Mining x 504 a.
COMPANY UNIONS—iv 123-26; Conciliation, Industrial iv 167 b; Industrial Democracy vii 691 b; Iron and Steel Industry viii 317 a; Labor Disputes viii 635 b.
COMPARATIVE LAW—iv 126-29; Introd. Vol. 1 (The Social Sciences as Disciplines, France) i 252 a; Jurisprudence viii 477-92; Jus Gentium viii 504 a; Law ix 202-67; Reception xiii 153-57.
COMPARATIVE PSYCHOLOGY — iv 129-31.
COMPARATIVE RELIGION—iv 131-34; Introd. Vol. 1 (The Social Sciences as Disciplines, France) i 253 a; Religion xiii 237 a; Smith, W. R. xiv 118 b; Tiele xiv 628 a.
COMPAYRÉ, G.—iv 134.
COMPENSATED DOLLAR—iv 134-35.
Compensation—Criminal Law iv 570 a.
COMPENSATION AND LIABILITY INSURANCE—iv 135-41; Automobile Insurance ii 330-32; Casualty Insurance iii 262-65; Employers' Liability v 517 b; Social Insurance xiv 134-38; Workmen's Compensation xv 488-92.
Compensation, Psychical — Abnormal Psychology i 364 a.
Compensatory Duty—xiv 519 b.
Compensatory Principle—Bimetallism and Monometallism ii 547 a.
COMPETITION—iv 141-47; Advertising i 469-75; Bargaining Power ii 460 b; Business iii 84 a, 86 a; Capitalism iii 197 a; Cartel iii 234-43; Combinations, Industrial iii 664-74; Conflict, Social iv 194-96; Construction Industry iv 267 b; Cut-Throat Competition iv 678-79; Economic Policy v 339 a; Economics (Classical School) v 356 a; Fair Return vi 56-58; Federal Trade Commission vi 165-69; Govt. Regulation of Industry vii 125 a, 127 a; Instalment Selling viii 76 b; Interlocking Directorates viii 150 a; Liberalism ix 438 b; Monopoly x 623-30; Price Discrimination xii 350-55; Railroads xiii 105 b; Restraint of Trade xiii 339-42; Social Christian Movements xiv 126 b; Stabilization, Economic xiv 314 b; Trade Associations xiv 670-76; Trusts xv 111-22; Unemployment xv 153 b; Unfair Competition xv 174-78; Wages xv 299 a.
Complex, Psychological—Abnormal Psychology i 364 a.
Composition—Blood Vengeance Feud ii 599 b; Damages iv 697 a; Fines vi 249 b; Liability ix 428 a.
COMPROMISE—iv 147-49; Coalition iii 600-02; Conflict, Social iv 195 b; Conformity iv 196-98; Opportunism xi 476-79; Statesmanship xiv 350 b.
Comptoir—Iron and Steel Industry viii 309 a; Trade Associations xiv 672 b.
Compulsory Voting—xv 289 b.

Index (Commons — Conservation)

COMPURGATION—iv 149–50; Benefit of Clergy ii 512 b; Procedure, Legal xii 442 b; Self-Incrimination xiii 651 b.

COMSTOCK, A.—iv 150; Birth Control ii 562 b; Censorship iii 293 a.

COMTE, I. A. M. F. X.—iv 151; Introd. Vol. 1 (Individualism and Capitalism) i 159 b; Bonald ii 631 a; Evolution, Social v 657 b; History and Historiography vii 379 a; Humanitarianism vii 548 b; Littré ix 544 a; Positivism xii 263 a; Progress xii 498 a; Saint-Simon and Saint-Simonianism xiii 509 b; Social Organism xiv 139 b; Social Process xiv 150 a; Sociology xiv 236 b; Statics and Dynamics xiv 352 b.

CONANT, C. A.—iv 153.

Concentration, Industrial — see COMBINATIONS, INDUSTRIAL.

Concerns, Industrial—Combinations, Industrial iii 665 a.

Concert of Europe—ix 288 a.

CONCERT OF POWERS—iv 153–54; Balance of Power ii 395–99; Great Powers vii 161 a; Internationalism viii 216 b; Isolation, Diplomatic viii 353 a.

CONCESSIONS—iv 154–60; Asiento ii 268–70; Backward Countries ii 381 a; Calvo and Drago Doctrines iii 153 b; Colonial Economic Policy iii 650 b; Far Eastern Problem vi 94 a; Imperialism vii 611 b; International Finance viii 162 b; Mining Law x 513–18; Oil Industry xi 450 a; Public Domain xii 622 b.

CONCILIAR MOVEMENT—iv 160–65; Introd. Vol. 1 (The Growth of Autonomy) i 82 a; Gallicanism vi 550 b; Gerson vi 640 a; Papacy xi 564 a; Reformation xiii 187 a; Religious Institutions (Roman Catholic) xiii 256 b.

CONCILIATION, INDUSTRIAL — iv 165–69. See ARBITRATION, INDUSTRIAL.

CONCORDAT—iv 169–71; Anticlericalism ii 112 b.

Concordat of Worms—viii 262 b.

CONCUBINAGE—iv 171–73; Illegitimacy vii 582 b.

Concurrent Majority—iii 144 b.

CONCURRENT POWERS—iv 173–74; Federation vi 174 b; Govt. (U. S.) vii 18 a.

Condemnation Proceedings—v 494 a.

CONDILLAC, É. B. DE—iv 175; Introd. Vol. 1 (The Revolutions) i 142 a; Encyclopédistes v 529 b; Human Nature vii 532 b.

CONDITIONED REFLEX—iv 175–76; Habit vii 237 a; Imitation vii 587 a.

CONDORCET, M. J. A. N. C.—iv 176; Education v 415 a; Literacy and Illiteracy ix 518 a.

CONDUCT—iv 177–79. See Classification of Articles (Conduct), p. 549.

Confectionery Industry — Food Industries vi 309–11.

Confederación Nacional de Trabajo—xv 29 b.

CONFÉDÉRATION GÉNÉRALE DU TRAVAIL—iv 179–81; Antimilitarism ii 115 b; Bourses du Travail ii 659 b; Labor Movement viii 689 b; Merrheim x 355 a; Socialization xiv 222 a; Syndicalism xiv 498 b; Trade Unions (France) xv 26 a.

Confederazione Generale del Lavoro—xv 31 a.

Conference for Progressive Political Action, U. S.—viii 707 b.

CONFESSION—iv 181–83.

CONFISCATION—iv 183–87; Alien Property i 636–38; Attainder ii 305 a; Eminent Domain v 493–97; Requisitions, Military xiii 324–26.

CONFLICT OF LAWS—iv 187–94; Argentré ii 183 a; Bankruptcy ii 450 b; Bartolus of Sassoferrato ii 470 b; Capitulations iii 213–15; Citizenship iii 472 b; Comity iii 678 a; Commercial Law iv 18 a; Common Law iv 54 a; Double Taxation v 224–27; Dual Citizenship v 257–59; Exterritoriality vi 36–39; Extradition vi 41–44; Foreign Corporations vi 354–58; Full Faith and Credit Clause vi 515–17; German Civil Code vi 635 b; Jus Gentium viii 504 a; Lainé ix 15 a; Pillet xii 134 b.

CONFLICT, SOCIAL—iv 194–96; Accommodation i 403–04; Civil War iii 523–25; Class Struggle iii 538–42; Compromise iv 147–49; Consensus iv 225–27; Discussion v 166–67; Feuds vi 220–21; Pressures, Social xii 344–48; Ratzenhofer xiii 121 b; Revolution and Counter-revolution xiii 367–76; Riot xiii 386–92; Social Process xiv 150 a; Violence xv 264–67; War xv 331–42.

CONFORMITY—iv 196–98; Americanization ii 33–35; Art ii 224 b; Censorship iii 290–94; Ceremony iii 313–16; Change, Social iii 333 a; Civic Education iii 496–98; Coercion iii 618 a; Collective Behavior iii 631–33; Conduct iv 178 b; Consensus iv 225 b; Conventions, Social iv 351–53; Custom iv 661 a; Fashion vi 139–44; Folkways vi 293–96; Imitation vii 586–87; Morals x 643–49; Pressures, Social xii 344–48; Sanction, Social xiii 531–34.

CONFUCIANISM—iv 198–201; Education v 404 a; History and Historiography vii 383 a; K'ang Yu-wei viii 537 b; Law (Chinese) ix 250 a; Mencius x 306 a; Sociology xiv 234 a.

Confucius—see CONFUCIANISM.

Congregationalism—Browne iii 16 a; Religious Institutions (Protestant) xiii 272 a; Sects xiii 628 a.

Congress, U. S.—Cannon iii 179 b; Legislative Assemblies ix 361–65.

CONGRESSIONAL GOVERNMENT—iv 201–03; Bicameral System ii 534 b; Budget iii 43 a; Cabinet iii 133 b; Deadlock v 17 a; Govt. (Hist. and Theory) vii 10 b, (Lat. Amer.) 91 b; Legislative Assemblies ix 360 a; Veto xv 247–49.

Congressional Record—ii 582 b.

CONIGLIANI, C. A.—iv 203.

CONJUNCTURE—iv 203–04.

CONNOLLY, J.—iv 204; Irish Question viii 293 a.

CONQUEST—iv 205–08; Annexation ii 68–69; Aristocracy ii 185 b; Disarmament v 159 b; Economic Policy v 338 a; Empire v 497–506; Ethnic Communities v 607 b; Filibustering vi 231–33; Imperialism vii 605 b; Indemnity, Military vii 641 a; Language ix 167 b; Metals x 368 a; Migrations x 425–29; Missions x 539 a; Native Policy xi 252–83; State Succession xiv 344–46; Tribute xv 102–04; War xv 332 b.

CONRAD, J.—iv 208.

CONRAT (COHN), M.—iv 208.

CONRING, H.—iv 209.

CONSALVI, E.—iv 210.

Conscience—Duty v 293 a.

CONSCIENTIOUS OBJECTORS — iv 210–12; Hunger Strike vii 554 a; Passive Resistance and Noncooperation xii 11 a.

CONSCIOUSNESS — iv 212–20; Gestalt vi 643 a; Helvétius vii 319 a; Materialism x 211 b, 213 b, 215 a; Psychoanalysis xii 580–88; Titchener xiv 639 b.

Consciousness of Kind—vi 654 b.

CONSCRIPTION—iv 220–23; Army ii 210–18; Conscientious Objectors iv 211 a; Impressment vii 614–16; Limitation of Armaments ix 483 b; Mobilization and Demobilization x 559 a; Mutiny xi 166 b; Navy xi 317 a.

Consecration Ceremonies—Death Customs v 23 a; Deification v 60 a.

CONSEIL D'ÉTAT—iv 223–25.

Consejo de Indias—see COUNCIL OF THE INDIES.

CONSENSUS—iv 225–27; Consideration iv 235 b; Discussion v 166–67.

CONSERVATION—iv 227–30; Fernow vi 185 b; Fisheries vi 268 b; Forests vi 384 a; Fur Trade and Industry vi 534 a; Game Laws vi 563 a; Oil Industry xi 445 b; Pulp and Paper Industry xii 710 b; Reclamation xiii 160–64; Waste xv 367–69.

CONSERVATISM—iv 230–33; Antiradicalism ii 116–18; Chambers of Commerce iii 327 b; Change, Social iii 333 a; Continuity, Social iv 317 b; Gerlach vi 632 b; Liberalism ix 435 b; Opportunism xi 477 b; Parties, Political (Bulgaria) xi 629 b, (Germany) 615 b, (Lat. Amer.) 633 a, (Sweden) 621 b; Philosophy xii 124 b; Radicalism xiii 53 a; Rentier xiii 298 b; Revolution and Counter-revolution xiii 367–76; Traditionalism xv 67–70.

Conservative Parties—see PARTIES, POLITICAL.

CONSIDÉRANT, V.—iv 233; Socialism xiv 194 b.

CONSIDERATION—iv 233–36; Contract iv 337 a; Mansfield x 103 a.

Consolato del Mare—ii 203 b.

Consolidations — see COMBINATIONS, INDUSTRIAL.

CONSPIRACY, CRIMINAL—iv 236–38; Labor Legislation and Law viii 668 b.

CONSPIRACY, POLITICAL—iv 238–41; Carbonari iii 220–23; Political Offenders xii 199–203; Political Police xii 203–07; Praetorianism xii 305–07; Treason xv 93–96.

Constable and Marshal's Court—iv 512 a.

Constabulary—see POLICE.

CONSTANT DE REBECQUE, H. B.—iv 241.

CONSTANTINE—iv 242; Introd. Vol. I (The Roman World) i 54 a.

CONSTITUENCY—iv 243–44; Gerrymander vi 638–39; Representation xiii 313 a; Rotten Boroughs xiii 443–44.

Constituent Assemblies—see CONSTITUTIONAL CONVENTIONS.

CONSTITUTIONAL CONVENTIONS—iv 244–47; Constitutions iv 261 a; Govt. (U. S.) vii 15 b; Russian Revolution xiii 482 b.

Constitutional Government — Centralization iii 309 b; Govt. vii 10 b; Legislative Assemblies (Hist. and Theory) ix 357 b, 361 a.

CONSTITUTIONAL LAW—iv 247–55; Advisory Opinions i 476 b; Comity iii 679 a; Constitutionalism iv 257 a; Constitutions iv 259–62; Cooley iv 356 b; Dicey v 131 b; Due Process of Law v 264–68; Eminent Domain v 493–97; Interstate Commerce viii 220–29; Judicial Review viii 457–64; Jurisdiction viii 474 b; Labor Injunction viii 656 a; Lefroy ix 319 a; Municipal Corporation xi 89 b; Police Power xii 190–93; Rate Regulation xiii 104–12; Reconstruction xiii 171 a; Supreme Court, United States xiv 474–82.

CONSTITUTIONALISM—iv 255–59; Introd. Vol. I (The Rise of Liberalism) i 107 b; Carbonari iii 221 b; Constitutional Law iv 247–55; Constitutions iv 261 b; Cooley iv 356 b; Democracy v 79 b; Govt. (U. S.) vii 17 a; Judicial Review viii 457–64; Law Enforcement ix 269 b; Monarchy x 583 a; Natural Rights xi 301 a; Police Power xii 191 a; Rule of Law xiii 463–66; Smith xiv 116 a; Supreme Court, U. S. xiv 474–82.

CONSTITUTIONS — iv 259–62; Agreement of the People i 516–18; Amendments, Constitutional ii 21–23; Armed Forces, Control of ii 200 a; Articles of Confederation ii 262–63; Bills of Rights ii 544–46; Bundesrat iii 65–67; Cánovas del Castillo iii 186 a; Carranza iii 233 b; Civil Liberties iii 510 b; Congressional Govt. iv 201 b; Constitutional Conventions iv 244–47; Constitutional Law iv 247–55; Constitutionalism iv 255–59; Federation vi 175 a; Govt. vii 9 a, (Argentina) 92 a, (Australia) 31 a, (Austria) 77 a, (Balkan States) 82 a, (Belgium) 47 b, (Brazil) 92 b, (Canada) 27 a, (Chile) 94 b, (China) 100 a, (Czechoslovakia) 78 b, (Denmark) 61 a, (Estonia) 71 a, (Finland) 64 b, (France) 45 a, (Germany) 53 b, (Iceland) 62 a, (Ireland) 36 b, (Italy) 48 b, (Japan) 95 b, (Jugoslavia) 80 b, (Latvia) 72 a, (Lithuania) 73 a, (Mexico) 93 a, (Netherlands) 59 a, (Norway) 62 b, (Poland) 74 a, (Rumania) 80 a, (Russia, Imperial) 65 b, (Russia, Soviet) 67 b, (S. Africa) 34 b, (Spain) 86 a, (Sweden) 63 a, (Turkey) 85 a, (U. S.) 15 a; Harrington vii 272 b; Hooker vii 460 a; Investigations, Governmental viii 258 b; League of Nations ix 288 b; Legislative Assemblies (Germany) ix 380 b, (Spain) 392 b; Levellers ix 422 a; Magna Carta x 44–46; Midhat Pasha x 418 a; Minority Rights x 526 a; Montesquieu x 639 a; State Govt., U. S. xiv 336 b.

Constitutions of Clarendon—see Clarendon, Constitutions of.

CONSTRUCTION INDUSTRY — iv 262–79; Architecture ii 167–75; Building Regulations iii 52–57; Business Agent iii 91 b; Cement iii 286–90; Guild Socialism vii 204 a; Housing vii 496–517; Producers' Cooperation xii 460 b; Public Contracts xii 597 b; Public Works xii 690 a; Quarrying xiii 14 b; Shipbuilding xiv 25–30.

Constructive Trust—xv 125 b.

CONSULAR SERVICE—iv 279–82; Business, Govt. Services for iii 114 b; Commercial Treaties iv 26 a; Diplomacy v 149 b; Exterritoriality vi 36–39; Hospitality vii 464 a; Immunity, Diplomatic vii 595–97.

Consulate of the Sea—x 123 b.

Consumer Credit—Retail Credit xiii 342–46; Small Loans xiv 105–11.

CONSUMER PROTECTION—iv 282–85; Adulteration i 466–68; Caveat Emptor iii 280–82; Consumers' Cooperation iv 285–91; Food and Drug Regulation vi 297–301; Freedom of Contract vi 453 b; Govt. Regulation of Industry vii 126 a; Grading vii 133 b; Inspection viii 71 a; Medical Materials Industry x 279 b; Trademarks and Names xv 58 a.

CONSUMERS' COOPERATION — iv 285–91; Agric. Cooperation i 524 a, 527 b; Consumer Protection iv 284 b; Cooperation iv 359–99; Cooperative Public Boards iv 399–400; Food Industries vi 303 a, 315 b, 321 b, 328 b; Housing, Cooperative vii 518 b; Labor Movement viii 690 b; Retail Trade xiii 353 a. See also COOPERATION.

CONSUMERS' LEAGUES—iv 291–93; Food Industries (Confectionery) vi 311 a.

CONSUMPTION—iv 293–301. See Classification of Articles (Consumption), p. 550. See also Advertising i 470 b, 474 b; Credit Cooperation iv 556 b; Dairy Industry iv 694 b; Food Industries vi 302 a, 305 b, 310 a; Food Supply vi 333 a; Fur Trade and Industry vi 534 a; Gas Industry vi 593 b; Grains vii 147 a; Hours of Labor vii 492 a; Iron and Steel Industry viii 310 b; Land Utilization ix 132 b; Leather Industries ix 302 b; Meat Packing and Slaughtering x 242 a; Medical Materials Industry x 280 b; Milk Supply x 476 a; National Economic Planning xi 203 b; Production (Theory) xii 463 a; Prohibition xii 507 a; Rentier xiii 298 b; Rubber xiii 455 b; Silver xiv 58 b; Wages xv 298 a; War Economics xv 345 a; Water Supply xv 373 b, 376 b.

Contagious Diseases—see COMMUNICABLE DISEASES, CONTROL OF.

CONTARINI, G.—iv 301.

CONTEMPT OF COURT—iv 302–08; Investigations, Governmental viii 254 b; Labor Injunction viii 654 a; Pardon xi 572 a.

CONTESTED ELECTIONS—iv 308–10; Elections v 455 b; Legislative Assemblies (Hist. and Theory) ix 358 a.

Conti, L. dei—see INNOCENT III.

CONTINENTAL SYSTEM—iv 310–11; Mercantilism x 335 b; Smuggling xiv 120 b.

Index (Conservatism — Corporation)

Contingent Fee—iv 311–13.
Continuation Schools—iv 313–15; Adult Education i 464 a; Apprenticeship ii 146 b; Child (Labor) iii 421 b; Education (Part Time) v 426 b.
Continuity, Social—iv 315–18; Custom iv 659 a; Human Nature vii 531–37; Initiation viii 49–50; Language ix 160 a; Social Process xiv 148–51; Tradition xv 62–67; Traditionalism xv 67–70.
Continuous Industry—iv 318–20; Cement iii 290 b; Hours of Labor vii 488 b; Iron and Steel Industry viii 304 a, 319 a.
Continuous Voyage—iv 320–21; Contraband of War iv 322 a; Declaration of London v 47 b.
Contraband of War—iv 321–23; Armed Neutrality ii 203 a; Arms and Munitions Traffic ii 207 a; Blockade ii 594–96; Continuous Voyage iv 320–21; Declaration of London iv 47 b; Declaration of Paris v 49 a; Prize xii 424–26; Smuggling xiv 119–23; Stowell xiv 415 a.
Contract—iv 323–39; Agency i 484 b; Breach of Marriage Promise ii 688–89; Business iii 84 a; Canon Law iii 184 a; Capitalism iii 199 a; Commercial Law iv 18 b; Compacts, Interstate iv 109–13; Competition iv 142 b; Conflict of Laws iv 191 b; Consideration iv 233–36; Contract Clause iv 339–42; Contract Labor iv 342–44; Corporation iv 417 b; Damages iv 699 a; Debt v 32–39; Due Process of Law v 266 b; Duress v 287–90; Feudalism vi 205 a; Frauds, Statute of vi 429–30; Freedom of Contract vi 450–55; Gifts vi 658–61; Labor Contract viii 629–33; Labor Legislation and Law viii 670 a; Landlord and Tenant ix 143–48; Law (Celtic) ix 249 a, (Greek) 228 a, (Hellenistic and Greco-Egyptian) 232 a, (Slavic) 244 b; Liability ix 427–29; Moratorium x 651 a; Municipal Corporation xi 91 a; Negligence xi 330 a; Partnership xii 3 a; Sales xiii 511–16; Specific Performance xiv 285–88; State Liability xiv 338–43; Tort xiv 653 b.
Contract Clause—iv 339–42; Freedom of Contract vi 451 b; Retroactive Legislation xiii 355 b.
Contract, Freedom of—see Freedom of Contract.
Contract Labor—iv 342–44; Migrations x 435 a; Oriental Immigration xi 490 a; Peonage xii 71 b; Prison Labor xii 416 b.
Contracting System—Construction Industry iv 266 b.
Contracts, Public—see Public Contracts.

Contributions, Military—see Requisitions, Military.
Contributory Negligence—v 515 a.
Control, Social—iv 344–49; Bargaining Power ii 462 a; Behaviorism ii 496 a, 498 a; Belief ii 501 a; Birth Control ii 560 b; Coercion iii 617–19; Fatalism vi 148 a; Govt. vii 8 a; Govt. Regulation of Industry vii 122–29; Human Nature vii 531–37; Jurisprudence viii 478 a; Law (Primitive) ix 202 a; Martial Law x 161–67; Morals x 643–49; Organization, Economic xi 487 a; Poverty xii 291 a; Pressures, Social xii 344–48; Rationalism xiii 113–17; Sanction, Social xiii 531–34; Science xiii 591–603; Value and Price xv 223 a.
Conubium—viii 152 a.
Convention, Constitutional—see Constitutional Conventions.
Convention, Political—iv 349–51; Nominations, Political xi 394 a; Parties, Political (U. S.) xi 600 b; Primaries, Political xii 396 a.
Convention for the Regulation of Aerial Navigation—ii 366 a.
Conventions, Social—iv 351–53; Ceremony iii 313–16; Conduct iv 177–79; Custom iv 658 b; Etiquette v 615–17; Fashion vi 139–44; Folkways vi 293–96; Habit vii 238 b; Innovation viii 58–61; Morals x 643–49; Taste xiv 523–25; Tradition xv 62–67.
Conversion of Debt—Public Debt xii 608 b.
Conversion, Religious—iv 353–55; Missions x 538 b; Proselytism xii 551–53; Revivals, Religious xiii 363–67.
Conveyances—see Land Transfer.
Convict Labor—see Prison Labor.
Cook, W. W.—Introd. Vol. I (War and Reorientation) i 221 a; Conflict of Laws iv 189 b.
Cooke, J.—iv 355; Morgan Family xi 11 b.
Cooley, C. H.—iv 355; Introd. Vol. I (The Trend to Internationalism) i 182 a; Economics v 392 a.
Cooley, T. M.—iv 356.
Coolie Labor—iv 342 a.
Cooper, A. A. (d. 1683)—see Shaftesbury, First Earl of.
Cooper, A. A. (d. 1713)—see Shaftesbury, Third Earl of.
Cooper, A. A. (d. 1885)—see Shaftesbury, Seventh Earl of.
Cooper, P.—iv 357.
Cooper, T. (d. 1839)—iv 358.
Cooper, T. (d. 1892)—iv 359.
Cooperation—iv 359–99 (General Survey 359–63, 398, Brit. Empire 363–71, 398, Germany and Austria 371–76, 398, France 376–79, 398, Belgium 379–80, 398, Switzerland 380–81, 398, Italy 381–82, 399, Scandinavian Countries 382–84, 399, Russia 384–90, 399, Succession States and Balkan Countries 390–93, 399, U. S. and Canada 393–95, 399, Japan 395–98). See Classification of Articles (Cooperation), p. 550. See also Agric. Marketing i 561 b, 563 a, 564 b; Agriculture, Govt. Services for i 603 a; Christian Socialism iii 450 b; Cotton iv 492 a; Folk High Schools vi 287 a; Food Industries vi 304 b, 306 b, 317 a, 321 a, 325 b; Grain Elevators vii 138 b; Handicraft vii 258 a, 259 a; Labor Exchange Banks viii 638 a; Labor Movement viii 690 b; Marketing x 136 a; Mormonism xi 17 b; Trade Unions xv 11 b; Wool xv 480 b. For biog. references see Classification of Articles (Cooperation), p. 559.
Cooperation, Agricultural — see Agricultural Cooperation.
Cooperation, Consumers' — see Consumers' Cooperation.
Cooperative Credit—see Credit Cooperation.
Cooperative Housing—see Housing, Cooperative.
Cooperative Public Boards—iv 399–400; Consumers' Cooperation iv 289 b.
Cooperative Schools—v 427 b.
Copeland, M. A.—xi 223 b.
Copernicus, N.—iv 400; Introd. Vol. I (Renaissance and Reformation) i 86 a; Astrology ii 288 a; Galileo Galilei vi 547 b; Science xiii 598 b.
Copleston, E.—iv 401.
Copper—x 364 b, 372 a, 385 a.
Copper Exporters, Inc.—x 374 b.
Copyhold—ix 88 a.
Copyright—iv 401–04; Industrial Arts vii 690 a.
Coquelin, C.—iv 405.
Coquille, G.—iv 405.
Core, D. E.—i 362 b.
Corn Laws—iv 405–08; Anti-Corn Law League ii 114–15; Food Supply vi 335 b; Free Trade vi 443 b; Peel xii 55 a; Tariff xiv 520 a; Villiers xv 261 b.
Corneille, P.—xiv 607 b.
Cornell University—xv 409 a.
Corner, Speculative—iv 408–10.
Cornwallis, C.—vii 661 b.
Coronation — see Consecration Ceremonies.
Coroner—iv 410–11; Medical Jurisprudence x 277 b.
Corporal Punishment—iv 411–13; Punishment xii 713 b.
Corporation—iv 414–23; Absentee Ownership i 377 a; Bargaining Power ii 460 a; Blue Sky Laws ii 602–05;

Business iii 83 b; By-Law iii 128 b; Combinations, Industrial iii 664-74; Contract Clause iv 340 b; Corporation Finance iv 423-30; Corporation Taxes iv 430-35; Domicile v 209 a; Foreign Corporations vi 354-58; Govt. Owned Corporations vii 106-11; Govt. Regulation of Industry vii 127 a; Holding Companies vii 403-12; Income Tax vii 632 a; Industrialism viii 22 b; Interlocking Directorates viii 148-51; Investment viii 264 a; Investment Banking viii 268 b; Joint Stock Company viii 412 a; Law Merchant ix 272 a; Management x 77 b; Massachusetts Trusts x 189-91; Money Market x 615 a; Mortmain xi 48 a; Municipal Corporation xi 86-94; Receivership xiii 149-53; Trusts xv 114 a; Trusts and Trustees xv 124 b; Voluntary Associations xv 283 b.

CORPORATION FINANCE—iv 423-30; Auditing ii 312-13; Blue Sky Laws ii 602-05; Bonds ii 635 a; Capitalization iii 208-11; Combinations, Industrial iii 664-74; Corporation iv 414-23; Debentures v 29-30; Debt v 35 b; Depreciation v 98-102; Electric Power v 465 b; Employee Stock Ownership v 506-09; Express Companies vi 29 a; Fair Return vi 56 b; Financial Statements vi 247-49; Gas Industry vi 591 a; Goodwill vi 700 a; Govt. Owned Corporations vii 106 a; Holding Companies vii 403-12; Interest viii 142 b; Investment viii 267 a; Investment Banking viii 268-77; Match Industry x 207 b; Municipal Transit xi 119 b; Promotion xii 518-21; Public Utilities (U. S.) xii 680 b; Radio xiii 56 a; Railroads xiii 80 b, 83 a; Receivership xiii 149-53; Shipbuilding xiv 29 b; Sinking Fund xiv 68 a; Stock Exchange xiv 397-402; Stocks and Stock Ownership xiv 403-07; Telephone and Telegraph xiv 565 a; Trust Companies xv 110 b; Trusts and Trustees xv 124 b.

Corporation, Foreign—see FOREIGN CORPORATIONS.

Corporation, Govt. Owned—see GOVT. OWNED CORPORATIONS.

Corporation, Municipal—see MUNICIPAL CORPORATION.

Corporation Schools—vii 696 a.

CORPORATION TAXES—iv 430-35; Business Taxes iii 123 a; Double Taxation v 226 b; Excess Profits Tax v 664-66; Income Tax vii 632 a, 633 b.

CORPUS JURIS CIVILIS—iv 435-38; Introd. Vol. I (The Roman World) i 58 a, (The Universal Church) 69 a; Civil Law iii 503 a, 505 a; Codification iii 607 a; Favre vi 152 b; Gaius vi 544 b; Glossators vi 680 a; Haloander vii 249 b; Irnerius viii 295 a; Law x 206 b; Legal Profession and Legal Education ix 328 b; Roman Law xiii 424 a; Usury xv 194 b.

CORRELATION—iv 438-44; Demand v 73 a; Method, Scientific x 392 a; Probability xii 434 b.

CORRESPONDENCE SCHOOLS — iv 444-47; Business Education iii 109 a; Chautauqua iii 360 b.

CORRUPT PRACTISES ACTS—iv 447-48.

CORRUPTION, POLITICAL—iv 448-55; Bail ii 387 b; Ballot ii 411 a; Bribery ii 690-92; Contested Elections iv 308-10; Corrupt Practises Acts iv 447-48; Investigations, Governmental viii 256 b; Lobby ix 565-68; Machine, Political ix 657-61; Municipal Government xi 113 b; Municipal Transit xi 118 b; Public Contracts xii 596-99; Publicity xii 699 a; Racketeering xiii 47 a; Rotten Boroughs xiii 443-44; Smuggling xiv 122 b; Spoils System xiv 301-05.

Cort, H.—viii 299 a.

Cortes — Legislative Assemblies (Spain) ix 391-93.

CORTÉS, H.—iv 455.

CORVÉE—iv 455-57.

Cosach—Nitrates xi 381 a.

Cosgrave, W. T.—Govt. (Ireland) vii 37 b; Parties, Political (Irish Free State) xi 610 a.

COSMOPOLITANISM — iv 457-61; Introd. Vol. I (Greek Culture and Thought) i 32 b; Cynics iv 680-85.

COSSA, E.—iv 461.

COSSA, L.—iv 462; Introd. Vol. I (The Social Sciences as Disciplines, Italy) i 276 b.

COSSACKS—iv 463-66; Khmelnitsky viii 562 a.

COST—iv 466-75; Advertising i 472 b; Appreciation ii 142 b; By-Product iii 129 b; Cost Accounting iv 475-78; Depreciation v 98 b; Diminishing Returns v 144-46; Distribution v 167-74; Economics (Classical School) v 353 a, (Marginal Utility Economics) 358 b, (Mathematical Economics) 365 b, (Cambridge School) 369 a, (Universalist Economics) 387 a; Efficiency v 437-39; Electric Power v 459 b; Fatigue vi 150 b; Food Industries (Baking, U. S.) vi 306 a, (Food Distribution, U. S.) 319 a; Increasing Returns vii 639-40; Interest viii 132 a, 135 a, 140 b; International Trade (Theory) viii 201 a; Just Price viii 505 b; Labor Exchange Banks viii 638 b; Laissez Faire ix 17 a; Large Scale Production ix 172 a; Location of Industry ix 589 a; Marketing x 138 b; Overhead Costs xi 511-13; Price Discrimination xii 353 b; Production (Statistics) xii 471 a; Profit xii 480-87; Retail Trade xiii 353 b; Supply xiv 471 b, 473 a; Valuation xv 214 a; Value and Price xv 218 b.

COST ACCOUNTING—iv 475-78; Accounting i 410 b; Accounts, Public i 413 b; Agricultural Economics i 537 a; By-Product iii 129 b; Municipal Finance xi 103 b.

COST OF LIVING—iv 478-83; Arbitration, Industrial ii 155 a; Consumption iv 295-301; Family Budgets vi 73-78; Poverty xii 286 a; Prices (Hist.) xii 375-81; Standards of Living xiv 322-25; Wages xv 304 a.

COSTA, A.—iv 483.

COSTA FERREIRA, A. A. DA—iv 484.

COSTA Y MARTINEZ, J.—iv 484.

COSTE, A.—iv 485.

COTTA, J. F.—iv 485.

COTTON—iv 486-93; Agricultural Marketing i 562 b; Commerce iv 10 a; Flax, Hemp and Jute vi 277 b; Gregg vii 165 b; Slavery xiv 87 b; Textile Industry xiv 582 b, 584 a; Whitney xv 410 b.

COTTON, J.—iv 493.

Coudenhove-Kalergi, R.—xi 552 b.

Council of Basel — Conciliar Movement iv 163 a; Religious Institutions (Roman Catholic) xiii 257 a.

Council of Chalcedon—xiii 248 b.

Council of Constance—Introd. Vol. I (The Growth of Autonomy) i 83 a; Conciliar Movement iv 161 b; Religious Institutions (Roman Catholic) xiii 257 a.

COUNCIL OF THE INDIES—iv 494-97.

Council of Legal Education—ix 336 b.

Council of Pisa—iv 161 b.

Council of Trent—Religious Institutions (Roman Catholic) xiii 257 b, 258 b; Sarpi xiii 544 b.

Counter-reformation — Introd. Vol. I (Renaissance and Reformation) i 96 b; Jesuits viii 385 a; Reformation xiii 190 a; Religious Institutions (Roman Catholic) xiii 257 b; Religious Orders xiii 278 a.

Counter-revolution — see REVOLUTION AND COUNTER-REVOLUTION.

COUNTRY LIFE MOVEMENT — iv 497-99; Back-to-the-Land Movements ii 378-79.

County Agent—see EXTENSION WORK, AGRICULTURAL.

COUNTY-CITY CONSOLIDATION—iv 499-501; Metropolitan Areas x 397 b.

Index (Corporation — Criminal Law)

COUNTY COUNCILS—iv 501–04; Local Govt. ix 574 b; Metropolitan Areas x 399 b; Municipal Govt. xi 108 a.

COUNTY GOVERNMENT, U. S.—iv 504–08; Administrative Areas i 450 b; County-City Consolidation iv 499–501; Grants-in-Aid vii 155 a; Home Rule vii 436 b; Local Govt. ix 578 a; Municipal Corporation xi 89 a; Sheriff xiv 22 a.

COUP D'ÉTAT—iv 508–10; Conspiracy, Political iv 238–41; Fraternizing vi 426 a.

COURCELLE-SENEUIL, J. G.—iv 510; Introd. Vol. 1 (The Social Sciences as Disciplines, Lat. Amer.) i 310 a.

COURNOT, A.-A.—iv 511; Demand v 72 b; Economics v 365 b; Monopoly x 627 a.

Court of Admiralty—ix 273 b.

Court of Chancery—Courts iv 522 b; Ellesmere v 481 a; Equity v 584 a; Mortgage xi 34 b.

Court of Common Pleas—iv 521 a.

Court of Exchequer—iv 521 a.

Court of King's Bench—iv 521 a.

COURT MARTIAL—iv 512–14; Military Law x 453–56.

COURT, P. DE LA—iv 514.

Court, Royal—see ROYAL COURT.

COURTNEY, LORD—iv 515.

COURTS—iv 515–29. See relevant titles in Classification of Articles (Administration of Justice), p. 548. See also Administration, Public i 448 a; Capitulations iii 214 b; Ellesmere v 481 a; Ellsworth v 482 a; Govt. (Brit. Commonwealth of Nations) vii 42 b, (Canada) 28 b, (Denmark) 61 b, (Estonia) 72 a, (Germany) 56 a, (Ireland) 38 a, (Japan) 97 b, (Latvia) 72 b, (Lithuania) 73 b, (Poland) 75 a, (Russia, Soviet) 69 a, (S. Africa) 35 a, (Sweden) 64 b; Henry II vii 321 a; Immunity, Political vii 598 a; Law (Primitive) ix 205 a, (Greek) 229 a, (Hellenistic and Greco-Egyptian) 233 b, (Hindu) 258 b, (Jewish) 221 b, 222 b; Maritime Law x 124 a, 129 b; Military Law x 455 a; Prize xii 424 b; Receivership xiii 149–53.

COURTS, ADMINISTRATIVE — iv 529–33; Audiencia ii 311–12; Certiorari iii 317 b; Conseil d'État iv 223–25; Contempt of Court iv 305 b; Judiciary viii 467 b.

COURTS, COMMERCIAL—iv 533–35; Arbitration, Commercial ii 152 a; Commercial Law iv 16 a; Fairs vi 60 a; Interstate Commerce Commission viii 231 a; Law Merchant ix 272 a.

Courts, Domestic Relations—see DOMESTIC RELATIONS COURTS.

Courts, Ecclesiastical—see ECCLESIASTICAL COURTS.

COURTS, INDUSTRIAL—iv 535–38; Arbitration, Industrial ii 154 b; Labor, Govt. Services for viii 647 a; Minimum Wage x 492 b.

Courts, Juvenile—see JUVENILE DELINQUENCY AND JUVENILE COURTS.

Courts, Municipal—see MUNICIPAL COURTS.

Courts, Small Claims—see SMALL CLAIMS COURTS.

COURTSHIP—iv 538–40; Culture iv 628 a; Dance iv 701 b.

COUSIN, V.—iv 540; Transcendentalism xv 76 b.

COUTTS, T.—iv 540.

Couvade—Birth Customs ii 566 a; Culture iv 630 b.

COVARRUBIAS Y LEIVA, D.—iv 541.

Covenant of the League of Nations—ix 288 a.

Coventry Ordnance Works—xi 130 a.

COWDRAY, LORD—iv 541.

COXE, T.—iv 542.

Craft Guilds—see GUILDS.

Craft Unions—Construction Industry iv 271 b; Labor Movement viii 683 a; Mechanic x 266 b. See also TRADE UNIONS.

Crafts—see INDUSTRIAL ARTS.

CRAIG, J.—iv 542.

CRAMB, J. A.—iv 543.

CRANE, W.—iv 543.

Cranial Index—xiii 26 b.

CRANMER, T.—iv 543.

CRAWLEY, A. E.—iv 544.

Crèche—see DAY NURSERY.

CREDIT—iv 545–50. See Classification of Articles (Credit), p. 550. See also Anthropology ii 84 b; Bank Reserves ii 420 a; Banks, Wildcat ii 454–56; Cieszkowski iii 470 a; Construction Industry iv 269 a; Contract (Institutional Aspects) iv 329–39; Corporation Finance iv 427 b; Crises iv 597 a; Interest viii 141 b; Investment Banking viii 275 a; Just Price viii 506 b; Law (Cuneiform) ix 217 b, (Jewish) 223 b; Livestock Industry ix 549 a; Lotteries ix 613 a; Mobilization and Demobilization x 561 a; Prices (Theory) xii 371 b; Public Works xii 696 b; Speculation xiv 292 b; Stock Exchange xiv 401 b; Unemployment xv 155 b, 159 b; War Economics xv 345 a.

Credit, Agricultural—see AGRICULTURAL CREDIT.

CREDIT CONTROL—iv 550–53; Central Banking iii 304 b; Compensated Dollar iv 134–35; Economic Policy v 343 a; Federal Reserve System vi 154–65; Money Market x 616 b; National Economic Planning xi 202 b.

CREDIT COOPERATION—iv 553–57; Agric. Credit i 533 a; Cattle Loans iii 277 b; Cooperation iv 359–99; Labor Banking viii 620 b; Land Mortgage Credit (Agric.) ix 44 b, (Urban) 50 a; Small Loans xiv 106 a.

Crédit Foncier—Agric. Credit i 534 a; Land Mortgage Credit (Agric.) ix 45 b.

Credit Information Bureaus—xiii 344 a.

CREDIT INSURANCE—iv 557–60; Business, Govt. Services for iii 117 b.

Credit, Land Mortgage—see LAND MORTGAGE CREDIT.

Credit Men's Associations — Bankruptcy ii 452 b; Mercantile Credit x 332 b.

Crédit Mobilier—Banking, Commercial ii 436 a; Investment Banking viii 270 b; Péreire xii 73 a; Railroads xiii 83 a.

Credit Unions—iv 394 b.

CREIGHTON, M.—iv 560.

Cremation—v 26 a.

CREMER, W. R.—iv 561; Peace Movements xii 44 a.

CRÉMIEUX, A. I. M.—iv 561.

CRÈVECOEUR, M.-G. J. DE—iv 562.

CRIME—iv 563–69. See Classification of Articles (Crime), p. 550. See also Alcohol i 626 a; Anthropology ii 89 a; Asylum ii 289 b; Child (Delinquent) iii 406–09; Deportation and Expulsion of Aliens v 96 b; Gangs vi 566 b; Imprisonment vii 616–19; Law Enforcement ix 267–70; Limitation of Actions ix 477 a; Police xii 186 b; Poverty xii 290 a; Suicide xiv 456 a; Venue xv 236 b.

Criminal Conspiracy—see CONSPIRACY, CRIMINAL.

Criminal Intent — see INTENT, CRIMINAL.

CRIMINAL LAW—iv 569–79; Introd. Vol. 1 (The Roman World) i 48 a; Arrest ii 221–22; Attainder ii 304–05; Bail ii 386–88; Benefit of Clergy ii 513 a; Canon Law iii 182 b; Carpzov iii 232 a; Comparative Law iv 127 b; Conspiracy, Criminal iv 236–38; Criminology iv 584 b; Duress v 287 b; Extortion vi 39–41; Extradition vi 41–44; Feuerbach vi 222 b; Fines vi 249–52; Grolman vii 174 a; Hälschner vii 250 a; Injunction viii 55 b; Intent, Criminal viii 126–31; Justice, Administration of viii 516 b, 521 b; Justice of the Peace viii 525 b; Law (Primitive) ix 202–06, (Cuneiform) 214 b, (Egyptian) 211 a, (Germanic) 237 a, (Greek) 228 b, (Hellenistic and Greco-Egyptian) 234 b, (Jewish) 220 b, (Slavic) 244 b; Law Enforcement ix 267–70; Limitation of Actions ix 477 a; Liszt ix 511 a; Medical Jurisprudence x 274-79; Merkel x 354 a; Mittermaier x 551 b; Prosecution xii 545-51; Retroactive Legislation xiii 356 a; Roman Law xiii 421 a; Romilly xiii 434 b; Schwarzenberg xiii 588 b. *See also* LAW.

Criminal Psychology—i 366 b.

CRIMINAL STATISTICS—iv 579-82; Homicide vii 455 a; Justice, Administration of viii 523 a; Juvenile Delinquency and Juvenile Courts viii 531 a; Police xii 187 b; Recidivism xiii 157 a.

CRIMINAL SYNDICALISM—iv 582-84; Industrial Workers of the World viii 15 b; Sabotage xiii 497 b.

CRIMINOLOGY—iv 584-92; Introd. Vol. I (What Are the Social Sciences?) i 5 a, (War and Reorientation) 208 b, (The Social Sciences as Disciplines, Lat. Amer.) 315 a; Abnormal Psychology i 366 b; Alienist i 641; Atavism ii 290-91; Capital Punishment iii 192-95; Commutation of Sentence iv 108-09; Crime iv 568 b; Criminal Law iv 576 b; Degeneration v 56 a; Identification vii 573-75; Juvenile Delinquency and Juvenile Courts viii 528-33; Law (Chinese) ix 252 a; Punishment xii 714 b; Recidivism xiii 158 a, 159 b; Utilitarianism xv 199 a. *For biog. references see* Classification of Articles (Criminology), p. 559.

CRIPPLES—iv 592-95; Rehabilitation xiii 221-25.

CRISES—iv 595-99; Business Cycles iii 92 b; Economics (Socialist Economics) v 379 b, (Universalist Economics) 387 a; Juglar viii 469 b; Moratorium x 649-52; Sismondi xiv 70 a; Socialism (Marxian) xiv 200 b.

CRISPI, F.—iv 599.

Criticism, Literary—ix 536 b.

CRITICISM, SOCIAL—iv 599-602; Freedom of Speech and of the Press vi 455-59; Literature ix 524 a; Radicalism xiii 51-54; Reformism xiii 194-95; Romanticism xiii 429 b; Socialism xiv 188-212; Utopia xv 200-03. *For biog. references see* Classification of Articles (Literature and Social Criticism), p. 564.

Croce, B.—Introd. Vol. I (The Social Sciences as Disciplines, Italy) i 277 a; Idealism vii 572 a.

Crofters—i 497 a.

CROFTON, W. F.—iv 602.

CROLY, H.—iv 603.

CROMBIE, A.—iv 603.

CROME, A. F. W.—iv 604.

CROMER, LORD—iv 604; Egyptian Problem v 442 b.

CROMWELL, O.—iv 605.

CROMWELL, T.—iv 606.

CRONHIELM, G.—iv 607.

Crop Damages—i 530 b.

Crop Insurance—i 546 a.

CROP AND LIVESTOCK REPORTING—iv 607-12; Production (Statistics) xii 468 a.

Cross Examination—*see* JUDICIAL INTERROGATION.

CROWD—iv 612-13; Collective Behavior iii 631 b; Le Bon ix 316 b; Masses x 200 a; Mob x 552 b; Social Psychology xiv 153 b.

CRUCÉ, É.—iv 613.

Cruelty to Animals—*see* ANIMAL PROTECTION.

CRUSADES—iv 614-17; Introd. Vol. I (The Universal Church) i 66 b, (Renaissance and Reformation) 84 b; Chivalry iii 438 a; City iii 476 a; Cluniac Movement iii 581 b; Commerce iv 5 b; Military Orders x 459 b; Missions x 539 a; Music xi 158 b; War xv 334 a.

Crystal Palace—vi 23 b.

Cubism—Art ii 257 a.

Cudahy, M.—x 245 b.

Cuer, J.—*see* COEUR, J.

CUJAS, J.—iv 617; Commentators iii 681 b; Doneau v 216 a.

CULPEPER, T.—iv 617.

CULTS—iv 618-21; Introd. Vol. I (Greek Culture and Thought) i 17 b, 21 b, 34 b; Christian Science iii 446-49; Intransigence viii 246 a; Judaism viii 434 a; Mormonism xi 14-18; Mysteries xi 172-75; Religion xiii 235 b; Shinto xiv 24 b.

Cultural Geography—*see* GEOGRAPHY.

CULTURE—iv 621-46. *See relevant titles in* Classification of Articles (Primitive Society), p. 554, (Social Organization), p. 556, (Social Process), p. 556, (Sociology), p. 556. *See also* Introd. Vol. I (War and Reorientation) i 202 a.

CULTURE AREA—iv 646-47; Introd. Vol. I (The Trend to Internationalism) i 185 b; Anthropology ii 105 b; Geography vi 622 b.

Cumann na nGaedhal—xi 610 a.

CUNARD, S.—iv 647.

Cunard Steam Ship Co., Ltd.—xiv 39 b.

Cuneiform Law—Law (Cuneiform) ix 211-19.

CUNNINGHAM, W.—iv 648.

CUOCO, V.—iv 648.

Curia, Roman—Banking, Commercial ii 425 b; Papacy xi 563 b, 564 b, 566 b.

CURRENCY—iv 649-51; Aldrich i 629 a; Attwood ii 307 a; Bamberger ii 413 a; Bank Deposits ii 416-17; Banknotes ii 447 b; Check iii 362-63; Cieszkowski iii 470 a; Compensated Dollar iv 134-35; Copleston iv 401 a; Cynics iv 683 a; Debt v 36 a; Free Silver vi 438-40; Gold vi 692 a; Graumann vii 157 b; Hoarding vii 394 a; Inflation and Deflation viii 28-33; International Trade viii 194 b, 205 b; Labor Exchange Banks viii 637-44; Land Bank Schemes ix 29-32; Money x 601-13; National Banks, U. S. xi 188 a; Paper Money xi 568-70; Rentenmark xiii 296; Silver xiv 59 a; Walker xv 323 b.

Curtesy—x 118 b.

CURTIS, G. W.—iv 651.

CURTIUS, E.—iv 652.

CURVE FITTING—iv 652-56; Demand v 73 b; Frequency Distribution iv 485 a.

CURZON, G. N.—iv 656; Indian Question vii 665 a.

Cusa, N. of—*see* NICHOLAS OF CUSA.

CUSHING, C.—iv 656.

CUSHING, F. H.—iv 657.

CUSTODI, P.—iv 658.

CUSTOM—iv 658-62; Avoidance ii 369-70; Belief ii 500 b; Birth Customs ii 565-68; Ceremony iii 313-16; Change, Social iii 330-34; Conduct iv 177-79; Continuity, Social iv 316 a; Control, Social iv 344-49; Conventions, Social iv 351-53; Crime iv 563 a; Culture iv 621-46; Customary Law iv 662-67; Death Customs v 21-27; Dialect v 123-26; Duty v 293-95; Etiquette v 615-17; Fashion vi 139-44; Fertility Rites vi 190-92; Festivals vi 198-201; Folkways vi 293-96; Innovation viii 58-61; Institution viii 84-89; Morals x 643-49; Sanction, Social xiii 531-34; Tabu xiv 502-05; Tradition xv 62-67.

CUSTOMARY LAW—iv 662-67; Introd. Vol. I (The Growth of Autonomy) i 74 a; Anthropology ii 88 b; Argentré ii 182 b; By-Law ii 128 b; Civil Law iii 504 a; Code Civil iii 605 a; Codification iii 606 a; Comity iii 679 a; Conflict of Laws iv 188 b; Constitutions iv 259 b; Contract iv 323-39; Coquille iv 405 b; Criminal Law iv 570 a, 573 a; Custom iv 661 b; Draco v 233 a; Family Law vi 81-85; International Law viii 167 a; Islamic Law viii 345 a, 347 a; Law (Chinese) ix 251 a, 253 b, (Germanic) 237 b, (Greek) 225 b, (Hindu) 257 b, (Jewish) 219 a, (Slavic) 240 b; Law Merchant ix 271 a; Loisel ix 603 b; Savigny xiii 547 a.

Customs Assimilation—Colonial Economic Policy iii 648 a.

CUSTOMS DUTIES—iv 667-73. *See* TARIFF.

CUSTOMS UNIONS—iv 673-77; Govt. (Austria) vii 78 a.

CUSUMANO, V.—iv 677.

Cut-Throat Competition — iv 678–79.
Cuvier, G. L. C. F. D.—Biology ii 551 b; Lamarck ix 21 b.
Cuza, A. J.—iv 679; Agrarian Movements i 503 a.
Cycloids—i 364 b.
Cygnaeus, U.—x 103 b.
Cynics—iv 680–85; Stoicism xiv 407 b.
Cyprian, T. C.—iii 465 a.
Cyrenaics—iv 685–87; Hedonism vii 307 a.
Czartoryski, A. J.—iv 687.
Czerkawski, W.—iv 688.
Czoernig von Czernhausen, K.—iv 688.

Daguesseau, H.-F.—iv 689.
Dahlmann, F. C.—iv 689; Waitz xv 322 a.
Dahn, F. L. S.—iv 690.
Dähnhardt, O.—vi 290 a.
Dail Eireann—Govt. (Ireland) vii 37 a; Legislative Assemblies ix 374 a.
Daimios—i 591 a.
Dairy Industry — iv 690–95; Agric. Cooperation i 523 b, 526 a; Agric. Marketing (Eur.) i 563 b, (U. S.) 563 a; Balakshin ii 394 b; Cattle Loans iii 276–77; Food Industries (Food Distribution, W. Eur.) vi 321 a; Milk Supply x 475–80.
Dalberg, J. E. E.—see Acton, Lord.
Dalhousie, Lord—iv 695; Indian Question vii 662 b.
Dalton, H.—National Income xi 221 a; Taxation xiv 536 b, 540 a.
Damages—iv 696–700; Eminent Domain v 495 a; Employers' Liability v 514–18; Judgments viii 444 b; Law (Primitive) ix 203 a, (Celtic) 248 b; Liability ix 428 a; Reprisals xiii 315–17; Sanction, Social xiii 533 b; Specific Performance xiv 285–88; Valuation xv 215 b; Workmen's Compensation xv 488–92.
Dana, C. A.—iv 700; Labor Exchange Banks viii 641 a.
Dance—iv 701–07; Anthropology ii 92 a.
Danielson, N. F.—iv 707.
Danielsson, A. F.—iv 707.
Danilevsky, N. Y.—iv 708.
Dante Alighieri—iv 708; Introd. Vol. 1 (The Growth of Autonomy) i 79 b, (Renaissance and Reformation) 90 b.
Danton, G.-J.—v 3.
Danube Shipping—viii 210 b.
Dargun, L. von—v 3.
Darius I—v 500 b.
Darjes, J. G.—v 4.
Darrein Presentment—ii 283 b.
Darwin, C. R.—v 4; Introd. Vol. 1 (Individualism and Capitalism) i 162 a; Adaptation i 436 a; Atavism ii 290 b; Behaviorism ii 496 a; Biology ii 552 a, 554 b; Butler iii 125 b;

Evolution v 651 a; Huxley vii 562 a; Lamarck ix 21 b; Malthus x 69 b; Materialism (Dialectical) x 215 a; Psychology xii 593 a; Spencer xiv 296 a.
Darwin, E.—v 650 b.
Das, C. R.—v 5.
Dato e Iradier, E.—v 6.
Dā'ūd al-Zāhiri—v 6.
Davanzati, B.—v 7.
Davenant, C.—v 7; Free Trade vi 441 a.
Davenport, C. B.—ii 112 a.
Davenport, H. J.—v 8; Diminishing Returns v 145 b.
David, E.—v 9.
David, J. L.—x 566 a.
Davids, T. W. R.—v 10.
Davidson, T.—v 10.
Davies, D.—v 11.
Davies, S. E.—v 11.
Davis, Jefferson—v 11; Benjamin ii 516 b.
Davis, John B.—iii 380 b.
Davis, John W.—xiv 475 b.
Davis, T.—viii 290 a.
Davitt, M.—v 12; Irish Question viii 291 b; Parnell xi 587 a.
Dawes Plan—Indemnity, Military vii 643 b; Reparations xiii 303 b.
Dawson, J. W.—v 13.
Day, B.—xii 328 b.
Day Nursery—v 13–16; Preschool Education xii 323 a.
Dayananda — see Saraswati, Swami D.
Dead Hand—see Mortmain.
Deadlock—v 16–18.
Deaf — v 18–20; Institutions, Public viii 91 b; Rehabilitation xiii 222 b.
Deák, F.—v 20.
Deakin, A.—v 21.
Death Customs—v 21–27; Culture iv 641 b; Dance iv 704 a; Funerals vi 527–29; Mysteries xi 172 b.
Death Duties—see Inheritance Taxation.
Death Penalty — see Capital Punishment.
Death Rates—see Mortality.
Debate, Parliamentary—v 28–29; Closure iii 570–73; Committees, Legislative iv 40–44; Immunity, Political vii 597–600; Procedure, Parliamentary xii 456 a.
Debentures—v 29–30; Bonds ii 635 b; Investment Trusts viii 279 b.
De Bow, J. D. B.—v 30.
De Brosses, C.—v 31; Fetishism vi 202 a.
Debs, E. V.—v 31; Berger ii 522 a; Boycott ii 664 b; Ruthenberg, xiii 493 a.
Debt—v 32–39; Bankruptcy ii 449–54; Credit iv 545–50; Credit Insurance iv 557–60; Devaluation v 115 b; Homestead Exemption Laws vii 441–44; Instalment Selling viii

74–81; Judgments viii 445 a; Justice, Administration of viii 521 b; Law (Celtic) ix 248 b, (Cuneiform) 218 a, (Greek) 227 a, (Hellenistic and Greco-Egyptian) 232 b, (Jewish) 220 b; Lien ix 456–60; Loans, Intergovernmental ix 556–61; Loans, Personal ix 561–65; Moratorium x 649–52; Mortgage xi 32–38; Pawnbroking xii 32–40; Peonage xii 69–72; Pledge xii 166–68; Public Debt xii 599–611; Sinking Fund xiv 68 a; Suretyship and Guaranty xiv 482–87; Usury xv 193–97.
Debt, Imprisonment for—Bankruptcy ii 449 a; Debt v 37 b; Judgments viii 445 b.
Debt, Public—see Public Debt.
Decadence — v 39–43; Art (Egyptian) ii 239 b, (French) 249 b, (Greek) 242 a, (Indian) 232 b, (Italian) 247 a; Change Social iii 331 b; City iii 476 a; Civilization iii 529 a; Degeneration v 56 a; Ibn-Khaldūn vii 564; Mysticism xi 177 a; Technology xiv 559 b.
Decentralization — v 43–44; Administration, Public i 444 a; Administrative Areas i 450–52; Autonomy ii 332–36; Centralization iii 309 a; City iii 479 b; Compacts, Interstate iv 109–13; Delegation of Powers v 65–67; Education (Public) v 419 b; Federalism vi 169–72; Federation vi 172–78; Feudalism vi 203–20; Home Rule vii 434–36; Local Govt. ix 580 b; Organization, Administrative xi 481 a; Regionalism xiii 208–18; States' Rights xiv 346–50.
De Cesare, C.—v 44.
Decker, M.—v 45.
Declaration of Independence—v 45–47; Civil Liberties iii 510 b; Enlightenment v 550 b; Republicanism xiii 319 a; Wilson xv 425 a.
Declaration of London—v 47–48; Blockade ii 594 b; Contraband of War iv 321 b; Freedom of the Seas vi 460 a; International Law viii 170 b; Prize xii 426 a; Warfare, Laws of xv 363 a.
Declaration of Paris—v 48–49; Blockade ii 594 b; Contraband of War iv 321 a; International Law viii 170 a; Privateering xii 423 b; Warfare, Laws of xv 360 a.
Declaration of the Rights of Man and the Citizen—v 49–51; Civil Liberties iii 512 a; Enlightenment v 550 b; Freethinkers vi 466 b; French Revolution vi 475 a.
Declaration of St. Petersburg—xv 360 b.
Declaratory Judgment—v 51–52.

Decorative and Industrial Arts—see INDUSTRIAL ARTS.
Decretals—iii 180 b.
Deductive Method—x 390 b.
DE FACTO GOVERNMENT—v 53–54; Military Occupation x 456–59; Municipal Corporation xi 90 a; Recognition, International xiii 165 a, 166 b.
Defender, Public—see PUBLIC DEFENDER.
Defense, National—see NATIONAL DEFENSE.
Deflation—see INFLATION AND DEFLATION.
DEFOE, D.—v 54.
De Forest, L.—xiii 54 b.
DE FOREST, R. W.—v 55.
DEGENERATION—v 55–57; Criminology iv 587 a; Decadence v 40 b.
DEGENKOLB, H.—v 57.
DE GREEF, G.—v 58; Sociology xiv 239 a.
DEIFICATION—v 58–60; Introd. Vol. I (Greek Culture and Thought) i 33 b, 35 a, (The Roman World) 53 a, 54 a; Ancestor Worship ii 53–55; Death Customs v 24 a; Divine Right of Kings v 176–77; Hero Worship vii 336 b; Idolatry vii 575–77; Lawgivers ix 275 a.
DEISM—v 61–63; Enlightenment v 551 b; Freethinkers vi 470 a; Reimarus xiii 226 b; Shaftesbury xiv 14 b; Tindal xiv 636 b; Toland xiv 647 a.
Dekker, E. D.—see DOUWES DEKKER, E.
DELANE, J. T.—v 63.
Delano, F. A.—iii 485 b.
DELANY, M. R.—v 63.
DELBRÜCK, H.—v 64.
DELCASSÉ, T.—v 64.
DELEGATION OF POWERS—v 65–67; By-Law iii 128–29; Compacts, Interstate iv 109–13; Constitutional Law iv 251 a; Eminent Domain v 494 a; Municipal Corporation xi 88 b, 90 b.
DE LEON, D.—v 67; Industrial Workers of the World viii 13 b; Knights of Labor viii 583 b; Socialism xiv 205 b.
DELFICO, M.—v 67.
Deligiannis, N.—xi 629 a.
Delinquency—see JUVENILE DELINQUENCY AND JUVENILE COURTS.
DELISLE, L. V.—v 68.
DELITZSCH, F.—v 68.
Della-Vos, V.—x 104 a.
De Lolme, J. L.—i 133 b.
Demagogy—ix 282 b.
DEMAND—v 69–75; Consumption iv 295–301; Economics (Marginal Utility Economics) v 359 a, (Cambridge School) 369 a; Interest viii 136 a; Laissez Faire ix 17 a; Luxury ix 637 a; Market x 131–33; Monopoly x 623–30; Supply xiv 470–74; Taxation xiv 536 b; Wages xv 294 a.

Demand Curves—Demand v 72–75; Forecasting, Business vi 349 b; Statics and Dynamics xiv 354 a.
Dementia Paralytica—Mental Disorders x 314 a.
Dementia Praecox—Abnormal Psychology i 362 a, 364 b; Mental Disorders x 314 b.
DÉMEUNIER, J.-N.—v 75.
Demilitarization—xi 365 a.
Demobilization — see MOBILIZATION AND DEMOBILIZATION.
DEMOCRACY—v 76–85; Introd. Vol. I (Greek Culture and Thought) i 12 a, (The Roman World) 50 a, (War and Reorientation) 216 b; Agreement of the People i 516–18; Aristocracy ii 188 b; Art ii 255 b; Bureaucracy iii 71 a; Campaign, Political iii 162–66; Capitalism iii 204 a; Career iii 225 a; Census iii 296 b; Centralization iii 312 b; Citizenship iii 473 b; Civic Organizations iii 498 b; Civil Liberties iii 509–13; Civil Service iii 517 b; Colonial Administration iii 642 a; Common Sense iv 60 b; Conscription iv 222 b; Conspiracy, Political iv 239 a; Declaration of Independence v 45–47; Declaration of the Rights of Man and the Citizen v 49–51; Dictatorship v 134 b; Education v 411 a; Elections v 450–56; Emancipation v 484 b; Equality v 577 b; Executive v 682 a; Expert v 10–13; French Revolution vi 471–83; Frontier vi 500–06; Functional Representation vi 518–23; Gosplan vi 712 b; Govt. vii 12 b, (Switzerland) 57 b; Industrial Democracy vii 691–92; Industrial Relations vii 711 b; Initiative and Referendum viii 50–52; Interests viii 144 b; Irredentism viii 325 a; Jaurès viii 374 b; Laveleye ix 198 b; Legislative Assemblies ix 361 a; Liberalism ix 437 b; Liberty ix 444 b; Literacy and Illiteracy ix 517 b; Madison x 34 b; Majority Rule x 57 a; Masses x 195 b; Minorities, National x 518 b; Minority Rights x 525–27; Monarchy x 583 a; Nationalism xi 242 b, 246 a; Natural Rights xi 299–302; Parties, Political xi 590–639; Petition, Right of xii 100 b; Pluralism xii 170–74; Plutocracy xii 176 b; Pobedonostsev xii 178 a; Political Offenders xii 201 b; Political Police xii 205 a; Popular Assemblies xii 236–39; Power, Political xii 304 b; Proportional Representation xii 541–45; Protestantism xii 574 a; Public Opinion xii 673 b; Representation xiii 311 b; Republicanism xiii 317–21; Tocqueville xiv 646 b; Voting xv 287–91.

Democratic Parties—see PARTIES, POLITICAL.
Democritus—Materialism x 209 b; Naturalism xi 303 a.
DEMOGRAPHY—v 85–86; Graunt vii 158 a; Moheau x 574 a; Mortality xi 22–32; Population xii 240–54; Sociology xiv 242 a; Statistics xiv 358 a.
DEMOLINS, E.—v 86; Social Surveys xiv 163 a.
DEMOLOMBE, J. C. F.—v 87.
DEMOSTHENES—v 88.
DENIFLE, H. S.—v 88.
DENIKER, J.—v 88; Race xiii 27 b.
DENIS, E.—v 89.
DENIS, H.—v 89.
Denison Act—xv 380 a.
Denison, E.—iii 343 b.
DENISON, G. T.—v 90.
Denizen—xi 307 a.
DENNY, W.—v 90.
Denominational Schools—v 421–25.
DENTISTRY—v 91–93.
DEPARCIEUX, A.—v 93.
Department Stores—Macy x 33 b; Marketing x 136 b; Retail Trade xiii 349 a; Stewart xiv 391 b.
DEPENDENCY—v 93–95; Almshouse ii 8–10; Begging ii 493–95; Blind ii 587–90; Child iii 373–431; Cripples iv 592–95; Legal Aid ix 319–24; Old Age xi 456 a; Poor Laws xii 230–34; Poverty xii 284–92; Rehabilitation xiii 221–25; Slavery xiv 73–92; Social Work xiv 165–83; Vagrancy xv 205–08.
DEPORTATION AND EXPULSION OF ALIENS—v 95–98; Mass Expulsion x 185–89.
DEPRECIATION—v 98–102; Accounting i 409 a; Armaments ii 197 b; Corporation Finance iv 428 a; Dumping v 277 b; Foreign Exchange vi 363 b; Goodwill vi 700 a; Income Tax vii 629 a, 631 a; Monetary Stabilization x 592 a; Paper Money xi 569 a; Public Debt xii 603 a.
Depression, Economic — see CRISES.
DEPRETIS, A.—v 102.
DE QUINCEY, T.—v 102; Drug Addiction v 245 a.
DERAISMES, M.—v 103.
DERBY, LORD—v 103.
DERNBURG, H.—v 104.
DEROIN, J.—v 104.
DÉROULÈDE, P.—v 105.
DE SANCTIS, F.—v 105.
DESCARTES, R.—v 106; Introd. Vol. I (The Rise of Liberalism) i 105 b; Humanism vii 541 b; Logic ix 601 a; Materialism x 211 a; Mechanism and Vitalism x 268 a; Newton xi 369 b; Psychology xii 589 a.
Deschanel, P.—Regionalism xiii 210 a.
Desertion, Family—see FAMILY DESERTION AND NON-SUPPORT.

Desertion, Military—see MILITARY DESERTION.
Desjardins, A.—iv 394 b.
Desmoulins, A.—xii 44 b.
DESMOULINS, C.—v 107.
Desnitsky, S.—i 280 b.
Despagnet, F.—iii 679 a.
DESPINE, P.—v 107.
Despotism—Montesquieu x 638 a.
DESTUTT DE TRACY, A. L. C.—v 108.
DETECTIVE AGENCIES, PRIVATE—v 108–10; Espionage v 596 b; Policing, Industrial xii 194 a.
DETERMINISM—v 110–14; Behaviorism ii 496 a; Child Psychology v 434 b; Climate iii 560 a; Consciousness iv 212–20; Environmentalism v 561–66; Evolution, Social v 656–62; Fatalism vi 146–48; Geography vi 621 b, 624 b; Laplace ix 169 b; Materialism (Dialectical) x 214 a, (Historical) 216 b; Method, Scientific x 392 a; Quetelet xiii 23 b.
Deusdedit, Cardinal—viii 261 b.
Deutsche Gesellschaft für Soziologie—i 263 a.
Deutsches Bürgerliches Gesetzbuch—see GERMAN CIVIL CODE.
De Valera, E.—Govt. (Ireland) vii 37 b; Parties, Political (Irish Free State) xi 610 a.
DEVALUATION—v 114–17; Monetary Stabilization x 592 b; Rentenmark xiii 296.
DEVAS, C. S.—v 117.
Devolution—see DECENTRALIZATION.
DEW, T. R.—v 117; Introd. Vol. I (The Social Sciences as Disciplines, U. S.) i 328 a.
Dewey, G.—xii 109 b.
Dewey, J.—Consciousness iv 215 a; Education v 413 b; Ethics v 605 b; Positivism xii 265 b; Pragmatism xii 309 b.
Dewing, A. S.—iii 209 b.
Dexter, E. G.—iv 589 a.
DEZAMY, T.—v 118.
Dharma—Art (Indian) ii 231 a; Asoka ii 270 b; Law (Hindu) ix 257 b.
Dharmasutras—Law (Hindu) ix 259 b.
Dhatu—Buddhism iii 33 b.
DIABOLISM—v 118–23.
DIALECT—v 123–26; Nationalism xi 235 a.
Dialectical Materialism—see MATERIALISM.
DIAMOND, H.—v 126.
Diamond Match Co.—x 206 a.
DIASPORA—v 126–30; Ghetto vi 646–50; Jewish Autonomy viii 391–94; Judaism viii 430–42; Law (Jewish) ix 223 b; Messianism x 358 b; Zionism xv 528–36.
DÍAZ, J. DE LA C. P.—v 130; Central American Federation iii 302 a; Madero x 33 b; Native Policy (Lat. Amer.) xi 258 a; Public Domain xii 625 b.

DICEY, A. V.—v 131; Rule of Law xiii 465 a.
DICKENS, C.—v 132.
DICKINSON, J.—v 133; Interests viii 146 a.
DICTATORSHIP—v 133–36; Introd. Vol. I (War and Reorientation) i 217 a; Autocracy ii 321–22; Coup d'État iv 509 b; Cromwell iv 605 a; Democracy v 82 b; Economic Policy v 341 b; Fascism vi 133–39; Force, Political vi 341 a; Freedom of Association vi 448 b; Freedom of Speech and of the Press vi 457 b; French Revolution vi 475 a, 477 b; Govt. (Italy) vii 51 b; Ku Klux Klan viii 608 b; Legislative Assemblies ix 360 b; Monarchy x 579–84; Parties, Political (Theory) xi 591 a, 594 a, (Organization) 594 a, (Jugoslavia) 627 b; Passport xii 16 a; Political Offenders xii 202 b; Political Police xii 205 b; Power, Political xii 304 b; Press xii 332 a; Representation xiii 312 b; State xiv 330 b; Succession, Political xiv 443 a.
Dictatorship of the Proletariat—Blanqui ii 585 a; Bolshevism ii 623–30; Communist Parties iv 88 a; Revolution and Counterrevolution xiii 375 a; Socialism (Marxian) xiv 202 a.
DIDEROT, D.—v 137; Anarchism ii 47 b; Encyclopédistes v 527 b.
Diehl, K.—Economics v 384 a; Hours of Labor vii 491 b.
DIESTERWEG, F. A. W.—v 137.
Diet—see LEGISLATIVE ASSEMBLIES.
Diet—see NUTRITION.
DIETERICI, K. F. W.—v 138.
DIETZEL, K. A.—v 138.
DIETZGEN, J.—v 139; Materialism x 219 a.
DIFFUSIONISM—v 139–42; Introd. Vol. I (The Trend to Internationalism) i 185 a, (War and Reorientation) 200 b; Anthropology ii 74 a, 103 a; Conquest iv 206 b; Culture iv 624 a; Evolution, Social v 661 a; Folklore vi 290 a; Language ix 164 a; Man x 76 a; Migrations x 420–41; Pottery xii 279 b; Prehistory xii 317 a; Reception xiii 156 a.
Digest of Justinian—see CORPUS JURIS CIVILIS.
Diggers—Levellers ix 422 b; Sects xiii 627 b; Socialism xiv 191 a.
DILKE, C. W.—v 142; Military Training x 467 a.
DILL, S.—v 143.
DILLON, J. F.—v 143.
Dilthey, P. H.—i 280 b.
DILTHEY, W.—v 144; Introd. Vol. I (War and Reorientation) i 204 b; Geisteswissenschaften vi 601 a; Political Science xii 213 a.

DIMINISHING RETURNS—v 144–46; Cost iv 469 a; Economics (Classical School) v 354 b; Increasing Returns vii 639 b.
DIOCLETIAN—v 146; Introd. Vol. I (The Roman World) i 54 a; Price Regulation xii 356 b.
Diogenes—iv 683 a.
DIPLOMACY—v 147–53; Alliance ii 3–4; Archives ii 177–81; Armaments ii 195 a; Concert of Powers iv 153–54; Consular Service iv 279–82; Gentili vi 616 a; Great Powers vii 161 a; Holy Alliance vii 417–19; Immunity, Diplomatic xv 595–97; International Organization viii 181 a; Intervention viii 236–39; Isolation, Diplomatic viii 352–55; Mediation x 272–74; Munitions Industry xi 132 a; Treaties xv 96–101.
Diplomatic Immunity—see IMMUNITY, DIPLOMATIC.
Diplomatic Isolation—see ISOLATION, DIPLOMATIC.
DIPLOMATIC PROTECTION—v 153–55; Calvo and Drago Doctrines iii 153 b; Capitulations iii 213–15.
DIRECT ACTION—v 155–58; Action Française i 424 b; Babouvism ii 375; Criminal Syndicalism iv 582–84; General Strike vi 608 b; Industrial Workers of the World viii 15 a; Sabotage xiii 495–97; Sorel xiv 262 b; Syndicalism xiv 496 b; Violence xv 266 a.
Direct Legislation—see INITIATIVE AND REFERENDUM.
Direct Taxes—xiv 533 b.
Disability Insurance—see HEALTH INSURANCE.
DISARMAMENT—v 158–61; Introd. Vol. I (The Trend to Internationalism) i 172 b; Antimilitarism ii 115–16; Armaments ii 198 b; Aviation ii 348 b; League of Nations ix 293 b; Limitation of Armaments ix 480–86; National Defense xi 192 a; Navy xi 317 b; War xv 338 b.
DISASTERS AND DISASTER RELIEF —v 161–66; Black Death ii 574–76; Epidemics v 569–72; Famine vi 85–89; Fire Protection vi 262–66; Floods and Flood Control vi 282–85; Nansen xi 181 b; Red Cross xiii 183 a, 184 a; Refugees xiii 200–05.
Discount Houses—see Bill Broker.
Discount Rate—Banking, Commercial ii 434 a; Central Banking iii 305 a; Credit Control iv 550 b; Economic Policy v 343 b; Money Market x 615 b, 616 b.
Discovery—Invention viii 247 a.
Discrimination, Price—see PRICE DISCRIMINATION.
Discrimination, Social—see SOCIAL DISCRIMINATION.
DISCUSSION—v 166–67.

Disease — see COMMUNICABLE DISEASES, CONTROL OF.
Disinfection—Water Supply xv 375 b.
Dispensaries—see CLINICS AND DISPENSARIES.
Displacement of Population—Conquest iv 205 a; War xv 332 a. See also MASS EXPULSION.
Disraeli, B.—see BEACONSFIELD, LORD.
Distress, Right of—ix 146 b.
DISTRIBUTION—v 167–74; Economics (Classical School) v 353 b, (Marginal Utility Economics) 360 a, (Cambridge School) 369 b; Entrepreneur v 559 a; Exploitation vi 16–17; George vi 630 b; Income vii 622–25; Industrialism viii 18 b; Interest viii 132 a; Labor viii 618 b; National Income xi 205–24; Poverty xii 284–92; Profit xii 480–87; Rent xiii 289–92; Rodbertus xiii 415 a; Wages xv 291–302.
DITHMAR, J. C.—v 174.
Dittemore, J. V.—iii 449 a.
DIVINATION—v 174–76; Astrology ii 287–89; Law (Egyptian) ix 210 a.
DIVINE RIGHT OF KINGS—v 176–77; Introd. Vol. 1 (Renaissance and Reformation) i 99 a; Absolutism i 381 a; Barclay ii 458 a; Deification v 58–60; Filmer vi 233 b; French Revolution vi 481 b; James I viii 367 a.
Division of Labor—see SPECIALIZATION.
DIVORCE—v 177–84; Alimony i 641–43; Christianity iii 459 b; Conflict of Laws iv 193 a; Detective Agencies, Private v 109 a; Domestic Relations Courts v 197 a; Domicile v 209 a; Family Desertion and Non-support vi 78–81; Insanity viii 70 a; Judaism viii 437 a; Marriage x 151 b.
DIX, D. L.—v 184.
DŁUGOSZ, J.—v 185.
DMITRIEV, V. K.—v 185.
DOBROGEANU-GHEREA, C. — v 186.
DOBROLUBOV, N. A.—v 186; Nihilism xi 377 b.
DOBROVSKÝ, J.—v 187.
Docks—see PORTS AND HARBORS; LONGSHOREMEN.
Dockwra, W.—xii 271 a.
DOCTRINAIRE—v 187–89.
DODGE, D. L.—v 189; Peace Movements xii 41 b.
Dodge, R.—i 621 a.
DOGMA—v 189–91; Belief ii 502 a; Church Fathers iii 464–68; Fundamentalism vi 526–27; Islam viii 334 b; Political Science xii 219 a; Sacred Books xiii 497–501; Secularism xiii 632 b.
DOHERTY, J.—v 191.

DOHM, H.—v 192.
Dole—Allowance System ii 7; Social Insurance xiv 137 a; Unemployment Insurance xv 166 a.
Dolichocephalism—Ammon ii 36 a; Anthropometry ii 111 a; Aryans ii 265 a.
DOLLFUS, J.—v 192.
DÖLLINGER, I. VON—v 193; Acton i 425 a.
Domain, Public—see PUBLIC DOMAIN.
DOMAT, J.—v 194; Civil Law iii 505 b.
Domestic Allotment Plan—vi 117 a.
DOMESTIC RELATIONS COURTS—v 194–98.
Domestic Relations, Law of—see FAMILY LAW.
Domestic Science—see HOME ECONOMICS.
DOMESTIC SERVICE—v 198–206; Negro Problem xi 342 a.
Domestic System—see PUTTING OUT SYSTEM.
DOMESTICATION—v 206–08; Anthropology ii 79 b, 83 a; Archaeology ii 165 a; Race xiii 29 b.
DOMICILE—v 208–10; Conflict of Laws iv 187–94; Double Taxation v 224–27; Nationality xi 250 b; Searches and Seizures xiii 619 b.
DOMINICAN FRIARS—v 210–11; Franciscan Movement vi 413 a; Religious Institutions (Roman Catholic) xiii 252 a.
DOMINION STATUS—v 211–16; Baldwin ii 407 b; Blake ii 583 a; Elgin v 478 a; Govt. (Brit. Commonwealth of Nations) vii 38–43; Indian Question vii 669 b; Legislative Assemblies (Gt. Brit. and Dominions) ix 372 b; Local Govt. ix 578 b; Naturalization xi 308 b.
DONEAU, H.—v 216; Commentators iii 681 b.
DONNELLY, I.—v 218.
Donnersmarck, Fürst von—see HENCKEL, G.
DONOSO CORTÉS, J.—v 218.
DORADO MONTERO, P.—v 218.
Dorchester, Lord—see CARLETON, G.
DORMER, D. J.—v 219.
DÖRPFELD, F. W.—v 219.
DOSTOEVSKY, F. M.—v 220.
DOUAI, A.—v 221.
DOUAREN, F. LE—v 221; Doneau v 216 a.
DOUBLE JEOPARDY—v 222–24.
Double Party System—xi 591 b.
DOUBLE TAXATION—v 224–27; Corporation Taxes iv 430–35; Dual Citizenship v 258 b; General Property Tax vi 604 b; Income Tax vii 630 b, 636 a; Mortgage Tax xi 39 b.
Douglas, C. H.—Guild Socialism vii 204 b; Labor Exchange Banks viii 642 b.

Douglas, P.—xv 295 b.
DOUGLAS, S. A.—v 227; Popular Sovereignty xii 239 b.
DOUGLASS, F.—v 228; Negro Problem xi 346 b.
Doumer, P.—xi 271 b.
DOUWES DEKKER, E.—v 228; Native Policy xi 271 b.
DOVE, P. E.—v 229.
Dow, N.—v 229.
Dower—x 118 b.
DOWRY—v 230–32; Law (Cuneiform) ix 216 a; Marriage x 148 a.
DOZY, R. P. A.—v 232.
DRACO—v 232.
Draft, Military—see CONSCRIPTION.
Drago Doctrine—see CALVO AND DRAGO DOCTRINES.
Drago, L.—iii 155 a.
DRAHOMANOV, M. P.—v 233.
Drainage—xiii 161 a.
Drake, F.—xii 138 a.
Drama—see THEATER.
DRAWBACK—v 233–35; Debentures v 29 b; International Trade viii 195 b.
Dreams—Abnormal Psychology i 363 b; Psychoanalysis xii 585 a.
Dred Scott Case—xiv 510 a.
DRESS—v 235–38; Anthropology ii 80 b; Fashion vi 139–44; Flax, Hemp and Jute vi 275 a; Garment Industries vi 573–85; Gentleman, Theory of the vi 619 b; Leather Industries ix 304 a; Ornament xi 496 a; Sumptuary Legislation xiv 464–66.
Dreyfus Affair—Action Française i 423 b; Anticlericalism ii 114 a; Antisemitism ii 123 a; Armed Forces, Control of ii 200 b; France, A. vi 407 b.
Driesch, H.—Gestalt vi 643 b; Mechanism and Vitalism x 269 a, 270 b.
DRINOV, M. S.—v 238.
DRIVES, MONEY RAISING—v 238–41.
DROYSEN, J. G.—v 241.
Drucki, Prince—see LUBECKI, F. X.
DRUG ADDICTION — v 242–52; Opium Problem xi 471–76.
Drugs, Public Regulation of—see FOOD AND DRUG REGULATION.
Drumont, E.—ii 123 a.
Dry Cleaning Industry — see LAUNDRY AND DRY CLEANING INDUSTRY.
DRY FARMING—v 252–56; Agriculture (India) i 592 b.
DRYDEN, J.—v 256.
Drysdale, G.—ii 561 a.
DUAL CITIZENSHIP—v 257–59; Military Desertion x 452 b.
DUAL UNIONISM — v 259–61; American Federation of Labor ii 27 a; Iron and Steel Industry viii 317 b; Knights of Labor viii 583 a.

Duaren—see DOUAREN, F. LE.
Dublin, L. I.—Child (Mortality) iii 385 b; Mortality xi 26 b.
Dubnow, S.—vi 650 b.
DUBOIS, G.—v 261.
DUBOIS, P.—v 262.
Du Bois, W. E. B.—xi 349 b.
DUBOS, J. B.—v 262.
DU CANE, E. F.—v 262.
DU CANGE, C. DU F.—v 263.
DUCHESNE, L. M. O.—v 263.
DUCPÉTIAUX, É.—v 264; Family Budgets vi 74 a.
Dudevant, Baronne—see SAND, G.
Dudley, S. F.—v 570 b.
DUE PROCESS OF LAW—v 264–68; Blacklist ii 577 b; Civil Liberties iii 511 a; Confiscation iv 186 b; Conflict of Laws iv 193 b; Constitutional Law iv 251 a; Cooley iv 357 a; Courts, Administrative iv 531 b; Double Jeopardy v 222–24; Eminent Domain v 493–97; Equal Protection of the Law v 573 a; Freedom of Contract vi 452 a; Full Faith and Credit Clause vi 516 a; Govt. Regulation of Industry vii 128 b; Judicial Review viii 461 b; Police Power xii 192 a; Rate Regulation xiii 107 b; Retroactive Legislation xiii 355 b; Searches and Seizures xiii 618 a; Supreme Court, U. S. xiv 479 b; Vested Interests xv 241 b.
DUELING—v 268–70; Sanction, Social xiii 533 a.
DUFF, A.—v 270.
DUFFERIN AND AVA, LORD—v 271; Egyptian Problem v 442 b.
DUGUIT, L.—v 272; Jurisprudence viii 483 a; Pluralism xii 170 b.
DÜHRING, E. K.—v 272; Distribution v 172 a; Socialism xiv 203 b.
Duke, J. B.—xiv 642 a.
Duma—Russian Revolution xiii 477 a.
Dumini, A.—x 230 b.
DUMONT, A.—v 273.
DUMONT FAMILY—v 274.
DUMOULIN, C.—v 274; Conflict of Laws iv 188 b; Loisel ix 603 b.
DUMPING—v 275–78; Bounties ii 653 a; Cartel iii 238 b; Price Discrimination xii 354 b; Tariff xiv 518 b.
Dun, R. G. and Co.—x 331 b.
DUNANT, J. H.—v 278; Red Cross xiii 182 a.
DUNBAR, C. F.—v 278.
DUNCKER, F. G.—v 279.
DUNCKER, M. W.—v 280.
Dunlop, M. W.—vii 552 b.
DUNNING, T. J.—v 280.
DUNNING, W. A.—v 280.
DUNOYER, B. C. P. J.—v 281.
DUNS SCOTUS, J.—v 282; Scholasticism xiii 580 a.
Dupin, A.—see SAND, G.
DUPLEIX, J.—v 282; Indian Question vii 660 b.

Duplessis-Mornay, P. — Introd. Vol. I (Renaissance and Reformation) i 96 b; Social Contract xiv 128 a.
DUPONT DE NEMOURS, P. S.—v 283.
DUPONT-WHITE, C. B.—v 284.
DUPRÉ DE SAINT MAUR, N. F.—v 285.
DUPUIT, A. J. É. J.—v 285; Economics v 365 b.
DURAN Y BAS, M.—v 286.
DURAND, G.—v 286.
DURESS—v 287–90.
DURHAM, LORD—v 290; Buller iii 60 a; Wages xv 322 b.
DURKHEIM, É.—v 291; Introd. Vol. I (Nationalism) i 169 b, (The Trend to Internationalism) 184 b, (War and Reorientation) 207 a, (The Social Sciences as Disciplines, France) 250 b; Animism ii 66 a; Belief ii 501 b; Criminology iv 588 a; Pluralism xii 171 b, 172 b; Positivism xii 264 a; Ritual xiii 396 b; Social Psychology xiv 154 a; Sociology xiv 239 a, 244 a.
DURUY, J. V.—v 292.
DUTOT, C. DE F.—v 292; Melon x 305 b.
Dutt, N. N.—see VIVEKĀNANDA, SWAMI.
DUTY—v 293–95.
Duvillard de Durand, E. É.—ii 525 b.
DWIGHT, L.—v 295.
DYAKONOV, M. A.—v 295.
DYE INDUSTRY—v 296–305; Industrial Arts vii 685 a.
Dyer, R. E. H.—vii 668 b.
Dynamics—see STATICS AND DYNAMICS.

Easements—Eminent Domain v 494 b; Servitudes xiv 4 b.
East India Companies—see CHARTERED COMPANIES.
Eastern Orthodox Church—xiii 262–67.
Eaton Co., T. B.—xiii 350 b.
EATON, D. B.—v 305.
EBBINGHAUS, H.—v 306.
EBERT, F.—v 306.
EBERT, M.—v 307.
Ecclesia—xii 236 b.
ECCLESIASTICAL COURTS—v 307–14; Benefit of Clergy ii 511–13; Breach of Marriage Promise ii 688 b; Canon Law iii 181 b, 183 b; Courts iv 519 a.
ECHEVERRIA, J. E. A.—v 314.
École Libre des Sciences Politiques—ii 661 a.
ECOLOGY, HUMAN—v 314–15; Community iv 102–05; Population xii 240–54; Sociology xiv 241 b.
Economic Councils — see NATIONAL ECONOMIC COUNCILS.
Economic Cycles—see BUSINESS CYCLES.
Economic Geography—see GEOGRAPHY.

Economic Geology—i 520 b.
ECONOMIC HISTORY—v 315–30; Introd. Vol. I (War and Reorientation) i 213 a, (The Social Sciences as Disciplines, Russia) 284 a; History and Historiography vii 369 b; Prices (Hist.) xii 375–81; Sociology xiv 242 b. For biog. references see Classification of Articles (History—Economic), p. 562.
ECONOMIC INCENTIVES—v 330–33; Abstinence i 382–83; Acquisition i 420–23; Altruism and Egoism ii 15 a; Economics (Classical School) v 351 b; Hedonism vii 309 a; Human Nature vii 535 b; Laissez Faire ix 19 a; Large Scale Production ix 178 b; Profit xii 486 a.
Economic Organization—see ORGANIZATION, ECONOMIC.
ECONOMIC POLICY—v 333–44. See Index, Government Regulation, and Classification of Articles (Economic Policy), p. 550, (Tariff), p. 556.
Economic Stabilization — see STABILIZATION, ECONOMIC.
ECONOMICS—v 344–95 (As a Discipline 344–46, Introd. to Hist. of Econ. Thought 346–48, 392, Physiocrats 348–51, 393, Classical School 351–57, 393, Marginal Utility Economics 357–63, 393, Mathematical Economics 364–68, 393, Cambridge School 368–71, 394, Historical School 371–77, 394, Socialist Economics 377–81, 394, Socio-Ethical Schools 381–85, 395, Romantic and Universalist Economics 385–87, 395, Institutional School 387–92, 395). See Classification of Articles (Economics), p. 550. See also Introd. Vol. I (What Are the Social Sciences?) i 3 b, (Greek Culture and Thought) 29 b, (The Roman World) 58 b, (The Rise of Liberalism) 122 a, (The Revolutions) 140 a, (Individualism and Capitalism) 153 a, (Nationalism) 166 a, (The Trend to Internationalism) 174 a, (War and Reorientation) 210 a, (The Social Sciences as Disciplines, Austria) 266 b, (France) 255 a, (Germany) 258 a, (Gt. Brit.) 235 a, 242 a, (Hungary) 270 b, (Italy) 274 a, (Japan) 322 a, (Lat. Amer.) 310 a, 317 b, (Russia) 281 b, 283 b, 284 b, 286 a, 287 b, (Scandinavia) 292 a, (Spain) 295 b, 299 b, (U. S.) 330 b, 336 b; Bounties ii 653 b; Christianity iii 457 a; Consumers' Cooperation iv 288 b; Economic Policy v 333 b; Efficiency v 437 a; Hedonism vii 309 a; Labor viii 617 a, 618 b; Liberalism ix 438 b; Location of Industry ix 585 a, 591 b;

Philosophy xii 127 a; Population xiv 249 b; Price Discrimination xii 350 b; Science xiii 600 a; Single Tax xiv 64 b; Sociology xiv 242 b; Statistics xiv 371 a; Utilitarianism xv 198 b. *For biog. references see* Classification of Articles (Economics), p. 559 *and* (History—Economic), p. 562.

Economics, Agricultural—*see* AGRICULTURAL ECONOMICS.

EDDY, M. B.—v 395; Christian Science iii 446 b.

EDELMANN, J. C.—v 396.

EDEN, F. M.—v 397; Economic History v 316 a; Family Budgets vi 73 b.

EDGEWORTH, F. Y.—v 397; Economics v 367 b; Index Numbers vii 653 b; Monopoly x 627 b.

Edgeworth, M.—v 398 b.

EDGEWORTH, R. L.—v 398.

EDMONDS, T. R.—v 399.

EDUCATION—v 403-32 (History 403-14, 431, Public 414-21, 431, Sectarian 421-25, 432, Part Time 425-28, 432, Educational Finance 428-32). *See* Classification of Articles (Education), p. 550. *See also* Introd. Vol. I (What Are the Social Sciences?) i 6 a, (Greek Culture and Thought) 22 b, 38 b, (The Universal Church) 67 b, (Individualism and Capitalism) 150 a, (The Social Sciences as Disciplines, Gt. Brit.) 231-349; Aviation ii 343 b; Belief ii 501 a; Blind ii 588 b; Career iii 226 a; Character iii 337 a; Charitable Trusts iii 339 b; Child (Labor) iii 421 a, (Welfare) 375 b; Civil Service iii 518 b; Colonial Administration iii 646 a; Company Towns iv 120 a; Continuity, Social iv 316 a; Deaf v 19 a; Endowments and Foundations v 532 b; Engineering v 544 a; Ethical Culture Movement v 601 b; Family vi 68 a; Fascism vi 138 a; Franciscan Movement vi 413 b; Fundamentalism vi 526 b; Habit vii 238 a; Insurance viii 106 a; Intellectuals viii 122 a; Jesuits viii 384 a; Journalism viii 422 a; Judaism viii 437 a; Land Grants (Brit. Empire) ix 39 a, (U. S.) 33 b; Mental Defectives x 312 a; Motion Pictures xi 67 b; Native Policy (N. Amer.) xi 266 a, 268 b; Negro Problem xi 347 a, 352 a; Penal Institutions xii 62 b; Philosophy xii 127 b; Pragmatism xii 310 a; Propaganda xii 522 a; Public Employment xii 633 a; Radio xiii 60 b; Symbolism xiv 494 b; Utilitarianism xv 199 a; Woman, Position in Society xv 449 b. *For biog. references see* Classification of Articles (Education), p. 560.

Education, Adult—*see* ADULT EDUCATION.

Education, Agricultural—*see* AGRICULTURAL EDUCATION.

Education, Health—*see* HEALTH EDUCATION.

Education, Industrial—*see* INDUSTRIAL EDUCATION.

EDUCATION, PRIMITIVE—v 399-403; Anthropology ii 102 a; Culture iv 633 b; Family vi 67 a; Initiation viii 49-50.

EDUCATIONAL PSYCHOLOGY — v 432-35; Mental Tests x 323-29.

EDWARD I—v 435; Mortmain xi 44 b.

Edward III—Justice of the Peace viii 524 b; Pole Family xii 182 b; Treason xv 94 b.

EDWARDS, J.—v 436.

EFFICIENCY—v 437-39; Alcohol i 627 a; Behaviorism ii 497 b; Business Administration iii 87-91; By-Product iii 129-30; Capitalism iii 198 a; Civil Service iii 520 a; Cost Accounting iv 475-78; Expert vi 10-13; Fatigue vi 148-51; Hours of Labor vii 491 a; Labor, Methods of Remuneration for viii 679 a; Large Scale Production ix 174 a; Management x 76-80; Organization, Administrative xi 483 a; Personnel Administration xii 88-90; Scientific Management xiii 603-08; Specialization xiv 284 a; Waste xv 367-69.

Efficiency Wage—viii 678 a.

EFIMENKO, A. Y.—v 439.

EGERTON, H. E.—v 440.

Egerton, T. — *see* ELLESMERE, LORD.

EGGLESTON, E.—v 440.

Egoism—*see* ALTRUISM AND EGOISM.

Egyptian Law—Law ix 209-11.

EGYPTIAN PROBLEM—v 441-44; Cromer iv 604 b; Dufferin and Ava v 271 b; Europeanization v 631 a; Mehemet Ali x 301 a; Mohammed ʿAbdu x 571 a; Muṣṭāfa Kamil xi 165 a; Pan-Islamism xi 542-44; Suez Canal xiv 444-47; Zaghlul Pasha xv 523 b.

Egyptology—Champollion iii 329 b; Lepsius ix 412 b; Maspero x 184 b; Rougé xiii 444 a.

EHRENBERG, R.—v 444.

EHRENBERG, V.—v 445.

Ehrenfels, C. von—vi 643 a.

EHRENREICH, P.—v 445; Folklore vi 289 a.

EHRLICH, E.—v 445.

EICHHORN, K. F.—v 446.

Eight Hours Movement—Hours of Labor vii 478-93; Short Hours Movement xiv 45 b.

Eighteenth Amendment — *see* PROHIBITION.

EINARSEN, E.—v 447.

Einhorn—*see* HORN, E. I.

EISELE, F.—v 447; Roman Law xiii 424 b.

EISELEN, J. F. G.—v 448.

EISNER, K.—v 448.

Elamitic Law—Law (Cuneiform) ix 211-19.

Elberfeld System—Münsterberg xi 135 b; Poor Laws xii 233 b.

ELDON, LORD—v 449.

ELECTIONS—v 450-56; Absent-Voting i 376; Ballot ii 410-12; By-Elections iii 127-28; Campaign, Political iii 162-66; Caucus iii 278 a; Contested Elections iv 308-10; Convention, Political iv 349-51; Corrupt Practises Acts iv 447-48; Executive v 684 a; Gerrymander vi 638-39; Initiative and Referendum viii 50-52; Judiciary viii 465 a; Legislative Assemblies ix 359 a, (France) 375 b; Machine, Political ix 660 b; Majority Rule x 55-60; Nominations, Political xi 392-95; Plebiscite xii 165 b; Primaries, Political xii 396-98; Proportional Representation xii 541-45; Registration of Voters xiii 218-21; Representation xiii 312 a; Short Ballot Movement xiv 43-44; Straw Vote xiv 417-19; Voting xv 287-91.

ELECTRIC POWER — v 456-70; Beck ii 490 a; Electrical Manufacturing Industry v 470 a; Gas Industry vi 589 b, 590 a; Govt. Owned Corporations vii 107 b; International Waterways viii 212 b; Interstate Commerce viii 224 a; Large Scale Production ix 175 a; Leather Industries ix 308 b; Machines and Tools x 25 a; Power, Industrial xii 296 b; Public Utilities xii 674-87; Waterways, Inland xv 383 a; Westinghouse xv 405 a.

Electrical Construction Industry —viii 628 a.

ELECTRICAL MANUFACTURING INDUSTRY—v 470-77; Motion Pictures xi 59 b; Radio xiii 54-59, 65 b; Siemens xiv 49 b; Telephone and Telegraph xiv 564 a; Westinghouse xv 405 a.

Elementargedanken—Anthropology ii 109 b; Bastian ii 476 a; Civilization iii 527 a.

Elevated Railways—xi 124 a.

ELGIN, LORD—v 478.

Elias, Brother—vi 411 b.

ELIOT, C. W.—v 478.

ELIOT, G.—v 478.

ELIOT, J.—v 479.

Élite—Fascism vi 134 b; Intellectuals viii 118-26; Minority Rights x 527 a.

ELIZABETH—v 480; Irish Question viii 286 b.

ELLESMERE, LORD—v 480; Equity v 586 a.

Ellis, H.—Abortion i 374 b; Genius vi 612 b.

Ellis, W.—i 240 a.

ELLSWORTH, O.—v 481.

ELM, A. VON—v 482.

Index (Economics — Environment)

Elmira System—Brockway iii 8 a.
ELPHINSTONE, M.—v 482.
EMANCIPATION—v 483–85; Catholic Emancipation iii 269–71; Cherkassky iii 369 a; Eminent Domain v 496 b; Jewish Emancipation viii 394–99; Kiselev viii 575 a; Kosciuszko viii 593 b; Land Tenure (Russia) ix 108 a; Landed Estates ix 141 b; Milutin x 490 a; Negro Problem xi 337 b; Peasantry xii 49 b; Serfdom xiii 670 a.
Embalming—vi 528 a.
EMBARGO—v 485–87; Angary ii 59 b; Blockade ii 594–96; Continental System iv 310–11.
Emergent Evolution—Evolution v 649 b; Materialism (Dialectical) x 214 a; Mechanism and Vitalism x 269 b.
Emerson Efficiency Bonus Plan—viii 679 a.
EMERSON, R. W.—v 487; Transcendentalism xv 76 b.
EMIGRATION—v 488–93; Far Eastern Problem vi 97 b; Immigration vii 587–95; Irish Question viii 290 b; Mass Expulsion x 185–89; Migrations x 420–41; Military Desertion x 452 b.
EMINENT DOMAIN—v 493–97; Alienation of Property i 639–41; Confiscation iv 183–87; Excess Condemnation v 663–64; Mining Law x 513 b; Municipal Corporation xi 91 b; State Liability xiv 339 a.
Emphyteusis—ix 144 a.
EMPIRE—v 497–506; Introd. Vol. I (The Roman World) i 52 b; Alexander the Great i 631 a; Colonial Administration iii 641–46; Colonies iii 653–63; Commerce iv 4 b; Conquest iv 205–08; Dominion Status v 211–16; Emigration v 491 b; Europeanization v 624 a; Federalism vi 170 b; Feudalism (Saracen and Ottoman) vi 210–13, (Chinese) 213–14; Govt. (Brit. Commonwealth of Nations) vi 38–43; Holy Roman Empire vii 422–27; Imperial Unity vii 602–05; Imperialism vii 605–13; Indian Question vii 659–74; Islam viii 338 b; Land Grants (Brit. Empire and Lat. Amer.) ix 36–43; Monarchy x 579 b; Navy xi 311 a; Rebellion xiii 144 b; Roads xiii 400 b; Royal Court xiii 448 a; Transportation xv 83 b; Tribute xv 102–04; War xv 332 b.
Empiricism—Locke ix 593 b; Logic ix 601 b.
Employee Representation—Company Unions iv 123–26; Conciliation, Industrial iv 167 b; Industrial Democracy vii 691 b; Industrial Relations Councils vii 722 a.
EMPLOYEE STOCK OWNERSHIP—v 506–09; Gas Industry vi 591 b; Hewitt vii 344 b; Iron and Steel Industry viii 317 a; Labor, Methods of Remuneration for viii 681 a; Profit Sharing xii 489 a.
EMPLOYERS' ASSOCIATIONS — v 509–14; Chambers of Commerce iii 325–29; Construction Industry iv 275 b; Iron and Steel Industry viii 321 b; Justi viii 507 b; Kirby viii 572 b; Laundry and Dry Cleaning Industry ix 196 a; Parry xi 588 b.
EMPLOYERS' LIABILITY—v 514–18; Compensation and Liability Insurance iv 135–41.
EMPLOYMENT EXCHANGES — v 518–23; Bourses du Travail ii 659–60; Casual Labor iii 261 b; Labor Legislation and Law viii 663 a; Unemployment Insurance xv 172 b.
ENCLOSURES—v 523–27; Agrarian Movements i 495 b; Agric. Labor i 548 a; Agriculture (Eng.) i 578 a, 580 b; Allotments ii 6 b; Bakewell ii 393 b; Freehold vi 463 b; Labourers, Statutes of ix 4 b; Land Tenure ix 88 b.
Encomienda — Land Grants (Latin America) ix 40 a; Native Policy (Latin America) xi 253 b.
ENCYCLOPÉDISTES—v 527–31; Introd. Vol. I (The Revolutions) i 131 a; Alembert i 629 b; Bayle ii 484 a; Condorcet iv 176; Diderot v 137 a; Enlightenment v 551 b; French Revolution vi 474 a; Helvétius vii 319 a; Holbach vii 401 a; Morellet xi 10 a; Passive Resistance and Non-cooperation xii 12 a; Rousseau xiii 445 b.
ENDEMANN, W.—v 531.
Endocrinology—i 197 a.
Endogamy—Anthropology ii 86 b; Aristocracy ii 187 a; Marriage x 146 b.
ENDOWMENTS AND FOUNDATIONS — v 531–37; Introd. Vol. I (The Social Sciences as Disciplines, Scandinavia) i 293 b; Charitable Trusts iii 338–40; Negro Problem xi 346 b; Research xiii 332 a.
ENEMY ALIEN—v 537–39; Alien Property i 636–38; Alien and Sedition Acts i 635 a; Domicile v 209 b; Prisoners of War xii 419–22.
ENFANTIN, B. P.—v 539; Bazard ii 484 b; Saint-Simon and Saint-Simonianism xiii 510 a.
ENGEL, C. L. E.—v 539; Cost of Living iv 480 b; Family Budgets vi 74 b.
ENGELS, F.—v 540; Introd. Vol. I (Individualism and Capitalism) i 157 a; Babouvism ii 375 b; Marx x 173 a; Materialism x 213 a; Socialism xiv 197 b; Sociology xiv 243 a; Utopia xv 201 a.
ENGINEERING—v 541–46; Architecture ii 172–75; Art (Roman) ii 243 a; Cement iii 286 b; Efficiency v 437–39; Irrigation viii 329 b; Professional Ethics xii 474 b; Roads xiii 400–11; Standardization xiv 320 a; Technology xiv 555 a; Traffic Regulation xv 72 a; Water Supply xv 372 b.
ENLIGHTENMENT—v 547–52; Introd. Vol. I (The Revolutions) i 138 a; Cosmopolitanism iv 460 b; Criticism, Social iv 601 a; Deism v 61–63; Encyclopédistes v 527–31; Fontenelle vi 297 a; Freethinkers vi 466 b; History and Historiography vii 375 a; Jesuits viii 386 a; Judaism viii 438 a; Legal Profession and Legal Education ix 335 a; Lessing ix 419 a; Mendelssohn x 308 a; Positivism xii 262 a; Rationalism xiii 115 b; Republicanism xiii 319 a; Secularism xiii 632 b.
Ennius, Q.—xiv 602 b.
Enquête — Investigations, Governmental viii 258 a.
ENSENADA, MARQUÉS DE LA—v 552.
ENTAIL—v 553–56; Alienation of Property i 640 a; Perpetuities xii 81 b.
Entelechy—x 267 b.
ENTICEMENT OF EMPLOYEES—v 556–58.
ENTREPRENEUR—v 558–60; Business iii 84 b; Capitalism iii 201–06; Captain of Industry iii 216–20; Combinations, Industrial iii 672 b; Corporation iv 418 b; Employers' Associations v 509–14; Fortunes, Private vi 399 a; Hawley vii 283 a; Middle Class x 407 b; Profit xii 480–87; Risk xiii 392–94; Wages xv 296 b.
ENVER PASHA—v 560.
Environment — Abnormal Psychology i 368 a; Acclimatization i 401–03; Adaptation i 435–37; Anthropology ii 76 a, 98 a; Anthropometry ii 112 a; Behaviorism ii 498 a; Biology ii 555 a; Bodin ii 615 a; Character iii 335 b; Climate iii 556–62; Criminology iv 588 a; Determinism v 112 b; Environmentalism v 561–66; Eugenics v 620 a; Evolution v 652 b; Genius vi 613 b; Geography vi 621–29; Heredity vii 332 b; Human Nature vii 532 b; Literature ix 538 b; Man x 75 b; Materialism (Historical) x 216 b; Mental Disorders x 315 a; Mental Tests x 324 b; Migrations x 421 b; Owen and Owenism xi 519 b; Personality xii 86 b; Political Science xii 217 b; Religion xiii 232 a; Ritter xiii 395 a; Social Psychology xiv 154 b; Sociology xiv 241 a; Soils xiv 250 b.

ENVIRONMENTALISM—v 561-66. See Environment.
Eoanthropus—x 74 b.
Eolithic Period—ii 164 a.
Eötvös, J.—v 566.
Ephebate—i 38 b.
EPICTETUS—v 567.
EPICUREANISM—v 567-69; Ethics v 602 b; Hedonism vii 307 b; Individualism vii 675 b; Lucretius Carus ix 627 a; Materialism x 210 a; Self-Preservation xiii 654 b; Valla xv 209 b.
Epicurus—see EPICUREANISM.
EPIDEMICS — v 569-72; Black Death ii 574-76; Communicable Diseases, Control of iv 66-78; Disasters and Disaster Relief v 161-66; Famine vi 87 a; Koch viii 586 a.
EQUAL PROTECTION OF THE LAW —v 572-74; Constitutional Law iv 250 b; Due Process of Law v 268 a.
EQUALITY—v 574-80; Introd. Vol. I (Individualism and Capitalism) i 150 a; Aristocracy ii 189 a; Common Sense iv 58-61; Communism iv 81-87; Cosmopolitanism iv 459 b; Declaration of Independence v 46 a; Democracy v 76-85; Education v 411 b; Emancipation v 483-85; Equal Protection of the Law v 572-74; Equality of States v 580-82; French Revolution vi 475 a; Govt. (Switzerland) vii 57 b; Human Nature vii 534 a; Individualism vii 677 b; Inheritance viii 38 b; Jewish Emancipation viii 394-99; Justice viii 509 b, 511 a; Justice, Administration of viii 521 a; Labor Legislation and Law viii 667 b; Liberalism ix 437 b; Liberty ix 442-47; Mably ix 644 b; Majority Rule x 55-60; Masses x 195 b; Natural Law xi 288 b; Natural Rights xi 299-302; Race Conflict xiii 37 a; Social Contract xiv 130 a; Social Discrimination xiv 131-34; Status xiv 376 a; Stoicism xiv 409 a; Taxation xiv 539 a.
EQUALITY OF STATES—v 580-82; Great Powers vii 161 b; International Organization viii 178 b.
Equalization Boards — General Property Tax vi 605 b.
Equalization Fee—Farm Relief vi 117 a.
Equilibrium, Economic — see STATICS AND DYNAMICS.
Equilibrium Price—x 131 b.
EQUITY—v 582-88; Introd. Vol. I (The Roman World) i 49 a; Canon Law iii 185 a; Courts iv 522 a; Declaratory Judgment v 52 a; Eldon v 449 b; Ellesmere v 481 a; Gibson vi 654 a; Guardianship vii 194 a; Hardwicke vii 269 b; Injunction viii 53-57; Jessel viii 381 a; Judgments viii 445 b; Langdell ix 151 b; Law (Hindu) ix 262 a; Lien ix 457 a; Marital Property x 119 a; Nottingham xi 401 a; Pomeroy xii 230 a; Procedure, Legal xii 446 b; Receivership xiii 150 a; Specific Performance xiv 286 a; Suretyship and Guaranty xiv 484 a; Trusts and Trustees xv 122 a.
Equity Stores—Warren xv 364 b.
ERASMUS, D.—v 588; Humanism vii 540 a.
Eratosthenes of Cyrene—i 35 b.
Erdman Act—xiii 95 b.
Ericsson, J.—xi 314 b.
Ericsson Telephone Co., Ltd.—xiv 566 b.
Erie Canal—iii 567 b.
ERNEST I—v 589.
ERSKINE, LORD—v 589.
ERSLEV, K.—v 590.
ERZBERGER, M.—v' 590.
ESCHEAT—v 591-93; Confiscation iv 184 b; Freehold vi 463 a.
Eskimo — Native Policy (N. Amer.) xi 269 a.
ESMEIN, A.—v 593.
Esperanto—ix 168 a.
ESPINAS, A.—v 593.
ESPIONAGE—v 594-96; Blacklist, Labor ii 579 a; Detective Agencies, Private v 108-10; Diplomacy v 148 b; Political Police xii 203-07.
ESQUIROL, J.-É. D.—v 596.
Essenes—Monasticism x 584 b; Religious Orders xiii 277 a.
ESTATES GENERAL—v 597-600; Bicameral System ii 533 b; French Revolution vi 474 b; Functional Representation vi 519 a; Govt. vii 11 b; Legislative Assemblies ix 357 a; Representation xiii 311 a.
Estoppel—viii 110 a.
ESTOURNELLES DE CONSTANT, BARON D'—v 600.
ETHICAL CULTURE MOVEMENT—v 600-02.
ETHICS—v 602-07; Introd. Vol. I (What Are the Social Sciences?) i 5 b, (Greek Culture and Thought) 26 b; Altruism and Egoism ii 14-16; Anthropology ii 97 b; Business Ethics iii 111-13; Casuistry iii 265-66; Christianity iii 460 b; Common Sense iv 58-61; Confucianism iv 198 b; Duty v 293-95; Economics (Socio-Ethical Economics) v 381-85; Enlightenment v 551 b; Epicureanism v 567-69; Equality v 574-80; Ethical Culture Movement v 600-02; Fraud vi 427 a; Freethinkers vi 470 b; Gentleman, Theory of the vi 619 b; Hedonism vii 307-10; Hegel vii 312 b; Honor vii 456-58; Humanitarianism vii 544-49; Judaism viii 440 a; Jurisprudence viii 485 a; Just Price viii 504 b; Justice viii 509-15; Kant viii 539 a; Labor Movement viii 687 a; Luxury ix 635 b; Morals x 649 a; Opportunism xi 476-79; Professional Ethics xii 472-76; Realism xiii 142 b; Religion xiii 236 b; Renouvier xiii 288 b; Service xiii 672-74; Sex Education and Sex Ethics xiv 8-13; Social Christian Movements xiv 123-27; Sociology xiv 233 b; Socrates xiv 247 b; War xv 339 b.
Ethics, Business—see BUSINESS ETHICS.
Ethics, Professional—see PROFESSIONAL ETHICS.
ETHNIC COMMUNITIES—v 607-13; Diaspora v 126-30; Foreign Language Press vi 378-82; Ghetto vi 646-50; Gypsies vii 231-32; Immigration vii 591 a; Intermarriage viii 154 a; Irredentism viii 325-28; Jewish Autonomy viii 391-94; Minorities, National x 518-25; Native Policy xi 252-83; Negro Problem xi 335-56; Segregation xiii 643-47.
ETHNOCENTRISM—v 613-14; Intermarriage viii 151-55; Minorities, National x 518-25; Nationalism xi 231-49; Pan-movements xi 544-54; Patriotism xii 26-29; Race Conflict xiii 36-41; Regionalism xiii 208-18.
Ethnology—see ANTHROPOLOGY; RACE.
ÉTIENNE, E.—v 614.
ETIQUETTE—v 615-17; Ceremony iii 316 a; Fictions vi 227 b; Gentleman, Theory of the vi 618 b; Honor vii 456 b; Hospitality vii 462-64; Morals x 643-49; Symbolism xiv 494 a.
Eucharist—xi 174 b.
EUCKEN, R. C.—v 617.
Eudoxus—vii 307 b.
EUGENICS—v 617-21; Aristocracy ii 187 a; Biology ii 557 a; Birth Control ii 564 b; Child (Marriage) iii 395-98; Galton vi 553 b; Heredity vii 334 b; Mendel x 307 b; Mental Defectives x 313 b; Science xiii 601 a.
Eugenius IV—iv 163 a.
EUHEMEROS—v 621.
Euhemerus of Messana—i 35 a.
Eunuchs—Slavery xiv 79 b.
EURIPIDES—v 622; Theater xiv 601 a.
EUROPEANIZATION—v 623-36; Art (Chinese) ii 234 b, (Indian) 233 a, (Japanese) 238 a; Chinese Problem iii 431 b; Colonies iii 661 b; Egyptian Problem v 441 b; Far Eastern Problem vi 92-100; Imperialism vii 609 a; Indian Question vii 659-74; International Advisers viii 155-59; Kuomintang viii 610-14; Law (Japanese) ix 256 a; Liang Ch'i-ch'ao ix 430 a; Macaulay ix 648 b; Mahmud II x 47 b; Manchurian Problem x 80-84; Missions x 540 a; Native Policy xi 252-83; Peter

Index (Environmentalism — Exploitation)

i xii 96 a; Russian Revolution xiii 474 a, 490 a; Youth Movements xv 518 a.
EUSEBIUS OF CAESAREA—v 636; Church Fathers iii 465 a; History and Historiography vii 370 b.
Evangelism—Booth Family ii 641 a; Revivals, Religious xiii 364 b; Sects xiii 629 a.
Evans, G. C.—v 367 b.
Evans, G. H.—v 636.
Evans, H. W.—viii 607 b.
Evans, J.—ii 163 b.
Evans, M. A.—see ELIOT, G.
Evelyn, J.—xii 398 b.
Everard, W.—xv 430 a.
EVIDENCE—v 637–49; Alienist i 641; Expert Testimony vi 13–16; Frauds, Statute of vi 429–30; Identification vii 573–75; Investigations, Governmental viii 252 b; Judicial Interrogation viii 448–50; Jury viii 492–502; Law (Jewish) ix 223 b, (Slavic) 246 a; Medical Jurisprudence x 274–79; Perjury xii 74–76; Searches and Seizures xiii 617–20; Self-Incrimination xiii 651–53; Thayer xiv 597 a; Valuation xv 213 b.
EVOLUTION—v 649–56; Introd. Vol. I (Individualism and Capitalism) i 162 a; Adaptation i 436 a; Atavism ii 290–91; Biology ii 552 a, 554 b; Butler iii 125 b; Consensus iv 226 a; Darwin v 4; Domestication v 206–08; Evolution, Social v 656–62; Freethinkers vi 468 a; Fundamentalism vi 526 a; Huxley vii 562 a; Lamarck ix 21 b; Logic ix 602 a; Lyell ix 639 a; Materialism (Dialectical) x 215 a; Mechanism and Vitalism x 269 b; Pragmatism xii 308 a; Psychology xii 592 b; Renouvier xiii 288 a; Science xiii 601 a.
EVOLUTION, SOCIAL—v 656–62; Introd. Vol. I (War and Reorientation) i 200 b; Ammon ii 36 a; Change, Social iii 330–34; Civilization iii 525–29; Comte iv 151; Control, Social iv 344–49; Culture iv 623 b; Decadence v 39–43; Determinism v 110–14; Economic History v 328 a; Economics (Historical School) v 373 b; Family vi 65 a; Fiske vi 271 a; Functionalism vi 523–26; Higher Criticism vii 347 b; History and Historiography vii 361 a; Mechanism and Vitalism x 270 b; Müller-Lyer xi 83 a; Positivism xii 263 a; Ritchie xiii 394 b; Social Organism xiv 139 b; Social Process xiv 149 a; Sociology xiv 237 b, 238 a; Spencer xiv 295 a; Statics and Dynamics xiv 352 b; Sternberg xiv 388 b.
EWERS, J. P. G. VON—v 663.
Exarch—xiii 262 a.

EXCESS CONDEMNATION—v 663–64; Eminent Domain v 494 b; Municipal Corporation xi 92 a.
EXCESS PROFITS TAX—v 664–66; Unearned Increment xv 147 a.
EXCHANGE—v 666–69; Anthropology ii 83 b; Economics (Classical School) v 353 a, (Marginal Utility Economics) 358 b, (Mathematical Economics) 366 a, (Socialist Economics) 378 a; Feudalism vi 204 a, 209 b; Foreign Exchange vi 358–64; Individualism vii 679 b; Labor Exchange Banks viii 637–44; Money x 601–13; Prices (Theory) xii 366–75; Production (Theory) xii 463 b; Society xiv 229 b.
Exchange Banks—viii 639 b.
Exchange of Populations—Mass Expulsion x 187 a; Minorities, National x 524 a.
Exchequer, Court of—see Court of Exchequer.
EXCISE—v 669–71; Aids i 608 b; Licensing ix 447 a; Liquor Traffic ix 505 a; Tobacco xiv 645 a.
EXCOMMUNICATION — v 671–80; Law (Jewish) ix 224 b; Outlawry xi 506 a; Religious Institutions (Roman Catholic) xiii 252 b.
EXECUTIVE—v 680–85; Administration, Public i 449 a; Advisory Opinions i 475–78; Armed Forces, Control of ii 201 a; Bicameral System ii 534 b; Budget iii 40 a; Cabinet iii 132 b, 133 b; Checks and Balances iii 363 b; Congressional Govt. iv 201–03; Executive Agreements v 685–86; Govt. (Argentina) vii 92 a, (Austria) 77 b, (Balkan States) 82 a, (Belgium) 47 b, (Brazil) 93 a, (Canada) 27 b, (Chile) 94 b, (China) 99 b, (Czechoslovakia) 79 a, (Estonia) 71 b, (Finland) 65 a, (France) 45 a, (Germany) 54 b, (Gt. Brit.) 22 a, (Greece) 83 b, (Hungary) 78 a, (Ireland) 37 a, (Italy) 49 a, 51 b, (Japan) 96 a, (Latvia) 72 a, (Lithuania) 73 a, (Netherlands) 59 b, (Norway) 62 b, (Poland) 74 a, (Russia, Imperial) 66 a, (S. Africa) 35 a, (Spain) 86 a, (Sweden) 63 b, (Switzerland) 58 a, (Turkey) 85 a, (Uruguay) 94 a, (U. S.) 19 b; Impeachment vii 600–02; Legislative Assemblies (Hist. and Theory) ix 358 b, 360 b, (Germany) 381 b, (Japan) 394 a, (U. S.) 363 b; Mandamus x 85 a; Martial Law x 162–67; Monarchy x 579–84; Pardon xii 571 b; Prerogative xii 319 b; Recognition, International xiii 166 a; Separation of Powers xiii 663–67; Succession, Political xiv 441–44; Treaties xv 98 a; Veto xv 247–49.

EXECUTIVE AGREEMENTS—v 685–86; Agreements, International i 518–20.
Exemptions, Tax—see TAX EXEMPTION.
Exhibitions—see MUSEUMS AND EXHIBITIONS.
EXILE—v 686–90; Foreign Language Press vi 381 a; Homicide vii 451 b; Ostracism xi 501–03; Refugees xiii 200–05; Transportation of Criminals xv 90–93.
Exogamy—Anthropology ii 86 a; Aristocracy ii 187 b; Culture iv 630 a; Lubbock ix 623 a; McLennan x 29 b; Marriage x 146 b.
EXPATRIATION—vi 3–5; Nationality xi 251 b; Naturalization xi 308 b.
EXPENDITURES, PUBLIC—vi 5–10; Armaments ii 196 b; Aviation ii 346 b; Budget iii 38–44; Financial Administration vi 234–41; Grants-in-Aid vii 152–55; Institutions, Public viii 94 b; Investigations, Governmental viii 256 b; Local Finance ix 568 b; Municipal Finance xi 98 a; Penal Institutions xii 59 a; Public Contracts xii 596–99; Public Employment xii 631 b; Public Finance xii 639 b; Public Health xii 652 a; Public Libraries xii 661 b; Public Works xii 691 a; Roads xiii 408 b; Social Insurance xiv 134–38; Subsidies xiv 430–33; War Finance xv 348 a; Waterways, Inland xv 380 a.
EXPERT—vi 10–13; Introd. Vol. I (War and Reorientation) i 211 a; Academic Freedom i 384 b; Administration, Public i 445 a, 448 b; Alienist i 641; Boards, Advisory ii 609–12; Bureaucracy iii 71 a; Centralization iii 310 b; Chemical Industries iii 366 a; Civil Service iii 517 b; Codification iii 610 b; Commissions iv 38 b; Common Sense iv 61 a; Customs Duties iv 670 b; Diplomacy v 152 b; Expert Testimony vi 13–16; Federal Trade Commission vi 165–69; Functional Representation vi 520 b; Gosplan vi 709 a; International Advisers viii 155–59; Judiciary viii 467 b; Labor, Govt. Services for viii 652 a; Labor Movement viii 686 a; Politics xii 226 b; Professions xii 476–80; Specialization xiv 281 b.
EXPERT TESTIMONY—vi 13–16; Insanity viii 65 a; Medical Jurisprudence x 274–79; Valuation xv 213 b.
EXPLOITATION—vi 16–17; Distribution v 170 a; Economics (Socialist Economics) v 378 a; Imperialism vii 606 a; Interest viii 133 a; Labor Exchange Banks viii 637 a.

Exploration—Introd. Vol. I (Renaissance and Reformation) i 87 b, (The Rise of Liberalism) 104 a.
EXPORT ASSOCIATIONS—vi 17–19.
EXPORT CREDITS — vi 19–21; Credit Insurance iv 559 b; Farm Relief vi 117 a.
EXPORT DUTIES—vi 21–23; Customs Duties iv 667 b; Raw Materials xiii 129 b.
Export Rebate—see DRAWBACK.
Exports — see INTERNATIONAL TRADE.
EXPOSITIONS, INTERNATIONAL— vi 23–27; Art (Modern) ii 255 a, 256 b; Fairs vi 58 b; Museums and Exhibitions xi 139 b.
Ex Post Facto Laws—see RETROACTIVE LEGISLATION.
Exposure—Introd. Vol. I (Greek Culture and Thought) i 25 b; Infanticide viii 27 b; Old Age xi 453 a.
EXPRESS COMPANIES—vi 27–31.
Express Trust—xv 125 b.
Expressionism—iii 544 b.
Expropriation—see EMINENT DOMAIN.
Extension Work, Academic—see UNIVERSITY EXTENSION.
EXTENSION WORK, AGRICULTURAL —vi 31–36; Agric. Education i 541 a; Agriculture, Govt. Services for i 602 a; Farm Bureau Federation, Amer. vi 105–06; Home Economics vii 429 a; Knapp viii 579 b.
EXTERRITORIALITY — vi 36–39; Asylum ii 289 b; Capitulations iii 213–15; Consular Service iv 279 b; Diplomacy v 148 b; Domicile v 209 b; Far Eastern Problem vi 94 b, 97 a; Immunity, Diplomatic vii 596 a; Segregation xiii 646 a.
EXTORTION—vi 39–41; Brigandage ii 694 b; Corruption, Political iv 448–55; Gifts vi 659 b; Racketeering xiii 45–50.
EXTRADITION—vi 41–44; Jurisdiction viii 476 a; Military Desertion x 452 a; Political Offenders xii 201 b.
Extravert—i 364 b.
EYTH, M.—vi 44.
EZPELETA, P. A. DE—vi 44.

FABBRONI, G.—vi 45.
Faber, A.—see FAVRE, A.
FABER FAMILY—vi 45.
FABIANISM—vi 46–49; Introd. Vol. I (The Social Sciences as Disciplines, Gt. Brit.) i 241 b; Class Struggle iii 539 b; Labor Parties viii 699 b; Reformism xiii 195 a; Socialism xiv 204 b.
Fact Finding Commissions—viii 257 a.
FACTION—vi 49–51; Insurgency, Political viii 113–16; Parties, Political xi 590 a.
Factory Acts—Labor, Govt. Services for viii 645 a; Labor Legislation and Law viii 658 a.

FACTORY SYSTEM—vi 51–55; Business iii 83 b; Continuous Industry iv 318–20; Garment Industries vi 574 a, 576 b; Gott vii 4 b; Handicraft vii 258 a; Hours of Labor vii 479 b; Industrial Relations vii 710 b; Industrial Revolution viii 3–13; Industrialism viii 18–26; Labor viii 619 b; Labor, Govt. Services for viii 645 a; Large Scale Production ix 173 b; Leather Industries ix 307 a; Occupation xi 427 b; Scientific Management xiii 603–08; Specialization xiv 281 b; Temperance Movements xiv 568 a; Textile Industry xiv 591 a.
FAHLBECK, P. E.—vi 55.
FAIDHERBE, L. L. C.—vi 55.
FAIR RETURN—vi 56–58; Municipal Transit xi 119 a; Profit xii 480–87; Rate Regulation xiii 108 b, 110 a; Valuation xv 216 b.
Fair Value—see VALUATION.
Fairhope, Alabama—iv 101 a.
FAIRS—vi 58–64; Agric. Fairs i 544–45; Agric. Marketing i 559 b; Banking, Commercial ii 425 a; Bill of Exchange ii 540 b; Expositions, International vi 23–27; Law Merchant ix 272 b; Marketing x 135 a; Mercantile Credit x 329 a.
Fairs, Agricultural—see AGRICULTURAL FAIRS.
Faisal, King of Iraq—Near Eastern Problem xi 326 a.
Falconer, H.—ii 648 a.
FALLMERAYER, J. P.—vi 64.
Fallopius, G.—ii 560 b.
Fallow Field System—Agriculture i 576 a, 595 b.
FAMILY—vi 65–70. See relevant titles in Classification of Articles (Marriage and the Family), p. 553. See also Introd. Vol. I (Greek Culture and Thought) i 14 b; Animal Societies i 63–65; Anthropology ii 85 a; City-State iii 489 b; Culture iv 629 a; Education, Primitive v 401 a; Inheritance viii 43 a; Inheritance Taxation viii 46 a; Judaism viii 436 b; Land Tenure (E. Eur. and Near East) ix 99 b; Law (Chinese) ix 252 b, (Cuneiform) 215 a, (Hindu) 258 b, (Japanese) 256 a; Mothers' Pensions xi 53–57; Organization, Economic xi 487 a; Peasantry xii 48 b; Proletariat xii 513 b; Service xiii 672 b; Social Organization xiv 143 a; Social Work (Case Work) xiv 178 b.
FAMILY ALLOWANCES—vi 70–73; Allowance System ii 7; Mothers' Pensions xi 53–57; Social Insurance xiv 134–38.
FAMILY BUDGETS—vi 73–78; Consumption iv 295–301; Cost of Living iv 480 b; Davies v 11 a; Ducpétiaux v 264 b; Eden v 397 a; Engel v 540 a; Lavoisier ix 200 b; Le Play ix 412 a; Poverty xii 286 a; Social Surveys xiv 162 b; Tourville xiv 664 b; Wages xv 303 b.
FAMILY DESERTION AND NON-SUPPORT—vi 78–81.
Family Endowment—see FAMILY ALLOWANCES.
FAMILY LAW—vi 81–85; Adoption i 460–63; Alimony i 641–43; Breach of Marriage Promise ii 688–89; Common Law Marriage iv 56–58; Concubinage iv 173 a; Conflict of Laws iv 192 a; Domestic Relations Courts v 194–98; Family Desertion and Non-support vi 79 b; Guardianship vii 192–95; Illegitimacy vii 582–86; Law (Celtic) ix 248 a, (Chinese) 252 b, (Cuneiform) 215 b, (Germanic) 236 a, (Hellenistic and Greco-Egyptian) 231 b, (Hindu) 258 b, (Japanese) 256 a, (Jewish) 223 a, (Slavic) 243 a; Marital Property x 116–22; Seduction xiii 639–41; Woman, Position in Society xv 449 a.
FAMINE—vi 85–89; Disasters and Disaster Relief v 161–66.
FANATICISM—vi 90–92; Intolerance viii 242–45.
FAR EASTERN PROBLEM—vi 92–100; Chinese Problem iii 431–36; Europeanization v 633 a; Govt. (China) vii 98–100, (Japan) 95–98; Imperialism vii 611 a; Industrial Revolution viii 10 a; League of Nations ix 293 a; Manchurian Problem x 80–84; Open Door xi 468–71; Opium Problem xi 471–76; Pan-movements xi 552 b; Philippine Problem xii 114 a; Raffles xiii 69 a; Recognition, International xiii 167 a; Russian Revolution xiii 485 a; Spheres of Influence xiv 297–99.
FĀRĀBĪ, AL-—vi 100.
FARM—vi 101–03; Agriculture (U. S.) i 586 b; Dry Farming v 255 b; Farm Management vi 111–14; Farm Tenancy vi 118–27; Frontier vi 501 a.
FARM BLOC, U. S.—vi 103–05; Agrarian Movements (U. S.) i 511 a; Bloc, Parliamentary ii 592.
FARM BUREAU FEDERATION, AMERICAN—vi 105–06; Agric. Cooperation i 525 a.
Farm Colony—ix 596 b.
Farm Costs—see FARM MANAGEMENT.
FARM LOAN SYSTEM, FEDERAL— vi 106–11; Agric. Credit i 533 a; Agriculture, Govt. Services for i 603 b; Land Mortgage Credit (Agric.) ix 48 a.
FARM MANAGEMENT—vi 111–14; Agric. Economics i 534–38; Agric. Education i 538–42; Agriculture i 597 a; Extension Work, Agric. vi 34 b; Family Budgets vi 76 b.

FARM RELIEF—vi 114–18; Farm Bloc, U. S. vi 103–05; Farm Loan System, Federal vi 106–11.
FARM TENANCY—vi 118–27; Introd. Vol. I (The Roman World) i 56 b; Agrarian Movements i 492–515; Agriculture (Eng.) i 578 a, (Japan) 591 b, (U. S.) 588 a; Colonate iii 639–41; Cotton iv 489 a; Enclosures v 524 a; Farm vi 101 b, 102 a; Fruit and Vegetable Industry vi 510 b; Irish Question viii 286 b; Land Tenure ix 73–127; Landlord and Tenant ix 143–48; Negro Problem xi 341 b; Peasantry xii 48–53.
Farmer-Labor Party, U. S.—Labor Parties (U. S.) viii 707 a; Parties, Political (U. S.) xi 599 b.
FARMERS' ALLIANCE—vi 127–29; Agric. Cooperation (U. S.) i 524 b; Farmers' Union vi 132 a; Free Silver vi 438 b.
Farmers' Institutes—Agriculture, Govt. Services for i 602 a; Extension Work, Agric. vi 32 a.
FARMERS' ORGANIZATIONS — vi 129–32; Agrarian Syndicalism i 515–16; Agric. Cooperation i 521–29; Agric. Societies i 570–71; Chambers of Agriculture iii 323–25; Extension Work, Agric. vi 33 b; Farm Bureau Federation, Amer. vi 105–06; Farmers' Alliance vi 127–29; Farmers' Union vi 132–33; Grange vii 150–51; Kelley viii 555 b.
FARMERS' UNION—vi 132–33; Agric. Cooperation (U. S.) i 525 a.
FARR, W.—vi 133.
FASCISM—vi 133–39; Introd. Vol. I (The Social Sciences as Disciplines, Italy) i 277 b; Civil Liberties iii 512 b; Democracy v 83 a; Economic Policy v 342 a; Force, Political vi 341 a; Functional Representation vi 521 a; Functionalism vi 525 a; Govt. (Italy) vii 51 a; Idealism vii 571 b; Ku Klux Klan viii 608 b; Labor Movement viii 691 a; Leadership ix 286 b; Matteotti x 230 b; National Economic Planning xi 202 a; National Socialism, German xi 224–27; Parties, Political xi 594 a, (Japan) 635 a; Romanticism xiii 433 a; Russian Revolution xiii 490 b; Sorel xiv 263 a; State xiv 330 b; Trade Unions xv 6 b, (Italy) 31 a, (Sweden) 20 b; Women in Industry xv 452 b; Youth Movements xv 519 a. See also Fascist Italy.
Fascist Italy—Introd. Vol. I (The Social Sciences as Disciplines, Italy) i 277 a; Administration, Public i 444 a; Agrarian Syndicalism i 516 a; Agric. Policy i 567 a; Amnesty ii 38 b; Arbitration, Industrial ii 154 b; Banking, Commercial ii 441 b; Cooperation iv 381 b, 382 b; Courts, Industrial iv 538 a; Employers' Associations v 511 a; Fascism vi 133–39; Functional Representation vi 521 a; Govt. (Italy) vii 51 a; Industrial Relations vii 716 a; Labor, Govt. Services for viii 650 b; Labor Movement viii 691 a; Learned Societies ix 297 b; Literacy and Illiteracy ix 521 b; Local Govt. ix 582 a; Mafia x 38 a; Merchant Marine x 349 a; Militarism x 450 a; Militia x 473 a; Motion Pictures xi 67 b; Municipal Finance xi 102 a; Municipal Govt. xi 111 a; Press xii 332 a; Regional Planning xiii 207 b; Representation xiii 312 b; Teaching Profession xiv 545 b; Trade Associations xiv 672 a; Trade Unions xv 32 a. See also FASCISM.
FASHION—vi 139–44; Clubs iii 576 a; Custom iv 659 a; Dress v 237 a; Luxury ix 635 a.
FASTING—vi 144–46; Holidays vii 413 a; Hunger Strike vii 552–55.
FATALISM—vi 146–48.
FATIGUE—vi 148–51; Absenteeism i 379 b; Accidents, Industrial i 399 a; Hours of Labor vii 491 a.
FAUCHER, J.—vi 151.
FAUCHILLE, P.—vi 152.
FAVRE, A.—vi 152.
FAWCETT, H.—vi 153.
FAWCETT, M. G.—vi 153.
Febronius, J.—see HONTHEIM, J. N. VON.
FECHNER, G. T.—vi 154; Behaviorism ii 496 b; Psychology xii 591 b.
Feder, G. — Labor Exchange Banks viii 643 a; National Socialism, German xi 225 b.
Federal Home Loan Banks—ix 52 b.
Federal Intermediate Credit Banks—iii 277 a.
Federal Radio Commission—xiii 58 b, 59 b, 63 a.
FEDERAL RESERVE SYSTEM—vi 154–65; Acceptance i 388 b; Agric. Credit i 533 a; Bank Reserves ii 420 a; Banking, Commercial ii 444 b; Branch Banking ii 680 a; Brokers' Loans iii 11 a, 12 b; Call Money iii 150 b; Cattle Loans iii 277 a; Central Banking iii 302–08; Clearing Houses iii 547 b; Credit Control iv 551 b; Export Credits vi 20 b; Financial Administration vi 240 a; Foreign Exchange vi 360 b; National Banks, U. S. xi 186–89; State Banks, U. S. xiv 333 b; War Finance xv 353 a.
FEDERAL TRADE COMMISSION—vi 165–69; Advertising i 473 a; Bargaining Power ii 462 a; Business Ethics iii 111 b; Business, Govt. Services for iii 119 a; Cut-Throat Competition iv 679 b; Trusts xv 118 a.
FEDERALISM—vi 169–72. See FEDERATION.
Federalist Party, U. S.—Agrarian Movements i 509 a; Parties, Political xi 597 b.
FEDERATION—vi 172–78; Introd. Vol. I (The Roman World) i 43 b; Articles of Confederation ii 262–63; Bicameral System ii 534 b; Bundesrat iii 65–67; Central American Federation iii 301–02; Centralization iii 309 b; Citizenship iii 473 a; Compacts, Interstate iv 109–13; Concurrent Powers iv 173–74; Constitutional Law iv 248 a; Dominion Status v 213 a; Double Jeopardy v 223 b; Double Taxation v 225 b; Education (Public) v 419 a; Extradition vi 43 b; Federalism vi 169–72; Foreign Corporations vi 354 a; Full Faith and Credit Clause vi 515–17; Govt. (Australia) vii 30 b, (Canada) 27 a, (Germany) 53 b, (Lat. Amer.) 91 b, (Russia, Soviet) 67 b, (Switzerland) 57 a, (U. S.) 15 a; Imperialism vii 605 b; Indian Question vii 671 a; International Organization viii 182 b; Interstate Commerce viii 220–29; Judicial Review viii 462 b; Labor Legislation and Law viii 664 b; Legislation ix 349 b; Metropolitan Areas x 398 b, 400 b; Popular Sovereignty xii 239–40; Regionalism xiii 208–18; Revenues, Public xiii 363 a; State Govt., U. S. xiv 335–38; States' Rights xiv 346–50; Supreme Court, U. S. xiv 474 b; Tax Administration xiv 528 a.
Fédération Aéronautique Internationale—ii 344 a.
Fédération Jurassienne—ii 51 b.
FEE SPLITTING—vi 178–79.
Fee Tail—see ENTAIL.
FEIJÓO Y MONTENEGRO, B. J.—vi 179.
Félibrige—xiii 210 b.
FELLENBERG, P. E. VON—vi 180.
Fellow Servant Doctrine—v 515 a.
Fellowship of the New Life—v 10 b.
FELS, J.—vi 180.
Feminism—Birth Control ii 563 a; Divorce v 184 a; Equality v 578 a; Family vi 68 b; Woman, Position in Society xv 445 a; Women's Organizations xv 460–65. See also WOMAN, POSITION IN SOCIETY. For biog. references see Classification of Articles (Feminism), p. 561.
FÉNELON, F. DE S. DE LA M.—vi 181; Introd. Vol. I (The Rise of Liberalism) i 117 a; Balance of Power ii 396 a.
Fenians—viii 291 a.
FÉNYES, E. C.—vi 182.
Feoffee to Uses—xv 123 a.
FERDINAND V AND ISABELLA—vi 183.

Ferdinand of Naples—iii 222 a.
Ferguson, A.—vi 184.
Fernald, W. E.—vi 184.
Fernández Navarrete, P.—vi 185.
Fernow, B. E.—vi 185.
Ferrara, F.—vi 186; Introd. Vol. I (The Social Sciences as Disciplines, Italy) i 275 b.
Ferrari, G.—vi 186.
Ferraris, C. F.—vi 187.
Ferreira Borges, J.—vi 187.
Ferreira, S. P.—see Pinheiro Ferreira, S.
Ferrero, G. L.—iv 587 a.
Ferri, E.—vi 188; Criminology iv 585 b, 588 b; Labor Movement viii 690 b.
Ferrini, C.—vi 189.
Ferry, J. F. C.—vi 189.
Fertility Rites—vi 190–92; Fasting vi 144 b; Mysteries xi 172 b.
Fertilizer Industry—vi 193–98; Liebig ix 454 a; Nitrates xi 379 b; Potash xii 274–77.
Festivals—vi 198–201; Calendar iii 140–44; Fertility Rites vi 191 a; Holidays vii 413 a.
Fetishism—vi 201–02; Idolatry vii 575–77.
Fetter, F. A.—x 628 b.
Feudalism—vi 203–20 (Europ. 203–10, 219, Saracen and Ottoman 210–13, 219, Chinese 213–14, 219, Japanese 214–20); Introd. Vol. I (The Universal Church) i 65 a, (The Growth of Autonomy) 74 a; Agrarian Movements i 495–504; Agriculture (Japan) i 591 a; Aids i 608 a; Alienation of Property i 639 b; Allegiance i 644 a; Appanage ii 130–31; Armed Forces, Control of ii 200 a; Army ii 210 b; Aubaine, Right of ii 307–08; Bail ii 386 b; Charlemagne iii 345 b; Chivalry (Europ.) iii 436–41; Civil Law iii 504 a; Civil Service iii 516 a; Class iii 533 b; Commune, Mediaeval iv 61–63; Confiscation iv 184 a; Conflict of Laws iv 188 a; Corvée iv 456 a; Courts iv 520 a; Crusades iv 614–17; Customary Law iv 664 a; Entail v 553 b; Escheat v 591 b; Farm Tenancy vi 119 a; Freehold vi 461–65; French Revolution vi 471 b; Game Laws vi 562 a; Govt. vii 11 a, (Japan) 95 b; Govt. Regulation of Industry vii 123 a; Guardianship vii 193 b; Guilds (Europ.) vii 210 a, (Japanese) 221 a; Henry IV vii 322 a; Kido viii 564 b; Labor viii 617 b; Land Tenure ix 82–99, 100 a, 107 a, 117 b; Land Transfer ix 129 a; Law (Cuneiform) ix 214 a; Legislative Assemblies ix 356 b, 369 a; Literacy and Illiteracy ix 514 a; Loans, Personal ix 562 b; Manorial System x 97–102; Mortmain xi 41 a; Municipal Courts xi 94 b; Music xi 158 a; Nobility xi 387 a; Pavlov-Silvansky xii 32 b; Peasantry xii 49 a; Political Offenders xii 200 b; Primogeniture xii 403 a; Property xii 533 b; Public Domain xii 615 b, 618 a; Religious Institutions (Roman Catholic) xiii 255 a; Rent Charge xiii 292; Serfdom xiii 667 b; Society xiv 226 b; State xiv 329 b; Status xiv 375 b; Woman, Position in Society xv 444 a.
Feuds—vi 220–21; Blood Vengeance Feud ii 598–99; Gangs vi 565 b; Law (Germanic) ix 237 a.
Feuerbach, L. A.—vi 221; Anarchism ii 48 a; Freethinkers vi 468 b; Grün vii 189 a.
Feuerbach, P. J. A. von—vi 222.
Fichte, J. G.—vi 223; Kant viii 540 b; Socialism xiv 196 a; Sociology xiv 235 b.
Ficker, C. J. von—vi 225.
Fictions—vi 225–28; Myth xi 178–81; Political Science xii 221 a; Social Organism xiv 138–41; Tradition xv 62–67; Utopia xv 200–03.
Fideicommissum—v 553 a.
Fidelity Insurance—ii 632 b.
Fiduciary Bonds—ii 633 a.
Field, C. W.—xiv 561 b.
Field, D. D.—vi 228; Codification iii 609 b; Pomeroy xii 230 a.
Field, M.—vi 229.
Fielding, W. S.—vi 229.
Fifth-Monarchy Men—Sects xiii 627 b.
Figgis, J. N.—vi 230; Pluralism xii 171 b, 172 b.
Filangieri, G.—vi 231; Introd. Vol. I (The Revolutions) i 137 b.
Filene, E. A.—iv 395 a.
Filibuster, Legislative—iii 572 a.
Filibustering—vi 231–33.
Filmer, R.—vi 233; Sidney xiv 49 b.
Filosofova, A. P.—vi 234.
Filtration — Water Supply xv 375 b.
Finance Companies—Investment Banking viii 270 b; Investment Trusts viii 280 a.
Finance, Public—see Public Finance.
Financial Administration—vi 234–41; Assessment of Taxes ii 276–79; Auditing i 312–13; Budget iii 38–44; Expenditures, Public vi 5–10; Federal Reserve System vi 154–65; Gosplan vi 711 a; Local Finance ix 568–74; Public Finance xii 637–46; Revenue Farming xiii 358–60; Revenues, Public xiii 360–63; Sinking Fund xiv 67–69; Tax Administration xiv 526–28; Taxation xiv 531–41. For biog. references see Classification of Articles (Financial Administration), p. 561.
Financial Organization — vi 241–47; Banking, Commercial ii 421–47; Credit iv 545–50; Credit Control iv 550–53; Credit Cooperation iv 553–57; Debt v 32–39; Federal Reserve System vi 154–65; Foreign Exchange vi 358–64; Investment viii 263–68; Investment Banking viii 268–77; Investment Trusts viii 277–84; Land Mortgage Credit ix 43–53; Loans, Personal ix 561–65; Mobilization and Demobilization x 561 a; Money x 601–13; Money Market x 613–18; Municipal Finance xi 101 a; National Banks, U. S. xi 186–89; Savings Banks xiii 552–58; Stock Exchange xiv 397–402; Trust Companies xv 109–11.
Financial Statements—vi 247–49.
Finch, H. — see Nottingham, Lord.
Finckelhaus, J.—see Finot, J.
Finer, H.—xiii 217 a.
Fines—vi 249–52.
Fink, A.—vi 252.
Finlay, G.—vi 253.
Finley, R.—vi 253.
Finney, C. G.—xiii 365 b.
Finot, J.—vi 254.
Fiore, P.—vi 254.
Fire, Discovery of—ii 80 b.
Fire Insurance—vi 255–62; Agric. Insurance i 546 b.
Fire Protection—vi 262–66; Building Regulations iii 52–57; Fire Insurance vi 259 a; Water Supply xv 374 a.
First International—Anarchism ii 51 a; Bakunin ii 394 a; General Strike vi 608 a; Marx x 174 a; Socialist Parties xiv 213 b.
Fiscal Science—vi 266; Public Finance xii 637 b, 641 b.
Fischer, E.—ii 111 b.
Fisher, I.—Distribution v 171 b; Income vii 624 b; Index Numbers vii 654 a, 655 a, 656 a; Interest viii 141 a; Money x 609 b; Price Stabilization xii 364 b.
Fisher, R. A.—vi 486 b, 488 a.
Fisheries—vi 266–70; Business, Govt. Services for iii 119 b; Conservation iv 227–30.
Fisk, J., Jr.—vi 270.
Fiske, J.—vi 271; History and Historiography vii 387 b.
Fison, L.—vi 272.
Fitting, H. H.—vi 272.
Fitzherbert, A.—vii 321 a.
Fitzherbert, J.—vi 273; Agriculture i 579 a.
Fitzhugh, G.—vi 273; Slavery xiv 90 a.
Five-Year Plan, Russian—vi 710 a.
Fixed Costs—Iron and Steel Industry viii 308 a; Price Discrimination xii 353 b.
Flach, J.—vi 274.
Flacius, M. (Illyricus)—x 38 a.
Flax, Hemp and Jute—vi 274–79.

Index (Ferdinand of Naples — France, A.)

Fleetwood, W.—vi 279.
Fleming, S.—vi 280.
Fleury, A. H. de—vi 280.
Fliedner, T.—xi 406 a.
Flint, R.—vi 281.
Flood, H.—vi 282.
Floods and Flood Control—vi 282–85; Disasters and Disaster Relief v 161–66; Irrigation viii 328 b; Waterways, Inland xv 383 a.
Flop House—ix 596 a.
Flores de Lemus, A.—i 299 b.
Flórez Estrada, A.—vi 285.
Floridablanca, Conde de—vi 285.
Flourens, J. P. M.—xii 590 b.
Folk High Schools—vi 286–88; Adult Education i 464 a; Agrarian Movements (Denmark) i 501 b; Bruun iii 21 b; Education (Part Time) v 426 b; Grundtvig vii 190 a; University Extension xv 188 b.
Folk Psychology—xiv 153 a.
Folketing—ix 388 a.
Folklore—vi 288–93; Gomme vi 696 b; Hero Worship vii 336 b; Literature ix 526 b; Myth xi 178–81; Sacred Books xiii 498 a.
Folkmoot—Government vii 11 a; Legislative Assemblies ix 356 b.
Folkways—vi 293–96; Ceremony iii 313–16; Conventions, Social iv 351–53; Custom iv 658–62; Démeunier v 76 a; Ethnocentrism v 613 a; Institution viii 84–89; Morals x 643–49; Pressures, Social xii 346 b; Sumner xiv 464 a.
Follen, C.—xii 131 b.
Follett, M. P.—Introd. Vol. i (War and Reorientation) i 207 a; Pluralism xii 172 b.
Fontanella, J. P.—vi 296.
Fontenelle, B. le B. de—vi 296.
Food Distribution—Food Industries vi 311–32; Markets, Municipal x 139–44.
Food and Drug Regulation—vi 297–301; Adulteration i 466–68; Assizes ii 283 b; Canning Industry iii 177 a; Consumer Protection iv 283 b; Drug Addiction v 249 a; Food Industries (Baking, Eur.) vi 303 b, (Baking, U. S.) 307 b; Grading vii 134 b; Medical Materials Industry x 279 b; Milk Supply x 475–80; Opium Problem xi 471–76.
Food Grains—see Grains.
Food Industries—vi 301–32 (Introd. 301–03, Baking, Eur. 303–05, 330, U. S. 305–07, 330, Beverages 307–09, 330, Confectionery 309–11, 330, Grocery Trade 311–15, 330, Food Distribution, U. S. 315–20, 331, W. Eur. 320–23, 331, Russia 323–30, 332). See Classification of Articles (Food and Drink), p. 551.

Food Supply—vi 332–38. See Classification of Articles (Food and Drink), p. 551. See also Anthropology ii 79 b; Commerce iv 10 b; International Trade viii 191 b; Irrigation viii 328–32; Migrations x 421 a; Soils xiv 250–54; War Economics xv 345 a.
Forbonnais, F. V. D. de—vi 338.
Force, Political—vi 338–41; Fascism vi 136 a; General Strike vi 607–12; Intolerance viii 243 b; Obedience, Political xi 416 b; Political Offenders xii 199–203; Political Police xii 203–07; Power, Political xii 300–05; Praetorianism xii 305–07; Revolution and Counter-revolution xiii 367–76; Violence xv 264 b.
Forced Labor—vi 341–46; Backward Countries ii 381 a; Corvée iv 455–57; Imperialism vii 611 a; Indenture vii 644–48; Land Tenure (Ancient World) ix 78 a; Native Policy (Lat. Amer.) xi 253 b; Peonage xii 69–72; Prison Labor xii 416 a; Rubber xiii 454 a; Slavery xiv 80 b; Transportation of Criminals xv 90–93.
Forced Loans—vi 346–47.
Forceful Blow—Action Française i 424 b.
Ford, H.—Antisemitism ii 124 b; Hours of Labor vii 492 b.
Ford, H. J.—vi 348.
Ford Motor Co.—ii 323 b.
Forecasting, Business—vi 348–54; Correlation iv 443 b; Crop and Livestock Reporting iv 609 b; Production xii 467–72.
Foreign Advisers—see International Advisers.
Foreign Corporations—vi 354–58; Full Faith and Credit Clause vi 516 b; Holding Companies vii 406 a.
Foreign Exchange—vi 358–64; Agio i 487; Arbitrage ii 150–51; Balance of Trade ii 403 b; Bimetallism and Monometallism ii 547 b; Bullionists iii 62 a; Dumping v 277 b; Goschen vi 705 b; Hedging vii 306 a; Inflation and Deflation viii 30 b; Monetary Stabilization x 591–95; Monetary Unions x 595–601; Paper Money xi 569 b.
Foreign Investment—vi 364–78; Backward Countries ii 381 a; Balance of Trade ii 403 b; Calvo and Drago Doctrines iii 153–56; Cement iii 287 b; Colonial Economic Policy iii 650 a; Colonies iii 659 b; Concessions iv 154–60; Double Taxation v 224 a; Electric Power v 466 b; Far Eastern Problem vi 92–100; Imperialism vii 610 a; Industrialism viii 21 b; International Advisers viii 156 a; International Finance viii 159–64; International Trade viii 191 a, 192 b; Investment Banking viii 276 a; Investment Trusts viii 281 b; Loans, Intergovernmental ix 559 a; Philippine Problem xii 113 a; Public Utilities xii 685 b; Raw Materials xiii 130 b; Repudiation of Public Debts xiii 323 b; Spheres of Influence xiv 298 b.
Foreign Language Press—vi 378–82.
Foreign Missions—x 541 b.
Foreign Policy — see International Relations.
Foreign Trade — see International Trade.
Forel, A. H.—vi 382.
Forensic Medicine—see Medical Jurisprudence.
Forests—vi 382–87; Conservation iv 227–30; Fernow vi 185 b; Fire Insurance vi 261 b; Floods and Flood Control vi 284 a; Game Laws vi 562 a; Land Utilization ix 134 b; Land Valuation ix 139 a; Lehr ix 399 a; Pulp and Paper Industry xii 711 a; Wood Industries xv 467 a, 470 b.
Forfeiture—Confiscation iv 184 b.
Forsman, G. Z.—see Yrjö-Koskinen, Y. S.
Forster, W. E.—vi 387.
Fortescue, J.—vi 388.
Fortunatov, A. F.—vi 388.
Fortunes, Private—vi 389–99; Inheritance viii 35–43; Inheritance Taxation viii 43–49; Landed Estates ix 140–43; Large Scale Production ix 178 b.
Foscolo, U.—vi 399.
Foster, W. A.—vi 400.
Foster, W. T.—Business Cycles iii 99 a; Price Stabilization xii 363 a.
Fouché, J.—vi 401.
Fouillée, A. J. É.—vi 401; Ardigò ii 181 b; Social Organism xiv 140 a.
Foundations—see Endowments and Foundations.
Four Doctors—vi 401; Glossators vi 680 b.
Four L.—Wood Industries xv 474 b.
Fourier and Fourierism—vi 402–04; Brisbane iii 5 a; Brook Farm iii 14 a; Channing iii 334 b; Communistic Settlements iv 99 b; Considérant iv 233 a; Cooperation iv 360 a; Godin vi 685 a; Socialism xiv 194 b.
Fournière, E.—vi 404.
Fourteenth Amendment—xiii 169 b.
Foville, A. de—vi 404; National Wealth xi 230 a.
Fowler, W. W.—vi 405.
Fox, C. J.—vi 405.
Fox, G.—vi 406; Quakers xiii 12 a.
Foy, W.—v 141 b.
Foynitsky, I. Y.—vi 407.
Fracastoro, G.—x 287 b.
France, A.—vi 407.

Franchise—see SUFFRAGE.
Franchises—Corporation iv 414 b; Licensing ix 447 a; Public Utilities xii 674-87.
FRANCIA, J. G. R.—vi 408.
Francis I—Balance of Power ii 395 b; Gallicanism vi 550 b.
Francis of Assisi—see FRANCISCAN MOVEMENT.
FRANCIS JOSEPH I—vi 408.
Francis, P.—vii 279 a.
FRANCIS XAVIER—vi 409.
FRANCISCAN MOVEMENT—vi 410-15; Charity iii 341 b; Dominican Friars v 210 a; Religious Institutions (Roman Catholic) xiii 252 a; Sabatier xiii 495 a.
FRANCK, S.—vi 415.
FRANCKE, A. H.—vi 416; Child (Welfare) iii 376 a; Preschool Education xii 320 b.
FRANCKE, E.—vi 416.
FRANCKE, J. P.—vi 417.
FRANK, L.—vi 417.
Frankalmoign—vi 461 a.
FRANKEL, L.—vi 418.
FRANKEL, Z.—vi 418.
Frankfurter Zeitung—xiv 257 b.
FRANKING—vi 419-20.
FRANKLIN, B.—vi 420; Articles of Confederation ii 262 a; Bicameral System ii 535 a; Child (Welfare) iii 376 a; Endowments and Foundations v 532 b.
FRANKO, I.—vi 422.
Frankpledge—xiv 482 a.
FRANTZ, K.—vi 422; Federalism vi 169 a.
Fraternal Insurance—see FRATERNAL ORDERS.
FRATERNAL ORDERS—vi 423-25; Friendly Societies vi 495 b; Insurance viii 100 a; Masonry x 177-84.
FRATERNIZING—vi 425-27.
FRAUD—vi 427-29; Adulteration i 466-68; Ad Valorem and Specific Duties i 468 b; Advertising i 473 a; Bankruptcy ii 453 a; Banks, Wildcat ii 455 a; Blue Sky Laws ii 602-05; Boom ii 639 b; Bucket Shops iii 30-31; Consumer Protection iv 282 b; Correspondence Schools iv 446 b; Corrupt Practises Acts iv 447-48; Debt v 37 b; Elections v 453 b; Food and Drug Regulation vi 297-301; Frauds, Statute of vi 429-30; Gambling vi 558 a; Judgments viii 446 a; Seduction xiii 640 b.
FRAUDS, STATUTE OF—vi 429-30; Contract iv 338 b.
Frazer, J. G.—x 40 a.
FREDERICK I—vi 430; Holy Roman Empire vii 424 a.
FREDERICK II—vi 430; Holy Roman Empire vii 424 b; Innocent III viii 57 b; Religious Institutions (Roman Catholic) xiii 255 b.
FREDERICK II (the Great)—vi 431; Holy Roman Empire vii 426 a; Military Training x 465 a.

FREDERICK WILLIAM—vi 432.
FREDERICK WILLIAM I—vi 433.
FREE LOVE—vi 433-36.
FREE PORTS AND FREE ZONES—vi 436-38; Transit, International xv 78 b.
FREE SILVER—vi 438-40; Agrarian Movements (U. S.) i 510 b; Silver xiv 57 b.
FREE TRADE—vi 440-47; Ad Valorem and Specific Duties i 468-69; Anti-Corn Law League ii 114-15; Bacalan ii 376 a; Bastiat ii 476 b; Commerce iv 11 a; Corn Laws iv 407 a; Customs Unions iv 675 a; Dormer v 219 b; Economics (Classical School) v 356 a; International Trade viii 194 b; Laissez Faire ix 18 b; Philippine Problem xii 113 b; Protection xii 561 b.
Freedom—see LIBERTY.
Freedom of Assembly—see ASSEMBLY, RIGHT OF.
FREEDOM OF ASSOCIATION—vi 447-50; Assembly, Right of ii 275-76; Association ii 284-86; Bargaining Power ii 460 a; Civil Service iii 521 a; Conspiracy, Criminal iv 236-38; Criminal Syndicalism iv 582-84; Labor Disputes viii 634 a; Labor Legislation and Law viii 673 b.
FREEDOM OF CONTRACT—vi 450-55; Bargaining Power ii 460 b; Competition iv 146 b; Constitutional Law iv 251 b; Labor Contract viii 630 a; Labor, Government Services for viii 648 b; Labor Legislation and Law viii 667 b; Police Power xii 192 a.
FREEDOM OF SPEECH AND OF THE PRESS—vi 455-59; Academic Freedom i 384-88; Alien and Sedition Acts i 635-36; Assembly, Right of ii 275-76; Blasphemy ii 586 a; Censorship iii 290-94; Contempt of Court iv 305 b; Criminal Syndicalism iv 582-84; Hetherington vii 343 b; Immunity, Political vii 597-600; Journalism viii 420 b; Libel and Slander ix 430-35; Press xii 326 a.
FREEDOM OF THE SEAS—vi 459-61; Armed Neutrality ii 203-04; Arms and Munitions Traffic ii 206-09; Blockade ii 594-96; Continuous Voyage iv 320-21; Merchantmen, Status of x 350 b; Navy xi 317 a.
FREEHOLD—vi 461-65; Land Tenure ix 73-127; Landlord and Tenant ix 144 b; Ownership and Possession xi 522 b.
FREEMAN, E. A.—vi 465.
Freemasons—see MASONRY.
FREETHINKERS—vi 465-71.
Freight Transportation—Motor Vehicle Transportation xi 75 b; Railroads xiii 85 b; Terminals xiv 572 a; Waterways, Inland xv 380 b.
Freiheit Weekly—xi 53 a.

French Civil Code—see CODE CIVIL.
French Confederation of Labor—see CONFÉDÉRATION GÉNÉRALE DU TRAVAIL.
FRENCH REVOLUTION—vi 471-83; Agrarian Movements i 497 b, 499 a; Alsace-Lorraine ii 10 b; Anticlericalism ii 112 b; Assignats ii 279-81; Aulard ii 316 a; Babouvism ii 375; Barère de Vieuzac ii 459 a; Barnave ii 463 b; Burke iii 75 b; Cachet, Lettre de iii 138 a; Cambon iii 157 a; Carlyle iii 229 b; Carnot iii 231 a; Catholic Parties iii 272 a; Civil Service iii 517 b; Cloots iii 568 b; Clubs, Political iii 577 b; Cochin iii 604 a; Condorcet iv 176; Conscription iv 221 a; Danton v 3 a; Declaration of the Rights of Man and the Citizen v 49-51; Desmoulins v 107 a; Economic History v 323 a; Education (Public) v 415 a; Encyclopédistes v 530 b; Estates General v 599 a; Freethinkers vi 466 b; Fréron vi 490 a; Gallicanism vi 551 b; Govt. (France) vii 44 a; Hébert vii 304 b; History and Historiography vii 378 a; Intellectuals viii 118 b; Jacobinism viii 360-63; Jewish Emancipation viii 396 a; Lafayette ix 11 a; Legal Profession and Legal Education ix 335 a; Liberalism ix 437 b; Mallet du Pan x 65 b; Marat x 107 a; Masonry x 182 b; Massacre x 193 a; Masses x 199 b; Mathiez x 228 a; Mobilization and Demobilization x 556 b; Modernism x 565 a; Montesquieu x 639 a; Mortmain xi 47 a; Napoleon I xi 182 b; Nationalism xi 243 a; Passport xii 14 b; Plebiscite xii 163 b; Political Offenders xii 201 a; Raynal xiii 134 b; Religious Freedom xiii 244 b; Religious Institutions (Roman Catholic) xiii 259 b; Republicanism xiii 319 b; Robespierre xiii 413 b; Roland de la Platière xiii 418 a; Rousseau xiii 446 b; Sieyès xiv 50 b; Sorel xiv 261 b; Soviet xiv 269 b; Stephens xiv 387 a; Stoicism xiv 409 b; Suffrage xiv 448 b; Tocqueville xiv 647 a; Vergniaud xv 238 b; Woman, Position in Society xv 445 a.
FRENEAU, P. M.—vi 483.
FREQUENCY DISTRIBUTION—vi 484-89; Average ii 336-38; National Income xi 219 b; Probability xii 433 a; Statistics xiv 370 a.
FRÉRET, N.—vi 489.
FRÉRON, É. C.—vi 489.
Fréron, S.-L.-M.—vi 490 a.
Freud, S.—Abnormal Psychology i 362 b, 363 b, 367 b; Character iii 336 b; Charcot iii 338 a; Genius vi 613 a; Incest vii 621 a; Magic x 43 a; Mental Dis-

Index (Franchise — Gauss)

orders x 315 a; Personality xii 87 a; Psychiatry xii 578 b; Psychoanalysis xii 581 a.
FREYCINET, C. DE—vi 490.
FREYTAG, G.—vi 490.
Friars—Monasticism x 588 a; Religious Orders xiii 278 a.
FRICK, H. C.—vi 491.
FRIED, A. H.—vi 492.
FRIEDBERG, E. A.—vi 492.
FRIEDJUNG, H.—vi 493.
FRIEDLÄNDER, L.—vi 493.
FRIEDLÄNDER, M.—vi 493.
Friedrich List Gesellschaft — i 263 b.
FRIENDLY SOCIETIES—vi 494–98; Benefits, Trade Union ii 513–16; Fraternal Orders vi 423 a; Health Insurance vii 296 a; Insurance viii 100 a; Life Insurance ix 463 a.
Fries, J. F.—Nelson xi 357 b; Psychology xii 590 b.
FRÖBEL, F.—vi 498; Child (Psychology) iii 391 b; Education v 413 b; Peabody xii 41 a; Preschool Education xii 321 b.
Frobenius, L.—ii 103 b.
Frohman, C.—xiv 613 a.
FROISSART, J.—vi 499; History and Historiography vii 373 a.
FRONTENAC, COMTE DE—vi 499.
FRONTIER—vi 500–06; Agriculture (U. S.) i 586 b; Boom ii 638 b; Boundaries ii 649–52; Brigandage ii 693 b; Cossacks iv 463–66; Fur Trade vi 531 b; Gangs vi 564 b; Homestead vii 436–41; Hunting vii 557 b; Justice of the Peace viii 526 b; Land Settlement ix 55 a; Lawlessness ix 278 b; Livestock Industry ix 547 a; Lynching ix 639 b; Migrations x 439 b; Militarism x 446 b; Nationalism xi 234 a; Native Policy (N. Amer.) xi 263 a; Pragmatism xii 307 b; Public Domain xii 618–23; Railroads xiii 75 a; Roads xiii 404 b; Turner xv 132 b.
FROUDE, J. A.—vi 506.
FRUIN, R. J.—vi 507.
FRUIT AND VEGETABLE INDUSTRY—vi 507–11; Agric. Cooperation (U. S.) i 525 b; Agric. Marketing (U. S.) i 563 a; Auctions ii 310 a; Food Industries (Russia) vi 328 a, (W. Eur.) 321 b; Keith viii 553 b; Refrigeration xiii 197 a.
Fruitlands—Alcott i 628 a; Transcendentalism xv 76 b.
FRY, E. G.—vi 511.
FUCHS, E.—vi 512.
Fueros—Civil Law iii 506 a; Customary Law iv 664 b.
FUETER, E.—vi 512.
FUGGER FAMILY—vi 513; Fortunes, Private vi 391 a; Loans, Personal ix 563 a.
FUKUZAWA, Y.—vi 514.
FULL FAITH AND CREDIT CLAUSE—vi 515–17; Conflict of Laws iv 193 b; Judgments viii 447 b.

FULLER, S. M.—vi 517; Transcendentalism xv 76 b.
FUNCTIONAL REPRESENTATION—vi 518–23; Introd. Vol. 1 (War and Reorientation) i 216 b; Bicameral System ii 536 a; Bloc, Parliamentary ii 592 a; Boards, Advisory ii 611 b; Chambers of Commerce iii 327 a; Functionalism vi 525 a; Guild Socialism vii 202–04; Interests viii 145 b; International Labor Organization viii 164 b; Legislative Assemblies ix 361 b; Lobby ix 567 b; Minority Rights x 526 b; National Economic Councils xi 192–97; Pluralism xii 170–74; Representation xiii 313 b; Soviet xiv 269–74.
FUNCTIONALISM — vi 523–26; Architecture ii 174 b; Behaviorism ii 496 b; Culture iv 625 a; Democracy v 83 b; Determinism v 114 a; Functional Representation vi 520 a; Furniture vi 538 b; Gestalt vi 642–46; Industrial Arts vii 689 b; Institution viii 89 a; Pragmatism xii 307–11; Psychology xii 593 a.
FUNDAMENTALISM—vi 526–27.
FUNERALS—vi 527–29.
FUNK, F. X. VON—vi 529.
FUOCO, F.—vi 530.
FUR TRADE AND INDUSTRY—vi 530–36; Astor ii 287 a; Auctions ii 310 b.
FURNITURE—vi 537–43; Industrial Arts vii 687 b.
FUSTEL DE COULANGES, N.-D.—vi 543; City-State iii 490 a; History and Historiography vii 378 a.

Gabelle—Salt xiii 523 b.
Gaelic Revival—viii 292 b.
Gaetani, B.—see BONIFACE VIII.
Gaëte, Duc de—see GAUDIN, M. M. C.
GAGERN, H. VON—vi 543.
GAIUS—vi 544.
GAJ, L.—vi 545; Karadžić viii 543 a.
GALES, J., JR.—vi 546.
GALIANI, F.—vi 546.
GALILEO GALILEI—vi 547; Astrology ii 288 a.
GALL, F. J.—vi 548; Criminal Law iv 578 a; Criminology iv 587 a; Psychology xii 590 a.
GALLATIN, A.—vi 549; Hamilton vii 253 a.
GALLICANISM—vi 550–52; Anticlericalism ii 112 b; Religious Institutions (Roman Catholic) xiii 259 a.
GALLIÉNI, J.-S.—vi 552; Native Policy xi 274 a.
GALLUPPI, P.—vi 552.
GALT, A. T.—vi 553.
GALTON, F.—vi 553; Correlation iv 443 a; Eugenics v 618 a; Genius vi 612 b, 613 b; Heredity vii 331 a, 333 b; Identification vii 573 b; Mental Tests x 323 a; Psychology xii 594 a.
GÁLVEZ, J. DE—vi 554.
GAMA BARROS, H. DE—vi 554.
GAMBETTA, L.—vi 555; Anticlericalism ii 114 a; Army ii 212 a.
GAMBLING—vi 555–62; Insurance viii 106 b; Lotteries ix 611–16; Speculation xiv 289 a, 290 a.
GAME LAWS—vi 562–64; Fur Trade and Industry vi 534 b; German Civil Code vi 635 b.
Games—see ATHLETICS.
Gamio, M.—xi 258 b.
Gandhi, Mahatma—Anarchism ii 50 a; Hunger Strike vii 554 b; Indian Question vii 667 b; Passive Resistance and Noncooperation xii 10 a, 13 a.
GANGS—vi 564–67; Camorra iii 161–62; Collective Behavior iii 632 a; Feuds vi 220 a; Intimidation viii 241 b; Liquor Industry ix 501 b; Mafia x 36–38; Racketeering xiii 46 b; Riot xiii 387 a.
GANIVET, A.—vi 567.
GANS, E.—vi 568.
GANTT, H. L.—vi 568; Scientific Management xiii 607 a.
Gantt Task and Bonus Formulae—viii 679 a.
GAPON, G. A.—vi 568.
GARCÍA MORENO, G.—vi 569.
GARDEN CITIES—vi 569–71; City and Town Planning iii 485 a; Housing (Eur.) vii 502 a.
GARDINER, S. R.—vi 571.
GARIBALDI, G.—vi 572.
GARMENT INDUSTRIES—vi 573–85; Conciliation, Industrial iv 167 b; Fashion vi 142 b; Fur Trade and Industry vi 535 a; Homework, Industrial vii 446 a; Labor-Capital Cooperation viii 628 b; Trade Agreements xiv 668 b.
GARNEAU, F. X.—vi 585.
GARNIER, G.—vi 585.
GARNIER, J. C.—vi 586.
Garofalo, R.—iv 586 a.
GARRETSON, A. B.—vi 586.
GARRISON, W. L.—vi 587; Abolition i 370 b; Birney ii 558 b.
Garton Foundation—xii 46 a.
Garvey, M.—Negro Problem xi 350 a; Pan-movements xi 549 b.
GARY, E. H.—vi 587.
GAS INDUSTRY—vi 588–94; Iron and Steel Industry viii 304 b; Public Utilities xii 674–87.
GASCA, P. DE LA—vi 594.
Gascoyne-Cecil, R. A. T.—see SALISBURY, LORD.
GASOLINE TAX—vi 595–96.
GASPARIN, COMTE DE—vi 596.
GATSCHET, A. S.—vi 597.
Gau—Land Tenure ix 83 b.
GAUDENZI, A.—vi 597.
GAUDIG, H.—vi 597.
GAUDIN, M. M. C.—vi 598.
Gauss, K. F.—Average ii 337 a; Frequency Distribution vi 480 a; Probability xii 429 b, 432 a.

Gavelkind—vi 462 b.
GEBHART, N. E.—vi 599.
Geddes, P.—i 237 b.
GEIGER, A.—vi 599; Judaism viii 439 a.
GEIJER, E. G.—vi 600.
GEISTESWISSENSCHAFTEN — vi 600–02; Introd. Vol. 1 (The Trend to Internationalism) i 184 a; Political Science xii 213 a.
GELASIUS I—vi 602.
Gemara—Law (Jewish) ix 222 a.
Gems—see PRECIOUS STONES.
General Average—Marine Insurance x 111 b; Maritime Law x 128 a.
General Electric Co.—Morgan Family xi 12 a; Radio xiii 55 a; Westinghouse xv 405 a.
General Federation of Trade Unions—xv 10 b.
General Federation of Women's Clubs—xv 461 b, 464 b.
General Motors Corp.—ii 325 a.
GENERAL PROPERTY TAX — vi 602–07; Assessment of Taxes ii 276–79; Double Taxation v 226 a; Income Tax vii 626 a, 636 a; Land Taxation ix 70 b; Local Finance ix 571 b; Mortgage Tax xi 38 a; Property Tax xii 538–41.
GENERAL STRIKE—vi 607–12; Antimilitarism ii 116 a; Benbow ii 509 b; Direct Action v 157 a; Passive Resistance and Noncooperation xii 12 b; Syndicalism xiv 497 b.
General Strike, 1926 — Labor Movement viii 688 b; Labor Parties (Gt. Brit.) viii 701 b.
General Will—Introd. Vol. 1 (The Revolutions) i 130 a; Absolutism i 381 a; Justice viii 511 b; Rousseau xiii 446 b; Social Contract xiv 130 b; Society xiv 230 a.
Geneva Convention—Atrocities ii 303 b; Red Cross xiii 182 a.
Genghis Khan—Introd. Vol. 1 (Renaissance and Reformation) i 85 a; Empire v 501 b.
GENIUS—vi 612–15; Aristocracy ii 187 b; Hero Worship vii 337 b; Maladjustment x 63 a; Mental Tests x 327 a.
GENOVESI, A.—vi 615; Introd. Vol. 1 (The Social Sciences as Disciplines, Italy) i 274 a.
Genteel Tradition—xii 307 b.
Gentile, G.—Fascism vi 138 a; Idealism vii 571 b; Teaching Profession xiv 545 b.
GENTILI, A.—vi 615; Neutrality xi 361 b.
GENTLEMAN, THEORY OF THE—vi 616–20; Aristocracy ii 188 b, 189 b.
GENTZ, F. VON—vi 620; Minority Rights x 525 b.
Gény, F.—xi 290 a.
GEOGRAPHY—vi 621–29 (Cultural 621–24, 629, Human 624–26, 629, Economic 626–29); Introd. Vol. 1 (What Are the Social Sciences?) i 7 a, (The Trend to Internationalism) 183 a, (War and Reorientation) 197 b, (The Social Sciences as Disciplines, Lat. Amer.) 309 b, (U. S.) 340 b; Adaptation i 436 b; Anthropology ii 98 b; Climate iii 556–62; Commercial Routes iv 19–24; Determinism v 112 b; Ecology, Human v 314–15; Economic History v 330 a; Environmentalism v 561–66; Frontier vi 500–06; Migrations x 421 b; Political Science xii 213 a; Sociology xiv 241 a. For biog. references see Classification of Articles (Geography), p. 561.
Geology—Evolution v 652 b; Lyell ix 639 a.
Geometric Mean—ii 338 a.
GEORGE III—vi 629.
GEORGE, H.—vi 630; Appreciation ii 143 b; Capitalization and Amortization of Taxes iii 211 b; Single Tax xiv 65 a; Unearned Increment xv 145 b.
Georgias of Leontini—xiv 259 b.
GERBER, K. F. W. VON—vi 631.
GERHOH OF REICHERSBERG—vi 632.
GERLACH, E. L. VON—vi 632.
GERLACH, O. A. J.—vi 633.
GERLAND, G.—vi 633.
GERMAN CIVIL CODE—vi 634–37; Civil Law iii 507 a; Codification iii 609 a, 610 b; Evidence v 648 a; Gierke vi 655 b; Illegitimacy vii 583 b; Legal Profession and Legal Education ix 335 b; Leonhard ix 410 a; Lien ix 458 a; Marital Property x 121 a; Menger x 310 b; Mortgage xi 36 b; Negligence xi 330 a; Planck xii 147 a; Windscheid xv 429 a.
German National Socialism—see NATIONAL SOCIALISM, GERMAN.
Germanic Law—Andlo ii 56 b; Beseler ii 529 a; Beyer ii 532 b; Brunner iii 19 b; Child (Delinquent) iii 407 a; Civil Law iii 506 a; Common Law iv 51 b; Conring iv 209 b; Eichhorn v 446 b; Family Law vi 82 a; Homeyer vii 449 b; Judgments viii 443 b; Land Transfer ix 128 b; Landlord and Tenant ix 146 a; Law ix 235–39; Law Merchant ix 272 b; Legal Profession and Legal Education ix 335 b; Lese Majesty ix 415 b; Mining Law x 515 b; Negligence xi 328 b; Procedure, Legal xii 442 a; Repgow xiii 309 a; Rule of Law xiii 463 b; Schröder xiii 584 b; Schwarzenberg xiii 588 b; Sohm xiv 250 a; Struve xiv 427 a; Succession, Laws of xiv 437 a; Treason xv 93 b.
GERONTOCRACY—vi 637–38.
GERRYMANDER—vi 638–39; Apportionment ii 139 b; Majority Rule x 58 a.
GERSHUNI, G. A.—vi 639.
GERSON, J.—vi 639; Introd. Vol. 1 (The Growth of Autonomy) i 82 b; Conciliar Movement iv 161 a.
Gertzenstein, M. Y.—see HERTZENSTEIN, M. Y.
GERVINUS, G. G.—vi 640.
GESELL, S.—vi 641; Labor Exchange Banks viii 643 a.
Gesetzbuch—see GERMAN CIVIL CODE.
GESHOV, I. E.—vi 641.
GESNER, J. M.—vi 642.
GESTALT—vi 642–46; Introd. Vol. 1 (War and Reorientation) i 197 b; Consciousness iv 216 a; Educational Psych. v 434 a.
Gesture—Communication iv 78 b.
GHAZZĀLĪ, AL—vi 646.
Ghent Plan—Unemployment Insurance xv 164 a.
GHETTO—vi 646–50; Alien i 633 b; Antisemitism ii 120 b; Ethnic Communities v 611 b; Jewish Autonomy viii 391–94; Segregation xiii 644 a.
GIANNI, F. M.—vi 650.
GIANNONE, P.—vi 651.
GIANNOTTI, D.—vi 652.
GIBBINS, H. DE B.—vi 652.
GIBBON, E.—vi 653; Introd. Vol. 1 (The Rise of Liberalism) i 120 b.
Gibrat, R.—xi 220 b.
GIBSON, J. B.—vi 654.
GIDDINGS, F. H.—vi 654; Accommodation i 403 a.
GIERKE, O. VON—vi 655; Beseler ii 529 b; Minority Rights x 525 b; Pluralism xii 171 a, 172 a; Public Law xii 659 a.
GIESELER, J. K. L.—vi 656.
GIESSWEIN, S.—vi 656.
GIFFEN, R.—vi 656.
Gift Tax—see INHERITANCE TAXATION.
GIFTS—vi 657–61; National Income xi 208 b.
GILBART, J. W.—vi 661.
Gilbert, J. H.—vi 193 b.
GILBERT, T.—vi 661.
GILBRETH, F. B.—vi 661; Scientific Management xiii 607 a.
Gilchrist, P. C.—viii 302 a.
Gill, C. A.—v 570 b.
GILMAN, D. C.—vi 662.
GINER DE LOS RÍOS, F.—vi 662; Introd. Vol. 1 (The Social Sciences as Disciplines, Spain) i 297 b.
Gini, C.—xi 220 b.
GINN, E.—vi 663.
GINSBERG, A.—vi 663.
GIOBERTI, V.—vi 664; Pius IX xii 142 b.
GIOIA, M.—vi 665.
GIOLITTI, G.—vi 665.
GIRARD, J.-B.—vi 666.
GIRARD, P. F.—vi 667.
GIRARDIN, É. DE—vi 667; Labor Exchange Banks viii 641 a.
GIRDLESTONE, E.—vi 668.
Girl Scouts—ii 667 b.
Girondists—Brissot de Warville iii 6 b; French Revolution vi 476 b; Marat x 107 b.

Index (Gavelkind — Government Publications)

Giry, A.—vi 668.
Giusti, G.—vi 669.
Gladstone, W. E.—vi 669; Free Trade vi 444 b; Irish Question viii 291 b.
Glands—i 365 a.
Glanvill, R. de—vi 670.
Glaser, J.—vi 670.
Glasier, J. B.—vi 671.
Glass and Pottery Industries—vi 671–78; Industrial Arts vii 687 a; Pottery xii 279–84.
Glasson, E. D.—vi 678.
Gleason, A. H.—vi 679.
Glenesk, Lord—see Borthwick, A.
Glossators—vi 679–82; Accursius i 418 b; Azo ii 372 b; Civil Law iii 505 a; Commentators iii 679 b; Fitting vi 272 b; Four Doctors vi 401 b; Irnerius viii 295 a; Jurisprudence viii 479 b; Legal Profession and Legal Education ix 329 a; Vacarius xv 204 a.
Glove Industry—ix 312 a.
Gneist, R. von—vi 682.
Gnosticism—x 585 a.
Gobineau, J. A. de—vi 683; Aryans ii 265 a.
Goblet d'Alviella, E. F. A.—vi 684.
Goddard, H. H.—x 312 b.
Godefroy, D. and J.—vi 684.
Godin, J. B. A.—vi 685.
Godkin, E. L.—vi 685.
Godwin, M. W.—see Wollstonecraft, M.
Godwin, W.—vi 686; Introd. Vol. I (The Revolutions) i 134 b; Anarchism ii 48 a; Passive Resistance and Non-cooperation xii 12 a; Social Psychology xiv 152 b; Wallace xv 326 b; Wollstonecraft xv 436 b.
Goethe, J. W.—vi 686; Möser xi 51 b; Romanticism xiii 429 a; Theater xiv 609 b; Traditionalism xv 68 b.
Gök Alp, Z.—vi 687.
Gokhale, G. K.—vi 688.
Gold—vi 689–93; Bimetallism and Monometallism ii 546–49; Coinage iii 622 b; Compensated Dollar iv 134–35; Credit Control iv 550–53; Foreign Exchange vi 361 a; Hoarding vii 394 a; International Finance viii 163 a; International Trade viii 207 a; Liquidity ix 495 a; Metals x 364 b, 385 b; Monetary Stabilization x 591–95; Monetary Unions x 595–601; Money x 601–13; Prices (Hist.) xii 377 b, 379 a; Public Debt xii 603 a; Public Works xii 696 b; Silver xiv 57 b; Soetbeer xiv 249 a.
Gold Exchange Standard—Bimetallism and Monometallism ii 547 b, 549 a; Foreign Exchange vi 362 b; Money x 605 b.
Gold Points—vi 358 b.
Gold Standard — see Gold; Money.

Golden Age—Communism iv 81 b; Primitivism xii 399 b; Progress xii 495 b.
Goldenweiser, A. S.—vi 693.
Goldie, G. D. T.—vi 694.
Goldsborough Bill—xii 365 a.
Goldschmidt, L.—vi 694.
Goldziher, I.—vi 695.
Golf—xiv 307 b.
Goliards—xi 158 a.
Goltz, T. von der—vi 695.
Gomel, C.—vi 696.
Gomme, G. L.—vi 696.
Gompers, S.—vi 696; Amer. Federation of Labor ii 24 a.
Gonner, E. C. K.—vi 697.
González de Cellorigo, M.—vi 698.
Gooch, G. P.—Introd. Vol. I (The Trend to Internationalism) i 187 a; Archives ii 177 b.
Good Offices—see Mediation.
Good Roads Movement—xiii 406 b.
Goodwill—vi 698–702; Accounting i 411 b; Monopoly x 628 b; Trademarks and Names xv 58 a.
Goodyear, C.—Leather Industries ix 307 b; Rubber xiii 453 b.
Googe, B.—i 579 a.
Goos, C.—vi 702.
Gordon, A. D.—vi 702; Zionism xv 533 a.
Gore, C.—iii 451 a.
Goring, C. B.—vi 703.
Gorky, M.—xi 20 a.
Gorostiaga, J. B.—vi 703.
Görres, J. von—vi 704.
Gorter, H.—vi 704.
Goschen, Lord—vi 705; Foreign Exchange vi 361 b.
Gosplan—vi 705–13; Govt. Owned Corporations vii 109 a; Owen and Owenism xi 520 a; Russian Revolution xiii 485 b. See also Soviet Russia.
Gossen, H. H.—vii 3; Economics v 366 a.
Gothein, E.—vii 3.
Gothenburg System—ix 507 a.
Goto, S.—vii 4.
Gott, B.—vii 4.
Gottl-Ottlilienfeld, F. von—xi 228 a.
Götz, W.—vi 627 a.
Gouges, O. de—vii 5; Woman, Position in Society xv 445 a.
Gould, J.—vii 5.
Gourlay, R. F.—vii 6.
Gournay, J. C. M. V. de—vii 6; Laissez Faire ix 16 a; Morellet xi 10 a.
Gouvêa, A. de—vii 7.
Gouze, M.—see Gouges, O. de.
Government—vii 8–106 (History and Theory 8–15, 100, U. S. 15–21, 101, Gt. Brit. 21–26, 101, Canada 27–29, 101, Australia 29–32, 101, New Zealand 32–33, 101, S. Africa 33–36, 102, Ireland 36–38, 102, Brit. Commonwealth of Nations 38–43, 102, France 43–47, 102, Belgium 47–48, 102, Italy 48–52, 102, Germany 52–56, 103, Switzerland 56–58, 102, Netherlands 58–60, 103, Scandinavian States, General 60–61, 103, Denmark, Iceland and Norway 61–63, 103, Sweden and Finland 63–65, 103, Imperial Russia 65–67, 103, Soviet Russia 67–70, 104, Baltic States 70–75, 104, Succession States 75–81, 104, Balkan States 81–84, 105, Turkey 84–86, 105, Spain and Portugal 86–88, 105, Lat. Amer. 88–95, 105, Japan 95–98, 105, China 98–100, 106). See Classification of Articles (Government), p. 551, and further references suggested there. See also Introd. Vol. I (Greek Culture and Thought) i 11 a, 12 a, 31 a, (The Roman World) 42 a, 50 a, 52 b, 59 a, (The Universal Church) 61 a, 69 a, (The Growth of Autonomy) 76 a, (Renaissance and Reformation) 88 b. For biog. references see Classification of Articles (Statecraft), p. 569, and further references suggested there.
Government Employment — see Public Employment.
Government Owned Corporations—vii 106–11; Cooperative Public Boards iv 399–400; Decentralization v 44 a; Foreign Corporations vi 354 b; Govt. Ownership vii 117 b; Municipal Transit xi 122 a; Public Office xii 668 a; Public Utilities (Eur.) xii 684 b; State Liability xiv 341 a.
Government Ownership — vii 111–19; Central Banking iii 308 a; Cooperative Public Boards iv 399–400; Electric Power v 464 b; Fire Insurance vi 261 a; Forests vi 384 a; Funerals vi 528 b; Gas Industry vi 588 b; Govt. Owned Corporations vii 106–11; Govt. Regulation of Industry vii 129 a; Hospitals and Sanatoria vii 467 b; Housing (Eur.) vii 504 a, (U. S.) 513 b; Insurance vii 100 b; Land Mortgage Credit (Urban) ix 50 a; Marine Insurance x 116 a; Maritime Law x 129 b; Markets, Municipal x 140 b; Merchantmen, Status of x 351 b; Municipal Corporation xi 92 b; Municipal Finance xi 100 b; Municipal Transit xi 121 a, 125 a; Pawnbroking xii 35 b, 38 a; Postal Savings Banks xii 269–74; Public Domain xii 613–28; Public Utilities (Eur.) xii 684 a; Railroads xiii 82 b; Rate Regulation xiii 111 b; Revenues, Public xiii 361 b; Savings Banks xiii 553 b; Socialization xiv 221–25; Transportation xv 90 a.
Government Publications—vii 120–22; Govt. Reporting vii 130–32; Investigations, Gov-

ernmental viii 253 a; Labor, Govt. Services for viii 649 a; Records, Historical xiii 176 a.
Government Regulation — see Classification of Articles (Economic Policy), p. 550. See also Introd. Vol. I (War and Reorientation) i 210 b; Adams i 432 b; Administration, Public i 441 b; Amusements, Public ii 45 a; Bonding ii 633 b; Business iii 86 a; Business Ethics iii 111 b; Capitalization iii 209 b; Cartel iii 241 a; Casualty Insurance iii 264 b; Censorship iii 290–94; Child (Hygiene) iii 383 a; Collectivism iii 634 a; Commissions iv 38 a; Commodity Exchanges iv 47 b; Compensation and Liability Insurance iv 140 b; Competition iv 146 a; Conciliation, Industrial iv 165 b; Cost iv 475 a; Dairy Industry iv 694 a; Economics (Classical School) v 356 a, (Historical School) 372 a; Electric Power v 464 b; Financial Organization vi 245 b; Fire Insurance vi 256 a, 262 a; Fisheries vi 269 a; Food Industries vi 319 b, 323 a; Foreign Exchange vi 362 a; Foreign Investment vi 375 a; Freedom of Contract vi 453 a; Garment Industries vi 580 a; Govt. (Ireland) vii 38 b, (New Zealand) 33 a; Grain Elevators vii 138 a; Guilds (Antiquity) vii 206 a, (Late Roman and Byzantine) 206–08, (Europ.) 210 a, (Japanese) 221 b; Holding Companies vii 405 a; Homework, Industrial vii 447 b; Housing vii 496–517; Industrial Alcohol vii 682 a; Industrial Hygiene vii 707 b; Industrialism viii 26 b; Insurance viii 104 b, 110 b; Interlocking Directorates viii 150 b; International Trade viii 194 a; Investment viii 267 b; Investment Banking viii 276 b; Investment Trusts viii 283 b; Land Mortgage Credit (Urban) ix 51 a; Land Utilization ix 136 a; Life Insurance ix 465 a; Liquor Industry ix 496 b; Lotteries ix 614 b; Marine Insurance x 115 b; Massachusetts Trusts x 191 a; Meat Packing and Slaughtering x 257 b; Medicine (Medical Education) x 289 b; Metals x 388 b; Migrations x 434 a; Motor Vehicle Transportation xi 77 a; National Defense xi 190 a; National Socialism, German xi 225 b; Natural Resources xi 298 a; Nitrates xi 380 b; Oil Industry xi 446 a; Pawnbroking xii 35 b; Police Power xii 190–93; Population xii 248 a; Potash xii 274–77; Press xii 326 a, 332 a, 341 b; Printing and Publishing xii 409 b; Professions xii 478 a; Prostitution xii 553–59; Radio xiii 58 b, 59 b, 62 a, 63 a; Railroads xiii 82 a, 85 b; Raw Materials xiii 129 b; Recreation xiii 177 b; Refrigeration xiii 198 a; Restaurants xiii 339 a; Roosevelt xiii 436 a; Russian Revolution xiii 485 b; Savings Banks xiii 555 b; Speculation xiv 292 b; Telephone and Telegraph xiv 565 b; Trade Associations xiv 674 a; Trade Unions xv 5 b; Unfair Competition xv 176 b; Value and Price xv 223 a.
Government Regulation of Industry — vii 122–29. See Government Regulation.
Government Reporting — vii 130–32; Gales vi 546 a; Govt. Publications vii 120–22; Labor, Govt. Services for viii 649 a; Legislation ix 353 b; Maclay x 29 a.
Government Services for Agriculture—see Agriculture, Govt. Services for.
Government Services for Business—see Business, Govt. Services for.
Government Services for Labor—see Labor, Govt. Services for.
Governmental Investigations — see Investigations, Governmental.
Goya y Lucientes, F. de—ii 250 b.
G. P. U.—xii 204 b.
Gracchus, T. *and* G.—vii 132; Introd. Vol. I (The Roman World) i 46 b; Agrarian Movements (Rome) i 494 b.
Grace, W. R.—vii 132.
Gradenwitz, O.—xiii 424 b.
Grading—vii 133–34; Business, Govt. Services for iii 118 a; Canning Industry iii 177 a; Commodity Exchanges iv 46 b; Consumer Protection iv 283 b; Cotton iv 491 a; Food Industries vi 317 a.
Gradovsky, A. D.—vii 134.
Grady, H. W.—vii 135.
Graebner, F.—Introd. Vol. I (The Trend to Internationalism) i 185 a; Anthropology ii 103 b; Diffusionism v 141 b.
Graetz, H.—vii 135.
Graft—see Spoils System.
Grain Elevators—vii 136–39; Agric. Marketing i 562 a; Food Industries (Food Distribution, Russia) vi 327 b.
Grains—vii 139–47; Agric. Co-operation (U. S.) i 526 b; Agric. Marketing (U. S.) i 562 a; Agriculture (General Problems) i 594 a, (Primitive) 572 b, (China) 589 b; Dry Farming v 252 b; Food Industries (Food Distribution, Russia) vi 323 b, 327 b; Food Supply vi 334 a; Grain Elevators vii 136–39; Livestock Industry ix 550 b; Milling Industry x 484–88; Soils xiv 252 a.
Grammar—Language ix 156 a.
Gramont, S. de—vii 147.
Grand Jury—vii 148–50.
Grand National Consolidated Trades Union—xv 7 b.
Grange—vii 150–51; Agric. Co-operation i 524 a.
Granger Cases—ii 460 b.
Granovsky, T. N.—vii 151.
Grants-in-Aid—vii 152–55; Allowance System ii 7; Child (Hygiene) iii 383 a; Day Nursery v 14 b; Local Finance ix 571 b; Public Works xii 693 b; Rehabilitation xiii 221 b; Roads xiii 407 b; States' Rights xiv 348 a.
Gras, N. S. B.—vii 256 a.
Graslin, J. J. L.—vii 155.
Grasslands—Soils xiv 251 b.
Gratian—vii 156; Canon Law iii 180 b; Excommunication v 675 a.
Grattan, H.—vii 156.
Graumann, J. P.—vii 157.
Graunt, J.—vii 158; Census iii 295 a; Petty xii 104 b; Statistics xiv 357 a.
Gravier, C. — see Vergennes, Comte de.
Gravina, G.—vii 158.
Gray, J.—vii 159; Socialism xiv 195 b; State xiv 331 a.
Gray, J. C.—vii 159.
Great Powers—vii 160–62; Imperialism vii 605–13; Isolation, Diplomatic viii 352–55; League of Nations ix 290 b; Natural Resources xi 295 a.
Greco-Egyptian Law—Law ix 229–35.
Greek Law—Law ix 225–29; Law Merchant ix 271 a.
Greeley, H.—vii 162; Press xii 329 a.
Green, E. F.—see Fiske, J.
Green, F. E.—vii 163.
Green, J. R.—vii 164.
Green, T. H.—vii 164; Idealism vii 572 a.
Greenback Labor Party, U. S.—Amer. Feder. of Labor ii 23 b.
Greenback Party, U. S.—Free Silver vi 438 b; Kellogg viii 556 b; Parties, Political xi 599 a.
Greene, W. B.—viii 641 a.
Greening, E. O.—vii 165.
Gregg, W.—vii 165.
Grégoire, Father—see Girard, J.-B.
Grégoire, H.—vii 166.
Gregory I—vii 166; Introd. Vol. I (The Universal Church) i 62 a; Slavery xiv 78 a; Tyranny xv 136 a.
Gregory VII—vii 167; Investiture Conflict viii 261 a; Papacy xi 561 a; Religious Institutions (Roman Catholic) xiii 254 b.
Gregory XIII—iii 143 a.
Gregory of Nazianzus—iii 465 b.
Gregory of Nyssa—iii 465 b.
Gregory of Tours—vii 371 b.
Grenville, G.—vii 168.
Gresham, T.—vii 169.

Gresham's Law—iii 61 b.
GREY, SECOND EARL—vii 169.
GREY, THIRD EARL—vii 170.
Grey, E.—Archives ii 177 b, 179 a; Balance of Power ii 396 b; Cambon iii 158 a; League of Nations ix 287 b.
GREY, G.—vii 170; Parties, Political (New Zealand) xi 607 b.
GRIESINGER, W.—vii 171.
GRIFFITH, A.—vii 171; Irish Question viii 293 a.
GRIFFITH, S. W.—vii 172.
GRIFFUELHES, V.—vii 172.
Grillparzer, F.—xiv 610 a.
GRIMM, J. L. K. and W. K.—vii 173; Folklore vi 288 b.
Grocery Trade—vi 311–15.
GROLMAN, K. VON—vii 174.
Groos, K.—xii 160 a.
Groot, H. de—see GROTIUS, H.
GROSS, C.—vii 174.
GROSS, H.—vii 175.
GROSSE, E.—vii 175.
GROSSETESTE, R.—vii 176.
GROTE, G.—vii 176; History and Historiography vii 378 b.
Grotefend, G. F.—ii 163 b.
GROTIUS, H.—vii 177; Introd. Vol. I (Renaissance and Reformation) i 100 a; Contraband of War iv 321 a; Enlightenment v 550 a; Equality of States v 581 a; Gentili vi 616 a; International Law viii 169 a; Jus Gentium viii 503 b; Justice viii 512 a; Natural Law xi 284 b, 287 b, 289 a; Neutrality xi 361 b; Social Contract xiv 129 a.
GROUP—vii 178–82; Introd. Vol. I (War and Reorientation) i 206 b; Association ii 284–86; Class iii 531–36; Clubs iii 573–77; Collective Behavior iii 631–33; Community iv 102–05; Consciousness iv 219 a; Crowd iv 612–13; Ethnocentrism v 613–14; Faction vi 49–51; Family vi 65–70; Gumplowicz vii 227 a; Honor vii 457 a; Interests viii 144–48; Intermarriage viii 151–55; Isolation viii 350–52; Language ix 159 b; Leadership ix 282–87; Morale x 641–42; Pressures, Social xii 344–48; Secret Societies xiii 621–23.
Group Buying—Retail Trade xiii 353 a.
GROUP INSURANCE—vii 182–88; Benefits, Trade Union ii 513–16; Health Insurance vii 299 a.
Group Marriage—x 150 a.
GROUSSAC, P.—vii 188.
GRUBER, J.—vii 188.
GRUEV, D.—vii 189.
GRÜN, K. T. F.—vii 189.
GRUNDTVIG, N. F. S.—vii 189; Agrarian Movements (Denmark) i 501 b; Folk High Schools vi 286 b.
GUARANTIES, INTERNATIONAL—vii 190–92; Neutralization xi 365–67.
Guaranty, Legal—see SURETYSHIP AND GUARANTY.

GUARDIANSHIP — vii 192–95; Adoption i 459–63; Conflict of Laws iv 193 a; Insanity viii 68 a, 69 a; Juvenile Delinquency and Juvenile Courts viii 529 a; Law (Hellenistic and Greco-Egyptian) ix 231 b; Majority, Age of x 54 b.
GÜDEMANN, M.—vii 195.
GÜELL Y FERRER, J.—vii 196.
Guenther, H.—xi 225 b.
GUÉRARD, B.—vii 196.
GUERRAZZI, F. D.—vii 196.
GUERRILLA WARFARE—vii 197–99.
GUESDE, J.—vii 199.
GUGGENHEIM FAMILY—vii 200.
Guggenheim Fund for the Promotion of Aeronautics—ii 343 b.
GUICCIARDINI, F.—vii 201.
Guido, Prince—see HENCKEL, G.
GUILD SOCIALISM—vii 202–04; Association ii 285 b; Construction Industry iv 277 a; Functional Representation vi 519 b; Functionalism vi 525 a; Labor Movement viii 688 a; Socialism xiv 204 b.
GUILDS—vii 204–24 (Antiquity 204–06, 222, Late Roman and Byzantine 206–08, 223, Europ. 208–14, 223, Islamic 214–16, 223, Indian 216–19, 224, Chinese 219–21, 224, Japanese 221–22, 224); Introd. Vol. I (The Growth of Autonomy) i 75 a; Apprenticeship ii 144–47; Art (Indian) ii 230 b; Boileau vi 619 b; Construction Industry iv 263 a; Copyright iv 402 a; Dye Industry v 299 a; Food Industries (Baking, Eur.) vi 303 b, (Grocery Trade) 312 a; Friendly Societies vi 494 b; Functional Representation vi 519 a; Fur Trade and Industry vi 531 b; Garment Industries vi 573 a; Gross vii 175 a; Guild Socialism vii 202–04; Handicraft vii 256 b, 257 b; Hanseatic League vii 262 a; Industrial Arts vii 686 b; Journeymen's Societies viii 424 b; Labor viii 616 a, 619 a; Labor Legislation and Law viii 673 b; Labor, Methods of Remuneration for viii 677 a; Law Merchant ix 272 a; Leather Industries (Labor) ix 312 b; Masonry x 177 b; Monopoly x 625 a; Mutual Aid Societies xi 168 a; Occupation xi 426 b; Plutocracy xii 176 b; Professions xii 477 a; Putting Out System xiii 9 a; Textile Industry xiv 590 b; Trade Associations xiv 670 b.
GUILLAUME, J.—vii 224.
GUILLAUME-SCHACK, G.—vii 225.
Guillotine, Parliamentary — iii 571 b.
GUIRAUD, P.—vii 225.
GUIZOT, F. P. G.—vii 225; Introd. Vol. I (The Social Sciences as Disciplines, France) i 249 a; Doctrinaire v 187 b.

GUMPLOWICZ, L.—vii 227; Introd. Vol. I (Nationalism) i 169 a; Conquest iv 207 b; Race xiii 36 a; Sociology xiv 238 b.
GUSTAVUS I—vii 227; Mortmain xi 46 a.
GUSTAVUS II—vii 228; Oxenstierna xi 526 a.
GUTIÉRREZ, J. M.—vii 228.
GUYAU, J. M.—vii 229.
GUYOT, Y.—vii 230.
GUZMÁN-BLANCO, A.—vii 230.
Gymnastics—see PHYSICAL EDUCATION.
GYPSIES—vii 231–32.

Ha-am, A.—xv 531 a.
Haarfager, H.—ix 85 a.
HAAS, W.—vii 232; Cooperation iv 374 a.
HAASE, H.—vii 233.
HABEAS CORPUS—vii 233–36; Arrest ii 222 a; Jurisdiction viii 472 b; Martial Law x 163 a.
Haber, F.—xi 382 a.
HABIT—vii 236–39; Comparative Psychology iv 131 a; Custom iv 658 b; Folkways vi 293–96; Human Nature vii 531–37.
Hacienda—ix 118 b.
Haddon, A. C.—Evolution, Social v 659 a; Ornament xi 497 a.
Hadith—viii 334 a.
HADLEY, A. T.—vii 239; Taxation xiv 538 b.
Hadrian—viii 471 a.
HAECKEL, E.—vii 240; Freethinkers vi 469 a.
HAGEN, K. H.—vii 241.
HAGGARD, H. R.—vii 241.
HAGUE CONFERENCES—vii 242–44; Introd. Vol. I (The Trend to Internationalism) i 173 a; Arms and Munitions Traffic ii 207 a; Belligerency ii 506 a; International Law viii 170 b; League of Nations ix 288 a; Limitation of Armaments ix 480 b; Neutrality xi 363 a; Permanent Court of Arbitration xii 76 b; Prisoners of War xii 420 b; Prize xii 426 a; Requisitions, Military xiii 325 b; Warfare, Laws of xv 361 a.
Hague Tribunal—see PERMANENT COURT OF ARBITRATION.
HAHN, E.—vii 244; Geography vi 623 b.
Haig, R. M.—vii 628 b.
Hail Insurance—i 546 a.
Halbwachs, M.—i 207 a.
Haldane, J. S.—x 269 a.
HALE, M.—vii 245.
HALES, J.—vii 245; Mercantilism x 336 b.
HALIFAX, LORD (d. 1695)—vii 246.
Halifax, Lord (d. 1715)—see MONTAGU, C.
HALL, C.—vii 246; Socialism xiv 195 b.
HALL, G. S.—vii 247; Adolescence i 458 a; Child (Psychology) iii 391 b; Haeckel vii 240 b; Play xii 160 b.

HALL, W. E.—vii 248; Belligerency ii 506 b; Intervention viii 237 b.
HALLAM, H.—vii 248.
HALLER, K. L. VON—vii 249.
Halles Centrales—x 142 b.
HALOANDER, G.—vii 249.
HÄLSCHNER, H.—vii 250.
Halsey Formula—viii 679 a.
Hamburg-American Line—ii 409 b.
HAMEL, G. A. VAN—vii 250.
HAMILTON, A.—vii 251; Introd. Vol. I (The Revolutions) i 136 a; Alien Property i 636 b; Judicial Review viii 458 b; Protection xii 562 a.
HAMILTON, G. G.—vii 252.
HAMILTON, R.—vii 252.
Hamilton, W. H.—v 172 b.
HAMMER-PURGSTALL, J. VON—vii 253.
Hammond, G. H.—x 245 b.
Hammurabi, Code of—see CODE OF HAMMURABI.
HAMPDEN, J.—vii 253.
HAN FEI-TZŬ—vii 254.
Hanassi, J.—ix 222 a.
Hanbalite School—vii 563 b.
HANCOCK, W. N.—vii 254.
Hand, L.—xiv 480 b.
HANDICRAFT—vii 255-60; Anthropology ii 89 b; Apprenticeship ii 144-47; Architecture ii 173 a; Art ii 223-59; Bourgeoisie ii 654 b; Crane iv 543 b; Dye Industry v 296-300; Furniture vi 537-43; Garment Industries vi 573 a; Guilds vii 204-24; Industrial Arts vii 684 a; Industrial Education vii 693 a; Journeymen's Societies viii 424-27; Leather Industries (Leather Products) ix 304 b, (Labor) 312 a; Manual Training x 103-05; Mechanic x 263 b; Middle Class x 410 b; Morris xi 21 a; Museums and Exhibitions xi 139 b; Occupation xi 426 b; Pottery xii 279-84; Precious Stones xii 313 a; Putting Out System xiii 8 a; Rural Industries xiii 466-69; Specialization xiv 281 b; Textile Industry xiv 581 a, 590 a; Wages xv 305 a.
HÄNEL, A.—vii 260.
HANNA, M. A.—vii 261.
HANSEATIC LEAGUE—vii 261-67; Military Orders x 462 b; Municipal Govt. xi 106 a.
HANSEMANN, D. J. L.—vii 267.
Hansen, A.—xii 374 a.
HANSSEN, G.—vii 267; Economic History v 317 b; Economics v 373 a.
Hapag—ii 409 b.
Hapoel Hazair—xv 533 a.
Hapsburgs—Fugger Family vi 514 a; Holy Roman Empire vii 425 b; Maria Theresa x 109 a.
Harbors—see PORTS AND HARBORS.
Hardenberg, F. von—see NOVALIS.

HARDENBERG, K. A. VON—vii 268; Agrarian Movements i 499 a.
HARDIE, J. K.—vii 268; Labor Parties (Gt. Brit.) viii 700 a.
HARDWICKE, LORD—vii 269.
Hare Plan—Proportional Representation xii 541 b, 543 b.
HARET, S.—vii 270.
HARMEL, L.—vii 270.
Harmonic Mean—ii 338 a.
Harmonists—Communistic Settlements iv 96 b.
Harmsworth, A. C. W.— see NORTHCLIFFE, LORD.
Harmsworth, H. S.—see Rothermere, Lord.
HARNACK, A. VON—vii 271.
HARNEY, G. J.—vii 271.
HARRIMAN, E. H.—vii 272; Railroads xiii 81 a.
HARRINGTON, J.—vii 272; Introd. Vol. I (Renaissance and Reformation) i 102 b; Balance of Trade ii 400 a; Utopia xv 201 a.
HARRIS, J.—vii 273.
HARRIS, W. T.—vii 274; Hegel vii 314 b; Preschool Education xii 322 a.
HARRISON, F.—vii 274.
Harrison, F. B.—xii 112 a.
HARRISON, J. E.—vii 275; Ritual xiii 396 b.
HART, R.—vii 275.
Hart, Schaffner and Marx Co.—viii 628 b.
Harter Act—x 128 b.
HARTLAND, E. S.—vii 276.
HARTLEY, D.—vii 276; Psychology xii 589 b.
HARTMANN, E. VON—vii 276.
HARTMANN, L. M.—vii 277.
HARVEY, G. B. McC.—vii 278.
Harvey, W.—ii 551 a.
HASBACH, W.—vii 278.
Hassan Sabah—ii 272 b.
HASTINGS, W.—vii 279; Burke iii 75 b; Indian Question vii 661 b.
Hatzfeldt, S.—ix 184 a.
HAUCK, A.—vii 279.
Hauer, J. W.—ii 66 a.
HAURIOU, M.—vii 280.
HÄUSSER, H.—vii 281.
Haüy, V.—ii 588 b, 589 a.
Havas—xii 336 b.
HAVEMEYER, H. O.—vii 281.
HAVERFIELD, F. J.—vii 282.
HAVLÍČEK, K.—vii 282.
HAWLEY, F. B.—vii 283.
Hawtrey, R. G.—Business Cycles iii 98 b; Money x 610 a; Price Stabilization xii 364 a.
HAXTHAUSEN, A. VON—vii 283.
Hay-Bunau-Varilla Treaty — xi 555 b.
Hay-Herrán Convention—xi 555 a.
HAY, J. M.—vii 284; Open Door xi 469 a; Spheres of Influence xiv 298 b.
Hay-Pauncefote Treaty—xi 554 b.
HAYES, E. C.—vii 285.
HAYM, R.—vii 285.

Haymarket Riot—Altgeld ii 12 b; Anarchism ii 52 a; General Strike vi 608 b; Knights of Labor viii 582 b; Parsons xi 598 b.
Hays, W. H.—xi 66 b.
HAYWOOD, W. D.—vii 285.
Hazelius, A.—vii 257 a.
HAZLITT, W.—vii 286.
HEADLAM, S. D.—vii 287; Christian Socialism iii 450 b.
Healing—Christian Science iii 446-49; Medicine (Hist.) x 283-89.
Health Administration—see PUBLIC HEALTH.
HEALTH CENTERS—vii 287-89; Medicine x 297 a.
HEALTH EDUCATION—vii 289-94; Child (Hygiene) iii 380-84; Health Centers vii 287-89; Life Extension Movement ix 460-62; Mental Hygiene x 322 b; Public Health xii 649 a; Sex Education and Sex Ethics xiv 8-13.
HEALTH INSURANCE—vii 294-300; Casualty Insurance iii 263 b; Clinics iii 564 a; Group Insurance vii 184 b; Labor, Govt. Services for viii 648 a; Labor Legislation and Law viii 664 a; Medicine x 297 b; Mutual Aid Societies xi 168-72; Social Insurance xiv 134-38.
Health, Public — see PUBLIC HEALTH.
Healy, W.—Child (Guidance) iii 394 a; Criminology iv 590 a.
HEARN, W. E.—vii 300.
Hearst, W. R.—xii 330 a.
HEAVY CHEMICALS—vii 300-04.
Hebbel, F.—xiv 610 a.
HÉBERT, J. R.—vii 304.
HECKER, J. J.—vii 305.
HEDGING — vii 305-07; Agric. Marketing (U. S.) i 562 b; Foreign Exchange vi 359 a.
HEDONISM—vii 307-10; Cyrenaics iv 685-87; Epicureanism v 568 a; Hume vii 551 a; Individualism vii 674-80; Utilitarianism xv 197-200; Valla xv 209 b; Value and Price xv 219 b.
HEEREN, A. H. L.—vii 310.
HEFELE, K. J. VON—vii 310.
HEFFTER, A. W.—vii 311.
HEGEL, G. W. F.—vii 311; Introd. Vol. I (Individualism and Capitalism) i 157 b; Absolutism i 381 b; Bauer ii 481 a; Berner ii 524 b; Bradley ii 673 a; History and Historiography vii 376 a; Idealism vii 571 a; Individualism vii 677 a; Kant viii 540 b; Lassalle ix 184 a; Logic ix 601 b; Marx x 172 a; Materialism x 212 a, (Dialectical) 213 b; Nationalism xi 233 b; Political Science xii 218 a, 220 b; Rationalism xiii 116 b; Spaventa xiv 275 a.
HEGEL, K.—vii 315.
Heidelberg Man—x 74 b.
HEINE, H.—vii 315.
HEINECCIUS, J. G.—vii 316.
HELD, A.—vii 317.

Helferich, J. A. R. von—vii 317.
Helfferich, K.—vii 317.
Hellenistic Law—Law ix 229–35.
Hellwald, F. von—ii 122 a.
Helmholtz, H. F. L. von—Behaviorism ii 496 b; Psychology xii 591 a.
Helper, H. R.—vii 318.
Helvétius, C. A.—vii 319; Human Nature vii 532 b; Social Psychology xiv 152 b.
Hemp—see Flax, Hemp and Jute.
Henckel, G.—vii 320.
Henderson, C. R.—vii 320.
Henderson, L. J.—v 652 b.
Henley, W. of—vii 320.
Henry II—vii 321; Religious Institutions (Roman Catholic) xiii 256 a.
Henry III—Investiture Conflict viii 261 a; Montfort x 639 b.
Henry IV (d. 1106)—vii 321; Gregory VII vii 168 a; Investiture Conflict viii 261 a; Religious Institutions (Roman Catholic) xiii 254 b.
Henry IV (d. 1610)—vii 322.
Henry V—viii 262 a.
Henry VII—vii 323.
Henry VIII—vii 323; Cranmer iv 544 a; Monasticism x 589 b; More xi 8 b.
Henry, E. R.—vii 573 b.
Henry of Langenstein—vii 324.
Henry the Navigator—vii 324; Introd. Vol. i (Renaissance and Reformation) i 87 b.
Heraldry—iii 442 b.
Herbart, J. F.—vii 325; Child (Psychology) iii 391 b; Education v 413 b; Psychology xii 590 b.
Herbert of Cherbury, Lord—vii 325; Enlightenment v 550 b.
Herculano de Carvalho e Araujo, A.—vii 326.
Herder, J. G. von—vii 327; History and Historiography vii 375 b.
Herding—Livestock Industry ix 545–51; Nomads xi 390 b; Soils xiv 251 b.
Heredity—vii 328–35; Anthropology ii 76 a; Anthropometry ii 112 a; Aristocracy ii 187 a; Atavism ii 290–91; Biology ii 554 b; Blind ii 588 a; Character iii 335 b; Criminology iv 585 a; Degeneration v 55–57; Determinism v 113 a; Drug Addiction v 246 b; Eugenics v 617–21; Evolution v 652 a; Genius vi 613 b; Gentleman, Theory of the vi 616 b; Human Nature vii 533 a; Instinct viii 82 a; Mendel x 307 a; Mental Disorders x 315 a; Mental Tests x 326 b; Personality xii 86 b; Race xiii 25–36; Race Mixture xiii 42 a; Weismann xv 392 a.
Heresy—see Apostasy and Heresy.
Hergenröther, J.—vii 335.

Hering, E.—ii 496 b.
Hermann, F. B. W. von—vii 336; Banfield ii 415 b; Income Tax vii 628 b.
Hero Worship—vii 336–38.
Herodotus of Halicarnassus—vii 339; Introd. Vol. i (Greek Culture and Thought) i 27 b; History and Historiography vii 368 b.
Herrenschwand, J.—vii 339.
Herriot, E.—ii 114 b.
Hertzberg, E. C. H.—vii 339.
Hertzenstein, M. Y.—vii 340.
Hertzka, T.—vii 340.
Hertzog, J. B. M.—xi 609 a.
Herzen, A. I.—vii 341.
Herzl, T.—vii 342; Zionism xv 531 a.
Hess, M.—vii 342; Zionism xv 530 a.
Hetaerae—xii 554 a.
Hetherington, H.—vii 343.
Heusler, A.—vii 344.
Hewitt, A. S.—vii 344.
Heyd, W. von—vii 345.
Heyn, O.—vii 345.
Hidalgo y Costilla, M.—vii 345.
Hide—Land Tenure ix 83 a, 87 b.
Hieroduloi—ix 216 b.
Hieronymus—iii 465 b.
Higgins, H. B.—vii 346.
Higher Criticism—vii 347–49; Freethinkers vi 468 a; Hegel vii 314 a; Sacred Books xiii 500 b; Smith xiv 118 a; Wellhausen xv 400 b.
Highways—see Roads.
Hildebrand—see Gregory VII.
Hildebrand, B.—vii 349; Economic History v 328 b; Economics v 371–77; Exchange v 667 a.
Hildreth, R.—vii 349.
Hilferding, R.—Bolshevism ii 626 a; Economics v 380 a.
Hill, J. J.—vii 350; Railroads xiii 81 a.
Hill, O.—vii 350; Charity iii 343 b; Social Work xiv 173 b.
Hill, R.—vii 351.
Hinayana—iii 36 b.
Hincmar of Reims—vii 351; Investiture Conflict viii 260 a.
Hindu Law—Jīmūtavāhana viii 403 a; Law ix 257–62; Nārada xi 184 b; Vijnaneṣvāra xv 252 a.
Hinduism—see Brahmanism and Hinduism.
Hinojosa y Naveros, E. de—vii 352.
Hinschius, P.—vii 352.
Hippias—Natural Law xi 285 b; Sophists xiv 260 a.
Hippocrates and the Hippocratic Collection—vii 353; Introd. Vol. i (Greek Culture and Thought) i 23 b; Climate iii 560 b; Communicable Diseases, Control of iv 67 a; Epidemics v 570 a; Medicine x 284 b.
Hire Purchase System—viii 75 b.
Hirsch, Maurice de—vii 354.

Hirsch, Max—vii 355; Duncker v 279 b.
Hirsch, S. R.—viii 439 a.
Hirschfeld, O.—vii 355.
Hirth, F.—vii 356.
Hispanic American Congresses—xi 539 a.
Historical Materialism—see Materialism.
Historical Records—see Records, Historical.
Historical School, Economics—Introd. Vol. i (Nationalism) i 167 a; Economics v 371–77.
History, Economic — see Economic History.
History and Historiography—vii 357–91 (History 357–68, 389, Historiography: Antiquity 368–70, 390, Mediaeval Eur. 370–74, 390, Modern Eur. 374–81, 391, Islam 381–83, 391, China and Japan 383–85, 391, U. S. 385–89, 391); Introd. Vol. I (What Are the Social Sciences?) i 4 a, (Greek Culture and Thought) 27 b, (The Roman World) 51 a, (Renaissance and Reformation) 93 a, (The Rise of Liberalism) 119 b, (The Revolutions) 142 a, (Individualism and Capitalism) 160 a, (Nationalism) 170 a, (The Trend to Internationalism) 186 a, (War and Reorientation) 222 a, (The Social Sciences as Disciplines, Austria) 267 b, (France) 251 b, (Gt. Brit.) 236 b, 245 a, (Hungary) 270 b, (Lat. Amer.) 301 a, 307 b, 315 b, (Russia) 282 b, (Scandinavia) 292 b, (U. S.) 326 b, 333 b; Archives ii 177–81; Comparative Religion iv 131–34; Continuity, Social iv 316 a; Economic History v 315–30; Economics (Historical School) v 376 a; Hero Worship vii 337 b; Higher Criticism vii 347–49; Jurisprudence viii 480 b; Method, Scientific x 392 b; Militarism x 448 a; Nationalism xi 238 b; Prehistory xii 316–18; Progress xii 495–99; Records, Historical xiii 173–76. *For biog. references see* Classification of Articles (History), p. 561.
Hitler, A.—Labor Movement viii 689 b; National Socialism, German xi 225 a.
Hittite Law—Law (Cuneiform) ix 211–19.
Hitze, F.—vii 391.
Hjärne, H.—vii 392.
Hoadly, B.—vii 393.
Hoarding—vii 393–94; Investment viii 264 b; Precious Stones xii 313 b; Saving xiii 549 b.
Hobbes, T.—vii 394; Introd. Vol. i (The Rise of Liberalism) i 109 b; Absolutism i 380 b; Altruism and Egoism ii 14 b; Authority ii 321 a; Enlightenment v 549 a; Equality of States v 581 a; Force, Political vi 340 a; Freedom of Associa-

tion vi 449 a; Hedonism vii 308 a; Human Nature vii 535 a; Individualism vii 677 b; Materialism x 211 a; Natural Law xi 288 a; Political Science xii 216 a; Psychology xii 589 a; Public Finance iii 643 b; Social Contract xiv 129 b; Social Organism xiv 138 a; Sovereignty xiv 267 a.
HOBHOUSE, L. T.—vii 396; Introd. Vol. I (The Trend to Internationalism) i 182 a; Mechanism and Vitalism x 269 b, 270 b.
Hobo—xv 206 a.
Hobson, J. A.—Introd. Vol. I (The Trend to Internationalism) i 176 b; Bolshevism ii 626 a; Business Cycles iii 98 b; Cost iv 474 a; Economics v 382 b; Income Tax vii 631 a.
Hobson, S. G.—vii 204 a.
Hock, K. F.—vii 397.
HODGSKIN, T.—vii 397; Socialism xiv 195 b.
HOERNES, M.—vii 398.
HOFFMANN, J. G.—vii 398.
Hoffmann, M.—xiii 627 a.
HOFMEYR, J. H.—vii 399.
HOHENLOHE-SCHILLINGSFÜRST, C. K. V.—vii 399.
Hohenstaufens—vii 424 a.
HOHFELD, W. N.—vii 400; Introd. Vol. I (War and Reorientation) i 221 a.
HOLBACH, BARON VON—vii 401; Introd. Vol. I (The Revolutions) i 131 a.
HOLBERG, L.—vii 402.
HOLBROOK, J.—vii 402.
HOLDHEIM, S.—vii 403.
HOLDING COMPANIES—vii 403–12; Combinations, Industrial iii 665 b; Corporation iv 419 a; Corporation Finance iv 429 a; Electric Power v 465 b; Gas Industry vi 593 b; Kreuger viii 600 b; Loewenstein ix 598 b; Municipal Transit xi 119 b; Public Utilities (U. S.) xii 680 b.
HOLIDAYS—vii 412–15; Blue Laws ii 600–02; Hours of Labor vii 479 a; Judaism viii 435 a; Leisure ix 403 b; Truce and Peace of God xv 108 a.
HOLLAND, H. S.—vii 415.
HOLLAND, T. E.—vii 415.
Holmes, O. W.—Ownership and Possession xi 524 a; Resale Price Maintenance xiii 328 a.
Holmes, R. H.—vi 613 b.
HOLST, H. E. VON—vii 415.
HOLSTEIN, F. VON—vii 416; Archives ii 177 b.
HOLT, J.—vii 416; Bailment ii 389 b.
HOLTZENDORFF, F. VON—vii 417.
HOLY ALLIANCE—vii 417–19; Alexander I i 630 a; Carbonari iii 220–23; Internationalism viii 215 a.
HOLY PLACES—vii 419–22; Sanctuary xiii 534–37.

HOLY ROMAN EMPIRE—vii 422–27; Introd. Vol. I (The Universal Church) i 64 a, (The Growth of Autonomy) 73–83; Charlemagne iii 345 a; Innocent III viii 57 b; Investiture Conflict viii 260 b; Monarchy x 581 a; Papacy xi 561 a; Religious Institutions (Roman Catholic) xiii 254 a.
Holy War—Islam viii 337 a; Jihad viii 401–03; Military Orders x 459 b.
HOLYOAKE, G. J.—vii 427.
HOME ECONOMICS—vii 427–31; Canning Industry iii 178 a; Domestic Service v 198–206; Laundry and Dry Cleaning Industry ix 191 b, 194 a.
Home Missions—x 545 a.
HOME OWNERSHIP—vii 431–34; Land Mortgage Credit (Urban) ix 53 a.
HOME RULE—vii 434–36; Administrative Areas i 450–52; City iii 479 b; City and Town Planning iii 484 a; Govt. (U. S.) vii 19 a; Irish Question viii 292 b; Municipal Corporation xi 89 b; Municipal Courts xi 97 b.
HOMESTEAD—vii 436–41; Frontier vi 504 b; Homestead Exemption Laws vii 441–44; Land Grants (U. S.) ix 35 b; Public Domain xii 621 a.
HOMESTEAD EXEMPTION LAWS—vii 441–44.
HOMEWORK, INDUSTRIAL — vii 444–49; Garment Industries vi 574 a, 576 b; Putting Out System xiii 7–11; Rural Industries xiii 466–69.
HOMEYER, K. G.—vii 449.
HOMICIDE—vii 450–56; Intent, Criminal viii 128 a.
Hondt, V. d'—xii 542 a.
HONOR—vii 456–58; Dueling v 269 b; Feudalism (Japanese) vi 217 b; Feuds vi 221 a; Gentleman, Theory of the vi 619 b; Seduction xiii 640 a.
HONTHEIM, J. N. VON—vii 458.
HOOKER, R.—vii 459; Cartwright iii 246 a.
HOOKER, T.—vii 459.
Hooton, E. A.—ii 111 b.
Hoplites—ix 79 a.
Hormand, J.—xi 274 b.
HORN, E. I.—vii 460.
Hornbostel, E. M. von—xi 151 b, 154 b.
HORNIGK, P. W. VON—vii 461; Cameralism iii 159 a.
Horse Racing—Lotteries ix 613 b; Sports xiv 307 b.
HORTON, S. D.—vii 461.
HORVÁTH, M.—vii 461.
Hosiery Industry—vi 575 b.
HOSPITAL, M. DE L'—vii 462.
Hospitallers—see Knights Hospitallers.
HOSPITALITY—vii 462–64.
HOSPITALS AND SANATORIA—vii 464–72; Clinics and Dispensaries iii 562–67; Medicine x

286 a, 298 b, (Medical Education) 290 b; Mental Disorders x 317 b; Mental Hygiene x 320 b; Military Orders x 460 a; Nursing xi 409 a; Resorts xiii 334–36; Social Work (Case Work) xiv 179 a.
Hostage—xiv 482 a.
HOSTOS, E. M. DE—vii 472.
HOTELS—vii 472–77; Bailment ii 390 a; Lodging Houses ix 596 b; Resorts xiii 334–36.
HOTMAN, F.—vii 477.
Hötzendorf, C. von—ii 178 a.
HOURS OF LABOR—vii 478–93; Abbe i 354 b; Automobile Industry ii 326 b; Child (Labor) iii 412–24; Clerical Occupations iii 553 a; Construction Industry iv 271 a; Continuous Industry iv 318 b; Domestic Service v 202 b; Factory System vi 54 a; Fatigue vi 149 a; Food Industries (Baking, Eur.) vi 304 b, (Confectionery) 311 a; Iron and Steel Industry viii 316 a, 319 a; Labor Legislation and Law viii 662 b; Laundry and Dry Cleaning Industry ix 195 b; Leisure ix 404 b; National Economic Planning xi 203 b; Oil Industry xi 446 b; Railroads xiii 95 b; Short Hours Movement xiv 44–47; Steward xiv 391 a; Strikes and Lockouts xiv 421 a.
HOURWICH, I. A.—vii 494.
HOUSE AND BUILDING TAXES—vii 494–96.
House of Commons—ix 369 b.
House of Lords—ix 369 b.
House of Representatives, U. S.—Apportionment ii 139 a; Legislative Assemblies ix 361–65.
HOUSING — vii 496–517 (Europe: Early Hist. 496–98, 517, From Industrial Revolution to World War 498–502, 517, War and Post-War Period 502–11, 517; U.S.: 511–17). See Classification of Articles (Housing), p. 551. See also Anthropology ii 80 a; Hill vii 350 b; Industrial Revolution viii 11 b; Negro Problem xi 345 b; Segregation xiii 645 a.
HOUSING, COOPERATIVE—vii 517–20; Housing (Eur.) vii 501 b, 505 b, (U. S.) 515 b.
HOUSSAYE, H.—vii 520.
Hove, van den—see COURT, P. DE LA.
Howard, E.—vi 569 b.
HOWARD, G. E.—vii 520.
HOWARD, J.—vii 521.
Howarth, C.—Consumers' Cooperation iv 286 a; Cooperation iv 364 a.
HOWE, J.—vii 521.
HOWE, J. W.—vii 522.
HOWE, S. G.—vii 523; Institutions, Public viii 91 b.
HOWELL, G.—vii 523.
HOWITT, A. W.—vii 524; Fison vi 272 a.
HOXIE, R. F.—vii 524; Trade Unions xv 5 a.

Index (Hobbes — Imperial Unity)

Hrabanus—see RABANUS MAURUS, M.
Hrdlička, A.—ii 111 b.
Hsing Chung Hui—viii 610 b.
Hsiung-nu—x 426 b.
Hsün Tzŭ—ix 250 b.
HUBE, R.—vii 525.
HUBER, E.—vii 525.
HUBER, U.—vii 526; Comity iii 678 a; Conflict of Laws iv 189 a.
HUBER, V. A.—vii 526.
HUBERT, H.—vii 527; Magic x 42 b.
HÜBNER, M.—vii 527.
HÜBNER, N. P.—vii 528.
HUDSON, G.—vii 528.
Hue and Cry—ii 221 b.
HUÉ, O.—vii 528.
Huei Tsung—ii 234 b.
HUFELAND, G.—vii 529.
Hugenberg, A.—xii 338 a.
Hughes, C. H.—x 632 b.
HUGHES, T.—vii 529.
Hugo—Four Doctors vi 401 b.
HUGO, G.—vii 530.
HUGO, V.-M.—vii 531.
Hugues, Viscount d'—ii 123 a.
Human Ecology—see ECOLOGY, HUMAN.
Human Geography—see GEOGRAPHY.
HUMAN NATURE—vii 531–37; Altruism and Egoism ii 14–16; Anthropology ii 109 b; Aristocracy ii 186 b; Behaviorism ii 496 a; Economic Incentives v 330–33; Encyclopédistes v 529 b; Equality v 579 b; Fourier and Fourierism vi 403 a; Hume vii 550 b; Individualism vii 678 a; Instinct viii 81–83; Laissez Faire ix 19 b; Machiavelli ix 656 a; Materialism (Historical) x 219 b; Personality xii 85–88.
HUMANISM—vii 537–44; Introd. Vol. I (Renaissance and Reformation) i 86 b, (Individualism and Capitalism) 149 a; Art (Renaissance) ii 246–53; Ascham ii 267; Child (Welfare) iii 376 a; Communism iv 84 b; Copernicus iv 400 b; Education v 409 b; Hume vii 551 a; Melanchthon x 302 b; Petrarch xii 102 a; Reformation xiii 188 a; Renaissance xiii 278–85; Theater xiv 604 a; Universities and Colleges xv 182 b; Utopia xv 200 b.
Humanist Jurisprudence—Alciati i 618 a; Commentators iii 681 a; Cujas iv 617 a; Doneau v 216 a; Gouvêa vii 7 b.
HUMANITARIANISM—vii 544–49; Abolition i 369–72; Animal Protection ii 61–63; Atrocities ii 303 b; Capital Punishment iii 193 b; Charity iii 342 b; Christianity iii 452 a; Corporal Punishment iv 413 a; Criminal Law iv 576 b; Game Laws vi 564 a; Humanism vii 541 a; Justice, Administration of viii 521 b; Labor, Govt. Services for viii 645 a; Labor Legislation and Law viii 658 b; Missions x 544 a; Quakers xiii 13 a; Red Cross xiii 181–86; Social Work xiv 166 b; Welfare Work, Industrial xv 396 b.
HUMBOLDT, A. VON—vii 549.
HUMBOLDT, F. W. VON—vii 549.
HUME, D.—vii 550; Introd. Vol. I (The Rise of Liberalism) i 120 a, (The Revolutions) 133 a, 140 b; Acquisition i 421 b; Balance of Trade ii 401 a; Belief ii 500 b; Capital Levy iii 190 b; Common Sense iv 59 a; Evolution, Social v 657 a; Foreign Exchange vi 361 a; Gestalt vi 645 a; Individualism vii 678 a; International Trade (Theory) viii 205 a; Leadership ix 283 b; Logic ix 601 b; Political Science xii 217 b; Positivism xii 262 a; Wallace xv 326 a.
Hundred—Land Tenure ix 87 a.
HUNG HSIU-CH'ÜAN—vii 552.
Hungarian Scientific Academy—i 271 b.
HUNGER STRIKE—vii 552–55.
Huns—Migrations x 427 a.
HUNT, F.—vii 555.
Hunter, W. S.—iv 214 b.
HUNTER, W. W.—vii 555.
HUNTING—vii 556–58; Game Laws vi 562–64; Land Tenure (Primitive) ix 76 a; Nomads xi 390 b; Sports xiv 305 b.
HUNTINGTON, C. P.—vii 558.
Huntington, E.—Climate iii 561 a; Materialism (Historical) x 217 b; Migrations x 420 b.
HUSAYN A'LI—vii 559.
HUSKISSON, W.—vii 559; Free Trade vi 443 b.
Huss, J.— vii 560; Conciliar Movement iv 162 b.
Husserl, E.—i 205 a.
Hutcheson, A.—iii 190 b.
HUTCHESON, F.—vii 561; Introd. Vol. I (The Revolutions) i 140 b.
Huterian Brethren—iv 96 b.
HUXLEY, T. H.—vii 562; Mechanism and Vitalism x 268 a.
Hyde, E.—see CLARENDON, LORD.
HYNDMAN, H. M.—vii 562; Bax ii 482 b.
Hypnotism—x 355 b.
Hypotheca—xi 33 b, 36 b.
Hysteria—Abnormal Psychology i 362 a; Charcot iii 337 b.

Ibn 'Abd al-Wahhāb—see MOHAMMED IBN 'ABD AL-WAHHĀB.
IBN-HANBAL—vii 563.
IBN-KHALDŪN—vii 564; History and Historiography vii 382 b.
Ibn-Miskawayhi — see MISKAWAYHI.
Ibn Rushd—see AVERROES.
Ibn-Sa'ūd—xi 326 a.
IBN-TAYMĪYA—vii 565; Islam viii 335 a.
IBSEN, H.—vii 565.
Icaria—Communistic Settlements iv 100 a.
ICONOCLASM—vii 566–68; Ceremony iii 315 b; Cynics iv 680–85.
IDEALISM—vii 568–72; Introd. Vol. I (Greek Culture and Thought) i 26 a; Art (Greek) ii 241 b; Chuang Tzu iii 462; Classicism iii 542–45; Consciousness iv 212–20; Ethics v 602–07; Jurisprudence viii 480 b; Kant viii 538 b; Materialism (Historical) x 217 a; Naturalism xi 304 a; Plato and Platonism xii 158 a, Transcendentalism xv 75–77.
IDENTIFICATION—vii 573–75; Bertillon ii 527 b; Passport xii 13–16; Police xii 187 a.
Idéologues—v 108 a.
IDOLATRY—vii 575–77; Hero Worship vii 336–38; Iconoclasm vii 566–68.
IDRĪSI, AL-—vii 577.
IGLESIAS POSSE, P.—vii 577; Parties, Political (Spain) xi 630 b.
Ignatius of Loyola—see LOYOLA, I. DE.
Ihering, R. von—see JHERING, R. VON.
IHRER, E.—vii 578.
ILBERT, C. P.—vii 578.
ILLEGITIMACY—vii 579–86; Abortion i 372–74; Adoption i 462 b; Child (Mortality) iii 389 b, (Welfare Legislation) 426 a; Infanticide viii 27 b; Miscegenation x 533 b.
Illiteracy—see LITERACY AND ILLITERACY.
IMITATION—vii 586–87; Communication iv 79 a; Diffusionism v 140 a; Fashion vi 139–44; Habit vii 238 b; Sociology xiv 239 b; Tarde xiv 513 b.
IMMIGRATION—vii 587–95; Americanization ii 33–35; Antisemitism ii 124 b; Assimilation, Social ii 281–83; Contract Labor iv 342–44; Deportation and Expulsion of Aliens v 95–98; Ethnic Communities v 608 b, 611 a; Foreign Language Press vi 378–82; Frontier vi 501 b; Gangs vi 565 b; Garment Industries vi 578 b; Indenture vii 644–48; Intermarriage viii 154 a; Labor Movement viii 694 a; Legal Aid ix 320 a; Migrations x 429–41; Oriental Immigration xi 490–94.
Immortality—ii 95 a.
IMMUNITY, DIPLOMATIC—vii 595–97; Asylum ii 289 b.
IMMUNITY, POLITICAL—vii 597–600; Consular Service iv 280 b; Diplomacy v 148 b.
IMPEACHMENT—vii 600–02; Pardon xii 571 b.
IMPERIAL UNITY—vii 602–05; Introd. Vol. I (The Roman World) i 59 b; Govt. (Brit. Commonwealth of Nations) vii 38–43; Imperialism vii 605–13; Navy xi 311 a; Roads xiii 400 b; War xv 332 b.

IMPERIALISM—vii 605–13; Abolition i 371 b; Art (Indian) ii 233 a; Autonomy ii 332 b; Aviation ii 349 b; Backward Countries ii 380 a; Balance of Power ii 397 b; Bolshevism ii 626 a; Boundaries ii 650 a; Boycott ii 663 a; Brigandage ii 695 b; Capitulations iii 213 b; Captain of Industry iii 218 b; Chamberlain iii 323 a; Chambers of Commerce iii 328 b; Chartered Companies iii 347–52; Colonial Economic Policy iii 646–51; Colonies iii 653–63; Commerce iv 7 a; Concessions iv 158 a; Conquest iv 205–08; Cotton iv 487 b; Democracy v 81 b; Egyptian Problem v 441–44; Empire v 497–506; Étienne v 614 b; Europeanization v 623–36; Exploitation vi 17 a; Far Eastern Problem vi 92–100; Filibustering vi 231–33; Forced Labor vi 342 b; Foreign Investment vi 374 a, 376 a, 377 b; Foreign Language Press vi 381 a; Fortunes, Private vi 394 b; Guerrilla Warfare vii 198 a; Imperial Unity vii 602–05; Indian Question vii 659–74; International Advisers viii 157 a; International Finance viii 162 b; Leopold II ix 411 b; Manchurian Problem x 80–84; Mandates x 87–93; Massacre x 192 b; Merchant Marine x 343 b; Messianism x 357 b; Metals x 368 a; Missions x 542 b; Monroe Doctrine x 630–33; Morocco Question xi 18–19; Native Policy xi 252–83; Natural Resources xi 293 b, 296 b; Navy xi 312 a; Near Eastern Problem xi 320–27; Oil Industry xi 449 b; Open Door xi 468–71; Opium Problem xi 471 b; Pan-Americanism xi 539 b; Pan-Islamism xi 542–44; Pan-movements xi 544–54; Philippine Problem xii 109–16; Plantation xii 148–53; Protectorate xii 569 a; Race Conflict xiii 37 b; Roosevelt xiii 436 a; Socialism xiv 207 b; Spheres of Influence xiv 297–99; Stanley xiv 325 b; Technology xiv 555 b; War xv 335 b; World War xv 493 b.

Import Duties—see CUSTOMS DUTIES.

IMPRESSMENT—vii 614–16.

IMPRISONMENT—vii 616–19; Fines vi 250 a; Habeas Corpus vii 233–36; Indeterminate Sentence vii 650–52; Penal Institutions xii 57–64; Prison Labor xii 415–19; Punishment xii 714 a; Recidivism xiii 157–60.

Imprisonment for Debt — see Debt, Imprisonment for.

INAMA-STERNEGG, K. T. VON—vii 619.

INCEST—vii 620–22; Anthropology ii 85 b; Culture iv 629 b; Marriage x 146 b.

Incidence of Taxation — Land Taxation ix 72 a; Taxation xiv 534 b.

INCOME—vii 622–25; Capital iii 187–90; Distribution v 167–74; Income Tax vii 628 b; Interest viii 131–44; Investment viii 263–68; Laissez Faire ix 18 a; Land Valuation ix 137 a; National Income xi 205–24; Wages xv 291–320.

Income, National—see NATIONAL INCOME.

INCOME TAX—vii 626–39; Assessment of Taxes ii 276–79; Double Taxation v 225 a, 226 a; General Property Tax vi 607 a; Income vii 625 a; Interstate Commerce viii 225 a; Mortgage Tax xi 38 a; Municipal Finance xi 100 b; Publicity xii 699 b.

INCREASING RETURNS—vii 639–40; Diminishing Returns v 145 a; Economics (Cambridge School) v 370 b.

Indemnification — Law (Primitive) ix 204 a; Sanction, Social xiii 533 b.

INDEMNITY, MILITARY—vii 640–44; Reparations xiii 300–08.

INDENTURE—vii 644–48; Child (Dependent) iii 399 b, 401 a; Contract Labor iv 342 a; Migrations x 431 a; Oriental Immigration xi 490 a.

Independency—Levellers ix 421 b; Religious Institutions (Protestant) xiii 271 a; Sects xiii 627 b.

Independent Labour Party (British)—Anderson ii 56 a; Glasier vi 671 b; Hardie vii 269 a; Labor Parties viii 700 a.

Independent National Party, U. S.—see Greenback Party, U. S.

INDEPENDENT VOTING—vii 648–49.

INDETERMINATE SENTENCE—vii 650–52; Brockway iii 7 b; Criminology iv 590 b.

INDEX NUMBERS—vii 652–58; Average ii 336–38; Compensated Dollar iv 134 b; Cost of Living iv 481 b; Laspeyres ix 183 b; Money x 609 b; Prices (Statistics) xii 384 a.

Indian National Congress—vii 665 b.

Indian Problem, N. Amer.—xi 260–69.

INDIAN QUESTION—vii 659–74; Bentinck ii 519 b; Boycott ii 663 b; Brahmanism and Hinduism ii 677 b; Burke iii 75 b; Caste iii 255 a; Clive iii 568 a; Cooperation (India) iv 368–70; Curzon iv 656 a; Dalhousie iv 696 a; Das v 5; Dominion Status v 215 b; Duff v 271 a; Dufferin and Ava v 271 b; Dupleix v 282 b; Europeanization v 632 a; Famine vi 86 b, 88 b; Flax, Hemp and Jute vi 278 b; Gokhale vi 688 a; Guilds (Indian) vii 218 b; Hastings vii 279 a; Hunger Strike vii 554 b; Ilbert vii 578 b; Industrial Revolution viii 9 b; Lajpat Rai ix 21 a; Lawrence ix 279 b; Local Govt. ix 579 a; Macaulay ix 648 b; Malabari x 60 a; Mohammed 'Ali x 572 b; Municipal Govt. xi 113 a; Naoroji xi 182 a; Opium Problem xi 471–76; Pan-Islamism xi 543 b; Passive Resistance and Non-cooperation xii 10 a, 13 a; Public Health xii 655 a; Ramabai xiii 100 a; Ranade xiii 101 b; Roy xiii 447 b; Saraswati xiii 543 b; Sayyid Ahmad Khan xiii 560 a; Tilak xiv 628 b; Trade Unions xv 37 b; Wellesley xv 399 b.

Indiana Limestone Corp.—xiii 19 a.

Indictment—see GRAND JURY; PROSECUTION.

Indirect Taxes—xiv 533 b.

Individual Differences—see MENTAL TESTS; PERSONALITY.

INDIVIDUALISM—vii 674–80; Introd. Vol. 1 (Greek Culture and Thought) i 19 b, 37 a, (Individualism and Capitalism) 145–63; Agric. Cooperation i 521 b; Bills of Rights ii 545 b; Bonald ii 631 a; Bourgeoisie ii 655 b; Calvin iii 152 a; Capitalism iii 197 a; Charity iii 343 a; Christianity iii 458 a; Civil Liberties iii 509–13; Collectivism iii 633 a; Competition iv 141–47; Conscientious Objectors iv 211 a; Constant de Rebecque iv 242 a; Control, Social iv 346 a; Cosmopolitanism iv 458 a; Cynics iv 680–85; Democracy v 79 b; Economics (Physiocrats) v 349 a, (Classical School) 351 b; Emerson v 487 b; Endowments and Foundations v 534 a; Engineering v 545 a; Freedom of Contract vi 450–55; French Revolution vi 475 a, 479 b; Frontier vi 500–06; Govt. Regulation of Industry vii 124 a; Hedonism vii 307–10; Jhering viii 400 b; Jourdan viii 419 b; Justice viii 511 a; Justice, Administration of viii 521 a; Kelly viii 557 a; Labor Legislation and Law viii 665 a; Laissez Faire ix 15–20; Liberalism ix 435–42; Liberty ix 442–47; Literature ix 535 b; Materialism (Historical) x 218 a; Michel x 403 b; Middle Class x 408 b; Mill x 481 a; Minority Rights x 526 a; Monasticism x 585 a; Natural Law xi 288 a; Natural Rights xi 299–302; Nihilism xi 377–79; Passive Resistance and Non-cooperation xii 11 b; Political Science xii 216 b; Property xii 534 b; Protestantism xii 572 b; Puritanism xiii 4 b; Rationalism xiii 116 a; Religion xiii 230 a; Religious Freedom xiii 241 b; Religious Institutions (Protestant) xiii 268 a; Renaissance xiii 278–85; Romanticism xiii 430 b; Smiles xiv 112 a; Social Christian Movements xiv 125 a; Social Process xiv 150 b; Socialism xiv 192 a; Society xiv 225–32; Utilitarianism xv 197–200.

Inductive Method—x 390 b.

Industrial Accidents—see ACCIDENTS, INDUSTRIAL.

INDUSTRIAL ALCOHOL—vii 680–84.

Industrial Arbitration—see ARBITRATION, INDUSTRIAL.

INDUSTRIAL ARTS—vii 684–90; Architecture ii 172–75; Art (Modern) ii 253–57; Furniture vi 537–43; Glass and Pottery Industries vi 671–78; Gold vi 691 a; Handicraft vii 255–60; Morris xi 21 a; Museums and Exhibitions xi 139 b; Patents xii 20 b; Pottery xii 279–84; Textile Industry xiv 581 a.

Industrial Banks—xiv 109 b.

Industrial Combinations — see COMBINATIONS, INDUSTRIAL.

Industrial Conciliation—see ARBITRATION, INDUSTRIAL.

Industrial Courts—see COURTS, INDUSTRIAL.

INDUSTRIAL DEMOCRACY — vii 691–92; Guild Socialism vii 202–04; Industrial Relations vii 710–17; Industrial Relations Councils vii 717–22.

Industrial Disease—see INDUSTRIAL HAZARDS.

Industrial Disputes—see LABOR DISPUTES.

INDUSTRIAL EDUCATION—vii 692–97; Apprenticeship ii 144–47; Continuation Schools iv 313–15; Vocational Educ. xv 272–75.

INDUSTRIAL HAZARDS—vii 697–705; Accidents, Industrial i 391–401; Automobile Industry ii 327 a; Cement iii 290 a; Child (Labor) iii 422 a; Clerical Occupations iii 552 b; Construction Industry iv 270 a; Fatigue vi 148–51; Flax, Hemp and Jute vi 277 b; Glass and Pottery Industries vi 677 a; Industrial Hygiene vii 705–10; Iron and Steel Industry viii 316 b; Laundry and Dry Cleaning Industry ix 195 a; Leather Industries ix 314 b; Match Industry x 204 a; Mining Accidents x 508–13; Paints and Varnishes xi 532 a; Safety Movement xiii 503–06.

INDUSTRIAL HYGIENE—vii 705–10; Absenteeism i 379 b; Fatigue vi 148–51; Health Centers vii 288 a; Homework, Industrial vii 447 b; Industrial Hazards vii 702 b.

Industrial Insurance—ix 471 a.

Industrial Machinery—see MACHINERY, INDUSTRIAL.

Industrial Museums—xi 139 a.

Industrial Poisons—see INDUSTRIAL HAZARDS.

Industrial Police—see POLICING, INDUSTRIAL.

Industrial Power—see POWER, INDUSTRIAL.

INDUSTRIAL RELATIONS—vii 710–17; Introd. Vol. I (War and Reorientation) i 214 b; Absentee Ownership i 378 a; Arbitration, Industrial ii 153–57; Blacklist, Labor ii 578–79; Business Agent iii 91–92; Cartel iii 237 b; Closed Shop and Open Shop iii 568–70; Collective Bargaining iii 628–31; Company Housing iv 115–19; Company Towns iv 119–23; Company Unions iv 123–26; Conciliation, Industrial iv 165–69; Courts, Industrial iv 535–38; Detective Agencies, Private v 109 b; Employee Stock Ownership v 506–09; Employers' Associations v 509–14; Factory System vi 53 b; Fascism vi 137 b; Fraternizing vi 426 a; Garment Industries vi 582 b; Gas Industry vi 591 b; Group Insurance vii 185 b; Industrial Democracy vii 691–92; Industrial Relations Councils vii 717–22; Intimidation viii 239 b; Iron and Steel Industry viii 315–22; Labor-Capital Cooperation viii 624–29; Labor Contract viii 629–33; Labor Disputes viii 633–37; Labor, Govt. Services for viii 646 b; Labor Injunction viii 653–57; Labor Legislation and Law viii 657–76; Labor Turnover viii 709–13; Leather Industries ix 312–16; Leo XIII ix 408 b; Melchett x 304 a; Personnel Administration xii 88–90; Profit Sharing xii 487–92; Public Contracts xii 598 a; Public Utilities (U. S.) xii 682 b; Railroads xiii 93–100; Sabotage xiii 495–97; Scientific Management xiii 603–08; Strikes and Lockouts xiv 419–26; Textile Industry xiv 590–96; Trade Agreements xiv 667–70; Trade Unions (Germany) xv 15 b, (Gt. Brit.) 10 b, (Scandinavian Countries) 22 a; Unemployment Insurance xv 162–74; Welfare Work, Industrial xv 395–99.

INDUSTRIAL RELATIONS COUNCILS —vii 717–22; Arbeitsgemeinschaft ii 150; Conciliation, Industrial iv 165 b; Labor, Govt. Services for viii 647 b; National Economic Councils xi 194 a; Trade Unions (Germany) xv 16 a.

INDUSTRIAL REVOLUTION—viii 3–13; Art ii 254 a; Business iii 82 a; Centralization iii 310 b; Charity iii 343 a; Child (Welfare) iii 376 b, (Labor) 413 b; Chinese Problem iii 433 a; City iii 476 b; Civil Service iii 517 b; Coal Industry iii 583 a; Coeducation iii 614 b; Colonies iii 659 b; Commerce iv 9 b; Companionate Marriage iv 113 b; Cotton iv 486 b; Dye Industry v 304 b; Engineering v 543 a; Factory System vi 52 a; Fortunes, Private vi 393 b; Guilds (Chinese) vii 220 b, (Europ.) 213 a, (Indian) 218 b, (Islamic) 216 a, (Japanese) 222 b; Hours of Labor vii 479 b; Housing vii 498 b; Industrialism viii 19 a; International Relations viii 186 b; Invention viii 249 a; Iron and Steel Industry viii 298 b; Leather Industries ix 301 b; Literacy and Illiteracy ix 518 a; Literature ix 535 a; Machines and Tools x 21 b; Migrations x 433 b; Mining x 497 a; Music xi 159 b; Nationalism xi 245 b; Proletariat xii 511 a; Socialism xiv 193 a; Textile Industry xiv 584 a, 591 a.

Industrial Unionism—see TRADE UNIONS.

INDUSTRIAL WORKERS OF THE WORLD—viii 13–18; American Legion ii 31 b; Casual Labor iii 261 a; Criminal Syndicalism iv 582 b; Debs v 32 a; Dual Unionism v 260 a; Haywood vii 286 a; Negro Problem xi 350 b; Sabotage xiii 496 a; Wood Industries xv 474 a.

INDUSTRIALISM—viii 18–26; Absenteeism i 378–80; Acquisition i 421 a; Agric. Marketing i 560 a; Agric. Policy i 566 a; Agriculture i 580 a, 584 b, 596 b; Aristocracy ii 188 a; Armaments ii 194 a; Art ii 226 a, (Modern) 253–57; Bourgeoisie ii 654–56; Business iii 82 b; Business Cycles iii 92–106; Capitalism iii 195–208; Captain of Industry iii 216–20; Cement iii 287 a; Chemical Industries iii 365–67; Child (Labor) iii 412–24; Chinese Problem iii 433 a; Christianity iii 457 a; City iii 477 a; Civic Art iii 492 b; Class iii 534 a; Clerical Occupations iii 551 a; Coal Industry iii 582 a; Combinations, Industrial iii 664–74; Commercialism iv 33 a; Company Housing iv 115–19; Company Towns iv 119–23; Competition iv 141–47; Consumer Protection iv 282 b; Corporation iv 415 b; Criticism, Social iv 601 b; Dye Industry v 301–05; Economic Policy v 333–44; Economics (Socialist Economics) v 378 a; Education v 411 b; Efficiency v 437–39; Electric Power v 456–70; Engineering v 543 a; Europeanization v 633 a, 634 a, 635 a; Expenditures, Public vi 7 b; Expositions, International vi

23–27; Factory System vi 51–55; Family vi 68 b; Far Eastern Problem vi 92–100; Foreign Investment vi 367 a; Fortunes, Private vi 394 a; Furniture vi 539 a; Garment Industries vi 573 b; Gosplan vi 705–13; Govt. vii 13 b; Handicraft vii 257 a; Hours of Labor vii 479 b; Imperialism vii 609 b; Indian Question vii 662 a; Industrial Arts vii 688 b; Industrial Hazards vii 698 a; Industrial Hygiene vii 705–10; Industrial Relations vii 710–17; Industrial Revolution viii 3–13; International Trade viii 190 b, 192 a; Iron and Steel Industry viii 296 a; Labor viii 618 a; Labor, Govt. Services for viii 644 a; Labor Legislation and Law viii 665 a; Laissez Faire ix 19 a; Large Scale Production ix 170–81; Leather Industries ix 301 a, 307 a, 313 a; Leisure ix 404 a; Liberalism ix 438 a; Literature ix 535 a; Machinery, Industrial x 3 a; Management x 77 b; Mechanic x 264 b; Metals x 369 b; Middle Class x 408 a; Mining x 497 a; Mobilization and Demobilization x 555–64; Nationalism xi 245 b; Natural Resources xi 292 b; Navy xi 311 b; Occupation xi 427 b; Old Age xi 454 a; Organization, Economic xi 486 a; Power, Industrial xii 293–300; Raw Materials xiii 123–32; Reconstruction xiii 170 a; Socialism xiv 193 a; Standardization xiv 319–22; Technology xiv 553–60; Unemployment xv 147–62; Women in Industry xv 451–59.

Industry—see Classification of Articles (Industry), p. 551. See also Census iii 300 a; National Income xi 215 b; Negro Problem xi 339 a, 344 a; Occupation xi 433 a; Pensions xii 68 b; Research xiii 331 a; Social Work (Case Work) xiv 180 a; Statistics xiv 361 a; Weights and Measures xv 390 b. See also Index, Government Regulation; INDUSTRIAL RELATIONS; INDUSTRIAL REVOLUTION; INDUSTRIALISM. For biog. references see Classification of Articles (Business and Finance), p. 558.

Infant Mortality—Child (Mortality) iii 384–90; Illegitimacy vii 580 b; Mortality xi 25 b.

INFANTICIDE—viii 27–28; Abortion i 372–74; Birth Control ii 559 a; McLennan x 29 b.

Infectious Diseases—see COMMUNICABLE DISEASES, CONTROL OF.

INFLATION AND DEFLATION—viii 28–33; Agio i 487; Assignats ii 279–81; Bills of Credit ii 542–44; Compensated Dollar iv 134–35; Confiscation iv 186 b; Debt v 36 b; Devaluation v 116 b; Economic Policy v 343 a; Foreign Exchange vi 364 a; Free Silver vi 438–40; Hoarding vii 394 a; Monetary Stabilization x 592 a; Paper Money xi 569 a; Price Regulation xii 356 a; Prices (Hist.) xii 375–81; Public Works xii 696 b; Rentenmark xiii 296; Speculation xiv 291 b; Spoils System xiv 312 a; Unearned Increment xv 147 a; Unemployment xv 152 a.

Inflective Languages—ix 161 b.

INGENIEROS, J.—viii 33.

INGERSOLL, R. G.—viii 33.

INGRAM, J. K.—viii 34.

INHERITANCE—viii 35–43; Alienation of Property i 639 b; Aubaine, Right of ii 307–08; Concubinage iv 171–73; Conflict of Laws iv 192 a; Entail v 553–56; Escheat v 591–93; Feudalism (Europ.) vi 207 b, (Ottoman) 212 a; Freehold vi 462 b; Gifts vi 659 b; Illegitimacy vii 582–86; Inheritance Taxation viii 43–49; Jīmūtavāhana viii 403 b; Land Tenure (Primitive) ix 77 a; Landed Estates ix 142 b; Law (Chinese) ix 253 a, (Cuneiform) 216 a, (Greek) 228 a, (Hellenistic and Greco-Egyptian) 231 b, (Japanese) 256 a, (Jewish) 220 a, (Slavic) 243 b; Marital Property x 116–22; Mortmain xi 41 b; Primogeniture xii 402–05; Succession, Laws of xiv 436–41.

INHERITANCE TAXATION—viii 43–49; Assessment of Taxes ii 277 b; Double Taxation v 226 a; Inheritance viii 39 b, 40 b.

INITIATION—viii 49–50; Dance iv 702 b; Death Customs iv 23 a; Education, Primitive v 401 b; Fasting vi 144 b; Mysteries xi 172–75; Secret Societies xiii 622 a.

INITIATIVE AND REFERENDUM—viii 50–52; Amendments, Constitutional ii 22 b; Govt. (Austria) vii 77 b, (Switzerland) 58 a, (U. S.) 20 b; Plebiscite xii 163–66.

INJUNCTION—viii 53–57; Arrest ii 222 a; Boycott ii 664 a; Jurisdiction viii 475 a; Labor Injunction viii 653–57; Patents xii 22 a.

Injunction, Labor—see LABOR INJUNCTION.

Inland Waterways—see WATERWAYS, INLAND.

INNOCENT III—viii 57; Holy Roman Empire vii 424 b; Religious Institutions (Roman Catholic) xiii 255 a.

INNOVATION—viii 58–61; Invention viii 247–51; Modernism x 564–68; Pragmatism xii 307 b.

Inns of Chancery—ix 332 a.

Inns of Court—ix 332 a, 336 b.

Inoculation—Jenner viii 381 a; Pasteur xii 18 b.

INQUISITION—viii 61–64; Apostasy and Heresy ii 129 b; Canon Law iii 183 a; Jury viii 493 a; Llorente ix 554 a; Military Orders x 461 b; Prosecution xii 546 a.

INSANITY—viii 64–71; Abnormal Psychology i 360–69; Alcohol i 625 a; Alienist i 641; Genius vi 612 b; Institutions, Public viii 91 a; Mental Disorders x 313–19.

Insects—Climate iii 560 b; Communicable Diseases, Control of iv 70 a; Cotton iv 490 a; Dye Industry v 297 a.

INSPECTION—viii 71–74; Adulteration i 467 a; Business, Govt. Services for iii 118 a; Canning Industry iii 177 a; Commissions iv 37 b; Commodity Exchanges iv 46 b; Labor, Govt. Services for viii 646 a, 652 a; Meat Packing and Slaughtering x 261 a; Public Contracts xii 598 a.

INSTALMENT SELLING—viii 74–81; Retail Credit xiii 342–46.

INSTINCT—viii 81–83; Introd. Vol. I (War and Reorientation) i 206 a; Cannibalism iii 173 a; Comparative Psychology iv 131 a; Darwin v 5 a; Habit vii 236 b; Human Nature vii 531–37; Psychology xii 593 b; Social Psychology xiv 154 a.

Institute of Human Relations, Yale—i 345 a.

Institutes of Justinian—see CORPUS JURIS CIVILIS.

INSTITUTION—viii 84–89; Association ii 284 b; Control, Social iv 345 b; Culture iv 626 a; Economic Policy v 337 a; Economics (Institutional School) v 388 b; Folkways vi 293–96; Functionalism vi 525 a; Hadley vii 240 a; Human Nature vii 531–37; Lacombe ix 8 a; Literature ix 523–43; Method, Scientific x 392 b; Organization, Economic xi 484–90; Religion xiii 230 b; Society xiv 231 a.

Institutional Economics—v 387–92.

INSTITUTIONS, PUBLIC—viii 90–95; Almshouse ii 8–10; Blind ii 588 b; Boards, Administrative ii 607 b; Boards, Advisory ii 611 a; Child (Dependent) iii 399 b, (Delinquent) 408 b, (Institutions) 410–12; Cripples iv 593 a; Dix v 184 b; Mental Defectives x 312–13; Mental Disorders x 317 b; Mental Hygiene x 319–23; Old Age xi 458 a; Penal Institutions xii 57–64.

Instrumentalism — Pragmatism xii 309 b.

INSURANCE—viii 95–113 (Principles and History 95–98, 112, Industry 98–106, 112, Law and Regulation 106–13). See Classification of Articles (Insurance),

Index (Industrialism — International Law)

p. 552. *See also* Aviation ii 357 a; Bonding ii 632 a; Broker iii 9 b; Corporation Taxes iv 433 b; Ehrenberg v 445 a; Land Mortgage Credit (Agric.) ix 48 b; Law (Japanese) ix 257 a; Money Market x 615 a; Negro Problem xi 348 a; Price, R. xii 350 a; Suretyship and Guaranty xiv 485 b; Trusts and Trustees xv 124 a; Veterans xv 246 a.

Insurgency, Political (*International Law*)—*see* INSURRECTION.

INSURGENCY, POLITICAL (*Party Politics*)—viii 113–16; Legislative Assemblies (U. S.) ix 363 b.

INSURRECTION—viii 116–18; Belligerency ii 506 a; Civil War iii 523 b; Guerrilla Warfare vii 198 a; Rebellion xiii 144–47; Terrorism xiv 577 a.

Integration, Industrial—*see* COMBINATIONS, INDUSTRIAL.

INTELLECTUALS—viii 118–26; Labor Movement viii 685 b; Machajski ix 654 a; Middle Class x 413 b; Nihilism xi 377–79; Professions xii 476–80; Renaissance xiii 280 b; Russian Revolution xiii 474 b, 480 b.

Intelligence—*see* MENTAL TESTS.

Intelligence Quotient—Abnormal Psychology i 365 b; Mental Tests x 323 b.

Intendants—Ardashev ii 181 a; Local Govt. ix 575 a; Louis XIV ix 619 a.

INTENT, CRIMINAL—viii 126–31; Homicide vii 453 a; Insanity viii 65 a; Juvenile Delinquency and Juvenile Courts viii 529 a.

Interallied Debts—Loans, Intergovernmental ix 557 a; Reparations xiii 307 a; War Finance xv 351 a.

Interdict — Excommunication v 675 b; Outlawry xi 506 a; Religious Institutions (Roman Catholic) xiii 252 b.

INTEREST—viii 131–44; Abstinence i 382–83; Böhm-Bawerk ii 618 b; Bonds ii 634 b, 636 a; Capital iii 189 b; Capitalization and Amortization of Taxes iii 212 a; Christianity iii 458 a; Church Fathers iii 467 b; Culpeper iv 617 b; Distribution v 171 a; Economics (Classical School) v 355 a, (Marginal Utility Economics) 362 a, (Cambridge School) 370 a; Fair Return vi 56–58; Gesell vi 641 a; Income vii 623 b; Judaism viii 435 b; Just Price viii 505 b; Labor Exchange Banks viii 637–44; Land Mortgage Credit (Urban) ix 51 b; Law (Jewish) ix 223 b; Life Insurance ix 469 a; Loans, Personal ix 562 a, 564 b; Location of Industry ix 587 a; National Income xi 210 a; Pawnbroking xii 34 a; Price Stabilization xii 363 b; Prices (Theory) xii 374 a; Profit xii 480–87; Public Debt xii 603 b; Saving xiii 552 a; Small Loans xiv 107 a, 109 a; Usury xv 193–97; Wages xv 296 a; Wicksell xv 418 a.

INTERESTS—viii 144–48; Bloc, Parliamentary ii 592 a; Bribery ii 690–92; Civic Organizations iii 498–502; Customs Duties iv 670 b; Discussion v 166–67; Functional Representation vi 520 a; Group vii 181 a; Jurisprudence viii 489 a; Legal Profession and Legal Education ix 341 a; Liberty ix 442 a; Lobby ix 565–68; Middle Class x 407–15; Militarism x 447 b; Munitions Industry xi 132 b; National Economic Planning xi 192–97; Parties, Political xi 590–639; Philippine Problem xii 111 a; Pluralism xii 170–74; Plutocracy xii 175–77; Political Science xii 219 b; Pressures, Social xii 347 a; Propaganda xii 521–28; Publicity xii 700 b; Ratzenhofer xiii 121 a; Reconstruction xiii 169 a; Representation xiii 313 a; Revolution and Counter-revolution xiii 367–76; Trusts xv 118 b; Vested Interests xv 240–43; Veterans xv 243–47.

Intergovernmental Loans — *see* LOANS, INTERGOVERNMENTAL.

INTERLOCKING DIRECTORATES— viii 148–51.

INTERMARRIAGE — viii 151–55; Aristocracy ii 187 b; Heredity vii 332 a; Jewish Emancipation viii 398 b; Miscegenation x 531–34; Race xiii 28 b; Race Mixture xiii 41–43.

Intermediate Credit — Agric. Credit i 532 a; Farm Loan System, Federal vi 110 a.

Interment—*see* Burial Customs.

Internal Revenue Taxes—*see* EXCISE.

International—*see* First International; Second International; Third International.

INTERNATIONAL ADVISERS—viii 155–59; International Finance viii 162 a.

International Agreements — *see* AGREEMENTS, INTERNATIONAL.

International Arbitration — *see* ARBITRATION, INTERNATIONAL.

International Convention for Air Navigation—ii 351 a, 357 a, 365 b.

International Expositions — *see* EXPOSITIONS, INTERNATIONAL.

International Federation of Teachers' Associations—xiv 552 a.

International Federation of Trade Unions — Labor Movement viii 695 a; Trade Unions xv 53 b. *See also* Amsterdam International.

INTERNATIONAL FINANCE — viii 159–64; Balance of Trade ii 399–406; Central Banking iii 306 a; Financial Organization vi 246 b; Foreign Exchange vi 358–64; Foreign Investment vi 364–78; Gold vi 692 b; Indemnity, Military vii 643 a; International Trade viii 198 b, (Theory) 204 a; Loans, Intergovernmental ix 556–61; Money Market x 617 a; Reparations xiii 300–08; Rothschild Family xiii 440 b; Self-Sufficiency, Economic xiii 657 b, 658 b; Silver xiv 59 a; Tourist Traffic xiv 663 a.

International Guaranties — *see* GUARANTIES, INTERNATIONAL.

International Harvester Co.—i 555 a.

International Institute of Agriculture—*see* AGRICULTURE, INTERNATIONAL INSTITUTE OF.

International Labor Office—*see* INTERNATIONAL LABOR ORGANIZATION.

INTERNATIONAL LABOR ORGANIZATION—viii 164–67; Child (Labor) iii 417 a; Coal Industry iii 599 b; Forced Labor vi 344 b; Health Insurance vii 295 b; Labor, Govt. Services for viii 652 b; Leisure ix 404 b; Statistics xiv 360 a; Wages xv 317 a.

International Ladies' Garment Workers' Union—Garment Industries vi 581 b; Schlesinger, B. xiii 573 a; Sigman, M. xiv 51 b.

International Language—ix 168 a.

INTERNATIONAL LAW—viii 167–75; Introd. Vol. 1 (The Roman World) i 49 b, 60 a, (Renaissance and Reformation) 100 a; Advisory Opinions i 478–80; Aggression, International i 486 a; Agreements, International i 518–20; Alabama Claims i 611–13; Alien i 634 b; Alien Property i 638 b; Amos ii 39 a; Annexation ii 68–69; Arbitration, International ii 162 a; Armed Merchantmen ii 201–03; Asylum ii 289–90; Bar ii 456 a; Bartolus of Sassoferrato ii 471 a; Belligerency ii 505–07; Bergbohm ii 521 b; Blockade ii 594–96; Boundaries ii 651 b; Bulmerincq iii 64 a; Bynkershoek iii 130 a; Calvo iii 153 a; Calvo and Drago Doctrines iii 153–56; Casus Belli iii 266 b; Cession iii 319–20; Citizenship iii 472 a; Clunet iii 580 a; Codification iii 609 b; Comity iii 678–79; Concessions iv 155 a; Conflict of Laws iv 187–94; Continuous Voyage iv 320–21; Contraband of War iv 321–23; Declaration of London v 47–48; Declaration of Paris v 48–49; Diplomatic Protection v 153–55; Duress v 289 b; Enemy Alien v 537–39; Equality of States v 580–82; Exterritoriality vi 36–39; Extradition vi 41–44; Fauchille vi 152 a;

Field vi 229 a; Fiore vi 254 b; Foreign Corporations vi 357 a; Freedom of the Seas vi 459–61; Gentili vi 616 a; Grotius vii 177 b; Hall vii 248 a; Heffter vii 311 b; Hübner vii 527 b; Immunity, Diplomatic vii 596 b; Insurrection viii 117 b; International Legislation viii 175–77; International Organization viii 181 a; International Waterways viii 212 a; Intervention viii 236–39; Jitta viii 405 a; Jus Gentium viii 502–04; Lainé ix 15 a; League of Nations ix 288 b; Martens, F. F. x 161 a; Martens, G. F. von x 161 b; Merchantmen, Status of x 350–52; Military Occupation x 456–59; Nationality xi 249–52; Neutrality xi 360–65; Oppenheim xi 476 a; Outlawry of War xi 508 b; Peace Movements xii 44 b; Permanent Court of Arbitration xii 76–78; Permanent Court of International Justice xii 78–81; Piracy xii 136 b; Prize xii 424–26; Pufendorf xii 702 b; Rachel xiii 44 a; Recognition, International xiii 165–68; Renault xiii 287 b; Reprisals xiii 315–17; Rivier xiii 399 b; Sanction, International xiii 528 b; Sovereignty xiv 265 b; Stoicism xiv 409 b; Stowell xiv 414 b; Suárez xiv 429 a; Treaties xv 96–101; Uniform Legislation xv 179 b; Vattel xv 232 a; Vitoria xv 268 b; Warfare, Laws of xv 359–64; Weiss xv 393 a; Westlake xv 405 b; Wheaton xv 408 a; Zitelmann xv 537 a; Zouche xv 540 b.

INTERNATIONAL LEGISLATION—viii 175–77; Arbitration, International ii 157–62; Declaration of London v 47–48; Declaration of Paris v 48–49; Hague Conferences vii 242–44; International Labor Organization viii 164–67; International Law viii 167–75; International Organization viii 177–85; Labor Legislation and Law viii 666 b; League of Nations ix 289 a; Treaties xv 96–101; Uniform Legislation xv 180 a.

International Management Institute—iii 90 a.

International Mercantile Marine Co.—Ballin ii 410 a; Shipping xiv 39 b.

International Miners' Federation —x 506 a.

International News Service—xii 336 a.

INTERNATIONAL ORGANIZATION—viii 177–85. *See relevant titles in* Classification of Articles (International Relations), p. 552. *See also* Index, INTERNATIONAL RELATIONS.

International Police Force—ix 485 b.

INTERNATIONAL RELATIONS—viii 185–89. *See* Classification of Articles (International Relations), p. 552. *See also* Introd. Vol. I (War and Reorientation) i 217 a; Boards, Administrative ii 608 a; Casus Belli iii 266–68; Embargo v 485–87; Executive v 683 a; Fascism vi 138 b; Govt. (Brit. Commonwealth of Nations) vii 38–43; Immigration vii 593 b; Investigations, Governmental viii 259 b; Protection xii 564 a. *See also* INTERNATIONALISM.

International Relief Union—xiii 183 b.

International Settlements, Bank for—*see* Bank for International Settlements.

International Statistical Institute —xiv 359 b.

International Telephone and Telegraph Corp.—xiv 566 b.

INTERNATIONAL TRADE—viii 189–208 (Institutional Framework 189–200, 208, Theory 200–08). *See relevant titles in* Classification of Articles (Commerce), p. 549. *See also* Automobile Industry ii 324 b, 325 b, 328 a; Aviation ii 364 b; Bill of Exchange ii 541 b; Business, Govt. Services for iii 114 a; Cartel iii 240 a; Cement iii 288 a; Credit Insurance iv 559 a; Drawback v 233–35; Dye Industry v 304 a; Economic Policy v 338 a; Economics (Classical School) v 355 b; Electric Power v 466 b; Electrical Manufacturing Industry v 475 b; Far Eastern Problem vi 92 b; Foreign Investment vi 365 b; Furniture vi 542 a; Glass and Pottery Industries vi 677 b; Gosplan vi 713 a; Grains vii 143 b; Heavy Chemicals vii 303 a; International Finance viii 160 a; Iron and Steel Industry viii 312 b; Meat Packing and Slaughtering x 252 b; Metals x 371 a, 387 b; Milling Industry x 486 b; Motion Pictures xi 64 b; National Econ. Planning xi 203 a; Oil Industry xi 449 b; Paints and Varnishes xi 532 b; Pan-Americanism xi 539 b; Philippine Problem xii 111 a, 113 b; Rubber xiii 459 b; Stabilization, Econ. xiv 314 a; Textile Industry xiv 587 b. *See also* COMMERCE.

International Transit — *see* TRANSIT, INTERNATIONAL.

International Union of Revolutionary Writers—ix 541 a.

INTERNATIONAL WATERWAYS — viii 208–14; Commercial Routes iv 19–24; Fisheries vi 270 a; Panama Canal xi 554–58; Suez Canal xiv 444–47; Transit, International xv 79 a.

International Working Men's Assoc. (1864)—*see* First International.

International Working Men's Assoc. (1922)—Labor Movement viii 695 b; Syndicalism xiv 499 a.

INTERNATIONALISM—viii 214–19. *See relevant titles in* Classification of Articles (International Relations), p. 552. *See also* Introd. Vol. I (The Trend to Internationalism) i 172 b; Autonomy ii 336 a; Chambers of Commerce iii 328 b; Communication iv 80 a; Cooperation iv 362 a; Copyright iv 403 a; Cosmopolitanism iv 458 a; Empire v 505 b; Employers' Associations v 513 b; Expositions, International vi 23–27; Federalism vi 169 a, 172 a; Federation vi 176 b; Financial Organization vi 246 b; Imperial Unity vii 605 a; Labor Movement viii 695 a; Learned Societies ix 299 a; Legal Aid ix 323 b; Maritime Law x 130 a; Maternity Welfare x 225 a; Minorities, National x 523 a; Monetary Unions x 600 a; Nationalism xi 239 b; Patents xii 22 b; Postal Service xii 273 b; Public Health xii 655 b; Radio xiii 59 a, 65 a; Railroads (Labor) xiii 98 a; Religious Institutions (Protestant) xiii 272 b; Socialist Parties xiv 216 a; Stabilization, Economic xiv 314 a; Teaching Profession xiv 552 a; Trade Unions xv 53–55; Trademarks and Names xv 60 a; Transportation xv 89 b; Weights and Measures xv 390 a.

INTERPELLATION — viii 219–20; Investigations, Governmental viii 258 a; Legislative Assemblies (France) ix 375 a, (Germany) 382 a.

Interpolation—Eisele v 447 b; Favre vi 152 b; Roman Law xiii 424 b.

INTERSTATE COMMERCE—viii 220–29; Concurrent Powers iv 174 a; Foreign Corporations vi 355 a; Interstate Commerce Commission viii 229–36; Radio xiii 63 b.

INTERSTATE COMMERCE COMMISSION—viii 229–36; Adams i 433 a; Express Companies vi 28 a; Knapp viii 579 a; Prouty xii 576 b; Railroads xiii 82 a, 85 b; Rate Regulation xiii 107 a.

Inter-State Commission, Australia—viii 228 a.

Interstate Compacts—*see* COMPACTS, INTERSTATE.

INTERVENTION — viii 236–39; Backward Countries ii 381 a; Calvo and Drago Doctrines iii 153–56; Capitulations iii 213 b; Civil War iii 525 a; Diplomatic Protection v 153–55; Far Eastern Problem vi 92–100; Foreign Investment vi 376 a; International Finance viii 161 b; Loans, Intergovernmental ix 556 b; Mediation x 272 a; Minorities,

National x 523 b; Monroe Doctrine x 630-33; Repudiation of Public Debts xiii 323 b.
Intestacy—Inheritance viii 37 a; Succession, Laws of xiv 437 a, 438 b.
Intieri, B.—i 274 a.
INTIMIDATION—viii 239-42; Ku Klux Klan viii 606 b; Policing, Industrial xii 193-96; Racketeering xiii 45-50; Terrorism xiv 576 a.
INTOLERANCE—viii 242-45. See relevant titles in Classification of Articles (Social Discrimination), p. 555. See also Anti-radicalism ii 116-18; Apostasy and Heresy ii 128-30; Belief ii 502 a; Blasphemy ii 586 b; Blue Laws ii 600-02; Censorship iii 290-94; Civil Liberties iii 511 a; Fanaticism vi 90-92; Freedom of Speech and of the Press vi 455-59; Inquisition viii 61-64; Jesuits viii 382 a.
INTRANSIGENCE — viii 245-47; Doctrinaire v 187-89; Faction vi 49-51; Opportunism xi 476 b; Radicalism xiii 53 b.
Intrastate Commerce—Interstate Commerce viii 225 a; Interstate Commerce Commission viii 232 b.
Introvert—i 364 b.
Invasion—x 457 a.
INVENTION — viii 247-51. See TECHNOLOGY.
Inveresk Press Interests—xii 333 b.
INVESTIGATIONS, GOVERNMENTAL—viii 251-60; Federal Trade Commission vi 165-69; Impeachment vii 600-02; Legislative Assemblies (U. S.) ix 363 b.
INVESTITURE CONFLICT—viii 260-63; Anselm ii 71 b; Gregory VII vii 167 b; Henry IV (d. 1106) vii 321 b; Holy Roman Empire vii 424 a; Religious Institutions (Roman Catholic) xiii 251 a; Yves of Chartres xv 522 a.
INVESTMENT—viii 263-68. See Classification of Articles (Investment and Speculation), p. 552. See also Appreciation ii 141-44; Debt v 35 a; Insurance viii 104 a; Laissez Faire ix 19 a; Life Insurance ix 470 b; Stabilization, Economic xiv 310 b.
INVESTMENT BANKING—viii 268-77; Banking, Commercial (Eur.) ii 435-41; Business Ethics iii 112 a; Corporation Finance iv 425 a; Financial Organization vi 241-47; Interlocking Directorates viii 150 b; International Finance viii 162 a; Investment viii 265 b; Money Market x 616 a; Morgan Family xi 11 a; Promotion xii 521 a; Schiff xiii 568 b; Stillman xiv 392 a.
Investment, Foreign—see FOREIGN INVESTMENT.
INVESTMENT TRUSTS—viii 277-84.

IONESCU, T.—viii 284.
Irish Labour Party—viii 705 b.
IRISH QUESTION—viii 285-95; Absentee Ownership i 377 a; Allegiance i 646 b; Butt iii 126 b; Catholic Emancipation iii 270 a; Collins iii 637 b; Connolly iv 204; Davitt v 12 a; Famine vi 86 a; Flax, Hemp and Jute vi 276 a; Flood vi 282 a; Govt. (Ireland) vii 36-38; Grattan vii 156 b; Griffith vii 171 b; Hunger Strike vii 553 b; Land Settlement ix 58 b; Land Tenure ix 89 a; Legislative Assemblies ix 374 a; O'Connell xi 436 a; Parties, Political (Irish Free State) xi 610 a; Terrorism xiv 577 b; Trade Unions xv 11 b.
IRNERIUS—viii 295; Glossators vi 680 b.
Iron—x 365 a, 370 a, 384 b.
Iron Age—ii 165 b.
Iron Law of Wages—xv 293 a.
IRON AND STEEL INDUSTRY—viii 295-324 (Hist. and Present Organization 295-315, 322, Labor 315-22, 324); Basing Point Prices ii 473-75; Carnegie iii 230 b; Cement iii 289 b; Coal Industry iii 583 a; Gary vi 588 a; Industrial Revolution viii 6 b; Krupp viii 605 a; Large Scale Production ix 176 b; Location of Industry ix 591 a; Metals x 370 a; Munitions Industry xi 128-34; Shipbuilding xiv 26 b.
IRREDENTISM—viii 325-28; Boundaries ii 651 a; Military Desertion x 453 a.
IRRIGATION—viii 328-32; Agric. Cooperation i 527 a; Agriculture i 574 a, 589 b, 595 a; Agriculture, Govt. Services for i 602 b; Fruit and Vegetable Industry vi 508 a; International Waterways viii 213 a; Reclamation xiii 161 b.
Irwin, Lord—vii 669 b.
Isabella of Castile—see FERDINAND V AND ISABELLA.
ISELIN, I.—viii 332.
ISIDORE OF SEVILLE—viii 332; Church Fathers iii 467 a; History and Historiography vii 371 a; Jus Gentium viii 503 a; Tyranny xv 136 a.
ISLAM—viii 333-44; Introd. Vol. I (The Universal Church) i 62 b; Art (Indian) ii 232 a; Caliphate iii 145-49; Chivalry (Arabic) iii 441-43; Commerce iv 5 b; Commercial Routes iv 21 a; Education v 409 a; Egyptian Problem v 441-44; Fatalism vi 147 b; Guilds vii 214-16; History and Historiography vii 381-83; Holidays vii 414 b; Indian Question vii 659 b; Intermarriage viii 153 a; Islamic Law viii 344-49; Jihad viii 401-03; Judaism viii 441 a; Law (Hindu) ix 261 a; Messianism x 363 a; Military Orders x 459 b; Missions x 536

a; Mysticism xi 175 b; Pan-Islamism xi 542-44; Printing and Publishing xii 408 a; Proselytism xii 551 b; Religious Freedom xiii 240 b; Religious Orders xiii 277 a; Slavery xiv 79 a. For biog. references see Classification of Articles (Religion—Islam), p. 568.
ISLAMIC LAW—viii 344-49; Caliphate iii 145-49. For biog. references see Classification of Articles (Law), p. 564, under heading Moslem.
Isly, Duc d'—see BUGEAUD DE LA PICONNERIE, T. R.
ISMAIL KEMAL BEY—viii 350.
ISMAY, T. H.—viii 350.
Isnard, A. N.—v 365 a.
Isocrates—i 29 b.
ISOLATION—viii 350-52; Feuds vi 220 b; Gypsies vii 231-32; Isolation, Diplomatic viii 352-55; Segregation xiii 643-47.
ISOLATION, DIPLOMATIC—viii 352-55.
Isolation, Medical—iv 67 a, 71 a.
Isomorphism—iv 215 b.
ITAGAKI, T.—viii 355.
Itard, J. E. M. G.—x 312 a.
ITO, H.—viii 356; Govt. (Japan) vii 95 b.
IVAN IV—viii 356.
Ivan the Terrible—see IVAN IV.
Ivo of Chartres—see YVES OF CHARTRES.
IXTLILXÓCHITL, F. DE A.—viii 357; Introd. Vol. I (The Social Sciences as Disciplines, Lat. Amer.) i 301 a.
IZVOLSKY, A. P.—viii 358; Aehrenthal i 481 a.

JABAVU, J. T.—viii 358.
Jabir ibn Hayyan—i 617 b.
JACINI, S. F.—viii 359.
JACKSON, A.—viii 359; Agrarian Movements (U. S.) i 509 b; Biddle ii 536 b; Spoils System xiv 303 a; Veto xv 247 b.
JACOBINISM—viii 360-63; Introd. Vol. I (The Revolutions) i 132 b; French Revolution vi 477 a; Masonry x 180 b.
JACOBS, J.—viii 363.
Jacobus—see FOUR DOCTORS.
JACOBY, J.—viii 364.
Jacquerie—x 108 b.
Jahangir—ii 232 a.
JAHN, F. L.—viii 365; Physical Education xii 130 b.
Jainism—xiii 276 b.
JAKOB, L. H. VON—viii 365.
JAKŠIĆ, V.—viii 365.
JAMÁL U'D-DÍN AL-ÁFGHÁNÍ—viii 366.
JAMES I—viii 366; Introd. Vol. I (Renaissance and Reformation) i 99 b; Allegiance i 645 a; Prerogative xii 319 a.
JAMES OF VITERBO—viii 367.
JAMES, W.—viii 368; Behaviorism ii 496 b; Consciousness iv 213 b; Lange ix 152 a; Pragmatism xii 309 a; Psychology xii 593 a.

JAMESON, A. B.—viii 369.
JANET, P.—viii 369; Psychiatry xii 578 b.
Janizaries—Military Orders x 460 a; Suleiman I xiv 459 b.
JANNET, C.—viii 370.
Jansen, C.—viii 371 a.
JANSENISM—viii 371–72; Jesuits viii 386 a; Religious Institutions (Roman Catholic) xiii 259 a.
Janson, E.—iv 97 a.
JANSSEN, J.—viii 373.
Japanese Immigration—xi 492 a.
Japanese Law—Law ix 254–57.
JARVIS, E.—viii 373.
JASTROW, M.—viii 374.
JAURÈS, J.—viii 374; Anticlericalism ii 114 a; French Revolution vi 471 a; Militarism x 449 b.
JAVID, M.—viii 375.
JAWORSKI, W. L.—viii 376.
JAY, J.—viii 376; Judicial Review viii 459 a.
Jean Paul—see RICHTER, J. P. F.
JEFFERSON, T.—viii 377; Introd. Vol. I (The Revolutions) i 136 b; Agrarian Movements (U. S.) i 509 b; Declaration of Independence v 45 b; Democracy v 80 b; Entail v 556 a; Isolation, Diplomatic viii 354 a; Legislative Assemblies (U. S.) ix 366 a; Liberalism ix 439 a; Popular Sovereignty xii 239 a; Recognition, International xiii 166 a.
JEKELFALUSSY, J.—viii 378.
JELAČIĆ, J.—viii 378.
Jelliffe, S. E.—x 315 b.
JELLINEK, G.—viii 379; Absolutism i 380 b; Declaration of the Rights of Man and the Citizen v 50 a; International Law viii 172 a; Minority Rights x 525 b; Public Law xii 659 a.
JENKIN, H. C. F.—viii 380.
JENKINS, L.—viii 380.
Jenkinson, C.—see LIVERPOOL, LORD.
JENNER, E.—viii 380; Pasteur xii 18 b.
Jennings, H. S.—vi 614 a.
Jerome of Prague—iv 162 b.
JESSEL, G.—viii 381.
JESUITS—viii 381–89; Introd. Vol. I (Renaissance and Reformation) i 97 a; Education v 410 b; Francis Xavier vi 409 b; Jansenism viii 371 a; Loyola ix 621 b; Missions x 540 b; Native Policy (Lat. Amer.) xi 253 a, 255 b; Religious Orders xiii 278 a.
JEVONS, W. S.—viii 389; Introd. Vol. I (Nationalism) i 166 b; Abstinence i 382 a; Business Cycles iii 98 a; Economics (Marginal Utility Economics) v 357–63, (Mathematical Economics) 366 a; Gossen vii 3 a; Index Numbers vii 653 a; Interest viii 133 b, 135 b; Laissez Faire ix 17 a.
Jewelry—see PRECIOUS STONES.
JEWISH AUTONOMY—viii 391–94.

Jewish Colonization Association—vii 354 b.
JEWISH EMANCIPATION—viii 394–99.
Jewish Law—Judaism viii 430–42; Law ix 219–25.
Jewish Problems—Antisemitism ii 119–25; Banking, Commercial ii 424 a, 426 a; Blood Accusation ii 597–98; Capitalism iii 205 a; Cooperation (Palestine) iv 371; Diaspora v 126–30; Fortunes, Private vi 390 b; Ghetto vi 646–50; Intellectuals viii 120 b; Jewish Autonomy viii 391–94; Jewish Emancipation viii 394–99; Loans, Personal ix 563 b; Mass Expulsion x 186 b; Pawnbroking xii 33 b; Refugees xiii 202 a; Status xiv 376 a; Zionism xv 528–36. See also JUDAISM and ZIONISM. For biog. references see Classification of Articles (Jewish Problems and Judaism), p. 563.
Jewish Territorial Organization—xv 524 b.
JEX-BLAKE, S.—viii 399.
JHERING, R. VON—viii 400; Interests viii 146 b; Jurisprudence viii 482 a; Ownership and Possession xi 523 b.
JIHAD—viii 401–03; Chivalry iii 441 b; Islam viii 337 a; Pan-Islamism xi 542 b.
JĪMŪTAVĀHANA—viii 403.
Jingoism—see CHAUVINISM.
JIREČEK, J. K.—viii 404.
JITTA, D. J.—viii 405.
JOACHIM OF FLORA—viii 405; Franciscan Movement vi 410 a; Messianism x 361 a.
João VI—xii 54 a.
Job Analysis—Labor, Methods of Remuneration for viii 678 b; Labor Turnover viii 712 a.
JOHANN MORITZ—viii 406.
John XXIII—iv 161 b.
John Duns Scotus—see DUNS SCOTUS, J.
John, King—Magna Carta x 44 b.
John of Leyden—xiii 627 a.
JOHN QUIDORT OF PARIS—viii 407.
JOHN OF SALISBURY—viii 407; Scholasticism xiii 579 a.
Johnson, A.—Amnesty ii 38 a; Reconstruction xiii 168 a.
JOHNSON, G.—viii 408.
JOHNSON, J. F.—viii 408.
JOHNSON, S.—viii 409.
JOHNSON, T. L.—viii 410.
JOHNSTON, H. H.—viii 410.
Joint Cost—Cost iv 473 a; Cost Accounting iv 477 a; Meat Packing and Slaughtering x 259 a; Overhead Costs xi 511–13; Price Discrimination xii 354 a.
Joint Family—Law (Hindu) ix 258 b.
JOINT STOCK COMPANY—viii 411–13; Chartered Companies iii 348 b; Corporation iv 414 b; Voluntary Associations xv 283 b.

JOLY, C.—viii 413; Introd. Vol. I (The Rise of Liberalism) i 115 b.
JONES, A.—viii 414.
JONES, E. C.—viii 414.
JONES, L.—viii 414.
Jones Law—xii 111 a.
JONES, M.—viii 415.
JONES, R.—viii 415.
Jonescu, T.—see IONESCU, T.
JORDAN, D. S.—viii 416.
JÖRG, J. E.—viii 416.
JOSEPH II—viii 417; Agrarian Movements (E. Eur.) i 502 b.
JOSEPHUS—viii 418.
JOST, I. M.—viii 419; Basnage ii 475 a.
JOURDAN, A.—viii 419.
Journal des Débats—ii 528 b.
JOURNALISM — viii 420–24. See PRESS.
JOURNEYMEN'S SOCIETIES — viii 424–27; Guilds (Europ.) vii 213 b; Labor Disputes viii 634 a.
JOVELLANOS, G. M. DE—viii 427.
JOWETT, B.—viii 428.
JUÁREZ, B. P.—viii 429.
JUBAINVILLE, H. D'ARBOIS DE—viii 429.
JUDAISM—viii 430–42; Birth Customs ii 567 a; Charity iii 341 a; Chassidism iii 354–57; Child (Dependent) iii 399 a; Diabolism v 119 a; Divorce v 177 b; Education v 404 b, 424 a; Holidays vii 414 a; Intermarriage viii 153 a; Islam viii 333 b; Justice viii 510 a; Law (Jewish) ix 219–25; Messianism x 356–64; Modernism x 566 a; Monasticism x 584 b; Mysticism xi 175 b; Progress xii 496 a; Proselytism xii 551 a; Religious Orders xiii 277 a; Sanctuary xiii 534 a; Suicide xiv 456 a. See also Jewish Problems and ZIONISM. For biog. references see Classification of Articles (Jewish Problems and Judaism), p. 563.
JUDD, O.—viii 442.
Judge Baker Foundation—ii 393 a.
JUDGMENTS—viii 442–48; Declaratory Judgment v 51–52; Full Faith and Credit Clause vi 515–17; Judicial Process viii 450–57; Jurisdiction viii 472 a; Small Claims Courts xiv 100 b; Summary Judgment xiv 461–62.
Judicature Acts—Appeals ii 133 a; Jessel viii 381 b.
Judicial Councils—viii 523 a.
JUDICIAL INTERROGATION — viii 448–50; Jury viii 499 a; Justice, Administration of viii 520 a.
JUDICIAL PROCESS—viii 450–57; Introd. Vol. I (The Trend to Internationalism) i 180 a; Case Law iii 249–51; Casuistry iii 265 b; Common Law iv 54 b; Consideration iv 233–36; Constitutional Law iv 247–55; Constitutionalism iv 256 b;

Contract iv 323-39; Contract Clause iv 339-42; Damages iv 697 a; Declaratory Judgment v 51-52; Equity v 582-88; Evidence v 637-49; Fictions vi 227 b; Freedom of Contract vi 450-55; Judicial Interrogation viii 448-50; Judicial Review viii 457-64; Labor Legislation and Law viii 671 b; Law (Chinese) ix 254 a; Lawgivers ix 275-77; Legal Profession and Legal Education ix 339 b; Legislation ix 347-54; Police Power xii 192 a; Procedure, Legal xii 439-54; Property xii 535 a; Rule of Law xiii 463-66; Supreme Court, U. S. xiv 480 a.

JUDICIAL REVIEW—viii 457-64; Advisory Opinions i 476 b; Appeals ii 131-36; Assessment of Taxes ii 278 a; Centralization iii 311 b; Certiorari iii 317-19; Civil Liberties iii 511 a; Commissions iv 40 a; Common Law iv 55 a; Conseil d'État iv 224 b; Constitutional Law iv 248 a; Constitutionalism iv 257 b; Constitutions iv 261 b; Cooley iv 356 b; Courts iv 525 b; Due Process of Law v 265 b; Federation vi 175 b; Freedom of Contract vi 450-55; Govt. (Canada) vii 28 b, (U. S.) 20 b; Injunction viii 56 b; Interstate Commerce viii 226 a; Interstate Commerce Commission viii 233 b; Labor Legislation and Law viii 671 b; Marshall x 157 b; Police Power xii 192 a; Rule of Law xiii 464 b; Supreme Court, U. S. xiv 474-82.

Judicial Statistics—viii 523 a.

JUDICIARY—viii 464-69; Introd. Vol. I (The Roman World) i 48 b; Advisory Opinions i 475-78; Appeals ii 131-36; Colonial Administration iii 645 b; Contempt of Court iv 302-08; Courts iv 515-29; Customary Law iv 663 a; Govt. (Canada) vii 28 b, (Denmark) 61 b, (Estonia) 72 a, (Gt. Brit.) 25 b, (Italy) 50 b, 52 a, (Japan) 97 b, (Latvia) 72 b, (New Zealand) 32 b, (Norway) 63 a, (Russia, Imperial) 66 b, (Switzerland) 58 a; Impeachment vii 600-02; Judicial Interrogation viii 448-50; Judicial Process viii 450-57; Jury viii 496 a; Justice, Administration of viii 515-24; Justice of the Peace viii 524-27; Juvenile Delinquency and Juvenile Courts viii 532 a; Law (Primitive) ix 205 a, (Celtic) 249 a; Lawgivers ix 275 b; Legal Profession and Legal Education ix 324-46; Municipal Courts xi 94-98; Penal Institutions xii 60 b; Recall xiii 147 b; Roman Law xiii 420 b; Rule of Law xiii 463-66; Separation of Powers xiii 663-67; Supreme Court, U. S. xiv 474-82.

JUGLAR, C.—viii 469.
Julian the Apostate—see JULIANUS.
JULIANUS—viii 470.
JULIANUS, S.—viii 470.
Jung, C. G.—Abnormal Psychology i 364 b; Character iii 336 a; Mental Disorders x 315 b; Personality xii 87 a; Psychoanalysis xii 585 b.
Junkers—i 499 b.
JURIEU, P.—viii 471.
JURISDICTION—viii 471-77; Benefit of Clergy ii 511-13; Calvo and Drago Doctrines iii 153-56; Canon Law iii 183 b; Capitulations iii 213-15; Comity iii 679 a; Conflict of Laws iv 187-94; Courts iv 515-29; Courts, Administrative iv 530 a; Domestic Relations Courts v 194-98; Ellesmere v 481 a; Exterritoriality vi 36-39; Extradition vi 41-44; Foreign Corporations vi 354-58; Freedom of the Seas vi 459-61; Full Faith and Credit Clause vi 516 b; Habeas Corpus vii 233 b; Immunity, Political vii 597-600; Justice of the Peace viii 525 b; Juvenile Delinquency and Juvenile Courts viii 531 a; Law (Celtic) ix 249 b, (Jewish) 222 b; Mandamus x 86 a; Maritime Law x 124 b, 129 b; Merchantmen, Status of x 350 b; Military Law x 455 a; Receivership xiii 151 b; Territorial Waters xiv 574-75; Venue xv 235 b.
Jurisdictional Disputes—see DUAL UNIONISM.
Jurisdictional Fact, Doctrine of—iii 318 b.
JURISPRUDENCE—viii 477-92. See LAW.
JURY—viii 492-502; Assizes ii 283-84; Attainder ii 304 b; Breach of Marriage Promise ii 688 b; Common Law iv 55 a; Criminal Law iv 575 b; Evidence v 638 b; Grand Jury vii 148-50; Henry II vii 321 a; Justice, Administration of viii 520 a; Labor Injunction viii 656 b; Procedure, Legal xii 445 b; Thayer xiv 597 b.
JUS GENTIUM—viii 502-04; Introd. Vol. I (The Roman World) i 48 b, (Renaissance and Reformation) 100 a; Conflict of Laws iv 187 b; Natural Law xi 286 b; Roman Law xiii 420 b.
Jus Naturale—see NATURAL LAW.
Jus Sanguinis—xi 250 b.
Jus Soli—xi 251 a.
JUST PRICE—viii 504-07; Aquinas ii 147 b; Augustine ii 315 a; Christianity iii 457 b; Church Fathers iii 467 b; Govt. Regulation of Industry vii 123 a; Henry of Langenstein vii 324 b; Interest viii 131 b; Price Regulation xii 361 b.
JUSTI, H.—viii 507.

JUSTI, J. H. G. VON—viii 508; Cameralism iii 159 b; Revenues, Public xiii 361 a.
JUSTICE—viii 509-15; Augustine ii 314 b; Christianity iii 456 b; Just Price viii 504 b; Justice, Administration of viii 515-24; Liberty ix 443 b; Natural Law xi 284-90.
JUSTICE, ADMINISTRATION OF—viii 515-24. See Classification of Articles (Administration of Justice), p. 548. See also Introd. Vol. I (Greek Culture and Thought) i 11 b; Equality v 577 a; Feudalism vi 206 b; Govt. (Canada) vii 28 b, (Soviet Russia) 69 a; Islamic Law viii 348 b; Jurisprudence viii 477-92; Law •(Primitive) ix 205 a, (Celtic) 249 a, (Cuneiform) 215 a, (Germanic) 237 a, (Greek) 229 a, (Hellenistic and Greco-Egyptian) 233 b, (Slavic) 245 b; Mafia x 36 b; Military Law x 455 a.
JUSTICE OF THE PEACE—viii 524-27; Arrest ii 221 b; County Councils iv 501 a; Lambarde ix 24 a.
JUSTINIAN I—viii 527; Religious Institutions (Roman Catholic) xiii 253 b, (Byzantine) 263 b; Silk Industry xiv 52 b. See also CORPUS JURIS CIVILIS.
Justinus Febronius—see HONTHEIM, J. N. VON.
JUSTO, J. B.—viii 527.
Jute—see FLAX, HEMP AND JUTE.
Juvenile Courts—see JUVENILE DELINQUENCY AND JUVENILE COURTS.
JUVENILE DELINQUENCY AND JUVENILE COURTS—viii 528-33; Baker ii 393 a; Child (Guidance) iii 393-95, (Delinquent) 406-09, (Labor) 423 b, (Welfare Legislation) 426 a; Domestic Relations Courts v 194 b; Family Desertion and Nonsupport vi 79 a; Gangs vi 566 b; Mothers' Pensions xi 55 a; Probation and Parole xii 435-39; Slums xiv 95 a.

Kabbala—viii 432 a.
KABLUKOV, N. A.—viii 533.
KADLEC, K.—viii 533.
KAGWA, A.—viii 534.
KAHL, W.—viii 534.
Kalanianaole, J. K.—xi 272 b.
Kalischer, O.—iv 176 a.
KÁLLAY, B.—viii 535.
KAMÁL MAḤMAD NÁMŬK—viii 535.
Kamenev, L. B.—ii 627 a.
KAMIEŃSKI, H. M.—viii 536.
K'ANG YU-WEI—viii 537; History and Historiography vii 384 a.
Kangaroo, Legislative—iii 572 a.
KANKRIN, E. F.—viii 538.
KANT, I.—viii 538; Beneke ii 516 a; Common Sense iv 59 a; Deism v 62 b; Enlightenment v 551 b; Humanism vii 541 b;

Idealism vii 569 a; Internationalism viii 215 a; Justice viii 511 a; Logic ix 601 a; Natural Law xi 289 a; Positivism xii 263 b; Psychology xii 590 a; Science xiii 599 b; Social Contract xiv 130 b.
Kapp Putsch—vi 610 a.
KARADŽIĆ, V. S.—viii 542.
KARAGEORGE, P.—viii 543.
Karageorgević, A.—viii 543 b.
KARAMZIN, N. M.—viii 543.
KARAVELOFF, L.—viii 544.
KAREYEV, N. I.—viii 545.
KARISHEV, N. A.—viii 546.
KARL FRIEDRICH—viii 546.
Karma—Brahmanism and Hinduism ii 675 b; Buddhism iii 33 b.
KÁRMÁN, M.—viii 547.
Karmathian Movement—vii 214 b.
KARO, J. BEN E.—viii 547; Law (Jewish) ix 224 a.
Karsten, R.—xi 496 a.
KASIM AMIN—viii 548.
KASKEL, W.—viii 548.
KATKOV, M. N.—viii 549.
Katz, S.—see DOBROGEANU-GHEREA, C.
KAUFMAN, A. A.—viii 549.
Kaulback, J. G.—iv 393 b.
KAUTILYA—viii 550; Law (Hindu) ix 260 a.
Kautsky Documents—ii 179 b.
Kautsky, K.—Socialism xiv 208 a; Socialization xiv 221 b.
KAUTZ, G.—viii 551.
KAVELIN, K. D.—viii 552.
KAY-SHUTTLEWORTH, J.—viii 552.
KEARNEY, D.—viii 553.
Kedleston, First Marquess Curzon of—see CURZON, G. N.
Keil, W.—iv 97 a.
KEITH, M. C.—viii 553.
KELETI, K.—viii 554.
KELLER, F. L.—viii 554.
KELLEY, F.—viii 555.
KELLEY, O. H.—viii 555; Grange vii 150 a.
KELLEY, W. D.—viii 555.
KELLOGG, E.—viii 556; Labor Exchange Banks viii 641 a.
Kellogg, F. B.—ii 178 b.
Kellogg, P. U.—xiv 163 b.
Kellogg Pact—i 485 b.
Kelly Act—Aviation ii 341 b, 353 a.
KELLY, E.—viii 557.
Kelsen, H.—Introd. Vol. I (War and Reorientation) i 216 a; Jurisprudence viii 484 b; Public Law xii 658 b; State xiv 328 b, 329 a.
Kémál Méhméd Námŭk—see KAMÁL MAḤMAD NÁMŬK.
KEMBLE, J. M.—viii 557.
Kemmerer, E. W.—viii 156 a.
Kemper, J. de B.—see BOSCH KEMPER, J. DE.
KENT, J.—viii 558; Common Law iv 52 b.
Keogh, J.—iii 270 b.
Kepler, J.—ii 288 a.
Kerensky, A. F.—xiii 479 b, 481 a.

KETTELER, W. E. VON—viii 559.
KEUFER, A.—viii 560.
KEY, E.—viii 560.
Keynes, J. M.—Economics v 371 a; Inflation and Deflation viii 29 a, 32 a; Money x 610 a; Price Stabilization xii 364 a; Prices (Theory) xii 374 a; Statistics xiv 369 b.
KEYSER, R. J.—viii 561.
KHAMA—viii 561.
Kharijites—viii 335 a.
KHMELNITSKY, B.—viii 562.
KHOMYAKOV, A. S.—viii 562.
KHRIMIAN, M.—viii 563.
KIDD, B.—viii 563; Belief ii 501 b.
Kidder, A. V.—ii 166 a.
KIDERLEN-WÄCHTER, A. VON—viii 564.
Kidnaping—Mafia x 37 a.
KIDO, T.—viii 564.
Kienthal, Conference of—xv 141 b.
Kilpatrick, W. H.—v 413 b.
Kimiyoshi—see ARAI HAKUSEKI.
Kindergarten — see PRESCHOOL EDUCATION.
KING, G.—viii 565; Population xii 241 a.
KING, L. W.—viii 565.
KING, W.—viii 566; Cooperation iv 363 b.
KING, W. A.—viii 567.
King, W. I.—vi 77 b.
King's Bench, Court of—see Court of King's Bench.
King's Peace—iv 572 b.
Kingship—Introd. Vol. I (Greek Culture and Thought) i 11 a, (The Universal Church) 69 b; Aristocracy ii 184 a; Deification v 58–60; Divine Right of Kings v 176–77; Empire v 497–506; Excommunication v 677 b; Game Laws vi 562 a; Govt. (Gt. Brit.) vii 21 b; Lese Majesty ix 415–17; Monarchy x 579–84; Parties, Political (Gt. Brit.) xi 604 b; Philip Augustus xii 108 a; Prerogative xii 319 a; Priesthood xii 391 b; Royal Court xiii 448–51; Succession, Political xiv 442 b.
KINGSLEY, C.—viii 567; Christian Socialism iii 450 a.
KINGSTON, C. C.—viii 568.
KINSHIP—viii 568–72; Adoption i 459–63; Ancestor Worship ii 53–55; Anthropology ii 85 b; Avoidance ii 369–70; Ceremony iii 313 a; Culture iv 628 b; Family ii 65–70; Feudalism vi 204 a; Fison vi 272 a; Incest vii 620–22; Law (Celtic) ix 248 a, (Jewish) 219 b; Marriage x 146–54; Morgan xi 13 a; Social Organization xiv 142 b; Succession, Laws of xiv 437 a.
KIRBY, J., JR.—viii 572.
KIRCHMANN, J. H. VON—viii 573.
KIREYEVSKY, I. V.—viii 573.
KIRK, J.—viii 574.
KISELEV, P. D.—viii 574.
KISTYAKOVSKY, A. F.—viii 575.
KISTYAKOVSKY, B. A.—viii 575.

Kiuprili Family—see KÖPRÜLÜ FAMILY.
KJELLÉN, R.—viii 576.
Kleefeld, E. von—see SCHUBART, J. C.
KLEIN, F.—viii 577.
Kleist, H. von—xiv 610 a.
KLUCHEVSKY, V. O.—viii 577.
Knaffl-Lenz, E. von—xi 475 a.
KNAPP, G. F.—viii 578; Bendixen ii 509 b; Economics v 371–77; Money x 604 a.
KNAPP, M. A.—viii 579.
KNAPP, S. A.—vii 579; Extension Work, Agric. vi 32 b.
KNIBBS, G. H.—viii 580.
Knickerbocker Village—xiv 97 b.
KNIES, K. G. A.—viii 580; Economics v 371–77.
Knight, F. H.—Entrepreneur v 558 b; Profit xii 484 a.
Knighthood—see CHIVALRY.
Knights Hospitallers—Chivalry iii 438 b; Military Orders x 460 a.
KNIGHTS OF LABOR—viii 581–84; Amer. Federation of Labor ii 24 a; Boycott ii 663 b; Farmers' Alliance vi 128 b; Industrial Workers of the World viii 13 b; Leather Industries (Labor) ix 313 b; Negro Problem xi 341 a; Powderly xii 292 b; Producers' Cooperation xii 459 a; Stephens xiv 387 b; Trade Unions xv 4 b.
Knights of St. Crispin—ix 313 b.
Knights Templar—Chivalry iii 438 b; Military Orders x 460 a; Philip IV xii 107 b.
Know Nothing Party—Ku Klux Klan viii 608 b; Parties, Political (U. S.) xi 600 a.
Knowledge—Alembert i 629 b; Anthropology ii 93 a; Aristotle ii 191 b; Culture iv 634 a; Kant viii 539 b; Locke ix 594 a; Logic ix 598–603; Materialism (Dialectical) x 213 b, 215 a; Method, Scientific x 389–96.
KNOWLES, L. C. A.—viii 584.
KNOWLTON, C.—viii 585; Birth Control ii 561 a.
KNOX, J.—viii 585.
Knox, P. C.—xi 509 a.
KOCH, R.—viii 586; Communicable Diseases, Control of iv 68 a.
Kocharovsky, K. R.—xv 255 b.
KOGĂLNICEANU, M.—viii 586.
KOHLER, J.—viii 587; Jurisprudence viii 482 b.
Köhler, W.—Consciousness iv 214 b, 216 a; Gestalt vi 644 a.
KOLLÁR, J.—viii 588.
KOŁŁĄTAJ, H.—viii 588.
KOLPING, A.—viii 589.
Komensky—see COMENIUS, J. A.
KONARSKI, S.—viii 589.
Kondratiev, N. D.—xii 371 b.
Koppers, W.—Anthropology ii 102 a; Diffusionism v 141 b.
KÖPRÜLÜ FAMILY—viii 590.
Kops, J. L. de B.—see BRUIJN Kops, J. L. DE.
KORAES, A.—viii 590.

Index (Kant — Labor Legislation and Law)

Koran—*see* SACRED BOOKS.
KORKUNOV, N. M.—viii 591.
KOROLENKO, V. G.—viii 592.
KŐRÖSY DE SZÁNTÓ, J.—viii 592.
KOŚCIUSZKO, T. A.—viii 593.
KOSSUTH, L.—viii 594.
KOSTOMAROV, N. I.—viii 594.
KOVÁCS, G.—viii 595.
KOVALEVSKY, M. M.—viii 595.
Krabbe, H.—Introd. Vol. 1 (The Trend to Internationalism) i 179 a; Interests viii 146 b; Public Law xii 658 b.
KRAEMER, A.—viii 596.
KRAEPELIN, E.—viii 597; Mental Disorders x 314 a.
KRAUS, C. J.—viii 597.
KRAUS, F. X.—viii 598.
Krause, K. C. F.—i 608 a.
KRAUZ-KELLES, K.—viii 598.
KREITTMAYR, BARON VON—viii 598.
KREK, J.—viii 599.
KREMER, A. VON—viii 600.
Kretschmer, E.—Abnormal Psychology i 364 b; Genius vi 612 b; Personality xii 86 b.
KREUGER, I.—viii 600; Match Industry x 206 b.
Kreuger and Toll—viii 273 b.
Kries, J. von—xiv 369 b.
KRIŽANIĆ, J.—viii 601.
KROCHMAL, N.—viii 602.
Kroeber, A. L.—Dress v 237 b; Kinship viii 568 b.
KRONVALDS, A.—viii 602.
KROPOTKIN, P. A.—viii 602; Anarchism ii 49 b.
KRUEGER, P.—viii 604.
KRUGER, S. J. P.—viii 604.
KRUMBACHER, K.—viii 605.
KRUPP, A.—viii 605; Fortunes, Private vi 394 b; Iron and Steel Industry viii 309 b; Munitions Industry xi 129 a, 132 a.
KRUTTSCHNITT, J.—viii 606.
Ku Chiang—*see* KU YEN-WU.
KU KLUX KLAN—viii 606-09; Antisemitism ii 124 b.
Ku T'inglin—*see* KU YEN-WU.
KU YEN-WU—viii 609.
KUENEN, A.—viii 609.
Kuhn, Loeb and Co.—xiii 568 b.
Kula—ii 468 b.
Kulaks—Land Tenure (Russia) ix 109 b; Russian Revolution xiii 487 a.
Kuliscioff, A.—xv 130 a.
KULIZHNY, A. E.—viii 609.
Kulturkreis—Anthropology ii 103 b; Diffusionism v 141 a.
KUNFI, Z.—viii 610.
Kung-sun Yang — *see* SHANG YANG.
Kunstgewerbeschule—ii 256 a.
KUOMINTANG—viii 610-14; Far Eastern Problem vi 96 b; Government (China) vii 99 a; Sun Yat Sen xiv 466 b; Trade Unions xv 36 b.

LABAND, P.—viii 614; Hänel vii 260 b; Public Law xii 659 a.
LA BOÉTIE, É. DE—viii 615; Anarchism ii 47 b.

LABOR—viii 615-20. *See* Classification of Articles (Labor), p. 552. *See also* Introd. Vol. 1 (War and Reorientation) i 214 b; Automobile Industry ii 326 a; Aviation (Industry) ii 362 b; Blind ii 589 b; Business, Govt. Services for iii 121 a; Cement iii 290 a; Coal Industry iii 588 b, 591 b, 595 a, 597 b; Construction Industry iv 265 b, 270 b; Consumers' Cooperation iv 287 a; Cooperation (Gt. Brit.) iv 365 b; Economics (Classical School) v 353 a, (Cambridge School) 370 a, (Socialist Economics) 378 a; Efficiency v 438 a; Electric Power v 467 a; Electrical Manufacturing Industry v 474 b; Equal Protection of the Law v 574 a; Fascism vi 137 b; Food Industries (Baking, Eur.) vi 304 b, (Baking, U. S.) 307 a, (Beverages) 309 a, (Confectionery) 311 a; Fur Trade and Industry vi 533 b, 536 a; Furniture vi 541 a; Garment Industries vi 576 b, 580 a; Gas Industry vi 591 b; Glass and Pottery Industries vi 675 a; Govt. Ownership vii 118 a; Heavy Chemicals vii 300 b; Hotels vii 475 b; Immigration vii 589 b; Industrial Revolution viii 11 b; Iron and Steel Industry viii 315-22; Laundry and Dry Cleaning Industry ix 195 a; Law (Cuneiform) ix 218 b; Leather Industries ix 312-16; Location of Industry ix 587 a, 589 a; Machines and Tools x 22 b; Match Industry x 205 a; Meat Packing and Slaughtering x 248 b, 261 a; Middle Class x 414 a; Migrations x 433 b, 437 a; Milling Industry x 486 a; Mining x 504 a; Monopoly x 626 b; Municipal Transit xi 120 b; Music xi 163 b; National Income xi 218 a; Oil Industry xi 446 b; Old Age xi 454 a; Pensions xii 68 b; Poverty xii 287 b; Printing and Publishing xii 412 a; Profit xii 481 b; Quarrying xiii 19 b; Racketeering xiii 46 a; Radio xiii 57 a; Railroads xiii 93-100; Restaurants xiii 338 b; Rubber xiii 458 a; Socialism xiv 199 b, 208 b; Statistics xiv 362 b; Technology xiv 557 a; Textile Industry xiv 590-96; Tobacco xiv 643 b; Value and Price xv 218 b; Wood Industries xv 473 a.
Labor, Agricultural—*see* AGRICULTURAL LABOR.
LABOR BANKING—viii 620-24.
Labor Blacklist—*see* BLACKLIST, LABOR.
LABOR-CAPITAL COOPERATION—viii 624-29; Abbe i 354 a; Arbeitsgemeinschaft ii 150; Company Unions iv 123-26; Construction Industry iv 276 b; Employee Stock Ownership v 506-09; Industrial Relations vii 713 b; Industrial Relations Councils vii 717-22; International Labor Organization viii 164-67; Labor Banking viii 622 b; Labor, Govt. Services for viii 647 b; Profit Sharing xii 487-92; Railroads xiii 96 b; Unemployment Insurance xv 162-74.
Labor Colleges—*see* WORKERS' EDUCATION.
LABOR CONTRACT—viii 629-33; Bargaining Power ii 461 a; Blacklist, Labor ii 578-79; Contract Labor iv 342-44; Duress v 288 a; Enticement of Employees v 557 b; Indenture vii 645 b; Labor Legislation and Law viii 667-76; Labourers, Statutes of ix 3-6; Law (Cuneiform) ix 218 b.
LABOR DISPUTES—viii 633-37; Boycott ii 663 b; Company Housing iv 116 b; Company Unions iv 125 a; Conciliation, Industrial iv 165-69; Conspiracy, Criminal iv 237 a; Construction Industry iv 270 b; Courts, Industrial iv 535-38; Detective Agencies, Private v 109 b; Direct Action v 156 b; Employers' Associations v 511 b; Iron and Steel Industry viii 317 a; Labor, Govt. Services for viii 646 b; Labor Injunction viii 653-57; Labor Legislation and Law viii 664 a; Martial Law x 164 a; Policing, Industrial xii 193-96; Railroads xiii 95 a; Strikes and Lockouts xiv 419-26.
LABOR EXCHANGE BANKS—viii 637-44.
Labor Exchanges—*see* EMPLOYMENT EXCHANGES.
LABOR, GOVERNMENT SERVICES FOR—viii 644-53; Bourses du Travail ii 659-60; Employment Exchanges v 518-23; International Labor Organization viii 164-67; Labor Legislation and Law viii 657-76; Migratory Labor x 444 a; Minimum Wage x 491-95; Producers' Cooperation xii 460 b; Social Insurance xiv 134-38; Unemployment Insurance xv 162-74.
Labor, Hours of—*see* HOURS OF LABOR.
LABOR INJUNCTION—viii 653-57; Labor Contract viii 631 b; Labor Legislation and Law viii 670 a.
LABOR LEGISLATION AND LAW—viii 657-76 (Legislation 657-67, 675, Law 667-76); Chartism iii 352-54; Child (Labor) iii 412-24; Consumers' Leagues iv 292 a; Dato e Iradier v 6 a; Domestic Service v 204 a; Due Process of Law v 266 a; Equal Protection of the Law v 574 a; Factory System vi 54 a;

Freedom of Contract vi 453 a; Govt. Regulation of Industry vii 124 b, 126 a; Homework, Industrial vii 447 b; Hours of Labor vii 480 a; Industrial Hazards vii 703 a; Industrial Hygiene vii 707–10; Industrial Relations vii 712 a; Inspection viii 72 b; International Labor Organization viii 164–67; Kaskel viii 548 b; Labor Contract viii 629–33; Labor Disputes viii 634 a; Labor, Govt. Services for viii 644–53; Labor Injunction viii 653–57; Labourers, Statutes of ix 3–6; Le Grand ix 398 a; Maternity Welfare x 223 b; Minimum Wage x 491–95; Mining Accidents x 512 a; Railroads xiii 95 a; Safety Movement xiii 504 b; Seamen xiii 615 a; Short Hours Movement xiv 46 a; Social Insurance xiv 134–38; Trade Unions (Germany) xv 16 a; Unemployment Insurance xv 162–74; Welfare Work, Industrial xv 398 b; Women in Industry xv 454 b; Workmen's Compensation xv 488–92.

LABOR, METHODS OF REMUNERATION FOR—viii 677–82; Profit Sharing xii 487–92; Wages xv 291–320.

LABOR MOVEMENT—viii 682–96; Agrarian Movements i 492 a; Agric. Labor i 550 b; American Federation of Labor ii 23–30; Bourses du Travail ii 659–60; Chartism iii 352–54; Christian Labor Unions iii 443–46; Christian Socialism iii 449–52; Civil Liberties iii 511 b; Closed Shop and Open Shop iii 568–70; Confédération Générale du Travail iv 179–81; Cooperation iv 360 a, (Belgium) 379–80, (Germany) 372 a; Criminal Syndicalism iv 582–84; Direct Action v 155–58; Dual Unionism v 259–61; Farmers' Union vi 132 b; Federation vi 177 a; Freedom of Association vi 448 a; Freedom of Contract vi 453 b; Friendly Societies vi 495 a; Garment Industries vi 581 b; General Strike vi 607–12; Hours of Labor vii 480 a; Immigration vii 590 a; Industrial Relations vii 711 b; Industrial Workers of the World viii 13–18; International Labor Organization viii 164–67; International Relations viii 187 b; Knights of Labor viii 581–84; Labor viii 619 b; Labor Banking viii 620–24; Labor-Capital Cooperation viii 624–29; Labor Disputes viii 633–37; Labor Legislation and Law viii 657–76; Labor Parties viii 697–709; Negro Problem xi 340 b, 347 b, 350 a; Peace Movements xii 42 b; Producers' Cooperation xii 458–62; Proletariat xii 516 a; Sabotage xiii 495–97; Short Hours Movement xiv 45 a; Socialist Parties xiv 212–21; Strikes and Lockouts xiv 419–26; Syndicalism xiv 496–500; Trade Unions xv 3–57; Workers' Education xv 484–88. See also TRADE UNIONS. For biog. references see Classification of Articles (Labor), p. 563.

LABOR PARTIES—viii 697–709 (General 697–99, 708, Gt. Brit. 699–703, 708, Brit. Dominions 703–05, 708, U. S. 706–09); Fabianism vi 48 a; Indian Question vii 669 b; Industrial Relations vii 715 b; Industrial Workers of the World viii 13 b; Labor Movement viii 688 a; Parties, Political xi 594 b, (Australia) 606 a, (Belgium) 614 a, (Gt. Brit.) 602 a, (Japan) 635 b, (New Zealand) 607 b, (U. S.) 599 b; Proletariat xii 516 b; Socialist Parties xiv 213 a, 218 b; Trade Unions (Australia) xv 46 a, (Belgium) 28 a, (Gt. Brit.) 11 a, (Norway) 21 a; Workers' Education xv 486 a.

Labor Press—viii 686 a.

Labor Psychology—Parker xi 579 b.

Labor Statistics—Labor, Govt. Services for viii 649 a; Wright xv 499 b.

Labor Tax—Forced Labor vi 342 b.

LABOR TURNOVER—viii 709–13; Casual Labor iii 260–62; Domestic Service v 202 a; Employment Exchanges v 518–23; Negro Problem xi 345 a; Profit Sharing xii 490 b.

LABOULAYE, É. R. L. DE—ix 3.

LABOURERS, STATUTES OF—ix 3–6; Agriculture i 578 b; Enticement of Employees v 557 a.

LABRA Y CADRANA, R. M. DE—ix 6.

LABRIOLA, A.—ix 7.

La Chalotais, L. R. de C. de—v 415 a.

LACOMBE, P.—ix 8.

LACORDAIRE, J. B. H. D.—ix 8.

LADD, G. T.—ix 9.

LADD, W.—ix 9; Peace Movements xii 42 a.

Ladies' Home Journal—ii 621 b.

LAFARGUE, P.—ix 10.

LAFAYETTE, MARQUIS DE—ix 11.

LAFERRIÈRE, É. L. J.—ix 11.

LAFFEMAS, B. DE—ix 12.

LAFITAU, J.-F.—ix 12.

LA FOLLETTE, R. M.—ix 13.

LAFONTAINE, L. H.—ix 13; Baldwin ii 407 b.

LAFUENTE Y ZAMALLOA, M.—ix 14.

LAGARDE, P. DE—ix 14.

LAINÉ, A.—ix 15.

LAISSEZ FAIRE—ix 15–20; Administration, Public i 441 b; Business iii 82 a; Business, Govt. Services for iii 114 a; Capitalism iii 198 b; Christianity iii 458 b; Chydenius iii 468 b; Collectivism iii 633 b; Competition iv 141–47; Control, Social iv 346 a; Dunoyer v 281 b; Economic Policy v 339 a; Economics (Cambridge School) v 368 b; Free Trade vi 442 a; Govt. vii 13 a; Govt. Regulation of Industry vii 124 a; Investment viii 267 b; Labor Legislation and Law viii 665 a; Liberalism ii 438 b; Liberty ix 443 b; Market x 131 a; Mercantilism x 338 b; Middle Class x 408 a; Protection xii 561 b; Smith vi 442 b; Trade Associations xiv 672 a; Utilitarianism xv 198 b.

LAJPAT RAI, L.—ix 20.

Lalor, F.—viii 290 a.

LAMARCK, CHEVALIER DE—ix 21; Adaptation i 436 a; Biology ii 551 b; Evolution v 651 a.

LAMARTINE, A. M. L. DE P. DE—ix 22.

LAMAS, A.—ix 23.

LAMBARDE, W.—ix 23.

Lambeth Conferences—xi 551 b.

Lambton, J. G.—see DURHAM, LORD.

Lame Ducks—ix 362 b.

LAMENNAIS, H. F. R. DE—ix 24.

LAMETTRIE, J. O. DE—ix 25.

LAMMASCH, H.—ix 26.

LAMOIGNON, G. DE—ix 26.

LAMPERTICO, F.—ix 27.

LAMPRECHT, K.—ix 27; Introd. Vol. 1 (The Trend to Internationalism) i 186 b; History and Historiography vii 380 a.

LAMPREDI, G. M.—ix 28.

LANCASTER, J.—ix 29; Bell ii 503 b.

LAND BANK SCHEMES—ix 29–32; Assignats ii 281 a; Hertzenstein vii 340 b; Law, J. ix 270 a; Rentenmark xiii 296.

Land Grant Colleges—Agric. Education i 540 a; Agric. Experiment Stations i 543 a; Agriculture, Govt. Services for i 602 a.

LAND GRANTS—ix 32–43 (U. S. 32–36, 43, Brit. Empire 36–39, 43, Lat. Amer. 39–43); Forests vi 385 a; Freehold vi 464 b; Homestead vii 436–41; Land Settlement ix 53–64; Land Tenure (Ancient World) ix 80 b; Negro Problem xi 337 b; Public Domain xii 613–28; Railroads xiii 78 b; Veterans xv 243 a.

LAND MORTGAGE CREDIT—ix 43–53 (Agric. 43–50, 53, Urban 50–53); Agric. Credit i 532 b; Construction Industry iv 269 a; Farm Loan System, Federal vi 106 b; Home Ownership vii 433 a; Housing (Eur.) vii 500 a, 508 b; Investment viii 266 a; Land Bank Schemes ix 29–32; Land Settlement ix 53–64.

Land Registration—Land Transfer ix 129 b; Law (Hellenistic and Greco-Egyptian) ix 233 b.

LAND SETTLEMENT—ix 53-64; Agriculture (U. S.) i 586 b; Agriculture, Govt. Services for i 603 a, 604 b; Back-to-the-Land Movements ii 378-79; Colonies iii 653-63; Frontier vi 500-06; Hirsch vii 354 b; Homestead vii 436-41; Irrigation viii 328 a; Land Grants ix 32-43; Land Mortgage Credit (Agric.) ix 47 a; Land Tenure ix 91 a; Land Utilization ix 132-37; Native Policy (Africa) xi 277 b, (N. Amer.) 262 b; Public Domain xii 613-28; Small Holdings xiv 103 b; Wages xv 322 a; Zionism xv 534 a.

LAND SPECULATION—ix 64-70; Boom ii 639 a; Land Grants (U. S.) ix 33 b; Real Estate xiii 136 a; Speculation xiv 291 a.

LAND TAXATION—ix 70-73; Appreciation ii 143 b; Capitalization and Amortization of Taxes iii 211 b; Forests vi 385 b; General Property Tax vi 603 a; George vi 631 a; Land Tenure (China and Japan) ix 114 b, (Russia) 107 a; Property Tax xii 538-41; Single Tax xiv 64-67; Unearned Increment xv 145 b.

LAND TENURE — ix 73-127 (Introd. 73-76, Primitive Societies 76-77, 122, Ancient World 77-82, 123, W. Eur., Brit. Empire and U. S. 82-99, 123, E. Eur. and Near East 99-106, 125, Russia 106-110, 126, India 110-112, 127, China and Japan 112-118, 127, Lat. Amer. 118-122, 127); Introd. Vol. I (Greek Culture and Thought) i 39 b, (The Roman World) 45 b, 56 b; Absentee Ownership i 376 b; Agrarian Movements i 492-515; Agriculture (Antiquity and Middle Ages) i 575 a, (Eng.) 577 b, (Europe) 582 b, (India) 592 a, (U. S.) 585 b; Alienation of Property i 639 b; Allotments ii 5-7; Appanage ii 130-31; Aranda ii 149 b; Assizes ii 283 b; Bright iii 3 a; Colonate iii 639-41; Enclosures v 523-27; Entail v 553-56; Escheat v 591-93; Farm vi 101-03; Farm Tenancy vi 118-27; Feudalism (Chinese) vi 213-14, (Europ.) 205 b, (Japanese) 215 b, (Saracen and Ottoman) 210-13; Freehold vi 461-65; Gracchus vii 132 a; Homestead vii 436-41; Irish Question viii 286 b; Knapp viii 578 b; Land Grants (Lat. Amer.) ix 40 a; Land Transfer ix 127-32; Landed Estates ix 140-43; Landlord and Tenant ix 143-48; Latifundia ix 186-89; Law (Cuneiform) ix 216 b, (Germanic) 236 a, (Hellenistic and Greco-Egyptian) 233 a, (Japanese) 256 b, (Jewish) 219 b, 222 b, (Slavic) 244 a; Manorial System x 97-102; Mining Law x 513-18; Mortgage xi 32-38; Mortmain xi 40-50; Nomads xi 390-92; Peasantry xii 48-53; Perpetuities xii 81-83; Plantation xii 148-53; Primogeniture xii 402-05; Public Domain xii 613-28; Serfdom xiii 667-71; Small Holdings xiv 101-05; Village Community xv 253-59.

LAND TRANSFER—ix 127-132; Alienation of Property i 639 b; Law (Cuneiform) ix 217 a, (Germanic) 236 a, (Hellenistic and Greco-Egyptian) 233 a; Native Policy (N. Amer.) xi 261 a; Real Estate xiii 135 a; Specific Performance xiv 286 b.

LAND UTILIZATION—ix 132-137; Natural Resources xi 292 a; Regional Planning xiii 205-08; Soils xiv 250-54.

LAND VALUATION—ix 137-39; Agric. Economics i 537 b; Assessment of Taxes ii 276-79; Land Mortgage Credit (Agric.) ix 49 b; Land Taxation ix 70-73; Special Assessments xiv 277 a.

LANDAUER, G.—ix 139.

LANDED ESTATES—ix 140-43; Agrarian Movements i 492-515; Agriculture (Eng.) i 577-81, (India) 592 a, (Rome) 575 a; Alienation of Property i 639 b; Aristocracy ii 186 b; Charlemagne iii 346 a; Colonate iii 639-41; Enclosures v 526 b; Entail v 553-56; Feudalism (Japanese) vi 215 a; Fortunes, Private vi 389-92; Land Tenure ix 73-127; Latifundia ix 186-89; Manorial System x 97-102; Nobility xi 386 a; Perpetuities xii 81 b; Plantation xi 148-53; Primogeniture xii 402-05; Rent Charge xiii 292; Rentier xiii 297 b; Slavery (Rome) xiv 77 a, (U. S.) 85 b; Spence xiv 293 b.

LANDLORD AND TENANT—ix 143-48; Farm Tenancy vi 118-27; Rent Regulation xiii 293-96.

Landschaft Associations—Agric. Credit i 533 b; Land Mortgage Credit (Agric.) ix 44 b.

Landsgemeinde—xii 237 a.

Landsting—ix 388 a.

LANE, W.—ix 148.

LANESSAN, J. M. A. DE—ix 148; Native Policy xi 271 b.

LANFRANC—ix 149.

LANG, A.—ix 150; Animism ii 66 a; Folklore vi 288 b.

Lang, J. T.—xi 606 b.

LÁNG, L.—ix 151.

LANGDELL, C. C.—ix 151; Ames ii 35 b; Case Method iii 252 a; Legal Profession and Legal Education ix 338 a.

LANGE, C. G.—ix 152.

LANGE, F. A.—ix 152.

LANGE, H.—ix 153.

Lange-Eichbaum, W.—vi 612 b.

LANGLAND, W.—ix 153.

LANGLOIS, C. V.—ix 154.

Langton, S.—x 44 b.

LANGUAGE—ix 155-169; Introd. Vol. I (What Are the Social Sciences?) i 7 b, (The Universal Church) 67 b; Anthropology ii 77-79, 100 a; Aryans ii 264 a; Attitudes, Social ii 305-07; Communication iv 78 b; Culture iv 622 a, 633 b; Dialect v 123-26; Ethnic Communities v 609 a; Gentleman, Theory of the vi 619 a; Indian Question vii 660 a; Kinship viii 568 b; Literature ix 528 a; Man x 72 a; Music xi 143 a; Nationalism xi 235 a; Records, Historical xiii 174 a; Regionalism xiii 210 b, 215 b; Symbolism xiv 493 b; Tradition xv 64 a. For biog. references see Classification of Articles (Philology), p. 565.

Lansquenets—x 342 a.

Lao Tzu—see TAOISM.

Lapeyre, P.—ii 123 a.

LAPLACE, MARQUIS DE—ix 169; Average ii 337 a; Frequency Distribution vi 486 a; Poisson xii 180 b; Probability xii 426 b, 429 b, 432 a.

Lapouge, G. V. de—xiv 238 b.

LAPPO-DANILEVSKY, A. S.—ix 169.

Lapua Movement—xi 624 a.

Large Numbers, Laws of—Probability xii 430-34.

LARGE SCALE PRODUCTION—ix 170-81; Agric. Credit i 531 a; Agric. Labor i 549 b; Agriculture i 583 b, 597 a; Agriculture, Govt. Services for i 606 a; Automobile Industry ii 324 a; By-Product iii 129 b; Combinations, Industrial iii 664-74; Continuous Industry iv 318-20; Cost iv 471 b; Dairy Industry iv 693 a; Electric Power v 462 b; Engineering v 545 a; Factory System vi 51-55; Farm vi 102 b; Increasing Returns vii 640 a; Industrial Revolution viii 3-13; Industrialism viii 18-26; Plantation xii 148-53; Scientific Management xiii 603-08; Small Holdings xiv 102 a; Specialization xiv 282 a; Standardization xiv 322 a; Trusts xv 111-22.

Larkin, J.—viii 293 b.

LA ROCHEFOUCAULD-LIANCOURT, F. DE—ix 181.

La Sagra y Périz, R. D. de—see SAGRA Y PÉRIZ, R. D. DE LA.

LA SALLE, J.-B. DE—ix 181; Literacy and Illiteracy ix 517 a.

LAS CASAS, B. DE—ix 182.

LASKER, E.—ix 183.

Laski, H. J.—xii 171 b, 172 b.

Łaski, J.—x 568 b.

LASPEYRES, É.—ix 183; Index Numbers vii 657 b; Mercantilism x 336 a.

LASSALLE, F.—ix 184; Abstinence i 382 a; Ateliers Nationaux ii 292 a; Cooperation iv 372 a;

Labor Movement viii 688 b; Socialism xiv 196 b; Socialist Parties xiv 213 b.
LASTARRIA, J. V.—ix 185.
LATANÉ, J. H.—ix 185.
Lathe—x 20 b.
LATHROP, J. C.—ix 186.
LATIFUNDIA—ix 186–89; Agrarian Movements (Ancient Rome) i 494 b, (E. Eur.) 502 b, (Italy) 500 a, (Lat. Amer.) 512 a; Colonate iii 639–41; Fortunes, Private vi 390 a; Land Tenure (Ancient World) ix 81 a; Manorial System x 97 b; Slavery (Rome) xiv 77 a.
Latin Monetary Union—Bimetallism and Monometallism ii 548 b; Monetary Unions x 596 a.
LA TOUR DU PIN CHAMBLY, R. DE —ix 189.
Latter Day Saints—see MORMONISM.
Lattes, L.—xiii 32 b.
LAU, T. L.—ix 190.
Lauck, W. J.—vii 692 a.
LAUD, W.—ix 190.
LAUDERDALE, LORD—ix 191.
Laughlin, J. L.—viii 29 b.
LAUNDRY AND DRY CLEANING INDUSTRY—ix 191–97.
Laur, E.—vi 112 b.
LAURIER, W.—ix 197.
LAVAL, F. X. DE—ix 198.
Lavater, J. K.—x 308 a.
LAVELEYE, É. L. V. DE—ix 198; Village Community xv 253 b.
LAVERGNE, L.-G. L. DE—ix 199.
LAVISSE, E.—ix 199.
LAVOISIER, A. L.—ix 200.
LAVROV, P. L.—ix 201.
LAW—ix 202–67 (Primitive 202–06, 262, General View of Ancient 206–09, 262, Egyptian 209–11, 263, Cuneiform 211–19, 263, Jewish 219–25, 264, Greek 225–29, 265, Hellenistic and Greco-Egyptian 229–35, 265, Germanic 235–39, 265, Slavic 240–46, 266, Celtic 246–49, 266, Chinese 249–54, 266, Japanese 254–57, 267, Hindu 257–62, 267). See Classification of Articles (Administration of Justice), p. 548, (Jurisprudence), p. 552, (Legal Relations), p. 553, *and relevant titles in* (Crime), p. 550. See also Introd. Vol. I (What Are the Social Sciences?) i 4 a, (Greek Culture and Thought) 18 a, (The Roman World) 47 a, 57 b, 59 b, (The Universal Church) 68 b, (The Growth of Autonomy) 74 a, 77 a, 80 b, (Renaissance and Reformation) 100 a, (Individualism and Capitalism) 161 b, (Nationalism) 170 b, (The Trend to Internationalism) 179 a, 180 a, (War and Reorientation) 219 a, (The Social Sciences as Disciplines, Austria) 267 a, (France) 252 a, 253 b, (Gt. Brit.) 239 a, 245 a, (Hungary) 269 b, (Japan) 321 a, (Lat. Amer.) 306 a, 313 b, 315 a, (Russia) 282 a, 283 b, (Scandinavia) 293 a, (U. S.) 324 a, 340 a, 344 b; Anthropology ii 88 b; Authority ii 319–21; Casuistry iii 265 b; Christianity iii 456 a; Colonial Administration iii 644 b; Consensus iv 226 b; Culture iv 633 b; Custom iv 661 b; Enlightenment v 550 a; Fictions vi 227 b; Folkways vi 295 b; Functionalism vi 525 b; Govt. vii 9 b; Liberty ix 444 a; Obedience, Political xi 415–18; Outlawry of War xi 509 b; Philosophy xii 126 b; Power, Political xii 304 a; Sociology xiv 242 b; State xiv 331 a; Utilitarianism xv 199 a; Vested Interests xv 240 b. *For biog. references see* Classification of Articles (Law), p. 563 *and* (History—Legal), p. 562.
LAW ENFORCEMENT—ix 267–70; Anthropology ii 89 a; Civic Education iii 496–98; Justice, Administration of viii 518 a; Labor, Govt. Services for viii 646 a; Lawlessness ix 277–79; Obedience, Political xi 416 b; Police xii 183–90; Prohibition xii 505 a; Racketeering xiii 47 a, 49 a.
LAW, J.—ix 270; Banking, Commercial ii 429 b; Bubbles, Speculative iii 24 b; Land Bank Schemes ix 31 a; Mercantilism x 338 a.
LAW MERCHANT—ix 270–74; Bill of Exchange ii 540 b; Commercial Law iv 15 a; Common Law iv 53 b; Fairs vi 60 b; Mansfield x 103 a; Negotiable Instruments xi 332 b.
Law of Nations—see INTERNATIONAL LAW.
Law of Nature—see NATURAL LAW.
Law Reform—Amer. Law Institute ii 30–31; Equity v 586 b; Judiciary viii 469 a; Justice, Administration of viii 522 b; Law (Chinese) ix 253 a; Legislation ix 350 a; Procedure, Legal xii 450 b.
Law of War—see WARFARE, LAWS OF.
LAWES, J. B.—ix 274; Fertilizer Industry vi 193 b.
LAWGIVERS—ix 275–77; Solon xiv 254 a.
LAWLESSNESS—ix 277–79; Brigandage ii 693–96; Camorra iii 161–62; Gangs vi 566 a; Justice, Administration of viii 518 b; Lynching ix 639–43; Mafia x 36–38; Policing, Industrial xii 193–96; Racketeering xiii 45–50; Smuggling xiv 119–23.
LAWRENCE, H. M. *and* LORD—ix 279.
LAZĂR, G.—ix 280.
Lazaristes—xv 262 b.

LAZARUS, M.—ix 280; Play xii 160 a; Social Psychology xiv 153 a.
Lazzari, C.—ix 281.
LEA, H. C.—ix 281; History and Historiography vii 387 b.
Lead—x 365 b, 378 a.
LEADERSHIP—ix 282–87; Aristocracy ii 187 b; Authority ii 319–21; Boutmy ii 660 b; Fascism vi 135 b; Genius vi 612–15; Hero Worship vii 336–38; Intellectuals viii 118–26; Journalism viii 421 a; Machine, Political ix 657–61; Mob x 553 a; Monarchy x 579–84; Oligarchy xi 464 a; Opportunism xi 479 a; Parties, Political xi 595 a, (Japan) 635 b; Politics xii 226 a; Statesmanship xiv 350–52.
League of Armed Neutrality— ii 203 b.
LEAGUE OF NATIONS—ix 287–95; Advisory Opinions i 478–80; Agreements, International i 519 a; Agriculture, Govt. Services for i 606 a; Alliance ii 4 b; Arms and Munitions Traffic ii 208 a; Aviation (Law) ii 366 b; Balance of Power ii 398 b; Balance of Trade ii 403 a; Business, Govt. Services for iii 117 a; Calendar iii 143 b; Child (Welfare) iii 379 a, (Neglected) 406 a, (Labor) 417 a; Coal Industry iii 599 b; Commercial Treaties iv 30 b; Diplomacy v 151 a; Disarmament v 160 a; Export Duties vi 23 a; Forced Labor vi 344 a; Great Powers vii 161 b; Guaranties, International vii 191 a; Immunity, Diplomatic vii 597 a; Imperialism vii 612 a; International Advisers viii 158 a; International Labor Organization viii 164 b; International Legislation viii 176 a; International Organization viii 183 b; International Waterways viii 211 b; Internationalism viii 217 a; Intervention viii 237 a; Investigations, Governmental viii 259 b; Limitation of Armaments ix 482 a; Loans, Intergovernmental ix 560 b; Manchurian Problem x 83 a; Mandates x 87–93; Minorities, National x 522 a; Monroe Doctrine x 632 a; Morbidity xi 4 a; Munitions Industry xi 133 b; Nansen xi 181 a; Opium Problem xi 474 a; Passport xii 16 a; Peace Movements xii 47 a; Permanent Court of International Justice xii 78–81; Prostitution xii 557 a; Public Health xii 655 b; Refugees xiii 203 a; Reprisals xiii 316 b; Sanction, International xiii 528 b; Statistics xiv 360 a; Transit, International xv 79 a; Treaties xv 99 b.
League of Universal Brotherhood —xii 42 a.

LEARNED SOCIETIES—ix 295–300; Introd. Vol. 1 (The Social Sciences as Disciplines, Austria) i 269 a, (Germany) 263 a, (Gt. Brit.) 242 a, (Hungary) 272 b, (Japan) 322 a, 323 a, (Russia) 289 b, (U. S.) 347 b; Research xiii 330 b, 331 b; Statistics xiv 359 a.
Lease—see LANDLORD AND TENANT.
Leasehold—Land Tenure ix 88 b.
LEATHER INDUSTRIES—ix 300–16 (Tanning 300–04, 315, Leather Products 304–12, 315, Labor 312–16).
Leblanc, N.—vii 301 b.
LE BON, G.—ix 316; Belief ii 500 b; Social Psychology xiv 153 b.
LECKY, W. E. H.—ix 316; Balance of Power ii 398 a.
LECLAIRE, E. J.—ix 317; Profit Sharing xii 488 a.
Le Corbusier, C. E. J.-G.—ii 256 b.
LEDRU-ROLLIN, A. A.—ix 317.
Lee, R. H.—v 45 b.
LEEUWEN, S. VAN—ix 318.
Leeuwenhoek A. van—ii 551 a.
LEFROY, A. H. F.—ix 319.
LEGAL AID—ix 319–24; Briesen ii 693 a; Legal Profession and Legal Education ix 344 b; Public Defender xii 611–13.
Legal Education—see LEGAL PROFESSION AND LEGAL EDUCATION.
Legal Medicine—see MEDICAL JURISPRUDENCE.
Legal Procedure—see PROCEDURE, LEGAL.
LEGAL PROFESSION AND LEGAL EDUCATION—ix 324–46 (Ancient and Mediaeval 324–34, 345, Modern Legal Education 334–40, 345, Modern Legal Profession 340–46); Introd. Vol. 1 (War and Reorientation) i 221 a, (The Social Sciences as Disciplines, France) 253 b, (Gt. Brit.) 233 a, 239 a, (Lat. Amer.) 306 a, (Russia) 287 a, (U. S.) 325 a; Administrative Law i 453 a; Amer. Law Institute ii 30–31; Ames ii 35 b; Anson ii 71 b; Blackstone ii 580 a; Case Method iii 251–54; Comparative Law iv 128 b; Contingent Fee iv 311–13; Coroner iv 410–11; Fee Splitting vi 178 a; Judicial Process viii 450–57; Judiciary viii 464–69; Justice of the Peace viii 524–27; Lawgivers ix 275–77; Legal Aid ix 322 a; Legislation ix 347 a; Notaries, Public xi 399–400; Professional Ethics xii 474 a; Professions xii 476–80; Public Defender xii 611–13; Roman Law xiii 421 b.
Legal Tender—see MONEY.
LEGIEN, C.—ix 346; Labor Movement viii 689 a.

LEGISLATION—ix 347–54; Begging ii 494 a; Blue Laws ii 600–02; Blue Sky Laws ii 602–05; By-Law iii 128–29; Child (Welfare) iii 376 b, (Hygiene) 383 a, (Delinquent) 406–09, (Welfare Legislation) 424–27; Committees, Legislative iv 40–44; Constitutional Law iv 247–55; Constitutionalism iv 257 b; Initiative and Referendum viii 50–52; International Legislation viii 175–77; Islamic Law viii 345 a; Judicial Review viii 457–64; Judiciary viii 469 a; Jurisprudence viii 486 a, 489 a; Labor Legislation and Law viii 657–67; Law (Chinese) ix 253 b, (Germanic) 238 b, (Greek) 225 b, (Hellenistic and Greco-Egyptian) 230 a; Legislative Assemblies (Hist. and Theory) ix 359 b, (France) 379 a, (Spain) 393 a, (U. S.) 364 b, 367 a; Lobby ix 565–68; Mining Law x 516 a; Petition, Right of xii 98 a; Poor Laws xii 230–34; Retroactive Legislation xiii 355–57; Roman Law xiii 420 a, 421 b, 423 b; Sumptuary Legislation xiv 464–66; Tariff xiv 521 b; Uniform Legislation xv 178–81; Veto xv 247–49.
Legislation, International — see INTERNATIONAL LEGISLATION.
LEGISLATIVE ASSEMBLIES — ix 355–98 (Hist. and Theory 355–61, 395, U. S. 361–69, 395, Gt. Brit. and Dominions 369–74, 396, France 374–79, 396, Germany and Austria 379–83, 396, Switzerland 384–85, 397, Netherlands 385–87, 397, Scandinavian States and Finland 387–89, 397, Hungary 389–90, 397, Spain and Portugal 391–93, 398, Japan 393–95, 398). See Classification of Articles (Legislation), p. 553. See also Introd. Vol. 1 (The Roman World) i 50 a; Administration, Public i 447 a; Armed Forces, Control of ii 201 a; Budget iii 40 a; By-Elections iii 127–28; Cabinet iii 132 b; Cabinet Govt. iii 135 b; Constitutional Conventions iv 246 b; Executive v 682 a; Govt. vii 11 a, (Argentina) 92 a, (Australia) 29 b, 31 a, (Austria) 77 a, (Austria-Hungary) 76 a, (Belgium) 48 a, (Brazil) 93 a, (Canada) 28 a, (Chile) 94 b, (Czechoslovakia) 79 a, (Denmark) 61 a, (Estonia) 71 b, (Finland) 65 a, (France) 45 a, (Germany) 53 b, (Gt. Brit.) 24 a, (Greece) 83 b, (Hungary) 78 a, (Iceland) 62 a, (Ireland) 37 a, (Italy) 49 a, 51 b, (Japan) 95 b, (Jugoslavia) 81 a, (Latvia) 72 b, (Lithuania) 73 a, (Mexico) 93 b, (Netherlands) 59 b, (New Zealand) 32 b, (Norway) 62 b, (Poland) 74 a, (Rumania) 80 a, (Russia, Imperial) 65 b, (Russia, Soviet) 68 b, (S. Africa) 34 a, (Spain) 86 a, (Sweden) 63 b, (Switzerland) 58 a, (Turkey) 85 a, (Uruguay) 94 a, (U. S.) 19 b; Govt. Publications vii 120 b; League of Nations ix 289 a; Organization, Administrative xi 481 b; Petition, Right of xii 98 a; Treaties xv 98 a.
Legislative Committees — see COMMITTEES, LEGISLATIVE.
Legislative Reference Bureaus—Legislation ix 353 b; Legislative Assemblies ix 359 b.
Legitim—viii 36 a.
LE GRAND, D.—ix 398.
LEHFELDT, R. A.—ix 398.
LEHR, J.—ix 399; Index Numbers vii 655 b.
LEIB, J. G.—ix 399.
LEIBNIZ, G. W. VON—ix 400; Enlightenment v 550 a; Humanism vii 541 b; Justice viii 512 a; Natural Law xi 289 a; Psychology xii 590 a.
Leicester, Lord—see MONTFORT, S. DE.
LEIST, B. W.—ix 402.
LEISURE—ix 402–06; Amateur ii 18–20; Anthropology ii 89 b, 100 b; Art ii 226 a; Career iii 225 a; Clubs iii 573–77; Gentleman, Theory of the vi 617 b; Hours of Labor vii 489 b; Industrialism viii 25 b; Parks xi 582–87; Play xii 160–61; Recreation xiii 176–81; Social Settlements xiv 160 b; Sports xiv 305–08; Tourist Traffic xiv 661–64.
LELEWEL, J.—ix 406.
Lemercier de la Rivière, P.-P.— see MERCIER DE LA RIVIÈRE, P.-P.
LEMIRE, J.—ix 406.
LEMONNIER, C. and É.—ix 407; Peace Movements xii 44 a.
Lemprière, J.—vi 288 b.
Lenin, N.—Bolshevism ii 623–30; Communist Parties iv 87 a; Gosplan vi 707 b; Literature ix 539 b; Russian Revolution xiii 481 b, 485 b; Socialism xiv 207 b; Ulyanov xv 140.
LEO III—ix 407; Introd. Vol. 1 (The Universal Church) i 64 a; Holy Roman Empire vii 423 a.
LEO XIII—ix 408; Harmel vii 270 b; Modernism x 567 b; Religious Institutions (Roman Catholic) xiii 260 a.
Leo the Great—xi 560 a.
LEO, H.—ix 409.
Leonardo da Vinci—Art ii 248 a; Industrial Revolution viii 6 a; Machines and Tools x 19 b.
LEONHARD, R. K. G.—ix 410.
Leontief, V.—v 73 b.
LEONTOVICH, F. I.—ix 410.
LEONTYEV, K. N.—ix 410.
LEOPOLD II—ix 411.
LE PLAY, P. G. F.—ix 411; Family Budgets vi 73 b; Social

Surveys xiv 162 b; Sociology xiv 236 b; Tourville xiv 664 b.
Lepsius, K. R.—ix 412.
Leroux, P.—ix 413.
Leroy-Beaulieu, P.—ix 414; Native Policy xi 273 b.
Lescure, J.—iii 99 a.
Lese Majesty—ix 415-17; Contempt of Court iv 303 a; Military Desertion x 451 b; Political Offenders xii 200 a.
Leslie, T. E. C.—ix 417.
Lesseps, F. de—xiv 444 b.
Lessing, G. E.—ix 418; Deism v 62 b; Enlightenment v 551 a; Romanticism xiii 428 b; Theater xiv 609 a.
Letelier, V.—ix 419.
Le Trosne, G. F.—ix 420.
Letters Patent—xi 307 a.
Lettre de Cachet—see Cachet, Lettre de.
Leuber, B.—ix 420.
Levasseur, P. É.—ix 421.
Levees—vi 283 b.
Levellers—ix 421-23; Agreement of the People i 516-18; Lilburne ix 473 a; Natural Law xi 287 b; Public Opinion xii 673 b; Sects xiii 627 b; Winstanley xv 430 a.
Lever, W. H.—see Leverhulme, Lord.
Leverhulme, Lord—ix 423; Garden Cities vi 570 a.
Levi, L.—ix 424.
Levinson, S. O.—xi 508 b.
Levirate—Kinship viii 570 b; Law (Jewish) ix 220 a.
Lévy-Bruhl, L.—Introd. Vol. i (The Trend to Internationalism) i 184 b; Animism ii 66 a; Magic x 41 a; Social Psychology xiv 154 a.
Levy Lawson Family—ix 425.
Lewiński, J. S.—ix 425.
Lewis, G. C.—ix 426.
Lexis, W.—ix 426; Probability xii 433 b; Statistics xiv 366 b.
Li Hung Chang—ix 427.
Liability—ix 427-29; Automobile Insurance ii 330-32; Bailment ii 388-90; Common Carrier iv 49 a; Compensation and Liability Insurance iv 136 a; Contract iv 323-39; Employers' Liability v 514-18; Fire Protection vi 264 b; Hotels vii 476 b; Law (Slavic) ix 245 b; Maritime Law x 128 b; Massachusetts Trusts x 190 a; Motor Vehicle Accidents xi 73 a; Municipal Corporation xi 92 b; Negligence xi 328-32; Negotiable Instruments xi 334 a; Riot xiii 391 a; State Liability xiv 338-43; Suretyship and Guaranty xiv 482-87; Tort xiv 653-57; Voluntary Associations xv 283-87.
Liability Insurance—see Casualty Insurance; Compensation and Liability Insurance.
Liang Ch'i-ch'ao—ix 430; Hist. and Historiography vii 384 a.

Libel and Slander—ix 430-35; Erskine v 589 b; Freedom of Speech and of the Press vi 456 b; Lese Majesty ix 416 a; Press xii 341 a; Searches and Seizures xiii 617 b; Sedition xiii 636 b.
Liberal Parties—Labor Parties (Brit. Dom's.) viii 705 a, (Gt. Brit.) 699 b; Parties, Political (Belgium) xi 613 b, (Canada) 605 a, (Gt. Brit.) 602 a, (Netherlands) 620 b, (New Zeal.) 607 b.
Liberalism—ix 435-42; Introd. Vol. i (The Rise of Liberalism) i 103-24; Anarchism ii 47 b; Baines ii 391 b; Capitalism iii 198 b; Civil Liberties iii 509-13; Constant de Rebecque iv 242 a; Consumers' Cooperation iv 289 b; Economic Policy v 339 a; Economics (Socio-Ethical Economics) v 381-85; French Revolution vi 481 b; Green vii 164 b; History and Historiography vii 378 a; Idealism vii 572 a; Imperialism vii 608 a; Indian Question vii 665 a; Individualism vii 678 a; Jacobinism viii 363 a; Jacoby viii 364 b; Laissez Faire ix 15-20; Liberty ix 443 b; Michel x 403 b; Middle Class x 408 a; Mill x 481 a; Nationalism xi 244 b; Natural Rights xi 299-302; Parties, Polit. (Bulgaria) xi 629 b, (Germany) 615 b, (Lat. Amer.) 633 a, (Sweden) 621 b; Proletariat xii 515 a; Reformism xiii 194 b; Ritchie xiii 394 b; Social Christian Movements xiv 124 b; Socialism xiv 192 a; Usury xv 196 b.
Liberty—ix 442-47; Citizenship iii 471 a; Civil Liberties iii 509-13; Declaration of Independence v 46 a; Declaration of the Rights of Man and the Citizen v 50 a; Democracy v 76-85; Due Process of Law v 267 a; Economics (Classical School) v 351 b; Freedom of Association vi 447-50; Freedom of Contract vi 450-55; Freedom of Speech and of the Press vi 455-59; French Revolution vi 475 a; Govt. vii 13 a; Idealism vii 570 b; Individualism vii 677 b; Justice viii 511 a; Kant viii 539 a; Liberalism ix 435-42; Mill x 482 a; Natural Law xi 287 b, 288 b; Natural Rights xi 299-302; Nihilism xi 377-79; Obedience, Political xi 415-18; Priestley xii 395 b; Religious Freedom xiii 239-46; Tradition xv 65 b; Value and Price xv 223 a.
Libraries—Introd. Vol. i (Greek Culture and Thought) i 39 a, (The Social Sciences as Disciplines, Lat. Amer.) 318 b; Blind ii 589 a; Govt. Publications vii 120 b; Public Libraries xii 659-65.

Licensing—ix 447-51; Administrative Law i 453 b; Arms, Right to Bear ii 209 b; Assembly, Right of ii 276 a; Aviation ii 357 a, 368 b; Blockade ii 595 a; Blue Sky Laws ii 603 a; Commissions iv 37 b; Copyright iv 402 a; Excise v 670 b; Liquor Traffic ix 505 b; Motor Vehicle Accidents xi 72 b; Professions xii 478 a; Prohibition xii 509 a; Prostitution xii 557 b; Radio xiii 64 a; Real Estate xiii 140 a; Teaching Profession xiv 546 b.
Lieben, R.—ix 451; Auspitz ii 317 b; Economics v 367 b.
Lieber, F.—ix 452; Introd. Vol. i (The Social Sciences as Disciplines, U. S.) i 328 b.
Liebermann, A. S.—ix 452.
Liebermann, F.—ix 453.
Liebig, J. von—ix 453; Agriculture i 584 a; Fertilizer Industry vi 193 a.
Liebknecht, K.—ix 454; Antimilitarism ii 115 b; General Strike vi 610 a.
Liebknecht, W.—ix 455; Socialist Parties xiv 213 b.
Lieh Tzu—xiv 511 a.
Lien—ix 456-60; Mortgage xi 35 a; Pledge xii 166-68.
Lietz, H.—ix 460.
Life Extension Movement—ix 460-62.
Life Insurance—ix 462-72; Annuities ii 69-71; Baily ii 390 b; Fraternal Orders vi 424 a; Group Insurance vii 182-88; Health Insurance vii 298 a; Insurance viii 98 a; Investment Banking viii 272 b; Life Extension Movement ix 461 b.
Likin—Transit Duties xv 77 b.
Lilburne, J.—ix 472; Levellers ix 421 b; Natural Law xi 287 b.
Lilienblum, M. L.—ix 473.
Lilienfeld, P. von—see Lilienfeld-Toailles, P. F.
Lilienfeld-Toailles, P. F.—ix 473; Social Organism xiv 140 a.
Limitation of Actions—ix 474-80; Land Transfer ix 129 b.
Limitation of Armaments—ix 480-86; Disarmament v 158-61; Far Eastern Problem vi 95 b; Hague Conferences vii 242 b; League of Nations ix 293 b; Munitions Industry xi 133 b; National Defense xi 192 a; Navy xi 317 b; War xv 338 b; Warfare, Laws of xv 363 a.
Limited Liability—viii 411 b.
Lincoln, A.—ix 486; Reconstruction xiii 168 a.
Lindsay, A. D.—xii 171 b.
Lindsey, B. B.—iv 115 a.
Linen—vi 277 a.
Ling, P. H.—xii 131 a.
Lingard, J.—ix 488.
Linguet, S. N. H.—ix 488; Mallet du Pan x 65 a.

Index (Le Play — Long Term Credit)

Linnaeus, C.—Biology ii 551 b; Race xiii 26 a.
Lipinsky, V.—ix 489.
Lipmann, O.—vii 491 b.
Lippert, J.—ix 490.
Lipsius, J. H.—ix 491.
Lipton, T. J.—ix 491.
Liquidity—ix 491–95.
Liquor Industry—ix 495–502; Alcohol i 619 a; Liquor Traffic ix 502–09; Monopolies, Public x 620 a; Prohibition xii 502 a.
Liquor Traffic — ix 502–09; Anti-Saloon League ii 118–19; Concurrent Powers iv 173 b; Industrial Alcohol vii 682 b; Liquor Industry ix 495–502; Prohibition xii 499–510; Smuggling xiv 121 a; Temperance Movements xiv 567–70.
List, F.—ix 509; Customs Unions iv 674 a; Economic History v 317 a; Economic Policy v 340 a; Economics v 371–77; Free Trade vi 445 b; Protection xii 562 a.
Lister, J.—ix 510; Communicable Diseases, Control of iv 68 a; Medicine x 288 b.
Liszt, F. E. von—ix 511.
Literacy and Illiteracy—ix 511–23; Introd. Vol. 1 (The Universal Church) i 68 a; Education v 411 b; Negro Problem xi 352 a.
Literary Digest—iii 166 a.
Literature—ix 523–43. See relevant titles in Classification of Articles (Literature and the Press), p. 553. See also Introd. Vol. 1 (The Revolutions) i 127 b; Anthropology ii 91 b; Art ii 251 b; Crusades iv 616 a; Decadence v 42 a; French Revolution vi 474 a; Gentleman, Theory of the vi 618 b; History and Historiography vii 358 a; Naturalism xi 305 a; Negro Problem xi 345 b. For biog. references see Classification of Articles (Literature and Social Criticism), p. 564.
Little Theater Movement—xiv 613 b.
Littleton, T. de—ix 543.
Littré, M. P. É.—ix 544.
Liverpool, Lord—ix 545.
Livestock Industry—ix 545–51; Agricultural Marketing (U. S.) i 562 b; Cattle Loans iii 276–77; Dry Farming v 255 b; Meat Packing and Slaughtering x 242–63; Milk Supply x 477 b; Stock Breeding xiv 394–97.
Livestock Insurance—i 546 b.
Livingston, E.—ix 552; Criminal Law iv 574 a.
Livingston, R. R.—ix 552.
Livingstone, D.—ix 552.
Livy—ix 553; Introd. Vol. 1 (The Roman World) i 52 a; History and Historiography vii 369 a.
Llorente, J. A.—ix 554.

Lloyd, H. D.—ix 554.
Lloyd, W. F.—ix 555.
Lloyd George, D.—Cabinet iii 132 a; Labor Parties (Gt. Brit.) viii 700 b.
Lloyd's — Marine Insurance x 112 b.
Loan Shark—xiv 107 b.
Loans, Intergovernmental—ix 556–61; Foreign Investment vi 365 a, 369 b; International Finance viii 159 b; Reparations xiii 307 a; Repudiation of Public Debts xiii 321–24; War Finance xv 351 a.
Loans, Personal—ix 561–65; Debt v 32–39; Pawnbroking xii 32–40; Small Loans xiv 105–11.
Lobby—ix 565–68; Anti-Saloon League ii 119 a; Chambers of Commerce iii 327 a; Civic Organizations iii 498–502; Legislative Assemblies ix 361 a; Munitions Industry xi 132 b; Propaganda xii 522 b; Veterans xv 245 a.
Local Finance—ix 568–74; Municipal Finance xi 98–104; Public Debt xii 610 a; Sinking Fund xiv 68 b; Special Assessments xiv 276–79; Tax Administration xiv 527 b.
Local Government—ix 574–85; Administrative Areas i 450–52; Autonomy ii 332–36; Centralization iii 308–13; County-City Consolidation iv 499–501; County Councils iv 501–04; County Govt., U. S. iv 504–08; Govt. (Argentina) vii 92 b, (Australia) 29 b, (Austria) 77 b, (Austria-Hungary) 76 b, (Belgium) 48 b, (Brazil) 93 a, (Bulgaria) 83 a, (Canada) 29 a, (China) 98 b, (Czechoslovakia) 79 a, (Denmark) 61 b, (Estonia) 72 a, (Finland) 65 a, (Germany) 54 a, (Gt. Brit.) 26 a, (Hungary) 78 b, (Ireland) 38 a, (Italy) 50 b, (Japan) 98 a, (Latvia) 73 a, (Lithuania) 73 b, (Netherlands) 59 b, (New Zealand) 33 b, (Norway) 63 a, (Poland) 74 b, (Russia, Imperial) 66 a, (Russia, Soviet) 68 a, (S. Africa) 36 a, (Spain) 86 b, (Sweden) 64 b, (U. S.) 18 b; Govt. Reporting vii 130 b; Grants-in-Aid vii 152–55; Home Rule vii 434–36; Justice of the Peace viii 525 a; Legislative Assemblies ix 360 a; Local Finance ix 568–74; Metropolitan Areas x 397 a; Municipal Corporation xi 86–94; Municipal Govt. xi 105–17; Organization, Administrative xi 482 b; Regionalism xiii 208–18; Sheriff xiv 20–23.
Local Option—see Prohibition.
Localism—see Regionalism.
Localization of Industry—see Location of Industry.
Locarno Treaties—ii 159 b.

Location of Industry—ix 585–93; Back-to-the-Land Movements ii 379 a; Increasing Returns vii 640 b; Industrial Revolution viii 11 a; Liquor Industry ix 497 a; Metals x 369 b; Munitions Industry xi 133 b; Power, Industrial xii 298 b; Pulp and Paper Industry xii 707 a; Quarrying xiii 17 b; Raw Materials xiii 126 b; Refrigeration xiii 197 b; Rural Industries xiii 466–69; Specialization xiv 283 a; Textile Industry xiv 586 b; Thünen xiv 627 a; Urbanization xv 190 a.
Loch, C. S.—ix 593; Charity iii 343 b; Social Work xiv 173 b.
Locke, J.—ix 593; Introd. Vol. 1 (The Rise of Liberalism) i 111 b; Bills of Rights ii 545 b; Blackstone ii 580 b; Checks and Balances iii 363 b; Child (Psychology) iii 391 a; Civil Liberties iii 510 b; Common Sense iv 59 a; Education v 413 a; Force, Political vi 340 b; Freedom of Association vi 449 a; Human Nature vii 532 b; Humanism vii 541 b; Logic ix 601 b; Materialism x 211 b; Natural Law xi 288 a; Natural Rights xi 300 b; Positivism xii 261 b; Prerogative xii 319 b; Psychology xii 589 a; Public Opinion xii 669 b; Religious Freedom xiii 242 a; Separation of Powers xiii 664 a, 665 b; Single Tax xiv 64 b; Social Contract xiv 129 b.
Lockout—see Strikes and Lockouts.
Lockwood, B. A. B.—ix 595.
Lodging Houses—ix 595–98; Begging ii 494 b.
Loewenstein, A.—ix 598.
Logic—ix 598–603; Jevons viii 390 b; Law (Chinese) ix 250 b; Method, Scientific x 389–96; Rationalism xiii 113–17.
Loisel, A.—ix 603.
Lollards—xiii 626 a.
Lombard, P.—see Peter Lombard.
Lombroso, C.—ix 603; Atavism ii 290 b; Baer ii 383 b; Benedikt ii 511 a; Carrara iii 234 a; Criminal Law iv 578 a; Criminology iv 585 a; Degeneration v 56 a; Genius vi 612 b.
Lomonosov, M. V.—ix 604.
London Morning Post—ii 644 a.
London Naval Conference—ix 482 b.
London School of Economics and Political Science—i 234 a, 236 a, 238 a.
London Times—Delane v 63 a; Walter Family xv 329 b.
Long Term Credit—Agric. Credit i 532 b; Credit iv 548 b; Farm Loan System, Federal vi 106 b; Foreign Investment vi 371 a; Investment Banking viii 268 a.

LONGE, F. D.—ix 605.
LONGFIELD, S. M.—ix 605; Absentee Ownership i 377 a.
LONGSHOREMEN—ix 606-09.
LÓPEZ DE PALACIOS RUBIOS, J.—ix 610.
LÓPEZ, V. F.—ix 609.
Lorenz, M. O.—xi 221 a.
Lorenzen, E.—iv 189 b.
LORIMER, J.—ix 610.
Lotka, A. J.—xi 26 b.
LOTTERIES—ix 611-16; Gambling vi 557 a; Public Debt xii 604 b.
LOTZ, J. F. E.—ix 616.
LOTZE, R. H.—ix 617; Mechanism and Vitalism x 268 b; Psychology xii 591 b.
LOUIS XI—ix 618.
LOUIS XIV—ix 619; Art (French) ii 249 a.
Louis Napoleon—see NAPOLEON III.
LOVETT, W.—ix 619; Workers' Education xv 484 a.
Lowe, J.—vii 657 a.
LOWELL, J. R.—ix 620.
LOWELL, J. S.—ix 621.
Lowie, R. H.—ii 285 b.
Lowther, J.—xiii 217 a.
Loyal Legion of Loggers and Lumbermen—see Four L.
Loyd, S. J.—see OVERSTONE, LORD.
LOYOLA, I. DE—ix 621; Jesuits viii 381 b.
LOYSEAU, C.—ix 622.
LUBBOCK, J.—ix 622; Anthropology ii 102 b; Archaeology ii 164 a.
LUBECKI, F. X.—ix 623.
LUBIN, D.—ix 623; Agriculture, International Institute of i 606 b.
LUCAS, C. P.—ix 624.
LUCHAIRE, A.—ix 624.
LUCHITSKY, I. V.—ix 625.
LUCIAN—ix 626.
LUCKENBILL, D. D.—ix 626.
LUCRETIUS CARUS, T.—ix 627; Materialism x 210 a; Naturalism xi 303 a.
LUDEN, H.—ix 627.
LUDLOW, J. M.—ix 628; Christian Socialism iii 450 a.
LUDOGOVSKY, A. P.—ix 629.
LUEDER, A. F.—ix 629.
LUEGER, K.—ix 629; National Socialism, German xi 225 b.
Lugard, F.—xi 275 a.
Lughinin Brothers—iv 387 a.
LULL, R.—ix 630.
Lumber Industry—see WOOD INDUSTRIES.
Lundborg, G.—ii 112 a.
LUSCHAN, F. VON—ix 631.
LUTHER, M.—ix 631; Introd. Vol. I (Renaissance and Reformation) i 94 b; Education (Public) v 415 a; Literacy and Illiteracy ix 515 b; Melanchthon x 302 b; Mysticism xi 176 b; Reformation xiii 188 b; Zwingli xv 542 a.
Lutheranism—Magdeburg Centuriators x 38 b; Protestantism xii 571 b; Reformation xiii 188 b; Religious Institutions (Protestant) xiii 268 b; Society xiv 227 b.
Luxembourg Labor Commission—ii 291 b.
LUXEMBURG, R.—ix 633; Economics v 380 a; General Strike vi 610 a, 611 b; Liebknecht ix 455 a.
LUXURY—ix 634-38; Leisure ix 404 a; Precious Stones xii 312-15; Sumptuary Legislation xiv 464-66; Taste xiv 523-25.
LUZZATTI, L.—ix 638; Cooperation iv 381 b; Monetary Unions x 600 a.
Lyautey, L. H. G.—xi 274 a.
Lyceums—vii 403 a.
Lycophron—xi 285 b.
LYELL, C.—ix 639.
LYNCHING—ix 639-43.
Lynd, R. S. and H. M.—xiv 164 b.
LYON, M.—ix 643.

MABILLON, J.—ix 643; Introd. Vol. 1 (The Revolutions) i 142 b.
MABLY, G. B. DE—ix 644.
MABUCHI, K.—ix 645.
MCADAM, J. L.—ix 645; Roads xiii 404 a.
Macaggi, G.—xiii 216 a.
MACANAZ, M. R. DE—ix 646.
MACARTHUR, J.—ix 646.
MACARTHUR, M. R.—ix 647.
MACAULAY, LORD—ix 647; Bentinck ii 520 a; Civil Service iii 519 a; History and Historiography vii 378 a; Indian Question vii 662 b; Liberty ix 442 b.
MCCORMICK, C. H.—ix 648.
McCrea, R. C.—xi 39 a.
MCCULLOCH, J. R.—ix 649; Absentee Ownership i 377 a; Barton ii 472 b; Inheritance viii 37 a.
MACDONALD, A.—ix 650.
MACDONALD, J. A.—ix 650.
MacDonald, J. R.—Indian Question vii 669 b; Labor Parties (Gt. Brit.) viii 700 b.
Macdonald, M.—xiii 217 a.
McDougall, W.—Introd. Vol. 1 (War and Reorientation) i 206 a; Educational Psychology v 433 b; Social Psychology xiv 154 a.
MCDUFFIE, G.—ix 651.
Macedonian Problem—Comitadji iii 675-78; Near Eastern Problem xi 323 a.
McFadden Act—ii 680 b.
MCGEE, T. D'A.—ix 652.
MCGEE, W. J.—ix 652.
MacGregor, W.—xi 270 b.
MACH, E.—ix 653; Consciousness iv 214 a, 215 b; Positivism xii 265 a; Pragmatism xii 308 b.
MACHAJSKI, W.—ix 654.
MACHIAVELLI, N.—ix 655; Introd. Vol. I (Renaissance and Reformation) i 90 b; Absolutism i 380 b; Belief ii 501 b; Checks and Balances iii 363 a; Force, Political vi 340 a; La Boétie viii 615 a; Reason of State xiii 143 a.
MACHINE, POLITICAL—ix 657-61; Campaign, Political iii 162-66; Caucus iii 277-79; Civic Organizations iii 498 b; Clubs, Political iii 578 b; Convention, Political iv 349-51; Corruption, Political iv 452 b; Gangs vi 566 b; Insurgency, Political viii 113-16; Intimidation viii 241 b; Nominations, Political xi 394 a; Parties, Political xi 594 a, (Balkan States) 628 b, (Canada) 605 b, (Czechoslovakia) 627 a, (Gt. Brit.) 603 b, (Irish Free State) 610 b, (Lat. Amer.) 633 b, (U. S.) 600 b; Racketeering xiii 47 a; Spoils System xiv 301-05.
Machinery, Agricultural—see AGRICULTURAL MACHINERY.
MACHINERY, INDUSTRIAL—x 3-14; Machines and Tools x 14-26.
MACHINES AND TOOLS—x 14-26. See TECHNOLOGY.
MACÍAS PICAVEA, R.—x 26.
MACIEJOWSKI, W. A.—x 27.
Mackay Companies—xiv 563 a.
McKay, G.—ix 307 b.
MCKENZIE, J.—x 28.
MACKENZIE, W.—x 28.
McKinley, W.—xii 109 b.
MACLAY, W.—x 29.
MCLENNAN, J. F.—x 29; Fison vi 272 a.
MACLEOD, H. D.—x 30.
MCMASTER, J. B.—x 31; History and Historiography vii 387 b.
McNary-Haugen Bill—i 511 b.
MCNEILL, G. E.—x 31.
MACONOCHIE, A.—x 32; Transportation of Criminals xv 92 a.
MACQUARIE, L.—x 32.
MacSwiney, T.—vii 553 b.
Macune, C. W.—vi 128 a.
MACVANE, S. M.—x 32.
Macy, R. H.—x 33.
MADERO, F. I.—x 33.
MADISON, J.—x 34; Checks and Balances iii 364 a.
MADOX, T.—x 35.
Maecenas—ix 534 a.
MAFFI, A.—x 36.
MAFIA—x 36-38.
MAGDEBURG CENTURIATORS — x 38-39.
MAGIC—x 39-44; Alchemy i 616-18; Animism ii 65-67; Anthropology ii 96 a; Architecture ii 167 b; Belief ii 501 b; Birth Customs ii 565-68; Blood Accusation ii 597-98; Blood Vengeance Feud ii 598 b; Cannibalism iii 173 a; Ceremony iii 313-16; Communicable Diseases, Control of iv 66 b; Confession iv 181 b; Culture iv 634 b; Dance iv 703 b; Death Customs v 21-27; Divination v 174-76; Dress v 236 a; Fasting vi 144-46; Fertility Rites vi 190-92; Festivals vi 198 b;

Fetishism vi 201-02; Folklore vi 288 a; Idolatry vii 575 a; Medicine x 283 b; Mysteries xi 172-75; Ornament xi 496 a; Priesthood xii 388 a; Religion xiii 229 b; Ritual xiii 396-98; Science xiii 594 b; Taoism xiv 512 a.
MAGNA CARTA—x 44-46; Civil Liberties iii 510 a; Mortmain xi 44 b.
Magnesium—x 385 b.
Magnum Concilium—ix 356 b.
MAHAFFY, J. P.—x 46.
MAHAN, A. T.—x 46.
Mahayana—iii 36 b.
Mahdi—Messianism x 363 a; Mohammed Ahmad x 572 a.
MAHMUD II—x 47.
Mail Order Houses—Marketing x 136 b; Retail Trade xiii 350 a.
MAIMONIDES, M.—x 48; Judaism viii 434 a; Karo viii 547 b; Law (Jewish) ix 224 a.
MAINE, H. J. S.—x 49; Introd. Vol. I (The Social Sciences as Disciplines, Gt. Brit.) i 239 b; Amos ii 39 a; Equity v 583 a; Jurisprudence viii 480 b; Natural Rights xi 300 a; Village Community xv 253 b.
MAISTRE, J. M. DE—x 50; Minority Rights x 525 b; Traditionalism xv 69 a.
MAITLAND, F. W.—x 52; Introd. Vol. I (The Social Sciences as Disciplines, Gt. Brit.) i 239 b; Economic History v 319 b; Pluralism xii 171 a; State xiv 331 a.
Maitland, J.—see LAUDERDALE, LORD.
MAJORITY, AGE OF—x 53-55; Juvenile Delinquency and Juvenile Courts viii 529 a.
MAJORITY RULE—x 55-60; Minority Rights x 525-27; Obedience, Political xi 415-18; Parties, Political xi 590-639; Voting xv 287-91.
MALABARI, B. M.—x 60.
MALADJUSTMENT—x 60-63; Abnormal Psychology i 366 a; Child (Guidance) iii 393-95; Emigration v 489 a; Fanaticism vi 92 a; Gangs vi 564-67; Juvenile Delinquency and Juvenile Courts viii 530 a; Labor Turnover viii 709 a; Mental Defectives x 312-13; Mental Disorders x 313-19; Mental Hygiene x 319-23; Psychiatry xii 578-80; Social Work (Case Work) xiv 174 b, 177 a; Suicide xiv 458 b.
Malaria—iii 243 a.
MALATESTA, E.—x 63.
Malguzars—ix 111 b.
MĀLIK IBN-ANAS—x 64; Islamic Law viii 345 b.
Malinovski, A. A.—see BOGDANOV, A.
Malinowski, B.—Family vi 65 b; Functionalism vi 525 a; Magic x 42 b.

MALKAM KHAN—x 64.
MALLET DU PAN, J.—x 65.
MALLINCKRODT, H. VON—x 66.
MALLOCK, W. H.—x 66.
MALMSTRÖM, C. G.—x 67.
Malnutrition—see NUTRITION.
MALON, B.—x 67.
MALTHUS, T. R.—x 68; Barton ii 472 a; Biology ii 555 a; Birth Control ii 560 b; Diminishing Returns v 145 a; Distribution v 168 b; Economic History v 316 b; Economics v 351-57; Education (Public) v 416 a; Evolution v 651 a; Hazlitt vii 286 b; Moheau x 574 a; Population xii 249 a; Price Stabilization xii 362 b; Townsend xiv 665 b; Wallace xv 326 b.
MALYNES, G. DE—x 69; Bullionists iii 62 b.
Mamelukes—Caliphate iii 147 a; Egyptian Problem v 441 a.
MAMIANI DELLA ROVERE, T.—x 70.
MAN—x 71-76; Anthropology ii 73-110; Anthropometry ii 110-12; Archaeology ii 163-67; Aryans ii 264-65; Biology ii 550-57; Civilization iii 525-29; Climate iii 560 a; Conduct iv 177-79; Culture iv 621-46; Darwin v 4; Domestication v 207 b; Environmentalism v 561-66; Eugenics v 617-21; Evolution v 649-56; Genius vi 612-15; Geography vi 621-26; Heredity vii 328-35; Human Nature vii 531-37; Maladjustment x 60-63; Migrations x 420-41; Old Age xi 452 b; Personality xii 85-88; Political Science xii 222 a; Prehistory xii 316-18; Race xiii 25-36; Self-Preservation xiii 653-55; Society xiv 225-32.
Mana—Religion xiii 234 b; Science xiii 594 b.
MANAGEMENT — x 76-80; Accounting i 404-12; Administration, Public i 440-50; Business Administration iii 87-91; Capitalism iii 198 a; Combinations, Industrial iii 672 b; Corporation iv 418 b; Financial Statements vi 247-49; Investment Banking viii 272 a; Labor-Capital Cooperation viii 624 b; Labor, Methods of Remuneration for viii 680 b; Labor Turnover viii 712 a; Large Scale Production ix 175 a; Mercantile Credit x 331 b; Personnel Administration xii 88-90; Profit xii 480-87; Promotion xii 518 b; Railroads xiii 90 a; Real Estate xiii 137 a; Scientific Management xiii 603-08; Stocks and Stock Ownership xiv 406 b; Waste xv 368 a; Welfare Work, Industrial xv 395-99.
Management, Farm—see FARM MANAGEMENT.
Manchester Guardian—xiii 609 a.

Manchester School (Economics)—Economic Policy v 339 a; Economics (Classical School) v 356 a.
Manchu Code—iii 606 b.
Manchu Dynasty—iii 431 b.
MANCHURIAN PROBLEM—x 80-84; Far Eastern Problem vi 97 a; Open Door xi 469 b.
MANCINI, P. S.—x 84.
Mancipatio—ix 128 b.
MANDAMUS—x 84-87.
Mandate, Legislative—iv 243 b.
MANDATES—x 87-93; Great Powers vii 161 a; Imperialism vii 612 a.
MANDEVILLE, B. DE—x 93; Altruism and Egoism ii 14 b.
MANEGOLD OF LAUTENBACH—x 94.
Manganese—x 384 b.
MANGOLDT, H. K. E. VON—x 95; Distribution v 169 b.
Manic Depressive Psychosis—Abnormal Psychology i 362 a, 364 b; Mental Disorders x 314 b.
Manichaeism—iv 81 a.
MANIN, D.—x 95.
MANN, H.—x 95.
MANNING, H. E.—x 96.
MANORIAL SYSTEM—x 97-102; Agrarian Movements (France) i 497 a, (Germany) 498 b, (Gt. Brit.) 495 a; Agric. Marketing i 559 b; Agriculture (Mediaeval) i 576 a, (Eng.) 577 b; Feudalism vi 206 b; Food Supply vi 335 a; Freehold vi 461-65; Guilds (Europ.) vii 209 b; Labourers, Statutes of ix 5 b; Land Tenure ix 82-99; Latifundia ix 188 b; Peasantry xii 49 a; Savin xiii 548 a; Serfdom xiii 667 b.
MANSFIELD, LORD—x 102; Commercial Law iv 16 a; Consideration iv 234 b; Insurance viii 108 a; Negotiable Instruments xi 333 b.
Manu, Code of—see Code of Manu.
MANUAL TRAINING—x 103-05; Industrial Education vii 694 b.
MANUILOV, A. A.—x 105.
Manumission—v 483 a.
MANZONI, A.—x 106; Romanticism xiii 431 b.
Maori—xi 272 a.
MAQRĪZĪ, AL-—x 106.
MARAT, J.-P.—x 107.
Marbeau, F.—v 13 b.
MARCEL, É.—x 108; Estates General v 598 a.
MARCET, J.—x 108.
Marconi, G.—xiii 54 a.
Marcus Aurelius—see AURELIUS ANTONINUS, M.
Marett, R. R.—Animism ii 66 a; Magic x 40 a.
Margin Transactions—xiv 399 b.
Marginal Utility Economics—Introd. Vol. I (Nationalism) i 166 a, (The Trend to Internationalism) 174 a, (The Social Sciences as Disciplines, Aus-

tria) 266 b; Cost iv 468 b; Dupuit v 285 b; Economics v 357–63, 366 a; Gossen vii 3 a; Jevons viii 390 b; Menger x 311 a; Money x 609 a; Value and Price xv 219 b; Walras xv 328 b.
MARIA THERESA—x 109; Agrarian Movements i 502 b.
MARIANA, J. DE—x 110; Introd. Vol. I (Renaissance and Reformation) i 97 a.
MARIÁTEGUI, J. C.—x 111.
MARINE INSURANCE—x 111–16; Insurance viii 97 b; Life Insurance ix 463 a.
MARITAL PROPERTY—x 116–22; Concubinage iv 171–73; Conflict of Laws iv 192 b; Dowry v 230–32; Family Law vi 81–85; Gifts vi 660 a; Marriage x 149 a; Succession, Laws of xiv 436–41; Trusts and Trustees xv 123 b; Woman, Position in Society xv 449 a.
MARITIME LAW—x 122–31; Armed Merchantmen ii 201–03; Continuous Voyage iv 320–21; Contraband of War iv 321–23; Declaration of London v 47–48; Declaration of Paris v 48–49; Fisheries vi 270 a; Freedom of the Seas vi 459–61; Hübner vii 527 b; International Waterways viii 208–14; Law Merchant ix 271 a; Lien ix 457 a; Merchantmen, Status of x 350–52; Piracy xii 136–39; Privateering xii 422–24; Prize xii 424–26; Procedure, Legal xii 449 a; Seamen xiii 615 a; Stowell xiv 414 b; Warfare, Laws of xv 362 b.
Mark—Land Tenure ix 83 b, 87 a; Village Community xv 253 a.
MARKET—x 131–33; Arbitrage ii 150–51; Broker iii 9–10; Combinations, Industrial iii 670 b; Commerce iv 3–13; Commodity Exchanges iv 44–48; Conjuncture iv 203–04; Credit iv 549 b; Demand v 69–75; Fairs vi 58–64; International Trade viii 198 a; Labor Exchange Banks viii 637–44; Land Tenure ix 78 b; Large Scale Production ix 171 a, 175 b; Law Merchant ix 272 b; Location of Industry ix 586 b, 588 a, 592 a; Marketing x 133–39; Markets, Municipal x 139–44; Price Discrimination xii 350–55; Prices (Theory) xii 366–75; Speculation xiv 289 a.
MARKETING—x 133–39; Advertising i 469–75; Agency i 483 b; Agric. Machinery Industry i 555 a; Agric. Marketing i 558–65; Auctions ii 309–11; Aviation (Industry) ii 364 a; Broker iii 9–10; Business Administration iii 89 b; Canning Industry iii 176 b; Cartel iii 234–43; Commodity Exchanges iv 44–48; Export Associations vi 17–19; Fairs vi 58–64; Food Industries (Baking, Eur.) vi 304 a, (Baking, U. S.) 306 a, (Beverages) 309 a, (Confectionery) 310 b, (Food Distribution) 311–32; Fur Trade and Industry vi 533 b; Furniture vi 540 b; Grading vii 133 b; Instalment Selling viii 74–81; Insurance viii 101 b; Life Insurance ix 468 b; Livestock Industry ix 548 a, 549 b, 550 b; Markets, Municipal x 139–44; Mercantile Credit x 329–33; Middleman x 415–17; Milk Supply x 478 a; Milling Industry x 486 b; Oil Industry xi 441 b; Printing and Publishing xii 413 b; Raw Materials xiii 127 a; Resale Price Maintenance xiii 326–30; Retail Trade xiii 346–55; Salesmanship xiii 519–21; Silk Industry xiv 55 b; Valorization xv 210–12; Warehousing xv 354–59; Wholesaling xv 411–17; Wool xv 480 a.
Marketing, Agricultural—see AGRICULTURAL MARKETING.
MARKETS, MUNICIPAL—x 139–44; Food Industries (Food Distribution, U. S.) vi 316 b, 320 a, (W. Eur.) 320 b.
MARKOVIĆ, S.—x 144.
Marlo, K.—x 145.
Marlowe, C.—xiv 604 b.
MARQUARDT, K. J.—x 145.
Marr, W.—ii 119 b.
MARRIAGE—x 146–54. See Classification of Articles (Marriage and the Family), p. 553. See also Introd. Vol. I (Greek Culture and Thought) i 15 b; Animal Societies ii 63–65; Anthropology ii 84 b; Canon Law iii 185 a; Chivalry iii 439 b; Christianity iii 459 b; Conflict of Laws iv 192 b; Crawley iv 544 b; Culture iv 628 a; Dual Citizenship v 257 b; Gypsies vii 231 b; Judaism viii 437 a; Law (Celtic) ix 248 a, (Cuneiform) 215 b, (Germanic) 236 a, (Greek) 228 a, (Hellenistic and Greco-Egyptian) 231 b, (Hindu) 259 a, (Slavic) 243 a; Lubbock ix 623 a; McLennan x 29 b.
Married Women's Property Acts —x 119 b.
Marro, A.—iv 587 b.
Marschak, J.—xi 199 b.
MARSCHALL VON BIEBERSTEIN, A. —x 155.
MARSHALL, A.—x 155; Bimetallism and Monometallism ii 547 a; Bounties ii 653 b; Cost iv 468 b, 472 b; Demand v 72 b; Economics v 362 a, 365 a, 368–71; Luxury ix 636 b; Money x 608 b; Rent xiii 291 a; Standards of Living xiv 322 b; Statics and Dynamics xiv 353 b.
MARSHALL, J.—x 157; Judicial Review viii 459 b; Treason vii 95 b; Vested Interests xv 241 a.
MARSHALL, L.—x 158.
MARSHALL, W.—x 159.

MARSILIUS OF PADUA—x 159; Introd. Vol. I (The Growth of Autonomy) i 81 a; Natural Law xi 287 b; Religious Freedom xiii 241 b; Representation xiii 311 b.
MARTELLO, T.—x 160.
MARTENS, F. F.—x 161.
MARTENS, G. F. VON—x 161.
MARTIAL LAW—x 162–67; Habeas Corpus vii 235 a; Military Law x 455 b.
Martignano (Lecce), Marquis of —see PALMIERI, G.
Martin v—iv 162 a.
MARTIN, B.-L.-H.—x 167.
Martin Brothers—viii 302 b.
Martin, P. W.—iii 99 a.
MARTIN, R.—x 167; Anthropometry ii 111 a, 112 a.
MARTINEAU, H.—x 168.
MARTINEAU, J.—x 168.
MARTÍNEZ DE LA MATA, F.—x 169.
MARTÍNEZ MARINA, F.—x 169.
MARTINOVICS, I. J.—x 170.
Martinus Gosia—see FOUR DOCTORS.
Martov, J. O.—ii 625 a.
Martov, L.—x 171.
Marvin, F. S.—i 222 b.
MARX, K.—x 172; Introd. Vol. I (Individualism and Capitalism) i 156 b; Atheism ii 294 b; Babouvism ii 375 b; Bax ii 482 a; Blanqui ii 585 a; Capital iii 188 b; Class Struggle iii 539 a; Communist Parties iv 87 a; Distribution v 170 a; Economic History v 319 a; Economics (Socialist) v 377 b; Engels v 540 b; Ethics v 604 b; Evolution, Social v 660 a; Exploitation vi 16 a; Force, Political vi 340 b; Hegel vii 314 a; History and Historiography vii 379 a; Industrialism viii 23 a; Internationalism viii 215 b; Labor viii 617 a; Labor Movement viii 683 a, 688 b; Large Scale Production ix 171 a; Lassalle ix 184 a; Logic ix 602 a; Malthus x 69 b; Materialism x 213 a; Mehring x 301 b; Political Science xii 220 b; Population xii 251 a; Progress xii 498 a; Proletariat xii 511 a; Socialism xiv 197 b; Socialization xiv 221 a; Sociology xiv 243 a; Statics and Dynamics xiv 353 a; Unearned Increment xv 144 b; Unemployment xv 156 a; Violence xv 266 a.
Marxism—see SOCIALISM.
Masaryk, T. G.—vii 79 a.
MASCOV, J. J.—x 175.
MASDEU, J. F.—x 176.
MASON, G.—x 176.
MASON, O. T.—x 177.
MASONRY—x 177–84; Fraternal Orders vi 423 a; French Revolution vi 473 a; Guilds (Islamic) vii 214 b; Journeymen's Societies viii 425 b.
MASPERO, G. C. C.—x 184.

Mass Expulsion—x 185–89; Exile v 688 b; Mormonism xi 15 b; Native Policy (N. Amer.) xi 264 b; Refugees xiii 201 b.
Mass Production — *see* Large Scale Production.
Massachusetts Trusts—x 189–91; Investment Trusts viii 282 a; Voluntary Associations xv 284 b.
Massacre—x 191–94; Atrocities ii 302–04; Indian Question vii 668 a.
Masses—x 195–201; Public Opinion xii 673 b; Russian Revolution xiii 474–93; Sports xiv 306 b.
Massie, J.—x 202.
Massingham, H. W.—x 202.
Masson, F.—x 203.
Mas'ūdī, al-—x 203; History and Historiography vii 382 a.
Match Industry — x 203–09; Kreuger viii 600 b.
Materialism—x 209–20; Introd. Vol. i (Individualism and Capitalism) i 145–63, (The Social Sciences as Disciplines, Russia) 290 a; Atheism ii 292–96; Büchner iii 30 a; Consciousness iv 212–20; Cynics iv 680–85; Determinism v 112 b; Engels v 541 a; Epicureanism v 567–69; Evolution v 654 b; Feuerbach vi 222 a; Freethinkers vi 468 b; Jurisprudence viii 488 a; Labriola ix 7 b; Lamettrie ix 25 a; Lange ix 152 b; Literature ix 539 b; Logic ix 602 a; Marx x 173 a; Mechanism and Vitalism x 267–71; Naturalism xi 303 b; Nihilism xi 377–79; Pecqueur xii 53 a; Socialism (Marxian) xiv 199 a; Sociology xiv 243 a.
Materialistic Interpretation of History—*see* Materialism.
Maternity Welfare—x 221–27; Abortion i 372–74; Child (Hygiene) iii 380–84, (Mortality) 386 b; Health Insurance vii 295 b; Illegitimacy vii 580 b; Mothers' Pensions xi 53–57.
Mathematical Economics—v 364–68.
Mathematics—Science xiii 595 b, 597 b.
Mather, I. *and* C.—x 227.
Mathiez, A.—x 228; Aulard ii 316 b.
Matlekovits, S.—x 229.
Matov, K.—x 229.
Matriarchate—ii 377 b.
Matriliny—xv 439 a.
Matteotti, G.—x 230.
Matthews, N., Jr.—xi 39 a.
Matthijsz, J.—xiii 627 a.
Mauá, I. E. de S. de—ix 23 a.
Maudsley, H.—x 231.
Maurer, G. L. von—x 231; Village Community xv 253 a.
Maurer, K. von—x 232.
Maurice, F. D.—x 233; Christian Socialism iii 450 a; Kingsley viii 567 a.
Maurice of Nassau—xi 462 b.

Maurras, C.—Action Française i 423 b; Intellectuals viii 123 b.
Mauss, M.—Introd. Vol. i (War and Reorientation) i 207 a; Magic x 42 b.
Mauvillon, J.—x 233.
Mavor, J.—x 234.
Māwardi, al-—x 234; Caliphate iii 146 b.
Maximilian—x 631 b.
Maxwell, W.—x 235.
Mayer, M. E.—x 236.
Mayer, O.—x 236; Public Law xii 659 a.
Mayo-Smith, R.—x 237.
Mayr, G. von—x 237.
Mazarin, J.—x 238.
Mazel, B.—viii 639 b.
Mažuranić, V.—x 239.
Mazzarini, G.—*see* Mazarin, J.
Mazzini, G.—x 240; Cooperation iv 381 b; Garibaldi vi 572 b; Romanticism xiii 430 b; Youth Movements xv 517 a.
Mazzola, U.—x 241.
Mead, G. H.—x 241.
Meat Packing and Slaughtering—x 242–63 (Hist. and Amer. Developments 242–49, 262, Foreign and International Aspects 249–55, 262, Social Aspects 255–63); Agric. Marketing (U. S.) i 562 b; Armour Family ii 205 a; Food Industries (Food Distribution, Russia) vi 328 a, (Food Distribution, W. Eur.) 320 b.
Mechanic—x 263–67.
Mechanic's Lien—ix 458 b.
Mechanism and Vitalism—x 267–71; Biology ii 554 a; Gestalt vi 643 a; Natural Law xi 288 a; Naturalism xi 303 b; Science xiii 592 a, 599 a.
Mechanization—Agric. Machinery i 552 a; Art ii 226 a; Capitalism iii 201 a; Clerical Occupations iii 552 a; Coal Industry iii 586 b; Electric Power v 456–70; Food Industries (Baking, Eur.) vi 305 a, (Beverages) 308 b, (Confectionery) 310 b; Fruit and Vegetable Industry vi 510 a; Furniture vi 539 a; Garment Industries vi 573 b; Gosplan vi 707 b, 712 a; Handicraft vii 255 b; Leather Industries ix 301 a, 307 a, 313 b; Liquor Industry ix 499 a; Mechanic x 265 b; Music xi 162 a, 164 a; Printing and Publishing xii 410 b; Quarrying xiii 17 b; Wood Industries xv 471 a. *See also* Technology.
Medem, W.—x 271.
Median—ii 337 b.
Mediation—x 272–74; Arbitration, International ii 157–62.
Mediation, Industrial—*see* Arbitration, Industrial.
Medical Examiner—Coroner iv 411 a; Medical Jurisprudence x 278 a.
Medical Jurisprudence—x 274–79; Coroner iv 410–11.

Medical Materials Industry—x 279–82; Food and Drug Regulation vi 300 a; Opium Problem xi 471–76.
Medici—x 282; Loans, Personal ix 563 a; Machiavelli ix 655 b.
Medicine—x 283–301 (Hist. 283–89, 299, Medical Education 289–92, 300, Economic Organization 292–301); Introd. Vol. i (What Are the Social Sciences?) i 7 b, (Greek Culture and Thought) 23 a; Alchemy i 617 a; Anderson ii 55 a; Baker ii 392 b; Biology ii 556 b; Blackwell ii 581 b; Clinics and Dispensaries iii 562–67; Communicable Diseases, Control of iv 66–78; Dentistry v 91–93; Drug Addiction v 242–52; Epidemics v 570 a; Fee Splitting vi 178 b; Gilman vi 662 b; Health Education vii 292 b; Hippocrates and the Hippocratic Collection vii 353 a; Hospitals and Sanatoria vii 464–72; Jex-Blake viii 399 b; Life Extension Movement ix 461 a; Lister ix 510 b; Medical Jurisprudence x 274–79; Medical Materials Industry x 279–82; Mental Disorders x 314 b; Mental Hygiene x 319–23; Nursing xi 405–12; Nutrition xi 413 a; Professional Ethics xii 474 a; Professions xii 476–80; Psychiatry xii 578–80; Public Health xii 649 b; Social Work (Case Work) xiv 179 a.
Mehemet Ali—x 301; Egyptian Problem v 441 b; Europeanization v 631 a.
Mehring, F.—x 301.
Meh-Ti—*see* Mo Ti.
Meinecke, F.—xiii 143 b.
Meitzen, A.—x 302; Agriculture i 576 a; Economic History v 317 b; Geography vi 623 b; Village Community xv 254 b.
Melanchthon, P.—x 302; Introd. Vol. i (Renaissance and Reformation) i 95 a; Literacy and Illiteracy ix 516 a.
Melchett, Lord—x 303; Industrial Relations Councils vii 721 b; Labor-Capital Cooperation viii 626 b.
Méline, J.—x 304.
Mellaerts, J. F.—x 304.
Mello Freire, P. J. de—x 305.
Melon, J. F.—x 305.
Meltzer, G.—*see* Haloander, G.
Melville, A.—iii 246 a.
Menander—xiv 601 b.
Mencius—x 306; Confucianism iv 199 a.
Mendel, D.—*see* Neander, A.
Mendel, G. J.—x 307; Atavism ii 291 a; Evolution v 652 a; Heredity vii 330 b.
Mendelssohn, M.—x 307; Judaism viii 438 a.
Mendicant Orders—*see* Friars.
Mendoza, A. de—x 308.
Menéndez y Pelayo, M.—x 309.
Meng K'o—*see* Mencius.

MENGER, A.—x 310.
MENGER, C.—x 311; Introd. Vol. I (Nationalism) i 166 b; Distribution v 171 a; Economics v 357–63, 366 a; Laissez Faire ix 17 b.
Mennonites—xiii 627 a.
Menshevism—Axelrod ii 370 b; Bolshevism ii 625 a; Martov 171 a; Russian Revolution xiii 476 b; Ulyanov xv 142 a.
MENTAL DEFECTIVES—x 312–13; Abnormal Psychology i 365 b; Costa Ferreira iv 484 b; Eugenics v 619 a; Fernald vi 184 b; Juvenile Delinquency and Juvenile Courts viii 530 b; Mental Disorders x 313–19; Mental Hygiene x 319–23; Mental Tests x 326 b; Pinel xii 135 a.
MENTAL DISORDERS—x 313–19; Genius vi 612 b; Insanity viii 64–71; Maudsley x 231 a; Mental Defectives x 312–13; Mental Hygiene x 319–23; Psychiatry xii 578–80; Seguin xiii 647 a.
MENTAL HYGIENE—x 319–23; Abnormal Psychology i 368 b; Child (Guidance) iii 393–95, (Labor) 423 a; Juvenile Delinquency and Juvenile Courts viii 530 a; Maladjustment x 60–63; Mental Defectives x 312–13; Mental Disorders x 313–19; Mental Tests x 323–29; Salmon xiii 522 a; Social Work (Case Work) xiv 174 a, 179 b.
MENTAL TESTS—x 323–29; Introd. Vol. I (War and Reorientation) i 197 a; Abnormal Psychology i 365 b; Administration, Public i 447 a; Binet ii 549 b; Character iii 336 b; Child (Psychology) iii 392 a; Correlation iv 444 a; Genius vi 614 a; Mental Defectives x 312 b; Negro Problem xi 354 a; Psychology xii 594 a; Race xiii 33 b; Social Psych. xiv 155 b.
Mental Traits — see National Characteristics.
MERCANTILE CREDIT—x 329–33; Credit Insurance iv 557–60; Instalment Selling viii 74–81; Warehousing xv 356 b.
MERCANTILISM—x 333–39; Introd. Vol. I (The Rise of Liberalism) i 121 b, (The Social Sciences as Disciplines, Spain) 295 b; Acts of Trade, Brit. i 426–29; Administration, Public i 441 a; Agriculture (Europ.) i 582 a; Asiento ii 268–70; Balance of Trade ii 399–401; Bounties ii 652 a; Business, Govt. Services for iii 113 b; Cameralism iii 158–61; Cary iii 246 a; Castro iii 259 b; Chartered Companies iii 347–52; Colbert iii 626 b; Colonial Economic Policy iii 647 a; Colonial System iii 651–53; Colonies iii 657 b; Continental System iv 310–11; Control, Social iv 346 a; Customs Duties iv 667 b; Economic Policy v 338 b; Economics v 347 b; Fisheries vi 269 a; Forbonnais vi 338 a; Free Trade vi 441 a; Govt. vii 13 a; Govt. Regulation of Industry vii 123 b; Imperialism vii 607 a; Indemnity, Military vii 641 b; Lau ix 190 a; Martínez de la Mata x 169 a; Melon x 305 b; Merchant Marine x 343 a; Moncada x 590 b; Mun xi 84 b; Production (Statistics) xii 468 a; Protection xii 560 b; Rural Industries xiii 468 a; Schroeder xiii 585 a; Shipping xiv 36 b; Smith xiv 113 b; Uztáriz xv 203 b; Wool xv 477 b.
MERCENARY TROOPS—x 339–43; Army ii 211 a; Brigandage ii 695 a; Feudalism (Moslem) vi 211 a; Military Desertion 452 a.
Merchant Fleet Corporation—x 347 a.
MERCHANT MARINE—x 343–50; Business, Govt. Services for iii 117 b; Merchantmen, Status of x 350–52; Seamen xiii 611–17; Shipbuilding xiv 25–30; Shipping xiv 30–43.
Merchantmen, Armed — see ARMED MERCHANTMEN.
MERCHANTMEN, STATUS OF—x 350–52; Armed Merchantmen ii 201–03; Armed Neutrality ii 203–04.
Merchants Adventurers—Balance of Trade ii 399 a; Chartered Companies iii 348 a; Misselden x 535 b.
MERCIER DE LA RIVIÈRE, P.-P.—x 353.
Mercury—x 386 b.
Merger—see COMBINATIONS, INDUSTRIAL.
Meriam, L.—xi 267 a.
Merit System—Civil Service iii 520 a; Spoils System xiv 303 b.
MERIVALE, H.—x 353.
MERKEL, A. J.—x 354.
MERRHEIM, A.—x 354.
Merrimac—xi 314 b.
MESMER, F. A.—x 355.
MESSEDAGLIA, A.—x 356; Introd. Vol. I (The Social Sciences as Disciplines, Italy) i 276 b.
MESSIANISM—x 357–64; Diaspora v 130 a; Islam viii 335 b; Mickiewicz x 406 b; Mohammed Aḥmad x 572 a; Progress xii 496 a; Wroński-Hoene xv 505 a.
Mesta—Campomanes iii 170 b; Wool xv 477 b.
METALS—x 364–89; Agricola i 520 a; Anthropology ii 81 b; Coinage iii 622 b; Gold vi 689–93; Guggenheim Family vii 200 b; Iron and Steel Industry viii 295–315; Large Scale Production ix 176 b; Machines and Tools x 22 a; Mining x 495–508; Mining Accidents x 508–13; Natural Resources xi 293 a; Silver xiv 57–60.
Métayage—ix 92 a.
METHOD, SCIENTIFIC—x 389–96. See relevant titles in Classification of Articles (Science), p. 555. See also Introd. Vol. I (What Are the Social Sciences?) i 3–7, (The Revolutions) 144 a, (The Trend to Internationalism) 174 b, (War and Reorientation) 226 b, (The Social Sciences as Disciplines, U. S.) 341 b; Case Method iii 251–54; Casuistry iii 266 a; Correlation iv 443 b; Culture Area iv 646–47; Determinism v 110–14; Doctrinaire v 187–89; Education v 414 a; Evolution, Social v 659 a; Forecasting, Business vi 352 a; Functionalism vi 523–26; Gestalt vi 642–46; Innovation viii 59 a; Institution viii 89 a; Mach ix 653 a; Mental Tests x 323–39; Newton xi 369 b; Social Surveys xiv 162–65; Time Series xiv 629–36; Value and Price xv 218–25.
Methodism — Religious Institutions (Protestant) xiii 272 a; Revivals, Religious xiii 365 b; Sects xiii 628 a; Wesley xv 403 b; Whitefield xv 409 b.
Metics—i 12 b.
METROPOLITAN AREAS—x 396–401; Administrative Areas i 450 b; City iii 478 b; County-City Consolidation iv 499–501; Local Govt. ix 584 a; Municipal Govt. xi 108 a, 110 a, 114 b; Municipal Transit xi 118–28; Regional Planning xiii 205 a; Suburbs xiv 433–35; Water Supply xv 372–77.
METTERNICH-WINNEBURG, C. W. L.—x 401; Nationalism xi 244 a.
Meyer, A.—Mental Disorders x 315 b; Psychiatry xii 578 b.
MEYER, E.—x 402.
MIASKOWSKI, A. VON—x 403.
Miasmatic Theory—v 570 a.
MICHEL, H.—x 403.
MICHEL, L.—x 404.
Michelangelo—ii 247 b.
MICHELET, J.—x 405; Anticlericalism ii 113 b.
Michels, R.—xi 464 a.
MICKIEWICZ, A.—x 406.
MIDDLE CLASS—x 407–15; Introd. Vol. I (The Rise of Liberalism) i 107 a, (The Revolutions) 126 b; Bourgeoisie ii 654–56; Censorship iii 292 b; Furniture vi 538 b; Humanitarianism vii 545 b; Jansenism viii 372 b; Literacy and Illiteracy ix 517 a; Literature ix 535 a; Natural Rights xi 300 a; Negro Problem xi 348 a; Poverty xii 288 a; Protestantism xii 574 b; Puritanism xiii 3 b; Rentier xiii 296–300; Revolution and Counterrevolution xiii 367–76.
MIDDLEMAN—x 415–17; Agric. Marketing i 561 b; Broker iii 9–10; Cartel iii 238 a; Food Industries (Grocery Trade) vi

313 a, (Food Distribution, U. S.) 316 a, (W. Eur.) 320 b; Instalment Selling viii 77 b; Labor Exchange Banks viii 637 a; Wholesaling xv 411–17.
MIDHAT PASHA—x 418.
Midwives—x 221–27.
MIELCZARSKI, R.—x 418.
MIEROSŁAWSKI, L.—x 419.
MIGNET, F. A. M. A.—x 419.
MIGRATIONS—x 420–41 (Primitive 420–25, 440, Ancient and Mediaeval 425–29, 440, Modern 429–41); Introd. Vol. 1 (The Roman World) i 42 a; Acclimatization i 401–03; Agriculture (Primitive) i 573 a; Alien i 633–35; Back-to-the-Land Movements ii 378–79; Civilization iii 528 a; Commercial Routes iv 21 b; Diaspora v 126–30; Emigration v 488–93; Ethnic Communities v 607 a; Famine vi 87 a; Frontier vi 500–06; Gypsies vii 231–32; Immigration vii 587–95; Land Settlement ix 53–64; Land Tenure ix 82 b; Man x 76 a; Migratory Labor x 441–45; Negro Problem xi 342 a; Nomads xi 390–92; Race xiii 30 b; Refugees xiii 200 b; Transportation xv 89 a.
MIGRATORY LABOR—x 441–45; Agric. Labor i 549 a; Begging ii 494 a; Canning Industry iii 178 a; Casual Labor iii 260–62; Contract Labor iv 342 b; Fruit and Vegetable Industry vi 511 a; Lodging Houses ix 595–98; Transportation xv 89 a; Vagrancy xv 205–08.
MIKHAILOVSKY, N. K.—x 445.
MILITARISM—x 446–51; Army ii 210–18; Art (Roman) ii 243 a; Business, Govt. Services for iii 122 a; Chauvinism iii 361; Cramb iv 543 a; Disarmament v 160 b; Empire v 497–506; Judaism viii 436 b; Limitation of Armaments ix 480–86; National Defense xi 189–92; Nationalism xi 246 a; Navy xi 310–19; Praetorianism xii 305 b; World War xv 494 a.
MILITARY DESERTION—x 451–53; Mutiny xi 166–68.
Military Indemnity—see INDEMNITY, MILITARY.
MILITARY LAW—x 453–56; Court Martial iv 512–14; Martial Law x 163 b; Military Desertion x 451–53; Mutiny xi 167 b.
MILITARY OCCUPATION—x 456–59; Indemnity, Military vii 640–44; Requisitions, Military xiii 324–26.
MILITARY ORDERS—x 459–64; Chivalry iii 438 b; Monasticism x 587 b.
Military Requisitions—see REQUISITIONS, MILITARY.
Military Service—Introd. Vol. 1 (The Roman World) i 54 b; American Legion ii 31–33; Armed Forces, Control of ii 199–201; Army ii 210–18; Chivalry iii 436–43; Conscientious Objectors iv 210–12; Conscription iv 220–23; Court Martial iv 512–14; Dual Citizenship v 258 b; Espionage v 594–96; Feudalism (Europ.) vi 207 a, (Moslem) 211 a; Fraternizing vi 425–27; Gentleman, Theory of the vi 618 a; Govt. (Switzerland) vii 57 a; Health Education vii 291 b; Hospitals and Sanatoria vii 466 a; Impressment vii 614–16; Land Grants (Brit. Empire) ix 36 b, (Lat. Amer.) 40 a, (U. S.) 32 b; Limitation of Armaments ix 483 b; Mercenary Troops x 339–43; Militarism x 448 a, 449 a; Military Desertion x 451–53; Military Law x 453–56; Military Orders x 459–64; Military Training x 464–71; Militia x 471–75; Mobilization and Demobilization x 555–64; Morale x 641 b; Moratorium x 651 b; Mutiny xi 166–68; Pensions xii 68 b; Praetorianism xii 305–07; Prisoners of War xii 419–22; Revolution and Counter-revolution xiii 369 b; Veterans xv 243–47; Warfare, Laws of xv 361 b.
MILITARY TRAINING—x 464–71; Army ii 210–18; Conscription iv 222 b.
MILITIA—x 471–75; Arms, Right to Bear ii 209–10; Army ii 210–18; Military Training x 470 b; Policing, Industrial xii 194 b.
Miliukov, P.—xiii 479 b.
MILK SUPPLY—x 475–80; Communicable Diseases, Control of iv 70 a; Dairy Industry iv 693 a.
MILL, J.—x 480; Cost iv 468 a; Economics v 351–57.
MILL, J. S.—x 481; Altruism and Egoism ii 14 b; Bentham ii 519 a; By-Product iii 129 b; Cairnes iii 140 a; Capital iii 188 b; Capital Levy iii 190 b; Democracy v 80 b; Distribution v 169 a; Economics v 351–57; Education v 416 b; Functional Representation vi 519 b; Geisteswissenschaften vi 600 b; Hedonism vii 309 a; Individualism vii 680 a; Inheritance viii 37 b; Interest viii 133 a; International Trade (Theory) viii 201 b; Justice viii 513 a; Legislative Assemblies ix 358 a; Logic ix 602 a; Longe ix 605 b; Method, Scientific x 391 b; National Wealth xi 228 b; Socialism xiv 210 a; Statics and Dynamics xiv 353 a; Taxation xiv 539 a; Unearned Increment xv 144 a; Utilitarianism xv 197 b; Woman, Position in Society xv 445 b.
MILLES, T.—x 483; Bullionists iii 60 a, 61 a.
Millet—Islamic Law viii 349 a; Near Eastern Problem xi 322 a.
Milligan Case—x 164 a.
MILLING INDUSTRY—x 484–88.
Mills, F. C.—xii 380 b.
MILNER, A.—x 488.
MILOVANOVIĆ, M.—x 489.
MILTON, J.—x 489; Academic Freedom i 386 b.
MILUTIN, N. A.—x 490.
Miners' National Association—xiv 63 b.
Minghetti, M.—xiii 215 b.
MINIMUM WAGE—x 491–95; Allowance System ii 7; Arbitration, Industrial ii 155 a; Cost of Living iv 479 b; Higgins vii 346 b; Homework, Industrial vii 448 a; Labor, Govt. Services for viii 648 b; Price Regulation xii 360 a.
MINING—x 495–508; Coal Industry iii 582–600; Conservation iv 227–30; Gas Industry vi 589 b; Gold vi 689 a; Guggenheim Family vii 201 a; Iron and Steel Industry viii 305 b; Metals x 364–89; Mining Accidents x 508–13; Mining Law x 513–18; Oil Industry xi 438–51; Potash xii 274–77; Precious Stones xii 314 b; Production (Statistics) xii 468 b; Quarrying xiii 14–21; Silver xiv 58 a.
MINING ACCIDENTS—x 508–13; Employers' Liability v 516 b.
MINING LAW—x 513–18; Land Valuation ix 139 a.
Ministerial Responsibility—iii 135 a.
MINORITIES, NATIONAL—x 518–25; Autonomy ii 334 b; Boundaries ii 650 b; Comitadji iii 675–78; Cossacks iv 463–66; Diaspora v 126–30; Ethnic Communities v 607–13; Federalism vi 171 a; Govt. (Balkan States) vii 81 b, (Czechoslovakia) 79 b, (Jugoslavia) 80 b, (Rumania) 80 b, (Soviet Russia) 67 b, (Switzerland) 57 a; Indian Question vii 666 b; Irredentism viii 325–28; Jewish Autonomy viii 393 b; Jewish Emancipation viii 394–99; Language ix 167 b; Mass Expulsion x 185–89; Nationalism xi 231 b, 247 a; Near Eastern Problem xi 320–27; Pan-movements xi 545 b, 548 b; Parties, Political (Baltic States) xi 624 b; Polish Corridor xii 196–99; Race Conflict xiii 36–41; Russian Revolution xiii 482 a, 490 b; Self-Determination, National xiii 649–51.
MINORITY RIGHTS—x 525–27; Education (Sectarian) v 423 b; Jewish Emancipation viii 395 a; Minorities, National x 518–25; Obedience, Political xi 417 a; Obstruction, Parliamentary xi 422–24; Proportional Representation xii 541–45; Regionalism xiii 208–18; Representation xiii 313 b.
Minseito—xi 634 b.
MIQUEL, J. VON—x 527.

Mir—Agrarian Movements (Russia) i 505 b; Land Tenure (Russia) ix 108 a; Peasantry xii 48 b; Village Community xv 255 a.
MIRABEAU, COMTE DE—x 528.
MIRABEAU, MARQUIS DE—x 529.
MIRANDA, F. DE—x 530.
Mirza Ghulām Ahmad—viii 341 b.
MISCEGENATION — x 531–34; Amalgamation ii 16–17; Aristocracy ii 187 b; Intermarriage viii 154 a; Race Mixture xiii 41–43; Slavery xiv 83 a.
Mises, L. von—Money x 603 b, 609 a; National Economic Planning xi 198 b.
Mises, R. M. von—xii 427 a.
Mishna—Law (Jewish) ix 222 a.
MISKAWAYHI—x 534.
MISSELDEN, E.—x 535; Balance of Trade ii 399 b; Bullionists iii 63 b.
MISSIONS—x 536–47; Backward Countries ii 380 a; Buddhism iii 34 b; Chinese Problem iii 432 b; Europeanization v 630 a; Jesuits viii 386 a; Native Policy (Latin America) xi 252–60, (North America) 260 a; Ricci xiii 380 a.
Mississippi Bubble—iii 24 b.
Mistral, F.—xiii 210 a.
Mitchel, J.—Irish Question viii 290 a.
MITCHELL, J.—x 547.
MITCHELL, J. T. W.—x 548.
MITCHELL, W.—x 548.
Mitchell, W. C.—Introd. Vol. I (The Trend to Internationalism) i 176 a; Statics and Dynamics xiv 354 a.
Mithraism—xi 173 b.
MITRE, B.—x 549.
MITSUI FAMILY—x 549–50.
MITTEIS, L.—x 550.
MITTEN, T. E.—x 551.
MITTERMAIER, K. J. A.—x 551.
Mixed Claims Commission—i 638 a.
Mkhetar—ii 265 b.
Mo TI—xi 57.
MOB—x 552–54; Lynching ix 639–43; Riot xiii 386–92.
MOBILITY, SOCIAL — x 554–55; Aristocracy ii 183–90; Back-to-the-Land Movements ii 378–79; Bourgeoisie ii 654 b; Camping iii 169 b; Class iii 531–36; Class Consciousness iii 537 b; Emigration v 488–93; Frontier vi 500–06; Home Ownership vii 432 b; Immigration vii 587–95; Location of Industry ix 590 a; Migrations x 420–41; Nomads xi 390–92; Occupation xi 424–35.
MOBILIZATION AND DEMOBILIZATION—x 555–64; Carnot iii 231 a; Conscription iv 220–23; Militia x 471–75; Veterans xv 243–47; War Economics xv 342 b.
MOCHNACKI, M.—x 564.
Mode, Mathematical—ii 338 a.

MODERNISM—x 564–68; Architecture ii 173 b; Art (Modern) ii 253–57; Fundamentalism vi 527 a; Higher Criticism vii 347–49; Industrial Arts vii 689 b; Islam viii 343 a, 347 b; Judaism viii 438 b.
Modesty—v 235 b.
MODRZEWSKI, A. F.—x 568.
Moellendorff, W. G. O. von—xi 200 b.
MOELLER VAN DEN BRUCK, A.—x 569.
MOHAMMED—x 569; Caliphate iii 145 a; Islam viii 333 a; Islamic Law viii 345 a; Jihad viii 401 b; Judaism viii 441 a.
MOHAMMED II—x 570; Empire v 503 a.
MOHAMMED 'ABDU—x 571.
MOHAMMED AHMAD—x 572.
Mohammed 'Ali (d. 1849)—see MEHEMET ALI.
MOHAMMED 'ALI (d. 1931)—x 572.
MOHAMMED IBN 'ABD AL-WAHHĀB —x 573.
Mohammedan Law—see ISLAMIC LAW.
Mohammedanism—see ISLAM.
MOHEAU—x 574.
MOHL, R. VON—x 574.
MÖHLER, J. A.—x 575.
Moiety—xiv 143 a.
Moivre, A. de—vi 486 a.
MOLESWORTH, W.—x 575.
Molière—xiv 607 b.
Molinaeus, C.—see DUMOULIN, C.
MOLINARI, G. DE—x 576; Bourses du Travail ii 659 a; Customs Unions iv 675 a.
MOMMSEN, T.—x 576; History and Historiography vii 379 b; Krueger viii 604 a; Marquardt x 146 a.
Monads—Leibniz ix 400 a.
MONARCHOMACHS—x 577–78; Anarchism ii 47 b; Assassination ii 273 b; Justice viii 511 a; Natural Law xi 287 b; Republicanism xiii 318 b; Social Contract xiv 128 a; Tyranny xv 136 b.
MONARCHY—x 579–84; Introd. Vol. I (Greek Culture and Thought) i 31 b, (The Roman World) 52 b, (Renaissance and Reformation) 88 b, (The Rise of Liberalism) 110 b; Abdication i 356–57; Absolutism i 380–82; Action Française i 423–25; Aristocracy ii 184 a; Assassination ii 271 a; Autocracy ii 321–22; Centralization iii 309 a; Civil Service iii 516 b; Deification v 58–60; Divine Right of Kings v 176–77; Empire v 497–506; Encyclopédistes v 530 a; Executive v 681 b; Govt. vii 12 a; Magna Carta x 44–46; Montesquieu x 638 a; Nobility xi 387 a; Political Offenders xii 201 a; Political Police xii 204 a; Prerogative xii 319 a; Primogeniture xii 402–05; Republi-

canism xiii 317–21; Royal Court xiii 448–51; Succession, Political xiv 442 b; Tyranny xv 135–37.
MONASTICISM—x 584–90; Introd. Vol. I (The Universal Church) i 65 b; Benedict ii 510 a; Buddhism iii 34 a, 35–38; Celibacy iii 284 a; Charity iii 341 b; Clerical Occupations iii 550 b; Cluniac Movement iii 580–82; Communism iv 83 b; Education v 407 b; History and Historiography vii 372 a; Jesuits viii 382 a; Mabillon ix 643 b; Medicine x 287 a; Military Orders x 460 a; Missions x 538 a; Montalembert x 635 a; Religious Orders xiii 276–78; Sects xiii 625 b; Taoism xiv 511 b.
MONCADA, S. DE—x 590.
Mond, A. M.—see MELCHETT, LORD.
Mond-Turner Report—Industrial Relations Councils vii 721 b; Melchett x 304 a.
Monet, J. B. de—see LAMARCK, CHEVALIER DE.
Moneta, E. T.—xii 45 a.
MONETARY STABILIZATION — x 591–95; Central Banking iii 304 a; Credit Control iv 550–53; Devaluation v 114–17; Foreign Exchange vi 362 a; Land Bank Schemes ix 31 a; Monetary Unions x 595–601; Paper Money xi 569 b; Price Regulation xii 356 a; Price Stabilization xii 363 a; Rentenmark xiii 296; Unemployment xv 160 a.
MONETARY UNIONS—x 595–601; Bimetallism and Monometallism ii 548 b.
MONEY—x 601–13; Introd. Vol. I (War and Reorientation) i 212 b; Agio i 487; Anthropology ii 84 a; Banknotes ii 447 b; Barter ii 469 a; Bendixen ii 509 b; Bill of Exchange ii 540 b; Bimetallism and Monometallism ii 546–49; Bullionists iii 60–64; Büsch iii 80 a; Carli iii 228 b; Coinage iii 622–25; Compensated Dollar iv 134–35; Credit iv 545 a; Currency iv 649–51; Devaluation v 114–17; Dutot v 292 b; Economics (Cambridge School) v 370 b, (Universalist Economics) 387 a; Fleetwood vi 279 b; Forbonnais vi 338 a; Foreign Exchange vi 358–64; Gesell vi 641 a; Gold vi 691 b; Gramont vii 147 b; Harris vii 273 b; Helferich vii 317 b; Helfferich vii 318 a; Heyn vii 345 b; Horton vii 461 b; Hume vii 551 b; Index Numbers vii 652–58; Inflation and Deflation viii 28–33; International Trade (Theory) viii 205 a; Kankrin viii 538 a; Kellogg viii 556 b; Knapp viii 578 b; Labor

Exchange Banks viii 637-44; Labor, Methods of Remuneration for viii 677 a; Land Bank Schemes ix 29-32; Law, J. ix 270 a; Melon x 305 b; Menger x 311 b; Mercantilism x 337 b; Monetary Stabilization x 591-95; Monetary Unions x 595-601; Montanari x 635 b; National Economic Planning xi 198 b; Oresme xi 479 b; Ornament xi 496 b; Paper Money xi 568-70; Prices (Theory) xii 370 b, (Hist.) 375-81; Protection xii 560 a; Public Works xii 696 b; Scaruffi xiii 561 a; Serra xiii 671 b; Silver xiv 57 b; Soetbeer xiv 249 a; Usury xv 194 b; Vasco xv 230 b; Vaughan xv 233 b.

Money Changers — Banking, Commercial (Hist.) ii 424 b, 427 a; Fortunes, Private vi 391 a.

MONEY MARKET — x 613-18; Banking, Commercial (Hist.) ii 425 a, (Eng.) 433 a; Broker iii 10 a; Brokers' Loans iii 10-13; Call Money iii 149-50; Central Banking iii 302-08; Corporation Finance iv 426 a; Credit iv 550 a; Financial Organization vi 244 a; Foreign Exchange vi 358-64; Foreign Investment vi 368 a, 373 b; Interest viii 138 b; International Finance viii 160 a; International Trade viii 199 a; Investment viii 266 b; Investment Banking viii 268-77; Stock Exchange xiv 397-402.

Money Raising Drives — see DRIVES, MONEY RAISING.

Moñino y Redondo, J.—see FLORIDABLANCA, CONDE DE.

Monitor—xi 314 b.

Monitorial System—ii 503 b.

Monocracy—x 579 a.

MONOD, G. J. J.—x 618.

Monogamy—Marriage x 149 a; Sex Education and Sex Ethics xiv 9 a.

Monometallism — see BIMETALLISM AND MONOMETALLISM.

MONOPOLIES, PUBLIC—x 619-23; Asiento ii 268-70; Govt. Ownership vii 111-19; Liquor Traffic ix 507 a; Match Industry x 205 b; Municipal Transit xi 118 b; Nitrates xi 380 b; Opium Problem xi 471-76; Raw Materials xiii 130 a; Tobacco xiv 644 b; Water Supply xv 373 b.

MONOPOLY—x 623-30; Cartel iii 234-43; Cement iii 289 a; Combinations, Industrial iii 671 a; Demand v 72 a; Dumping v 275 b; Economic Policy v 339 b; Economics (Mathematical Economics) v 365 b; Fair Return vi 56-58; Govt. Regulation of Industry vii 125 a, 127 a; Guilds (Europ.) vii 208-14, (Japanese) 221 a; Holding Companies vii 406 b, 410 b;

Increasing Returns vii 640 a; Invention viii 249 b; Iron and Steel Industry viii 308 a; Market x 132 b; Match Industry x 207 b; Middle Class x 409 a; Monopolies, Public x 619-23; National Economic Planning xi 197 b; Oil Industry xi 442 b; Patents xii 19-25; Potash xii 274 b; Price Discrimination xii 352 b; Price Regulation xii 355 b, 359 a; Prices (Theory) xii 370 a; Public Utilities xii 674-87; Radio xiii 65 b; Rate Regulation xiii 105 b; Trusts xv 111-22; Unearned Increment xv 144 b.

MONROE DOCTRINE—x 630-33; Adams i 434 b; Arbitration, International ii 158 b; Calvo and Drago Doctrines iii 155 a; Monroe x 633 b; Olney xi 466 b; Pan-Americanism xi 539 a.

MONROE, J.—x 633; Monroe Doctrine x 630 b.

Montagnards—vi 476 b.

MONTAGU, C.—x 634.

MONTAIGNE, M. DE—x 634; La Boétie viii 615 a.

MONTALEMBERT, COMTE DE—x 635.

MONTANARI, G.—x 635.

MONTCHRÉTIEN, A. DE—x 636; Introd. Vol. 1 (The Rise of Liberalism) i 122 a.

MONTEFIORE, M.—x 636.

MONTEMARTINI, G.—x 637.

Montes Pietatis—xii 34 b.

Montesa — Military Orders x 463 b.

MONTESQUIEU, BARON DE—x 637; Introd. Vol. 1 (The Revolutions) i 129 a; Bicameral System ii 534 a; Blackstone ii 580 b; Checks and Balances iii 363 b; Climate iii 560 b; Congressional Govt. iv 201 b; Criminology iv 588 b; History and Historiography vii 375 a; Political Science xii 217 a; Primitivism xii 400 b; Prisoners of War xii 420 a; Republicanism xiii 319 a; Separation of Powers xiii 664 a, 665 b; Sociology xiv 235 b; Traditionalism xv 68 a.

MONTFORT, S. DE—x 639; Massacre x 193 b.

Montgomery Ward Co.—xiii 350 b.

Monts de Piété—xii 35 b.

Montyon, Baron—x 574 a.

Monzambano, S. von—see PUFENDORF, S. VON.

Moody, D. L.—xiii 365 b.

MOONEY, J.—x 640.

Moore, G. E.—xiii 141 b.

Moore, H. L.—Business Cycles iii 98 a; Demand v 73 a; Economics v 368 a; Forecasting, Business vi 350 b; Prices (Statistics) xii 384 a.

Moore, J. B.—i 479 a.

MORALE—x 641-42; Introd. Vol. 1 (War and Reorientation) i 190 b; Administration, Public i 446 b; Military Desertion x 451-53; Military Training x 465 b; Mutiny xi 166-68.

MORALS—x 643-49; Abortion i 373 b; Art ii 224 b; Berkeley ii 523 a; Birth Control ii 563 a; Casuistry iii 265-66; Censorship iii 290-94; Character iii 335-37; Chastity iii 357-58; Chinese Problem iii 434 a; Christianity iii 452-61; Common Sense iv 58-61; Confucianism iv 198 b; Conventions, Social iv 352 a; Duty v 293-95; Enlightenment v 551 b; Ethical Culture Movement v 600-02; Ethics v 602-07; Folkways vi 295 a; Fraud vi 427 a; Freethinkers vi 470 b; Gambling vi 558 a; Gentleman, Theory of the vi 619 a; Guyau vii 229 b; Judaism viii 423 a; Jurisprudence viii 487 b; Justice viii 509-15; Kant viii 539 a; Leibniz ix 400 b; Literature ix 537 b; Luther ix 632 b; Materialism x 210 a; Opportunism xi 476-79; Sophists xiv 260 a.

MORATORIUM—x 649-52.

Moravians — Religious Institutions (Protestant) xiii 271 b; Sects xiii 626 a; Zinzendorf xv 527 b.

MORBIDITY—xi 3-7; Blind ii 587-90; Communicable Diseases, Control of iv 66-78; Industrial Hazards vii 697-705; Life Extension Movement ix 460-62; Mining Accidents x 508 a; Negro Problem xi 354 a; Old Age xi 452 b; Urbanization xv 191 b.

MORE, H.—xi 8.

More, L. B.—vi 75 a.

More, P. E.—vii 543 b.

MORE, T.—xi 8; Introd. Vol. 1 (Renaissance and Reformation) i 102 a; Communism iv 84 b; Socialism xiv 191 a; Utopia xv 200 b.

MOREL, E. D.—xi 9.

Morel, M.—iii 380 b.

MORELLET, A.—xi 10.

MORELLY—xi 10; Introd. Vol. 1 (The Revolutions) i 132 a.

Mores—see FOLKWAYS.

Morgan, C. L.—x 269 b.

MORGAN FAMILY—xi 11.

MORGAN, L. H.—xi 13; Introd. Vol. 1 (The Social Sciences as Disciplines, U. S.) i 338 a; Anthropology ii 102 b; Evolution, Social v 658 b; Family vi 65 a; Fison vi 272 a; Howitt vii 524 a; Kinship viii 569 b; Social Organization xiv 143 a.

Morgan, W.—x 179 b.

MORLEY, J.—xi 13; Compromise iv 148 b; Indian Question vii 666 b.

Mormonism—xi 14–18; Communistic Settlements iv 97 b; Religious Institutions (Protestant) xiii 271 b; Sects xiii 629 b; Smith xiv 117 a; Young xv 516 a.
Morocco Question—xi 18–19; Protectorate xii 569 b; Spheres of Influence xiv 299 a.
Morozov, S.—xi 19.
Morphology—v 653 a.
Morris, N.—x 245 b.
Morris Plan—Small Loans xiv 109 b.
Morris, R.—xi 20.
Morris, W.—xi 21; Art ii 255 a; Bax ii 482 b; Crane iv 543 b; Industrial Arts vii 689 a; Printing and Publishing xii 409 a.
Morrison, H.—xiv 222 b.
Morrison, J. (d. 1835)—xi 22.
Morrison, J. (d. 1857)—xi 21.
Morse, S. F. B.—xiv 561 a.
Mort d'Ancestor—Assizes ii 283 b.
Mortality—xi 22–32; Accidents i 389–91; Accidents, Industrial i 391–401; Alcohol i 624 a; Child (Hygiene) iii 384 a, (Mortality) 384–90; Famine vi 86 b; Kőrösy de Szántó viii 593 a; Life Extension Movement ix 460–62; Life Insurance ix 463 a; Maternity Welfare x 221–27; Mining Accidents x 509 b; Motor Vehicle Accidents xi 70 a; Negro Problem xi 354 a; Old Age xi 455 a; Population xii 246 a; Poverty xii 290 a; Slums xiv 94 b; Suicide xiv 456 b; Urbanization xv 191 b.
Mortgage—xi 32–38; Bonds ii 635 a; Debentures v 30 a; Debt v 34 b; Home Ownership vii 432 b; Land Mortgage Credit ix 43–53; Law (Hellenistic and Greco-Egyptian) ix 232 b; Lien ix 456 b; Mortgage Tax xi 38–40; Real Estate xiii 138 a.
Mortgage Tax—xi 38–40.
Mortillet, G. de—ii 163 b.
Mortmain—xi 40–50; Charitable Trusts iii 338–40; Endowments and Foundations v 535 b; Land Tenure (E. Eur. and Near East) ix 102 b, (Lat. Amer.) 121 a.
Moscow Art Theater—xiv 611 b.
Moser, Johann J. and F. K. von—xi 50; Pütter xiii 7 a.
Möser, Justus—xi 51; Introd. Vol. i (The Revolutions) i 138 b.
Mosheim, J. L.—xi 52.
Moshesh—xi 52.
Most, J.—xi 53; Anarchism ii 52 a.
Most-Favored-Nation Clause—Commercial Treaties iv 27 a; Customs Duties iv 668 b; Tariff xiv 515 b.
Mothers' Pensions—xi 53–57; Child (Dependent) iii 402 a.

Motion Pictures — xi 58–69; Censorship iii 293 b.
Motley, J. L.—xi 69; History and Historiography vii 386 a.
Moton, R. R.—xi 348 a.
Motoöri, N.—xi 69.
Motor Bus — Motor Vehicle Transportation xi 74 b; Municipal Transit xi 123 a.
Motor Vehicle Accidents—xi 70–74; Automobile Insurance ii 330–32; Railroad Accidents xiii 72 b; Traffic Regulation xv 71 a.
Motor Vehicle Transportation—xi 74–78; Automobile Industry ii 322 a, 328 b; Express Companies vi 29 b; Motor Vehicle Accidents xi 70–74; Municipal Transit xi 123 a, 126 a; Quarrying xiii 17 b; Traffic Regulation xv 70–75; Transit, International xv 79 b; Transportation xv 87 a.
Mott, L.—xi 78.
Mount Stephen, Lord—xi 78.
Mouton, G.—xv 390 a.
Muʻāwiyah—xi 79.
Mulcaster, R.—xi 79.
Müller, A. H.—xi 80; Economics v 385 b; Minority Rights x 525 b; National Socialism, German xi 225 a.
Müller, F. M.—xi 81; Antisemitism ii 122 a; Aryans ii 264 b; Folklore vi 288 b.
Müller, Fritz—v 651 b.
Müller, G. E.—Behaviorism ii 496 b; Consciousness iv 215 b.
Muller, H. J.—vii 332 a.
Müller, J. von—xi 81; Psychology xii 591 a.
Müller, K. O.—xi 82.
Müller-Lyer, F. C.—xi 83.
Multatuli—see Douwes Dekker, E.
Multiple Party System—xi 592 b.
Mun, A. de—xi 84; Harmel vii 270 b; La Tour du Pin Chambly ix 189 a.
Mun, T.—xi 84; Introd. Vol. i (The Rise of Liberalism) i 122 b; Balance of Trade ii 399 b; Chartered Companies iii 350 a; Mercantilism x 336 b.
Munch, P. A.—xi 85.
Mundella, A. J.—xi 85.
Municipal Corporation—xi 86–94; By-Law iii 128 b; City iii 475 b, 480 b; Commune, Mediaeval iv 61–63; Dillon v 143 b; Home Rule vii 434–36; State Liability xiv 341 a.
Municipal Councils—xi 107 a.
Municipal Courts—xi 94–98; Small Claims Courts xiv 99–101.
Municipal Finance—xi 98–104; Budget iii 40 b; Municipal Corporation xi 91 b; Municipal Transit xi 118–28; Sinking Fund xiv 68 b; Slums xiv 95 b; Special Assessments xiv 276–79.

Municipal Government — xi 105–17; Bicameral System ii 535 b; Boards, Administrative ii 607 a; Budget iii 40 b; City iii 479 b; City Manager iii 488–89; Civil Service (Hist.) iii 516 b; Clubs, Political iii 578 b; Commission System of Govt. iv 35–36; Commune, Mediaeval iv 61–63; Corruption, Political iv 452 b; County-City Consolidation iv 499–501; County Councils iv 502 b; Govt. (Canada) vii 29 a, (Japan) 98 a; Guilds (Chinese) vii 220 b, (Europ.) 212 a; Home Rule vii 434–36; Investigations, Governmental viii 257 b; Local Govt. ix 574–85; Municipal Corporation xi 86–94; Municipal Finance xi 98–104; Public Works xii 691 b, 692 a; Veto xv 248 b.
Municipal Housing—vii 504 a.
Municipal Lodging Houses—ix 597 b.
Municipal Markets—see Markets, Municipal.
Municipal Ownership—vii 114 a.
Municipal Reform Movement—xi 114 a.
Municipal Research, Bureaus of—xi 116 a.
Municipal Trading—see Municipal Ownership.
Municipal Transit—xi 118–28; Johnson viii 410 a; Mitten x 551 a; Motor Vehicle Transportation xi 74 b; Public Utilities xii 674–87; Ryan xiii 494 a; Yerkes xv 513 b.
Munitions Industry—xi 128–34; Armaments ii 198 a; Arms and Munitions Traffic ii 206–09; Krupp viii 605 b; Limitation of Armaments ix 484 a; Militarism x 447 a; Mobilization and Demobilization x 555–64; Nitrates xi 381 b; Nobel xi 384 b.
Munro, T.—xi 134; Bentinck ii 519 b.
Munroe Smith, E.—see Smith, E. Munroe.
Munsey, F. A.—xi 135.
Münsterberg, E.—xi 135.
Münsterberg, H.—xi 136; Behaviorism ii 497 b.
Münzer, T.—xi 136; Sects xiii 627 a.
Muratori, L. A.—xi 137.
Muraviev, M.—vii 242 a.
Muraviev, N.—xii 95 b.
Mureaux, Abbé de—see Condillac, É. B. de.
Muscle Shoals — Nitrates xi 382 b.
Muscovy Co.—iii 348 b.
Museums and Exhibitions—xi 138–42; Introd. Vol. i (Greek Culture and Thought) i 39 a; Art Collecting ii 259–60; Expositions, International vi 23–27; Pitt-Rivers xii 141 b; Putnam xiii 6 b.

Index (Mormonism — National Workshops)

Music—xi 143-65 (Music and Musicology 143-50, 64, Primitive 150-52, 65, Oriental 152-55, 65, Occidental 155-65); Anthropology ii 91 b; Dance iv 704 b; Language ix 155 b; Modernism x 567 a.

Musicology—xi 144 a, 155 a.

Mussolini, B.—Fascism vi 135 a; General Strike vi 610 a; Lazzari ix 281 a; Leadership ix 286 b; Matteotti x 230 b; Press xii 332 a.

Mustafa Kāmil—xi 165; Egyptian Problem v 442 b.

Mutation—vii 331 b.

Mutiny—xi 166-68.

Mutiny Act—Armed Forces, Control of ii 200 a; Army ii 214 b.

Mutual Aid Societies—xi 168-72; Benefits, Trade Union ii 513-16; Farmers' Organizations vi 130 b; Fraternal Orders vi 423-25; Friendly Societies vi 494-98; Funerals vi 529 b; Health Insurance vii 294 b, 298 a; Hospitals and Sanatoria vii 468 a; Police xii 185 b.

Mutual Insurance — Benefits, Trade Union ii 513-16; Mutual Aid Societies xi 168-72.

Mutualism — Labor Exchange Banks viii 641 a.

Mysteries—xi 172-75; Theater xiv 603 b.

Mysticism—xi 175-78; Asceticism ii 266; Chassidism iii 354-57; Islam viii 334 b; Judaism viii 432 a; Passive Resistance and Non-cooperation xii 10 a.

Myszkowski, Marquis—see Wielopolski, A.

Myth—xi 178-81; Anthropology ii 92 b, 95 b; Art (Greek) ii 241 a; Culture iv 640 b; Ehrenreich v 445 a; Fictions vi 225-28; Folklore vi 288-93; Hero Worship vii 336-38; Lang ix 150 b; Mysteries xi 172-75; Utopia xv 200-03.

Mythology—see Myth.

Naevius, C.—xiv 602 b.

Nansen, F.—xi 181; Passport xii 16 a; Prisoners of War xii 421 b; Refugees xiii 203 a.

Nansen Passport—Expatriation vi 4 b; Passport xii 16 b; Refugees xiii 203 b.

Naoroji, D.—xi 182.

Napoleon I—xi 182; Introd. Vol. i (Individualism and Capitalism) i 150 b; Centralization iii 311 b; Code Civil iii 604 b; Conciliation, Industrial iv 165 b; Consalvi iv 210 a; Education (Public) v 415 b; Gallicanism vi 551 b; Govt. (France) vii 44 a; Holy Roman Empire vii 426 a; Houssaye vii 520 b; Indemnity, Military vii 642 a; Jewish Emancipation viii 396 a; Judaism viii 438 b; Masson x 203 a; Military Training x 466 a; Nationalism xi 243 b; Pan-movements xi 552 b; Requisitions, Military xiii 325 a.

Napoleon III—xi 184; Plebiscite xii 164 a.

Nārada—xi 184.

Narcotics—see Drug Addiction; Opium Problem.

Nariño, A.—i 304 a.

Narodniki—Axelrod ii 370 b; Bolshevism ii 624 a; Masses x 196 b; Terrorism xiv 578 a.

Nassau-Siegen, Fürst von—see Johann Moritz.

Nasse, E.—xi 185.

National Advisory Committee for Aeronautics—ii 344 a.

National Advisory Council on Radio in Education—xiii 60 b.

National Assoc. for the Advancement of Colored People—xi 349 b.

National Assoc. of Credit Men—see Credit Men's Associations.

National Assoc. for the Promotion of Social Science—Introd. Vol. i (The Social Sciences as Disciplines, Gt. Brit.) i 244 a; Learned Societies ix 296 b.

National Banks, U. S.—xi 186-89; Banking, Commercial ii 443 b.

National Board of Review—xi 66 b.

National Broadcasting Co.—xiii 58 a.

National Characteristics—Bodley ii 617 a; Conservatism iv 232 a; Heredity vii 333 b; Nationalism xi 232 b; Race xiii 33 b; Tradition xv 64 a.

National City Bank—Small Loans xiv 110 a; Stillman xiv 392 a.

National Committee on Education by Radio—xiii 60 b.

National Conference of Commissioners on Uniform State Laws—xv 179 a.

National Debt—see Public Debt.

National Defense—xi 189-92; Armaments ii 193-99; Army ii 210-18; Aviation ii 340 a, 346 a, 347 b; Disarmament v 158-61; Militarism x 446 b; Militia x 471-75; Mobilization and Demobilization x 555-64; Munitions Industry xi 128-34; Navy xi 310-19; Pacifism xi 527 b; War xv 338 b.

National Economic Councils—xi 192-97; Functional Representation vi 521 b; Govt. (Germany) vii 56 a; Pluralism xii 172 a.

National Economic Planning—xi 197-205; Economic Policy v 341 b; Engineering v 546 b; Fascism vi 137 a; Gosplan vi 705-13; Govt. Owned Corporations vii 106-11; Mobilization and Demobilization x 555-64; Socialization xiv 221-25; Stabilization, Economic xiv 312 b.

National Education Assoc.—xiv 551 b.

National Guard—Army ii 215 b; Military Training x 470 b; Militia x 474 b.

National Income—xi 205-24; Consumption iv 295-301; Distribution v 173 a; Fortunes, Private vi 389-99; Gosplan vi 711 b; Income vii 623 a; Lavoisier ix 200 b; National Wealth xi 227-31; Profit xii 480-87; Statistics xiv 362 a.

National Industrial Council—xv 226 a.

National Industrial Recovery Act—Oil Industry xi 446 a; Stabilization, Economic xiv 313 a; Trade Agreements xiv 670 a; Trade Associations xiv 675 b; Trade Unions xv 43 b; Trusts xv 121 a; Unfair Competition xv 177 a.

National Labor Union, U. S.—Amer. Federation of Labor ii 23 b; Knights of Labor viii 581 b; Labor Parties (U. S.) viii 706 a; Negro Problem xi 340 b.

National Liberal Party, Germany—Bassermann ii 475 a; Bennigsen ii 518 a; Parties, Political (Germany) xi 615 b.

National Minorities—see Minorities, National.

National Non-partisan League—Agriculture, Govt. Services for i 604 a; Labor Parties (U. S.) viii 706 b; Parties, Political (U. S.) xi 601 a.

National Parks—xi 583 b, 585 b.

National Recovery Administration—see National Industrial Recovery Act.

National Research Council—xiii 331 b.

National Self-Determination—see Self-Determination, National.

National Socialism, German—xi 224-27; Labor Exchange Banks viii 643 a; Labor Movement viii 689 b; Middle Class x 414 b; Moeller van den Bruck x 569 b; Müller xi 80 b; Parties, Political (Austria) xi 627 a, (Germany) 617 b; Peasantry xii 51 a; Plutocracy xii 175 b; Public Employment xii 634 a; Race Conflict xiii 37 a; Representation xiii 312 b; Romanticism xiii 433 a; Socialism xiv 189 a; Theater xiv 611 b; Youth Movements xv 519 a.

National Theater—xiv 608 a, 610 a.

National Tuberculosis Association—vii 290 a.

National Wealth—xi 227-31; Economics (Hist.) v 347 b; Mercantilism x 337 b; National Income xi 205-24; Natural Resources xi 290-99.

National Wool Marketing Corp.—xv 481 a.

National Workshops—see Ateliers Nationaux.

NATIONALISM—xi 231-49; Introd. Vol. I (Greek Culture and Thought) i 19 a, (The Growth of Autonomy) 73 b, (Renaissance and Reformation) 89 a, 94 a, (Individualism and Capitalism) 159 a, 160 b, (Nationalism) 164 b, (The Trend to Internationalism) 172 b; Action Française i 423-25; Agrarian Movements i 502 b, 507 a; Alsace-Lorraine ii 10-12; American Legion ii 31 b; Art (Indian) ii 233 a; Aryans ii 264-65; Boundaries ii 650 b; Brigandage ii 695 a; Carbonari iii 220-23; Chauvinism iii 361; Chinese Problem iii 434 a; Civic Education iii 496-98; Codification iii 611 a; Comitadji iii 675-78; Cosmopolitanism iv 460 b; Customs Unions iv 673-77; Democracy v 81 b; Dialect v 125 a; Diplomacy v 148 a; Dominion Status v 211-16; Education (Public) v 415 a; Egyptian Problem v 441-44; Ethnic Communities v 610 b; Ethnocentrism v 613 b; Europeanization v 623-36; Far Eastern Problem vi 96 a; Fascism vi 133-39; Federalism vi 171 a; French Revolution vi 481 a; Govt. (Baltic States) vii 70 a; History and Historiography vii 377 a; Holy Roman Empire vii 426 b; Idealism vii 571 a; Imperialism vii 609 a; Indian Question vii 665 b; Intellectuals viii 119 a; International Relations viii 185 b; Irish Question viii 285-95; Irredentism viii 325-28; Islam viii 338 b; Jewish Autonomy viii 393 a; Kuomintang viii 610-14; Labor Movement viii 686 b; Language ix 166 b; Mercantilism x 333-39; Messianism x 362 b; Minorities, National x 518-25; Music xi 160 a; National Defense xi 189-92; National Socialism, German xi 224-27; Native Policy (Africa) xi 278 a, (Lat. Amer.) 257 a; Natural Resources xi 298 b; Near Eastern Problem xi 320-27; Pan-Islamism xi 543-44; Pan-movements xi 544-54; Patriotism xii 27 a; Philippine Problem xii 109-16; Polish Corridor xii 196-99; Protestantism xii 573 b; Romanticism xiii 432 a; Russian Revolution xiii 490 b; Shinto xiv 24-25; Social Organism xiv 140 a; Stabilization, Economic xiv 314 a; Tradition xv 64 a; Traditionalism xv 69 a; Transportation xv 89 b; War xv 335 a; World War xv 492 b; Youth Movements xv 519 a; Zionism xv 528-36. For biog. references see Classification of Articles (Nationalism), p. 565.

Nationalist Parties—see PARTIES, POLITICAL.

NATIONALITY—xi 249-52; Autonomy ii 334 b; Boundaries ii 649-52; Citizenship iii 471-74; Conflict of Laws iv 190 a; Dual Citizenship v 257-59; Ethnic Communities v 609 a; Expatriation vi 3-5; Foreign Corporations vi 357 a; Mancini x 84 a; Merchantmen, Status of x 350 a; Minorities, National x 518-25; Nationalism xi 231 b, 240 b; Naturalization xi 305-09; Passport xii 13-16; Public Employment xii 633 b.

Nationalization—see SOCIALIZATION.

NATIVE POLICY—xi 252-83 (Lat. Amer. 252-60, 281, N. Amer. 260-69, 281, The Pacific and Africa 269-79, 282, General Summary 279-83); Colonial Administration iii 641-46; Colonial Economic Policy iii 650 b; Colonies iii 653-63; Forced Labor vi 342 b; Galliéni vi 552 a; Govt. (New Zealand) vii 33 b, (S. Africa) 36 a; Imperialism vii 610 a; Indian Question vii 659-74; Jabavu viii 358 b; Land Grants (Lat. Amer.) ix 39-43; Las Casas ix 182 a; Livingstone ix 552 b; Miscegenation x 531 a; Missions x 539 a; Peonage xii 70 a; Philippine Problem xii 109-16; Public Employment xii 634 a; Race Conflict xiii 37 b; Rubber xiii 454 a; Shepstone xiv 20 b; Slavery xiv 80 b; Standards of Living xiv 324 a.

NATORP, P.—xi 283; Kant viii 541 b.

NATURAL LAW—xi 284-90; Introd. Vol. I (The Roman World) i 49 b, (Renaissance and Reformation) 100 a, (The Rise of Liberalism) 110 a, 112 a; Absolutism i 380 b; Ahrens i 608 a; Bills of Rights ii 545 b; Burlamaqui iii 76 a; Checks and Balances iii 363 b; Christianity iii 454 a, 457 a; Church Fathers iii 466 b; Cicero iii 469 a; Cocceji iii 603 b; Cocceji iii 604 a; Communism iv 81-87; Criminology iv 586 a; Divine Right of Kings v 176 a; Duty v 293 b; Enlightenment v 547-52; Equality v 575 b; Equality of States v 581 a; Grotius vii 177 b; Hobbes vii 395 a; Human Nature vii 535 a; Humanitarianism vii 547 b; International Law viii 169 a; Jurisprudence viii 479 a; Jus Gentium viii 503 a; Justice viii 511 a; Kant viii 540 b; Law (Chinese) ix 250 a; Leibniz ix 400 b; Lorimer ix 610 b; Mably ix 644 b; Natural Rights xi 299-302; Political Science xii 214 a, 219 b; Progress xii 497 a; Secularism xiii 632 a; Society xiv 228 b; Sovereignty xiv 267 a; Stoicism xiv 409 a; Suárez xiv 429 a; Tyranny xv 135 b.

Natural Order—see NATURAL LAW.

NATURAL RESOURCES—xi 290-99; Agric. Policy i 565-69; Boom ii 639 a; Coal Industry iii 582-600; Conservation iv 227-30; Fisheries vi 266-70; Forests vi 382-87; Fortunes, Private vi 395 b; Fur Trade and Industry vi 530-36; Game Laws vi 562-64; Gas Industry vi 589 b; Gold vi 689 a; Iron and Steel Industry viii 311 b; Land Utilization ix 132-37; Metals x 364-89; Mining x 495-504; Mining Law x 513-18; Nitrates xi 379 b; Oil Industry xi 450 b; Potash xii 274-77; Power, Industrial xii 293-300; Precious Stones xii 312-15; Quarrying xiii 15 b; Raw Materials xiii 123-32; Self-Sufficiency, Economic xiii 658 a; Soils xiv 250-54; Waste xv 367-69; Water Law xv 369-72; Water Supply xv 374 b; Wood Industries xv 465-75.

NATURAL RIGHTS—xi 299-302; Introd. Vol. I (The Rise of Liberalism) i 112 a, (Individualism and Capitalism) 150 a; Bills of Rights ii 545 b; Cameralism iii 159 b; Civil Liberties iii 509-13; Confiscation iv 183 b; Constant de Rebecque iv 242 a; Constitutional Law iv 251 b; Constitutionalism iv 255 b; Declaration of Independence v 45-47; Declaration of the Rights of Man and the Citizen v 49-51; Duty v 293 b; Enlightenment v 548 b; Individualism vii 674-80; Kant viii 540 a; Liberalism ix 435-42; Liberty ix 442-47; Literacy and Illiteracy ix 517 b; Minority Rights x 526 a; Natural Law xi 288 b; Naturalization xi 307 a; Ritchie xiii 394 b; Slavery xiv 85 a; Society xiv 228 b; Sophists xiv 260 b; Suffrage xiv 448 b; Vested Interests xv 240 b.

Natural Selection—Acclimatization i 402 b; Biology ii 552 a, 554 b; Evolution v 652 b; Standardization xiv 319 a.

NATURALISM—xi 302-05; Epicureanism v 567-69; Evolution v 654 b; Humanism vii 541 b; Idealism vii 569 a; Natural Law xi 284-90; Primitivism xii 398-402.

NATURALIZATION — xi 305-09; Alien and Sedition Acts i 635 a; Aubaine, Right of ii 308 a; Citizenship iii 472 a; Domicile v 209 b; Dual Citizenship v 257-59; Expatriation vi 3-5; Nationality xi 251 b.

NAUMANN, F.—xi 310; National Socialism, German xi 225 a.

Naval Bases—Armaments ii 194 b; Navy xi 318 a; Philippine Problem xii 114 a.
Navigation—see SHIPPING.
Navigation Acts—Acts of Trade, Brit. i 426–29; Merchant Marine x 343 a; Smuggling xiv 120 a
NAVY—xi 310–19; Armaments ii 193–99; Armed Forces, Control of ii 199–201; Impressment vii 614–16; Limitation of Armaments ix 480 b; Mahan x 47 a; Merchant Marine x 343 b; Mutiny xi 166–68; Privateering xii 422–24; Shipbuilding xiv 25–30; Wood Industries xv 468 b.
Nazarites—xiii 277 a.
Nazi Germany—see NATIONAL SOCIALISM, GERMAN.
NEALE, E. V.—xi 319.
NEANDER, A.—xi 320.
Neandertal Skeletons—x 74 b.
NEAR EASTERN PROBLEM — xi 320–27; Aehrenthal i 481 a; Caliphate iii 145–49; Canning iii 174 a; Capitulations iii 213–15; Colonies iii 660 a; Comitadji iii 675–78; Concert of Powers iv 153 b; Enver Pasha v 560; Europeanization v 626 a, 631 b; Fallmerayer vi 64 b; Govt. (Balkan States and Turkey) vii 81–86, (Jugoslavia) 80 b; Gruev vii 189 a; Holy Places vii 421 b; Islam viii 338 b; Ismail Kemal Bey viii 350 a; Mass Expulsion x 187 a; Massacre x 194 a; Matov x 229 b; Midhat Pasha x 418 a; Minorities, National x 521 b; Obrenović Dynasty xi 420 a; Pan-Islamism xi 542–44; Pan-movements xi 545 b, 548 a; Parties, Political (Balkan States) xi 628 a; Pašić xii 9 a; Pelagić xii 56 a; Refugees xiii 202 b; Rhigas xiii 376 b; Religious Institutions (Byzantine) xiii 264 b; Zionism xv 534 a.
NEBENIUS, K. F.—xi 327.
NECKER, J.—xi 327.
Neft, H.—xiv 611 a.
NEGLIGENCE—xi 328–32; Automobile Insurance ii 331 a; Bailment ii 389 b; Caveat Emptor iii 281 a; Compensation and Liability Insurance iv 136 a; Employers' Liability v 514–18; Intent, Criminal viii 128 b; Tort xiv 655 a.
NEGOTIABLE INSTRUMENTS — xi 332–35; Acceptance i 388–89; Bill of Exchange ii 539–41; Central Banking iii 303 b; Check iii 362–63; Credit iv 546 a; Drawback v 235 a; Financial Organization vi 241 b; Mercantile Credit x 330 a; Moratorium x 649–52; Speculation xiv 289 a; Suretyship and Guaranty xiv 485 a; Warehousing xv 358 b.
NEGRO PROBLEM—xi 335–56; Abolition i 369–72; Civil Liberties iii 511 b; Civil Rights iii 513–15; Emancipation v 485 a;

Equal Protection of the Law v 573 b; Homicide vii 455 b; Ku Klux Klan viii 606–09; Lynching ix 640 a; Maternity Welfare x 225 b; Migrations x 440 a; Miscegenation x 531–34; Pan-movements xi 549 a; Parties, Political (U. S.) xi 600 b; Peonage xii 71 a; Prohibition xii 504 b; Race Conflict xiii 38 a; Reconstruction xiii 168–73; Segregation xiii 644 a; Slavery (S. Amer.) xiv 81 a, (U. S.) 84–92. For biog. references see Classification of Articles (Negro Problem and Slavery), p. 565.
NEIGHBORHOOD—xi 356–57; Social Settlements xiv 157–62.
NELSON, L.—xi 357; Introd. Vol. I (War and Reorientation) i 216 b.
Nelson, N. C.—ii 166 a.
Neoclassical Economics—v 368–71.
Neolithic Period—ii 164 a.
Neo-Malthusianism—ii 561 a.
Neo-Thomism—ii 148 a.
NEP—see New Economic Policy.
Nepotism—xiv 302 a.
NERI, PHILIP—xi 358.
NERI, POMPEO—xi 359; Bandini ii 415 b.
Netchayev, S. G.—ii 49 b.
Nettelbladt, D.—xi 284 b, 289 a.
Neuberin, F. K.—xiv 609 a.
NEUMANN, F. J.—xi 360.
Neurasthenia—i 363 b.
Neurath, O.—xiv 240 b.
NEUTRALITY—xi 360–65; Alabama Claims i 611–13; Angary ii 59–60; Armed Neutrality ii 203–04; Arms and Munitions Traffic ii 206–09; Blockade ii 594–96; Buffer State iii 45–46; Continuous Voyage iv 320–21; Contraband of War iv 321–23; Declaration of London v 48 a; Declaration of Paris v 49 a; Embargo v 486 b; Filibustering vi 231–33; Freedom of the Seas vi 459 b; Govt. (Brit. Commonwealth of Nations) vii 41 a, (Switzerland) 57 a; Hübner vii 527 b; Merchantmen, Status of x 352 a; Military Occupation x 457 b; Neutralization xi 365–67; Prize xii 424–26.
NEUTRALIZATION — xi 365–67; Buffer State iii 45 a.
New Economic Policy—Bolshevism ii 628 b; Gosplan vi 706 b; Russian Revolution xiii 485 b.
New Harmony — Communistic Settlements iv 99 a; Owen and Owenism xi 518 b.
New Lanark—xi 518 a.
New Llano—iv 100 b.
NEWMAN, J. H.—xi 367.
NEWMARCH, W.—xi 368.
New School for Social Research—v 428 a.
New York Central Railroad—xv 227 b.
New York Code of Procedure—xii 448 a.

New York Herald—ii 517 a.
New York Public Library—Astor ii 287 a; Billings ii 542 a.
New York Telegram—ii 517 b.
New York Times—xiii 133 b.
New York Tribune—xiii 225 b.
New York World—Press xii 334 b; Pulitzer xii 703 a.
Newlands Act—xiii 95 b.
News Agencies—see Press Associations.
Newspapers—see PRESS.
NEWTON, I.—xi 369.
Ngata, A.—xi 272 b.
Nicholas I—xi 546 a.
Nicholas II—ii 396 a.
NICHOLAS OF CUSA—xi 370; Introd. Vol. I (The Growth of Autonomy) i 82 b; Conciliar Movement iv 163 b.
Nickel—x 384 a.
Nicole, P.—viii 372 b.
NICOLSON, A.—xi 371.
NIEBOER, H. J.—xi 372.
NIEBUHR, B. G.—xi 372; History and Historiography vii 376 b.
NIETZSCHE, F. W.—xi 373; Freethinkers vi 470 b.
NIEUWENHUIS, F. D.—xi 375.
NIGHTINGALE, F.—xi 376; Nursing xi 406 a.
NIHILISM—xi 377–79; Assassination ii 274 a; Youth Movements xv 517 a.
Nikolay-on—see DANIELSON, N. F.
NILES, H.—xi 379.
Nilus, S.—ii 124 a.
Ninomiya Sontoku—iv 396 a.
NITRATES—xi 379–84; Fertilizer Industry vi 193–98; Raw Materials xiii 130 a.
NITZSCH, K. W.—xi 384.
NOBEL, A. B.—xi 384.
NOBILITY—xi 385–89; Feudalism (Europ.) vi 209 a, (Japanese) 215 a; French Revolution vi 471 b; Sports xiv 305 b. See also ARISTOCRACY.
Noble Order of the Knights of Labor—see KNIGHTS OF LABOR.
Nogaro, B.—Foreign Exchange vi 364 a; Inflation and Deflation viii 32 a.
NÖLDEKE, T.—xi 389.
NOMADS—xi 390–92; Gypsies vii 231–32; Hunting vii 556 b; Land Tenure (Primitive Societies) ix 77 b, (W. Eur.) 82 b; Migrations x 421 a, 425–29; Soils xiv 251 b.
Nominalism—Materialism x 210 b; Natural Law xi 287 a; Scholasticism xiii 580 a.
NOMINATIONS, POLITICAL — xi 392–95; Parties, Political (U. S.) xi 600 b; Primaries, Political xii 396–98.
Non-cooperation — see PASSIVE RESISTANCE AND NON-COOPERATION.
Non-partisan League—see National Non-partisan League.
Non-resistance—see PASSIVE RESISTANCE AND NON-COOPERATION.

Non-support—see FAMILY DESERTION AND NON-SUPPORT.
Non-violence—see Ahimsa.
NORDAU (SÜDFELD), M. S.—xi 395; Criminology iv 588 b; Degeneration v 56 a.
Norden Movement—xi 551 a.
NORDENSKIÖLD, N. E.—xi 396.
Normal Schools—Home Economics vii 429 b; Mann x 96 a; Teaching Profession xiv 544 b.
Normal Unemployment—xv 151 a.
NORMAN, G. W.—xi 397.
Norris-La Guardia Act—viii 671 a.
North Atlantic Steamship Lines Assoc.—ii 410 a.
NORTH, D.—xi 397; Free Trade vi 441 a.
NORTHCLIFFE, LORD—xi 398; Press xii 330 b.
Norton, C. D.—iii 485 b.
NOTARIES, PUBLIC—xi 399-400; Real Estate xiii 139 b.
NOTTINGHAM, LORD—xi 400.
NOVALIS—xi 401.
Novel Disseisin—ii 283 b.
Novels of Justinian—see CORPUS JURIS CIVILIS.
Novikov, N. I.—i 281 a.
NOVIKOV, Y. A.—xi 402.
Noyes, J. H.—iv 97 a.
NUISANCE—xi 402-04; Injunction viii 55 b.
Nullification—xiv 347 a.
NÚÑEZ, R.—xi 404.
Nunneries—x 588 b.
Nurseries, Day—see DAY NURSERY.
Nursery Schools—xii 322 b.
NURSING—xi 405-12; Hospitals and Sanatoria vii 470 b; Nightingale xi 376 b; Public Health xii 649 b; Social Settlements xiv 160 b.
NUTRITION—xi 412-15; Food Industries vi 302 a; Food Supply vi 333 a; Grains vii 143 a; Home Economics vii 430 a; Salt xiii 523 a.

OASTLER, R.—xi 415.
OBEDIENCE, POLITICAL—xi 415-18; Introd. Vol. 1 (Renaissance and Reformation) i 96 b, (The Rise of Liberalism) 112 a, (The Revolutions) 130 a; Authority ii 319-21; Citizenship iii 471-74; Civic Education iii 496-98; Conscientious Objectors iv 210-12; Force, Political vi 338-41; Law Enforcement ix 267-70; Lawlessness ix 277-79; Monarchomachs x 577-78; Mutiny xi 166-68; Passive Resistance and Non-cooperation xii 9-13; Pluralism xii 170-74; Power, Political xii 300-05; Rebellion xiii 144-47; Revolution and Counter-revolution xiii 367-76; Social Contract xiv 127-31; Tyranny xv 136 a.
Oberlin, J. F.—xii 321 a.
OBRADOVIĆ, D.—xi 418.
OBRECHT, G. VON—xi 418.

OBREGÓN, A.—xi 419.
OBRENOVIĆ DYNASTY—xi 420.
O'BRIEN, J.—xi 421.
OBSTRUCTION, PARLIAMENTARY—xi 422-24; Closure iii 570-73; Deadlock v 16-18; Legislative Assemblies (U. S.) ix 363 b; Socialist Parties xiv 215 a.
Occam, W. of—see OCKHAM, W. OF.
OCCUPATION—xi 424-35. See Classification of Articles (Occupations), p. 553. See also Business iii 85 a; Jewish Emancipation viii 398 b; Marketing x 137 b; Middle Class x 407-15; Negro Problem xi 339 a; Old Age xi 454 b, 455 b; Proletariat xii 511-18.
Occupational Diseases and Poisons—see INDUSTRIAL HAZARDS.
Occupational Therapy—see REHABILITATION.
OCKHAM, W. OF—xi 435; Franciscan Movement vi 414 b; Representation xiii 311 b; Scholasticism xiii 580 a.
O'CONNELL, D.—xi 436; Catholic Emancipation iii 270 b; Irish Question viii 289 a.
O'CONNOR, F.—xi 436; Chartism iii 352 b.
Octavianus—see AUGUSTUS.
Octroi—Local Finance ix 570 a; Municipal Finance xi 100 a.
ODGER, G.—xi 437.
Odo of Cluny—iii 580 b.
Oecumenical Councils—xiii 248 a, 257 a.
Oedipus Complex—xii 583 a.
O'Farrell, H. H.—vii 643 a.
OGILVIE, W.—xi 438; Single Tax xiv 65 a.
Ohio Plan—Unemployment Insurance xv 170 b.
Ohlin, B.—viii 206 b.
OIL INDUSTRY—xi 438-51; Concessions iv 158 a; Conservation iv 227-30; Cowdray iv 542 a; Electric Power v 461 a; Natural Resources xi 297 a; Shipping xiv 40 b.
Okhrana—xii 204 a.
ŌKUBO, T.—xi 451.
ŌKUMA, S.—xi 452.
OLD AGE—xi 452-62; Institutions, Public viii 90-95; Pensions xii 65-69; Social Insurance xiv 134-38.
OLDENBARNEVELDT, J. VAN—xi 462.
OLIGARCHY—xi 462-65; Aristocracy ii 183-90; Plutocracy xii 175-77.
OLIVEIRA MARTINS, J. P. DE—xi 465.
Olivi, P. J.—vi 414 b.
OLMSTED, F. L.—xi 465.
Olympic Games—ii 300 a.
OLNEY, R.—xi 466.
OMAR IBN AL-KHATTAB—xi 467; Caliphate iii 145 b.
Ommiad Dynasty—Caliphate iii 146 a; Islam viii 338 b; Mu'āwiyah xi 79 a.

ONCKEN, A.—xi 467.
ONCKEN, W.—xi 468.
Oneida Community—iv 97 b.
OPEN DOOR—xi 468-71; Colonial Economic Policy iii 648 a; Far Eastern Problem vi 94 b; Imperialism vii 611 a; Manchurian Problem x 83 a; Spheres of Influence xiv 299 a.
Open Market Operations—Credit Control iv 552 a; Federal Reserve System vi 161 a; Money Market x 617 a.
Open Shop—see CLOSED SHOP AND OPEN SHOP.
Opera—xiv 606 a.
Opinion—see Classification of Articles (Opinion), p. 553.
Opinion, Legal—viii 454 b.
OPIUM PROBLEM—xi 471-76; Drug Addiction v 242-52; Far Eastern Problem vi 93 a; Food and Drug Regulation vi 300 a.
OPPENHEIM, L. F. L.—xi 476.
Oppenheimer, F.—Anarchism ii 51 a; Race Conflict xiii 36 a; Socialism xiv 204 a; Sociology xiv 242 b.
OPPORTUNISM—xi 476-79; Compromise iv 147-49; Conformity iv 196-98; Duty v 294 a; Statesmanship xiv 350 b.
Optimism—see PROGRESS.
Optimum Population—xii 246 a, 252 a.
Option Trading—xiv 400 a.
Orage, A. R.—vii 203 a.
Oratory, Congregation of the—xi 358 b.
Order of Christ—x 463 b.
Order of the Coif—ix 332 a.
Order of Santiago de Compostela—x 463 a.
Orders, Fraternal—see FRATERNAL ORDERS.
Orders, Religious—see RELIGIOUS ORDERS.
Ordonnance de la Marine—x 123 b.
ORESME, N.—xi 479.
Organism, Social—see SOCIAL ORGANISM.
ORGANIZATION, ADMINISTRATIVE—xi 480-84. See ADMINISTRATION, PUBLIC.
ORGANIZATION, ECONOMIC—xi 484-90; Introd. Vol. 1 (Greek Culture and Thought) i 8 b, 15 b, 28 b, (The Roman World) 46 a, 55 b, (The Growth of Autonomy) 75 a, (Renaissance and Reformation) 101 a, (The Rise of Liberalism) 108 a, 121 a, (Individualism and Capitalism) 146 a, (Nationalism) 165 a, (War and Reorientation) 210 a; Agriculture i 572-600; Anthropology ii 82 b, 100 a; Backward Countries ii 379-81; Business iii 80-87; Capitalism iii 195-208; Class iii 531-36; Collectivism iii 633-37; Commerce iv 3-13; Commercialism iv 31-34; Communism iv 81-87; Competition iv 141-47; Consumption

iv 295-301; Cooperation iv 359-99; Economic Policy v 333-44; Economics v 344-95; Evolution, Social v 659 a, 660 a; Exchange v 666-69; Factory System vi 51-55; Feudalism vi 204 a, 209 b; Financial Organization vi 241-47; Geography (Economic) vi 626-29; Govt. Ownership vii 111-19; Guilds vii 204-24; Handicraft vii 255-60; Hunting vii 556 a; Industrialism viii 18-26; International Trade viii 196 b; Labor viii 615-20; Land Tenure ix 73-127; Manorial System x 97-102; Market x 131-33; Marketing x 133-39; Medicine (Economic Organization) x 292-301; National Economic Planning xi 197-205; Occupation xi 424-35; Power, Political xii 302 a; Property xii 528-38; Rationalization xiii 117-20; Self-Sufficiency, Economic xiii 655-60; Socialism xiv 188-212; Socialization xiv 221-25; Specialization xiv 279-85; Stabilization, Economic xiv 309-15. *For more specific references see further titles in* Classification of Articles (Agriculture), p. 548, (Banking), p. 548, (Business), p. 548, (Commerce), p. 549, (Economic Policy), p. 550, (Economics), p. 550, (Industry), p. 551.
Organization, Financial—*see* FINANCIAL ORGANIZATION.
Organization, Social—*see* SOCIAL ORGANIZATION.
Organized Reserves, Military—ii 216 a.
Oria, J. d'—vii 373 a.
Oribasius—iii 380 b.
ORIENTAL IMMIGRATION—xi 490-94; Immigration vii 592 b; Migrations x 435 b.
ORIGEN—xi 494; Church Fathers iii 465 a.
Original Package Doctrine—viii 222 b, 225 a.
ORLOV, V. I.—xi 495.
ORNAMENT — xi 496-98; Art (Primitive) ii 226-29; Dress v 235-38; Precious Stones xii 312-15.
Orosius—vii 371 a.
Orphan Asylums—iii 410-12.
ORTES, G.—xi 498.
Orzęcki, R.—*see* ORZHENTSKY, R. M.
ORZHENTSKY, R. M.—xi 499.
OSBORNE, T. M.—xi 499.
OSGOOD, H. L.—xi 500.
OSSE, M. VON—xi 501.
Ossoli, Marchesa d'—*see* FULLER, S. M.
OSTRACISM—xi 501-03; Exile v 687 b.
OSTROGORSKY, M. Y.—xi 503.
OTTO I—xi 504; Holy Roman Empire vii 423 b; Monarchy x 581 b.
Otto IV—viii 57 b.
OTTO OF FREISING—xi 504.

Ottoman Empire—Caliphate iii 147 b; Capitulations iii 213-15; Egyptian Problem v 441 a; Islam viii 340 b; Land Tenure (E. Eur. and Near East) ix 100 a; Mohammed II x 570 b; Near Eastern Problem xi 320 b; Pan-Islamism xi 542 a; Religious Freedom xiii 240 b; Suleiman I xiv 459 b.
OTTO-PETERS, L.—xi 505.
OUTLAWRY—xi 505-08; Excommunication v 672 a, 677 a; Punishment xii 713 a.
OUTLAWRY OF WAR—xi 508-10. *See* PEACE MOVEMENTS.
OVERHEAD COSTS—xi 511-13; Cost iv 469 b, 473 a; Cost Accounting iv 476 b; Cut-Throat Competition iv 678 a.
OVERPRODUCTION — xi 513-17; Unemployment xv 155 b; Valorization xv 210-12.
OVERSTONE, LORD—xi 517.
Owen, A. K.—iv 100 b.
Owen, Robert—*see* OWEN AND OWENISM.
OWEN, ROBERT D.—xi 517.
OWEN AND OWENISM—xi 518-21; Child (Psychology) iii 391 b; Communistic Settlements iv 99 a; Consumers' Cooperation iv 286 a; Cooperation iv 359 a, 363 b; Fourier and Fourierism vi 403 b; Hours of Labor vii 490 b; Labor Exchange Banks viii 637 b; Preschool Education xii 320 b; Producers' Cooperation xii 458 b; Short Hours Movement xiv 45 a; Socialism xiv 195 b.
OWNERSHIP AND POSSESSION—xi 521-25; Assizes ii 283-84; Bailment ii 388-90; Canon Law iii 184 a; Land Tenure ix 73-127; Land Transfer ix 127-32; Landlord and Tenant ix 143-48; Law (Germanic) ix 236 b, (Greek) 227 b, (Hindu) 258 b, (Jewish) 223 a, (Slavic) 244 b; Lien ix 456-60; Limitation of Actions ix 474 b, 478 a; Mortgage xi 32-38; Pledge xii 166-68; Property xii 528-38; Sales xiii 511-16; Specific Performance xiv 286 a; Trusts and Trustees xv 122-26; Water Law xv 369-72.
OXENSTIERNA, A. G.—xi 525.
Oxford Movement—xi 367 b.
Oxford University—i 231 b, 235 b.
OZANAM, F.—xi 526.

Paasche, H.—vii 657 b.
Pachomius—x 585 b.
PACIFISM—xi 527-28. *See* PEACE MOVEMENTS.
Pacuvius, M.—xiv 602 b.
Padrone System—Contract Labor iv 343 b; Employment Exchanges v 521 a.
PAEPE, C. DE—xi 528.
PAGANO, F. M.—xi 529.
PAINE, T.—xi 530; Single Tax xiv 65 a.

PAINTS AND VARNISHES—xi 530-34.
PAISII OF KHILENDAR—xi 534.
PALACKÝ, F.—xi 534; Pan-movements xi 546 b.
Palaeolithic Period—ii 163 b.
Pale of Settlement—ii 123 b.
PALEY, W.—xi 535; Commutation of Sentence iv 108 b.
PALGRAVE, F.—xi 536.
PALGRAVE, R. H. I.—xi 536.
Pall Mall Gazette—xiv 378 a.
Palmer, R.—*see* SELBORNE, LORD.
PALMERSTON, LORD—xi 537.
PALMIERI, G.—xi 537.
Pan-Africanism—Negro Problem xi 350 a; Pan-movements xi 549 a.
Pan-American Air Convention—ii 351 b, 367 a.
Pan-American Treaty of Arbitration—ii 161 a.
PAN-AMERICANISM — xi 538-41; Arbitration, International ii 159 b; Central American Federation iii 301-02; Customs Unions iv 676 a; International Law viii 170 b; Monroe Doctrine x 630-33; Pan-movements xi 552 a.
Pan-Anglicanism—xi 551 b.
Pan-Arabism—Caliphate iii 148 b; Pan-movements xi 548 b.
Pan-Asianism—xi 552 b.
Pan-Europeanism—Customs Unions iv 676 b; Pan-movements xi 552 b.
Pan-Germanism — Pan-movements xi 547 b; World War xv 493 a.
Pan-Hispanism — Labra y Cadrana ix 7 a; Pan-movements xi 550 b.
PAN-ISLAMISM—xi 542-44; Caliphate iii 148 b; Enver Pasha v 560 b; Islam viii 342 a; Jihad viii 402 b; Mohammed 'Ali x 572 b; Pan-movements xi 551 b.
Pan-Latinism—xi 551 a.
PAN-MOVEMENTS — xi 544-54; Federalism vi 172 b; Pan-Americanism xi 538-41; Pan-Islamism xi 542-44.
Pan-Slavism—Dobrovský v 187 a; Križanić viii 601 b; Pan-movements xi 545 b; Rački xiii 50 b; Šafařík xiii 503 b; Starčević xiv 326 b; Strossmayer xiv 426 b; Supilo xiv 469 a; World War xv 493 a.
Pan-Turanism—Caliphate iii 148 b; Enver Pasha v 560 b; Islam viii 342 a; Pan-movements xi 548 b.
PANAMA CANAL—xi 554-58; Aviation ii 351 b; Location of Industry ix 589 a; Monroe Doctrine x 631 b.
Panchayat—ix 579 a.
Pandects—*see* CORPUS JURIS CIVILIS.
Panics—*see* BUSINESS CYCLES; CRISES.
PANKHURST, E. G.—xi 558.
Pansophism—iii 674 b.
PANTALEONI, M.—xi 558.

PAPACY—xi 559–68; Introd. Vol. I (The Universal Church) i 61–72, (The Growth of Autonomy) 73–83; Arnold of Brescia ii 219 a; Boniface VIII ii 636 b; Bull, Papal iii 57–59; Canon Law iii 181 b; Conciliar Movement iv 160–65; Creighton iv 560 b; Ecclesiastical Courts v 308 b; Excommunication v 678 a; Fascism vi 138 a; Franciscan Movement vi 414 b; Frederick I vi 430 b; Gallicanism vi 550–52; Gelasius I vi 602 a; Gerson vi 640 a; Ghetto vi 648 a; Gregory I vii 167 a; Gregory VII vii 167 b; Holy Roman Empire vii 423 a; Huss vii 560 a; Innocent III viii 57 b; Investiture Conflict viii 260–63; Irish Question viii 285 a; James of Viterbo viii 367 b; Jesuits viii 384 a; Leo XIII ix 408 a; Otto I xi 504 a; Pastor xii 19 a; Paul IV xii 30 a; Pius II xii 142 a; Pius IX xii 142 b; Political Science xii 214 b; Reformation xiii 186–94; Religious Freedom xiii 244 b; Religious Institutions (Roman Catholic) xiii 249 b, 253 b, (Byzantine) 262 b.

Papal Legates—xiii 250 b.

Papal States—xi 565 a.

Paper Industry—see PULP AND PAPER INDUSTRY.

PAPER MONEY—xi 568–70; Assignats ii 279–81; Bills of Credit ii 542–44; Currency iv 649–51; Devaluation v 116 a; Land Bank Schemes ix 29–32; Law, J. ix 270 a; Monetary Stabilization x 591 b; Money x 601–13.

PAPINIANUS, A.—xi 570.

Papyri—Law ix 208 b, 230 a.

Par Value—iv 424 b.

Paracelsus—x 287 b.

Paradisi, A.—i 274 b.

Paranoia—x 314 b.

Parcel Post—vi 28 b.

PARDON—xi 570–72; Amnesty ii 36 b; Commutation of Sentence iv 108–09.

PARENT EDUCATION—xi 573–76.

PARETO, V.—xi 576; Introd. Vol. I (War and Reorientation) i 205 b, (The Social Sciences as Disciplines, Italy) 277 a; Economics v 365 a, 367 a; National Income xi 220 a; Political Science xii 220 b, 221 a; Sociology xiv 240 b.

Paris Commune—see COMMUNE OF PARIS.

PARIS, M.—xi 578; History and Historiography vii 373 a.

Paris Pact, 1928—xi 508 b.

Paris Peace Conference — see Treaty of Versailles, 1919.

Park, R. E.—i 403 a.

PARKER, C. H.—xi 579.

PARKER, F. W.—xi 580.

PARKER, T.—xi 580.

PARKES, H.—xi 581.

PARKMAN, F.—xi 581; History and Historiography vii 386 a.

PARKS—xi 582–87; Olmsted xi 465 b; Playgrounds xii 162 b.

Parliament—see LEGISLATIVE ASSEMBLIES.

Parliamentary Debate—see DEBATE, PARLIAMENTARY.

Parliamentary Obstruction — see OBSTRUCTION, PARLIAMENTARY.

Parliamentary Procedure — see PROCEDURE, PARLIAMENTARY.

PARNELL, C. S.—xi 587; Irish Question viii 291 b.

Parole—Criminology iv 591 a; Prisoners of War xii 420 a; Probation and Parole xii 437 b.

PARRINGTON, V. L.—xi 587.

PARRY, D. M.—xi 588.

PARSONS, A. R.—xi 588.

Parsons, F.—xv 277 b.

Parsons, T.—ii 546 a.

Part Time Education—v 425–28.

PARTIES, POLITICAL—xi 590–639 [Theory 590–94, 636, Organization 594–96, 636, U. S. 596–601, 636, Gt. Brit. 601–04, 636, Canada 604–05, 637, Australia 605–07, 637, New Zealand 607–08, 637, Union of S. Africa 608–10, 637, Irish Free State 610–11, 637, France 611–13, 637, Belgium 613–15, 637, Italy see FASCISM and GOVT. (Italy), Germany 615–19, 637, Switzerland 619–20, 638, Netherlands 620–21, 638, Scandinavian States and Finland 621–24, 638, Baltic States 624–26, 638, Russia see COMMUNIST PARTIES, Succession States 626–28, 638, Balkan States 628–30, 639, Turkey see GOVT. (Turkey), Spain and Portugal 630–32, 639, Lat. Amer. 632–34, 639, Japan 634–35, 639, China see KUOMINTANG and GOVT. (China)]. See Classification of Articles (Political Parties), p. 554. See also Agrarian Movements (U. S.) i 508–11; Alien and Sedition Acts i 635–36; Cabinet Govt. iii 135 b; Christian Labor Unions iii 445 a; Congressional Govt. iv 202 a; Constituency iv 244 a; Cooperation (Gt. Brit.) iv 366 a; Deadlock v 17 b; Democracy v 81 b; Elections v 454 a; Farmers' Alliance vi 129 a; Fascism vi 136 a; Govt. (Australia) vii 32 a, (Balkan States) 82 b, (Germany) 55 b, (Ireland) 37 a, (Portugal) 88 a, (U. S.) 19 b; Investigations, Governmental viii 256 a; Journalism viii 420 b; Legislative Assemblies (Hist. and Theory) ix 360 a, (France) 376 b, (Germany) 381 a, 383 a, (Gt. Brit. and Dominions) 372 a, (U. S.) 364 b; Majority Rule x 58 b; National Socialism, German xi 226 a; Negro Problem xi 353 a; Ostrogorsky xi 503 a; Philippine Problem xii 110 b; Procedure, Parliamentary xii 456 a; Proportional Representation xii 541–45; Radio xiii 61 b; Russian Revolution xiii 476 a; Separation of Powers xiii 665 a; State Govt., U. S. xiv 337 b. For biog. references see Classification of Articles (Political Affairs), p. 566.

PARTNERSHIP — xii 3–6; Joint Stock Company viii 412 a; Law (Jewish) ix 223 b; Massachusetts Trusts x 190 b; Usury xv 195 b; Voluntary Associations xv 283 b.

PARUTA, P.—xii 6.

PASCAL, B.—xii 7; Jesuits viii 386 b.

Paschal II—viii 262 a.

Paschal, L.—vi 612 b.

PASCOLI, L.—xii 8.

PAŠIĆ, N.—xii 9.

PASSIVE RESISTANCE AND NONCOOPERATION—xii 9–13; Anarchism ii 50 a; Boycott ii 662–66; Conscientious Objectors iv 210–12; Force, Political vi 341 b; Hunger Strike vii 552–55; Indian Question vii 667 b; Pacifism xi 527–28; Reparations xiii 302 a.

PASSPORT—xii 13–16.

PASSY, F.—xii 16.

PASTEUR, L.—xii 17; Biology ii 551 b; Communicable Diseases, Control of iv 68 a, 72 a.

Pasteurization—x 475 b.

PASTOR, L. VON—xii 18.

Patch Agriculture—i 594 b.

PATENTS—xii 19–25; Combinations, Industrial iii 669 b; Electrical Manufacturing Industry v 471 b; Holding Companies vii 411 a; Invention viii 249 b; Radio xiii 54 b, 65 b.

Paterson, D. G.—x 324 a.

PATERSON, E.—xii 25.

PATERSON, W.—xii 25; Banking, Commercial ii 429 b.

Patriarchate—Religious Institutions (Byzantine) xiii 262 b, (Russian) 265 a.

Patrick—x 538 a.

Patriotic Societies—xii 27 b.

PATRIOTISM—xii 26–29; Introd. Vol. I (Greek Culture and Thought) i 19 a; Chauvinism iii 361; Civic Education iii 496–98; Ethnocentrism v 613 b; Nationalism xi 231–49; Regionalism xiii 208–18; Shinto xiv 24–25.

Patronage—Art (Chinese) ii 234 a, (French) 248 b, (Indian) 231 b, 232 a, (Italian) 246 b, (Japanese) 238 b, (Roman) 242 b, (Modern) 255 b; Art Collecting ii 259–60; Literature ix 532 b; Music xi 163 a; Royal Court xiii 449 a.

Patronage, Political—see SPOILS SYSTEM.

PATTEN, S. N.—xi 29; Protection xii 562 a; Standards of Living xiv 323 a.

Patterson, J. H.—xiii 520 b.

PAUL IV—xii 30.

Paul-Boncour, J.—xii 171 a, 172 b.
PAULSEN, F.—xii 30.
PAULUS, J.—xii 31.
Pauperism—see POOR LAWS.
Pavlov, I. P.—Behaviorism ii 497 a; Bekhterev ii 499 a; Conditioned Reflex iv 175 b.
PAVLOV-SILVANSKY, N. P.—xii 32.
PAWNBROKING—xii 32–40; Loans, Personal ix 564 b.
PEABODY, E. P.—xii 40; Pre-school Education xii 322 a.
Peabody, G.—Endowments v 532 b; Morgan Family xi 11 a.
Peace Conferences—xii 43 a, 45 b.
Peace of God—see TRUCE AND PEACE OF GOD.
PEACE MOVEMENTS—xii 41–48; Introd. Vol. I (Trend to Internationalism) i 172 b; Aggression, International i 485–86; Antimilitarism ii 115–16; Armaments ii 198 b; Casus Belli iii 268 a; Concert of Powers iv 153–54; Conscientious Objectors iv 210–12; Hague Conferences vii 242–44; International Law viii 172 b; International Organization viii 180 b; Internationalism viii 214–19; Judaism viii 436 b; League of Nations ix 287 b, 293 b; Limitation of Armaments ix 480–86; Mediation x 272–74; National Defense xi 191 a; Outlawry of War xi 508–10; Pacifism xi 527–28; Pan-Americanism xi 538–41; Passive Resistance and Non-cooperation xii 11 a; Permanent Court of Arbitration xii 76–78; Permanent Court of International Justice xii 78–81; Quakers xiii 14 a; Sanction, International xiii 528–31; Truce and Peace of God xv 107–09; Women's Organizations xv 461 a. For biog. references see Classification of Articles (Pacifism), p. 565.
Pearl, R.—i 622 a.
Pearson, C. A.—xii 334 a.
PEARSON, C. H.—xii 48.
Pearson, K.—Correlation iv 443 b; Eugenics v 618 a; Frequency Distribution vi 485 b, 487 b; Race xiii 34 b; Statistics xiv 366 b.
Pearson, W. D.—see COWDRAY, LORD.
PEASANTRY—xii 48–53; Agrarian Movements i 492–515; Agric. Labor i 548 a; Agriculture (Japan) i 591 a; Bolshevism ii 623–30; Corvée iv 456 a; Cossacks iv 463–66; Enclosures v 523–27; Farm vi 102 a; Govt. (Balkan States) vii 82 a, (Imperial Russia) 67 a; Labor viii 617 b; Land Tenure ix 73–127; Landed Estates ix 141 a; Latifundia ix 186 b; Literature ix 526 b; Manorial System x 97–102; Middle Class x 411 b; Parties, Political (Succession States) xi 626 a; Peshekhonov xii 93 a; Poverty xii 288 a; Primogeniture xii 402–05; Proletariat xii 511 a; Radić xiii 51 a; Russian Revolution xiii 475 b; Semevsky xiii 661 a; Serfdom xiii 667–71; Small Holdings xiv 101–05; Soviet xiv 272 a; Trade Unions (Sweden) xv 20 b; Village Community xv 253–59.
PECQUEUR, C.—xii 53.
PEDRO I and PEDRO II—xii 54.
PEEL, R.—xii 54; Anti-Corn Law League ii 115 a; Beaconsfield ii 485 a; Corn Laws iv 407 a; Free Trade vi 444 a.
Peers, House of—Legislative Assemblies (France) ix 375 a, (Gt. Brit.) 369 b, (Japan) 395 a.
PÉGUY, C.—xii 55.
Peirce, C.—xii 309 a.
PELAGIĆ, V.—xii 56.
PELLOUTIER, F.-L.-É.—xii 56; Bourses du Travail ii 659 b.
Penal Colonies—see TRANSPORTATION OF CRIMINALS.
PENAL INSTITUTIONS—xii 57–64; Child (Delinquent) iii 408 b; Institutions, Public viii 90–95; Juvenile Delinquency and Juvenile Courts viii 531 b; Prison Labor xii 415–19. For biog. references see Classification of Articles (Criminology), p. 559.
Penal Transportation—see TRANSPORTATION OF CRIMINALS.
Peninsular and Oriental Steam Navigation Co.—xiv 39 b.
PENN, W.—xii 64.
Penology—see CRIMINOLOGY.
PENSIONS—xii 65–69; Blind ii 590 a; Mothers' Pensions xi 56 a; Old Age xi 457 a, 459 a; Social Insurance xiv 134–38; Veterans xv 244 a.
Pensions, Mothers'—see MOTHERS' PENSIONS.
Penty, A. J.—vii 203 a.
PEONAGE—xii 69–72.
People's Diplomacy—iii 78 a.
People's Parties—see PARTIES, POLITICAL.
Pepe, G.—iii 222 a.
PÉREIRE, J.-É.—xii 73.
Pericles—Introd. Vol. I (Greek Culture and Thought) i 19 a; Classicism iii 543 a.
PÉRIN, H. X. C.—xii 73.
PERJURY—xii 74–76.
PERMANENT COURT OF ARBITRATION—xii 76–78; Arbitration, International ii 157 b; Hague Conferences vii 242 a.
PERMANENT COURT OF INTERNATIONAL JUSTICE—xii 78–81; Advisory Opinions i 479 a; Arbitration, International ii 159 a; Irredentism viii 327 a; League of Nations ix 292 a; Permanent Court of Arbitration xii 77 b.
Permanent Mandates Commission—x 90 b.
PERPETUITIES—xii 81–83; Alienation of Property i 639–41; Entail v 555 b; Mortmain xi 40–50; Municipal Transit xi 118 b.
Perry, W. J.—v 141 b.
PERSECUTION—xii 83–85; Apostasy and Heresy ii 128–30; Atrocities ii 302–04; Fanaticism vi 90 b; Ghetto vi 647 b; Intolerance viii 242–45; Mass Expulsion x 185–89; Race Conflict xiii 36–41; Refugees xiii 201 b.
Persian Empire—Tribute xv 103 a; War xv 332 b.
Personal Law—Civil Law iii 503 b; Conflict of Laws iv 187 b; Minorities, National x 520 b.
Personal Loans—see LOANS, PERSONAL.
PERSONALITY—xii 85–88; Introd. Vol. I (War and Reorientation) i 206 b; Abnormal Psychology i 364 b; Adolescence i 455–59; Behaviorism ii 498 a; Character iii 335–37; Child (Psychology) iii 391–93, (Guidance) 393–95; Conduct iv 177–79; Conversion, Religious iv 353–55; Dialect v 126 a; Habit vii 237 b; Idealism vii 570 a; Juvenile Delinquency and Juvenile Courts viii 530 a; Language ix 160 b; Leadership ix 282–87; Liberty ix 442–47; Maladjustment x 62 a; Mental Disorders x 313–19; Mental Tests x 323–29; Psychiatry xii 578–80; Psychoanalysis xii 580–88; Psychology xii 588–96; Race xiii 33 b; Radicalism xiii 53 b; Social Psychology xiv 154 a; Social Work (Case Work) xiv 174 a.
PERSONNEL ADMINISTRATION—xii 88–90; Absenteeism i 379 b; Capitalism iii 201 b; Civil Service iii 519 b; Continuous Industry iv 318 b; Fatigue vi 148–51; Labor Turnover viii 710 a, 712 a; Public Employment xii 634 a; Scientific Management xiii 603–08; Welfare Work, Industrial xv 395–99.
Persons, W. M.—vi 350 a.
PERTZ, G. H.—xii 91; History and Historiography vii 377 b.
Peruzzi—ix 563 a.
PESCH, H.—xii 91; Economics v 384 b.
PESCHEL, O.—xii 92.
PESHEKHONOV, A. V.—xii 92.
Pessimism—see PROGRESS.
PESSINA, E.—xii 93.
PESTALOZZI, J. H.—xii 94; Child (Psychology) iii 391 a; Education v 413 a; Teaching Profession xiv 544 b.
PESTEL, P. I.—xii 95.
PETER I—xii 96; Religious Institutions (Russian) xiii 266 a; Russian Revolution xiii 474 a.
Peter I (Serbia)—viii 543 b.

Peter of Andlo—see ANDLO, P. OF.
PETER LOMBARD—xii 97.
PETERS, C.—xii 97.
Petition, Electoral—xi 393 b.
Petition of Right—xii 99 a.
PETITION, RIGHT OF—xii 98–101.
PETRARCH, F.—xii 102; Renaissance xiii 279 a.
PETRAZHITSKY, L. I.—xii 103.
Petroleum—see OIL INDUSTRY.
Pettenkofer, M. von—v 570 a.
PETTY, W.—xii 104.
PEUTINGER, K.—xii 105.
PFEIFFER, E. VON—xii 106.
PFEIFFER, J. F. VON—xii 106.
Phalanx—see FOURIER AND FOURIERISM.
Pharisees—Judaism viii 431 a; Law (Jewish) ix 221 a.
Pharmacy—see MEDICAL MATERIALS INDUSTRY.
Philanthropy — Child (Institutions) iii 410 a; Christian Science iii 448 a; Endowments and Foundations v 531–37; Negro Problem xi 346 b.
Philip II (Macedon)—i 31 b.
PHILIP II (Spain)—xii 107.
PHILIP IV (the Fair)—xii 107; Aids i 608 b; Religious Institutions (Roman Catholic) xiii 256 a.
PHILIP AUGUSTUS—xii 108; Innocent III viii 58 a.
PHILIPPINE PROBLEM—xii 109–16; Oriental Immigration xi 494 a; Peonage xii 72 a.
PHILIPPOVICH VON PHILIPPSBERG, E.—xii 116.
PHILIPPSON, L.—xii 116.
Philips, D.—xiii 627 a.
Phillimore Committee—ix 287 b.
PHILLIP, A.—xii 117.
PHILLIPS, W.—xii 117.
Philo of Byzantium—x 17 a.
PHILO JUDAEUS—xii 118.
Philology—For biog. references see Classification of Articles (Philology), p. 565.
Philosophes—Encyclopédistes v 527–31; Positivism xii 262 b; Roland de la Platière xiii 418 a; Sieyès xiv 50 b.
PHILOSOPHY — xii 118–29. See Classification of Articles (Philosophy), p. 553. See also Introd. Vol. I (What Are the Social Sciences?) i 6 b, (Greek Culture and Thought) 22 a, 26 a, (The Rise of Liberalism) 105 b, (Individualism and Capitalism) 157 b; Alchemy i 617 a; Art (Greek) ii 241 a; Christian Science iii 446–49; Geisteswissenschaften vi 600–02; History and Historiography vii 360 a; Instinct viii 81 b; Jurisprudence viii 478 b; Psychology xii 588 b; Romanticism xiii 427 b; Science xiii 591 b, 596 b. For biog. references see Classification of Articles (Philosophy), p. 566.
Phonemes—ix 155 b.
Phosphorus—x 203 b.

PHOTIUS—xii 129.
Phratry—xiv 142 b.
Phrenology—vi 548 b.
PHYSICAL EDUCATION—xii 129–33; Athletics ii 296–300; Jahn viii 365 a; Playgrounds xii 161–63.
Physics—xiii 599 a.
Physiocrats—Introd. Vol. I (The Rise of Liberalism) i 123 a; Anarchism ii 47 b; Baudeau ii 479 b; Cantillon iii 186 b; Distribution v 168 a; Dupont de Nemours v 283 b; Economics (Physiocrats) v 348–51; Free Trade vi 442 a; French Revolution vi 472 a; Gournay vii 7 a; Karl Friedrich viii 546 b; Laissez Faire ix 16 a; Land Taxation ix 70 b; Mauvillon 233 b; Melon x 305 b; Mercier de la Rivière x 353 a; Popławski xii 235 a; Quesnay xiii 22 a; Rent xiii 290 a; Schlettwein xiii 573 b; Self-Sufficiency, Economic xiii 656 b; Single Tax xiv 64 b; Strojnowski xiv 426 a.
PI Y MARGALL, F.—xii 133; Castelar y Ripoll iii 257 a; Regionalism xiii 214 a.
Piatiletka—vi 710 b.
Picasso, P.—ii 257 a.
Picavea, R. M.—see MACÍAS PICAVEA, R.
Picketing—Intimidation viii 239 b; Labor Legislation and Law viii 668 b; Strikes and Lockouts xiv 422 b.
Piece Wage—viii 678 a.
PIERSON, N. G.—xii 133.
Pietism—Francke vi 416 a; Missions x 541 b; Preschool Education xii 320 b; Sects xiii 628 a; Zinzendorf xv 527 b.
Pig Iron—x 371 b.
Pigou, A. C.—Introd. Vol. I (The Trend to Internationalism) i 176 a; Armaments ii 197 b; Business Cycles iii 98 a; Cost iv 474 b; Economics v 370 b; Money x 610 a.
Pilgrimages—Crusades iv 614 a; Holy Places vii 421 a.
PILLET, A.—xii 134.
Pilsudski, J.—vii 74 a.
Piltdown Skull—x 75 a.
PINEL, P.—xii 135; Esquirol v 597 a; Mental Hygiene x 319 b.
PINHEIRO FERREIRA, S.—xii 135.
PINSKER, J. L.—xii 136; Zionism xv 530 b.
Pintner, R.—x 324 a.
Pioneer Youth of America—ii 667 b.
Pipe Lines—xi 440 b.
Pipe Roll—ii 575 b.
PIRACY—xii 136–39; Armed Merchantmen ii 201 b; Commerce iv 3 a; Filibustering vi 231–33; Maritime Law x 124 a; Privateering xii 422–24.
PIRRIE, W. J.—xii 139.
PISAN, C. DE—xii 140.
Pisarev, D. I.—xi 377 b.
Pithecanthropus Erectus—x 74 b.

PITKIN, T.—xii 140.
PITT, W. (d. 1778) and W. (d. 1806)—xii 140; Catholic Emancipation iii 270 b.
PITT-RIVERS, A. H. L. F.—xii 141.
Pittsburgh-Plus — Basing Point Prices ii 473 b; Iron and Steel Industry viii 308 a.
PIUS II—xii 142. See also Aeneas Silvius.
PIUS IX—xii 142.
Pius X—x 567 b.
Pius XI—xiii 260 b.
PLACE, F.—xii 143; Birth Control ii 561 a.
PLACENTINUS—xii 144.
PLACING OUT—xii 144–46; Brace ii 671 a; Child (Dependent) iii 398–403.
Plague—see COMMUNICABLE DISEASES, CONTROL OF.
PLANCK, G.—xii 146.
PLANCK, G. J.—xii 147.
PLANCK, J. J. W. VON—xii 148.
Plankton—vi 268 a.
PLANTATION—xii 148–53; Introd. Vol. I (The Roman World) i 45 b, 56 b; Agriculture i 587 a, 594 b; Cotton iv 489 a; Land Tenure (Lat. Amer.) ix 118 b; Landed Estates ix 142 b; Peonage xii 70 b; Plantation Wares xii 153–58; Rubber xiii 454 a; Slavery (S. Amer.) xiv 81 a, (U. S.) 84 b, 85 b.
PLANTATION WARES—xii 153–58; International Trade viii 191 b; Plantation xi 148–53; Raw Materials xiii 123–32; Rubber xiii 454 a; Sugar xiv 450–55; Valorization xv 210–12.
Plat, H.—i 579 b.
Platform, Political—iii 164 a.
Platinum—x 386 a.
PLATO AND PLATONISM—xii 158; Introd. Vol. I (Greek Culture and Thought) i 26 a, 30 a, 31 a; Aristocracy ii 183 a; Aristotle ii 191 a; Art ii 224 b; Averroes ii 338 b; Communism iv 81 b; Economics v 346 b; Education v 406 a; Eugenics v 618 a; Evolution, Social v 657 a; Idealism vii 568 a; Individualism iii 675 b; Justice viii 509 b; Logic ix 599 a; Natural Law xi 286 a; Philosophy xii 120 b, 124 b; Political Science xii 207 b; Population xii 248 b; Realism xiii 140 b; Socialism xiv 190 b; Sociology xiv 232 b; Utopia xv 200 b; Woman, Position in Society xv 443 b.
PLAY—xii 160–61; Amusements, Public ii 39–46; Anthropology ii 89 b; Athletics ii 296–300; Culture iv 642 a; Dance iv 701 b; Gambling vi 555–62; Gangs vi 564–67; Physical Education xii 129–33; Playgrounds xii 161–63; Preschool Education xii 321 a; Recreation xiii 176–81.
PLAYGROUNDS—xii 161–63.

Index (Peter of Andlo — Popławski)

PLEBISCITE — xii 163–66; Self-Determination, National xiii 650 b.
PLEDGE—xii 166–68; Debt v 33 a; Law (Cuneiform) ix 218 a, (Greek) 227 b; Lien ix 456 b; Loans, Personal ix 562 b; Mortgage xi 32–38; Pawnbroking xii 32–40; Suretyship and Guaranty xiv 482 a.
Plehn, C. C.—xi 39 a.
PLEKHANOV, G. V.—xii 168; Axelrod ii 370 b; Bolshevism ii 625 a.
Pliny—i 57 a.
Plotinus—ii 224 b.
Plumb Plan—xiii 96 b.
PLUNKETT, H. C.—xii 169.
PLURALISM—xii 170–74; Introd. Vol. I (The Trend to Internationalism) i 179 b, (War and Reorientation) 216 a; Absolutism i 381 b; Allegiance i 646 b; Anarchism ii 51 a; Association ii 285 b; Autonomy ii 335 a; Centralization iii 312 b; Civic Organizations iii 498–502; Civil Liberties iii 512 b; Democracy v 83 b; Figgis vi 230 b; Force, Political vi 341 a; Functional Representation vi 518–23; Functionalism vi 525 a; Guild Socialism vii 202–04; Interests viii 147 b; Liberty ix 445 a; National Economic Councils xi 192–97; Obedience, Political xi 417 a; Power, Political xii 300–05; Pragmatism xii 307–11; Representation xiii 314 b.
PLUTARCH—xii 174; Belief ii 501 b.
PLUTOCRACY—xii 175–77; Aristocracy ii 188 a; Captain of Industry iii 219 b; Endowments and Foundations v 534 a; Fashion vi 142 a; Fortunes, Private vi 389–99; Gentleman, Theory of the vi 617 a; Inheritance viii 39 a; Oligarchy xi 563 b.
Poale Zion—Boruchov ii 644 a; Zionism xv 533 a.
POBEDONOSTSEV, K. P.—xii 177.
Pocket Boroughs—xiii 443 b.
Podestà—ix 582 a.
POGODIN, M. P.—xii 178.
Pogrom—x 194 a.
POHLE, L.—xii 179.
PÖHLMANN, R. VON—xii 180.
Poincaré, H.—xii 308 b.
POISSON, S.-D.—xii 180; Probability xii 429 b.
POKROVSKY, M. N.—xii 181.
POLE FAMILY—xii 182.
POLICE — xii 183–90; Armed Forces, Control of ii 199–201; Arrest ii 221–22; Criminal Statistics iv 581 a; Juvenile Delinquency and Juvenile Courts viii 532 b; Police Power xii 190 a; Policing, Industrial xii 193–96; Political Police xii 203–07; Riot xiii 388 a; Traffic Regulation xv 73 b.
Police Courts—xi 96 a.

POLICE POWER — xii 190–93; Building Regulations iii 53 b; Civic Art iii 493 b; Constitutional Law iv 252 b; Contract Clause iv 341 a; Due Process of Law v 266 a; Eminent Domain v 495 b; Freedom of Contract vi 452 a; Govt. Regulation of Industry vii 128 a; Municipal Corporation xi 92 a.
POLICING, INDUSTRIAL—xii 193–96; Company Towns iv 121 b.
Polis—see CITY-STATE.
POLISH CORRIDOR—xii 196–99.
Political Arithmetic—xiv 357 a.
Political Clubs—see CLUBS, POLITICAL.
Political Conspiracy—see CONSPIRACY, POLITICAL.
Political Convention—see CONVENTION, POLITICAL.
Political Corruption—see CORRUPTION, POLITICAL.
Political Economy—see ECONOMICS.
Political Economy Club—i 242 a.
Political Force—see FORCE, POLITICAL.
Political Immunity—see IMMUNITY, POLITICAL.
Political Machine—see MACHINE, POLITICAL.
Political Nominations—see NOMINATIONS, POLITICAL.
Political Obedience—see OBEDIENCE, POLITICAL.
POLITICAL OFFENDERS—xii 199–203; Amnesty ii 36–39; Asylum ii 289 b; Attainder ii 304–05; Cachet, Lettre de iii 137–38; Camorra iii 161 b; Conspiracy, Political iv 241 a; Exile v 687 b; Extradition vi 43 a; Hunger Strike vii 552–55; Ostracism xi 501–03; Political Police xii 203–07; Sanctuary xiii 537 a; Treason xv 93–96.
Political Parties—see PARTIES, POLITICAL.
POLITICAL POLICE—xii 203–07; Police xii 188 a.
Political Power—see POWER, POLITICAL.
Political Refugees — see REFUGEES.
POLITICAL SCIENCE—xii 207–24 (Content and Method 207–14, 223, Hist. 214–18, 223, Function 218–24); Introd. Vol. I (What Are the Social Sciences?) i 3 b, (Greek Culture and Thought) 26 b, (The Universal Church) 70 b, (The Growth of Autonomy) 80 a, (Renaissance and Reformation) 90 b, 94 b, 96 b, (The Rise of Liberalism) 108 b, (The Revolutions) 129 a, (Individualism and Capitalism) 161 a, (The Trend to Internationalism) 178 a, (War and Reorientation) 215 a, (The Social Sciences as Disciplines, Gt. Brit.) 238 a, (Japan) 321 b, (Lat. Amer.) 312 a, (Scandinavia) 292 b, (U. S.) 329 a, 335 b, 343 b; Absolutism i 380–82; Divine Right of Kings v 176–77; Ethics v 603 b; Executive v 680 b; Force, Political vi 338–41; Govt. vii 8–15; Individualism vii 674–80; Philosophy xii 127 a; Pluralism xii 170–74; Scholasticism xiii 579 a; Social Contract xiv 127–31; Social Organism xiv 138 a; Sociology xiv 235 b, 242 a; Sovereignty xiv 265–69; State xiv 328–32; Statistics xiv 356 a. For biog. references see Classification of Articles (Political Science), p. 566.
Political Succession—see SUCCESSION, POLITICAL.
POLITICS—xii 224–27; Bribery ii 690–92; Caucus iii 277–79; Civic Organizations iii 498–502; Civil Service iii 522 a; Clubs, Political iii 577–80; Coalition iii 600–02; Convention, Political iv 349–51; Customs Duties iv 671 a; Labor viii 620 a; Legislation ix 348 a; Machine, Political ix 657–61; Negro Problem xi 353 a; Ostracism xi 501–03; Political Science xii 207–24; Statesmanship xiv 350 b; Universities and Colleges xv 184 a.
Polk, J. K.—x 631 a.
POLL TAX—xii 227–28.
Polls—see ELECTIONS.
Polyandry—x 150 a.
POLYBIUS—xii 228; Introd. Vol. I (The Roman World) i 50 b, 51 b; Balance of Power ii 395 b; Checks and Balances iii 363 a; Cicero iii 469 a; Force, Political vi 339 b; History and Historiography vii 369 a.
Polygamy—xi 16 b.
Polygyny—x 149 b.
POMBAL, MARQUEZ DE—xii 229.
Pomeranus—see BUGENHAGEN, J.
POMEROY, J. N.—xii 229.
Pompey—i 44 a.
Pomponazzi, P.—Enlightenment v 552 a; Renaissance xiii 281 a.
Pools—Employers' Associations v 510 b; Meat Packing and Slaughtering x 259 b; Trusts xv 112 a.
POOR LAWS—xii 230–34; Acland i 420 a; Allotments ii 5–7; Allowance System ii 7; Almshouse ii 8 a; Begging ii 494 a; Charity iii 342 b; Child (Dependent) iii 399 b; Davies v 11 a; Gilbert vi 661 b; Villiers xv 261 b.
Poor Relief—Almshouse ii 8–10; Charity iii 340–45; Institutions, Public viii 90–95; Mothers' Pensions xi 53–57; Social Insurance xiv 137 a; Social Work xiv 165 b, 173 a. See also POOR LAWS.
Poorhouse—see ALMSHOUSE.
Pope, A.—ii 622 b.
POPŁAWSKI, A.—xii 235.

Popov, K.—xii 235.
POPULAR ASSEMBLIES—xii 236–39.
POPULAR SOVEREIGNTY—xii 239–40; Bicameral System ii 535 a; Political Science xii 215 b; Representation xiii 311 b; Rousseau xiii 446 a.
POPULATION—xii 240–54; Introd. Vol. I (War and Reorientation) i 208 a; Acclimatization i 401–03; Agriculture (China) i 589 a, (Japan) 591 a; Anthropology ii 99 b; Balance of Power ii 397 b; Biology ii 555 a; Birth Control ii 560 b; Births ii 568–72; Botero ii 647 a; Census iii 295–300; Child (Mortality) iii 384–90; Demography v 85–86; Ecology, Human v 314–15; Economic Policy v 337 a; Economics (Classical School) v 354 a; Emigration v 488–93; Famine vi 89 b; Far Eastern Problem vi 98 a, 99 b; Food Supply vi 332–38; Ghetto vi 649 b; Infanticide viii 27–28; International Trade viii 190 b; King viii 565 b; Land Utilization ix 132 b; Life Insurance ix 463 a; Location of Industry ix 588 a; Malthus x 68 a; Mass Expulsion x 185–89; Mental Defectives x 312 b; Mental Hygiene x 320 b; Metropolitan Areas x 396 a; Migrations x 420–41; Moheau x 574 a; Mortality xi 22–32; Negro Problem xi 342 b, 354 a; Occupation (Statistics) xi 429 a; Old Age xi 455 a; Oriental Immigration xi 490–94; Ortes xi 498 b; Race xiii 31 a; Refugees xiii 200–05; Statistics xiv 358 a, 361 a; Suicide xiv 455–59; Unemployment xv 159 a; Urbanization xv 191 b; Wages xv 295 a; Wallace xv 326 a; War xv 336 b.
Populism—La Follette ix 13 a; Parties, Political (U. S.) xi 599 a.
Porcelain—ii 235 b.
Port of New York Authority—x 398 b.
Port Sunlight—Company Housing iv 117 b; Leverhulme ix 423 b.
PORTALES, D.—xii 255.
PORTALIS, J. É. M.—xii 255.
Porter, H.—iii 156 a.
Porter, S. G.—xi 474 a.
PORTS AND HARBORS—xii 255–60; Commercial Routes iv 19–24; Free Ports and Free Zones vi 436–38; Longshoremen ix 606–09; Navy xi 318 a.
POSITIVISM—xii 260–66; Ardigò ii 181 b; Comte iv 151; Harrison vii 274 b; History and Historiography vii 379 a; Humanitarianism vii 548 b; Jurisprudence viii 483 b; Natural Law xi 290 a; Political Science xii 218 a; Saint-Simon and Saint-Simonianism xiii 509 b; Social Organism xiv 139 b; Society xiv 230 b; Sociology xiv 237 a.
POSOSHKOV, I. T.—xii 266.
Possession—see OWNERSHIP AND POSSESSION.
Possibilism—Brousse iii 15 b; Renaissance xiii 283 b.
POST, A. H.—xii 267.
POST, L. F.—xii 267.
POSTAL SAVINGS BANKS—xii 268–69; Savings Banks xiii 553 b.
POSTAL SERVICE—xii 269–74; Express Companies vi 28 b; Franking vi 419–20; Hill vii 351 a; Postal Savings Banks xii 268–69. See also Air Mail.
Postal Telegraph and Cable Corp.—xiv 563 a.
POTASH—xii 274–77; Business, Govt. Services for iii 120 a; Fertilizer Industry vi 193–98.
POTHIER, R.-J.—xii 277; Civil Law iii 505 b.
POTTER, G.—xii 278.
POTTERY—xii 279–84; Anthropology ii 81 a; Archaeology ii 165 a; Glass and Pottery Industries vi 671–78.
Pouget, É.—ii 115 b.
Pound, R.—Introd. Vol. I (The Trend to Internationalism) i 181 a, (The Social Sciences as Disciplines, U. S.) 344 b.
POVERTY—xii 284–92; Alcohol i 626 b; Begging ii 493–95; Charitable Trusts iii 339 a; Child iii 373–431; Dependency v 93–95; Family Desertion and Non-support vi 78–81; Franciscan Movement vi 411 a; Indian Question vii 664 a; Legal Aid ix 319–24; Old Age xi 456 a; Pawnbroking xii 36 b; Poor Laws xii 230–34; Slums xiv 93–98; Social Work xiv 165–83; Unemployment xv 148 b.
POWDERLY, T. V. — xii 292; Knights of Labor viii 581 b.
POWELL, J. W.—xii 293.
POWER, INDUSTRIAL—xii 293–300; Coal Industry iii 583 a; Compacts, Interstate iv 112 a; Electric Power v 456–70; Engineering v 542 a; Factory System vi 51 b; Gas Industry vi 588–94; Industrialism viii 19 a; Large Scale Production ix 174 b; Location of Industry ix 587 a; Machines and Tools x 25 a; Natural Resources xi 292 a; Oil Industry xi 438 b.
POWER POLITICAL—xii 300–05; Assassination ii 271–75; Authority ii 319–21; Autocracy ii 321–22; Checks and Balances iii 363–65; Civic Organizations iii 498–502; Democracy v 76–85; Dictatorship v 133–36; Faction vi 49–51; Force, Political vi 338–41; Laissez Faire ix 19 b; Landed Estates ix 140 b; Leadership ix 283 b; Masses x 195–201; Oligarchy xi 462–65; Political Science xii 207–24; Praetorianism xii 305–07; Reason of State xiii 143–44; Sovereignty xiv 265–69; War xv 337 a; Woman, Position in Society xv 440 a, 448 b.
Praedial Servitudes—xiv 3 b.
PRAETORIANISM — xii 305–07; Armed Forces, Control of ii 199 b.
Pragmatic Sanction of Bourges—Gallicanism vi 550 b; Religious Institutions (Roman Catholic) xiii 257 b.
PRAGMATISM—xii 307–11; Common Sense iv 58–61; Conduct iv 179 b; Duty v 294 b; Ethics v 605 b; Functionalism vi 524 a; Humanism vii 542 b; James viii 368 b; Logic ix 602 b; Opportunism xi 477 b; Positivism xii 265 b.
Prat de la Riba, E.—xiii 214 a.
PRATO, G.—xii 311.
Pratt, H.—xii 45 a.
Pratt, T.—vi 496 a.
Precedent, Judicial—see CASE LAW.
PRECIOUS STONES—xii 312–15.
Predestination—iii 152 a.
Preemption, Right of—see PUBLIC DOMAIN; HOMESTEAD.
Preferred Stock—xiv 404 b.
PREHISTORY—xii 316–18; Introd. Vol. I (War and Reorientation) i 224 a; Archaeology ii 163–67; Man x 72 b; Records, Historical xiii 173 b.
Premium System of Remuneration—viii 678 b, 680 a.
Preparedness—see NATIONAL DEFENSE.
PREROGATIVE—xii 318–20.
Presbyterianism—xiii 270 b.
PRESCHOOL EDUCATION—xii 320–24; Aporti ii 128 a; Blow ii 600 a; Brunswick iii 21 a; Day Nursery v 16 a; Fröbel vi 498 b.
PRESCOTT, W. H.—xii 324; History and Historiography vii 386 a.
Prescription, Legal—Canon Law iii 184 a; Land Transfer ix 129 b; Limitation of Actions ix 474 b.
PRESS—xii 325–44; Campaign, Political iii 165 a; Censorship iii 293 b; Diplomacy v 149 a; Foreign Language Press vi 378–82; Freedom of Speech and of the Press vi 455–59; Health Insurance vii 299 a; History and Historiography vii 380 b; Journalism viii 420–24; Learned Societies ix 298 b; Libel and Slander ix 432 b; Printing and Publishing xii 406–15; Public Opinion xii 672 a, 673 a, 674 a; Publicity xii 701 a; Pulp and Paper Industry xii 709 a; Radio xiii 61 a; Straw Vote xiv 417 b; World War xv 494 a. For biog. references see Classification of Articles (Journalism), p. 563.

Press Associations—Press xii 329 b, 331 a, 335 b; Reuter xiii 357 b.
Press, Foreign Language — see FOREIGN LANGUAGE PRESS.
Pressure Groups—see LOBBY.
PRESSURES, SOCIAL—xii 344–48; Sanction, Social xiii 531–34.
Prestige—see HONOR.
PREUSS, H.—xii 349.
Prévost-Paradol—xiii 210 a.
PREYER, W. T.—xii 349; Child (Psychology) iii 391 b.
Pribram, A. F.—ii 179 b.
Price—see VALUE AND PRICE.
PRICE, R.—xii 350; Sinking Fund xiv 67 b.
PRICE DISCRIMINATION—xii 350–55; Basing Point Prices ii 473–75; Dumping v 275–78; Railroads xiii 87 b; Resale Price Maintenance xiii 329 b.
PRICE REGULATION—xii 355–62; Consumer Protection iv 283 b; Cost of Living iv 478 b; Economic Policy v 342 b; Just Price viii 504–07; Prices xii 368 a; Profiteering xii 492 b; Rate Regulation xiii 104–12; Rent Regulation xiii 293–96; Resale Price Maintenance xiii 326–30; Valorization xv 210–12.
PRICE STABILIZATION—xii 362–66; Bimetallism and Monometallism ii 547 b; Central Banking iii 305 b; Compensated Dollar iv 134–35; Economic Policy v 343 a; Farm Relief vi 116 b; Foreign Exchange vi 362 a; Iron and Steel Industry viii 308 a; Monetary Stabilization x 591–95; Prices xii 370 a; Rubber xiii 456 a; Stabilization, Economic xiv 309–15.
PRICES—xii 366–87 (Theory 366–75, 385, History 375–81, 386, Statistics 381–85, 387). See VALUE AND PRICE.
PRICHARD, J. C.—xii 388.
PRIESTHOOD—xii 388–95; Introd. Vol. I (Greek Culture and Thought) i 17 b; Benefit of Clergy ii 511–13; Brahmanism and Hinduism ii 674 b; Buddhism iii 37 a; Calendar iii 142 a; Celibacy iii 283 b; Christian Labor Unions iii 445 a; Confession iv 182 b; Divination v 174 b; Judaism viii 430 b; Law (Egyptian) ix 210 a; Legal Profession and Legal Education ix 324 b; Papacy xi 559–68; Professions xii 476 a; Reformation xiii 189 a; Religious Institutions (Roman Catholic) xiii 246 a, (Byzantine) 262 a, (Russian) 265 a; Woman, Position in Society (Primitive) xv 441 b.
PRIESTLEY, J.—xii 395.
PRIMARIES, POLITICAL—xii 396–98; Convention, Polit. iv 349–51; Machine, Polit. ix 659 a; Nominations, Polit. xi 394 a; Parties, Polit. (U. S.) xi 600 b.

Primitive Law—Anthropology ii 88 b; Blood Vengeance Feud ii 598–99; Criminal Law iv 570 a; Damages iv 696 b; Law (Primitive) ix 202–06; Procedure, Legal xii 439 b.
Primitive Society—see Classification of Articles (Primitive Society), p. 554. See also Adolescence i 458 b; Alcohol i 619 a; Ancestor Worship ii 54 a; Barter ii 468 b; Capital Punishment iii 192 b; Caste xiii 256 b; Celibacy iii 283 a; Chastity iii 357 a; Child (Marriage) iii 395 b, (Welfare) 374 b; Class iii 533 a; Clubs iii 574 a; Commercial Routes iv 20 a; Communism iv 85 b; Concubinage iv 171 b; Confession iv 181 b; Corruption, Political iv 449 a; Courts iv 516 b; Courtship iv 539 a; Criminal Law iv 570 a; Custom iv 660 b; Dance iv 701 b; Debt v 33 a; Divorce v 177 a; Dueling v 268 b; Empire v 497 b; Equality v 574 b; Exchange v 667 a; Executive v 681 a; Famine iv 87 b; Festivals vi 198 b; Food Supply vi 333 b; Furniture vi 537 a; Gambling vi 555 b; Hoarding vii 393 b; Hospitality vii 462 b; Housing vii 496 b; Humanitarianism vii 544 b; Illegitimacy vii 579 a; Justice viii 509 a; Labor viii 619 a; Legislative Assemblies ix 355 a; Leisure ix 402 b; Liquor Industry ix 495 b; Literature ix 532 a; Machines and Tools x 14 b; Maladjustment x 61 b; Monarchy x 579 b; Old Age xi 453 a; Organization, Economic xi 485 b; Property xii 530 a; Religion xiii 234 b; Religious Orders xiii 276 b; Science xiii 594 a; Specialization xiv 280 a; Village Community xv 254 b, 257 b; War xv 331 b. See also ANTHROPOLOGY.
PRIMITIVISM—xii 398–402; Literature ix 526 b; Rousseau xiii 445 b.
PRIMOGENITURE — xii 402–05; Alienation of Property i 639 b; Appanage ii 130–31; Entail v 553–56; Freehold vi 462 b; Inheritance viii 37 a.
PRINCE, M.—xii 405.
PRINCE-SMITH, J.—xii 405.
Principal and Agent—see AGENCY.
PRINS, A.—xii 406.
PRINTING AND PUBLISHING—xii 406–15; Copyright iv 401–04; Govt. Publications vii 120–22; Humanism vii 539 a; Literacy and Illiteracy ix 515 b; Press xii 325–44; Public Opinion xii 672 b.
Prison Discipline—see PENAL INSTITUTIONS.
PRISON LABOR—xii 415–19; Public Contracts xii 597 a.

Prison Reform—see PENAL INSTITUTIONS.
PRISONERS OF WAR—xii 419–22; Warfare, Laws of xv 363 b.
Prisons—see PENAL INSTITUTIONS.
Privatdocent—i 262 a.
Private Bankers—Banking, Commercial (Hist.) ii 425 b; Bardi ii 458 a; Investment Banking viii 270 b.
Private Property—see PROPERTY.
PRIVATEERING—xii 422–24; Armed Merchantmen ii 201 b; Declaration of Paris v 49 a; Merchantmen, Status of x 352 a; Reprisals xiii 316 a.
Privilege, Parliamentary—see IMMUNITY, POLITICAL.
PRIZE—xii 424–26; Declaration of London v 47 b; Neutrality xi 363 b; Privateering xii 422–24; Stowell xiv 414 b; Warfare, Laws of xv 362 b.
PROBABILITY—xii 426–35; Annuities ii 70 b; Bernoulli ii 525 a; Frequency Distribution vi 484–89; Laplace ix 169 a; Lotteries ix 611–16; Poisson xii 180 b; Statistics xiv 369 a.
PROBATION AND PAROLE—xii 435–39; Criminology iv 590 b; Social Work (Case Work) xiv 179 b.
PROCEDURE, LEGAL—xii 439–54. See relevant titles in Classification of Articles (Administration of Justice), p. 548. See also Arbitration, International ii 160 a; Bentham ii 519 a; Canon Law iii 185 a; Child (Delinquent) iii 409 a; Christianity iii 456 a; Common Law iv 54 b; Conflict of Laws iv 193 a; Criminology iv 590 b; Dueling v 269 a; Glaser vi 670 b; Investigations, Governmental viii 252 a; Law (Primitive) ix 205 a, (Cuneiform) 215 a, (Germanic) 237 a, (Greek) 229 a, (Hellenistic and Greco-Egyptian) 233 b, (Slavic) 246 a; Lawlessness ix 278 b; Planck xii 148 a; Roman Law xiii 421 a.
PROCEDURE, PARLIAMENTARY — xii 454–58; Closure iii 570–73; Committees, Legislative iv 40–44; Debate, Parliamentary v 28–29; Interpellation viii 219–20; League of Nations ix 290 a; Legislation ix 353 b; Legislative Assemblies (France) ix 378 b, (Germany) 382 a, (Gt. Brit. and Dominions) 370 b, (Japan) 394 b, (U. S.) 362 a, 368 a; Majority Rule x 55–60; Obstruction, Parliamentary xi 422–24; Petition, Right of xii 100 a.
Prodicus—xiv 260 a.
PRODUCERS' COOPERATION — xii 458–62; Agric. Cooperation i 522 a, 524 a; Ateliers Nationaux ii 291–92; Cooperation iv 359–99; Labor, Methods of Remuneration for viii 681 a; Labor Movement viii 690 b. See also COOPERATION.

PRODUCTION—xii 462–72; Advertising i 470 b, 474 b; Consumers' Cooperation iv 286 b; Consumption iv 293 b; Cost iv 466–75; Diminishing Returns v 144–46; Economics (Socialist Economics) v 379 a; Electric Power v 458 a; Electrical Manufacturing Industry v 472 a; Factory System vi 51–55; Increasing Returns vii 639–40; Labor viii 618 b; Laissez Faire ix 16 b; Large Scale Production ix 170–81; Machinery, Industrial x 3–14; Machines and Tools x 14–26; Materialism (Historical) x 217 b; Mercantilism x 337 a; National Economic Planning xi 199 a; National Income xi 205–24; Overhead Costs xi 511–13; Overproduction xi 513–17; Prices (Theory) xii 366–75; Producers' Cooperation xii 458–62; Promotion xii 518–21; Protection xii 560 b; Specialization xiv 279–85; Standardization xiv 319–22; Supply xiv 470–74; Technology xiv 553–60; Wages xv 291–302, 311 b; Waste xv 368 a.

Production, Large Scale — see LARGE SCALE PRODUCTION.

PROFESSIONAL ETHICS—xii 472–76; Business Ethics iii 111 a; Civil Service iii 520 b; Engineering v 544 b; Fee Splitting vi 178–79; Journalism viii 421 a, 423 b; Legal Profession and Legal Education ix 340–46; Medicine x 296 a; Professions xii 479 a.

Professionalism—Amateur ii 19 b; Architecture ii 172 a; Athletics ii 299 b; Commercialism iv 32 b; Sports xiv 308 a. See also PROFESSIONS; PROFESSIONAL ETHICS.

PROFESSIONS—xii 476–80; Introd. Vol. I (The Social Sciences as Disciplines, Gt. Brit.) i 233 a, (U.S.) 333 a, 345 b; Accounting i 406 a; Administration, Public i 446 a; Apprenticeship ii 144–47; Architecture ii 174 a, 175 a; Art ii 223–59; Career iii 225 b; Civil Service iii 515–23; Dentistry v 91–93; Diplomacy v 147 b; Engineering v 543 b; Fee Splitting vi 178–79; Gentleman, Theory of the vi 618 a; Home Economics vii 430 b; Intellectuals viii 118–26; Journalism viii 420–24; Labor viii 617 b; Learned Societies ix 295–300; Legal Profession and Legal Education ix 324–46; Literature ix 532 a; Medicine x 283–301; Middle Class x 413 a; Music xi 162 b; Nursing xi 411 b; Occupation xi 424–35; Professional Ethics xii 472–76; Research xiii 330–34; Social Work (Training) xiv 183–87; Teaching Profession xiv 543–53.

PROFIT—xii 480–87; Business iii 80–87; Capitalism iii 195–208; Christianity iii 457 b; Competition iv 142 b; Consumers' Cooperation iv 285 b; Distribution v 167–74; Economics (Classical School) v 355 a, (Cambridge School) 370 a, (Socialist Economics) 379 a; Entrepreneur v 558–60; Excess Profits Tax v 664–66; Fair Return vi 56–58; Goodwill vi 699 b; Income Tax vii 637 a; Interest viii 132 a; Iron and Steel Industry viii 308 b; Laissez Faire ix 19 a; National Economic Planning xi 199 a; Profit Sharing xii 491 a; Profiteering xii 494 a; Speculation xiv 288–93.

PROFIT SHARING — xii 487–92; Employee Stock Ownership v 507 a; Leclaire ix 317 b.

PROFITEERING—xii 492–95; War Economics xv 346 b.

Profits, Legal—xiv 5 a.

PROGRESS—xii 495–99; Backward Countries ii 379–81; Bodin ii 615 a; Bury iii 79 a; Change, Social iii 330–34; Civilization iii 525–29; Condorcet iv 176 b; Decadence v 39–43; Encyclopédistes v 529 b; Evolution v 649 b; Evolution, Social v 659 a, 660 b; History and Historiography vii 370 b, 375 b; Innovation viii 58–61; Invention viii 250 a; Luxury ix 635 a; Reformism xiii 194–95; Social Process xiv 148–51; Sorel xiv 262 a.

Progressive Parties—see PARTIES, POLITICAL.

Progressive Party, U. S.—Beveridge ii 532 a; Parties, Political xi 599 b; Roosevelt xiii 436 b.

Progressive Taxation — Cohen Stuart iii 621 a; Taxation xiv 539 b.

PROHIBITION—xii 499–510; Alcohol i 620 a; Anti-Saloon League ii 118–19; Blue Laws ii 602 a; Concurrent Powers iv 173 b; Consensus iv 226 b; Corruption, Political iv 453 a; Double Jeopardy v 223 b; Dow v 229 b; Food Industries (Beverages) vi 308 a, (Confectionery) 310 a; Liquor Industry ix 500 a; Liquor Traffic ix 503 b; Racketeering xiii 47 b; Searches and Seizures xiii 519 a; Temperance Movements xiv 569 b.

Prokopovich, F.—xiii 527 a.

PROLETARIAT—xii 510–18; Bolshevism ii 623–30; Commune of Paris iv 63–66; Communist Parties iv 88 a; French Revolution vi 476 a; Intellectuals viii 121 b; Labor viii 618 a; Labor Movement viii 684 a; Literature ix 539 b; Masses x 196 a; Revolution and Counter-revolution xiii 367–76; Socialism (Marxian) xiv 201 b; Trade Unions xv 3–57; Unemployment xv 147–62.

Promissory Note—iv 546 a.

PROMOTION—xii 518–21; Blue Sky Laws ii 602–05; Boom ii 639 b; Corporation Finance iv 424 b; Correspondence Schools iv 446 a; Investment Banking viii 275 a; Salesmanship xiii 519–21.

PROPAGANDA—xii 521–28; Advertising i 469–75; Antiradicalism ii 117 b; Anti-Saloon League ii 119 a; Atrocities ii 304 a; Birth Control ii 561 a; Boys' and Girls' Clubs ii 668 b; Campaign, Political iii 164 a; Civic Education iii 497 b; Civic Organizations iii 498–502; Communist Parties iv 91 a; Drives, Money Raising v 238–41; Education (Public) v 420 b; Foreign Language Press vi 380 a; Fraternizing vi 425–27; Habit vii 238 a; Health Education viii 290 b, 291 b, 293 b; Irredentism viii 325 a; Literature ix 539 b; Lobby ix 567 a; Masses x 198 a; Motion Pictures xi 67 b; Nationalism xi 237 b; Patriotism xii 27 b; Proselytism xii 551 b; Public Opinion xii 673 b; Publicity xii 700 b; Terrorism xiv 575–80.

PROPERTY—xii 528–38. See Classification of Articles (Property), p. 554. See also Introd. Vol. I (The Growth of Autonomy) i 76 a; Anthropology ii 83 b; Aquinas ii 147 b; Aristocracy ii 185 b; Bargaining Power ii 460 a; Begging ii 493 a; Business iii 84 a; Capitalism iii 195–208; Christianity iii 457 a; Church Fathers iii 466 b; Competition iv 142 b; Conflict of Laws iv 191 b; Diplomatic Protection v 154 b; Economics (Physiocrats) v 349 a, (Classical School) 351 b; Freedom of Contract vi 452 b; Gambling vi 557 b; Game Laws vi 563 a; Guardianship vii 192 b; Jhering viii 400 b; Law (Cuneiform) ix 217 a, (Germanic) 236 a, (Greek) 227 b, (Hellenistic and Greco-Egyptian) 233 a, (Slavic) 244 a; Libel and Slander ix 433 a; Madison x 34 b; Mass Expulsion x 188 a; Materialism (Historical) x 218 a; Morals x 645 b; National Income xi 212 b, 218 a; Natural Rights xi 300 b; Specific Performance xiv 286 a; Status xiv 373 b; Tort xiv 653 a.

PROPERTY TAX—xii 538–41; Capitalization and Amortization of Taxes iii 211–13; Local Finance ix 571 a; Valuation xv 216 a.

Prophets—Judaism viii 430 b.

PROPORTIONAL REPRESENTATION —xii 541–45; Gerrymander vi 638 b; Minority Rights x 526 b; Representation xiii 314 a.

PROSECUTION—xii 545–51; Arrest ii 221–22; Criminal Law iv 575 b; Double Jeopardy v 222–24; Grand Jury vii 148–50; Justice,

Index (Production — Public Finance)

Administration of viii 516 b; Law (Greek) ix 228 b; Law Enforcement ix 267–70; Public Defender xii 611–13; Racketeering xiii 49 a; Searches and Seizures xiii 617–20; Self-Incrimination xiii 651–53; State Liability xiv 343 a.

PROSELYTISM—xii 551–53; Backward Countries ii 379 b; Buddhism iii 34 b; Conversion, Religious iv 353 b; Cults iv 619 b; Islam viii 339 a; Jihad viii 401 b; Judaism viii 433 a; Missions x 536–47; Religious Institutions (Roman Catholic) xiii 249 a; Revivals, Religious xiii 363–67.

PROSTITUTION—xii 553–59; Butler iii 124 b; Corruption, Political iv 453 a; Guillaume-Schack vii 225 a.

Protagoras—Introd. Vol. I (Greek Culture and Thought) i 24 b; Humanism vii 542 b; Natural Law xi 285 b; Sophists xiv 259 b.

PROTECTION—xii 559–67; Ad Valorem and Specific Duties i 468–69; Balance of Trade ii 400 b; Bounties ii 653 a; Cartel iii 241 a; Commerce iv 11 a; Commercial Treaties iv 29 b; Continental System iv 310–11; Corn Laws iv 405–08; Customs Duties iv 667–73; Customs Unions iv 675 b; Drawback v 233–35; Economic Policy v 339 a; Free Ports and Free Zones vi 436–38; Free Trade vi 440–47; International Trade viii 194 b; Kelley viii 556 a; Mercantilism x 337 a; Metals x 375 b; Price Regulation xii 360 b; Tariff xiv 514–23; Textile Industry xiv 586 a.

Protection, Diplomatic—see DIPLOMATIC PROTECTION.

PROTECTORATE—xii 567–71; Chartered Companies iii 351 a; Egyptian Problem v 443 a; Loans, Intergovernmental ix 560 a.

PROTESTANTISM—xii 571–75; Introd. Vol. I (Individualism and Capitalism) i 149 a; Bourgeoisie ii 655 b; Calvin iii 151 b; Christianity iii 458 a; Commercialism iv 32 b; Cranmer iv 543 b; Diabolism v 120 b; Divorce v 179 b; Dogma v 190 b; Excommunication v 680 a; Festivals vi 200 b; Fundamentalism vi 526–27; Higher Criticism vii 347 a; Intermarriage viii 152 b; Jesuits viii 382 a, 384 a; Labor viii 616 b; Literacy and Illiteracy ix 516 a; Magdeburg Centuriators x 38 b; Melanchthon x 302 b; Missions x 541 a; Modernism x 565 b; Puritanism xiii 3–6; Quakers xiii 12–14; Reformation xiii 187–94; Religious Institutions (Protestant) xiii 267–72; Sects xiii 626 b; Social Christian Movements xiv 124 a; Society xiv 227 b; Weber xv 387 b.

Protocols of the Elders of Zion—ii 124 a.

PROUDHON, P. J.—xii 575; Introd. Vol. I (Individualism and Capitalism) i 158 a; Anarchism ii 48 b; Anticlericalism ii 113 b; Cooperation iv 377 b; Federalism vi 169 a; Justice viii 512 b; Labor Exchange Banks viii 640 b; Socialism xiv 194 b.

PROUTY, C. A.—xii 576.

Provident Loan Society of N. Y.—xii 38 b.

Provisions of Oxford—Montfort x 640 a.

Provisions of Westminster—Montfort x 640 a.

PRYNNE, W.—xii 577.

PSELLOS, M.—xii 577.

PSYCHIATRY—xii 578–80; Abnormal Psychology i 360–69; Adjustment i 439 a; Alienist i 641; Bourneville ii 658 b; Charcot iii 337 b; Child (Guidance) iii 393–95; Criminology iv 590 a; Esquirol v 597 a; Fernald vi 184 b; Griesinger vii 171 a; Kraepelin viii 597 a; Maudsley x 231 a; Mental Disorders x 313–19; Mental Hygiene x 319–23; Personality xii 86 a; Pinel xii 135 a; Prince xii 405 a; Psychoanalysis xii 580–88; Psychology xii 594 b; Rush xiii 472 a; Salmon xiii 522 a; Seguin xiii 647 a; Social Work (Case Work) xiv 174 a, 179 b.

PSYCHOANALYSIS—xii 580–88; Introd. Vol. I (War and Reorientation) i 195 b; Abnormal Psychology i 363 b; Character iii 336 b; Confession iv 183 a; Consciousness iv 217 a; Educational Psychology v 433 b; Folklore vi 289 b; Genius v 613 a; Mental Disorders x 313–19; Mental Hygiene x 322 b; Personality xii 87 a; Play xii 160 b; Psychiatry xii 578 b; Psychology xii 594 b, 595 b; Social Psychology xiv 154 a.

PSYCHOLOGY—xii 588–96. See Classification of Articles (Psychology), p. 554. See also Introd. Vol. I (What Are the Social Sciences?) i 7 a, (The Trend to Internationalism) 174 a, 183 a, (War and Reorientation) 195 a, (The Social Sciences as Disciplines, Gt. Brit.) 238 a; Adjustment i 438 b; Anthropology ii 77 a, 107 a; Chastity iii 358 a; Confession iv 183 a; Conversion, Religious iv 354 a; Corporal Punishment iv 413 b; Determinism v 113 a; Environmentalism v 564 b; Evidence v 645 a; Evolution, Social v 659 a, 660 b; Functionalism vi 524 a; Group vii 182 a; History and Historiography vii 365 a; Human Nature vii 535 b; Mechanism and Vitalism x 270 a; Social Work (Case Work) xiv 174 a; Sociology xiv 240 a. For biog. references see Classification of Articles (Psychology), p. 567.

Psycho-Physical Parallelism—iv 215 b.

Psychophysics—vi 154 a.

Ptolemy, C. P.—xiii 597 b.

Public Accounts—see ACCOUNTS, PUBLIC.

Public Administration—see ADMINISTRATION, PUBLIC.

PUBLIC CONTRACTS—xii 596–99; Corruption, Political iv 450 a; Municipal Corporation xi 91 a; Producers' Cooperation xii 460 b.

PUBLIC DEBT—xii 599–611; Banking, Commercial (Hist.) ii 427 b; Calvo and Drago Doctrines iii 155 a; Capital Levy iii 190–92; Debt v 36 b; Devaluation v 116 a; Expenditures, Public vi 8 a; Forced Loans vi 346–47; Indemnity, Military vii 642 a; International Finance viii 159–64; Loans, Intergovernmental ix 556–61; Local Finance ix 572 b; Municipal Finance xi 99 a; Rentier xiii 297 b; Repudiation of Public Debts xiii 321–24; Revenues, Public xiii 362 a, 363 a; Sinking Fund xiv 67–69; Special Assessments xiv 278 a; Tax Exemption xiv 529 b; War Finance xv 350 a.

PUBLIC DEFENDER—xii 611–13.

PUBLIC DOMAIN—xii 613–28; Introd. Vol. I (Greek Culture and Thought) i 39 b; Agrarian Movements (Ancient Rome) i 494 a; Conservation iv 227–30; Corruption, Political iv 453 a; Forests vi 385 a; Frontier vi 500–06; Homestead vii 436–41; Land Grants ix 32–43; Mining Law x 513–18; Revenues, Public xiii 361 a; Water Law xv 371 a.

Public Education—v 414–21.

PUBLIC EMPLOYMENT—xii 628–37; Administration, Public i 442–47; Civil Service iii 515–23; Fire Protection vi 265 a; Govt. Ownership vii 118 a; Labor Disputes viii 635 b; Labor Turnover viii 710 b; Pensions xii 66 b; Personnel Administration xii 89 b; Police xii 185 a; Public Contracts xii 596–99; Public Office xii 665–69; Public Works xii 693 b; Spoils System xiv 301–05; State Liability xiv 338–43; Teaching Profession xiv 543–53; Wages xv 315 b.

Public Expenditures — see EXPENDITURES, PUBLIC.

PUBLIC FINANCE—xii 637–46. See Classification of Articles (Public Finance), p. 554, (Taxation), p. 556. See also Introd. Vol. I (Greek Culture and Thought) i 29 b; Adams i 432 b; Banking, Commercial (Hist.) ii 425 b, 429 b; Bonds ii 634 a; Civic Organizations iii 500 a; Cohn iii 622 a; Dietzel v 138 b; Indian

664 Encyclopaedia of the Social Sciences

Question vii 664 a; Investment Banking viii 268 b; Mazzola x 241 a; Mobilization and Demobilization x 561 a; Money Market x 616 a; Schanz xiii 563 b; Social Work xiv 170 a; Water Supply xv 377 a. *For further biog. references see* Classification of Articles (Financial Administration), p. 561; *also* (Economics), p. 559, *passim*.

PUBLIC HEALTH—xii 646–57. *See* Classification of Articles (Public Health), p. 554. *See also* Biology ii 556 b; Birth Control ii 563 b; Inspection viii 72 b; Institutions, Public viii 90–95; Negro Problem xi 354 a; Nuisance xi 403 b; Poverty xii 289 b; Sex Education and Sex Ethics xiv 9 b; Slums xiv 94 b; Social Work (Case Work) xiv 179 a. *For biog. references see* Classification of Articles (Public Health), p. 567.

Public Institutions—*see* INSTITUTIONS, PUBLIC.

Public Interest—Eminent Domain v 494 a; Rate Regulation xiii 104 b, 106 a; Resale Price Maintenance xiii 329 a.

Public Lands—*see* PUBLIC DOMAIN.

PUBLIC LAW—xii 657–59; Administrative Law i 452–55; Advisory Opinions i 475–78; Constitutional Law iv 247–55; Constitutions iv 259–62; Law ix 202–67.

PUBLIC LIBRARIES—xii 659–65. *See* Libraries.

Public Monopolies—*see* MONOPOLIES, PUBLIC.

PUBLIC OFFICE—xii 665–69. *See* Classification of Articles (Public Office), p. 554. *See also* Campaign, Political iii 162–66; Civic Organizations iii 499 a; County Govt., U. S. iv 506 b; Domicile v 209 a; Masses x 197 b; Woman, Position in Society xv 448 b.

Public Official Bonds—ii 632 b.

PUBLIC OPINION—xii 669–74; Antiradicalism ii 116–18; Anti-semitism ii 119–25; Attitudes, Social ii 305–07; Belief ii 500–03; Campaign, Political iii 165 b; Civic Education iii 496–98; Civic Organizations iii 498–502; Collective Behavior iii 632 a; Common Sense iv 58–61; Consensus iv 225–27; Control, Social iv 344–49; Criminal Law iv 573 a; Discussion v 166–67; Hunger Strike vii 552–55; Leadership ix 284 a; Militarism x 446–51; Morals x 643–49; Press xii 325–44; Pressures, Social xii 344–48; Propaganda xii 521–28; Publicity xii 698–701; Sanction, Social xiii 531–34.

Public Relations Counsels—Propaganda xii 526 b; Publicity xii 700 b.

Public Revenues—*see* REVENUES, PUBLIC.

PUBLIC UTILITIES—xii 674–87; Accounting i 408 b; Bargaining Power ii 460 b; Capitalization iii 209 a, 210 a; Commissions iv 38 a; Common Carrier iv 48–50; Compacts, Interstate iv 112 a; Corporation Taxes iv 432 b; Electric Power v 456–70; Electrical Manufacturing Industry v 470–77; Express Companies vi 27–31; Fair Return vi 56 b; Gas Industry vi 588–94; Govt. Owned Corporations vii 107 b; Govt. Ownership vii 113 b; Holding Companies vii 407 b; Interstate Commerce viii 223 b; Labor Disputes viii 635 b; Labor Turnover viii 710 b; Municipal Transit xi 118–28; Price Discrimination xii 352 b; Railroads xiii 74–100; Rate Regulation xiii 104–12; Telephone and Telegraph xiv 560–67; Valuation xv 216 a.

PUBLIC WELFARE—xii 687–90. *See* Classification of Articles (Public Welfare), p. 555. *See also* City iii 480 b; Economic Policy v 333–44; Expenditures, Public vi 8 b.

PUBLIC WORKS — xii 690–98; Bonding ii 633 a; Civic Art iii 492–95; Civic Centers iii 495–96; Construction Industry iv 262 b; Corvée iv 456 a; Engineering v 542 b; Forced Labor vi 341–46; Producers' Cooperation xii 460 b; Public Contracts xii 597 b; Public Debt xii 600 b; Roads xiii 400–11; Special Assessments xiv 276–79; Unemployment xv 161 b; Waterways, Inland xv 380 a.

PUBLICITY — xii 698–701; Law (Greek) ix 226 b; Press xii 325–44. *See also* ADVERTISING.

Publishing—*see* PRINTING AND PUBLISHING.

PUCHTA, G. F.—xii 702; Natural Law xi 289 b.

Puerperal Septicaemia—x 221 b.

PUFENDORF, S. VON—xii 702; Introd. Vol. I (The Rise of Liberalism) i 118 a; Equality of States v 581 a; Natural Law xi 288 a.

Pujo Investigation—xi 12 a.

PULITZER, J.—xii 703; Press xii 330 a, 334 b.

PULLMAN, G. M.—xii 704.

Pullman Strike—Debs v 31 b; Olney xi 466 b.

PULP AND PAPER INDUSTRY—xii 705–11; Introd. Vol. I (Greek Culture and Thought) i 39 a; Business, Govt. Services for iii 120 a; Forests vi 386 a.

PULSZKY, Á.—xii 711.

PUNISHMENT—xii 712–16; Attainder ii 304–05; Blood Vengeance Feud ii 598–99; Canon Law iii 183 a; Capital Punishment iii 192–95; Child (Delinquent) iii 406–09; Christianity iii 456 a; Commutation of Sentence iv 108–09; Confession iv 182 a; Corporal Punishment iv 411–13; Criminal Law iv 569–79; Criminology iv 584 b; Excommunication v 671–80; Exile v 686–90; Fines vi 249–52; Imprisonment vii 616–19; Indeterminate Sentence vii 650–52; Insanity viii 67 a; Intent, Criminal viii 129 b; Law (Primitive) ix 202 a, (Cuneiform) 214 b, (Germanic) 237 a, (Greek) 229 a, (Hellenistic and Greco-Egyptian) 234 b, (Jewish) 220 b, (Slavic) 244 b; Lynching ix 639–43; Ostracism xi 501–03; Outlawry xi 505–08; Pardon xi 570–72; Penal Institutions xii 57–64; Prison Labor xii 415–19; Probation and Parole xii 435–39; Recidivism xiii 159 a; Sanction, Social xiii 532 b; Transportation of Criminals xv 90–93.

Purchasing Power Parity — viii 31 b.

PURITANISM—xiii 3–6; Introd. Vol. I (The Rise of Liberalism) i 109 a; Art ii 224 b; Blue Laws ii 601 a; Bradford ii 672 a; Calvin iii 151 b; Christianity iii 458 b; Common Law iv 52 b, 55 b; Cotton iv 493 b; Cromwell iv 605 a; Edwards v 436 b; Free Love vi 434 b; Gambling vi 558 a; Judaism viii 441 a; Justice, Administration of viii 518 b; Leisure ix 404 a; Levellers ix 421 b; Mather x 227 b; Williams xv 424 b.

PUTNAM, F. W.—xiii 6.

PÜTTER, J. S.—xiii 7.

PUTTING OUT SYSTEM—xiii 7–11; Labor Movement viii 682 b; Large Scale Production ix 173 a; Leather Industries ix 306 b, 313 a; Occupation xi 427 b; Rural Industries xiii 467 b.

Puységur, Marquis de—x 355 b.

PYM, J.—xiii 11.

Quadruple Alliance—Holy Alliance vii 418 a.

QUAKERS—xiii 12–14; Corporal Punishment iv 413 a; Fox vi 406 b; Individualism vii 676 b; Mott xi 78 a; Passive Resistance and Non-cooperation xii 11 a; Religious Institutions (Protestant) xiii 271 a; Sects xiii 628 a.

Quantity Theory of Money—Money x 608 b; Price Stabilization xii 364 b; Prices (Theory) xii 371 a.

Quarantine—iv 67 a, 71 b.

QUARRYING—xiii 14–21; Mining Accidents x 508–13.

Quartiles—ii 337 b.

QUATREFAGES DE BRÉAU, J.-L. A. DE—xiii 21.

Quebec Act—iii 228 a.

QUENTAL, A. T. DE—xiii 21.

Index (Public Finance — Rationalism)

QUESNAY, F.—xiii 22; Distribution v 168 a; Dupont de Nemours v 283 b; Economics v 348 b; Increasing Returns vii 639 b.
Questions, Parliamentary — viii 219 a.
Quet Consumption Unit—Consumption iv 298 b; Cost of Living iv 480 b; Engel v 540 a; Family Budgets vi 74 b.
QUETELET, A.—xiii 23; Average ii 337 a; Census iii 296 a, 297 b; Criminology iv 588 b; Láng ix 151 a; Statistics xiv 357 a, 359 a, 366 a.
Quimby, P. P.—v 395 b.
QUINET, E.—xiii 24; Anticlericalism ii 113 b.
Quintilian—v 407 a.
Quota System, Immigration—vii 593 a.
Quota System, Tariff—xiv 518 b.

RABANUS MAURUS, M.—xiii 24.
RABELAIS, F.—xiii 25; Introd. Vol. I (Renaissance and Reformation) i 685 a.
Rabkrin—viii 259 a.
RACE—xiii 25–36; Introd. Vol. I (War and Reorientation) i 199 b; Adaptation i 436 b; Alcohol i 622 a, 624 b; Anthropology ii 75–76, 98 a; Anthropometry ii 111 a; Antisemitism ii 119 b, 122 a; Aristocracy ii 187 a; Aryans ii 264–65; Blumenbach ii 605 a; Caste iii 255 b; Chamberlain iii 322 b; Civilization iii 527 a; Degeneration v 57 a; Determinism v 113 a; Domestication v 208 a; Equality v 578 a; Ethnic Communities v 609 a; Finot vi 254 a; Genius vi 613 b; Gobineau vi 683 b; Heredity vii 333 b; Language ix 166 b; Le Bon ix 316 a; Man x 75 b; Mental Tests x 325 b; Nationalism xi 233 a; Negro Problem xi 335–56; Pan-movts. xi 544–54; Political Science xii 212 b; Race Conflict xiii 36–41; Race Mixture xiii 41–43; Ratzenhofer xiii 121 b; Waitz xv 321 a.
RACE CONFLICT—xiii 36–41; Aryans ii 264–65; Blood Accusation ii 597 a; Ethnocentrism v 613 b; Imperialism vii 610 a; Indian Question vii 663 b; Ku Klux Klan viii 606–09; Lynching ix 640 a; Native Policy xi 252–83; Negro Problem xi 335–56; Oriental Immigration xi 490–94; Reconstruction xiii 168–73; Segregation xiii 644 a; Slavery xiv 82 a; Venue xv 236 b.
RACE MIXTURE — xiii 41–43; Amalgamation ii 16–17; Concubinage iv 172 a; Heredity vii 332 a; Intermarriage viii 153 b; Migrations x 429 a; Miscegenation x 531–34; Negro Problem xi 336 a; Race xiii 25–36.
Race Prejudice—see RACE CONFLICT.

RACHEL, S.—xiii 43.
RACHFAHL, F.—xiii 44.
Racine, J. P.—xiv 607 b.
RACKETEERING—xiii 45–50; Brigandage ii 694 b; Extortion vi 41 a; Feuds vi 220 a; Gangs vi 565 a; Intimidation viii 241 b; Laundry and Dry Cleaning Industry ix 196 b; Liquor Industry ix 501 b; Mafia x 37 a; Prohibition xii 505 a.
RAČKI, F.—xiii 50.
Radcliffe-Brown, A. R.—Family vi 65 b; Kinship viii 570 a.
RADIĆ, S.—xiii 51.
RADICALISM—xiii 51–54; Assassination ii 273 b; Change, Social iii 333 b; Intellectuals viii 118 b; Intransigence viii 245 a; Opportunism xi 478 a; Philosophy xii 124 b; Revolution and Counter-revolution xiii 367–76; Youth Movements xv 516–21.
RADIO—xiii 54–67; Campaign, Political iii 164 b; Copyright iv 404 a; Debate, Parliamentary v 29 a; Police xii 186 b; Public Utilities (Eur.) xii 685 a; Telephone and Telegraph xiv 564 b.
RADISHCHEV, A. N.—xiii 67.
RADOWITZ, J. M. VON—xiii 67.
RAE, J.—xiii 68; Distribution v 171 b.
RAFFI, H. M. H.—xiii 69.
RAFFLES, T. S.—xiii 69.
Ragas—Music xi 152 b.
Rai, L. L.—see LAJPAT RAI, L.
RAIFFEISEN, F. W.—xiii 69; Agric. Credit i 533 b; Cooperation iv 373 b; Credit Coop. iv 554 b.
RAIKES, R.—xiii 70.
RAILROAD ACCIDENTS—xiii 71–74; Employers' Liability v 516 b.
Railroad Labor Board—xiii 96 a.
RAILROADS — xiii 74–100; Accounting i 408 b; Acworth i 429 a; Adams, C. F. (d. 1915) i 430 a; Adams, H. C. i 433 a; Arthur ii 261 b; Aviation (Industry) ii 365 b; Brassey ii 684 b; Brice ii 692 a; Commerce iv 10 b; Commercial Routes iv 23 a; Concessions iv 158 b; Customs Duties iv 670 a; Electric Power v 458 a; Eminent Domain v 494 a; Express Companies vi 27–31; Fink vi 252 b; Fisk vi 271 b; Fleming vi 280 a; Fortunes, Private vi 396 a; Gomel vi 696 a; Gould vii 5 b; Grain Elevators vii 137 b; Hadley vii 239 b; Harriman vii 272 a; Hill vii 350 a; Holding Companies vii 409 a; Hudson vii 528 b; Huntington vii 558 b; International Trade viii 191 a; Interstate Commerce Commission viii 229–36; Investment Banking viii 271 b; Kruttschnitt viii 606 a; Labor-Capital Cooperation viii 627 b; Land Grants (Brit. Empire) ix 38 b, (Lat. Amer.) 42 a, (U. S.) 35 a; Machinery, Industrial x 5 a; Mackenzie x 28 b; Meat Packing and Slaughtering (U.

S.) x 245 a; Morgan Family xi 11 b; Morrison xi 22 a; Motor Vehicle Transportation xi 75 a; Péreire xii 73 a; Price Discrimination xii 352 b; Price Regulation xii 359 b; Prouty xii 576 b; Pullman xii 704 a; Railroad Accidents xiii 71–74; Rate Regulation xiii 104 b, 107 a; Receivership xiii 149 b; Shipping xiv 40 b; Socialization xiv 222 a; Stanford xiv 325 a; Stephenson xiv 388 a; Sterne xiv 389 a; Stevens xiv 390 a; Terminals xiv 571–74; Trade Agreements xiv 669 a; Transit, International xv 79 a; Transportation xv 84 b; Valuation xv 216 a; Vanderbilt Family xv 227 a; Villard xv 259 b; War Economics xv 345 a; Warehousing xv 355 a; Waterways, Inland xv 379 b; Watkin xv 384 a; Westinghouse xv 405 a.
Raison d'État—see REASON OF STATE.
RAMABAI, P.—xiii 100.
Rāmakrishna—xv 270 a.
Ramazzini, B.—Industrial Hazards vii 698 a; Industrial Hygiene vii 705 b.
RAMBAUD, A.—xiii 100.
RAMSAY, G.—xiii 101.
Ramsay, J. A.—see DALHOUSIE, LORD.
RANADE, M. G.—xiii 101.
Ranade, R.—xiii 101 b.
Rand School of Social Science—xv 485 a.
RANKE, L. VON—xiii 102; Hauck vii 280 a; History and Historiography vii 376 b.
RANTOUL, R., JR.—xiii 103.
Rapid Transit—xi 124 a.
Rapin-Thoyras, P. de—see Thoyras, P. de.
Rapp, G.—iv 96 b.
RAŠÍN, A.—xiii 103.
Rate Making—Compensation and Liability Insurance iv 139 a.
RATE REGULATION—xiii 104–12; Accounting i 408 b; Adams i 433 a; Corporation Taxes iv 433 b; Due Process of Law v 267 b; Fair Return vi 56 b; Fink vi 252 b; Interstate Commerce Commission viii 230 a; Municipal Transit xi 119 a; Price Discrimination xii 352 b; Price Regulation xii 359 b; Public Utilities (U. S.) xii 681 b; Railroads xiii 85 b; Valuation xv 216 a; Water Supply xv 377 a; Waterways, Inland xv 380 b.
RATHENAU, W.—xiii 112; Mobilization and Demobilization x 560 a; National Economic Planning xi 200 b.
Ratichius—see RATKE, W.
Ratification of Treaties—xv 98 a.
RATIONALISM—xiii 113–17; Introd. Vol. I (The Rise of Liberalism) i 103–24, (The Revolutions) 127 a; Atheism

ii 292–96; Bury iii 79 a; Classicism iii 542–45; Common Sense iv 58–61; Copernicus iv 400 b; Cynics iv 680–85; Deism v 61–63; Descartes v 106 a; Encyclopédistes v 529 a; Enlightenment v 547–52; Epicureanism v 568 b; Equality v 576 b, 579 b; Ethics v 602–07; Fourier and Fourierism vi 402–04; Freethinkers vi 465–71; Higher Criticism vii 347 a; Hobbes vii 395 a; Human Nature vii 535 a; Liberalism ix 436 a; Logic ix 601 a; Mill, J. S. x 481 a; Natural Law xi 284–90; Natural Rights xi 299–302; Naturalism xi 302–05; Political Science xii 216 b; Technology xiv 554 a; Utilitarianism xv 197–200.

RATIONALIZATION — xiii 117–20; Bolshevism ii 627 b; Business Administration iii 88 b; Capitalism iii 198 a; Cartel iii 234–43; Coal Industry iii 591 a; Combinations, Industrial iii 664–74; Cost Accounting iv 475–78; Engineering v 546 a; Gosplan vi 705–13; Melchett x 304 a; Potash xii 275 b; Scientific Management xiii 603–08; Textile Industry xiv 594 a; Unemployment xv 157 b.

Rationing—Blockade ii 595 b; War Economics xv 345 b.

RATKE, W.—xiii 120.

Rattray, R. S.—vi 201 b.

RATZEL, F.—xiii 120; Climate iii 561 a; Geography vi 621 b; Semple xiii 661 b.

RATZENHOFER, G.—xiii 121; Sociology xiv 238 b.

Ratzenhofer, W.—i 169 a.

RATZINGER, G.—xiii 122.

RAU, K. H.—xiii 122; Economics v 373 b.

Ravanis, J. de—see Revigny, J. de.

RAVENSTONE, P.—xiii 122.

RAW MATERIALS—xiii 123–32; Backward Countries ii 380 a; Colonial Economic Policy iii 650 b; Colonies iii 659 b; Concessions iv 158 a; Cotton iv 486–93; Export Duties vi 21–23; Flax, Hemp and Jute vi 274–79; International Trade viii 192 a; Leather Industries ix 303 b; Location of Industry ix 590 b; Match Industry x 205 b; Metals x 364–89; Mining x 495–504; Nitrates xi 379–84; Oil Industry xi 438–51; Potash xii 274–77; Pulp and Paper Industry xii 705 b; Rubber xiii 453–61; Silk Industry xiv 54 a; Sugar xiv 450–55; Valorization xv 210–12; War Economics xv 343 b; Wool xv 476–82.

Rawlinson, G.—ii 163 b.

RAWLINSON, H. C.—xiii 132.

RAYMOND, D.—xiii 133.

RAYMOND, H. J.—xiii 133.

RAYMOND DE PENNAFORT—xiii 134.

RAYNAL, G. T. F.—xiii 134.

Rayon—Silk Industry xiv 55 b; Textile Industry xiv 588 b, 594 a.

REAL ESTATE—xiii 135–40; Home Ownership vii 431–34; House and Building Taxes vii 494–96; Income Tax vii 636 a; Land Mortgage Credit ix 43–53; Land Speculation ix 64–70; Land Valuation ix 137–39; Mortgage xi 32–38; Rent Regulation xiii 293–96; Servitudes xiv 3–7; Slums xiv 93–98; Valuation xv 213 a.

Real Estate Brokers—iii 9 b.

Real Estate Taxation—see PROPERTY TAX.

Real Property Limitation Act—ii 284 b.

REALISM—xiii 140–43; Art ii 227 b, 254 a; Materialism (Dialectical) x 213 a; Nationalism xi 246 b; Naturalism xi 305 a.

REASON OF STATE—xiii 143–44; Boccalini ii 612 a; Opportunism xi 477 a; Rationalism xiii 116 a; Statesmanship xiv 351 b.

REBELLION—xiii 144–47; Insurrection viii 116 b.

RECALL—xiii 147–49.

RECEIVERSHIP — xiii 149–53; Bankruptcy ii 452 b; Corporation Finance iv 430 a; Labor Injunction viii 654 a.

RECEPTION—xiii 153–57; Civil Law iii 505 a; Common Law iv 52 a; Conring iv 209 b; Corpus Juris Civilis iv 437 b; Glossators vi 682 a; Justice, Administration of viii 519 a; Law (Ancient) ix 206 a, (Germanic) 239 b, (Hindu) 261 b; Schwarzenberg xiii 588 b.

Rechabites—xiii 277 a.

RECIDIVISM—xiii 157–60; Bertillon ii 527 b; Penal Institutions xii 63 b.

Reciprocity — see COMMERCIAL TREATIES.

RECLAMATION—xiii 160–64; Agriculture, Govt. Services for i 602 b; Conservation iv 227–30; Land Grants (U. S.) ix 34 b; Land Tenure ix 116 a.

Reclus, E. M.—ii 694 b.

RECLUS, J. É.—xiii 164.

RECOGNITION, INTERNATIONAL—xiii 165–68; Civil War iii 525 a; De Facto Govt. v 53 a.

RECONSTRUCTION — xiii 168–73; Ku Klux Klan viii 606 b; Lincoln ix 487 b; Negro Problem xi 337 b; Stevens xiv 390 b; Sumner xiv 462 b.

RECORDS, HISTORICAL—xiii 173–76; Archaeology ii 163–67; Archives ii 176–81; Economic History v 327 a; Govt. Publications vii 120–22; History and Historiography vii 358 b, 363 b, (China) 383 a, (Islam) 381 b, (Japan) 384 b, (Mediaeval Eur.) 372 a, (Modern Eur.) 377 b; Law (Cuneiform) ix 213 a, (Egyptian) 209 b, (Greek) 225 a, (Hellenistic and Greco-Egyptian) 230 a; Prehistory xii 316–18; Statistics xiv 358 a.

RECREATION— xiii 176–81. See Classification of Articles (Recreation and Amusement), p. 555. See also Culture iv 643 a.

RED CROSS—xiii 181–86; Barton ii 471 b; Biggs ii 539 a; Child (Dependent) iii 402 b; Disaster Relief v 164 a; Dunant v 278 b; Health Centers vii 287 b; Health Education vii 290 b; Nursing xi 407 a, 409 b; Prisoners of War xii 421 b; Public Health xii 655 b; Warfare, Laws of xv 360 a, 363 b.

Red Flag Laws—xiii 638 b.

Red International of Labor Unions—Labor Movement viii 695 b; Trade Unions xv 54 a.

Redmond, J. E.—viii 293 a.

Redslob, R.—v 50 b.

REEVES, W. P.—xiii 186.

Referendum—see INITIATIVE AND REFERENDUM.

Refining—Metals x 373 a; Oil Industries xi 440 b; Potash xii 274 a; Sugar xiv 452 b.

Reforestation—Forests vi 385 b; Wood Industries xv 467 a.

REFORMATION—xiii 186–94; Introd. Vol. I (Renaissance and Reformation) i 93 b, (The Rise of Liberalism) 121 a; Calvin iii 151 b; Cranmer iv 543 b; Education v 410 a, 415 a; Holy Roman Empire vii 425 b; Humanism vii 540 b; Iconoclasm vii 567 a; Individualism vii 676 b; Jesuits viii 382 a; Knox viii 585 b; Literacy and Illiteracy ix 515 b; Luther ix 631 b; Melanchthon x 302 b; Messianism x 362 a; Mortmain xi 46 a; Münzer xi 136 b; Puritanism xiii 3 a; Religious Freedom xiii 241 b; Republicanism xiii 318 b; Sects xiii 626 b; Secularism xiii 633 a; Service xiii 673 b; Sleidan xiv 92 b; Social Contract xiv 127 b; Society xiv 227 b; Universities and Colleges xv 182 b; Zwingli xv 542 a.

Reformatories—see PENAL INSTITUTIONS.

REFORMISM—xiii 194–95; Clubs iii 575 a; Clubs, Political iii 579 b; Doctrinaire v 187–89; Fabianism vi 46–49; Human Nature vii 531–37; Humanitarianism vii 544–49; Labor Legislation and Law viii 658 a, 666 a; Machine, Political ix 660 b; Missions x 544 a; Opportunism xi 478 a; Poverty xii 291 a; Publicity xii 699 a; Quakers xiii 13 a; Social Christian Movements xiv 123–27; Social Work xiv 171 a; Utilitarianism xv 197–200; Utopia xv 200–03; Vested Interests xv 242 a. For biog.

Index (Rationalism — Representation)

references see Classification of Articles (Social Reform), p. 568.
REFRIGERATION — xiii 196–200; Fisheries vi 267 a; Food Industries vi 315 b; Fruit and Vegetable Industry vi 508 b; Meat Packing and Slaughtering x 245 a, 249 b.
REFUGEES—xiii 200–05; Passport xii 16 a.
REGIONAL PLANNING—xiii 205–08; Administrative Areas i 450–52; Agriculture i 598 b; Garden Cities vi 569–71; Housing (U. S.) vii 515 b; Metropolitan Areas x 396–401.
REGIONALISM—xiii 208–18; Introd. Vol. I (War and Reorientation) i 198 a; Administrative Areas i 450–52; Autonomy ii 332–36; Bloc, Parliamentary ii 592 b; Compacts, Interstate iv 111 b; Dialect v 123–26; Federalism vi 172 a; Frontier vi 505 a; Geography vi 622 a, 625 b; Gosplan vi 710 a; Govt. (Soviet Russia) vii 68 b; National Income xi 215 b; Nationalism xi 234 a; Parties, Political (U. S.) xi 598 a; States' Rights xiv 346 b.
Registration—Census iii 295–300; Merchantmen, Status of x 350 a; Mortality xi 23 a; Statistics xiv 358 b; Trademarks and Names xv 59 a.
Registration of Titles—ix 130 a.
REGISTRATION OF VOTERS—xiii 218–21; Absent-Voting i 376; Elections v 454 a.
REHABILITATION — xiii 221–25; American Legion ii 32 a; Begging ii 495 a; Blind ii 590 a; Cripples iv 592–95; Social Work (Case Work) xiv 173–83; Vagrancy xv 207 a; Veterans xv 244 a.
REICHENSPERGER, A. *and* P. F.—xiii 225.
Reichsbank—vi 238 b.
Reichskammergericht—iv 525 a.
Reichsrat—ix 382 b.
Reichstag—ix 380 b.
REID, W.—xiii 225.
REIMARUS, H. S.—xiii 226; Lessing ix 418 b.
REINACH, S.—xiii 227.
REINACH, T.—xiii 228.
Reinsurance—Fire Insurance vi 258 a; Insurance viii 103 a.
RELIGION—xiii 228–39. *See* Classification of Articles (Religion), p. 555. *See also* Introd. Vol. I (Greek Culture and Thought) i 17 b, 34 a, (Renaissance and Reformation) 93 b, (The Social Sciences as Disciplines, France) 253 a; Amusements, Public ii 40 b; Anthropology ii 94 a, 101 b; Aristocracy ii 186 a; Art (Egyptian) ii 238 b, (Greek) 241 a, (Indian) 230 a, (Japanese) 236 b, (Mediaeval) 243–45; Begging ii 493 b; Belief ii 501 b; Charity iii 340 b;

Chateaubriand iii 358 b; Crime iv 563 b; Criminal Law iv 571 a; Culture iv 641 a; Dance iv 702 a; Duty v 293 a; Enlightenment v 550 b; Ethnic Communities v 609 b; Evolution, Social v 658 b, 660 a; Frontier vi 505 b; Guyau vii 229 b; Herbert of Cherbury vii 326 a; Holbach vii 401 b; Imperial Unity vii 602 a; Individualism vii 676 a; Intermarriage viii 152 a; Labor Movement viii 687 a; Lang ix 150 b; Law (Japanese) ix 254 b; Masonry x 179 b; Mass Expulsion x 186 b; Morals x 646 a, 647 b; Nationalism xi 236 a; Panmovements xi 545 a, 551 a; Prostitution xii 553 a; Rationalism xiii 115 a; Ritual xiii 396 b; Russian Revolution xiii 475 b; Sanction, Social xiii 531 b; Science xiii 595 a; Sex Education and Sex Ethics xiv 8 b; Suicide xiv 456 a; Totemism xiv 659 a; Tradition xv 63 a; War xv 334 b; Weber xv 387 b; Woman, Position in Society (Primitive) xv 441 b. *See also* Church. *For further biog. references see* Classification of Articles (Religion), p. 567 *and* (History—Religious), p. 562.
Religious Education—Chautauqua iii 359–60; Civic Education iii 496 b; Education (Sectarian) v 421–25.
RELIGIOUS FREEDOM—xiii 239–46; Introd. Vol. I (Greek Culture and Thought) i 17 b, (Renaissance and Reformation) 94 b, (The Rise of Liberalism) 103–24; Academic Freedom i 385 a; Catholic Emancipation iii 269–71; Charitable Trusts iii 339 a; Enlightenment v 551 a; Jewish Emancipation viii 394–99; Monarchomachs x 577–78; Mysticism xi 178 a; Penn xii 65 a; Puritanism xiii 3–6; Quakers xiii 12 a; Reformation xiii 186–94; Refugees xiii 201 b; Religious Institutions (Roman Catholic) xiii 260 b; Social Contract xiv 128 a; Status xiv 376 b; Williams xv 424 b.
RELIGIOUS INSTITUTIONS, CHRISTIAN — xiii 246–76 (Roman Catholic 246–62, 273, Byzantine 262–65, 275, Russian 265–67, 275, Protestant 267–72, 274). *See* Church.
RELIGIOUS ORDERS—xiii 276–78; Chivalry iii 438 b, 442 a; Dominican Friars v 210–11; Franciscan Movement vi 410–15; Hospitals and Sanatoria vii 465 a; Jesuits viii 381–89; Military Orders x 459–64; Monasticism x 584–90; Nursing xi 405 b; Records, Historical xiii 175 b.
Religious Revivals—*see* REVIVALS, RELIGIOUS.

Remedial Loan Societies — xii 38 b.
RENAISSANCE—xiii 278–85; Introd. Vol. I (Renaissance and Reformation) i 84 a; Architecture ii 171 b; Art (Renaissance) ii 246–53; Assassination ii 273 a; Bodin ii 614 b; Burckhardt iii 69 a; Child (Welfare) iii 376 a; Civic Art iii 492 b; Classicism iii 543 a; Communism iv 84 b; Criticism, Social iv 600 b; Education v 409 a; Furniture vi 538 a; Gebhart vi 599 a; Humanism vii 537 a; Invention viii 248 b; Justice viii 511 a; Music xi 158 b; Primitivism xii 400 a; Printing and Publishing xii 408 b; Rationalism xiii 115 b; Reformation xiii 188 a; Science xiii 598 a; Symonds xiv 495 b; Theater xiv 605 b; Universities and Colleges xv 182 b.
RENAN, E. — xiii 285; Antisemitism ii 122 a.
RENAUDOT, T.—xiii 287.
RENAULT, L.—xiii 287.
Renner, K.—x 521 a.
RENOUVIER, C. B.—xiii 288; James viii 368 b.
Renouvin, P.—xv 495 b.
RENT — xiii 289–92; Absentee Ownership i 376–78; Anderson ii 56 a; Cost iv 471 a; Diminishing Returns iv 145 a; Distribution v 167–74; Economics (Classical School) v 354 b, (Cambridge School) 370 a; Fabianism vi 46 b; George vi 630 b; Jones viii 415 b; Land Taxation ix 71 b; Land Valuation ix 137 a; Location of Industry ix 587 a; Profit xii 480–87; Rent Charge xiii 292; Rent Regulation xiii 293–96; Rodbertus xiii 415 a; Single Tax xiv 64 b; Unearned Increment xv 144 a.
RENT CHARGE—xiii 292.
RENT REGULATION—xiii 293–96; Housing (Eur.) vii 502–11, (U. S.) 514 b.
Rentenbank, German— ix 31 b.
RENTENMARK—xiii 296; Helfferich vii 318 b; Land Bank Schemes ix 31 b.
RENTIER—xiii 296–300; Interest viii 142 b; Landed Estates ix 141 a; Stabilization, Economic xiv 310 b.
Renvoi—Conflict of Laws iv 189 b; Lainé ix 15 b.
REPARATIONS—xiii 300–08; Central Banking iii 306 b; Indemnity, Military vii 643 b; International Trade (Theory) viii 204 b; Loans, Intergovernmental ix 559 a.
REPGOW, E. VON—xiii 308.
Replacement Insurance—vi 262 a.
REPRESENTATION—xiii 309–15. *See* Classification of Articles (Representation), p. 555. *See also* Althusius ii 13 b; Census iii

296 b; Democracy v 79 a; Dictatorship v 134 b; Estates General v 597–600; Govt. (Belgium) vii 47 b, (Italy) 49 b, 51 b, (Russia, Imperial) 65 b, (Russia, Soviet) 68 b; Interests viii 144 a; Legislation ix 348 a; Legislative Assemblies (Hist. and Theory) ix 359 a, (Switzerland) 384 b, (U. S.) 361 b, 367 b; Parties, Political xi 590–639.

Representation, Functional—see FUNCTIONAL REPRESENTATION.

Representation, Proportional — see PROPORTIONAL REPRESENTATION.

REPRISALS—xiii 315–17; Intervention viii 236 b; Prisoners of War xii 421 a; Privateering xii 422 a; Sanction, International xiii 529 b.

Republican Party, U. S.—Abolition i 371 a; Agrarian Movements (U. S.) i 510 a; Hay vii 284 b; Negro Problem xi 338 a; Parties, Political (U. S.) xi 598 b; Philippine Problem xii 110 b; Raymond xiii 133 b; Reconstruction xiii 169 a.

REPUBLICANISM—xiii 317–21; Introd. Vol. I (The Roman World) i 44 b, 50 a; Carbonari iii 220–23; Succession, Political xiv 442 b. See also DEMOCRACY.

REPUDIATION OF PUBLIC DEBTS—xiii 321–24; Public Debt xii 609 a.

REQUISITIONS, MILITARY — xiii 324–26; Angary ii 59–60; Indemnity, Military vii 641 a.

RESALE PRICE MAINTENANCE—xiii 326–30.

RESEARCH—xiii 330–34; Introd. Vol. I (The Social Sciences as Disciplines, Germany) i 262 b, (Gt. Brit.) 245 b, (Hungary) 272 a, (Lat. Amer.) 219 a, (Russia) 289 b, (Scandinavia) 293 b, (U. S.) 347 b; Academic Freedom i 384–88; Agric. Economics i 534–38; Agric. Education i 538–42; Agric. Experiment Stations i 542–44; Alchemy i 616–18; Chemical Industries iii 365–67; Civic Organizations iii 499 b; Combinations, Industrial iii 669 b; Communicable Diseases, Control of iv 68 a; Comparative Psychology iv 129–31; Economic History v 315–30; Endowments and Foundations v 535 a; Freethinkers vi 468 a; Higher Criticism vii 347–49; History and Historiography vii 357–68, (China) 384 a, (Modern Eur.) 374–81, (U. S.) 388 b; Laundry and Dry Cleaning Industry ix 193 b; Learned Societies ix 298 b; Method, Scientific x 389–96; Museums and Exhibitions xi 139 a.

Reservations, Indian—xi 262 b.

Reserve Officers' Training Corps—x 470 b.

Reserved Powers, Doctrine of—ix 422 a.

Reserves, Banking—see BANK RESERVES.

RESORTS—xiii 334–36.
RESTAURANTS—xiii 336–39.
RESTRAINT OF TRADE—xiii 339–42; Bargaining Power ii 460 b; Labor Legislation and Law viii 670 b.

Resulting Trust—xv 125 b.
RETAIL CREDIT—xiii 342–46.
RETAIL TRADE—xiii 346–55; Consumers' Cooperation iv 285–91; Food Industries (Grocery Trade) vi 313 b, (Food Distribution, U. S.) 318 a, (W. Eur.) 321 b, (Russia) 328 b; Furniture vi 541 a; Instalment Selling viii 74–81; Marketing x 136 b; Middleman x 415–17; Resale Price Maintenance xiii 326–30; Retail Credit xiii 342–46; Wholesaling xv 411–17.

Retaliation—Law (Primitive) ix 203 b; Reprisals xiii 315 b; Sanction, Social xiii 533 a; Tariff xiv 516 b.

Retorsion—xiii 315 b.
RETROACTIVE LEGISLATION—xiii 355–57.
RETZIUS, A. A.—xiii 357.
REUTER, BARON VON—xiii 357.
REVENUE FARMING—xiii 358–60; Introd. Vol. I (The Roman World) i 44 b; Aids i 609 a; Alcabala i 616 a; Feudalism (Moslem) vi 210 b; Fortunes, Private vi 390 a; Land Tenure (India) ix 110 b; Latifundia ix 187 b.

REVENUES, PUBLIC—xiii 360–63; Aids i 608–10; Budget iii 38–44; Coinage iii 622–25; Customs Duties iv 668 a; Excise v 669–71; Export Duties vi 22 a; Financial Administration vi 234–41; Fines vi 251 b; Franking vi 419 b; Gasoline Tax vi 595–96; Income Tax vii 626 b; Local Finance ix 570 a; Lotteries ix 611–16; Monopolies, Public x 619–23; Municipal Finance xi 99 b; Public Finance xii 640 a; Revenue Farming xiii 358–60; Roads xiii 408 b; Special Assessments xiv 276–79; Taxation xiv 531–41; Tribute xv 102–04; War Finance xv 350 a.

Revigny, J. de—iii 680 a.
REVILLAGIGEDO, CONDE DE—xiii 363.
Revisionism (Socialism) — Economics (Socialist Economics) v 380 a; Socialism xiv 203 a; Socialist Parties xiv 215 b; Syndicalism xiv 497 a.

REVIVALS, RELIGIOUS—xiii 363–67; Edwards v 436 b; Sects xiii 629 a.

REVOLUTION AND COUNTER-REVOLUTION—xiii 367–76. See Classification of Articles (Civil Opposition), p. 549. See also Bakunin ii 393 b; Blanqui ii 584 b; Chateaubriand iii 358 b; Chinese Problem iii 434 a; Class Struggle iii 541 a; Evolution, Social v 660 b; Faction vi 50 a; Ferrari vi 186 b; Freedom of Association vi 449 b; Intellectuals viii 118 b; Labor Movement viii 692 b; Marx x 173 b; Masses x 199 a; Military Desertion x 453 a; Proletariat xii 516 b; Reformism xiii 194 b; Sorel xiv 262 b; Spoils System xiv 302 b; Traditionalism xv 67–70; Ulyanov xv 140 b.

Revolutionary Syndicalism—see SYNDICALISM.

Reyher, A.—v 589 a.
Rhabanus—see RABANUS MAURUS, M.
RHETT, R. B.—xiii 376.
RHIGAS, K.—xiii 376.
RHODES, C. J.—xiii 377; Fortunes, Private vi 395 a.
RHODES, J. F.—xiii 377; History and Historiography vii 388 a.
Rhodesian Man—x 74 b.
Rhodian Sea Law—x 122 a.
Rhys Davids, T. W.—see DAVIDS, T. W. R.
RICARDO, D.—xiii 378; Introd. Vol. I (Individualism and Capitalism) i 154 b; Abstinence i 382 a; Barton ii 472 a; Baumstark ii 481 b; Capital iii 188 b; Capital Levy iii 190 b; Cost iv 467 b; Diminishing Returns v 145 a; Distribution v 168 b; Economics v 351–57; Exploitation vi 16 a; Fabianism vi 46 b; International Trade (Theory) viii 201 b; Malthus x 69 a; Price Stabilization xii 362 b; Rent xiii 290 b; Socialism xiv 195 b; Unearned Increment xv 144 a.

RICCA-SALERNO, G.—xiii 379.
RICCI, M.—xiii 380.
Riccioli, G. B.—Census iii 295 a; Population xii 241 a.
Riccobono, S.—xiii 425 b.
RICHARD, H.—xiii 380; Peace Movements xii 44 a.
RICHELIEU, A.-J. DU P. DE—xiii 381; Introd. Vol. I (The Rise of Liberalism) i 115 a; Local Govt. ix 575 a; Press xii 326 a; Roads xiii 402 b.

RICHMOND, M. E.—xiii 382; Social Work xiv 174 a.
Richter, C. P.—i 621 a.
RICHTER, E.—xiii 382.
RICHTER, J. P. F.—xiii 383.
Rickert, H.—vi 601 a.
RIDGEWAY, W.—xiii 383.
RIDOLFI, C.—xiii 384.
RIEGER, F. L.—xiii 384.
RIEHL, W. H.—xiii 385.
RIESSER, G.—xiii 385.
Rigdon, S.—xi 15 a.
Rignano, E.—viii 47 a.

Rigsbank, Danish—ix 31 a.
Riksdag—ix 387 a.
RIOT—xiii 386–92; Martial Law x 162 b.
Riparian Rights — see WATER LAW.
Ripley, G.—Brook Farm iii 13 b; Transcendentalism xv 76 b.
Riquetti, H. G.—see MIRABEAU, COMTE DE.
Riquetti, V. — see MIRABEAU, MARQUIS DE.
RISK—xiii 392–94; Entrepreneur v 558–60; Fashion vi 142 b; Hedging vii 305–07; Insurance viii 95–113; Interest viii 141 a; Investment Banking viii 274 a; Joint Stock Company viii 412 b; Middleman x 416 a; Profit xii 483 b; Speculation xiv 288–93.
Rist, C.—vi 364 a.
RITCHIE, D. G.—xiii 394.
RITTER, K.—xiii 395; Climate iii 561 a; Geography vi 621 a.
RITTER, M.—xiii 395.
RITUAL—xiii 396–98; Agriculture (Primitive) i 574 a; Anthropology ii 96 b; Birth Customs ii 566 b; Brahmanism and Hinduism ii 675 a; Ceremony iii 313–16; Cults iv 618–21; Death Customs v 21–27; Etiquette v 615–17; Famine vi 87 b; Fasting vi 144–46; Fertility Rites vi 190–92; Festivals vi 198–201; Fictions vi 227 b; Holidays vii 413 a; Iconoclasm vii 567 b; Initiation viii 49–50; Islam viii 337 a; Journeymen's Societies viii 425 b; Judaism viii 434 a; Law (Primitive) ix 202 b; Marriage x 151 a; Masonry x 179 a; Mysteries xi 172–75; Procedure, Legal xii 440 a; Religion xiii 235 b; Sacrifice xiii 501–03; Secret Societies xiii 622 a.
Ritual Murder Accusation—see BLOOD ACCUSATION.
RIVADAVIA, B.—xiii 398; Introd. Vol. I (The Social Sciences as Disciplines, Lat. Amer.) i 305 a; Land Grants (Lat. Amer.) ix 42 a.
Rivera, P. de—ix 392 b.
RIVERS, W. H. R.—xiii 398; Introd. Vol. I (The Trend to Internationalism) i 185 a; Assimilation, Social ii 282 b; Diffusionism v 141 b; Folklore vi 290 a; Gerontocracy vi 637 b; Kinship viii 570 b.
RIVIER, A.-P.-O.—xiii 399.
ROADS—xiii 400–11; Introd. Vol. I (The Roman World) i 56 a; Corvée iv 456 a; Eminent Domain v 494 b; Gasoline Tax vi 595–96; McAdam ix 645 b; Motor Vehicle Accidents xi 71 a; Public Works xii 691 b; Quarrying xiii 14 b; Railroad Accidents xiii 72 a; Transportation xv 82 b, 86 b.
Robert, C.—xii 488 a.

Robertson, D. H.—viii 29 b.
ROBERTSON, J. M.—xiii 411.
ROBERTSON, W.—xiii 412; Introd. Vol. I (The Rise of Liberalism) i 120 a.
ROBERTY, E. DE—xiii 412; Sociology xiv 239 a.
ROBESPIERRE, M.—xiii 413; Introd. Vol. I (The Revolutions) i 132 b; French Revolution vi 478 a.
Robinson, J. H.—Introd. Vol. I (The Trend to Internationalism) i 187 b, (War and Reorientation) 223 a.
Rochdale Pioneers—Anarchism ii 48 b; Consumers' Cooperation iv 286 a; Cooperation iv 363 b.
Rockefeller, J. D.—v 533 b.
Rockefeller Foundation — xii 655 b.
RODBERTUS, J. K.—xiii 414; Distribution v 170 a; Economics v 383 a; Labor Exchange Banks viii 641 b; Price Stabilization xii 363 a; Socialism xiv 196 b.
Rodin, A.—ii 255 a.
RODÓ, J. E.—xiii 416.
Rodriguez Francia, J. G.—see FRANCIA, J. G. R.
Roebuck, A. C.—xiii 350 b.
ROGERS, J. E. T.—xiii 417; Black Death ii 574 b; Economic History v 318 a; Gibbins vi 652 b; Wages xv 306 b.
ROHDE, E.—xiii 417.
Roland, Madame—see ROLAND DE LA PLATIÈRE, M. J.
ROLAND DE LA PLATIÈRE, M. J.—xiii 418.
Rolland, R.—xii 47 a.
Rolls of Oléron—x 123 a.
ROMAGNOSI, G. D.—xiii 419.
Roman Catholic Church — Religious Institutions (Roman Catholic) xiii 246–62.
Roman Curia—see Curia, Roman.
Roman Empire—Introd. Vol. I (The Roman World) i 42–60, (The Universal Church) 61 a; Augustus ii 315 b; Empire v 504 b; War xv 332 b.
ROMAN LAW—xiii 419–26; Introd. Vol. I (The Roman World) i 47 a, (The Universal Church) 69 a; Accursius i 418 b; Agustín i 607 b; Alciati i 618 a; Bailment ii 389 a; Bruns iii 20 b; Budé iii 38 b; Child (Delinquent) iii 407 a; Civil Law iii 502–09; Code Civil iii 605 a; Codification iii 607 a; Commentators iii 679–81; Commercial Law iv 14 b; Common Law iv 51 b; Confiscation iv 183 b; Conflict of Laws iv 187 b; Conrat (Cohn) iv 208 b; Consideration iv 235 b; Contract iv 325 b; Corpus Juris Civilis iv 435–38; Criminal Law iv 571 b; Cujas iv 617 a; Domat v 194 a; Doneau v 216 a; Douaren v 221 b; Eisele v 447 b; Equity v 583 a; Family Law vi 81 b; Favre vi 152 b; Gaius vi

544 b; Gambling vi 559 a; Gifts vi 658–61; Girard vi 667 a; Glossators vi 679–82; Gouvêa vii 7 b; Guardianship vii 192 b; Intent, Criminal viii 126 b; Judgments viii 442 b; Jus Gentium viii 502–04; Just Price viii 504 b; Labor Legislation and Law viii 672 b; Land Transfer ix 128 b; Landlord and Tenant ix 143 b; Law (Ancient) ix 206 a, (Germanic) 239 a; Law Merchant ix 271 a; Legal Profession and Legal Education ix 325 b, 335 a; Lese Majesty ix 415 a; Maine x 49 b; Mining Law x 515 a; Mitteis x 550 b; Mommsen x 577 a; Negligence xi 328 b; Ownership and Possession xi 521 b, 523 b; Procedure, Legal xii 440 b; Reception xiii 153–57; Specific Performance xiv 287 a; Stoicism xiv 409 a; Succession, Laws of xiv 436 a; Suretyship and Guaranty xiv 482 b; Tort xiv 656 a; Treason xv 93 b; Water Law xv 369 a. See also LAW.
Romantic Economics—v 385–87.
ROMANTICISM—xiii 426–34; Introd. Vol. I (The Revolutions) i 127 a; Art ii 253 b; Classicism iii 544 a; Diabolism v 121 b; Dialect v 125 a; Economics (Socio-Ethical Economics) v 381 a, (Romantic Economics) 385 a; History and Historiography vii 376 a; Literature ix 530 a; Müller xi 80 a; National Socialism, German xi 225 a; Nationalism xi 242 b; Novalis xi 401 a; Primitivism xii 398–402; Schlegel xiii 571 a; Social Organism xiv 138 b; Traditionalism xv 69 a.
ROMILLY, S.—xiii 434.
RONCALI, A.—xiii 435.
Rooming House—ix 596 a.
Roos, C. F.—v 367 b.
ROOSEVELT, T.—xiii 435; Central American Federation iii 302 a; Monroe Doctrine x 632 a; Panama Canal xi 555 b; Publicity xii 699 a.
Root, E.—Amer. Law Institute ii 30 a; Arbitration, International ii 158 a.
Röpke, W.—xiii 549 a.
ROSAS, J. M. DE—xiii 436; Lamas ix 23 a; Land Grants ix 42 a.
ROSCHER, W. G. F.—xiii 437; Economics v 371–77; Location of Industry ix 585 b.
Rosenberg, A.—xi 225 b.
ROSENWALD, J.—xiii 438; Endowments and Foundations v 536 a.
ROSMINI-SERBATI, A.—xiii 438.
Ross, E. A.—Belief ii 501 b; Imitation vii 587 a; Social Psychology xiv 153 b.
Rossi, C.—x 230 b.
ROSSI, G. B. DE—xiii 439.
ROSSI, P. L. E.—xiii 439.

Encyclopaedia of the Social Sciences

Rössler, C.—xiii 440.
Rotation in Office—xiv 303 a.
Rothermere, Lord—xii 333 b.
Rothschild Family—xiii 440; Banking, Commercial ii 426 b; Fortunes, Private vi 394 a.
Rotteck, K. W. R. von—xiii 442.
Rotten Boroughs—xiii 443–44; Gerrymander vi 639 a.
Rougé, O. C. E. de—xiii 444.
Round, J. H.—xiii 444.
Round Table Conferences—Indian Question vii 669 b, 671 a.
Rousseau, J.-J.—xiii 445; Introd. Vol. I (The Rise of Liberalism) i 114 a, (The Revolutions) 130 a, (Individualism and Capitalism) 150 a; Absolutism i 381 a; Bicameral System ii 535 a; Child (Welfare) iii 376 a, (Psychology) 391 a; Declaration of the Rights of Man and the Citizen v 50 a; Education v 413 a; Enlightenment v 549 b; Force, Political vi 340 b; Freedom of Association vi 449 a; Humanism vii 541 b; Justice viii 511 a; Natural Law xi 288 a; Natural Rights xi 300 b; Naturalism xi 304 b; Preschool Education xii 321 b; Prisoners of War xii 420 a; Representation xiii 311 b; Republicanism xiii 319 b; Romanticism xiii 428 b; Social Contract xiv 130 a; Socialism xiv 192 b; Society xiv 230 a; Sovereignty xiv 267 a.
Rouvroy, C.-H. de—see Saint-Simon and Saint-Simonianism.
Rouvroy, L. de—see Saint-Simon, Duc de.
Rowan Formula—viii 679 a.
Rowntree, B. S.—vi 75 a.
Roy, R. M.—xiii 447.
Royal Canadian Mounted Police—xii 188 a.
Royal Court—xiii 448–51; Art (French) ii 248 b, (Indian) 231 b, 232 a; Dance iv 705 b; Nobility xi 385–89.
Royal Dutch-Shell—xi 448 a.
Royal Mail Lines, Ltd.—xiv 39 a.
Royal Society—xii 104 b.
Royce, J.—xiii 451.
Royer-Collard, P. P.—xiii 452; Doctrinaire v 187 b.
Rubber—xiii 453–61; Business, Govt. Services for iii 120 a; Concessions iv 158 b; Raw Materials xiii 130 b.
Rubens, P. P.—ii 251 b.
Rubin, M.—xiii 461.
Ruffin, E.—xiii 461.
Ruffini, F.—xiii 462.
Rufinus—iii 465 b.
Ruge, A.—xiii 462.
Ruhr Occupation—xiii 302 a.
Rule of Certainty—iv 575 a.
Rule of Law—xiii 463–66; Introd. Vol. I (Greek Culture and Thought) i 18 b, (The Growth of Autonomy) 77 a; Common Law iv 55 a; Constitutionalism iv 255–59; Due Process of Law v 264–68; Force, Political vi 340 b; Judicial Process viii 450–57; Shang Yang xiv 16 a; State Liability xiv 338–43.
Rule of St. Benedict—ii 510 b.
Rule of Warranty—iii 280 b.
Rümelin, G.—xiii 466.
Runkle, J. D.—x 104 a.
Runrig System—ix 89 b.
Rural Exodus—see Urbanization.
Rural Industries—xiii 466–69; Handicraft vii 257 a, 259 a.
Rural Society—xiii 469–71; Agrarian Movements i 489–92; Agric. Fairs i 544–45; Agric. Labor i 550 b; Automobile Industry ii 329 a; Chautauqua iii 360 a; City iii 479 a; Country Life Movement iv 497–99; Dry Farming v 256 a; Farm Tenancy vi 122 a, 126 b; Farmers' Organizations vi 129–32; Folk High Schools vi 286 b; Fundamentalism vi 527 a; Haxthausen vii 283 b; Hospitals and Sanatoria vii 471 b; Housing (U. S.) vii 512 a; Peasantry xii 48–53; Poverty xii 288 a; Prohibition xii 504 a; Public Health xii 652 a; Rural Industries xiii 466–69; Social Work (Case Work) xiv 180 a; Village Community xv 253–59; Women's Organizations xv 464 b.
Rush, B.—xiii 471.
Ruskin College—xv 484 a.
Ruskin Commonwealth—iv 100 b.
Ruskin, J.—xiii 472; Introd. Vol. I (Individualism and Capitalism) i 155 b; Economics v 381 b.
Russell, B.—Companionate Marriage iv 115 a; Consciousness iv 214 b; Realism xiii 142 a.
Russell, H. H.—ii 118 a.
Russell, J.—xiii 473.
Russell Sage Foundation—xiv 163 b.
Russian Church—Religious Institutions (Russian) xiii 265–67; Sects xiii 630 a.
Russian Revolution—xiii 474–93; Agrarian Movements (Russia) i 506 b; Antisemitism ii 122 b, 124 b; Axelrod ii 370 b; Bolshevism ii 623–30; Chaykovsky iii 362 a; Communist Parties iv 88 b; Cossacks iv 466 b; Gosplan vi 705–13; Govt. (Soviet Russia) vii 67–70; Labor Parties (Gt. Brit.) viii 701 a; Land Tenure (Russia) ix 109 b; Machajski ix 654 a; Martov x 171 a; Masses x 196 b; Morozov xi 20 a; Nihilism xi 378 b; Plekhanov xii 168 b; Pokrovsky xii 181 a; Refugees xiii 203 a; Religious Institutions (Russian) xiii 266 b; Socialism xiv 205 a, 206 b; Socialist Parties xiv 217 b; Soviet xiv 269 b; Terrorism xiv 578 a; Ulyanov xv 140 b.
Ruthenberg, C. E.—xiii 493.
Rutherford, S.—xiii 493.
Ryan, T. F.—xiii 494.
Ryotwari System—xi 134 b.

S. A.—see Sturm-Abteilungen.
S. S.—see Schutz-Staffeln.
Sabatier, P.—xiii 495.
Sabotage—xiii 495–97; Criminal Syndicalism iv 582–84.
Sacco, N.—vii 554 a.
Sachsenspiegel—xiii 308 b.
Sacred Books—xiii 497–501; Freethinkers vi 468 a; Fundamentalism vi 526–27; Higher Criticism vii 347–49; History and Historiography vii 368 a; Islam viii 333 a; Islamic Law viii 345 a; Jihad viii 401 b; Judaism viii 431 a, 440 b; Law (Jewish) ix 219–25; Literacy and Illiteracy ix 515 b; Maimonides x 48 a; Religious Institutions (Protestant) xiii 267 b; Smith xiv 117 a; Tradition xv 63 a.
Sacrifice—xiii 501–03; Blood Accusation ii 597–98; Fasting vi 144 b.
Sacrilege—see Blasphemy.
Saddlery—ix 311 a.
Sadducees—Law (Jewish) ix 221 a.
Šafařík, P. J.—xiii 503.
Safety Movement—xiii 503–06; Accidents i 391 a; Accidents, Industrial i 400 a; Building Regulations iii 52–57; Casualty Insurance iii 264 a; Industrial Hazards vii 702 b; Industrial Hygiene vii 707–10; Labor, Govt. Services for viii 646 a; Labor Legislation and Law viii 663 a; Match Industry x 204 a; Mining Accidents x 512 a; Motor Vehicle Accidents xi 71 b; Railroad Accidents xiii 71–74; Traffic Regulation xv 70–75.
Sagra y Périz, R. D. de la—xiii 506.
Sainte-Beuve, C. A.—xiii 507.
St. John, H.—see Bolingbroke, Lord.
Saint-Just, L. A. L.—i 132 b.
St. Lawrence Waterway Project—xv 381 b.
Saint-Pierre, C. I. C. de—xiii 507.
Saint-Simon, Comte de—see Saint-Simon and Saint-Simonianism.
Saint-Simon, Duc de—xiii 508.
Saint-Simon and Saint-Simonianism—xiii 509; Introd. Vol. I (The Rise of Liberalism) i 117 a; (Individualism and Capitalism) 156 a; Bazard ii 484 b; Boissel ii 620 b; Economic History v 317 a; Economics v 377 b; Enfantin v 539 a; Heine vii 315 b; Lamas ix 23 a; Lemonnier ix 407 a; Leroux ix 413 b; Péreire xii 73 a; Romanticism xiii 430 b; Socialism xiv 194 a.
Saladin—iii 442 a.

Index (Rössler — Schwarzenberg)

Salaries—*see* WAGES.
SALEILLES, R.—xiii 511.
SALES—xiii 511–16; Caveat Emptor iii 280–82; Frauds, Statute of vi 429–30; Law (Cuneiform) ix 217 a, (Hellenistic and Greco-Egyptian) 232 a; Specific Performance xiv 286 b.
SALES TAX—xiii 516–19; Alcabala i 615–16; Business Taxes iii 123 a.
Salesian Order—ii 646 a.
SALESMANSHIP—xiii 519–21; Advertising i 469–75; Proselytism xii 551 b.
Salillas, R.—iv 588 b.
SALISBURY, LORD—xiii 521; Archives ii 178 a; Peace Movements xii 44 b.
SALMON, T. W.—xiii 522; Mental Hygiene x 321 a.
Salomon, O.—x 103 b.
Salon—Amateur ii 19 a; Revolution and Counter-revolution xiii 369 b.
Saloon—Liquor Industry ix 499 b; Liquor Traffic ix 505 b; Prohibition xii 501 b.
SALT—xiii 522–26.
SALT, T.—xiii 526.
Saltaire—xiii 526 a.
Salvandy, N. A.—i 249 a.
Salvation Army—ii 641 a.
SALVIOLI, G.—xiii 526.
SAMARIN, Y. F.—xiii 527.
Samuel, H.—vi 611 a.
Samurai—Agriculture (Jap.) i 591 a; Feudalism (Jap.) vi 217 b.
SAN MARTÍN, J. DE—xiii 527.
Sanatoria—*see* HOSPITALS AND SANATORIA.
SANCTION, INTERNATIONAL—xiii 528–31; Guaranties, International vii 191 b; International Organization viii 180 a, 184 a; League of Nations ix 293 a; Mandates x 91 a; Recognition, International xiii 167 a; Sovereignty xiv 265 b; Treaties xv 99 a.
SANCTION, SOCIAL—xiii 531–34; Coercion iii 618 a; Conduct iv 179 a; Debt v 33 a; Duty v 293–95; Law ix 202 a; Morals x 647 b; Pressures, Social xii 344–48; Punishment xii 712–16; Tabu xiv 502–05.
SANCTUARY—xiii 534–37; Asylum ii 289–90; Exile v 687 a; Holy Places vii 419–22.
SAND, G.—xiii 537.
Sandino, A.—vii 198 a.
Sanger, M.—ii 562 a.
Sangha—iii 34 a.
SANITATION—xiii 538–42; Building Regulations iii 52–57; Communicable Diseases, Control of iv 67 b, 69 a; Inspection viii 72 b; Laundry and Dry Cleaning Industry ix 194 b; Maternity Welfare x 221 b; Meat Packing and Slaughtering x 260 b; Milk Supply x 475 b; Public Health xii 647 b; Water Supply xv 372–77.

Sankey, I. D.—xiii 365 b.
Sans-culottes—vi 480 a.
SANTA CRUZ, A.—xiii 542.
Sarafov, B.—iii 676 a.
SARASWATI, D.—xiii 543.
Sarcey, F.—ii 114 a.
Sargent, D. A.—xii 132 a.
SARMIENTO, D. F.—xiii 543.
SARPI, P.—xiii 544.
SARS, J. E. W.—xiii 545.
SARTORIUS VON WALTHERSHAUSEN, G.—xiii 545.
SAVIGNY, F. C. VON—xiii 546; Introd. Vol. I (Individualism and Capitalism) i 161 b; Bar ii 456 a; Codification iii 611 a; Jurisprudence viii 480 b; Natural Law xi 289 b; Puchta xii 702 a.
Savile, G.—*see* HALIFAX, LORD (d. 1695).
SAVIN, A. N.—xiii 548.
SAVING—xiii 548–52; Abstinence i 382–83; Accumulation i 415–18; Building and Loan Associations iii 47–52; Hoarding vii 393 b; Income vii 623 b; Income Tax vii 630 b; Inheritance viii 40 a; Instalment Selling viii 79 b; Interest viii 136 a; Investment viii 263 b; Postal Savings Banks xii 268 b; Rentier xiii 299 b; Savings Banks xiii 552–58; Stabilization, Economic xiv 310 b; Thrift xiv 623–26; Wages xv 296 a.
SAVINGS BANKS—xiii 552–58; Bank Deposits ii 416 b; Building and Loan Associations iii 49 b; Financial Organization vi 244 a; Investment viii 264 b; Postal Savings Banks xii 268–69.
SAVONAROLA, G.—xiii 558.
SAX, E.—xiii 558.
SAY, J.-B.—xiii 559; Economics v 351–57; Price Discrimination xii 351 a.
SAY, L.—xiii 559.
SAYYID AHMAD KHAN—xiii 560.
SAZONOV, S. D.—xiii 560.
Scaccia, S.—viii 507 a.
Scandinavian Unity Movement—xi 551 a.
SCARUFFI, G.—xiii 561.
SCHÄFER, D.—xiii 561.
SCHAFF, P.—xiii 562.
SCHÄFFLE, A. E. F.—xiii 562.
SCHANZ, G. VON—xiii 563; Income Tax vii 628 b.
SCHÄR, J. F.—xiii 564.
SCHARLING, H. W.—xiii 564.
SCHECHTER, S.—xiii 565.
SCHEEL, H. VON—xiii 566.
SCHELER, M.—xiii 566; Introd. Vol. I (War and Reorientation) i 205 a; Invention viii 248 b.
SCHELLING, F. W. J.—xiii 567.
Scher, H.—xiii 9 b.
SCHIFF, J. H.—xiii 568.
Schiller, F. C. S.—Humanism vii 542 b; Pragmatism xii 310 a.
SCHILLER, J. C. F.—xiii 569; Theater xiv 609 b.
SCHIPPEL, M.—xiii 570.

SCHIRMACHER, K.—xiii 570.
Schism — Religious Institutions (Roman Catholic) xiii 248 b; (Byzantine) 262 b, (Russian) 265 b.
Schizoids—i 364 b.
SCHLEGEL, K. W. F. VON *and* A. W. VON—xiii 571.
Schleiden, M. J.—ii 551 b.
SCHLEIERMACHER, F. E. D.—xiii 572.
SCHLESINGER, B.—xiii 573.
SCHLETTWEIN, J. A.—xiii 573.
Schliemann, H.—ii 163 b.
SCHLOSS, D. F.—xiii 574.
SCHLOSSER, F. C.—xiii 574.
SCHLÖZER, A. L. VON—xiii 575; Natural Law xi 289 b.
SCHMIDT, A.—xiii 576.
Schmidt, J. K.—*see* STIRNER, M.
Schmidt, W.—Anthropology ii 102 a, 103 b; Diffusionism v 141 b.
Schmitt, C.—Introd. Vol. I (War and Reorientation) i 216 b; Political Science xii 221 b.
SCHMOLLER, G. VON—xiii 576; Introd. Vol. I (Nationalism) i 167 a; Class iii 535 a; Economic History v 318 b; Economics v 371–77; Income Tax vii 628 b; Mercantilism x 333 b; Wages xv 307 a.
SCHNEIDER, J.-E.—xiii 577; Munitions Industry xi 132 a.
SCHOLASTICISM—xiii 578–81; Introd. Vol. I (The Universal Church) i 66 a; Aristotle ii 192 a; Commentators iii 680 a; Education v 408 a; Legal Profession and Legal Education ix 329 b; Logic ix 600 b; Peter Lombard xii 97 a; Realism xiii 141 a.
SCHÖNBERG, G. F. VON—xiii 581.
School Hygiene—xii 652 b.
Schools—*see* EDUCATION.
SCHOPENHAUER, A.—xiii 582.
SCHOULER, J.—xiii 583.
SCHRADER, E.—xiii 583.
SCHREINER, O. E. A.—xiii 584.
SCHRÖDER, R.—xiii 584.
SCHROEDER, W. VON—xiii 585; Cameralism iii 159 a.
SCHUBART, J. C.—xiii 586.
Schulze, J.—ii 12 b.
SCHULZE-DELITZSCH, H.—xiii 586; Agric. Credit i 533 b; Ateliers Nationaux ii 292 a; Cooperation iv 371 b, 373 b; Credit Cooperation iv 554 a.
SCHULZE-GÄVERNITZ, F. G.—xiii 587.
Schumpeter, J. A.—Business Cycles iii 100 a; Interest viii 134 a; Prices (Theory) xii 375 a.
SCHURTZ, H.—xiii 587; Age Societies i 482 a.
SCHURZ, C.—xiii 588.
Schutz-Staffeln—xi 226 a.
Schwann, T.—ii 551 b.
SCHWARZENBERG, F. VON—xiii 589.
SCHWARZENBERG, J. VON—xiii 588.

SCHWEIGAARD, A. M.—xiii 589.
SCHWEITZER-ALLESINA, J. B. VON—xiii 590; Trade Unions (Germany) xv 12 b.
SCIALOJA, A.—xiii 590; Introd. Vol. I (The Social Sciences as Disciplines, Italy) i 275 a.
SCIENCE—xiii 591–603. See Classification of Articles (Science), p. 555. See also Academic Freedom i 384 b; Art ii 254 b; Authority ii 320 a; Chemical Industries iii 365–67; Culture iv 636 b; Determinism v 112 b; Dogma v 191 a; Fatalism vi 148 a; Humanitarianism vii 546 a; Individualism vii 677 a; Magic x 40 a; Modernism x 564–68; Music xi 144 b; Patents xii 24 a; Progress xii 497 a; Rationalism xiii 115 b; Realism xiii 142 a. For biog. references see Classification of Articles (Natural Science), p. 565.
SCIENTIFIC MANAGEMENT—xiii 603–08; Administration, Public i 442 b; Automobile Industry ii 324 a; Business Administration iii 88 b; Efficiency v 437–39; Engineering v 546 a; Farm Management vi 111–14; Gantt vi 568 b; Gilbreth vi 662 a; Industrial Relations vii 711 a; Labor-Capital Cooperation viii 627 a; Labor, Methods of Remuneration for viii 678 b; Large Scale Production ix 172 b; Management x 78 b; Mechanic x 265 a; Personnel Administration xii 88 b; Rationalization xiii 118 a; Safety Movement xiii 504 a; Taylor xiv 542 a; Waste xv 368 a.
Scientific Method—see METHOD, SCIENTIFIC.
SCLOPIS DI SALERANO, F.—xiii 608.
SCOTT, C. P.—xiii 609.
Scott, J.—see ELDON, LORD.
SCOTT, W.—xiii 610.
Scott-Holland, H.—iii 451 a.
Scottsboro Case—xi 351 b.
Scotus Erigena, J.—xiii 578 b.
Scotus, J. D.—see DUNS SCOTUS, J.
Scrap—Iron and Steel Industry viii 306 b; Metals (Iron) x 371 b, (Copper) 373 b; Mining x 501 b; Rubber xiii 459 b.
SCRIPPS, E. W.—xiii 610; Press xii 331 b, 340 b.
Scripps-Howard—xii 334 b.
SCROPE, G. J. P.—xiii 610.
Scutage—vi 461 b.
Sea Power—see NAVY.
SEAGER, H. R.—xiii 611.
SEAMEN—xiii 611–17; Impressment vii 614–16; Maritime Law x 128 a, 129 b; Mutiny xi 166–68; Wilson xv 426 a.
SEARCHES AND SEIZURES—xiii 617–20; Continuous Voyage iv 320–21; Contraband of War iv 321–23.
Sears, R. W.—xiii 350 b.

Sears, Roebuck and Co.—Retail Trade xiii 350 b; Rosenwald xiii 438 a.
Seasonal Employment—Construction Industry iv 268 a; Labor Turnover viii 712 b; Meat Packing and Slaughtering (U. S.) x 249 a; Unemployment xv 150 a. See also MIGRATORY LABOR.
Seasonal Fluctuations—Time Series xiv 633 b.
Seaton, W. W.—vi 546 a.
SECKEL, E.—xiii 620.
SECKENDORFF, V. L. VON—xiii 620.
Second International—Communist Parties iv 88 b; General Strike vi 609 a; Internationalism viii 216 a; Socialism xiv 202 a; Socialist Parties xiv 214 a.
Secondat, C. de—see MONTESQUIEU, BARON DE.
Secret Service—Espionage v 594–96; Political Police xii 203–07.
SECRET SOCIETIES—xiii 621–23; Anthropology ii 87 b; Camorra iii 161–62; Carbonari iii 220–23; Comitadji iii 675–78; Conspiracy, Political iv 240 a; Fraternal Orders vi 423–25; Irish Question viii 288 a; Ku Klux Klan viii 606–09; Mafia x 36–38; Masonry x 177–84; Minorities, National x 519 b; Mysteries xi 172–75; Religious Orders xiii 276 b; Social Organization xiv 146 a.
Secret Treaties—Alliance ii 4 a; Diplomacy v 150 b; Treaties xv 98 b; World War xv 494 b, 496 b.
SECRÉTAN, C.—xiii 623.
Sectarian Education—v 421–25.
Sectarianism—see SECTS.
Sectionalism—see REGIONALISM.
SECTS—xiii 624–31; Buddhism iii 36 b; Christian Science iii 446–49; Communism iv 83 b; Communistic Settlements iv 95 b; Conscientious Objectors iv 210 b; Cults iv 620 a; Education (Sectarian) v 421–25; Faction vi 49–51; Husayn A'li vii 559 a; Huss vii 561 a; Intransigence viii 246 a; Islam viii 335 a; Judaism viii 431 a; Messianism x 361 a; Missions x 541 b; Mormonism xi 14–18; Pacifism xi 527 a; Protestantism xii 571–75; Puritanism xiii 3–6; Quakers xiii 12–14; Reformation xiii 186–94; Religious Institutions (Protestant) xiii 268 b; Russian Revolution xiii 475 b; Sacred Books xiii 500 a; Shinto xiv 25 a; Socialism xiv 190 b; Society xiv 228 a.
Secular Trend—see TIME SERIES.
SECULARISM—xiii 631–35; Introd. Vol. I (The Rise of Liberalism) i 103–24; Anticlericalism ii 112–14; Antisemitism ii 121 a; Art (Indian) ii 232 b, (Japanese) 238 a; Deism v 61–63; Educa-

tion v 411 a; Enlightenment v 547–52; Ethical Culture Movement v 600–02; Freethinkers vi 465–71; French Revolution vi 481 b; Humanism vii 538 a; Islam viii 342 b; Marsilius of Padua x 160 a; Mortmain xi 45 b; Priesthood xii 394 b; Professions xii 477 a; Reformation xiii 186–94; Renaissance xiii 280 b, 282 b; Society xiv 228 b.
Securities Act, 1933—xiv 406 b.
Securities Exchange Act, 1934—Stock Exchange xiv 398 a; Stocks and Stock Ownership xiv 406 b.
SEDDON, R. J.—xiii 635.
SEDGWICK, W. T.—xiii 635.
Sedimentation—Water Supply xv 375 a.
SEDITION—xiii 636–39; Alien and Sedition Acts i 635–36; Blasphemy ii 586 b; Criminal Syndicalism iv 582–84; Freedom of Speech and of the Press vi 456 b; Mutiny xi 166 a; Political Offenders xii 199–203.
Sedition Acts—see ALIEN AND SEDITION ACTS.
SEDUCTION—xiii 639–41.
SEEBOHM, F.—xiii 641.
SEECK, O.—xiii 642.
SEELEY, J. R.—xiii 642.
SEGREGATION—xiii 643–47; Alien i 633 b; Assimilation, Social ii 281 b; Foreign Language Press vi 378 b; Ghetto vi 646–50; Isolation viii 350–52; Native Policy (N. Amer.) xi 262 b; Negro Problem xi 335–56.
SEGUIN, E.—xiii 647; Mental Defectives x 312 a.
Seisin—xi 522 a.
Seiyukai—xi 634 b.
SELBORNE, LORD—xiii 647.
SELDEN, J.—xiii 648.
SELER, E. G.—xiii 649.
Seleucid Kingdom—Introd. Vol. I (Greek Culture and Thought) i 32 a; Land Tenure (Ancient World) ix 80 a.
SELF-DETERMINATION, NATIONAL—xiii 649–51; Autonomy ii 334 b; Cession iii 319 b; Federalism vi 171 a; Irredentism viii 325 a; Plebiscite xii 163–66.
SELF-INCRIMINATION—xiii 651–53; Investigations, Governmental viii 252 b.
SELF-PRESERVATION—xiii 653–55.
SELF-SUFFICIENCY, ECONOMIC—xiii 655–60; Natural Resources xi 295 a; Raw Materials xiii 129 a; Stabilization, Economic xiv 314 a.
Seligman, B.—vii 621 b.
Seligman, E. R. A.—Capitalization and Amortization of Taxes iii 212 a; Mortgage Tax xi 39 a; Revenues, Public xiii 362 b; Taxation xiv 532 a, 534 b, 535 b, 538 b, 539 b.
Seljuks—viii 340 b.
SEMBAT, M. É.—xiii 660.
SEMENOV, P. P.—xiii 660.

Index (Schweigaard — Simmel)

SEMEVSKY, V. I.—xiii 661.
SEMPLE, E. C.—xiii 661.
Senate, U. S.—ix 361–65.
SENECA, L. A.—xiii 662.
Seneuil, J. G. C.—see COURCELLE-SENEUIL, J. G.
SENIOR, N. W.—xiii 662; Absentee Ownership i 377 a; Abstinence i 382 a; Cost iv 468 a; Diminishing Returns v 145 a; Distribution v 169 a; Economics v 357 b; Increasing Returns vii 639 b; Interest viii 132 b.
SEPARATION OF POWERS — xiii 663–67; Introd. Vol. I (The Roman World) i 51 a; Advisory Opinions i 476 b; Appointments ii 137 b; Checks and Balances iii 363–65; Congressional Govt. iv 201–03; Constitutional Law iv 251 a; Corruption, Political iv 452 a; Courts iv 525 b; Delegation of Powers v 65–67; Govt. (Norway) vii 62 b, (U. S.) 19 a; Investigations, Governmental viii 255 b; Judicial Review viii 457 b; Judiciary viii 464 a; Justice, Administration of viii 517 a; Legislative Assemblies (U. S.) ix 366 a; Levellers ix 422 a; Prerogative xii 319 b; Veto xv 247–49.
Sepoy Mutiny—vii 662 b.
SERFDOM—xiii 667–71; Introd. Vol. I (Individualism and Capitalism) i 152 a; Agrarian Movements i 492–515; Agric. Labor i 547 b; Chavchavadze iii 361 b; Colonate iii 639–41; Emancipation v 483–85; Labor viii 618 a; Labourers, Statutes of ix 5 b; Land Tenure ix 82–99, 100 a, 107 a.
SERGEYEVICH, V. I.—xiii 671.
Sergio, V. E.—i 275 a.
Sericulture—xiv 52 a, 56 a.
Sering, M.—xiv 102 b.
Serjeants—ix 331 b.
Serjeanty—vi 461 b.
SERRA, A.—xiii 671.
SERVICE—xiii 672–74; Chivalry iii 436–41; Christianity iii 452 b; Tourist Traffic xiv 661 b.
SERVITUDES—xiv 3–7.
Settlements, Social—see SOCIAL SETTLEMENTS.
SEWALL, M. W.—xiv 7.
SEWARD, W. H.—xiv 7; Monroe Doctrine x 631 b.
Sewers—xiii 538 b.
SEX EDUCATION AND SEX ETHICS—xiv 8–13; Introd. Vol. I (Greek Culture and Thought) i 25 b; Abortion i 372–74; Birth Control ii 561 a; Celibacy iii 283–86; Chastity iii 357–58; Child (Marriage) iii 395–98; Chivalry iii 439 a; Christianity iii 459 b; Education, Primitive v 401 a; Fertility Rites vi 191 a; Free Love vi 433–36; Marriage x 146–54; Morals x 645 a; Prostitution xii 553–59; Psychoanalysis xii 580–88; Spencer xiv 295 a.

Sex Heredity—vii 331 a.
SEYDEL, M. VON—xiv 13.
SHĀFI'I, AL-—xiv 13; Islamic Law viii 346 a.
SHAFTESBURY, FIRST EARL OF—xiv 14; Dryden v 257 a.
SHAFTESBURY, THIRD EARL OF—xiv 14.
SHAFTESBURY, SEVENTH EARL OF—xiv 15.
Shakers — Communistic Settlements iv 96 a; Sects xiii 629 b.
Shakespeare—xiv 604 b.
Shand, A.—xii 160 b.
SHANG YANG—xiv 15; Land Tenure ix 113 b.
Share Croppers—Cotton iv 489 a; Farm Tenancy (U. S.) vi 123 a; Negro Problem xi 341 b.
Sharī'a—see ISLAMIC LAW.
Sharp, G.—i 369 a.
SHATTUCK, L.—xiv 16; Census iii 298 a.
SHAW, A. H.—xiv 16.
Shaw, G. B.—vi 46 a.
SHAW, L.—xiv 17.
Shays' Rebellion—Agrarian Movements (U. S.) i 509 a; Armed Forces, Control of ii 200 a; Army ii 213 b; Articles of Confederation ii 263 a.
SHCHAPOV, A. P.—xiv 18.
SHCHERBATOV, M. M.—xiv 18.
Sheldon, A. E.—xiii 520 b.
SHELLEY, P. B.—xiv 19; Passive Resistance and Non-cooperation xii 12 a.
Sheppard-Towner Act — Maternity Welfare x 226 a.
SHEPSTONE, T.—xiv 20.
SHERIFF—xiv 20–23; Police xii 187 b.
Sherman Act—Labor Legislation and Law viii 670 b; National Banks, U. S. xi 187 b; Olney xi 466 a; Trusts xv 113 b.
SHEVCHENKO, T.—xiv 23.
Shifting of Taxes—xiv 534 b.
Shih-chai—see CHANG HSÜEH-CH'ENG.
Shih Huang Ti—v 501 b.
Shiites—Islam viii 335 b; Islamic Law viii 346 a; Messianism x 363 a.
SHINASI, I.—xiv 23.
SHINTO—xiv 24–25; Art (Japanese) ii 236 b; Motoöri xi 69 b.
Ship Brokers—iii 9 b.
SHIPBUILDING—xiv 25–30; Merchant Marine x 343–50; Navy xi 315 b; Pirrie xii 139 b; Wood Industries xv 468 b.
SHIPPING—xiv 30–43; Acts of Trade, British i 426–29; Allan i 643 b; Ballin ii 409 b; Colonial Economic Policy iii 649 b; Commerce iv 3–13; Commercial Routes iv 19–24; Cunard iv 647 b; Embargo v 485–87; Govt. Owned Corporations vii 109 b; International Trade viii 193 a; International Waterways viii 208–14; Ismay viii 350 a; Longshoremen ix 606–09; Marine Insurance x 111–16; Maritime Law x 122–31; Merchant Marine x 343–50; Piracy xii 136–39; Ports and Harbors xii 255–60; Power, Industrial xii 298 c; Privateering xii 422–24; Seamen xiii 611–17; Shipbuilding xiv 25–30; Transit, International xv 79 a; Transportation xv 81 b, 84 b; War Economics xv 344 b.
Shiva—ii 676 b.
Shoe Industry—see LEATHER INDUSTRIES.
Shoe Workers Protective Union—ix 314 a.
Shogunate—vi 216 a.
Shōin—see YOSHIDA TORAJIRŌ.
Shop Councils—see INDUSTRIAL RELATIONS COUNCILS.
Shop Stewards—Industrial Relations Councils vii 720 b; Labor, Government Services for viii 647 b.
SHORT BALLOT MOVEMENT—xiv 43–44; Ballot ii 411 b.
SHORT HOURS MOVEMENT—xiv 44–47; Hours of Labor vii 480 a.
Short Selling—Speculation xiv 290 b; Stock Exchange xiv 400 a.
Short Term Credit—Agric. Credit i 531 b; Credit iv 548 a; Foreign Investment vi 371 b; Investment viii 266 b.
Sib—see Clan.
SICKEL, T.—xiv 47.
Sickness—see MORBIDITY.
Sickness Insurance—see HEALTH INSURANCE.
SIDGWICK, H.—xiv 48; Altruism and Egoism ii 14 b.
SIDIS, B.—xiv 48.
SIDNEY, A.—xiv 49.
Siegfried, A.—xi 613 a.
Siegmund-Schultze, F.—xiv 159 b.
SIEMENS, E. W. VON—xiv 49.
Siemens' Regenerative Furnace—vi 672 a.
Siemens, W.—viii 302 b.
Siete Partidas—iii 607 b.
SIEYÈS, J. E.—xiv 50; Race Conflict xiii 36 b.
SIGHELE, S.—xiv 51; Social Psychology xiv 153 b.
Sigismund—iv 161 b.
SIGMAN, M.—xiv 51.
SILK INDUSTRY—xiv 52–57; Textile Industry xiv 582 a, 584 b, 588 a.
Sills, M.—Motion Pictures xi 67 a.
SILVER—xiv 57–60; Bimetallism and Monometallism ii 546–49; Foreign Exchange vi 363 b; Free Silver vi 438–40; Metals x 366 a, 378 a; Monetary Unions x 596 a; Prices (Hist.) xii 377 b, 379 a.
ŠIMÁČEK, F.—xiv 60.
Simiand, F.—xv 308 a.
SIMMEL, G.—xiv 61; Introd. Vol. I (The Trend to Internationalism) i 183 b; Accommodation i 403 a; Sociology xiv 244 b.

Simmons, W. J.—viii 607 a.
SIMON, JOHN (d. 1904)—xiv 62; Communicable Diseases, Control of iv 67 b; Public Health xii 648 a.
Simon, John—Indian Question vii 669 a.
SIMON, JULES—xiv 61; Anticlericalism ii 113 b.
Simon, T.—x 323 b.
Simons, M.—xiii 627 a.
Simony—viii 261 a.
Sinanthropus—x 74 b.
SINCLAIR, J.—xiv 62; Statistics xiv 356 b.
Sinclair, U.—x 261 a.
SINEY, J.—xiv 63.
SINGER, P.—xiv 63.
Single Party System—xi 591 a.
SINGLE TAX—xiv 64–67; Capitalization and Amortization of Taxes iii 211 b; Communistic Settlements iv 101 a; Dove v 229 a; Fabianism vi 46 b; Fels vi 180 b; George vi 631 a; Land Taxation ix 70 b; Post xii 267 b; Unearned Increment xv 145 b.
SINKING FUND—xiv 67–69; Price, R. xii 350 b; Public Debt xii 607 b.
Sinn Fein—Irish Question viii 293 a; Parties, Political xi 610 a.
SISMONDI, J. C. L. S. DE—xiv 69; Introd. Vol. I (Individualism and Capitalism) i 156 a; Distribution v 170 a; Proletariat xii 514 b; Statics and Dynamics xiv 352 b.
SKARBEK, F. F.—xiv 71.
SKARGA POWĘSKI, P.—xiv 71.
SKIDMORE, T.—xiv 72.
SKINNER, J. S.—xiv 72.
Slander—see LIBEL AND SLANDER.
Slave Trade—see SLAVERY.
SLAVERY—xiv 73–92 (Primitive 73–74, 90, Ancient 74–77, 90, Mediaeval 77–80, 91, Modern 80–84, 91, U. S. 84–92); Introd. Vol. I (Greek Culture and Thought) i 13 b; Abolition i 369–72; Agrarian Movements (Ancient Rome) i 494 a; Agric. Labor i 547 b; Aquinas ii 147 b; Aristocracy ii 185 b; Asiento ii 268–70; Christianity iii 454 b; Commerce iv 8 a; Debt v 33 b; Dew v 117 b; Douglas v 227 b; Emancipation v 483–85; Euripides v 622 b; Fitzhugh vi 274 a; Judaism viii 435 a; Kirk viii 574 b; Labor viii 616 a; Latifundia ix 186 b; Law (Greek) ix 227 a, (Hellenistic and Greco-Egyptian) 231 a, (Jewish) 220 a; Lincoln ix 486 b; Livingstone ix 552 b; Lynching ix 640 a; Migrations x 433 a; Mining x 504 b; Miscegenation x 532 a; Negro Problem xi 335 b; Nieboer xi 372 a; Popular Sovereignty xii 239 b; Smuggling xiv 120 b; Status xiv 376 b. *For further biog. references see* Classification of Articles (Negro Problem and Slavery), p. 565.

SLAVEYKOV, P. R.—xiv 92.
Slavic Law—Bogišić ii 618 a; Kadlec viii 534 a; Law ix 240–46; Maciejowski x 27 a; Mažuranic x 239 a.
Slavophiles—Aksakovs i 610 b; Danilevsky iv 708 a; Khomyakov viii 562 b; Kireyevsky viii 573 b; Russian Revolution xiii 474 b; Samarin xiii 527 a.
SLEIDAN, J.—xiv 92.
Sloyd—x 103 b.
Slum Clearance—xiv 96 a.
SLUMS—xiv 93–98; Housing (Eur.) vii 499 a, (U. S.) 513 a; Social Settlements xiv 157–62.
SMALL, A. W.—xiv 98; Interests viii 146 b; Social Process xiv 148 b.
SMALL CLAIMS COURTS—xiv 99–101; Legal Aid ix 320 a.
SMALL HOLDINGS—xiv 101–05; Agrarian Movements i 492–515; Agric. Labor i 548 b; Agriculture (Eng.) i 577–81, (Europ.) 582 a; Allotments ii 6 a; Farm Tenancy vi 123 a; Land Settlement ix 53–64; Land Tenure ix 73–127; Primogeniture xii 402–05; Village Community xv 253–59.
SMALL LOANS—xiv 105–11; Debt v 32–39; Loans, Personal ix 561–65; Pawnbroking xii 32–40.
SMART, W.—xiv 111.
Smelting—see METALS; IRON AND STEEL INDUSTRY.
SMILES, S.—xiv 111.
SMITH, A.—xiv 112; Introd. Vol. I (The Revolutions) i 140 b; Absentee Ownership i 377 a; Acquisition i 421 b; Balance of Trade ii 401 a; Bargaining Power ii 459 b; Buchanan iii 27 b; Capital iii 188 a; Christianity iii 459 a; Cost iv 467 b; Distribution v 168 a; Drawback v 233 b; Economic History v 316 a; Economics v 351–57; Education (Public) v 416 a; Efficiency v 437 a; Expenditures, Public vi 6 b; Exploitation vi 16 a; Free Trade vi 442 b. Income vii 625 a; Increasing Returns vii 639 b; Individualism vii 678 a; Laissez Faire ix 16 a; Large Scale Production ix 171 a; Malthus x 69 a; Mercantilism x 333 b; Monopoly x 626 b; Public Finance xii 644 a; Rent xiii 290 a; Revenues, Public xiii 361 a; Soden xiv 248 b; Specialization xiv 283 b; Statics and Dynamics xiv 352 b; Storch xiv 412 b; Taxation xiv 538 a; Value and Price xv 218 a.
SMITH, E. MUNROE—xiv 114; Amendments, Constitutional ii 22 a; Codification iii 611 b.
Smith, G. Elliot—v 141 b.
SMITH, GOLDWIN—xiv 115.
Smith-Hughes Act — Industrial Education vii 695 a; Vocational Education xv 275 a.

SMITH, JAMES A.—xiv 116.
Smith, John Prince—see PRINCE-SMITH, J.
SMITH, JOSEPH — xiv 117; Mormonism xi 14 b.
Smith, T. V.—xiv 304 a.
SMITH, THOMAS—xiv 117; Prerogative xii 319 a.
SMITH, W. R.—xiv 118.
SMITH, Z. D.—xiv 118.
SMUGGLING—xiv 119–23; Asiento ii 268–70; Continental System iv 311 a; Liquor Traffic ix 503 b.
Smuts, J. C.—Gestalt vi 645 b; Mandates x 88 a; Parties, Political (S. Africa) xi 609 a.
SNELLMAN, J. V.—xiv 123.
Snowden, P.—viii 701 a.
Socage—vi 462 a.
Social Case Work—Social Work (Case Work) xiv 173–83.
Social Change—see CHANGE, SOCIAL.
SOCIAL CHRISTIAN MOVEMENTS—xiv 123–27; Barnett ii 464 a; Christian Labor Unions iii 443–46; Christian Socialism iii 449–52; Christianity iii 460 b; Cooperation (Belgium) iv 380 a, (Germany) 372 b, (Italy) 382 a; Devas v 117 a; Economics (Socio-Ethical Economics) v 384 b; Harmel vii 270 b; Headlam vii 287 a; Hitze vii 392 a; Holland vii 415 a; Ketteler viii 559 a; Kolping viii 589 b; La Tour du Pin Chambly ix 189 a; Leo XIII ix 408 b; Mun xi 84 a; Ozanam xi 526 b.
Social Conflict—see CONFLICT, SOCIAL.
Social Consciousness—Consciousness iv 219 a.
Social Continuity—see CONTINUITY, SOCIAL.
SOCIAL CONTRACT—xiv 127–31; Introd. Vol. I (The Rise of Liberalism) i 112 b, (The Revolutions) 130 a; Constitutional Conventions iv 245 a; Constitutionalism iv 255 b; Declaration of the Rights of Man and the Citizen v 50 a; Democracy v 79 a; Duns Scotus v 282 a; Enlightenment v 548 b; Feudalism vi 210 a; Fouillée vi 401 b; Hume vii 551 a; Individualism vii 675 a; Kant viii 540 a; Manegold of Lautenbach x 94 b; Monarchomachs x 578 a; Natural Law xi 288 b; Natural Rights xi 300 a; Political Science xii 215 b; Rousseau xiii 446 a; Sociology xiv 235 b.
Social Control—see CONTROL, SOCIAL.
Social Conventions—see CONVENTIONS, SOCIAL.
Social Cost—iv 473 b.
Social Credit—viii 642 b.
Social Criticism—see CRITICISM, SOCIAL.

Social Democratic Party, Germany—Auer ii 313 b; Bebel ii 487 a; David v 9 b; Frank vi 417 b; Haase vii 233 a; Labor Movement viii 689 a; Liebknecht ix 454 b; Mehring x 301 b; Parties, Political (Germany) xi 616 a; Schweitzer-Allesina xiii 590 a; Singer xiv 63 b; Socialist Parties xiv 213 b, 218 a; Trade Unions (Germany) xv 13 b; Workers' Education xv 486 a.

SOCIAL DISCRIMINATION — xiv 131–34. See Classification of Articles (Social Discrimination), p. 555. See also Game Laws vi 562 a; Gypsies vii 231 b; Immigration vii 590 a; Tax Exemption xiv 529 a.

Social Evolution—see EVOLUTION, SOCIAL.

SOCIAL INSURANCE—xiv 134–38; Benefits, Trade Union ii 515 b; Bismarck ii 573 a; Blind ii 590 b; Bödiker ii 614 a; Compensation and Liability Insurance iv 137 a; Friendly Societies vi 497 a; Funerals vi 529 b; Group Insurance vii 187 a; Health Insurance vii 294–300; Insurance viii 98 b; Kaskel viii 548 b; Labor, Govt. Services for viii 648 a; Labor Legislation and Law viii 663 b; Maternity Welfare x 223 a; Mothers' Pensions xi 56 a; Mutual Aid Societies xi 169 a; Old Age xi 459 a; Pensions xii 69 a; Sörensen xiv 263 b; Unemployment Insurance xv 162–74; Workmen's Compensation xv 488–92.

Social Legislation—see LABOR LEGISLATION AND LAW; PUBLIC WELFARE; SOCIAL INSURANCE.

Social Mobility—see MOBILITY, SOCIAL.

SOCIAL ORGANISM—xiv 138–41; Biology ii 555 b, 557 a; Culture iv 623 a; Functionalism vi 524 b; Lilienfeld-Toailles ix 473 b; Müller xi 80 a; Positivism xii 263 b; Social Process xiv 149 a; Sociology xiv 237 b; Spencer xiv 295 a; Worms xv 498 b.

SOCIAL ORGANIZATION—xiv 141–48. See Classification of Articles (Social Organization), p. 556. See also Introd. Vol. 1 (Greek Culture and Thought) i 8 a, 12 b, (The Roman World) 44 b, 57 a, (The Universal Church) 65 a, (The Growth of Autonomy) 73 b, 75 a, (Renaissance and Reformation) 101 a, (The Rise of Liberalism) 107 a, (The Revolutions) 126 b; Anthropology ii 84 b; Chinese Problem iii 433 b; Evolution, Social v 658 b, 660 a; Law (Celtic) ix 247 b, (Chinese) 252 b, (Germanic) 236 a, (Hindu) 258 b, (Japanese) 254 a, Maladjustment x 60 b;

Plantation xii 152 a; Sociology xiv 232–47; Specialization xiv 280 a; Technology xiv 556 a.

Social Pressures—see PRESSURES, SOCIAL.

SOCIAL PROCESS—xiv 148–51. See Classification of Articles (Social Process), p. 556, and further references suggested there.

SOCIAL PSYCHOLOGY—xiv 151–57; Introd. Vol. 1 (The Trend to Internationalism) i 183 a, (War and Reorientation) 205 b, 218 a; Attitudes, Social ii 305–07; Bagehot ii 385 a; Behaviorism ii 498 a; Chauvinism iii 361; Collective Behavior iii 631–33; Consciousness iv 219 a; Cosmopolitanism iv 457–61; Crowd iv 612–13; Group vii 182 a; Imitation vii 586–87; Instinct viii 82 a; Language ix 155–69; Le Bon ix 316 a; Mob x 552–54; Psychology xii 595 a; Sociology xiv 239 a.

Social Reform—see REFORMISM.

Social Sanctions—see SANCTION, SOCIAL.

Social Science Research Council—Agric. Economics i 535 b; Learned Societies ix 299 b; Research xiii 331 b.

Social Sciences—see especially Introd. Vol. 1 (The Development of Social Thought and Institutions) i 3–228, (The Social Sciences as Disciplines) 231–349. See also Classification of Articles (Science), p. 555, and further references suggested there.

SOCIAL SETTLEMENTS—xiv 157–62; Barnett ii 464 a; Toynbee xiv 667 a; Woods xv 476 a.

SOCIAL SURVEYS—xiv 162–65; Booth ii 642 a; Cost of Living iv 480 b; Criminal Law iv 576 a; Eden v 397 a; Family Budgets vi 73–78; Land Utilization ix 135 a; Le Play ix 412 a.

Social Welfare—see PUBLIC WELFARE.

SOCIAL WORK—xiv 165–87 (General 165–73, 187, Case Work 173–83, 187, Training 183–87); Introd. Vol. 1 (What Are the Social Sciences?) i 5 b, (War and Reorientation) 209 a, (The Social Sciences as Disciplines, Gt. Brit.) 234 a, (U. S.) 346 a; Adoption i 461 b; Begging ii 494 b; Boys' and Girls' Clubs ii 669 a; Brinkerhoff iii 4 a; Chalmers iii 321 b; Charity iii 343 b; Child iii 373–431; Clinics and Dispensaries iii 565 a; Community Organization iv 106–08; Dependency v 94 b; Ethical Culture Movt. v 601 b; Family Desertion and Non-support vi 78–81; Health Centers vii 287–89; Health Education vii 289–94; Legal Aid ix 323 b; Lodging Houses ix 597 a; Maladjustment x 62 b; Placing Out xii 145 b; Public

Welfare xii 687–90; Rehabilitation xiii 221–25; Richmond xiii 382 a; Social Settlements xiv 157–62; Social Surveys xiv 162–65.

SOCIALISM—xiv 188–212 (General 188–90, 210, Pre-Marxian 190–97, 210, Marxian 197–202, 211, After Marx 202–08, 210, Retrospect and Prospect 208–212). See Classification of Articles (Socialism), p. 556. See also Introd. Vol. 1 (The Revolutions) i 131 b, (Individualism and Capitalism) 156 b, (The Trend to Internationalism) 178 a; Amer. Federation of Labor ii 24 a; Anarchism ii 49 b, 51 a; Antimilitarism ii 116 a; Bargaining Power ii 460 a; Bourgeoisie ii 655 b; Capitalism iii 195 b; Chartism iii 353 b; Communism iv 81 b, 85 a; Confédération Générale du Travail iv 180 a; Conscientious Objectors iv 211 a; Consensus iv 226 a; Consumers' Cooperation iv 289 a; Cooperation (Belgium) iv 379–80, (France) 376 b, (Germany) 372 a; Criminology iv 588 b; Democracy v 82 b; Economic Policy v 340 b; Equality v 579 a; Europeanization v 627 a; Exploitation vi 16 b; Far Eastern Problem vi 99 a; Force, Political vi 341 a; French Revolution vi 478 b; Functionalism vi 525 a; Garment Industries vi 581 b; Govt. vii 13 b, (Soviet Russia) 67–70; Industrialism viii 24 b; Inheritance viii 38 a, 41 b; Intellectuals viii 120 a; Interest viii 143 a; International Relations viii 188 a; Internationalism viii 215 b; Jacobinism viii 363 a; Justice viii 512 b; Kant viii 541 b; Labor-Capital Co-operation viii 626 a; Labor Exchange Banks viii 642 a; Labor, Methods of Remuneration for viii 681 a; Labor Parties viii 697–99; Laissez Faire ix 19 a; Liberty ix 445 a; Literature ix 539 a; Minority Rights x 527 a; Nationalism xi 247 b; Pan-movements xi 550 a; Patriotism xii 28 b; Peace Movements xii 46 b; Peasantry xii 51 a; Political Offenders xii 202 a; Race Conflict xiii 40 a; Republicanism xiii 320 b; Revolution and Counter-revolution xiii 370 a; Romanticism xiii 432 a; Seamen xiii 614 a; Small Holdings xiv 102 b; Social Insurance xiv 136 b; Social Process xiv 150 a; State xiv 330 b, 331 b; Terrorism xiv 577 a; Trade Unions xv 6 b, 29 b; Violence xv 266 a; Woman, Position in Society xv 446 a. For biog. references see Classification of Articles (Socialism), p. 569.

SOCIALIST PARTIES—xiv 212–21; Bolshevism ii 623–30; Fascism vi 135 a; Labor Movement viii 689 a; Labor Parties viii 697 b, 698 b; Parties, Political xi 594 b, (France) 611 b, (Germany) 616 a, (Spain) 630 b, (Switzerland) 619 b; Sabotage xiii 497 a; Socialism xiv 202 a, 206 a; Soviet xiv 269–74; Trade Unions (Finland) xv 21 a, (Germany) 12 b, (Sweden) 20 a; Workers' Education xv 486 a. *See also* SOCIALISM.

SOCIALIZATION—xiv 221–25; Bolshevism ii 627 b; Confiscation iv 186 a; Electric Power v 465 a, 469 a; Express Companies vi 29 a; Food Industries (Food Distribution, Russia) vi 325 b; Funerals vi 528 b; Gosplan vi 706 a; Govt. Owned Corporations vii 106–11; Govt. Ownership vii 111–19; Housing (Eur.) vii 504 a; Legal Profession and Legal Education ix 344 b; National Economic Planning xi 197–205.

SOCIETY—xiv 225–32. See Classification of Articles (Social Organization), p. 556, (Social Process), p. 556, (Sociology), p. 556.

Society of Automotive Engineers —ii 344 a.

Society of Friends—*see* QUAKERS.

Society of Jesus—*see* JESUITS.

Society for the Prevention of Cruelty to Animals—Animal Protection ii 62 a; Bergh ii 522 b.

Society for the Prevention of Cruelty to Children—Bergh ii 522 b; Child (Neglected) iii 404 a; Waugh xv 385 b.

Socinians—xiii 242 a.

SOCIOLOGY—xiv 232–47. See Classification of Articles (Sociology), p. 556. *See also* Introd. Vol. I (What Are the Social Sciences?) i 5 a, (Individualism and Capitalism) 159 b, (Nationalism) 168 b, (The Trend to Internationalism) 181 b, (War and Reorientation) 204 a, (The Social Sciences as Disciplines, Austria) 267 a, (France) 251 a, (Germany) 260 b, (Gt. Brit.) 237 b, 244 b, (Hungary) 271 a, (Japan) 321 b, (Lat. Amer.) 311 a, 316 b, (Russia) 284 b, (Scandinavia) 292 b, (U. S.) 338 b, 344 a; Accommodation i 403 a; Adaptation i 435 b; Adjustment i 439 a; History and Historiography vii 364 b, 379 a; Jurisprudence viii 483 a; Mechanism and Vitalism x 270 a; Positivism xii 263 b; Statics and Dynamics xiv 352 a. *For biog. references see* Classification of Articles (Social Philosophy and Sociology), p. 568.

SOCRATES—xiv 247; Introd. Vol. I (Greek Culture and Thought) i 25 a; Education v 406 a; Hedonism vii 307 b; Philosophy xii 120 a; Plato and Platonism xii 158 a; Political Science xii 207 b; Realism xiii 140 b.

SODEN, F. J. H. VON—xiv 248.

SOETBEER, A. G.—xiv 249.

Sohm, F.—xi 524 a.

SOHM, R.—xiv 249.

SOILS—xiv 250–54; Agriculture i 593 b; Dry Farming v 254 a; Fertilizer Industry vi 193 a.

Solidarism—Bourgeois ii 654 a; Economics (Socio-Ethical Economics) v 384 a; Justice viii 512 b; Secrétan xiii 623 b.

SOLON—xiv 254; Agrarian Movements i 493 a; Appeals ii 131 b.

SOLOVYEV, S. M.—xiv 255.

SOLOVYEV, V. S.—xiv 256.

SOLVAY, E.—xiv 256; Introd. Vol. I (The Social Sciences as Disciplines, Belgium) i 257 b; Heavy Chemicals vii 302 a.

Sombart, W.—Introd. Vol. I (The Social Sciences as Disciplines, Germany) i 260 a; Capitalism iii 195 b; Class iii 532 b; Economic History v 319 a; Economics v 375 b, 391 b; Geisteswissenschaften vi 601 b; Judaism viii 437 b; Statics and Dynamics xiv 355 a.

Somodevilla, Z. de—*see* ENSENADA, MARQUÉS DE LA.

SONNEMANN, L.—xiv 257.

SONNENFELS, J. VON—xiv 258; Cameralism ii 159 b.

Sonora, Marqués de—*see* GÁLVEZ, J. DE.

SOPHISTS—xiv 259–61; Introd. Vol. I (Greek Culture and Thought) i 24 b; Logic ix 599 a; Natural Law xi 285 b; Philosophy xii 119 b; Political Science xii 207 b; Social Psychology xiv 152 a; Sociology xiv 232 b.

Sophocles—xiv 600 b.

Soranus of Ephesus—Child (Hygiene) iii 380 b; Medicine x 285 b.

SOREL, A.—xiv 261.

SOREL, G.—xiv 262; Anarchism ii 50 b; Belief ii 501 b; Fascism vi 134 b; Force, Political vi 341 a; General Strike vi 608 b; Labor Movement viii 689 b; Masses x 196 b; Myth xi 181 a; Political Science xii 220 b; Sabotage xiii 496 b; Syndicalism xiv 497 a.

SÖRENSEN, T.—xiv 263.

SÖRGE, F. A.—xiv 264.

Sororate—viii 570 b.

SOTO, D. DE—xiv 264.

South Manchuria Railway—x 80 b.

South Sea Bubble—iii 25 a.

SOUTHEY, R.—xiv 265.

SOVEREIGNTY—xiv 265–69; Introd. Vol. I (The Universal Church) i 69 a, (The Growth of Autonomy) 73–83, (Renaissance and Reformation) 95 a, 96 b, (The Rise of Liberalism) 109 a, (The Trend to Internationalism) 178 b, (War and Reorientation) 216 a; Absolutism i 380–82; Aegidius Colonna i 481 a; Agreements, International i 518–20; Allegiance i 644–46; Althusius ii 13 b; Annexation ii 68–69; Association ii 285 b; Asylum ii 289–90; Austin ii 318 b; Authority ii 319–21; Autocracy ii 321–22; Autonomy ii 332–36; Aviation ii 351 a, 368 a; Barclay ii 458 a; Bodin ii 615 a; Boundaries ii 649–52; Capitulations iii 213–15; Centralization iii 308 b; Cession iii 319–20; Civil War iii 523–25; Comity iii 678–79; Compacts, Interstate iv 109–13; Conciliar Movement iv 160–65; Concordat iv 169–71; Concurrent Powers iv 173–75; Confiscation iv 183–87; Conflict of Laws iv 187–94; Constant de Rebecque iv 242 a; De Facto Govt. v 53–54; Diplomatic Protection v 153–55; Dominion Status v 211–16; Duguit v 272 a; Eminent Domain v 493–97; Enlightenment v 549 a; Excommunication v 678 a; Exterritoriality vi 36–39; Extradition vi 41–44; Far Eastern Problem vi 92–100; Fascism vi 134 a; Feudalism vi 203–20; Figgis vi 230 b; Force, Political vi 338–41; Freedom of Association vi 447–50; Gelasius I vi 602 a; Govt. vii 8–15; Hobbes vii 395 a; International Law viii 171 b; International Organization viii 178 b; Intervention viii 236–39; Investiture Conflict viii 260–63; Irredentism viii 325–28; James of Viterbo viii 367 b; Judicial Review viii 458 a; Levellers ix 422 a; Mandates x 91 b; Minorities, National x 524 b; Monarchomachs x 577–78; Native Policy (N. Amer.) xi 261 a; Obedience, Political xi 415–18; Philosophy xii 127 a; Pius II xii 142 a; Plebiscite xii 163–66; Pluralism xii 170–74; Polish Corridor xii 196–99; Political Science xii 214 b; Popular Sovereignty xii 239–40; Prerogative xii 318–20; Protectorate xii 567–71; Recognition, International xiii 165–68; Self-Determination, National xiii 649–51; Seydel xiv 13 a; Social Contract xiv 127–31; Society xiv 230 a; State xiv 328–32; State Liability xiv 338–43; State Succession xiv 344–46; States' Rights xiv 346–50; Suárez xiv 429 b; Territorial Waters xiv 574–75.

SOVIET—xiv 269–74; Bolshevism ii 625 b, 626 b; Gosplan vi 712 b; Govt. (Soviet Russia) vii 68 a; Labor Movement viii

692 a; Local Govt. ix 577 a; National Economic Councils xi 194 a; Russian Revolution xiii 476 b, 480 a, 481 b.

Soviet Russia—Introd. Vol. I (The Social Sciences as Disciplines, Russia) i 287 a; Abortion i 374 a; Agrarian Syndicalism i 516 a; Agric. Policy i 567 a; Agriculture, Govt. Services for i 605 b; Amnesty ii 38 b; Arbitration, Industrial ii 154 b; Archives ii 179 a; Artel ii 261 a; Atheism ii 295 b; Behaviorism ii 498 b; Bolshevism iii 623–30; Calendar iii 143 b; Child (Welfare) iii 379 b, (Dependent) 402 b, (Neglected) 406 a; Coal Industry iii 593 b; Codification iii 608 a; Cooperation (Consumers') iv 385 b, (Credit) 388 a, (Agric.) 389 a; Copyright iv 403 b; Corruption, Political iv 451 b; Courts, Industrial iv 538 a; Criminology iv 590 a; Day Nursery v 16 a; Divorce v 180 b; Domestic Service v 204 a; Economic Policy v 342 a; Education v 412 b, (Part Time) 426 a; Exile v 689 a; Exploitation vi 17 a; Fairs vi 63 b; Far Eastern Problem vi 96 a; Farm Management vi 113 a; Federalism vi 171 b; Fire Insurance vi 261 b; Food Industries (Food Distribution) vi 325 b; Forced Labor vi 342 a; Free Love vi 435 a; Gosplan vi 705–13; Govt. vii 67–70; Govt. Owned Corporations vii 109 a; Handicraft vii 258 a; Health Education vii 293 b; Homework, Industrial vii 447 a, 448 a; Homicide vii 454 b; Hospitals and Sanatoria vii 468 a; Hours of Labor vii 488 b; Housing vii 504 a; Imperial Unity vii 605 a; Industrial Education vii 694 b; Industrial Hygiene vii 708 b; Industrial Revolution viii 10 b; Industrialism viii 24 a; Inheritance viii 42 a; Institutions, Public viii 90 b; Internationalism viii 216 a; Investigations, Governmental viii 259 a; Iron and Steel Industry viii 310 a; Jewish Emancipation viii 398 b; Labor, Govt. Services for viii 650 b; Labor, Methods of Remuneration for viii 681 a; Labor Movement viii 691 b; Labor Turnover viii 710 b; Land Settlement xi 58 b; Land Tenure ix 109 b; Large Scale Production ix 177 b; Learned Societies ix 297 b; Legal Profession and Legal Education ix 339 a; Leisure ix 404 b; Literacy and Illiteracy ix 521 a; Literature ix 539 a; Local Govt. ix 577 a; Management x 79 a; Match Industry x 208 a; Maternity Welfare x 224 a; Meat Packing and Slaughtering x 252 a; Medicine x 299 a; Migrations x 440 b; Mining Law x 517 b; Minorities, National x 523 a; Motion Pictures xi 67 b; Municipal Finance xi 100 b; Municipal Govt. xi 112 a; Museums and Exhibitions xi 141 a; Naturalization xi 309 a; Near Eastern Problem xi 325 a; Nursing xi 411 a; Oil Industry xi 449 a; Parent Education xi 575 a; Parks xi 585 b; Peasantry xii 51 b; Political Police xii 204 b; Poor Laws xii 234 a; Poverty xii 287 a, 291 a; Preschool Education xii 323 a; Press xii 332 b; Printing and Publishing xii 414 b; Prison Labor xii 417 a; Procedure, Legal xii 445 a; Proletariat xii 518 a; Public Domain xii 616 b; Public Health xii 654 b; Public Libraries xii 664 a; Race Conflict xiii 40 a; Rationalization xiii 118 b; Recognition, International xiii 167 a; Recreation xiii 180 b; Regional Planning xiii 208 a; Religious Institutions (Russian) xiii 267 a; Repudiation of Public Debts xiii 322 a; Research xiii 333 a; Russian Revolution xiii 481 b; Self-Sufficiency, Economic xiii 657 b; Sex Education and Sex Ethics xiv 12 a; Shipping xiv 41 b; Silk Industry xiv 54 b; Socialization xiv 224 a; Soviet xiv 272 b; Succession, Laws of xiv 441 a; Teaching Profession xiv 546 a; Theater xiv 612 a; Trade Agreements xiv 669 b; Trade Unions xv 33 a; Vocational Education xv 274 b; Vocational Guidance xv 278 b; Wages xv 310 a; Women in Industry xv 452 b, 457 a; Women's Organizations xv 464 a; Wood Industries xv 472 a.

Spann, O.—Economics v 385 b; National Wealth xi 228 a.

Sparkes, M.—vii 204 a.

SPARKS, J.—xiv 274.

Spartacist Workers' and Soldiers' Council—vi 610 a.

Spasowicz, W.—xiv 274.

SPAVENTA, B.—xiv 275.

SPAVENTA, S.—xiv 275.

Speaker—Debate, Parliamentary v 28 a; Procedure, Parliamentary xii 456 a.

SPECIAL ASSESSMENTS—xiv 276–79; Excess Condemnation v 663 b; Municipal Corporation xi 91 b; Taxation xiv 532 a.

SPECIALIZATION—xiv 279–85; Administration, Public i 445 a; Amateur ii 18 b; Anthropology ii 82 b, 101 a; Art ii 226 b; Automobile Industry ii 326 a; Aviation (Industry) ii 363 a; Capitalism iii 199 a, 203 a; Commerce iv 10 a; Fee Splitting vi 178–79; Fruit and Vegetable Industry vi 509 a; Journalism viii 421 b; Labor viii 619 a; Large Scale Production ix 171 a, 172 b; Machines and Tools x 24 b; Management x 78 a; Medicine x 295 a; Middleman x 416 a; Occupation xi 426 a; Professions xii 476–80; Retail Trade xiii 347 a; Scientific Management xiii 603–08; Technology xiv 559 a; Woman, Position in Society (Primitive) xv 439 b, 442 a.

SPECIFIC PERFORMANCE — xiv 285–88.

SPECULATION—xiv 288–93. See Classification of Articles (Investment and Speculation), p. 552. See also Appreciation ii 141–44; Construction Industry iv 269 b; Crises iv 596 a; Debt v 36 a; Gambling vi 556 a; Prices (Theory) xii 371 b; Promotion xii 519 b; Wages xv 299 b.

Speculation, Land — see LAND SPECULATION.

Speenhamland System — Allowance System ii 7 a; Poor Laws xii 231 a.

SPENCE, T.—xiv 293; Single Tax xiv 65 a.

SPENCE, W. G.—xiv 294.

SPENCER, A. G.—xiv 294.

SPENCER, H.—xiv 295; Introd. Vol. I (Individualism and Capitalism) i 159 b; Adaptation i 436 a; Animism ii 66 a; Anthropology ii 102 b; Education v 413 b; Evolution v 651 b; Evolution, Social v 657 b; Justice viii 513 a; Play xii 160 a; Sociology xiv 237 b; Statics and Dynamics xiv 353 a.

Spendthrift Trust—Alienation of Property i 640 b; Trusts and Trustees xv 124 b.

Spener, P. J.—vi 416 a.

Spengler, O.—Decadence v 40 b; Evolution, Social v 661 b; National Socialism, German xi 225 b; Polit. Science xii 221 b.

SPERANSKY, M. M.—xiv 296; Alexander I i 630 a.

SPHERES OF INFLUENCE—xiv 297–99; Far Eastern Problem vi 94 a; Open Door xi 468 b.

Spices—xii 154 a.

Spiess, A.—xii 130 b.

Spiethoff, A.—iii 99 a.

Spinner, J.—ii 47 a.

SPINOZA, B.—xiv 299; Introd. Vol. I (The Rise of Liberalism) i 118 b; Academic Freedom i 387 a; Freethinkers vi 466 b; Natural Law xi 288 a; Self-Preservation xiii 655 a.

SPITTLER, L. T.—xiv 301.

SPOILS SYSTEM—xiv 301–05; Appointments ii 137–38; Clubs, Political iii 578 b; Judiciary viii 465 b; Machine, Political ix 659 b; Municipal Govt. xi 113 b; Parties, Political (Balkan States) xi 628 b; Rotten Boroughs xiii 443–44.

SPORTS—xiv 305–08; Amateur ii 20 a; Athletics ii 296–300; Gambling vi 556 b; Game Laws vi 562–64; Hunting vii 557 a; Physical Education xii 129–33.
Spranger, E.—iii 336 b.
Springer, G.—xiv 611 a.
SSŬ-MA CH'IEN—xiv 308; History and Historiography vii 383 b.
SSŬ-MA KUANG—xiv 309.
STABILIZATION, ECONOMIC — xiv 309–15; Bargaining Power ii 461 a; Labor Turnover viii 712 b; National Economic Planning xi 198 a; Price Regulation xii 355–62; Price Stabilization xii 362–66; Public Works xii 694 a; Rationalization xiii 117–20; Trade Associations xiv 670–76; Unemployment xv 161 b; Valorization xv 210–12.
Stabilization, Monetary — see MONETARY STABILIZATION.
Stabilization, Price—see PRICE STABILIZATION.
Stadtschaften—ix 50 a.
STAËL-HOLSTEIN, A. L. G. N. DE —xiv 315.
Stagecoach—xiii 406 b.
STAHL, F. J.—xiv 316; Public Law xii 659 a.
Stahl, G. E.—x 268 a.
Stalin, I. V.—Gosplan vi 708 a; Russian Revolution xiii 486 b.
STAMBOLIĬSKI, A. S.—xiv 317.
STAMBULOV, S. N.—xiv 318.
Stammler, R.—Economics v 383 b; Jurisprudence viii 482 a; Natural Law xi 290 a; Kant viii 541 b.
Stamp, J.—ii 197 b.
Standard Oil Co.—Oil Industry xi 442 b, 448 a; Trusts xv 113 a.
STANDARDIZATION — xiv 319–22; Adulteration i 467 b; Automobile Industry ii 324 a; Aviation (Industry) ii 363 a; Business, Govt. Services for iii 119 b; Capitalism iii 198 a; Consumer Protection iv 284 a; Factory System vi 53 a; Food and Drug Regulation vi 299 b; Grading vii 133 a; Inspection viii 73 b; Iron and Steel Industry viii 304 a; Labor, Methods of Remuneration for viii 679 a; Large Scale Production ix 174 a; Medical Materials Industry x 280 a; Scientific Management xiii 603–08; Specialization xiv 282 b; Weights and Measures xv 389–92.
STANDARDS OF LIVING—xiv 322–25; Child (Mortality) iii 388 b; Consumption iv 295–301; Cost of Living iv 481 a; Family Budgets vi 76 b; Furniture vi 537 a; Home Ownership vii 431 b; Housing vii 496–517; Luxury ix 634–38; Malthus x 68 a; Minimum Wage x 493 b; Poverty xii 284–92; Slums xiv 93–98; Technology xiv 555 b.
STANFORD, L.—xiv 325.
Stanislavsky, C.—xiv 611 b.

Stanley, E. H.—see DERBY, LORD.
STANLEY, H. M.—xiv 325.
STANTON, E. C.—xiv 326; Mott xi 78 b.
STARČEVIĆ, A.—xiv 326.
Stare Decisis—Advisory Opinions i 478 a; Judicial Process viii 452 b.
Starling, E. H.—i 621 a.
STASZIC, S. W.—xiv 327.
STATE—xiv 328–32; Introd. Vol. I (Renaissance and Reformation) i 88 b, 98 a, (The Rise of Liberalism) 109 a, (The Trend to Internationalism) 178 b, (War and Reorientation) 215 b; Absolutism i 380–82; Agreements, International i 518–20; Aksakovs i 610 b; Allegiance i 644–46; Anarchism ii 46–53; Aquinas ii 147 a; Aristotle ii 193 a; Association ii 285 b, 286 a; Authority ii 319–21; Autocracy ii 321–22; Autonomy ii 332–36; Bacon ii 382 b; Bodin ii 615 a; Bonald ii 631 a; Bosanquet ii 645 a; Cameralism iii 158–61; Catholic Parties iii 272 a; Centralization iii 308–13; Charity iii 342 a; Charles v iii 347 a; Checks and Balances iii 363–65; Christianity iii 453 b; Church Fathers iii 466 a; Cicero iii 469 a; Citizenship iii 471–74; City-State iii 489–92; Civic Education iii 496–98; Civil Liberties iii 509–13; Civil Service iii 515–23; Civilization iii 528 a; Collectivism iii 633–37; Confiscation iv 183–87; Consumers' Cooperation iv 289 b; Control, Social iv 347 b; Corporation iv 422 b; Duguit v 272 a; Education v 410 b, (Public) 414–21, (Sectarian) 421–25; Empire v 497–506; Engels v 541 b; Enlightenment v 548 a; Equality of States v 580–82; Executive v 680 b; Fascism vi 134 a; Federalism vi 169–72; Federation vi 172–78; Feudalism vi 203 b, 209 b; Fichte vi 224 a; Force, Political vi 338–41; Govt. vii 8–15; Green vii 164 b; Guild Socialism vii 203 a; Hedonism vii 308 b; Hegel vii 313 a; Idealism vii 570 a; Interests viii 145 a; Intolerance viii 243 b; Iselin viii 332 a; Islam viii 338 a; James of Viterbo viii 367 b; Justice viii 509 b; Justice, Administration of viii 516 a; Kant viii 540 a; Korkunov viii 591 b; Liberty ix 443 a; Marsilius of Padua x 160 a; Mercantilism x 335 b; Money x 604 b; Nationalism xi 231–49; Natural Law xi 285 b, 288 a; Obedience, Political xi 415–18; Organization, Economic xi 487 a; Pluralism xii 170–74; Political Offenders xii 199–203; Political Science xii 207–24; Power, Political xii 300–05;

Protestantism xii 573 b; Public Finance xii 638 a; Reason of State xiii 143–44; Recognition, International xiii 165–68; Republicanism xiii 317–21; Revolution and Counter-revolution xiii 367–76; Social Contract xiv 127–31; Social Organism xiv 138 a; Social Organization xiv 147 a; Socialism (Marxian) xiv 201 a; Society xiv 225–32; Sociology xiv 242 a; Sovereignty xiv 265–69; Spencer xiv 295 b.
STATE BANKS, U. S.—xiv 332–35; Bank Deposits, Guaranty of ii 417–19; Banking, Commercial ii 443 a; National Banks, U. S. xi 188 a.
State and County Fairs—i 545 a.
STATE GOVERNMENT, U. S.—xiv 335–38; Advisory Opinions i 476 b; Bicameral System ii 535 b; Boards, Administrative ii 607 b; Budget iii 42 b; Corruption, Political iv 452 a; Govt. (U. S.) vii 15–21; Govt. Reporting vii 130 b; Grants-in-Aid vii 154 b; State Liability xiv 340 a; States' Rights xiv 346–50; Tax Administration xiv 527 b; Veto xv 248 a.
State Legislatures, U. S.—ix 365–69.
STATE LIABILITY—xiv 338–43; Civil Service iii 522 b; De Facto Govt. v 53 b.
State Parks—xi 583 b.
State Police—Police xii 188 a; Policing, Industrial xii 195 a.
State Press—see GOVERNMENT PUBLICATIONS.
State Responsibility—see STATE LIABILITY.
State Socialism—see SOCIALISM.
STATE SUCCESSION—xiv 344–46; Cession iii 319–20; Concessions iv 157 a; De Facto Govt. v 53–54; Public Debt xii 610 a; Recognition, International xiii 165–68.
State Theater — see National Theater.
States General — see ESTATES GENERAL.
STATES' RIGHTS—xiv 346–50; Articles of Confederation ii 262–63; Aviation (Law) ii 367 b; Bicameral System ii 534 b; Calhoun iii 144 a; Centralization iii 310 a; Concurrent Powers iv 173–74; Extradition vi 43 b; Federation vi 174 b; Floods and Flood Control vi 284 a; Interstate Commerce viii 220–29; Interstate Commerce Commission viii 232 b; Labor Legislation and Law viii 664 b; Militia x 474 a; Police Power xii 191 a; Popular Sovereignty xii 239–40; State Government, U. S. xiv 335–38.
STATESMANSHIP—xiv 350–52.
STATICS AND DYNAMICS—xiv 352–56; Economics (Classical School) v 351 b, (Marginal

Index (Sports — Strikes and Lockouts)

Utility Economics) 362 b, (Mathematical Economics) 366 b, (Cambridge School) 369 a, (Socialist Economics) 379 b, (Universalist Economics) 386 a, (Institutional School) 388 b; Entrepreneur v 559 a; Market x 131 b; Production (Theory) xii 466 a; Profit xii 483 b; Social Process xiv 148-51; Walras xv 328 b.

Statistical Society of London—Introd. Vol. I (The Social Sciences as Disciplines, Gt. Brit.) i 242 b; Learned Societies ix 296 b.

STATISTICS—xiv 356-73 (Hist. 356-60, 372, Practise 360-66, 373, Method 366-73). See Classification of Articles (Statistics), p. 556. See also Introd. Vol. I (War and Reorientation) i 213 b, (The Social Sciences as Disciplines, Austria) 267 b, (Gt. Brit.) 242 b, (Hungary) 271 a, (Russia) 283 b, 284 b, (U. S.) 337 a, 343 a; Accidents i 389 b; Accidents, Industrial i 391 b; Annuities ii 70 b; Anthropometry ii 111 b; Business Cycles iii 93 a; Cost of Living iv 480 b; Economic History v 328 a; Economics (Mathematical Economics) v 368 a, (Historical School) 374 a, 376 b; Financial Statements vi 247-49; Method, Scientific x 392 a; Profit xii 484 b; Race xiii 27 b; Social Psychology xiv 155 b; Social Work (Case Work) xiv 183 a; Unemployment xv 149 a; Wages xv 302 a. For biog. references see Classification of Articles (Statistics), p. 571.

Statistics, Criminal—see CRIMINAL STATISTICS.

STATUS—xiv 373-78; Alien i 633-35; Anthropology ii 88 a; Aristocracy ii 185 a; Career iii 225 a; Caste iii 254-57; Class iii 531-36; Emancipation v 483-85; Equality v 574-80; Family vi 66 a; Feudalism (Europ.) vi 204 b, (Ottoman) 212 a; Guilds vii 207 b, 213 b; Labor Legislation and Law viii 672 b; Mobility, Social x 554-55; Nobility xi 385-89; Ornament xi 496 b; Race Conflict xiii 36-41; Serfdom xiii 667-71; Slavery xiv 73-92; Social Discrimination xiv 131-34; Suffrage xiv 448 a; Woman, Position in Society xv 439-51.

Statute of Artificers—see Artificers, Statute of.

Statute of Frauds—see FRAUDS, STATUTE OF.

Statutes of Labourers—see LABOURERS, STATUTES OF.

Statutes of Limitations—see LIMITATION OF ACTIONS.

Staunford, W.—xii 319 a.
STEAD, W. T.—xiv 378.

Steam Engine—Machinery, Industrial x 4 a; Machines and Tools x 22 a; Power, Industrial xii 295 a.
Stearns, W. A.—xii 131 b.
Steel—x 385 a.
Steel Industry—see IRON AND STEEL INDUSTRY.
STEELE, R.—xiv 378; Addison i 437 a.
STEFAN DUŠAN—xiv 379.
STEFFEN, G. F.—xiv 379.
STEIN, H. F. K. VOM UND ZUM—xiv 380; Agrarian Movements i 499 a; Army ii 212 a; Hardenberg vii 268 a; Local Govt. ix 575 b; Municipal Govt. xi 108 b; Pertz xii 91 a.
STEIN, LORENZ VON—xiv 381.
STEIN, LUDWIG—xiv 382.
STEINER, R.—xiv 382.
STEINHAUSEN, G.—xiv 383.
STEINKELLER, P. A.—xiv 384.
STEINTHAL, H.—xiv 384; Social Psychology xiv 153 a.
Stephan, H. von—xii 272 a.
Stephen I—xi 560 a.
Stephen, G. — see MOUNT STEPHEN, LORD.
STEPHEN, J. F.—xiv 385; Sedition xiii 626 b.
STEPHEN, L.—xiv 385.
STEPHENS, A. H.—xiv 386.
STEPHENS, H. M.—xiv 386.
STEPHENS, U. S. — xiv 387; Knights of Labor viii 581 b.
STEPHENSON, G.—xiv 387.
Sterilization—Criminology iv 591 a; Eugenics v 619 a; Mental Defectives x 313 b; Recidivism xiii 160 a.
Stern, W.—x 323 b.
STERNBERG, L. Y.—xiv 388.
STERNE, S.—xiv 389.
Stetson, A.—iii 448 b.
STEUART, J. D.—xiv 389.
STEVENS, J.—xiv 389.
STEVENS, T.—xiv 390; Negro Problem xi 338 a.
Stevenson Rubber Restriction Act—xiii 456 a.
STEWARD, I.—xiv 391; Hours of Labor vii 492 b; Short Hours Movement xiv 45 b.
STEWART, A. T.—xiv 391; Garden Cities vi 570 a.
Stieber, W.—v 594 b.
STILLMAN, J.—xiv 392.
STINNES, H.—xiv 392.
STIRNER, M.—xiv 393; Anarchism ii 48 a.
STO—Gosplan vi 706 a, 709 a.
STOCK BREEDING—xiv 394-97; Agriculture i 582 b, 584 b; Bakewell ii 393 b; Dairy Industry iv 692 a; Livestock Industry ix 545-51; Meat Packing and Slaughtering x 242 b.
STOCK EXCHANGE—xiv 397-402; Arbitrage ii 150-51; Broker iii 10 a; Brokers' Loans iii 10-13; Business Ethics iii 112 b; Call Money iii 149-50; Corner, Speculative iv 408-10; Financial Organization vi 242 a, 244 a; Investment viii 266 a; Investment Trusts viii 283 a; Speculation xiv 290 b.
STÖCKER, A.—xiv 402; Anti-semitism ii 122 b.
STOCKS AND STOCK OWNERSHIP—xiv 403-07; Blue Sky Laws ii 602-05; Corporation iv 420 a; Corporation Finance iv 423-30; Employee Stock Ownership v 506-09; Income vii 624 a; Income Tax vii 630 a; Joint Stock Company viii 411-13; Speculation xiv 290 b; Stock Exchange xiv 397-402.
Stockyards—i 562 b.
STOICISM—xiv 407-10; Introd. Vol. I (Greek Culture and Thought) i 36 a, (The Roman World) 49 a; Astrology ii 287 b; Aurelius Antoninus ii 317 a; Communism iv 82 a; Democracy v 78 b; Epictetus v 567 a; Equality v 575 a; Ethics v 602 b; Human Nature vii 534 a; Justice viii 510 a; Materialism x 210 a; Natural Law xi 286 b; Naturalism xi 304 b; Passive Resistance and Non-cooperation xii 10 b; Rationalism xiii 114 b; Self-Preservation xiii 654 b.
STOLIPIN, P. A.—xiv 410; Small Holdings xiv 104 a.
Stolzmann, R.—v 384 a.
Stone Age—Machines and Tools x 14 b; Prehistory xii 316 b.
Stone Industry—see QUARRYING.
STONE, L.—xiv 411.
STONE, M. E.—xiv 411.
STONE, W. S.—xiv 412; Labor Banking viii 622 b.
Stopes, M.—ii 561 b.
Storage—see WAREHOUSING.
STORCH, H. F. VON—xiv 412.
Storting—ix 387 b.
STORY, J.—xiv 413; Comity iii 678 b; Common Law iv 53 a; Conflict of Laws iv 189 a; Kent viii 558 b; Negotiable Instruments xi 333 b.
STOURM, R.—xiv 413.
STOWE, H. B.—xiv 414.
STOWELL, LORD—xiv 414.
STRACCA DI ANCONA, B.—xiv 415.
STRACHEY, J. ST. L.—xiv 415.
Strasser, A.—ii 24 a.
Strasser, O.—xi 226 a.
Stratz, C. H.—xiii 26 a.
STRAUS, N.—xiv 416.
STRAUSS, D. F.—xiv 416.
STRAW VOTE—xiv 417-19.
Street Railways—xi 118 a.
STRESEMANN, G.—xiv 419; Parties, Political (Germany) xi 616 b.
STRIKES AND LOCKOUTS—xiv 419-26; Benefits, Trade Union ii 513-16; Boycott ii 664 a; Civil Service iii 521 b; Company Housing iv 116 b; Company Unions iv 125 b; General Strike vi 607-12; Industrial Workers of the World viii 15 a;

Intimidation viii 240 a; Jones viii 415 a; Journeymen's Societies viii 426 a; Knights of Labor viii 582 b; Labor Disputes viii 633–37; Labor, Govt. Services for viii 646 b; Labor Injunction viii 653–57; Labor Legislation and Law viii 668 b; Longshoremen ix 608 a; Mining x 505 a; Policing, Industrial xii 193–96; Public Employment xii 635 a; Railroads xiii 95 a; Unemployment Insurance xv 172 b.

Strip System of Agriculture—Land Tenure ix 82 b; Manorial System x 98 b.

STROJNOWSKI, H.—xiv 426.

STROSSMAYER, J. J.—xiv 426.

Struggle for Existence—Acclimatization i 401–03; Adaptation i 435–37; Biology ii 555 a; Evolution v 651 a; Humanitarianism vii 547 b; Self-Preservation xiii 653–55.

STRUVE, G. A.—xiv 427.

STUBBS, W.—xiv 427.

STUCKENBERG, J. H. W.—xiv 428.

Stundists—xiii 630 a.

Sturm-Abteilungen—xi 226 a.

Sturm und Drang—Romanticism xiii 429 a; Theater xiv 609 b.

SUÁREZ, F.—xiv 429; Introd. Vol. 1 (The Social Sciences as Disciplines, Spain) i 295 a; Social Contract xiv 128 b.

SUAREZ, K. G.—xiv 430.

Subaraean Law—ix 211–19.

Submarine Warfare—Armed Merchantmen ii 201–03; Blockade ii 595 b; Navy xi 315 a; Piracy xii 139 a.

SUBSIDIES—xiv 430–33; Aviation ii 340 b, 346 a, 350 b, 353 b; Bounties ii 652 a; Business, Govt. Services for iii 120 b; Export Credits vi 20 a; Grants-in-Aid vii 152–55; Housing (Eur.) vii 508 a; Land Grants ix 32–43; Loans, Intergovernmental ix 556 a; Local Finance ix 572 a; Merchant Marine x 343–50; Railroads xiii 78 a; Shipbuilding xiv 29 b; Slums xiv 96 a; Universities and Colleges xv 185 b.

SUBURBS—xiv 433–35; Back-to-the-Land Movements ii 379 a; City iii 478 a; Garden Cities vi 569–71; Home Ownership vii 432 a; Land Utilization ix 134 a; Regional Planning xiii 205 a.

Subvention—see GRANTS-IN-AID; SUBSIDIES.

Subways—xi 124 a.

SUCCESSION, LAWS OF—xiv 436–41. See INHERITANCE.

SUCCESSION, POLITICAL—xiv 441–44; Chinese Problem iii 431 b; Coalition iii 600–02; Conspiracy, Political iv 238–41; Coup d'État iv 508–10; Fascism vi 137 a.

Succession, State—see STATE SUCCESSION.

SUEZ CANAL—xiv 444–47.

SUFFRAGE—xiv 447–50; Absentee-Voting i 376; Catholic Emancipation iii 269–71; Chartism iii 352–54; Elections iv 451 a; Equality v 577 b; Freehold vi 464 a; Govt. (Belgium) vii 47 b, (Italy) 49 b, (Japan) 97 a, (U. S.) 17 a; Law (Celtic) ix 247 b; Literacy and Illiteracy ix 520 a; Negro Problem xi 338 b, 353 a. See also Woman Suffrage.

SUGAR—xiv 450–55; Business, Govt. Services for iii 120 a; Havemeyer vii 281 b.

SUICIDE—xiv 455–59; Self-Preservation xiii 654 b.

SULEIMAN I—xiv 459.

SULLY, DUC DE—xiv 460; Henry IV vii 322 b.

Sulphur—x 497 b.

Sulphuric Acid—x 382 a.

Sultanate—viii 340 a.

Sumerian Law—Law (Cuneiform) ix 211–19.

SUMMARY JUDGMENT—xiv 461–62; Small Claims Courts xiv 99–101.

SUMNER, C.—xiv 462; Negro Problem xi 338 a.

SUMNER, W. G.—xiv 463; Folkways vi 293 b.

SUMPTUARY LEGISLATION — xiv 464–66; Baudrillart ii 480 b; Blue Laws ii 600–02; Consumption iv 293 b; Liquor Traffic ix 504 b; Luxury ix 634 b; Prohibition xii 499–510.

SUN YAT SEN—xiv 466; Chinese Problem iii 434 b; Far Eastern Problem vi 96 b; Govt. (China) vii 98 b; Kuomintang viii 610 b; Law (Chinese) ix 253 b.

Sunday Laws—see BLUE LAWS.

Sunday School—xiii 70 b.

SUNDBÄRG, A. G.—xiv 467.

Sundstroem, E. S.—i 402 a.

SUNDT, E. L.—xiv 468.

Sunna—Islam viii 334 a; Islamic Law viii 345 b.

Superstition—see MAGIC.

SUPILO, F.—xiv 469.

SUPINO, C.—xiv 469.

SUPIŃSKI, J.—xiv 470.

SUPPLY—xiv 470–74; Demand v 69 b; Economics (Marginal Utility Economics) v 359 a, (Cambridge School) 369 a; Interest viii 136 a; Luxury ix 637 a; Market x 131–33; Monopoly x 623–30; Taxation xiv 536 b; Value and Price xv 219 a; Wages xv 295 a.

Supremacy of Law—see RULE OF LAW.

SUPREME COURT, U. S.—xiv 474–82; Introd. Vol. 1 (War and Reorientation) i 220 a; Certiorari iii 318 b; Constitutionalism iv 256 b; Criminal Syndicalism iv 583 a; Ellsworth v 482 a; Freedom of Contract vi 454 a; Judicial Review viii 457–64; Rate Regulation xiii 106 a; Reconstruction xiii 172 a; Resale Price Maintenance xiii 328 a.

Surety Association of America—ii 633 b.

SURETYSHIP AND GUARANTY—xiv 482–87; Bail ii 386–88; Bonding ii 631–34; Law (Celtic) ix 249 a, (Cuneiform) 218 a, (Greek) 228 a; Pledge xii 166–68.

Surplus Value—Distribution v 170 b; Economics (Socialist Economics) v 378 b; Exploitation vi 16 b; Socialism (Marxian) xiv 200 a; Unearned Increment xv 144 b.

Survival of the Fittest—see Struggle for Existence.

SÜSSMILCH, J. P.—xiv 487.

Suttee—v 23 b.

SUTTNER, B. VON—xiv 487.

Svenska Tändsticksaktiebolag—x 207 a.

SVERDRUP, J.—xiv 488.

Sveriges Rikes Lag—iv 607 a.

Swadeshi—ii 663 b.

SWAINSON, W.—xiv 488.

Sweatshop—Homework, Industrial vii 445 b, 447 b; Labor Movement xiii 682 b; Minimum Wage x 491 b.

Sweepstakes—ix 613 b.

Swift, G. F.—x 245 b.

SWIFT, J.—xiv 489.

SWINTON, J.—xiv 490.

Swiss Civil Code—vii 525 b.

Swope Plan—Stabilization, Economic xiv 312 b.

Sword-Bearers—x 462 b.

SYBEL, H. VON—xiv 491.

Sydenham, T.—v 570 a.

Sydenstricker, E.—Family Budgets vi 77 b; Morbidity xi 6 a.

Sydney, A.—see SIDNEY, A.

SYLVIS, W. H.—xiv 492.

SYMBOLISM—xiv 492–95; Anthropology ii 90 b; Art (Primitive) ii 227 a, (Egyptian) 238 b, (Indian) 230 b, (Japanese) 237 b, (Mediaeval) 243–45; Ceremony iii 313–16; Communication iv 78–81; Death Customs v 22 b; Fashion vi 141 a; Fertility Rites vi 190–92; Fictions vi 225–28; Folklore vi 289 a; Language ix 155–169; Leadership ix 285 b; Nationalism xi 234 b; Ornament xi 496–98; Ritual xiii 396–98; Sacrifice xiii 502 a; Utopia xv 200–03; Writing xv 500–03.

SYMONDS, J. A.—xiv 495.

Sympathetic Strike—xiv 421 a.

SYNDICALISM—xiv 496–500; Introd. Vol. 1 (The Trend to Internationalism) i 178 b; Administration, Public i 446 a; Agrarian Syndicalism i 515–16; Anarchism ii 50 b; Antimilitarism ii 115 b; Blanqui ii 585 a; Bourses du Travail ii 659 b; Class Struggle iii 540 a; Confédération Générale du Travail iv 180 a; Criminal Syndicalism iv 582–84; Direct Action v 156

b; Fascism vi 135 b; Functional Representation vi 519 b; Functionalism vi 525 a; General Strike vi 608 b; Griffuelhes vii 172 b; Industrial Workers of the World viii 15 a; Labor Movement viii 688 a, 689 b; Labor Parties viii 698 a; Morrison xi 22 b; Pelloutier xii 56 b; Sabotage xiii 495–97; Socialism xiv 205 a, 216 b; Sorel xiv 262 b; Trade Unions (France) xv 26 a, (Italy) 31 b, (Spain) 29 b, (Sweden) 20 a.
Syndicalism, Agrarian—see AGRARIAN SYNDICALISM.
Syndicalism, Criminal—see CRIMINAL SYNDICALISM.
SYRKIN, N.—xiv 500.
SZABÓ, E.—xiv 501.
SZCZEPANOWSKI, A. P. S.—xiv 501.
SZÉCHENYI, I.—xiv 502.

Ṭabari, al-—History and Historiography vii 382 a; Miskawayhi x 535 a.
Tabloid Journalism—xii 334 b.
Taborites—xiii 626 a.
TABU—xiv 502–05; Avoidance ii 369–70; Birth Control ii 559 b; Birth Customs ii 565 b; Cannibalism iii 173 a; Censorship iii 290 b; Folkways vi 295 b; Holidays vii 413 b; Incest vii 620–22; Language ix 166 a; Marriage x 146 b; Meat Packing and Slaughtering x 242 a; Morals x 643–49; Priesthood xii 389 a; Religion xiii 234 b.
TACITUS, P. C.—xiv 505; Introd. Vol. I (The Roman World) i 52 b.
Taft, W. H.—Philippine Problem xii 110 b; Rate Regulation xiii 106 b.
TAGÁNYI, K.—xiv 506.
Tagore, R.—vii 666 a.
Taiho Statutes—ix 116 b.
Taikwa Reforms—v 502 a.
Taille—i 608 b.
TAINE, H.-A.—xiv 506; French Revolution vi 471 a.
Taiping Rebellion—xiii 145 a.
TALLEYRAND-PÉRIGORD, C.-M. DE —xiv 507; Education (Public) v 415 a.
Talmud—see SACRED BOOKS.
Tammany Society—iii 578 b.
TÁNCSICS, M.—xiv 508.
TANEY, R. B.—xiv 509.
Tanning—ix 300–04.
TAOISM—xiv 510–13; Art (Japanese) ii 237 b; Chuang Tzu iii 462 a; Confucianism iv 198 a; Fatalism vi 147 b.
Tappan, L.—x 331 a.
Tapparelli d'Azeglio, M. — see AZEGLIO, M. D'.
TARDE, G.—xiv 513; Introd. Vol. I (Nationalism) i 169 b; Accommodation i 403 a; Criminology iv 588 a; Imitation vii 586 b; Social Psychology xiv 153 b; Sociology xiv 239 b.

TARIFF—xiv 514–23. See Classification of Articles (Tariff), p. 556. See also Agrarian Movements i 491 b; Bounties ii 653 a; Colonial Economic Policy iii 648 a; Commercial Treaties iv 28 a; Dumping v 276 b; Forced Labor vi 345 a; International Trade (Theory) viii 201 a; Iron and Steel Industry viii 314 a; Meat Packing and Slaughtering x 255 a; Mercantilism x 334 a; Metals (Copper) x 375 b; Price Regulation xii 356 a; Raw Materials xiii 129 b; Smuggling xiv 119–23; Textile Industry xiv 586 a.
TASTE—xiv 523–25; Art ii 223–59; Fashion vi 139 a.
TATISHCHEV, V. N.—xiv 525.
Taussig, F. W.—viii 204 a.
TAX ADMINISTRATION—xiv 526–28; Assessment of Taxes ii 276–79; Customs Duties iv 671 b; Feudalism (Moslem) vi 210 b; Gasoline Tax vi 595 b; General Property Tax vi 603 b; Income Tax vii 634 a; Inheritance Taxation viii 47 b; Revenue Farming xiii 358–60.
TAX EXEMPTION—xiv 528–30; Bonds ii 634 b; Business, Govt. Services for iii 120 b; Housing (Eur.) vii 508 b, (U. S.) 515 a; Public Debt xii 604 b; Public Utilities (Eur.) xii 685 a.
Tax Farming — see REVENUE FARMING.
TAXATION—xiv 531–41. See Classification of Articles (Taxation), p. 556. See also Absentee Ownership i 378 a; Bodin ii 616 a; Broggia iii 8 a; Bunge iii 68 a; Canard iii 171 b; Civic Organizations iii 500 a; Colonial Administration iii 644 a; Expenditures, Public vi 10 a; Govt. Owned Corporations vii 110 b; Interstate Commerce viii 224 a; Land Tenure (China and Japan) ix 116 b, (India) 110 b; Landed Estates ix 142 b; Liquor Traffic ix 505 a; Local Finance ix 570 a; Municipal Corporation xi 91 b; Municipal Finance xi 100 a; Revenues, Public xiii 360 b; Salt xiii 523 b; Schanz xiii 564 a; Valuation xv 216 a; War Finance xv 350 a, 351 a.
Taxis, J. von—xii 270 b.
Taylor Differential Piece Rate— viii 679 a.
TAYLOR, F. M.—xiv 541; Diminishing Returns v 145 b.
TAYLOR, F. W.—xiv 542; Administration, Public i 442 b; Business Administration iii 88 b; Efficiency v 437 b; Engineering v 545 b; Scientific Management xiii 603 b.
Taylor, Harriet H.—x 481 b.
Taylor, Henry C.—i 535 a.
TAYLOR, J.—xiv 542.
Taylor Society—iii 90 a.

Tea—Art (Japanese) ii 237 b; Plantation Wares xii 156 a.
TEACHING PROFESSION—xiv 543–53; Introd. Vol. I (The Social Sciences as Disciplines, Gt. Brit.) i 231 b, (Germany) 262 a, (Italy) 278 a, (Russia) 282 a, 286 a, 289 a; Academic Freedom i 384–88; Learned Societies ix 298 b; Legal Profession and Legal Education ix 342 b.
Technical Education—see VOCATIONAL EDUCATION.
Technocrats—xiv 558 b.
Technological Unemployment— Invention viii 250 a; Labor viii 619 b; Labor Movement viii 684 b; Mechanic x 265 b; Technology xiv 557 a; Unemployment xv 153 b, 157 a.
TECHNOLOGY—xiv 553–60. See Classification of Articles (Industry), p. 551, especially INDUSTRIAL REVOLUTION, INVENTION, MACHINES AND TOOLS. See also Introd. Vol. I (The Revolutions) i 125 b, (Individualism and Capitalism) 152 b, (The Trend to Internationalism) 172 a, 177 b; Agric. Machinery i 551–54; Agriculture (Primitive) i 573 a, (Mediaeval) 577 a; Anthropology ii 80 b, 89 b; Architecture ii 172 b; Change, Social iii 331 a; Communication iv 80 a; Cotton iv 489 b; Economics (Socialist Economics) v 379 b; Engineering v 541–46; Expositions, International vi 26 a; Fire Protection vi 265 a; Floods and Flood Control vi 283 b; Food Supply vi 332 b; Fortunes, Private vi 396 a; Grains vii 141 a; Hunting vii 556 b; Innovation viii 58–61; Labor viii 619 b; Limitation of Armaments ix 484 a; Literature ix 527 b; Magic x 39–44; Man x 73 a; Materialism (Historical) x 218 a; Method, Scientific x 389–96; Patents xii 19–25; Research xiii 331 a; Roads xiii 400–11; Science xiii 591–603; Shipping xiv 32 a; Urbanization xv 190 b; Wages xv 297 a; Weights and Measures xv 389–92.
TELEPHONE AND TELEGRAPH— xiv 560–67; Electrical Manufacturing Industry v 470–77; Postal Service xii 273 a; Public Utilities xii 674–87; Radio xiii 54 a; Reuter xiii 357 b; Vail xv 208 a.
Teletypewriter—xiv 565 b.
Telford, T.—xiii 403 b.
TEMPERANCE MOVEMENTS—xiv 567–70; Anti-Saloon League ii 118–19; Dow v 229 b; Liquor Traffic ix 504 b; Prohibition xii 500 a; Willard xv 423 a.
Temperley, H.—ii 177 b.
Temple, H. J.—see PALMERSTON, LORD.

TEMPLE, W.—xiv 570.
Temporalism—Materialism (Dialectical) x 214 b.
Tenancy, Farm—see FARM TENANCY.
Tennessee Valley—xiii 206 b.
Terman, L. M.—vi 614 a.
TERMINALS—xiv 571–74; Markets, Municipal x 143 b; Ports and Harbors xii 255–60.
TERRITORIAL WATERS—xiv 574–75; Boundaries ii 651 b; Fisheries vi 267 b; Merchantmen, Status of x 351 a; Water Law xv 369 a.
TERRORISM—xiv 575–80; Antiradicalism ii 117 b; Assassination ii 271–75; Brigandage ii 693–96; Camorra iii 161–62; Gershuni vi 639 b; Ku Klux Klan viii 607 a; Policing, Industrial xii 193–96; Violence xv 266 b.
TERTULLIAN—xiv 580; Church Fathers iii 465 a.
Tests, Mental—see MENTAL TESTS.
Tetens, J. N.—ii 390 b.
Teutonic Knights—Chivalry iii 439 a; Hanseatic League vii 264 a; Military Orders x 460 a.
TEXTILE INDUSTRY—xiv 580–96; Arkwright ii 193 a; Company Housing iv 115–19; Flax, Hemp and Jute vi 274–79; Gott vii 4 b; Gregg vii 165 b; Heavy Chemicals vii 301 a; Industrial Arts vii 685 b; Industrial Revolution viii 6 b; Large Scale Production ix 176 b; Laundry and Dry Cleaning Industry ix 193 b; Machines and Tools x 21 b; Silk Industry xiv 52–57.
THAER, A. D.—xiv 596; Agriculture i 583 b.
THAYER, J. B.—xiv 597.
THAYER, W. R.—xiv 597.
THEATER—xiv 598–615; Introd. Vol. I (Greek Culture and Thought) i 22 b; Censorship iii 290–94; Literature ix 533 b; Motion Pictures xi 58–69; Mysteries xi 172–75; Public Opinion xii 671 b.
Théâtre Français—xiv 608 a.
Theocracy—Blue Laws ii 602 a; Bradford ii 672 a; Cotton iv 494 a; Hooker vii 460 a; Islam viii 333 a; Mather x 227 b; Puritanism xiii 5 b; Reformation (Calvinism) xiii 191 a; Religious Freedom xiii 244 a; Religious Institutions (Protestant) xiii 270 b.
THEODOSIUS I—xiv 615; Introd. Vol. I (The Universal Church) i 61 a.
THEODOSIUS II—xiv 616; Civil Law iii 503 a.
Theology—Comparative Religion iv 131–34; Ethics v 602 a; Evolution v 654 a; Jurisprudence viii 479 b.
Theophilus—x 18 b.

THIBAUT, A. F. J.—xiv 616.
THIERRY, J.-N.-A.—xiv 617.
THIERS, L. A.—xiv 617; Anticlericalism ii 113 b; Commune of Paris iv 64 a.
Third Degree—xii 187 a.
Third International—Communist Parties iv 89 a; Direct Action v 157 b; Socialism xiv 206 b, 217 b.
THÖL, J. H.—xiv 618.
THOMAS, A. A.—xiv 619.
Thomas, J. H.—viii 701 a.
Thomas, P. É.—ii 291 b.
Thomas, S. G.—viii 302 a.
Thomas, W. I.—Introd. Vol. I (War and Reorientation) i 206 a; Adolescence i 458 a.
THOMASIUS, C.—xiv 619.
THOMPSON, W.—xiv 620; Socialism xiv 195 b.
Thomsen, C. J.—Archaeology ii 163 b; Records, Hist. xiii 173 b.
THONISSEN, J. J.—xiv 621.
THOREAU, H. D.—xiv 621; Passive Resistance and Non-cooperation xii 12 a; Transcendentalism xv 76 b.
Thorndike, E. L.—v 433 a.
Thornton, H.—Longe ix 605 b; Price Stabilization xii 363 a.
THOU, J. A. DE—xiv 622.
Thoyras, P. de—i 143 a.
THRANE, M. M.—xiv 623.
Thrasybulus—ii 37 b.
Thrasymachus—Natural Law xi 286 a; Sophists xiv 260 b.
Three-Field System—Agriculture i 576 b; Soils xiv 253 a; Village Community xv 258 a.
Three Mile Limit—iii 130 b.
THRIFT—xiv 623–26; Accumulation i 417 a; Bourgeoisie ii 655 a; Calvin iii 152 b; Christianity iii 458 b; Labor Movement viii 685 b, 687 a; Rentier xiii 299 b.
Thuanus—see THOU, J. A. DE.
THUCYDIDES—xiv 626; Introd. Vol. I (Greek Culture and Thought) i 23 b, 28 a; History and Historiography vii 369 a.
THÜNEN, J. H. VON—xiv 627; Distribution v 171 a; Economics v 365 b.
Thurn and Taxis—xii 270 b.
TIELE, C. P.—xiv 628.
Tien-wang—xiii 145 a.
Tikhon—xiii 266 b.
TILAK, B. G.—xiv 628; Indian Question vii 665 b.
Timber—see WOOD INDUSTRIES.
Time Preference Theory—Interest viii 134 b.
TIME SERIES—xiv 629–36; Business Cycles iii 93 a; Statistics xiv 370 b.
Time Wage—viii 678 a, 679 b.
Tin—x 382 b.
TINDAL, M.—xiv 636.
Tipping—Restaurants xiii 339 a.
Tires and Tubes—xiii 458 a.
TIRPITZ, A. VON—xiv 637; Archives ii 178 a.
TISZA, I.—xiv 637.
TISZA, K.—xiv 638.

TITCHENER, E. B.—xiv 639; Psychology xii 592 b.
Title Insurance Companies—ix 131 b.
Titus Livius—see LIVY.
TOBACCO—xiv 640–46; Blue Laws ii 601 b; Monopolies, Public x 620 b.
Tobacco Workers' International Union— xiv 643 b.
TOCQUEVILLE, A. C. H. M. C. DE—xiv 646; Democracy v 80 b; French Revolution vi 471 a; Individualism vii 674 b; Liberty ix 445 a.
Todd, T. W.—ii 111 b.
Token Coins—iv 649–51.
TOLAND, J.—xiv 647.
TOLEDO, F. DE—xiv 648.
Toleration—see INTOLERANCE; RELIGIOUS FREEDOM.
Tolls—Mercantilism x 334 a; Roads xiii 404 a, 405 a.
TOLSTOY, L. N.—xiv 648; Anarchism ii 47 a, 50 a; Art ii 224 b; Passive Resistance and Non-cooperation xii 11 b.
TOMEK, V. V.—xiv 649.
TOMMASEO, N.—xiv 650.
Tomn—see KNOWLES, L. C. A.
Tone, T. W.—Irish Question viii 288 a; Martial Law x 164 b.
Tönnies, F.—Introd. Vol. I (Nationalism) i 168 b; Sociology xiv 244 a.
Tonti, L.—ii 70 a.
Tontine — Annuities ii 70 a; Friendly Societies vi 496 b; Life Insurance ix 465 b.
TOOKE, T.—xiv 651; Newmarch xi 368 b.
Tools—see TECHNOLOGY.
TOOMBS, R.—xiv 651.
TOPINARD, P.—xiv 652.
TORRENS, R.—xiv 652; Crombie iv 604 a.
Torrens System—Land Transfer ix 130 a.
Torrey, H. W.—i 333 b.
TORT—xiv 653–57; Conflict of Laws iv 191 b; Damages iv 698 a; Injunction viii 55 a; Labor Legislation and Law viii 669 a; Liability ix 427–29; Maritime Law x 128 a; Negligence xi 329 b; Nuisance xi 402–04; State Liability xiv 338–43.
Tory Party, Gt. Brit.—Beaconsfield ii 484 b; Bolingbroke ii 622 a; Parties, Political (Gt. Brit.) xi 601 b; Shaftesbury xiv 14 a.
Totalitarian State—xiv 330 b.
TOTEMISM—xiv 657–61.
TOURIST TRAFFIC—xiv 661–64; Foreign Language Press vi 381 a; Passport xii 13–16; Resorts xiii 334–36.
TOURVILLE, H. DE—xiv 664.
TOUT, T. F.—xiv 665.
Town Meeting—xii 237 b.
Town Planning—see CITY AND TOWN PLANNING.
Towne-Halsey Formula — viii 679 a.
Towner Rating Bureau—ii 633 b.

TOWNSEND, J.—xiv 665.
TOWNSHEND, C.—xiv 666; Agriculture i 579 b.
TOYNBEE, A.—xiv 666.
Toynbee Hall—Social Settlements xiv 157 b; Toynbee xiv 666 b.
Tracy, D. de—see DESTUTT DE TRACY, A. L. C.
TRADE AGREEMENTS—xiv 667–70; Amer. Federation of Labor ii 27 b; Collective Bargaining iii 629 b; Conciliation, Industrial iv 167 b; Justi viii 507 b; Labor Contract viii 631 a; Labor Movement viii 683 b; Strikes and Lockouts xiv 422 a; Trade Unions (Germany) xv 16 b.
TRADE ASSOCIATIONS—xiv 670–76; Arbitration, Commercial ii 152 a; Boycott ii 664 b; Cartel iii 235 a, 239 b; Cement iii 289 b; Dairy Industry iv 693 a; Employers' Associations v 510 b; Food Industries (Grocery Trade) vi 314 b; Iron and Steel Industry viii 307 b; Laundry and Dry Cleaning Industry ix 196 a; Liquor Industry ix 499 b; Mercantile Credit x 332 a; Milling Industry x 486 a; Paints and Varnishes xi 533 b; Printing and Publishing xii 412 b; Production (Statistics) xii 469 b; Resale Price Maintenance xiii 327 b; Rubber xiii 455 b; Shipping xiv 38 a; Trusts xv 120 a.
Trade Routes—see COMMERCIAL ROUTES.
TRADE UNIONS—xv 3–57 (Introd. 3–7, 55, United Kingdom and Irish Free State 7–12, 55, Germany 12–17, 55, Austria, Switzerland and Holland 17–19, 55, Scandinavian Countries and Finland 19–22, 55, Succession States and Balkan Countries 22–25, 56, France 25–27, 56, Belgium 27–29, 56, Spain and Portugal 29–31, 56, Italy 31–32, 56, Russia 32–35, 56, Far and Near East 35–40, 56, U. S. and Canada 40–45, 56, Australia, New Zealand and S. Africa 45–48, 57, Lat. Amer. 48–53, 57, International Organization 53–55). See LABOR MOVEMENT. See also Agrarian Movements (Germany) i 499 b, (Gt. Brit.) 496 a, (Italy) 500 b; Apprenticeship ii 146 a; Arbitration, Industrial ii 153–57; Automobile Industry ii 327 a; Bargaining Power ii 460 a; Benefits, Trade Union ii 513–16; Blacklist, Labor ii 578–79; Business Agent iii 91–92; Casual Labor iii 261 a; Civil Service iii 521 a; Clerical Occupations iii 553 a; Collective Bargaining iii 628–31; Communist Parties iv 92 a; Company Unions iv 123–26; Conciliation, Industrial iv 169 a; Conspiracy, Criminal iv 237 a; Construction Industry iv 271 a, 278 a; Consumers'

Cooperation iv 287 a; Cooperation (Gt. Brit.) iv 365 b; Domestic Service v 204 a; Electric Power v 467 b; Electrical Manufacturing Industry v 475 a; Employers' Associations v 511 a; Fabianism vi 47 b; Factory System vi 54 a; Family Allowances vi 72 b; Food Industries (Baking, U. S.) vi 307 a; Fur Trade and Industry vi 536 a; Furniture vi 541 b; Garment Industries vi 580 b; Glass and Pottery Industries vi 675 b; Group Insurance vii 186 b; Guild Socialism vii 202–04; Health Insurance vii 296 a; Hotels vii 476 a; Housing vii 516 b; Industrial Democracy vii 691–92; Industrial Relations Councils vii 717–22; Intimidation viii 239 b, 242 a; Irish Question viii 293 a; Iron and Steel Industry viii 317 a, 320 b; Journalism viii 422 b; Journeymen's Societies viii 427 a; Labor Contract viii 631 a; Labor Injunction viii 653–57; Labor Legislation and Law viii 671 a; Labor, Methods of Remuneration for viii 678 a; Laundry and Dry Cleaning Industry ix 195 b; Leather Industries ix 313 b; Longshoremen ix 607 b; Match Industry x 205 a; Meat Packing and Slaughtering x 261 a; Mechanic x 266 b; Milling Industry x 486 a; Minimum Wage x 491 a; Mining x 505 a; Mutual Aid Societies xi 170 a; Oil Industry xi 447 a; Owen and Owenism xi 518 b; Personnel Administration xii 90 a; Printing and Publishing xii 412 a; Producers' Cooperation xii 459 a; Public Employment xii 635 a; Pulp and Paper Industry xii 710 a; Quarrying xiii 20 a; Racketeering xiii 46 a; Railroads xiii 97 a; Restaurants xiii 338 b; Scientific Management xiii 607 b; Seamen xiii 614 a; Socialist Parties xiv 216 b; Socialization xiv 222 b; Strikes and Lockouts xiv 420 a, 421 a; Teaching Profession xiv 550 b; Textile Industry xiv 591 b, 593 b, 594 b; Theater xiv 613 b; Trade Agreements xiv 667–70; Unemployment Insurance xv 163 a; Voluntary Associations xv 286 a; Women in Industry xv 454 a, 456 b; Women's Organizations xv 465 a; Wood Industries xv 474 a. For biog. references see Classification of Articles (Labor), p. 563.
Trademark, National—iii 118 a.
TRADEMARKS AND NAMES—xv 57–61.
Trades Union Congress, Brit.—xv 9 b.
TRADING WITH THE ENEMY—xv 61–62; Blockade ii 594–96.
Traditio—ix 128 b.

TRADITION—xv 62–67; Antiradicalism ii 116–18; Aristocracy ii 189 b; Art ii 223–59; Belief ii 500 b; Bureaucracy iii 71 a; Ceremony iii 313–16; Change, Social iii 333 a; Common Sense iv 58–61; Conduct iv 177–79; Conservatism iv 230–33; Continuity, Social iv 316 a; Conventions, Social iv 351–53; Culture iv 621–46; Custom iv 658 b; Diffusionism v 139 b; Duty v 293–95; Ethnic Communities v 610 a; Etiquette v 615–17; Folklore vi 288–93; Folkways vi 293–96; Habit vii 239 a; Jansenism viii 371 b; Judaism viii 431 a; Jurisprudence viii 486 a; Law (Celtic) ix 247 a, (Germanic) 237 b, (Jewish) 221 a; Liberalism ix 436 a; Materialism (Historical) x 217 b; Modernism x 564–68; Regionalism xiii 208–18; Renaissance xiii 282 a; Sacred Books xiii 498 b; Traditionalism xv 67–70.
TRADITIONALISM—xv 67–70; Bonald ii 631 a; Jacobinism viii 363 b; Maistre x 51 a. See also TRADITION.
Traditions of Mohammed—Būkhāri iii 57 a; History and Historiography (Islam) vii 381 b; Islam viii 334 a; Islamic Law viii 345 b; Mālik ibn-Anas x 64 a; Mohammed ibn 'Abd al-Wahhāb x 573 b.
TRAFFIC REGULATION—xv 70–75; Motor Vehicle Accidents xi 72 a; Police xii 187 b.
Tramp Shipping—xiv 37 a.
TRANSCENDENTALISM—xv 75–77; Alcott i 628 a; Christian Science iii 446–49; Kant viii 539 a.
TRANSIT DUTIES—xv 77–78; Customs Duties iv 667 b; International Waterways viii 209 a; Mercantilism x 334 a; Transit, International xv 78 a.
TRANSIT, INTERNATIONAL—xv 78–80; Transit Duties xv 78 a.
Transmigration—ii 675 b.
TRANSPORTATION—xv 80–90. See Classification of Articles (Transportation), p. 557. See also Anthropology ii 82 a; Concessions iv 158 b; Economics (Historical School) v 372 b; Food Industries (Food Distribution, Russia) vi 327 b; Fruit and Vegetable Industry vi 508 b; Gas Industry vi 593 a; International Trade viii 191 a, 195 a; Land Grants (U. S.) ix 35 a; Location of Industry ix 586 b; Metrop. Areas x 396 b; Power, Industrial xii 297 b; Refrigeration xiii 197 a; Statistics xiv 361 b.
TRANSPORTATION OF CRIMINALS—xv 90–93; Molesworth x 575 b; Punishment xii 714 a.
Transportation, Motor Vehicle—see MOTOR VEHICLE TRANSPORTATION.
Travel—see TOURIST TRAFFIC.

TREASON—xv 93–96; Allegiance i 645 a; Attainder ii 305 a; Confiscation iv 184 b; Conspiracy, Political iv 238–41; Lese Majesty ix 415 b; Military Desertion x 451 b; Political Offenders xii 199–203; Riot xiii 388 b; Sedition xiii 636 a.
TREATIES—xv 96–101; Aggression, International i 485 b; Agreements, International i 518–20; Arbitration, International ii 157–62; Armistice ii 204 b; Aviation ii 351 a, 366 a; Balance of Power ii 395 b; Commercial Treaties iv 23–31; Diplomacy v 150 b; Duress v 289 b; Executive Agreements v 685–86; Guaranties, International vii 190–92; International Law viii 167 b, 169 b; International Legislation viii 175–77; International Organization viii 181 a; Intervention viii 238 a; Limitation of Armaments ix 480 a; Mediation x 272 b; Native Policy (N. Amer.) xi 262 a.
Treaties, Commercial—see COMMERCIAL TREATIES.
Treaty of Lausanne—xi 324 a.
Treaty of Sèvres—xi 324 a.
Treaty of Versailles, 1919—Alien Property i 637 a; Clemenceau iii 548 b; Disarmament v 159 b; Indemnity, Military vii 643 b; International Labor Organization viii 164 b; International Law viii 171 a; Limitation of Armaments ix 480 b; Minorities, National x 521 a; Monroe Doctrine x 632 a; Polish Corridor xii 196 b; Reparations xiii 300 a; Treaties xv 97 a; Wilson xv 427 b.
Treaty of Vienna—iii 220 b.
TREITSCHKE, H. VON—xv 101.
Trespass—xv 504 a.
Tretiakov, I. A.—i 280 b.
TREVELYAN, G. O.—xv 102.
Trial by Ordeal—v 269 a.
TRIBUTE—xiv 102–04; Introd. Vol. I (The Roman World) i 54 b; Brigandage ii 694 b; Indemnity, Military vii 641 a; Islam viii 339 a; Machine, Political ix 660 a.
TRIKOUPIS, C.—xv 104; Parties, Political (Greece) xi 629 a.
Triple Alliance—Alliance ii 3 b; Balance of Power ii 398 b.
Triple Entente—Alliance ii 3 b; Balance of Power ii 398 b.
TRISTAN, F. C. T. H.—xv 105.
TROELSTRA, P. J.—xv 106.
TROELTSCH, E.—xv 106; Mechanism and Vitalism x 270 b.
TRONCHET, F.-D.—xv 107.
Tropical Medicine—Acclimatization i 402 a; Colonial Administration iii 646 a; Communicable Diseases, Control of iv 70 b.
Trotsky, L.—Bolshevism ii 625 a, 628 b; General Strike vi 611 b; Gosplan vi 708 a; Russian Revolution xiii 481 b, 486 b.

TRUCE AND PEACE OF GOD—xv 107–09; Cluniac Movt. iii 581 b; Excommunication v 677 a.
Trucking—xi 75 b.
TRUST COMPANIES—xv 109–11; Investment Trusts viii 282 a; Trusts and Trustees xv 125 a.
TRUSTS—xv 111–22; Agrarian Movements (U. S.) i 511 a; Bargaining Power ii 460 a; Basing Point Prices ii 474 b; Cartel iii 235 a; Combinations, Industrial iii 664–74; Commercial Law iv 18 b; Crises iv 598 a; Dumping v 275 b; Federal Trade Commission vi 165–69; Gosplan vi 707 a; Holding Companies vii 406 b; Iron and Steel Industry viii 307 a; Massachusetts Trusts x 189–91; Match Industry x 207 a; Meat Packing and Slaughtering x 257 a; Middle Class x 409 a; National Economic Planning xi 201 b; Oil Industry xi 442 b; Price Discrimination xii 352 b; Tobacco xiv 642 a; Trade Associations xiv 674 a; Trusts and Trustees xv 125 a; Unfair Competition xv 176 a.
TRUSTS AND TRUSTEES—xv 122–26; Charitable Trusts iii 338–40; Endowments and Foundations v 535 b; Investment Trusts viii 281 b; Massachusetts Trusts x 189–91; Perpetuities xii 82 b; Trust Companies xv 109–11; Trusts xv 113 a; Voluntary Assoc's. xv 284 b.
Tryon, C. F. R. de—see MONTALEMBERT, COMTE DE.
Tsin Tien—ix 113 a.
Tsonchev, General—iii 676 a.
TUCKER, G.—xv 126.
TUCKER, J.—xv 127; Introd. Vol. I (The Revolutions) i 140 b.
TUCOVIĆ, D.—xv 128.
Tudor, F.—xiii 196 a.
TUGAN-BARANOVSKY, M. I.—xv 128; Distribution v 172 a.
Tulip Bubble—iii 24 b.
TULL, J.—xv 129; Agriculture (Eng.) i 579 b.
T'ung Meng Hui—viii 610 b.
Tungsten—x 387 a.
TURATI, F.—xv 130.
TURGENEV, N. I.—xv 131.
TURGOT, R. J.—xv 131; Roads xiii 402 b; Specialization xiv 279 b.
Turner, B.—viii 626 b.
TURNER, F. J.—xv 132; Frontier vi 500 a; Knights of Labor viii 582 a; Regionalism xiii 217 a.
TURNER, J. M.—xv 133.
Turnpikes—xiii 404 a, 405 a.
Turnvereine—xii 130 b.
Tusser, T.—i 579 a.
Twelve Tables—Introd. Vol. I (The Roman World) i 47 b; Roman Law xiii 419 b.
Two-Party System—see Double Party System.
Tyler, E.—viii 607 a.
TYLER, M. C.—xv 133.

TYLOR, E. B.—xv 134; Animism ii 65 b; Anthropology ii 102 b; Avoidance ii 370 a; Fetishism vi 202 a; Folklore vi 289 a.
Tyndall, J.—ii 551 b.
Tyrannicide—Anarchism ii 47 b; Mariana x 110 a.
TYRANNY—xv 135–37; Introd. Vol. I (Renaissance and Reformation) i 96 b; Monarchy x 580 a; Social Contract xiv 128 a.
Tyszka, C. von—xv 316 b.
Tz'ŭ Hsi—xv 137.

Ugolino of Ostia—vi 411 b.
Uhle, M.—ii 166 b.
'Ulama—iii 146 b.
ULLOA, B. DE—xv 138.
ULLSTEIN FAMILY—xv 138.
ULPIAN—xv 139.
Ultra Vires—ix 582 b.
ULYANOV, V. I.—xv 140. See Lenin, N.
Undue Influence—Duress v 289 b.
UNEARNED INCREMENT—xv 144–47; Appreciation ii 141–44; Land Speculation ix 69 a; Land Taxation ix 70 b.
UNEMPLOYMENT—xv 147–62; Ateliers Nationaux ii 291–92; Begging ii 493–95; Benefits, Trade Union ii 513–16; Casual Labor iii 260–62; Employment Exchanges v 518–23; Iron and Steel Industry viii 320 a; Journalism viii 423 b; Labor Movement viii 684 b; Longshoremen ix 607 b; Mechanic x 265 b; Public Works xii 694 b; Rehabilitation xiii 221–25; Social Settlements xiv 161 a; Socialism (Marxian) xiv 200 a; Technology xiv 557 a; Unemployment Insurance xv 162–74.
UNEMPLOYMENT INSURANCE—xv 162–74; Garment Industries vi 584 a; Labor, Govt. Services for viii 649 a; Labor Movement viii 685 a; Social Insurance xiv 134–38.
UNFAIR COMPETITION—xv 174–78; Adulteration i 466–68; Bargaining Power ii 461 b; Dumping v 275–78; Espionage v 596 b; Federal Trade Commission vi 165–69; Patents xii 23 b; Price Discrimination xii 350–55; Resale Price Maintenance xiii 326–30; Restraint of Trade xiii 339–42; Trademarks and Names xv 58 a.
Unfair List—see BOYCOTT.
UNGER, J.—xv 178.
Unicameral System—ii 535 a.
UNIFORM LEGISLATION—xv 178–81; Business, Govt. Services for iii 121 b; Codification iii 609 b; Commercial Law iv 16 b; Compacts, Interstate iv 112 b; Conflict of Laws iv 194 a; Foreign Corporations vi 357 b; Full Faith and Credit Clause vi 517 a; Govt. (U. S.) vii 18 b; Law Merchant ix 274 a.

Index (Treason — Value and Price)

Uniform Small Loan Law—xiv 108 a.
Uniform State Law of Aeronautics—ii 368 a.
Unincorporated Associations—see VOLUNTARY ASSOCIATIONS.
Union Académique Internationale—ix 299 b.
Unión General de Trabajadores—xv 29 b.
Union Label—ii 25 a.
Union-Management Cooperation—see LABOR-CAPITAL COOPERATION.
Union of Soviet Socialist Republics—see Soviet Russia.
Unitarianism—xv 76 a.
United Front—Communist Parties iv 92 a.
United Irishmen—viii 288 a.
United Mine Workers of America—Coal Industry iii 595 a, 598 a; Mining x 505 b.
United Press—xii 331 a, 336 a.
United Shoe Machinery Co.—Leather Industries ix 308 a; Trusts xv 117 a.
United States Congress—see Congress, U. S.
United States Steel Corp.—Iron and Steel Industry viii 307 a; Morgan Family xi 12 a; Trusts xv 117 a.
Universalism (Economics) — v 386 a.
UNIVERSITIES AND COLLEGES—xv 181–87; Introd. Vol. I (The Social Sciences as Disciplines, Gt. Brit.) i 231–349; Academic Freedom i 384–88; Business Education iii 109 a; Coeducation iii 615 b; Correspondence Schools iv 445 a; Education (Hist.) v 408 a, (Sectarian) 423 b, (Part Time) 427 b, (Finance) 429 a; Endowments v 532 b; Forecasting, Business vi 351 a; Health Education vii 293 a; Home Economics vii 429 a; Humanism vii 540 a; Intellectuals viii 122 a; Journalism viii 422 a; Land Grants (U. S.) ix 34 a; Legal Profession and Legal Education ix 329 a, 337 a, 338 a; Medical Jurisprudence x 276 b; Medicine x 289–92; Military Training x 470 a; Monasticism x 587 b; Physical Education xii 131 b; Professions xii 476 b; Research xiii 331 a; University Extension xv 187–89; Woman, Position in Society xv 449 b.
University of Berlin—xv 184 a.
University of Bologna—xv 181 b.
UNIVERSITY EXTENSION—xv 187–89; Correspondence Schools iv 445 a; Education v 426 a; Extension Work, Agric. vi 32 a.
University of France—xv 185 a.
University of Michigan—ii 60 b.
University of Montpellier—xv 181 b.
University of Paris—iv 161 a.
University of Vienna—i 268 a.

UNWIN, G.—xv 189.
Urban vi—xiii 256 b.
URBANIZATION—xv 189–92; Amusements, Public ii 42 a; Automobile Industry ii 328 b; Back-to-the-Land Movements ii 379 a; City iii 474–82; City-State iii 489–92; City and Town Planning iii 482–88; Civic Art iii 492–95; Civic Centers iii 495–96; Divorce v 183 b; Industrial Revolution viii 11 b; Industrialism viii 25 a; Land Speculation ix 66 a; Negro Problem xi 342 a; Specialization xiv 280 b; Transportation xv 89 a.
Use—Trusts and Trustees xv 122 b.
USENER, H.—xv 192.
USPENSKY, F. I.—xv 193.
Usucapio—Limitation of Actions ix 475 a.
Usufruct—Servitudes xiv 4 a.
USURY—xv 193–97; Introd. Vol. I (Individualism and Capitalism) i 148 a; Antisemitism ii 120 b; Christianity iii 458 a; Fraud vi 428 a; Funk vi 530 a; Interest viii 131 a; Just Price viii 505 b; Pawnbroking xii 33 a; Small Loans xiv 107 a.
UTILITARIANISM—xv 197–200; Introd. Vol. I (The Revolutions) i 134 a, (Individualism and Capitalism) 153 b; Art (Egyptian) ii 238 b, (Roman) 242 b; Bentham ii 518 b; Duty v 294 a; Encyclopédistes v 530 a; Epicureanism v 569 a; Ethics v 603 b; Fabianism vi 47 a; Hedonism vii 308 b; Hume vii 551 a; Individualism vii 678 b; Jurisprudence viii 481 a; Laissez Faire ix 17 a; Malthus x 68 b; Mill, J. x 480 b; Mill, J. S. x 481 a; Paley xi 535 b; Positivism xii 262 b; Priestley xii 395 b; Society xiv 229 a; Sovereignty xiv 267 b.
Utility—see Marginal Utility Economics.
UTOPIA—xv 200–03; Introd. Vol. I (Renaissance and Reformation) i 101 b, (Individualism and Capitalism) 156 b; Bellamy ii 504 a; Cabet iii 131 b; Campanella iii 166 b; Communism iv 84 b; Communistic Settlements iv 95–102; Fourier and Fourierism vi 403 b; Harrington vii 272 b; Hertzka vii 341 a; Idealism vii 570 a; Levellers ix 423 a; More xi 8 b; Morelly xi 11 a; Primitivism xii 398–402; Shcherbatov xiv 19 a; Socialism xiv 191 a.
UVAROV, S. S.—xv 203.
UZTÁRIZ, J. DE—xv 203; Introd. Vol. I (The Social Sciences as Disciplines, Spain) i 296 a.

V. A. P. P.—Literature ix 540 a.
V. V.—see VORONTSOV, V. P.
VACARIUS—xv 204.
Vaccaro, M. A.—iv 588 a.

Vaccination—Communicable Diseases, Control of iv 72 a; Jenner viii 381 a; Kőrösy de Szántó viii 593 a; Pasteur xii 18 b.
VAGRANCY—xv 205–08; Begging ii 494 a; Lodging Houses ix 595–98.
Vaihinger, H.—vi 225 b.
VAIL, T. N.—xv 208.
Vaillant, É.—ii 585 a.
Vakuf—ix 102 b.
Valdegamas, Marqués de—see DONOSO CORTÉS, J.
VALENTI, G.—xv 208.
Valeriani, L.—i 275 a.
VALLA, L.—xv 209.
Vallaux, C.—vi 622 b.
VALORIZATION—xv 210–12; Business, Govt. Services for iii 120 a; Devaluation v 115 b; Farm Relief vi 116 b; International Trade viii 196 b.
VALUATION—xv 212–18; Accounting i 410 b; Appreciation ii 143 b; Assessment of Taxes ii 276–79; Capitalization iii 208–11; Customs Duties iv 671 b; Fair Return vi 56–58; Goodwill vi 699 b; Interest viii 134 b; Interstate Commerce Commission viii 231 b; Land Valuation ix 137–39; Rate Regulation xiii 108 b; Real Estate xiii 138 a.
Valuation, Land—see LAND VALUATION.
VALUE AND PRICE—xv 218–25; Abstinence i 382–83; Antonino ii 126 b; Appreciation ii 141–44; Barter ii 468–69; By-Product iii 129 b; Capital iii 187–90; Carey iii 226 b; Christianity iii 457 b; Church Fathers iii 467 b; Consumption iv 294 b; Cost iv 467 a; Cost of Living iv 478–83; Davenport v 8 b; Demand v 69–75; Depreciation v 98 b; Distribution v 167–74; Dumping v 276 a; Economic Policy v 336 b; Economics (Classical School) v 353 a, (Marginal Utility Economics) 358 b, (Mathematical Economics) 365 b, (Cambridge School) 369 a, (Socialist Economics) 378 b, (Universalist Economics) 386 b; Exchange v 668 a; Excise v 670 b; Exploitation vi 16–17; Fair Return vi 56–58; Fleetwood vi 279 b; Food Industries (Baking, U. S.) vi 306 b; Foreign Exchange vi 361 a, 364 a; Galiani vi 546 b; Goodwill vi 698–702; Gossen vii 3 a; Graslin vii 156 a; Hedging vii 305–07; Hermann vii 336 a; Index Numbers vii 652–58; Inflation and Deflation viii 28–33; Interest viii 134 a, 141 a; International Trade (Theory) viii 206 a; Just Price viii 504–07; Labor viii 617 a, 618 b; Labor Exchange Banks viii 637–44; Laissez Faire ix 17 a; Land Valuation ix 137–39; Laspeyres ix 183 b; Location of Industry ix 592 a; Market x

131–33; Marshall x 156 a; Menger x 311 a; Money x 601–13; Monopoly x 623–30; National Economic Planning xi 199 a; Overproduction xi 513–17; Price Discrimination xii 350–55; Price Regulation xii 355–62; Price Stabilization xii 362–66; Prices xii 366–87; Production (Theory) xii 463 a, (Statistics) 470 b; Rent xiii 289–92; Rubber xiii 455 b; Smith xiv 113 a; Socialism xiv 199 b, 208 b; Speculation xiv 290 a; Supply xiv 470–74; Taxation xiv 536 a; Transportation xv 88 a; Unearned Increment xv 144–47; Unemployment xv 152 a, 160 b; Valorization xv 210–12; Valuation xv 212–18; Wages xv 311 b.
Values—Introd. Vol. 1 (The Social Sciences as Disciplines, Germany) i 260 a; Cyrenaics iv 685 a; Ethics v 602–07; Geisteswissenschaften vi 601 a; Jurisprudence viii 489 b; Justice viii 513 b; Philosophy xii 121 b; Political Science xii 219 b, 221 a; State xiv 330 b; Value and Price xv 218–25; Weber xv 387 a.
VÁMBÉRY, A.—xv 225.
VAN CLEAVE, J. W.—xv 225.
VANDAL, A.—xv 226.
VANDERBILT FAMILY—xv 227.
VANDERKINDERE, L.—xv 228.
VANDERLINT, J.—xv 228.
VANE, H.—xv 229.
VARLIN, L. E.—xv 229.
Varro—i 575 b.
Vasa, G.—see GUSTAVUS I.
VASCO, G.—xv 230.
Vasconcelos, J.—xi 419 b.
VASILCHIKOV, A. I.—xv 231.
VASILEVSKY, V. G.—xv 231.
Vasquez—xi 287 a.
VATTEL, E. DE—xv 232; Casus Belli iii 266 b; Diplomatic Protection v 154 a; Equality of States v 581 a; Intervention viii 236 a; Neutrality xi 361 b.
Vatteville, Sieur de—see MONTCHRÉTIEN, A. DE.
VAUBAN, S. LE P. DE—xv 232; Introd. Vol. 1 (The Rise of Liberalism) i 123 a.
Vaugeois, H.—i 423 b.
VAUGHAN, R.—xv 233.
VEBLEN, T. B.—xv 234; Introd. Vol. 1 (The Trend to Internationalism) i 177 a; Absentee Ownership i 377 b; Academic Freedom i 387 b; Business Cycles iii 99 a; Career iii 225 a; Conservatism iv 232 a; Economics v 388 b, 392 a; Functionalism vi 525 a; Vested Interests xv 242 a.
Vedism—Brahmanism and Hinduism ii 673 b.
Veeder Pool—x 259 b.
Vega, L. de—xiv 607 a.
Vegetable Industry—see FRUIT AND VEGETABLE INDUSTRY.
Velasquez, D. R. de S.—ii 250 b.

Venereal Diseases—Blind ii 587 b; Prostitution xii 555 a; Sex Education and Sex Ethics xiv 9 b.
Venizelos, E.—xi 629 a.
VENUE—xv 235–37; Jurisdiction viii 473 b.
VERBŐCZY, I.—xv 237.
Verein für Sozialpolitik—i 263 a.
VERGENNES, COMTE DE—xv 238.
VERGNIAUD, P. V.—xv 238.
Verri, A.—ii 488 a.
VERRI, P.—xv 239; Beccaria ii 488 a.
Versailles, Treaty of—see Treaty of Versailles, 1919.
Verworn, M.—x 268 a.
Vesalius, A.—ii 551 a.
Vesenha—Gosplan vi 709 a.
VESTED INTERESTS—xv 240–43.
Vested Rights—see VESTED INTERESTS.
VETERANS—xv 243–47; Amer. Legion ii 31–33; Housing (U. S.) vii 516 a; Land Grants (Brit. Empire) ix 36 b, (Lat. Amer.) 40 a, (U. S.) 32 b; Pensions xii 68 b; Public Employment xii 633 b; Land Settlement ix 62 b; Rehabilitation xiii 221–25.
VETO—xv 247–49; Legislative Assemblies (U. S.) ix 367 a.
VEUILLOT, L.—xv 249.
Vickers, A.—xi 130 a.
Vickers-Armstrongs, Ltd.—xi 132 a.
VICO, G. B.—xv 249; Introd. Vol. 1 (The Revolutions) i 139 a; Romanticism xiii 428 a; Social Psychology xiv 152 a.
VICTOR EMMANUEL II—xv 251.
VIDAL DE LA BLACHE, P. M. J.—xv 251.
Vidal, F.—iv 378 a.
Vienna, Congress of—ii 398 b.
Vierkandt, A.—Introd. Vol. 1 (War and Reorientation) i 205 a; Sociology xiv 244 b.
VIJNANESVĀRA—xv 252; Jīmūtavāhana viii 403 b.
Vilain XIII—iv 108 b.
VILLAGE COMMUNITY—xv 253–59; Agrarian Movements (Lat. Amer.) i 511 b; Agriculture (Mediaeval) i 575 b, (China) 590 a, (Eng.) 577 b, (Japan) 591 b; Enclosures v 523 a; Land Tenure (E. Eur. and Near East) ix 99 b, (India) 110 b, (Lat. Amer.) 119 a, (Russia) 108 a, (W. Eur., Brit. Empire and U. S.) 83 a, 87 b; Manorial System x 98 a; Representation xiii 310 a; Rural Society xiii 471 a; Seebohm xiii 641 b.
Villani, G.—vii 373 a.
VILLARD, H.—xv 259.
VILLARI, P.—xv 260.
VILLENEUVE-BARGEMONT, VICOMTE DE—xv 260.
VILLERMÉ, L. R.—xv 261.
VILLIERS, C. P.—xv 261.
VILLIERS, J. H. DE—xv 262.
VINCENT, H.—xv 263.
VINCENT DE PAUL—xv 262; Ozanam xi 526 b.

VINOGRADOFF, P.—xv 263; Introd. Vol. 1 (The Social Sciences as Disciplines, Gt. Brit.) i 239 b; Jurisprudence viii 483 a.
VIOLENCE—xv 264–67; Anarchism ii 48 a; Antiradicalism ii 117 b; Assassination ii 271–75; Atrocities ii 302–04; Babouvism ii 375; Brigandage ii 693–96; Conspiracy, Political iv 238–41; Criminal Syndicalism iv 582–84; Elections v 455 b; Ethics v 605 a; Feuds vi 220–21; Filibustering vi 231–33; Force, Political vi 341 a; General Strike vi 608 b; Gershuni vi 639 b; Insurrection viii 116–18; Intimidation viii 239–42; Ku Klux Klan viii 607 b; Labor Legislation and Law viii 668 b; Lese Majesty ix 416 b; Lynching ix 639–43; Massacre x 191–94; Masses x 199 b; Novikov xi 402 a; Policing, Industrial xii 193–96; Racketeering xiii 45–50; Revolution and Counter-revolution xiii 367 a, 370 b; Riot xiii 386–92; Sabotage xiii 495 b; Sorel xiv 262 b; Strikes and Lockouts xiv 422 b; Terrorism xiv 575–80.
VIOLLET, P.—xv 267.
VIRCHOW, R.—xv 267.
Visa—xii 15 b.
Vishnu—ii 676 b.
Vital Statistics—see BIRTHS; MORTALITY; POPULATION; DEMOGRAPHY.
Vitalism—see MECHANISM AND VITALISM.
VITORIA, F. DE—xv 268; Introd. Vol. 1 (The Social Sciences as Disciplines, Spain) i 295 a.
Vitruvius, M.—ii 242 a.
VITTORINO DA FELTRE—xv 269.
VIVEKĀNANDA, SWAMI—xv 270.
VIVES, J. L.—xv 270.
Vladimir of Kiev—xiii 265 a.
VLADIMIRSKY-BUDANOV, M. F.—xv 271.
VOCATIONAL EDUCATION—xv 272–75; Agric. Education i 538–42; Apprenticeship ii 144–47; Business Education iii 107–10; Continuation Schools iv 313–15; Correspondence Schools iv 445 b; Cripples iv 594 a; Home Economics vii 429 a; Industrial Education vii 692–97; Manual Training x 103–05; Rehabilitation xiii 221–25; Social Work xiv 178 a, 183–87; Teaching Profession xiv 547 b; Unemployment Insurance xv 172 b.
VOCATIONAL GUIDANCE—xv 276–79; Labor Turnover viii 712 a; Mental Tests x 328 a.
Voet, J.—iv 189 a.
VOGEL, J.—xv 279; Parties, Political (New Zealand) xi 607 b.
VOGELSANG, K. VON—xv 280.
Voldemaras, A.—vii 73 a.
Volksbühne—xiv 611 a.
Volksgeist—xi 233 b.
VOLLMAR, G. VON—xv 281.

Volski, A.—see MACHAJSKI, W.
Volstead Act—xii 504 a.
VOLTAIRE, F.-M. A. DE—xv 281; Introd. Vol. I (The Rise of Liberalism) i 120 a, (The Revolutions) 129 b; Bayle ii 484 a; Enlightenment v 551 b; Fréron vi 489 b; History and Historiography vii 375 a.
Voluntarism—xii 310 a.
VOLUNTARY ASSOCIATIONS — xv 283–87; Introd. Vol. I (The Growth of Autonomy) i 74 b, (The Trend to Internationalism) 178 b; Association ii 284–86; Clubs iii 573–77; Clubs, Political iii 577–80; Collectivism iii 634 b; Cooperation iv 359–99; Federation vi 177 a; Guilds vii 204–24; Legal Aid ix 322 b; Majority Rule x 59 a; Religious Institutions (Protestant) xiii 271 b; Social Organization xiv 146 a; Unwin xv 189 a.
VORONTSOV, V. P.—xv 287.
Vorwärts—ii 522 b.
VOTING—xv 287–91; Absent-Voting i 376; Ballot ii 410–12; Elections v 450–56; Independent Voting vii 648–49; Initiative and Referendum viii 50–52; Intimidation viii 241 a; Literacy and Illiteracy ix 520 a; Machine, Political ix 660 b; Majority Rule x 55–60; Minority Rights x 526 b; Native Policy (N. Amer.) xi 266 a; Plebiscite xii 165 b; Primaries, Political xii 396 b; Proportional Representation xii 541–45; Registration of Voters xiii 218–21; Short Ballot Movement xiv 43–44; Straw Vote xiv 417–19; Suffrage xiv 447–50.
Voting Machines—Ballot ii 411 a; Elections v 455 a.
Vucetich, J.—vii 573 b.

WACH, A.—xv 291.
Wafd—Zaghlul Pasha xv 523 b.
Wage Fund Theory—Longe ix 605 b; Wages xv 294 b.
Wage Regulation—Labor Legislation and Law viii 662 b; Labourers, Statutes of ix 3–6; Minimum Wage x 491–95.
WAGES—xv 291–320; Agric. Labor i 549 b, 550 a; Automobile Industry ii 326 b; Black Death ii 575 b; Clerical Occupations iii 552 a; Construction Industry iv 270 b; Distribution v 167–74; Domestic Service v 202 b; Economics (Classical School) v 353 b, (Cambridge School) 370 a; Electrical Manufacturing Industry v 475 a; Family Allowances vi 71–73; Fisheries vi 269 b; Food Industries (Baking, Eur.) vi 304 b, (U. S.) 307 b, (Beverages) 309 a, (Confectionery) 311 a; Furniture vi 541 b; Garment Industries vi 580 a, 583 a; Gas Industry vi 591 b; Glass and Pottery Industries vi 675 a; Hotels vii 476 a; Hours of Labor vii 481 b, 483 a; International Trade (Theory) viii 202 a; Iron and Steel Industry viii 315 b, 319 a; Journalism viii 423 a; Labor Disputes viii 634 b; Labor Exchange Banks viii 637–44; Labor, Methods of Remuneration for viii 672–82; Labourers, Statutes of ix 3–6; Laundry and Dry Cleaning Industry ix 195 b; Leather Industries ix 314 b; Location of Industry ix 589 a; Longshoremen ix 607 a; Match Industry x 205 a; Meat Packing and Slaughtering (U. S.) x 248 b; Minimum Wage x 491–95; Oil Industry xi 447 a; Prices (Hist.) xii 378 a; Printing and Publishing xii 413 a; Public Employment xii 630 b; Pulp and Paper Industry xii 710 b; Quarrying xiii 19 b; Railroads xiii 94 a; Rodbertus xiii 415 'a; Seamen xiii 614 a; Social Insurance xiv 136 a; Standards of Living xiv 324 b; Statistics xiv 262 b; Strikes and Lockouts xiv 420 b; Trade Unions (Russia) xv 34 b; Unemployment xv 153 a; Women in Industry xv 455 a, 458 a; Wood Industries xv 473 b.
WAGNER, A. H. G.—xv 320; Economics v 383 b; Taxation xiv 533 a.
Wagner, O.—ii 256 a.
Wagner, R.—xi 374 a.
Wahhabites—Islamic Law viii 347 a; Mohammed ibn 'Abd al-Wahhāb x 573 b.
Wailly, J. N. de—ii 176 a.
Waite, M. R.—xiii 106 a.
WAITZ, F. T.—xv 321.
WAITZ, G.—xv 321.
Waiver, Doctrine of—Insurance viii 110 a.
WAKEFIELD, E. G.—xv 322; Homestead vii 439 a; Land Grants (Brit. Empire) ix 38 a; Land Settlement ix 59 b; Public Domain xii 620 a.
WAKLEY, T.—xv 322.
Wald, L.—xi 408 b.
Waldeck-Rousseau, P. M. — ii 114 a.
Waldenses—Messianism x 361 b; Sects xiii 626 a.
WALKER, A.—xv 323.
WALKER, F. A.—xv 323; Introd. Vol. I (The Social Sciences as Disciplines, U. S.) i 336 b; Distribution v 169 b.
Walker, W.—vi 232 a.
Wall Street Journal—ii 467 a.
WALLACE, A. R.—xv 325; Biology ii 555 a; Evolution v 651 a.
WALLACE, H. and H. C.—xv 325.
WALLACE, R.—xv 326.
WALLAS, G.—xv 326; Introd. Vol. I (The Trend to Internationalism) i 182 b.
Wallenstein, A. E. W. von—vii 641 a.
WALPOLE, R.—xv 327.
WALRAS, A. A.—xv 328.
WALRAS, M. E. L.—xv 328; Introd. Vol. I (Nationalism) i 166 a; Economics v 357–63, 365 a, 366 a.
Walsh, C. M.—vii 653 b.
WALTER FAMILY—xv 329.
Wanamaker, J.—xii 273 b.
WANG AN-SHI—xv 330.
Wang Mang—ix 114 a.
WAR—xv 331–42. See Classification of Articles (War), p. 557. See also Agreements, International i 519 a; Anthropology ii 84 b; Balance of Power ii 395–99; Christianity iii 456 a; Cluniac Movement iii 581 b; Corruption, Political iv 450 a; Dance iv 703 a; Diplomacy v 151 b; Drug Addiction v 244 a; Food Supply vi 336 b; International Law viii 168 a; Intervention viii 237 a; Labor Movement viii 686 b; Marine Insur. x 116 a; Mass Expulsion x 186 a; Massacre x 192 a; Metals x 367 a; Migrations x 421 a; Propaganda xii 524 b; Waterways, Inland xv 382 b.
War Debts—Debt v 36 b; War Finance xv 350 a.
WAR ECONOMICS—xv 342–47; Introd. Vol. I (War and Reorientation) i 210 a; Gosplan vi 706 a; Govt. Owned Corporations vii 109 b; Govt. Regulation of Industry vii 128 b; Housing (Eur.) vii 502 a, (U. S.) 513 b; Inflation and Deflation viii 30 a; National Economic Planning xi 200 a; Price Regulation xii 357 b; Profiteering xii 492 b; Regionalism xiii 212 a; Rent Regulation xiii 293 a; Requisitions, Military xiii 324–26; War Finance xv 347–52; Women in Industry xv 455 a.
WAR FINANCE — xv 347–52; Drives, Money Raising v 239 a; Excess Profits Tax v 664–66; Federal Reserve System vi 158 a; Forced Loans vi 347 a; Loans, Intergovernmental ix 556 b; Mobilization and Demobilization x 561 a; War Economics xv 345 a.
War Guilt—Aggression, International i 485–86; Archives ii 179 a; War xv 340 a; World War xv 495 b.
War Profits Tax—see EXCESS PROFITS TAX.
War Risk Insurance—Life Insurance ix 467 a; Veterans xv 246 a.
WARBURG, P. M.—xv 352.
Ward, A. M.—xiii 350 b.
WARD, L. F.—xv 353; Introd. Vol. I (Nationalism) i 169 b; Genius vi 613 b; Statics and Dynamics xiv 353 a.

WAREHOUSING — xv 354–59; Agric. Marketing (U. S.) i 561 a, 562 a; Auctions ii 309–11; Famine vi 87 b; Food Industries (Food Distribution, Russia) vi 327 b; Free Ports and Free Zones vi 437 b; Grain Elevators vii 136–39; Ports and Harbors viii 257 a; Refrigeration xiii 197 b.
WARFARE, LAWS OF—xv 359–64; Armed Merchantmen ii 201–03; Armistice ii 204–05; Aviation ii 348 a; Blockade ii 594–96; Declaration of London v 47–48; Declaration of Paris v 48–49; Hague Conferences vii 243 a; International Law viii 169 b; Merchantmen, Status of x 352 a; Prisoners of War xii 419–22; Prize xii 424–26; Reprisals xiii 317 a.
Warner, W.—viii 570 a.
Warrants — Arrest ii 221 b; Searches and Seizures xiii 617 a.
Warren, G. F.—i 534 b.
WARREN, J.—xv 364; Anarchism ii 49 a; Communistic Settlements iv 100 b; Labor Exchange Banks viii 638 b.
WARYŃSKI, L. T.—xv 365.
WASHINGTON, B. T.—xv 365; Negro Problem xi 347 a.
Washington Conference—Armaments ii 196 a; Armed Merchantmen ii 202 a; Far Eastern Problem vi 95 b; Limitation of Armaments ix 480 b.
WASHINGTON, G.—xv 366; Agriculture, Govt. Services for i 600 b; Isolation, Diplomatic viii 354 b.
WASTE—xv 367–69; Advertising i 474 a; By-Product iii 129–30; Conservation iv 227–30; Construction Industry iv 266 b; Fatigue vi 148–51; Heavy Chemicals vii 302 a; Management x 79 a; Oil Industry xi 445 b; Quarrying xiii 18 a; Water Supply xv 374 b.
Waste Disposal—see SANITATION.
WATER LAW—xv 369–72.
Water Power—Electric Power v 460 a; Power, Industrial xii 294 a.
WATER SUPPLY — xv 372–77; Communicable Diseases, Control of iv 69 b; Water Law xv 369–72.
Waterman, T. T.—vi 290 a.
WATERWAYS, INLAND—xv 377–84; Commercial Routes iv 19–24; Compacts, Interstate iv 110 b; Floods and Flood Control vi 282–85; International Waterways viii 208–14; Interstate Commerce viii 221 a; Panama Canal xi 554–58; Ports and Harbors xii 255–60; Railroads xiii 78 a; Suez Canal xiv 444–47; Transportation xv 81 b, 85 b; Water Law xv 369–72.
Waterways, International — see INTERNATIONAL WATERWAYS.

WATKIN, E. W.—xv 384.
Watres Bill—ii 342 b, 356 a.
WATSON, E.—xv 384; Agric. Societies i 570 b.
WATSON, J.—xv 385.
Watson, J. B.—Abnormal Psychology i 361 b; Adjustment i 438 b; Behaviorism ii 495 b, 497 b; Educational Psychology v 433 b; Psychology xii 594 a.
Watson-Parker Act—xiii 96 b.
Watt, J.—x 4 a.
WAUGH, B.—xv 385.
Wazo—viii 261 a.
Wealth, National—see NATIONAL WEALTH.
Weather—iii 559 a.
WEAVER, J. B.—xv 386.
Webb, B. and S.—Fabianism vi 46 a, 47 b; Industrial Democracy vii 691 a.
Webb-Pomerene Export Trade Act—vi 17 b.
Weber, A.—Location of Industry ix 586 a; Sociology xiv 243 b.
Weber, E. H.—Behaviorism ii 496 b; Psychology xii 591 a.
WEBER, M.—xv 386; Introd. Vol. I (The Social Sciences as Disciplines, Germany) i 260 a; Belief ii 501 b; Bourgeoisie ii 655 b; Class iii 532 a; Economic History v 322 a; Economics v 375 a, 390 a, 392 a; Geisteswissenschaften vi 601 b; Judaism viii 438 a; National Economic Planning xi 198 b; Sociology xiv 242 b, 244 b; Technology xiv 554 a.
WEBSTER, D.—xv 389.
Wei Yang—see SHANG YANG.
WEIGHTS AND MEASURES—xv 389–92; Assizes ii 283 b; Consumer Protection iv 283 a.
Weimar Constitution—Budget iii 43 b; Govt. (Germany) vii 53 b; Labor Legislation and Law viii 661 a; National Economic Councils xi 194 a; Preuss xii 349 a.
WEISMANN, A.—xv 392; Biology ii 554 b; Lamarck ix 22 a.
WEISS, A.—xv 393.
WEITLING, W.—xv 393; Labor Exchange Banks viii 641 b.
Weizmann, C.—xv 534 b.
WELCH, W. H.—xv 394.
WELCKER, K. T.—xv 394.
WELD, T. D.—xv 395.
WELFARE WORK, INDUSTRIAL—xv 395–99; Brandts ii 683 a; Company Housing iv 117 b; Denny v 90 b; Dollfus v 192 b; Employers' Associations v 514 a; Factory System vi 53 b; Group Insurance vii 182–88; Harmel vii 270 b; Hospitals and Sanatoria vii 468 a; Industrial Hygiene vii 707–10; Industrial Relations vii 715 b; Iron and Steel Industry viii 317 a; Labor Disputes viii 635 b; Labor, Methods of Remuneration for viii 677 b; Leclaire ix 317 b; Leverhulme ix 424 a;

Quakers xiii 13 b; Salt xiii 526 a; Social Work (Case Work) xiv 180 a.
Wellesley, A.—see WELLINGTON, LORD.
WELLESLEY, R. C.—xv 399.
WELLHAUSEN, J. — xv 400; Kuenen viii 609 a.
WELLINGTON, LORD—xv 401.
WELLS, D. A.—xv 402.
Wentworth, P.—xiii 3 b.
WENTWORTH, W. C.—xv 402.
WERGELAND, H. A.—xv 403.
Wertheimer, M.—Consciousness iv 216 a; Gestalt vi 644 a.
WESLEY, J.—xv 403; Literacy and Illiteracy ix 516 b; Revivals, Religious xiii 366 a.
Westergaard, H.—vii 653 b.
Westermarck, E. A.—Family vi 65 a; Incest vii 621 a; Ornament xi 496 a.
Western Associated Press—xii 331 a.
Western Electric Co.—xiv 564 a.
Western Fed. of Miners—x 506 b.
Western Union Telegraph Co.—xiv 562 b.
Westernization—see EUROPEANIZATION.
Westinghouse Electric and Manufacturing Co.—xv 405 a.
WESTINGHOUSE, G.—xv 405.
WESTLAKE, J.—xv 405.
Weston, R.—i 579 a.
WEYDEMEYER, J.—xv 406.
WEYL, W. E.—xv 406.
WHATELY, R.—xv 407.
WHEATLEY, J.—xv 407.
WHEATON, H.—xv 408; Calvo iii 153 a.
Wheel—x 15 b.
Whigs—Parties, Political (Gt. Brit.) xi 601 b, (U. S.) 598 b; Shaftesbury xiv 14 a.
WHITE, A. D.—xv 408; Introd. Vol. I (The Social Sciences as Disciplines, U. S.) i 334 a.
White Collar Worker—Labor Movement viii 686 b; Middle Class x 412 a.
White List—iv 291 b.
White Man's Burden—ii 381 a.
White Slave Traffic—xii 556 b.
White, W. A.—x 315 b.
Whiteboy Disturbances—viii 287 b.
WHITEFIELD, G.—xv 409.
Whitehead, A. N.—Gestalt vi 645 b; Mechanism and Vitalism x 269 b.
Whitley Councils—Industrial Relations Councils vii 721 a; Labor-Capital Cooperation viii 626 a; Labor, Govt. Services for viii 648 a.
WHITMAN, W.—xv 410.
Whitney, C. A.—iv 583 a.
WHITNEY, E.—xv 410; Standardization xiv 320 a.
WHOLESALING—xv 411–17; Food Industries (Grocery Trade) vi 313 a; Marketing x 136 a; Mercantile Credit x 330 a; Middleman x 415–17.

WICHERN, J. H.—xv 417.
WICKSELL, K.—xv 417; Economics v 367 b; International Trade (Theory) viii 206 a; Price Stabilization xii 363 b, 365 a; Prices (Theory) xii 374 a.
WICKSTEED, P. H.—xv 418; Distribution v 171 a.
Wido of Ferrara—viii 261 b.
Widows' Pensions—see MOTHERS' PENSIONS.
WIELOPOLSKI, A.—xv 419.
Wiese, L. von—Introd. Vol. I (War and Reorientation) i 205 b; Sociology xiv 244 b.
WIESER, F. VON—xv 419; Distribution v 171 a; Laissez Faire ix 17 b; Money x 608 b.
WILAMOWITZ-MOELLENDORFF, U. VON—xv 420.
WILBERFORCE, W.—xv 421.
Wiley, H. W.—vi 298 b.
Wilfan, J.—x 523 b.
Wilhelm I—see WILLIAM I (Germany).
Wilhelmsdorf Colony—xv 206 b.
WILKES, J.—xv 422; Searches and Seizures xiii 617 b.
WILLARD, E. H.—xv 422.
WILLARD, F. E.—xv 423.
Willcox, W. F.—xii 240 b.
Wille, B.—xiv 611 a.
WILLIAM I (England)—xv 423.
WILLIAM I (Germany)—xv 424.
William of Champeaux — xiii 141 a.
William of Normandy—ix 149 a.
William of Orange—viii 287 a.
William of Tyre—vii 372 b.
WILLIAMS, R.—xv 424; Natural Law xi 287 b; Religious Freedom xiii 244 a.
Wills—see INHERITANCE.
WILSON, J.—xv 425; Contract Clause iv 340 a.
WILSON, J. H.—xv 426.
WILSON, T. W.—xv 426; Amendments, Constitutional ii 22 a; Checks and Balances iii 364 b; Congressional Govt. iv 202 a; Harvey vii 278 a; Isolation, Diplomatic viii 355 a; Monroe Doctrine x 632 a; Open Door xi 470 a; Publicity xii 699 a; Reparations xiii 300 a.
WINCKELMANN, J. J.—xv 428.
Windelband, W.—vi 601 a.
Window Tax—vii 494 b.
WINDSCHEID, B.—xv 429.
Windstorm Insurance—i 547 a.
WINDTHORST, L.—xv 429.
Winkelblech, K. G. — see MARLO, K.
WINSTANLEY, G.—xv 430; Levellers ix 423 a; Socialism xiv 191 a.
WINTHROP, J.—xv 430; History and Historiography vii 385 b.
WIRTH, M.—xv 431.
WISE, I. M.—xv 432.
Wishart, G.—viii 585 b.
Wissell, R.—xi 200 b.
Wissler, C.—Anthropology ii 105 b; Culture Area iv 646 a.

Witchcraft—Magic x 43 b; Persecution xii 84 a.
Witenagemot—Govt. vii 11 a; Legislative Assemblies ix 356 b.
WITT, J. DE—xv 432; Annuities ii 70 a.
WITTE, S. Y.—xv 433; Archives ii 177 b.
WOLF, F. A.—xv 434.
WOLFF, C.—xv 435; Introd. Vol. I (The Revolutions) i 138 a; Enlightenment v 550 a; Natural Law xi 284 b, 289 a; Psychology xii 590 a; Vattel xv 232 a.
WOLFF, H. W.—xv 435.
Wollemborg, L.—iv 382 a.
WOLLSTONECRAFT, M.—xv 436.
WOLOWSKI, L. F. M. R.—xv 437.
WOLSEY, T.—xv 437.
WOLTMANN, L.—xv 438.
Wolzendorff, K.—i 216 b.
WOMAN, POSITION IN SOCIETY—xv 439–51. See Classification of Articles (Marriage and the Family), p. 553. See also Introd. Vol. I (Greek Culture and Thought) i 14 b, 36 b; Amateur ii 19 b; Anthropology ii 82 b; Art (Chinese) ii 236 a; Bok ii 621 b; Career iii 226 a; Chinese Problem iii 434 a; Chivalry iii 439 a; Christianity iii 460 a; Coeducation iii 614–17; Domestic Service v 198–206; Euripides v 623 a; Fashion vi 142 b; Gentleman, Theory of the vi 619 a; Judaism viii 437 a; Law (Celtic) ix 248 a, (Hindu) 259 a, (Jewish) 223 a, (Slavic) 243 b; Literature ix 526 a; Morals x 645 a; Nursing xi 405–12; Occupation xi 429 a; Public Employment xii 633 a; Specialization xiv 280 a; Status xiv 375 a; Stoicism xiv 409 a; Teaching Profession xiv 548 a; Women in Industry xv 451–59; Women's Organizations xv 460–65. For further biog. references see Classification of Articles (Feminism), p. 561.
Woman Suffrage—Anthony ii 73 a; Auclert ii 308 b; Cauer iii 279 a; Dohm v 192 a; Fawcett vi 153 b; Hunger Strike vii 552 b; Lockwood ix 549 b; Mott xi 78 b; Pankhurst xi 558 a; Sewall xiv 7 a; Shaw xiv 17 a; Stanton xiv 326 a; Woman, Position in Society xv 445 a; Women's Organizations xv 462 b; Woodhull xv 475 b.
Woman's Christian Temperance Union—Prohibition xii 501 b; Temperance Movements xiv 569 a.
WOMEN IN INDUSTRY—xv 451–59; Bagley ii 385 b; Clerical Occupations iii 551 b; Day Nursery v 13–16; Domestic Service v 199 b; Factory System vi 54 b; Food Industries (Baking, U. S.) vi 307 b, (Confectionery) 311 a; Hours of Labor vii 481 b, 489 b;

Ihrer vii 578 a; Industrial Hazards vii 700 b; Jameson viii 369 b; Labor Turnover viii 711 a; Laundry and Dry Cleaning Industry ix 195 a; Macarthur, M. R. ix 647 a; Match Industry x 205 a; Maternity Welfare x 223 b; Meat Packing and Slaughtering (U. S.) x 248 b; Occupation xi 431 b; Paterson xii 25 a; Textile Industry xiv 592 a; Vocational Education xv 273 b; Wages xv 315 a; Woman, Position in Society xv 444 b.
Women's Education—Anderson ii 55 a; Blackwell ii 581 b; Bodichon ii 613 b; Coeducation iii 614–17; Davies v 11 a; Filosofova vi 234 a; Jex-Blake viii 399 b; Lange ix 153 a; Lyon ix 643 a; Ramabai xiii 100 a; Schmidt xiii 576 a; Sewall xiv 7 a; Willard xv 422 b; Woman, Position in Society xv 449 b.
WOMEN'S ORGANIZATIONS — xv 460–65.
WOOD INDUSTRIES—xv 465–75; Conservation iv 227 b; Forests vi 382–87; Pulp and Paper Industry xii 705–11; Shipbuilding xiv 26 b.
Wood, S.—v 171 a.
WOODHULL, V. C.—xv 475.
WOODS, R. A.—xv 476.
Woodward, C. M.—x 104 a.
WOOL—xv 476–82; Auctions ii 310 a; Land Settlement ix 59 b; Livestock Industry ix 548 b; Macarthur ix 646 b; Mercantile Credit x 329 b; Parties, Political (Australia) xi 605 b; Textile Industry xiv 581 b, 584 b, 588 a.
Woolley, H. T.—i 457 a.
WOOLMAN, J.—xv 482.
Worcester, N.—xii 41 b.
WORDSWORTH, W.—xv 483; Transcendentalism xv 76 a.
WORKERS' EDUCATION—xv 484–88; Introd. Vol. I (The Social Sciences as Disciplines, France) i 256 b; Adult Education i 464 a; Education (Part Time) v 425–28; Industrial Education vii 692–97.
Workhouse—ii 8 a.
WORKMEN'S COMPENSATION—xv 488–92; Automobile Insurance ii 331 b; Casualty Insurance iii 262 a; Compensation and Liability Insurance iv 135–41; Employers' Liability v 518 a; Industrial Hazards vii 702 a, 703 b; Labor, Govt. Services for viii 648 b; Labor Legislation and Law viii 663 b; Maritime Law x 127 a; Rehabilitation xiii 223 b; Safety Movement xiii 504 b; Social Insurance xiv 134–38; Social Work (Case Work) xiv 180 a.
Works Councils—see INDUSTRIAL RELATIONS COUNCILS.

World Court—see PERMANENT COURT OF INTERNATIONAL JUSTICE.
World Disarmament Conference—ix 485 b.
World Federation of Education Associations—xiv 552 a.
WORLD WAR—xv 492–98; Introd. Vol. 1 (War and Reorientation) i 189 a; Aehrenthal i 481 b; Aggression, International i 485–86; Agrarian Movements (E. Central Eur. and the Balkans) i 503 b; Agric. Education i 539 a; Agric. Policy (Eur.) i 566 a; Alien Property i 636 b; Alsace-Lorraine ii 11 b; American Legion ii 31–33; Archives ii 177–81; Aviation ii 340 a; Bethmann Hollweg ii 530 b; Blockade ii 594 b; Bolshevism ii 625 b; Boundaries ii 651 a; Brigandage ii 695 a; Brokers' Loans iii 12 b; Cambon iii 158 a; Civil Liberties iii 511 b; Conscientious Objectors iv 211 a; Conscription iv 222 a; Continuous Voyage iv 320 b; Contraband of War iv 322 b; Cripples iv 593 b; Declaration of London v 48 a; Delcassé v 64 b; Disarmament v 159 b; Dye Industry v 303 a; Economic History v 324 b; Egyptian Problem v 442 b; Enemy Alien v 538 a; Enver Pasha v 560 b; Espionage v 594 b; Far Eastern Problem vi 94 b; Fascism vi 134 b; Fortunes, Private vi 397 a; Indian Question vii 667 a; Industrial Relations vii 713 a; Intolerance viii 244 a; Irredentism viii 326 a; Labor Legislation and Law viii 660 a; League of Nations ix 287 a; Literacy and Illiteracy ix 520 b; Loans, Intergovernmental ix 557 a; Meat Packing and Slaughtering (U. S.) x 246 a; Mobilization and Demobilization x 557 a; Morgan Family xi 12 b; Munitions Industry xi 131 a; Mutiny xi 167 a; National Socialism, German xi 224 b; Nationalism xi 247 a; Neutralization xi 366 a; Prisoners of War xii 421 a; Protection xii 565 b; Reparations xiii 300–08; Republicanism xiii 320 b; Requisitions, Military xiii 326 a; Russian Revolution xiii 478 b; Sazonov xiii 560 b; Self-Determination, National xiii 649–51; Socialism xiv 206 a; Socialist Parties xiv 217 a; Textile Industry xiv 587 a; Tirpitz xiv 637 a; Trusts xv 118 b; War xv 335 b, 340 a; War Economics xv 342–47; War Finance xv 348 a; Welfare Work, Industrial xv 398 a; Wilson xv 427 a.
WORMS, R.—xv 498.
WRIGHT, C. D.—xv 499; Family Budgets vi 75 a.
Wright, E.—ix 465 b.
WRIGHT, F.—xv 500.
Wright, J. L.—viii 582 a.
Writ of Deceit—xiv 654 a.
Writ of Error—ii 133 a.
Writ of False Judgment—ii 132 b.
Writ of Trespass—xiv 653 b.
Writ of Trover—xiv 654 a.
WRITING — xv 500–03; Introd. Vol. 1 (Greek Culture and Thought) i 38 a; Art (Chinese) ii 233–36; Communication iv 79 b; Language ix 158 a; Literacy and Illiteracy ix 512 b; Nationalism xi 235 b; Printing and Publishing xii 406 b; Symbolism xiv 493 a.
WRITS—xv 503–04; Certiorari iii 317–19; Habeas Corpus vii 233–36; Injunction viii 53–57; Mandamus x 84–87.
WROŃSKI-HOENE, J. M.—xv 504.
WU T'ING FANG—xv 505.
WUNDT, W. M.—xv 506; Behaviorism ii 496 b; Consciousness iv 213 b, 216 a; Evolution, Social v 660 b; Psychology xii 592 a; Social Psychology xiv 153 a.
WYCLIFFE, J.—xv 506; Huss vii 560 a; Monasticism x 589 b; Sects xiii 626 a.
WYTHE, G.—xv 507.

X-Construction Plan — Labor-Capital Cooperation viii 628 b.
Xavier, F.—see FRANCIS XAVIER.
XENOPHON—xv 508; Economics v 346 b; History and Historiography vii 369 a.
XENOPOL, A.—xv 509.
XIMÉNES DE CISNEROS, F.—xv 510.

YAMAGATA, A.—xv 510.
YANG CHU—xv 511.
YANSON, Y. E.—xv 511.
YANZHUL, I. I.—xv 512.
YĀQŪT—xv 512.
YARRANTON, A.—xv 513.
Yavorsky, S.—xiii 527 a.
Yellow Dog Contract — Labor Contract viii 631 b; Labor Injunction viii 656 a; Labor Legislation and Law viii 670 a.
Yellow Fever—iii 243 a.
YERKES, C. T.—xv 513.
Yoga—Art (Indian) ii 230 b, (Japanese) 236 b; Passive Resistance and Non-cooperation xii 10 a.
Yoritomo—vi 216 a.
Yorke, P. — see HARDWICKE, LORD.
YOSHIDA TORAJIRŌ—xv 514.
YOUNG, A. A.—xv 514.
YOUNG, ARTHUR—xv 515; Agriculture i 580 a; Agriculture, Govt. Services for i 600 b; Poverty xii 286 a.
YOUNG, B.—xv 516; Mormonism xi 16 a.
Young Germany—ii 643 a.
Young Ireland—viii 290 a.
Young Italy—iii 222 b.
Young Men's Christian Assoc.—Boys' and Girls' Clubs ii 667 b; Physical Education xii 131 b.
Young Pioneers—ii 668 a.
Young Plan—Indemnity, Military vii 643 b; Reparations xiii 305 a.
Young Turks—Kamál Maḥmad Námŭk viii 536 a; Pan-Islamism xi 543 a; Pan-movements xi 548 b.
Young Women's Christian Assoc.—xii 131 b.
YOUTH MOVEMENTS—xv 516–21; Nihilism xi 377–79.
YRJÖ-KOSKINEN, Y. S.—xv 521.
YUAN SHIH-KAI—xv 521; Kuomintang viii 611 a.
Yüan Shu—vii 384 a.
Yü-chung—see CHENG CH'IAO.
YVES OF CHARTRES—xv 522; Investiture Conflict viii 262 a.
Yvetot, G.—ii 115 b.

ZACHARIAE VON LINGENTHAL, K.-E.—xv 522.
ZACHARIAE VON LINGENTHAL, K. S.—xv 523.
Zadruga—Land Tenure ix 99 b; Law (Slavic) ix 244 a; Leontovich ix 410 b; Marković x 144 b; Village Community xv 256 a.
ZAGHLUL PASHA, S.—xv 523; Egyptian Problem v 443 a.
Zaharoff, B.—xi 130 a.
Zahirite School—v 6 b.
Zamindars—ix 110 b.
ZANGWILL, I.—xv 524; Zionism xv 532 b.
ZAPATA, E.—xv 524.
Zederbaum, Y. O. — see MARTOV, L.
ZELGEIM, V. N.—xv 525.
Zemstvo—ix 576 b.
Zenism—ii 237 b.
Zeno—Introd. Vol. 1 (Greek Culture and Thought) i 36 a; Anarchism ii 47 a; Communism iv 82 a; Stoicism xiv 408 a.
Zeppelins—ii 344 b.
ZETKIN, C.—xv 526.
Zeuthen, F.—x 628 a.
ZIA PASHA—xv 526.
Zimmerwald, Conference of—Socialist Parties xiv 217 a; Ulyanov xv 141 b.
Zinc—x 379 b.
ZINCKE, G. H.—xv 527.
ZINZENDORF, N. L. VON—xv 527.
ZIONISM—xv 528–36; Aaronson i 353 a; Boruchov ii 644 b; Communistic Settlements iv 101 a; Cooperation (Palestine) iv 371 a; Diaspora v 130 a; Ghetto vi 650 b; Ginsberg vi 664 a; Herzl vii 342 b; Hess vii 343 b; Jewish Emancipation viii 399 a; Land Settlement ix 61 a; Lilienblum ix 473 b; Mandates x 90 a; Melchett x 304 a; Near Eastern Problem xi 325 b; Nordau xi 396 b; Pinsker xii 136 b; Syrkin xiv 500 a; Trade Unions (Palestine) xv 39 a; Zangwill xv 524 a.

Zionist Congress—xv 531 b.
Zionist Organization—xv 531 b.
Zionist Labour Party—xv 534 b.
ZITELMANN, E.—xv 536.
Znaniecki, F.—i 206 a.
Zoarites—iv 97 a.
ZOLA, É.—xv 537.

ZONING—xv 538–39; City and Town Planning iii 486 a; Civic Art iii 494 a; Eminent Domain v 496 a; Housing vii 515 a.
ZORN, P.—xv 539.
Zoroastrianism — Messianism x 357 b; Religion xiii 231 b.

ZOUCHE, R.—xv 540.
ZUNZ, L.—xv 541; Judaism viii 439 a.
ZWINGLI, H.—xv 542; Introd. Vol. 1 (Renaissance and Reformation) i 95 b; Reformation xiii 190 b.

Index of Contributors

ABBOTT, EDITH—Barton, C.; Booth, C.; Butler, J.; Carpenter, M.; Dix, D. L.; Hill, O.; Howe, S. G.
ABBOTT, GRACE—Adoption (Modern).
ABEL, THEODORE—Novikov, Y. A.
ABENSOUR, LÉON—Gouges, O. de.
ABRAMOWITSCH, R.—Martov, L.
ADAM, LEONHARD—Cohn, G. L.; Dahn, F. L. S.
ADAMS, FRANK—Reclamation.
ADAMS, THOMAS—City and Town Planning; Garden Cities.
ADAMS, T. S.—Excess Profits Tax.
ADLER, MAX—Adler, V.; Lange, F. A.; Stirner, M.
AKZIN, B.—Martens, F. F.
ALBION, ROBERT G.—Privateering; Smuggling.
ALBRECHT, G.—Dühring, E. K.
ALBRIGHT, W. F.—Clermont-Ganneau, C.; Delitzsch, F.; Kuenen, A.; Rawlinson, Sir H. C.; Rougé, Vicomte O. C. E. de; Tiele, C. P.
ALLEN, G. C.—Guilds (Japanese).
ALLISON, JOHN M. S.—Bodley, J. E. C.; Gambetta, L.
ALLIX, EDGARD—Péreire, J.-É.
ALLYN, EMILY—Rotten Boroughs.
ALSBERG, CARL L.—Food and Drug Regulation.
ALTAVILLA, ENRICO—Pessina, E.
ALVERDES, F.—Animal Societies.
AMERY, G. D.—Marshall, W.; Young, A.
AMES, EDWARD SCRIBNER—Confession.
AMZALAK, MOSES BENSABAT—Ferreira Borges, J.
ANDERSON, NELS—Lodging Houses; Smith, J.; Vagrancy; Young, B.
ANDERSON, OSKAR M.—Statistics (Statistical Method).
ANDLER, CHARLES—Nietzsche, F. W.
ANDREAS, WILLY—Contarini, G.
ANDRÉN, GEORG—Government (Sweden and Finland).
ANDREWS, C. F.—Gokhale, G. K.; Ramabai, P.
ANDREWS, CHARLES M.—Acts of Trade (British); Beer, G. L.; Osgood, H. L.
ANESAKI, M.—Buddhism (Doctrines and Influence); Shinto.
ANGELL, JAMES W.—Foreign Exchange; Reparations.
ANGELL, NORMAN — Pacifism; Peace Movements.
ANSTEY, VERA — Cooperation (Brit. Empire: India); Guilds (Indian).
ANTHONY, KATHARINE — Eliot, George.

ANTONELLI, ÉTIENNE — Walras, A. A.; Walras, M. E. L.
ANTSIFEROV, A. N.—Cooperation (Russia: Credit Coop.); Hübner, N. P.
ARBUSOW, L. H.—Bunge, F. G. von.
ARDZROONI, LEON—Abovian, K.
ARMSTRONG, BARBARA NACHTRIEB—Workmen's Compensation.
ARNEKKER, EDWARD—Supiński, J.
ARNOLD, JOHN R.—Leather Industries (Tanning).
ARNOLD, THURMAN—Court Martial; Law Enforcement; Martial Law; Military Law.
ARONSON, MOSES J.—Cheysson, É.
AROSENIUS, E.—Sundbärg, A. G.
ARTZ, FREDERICK B.—Consalvi, E.
ASAKAWA, K.—Feudalism (Japanese).
ASCHAFFENBURG, GUSTAV—Gross, H.
ASHBY, A. W.—Allotment; Farm Tenancy (General and Historical).
ASPELIN, GUNNAR—Fahlbeck, P. E.
ASPINALL, ARTHUR—Brougham, Lord.
ATKINS, WILLARD E.—Taylor, F. W.
AUBIN, GUSTAV—Conrad, J.
AUBIN, HERMANN—Hegel, K.
AUBURTIN, JEAN—Jannet, C.
AUGÉ-LARIBÉ, MICHEL—Cooperation (France: Credit Coop. and Agric. Coop.); Gasparin, Comte de.
AYRES, EDITH—Inspection.

BAB, JULIUS—Theater.
BABINGER, FRANZ—Dozy, R. P. A.; Jihad; Kremer, Baron A. von; Mahmud II; Mohammed II; Vámbéry, A.
BACHI, RICCARDO—Agazzini, M.; Vasco, G.
BAILEY, K. H.—Deakin, A.; Griffith, Sir S. W.
BAIRD-SMITH, DAVID—Hotman, F.
BAKELESS, JOHN—Armaments.
BAKER, O. E.—Dry Farming; Land Utilization.
BALABANOFF, ANGELICA—Lazzari, C.
BALDENSPERGER, FERNAND—Hugo, V.-M.; Sainte-Beuve, C. A.; Sand, G.
BALDWIN, ROGER N.—Andrews, S. P.; Political Police.
BALDWIN, SUMMERFIELD—Game Laws.
BALL, CARLETON R.—Grains.

BALOGH, ELEMÉR—Bergbohm, K. M.; Berner, A. F.; Bierling, E. R.
BALOGH, THOMAS—Devaluation.
BANSE, EWALD—Humboldt, A. von.
BARBAGALLO, CORRADO—Salvioli, G.
BARBOUR, VIOLET—Hallam, H.
BARKER, ERNEST—Aristotle; Arnold of Brescia; Bryce, J.; Paine, T.; Pearson, C. H.; Sidgwick, H.; Stoicism.
BÄRMANN, JOHANNES—Hugo, G.; Mayer, O.; Struve, G. A.
BARNARD, H. C.—La Salle, Saint J.-B. de.
BARNES, GILBERT HOBBS—Weld, T. D.
BARNES, HARRY E.—Beccaria, C. B.; Corporal Punishment; Criminology; Dwight, L.; Fry, E. G.; Howard, J.; Ingersoll, R. G.; Kidd, B.; Le Bon, G.; Transportation of Criminals.
BARNIKOL, ERNST—Edelmann, J. C.; Hauck, A.; Huss, J.
BARON, HANS—Bruni, L.
BARON, SALO—Berliner, A.; Frankel, Z.; Jewish Emancipation; Karo, J. B. E.
BASHAM, W. A.—Giffen, Sir R.
BATES, M. SEARLE—Kuomintang.
BATSON, H. E.—Wicksteed, P. H.
BAUER, CLEMENS—Fortunes, Private (Antiquity); Papacy.
BAUER, JOHN—Accounting; Depreciation; Public Utilities (U. S. and Canada).
BAUER, STEPHEN—Casaux, C.; Engel, C. L. E.; Lavoisier, A. L.; Le Grand, D.; Oncken, A.
BAUER, WILHELM—Public Opinion; Sickel, T.
BAUMSTARK, ANTON—Ibn-Ḥanbal; Mālik ibn-Anas.
BAXTER, JAMES P., 3RD—Alabama Claims; Ashburton, Lord.
BAYNES, NORMAN H.—Bury, J. B.; Haverfield, F. J.; Julianus, F. C.
BEALE, HOWARD K.—Reconstruction.
BEALE, JOSEPH H.—Argentré, B. d'; Bar, K. L. von; Clunet, É.; Conflict of Laws (Historical and Theoretical Aspects); Domicile; Dumoulin, C.
BEALES, H. L.—Burnett, J.
BEALS, CARLETON—Brigandage; Carranza, V.; Guerrilla Warfare.
BEARD, CHARLES A.—Introduction (Individualism and Capitalism).
BEARD, MARY R.—Anthony, S. B.; Howe, J. W.; Knights of Labor; Pankhurst, E. G.

Index of Contributors (Abbott — Boudin)

BEARDWOOD, ALICE—Pole Family
BECKER, CARL—Adams, H.; Adams, S.; Declaration of Independence; Franklin, B.; Jefferson, T.; Napoleon I; Progress; Roland de la Platière, M. J.; Voltaire, F.-M. A. de.
BECKER, HOWARD—Lilienfeld-Toailles, P. F.
BECKERATH, ERWIN VON—Bendixen, F.; Fascism.
BECKHART, BENJAMIN HAGGOTT—Banking, Commercial (Canada).
BECKMAN, THEODORE N.—Mercantile Credit; Wholesaling.
BECKMANN, F.—Goltz, T. von der.
BEER, MAX—Bray, J. F.; Colquhoun, P.; Communism; Glasier, J. B.; Gray, J.; Hall, C.; Holyoake, G. J.; Hyndman, H. M.; Liebknecht, W.; Ogilvie, W.; Paepe, C. de; Spence, T.; Vincent, H.; Watson, J.
BEHA, JAMES A.—Casualty Insurance.
BELASCO, PHILIP S.—Bellers, J.; Fox, G.; Penn, W.
BELING, ERNST VON—Binding, K.; Hälschner, H.
BELL, BERNARD IDDINGS—Gilman, D. C.
BELL, HERBERT C.—Palmerston, Viscount.
BENEDICT, BERTRAM—Express Companies.
BENEDICT, RUTH—Animism; Child (Marriage: General); Dress; Ehrenreich, P.; Folklore; Magic; Myth; Ritual.
BENNER, CLAUDE L.—Farm Loan System, Federal.
BENNETT, CHARLES A.—Asceticism.
BENT, SILAS—Abell, A. S.; Bennett, J. G.; Bok, E. W.; Bowles Family; Dana, C. A.; Harvey, G. B. McC.; Scripps, E. W.; Stone, M. E.
BEREND, EDUARD—Richter, J. P. F.
BERGENGREN, ROY F.—Cooperation (U. S. and Canada: Credit Coop.).
BERGLUND, ABRAHAM—Merchant Marine; Pirrie, Viscount W. J.; Shipping.
BERGSTRÄSSER, LUDWIG—Bassermann, E.; Catholic Parties; Gagern, H. von; Mallinckrodt, H. von.
BERL, EMMANUEL—Péguy, C.
BERLE, A. A., JR.—American Legion; Corporation; Legal Profession and Legal Education (Modern Legal Prof.); Receivership.
BERLIN, KNUD—Government (Scandinavian States: General and Denmark, Iceland and Norway).
BERMAN, EDWARD—Cooper, P.; Employers' Liability.

BERNÁCER, GERMÁN—Arriquibar, N. de; Flórez Estrada, A.; Floridablanca, Conde de.
BERNALDO DE QUIRÓS, C.—Costa Ferreira, A. A. da; Dato e Iradier, E.; Dorado Montero, P.; Ferri, E.; Giner de los Ríos, F.; Iglesias Posse, P.; Ingenieros, J.; Jovellanos, G. M. de; Lombroso, C.; Sagra y Périz, R. D. de la.
BERNARD, L. L.—Introduction (The Social Sciences as Disciplines: Lat. Amer. and U. S.); Alberdi, J. B.; Alvarez, A.; Attitudes, Social; Barros, J. de; Bello, A.; Bunge, C. O.; Crowd; Echeverria, J. E. A.; Instinct; Mob; Rivadavia, B.; Sarmiento, D. F.; Sidis, B.; Social Psychology; Stuckenberg, J. H. W.
BERNARDI, MARIO DE—Botero, G.
BERNEY, ARNOLD—Heeren, A. H. L.
BERNSTEIN, EDUARD—Auer, I.
BERR, HENRI—History and Historiography (History); Lacombe, P.
BERRIEN, LAURA M.—Lockwood, B. A. B.
BERTHOLET, ALFRED—Priesthood; Religion; Religious Orders.
BERTRAND, LOUIS—Denis, H.
BESNIER, MAURICE—Boissier, G.
BEST, HARRY—Blind; Deaf.
BESTERMAN, THEODORE—Crawley, A. E.
BETTERMANN, WILHELM—Zinzendorf, Count N. L. von.
BEVERIDGE, W. H.—Employment Exchanges (Eur.).
BIBL, VIKTOR—Friedjung, H.
BICHON VAN IJSSELMONDE, F. PH.—Ackersdijck, J.; Bruijn Kops, J. L. de.
BIDDLECOMBE, C. H.—Aviation (Historical Development).
BIDWELL, PERCY WELLS—Drawback.
BIGELOW, KARL W.—Hawley, F. B.; Ramsay, Sir G.; Scrope, G. J. P.
BIGELOW, M. A.—Sex Education and Sex Ethics.
BIGONGIARI, DINO—Amari, M.
BINDER, RUDOLPH M.—Bliss, W. D. P.
BIRD, FREDERICK L.—Recall.
BIZILLI, PETER—Lappo-Danilevsky, A. S.
BLACHLY, FREDERICK F.—Aucoc, J. L.; Courts, Administrative.
BLACK, A. G.—Land Mortgage Credit (Agric.: U. S. and Canada).
BLACK, J. B.—Gibbon, E.; Robertson, W.
BLACK, JOHN D.—Agricultural Credit.
BLANSHARD, PAUL—Municipal Transit.
BLATCH, HARRIET STANTON—Stanton, E. C

BLEULER, EUGEN—Kraepelin, E.
BLIND, ADOLF—Süssmilch, J. P.
BLIVEN, BRUCE—Munsey, F. A.
BLOCH, MARC—Feudalism (Europ.); Fustel de Coulanges, N.-D.
BLOCK, ALEXANDER—Building and Loan Associations.
BLOM, D. VAN—Troelstra, P. J.
BOAK, A. E. R.—Caesar, G. J.; Constantine; Diocletian; Guilds (Late Roman and Byzantine).
BOAS, FRANZ—Anthropology; Race.
BOAS, GEORGE—Berkeley, G.
BODFISH, MORTON—Real Estate.
BOEHM, MAX HILDEBERT—Autonomy; Cosmopolitanism; Federalism; Irredentism; Isolation; Minorities, National; Moeller van den Bruck, A.; Nationalism (Theoretical Aspects).
BOGART, E. L.—Huntington, C. P.
BOGEN, JULES I.—Investment Banking.
BOGIČEVIĆ, MILOŠ—Milovanović, M.
BONBRIGHT, JAMES C.—Holding Companies (U. S.); Valuation.
BONGER, WILLIAM ADRIAN—Bosch Kemper, J. de; Hamel, G. A. van.
BONHAM, MILLEDGE L., JR.—Livingston, E.; Livingston, R. R.
BONN, MORITZ JULIUS—Economic Policy; Imperialism; International Finance; Price Regulation; Rationalization; Self-Sufficiency, Economic.
BONNARD, ROGER—Duguit, L.
BONNECASE, JULIEN—Demolombe, J. C. F.
BONNETT, CLARENCE E.—Employers' Associations.
BONOLIS, GUIDO—Stracca di Ancona, B.
BONTECOU, ELEANOR—By-Law; Delegation of Powers.
BOONE, GLADYS—Anderson, W. C.; MacArthur, M. R.
BORCHARD, EDWIN M.—Alien Property; Arbitration, International; Calvo and Drago Doctrines; Declaratory Judgment; Diplomatic Protection; Fiore, P.; International Law; Sanction, International; State Liability.
BORDEWIJK, H. W. C.—Pierson, N. G.
BORDWELL, PERCY—Land Transfer.
BORGESE, G. ANT.—Muratori, L. A.; Primitivism; Romanticism.
BORING, EDWIN G.—Titchener, E. B.
BORRIES, KURT—Frantz, K.
BORTKIEWICZ, L. VON—Dmitriev, V. K.
BOTSFORD, JAY BARRETT—Impressment; Piracy.
BOUDIN, LOUIS B.—Taney, R. B.

BOUGLÉ, C.—Considérant, V.; Cournot, A.-A.; Durkheim, É.; Espinas, A.; Proudhon, P. J., Roberty, E. de.
BOURGEOIS, ÉMILE—Broglie, A. V.; Dubois, G.; Fleury, A. H. de.
BOURGIN, GEORGES—Barnave, A. P. J. M.; Bazard, Saint-Amand; Blanc, L.; Carbonari; Commune of Paris; Thomas, A. A.; Trade Unions (France *and* Belgium *and* Spain and Portugal *and* Italy).
BOURNE, HENRY E.—Mignet, F. A. M. A.; Sorel, A.
BOURTZEFF, VLADIMIR—Gapon, G. A.
BOUSQUET, G. H.—Barone, E.
BOWERS, CLAUDE G.—Beveridge, A. J.
BOWLEY, MARIAN—Senior, N. W.
BOYER, GEORGES—Boutillier, J; Budé, G.; Loisel, A.; Loyseau, C.
BOYLE, JAMES E.—Agricultural Marketing (Hist. *and* U. S.).
BRACKETT, JEFFREY R.—Smith, Z. D.
BRADLEY, PHILLIPS—Administrative Areas; Great Powers; Transit, International.
BRADY, ALEXANDER—Huskisson, W.; Liverpool, First Earl of; McGee, T. D'A.; Morrison, J.
BRAILSFORD, H. N.—Atrocities; Godwin, W.; Indian Question; Internationalism; Labor Parties (Gt. Brit.); Massacre; Massingham, H. W.; Passive Resistance and Non-cooperation; Strachey, J. St. L.; Wollstonecraft, M.
BRAND, C. E.—Military Law.
BRANDI, K.—Möser, J.
BRANDT, WALTHER I.—Dubois, P.; Philip IV.
BRATTER, HERBERT M.—Silver.
BRÄUER, KARL—Excise; Gerlach, O. A. J.; House and Building Taxes; Land Taxation.
BRAUER, THEODOR—Brandts, F.; Kolping, A.
BRAUN, ROBERT—Frankel, L.; Government (Succession States); Kállay, B.; Legislative Assemblies (Hungary); Parties, Political (Succession States); Táncsics, M.
BRAWLEY, BENJAMIN—Armstrong, S. C.; Delany, M. R.
BREASTED, JAMES HENRY—Lepsius, K. R.
BREBNER, J. BARTLET—Dawson, Sir J. W.; Foster, W. A.; Mavor, J.
BRECKINRIDGE, S. P.—Institutions, Public; Maternity Welfare.
BRÉHIER, LOUIS—Leo III; Photius.
BREWER, JOHN M.—Vocational Guidance.
BREYSIG, KURT—Empire; Haeckel, E.; Lamprecht, K.
BRIEFS, G.—Duncker, F. G.; Funk, F. X. von; Hirsch, M.; Hué, O.; Ketteler, Baron W. E. von; Pesch, H.; Ratzinger, G.; Reichensperger, A. and P. F.; Social Christian Movements.
BRIERLY, J. L.—Holland, Sir T. E.; Zouche, R.
BRIFFAULT, ROBERT—Abduction; Birth Customs; Chastity; Concubinage; De Brosses, C.; Fertility Rites; Festivals; Forel, A. H.; Free Love; Holy Places.
BRIGGS, HERBERT W.—Continuous Voyage.
BRINKMANN, CARL—Introduction (Nationalism); Alien; Arndt, E. M.; Arnold, W.; Barth, P.; Below, G. A. H. von; Bluntschli, J. K.; Bourgeoisie; Citizenship; Civic Education; Civilization; Economic Incentives; Economics (Socio-Ethical Schools); Family (Social Aspects); Geisteswissenschaften; Gothein, E.; Held, A.; Invention; Land Tenure (Introd.); Landed Estates; Luxury; Maurer, G. L. von; Nasse, E.; Nobility; Primogeniture; Public Utilities (General *and* Eur.); Roscher, W. G. F.; Rotteck, K. W. R. von; Rural Industries; Standards of Living.
BRINTON, CRANE—Introduction (The Revolutions); Aulard, F. V. A.; Bolingbroke, Lord; Buckle, H. T.; Byron, Lord; Carlyle, T.; Chateaubriand, F. A. R.; Cloots J. B.; Clubs; Cochin, A.; Danton, G.-J.; Declaration of the Rights of Man and the Citizen; Desmoulins, C.; Doctrinaire; Equality; Figgis, J. N.; Flint, R.; Fouché, J.; Green, T. H.; Hébert, J. R.; Humanitarianism; Jacobinism; Macaulay, First Baron; Mathiez, A.; Natural Rights; Quinet, E.; Ritchie, D. G.; Scott, Sir W.; Shelley, P. B.; Sidney, A.; Stephens, H. M.; Utilitarianism.
BRISSENDEN, PAUL F.—Casual Labor; Industrial Workers of the World; Sabotage.
BROGAN, D. W.—Statesmanship.
BROOKES, EDGAR H.—Government (Union of S. Africa); Parties, Political (Union of S. Africa); Shepstone, Sir T.
BROOKS, VAN WYCK—Alcott, A. B.; Bourne, R. S.
BROWN, LOUISE FARGO—Burnet, G.
BROWN, PHILIP MARSHALL—Capitulations; Exterritoriality (General).
BROWNLEE, ALETA—Disasters and Disaster Relief.
BRUBAKER, HOWARD—Weyl, W. E.
BRUBECK, PAUL E.—Coroner.
BRÜGGEMANN, FRITZ—Lessing, G. E.
BRUNO, FRANK J.—Barrows, S. J.
BRUNSCHVICG, LÉON—Boutroux, É.; Cousin, V.; Janet, P.; Pascal, B.; Plato and Platonism.
BUCHANAN, D. H.—Agriculture (India).
BUCK, A. E.—Accounts, Public; Municipal Finance.
BUCK, SOLON J.—Alvord, C. W.; Donnelly, I.; Grange; Kelley, O. H.
BUDGE, SIEGFRIED—Pohle, L.; Prince-Smith, J.; Wirth, M.
BUEHLER, ALFRED G.—Sales Tax.
BUELL, RAYMOND LESLIE—Disarmament; Forced Labor; International Advisers; Limitation of Armaments.
BÜHLER, CHARLOTTE—Preyer, W. T.
BUJAK, FRANCISZEK—Cieszkowski, A.; Kamieński, H. M.
BULL, FRANCIS—Holberg, Baron L.; Sundt, E. L.
BUNZEL, BESSIE—Suicide.
BUNZEL, RUTH—Ornament.
BUONAIUTI, ERNESTO—Joachim of Flora.
BURGESS, ERNEST W.—Accommodation.
BURHENNE, KARL—Siemens, E. W. von.
BURNETT, MARY CLARKE—Social Work (Training for).
BURNHAM, WILLIAM H.—Mann, Horace.
BURNS, ARTHUR ROBERT—Babelon, E.; Joint Stock Company; Partnership.
BURNS, C. DELISLE—Agreements, International; Ceremony (Historical); Commercialism; Diplomacy; Militarism.
BURNS, E. M.—Introduction (The Social Sciences as Disciplines: Gt. Brit.); Fawcett, H.; Jones, R.; Minimum Wage.
BURR, GEORGE L.—White, A. D.
BURT, A. L.—Carleton, G.
BUSCH, HENRY M.—Camping.
BUSSE, MARTIN—Gans, E.
BUSTAMANTE, A. S. DE—Calvo, C.
BUTLER, J. R. M.—Grey, Second Earl.
BUTLER, PIERCE—Public Libraries (Hist. and Institutional Types).
BUXTON, L. H. DUDLEY—Prichard, J. C.
BYERS, JOSEPH P.—Brinkerhoff, R.

CABLE, J. RAY—State Banks, United States.
CABRAL DE MONCADA, LUIS—Gouvêa, A. de; Mello Freire, P. J. de; Pinheiro Ferreira, S.
CAHEN, LÉON—Grégoire, H.
CALKER, FRITZ VAN—Lese Majesty.
CALLANDER, WILLIAM F.—Crop and Livestock Reporting.
CALMAN, ALVIN R.—Ledru-Rollin, A.-A.

CAMPAGNAC, E. T.—Mulcaster, R.
CANNING, JOHN B.—Cost Accounting.
CANNON, W. B.—Lange, C. G.
CANTOR, NATHANIEL — Recidivism.
CAPITANT, MAURICE—Clunet, É.
CARANO-DONVITO, GIOVANNI—Palmieri, G.
CARBIA, RÓMULO D.—Groussac, P.; Gutiérrez, J. M.; López, V. F.
CARLYLE, A. J.—Aegidius Colonna; Gelasius I; Gerhoh of Reichersberg; Hincmar of Reims; Investiture Conflict; Manegold of Lautenbach; Yves of Chartres.
CARPENTER, NILES — Neighborhood; Social Surveys.
CARPENTER, WILLIAM SEAL—Apportionment; Armed Neutrality; Calhoun, J. C.; Constituency; Gerrymander; Madison, J.
CARR-SAUNDERS, A. M.—Professions.
CARRA DE VAUX, B.—Ghazzālī, al-; Husayn A'li; Maqrīzi, al-.
CARRIER, E. H.—Irrigation.
CARSTENS, C. C.—Child (Neglected); Waugh, B.
CARTER, KEITH—Extortion.
CASE, CLARENCE MARSH—Conscientious Objectors.
CASON, CLARENCE E.—Grady, H. W.
CASSAU, THEODOR—Cooperation (Germany and Austria: Consumers' Coop.); Elm, A. von; Pfeiffer, E. von; Trade Unions (Germany and Austria, Switzerland and Holland).
CASSIDY, HARRY M.—Benefits, Trade Union.
CASSIRER, ERNST — Enlightenment; Kant, I.; Leibniz, Freiherr von.
CATLIN, GEORGE E. G.—Alcohol (Alcoholism); Expert; Hobbes, T.
CAUDEL, MAURICE—Government (France and Belgium).
CAVERLY, H. L.—Fink, A.
CHADDOCK, ROBERT E.—Average; Billings, J. S.
CHAFEE, ZECHARIAH, JR.—Arms, Right to Bear; Assembly, Right of; Injunction; Sedition.
CHALUPNÝ, EMMANUEL—Havlíček, K.; Kollár, J.; Rieger, F. L.
CHAMBERLAIN, J. P.—Deadlock; International Waterways.
CHAMPION, PIERRE—Louis XI.
CHANDLER, LESTER V.—Inflation and Deflation.
CHAPMAN, CHARLES E.—Alberoni, J.; Bucareli y Ursúa, A. M.
CHAPPELL, A. F.—Rabelais, F.
CHERINGTON, PAUL T.—Auctions.
CHEYNEY, EDWARD P.—Elizabeth; Froude, J. A.; Henry VII; Henry VIII; Humanism (Historical Aspects); Lingard, J.; Seeley, Sir J. R.; Shaftesbury, First Earl of; Smith, G.; Stubbs, W.; Wolsey, T.
CHILDE, V. GORDON—Prehistory.
CHLEPNER, B. S.—Capital Levy; Loewenstein, A.
CHUBINSKY, M. — Foynitsky, I. Y.; Kistyakovsky, A. F.
CLAPHAM, J. H.—Economic History (Survey of Devel. to the 20th Cent. and Study and Research in the 20th Cent.: Gt. Brit. and As a Discipline).
CLARK, CHARLES E.—Servitudes; Summary Judgment.
CLARK, HAROLD F.—Education (Educational Finance).
CLARK, HORACE F.—Building and Loan Associations.
CLARK, JOHN MAURICE — By-Product; Diminishing Returns; Distribution; Government Regulation of Industry; Increasing Returns; Monopoly; Overhead Costs; Smith, A.; Statics and Dynamics.
CLARKSON, JESSE DUNSMORE—Irish Question; Parnell, C. S.; Plunkett, Sir H. C.
CLAUSING, ROTH—Colonate.
CLAYTON, JOSEPH—Isidore of Seville.
CLEMEN, RUDOLF A.—Livestock Industry.
CLEVELAND-STEVENS, EDWARD—Hudson, G.; Stephenson, G.
CLEVEN, N. ANDREW N.—Barbosa, R.; Santa Cruz, A.
COATS, R. H.—Johnson, G.
COBBAN, ALFRED—Coleridge, S. T.; Crane, W.; Hazlitt, W.; Johnson, S.; Paley, W.; Southey, R.; Wordsworth, W.
COCHRAN, M. H.—Bethmann Hollweg, T. von.
COCHRANE, C. N.—Thucydides.
CODIGNOLA, ERNESTO—Capponi, G. A.; Cuoco, V.; Vittorino da Feltre.
COHEN, FELIX S. — Casuistry; Lorimer, J.
COHEN, JOSEPH L.—Allowance System; Health Insurance.
COHEN, MORRIS R.—Atheism (Hist. and Doctrine); Austin, J.; Belief; Bradley, F. H.; Davidson, T.; Descartes, R.; Fictions; Hegel, G. W. F.; Method, Scientific.
COKER, FRANCIS W.—Abdication; Ahrens, H.; Lieber, F.; Lynching; Mallock, W. H.; Patriotism; Pluralism; Representation; Sovereignty.
COLBY, ELBRIDGE—Army; Conscription; Military Training; Militia (Anglo-American).
COLCORD, JOANNA C.—Family Desertion and Non-support.
COLE, ARTHUR C.—Benjamin, J. P.; Lincoln, A.; Schouler, J.
COLE, G. D. H.—Fabianism; Guild Socialism; Hardie, J. K.; Industrialism; Inheritance; Kingsley, C.; Laissez Faire; MacDonald, A.; Maurice, F. D.; Melchett, Lord; Mobilization and Demobilization; Morris, W.; Owen and Owenism; Place, F.; Ruskin, J.; Salt, Sir T.; Socialization; Thompson, W.; Trade Unions (United Kingdom and Irish Free State).
COLE, TAYLOR—Recognition, International.
COLEMAN, MCALISTER—Phillips, W.
COLLIN, FERNAND—Prins, A.; Thonissen, J. J.
COLLINET, PAUL—Ferrini, C.; Girard, P. F.; Jubainville, H. d'A. de; Zachariae von Lingenthal, K.-E.
COLM, GERHARD — Production (Statistics); Unearned Increment; Wagner, A. H. G.; War Finance.
COLMO, ALFREDO—Rodó, J. E.
COLVIN, H. MILTON—Casus Belli.
COMMAGER, HENRY STEELE—Gallatin, A.; Hildreth, R.; Parker, T.; Prescott, W. H.
COMMONS, JOHN R.—American Federation of Labor; Bargaining Power; Fair Return; Justi, H.; Kellogg, E.; Labor Movement; Price Stabilization.
COMSTOCK, ALZADA — Expenditures, Public.
CONDLIFFE, J. B.—Government (New Zealand); Grey, Sir G.; McKenzie, Sir J.; Parties, Political (New Zealand); Reeves, W. P.; Seddon, R. J.; Vogel, Sir J.
CONKLIN, ROBERT J.—Cooper, T.
COOK, CARA — Cameron, A. C.
COOK, THOMAS I.—Filmer, Sir R.
COOK, WALTER WHEELER — Equity; Hardwicke, First Earl of; Langdell, C. C.; Ownership and Possession; Special Performance.
COOPER, JOHN M.—Lafitau, J.-F.
COOPER, LYLE W.—Profit Sharing.
COPELAND, MELVIN T.—Resale Price Maintenance.
CORALNIK, A.—Friedländer, M.; Marshall, L.
CORBIN, ARTHUR L.—Frauds, Statute of.
COREY, LEWIS—Field, M.; Fortunes, Private (Modern Period); Gould, J.; Harriman, E. H.; Hewitt, A. S.; Hill, J. J.; Kelly, E.; Machines and Tools (Modern); Morgan Family.
CORWIN, EDWARD S.—Judicial Review; Marshall, J.
COULTON, G. G.—Froissart, J.; Green, J. R.; History and Historiography (Historiography: Med. Eur.); Langland, W.; Mabillon, J.
COUNTS, GEORGE S.—Education (Hist.).
COUPLAND, R.—Egerton, H. E.; George III; Kirk, Sir J.;

Livingstone, D.; Wilberforce, W.
COUSINET, ROGER—Bréal, M.; Compayré, G.
COWELL, HENRY—Music (Oriental).
COX, A. B.—Cotton.
COX, GARFIELD V.—Forecasting, Business.
COX, ISAAC JOSLIN—Balmaceda, J.
CRANE, R. S.—Steele, Sir R.
CRANE, ROBERT T.—Agobard.
CRAVEN, AVERY—Ruffin, E.
CRAVEN, IDA (*see also* Merriam, Ida Craven) — Amusements, Public; Dye Industry (Early Dye Trade); Home Ownership; Leisure.
CRAVEN, THOMAS—Art Collecting.
CRAWFORD, NELSON ANTRIM—Agricultural Societies; Agriculture, Government Services for.
CRAWLEY, C. W.—Canning, G.; Hamilton, G. G.
CREER, L. H.—Mormonism.
CROCE, BENEDETTO — Carducci, G.; Dante Alighieri; Vico, G. B.
CROISET, MAURICE—Lucian.
CROOK, WILFRED HARRIS—General Strike.
CROSS, ARTHUR LYON—Gardiner, S. R.
CULBERTSON, W. S.—Commercial Treaties.
CUNNINGHAM, WILLIAM J.—Terminals.
CUNOW, HEINRICH—Bachofen, J. J.; Bebel, A.; Blumenbach, J. F.; Land Tenure (W. Eur., Brit. Empire and U. S.); Schippel, M.; Vollmar, G. von.
CURTI, MERLE E.—Bloch, J. de; Burritt, E.; Cremer, Sir W. R.; Dodge, D. L.; Ginn, E.; Jordan, D. S.; Ladd, W.; Rantoul, R., Jr.; Richard, H.; Webster, D.
CURTIS, Anna L.—Holbrook, J.
CUSHMAN, JOAN ROSE—Cripples.
CUSHMAN, ROBERT E.—Adams, J.; Alien and Sedition Acts; Amendments, Constitutional; Civil Liberties; Contract Clause; Due Process of Law; Equal Protection of the Law.

DAGGETT, STUART — Aviation (Commercial); Villard, H.
DAHL, FRANTZ—Goos, C.; Hertzberg, E. C. H.
DALLA VOLTA, RICCARDO—Fuoco, F.
DANA, H. W. L.—Clarté Movement.
DANIELIAN, N. R. — Westinghouse, G.
DANIELS, G. W.—Doherty, J.; Unwin, G.
DASZYŃSKA GOLIŃSKA, ZOFJA—Kołłataj, H.; Popławski, A.
DAVIE, MAURICE R.—Folkways.
DAVIES, STANLEY P.—Seguin, E.
DAVIS, HORACE B. — Business Agent; Company Towns; Iron and Steel Industry (Labor Conditions outside U. S.); Policing, Industrial.
DAVIS, MICHAEL M.—Clinics and Dispensaries.
DAWSON, ROBERT MACGREGOR—Fielding, W. S.
DAWSON, W. H.—Abbot, C.; Acland, J.; Alison, A.; Anderson, J.; Anti-Corn Law League; Atkinson, W.; Attwood, T.; Babbage, C.; Barton, J.; Baxter, R. D.; Bismarck, O. E. L.; Bödiker, T.; Bosanquet, B.; Brassey, T.; Bruce, H. A.; Bruck, K. L. von; Buchanan, D.; Burdett, F.; Butt, I.; Buxton, T. F.; Caird, J.; Cassell, E. J.; Chadwick, E ; Chalmers, T.; Chartism; Clarendon, Lord; Copleston, E.; Crombie, A.; Friendly Societies; Mutual Aid Societies.
DEÁK, FRANCIS—Immunity, Diplomatic; Merchantmen, Status of; Notaries, Public; Reprisals.
DEARDORFF, NEVA R.—Child (Welfare).
DECLAREUIL, J.—Cambacérès, J. J. R. de; Charmont, J.; Civil Law; Douaren, F. le; Durand, G.
DEHN, VLADIMIR E.—Chuprov, A. I.
DELEITO Y PIÑUELA, JOSÉ—Lafuente y Zamalloa, M.
DE LEON, SOLON—McAdam, J. L.
DE LOS RÍOS, FERNANDO—Introduction (The Social Sciences as Disciplines: Spain and Portugal); Agustín, A.; Aranda, P. P. A. de B.; Ayala, B.; Azcárate, G. de; Campillo y Cossio, J.; Campomanes, P. R.; Canalejas y Mendez, J.; Canga Arguelles, J.; Cánovas del Castillo, A.; Cárdenas, F. de; Colmeiro, M.; Costa y Martinez, J.; Donoso Cortés, J.; Duran y Bas, M.; Las Casas, B. de; Vives, J. L.
DELPECH, JOSEPH—Brissaud, J. B.
DEL RÍO, ANGEL—Balmes, J. L.
DEL VECCHIO, GUSTAVO—Ferrara, F.
DENNY, LUDWELL — Cowdray, First Viscount.
DERSCH, HERMANN—Courts, Industrial.
DE SANCTIS, GAETANO—Livy.
DESSION, GEORGE H.—Perjury.
DEVAUX, JEAN—Renault, L.; Rivier, A.-P.-O.
DEWEY, DAVIS R.—Atkinson, Edward; Banks, Wildcat; Bills of Credit; Walker, F. A.
DEWEY, JOHN—Human Nature; Logic; Outlawry of War; Philosophy.
DEWING, ARTHUR S.—Corporation Finance.
DICKINSON, EDWIN D.—Belligerency; Comity; Equality of States; Extradition.
DICKINSON, JOHN—Andreae, J.; Buchanan, G.; Burchard of Worms; Certiorari; Checks and Balances; Civil Rights; Commissions.
DIEHL, CHARLES—Justinian I; Psellos, M.; Rambaud, A.
DIEHL, KARL—Adler, G.; Bernhardi, T. von; Economics (Classical School); Labor Exchange Banks; Mangoldt, H. K. E. von.
DIETRICH, E. L.—Mohammed Aḥmad.
DIETRICH, ETHEL B.—Textile Industry (Hist. and Organization).
DIETZ, FREDERICK — Salisbury, Third Marquis of; Walpole, R.
DIETZE, C. VON—Peasantry; Small Holdings.
DIGBY, MARGARET—Cooperation (Brit. Empire: Agric. Coop. *and* Switzerland *and* Scandinavian Countries *and* Russia: Agric. Coop. *and* Succession States and Balkan Countries).
DILLIARD, IRVING—Post, L. F.; Rosenwald, J.; Turner, J. M.
DINGLER, HUGO—Mach, E.
DINWIDDIE, COURTENAY—Child (Hygiene).
DIONEO-SHKLOVSKY, I. V.—Chernyshevsky, N. G.; Leontyev, K. N.
DIXON, ROLAND B.—Migrations (Primitive).
DOBB, MAURICE — Bolshevism; Economics (Cambridge School); Entrepreneur; Gosplan; Middleman.
DODD, WALTER F.—Concurrent Powers; Constitutional Conventions.
DODD, WILLIAM E.—Wilson, (T.) Woodrow.
DODWELL, H. H.—Elphinstone, M.; Hastings, W.; Lawrence, Sir H. M. and First Baron; Munro, Sir T.
DONALDSON, JOHN — Colonial Economic Policy.
DONNAN, ELIZABETH—Child, L. M.
DOPSCH, ALFONS—Anton, K. G. von; Inama-Sternegg, K. T. von.
DOROSHENKO, D.—Shevchenko, T.
DOUGHTY, FRANK H.—Arnold, T.
DOUGLAS, DOROTHY W.—Colins, J. H.; Communistic Settlements; Cost of Living; Davies, D.; De Greef, G.; Dove, P. E.; Ducpétiaux, É.; Eden, Sir F. M.; Family Budgets; Fels, J.; Warren, J.
DOUGLAS, PAUL H.—Apprenticeship; Labor Turnover.
DOUGLAS, WILLIAM O.—Automobile Insurance; Bankruptcy.
DOUGLASS, H. PAUL—Suburbs.
DOYLE, PHYLLIS—Pym, J.
DRIESCH, MARGARETE — Otto-Peters, L.
DRIVER, C. H.—Barclay, W.; Edmonds, T. R.
DUBLIN, LOUIS I.—Mortality.

Index of Contributors (Coupland — Flexner)

Dubnow, Simon — Diaspora; Graetz, H.; Jewish Autonomy; Josephus, F.
Du Bois, W. E. B.—Washington, B. T.
Duffus, R. L.—Printing and Publishing.
Duncan-Jones, A. S.—Laud, W.
Dunn, Robert W.—Automobile Industry (U. S.: Labor Conditions); Detective Agencies, Private; Food Industries (Beverage Industry and Confectionery Industry).
Dunoyer, L.-H.—Pothier, R.-J.
Duprat, G. L.—Coste, A.; Fouillée, A. J. É.
Durfee, Edgar N.—Pomeroy, J. N.
Dürr, Emil—Burckhardt, J. C.; Fueter, E.
Duyvendak, J. J. L.—Han Fei-tzǔ; Mencius; Shang Yang; Taoism.
Dziewulski, Stefan—Strojnowski, H.

Eastman, Max—Axelrod, P. B.
Ebersole, J. Franklin—Cattle Loans.
Eby, E. H.—Parrington, V. L.
Eckel, Edwin C.—Cement; Salt.
Eckhart, Franz—Tagányi, K.; Verbőczy, I.
Edie, Lionel D.—Investment.
Edman, Irwin—Art (Introd.); Naturalism.
Edminster, Lynn Ramsay—Export Duties; Meat Packing and Slaughtering (Hist. and Amer. Developments).
Edwards, George W.—Bonds.
Edwards, Lyford Paterson—Civil War.
Einaudi, Luigi—Bandini, S. A.; Capitalization and Amortization of Taxes; Custodi, P.; Davanzati, B.; De Cesare, C.; Gianni, F. M.; Lampertico, F.; Luzzatti, L.; Prato, G.; Scialoja, A.
Eisenmann, Charles—Hauriou, M.; Laferrière, É. L. J.
Eisenmann, Louis—Denis, E.
Eisler, Robert—Cynics; Cyrenaics; Epictetus; Freethinkers.
Elbogen, Ismar—Geiger, A.; Holdheim, S.; Judaism; Zunz, L.
Elliott, W. Y.—Amnesty; Force, Political; Government (Brit. Commonwealth of Nations).
Ellis, Ellen Deborah—Autocracy.
Ellwood, Charles A.—Hayes, E. C.
Emerson, Haven—Health Centers.
Emerton, Ephraim—Bartolus of Sassoferrato.
Emin, Ahmet—Gök Alp, Z.; Kamál, M. N.; Malkam Khan; Shinasi, I.; Zia Pasha.
Endres, Max—Lehr, J.
Engliš, Charles—Rašín, A.

Englund, Eric — Agricultural Experiment Stations.
Epstein, F.—Pokrovsky, M. N.
Ernle—Agriculture (England); Bakewell, R.; Fitzherbert, J.; Henley, W. of; Lawes, Sir J. B.
Errera, Carlo—Balbi, A.
Escarra, Jean—Law (Chinese).
Esmonin, Ed.—Aubaine, Right of; Baudrillart, H. J. L.; Boncerf, P. F.; Boulainvilliers, H.; Cachet, Lettre de; Chuquet, A. M.; Clément, J.-P.; Corvée; Duruy, J. V.; Martin, B.-L.-H.
Eulenberg, Franz — International Trade (Institutional Framework).
Evans, Austin P.—Bull, Papal; Records, Historical.
Evans, I. L.—Agrarian Movements (E. C. Eur. and the Balkan Countries); Lucas, Sir C. P.
Everard, L. C.—Museums and Exhibitions.
Everett, C. W.—Molesworth, Sir W.
Everett, Helen—Career; Control, Social.
Evreinov, Boris—Beliayev, I. D.
Ewing, J.—Hofmeyr, J. H.
Ezekiel, Mordecai—Correlation.

Fainsod, Merle—Soviet.
Fairchild, David—Aaronson, A.
Fairlie, John A.—Boards, Administrative; County-City Consolidation; County Government, United States.
Falconer, Martha P.—Child (Institutions).
Falnes, Oscar J.—Wergeland, H. A.
Fanno, Marco—Ferraris, C. F.; Supino, C.
Farnell, Lewis Richard—Fowler, W. W.
Farrand, Max—Articles of Confederation.
Faulkner, Harold U.—Coxe, T.; Hanna, M. A.; Newman, Cardinal J. H.; Pitkin, T.; Stanford, L.; Stillman, J.; Tucker, G.
Faÿ, Bernard—Fréron, É. C.; Vergennes, Comte de.
Fay, Sidney B.—Alliance; Alsace-Lorraine; Archives (National); Balance of Power; Bülow, B. H. M.; Concert of Powers; Izvolsky, A. P.; Marschall von Bieberstein, Baron A.; Nicolson, Sir A.; Oldenbarneveldt, J. van; Sazonov, S. D.; World War.
Febvre, Lucien—History and Historiography (History); Michelet, J.
Fedozzi, Prospero—Lampredi, G. M.
Fehr, Hans—Beyer, G.; Heineccius, J. G.; Leist, B. W.; Schröder, R.

Feilchenfeld, Ernst H.—Concessions; State Succession.
Feldhaus, F. M.—Machines and Tools (Ancient, Mediaeval and Early Modern).
Feldman, Herman — Business Administration.
Feller, A. H.—Evidence (Modern Civil Law); Majority, Age of; Moratorium; Protectorate; Self-Incrimination; Shaw, L.; Uniform Legislation; Westlake, J.
Fellner, Frédéric de—Jekelfalussy, J.; Láng, Baron L.
Fenwick, Charles G.—Aviation (Law).
Ferenczi, Imre — Migrations (Modern).
Ferguson, William Scott—Alexander the Great; Beloch, K. J.; Demosthenes; Grote, G.; Mahaffy, Sir J. P.
Fernández de Velasco, Recaredo—Mariana, J. de.
Ferrière, Adolphe—Brunswick, T.; Lietz, H.
Fetter, Frank A.—Cairnes, J. E.; Capital; Rent; Rent Charge.
Fetter, Frank Whitson—Wheatley, J.
Feugère, Anatole—Raynal, G. T. F.
Figueiredo, Fidelino de—Gama Barros, H. de; Henry the Navigator; Herculano de Carvalho e Araujo, A.; Morales, A. de; Oliveira Martins, J. P. de; Pedro I and Pedro II; Pombal, Marquez de; Quental, A. T. de.
Fineman, Hayim—Boruchov, B.; Syrkin, N.
Finer, Herman—Civil Service; Grants-in-Aid; Organization, Administrative.
Finkelstein, Maurice—Amos, S.; Bailment.
Finkelstein, Moses I.—Wellhausen, J.
Fischelis, Robert P.—Medical Materials Industry.
Fischer, Eugen—Martin, R.
Fish, Carl Russell—Adams, C. F. (d. 1886); Adams, J. Q.; Fiske, J.
Fisher, Irving — Compensated Dollar; Income.
Fisher, Lillian Estelle—Gálvez, J. de; Revillagigedo, Conde de.
Fisher, Mary S.—Parent Education.
Fitch, John A.—Blacklist, Labor; Labor Disputes; Strikes and Lockouts.
Fitzpatrick, John C.—Washington, G.
Flanagan, James A.—Maxwell, Sir W.
Fleischmann, Max—Heffter, A. W.
Flenley, R.—Champlain, S. de.
Flexner, Jean Atherton—Kirby, J., Jr.; Van Cleave, J. W.

FLICHE, AUGUSTIN—Gregory VII; Religious Institutions, Christian (Roman Catholic).
FLORENCE, P. SARGANT—Absenteeism (Labor); Fatigue.
FLOURNOY, RICHARD W., JR.—Dual Citizenship; Expatriation; Nationality.
FLÜGEL, FELIX—Clinton, De Witt.
FLÜGGE, EVA—Ballin, A.
FOERSTER, ROBERT F.—Employee Stock Ownership.
FOLEY, HENRY E.—Foreign Corporations.
FORBES, RUSSELL—Public Contracts.
FORD, GRACE—Jex-Blake, S.; Paterson, E.; Wilson, J. H.
FORD, GUY STANTON—Expositions, International.
FORD, PERCY—Jones, L.; Ravenstone, P.
FORD, W. W.—Frank, J. P.
FOREST, ILSE—Preschool Education.
FORKE, A.—Mo Ti.
FORSTER, G. W.—Farm.
FORTUNE, REO F.—Divination; Incest.
FOSTER, ROGER S.—Jurisdiction.
FOX, DIXON RYAN—Birney, J. G.
FRANCKE, KUNO—Biedermann, F. K.
FRANK, JEROME—Lawlessness.
FRANK, TENNEY—Introduction (The Roman World); Abbott, F. F.; Dill, Sir S.
FRANKE, OTTO—Feudalism (Chinese); Hirth, F.; Wang An-shi.
FRANKEL, S. HERBERT—Lehfeldt, R. A.
FRANKFURTER, FELIX—Advisory Opinions (National); Interstate Commerce (U. S.); Labor Injunction; Rate Regulation; Supreme Court, United States.
FRASER, HERBERT F.—Indemnity, Military.
FRASER, LINDLEY M.—Goschen, First Viscount; Ingram, J. K.; Leslie, T. E. C.; Marcet, J.; Martineau, H.; Newmarch, W.; Palgrave, Sir R. H. I.; Steuart, Sir J. D.; Tooke, T.; Torrens, R.; Whately, R.
FRÉCHET, MAURICE—Poisson, S.-D.
FREDERICK, JOHN H.—Brice, C. S.
FREEMAN, JOSEPH—Ruthenberg, C. E.
FREUND, ERNST—Administrative Law; Constitutional Law; Eminent Domain; Legislation; Licensing; Mandamus.
FREUND, MICHAEL—Melanchthon, P.; Münzer, T.; Neander, A.; Oncken, W.; Reimarus, H. S.
FREUND, PAUL A.—Interstate Commerce (U. S.).
FRIDAY, DAVID—Brokers' Loans.
FRIEDRICH, A. A.—Liquor Industry; Rent Regulation; Stocks and Stock Ownership; Veterans.
FRIEDRICH, CARL JOACHIM—Allegiance; Althusius, J.; Charles V; Confiscation; Cromwell, Oliver; Gierke, O. von; Monarchy; Naturalization; Oligarchy; Plutocracy; Prerogative; Reason of State; Separation of Powers.
FRIESS, HORACE L.—Eucken, R. C.; Natorp, P.; Nelson, L.; Sacred Books; Scheler, M.; Steiner, R.; Strauss, D. F.
FRITZSCHE, HANS—Bülow, O.; Keller, F. L.; Wach, A.
FRÖLICH, PAUL—Luxemburg, R.
FUCHS, RALPH F.—Labor Contract.
FUESS, CLAUDE MOORE—Cushing, C.
FULLER, B. A. G.—Sophists.
FULLER, RAYMOND G.—Child (Labor).
FURST, HENRY—Government Publications.

GABRIEL, RALPH HENRY—Bourne, E. G.; Crèvecoeur, M.-G. J. de; Parkman, F.
GALDAMES, LUIS—Letelier, V.; Portales, D.
GALDSTON, IAGO—Health Education.
GALITZI, CHRISTINE—Ionescu, T.; Kogălniceanu, M.; Lazăr, G.
GALLOWAY, GEORGE B.—Investigations, Governmental.
GALLOWAY, LEE—Salesmanship.
GALTON, F. W.—By-Elections.
GAMIO, MANUEL—Ixtlilxóchitl, F. de A.
GARDINER, A. G.—Cadbury, G.; Scott, C. P.
GARDINER, RAYNOR M.—Small Claims Courts.
GARDNER, HELEN—Art (Mediaeval).
GARNER, JAMES WILFORD—Conseil d'État; Dunning, W. A.; Latané, J. H.; Warfare, Laws of.
GARRISON, F. H.—Welch, W. H.
GAUS, JOHN M.—Stead, W. T.; Wilkes, J.
GAY, EDWIN F.—Putting Out System.
GAYER, ARTHUR D.—Public Works.
GEBHART, JOHN C.—Funerals.
GEHRIG, HANS—Böhmert, K. V.; Hildebrand, B.; Knies, K. G. A.; Schmoller, G. von.
GELESNOFF, V.—Jakob, L. H. von; Storch, F. von; Turgenev, N. I.
GEMÄHLING, PAUL—Bureau, P.
GEORGIEVSKY, P. I.—Semenov, P. P.; Yanson, Y. E.
GERHARD, DIETRICH—Niebuhr, B. G.
GERLAND, H. B.—Mayer, M. E.
GERLOFF, WILHELM—Hock, Baron K. F.; Neumann, F. J.
GERSHOY, LEO—Barère de Vieuzac, B.; Sieyès, Abbé Joseph Emmanuel.
GESELL, ARNOLD—Child (Psychology).
GETTELL, R. G.—Pius II.
GHIULEA, N.—Dobrogeanu-Gherea, C.
GHOSHAL, U. N.—Kautilya.
GIBBONS, HERBERT ADAMS—Boundaries.
GIDE, CHARLES—Boyve, É. de; Consumers' Cooperation; Cooperation (France: Consumers' Coop. and Italy: Consumers' Coop. and Belgium).
GIDEONSE, HARRY D.—Cohen Stuart, A. J.
GIESECKE, FRITZ—Liebig, Freiherr J. von.
GILL, C. A.—Epidemics.
GILLESPIE, FRANCES E.—Broadhurst, H.; Campbell, A.; Dunning, T. J.; Jones, E. C.; Odger, G.; Potter, G.
GILLIN, JOHN L.—Begging.
GILLOUIN, RENÉ—Barrès, M.
GILSON, MARY BARNETT—Unemployment Insurance.
GINSBERG, MORRIS—Association; Class Consciousness; Conventions, Social; Courtship; Hobhouse, L. T.; Mechanism and Vitalism.
GINZBURG, BENJAMIN—About, E.; Antisemitism; Bonald, L. G. A.; Galileo Galilei; Lamarck, Chevalier de; Lomonosov, M. V.; Newton, Sir I.; Pasteur, L.; Price, R.; Priestley, J.; Science; Socrates; Spinoza, B.
GIUSTI, ROBERTO F.—Justo, J. B.; Mariátegui, J. C.; Mitre, B.
GIVENS, MEREDITH—Gary, E. H.; Iron and Steel Industry (General).
GLAESER, M. G.—Capitalization.
GLOTZ, GUSTAVE—Guiraud, P.; Reinach, T.; Solon.
GLOVER, T. R.—Herodotus of Halicarnassus; History and Historiography (Historiography: Antiquity); Polybius.
GLÜCK, ELSIE—Anderson, E. G.; Child (Welfare Legislation); Cooperation (General Survey); Industrial Democracy; Mitchell, J.; Schlesinger, B.; Sigman, M.; Trade Unions (Introd.); Women in Industry (Problems of Organization).
GLUECK, BERNARD—Child (Guidance); Mental Hygiene.
GLUECK, SHELDON—Crofton, Sir W. F.; Insanity (Criminal Law); Maconochie, A.
GOBBI, ULISSE—Bocchi, R.; Scaruffi, G.
GOETZ, WALTER—History and Historiography (Historiography: Modern Eur.); Jesuits; Loyola, I. de; Pastor, Freiherr L. von; Philip II; Riehl, W. H.; Ritter, M.; Spittler, L. T.; Steinhausen, G.
GOLD, NORMAN LEON—Roads

Index of Contributors (Fliche — Hammond)

(Ancient, Mediaeval and Early Modern).
GOLDENWEISER, ALEXANDER—Bastian, A.; Evolution, Social; Goldenweiser, A. S.; Huxley, T. H.; Rivers, W. H. R.; Totemism.
GOLDSCHMIDT, JAMES—Planck, J. J. W. von.
GÖNCZI, EUGENE—Hertzka, T.
GONNARD, RENÉ—Dumont, A.; Moheau.
GONZÁLEZ CALDERÓN, JUAN A.—Gorostiaga, J. B.
GONZÁLEZ PALENCIA, ANGEL—Lull, R.
GOOCH, R. K.—Bloc, Parliamentary; Daguesseau, H.-F.
GOODHART, ARTHUR—Campbell, J.
GOODMAN, PAUL—Montefiore, Sir M.
GOODRICH, CARTER—Arbitration, Industrial; Contract Labor; Hoxie, R. F.; Indenture; Migratory Labor; Parker, C. H.; Trade Unions (Australia, New Zealand and S. Africa).
GOODRICH, L. C.—Yang Chu.
GOODSELL, WILLYSTINE—Coeducation; Willard, E. H.
GOSNELL, HAROLD F.—Aldrich, N. W.; Ballot; Parties, Political (Organization); Proportional Representation; Voting.
GOTTSCHALK, LOUIS—Carnot, L. N. M.; Lafayette, Marquis de; Marat, J.-P.; Vandal, Comte A.
GOURVITCH, ALEXANDER—Ardashev, P. N.; Food Industries (Food Distribution: Russia); Gershuni, G. A.
GOYAU, GEORGES—Baronius, C.; Cluniac Movement; Gregory I; Montalembert, Comte de; Ozanam, F.; Paul IV; Périn, H. X. C.; Veuillot, L.; Vincent de Paul, Saint.
GRABOWER, ROLF—Alcabala.
GRABOWSKI, TADEUSZ — Skarga Poweski, P.
GRAHAM, FRANK D.—Monetary Stabilization.
GRAHAM, MALBONE W.—Government (Baltic States); Parties, Political (Baltic States); Polish Corridor.
GRANT, ELLIOTT M.—Brissot de Warville, J.-P.
GRAS, N. S. B.—Agriculture (Antiquity and Middle Ages); Barter; Bill of Exchange (Historical); Economic History (U. S.); Gross, C.
GRATTAN, C. HARTLEY—Botha, L.; Bryan, W. J.
GRAVES, W. BROOKE—Curtis, G. W.
GRAY, LEWIS CECIL—Agricultural Machinery; Land Speculation.
GRAZIANI, AUGUSTO—Introduction (The Social Sciences as Disciplines: Italy to the end of the World War); Augustinis,
M. de; Bianchini, L.; Broggia, C. A.; Cossa, E.; Cossa, L.; Cusumano, V.; Pascoli, L.; Ricca-Salerno, G.; Serra, A.
GREAVES, H. R. G.—Linguet, S. N. H.
GREENE, NATHAN—Labor Injunction.
GREENSTONE, JULIUS H.—Abrahams, I.; Güdemann, M.; Schechter, S.
GREGORY, ALYSE—Blunt, W. S.
GREGORY, T. E.—Currency; Gilbart, J. W.; Money.
GRINBERG, SUZANNE — Auclert, H.; Deraismes, M.
GRISWOLD, H. D.—Brahmanism and Hinduism.
GRIZIOTTI, BENVENUTO—Montemartini, G.; Roncali, A.
GROBA, KURT—Gentz, F. von.
GROETHUYSEN, B. — Jansenism; Lotze, R. H.; Montaigne, M. de; Mysticism; Rationalism; Renaissance; Secularism.
GRONSKI, PAUL — Government (Imperial Russia).
GROSS, HERBERT — Monopolies, Public.
GROSSMAN, HENRYK—Sismondi, J. C. L. S. de.
GROTKOPP, WILHELM—Branting, K. H.; Kreuger, I.; Match Industry.
GRUBB, ISABEL—Quakers.
GRUENING, ERNEST—Publicity.
GRÜNFELD, ERNST—Cooperation (Germany and Austria: Credit Coop. *and* Italy: Credit Coop.); Credit Cooperation; Haas, W.; Raiffeisen, G. W.; Schulze-Delitzsch, H.
GRÜNHUT, MAX—Feuerbach, P. J. A. von; Merkel, A. J.
GRÜNTHAL, ADOLF—Resorts.
GRUNTZEL, JOSEF—Customs Duties.
GRUYTER, J. DE—Douwes Dekker, E.
GUILDAY, PETER— Denifle, H. S.
GUILLEBAUD, C. W.—Industrial Relations Councils.
GULAK, ASHER—Law (Jewish).
GULICK, CHARLES A., JR.—Seager, H. R.
GÜNTHER, ADOLF — Arbeitsgemeinschaft.
GURFEIN, MURRAY I.—Racketeering.
GURIAN, WALDEMAR—Jörg, J. E.
GURVITCH, GEORGES—Chicherin, B. N.; Fichte, J. G.; Gradovsky, A. D.; Justice; Kistyakovsky, B. A.; Korkunov, N. M.; Menger, A.; Natural Law; Petrazhitsky, L. I.; Secrétan, C.
GUTMANN, FRANZ—Heyn, O.; Knapp, G. F.
GUTMANN, JAMES—Schelling, F. W. J.
GUTTMANN, JULIUS — Maimonides, M.
GUY-GRAND, GEORGES—Tarde, G.
GUYOT, RAYMOND—Masson F.
GWYNN, DENIS—Catholic Emancipation; Manning, H. E.; O'Connell, D.

HAAS, J. ANTON DE—Business, Government Services for.
HABER, FRANZ—Gesell, S.
HABER, WILLIAM—Construction Industry.
HACKER, LOUIS M.—Food Supply; Lloyd, H. D.; Schiff, J. H.; Schurz, C.
HACKETT, FRANCIS—Collins, M.; Grattan, H.; Griffith, A.
HADDON, A. C.—Beddoe, J.
HAENSEL, PAUL—Local Finance.
HAHNE, ERNST HERMAN—Special Assessments.
HAIG, ROBERT MURRAY—Corporation Taxes; Taxation.
HAIL, WILLIAM JAMES—Chang Chih-tung; Li Hung Chang; Yuan Shih-kai.
HAINES, ANNA J.—Nursing.
HALBWACHS, MAURICE—Bernoulli; Laplace, Marquis de; Quetelet, A.
HALE, ROBERT L.—Labor Legislation and Law (Law: Anglo-American).
HALÉVY, ÉLIE—Mill, J.
HALFTER, FRITZ—Fröbel, F.
HALL, FRED—Cooperation (Consumers' Coop. in Gt. Brit. and Ireland).
HALL, FRED S.—Child (Marriage: U. S.).
HALL, T. D. H.—Swainson, W.
HALL, WALTER PHELPS—Balfour, A. J.; Peel, Sir R.
HALLBERG, CHARLES W.—Suez Canal.
HALLINAN, C. T.—Booth Family.
HALPHEN, LOUIS—Charlemagne; Delisle, L. V.; Du Cange, C. du F.; Estates General; Giry, A.; Guérard, B.; Langlois, C. V.; Luchaire, A.; Migrations (Ancient and Mediaeval); Monod, G. J. J.; Philip Augustus; Sabatier, P.; Thierry, J.-N.-A.; Truce and Peace of God.
HAMILTON, EARL J.—Anzano, T. de; Cantos y Benitez, P. de; Carranza, A.; Castro, J. de; Ezpeleta, P. A. de; Fernández Navarrete, P.
HAMILTON, WALTON H.—Accumulation; Acquisition; Caveat Emptor; Celibacy; Collective Bargaining; Collectivism; Competition; Constitutionalism; Cooley, C. H.; Damages; Freedom of Contract; Institution; Judicial Process; Mill, J. S.; Organization, Economic; Police Power; Property.
HAMMOND, JOHN LAWRENCE—Agrarian Movements (Gt. Brit.); Cobbett, W.; Commerce; Courtney, First Baron; Factory System; Fox, C. J.; Gilbert, T.; Green, F. E.; Oastler, R.; Shaftesbury, Seventh Earl of; Toynbee, A.; Trevelyan, G. O.

HAMPE, KARL—Frederick II; Henry IV; Holy Roman Empire; Otto I.
HANBURY, H. G.—Jessel, Sir G.
HANCOCK, W. K.—Government (Commonwealth of Australia); Parkes, Sir H.; Parties, Political (Australia); Phillip, A.
HANDELSMAN, MARCELI—Czartoryski, A. J.; Długosz, J.; Lelewel, J.; Wielopolski, A.
HANDLER, MILTON—Restraint of Trade.
HANDMAN, MAX SYLVIUS—Abortion; Boom; Gypsies; Ku Klux Klan.
HANKINS, FRANK H.—Achenwall, G.; Adaptation; Aryans; Atavism; Bateson, W.; Birth Control; Chamberlain, H. S.; Darwin, C. R.; Degeneration; Divorce; Finot, J.; Fraternal Orders; Hall, G. S.; Illegitimacy (Social Aspects); Masonry; Social Discrimination; Woltmann, L.
HANMER, LEE F.—Recreation.
HANSON, ALICE C.—Laundry and Dry Cleaning Industry; Restaurants.
HANTOS, ELEMÉR—Matlekovits, S.
HANUŠ, JOSEPH—Dobrovský, J.
HARDMAN, J. B. S.—Berger, V. L.; Debs, E. V.; De Leon, D.; Intimidation; Labor Banking; Labor-Capital Cooperation; Labor Parties (General *and* U. S.); Masses; Terrorism.
HARDY, CHARLES O.—Broker; Bucket Shops; Hedging; Market; Speculation.
HARING, CLARENCE H.—Audiencia; Casa de Contratación; Cortés, H.; Council of the Indies; Juárez, B. P.; Mendoza, A. de.
HARING, H. A.—Warehousing.
HARRIS, ABRAM L.—Finley, R.; Helper, H. R.; Negro Problem.
HARRIS, C. R. S.—Duns Scotus.
HARRIS, JOSEPH P.—Elections; Registration of Voters.
HARROD, R. F.—Lloyd, W. F.
HARSIN, PAUL—Agoult, Charles d'; Ailly, P. d'; Gramont, S. de; Laffemas, B.; Law, J.; Montchrétien, A. de; Necker, J.; Oresme, N.; Richelieu, A.-J. du P. de; Saint-Simon, Duc de; Sully, Duc de; Turgot, R. J.; Wolowski, L. F. M. R.
HART, HENRY M., JR.—Rate Regulation.
HART, JOSEPH K.—Folk High Schools.
HART, RICHARD H.—Public Libraries (Modern Library Systems).
HARTMANN, RICHARD—Mohammed ibn 'Abd al-Wahhāb; Omar ibn al-Khattab.
HARTSOUGH, MILDRED L.—Lipton, Sir T. J.; Stinnes, H.
HARTUNG, FRITZ—Waitz, G.
HARTZOG, JUSTIN R.—Parks.

HASBROUCK, PAUL DEWITT—Caucus.
HAUSER, HENRI—Bardi; Coeur, J.; Colbert, J.-B.; Henry IV; Journeymen's Societies; Levasseur, P. É.; Marcel, É.; Mazarin, J.; Morellet, Abbé A.; Thou, J. A. de.
HAWTREY, R. G.—Banking, Commercial (United Kingdom); Credit.
HAYDON, A. EUSTACE—Comparative Religion; Fatalism; Goblet d'Alviella, E. F. A.; Reinach, S.; Smith, W. R.
HAYEK, FRIEDRICH A.—Gossen, H. H.; MacLeod, H. D.; Norman, G. W.; Philippovich von Philippsberg, E.; Saving.
HAYES, CARLTON J. H.—Action Française; Acton, Lord; Cavour, C. B. di; Nationalism (Historical Development).
HAZELTINE, H. D.—Blackstone, W.; Canon Law; Commentators; Doneau, H.; Ecclesiastical Courts; Eldon, First Earl of; Ellesmere, Baron; Excommunication; Gaius; Glossators; Lanfranc; Legal Profession and Legal Education (Ancient and Mediaeval); Liebermann, F.; Maitland, F. W.; Mansfield, First Earl of; Mortmain.
HAZEN, CHARLES DOWNER—Thayer, W. R.
HEALY, WILLIAM—Maudsley, H.
HEARNSHAW, F. J. C.—Introduction (Renaissance and Reformation); Beaconsfield, Earl of; Burke, E.; Chivalry (Europ.); Churchill, R. H. S.; Smith, Sir T.; Vane, Sir H.; Wellington, First Duke of.
HEATON, HERBERT—Angas, G. F.; Ballance, J.; Bourke, R.; Enclosures; Gott, B.; Hales, J.; Industrial Revolution; Kingston, C. C.; Labor Parties (Brit. Dominions); Land Grants (Brit. Empire); Public Domain (New Countries); Wool.
HEATON, JOHN L.—Cobb. F. I.
HEBER, LILY—Bruun, C. A.
HEBERLE, RUDOLF—Trade Unions (Scandinavian Countries and Finland).
HECKER, J. F.—Bogdanov, A.
HECKSCHER, ELI F.—Berch, A.; Chydenius, A.; Continental System; Mercantilism; Protection.
HEDDEN, W. P.—Food Industries (Food Distribution: Perishable Products, U. S.); Refrigeration.
HEDEMANN, J. WILHELM—Fuchs, E.; German Civil Code, Jhering, R. von.
HEDGES, M. H.—Mechanic.
HEICHELHEIM, FRITZ—Land Tenure (Ancient World); Public Domain (General); Tribute.
HEINBERG, J. G.—Lewis, Sir G. C.

HELANDER, SVEN—Free Ports and Free Zones.
HELLER, HERMANN—Jellinek, G.; Political Science; Power, Political; Stahl, F. J.
HELLER, WOLFGANG—Horn, E. I.
HEMMEON, J. C.—Hill, Sir R.; Postal Savings Banks; Postal Service.
HENTIG, HANS VON—Punishment.
HERRE, PAUL—Holstein, F. von.
HERRING, E. PENDLETON—Farm Bloc, United States; Garrison, W. L.; Lobby.
HERRING, JOHN W.—Apostasy and Heresy.
HERSKOVITS, MELVILLE J.—Anthropometry; Broca, P.-P.; Domestication; Race Mixture; Retzius, A. A.
HERTZLER, J. O.—Andreae, J. V.; Bellamy, E.
HERZFELD, HANS—Miquel, J. von.
HEUSS, THEODOR—Bamberger, L.; Barth, T.; Bundesrat; Lasker, E.; Lueger, K.; National Socialism, German; Naumann, F.; Preuss, H.; Richter, E.; Stöcker, A.; Virchow, R.; Welcker, K. T.; Wichern, J. H.; Zorn, P.
HEWES, AMY—Clerical Occupations.
HEYDE, LUDWIG—Francke, E.
HEYMANN, ERNST—Endemann, W.; Goldschmidt, L.
HIBBARD, B. H.—Agricultural Cooperation; Farm Bureau Federation, American; Homestead; Land Grants (U. S.).
HICKS, GRANVILLE—Abbott, L.; Channing, W. E.; Channing, W. H.; Fuller, S. M.; Whitman, W.
HICKS, J. R.—Mundella, A. J.
HIGGINS, A. PEARCE—Hall, W. E.
HIGGS, HENRY—Bailey, S.; Banfield, T. C.; Child, J.
HIGHT, JAMES—Atkinson, H. A.
HILFERDING, RUDOLF—Haase, H.
HILL, NORMAN L.—Guaranties, International.
HILL, PATTY S.—Blow, S. E.; Peabody, E. P.
HIMES, NORMAN E.—Carlile, R.; Knowlton, C.; Owen, R. D.; Wakley, T.
HINTZE, HEDWIG—Regionalism; Schlosser, F. C.; Staël-Holstein, Baronne A. L. G. N. de; Sybel, H. von; Vergniaud, P. V.
HIPPEL, ERNST VON—Gerber, K. F. W. von; Gneist, R. von; Hänel, A.; Laband, P.; Mohl, R. von; Moser, J. J. and F. K. von; Pütter, J. S.
HIPPEL, ROBERT VON—Liszt, F. E. von; Schwarzenberg, Freiherr J. von.
HIRST, FRANCIS W.—Asquith, H. H.; Delane, J. T.; Gladstone, W. E.
HIS, EDUARD—Heusler, A.; Huber, E.

HITTI, PHILIP K.—Chivalry (Arabic); History and Historiography (Historiography: Islam); Idrīsi, al-; Mas'ūdi, al-; Mu-'āwiyah; Yāqūt.
HOBHOUSE, L. T.—Aristocracy; Christianity.
HOBSON, ASHER—Agricultural Economics (Eur.); Agriculture, International Institute of; Chambers of Agriculture; Lubin, D.
HOCART, A. M.—Death Customs; Deification; Etiquette; Fasting; Iconoclasm; Idolatry; Infanticide; Ridgeway, Sir W.; Sacrifice.
HOCKING, WILLIAM ERNEST—Royce, J.
HOETZSCH, OTTO—Government (Soviet Russia).
HOFMEYR, JAN H.—Kruger, S. J. P.
HOHMAN, ELMO P.—Fisheries; Longshoremen; Seamen.
HOLCOMBE, ARTHUR N.—Chinese Problem; Exterritoriality (China); Government (China); Legislative Assemblies (U. S.: State Legislatures); Parties, Political (Theory); State Government, United States.
HOLLANDER, JACOB H.—Dunbar, C. F.; Lauderdale, Eighth Earl of; Longe, F. D.; Massie, J.; Ricardo, D.
HOLMES, C. L.—Farm Management.
HOLMES, S. J.—Biology.
HOLST, HENRIETTE ROLAND—Gorter, H.; Nieuwenhuis, F. D.
HOLTZMANN, WALTHER—Frederick I.
HOMAN, PAUL T.—Bastiat, F.; Blanqui, J. A; Carey, H. C.; Consumption (Economic Theory); Economics (Institutional School); Trusts.
HOOK, SIDNEY—Bauer, B.; Büchner, L.; Determinism; Dietzgen, J.; Engels, F.; Feuerbach, L. A.; Materialism; Ruge, A.; Violence.
HOOTON, EARNEST A.—Man.
HORMELL, ORREN C.—Popular Assemblies.
HORNER, JOHN T.—Dairy Industry.
HOTELLING, HAROLD—Frequency Distribution.
HOUGH, WALTER—Mason, O. T.
HOWARD, PENDLETON—Habeas Corpus; Prosecution; Romilly, Sir S.
HOWE, FREDERIC C.—Agrarian Movements (Denmark).
HOWE, HARRISON E.—Industrial Alcohol.
HRUŠEVSKY, M.—Drahomanov, M. P.; Khmelnitsky, B.; Kostomarov, N. I.
HU SHIH—Confucianism; K'ang Yu-wei.
HUART, FREDERICK J. A.—Parties, Political (Netherlands).

HUBERT, RENÉ—Alembert, J. L. d'; Ballanche, P. S.; Bayle, P.; Boccardo, G.; Bosco, Don G.; Bossuet, J. B.; Buffon, G. L. L.; Comte, I. A. M. F. X.; Condillac, É. B. de; Dubos, J. B.; Encyclopédistes; Fénelon, F. de S. de la M.; Guyau, J. M.; Helvétius, C. A.; Holbach, Baron von; Lamettrie, J. O. de; Littré, M. P. É.; Saint-Pierre, Abbé C. I. C. de; Tourville, H. de.
HÜBNER, RUDOLF—Beseler, K. G. C.; Eichhorn, K. F.
HUDSON, MANLEY O.—Hague Conferences; International Legislation; Permanent Court of Arbitration; Permanent Court of International Justice.
HUEBNER, S. S.—Arbitrage; Corner, Speculative; Fire Insurance (American).
HUGELMANN, KARL GOTTFRIED—Klein, F.; Unger, J.
HUIZINGA, J.—Erasmus, D.
HULME, EDWARD M.—Gebhart, N. É.; Otto of Freising.
HULTGREN, THOR—Adams, C. F. (d. 1915); Cooke, J.; Fisk, J., Jr.
HUMMEL, ARTHUR W.—Chang Hsüeh-ch'eng; Cheng Ch'iao; History and Historiography (Historiography: China and Japan); Ku Yen-wu; Ssŭ-ma Ch'ien.
HUNTINGTON, ELLSWORTH—Acclimatization.
HUSIK, ISAAC—Philo Judaeus.
HUSTVEDT, S. B.—Grundtvig, N. F. S.
HUTCHINSON, WILLIAM T.—McCormick, C. H.; McMaster, J. B.
HUTTON, W. H.—Becket, T.
HYDE, CHARLES CHENEY—Armed Merchantmen.
HYMA, ALBERT—Blok, P. J.; Motley, J. L.; Witt, J. de.

ILTIS, HUGO—Mendel, G. J.
INGBERG, S. H.—Fire Protection.
INNIS, HAROLD A.—Allan, H.; Fur Trade and Industry; Mackenzie, Sir W.; Mount Stephen, First Baron.
IRSAY, STEPHEN D'—Universities and Colleges.
ISAACS, NATHAN—Commercial Law; Holt, Sir J.; Levi, Leone; Negotiable Instruments; Pledge; Sales.
ISAY, RUDOLF—Mining Law.
IVERSEN, CARL—Scharling, H. W.

JÄCKH, ERNST—Kiderlen-Wächter, A. von; Stresemann, G.
JACOB, E. F.—Introduction (The Growth of Autonomy); Conciliar Movement; Innocent III; Inquisition; John of Salisbury; Lea, H. C.; Montfort, S. de; Paris, M.
JACOBI, ERNST—Thöl, J. H.

JACOBS, A. C.—Common Law Marriage; Guardianship; Illegitimacy (Legal Aspects); Landlord and Tenant; Marital Property.
JAFFE, L. L.—Venue.
JAMES, F. CYRIL—Overstone, Lord; Shipbuilding.
JAMES, HERMAN G.—Government (Lat. Amer.).
JAMES, M.—Levellers; Lilburne, J.; Puritanism; Winstanley, G.
JAMESON, J. F.—Adams, H. B.; Archives (U. S.).
JANNACCONE, P.—Cognetti de Martiis, S.
JANOWSKY, OSCAR I.—Zangwill, I.
JARRETT, BEDE, O.P.—Introduction (The Universal Church); Antonino; Chrysostom, J.; Dominican Friars; Grosseteste, R.
JASTROW, JOSEPH—Abnormal Psychology; Conversion, Religious; Ladd, G. T.; Mesmer, F. A.; Prince, M.; Psychology.
JÁSZI, OSCAR—Anarchism; Atheism (Modern); Bach, A.; Francis Joseph I; Horváth, M.; Kossuth, L.; Kunfi, Z.; La Boétie, É. de; Socialism; Szabó, E.; Széchenyi, Count I.; Tisza, I.; Tisza, K.
JELLIFFE, SMITH ELY—Esquirol, J.-É. D.; Griesinger, W.
JENKINSON, HILARY—Archives (Hist. and Admin.).
JENKS, LELAND H.—Armed Forces, Control of; Brassey, T.; Brooke, J.; Curzon, G. N.; Dalhousie, Tenth Earl and Marquess of; Emancipation; Goldie, Sir G. D. T.; Grace, W. R.; Johnston, Sir H. H.; Milner, Viscount A.; Rhodes, C. J.; Stanley, Sir H. M.
JENNINGS, H. S.—Eugenics.
JENSEN, CHRISTEN—Pardon.
JESSUP, PHILIP C.—Neutrality; Prize; Reprisals.
JEVONS, H. STANLEY—Jevons, W. S.
JÈZE, GASTON—Block, M.; Boiteau, D. A. P.; Financial Administration; Loans, Intergovernmental; Public Debt; Stourm, R.
JITTA, A. C. JOSEPHUS—Government (Netherlands); Legislative Assemblies (Netherlands).
JOAD, C. E. M.—Hume, D.; Realism; Robertson, J. M.; Spencer, H.; Stephen, Sir L.; Wallace, A. R.
JOCHELSON, WALDEMAR—Anuchin, D. N.
JOHNSON, ALEXANDER—Almshouse.
JOHNSON, ALVIN—Agrarian Movements (Introd.); Antiradicalism; Veblen, T. B.; War; War Economics.
JOHNSON, E.-A. J.—Malynes, G. de; Misselden, E.; Rae, J.
JOKL, NORBERT—Ismail Kemal Bey.

JOLOWICZ, H. F.—Windscheid, B.
JONES, BARBARA—Life Extension Movement; Medicine (Econ. Organization).
JONES, CHESTER LLOYD—Panama Canal.
JONES, ELLIOT—Kruttschnitt, J.
JONES, HOWARD MUMFORD—Tyler, M. C.
JONES, J. D. RHEINALLT—Jabavu, J. T.
JONES, LEWIS WEBSTER—Dentistry; Medicine (Econ. Organization).
JONES, RICHARD F.—Classicism.
JONES, RUFUS M.—Woolman, J.
JONES, THOMAS—Smart, W.
JORDAN, H. DONALDSON—Borthwick, A.; Levy Lawson Family; Reuter, Baron von; Walter Family.
JOSEPHSON, MATTHEW—France, A.
JOVANOVIĆ, DRAGOLJUB—Bukšeg, V.; Marković, S.
JUDGES, A. V.—Burlamachi, P.; Culpeper, Sir T.; Eliot, Sir J.
JUYNBOLL, TH. W.—Būkhāri, al-.

KALKEN, FRANS VAN—Parties, Political (Belgium).
KALLEN, HORACE M.—Behaviorism; Blasphemy; Coercion; Conditioned Reflex; Conformity; Consensus; Cults; Functionalism; Innovation; Intransigence; James, W.; Modernism; Morals; Persecution; Pragmatism; Psychoanalysis; Radicalism; Reformism; Self-Preservation.
KAMPFFMEYER, PAUL—Eisner, K.
KANDEL, I. L.—Altenstein, K.; Angell, J. B.; Bonitz, H.; Bray, T.; Buchenhagen, A.; Carter, J. G.; Comenius, J. A.; Continuation Schools; Diesterweg, F. A. W.; Education (Public); Ernest I; Hecker, J. J.; Vocational Education.
KANELLOPOULOS, PANAJOTIS — Koraes, A.; Rhigas, K.
KANTOR, J. R.—Bekhterev, V.
KANTOROWICZ, HERMANN — Puchta, G. F.; Savigny, F. C. von; Thibaut, A. F. J.
KAPLAN, A. D. H.—Baird, H. C.; Carey, M.; Colwell, S.; Kelley, W. D.; Raymond, D.
KAREYEV, N.—Danilevsky, N. Y.
KATZ, LEO—Art (Japan).
KAWAKAMI, KIYOSHI K.—Fukuzawa, Y.; Government (Japan); Ito, Prince H.; Kido, T.
KAYDEN, EUGENE M.—Cooperation (Russia: Consumers' Coop.).
KEEZER, DEXTER MERRIAM — Business; Federal Trade Commission; Press.
KEHR, ECKART—Clausewitz, C. von; Graumann, J. P.; Krupp, A.; Munitions Industry; Nobel, A. B.
KEILHAU, WILHELM—Aarum, P. T.; Einarsen, E.; Schweigaard, A. M.
KEITH, A. BERRIEDALE—Dominion Status; Ilbert, Sir C. P.
KELLOGG, PAUL U.—Gleason, A. H.; Social Settlements.
KENDRICK, BENJAMIN B.—Agrarian Movements (U. S.); Stephens, A. H.; Stevens, T.; Sumner, C.
KENNEDY, W. P. M.—Baldwin, R.; Blake, E.; Flood, H.; Howe, J.; Lafontaine, Sir L. H.; Lefroy, A. H. F.
KENWORTHY, J. M.—Mahan, A. T.; Navy.
KENYON, RUTH—Headlam, S. D.; Holland, H. S.
KEYNES, J. M.—Credit Control; Edgeworth, F. Y.
KHAIRALLAH, K. T.—Buṭrus al-Bustāni.
KIANG KANG-HU—Art (China).
KIESEWETTER, A. A.—Alexander I; Betsky, I. I.; Cherkassky, V. A.; Ivan IV; Kiselev, Count P. D.; Milutin, N. A.
KIESSLING, O. E.—Quarrying.
KILPATRICK, WYLIE — Government Reporting.
KING, BOLTON — Government (Italy).
KIPP, THEODOR—Dernburg, H.
KIRBY, ETHYN WILLIAMS—Prynne, W.; Rutherford, S.
KIRBY, RICHARD SHELTON — Motor Vehicle Accidents.
KIRCHWEY, GEORGE W.—Capital Punishment; Criminal Law; Osborne, T. M.
KIRKALDY, A. W.—Cunard, Sir S.; Ismay, T. H.
KIRKLAND, EDWARD C.—Niles, H.
KITCHIN, JOSEPH—Gold.
KLAPPER, PAUL—Ascham, R.
KLEECK, MARY VAN—Women in Industry (General Principles).
KLEIN, PHILIP—Child (Delinquent); De Forest, R. W.; Drives, Money Raising; Loch, C. S.; Lowell, J. S.; Richmond, M. E.; Social Work (General Discussion *and* Social Case Work); Straus, N.
KLINEBERG, OTTO — Genius; Mental Tests.
KLINGBERG, FRANK J.—Abolition; Clarkson, T.
KNIGHT, EDGAR W.—Aycock, C. B.; Lyon, M.
KNIGHT, FRANK H.—Absentee Ownership; Abstinence; Davenport, H. J.; Demand (Theory); Economics (Marginal Utility Economics); Exchange; Interest; Profit; Risk; Supply; Taylor, F. M.; Value and Price.
KNIGHT, HOWARD LAWSON—Atwater, W. O.
KNIGHT, MELVIN M.—Backward Countries; Chartered Companies; Colonies; Commercial Routes; Companionate Marriage; Cunningham, W.; Handicraft; Morocco Question; Plantation Wares; Precious Stones; Roads (Ancient, Mediaeval and Early Modern); Serfdom; Slavery (Mediaeval).
KNIGHT, W. S. M.—Gentili, A.
KNUBBEN, ROLF—Hübner, M.; Martens, G. F. von; Vattel, E. de.
KOCH, WOLDEMAR—Trade Unions (Russia).
KOCHAROVSKY, K.—Haxthausen, A. von; Karishev, N. A.; Kaufman, A. A.; Orlov, V. I.; Shchapov, A. P.; Vasilchikov, Prince A. I.; Vorontsov, V. P.
KOELLREUTTER, OTTO—Legislative Assemblies (Germany and Austria).
KOFFKA, K.—Consciousness; Gestalt.
KÖHLER, W.—Castellio, S.; Harnack, A. von; Reformation (Lutheran); Zwingli, H.
KOHN, HANS—Ginsberg, A.; Gordon, A. D.; Herzl, T.; Jamāl u'd Dín al-Áfghāní; Lajpat Rai, L.; Messianism; Mohammed 'Abdu; Mohammed 'Ali; Muṣtafa Kāmil; Naoroji, D.; Near Eastern Problem; Pan-movements; Pinsker, J. L.; Race Conflict; Ranade, M. G.; Riesser, G.; Roy, R. M.; Russian Revolution; Saraswati, Swami D.; Sayyid Ahmad Khan, Sir; Tilak, B. G.; Youth Movements; Zaghlul Pasha, S.; Zionism.
KOHN, STANISLAS—Chuprov, A. A.
KOHT, HALVDAN—Erslev, K.; Ibsen, H.; Keyser, R. J.; Sars, J. E. W.; Sverdrup, J.; Thrane, M. M.
KOMORA, PAUL O.—Salmon, T. W.
KONKLE, BURTON ALVA—Rush, B.; Wilson, J.
KONOPCZYŃSKI, LADISLAS—Majority Rule; Minority Rights.
KOPF, EDWIN W.—Annuities; Baily, F.
KORFF, HERMANN A.—Goethe, J. W.
KORSCH, KARL—Marx, K.
KOSCHAKER, PAUL—Law (Cuneiform).
KOSMINSKY, E. A.—Savin, A. N.; Yanzhul, I. I.
KOSSINSKY, V. A.—Fortunatov, A. F.
KOSSINSKY, W.—Ludogovsky, A. P.
KOSTERS, J.—Jitta, D. J.
KÖTZSCHKE, RUDOLF—Manorial System; Nitzsch, K. W.
KOYRÉ, ALEXANDRE — Pobedonostsev, K. P.; Pogodin, M. P.; Samarin, Y. F.
KRACAUER, S. — Sonnemann, L.
KREPS, THEODORE J.—Chemical Industries; Dye Industry (Modern Dyestuffs Industry); Heavy Chemicals.
KRISZTICS, ALEXANDER L.—Be-

öthy de Bessenyo, L.; Fényes, E. C.
KROEBER, A. L.—Archaeology; Art (Primitive); Caste; Culture Area; Cushing, F. H.; Diffusionism.
KROUT, JOHN A.—Dow, N.
KRUGER, F.-K.—Stuckenberg, J. H. W.
KRUSPI, FRIEDRICH—Machinery, Industrial.
KRZECKZKOWSKI, K. — Skarbek, Count F. F.
KRZYWICKI, LUDWIK — Krauz-Kelles, Baron K.; Waryński, L. T.
KRZYŻANOWSKI, ADAM—Lewiński, J. S.
KUCZYNSKI, JÜRGEN — Homework, Industrial.
KUCZYNSKI, R. R.—Births; Population (Hist. and Statistics).
KUHLMANN, C. B.—Milling Industry.
KÜHN, HERBERT—Grosse, E.
KÜHNE, OTTO—Dupuit, A. J. É. J.
KULISCHER, JOSEPH—Fairs.
KULP, C. A.—Compensation and Liability Insurance.
KUMANIECKI, KAZIMIERZ W.—Jaworski, W. L.
KÜNSSBERG, EBERHARD VON—Andlo, Peter of; Brunner, H.; Carpzov, B.; Ficker, C. J. von; Law (Germanic); Maurer, K. von; Repgow, E. von; Suarez, K. G.
KÜNTZEL, GEORG — Frederick William; Frederick William I.
KURKJIAN, V. M.—Khrimian, M.
KUSKOVA, E.—Filosofova, A. P.
KUTRZEBA, STANISŁAW — Law (Slavic); Maciejowski, W. A.
KUZNETS, SIMON—Conjuncture; Curve Fitting; National Income; Time Series.
KUZNETS, SOLOMON—Agricultural Machinery Industry; Cernuschi, H.; Hoffmann, J. G., Kankrin, Count E. F.; Kavelin, K. D.; Khomyakov, A. S.; Kireyevsky, I. V.; Orzhentsky, R. M.; Pavlov-Silvansky, N. P.; Pawnbroking.
KYRK, HAZEL—Home Economics.

LABOURET, HENRI—Lanessan, J. M. A. de.
LABRIOLA, ARTURO—Matteotti, G.
LABRIOLLE, PIERRE DE—Batiffol, P.; Eusebius of Caesarea; Rossi, G. B. de.
LADAS, STEPHEN P.—Patents; Trademarks and Names.
LAIDLER, HARRY W.—Boycott.
LAISTNER, M. L. W.—Alcuin; Benedict; Seneca, L. A.; Xenophon.
LAMBERT, ÉDOUARD—Comparative Law.
LA MONTE, JOHN L.—Military Orders.
LANCTOT, GUSTAVE—Frontenac, C. de P. et de; Garneau, F. X.
LANDGREBE, LUDWIG—Dilthey, W.
LANDIS, J. M.—Deportation and Expulsion of Aliens; Ellsworth, O.; Freedom of Speech and of the Press.
LANDMANN, JULIUS — Banking, Commercial (History).
LANDTMANN, GUNNAR — Yrjö-Koskinen, Y. S.
LANE, WINTHROP D.—Brockway, Z. R.
LANGER, GOTTFRIED—Friedberg, E. A.
LANGER, WILLIAM L.—Aehrenthal, A. L.; Cambon, P. P.; Delcassé, T.; Ferry, J. F. C.; Isolation, Diplomatic; Metternich-Winneburg, Fürst C. W. L.
LANNOY, CHARLES DE—Coen, J. P.; Faidherbe, L. L. C.
LA PRADELLE, A. DE GEOUFFRE DE—Fauchille, P.
LARRABEE, HAROLD A.—Saint-Simon and Saint-Simonianism.
LARSEN, HANNA ASTRUP—Björnson, B.; Bremer, F.; Collett, C.
LARSON, LAURENCE M.—Geijer, E. G.
LASKI, HAROLD J.— Introduction (The Rise of Liberalism); Bureaucracy; Democracy; Freedom of Association; Government (Gt. Brit.); James I; Judiciary; Liberty; Monarchomachs; Social Contract; Ulyanov, V. I.
LASLOWSKI, ERNST—Janssen, J.
LASSWELL, HAROLD D.—Adams, B.; Agitation; Bribery; Censorship; Chauvinism; Compromise; Conflict, Social; Faction; Feuds; Fraternizing; Morale; Propaganda.
LATOURETTE, K. S. — Francis Xavier; Hung Hsiu-ch'üan; Missions; Ricci, M.
LAUR, ERNST—Kraemer, A.
LAUTERPACHT, H.—Oppenheim, L. F. L.
LAVERGNE, BERNARD—Bourguin, M.; Cooperative Public Boards.
LE BRAS, GABRIEL—Gratian.
LEDERER, EMIL — Agriculture (China and Japan); Economics (Socialist Economics); Labor; National Economic Councils; National Economic Planning; Rathenau, W.; Singer, P.; Technology.
LEDERMANN, L.—Rossi, P. L. E.
LEDNICKI, W.—Spasowicz, W.
LEE, ROBERT WARDEN—Leeuwen, S. van; Villiers, First Baron J. H. de.
LEFEBVRE, G.—Robespierre, M.
LEHMANN, FRITZ—Wicksell, K.
LEHMANN, HEINRICH—Planck, G.
LEHMANN, W. C.—Ferguson, A.
LEHMANN, WALTER—Seler, E. G.
LEISERSON, WILLIAM M.—Closed Shop and Open Shop; Company Unions.
LELAND, SIMEON E.—Mortgage Tax.
LEMOINE, R. J.—Solvay, E.
LENGYEL, EMIL—Andrássy, G.
LEONARD, WILLIAM R.—Abbott, S. W.
LEONTOVICH, V.—Religious Institutions, Christian (Byzantine).
LERNER, MAX—Adams, G. B.; Assassination; Bagehot, W.; Beecher, H. W.; Emerson, R. W.; Guggenheim Family; Hadley, E.; Literature; Political Offenders; Social Process; Swift, J.; Thoreau, H. D.; Vested Interests.
LEROY, MAXIME—Enfantin, B. P.; Lemonnier, C. and É.; Leroux, P.; Pecqueur, C.
LESCOHIER, DON D.—Employment Exchanges (U. S.).
LESCURE, JEAN—Crises; Juglar, C.
LESTSCHINSKY, JAKOB—Ghetto; Liebermann, A. S.; Medem, W.
LETHABY, W. R.—Architecture (Through the Renaissance).
LEVETT, A. E.—Black Death; Harrington, J.
LEVI, ALESSANDRO—Ardigò, R.; Cattaneo, C.; Mamiani della Rovere, Conte T.; Mancini, P. S.; Romagnosi, G. D.; Sighele, S.
LEVIN, MAX—Bell, Andrew; Fernow, B. E.; Llorente, J. A.; Madero, F.; Tacitus, P. C.; Trade Unions (Lat. Amer.).
LEVINSON, S. O.—Aggression, International.
LEVY, DAVID M.—Mental Defectives.
LEVY, ERNST—Paulus, J.
LEVY, HERMANN—Hasbach, W.
LEVY, NEWMAN—Contingent Fee.
LEVY, RAPHAEL—Renaudot, T.
LÉVY-BRUHL, HENRI—Introduction (The Social Sciences as Disciplines: France, Belgium and Romanic Switzerland); Coquille, G.; Esmein, A.; Viollet, P.
LÉVY-ULLMANN, HENRI — Glasson, E. D.
LEWAK, ADAM—Mierosławski, L.
LEWINSKI-CORWIN, E. H.—Hospitals and Sanatoria.
LEWIS, HOWARD T.—Motion Pictures (Industrial Development); Radio (Hist. and Econ. Organization).
LEWIS, READ —Americanization.
LHÉRITIER, MICHEL—Trikoupis, C.
LIBELLI, MARIO MARSILI—Fabbroni, G.
LICHTENBERGER, ANDRÉ—Beaumarchais, P. A. C. de; Cabet, É.
LIEFMANN, ROBERT — Cartel; Holding Companies (Eur.).
LIEFTINCK, P.—Beaujon, A.
LIESSE, ANDRÉ — Courcelle-Seneuil, J. G.; Villermé, L. R.
LILJEGREN, S. B.—Milton, J.

LIMENTANI, LUDOVICO—Delfico, M.
LINDAHL, ERIK—Sax, E.
LINDEMAN, E. C.—Adult Education; Community; Discussion; Public Welfare.
LINDSAY, A. D.—Absolutism; Individualism.
LINGELBACH, WILLIAM E.—Talleyrand-Périgord, C.-M. de; Thiers, L. A.
LIPSON, E.—Arkwright, R.
LITTLEFIELD, WALTER—Camorra.
LITTMANN, ENNO—Nöldeke, T.
LIVINGSTON, ARTHUR—Gentleman, Theory of the.
LIVINGSTON, J. A.—Yarranton, A.
LLEWELLYN, K. N.—Agency; Carter, J. C.; Case Law; Case Method; Contract (Institutional Aspects); Hohfeld, W. N.
LLOYD, C. M.—Arabi, Ahmed; Benbow, W.
LLOYD, WILLIAM ALLISON—Extension Work, Agricultural.
LOBINGIER, CHARLES SUMNER—Alfonso X; Asoka; Bogišić, V. A.; Code Civil; Codification; Colonial Administration; Corpus Juris Civilis; Cronheim, G.; Customary Law; Draco; Limitation of Actions; Stefan Dušan.
LOCKLIN, D. PHILIP—Prouty, C. A.
LOEB, EDWIN M.—Cannibalism.
LOEVENSTEIN, JAN—Bráf, A.
LOISY, A.—Duchesne, L. M. O.
LOMAN, H. J.—Credit Insurance.
LOMBARDO-RADICE, GIUSEPPE—Alberti, L. B.; Angiulli, A.; Aporti, F.
LORE, LILY—Ihrer, E.
LORE, LUDWIG—Most, J.; Textile Industry (Labor); Weydemeyer, J.
LORENZ, REINHOLD—Maria Theresa.
LORENZEN, ERNEST G.—Conflict of Laws (Modern Rules); Huber, U.
LORWIN, LEWIS L.—Antimilitarism; Blanqui, L. A.; Class Struggle; Communist Parties; Confédération Générale du Travail; Criminal Syndicalism; Direct Action; Exploitation; Syndicalism; Trade Unions (International Organization).
LOTZ, W.—Forced Loans; Revenue Farming.
LOUIS, PAUL—Agrarian Movements (Greece *and* Rome); Babouvism; Brousse, P.; Fournière, E.; Gracchus, T. and G.; Guesde, J.; Pelloutier, F.-L.-É.
LOVEJOY, ARTHUR O.—Academic Freedom.
LOVEJOY, OWEN R.—Brace, C. L.
LOVETT, ROBERT MORSS—Arnold, M.; Criticism, Social.
LOWENTHAL, ESTHER—Hodgskin, T.
LOWIE, ROBERT H.—Adoption (Primitive); Age Societies; Avoidance; Ceremony (Primitive); Kinship; Land Tenure (Primitive Societies); Marriage; Nordenskiöld, N. E.; Schurtz, H.; Social Organization; Waitz, F. T.
LUBIN, ISADOR—Coal Industry; Mining (Labor).
LÜDERS, ELSE—Cauer, M.
LUMPKIN, KATHARINE DU PRE—Communistic Settlements.
LUNDBERG, EMMA OCTAVIA—Mothers' Pensions.
LUNDBERG, GEORGE A.—Jarvis, E.; Mayo-Smith, R.
LUNT, EDWARD C.—Bonding.
LUTZ, HARLEY L.—Assessment of Taxes; General Property Tax; Revenues, Public; Tax Administration.
LUYTGAERENS, E.—Mellaerts, J. F.
LYBYER, ALBERT H.—Caliphate; Enver Pasha; Feudalism (Saracen and Ottoman); Government (Turkey); Hammer-Purgstall, J. von; Javid, Maḥmad; Köprülü Family; Mehemet Ali; Midḥat Pasha; Suleiman I.
LYON, LEVERETT S.—Advertising; Broker; Business Education; Commodity Exchanges; Grading; Marketing.

McARTHUR, DUNCAN—Beck, A.
MACARTNEY, CARLILE A.—Refugees.
McBAIN, HOWARD LEE—Appointments; Constitutions; Double Jeopardy; Searches and Seizures.
McBRIDE, GEORGE McCUTCHEN—Agrarian Movements (Lat. Amer.); Land Grants (Lat. Amer.); Land Tenure (Lat. Amer.); Peonage; Plantation; Public Domain (Lat. Amer.); Toledo, F. de; Zapata, E.
McBRIDE, RUSSELL S.—Gas Industry.
McCABE, JOSEPH—Abelard, P.; Bradlaugh, C.
McCLINTOCK, MILLER—Traffic Regulation.
MACCOBY, S.—Azuni, D. A.; Baldus, P.
McCONNELL, D. W.—Liquor Traffic; Temperance Movements.
McCORMICK, CHARLES T.—Evidence (General Aspects).
MACCURDY, GEORGE GRANT—Boucher de Crèvecoeur de Perthes, J.
MACDONALD, WILLIAM—Bassett, J. S.; Chase, S. P.; Clay, H.; Jackson, A.; Jay, J.
MACEK, JOSEF—Gruber, J.
MACELWEE, ROY S.—Ports and Harbors.
McFAYDEN, DONALD—Augustus.
McGOLDRICK, JOSEPH—Clubs, Political.

McILWAIN, C. H.—Agreement of the People; Attainder; Bills of Rights; Divine Right of Kings; Hampden, J.
MACIVER, R. M.—Introduction (The Trend to Internationalism); Bodin, J.; Interests; Maladjustment; Pressures, Social; Sociology; Wallas, G.
MACKAY, ROBERT A.—Government (Dominion of Canada).
MACKENZIE, CATHERINE—Vail, T. N.
McKENZIE, R. D.—Ecology, Human; Oriental Immigration.
McKEON, RICHARD—Albertus Magnus; Anselm; Averroes; Peter Lombard.
McLAUGHLIN, A. C.—Holst, H. E. von.
MACLEOD, W. C.—Alcohol (Historical Aspects); Conquest; Gerontocracy; Hoarding; Native Policy (N. Amer.).
MACMAHON, ARTHUR W.—Boards, Advisory; Compacts, Interstate; Federation; Government (U. S.); Ostrogorsky, M. Y.; Parties, Political (U. S.); Public Office; States' Rights.
McMURRAY, ORRIN K.—Ames, J. B.; Gibson, J. B.; Mitchell, W.; Succession, Laws of; Water Law.
MACNAIR, HARLEY FARNSWORTH—Goto, S.
MacNEILL, EOIN—Law (Celtic).
McPHEE, E. T.—Knibbs, Sir G. H.
MADARIAGA, S. DE—Arms and Munitions Traffic.
MADDEN, MARIE R.—Agia, M. de; Antequera, J. M.; Covarrubias y Leiva, D.
MAGNUSSON, GERHARD—Danielsson, A. F.; Steffen, G. F.
MAGNUSSON, LEIFUR—Company Housing.
MAGUIRE, JOHN MACARTHUR—Expert Testimony; Legal Aid; Public Defender.
MAHAIM, ERNEST—Brants, V.; Lavaleye, É. L. V. de.
MALINIAK, WŁADYSŁAW—Hube, R.; Modrzewski, A. F.
MALINOWSKI, BRONISLAW—Culture.
MALLON, J. J.—Aves, E.
MALONE, ANDREW E.—Government (Irish Free State).
MALOTT, E. ORTH—Mitten, T. E.
MAN, HENRY DE—Christian Labor Unions.
MANES, ALFRED—Ehrenberg, V.; Fire Insurance (Europ.); Insurance (Principles and Hist.).
MANFREDI, FELICE—Maffi, A.
MANGEL, ESTHER R.—Agrarian Movements (Poland and Lithuania *and* Latvia and Estonia).
MANIGK, ALFRED—Leonhard, R. K. G.
MANN, A. R.—Agricultural Education.

Mann, Fritz Karl—Schäffle, A. E. F.
Mannheim, Karl — Troeltsch, E.; Utopia.
Manson, A.—Neri, Saint P.
Manyon, Leonard—Benefit of Clergy.
Manzini, Vincenzo — Carmignani, G.; Carrara, F.
Marbut, C. F.—Soils.
Marcus, Alfred—Metals (Modern).
Marczali, Henry—Deák, F.
Marett, R. R.—Codrington, R. H.; Fetishism; Gomme, Sir G. L.; Hartland, E. S.; Lang, A.; Tylor, Sir E. B.
Margoliouth, David S.—Fārābi, al-; Ibn-Khaldūn; Ibn-Taymīya; Miskawayhi.
Margouliès, G.—Ssŭ-ma Kuang.
Marion, Marcel—Aids; Cambon, P. J.; Gaudin, M. M. C.; Gomel, C.
Markham, R. H.—Geshov, I. E.; Government (Balkan States); Parties, Political (Balkan States).
Marschak, Jakob — Consumption (Problems of Measurement); Wages (Theory and Policy).
Marsh, A. W.—Athletics.
Marsh, Margaret Alexander—Keith, M. C.
Marshall, George — Bridgewater, F. E.; Denny, W.; Furniture (Industry); Parry, D. M.; Ryan, T. F.; Sterne, S.; Stevens, J.; Stewart, A. T.; Yerkes, C. T.
Marshall, J. Howard, II—Massachusetts Trusts.
Marshall, T. H.—Sinclair, Sir J.; Townshend, Second Viscount C.; Tull, J.
Martin, Alfred von—Gerlach, E. L. von; Haller, K. L. von; Leo, H.
Martin, John—Dance.
Martin, Kingsley — Halifax, First Marquis of; Morel, E. D.; Morelly; Morley, J.; Northcliffe, First Viscount.
Martin St.-Léon, Et. — Barberet, J.-J.; Boileau, É.
Martino, Pierre—Zola, É.
Mason, Edward S.—Dezamy, T.; Fourier and Fourierism.
Massignon, Louis — Goldziher, I.; Guilds (Islamic).
Masterson, W. E.—Territorial Waters.
Mata, Enrique Rodriguez—Güell y Ferrer, J.
Mather, Kirtley F.—Lyell, C.
Mathews, John M.—Executive Agreements.
Mathiez, Albert—French Revolution.
Matl, Josef—Drinov, M. S.; Gaj, L.; Jakšić, V.; Jireček, J. K.; Karaveloff, L.; Matov, K.; Mažuranić, V.; Paisii of Khilendar; Rački, F.; Radić, S.; Slaveykov, P. R.; Stambulov, S. N.; Supilo, F.
Matsui, Shichiro—Silk Industry.
Mattern, Johannes—Bähr, O.
Maunier, René—Cabanis, P. J. G.; Démeunier, J.-N.
Mauss, Marcel—Hubert, H.
Maxton, John P.—Agricultural Marketing (Eur.).
May, Geoffrey—Prostitution; Small Loans.
May, Stacy—Government Ownership.
Mayer, Clara W.—Albuquerque, A. de.
Mayer, Gustav—Frank, L.; Jacoby, J.; Lassalle, F.; Schweitzer-Allesina, J. B. von; Weitling, W.
Mayers, Lewis—Impeachment.
Mazzei, Jacopo—Ridolfi, Marchese C.
Mead, Elizabeth — University Extension.
Mead, Elwood—Land Settlement.
Mead, Margaret—Education, Primitive; Family (Primitive); Tabu; Woman, Position in Society (Primitive).
Means, Gardiner C. — Corporation; Holding Companies (United States); Interlocking Directorates.
Meeker, Royal—Labor, Government Services for; Mining Accidents.
Meerwarth, Rudolf—Dieterici, K. F. W.; Laspeyres, É.; Mayr, G. von; Rümelin, G.; Scheel, H. von.
Megaro, Gaudence—Alfieri, V.; Ruffini, F.
Meiklejohn, Alexander—Andrews, E. B.
Meisel, Franz—Biliński, Leon; Dietzel, K. A.
Meissner, Bruno—Schrader, E.
Mellone, S. H.—Martineau, J.
Mendel, Lafayette B.—Nutrition.
Mendelssohn Bartholdy, A.—Government (Germany).
Menghin, Oswald—Hoernes, M.
Mercer, T. W.—Neale, E. V.
Mereness, Newton D.—Calvert Family.
Merriam, Ida Craven (see also Craven, Ida) — Profiteering; Rentier.
Mestre, Achille—Saleilles, R.
Meusel, Alfred—Middle Class; Proletariat; Revolution and Counter-revolution.
Meyendorff, A. — Agrarian Movements (Europ. Russia).
Meyerand, Gladys E.—Home Ownership; Red Cross; Sewall, M. W.; Shaw, A. H.; Women's Organizations; Woodhull, V. C.; Woods, R. A.
Meyers, Norman L.—Consideration; Kent, J.

Meynial, Ed.—Beaumanoir, P. de R.
Miakotin, V.—Annensky, N. F.; Antonovich, V. B.; Bestuzhev-Riumin, K. N.; Chaykovsky, N. V.; Cossacks; Dobrolubov, N. A.; Efimenko, A. Y.; Granovsky, T. N.; Leontovich, F. I.; Semevsky, V. I.; Shcherbatov, Prince M. M.; Speransky, M. M.; Stolipin, P. A.
Michael, Louis G.—Agrarian Syndicalism.
Michels, Roberto—Authority; Bissolati, L.; Carli, G. R.; Colajanni, N.; Conservatism; Intellectuals.
Mikol, Vera—Boulanger, G. E.; Déroulède, P.
Mikusch, Gustav—Sugar.
Miliukov, Paul—Appanage; Arsenyev, K. K.; Catherine II; Chaadayev, P. Y.; Herzen, A. I.; Karamzin, N. M.; Kareyev, N. I.; Katkov, M. N.; Kluchevsky, V. O.; Pestel, P. I.; Peter I; Pososhkov, I. T.; Radischev, A. N.; Religious Institutions, Christian (Russian); Solovyev, S. M.; Solovyev, V. S.; Tatishchev, V. N.; Witte, Graf S. Y.
Millar, Robert W. — Judgments; Procedure, Legal.
Miller, Harry E.—Bollmann, J. E.; Walker, A.
Miller, Nathan — Initiation; Secret Societies.
Miller, Perry G.—Hooker, T.
Mills, Frederick C.—Prices (Statistics).
Mills, R. C.—Hearn, W. E.; Wakefield, E. G.
Milsom, Georges—Dunant, J. H.
Mims, Edwin, Jr.—Bodio, L.; Constant de Rebecque, H. B.; Cooper, T.; Literature; More, Sir T.
Mises, R. von—Probability.
Mishnun, Florence — Judicial Interrogation; Labourers, Statutes of; Ostracism; Vivekānanda, Swami; Voluntary Associations; Xenopol, A.; Ximénes de Cisneros, F.
Mitchell, Broadus—Cardozo, J. N.; DeBow, J. D. B.; Dew, T. R.; Gregg, W.; Olmsted, F. L.; Single Tax; Skidmore, T.; Whitney, E.
Mitchell, Waldo F. — Bank Reserves.
Mitchell, Wesley C.—Business Cycles; Marshall, A.
Mitrany, David—Cuza, A. J.; Haret, S.; Land Tenure (E. Eur. and Near East).
Mittermaier, Wolfgang—Holtzendorff, F. von.
Moeller, Hero—Soetbeer, A. G.
Moir, Henry—Life Insurance.
Moley, Raymond—Bail; Extortion; Grand Jury.
Mombert, Paul—Braun, K.; Class; Crome, A. F. W.; Nebenius, K. F.

MOMMSEN, WILHELM—Delbrück, H.; Schäfer, D.
MONDOLFO, RODOLFO — Campanella, T.; Costa, A.; Epicureanism; Ferrari, G.; Filangieri, G.; Galuppi, P.; Gioia, M.; Gravina, G.; Grün, K. T. F.; Kropotkin, Prince P. A.; Labriola, A.; Lucretius Carus, T.; Marlo, K.; Paruta, P.
MONROE, A. E.—Harris, J.; Montanari, G.; Vaughan, R.
MONROE, WILL S.—Barnard, H.
MONTGELAS, MAX GRAF—Stein, Freiherr H. F. K. vom und zum.
MONTGOMERY, J. A.—Jastrow, M.
MONTGOMERY, R. H.—Auditing.
MOORHEAD, HELEN HOWELL — Opium Problem.
MOREHOUSE, E. W.—Appreciation; Land Valuation.
MORET, ALEXANDRE—Champollion, J. F.
MORGAN, E. M.—Appeals.
MORGENSTERN, OSKAR — Economics (Mathematical Economics).
MORISON, S. E. — Ames, F.; Sparks, J.; Winthrop, J.
MORIZE, ANDRÉ—Bertin, L. F.; Brunetière, F.
MORNET, DANIEL—Fontenelle, B. le B. de.
MORREL, W. P.—Grey, Third Earl.
MORRIS, C. R.—Locke, J.
MORRIS, RICHARD B.—Entail; Freehold; Wythe, G.
MORROW, FELIX—Williams, R.
MORROW, GLENN R.—Mandeville, B. de.
MOSCA, GAETANO—Giusti, G.; Machiavelli, N.; Mafia; Manzoni, A.
MOSS, WARNER—Parties, Political (Irish Free State).
MOTT, LEWIS F.—Renan, E.
MOULTON, HAROLD G.—Waterways, Inland.
MOWAT, R. B.—Canning, S.
MOWBRAY, A. H.—Insurance (Industry).
MÜHLMANN, W. E.—Gerland, G.; Hahn, E.; Hospitality.
MUIRHEAD, J. H.—Barnett, S. A.
MUKERJEE, RADHAKAMAL—Land Tenure (India); Malabari, B. M.
MULERT, HERMANN—Concordat; Hontheim, J. N. von.
MÜLLER, FRANZ—Hitze, F.
MUMFORD, LEWIS—Architecture (Since the Renaissance); Civic Art.
MUNRO, DANA C.—Crusades.
MUNRO, WILLIAM B.—City; Civic Organizations; Commission System of Government; Excess Condemnation; Home Rule; Initiative and Referendum; Municipal Courts; Municipal Government; Short Ballot Movement; Veto.
MURDOCK, GEORGE P.—Ethnocentrism; Lippert, J.

MURPHY, GARDNER—Charcot, J. M.; Fechner, G. T.; Habit.
MURPHY, J. T.—Morrison, J.
MURRAY, ROBERT H.—Bellarmine, R. F. R.; Knox, J.
MURRAY, W. G.—Land Mortgage Credit (Agric.: U. S. and Canada).
MUTSCHLER, C.—Schär, J. F.
MUZZEY, DAVID S.—Bancroft, G.
MYERS, GUSTAVUS—Blue Laws.

NADLER, MARCUS—Conant, C. A.; Financial Organization; Land Mortgage Credit (Urban); Money Market; Stock Exchange.
NASH, JAY B.—Playgrounds.
NATHAN, OTTO—David, E.; Subsidies; Transit Duties.
NEEDHAM, JOSEPH—Evolution.
NEFF, WANDA FRAIKEN—Jameson, A. B.
NEILSON, WILLIAM ALLEN—Eliot, C. W.
NELLES, WALTER—Blacklist.
NETTLAU, MAX—Bakunin, M.; Reclus, J. É.
NEU, KURT—Electrical Manufacturing Industry.
NEUMANN, SIGMUND — Parties, Political (Germany); Radowitz, J. M. von; Seydel, M. von; Sorel, G.; Tirpitz, A. von; Treitschke, Heinrich von; Zachariae von Lingenthal, K. S.
NEVINS, ALLAN—Bryant, W. C.; Cleveland, S. G.; Freneau, P. M.; Gales, J., Jr.; Godkin, E. L.; Greeley, H.; Hamilton, A.; History and Historiography (Historiography: United States); Journalism; Lowell, J. R.; Olney, R.; Pulitzer, J.; Raymond, H. J.
NEW, CHESTER W.—Durham, First Earl of; Elgin, Eighth Earl of.
NEWMAN, BERNHARD J.—Slums.
NEWSHOLME, ARTHUR — Baker, G.; Buchanan, G.; Farr, W.
NEWSTETTER, W. I.—Boys' and Girls' Clubs.
NEWTON, ARTHUR PERCIVAL—Bentinck, Lord.
NIBOYET, J. P.—Lainé, A.; Pillet, A.; Weiss, A.
NICOLINI, FAUSTO—Galiani, F.
NIEBUHR, H. RICHARD—Dogma; Education (Sectarian); Fundamentalism; Higher Criticism; Protestantism; Reformation (Non-Lutheran); Religious Institutions, Christian (Protestant); Schaff, P.; Sects.
NIELSEN, AXEL—Monetary Unions.
NILSSON, MARTIN P.—Calendar; Rohde, E.; Usener, H.
NIXON, H. C.—Judd, O.
NOCK, ARTHUR DARBY—Mysteries; Proselytism.
NOEL BAKER, PHILIP—League of Nations; Nansen, F.; National Defense.

NOFFSINGER, JOHN S.—Chautauqua.
NOLEN, JOHN—Civic Centers; Regional Planning.
NOMAD, MAX—Machajski, W.; Malatesta, E.
NORMANO, J. F.—Lamas, A.
NOSADZÉ, V.—Chavchavadze, I.
NOTZ, WILLIAM F.—Export Associations; Raw Materials.
NOURSE, E. G.—Agricultural Economics (U. S.); Agricultural Policy.
NYSTROM, PAUL H.—Food Industries (Food Distribution: Grocery Trade); Retail Trade.

OATMAN, MIRIAM E.—Courts, Administrative.
OBATA, SHIGEYOSHI—Arai Hakuseki.
O'BRIEN, GEORGE—Connolly, J.; Davitt, M.; Hancock, W. N.; Henry of Langenstein.
ODEBRECHT, RUDOLF—Schleiermacher, F. E. D.
ODEGARD, PETER H. — Anti-Saloon League; Corruption, Political (U. S.).
ODINETZ, D.—Sergeyevich, V. I.
OERTEL, FRIEDRICH—Euhemeros; Pohlmann, R. von.
OGATA, K.—Cooperation (Japan).
OGBURN, WILLIAM F.—Change, Social.
OGDEN, R. M. — Educational Psychology.
OGG, DAVID—Selden, J.
OGG, FREDERIC A.—Coalition; Franking; Learned Societies.
OGILVIE, F. W.—Tourist Traffic.
OHLIN, BERTIL — Introduction (The Social Sciences as Disciplines: Scandinavia).
OLDENBERG, KARL—Lexis, W.
OLDFATHER, W. A.—Beaufort, L. de; Curtius, E.
OLIVER, THOMAS—Industrial Hygiene (Hist. and Description).
OLIVIER-MARTIN—Chénon, É.
OLMSTEAD, A. T.—King, L. W.; Luckenbill, D. D.
O'MALLEY, IDA BEATRICE — Nightingale, F.
ONCKEN, HERMANN—Bennigsen, R. von; Rachfahl, F.
OPIE, REDVERS—Jenkin, H. C. F.
ORCHARD, DOROTHY JOHNSON—Trade Unions (Far and Near East).
ORCHARD, JOHN E.—Flax, Hemp and Jute; Mitsui.
ORTON, WILLIAM A.—Ateliers Nationaux; Endowments and Foundations; Motion Pictures (Social Implications); Radio (Cultural Aspects).
OSTRORÓG, LÉON—Māwardi, al-.
OTS Y CAPDEQUI, JOSÉ—Feijóo y Montenegro, B. J.; Ferdinand and Isabella; Francia, J. G. R.; Ganivet, A.; Government (Spain and Portugal); Hinojosa y Naveros, E. de; Labra y Cadrana, R. M. de; Legislative

Assemblies (Spain and Portugal); Martínez Marina, F.; Masdeu, J. F.; Native Policy (Lat. Amer.).
OTTO, M. C.—Fanaticism; Hedonism; Intolerance.
OUALID, WILLIAM—Bérenger, A. M. M. T.; Cauwes, P. L.; Coquelin, C.
OVERACKER, LOUISE—Primaries, Political.
OVERBECK, ALFRED VON—Birkmeyer, K. von.

PACKARD, LAURENCE B.—Dupleix, J.
PAGÈS, G.—Louis XIV.
PAGNI, CARLO—Martello, T.; Mazzola, U.; Verri, P.
PALM, FRANKLIN C.—Hospital, M. de l'; Jurieu, P.
PALYI, M.—Agio; Coinage; Foreign Investment; Helferich, J. A. R. von; Helfferich, K.; Hermann, F. B. W. von; Hufeland, G.; Lotz, J. F. E.
PANTIN, W. A.—Bernard of Clairvaux.
PARK, EDWIN AVERY—Art (Modern); Furniture (General and Historical).
PARK, ROBERT E.—Assimilation, Social; Collective Behavior.
PARKES, H. B.—Mather, I. and C.
PARMELEE, MAURICE—Blockade.
PARODI, D.—Renouvier, C. B.
PARRINGTON, VERNON LOUIS—Brook Farm.
PARRY, ALBERT—Morozov, S.; Sports.
PARSONS, TALCOTT—Calvin, J.; Malthus, T. R.; Pareto, V.; Service; Smiles, S.; Society; Thrift.
PASSOW, RICHARD—Ehrenberg, R.
PATON, WILLIAM—Duff, A.
PATTERSON, EDWIN W.—Ehrlich, E.; Insanity (Civil Law); Insurance (Law and Regulation).
PATTERSON, ERNEST MINOR—Patten, S. N.
PATTON, HARALD S.—Grain Elevators.
PAULSEN, INGWER—Huber, V. A.
PAXSON, FREDERIC L.—Benton, T. H.; Frontier (American History); Turner, F. J.
PEAKE, HAROLD J. E.—Village Community.
PEARDON, THOMAS P.—Kemble, J. M.
PEARL, RAYMOND—Alcohol (Biological Aspects).
PEARSON, A. F. SCOTT—Cartwright, T.
PECK, GUSTAV—Bright, J.; McCulloch, J. R.
PEFFER, NATHANIEL—Far Eastern Problem; Manchurian Problem; Open Door.
PENTMANN, J.—Customs Unions.
PEREYRA, CARLOS—García Moreno, G.; Gasca, P. de la; Hostos, E. M. de.

PERKINS, DEXTER—Monroe Doctrine; Monroe, J.; Seward, W. H.
PERLMAN, JACOB—Arthur, P. M.; Railroads (Labor); Stone, W. S.
PERLMAN, SELIG—Brisbane, A.; Douai, A.; Kearney, D.; Short Hours Movement; Sorge, F. A.; Steward, I.; Swinton, J.; Sylvis, W. H.; Trade Agreements; Workers' Education.
PERREAU, E.-H.—Portalis, J. É. M.; Tronchet, F.-D.
PERSON, H. S.—Continuous Industry; Engineering; Gantt, H. L.; Gilbreth, F. B.; Industrial Education; Labor, Methods of Remuneration for; Safety Movement; Scientific Management; Waste; Welfare Work, Industrial.
PETERS, HANS—Kaskel, W.
PETERSON, SHOREY—Motor Vehicle Transportation; Railroads (General).
PFISTER, CH.—Flach, J.
PHALEN, JAMES M.—Carter, H. R.
PHILLIPS, ULRICH B.—Davis, J.; Douglas, S. A.; Popular Sovereignty; Slavery (Modern: U. S.); Toombs, R.
PHILLIPS, W. ALISON—Capodistrias, J.
PHILLIPSON, COLEMAN—Alciati, A.
PHYTHIAN, MABEL—Birkbeck, G.
PICARD, ROGER—Bacalan, A. T. I. de; Bellet, D.; Bourses du Travail; Chevalier, M.; Clément, A.; Dupont de Nemours, P. S.; Dutot, C. de F.; Melon, J. F.; Molinari, G. de.
PIERSON, W. W., JR.—Castilla, R.
PIETRA, GAETANO—Popov, K.
PIGANIOL, ANDRÉ—City-State; Fréret, N.; Latifundia.
PIGÓN, STANISLAW—Mickiewicz, A.
PINSON, KOPPEL S.—Adelung, J. C.; Chassidism; Chuang Tzu; Creighton, M.; Francke, A. H.; Freytag, G.; Fruin, R. J.; Görres, J. von; Müller, F. M.; Novalis; Schlegel, K. W. F. von and A. W. von; Symonds, J. A.; Wolff, C.
PINTNER, R.—Binet, A.
PIPKIN, CHARLES W.—Poor Laws.
PIPPING, HUGO E.—Snellman, J. V.
PIRENNE, HENRI—Commines, P. de; Commune, Mediaeval; Economic History (Study and Research in the 20th Cent.: Continental Eur.); Guilds (Europ.); Vanderkindere, L.
PIROU, GAÉTAN—Jourdan, A.
PITTARD, EUGÈNE—Deniker, J.
PLATZ, HERMANN—Lagarde, P. de.
PLOMER, WILLIAM—Schreiner, O. E. A.
PLOSCOWE, MORRIS—Treason.

PLUCKNETT, THEODORE F. T.—Bracton, H. de; Coke, E.; Compurgation; Escheat; Fortescue, Sir J.; Glanvill, R. de; Hale, Sir M.; Libel and Slander; Nottingham, First Earl of; Outlawry; Selborne, First Earl of; Sheriff; Writs.
PLUMMER, ALFRED—Hetherington, H.; Lovett, W.; O'Brien, J. (Bronterre).
PLUMMER, W. C.—Instalment Selling; Retail Credit.
POKROVSKY, M.—Introduction (The Social Sciences as Disciplines: Soviet Russia).
POLLACZEK-GEIRINGER, H.—Probability.
POLLAK, INEZ—Food Industries (Introd. and Food Distribution: W. Eur.); Harney, G. J.
POLLOCK, JAMES K.—Corrupt Practises Acts.
POOLE, AUSTIN L.—Bateson, M.; Bede.
POPESCU, AURELIU ION—Bratianu.
POPITZ, E. H. JOHANNES—Erzberger, M.
POPOVIĆ, DUŠAN J.—Jelačić, Count J.
PORTUS, G. V.—Higgins, H. B.; Lane, W.; Spence, W. G.
POSCH, ANDREAS—Nicholas of Cusa.
POSTGATE, R. W.—King, W.
POTRESOFF, A.—Plekhanov, G. V.
POTTER, PITMAN B.—Annexation; Buffer State; Cession; Field, D. D.; Freedom of the Seas; International Organization; Mediation; Military Occupation.
POUND, ROSCOE—American Law Institute; Anson, W. R.; Common Law; Contract (Legal Doctrine and Hist.); Jurisprudence; Jury (Eng. and U. S.); Liability; Rule of Law; Story, J.
POUTHAS, CHARLES H.—Guizot, F. P. G.; Royer-Collard, P. P.
POWELL, RICHARD R.—Perpetuities.
POWER, EILEEN—Knowles, L. C. A.; Pisan, C. de.
PRATT, JULIUS W.—Reid, W.
PRAY, KENNETH L. M.—Charity.
PREWETT, F. J.—Greening, E. O.
PREZZOLINI, GIUSEPPE—Boccalini, T.
PRIBRAM, ALFRED FRANCIS—Hartmann, L. M.; Schwarzenberg, Prince F. von.
PRIBRAM, KARL—Czoernig von Czernhausen, K.; Housing (Eur.); Kraus, C. J.; Lueder, A. F.; Rau, K. H.; Sartorius von Walthershausen, Freiherr G.; Soden, Graf F. J. H. von; Trade Unions (Succession States and Balkan Countries); Unemployment.
PRICE, FRANK WILSON—Kuomintang; Sun Yat Sen.

PRICE, L. L.—Gonner, Sir E. C. K.
PRIEST, GEORGE H., JR.—Paints and Varnishes.
PRINGLE, HENRY F.—Roosevelt, T.
PROCOPOVICZ, S.—Kablukov, N. A.; Kulizhny, A. E.; Peshekhonov, A. V.; Zelgeim, V. N.
PRUETTE, LORINE—Blackwell, E.; Stone, L.; Willard, F. E.
PUCKETT, HUGH WILEY—Guillaume-Schack, G.; Lange, H.; Schirmacher, K.; Schmidt, A.
PUECH, J. L.—Guillaume, J.; Tristan, F. C. T. H.
PUGLIESE, SALVATORE—Jacini, S. F.; Neri, P.

QUARCK, GERTRUD—Born, S.
QUEEN, STUART A.—Henderson, C. R.
QUIGLEY, HAROLD S.—Asylum; Parties, Political (Japan).
QUIGLEY, HUGH—Electric Power; Power, Industrial.

RADBRUCH, GUSTAV—Ebert, F.
RADCLIFFE-BROWN, A. R.—Law (Primitive); Sanction, Social.
RADIN, MAX — Aristophanes; Baudouin, F.; Cato, M. P.; Courts; Debt; Domat, J.; Dowry; Duress; Fraud; Intent, Criminal; Jus Gentium; Legal Profession and Legal Education (Modern Legal Educ.); Placentinus; Seduction; Status; Tradition.
RADIN, PAUL—Ancestor Worship.
RÁDL, EMMANUEL—Palacký, F.; Šafařík, P. J.
RANDALL, JOHN H., JR.—Copernicus, N.; Deism.
RANDALL, WILLIAM M.—Dā'ūd al-Zāhiri.
RAPACKI, MARJAN—Mielczarski, R.
RAPPARD, W. E.—Ador, G.; Government (Switzerland); Legislative Assemblies (Switzerland); Parties, Political (Switzerland).
RAPPOPORT, CHARLES — Jaurès, J.; Merrheim, A.
RAS, G.—Heine, H.
RATCLIFFE, S. K.—Clive, Robert; Hunger Strike.
RATHBUN, SEWARD HUME—Art (Near Eastern and Classical).
RAUP, R. B.—Harris, W. T.
RAUSHENBUSH, WINIFRED—Macy, R. H.
RAVEN, CHARLES E.—Hughes, T.; Ludlow, J. M.
RAWIDOWICZ, S.—Krochmal, N.; Mendelssohn, M.; Nordau (Südfeld), M. S.
RAWLINSON, H. G.—Abul Fazl Allami.
RAY, P. ORMAN— Absent-Voting.
READ, CONYERS—Burghley, Lord.
READ, THOMAS T.—Agricola, G.
REALE, EGIDIO—Passport.
RECKITT, MAURICE B.—Bax, E. B.; Christian Socialism (Gt. Brit.).
REDDAWAY, W. F.—Bernstorff, A. P.; Bernstorff, J. H. E.; Russell, J.
REDFERN, P.—Mitchell, J. T. W.
REDSLOB, ROBERT—Burlamaqui, J. J.
REED, HAROLD L.—Bimetallism and Monometallism; Free Silver; Horton, S. D.; National Banks, United States; Rentenmark.
REED, LOUIS S.—Fee Splitting.
REED, ROBERT R.—Blue Sky Laws.
REED, THOMAS H.—Metropolitan Areas; Sanitation; Water Supply.
REES, J. F.—Cary, J.; Colonial System; Davenant, C.; Decker, Sir M.; Free Trade; Gibbins, H. de B.; Grenville, G.; Gresham, Sir T.; King, G.; Petty, Sir W.; Rogers, J. E. T.; Temple, Sir W.; Tucker, J.; Vanderlint, J.; Villiers, C. P.; Wallace, R.
REICH, NATHAN—Diamand, H.; Lipinsky, V.; Pulp and Paper Industry; Staszic, S. W.; Wroński-Hoene, J. M.
REIGBERT, ROBERT—Fellenberg, P. E. von; Gesner, J. M.; Ratke, W.
REISNER, EDWARD H.—Forster, W. E.; Pestalozzi, J. H.; Raikes, R.
REUTER, E. B.—Amalgamation.
RIAZA, ROMÁN—López de Palacios Rubios, J.; Macanaz, M. R. de; Pi y Margall, F.; Soto, D. de.
RICCI, UMBERTO—Pantaleoni, M.; Valenti, Gh.
RICE, EMMETT A.—Physical Education.
RICHARDS, CHARLES R.—Industrial Arts.
RICHARDS, R. D.—Barbon, N.; Montagu, C.; Paterson, W.
RICHARDSON, CAROLINE FRANCIS—Baxter, R.
RICHARDSON, J. H.—Allan, W.; Applegarth, R.; Arch, J.; Family Allowances; Schloss, D. F.
RICHBERG, DONALD R.—Garretson, A. B.
RIDDELL, WALTER A.—Laval, F. X. de.
RIEFLER, WINFIELD W. — Call Money.
RIPPY, J. FRED—Castro, C.; Díaz, J. de la C. P.; Guzmán-Blanco, A.; Hidalgo y Costilla, M.; Pan-Americanism.
RITTENHOUSE, IRMA—Industrial Hygiene (Legislation and Reform).
RITTER, GERHARD—Luther, M.
ROA, JORGE—Bachiller y Morales, A.
ROBACK, A. A.—Character; Ebbinghaus, H.; Gall, F. J.; Galton, Sir F.; Hartmann, E. von; Lazarus, M.; Münsterberg, H.; Steinthal, H.
ROBB, T. BRUCE—Bank Deposits, Guaranty of.
ROBBINS, LIONEL — Production (Theory).
ROBERTS, HELEN H. — Music (Primitive).
ROBERTS, STEPHEN H.—Bert, P.; Bugeaud de la Piconnerie, T. R.; Étienne, E.; Gallieni, J.-S.; Leopold II; MacQuarie, L.; Native Policy (Pacific and Africa and General Summary).
ROBERTSON, WILLIAM SPENCE—Artigas, J. G.; Barrios, J. R.; Bolívar, J.; Central American Federation; Miranda, F. de; Parties, Political (Spain and Portugal).
ROBINSON, CLAUDE E.—Straw Vote.
ROBINSON, EDWARD S.—Play.
ROBINSON, HOWARD—Freeman, E. A.; Harrison, F.; Pitt, W. and W.; Raffles, Sir T. S.; Shaftesbury, Third Earl of; Tindal M.; Toland, J.; Wellesley, Marquis R. C.; Wentworth, W. C.
ROBINSON, JAMES HARVEY—Butler, S.
ROBINSON, LELAND REX—Investment Trusts.
ROBINSON, LOUIS N.—Criminal Statistics; Prison Labor.
ROBINSON, RALPH M.—Coutts, T.
ROBINSON, W. A.—Buller, C.
ROBSON, WILLIAM A.—County Councils; DuCane, Sir E. F.; Functional Representation; Local Government.
RODEE, CARLTON C. — Police Power; Representation.
RODKEY, ROBERT G.—Bank Deposits.
ROGERS, H. O.—Mining (Hist., Technology and Economics).
ROGERS, JAMES HARVEY—Inflation and Deflation.
ROGERS, LINDSAY—Cabinet; Cannon, J. G.; Closure; Committees, Legislative; Congressional Government; Debate, Parliamentary; Insurgency, Political; Interpellation; Legislative Assemblies (U. S.: Congress); Obstruction, Parliamentary; Parties, Political (France); Politics.
ROHDEN, PETER RICHARD — Maistre, Comte J. M. de; Montesquieu, Baron de la Brède et de; Republicanism; Royal Court; Traditionalism.
RÖPKE, WILHELM—Faucher, J.; Hagen, K. H.; Hansemann, D. J. L.
RÖRIG, FRITZ—Hanseatic League.
ROSE, H. J.—Harrison, J. E.
ROSE, WILLIAM J.—Konarski, S.
ROSENBAUM, EDUARD — Export Credits.
ROSENBERG, ARTHUR—Hohen-

Index of Contributors (Price, L. L. — Scott)

lohe-Schillingsfürst, C. K. V.; Landauer, G.; Legien, C.; Liebknecht, K.; Mehring, F.; Socialist Parties; Windthorst, L.; Zetkin, C.

ROSENBERG, VLADIMIR — Korolenko, V. G.

ROSMARIN, TRUDE W.—Philippson, L.

ROSNER, HENRY J.—Municipal Transit.

ROSS, MARY—More, Hannah; Mott, L.; Spencer, A. G.

ROSTOVTZEFF, M.—Meyer, E.

ROTH, CECIL—Basnage, J. C.; Jacobs, J.

ROUBAKINE, N.—Dörpfeld, F. W.; Girard, J.-B.; Uvarov, Count S. S.

ROURKE, CONSTANCE — Stowe, H. B.

ROWAN, RICHARD WILMER—Espionage.

ROYO VILLANOVA, ANTONIO — Fontanella, J. P.

RUBINOW, I. M.—Group Insurance; Hourvich, I. A.; Industrial Hazards; Old Age; Poverty; Social Insurance.

RUBIO, JOSÉ ANTONIO — Castelar y Ripoll, E.

RUDLIN, W. A.—Obedience, Political; Parties, Political (Gt. Brit.).

RUDWIN, MAXIMILIAN — Diabolism.

RUGG, HAROLD—Parker, F. W.

RUGGIERO, GUIDO DE—Crispi, F.; Depretis, A.; De Sanctis, F.; Exile; Foscolo, U.; Genovesi, A.; Giannone, P.; Giannotti, D.; Gioberti, V.; Guicciardini, F.; Idealism; Laboulaye, É. R. L. de; Liberalism; Pagano, F. M.; Petrarch, F.; Positivism; Religious Freedom; Rosmini-Serbati, A.; Sarpi, P.; Sclopis di Salerano, Conte F.; Spaventa, B.; Spaventa, S.; Tocqueville, A. C. H. M. C. de; Tommaseo, N.; Valla, L.

RÜHLAND, CURT—Rachel, S.

RUSANOV, NICHOLAS—Lavrov, P. L.; Mikhailovsky, N. K.

RUTKOWSKI, JAN—Lubecki, F. X.; Steinkeller, P. A.

RUYSSEN, TH.—Estournelles de Constant, Baron d'; Passy, F.

RYAN, JOHN A.—Aquinas, T.; Biel, G.; Devas, C. S.; Leo XIII.

SABINE, GEORGE H.—Aurelius Antoninus, M.; Cicero, M. T.; State.

SADLER, MICHAEL E.—Baines, E.; Edgeworth, R. L.; Jowett, B.; Kay-Shuttleworth, Sir J.

SAGNAC, PHILIPPE — Lavisse, E.; Mallet du Pan, J.; Mirabeau, Comte de; Mirabeau, Marquis de.

SAIT, EDWARD MCCHESNEY — Campaign, Political; Contested Elections; Convention, Political; Machine, Political; Nominations, Political.

SAKOLSKI, A. M.—Debentures.

SALIN, EDGAR — Introduction (The Social Sciences as Disciplines: Germany); Ambrose; Augustine; Church Fathers; Clement of Alexandria; Economics (Romantic and Universalist Economics); Just Price; List, F.; Origen; Schönberg, G. F. von; Tertullian; Thünen, J. H. von; Usury.

SALOMON, ALICE — Braun, L.; Dohm, H.; Münsterberg, E.

SALOMON, GOTTFRIED—Baader, F. X. von; Demolins, E.; Gobineau, J. A. de; Hero Worship; Le Play, P. G. F.; Müller-Lyer, F. C.; Ratzenhofer, G.; Social Organism; Stein, Lorenz von; Stein, Ludwig.

SALVATORELLI, LUIGI — Giolitti, G.

SALVEMINI, GAETANO—Assignats; Mazzini, G.; Turati, F.; Villari, P.

SALZ, ARTHUR—Müller, A. H.; Occupation; Rodbertus, J. K.; Rössler, C.; Specialization.

SALZMAN, L. F.—Metals (Ancient, Mediaeval and Early Modern).

SAN NICOLÒ, MARIANO—Guilds (Antiquity).

SANBORN, FREDERIC ROCKWELL —Jenkins, Sir L.; Law Merchant; Lien; Maritime Law; Stowell, First Baron.

SÁNCHEZ ALONSO, B.—Macías Picavea, R.; Menéndez y Pelayo, M.

SAND, RENÉ—Bourneville, D. M.; Budin, P.

SAPIR, EDWARD — Communication; Custom; Dialect; Fashion; Group; Language; Personality; Symbolism.

SAPOSS, DAVID J.—Dual Unionism; Evans, G. H.; Producers' Cooperation.

SAPPER, KARL—Geography (Economic).

SARFATTI, MARIO—Chironi, G.

SARKAR, BENOY KUMAR—Nārada.

SAUER, CARL—Geography (Cultural); Peschel, O.; Ratzel, F.; Ritter, K.; Semple, E. C.

SAUNDERS, K. J.—Buddhism (Institutional Organization); Davids, T. W. R.

SAYRE, FRANCIS B.—Arrest; Conspiracy, Criminal.

SAYRE, WALLACE S.—La Follette, R. M.

SCELLE, GEORGES — Asiento; Bourgeois, L. V. A.

SCHACHT, JOSEPH—Islam; Islamic Law; Mohammed; Shāfi'i, al-.

SCHAPERA, I. — Kagwa, A.; Khama; Moshesh.

SCHAPIRO, J. SALWYN—Anticlericalism; Condorcet, M. J. A. N. C.; Diderot, D.; Lamartine, A. M. L. de Prat de; Lecky, W. E. H.

SCHAPIRO, MEYER — Pottery (Historical); Taste.

SCHEVILL, FERDINAND—Frederick II; Marsilius of Padua; Medici; Savonarola, G.

SCHILLER, A. ARTHUR—Conrat (Cohn), M.; Degenkolb, H.; Eisele, F.; Favre, A.; Fitting, H. H.; Irnerius; Law (Hellenistic and Greco-Egyptian); Lawgivers; Papinianus, A.; Roman Law; Ulpian.

SCHILLER, F. C. S.—Humanism (Philosophical Aspects).

SCHINZ, ALBERT—Rousseau, J.-J.

SCHLESINGER, A. M.—Eggleston, E.

SCHLINK, F. J.—Adulteration.

SCHMIDT, LOUIS BERNARD—Agriculture (U. S.); Skinner, J. S.; Wallace, H. and H. C.; Watson, E.; Weaver, J. B.

SCHMIDT, RICHARD—Leadership.

SCHMITTHENNER, PAUL—Mercenary Troops; Military Desertion; Militia (Continental).

SCHNABEL, FRANZ—Hardenberg, K. A. von; Jahn, F. L.; Luden, H.; Pertz, G. H.; William I.

SCHNEIDER, FEDOR—Bezold, F. von.

SCHNEIDER, HERBERT W.—Introduction (The Social Sciences as Disciplines: Italy under Fascism); Bradford, W.; Brownson, O. A.; Christian Socialism; Cotton, J.; Eddy, M. B.; Edwards, J.; Ethical Culture Movement; Revivals, Religious; Transcendentalism.

SCHOLZ, RICHARD—Boniface VIII; Gerson, J.; James of Viterbo; John Quidort of Paris.

SCHÜCKING, WALTHER—Fried, A. H.; Lammasch, H.

SCHULTE, FRITZ—Land Mortgage Credit (Agric.: General).

SCHUMACHER, HERMANN — Economics (Historical School); Location of Industry.

SCHUMAN, FREDERICK L.—De Facto Government; Enemy Alien; Hay, J. M.; Insurrection; Mutiny; Spheres of Influence; Trading with the Enemy; Treaties.

SCHUMPETER, JOSEPH A.—Auspitz, R.; Böhm-Bawerk, E. von; Young, A. A.

SCHWARTZ, PH.—Böckh, R.

SCHWERIN, CLAUDIUS VON — Homeyer, K. G.

SCHWERTFEGER, BERNHARD—Caprivi (de Caprara de Montecuculi), G. L. von.

SCHWINGE, ERICH—Glaser, J.; Grolman, K. von; Mittermaier, K. J. A.

SCOTT, AUSTIN W.—Charitable Trusts; Trusts and Trustees.

SCOTT. JAMES BROWN—Vitoria, F. de.

SCOTT, W. R.—Hutcheson, F.

SCROGGS, WILLIAM O.—Filibustering.
SCUDDER, VIDA D.—Christian Socialism (U. S.).
SEAGLE, WILLIAM — Alimony; Bekker, E. I.; Bulmerincq, A. von; Contempt of Court; Cooley, T. McI.; Domestic Relations Courts; Erskine, Baron; Family Law; Fines; Gambling (Legal Aspects); Homicide; Jury (Outside Eng. and U. S.); Justice, Administration of; Kohler, J.; Labor Legislation and Law (Law: Continental); Reception; Riot (Legal Aspects); Smith, J. A.; Thayer, J. B.; Vinogradoff, Sir P.; Zitelmann, E.
SÉE, HENRI—Agrarian Movements (France *and* Germany and Austria *and* Italy); Buchez, P. J. B.; Chaptal, J. A.; Joly, C.; Lavergne, L.-G. L. de; Luchitsky, I. V.
SEEDORF, WILHELM—Eyth, M.
SEEGER, CHARLES—Music (Music and Musicology *and* Occidental).
SEELIG, ERNST—Lotteries.
SEIDL, ERWIN—Law (Egyptian).
SELEKMAN, B. M.—Leverhulme, Viscount.
SELIGMAN, EDWIN R. A.—Introduction (What Are the Social Sciences?); Boisguillebert, P. le P.; Boyd, W.; Bullionists; Canard, N. F.; Cohn, G.; Craig, J.; De Quincey, T.; Double Taxation (Domestic); Economics (As a Discipline *and* Hist. of Econ. Thought: Introd.); Fiscal Science; Hamilton, R.; Income Tax; Leroy-Beaulieu, P.; Milles, T.; Property Tax; Public Finance; Vauban, Seigneur S. le P. de; Warburg, P. M.; Wells, D. A.
SELLIN, THORSTEN—Baer, A. A.; Benedikt, M.; Bertillon, A.; Bonneville de Marsangy, A.; Commutation of Sentence; Crime; Despine, P.; Goring, C. B.; Identification; Imprisonment; Indeterminate Sentence; Penal Institutions; Probation and Parole.
SELTZER, LAWRENCE H.—Automobile Industry (U. S.: Manufacture and Sale *and* Eur. Countries *and* Social Incidence).
SENTURIA, JOSEPH J.—Clamageran, J. J.; Conspiracy, Political; Corruption, Political (General); Embargo; Interstate Commerce (Federal States other than U. S.); Mass Expulsion; Procedure, Parliamentary; Trade Unions (Lat. Amer.).
SEWNY, V. D.—Worms, R.
SEYBOLT, ROBERT FRANCIS — Rabanus Maurus, M.
SHANN, E. O. G.—MacArthur, J.
SHAPIRO, H. L.—Topinard, P.

SHARENKOFF, VICTOR N.—Stamboliĭski, A. S.
SHARFMAN, I. L.—Adams, H. C.; Interstate Commerce Commission; Knapp, M. A.; Motor Vehicle Transportation; Railroads (General).
SHARP, WALTER R.—Public Employment; Teaching Profession.
SHATZKY, JACOB—Jost, I. M.
SHAW, F. J.—Cobden, R.; Corn Laws; Derby, Earl of.
SHAW, PAUL VANORDEN—Batlle y Ordóñez, J.; Bonifacio de Andrada e Silva, J.; Lastarria, J. V.
SHELDON, OLIVER—Management.
SHEPARD, MAX A.—Ockham, William of.
SHEPARD, W. J.—Bicameral System; Cabinet Government; Centralization; Dicey, A. V.; Executive; Government (Hist. and Theory); Legislative Assemblies (Hist. and Theory); Suffrage.
SHERMAN, CAROLINE B.—Markets, Municipal.
SHERMAN, WELLS ALVORD—Fruit and Vegetable Industry.
SHERRINGTON, CHARLES ELY ROSE—Acworth, W. M.
SHIPPEE, L. B.—Blaine, J. G.; Rhodes, J. F.
SHIRRAS, G. FINDLAY—Baines, J. A.; Hunter, Sir W. W.
SHOUP, CARL—Business Taxes; Poll Tax; Tax Exemption.
SHUB, DAVID—Barondess, J.
SHULMAN, HARRY—Radio (Legal Aspects); Retroactive Legislation.
SHULTZ, WILLIAM J.—Animal Protection; Bergh, H.; Inheritance Taxation.
SIEBOLD, MARTIN—Sanctuary.
SIEGFRIED, ANDRÉ—Boutmy, É. G.; Clemenceau, G.; Guyot, Y.
SIEVEKING, HEINRICH — Loans, Personal.
SILVA, PIETRO—Azeglio, M. d'; Garibaldi, G.; Guerrazzi, F. D.; Manin, D.; Pius IX; Victor Emmanuel II.
SILVERMASTER, NATHAN G.—Plantation Wares.
SIMIAND, FRANÇOIS—Foville, A. de.
SIMMS, HENRY HARRISON—Taylor, J.
SIMON, ERNST—Ranke, L. von.
SIMPSON, KEMPER—Goodwill.
SINGER, CHARLES — Astrology; Hippocrates and the Hippocratic Collection.
SINGER, EDGAR A., JR.—Bruno, G.
ŠIŠIĆ, FERDO—Karageorge, P.
SKALKOWSKI, A. M.—Kościuszko, T. A.
SKALWEIT, AUGUST—Agriculture (Europ. Continent); Buchenberger, A.; Hanssen, G.; Meitzen, A.; Miaskowski, A. von; Schubart, J. C.; Schulze-

Gävernitz, F. G.; Thaer, A. D.
ŠKATULA, EMANUEL—Chleborád, F. L.
SKELTON, O. D.—Galt, Sir A. T.; Laurier, Sir W.
SLESINGER, DONALD—Breach of Marriage Promise; Research; University Extension.
SLICHTER, SUMNER H.—Efficiency.
ŚLIWIŃSKI, ARTUR—Mochnacki, M.
SLOCHOWER, HARRY—Schiller, J. C. F.; Schopenhauer, A.
SLONIMSKY, H.—Wise, I. M.
SLOSSON, PRESTON W.—Harney, G. J.; O'Connor, F.
SMALL, SARA—Michel, L.
SMELLIE, K.—Legislative Assemblies (Gt. Brit. and Dominions); Maine, Sir H. J. S.; Petition, Right of; Rebellion; Riot (General and Historical Aspects); Seebohm, F.; Stephen, Sir J. F.
SMEND, RUDOLF—Kahl, W.
SMITH, BRUCE—Police.
SMITH, CHESTER H.—Justice of the Peace.
SMITH, FRANK—Lancaster, J.
SMITH, H. LLEWELLYN—Bateman, A. E.
SMITH, J. RUSSELL—Agriculture (General Problems); Climate.
SMITH, REGINALD H.—Briesen, A. v.
SMITH, ROBERT S.—Centani, F.; Dormer, D. J.; Ensenada, Marqués de la; González de Collorigo, M.; Martínez de la Mata, F.; Moncada, S. de; Ulloa, B. de; Uztáriz, J. de.
SMITH, SYDNEY A.—Medical Jurisprudence.
SMITH, T. V.—Common Sense; Conduct; Duty; Ethics; Honor; Mead, G. H.
ŠMURLO, E.—Ewers, J. P. G. von; Križanić, J.
SNELLER, Z. W.—Court, P. de la.
SOLARI, G.—Balbo, C.; Carle, G.
SOLMI, ARRIGO—Gaudenzi, A.
SOLNTSEV, S.—Tugan-Baranovsky, M. I.
SOLOW, HERBERT—Blood Accusation; Chamberlain, J.; Correspondence Schools; Crémieux, A. I. M.; Haywood, W. D.
SOLTAU, ROGER—Lacordaire, J. B. H. D.; Lamennais, H. F. R. de; Legislative Assemblies (France); Michel, H.
SOMBART, WERNER—Capitalism.
SOMMER, FRANZ—Brinz, A. von; Bruns, K. G.; Haloander, G.; Krueger, P.; Seckel, E.; Sohm, R.
SOMMER, LOUISE — Arnd, K.; Becher, J. J.; Bornitz, J.; Cameralism; Darjes, J. G.; Forbonnais, F. V. D. de; Graslin, J. J. L.; Herrenschwand, J.; Iselin, I.; Justi, J. H. G. von; Karl, F.; Mauvillon, J.; Pfeiffer, J. F. von;

Index of Contributors (Scroggs — Thompson)

Schlettwein, J. A.; Zincke, G. H.
Sonnichsen, Albert—Comitadji; Cooperation (U. S. and Canada: Consumers' Coop.); Gruev, D.
Sorokin, P. A.—Ammon, A. O.; Artel; Mobility, Social.
Soule, George—Consumer Protection; Consumers' Leagues; Croly, H.; Stabilization, Economic; Standardization.
Southard, Frank A., Jr.—Famine.
Souvarine, Boris—Boissel, F.; Lafargue, P.; Varlin, L. E.
Spahr, Walter E. — Check; Clearing Houses.
Speier, Hans—Vogelsang, Freiherr K. von; Weber, M.
Spektorski, E.—Kovalevsky, M. M.
Spencer, Henry R.—Dictatorship.
Spengler, Joseph J.—Bertillon, J.; Graunt, J.; Ortes, G.
Spero, Sterling D. — Negro Problem.
Spiegel, Shalom — Lilienblum, M. L.
Spiethoff, A.—Overproduction.
Sprague, Blanche Hazard — Leather Industries (Leather Products and Labor).
Sprague, O. M. W.—Banking, Commercial (Theory and U. S.); Banknotes.
Spranger, Eduard—Humboldt, F. W. von; Paulsen, F.
Sprockhoff, Ernst—Ebert, M.
Squires, B. M.—Conciliation, Industrial.
Stadelmann, Rudolf—Grimm, J. L. K. and W. K.; Herder, J. G. von; Joseph ii; Mascov, J. J.; Müller, J. von.
Stamp, J. C.—Double Taxation (International).
Stavenow, Ludvig—Hjärne, H.; Malmström, C. G.
Steen, Sverre—Munch, P. A.
Steenhoff, Frida—Key, E.
Stefani, Alberto de'—Messedaglia, A.
Stehman, J. Warren—Telephone and Telegraph.
Steiger, G. Nye—Burlingame, A.
Steinen, Wolfram von den—Döllinger, I. von; Hefele, K. J. von; Hergenröther, J.; Kraus, F. X.; Möhler, J. A.
Steiner, Jesse Frederick—Community Centers; Community Organization.
Steiner, W. H.—Savings Banks; Trust Companies.
Steinmetz, S. R.—Nieboer, H. J.
Stenton, F. M.—Madox, T.; Palgrave, Sir F.; Round, J. H.; Tout, T. F.; William i.
Stephen, Barbara—Bodichon, B. L. S.; Davies, S. E.
Stephens, G. A.—Basing Point Prices; Food Industries (Baking Industry: U. S.).

Stephenson, Mary — Research.
Stephenson, N. W.—Rhett, R. B.
Stern, Alfred—Dahlmann, F. C.; Droysen, J. G.; Gervinus, G. G.
Stern, Bernhard J.—Bancroft, H. H.; Fison, L.; Giddings, F. H.; Howitt, A. W.; Intermarriage; Jenner, E.; Lister, First Baron; Lubbock, Sir J.; McLennan, J. F.; Morgan, L. H.; Pottery (Primitive); Powell, J. W.; Slavery (Primitive); Sumner, W. G.; Ward, L. F.; Woman, Position in Society (Historical); Writing.
Stern, Boris—Glass and Pottery Industries.
Sternberg, Theodor — Kirchmann, J. H. von.
Stewart, Charles L.—Farm Relief.
Stewart, Ethelbert—Wright, C. D.
Stewart, Robert—Floods and Flood Control.
Stieda, Wilhelm—Dithmar, J. C.; Eiselen, J. F. G.; Heyd, W. von.
Stocking, Collis — Gambling (General and Historical).
Stocking, George Ward—Fertilizer Industry; Nitrates; Oil Industry; Potash.
Stone, Ursula Batchelder — Food Industries (Baking Industry: Eur.); Hotels.
Stowell, Ellery C.—Consular Service.
Strachey, Ray—Fawcett, Dame M. G.
Strickland, C. F.—Wolff, H. W.
Strieder, Jakob—Fortunes, Private (Mediaeval and Early Modern); Fugger Family; Henckel, G.; Peutinger, K.; Rothschild Family.
Struck, F. Theodore—Manual Training.
Struve, Peter — Introduction (The Social Sciences as Disciplines: Imperial Russia); Aksakovs; Bunge, N. C.; Danielson, N. F.; Land Tenure (Russia).
Stuart, Henry W.—Altruism and Egoism.
Studenski, Paul—Chambers of Commerce; Pensions; Repudiation of Public Debts.
Sturges, Wesley A.—Arbitration, Commercial; Courts, Commercial; Mortgage; Suretyship and Guaranty.
Subercaseaux, Guillermo — Paper Money.
Sudhoff, Karl—Koch, R.; Medicine (History).
Suffern, Arthur E.—Siney, J.
Sullivan, Harry Stack—Mental Disorders; Psychiatry.
Sullivan, Helen — Franciscan Movement; Literacy and Illiteracy.

Sullivan, Oscar M.—Rehabilitation.
Supino, Camillo—Conigliani, C. A.
Surányi-Unger, Theo—Introduction (The Social Sciences as Disciplines: Austria and Hungary); Kautz, G.
Surface, Frank M. — Meat Packing and Slaughtering (Foreign and International Aspects).
Šusta, Josef—Tomek, V. V.
Swanton, John R.—Gatschet, A. S.; Mooney, J.
Sydenstricker, Edgar — Morbidity.
Sykes, Norman — Herbert of Cherbury, First Lord; Hoadly, B.; Hooker, R.
Szczepanowski, S. Prus — Szczepanowski, A. P. S.
Szekfü, Julius—Acsady, I.
Széll, Theodore—Keleti, K.; Kőrösy de Szántó, J.

Taeusch, C. F.—Business Ethics; Professional Ethics.
Takekoshi, Tosaburo — Land Tenure (China and Japan).
Takikawa, Masajiro — Law (Japanese).
Taranovsky, Theodor — Kadlec, K.; Vladimirsky-Budanov, M. F.
Taussig, Frank W.—Bounties; MacVane, S. M.
Taylor, A. Wellington—Johnson, J. F.
Taylor, Carl C.—Country Life Movement; Farmers' Organizations.
Taylor, Ethel—Barnardo, T.
Taylor, George R.—Prices (History).
Taylor, Rachel Annand—Art (Renaissance).
Taylor, W. S.—Pinel, P.
Tead, Ordway—Personnel Administration.
Teilhac, Ernest—Dunoyer, B. C. P. J.; Garnier, G.; Garnier, J. C.; Say, J.-B.; Say, L.
Ter Meulen, Jacob—Crucé, É.
Terry, C. E.—Drug Addiction.
Teschemacher, Hans—Schanz, G. von.
Thayer, James Bradley—Gifts (Law).
Theis, Sophie van S.—Placing Out.
Thibaudet, Albert—Taine, H.-A.
Thibert, Marguerite—Deroin, J.
Thomas, E. L.—Meat Packing and Slaughtering (Foreign and International Aspects).
Thomas, Paul—Lamoignon, G. de.
Thompson, George Jarvis — Common Carrier.
Thompson, George Norwell—Building Regulations.
Thompson, Warren S.—Urbanization.

THOMSON, J. A. K.—Euripides; Plutarch.
THORNDIKE, LYNN—Alchemy; Bacon, R.
THORP, WILLARD L.—Bubbles, Speculative; Prices (History).
THRASHER, FREDERIC M.—Gangs.
THURNWALD, R.—Achelis, T.; Andrée, R.; Blood Vengeance Feud; Nomads.
THURSTON, HENRY W.—Child (Dependent).
TILL, IRENE—Property.
TING, V. K.—Liang Chi'i-ch'ao.
TINGLUM, OTTAR—Aasen, I. A.
TINGSTEN, HERBERT—Legislative Assemblies (Scandinavian States and Finland); Parties, Political (Scandinavian States and Finland).
TIPPETT, TOM—Jones, M.
TOBEY, JAMES A.—Nuisance.
TOBIN, HAROLD—Opium Problem.
TODA, TEIZO—Introduction (The Social Sciences as Disciplines: Japan).
TODD, ARTHUR J.—Howard, G. E.
TODD, ELIZABETH—Amateur; Art (India); Brandes, G. M. C.; Decadence; Dickens, C.; Red Cross.
TODD, T. WINGATE—Quatrefages de Bréau, J.-L. A. de.
TOOKE, CHARLES W.—Dillon, J. F.; Municipal Corporation.
TOTOMIANZ, V.—Arzruni, G.; Balakshin, A. N.; Busch, E.; Godin, J. B. A.; Raffi, H. M. H.; Šimáček, F.
TOWNSEND, MARY E.—Peters, C.
TOZZER, ALFRED M.—Putman, F. W.
TRAUB, HANS—Bachem, J. and J.; Börne, L.; Cotta, J. F.; Dumont Family; Faber Family.
TRIMBLE, E. G.—Prisoners of War; Requisitions, Military.
TRIMBORN, HERMANN—Dargun, L. von; Post, A. H.
TROTTER, REGINALD G.—Cartier, G. É.; Denison, G. T.; Watkin, Sir E. W.
TROXELL, JOHN P.—Tobacco.
TRUESDELL, LEON E.—Farm Tenancy (U. S.).
TRUMBOWER, HENRY R.—Roads (Modern).
TRYON, F. G.—Conservation; Mining (Hist., Technology and Economics).
TSCHERIKOWER, E.—Hirsch, Baron M. de.
TSUNODA, RYUSAKU—Itagaki, Count T.
TSURUMI, YUSUKÉ—Legislative Assemblies (Japan); Mabuchi, K.; Motoöri, N.
TUGWELL, R. G.—George, H.
TURIN, S. P.—Manuilov, A. A.
TURNER, JENNIE MCMULLIN—Education (Part Time).
TVERDOKHLEBOV, V.—Hertzenstein, M. Y.

TYSON, HELEN GLENN—Day Nursery.

UNDERHILL, FRANK H.—Brown, G.; Fleming, Sir S.; Gourlay, R. F.; Parties, Political (Canada).
USHER, ABBOTT PAYSON—Ashley, W. J.
USHER, ROLAND G.—Atkyns, R.; Bacon, F.; Bancroft, R.; Browne, R.; Camden, W.; Cranmer, T.; Cromwell, T.

VAILLANT, RENÉ E. G.—Arenal, C.
VALGREN, VICTOR N.—Agricultural Insurance.
VALLAUX, CAMILLE—Geography (Human); Vidal de la Blache, P. M. J.
VALTERS, M.—Kronvalds, A.
VAMBÉRY, RUSZTEM—Eötvös, J.; Giesswein, S.; Kovács, G.; Martinovics, I. J.; Pulszky, A.
VAN BUREN, GEORGE H.—King, W. A.
VANCE, RUPERT B.—Frontier (Geographical and Social Aspects).
VANCE, W. R.—Alienation of Property; Gray, J. C.; Homestead Exemption Laws; Littleton, Sir T. de.
VAN HOVE, A.—Raymond de Pennafort.
VAN METRE, T. W.—Vanderbilt Family.
VAN WATERS, MIRIAM—Adolescence; Baker, H. H.; Juvenile Delinquency and Juvenile Courts.
VASILIEV, A. A.—Fallmerayer, J. P.; Finlay, G.; Krumbacher, K.; Theodosius I; Theodosius II; Uspensky, F. I.; Vasilevsky, V. G.
VEATCH, ROY—Philippine Problem.
VEITCH, GEORGE STEAD—Cartwright, J.
VELASCO, RECAREDO F. DE—Parties, Political (Spain and Portugal).
VENN, J. A.—Agricultural Labor; Collings, J.; Girdlestone, E.; Haggard, Sir H. R.
VERNADSKY, GEORGE—Alexander II; Dyakonov, M. A.
VERSHOFEN, WILHELM—Land Bank Schemes.
VESEY-FITZGERALD, SEYMOUR—Jīmūtavāhana; Law (Hindu); Vijnaneṣvāra.
VIAL, EDMUND E.—Milk Supply.
VIERKANDT, A.—Simmel, G.; Wundt, W. M.
VIGOROUX, LOUIS—Benoiston de Chateauneuf, L. F.; Cherbuliez, A. É.; Deparcieux, A.; Dupré de Saint Maur, N. F.
VIJAYA-TUNGA, J.—Das, "Deshbandhu" C. R.
VILLARD, OSWALD GARRISON—Blair, F. P.

VINACKE, HAROLD M.—Guilds (Chinese); Ōkubo, T.; Ōkuma, Marquis S.; Tz'ŭ Hsi; Yamagata, Prince A.; Yoshida Torajirō.
VINCENT, J. M.—Sumptuary Legislation.
VINER, JACOB—Balance of Trade; Cost; Dumping; International Trade (Theory); Longfield, S. M.; Mun, T.; North, Sir D.; Tariff.
VINNIKOV, I.—Sternberg, L. Y.
VIRTUE, GEORGE O.—Gasoline Tax; McDuffie, G.
VITELES, HARRY—Cooperation (Palestine).
VLEUGELS, WILHELM—Wieser, F. von.
VOGEL, WALTHER—Kjellén, R.
VÖLKER, KARL—Baur, F. C.; Franck, S.; Gieseler, J. K. L.; Magdeburg Centuriators; Mosheim, J. L.; Planck, G. J.; Sleidan, J.
VOLLENHOVEN, CORNELIUS VAN—Grotius, H.
VREELAND, HAMILTON, JR.—Bynkershoek, C. van.

WADE, HERBERT T.—Weights and Measures.
WAGNER, DONALD O.—Merivale, H.
WALL, ALEXANDER—Financial Statements.
WALLACE, W. S.—Bourinot, J. G.; MacDonald, Sir J. A.
WALLAS, GRAHAM—Bentham, J.
WALLIS, WILSON D.—Dueling; Environmentalism; Hunting; Luschan, F. von.
WALSH, C. M.—Fleetwood, W.; Index Numbers (Price Index Numbers: History and Theory).
WALZ, GUSTAV ADOLF—Public Law.
WAMBAUGH, SARAH—Plebiscite; Self-Determination, National.
WAPLES, DOUGLAS—Public Libraries (Social Implications).
WARBASSE, JAMES PETER—Housing, Cooperative.
WARBURTON, CLARK—Prohibition.
WARDLE, H. NEWELL—Gifts (Primitive).
WARE, CAROLINE F.—Appleton, N.; Emigration; Ethnic Communities; Foreign Language Press; Hunt, F.; Immigration.
WARE, NORMAN J.—Bagley, S.; Buchanan, J. R.; Gompers, S.; McNeill, G. E.; Parsons, A. R.; Powderly, T. V.; Stephens, U. S.; Trade Unions (U. S. and Canada).
WARNE, COLSTON E.—Frick, H. C.; Iron and Steel Industry (Labor Conditions: U. S.); Pullman, G. M.
WARNER, EDWARD P.—Aviation (International Aspects).
WARNER, WELLMAN J.—Wesley, J.; Whitefield, G.

Index of Contributors (Thomson — Wozniak)

WARREN, HOWARD C.—Bain, Alexander; Hartley, D.
WATERMAN, T. T.—Bandelier, A. F. A.
WÄTJEN, HERMANN—Johann Moritz.
WATKINS, FREDERICK MUNDELL—Monarchy; Opportunism; Praetorianism; Succession, Political; Tyranny.
WATKINS, MYRON W.—Aviation (Industry); Cut-Throat Competition; Havemeyer, H. O.; Large Scale Production; Meat Packing and Slaughtering (Social Aspects); Price Discrimination; Prices (Theory: Price System); Promotion; Trade Associations; Trusts; Unfair Competition.
WATSON, AMEY E.—Domestic Service.
WEBBINK, PAUL—Astor, J. J.; Baer, G. F.; Biddle, N.; Carnegie, A.; Government Owned Corporations.
WEBER, ADOLF—Banking, Commercial (Continental Eur.).
WEBER, WILHELM—Böckh, A.; Duncker, M. W.; Friedländer, L.; Hirschfeld, O.; Marquardt, K. J.; Mommsen, T.; Müller, K. O.; Seeck, O.; Wilamowitz-Moellendorff, U. von; Winckelmann, J. J.; Wolf, F. A.
WEBSTER, CHARLES K.—Castlereagh, R. S.; Holy Alliance.
WEBSTER, HUTTON—Holidays.
WEHBERG, HANS—Pufendorf, S. von; Suttner, Baroness B. von.
WEILL, GEORGES—Acollas, É.; Barrot, C. H. O.; Beluze, J. P.; Destutt de Tracy, A. L. C.; Dollfus, J.; Dupont-White, C. B.; Freycinet, C. de; Gallicanism; Girardin, É. de; Griffuelhes, V.; Harmel, L.; Houssaye, H.; Keufer, A.; La Rochefoucauld-Liancourt, Duc F. de; La Tour du Pin Chambly, R. de; Leclaire, E. J.; Lemire, Abbé J.; Méline, J.; Mun, A. de; Napoleon III; Schneider, J.-E.; Simon, J.; Villeneuve-Bargemont, Vicomte de.
WEINBERGER, OTTO—Lieben, R.
WEINER, A.—Howell, G.
WEINSTEIN, ALEXANDER—Heredity; Weismann, A.
WEISS, EGON—Law (Greek); Lipsius, J. H.
WEISS, FRANZ X.—Menger, C.
WELBOURNE, E.—Burt, T.
WENDEL, HERMANN—Karadžić, Vuk S.; Krek, J.; Obradović, D.; Obrenović Dynasty; Pašić, N.; Pelagić, V.; Starčević, A.; Strossmayer, J. J.; Tucović, D.
WENGER, LEOPOLD—Law (Gen. View of Ancient); Mitteis, L.
WERTHEIMER, EDUARD VON—Beust, F. F. von.
WESLEY, CHARLES H.—Jones, A.
WESSELY, PETER K. H.—Leuber, B.

WESTERFIELD, RAY B.—Liquidity.
WESTERGAARD, HARALD—Aschehoug, T. H.; Rubin, M.; Sörensen, T.
WESTERGAARD, WALDEMAR—Gustavus I; Gustavus II; Oxenstierna, A. G.
WESTERMANN, WILLIAM LINN—Introduction (Greek Culture and Thought); Slavery (Ancient).
WESTPHAL, OTTO—Häusser, L.; Haym, R.
WETTEREAU, JAMES O.—Morris, R.
WEULERSSE, G.—Abeille, L. P.; Argenson, R. L. de V. de P.; Baudeau, N.; Cantillon, R.; Clicquot-Blervache, S. de; Economics (The Physiocrats); Gournay, J. C. M. V. de; Le Trosne, G. F.; Mercier de la Rivière, P.-P.; Quesnay, F.
WEYERMANN, M. R.—National Wealth.
WHIPPLE, LEON—Addison, J.; Comstock, A.; Copyright; Defoe, D.
WHITAKER, A. C.—Acceptance; Bill of Exchange (Modern).
WHITAKER, ARTHUR P.—Maclay, W.
WHITE, ALBERT BEEBE—Assizes; Edward I; Henry II; Magna Carta.
WHITE, LEONARD D.—Administration, Public; City Manager; Decentralization; Eaton, D. B.; Spoils System.
WHITE, WALTER—Douglass, F.
WHITE, WILLIAM A.—Alienist.
WHITFIELD, ERNEST A.—Mably, Abbé G. B. de.
WHITTEN, ROBERT—Zoning.
WHITTLESEY, CHARLES R.—Rubber; Valorization.
WICKENS, CHARLES H.—Coghlan, T. A.
WIEDENFELD, KURT—Combinations, Industrial; Transportation.
WIESE, HELMUT—Basedow, J. B.; Beneke, F. E.; Gaudig, H.; Herbart, J. F.; Kármán, M.
WIEST, EDWARD — Agricultural Fairs; Farmers' Alliance; Farmers' Union; Knapp, S. A.
WILBRANDT, ROBERT—Abbé, E.
WILLCOX, WALTER F.—Census; Shattuck, L.; Statistics (Hist.).
WILLEY, MALCOLM M.—Atkinson, W.; Continuity, Social.
WILLIAMS, E. T.—Hart, Sir R.; Wu T'ing Fang.
WILLIAMS, FAITH M.—Canning Industry.
WILLIAMS, FRANKWOOD E.—Fernald, W. E.
WILLIAMS, MARY WILHELMINE—Núñez, R.; Obregón, A.; Rosas, J. M. de; San Martín, J. de; Slavery (Modern: General).
WILLIAMS, SIDNEY J.—Accidents.
WILLIS, H. PARKER—Barron, C.

W.; Branch Banking; Central Banking; Federal Reserve System.
WILLOUGHBY, W. F.—Budget.
WILSON, FRANCIS G.—Ford, H. J.; Independent Voting; International Labor Organization.
WILSON, GEORGE GRAFTON — Angary; Contraband of War; Declaration of London; Declaration of Paris; Neutralization, Wheaton, H.
WILSON, JOHN A.—Maspero, G. C. C.
WILSON, M. L.—Dry Farming.
WILSON, P. A.—Professions.
WINFIELD, PERCY H.—Intervention; Lambarde, W.; Negligence; Tort.
WINGFIELD-STRATFORD, ESMÉ—Cramb, J. A.; Dryden, J.
WINSLOW, C.-E. A.—Biggs, H. M.; Communicable Diseases, Control of; Public Health; Sedgwick, W. T.; Simon, Sir J.
WINTER, WILLIAM D.—Marine Insurance.
WINTERS, LAURENCE M.—Stock Breeding.
WIRTH, LOUIS — Segregation; Small, A. W.
WISSLER, CLARK—Abbott, C. C.; Agriculture (Primitive); Brinton, D. G.; McGee, W. J.; Pitt-Rivers, A. H. L.-F.
WITHERS, WILLIAM — Sinking Fund.
WITTE, EDWIN E.—Labor Legislation and Law (Legislation).
WITTENBERG, PHILIP — Enticement of Employees; Miscegenation.
WITTKE, CARL—Immunity, Political.
WOHLHAUPTER, EUGEN — Hinschius, P.; Kreittmayr, Baron von.
WOLF, ERIK—Cocceji, H. von; Cocceji, S. von; Thomasius, C.
WOLFE, A. B.—Demography; Population (Theory); Townsend, J.
WOLFF, HELLMUTH — Büsching, A. F.
WOLFSON, THERESA—Wright, F.
WOLMAN, LEO—Garment Industries; Industrial Relations.
WOOD, EDITH ELMER—Housing (U. S.).
WOODBURY, HELEN SUMNER—Altgeld, J. P.
WOODBURY, ROBERT M.—Accidents, Industrial; Child (Mortality); Railroad Accidents; Statistics (Statistical Practise).
WOODDY, CARROLL H.—Johnson, T. L.
WORKING, E. J.—Demand (Statistical Demand Curves).
WORKMAN, H. B.—Monasticism; Wycliffe, J.
WOYTINSKY, WLADIMIR—Hours of Labor; Wages (Hist. and Statistics).
WOZNIAK, M.—Franko, I.

WRIGHT, B. F., JR.—Dickinson, J.; Fitzhugh, G.; Mason, G.
WRIGHT, HELEN R.—Armour Family; Callender, G. S.; Captain of Industry; Dependency; Kelley, F.; Lathrop, J. C.; Medicine (Medical Educ.).
WRIGHT, HERBERT—Suárez, F.
WRIGHT, LUCY—Braille, L.
WRIGHT, PHILIP G.—Ad Valorem and Specific Duties.
WRIGHT, QUINCY—Advisory Opinions (International); Armistice; Mandates.
WULF, MAURICE DE—Scholasticism.
WUORINEN, JOHN H.—Arwidsson, A. I.

YARMOLINSKY, AVRAHM—Belinsky, V. G.; Dostoevsky, F. M.; Nihilism; Tolstoy, L. N.

YERKES, ROBERT M.—Comparative Psychology.
YNTEMA, HESSEL E.—Full Faith and Credit Clause; Smith, E. M.
YOUNG, GEORGE—Cromer, First Earl of; Dilke, Sir C. W.; Dufferin and Ava, First Marquis of; Egyptian Problem; Europeanization; Imperial Unity; International Relations; Kasim Amin; Pan-Islamism.
YOUNG, KIMBALL—Adjustment; Imitation.

ZAWADZKI, LADISLAUS—Czerkawaki, W.
ZEHRFELD, REINOLD—Conring, H.
ZÉVAÈS, ALEXANDRE—Malon, B.; Sembat, M. É.
ZIELENZIGER, KURT—Baumstark. E.: Bernstein, A.; Besold, C.; Büsch, J. G.; Hornigk, P. W. von; Lau, T. L.; Leib, J. G.; Obrecht, G. von; Osse, M. von; Schlözer, A. L. von; Schroeder, Freiherr W. von; Seckendorff, V. L. von; Sonnenfels, Freiherr J. von; Ullstein Family.
ZIMMERMAN, CARLE C.—Back-to-the-Land Movements; Rural Society.
ZIMMERMANN, ERICH W.—Natural Resources; Wood Industries.
ŽIŽEK, FRANZ—Süssmilch, J. P.
ZLOCISTI, THEODOR—Hess, M.
ZNANIECKI, E. AND F.—Gumplowicz, L.
ZON, RAPHAEL—Forests.
ZULUETA, F. DE—Accursius; Azo; Cino da Pistoia; Cujas, J.; Four Doctors; Godefroy, D. and J.; Julianus, S.; Vacarius.

UNION UNIVERSITY
LIBRARY